Leonard G

64 St

Cresslyn Ray,

Nr Walsall,

Staffs

CW01614870

BURLINGTON UNIVERSAL CONCISE DICTIONARY

BURLINGTON UNIVERSAL CONCISE DICTIONARY

Brown Watson
ENGLAND

Printed in USSR for the publishers
Peter Haddock Ltd., Bridlington, England

CONTENTS

ABBREVIATIONS
used in this Dictionary

a.	adjective
adv.	adverb
conj.	conjunction
int.	interjection
n.	noun
n.pl.	noun plural
p.a.	participial adjective
pl.	plural
pp.	past participle
prep.	preposition
pret.	preterit
pron.	pronoun
vi.	verb intransitive
vt.	verb transitive

A, the indefinite article, used before a consonant. *See* AN.
Aaron's-beard, ā'ronz-bērd, *n.* A name of several plants.
Aback, a-bak', *adv.* Backwards; by surprise.
Abacus, ab'a-kus, *n.*; pl. **-ci,** or **-cuses.** A square slab forming the crowning of a column.
Abaft, a-bäft', *adv.* or *prep.* On or towards the aft or hinder part of a ship.
Abandon, a-ban'dun, *vt.* To forsake entirely; to desert.
Abandoned, a-ban'dund, *p.a.* Depraved.
Abandonment, a-ban'dun-ment, *n.* A total desertion.
Abase, a-bās', *vt.* (abasing, abased). To bring low; degrade; disgrace.
Abasement, a-bās'ment, *n.* State of being abased; degradation.
Abash, a-bash', *vt.* To put to confusion; to make ashamed.
Abate, a-bāt', *vt.* (abating, abated). To lessen. *vi.* To become less.
Abatement, a-bāt'ment, *n.* Act of abating; a mitigation; deduction.
Abattis, Abatis, ab'a-tis or ab-a-tē', *n.*; pl. the same. A fortification consisting of felled trees with the smaller branches cut off.
Abattoir, a-ba-twär', *n.* A public slaughter-house.
Abbacy, ab'a-si, *n.*; pl. **-cies.** The dignity, rights, and privileges of an abbot.
Abbé, ab-ā, *n.* An inferior R. Catholic ecclesiastic with no benefice.
Abbess, ab'es, *n.* A female superior of a nunnery.
Abbey, ab'i, *n.*; pl. **-eys.** A monastery, or convent.
Abbot, ab'ut, *n.* The male superior of an abbey.
Abbreviate, ab-brē'vi-āt, *vt.* To shorten.
Abbreviation, ab-brē'vi-ā"shon, *n.* A shortening; contraction.
Abbreviator, ab-brē'vi-ā-tėr, *n.* One who abbreviates or abridges.
Abdicate, ab'di-kāt, *vt.* (abdicating, abdicated). To resign voluntarily; to relinquish. *vi.* To resign power.
Abdication, ab-di-kā'shon, *n.* Act of abdicating an office.
Abdomen, ab-dō'men, *n.* The lower belly.
Abdominal, ab-dom'in-al, *a.* Pertaining to the lower belly.
Abduct, ab-dukt', *vt.* To entice or lead away wrongly.
Abduction, ab-duk'shon, *n.* The felonious carrying off a man's daughter, wife, &c.
Abeam, a-bēm', *adv.* or *pred.a.* At right angles to the length of a ship.
Abed, a-bed', *adv.* On or in bed.
Aberrant, ab-e'rant, *a.* Wandering from; deviating from an established rule.
Aberration, ab-e-rā'shon, *n.* A wandering from; alienation of the mind.
Abet, a-bet', *vt.* (abetting, abetted). To urge on; to encourage. (Chiefly in a bad sense.)
Abetment, a-bet'ment, *n.* Act of abetting.
Abetter, Abettor, a-bet'ėr, *n.* One who abets.
Abeyance, a-bā'ans, *n.* Temporary extinction. (With *in* before it.)
Abhor, ab-hor', *vt.* (abhorring, abhorred). To shrink from with horror; to loathe, detest.
Abhorrence, ab-hor'rens, *n.* Detestation.
Abhorrent, ab-hor'rent, *a.* Hating; inconsistent with. (With *to.*)
Abide, a-bīd', *vi.* (abiding, abode or abided). To stay in a place; to dwell.—*vt.* To wait for; to endure.
Abiding, a-bīd'ing, *p.a.* Permanent.
Abigail, ab'i-gāl, *n.* A familiar name for a waiting woman or lady's-maid.
Ability, a-bil'li-ti, *n.* Power to do anything; talent; skill; in *pl.* the powers of the mind.
Abiogenesis, ab'i-ō-jen"e-sis, *n.* The doctrine that living matter may be produced by not-living matter.
Abiogenetic, ab'i-o-jen-et"ik, *a.* Pertaining to abiogenesis.
Abject, ab'jekt, *a.* Mean; despicable.
Abjuration, ab-jū-rā'shon, *n.* Act of abjuring; oath taken for that end.
Abjure, ab-jūr', *vt.* (abjuring, abjured). To renounce upon oath; to reject.
Ablative, ab'lat-iv, *a.* or *n.* Applied to a case of nouns in Latin and other languages.
Ablaze, a-blāz', *adv.* On fire; in a blaze.
Able, ā'bl, *a.* Having power sufficient; capable; skilful.
Ablution, ab-lū'shon, *n.* A washing away from; a purification by water.
Ably, ā'bli, *adv.* With ability.
Abnegate, ab'nē-gāt, *vt.* To deny; to renounce.
Abnegation, ab-nē-gā'shon, *n.* A denial.
Abnormal, ab-norm'al, *a.* Deviating from a fixed rule; irregular.
Aboard, a-bōrd', *adv.* or *prep.* On board; in a ship or vessel.

Abode, a-bōd′, *n.* Residence; habitation.
Abolish, a-bol′ish, *vt.* To destroy; to abrogate.
Abolition, ab-ō-li′shon, *n.* Act of abolishing; state of being abolished.
Abolitionist, ab-ō-li′shon-ist, *n.* One who seeks to abolish anything, especially slavery.
Abominable, a-bom′in-a-bl, *a.* Loathsome.
Abominably, a-bom′in-a-bli, *adv.* Odiously.
Abominate, a-bom′in-āt, *vt.* (abominating, abominated). To hate extremely; to abhor.
Abomination, a-bom′in-ā″shon, *n.* Hatred; object of hatred; loathsomeness.
Aboriginal, ab-ō-rij′in-al, *a.* Primitive.
Aborigines, ab-ō-rij′in-ēz, *n.pl.* The original inhabitants of a country.
Abort, a-bort′, *vi.* To miscarry in giving birth.
Abortion, a-bor′shon, *n.* A miscarriage.
Abortive, a-bort′iv, *a.* Immature; causing abortion; coming to nought.
Abortively, a-bort′iv-li, *adv.* Immaturely.
Abound, a-bound′, *vi.* To be, or have, in great plenty.
Abounding, a-bound′ing, *p.a.* In great plenty; prevalent.
About, a-bout′, *prep.* Around; near to; relating to; engaged in.—*adv.* Around; round; nearly; here and there.
Above, a-buv′, *prep.* To or in a higher place than; superior to; more than; beyond; before.—*adv.* To or in a higher place; chiefly.
Above-board, a-buv′bōrd, *adv.* Without concealment or deception.
Abrade, a-brād′, *vt.* (abrading, abraded). To scrape off; to waste by friction.
Abrasion, ab-rā′zhon, *n.* A rubbing off; substance worn off by rubbing.
Abreast, a-brest′, *adv.* In a line; side by side.
Abridge, a-brij′, *vt.* To shorten; to condense.
Abridgment, a-brij′ment, *n.* An epitome; a summary.
Abroach, a-brōch′, *adv.* In a posture to flow out; set afloat; ready to be diffused.
Abroad, a-brąd′, *adv.* At large; away from home; in a foreign country.
Abrogate, ab′rō-gāt, *vt.* (abrogating, abrogated). To repeal; to make void.
Abrogation, ab-rō-gā′shon, *n.* Act of abrogating; a repeal; annulment.
Abrupt, ab-rupt′, *a.* Broken off; steep; sudden; unceremonious.
Abruptly, ab-rupt′li, *adv.* Suddenly; unceremoniously.
Abruptness, ab-rupt′nes, *n.* Suddenness; unceremonious haste.
Abscess, ab′ses, *n.* A gathering of purulent matter in some part of the body.
Abscind, ab-sind′, *vt.* To cut off.
Abscission, ab-si′zhon, *n.* The act of cutting off; severance; removal.
Abscond, ab-skond′, *vi.* To hide oneself; to fly from justice.
Absence, ab′sens, *n.* State of being absent; inattention to things present.
Absent, ab′sent, *a.* Being away from; not present; wanting in attention.
Absent, ab-sent′, *vt.* To keep away from. (With refl. pron.)
Absentee, ab-sen-tē′, *n.* One who absents himself.
Absenteeism, ab-sen-tē′izm, *n.* State or habit of an absentee.
Absently, ab′sent-li, *adv.* With absence of mind.
Absinthe, ab′sinth, *n.* A liqueur consisting of spirit flavoured with wormwood.
Absolute, ab′sō-lūt, *a.* Unlimited; unconditional; certain; despotic.
Absolutely, ab′sō-lūt-li, *adv.* Unconditionally; peremptorily.
Absoluteness, ab′sō-lūt-nes, *n.* State or quality of being absolute.
Absolution, ab-sō-lū′shon, *n.* A loosing from guilt, or its punishment.
Absolutism, ab′sō-lūt-izm, *n.* The principles of absolute government.
Absolve, ab-solv′, *vt.* To free from, as from guilt or punishment; acquit; pardon.
Absorb, ab-sorb′, *vt.* To drink in; to engross.
Absorbable, ab-sorb′a-bl, *a.* That may be absorbed or swallowed up.
Absorbent, ab-sorb′ent, *a.* Imbibing; swallowing.—*n.* That which absorbs.
Absorption, ab-sorp′shon, *n.* Act or process of imbibing or swallowing up.
Abstain, ab-stān′, *vi.* To keep back from; to refrain; to forbear.
Abstemious, ab-stē′mi-us, *a.* Sparing in food or drink; temperate; sober.
Absterge, ab-stėrj′, *vt.* To rub or wipe off; to cleanse.
Abstergent, ab-stėrj′ent, *a.* Having absterging properties.—*n.* Whatever absterges.
Abstinence, ab′sti-nens, *n.* A keeping from the indulgence of the appetities, especially from intoxicating liquors.
Abstinent, ab′sti-nent, *a.* Abstaining from; refraining from indulgence.
Abstinently, ab′sti-nent-li, *adv.* With abstinence.
Abstract, ab-strakt′, *vt.* To draw from; to separate and consider by itself; to epitomize.
Abstract, ab′strakt, *a.* Existing in the mind only; not concrete; general in language or in reasoning.—*n.* A summary; an abridgment.
Abstracted, ab-strakt′ed, *a.* Absent in mind.
Abstractedly, ab-strakt′ed-li, *adv.* In an absent manner.
Abstraction, ab-strak′shon, *n.* Act of abstracting; deep thought; absence of mind.
Abstractive, ab-strakt′iv, *a.* Having the power or quality of abstracting.
Abstractly, ab-strakt′li, *adv.* Separately; absolutely.
Abstruse, ab-strūs′, *a.* Difficult of comprehension; profound in meaning; obscure.
Absurd, ab-sėrd′, *a.* Contrary to reason or common sense; ridiculous.
Absurdity, ab-sėrd′i-ti, *n.* Quality of being absurd; that which is absurd.
Absurdly, ab-sėrd′li, *adv.* In an absurd manner; against common sense; ridiculously.
Abundance, a-bun′dans, *n.* Plenteousness; copiousness; wealth.
Abundant, a-bun′dant, *a.* Abounding; plentiful; ample.
Abundantly, a-bun′dant-li, *adv.* Fully; amply; plentifully.
Abuse, a-būz′, *vt.* (abusing, abused). To turn from the proper use; to ill-use; to deceive; to vilify; to violate.
Abuse, a-būs′, *n.* Misuse; bad language addressed to a person; insulting words; violation.
Abusive, a-būs′iv, *a.* Practising abuse; containing abuse; insulting.
Abut, a-but′, *vi.* (abutting, abutted). To border; to meet. (With *upon.*)

Abutment, a-but'ment, *n.* That which abuts; solid support for the extremity of a bridge, arch, &c.
Abyss, a-bis', *n.* A bottomless gulf; a deep pit or mass of waters; hell.
Acacia, a-kā'shi-a, *n.* A genus of ornamental plants, yielding catechu, gum-arabic, &c.
Academic, Academical, ak-a-dem'ik, ak-a-dem'ik-al, *a.* Belonging to an academy or university.
Academician, ak'a-dē-mi''shi-an, *n.* A member of an academy.
Academy, a-kad'ē-mi, *n.* A seminary of arts or sciences; a society of persons for the cultivation of arts and sciences.
Acajou, ak'a-jö, *n.* A heavy red mahogany.
Acanthus, a-kan'thus, *n.* A prickly plant, the model of the foliage of the Corinthian order.
Acaridan, a-kar'i-dan, *n.* A mite, tick, or allied animal.
Accede, ak-sēd', *vi.* (acceding, acceded). To assent to; to comply with.
Accelerate, ak-sel'lė-rāt, *vt.* (accelerating, accelerated). To hasten; to quicken the speed of.
Acceleration, ak-sel'lė-rā''shon, *n.* Act of accelerating; increase of velocity.
Accelerative, ak-sel'lė-rāt-iv, *a.* Adding to velocity; accelerating.
Accent, ak'sent, *n.* A tone or modulation of the voice; stress of the voice on a syllable or word; the mark which indicates this stress; manner of speaking.
Accent, ak-sent', *vt.* To express or note the accent of.
Accented, ak-sent'ed, *p.a.* Uttered or marked with accent.
Accentual, ak-sent'ū-al, *a.* Pertaining to accent.
Accentuate, ak-sent'ū-āt, *vt.* (accentuating, accentuated). To mark or pronounce with an accent or accents; to emphasize.
Accentuation, ak-sent'ū-ā''shon, *n.* Act of marking with the proper accents.
Accept, ak-sept', *vt.* To receive; to admit; to promise to pay, by attaching one's signature.
Acceptability, ak-sept'a-bil''li-ti, *n.* Quality of being acceptable.
Acceptable, ak-sept'a-bl, *a.* That may be accepted; pleasing; gratifying.
Acceptably, ak-sept'a-bli, *adv.* In an acceptable manner.
Acceptance, ak-sept'ans, *n.* Reception; reception with approbation; a bill of exchange accepted.
Acceptation, ak-sep-tā'shon, *n.* Kind reception; meaning in which a word is understood.
Accepter, Acceptor, ak-sept'ėr, ak-sept'or, *n.* A person who accepts.
Access, ak'ses, *n.* Approach; admission; means of approach; increase.
Accessary, ak'ses-a-ri. *See* ACCESSORY.
Accessibility, ak-ses'i-bil''li-ti, *n.* Quality of being accessible.
Accessible, ak-ses'i-bl, *a.* Easy of approach; affable.
Accessibly, ak-ses'i-bli, *adv.* So as to be accessible.
Accession, ak-se'shon, *n.* The act of acceding; augmentation; succession to a throne.
Accessorial, ak-ses-sō'ri-al, *a.* Pertaining to an accessory.
Accessory, ak'ses-sō-ri, *a.* Additional, contributing to.—*n.* An accomplice; an adjunct.
Accidence, ak'si-dens, *n.* The changes which inflected parts of speech undergo; a work exhibiting such changes.
Accident, ak'si-dent, *n.* Quality of a being not essential to it; an unfortunate event occurring casually.
Accidental, ak-si-dent'al, *a.* Happening by chance; not necessarily belonging to.—*n.* A property or thing not essential.
Accidentally, ak-si-dent'al-li, *adv.* By accident or chance; casually.
Acclaim, ak-klām', *n.* Acclamation.—*vt.* To applaud; to declare by acclamation.
Acclamation, ak-kla-mā'shon, *n.* A shout of applause, assent, or approbation.
Acclimatize, ak-klī'mat-īz, *vt.* To habituate to a climate different from the native one.
Acclivity, ak-kliv'i-ti, *n.* A rise, as of a hill, viewed from below; ascent.
Accolade, ak-kō-lād', *n.* A ceremony used in conferring knighthood, usually a blow on the shoulder with the flat of a sword.
Accommodate, ak-kom'mō-dāt, *vt.* (accommodating, accommodated). To make suitable; to adjust; to furnish with.
Accommodating, ak-kom'mō-dāt-ing, *p.a.* Obliging; complying.
Accommodation, ak-kom'mō-dā''shon, *n.* Act of accommodating; a convenience; lodgings; loan.
Accompaniment, ak-kum'pa-ni-ment, *n.* That which accompanies; the subordinate part or parts, in music.
Accompany, ak-kum'pa-ni, *vt.* (accompanying, accompanied). To go with; to associate with; to perform music along with.
Accomplice, ak-kom'plis, *n.* An associate, especially in a crime.
Accomplish, ak-kom'plish, *vt.* To fulfil; to execute fully; to perfect.
Accomplishable, ak-kom'plish-a-bl, *a.* That may be accomplished.
Accomplished, ak-kom'plisht, *p.a.* Elegant; having a finished education.
Accomplishment, ak-kom'plish-ment, *n.* Fulfilment; acquirement; embellishment.
Accord, ak-kord', *n.* Harmony; agreement; will.—*vt.* To make to agree; to grant, or concede.—*vi.* To agree; to be in correspondence.
Accordance, ak-kord'ans, *n.* Agreement; conformity; harmony.
Accordant, ak-kord'ant, *a.* Corresponding; consonant; agreeable.
According, ak-kord'ing, *p.a.* Agreeing; harmonizing; agreeable.
Accordingly, ak-kord'ing-li, *adv.* Agreeably; consequently.
Accordion, ak-kord'i-on, *n.* A small melodious, keyed wind-instrument.
Accost, ak-kost', *vt.* To speak to first; to address.
Accouchement, ak-kösh'mong, *n.* Delivery in child-bed.
Accoucheur, ak-kö-shėr', *n.* A man who assists women in child-birth.
Account, ak-kount', *n.* A reckoning; a register of facts relating to money; narration; advantage; end; importance.—*vt.* To reckon; to consider; to deem; to value.—*vi.* To give or render reasons; to explain (with *for*).

Accountability, ak-kount'a-bil''li-ti, *n.* State of being accountable; liability.
Accountable, ak-kount'a-bl, *a.* Liable to be called to account; amenable.
Accountably, ak-kount'a-bli, *adv.* In an accountable manner.
Accountant, ak-kount'ant, *n.* One skilled or employed in accounts; one whose profession is to examine accounts.
Accountantship, ak-kount'ant-ship, *n.* The office or duties of an accountant.
Accoutre, ak-kö'tėr, *vt.* (accoutring, accoutred). To furnish with a military dress and arms.
Accoutrements, ak-kö'tėr-ments, *n.pl.* Military dress and arms; dress.
Accredit, ak-kred'it, *vt.* To give credit or authority to; to receive, as an envoy; to bring into vogue, as a word.
Accredited, ak-kred'it-ed, *p.a.* Authorized; sanctioned.
Accresce, ak-kres', *vi.* To accrue.
Accrescent, ak-kres'ent, *a.* Increasing.
Accretion, ak-krē'shon, *n.* A growing to, or increase by natural growth.
Accretive, ak-krēt'iv, *a.* Increasing by growth.
Accrue, ak-krö', *vi.* (accruing, accrued). To arise or come; to be added.
Accumulate, ak-kū'mū-lāt, *vt.* (accumulating, accumulated). To heap up; to amass.—*vi.* To increase.
Accumulation, ak-kū'mū-lā''shon, *n.* Act of accumulating; a heap; a collection.
Accumulative, ak-kū'mū-lāt-iv, *a.* That accumulates, or is accumulated.
Accumulator, ak-kū'mū-lāt-ėr, *n.* A kind of battery which stores electric energy.
Accuracy, ak'kū-rā-si, *n.* State of being accurate; precision; exactness.
Accurate, ak'kū-rāt, *a.* Done with care; exact; without error.
Accurately, ak'kū-rāt-li, *adv.* Exactly.
Accursed, ak-kėrs'ed, *a.* Lying under a curse; doomed; wicked.
Accusable, ak-kūz'a-bl, *a.* That may be accused.
Accusation, ak-kū-zā'shon, *n.* Act of accusing; impeachment; that of which one is accused.
Accusative, ak-kūz'at-iv, *a.* or *n.* A case in grammar, in English the objective.
Accuse, ak-kūz', *vt.* (accusing, accused). To charge with a crime; to impeach; to censure.
Accused, ak-kūzd', *n.* A person charged with a crime or offence.
Accuser, ak-kūz'ėr, *n.* One who accuses.
Accustom, ak-kus'tum, *vt.* To inure to a custom; to make familiar with by use.
Accustomed, ak-kus'tumd, *p.a.* Familiar by custom; usual; often practised.
Ace, ās, *n.* A unit; a single point on cards or dice; a distinguished airman, who has destroyed many enemy planes.
Acephalous, a-sef'al-us, *a.* Without a head.
Acerbity, a-sėrb'i-ti, *n.* Sourness; bitterness or severity of language.
Acetic, a-set'ik, *a.* Relating to vinegar; sour.
Acetify, a-set'i-fī, *vt.* or *i.* (acetifying, acetified). To turn into acid or vinegar.
Acetous, as-ēt'us, *a.* Having the quality of vinegar; sour; acid.
Acetylene, a-set'i-lēn, *n.* A gas used for lighting houses, &c.
Ache, āk, *vi.* (aching, ached). To be in pain; to be distressed.—*n.* Continued pain.
Achieve, a-chēv, *vt.* (achieving, achieved). To bring to an end; to accomplish; to obtain by effort.
Achievement, a-chēv'ment, *n.* Act of achieving; exploit; an escutcheon.
Aching, āk'ing, *p.a.* Being in continued pain. —*n.* Pain.
Achromatic, ak-rō-mat'ik, *a.* Free from colour.
Acid, as'id, *a.* Sharp, or sour to the taste.—*n.* A sour substance; a substance that with certain other substances forms salts.
Acidifiable, as-id'i-fī-a-bl, *a.* Capable of being acidified.
Acidification, as-id'i-fi-kā''shon, *n.* The act or process of acidifying.
Acidifier, as-id'i-fī-ėr, *n.* A principle whose presence is necessary for acidity.
Acidify, as-id'i-fī, *vt.* (acidifying, acidified). To make acid; to convert into an acid.
Acidity, as-id'i-ti, *n.* Sourness.
Acidulate, as-id'ū-lāt, *vt.* To make moderately acid.
Acidulous, as-id'ū-lus, *a.* Slightly acid.
Acknowledge, ak-nol'lej, *vt.* (acknowledging, acknowledged). To own the knowledge of; to avow; to own or confess.
Acknowledgment, ak-nol'lej-ment, *n.* Act of acknowledging; recognition.
Acme, ak'mē, *n.* The top or highest point.
Acolyte, ak'ol-īt, *n.* One of the lowest order in the Roman church; an attendant.
Aconite, ak'on-īt, *n.* The herb wolf's-bane.
Acorn, ā'korn, *n.* The fruit of the oak.
Acotyledon, a-kot'il-ē''don, *n.* A plant whose seeds have no seed-lobes.
Acotyledonous, a-kot'il-ē''don-us, *a.* Having no seed-lobes.
Acoustic, a-kous'tik, *a.* Pertaining to the sense of hearing, or to the doctrine of sounds.
Acoustics, a-kous'tiks, *n.* The science of sound.
Acquaint, ak-kwānt', *vt.* To make to know; to make familiar; to inform.
Acquaintance, ak-kwānt'ans, *n.* Familiar knowledge; intimacy; a person well known.
Acquaintanceship, ak-kwānt'ans-ship, *n.* State of being acquainted.
Acquiesce, ak-kwi-es', *vi.* (acquiescing, acquiesced). To rest satisfied; to admit without opposition; to comply.
Acquiescence, ak-kwi-es'ens, *n.* Assent.
Acquiescent, ak-kwi-es'ent, *a.* Resting satisfied; submitting.
Acquirable, ak-kwīr'a-bl, *a.* That may be acquired.
Acquire, ak-kwīr', *vt.* (acquiring, acquired). To obtain; to procure.
Acquirement, ak-kwīr'ment, *n.* Act of acquiring; the thing acquired; attainment.
Acquisition, ak-kwi-zi'shon, *n.* Act of acquiring; the thing acquired; gain.
Acquisitive, ak-kwiz'it-iv, *a.* Prone or eager to acquire.
Acquit, ak-kwit', *vt.* (acquitting, acquitted). To set free from a charge or blame; to absolve; to bear or conduct (with refl. pron.).
Acquittal, ak-kwit'al, *n.* A setting free from a charge; a judicial discharge.
Acquittance, ak-kwit'ans, *n.* Discharge or release from a debt.

Acre, ā'kėr, *n.* A quantity of land, containing 4840 square yards.
Acreage, ā'kėr-āj, *n.* The number of acres in a piece of land.
Acred, ā'kėrd, *a.* Possessing acres or landed property.
Acrid, ak'rid, *a.* Sharp; hot or biting to the taste; corroding; harsh.
Acridity, ak-rid'i-ti, *n.* Acrid quality.
Acrimonious, ak-ri-mō'ni-us, *a.* Full of acrimony; severe; sarcastic.
Acrimoniously, ak-ri-mō'ni-us-li, *adv.* With sharpness or acrimony.
Acrimony, ak'ri-mo-ni, *n.* Sharpness; harshness; severity.
Acrobat, ak'rō-bat, *n.* A rope-dancer; one who practises vaulting, tumbling, &c.
Acrobatic, ak'rō-bat-ik, *a.* Pertaining to an acrobat or his performance.
Acrocephalic, ak'rō-se-fal"ik, *a.* High-skulled.
Acrogen, ak'rō-jen, *n.* A plant increasing by extension of the stem at the top.
Acrogenous, a-kroj'en-us, *a.* Pertaining to acrogens.
Acropolis, a-krop'o-lis, *n.* The citadel of a Greek city, as of Athens.
Across, a-kros', *prep.* or *adv.* From side to side; transversely; crosswise.
Acrostic, a-kros'tik, *n.* A composition in verse, in which the first (or other) letters of the lines form the name of a person, &c.
Act, akt, *vi.* To be in action; to exert power; to conduct oneself.—*vt.* To do; to perform, as an assumed part; to counterfeit.—*n.* A deed; power, or the effect of power, put forth; a state of reality; a part of a play; law, as an act of parliament.
Acting, akt'ing, *n.* Action; mode of performing a part of a play.
Actinia, ak-tin'i-a, *n.*; pl. **-iæ.** A sea-anemone.
Actinic, ak-tin'ik, *a.* Pertaining to actinism.
Actinism, ak'tin-izm, *n.* The chemical action of the sun's rays.
Action, ak'shon, *n.* A deed; operation; a series of events; gesture; a suit or process; an engagement, battle.
Actionable, ak'shon-a-bl, *a.* Furnishing ground for an action at law.
Active, ak'tiv, *a.* That acts or is in action; busy; quick; denoting action.
Actively, ak'tiv-li, *adv.* In an active manner.
Activity, ak-tiv'i-ti, *n.* Quality of being active; agility; nimbleness.
Actor, akt'ėr, *n.* One who acts; an active agent; a stage-player.
Actress, akt'res, *n.* A female stage-player.
Actual, ak'tū-al, *a.* Existing in act; real; certain; positive.
Actuality, ak-tū-al'li-ti, *n.* State of being actual; reality.
Actually, ak'tū-al-li, *adv.* In fact; really.
Actuary, ak'tū-a-ri, *n.* A registrar or clerk; a specially able accountant.
Actuate, ak'tū-āt, *vt.* (actuating, actuated). To put into action; to incite.
Aculeate, a-kū'lē-āt, *a.* Having prickles or sharp points.
Acumen, a-kū'men, *n.* Sharpness of perception; sagacity.
Acupressure, ak-ū-pre'shūr, *n.* The stopping of hæmorrhage from arteries, in surgical operations, by needles or wires.
Acute, a-kūt', *a.* Sharpened; sharp; ending in a sharp point; penetrating; having nice sensibility; sharp in sound.
Acutely, a-kūt'li, *adv.* Sharply.
Acuteness, a-kūt'nes, *n.* Sharpness; shrewdness; faculty of nice perception.
Adage, ad'āj, *n.* A proverb; a maxim.
Adagio, a-dä'jō, *a.* and *adv.* In *music*, slow; with grace.—*n.* A slow movement.
Adamant, ad'a-mant, *n.* Any substance of impenetrable hardness; the diamond.
Adamantine, ad-a-mant'in, *a.* Made of adamant; very hard.
Adam's-apple, ad'amz-ap'l, *n.* The prominence on the forepart of the throat.
Adapt, a-dapt', *vt.* To fit; to adjust; to suit.
Adaptability, a-dapt'a-bil"li-ti, *n.* Capability of being adapted.
Adaptable, a-dapt'a-bl, *a.* That may be adapted.
Adaptation, a-dap-tā'shon, *n.* Act of adapting; the result of adapting.
Add, ad, *vt.* To join to; to annex; to say further.
Addendum, ad-den'dum, *n.*; pl. **-da.** A thing to be added; an appendix.
Adder, ad'ėr, *n.* A venomous serpent.
Addict, ad-dikt', *vt.* To apply habitually: generally in a bad sense, with refl. pron.
Addicted, ad-dikt'ed, *p.a.* Habitually given to a practice; inclined; prone.
Addiction, ad-dik'shon, *n.* The state of being addicted; devotion.
Addition, ad-di'shon, *n.* Act of adding; the thing added; increase.
Additional, ad-di'shon-al, *a.* Added on.
Additive, ad'it-iv, *a.* That is to be or may be added.
Addle, ad'l, *a.* Rotten; barren.—*vt.* (addling, addled). To make corrupt or barren.
Addle-headed, ad'l-hed-ed, *a.* Having barren brains; of weak intellect.
Address, ad-dres', *vt.* To direct; to apply to by words or writing; to speak to; to apply (oneself); to write a name and destination on.—*n.* Verbal or written application; speech or discourse to a person; tact; courtship (generally in *plural*); direction of a letter.
Addressee, ad-dres'ē, *n.* One addressed.
Adduce, ad-dūs', *vt.* (adducing, adduced). To bring forward; to cite.
Adducible, ad-dūs'i-bl, *a.* That may be adduced.
Adductor, ad-dukt'ėr, *n.* A muscle which draws one part to another.
Adenoid, ad'en-oid, *a.* Glandular.—*n.pl.* Gland-like morbid growths in the throat behind the soft palate.
Adept, a-dept', *n.* One fully skilled in any art.—*a.* Well skilled; completely versed or acquainted.
Adequacy, ad'ē-kwa-si, *n.* State or quality of being adequate.
Adequate, ad'ē-kwāt, *a.* Equal to; proportionate; fully sufficient.
Adequately, ad'ē-kwāt-li, *adv.* In an adequate manner.
Adhere, ad-hēr', *vi.* (adhering, adhered). To stick; to cling; to remain firm.
Adherence, ad-hēr'ens, *n.* State of adhering; attachment; fidelity.
Adherent, ad-hēr'ent, *a.* Sticking to; united with.—*n.* A follower; a partisan.

Adhesion, ad-hē'zhon, *n.* Act or state of sticking to; adherence.
Adhesive, ad-hē'siv, *a.* Apt or tending to adhere; sticky; tenacious.
Adhibit, ad-hib'it, *vt.* To attach (one's signature).
Adhortatory, ad-hor'ta-tō-ri, *a.* Containing counsel or warning.
Adieu, a-dū', *interj.* Farewell.—*n.*; pl. **-us** or **-ux.** A farewell.
Adipose, ad'i-pōs, *a.* Consisting of or resembling fat; fatty.
Adit, ad'it, *n.* An approach; the horizontal opening into a mine.
Adjacence, Adjacency, ad-jā'sens, ad-jā'sen-si, *n.* State of lying close or contiguous.
Adjacent, ad-jā'sent, *a.* Lying near; adjoining; contiguous; neighbouring.
Adjectival, ad'jek-tiv-al, *a.* Belonging to or like an adjective.
Adjective, ad'jek-tiv, *n.* A word used with a noun, to express some quality or circumstance.
Adjoin, ad-join', *vt.* To join to.—*vi.* To lie or be next; to be contiguous.
Adjoining, ad-join'ing, *p.a.* Adjacent.
Adjourn, ad-jėrn', *vt.* To put off to a future day; to postpone.—*vi.* To leave off for a future meeting.
Adjournment, ad-jėrn'ment, *n.* Act of adjourning; interval during which a public body defers business.
Adjudge, ad-juj', *vt.* To decree judicially; to decide.
Adjudicate, ad-jū'di-kāt, *vt.* To adjudge; to determine judicially.
Adjudication, ad-jū'di-kā''shon, *n.* Judicial sentence; judgment or decision.
Adjudicator, ad-jū'di-kāt-or, *n.* One who adjudicates.
Adjunct, ad'jungkt, *n.* A thing (or person) joined to another.—*a.* United with.
Adjuration, ad-jū-rā'shon, *n.* Act of adjuring; an oath or solemn charge.
Adjure, ad-jūr', *vt.* (adjuring, adjured). To charge on oath; to charge earnestly and solemnly.
Adjust, ad-just', *vt.* To rectify; to make exact; to regulate; to adapt; to settle.
Adjustable, ad-just'a-bl, *a.* That may or can be adjusted.
Adjustment, ad-just'ment, *n.* Act of adjusting; arrangement; settlement.
Adjutancy, ad'jū-tan-si, *n.* Office of an adjutant.
Adjutant, ad'jū-tant, *n.* An officer who assists a commanding officer; a large species of bird allied to the stork.
Admeasure, ad-me'zhūr, *vt.* To ascertain the size or capacity of.
Admeasurement, ad-me'zhūr-ment, *n.* Act of admeasuring; dimensions.
Adminicle, ad-min'i-kl, *n.* Support; aid.
Administer, ad-min'is-tėr, *vt.* To manage; to dispense; to distribute.
Administration, ad-min'is-trā''shon, *n.* Management; executive part of a government.
Administrative, ad-min'is-trāt-iv, *a.* That administers.
Administrator, ad-min-is-trāt'or, *n.* One who manages an intestate estate.
Admirable, ad'mi-ra-bl, *a.* Worthy of admiration; excellent.
Admirably, ad'mi-ra-bli, *adv.* In an admirable manner.
Admiral, ad'mi-ral, *n.* The chief commander of a fleet or navy.
Admiralty, ad'mi-ral-ti, *n.* A board of officials for administering naval affairs; the official buildings of this board.
Admiration, ad-mi-rā'shon, *n.* Wonder mingled with delight; esteem.
Admire, ad-mīr', *vt.* (admiring, admired). To regard with delight or affection.
Admirer, ad-mīr'ėr, *n.* One who admires; a lover.
Admiringly, ad-mīr'ing-li, *adv.* With admiration.
Admissibility, ad-mis'i-bil''li-ti, *n.* Quality of being admissible.
Admissible, ad-mis'i-bl, *a.* That may be admitted.
Admission, ad-mi'shon, *n.* Admittance; access; introduction; concession.
Admit, ad-mit', *vt.* (admitting, admitted). To allow to enter; to grant; to concede.
Admittance, ad-mit'ans, *n.* Permission to enter; entrance; allowance.
Admixture, ad-miks'tūr, *n.* That which is mixed with something else; a mixing.
Admonish, ad-mon'ish, *vt.* To warn; to reprove solemnly or quietly; to exhort.
Admonisher, ad-mon'ish-ėr, *n.* One who admonishes.
Admonition, ad-mō-ni'shon, *n.* Gentle or solemn reproof; instruction; caution.
Admonitory, ad-mon'i-tō-ri, *a.* Containing admonition.
Ado, a-dö', *n.* Stir; bustle; difficulty.
Adobe, a-dō'be, *n.* A sun-dried brick.
Adolescence, ad-ō-les'ens, *n.* A growing up to manhood; the age of youth.
Adolescent, ad-ō-les'ent, *a.* Advancing to manhood.
Adopt, a-dopt', *vt.* To take and treat as a child, giving a title to the rights of a child; to embrace.
Adoption, a-dop'shon, *n.* Act of adopting; state of being adopted.
Adoptive, a-dopt'iv, *a.* Adopting or adopted.
Adorable, a-dōr'a-bl, *a.* Worthy to be adored.
Adorably, a-dōr'a-bli, *adv.* In a manner worthy of adoration.
Adoration, a-dōr-ā'shon, *n.* Worship paid to God; profound reverence.
Adore, a-dōr', *vt.* (adoring, adored). To address in prayer; to worship with reverence and awe; to love intensely.
Adorer, a-dōr'ėr, *n.* One who adores.
Adoringly, a-dōr'ing-li, *adv.* With adoration.
Adorn, a-dorn', *vt.* To deck with ornaments; to embellish; to beautify.
Adown, a-doun', *prep.* Down; towards the lower part of.—*adv.* Down; on the ground.
Adrift, a-drift', *adv.* Floating at random; at the mercy of any impulse.
Adroit, a-droit', *a.* Dexterous; skilful; ready.
Adroitly, a-droit'li, *adv.* With dexterity.
Adroitness, a-droit'nes, *n.* Dexterity.
Adscititious, ad'si-ti''shus, *a.* Additional; not requisite.
Adstriction, ad-strik'shon, *n.* A binding fast.
Adulation, ad-ū-lā'shon, *n.* Servile flattery; excessive praise.

Adulatory, ad'ū-lā-tō-ri, *a.* Flattering; praising excessively or servilely.
Adult, a-dult', *a.* Grown to maturity.—*n.* A person grown to manhood.
Adulterate, a-dul'tėr-āt, *vt.* (adulterating, adulterated). To change to a worse state by mixing; to contaminate with base matter.
Adulterate, a-dul'tėr'āt, *a.* Adulterated.
Adulterated, a-dul'tėr-āt-ed, *p.a.* Debased by admixture.
Adulteration, a-dul'tėr-ā"shon, *n.* Act of adulterating, or state of being adulterated.
Adulterer, a-dul'tėr-ėr, *n.* A man guilty of adultery.
Adulteress, a-dul'tėr-es, *n.* A woman guilty of adultery.
Adulterine, a-dul'tėr-īn, *a.* Proceeding from adulterous commerce; spurious.
Adulterous, a-dul'tėr-us, *a.* Guilty of adultery; pertaining to adultery.
Adulterously, a-dul'tėr-us-li, *adv.* In an adulterous manner.
Adultery, a-dul'tė-ri, *n.* Unfaithfulness to the marriage-bed.
Adumbrate, ad-um'brāt, *vt.* (adumbrating, adumbrated). To give a faint shadow of; to shadow out; to describe faintly.
Adumbration, ad-um-brā'shon, *n.* Act of adumbrating; a faint sketch.
Adust, a-dust', *a.* Burnt up; scorched.
Advance, ad-vans', *vt.* (advancing, advanced). To put forward; to promote; (in *commerce*) to pay beforehand; to supply.—*vi.* To go forward; to be promoted.—*n.* A going forward; preferment; first hint or step; rise in value; a giving beforehand.
Advanced, ad-vanst', *p.a.* In the van of intellectual or religious progress.
Advancement, ad-vans'ment, *n.* Act of moving forward; improvement.
Advantage, ad-van'tāj, *n.* Favourable state; superiority; gain.—*vt.* (advantaging, advantaged). To benefit ; to promote.
Advantageous, ad-van-tāj'us, *a.* Profitable; beneficial; useful.
Advantageously, ad-van-tāj'us-li, *adv.* In an advantageous manner.
Advent, ad'vent, *n.* Arrival; the coming of Christ; the four weeks before Christmas.
Adventitious, ad-ven-ti'shi-us, *a.* Accidental; casual; accessory; foreign.
Adventure, ad-ven'tūr, *n.* Hazardous enterprise; a bold undertaking.—*vt.* To risk or hazard.—*vi.* To dare; to venture.
Adventurer, ad-ven'tūr-ėr, *n.* One who risks, hazards, or braves.
Adventuress, ad-ven'tūr-es, *n.* A female adventurer.
Adventurous, ad-ven'tūr-us, *a.* Prone to incur hazard; daring; full of hazard.
Adventurously, ad-ven'tūr-us-li, *adv.* In a manner to incur hazard.
Adverb, ad'vėrb, *n.* A word which modifies a verb, adjective, or another adverb.
Adverbial, ad-vėrb'i-al, *a.* Pertaining to an adverb.
Adverbially, ad-vėrb'i-al-li, *adv.* In the manner of an adverb.
Adversary, ad'vėr-sa-ri, *n.* An enemy; an antagonist.
Adversative, ad-vėrs'at-iv, *a.* Noting or causing opposition.—*n.* A word denoting opposition.
Adverse, ad'vėrs, *a.* Hostile; unprosperous.
Adversely, ad-vėrs'li, *adv.* In an adverse manner.
Adversity, ad-vėrs'i-ti, *n.* Misfortune; affliction; calamity; distress.
Advert, ad-vėrt', *vi.* To refer or allude to; to regard. (With *to.*)
Advertence, ad-vėrt'ens, *n.* Regard; attention; heedfulness.
Advertent, ad-vėrt'ent, *a.* Attentive.
Advertise, ad-vėr-tīz', *vt.* (advertising, advertised). To inform; to announce; to publish a notice of.
Advertisement, ad-vėr'tiz-ment, *n.* Information; public notice.
Advertiser, ad-vėr-tīz'ėr, *n.* One who advertises.
Advertising, ad-vėr-tīz'ing, *p.a.* Containing or furnishing advertisements.
Advice, ad-vīs', *n.* Opinion offered; counsel; information.
Advisable, ad-vīs'a-bl, *a.* Fitting or proper to be done; expedient; fit.
Advise, ad-vīz', *vt.* (advising, advised). To counsel; to warn; to inform.—*vi.* To deliberate or consider.
Advised, ad-vīzd', *p.a.* Cautious; done with advice.
Advisedly, ad-vīz'ed-li, *adv.* With deliberation or advice.
Adviser, ad-vīz'ėr, *n.* One who advises.
Advocacy, ad'vō-kā-si, *n.* Act of pleading for; defence; vindication.
Advocate, ad'vō-kāt, *n.* One who pleads for another; an intercessor.—*vt.* (advocating, advocated). To plead in favour of; to vindicate.
Advocateship, ad'vō-kāt-ship, *n.* The office or duty of an advocate.
Advowson, ad-vou'sn, *n.* Right or presentation to a benefice in the Church of England.
Adze, adz, *n.* A kind of axe, with the edge at right angles to the handle.
Ædile, ē'dīl, *n.* A Roman magistrate who had the care of public buildings, &c.
Ægis, ē'jis, *n.* A shield; protection.
Æolian, ē-ō'li-an, *a.* Pertaining to Æolus, the god of the winds; played upon by the wind.
Aerate, ā'ėr-āt, *vt.* (aerating, aerated). To put air into; to combine with carbonic acid.
Aeration, ā-ėr-ā'shon, *n.* Impregnation of a liquid with carbonic acid gas.
Aerial, ā-ē'ri-al, *a.* Belonging to the air; high; lofty.—*n.* The overhead structure of a wireless station, used for transmitting and receiving electrical oscillations.
Aerie, ē'rē, *n.* The nest of a bird of prey; a brood of such birds.
Aerify, ā'ėr-i-fī, *vt.* (aerifying, aerified). To infuse air into.
Aerodrome, ār'o-drōm, *n.* An area of land or water set apart for aircraft to land at or take off from.
Aerolite, ā'ėr-ō-līt, *n.* A meteoric stone; a meteorite.
Aerology, ā-ėr-ol'o-ji, *n.* The science of atmospheric phenomena.
Aerometer, ā-ėr-om'et-ėr, *n.* An instrument for finding the density of air and gases.
Aerometry, ā-ėr-om'et-ri, *n.* The science of measuring the density of air and gases.
Aeronaut, ā-ėr-ō-nąt, *n.* One who sails or floats in the air.
Aeronautic, ā'ėr-ō-nąt"ik, *a.* Pertaining to aerial sailing.

Aeronautics, ā′ėr-ō-nạt″iks, *n.* The science or art of flying in aircraft.

Aeroplane, ār′o-plān, *n.* A heavier-than-air power-driven flying-machine having one or two pairs of wings (monoplane or biplane) which support it owing to the reaction of the air.

Aerostatic, ā′ėr-ō-stat″ik, *a.* Pertaining to aerostatics.

Aerostatics, ā′ėr-ō-stat″iks, *n.* The science which treats of air in a state of rest.

Æsculapian, es-kū-lā′pi-an, *a.* Pertaining to Æsculapius, the god of medicine.

Æsthetic, Æsthetical, ēs-thet′ik, ēs-thet′ik-al, or es-, *a.* Pertaining to æsthetics.

Æsthetics, ēs-thet′iks, or es-, *n.* The science of the beautiful; the philosophy of taste.

Ætiology, ē-ti-ol′o-ji, *n.* The doctrine of causation; the assigning of causes or reasons.

Afar, a-fär′, *adv.* At, to, or from a distance.

Affability, af-fa-bil′i-ti, *n.* Courteousness; civility; urbanity.

Affable, af′fa-bl, *a.* Easy to be spoken to; courteous; accessible.

Affably, af′fa-bli, *adv.* In an affable manner.

Affair, af-fār′, *n.* That which is to do, or which is done; business.

Affect, af-fekt′, *vt.* To act upon; to move the feelings of; to aim at; to pretend.

Affectation, af-fek-tā′shon, *n.* False pretence; an artificial air put on by a person.

Affected, af-fekt′ed, *p.a.* Inclined to; full of affectation; assumed artificially.

Affectedly, af-fekt′ed-li, *adv.* In an affected manner; feignedly.

Affecting, af-fekt′ing, *p.a.* Pathetic; tender; exciting.

Affectingly, af-fekt′ing-li, *adv.* In an affecting manner.

Affection, af-fek′shon, *n.* The state of being affected; fondness; love.

Affectionate, af-fek′shon-āt, *a.* Tender; loving; fond.

Affectionately, af-fek′shon-āt-li, *adv.* Fondly.

Affectioned, af-fek′shond, *a.* Inclined.

Affeer, af-fēr′, *vt.* To assess or settle, as an arbitrary fine.

Afferent, af′fėr-ent, *a.* Carrying to or inwards.

Affiance, af-fī′ans, *n.* Faith pledged; marriage contract; reliance.—*vt.* (affiancing, affianced). To pledge one's faith to; to betroth.

Affianced, af-fī′anst, *p.a.* Betrothed.

Affidavit, af-fi-dā′vit, *n.* A written declaration upon oath.

Affiliate, af-fil′li-āt, *vt.* (affiliating, affiliated). To adopt; to assign to a father; to unite to a chief society or body.

Affiliation, af-fil′li-ā″shon, *n.* Act of affiliating; association.

Affinity, af-fin′i-ti, *n.* Relation by marriage; resemblance; chemical attraction.

Affirm, af-fėrm′, *vt.* To assert; to declare; to ratify.—*vi.* To declare solemnly.

Affirmable, af-fėrm′a-bl, *a.* That may be affirmed.

Affirmation, af-fėrm-ā′shon, *n.* Act of affirming; declaration; ratification.

Affirmative, af-fėrm′at-iv, *a.* That affirms; positive.—*n.* That which expresses assent.

Affirmatively, af-fėrm′at-iv-li, *adv.* In an affirmative manner.

Affix, af-fiks′, *vt.* To fasten to; to subjoin.—*n.* af′fiks. A syllable or letter added to a word.

Afflatus, af-flā′tus, *n.* Inspiration.

Afflict, af-flikt′, *vt.* To distress; to grieve; to harass.

Afflicting, af-flikt′ing, *p.a.* Distressing.

Affliction, af-flik′shon, *n.* State of being afflicted; distress; grief.

Afflictive, af-flikt′iv, *a.* Containing affliction; painful.

Affluence, af′flū-ens, *n.* A flowing to; abundance; opulence; wealth.

Affluent, af′flū-ent, *a.* Flowing to; wealthy; abundant.—*n.* A river that flows into another river.

Afflux, af′fluks, *n.* A flowing to; that which flows to.

Afford, af-fōrd′, *vt.* To yield; to supply; to be able to give, grant, buy, or expend.

Afforest, af-for′est, *vt.* To convert into forest.

Affranchise, af-fran′chiz, *vt.* To make free.

Affray, af-frā′, *n.* A tumult; brawl.

Affright, af-frīt′, *vt.* To frighten; to terrify. —*n.* Sudden or great fear.

Affront, af-frunt′, *vt.* To insult; to offend.—*n.* Open defiance; insult.

Affronting, af-frunt′ing, *p.a.* Contumelious; abusive; insulting.

Afield, a-fēld′, *adv.* To or in the field.

Afloat, a-flōt′, *adv.* or *a.* Floating; in circulation (as a rumour).

Afoot, a-fụt′, *adv.* On foot; in action.

Aforehand, a-fōr′hand, *adv.* Beforehand; before.

Aforementioned, a-fōr′men-shond, *a.* Mentioned before.

Aforenamed, a-fōr′nāmd, *a.* Named before.

Aforesaid, a-fōr′sād, *a.* Said before.

Afraid, a-frād′, *a.* Struck with fear; fearful.

Afresh, a-fresh′, *adv.* Anew; again.

African, af′rik-an, *a.* Belonging to Africa.—*n.* A native of Africa.

Afrikander, af′rik-an-dėr, *n.* A native of South Africa, born of white, especially of Dutch, parents.

Aft, äft, *a.* or *adv.* Abaft; astern.

After, äft′ėr, *a.* Later in time; subsequent.—*prep.* Later in time than; behind; according to; in imitation of.—*adv.* Later in time.

After-birth, äft′ėr-bėrth, *n.* That which is expelled from the uterus after the birth of a child.

After-crop, äft′ėr-krop, *n.* A second crop in the same year.

After-damp, äft′ėr-damp, *n.* Choke-damp arising from an explosion of fire-damp.

Aftermath, äft′ėr-math, *n.* A second crop of grass in the same season; consequences; results.

Aftermost, äft′ėr-mōst, *a.* Hindmost.

Afternoon, äft′ėr-nön, *n.* The part of the day which follows noon.

After-piece, äft′ėr-pēs, *n.* A piece performed after a play; a farce.

After-thought, äft′ėr-thạt, *n.* Reflection after an act.

Afterward, Afterwards, äft′ėr-wėrd, äft′ėr-wėrdz, *adv.* In subsequent time.

Again, a-gen′, *adv.* Once more; further.

Against, a-genst′, *prep.* In opposition to; in expectation of.

Agape, a-gāp′, *a.* With the mouth wide open.

Agate, ag′āt, *n.* A semi-pellucid mineral.

Age, āj, *n.* A period of time; an epoch; number of years during which a person has lived;

decline of life; oldness; legal maturity.—*vi.* and *t.* (aging, aged). To grow or make old; to show signs of advancing age.

Aged, āj'ed, *a.* Old; having a certain age.

Agency, ā'jen-si, *n.* Instrumentality; office or business of an agent.

Agenda, a-jen'da, *n.pl.* Memoranda; business to be transacted at a meeting.

Agent, ā'jent, *n.* One who acts; a deputy; an active cause or power.

Agglomerate, ag-glom'mė-rāt, *vt.* To gather into a mass.—*vi.* To grow into a mass.

Agglomeration, ag-glom'mė-rā''shon, *n.* Act of agglomerating; heap.

Agglutinant, ag-glū'tin-ant, *n.* Any viscous or gluey substance.

Agglutinate, ag-glū'tin-āt, *vt.* To glue to; to cause to adhere.

Agglutination, ag-glū'tin-ā''shon, *n.* Act of agglutinating; in *philology*, the loose combination of roots to form words.

Aggrandize, ag'gran-dīz, *vt.* To make great; to magnify.

Aggrandizement, ag'gran-dīz-ment, *n.* Act of aggrandizing; augmentation.

Aggravate, ag'gra-vāt, *vt.* (aggravating, aggravated). To intensify; to exasperate.

Aggravating, ag'gra-vāt'ing, *p.a.* Making worse; provoking.

Aggravation, ag-gra-vā'shon, *n.* Act of aggravating; provocation.

Aggregate ag'grē-gāt, *vt.* To bring together; to heap up.—*a.* Formed of parts collected.—*n.* A sum, mass, or assemblage of particulars.

Aggregately, ag'grē-gāt-li, *adv.* Collectively.

Aggregation, ag-grē-gā'shon, *n.* Act of aggregating; an aggregate or collection.

Aggression, ag-gre'shon, *n.* The first act of hostility; attack.

Aggressive, ag-gres'iv, *a.* Taking the first step against; prone to encroachment.

Aggressor, ag-gres'or, *n.* The person who commences hostilities.

Aggrieve, ag-grēv', *vt.* To pain, oppress, or injure.

Aghast, a-gast', *a.* or *adv.* Amazed; stupefied. Also *agast.*

Agile, aj'il, *a.* Ready to act; nimble.

Agility, a-jil'i-ti, *n.* Nimbleness; activity.

Agio, ā'ji-ō, *n.* The difference in value between paper and metallic money.

Agitate, aj'it-āt, *vt.* (agitating, agitated). To put in violent motion; to shake briskly; to excite; to consider; to discuss.

Agitated, aj'it-āt-ed, *p.a.* Disturbed.

Agitation, aj-it-ā'shon, *n.* Excitement; emotion; discussion.

Agitator, aj'it-āt-or, *n.* One who excites discontent, sedition, or revolt.

Aglet, ag'let, *n.* A point or tag at the ends of fringes or of lace.

Agnate, ag'nāt, *a.* Related by the father's side.

Agnomen, ag-nō'men, *n.* An additional name or epithet conferred on a person.

Agnostic, ag-nos'tik, *n.* One who disclaims any knowledge of God or of anything but material phenomena.—*a.* Pertaining to agnostics or their doctrines.

Agnosticism, ag-nos'ti-sizm, *n.* The doctrines or belief of agnostics.

Ago, a-gō', *adv.* or *a.* Past; gone.

Agog, a-gog', *adv.* In eager excitement.

Agoing, a-gō'ing, *adv.* In motion.

Agonize, ag'ō-nīz, *vi.* (agonizing, agonized). To writhe with extreme pain.—*vt.* To distress with extreme pain; to torture.

Agonizing, ag'ō-nīz-ing, *p.a.* Giving extreme pain.

Agonizingly, ag'ō-nīz-ing-li, *adv.* With extreme anguish.

Agony, ag'ō-ni, *n.* Extreme pain of body or mind; anguish; the pangs of death.

Agora, ag'o-ra, *n.* A public assembly in ancient Greece; the market-place.

Agrarian, a-grā'ri-an, *a.* Relating to lands.

Agrarianism, a-grā'ri-an-izm, *n.* The principles of those who favour an equal division of lands.

Agree, a-grē', *vi.* (agreeing, agreed). To be in concord; to correspond; to suit.

Agreeable, a-grē'a-bl, *a.* Suitable to; pleasing; grateful.

Agreeableness, a-grē'a-bl-nes, *n.* Quality of being agreeable; suitableness.

Agreeably, a-grē'a-bli, *adv.* In an agreeable manner; conformably.

Agreement, a-grē'ment, *n.* Harmony; conformity; stipulation.

Agrestic, a-gres'tik, *a.* Rural; rustic.

Agricultural, ag-ri-kul'tūr-al, *a.* Pertaining to agriculture.

Agriculture, ag'ri-kul-tūr, *n.* The art or science of cultivating the ground.

Agriculturist, ag-ri-kul'tūr-ist, *n.* One skilled in agriculture.

Aground, a-ground', *adv.* Stranded.

Ague, ā'gū, *n.* An intermittent fever, with cold fits and shivering.

Agued, ā'gūd, *p.a.* Having a fit of ague.

Aguish, ā'gū-ish, *a.* Having the qualities of an ague; shivering.

Ah, ä, *interj.* Expressing surprise, pity, &c.

Aha, ä-hä', *interj.* Expressing triumph or contempt.

Ahead, a-hed', *adv.* Before; onward.

Ahoy, a-hoi', *exclam.* A sea-term used in hailing.

Aid, ād, *vt.* To help; to relieve.—*n.* Help; assistance; a helper.

Aide-de-camp, ād-de-kong, *n.*; pl. **Aides-de-camp.** An officer attendant on a general.

Aigret, Aigrette, ā'gret, ā-gret', *n.* A plume or ornament for the head composed of feathers or precious stones.

Aiguille, ā'gwil, *n.* A needle-like pointed rock or mountain mass, or mass of ice.

Ail, āl, *vt.* To pain; to affect with uneasiness.—*vi.* To be in pain or trouble.

Ailment, āl'ment, *n.* Pain; disease.

Aim, ām, *vi.* To point with a missive weapon; to intend; to endeavour.—*vt.* To level or direct as a firearm.—*n.* That which is aimed at; direction; purpose; drift.

Aimless, ām'les, *a.* Without aim.

Air, ār, *n.* The fluid which we breathe; a light breeze; a tune; mien; *pl.* affected manner.—*vt.* To expose to the air; to ventilate; to dry. **Air Chief Marshal,** *n.* Officer in the Royal Air Force ranking with an Admiral in the Navy, or a General in the Army. **Air Commodore,** *n.* Officer in the Royal Air Force ranking with a Commodore in the Navy, or a Brigadier in the Army. **Air Marshal,** *n.* Officer in the Royal Air Force ranking with a Vice-Admiral in the Navy, or a Lieutenant-General in the Army. **Air Vice-**

Marshal, *n*. Officer in the Royal Air Force ranking with a Rear-Admiral in the Navy, or a Major-General in the Army.

Air-bladder, ãr'blad-dėr, *n*. The bladder of a fish containing air.

Aircraft, ãr-kraft, *n*. A general name for craft designed for the navigation of the air, such as aeroplanes, airships or balloons.

Air-cushion, ãr'kush-on, *n*. An inflated bag of air-tight cloth or indiarubber.

Airgraph, ãr'graf, *n*. A letter reproduced as a micro-film, sent home by air, and enlarged before delivery to the addressee.

Air-gun, ãr'gun, *n*. A gun to discharge bullets by means of condensed air.

Airily, ãr'i-li, *adj*. In an airy manner.

Airiness, ãr'i-nes, *n*. Openness; gaiety.

Airing, ãr'ing, *n*. An exposure to the air or to a fire; an excursion in the open air.

Airport, ãr'pōrt, *n*. A large aerodrome, usually having customs houses, servicing facilities, &c.

Air-pump, ãr'pump, *n*. A machine for pumping the air out of a vessel.

Air-shaft, ãr'shaft, *n*. A passage for air into a mine.

Air-tight, ãr'tīt, *a*. So tight or compact as not to let air pass.

Airy, ā'ri, *a*. Open to the free air; high in air; light; thin; vain; gay.

Aisle, īl, *n*. A wing or side of a church; a passage in a church.

Aitchbone, āch'bōn, *n*. An ox's rump-bone.

Ajar, a-jär', *adv*. Partly open, as a door.

Akee, a-kē', *n*. The fruit of a W. African tree, now common in the W. Indies, &c.

Akimbo, a-kim'bō, *pred.a.* or *adv*. With the elbow outwards and the hand on the hip.

Akin, a-kin', *a*. Of kin; related to; partaking of the same properties.

Alabaster, al'a-bas-tėr, *n*. A soft marble-like mineral.—*a*. Made of alabaster.

Alack, a-lak', *interj*. Expressing sorrow.

Alacrity, a-lak'ri-ti, *n*. Liveliness; cheerful readiness; promptitude.

Alamode, ä-lä-mōd', *adv*. According to fashion.

Alarm, a-lärm', *n*. A call to arms; sudden surprise; fright; a notice of danger.—*vt*. To give notice of danger; to disturb.

Alarm-bell, a-lärm'bel, *n*. A bell that gives notice of danger.

Alarm clock, a-lärm' klok, *n*. A clock which can be set to awaken sleepers at a given time by ringing a small gong.

Alarm-gun, a-lärm'gun, *n*. A gun fired as a signal of alarm.

Alarming, a-lärm'ing, *p.a*. Terrifying.

Alarmingly, a-lärm'ing-li, *adv*. So as to excite apprehension.

Alarmist, a-lärm'ist, *n*. One prone to excite alarm.—*a*. Exciting unnecessary alarm.

Alarum, a-lär'um, *n*. Alarm. (Poet.)

Alas, a-las', *interj*. Expressing grief, pity, &c.

Alb, alb, *n*. A long robe of white linen.

Albata, al-bā'ta, *n*. German silver.

Albatross, al'ba-tros, *n*. An aquatic bird of southern seas, the largest sea-bird known.

Albeit, al'bē'it, *adv*. Be it so; although.

Albino, al-bī'nō, *n*. A person with abnormally white skin and hair, and pink eyes.

Album, al'bum, *n*. A book for autographs, sketches, &c.

Albumen, al-bū'men, *n*. The white of an egg; a substance of the same kind found in animals and vegetables.

Albuminous, al-bū'min-us, *a*. Pertaining to or having the properties of albumen.

Alburnum, al-bėr'num, *n*. Sap-wood of a tree.

Alchemist, al'kem-ist, *n*. One who practised alchemy.

Alchemy, al'ke-mi, *n*. An obsolete science, aiming at changing metals into gold, &c.

Alcohol, al'kō-hol, *n*. Pure spirit of a highly intoxicating nature.

Alcoholic, al-kō-hol'ik, *a*. Pertaining to alcohol.

Alcoholism, al'kō-hol-izm, *n*. The condition of habitual drunkards.

Alcove, al'kov, *n*. A recess.

Aldehyde, al'dē-hīd, *n*. A colourless liquid produced by oxidation of alcohol.

Alder, al'dėr, *n*. A tree generally growing in moist land.

Alderman, al'dėr-man, *n*.; pl. **-men.** A magistrate of a town.

Ale, āl, *n*. A fermented malt liquor; beer.

Alee, a-lē', *adv*. On the lee side of a vessel.

Alembic, a-lem'bik, *n*. A vessel used in chemical distillation.

Alert, a-lėrt', *a*. Vigilant; quick; prompt.—*n*. An air-raid warning.

Alertness, a-lėrt'nes, *n*. Briskness; activity.

Alexandrine, al'legz-an"drin, *n*. A line with six stresses.

Alga, al'ga, *n*.; pl. **-gæ,** A sea-weed.

Algebra, al'je-bra, *n*. The science of computing by symbols.

Algebraic, Algebraical, al-jē-brā'ik, al-jē-brā'ik-al, *a*. Pertaining to algebra.

Algebraically, al-jē-brā'ik-al-li, *adv*. By algebraic process.

Algebraist, al'jē-brā-ist, *n*. One versed in algebra.

Alias, ā'li-as, *adv*. Otherwise.—*n*.; pl. **-ses,** An assumed name.

Alibi, al'i-bī, *n*. The plea of a person who, charged with a crime, alleges that he was elsewhere when the crime was committed.

Alien, āl'yen, *a*. Foreign; estranged from.—*n*. A foreigner.

Alienable, āl'yen-a-bl, *a*. That may be alienated or transferred to another.

Alienate, āl'yen-āt, *vt*. (alienating, alienated). To transfer to another; to estrange.

Alienation, āl'yen-ā'shon, *n*. Act of alienating.

Alight, a-līt', *vi*. To get down; to settle on.

Alight, a-līt', *pred.a.* or *adv*. Lighted; kindled

Alike, a-līk', *a*. Like; similar.—*adv*. In the same manner, form, or degree.

Aliment, al'i-ment, *n*. Nourishment; food.

Alimental, al-i-ment'al, *a*. Nourishing.

Alimentary, al-i-ment'a-ri, *a*. Pertaining to aliment or food.

Alimony, al'i-mo-ni, *n*. Allowance to a woman legally separated from her husband.

Aliped, al'i-ped, *n*. A wing-footed animal.

Aliquot, al'i-kwot, *a*. A part of a number which divides the whole without remainder.

Alive, a-līv', *a*. Living; lively; susceptible.

Alkalescent, al-ka-les'ent, *a*. Slightly alkaline.

Alkali, al'ka-li, *n*.; pl. **-ies** or **-is.** A substance, as potash and soda, which neutralizes acids and unites with oil or fat to form soap.

Alkaline, al'ka-lin, *a*. Having the properties of an alkali.

Alkaloid, al'ka-loid, *n.* A substance resembling an alkali, or having alkaline properties.
Alkoran, al-kō'ran, *n.* The Koran.
All, al, *a.* Every part; every one.—*n.* The whole; everything.—*adv.* Wholly; entirely.
Allah, al'la, *n.* The Arabic name of God.
Allay, al-lā', *vt.* To repress; to assuage.
Allegation, al-lē-gā'shon, *n.* Affirmation; declaration.
Allege, al-lej', *vt.* (alleging, alleged). To adduce; to assert; to plead in excuse.
Allegiance, al-lē'ji-ans, *n.* Loyalty.
Allegoric, Allegorical, al-li-gor'ik, al-li-gor'ik-al, *a.* Pertaining to allegory; figurative.
Allegorically, al-lē-gor'ik-al-li, *adv.* By way of allegory.
Allegorist, al'li-gō-rist, *n.* One who allegorizes.
Allegorize, al'li-gō-rīz, *vt.* To turn into allegory.—*vi.* To use allegory.
Allegory, al'li-gō-ri, *n.* A speech or discourse which conveys a meaning different from the literal one.
Allegro, al-lā'grō. A word denoting a brisk sprightly movement.
Alleluiah, al-lē-lū'ya, *n.* Praise to Jehovah; a word used to express pious joy.
Allergic, a-ler'jik, *a.* Possessing allergy.
Allergy, al'er-je, *n.* A state of the body in which the cells are specially sensitive to certain substances, usually proteins.
Alleviate, al-lē'vi-āt, *vt.* (alleviating, alleviated). To make light; to assuage.
Alleviation, al-lē-vi-ā'shon, *n.* Act of alleviating; mitigation.
Alley, al'i, *n.* A narrow walk or passage.
All-fools' Day, al'fölz'dā, *n.* 1st April.
All-hallow, All-hallows, al-hal'lō, al-hal'lōz, *n.* All-Saints' Day.
Alliance, al-lī'ans, *n.* State of being allied; confederacy; league.
Allied, al-līd', *p.a.* United by treaty.
Alligation, al-li-gā'shon, *n.* Act of tying together; a rule of arithmetic.
Alligator, al'li-gā-tor, *n.* The American crocodile.
Alliteration, al-lit-ėr-ā'shon, *n.* The repetition of a letter at the beginning of two or more words in close succession.
Alliterative, al-lit'ėr-at-iv, *a.* Pertaining to alliteration.
Allocate, al'lō-kāt, *vt.* (allocating, allocated). To distribute; to assign to each his share.
Allocation, al-lō-kā'shon, *n.* Distribution; assignment.
Allocution, al-lō-kū'shon, *n.* The act or manner of speaking; a formal address.
Allodial, al-lō'di-al, *a.* Held independent of a lord paramount.
Allodium, al-lō'di-um, *n.* Freehold estate.
Allomorphism, al-lo-mor'fizm, *n.* Difference of form, with sameness of substance.
Allopathic, al-lō-path'ik, *a.* Pertaining to allopathy.
Allopathy, al-lop'a-thi, *n.* The ordinary mode of curing diseases, by using medicines which produce a condition contrary to that of the disease.
Allot, al-lot', *vt.* (allotting, allotted). To give by lot; to apportion.
Allotment, al-lot'ment, *n.* Act of allotting; a share allotted.
Allotropy, al-lot'ro-pi, *n.* The capability of substances of existing in more than one form.
Allow, al-lou', *vt.* To grant; to admit; to abate; to bestow, as compensation.
Allowable, al-lou'a-bl, *a.* That may be allowed.
Allowably, al-lou'a-bli, *adv.* In an allowable manner.
Allowance, al-lou'ans, *n.* Act of allowing; that which is allowed; abatement.
Alloy, al-loi', *vt.* To mix with baser metals; to abate by mixture.—*n.* A baser metal mixed with a finer; a metallic compound.
All-saints' Day, al'sānts dā, *n.* 1st November.
All-souls' Day, al'sōlz dā, *n.* 2nd November.
All-spice, al-spīs, *n.* Pimento or Jamaica pepper, supposed to combine many different flavours.
Allude, al-lūd', *vi.* (alluding, alluded). To refer to; to hint at.
Allure, al-lūr', *vt.* (alluring, allured). To draw by some lure; to entice; to decoy.
Allurement, al-lūr'ment, *n.* That which allures; temptation; enticement.
Alluring, al-lūr'ing, *p.a.* Attractive.
Alluringly, al-lūr'ing-li, *adv.* In an alluring manner.
Allusion, al-lū'zhon, *n.* The act of alluding; a hint; a reference.
Allusive, Allusory, al-lū'siv, al-lū'so-ri, *a.* Containing allusion.
Alluvial, al-lū'vi-al, *a.* Deposited by water.
Alluvion, al-lū'vi-on, *n.* Land added to a property by soil washed up by the sea or a river.
Alluvium, al-lū'vi-um, *n.*; pl. **-via.** Soil deposited by the action of water.
Ally, al-lī', *vt.* (allying, allied). To unite by friendship, marriage, or treaty; to associate. *n.* One related by marriage or other tie; an associate.
Almanac, al'ma-nak, *n.* A calendar of days, weeks, and months, &c.
Almightiness, al-mī'ti-nes, *n.* Omnipotence.
Almighty, al-mī'ti, *a.* Omnipotent.—*n.* God.
Almond, ä'mund, *n.* The nut of the almond-tree; *pl.* the tonsils of the throat.
Almoner, al'mon-ėr, *n.* A dispenser of alms.
Almonry, al'mon-ri, *n.* The place where alms are distributed.
Almost, al'most, *adv.* Nearly; well-nigh; for the greatest part.
Alms, ämz, *n.pl.* A charitable gift.
Alms-deed, ämz'dēd, *n.* An act of charity.
Alms-house, ämz'hous, *n.* A house where poor persons are lodged and supported.
Alms-man, ämz'man, *n.* One supported by alms.
Aloe, al'ō, *n.* A succulent plant; *pl.* a bitter purgative medicine.
Aloetic, al-ō-et'ik, *a.* Pertaining to aloes.
Aloft, a-loft', *adv.* In the sky; on high.
Alone, a-lōn', *a.* Solitary.—*adv.* Separately.
Along, a-long', *adv.* Lengthwise; forward.—*prep.* By the side of; lengthwise.
Aloof, a-löf', *adv.* At a distance; apart.
Aloud, a-loud', *adv.* Loudly.
Alp, alp, *n.* A high mountain.
Alpaca, al-pak'a, *n.* A Peruvian animal, with long, soft, and woolly hair; cloth made of its hair, or a similar cloth.
Alpenstock, al'pen-stok, *n.* A long stick shod with iron, used in climbing mountains.
Alpha, al'fa, *n.* The first letter in the Greek alphabet; the first or beginning.

Alphabet, al'fa-bet, *n.* The letters of a language arranged in the customary order.
Alphabetical, al-fa-bet'ik-al, *a.* In the order of an alphabet.
Alphabetically, al-fa-bet'ik-al-li, *adv.* In an alphabetical manner or order.
Alpine, al'pīn, *a.* Pertaining to high mountains.
Already, al-red'i, *adv.* Before or by this time; even now.
Also, al'sō, *adv.* Likewise; in the same manner, further.
Altar, al'tėr, *n.* An elevated place on which sacrifices were offered; the communion table.
Altar-cloth, al'tėr-kloth, *n.* A cloth to lay upon an altar in churches.
Altar-piece, al'tėr-pēs, *n.* A painting placed over the altar in a church.
Alter, al'tėr, *vt.* To make some change in; to vary.—*vi.* To vary.
Alterable, al'tėr-a-bl, *a.* That may alter, or be altered.
Alteration, al-tėr-ā'shon, *n.* Partial change or variation.
Alterative, al'tėr-at-iv, *a.* Causing alteration. —*n.* A medicine which induces a change in the habit or constitution.
Altercate, al'tėr-kāt, *vi.* (altercating, altercated). To dispute; to wrangle.
Altercation, al-tėr-kā'shon, *n.* Heated dispute; wrangle.
Alternate, al-tėr'nāt, *a.* Being by turns.—*vt.* (alternating, alternated). To cause to follow by turns; to interchange.—*vi.* To happen or act by turns.
Alternately, al-tėrn'āt-li, *adv.* By turns.
Alternation, al-tėrn-ā'shon, *n.* Reciprocal succession; interchange.
Alternative, al-tėrn'at-iv, *n.* A choice of two things.
Alternatively, al-tėrn'at-iv-li, *adv.* In the manner of alternatives.
Although, al'ᴛʜō', *conj.* Be it so; admit all that.
Altitude, al'ti-tūd, *n.* Height; eminence; elevation.
Alto, al'tō, *a.* High.—*n.* In *music*, contralto.
Altogether, al-tö-geᴛʜ'ėr, *adv.* Wholly; entirely; without exception.
Alto-rilievo (or -re-), al'tō-rē-lyā"vō, re-lyā", *n.* High relief: a term in sculpture.
Altruism, al'trö-izm, *n.* Devotion to others or to humanity; the opposite of selfishness.
Altruistic, al-trö-ist'ik, *a.* Pertaining or relating to altruism.
Alum, al'um, *n.* An astringent salt of great use in medicine and the arts.
Alumina, al-ū'min-a, *n.* The oxide of aluminium; the chief ingredient of clay.
Aluminium, al-ū-min'i-um, *n.* A very light metal of a silvery white colour.
Alumnus, a-lum'nus, *n.*; pl. **-ni.** A pupil; a graduate of a university.
Alveolar, Alveolate, al-vē'o-lėr, al-vē'o-lāt, *a.* Containing sockets; resembling a honeycomb.
Alvine, al'vīn, *a.* Belonging to the lower belly.
Always, al'wāz, *adv.* At all times; continually.
Am, am. The first person singular, present tense, indicative mood, of the verb *to be*.
Amain, a-mān', *adv.* Vigorously.
Amalgam, a-mal'gam, *n.* A compound of quicksilver with another metal; a compound.
Amalgamate, a-mal'gam-āt, *vt.* To mix, as quicksilver with another metal.—*vi.* To unite in an amalgam; to blend.
Amalgamation, a-mal'gam-ā"shon, *n.* The act or operation of amalgamating.
Amanuensis, a-man'ū-en"sis, *n.*; pl. **-ses.** One who writes what another dictates.
Amaranth, am'a-ranth, *n.* The unfading flower; a colour inclining to purple.
Amaranthine, am-a-ran'thin, *a.* Unfading.
Amaryllis, am-a-ril'lis, *n.* Lily-asphodel.
Amass, a-mas', *vt.* To form into a mass; to accumulate; to heap up.
Amateur, am-a-tūr', *n.* A lover of any art or science, not a professor.
Amatory, am'a-tō-ri, *a.* Relating to love; causing love; amorous.
Amaze, a-māz', *vt.* (amazing, amazed). To astonish; to bewilder.
Amazedly, a-māz'ed-li, *adv.* With amazement.
Amazement, a-māz'ment, *n.* Wonder; perplexity.
Amazing, a-māz'ing, *p.a.* Very wonderful.
Amazingly, a-māz'ing-li, *adv.* In an astonishing degree.
Amazon, am'a-zon, *n.* A warlike or masculine woman; a virago.
Amazonian, am-a-zō'ni-an, *a.* Relating to the Amazons.
Ambassador, am-bas'sa-dor, *n.* A representative of a sovereign or state at a foreign court.
Ambassadress, am-bas'sa-dres, *n.* The wife of an ambassador.
Amber, am'bėr, *n.* A mineralized pale-yellow resin of extinct pine-trees.
Ambergris, am'bėr-grēs, *n.* A fragrant, solid, opaque, ash-coloured substance, obtained from the spermaceti whale.
Ambidexter, am-bi-deks'tėr, *n.* One who uses both hands with equal facility.
Ambidextrous, am-bi-deks'trus, *a.* Using both hands alike.
Ambient, am'bi-ent, *a.* Encompassing.
Ambiguity, am-bi-gū'i-ti, *n.* Doubtfulness of signification.
Ambiguous, am-big'ū-us, *a.* Of uncertain signification; doubtful.
Ambiguously, am-big'ū-us-li, *adv.* In an ambiguous manner.
Ambit, am'bit, *n.* Compass; scope.
Ambition, am-bi'shon, *n.* Desire of preferment or power.
Ambitious, am-bi'shus, *a.* Aspiring.
Ambitiously, am-bi'shus-li, *adv.* In an ambitious manner.
Amble, am'bl, *vi.* (ambling, ambled). To move, as a horse, by lifting the two legs on each side alternately; to go between a walk and a trot.—*n.* A peculiar motion of a horse; a pace between a walk and a trot.
Ambler, am'blėr, *n.* A horse which ambles.
Ambrosia, am-brō'zhi-a, *n.* The imaginary food of the gods, which conferred immortality.
Ambrosial, am-brō'zhi-al, *a.* Of the nature of ambrosia; fragrant; delicious.
Ambulance, am'bū-lans, *n.* An itinerant hospital; a wagon for the sick or wounded.
Ambulatory, am'bū-lā-tō-ri, *a.* Movable.—*n.* A part of a building to walk in.
Ambuscade, am-bus-kād', *n.* The act or place of lying in wait in order to surprise; the troops lying in wait; ambush.
Ambush, am'bush, *n.* Ambuscade.

Ameliorate, a-mēl'yor-āt, *vt.* To make better.
Amelioration, a-mēl'yor-ā"shon, *n.* A making better; improvement.
Amen, ā-men', *adv.* So be it.
Amenable, a-mēn'a-bl, *a.* Accountable; responsible.
Amend, a-mend', *vt.* To correct; to improve. —*vi.* To grow better.
Amende, ā-mängd, *n.* A fine; reparation.
Amendment, a-mend'ment, *n.* A change for the better; correction; reformation.
Amends, a-mendz', *n.pl.* Compensation; satisfaction; recompense.
Amenity, a-men'i-ti, *n.* Pleasantness; agreeableness of situation.
Amerce, a-mėrs', *vt.* (amercing, amerced). To punish by fine.
Amerceable, a-mėrs'a-bl, *a.* Liable to amercement.
Amercement, a-mėrs'ment, *n.* A pecuniary penalty inflicted on an offender.
American, a-me'ri-kan, *n.* A native of America. —*a.* Pertaining to America.
Americanism, a-me'ri-kan-izm, *n.* An American idiom or custom.
Amethyst, am'ē-thist, *n.* A variety of quartz, a precious stone of a violet or purple colour.
Amethystine, a-mē-thist'in, *a.* Pertaining to or resembling amethyst.
Amiability, ā'mi-a-bil"i-ti, *n.* Sweetness of temper.
Amiable, ā'mi-a-bl, *a.* Lovable; sweet-tempered.
Amiably, ā'mi-a-bli, *adv.* In an amiable manner.
Amianth, Amianthus, am'i-anth, am-i-an'thus, *n.* Mountain-flax, flexible asbestos.
Amicable, am'ik-a-bl, *a.* Friendly; kind.
Amicably, am'ik-a-bli, *adv.* In a friendly manner.
Amice, am'is, *n.* A cloth worn by priests about the shoulders.
Amid, Amidst, a-mid', a-midst', *prep.* In the midst of; enveloped with.
Amidships, a-mid'ships, *adv.* or *pred.a.* In or towards the middle of a ship.
Amiss, a-mis', *a.* In error; improper.—*adv.* In a faulty manner; improperly.
Amity, am'i-ti, *n.* Friendship; harmony.
Ammeter, am'met-ėr, *n.* An instrument for measuring an electric current (in AMPERES).
Ammonia, am-mō'ni-a, *n.* Volatile alkali.
Ammoniac, Ammoniacal, am-mō'ni-ak, am-mo-nī'ak-al, *a.* Pertaining to ammonia.
Ammoniac, am-mō'ni-ak, *n.* A gum obtained from a plant.
Ammonite, am'mon-īt, *n.* The fossil shell of extinct cuttle-fishes.
Ammunition, am-mū-ni'shon, *n.* Military projectiles; formerly military stores generally.
Amnesty, am'nes-ti, *n.* A general pardon of offences against a government.
Amnion, am'ni-on, *n.* The innermost membrane surrounding the fetus of mammals, birds, and reptiles.
Amœba, a-mē'ba, *n.*; pl. **-bæ.** A microscopic animal commonly found in fresh water.
Amœbean, am-ē-bē'an, *a.* Exhibiting persons speaking alternately (an amœbean poem).
Among, Amongst, a-mung', a-mungst', *prep.* Amidst; throughout; of the number.
Amorous, am'or-us, *a.* Inclined to love; enamoured; fond; relating to love.
Amorously, am'or-us-li, *adv.* In an amorous manner.
Amorphous, a-mor'fus, *a.* Without shape; of irregular shape.
Amount, a-mount', *vi.* To mount up to; to result in.—*n.* The sum total; effect or result.
Amour, a-mör', *n.* A love intrigue.
Ampere, am-pār', *n.* The unit in measuring the strength of an electric current.
Amphibian, am-fib'i-an, *n.*; pl. **Amphibia,** am-fib'i-a. An animal capable of living both in water and on land; an animal that has both lungs and gills.
Amphibious, am-fib'i-us, *a.* Able to live under water and on land.
Amphibology, am-fi-bol'o-ji, *n.* Speech susceptible of two interpretations.
Amphibrach, am'fi-brak, *n.* A poetical foot of three syllables, the first and third short, and the second long.
Amphitheatre, am-fi-thē'a-tėr, *n.* An edifice of an oval form, with rows of seats all round, rising higher as they recede from the area.
Ample, am'pl, *a.* Spacious; copious; rich.
Ampleness, am'pl-nes, *n.* Spaciousness; abundance.
Amplification, am'pli-fi-kā"shon, *n.* Act of amplifying; enlargement; discussion.
Amplifier, am'pli-fi-ėr, *n.* One who or that which amplifies or enlarges.
Amplify, am'plif-ī, *vt.* (amplifying, amplified). To enlarge; to treat copiously.—*vi.* To speak copiously; to be diffuse.
Amplitude, am'pli-tūd, *n.* Ampleness; extent; abundance.
Amply, am'pli, *adv.* Largely; liberally; fully; copiously.
Amputate, am'pū-tāt, *vt.* (amputating, amputated). To cut off, as a limb.
Amputation, am-pū-tā'shon, *n.* Act of amputating.
Amuck, a-muk', *n.* or *adv.* Only in phrase *to run amuck*, to rush about frantically, to attack all and sundry.
Amulet, am'ū-let, *n.* A charm against evils or witchcraft.
Amuse, a-mūz', *vt.* (amusing, amused). To entertain; to beguile.
Amusement, a-mūz'ment, *n.* Diversion; entertainment.
Amusing, a-mūz'ing, *a.* Giving amusement; diverting.
Amusingly, a-mūz'ing-li, *adv.* In an amusing manner.
Amygdalate, a-mig'da-lāt, *n.* Milk of almonds.
Amygdaloid, a-mig'da-loid, *n.* A kind of igneous rock, containing cavities filled with various minerals.
Amyl, am'il, *n.* A hypothetical radical said to exist in many substances.
Amyloid, am'il-oid, *a.* Resembling or of the nature of starch.—*n.* A starchy substance.
An, an, *a.* The indefinite article, used before words beginning with a vowel-sound.
Anabaptist, an-a-bap'tist, *n.* One who maintains that adults only should be baptized.
Anachronism, an-ak'ron-izm, *n.* An error in chronology.
Anaconda, an-a-kon'da, *n.* A large species of the serpent tribe.
Anacreontic, a-nak'rē-on"tik, *a.* Pertaining to Anacreon; noting a kind of verse or measure; amatory.

Anæmia, a-nē'mi-a, *n.* Bloodlessness.
Anæsthetic, an-es-thet'ik, *a.* Producing insensibility.—*n.* A substance, as chloroform, which produces insensibility.
Anagram, an'a-gram, *n.* A transposition of the letters of a name or sentence, by which a new word or sentence is formed.
Anal, ā'nal, *a.* Pertaining to the anus.
Analogical, an-a-loj'ik-al, *a.* According to analogy.
Analogous, an-al'og-us, *a.* Having analogy; corresponding.
Analogy, an-al'o-ji, *n.* Likeness; similarity.
Analyse, an'a-līz, *vt.* (analysing, analysed). To subject to analysis; to resolve into its elements.
Analysis, an-al'i-sis, *n.*; pl. **-ses.** A resolution of a thing into its elements; synopsis.
Analyst, an'a-list, *n.* One who analyses.
Analytic, Analytical, an-a-lit'ik, an-a-lit'ik-al, *a.* Pertaining to analysis.
Analytically, an-a-lit'ik-al-li, *adv.* In the manner of analysis.
Analytics, an-a-lit'iks, *n.* The science of analysis.
Anapest, an'a-pest, *n.* A poetical foot of three syllables, the first two short, the last long.
Anapestic, an-a-pes'tik, *a.* Pertaining to an anapest; consisting of anapests.
Anarchic, Anarchical, an-ärk'ik, an-ärk'ik-al, *a.* Without rule or government.
Anarchist, an'ärk-ist, *n.* An author or promoter of anarchy; one who opposes all existing systems of government.
Anarchy, an'är-ki, *n.* State of being without rule; political confusion.
Anathema, a-nath'e-ma, *n.* An ecclesiastical denunciation; curse.
Anathematize, a-nath'e-mat-īz, *vt.* (anathematizing, anathematized). To pronounce an anathema against; to excommunicate.
Anatomical, an-a-tom'ik-al, *a.* Relating to anatomy.
Anatomist, a-nat'ō-mist, *n.* One skilled in anatomy.
Anatomize, a-nat'ō-mīz, *vt.* (anatomizing, anatomized). To cut up or dissect.
Anatomy, a-nat'ō-mi, *n.* The art of dissection; doctrine of the structure of the body learned by dissection.
Ancestor, an'ses-tėr, *n.* A progenitor; forefather.
Ancestral, an-ses'tral, *a.* Relating or belonging to ancestors.
Ancestry, an'ses-tri, *n.* Lineage; descent.
Anchor, ang'kėr, *n.* An iron instrument for holding a ship at rest in water. *vt.* To hold fast by an anchor.—*vi.* To cast anchor.
Anchorage, ang'ker-āj, *n.* A place where a ship can anchor; duty on ships for anchoring.
Anchorite, ang'kō-rīt, *n.* A hermit.
Anchovy, an-chō'vi, *n.* A small fish of the herring kind, furnishing a fine sauce.
Ancient, ān'shent, *a.* That happened in former times; old, antique.
Anciently, ān'shent-li, *adv.* In old times.
Ancientness, ān'shent-nes, *n.* Antiquity.
Ancillary, an'sil-la-ri, *a.* Pertaining to a maidservant; subservient or subordinate.
And, and, *conj.* A particle which connects words and sentences together.
Andante, an-dan'te, *a.* In *music*, with slow, graceful movement.
Andiron, and'ī-ėrn, *n.* A metallic support for logs of wood burned on an open hearth.
Anecdote, an'ek-dōt, *n.* A short story.
Anecdotical, an-ek-dot'ik-al, *a.* Pertaining to an anecdote.
Anele, a-nēl', *vt.* To give extreme unction.
Anemometer, an-e-mom'et-ėr, *n.* An instrument for measuring the force of the wind.
Anemone, a-nem'o-nē, *n.* Wind-flower, a genus of plants.
Anent, a-nent', *prep.* About; regarding.
Aneroid, an'ē-roid, *a.* Dispensing with fluid, said of a kind of barometer.
Aneurism, an'ū-rizm, *n.* Dilatation of an artery.
Aneurismal, an-ū-riz'mal, *a.* Pertaining to an aneurism.
Anew, a-nū', *adv.* On new; fresh.
Angel, ān'jel, *n.* A divine messenger; a spirit; an old English gold coin worth ten shillings.
Angelic, Angelical, an-jel'ik, an-jel'ik-al, *a.* Belonging to or resembling an angel.
Angelically, an-jel'ik-al-li, *adv.* Like an angel.
Anger, ang'gėr, *n.* A violent passion, excited by real or supposed injury; resentment.—*vt.* To excite anger; to irritate.
Angina, an-jī'na, *n.* Angina pectoris, a fatal disease characterized by paroxysms of intense pain and a feeling of constriction in the chest.
Angle, ang'gl, *n.* The inclination of two lines which meet in a point but have different directions; a corner.
Angle, ang'gl, *n.* A fishing-hook, or hook with line and rod.—*vi.* (angling, angled). To fish with an angle.
Angler, ang'glėr, *n.* One that fishes with an angle.
Anglican, ang'glik-an, *a.* Pertaining to England, or to the English Church.
Anglicism, ang'gli-sizm, *n.* An English idiom.
Anglicize, ang'gli-sīz, *vt.* To make English.
Anglomania, ang-glō-mā'ni-a, *n.* Excessive attachment to English people, customs, &c.
Anglophobia, ang-glō-fō'bi-a, *n.* Excessive hatred of English people, customs, &c.
Anglo-Saxon, ang-glō-sak'son, *n.* One of the English race; the English language in its first stage.—*a.* Pertaining to the Anglo-Saxons, or their language.
Angrily, ang'gri-li, *adv.* In an angry manner.
Angry, ang'gri, *a.* Affected with anger; provoked; wrathful; resentful.
Anguish, ang'gwish, *n.* Extreme pain, either of body or mind; agony; grief.
Angular, ang'gū-lėr, *a.* Having an angle; stiff.
Angularity, ang-gū-la'ri-ti, *n.* Quality of being angular.
Anile, an'īl, *a.* Aged; imbecile.
Aniline, an'i-lin, *n.* A substance obtained from coal-tar, used in dyeing.
Anility, a-nil'i-ti, *n.* State of being anile.
Animadversion, an'i-mad-vėr"shon, *n.* Censure; criticism.
Animadvert, an'i-mad-vėrt", *vi.* To criticise; to censure (with *upon*).
Animal, an'i-mal, *n.* A living being having sensation and voluntary motion; a quadruped.—*a.* Belonging to animals; gross.
Animalcular, an-i-mal'kūl-ėr, *a.* Pertaining to animalcules.
Animalcule, an-i-mal'kūl, *n.* A minute animal seen by means of a microscope.
Animalism, an'i-mal-izm, *n.* Sensuality.
Animate, an'i-māt, *vt.* (animating, animated). To give natural life to; to enliven.

Animated, an'i-māt-ed, *p.a.* Lively; living.
Animating, an'i-māt-ing, *p.a.* Enlivening.
Animation, an-i-mā'shon, *n.* Life; vigour.
Animism, an'i-mizm, *n.* The belief that natural phenomena are due to spirits, and that inanimate objects have spirits.
Animosity, an-i-mos'i-ti, *n.* Violent hatred; active enmity; malignity.
Animus, an'i-mus, *n.* Intention; hostile spirit.
Anise, an'is, *n.* An aromatic plant, the seeds of which are used in making cordials.
Aniseed, an'i-sēd, *n.* The seed of the anise.
Anker, ang'kėr, *n.* A liquid measure of eight and a half imperial gallons.
Ankle, ang'kl, *n.* The joint which connects the foot with the leg.
Anna, an'na, *n.* An Indian coin worth 1½*d.*
Annalist, an'nal-ist, *n.* A writer of annals.
Annals, an'nalz, *n.pl.* A record of events under the years in which they happened.
Anneal, an-nēl', *vt.* To temper glass or metals by heat; to fix colours laid on glass.
Annelid, an'ne-lid, *n.* An invertebrate animal whose body is formed of numerous small rings, as the worm, leech, &c.
Annex, an-neks', *vt.* To unite at the end; to subjoin; to take possession of.
Annexation, an-neks-ā'shon, *n.* Act of annexing.
Annihilable, an-nī'hil-a-bl, *a.* That may be annihilated.
Annihilate, an-nī'hil-āt, *vt.* (annihilating, annihilated). To reduce to nothing; to destroy the existence of.
Annihilation, an-nī'hil-ā"shon, *n.* Act of annihilating; state of being annihilated.
Anniversary, an-ni-vėrs'a-ri, *n.* A day on which some event is annually celebrated.
Annotate, an'nō-tāt, *vt.* (annotating, annotated). To write notes upon.
Annotation, an-nō-tā'shon, *n.* A remark on some passage of a book, &c.
Annotator, an'nō-tāt-ėr, *n.* A writer of notes.
Announce, an-nouns', *vt.* (announcing, announced). To declare; to proclaim.
Announcement, an-nouns'ment, *n.* Declaration.
Annoy, an-noi', *vt.* To hurt; to molest; to vex.
Annoyance, an-noi'ans, *n.* Act of annoying; state of being annoyed.
Annual, an'nū-al, *a.* Yearly; lasting a year.—*n.* A plant whose root dies yearly; a book published yearly.
Annually, an'nū-al-li, *adv.* Yearly.
Annuitant, an-nū'it-ant, *n.* One who receives an annuity.
Annuity, an-nū'i-ti, *n.* A sum of money payable yearly, &c.
Annul, annul', *vt.* (annulling, annulled). To make void or of no effect; to repeal.
Annular, an'nū-lėr, *a.* Having the form of a ring; pertaining to a ring.
Annulment, an-nul'ment, *n.* Act of annulling.
Annulose, an'nū-lōs, *a.* Having a body composed of rings; applied to annelids.
Annunciation, an-nun'si-ā"shon, *n.* The angel's salutation to the Virgin Mary, and its anniversary, the 25th of March.
Anode, an'ōd, *n.* The positive pole of a voltaic current.
Anodyne, an'ō-dīn, *n.* Any medicine which allays or mitigates pain.—*a.* Assuaging pain.
Anoint, a-noint', *vt.* To rub over with oil; to consecrate by unction.
Anointed, a-noint'ed, *n.* The Messiah.
Anomalous, a-nom'a-lus, *a.* Deviating from common rule.
Anomaly, a-nom'a-li, *n.* Irregularity; deviation from common rule.
Anon, a-non', *adv.* Immediately.
Anonymous, a-non'im-us, *a.* Nameless; without the real name of the author.
Anonymously, a-non'im-us-li, *adv.* Without a name.
Another, an-uᴛʜ'ėr, *a.* Not the same; different; any other.
Anserine, an'sėr-īn, *a.* Relating to the goose.
Answer, an'sėr, *vt.* To reply to; to satisfy; to suit.—*vi.* To reply; to be accountable; to succeed.—*n.* A reply; a solution.
Answerable, an'sėr-a-bl, *a.* That may be answered; accountable; suitable.
Answerably, an'sėr-a-bli, *adv.* In due proportion; suitably.
Ant, ant, *n.* An emmet; a pismire.
Antagonism, an-tag'ō-nizm, *n.* Opposition; contest.
Antagonist, an-tag'ō-nist, *n.* One who struggles with another in combat; an opponent; that which acts in opposition.
Antagonistic, an-tag'ō-nist"ik, *a.* Opposing in combat; contending against.
Antarctic, ant-ärk'tik, *a.* Relating to the south pole, or to the region near it.
Antecedent, an-tē-sē'dent, *a.* Going before; prior.—*n.* That which goes before; the noun to which a relative refers; *pl.* a man's previous history, &c.
Ante-chamber, an'tē-chām-bėr, *n.* An apartment leading into a chief apartment.
Antedate, an'tē-dāt, *n.* Prior date.—*vt.* To date before the true time.
Antediluvian, an'tē-di-lū"vi-an, *a.* Before the flood.—*n.* One who lived before the flood.
Antelope, an'tē-lōp, *n.* An animal resembling the deer, but with hollow, unbranched horns.
Antemeridian, an'tē-mē-rid"i-an, *a.* Before mid-day; pertaining to the forenoon.
Antemundane, an-tē-mun'dān, *a.* Before the creation of the world.
Antenna, an-ten'na, *n.*; pl. **Antennæ,** an-ten'nē. The feeler of an insect; an aerial.
Antenuptial, an-tē-nup'shi-al, *a.* Before nuptials or marriage.
Antepenult, an'tē-pē-nult", *n.* The last syllable of a word except two.
Antepenultimate, an'tē-pē-nul"ti-māt, *a.* Pertaining to the antepenult.—*n.* Antepenult.
Anterior, an-tē'ri-ėr, *a.* Before; prior; in front.
Anteroom, an'tē-röm, *n.* A room in front of a principal apartment.
Anthem, an'them, *n.* A sacred song sung in alternate parts; a piece of Scripture set to music.
Anther, an'thėr, *n.* The summit of the stamen in a flower, containing the pollen.
Anthological, an-tho-loj'ik-al, *a.* Pertaining to anthology.
Anthology, an-thol'o-ji, *n.* A collection of poems.
Anthracite, an'thra-sīt, *n.* A hard, compact coal which burns almost without flame.
Anthropoid, an'thrō-poid, *a.* Resembling man: applied to the higher apes.

Anthropology, an-thrō-pol'o-ji, *n.* The science of man and mankind; the study of the physical and mental constitution of man.
Anthropomorphism, an-thrō'pō-mor"fizm, *n.* The representation of a deity in human form, or with human attributes.
Anthropophagi, an-thrō-pof'a-ji, *n.pl.* Man-eaters; cannibals.
Anthropophagy, an-thrō-pof'a-ji, *n.* Cannibalism.
Anti-aircraft, an'ti-ār-kraft, *a.* Used in defence against attacks from the air, as guns, searchlights, &c.
Antic, an'tik, *a.* Grotesque; fantastic.—*n.* A buffoon; buffoonery.
Antichrist, an'ti-krist, *n.* The great adversary of Christ.
Antichristian, an-ti-kris'ti-an, *a.* Pertaining to Antichrist.
Anticipate, an-tis'i-pāt, *vt.* (anticipating, anticipated). To forestall; to foretaste; to preclude; to expect.
Anticipation, an-tis'i-pā"shon, *n.* Act of anticipating; foretaste; expectation.
Anti-climax, an-ti-klī'maks, *n.* A sentence in which the ideas become less striking at the close.
Anticlinal, an-ti-klī'nal, *a.* Marking inclination in opposite directions.
Anticyclone, an'ti-si-klōn, *n.* An opposite state of atmospheric or meteorological conditions to what exists in a cyclone.
Antidotal, an'ti-dōt-al, *a.* Acting as an antidote.
Antidote, an'ti-dōt, *n.* A remedy for poison or any evil.
Anti-macassar, an'ti-ma-kas"ār, *n.* A movable covering for chairs, sofas, &c.
Antimonial, an-ti-mō'ni-al, *a.* Pertaining to antimony.
Antimony, an'ti-mo-ni, *n.* A brittle, white-coloured metal, used in the arts and in medicine.
Antinomian, an-ti-nō'mi-an, *n.* One who opposes the moral law.
Antipathy, an-tip'a-thi, *n.* Instinctive aversion; dislike; opposition.
Antiphlogistic, an'ti-flo-jis"tik, *a.* Counteracting inflammation.
Antiphon, an'ti-fōn, *n.* The chant or alternate singing in choirs of cathedrals.
Antiphrasis, an-tif'ra-sis, *n.* The use of words in a sense opposite to the proper one.
Antipodal, an-tip'od-al, *a.* Pertaining to the antipodes.
Antipodes, an-tip'o-dēz, *n.pl.* Those who live on opposite sides of the globe; the opposite side of the globe.
Antipope, an'ti-pōp, *n.* An opposition pope
Antipyrin, an-ti-pī'rin, *n.* A drug used to reduce fever and relieve pain.
Antiquarian, an-ti-kwā'ri-an, *a.* Pertaining to antiquaries.—*n.* One versed in antiquities.
Antiquarianism, an-ti-kwā'ri-an-izm, *n.* Love or knowledge of antiquities.
Antiquary, an'ti-kwa-ri, *n.* One versed in antiquities.
Antiquated, an'ti-kwāt-ed, *a.* Grown old; obsolete.
Antique, an-tēk', *a.* Old; of genuine antiquity.—*n.* Anything very old; an ancient relic.
Antiquity, an-tik'wi-ti, *n.* Ancient times; great age; *pl.* remains of ancient times.
Antiseptic, an-ti-sep'tik, *a.* Counteracting putrefaction.—*n.* A substance which resists or corrects putrefaction.
Antistrophe, an-tis'tro-fi, *n.* The stanza of an ode, succeeding the strophe.
Antithesis, an-tith'e-sis, *n.*; pl. **-theses.** Opposition of thoughts or words; contrast.
Antithetical, an-ti-thet'ik-al, *a.* Pertaining to antithesis.
Antitype, an'ti-tīp, *n.* That which is shadowed out by a type or emblem.
Antitypical, an-ti-tip'ik-al, *a.* Pertaining to an antitype; explaining the type.
Antler, ant'lėr, *n.* A branch of a stag's horn.
Antonym, ant'ō-nim, *n.* A word of directly contrary signification to another: the opposite of a synonym.
Anus, ā'nus, *n.* The opening of the body by which excrement is expelled.
Anvil, an'vil, *n.* An iron block on which smiths hammer and shape their work.
Anxiety, ang-zī'e-ti, *n.* State of being anxious; concern.
Anxious, angk'shus, *a.* Suffering mental distress; solicitous; concerned.
Anxiously, angk'shus-li, *adv.* In an anxious manner.
Anxiousness, angk'shus-nes, *n.* Anxiety.
Any, en'i, *a.* One indefinitely; whatever; some.—*adv.* At all; in any degree.
Anzac, an'zak, *n.* The Australian New Zealand Army Corps; an Australasian Expeditionary soldier.
Aorist, ā'or-ist, *n.* An indefinite past tense in the Greek verb.
Aorta, ā-ort'a, *n.* The great artery which rises up from the left ventricle of the heart.
Aortal, Aortic, ā-ort'al, ā-ort'ik, *a.* Pertaining to the aorta or great artery.
Apace, a-pās', *adv.* Quick; fast; speedily.
Apart, a-pärt', *adv.* Separately; aside.
Apartment, a-pärt'ment, *n.* A room.
Apathetic, ap-a-thet'ik, *a.* Void of feeling; free from passion; indifferent.
Apathy, ap'a-thi, *n.* Want of feeling; insensibility; indifference.
Ape, āp, *n.* A monkey; an imitator.—*vt.* (aping, aped). To imitate servilely; to mimic.
Aperient, a-pē'ri-ent, *a.* Mildly purgative.—*n.* A laxative; a mild purgative.
Aperture, ap'ėr-tūr, *n.* An opening; a hole.
Apex, ā'peks, *n.*; pl. **-exes** and **-ices.** The summit of anything.
Aphæresis, Apheresis, a-fē're-sis, *n.* The taking of a letter or syllable from the beginning of a word.
Aphelion, a-fē'li-on, *n.*; pl. **-lia.** The point of a planet's orbit farthest from the sun.
Aphorism, af'or-izm, *n.* A precept expressed in few words; a maxim.
Apiary, ā'pi-a-ri, *n.* A place where bees are kept.
Apiece, a-pēs', *adv.* In a separate share; to each; noting the share of each.
Apish, āp'ish, *a.* Resembling an ape.
Aplomb, a-plong, *n.* Self-possession.
Apocalypse, a-pok'a-lips, *n.* Revelation; the last book of the New Testament.
Apocalyptic, a-pok'a-lip"tik, *a.* Pertaining to the Apocalypse.
Apocope, a-pok'ō-pē, *n.* The cutting off of the last letter or syllable of a word.
Apocrypha, a-pok'ri-fa, *n.pl.* Certain books

whose authenticity as inspired writings is not generally admitted.
Apocryphal, a-pok'ri-fal, *a.* Pertaining to the Apocrypha; not canonical; fictitious.
Apogee, ap'ō-jē, *n.* The point in the moon's orbit farthest from the earth.
Apologetic, a-pol'ō-jet"ik, *a.* Containing apology; defending; excusing.
Apologetics, a-pol'ō-jet"iks, *n.pl.* The branch of theology which defends Christianity.
Apologist, a-pol'ō-jist, *n.* One who apologizes; an excuser, or defender.
Apologize, a-pol'ō-jīz, *vi.* (apologizing, apologized). To make an apology.
Apologue, ap'o-log, *n.* A moral fable.
Apology, a-pol'ō-ji, *n.* That which is said in defence; vindication; excuse.
Apophthegm, Apothegm, ap'o-them, *n.* A terse, pointed saying.
Apoplectic, ap-o-plek'tik, *a.* Pertaining to apoplexy.
Apoplexy, ap'ō-plek-si, *n.* A sudden privation of sense and voluntary motion.
Apostasy, a-pos'ta-si, *n.* Departure from one's faith; desertion of a party.
Apostate, a-pos'tāt, *n.* One who renounces his religion or his party.—*a.* False; traitorous.
Apostatize, a-pos'ta-tīz, *vi.* To abandon one's religion or party.
Aposteme, ap'os-tēm, *n.* An abscess.
Apostle, a-pos'l, *n.* One sent to preach the gospel; one of the twelve disciples.
Apostleship, a-pos'l-ship, *n.* Office of an apostle.
Apostolic, Apostolical, ap-os-tol'ik, ap-os-tol'ik-al, *a.* Pertaining to an apostle.
Apostrophe, a-pos'tro-fē, *n.* An addressing of the absent or the dead as if present; a mark (') indicating contraction of a word, or the possessive case.
Apostrophize, a-pos'trof-īz, *vi.* To make an apostrophe.—*vt.* To address by apostrophe.
Apothecary, a-poth'e-ka-ri, *n.* One who prepares and sells drugs or medicines.
Apothegm, ap'o-them, *n.* *See* APOPHTHEGM.
Apotheosis, ap-o-thē'ō-sis or -thē-ō'sis, *n.* A deification; a placing among the gods.
Appal, ap-pal', *vt.* (appalling, appalled). To depress with fear; to dismay.
Appalling, ap-pal'ing, *a.* Causing dread or terror.
Appanage, ap'pan-āj, *n.* Lands or revenue settled on the younger son of a ruler; an adjunct; appendage.
Apparatus, ap-pa-rā'tus, *n.*; pl. **-tus,** or **-tuses,** Set of instruments or utensils for performing any operation.
Apparel, ap-pa'rel, *n.* Equipment; clothing. *vt.* (apparelling, apparelled). To dress; to array.
Apparent, ap-pā'rent, *a.* That may be seen; evident; seeming, not real.
Apparently, ap-pā'rent-li, *adv.* Openly; seemingly.
Apparition, ap-pa-ri'shon, *n.* An appearance; a spectre; a ghost or phantom.
Appeal, ap-pēl', *vi.* To call; to refer to a superior court; to have recourse.—*vt.* To remove to a superior court.—*n.* The removal of a cause to a higher tribunal; a reference to another.
Appear, ap-pēr', *vi.* To be or become visible; to seem.
Appearance, ap-pēr'ans, *n.* Act of coming into sight; semblance; likelihood.
Appeasable, ap-pēz'a-bl, *a.* That may be appeased.
Appease, ap-pēz', *vt.* (appeasing, appeased). To pacify; to tranquillize.
Appellant, ap-pel'ant, *n.* One who appeals.
Appellate, ap-pel'āt, *a.* Pertaining to appeals.
Appellation, ap-pel-ā'shon, *n.* Name; title.
Appellative, ap-pel'at-iv, *a.* Naming; designating.—*n.* A name; an appellation.
Append, ap-pend', *vt.* To add; to annex.
Appendage, ap-pend'āj, *n.* Something added; a subordinate part.
Appendant, ap-pend'ant, *a.* Annexed.—*n.* Something subordinate or incidental.
Appendix, ap-pen'diks, *n.*; pl. **-ixes** or **-ices.** An adjunct or appendage; a supplement; a narrow tube with blind end leading out of intestine.
Appertain, ap-pėr-tān', *vi.* To belong; to relate.
Appetence, Appetency, ap'pē-tens, ap'pē-ten-si, *n.* Desire; sensual appetite.
Appetite, ap'pē-tīt, *n.* A desire or relish for food or other sensual gratifications.
Appetize, ap'pē-tīz, *vt.* (appetizing, appetized). To give an appetite to; to whet the appetite.
Appetizer, ap'pē-tīz-ėr, *n.* That which appetizes.
Applaud, ap-plad', *vt.* To praise by clapping the hands, &c.; to extol.
Applause, ap-plaz', *n.* Praise loudly expressed; acclamation.
Apple, ap'l, *n.* The fruit of the apple-tree; the pupil of the eye.
Appliance, ap-plī'ans, *n.* Act of applying; thing applied; article of equipment.
Applicability, ap'pli-ka-bil"li-ti, *n.* Quality of being applicable.
Applicable, ap'pli-ka-bl, *a.* That may be applied; suitable.
Applicably, ap'pli-ka-bli, *adv.* In an applicable manner.
Applicant, ap'pli-kant, *n.* One who applies.
Application, ap-pli-kā'shon, *n.* Act of applying; request; close study; assiduity; the thing applied.
Apply, ap-plī', *vt.* (applying, applied). To fasten or attach; to use; to employ with assiduity.—*vi.* To suit; to solicit; to have recourse to.
Appoint, ap-point', *vt.* To fix; to allot; to nominate; to equip.—*vi.* To determine.
Appointment, ap-point'ment, *n.* Act of appointing; office held; arrangement; decree; *pl.* equipments.
Apportion, ap-pōr'shon, *vt.* To portion out; to assign in just proportion.
Apportioner, ap-pōr'shon-ėr, *n.* One who apportions.
Apportionment, ap-pōr'shon-ment, *n.* Act of apportioning.
Apposite, ap'pō-zit, *a.* Suitable; applicable; pat.
Appositely, ap'pō-zit-li, *adv.* Suitably.
Appositeness, ap'pō-zit-nes, *n.* Fitness.
Apposition, ap-pō-zi'shon, *n.* In *grammar*, the relation of one noun to another, when it explains its meaning, while agreeing in case.
Appraise, ap-prāz', *vt.* (appraising, appraised). To fix or set a price on; to estimate.
Appraisement, ap-prāz'ment, *n.* Valuation.

Appraiser, ap-prāz'ėr, *n.* One who values; a valuator.
Appreciable, ap-prē'shi-a-bl, *a.* That may be appreciated.
Appreciate, ap-prē'shi-āt, *vt.* (appreciating, appreciated). To value; to estimate justly.
Appreciation, ap-prē'shi-ā"shon, *n.* Act of appreciating; a just valuation.
Apprehend, ap-prē-hend', *vt.* To take hold of; to arrest; to conceive; to fear.—*vi.* To think; to imagine.
Apprehensible, ap-prē-hen'si-bl, *a.* That may be apprehended or conceived.
Apprehension, ap-prē-hen'shon, *n.* Seizure; faculty of conceiving ideas; dread.
Apprehensive, ap-prē-hen'siv, *a.* Fearful; suspicious.
Apprentice, ap-pren'tis, *n.* One who is indentured to a master to learn a trade, an art, &c.—*vi.* To bind as an apprentice.
Apprenticeship, ap-pren'tis-ship, *n.* The term an apprentice serves; state or condition of an apprentice.
Apprise, ap-prīz', *vt.* (apprising, apprised). To inform; to make known to.
Approach, ap-prōch', *vi.* To come near; to approximate.—*vt.* To come near to; to resemble.—*n.* Act of drawing near; an avenue; access.
Approachable, ap-prōch'a-bl, *a.* That may be approached.
Approbation, ap-prō-bā'shon, *n.* Approval; attestation; a liking.
Appropriable, ap-prō'pri-a-bl, *a.* That may be appropriated.
Appropriate, ap-prō'pri-āt, *vt.* (appropriating, appropriated). To take to oneself as one's own; to set apart for.—*a.* Set apart for a particular use or person; suitable; adapted.
Appropriately, ap-prō'pri-āt-li, *adv.* In an appropriate manner.
Appropriateness, ap-prō'pri-āt-nes, *n.* Peculiar fitness.
Appropriation, ap-prō'pri-ā"shon, *n.* Act of apropriating; application to special use.
Approvable, ap-prov'a-bl, *a.* That may be approved.
Approval, ap-prōv'al, *n.* Approbation.
Approve, ap-prōv', *vt.* (approving, approved). To deem good; to like; to sanction.—*vi.* To feel or express approbation (with *of*).
Approver, ap-prōv'ėr, *n.* One who approves.
Approximate, ap-prok'si-māt, *a.* Near; approaching.—*vt.* (approximating, approximated). To bring near.—*vi.* To come near; to approach.
Approximately, ap-prok'si-māt-li, *adv.* Nearly.
Approximation, ap-prok'si-mā"shon, *n.* Act of approximating; approach.
Appurtenance, ap-pėr'ten-ans, *n.* That which pertains to; an appendage.
Apricot, ā'pri-kot, *n.* Stone-fruit, resembling the peach.
April, ā'pril, *n.* The fourth month of the year.
Apron, ā'prun, *n.* A cloth, or piece of leather, worn in front to protect the clothes.
Apropos, ap'rō-pō, *adv.* To the purpose; opportunely.
Apsis, ap'sis, *n.*; pl. **-sides,** -si-dēz. One of the two points in a planet's orbit which mark its greatest and least distance from the body round which it revolves.
Apt, apt, *a.* Suitable; liable; ready.
Apterous, ap'tėr-us, *a.* Destitute of wings.
Apteryx, ap'tė-riks, *n.* A bird of New Zealand, with rudimentary wings, and no tail.
Aptitude, ap'ti-tūd, *n.* Fitness; readiness.
Aptly, apt'li, *adv.* In an apt manner.
Aptness, apt'nes, *n.* Aptitude.
Aqua, ak'wa, *n.* Water.
Aqua fortis, ak'wa for-tis, *n.* Weak and impure nitric acid.
Aquarium, a-kwā'ri-um, *n.*; pl. **-iums** or **-ia.** A vessel or tank for aquatic plants and animals; a collection of such vessels.
Aquarius, a-kwā'ri-us, *n.* The water-bearer, a sign in the zodiac.
Aquatic, a-kwat'ik, *a.* Living or growing in water.—*n.* A plant which grows in water; *pl.* sports or exercises in water.
Aquatint, ak'wa-tint, *n.* A method of etching which gives effects resembling drawing in water-colours or Indian ink.
Aqueduct, ak'wē-dukt, *n.* A conduit made for conveying water.
Aqueous, ā'kwē-us, *a.* Watery.
Aquiline, ak'wil-īn, *a.* Belonging to the eagle; hooked like the beak of an eagle.
Arab, a'rab, *n.* A native of Arabia; a street urchin; an Arabian horse.
Arabesque, ar'ab-esk, *n.* A species of ornamentation consisting of fanciful figures and floral forms.
Arabian, a-rā'bi-an, *a.* Pertaining to Arabia. —*n.* A native of Arabia.
Arabic, a'rab-ik, *a.* Belonging to Arabia.—*n.* The language of the Arabians.
Arable, a'ra-bl, *a.* Fit for ploughing.
Arachnida, a-rak'ni-da, *n.pl.* A class of annulose wingless animals, such as spiders.
Aramaic, Aramean, a-ra-mā'ik, a-ra-mē'an, *a.* Pertaining to the language, &c., of the Syrians and Chaldeans.
Araucaria, ar-a-kā'ri-a, *n.* A coniferous prickly tree, the monkey-puzzle.
Arbiter, är'bit-ėr, *n.* A person appointed by parties in controversy to decide their differences; an umpire.
Arbitrament, är-bit'ra-ment, *n.* Decision.
Arbitrarily, är'bi-tra-ri-li, *adv.* By will only; despotically.
Arbitrary, är'bi-tra-ri, *a.* Depending on one's will; despotic.
Arbitrate, är'bi-trāt, *vi.* (arbitrating, arbitrated). To act as an arbiter; to decide.
Arbitration, är-bi-trā'shon, *n.* The act of arbitrating.
Arbitrator, är'bi-trāt-ėr, *n.* A person chosen to decide a dispute; umpire.
Arboreous, är-bō'rē-us, *a.* Belonging to trees.
Arborescence, är-bor-es'sens, *n.* The state of being arborescent.
Arborescent, är-bor-es'sent, *a.* Growing like a tree; becoming woody.
Arboretum, är-bo-rē'tum, *n.* A place where trees are cultivated for scientific purposes.
Arboriculture, är-bo'ri-kul"tūr, *n.* The art of cultivating trees and shrubs.
Arbour, Arbor, är'bėr, *n.* A bower; a shelter in a garden, formed of trees, &c.
Arbutus, är'bū-tus, *n.* An evergreen shrub, with berries like the strawberry.
Arc, ärk, *n.* A part of a circle or curve.
Arcade, är-kād', *n.* A walk arched above; an arched gallery; a covered passage containing shops.

Arcadian, är-kā'di-an, *a.* Pertaining to Arcadia.
Arcanum, är-kān'um, *n.*; pl. **-na.** Mystery.
Arch, ärch, *a.* Chief; cunning; sly; roguish.
Arch, ärch, *n.* A concave structure supported by its own curve; a vault.—*vt.* To cover with an arch; to form with a curve.
Archæological, är-kē-ō-loj'ik-al, *a.* Relating to archæology.
Archæologist, är-kē-ol'o-jist, *n.* One versed in archæology.
Archæology, är-kē-ol'o-ji, *n.* The science of antiquities; knowledge of ancient art.
Archaic, är-kā'ik, *a.* Antiquated; obsolete.
Archaism, är'kā-izm, *n.* Obsolete word or expression.
Archangel, ärk-ān'jel, *n.* An angel of the highest order.
Archangelic, ärk-an-jel'ik, *a.* Belonging to archangels.
Archbishop, ärch-bish'up, *n.* A chief bishop; a bishop who superintends other bishops, his suffragans, in his province.
Archbishopric, ärch-bish'up-rik, *n.* The province of an archbishop.
Archdeacon, ärch-dē'kn, *n.* A church dignitary next in rank below a bishop.
Archdeaconry, ärch-dē'kn-ri, *n.* The office or residence of an archdeacon.
Archdeaconship, ärch-dē'kn-ship, *n.* The office of an archdeacon.
Archduke, ärch-dūk', *n.* Formerly a title of princes of the House of Austria.
Archer, ärch'ėr, *n.* A bowman; one who shoots with a bow and arrow.
Archery, ärch'ė-ri, *n.* The practice, art, or skill of archers.
Archetype, är'kē-tīp, *n.* The original model from which a thing is made.
Archidiaconal, är'ki-dī-ak"on-al, *a.* Pertaining to an archdeacon.
Archiepiscopal, är'ki-ē-pis"kō-pal, *a.* Belonging to an archbishop.
Archipelago, är-ki-pel'a-gō, *n.* The Ægean Sea; a sea abounding in small islands.
Architect, är'ki-tekt, *n.* One who plans buildings, &c.; a contriver.
Architectural, är-ki-tek'tūr-al, *a.* Pertaining to architecture.
Architecture, är'ki-tek-tūr, *n.* The art or science of building; structure.
Architrave, är'ki-trāv, *n.* In *architecture*, the part of an entablature resting on a column.
Archive, är'kīv, *n.* A record; generally *pl.*, records of a kingdom, city, family, &c.
Archly, ärch'li, *adv.* Shrewdly; roguishly.
Archness, ärch'nes, *n.* Roguishness.
Archon, är'kon, *n.* One of the chief magistrates of ancient Athens.
Archway, ärch'wā, *n.* A way or passage under an arch.
Arctic, ärk'tik, *a.* Pertaining to the regions about the north pole; frigid; cold.
Ardency, är'den-si, *n.* Ardour; eagerness.
Ardent, är'dent, *a.* Burning; fervent; eager.
Ardently, är'dent-li, *adv.* With ardour.
Ardour, är'dėr, *n.* Warmth; fervency; eagerness.
Arduous, är'dū-us, *a.* Difficult; laborious.
Arduously, är'dū-us-li, *adv.* In an arduous manner; with effort.
Are, är. The plural pres. indic. of the verb *to be.*
Area, ā'rē-a, *n.* Any open surface; superficial contents; any inclosed space.
Arena, a-rē'na, *n.* An open space of ground, strewed with sand or saw-dust, for combatants; any place of public contest.
Arenaceous, a-rē-nā'shus, *a.* Sandy.
Areopagus, ar-ē-op'a-gus, *n.* The supreme court of ancient Athens, held on a hill of this name.
Argent, är'jent, *a.* Silvery; like silver.
Argil, är'jil, *n.* White clay; potter's earth.
Argillaceous, är-jil-lā'shus, *a.* Clayey.
Argon, är'gon, *n.* A gas existing in the atmosphere in very small quantities; an inert chemical element.
Argonaut, är'go-nąt, *n.* One who sailed in the ship *Argo* in quest of the golden fleece.
Argue, är'gū, *vi.* (arguing, argued). To offer reasons; to dispute.—*vt.* To show reasons for; to discuss.
Argument, är'gū-ment, *n.* A reason offered; a plea; subject of a discourse; heads of contents; controversy.
Argumentation, är-gū-ment-ā"shon, *n.* Act, art, or process of arguing.
Argumentative, är-gū-ment'at-iv, *a.* Consisting of or prone to argument.
Argus, är'gus, *n.* A fabulous being with a hundred eyes; a watchful person.
Arian, ā'ri-an, *a.* Pertaining to Arius, who denied the divinity of Christ.—*n.* One who adheres to the doctrines of Arius.
Arianism, ā'ri-an-izm, *n.* The doctrines of the Arians.
Arid, a'rid, *a.* Dry; dried; parched.
Aridity, a-rid'i-ti, *n.* Dryness.
Aries, ā'ri-ēz, *n.* The Ram, the first of the twelve signs in the zodiac.
Aright, a-rīt', *adv.* Rightly; justly.
Arise, a-rīz', *vi.* (arising, pret. arose, pp. arisen). To rise up; to proceed from.
Aristocracy, a-ris-tok'ra-si, *n.* Government by the nobility; the nobility.
Aristocrat, a'ris-to-krat, *n.* A noble; one who favours aristocracy.
Aristocratic, a-ris-to-krat'ik, *a.* Pertaining to aristocracy.
Aristocratically, a-ris-to-krat'ik-al-li, *adv.* In an aristocratic manner.
Aristotelian, a-ris-to-tē'li-an, *a.* Pertaining to Aristotle, or to his philosophy.
Arithmetic, a-rith'met-ik, *n.* The science of numbering; the art of computation.
Arithmetical, a-rith-met'ik-al, *a.* Pertaining to arithmetic.
Arithmetically, a-rith-met'ik-al-li, *adv.* By means of arithmetic.
Arithmetician, a-rith'me-ti"shan, *n.* One skilled in arithmetic.
Ark, ärk, *n.* A chest; a large floating vessel.
Arm, ärm, *n.* The limb from the shoulder to the hand; anything extending from a main body; a weapon; *pl.* war; armour; armorial bearings.—*vt.* To furnish with arms; to fortify.—*vi.* To take up arms.
Armada, är-mā'da, *n.* A fleet of armed ships; a squadron.
Armadillo, är-ma-dil'lō, *n.* A quadruped of S. America with a hard bony shell.
Armament, ärm'a-ment, *n.* A force armed for war; war-munitions of a ship.
Armenian, är-mē'ni-an, *a.* Pertaining to Armenia.—*n.* A native of Armenia; the language of the country.

Arminian, är-min'i-an, *a.* Pertaining to Arminius.—*n.* A Protestant who denies the doctrine of predestination.
Arminianism, är-min'i-an-izm, *n.* The peculiar doctrines of the Arminians.
Armipotent, är-mip'ō-tent, *a.* Powerful in arms.
Armistice, är'mis-tis, *n.* A cessation of hostilities for a short time; a truce.
Armlet, ärm'let, *n.* A bracelet.
Armorial, är-mō'ri-al, *a.* Belonging to armour, or to the arms of a family.
Armoric, är-mo'rik, *a.* Pertaining to Brittany.—*n.* The language of Brittany.
Armour, ärm'ėr, *n.* Defensive arms.
Armourer, ärm'ėr-ėr, *n.* One who makes or has the care of arms.
Armoury, ärm'ė-ri, *n.* A repository of arms.
Armpit, ärm'pit, *n.* The hollow place under the shoulder.
Army, är'mi, *n.* A body of men armed for war; a great number.
Aroma, a-rō'ma, *n.* Perfume; the fragrant principle in plants, &c.
Aromatic, a-rō-mat'ik, *a.* Fragrant; spicy.—*n.* A fragrant plant or drug.
Around, a-round', *prep.* About; on all sides of; encircling.—*adv.* On every side.
Arouse, a-rouz', *vt.* (arousing, aroused). To rouse; to stir up.
Arquebus, Arquebuse, är'kwē-bus, *n.* An old-fashioned hand-gun.
Arrack, a'rak, *n.* A spirituous liquor distilled in the E. Indies from rice, &c.
Arraign, a-rān', *vt.* To indict; to censure.
Arraigner, a-rān'ėr, *n.* One who arraigns.
Arraignment, a-rān'ment, *n.* Act of arraigning; accusation.
Arrange, a-rānj', *vt.* (arranging, arranged). To put in order; to classify.
Arrangement, a-rānj'ment, *n.* Orderly disposition; adjustment; classification.
Arrant, a'rant, *a.* Downright; thorough.
Arras, a'ras, *n.* Tapestry.
Array, a-rā', *n.* Order; order of battle; apparel.—*v.t.* To draw up in order; to adorn.
Arrear, a-rēr', *n.* That which remains unpaid. Generally in plural.
Arrest, a-rest', *vt.* To stop; to apprehend.—*n.* A seizure by warrant; stoppage.
Arrival, a-rīv'al, *n.* Act of coming to a place; persons or things arriving.
Arrive, a-rīv', *vi.* (arriving, arrived). To come; to reach; to attain.
Arrogance, a'rō-gans, *n.* Assumption; haughtiness; insolent bearing.
Arrogant, a'rō-gant, *a.* Assuming; haughty.
Arrogantly, a'rō-gant-li, *adv.* In an arrogant manner.
Arrogate, a'rō-gāt, *vt.* (arrogating, arrogated). To claim unduly; to assume.
Arrow, a'rō, *n.* A straight-pointed weapon, to be discharged from a bow.
Arrow-headed, a'rō-hed-ed, *a.* Shaped like the head of an arrow.
Arrowroot, a'rō-röt, *n.* A W. Indian plant; the starch of the plant, a medicinal food.
Arrowy, a'rō-i, *a.* Of or like arrows.
Arsenal, är'sē-nal, *n.* A public establishment where ammunition and guns are manufactured or stored.
Arsenic, är'sen-ik, *n.* A virulent mineral poison; an oxide of a brittle metal, called also arsenic.
Arsenical, är-sen'ik-al, *a.* Consisting of or containing arsenic.
Arson, är'son, *n.* The malicious setting on fire of a house, &c.
Art, ärt, *v.* The second person, present indicative of the verb *to be.*
Art, ärt, *n.* Practical skill; a system of rules for certain actions; cunning; profession of a painter, &c.
Arterial, är-tē'ri-al, *a.* Pertaining to an artery or the arteries.
Artery, är'tė-ri, *n.* A tube which conveys blood from the heart.
Artesian, är-tē'zi-an, *a.* Designating a well made by boring till water is reached.
Artful, ärt'ful, *a.* Full of art; skilful; crafty.
Artfully, ärt'ful-li, *adv.* With art.
Artfulness, ärt'ful-nes, *n.* Craft; address.
Arthritis, är-thrī'tis, *n.* Gout.
Artichoke, är'ti-chōk, *n.* An esculent plant somewhat resembling a thistle.
Article, är'ti-kl, *n.* A separate item; stipulation; a particular commodity; a part of speech used before nouns, as *the.*—*vt.* To bind by articles.—*vi.* To stipulate.
Articulate, är-tik'ū-lāt, *a.* Distinct; clear.—*vi.* To utter distinct sounds, syllables, or words.—*vt.* To speak distinctly.
Articulately, är-tik'ū-lāt-li, *adv.* Distinctly.
Articulation, är-tik'ū-lā''shon, *n.* Juncture of bones; joint; distinct utterance.
Artifice, ärt'i-fis, *n.* An artful device; fraud; stratagem.
Artificer, är-tif'is-ėr, *n.* A contriver; a mechanic.
Artificial, ärt-i-fi'shal, *a.* Made by art; not natural.
Artificially, ärt-i-fi'shal-li, *adv.* In an artificial manner.
Artillery, är-til'lė-ri, *n.* Cannon; the troops who manage them; gunnery.
Artisan, ärt'i-zan, *n.* One trained to manual dexterity; a mechanic.
Artist, ärt'ist, *n.* One skilled in some art, especially the fine arts, as painting, &c.
Artiste, är-tēst, *n.* One skilled in some art not one of the fine arts, as singing, dancing.
Artistic, är-tist'ik, *a.* Conformed to art.
Artistically, är-tist'ik-al-li, *adv.* In an artistic manner.
Artless, ärt'les, *a.* Wanting art; unaffected.
Artlessly, ärt'les-li, *adv.* In an artless manner.
Artlessness, ärt'les-nes, *n.* Quality of being artless; simplicity.
Aryan, är'i-an or ā'ri-an, *a.* Indo-European; belonging to the Hindus, Persians, and most Europeans (except Turks, Hungarians, Finns, &c.), and to their languages.
As, az, *adv.* and *conj.* Like; even; equally; while; since; for example.
Asbestos, as-bes'tos, *n.* A mineral fibrous substance which is incombustible.
Ascend, as-send', *vi.* To rise; to go backward in order of time.—*vt.* To move upward upon; to climb.
Ascendancy, Ascendency, as-send'an-si, as-send'en-si, *n.* Controlling power; sway.
Ascendant, as-send'ant, *a.* Rising; superior; predominant.—*n.* Ascendancy; superiority.
Ascension, as-sen'shon, *n.* Act of ascending.
Ascension Day, as-sen'shon dā, *n.* The Thursday but one before Whitsuntide, to commemorate Christ's ascension into heaven.

Ascent, as-sent′, *n.* Rise; a mounting upward; the means of ascending.
Ascertain, as-sėr-tān′, *vt.* To make certain; to find out.
Ascertainable, as-sėr-tān′a-bl, *a.* That may be ascertained.
Ascetic, as-set′ik, *a.* Unduly rigid in devotion. —*n.* One rigidly austere.
Asceticism, as-set′i-sizm, *n.* State or practice of ascetics.
Ascribable, as-krīb′a-bl, *a.* That may be ascribed.
Ascribe, as-krīb′, *vt.* (ascribing, ascribed). To attribute; to assign.
Ascription, as-krip′shon, *n.* Act of ascribing; the thing ascribed.
Asdic, as′dik, *n.* A kind of hydrophone for detecting submarines (*A*llied *S*ubmarine *D*etection *I*nvestigation *C*ommittee).
Aseptic, a-sep′tik, *a.* Not liable to putrefy.
Ash, ash, *n.* A well-known timber tree.
Ashamed, a-shāmd′, *a.* Affected by shame.
Ashen, ash′en, *a.* Pertaining to ash; made of ash.
Ashes, ash′ez, *n.pl.* The dust produced by combustion; the remains of a dead body.
Ashlar, Ashler, ash′lėr, *n.* A facing of dressed stones on a wall; hewn stone.
Ashore, a-shōr′, *adv.* or *pred.a.* On shore.
Ash-Wednesday, ash-wenz′dā, *n.* The first day of Lent, so called from a custom of sprinkling ashes on the head.
Ashy, ash′i, *a.* Resembling or composed of ashes.
Asiatic, ā-shi-at′ik, *a.* Belonging to Asia.—*n.* A native of Asia.
Aside, a-sīd′, *adv.* On one side; apart; at a small distance.
Asinine, as′i-nīn, *a.* Belonging to or resembling the ass.
Ask, ask, *vt.* To request; to question; to invite.—*vi.* To request or petition; to make inquiry.
Askance, Askant, a-skans′, a-skant′, *adv.* Awry; obliquely.
Askew, a-skū′, *adv.* or *pred.a.* Awry.
Aslant, a-slant′, *pred.a.* or *adv.* On slant; obliquely; not perpendicularly.
Asleep, a-slēp′, *pred.a.* or *adv.* Sleeping; at rest.
Aslope, a-slōp′, *pred.a.* or *adv.* On slope; obliquely.
Asp, asp, *n.* A small venomous serpent of Egypt.
Asparagus, as-pa′ra-gus, *n.* A well-known esculent plant.
Aspect, as′pekt, *n.* Appearance; situation.
Aspen, asp′en, *n.* A species of the poplar.
Asperity, as-pe′ri-ti, *n.* Roughness; harshness.
Asperse, as-pėrs′, *vt.* (aspersing, aspersed). To calumniate; to slander.
Aspersion, as-pėr′shon, *n.* Calumny.
Asphalt, as-falt′, *n.* A bituminous, hard substance, used for pavement, &c.
Asphaltic, as-falt′ik, *a.* Pertaining to asphalt.
Asphodel, as′fō-del, *n.* A kind of lily.
Asphyxia, as-fik′si-a, *n.* Suspended animation from suffocation, &c.
Asphyxiate, as-fik′si-āt, *vt.* To bring to a state of asphyxia.
Aspirant, as-pīr′ant, *n.* A candidate.
Aspirate, as′pi-rāt, *vt.* (aspirating, aspirated). To pronounce with an audible breath; to add an *h*-sound to.—*n.* An aspirated letter.
Aspiration, as-pi-rā′shon, *n.* Ardent desire; an aspirated sound.
Aspire, as-pīr′, *vi.* (aspiring, aspired). To aim at high things; to soar.
Asquint, a-skwint′, *adv.* Out of the corner or angle of the eye; obliquely.
Ass, as, *n.* A well-known animal akin to the horse; a dolt.
Assagai, as′sa-gā, *n.* A Kaffir throwing spear; a species of javelin. Also *Assegai.*
Assail, as-sāl′, *vt.* To attack; to assault.
Assailable, as-sāl′a-bl, *a.* That may be assailed.
Assailant, as-sāl′ant, *n.* One who assails.
Assassin, as-sas′sin, *n.* One who kills, or attempts to kill, by surprise or secretly.
Assassinate, as-sas′sin-āt, *vt.* (assassinating, assassinated). To murder by surprise or secretly.
Assassination, as-sas′sin-ā″shon, *n.* Act of murdering by surprise.
Assault, as-sạlt′, *n.* An attack; a storming.—*vt.* To assail; to storm.
Assaulter, as-sạlt′ėr, *n.* One who assaults.
Assay, as-sā′, *n.* Proof; trial; determination of the quantity of metal in an ore or alloy.—*vt.* To try; to ascertain the purity or alloy of. —*vi.* To try or endeavour.
Assayer, as-sā′ėr, *n.* One who assays.
Assaying, as-sā′ing, *n.* Act of ascertaining the purity of the precious metals.
Assemblage, as-sem′blāj, *n.* A collection of individuals or things.
Assemble, as-sem′bl, *vt.* (assembling, assembled). To bring together.—*vi.* To come together.
Assembly, as-sem′bli, *n.* An assemblage; a convocation.
Assent, as-sent′, *n.* Act of agreeing to anything; consent.—*vi.* To agree; to yield.
Assert, as-sėrt′, *vt.* To affirm; to maintain; to vindicate.
Assertion, as-sėr′shon, *n.* Act of asserting.
Assertive, as-sėrt′iv, *a.* Affirming confidently; peremptory.
Assess, as-ses′, *vt.* To fix a charge to be paid upon; to rate.
Assessable, as-ses′a-bl, *a.* That may be assessed.
Assessment, as-ses′ment, *n.* Act of assessing; the sum levied; a tax.
Assessor, as-ses′ėr, *n.* A legal adviser who assists a magistrate or judge.
Assets, as′sets, *n.pl.* Goods available to pay debts.
Asseverate, as-sev′ė-rāt, *vt.* (asseverating, asseverated). To declare seriously or solemnly; to protest.
Asseveration, as-sev′ė-rā″shon, *n.* Positive and solemn declaration.
Assiduity, as-si-dū′i-ti, *n.* Close application; diligence.
Assiduous, as-sid′ū-us, *a.* Constantly diligent.
Assign, as-sīn′, *vt.* To designate; to allot; to make over to another.—*n.* A person to whom property or any right may be or is transferred.
Assignable, as-sīn′a-bl, *a.* That may be assigned.
Assignation, as-sig-nā′shon, *n.* An appointment to meet, as of lovers; a making over by transfer of title.
Assignee, as-sī-nē′, *n.* One to whom an assignment is made.

Assigner, as-sīn'ėr, *n.* One who assigns.
Assignment, as-sīn'ment, *n.* Act of assigning; thing assigned; a writ of transfer.
Assimilate, as-sim'il-āt, *vt.* (assimilating, assimilated). To make like to; to digest.—*vi.* To become similar or of the same substance.
Assimilation, as-sim'il-ā"shon, *n.* Act of assimilating.
Assist, as-sist', *vt.* To help.—*vi.* To lend help; to contribute.
Assistance, as-sist'ans, *n.* Help; aid.
Assistant, as-sist'ant, *n.* One who assists.
Assize, as-sīz', *n.* A statute regulating weights, measures, or prices; in *pl.* the periodical courts held in the counties of England and Wales.
Associable, as-sō'shi-a-bl, *a.* Companionable.
Associate, as-sō'shi-āt, *vt.* (associating, associated). To join in company with; to combine.—*vi.* To keep company with.—*n.* A companion; friend.
Association, as-sō'si-ā"shon, *n.* Act of associating; union; confederacy; one of the two principal varieties of football, played by eleven men a side, with a round ball, handling (except by the goalkeeper) being forbidden.
Assoil, as-soil', *vt.* To release; to absolve.
Assonance, as'sō-nans, *n.* Resemblance of sounds.
Assort, as-sort', *vt.* To sort; to arrange.—*vi.* To suit; to agree.
Assortment, as-sort'ment, *n.* Act of assorting; quantity of things assorted; variety.
Assuage, as-swāj', *vt.* (assuaging, assuaged). To allay; to calm.—*vi.* To abate or subside.
Assuagement, as-swāj'ment, *n.* Mitigation.
Assume, as-sūm', *vt.* (assuming, assumed). To take for granted; to usurp.—*vi.* To claim more than is due; to be arrogant.
Assuming, as-sūm'ing, *a.* Arrogant.
Assumption, as-sum'shon, *n.* Act of assuming; the thing assumed; the taking up of any person into heaven.
Assurance, a-shör'ans, *n.* Act of assuring; secure confidence; impudence; positive declaration; insurance.
Assure, a-shör', *vt.* (assuring, assured). To make sure; to confirm; to insure.
Assuredly, a-shör'ed-li, *adv.* Certainly.
Assuredness, a-shör'ed-nes, *n.* State of being assured.
Assurer, a-shör'ėr, *n.* One who assures or insures.
Assyrian, as-sir'i-an, *a.* Pertaining to Assyria or its inhabitants.—*n.* A native of Assyria; the language of the Assyrians.
Astatic, a-stat'ik, *a.* Being without polarity, as a magnetic needle.
Aster, as'tėr, *n.* A genus of composite plants, with flowers somewhat like stars.
Asterisk, as'tė-risk, *n.* The figure of a star, thus *, used in printing.
Astern, a-stėrn', *adv.* In or at the hinder part of a ship.
Asteroid, as'tėr-oid, *n.* A small planet.
Asthma, as'ma or as'thma, *n.* A disorder of respiration, characterized by difficulty of breathing, cough, and expectoration.
Asthmatic, as-mat'ik, *a.* Pertaining to asthma; affected by asthma.
Astigmatism, a-stig'mat-izm, *n.* A malformation of the eye, in which rays of light do not properly converge to one point.
Astir, a-stėr', *adv.* or *pred.a.* On stir; active.
Astonish, as-ton'ish, *vt.* To surprise; to astound.
Astonishing, as-ton'ish-ing, *a.* Marvellous.
Astonishment, as-ton'ish-ment, *n.* Amazement.
Astound, as-tound', *vt.* To astonish; to stun; to strike dumb with amazement.
Astounding, as-tound'ing, *a.* Adapted to astonish; most astonishing.
Astraddle, a-strad'l, *adv.* or *pred.a.* Astride.
Astragal, as'tra-gal, *n.* A moulding surrounding the top or bottom of a column.
Astrakhan, as'tra-kan, *n.* A rough kind of cloth with a curled pile.
Astral, as'tral, *a.* Belonging to the stars.
Astray, a-strā', *adv.* or *pred.a.* Straying.
Astrict, as-trikt', *vt.* To contract; to limit.
Astriction, as-trik'shon, *n.* Contraction.
Astride, a-strīd', *adv.* or *pred.a.* With the legs apart or across a thing.
Astringency, as-trinj'en-si, *n.* Power of contracting, or of giving firmness.
Astringent, as-trinj'ent, *a.* Contracting tissues of the body; strengthening.—*n.* A medicine which contracts and strengthens.
Astrolabe, as'trō-lāb, *n.* An old instrument for taking the altitude at sea.
Astrologer, as-trol'o-jėr, *n.* One versed in astrology.
Astrological, as-trō-loj'ik-al, *a.* Pertaining to astrology.
Astrology, as-trol'o-ji, *n.* The pretended art of foretelling future events from the stars.
Astronomer, as-tron'ō-mėr, *n.* One versed in astronomy.
Astronomical, as-trō-nom'ik-al, *a.* Pertaining to astronomy.
Astronomy, as-tron'o-mi, *n.* The science of the heavenly bodies.
Astrut, a-strut', *adv.* or *pred.a.* In a strutting manner.
Astute, as-tūt', *a.* Shrewd; crafty.
Astutely, as-tūt'li, *adv.* Shrewdly.
Astuteness, as-tūt'nes, *n.* Shrewdness.
Asunder, a-sun'dėr, *adv.* or *pred.a.* Apart; into parts; in a divided state.
Asylum, a-sī'lum, *n.* A place of refuge; an institution for the care or relief of the unfortunate.
Asyndeton, a-sin'de-ton, *n.* The dispensing with conjunctions in speech.
At, at, *prep.* Denoting presence or nearness; in a state of; employed in, on, or with; with direction towards.
Atavism, at'a-vizm, *n.* The resemblance of offspring to a remote ancestor.
Atelier, ä-tl-yā, *n.* A workshop; a studio.
Athanasian, ath-a-nā'si-an, *a.* Pertaining to Athanasius or to his creed.
Atheism, ā'thē-izm, *n.* The disbelief in the existence of a God.
Atheist, ā'thē-ist, *n.* One who disbelieves the existence of a God.
Atheistic, Atheistical, ā-thē-ist'ik, ā-thē-ist'-ik-al, *a.* Pertaining to atheism.
Athenæum, ath-e-nē'um, *n.* An establishment connected with literature, science, or art.
Athenian, a-thēn'i-an, *a.* Pertaining to Athens.—*n.* A native of Athens.
Athirst, a-thėrst', *pred.a.* Thirsty.
Athlete, ath-lēt', *n.* One skilled in exercises of agility or strength.

Athletic, ath-let'ik, *a.* Pertaining to an athlete; strong; robust; vigorous.
Athleticism, ath-let'i-sizm, *n.* The practice of athletics.
Athletics, ath-let'iks, *n.pl.* Athletic exercises.
Athwart, a-thwart', *prep.* Across; from side to side.—*adv.* Crossly; wrong.
Atlantean, at-lan-tē'an, *a.* Gigantic.
Atlantic, at-lan'tik, *a.* Pertaining to the ocean between Europe, Africa, and America.—*n.* This ocean.
Atlas, at'las, *n.* A collection of maps.
Atmosphere, at'mos-fēr, *n.* The mass of gas around the earth; air; pervading influence.
Atmospheric, at-mos-fe'rik, *a.* Pertaining to the atmosphere.—*n.* (plural). In wireless telegraphy, disturbances produced in the receiving circuits by electrical action in the atmosphere or in the earth's crust.
Atoll, a-tol', *n.* A ring-shaped coral island.
Atom, a'tom, *n.* A minute particle of matter; anything extremely small.
Atomic, a-tom'ik, *a.* Pertaining to or consisting of atoms.
Atomic bomb, a-tom'ik bom, *n.* A bomb in which the splitting of atoms causes vast heating and explosion on a catastrophic scale.
Atomism, at'om-izm, *n.* Atomic philosophy; the doctrine that atoms of themselves formed the universe.
Atone, a-tōn', *vi.* (atoning, atoned). To make satisfaction.—*vt.* To expiate.
Atonement, a-tōn'ment, *n.* Reconciliation; satisfaction.
Atrabilious, at-ra-bil'i-us, *a.* Melancholic or hypochondriacal. Also *Atrabiliar, Atrabilarious.*
Atrip, a-trip', *adv.* or *pred.a.* Just raised from the ground, as an anchor.
Atrocious, a-trō'shus, *a.* Extremely cruel or wicked; flagitious.
Atrociously, a-trō'shus-li, *adv.* In an atrocious manner.
Atrocity, a-tros'i-ti, *n.* Horrible wickedness.
Atrophy, at'rō-fi, *n.* A wasting away; emaciation.
Attach, at-tach', *vt.* To affix; to connect; to arrest; to win.—*vi.* To adhere.
Attaché, at-ta-shā', *n.* One attached to the suite of an ambassador. **Attaché case,** *n.* A small oblong case of leather or fibre, for carrying documents, books, &c.
Attachment, at-tach'ment, *n.* State of being attached; fidelity; tender regard.
Attack, at-tak', *vt.* To assault; to assail.—*n.* An assault; seizure by a disease.
Attain, at-tān', *vi.* To come or arrive.—*vt.* To reach; to gain; to obtain.
Attainable, at-tān'a-bl, *a.* That may be attained.
Attainder, at-tān'dėr, *n.* Extinction of civil rights, in consequence of a capital crime.
Attainment, at-tān'ment, *n.* Act of attaining; acquirement; accomplishment.
Attaint, at-tānt', *vt.* To affect with attainder.
Attar, at'tär, *n.* An essential oil made from roses, forming a valuable perfume.
Attemper, at-tem'pėr, *vt.* To temper; to modify; to accommodate.
Attempt, at-temt', *vt.* To try to do; to make an effort upon.—*n.* An essay; enterprise.
Attend, at-tend', *vt.* To wait on; to accompany or be present at.—*vi.* To pay regard; to hearken; to wait.
Attendance, at-tend'ans, *n.* Act of attending; service; retinue.
Attendant, at-tend'ant, *a.* Accompanying, as subordinate.—*n.* One who waits on, is present, or accompanies.
Attention, at-ten'shon, *n.* Act of attending; heed; courtesy.
Attentive, at-tent'iv, *a.* Heedful.
Attentively, at-tent'iv-li, *adv.* With attention.
Attentiveness, at-tent'iv-nes, *n.* State of being attentive; heedfulness.
Attenuate, at-ten'ū-āt, *vt.* (attenuating, attenuated). To make slender or thin (as liquids).—*vi.* To diminish.
Attenuation, at-ten'ū-ā"shon, *n.* Act of attenuating; thinness; slenderness.
Attest, at-test', *vt.* To bear witness to; to certify; to call to witness.
Attestation, at-test-ā'shon, *n.* Testimony.
Attic, at'tik, *a.* Pertaining to Attica or to Athens; pure; elegant in style or language.—*n.* The dialect of Attica or Athens; the uppermost story of a building; garret.
Attire, at-tīr', *vt.* (attiring, attired). To dress; to array.—*n.* Dress.
Attitude, at'ti-tūd, *n.* Posture.
Attitudinize, at-ti-tūd'in-īz, *vi.* To assume affected attitudes or airs.
Attorney, at-tėr'ni, *n.* One who acts in place of another; one who practises in law-courts. **Attorney-general,** *n.* The first ministerial law officer of the British crown.
Attorneyship, at-tėr'ni-ship, *n.* The office of an attorney.
Attract, at-trakt', *vt.* To draw to; to entice.
Attractable, at-trakt'a-bl, *a.* That may be attracted.
Attraction, at-trak'shon, *n.* Act of attracting; allurement; charm.
Attractive, at-trakt'iv, *a.* Having the power of attracting; enticing.
Attractively, at-trakt'iv-li, *adv.* In an attractive manner.
Attributable, at-trib'ūt-a-bl, *a.* That may be attributed.
Attribute, at-trib'ūt, *vt.* (attributing, attributed). To ascribe; to impute.—*n.* at'tri-būt. Inherent property; characteristic; an adjectival word or clause.
Attribution, at-tri-bū'shon, *n.* Act of attributing, or the quality ascribed.
Attributive, at-trib'ūt-iv, *a.* That attributes.—*n.* That which is attributed.
Attrition, at-tri'shon, *n.* Act of wearing, or state of being worn, by rubbing.
Attune, at-tūn', *vt.* (attuning, attuned). To put in tune; to adjust to another sound.
Auburn, a'bėrn, *a.* Reddish-brown.
Auction, ąk'shon, *n.* A public sale in which the article falls to the highest bidder.
Auctioneer, ąk-shon-ēr', *n.* The person who sells at auction.
Audacious, ą-dā'shus, *a.* Daring; impudent.
Audacity, ą-das'i-ti, *n.* Daring; reprehensible boldness; impudence.
Audible, ą'di-bl, *a.* That may be heard.
Audibly, ą'di-bli, *adv.* In an audible manner.
Audience, ą'di-ens, *n.* Act of hearing; an assembly of hearers; admittance to a hearing; ceremonial interview.
Audit, ą'dit, *n.* An official examination of accounts.—*vt.* To examine and adjust, as accounts.

Auditor, a'dit-ėr, *n.* One who examines and adjusts accounts.
Auditorship, a'dit-ėr-ship, *n.* The office of auditor.
Auditory, a'di-tō-ri, *a.* Pertaining to the sense or organs of hearing.—*n.* An audience; an auditorium.
Augean, a-jē'an, *a.* Pertaining to Augeas, King of Elis, in Greece, whose stable for 3000 oxen, uncleaned for thirty years, was cleaned by Hercules in one day.
Auger, a'gėr, *n.* An instrument for boring holes.
Aught, at, *n.* Anything; any part; a whit.
Augment, ag-ment', *vt.* To make larger; to add to.—*vi.* To grow larger.
Augment, ag'ment, *n.* Increase; a prefix to a word.
Augmentable, ag-ment'a-bl, *a.* Capable of augmentation.
Augmentation, ag-ment-ā'shon, *n.* Act of augmenting; increase; addition.
Augmentative, ag-ment'at-iv, *a.* Having the quality of augmenting.—*n.* A word formed to express greatness.
Augur, a'gėr, *n.* One who foretold the future by observing the flight of birds; a soothsayer.—*vi.* To predict; to bode.—*vt.* To predict or foretell.
Augural, a'gū-ral, *a.* Pertaining to an augur or augury.
Augurer, a'gėr-ėr, *n.* One who augurs.
Augury, a'gū-ri, *n.* Omen; prediction.
August, a-gust', *a.* Grand; majestic; awful.
August, a'gust, *n.* The eighth month of the year.
Augustan, a-gust'an, *a.* Pertaining to Augustus, or to his reign; classic.
Augustness, a-gust'nes, *n.* Quality of being august; dignity of mien.
Auk, ak, *n.* A swimming bird found in the British seas, with very short wings.
Aulic, a'lik, *a.* Pertaining to a royal court.
Aunt, änt, *n.* The sister of one's father or mother.
Aureate, a-rē'āt, *a.* Golden.
Aurelia, a-rē'li-a, *n.* The chrysalis of an insect.
Aureola, Aureole, a-rē'o-la, a'rē-ōl, *n.* An illumination represented as surrounding a holy person, as Christ; a halo.
Auricle, a'ri-kl, *n.* The external ear; either of the two ear-like cavities over the two ventricles of the heart.
Auricula, a-rik'ū-la, *n.* Species of primrose.
Auricular, a-rik'ū-lėr, *a.* Pertaining to the ear; confidential.
Auriferous, a-rif'ėr-us, *a.* Yielding gold.
Aurist, a'rist, *n.* One skilled in disorders of the ear.
Aurochs, a'roks, *n.* A species of wild ox, once abundant in Europe.
Aurora, a-rō'ra, *n.* The dawn; the goddess of the dawn.
Aurora Borealis, a-rō'ra bō-rē-ā'lis, *n.* The northern lights or streamers.—**Aurora Australis,** a similar phenomenon in the S. hemisphere.
Auscultation, as-kul-tā'shon, *n.* A method of discovering diseases of the lungs, &c., by listening for the sounds arising there.
Auspice, a'spis, *n.* Augury from birds; protection; influence.
Auspicious, a-spi'shus, *a.* Fortunate; propitious.
Auspiciously, a-spi'shus-li, *adv.* Prosperously; favourably.
Austere, a-stēr', *a.* Rigid; sour; stern; severe.
Austerely, a-stēr'li, *adv.* In an austere manner.
Austerity, a-ste'ri-ti, *n.* Severity of manners or life; rigour.
Austral, as'tral, *a.* Southern.
Autarky, a'tar-ki, *n.* Self sufficiency; economic independence.
Authentic, a-then'tik, *a.* Genuine; authoritative.
Authentically, a-then'tik-al-li, *adv.* In an authentic manner.
Authenticate, a-then'ti-kāt, *vt.* To render or prove authentic.
Authentication, a-then'ti-kā"shon, *n.* Act of authenticating; confirmation.
Authenticity, a-then-tis'i-ti, *n.* Quality of being authentic; genuineness.
Author, a'thėr, *n.* One who creates; an originator; the writer of a book, &c.
Authoress, a'thėr-es, *n.* A female author.
Authoritative, a-tho'ri-tā-tiv, *a.* Having due authority; peremptory.
Authoritatively, a-tho'ri-tā-tiv-li, *adv.* In an authoritative manner.
Authority, a-tho'ri-ti, *n.* Legal power or right; influence conferred by character or station; person in power; testimony; credibility; precedent.
Authorize, a'thor-īz, *vt.* (authorizing, authorized). To give authority to; to make legal; to sanction.
Authorship, a'thėr-ship, *n.* Quality or state of being an author.
Autobiographical, a-tō-bī'ō-graf"ik-al, *a.* Pertaining to or containing autobiography.
Autobiography, a'tō-bi-og"ra-fi, *n.* Memoirs of a person written by himself.
Autocracy, a-tok'ra-si, *n.* Absolute government by one man.
Autocrat, a'tō-krat, *n.* An absolute prince or sovereign.
Auto-de-fe, au'tō-de-fā", *n.*; pl. **Autos-de-fe.** The burning of heretics by authority of the Inquisition. **Auto-da-fe,** ou'tō-dä-fā", is the Portuguese form.
Autogiro, a-tō-jī'rō, *n.* Trade name for a type of aircraft with rotating blades hinged at one end to a vertical shaft.
Autograph, a'tō-graf, *n.* A person's own handwriting; signature.
Automatic, a-tō-mat'ik.—*a.* Self-acting; moving spontaneously.—*n.* A pistol which is reloaded by force of the recoil.
Automaton, a-tom'a-ton, *n.*; pl. **-ta.** A self-moving machine, or one which moves by invisible machinery.
Automobile, a'tō-mō-bēl", *n.* A motor-car or similar vehicle.
Autonomy, a-ton'o-mi, *n.* The power or right of self-government.
Autopsy, a'top-si, *n.* Personal observation; post-mortem examination.
Autumn, a'tum, *n.* The third season of the year, between summer and winter.
Autumnal, a-tum'nal, *a.* Belonging or peculiar to autumn.
Auxiliary, ag-zil'i-a-ri, *a.* Aiding.—*n.* One who aids; a verb which helps to form the

moods and tenses of other verbs; *pl.* foreign troops employed in war.
Avail, a-vāl', *vt.* To profit; to promote.—*vi.* To be of use; to answer the purpose.—*n.* Advantage; use.
Available, a-vāl'a-bl, *a.* That may be used; attainable.
Avalanche, av'a-lansh, *n.* A large body of snow or ice sliding down a mountain.
Avarice, av'a-ris, *n.* Covetousness.
Avaricious, av-a-ri'shus, *a.* Covetous; greedy of gain; niggardly.
Avariciously, av-a-ri'shus-li, *adv.* In an avaricious manner.
Avast, a-väst', *exclam.* Hold! stop! (Nautical.)
Avatar, av-a-tär', *n.* A descent of a Hindu deity; a remarkable appearance of any kind.
Avaunt, a-vạnt', *exclam.* Hence! begone!
Ave, ā'vē, *n.* Hail; an abbreviation of the Ave-Maria, or Hail-Mary.
Avenge, a-venj', *vt.* (avenging, avenged). To vindicate; to take satisfaction for.
Avenger, a-venj'ėr, *n.* One who avenges.
Avenue, av'e-nū, *n.* An approach to; an alley of trees leading to a house, &c.
Aver, a-vėr', *vt.* (averring, averred). To declare positively; to assert.
Average, av'ėr-āj, *n.* Medium; mean proportion.—*a.* Medial; containing a mean proportion.—*vt.* To find the mean of.—*vi.* To form a mean.
Averment, a-vėr'ment, *n.* Affirmation; declaration.
Averruncator, av-e-rung'kāt-ėr, *n.* Shears for pruning trees.
Averse, a-vėrs', *a.* Disinclined; not favourable.
Averseness, a-vėrs'nes, *n.* Aversion.
Aversion, a-vėr'shon, *n.* Dislike; antipathy.
Avert, a-vėrt', *vt.* To turn aside or away from; to keep off or prevent.
Aviary, ā'vi-a-ri, *n.* A place for keeping birds.
Aviation, ā'vi-ā-shon, *n.* Aerial navigation by machines heavier than air.
Avidity, a-vid'i-ti, *n.* Eager desire; greediness; strong appetite.
Avizandum, av-i-zan'dum, *n.* In Scotland, the private consideration by a judge of a case which has been heard in court.
Avocation, av-ō-kā'shon, *n.* Business; occupation.
Avoid, a-void', *vt.* To shun; to evade; to make void.
Avoidable, a-void'a-bl, *a.* That may be avoided.
Avoidance, a-void'ans, *n.* Act of avoiding; the state of being vacant.
Avoirdupois, av'ėr-dū-poiz", *n.* or *a.* A system of weight, in which a pound contains sixteen ounces.
Avouch, a-vouch', *vt.* To affirm; to avow.
Avow, a-vou', *vt.* To declare with confidence; to confess frankly.
Avowable, a-vou'a-bl, *a.* That may be avowed.
Avowal, a-vou'al, *n.* An open declaration; frank acknowledgment.
Avowedly, a-vou'ed-li, *adv.* In an open manner; with frank acknowledgment.
Await, a-wāt', *vt.* To wait for; to expect; to be in store for.
Awake, a-wāk', *vt.* (awaking, pret. woke, awaked, pp. awaked). To rouse from sleep or from a state of inaction.—*vi.* To cease from sleep; to rouse oneself.—*a.* Not sleeping; vigilant.
Awaken, a-wāk'n, *vt.* and *i.* To awake.
Awakening, a-wāk'n-ing, *n.* Act of awaking.
Award, a-wạrd', *vt.* To adjudge.—*vi.* To make an award.—*n.* A judgment; decision of arbitrators.
Aware, a-wār', *a.* Informed; conscious.
Away, a-wā', *adv.* Absent; at a distance; in motion from; by degrees; in continuance.—*exclam.* Begone!
Awe, ạ, *n.* Fear; fear mingled with reverence.—*vt.* (awing, awed). To strike with fear and reverence.
Aweary, a-wē'ri, *pred.a.* Weary; tired.
Aweigh, a-wā', *adv.* or *pred.a.* Atrip.
Awful, ạ'fụl, *a.* Filling with awe; terrible.
Awfully, a'fụl-li, *adv.* In an awful manner.
Awfulness, ạ'fụl-nes, *n.* Quality or state of being awful.
Awhile, a-whīl', *adv.* For some time.
Awkward, ak'wėrd, *a.* Inexpert; inelegant.
Awkwardly, ạk'wėrd-li, *adv.* In a bungling manner; inelegantly.
Awl, ạl, *n.* A pointed iron instrument for piercing small holes in leather.
Awn, ạn, *n.* The beard of corn or grass.
Awned, ạnd, *a.* Furnished with an awn.
Awning, ạn'ing, *n.* A cover of canvas, &c., to shelter from the sun or wind.
Awry, a-rī, *pred.a.* or *adv.* Twisted toward one side; distorted; asquint.
Axe, aks, *n.* An instrument for hewing and chopping.
Axial, aks'i-al, *a.* Pertaining to an axis.
Axilla, aks-il'la, *n.* The arm-pit.
Axiom, aks'i-om, *n.* A self-evident truth; an established principle.
Axiomatic, aks'i-ō-mat"ik, *a.* Pertaining to an axiom.
Axiomatically, aks'i-ō-mat"ik-al-li, *adv.* By the use of axioms.
Axis, aks'is, *n.*; pl. **Axes,** aks'ēz. The straight line, real or imaginary, passing through a body, on which it revolves.
Axle, Axle-tree, aks'l, aks'l-trē, *n.* The pole on which a wheel turns.
Ay, Aye, ī, *adv.* Yea; yes.—*n.* An affirmative vote.
Ayah, ā'yä, *n.* A native Indian waiting woman.
Aye, ā, *adv.* Always; ever; continually.
Azalea, a-zā'lē-a, *n.* The generic name of certain showy plants of the heath family.
Azimuth, az'i-muth, *n.* An arc of the horizon between the meridian of a place and a vertical circle.
Azoic, a-zō'ik, *a.* Destitute of organic life.
Azote, az'ōt, *n.* Nitrogen.
Azure, ā'zhūr, *a.* Sky-coloured.—*n.* The fine blue colour of the sky; the sky.

B

Baa, bä, *n.* The cry of a sheep.—*vi.* To cry or bleat as sheep.
Babble, bab'bl, *vi.* (babbling, babbled). To talk idly; to prate.—*vt.* To utter idly.—*n.* Idle talk; murmur, as of a stream.
Babblement, bab'bl-ment, *n.* Babble.
Babbler, bab'bl-ėr, *n.* One who babbles.
Babe, bāb, *n.* An infant; a young child.

Babel, bā'bel, *n.* Confusion; disorder.

Baboon, ba-bön', *n.* A large kind of monkey.

Baby, bā'bi, *n.* A babe; a young child.—*a.* Pertaining to a baby.

Baby-farmer, bā'bi-fär-mėr, *n.* One who makes a trade of rearing infants.

Babylonian, Babylonish, ba-bi-lōn'i-an, ba-bi-lōn'ish, *a.* Pertaining to Babylon.

Baccarat, bak-ka-rä', *n.* A game of cards played by any number and a banker.

Bacchanal, bak'ka-nal, *n.* A votary of Bacchus; a revel.—*a.* Characterized by intemperate drinking.

Bacchanalia, bak-a-nā'li-a, *n.pl.* Feasts in honour of Bacchus.

Bacchanalian, bak-ka-nā'li-an, *a.* Bacchanal. —*n.* A reveller; a votary of Bacchus.

Bachelor, bach'el-ėr, *n.* An unmarried man; one who has taken the university degree below that of Master or Doctor.

Bachelorhood, Bachelorship, bach'el-ėr-hu̇d, bach'el-ėr-ship, *n.* The state of being a bachelor.

Bacillus, ba-sil'lus, *n.*; pl. **-illi.** A microscopic organism which causes disease.

Back, bak, *n.* The hinder part of the body in man and the upper part in beasts; the hinder part.—*vt.* To support; to cause to recede; to endorse.—*vi.* To move back.—*adv.* To the rear; to a former state; in return.

Backbite, bak'bīt, *vt.* To speak evil of secretly.

Backbone, bak'bōn, *n.* The spine; strength.

Back-door, bak'dōr, *n.* A door in the back part of a building.

Backer, bak'ėr, *n.* One who backs or supports another in a contest.

Backgammon, bak-gam'mon, *n.* A game played by two persons on a board, with men and dice.

Background, bak'ground, *n.* The part of a picture represented as farthest away; a situation little noticed.

Backhand, Backhanded, bak'hand, bak'-hand-ed, *a.* With the hand turned backward; indirect.

Backslide, bak-slīd', *vt.* To apostatize; to relapse.

Backslider, bak-slīd'ėr, *n.* An apostate.

Backward, Backwards, bak'wėrd, bak'-wėrdz, *adv.* With the back forwards; towards past times; back; from better to worse.

Backward, bak'wėrd, *a.* Lagging behind; reluctant; late; dull.

Backwardly, bak'wėrd-li, *adv.* In a backward manner; unwillingly.

Backwardness, bak'wėrd-nes, *n.* Unwillingness; reluctance; dilatoriness.

Backwoods, bak'wu̇dz, *n.pl.* Outlying forest districts.

Bacon, bā'kn, *n.* Swine's flesh cured and dried.

Bacteriology, bak-tē'ri-ol''o-ji, *n.* The doctrine or study of bacteria.

Bacterium, bak-tē'ri-um, *n.*; pl. **-ia.** A disease germ.

Bad, bad, *a.* Not good; wicked; immoral; injurious; incompetent.

Badge, baj, *n.* A mark or cognizance worn.

Badger, baj'ėr, *n.* A burrowing quadruped, nocturnal in habits.—*vt.* To worry; to pester.

Badinage, bä'di-näzh, *n.* Raillery; banter.

Badly, bad'li, *adv.* In a bad manner.

Badminton, bad'min-ton, *n.* A game like lawn-tennis played with shuttlecocks.

Baffle, baf'fl, *vt.* (baffling, baffled). To elude; to frustrate; to defeat.

Bag, bag, *n.* A sack; what is contained in a bag; a certain quantity of a commodity.—*vt.* (bagging, bagged). To put into a bag; to distend.—*vi.* To swell like a full bag.

Bagatelle, bag-a-tel', *n.* A trifle; a game somewhat like billiards.

Baggage, bag'āj, *n.* The necessaries of an army; luggage; lumber.

Bagging, bag'ing, *p.n.* The cloth for bags.

Bagnio, ban'yō, *n.* A bath; brothel; prison.

Bagpipe, bag'pīp, *n.* A musical wind-instrument.

Bail, bāl, *vt.* To liberate from custody on security for reappearance; to free (a boat) from water; to bale.—*n.* Security given for release; the person who gives such security.

Bailable, bāl'a-bl, *a.* That may be bailed.

Bailie, Baillie, bā'li, *n.* A magistrate in Scotland, corresponding to an alderman.

Bailiff, bā'lif, *n.* A subordinate civil officer; a steward.

Bailiwick, bā'li-wik, *n.* The extent or limit of a bailiff's jurisdiction.

Bait, bāt, *n.* A substance used to allure fish, &c.; an enticement.—*vt.* To furnish with a lure; to give food and drink to a beast when travelling; to harass; to annoy.—*vi.* To take refreshment on a journey.

Baize, bāz, *n.* A coarse woollen stuff with a long nap.

Bake, bāk, *vt.* (baking, baked). To heat, dry, and harden by fire or the sun's rays; to cook in an oven.—*vi.* To do the work of making bread; to be baked.

Bakelite, bāk'l-īt, *n.* Trade name for a hard, insoluble, infusible substance derived by heat treatment from phenol and formaldehyde.

Baker, bāk'ėr, *n.* One whose occupation is to bake bread, &c.

Bakery, bāk'ė-ri, *n.* A place for baking.

Baking, bāk'ing, *p.n.* The action of the verb *to bake*; the quantity baked at once.

Bakshish, bak'shēsh, *n.* A gratuity of money.

Balance, bal'ans, *n.* A pair of scales; equilibrium; surplus; difference of two sums; the sum due on an account.—*vt.* (balancing, balanced). To bring to an equilibrium; to weigh, as reasons; to settle, as an account.—*vi.* To be in equilibrium; to be equal when added up; to hesitate.

Balance-sheet, bal'ans-shēt, *n.* A statement of assets and liabilities.

Balcony, bal'ko-ni, *n.* A platform projecting from a window.

Bald, ba̤ld, *a.* Wanting hair; unadorned; bare; paltry.

Baldachin, bal'da-kin, *n.* A canopy held over the pope; a canopy over an altar or throne.

Balderdash, ba̤l'dėr-dash, *n.* Senseless prate; jargon.

Baldly, ba̤ld'li, *adv.* Nakedly; meanly.

Baldness, ba̤ld'nes, *n.* State of being bald; inelegance of style; want of ornament.

Baldrick, Baldric, ba̤ld'rik, *n.* A broad belt worn diagonally across the body.

Bale, bāl, *n.* A bundle or package of goods.—*vt.* (baling, baled). To make up in a bale; to free from water; to bail. **Bale out,** *vi.* To leave aircraft by parachute.

Baleen, ba-lēn′, *n.* The whalebone of commerce.
Baleful, bāl′fụl, *a.* Calamitous; deadly.
Balk, bạk, *n.* A ridge of land left unploughed; a great beam; a barrier; a disappointment.—*vt.* To baffle; to disappoint.
Ball, bạl, *n.* A round body; a globe; a bullet; an entertainment of dancing.—*vi.* To form, as snow, into balls, as on horses' hoofs.
Ballad, bal′lad, *n.* A short narrative poem; a popular song.
Ballade, ba-läd′, *n.* A poem of three stanzas of eight lines and an envoy of four lines.
Ballast, bal′last, *n.* Heavy matter carried in a ship to keep it steady; that which confers steadiness.—*vt.* To load with ballast; to make or keep steady.
Ball-cock, bạl′kok, *n.* A kind of self-acting stop-cock, used in cisterns.
Ballet, bal′lā, *n.* A theatrical dance.
Ballista, bal-lis′ta, *n.* A military engine used by the ancients for throwing stones.
Ballistic, bal-lis′tik, *a.* Pertaining to projectiles.—*n.pl.* The science of projectiles in motion.
Balloon, bal-lön′, *n.* A spherical hollow body; a large bag filled with a gas which makes it rise and float in the air.
Ballot, bal′lot, *n.* A ball, paper, &c., used for voting in private; the system of voting by such means.—*vi.* To vote by ballot.
Balm, bäm, *n.* Balsam; that which heals or soothes; the name of several aromatic plants.—*vt.* To anoint with balm; to soothe.
Balmoral, bal-mo′ral, *n.* A kind of Scottish bonnet.
Balmy, bäm′i, *a.* Aromatic; soothing.
Balsam, bạl′sam, *n.* An oily, aromatic substance got from trees; a soothing ointment.
Balsamic, bạl- or bal-sam′ik, *a.* Balmy; mitigating.
Baluster, bal′us-tėr, *n.* A small column or pillar, used for balustrades.
Balustrade, bal-us-trād′, *n.* A row of balusters joined by a rail.
Bamboo, bam-bö′, *n.* A tropical plant of the reed kind.
Bamboozle, bam-bö′zl, *vt.* (bamboozling, bamboozled). To hoax; to humbug; to perplex.
Ban, ban, *n.* A public proclamation; curse; excommunication; *pl.* proclamation of marriage.—*vt.* (banning, banned). To curse.
Banal, ban′al, or ba nal′, *a.* Hackneyed; vulgar.
Banality, ba-nal′i-ti, *n.* State of being banal.
Banana, ba-nä′na, *n.* A plant allied to the plantain, with soft luscious fruit.
Band, band, *n.* That which binds; a bond; a fillet; a company; a body of musicians.—*vt.* To bind together; to unite in a troop or confederacy.—*vi.* To unite in a band.
Bandage, band′āj, *n.* A band; a cloth for a wound, &c.—*vt.* (bandaging, bandaged). To bind with a bandage.
Bandbox, band′boks, *n.* A slight box for caps, bonnets, &c.
Banded, band′ed, *p.a.* United in a band.
Banderole, ban′de-rōl, *n.* A little flag.
Bandit, ban′dit, *n.*; pl. **-itti, -its.** An outlaw; a robber; a highwayman.
Bandog, ban′dog, *n.* A large fierce dog, usually kept chained.
Bandolier, ban-dō-lēr′, *n.* A shoulder-belt for carrying cartridges.
Bandrol, band′rōl, *n.* Same as *Banderole.*
Bandy, ban′di, *n.* A bent club for striking a ball; a play at ball with such a club.—*vt.* (bandying, bandied). To strike to and fro; to exchange (compliments, &c.).
Bandy-legged, ban′di-legd, *a.* Having crooked legs.
Bane, bān, *n.* That which causes hurt or death; ruin; poison; mischief.
Baneful, bān′fụl, *a.* Pernicious; poisonous.
Bang, bang, *vt.* To thump; to treat with violence.—*n.* A heavy blow.
Bangle, bang′gl, *n.* An ornamental ring worn upon the arms and ankles.
Banian, ban′yan, *n.* *See* BANYAN.
Banish, ban′ish, *vt.* To drive away; to exile.
Banishment, ban′ish-ment, *n.* Act of banishing; exile.
Banister, ban′is-tėr, *n.* A baluster.
Banjo, ban′jō, *n.* A six-stringed musical instrument.
Bank, bangk, *n.* Ground rising from the side of a river, lake, &c.; any heap piled up; a bench of rowers; place where money is deposited; a banking company.—*vt.* To fortify with a bank; to deposit in a bank.
Banker, bangk′ėr, *n.* One who deals in money.
Banking, bangk′ing, *p.n.* The business of a banker.
Bank-note, bangk′nōt, *n.* A promissory note issued by a banking company.
Bankrupt, bangk′rupt, *n.* One who cannot pay his debts.—*a.* Unable to pay debts.
Bankruptcy, bangk′rupt-si, *n.* State of being a bankrupt; failure in trade.
Bank-stock, bangk′stok, *n.* A share or shares in the capital stock of a bank.
Banner, ban′nėr, *n.* A flag bearing a device or national emblem; a standard.
Banneret, ban′nėr-et, *n.* An old rank between that of knight and baron.
Banns, banz, *n.pl.* The proclamation in church necessary for a regular marriage.
Banquet, bang′kwet, *n.* A feast; a sumptuous entertainment.—*vt.* To treat with a feast.—*vi.* To feast.
Banshee, ban′shē, *n.* An Irish fairy believed to attach herself to a house or family.
Bantam, ban′tam, *n.* A small breed of domestic fowl with feathered shanks.
Banter, ban′tėr, *vt.* To attack with jocularity; to rally.—*n.* Raillery; pleasantry.
Bantling, bant′ling, *n.* An infant.
Banyan, ban′yan, *n.* An Indian tree of the fig genus.
Baptism, bap′tizm, *n.* An immersing in or sprinkling with water, as a religious ceremony.
Baptismal, bap-tiz′mal, *a.* Pertaining to baptism.
Baptist, bap′tist, *n.* One of those Protestants who believe in adult baptism by immersion.
Baptistery, bap′tis-te-ri, *n.* A place where baptisms take place.
Baptize, bap-tīz′, *vt.* (baptizing, baptized). To administer baptism to; to christen.
Bar, bär, *n.* A bolt; obstacle; a long piece of wood or metal; inclosure in an inn or court; a tribunal; body of barristers; obstruction at the mouth of a river; a counter where liquors are served.—*vt.* (barring, barred). To secure; to hinder; to prohibit; to except.

Barb, bärb, *n.* The points which stand backward in an arrow, hook, &c.; a Barbary horse.—*vt.* To furnish with barbs or points.
Barbarian, bär-bā′ri-an, *a.* Belonging to savages; uncivilized.—*n.* A savage.
Barbarism, bär′bär-izm, *n.* Barbarity; an impropriety of speech.
Barbarity, bär-ba′ri-ti, *n.* The state or qualities of a barbarian; ferociousness.
Barbarize, bär′bär-iz, *vt.* (barbarizing, barbarized). To make barbarous.
Barbarous, bär′bär-us, *a.* In a state of barbarism; cruel; inhuman.
Barbarously, bär′bär-us-li, *adv.* In a savage, cruel, or inhuman manner.
Barbecue, bär′be-kū, *n.* A hog, &c., roasted whole; a feast in the open air.—*vt.* To dress and roast whole.
Barbed, bärbd, *a.* Jagged with hooks or points.
Barbel, bär′bel, *n.* A fish having on its upper jaw four beard-like appendages.
Barber, bär′bėr, *n.* One who shaves beards and dresses hair.
Barberry, bär′be-ri, *n.* A thorny shrub bearing red berries.
Barbette, bär-bet′, *n.* A platform from which cannon may be fired over the parapet instead of through an embrasure; circular armoured platform for guns in warships.
Barbican, bär′bi-kan, *n.* An outer-work defending a castle, &c.
Barcarolle, bär′ka-rōl, *n.* A melody sung by Venetian gondoliers.
Bard, bärd, *n.* A Celtic minstrel; a poet.
Bardic, bärd′ik, *a.* Pertaining to bards.
Bare, bār, *a.* Uncovered; empty; scanty; worn.—*vt.* (baring, bared). To make naked.
Barebacked, bār′bakt, *a.* Unsaddled.
Barefaced, bār′fāst, *a.* Shameless; glaring.
Barefoot, bār′fụt, *a.* or *adv.* With the feet bare.
Barely, bār′li, *adv.* Nakedly; scarcely.
Bargain, bär′gin, *n.* A contract; a gainful transaction; a thing bought or sold.—*vi.* To make a bargain.—*vt.* To sell.
Bargainer, bär′gin-ėr, *n.* One who makes a bargain.
Barge, bärj, *n.* A boat of pleasure or state; a flat-bottomed boat of burden.
Bargee, bärj-ē′, *n.* One of a barge's crew.
Bargeman, bärj′man, *n.* The man who manages a barge.
Barilla, ba-ril′la, *n.* An impure soda obtained by burning several species of plants.
Bar-iron, bär′ī-ėrn, *n.* Iron in bars.
Bark, bärk, *n.* The outer rind of a tree; a barque; the noise made by a dog, wolf, &c.—*vt.* To strip bark off; to treat with bark; to make the cry of dogs, &c.
Barley, bär′li, *n.* A species of grain used especially for making malt.
Barley-corn, bär′li-korn, *n.* A grain of barley; the third part of an inch.
Barley-sugar, bär-li-shụg′ėr, *n.* Sugar boiled till it is brittle and candied.
Barm, bärm, *n.* Yeast.
Barmaid, bär′mād, *n.* A woman who tends a bar where liquors are sold.
Barmy, bärm′i, *a.* Containing barm; light-headed; mad.
Barn, bärn, *n.* A building for grain, hay, &c.
Barnacle, bär′na-kl, *n.* A shell-fish, often found on ships' bottoms; a species of goose.
Barnacles, bär′na-klz, *n.pl.* An instrument put on a horse's nose; a pair of spectacles.
Barograph, ba′rō-graf, *n.* An instrument for recording changes in the atmosphere.
Barometer, ba-rom′et-ėr, *n.* An instrument for measuring the weight of the atmosphere.
Barometric, ba-rō-met′rik, *a.* Pertaining or relating to the barometer.
Barometrically, ba-rō-met′rik-al-li, *adv.* By means of a barometer.
Baron, ba′ron, *n.* A peer of the lowest rank; a title of certain judges, &c.
Baronage, ba′ron-āj, *n.* The whole body of barons; the dignity or estate of a baron.
Baroness, ba′ron-es, *n.* A baron's wife.
Baronet, ba′ron-et, *n.* One of the hereditary rank next below a baron.
Baronetage, ba′ron-et-āj, *n.* The collective body of baronets.
Baronetcy, ba′ron-et-si, *n.* The condition or rank of a baronet.
Baronial, ba-rō′ni-al, *a.* Pertaining to a baron.
Barony, ba′ron-i, *n.* The lordship, honour, or fee of a baron.
Barouche, ba-rösh′, *n.* A four-wheeled carriage with a collapsible top.
Barque, bärk, *n.* A sailing vessel; a three-masted ship, the mizzen-mast without yards.
Barrack, ba′rak, *n.* A building for soldiers, especially in garrison (generally in *pl.*).
Barrage, bar′aj, *n.* The discharge of artillery in such a manner as to keep a selected zone under continuous fire.
Barrator, ba′rat-ėr, *n.* One who excites law suits.
Barratry, ba′ra-tri, *n.* The practice of a barrator; fraud by a shipmaster.
Barrel, ba′rel, *n.* A round wooden cask; the quantity which a barrel holds; a hollow cylinder.—*vt.* (barrelling, barrelled). To pack in a barrel.
Barrelled, ba′reld, *a.* Having a barrel or barrels.
Barren, ba′ren, *a.* Sterile; unfruitful; unsuggestive.
Barrenness, ba′ren-nes, *n.* The state or quality of being barren.
Barricade, ba-ri-kād′, *n.* A temporary fortification to obstruct an enemy; a barrier.—*vt.* To obstruct; to bar.
Barrier, ba′ri-ėr, *n.* Fence; obstruction.
Barrister, ba′ris-tėr, *n.* A counsellor at law; a lawyer whose profession is to speak in court on behalf of clients.
Barrow, ba′rō, *n.* A small hand or wheel carriage; a sepulchral mound.
Barter, bär′tėr, *vi.* To traffic by exchange.—*vt.* To exchange in commerce.—*n.* Traffic by exchange.
Bartizan, bär′ti-zan, *n.* A small overhanging turret with apertures to shoot through.
Baryta, Barytes, ba-rī′ta, ba-rī′tēz, *n.* The heaviest of the alkaline earths.
Barytone, ba′ri-tōn, *a.* Having a voice ranging between tenor and bass.—*n.* A male voice between tenor and bass.
Basalt, ba-zạlt′, *n.* A dark volcanic rock, often found in columnar form.
Basaltic, ba-zạlt′ik, *a.* Pertaining to basalt.
Bascule, bas′kūl, *n.* An arrangement in bridges by which one part balances another.
Base, bās, *a.* Low in value or station; worthless; despicable.—*n.* Foundation; lower side;

support; chief ingredient of a compound; the gravest part in music.—*vt.* (basing, based). To place on a basis; to found.
Base-ball, bās'bạl, *n.* The national game of the U.S.A. played with bat and ball by two sides of nine men each.
Base-born, bās'born, *a.* Illegitimate.
Baseless, bās'les, *a.* Without base; groundless.
Base-line, bās'lin, *n.* A line taken as a base of operations.
Basely, bās'li, *adv.* In a base manner.
Basement, bās'ment, *n.* The ground floor of a building.
Baseness, bās'nes, *n.* Lowness; meanness; vileness.
Bash, bash, *vt.* To beat violently.
Bashaw, ba-shạ', *n.* A pasha; a proud, overbearing person.
Bashful, bash'fụl, *a.* Modest; wanting confidence.
Bashfully, bash'fụl-li, *adv.* In a shy manner.
Bashfulness, bash'fụl-nes, *n.* Quality of being bashful; extreme modesty.
Basic, bās'ik, *a.* Relating to a base.
Basil, baz'il, *n.* An aromatic pot-herb.
Basilica, ba-sil'i-ka, *n.* An ancient Roman public hall; a church in imitation thereof.
Basilisk, baz'il-isk, *n.* A fabulous serpent, lizard, or cockatrice; a genus of crested lizards; an old kind of cannon.
Basin, bā'sn, *n.* A broad circular dish; a reservoir; a dock; tract of country drained by a river.
Basis, bās'is, *n.*; pl. **-ses.** A base; foundation; groundwork.
Bask, bask, *vi.* To lie in warmth, or in the sun; to enjoy ease and prosperity.—*vt.* To warm by exposure to heat.
Basket, bas'ket, *n.* A domestic vessel made of twigs, &c.; the contents of a basket.—*vt.* To put in a basket.
Bas-relief, bas'rē-lēf, or bä', *n.* Low relief; sculpture in which the figures do not stand out prominently.
Bass, bäs, *n.* The American linden; a mat made of bast; a fish allied to the perch.
Bass, bās, *n.* The lowest part in musical harmony; the lowest male voice.
Basset, bas'set, *n.* The outcrop of a stratum.
Bassinet, bas'si-net, *n.* A wicker cradle; a type of perambulator.
Bassoon, bas-sön', *n.* A musical wind-instrument which serves for a bass.
Bass-relief, bäs'rē-lēf, *n.* Bas-relief.
Bast, bast, *n.* The inner bark of the lime tree.
Bastard, bas'tėrd, *n.* An illegitimate child.—*a.* Illegitimate; not genuine.
Bastardize, bas'tėrd-īz, *vt.* (bastardizing, bastardized). To prove to be a bastard.
Bastardy, bas'tėrd-i, *n.* The state of being a bastard.
Baste, bāst, *vt.* (basting, basted). To beat with a stick; to drip fat or butter on meat while roasting; to sew with temporary stitches.
Bastinado, bas-ti-nā'dō, *n.* A beating with a cudgel on the soles of the feet.—*vt.* To beat thus.
Bastion, bas'ti-on, *n.* A large mass of earth or masonry standing out from a rampart.
Bat, bat, *n.* A flying mammal, like a mouse; a heavy stick; a club used to strike the ball in cricket, &c.—*vi.* (batting, batted). To play with a bat.
Batch, bach, *n.* Quantity of bread baked at one time; a quantity.
Bate, bāt, *vt.* (bating, bated). To abate.
Bath, bäth, *n.* Place to bathe in; immersion in water, &c.; a Jewish measure.
Bath-brick, bäth'brik, *n.* A brick of siliceous earth for cleaning knives, &c.
Bath-chair, bäth'chār, *n.* A wheeled chair for invalids.
Bathe, bāᴛʜ, *vt.* (bathing, bathed). To immerse in water, &c.—*vi.* To take a bath.
Bathometer, ba-thom'et-ėr, *n.* An apparatus for taking soundings.
Bathos, bā'thos, *n.* A ludicrous sinking in writing or speech; anti-climax.
Batist, Batiste, ba-tēst', *n.* A kind of cambric.
Batman, bat'man, *n.* An officer's servant.
Baton, ba'ton, *n.* A staff; a truncheon; a badge of office carried by field-marshals.
Battalion, bat-ta'li-on, *n.* A body of infantry, consisting of from 300 to 1000 men.
Batten, bat'n, *n.* A piece of wood from 1 to 7 inches broad, and from ½ to 2½ thick; a plank.—*vt.* To fasten with battens; to fatten.
Batter, bat'tėr, *vt.* To beat with violence; to wear by hard usage.—*n.* A mixture beaten together with some liquid.
Battering-ram, bat'tėr-ing-ram, *n.* An ancient engine for battering down walls.
Battery, bat'tė-ri, *n.* A number of cannon prepared for field operations; a parapet covering guns; an apparatus for originating an electric current; a violent assault.
Battle, bat'l, *n.* Encounter of two armies; a combat.—*vi.* (battling, battled). To contend in fight.
Battle-axe, bat'l-aks, *n.* An axe anciently used as a weapon of war.
Battledore, bat'l-dōr, *n.* An instrument to strike a ball or shuttlecock.
Battlement, bat'l-ment, *n.* A parapet with openings to discharge missiles through.
Battue, bat'tụ, *n.* The shooting of game that is driven towards the sportsmen.
Bauble, bạ'bl, *n.* A trifling piece of finery; a gewgaw.
Bawd, bạd, *n.* A procurer or procuress; a pimp.
Bawdy, bạ'di, *a.* Obscene; unchaste.
Bawl, bạl, *vi.* To shout; to clamour.
Bay, bā, *a.* Reddish-brown.—*n.* An arm of the sea; the laurel tree; a laurel-crown, fame (generally in *pl.*); a deep-toned bark of a dog.—*vi.* To bark.—*vt.* To bark at; to follow with barking. **At bay,** so pressed by enemies as to be compelled to face them.
Bayadere, bā-ya-dēr', *n.* In the East Indies, a professional dancing girl.
Bayonet, bā'on-et, *n.* A dagger-like weapon fixed to a rifle.—*vt.* (bayoneting, bayoneted). To stab with a bayonet.
Bay-rum, bā'rum, *n.* A spirituous liquor containing the oil of the bayberry of Jamaica.
Bay-window, bā'win-dō, *n.* A projecting window which forms a recess within.
Bazaar, ba-zär', *n.* A place of sale; a sale of articles for a charitable purpose.
Bdellium, del'li-um, *n.* An aromatic gum-resin.
Be, bē, *vi. substantive* (being, been; pres. am, art, is, are; pret. was, wast or wert, were). To exist; to become; to remain.

Beach, bēch, *n.* The shore of the sea.—*vt.* To run (a vessel) on a beach.
Beached, bēcht, *p.a.* Having a beach; stranded.
Beacon, bē'kn, *n.* A light to direct seamen; a signal of danger.—*vt.* To afford light, as a beacon; to light up.
Bead, bēd, *n.* A little ball strung on a thread, any small globular body; a small moulding.
Beadle, bē'dl, *n.* A messenger or crier of a court; a petty officer in a parish, church, university, &c.
Bead-roll, bēd'rōl, *n.* A list of persons to be prayed for.
Beadsman, bēdz'man, *n.* One who prays for others; a privileged beggar.
Beagle, bē'gl, *n.* A small hunting dog.
Beak, bēk, *n.* The bill of a bird; anything like a bird's beak.
Beaked, bēkt, *a.* Having a beak.
Beaker, bēk'ėr, *n.* A large drinking-cup.
Beam, bēm, *n.* A main timber in a building; part of a balance which sustains the scales; pole of a carriage; a ray of light.—*vt.* To send forth, as beams; to emit.—*vi.* To shine.
Beaming, bēm'ing, *a.* Emitting beams or rays; radiant; expressing joy in the face.
Beamy, bēm'i, *a.* Emitting beams or rays; radiant; shining.
Bean, bēn, *n.* A name of several kinds of pulse.
Bear, bār, *vt.* (bearing, pret. bore, pp. borne). To carry; to suffer; to produce; to have; to permit; to behave (oneself).—*vi.* To suffer; to be patient; to produce; to take effect; to be situated as to the point of the compass; to refer (with *upon*).
Bear, bār, *n.* A large carnivorous plantigrade quadruped; one of two constellations, the Greater and Lesser; an uncouth person; one who tries to bring down the price of stock.
Bearable, bār'a-bl, *a.* That can be borne.
Beard, bērd, *n.* The hair on the chin, &c.; the awn of corn.—*vt.* To defy to the face.
Bearded, bērd'ed, *a.* Having a beard.
Beardless, bērd'les, *a.* Without a beard.
Bearer, bār'ėr, *n.* One who bears; one who carries a letter, &c.; a support.
Bear-garden, bār'gär-dn, *n.* A place where bears were kept; a place of disorder.
Bearing, bār'ing, *n.* A carrying; deportment; mien; relation; tendency.
Bearing-rein, bār'ing-rān, *n.* The rein by which a horse's head is held up.
Bearish, bār'ish, *a.* Partaking of the qualities of a bear.
Beast, bēst, *n.* Any four-footed animal; a brutal man.
Beastly, bēst'li, *a.* Brutal; filthy; bestial.
Beat, bēt, *vt.* (beating, pret. beat, pp. beat, beaten). To strike repeatedly; to overcome; to crush; to harass.—*vi.* To throb, as a pulse; to sail against the wind.—*n.* A stroke; a pulsation; a course frequently trodden.
Beater, bēt'ėr, *n.* One who beats; that which beats; one who rouses game from coverts.
Beatific, bē-a-tif'ik, *a.* Blessing or making happy.
Beatification, bē-at'i-fi-kā"shon, *n.* Act of beatifying; a kind of canonization.
Beatify, bē-at'i-fī, *vt.* (beatifying, beatified). To make happy; to declare a person blessed.
Beating, bēt'ing, *n.* Act of striking; chastisement by blows; a conquering; defeat.
Beatitude, bē-at'i-tūd, *n.* Blessedness; bliss; one of the declarations of blessedness to particular virtues made by Christ.
Beau, bō, *n.*; pl. **-aux** or **-aus,** bōz. A man fond of fine dress; a gallant; a lover.
Beau-ideal, bō-ī-dē'al, *n.* An imagined standard of perfection.
Beauteous, bū'tē-us, *a.* Beautiful; fair.
Beautiful, bū'ti-fu̥l, *a.* Full of beauty; lovely. —*n.* That which possesses beauty.
Beautifully, bū'ti-fu̥l-li, *adv.* In a beautiful manner.
Beautify, bū'ti-fī, *vt.* (beautifying, beautified). To make beautiful; to adorn.—*vi.* To become beautiful.
Beauty, bū'ti, *n.* Loveliness; elegance; grace; a beautiful woman.
Beauty-spot, bū'ti-spot, *n.* A patch placed on the face to heighten beauty.
Beaver, bē'vėr, *n.* A rodent quadruped; beaver-fur, or a hat made of it; the face-guard of a helmet; a visor.—*a.* Made of beaver, or of its fur.
Beavered, bē'vėrd, *a.* Having a visor.
Bebeeru, bē-bē'rö, *n.* A tree of British Guiana, called also *green-heart.*
Becalm, bē-käm', *vt.* To make calm.
Because, bē-ka̤z'. By cause; on this account that.
Beccafico, bek-a-fē'kō, *n.* A bird resembling the nightingale; the garden-warbler.
Bechamel, besh'a-mel, *n.* A fine white sauce thickened with cream.
Beck, bek, *n.* A sign with the hand or head. —*vi.* To make a sign or nod.—*vt.* To notify by a sign or nod.
Beckon, bek'n, *vi.* To make a sign by nodding, &c.—*vt.* To make a sign to.
Becloud, bē-kloud', *vt.* To cloud; to obscure.
Become, bē-kum', *vi.* (becoming, pp. become, pret. became). To come to be; to change to. —*vt.* To suit; to add grace to; to be worthy of.
Becoming, bē-kum'ing, *a.* Fit; graceful.
Becomingly, bē-kum'ing-li, *adv.* In a becoming or proper manner.
Bed, bed, *n.* Something to sleep or rest on; the channel of a river; place where anything is deposited; a layer; a stratum.—*vt.* (bedding, bedded). To lay in a bed; to sow; to stratify. —*vi.* To go to bed.
Bedaub, bē-da̤b', *vt.* To daub over; to besmear.
Bedchamber, bed'chām-bėr, *n.* An apartment for a bed.
Bedding, bed'ing, *n.* The materials of a bed.
Bedeck, bē-dek', *vt.* To deck; to adorn.
Bedesman, bēdz'man, *n.* A beadsman.
Bedew, bē-dū', *vt.* To moisten, as with dew.
Bedight, bē-dīt', *vt.* To array; to dress.
Bedim, bē-dim', *vt.* To make dim.
Bedizen, bē-dī'zn, *vt.* To adorn gaudily.
Bedlam, bed'lam, *n.* A madhouse; a place of uproar.—*a.* Belonging to a madhouse.
Bedouin, bed'ö-in, *n.* A nomadic Arab living in tents in Arabia, Syria, Egypt, &c.
Bedraggle, bē-drag'l, *vt.* To soil by drawing along on mud.
Bedrid, Bedridden, bed'rid, bed'rid-n, *a.* Confined to bed by age or infirmity.
Bedroom, bed'röm, *n.* A sleeping apartment.
Bedrop, bē-drop', *vt.* (bedropping, bedropped). To sprinkle, as with drops.

Bedstead, bed'sted. *n.* A frame for supporting a bed.
Bee, bē, *n.* The insect that makes honey.
Beech, bēch, *n.* A large smooth-barked tree yielding a hard timber and nuts.
Beechen, bēch'en, *a.* Consisting of the wood or bark of the beech.
Beef, bēf, *n.* The flesh of an ox, bull, or cow. —*a.* Consisting of such flesh.
Beef-eater, bēf'ēt-ėr, *n.* A yeoman of the royal guard of England.
Beef-tea, bēf'tē, *n.* A soup made from beef.
Beef-wood, bēf'wụd, *n.* The wood of some Australian trees.
Bee-line, bē'līn, *n.* The direct line between two places.
Beer, bēr, *n.* A fermented alcoholic liquor made from barley and hops.
Bees'-wax, bēz'waks, *n.* The wax collected by bees, of which their cells are made.
Bees'-wing, bēz'wing, *n.* A film in port-wines showing age and quality.
Beet, bēt, *n.* A vegetable with thick, fleshy roots, yielding sugar.
Beetle, bē'tl, *n.* A coleopterous insect; a heavy wooden mallet.—*vi.* (beetling, beetled). To jut; to hang over.
Beetle-browed, bē'tl-broud, *a.* Having prominent brows.
Beetling, bē'tl-ing, *a.* Jutting; overhanging.
Beeves, bēvz, *n.pl.* of beef. Cattle; black cattle.
Befall, bē-fạl', *vt.* To happen to.—*vi.* To happen.
Befit, bē-fit', *vt.* To suit; to become.
Befitting, bē-fit'ing, *a.* Suitable.
Befog, bē-fog', *vt.* (befogging, befogged). To involve in fog; to confuse.
Befool, bē-föl', *vt.* To fool; to delude.
Before, bē-fōr', *prep.* In front of; in presence of; earlier than; in preference to.—*adv.* In time preceding; further; onward; in front.
Beforehand, bē-fōr'hand, *a.* In good pecuniary circumstances.—*adv.* In advance.
Befoul, bē-foul', *vt.* To make foul.
Befriend, bē-frend', *vt.* To act as a friend to.
Beg, beg, *vt.* (begging, begged). To ask in charity; to ask earnestly; to take for granted. —*vi.* To ask or live upon alms.
Beget, bē-get', *vt.* (begetting, pp. begot, begotten, pret. begot). To procreate; to produce.
Begetter, bē-get'ėr, *n.* One who begets.
Beggar, beg'gėr, *n.* One who begs.—*vt.* To impoverish.
Beggarliness, beg'gėr-li-nes, *n.* Meanness; extreme poverty.
Beggarly, beg'gėr-li, *a.* Like a beggar; poor. —*adv.* Meanly; despicably.
Beggary, beg'gė-ri, *n.* Extreme indigence.
Begin, bē-gin', *vi.* (pp. begun, pret. began). To take rise; to do the first act; to commence.—*vt.* To enter on; to originate.
Beginner, bē-gin'ėr, *n.* One who begins; a novice.
Beginning, bē-gin'ing, *n.* The first cause, act, or state; origin; commencement.
Begird, bē-gėrd', *vt.* To gird round about; to bind.
Begone, bē-gon', *interj.* Get you gone! go away!
Begonia, bē-gō'ni-a, *n.* A showy tropical plant much cultivated in hothouses.
Begrudge, bē-gruj', *vt.* To envy the possession of.
Beguile, bē-gīl', *vt.* (beguiling, beguiled). To practise guile on; to dupe; to while away.
Beguilement, bē-gīl'ment, *n.* Act of beguiling.
Beguiler, bē-gīl'ėr, *n.* One who or that which beguiles.
Begum, bē'gum, *n.* An Indian lady of rank.
Behalf, bē-haf', *n.* Interest; support.
Behave, bē-hāv', *vt.* (behaving, behaved). To conduct (oneself).—*vi.* To act; to conduct oneself.
Behaviour, bē-hāv'i-ėr, *n.* Conduct; deportment.
Behead, bē-hed', *vt.* To cut off the head of.
Behemoth, bē-hē'moth, *n.* A huge beast mentioned in the Book of Job and supposed to be an elephant or hippopotamus.
Behest, bē-hest', *n.* Command; precept.
Behind, bē-hīnd', *prep.* In the rear of; remaining after; inferior to.—*adv.* In the rear; backwards; remaining.
Behindhand, bē-hīnd'hand, *adv.* or *pred.a.* Backwards; in arrears.
Behold, bē-hōld', *vt.* (beholding, beheld). To look upon; to regard with attention.—*vi.* To look; to fix the mind.
Beholden, bē-hōld'n, *a.* Obliged; indebted.
Behoof, bē-höf', *n.* Behalf; profit.
Behove, bē-höv', *vt.* (behoving, behoved). To be meet or necessary for (used impersonally).
Beige, bāzh, *n.* A fabric made of unbleached or undyed wool; a greyish-brown colour.
Being, bē'ing, *n.* Existence; a creature.
Belabour, bē-lā'bėr, *vt.* To beat soundly; to thump.
Belated, bē-lāt'ed, *p.a.* Made late; benighted.
Belay, bē-lā', *vt.* *Nautical*, to fasten by winding round something.
Belch, belch, *vt.* To eject, as wind from the stomach; to cast forth violently.—*vi.* To eject wind from the stomach; to issue out, as by eructation.—*n.* Eructation.
Beldam, bel'dam, *n.* An old woman; a hag.
Beleaguer, bē-lē'gėr, *vt.* To surround with an army; to blockade; to besiege.
Belemnite, bel'em-nīt, *n.* A dart-shaped fossil common in the chalk formation.
Belfry, bel'fri, *n.* A bell-tower; place where a bell is hung.
Belial, bē'li-al, *n.* An evil spirit; Satan.
Belie, bē-lī', *vt.* (belying, belied). To represent falsely; to be in contradiction to; to fail to equal.
Belief, bē-lēf', *n.* Assent of the mind; persuasion; creed; opinion.
Believe, bē-lēv', *vt.* (believing, believed). To give belief to; to credit; to expect with confidence.—*vi.* To have a firm persuasion.
Believer, bē-lēv'ėr, *n.* One who believes.
Belittle, bē-lit'l, *vt.* To make smaller; to speak disparagingly of.
Bell, bel, *n.* A metallic vessel used for giving sounds by being struck; anything in form of a bell.—*vi.* To flower.—*vt.* To put a bell on.
Belladonna, bel-la-don'na, *n.* A European plant yielding a powerful medicine.
Belle, bel, *n.* A lady of great beauty.
Belles-lettres, bel-let'tr, *n.pl.* Polite literature, including poetry, rhetoric, history, &c.
Bell-founder, bel'found-ėr, *n.* A man who casts bells.

Bellicose, bel'li-kōs, *a.* Warlike; pugnacious.
Bellied, bel'lid, *a.* Swelled in the middle.
Belligerent, bel-lij'ėr-ent, *a.* Waging war.—*n.* A nation or state waging war.
Bell-metal, bel'me-tal, *n.* A mixture of copper and tin, used for bells.
Bellow, bel'ō, *vi.* To make a hollow loud noise, as a bull; to roar.—*n.* A roar.
Bellows, bel'ōz, *n.sing.* and *pl.* An instrument for blowing fires, supplying wind to organ-pipes, &c.
Bell-ringer, bel'ring-ėr, *n.* One whose business is to ring a church or other bell.
Bell-wether, bel'weᴛʜ-ėr, *n.* A sheep which leads the flock with a bell on his neck.
Belly, bel'li, *n.* That part of the body which contains the bowels.—*vt.* and *i.* (bellying, bellied). To swell, bulge.
Belly-band, bel'li-band, *n.* A band that goes round the belly of a horse.
Belong, bē-long', *vi.* To be the property; to appertain; to be connected; to have original residence.
Belonging, bē-long'ing, *n.* That which pertains to one: generally in *pl.*
Beloved, bē-luvd', bē-luv'ed, *a.* Greatly loved.
Below, bē-lō', *prep.* Under in place; beneath; unworthy of.—*adv.* In a lower place; beneath; on earth; in hell.
Belt, belt, *n.* A girdle; a band.—*vt.* To encircle.
Beltane, bel'tān, *n.* An ancient festival on 1st May (Scotland) or 21st June (Ireland).
Belted, belt'ed, *a.* Having a belt.
Belvedere, bel've-dēr, *n.* An open erection on the top of a house; a summer-house.
Bemire, bē-mīr', *vt.* (bemiring, bemired). To drag in or cover with mire.
Bemoan, bē-mōn', *vt.* To lament; bewail.
Bemused, bē-mūzd', *a.* Muddled; stupefied.
Ben, ben, *n.* A mountain peak.
Bench, bensh, *n.* A long seat; seat of justice; body of judges.—*vt.* To furnish with benches.
Bencher, bensh'ėr, *n.* A senior barrister in an inn of court.
Bend, bend, *vt.* (pp. and pret. bent and bended). To curve; to direct to a certain point; to subdue.—*vi.* To become crooked; to lean or turn; to yield.—*n.* A curve.
Beneath, bē-nēth', *prep.* Under; lower in place, rank, dignity, &c.; unworthy of.—*adv.* In a lower place; below.
Benediction, ben-ē-dik'shon, *n.* Act of blessing; invocation of happiness.
Benefaction, ben-ē-fak'shon, *n.* The doing of a benefit; a benefit conferred.
Benefactor, ben-ē-fak'tėr, *n.* He who confers a benefit.
Benefactress, ben-ē-fak'tres, *n.* A female who confers a benefit.
Benefice, ben'ē-fis, *n.* An ecclesiastical living.
Beneficed, ben'ē-fist, *p.a.* Possessed of a benefice or church preferment.
Beneficence, bē-nef'i-sens, *n.* Active goodness.
Beneficent, bē-nef'i-sent, *a.* Kind; bountiful.
Beneficently, bē-nef'i-sent-li, *adv.* In a beneficent manner.
Beneficial, ben-ē-fi'shal, *a.* Conferring benefit.
Beneficially, ben-ē-fi'shal-li, *adv.* Helpfully.
Beneficiary, ben-ē-fi'shi-a-ri, *n.* A person who is benefited or assisted.
Benefit, ben'ē-fit, *n.* An act of kindness; a favour; advantage.—*vt.* To do a service to.—*vi.* To gain advantage.
Benevolence, bē-nev'ō-lens, *n.* Kindness; active love of mankind.
Benevolent, bē-nev'ō-lent, *a.* Kind; charitable.
Benevolently, bē-nev'ō-lent-li, *adv.* In a kind manner; with good-will.
Bengalee, Bengali, ben-gal-ē', *n.* The language of Bengal; a native of Bengal.
Benight, bē-nīt', *vt.* To involve in night; to overwhelm in moral darkness or ignorance.
Benign, bē-nīn', *a.* Gracious; kind; mild.
Benignant, bē-nig'nant, *a.* Gracious; favourable.
Benignantly, bē-nig'nant-li, *adv.* In a benignant manner.
Benignity, bē-nig'ni-ti, *n.* Kindness; graciousness; beneficence.
Benignly, bē-nīn'li, *adv.* Graciously.
Benison, ben'i-zn, *n.* A blessing, benediction.
Bent, bent, pret. and pp. of *bend.*—*n.* Bias of mind; inclination; a wiry grass; a wild piece of land.
Benumb, bē-num', *vt.* To deprive of sensation; to make torpid; to stupefy.
Benzene, ben'zēn, *n.* A liquid used to remove grease spots, &c.
Benzoin, Benzoine, ben-zō'in or ben'zoin, *n.* A fragrant resinous juice.
Benzole, Benzoline, ben'zōl, ben'zō-lin. Same as *Benzene.*
Bepraise, bē-prāz', *vt.* To praise greatly or extravagantly.
Bequeath, bē-kwēᴛʜ', *vt.* To leave by will; to hand down.
Bequest, bē-kwest', *n.* A legacy.
Bere, bēr, *n.* A species of barley.
Bereave, bē-rēv', *vt.* (bereaving, pp. and pret. bereaved and bereft). To deprive of.
Bereavement, bē-rēv'ment, *n.* Act of bereaving; state of being bereft.
Beret, be'ri, *n.* A close-fitting round woollen cap.
Beretta. *See* Biretta.
Bergamot, bėrg'a-mot, *n.* A species of pear; perfume from the fruit of the lime; a coarse tapestry.
Beri-beri, ber'i-ber'i, *n.* A dangerous disease endemic in parts of India and Ceylon, characterized by paralysis, difficult breathing, and other symptoms.
Berlin, bėr'lin or bėr-lin', *n.* A four-wheeled vehicle; a wool for fancy work.
Berry, be'ri, *n.* A pulpy fruit containing many seeds.
Berserker, bėr'sėr-kėr, *n.* A furious Scandinavian warrior of heathen times.
Berth, bėrth, *n.* A station in which a ship lies; a place for sleeping in a ship, &c.—*vt.* To allot a berth to.
Beryl, be'ril, *n.* A hard greenish mineral.
Beseech, bē-sēch', *vt.* (beseeching, besought). To entreat; to solicit.
Beseechingly, bē-sēch'ing-li, *adv.* In a beseeching manner.
Beseem, bē-sēm', *vt.* To become; to be fit.
Beseeming, bē-sēm'ing, *a.* Becoming.
Beset, bē-set', *vt.* (besetting, beset). To surround; to press on all sides.
Besetting, bē-set'ing, *a.* Habitually assailing.
Beshrew, bē-shrö', *vt.* To wish a curse to.
Beside, Besides, bē-sīd', bē-sīdz', *prep.* By

the side of; near; over and above; distinct from.—*adv*. Moreover; in addition.
Besiege, bē-sēj′, *vt*. (besieging, besieged). To lay siege to; to beset.
Besieger, bē-sēj′ėr, *n*. One who besieges.
Besmear, bē-smēr′, *vt*. To smear; to soil.
Besom, bē′zum, *n*. A brush of twigs; a broom.
Besot, bē-sot′, *vt*. (besotting, besotted). To make sottish.
Besotted, bē-sot′ed, *p.a*. Made sottish; stupid.
Bespangle, bē-spang′gl, *vt*. To adorn with spangles.
Bespatter, bē-spat′tėr, *vt*. To spatter over.
Bespeak, bē-spēk′, *vt*. (pp. bespoke, bespoken, pret. bespoke). To speak for beforehand; to indicate.
Bespread, bē-spred′, *vt*. To spread over.
Besprinkle, bē-spring′kl, *vt*. To sprinkle over.
Bessemer-steel, bes′e-mėr-stēl, *n*. Steel made directly from molten cast-iron by driving through it air to carry off impurities.
Best, best, *a.superl*. Most good; having good qualities in the highest degree; exceeding all. —*n*. The utmost; highest endeavour.—*adv*. In the highest degree; beyond all others.
Bestead, bē-sted′, *pp*. or *a*. Placed, circumstanced; with *ill*, &c.
Bestial, bes′ti-al, *a*. Belonging to a beast; brutish; vile.
Bestiality, bes-ti-al′i-ti, *n*. The quality of being bestial; brutal conduct.
Bestially, bes′ti-al-li, *adv*. Brutally.
Bestiary, bes′ti-a-ri, *n*. A book of the middle ages treating fancifully of beasts.
Bestir, bē-stėr′, *vt*. To stir up; to put into brisk action. (Usually with *refl*. pron.)
Bestow, bē-stō′, *vt*. To lay up; to give; to confer; to dispose of; to apply.
Bestowal, bē-stō′al, *n*. Act of bestowing; disposal.
Bestower, bē-stō′ėr, *n*. One who bestows; a giver; a disposer.
Bestraddle, bē-strad′dl, *vt*. To bestride.
Bestrew, bē-strö′, *vt*. To scatter over.
Bestride, bē-strīd′, *vt*. (pp. bestrid, bestridden, pret. bestrid, bestrode). To stride over; to place a leg on each side of.
Bestud, bē-stud′, *vt*. To set with studs; to adorn with bosses.
Bet, bet, *n*. A wager; that which is pledged in a contest.—*vt*. (betting, betted). To wager.
Betake, bē-tāk′, *vt*. To apply (oneself); to have recourse to.
Bethink, bē-thingk′, *vt*. To call to mind; to recollect.
Betide, bē-tīd′, *vt*. (pp. betid, pret. betid, betided). To happen to; to befall.—*vi*. To happen.
Betimes, bē-tīmz′, *adv*. Seasonably; early.
Betoken, bē-tō′kn, *vt*. To portend; to signify.
Betray, bē-trā′, *vt*. To disclose treacherously; to entrap.
Betrayal, bē-trā′al, *n*. Act of betraying.
Betrayer, bē-trā′ėr, *n*. One who betrays.
Betroth, bē-trōᴛʜ′, *vt*. To affiance; to pledge to marriage.
Betrothal, bē-trōᴛʜ′al, *n*. Mutual contract of marriage.
Better, bet′tėr, *a.comp*. More good; improved.—*adv*. More excellently; in a higher degree.—*vt*. To make better; to advance.—*n*. A superior (generally in *pl*.).
Bettor, bet′ėr, *n*. One who bets.
Between, bē-twēn′, *prep*. In the middle; from one to another of; belonging to two.
Betwixt, bē-twikst′, *prep*. Between.
Bevel, be′vel, *n*. An instrument for taking angles; an angle not a right angle.—*a*. Slant; oblique.—*vt*. (bevelling, bevelled). To cut to a bevel angle.
Beverage, bev′ėr-āj, *n*. Drink; liquor.
Bevy, be′vi, *n*. A flock of birds; a company of females.
Bewail, bē-wāl′, *vt*. To lament.—*vi*. To utter deep grief.
Beware, bē-wār′, *vi*. To take care (with *of*).
Bewilder, bē-wil′dėr, *vt*. To confuse; to perplex.
Bewilderment, bē-wil′dėr-ment, *n*. State of being bewildered.
Bewitch, bē-wich′, *vt*. To enchant; to fascinate; to overpower by charms.
Bewitchery, bē-wich′ėr-i, *n*. Fascination.
Bewitching, bē-wich′ing, *p.a*. Fascinating; captivating.
Bewitchingly, bē-wich′ing-li, *adv*. In a fascinating manner.
Bewitchment, bē-wich′ment, *n*. Fascination.
Bewray, bē-rā′, *vt*. To betray.
Bey, bā, *n*. A Turkish governor.
Beyond, bē-yond′, *prep*. On the further side of; farther onward than; out of the reach of; above.—*adv*. At a distance.
Bezel, bez′el, *n*. The part of a ring which holds the stone.
Bezique, be-zēk′, *n*. A game at cards.
Bhang, bang, *n*. A narcotic drug prepared from an Indian hemp.
Biangular, bī-ang′gū-lėr, *a*. Having two angles.
Bias, bī′as, *n*.; pl. **-ses.** Weight on one side; a leaning of the mind; bent.—*vt*. To incline to one side; to prejudice.
Biased, Biassed, bī′ast, *p.a*. Prejudiced.
Bib, bib, *n*. A cloth worn by children over the breast.
Bibber, bib′ėr, *n*. A drinker; a tippler.
Bible, bī′bl, *n*. The Holy Scriptures.
Biblical, bib′lik-al, *a*. Pertaining to the Bible.
Biblically, bib′lik-al-li, *adv*. In accordance with the Bible.
Biblicist, bib′li-sist, *n*. One skilled in biblical knowledge.
Bibliographical, bib′li-ō-graf″ik-al, *a*. Pertaining to bibliography.
Bibliography, bib-li-og′ra-fi, *n*. A history of books and their editions; list of books by one author or on one subject.
Bibliomania, bib′li-ō-mā″ni-a, *n*. A rage for possessing rare books.
Bibliophile, bib′li-ō-fīl, *n*. A lover of books.
Bibliopolist, bib-li-op′ol-ist, *n*. A bookseller.
Bibulous, bib′ū-lus, *a*. Spongy; addicted to intoxicants.
Bicarbonate, bī-kär′bon-āt, *n*. A carbonate containing two equivalents of carbonic acid to one of a base.
Bicentenary, bī-sen′te-na-ri, *n*. Two hundred years.
Biceps, bī′seps, *n*. A muscle of the arm and of the thigh.
Bicker, bik′ėr, *vi*. To skirmish; to quarrel.
Bicycle, bī′si-kl, *n*. A two-wheeled vehicle propelled by the rider.
Bicyclist, bī′sik-list, *n*. One who rides a bicycle.

Bid, bid, *vt.* (bidding, pp. bid, bidden, pret. bid, bade). To ask; to order; to offer.—*n.* An offer, as at an auction.
Biddable, bid'a-bl, *a.* Obedient; docile.
Bidding, bid'ing, *n.* Invitation; order; offer.
Bide, bīd, *vi.* (biding, bode). To dwell; to remain.—*vt.* To endure; to abide.
Bidental, bī-dent'al, *a.* Having two teeth.
Bidet, bi-det' or bē-dā, *n.* A baggage horse.
Biennial, bī-en'ni-al, *a.* Continuing for two years; taking place once in two years.—*n.* A plant which lives two years.
Biennially, bī-en'ni-al-li, *adv.* Once in two years; at the return of two years.
Bier, bēr, *n.* A carriage or frame for conveying a corpse to the grave.
Bifid, bī'fid, *a.* Cleft into two parts; forked.
Bifurcate, bī-fėr'kāt, *a.* Forked.
Big, big, *a.* Great; large; pregnant; arrogant.
Bigamist, big'am-ist, *n.* One who has two wives or husbands at once.
Bigamy, big'a-mi, *n.* The crime of having two wives or husbands at once.
Bigg, big, *n.* A variety of winter barley.
Bight, bīt, *n.* A small bay; a loop.
Bigness, big'nes, *n.* Quality of being big; size.
Bigot, big'ot, *n.* A person obstinately wedded to a particular creed.
Bigoted, big'ot-ed, *a.* Obstinately attached to some creed.
Bigotry, big'ot-ri, *n.* Blind zeal in favour of a creed, party, sect, or opinion.
Bijou, bē-zhö', *n.*; pl. **-joux,** -zhö. A trinket; a jewel.
Bilander, bī'lan-dėr, *n.* A Dutch two-masted vessel.
Bilateral, bī-lat'ėr-al, *a.* Two-sided.
Bilberry, bil'be-ri, *n.* The whortleberry or blaeberry.
Bilbo, bil'bō, *n.* A rapier; a sword.
Bilboes, bil'bōz, *n.pl.* A sort of stocks for offenders on board of ships.
Bile, bīl, *n.* A yellow bitter liquid secreted in the liver; spleen; anger.
Bilge, bilj, *n.* The protuberant part of a cask; the breadth of a ship's bottom.—*vi.* (bilging, bilged). To leak in the bilge.
Bilge-water, bilj'wa-tėr, *n.* Water on the bilge or bottom of a ship.
Biliary, bil'i-a-ri, *a.* Belonging to the bile.
Bilingual, bī-lin'gwal, *a.* In two languages.
Bilious, bil'i-us, *a.* Affected by bile.
Biliteral, bī-lit'ėr-al, *a.* Consisting of two letters.
Bilk, bilk, *vt.* To defraud; to elude.
Bill, bil, *n.* The beak of a bird; anything resembling a bird's beak; an instrument for pruning, &c.; a military weapon now obsolete; an account of money due; draught of a proposed new law; a placard.—*vi.* To join bills, as doves; to fondle.—*vt.* To announce by bill; to stick bills on.
Billet, bil'et, *n.* A small note in writing; a ticket directing soldiers where to lodge; a situation; a stick of wood.—*vt.* To quarter, as soldiers.—*vi.* To be quartered.
Billet-doux, bil-e-dö', *n.* A love-letter.
Billiards, bil'yėrdz, *n.pl.* A game played on a table with balls and cues.
Billingsgate, bil'lingz-gāt, *n.* Foul language.
Billion, bil'yon, *n.* A million of millions.
Billow, bil'lō, *n.* A great wave of the sea.—*vi.* To roll in large waves.
Billowy, bil'lō-i, *a.* Swelling into large waves.
Bimanous, bī'man-us, *a.* Having two hands.
Bimensal, bī-men'sal, *a.* Occurring every two months.
Bimetallism, bī-met'al-izm, *n.* A system of currency which recognizes silver and gold as legal tender to any amount.
Bimetallist, bī-met'al-ist, *n.* One who favours bimetallism.
Bimonthly, bī-munth'li, *a.* Occurring every two months.
Bin, bin, *n.* A receptacle for corn, &c.; a partition in a wine-cellar.
Binary, bī'na-ri, *a.* Twofold.
Bind, bīnd, *vt.* (binding, bound). To tie; to confine; to oblige; to cover (a book); to render costive; to make firm.—*vi.* To grow hard; to be obligatory.
Binder, bīnd'ėr, *n.* One who binds books or sheaves; a bandage.
Binding, bīnd'ing, *p.n.* Act of binding; the cover and sewing, &c., of a book.
Bind-weed, bīnd'wēd, *n.* Convolvulus.
Bing, bing, *n.* A large heap.
Binnacle, bin'a-kl, *n.* A case in which a ship's compass is kept.
Binocular, bi-nok'ū-lėr, *a.* Adapted for both eyes.—*n.* A small telescope for using with both eyes at once.
Binomial, bī-nō'mi-al, *a.* or *n.* An algebraic expression consisting of two terms.
Biochemistry, bī-ō-kem'ist-ri, *n.* The study of the chemistry of living things.
Biogenesis, bī-ō-jen'e-sis, *n.* The doctrine that living organisms can spring only from living parents.
Biographer, bī-og'ra-fėr, *n.* A writer of biography.
Biographical, bī-ō-graf'ik-al, *a.* Pertaining to biography.
Biography, bī-og'ra-fi, *n.* An account of one's life and character.
Biologist, bī-ol'o-jist, *n.* One skilled in biology.
Biology, bī-ol'o-ji, *n.* The science of life.
Bioplasm, bī'ō-plazm, *n.* The germinal matter in plants and animals.
Bipartite, bī-pärt'īt, *a.* Having two parts.
Biped, bī'ped, *n.* An animal with two feet.
Birch, bėrch, *n.* A tree having small leaves, white bark, and a fragrant odour.
Birch, Birchen, bėrch, bėrch'en, *a.* Made of birch; consisting of birch.
Bird, bėrd, *n.* One of the feathered race.
Bird-lime, bėrd'līm, *n.* A viscous substance used to catch birds.
Bird's-eye, bėrdz'ī, *a.* Seen as by a flying bird; wide and rapid.—*n.* A finely cut tobacco.
Bireme, bī'rēm, *n.* An ancient Greek or Roman vessel with two banks of oars.
Biretta, Beretta, bi-ret'ta, be-ret'ta, *n.* A square cap worn by ecclesiastics.
Birth, bėrth, *n.* Act of bearing or coming into life; extraction.
Birthday, bėrth'dā, *n.* The day on which a person is born, or its anniversary.
Birthplace, bėrth'plās, *n.* Place where one is born.
Birthright, bėrth'rīt, *n.* Any right to which a person is entitled by birth.
Biscuit, bis'ket, *n.* Hard bread made into cakes; unglazed porcelain.
Bisect, bī-sekt', *vt.* To cut into two equal parts.

Bisection, bī-sek'shon, *n.* Act of bisecting; division into two equal parts.
Bishop, bish'up, *n.* Head of a diocese; a piece in chess which moves diagonally.
Bishopric, bish'up-rik, *n.* Office of a bishop; a diocese.
Bismuth, bis'muth, *n.* A brittle yellowish or reddish-white metal.
Bison, bī'zon, *n.* A quadruped of the ox family; the American buffalo.
Bisque, bisk, *n.* Unglazed white porcelain; odds given at tennis, &c.
Bissextile, bis-seks'til, *n.* Leap-year.
Bistre, bis'tėr, *n.* A dark-brown pigment.
Bisulcate, bī-sul'kāt, *a.* Cloven-footed.
Bit, bit, *n.* A morsel; fragment; the metal part of a bridle inserted in a horse's mouth; a boring tool.—*vt.* (bitting, bitted). To put the bit in the mouth.
Bitch, bich, *n.* A female dog; a name of reproach for a woman.
Bite, bīt, *vt.* (biting, pp. bit, bitten, pret. bit). To crush or sever with the teeth; to cause to smart; to wound by reproach, &c.; to corrode.—*n.* Act of biting; wound made by biting; a mouthful.
Biting, bīt'ing, *p.a.* Sharp; severe; sarcastic.
Bitingly, bīt'ing-li, *adv.* In a biting or sarcastic manner.
Bitter, bit'ėr, *a.* Sharp to the taste; severe; painful; calamitous; distressing.
Bitterish, bit'ėr-ish, *a.* Somewhat bitter.
Bitterly, bit'ėr-li, *adv.* In a bitter manner.
Bittern, bit'ėrn, *n.* A bird of the heron kind.
Bitterness, bit'ėr-nes, *n.* Quality of being bitter; hatred; deep distress.
Bitters, bit'ėrz, *n.pl.* A liquor in which bitter herbs or roots are steeped.
Bitumen, bi-tū'men, *n.* A mineral, pitchy, inflammable substance.
Bituminous, bi-tū'min-us, *a.* Having the qualities of or containing bitumen.
Bivalve, bī'valv, *n.* A molluscous, bivalvular animal.
Bivalve, Bivalvular, bī'valv, bī-valv'ū-lėr, *a.* Having two shells which open and shut, as the oyster.
Bivouac, bi'vö-ak, *n.* Encampment of soldiers for the night in the open air.—*vi.* (bivouacking, bivouacked). To encamp during the night without covering.
Biweekly, bī-wēk'li, *a.* Occurring every two weeks.
Bizarre, bi-zär', *a.* Odd; fantastical.
Blab, blab, *vt.* (blabbing, blabbed). To tell indiscreetly.—*vi.* To talk indiscreetly.
Black, blak, *a.* Destitute of light; dark; gloomy; sullen; atrocious; wicked.—*n.* The darkest colour; a negro.—*vt.* To make black.
Blackamoor, blak'a-mör, *n.* A negro.
Black-ball, blak'bal, *n.* A composition for blacking shoes; a ball used as a negative in voting.—*vt.* To reject by private voting.
Blackberry, blak'be-ri, *n.* A plant of the bramble kind, and its fruit.
Blackbird, blak'bėrd, *n.* A species of thrush.
Blackboard, blak'bōrd, *n.* A board for writing on with chalk for instruction.
Black-cap, blak'kap, *n.* A British song-bird.
Blackcock, blak'kok, *n.* A species of grouse.
Blacken, blak'n, *vt.* To make black; to defame.—*vi.* To grow black or dark.
Black-friar, blak'frī-ėr, *n.* A friar of the Dominican order.
Blackguard, blak'gärd or bla'gärd, *n.* A scoundrel.—*vt.* To revile in scurrilous language.
Blackguardly, blak'gärd-li or bla'gärd-li, *a.* Rascally; villainous.
Blacking, blak'ing, *n.* A substance used for blacking shoes.
Black-lead, blak'led, *n.* A dark mineral substance used for pencils; plumbago.
Black-leg, blak'leg, *n.* A swindler; one who works during a strike.
Black-letter, blak'let-tėr, *n.* The old English letter or character.
Black-list, blak-list, *n.* A list of bankrupts.
Black-mail, blak'māl, *n.* Money paid for protection; extortion by intimidation.
Black-market, blak-mär'ket, *n.* Illegal dealing in goods or currencies which are scarce or controlled.
Black-out, blak'out, *n.* In war-time, the period between dusk and dawn during which no light must be visible through windows and doors.
Black-sheep, blak'shēp, *n.* One whose conduct is discreditable.
Blacksmith, blak'smith, *n.* A smith who works in iron.
Blackthorn, blak'thorn, *n.* The sloe.
Bladder, blad'ėr, *n.* A thin sac in animals containing the urine, bile, &c.; a blister; anything like the animal bladder.
Bladder-wrack, blad'ėr-rak, *n.* A common large kind of seaweed.
Blade, blād, *n.* A leaf; cutting part of a sword, knife, &c.; flat part of an oar.
Blaeberry, blā'be-ri, *n.* The bilberry.
Blamable, blām'a-bl, *a.* Deserving of blame.
Blame, blām, *vt.* (blaming, blamed). To censure; to reprimand.—*n.* Censure; fault.
Blameless, blām'les, *a.* Free from blame.
Blanch, blansh, *vt.* To make white.—*vi.* To grow white; to bleach.
Blanc-mange, bla-mängzh', *n.* A dish of arrow-root or maize-flour boiled with milk.
Bland, bland, *a.* Mild; soothing; gentle.
Blandish, bland'ish, *vt.* To soothe; to caress; to flatter.
Blandishment, bland'ish-ment, *n.* Soft words; artful caresses; flattery.
Blank, blangk, *a.* White; pale; void; void of writing; without rhyme.—*n.* A white unwritten paper; a void space; the white mark which a shot is to hit.
Blanket, blang'ket, *n.* A woollen covering for a bed, horses, &c.
Blanketing, blang'ket-ing, *n.* Cloth for blankets.
Blankly, blangk'li, *adv.* In a blank manner; with paleness or confusion.
Blank-verse, blangk'vėrs, *n.* Ten-syllabled line without rhyme.
Blare, blār, *vi.* (blaring, blared). To give forth a loud sound.—*vt.* To sound loudly; to proclaim noisily.—*n.* Sound like that of a trumpet; roar.
Blarney, blär'ni, *n.* Excessively complimentary language; gammon.—*vt.* To flatter.
Blasé, blä-zā, *a.* Satiated; used up; bored.
Blaspheme, blas-fēm', *vt.* (blaspheming, blasphemed). To speak irreverently of, as of God; to speak evil of.—*vi.* To utter blasphemy.
Blasphemer, blas-fēm'ėr, *n.* One who blasphemes.

Blasphemous, blas'fēm-us, *a.* Impiously irreverent.
Blasphemy, blas'fēm-i, *n.* Profane speaking; an indignity offered to God.
Blast, blast, *n.* A gust of wind; sound of a wind-instrument; violent explosion of gunpowder; pernicious influence, as of wind; blight.—*vt.* To blight; to strike with some sudden plague, &c.; to destroy; to blow up by gunpowder.—*vi.* To wither; to be blighted.
Blatant, blā'tant, *a.* Bellowing; noisy.
Blaze, blāz, *n.* A flame; brilliance; a bursting out; a white spot.—*vi.* (blazing, blazed). To flame; to send forth a bright light.—*vt.* To noise abroad; to proclaim.
Blazer, blāz'ėr, *n.* A bright-coloured coat suited for sports.
Blazon, blāz'on, *vt.* To display; to adorn; to explain in heraldic terms.—*n.* A coat of arms; description of coats of arms.
Blazoner, blāz'on-ėr, *n.* A herald.
Blazonry, blāz'on-ri, *n.* The art of explaining coats of arms in proper terms.
Bleach, blēch, *vt.* To make white or whiter.—*vi.* To grow white.
Bleacher, blēch'ėr, *n.* One whose occupation is to whiten cloth.
Bleachery, blēch'ėr-i, *n.* A place for bleaching.
Bleak, blēk, *a.* Exposed; chill; dreary.
Blear, blēr, *a.* Sore; dimmed, as the eyes.—*vt.* To dim or impair.
Blear-eyed, blēr'īd, *a.* Having sore eyes; having the eyes dim with rheum.
Bleat, blēt, *vi.* To cry as a sheep.—*n.* The cry of a sheep.
Bleed, blēd, *vi.* (bleeding, bled). To emit blood; to die by slaughter; to feel agony, as from bleeding; to drop, as blood.—*vt.* To take blood from; to extort money from.
Bleeding, blēd'ing, *n.* A discharge of blood; the operation of letting blood; the drawing of sap from a tree.
Blemish, blem'ish, *vt.* To mar; to tarnish.—*n.* A mark of imperfection; dishonour.
Blench, blensh, *vi.* To shrink; to flinch.
Blend, blend, *vt.* To mix together.—*vi.* To be mixed.—*n.* A mixture.
Blenheim, blen'em, *n.* A spaniel.
Blenny, blen'ni, *n.* A small sea fish.
Bless, bles, *vt.* (blessing, blessed or blest). To make happy; to wish happiness to; to consecrate.
Blessed, bles'ed, *a.* Happy; prosperous; holy and happy; happy in heaven.
Blessedness, bles'ed-nes, *n.* Sanctity; joy.
Blessing, bles'ing, *n.* A prayer imploring happiness upon; piece of good fortune.
Blest, blest, *a.* Blessed; cheering.
Blight, blīt, *n.* That which withers up; mildew.—*vt.* To wither up; to corrupt with mildew; to frustrate.
Blighty, blī'ti, *n.* Home; Great Britain; a wound which ensures its recipient going home.
Blind, blīnd, *a.* Destitute of sight; wanting discernment; having no outlet.—*n.* A screen; something to mislead; a pretext.—*vt.* To make blind; to obstruct the view.
Blindfold, blīnd'fōld, *a.* Having the eyes covered.—*vt.* To cover the eyes of.
Blindly, blīnd'li, *adv.* Heedlessly.
Blindness, blīnd'nes, *n.* Want of sight or discernment; ignorance.
Blind-worm, blīnd'wėrm, *n.* A small harmless reptile; the slow-worm.
Blink, blingk, *vi.* To wink; to twinkle.—*vt.* To shut the eyes upon; to avoid.—*n.* A twinkle; a glimpse or glance.
Blinker, bling'kėr, *n.* A flap to prevent a horse from seeing sideways.
Bliss, blis, *n.* Blessedness; perfect happiness.
Blissful, blis'ful, *a.* Full of bliss.
Blister, blis'tėr, *n.* A thin bladder on the skin; a pustule; something to raise a blister.—*vi.* To rise in blisters.—*vt.* To raise a blister or blisters on; to apply a blister to.
Blister-fly, blis'tėr-flī, *n.* The Spanish fly, used in raising a blister.
Blistery, blis'tėr-i, *a.* Full of blisters.
Blithe, blīTH, *a.* Joyful; gay; mirthful.
Blithely, blīTH'li, *adv.* In a blithe manner.
Blithesome, blīTH'som, *a.* Gay; merry.
Blitz, blitz, *n.* A concentrated attack by air.
Blizzard, bliz'ėrd, *n.* A violent snow-storm, with high wind and intense cold.
Bloat, blōt, *vt.* To make turgid; to cure by salting and smoking.—*vi.* To grow turgid.
Bloated, blōt'ed, *p.a.* Inflated; overgrown.
Bloater, blōt'ėr, *n.* A smoke-dried herring.
Blob, blob, *n.* A small globe of liquid.
Block, blok, *n.* A heavy piece of wood or stone; a lump of solid matter; piece of wood in which a pulley is placed; a mass of buildings; an obstacle; a stupid person.—*vt.* To shut up; to obstruct; to form into blocks.
Blockade, blok-ād', *n.* A close siege by troops or ships.—*vt.* (blockading, blockaded). To besiege closely.
Blockhead, blok'hed, *n.* A stupid fellow.
Block-house, blok'hous, *n.* A building used for defence, chiefly of timber.
Blockish, blok'ish, *a.* Stupid; dull.
Block-tin, blok'tin, *n.* Tin cast into blocks.
Blond, Blonde, blond, *a.* Of a fair complexion.—*n.* A person of fair complexion.
Blood, blud, *n.* The fluid which circulates in animals; kindred; high birth; the juice of fruits.—*a.* Pertaining to blood; of a superior breed.—*vt.* To bleed; to stain with blood; to inure to blood.
Blood-heat, blud'hēt, *n.* The heat of the human blood, about 98° Fah.
Blood-horse, blud'hors, *n.* A horse of the purest breed.
Blood-hound, blud'hound, *n.* A hound of remarkably acute smell.
Bloodily, blud'i-li, *adv.* Cruelly.
Bloodiness, blud'i-nes, *n.* State of being bloody; disposition to shed blood.
Bloodless, blud'les, *a.* Without blood; without shedding blood.
Blood-money, blud'mu-ni, *n.* Money earned by the shedding of blood or murder.
Bloodshed, blud'shed, *n.* The shedding of blood; slaughter.
Blood-shot, blud'shot, *a.* Inflamed.
Blood-stone, blud'stōn, *n.* A greenish stone with red spots.
Blood-sucker, blud'suk-ėr, *n.* Any animal that sucks blood; an extortioner.
Bloodthirsty, blud'thėrs-ti, *a.* Eager to shed blood.
Blood-vessel, blud'ves-sel, *n.* An artery or a vein.
Bloody, blud'i, *a.* Stained with blood; cruel; given to the shedding of blood.

Bloody-flux, blud'i-fluks, *n.* The dysentery.
Bloom, blöm, *n.* A blossom; a flower; state of youth; native flush on the cheek; the powdery coating on plums, &c.; a lump of puddled iron.—*vi.* To blossom; to flourish; to show the freshness of youth.
Bloomy, blöm'i, *a.* Full of bloom.
Blossom, blos'om, *n.* The flower of a plant.—*vi.* To bloom; to flower; to flourish.
Blot, blot, *vt.* (blotted, blotting). To spot; to stain; to cancel (with *out*); to dry.—*n.* A spot or stain; an obliteration.
Blotch, bloch, *n.* Pustule upon the skin; an eruption; a confused patch of colour.
Blotchy, bloch'i, *a.* Having blotches.
Blotter, blot'ėr, *n.* One who blots; a piece of blotting-paper.
Blotting-paper, blot'ing-pā-pėr, *n.* Unsized paper, serving to absorb ink.
Blouse, blouz, *n.* A light loose upper garment.
Blow, blō, *vi.* (blowing, pp. blown, pret. blew). To make a current of air; to emit air or breath; to pant · to sound by being blown; to bloom; to flourish.—*vt.* To impel by wind; to inflate; to sound by the breath; to infect with the eggs of flies.—*n.* A blast; a blossoming; bloom; a stroke; a calamitous event.
Blower, blō'ėr, *n.* One who blows; a contrivance to increase the draught of a chimney.
Blowpipe, blō'pīp, *n.* A tube by which a current of air is driven through a flame.
Blowze, blouz, *n.* A ruddy, fat-faced woman.
Blowzy, blouz'i, *a.* Fat and ruddy.
Blubber, blub'bėr, *n.* The fat of whales and other large sea-animals; the sea-nettle.—*vi.* To weep in a noisy manner.
Blucher, bluch'ėr or blö'kėr, *n.* A strong half-boot.
Bludgeon, blud'jon, *n.* A short club with one end loaded.
Blue, blü, *n.* The colour which the sky exhibits; one of the seven primary colours; one who represents his University (especially Oxford and Cambridge) at rowing, cricket, football, &c.; (*pl.*) depression, the dumps.—*a.* Of a blue colour; sky-coloured.—*vt.* (bluing, blued). To dye of a blue colour.
Bluebell, blü'bel, *n.* The wild hyacinth (in England), the harebell (in Scotland).
Blue-book, blü'buk, *n.* A name applied to British government official reports and other papers.
Blue-bottle, blü'bot-l, *n.* A fly with a large blue belly.
Blue-jacket, blü'jak-et, *n.* A sailor.
Blue-pill, blü'pil, *n.* Mercurial pill.
Blue-print, blü'print, *n.* A print obtained by the action of light on prepared paper over which a transparent drawing is laid. The exposed part of the paper becomes covered with Prussian blue, and the drawing is shown in white.
Blue-stocking, blü'stok-ing, *n.* A learned and pedantic lady.
Blue-stone, blü'stōn, *n.* Sulphate of copper.
Bluff, bluf, *a.* Steep; blustering; burly; hearty.—*n.* A steep projecting bank.—*vt.* and *i.* To impose on by a show of boldness or strength.
Bluish, blü'ish, *a.* Blue in a small degree.
Blunder, blun'dėr, *vi.* To err stupidly; to stumble.—*vt.* To confound.—*n.* A gross mistake; error.
Blunderbuss, blun'dėr-bus, *n.* A short gun with a large bore.
Blunt, blunt, *a.* Dull on the edge or point; not sharp; dull in understanding; unceremonious.—*vt.* To make blunt or dull.
Bluntly, blunt'li, *adv.* In a blunt manner.
Bluntness, blunt'nes, *n.* Dullness of edge or point; rude sincerity or plainness.
Blur, blėr, *n.* A stain; a blot.—*vt.* (blurring, blurred). To stain; to obscure; to render indistinct.
Blurb, blėrb, *n.* A brief epitome or eulogy of a book, often printed on its jacket.
Blurt, blėrt, *vt.* To utter suddenly or unadvisedly.
Blush, blush, *vi.* To redden in the face; to bear a blooming red colour.—*n.* A red colour caused by shame, confusion, &c.; sudden appearance or glance.
Blushing, blush'ing, *a.* Reddening in the cheeks or face; roseate.
Bluster, blus'tėr, *vi.* To roar like wind; to swagger.—*n.* A violent gust of wind; swagger.
Blusterer, blus'tėr-ėr, *n.* A swaggerer.
Blustering, blus'tėr-ing, *a.* Noisy; windy.
Boa, bō'a, *n.* A genus of large serpents without fangs and venom; a long piece of fur, &c., worn round the neck.
Boar, bōr, *n.* The male of swine.
Board, bōrd, *n.* A piece of timber broad and thin; a table; food; persons seated round a table; a council; the deck of a ship; a thick stiff paper.—*vt.* To cover with boards; to supply with food; to place as a boarder; to enter a ship by force.—*vi.* To live in a house at a certain rate.
Boarder, bōrd'ėr, *n.* One who receives food and lodging at a stated charge; one who boards a ship in action.
Boarding, bōrd'ing, *n.* Act of one who boards; boards collectively.
Boarding-house, bōrd'ing-hous, *n.* A house where board and lodging is furnished.
Boarding-school, bōrd'ing-sköl, *n.* A school which supplies board as well as tuition.
Board-school, bōrd'sköl, *n.* A school under the management of a school-board.
Boarish, bōr'ish, *a.* Like a boar; swinish.
Boast, bōst, *vi.* To brag; to talk ostentatiously.—*vt.* To brag of; to magnify.—*n.* A vaunting; the cause of boasting.
Boaster, bōst'ėr, *n.* One who boasts.
Boastful, bōst'ful, *a.* Given to boasting.
Boastingly, bōst'ing-li, *adv.* In an ostentatious manner; with boasting.
Boat, bōt, *n.* A small open vessel, usually impelled by oars; a small ship.—*vt.* To transport in a boat.—*vi.* To go in a boat.
Boatman, bōt'man, *n.* One who manages a boat.
Boatswain, bō'sn, *n.* A ship's officer who has charge of boats, sails, &c.
Bob, bob, *n.* A pendant; something that plays loosely; a short jerking motion; a docked tail; (slang) a shilling.—*vt.* (bobbing, bobbed). To move with a short jerking motion.—*vi.* To play backward and forward, or loosely.
Bobbin, bob'in, *n.* A small pin of wood to wind the thread on in weaving lace, &c.
Bobbinet, bob-in-et', *n.* A machine-made cotton net.

Boche, bosh, *n.* A German.
Bode, bōd, *vt.* (boding, boded). To portend; to be the omen of.—*vi.* To presage.
Bodice, bod'is, *n.* Something worn round the waist; a corset.
Bodied, bo'did, *a.* Having a body.
Bodiless, bo'di-les, *a.* Having no body.
Bodily, bo'di-li, *a.* Relating to the body; actual.—*adv.* Corporeally; entirely.
Bodkin, bod'kin, *n.* An instrument for piercing holes; a kind of large needle.
Body, bo'di, *n.* The trunk of an animal; main part; matter; a person; a system; strength; reality; any solid figure.—*vt.* (bodying, bodied). To give a body to; to embody (with *forth*).
Body-guard, bo'di-gärd, *n.* The guard that protects or defends the person.
Boer, bör, *n.* A Dutch colonist of S. Africa.
Bog, bog, *n.* A quagmire; a morass.—*vt.* (bogging, bogged). To whelm, as in mud.
Bogey, Bogy, bō'gi, *n.* A goblin.
Boggle, bog'l, *vi.* (boggling, boggled). To stop; to hesitate; to waver.
Boggling, bog'l-ing, *a.* Hesitating; bungling.
Boggy, bog'i, *a.* Containing bogs.
Bogie, Bogey, bō'gi, *n.* A four-wheeled truck supporting the front of a locomotive.
Bogus, bō'gus, *a.* Counterfeit; sham.
Bohea, bō-hē', *n.* A special kind of black tea.
Bohemian, bō-hē'mi-an, *n.* A native of Bohemia; a gypsy; an artist who leads an unconventional life.
Boil, boil, *vi.* To bubble from the action of heat; to seethe; to be cooked by boiling; to be in a state of agitation.—*vt.* To heat to a boiling state; to prepare by boiling.—*n.* A sore swelling or tumour.
Boiler, boil'ėr, *n.* One who boils; a vessel in which a thing is boiled, or steam generated.
Boisterous, bois'tėr-us, *a.* Stormy; noisy.
Boisterously, bois'tėr-us-li, *adv.* In a boisterous manner.
Bold, bōld, *a.* Daring; courageous; impudent; steep and abrupt.
Boldly, bōld'li, *adv.* In a bold manner.
Boldness, bōld'nes, *n.* Quality of being bold; intrepidity; assurance.
Bole, bōl, *n.* The body or stem of a tree; a kind of fine clay.
Bolero, bō-lār'ō, *n.* A Spanish dance.
Boll, bōl, *n.* A pod; an old Scottish dry measure of 6 bushels.—*vi.* To form into a pericarp.
Bolshevik, bol'shev-ik, *n.* The Russian name for the majority party in the 1903 split of the Social Democrats; revolutionists; extreme Socialists.
Bolster, bōl'stėr, *n.* A long pillow; a pad.—*vt.* To support with a bolster; to hold up; to maintain.
Bolt, bōlt, *n.* An arrow; a thunderbolt; a bar of a door; anything which fastens or secures.—*vi.* To leave suddenly.—*vt.* To fasten; to swallow hurriedly; to sift.
Bolter, bōlt'ėr, *n.* A machine for separating bran from flour.
Bolt-upright, bōlt'up-rīt, *a.* Perfectly upright.
Bomb, bom, *n.* An iron shell filled with explosive material.
Bombard, bom-bärd', *vt.* To attack with shot and shell.—*n.* An old short cannon.
Bombardier, bom-bärd-ēr', *n.* A non-commissioned officer who serves artillery.
Bombardment, bom-bärd'ment, *n.* The act of bombarding.
Bombardon, bom-bär'don, *n.* A large grave-toned trumpet.
Bombast, bom'bast, *n.* High-sounding words.
Bombastic, bom-bast'ik, *a.* Inflated; turgid.
Bombastically, bom-bas'tik-al-li, *adv.* In a bombastic or inflated manner.
Bombazine, Bombasine, bom-ba-zēn', *n.* A twilled fabric, with the warp silk and the weft worsted.
Bona fide, bō'na fī'dē, *adv.* and *a.* With good faith.
Bon-bon, bong-bong, *n.* A sweetmeat.
Bond, bond, *n.* That which binds; obligation; state of being bonded; a writing by which a person binds himself; in *pl.* chains; imprisonment.—*a.* In a servile state.—*vt.* To grant a bond in security for money; to store till duty is paid.
Bondage, bond'āj, *n.* Slavery; thraldom.
Bonded, bond'ed, *a.* Secured by bond; under a bond to pay duty; containing goods liable to duties.
Bonder, bon'dėr, *n.* One who bonds; one who deposits goods in a bonded warehouse.
Bond-holder, bond'hōld-ėr, *n.* A person who holds a bond for money lent.
Bondman, Bondsman, bond'man, bondz'-man, *n.* A man slave.
Bone, bōn, *n.* A hard substance, forming the framework of an animal; something made of bone.—*vt.* (boning, boned). To take out bones from.
Boned, bōnd, *a.* Having bones; deprived of bones.
Bonfire, bon'fīr, *n.* A large fire in the open air expressive of joy.
Bon-mot, bong-mō, *n.* A witticism.
Bonne, bon, *n.* A French nursemaid.
Bonnet, bon'net, *n.* A dress for the head.
Bonny, bon'ni, *a.* Beautiful; blithe.
Bonus, bō'nus, *n.* A premium; extra dividend to shareholders.
Bony, bōn'i, *a.* Pertaining to or consisting of bones; full of bones; stout; strong.
Bonze, bonz, *n.* A Buddhist priest.
Booby, bö'bi, *n.* A dunce; a water-bird.
Book, bųk, *n.* A printed or written ilterary work; a volume; division of a literary work.—*vt.* To enter in a book.
Booking-office, bųk'ing-of-is, *n.* An office where passengers receive tickets, &c.
Bookish, bųk'ish, *a.* Given to books or reading; fond of study.
Book-keeper, bųk'kēp-ėr, *n.* One who keeps the accounts of a business house.
Booklet, bųk'let, *n.* A little book.
Book-maker, bųk'māk-ėr, *n.* One who compiles books; one who bets systematically.
Bookseller, bųk'sel-ėr, *n.* One who sells books.
Bookworm, bųk'wėrm, *n.* A worm that eats holes in books; a close student of books.
Boom, böm, *n.* A long pole to extend the bottom of a sail; a chain or bar across a river or mouth of a harbour; a hollow roar; briskness in commerce.—*vi.* To make a humming sound; to roar, as waves or cannon.
Boomerang, böm'e-rang, *n.* An Australian missile of hard wood, which can return to hit an object behind the thrower.

Boon, bön, *n.* Answer to a prayer; a favour, gift, or grant.—*a.* Merry; pleasant.
Boor, bör, *n.* A rustic; an ill-mannered or illiterate fellow.
Boorish, bör'ish, *a.* Clownish; rustic.
Boose, Booze, böz, *vi.* To drink largely.
Boosy, Boozy, bö'zi, *a.* A little intoxicated.
Boot, böt, *vt.* To benefit; to put on boots.—*n.* Profit; a covering for the foot and leg; *pl.* a male servant in a hotel.
Booted, böt'ed, *a.* Having boots on.
Booth, böTH, *n.* A temporary shed.
Boot-jack, böt'jak, *n.* An instrument for drawing off boots.
Bootless, böt'les, *a.* Unavailing; without boots.
Boot-tree, Boot-last, böt'trē, böt'last, *n.* An instrument for stretching a boot.
Booty, bö'ti, *n.* Spoil; plunder.
Boracic, bō-ras'ik, *a.* Relating to borax.
Borax, bō'raks, *n.* A salt found crude, or prepared from boracic acid and soda.
Border, bor'dėr, *n.* The outer edge of anything; boundary; margin.—*vi.* To approach near; to touch at the confines; to be contiguous.—*vt.* To surround with a border.
Borderer, bor'dėr-ėr, *n.* One who dwells on a border.
Bore, bōr, *vt.* (boring, bored). To make a hole in; to weary.—*vi.* To pierce.—*n.* The hole made by boring; the diameter of a round hole; a person or thing that wearies; a sudden rise of the tide in certain estuaries.
Boreal, bō'rē-al, *a.* Northern.
Boreas, bō'rē-as, *n.* The north wind.
Borer, bōr'ėr, *n.* One who or that which bores.
Boric, bō'rik, *a.* Same as *Boracic.*
Born, born, *pp.* of *bear,* to bring forth.
Borne, bōrn, *pp.* of *bear,* to carry.
Borough, bu'ro, *n.* A town with a municipal government.
Borrow, bo'rō, *vt.* To ask or receive as a loan; to appropriate.
Borrower, bo'rō-ėr, *n.* One who borrows.
Bort, bort, *n.* Fragments of diamonds.
Boscage, Boskage, bos'kāj, *n.* A mass of growing trees, groves, or thickets.
Bosh, bosh, *n.* Nonsense.
Bosky, bosk'i, *a.* Woody or bushy.
Bosom, bö'zum, *n.* The breast; the seat of the affections.—*vt.* To conceal.—*a.* Much beloved; confidential.
Boss, bos, *n.* A knob; an ornamental projection; a master.
Bossy, bos'i, *a.* Ornamented with bosses.
Botanic, Botanical, bō-tan'ik, bō-tan'ik-al, *a.* Pertaining to botany.
Botanist, bot'an-ist, *n.* One skilled in botany.
Botanize, bot'an-īz, *vi.* (botanizing, botanized). To study botany.
Botany, bot'a-ni, *n.* The science which treats of plants.
Botch, boch, *n.* A swelling on the skin; a clumsy patch; bungled work.—*vt.* To mend or perform clumsily.
Botcher, boch'ėr, *n.* One who botches.
Botchy, boch'i, *a.* Marked with botches.
Both, bōth, *a.* and *pron.* The two, taken by themselves; the pair.—*conj.* As well; on the one side.
Bother, boTH'ėr, *vt.* To annoy.—*vi.* To trouble oneself.—*n.* A trouble, vexation.
Botheration, boTH-ėr-ā'shon, *n.* The act of bothering; state of being bothered.
Bothersome, boTH'ėr-sum, *a.* Causing trouble.
Bothie, Bothy, both'i, *n.* In Scotland, a farm building for servants.
Bott, Bot, bot, *n.* A maggot found in the intestines of horses, &c.: generally in *pl.*
Bottle, bot'l, *n.* A narrow-mouthed vessel of glass, leather, &c., for liquor; the contents of a bottle.—*vt.* (bottling, bottled). To put into a bottle or bottles.
Bottle-holder, bot'l-hōld-ėr, *n.* A backer in a boxing match.
Bottle-nose, bot'l-nōz, *n.* A kind of whale.
Bottom, bot'tom, *n.* The lowest part; the ground under water; foundation; a valley; native strength; a ship; dregs.—*vt.* To found or build upon.
Bottomless, bot'tom-les, *a.* Without a bottom; fathomless.
Bottomry, bot'tom-ri, *n.* The act of borrowing money on a ship.
Boudoir, bö-dwär', *n.* A lady's private room.
Bough, bou, *n.* A branch of a tree.
Bougie, bö-zhē, *n.* A wax-taper; a medical instrument.
Bouilli, bö-yē, *n.* Boiled or stewed meat.
Boulder, bōl'dėr, *n.* A large roundish stone.
Boulevard, böl-vär, *n.* A wide street planted with trees.
Bounce, bouns, *vi.* (bouncing, bounced). To spring or rush out suddenly; to thump; to boast or bully.—*n.* A strong sudden thump; a rebound; a boast.
Bouncer, bouns'ėr, *n.* A boaster; a liar.
Bouncing, bouns'ing, *p.a.* Big; strong; boasting.
Bound, bound, *n.* A boundary; a leap.—*vt.* To limit; to restrain.—*vi.* To leap; to rebound.—*p.a.* Obliged; sure.—*a.* Ready; destined.
Boundary, bound'a-ri, *n.* A mark designating a limit; border.
Bounden, bound'en, *a.* Obligatory.
Bounder, boun'dėr, *n.* A loud-mannered and vulgar person.
Boundless, bound'les, *a.* Unlimited.
Bounteous, boun'tē-us, *a.* Liberal; bountiful.
Bounteously, boun'tē-us-li, *adv.* Liberally; generously; largely.
Bountiful, boun'ti-ful, *a.* Munificent; generous.
Bounty, boun'ti, *n.* Liberality; generosity; a gratuity; premium to encourage trade.
Bouquet, bö-kā', *n.* A bunch of flowers; a nosegay; an agreeable aromatic odour.
Bourgeois, bur-jō', *n.* A small printing type.
Bourgeois, börzh-wä, *n.* A citizen; a man of middle rank.
Bourgeoisie, börzh-wä-zē, *n.* The middle classes, especially those dependent on trade.
Bourn, bōrn, *n.* A bound; a limit.
Bourse, börs, *n.* An exchange; a merchants' meeting-place for business.
Bout, bout, *n.* As much of an action as is performed at one time; turn; debauch.
Bovine, bō'vīn, *a.* Pertaining to oxen.
Bow, bou, *vt.* To bend; to bend the head or body in token of respect; to depress.—*vi.* To bend; to make a reverence; to yield.—*n.* A bending of the head or body, in token of respect; the rounding part of a ship's side forward.
Bow, bō, *n.* An instrument to shoot arrows;

the rainbow; a curve; a fiddlestick; an ornamental knot.
Bowdlerize, bōd'lėr-īz, *vt.* To expurgate.
Bowed, bōd, *p.a.* Bent like a bow.
Bowel, bou'el, *n.* One of the intestines; *pl.* the intestines; the seat of pity; compassion.
Bower, bou'ėr, *n.* An anchor carried at the bow; a shady recess; an arbour.
Bowery, bou'ėr-i, *a.* Containing bowers; leafy.
Bowie-knife, bō'i-nīf, *n.* A knife from 10 to 15 inches long and about 2 inches broad.
Bowl, bōl, *n.* A large roundish cup; a ball, of wood, &c., used for rolling on a level plat of ground; *pl.* the game played with such bowls.—*vi.* To play with bowls; to deliver a ball at cricket; to move rapidly.—*vt.* To roll as a bowl; to deliver (a ball) at cricket, &c.
Bow-legged, bō'legd, *a.* With crooked legs.
Bowler, bōl'ėr, *n.* One who bowls; a round-shaped felt hat.
Bowline, bō'lin, *n.* A rope to make a sail stand towards the bow to catch the wind.
Bowling, bōl'ing, *n.* Act or art of playing with bowls; art or style of a bowler.
Bowling-green, bōl'ing-grēn, *n.* A level piece of ground for bowling.
Bowman, bō'man, *n.* An archer.
Bowshot, bō'shot, *n.* The distance which an arrow flies when shot from a bow.
Bowsprit, bō'sprit, *n.* A large spar which projects over the bow of a ship.
Bow-window, bō'win-dō, *n.* A bay-window.
Box, boks, *n.* A case of wood, metal, &c.; quantity that a case contains; a seat in a play-house, &c.; driver's seat on a coach; a sportsman's house; a blow on the ear; a tree or shrub, yielding a hard wood.—*vt.* To put in a box; to strike with the hand.—*vi.* To fight with the fists.
Boxen, boks'en, *a.* Made of boxwood.
Boxer, boks'ėr, *n.* One who boxes; a pugilist.
Boxing, boks'ing, *n.* The act or art of fighting with the fists; pugilism.
Boxwood, boks'wụd, *n.* The hard-grained wood of the box-tree; the plant itself.
Boy, boi, *n.* A male child; a lad.
Boycott, boi'kot, *vt.* To combine in refusing to have dealings with.
Boyhood, boi'hụd, *n.* The state of a boy.
Boyish, boi'ish, *a.* Like a boy; puerile.
Boy Scout, boi skout, *n.* A member of an organization founded in England in 1908 by Lord Baden-Powell with the object of promoting good citizenship.
Brace, brās, *n.* That which holds; a bandage; a couple.—*vt.* (bracing, braced). To tighten; to strain up; to strengthen.
Bracelet, brās'let, *n.* An ornament for the wrist.
Brachial, brā'ki-al, *a.* Belonging to the arm.
Bracing, brās'ing, *a.* Invigorating.
Bracken, brak'en, *n.* A kind of large fern.
Bracket, brak'et, *n.* A support for something fixed to a wall; a mark in printing to inclose words, &c.—*vt.* To place within or connect by brackets.
Bracketing, brak'et-ing, *n.* A series of brackets for the support of something.
Brackish, brak'ish, *a.* Salt; saltish.
Bract, brakt, *n.* An irregularly developed leaf at the base of a flower.
Brad, brad, *n.* A small nail with no head.
Brae, brā, *n.* A slope; an acclivity.
Brag, brag, *vi.* (bragging, bragged). To bluster; to talk big.—*n.* A boast.
Braggadocio, brag-a-dō'shi-ō, *n.* A boasting fellow; boastful words.
Braggart, brag'ärt, *a.* Boastful.—*n.* A boaster.
Brahman, Brahmin, brä'man, brä'min, *n.* A Hindu of the sacerdotal caste.
Brahmanism, Brahminism, brä'man-izm, brä'min-izm, *n.* The religion of the Brahmans.
Braid, brād, *vt.* To weave, knit, or wreathe; to intertwine.—*n.* A narrow woven band of silk, cotton, &c.; something braided.
Braided, brād'ed, *a.* Edged with braid.
Brail, brāl, *n.* A small rope attached to sails.—*vt.* To haul in by means of brails (with *up*).
Braille, brāl, *n.* A system of reading with raised letters for the blind.
Brain, brān, *n.* The nervous matter within the skull; seat of sensation and of the intellect; the understanding.—*vt.* To dash out the brains of.
Brainless, brān'les, *a.* Silly; thoughtless.
Brain-sick, brān'sik, *a.* Disordered in the understanding; crazed.
Braise, Braize, brāz, *vt.* (braising, braised). To cook with herbs, &c., in a close pan.
Brake, brāk, *n.* A place overgrown with brushwood, &c.; a thicket; the bracken; an instrument to break flax; a harrow for breaking clods; a contrivance for retarding the motion of wheels; a large wagonette.
Braky, brāk'i, *a.* Full of brakes; thorny.
Bramble, bram'bl, *n.* A prickly shrub of the rose family; its berry.
Brambling, bram'bling, *n.* A British finch, like the chaffinch, but larger.
Bran, bran, *n.* The husks of ground corn.
Branch, bransh, *n.* The shoot of a tree or plant; the offshoot of anything, as of a river, family, &c.; a limb.—*vi.* To spread in branches.—*vt.* To divide or form into branches.
Branchy, bransh'i, *a.* Full of branches.
Brand, brand, *n.* A burning piece of wood; a sword; a mark made with a hot iron; a note of infamy; a trade-mark; a kind or quality.—*vt.* To mark with a hot iron; to stigmatize as infamous.
Brandish, brand'ish, *vt.* To shake, wave, or flourish.—*n.* A waving; a flourish.
Brandling, brand'ling, *n.* The parr of the salmon; a small red worm.
Brand-new, Bran-new, brand'nū, bran'nū, *a.* Quite new.
Brandy, bran'di, *n.* An ardent spirit distilled from wine.
Brangle, brang'gl, *n.* A squabble; a wrangle.—*vi.* (brangling, brangled). To wrangle.
Brank, brangk, *n.* Buckwheat.
Branks, brangks, *n.* A bridle for scolds.
Brash, brash, *n.* A confused heap of fragments; small fragments of crushed ice.
Brasier, brā'zhėr, *n.* One who works in brass; a pan for holding coals.
Brass, bras, *n.* A yellow alloy of copper and zinc; a utensil, &c., made of brass; impudence.
Brassard, bras'ard, *n.* A badge worn on the arm; an armlet.
Brassy, bras'i, *a.* Made of brass; like brass.
Brat, brat, *n.* A child, so called in contempt.
Brattice, brat'is, *n.* A partition in coal-mines for ventilation; a fence round machinery.

Bravado, bra-vä'dō, *n.* A boast or brag; would-be boldness.
Brave, brāv, *a.* Daring; bold; valiant; noble.—*n.* A daring person; a savage warrior.—*vt.* (braving, braved). To challenge; to defy; to encounter with courage.
Bravely, brāv'li, *adv.* Courageously.
Bravery, brāv'ė-ri, *n.* Courage; heroism.
Bravo, brä'vō, *n.* A bandit; an assassin.—*interj.* Well done!
Brawl, bral, *vi.* To quarrel noisily.—*n.* A noisy quarrel; uproar.
Brawler, bral'er, *n.* A noisy fellow.
Brawling, bral'ing, *p.a.* Quarrelsome.
Brawn, bran, *n.* The flesh of a boar; the muscular part of the body; muscle.
Brawny, bran'i, *a.* Muscular; fleshy.
Bray, brā, *vt.* To beat or grind small.—*vi.* To make a loud harsh sound, as an ass.—*n.* The cry of an ass.
Braze, brāz, *vt.* (brazing, brazed). To cover with brass; to solder with brass.
Brazen, brāz'n, *a.* Made of brass; impudent.—*vt.* To behave with insolence (with *it*).
Brazen-faced, brāz'n-fāst, *a.* Impudent; bold to excess; shameless.
Brazier, brā'zi-ėr, *n.* See BRASIER.
Breach, brēch, *n.* The act of breaking, or state of being broken; infringement; quarrel.—*vt.* To make a breach or opening in.
Bread, bred, *n.* Food made of flour or meal baked; food; sustenance.
Bread-corn, bred'korn, *n.* Corn of which bread is made.
Breadfruit-tree, bred'fröt-trē, *n.* A tree of the Pacific Islands, producing a fruit which forms a substitute for bread.
Breadstuff, bred'stuf, *n.* Bread-corn; that from which bread is made.
Breadth, bredth, *n.* The measure across any plane surface; width; liberality.
Break, brāk, *vt.* (breaking, pret. broke, pp. broke, broken). To sever by fracture; to rend; to open; to tame; to make bankrupt; to discard; to interrupt; to dissolve any union; to tell with discretion.—*vi.* To come to pieces; to burst; to burst forth; to dawn; to become bankrupt; to decline in vigour; to change in tone.—*n.* An opening; breach; pause; the dawn; a brake for vehicles; a large wagonette.
Breakage, brāk'āj, *n.* A breaking; damage by breaking; allowance for things broken.
Break-down, brāk'doun, *n.* An accident; a downfall; a lively dance.
Breaker, brāk'ėr, *n.* One who or that which breaks; a rock; a wave broken by rocks.
Breakfast, brek'fast, *n.* The first meal in the day.—*vi.* To eat the first meal in the day.—*vt.* To furnish with breakfast.
Break-neck, brāk'nek, *a.* Steep and dangerous; dangerously fast.
Break-up, brāk'up, *n.* Disruption; dissolution.
Breakwater, brāk'wa-tėr, *n.* A mole to break the force of the waves.
Bream, brēm, *n.* A fish.—*vt.* To clean a ship's bottom by means of fire.
Breast, brest, *n.* The fore part of the body, between the neck and the belly; the heart; the conscience; the affections.—*vt.* To bear the breast against; to meet in front.
Breast-bone, brest'bōn, *n.* The bone of the breast.
Breast-knot, brest'not, *n.* A knot of ribbons worn on the breast.
Breastplate, brest'plāt, *n.* Armour for the breast.
Breath, breth, *n.* The air drawn into and expelled from the lungs; life; a single respiration; pause; a gentle breeze.
Breathe, brēTH, *vi.* (breathing, breathed). To draw into and eject air from the lungs; to live; to take breath; to rest.—*vt.* To inspire and exhale; to infuse; to utter softly or in private; to suffer to take breath.
Breathing, brēTH'ing, *n.* Respiration; inspiration; breathing-place; an aspirate.
Breathless, breth'les, *a.* Being out of breath; spent with labour; dead.
Breccia, brech'i-a, *n.* A compound of fragments of rock united by a matrix or cement.
Bred, bred, *pp.* of *breed.*
Breech, brēch, *n.* The lower part of the body behind; the hinder part of a gun, &c.—*vt.* To put into breeches.
Breeches, brēch'ez, *n.pl.* A garment worn by men on the legs.
Breed, brēd, *vt.* (breeding, bred). To bring up; to educate; to engender; to bring forth; to occasion; to rear, as live stock.—*vi.* To produce offspring; to be with young; to be produced.—*n.* Offspring; kind; a brood.
Breeder, brēd'ėr, *n.* One that breeds.
Breeding, brēd'ing, *n.* The raising of a breed or breeds; education; deportment.
Breeze, brēz, *n.* A light wind.
Breezy, brēz'i, *a.* Subject to breezes; airy.
Bren gun, bren gun, *n.* A light machine-gun, fired from a bipod or tripod, and capable of firing 120 rounds a minute.
Brethren, breTH'ren, *n.pl.* of *brother.*
Breton, bret'on, *a.* Relating to Brittany.—*n.* The native language of Brittany.
Brettice, bret'is, *n.* See BRATTICE.
Breve, brēv, *n.* A written mandate; a note of time equal to four minims.
Brevet, brev'et, *n.* A commission entitling an officer to rank above his actual rank or pay.—*a.* Taking rank by brevet.
Breviary, brē'vi-a-ri, *n.* A book containing the daily service of the R. Catholic Church.
Brevier, brē-vēr', *n.* A small printing type.
Brevity, bre'vi-ti, *n.* Shortness; conciseness.
Brew, brö, *vt.* To prepare, as ale or beer, from malt, &c.; to concoct; to plot.—*vi.* To make beer; to be forming.—*n.* The mixture formed by brewing.
Brewage, brö'āj, *n.* Drink brewed.
Brewer, brö'ėr, *n.* One who brews.
Brewery, brö'ė-ri, *n.* A house where brewing is carried on.
Brewing, brö'ing, *n.* The act of making beer; the quantity brewed at once.
Briar, brī'ar, *n.* The root of the white heath, used extensively in the manufacture of tobacco-pipes.
Bribe, brīb, *n.* A gift to corrupt the conduct or judgment.—*vt.* (bribing, bribed). To gain over by bribes.
Briber, brīb'ėr, *n.* One who gives bribes.
Bribery, brīb'ė-ri, *n.* The act or practice of giving or taking bribes.
Bric-à-brac, brik-a-brak, *n.* Articles of interest or value from rarity, antiquity, &c.
Brick, brik, *n.* A rectangular mass of burned clay, used in building, &c.; a loaf shaped like

a brick.—*a.* Made of brick.—*vt.* To lay with bricks.

Brickbat, brik'bat, *n.* A piece of a brick.

Brick-field, brik'fēld, *n.* A field or yard where bricks are made.

Brick-kiln, brik'kiln, *n.* A kiln or furnace in which bricks are burned.

Bricklayer, brik'lā-ėr, *n.* One who builds with bricks.

Brickwork, brik'wėrk, *n.* Built work of bricks; place where bricks are made.

Bridal, brīd'al, *n.* A wedding-feast; a wedding.—*a.* Belonging to a bride or to a wedding.

Bride, brīd, *n.* A woman about to be or newly married.

Brides-cake, brīdz'kāk, *n.* The cake made for a wedding.

Bridegroom, brīd'gröm, *n.* A man about to be or newly married.

Bride's-maid, brīdz'mād, *n.* A woman who attends on a bride at her wedding.

Bridewell, brīd'wel, *n.* A house of hard labour for offenders.

Bridge, brij, *n.* A structure across a river, &c., to furnish a passage; the upper part of the nose.—*vt.* (bridging, bridged). To build a bridge over.

Bridge, brij, *n.* A game of cards resembling whist.

Bridgehead, brij'hed, *n.* Defensive work protecting approach to a bridge on side nearest to the enemy.

Bridle, brī'dl, *n.* The part of harness with which a horse is governed; a curb; a check. —*vt.* (bridling, bridled). To put a bridle on; to restrain.—*vi.* To hold up the head and draw in the chin.

Brief, brēf, *a.* Short; concise.—*n.* A short writing; a writ or precept; an abridgment of a client's case.

Briefless, brēf'les, *a.* Having no brief.

Briefly, brēf'li, *adv.* Concisely.

Brier, brī'ėr, *n.* A prickly shrub, species of the rose.

Briery, brī'ėr-i, *a.* Full of briers; rough.

Brig, brig, *n.* A vessel with two masts, square-rigged.

Brigade, bri-gād', *n.* A body of troops consisting of several battalions. **Brigade-major,** *n.* The principal staff-officer of a brigadier, usually a captain in rank.

Brigadier, bri-ga-dēr', *n.* The officer who commands a brigade.

Brigand, bri'gand, *n.* A freebooter.

Brigandage, bri'gand-āj, *n.* The practice of brigands; highway robbery; plunder.

Brigantine, brig'an-tīn, *n.* A light swift vessel, two-masted and square-rigged.

Bright, brīt, *a.* Clear; shining; glittering; acute· witty; lively; cheerful.

Brighten, brīt'n, *vt.* To make bright or brighter.—*vi.* To become bright; to clear up.

Brightly, brīt'li, *adv.* With lustre; cheerfully.

Brill, bril, *n.* A fish allied to the turbot.

Brilliance, Brilliancy, bril'yans, bril'yan-si, *n.* State of being brilliant; splendour.

Brilliant, bril'yant, *a.* Shining; sparkling; spendid; of great talents.—*n.* A diamond of the finest cut; a small printing type.

Brilliantly, bril'yant-li, *adv.* Splendidly.

Brim, brim, *n.* The rim of anything; the upper edge of the mouth of a vessel.—*vi.* (brimming, brimmed). To be full to the brim.

Brimful, brim'fu̦l, *a.* Full to the brim.

Brimmer, brim'ėr, *n.* A bowl full to the top.

Brimstone, brim'stōn, *n.* Sulphur.

Brindled, brind'ld, *a.* Marked with brown streaks.

Brine, brīn, *n.* Salt water; the sea.

Bring, bring, *vt.* (bringing, brought). To lead or cause to come; to fetch; to produce; to attract; to prevail upon.

Bringer, bring'ėr, *n.* One who brings.

Brink, bringk, *n.* The edge of a steep place.

Briny, brīn'i, *a.* Pertaining to brine.

Briquette, bri-ket', *n.* A lump of fuel, in the form of a brick, made from coal-dust.

Brisk, brisk, *a.* Lively; bright; effervescing.

Brisket, brisk'et, *n.* The breast of an animal, or that part next to the ribs.

Briskly, brisk'li, *adv.* Actively; vigorously.

Bristle, bris'l, *n.* A stiff hair of swine; stiff hair of any kind.—*vt.* (bristling, bristled). To erect in bristles.—*vi.* To stand erect, as bristles; to show anger, &c.

Bristly, bris'li, *a.* Thick set with bristles.

Britannia-metal, bri-tan'i-a-met-al, *n.* An alloy of tin, with copper and antimony.

Britannic, bri-tan'ik, *a.* Pertaining to Britain.

British, brit'ish, *a.* Pertaining to Britain or its inhabitants.

Briton, brit'on, *n.* A native of Britain.

Brittle, brit'l, *a.* Apt to break; not tough or tenacious.—*vt.* To cut up a deer.

Broach, brōch, *n.* A spit; a brooch.—*vt.* To pierce, as with a spit; to tap; to open up; to publish first.

Broacher, brōch'ėr, *n.* One who broaches; a spit.

Broad, brạd, *a.* Having extent from side to side; wide; unrestricted; indelicate.

Broadcasting, brạd'kast-ing, *n.* In wireless telegraphy, a system by which listeners provided with suitable receivers can hear items of music and speech transmitted at definite wave-lengths from certain central stations.

Broaden, brạd'n, *vi.* To grow broad.—*vt.* To make broad.

Broadside, brạd'sīd, *n.* A discharge of all the guns on one side of a ship; a sheet of paper printed on one side.

Broadsword, brạd'sōrd, *n.* A sword with a broad blade and a cutting edge.

Brocade, brō-kād', *n.* A silk or satin stuff variegated with gold and silver.

Brocaded, brō-kād'ed, *a.* Worked like brocade; dressed in brocade.

Brocard, bro-kärd', *n.* A law maxim; a canon.

Broccoli, brok'o-li, *n.* A kind of cauliflower.

Brochure, brō-shör', *n.* A pamphlet.

Brock, brok, *n.* A badger.

Brocket, brok'et, *n.* A stag in its second year.

Brogue, brōg, *n.* A shoe of raw hide; the pronunciation of English peculiar to the Irish.

Broider, broid'ėr, *vt.* To embroider.

Broil, broil, *n.* A brawl; a noisy quarrel.—*vt.* To cook over a fire; to subject to strong heat. —*vi.* To be subjected to heat; to be greatly heated.

Broken, brōk'n, *a.* Subdued; bankrupt.

Broker, brō'kėr, *n.* An agent who buys and sells for others; a pawn-broker.

Brokerage, bro'kėr-āj, *n.* The business of a broker; the pay or commission of a broker.

Bromide, brō'mid, *n.* A compound of bromine with another element.

Bromine, brō'min or brō'min, *n.* A simple non-metallic element with a rank odour.

Bronchial, brong'ki-al, *a.* Belonging to the tubes branching from the windpipe through the lungs.

Bronchitis, brong-kī'tis, *n.* Inflammation of the bronchial tubes.

Bronze, bronz, *n.* An alloy of copper and tin; a colour to imitate bronze; a figure made of bronze.—*vt.* (bronzing, bronzed). To make appear on the surface like bronze.

Bronzed, bronzd, *p.a.* Made to resemble bronze.

Brooch, brōch, *n.* An ornamental pin or buckle used to fasten dress.

Brood, bröd, *vi.* To sit on eggs; to ponder anxiously (with *over* or *on*).—*n.* That which is bred; birds of one hatching; offspring.

Brook, brụk, *n.* A natural stream smaller than a river.—*vt.* To bear; to endure.

Brooklet, brụk'let, *n.* A small brook.

Broom, bröm, *n.* A shrub with yellow flowers and angular branches; a brush.

Broomy, bröm'i, *a.* Full of broom.

Broth, broth, *n.* Liquor in which flesh, or some other substance, has been boiled.

Brothel, broth'el, *n.* A house of ill-fame.

Brother, bruᴛʜ'ėr, *n.*; pl. **Brothers, Brethren,** bruᴛʜ'ėrz, breᴛʜ'ren. A male born of the same parents; an associate; a fellow-creature.

Brotherhood, bruᴛʜ'ėr-hụd, *n.* The state or quality of being a brother; an association.

Brotherly, bruᴛʜ'ėr-li, *a.* Like a brother.

Brougham, bröm or brö'am, *n.* A one-horse close carriage.

Brow, brou, *n.* The ridge over the eye; the forehead; the edge of a steep place.

Browbeat, brou'bēt, *vt.* To bear down with stern looks or arrogant speech.

Brown, broun, *a.* Of a dusky colour, inclining to red.—*n.* A colour resulting from the mixture of red, black, and yellow.—*vt.* To make brown.

Brownie, brou'ni, *n.* A domestic spirit of benevolent character; a junior Girl Guide, between the ages of 8 and 11.

Brownish, broun'ish, *a.* Somewhat brown.

Brown-study, broun'stu-di, *n.* Deep meditation; reverie.

Browse, brouz, *vt.* (browsing, browsed). To pasture or feed upon.—*vi.* To crop and eat food.

Bruin, brö'in, *n.* A familiar name of a bear.

Bruise, bröz, *vt.* (bruising, bruised). To crush; to make a contusion on.—*n.* A contusion; a hurt from a blow.

Bruiser, bröz'ėr, *n.* A boxer; a prize-fighter.

Bruit, bröt, *n.* Report; rumour.—*vt.* To noise abroad.

Brumal, brö'mal, *a.* Belonging to winter.

Brunette, brö-net', *n.* A woman with a brownish or dark complexion.

Brunt, brunt, *n.* The heat of battle; onset; shock.

Brush, brush, *n.* An instrument to clean by rubbing or sweeping; a painter's large pencil; a skirmish; a thicket; the tail of a fox.—*vt.* To sweep, rub, or paint with a brush; to touch lightly in passing.—*vi.* To move nimbly or in haste; to skim.

Brushwood, brush'wụd, *n.* Small trees and shrubs growing together.

Brushy, brush'i, *a.* Rough; shaggy.

Brusque, brusk, *a.* Abrupt in manner; rude.

Brussels-sprouts, brus'elz-sprouts, *n.pl.* A variety of cabbage.

Brutal, bröt'al, *a.* Cruel; ferocious.

Brutality, bröt-al'i-ti, *n.* Quality of being brutal; savageness; cruelty.

Brutalize, bröt'al-īz, *vt.* (brutalizing, brutalized). To make brutal.—*vi.* To become brutal.

Brutally, bröt'al-li, *adv.* In a brutal manner.

Brute, bröt, *a.* Senseless; bestial; uncivilized.—*n.* A beast; a brutal person.

Brutish, bröt'ish, *a.* Brutal; grossly sensual.

Bubble, bub'bl, *n.* A small vesicle of fluid inflated with air; a vain project; a swindle.—*vi.* (bubbling, bubbled). To rise in bubbles.—*vt.* To cheat; to swindle.

Bubo, bū'bō, *n.*; pl. **-oes.** A swelling or abscess in a glandular part of the body.

Bubonic, bū-bon'ik, *a.* Pertaining to bubo.

Buccaneer, buk-a-nēr', *n.* A pirate.

Buccaneering, buk-a-nēr'ing, *n.* The employment of buccaneers.

Buck, buk, *n.* The male of deer, goats, &c.; a gay young fellow; a lye for steeping clothes in.—*vt.* To steep in lye.—*vi.* To leap, as a horse, so as to dismount the rider.

Bucket, buk'et, *n.* A vessel in which water is drawn or carried.

Buck-jumper, buk'jump-ėr, *n.* A horse that bucks so as to dismount its rider.

Buckle, buk'l, *n.* An instrument to fasten straps, &c.—*vt.* (buckling, buckled). To fasten with a buckle; to bend or warp.—*vi.* To apply with vigour (with *to*).

Buckler, buk'lėr, *n.* A small round shield.—*vt.* To shield; to defend.

Buckram, buk'ram, *n.* A coarse linen cloth stiffened with glue.—*a.* Stiff; formal.

Buck-shot, buk'shot, *n.* A large kind of shot used for killing large game.

Buckthorn, buk'thorn, *n.* A shrub bearing a purging berry, also used in dyeing.

Buckwheat, buk'whēt, *n.* A plant bearing small seeds which are ground into meal.

Bucolic, bū-kol'ik, *a.* Pastoral.—*n.* A pastoral poem.

Bud, bud, *n.* The first shoot of a leaf, &c.; a germ.—*vi.* (budding, budded). To put forth buds or germs; to begin to grow.—*vt.* To graft by inserting a bud.

Buddhism, bụd'izm, *n.* The religion founded in India by Buddha.

Buddhist, bụd'ist, *n.* One who adheres to Buddhism.

Budding, bud'ing, *n.* A mode of grafting buds.

Budge, buj, *vt.* (budging, budged). To move; to stir.

Budgerigar, bud'jer-ē-gär'', *n.* The grass or zebra parakeet; the Australian love-bird.

Budget, buj'et, *n.* A little sack with its contents; a stock; the annual statement respecting the British finances.

Buff, buf, *n.* Leather prepared from the skin of the buffalo, elk, &c.; a dull light yellow.—*a.* Light yellow; made of buff.

Buffalo, buf'fa-lō, *n.* A species of ox, larger than the common ox; the American bison.

Buffer, buf'ėr, *n.* An apparatus for deadening concussion.

4–859

Buffet, buf'et, *n.* A cupboard for wine, glasses, &c.; a place for refreshments (pron. bu̦-fe).
Buffet, buf'et, *n.* A blow; a slap.—*vt.* To beat; to box; to contend against.
Buffo, bu̦f'fō, *n.* A comic actor in an opera.
Buffoon, buf-fön', *n.* One who makes sport by low jests and antic gestures; a droll.
Buffoonery, buf-fön'ė-ri, *n.* The arts and practices of a buffoon.
Bug, bug, *n.* A name for various insects, particularly one infesting houses and inflicting severe bites.
Bugbear, bug'bār, *n.* Something real or imaginary that causes terror.
Buggy, bug'i, *n.* A light one-horse carriage.
Bugle, bū'gl, *n.* A hunting-horn; a military instrument of music; a long glass bead, commonly black.
Bugler, būg'lėr, *n.* A soldier who conveys officers' commands by sounding a bugle.
Buhl, böl, *n.* Unburnished gold or brass used for inlaying; articles so ornamented.
Build, bild, *vt.* (building, built). To construct; to raise on a foundation; to establish.—*vi.* To form a structure.—*n.* Construction; make; form.
Builder, bild'ėr, *n.* One who builds.
Building, bild'ing, *n.* The art of constructing edifices; an edifice.
Bulb, bulb, *n.* A round root; a round protuberance.
Bulbous, bulb'us, *a.* Pertaining to a bulb; swelling out.
Bulbul, bu̦l'bu̦l, *n.* The Persian nightingale.
Bulge, bulj, *n.* A swelling; bilge.—*vi.* (bulging, bulged). To swell out; to be protuberant.
Bulk, bulk, *n.* Magnitude; the majority; extent.
Bulky, bulk'i, *a.* Of great bulk.
Bull, bu̦l, *n.* The male of cattle; a sign of the zodiac; one who raises the price of stock; a letter or edict of the pope; a ludicrous contradiction in language.
Bullace, bu̦l'ās, *n.* A British wild plum.
Bull-baiting, bu̦l'bāt-ing, *n.* The practice of baiting or attacking bulls with dogs.
Bull-dog, bu̦l'dog, *n.* A species of dog.
Bulldozer, bu̦l'dōz-ėr, *n.* A machine provided with a blade for spreading and levelling material.
Bullet, bu̦l'et, *n.* A small ball; a conical projectile generally of lead intended to be discharged from small-arms.
Bulletin, bu̦l'e-tin, *n.* An official report.
Bull-fight, bu̦l'fīt, *n.* A combat between armed men and bulls in a closed arena.
Bullfinch, bu̦l'finsh, *n.* A British song-bird.
Bull-frog, bu̦l'frog, *n.* A large species of frog in N. America, with a loud bass voice.
Bullion, bu̦l'yon, *n.* Uncoined gold or silver.
Bullock, bu̦l'ok, *n.* An ox or castrated bull.
Bull's-eye, bu̦lz'ī, *n.* A circular opening for light or air; the centre of a target.
Bull-trout, bu̦l'trout, *n.* A large species of trout.
Bully, bu̦l'i, *n.* An overbearing quarrelsome fellow.—*vt.* (bullying, bullied). To insult and overbear.—*vi.* To bluster or domineer.
Bulrush, bu̦l'rush, *n.* A large, strong kind of rush.
Bulwark, bu̦l'wėrk, *n.* A bastion; a fortification; a means of defence or safety.
Bumbailiff, bum-bā'lif, *n.* An under-bailiff.
Bumble-bee, bum'bl-bē, *n.* A large bee.
Bum-boat, bum'bōt, *n.* A small boat for carrying provisions to a ship.
Bump, bump, *n.* A heavy blow, or the noise of it; a lump produced by a blow.—*vi.* To make a loud, heavy, or hollow noise.—*vt.* To strike heavily against.
Bumper, bump'ėr, *n.* A cup or glass filled to the brim; something completely filled.
Bumpkin, bump'kin, *n.* An awkward rustic; a lout.
Bumptious, bump'shus, *a.* Self-assertive.
Bun, bun, *n.* A kind of cake or sweet bread.
Bunch, bunsh, *n.* A knob or lump; a cluster.—*vi.* To swell out in a protuberance; to cluster.
Bunchy, bunsh'i, *a.* Like a bunch.
Bundle, bun'dl, *n.* A number of things bound together; a package.—*vt.* (bundling, bundled). To tie in a bundle; to dispose of hurriedly.—*vi.* To depart hurriedly (with *off*).
Bung, bung, *n.* The stopper of a cask.—*vt.* To stop with a bung; to close up.
Bungalow, bung'ga-lō, *n.* A single-storied house.
Bungle, bung'gl, *vi.* (bungling, bungled). To perform in a clumsy manner.—*vt.* To make or mend clumsily; to manage awkwardly.—*n.* A clumsy performance.
Bungler, bung'gl-ėr, *n.* A clumsy workman.
Bungling, bung'gl-ing, *p.a.* Clumsy; awkwardly done.
Bunion. *See* BUNYON.
Bunk, bungk, *n.* A wooden box serving as a seat and bed; a sleeping berth.
Bunker, bung'kėr, *n.* A large bin or receptacle; a sandy hollow on a golf course.
Bunkum, Buncombe, bung'kum, *n.* Talking for talking's sake; mere words.
Bunting, bunt'ing, *n.* A bird allied to finches and sparrows; stuff of which flags are made; flags.
Bunyon, Bunion, bun'yon, *n.* An excrescence on some of the joints of the feet.
Buoy, boi, *n.* A floating mark to point out shoals, &c.; something to keep a person or thing up in the water.—*vt.* To keep afloat; to bear up.—*vi.* To float.
Buoyancy, boi'an-si, *n.* The quality of being buoyant; vivacity; cheerfulness.
Buoyant, boi'ant, *a.* Floating; light; elastic.
Bur, bėr, *n.* The rough prickly head of the burdock, chestnut, &c. *See* BURR.
Burden, Burthen, bėr'dn, bėr'THn, *n.* That which is borne; load; freight; that which is oppressive; chorus of a song; that which is often repeated.—*vt.* To load; to oppress.
Burdensome, bėr'dn-sum, *a.* Heavy; oppressive.
Burdock, bėr'dok, *n.* A plant with a rough prickly head.
Bureau, bū-rō', *n.*; pl. **-eaux, -rōz, or -eaus.** A writing table with drawers; an office or court; a government office.
Bureaucracy, bū-rō'kra-si, *n.* Centralized administration of a country, through regularly graded officials; such officials collectively.
Burgage, bėrg'āj, *n.* A species of tenure of lands or tenements in boroughs.
Burgeon, bėr'jon, *n.* A bud, shoot, sprout.
Burgess, bėr'jes, *n.* An inhabitant, freeman, or parliamentary representative of a borough.

Burgh, bu'rė, *n.* The Scots term for borough.
Burglar, bėrg'lėr, *n.* One who robs a house by night.
Burglarious, bėrg-lā'ri-us, *a.* Pertaining to burglary.
Burglary, bėrg'la-ri, *n.* Act of nocturnal house-breaking.
Burgomaster, bėr'gō-mas-tėr, *n.* The chief magistrate of a Dutch and German town.
Burgundy, bėr'gun-di, *n.* A kind of wine, so called from Burgundy in France.
Burial, be'ri-al, *n.* Act of burying; interment.
Burin, bū'rin, *n.* A tool for engraving.
Burlesque, bėr-lesk', *a.* Tending to excite laughter.—*n.* A composition tending to excite laughter; caricature.—*vt.* (burlesquing, burlesqued). To turn into ridicule; to make ludicrous.
Burly, bėr'li, *a.* Great in size; boisterous.
Burmese, bur'mēz, *a.* Pertaining to Burma.—*n.* An inhabitant or inhabitants of Burma; their language.
Burn, bėrn, *vt.* (burning, burnt or burned). To consume with fire; to scorch; to inflame; to harden by fire.—*vi.* To be on fire; to be inflamed with desire; to rage fiercely.—*n.* A hurt caused by fire; a rivulet.
Burner, bėrn'ėr, *n.* One who burns; that which gives out light or flame.
Burning, bėrn'ing, *p.a.* Fiery; vehement.
Burning-glass, bėrn'ing-glas, *n.* A glass which collects the rays of the sun into a focus, producing an intense heat.
Burnish, bėr'nish, *vt.* To polish.—*vi.* To grow bright or glossy.—*n.* Gloss; lustre.
Burnt-offering, bėrnt'of-fėr-ing, *n.* A sacrifice burnt on an altar.
Burr, bėr, *n.* A guttural sounding of the letter *r*; a rough or projecting ridge; bur.
Burrow, bu'rō, *n.* A hole in the earth made by rabbits, &c.—*vi.* To excavate a hole underground; to hide.
Bursar, bėrs'ėr, *n.* A treasurer of a college or monastery; a student to whom a bursary is paid.
Bursary, bėrs'a-ri, *n.* A scholarship in a Scottish school or university.
Burst, bėrst, *vi.* (bursting, burst). To fly or break open; to rush forth; to come with violence.—*vt.* To break by force; to open suddenly.—*n.* A violent disruption; a rupture.
Burthen, bėr'THn. *See* BURDEN.
Bury, be'ri, *vt.* (burying, buried). To put into a grave; to overwhelm; to hide.
Bus, bus, *n.*; pl. **Buses.** An omnibus.
Busby, buz'bi, *n.* A military head-dress.
Bush, bush, *n.* A shrub with branches; a thicket; the backwoods of Australia; a lining of hard metal in the nave of a wheel, &c.—*vi.* To grow bushy.
Bushel, bush'el, *n.* A dry measure containing eight gallons or four pecks.
Bushman, bush'man, *n.* A settler in the bush or forest districts of a new country.
Bush-ranger, bush'rān-jėr, *n.* Formerly in Australia, one who lived in the 'bush' by robbery.
Bushy, bush'i, *a.* Full of bushes; like a bush.
Busily, bi'zi-li, *adv.* In a busy manner.
Business, biz'nes, *n.* Occupation; concern; trade.—*a.* Pertaining to traffic, trade, &c.
Busk, busk, *n.* A piece of steel or whalebone worn in corsets.—*vt.* To equip; dress.
Buskin, bus'kin, *n.* A kind of half boot; the high shoe worn by ancient tragedians.
Buskined, bus'kind, *a.* Wearing buskins.
Buss, bus, *n.* A kiss.—*vt.* To kiss.
Bust, bust, *n.* The chest and thorax; a sculptured figure of the head and shoulders.
Bustard, bus'tėrd, *n.* A large heavy bird of the order of runners.
Bustle, bus'l, *vi.* (bustling, bustled). To hurry and be busy.—*n.* Hurry; tumult; a pad formerly worn by ladies at the back below the waist.
Busy, bi'zi, *a.* Occupied; actively engaged; officious.—*vt.* (busying, busied). To make or keep busy.
Busy-body, bi'zi-bo-di, *n.* An officious meddling person.
But, but, *conj. prep. adv.* Except; unless; only; however; nevertheless.
Butcher, buch'ėr, *n.* One who kills animals for market; one who sells meat; one who delights in bloody deeds.—*vt.* To kill animals for food; to slaughter cruelly.
Butchery, buch'ėr-i, *n.* A slaughter-house; massacre.
Butler, but'lėr, *n.* A male servant who has the care of wines, &c.
Butt, but, *n.* The end of a thing; a mark to be shot at; the person at whom ridicule, &c., is directed; a cask holding 126 gallons of wine.—*vi.* To thrust the head forward.—*vt.* To strike with the head or horns.
Butter, but'tėr, *n.* An oily substance obtained from cream by churning; any substance resembling butter.—*vt.* To spread with butter; to flatter grossly.
Butter-cup, but'tėr-kup, *n.* A wild yellow cup-shaped flower.
Butterfly, but'tėr-flī, *n.* The name of a group of winged insects.
Buttermilk, but'ėr-milk, *n.* The milk that remains after the butter is separated.
Buttery, but'tėr-i, *n.* An apartment where provisions are kept.—*a.* Like butter; smeared with butter.
Buttock, but'tok, *n.* The protuberant part of the body behind; the rump.
Button, but'n, *n.* A knob to fasten the parts of dress; a knob or stud; *pl.* a page-boy.—*vt.* To fasten with buttons.
Button-hole, but'n-hōl, *n.* A hole for a button; a flower for putting in this.—*vt.* To detain in conversation against one's will.
Buttress, but'tres, *n.* A projecting support for a wall; a prop.—*vt.* To support by a buttress; to prop.
Buxom, buks'um, *a.* Gay; brisk; wanton.
Buy, bī, *vt.* (buying, bought). To acquire by payment; to purchase; to bribe.—*vi.* To negotiate or treat about a purchase.
Buyer, bī'ėr, *n.* One who buys.
Buzz, buz, *vi.* To hum, as bees; to whisper.—*vt.* To whisper.—*n.* The noise of bees; a confused humming noise.
Buzzard, buz'ėrd, *n.* A species of hawk; a blockhead.
By, bī, *prep.* Used to denote the instrument, agent, or manner; at; near; beside; through or with; in; for; according to; at the rate of; not later than.—*adv.* Near; passing. In *composition*, secondary, side.
By-and-by, bī-and-bī. In the near future.
Bye, bī, *n.* A term in certain games; e.g. in

cricket an odd or side run; the odd man in a game where the players pair off in couples.
By-end, bī'end, *n.* Private end; secret purpose.
By-gone, bī'gon, *a.* Past; gone by.
By-gones, bī'gonz, *n.pl.* Past troubles, offences, &c.
By-law, bī'la̤, *n.* A local law of a city, society, &c.; an accessory law.
By-path, bī'path, *n.* A private or side path.
By-play, bī'plā, *n.* Action carried on aside, and commonly in dumb-show.
Byre, bīr, *n.* A cow-house.
By-stander, bī'stand-ėr, *n.* One who stands near; a spectator; a mere looker-on.
By-the-by (or **bye**), bī-THē-bī. By the way; in passing.
By-way, bī'wā, *n.* A private or obscure way.
By-word, bī'wėrd, *n.* A common saying; a proverb.
Byzantine, biz-an'tīn or biz', *a.* Pertaining to Byzantium or Constantinople and the Greek Empire of which it was the capital.

C

Cab, kab, *n.* A covered one-horse carriage.
Cabal, ka-bal', *n.* An intrigue; persons united in some intrigue.—*vi.* (caballing, caballed). To combine in plotting.
Caballer, ka-bal'ėr, *n.* An intriguer.
Cabaret, kab'a-ret, ka-ba-rā, *n.* A tavern; a restaurant in which singing and dancing performances are given.
Cabbage, kab'āj, *n.* A culinary vegetable.—*vt.* (cabbaging, cabbaged). To purloin, especially pieces of cloth.
Cabbage-rose, kab'āj-rōz, *n.* A species of rose; called also *Provence rose.*
Cabbala, Cabala, kab'a-la, *n.* A mysterious tradition among Jewish rabbins.
Cabby, kab'i, *n.* A cabman.
Caber, kā'bėr, *n.* In Highland games, a long undressed stem of a tree, used for tossing as a feat of strength.
Cabin, kab'in, *n.* A hut; an apartment in a ship.—*vt.* To confine, as in a cabin.
Cabinet, kab'in-et, *n.* A closet; a small room; a set of drawers for curiosities; the ministers of state.
Cabinet-council, kab'in-et-koun-sil, *n.* A council of state.
Cabinet-maker, kab'in-et-māk-ėr, *n.* One who makes articles of furniture.
Cable, kā'bl, *n.* The strong rope or chain to hold a ship at anchor; a large rope or chain; a submarine telegraph wire.—*vt.* (cabling, cabled). To furnish with a cable; to send by ocean telegraph.
Cablegram, kā'bl-gram, *n.* A message sent by an oceanic telegraph cable.
Cabman, kab'man. *n.* The driver of a cab.
Cabriolet, kab'ri-ō-lā'', *n.* A one-horse chaise.
Cacao, ka-kā'ō, *n.* The chocolate-tree.
Cachalot, kash'a-lot, *n.* The sperm-whale.
Cachinnation, kak-in-nā'shon, *n.* Loud or immoderate laughter.
Cackle, kak'l, *vi.* (cackling, cackled). To make the noise of a goose or hen; to chatter. —*n.* The noise of a hen, &c.; idle talk.
Cacophony, ka-kof'ō-ni, *n.* Unpleasant vocal sound; a discord.
Cactus, kak'tus, *n.*; pl. **-tuses** or **-ti.** A spiny shrub of numerous species.
Cad, kad, *n.* A mean, vulgar fellow.
Cadaverous, ka-dav'ėr-us, *a.* Resembling a dead human body; pale; ghastly.
Caddie, kad'i, *n.* A golfer's attendant.
Caddy, kad'i, *n.* A small box for tea.
Cadence, kā'dens, *n.* A fall of the voice at the end of a sentence; rhythm; the close of a musical passage or phrase.
Cadet, ka-det', *n.* A younger brother; a young man in a military school.
Cadge, kaj, *vt.* and *i.* (cadging, cadged). To carry about for sale; to go about begging.
Cadger, kaj'ėr, *n.* An itinerant hawker.
Cadmium, kad'mi-um, *n.* A whitish metal.
Caduceus, ka-dū'sē-us, *n.* Mercury's rod.
Cæsura, sē-zū'ra, *n.* A pause in a verse.
Café, kaf-ā, *n.* A coffee-house; a restaurant.
Cafeteria, kaf-e-tēr'i-a, *n.* A restaurant in which customers serve themselves.
Caffeine, ka-fē'in, *n.* A slightly bitter alkaloid found in coffee, tea, &c.
Cage, kāj, *n.* An inclosure of wire, &c., for birds and beasts.—*vt.* (caging, caged). To confine in a cage.
Cairn, kārn, *n.* A rounded heap of stones.
Cairngorm, kārn'gorm, *n.* A yellow or brown rock-crystal found in Scotland.
Caisson, kās'son, *n.* An ammunition chest; a structure to raise sunken vessels; a structure used in laying foundations in deep water.
Caitiff, kā'tif, *n.* A mean villain; a despicable knave.
Cajole, ka-jōl', *vt.* (cajoling, cajoled). To coax; to court; to deceive by flattery.
Cajolery, ka-jōl'ė-ri, *n.* Flattery.
Cake, kāk, *n.* A composition of flour, butter, sugar, &c., baked; a mass of matter concreted.—*vt.* (caking, caked). To form into a cake or mass.—*vi.* To form into a hard mass.
Calabash, kal'a-bash, *n.* A gourd shell dried.
Calamitous, ka-lam'it-us, *a.* Miserable; afflictive.
Calamity, ka-lam'i-ti, *n.* Misfortune; disaster.
Calash, ka-lash', *n.* A light carriage with low wheels and a hood; a kind of head-dress for ladies.
Calcareous, kal-kā'rē-us, *a.* Of the nature of lime or chalk; containing lime.
Calcination, kal-sin-ā'shon, *n.* Act or operation of calcining.
Calcine, kal-sīn', *vt.* (calcining, calcined). To reduce to a powder by fire.—*vi.* To be converted by heat into a powder.
Calculable, kal'kū-la-bl, *a.* That may be calculated.
Calculate, kal'kū-lāt, *vt.* (calculating, calculated). To compute; to adjust; to make suitable.—*vi.* To make a computation.
Calculating, kal'kū-lāt-ing, *p.a.* Scheming.
Calculation, kal-kū-lā'shon, *n.* Estimate.
Calculator, kal'kū-lāt-ėr, *n.* One who calculates.
Calculus, kal'kū-lus, *n.*; pl. **-li.** The stone in the bladder, kidneys, &c.; a method of calculation in mathematics.
Caldron, ka̤l'dron, *n.* A large kettle or boiler.
Caledonian, kal-i-dō'ni-an, *a.* Pertaining to Scotland.—*n.* A Scot.

Calendar, ka'len-dėr, *n.* A register of the months and days of the year; an almanac.
Calender, ka'len-dėr, *n.* A machine for smoothing and glazing cloth.—*vt.* To press between rollers to make smooth, glossy, wavy, &c.
Calends, ka'lendz, *n.pl.* Among the Romans, the first day of each month.
Calf, käf, *n.*; pl. **Calves,** kävz. The young of the cow; a kind of leather; the fleshy part of the leg below the knee.
Calibre, ka'li-bėr, *n.* Diameter of the bore of a gun; extent of mental qualities; a sort or kind.
Calico, ka'li-kō, *n.* Cotton cloth.
Calipers. *See* CALLIPERS.
Caliph, kā'lif, *n.* A title given to the successors of Mohammed.
Calk, kạk, *vt.* *See* CAULK.
Calkin, Calker, kạk'in, kạk'ėr, *n.* The part of a horse-shoe bent downwards and pointed.
Call, kạl, *vt.* To name; to style; to summon; to ask, or command to come; to appoint; to appeal to; to utter aloud; to awaken.—*vi.* To utter a loud sound; to make a short visit. —*n.* A vocal utterance; summons; demand; divine vocation; a short visit.
Calligraphy, kal-lig'ra-fi, *n.* The art of beautiful writing; penmanship.
Calling, kạl'ing, *n.* Vocation; profession.
Callipers, kal'i-pėrz, *n.pl.* Compasses for measuring calibre.
Callisthenics, kal-is-then'iks, *n.* Exercise for health, strength, or grace of movement.
Callosity, ka-los'i-ti, *n.* Hardness of skin; horny hardness.
Callous, kal'us, *a.* Hardened; unfeeling; obdurate.
Callow, kal'ō, *a.* Destitute of feathers; unfledged.
Calm, käm, *a.* Still; free from wind; peaceable; composed.—*n.* Absence of wind; tranquillity.—*vt.* To make calm; to still; to assuage.—*vi.* To become calm.
Calmly, käm'li, *adv.* In a calm manner.
Calmness, käm'nes, *n.* Quietness; composure.
Calomel, ka'lō-mel, *n.* A preparation of mercury, much used in medicine.
Caloric, ka-lo'rik, *n.* The principle or simple element of heat; heat.
Calorific, ka-lo-rif'ik, *a.* Causing heat.
Calotype, ka'lō-tīp, *n.* A process of photography.
Caltrop, kal'trop, *n.* An iron ball with iron points to wound horses' feet.
Calumet, kal'ū-met, *n.* The North American Indians' pipe of peace.
Calumniate, ka-lum'ni-āt, *vt.* (calumniating, calumniated). To defame maliciously; to slander.—*vi.* To utter calumnies.
Calumniation, ka-lum'ni-ā''shon, *n.* False and malicious accusation.
Calumniator, ka-lum'ni-āt-ėr, *n.* One who calumniates.
Calumnious, ka-lum'ni-us, *a.* Partaking of calumny.
Calumniously, ka-lum'ni-us-li, *adv.* Slanderously.
Calumny, ka'lum-ni, *n.* False and malicious defamation; backbiting.
Calvary, kal'va-ri, *n.* A place of skulls, particularly the place where Christ was crucified.
Calve, käv, *vi.* (calving, calved). To give birth to a calf.
Calvinism, kal'vin-izm, *n.* The theological tenets of Calvin.
Calvinist, kal'vin-ist, *n.* One who embraces the doctrines of Calvin.
Calvinistic, kal-vin-is'tik, *a.* Pertaining to Calvin, or to his tenets.
Calyx, kā-liks, *n.*; pl. **-yces** or **-yxes.** The outer covering of a flower; the flower-cup.
Cam, kam, *n.* A projection on a wheel to give alternating motion to another wheel, &c.
Camber, kam'bėr, *n.* A convexity upon an upper surface, as a ship's deck, a bridge, a road, a beam.
Cambrian, kam'bri-an, *a.* Pertaining to Wales.—*n.* A Welshman.
Cambric, kām'brik, *n.* A fine white linen.
Camel, kam'el, *n.* A large ruminant hoofed quadruped used in Asia and Africa for carrying burdens.
Camellia, ka-mel'i-a or ka-mēl'ya, *n.* A genus of beautiful shrubs of the tea family.
Camelopard, kam-el'ō-pärd, *n.* The giraffe.
Cameo, kam'ē-ō, *n.* A stone or shell of different coloured layers cut in relief.
Camera, kam'ė-ra, *n.* An arched roof; a council chamber; an apparatus for taking photographs.
Camlet, kam'let, *n.* A stuff of various mixtures of wool, silk, hair, &c.
Camomile, kam'ō-mil, *n.* A bitter medicinal plant.
Camouflage, kạm-ö-fläzh, *n.* The art of disguising; especially the art of disguising material in warfare.
Camp, kamp, *n.* The ground on which an army pitch their tents; an encampment.—*vi.* To pitch a camp; to encamp.
Campaign, kam-pān', *n.* The time an army keeps the field every year, during a war; its operations.—*vi.* To serve in a campaign.
Campaigner, kam-pān'ėr, *n.* An old soldier; a veteran.
Campanile, kam-pa-nē'lā or 'kam'pa-nil, *n.*; pl. **-ili** or **-iles.** A bell-tower.
Campanology, kam-pa-nol'o-ji, *n.* The art or principles of ringing bells.
Camphor, kam'fėr, *n.* A whitish, bitter, strong-smelling substance used in medicine.
Camphorate, kam'fėr-āt, *vt.* (camphorating, camphorated). To impregnate with camphor.
Campion, kam'pi-on, *n.* A popular name of certain plants of the Pink family.
Can, kan, *n.* A cup or vessel for liquors.
Can, kan, *vi.* (pret. could). To be able; to have sufficient moral or physical power.
Canal, ka-nal', *n.* A channel; an artificial water-course for boats; a duct of the body.
Canard, ka-när or ka-närd', *n.* An absurd story; a false rumour.
Canary, ka-nā'ri, *n.* Wine made in the Canary Isles; a finch from the Canary Isles.
Cancel, kan'sel, *vt.* (cancelling, cancelled). To obliterate; to revoke; to set aside.—*n.* Act of cancelling.
Cancer, kạn'sėr, *n.* One of the signs of the zodiac; a malignant growth in the body.
Cancerous, kan'sėr-us, *a.* Having the qualities of a cancer.
Candelabrum, kan-de-lā'brum, *n.*; pl. **-ra.** A branched ornamental candlestick.
Candid, kan'did, *a.* Sincere; ingenuous.

Candidate, kan'di-dāt, *n.* One who proposes himself, or is proposed, for some office; one who aspires after preferment.
Candied, kan'did, *a.* Preserved with sugar, or incrusted with it.
Candle, kan'dl, *n.* A cylindrical body of tallow, wax, &c., surrounding a wick, and used for giving light.
Candlemas, kan'dl-mas, *n.* A church festival on 2nd February, in honour of the purification of the Virgin Mary.
Candlestick, kan'dl-stik, *n.* An instrument to hold a candle.
Candour, kan'dėr, *n.* Frankness; sincerity.
Candy, kan'di, *vt.* (candying, candied). To conserve with sugar; to form into crystals.—*vi.* To take on the form of candied sugar.—*n.* Crystallized sugar; a sweetmeat.
Cane, kān, *n.* A reed; a walking-stick.—*vt.* (caning, caned). To beat with a cane.
Canine, ka'nīn, *a.* Pertaining to dogs.
Caning, kān'ing, *n.* A beating with a cane.
Canister, kan'is-tėr, *n.* A small box for tea, coffee, &c.; a case containing shot which bursts on being discharged.
Canker, kang'kėr, *n.* A malignant ulcer; a disease of trees; a disease in horses' feet; something that gnaws or corrodes.—*vt.* and *i.* To corrode or corrupt.
Cankerous, kang'kėr-us, *a.* Corroding.
Canker-worm, kang'kėr-wėrm, *n.* A worm destructive to trees or plants.
Cannel-coal, Candle-coal, kan'el-kōl, kan'-dl-kōl, *n.* A coal which burns readily and brightly, used in making gas.
Cannibal, kan'ni-bal, *n.* A savage who eats human flesh.—*a.* Relating to cannibalism.
Cannibalism, kan'ni-bal-izm, *n.* The eating human flesh by mankind.
Cannon, kan'un, *n.* A great gun; the striking of a ball on two other balls successively.—*vi.* To strike with rebounding collision; to make a cannon at billiards.
Cannonade, kan-un-ād', *n.* An attack with cannon.—*vt.* (cannonading, cannonaded). To attack with cannon; to batter with cannon-shot.
Cannot, kan'not. The negative of *can*.
Canny, Cannie, kan'i, *a.* Cautious; wary.
Canoe, ka-nö', *n.* A boat made of the trunk of a tree, or of bark or skins; a light boat propelled by paddles.
Cañon, kan'on, *n.* A rule of doctrine or discipline; a law in general; the genuine books of the Holy Scriptures; a member of the cathedral chapter; a catalogue of saints canonized; a formula; a large kind of printing type.
Canon, Canyon, kan'yun, *n.* A long and narrow mountain gorge.
Canonical, kan-on'ik-al, *a.* According to the canon; ecclesiastical.
Canonicals, kan-on'ik-alz, *n.pl.* The full dress of the clergy worn when they officiate.
Canonist, kan'on-ist, *n.* One versed in canon or ecclesiastical law.
Canonization, kan'on-īz-ā"shon, *n.* Act of canonizing; state of being canonized.
Canonize, kan'on-īz, *vt.* (canonizing, canonized). To enroll in the canon as a saint.
Canonry, Canonship, kan'on-ri, kan'on-ship, *n.* The office of a canon in a cathedral or collegiate church.
Canopy, kan'ō-pi, *n.* A covering over a throne, bed, or person's head, &c.—*vt.* (canopying, canopied). To cover with a canopy.
Cant, kant, *vi.* To speak in a whining tone; to sham piety.—*vt.* To tilt up; to bevel.—*n.* A whining hypocritical manner of speech; jargon; slang; inclination from a perpendicular or horizontal line; a toss or jerk.—*a.* Of the nature of cant or slang.
Cantankerous, kan-tang'kėr-us, *a.* Ill-natured; cross; contentious.
Cantata, kan-tä'ta, *n.* A short musical composition in the form of an oratorio.
Cantatrice, kan-ta-trē'chā, *n.* A female singer.
Canteen, kan-tēn', *n.* A vessel used by soldiers for carrying liquor; a place in barracks where provisions, &c., are sold.
Canter, kan'tėr, *n.* A moderate gallop.—*vi.* To move in a moderate gallop.
Cantharides, kan-tha'ri-dēz, *n.pl.* Spanish flies, used to raise a blister.
Canticle, kan'ti-kl, *n.* A song; a passage of Scripture for chanting; in *pl.* the Song of Solomon.
Cantilever, kan'ti-lēv-ėr, *n.* A bracket to carry mouldings, eaves, balconies, &c.; one of two long arms projecting toward each other from opposite banks or piers, used in bridge-making.
Cantle, kan'tl, *n.* A corner; a piece; the hind part of a saddle.
Canto, kan'tō, *n.* A division of a poem; the treble part of a musical composition.
Canton, kan'ton, *n.* A division of territory or its inhabitants.—*vt.* To divide into cantons; to allot separate quarters to different parts of an army. (In *milit. lan.* pron. kan-tön'.)
Cantonal, kan'ton-al, *a.* Pertaining to a canton.
Cantonment, kan-ton'ment, *n.* A part of a town occupied by troops; a military town.
Canvas, kan'vas, *n.* A coarse cloth; sail-cloth; sails of ships; cloth for painting on; a painting.
Canvass, kan'vas, *vt.* To scrutinize; to solicit the votes of.—*vi.* To solicit votes or interest; to use efforts to obtain.—*n.* Scrutiny; solicitation of votes.
Canvasser, kan'vas-ėr, *n.* One who solicits votes, &c.
Canzonet, kan-zō-net', *n.* A little song.
Caoutchouc, kou'chök or kö'chök, *n.* India-rubber; a very elastic gum.
Cap, kap, *n.* A covering for the head; something used as a cover; a top piece.—*vt.* (capping, capped). To put a cap on; to complete; to crown; to excel.
Capability, kā-pa-bil'i-ti, *n.* Quality of being capable.
Capable, kā'pa-bl, *a.* Having sufficient skill or power; competent; susceptible.
Capacious, ka-pā'shus, *a.* Wide; large; comprehensive.
Capacitate, ka-pas'i-tāt, *vt.* To make able; to qualify.
Capacity, ka-pas'i-ti, *n.* Power of holding; extent of space; ability; state.
Cap-a-pie, kap-a-pē', *adv.* From head to foot.
Caparison, ka-pa'ri-son, *n.* A covering laid over the saddle of a horse; clothing.—*vt.* To cover with a cloth; to dress richly.
Cape, kāp, *n.* The point of a neck of land ex-

tending into the sea; a loose cloak hung from the shoulders.
Caper, kā'pėr, *vi*. To prance; to spring.—*n*. A skip, spring, jump; the flower-bud of the caper-bush, much used for pickling.
Capercailzie, kā-pėr-kal'yi, *n*. The wood-grouse or cock of the woods, the largest of the gallinaceous birds of Europe.
Capillary, ka-pil'la-ri, or kap'il-la-ri, *a*. Resembling a hair; having a bore of very small diameter.—*n*. A tube with a very small bore; a fine vessel or canal in an animal body.
Capital, kap'it-al, *a*. First in importance; metropolitan; affecting the head; punishable with death.—*n*. The uppermost part of a column; the chief city; the stock of a bank, tradesman, &c.; a large letter or type.
Capitalist, kap'it-al-ist, *n*. A man who has a capital or wealth.
Capitalize, kap'it-al-īz, *vt*. (capitalizing, capitalized). To convert into capital.
Capitally, kap'it-al-i, *adv*. In a capital manner; so as to involve life.
Capitation, kap-it-ā'shon, *n*. Numeration by heads or individuals.
Capitol, kap'it-ol, *n*. The temple of Jupiter in Rome; a citadel; a state-house.
Capitular, Capitulary, ka-pit'ū-lėr, ka-pit'ū-la-ri, *n*. An act passed in an ecclesiastical chapter; body of laws or statutes of a chapter; the member of a chapter.
Capitular, ka-pit'ū-lėr, *a*. Belonging to a chapter or capitulary.
Capitulate, ka-pit'ū-lāt, *vi*. (capitulating, capitulated). To surrender on conditions.
Capitulation, ka-pit'ū-lā"shon, *n*. Surrender on certain conditions.
Capon, kā'pon, *n*. A young castrated cock.
Caprice, ka-prēs', *n*. A freak; a sudden or unreasonable change of opinion or humour.
Capricious, ka-pri'shus, *a*. Full of caprice.
Capriciously, ka-pri'shus-li, *adv*. In a capricious manner; whimsically.
Capricorn, ka'pri-korn, *n*. The he-goat, one of the signs of the zodiac; the southern tropic.
Capsicum, kap'si-kum, *n*. The generic name of some tropical plants yielding chillies and cayenne pepper.
Capsizal, kap-sīz'al, *n*. The act of capsizing.
Capsize, kap-sīz', *vt*. (capsizing, capsized). To upset or overturn.
Capstan, kap'stan, *n*. An apparatus in ships to raise great weights, weigh anchors, &c.
Capsular, kap'sūl-ėr, *a*. Pertaining to a capsule; hollow like a capsule.
Capsule, kap'sūl, *n*. A dry, many-seeded seed-vessel; an envelope for drugs.
Captain, kap'tin, *n*. A head officer; the commander of a ship, troop of horse, or company of infantry; a leader.
Captaincy, kap'tin-si, *n*. The rank, post, or commission of a captain.
Caption, kap'shon, *n*. Seizure; arrest; heading or short title of a division of a book, or of a scene in a cinematograph film.
Captious, kap'shus, *a*. Ready to find fault; carping.
Captiously, kap'shus-li, *adv*. In a captious manner.
Captivate, kap'ti-vāt, *vt*. (captivating, captivated). To take captive; to fascinate.
Captive, kap'tiv, *n*. One taken in war; one insnared by love, beauty, &c.—*a*. Made prisoner; kept in bondage.
Captivity, kap-tiv'i-ti, *n*. State or condition of being a captive; slavery.
Captor, kap'tėr, *n*. One who captures.
Capture, kap'tūr, *n*. Act of taking; the thing taken.—*vt*. (capturing, captured). To take by force or stratagem.
Capuchin, ka-pū-shēn', *n*. A Franciscan monk; a cloak with a hood.
Car, kär, *n*. A chariot; a vehicle in pageants; a railway or tramway carriage.
Caracole, ka'ra-kōl, *n*. A half-turn which a horseman makes.—*vi*. (caracoling, caracoled). To move in a caracole; to wheel.
Carafe, ka'raf, *n*. A glass water-bottle.
Caramel, ka'ra-mel, *n*. Burnt sugar, used to colour spirits.
Carat, ka'rat, *n*. A weight of four grains, for weighing diamonds, &c.; a word employed to denote the fineness of gold, pure gold being of twenty-four carats.
Caravan, ka'ra-van, *n*. A company of travellers associated together for safety; a large close carriage.
Caravanserai, ka-ra-van'se-ri, *n*. A house in the East, where caravans rest at night.
Caraway, ka'ra-wā, *n*. A biennial, aromatic plant whose seeds are used in baking, &c.
Carbide, kär'bīd, *n*. A compound of carbon with a metal.
Carbine, kär'bīn, *n*. A short-barrelled rifle used by cavalry, police, &c.
Carbolic, kär-bol'ik, *a*. An antiseptic and disinfecting acid obtained from coal-tar.
Carbon, kär'bon, *n*. Pure charcoal; an elementary substance, bright and brittle.
Carbonaceous, kär-bon-ā'shus, *a*. Pertaining to or containing carbon.
Carbonate, kär'bon-āt, *n*. A salt formed by the union of carbonic acid with a base.
Carbonic, kär-bon'ik, *a*. Pertaining to carbon, or obtained from it.
Carboniferous, kär-bon-if'ėr-us, *a*. Producing or containing carbon.
Carbonize, kär'bon-īz, *vt*. (carbonizing, carbonized). To convert into carbon.
Carboy, kär'boi, *n*. A globular bottle protected by a wicker covering.
Carbuncle, kär'bung-kl, *n*. A fiery red precious stone; an inflammatory tumour.
Carburetted, kär'bū-ret-ed, *a*. Combined with carbon.
Carburettor, kär'bū-ret-ėr, *n*. A device for vaporizing the light oil fuel used in the engines of motor-cars, aeroplanes, &c.
Carcanet, kär'ka-net, *n*. A jewelled collar.
Carcass, kär'kas, *a*. A dead body; anything decayed; a framework; a kind of bomb.
Card, kärd, *n*. A piece of pasteboard with figures, used in games; a piece of pasteboard containing a person's name, &c.; a printed invitation; a note; the dial of a compass; a large comb for wool or flax.—*vt*. To comb wool, flax, hemp, &c.
Cardamom, kär'da-mum, *n*. The aromatic capsule of various plants of the ginger family.
Cardboard, kärd'bōrd, *n*. A stiff kind of paper or pasteboard for making cards, &c.
Carder, kärd'ėr, *n*. One who cards wool.
Cardiac, kär'di-ak, *a*. Pertaining to the heart; stimulating.—*n*. A cordial.
Cardigan, kär'di-gan, *n*. A knitted waistcoat.

Cardinal, kär'din-al, *a.* Chief; fundamental.—*n.* A dignitary in the Roman Catholic Church next to the pope; a lady's short cloak.
Cardinalate, Cardinalship, kär'din-al-āt, kär'din-al-ship, *n.* The office, rank, or dignity of a cardinal.
Care, kãr, *n.* Solicitude; attention; object of watchful regard.—*vi.* (caring, cared). To be solicitous; to be inclined; to have regard.
Careen, ka-rēn', *vt.* To lay (a ship) on one side, for the purpose of repairing.—*vi.* To incline to one side.
Career, ka-rēr', *n.* A race; course of action.—*vi.* To move or run rapidly.
Careful, kãr'fụl, *a.* Solicitous; cautious.
Carefully, kãr-fụl-li, *adv.* In a careful manner.
Carefulness, kãr'fụl-nes, *n.* Quality of being careful.
Careless, kãr'les, *a.* Heedless; incautious.
Carelessly, kãr'les-li, *adv.* In a careless way.
Carelessness, kãr'les-nes, *n.* Quality of being careless.
Caress, ka-res', *vt.* To fondle; to embrace affectionately.—*n.* An act of endearment.
Caressingly, ka-res'ing-li, *adv.* In a caressing manner.
Caret, kā'ret, *n.* In writing, this mark, ʌ, noting insertion.
Care-taker, kãr'tā-kėr, *n.* A person put in charge of a house, farm, or the like.
Cargo, kär'gō, *n.* The freight of a ship.
Cariboo, Caribou, ka'ri-bö, *n.* An American variety of the reindeer.
Caricature, ka-ri-ka-tūr', *n.* A portrait or description so exaggerated as to excite ridicule.—*vt.* (caricaturing, caricatured). To represent by caricature.
Caries, kā'ri-ēz, *n.* Ulceration of a bone.
Carillon, ka'ril-lon, *n.* A chime of bells; simple air adapted to a set of bells.
Carious, kā'ri-us, *a.* Ulcerated; decayed.
Cark, kärk, *n.* Anxiety.—*vi.* To be anxious.
Carl, Carle, kärl, *n.* A robust hardy man.
Carman, kär'man, *n.* A man who drives a car.
Carminative, kär'min-āt-iv, *n.* A medicine for flatulence, &c.
Carmine, kär'mīn, *n.* A bright crimson colour.
Carnage, kär'nāj, *n.* Great slaughter in war; massacre; butchery.
Carnal, kär'nal, *a.* Fleshly; sensual.
Carnality, kär-nal'i-ti, *n.* Sensuality.
Carnally, kär'nal-li, *adv.* In a carnal manner; according to the flesh.
Carnation, kär-nā'shon, *n.* Flesh-colour; a sweet-scented plant with pink flowers.
Carnelian, kär-nē'li-an, *n.* A red or flesh-coloured stone, a variety of chalcedony.
Carnival, kär'ni-val, *n.* A festival during the week before Lent; a revel.
Carnivora, kär-niv'ō-ra, *n.pl.* Animals that feed on flesh.
Carnivorous, kär-niv'ō-rus, *a.* Feeding on flesh.
Carob, ka'rob, *n.* A tree with sweet nutritious pods called locust-beans.
Carol, ka'rol, *n.* A song of joy or devotion; a warble.—*vi.* (carolling, carolled). To sing; to warble.—*vt.* To celebrate in song.
Carotid, ka-rot'id, *a.* Pertaining to the two great arteries in the neck conveying the blood to the head.
Carousal, ka-rouz'al, *n.* A noisy revel.
Carouse, ka-rouz', *vi.* (carousing, caroused). To drink freely with noisy jollity.—*n.* A drinking bout.
Carp, kärp, *vi.* To cavil; to find fault.—*n.* A voracious fish, found in rivers and ponds.
Carpenter, kär'pen-tėr, *n.* One who works in timber.
Carpentry, kär'pen-tri, *n.* The trade, art, or work of a carpenter.
Carpet, kär'pet, *n.* A woven fabric for covering floors, &c.—*vt.* To cover with a carpet.
Carpet-bag, kär'pet-bag, *n.* A travelling bag made of the same material as carpets.
Carpet-bagger, kär'pet-bag-ėr, *n.* An outsider who takes part in political affairs.
Carpeting, kär'pet-ing, *n.* Cloth for carpets; carpets in general.
Carping, kärp'ing, *a.* Cavilling.
Carriage, ka'rij, *n.* Act of carrying; that which carries; a vehicle; conveyance; price of carrying; behaviour; demeanour.
Carrier, ka'ri-ėr, *n.* One who carries for hire.
Carrion, ka'ri-on, *n.* Dead and putrefying flesh.—*a.* Relating to putrefying carcasses; feeding on carrion.
Carrot, ka'rot, *n.* A yellowish or reddish esculent root of a tapering form.
Carroty, ka'rot-i, *a.* Like a carrot in colour.
Carry, ka'ri, *vt.* (carrying, carried). To bear, convey, or transport; to gain; to capture; to import; to behave.—*vi.* To convey; to propel.—*n.* Onward motion.
Cart, kärt, *n.* A carriage of burden with two wheels.—*vt.* To carry or place on a cart.
Cartage, kärt'āj, *n.* Act of carrying in a cart; the price paid for carting.
Carte, kärt, *n.* A card; a bill of fare.
Carte-blanche, kärt-blänsh, *n.* A blank paper; unconditional terms.
Cartel, kär'tel, *n.* A challenge; an agreement for the exchange of prisoners.
Carter, kärt'ėr, *n.* One who drives a cart.
Cartilage, kär'ti-lāj, *n.* Gristle; an elastic substance from which bone is formed.
Cartilaginous, kär-ti-laj'in-us, *a.* Pertaining to or resembling a cartilage.
Cartography, kär-tog'ra-fi, *n.* The art or practice of drawing up charts.
Cartoon, kär-tön', *n.* A drawing for a fresco or tapestry; a pictorial sketch relating to a prevalent topic.
Cartouch, kär-tösh', *n.* A cartridge or cartridge-box; a sculptured ornament.
Cartridge, kär'trij, *n.* A case containing the charge of a gun or any firearm.
Cartridge-paper, kär'trij-pā-pėr, *n.* Thick paper, of which cartridges were made.
Cartulary, kär'tū-la-ri, *n.* *See* CHARTULARY.
Carve, kärv, *vt.* (carving, carved). To cut; to engrave; to shape by cutting.—*vi.* To cut up meat; to sculpture.
Carver, kärv'ėr, *n.* One who carves; a large table-knife for carving.
Carving, kärv'ing, *n.* The act or art of cutting meat or sculpturing figures; sculpture.
Caryatid, ka'ri-at-id, *n.*; pl. **-ids** or **-ides.** A figure of a woman serving as a column.
Cascade, kas'kād, *n.* A waterfall.
Case, kās, *n.* That which contains; a box; a receptacle; covering; an event; condition; a suit in court; a form in the inflection of nouns, &c.—*vt.* (casing, cased). To cover with a case; to put in a case.

Case-harden, kās'hárd-n, *vt.* To harden on the outside, as iron.
Casein, Caseine, kā'sē-in, *n.* That ingredient in milk which forms curd and cheese.
Casemate, kās'māt, *n.* A bomb-proof vault.
Casement, kāz'ment, *n.* A case for a window.
Caseous, kā'sē-us, *a.* Pertaining to cheese.
Casern, ka-zėrn', *n.* Small barracks.
Case-shot, kās'shot, *n.* Shot, old iron, &c., put in cases to be discharged from cannon.
Cash, kash, *n.* Money; ready money; coin.—*vt.* To turn into money.
Cashier, kash-ēr', *n.* One who has charge of money.—*vt.* To deprive of office; to dismiss; to break.
Cashmere, kash'mēr, *n.* A rich kind of shawl; a fine woollen stuff.
Casing, kās'ing, *n.* Act of putting in a case; a covering.
Casino, ka-sē'nō, *n.* A public dancing, singing, or gaming saloon.
Cask, kask, *n.* A vessel for containing liquors.
Casket, kask'et, *n.* A small chest for jewels.
Casque, kask, *n.* A head-piece; a helmet.
Cassava, kas-sā'va or sä'va, *n.* A tropical shrub yielding a nutritious starch formed into tapioca, &c.
Casserole, kas'e-rōl, *n.* A sauce-pan; a kind of stew.
Cassia, kash'i-a, *n.* A sweet spice; wild cinnamon; a plant which yields senna.
Cassimere, kas'si-mēr, *n.* A twilled woollen cloth.
Cassock, kas'ok, *n.* A close garment worn by clergymen under the surplice.
Cassowary, kas'sō-wa-ri, *n.* A running bird allied to the ostrich.
Cast, kast, *vt.* (casting, cast). To throw; to impel; to throw off; to let fall; to condemn; to compute; to model; to found; to scatter (seed); to bring forth immaturely.—*vi.* To revolve in the mind; to contrive (with *about*); to warp.—*n.* A throw; the thing thrown; manner of throwing; distance passed by a thing thrown; a squint; form; a tinge; manner; that which is formed from a mould; the actors to whom the parts of a play are assigned.
Castanet, kas'ta-net, *n.* Small pieces of wood or ivory struck together in dancing.
Castaway, kast'a-wā, *n.* A person abandoned; a reprobate.
Caste, kast, *n.* A distinct hereditary order among the Hindus; a class of society.
Castellated, kas'tel-lāt-ed, *a.* Adorned with turrets and battlements.
Caster, kast'ėr, *n.* A founder; one employed in shovelling; a castor.
Castigate, kas'ti-gāt, *vt.* (castigating, castigated). To chastise; to punish by stripes.
Castigation, kas-ti-gā'shon, *n.* Chastisement.
Castigator, kas'ti-gāt-ėr, *n.* One who corrects.
Casting, kast'ing, *n.* Act of casting; that which is cast in a mould.
Cast-iron, kast'ī-ėrn, *n.* Iron which has been cast into pigs or moulds.
Castle, kas'l, *n.* A fortified building; a large and imposing mansion; a piece in chess.
Castled, kas'ld, *a.* Furnished with castles; castellated.
Cast-off, kast'of, *a.* Laid aside; rejected.
Castor, kas'tėr, *n.* A small cruet; a small wheel on the leg of a table, &c.
Castor-oil, kas'tėr-oil, *n.* A medicinal oil obtained from a tropical plant.
Castrametation, kas'tra-me-tā"shon, *n.* The art or act of planning a camp.
Castrate, kas'trāt, *vt.* (castrating, castrated). To geld; to emasculate; to expurgate.
Castration, kas-trā'shon, *n.* Act of castrating.
Cast-steel, kast'stēl, *n.* Steel melted and cast into ingots and rolled into bars.
Casual, ka'zhū-al, *a.* Happening by chance; occasional; contingent.
Casually, ka'zhū-al-li, *adv.* In a casual manner; by chance.
Casualty, ka'zhū-al-ti, *n.* Accident, especially one resulting in death or injury; death or injury caused by enemy action.
Casuist, ka'zū-ist, *n.* One who studies and resolves cases of conscience.
Casuistic, ka-zū-ist'ik, *a.* Relating to cases of conscience or conduct.
Casuistry, ka'zū-is-tri, *n.* The science of determining cases of conscience; sophistry.
Cat, kat, *n.* A domestic animal of the feline tribe; a strong tackle; a double tripod; an instrument for flogging.
Catachresis, kat-a-krē'sis, *n.* The wresting of a word from its true sense.
Cataclysm, kat'a-klizm, *n.* A deluge; a sudden overwhelming catastrophe.
Catacomb, ka'ta-kōm, *n.* A subterranean place for the burial of the dead.
Catafalque, kat'a-falk, *n.* A temporary structure representing a tomb.
Catalectic, kat-a-lek'tik, *a.* Incomplete.
Catalepsy, ka'ta-leps-i, *n.* A nervous affection suspending motion and sensation.
Cataleptic, ka-ta-lep'tik, *a.* Pertaining to catalepsy.
Catalogue, ka'ta-log, *n.* A list; a register.—*vt.* (cataloguing, catalogued). To make a list of.
Catamaran, kat'a-ma-ran", *n.* A kind of raft; a cross-grained woman.
Cataplasm, ka'ta-plazm, *n.* A poultice.
Catapult, kat'a-pult, *n.* An apparatus for throwing stones, &c.
Cataract, kat'a-rakt, *n.* A great waterfall; a disease of the eye.
Catarrh, ka-tär', *n.* A flow of mucus from the nose, &c.; a cold.
Catarrhal, ka-tär'al, *a.* Pertaining to or produced by catarrh.
Catastrophe, ka-tas'trō-fē, *n.* Calamity or disaster; final event.
Catch, kach, *vt.* (catching, caught). To lay hold on; to stop the falling of; to grasp; to entangle; to receive by contagion; to be seized with; to get.—*vi.* To lay hold; to be contagious.—*n.* Act of seizing; anything that takes hold; a sudden advantage taken; something desirable; a capture; a song.
Catching, kach'ing, *a.* Infectious; charming.
Catch-penny, kach'pen-ni, *n.* A thing of little value intended to gain money in market.
Catch-word, kach'wėrd, *n.* A word under the last line of a page, repeated at the top of the next; the last word of a preceding speaker.
Cate, kāt, *n.* Rich food; a delicacy: generally in *pl.*
Catechetic, ka-tē-ket'ik, *a.* Relating to a catechism or catechisms.
Catechetically, ka-tē-ket'ik-al-li, *adv.* In a catechetic manner.

Catechise, ka'tē-kīz, *vt.* (catechising, catechised). To instruct by question and answer; to question.
Catechism, ka'tē-kizm, *n.* A manual of instruction by questions and answers, especially in religion.
Catechist, ka'tē-kist, *n.* One who catechises.
Catechu, kat'ē-shū, *n.* An astringent vegetable extract.
Catechumen, ka-tē-kū'men, *n.* One who is being instructed in the first rudiments of Christianity.
Categorical, ka-tē-go'ri-kal, *a.* Pertaining to a category; absolute; positive.
Categorically, ka-tē-go'ri-kal-li, *adv.* Absolutely; directly; positively.
Category, kat'ē-go-ri, *n.* One of the highest classes to which objects of thought can be referred; class; a general head.
Catena, ka-tē'na, *n.* A chain; series of extracts, arguments, &c.
Catenation, kat-ē-nā'shon, *n.* Connection; union of parts; concatenation.
Cater, kā'tėr, *vi.* To buy or procure provisions, food, entertainment, &c.
Caterer, kā'tėr-ėr, *n.* One who caters.
Cateress, kā'tėr-es, *n.* A woman who caters.
Caterpillar, kat'ėr-pil-ėr, *n.* The hairy wormlike grub of butterflies and moths; a traction device consisting of an endless chain encircling the wheels of the tractor.
Caterwaul, kat'ėr-wạl, *vi.* To cry as cats.
Catgut, kat'gut, *n.* The intestines of a cat; intestines made into strings for musical instruments, &c.; a kind of linen or canvas.
Cathartic, ka-thär'tik, *a.* Purging.—*n.* A medicine that purges.
Cat-head, kat'hed, *n.* A projecting beam with tackle for lifting the anchor.
Cathedra, ka-thē'dra or kath'e-dra, *n.* The throne or seat of a bishop.
Cathedral, ka-thē'dral, *n.* The principal church in a diocese.
Catheter, kath'e-tėr, *n.* A tubular instrument, to be introduced into the bladder.
Cathode, kath'ōd, *n.* The negative pole of an electric current.
Catholic, ka'thol-ik, *a.* Universal; liberal; pertaining to the universal Church; pertaining to the Roman Catholic Church.—*n.* A member of the universal Christian Church; an adherent of the Roman Catholic Church.
Catholicism, ka-thol'i-sizm, *n.* Adherence to the Catholic Church; adherence to the Roman Catholic Church; the Roman Catholic religion.
Catholicity, ka-thol-is'i-ti, *n.* Universality; liberality.
Catholicon, ka-thol'i-kon, *n.* Panacea.
Catkin, kat'kin, *n.* The blossom of the willow, birch, &c., resembling a cat's tail.
Catmint, Catnip, kat'mint, kat'nip, *n.* A strong-scented labiate plant.
Catoptrics, kat-op'triks, *n.* The part of optics treating of vision by reflected light.
Cat's-eye, kats'ī, *n.* A variety of chalcedony.
Cat's-paw, kats'pạ, *n.* A light breeze; a dupe; a tool.
Cattle, kat'tl, *n.pl.* Domestic quadrupeds serving for tillage or food; bovine animals.
Caucus, kạ'kus, *n.* A private committee to manage election matters.
Caudal, kạ'dal, *a.* Pertaining to a tail.
Caudle, kạ'dl, *n.* A warm drink for the sick.
Caul, kạl, *n.* A net for the hair; a membrane investing some part of the intestines.
Cauliflower, kạ'li-flou-ėr, *n.* A variety of cabbage.
Caulk, kạk, *vt.* To drive oakum into the seams of (a ship) to prevent leaking.
Causal, kạz'al, *a.* Implying cause.
Causality, kạz-al'i-ti, *n.* The agency of a cause.
Causation, kạz-ā'shon, *n.* The act or agency by which an effect is produced.
Causative, kạz'a-tiv, *a.* That expresses a cause or reason· that effects.
Cause, kạz, *n.* That which produces an effect; reason; origin; sake; purpose; a suit in court; that which a person or party espouses. —*vt.* (causing, caused). To effect; to bring about.
Causeless, kạz'les, *a.* Having no cause.
Causeway, Causey, kạz'wā, kạz'i, *n.* A raised road; a paved way.
Caustic, kạs'tik, *a.* Burning; corroding; cutting.—*n.* A substance which burns the flesh.
Caustically, kạs'tik-al-li, *adv.* In a caustic manner; severely.
Causticity, kạs-tis'i-ti, *n.* Quality of being caustic; severity; cutting remarks.
Cautelous, kạ'tel-us, *a.* Cautious; wary.
Cauterization, kạ'tėr-īz-ā"shon, *n.* Act of cauterizing.
Cauterize, kạ'tėr-īz, *vt.* To burn with caustics, or hot iron, as morbid flesh.
Cautery, kạ'tė-ri, *n.* A burning or searing by a hot iron, or caustic substances.
Caution, kạ'shon, *n.* Care; wariness; warning; pledge.—*vt.* To warn.
Cautionary, kạ'shon-a-ri, *a.* Containing caution; given as a pledge.
Cautious, kạ'shus, *a.* Using caution; wary; circumspect; prudent.
Cautiously, kạ'shus-li, *adv.* With caution.
Cavalcade, ka'val-kād, *n.* A procession of persons on horseback.
Cavalier, ka-va-lēr', *n.* A horseman; a gay military man; a beau.—*a.* Gay; brave; haughty; supercilious.
Cavalierly, ka-va-lēr'li, *adv.* Haughtily.
Cavalry, ka'val-ri, *n.* A body of troops mounted.
Cave, kāv, *n.* A hollow place in the earth; a den.
Caveat, kā'vē-at, *n.* A warning; a process to stop proceedings in a court.
Cavern, ka'vėrn, *n.* A large cave.
Caverned, ka'vėrnd, *a.* Full of caverns; forming or inhabiting a cavern.
Cavernous, ka'vėrn-us, *a.* Hollow; full of caverns.
Caviare, Caviar, ka-vi-är', *n.* The roe of the sturgeon salted and prepared for food.
Cavil, ka'vil, *vi.* (cavilling, cavilled). To carp; to find fault with insufficient reason.—*n.* A captious objection.
Caviller, ka'vil-ėr, *n.* One who cavils.
Cavity, ka'vi-ti, *n.* A hollow place.
Caw, kạ, *vi.* To cry like a crow, rook, or raven.—*n.* The cry of the rook or crow.
Cayenne, kā-en', *n.* A pepper made from capsicum seeds.
Cease, sēs, *vi.* (ceasing, ceased). To leave off; to fail; to stop; to become extinct.—*vt.* To put a stop to.
Ceaseless, sēs'les, *a.* Incessant; perpetual.

Ceaselessly, sēs'les-li, *adv.* Incessantly.
Cedar, sē'dėr, *n.* A large coniferous tree.—*a.* Made of cedar; belonging to cedar.
Cede, sēd, *vt.* (ceding, ceded). To give up; to surrender.—*vi.* To yield; to lapse.
Cedilla, sē-dil'la, *n.* A mark under *c* (thus ç), to show that it is to be sounded like *s*.
Ceil, sēl, *vt.* To cover the inner roof of a building; to cover with a ceiling.
Ceiling, sēl'ing, *n.* The upper inside surface of a room.
Celandine, sel'an-dīn, *n.* A British poppy or ranunculus.
Celebrant, sel'ē-brant, *n.* One who performs a public religious rite.
Celebrate, sel'ē-brāt, *vt.* (celebrating, celebrated). To honour by solemn rites; to praise; to commemorate.
Celebrated, se'lē-brāt-ed, *a.* Famous.
Celebration, se-lē-brā'shon, *n.* The act of celebrating; ceremonious performance.
Celebrity, se-leb'ri-ti, *n.* Fame; eminence.
Celerity, sē-le'ri-ti, *n.* Speed; quickness.
Celery, se'le-ri, *n.* An umbelliferous plant cultivated for the table.
Celestial, sē-les'ti-al, *a.* Heavenly; pertaining to heaven.—*n.* An inhabitant of heaven.
Celibacy, se'li-ba-si, *n.* The unmarried state; a single life.
Celibate, se'li-bāt, *n.* One who intentionally remains unmarried.—*a.* Unmarried.
Cell, sel, *n.* A small room; a cave; a small mass of protoplasm forming the structural unit in animal tissues.
Cellar, sel'lėr, *n.* An apartment underground used for storage.
Cellarage, sel'lėr-āj, *n.* Space for cellars; cellars; charge for cellar-room.
Cellarer, sel'lėr-er, *n.* The monk who has the care of the cellar; a butler.
Cellaret, sel-la-ret', *n.* A case of cabinet-work, for holding bottles of liquors.
Cellophane, sel'ō-fān, *n.* Trade name for a thin, waterproof solidification of viscose, much used for wrapping.
Cellular, sel'ū-lėr, *a.* Consisting of cells.
Celluloid, sel'lū-loid, *n.* An artificial substitute for ivory, bone, coral, &c.
Cellulose, sel'lū-lōs, *n.* The substance of which the permanent cell membranes of plants are always composed, in many respects allied to starch.
Celt, selt, *n.* One of a race of Western Europe; a prehistoric cutting instrument.
Celtic, selt'ik, *a.* Pertaining to the Celts.—*n.* Their language.
Cement, sē-ment', *n.* An adhesive substance which unites bodies; mortar; bond of union.—*vt.* To unite closely.—*vi.* To unite and cohere.
Cementation, sē-ment-ā'shon, *n.* Act of cementing.
Cemetery, se'mē-te-ri, *n.* A burial-place.
Cenobite, sē'nō-bīt, *n.* One of a religious order living in common.
Cenotaph, sen'ō-taf, *n.* A monument to one who is buried elsewhere.
Censer, sens'ėr, *n.* A vase or pan in which incense is burned.
Censor, sen'sėr, *n.* One who examines manuscripts, &c., before they are published; one who censures; in war-time, an official who controls the public press, &c., and who also supervises private correspondence.
Censorious, sen-sō'ri-us, *a.* Addicted to censure.
Censorship, sen'sėr-ship, *n.* The office or dignity of a censor.
Censurable, sen'shūr-a-bl, *a.* Blamable.
Censurably, sen'shūr-a-bli, *adv.* In a manner worthy of blame.
Censure, sen'shūr, *n.* Severe judgment; reproof.—*vt.* (censuring, censured). To judge unfavourably of; to blame.
Census, sen'sus, *n.* An enumeration of the inhabitants of a country.
Cent, sent, *n.* A hundred; a copper coin in America, &c.; the hundredth part of a dollar. *Per cent*, a certain rate by the hundred.
Centage, sent'āj, *n.* Rate by the hundred.
Cental, sen'tal, *n.* A weight of 100 lbs.
Centaur, sen'tạr, *n.* A fabulous being, half man and half horse.
Centenarian, sen-ten-ā'ri-an, *n.* A person a hundred years old.
Centenary, sen'ten-a-ri, *a.* Pertaining to a hundred.—*n.* Period of a hundred years; commemoration of an event a hundred years earlier.
Centennial, sen-ten'ni-al, *a.* Consisting of a hundred years; happening every hundred years.
Centesimal, sen-tes'i-mal, *a.* The hundredth.—*n.* The hundredth part.
Centigrade, sen'ti-grād, *a.* Divided into a hundred degrees.
Centimetre, sen'ti-mē-tr, *n.* The hundredth part of a metre, about two-fifths of an inch.
Centipede, sen'ti-pēd, *n.* An insect having a great number of feet.
Cento, sen'tō, *n.* A composition, literary or musical, formed by selections from different authors or composers.
Central, sen'tral, *a.* Placed in the centre; relating to the centre.
Centralization, sen'tral-īz-ā'shon, *n.* Act of centralizing.
Centralize, sen'tral-īz, *vt.* (centralizing, centralized). To render central; to concentrate.
Centrally, sen'tral-li, *adv.* In a central manner.
Centre, sen'tėr, *n.* The middle point; a nucleus.—*vt.* (centring, centred). To fix on a centre; to collect to a point.—*vi.* To be collected to a point; to have as a centre.
Centre-board, sen'tėr-bōrd, *n.* A movable keel in yachts.
Centric, Centrical, sen'trik, sen'trik-al, *a.* Placed in the centre; central; middle.
Centrifugal, sen-trif'ū-gal, *a.* Tending to fly from a centre.
Centripetal, sen-trip'et-al, *a.* Tending toward the centre.
Centuple, sen'tū-pl, *a.* Hundredfold.
Centurion, sen-tū'ri-on, *n.* Among the Romans the captain of a hundred men.
Century, sen'tū-ri, *n.* A hundred; the period of a hundred years.
Cephalic, se-fal'ik, *a.* Pertaining to the head.
Ceramic, se-ram'ik, *a.* Pertaining to the manufacture of porcelain and earthenware.
Cerate, sē'rāt, *n.* A thick ointment, composed of wax and oil.
Cere, sēr, *n.* The wax-like skin that covers the base of the bill in some birds.—*vt.* (cering, cered). To wax or cover with wax.
Cereal, sē'rē-al, *a.* Pertaining to corn.—*n.* A grain plant.

Cerebral, se'rē-bral, *a.* Pertaining to the brain.
Cerebration, se-rē-brā'shon, *n.* Action of the brain, conscious or unconscious.
Cerecloth, Cerement, sēr'kloth, sēr'ment, *n.* Cloth dipped in melted wax, used in embalming; *pl.* grave-clothes.
Ceremonial, se-rē-mō'ni-al, *a.* Relating to ceremony.—*n.* Sacred rite; outward form.
Ceremonious, se-rē-mō'ni-us, *a.* Formal.
Ceremony, se'rē-mō-ni, *n.* Outward rite; form; observance; formality.
Cerise, se-rēz', *n.* Cherry-colour.
Certain, sėr'tān, *a.* Sure; undeniable; decided; particular; some; one.
Certainly, sėr'tān-li, *adv.* Without doubt.
Certainty, sėr'tān-ti, *n.* A fixed or real state; truth; fact; regularity.
Certificate, sėr-tif'i-kāt, *n.* A written testimony; a credential.
Certifier, sėr'ti-fī-ėr, *n.* One who certifies.
Certify, sėr'ti-fī, *vt.* (certifying, certified). To give certain information; to testify to in writing.
Cerulean, sē-rū'lē-an, *a.* Sky-coloured.
Cerumen, sē-rū'mēn, *n.* The wax or yellow matter secreted by the ear.
Ceruse, sē'rūz, *n.* White-lead; a cosmetic prepared from white-lead.
Cervine, sėr'vīn, *a.* Pertaining to deer.
Cess, ses, *n.* A rate or tax.—*vt.* To rate, or impose a tax on.
Cessation, ses-ā'shon, *n.* Stoppage.
Cession, se'shon, *n.* Surrender; a yielding up.
Cesspool, ses'pöl, *n.* A receptacle for sewage.
Cestus, ses'tus, *n.* The girdle of Venus; a loaded boxing-glove.
Cesura, sē-zū'ra, *n.* *See* CÆSURA.
Cetaceous, sē-tā'shus, *a.* Pertaining to animals of the whale kind.
Chafe, chāf, *vt.* (chafing, chafed). To make warm by rubbing; to fret by rubbing; to enrage.—*vi.* To be fretted by friction; to rage.—*n.* A heat; a fretting.
Chafer, chāf'ėr, *n.* A beetle that eats roots, leaves, and young shoots.
Chaff, chaf, *n.* The husk of corn and grasses; banter.—*vt.* To banter.
Chaffer, chaf'fėr, *vi.* To bargain; to haggle.
Chafferer, chaf'fėr-ėr, *n.* One who chaffers.
Chaffinch, chaf'finsh, *n.* A British song-bird.
Chaffy, chaf'i, *a.* Full of chaff; light.
Chagrin, sha-grēn', *n.* Ill-humour; vexation.—*vt.* To vex; to mortify.
Chain, chān, *n.* A series of links; a line of things connected; that which binds; a line formed of links, 66 feet long; (*pl.*) bondage; slavery.—*vt.* To bind with a chain; to confine.
Chain-pump, chān'pump, *n.* A pump consisting of an endless chain equipped with buckets, &c.
Chain-shot, chān'shot, *n.* Two cannon-balls connected by a chain.
Chair, chār, *n.* A movable seat; an official seat; professorship.—*vt.* To place or carry in a chair.
Chairman, chār'man, *n.* The presiding officer of an assembly; a president.
Chairmanship, chār'man-ship, *n.* The office of a chairman.
Chaise, shāz, *n.* A light horse carriage.
Chalcedony, kal-sed'ō-ni, *n.* A variety of quartz, having a whitish colour.
Chaldaic, Chaldean, Chaldee, kal-dā'ik, kal-dē'an, kal'dē, *a.* Pertaining to Chaldea.—*n.* The language of the Chaldeans.
Chaldron, chąl'dron, *n.* A measure of coals, consisting of 36 bushels.
Chalice, cha'lis, *n.* A drinking-cup.
Chalk, chąk, *n.* A white calcareous earth or carbonate of lime.—*vt.* To mark with chalk.
Chalky, chąk'i, *a.* Resembling chalk; consisting of or containing chalk.
Challenge, chal'lenj, *n.* A summons to fight; a calling in question; an exception taken.—*vt.* (challenging, challenged). To summon to a fight; to defy; to call in question; to object to.
Challengeable, chal'lenj-a-bl, *a.* That may be challenged.
Challenger, chal'lenj-ėr, *n.* One who challenges.
Chalybeate, ka-lib'ē-āt, *a.* Impregnated with particles of iron.—*n.* A liquid into which iron or steel enters.
Chamber, chām'bėr, *n.* An apartment; an office; a hall of justice or legislation; a legislative body.
Chambered, chām'bėrd, *a.* Having chambers; shut up in a chamber.
Chamberlain, chām'bėr-lān, *n.* One who has charge of the chambers of a monarch or noble; an officer of state; a city treasurer; a steward.
Chamber-maid, chām'bėr-mād, *n.* A female servant who has the care of chambers.
Chameleon, ka-mē'lē-on, *n.* A species of lizard, whose colour changes.
Chamfer, cham'fėr, *n.* A small furrow in wood, &c.; a bevel.—*vt.* To cut a chamfer in; to bevel.
Chamois, sham'i or sham'wą, *n.* A species of antelope; a soft leather.
Chamomile, ka'mō-mīl, *n.* *See* CAMOMILE.
Champ, champ, *vt.* To devour with violent action of the teeth; to bite the bit, as a horse.—*vi.* To keep biting.
Champagne, sham-pān', *n.* A kind of brisk sparkling wine.
Champaign, sham'pān, *a.* Open; level.—*n.* A flat open country.
Champion, cham'pi-on, *n.* A combatant for another, or for a cause; a hero; one victorious in contest.—*vt.* To fight for.
Championship, cham'pi-on-ship, *n.* State of being a champion; support of a cause.
Chance, chans, *n.* That which happens; accident; possibility of an occurrence; opportunity.—*vi.* (chancing, chanced). To happen.—*a.* Happening by chance; casual.
Chancel, chan'sel, *n.* That part of a church where the altar is placed.
Chancellor, chan'sel-lėr, *n.* A high judicial officer who presides over a court of chancery, &c.; a presiding official.
Chancellorship, chan'sel-lėr-ship, *n.* The office of a chancellor.
Chancery, chan'se-ri, *n.* A court of public affairs; in England, a division of the High Court of Justice.
Chancre, shang'kėr, *n.* An ulcer which arises from the venereal virus.
Chandelier, shan-dē-lēr', *n.* A frame with branches for candles or lamps.
Chandler, chand'lėr, *n.* A maker and seller of candles; a retail dealer.
Chandlery, chand'lė-ri, *n.* Goods sold by a chandler.

Change, chānj, *vt.* (changing, changed). To cause to turn from one state to another; to substitute; to give one kind of money for another.—*vi.* To be altered.—*n.* Variation; small money.
Changeable, chānj'a-bl, *a.* Subject to alteration; fickle; wavering.
Changeably, chānj'a-bli, *adv.* Inconstantly.
Changeful, chānj'fụl, *a.* Full of change; inconstant; mutable; fickle; uncertain.
Changeling, chānj'ling, *n.* A child substituted for another; a fool; one apt to change.
Changer, chānj'ėr, *n.* One who changes.
Channel, chan'nel, *n.* A water-course; a narrow sea; means of passing or transmitting.—*vt.* (channelling, channelled). To form into a channel; to groove.
Channelled, chan'neld, *a.* Grooved longitudinally.
Chant, chant, *vt.* and *i.* To sing; to sing after the manner of a chant.—*n.* Song; a kind of sacred music; a part of church service.
Chanter, chant'ėr, *n.* A singer; a bagpipe tube with finger-holes.
Chanticleer, chan'ti-klēr, *n.* A cock.
Chantry, chant'ri, *n.* A chapel where priests sing or say mass for the souls of others.
Chaos, kā'os, *n.* Confused mass; disorder.
Chaotic, kā-ot'ik, *a.* Pertaining to chaos.
Chap, chap, *vt.* (chapping, chapped). To cause to crack.—*vi.* To open in slits.—*n.* A crack in the skin; the jaw; a young fellow.
Chap-book, chap'bụk, *n.* A small book such as were hawked by chapmen.
Chapel, chap'el, *n.* A place of worship; a church; a sanctuary.
Chaperon, sha'pe-rōn, *n.* A married lady who attends a young lady to public places.—*vt.* To act as chaperon to.
Chap-fallen, chap'fạln, *a.* Dejected.
Chapiter, chap'i-tėr, *n.* The head of a column.
Chaplain, chap'lān, *n.* A clergyman of the army, navy, court, &c.
Chaplaincy, chap'lān-si, *n.* The office of a chaplain.
Chaplet, chap'let, *n.* A garland or wreath; a string of beads; a rosary.
Chapman, chap'man, *n.*; pl. **-men.** A dealer; a hawker or pedlar.
Chapter, chap'tėr, *n.* Division of a book; a society of clergymen belonging to a cathedral or collegiate church; an organized branch of some fraternity.
Char, chār, *vt.* (charring, charred). To reduce to carbon by burning; to burn slightly.—*n.* A charred body; a lake fish of the salmon kind.
Char-à-banc, shar'a-baṅ, *n.* A vehicle with transverse seats facing forwards, now usually motor-driven.
Character, ka'rak-tėr, *n.* A mark engraved; a letter or figure; manner of writing; distinctive qualities of a person or thing; certificate of qualifications; a person in fiction or drama; a peculiar person.
Characteristic, ka'rak-tėr-is"tik, *a.* Constituting character; marking distinctive qualities.—*n.* That which constitutes character.
Characterize, ka'rak-tėr-īz, *vt.* To give a character to; to designate.
Charade, sha-rād', *n.* A species of riddle upon the syllables of a word.
Charcoal, chār'kōl, *n.* Coal made by charring wood; the residue of animal, vegetable, and many mineral substances, when heated to redness in close vessels.
Chare, chār, *n.* A single job; a day's work.—*vi.* (charing, chared). To work by the day; to do small jobs.
Charge, chārj, *vt.* (charging, charged). To load; to put a price on; to intrust; to impute, as a debt or crime; to command; to confide; to attack.—*vi.* To make a charge or onset.—*n.* That which is laid on; that which loads a rifle, &c.; an assault or onset; order; instruction; person or thing committed to another's care; accusation; cost.
Chargeable, chārj'a-bl, *a.* That may be charged.
Chargé d'affaires, shār-zhā dā-fār, *n.* One who transacts diplomatic business in place of an ambassador.
Charger, chārj'ėr, *n.* A large dish; a war-horse.
Charily, chā'ri-li, *adv.* Carefully; frugally.
Chariot, cha'ri-ot, *n.* A stately carriage with four wheels.
Charioteer, cha'ri-ot-ēr", *n.* The person who drives or conducts a chariot.
Charitable, cha'rit-a-bl, *a.* Liberal to the poor; pertaining to charity; indulgent.
Charitably, cha'rit-a-bli, *adv.* In a charitable manner; kindly; liberally.
Charity, cha'ri-ti, *n.* A disposition to relieve the wants of others; benevolence; alms; a charitable institution.
Charlatan, shār'la-tan, *n.* A quack.
Charm, chārm, *n.* A spell; fascination; a locket, &c.—*vt.* To enthral; to delight.
Charmer, chārm'ėr, *n.* One who charms.
Charming, chārm'ing, *a.* Enchanting.
Charnel-house, chār'nel-hous, *n.* A place for bones of the dead.
Chart, chārt, *n.* A map; delineation of coasts, &c.; tabulated facts.
Charter, chār'tėr, *n.* A writing given as evidence of a grant, contract, &c.—*vt.* To establish by charter; to hire or to let (a ship).
Chartered, chār'tėrd, *a.* Granted by charter; privileged.
Chartist, chār'tist, *n.* One of a body of radical reformers in England about 1838.
Chartulary, kār'tū-la-ri, *n.* A collection of charters; a register, as of a monastery.
Char-woman, chār'wụm-un, *n.* A woman hired for odd work, or for single days.
Chary, chā'ri, *a.* Careful; wary; frugal.
Chase, chās, *vt.* (chasing, chased). To pursue; to hunt; to enchase; to cut into the form of a screw.—*n.* Pursuit; hunt; that which is pursued; a printer's frame.
Chaser, chās'ėr, *n.* One who chases; a gun at the bow or stern of a ship; an enchaser.
Chasm, kazm, *n.* A wide opening; an abyss.
Chaste, chāst, *a.* Free from impure desires; undefiled; pure in taste and style.
Chasten, chās'n, *vt.* To afflict in order to reclaim; to chastise; to correct.
Chastise, chas-tīz', *vt.* (chastising, chastised). To correct by punishment.
Chastisement, chas'tiz-ment, *n.* Correction.
Chastity, chas'ti-ti, *n.* Purity of the body, mind, language, or style.
Chasuble, chas'ū-bl, *n.* A priest's uppermost vestment when celebrating the eucharist.
Chat, chat, *vi.* (chatting, chatter). To talk familiarly.—*n.* Familiar talk; a small song-bird.

Château, shä'tō, *n.* A castle; a country seat.
Chatelaine, shat'ė-lān, *n.* A chain with keys, &c., worn at a lady's waist.
Chattel, chat'el, *n.* Any article of movable goods; in law, all goods except such as have the nature of freehold.
Chatter, chat'ėr, *vi.* To make a noise by repeated clashing of the teeth; to jabber.—*n.* Sounds like those of a magpie or monkey; idle talk.
Chatter-box, chat'ėr-boks, *n.* One that talks incessantly: applied chiefly to children.
Chatterer, chat'ėr-ėr, *n.* A prater; a bird that makes a chattering sound.
Chatty, chat'i, *c.* Talkative.
Chauffeur, shō'fėr, *n.* A person regularly employed to drive a private motor-car.
Chauvinism, shō'vin-izm, *n.* Absurdly exaggerated patriotism or military enthusiasm.
Cheap, chēp, *a.* Of a low price; common; not respected.
Cheapen, chēp'n, *vt.* To beat down in price; to depreciate.
Cheaply, chēp'li, *adv.* At a small price.
Cheapness, chēp'nes, *n.* State or quality of being cheap; lowness in price.
Cheat, chēt, *vt.* To defraud; to deceive.—*n.* A deceitful act; a swindler.
Check, chek, *vt.* To stop; to curb; to chide; to compare with corresponding evidence.—*vi.* To stop; to clash or interfere.—*n.* An attack made on the king in chess; a stop; control; a counterfoil; a token; a cheque; cloth with a square pattern.
Checker, chek'ėr, *n.* One who checks. *See* CHEQUER.
Checkmate, chek'māt, *n.* A move in chess which ends the game; defeat.—*vt.* To give checkmate to; to frustrate; to defeat.
Cheddar, ched'ėr, *n.* A rich English cheese.
Cheek, chēk, *n.* The side of the face below the eyes on each side; impudence.
Cheep, chēp, *vi.* and *t.* To pule; to chirp.—*n.* A chirp.
Cheer, chēr, *n.* Expression of countenance; gaiety; viands; a shout of joy.—*vt.* To brighten the countenance of; to gladden; to applaud.—*vi.* To grow cheerful.
Cheerful, chēr'ful, *a.* Gay; sprightly; willing.
Cheerily, chēr'i-li, *adv.* With cheerfulness.
Cheering, chēr'ing, *a.* Encouraging.
Cheerless, chēr'les, *a.* Gloomy; dejected.
Cheery, chēr'i, *a.* Blithe; sprightly; promoting cheerfulness.
Cheese, chēz, *n.* Coagulated milk pressed into a firm mass, and used as food; anything in the form of cheese.
Cheesemonger, chēz'mung-gėr, *n.* One who deals in or sells cheese.
Cheese-paring, chēz'pār-ing, *n.* The rind of cheese.—*a.* Meanly economical.
Cheese-press, chēz'pres, *n.* A press or engine for making cheese.
Cheesy, chēz'i, *a.* Resembling cheese.
Chef, shef, *n.* A head cook.
Chef-d'œuvre, shā-dē-vr, *n.*; pl. **Chefs-d'œuvre,** shā-dē-vr. A master-piece.
Chemical, kem'ik-al, *a.* Pertaining to chemistry.
Chemically, kem'ik-al-li, *adv.* By chemical process or operation.
Chemise, she-mēz', *n.* An under garment worn by women.
Chemist, kem'ist, *n.* One versed in chemistry.
Chemistry, kem'ist-ri, *n.* The science which treats of the properties and nature of elementary substances.
Cheque, chek, *n.* An order for money.
Chequer, Checker, chek'ėr, *n.* A square pattern; an exchequer or treasury.—*vt.* To mark with little squares; to variegate.
Chequered, Checkered, chek'ėrd, *p.a.* Marked with squares; crossed with good and bad fortune.
Cherish, che'rish, *vt.* To treat with tenderness; to encourage.
Cheroot, shē-röt', *n.* A kind of cigar with both ends cut square off.
Cherry, che'ri, *n.* A tree and its fruit, of the plum family.—*a.* Like a cherry in colour.
Cherub, che'rub, *n.*; pl. **-ubs** and **-ubim.** An angel of the second order; a beautiful child.
Cherubic, che-rū'bik, *a.* Angelic.
Chess, ches, *n.* A game played by two, with 16 pieces each on a board of 64 squares.
Chess-board, ches'bōrd, *n.* The checkered board used in the game of chess.
Chess-man, ches'man, *n.* A piece used in the game of chess.
Chest, chest, *n.* A large close box; the part of the body containing the heart, lungs, &c.—*vt.* To reposit in a chest.
Chestnut, ches'nut, *n.* A kind of tree; its fruit or nut; a stale joke or anecdote.—*a.* Of the colour of a chestnut; reddish-brown.
Chevalier, she'va-lēr, *n.* A horseman; a knight.
Chevron, shev'run, *n.* A heraldic figure representing two rafters of a house meeting at the top; similar mark on uniform, worn by an N.C.O.
Chew, chö, *vt.* To grind with the teeth; to masticate.
Chic, shēk, *n.* Easy elegance; smartness.
Chicane, Chicanery, shi-kān', shi-kān'ė-ri, *n.* Trickery; artifice.—**Chicane,** *vi.* (chicaning, chicaned). To use chicane or artifices.
Chick, Chicken, chik, chik'en, *n.* The young of various birds; a child.
Chicken-hearted, chik'en-härt-ed, *a.* Timid; fearful; cowardly.
Chicken-pox, chik'en-poks, *n.* An eruptive disease, generally appearing in children.
Chickweed, chik'wēd, *n.* A weed of which chickens and birds are fond.
Chicory, chik'o-ri, *n.* A common English plant, often used to mix with coffee.
Chide, chīd, *vt.* and *i.* (chiding, pret. chid, pp. chid, chidden). To reprove; to scold.
Chief, chēf, *a.* Being at the head; first; leading.—*n.* A principal person; a leader.
Chiefly, chēf'li, *adv.* Mainly; especially.
Chieftain, chēf'tān, *n.* A chief; the head of a troop, army, or clan.
Chieftaincy, Chieftainship, chēf'tān-si, chēf'tān-ship, *n.* Rank or office of a chieftain.
Chiffonier, shif'fon-ēr, *n.* A small side-board.
Chilblain, chil'blān, *n.* A blain or sore produced on the hands or feet by cold.
Child, chīld, *n.*; pl. **Children.** An infant; one very young; a son or daughter; offspring.
Child-bearing, chīld'bār-ing, *n.* The act of bringing forth children.
Childbed, chīld'bed, *n.* The state of a woman in labour.

Childbirth, chīld'bėrth, *n.* The act of bringing forth a child; travail; labour.
Childe, chīld, *n.* A noble youth; a squire.
Childhood, chīld'hụd, *n.* State of a child.
Childish, chīld'ish, *a.* Like a child; trifling.
Childless, chīld'les, *a.* Destitute of children.
Childlike, chīld'līk, *a.* Like a child; innocent.
Chill, chil, *n.* A shivering with cold; a cold fit; that which checks or disheartens.—*a.* Cold; tending to cause shivering; dispiriting. —*vt.* To make cold; to discourage.
Chilling, chil'ing, *a.* Causing to shiver; tending to repress enthusiasm.
Chilly, chil'i, *a.* Moderately chill.
Chime, chīm, *n.* A set of bells tuned to each other; their sound; harmony; the brim of a cask.—*vi.* (chiming, chimed). To sound in consonance; to agree.—*vt.* To cause to sound in harmony; to cause to sound.
Chimera, ki-mē'ra, *n.* A fire-breathing monster of fable; a vain or idle fancy.
Chimere, shi-mēr', *n.* A bishop's upper robe, to which the lawn sleeves are attached.
Chimerical, ki-me'rik-al, *a.* Wildly or vainly conceived.
Chimney, chim'nē, *n.* The funnel through which the smoke is conveyed; a flue; a glass funnel for a lamp, &c.
Chimney-piece, chim'nē-pēs, *n.* An ornamental structure round a fireplace.
Chimpanzee, chim'pan-zē, *n.* A large W. African ape.
Chin, chin, *n.* The lower part of the face; the point of the under jaw.
China, chī'na, *n.* A species of fine porcelain.
Chinchilla, chin-chil'la, *n.* A genus of S. American rodent animals; their fur.
Chincough, chin'kof, *n.* Hooping-cough.
Chine, chīn, *n.* The backbone; a piece of the backbone of an animal, cut for cooking.
Chinese, chī-nēz', *n. sing.* and *pl.* A native of China; the language of China.
Chink, chingk, *n.* A narrow opening; a cleft; a sharp metallic sound; money.—*vi.* To crack; to make a sound as by the collision of coins.—*vt.* To jingle, as coins.
Chinky, chingk'i, *a.* Full of fissures.
Chintz, chints, *n.* Cotton cloth printed with coloured designs.
Chip, chip, *n.* A fragment; a small piece.—*vt.* (chipping, chipped). To cut into chips; to cut off chips.—*vi.* To fly off in small pieces.
Chirm, chėrm, *vi.* To chatter, as birds.
Chirography, kī-rog'ra-fi, *n.* Handwriting; fortune-telling by examination of the hand.
Chiromancy, kī'rō-man-si, *n.* Palmistry.
Chiropodist, kīr-op'od-ist, *n.* One who extracts corns, removes bunions, &c.
Chirp, chėrp, *vi.* To make the lively noise of small birds.—*n.* A short, shrill note of birds.
Chirrup, chi'rup, *vi.* To chirp.
Chisel, chiz'el, *n.* A cutting tool, used in wood-work, masonry, sculpture, &c.—*vt.* chiselling, chiselled). To cut, gouge, or engrave with a chisel.
Chiselled, chiz'eld, *p.a.* Cut with a chisel; clear-cut.
Chit, chit, *n.* A child; a shoot or sprout; a note; an order or pass.
Chit-chat, chit'chat, *n.* Prattle.
Chivalric, Chivalrous, shi'val-rik, shi'valrus, *a.* Pertaining to chivalry; gallant.
Chivalry, shi'val-ri, *n.* Knighthood; customs pertaining to the orders of knighthood; heroic defence of life and honour.
Chive, chīv, *n.* Same as *Cive.*
Chloral, klō'ral, *n.* An oily liquid produced from chlorine and alcohol; a narcotic.
Chloric, klō'rik, *a.* Pertaining to chlorine.
Chloride, klō'rīd, *n.* A compound of chlorine and some other substance.
Chlorine, klō'rīn, *n.* A gaseous substance obtained from common salt, used in bleaching and disinfecting.
Chlorodyne, klō'rō-dīn, *n.* An anodyne, containing morphia, chloroform, and prussic acid.
Chloroform, klō'rō-form, *n.* A volatile thin liquid, used as an anæsthetic.
Chlorophyll, klō'rō-fil, *n.* The green colouring matter of plants.
Chocolate, cho'kō-lāt, *n.* A preparation from the kernels of the cacao-nut.—*a.* Dark, glossy brown.
Choice, chois, *n.* Act of choosing; option; the thing chosen; best part of anything; the object of choice.—*a.* Select; precious.
Choir, kwīr, *n.* A body of singers in a church; part of a church set apart for the singers.
Choke, chōk, *vt.* (choking, choked). To strangle by compressing the throat of; to block up; to stifle.—*vi.* To be suffocated; to be blocked up.
Choke-damp, chōk'damp, *n.* Carbonic acid gas; a suffocating vapour in coal-mines, &c.
Choky, chōk'i, *a.* That tends to or has power to choke or suffocate.
Choler, ko'lėr, *n.* Anger; wrath.
Cholera, ko'lė-ra, *n.* A disease accompanied by purging and vomiting.
Choleric, ko'lė-rik, *a.* Irascible; peevish.
Choose, chöz, *vt.* (choosing, pret. chose, pp. chosen). To take by preference.—*vi.* To make choice; to prefer.
Chooser, chöz'ėr, *n.* One who chooses.
Chop, chop, *vt.* (chopping, chopped). To cut into small pieces; to barter or exchange.—*vi.* To change; to turn suddenly.—*n.* A piece chopped off; a small piece of meat; a crack or cleft; a turn or change; the jaw; the mouth.
Chop-fallen, chop'fạl-en, *a.* Dejected.
Choppy, chop'i, *a.* Full of clefts; having short abrupt waves.
Chopsticks, chop'stiks, *n.* Two sticks of wood, ivory, &c., used by the Chinese in eating.
Choral, kō'ral, *a.* Belonging to a choir.
Chord, kord, *n.* String of a musical instrument; the simultaneous combination of different sounds; a straight line joining the ends of the arc of a circle or curve.
Chorister, ko'rist-ėr, *n.* A singer in a choir.
Chorus, kō'rus, *n.* A company of singers; a piece performed by a company in concert; verses of a song in which the company join the singer; any union of voices in general.
Chosen, chōz'n, *a.* Select; eminent.
Chough, chuf, *n.* A bird of the crow family.
Chouse, chous, *vt.* (chousing, choused). To cheat; to trick.—*n.* A trick; imposition.
Chrism, krizm, *n.* Consecrated oil.
CHRIST, krīst, *n.* THE ANOINTED; the Messiah; the Saviour.
Christen, kris'n, *vt.* To baptize; to name.
Christendom, kris'n-dum, *n.* The countries

inhabited by Christians; the whole body of Christians.
Christening, kris'n-ing, *n.* Baptism.
Christian, kris'ti-an, *n.* A professed follower of Christ.—*a.* Pertaining to Christ or Christianity.
Christianity, kris-ti-an'i-ti, *n.* The religion of Christians.
Christianize, kris'ti-an-īz, *vt.* (christianizing, christianized). To convert to Christianity.
Christmas, kris'mas, *n.* The festival of Christ's nativity, observed annually on 25th December.—*a.* Belonging to Christmas time.
Chromatic, krō-mat'ik, *a.* Relating to colour; proceeding by semitones.
Chrome, Chromium, krōm, krō'mi-um, *n.* A steel-gray, hard metal, from which coloured preparations are made.
Chromic, krōm'ik, *a.* Pertaining to chrome.
Chronic, kron'ik, *a.* Continuing a long time; lingering; continuous.
Chronicle, kron'i-kl, *n.* An historical account of events in order of time.—*vt.* (chronicling, chronicled). To record.
Chronicler, kron'i-klėr, *n.* An historian.
Chronological, kron-ō-loj'ik-al, *a.* Relating to chronology; in order of time.
Chronologist, kro-nol'o-jist, *n* One who studies or is versed in chronology.
Chronology, kro-nol'o-ji, *n.* Arrangement of events according to their dates.
Chronometer, kro-nom'et-ėr, *n.* An instrument that measures time.
Chrysalis, kris'a-lis, *n.*; pl. **-ides** or **-ises.** The form of certain insects before they arrive at their winged state.
Chrysanthemum, kri-san'thē-mum, *n.* The name of numerous composite plants.
Chrysoberyl, kris'o-be-ril, *n.* A yellowish-green gem.
Chrysolite, kris'ō-līt, *n.* A gem of a yellowish or greenish colour.
Chrysoprase, kris'o-prāz, *n.* A yellowish-green mineral, a variety of chalcedony.
Chub, chub, *n.* A small river fish of the carp family.
Chubby, chub'i, *a.* Round or full-cheeked; plump; having a large fat face.
Chuck, chuk, *vi.* To make the noise of a hen.—*vt.* To call, as a hen her chickens; to tap under the chin; to throw with quick motion; to pitch.—*n.* The call of a hen; a slight blow under the chin; a short throw.
Chuckle, chuk'l, *vi.* (chuckling, chuckled). To laugh in the throat; to feel inward triumph or exultation.—*n.* A short and suppressed laugh in the throat.
Chum, chum, *n.* A sharer of one's rooms; an intimate friend.
Chump, chump, *n.* A short, thick piece of wood.
Chunk, chungk, *n.* A short, thick piece.
Church, chėrch, *n.* A house consecrated to the worship of God among Christians; the collective body of Christians; a particular body of Christians; the body of clergy; ecclesiastical authority. — *vt.* To give or receive a service in church, as after childbirth.
Churching, chėrch'ing, *n.* The offering of thanks in church, as after childbirth.
Churchman, chėrch'man, *n.* An ecclesiastic; an adherent of the Church.
Church-rate, chėrch'rāt, *n.* A tax levied on parishes for maintaining the church, &c.
Churchwarden, chėrch-wạr'den, *n.* An official who manages the affairs of the church, and represents parish interests; a clay tobacco-pipe with a long stem.
Churchyard, chėrch'yärd, *n.* The ground adjoining a church, in which the dead are buried.
Churl, chėrl, *n.* A rude, ill-bred man; a rustic labourer; a miser.
Churlish, chėrl'ish, *a.* Surly; sullen.
Churn, chėrn, *n.* A vessel in which butter is made.—*vt.* To agitate cream for making butter; to shake with violence.
Chyle, kīl, *n.* A milky fluid separated from aliments in the intestines and entering the blood.
Chyme, kīm, *n.* The pulp of partially digested food before the chyle is extracted.
Cicatrix, Cicatrice, si-kā'triks, sik'a-tris, *n.* A scar; a mark of a wound or ulcer.
Cicatrize, si'ka-triz, *vt.* (cicatrizing, cicatrized). To induce the formation of a scar.—*vi.* To heal or be healed; to skin over.
Cicely, sis'e-li, *n.* An umbelliferous plant.
Cicerone, chi-che-rō'ne, sis-e-rō'ne, *n.* A guide.
Cider, sī'dėr, *n.* A fermented drink prepared from the juice of apples.
Cigar, si-gär', *n.* A roll of tobacco for smoking.
Cigarette, sig-a-ret', *n.* A little cut tobacco rolled up in rice paper, used for smoking.
Cilia, sil'i-a, *n.pl.* Minute hairs on plants or animals.
Ciliary, sil'i-a-ri, *a.* Belonging to or of the nature of eyelashes.
Cimmerian, sim-mē'ri-an, *a.* Pertaining to the fabulous Cimmerians, who dwelt in perpetual darkness; extremely dark.
Cinchona, sin-kō'na, *n.* A genus of S. American trees whose bark yields quinine; Peruvian bark.
Cincture, singk'tūr, *n.* A girdle.
Cinder, sin'dėr, *n.* A burned coal; an ember; a piece of dross or slag.
Cinema, sin'e-ma, *n.* A picture-house or theatre for the exhibition of moving pictures.
Cinematograph, sin-e-mat'o-graf, *n.* A machine for projecting on a screen a series of photographs of changing scenes and moving objects, so as to produce the illusion of continuous motion.
Cinerary, si'ne-ra-ri, *a.* Pertaining to ashes.
Cingalese, sing'ga-lēz, *a.* Pertaining to Ceylon.
Cinnabar, sin'na-bär, *n.* Red sulphide of mercury; vermilion.
Cinnamon, sin'na-mon, *n.* The inner bark of a tree, a native of Ceylon; a spice.
Cipher, sī'fėr, *n.* The figure 0 or nothing; any numeral; a person or thing of no importance; a device; a secret writing.—*vi.* To use figures.—*vt.* To write in secret characters.
Circle, sėr'kl, *n.* A plane figure contained by a curved line, every point of which is equally distant from a point within the figure, called the centre; the curved line itself; a ring; inclosure; a class; a coterie.—*vt.* (circling, circled). To move round; to inclose.—*vi.* To move circularly.
Circlet, sėr'klet, *n.* A little circle; a chaplet.
Circuit, sėr'kit, *n.* Act of going round; space measured by travelling round; the journey of judges to hold courts; the district visited by judges; path of an electric current.

Circuitous, sėr-kū'it-us, *a.* Going in a circuit; round about; not direct.
Circular, sėr'kū-lėr, *a.* Round; addressed to a number of persons.—*n.* A paper addressed to a number of persons.
Circulate, sėr'kū-lāt, *vi.* (circulating, circulated). To move in a circle; to have currency.—*vt.* To spread; to give currency to.
Circulating, sėr'kū-lāt-ing, *a.* That circulates; repeating, as figures in decimals.
Circulation, sėr-kū-lā'shon, *n.* Act of circulating; diffusion; currency.
Circumambient, sėr-kum-am'bi-ent, *a.* Surrounding; encompassing.
Circumcise, sėr'kum-sīz, *vt.* (circumcising, circumcised). To cut off the foreskin, according to Jewish and Mohammedan law.
Circumcision, sėr-kum-si'zhon, *n.* The act of circumcising.
Circumference, sėr-kum'fė-rens, *n.* The bounding line of a circle.
Circumflex, sėr'kum-fleks, *n.* An accent on long vowels, generally marked thus (^).
Circumfuse, sėr-kum-fūz', *vt.* To pour round; to spread round.
Circumjacent, sėr-kum-jā'sent, *a.* Lying round about.
Circumlocution, sėr-kum'lō-kū''shon, *n.* A roundabout mode of speaking.
Circumlocutory, sėr-kum-lok'ū-to-ri, *a.* Pertaining to circumlocution; periphrastic.
Circumnavigate, sėr-kum-na'vi-gāt, *vt.* To sail round.
Circumnavigation, sėr-kum-na'vi-gā''shon, *n.* Act of circumnavigating.
Circumnavigator, sėr-kum-na'vi-gāt-ėr, *n.* One who sails round.
Circumscribe, sėr'kum-skrīb, *vt.* To draw a line round; to limit; to restrict.
Circumspect, sėr'kum-spekt, *a.* Watchful on all sides; wary; thoughtful.
Circumspection, sėr-kum-spek'shon, *n.* Watchfulness; deliberation; wariness.
Circumstance, sėr'kum-stans, *n.* Something attending, or relative to a main fact or case; event; (*pl.*) state of affairs; condition.
Circumstantial, sėr-kum-stan'shal, *a.* Consisting in or pertaining to circumstances; attending; detailed.
Circumstantiality, sėr-kum-stan'shi-al''i-ti, *n.* Minuteness; fullness of detail.
Circumstantially, sėr-kum-stan'shal-li, *adv.* With full detail; minutely.
Circumstantiate, sėr-kum-stan'shi-āt, *vt.* To confirm by circumstances.
Circumvallation, sėr-kum'val-lā''shon, *n.* The act of surrounding with fortifications; a line of field fortifications.
Circumvent, sėr-kum-vent', *vt.* To encompass; to outwit.
Circumvention, sėr-kum-ven'shon, *n.* Outwitting; overreaching.
Circumvolution, sėr-kum'vō-lū''shon, *n.* Act of turning or rolling round.
Circus, sėr'kus, *n.*; pl. **-ses.** Among the Romans, a place for horse-races; a place for feats of horsemanship and acrobatic displays.
Cirrus, sir'rus, *n.*; pl. **Cirri.** A tendril; a light fleecy cloud at a high elevation.
Cist, sist, *n.* A prehistoric place of interment formed of flat stones.
Cistern, sis'tėrn, *n.* An artificial receptacle for water, &c.; a natural reservoir.
Citable, sīt'a-bl, *a.* That may be cited.
Citadel, si'ta-del, *n.* A fortress in or near a city.
Citation, sī-tā'shon, *n.* Quotation; a summons.
Cite, sīt, *vt.* (citing, cited). To summon to appear in a court; to quote; to adduce.
Citizen, si'ti-zen, *n.* An inhabitant of a city; one who has full municipal and political privileges.—*a.* Having the qualities of a citizen.
Citizenship, si'ti-zen-ship, *n.* State of being vested with the rights of a citizen.
Citric, sit'rik, *a.* Belonging to citrons, or to lemons or limes.
Citrine, sit'rin, *n.* A yellow pellucid variety of quartz.
Citron, sit'ron, *n.* The fruit of the citron tree, a large species of lemon; the tree itself.
City, si'ti, *n.* A large town; a borough or town corporate; the inhabitants of a city.
Cive, sīv, *n.* A small species of leek.
Civet, si'vet, *n.* A perfume taken from the anal glands of the civet-cat.
Civet-cat, si'vet-kat, *n.* A carnivorous animal, native of N. Africa and Asia.
Civic, si'vik, *a.* Pertaining to a city or citizen; relating to civil affairs.
Civil, si'vil, *a.* Relating to the government of a city or state; polite; political; lay; legislative, not military; intestine, not foreign.
Civilian, si-vil'i-an, *n.* One skilled in the civil law; one engaged in civil, not military or clerical pursuits.
Civility, si-vil'i-ti, *n.* Quality of being civil; good breeding; (*pl.*) acts of politeness.
Civilization, si'vil-iz-ā''shon, *n.* Act of civilizing, or the state of being civilized.
Civilize, si'vil-īz, *vt.* (civilizing, civilized). To reclaim from a savage state.
Civilized, si'vil-īzd, *a.* Having civilization; refined.
Clack, klak, *n.* A sharp, abrupt noise; continual or excessive talk; an instrument that clacks.—*vi.* To make a sudden, sharp noise; to talk incessantly.
Clad, klad, pp. of *clothe.*
Claim, klām, *vt.* To ask; to demand as due.—*n.* A demand as of right; a title to something in the possession of another; a pretension.
Claimable, klām'a-bl, *a.* That may be claimed.
Claimant, klām'ant, *n.* One who claims.
Clairvoyance, klār-voi'ans, *n.* A power attributed to a mesmerised person, by which he discerns objects concealed from sight, &c.
Clam, klam, *vt.* (clamming, clammed). To smear with viscous matter.—*n.* A clamp; a bivalve shell-fish.
Clamant, klam'ant, *a.* Crying aloud; urgent.
Clamber, klam'bėr, *vi.* To climb with difficulty, or with hands and feet.
Clammy, klam'i, *a.* Sticky; adhesive.
Clamorous, klam'ėr-us, *a.* Noisy.
Clamour, klam'ėr, *n.* Loud and continued noise; uproar.—*vi.* To call aloud; to make importunate demands.
Clamp, klamp, *n.* A piece of timber or iron, used to strengthen or fasten; a heavy footstep.—*vt.* To fasten or strengthen with clamps; to tread heavily.
Clan, klan, *n.* A family; a tribe; a sect.
Clandestine, klan-des'tin, *a.* Secret; underhand.
Clang, klang, *vt.* or *i.* To make a sharp sound,

as by striking metallic substances.—*n.* A loud sound made by striking together metallic bodies.

Clangour, klang'gėr, *n.* A clang; a ringing sound.

Clank, klangk, *n.* The loud sound made by the collision of metallic bodies.—*vi.* or *t.* To sound or cause to sound with a clank.

Clannish, klan'ish, *a.* Devoted to the members of one's own clan and illiberal to others.

Clansman, klanz'man, *n.* One belonging to the same clan.

Clap, klap, *vt.* (clapping, clapped or clapt). To strike together so as to make a noise; to strike with something broad; to shut hastily; to pat.—*vi.* To move together suddenly with noise; to strike the hands together in applause. —*n.* A noise made by sudden collision; a sudden explosive sound; a striking of hands in applause.

Clapper, klap'ėr, *n.* He or that which claps; the tongue of a bell.

Claptrap, klap'trap, *n.* Words used merely to gain applause.—*a.* Showy in sentiment.

Claret, kla'ret, *n.* A French red wine.—*a.* Of the colour of claret wine.

Clarification, kla'ri-fi-kā"shon, *n.* The clearing of liquids by chemical means.

Clarifier, kla'ri-fī-ėr, *n.* That which clarifies.

Clarify, kla'ri-fī, *vt.* (clarifying, clarified). To purify; to make clear.—*vi.* To become clear, pure, or fine.

Clarion, kla'ri-on, *n.* A kind of trumpet with a shrill tone.

Clarionet, Clarinet, kla'ri-on-et, kla'rin-et, *n.* A musical wind instrument of wood.

Clary, klā'ri, *n.* A plant of the sage genus.

Clash, klash, *vi.* To make a noise by collision; to meet in opposition; to interfere.—*vt.* To strike noisily together.—*n.* Noisy collision; opposition.

Clasp, klasp, *n.* An embrace; a hook for fastening; a catch; a bar added to a military medal to commemorate a particular battle or campaign.—*vt.* To fasten together with a clasp; to inclose in the hand; to embrace closely.

Clasper, klasp'ėr, *n.* One who or that which clasps; the tendril of a vine.

Clasp-knife, klasp'nīf, *n.* A knife the blade of which folds into the handle.

Class, klas, *n.* A rank of persons or things; an order; a group.—*vt.* To arrange in classes.

Classic, klas'ik, *a.* Of the first rank; standard in literary quality; pertaining to Greek and Roman antiquity; pure in style.—*n.* An author of the first rank; a Greek or Roman author of this character; a work of the first rank.

Classical, klas'ik-al, *a.* Pertaining to writers of the first rank; pertaining to ancient Greece or Rome; correct; refined (taste, style, &c.).

Classicism, klas'i-sizm, *n.* A classic idiom or style.

Classicist, klas'i-sist, *n.* One versed in the classics; one imbued with classicism.

Classification, klas'i-fi-kā"shon, *n.* Act of forming into a class or classes.

Classify, klas'i-fī, *vt.* (classifying, classified). To distribute into classes.

Clatter, klat'tėr, *vi.* To make repeated rattling noises; to talk fast and idly.—*vt.* To cause to rattle.—*n.* A rattling, confused noise.

Clause, klạz, *n.* A member of a sentence; a distinct part of a contract, will, &c.

Claustrophobia, klạs'trō-fo"bē-a, *n.* Morbid fear of confined spaces.

Clavicle, klav'i-kl, *n.* The collar-bone.

Clavier, klav'i-ėr, *n.* The key-board of the pianoforte, &c.

Claw, klạ, *n.* The sharp hooked nail of an animal; that which resembles a claw.—*vt.* To scrape, scratch, or tear.

Clay, klā, *n.* A tenacious kind of earth; earth in general; the body.—*vt.* To cover with clay; to purify and whiten with clay, as sugar.

Clayey, klā'ē, *a.* Partaking of clay; like clay.

Claymore, klā'mōr, *n.* A large two-edged sword; a basket-hilted broadsword.

Clean, klēn, *a.* Free from dirt; pure.—*adv.* Quite; fully.—*vt.* To purify; to cleanse.

Cleanliness, klen'li-nes, *n.* State of being cleanly; purity.

Cleanly, klen'li, *a.* Clean in habits; neat.—*adv.* In a clean manner; neatly.

Cleanness, klēn'nes, *n.* Freedom from dirt; purity; innocence.

Cleanse, klenz, *vt.* (cleansing, cleansed). To make clean or pure; to free from guilt.

Cleanser, klenz'ėr, *n.* One who or that which cleanses.

Clear, klēr, *a.* Bright; shining; open; fair; plain; shrill; cheerful; acute; free from debt; free from guilt; exempt.—*adv.* Manifestly; quite; indicating entire separation.—*vt.* To make clear; to free from obstructions or obscurity; to cleanse; to justify; to make gain as profit; to prepare, as waste land, for tillage or pasture; to leap over; to pay customs on a cargo.—*vi.* To become clear; to become fair; to exchange cheques.

Clearance, klēr'ans, *n.* Act of clearing; a certificate that a ship has been cleared at the custom-house.

Clearer, klēr'ėr, *n.* One who or that which clears.

Clear-headed, klēr'hed-ed, *a.* Having a clear understanding.

Clearing, klēr'ing, *n.* Act of making clear; act of distributing the proceeds of traffic passing over several railways; among bankers, the act of exchanging drafts on each other's houses; a tract of land cleared of wood.

Clearly, klēr'li, *adv.* In a clear manner.

Clear-story, Clere-story, klēr'stō-ri, *n.* The upper story of a cathedral or church.

Cleat, klēt, *n.* A piece of wood or iron in a ship to fasten ropes upon; a wedge.

Cleavable, klēv'a-bl, *a.* That may be cloven.

Cleavage, klēv'āj, *n.* The act or manner of cleaving.

Cleave, klēv, *vi.* (pret. clave, cleaved, pp. cleaved). To stick; to adhere.

Cleave, klēv, *vt.* (pret. clove, cleaved, cleft, pp. cloven, cleaved, cleft). To split; to sever. —*vi.* To part asunder.

Cleaver, klēv'ėr, *n.* One who cleaves; that which cleaves; a butcher's axe.

Cleek, klēk, *n.* A large hook; an iron-headed club used in golf.

Clef, klef, *n.* A character prefixed to a staff in music to determine the pitch.

Cleft, kleft, *n.* A crevice; a fissure.

Cleg, kleg, *n.* A gadfly; a horse-fly.

Clematis, klem'a-tis, *n.* The generic name of woody climbing plants.

Clemency, kle'men-si, *n.* Mercifulness; mildness; tenderness.
Clement, kle'ment, *a.* Mild; humane.
Clench, klensh, *vt.* To secure; to confirm; to grasp.
Clepsydra, klep'si-dra, *n.* A water-clock.
Clergy, klėr'ji, *n.pl.* The body or order of men set apart to the service of God, in the Christian church.
Clergyman, klėr'ji-man, *n.* A man in holy orders; a minister of the gospel.
Cleric, kle'rik, *a.* Clerical.—*n.* A clergyman.
Clerical, kle'rik-al, *n.* Pertaining to the clergy, or to a clerk.
Clericalism, kle'rik-al-izm, *n.* Clerical power or influence; sacerdotalism.
Clerk, klärk, *n.* A clergyman; one who reads the responses in church; one who is employed under another as a writer.
Clerkship, klärk'ship, *n.* The office or business of a clerk.
Clever, kle'vėr, *a.* Adroit; talented; executed with ability.
Cleverness, kle'vėr-nes, *n.* Quality of being clever; smartness; skill.
Clew, klū, *n.* A clue; the corner of a sail.—*vt.* To truss up (sails) to the yard.
Cliché, klē'shā, *n.* A hackneyed phrase.
Click, klik, *vi.* To make a small sharp noise, or a succession of such sounds.—*n.* A small sharp sound.
Client, klī'ent, *n.* A person under patronage; one who employs a lawyer.
Clientele, klī'en-tēl, *n.* One's clients collectively.
Cliff, klif, *n.* A precipice; a steep rock.
Cliffy, klif'i, *a.* Having cliffs; craggy.
Climacteric, kli-mak-te'rik, *n.* A critical period in human life.
Climate, klī'māt, *n.* The condition of a country in respect of temperature, dryness, wind, &c.
Climatic, klī-mat'ik, *a.* Pertaining to a climate; limited by a climate.
Climax, klī'maks, *n.* A figure of rhetoric, in which the language gradually rises in strength and dignity; culmination; acme.
Climb, klīm, *vi.* To creep up step by step; to ascend.—*vt.* To ascend.
Climber, klīm'ėr, *n.* One who climbs; a plant that rises on a support.
Clime, klīm, *n.* A region of the earth.
Clinch, klinsh, *vt.* To rivet; to clench; to make conclusive.—*n.* A catch; a pun.
Clincher, klinsh'ėr, *n.* A kind of nail; a conclusive argument.
Cling, kling, *vi.* (clinging, clung). To hang by twining round; to adhere closely.
Clinic, Clinical, klin'ik, klin'ik-al, *a.* Pertaining to a sick-bed.—*n.* One confined to bed.
Clink, klingk, *vt.* To cause to ring or jingle.—*vi.* To ring.—*n.* A sound made by the collision of small sonorous bodies.
Clinker, klingk'ėr, *n.* A partially vitrified brick; a mass of incombustible slag.
Clinometer, klīn-om'et-ėr, *n.* An instrument for measuring the dip of rock strata.
Clip, klip, *vt.* (clipping, clipped). To shear; to trim with scissors; to cut short.—*n.* Act or product of sheep-shearing.
Clipper, klip'ėr, *n.* One who clips; a sharp fast-sailing vessel.
Clipping, klip'ing, *n.* The act of cutting off; a piece separated by clipping.
Clique, klēk, *n.* A party; a coterie; a set.
Cloak, klōk, *n.* A loose outer garment; a disguise; a pretext.—*vt.* To cover with a cloak; to hide; to veil.
Clock, klok, *n.* An instrument which measures time.
Clock-work, klok'wėrk, *n.* The machinery of a clock; well-adjusted mechanism.
Clod, klod, *n.* A lump of earth; a stupid fellow.—*vt.* (clodding, clodded). To pelt with clods.
Cloddy, klod'i, *a.* Consisting of clods; earthy; gross.
Clodhopper, klod'hop-ėr, *n.* A clown, dolt.
Clog, klog, *vt.* (clogging, clogged). To hinder; to impede; to trammel.—*vi.* To be loaded.—*n.* Hindrance; a shoe with a wooden sole.
Cloister, klois'tėr, *n.* A monastery or nunnery; an arcade round an open court.—*vt.* To shut up in a cloister; to immure.
Close, klōz, *vt.* (closing, closed). To shut; to finish.—*vi.* To come close together; to end; to grapple; to come to an agreement.—*n.* End.
Close, klōs, *a.* Shut fast; tight; dense; near; stingy; trusty; intense; without ventilation; disposed to keep secrets.—*adv.* Tightly; in contact, or very near.—*n.* An inclosed place; precinct of a cathedral.
Close-fisted, klōs'fist-ed, *a.* Niggardly.
Closely, klōs'li, *adv.* In a close manner.
Closet, kloz'et, *n.* A small private apartment.—*vt.* To take into a private apartment.
Closing, klōz'ing, *p.a.* That concludes.
Closure, klōz'ūr, *n.* The act of closing; the act of ending a parliamentary debate.
Clot, klot, *n.* A mass of soft or fluid matter concreted.—*vi.* (clotting, clotted). To become thick; to coagulate.
Cloth, kloth, *n.* A woven material or fabric; the covering of a table; the clerical profession.
Clothe, klōTH, *vt.* (clothing, clothed or clad). To put clothes on; to cover or spread over.
Clothes, klōTHz, *n.pl.* of *cloth.* Garments for the body; blankets, &c., on a bed.
Clothes-horse, klōTHz'hors, *n.* A frame to hang clothes on.
Clothier, klōTH'i-ėr, *n.* A maker or seller of cloths or clothes.
Clothing, klōTH'ing, *n.* Garments in general.
Clotty, klot'i, *a.* Full of clots.
Cloud, kloud, *n.* A collection of visible vapour, suspended in the air; something similar to this; what obscures, threatens, &c.; a great multitude; a mass.—*vt.* To obscure; to darken; to sully; to make to appear sullen.—*vi.* To grow cloudy.
Cloudiness, kloud'i-nes, *n.* State of being cloudy; gloom.
Cloudless, kloud'les, *a.* Without a cloud; clear.
Cloudlet, kloud'let, *n.* A little cloud.
Cloudy, kloud'i, *a.* Overcast with clouds; dark; not easily understood; indicating gloom.
Clout, klout, *n.* A patch of cloth, leather, &c.; a rag; a blow.—*vt.* To patch; to join clumsily.
Clove, klōv, *n.* The dried spicy bud of an East Indian tree; the tree itself; a small bulb in a compound bulb, as in garlic.

Cloven-footed, Cloven-hoofed, klōv'n-fụt-ed, klōv'n-hōft, *a.* Having the foot or hoof divided into two parts, as the ox.
Clove-pink, klōv'pingk, *n.* A species of carnation with an odour like that of cloves.
Clover, klō'vėr, *n.* A leguminous plant with three-lobed leaves.
Clown, kloun, *n.* An awkward country fellow; a lout; a professional jester.
Clownish, kloun'ish, *a.* Coarse; rude.
Cloy, kloi, *vt.* To glut; to fill to loathing.
Club, klub, *n.* A cudgel; a card of the suit marked with trefoils; a staff with a heavy head for driving the ball in golf, &c.; an association for some common object; the meeting-place of such an association.—*vt.* To beat with a club.—*vi.* To join for some common object.
Clubbable, klub'a-bl, *a.* Having the qualities that fit a man for a club; social.
Club-footed, klub'fụt-ed, *a.* Having short, crooked, or deformed feet.
Club-house, klub'hous, *n.* A house where a club meets.
Club-law, klub'lạ, *n.* Government by violence; the law of brute force.
Club-room, klub'röm, *n.* The apartment in which a club meets.
Cluck, kluk, *vi.* To make the noise of the hen when calling chickens.—*n.* Such a sound.
Clue, klö, *n.* A ball of thread; a thread serving to guide; something helping to unravel a mystery.
Clump, klump, *n.* A lump; a cluster of trees or shrubs.
Clumsily, klum'zi-li, *adv.* In a clumsy manner.
Clumsiness, klum'zi-nes, *n.* Quality of being clumsy.
Clumsy, klum'zi, *a.* Unwieldy; ungainly; rude in make.
Cluster, klus'tėr, *n.* A bunch, as of grapes; a knot; a small crowd.—*vi.* To be or to keep close together; to grow in bunches; to collect in masses.—*vt.* To collect into a body.
Clutch, kluch, *vt.* To seize hold of; to grasp. —*n.* A grasp; talon; a merciless hand; something that holds fast.
Clutter, klut'tėr, *n.* A confused noise; a bustle.—*vt.* To crowd together in disorder. —*vi.* To make a bustle.
Clyster, klis'tėr, *n.* An injection to cleanse the bowels, &c.
Coach, kōch, *n.* A large four-wheeled close vehicle; a tutor.—*vi.* To ride in a coach; to tutor.
Coach-box, kōch'boks, *n.* The seat on which the driver of a coach sits.
Coachman, kōch'man, *n.* The person who drives a coach.
Coadjutor, kō-ad-jū'tėr, *n.* An assistant; a colleague.
Coadjutrix, kō-ad-jū'triks, *n.* A female assistant.
Coagent, kō-ā'jent, *n.* A fellow-agent; an assistant or associate in an act.
Coagulable, kō-ag'ū-la-bl, *a.* Capable of being coagulated.
Coagulate, kō-ag'ū-lāt, *vt.* (coagulating, coagulated). To change from a fluid into a fixed state.—*vi.* To curdle; to congeal.
Coagulation, kō-ag'ū-lā''shon, *n.* Act of coagulating; mass coagulated.
Coal, kōl, *n.* Any combustible substance in a state of ignition; charcoal; a solid, black, fossil substance used as fuel.—*vt.* or *i.* To supply with coals; to take in coals.
Coal-black, kōl'blak, *a.* Black as coal.
Coalesce, kō-al-es', *vi.* (coalescing, coalesced). To grow together; to unite.
Coalescence, kō-al-es'ens, *n.* Act of coalescing; state of being united; union.
Coalescent, kō-al-es'ent, *a.* Coalescing.
Coalition, kō-al-i'shon, *n.* Act of coalescing; union of persons, parties, &c., into one body; alliance; confederation.
Coal-mine, kōl'mīn, *n.* A mine or pit containing mineral coal.
Coal-pit, kōl'pit, *n.* A pit where coal is dug.
Coal-tar, kōl'tär, *n.* A thick, black liquid condensed in the distillation of gas from coal.
Coaly, kōl'i, *a.* Like coal; containing coal.
Coarse, kōrs, *a.* Rude; not refined; crude; inelegant; gross.
Coarsely, kōrs'li, *adv.* In a coarse manner.
Coast, kōst, *n.* The sea-shore; the country near the sea.—*vi.* To sail along a shore; to sail from port to port.
Coaster, kōst'ėr, *n.* A trading vessel which trades from port to port.
Coast-guard, kōst'gärd, *n.* A force employed to guard the coast.
Coasting, kōst'ing, *a.* Sailing along a coast; employed in trade along a coast.
Coastwise, kōst'wīz, *adv.* By way of or along the coast.
Coat, kōt, *n.* An upper garment; vesture, as indicating office; hair or fur covering of animals; a layer; a covering; that on which ensigns armorial are portrayed.—*vt.* To cover; to spread over.
Coating, kōt'ing, *n.* A covering; a thin external layer; cloth for coats.
Coax, kōks, *vt.* To wheedle; to persuade by fondling and flattering.
Coaxer, kōks'ėr, *n.* A wheedler.
Cob, kob, *n.* A round knob; the head of clover or wheat; a smallish thick-set horse; a male swan.
Cobalt, kō'bạlt, *n.* A mineral of grayish colour, and a metal obtained from it yielding a permanent blue; the blue itself.
Cobble, kob'l, *vt.* (cobbling, cobbled). To mend coarsely, as shoes; to botch.—*n.* A roundish stone.
Cobbler, kob'l-ėr, *n.* A mender of shoes; a clumsy workman; a cooling beverage.
Coble, kō'bl, *n.* A flattish-bottomed boat.
Cobra, Cobra-de-capello, kob'ra, kob'ra-de-ka-pel'lō, *n.* A hooded venomous snake.
Cobweb, kob'web, *n.* A spider's net; something flimsy.
Coca, kō'ka, *n.* The dried leaf of a S. American plant which gives power of enduring fatigue.
Cocaine, kō'ka-in, *n.* The active principle of coca, used as a local anæsthetic.
Cochineal, ko'chi-nēl, *n.* An insect which forms a scarlet dye; a dye-stuff consisting of the bodies of these insects.
Cock, kok, *n.* The male of the domestic fowl; the male of other birds; a vane; a person or thing having resemblance to a cock; a chief man; a tap for drawing off liquids; the hammer of a gun; a small pile of hay.—*vt.* To set erect; to set on the head with an air of pertness; to draw back the cock of a gun.

Cockade, kok-ād′, *n.* A knot of ribbon worn on the hat.
Cock-a-hoop, kok′a-hụp, *a.* Strutting like a cock; triumphant.
Cock-and-bull, kok′and-bụl, *a.* Idle; without foundation (applied to stories).
Cockatoo, kok-a-tö′, *n.* A crested bird of the parrot kind.
Cockatrice, kok′a-trīs, *n.* A fabulous monster hatched from a cock's egg; a basilisk.
Cock-boat, kok′bōt, *n.* A small boat.
Cockchafer, kok′chāf-ėr, *n.* The May-bug, an insect destructive to vegetation.
Cock-crow, Cock-crowing, kok′krō, kok′-krō-ing, *n.* Early morning.
Cocker, kok′ėr, *vt.* To pamper.
Cockle, kok′l, *n.* A weed that chokes corn; a small shell-fish.—*vi.* or *t.* To wrinkle; to shrink.
Cock-loft, kok′loft, *n.* A small loft close under a roof.
Cockney, kok′nē, *n.* An effeminate citizen; a native of London.—*a.* Pertaining to a cockney.
Cockneyism, kok′nē-izm, *n.* The peculiar dialect, pronunciation, &c., of a cockney.
Cockpit, kok′pit, *n.* A pit where game-cocks fight.
Cockroach, kok′rōch, *n.* The black beetle.
Cock's-comb, koks′kōm, *n.* The comb of a cock; a plant. *See* COXCOMB.
Cocktail, kok′tāl, *n.* A species of beetle; a half-bred horse; a short drink or appetizer, usually consisting of gin, bitters, and some flavouring, and often iced.
Coco, Cocoa, kō′kō, *n.* A tropical palm-tree.
Cocoa, kō′kō, *n.* The seed of the cacao prepared for a beverage; the beverage itself.
Coco-nut, Cocoa-nut, kō′kō-nut, *n.* The fruit of the coco palm.
Cocoon, kō′kön′, *n.* The silky case in which the silkworm involves itself when still a larva; the envelope of other larvæ.
Cod, kod, *n.* A species of sea fish allied to the haddock; a husk; a pod.
Coddle, kod′l, *vt.* (coddling, coddled). To fondle.
Code, kōd, *n.* A digest of laws; a collection of rules; a system of signals, &c.
Codicil, ko′di-sil, *n.* A writing by way of supplement to a will.
Codification, kōd′i-fi-kā″shon, *n.* Act or process of reducing laws to a code.
Codify, kōd′i-fī, *vt.* (codifying, codified). To reduce to a code.
Codling, Codlin, kod′ling, kod′lin, *n.* A variety of cooking apple.
Codling, kod′ling, *n.* A young codfish.
Cod-liver oil, kod′li-vėr oil, *n.* A medicinal oil obtained from the livers of the cod.
Coefficient, kō-ef-fi′shent, *a.* Jointly efficient; co-operating.—*n.* That which co-operates; a number or quantity that multiplies or measures another.
Coequal, kō-ē′kwal, *a.* Jointly equal.—*n.* One who is equal to another.
Coerce, kō-ėrs′, *vt.* (coercing, coerced). To restrain by force; to compel.
Coercion, kō-ėr′shon, *n.* Act of coercing; restraint; compulsion.
Coercive, kō-ėrs′iv, *a.* That has power to coerce; constraining; compulsory.
Coessential, kō-es-sen′shal, *a.* One in essence; partaking of the same essence.
Coeternal, kō-ē-tėr′nal, *a.* Equally eternal with another.
Coeval, kō-ē′val, *a.* Of the same age; contemporary.—*n.* One of the same age.
Coexecutor, kō-eks-ek′ū-tėr, *n.* A joint executor.
Coexist, kō-egz-ist′, *vi.* To live at the same time with another.
Coexistence, kō-egz-ist′ens, *n.* Existence at the same time with another.
Coexistent, kō-egz-ist′ent, *a.* Existing at the same time with another.
Coextend, kō-eks-tend′, *vi.* To extend through the same space or duration with another.
Coextensive, kō-eks-ten′siv, *a.* Equally extensive.
Coffee, kof′i, *n.* A tree and its fruit or berries; a beverage made from the seeds.
Coffee-house, kof′i-hous, *n.* A house where coffee and refreshments are supplied.
Coffee-room, kof′i-röm, *n.* A public room in an inn where coffee, &c., is supplied.
Coffer, kof′ėr, *n.* A chest for holding gold, jewels, &c.
Coffer-dam, kof′ėr-dam, *n.* A case of piling, water-tight, serving to exclude water in laying the foundations of piers, bridges, &c.
Coffin, kof′fin, *n.* The chest in which a dead human body is buried.—*vt.* To inclose in a coffin.
Cog, kog, *n.* The tooth of a wheel.—*vt.* (cogging, cogged). To furnish with cogs; to trick, deceive; to manipulate dice unfairly.—*vi.* To cheat; to lie.
Cogency, kō′jen-si, *n.* Force; persuading power.
Cogent, kō′jent, *a.* Forcible; convincing.
Cogently, kō′jent-li, *adv.* In a cogent manner.
Cogitate, ko′jit-āt, *vi.* (cogitating, cogitated). To ponder; to meditate.
Cogitation, ko-jit-ā′shon, *n.* Act of thinking much or deeply; reflection.
Cogitative, ko′jit-āt-iv, *a.* Having the power of thinking; given to thought.
Cognac, kō′nyak, *n.* A kind of brandy.
Cognate, kog′nāt, *a.* Born of the same stock; akin; of the same nature.
Cognition, kog-ni′shon, *n.* Knowledge from personal view or experience.
Cognizable, kog′niz-a-bl, *a.* That may be known; that may be tried and determined.
Cognizance, kog′niz-ans, *n.* Knowledge; judicial notice; trial, or right to try; a badge.
Cognizant, kog′niz-ant, *a.* Having knowledge of.
Cognomen, kog-nō′men, *n.* A name added to a family name; a surname.
Cohabit, kō-hab′it, *vi.* To dwell together; to live as husband and wife, though not married.
Cohabitation, kō-hab′it-ā″shon, *n.* Act or state of cohabiting.
Coheir, kō-ār′, *n.* A joint heir.
Coheiress, kō-ār′es, *n.* A joint heiress.
Cohere, kō-hēr′, *vi.* (cohering, cohered). To stick together; to be consistent.
Coherence, Coherency, kō-hēr′ens, kō-hēr′-en-si, *n.* The state of being coherent; cohesion; congruity.
Coherent, kō-hēr′ent, *a.* Sticking together; consistent.
Coherently, kō-hēr′ent-li, *adv.* In a coherent manner.

Cohesion, kō-hē'zhon, *n.* Act of sticking together; the attraction by which bodies are kept together; coherence.
Cohesive, kō-hē'siv, *a.* That has the power of cohering; tending to unite in a mass.
Cohort, kō'hort, *n.* A company of soldiers, among the Romans the tenth part of a legion.
Coif, koif, *n.* A kind of caul or cap.—*vt.* To cover or dress with a coif.
Coiffure, koif'ūr, *n.* Mode of dressing the hair in women.
Coil, koil, *vt.* To wind into a ring.—*n.* A ring or rings into which a rope, &c., is wound.
Coin, koin, *n.* A piece of metal stamped, as money; that which serves for payment.—*vt.* To stamp and convert metal into money; to mint; to invent; to fabricate.
Coinage, koin'āj, *n.* The act or art of coining; coined money; fabrication.
Coincide, kō-in-sīd', *vi.* (coinciding, coincided). To agree in position; to happen at the same time; to concur.
Coincidence, kō-in'si-dens, *n.* Concurrence; agreement.
Coincident, kō-in'si-dent, *a.* Having coincidence; concurrent; corresponding.
Coiner, koin'ėr, *n.* One who coins; a minter; a forger; an inventor.
Coition, kō-i'shon, *n.* Sexual intercourse.
Coke, kōk, *n.* Coal charred and deprived of gas.—*vt.* (coking, coked). To turn into coke.
Cola, kō'la, *n.* An African tree with nuts containing much caffeine and yielding an invigorating beverage.
Colander, ko'lan-dėr, *n.* A strainer; sieve.
Cold, kōld, *a.* Not hot; chill; indifferent; reserved; stoical; unaffecting.—*n.* Absence of heat; sensation produced by the escape of heat; an ailment occasioned by cold.
Cold-blooded, kōld'blud-ed, *a.* Having cold blood; without sensibility or feeling.
Coldish, kōld'ish, *a.* Somewhat cold.
Coldly, kōld'li, *adv.* In a cold manner.
Coldness, kōld'nes, *n.* Want of heat; unconcern; frigidity of temper; reserve.
Cole, kōl, *n.* A kind of cabbage.
Coleoptera, ko-lē-op'te-ra, *n.pl.* The beetle order of insects.
Coleopterous, ko-lē-op'te-rus, *a.* Having the wings and wing-covers of the beetle family.
Colewort, kōl'wėrt, *n.* A species of cabbage.
Colic, kol'ik, *n.* A painful affection of the intestines.
Colitis, kō-lī'tis, *n.* Inflammation of the large intestine, especially of its mucous membrane.
Collaborator, kol-la'bo-rāt-ėr, *n.* An associate in literary or scientific labour.
Collapse, kol-laps', *n.* A wasting of the body; a sudden and complete failure.—*vi.* (collapsing, collapsed). To fall together, as the sides of a vessel; to break down.
Collar, kol'ėr, *n.* A part of dress that surrounds the neck; something worn round the neck.—*vt.* To seize by the collar; to put a collar on; to roll up and bind with a cord.
Collar-bone, kol'ėr-bōn, *n.* Each of the two bones of the neck.
Collate, kol-lāt', *vt.* (collating, collated). To lay together and compare, as books, &c.; to place in a benefice; to gather and place in order.—*vi.* To place in a benefice.
Collateral, kol-lat'ėr-al, *a.* Placed side by side; running parallel; descending from the same stock, but not one from the other; connected.—*n.* A kinsman.
Collation, kol-lā'shon, *n.* Act of collating; that which is collated; a light repast.
Collator, ko-lāt'ėr, *n.* One who collates.
Colleague, kol'lēg, *n.* An associate in office.
Collect, kol-lekt', *vt.* To bring together; to gain by information; to infer or deduce.—*vi.* To run together; to accumulate.
Collect, kol'ekt, *n.* A short comprehensive prayer; a short prayer adapted to a particular occasion.
Collected, kol-lekt'ed, *p.a.* Cool; self-possessed.
Collectedly, kol-lekt'ed-li, *adv.* In a collected state or manner.
Collection, kol-lek'shon, *n.* Act of collecting; that which is collected.
Collective, kol-lekt'iv, *a.* Gathered into a mass; congregated; united.
Collectively, kol-lekt'iv-li, *adv.* In a collected state; in a mass or body.
Collectivism, kol-lek'tiv-izm, *n.* The doctrine that the state should own or control the land and all means of production.
Collector, kol-lekt'ėr, *n.* One who collects; one who collects customs or taxes.
College, kol'lej, *n.* A society of men, invested with certain powers, engaged in some common pursuit; a seminary of the higher learning; the building occupied for such purposes.
Collegian, kol-lē'ji-an, *n.* A member of a college; a student.
Collegiate, kol-lē'ji-āt, *a.* Pertaining to a college.
Collide, kol-līd', *vi.* (colliding, collided). To strike against each other; to meet in opposition.
Collie, kol'i, *n.* A dog common in Scotland, much used for sheep.
Collier, kol'yėr, *n.* One who works in a coal-mine; a ship that carries coals.
Colliery, kol'yėr-i, *n.* A coal-mine.
Collimate, kol'li-māt, *vt.* To adjust to the proper line of sight.
Collingual, kol-ling'gwal, *a.* Speaking the same language.
Collision, kol-li'zhon, *n.* Act of striking together; state of contrariety; conflict.
Collocate, kol'lō-kāt, *vt.* To place; to set; to station.
Collocation, kol-lō-kā'shon, *n.* Act of collocating; disposition.
Collodion, kol-lō'di-on, *n.* A solution of guncotton in ether, forming a thin film.
Colloid, kol'loid, *a.* Like glue or jelly; *chem.* applied to uncrystallizable liquids.
Collop, kol'lop, *n.* A slice of meat.
Colloquial, kol-lō'kwi-al, *a.* Pertaining to common conversation or discourse.
Colloquialism, kol-lō'kwi-al-izm, *n.* A colloquial form of expression.
Colloquy, kol'lō-kwi, *n.* A speaking together; mutual discourse; dialogue.
Collude, kol-lūd', *vi.* (colluding, colluded). To conspire in a fraud; to connive.
Collusion, kol-lū'zhon, *n.* Fraud by concert.
Collusive, kol-lū'siv, *a.* Fraudulently concerted.
Colocynth, kol'ō-sinth, *n.* A kind of gourd and a purgative got from it.
Colon, kō'lon, *n.* A mark of punctuation, thus (:); the largest of the intestines.

Colonel, kėr'nel, *n.* The chief commander of a regiment of troops.
Colonelcy, kėr'nel-si, *n.* The office, rank, or commission of a colonel.
Colonial, ko-lō'ni-al, *a.* Pertaining to a colony.—*n.* A person belonging to a colony.
Colonialism, ko-lō'ni-al-izm, *n.* A phrase, idiom, or practice peculiar to a colony.
Colonist, ko'lon-ist, *n.* An inhabitant of a colony.
Colonization, ko'lon-īz-ā"shon, *n.* Act of colonizing, or state of being colonized.
Colonize, ko'lon-īz, *vt.* (colonizing, colonized). To establish a colony in; to migrate to and settle in as inhabitants.
Colonnade, ko-lon-ād', *n.* A range of columns placed at regular intervals.
Colony, ko'lō-ni, *n.* A body of people transplanted from their mother country to inhabit some distant place; the country colonized.
Colophon, ko'lo-fōn, *n.* An inscription or device formerly on the last page of a book, now usually in its preliminary pages.
Colossal, kō-los'al, *a.* Huge; gigantic.
Colossus, kō-los'us, *n.*; *pl.* **-lossi.** A statue of gigantic size.
Colour, kul'ėr, *n.* That which gives bodies different appearances independently of form; a pigment; complexion; appearance to the mind; pretence; (*pl.*) a flag.—*vt.* To give some kind of colour to; to give a specious appearance to; to exaggerate in representation.—*vi.* To show colour; to blush.
Colourable, kul'ėr-a-bl, *a.* Designed to cover or conceal; specious; plausible.
Colour-blindness, kul'ėr-blīnd-nes, *n.* Inability to distinguish colours.
Coloured, kul'ėrd, *a.* Tinged; having a specious appearance; of a dark skin.
Colouring, kul'ėr-ing, *n.* Act of giving a colour; colour applied; a specious appearance; fair artificial representation.
Colourist, kul'ėr-ist, *n.* One who colours; a painter who excels in colouring.
Colourless, kul'ėr-les, *a.* Destitute of colour.
Colporteur, kol'pōr-tėr, *n.* One who travels for the sale or distribution of moral books, &c.
Colt, kōlt, *n.* A young male of the horse kind; a young foolish fellow.
Coltish, kōlt'ish, *a.* Like a colt; wanton; gay.
Columbine, ko'lum-bīn, *n.* A plant of the buttercup family; the female companion of Harlequin in pantomimes.
Columbium, kō-lum'bi-um, *n.* A rare metal.
Column, ko'lum, *n.* A pillar; a formation of troops, narrow in front, and deep from front to rear; a perpendicular section of a page; a perpendicular line of figures.
Columnar, ko-lum'nėr, *a.* Formed in columns; having the form of columns.
Colure, kō-lūr', *n.* Either of two great circles of the heavens, passing through the solstitial and the equinoctial points of the ecliptic.
Coma, kō'ma, *n.* Deep sleep; stupor; the hair-like envelope round the nucleus of a comet.
Comatose, kō'ma-tōs, *a.* Pertaining to coma; lethargic.
Comb, kōm, *n.* An instrument for separating hair, wool, &c.; the crest of a cock; honeycomb.—*vt.* To separate and adjust with a comb.
Combat, kom'bat, *vi.* To fight; to act in opposition.—*vt.* To oppose; to resist.—*n.* A fighting; an engagement; a duel.
Combatable, kom-bat'a-bl, *a.* That may be combated, disputed, or opposed.
Combatant, kom'bat-ant, *a.* Contending.—*n.* One who combats.
Combative, kom'bat-iv, *a.* Disposed to combat.
Combinable, kom-bīn'a-bl, *a.* Capable of combining.
Combination, kom-bin-ā'shon, *n.* Act of combining; state of being combined; union; confederacy; (*pl.*) a close-fitting undergarment.
Combine, kom-bīn', *vt.* (combining, combined). To cause to unite; to join.—*vi.* To come into union; to coalesce; to league together.—kom'bīn, *n.* A union.
Combined, kom-bīnd', *a.* United closely; produced by combination.
Combustible, kom-bust'i-bl, *a.* Capable of catching fire; inflammable.—*n.* A substance easily set on fire.
Combustion, kom-bust'shon, *n.* A burning; chemical combination, attended with heat and light.
Come, kum, *vi.* (coming, pret. came, pp. come). To move hitherward; to draw nigh; to arrive; to happen; to appear; to rise; to result.
Comedian, ko-mē'di-an, *n.* An actor in or writer of comedies.
Comedy, ko'mē-di, *n.* A drama of the lighter kind.
Comeliness, kum'li-nes, *n.* The quality of being comely; good looks.
Comely, kum'li, *a.* Good-looking; handsome; becoming.
Comestible, kom'es-ti-bl, *n.* An eatable.
Comet, kom'et, *n.* A heavenly body having a luminous tail or train.
Cometary, kom'et-a-ri, *a.* Pertaining to or like a comet.
Comfit, kum'fit, *n.* A sweetmeat.
Comfort, kum'fėrt, *vt.* To console; to gladden.—*n.* Consolation; relief; moderate enjoyment.
Comfortable, kum'fėrt-a-bl, *a.* Enjoying or giving comfort.
Comfortably, kum'fėrt-a-bli, *adv.* In a comfortable manner.
Comforter, kum'fėrt-ėr, *n.* One who comforts; the Holy Spirit; a woollen scarf.
Comfortless, kum'fėrt-les, *a.* Destitute of comfort; forlorn; wretched.
Comic, kom'ik, *a.* Relating to comedy; comical.
Comical, kom'ik-al, *a.* Raising mirth; funny.
Comically, kom'ik-al-li, *adv.* In a comical manner.
Coming, kum'ing, *p.a.* Future.—*n.* Approach.
Comity, ko'mi-ti, *n.* Courtesy; civility.
Comma, kom'ma, *n.* A mark of punctuation, thus (,); an interval in music.
Command, kom-mand', *vt.* To order; to govern; to have at one's disposal.—*vi.* To have chief power.—*n.* Order; control; power of overlooking; power of defending.
Commandant, kom-man-dant', *n.* A commanding officer of a place or forces.
Commander, kom-mand'ėr, *n.* One who commands; an officer in the navy, between a lieutenant-commander and captain.

Commandery, kom-man'dėr-i, *n.* Among certain knights and religious orders, a district under a member called a commander.
Commanding, kom-mand'ing, *a.* Exercising command; overlooking a wide view.
Commandment, kom-mand'ment, *n.* A command; a precept of the moral law.
Commando, kom-man'dō, *n.* A member of a body of troops specially trained and selected for hazardous enterprises.
Commemorable, kom-mem'o-ra-bl, *a.* Worthy to be commemorated.
Commemorate, kom-mem'o-rāt, *vt.* To call to remembrance by a solemn act; to celebrate with honour and solemnity.
Commemoration, kom-mem'o-rā"shon, *n.* Solemn celebration.
Commemorative, kom-mem'o-rāt-iv, *a.* Tending to preserve in remembrance.
Commence, kom-mens', *vi.* (commencing, commenced). To take the first step; to begin to be.—*vt.* To begin; to originate.
Commencement, kom-mens'ment, *n.* Beginning; rise; origin; first existence.
Commend, kom-mend', *vt.* To commit to the care of; to recommend; to praise.
Commendable, kom-mend'a-bl, *a.* Worthy of praise.
Commendam, kom-men'dam, *n.* An ecclesiastical benefice intrusted to a qualified person till an incumbent is provided.
Commendation, kom-men-dā'shon, *n.* Praise; recommendation; compliments.
Commendatory, kom-mend'a-to-ri, *a.* That serves to commend; containing praise.
Commensal, kom-men'sal, *n.* One that eats at the same table; one living with another.
Commensurability, kom-men'sūr-a-bil"i-ti, *n.* The capacity of having a common measure.
Commensurable, kom-men'sūr-a-bl, *a.* Having a common measure.
Commensurate, kom-men'sūr-āt, *a.* Proportional; having equal measure.
Commensurately, kom-men'sūr-āt-li, *adv.* Correspondingly; adequately.
Comment, kom-ment', *vi.* To make remarks or criticisms.—*vt.* To annotate.—*n.* kom'-ment. An explanatory note; criticism.
Commentary, kom'ment-a-ri, *n.* Book of comments; an historical narrative.
Commentator, kom'ment-āt-ėr, *n.* One who writes annotations; an expositor.
Commerce, kom'mėrs, *n.* Exchange of goods by barter or purchase; trade; intercourse.
Commercial, kom-mėr'shal, *a.* Pertaining to commerce; trading; mercantile.
Commercially, kom-mėr'shal-li, *adv.* In a commercial manner or view.
Commination, kom-mi-nā'shon, *n.* A threat; recital of God's threatenings on stated days.
Comminatory, kom-mi'na-to-ri, *a.* Threatening.
Commingle, kom-ming'gl, *vt.* To blend.—*vi.* To unite together.
Comminute, kom'mi-nūt, *vt.* To make small or fine; to pulverize.
Comminution, kom-mi-nū'shon, *n.* Act of comminuting; pulverization.
Commiserate, kom-miz'ė-rāt, *vt.* (commiserating, commiserated). To pity; to condole with.
Commiseration, kom-miz'ė-rā"shon, *n.* Act of commiserating; pity.
Commissariat, kom-mis-sā'ri-at, *n.* The department of an army which supplies provisions, &c.; the officers in this department.
Commissary, kom'mis-sa-ri, *n.* A delegate; an officer of a bishop; an officer who has the charge of furnishing provisions, clothing, &c., for an army.
Commission, kom-mi'shon, *n.* Trust; warrant; a written document, investing one with an office; allowance made to an agent, &c., for transacting business; a body of men joined in an office or trust, or their appointment; perpetration.—*vt.* To appoint; to depute.
Commissionaire, kom-mi-shon-ār', *n.* A porter or messenger.
Commissioned, kom-mi'shond, *a.* Furnished with a commission.
Commissioner, kom-mi'shon-ėr, *n.* One commissioned to perform some office.
Commissure, kom'mis-sūr, *n.* A joint or seam; juncture.
Commit, kom-mit', *vt.* (committing, committed). To intrust; to consign; to send to prison; to perpetrate; to endanger or compromise (oneself).
Commitment, kom'mit'ment, *n.* The act of committing; a sending to prison.
Committal, kom-mit'al, *n.* The act of committing in the various senses of the verb.
Committee, kom-mit'tē, *n.* A body of persons appointed to manage any matter.
Commix, kom-miks', *vt.* To blend; to mix.
Commixture, kom-miks'tūr, *n.* Act of mixing together; compound.
Commode, kom-mōd', *n.* A kind of small sideboard; a lady's head-dress; a night-stool.
Commodious, kom-mō'di-us, *a.* Convenient; spacious and suitable.
Commodiously, kom-mō'di-us-li, *adv.* In a commodious manner; suitably.
Commodity, kom-mo'di-ti, *n.* Something useful; any article of commerce; (*pl.*) goods; merchandise.
Commodore, kom'mo-dōr, *n.* A captain in the Royal Navy who is discharging duties rather more important than those usually assigned to a captain.
Common, kom'mon, *a.* Having no separate owner; general; usual; of no rank; of little value.—*n.* An open public ground; *pl.* the untitled people; the lower House of Parliament; food at a common table; food in general.
Commonage, kom'mon-āj, *n.* The right of pasturing on a common.
Commonalty, Commonality, kom'on-al-ti, kom-on-al'i-ti, *n.* The common people.
Commoner, kom'on-ėr, *n.* One of the common people; a member of the House of Commons; a student of Oxford, not dependent for support on the foundation.
Commonly, kom'mon-li, *adv.* Usually.
Commonplace, kom'mon-plās, *n.* A usual topic; a trite saying.—*a.* Ordinary; trite.
Common sense, kom'mon sens, *n.* Sound practical judgment.
Commonweal, kom'on-wēl, *n.* A commonwealth; the state.
Commonwealth, kom'mon-welth, *n.* The public good; the state; body politic; a form of government; a republic.
Commotion, kom-mō'shon, *n.* Violent agitation; tumultuous disorder.

Commune, kom-mūn′, *vi.* (communing, communed). To confer; to meditate.
Commune, kom′mūn, *n.* A small administrative district in France; a socialist body which ruled over Paris in 1871.
Communicable, kom-mū′ni-ka-bl, *a.* Capable of being imparted to another.
Communicant, kom-mū′ni-kant, *n.* One who communicates; a partaker of the Lord's supper.
Communicate, kom-mū′ni-kāt, *vt.* (communicating, communicated). To cause to be common to others; to impart, as news, disease, &c.; to bestow; to reveal.—*vi.* To share with others; to partake of the Lord's supper; to have intercourse; to correspond.
Communication, kom-mū′ni-kā″shon, *n.* Act of communicating; that which is communicated; a letter or despatch received; a passage from one place to another.
Communicative, kom-mū′ni-kāt-iv, *a.* Ready to communicate; not reserved.
Communion, kom-mūn′yon, *n.* A mutual participation in anything; mutual intercourse; concord; celebration of the Lord's supper.
Communism, kom′mūn-izm, *n.* The doctrine of a community of property.
Communist, kom′mūn-ist, *n.* One who holds the doctrines of communism.
Community, kom-mū′ni-ti, *n.* Mutual participation; the public; a society of persons under the same laws.
Commutability, kom-mūt′a-bil″i-ti, *n.* Quality of being commutable.
Commutable, kom-mūt′a-bl, *a.* That may be exchanged; convertible into money.
Commutation, kom-mū-tā′shon, *n.* Exchange; change; substitution of a less for a greater penalty.
Commute, kom-mūt′, *vt.* (commuting, commuted). To exchange; to put one thing for another.
Compact, kom-pakt′, *a.* Closely united; solid; dense; brief.—*vt.* To consolidate; to unite firmly.—*n.* kom′pakt. An agreement; a contract.
Compactly, kom-pakt′li, *adv.* Closely; densely; tersely.
Companion, kom-pan′yon, *n.* A comrade; an associate; one of the third rank in an order of knighthood; a raised cover to the cabin stair of a merchant vessel.
Companionable, kom-pan′yon-a-bl, *a.* Fitted to be an agreeable companion; sociable.
Companionship, kom-pan′yon-ship, *n.* Fellowship; association.
Company, kum′pa-ni, *n.* Companionship; an assembly of persons; partners in a firm; a division of a battalion, consisting of four platoons, and commanded by a major or mounted captain, with a captain as second-in-command; the crew of a ship.—*vi.* To associate with.
Comparable, kom′pa-ra-bl, *a.* That may be compared; being of equal regard.
Comparably, kom′pa-ra-bli, *adv.* By comparison; so as to be compared.
Comparative, kom-pa′ra-tiv, *a.* Estimated by comparison; not positive or absolute.
Comparatively, kom-pa′ra-tiv-li, *adv.* By comparison.
Compare, kom-pār′, *vt.* (comparing, compared). To bring together and examine the relations between; to estimate one by another; to inflect in the degrees of comparison.—*vi.* To hold comparison.
Comparison, kom-pa′ri-son, *n.* Act of comparing; state of being compared; relation; the formation of an adjective in its degrees of signification; a simile.
Compartment, kom-pärt′ment, *n.* A division or part of a general design.
Compass, kum′pas, *n.* A round; a circuit; limit; extent; range; an instrument for directing the course of ships; an instrument for describing circles (often in *pl.*).—*vt.* To pass round; to inclose; to obtain; to contrive.
Compassable, kum′pas-a-bl, *a.* Capable of being accomplished.
Compassion, kom-pa′shon, *n.* Fellow-suffering; pity; sympathy.
Compassionate, kom-pa′shon-āt, *a.* Ready to pity; sympathizing.—*vt.* To pity.
Compassionately, kom-pa′shon-āt-li, *adv.* With compassion; mercifully.
Compatibility, kom-pat′i-bil″i-ti, *n.* Quality of being compatible.
Compatible, kom-pat′i-bl, *a.* Consistent; suitable; not incongruous.
Compatibly, kom-pat′i-bli, *adv.* Fitly.
Compatriot, kom-pā′tri-ot, *n.* One of the same country.
Compeer, kom-pēr′, *n.* An equal; an associate.
Compel, kom-pel′, *vt.* (compelling, compelled). To drive; to urge; to necessitate.
Compellable, kom-pel′a-bl, *a.* That may be compelled.
Compellation, kom-pel-lā′shon, *n.* An addressing; a ceremonious appellation.
Compendious, kom-pen′di-us, *a.* Short; comprehensive; concise.
Compendiously, kom-pen′di-us-li, *adv.* In a short or brief manner; summarily.
Compendium, kom-pen′di-um, *n.* An abridgment; a summary; an epitome.
Compensate, kom-pens′āt, *vt.* (compensating, compensated). To give equal value to; to make amends for; to requite.—*vi.* To make amends; to supply an equivalent.
Compensation, kom-pens-ā′shon, *n.* Act of compensating; recompense.
Compensatory, kom-pens′ā-to-ri, *a.* Serving for compensation; making amends.
Compete, kom-pēt′, *vi.* (competing, competed). To strive for the same thing as another; to contend.
Competence, Competency, kom′pē-tens, kom′pē-ten-si, *n.* Suitableness; sufficiency; legal capacity or right.
Competent, kom′pē-tent, *a.* Suitable; sufficient; qualified; having adequate right.
Competently, kom′pē-tent-li, *adv.* Sufficiently; adequately.
Competition, kom-pē-ti′shon, *n.* Contest for the same object; rivalry.
Competitive, kom-pet′it-iv, *a.* Relating to competition; carried out by competition.
Competitor, kom-pet′it-ėr, *n.* One who competes; a rival; an opponent.
Compilation, kom-pi-lā′shon, *n.* Act of compiling; that which is compiled; a work made up of parts from various authors.
Compile, kom-pīl′, *vt.* (compiling, compiled). To gather from various sources; to draw up by collecting parts from different authors.

Compiler, kom-pīl'ėr, *n.* One who compiles.
Complacence, Complacency, kom-plā'sens, kom-plā'sen-si, *n.* A feeling of quiet satisfaction; complaisance.
Complacent, kom-plā'sent, *a.* Showing complacency; complaisant.
Complacently, kom-plā'sent-li, *adv.* In a complacent manner; softly.
Complain, kom-plān', *vi.* To express grief or distress; to lament; to express dissatisfaction; to make a formal accusation.
Complainant, kom-plān'ant, *n.* One who complains; a plaintiff.
Complaint, kom-plānt', *n.* Expression of grief, censure, &c.; accusation; malady.
Complaisance, kom'plā-zans, *n.* A pleasing deportment; courtesy; urbanity.
Complaisant, kom'plā-zant, *a.* Pleasing in manners; desirous to please; courteous.
Complaisantly, kom'plā-zant-li, *adv.* With complaisance.
Complement, kom'plē-ment, *n.* That which fills up; full quantity or number.
Complementary, kom-plē-ment'a-ri, *a.* Completing; supplying a deficiency.
Complete, kom-plēt', *a.* Having no deficiency; finished; total; absolute.—*vt.* (completing, completed). To make complete; to finish; to fulfil.
Completely, kom-plēt'li, *adv.* Fully.
Completeness, kom-plēt'nes, *n.* State of being complete; perfection.
Completion, kom-plē'shon, *n.* Act of completing; state of being complete; fulfilment; accomplishment.
Complex, kom'pleks, *a.* Of various parts; involved; composite.—*n.* A series of emotionally accentuated ideas in a repressed state.
Complexion, kom-plek'shon, *n.* The colour of the face; general appearance.
Complexional, kom-plek'shon-al, *a.* Pertaining to complexion.
Complexity, kom-pleks'i-ti, *n.* State of being complex; intricacy.
Compliance, kom-plī'ans, *n.* Submission; consent.
Compliant, kom-plī'ant, *a.* Yielding; bending; submissive; obliging.
Complicacy, kom'pli-ka-si, *n.* A state of being complex or intricate.
Complicate, kom'pli-kāt, *vt.* (complicating, complicated). To make complex or intricate; to entangle.
Complicated, kom'pli-kāt-ed, *p.a.* Involved; intricate.
Complication, kom-pli-kā'shon, *n.* That which consists of many things involved; entanglement; intricacy.
Complicity, kom-plis'i-ti, *n.* State or condition of being an accomplice.
Compliment, kom'pli-ment, *n.* Act or expression of civility or regard; delicate flattery; a favour bestowed.—*vt.* To pay a compliment to; to congratulate; to praise.
Complimentary, kom-pli-ment'a-ri, *a.* Containing compliment; flattering.
Compline, kom'plin, *n.* In the Roman Catholic Church, the last service at night.
Complot, kom'plot, *n.* A joint plot.—*vt.* and *i.* To plot together.
Comply, kom-plī', *vi.* (complying, complied). To yield; to assent; to acquiesce.
Component, kom-pōn'ent, *a.* Composing; forming an element of a compound.—*n.* A constituent part; ingredient.
Comport, kom-pōrt', *vi.* To agree; to suit.—*vt.* To bear or carry (oneself); to behave.
Compose, kom-pōz', *vt.* (composing, composed). To form by uniting; to constitute; to write; to calm; to set types in printing.
Composed, kom-pōzd', *p.a.* Calm; sedate.
Composer, kom-pōz'ėr, *n.* An author, especially a musical author.
Composite, kom'po-zīt or -zit, *a.* Compound; noting a rich order of architecture; noting plants whose flowers are arranged in dense heads.
Composition, kom-pō-zi'shon, *n.* Act of composing; a mixture; a literary or musical work; arrangement; agreement to receive or pay part of a debt in place of the whole; the part paid; act of setting types.
Compositor, kom-poz'it-ėr, *n.* One who sets types.
Compost, kom'pōst, *n.* A mixture for manure.
Composure, kom-pō'zhūr, *n.* A settled frame of mind; calmness; tranquillity.
Compound, kom-pound', *vt.* and *i.* To put together; to mix; to adjust; to discharge a debt by paying a part.—*a.* kom'pound. Composed of two or more ingredients, words, or parts.—*n.* A mass composed of two or more elements; inclosure in which houses stand.
Compounder, kom-pound'ėr, *n.* One who compounds.
Comprehend, kom-prē-hend', *vt.* To embrace within limits; to understand.
Comprehensible, kom-prē-hens'i-bl, *a.* That may be comprehended; intelligible.
Comprehension, kom-prē-hen'shon, *n.* Act of comprehending; power of comprehending; understanding.
Comprehensive, kom-prē-hens'iv, *a.* Comprising much; capacious; able to understand.
Comprehensively, kom-prē-hens'iv-li, *adv.* In a comprehensive manner.
Compress, kom-pres', *vt.* To press together; to squeeze; to condense.—*n.* kom'pres. A soft mass or bandage used in surgery.
Compressed, kom-prest', *p.a.* Pressed together; flattened; condensed.
Compressibility, kom-pres'i-bil"i-ti, *n.* The quality of being compressible.
Compressible, kom-pres'i-bl, *a.* Capable of being compressed.
Compression, kom-pre'shon, *n.* Act of compressing; state of being compressed.
Comprise, kom-prīz', *vt.* (comprising, comprised). To embrace; to contain; to inclose.
Compromise, kom'prō-mīz, *n.* An amicable agreement to settle differences; mutual concession.—*vt.* To settle by mutual concessions; to involve; to endanger the interests of.
Comptroller, kon-trōl'ėr, *n.* A controller; an officer who examines the accounts of collectors of public money.
Compulsion, kom-pul'shon, *n.* Act of compelling; state of being compelled; force.
Compulsive, kom-pul'siv, *a.* Having power to compel.
Compulsory, kom-pul'so-ri, *a.* Constraining; coercive; obligatory.
Compunction, kom-pungk'shon, *n.* Remorse; contrition.
Compunctious, kom-pungk'shus, *a.* Implying or feeling compunction.

Compurgation, kom-pėr-gā'shon, *n.* Act of justifying a man by the oath of others.
Compurgator, kom-pėr'gāt-ėr, *n.* One who swears to another's innocence.
Computable, kom-pūt'a-bl, *a.* Capable of being computed.
Computation, kom-pū-tā'shon, *n.* Act or process of computing; reckoning.
Compute, kom-pūt', *vt.* (computing, computed). To count; to estimate.
Comrade, kom'rād, *n.* A mate: a companion; an associate.
Comradeship, kom'rād-ship, *n.* State of being a comrade or comrades.
Con, kon, *vt.* (conning, conned). To learn; to fix in the mind; to peruse carefully; to direct the steering of (a ship).
Concatenate, kon-ka'tē-nāt, *vt.* To link together; to unite in a series.
Concatenation, kon-ka'tē-nā"shon, *n.* A series of things depending on each other.
Concave, kon'kāv, *a.* Hollow, as the inner surface of a sphere; opposed to convex.—*n.* A hollow; an arch or vault.
Concavity, kon-kav'i-ti, *n.* Hollowness; a concave surface.
Conceal, kon-sēl', *vt.* To hide; to secrete; to disguise.
Concealable, kon-sēl'a-bl, *a.* That may be concealed.
Concealment, kon-sēl'ment, *n.* Act of concealing; state of being concealed; a hiding-place.
Concede, kon-sēd', *vt.* (conceding, conceded). To yield; to grant.—*vi.* To make concession.
Conceit, kon-sēt', *n.* Conception; fancy; self-flattering opinion; vanity.
Conceited, kon-sēt'ed, *a.* Vain; egotistical.
Conceivable, kon-sēv'a-bl, *a.* That may be imagined or understood.
Conceivably, kon-sēv'a-bli, *adv.* In a conceivable or intelligible manner.
Conceive, kon-sēv', *vt.* (conceiving, conceived). To form in the womb; to take into the mind; to comprehend.—*vi.* To become pregnant; to have or form an idea.
Concentrate, kon'sen-trāt, *vt.* (concentrating, concentrated). To bring together; to direct to one object; to condense.
Concentration, kon-sen-trā'shon, *n.* Act of concentrating; state of being concentrated.
Concentrative, kon-sen'trāt-iv, *a.* Tending to concentrate.
Concentric, kon-sen'trik, *a.* Having a common centre.
Concept, kon'sept, *n.* An object conceived by the mind; a general notion of a class of objects.
Conception, kon-sep'shon, *n.* Act of conceiving; state of being conceived; thing conceived; image in the mind; mental faculty which originates ideas.
Conceptualist, kon-sep'tū-al-ist, *n.* One who holds that the mind can give independent existence to general conceptions.
Concern, kon-sėrn', *vt.* To belong to; to affect the interest of; to make anxious.—*n.* That which relates to one; affair; care; anxiety; a commercial establishment.
Concerned, kon-sėrnd', *a.* Interested; anxious.
Concerning, kon-sėrn'ing, *prep.* Having relation to; respecting.
Concernment, kon-sėrn'ment, *n.* Affair; concern; solicitude.
Concert, kon-sėrt', *vt.* To plan together; to contrive.—*n.* kon'sėrt. Agreement in a design; harmony; performance of a company of players, singers, &c.
Concerted, kon-sėrt'ed, *p.a.* Mutually contrived; done in concert.
Concertina, kon-sėrt-ē'na, *n.* A musical instrument of the accordion species.
Concerto, kon-chăr'tō, *n.* A musical composition for one principal instrument, with accompaniments for a full orchestra.
Concession, kon-se'shon, *n.* Act of conceding; the thing yielded; a grant.
Concessive, kon-ses'iv, *a.* Implying concession.
Conch, kongk, *n.* A marine shell.
Conchoidal, kong-koi'dal, *a.* With curves like shells.
Conchology, kong-kol'o-ji, *n.* The doctrine or science of shells.
Conciliate, kon-si'li-āt, *vt.* (conciliating, conciliated). To bring to friendliness; to win the favour or consent; to reconcile; to propitiate.
Conciliation, kon-si'li-ā"shon, *n.* Act of gaining favour or affection.
Conciliator, kon-si'li-āt-ėr, *n.* One who conciliates or reconciles.
Conciliatory, kon-si'li-a-to-ri, *a.* Tending to conciliate; pacific.
Concise, kon-sīs', *a.* Brief; abridged; comprehensive.
Concisely, kon-sīs'li, *adv.* Briefly.
Conciseness, kon-sīs'nes, *n.* Brevity.
Concision, kon-si'zhon, *n.* A cutting off; conciseness.
Conclave, kon'klāv, *n.* A private apartment; the assembly of cardinals for the election of a pope; a close assembly.
Conclude, kon-klūd', *vt.* (concluding, concluded). To end; to decide; to deduce.—*vi.* To end; to form a final judgment.
Conclusion, kon-klū'zhon, *n.* Act of concluding; that which is concluded; inference; consequence; final decision; end.
Conclusive, kon-klū'siv, *a.* That concludes or determines; final; convincing.
Conclusively, kon-klū'siv-li, *adv.* Decisively; with final determination.
Concoct, kon-kokt', *vt.* To devise; to plot.
Concoction, kon-kok'shon, *n.* Act of concocting; a mixture or preparation.
Concomitance, Concomitancy, kon-kom'-i-tans, kon-kom'i-tan-si, *n.* A being together or in connection with another thing.
Concomitant, kon-kom'it-ant, *a.* Accompanying; concurrent.—*n.* An accompaniment; a connected circumstance.
Concord, kong'kord, *n.* Union in feelings, opinions, &c.; harmony; agreement of words in construction.
Concordance, kon-kord'ans, *n.* Agreement; index of the principal words of a book.
Concordant, kon-kord'ant, *a.* Agreeing together; correspondent; harmonious.
Concordat, kon-kord'at, *n.* An agreement made by a sovereign with the pope relative to ecclesiastical matters.
Concourse, kong'kōrs, *n.* Confluence; an assembly; crowd.
Concrete, kon'krēt, *a.* Composed of particles united in one mass; congealed; existing in a subject; not abstract.—*n.* A mass formed by concretion; a hard mass formed of lime, sand,

&c.—*vi.* kon-krēt' (concreting, concreted). To unite in a mass; to become solid.
Concretion, kon-krē'shon, *n.* Act of concreting; state of being concreted; a mass concreted.
Concubinage, kon-kū'bin-āj, *n.* The living together as husband and wife without being married.
Concubine, kong'kū-bīn, *n.* A woman who cohabits with a man; a mistress.
Concupiscence, kon-kū'pis-ens, *n.* Lust.
Concupiscent, kon-kū'pis-ent, *a.* Lustful.
Concur, kon-kėr', *vi.* (concurring, concurred). To unite; to agree; to assent.
Concurrence, kon-ku'rens, *n.* Act of concurring; union; joint action.
Concurrent, kon-ku'rent, *a.* Acting together. —*n.* That which concurs; joint cause.
Concurrently, kon-ku'rent-li, *adv.* With concurrence; unitedly.
Concussion, kon-ku'shon, *n.* A violent shock.
Concussive, kon-kus'iv, *a.* Having the power or quality of shaking; agitating.
Condemn, kon-dem', *vt.* To pronounce to be wrong; to censure; to sentence.
Condemnation, kon-dem-nā'shon, *n.* Act of condemning; state of being condemned; sentence; cause of blame.
Condemnatory, kon-dem'na-to-ri, *a.* Condemning; bearing condemnation.
Condensable, kon-dens'a-bl, *a.* Capable of being condensed.
Condensation, kon-dens-ā'shon, *n.* Act of condensing; state of being condensed.
Condense, kon-dens', *vt.* (condensing, condensed). To reduce in compass; to reduce from a gaseous to a liquid or solid state.—*vi.* To become dense; to grow thick.
Condenser, kon-dens'ėr, *n.* One who or that which condenses; a vessel in which vapours are reduced to liquid by coldness; a chamber in which steam is condensed; an instrument for storing an electric charge.
Condescend, kon-dē-send', *vi.* To descend from the privileges of superior rank; to deign.
Condescending, kon-dē-send'ing, *a.* Yielding to inferiors; patronizing.
Condescension, kon-de-sen'shon, *n.* Act of condescending; courtesy; complaisance.
Condign, kon-dīn', *a.* Deserved; suitable.
Condiment, kon'di-ment, *n.* Seasoning; relish.
Condition, kon-di'shon, *n.* State; case; external circumstances; temper; stipulation.
Conditional, kon-di'shon-al, *a.* Depending on conditions; not absolute.
Conditionally, kon-di'shon-al-li, *adv.* With certain limitations.
Conditioned, kon-di'shond, *a.* Having a certain condition, state, or qualities.
Condole, kon-dōl', *vi.* (condoling, condoled). To grieve with another; to sympathize.
Condolement, kon-dōl'ment, *n.* Sympathetic grief; sorrow with others.
Condolence, kon-dōl'ens, *n.* Act of condoling; expression of sympathy.
Condone, kon-dōn', *vt.* (condoning, condoned). To pardon; to imply forgiveness of.
Condor, kon'dor, *n.* A S. American vulture.
Conduce, kon-dūs', *vi.* (conducing, conduced). To lead; to tend; to contribute.
Conducive, kon-dūs'iv, *a.* Having a tendency to promote.
Conduct, kon'dukt, *n.* Personal behaviour; management; escort.—*vt.* kon-dukt'. To lead or guide; to escort; to manage; to behave (oneself); to transmit, as heat, &c.
Conductible, kon-dukt'i-bl, *a.* That may be conducted.
Conduction, kon-duk'shon, *n.* Property by which bodies transmit heat or electricity.
Conductive, kon-dukt'iv, *a.* Having the physical property of conducting.
Conductor, kon-dukt'ėr, *n.* A leader; a director; a body that transmits heat, electricity, &c.
Conductress, kon-duk'tres, *n.* A female conductor.
Conduit, kon'dit or kun'dit, *n.* A channel or pipe to convey water, &c., or to drain off filth; a channel or passage.
Cone, kōn, *n.* A solid body having a circle for its base, and tapering to a point; the fruit of firs, pine-trees, &c.
Confabulate, kon-fab'ū-lāt, *vi.* (confabulating, confabulated). To talk familiarly.
Confabulation, kon-fab'ū-lā"shon, *n.* Easy conversation; familiar talk.
Confection, kon-fek'shon, *n.* A mixture; a sweetmeat.
Confectioner, kon-fek'shon-ėr, *n.* One who makes or sells sweetmeats.
Confectionery, kon-fek'shon-ė-ri, *n.* Sweetmeats in general; confections.
Confederacy, kon-fe'de-ra-si, *n.* A confederation; the parties united by a league.
Confederate, kon-fe'de-rāt, *a.* Allied by treaty.—*n.* One united with others in a league. —*vt.* and *i.* (confederating, confederated). To unite in a league.
Confederation, kon-fe'de-rā"shon, *n.* A league; alliance, particularly of states, &c.
Confer, kon-fėr', *vi.* (conferring, conferred). To consult together.—*vt.* To give or bestow.
Conference, kon'fėr-ens, *n.* A meeting for consultation, or for the adjustment of differences; bestowal.
Confess, kon-fes', *vt.* To own, as a crime, debt, &c.; to admit; publicly to declare adherence to; to hear a confession, as a priest. —*vi.* To make confession.
Confessedly, kon-fes'ed-li, *adv.* Avowedly.
Confession, kon-fe'shon, *n.* Act of confessing; that which is confessed; a formulary of articles of faith; a creed.
Confessional, kon-fe'shon-al, *n.* The place where a priest sits to hear confessions.
Confessor, kon-fes'ėr, *n.* One who confesses; a priest who hears confession.
Confetti, kon-fet'i, *n.* Small pieces of coloured paper thrown at each other by revellers at carnivals, or at the bride and groom by wedding guests.
Confidant, kon'fi-dant, *n.m.*; **Confidante,** kon-fi-dant', *n.f.* A confidential friend.
Confide, kon-fīd', *vi.* (confiding, confided). To trust wholly; to have firm faith (with *in*). —*vt.* To intrust; to commit to the charge of.
Confidence, kon'fi-dens, *n.* Firm belief or trust; self-reliance; boldness; assurance; a secret.
Confident, kon'fi-dent, *a.* Having confidence; trusting; assured; dogmatical.
Confidentia kon-fi-den'shal, *a.* Enjoying confidence; trusty; private; secret.
Confidentially, kon-fi-den'shal-li, *adv.* In confidence.

Confidently, kon'fi-dent-li, *adv.* In a confident manner; positively.
Confiding, kon-fīd'ing, *a.* Trusting; reposing confidence.
Configuration, kon-fig'ūr-ā"shon, *n.* External form; contour.
Confinable, kon-fīn'a-bl, *a.* That may be confined.
Confine, kon'fīn, *n.* Boundary; territory near the end; border (generally in *pl.*).—*vt.* kon-fīn' (confining, confined). To restrain; to limit; to shut up; to imprison.—**To be confined,** to be in childbed.
Confined, kon-fīnd', *a.* Limited; secluded; close.
Confinement, kon-fīn'ment, *n.* Imprisonment; seclusion; childbirth.
Confirm, kon-fėrm', *vt.* To make firm or more firm; to establish; to make certain; to administer the rite of confirmation to.
Confirmation, kon-fėrm-ā'shon, *n.* Act of confirming; additional evidence; ratification; the laying on of a bishop's hands in the rite of admission to the privileges of a Christian.
Confirmative, kon-fėr'ma-tiv, *a.* Tending to confirm or establish; confirmatory.
Confirmatory, kon-fėrm'ā-to-ri, *a.* That serves to confirm.
Confirmed, kon-fėrmd', *a.* Fixed; settled in certain habits, state of health, &c.
Confiscable, kon-fis'ka-bl, *a.* That may be confiscated; liable to forfeiture.
Confiscate, kon'fis-kāt, *vt.* (confiscating, confiscated). To seize as forfeited to the public treasury.
Confiscation, kon-fis-kā'shon, *n.* Act of confiscating.
Confiscator, kon'fis- or kon-fis'kāt-ėr, *n.* One who confiscates.
Conflagration, kon-fla-grā'shon, *n.* A great fire.
Conflict, kon'flikt, *n.* A struggle; clashing of views or statements.—*vi.* kon-flikt'. To meet in opposition; to be antagonistic.
Conflicting, kon-flikt'ing, *a.* Contradictory.
Confluence, kon'flū-ens, *n.* A flowing together; meeting, or place of meeting, of rivers; a concourse; a crowd.
Confluent, kon'flū-ent, *a.* Flowing together; running into each other; united.
Conflux, kon'fluks, *n.* A flowing together; a concourse; a crowd.
Conform, kon-form', *vt.* To cause to be of the same form; to adapt.—*vi.* To comply.
Conformable, kon-for'ma-bl, *a.* In harmony or conformity; suitable; compliant; *geol.* lying in parallel planes.
Conformably, kon-for'ma-bli, *adv.* Suitably.
Conformation, kon-for-mā'shon, *n.* The act of conforming; structure; configuration.
Conformist, kon-for'mist, *n.* One who conforms; one who complies with the worship of the established church.
Conformity, kon-for'mi-ti, *n.* Agreement; resemblance; compliance with.
Confound, kon-found', *vt.* To confuse; to astound; to overthrow; to mistake.
Confounded, kon-foun'ded, *a.* Excessive; odious; detestable; reprehensible.
Confoundedly, kon-foun'ded-li, *adv.* Shamefully; odiously; detestably.
Confraternity, kon-fra-tėr'ni-ti, *n.* A brotherhood; a society or body of men.
Confrère, kong-frār, *n.* A colleague.
Confront, kon-frunt', *vt.* To face; to oppose; to bring into the presence of; to set together for comparison.
Confucian, kon-fū'shi-an, *a.* and *n.* Pertaining to, or a follower of, Confucius, the famous Chinese philosopher.
Confuse, kon-fūz', *vt.* (confusing, confused). To mix without order; to derange; to confound; to disconcert.
Confused, kon-fūzd', *p.a.* Perplexed; disconcerted.
Confusedly, kon-fūz'ed-li, *adv.* In a confused manner.
Confusion, kon-fū'zhon, *n.* Disorder; embarrassment.
Confutable, kon-fūt'a-bl, *a.* That may be confuted.
Confutation, kon-fūt-ā'shon, *n.* Act of confuting; refutation; overthrow.
Confute, kon-fūt', *vt.* (confuting, confuted). To prove to be false; to refute.
Congé, kon'jē, *n.* Leave to depart; leave-taking; a bow. Also the form **Congee** (kon'-jē), and sometimes as a verb: to take leave; to make a bow (congeeing, congeed).
Congeal, kon-jēl', *vt.* To freeze; to coagulate.—*vi.* To pass from a fluid to a solid state.
Congelation, kon-jēl-ā'shon, *n.* Act or process of congealing; mass congealed.
Congener, kon'je-nėr, *n.* One of the same origin or kind.
Congenial, kon-jē'ni-al, *a.* Of like taste or disposition; kindly; adapted.
Congeniality, kon-jē'ni-al"i-ti, *n.* Natural affinity; suitableness.
Congenital, kon-jen'it-al, *a.* Pertaining to an individual from his birth.
Conger, kong'gėr, *n.* The sea-eel.
Congeries, kon-jē'ri-ēz, *n.* A heap or pile; a collection of several bodies in one mass.
Congest, kon-jest', *vt.* and *i.* To accumulate to excess, as blood, population, &c.
Congestion, kon-jest'shon, *n.* Excessive accumulation; undue fullness of blood-vessels in an organ.
Conglobate, kon-glōb'āt, *a.* Formed into a globe.—*vt.* To form into a ball.
Conglobation, kon-glōb-ā'shon, *n.* Act of forming into a ball; a round body.
Conglomerate, kon-glom'ėr-āt, *a.* Gathered into a ball; composed of fragments of rock cemented together.—*n.* A rock composed of pebbles cemented together.—*vt.* To gather into a ball or round mass.
Conglomeration, kon-glom'ėr-ā"shon, *n.* Act of conglomerating; state of being conglomerated; a mixed mass.
Conglutinate, kon-glū'tin-āt, *vt.* To glue together; to heal by uniting.
Conglutination, kon-glū'tin-ā"shon, *n.* Act of conglutinating; union.
Conglutinative, kon-glū'tin-āt-iv, *a.* Having the power of conglutinating.
Congratulate, kon-grat'ū-lāt, *vt.* (congratulating, congratulated). To express sympathy to in good fortune; to felicitate.
Congratulation, kon-grat'ū-lā"shon, *n.* Act of congratulating; expression of sympathetic joy at another's good fortune.
Congratulator, kon-grat'ū-lāt-ėr, *n.* One who offers congratulations.
Congratulatory, kon-grat'ū-lā-to-ri, *a.* Expressing congratulation.

Congregate, kong'grē-gāt, *vt.* (congregating, congregated). To collect together.—*vi.* To come together; to assemble.
Congregation, kong-grē-gā'shon, *n.* Act of congregating; an assembly; an assembly met for divine worship.
Congregational, kong-grē-gā'shon-al, *a.* Pertaining to a congregation, or to the Congregationalists.
Congregationalist, kong-grē-gā'shon-al-ist, *n.* One who adheres to the system in which each separate congregation or church forms an independent body.
Congress, kong'gres, *n.* An assembly; a meeting of ambassadors, &c., for the settlement of affairs between different nations; the legislature of the United States.
Congressional, kon-gre'shon-al, *a.* Pertaining to a congress.
Congreve, kong'grēv, *n.* A kind of lucifer match.—**Congreve rocket,** an iron rocket for use in war.
Congruence, Congruency, kong'grụ-ens, kong'grụ-en-si, *n.* Accordance; consistency.
Congruent, kong'grụ-ent, *a.* Suitable; agreeing; correspondent.
Congruity, kon-grụ'i-ti, *n.* Suitableness; accordance; consistency.
Congruous, kong'grụ-us, *a.* Accordant; suitable; consistent.
Conic, Conical, kon'ik, kon'ik-al, *a.* Having the form of a cone; pertaining to a cone.
Conically, kon'ik-al-li, *adv.* In the form of a cone.
Conics, kon'iks, *n.* That part of geometry which treats of the cone.
Coniferous, kōn-if'ėr-us, *a.* Bearing cones, as the pine, fir, &c.
Conirostral, kōn-i-ros'tral, *a.* Having a thick conical beak, as crows and finches.
Conjecturable, kon-jek'tūr-a-bl, *a.* That may be conjectured or guessed.
Conjectural, kon-jek'tūr-al, *a.* Depending on conjecture.
Conjecture, kon-jek'tūr, *n.* Supposition; opinion without proof; surmise.—*vt.* (conjecturing, conjectured). To judge by guess; to surmise.—*vi.* To form conjectures.
Conjoin, kon-join', *vt.* To join together; to unite; to associate.
Conjoint, kon-joint', *a.* United; connected; associated.
Conjointly, kon-joint'li, *adv.* Jointly.
Conjugal, kon'jū-gal, *a.* Pertaining to marriage; connubial.
Conjugally, kon'jū-gal-li, *adv.* Matrimonially; connubially.
Conjugate, kon'jū-gāt, *vt.* (conjugating, conjugated). To join together; to inflect (a verb) through its several forms.—*a.* Joined in pairs; kindred in origin and meaning.
Conjugation, kon-jū-gā'shon, *n.* The act of conjugating; the inflection of verbs; a class of verbs similarly conjugated.
Conjunct, kon-jungkt', *a.* Conjoined; concurrent.
Conjunction, kon-jungk'shon, *n.* Act of joining; state of being joined; connection; a connecting word.
Conjunctive, kon-jungk'tiv, *a.* Serving to unite; subjunctive.
Conjuncture, kon-jungk'tūr, *n.* A combination of important events; a crisis.
Conjuration, kon-jū-rā'shon, *n.* The act of conjuring; an incantation; a spell.
Conjure, kon-jūr', *vt.* (conjuring, conjured). To call upon solemnly; to beseech.
Conjure, kun'jėr, *vt.* (conjuring, conjured). To summon up by enchantments.—*vi.* To practise the arts of a conjurer.
Conjurer, Conjuror, kun'jėr-ėr, *n.* An enchanter; one who practises legerdemain.
Connate, kon'nāt, *a.* Born with another; being of the same birth; united in origin.
Connatural, kon-na'tūr-al, *a.* Connected by nature; innate; congenital.
Connect, kon-nekt', *vt.* To conjoin; to combine; to associate.—*vi.* To unite or cohere together; to have a close relation.
Connectedly, kon-nekt'ed-li, *adv.* In a connected manner.
Connection, Connexion, kon-nek'shon, *n.* Act of connecting; state of being connected; a relation by blood or marriage; relationship.
Connective, kon-nekt'iv, *a.* Having the power of connecting; tending to connect.—*n.* A word that connects other words and sentences; a conjunction.
Connector, kon-nekt'ėr, *n.* One who or that which connects.
Connivance, kon-nīv'ans, *n.* Voluntary blindness to an act; pretended ignorance.
Connive, kon-nīv', *vi.* (conniving, connived). To wink; to pretend ignorance or blindness; to forbear to see (with *at*).
Conniver, kon-nīv'ėr, *n.* One who connives.
Connoisseur, kon'i-sūr, *n.* A judge of any art, particularly painting and sculpture.
Connotation, kon-ō-tā'shon, *n.* That which constitutes the meaning of a word.
Connote, kon-nōt', *vt.* (connoting, connoted). To include in the meaning; to imply.
Connubial, kon-nū'bi-al, *a.* Pertaining to marriage; conjugal; matrimonial.
Conoid, kōn'oid, *n.* A body resembling a cone.—*a.* Resembling a cone. Also *conoidal.*
Conquer, kong'kėr, *vt.* To gain by force; to vanquish; to subjugate; to surmount.—*vi.* To overcome; to gain the victory.
Conquerable, kong'kėr-a-bl, *a.* That may be conquered or subdued.
Conqueror, kong'kėr-ėr, *n.* A victor.
Conquest, kong'kwest, *n.* Act of conquering; that which is conquered; a gaining by struggle.
Consanguineous, kon-san-gwin'ē-us, *a.* Of the same blood; related by birth.
Consanguinity, kon-san-gwin'i-ti, *n.* Relationship by blood.
Conscience, kon'shens, *n.* Internal knowledge or judgment of right and wrong; the moral sense; morality.
Conscientious, kon-shi-en'shus, *a.* Regulated by conscience; crupulous.
Conscientiously, kon-shi-en'shus-li, *adv.* In a conscientious manner.
Conscionable, kon'shon-a-bl, *a.* Reasonable.
Conscious, kon'shus, *a.* Knowing in one's own mind; knowing by sensation or perception; aware; sensible; self-conscious.
Consciously, kon'shus-li, *adv.* In a conscious manner.
Consciousness, kon'shus-nes, *n.* State of being conscious; perception of what passes in one's own mind; sense of guilt or innocence.
Conscript, kon'skript, *a.* Registered; en-

rolled.—*n.* One compulsorily enrolled to serve in the army or navy.

Conscription, kon-skrip′shon, *n.* A compulsory enrolment for military or naval service.

Consecrate, kon′sē-krāt, *vt.* (consecrating, consecrated). To appropriate to sacred uses; to dedicate to God.—*a.* Sacred; consecrated.

Consecration, kon-sē-krā′shon, *n.* Act of consecrating; ordination of a bishop.

Consecutive, kon-sek′ū-tiv, *a.* Following in regular order; following logically.

Consecutively, kon-sek′ū-tiv-li, *adv.* In a consecutive manner.

Consent, kon-sent′, *n.* Agreement to what is proposed; concurrence; compliance.—*vi.* To be of the same mind; to assent; to comply.

Consentient, kon-sen′shi-ent, *a.* Consenting; agreeing; accordant.

Consequence, kon′sē-kwens, *n.* That which follows as a result; inference; importance.

Consequent, kon′sē-kwent, *a.* Following, as the natural effect, or by inference.—*n.* Effect; result; inference.

Consequential, kon-sē-kwen′shal, *a.* Following as the effect; pompous.

Consequentially, kon-sē-kwen′shal-li, *adv.* By consequence; pompously.

Consequently, kon′sē-kwent-li, *adv.* By consequence; therefore.

Conservancy, kon-sėrv′an-si, *n.* Conservation; preservation; official supervision.

Conservation, kon-sėrv-ā′shon, *n.* Preservation; the keeping of a thing entire.

Conservatism, kon-sėrv′at-izm, *n.* The political principles of Conservatives.

Conservative, kon-sėrv′at-iv, *a.* Preservative; adhering to existing institutions.—*n.* One opposed to political changes of a radical nature; a Tory.

Conservatoire, kong-sėr-vä-twär, *n.* A public establishment for the study of music.

Conservator, kon′sėrv-āt-ėr, *n.* A preserver; a custodian; a guardian.

Conservatory, kon-sėrv′a-to-ri, *n.* A greenhouse for exotics.

Conserve, kon-sėrv′, *vt.* (conserving, conserved). To keep in a sound state; to candy or pickle.—*n.* kon′sėrv. That which is conserved, particularly fruits.

Consider, kon-si′dėr, *vt.* To fix the mind on; to ponder; to have respect to; to regard to be.—*vi.* To think seriously; to ponder.

Considerable, kon-si′dėr-a-bl, *a.* Worthy of consideration; moderately large.

Considerably, kon-si′dėr-a-bli, *adv.* In a considerable degree.

Considerate, kon-si′dėr-āt, *a.* Given to consideration; mindful of others; deliberate.

Considerately, kon-si′dėr-āt-li, *adv.* In a considerate manner.

Consideration, kon-si′dėr-ā″shon, *n.* Mental view; serious deliberation; importance; motive of action; an equivalent.

Considering, kon-si′dėr-ing, *prep.* Taking into account; making allowance for.

Consign, kon-sīn′, *vt.* To deliver over to another by agreement; to intrust; to commit; to deposit.

Consignee, kon-sīn-ē′, *n.* The person to whom goods are consigned.

Consignment, kon-sīn′ment, *n.* Act of consigning; the thing consigned.

Consignor, kon-sī′nor, *n.* The person who consigns.

Consist, kon-sist′, *vi.* To be in a fixed state; to be comprised; to be made up; to be compatible; to agree.

Consistence, Consistency, kon-sis′tens, kon-sis′ten-si, *n.* A degree of density; firmness or coherence; harmony; agreement.

Consistent, kon-sis′tent, *a.* Fixed; firm; not contradictory; compatible.

Consistently, kon-sis′tent-li, *adv.* In a consistent manner.

Consistorial, kon-sis-tō′ri-al, *a.* Pertaining or relating to a consistory.

Consistory, kon′sis-to-ri, *n.* A spiritual court; the court of a diocesan bishop; college of cardinals.

Consociation, kon-sō′shi-ā″shon, *n.* Association; alliance; fellowship.

Consolable, kon-sōl′a-bl, *a.* That may be consoled or comforted.

Consolation, kon-sōl-ā′shon, *n.* A solace; alleviation of misery; what helps to cheer; what gives comfort.

Consolatory, kon-sol′a-to-ri, *a.* Tending to give solace; assuaging grief.

Console, kon-sōl′, *vt.* (consoling, consoled). To comfort; to soothe; to cheer.

Console, kon′sōl, *n.* A bracket to support a cornice, vase, &c.

Consolidate, kon-sol′id-āt, *vt.* (consolidating, consolidated). To make solid or firm; to unite into one; to compact.—*vi.* To grow firm and solid.

Consolidation, kon-sol′id-ā″shon, *n.* Act of consolidating; state of being consolidated.

Consols, kon′solz, *n.pl.* A portion of the public debt of Great Britain.

Consonance, kon′sō-nans, *n.* Concord; agreement; consistency.

Consonant, kon′sō-nant, *a.* Having agreement; accordant; consistent.—*n.* A letter always sounded with a vowel.

Consonantal, kon-sō-nant′al, *a.* Partaking of the nature of a consonant.

Consort, kon′sort, *n.* A partner; a wife or husband; a companion.—*vi.* kon-sort′. To associate; to accord.

Conspectus, kon-spek′tus, *n.* A comprehensive view of a subject; abstract or sketch.

Conspicuous, kon-spik′ū-us, *a.* Standing clearly in view; manifest; distinguished.

Conspicuously, kon-spik′ū-us-li, *adv.* In a conspicuous manner.

Conspiracy, kon-spi′ra-si, *n.* A plot; a treasonable combination.

Conspirator, kon-spi′rāt-ėr, *n.* One who engages in a plot or conspiracy.

Conspire, kon-spīr′, *vi.* (conspiring, conspired). To plot; to combine for some evil purpose; to tend to one end.

Constable, kun′sta-bl, *n.* An officer of the peace; a policeman.

Constabulary, kon-stab′ū-la-ri, *a.* Pertaining to constables.—*n.* The body of constables in a city, county, &c.

Constancy, kon′stan-si, *n.* Uniformity; steadfastness; lasting affection.

Constant, kon′stant, *a.* Steadfast; perpetual; assiduous; resolute.—*n.* That which remains unchanged; a fixed quantity.

Constantly, kon′stant-li, *adv.* In a constant manner.

Constellation, kon-stel-lā'shon, *n.* A group of fixed stars; an assemblage of splendours or excellences.
Consternation, kon-stėr-nā'shon, *n.* Prostration of the mind by terror, dismay, &c.
Constipate, kon'sti-pāt, *vt.* (constipating, constipated). To make costive.
Constipation, kon-sti-pā'shon, *n.* Costiveness.
Constituency, kon-stit'ū-en-si, *n.* The body of constituents.
Constituent, kon-stit'ū-ent, *a.* Forming; existing as an essential part.—*n.* An elector; an essential part.
Constitute, kon'sti-tūt, *vt.* (constituting, constituted). To set up or establish; to compose; to appoint; to make and empower.
Constitution, kon-sti-tū'shon, *n.* The particular frame or character of the body or mind; established form of government; a system of fundamental laws; a particular law.
Constitutional, kon-sti-tū'shon-al, *a.* Adherent in the human constitution; consistent with the civil constitution; legal.—*n.* A walk for the sake of health.
Constitutionalism, kon-sti-tū'shon-al-izm, *n.* The theory of constitutional rule; adherence to a constitution.
Constitutionalist, Constitutionist, kon-sti-tū'shon-al-ist, kon-sti-tū'shon-ist, *n.* An adherent to the constitution.
Constitutionally, kon-sti-tū'shon-al-li, *adv.* In consistency with the constitution.
Constitutive, kon'sti-tūt-iv, *a.* That constitutes; having power to enact, establish, &c.
Constrain, kon-strān', *vt.* To urge by force; to necessitate; to restrain.
Constrainable, kon-strān'a-bl, *a.* That may be constrained.
Constrained, kon-strānd', *a.* With a certain constraint or want of freedom; forced.
Constraint, kon-strānt', *n.* Necessity; reserve; restraint.
Constrict, kon-strikt', *vt.* To draw together; to contract.
Constriction, kon-strik'shon, *n.* Contraction.
Constrictive, kon-strik'tiv, *a.* Tending to contract or compress.
Constrictor, kon-strik'tėr, *n.* That which constricts; a muscle that closes an orifice; a serpent which crushes its prey.
Construct, kon-strukt', *vt.* To build; to frame with contrivance; to devise.
Construction, kon-struk'shon, *n.* Structure; arrangement of words in a sentence; sense; interpretation.
Constructional, kon-struk'shon-al, *a.* Pertaining to construction.
Constructive, kon-strukt'iv, *a.* Having ability to construct; created or deduced by construction; inferred.
Constructively, kon-strukt'iv-li, *adv.* In a constructive manner; by fair inference.
Construe, kon'strū, *vt.* (construing, construed). To arrange words so as to discover the sense of a sentence; to interpret.
Consubstantial, kon-sub-stan'shal, *a.* Having the same substance; co-essential.
Consubstantiality, kon-sub-stan'shi-al"i-ti, *n.* Participation of the same nature.
Consubstantiation, kon-sub-stan'shi-ā"shon, *n.* The doctrine of the presence of the body and blood of Christ in the sacramental elements.
Consuetude, kon'swē-tūd, *n.* Custom.
Consul, kon'sul, *n.* One of the two chief magistrates of ancient Rome; a person appointed by government to reside in a foreign country, and protect the commercial interests of his own country.
Consular, kon'sūl-ėr, *a.* Pertaining to a consul.
Consulate, kon'sūl-āt, *n.* The office, jurisdiction, or residence of a consul.
Consulship, kon'sul-ship, *n.* The office of a consul, or the term of his office.
Consult, kon-sult', *vi.* To seek the opinion of another; to deliberate in common; to consider.—*vt.* To ask advice of; to refer to for information; to have regard to.
Consultation, kon-sult-ā'shon, *n.* Act of consulting; a meeting for deliberation.
Consulter, kon-sult'ėr, *n.* One who consults.
Consulting, kon-sult'ing, *a.* Giving advice; used for consultations.
Consumable, kon-sūm'a-bl, *a.* That may be consumed.
Consume, kon-sūm', *vt.* (consuming, consumed). To reduce to nothing; to burn up; to squander.—*vi.* To waste away slowly; to be exhausted.
Consumer, kon-sūm'ėr, *n.* One who consumes.
Consummate, kon'sum-āt, *vt.* To finish; to perfect.—*a.* kon-sum'āt. Complete; perfect.
Consummately, kon-sum'āt-li, *adv.* Completely; perfectly.
Consummation, kon-sum-ā'shon, *n.* Act of consummating; end; perfection.
Consumption, kon-sum'shon, *n.* Act of consuming; quantity consumed; a gradual wasting away of the body; phthisis.
Consumptive, kon-sum'tiv, *a.* Affected with or inclined to consumption or phthisis.
Contact, kon'takt, *n.* A touching together; close union or juncture of bodies.
Contagion, kon-tā'jon, *n.* Communication of a disease by contact; poisonous emanation; infection.
Contagious, kon-tā'jus, *a.* Caught or communicated by contact; infectious.
Contagiously, kon-tā'jus-li, *adv.* In a contagious manner; by contagion.
Contain, kon-tān', *vt.* To hold; to be able to hold; to comprise; to restrain.
Containable, kon-tān'a-bl, *a.* That may be contained or comprised.
Container, kon-tā'nėr, *n.* That which contains.
Contaminate, kon-tam'in-āt, *vt.* To corrupt; to taint; to vitiate.
Contamination, kon-tam'in-ā"shon, *n.* Pollution; defilement; taint.
Contango, kon-tang'gō, *n.* A sum of money paid to a seller of stock for accommodating a buyer by putting off the time of payment.
Contemn, kon-tem', *vt.* To despise; to scorn.
Contemner, kon-tem'ėr, *n.* One who contemns; a despiser; a scorner.
Contemplate, kon'tem-plāt, *vt.* To view with continued attention; to meditate on; to design; to purpose.—*vi.* To study; to meditate.
Contemplation, kon-tem-plā'shon, *n.* Act of contemplating; meditation.
Contemplative, kon-tem'plāt-iv, *a.* Given to contemplation; thoughtful.
Contemporaneous, kon-tem'pō-rā"nē-us, *a.* Living or being at the same time.

Contemporaneously, kon-tem'pō-rā"nē-us-li, *adv.* At the same time.
Contemporary, kon-tem'pō-ra-ri, *a.* Living or occurring at the same time.—*n.* One who lives at the same time with another.
Contempt, kon-temt', *n.* Act of contemning; scorn; disregard; disobedience to the rules, &c., of a court.
Contemptible, kon-tem'ti-bl, *a.* Worthy of contempt; despicable; vile; mean.
Contemptibly, kon-tem'ti-bli, *adv.* In a contemptible manner; meanly.
Contemptuous, kon-tem'tū-us, *a.* Manifesting contempt; scornful; insolent.
Contemptuously, kon-tem'tū-us-li, *adv.* In a contemptuous manner.
Contend, kon-tend', *vi.* To strive; to vie; to dispute; to wrangle.
Contender, kon-tend'ėr, *n.* One who contends.
Content, kon-tent', *a.* Easy in mind; satisfied.—*vt.* To satisfy the mind of; to please or gratify.—*n.* State of being contented; contentment. Kon-tent' or kon'tent, things contained in a vessel, book, &c.: in these senses *pl.*; capacity; space occupied: in these senses *sing.*
Contented, kon-tent'ed, *a.* Satisfied; easy in mind.
Contentedly, kon-tent'ed-li, *adv.* In a contented manner.
Contention, kon-ten'shon, *n.* Struggle; quarrel; debate; emulation.
Contentious, kon-ten'shus, *a.* Quarrelsome.
Contentment, kon-tent'ment, *n.* State of being contented; satisfaction; content.
Conterminous, Conterminal, kon-tėr'min-us, kon-tėr'min-al, *a.* Having the same bounds; contiguous.
Contest, kon-test', *vt.* To call in question; to strive for.—*vi.* To strive; to contend; to emulate.—*n.* kon'test. Struggle for victory; encounter; debate; competition.
Contestable, kon-test'a-bl, *a.* That may be contested; disputable; controvertible.
Context, kon'tekst, *n.* The parts which precede or follow a passage quoted.
Contexture, kon-teks'tūr, *n.* The interweaving of several parts into one body; disposition of parts; texture.
Contiguity, kon-ti-gū'i-ti, *n.* State of being contiguous; proximity.
Contiguous, kon-tig'ū-us, *a.* Touching one another; in contact; adjacent.
Contiguously, kon-tig'ū-us-li, *adv.* In a contiguous manner or position.
Continence, Continency, kon'ti-nens, kon'ti-nen-si, *n.* Restraint of the desires and passions; chastity; temperance.
Continent, kon'ti-nent, *a.* Chaste; moderate.—*n.* A connected tract of land of great extent; the mainland of Europe.
Continental, kon-ti-nent'al, *a.* Pertaining to a continent, particularly Europe.
Continently, kon'ti-nent-li, *adv.* In a continent manner; chastely.
Contingence, Contingency, kon-tin'jens, kon-tin'jen-si, *n.* Quality of being contingent; an event which may occur; chance; juncture.
Contingent, kon-tin'jent, *a.* Happening by chance; incidental; dependent upon an uncertainty.—*n.* A contingency; a quota; a quota of troops for a joint enterprise.
Contingently, kon-tin'jent-li, *adv.* Accidentally; dependently.
Continual, kon-tin'ū-al, *a.* Not intermitting; uninterrupted; often repeated.
Continually, kon-tin'ū-al-li, *adv.* Constantly; always.
Continuance, kon-tin'ū-ans, *n.* Permanence in one state; duration.
Continuation, kon-tin'ū-ā"shon, *n.* Succession; extension; prolongation.
Continuator, kon-tin'ū-āt-ėr, *n.* One who continues anything begun by another.
Continue, kon-tin'ū, *vi.* (continuing, continued). To remain in a state or place; to be durable; to persevere; to be steadfast.—*vt.* To prolong; to extend; to persevere in.
Continuity, kon-ti-nū'i-ti, *n.* Close union of parts; unbroken texture; cohesion.
Continuous, kon-tin'ū-us, *a.* Joined together closely; conjoined; continued.
Continuously, kon-tin'ū-us-li, *adv.* Without interruption.
Contort, kon-tort', *vt.* To twist; to writhe; to draw or pull awry.
Contortion, kon-tor'shon, *n.* A twisting.
Contortionist, kon-tor'shon-ist, *n.* An acrobat who practises contortions of the body.
Contour, kon-tör', *n.* The line that bounds a body; outline.
Contour-map, kon-tör' map, *n.* A map showing elevations above sea-level by curves (*contour lines*) drawn through places of equal elevation.
Contraband, kon'tra-band, *n.* Illegal traffic; smuggling.—*a.* Prohibited.
Contrabandist, kon'tra-band-ist, *n.* One who deals in contraband goods; a smuggler.
Contract, kon-trakt', *vt.* To draw together; to cause to shrink; to reduce; to betroth; to bring on; to incur.—*vi.* To shrink up; to make a mutual agreement.—*n.* kon'trakt. Agreement; bond; the writing which contains stipulations; betrothment.
Contracted, kon-trakt'ed, *a.* Limited; narrow; mean.
Contractedly, kon-trakt'ed-li, *adv.* In a contracted manner.
Contractibility, kon-trakt'i-bil"i-ti, *n.* Capability of being contracted.
Contractible, kon-trakt'i-bl, *a.* Capable of contraction.
Contractile, kon-trakt'īl, *a.* Having the power of contracting, as living fibres.
Contraction, kon-trak'shon, *n.* Shrinking; shortening; abbreviation.
Contractor, kon-trakt'ėr, *n.* One who contracts to perform any work or service, or to furnish supplies, at a certain price or rate.
Contradict, kon-tra-dikt', *vt.* To assert to be the contrary; to deny; to oppose.
Contradiction, kon-tra-dik'shon, *n.* A contrary assertion; inconsistency with itself.
Contradictorily, kon-tra-dik'to-ri-li, *adv.* In a contradictory manner.
Contradictory, kon-tra-dik'to-ri, *a.* Implying contradiction; inconsistent.
Contradistinction, kon'tra-dis-tingk"shon, *n.* Distinction by opposites.
Contradistinctive, kon'tra-dis-tingkt"iv, *a.* Distinguishing by contrast.
Contradistinguish, kon'tra-dis-ting"gwish, *vt.* To distinguish by opposite qualities.

Contralto, kon-tral'tō, *n.* The lowest voice of a woman or boy.
Contraposition, kon'tra-pō-zi'shon, *n.* A placing over against; opposite position.
Contrapuntal, kon-tra-punt'al, *a.* Pertaining to counterpoint.
Contrapuntist, kon-tra-punt'ist, *n.* One skilled in counterpoint.
Contrariety, kon-tra-rī'e-ti, *n.* Opposition; repugnance; inconsistency.
Contrarily, kon'tra-ri-li, *adv.* In a contrary manner; on the other hand.
Contrariwise, kon'tra-ri-wīz, *adv.* On the contrary; on the other hand.
Contrary, kon'tra-ri, *a.* Opposite; repugnant; inconsistent.—*adv.* In an opposite manner; in opposition.—*n.* A thing that is contrary.
Contrast, kon-trast', *vt.* To set in opposition; to show the difference or heighten the effect.—*vi.* To stand in contrast to.—*n.* kon'trast. Opposition or comparison of things; a person or thing strikingly different.
Contravallation, kon'tra-val-lā''shon, *n.* A chain of redoubts raised by besiegers.
Contravene, kon-tra-vēn', *vt.* (contravening, contravened). To oppose; to transgress.
Contravention, kon-tra-ven'shon, *n.* Transgression; violation.
Contretemps, kong-tr-tong, *n.* An unexpected and untoward accident.
Contribute, kon-trib'ūt, *vt.* (contributing, contributed). To give in common with others.—*vi.* To give a part; to conduce.
Contribution, kon-tri-bū'shon, *n.* Act of contributing; that which is contributed; an article sent to a periodical, &c.
Contributive, kon-trib'ūt-iv, *a.* Tending to contribute; lending aid to promote.
Contributor, kon-trib'ūt-ėr, *n.* One who contributes; a writer to a periodical.
Contributory, kon-trib'ū-to-ri, *a.* Contributing to the same end.
Contrite, kon'trīt, *a.* Broken-hearted for sin; penitent.
Contrition, kon-tri'shon, *n.* Grief of heart for sin.
Contrivable, kon-trīv'a-bl, *a.* That may be contrived, invented, or devised.
Contrivance, kon-trīv'ans, *n.* Scheme; invention; artifice.
Contrive, kon-trīv', *vt.* (contriving, contrived). To invent; to devise.—*vi.* To form or design.
Contriver, kon-trīv'ėr, *n.* Inventor; schemer.
Control, kon-trōl', *n.* Restraint; superintendence; authority.—*vt.* (controlling, controlled). To restrain; to regulate.
Controllable, kon-trōl'a-bl, *a.* That may be controlled; subject to command.
Controller, kon-trōl'ėr, *n.* An officer who checks the accounts of collectors of public moneys.
Controlment, kon-trōl'ment, *n.* Power or act of controlling; control; restraint.
Controversial, kon-trō-vėr'shal, *a.* Relating to controversy.
Controversialist, kon-trō-vėr'shal-ist, *n.* One who carries on a controversy.
Controversy, kon'trō-vėr-si, *n.* A disputation, particularly in writing; litigation.
Controvert, kon'trō-vėrt, *vt.* To dispute by reasoning; to attempt to disprove or confute.
Controvertible, kon-trō-vėrt'i-bl, *a.* That may be controverted.
Controvertibly, kon-trō-vėrt'i-bli, *adv.* In a controvertible manner.
Contumacious, kon-tū-mā'shus, *a.* Opposing rightful authority; obstinate.
Contumaciously, kon-tū-mā'shus-li, *adv.* Obstinately; stubbornly.
Contumacy, kon'tū-mā-si, *n.* Resistance to authority; perverseness.
Contumelious, kon-tū-mē'li-us, *a.* Contemptuous; insolent; proudly rude.
Contumely, kon'tū-me-li, *n.* Haughty insolence; contemptuous language.
Contuse, kon-tūz', *vt.* (contusing, contused). To bruise; to injure without breaking the skin or substance.
Contusion, kon-tū'zhon, *n.* A severe bruise; injury without breaking of the skin.
Conundrum, kō-nun'drum, *n.* A sort of riddle turning on some odd resemblance between things quite unlike.
Convalesce, kon-va-les', *vi.* (convalescing, convalesced). To recover health.
Convalescence, kon-va-les'ens, *n.* The state of one convalescent; gradual recovery after illness.
Convalescent, kon-va-les'ent, *a.* Recovering health after sickness.—*n.* One recovering from sickness.
Convenable, kon-vēn'a-bl, *a.* That may be convened or assembled.
Convene, kon-vēn', *vi.* (convening, convened). To assemble.—*vt.* To cause to assemble; to convoke.
Convener, kon-vēn'ėr, *n.* One who calls an assembly together.
Convenience, Conveniency, kon-vē'ni-ens, kon-vē'ni-en-si, *n.* Ease; comfort; suitable opportunity; an appliance or utensil.
Convenient, kon-vē'ni-ent, *a.* Suitable; adapted; opportune.
Conveniently, kon-vē'ni-ent-li, *adv.* Suitably; with ease.
Convent, kon'vent, *n.* A body of monks or nuns; a monastery; a nunnery.
Conventicle, kon-ven'ti-kl, *n.* A secret meeting; a meeting of religious dissenters; their meeting-place.
Convention, kon-ven'shon, *n.* An assembly; an agreement; recognized social custom.
Conventional, kon-ven'shon-al, *a.* Formed by agreement; tacitly understood; resting on mere usage.
Conventionalism, kon-ven'shon-al-izm, *n.* Arbitrary custom; a conventional phrase, ceremony, &c.
Conventionally, kon-ven'shon-al-li, *adv.* In a conventional manner.
Conventual, kon-ven'tū-al, *a.* Belonging to a convent.—*n.* A monk or nun.
Converge, kon-vėrj', *vi.* (converging, converged). To tend to the same point; to approach in position or character.
Convergence, Convergency, kon-vėrj'ens, kon-vėrj'en-si, *n.* Tendency to one point.
Convergent, kon-vėrj'ent, *a.* Tending to one point or object; approaching.
Conversable, kon-vėrs'a-bl, *a.* Disposed to converse; communicative; sociable.
Conversably, kon-vėrs'a-bli, *adv.* In a conversable manner.
Conversant, kon'vėrs-ant, *a.* Having inter-

course or familiarity; versed in; proficient; occupied or concerned.
Conversation, kon-vėr-sā'shon, *n.* Familiar intercourse; easy talk.
Conversational, kon-vėr-sā'shon-al, *a.* Pertaining to conversation.
Conversationalist, Conversationist, kon-vėr-sā'shon-al-ist, kon-vėr-sā'shon-ist, *n.* One who excels in conversation.
Conversazione, kon-vėr-sat'si-ō"nā, *n.* A social meeting for promoting literary, scientific, or artistic matters.
Converse, kon-vėrs', *vi.* (conversing, conversed). To hold intercourse; to talk familiarly; to commune.—*n.* kon'vėrs. Conversation; familiarity; something forming a counterpart.—*a.* Put the opposite or reverse way.
Conversely, kon'vėrs-li, *adv.* In a converse manner; with inversion of order.
Conversion, kon-vėr'shon, *n.* Change from one state, religion, or party to another; interchange of terms in logic.
Convert, kon-vėrt', *vt.* and *i.* To change from one state, use, religion, or party to another; to turn from a bad life to a good; to interchange conversely.—*n.* kon'vėrt. One who has changed his opinion, practice, or religion.
Convertibility, kon-vėrt'i-bil"i-ti, *n.* Condition or quality of being convertible.
Convertible, kon-vėrt'i-bl, *a.* Transformable; interchangeable.
Convertibly, kon-vėrt'i-bli, *adv.* With interchange of terms.
Convex, kon'veks, *a.* Rising on the exterior surface into a round form: opposed to *concave.*
Convexity, kon-veks'i-ti, *n.* State of being convex; roundness.
Convexly, kon'veks-li, *adv.* In a convex form.
Convey, kon-vā', *vt.* To transport; to deliver; to impart.
Conveyable, kon-vā'a-bl, *a.* That may be conveyed.
Conveyance, kon-vā'ans, *n.* Act or means of conveying; a carriage; transference; a deed which transfers property.
Conveyancer, kon-vā'ans-ėr, *n.* One who draws deeds by which property is transferred.
Conveyancing, kon-vā'ans-ing, *n.* The act or practice of drawing deeds, &c., for transferring the title to property.
Conveyer, kon-vā'ėr, *n.* One who or that which conveys.
Convict, kon-vikt', *vt.* To prove or decide to be guilty.—*n.* kon'vikt. A person found guilty; one undergoing penal servitude.
Conviction, kon-vik'shon, *n.* Act of finding a person guilty; strong belief; state of being sensible of wrong-doing.
Convince, kon-vins', *vt.* (convincing, convinced). To persuade by argument; to satisfy by evidence or proof.
Convincing, kon-vins'ing, *a.* Compelling assent; leaving no doubt.
Convincingly, kon-vins'ing-li, *adv.* In a convincing manner.
Convivial, kon-vi'vi-al, *a.* Festive; festal; jovial; social.
Conviviality, kon-vi'vi-al"i-ti, *n.* Convivial disposition; mirth at an entertainment.
Convocation, kon-vō-kā'shon, *n.* Act of convoking; an assembly, particularly of clergy or heads of a university.
Convoke, kon-vōk', *vt.* (convoking, convoked). To call together; to summon to meet.
Convolute, Convoluted, kon'vō-lūt, kon'-vō-lūt-ed, *a.* Rolled on itself; presenting convolutions.
Convolution, kon-vō-lū'shon, *n.* Act of rolling together or on itself; a winding; a spiral.
Convolve, kon-volv', *vt.* To roll together or on itself; to coil up.
Convolvulus, kon-volv'ū-lus, *n.* Bind-weed; a genus of slender twining plants.
Convoy, kon-voi', *vt.* To accompany for defence; to escort.—*n.* kon'voi. A protecting force; escort.
Convulse, kon-vuls', *vt.* (convulsing, convulsed). To contract violently, as the muscles; to affect by irregular spasms; to disturb.
Convulsion, kon-vul'shon, *n.* A violent involuntary contraction of the muscles; a violent irregular motion; disturbance.
Convulsive, kon-vuls'iv, *a.* Tending to convulse; spasmodic; agitating.
Cony, Coney, kō'ni, *n.* A rabbit; simpleton.
Coo, kö, *vi.* (cooing, cooed). To make a low sound, as doves; to act in a loving manner.
Cook, kųk, *vt.* To prepare food by fire or heat; to concoct; to tamper with.—*n.* One who prepares victuals for the table.
Cookery, kųk'ė-ri, *n.* The art of preparing victuals for the table.
Cool, köl, *a.* Moderately cold; dispassionate; self-possessed; impudent.—*n.* A moderate degree or state of cold.—*vt.* To make cool; to moderate; to calm; to render indifferent.—*vi.* To lose heat, ardour, affection, &c.
Cooler, köl'ėr, *n.* That which cools; anything which abates heat or excitement.
Cool-headed, köl'hed-ed, *a.* Having a temper not easily excited.
Coolie, kö'li, *n.* An Oriental porter.
Coolish, köl'ish, *a.* Somewhat cool.
Coolly, köl'li, *adv.* In a cool or indifferent manner; with calm assurance.
Coolness, köl'nes, *n.* Moderate degree of cold; indifference; calm assurance.
Coop, köp, *n.* A barrel or cask; a box for poultry, &c.—*vt.* To confine in a coop; to shut up in a narrow compass.
Cooper, kö'pėr, *n.* One who makes barrels.—*vt.* and *i.* To do the work of a cooper.
Cooperage, kö'pėr-āj, *n.* The work of a cooper; workshop of a cooper.
Co-operate, kō-op'ėr-āt, *vi.* To act with another; to concur in producing the same effect.
Co-operation, kō-op'ėr-ā"shon, *n.* Act of co-operating; concurrent effort or labour.
Co-operative, kō-op'ėr-āt-iv, *a.* Operating jointly to the same end.
Co-operator, kō-op'ėr-āt-ėr, *n.* One who co-operates.
Co-ordinate, kō-or'din-āt, *a.* Holding the same rank or degree.—*vt.* To arrange in due order.
Co-ordination, kō-or'din-ā"shon, *n.* State of being co-ordinate; act of co-ordinating.
Coot, köt, *n.* A black wading bird.
Copal, kō-pal', *n.* The juice of certain trees, used as a varnish.
Coparcener, kō-pär'sen-ėr, *n.* One who has an equal portion of an inheritance.
Copartner, kō-pärt'nėr, *n.* An associate.
Cope, kōp, *n.* A sacerdotal cloak; the arch of

the sky; the roof of a house; the arch over a door, &c.—*vt.* (coping, coped). To cover, as with a cope; to strive, or contend; to oppose with success (with *with*).

Copernican, kō-pėr'ni-kan, *a.* Pertaining to Copernicus, or to his astronomical system.

Copestone, kōp'stōn, *n.* Head or top stone; hence, what finishes off.

Copier, Copyist, ko'pi-ėr, ko'pi-ist, *n.* One who copies; a transcriber; an imitator.

Coping, kōp'ing, *n.* The covering course of a wall, parapet, &c.

Copious, kō'pi-us, *a.* Abundant; exuberant; diffuse.

Copiously, kō'pi-us-li, *adv.* Abundantly.

Copper, kop'ėr, *n.* A reddish coloured ductile and malleable metal; a large boiler; a copper coin.—*a.* Consisting of or resembling copper. —*vt.* To cover with sheets of copper.

Copperas, kop'ėr-as, *n.* Green vitriol or sulphate of iron.

Copperplate, kop'ėr-plāt, *n.* A plate of polished copper, on which designs are engraved; a print from a copperplate.

Coppersmith, kop'ėr-smith, *n.* One who works in copper.

Coppery, kop'ėr-i, *a.* Mixed with or made of copper; like copper in taste, smell, &c.

Coppice, Copse, kop'is, kops, *n.* A wood of small growth; a thicket.

Coprolite, kop'ro-līt, *n.* The petrified dung of extinct animals.

Coptic, kop'tik, *a.* Pertaining to the descendants of the ancient Egyptians, called *Copts.*—*n.* The language of the Copts.

Copula, kop'ū-la, *n.* The word which unites the subject and predicate of a proposition, part of *to be*; a bond; a link.

Copulate, kop'ū-lāt, *vi.* (copulating, copulated). To come together, as different sexes.

Copulation, kop-ū-lā'shon, *n.* Coition.

Copulative, kop'ū-lāt-iv, *a.* That unites.—*n.* A conjunction.

Copy, ko'pi, *n.* An imitation; a transcript; a pattern; a single example of a book, &c.; matter to be set up in type.—*vt.* (copying, copied). To imitate; to transcribe.

Copyhold, ko'pi-hōld, *n.* A tenure for which the tenant has nothing to show except the rolls made by the steward of the lord's court; land held in copyhold.

Copyholder, ko'pi-hōld-ėr, *n.* One who is possessed of land in copyhold.

Copyist, ko'pi-ist, *n.* A transcriber; imitator.

Copyright, kop'i-rit, *n.* The exclusive right to print or produce, given for a limited number of years to an author, artist, &c., or his assignee.—*a.* Relating to, or protected by copyright.—*vt.* To secure by copyright.

Coquet, kō-ket', *vi.* (coquetting, coquetted). To trifle in love; to endeavour to excite admiration from vanity.

Coquetry, kō'ket-ri, *n.* The arts of a coquette; trifling in love.

Coquette, kō-ket', *n.* A vain, trifling woman; a flirt.

Coquettish, kō-ket'ish, *a.* Practising coquetry.

Coracle, kor'a-kl, *n.* A boat made of wicker-work covered with leather or oil-cloth.

Coral, ko'ral, *n.* A hard calcareous substance found in the ocean; a piece of coral.—*a.* Made of coral; resembling coral.

Coralliferous, ko-ral-if'ėr-us, *a.* Producing or containing coral.

Coralline, ko'ral-īn, *a.* Consisting of, like, or containing coral.—*n.* A sea-weed; an orange-red colour; a coral zoophyte.

Coralloid, ko'ral-oid, *a.* Having the form of coral; branching like coral.

Corbel, kor'bel, *n.* A piece projecting from a wall as a support.—*vt.* (corbelling, corbelled). To support on corbels; to provide with corbels.

Cord, kord, *n.* A small rope; a band; a sinew; a pile of wood, 8 feet long, 4 high, and 4 broad.—*vi.* To bind with a cord.

Cordage, kord'āj, *n.* Cords collectively; the ropes used in the rigging of a ship.

Cordate, kor'dāt, *a.* Heart-shaped.

Cordelier, kord'el-ēr, *n.* A Franciscan friar.

Cordial, kor'di-al, *a.* Hearty; heartfelt; invigorating.—*n.* A medicine or beverage which increases strength; anything that gladdens or exhilarates.

Cordiality, kor-di-al'i-ti, *n.* Heartiness; sincerity.

Cordially, kor'di-al-li, *adv.* Heartily.

Cordite, kor'dīt, *n.* A smokeless explosive introduced in 1889.

Cordon, kor'don, *n.* A line of military posts; a ribbon worn across the breast by knights.

Cordovan, kor'dō-van, *n.* Spanish leather.

Corduroy, kor-dė-roi', *n.* A thick cotton stuff corded or ribbed.

Cordwain, kord'wān, *n.* Spanish leather.

Cordwainer, kord'wān-ėr, *n.* A shoemaker.

Core, kōr, *n.* The heart or inner part; the central part of fruit.

Co-respondent, kō-rē-spond'ent, *n.* A joint respondent; a man charged with adultery in a divorce case.

Corf, korf, *n.*; pl. **Corves.** A basket used in mines.

Corgi, kor'ji, *n.* A small Welsh breed of dog.

Coriander, ko-ri-an'dėr, *n.* A plant which produces aromatic seeds.

Corinthian, ko-rin'thi-an, *a.* Pertaining to Corinth; denoting an order in architecture, distinguished by fluted columns and ornamental capitals.—*n.* A gay fellow.

Cork, kork, *n.* The bark of a species of oak; the tree itself; a stopple made of cork.—*vt.* To stop with a cork.

Corked, korkt, *a.* Stopped with a cork; tasting of cork; blackened with burnt cork.

Corky, kork'i, *a.* Consisting of or like cork.

Cormorant, kor'mō-rant, *n.* A large voracious sea-bird; a glutton.

Corn, korn, *n.* Grain; the seeds of plants which grow in ears, and are made into bread; a horny excrescence on a toe or foot.—*vt.* To preserve with salt in grains; to granulate.

Corn-crake, korn'krāk, *n.* The landrail.

Cornea, kor'nē-a, *n.* The horny transparent membrane in the fore part of the eye.

Corned, kornd, *a.* Cured by salting.

Cornelian, kor-nē'li-an. Same as *Carnelian.*

Corneous, kor'nē-us, *a.* Horny; hard.

Corner, kor'nėr, *n.* A projecting extremity; angle; a secret or retired place; a nook.—*vt.* To buy up the whole stock of a commodity.

Corner-stone, kor'nėr-stōn, *n.* The stone which lies at the corner of two walls, and unites them; the principal stone.

Cornet, kor'net, *n.* A sort of trumpet;

formerly a cavalry officer, of the lowest commissioned rank, who bore the standard.
Cornice, kor'nis, *n.* A moulded projection crowning a part; uppermost moulding of a pediment, room, &c.
Cornish, korn'ish, *a.* Pertaining to Cornwall. —*n.* The language of Cornwall.
Cornucopia, kor-nū-kō'pi-a, *n.* The representation of a horn filled with fruit, flowers, and grain, a symbol of plenty and peace.
Cornuted, kor-nūt'ed, *a.* Horned.
Corny, kor'ni, *a.* Producing corn; containing corn; tasting of corn or malt.
Corolla, ko-rol'la, *n.* The inner covering of a flower.
Corollary, ko'rol-la-ri, ko-rol'a-ri, *n.* Something added to a proposition demonstrated; an inference, deduction.
Coronal, ko'rō-nal, *a.* Belonging to the crown of the head.—*n.* A crown, garland.
Coronation, ko-rō-nā'shon, *n.* Act or solemnity of crowning a sovereign.
Coroner, ko'rō-nėr, *n.* An officer who holds a court of inquiry in a case of sudden death.
Coronet, ko'rō-net, *n.* A small crown worn by peers and peeresses; an ornamental head-dress; something that surmounts.
Corporal, kor'po-ral, *n.* A non-commissioned officer ranking below a sergeant.—*a.* Belonging or relating to the body; material.
Corporally, kor'po-ral-li, *adv.* Bodily.
Corporate, kor'po-rāt, *a.* Formed into a legal body, and empowered to act in legal processes as an individual.
Corporately, kor'po-rāt-li, *adv.* In a corporate capacity.
Corporation, kor-po-rā'shon, *n.* A body corporate, empowered to act as an individual; the human body or frame.
Corporeal, kor-pō'rē-al, *a.* Having a body; material; opposed to spiritual.
Corporeally, kor-pō'rē-al-li, *adv.* In a bodily form or manner.
Corps, kōr, *n.*; pl. **Corps,** kōrz. A body of troops. *Army Corps.* Two or more divisions.
Corpse, korps, *n.* The dead body of a human being; a carcass; remains.
Corpulence, Corpulency, kor'pū-lens, kor'pū-len-si, *n.* The state of being corpulent; excessive fatness.
Corpulent, kor'pū-lent, *a.* Having a gross or fleshy body; very fat; stout; lusty.
Corpuscle, kor'pus-l, *n.* A minute particle or physical atom; a minute animal cell.
Corpuscular, kor-pus'kū-lėr, *a.* Pertaining to corpuscles.
Corral, kor-räl', *n.* A pen for cattle; an inclosure formed by wagons; a stockade for capturing elephants.
Correct, ko-rekt', *a.* Right; accurate; exact. —*vt.* To make right; to chastise; to counteract.
Correction, ko-rek'shon, *n.* Act of correcting; state of being corrected; discipline; chastisement; counteraction.
Correctional, ko-rek'shon-al, *a.* Tending or pertaining to correction.
Corrective, ko-rekt'iv, *a.* Having the power to correct; tending to rectify.—*n.* That which corrects; restriction.
Correctly, ko-rekt'li, *adv.* Exactly; accurately.
Correctness, ko-rekt'nes, *n.* Freedom from faults or errors; accuracy; exactness.
Corrector, ko-rekt'ėr, *n.* One who or that which corrects.
Correlative, kor'ē-lāt, *n.* A correlative.—*vi.* (correlating, correlated). To be reciprocally related.—*vt.* To place in reciprocal relation; to determine the relations between.
Correlation, ko-rē-lā'shon, *n.* Reciprocal relation.
Correlative, ko-rel'at-iv, *a.* Having a mutual relation, as father and son.—*n.* One who or that which stands in reciprocal relation.
Correspond, ko-rē-spond', *vi.* To answer one to another; to be congruous; to fit; to hold intercourse by letters.
Correspondence, ko-rē-spond'ens, *n.* Act or state of corresponding; fitness; congruity; intercourse by letters; the letters interchanged.
Correspondent, ko-rē-spond'ent, *a.* Corresponding; suitable; congruous.—*n.* One who has intercourse by letters.
Corresponding, ko-rē-spond'ing, *a.* Answering; agreeing; suiting.
Correspondingly, ko-rē-spond'ing-li, *adv.* In a corresponding manner.
Corridor, ko'ri-dōr, *n.* A passage in a building, or round a court.
Corrigenda, ko-ri-jen'da, *n.pl.* Things to be corrected.
Corrigible, ko'ri-ji-bl, *a.* That may be corrected or reformed; punishable.
Corrival, ko-rī'val, *n.* A competitor.
Corroborant, ko-rob'ō-rant, *a.* Strengthening.
Corroborate, ko-rob'ō-rāt, *vt.* (corroborating, corroborated). To strengthen; to confirm.
Corroboration, ko-rob'ō-rā''shon, *n.* Act of corroborating; confirmation.
Corroborative, ko-rob'ō-rāt-iv, *a.* Tending to strengthen or confirm.
Corrode, ko-rōd', *vt.* (corroding, corroded). To eat or wear away by degrees; to prey upon; to poison, blight, canker.
Corrodent, ko-rō'dent, *a.* Having the power of corroding.—*n.* A substance that corrodes.
Corrodible, ko-rōd'i-bl, *a.* That may be corroded.
Corrosion, ko-rō'zhon, *n.* Action of corroding; state of being corroded.
Corrosive, ko-rōs'iv, *a.* Having the power of corroding; vexing; blighting.—*n.* That which has the quality of corroding.
Corrugate, ko'rū-gāt, *vt.* To wrinkle; to contract into folds or furrows.
Corrugated, ko'rū-gāt-ed, *a.* Wrinkled; having prominent ridges and grooves.
Corrugation, ko-rū-gā'shon, *n.* A wrinkling; contraction into wrinkles.
Corrupt, ko-rupt', *vt.* To make putrid; to deprave; to taint; to bribe; to infect with errors.—*vi.* To become putrid or vitiated.—*a.* Tainted; depraved; infected with errors.
Corrupter, ko-rupt'ėr, *n.* One who or that which corrupts.
Corruptibility, ko-rupt'i-bil''i-ti, *n.* The possibility of being corrupted.
Corruptible, ko-rupt'i-bl, *a.* That may be corrupted; subject to decay, destruction, &c.
Corruptibly, ko-rupt'i-bli, *adv.* In such a manner as to be corrupted.
Corruption, ko-rup'shon, *n.* Act or process of corrupting; depravity; pollution; taint of blood; bribe-taking; bribery.

Corruptive, ko-rupt'iv, *a.* Having the quality of corrupting or vitiating.
Corruptly, ko-rupt'li, *adv.* In a corrupt manner; with corruption; viciously.
Corsair, kor'sār, *n.* A pirate; a piratical vessel.
Corse, kors, *n.* A corpse (a poetical word).
Corselet, Corslet, kors'let, *n.* A cuirass to cover the body.
Corset, kor'set, *n.* An article of dress laced closely round the body; stays.
Cortège, kor'tāzh, *n.* A train of attendants.
Cortes, kor'tes, *n.pl.* The legislative assembly of Spain and of Portugal.
Cortex, kor'teks, *n.* The bark of a tree; a membrane enveloping part of the body.
Cortical, kor'tik-al, *a.* Belonging to, consisting of, or resembling bark; belonging to the external covering.
Coruscant, ko-rus'kant, *a.* Flashing.
Coruscate, ko-rus'kāt, *vi.* (coruscating, coruscated). To flash intermittently; to glitter.
Coruscation, ko-rus-kā'shon, *n.* A glittering or flashing; a quick vibration of light; intellectual brilliancy.
Corvette, kor-vet', *n.* A sloop of war with only one tier of guns; a small vessel used for escort duty.
Corvine, kor'vīn, *a.* Pertaining to the crow.
Corymb, kō'rimb, *n.* A form of inflorescence in which the blossoms form a mass with a convex or level top.
Coryphæus, ko-ri-fē'us, *n.*; pl. **-æi.** The leader of the chorus; the chief of a company.
Cosh, kosh, *n.* A bludgeon; a flexible tube filled with some heavy substance for use as a weapon.
Cosmetic, koz-met'ik, *a.* Improving beauty.—*n.* An application to improve the complexion.
Cosmic, Cosmical, koz'mik, koz'mik-al, *a.* Relating to the whole frame of the universe.
Cosmic rays, koz-mik rāz', *n.pl.* Penetrating radiation of shorter wavelength than X-rays, believed to reach the earth from outer space.
Cosmogony, koz-mog'on-i, *n.* The origin, or doctrine of the origin, of the universe.
Cosmographer, koz-mog'ra-fėr, *n.* One versed in cosmography.
Cosmography, koz-mog'ra-fi, *n.* A description of the world; the science of the construction of the universe.
Cosmology, koz-mol'o-ji, *n.* The science of the world or universe; cosmogony.
Cosmopolitan, Cosmopolite, koz-mō-pol'i-tan, koz-mop'o-līt, *n.* One who is at home in every place.—*a.* Free from local prejudices; common to all the world.
Cosmopolitanism, Cosmopolitism, koz-mō-pol'i-tan-izm, koz-mop'o-līt-izm, *n.* The state of being a cosmopolitan; disregard of local prejudices, &c.
Cosmos, koz'mos, *n.* The universe; the system of order and harmony in creation.
Cost, kost, *vt.* (costing, cost). To be bought for; to require to be laid out or borne.—*n.* That which is paid for anything; expenditure; loss; (*pl.*) expenses of a lawsuit.
Costal, kos'tal, *a.* Pertaining to the ribs.
Costard, kos'tärd, *n.* A large apple.
Coster, Costermonger, kos'tėr, kos'tėr-mung-gėr, *n.* A hawker of fruit or vegetables.
Costive, kos'tiv, *a.* Having the bowels bound; constipated.
Costliness, kost'li-nes, *n.* State of being costly; expensiveness; sumptuousness.
Costly, kost'li, *a.* Of a high price; valuable, precious; dear; sumptuous.
Costmary, kost'ma-ri, *n.* A perennial fragrant plant, a native of S. Europe.
Costume, kos'tūm, *n.* An established mode of dress; garb; attire.
Costumier, kos-tū'mi-ėr, *n.* One who prepares costumes; one who deals in costumes.
Co-surety, kō-shūr'ti, *n.* A joint surety; one who is surety with another.
Cosy, kō'zi, *a.* Snug; comfortable.—*n.* Padded covering put over a teapot to keep in the heat after the tea has been infused.
Cot, kot, *n.* A small house; a hut; a small bed.
Cote, kōt, *n.* A shelter for animals (as a dove-*cote*); a sheepfold; a cottage or hut.
Coterie, kō'te-rē, *n.* A circle of familiar friends who meet for social or literary intercourse; an exclusive society; a clique.
Cothurnus, kō-thėr'nus, *n.* A buskin; a high-laced shoe, such as was worn by tragic actors; tragedy.
Cotidal, kō-tīd'al, *a.* Marking an equality of tide.
Cotillion, ko-til'yon, *n.* A brisk dance; a kind of quadrille.
Cottage, kot'tāj, *n.* A cot; a small country or suburban house.
Cottager, kot'tāj-ėr, *n.* One who lives in a cottage.
Cottar, Cotter, kot'ėr, *n.* A cottager; a farm-servant.
Cotton, kot'tn, *n.* A soft, downy substance in the pods of several plants; cloth made of cotton.—*a.* Pertaining to, or consisting of cotton.—*vi.* To agree; to become friendly.
Cotton-wood, kot'tn-wụd, *n.* A large tree of the poplar kind.
Cotton-wool, kot'tn-wụl, *n.* Cotton in the raw state.
Cottony, kot'tn-i, *a.* Soft like cotton; downy.
Cotyledon, kot-i-lē'don, *n.* The seed-leaf, or first leaf or leaves, of the embryo plant.
Couch, kouch, *vi.* To lie down; to bend down; to lie close and concealed.—*vt.* To lay down; to place upon a bed; to comprise; to express; to fix a spear in rest; to depress a cataract in the eye.—*n.* A bed; a place for rest and ease.
Couchant, kouch'ant, *a.* Lying down.
Cougar, kö'gär, *n.* A large carnivorous quadruped of the cat kind; the puma.
Cough, kof, *n.* A violent convulsive effort of the lungs to throw off offending matter.—*vi.* To make a violent effort, with noise, to expel the air from the lungs, and throw off any offensive matter.—*vt.* To expel from the lungs by a violent effort with noise; to expectorate.
Could, kụd, *pret.* of *can.* Was able.
Coulter, kōl'tėr, *n.* The blade of a plough that cuts the earth in advance of the share.
Council, koun'sil, *n.* An assembly for consultation; a body of men designated to advise a sovereign or chief magistrate; a convocation.
Council-board, koun'sil-bōrd, *n.* The table round which a council holds consultation; the council itself.
Councillor, koun'sil-ėr, *n.* A member of a council.
Counsel, koun'sel, *n.* Deliberation; consulta-

tion; advice; design; a barrister.—*vt.* (counselling, counselled). To advise; to warn.
Counsellable, koun'sel-a-bl, *a.* That may be counselled; willing to receive counsel.
Counsellor, koun'sel-ėr, *n.* A person who gives counsel; an adviser; a barrister.
Count, kount, *vt.* To enumerate; to compute; to consider; to judge.—*vi.* To reckon; to rely; to be reckoned.—*n.* Reckoning; a particular charge in an indictment; a continental title of nobility, equivalent to the English earl.
Countable, kount'a-bl, *a.* That may be numbered.
Countenance, koun'ten-ans, *n.* The human face; air; aspect; favour; encouragement.—*vt.* To favour; to encourage; to vindicate.
Counter, kount'ėr, *n.* One who or that which counts; anything used to reckon, as in games; a shop table.—*adv.* Contrary; in an opposite direction.—*a.* Adverse; opposing.
Counteract, koun-tėr-akt', *vt.* To act in opposition to; to render ineffectual.
Counteraction, koun'tėr-ak-shon, *n.* Action in opposition; hindrance.
Counteractive, koun'tėr-akt-iv, *a.* Tending to counteract.—*n.* That which counteracts.
Counterbalance, koun-tėr-bal'ans, *vt.* To weigh against with an equal weight; to act against with equal power.—*n.* Equal weight, power, or agency, acting in opposition.
Countercharm, koun'tėr-chärm, *n.* That which can oppose the effect of a charm.
Countercheck, koun-tėr-chek', *vt.* To oppose by some obstacle; to check.—*n.* Check; check that controls another check.
Counterfeit, koun'tėr-fit, *vt.* and *i.* To forge; to copy; to feign.—*a.* Made in imitation; fraudulent.—*n.* An impostor; a forgery.
Counterfeiter, koun'tėr-fit-ėr, *n.* A forger.
Counterfoil, koun'tėr-foil, *n.* A portion of a document retained as a check.
Counter-irritant, koun'tėr-i-rit-ant, *n.* An irritant employed to relieve another irritation or inflammation.
Countermand, koun-tėr-mand', *vt.* To annul or revoke a former command.—*n.* A contrary order; revocation of a former order.
Countermarch, koun'tėr-märch, *vi.* To march back.—*n.* A marching back; a returning; a change of measures.
Countermark, koun'tėr-märk, *n.* An additional mark made for greater security.—*vt.* To add a countermark to.
Countermine, koun'tėr-mīn, *n.* A mine formed to defeat the purpose of one made by an enemy; a counterplot.—*vt.* To defeat by a countermine; to frustrate by secret and opposite measures.
Countermotion, koun'tėr-mō-shon, *n.* An opposite motion.
Counterpane, koun'tėr-pān, *n.* A bed-cover.
Counterpart, koun'tėr-pärt, *n.* A corresponding part; a duplicate; a supplement.
Counterplot, koun-tėr-plot', *vi.* To oppose one plot by another.—*vt.* To plot against in order to defeat another plot; to baffle by an opposite plot.—*n.* A plot to frustrate another.
Counterpoint, koun'tėr-point, *n.* The art, in music, of adding to a given melody one or more melodies.
Counterpoise, koun'tėr-poiz, *vt.* To counterbalance.—*n.* A weight which balances another; equivalence of power or force; equilibrium.
Counterscarp, koun'tėr-skärp, *n.* The exterior slope of the ditch of a fortification.
Counterseal, koun-tėr-sēl', *vt.* To affix a seal beside another seal.
Countersign, koun-tėr-sīn', *vt.* To sign with an additional signature.—*n.* A military watchword.
Counter-signature, koun'tėr-sig-na-tūr, *n.* The name of a secretary countersigned to a writing.
Counter-tenor, koun'tėr-ten-ėr, *n.* In *music*, same as *Alto* or *Contralto*.
Countervail, koun-tėr-vāl', *vt.* To act against with equal power or effect.
Counterwork, koun-tėr-wėrk', *vt.* To work in opposition to; to counteract.
Countess, kount'es, *n.* The wife or widow of an earl or count.
Countless, kount'les, *a.* Innumerable.
Country, kun'tri, *n.* A large tract of land; a region; a kindgom or state; the inhabitants of a region; the public; rural parts.—*a.* Pertaining to the country; rural.
Country-dance, kun'tri-dans, *n.* A dance in which the partners are arranged opposite to each other in lines.
Countryman, kun'tri-man, *n.* One born in the same country with another; one who dwells in the country; a rustic.
Country-side, kun'tri-sīd, *n.* A tract of country, or the people inhabiting such.
County, koun'ti, *n.* A particular portion of a state or kingdom; a shire.—*a.* Pertaining to a county.
Coupé, kö-pā, *n.* A railway compartment seated on one side only; a closed motor car, usually a two-seater.
Couple, ku'pl, *n.* A band or leash; a pair; a brace; a man and his wife.—*vt.* and *i.* (coupling, coupled). To join together; to unite.
Couplet, kup'let, *n.* Two lines that rhyme.
Coupling, kup'ling, *n.* The act of one who couples; that which couples; a hook, chain, or other contrivance forming a connection.
Coupon, kö'pon, *n.* An interest certificate attached to a bond; one of a series of tickets which guarantee the holder to obtain a certain value or service for each at different periods.
Courage, ku'rij, *n.* Intrepidity; dauntlessness; hardihood.
Courageous, ku-rā'jē-us, *a.* Bold; brave; heroic; fearless.
Courageously, ku-rā'jē-us-li, *adv.* With courage; bravely; boldly; stoutly.
Courier, kö'rē-ėr, *n.* A messenger sent express with despatches; a travelling attendant.
Course, kōrs, *n.* A running; passage; route; career; ground run over; line of conduct; order of succession; series of lectures, &c.; range of subjects taught; a layer of stones in masonry; part of a meal served at one time.—*vt.* (coursing, coursed). To hunt; to run through or over.—*vi.* To move with speed.
Courser, kōrs'ėr, *n.* A swift horse.
Coursing, kōrs'ing, *n.* The act or sport of chasing and hunting hares with greyhounds.
Court, kōrt, *n.* An inclosed area; residence of a sovereign; the family and retinue of a sovereign; judges assembled for deciding causes; the place where judges assemble; a judicial body; attention directed to gain favour; flattery.—*vt.* To endeavour to please by civilities; to woo; to seek.

Court-day, kōrt'dā, *n.* A day in which a court sits to administer justice.
Courteous, kōrt'ē-us, *a.* Polite; complaisant; affable; respectful.
Courteously, kōrt'ē-us-li, *adv.* In a courteous manner.
Courter, kōrt'ėr, *n.* One who courts; a wooer.
Courtesan, Courtezan, kōr'te-zan, *n.* A loose woman; a prostitute.
Courtesy, kōrt'e-si, *n.* Urbanity; complaisance; act of kindness or civility.
Courthand, kōrt'hand, *n.* The old manner of writing used in records, &c.
Courthouse, kōrt'hous, *n.* A house in which established courts are held.
Courtier, kōrt'i-ėr, *n.* A man who attends courts; a person of courtly manners; one who solicits favours.
Courtliness, kōrt'li-nes, *n.* Quality of being courtly; complaisance with dignity.
Courtly, kōrt'li, *a.* Relating to a court; elegant; polite with dignity; flattering.
Court - martial, kōrt-mär'shal, *n.*; pl. **Courts-martial.** A court consisting of military or naval officers for the trial of offences of a military or naval character.
Court-plaster, kōrt'plas-tėr, *n.* Sticking plaster made of black silk.
Courtship, kōrt'ship, *n.* Act of courting a woman in view of marriage; wooing.
Courtyard, kōrt'yärd, *n.* A court or inclosure round or near a house.
Cousin, kuz'n, *n.* The son or daughter of an uncle or aunt; a kinsman.
Cove, kōv, *n.* A small inlet or bay; a sheltered recess in the sea-shore; a concave moulding; a man, fellow.—*vt.* To arch over.
Covenant, kuv'en-ant, *n.* A contract; compact; a writing containing the terms of an agreement.—*vi.* To enter into a formal agreement; to stipulate.—*vt.* To grant by covenant.
Covenanter, kuv'en-ant-ėr, *n.* One who makes a covenant; a subscriber to the Solemn League and Covenant in Scotland in 1643.
Cover, kuv'ėr, *vt.* To overspread; to cloak; to secrete; to defend; to wrap up; to brood on; to be sufficient for; to include.—*n.* Anything spread over another thing; disguise; shelter; articles laid at table for one person.
Covering, kuv'ėr-ing, *n.* Envelope; cover.
Coverlet, kuv'ėr-let, *n.* The cover of a bed.
Covert, kuv'ėrt, *a.* Kept secret; private; insidious.—*n.* A shelter; a thicket.
Covertly, kuv'ėrt-li, *adv.* Secretly; insidiously.
Coverture, kuv'ėrt-ūr, *n.* Shelter; defence; the legal state of a married woman.
Covet, kuv'et, *vt.* To long for (in a good sense); to desire unlawfully; to hanker after.—*vi.* To have inordinate desire.
Covetable, kuv'et-a-bl, *a.* That may be coveted.
Covetous, kuv'et-us, *a.* Eager to obtain; inordinately desirous; avaricious.
Covetously, kuv'et-us-li, *adv.* In a covetous manner.
Covetousness, kuv'et-us-nes, *n.* Cupidity.
Covey, kuv'i, *n.* A hatch of birds; a small flock of birds (especially partridges) together; a company.
Cow, kou, *n.* The female of the bull, or of bovine animals generally.—*vt.* To sink the spirits or courage of; to dishearten.
Coward, kou'ėrd, *n.* A person who wants courage to meet danger; a craven; a dastard.—*a.* Destitute of courage; dastardly.
Cowardice, kou'ėrd-is, *n.* Want of courage to face danger.
Cowardliness, kou'ėrd-li-nes, *n.* Cowardice.
Cowardly, kou'ėrd-li, *a.* Wanting courage to face danger; faint-hearted; mean; base.—*adv.* In the manner of a coward.
Cow-bane, kou'bān, *n.* Water-hemlock.
Cow-catcher, kou'kach-ėr, *n.* A frame in front of locomotives to remove obstructions.
Cower, kou'ėr, *vi.* To crouch; to sink by bending the knees; to shrink through fear.
Cowherd, kou'hėrd, *n.* One who tends cows.
Cowhide, kou'hīd, *n.* The hide of a cow; a leather whip.—*vt.* To flog with a leather whip.
Cowl, koul, *n.* A monk's hood; a chimney cover which turns with the wind; a vessel carried on a pole by two persons.
Cowled, kould, *a.* Hooded; in shape of a cowl.
Cow-pox, kou'poks, *n.* The vaccine disease, which appears on the teats of the cow.
Cowry, kou'ri, *n.* A small shell used for coin in parts of Africa and S. Asia.
Cowslip, kou'slip, *n.* A species of primrose.
Coxcomb, koks'kōm, *n.* The comb worn by fools in their caps; the cap itself; a fop; a vain, showy fellow.
Coxcombry, koks'kōm-ri, *n.* Foppishness.
Coxswain, kok'sn, *n.* The man who steers a boat, or who has the care of a boat and its crew.
Coy, koi, *a.* Shy; reserved; bashful.
Coyly, koi'li, *adv.* With reserve; shyly.
Coyness, koi'nes, *n.* Shyness; bashfulness.
Coz, koz, *n.* A familiar contraction of *cousin.*
Cozen, kuz'n, *vt.* To cheat; to defraud; to beguile.—*vi.* To act deceitfully.
Cozenage, kuz'n-āj, *n.* Trickery; fraud.
Cozener, kuz'n-ėr, *n.* One who cheats.
Crab, krab, *n.* A crustaceous fish with strong claws; a portable windlass, &c.; Cancer, a sign of the zodiac; a wild sour apple; a morose person.
Crabbed, krab'ed, *a.* Perverse; peevish; perplexing.
Crabbedly, krab'ed-li, *adv.* Peevishly.
Crack, krak, *n.* A chink or fissure; a sudden or sharp sound; a sounding blow; a chat.—*vt.* and *i.* To break with a sharp, abrupt sound; to break partially; to snap; to boast of; to utter with smartness; to chat.
Crack-brained, krak'brānd, *a.* Crazy.
Cracked, krakt, *a.* Having fissures but not in pieces; impaired; crazy.
Cracker, krak'ėr, *n.* One who or that which cracks; a small firework; a hard biscuit.
Crackle, krak'l, *vi.* (crackling, crackled). To make small abrupt noises rapidly repeated.
Crackling, krak'ling, *n.* The act or noise of the verb to crackle; the brown skin of roasted pork.
Cracknel, krak'nel, *n.* A hard brittle cake or biscuit.
Cradle, krā'dl, *n.* A small bed in which infants are rocked; a frame to support or hold together.—*vt.* (cradling, cradled). To lay or rock in a cradle.
Craft, kraft, *n.* Ability; skill; artifice; guile; manual art; trade; a vessel or ship.
Craftily, kraf'ti-li, *adv.* Artfully; cunningly.

Craftiness, kraf'ti-nes, *n.* Artfulness.
Craftsman, krafts'man, *n.* An artificer.
Crafty, kraf'ti, *a.* Skilful; artful.
Crag, krag, *n.* A steep rugged rock; a cliff; gravel or sand mixed with shells.
Cragged, krag'ed, *a.* Full of crags; rugged.
Craggy, krag'i, *a.* Cragged.
Crake, krāk, *n.* The corn-crake or landrail.
Cram, kram, *vt.* (cramming, crammed). To thrust in by force; to stuff; to coach for an examination.—*vi.* To stuff; to eat beyond satiety; to prepare for an examination.
Crambo, kram'bō, *n.* A game of rhymes.
Cramp, kramp, *n.* A spasmodic contraction of a limb or muscle; restraint; piece of iron bent at the ends, to hold together pieces of timber, stones, &c.—*vt.* To affect with spasms; to restrain, hinder.
Cramped, krampt, *a.* Affected with spasm; restrained.
Cran, kran, *n.* A measure of capacity for herrings, averaging about 750 herrings.
Cranberry, kran'be-ri, *n.* A wild sour berry.
Crane, krān, *n.* A migratory bird with long legs and neck; a machine for raising great weights; a crooked pipe for drawing liquor out of a cask.—*vi.* To stretch out one's neck.
Crane's-bill, krānz'bil, *n.* The geranium.
Cranial, krā'ni-al, *a.* Relating to the skull.
Craniology, krā-ni-ol'o-ji, *n.* The knowledge of the cranium or skull.
Cranium, krā'ni-um, *n.* The skull; the bones which inclose the brain.
Crank, krangk, *n.* A contrivance for producing a horizontal or perpendicular motion by means of a rotary motion, or the contrary; a bend or turn.—*a.* Liable to be overset; loose.
Cranky, krangk'i, *a.* Liable to overset; full of whims; crazy.
Crannied, kran'id, *a.* Having crannies.
Cranny, kran'ni, *n.* A narrow opening; chink.
Crape, krāp, *n.* A thin, transparent stuff of a crisp texture, much used in mourning.
Crapulence, krap'ū-lens, *n.* Drunkenness; sickness occasioned by intemperance.
Crash, krash, *vi.* To make the loud, clattering sound of many things falling and breaking at once.—*n.* The sound of things falling and breaking; a commercial collapse.
Crasis, krā'sis, *n.* The mixture of bodily constituents; temperament; constitution; the contraction of vowels into one long vowel.
Crass, kras, *a.* Gross; coarse; dense.
Crate, krāt, *n.* A basket of wicker-work, for crockery, &c.
Crater, krā'tėr, *n.* A bowl; the circular cavity or mouth of a volcano; hole in the ground caused by the explosion of a shell, bomb, or mine.
Cravat, kra-vat', *n.* A neck-cloth.
Crave, krāv, *vt.* (craving, craved). To ask earnestly or submissively; to desire strongly. —*n.* Strong desire.
Craven, krā'vn, *n.* A coward; a weak-hearted, spiritless fellow.—*a.* Cowardly.
Craver, krāv'ėr, *n.* One who craves or begs.
Craving, krāv'ing, *n.* Vehement desire; morbid demand of appetite.
Craw, kra̤, *n.* The crop or first stomach of fowls.
Crawfish, kra̤'fish, *n.* *See* CRAYFISH.
Crawl, kra̤l, *vi.* To creep; to advance slowly, slyly, or weakly.
Crawler, kra̤l'ėr, *n.* One who or that which crawls; a creeper; a reptile.
Crayfish, Crawfish, krā'fish, kra̤'fish, *n.* A crustacean found in streams; also the spiny lobster, a sea crustacean.
Crayon, krā'on, *n.* A pencil of coloured clay, chalk, or charcoal, used in drawing; a drawing made with crayons.—*vt.* To sketch.
Craze, krāz, *vt.* (crazing, crazed). To shatter; to impair the intellect of.—*vi.* To become crazy.—*n.* An inordinate desire.
Crazed, krāzd, *a.* Decrepit; crazy.
Crazy, krāz'i, *a.* Decrepit; deranged; weakened or disordered in intellect.
Creak, krēk, *vi.* To make a grating sound.—*n.* A sharp, harsh, grating sound.
Cream, krēm, *n.* That part of a liquor which collects on the surface; the richer part of milk; best part of a thing.—*vt.* To take off cream from.—*vi.* To gather cream; to mantle.
Creamery, krē'mėr-i, *n.* A place where milk is made into butter and cheese.
Creamy, krēm'i, *a.* Full of cream; like cream; luscious.
Crease, krēs, *n.* A mark made by folding; a hollow streak like a groove; lines near the wickets in cricket.—*vt.* (creasing, creased). To make a mark in by compressing or folding.
Create, krē-āt', *vt.* (creating, created). To bring into being from nothing; to cause to be; to shape; to beget; to bring about; to invest with a new character; to constitute or appoint.
Creation, krē-ā'shon, *n.* Act of creating; the aggregate of created things; the universe; conferring of a title or dignity.
Creative, krē-āt'iv, *a.* Having the power to create, or exerting the act of creation.
Creator, krē-āt'ėr, *n.* The being that creates; a producer; the Supreme Being.
Creature, krē'tūr, *n.* Something created; a human being; something imagined; a person who owes his rise to another; a mere tool.
Crèche, krāsh, *n.* A public nursery for children.
Credence, krē'dens, *n.* The act of believing; credit; trust.
Credential, krē-den'shi-al, *n.* That which gives a title to credit; (*pl.*) documents showing that one is entitled to credit, or is invested with authority.
Credibility, kred-i-bil'i-ti, *n.* State or quality of being credible.
Credible, kred'i-bl, *a.* Worthy of credit.
Credit, kred'it, *n.* Reliance on testimony; faith; reputed integrity; transfer of goods, &c., in confidence of future payment; reputation for pecuniary worth; time given for payment of goods sold on trust; side of an account in which payment is entered; money possessed or due.—*vt.* To trust; to believe; to sell or lend to, in confidence of future payment; to procure credit or honour to; to enter on the credit side of an account; to attribute.
Creditable, kred'it-a-bl, *a.* Estimable.
Creditably, kred'it-a-bli, *adv.* In a creditable manner; with credit.
Creditor, kred'it-ėr, *n.* One to whom a debt is due.
Credulity, kre-dū'li-ti, *n.* A disposition to believe on slight evidence.
Credulous, kred'ū-lus, *a.* Apt to believe without sufficient evidence; unsuspecting.

Creed, krēd, *n.* A system of principles believed or professed; a brief summary of the articles of Christian faith.
Creek, krēk, *n.* A small bay; a small harbour; a brook (American and colonial).
Creel, krēl, *n.* An osier basket or pannier.
Creep, krēp, *vi.* (creeping, crept). To move as a reptile; to crawl; to grow along the ground, or on another body; to move secretly, feebly, or timorously; to be servile; to shiver.
Creeper, krēp'ėr, *n.* A creeping plant; a small bird; a kind of grapnel for dragging.
Creepy, krēp-i, *a.* Producing horror or fear.
Cremate, krē-māt', *vt.* To burn; to dispose of (a human body) by burning.
Cremation, krē-mā'shon, *n.* The act or custom of cremating.
Cremona, krē-mō'na, *n.* A general name for violins made at Cremona in N. Italy.
Crenate, Crenated, krē'nāt, krē'nāt-ed, *a.* Notched; indented.
Crenelle, kre-nel', *n.* An embrasure in an embattled parapet to fire through.
Creole, krē'ōl, *n.* A native of the W. Indies or Spanish America, but not of indigenous blood.
Creosote, krē'ō-sōt, *n.* An antiseptic liquid obtained from wood-tar.
Crepitate, krep'i-tāt, *vi.* To crackle.
Crepitation, krep-it-ā'shon, *n.* A sharp crackling sound or rattle.
Crepuscular, krē-pus'kūl-ėr, *a.* Pertaining to twilight.
Crescent, kres'ent, *n.* The moon in her state of increase; anything resembling the shape of the new moon; the Turkish standard; buildings in the form of a crescent.
Cress, kres, *n.* The name of various plants, mostly cruciferous, used as a salad.
Cresset, kres'et, *n.* A fire-pan fixed on the top of a pole.
Crest, krest, *n.* A tuft on the head of certain birds; the plume of feathers or tuft on a helmet; the helmet itself; the top; a lofty mien; a sort of heraldic badge.—*vt.* To furnish with a crest.
Crested, krest'ed, *p.a.* Having a crest.
Crestfallen, krest'fąl-en, *a.* Dejected.
Cretaceous, krē-tā'shus, *a.* Chalky.
Cretin, krē'tin, *n.* One afflicted with cretinism.
Cretinism, krē'tin-izm, *n.* A disease resembling rickets, but accompanied with idiocy.
Cretonne, kre-ton', *n.* A cotton cloth printed with coloured patterns.
Crevice, kre'vis, *n.* A crack; cleft; cranny.
Crew, krö, *n.* A company; a gang; the company of sailors belonging to a vessel.
Crewel, krö'el, *n.* A kind of fine worsted.
Crib, krib, *n.* A child's bed; a small habitation; a rack; a stall for oxen; a framework; a literal translation.—*vt.* (cribbing, cribbed). To shut up in a narrow habitation; to pilfer.
Cribbage, krib'āj, *n.* A game at cards.
Cribble, krib'l, *n.* A coarse sieve; coarse flour or meal.
Crick, krik, *n.* A local spasm or cramp; a stiffness of the neck.
Cricket, krik'et, *n.* An insect which makes a creaking or chirping sound; an open-air game played with bats, ball, and wickets.
Cricketer, krik'et-ėr, *n.* One who plays cricket.
Crier, krī'ėr, *n.* One who cries; one who makes proclamation.
Crime, krīm, *n.* A breach of law, divine or human; any great wickedness.
Criminal, krim'in-al, *a.* Guilty; wicked; relating to crime.—*n.* A malefactor; a convict.
Criminality, krim-in-al'i-ti, *n.* The quality of being criminal; guiltiness.
Criminally, krim'in-al-li, *adv.* In a criminal manner; wickedly.
Criminate, krim'in-āt, *vt.* To charge with or involve in a crime.
Crimination, krim-in-ā'shon, *n.* Accusation.
Criminative, Criminatory, krim'in-āt-iv, krim'in-a-to-ri, *a.* Relating to or involving crimination or accusation.
Criminous, krim'in-us, *a.* Criminal.
Crimp, krimp, *a.* Easily crumbled; friable; brittle.—*vt.* To curl or crisp; to seize; to pinch; to decoy for the army or navy.
Crimple, krimp'l, *vt.* (crimpling, crimpled). To contract; to cause to shrink; to curl.
Crimson, krim'zn, *n.* A deep-red colour; a red tinged with blue.—*a.* Of a beautiful deep-red.—*vt.* To dye of a deep-red colour.—*vi.* To become of a deep-red colour; to blush.
Cringe, krinj, *vi.* (cringing, cringed). To bend; to bend with servility; to fawn.—*n.* A bow; servile civility.
Cringle, kring'gl, *n.* A withe for fastening a gate; a ring or eye in a rope of a sail.
Crinkle, kring'kl, *vi.* (crinkling, crinkled). To bend in little turns; to wrinkle.—*vt.* To form with short turns or wrinkles.—*n.* A winding or turn; a wrinkle.
Crinoline, krin'o-lin, *n.* A fabric of horsehair and linen thread; a hooped petticoat.
Cripple, krip'l, *n.* A lame person.—*vt.* (crippling, crippled). To lame; to disable.
Crisis, krī'sis, *n.*; pl. **-ses.** Turning-point of a disease; a decisive stage; time when anything is at its height; conjuncture.
Crisp, krisp, *a.* Brittle; easily broken or crumbled; fresh; brisk.—*vt.* To curl; to make wavy.—*vi.* To form little curls.
Crisper, krisp'ėr, *n.* One who or that which crisps; an instrument for crisping cloth.
Crisply, krisp'li, *adv.* With crispness.
Crispy, krisp'i, *a.* Crisp; curled; brittle.
Cristate, kris'tāt, *a.* Crested; tufted.
Criterion, krī-tē'ri-un, *n.*; pl. **-ia.** Standard of judging; a measure; test.
Critic, kri'tik, *n.* One skilled in judging literary or artistic work; a reviewer; a severe judge.—*a.* Relating to criticism.
Critical, kri'tik-al, *a.* Relating to or containing criticism; nicely judicious; inclined to find fault; relating to a crisis; momentous.
Critically, kri'tik-al-li, *adv.* In a critical manner; at the crisis.
Criticism, kri'ti-sizm, *n.* Act or art of criticizing; exhibition of the merits of a literary or artistic work; a critical essay; censure.
Criticize, kri'ti-sīz, *vi.* and *t.* (criticizing, criticized). To examine or judge critically; to pick out faults; to animadvert upon.
Critique, kri-tēk', *n.* A written estimate of the merits of a literary or artistic work.
Croak, krōk, *vi.* To make a low hoarse noise in the throat, as a frog or crow; to forebode evil without much cause; to murmur.—*n.* The low harsh sound of a frog, raven, &c.

Croaker, krōk'ėr, *n.* A grumbler.
Croaking, Croaky, krōk'ing, krōk'i, *a.* Uttering a croak; foreboding evil; grumbling.
Crochet, krō'shā, *n.* A species of knitting performed by means of a small hook.
Crock, krok, *n.* An earthen vessel; a pot; a person broken down in health.
Crockery, krok'ė-ri, *n.* Earthenware; vessels formed of clay, glazed and baked.
Crocodile, kro'kō-dīl, *n.* A large aquatic reptile of the lizard kind.—*a.* Pertaining to or like a crocodile; affected (tears).
Crocus, krō'kus, *n.* A bulbous plant of the iris family; saffron.
Croft, kroft, *n.* A little field adjoining a dwelling-house; a little farm.
Crofter, krof'tėr, *n.* One who occupies a croft; a tenant of a small holding in the Highlands of Scotland.
Cromlech, krom'lek, *n.* An ancient structure of large stones set on end, supporting a stone laid horizontally.
Crone, krōn, *n.* An old woman.
Crony, krō'ni, *n.* A familiar friend.
Crook, krök, *n.* A bend; a curving instrument; a shepherd's staff; a pastoral staff; a criminal, swindler.—*vt.* and *i.* To bend; to make a hook on.
Crooked, krök'ed, *a.* Bent; wry; deceitful.
Crop, krop, *n.* The first stomach of birds; the craw; harvest; corn, &c., while growing; act of cutting, as hair; a short whip without a lash.—*vt.* (cropping, cropped or cropt). To cut off the ends of; to cut close; to browse; to gather before it falls; to cultivate.
Crop-eared, krop'ērd, *a.* Having the ears cut short.
Cropper, krop'ėr, *n.* A breed of pigeons with a large crop; a fall as from horseback.
Croquet, krō'kā, *n.* An open-air game played with mallets, balls, hoops, and pegs.
Crore, krōr, *n.* In the E. Indies, ten millions.
Crosier, Crozier, krō'zhi-ėr, *n.* A bishop's crook or pastoral staff.
Cross, kros, *n.* An instrument of death, consisting of two pieces of timber placed transversely; the symbol of the Christian religion; the religion itself; a monument or sign in the form of a cross; anything that thwarts; a hybrid.—*a.* Athwart; adverse; fretful.—*vt.* To draw a line or lay a body across; to mark with a cross; to cancel; to pass from side to side of; to thwart; to perplex; to interbreed.—*vi.* To be athwart; to move across.
Cross-bones, kros'bōnz, *n.pl.* A symbol of death; two human thigh-bones placed crosswise, generally in conjunction with a skull.
Crossbow, kros'bō, *n.* A weapon for shooting, formed by fixing a bow crosswise on a stock.
Cross-breed, kros'brēd, *n.* A breed from a male and female of different breeds.
Cross-examination, kros'egz-am-in-ā-shon, *n.* The examination of a witness called by one party by the opposite party.
Cross-examine, kros'egz-am-in, *vt.* To examine a witness of the opposite party.
Cross-grained, kros'grānd, *a.* Having the fibres across or irregular; perverse.
Crossing, kros'ing, *n.* Act of one who or that which crosses; a place where passengers cross.
Crossly, kros'li, *adv.* Peevishly; adversely.
Cross-purpose, kros'pėr-pus, *n.* A contrary purpose; a misunderstanding.
Cross-question, kros'kwes-chon, *vt.* To cross-examine.
Cross-road, kros'rōd, *n.* A road which crosses other roads.
Cross-trees, kros'trēz, *n.pl.* Horizontal pieces of timber on masts, to sustain the tops and extend the shrouds.
Crosswise, kros'wīz, *adv.* Transversely.
Crossword puzzle, kros'wėrd puz'l, *n.* A diagram of squares, each of which, except certain blanks, is to be filled with a letter so that the words formed, when read down and across, correspond to definitions given.
Crotch, kroch, *n.* A fork or forking.
Crotchet, kroch'et, *n.* A note in music, half the length of a minim; a whim; a perverse conceit; a bracket in printing.
Crotchety, kroch'et-i, *a.* Whimsical.
Croton, krō'ton, *n.* An E. Indian shrub whose seeds yield a violently purgative oil.
Crouch, krouch, *vi.* To bend low; to lie close to the ground; to cringe.
Croup, kröp, *n.* A disease of the windpipe in children; the rump of certain animals; the place behind the saddle.
Croupier, krö'pē-ėr, *n.* One who at a public dinner sits at the lower end of the table; person in charge of the money at a gaming table.
Crow, krō, *n.* A black bird of the genus Corvus, including the raven, rook, jackdaw, &c.; a crowbar; the sound which a cock utters.—*vi.* (crowing, *pret.* crew, crowed, *pp.* crowed). To cry as a cock; to exult; to boast.
Crowbar, krō'bär, *n.* A bar of iron with a bent or forked end, used as a lever.
Crowd, kroud, *n.* A number of persons or things; a throng; the populace.—*vt.* To fill by pressing together; to fill to excess.—*vi.* To press in numbers; to throng.
Crowded, kroud'ed, *a.* Filled by a promiscuous multitude.
Crow-flower, krō'flou-ėr, *n.* A name of the buttercup and other plants.
Crowfoot, krō'fu̦t, *n.* Cords used in ships to suspend the awnings, &c.; a buttercup.
Crown, kroun, *n.* An ornament for the head in the form of a wreath; a diadem; a badge of royalty; perfection; completion; the top of anything, especially the head; a coin five shillings in value.—*vt.* To invest with a crown; to cover; to adorn; to finish; to perfect.
Crowned, kround, *p.a.* Invested with a crown; surmounted.
Crown-glass, kroun'glas, *n.* The finest sort of window-glass.
Crowning, kroun'ing, *p.a.* Highest; perfecting; final.
Crown-prince, kroun'prins, *n.* The prince who is apparently successor to the crown.
Crow-quill, krō'kwil, *n.* The quill of the crow, formerly used in fine writing.
Crow's-feet, krōz'fēt, *n.pl.* The wrinkles at corners of the eyes, the effects of age.
Crucial, krö'shi-al, *a.* Relating to a cross; severe; searching; decisive.
Crucible, krö'si-bl, *n.* A melting pot, used by chemists and others.
Cruciferous, krö-sif'ėr-us, *a.* Having four petals in the form of a cross.

Crucifix, krö'si-fiks, *n.* A cross with the figure of Christ crucified on it.
Crucifixion, krö-si-fik'shon, *n.* The act of crucifying; the death of Christ.
Cruciform, krö'si-form, *a.* Cross-shaped.
Crucify, krö'si-fī, *vt.* (crucifying, crucified). To put to death by nailing the hands and feet of to a cross, to mortify; to torment.
Crude, kröd, *a.* Raw; unripe; in its natural state; not brought to perfection.
Crudely, kröd'li, *adv.* In a crude manner.
Crudity, kröd'i-ti, *n.* State of being crude; something in a crude state.
Cruel, krö'el, *a.* Unmerciful; hard-hearted; ferocious; brutal; severe.
Cruelly, krö'el-li, *adv.* In a cruel manner.
Cruelty, krö'el-ti, *n.* Quality of being cruel; inhumanity; barbarity; a cruel act.
Cruet, krö'et, *n.* A vial or small glass bottle for holding vinegar, oil, &c.
Cruise, kröz, *vi.* (cruising, cruised). To sail hither and thither.—*n.* A sailing to and fro in search of an enemy's ships, or for pleasure.
Cruiser, kröz'ėr, *n.* A person or a ship that cruises; a swift armed vessel to protect or destroy shipping.
Crumb, krum, *n.* A fragment; a small piece of bread broken off; the soft part of bread.—*vt.* To break into small pieces with the fingers; to cover with bread-crumbs.
Crumble, krum'bl, *vt.* (crumbling, crumbled). To break into small fragments; to pulverize.—*vi.* To part into small fragments; to decay.
Crumby, Crummy, krum'i, *a.* Full of crumbs; soft like the crumb of bread.
Crump, krump, *a.* Crooked; bent.
Crumpet, krum'pet, *n.* A sort of muffin.
Crumple, krum'pl, *vt.* (crumpling, crumpled). To press into wrinkles; to rumple.—*vi.* To shrink; to shrivel.
Crumpled, krum'pld, *p.a.* Wrinkled; curled.
Crunch, krunch, *vt.* To crush between the teeth.
Crupper, krup'ėr, *n.* A strap of leather to prevent a saddle from shifting forward; the buttocks.
Crural, krör'al, *a.* Belonging to the leg; shaped like a leg or root.
Crusade, krö-sād', *n.* A military expedition against the infidels of the Holy Land; a romantic or enthusiastic enterprise.
Crusader, krö-sād'ėr, *n.* A person engaged in a crusade.
Cruse, kröz, *n.* A small cup; cruet.
Crush, krush, *vt.* To squeeze; to bruise; to pound; to overpower; to oppress.—*vi.* To be pressed; to force one's way amid a crowd.—*n.* A violent pressing or squeezing; a crowding.
Crushing, krush'ing, *p.a.* Overwhelming.
Crust, krust, *n.* The hard outer coat of anything; the outside of a loaf; a piece of hard bread; a deposit from wine.—*vt.* and *i.* To cover with a crust or hard coat.
Crustacea, krus-tā'shē-a, *n.pl.* A division of animals, comprising crabs, shrimps, &c., having an external skeleton or shell.
Crustacean, krus-tā'shė-an, *n.* and *a.* One of, or pertaining to, the crustaceans.
Crustaceous, krus-tā'shus, *a.* Having a shell; belonging to the Crustacea.
Crustily, krust'i-li, *adv.* Peevishly.
Crusty, krust'i, *a.* Pertaining to, having, or like a crust; snappish; surly.
Crutch, kruch, *n.* A staff with a cross-piece used by cripples; a support.
Crutched, krucht, *p.a.* Furnished with a crutch; badged with a cross.
Cry, krī, *vi.* (crying, cried). To utter the loud shrill sounds of weeping, joy, fear, surprise, &c.; to clamour; to weep.—*vt.* To shout; to proclaim.—*n.* The loud voice of man or beast; a shriek or scream; acclamation; weeping; importunate call; a political catch-word.
Crying, krī'ing, *p.a.* Calling for vengeance or punishment; notorious; clamant.
Crypt, kript, *n.* A subterranean cell for burying purposes; a subterranean chapel.
Cryptic, Cryptical, krip'tik, krip'tik-al, *a.* Hidden; secret; occult.
Cryptogam, krip'tō-gam, *n.* One of those plants which do not bear true flowers, such as lichens, mosses, ferns, &c.
Cryptogamy, krip-tog'a-mi, *n.* Concealed fructification, as in cryptogams.
Cryptogram, Cryptograph, krip'tō-gram, krip'tō-graf, *n.* Something written in secret characters.
Cryptography, krip-tog'ra-fi, *n.* Art of writing in secret characters; cipher.
Crystal, kris'tal, *n.* Pure transparent quartz; a superior kind of glass; articles, collectively, made of this material; a regular solid mineral body with smooth surfaces.—*a.* Consisting of or like crystal; clear; pellucid.
Crystalline, kris'tal-īn, *a.* Pure; pellucid.
Crystallization, kris'tal-īz-ā"shon, *n.* Act or process of crystallizing.
Crystallize, kris'tal-īz, *vt.* and *i.* To form into crystals; to unite, and form a regular solid.
Ctenoid, ten'oid, *a.* Comb-shaped; having the posterior edge with teeth: said of the scales of fishes; having scales of this kind.
Cub, kub, *n.* The young of certain quadrupeds, as the bear and fox.—*vi.* (cubbing, cubbed). To bring forth cubs.
Cube, kūb, *n.* A regular solid body, with six equal square sides; the third power, or the product from multiplying a number twice by itself.—*vt.* To raise to the third power.
Cubic, Cubical, kūb'ik, kūb'ik-al, *a.* Having the form or properties of a cube.
Cubicle, kū'bi-kl, *n.* A sleeping-place; a compartment for one bed in a dormitory.
Cubit, kū'bit, *n.* The forearm; the length from the elbow to the extremity of the middle finger, usually taken as 18 inches.
Cuckold, kuk'old, *n.* A man whose wife is false to his bed.—*vt.* To make a cuckold of.
Cuckoo, ku̧'kö, *n.* A migratory bird, so named from the sound of its note.
Cucumber, kū'kum-bėr, *n.* An annual plant of the gourd family.
Cud, kud, *n.* The food which ruminating animals bring up from the first stomach to chew.
Cuddle, kud'dl, *vi.* (cuddling, cuddled). To lie close and snug.—*vt.* To hug; to embrace; to fondle.
Cuddy, kud'i, *n.* A ship's cabin towards the stern; an ass; donkey.
Cudgel, kuj'el, *n.* A short thick stick; a club.—*vt.* (cudgelling, cudgelled). To beat with a cudgel; to beat in general.
Cue, kū, *n.* The last words of an actor's speech; catch-word; hint; the part which

any man is to play in his turn; humour; the straight rod used in billiards.
Cuff, kuf, *n.* A blow; slap; part of a sleeve near the hand.—*vt.* To beat; to strike with talons or wings, or with fists.
Cuirass, kwi-ras', *n.* A breastplate.
Cuirassier, kwi-ras-sēr', *n.* A cavalryman who wears a cuirass or breastplate.
Cuisine, kwē-zēn', *n.* Style of cooking.
Cul-de-sac, köl'de-sak, *n.* A blind alley.
Culinary, kū'lin-a-ri, *a.* Relating to the kitchen, or cookery; used in kitchens.
Cull, kul, *vt.* To pick out; to gather.
Cullender, kul'en-dėr, *n.* A colander.
Cullion, kul'i-un, *n.* A mean wretch; a cully.
Cully, kul'li, *n.* A person easily deceived; a dupe.—*vt.* To deceive.
Culm, kulm, *n.* The straw of corn and grasses; anthracite shale.
Culminate, kul'min-āt, *vi.* To come or be in the meridian; to reach the highest point, as of rank, power, size, &c.
Culmination, kul-min-ā'shon, *n.* The transit of a heavenly body over the meridian; highest point; consummation.
Culpability, kulp-a-bil'i-ti, *n.* Blamableness; guiltiness.
Culpable, kulp'a-bl, *a.* Blameworthy; guilty; criminal; immoral; sinful.
Culpably, kulp'a-bli, *adv.* In a culpable manner; blamably.
Culprit, kul'prit, *n.* A person arraigned in court for a crime, or convicted of a crime; a criminal; an offender.
Cult, kult, *n.* A system of belief and worship; a subject of devoted study.
Cultivable, kul'ti-va-bl, *a.* Capable of being cultivated.
Cultivate, kul'ti-vāt, *vt.* To till; to refine; to foster; to improve.
Cultivation, kul-ti-vā'shon, *n.* Tillage; practice, care, or study directed to improvement; refinement; advancement.
Cultivator, kul'ti-vāt-ėr, *n.* One who cultivates; a kind of harrow.
Culture, kul'tūr, *n.* Cultivation; the rearing of certain animals, as oysters; the application of labour, or other means of improvement; the result of such efforts; refinement.—*vt.* To cultivate.
Cultured, kul'tūrd, *a.* Having education and taste; refined.
Culverin, kul'vėr-in, *n.* A long slender piece of ordnance formerly used.
Culvert, kul'vėrt, *n.* An arched drain under a road, railway, &c., for the passage of water.
Cumber, kum'bėr, *vt.* To embarrass; to entangle; to obstruct; to distract.
Cumbersome, kum'bėr-sum, *a.* Troublesome; unwieldy; unmanageable.
Cumbrous, kum'brus, *a.* Burdensome; troublesome; oppressive.
Cumin, Cummin, kum'in, *n.* An annual umbelliferous plant, whose seeds have stimulating and carminative properties.
Cummer-bund, kum'ėr-bund, *n.* A girdle or waistband.
Cumulate, kū'mū-lāt, *vt.* (cumulating, cumulated). To form a heap; to heap together.
Cumulation, kū-mū-lā'shon, *n.* A heaping up; a heap; accumulation.
Cumulative, kū'mū-lāt-iv, *a.* Forming a mass; that augments by addition.
Cumulus, kū'mū-lus, *n.*; pl. **-li.** A cloud in the form of dense convex or conical heaps.
Cuneate, Cuneated, kū'nē-āt, kū'nē-āt-ed, *a.* Wedge-shaped.
Cuneiform, kū-nē'i-form, *a.* Wedge-shaped; applied to the arrow-headed characters on old Babylonian and Persian inscriptions.
Cunning, kun'ing, *a.* Astute; artful.—*n.* Faculty or act of using stratagem; craftiness; artifice.
Cunningly, kun'ing-li, *adv.* In a cunning manner; craftily.
Cup, kup, *n.* A small vessel to drink out of; anything hollow, like a cup; a glass vessel for drawing blood; liquor in a cup.—*vt.* (cupping, cupped). To apply a cupping-glass.
Cup-bearer, kup'bār-ėr, *n.* An attendant at a feast, who serves the wine.
Cupboard, kup'bōrd, *n.* A case or inclosure for cups, plates, dishes, &c.
Cupel, kū'pel, *n.* A small cup or vessel used in refining precious metals.
Cupellation, kū-pel-lā'shon, *n.* The process of refining gold or silver in a cupel.
Cupid, kū'pid, *n.* The god of love.
Cupidity, kū-pid'i-ti, *n.* A longing to possess; inordinate or unlawful desire; covetousness.
Cupola, kū'pō-la, *n.* A spherical vault on the top of a building; a dome.
Cupping, kup'ing, *n.* A drawing of blood with a cupping-glass.
Cupping-glass, kup'ing-glas, *n.* A glass vessel like a cup, for drawing blood.
Cupreous, kū'prē-us, *a.* Coppery.
Cur, kėr, *n.* A mongrel dog; a contemptible man.
Curable, kūr'a-bl, *a.* That may be cured.
Curaçoa, Curaçao, kö-ra-sō'a, kö-ra-sä'o, *n.* A liqueur flavoured with orange-peel, &c.
Curacy, Curateship, kū'ra-si, kū-rāt-ship, *n.* The office of a curate.
Curate, kū'rāt, *n.* One to whom the cure of souls is committed; a clergyman employed to assist in the duties of a rector or vicar.
Curative, kū'rāt-iv, *a.* Relating to the cure of diseases; tending to cure.
Curator, kū-rāt'ėr, *n.* A superintendent; custodian; guardian.
Curb, kėrb, *vt.* To control; to check; to restrain with a curb, as a horse; to strengthen by a curb-stone.—*n.* Check; restraint; part of a bridle; a curb-stone.
Curb-stone, kėrb'stōn, *n.* The outer edge of a foot-pavement; a kerb-stone.
Curd, kėrd, *n.* Coagulated milk.—*vt.* and *i.* To curdle; to congeal.
Curdle, kėrd'l, *vt.* and *i.* (curdling, curdled). To change into curds; to coagulate.
Curdy, kėrd'i, *a.* Like curd; coagulated.
Cure, kūr, *n.* Act of healing; a remedy; the care of souls; spiritual charge.—*vt.* (curing, cured). To heal; to remedy; to pickle.—*vi.* To effect a cure.
Curé, kū-rā, *n.* A curate; a parson.
Cureless, kūr'les, *a.* Incurable.
Curer, kūr'ėr, *n.* One who cures; a physician; one who preserves provisions.
Curfew, kėr'fū, *n.* An evening bell; an old utensil for covering a fire.
Curia, kū'ri-a, *n.* The Roman see in its temporal aspect.
Curio, kū'ri-ō, *n.*; pl. **-os,** A curiosity; an interesting and curious article.

Curiosity, kū-ri-os'i-ti, *n.* Inquisitiveness; a thing unusual; a rarity.
Curious, kū'ri-us, *a.* Inquisitive; addicted to research or inquiry; strange; singular.
Curiously, kū'ri-us-li, *adv.* In a curious manner; inquisitively; unusually.
Curl, kėrl, *vt.* To form into ringlets.—*vi.* To take a twisted or coiled form; to play at the game of curling.—*n.* A ringlet of hair, or anything of a like form; a waving; flexure.
Curler, kėr'lėr, *n.* One who or that which curls; one who plays the game of curling.
Curlew, kėr'lū, *n.* A bird allied to the snipe and woodcock.
Curling, kėrl'ing, *n.* A winter game in which large smooth stones are propelled on the ice.
Curly, kėrl'i, *a.* Having curls; tending to curl.
Curmudgeon, kėr-muj'on, *n.* An avaricious churlish fellow; a miser; a churl.
Currant, ku'rant, *n.* A small dried grape; the name of several shrubs and of their fruit.
Currency, ku'ren-si, *n.* Circulation; circulating medium; the aggregate of coin, notes, &c., in circulation; general esteem; vogue.
Current, ku'rent, *a.* Running; circulating; general; present in its course.—*n.* A running; a stream; progressive motion of water; successive course; the passage of electricity from one pole of an apparatus to the other; often used for strength, amount, or intensity of current.
Currently, ku'rent li, *adv.* In a current manner; generally.
Curricle, ku'ri-kl, *n.* A chaise with two wheels, drawn by two horses.
Curriculum, ku-rik'ū-lum, *n.* A course of study in a university, school, &c.
Currier, ku'ri-ėr, *n.* A man who dresses leather after it is tanned.
Currish, kėr'ish, *a.* Like a cur; snappish.
Curry, ku'ri, *n.* A highly spiced sauce or mixture; a dish cooked with curry.—*vt.* (currying, curried). To flavour with curry; to dress leather; to rub and clean (a horse) with a comb; to seek (favour).
Curry-comb, ku'ri-kōm, *n.* A comb for rubbing and cleaning horses.
Curse, kėrs, *vt.* (cursing, cursed or curst). To utter a wish of evil against; to blight; to torment with calamities.—*vi.* To utter imprecations; to blaspheme.—*n.* Imprecation of evil; execration; torment.
Cursed, kėrs'ed, *a.* Deserving a curse; under a curse; execrable; detestable.
Cursedly, kėrs'ed-li, *adv.* In a cursed manner; confoundedly.
Cursing, kėrs'ing, *n.* The uttering of a curse; execration.
Cursive, kėr'siv, *a.* Running; flowing.
Cursores, kėr-sō'rēz, *n.pl.* The runners, an order of birds, such as the ostrich.
Cursorily, kėr'sō-ri-li, *adv.* In a hasty manner; slightly; hastily.
Cursory, kėr'sō-ri, *a.* Hasty; superficial.
Curst, kėrst, *a.* Snarling; peevish.
Curt, kėrt, *a.* Short; concise; somewhat rude.
Curtail, kėr-tāl', *vt.* To cut short; to abridge.
Curtain, kėr'tan, *n.* A hanging cloth for a window, bed, &c.; a screen in a theatre.—*vt.* To inclose or furnish with curtains.
Curtain-lecture, kėr'tan-lek-tūr, *n.* Lecture given in bed by a wife to her husband.
Curtly, kėrt'li, *adv.* Shortly; briefly.
Curtsy, Curtsey, kėrt'si, *n.* A gesture of respect by a female.—*vi.* (curtsying or curtseying, curtsied or curtseyed). To drop or make a curtsy.
Curvature, kėrv'a-tūr, *n.* A curving.
Curve, kėrv, *a.* Bending; inflected.—*n.* A bending without angles; a bent line.—*vt.* (curving, curved). To bend.
Curvet, kėr-vet', *n.* A leap of a horse, in which he raises his fore-legs together.—*vi.* (curvetting, curvetted). To leap and frisk.
Curvilinear, Curvilineal, kėrv-i-lin'ē-ėr, kėrv-i-lin'ē-al, *a.* Consisting of curved lines; bounded by curved lines.
Curvirostral, kėrv-i-ros'tral, *a.* Having a crooked beak.
Cushat, kush'at, *n.* The ring-dove.
Cushion, kush'on, *n.* A pillow for a seat; something resembling a pillow.—*vt.* To seat on a cushion; to furnish with cushions.
Cusp, kusp, *n.* The point of the moon, or other luminary; a point formed by the meeting of two curves.
Custard, kus'tėrd, *n.* A composition of milk and eggs, sweetened, and baked or boiled.
Custard-apple, kus'tėrd-ap-pl, *n.* A West Indian tree or fruit.
Custodial, kus-tō'di-al, *a.* Relating to custody or guardianship.
Custodian, kus-tō'di-an, *n.* One who has care of a library, public building, &c.
Custodier, kus-tō'di-ėr, *n.* One who has something in custody; a keeper; a guardian.
Custody, kus'tō-di, *n.* A keeping; guardianship; imprisonment; security.
Custom, kus'tum, *n.* Habit; established practice; fashion; a buying of goods; business support; a tax on goods; *pl.* duties on merchandise imported or exported.
Customable, kus'tum-a-bl, *a.* Subject to the payment of customs.
Customarily, kus'tum-a-ri-li, *adv.* Habitually.
Customary, kus'tum-a-ri, *a.* According to custom; habitual; usual.
Customer, kus'tum-ėr, *n.* An accustomed buyer at a shop, &c.; one who buys goods.
Custom-house, kus'tum-hous, *n.* The office where customs are paid.
Cut, kut, *vt.* (cutting, cut). To divide into pieces; to fell or mow; to clip; to carve; to affect deeply; to intersect; to castrate; to divide, as cards; to refuse to recognize.—*vi.* To make an incision; to be severed by a cutting instrument; to pass straight and rapidly.—*a.* Gashed; carved; intersected; deeply affected.—*n.* The action of an edged instrument; a wound; a stroke with a whip; a severe remark; a channel; any small piece; a lot; a near passage; a carving or engraving; act of dividing a pack of cards; form; fashion; refusal to recognize a person.
Cutaneous, kū-tā'nē-us, *a.* Pertaining to the skin.
Cuticle, kū'ti-kl, *n.* The thin exterior coat of the skin; a vesicular membrane in plants.
Cutlass, kut'las, *n.* A broad, curving sword.
Cutler, kut'lėr, *n.* One who makes or sharpens knives and other cutting instruments.
Cutlery, kut'lė-ri, *n.* Knives and edged instruments collectively.
Cutlet, kut'let, *n.* A small piece of meat for cooking, generally off the ribs.

Cutpurse, kut'pėrs, *n.* A thief; pickpocket.
Cutter, kut'ėr, *n.* One who or that which cuts; a vessel with one mast and a straight running bowsprit.
Cut-throat, kut'thrōt, *n.* A murderer.
Cutting, kut'ing, *p.a.* Serving to cut; wounding the feelings; severe.—*n.* A piece cut off; an incision; an excavation; a twig or scion.
Cuttle, Cuttle-fish, kut'tl, kut'tl-fish, *n.* A mollusc which ejects a black fluid to conceal itself.
Cutwater, kut'wạ-tėr, *n.* The fore part of a ship's prow, which cuts the water.
Cyanean, sī-ā'nē-an, *a.* Of a dark-blue colour.
Cyanide, sī'an-id, *n.* A combination of cyanogen with a metallic base.
Cyanogen, sī-an'ō-jen, *n.* A poisonous gas of a strong and peculiar odour.
Cycle, sī'kl, *n.* An orbit in the heavens; a circle of years; a bicycle or tricycle.—*vi.* To recur in a cycle; to ride a bicycle.
Cyclic, Cyclical, sī'klik, sī'klik-al, *a.* Pertaining to a cycle; connected with a series of legends.
Cyclist, sīk'list, *n.* One who uses a cycle.
Cycloid, sī'kloid, *n.* A geometrical curve.
Cyclometer, sī-klom'et-ėr, *n.* An instrument for measuring circles, or for giving the distance travelled by a cycle.
Cyclone, sī'klōn, *n.* A circular storm; a rotatory system of winds revolving round a calm centre, and advancing.
Cyclopædia, Cyclopedia, sī-klō-pē'di-a, *n.* A kind of dictionary, giving accounts on a branch or all branches of science, art, or learning.
Cyclopædic, Cyclopedic, sī-klō-pē'dik, *a.* Belonging to a cyclopædia.
Cyclopean, sī-klō-pē'an, *a.* Pertaining to the Cyclops; gigantic; vast.
Cyclops, sī'klops, *n.sing.* and *pl.*; pl. also **Cyclopes,** sī-klō'pēz. A one-eyed race of giants in Greek fable.
Cygnet, sig'net, *n.* A young swan.
Cylinder, si'lin-dėr, *n.* An elongated round body of uniform diameter.
Cylindric, Cylindrical, si-lin'drik, si-lin'drik-al, *a.* Having the form of a cylinder, or partaking of its properties.
Cymbal, sim'bal, *n.* A basin-shaped musical instrument of brass, used in pairs.
Cymric, kim'rik, *a.* Pertaining to the Cymry (kim'ri) or Welsh.—*n.* The language of the Cymry or ancient Britons.
Cynic, sin'ik, *n.* One of a sect of Greek philosophers who professed contempt of riches, arts, &c.; a morose man.
Cynic, Cynical, sin'ik, sin'i-kal, *a.* Belonging to the Cynics; surly; sneering; captious.
Cynicism, sin'i-sizm, *n.* A morose contempt of the pleasures and arts of life.
Cynosure, sī'nō-zhör, *n.* The constellation of the Little Bear; a centre of attraction.
Cypher, sī'fėr, *n.* Same as *Cipher*.
Cypress, sī'pres, *n.* An evergreen tree; the emblem of mourning.
Cyst, sist, *n.* A bag in animal bodies containing matter.
Cytherean, sith-e-rē'an, *a.* Pertaining to Venus.
Czar, tsär or zär, *n.* Formerly, the title of the Emperor of Russia.
Czarevitch, tsä're-vich, *n.* Formerly, the eldest son of the Czar: also *Cesarevitch* (tsā-zä-rā'vich).
Czarina, tsä-rē'na or zä-rē'na, *n.* Formerly, the title of the Empress of Russia.
Czech, chek, *n.* One of the Slavonic inhabitants of Bohemia; the language of the Czechs.

D

Dab, dab, *vt.* (dabbing, dabbed). To hit lightly with something soft or moist.—*n.* A gentle blow; a small mass of anything soft or moist; a small flat fish; an adept or expert.
Dabble, dab'bl, *vt.* (dabbling, dabbled). To wet; to sprinkle.—*vi.* To play in water; to do anything in a superficial manner; to meddle.
Dabbler, dab'bl-ėr, *n.* One who dabbles; a superficial meddler.
Dace, dās, *n.* A small river fish.
Dachshund, däks'hụnt, *n.* A long-bodied, short-legged dog, with short hair.
Dacoit, da-koit', *n.* An Indian name for a robber who is a member of a band of thieves.
Dactyl, dak'til, *n.* A poetical foot of one long or accented syllable followed by two short.
Dactylic, dak-til'ik, *a.* Pertaining to or consisting of dactyls.
Dad, Daddy, dad, dad'di, *n.* A childish or pet name for father.
Dado, dā'dō, *n.* That part of a pedestal between the base and the cornice; the finishing of the lower part of the walls in rooms.
Daffodil, daf'fō-dil, *n.* A plant of the amaryllis family with yellow flowers.
Dagger, dag'ėr, *n.* A short sharp-pointed sword.
Daggle, dag'gl, *vt.* (daggling, daggled). To trail in mud or wet grass; to dirty.
Dago, dā'gō, *n.* A contemptuous term for an Italian or Spaniard.
Daguerreotype, da-ger'ō-tīp, *n.* A photograph fixed on a metallic plate.
Dahabieh, da-ha-bē'ā, *n.* A Nile passenger boat.
Dahlia, da'li-a, *n.* A genus of composite plants, consisting of tuberous-rooted herbs.
Daily, dā'li, *a.* Happening or being every day; diurnal.—*adv.* Day by day.
Daintily, dān'ti-li, *adv.* Nicely; delicately.
Dainty, dān'ti, *a.* Toothsome; nice; delicate; elegant.—*n.* Something nice; a delicacy.
Dairy, dā'ri, *n.* The place where milk is converted into butter or cheese; a shop where milk, butter, &c., are sold.—*a.* Pertaining to the keeping of cows, managing of milk, &c.
Dais, dā'is, *n.* The high table at the upper end of the dining-hall; the raised floor on which the table stood; a canopy.
Daisy, dā'zi, *n.* The day's eye; a well-known plant, bearing a white flower with a tinge of red, and a yellow centre.
Dale, dāl, *n.* A valley; a place between hills.
Dalliance, dal'yans, *n.* Acts of fondness; interchange of caresses; toying.
Dally, dal'li, *vi.* (dallying, dallied). To trifle; to wanton; to linger.
Dalmatic, dal-mat'ik, *n.* The ecclesiastical vestment used by deacons at mass, and worn also by bishops under the chasuble.
Daltonism, dal'ton-izm, *n.* Colour-blindness.

Dam, dam, *n.* A female parent; a bank to confine or raise water.—*vt.* (damming, dammed). To obstruct or confine by a dam.
Damage, dam'āj, *n.* Hurt; injury; money compensation (generally in *pl.*).—*vt.* (damaging, damaged). To injure; to impair.
Damageable, dam'āj-a-bl, *a.* That may be damaged.
Damask, dam'ask, *n.* A fabric, of various materials, with figures of flowers, &c.; a pink colour.—*a.* Pink or rosy.—*vt.* To form or imprint flowers or figures on.
Damaskeen, dam'as-kēn, *vt.* To inlay iron, steel, &c., with another metal, as gold or silver.
Dame, dām, *n.* A lady; the wife of a knight or baronet; title given to a woman who belongs to the first or second class of the Victorian Order or the Order of the British Empire.
Damn, dam, *vt.* To send to hell; to condemn.
Damnable, dam'na-bl, *a.* Deserving damnation; odious; pernicious.
Damnably, dam'na-bli, *adv.* In a damnable manner.
Damnation, dam-nā'shon, *n.* Condemnation; sentence to punishment in the future state.
Damnatory, dam'na-to-ri, *a.* Containing condemnation; condemnatory.
Damned, damd, *a.* Hateful; detestable.
Damning, dam'ing or dam'ning, *a.* That condemns or exposes to damnation.
Damp, damp, *a.* Moist; humid.—*n.* Moist air; fog; noxious exhalation from the earth; depression of spirits; discouragement.—*vt.* To moisten; to dispirit; to restrain.
Dampen, dam'pen, *vt.* and *i.* To make or become damp or moist.
Damper, dam'pėr, *n.* One who or that which damps; a plate across a flue of a furnace, &c., to regulate the draught of air.
Dampish, damp'ish, *a.* Moderately damp.
Dampness, damp'nes, *n.* Moisture; fogginess; moistness; moderate humidity.
Damsel, dam'zel, *n.* A young unmarried woman; a girl.
Damson, dam'zn, *n.* A small dark plum.
Dance, dans, *vi.* (dancing, danced). To move with measured steps, regulated by a tune; to leap and frisk.—*vt.* To make to dance; to dandle.—*n.* A leaping or stepping to the measure of a tune; the tune itself.
Dancer, dans'ėr, *n.* One who dances.
Dancing-girl, dans'ing-gėrl, *n.* A girl who dances professionally, as in Egypt or India.
Dandelion, dan'di-lī-un, *n.* A composite plant bearing a bright yellow flower.
Dandle, dan'dl, *vt.* (dandling, dandled). To shake on the knee, as an infant; to fondle; to trifle with.
Dandruff, dan'druff, *n.* A scurf on the head.
Dandy, dan'di, *n.* A fop; a coxcomb.
Dandyish, dan'di-ish, *a.* Like a dandy.
Dandyism, dan'di-izm, *n.* The manners and dress of a dandy.
Danger, dān'jėr, *n.* Exposure to injury; jeopardy; risk.
Dangerous, dān'jėr-us, *a.* Perilous; causing risk of harm; unsafe; insecure.
Dangerously, dān'jėr-us-li, *adv.* With danger; perilously.
Dangle, dang'gl, *vi.* (dangling, dangled). To hang loose; to follow officiously.—*vt.* To carry suspended loosely; to swing.
Dangler, dang'gl-ėr, *n.* One who dangles; a man who hangs about women.
Dank, dangk, *a.* Damp; moist; humid.
Danseuse, däng-sėz, *n.* A female stage-dancer.
Dapper, dap'ėr, *a.* Little and active; neat.
Dapple, dap'l, *n.* A spot.—*a.* Marked with spots.—*vt.* (dappling, dappled). To variegate with spots.
Dappled, dap'pld, *a.* Spotted.
Dare, dār, *vi.* (daring, *pret.* dared or durst, *pp.* dared). To have courage; to be bold enough; to venture.—*vt.* To challenge; to defy; to venture on.
Dare-devil, dār'de-vil, *n.* A desperado; one who will fearlessly attempt anything.
Daring, dār'ing, *a.* Bold; intrepid; fearless.—*n.* Courage; audacity.
Daringly, dār'ing-li, *adv.* Boldly; fearlessly.
Dark, därk, *a.* Destitute of light; clouded; black or blackish; disheartening; involved in mystery; keeping designs in concealment.—*n.* Darkness; obscurity; secrecy; a state of ignorance.
Darken, därk'n, *vt.* To make dark.—*vi.* To grow dark or darker.
Darkish, därk'ish, *a.* Somewhat dark.
Darkling, därk'ling, *adv.* In the dark.—*a.* Black-looking; lowering; gloomy.
Darkly, därk'li, *adv.* Obscurely; dimly.
Darkness, därk'nes, *n.* Absence of light; blackness; gloom; ignorance; privacy.
Darksome, därk'sum, *a.* Dark; gloomy.
Darling, där'ling, *a.* Dearly beloved.—*n.* One much beloved; a favourite.
Darn, därn, *vt.* To mend by imitating the texture of the stuff with thread and needle; to sew together.—*n.* A place so mended.
Darnel, där'nel, *n.* A plant injurious to corn.
Dart, därt, *n.* A pointed missile thrown by the hand; a sudden rush or bound.—*vt.* To throw with a sudden thrust; to shoot.—*vi.* To fly or shoot, as a dart; to start and run.
Darter, därt'ėr, *n.* One who darts; a bird of the pelican tribe that darts after fish.
Darwinism, där'win-izm, *n.* The doctrine as to the origin and modifications of species taught by Darwin; evolution.
Dash, dash, *vt.* To cause to strike suddenly or violently; to throw or cast; to sprinkle; to mix slightly; to sketch out hastily; to obliterate; to frustrate; to abash.—*vi.* To rush with violence; to strike or be hurled.—*n.* A violent striking of two bodies; admixture; a rushing or onset; vigour in attack; bluster; a mark in writing or printing (—).
Dash-board, dash'bōrd, *n.* A board on a vehicle to keep off mud, &c., thrown by the horses' heels.
Dashing, dash'ing, *a.* Spirited; showy.
Dastard, das'tėrd, *n.* A coward.—*a.* Cowardly.
Dastardly, das'tėrd-li, *a.* Cowardly; base.
Data, dā'ta, *n.pl.* *See* DATUM.
Date, dāt, *n.* The time when any event happened; era; age; a soft fleshy drupe, the fruit of the date-palm.—*vt.* (dating, dated). To note the time of.—*vi.* To reckon time; to have origin.
Date-palm, Date-tree, dāt'päm, dāt'trē, *n.* The kind of palms which bear dates.
Dative, dāt'iv, *a.* or *n.* A grammatical case, following verbs that express giving, &c.
Datum, dā'tum, *n.*; pl. **-ta.** A fact, proposi-

tion, &c., granted or known, from which other facts, &c., are to be deduced.

Daub, dạb, *vt.* To smear; to cover with mud or other soft substance; to paint coarsely; to flatter grossly.—*n.* Coarse painting; a smear.

Dauber, dạb'ėr, *n.* One who daubs; a coarse painter; a gross flatterer.

Dauby, dạb'i, *a.* Viscous; glutinous.

Daughter, dạ'tėr, *n.* A female child or descendant.

Daughter-in-law, dạ'tėr-in-lạ, *n.* A son's wife.

Daughterly, dạ'tėr-li, *a.* Becoming a daughter.

Daunt, dạnt, *vt.* To subdue the courage of; to intimidate; to discourage.

Dauntless, dạnt'les, *a.* Fearless; intrepid.

Dauphin, dạ'fin, *n.* Formerly, the eldest son of the king of France.

Davenport, dav'en-port, *n.* A small ornamental writing-table fitted with drawers, &c.

Davit, dā'vit, *n.* One of a pair of projecting pieces over a ship's side, with tackle to hoist or lower a boat by.

Daw, dạ, *n.* A bird of the crow kind.

Dawdle, dạ'dl, *vi.* (dawdling, dawdled). To waste time; to trifle; to saunter.

Dawn, dạn, *vi.* To begin to grow light in the morning; to glimmer obscurely; to begin to open or appear.—*n.* The break of day; beginning; first appearance.

Dawning, dạn'ing, *n.* The first appearance of light in the morning; beginning.

Day, dā, *n.* The time between the rising and setting of the sun; the time of one revolution of the earth, or 24 hours; light; time specified; age; time; anniversary.

Day-book, dā'bụk, *n.* A book in which are recorded the debts and credits of the day.

Daybreak, dā'brāk, *n.* The dawn; first appearance of light in the morning.

Day-dream, dā'drēm, *n.* A vision to the waking senses; a reverie.

Daylight, dā'līt, *n.* The light of the day.

Daysman, dāz'man, *n.* An umpire; mediator.

Dayspring, dā'spring, *n.* The dawn.

Day-star, dā'stär, *n.* The star that ushers in the day; the morning-star, Lucifer.

Daytime, dā'tīm, *n.* The time of daylight.

Daze, dāz, *vt.* (dazing, dazed). To stupefy; to stun.

Dazzle, daz'zl, *vt.* (dazzling, dazzled). To overpower with light or splendour.—*vi.* To be intensely bright; to be overpowered by light.—*n.* A dazzling light; glitter.

Deacon, dē'kon, *n.* A person in the lowest degree of holy orders; a church officer; the president of an incorporated trade.

Deaconess, dē'kon-es, *n.* A female deacon.

Deaconhood, dē'kon-hụd, *n.* The state or office of a deacon; deacons collectively.

Deaconship, Deaconry, dē'kon-ship, dē'kon-ri, *n.* The office of a deacon.

Dead, ded, *a.* Without life; deceased; perfectly still; dull; cold; tasteless; spiritless; utter; unerring.

Deaden, ded'n, *vt.* To abate in vigour, force, or sensation; to darken, dull, or dim.

Dead-heat, ded'hēt, *n.* A race in which the competitors finish at the same time.

Dead-letter, ded'let-tėr, *n.* A letter which cannot be delivered, and is returned to the sender; a law, treaty, &c., which has ceased to be acted on.

Dead-light, ded'līt, *n.* A kind of shutter in ships for a cabin-window.

Dead-lock, ded'lok, *n.* Complete stand-still.

Deadly, ded'li, *a.* That may cause death; mortal; implacable.—*adv.* In a deadly manner.

Dead-march, ded'märch, *n.* A piece of solemn music played at funerals.

Dead-set, ded'set, *n.* The fixed position of a dog in pointing game; a pointed attack.

Dead-weight, ded'wāt, *n.* A heavy or oppressive burden.

Deaf, def, *a.* Wanting the sense of hearing; not listening or regarding.

Deafen, def'n, *vt.* To make deaf; to render impervious to sound.

Deafening, def'n-ing, *n.* Matter to prevent the passage of sound through floors, &c.

Deaf-mute, def'mūt, *n.* A deaf and dumb person.

Deal, dēl, *n.* A part; an indefinite quantity, degree, or extent; the distribution of playing cards; a board or plank; fir or pine timber.—*vt.* (dealing, dealt). To distribute.—*vi.* To traffic; to behave; to distribute cards.

Dealer, dēl'ėr, *n.* A trader; one who distributes cards.

Dealing, dēl'ing, *n.* Conduct; behaviour; intercourse; traffic.

Dean, dēn, *n.* A dignitary in cathedral and collegiate churches who presides over the chapter; an officer in a university or college.

Deanery, dēn'ė-ri, *n.* The revenue, office, jurisdiction, or house of a dean.

Deanship, dēn'ship, *n.* The office of a dean.

Dear, dēr, *a.* Bearing a high price; valuable; expensive; in high estimation; beloved.—*n.* A darling.—*adv.* Dearly.

Dearly, dēr'li, *adv.* At a high price; with great fondness.

Dearth, dėrth, *n.* Scarcity; want; famine.

Death, deth, *n.* Extinction of life; decease; cause of decease; damnation.

Death-bed, deth'bed, *n.* The bed on which a person dies.

Deathless, deth'les, *a.* Not subject to death.

Deathlike, deth'līk, *a.* Resembling death; gloomy; quiet; motionless.

Deathly, deth'li, *a.* Deadly; fatal.

Death-rate, deth'rāt, *n.* The proportion of deaths in a town, country, &c.

Death's-head, deths'hed, *n.* A figure of a human skull; a kind of moth.

Debacle, de-bak'l, *n.* A sudden breaking up of ice; a confused rout; a crash in the social or political world.

Debar, dē-bär', *vt.* (debarring, debarred). To hinder from approach, entry, or enjoyment.

Debark, dē-bärk', *vt.* To disembark.

Debase, dē-bās', *vt.* (debasing, debased). To lower; to degrade; to vitiate.

Debased, dē-bāst', *p.a.* Adulterated; degraded; vile.

Debasement, dē-bās'ment, *n.* Act of debasing; state of being debased.

Debatable, dē-bāt'a-bl, *a.* Disputable.

Debate, dē-bāt', *n.* Contention in words or arguments; discussion; controversy.—*vt.* (debating, debated). To dispute; to argue; to discuss.—*vi.* To examine different arguments in the mind; to deliberate.

Debater, dē-bāt'ėr, *n.* One who debates.

Debauch, dē-bạch', *vt.* To corrupt; to per-

vert.—*vi.* To riot; to revel.—*n.* Excess in eating or drinking; lewdness.
Debauched, dē-bạcht', *p.a.* Vitiated in morals; profligate.
Debauchee, deb-o-shē', *n.* One addicted to debauchery; a libertine; a rake.
Debaucher, dē-bạch'ėr, *n.* One who debauches or corrupts others.
Debauchery, dē-bạch'ė-ri, *n.* Gluttony; intemperance; habitual lewdness.
Debenture, dē-ben'tūr, *n.* A deed charging property with the repayment of money lent, and with interest; a certificate of drawback.
Debilitate, dē-bil'i-tāt, *vt.* (debilitating, debilitated). To enfeeble; to enervate.
Debility, dē-bil'i-ti, *n.* Weakness; feebleness.
Debit, deb'it, *n.* A recorded item of debt; the left-hand page or debtor side of a ledger or account.—*vt.* To charge with debt.
Debonair, de-bō-nār', *a.* Gracious; courteous.
Debouch, dē-bösh', *vi.* To issue, or march out of a narrow place.
Debris, dē-brē', *n.sing.* or *pl.* Fragments; rubbish.
Debt, det, *n.* That which is due from one person to another; obligation; guilt.
Debtor, det'ėr, *n.* One who owes money, goods, or services; one indebted.
Début, dā-bu', *n.* First appearance in public.
Débutant, dā-bu-täng; *fem.* **Débutante,** dā-bu-tängt, *n.* One who makes a début.
Decade, de'kād, *n.* The number of ten; a period of ten years.
Decadence, Decadency, dē-kā'dens, dē-kā'den-si or dek'a-, *n.* A falling off; decay.
Decadent, dē-kā'dent or dek'a-, *a.* Decaying; deteriorating.
Decagon, de'ka-gon, *n.* A figure having ten sides.
Decahedron, de-ka-hē'dron, *n.* A solid figure or body having ten sides.
Decalogue, de'ka-log, *n.* The ten commandments given by God to Moses.
Decamp, dē-kamp', *vi.* To depart from a camp; to march off; to take oneself off.
Decampment, dē-kamp'ment, *n.* Departure from a camp; a marching off.
Decant, dē-kant', *vt.* To pour from one vessel into another.
Decanter, dē-kant'ėr, *n.* A glass bottle used for holding wine or other liquors.
Decapitate, dē-kap'it-āt, *vt.* (decapitating, decapitated). To behead.
Decapitation, dē-kap'it-ā"shon, *n.* Act of beheading.
Decapod, dek'a-pod, *n.* A crustacean having ten feet, as a crab; also a cuttle-fish with ten prehensile arms.
Decarbonize, decarburize, dē-kär'bon-īz, dē-kär'bū-rīz, *vt.* To deprive of carbon.
Decay, dē-kā', *vi.* To pass from a sound or prosperous state; to waste; to wither; to fail.—*n.* Gradual loss of strength, excellence, &c.; corruption; putrefaction.
Decease, dē-sēs', *n.* Departure from this life; death.—*vi.* (deceasing, deceased). To die.
Deceased, dē-sēst', *a.* Dead; often as a noun (with *the*).
Deceit, dē-sēt', *n.* Fraud; guile; cunning.
Deceitful, dē-sēt'fụl, *a.* Fraudulent; delusive; false; hollow.
Deceitfully, dē-sēt'fụl-li, *adv.* In a deceitful manner.
Deceivable, dē-sēv'a-bl, *a.* Capable of being deceived; exposed to imposture.
Deceive, dē-sēv', *vt.* (deceiving, deceived). To mislead the mind of; to impose on; to delude; to frustrate (hopes, &c.).
Deceiver, dē-sēv'ėr, *n.* One who deceives.
December, dē-sem'bėr, *n.* The twelfth and last month of the year.
Decemvir, dē-sem'vėr, *n.*; pl. **-viri** or **-virs.** One of ten magistrates, who had absolute authority in Rome from B.C. 449 to 447.
Decency, dē'sen-si, *n.* The state or quality of being decent; decorum; modesty.
Decennial, dē-sen'ni-al, *a.* Consisting of ten years; happening every ten years.
Decent, dē'sent, *a.* Becoming; seemly; respectable; modest; moderate.
Decently, dē'sent-li, *adv.* In a decent manner.
Decentralize, dē-sen'tral-īz, *vt.* To remove from direct dependence on a central authority.
Deception, dē-sep'shon, *n.* Act of deceiving; state of being deceived; artifice practised; fraud; double-dealing.
Deceptive, dē-sep'tiv, *a.* Tending to deceive; misleading; false; delusive.
Decidable, dē-sīd'a-bl, *a.* That may be decided.
Decide, dē-sīd', *vt.* (deciding, decided). To determine; to settle; to resolve.—*vi.* To determine; to pronounce a judgment.
Decided, dē-sīd'ed, *a.* Clear; resolute.
Decidedly, dē-sīd'ed-li, *adv.* Clearly; indisputably.
Deciduous, dē-sid'ū-us, *a.* Not permanent; having leaves that fall in autumn.
Decimal, de'si-mal, *a.* Tenth; reckoned by ten.—*n.* A tenth.
Decimate, de'si-māt, *vt.* (decimating, decimated). To kill every tenth man of; to tithe; to destroy a large number of.
Decimation, de-si-mā'shon, *n.* Act of decimating; a tithing.
Decipher, dē-sī'fėr, *vt.* To explain what is written in ciphers; to read what is not clear; to interpret.
Decipherable, dē-sī'fėr-a-bl, *a.* That may be deciphered.
Decipherer, dē-sī'fėr-ėr, *n.* One who deciphers.
Decision, dē-si'zhon, *n.* Determination of a difference, doubt, or event; final judgment; firmness of purpose or character.
Decisive, dē-sī'siv, *a.* Conclusive; absolute; marked by prompt determination.
Decisively, dē-sī'siv-li, *adv.* Conclusively.
Deck, dek, *vt.* To clothe; to adorn; to furnish with a deck, as a vessel.—*n.* The platform or floor of a ship.
Decker, dek'ėr, *n.* One who decks; a ship having decks; as, a three-decker.
Declaim, dē-klām', *vi.* To make a formal speech; to harangue; to inveigh.
Declaimer, dē-klām'ėr, *n.* One who declaims.
Declamation, de-kla-mā'shon, *n.* The art or act of declaiming; a harangue.
Declamatory, dē-klam'a-to-ri, *a.* Relating to the practice of declaiming; rhetorical, without solid sense or argument.
Declarable, dē-klār'a-bl, *a.* That may be declared or proved.
Declaration, de-kla-rā'shon, *n.* Act of declaring; that which is declared; an explicit statement; a solemn affirmation.

Declarative, dē-klār'at-iv, *a.* Explanatory; making proclamation.
Declaratory, dē-kla'ra-to-ri, *a.* Making declaration or manifestation; expressive.
Declare, dē-klār', *vt.* (declaring, declared). To show clearly; to tell explicitly; to testify; to reveal.—*vi.* To make a declaration.
Declared, dē-klārd', *p.a.* Made known; avowed; openly professed.
Declension, dē-klen'shon, *n.* The act or state of declining; refusal; the change of the terminations of nouns, adjectives, and pronouns to form the oblique cases.
Declinable, dē-klīn'a-bl, *a.* That may be declined.
Declination, de-klin-ā'shon, *n.* A bending downwards; decay; deviation from rectitude; angular distance of a heavenly body north or south from the equator; variation of the magnetic needle from the true meridian of a place.
Decline, dē-klīn', *vi.* (declining, declined). To bend downwards; to serve; to fail; not to comply.—*vt.* To bend downward; to refuse; to change the termination of a noun, &c.—*n.* A falling off; decay; deterioration; consumption.
Declinometer, dek-lī-nom'et-ėr, *n.* An instrument for measuring the declination of the magnetic needle.
Declivity, dē-kli'vi-ti, *n.* Inclining downward; a downward slope.
Decoct, dē-kokt', *vt.* To prepare by boiling; to digest by heat.
Decoction, dē-kok'shon, *n.* The act of boiling a substance in water to extract its virtues; the preparation thus obtained.
Decollate, dē-kol'āt, *vt.* To behead.
Decolorate, Decolorize, dē-kul'ėr-āt, dē-kul'ėr-īz, *vt.* To deprive of colour.
Decomposable, dē-kom-pōz'a-bl, *a.* That may be decomposed.
Decompose, dē-kom-pōz', *vt.* To resolve into original elements.—*vi.* To become resolved into elementary particles; to decay.
Decomposition, dē-kom'pō-zi"shon, *n.* Act or process of decomposing; analysis; decay.
Decompound, dē-kom-pound', *a.* Compounded a second time.
Decorate, dek'ō-rāt, *vt.* (decorating, decorated). To adorn; to embellish.
Decoration, dek-ō-rā'shon, *n.* Act of decorating; that which adorns; a badge or medal.
Decorative, dek'ō-rāt-iv, *a.* Suited to adorn.
Decorator, dek'ō-rāt-ėr, *n.* One who decorates buildings by painting, &c.
Decorous, dē-kō'rus, *a.* Seemly; becoming; behaving with strict propriety.
Decorum, dē-kō'rum, *n.* Propriety of speech or behaviour; seemliness.
Decoy, dē-koi', *n.* An inclosure for catching ducks or wild fowls; a lure.—*vt.* To lure into a snare; to entice.
Decrease, dē-krēs', *vi.* (decreasing, decreased). To grow less.—*vt.* To cause to become less.—*n.* Gradual diminution; decay; the wane of the moon.
Decree, dē-krē', *n.* An edict; an order or law; predetermined purpose; judicial decision.—*vt.* (decreeing, decreed). To enact; to award; to determine judicially.—*vi.* To make an edict; to appoint by edict.
Decrement, de'krē-ment, *n.* Decrease; quantity lost by diminution or waste.
Decrepit, dē-krep'it, *a.* Broken down with age; being in the last stage of decay.
Decrepitate, dē-krep'it-āt, *vt.* To calcine in a strong heat, with a continual crackling of the substance.—*vi.* To crackle when roasting.
Decrepitation, dē-krep'it-ā"shon, *n.* The separation of parts with a crackling noise.
Decrepitude, dē-krep'it-ūd, *n.* The crazy state of the body produced by decay or age.
Decretal, dē-krēt'al, *a.* Containing a decree —*n.* A decree of the pope; a collection of papal decrees.
Decretive, dē-krēt'iv, *a.* Having the force of a decree; making a decree.
Decretory, de'krē-to-ri, *a.* Established by a decree; judicial; definitive.
Decrial, dē-krī-al, *n.* The act of decrying.
Decry, dē-krī', *vt.* To cry down; to rail against; to censure; to depreciate.
Decumbent, dē-kum'bent, *a.* Lying down; recumbent; prostrate.
Decuple, de'kū-pl, *a.* Tenfold.—*n.* A number ten times repeated.
Decussate, dē-kus'āt, *vt.* and *i.* To intersect; to cross.—*a.* Crossing; intersected.
Dedicate, ded'i-kāt, *vt.* (dedicating, dedicated). To consecrate to a sacred purpose; to devote (often refl.); to inscribe to a friend.
Dedication, ded-i-kā'shon, *n.* Act of devoting to some person, use, or thing; inscription or address.
Dedicator, ded'i-kāt-ėr, *n.* One who dedicates.
Dedicatory, ded'i-kā-to-ri, *a.* Serving to dedicate, or as a dedication.
Deduce, dē-dūs', *vt.* (deducing, deduced). To draw or bring; to gather from premises; to infer; to derive.
Deducible, dē-dūs'i-bl, *a.* That may be deduced or inferred.
Deduct, dē-dukt', *vt.* To subtract.
Deduction, dē-duk'shon, *n.* Inference; abatement; discount.
Deductive, dē-duk'tiv, *a.* That is or may be deduced from premises.
Deductively, dē-duk'tiv-li, *adv.* In a deductive manner; by deduction.
Deed, dēd, *n.* That which is done; an act; feat; reality; a written agreement; an instrument conveying real estate.
Deem, dēm, *vt.* To judge; to think.—*vi.* To judge; to be of opinion; to estimate.
Deemster, dēm'stėr, *n.* One of the two chief justices of the Isle of Man.
Deep, dēp, *a.* Being far below the surface; descending far downward; low in situation; not obvious; sagacious; designing; grave in sound; very still or solemn; thick; strongly coloured; mysterious; heartfelt; absorbed. —*n.* The sea; the abyss of waters; any abyss.
Deepen, dēp'n, *vt.* To make deep or deeper. *vi.* To become more deep.
Deep-laid, dēp'lād, *a.* Formed with great skill or artifice.
Deeply, dēp'li, *adv.* At or to a great depth; profoundly.
Deer, dēr, *n. sing.* and *pl.* A quadruped of several species, as the stag, the fallow-deer, the roebuck, the reindeer, &c.
Deer-stalking, dēr'stak-ing, *n.* The hunting of deer on foot, by stealing within shot of them unawares.
Deface, dē-fās', *vt.* To destroy or mar the surface of a thing; to disfigure; to erase.

Defacement, dē-fās'ment, *n.* Injury to the surface or beauty; obliteration; that which mars or disfigures.
Defalcate, dē-fal'kāt, *vt.* To take away or deduct.
Defalcation, dē-fal-kā'shon, *n.* A deficit; a fraudulent abstraction of money.
Defalcator, def'al-kāt-ėr, *n.* One guilty of defalcation or embezzlement.
Defamation, de-fa-mā'shon, *n.* Act of defaming; slander; calumny.
Defamatory, dē-fam'a-to-ri, *a.* Calumnious; slanderous.
Defame, dē-fām', *vt.* (defaming, defamed). To accuse falsely and maliciously; to slander.
Defamer, dē-fām'ėr, *n.* A slanderer.
Default, dē-fạlt', *n.* An omission; neglect to do what duty or law requires; failure to appear in court.—*vi.* To fail in fulfilling an engagement, contract, &c.
Defaulter, dē-fạlt'ėr, *n.* One who makes default; one who fails to account for money intrusted to his care; a delinquent.
Defeat, dē-fēt', *n.* Frustration; overthrow; loss of battle.—*vt.* To frustrate; to foil, to overthrow; to conquer.
Defecate, de'fē-kāt, *vt.* To clear from lees; to purify.—*vi.* To void excrement.
Defecation, de-fē-kā'shon, *n.* Act of separating from lees; purification.
Defect, dē-fekt', *n.* Want; a blemish; fault; flaw.
Defection, dē-fek'shon, *n.* Act of abandoning a person or cause; apostasy.
Defective, dē-fekt'iv, *a.* Having a defect; deficient; faulty.
Defectively, dē-fekt'iv-li, *adv.* In a defective manner.
Defence, dē-fens', *n.* A guarding against danger; protection; fortification; vindication; apology; plea; method adopted by one against whom legal proceedings are taken; skill in fencing.
Defenceless, dē-fens'les, *a.* Without defence; unprotected; weak.
Defend, dē-fend', *vt.* To guard; to support; to resist; to vindicate; to act as defendant.—*vi.* To make defence or opposition.
Defendant, dē-fend'ant, *n.* A defender; in *law*, the person that opposes a charge, &c.
Defender, dē-fend'ėr, *n.* One who defends; a protector, supporter, or vindicator.
Defensible, dē-fens'i-bl, *a.* That may be vindicated, maintained, or justified.
Defensive, dē-fens'iv, *a.* Proper for defence; carried on in resisting attack; in a state or posture to defend.—*n.* That which defends; state or posture of defence.
Defensory, dē-fens'o-ri, *a.* Tending to defend.
Defer, dē-fėr', *vt.* (deferring, deferred). To put off to a future time; to postpone.—*vi.* To yield to another's opinion; to submit courteously or from respect.
Deference, de'fėr-ens, *n.* A yielding in opinion; regard; respect; submission.
Deferential, de-fėr-en'shal, *a.* Expressing or implying deference; respectful.
Deferentially, de-fėr-en'shal-li, *adv.* With deference.
Deferment, dē-fėr'ment, *n.* Postponement.
Defiance, dē-fī'ans, *n.* Act of defying; a challenge to fight; contempt of opposition or danger.
Defiant, dē-fī'ant, *a.* Characterized by defiance, boldness, or insolence.
Deficiency, Deficience, de-fi'shen-si, de-fi'shens, *n.* Want; defect.
Deficient, de-fi'shent, *a.* Defective; imperfect; not adequate.
Deficit, de'fi-sit, *n.* Deficiency of revenue.
Defile, dē-fīl', *vt.* (defiling, defiled). To make foul; to pollute; to violate the chastity of; to march off in a line, or file by file.—*n.* A narrow way in which troops may march only in a line, or with a narrow front; a long narrow pass.
Defilement, dē-fīl'ment, *n.* Act of defiling, or state of being defiled.
Defiler, dē-fīl'ėr, *n.* One who defiles.
Definable, dē-fīn'a-bl, *a.* That may be defined.
Define, dē-fīn', *vt.* (defining, defined). To limit; to explain exactly.
Definite, de'fin-it, *a.* Having fixed limits; precise; exact; clear.
Definitely, de'fin-it-li, *adv.* Precisely.
Definition, de-fi-ni'shon, *n.* The act of defining; a brief description of a thing by its properties; an explanation in words.
Definitive, dē-fin'it-iv, *a.* Limiting; positive; determining; final.—*n.* A word used to limit the signification of a noun.
Definitively, dē-fin'it-iv-li, *adv.* In a definitive manner.
Deflagrate, de'flā-grāt, *vi.* To burn with a sudden and violent combustion.—*vt.* To set fire to.
Deflagration, de-flā-grā'shon, *n.* A sudden and violent combustion.
Deflagrator, de'flā-grāt-ėr, *n.* An instrument for producing rapid combustion.
Deflect, dē-flekt', *vi.* To deviate; to swerve. —*vt.* To cause to turn aside.
Deflection, Deflexion, Deflexure, dē-flek'-shon, dē-flek'sūr, *n.* Deviation; a turning from a true line or regular course.
Defloration, dē-flōr-ā'shon, *n.* Act of deflowering; rape.
Deflower, Deflour, dē-flou'ėr, dē-flour', *vt.* To strip of flowers, or of bloom and beauty; to deprive of virginity.
Defluxion, dē-fluk'shon, *n.* A discharge of fluid from a mucous membrane.
Defoliation, dē-fō'li-ā"shon, *n.* The fall of the leaf, or shedding of leaves.
Deforce, dē-fōrs', *vt.* To keep out of lawful possession; to resist (an officer of the law) in the execution of official duty.
Deforcement, dē-fōrs'ment, *n.* The act of deforcing.
Deform, dē-form', *vt.* To mar in form; to disfigure.
Deformation, dē-form-ā'shon, *n.* A disfiguring or defacing.
Deformed, dē-formd', *a.* Disfigured; distorted; misshapen.
Deformity, dē-form'i-ti, *n.* Want of proper form; distortion; gross deviation from propriety.
Defraud, dē-frạd', *vt.* To deprive of or withhold from wrongfully.
Defray, dē-frā', *vt.* To discharge or pay, as the expenses of anything.
Defrayal, Defrayment, dē-frā'al, dē-frā'-ment, *n.* The act of defraying.
Deft, deft, *a.* Apt; clever.
Deftly, deft'li, *adv.* Aptly; fitly; neatly.

Defunct, dē-fungkt′, *a.* Dead; deceased.—*n.* A dead person; one deceased.
Defy, dē-fī′, *vt.* (defying, defied). To provoke to combat; to dare; to challenge; to set at nought.
De-gauss, dē-gous, *vt.* To neutralize the magnetization of a ship so as to prevent it from exploding magnetic mines.
Degeneracy, dē-jen′ė-ra-si, *n.* A growing worse or inferior; decline in good qualities; departure from the virtue of ancestors.
Degenerate, dē-jen′ė-rāt, *vi.* To become worse than one's kind; to decay in good qualities.—*a.* Fallen from primitive or natural excellence; mean; corrupt.
Degeneration, dē-jen′ė-rā″shon, *n.* A degenerate state; degeneracy; deterioration.
Deglutition, dē-glū-ti′shon, *n.* Act or power of swallowing.
Degradation, de-gra-dā′shon, *n.* Act of degrading; state of being degraded; debasement; disgrace; a gradual wasting away.
Degrade, dē-grād′, *vt.* (degrading, degraded). To reduce to a lower rank; to strip of honours, to debase; to depose; to dishonour.
Degraded, dē-grād′ed, *p.a.* Sunk to an abject state; exhibiting degradation; debased.
Degrading, dē-grād′ing, *p.a.* Dishonouring.
Degree, dē-grē′, *n.* A step; step in relationship, rank, quality, &c.; measure; extent; the 360th part of the circumference of a circle; a mark of distinction conferred by universities; divisions marked on scientific instruments.
Dehisce, dē-his′, *vi.* To open, as seed-vessels.
Dehort, dē-hort′, *vt.* To dissuade.
Dehydration, dē-hī-drā′shon, *n.* Process of freeing a compound from water.
Deification, dē′if-ik-ā″shon, *n.* Act of deifying.
Deiform, dē′i-form, *a.* Of a god-like form.
Deify, dē′i-fī, *vt.* (deifying, deified). To exalt to the rank of a deity; to extol as an object of supreme regard.
Deign, dān, *vi.* To vouchsafe; to condescend. —*vt.* To condescend to give.
Deism, dē′izm, *n.* The doctrine of a deist.
Deist, dē′ist, *n.* One who acknowledges the existence of a God, but denies revealed religion; a freethinker.
Deistic, Deistical, dē-ist′ik, dē-ist′ik-al, *a.* Pertaining to deism or to deists.
Deity, dē′i-ti, *n.* Godhead; the Supreme Being; a fabulous god or goddess; a divinity.
Deject, dē-jekt′, *vt.* To dispirit; to depress.
Dejected, dē-jekt′ed, *p.a.* Cast down; depressed; grieved; discouraged.
Dejection, dē-jek′shon, *n.* Depression; melancholy; lowness of spirits.
Déjeuner, dā-zhö-nā, *n.* Breakfast; luncheon.
Delaine, dē-lān′, *n.* A figured muslin made of cotton and wool.
Delay, dē-lā′, *vt.* To defer; to retard; to stop; to protract.—*vi.* To linger; to stop for a time.—*n.* A lingering; stay; hindrance.
Delectable, dē-lekt′a-bl, *a.* Delightful.
Delectation, dē-lek-tā′shon, *n.* A giving of pleasure or delight.
Delegate, de′lē-gāt, *vt.* (delegating, delegated). To send as a representative; to depute; to commit to another's care.—*n.* A representative; a deputy.
Delegation, de-lē-gā′shon, *n.* Act of delegating; persons delegated; a commission.
Delete, dē-lēt′, *vt.* (deleting, deleted). To blot out; to erase; to efface.
Deleterious, de-lē-tē′ri-us, *a.* Hurtful; poisonous; pernicious.
Deletion, dē-lē′shon, *n.* Act of deleting; an erasure; passage deleted.
Delf, delf, *n.* Earthenware, covered with enamel or white glazing in imitation of china-ware or porcelain.
Deliberate, dē-lib′ė-rāt, *vi.* To weigh well in one's mind; to consider; to consult; to debate.—*vt.* To balance well in the mind; to consider.—*a.* Cautious; discreet; well advised.
Deliberately, dē-lib′ė-rāt-li, *adv.* In a deliberate manner; slowly; cautiously.
Deliberation, dē-lib′ė-rā″shon, *n.* Thoughtful consideration; prudence; discussion of reasons for and against a measure.
Deliberative, dē-lib′ė-rāt-iv, *a.* Proceeding or acting by deliberation; having a right to deliberate.
Delicacy, de′li-ka-si, *n.* The quality of being delicate; fineness of texture; tenderness; minute accuracy; refined taste; a dainty.
Delicate, de′li-kāt, *a.* Pleasing to the taste or senses; choice; fine; soft; smooth; nice in forms; minute; easily hurt or affected; tender; not robust.
Delicately, de′li-kāt-li, *adv.* In a delicate manner; finely.
Delicious, dē-li′shus, *a.* Highly pleasing to the taste; delightful.
Delight, dē-līt′, *n.* That which yields great pleasure; a high degree of pleasure; joy.—*vt.* To affect with great pleasure; to give high satisfaction to.—*vi.* To take great pleasure; to be rejoiced.
Delighted, dē-līt′ed, *a.* Experiencing delight; charmed.
Delightful, dē-līt′fụl, *a.* Affording great pleasure and satisfaction; charming.
Delimit, dē-lim′it, *vt.* To mark or settle distinctly the limits of.
Delimitation, dē-lim′i-tā″shon, *n.* The act of delimiting; fixing of boundaries.
Delineate, dē-lin′ē-āt, *vt.* To draw the lines showing the form of; to sketch; to describe.
Delineation, dē-lin′ē-ā″shon, *n.* Act of delineating; outline; sketch; description.
Delineator, dē-lin′ē-āt-ėr, *n.* One who delineates.
Delinquency, dē-lin′kwen-si, *n.* An omission of duty; fault; offence; crime.
Delinquent, dē-lin′kwent, *a.* Neglecting duty.—*n.* One who fails to perform his duty; one who commits a fault or crime.
Deliquesce, dē-li-kwes′, *vi.* To melt by absorbing moisture from the air.
Deliquescence, dē-li-kwes′ens, *n.* Act or process of deliquescing.
Deliquescent, dē-li-kwes′ent, *a.* That deliquesces; liquefying in the air.
Delirious, dē-li′ri-us, *a.* Disordered in intellect; raving; frenzied; insane.
Delirium, dē-li′ri-um, *n.* Temporary disorder of the mind; violent excitement.
Delitescence. Delitescency, del-i-tes′ens, del-i-tes′en-si, *n.* The state of being concealed, or not active or manifest.
Deliver, dē-liv′ėr, *vt.* To free, as from danger or bondage; to disburden a woman of a child; to surrender; to commit; to give forth in words or in action.

Deliverance, dē-liv'ėr-ans, *n.* Release; rescue; an authoritative judgment.
Deliverer, dē-liv'ėr-ėr, *n.* One who delivers.
Delivery, dē-liv'ė-ri, *n.* Act of delivering; childbirth; rescue; surrender; distribution (of letters); manner of speaking.
Dell, del, *n.* A small valley; a glen.
Delta, del'ta, *n.* The space between diverging mouths of a river, as the Nile.
Deltoid, del'toid, *a.* Triangular.
Delude, dē-lūd', *vt.* (deluding, deluded). To impose on; to deceive; to circumvent.
Deluge, del'ūj, *n.* A flood; an inundation; the flood in the days of Noah; a sweeping or overwhelming calamity.—*vt.* (deluging, deluged). To inundate; to drown; to overwhelm.
Delusion, dē-lū'zhon, *n.* Act of deluding; a false belief; illusion; fallacy.
Delusive, dē-lū'siv, *a.* Apt to deceive.
Delusory, dē-lū'so-ri, *a.* Delusive.
Delve, delv, *vt.* and *i.* (delving, delved). To dig.
Delver, delv'ėr, *n.* One who delves.
Demagnetize, dē-mag'net-īz, *vt.* To deprive of magnetic polarity.
Demagogue, dem'a-gog, *n.* A leader of the people; a factious orator.
Demand, dē-mand', *vt.* To seek as due by right; to require; to interrogate.—*n.* A claim by virtue of a right; an asking with authority; debt; the calling for in order to purchase; desire to purchase or possess.
Demandable, dē-mand'a-bl, *a.* That may be demanded.
Demandant, dē-mand'ant, *n.* One who demands; the plaintiff in a real action.
Demarcation, dē-mär-kā'shon, *n.* Act of setting a limit; a limit fixed.
Demean, dē-mēn', *vt.* To conduct; to behave; to debase (oneself).
Demeanour, dē-mēn'ėr, *n.* Manner of conducting oneself; behaviour.
Demented, dē-ment'ed, *a.* Insane; infatuated.
Demerit, dē-me'rit, *n.* Fault; vice.
Demesne, de-mān', *n.* The land adjacent to a manor-house kept in the proprietor's own hands; a domain or region.
Demi-god, de'mi-god, *n.* Half a god; one partaking of the divine nature.
Demi-monde, demi'-mongd, *n.* The class of fashionable courtesans.
Demirep, dem'i-rep, *n.* A woman of doubtful reputation.
Demisable, dē-mīz'a-bl, *a.* That may be demised.
Demise, dē-mīz', *n.* Death; conveyance of an estate by lease or will.—*vt.* (demising, demised). To transfer; to lease; to bequeath.
Demission, dē-mi'shon, *n.* A laying down office; resignation; transference.
Demit, dē-mit', *vt.* (demitting, demitted). To lay down formally, as an office.
Demiurge, Demiurgus, dē'mi-ėrj, dē-mi-ėr-gus, *n.* A maker; the Creator.
Demobilize, dē-mō'bil-īz, *vt.* To disband.
Democracy, dē-mok'ra-si, *n.* A form of government in which the supreme power is vested in the people.
Democrat, dem'ō-krat, *n.* One who adheres to democracy.
Democratic, Democratical, dem-ō-krat'ik, dem-ō-krat'ik-al, *a.* Pertaining to democracy.
Demogorgon, dē-mō-gor'gon, *n.* A terrifying divinity in ancient mythology.
Demoiselle, dem-wä-zel', *n.* A damsel.
Demolish, dē-mol'ish, *vt.* To pull down; to destroy.
Demolition, dē-mō-li'shon, *n.* Act of demolishing; ruin; destruction.
Demon, dē'mon, *n.* A spirit, holding a place below the celestial deities of the pagans; an evil spirit; a devil; a fiend-like man.
Demonetize, dē-mon'e-tīz, *vt.* To deprive of standard value, as money; to withdraw from circulation.
Demoniac, dē-mō'ni-ak, *n.* A human being possessed by a demon.
Demoniac, Demoniacal, dē-mō'ni-ak, dē-mō-nī'ak-al, *a.* Pertaining to demons; influenced or produced by demons.
Demonism, dē'mon-izm, *n.* Belief in demons.
Demonize, dē'mon-īz, *vt.* To fill with the spirit of a demon.
Demonology, dē-mon-ol'o-ji, *n.* Knowledge of, or a treatise on, evil spirits.
Demonstrable, de-mon'stra-bl, *a.* That may be demonstrated or proved.
Demonstrably, de-mon'stra-bli, *adv.* In a manner to preclude doubt.
Demonstrate, de-mon'strāt, *vt.* (demonstrating, demonstrated). To prove beyond doubt; to make evident; to exhibit.
Demonstration, de-mon-strā'shon, *n.* Act or process of demonstrating; proof; massing of troops to deceive the enemy; a gathering to exhibit sympathy with a person or cause.
Demonstrative, de-mon'strāt-iv, *a.* Serving to demonstrate; outwardly expressive of feelings; indicating clearly.
Demonstrator, de'mon-strāt-ėr, *n.* One who demonstrates.
Demoralization, dē-mo'ral-īz-ā''shon, *n.* Act of demoralizing.
Demoralize, dē-mo'ral-īz, *vt.* To corrupt the morals of; to deprave.
Demoralizing, dē-mo'ral-īz-ing, *p.a.* Tending to destroy morals or moral principles.
Demos, dē'mos, *n.* The people at large.
Demotic, dē-mot'ik, *a.* Pertaining to the common people; applied to the popular alphabet of the ancient Egyptians, as distinguished from the *hieratic*.
Demulcent, dē-mul'sent, *a.* Softening; mollifying.—*n.* A medicine to soothe irritation.
Demur, dē-mėr', *vi.* (demurring, demurred). To hesitate; to object.—*n.* Pause; suspense of proceeding or decision; objection stated.
Demure, dē-mūr', *a.* Consciously grave; affectedly modest.
Demurrage, dē-mu'rāj, *n.* Delay of a vessel, railway wagon, &c., in loading or unloading; compensation for such delay; charge for the exchange of notes or coin into bullion.
Demurrer, dē-mėr'ėr, *n.* One who demurs; a stop at som point in law pleadings; an issue on matter of law.
Demy, dē-mī', *n.* A particular size of paper, generally 22 × 17 inches.
Den, den, *n.* A cave; a dell; a haunt.
Denary, dē'na-ri, *a.* Containing ten; proceeding by tens.—*n.* The number ten.
Denationalize, dē-na'shon-al-īz, *vt.* To divest of national character or rights.
Denaturalize, dē-na'tūr-al-īz, *vt.* To render unnatural; to deprive of naturalization.

Dendriform, den'dri-form, *a.* Having the form or appearance of a tree.
Dendritic, Dendritical, den-drit'ik, den-drit'i-kal, *a.* Resembling a tree; marked by figures resembling shrubs, moss, &c.
Denial, dē-nī'al, *n.* Act of denying; contradiction; refusal to grant or acknowledge.
Denigrate, den'i-grāt, *vt.* To blacken; to sully.
Denim, den'im, *n.* A coarse cotton drill used for making aprons, overalls, &c.
Denizen, de'ni-zn, *n.* A stranger admitted to residence in a foreign country.
Denominate, dē-nom'in-āt, *vt.* (denominating, denominated). To name; to designate.
Denomination, dē-nom'in-ā''shon, *n.* Act of naming; title; class; religious sect.
Denominational, dē-nom'in-ā''shon-al, *a.* Pertaining to a denomination.
Denominationalism, dē-nom'in-ā''shon-al-izm, *n.* A class spirit; system of religious sects having each their own schools.
Denominative, dē-nom'in-āt-iv, *a.* That confers a distinct appellation.
Denominator, dē-nom'in-āt-ėr, *n.* One who or that which denominates; that number placed below the line in vulgar fractions.
Denotable, dē-nōt'a-bl, *a.* That may be denoted or marked.
Denote, dē-nōt', *vt.* To indicate; to imply.
Dénouement, dā-nö'mäng, *n.* The winding up of a plot in a novel or drama; solution of a mystery; issue; the event.
Denounce, dē-nouns', *vt.* (denouncing, denounced). To threaten; to accuse publicly; to stigmatize.
Denouncement, dē-nouns'ment, *n.* Act of denouncing; denunciation.
Dense, dens, *a.* Thick; close; compact.
Density, dens'i-ti, *n.* Closeness of constituent parts; compactness.
Dent, dent, *n.* A mark made by a blow on a solid body.—*vt.* To make a dent on.
Dental, den'tal, *a.* Pertaining to the teeth; pronounced by the teeth and the tip of the tongue.—*n.* A dental letter or sound, as *d*, *t*, *th*.
Dentate, Dentated, den'tāt, den'tāt-ed, *a.* Toothed; notched.
Denticle, den'ti-kl, *n.* A small tooth or projecting point.
Denticulate, Denticulated, den-tik'ū-lāt, den-tik'ū-lāt-ed, *a.* Having small teeth.
Dentiform, den'ti-form, *a.* Having the form of a tooth.
Dentifrice, den'ti-fris, *n.* A powder or other substance for cleansing the teeth.
Dentine, den'tin, *n.* The ivory tissue forming the body of the tooth.
Dentist, den'tist, *n.* One whose occupation is to extract, repair, or replace teeth.
Dentition, den-ti'shon, *n.* The cutting of teeth in infancy; the system of teeth peculiar to an animal.
Denture, den'tūr, *n.* A set of false teeth.
Denudation, dē-nūd-ā'shon, *n.* Act of denuding; exposure of rocks by the action of water.
Denude, dē-nūd', *vt.* (denuding, denuded). To make bare; to divest; to uncover.
Denunciation, dē-nun'si-ā''shon, *n.* Act of denouncing; public menace; arraignment.
Denunciator, dē-nun'si-āt-ėr, *n.* One who denounces or threatens publicly.
Denunciatory, dē-nun'si-a-to-ri, *a.* Characterized by denunciation; ready to denounce.
Deny, dē-nī', *vt.* (denying, denied). To declare not to be true; to disavow; to refuse to grant or acknowledge; not to afford or yield.
Deodorize, dē-ō'dėr-īz, *vt.* (deodorizing, deodorized). To deprive of fetid odour.
Deodorizer, Deodorant, dē-ō'dėr-ī-zėr, dē-ō'dėr-ant, *n.* A substance which destroys fetid effluvia.
Deoxidate, Deoxidize, dē-ok'sid-āt, dē-ok'-sid-īz, *vt.* To reduce from the state of an oxide.
Deoxidation, dē-ok'sid-ā''shon, *n.* The act or process of deoxidating.
Depart, dē-pärt', *vi.* To go away; to desist; to abandon; to deviate; to die.
Department, dē-pärt'ment, *n.* A separate part; a division of territory; a distinct branch, as of science, &c.
Departmental, dē-pärt'ment-al, *a.* Pertaining to a department.
Departure, dē-pärt'ūr, *n.* Act of going away; withdrawal; abandonment; death.
Depasture, dē-pas'tūr, *vt.* To eat up; to consume.—*vi.* To feed; to graze.
Depend, dē-pend', *vi.* To hang from; to be contingent or conditioned; to rest or rely solely; to trust.
Dependant, Dependent, dē-pend'ant, dē-pend'ent, *n.* One who depends on another; a retainer. (The spelling with *-ant* is more common in the noun, with *-ent* in the adj.)
Dependence, Dependance, dē-pend'ens, dē-pend'ans, *n.* State of being dependent; connection and support; reliance; trust.
Dependency, dē-pend'en-si, *n.* State of being dependent; that which is dependent; a subject territory.
Dependent, Dependant, dē-pend'ent, dē-pend'ant, *a.* Hanging down; subordinate; relying solely on another; contingent.
Dependently, Dependantly, dē-pend'ent-li, dē-pend'ant-li, *adv.* In a dependent manner.
Depict, dē-pikt', *vt.* To paint; to delineate; to represent in words.
Depilate, dep'i-lāt, *vt.* To strip of hair.
Depilatory, dē-pil'ā-to-ri, *n.* An application to remove hair from the skin.
Deplete, dē-plēt', *vt.* (depleting, depleted). To empty, reduce, or exhaust.
Depletion, dē-plē'shon, *n.* Act of depleting; act of diminishing the quantity of blood by blood-letting.
Deplorable, dē-plōr'a-bl, *a.* To be deplored; lamentable; grievous; pitiable.
Deplorably, dē-plōr'a-bli, *adv.* In a manner to be deplored.
Deplore, dē-plōr', *vt.* (deploring, deplored). To feel or express deep grief for; to bewail.
Deploy, dē-ploi', *vt.* To open out; to extend from column to line as a body of troops.—*vi.* To form a more extended front or line.
Deployment, dē-ploi'ment. The act of deploying.
Deplume, dē-plūm', *vt.* To strip of feathers.
Depolarize, dē-pō'lär-īz, *vt.* To deprive of polarity.
Depone, dē-pōn', *vi.* (deponing, deponed). To give testimony; to depose.
Deponent, dē-pōn'ent, *a.* Laying down; that has a passive form but an active signification.—*n.* One who gives testimony under oath; a deponent verb.

Depopulate, dē-po′pū-lāt, *vt.* To deprive of inhabitants; to dispeople.
Depopulation, dē-po′pū-lā″shon, *n.* Act or process of depopulating; decrease of population.
Depopulator, dē-po′pū-lāt-ėr, *n.* One who or that which depopulates.
Deport, dē-pōrt′, *vt.* To transport; to demean; to conduct (oneself).
Deportation, dē-pōrt-ā′shon, *n.* Removal from one country to another; exile.
Deportment, dē-pōrt′ment, *n.* Carriage; demeanour; manner of acting.
Deposable, dē-pōz′a-bl, *a.* That may be deposed or deprived of office.
Depose, dē-pōz′, *vt.* (deposing, deposed). To dethrone; to divest of office; to degrade.—*vi.* To bear witness; to give testimony in writing.
Deposit, dē-poz′it, *vt.* To lay down; to lodge in a place; to lay in a place for preservation; to intrust; to commit as a pledge.—*n.* Any matter laid down or lodged; anything intrusted to another; a thing given as security.
Depositary, dē-poz′it-a-ri, *n.* One to whom a thing is lodged in trust; a guardian.
Deposition, dē-pō-zi′shon, *n.* Act of depositing and of deposing; attested written testimony; declaration; act of dethroning a king, or degrading an official.
Depositor, dē-poz′it-ėr, *n.* One who makes a deposit; one who lodges money in a bank.
Depository, dē-poz′it-o-ri, *n.* A place where anything is lodged for safe-keeping.
Depot, dep′ō, *n.* A place of deposit; headquarters of a regiment; a railway-station.
Depravation, de-pra-vā′shon, *n.* Act of depraving; deterioration; degeneracy.
Deprave, dē-prāv′, *vt.* (depraving, depraved). To make bad or worse; to impair the good qualities of; to corrupt; to vitiate.
Depraved, dē-prāvd′, *a.* Given to evil courses; profligate; vitiated.
Depravity, dē-prav′i-ti, *n.* Corruption of moral principles; wickedness; profligacy.
Deprecate, de′prē-kāt, *vt.* (deprecating, deprecated). To pray for deliverance from; to plead against; to express regret or disapproval.
Deprecation, de-prē-kā′shon, *n.* Act of deprecating; protest; disapproval.
Deprecatory, Deprecative, de′prē-kā-to-ri, de′prē-kāt-iv, *a.* That serves to deprecate; containing protest or entreaty.
Depreciate, dē-prē′shi-āt, *vt.* (depreciating, depreciated). To bring down the price or value of; to undervalue; to disparage; to traduce.—*vi.* To fall in value.
Depreciation, dē-prē′shi-ā″shon, *n.* Act of depreciating; the falling of value.
Depreciative, Depreciatory, dē-prē′shi-āt-iv, dē-prē′shi-ā-to-ri, *a.* Tending to depreciate or undervalue.
Depredate, de′prē-dāt, *vt.* To plunder; to waste.
Depredation, de-prē-dā′shon, *n.* Act of plundering; pillaging.
Depredator, de′prē-dāt-ėr, *n.* One who plunders or pillages; a spoiler.
Depress, dē-pres′, *vt.* To press down; to lower; to humble; to deject.
Depressed, dē-prest′, *a.* Dejected; dispirited; flattened in shape.
Depression, dē-pre′shon, *n.* Act of depressing; state of being depressed; a low state; a sinking of a surface; a hollow; abasement; dejection; a state of dulness.
Depressive, dē-pres′iv, *a.* Able or tending to depress or cast down.
Deprivation, de-pri-vā′shon, *n.* Act of depriving; state of being deprived; want; bereavement; deposition of a clergyman.
Deprive, dē-priv′, *vt.* (depriving, deprived). To take from; to dispossess; to hinder from possessing or enjoying.
Depth, depth, *n.* Deepness; a deep place; the darkest or stillest part, as of the night; the inner part; abstruseness; unsearchableness; intensity; extent of penetration.
Deputation, de-pū-tā′shon, *n.* Act of deputing; the person or persons sent to transact business for another.
Depute, dē-pūt′, *vt.* (deputing, deputed). To appoint as a substitute; to send with authority to act for the sender; to assign to a deputy.
Deputy, de′pū-ti, *n.* A person appointed to act for another; a substitute; a delegate; an agent.
Deracinate, dē-ras′in-āt, *vt.* To pluck up by the roots; to extirpate.
Derange, dē-rānj′, *vt.* (deranging, deranged). To disturb the regular order of; to displace; to disconcert; to disorder the mind of.
Deranged, dē-rānjd′, *p.a.* Disordered in mind; distracted.
Derangement, dē-rānj′ment, *n.* A putting out of order; disorder; insanity.
Derelict, de′re-likt, *a.* Abandoned.—*n.* Anything forsaken or left, especially a ship.
Dereliction, de-re-lik′shon, *n.* Act of forsaking; state of being forsaken; neglect.
Deride, dē-rid′, *vt.* (deriding, derided). To laugh at in contempt; to ridicule; to jeer.
Derider, dē-rīd′ėr, *n.* A mocker; scoffer.
Deridingly, dē-rīd′ing-li, *adv.* By way of derision or mockery.
Derision, dē-ri′zhon, *n.* Act of deriding; scorn; ridicule; mockery.
Derisive, dē-rīs′iv, *a.* Mocking; ridiculing.
Derivable, dē-rīv′a-bl, *a.* That may be drawn or derived; deducible.
Derivably, dē-rīv′a-bli, *adv.* By derivation.
Derivation, de-ri-vā′shon, *a.* Act of deriving; the tracing of a word from its root; deduction.
Derivative, de-riv′āt-iv, *a.* Derived; secondary.—*n.* That which is derived; a word which takes its origin in another word.
Derivatively, de-riv′āt-iv-li, *adv.* In a derivative manner; by derivation.
Derive, de-rīv′, *vt.* (deriving, derived). To draw or receive, as from a source or origin; to trace the etymology of.—*vi.* To come from.
Derma, Dermis, Derm, dėr′ma, dėr′mis, dėrm, *n.* The true skin, or under layer of the skin.
Dermal, dėr′mal, *a.* Pertaining to skin; consisting of skin.
Dermatology, dėr-ma-tol′o-ji, *n.* The science which treats of skin and its diseases.
Dermo-skeleton, dėr′mo-skel″e-ton, *n.* The covering of scales, plates, shells, &c., of many animals, as crabs, crocodiles, &c.
Derogate, de′rō-gāt, *vt.* (derogating, derogated). To detract from; to disparage.—*vi.* To detract.
Derogation, de-rō-gā′shon, *n.* Act of derogating; detraction; disparagement.

Derogatory, dē-rog′ā-to-ri, *a.* Tending to lessen in repute, effect, &c.; disparaging.
Derrick, de′rik, *n.* A kind of crane for hoisting heavy weights.
Dervish, dėr′vish, *n.* A poor Mohammedan priest or monk.
Descant, des′kant, *n.* A discourse; discussion; a song or tune with various modulations.—*vi.* des-kant′. To discourse or animadvert freely; to add a part to a melody.
Descend, dē-send′, *vi.* To pass or move down; to invade; to be derived; to pass to an heir. —*vt.* To pass or move down, on, or along.
Descendant, dē-send′ant, *n.* Offspring from an ancestor; issue.
Descendent, dē-send′ent, *a.* Descending; proceeding from an original or ancestor.
Descendible, dē-send′i-bl, *a.* That may be descended or passed down; that may descend from an ancestor to an heir.
Descending, dē-send′ing, *p.a.* Moving or bent downward; gradually decreasing.
Descent, dē-sent′, *n.* Act of descending; declivity; invasion; a passing from an ancestor to an heir; lineage; distance from the common ancestor; descendants; a rank in the scale of subordination.
Describable, dē-skrīb′a-bl, *a.* That may be described.
Describe, dē-skrīb′, *vt.* (describing, described). To mark or trace out; to represent on paper, &c.; to portray; to relate.
Description, dē-skrip′shon, *n.* Act of describing; account; relation; class, species, kind.
Descriptive, dē-skrip′tiv, *a.* Containing description; having the quality of representing.
Descry, dē-skrī′, *vt.* (descrying, descried). To espy; to discover from a distance.
Desecrate, de′sē-krāt, *vt.* (desecrating, desecrated). To divert from a sacred purpose; to profane.
Desecration, de-sē-krā′shon, *n.* Act of desecrating; profanation.
Desert, de′zėrt, *a.* Waste; uncultivated.—*n.* An uninhabited tract; a vast sandy plain.
Desert. dē-zėrt′, *vt.* To leave, as service; to abandon; to quit.—*vi.* To run away; to quit a service without permission.—*n.* That which is deserved; merit or demerit; reward.
Deserter, dē-zėrt′ėr, *n.* One who deserts; a soldier or seaman who quits the service without permission.
Desertion, dē-zėr′shon, *n.* Act of deserting; state of being deserted.
Deserve, dē-zėrv′, *vt.* (deserving, deserved). To merit by qualities or services; to be worthy of.—*vi.* To merit; to be worthy of.
Deservedly, dē-zėrv′ed-li, *adv.* Justly; according to desert.
Deserving, dē-zėrv′ing, *a.* Worthy of reward or praise; meritorious.
Deshabille, dez-a-bēl′, *n.* The state of being in undress, or not fully dressed.
Desiccant, Desiccative, des′i-kant, or dē-sik′ant, dē-sik′a-tiv, *a.* Drying.—*n.* An application that dries a sore.
Desiccate, dē-sik′āt, *vt.* To exhaust of moisture; to dry.
Desiderate, dē-sid′ėr-āt, *vt.* To desire; to want; to miss.
Desiderative, dē-sid′ėr-āt-iv, *a.* Having, implying, or denoting desire.
Desideratum, dē-sid′ėr-ā″tum, *n.*; pl. **-ata.** That which is not possessed, but is desirable; something much wanted.
Design, dē-sīn′, *vt.* To delineate by drawing the outline of; to form in idea; to plan; to propose; to mean.—*vi.* To intend.—*n.* A representation of a thing by an outline; first idea represented by lines; a plan drawn out in the mind; purpose; aim; project.
Designate, de′sig-nāt, *vt.* (designating, designated). To point out; to name; to characterize; to appoint; to allot.
Designation, de-sig-nā′shon, *n.* Act of designating; appointment; assignment; appellation.
Designedly, dē-sīn′ed-li, *adv.* By design; purposely; intentionally.
Designer, dē-sīn′ėr, *n.* One who designs; a contriver; a plotter.
Designing, dē-sīn′ing, *a.* Artful; intriguing; deceitful; treacherous.
Desirability, dē-zīr′a-bil″i-ti, *n.* The state or quality of being desirable.
Desirable, dē-zīr′a-bl, *a.* Worthy of desire; pleasing; agreeable.
Desirably, dē-zīr′a-bli, *adv.* In a desirable manner.
Desire, dē-zīr′, *n.* Eagerness to obtain or enjoy; aspiration; longing; a request to obtain; the object of desire; love; lust.—*vt.* (desiring, desired). To wish for the possession or enjoyment of; to covet; to ask; to petition.
Desirous, dē-zīr′us, *a.* Full of desire; solicitous to possess and enjoy; eager.
Desist, dē-sist′, *vi.* To cease to act or proceed; to forbear; to leave off. (With *from*.)
Desk, desk, *n.* An inclining table to write or read upon; a portable case for the same purpose; a lectern; a pulpit.
Desolate, de′sō-lāt, *a.* Destitute of inhabitants; waste; laid waste; afflicted; forlorn. —*vt.* (desolating, desolated). To deprive of inhabitants; to make desert; to ravage.
Desolately, de′sō-lāt-li, *adv.* In a desolate manner.
Desolation, de-sō-lā′shon, *n.* Act of desolating; a desolate state or place; melancholy.
Despair, dē-spār′, *n.* A hopeless state; despondency; that which causes despair; loss of hope.—*vi.* To give up all hope; to despond.
Despatch, Dispatch, des-pach′, dis-pach′, *vt.* To send away in haste; to put to death; to perform quickly; to conclude.—*n.* Act of despatching; communication on public business; speedy performance; due diligence.
Desperado, des-pė-rā′dō, *n.* A desperate fellow; a reckless ruffian.
Desperate, des′pė-rāt, *a.* Without care of safety; reckless; frantic; beyond hope; past cure.
Desperately, des′pė-rāt-li, *adv.* In a desperate manner.
Desperation, des-pė-rā′shon, *n.* A giving up of hope; fury; disregard of danger; despair.
Despicable, des′pik-a-bl, *a.* Contemptible; vile; base; mean.
Despicably, des′pik-a-bli, *adv.* Meanly.
Despisable, dē-spīz′a-bl, *a.* That may be despised; despicable; contemptible.
Despise, dē-spīz′, *vt.* (despising, despised). To hold in contempt; to scorn; to disdain.
Despiser, dē-spīz′ėr, *n.* A contemner; scorner.
Despite, dē-spīt′, *n.* Extreme malice; de-

fiance with contempt; an act of malice.—*vt.* To despise; to spite.—*prep.* In spite of; notwithstanding.
Despiteful, dē-spit'fụl, *a.* Full of spite; malignant.
Despoil, dē-spoil', *vt.* To take from by force; to rob; to bereave; to rifle.
Despond, dē-spond', *vi.* To be cast down or dejected; to lose heart, hope, or resolution.
Despondence, Despondency, dē-spond'ens, dē-spond'en-si, *n.* Hopelessness; dejection.
Despondent, dē-spond'ent, *a.* Depressed and inactive in despair; desponding.
Despondently, Despondingly, dē-spond'-ent-li, dē-spond'ing-li, *adv.* In a despondent manner; without hope.
Despot, des'pot, *n.* An absolute ruler (generally in a bad sense); a tyrant.
Despotic, Despotical, des-pot'ik, des-pot'ik-al, *a.* Belonging to a despot; absolute in power; arbitrary; tyrannical.
Despotically, des-pot'ik-al-li, *adv.* In a despotic manner; arbitrarily.
Despotism, des'pot-izm, *n.* The rule of a despot; autocracy; tyranny.
Desquamate, dē-skwā'māt, *vt.* or *i.* To come off in scales; to peel off.
Dessert, dē-zėrt', *n.* That which is served at the close of a dinner, as fruits, &c.
Destination, des-tin-ā'shon, *n.* Act of destining; ultimate design; predetermined end.
Destine, des'tin, *vt.* (destining, destined). To set or appoint to a purpose; to design; to doom; to ordain.
Destiny, des'ti-ni, *n.* State appointed or predetermined; fate; invincible necessity.
Destitute, des'ti-tūt, *a.* Wanting; needy; comfortless; forlorn.
Destitution, des-ti-tū'shon, *n.* Want; poverty; indigence.
Destroy, dē-stroi', *vt.* To pull down; to overthrow; to devastate; to annihilate.
Destroyer, dē-stroi'ėr, *n.* One who or that which destroys; a swift class of vessel intended for the destruction of torpedo-craft, and itself armed with guns and torpedoes.
Destructible, dē-strukt'i-bl, *a.* Liable to destruction.
Destruction, dē-struk'shon, *n.* A pulling down; demolition; overthrow; death; slaughter; cause of destruction.
Destructive, dē-strukt'iv, *a.* Causing destruction; pernicious; mischievous.
Destructively, dē-strukt'iv-li, *adv.* With destruction; ruinously.
Desuetude, des'wē-tūd, *n.* Disuse.
Desultorily, de'sul-to-ri-li, *adv.* In a desultory manner; without method.
Desultory, de'sul-to-ri, *a.* Passing from one subject to another, without order; unconnected; rambling.
Detach, dē-tach', *vt.* To separate; to disengage.
Detached, dē-tacht', *p.a.* Separate.
Detachment, dē-tach'ment, *n.* Act of detaching; a body of troops, or number of ships, sent from the main army or fleet.
Detail, dē-tāl', *vt.* To relate in particulars; to specify; in military affairs, to appoint to a particular service.—*n.* dē-tāl' or dē'tāl. An individual fact, circumstance, or portion; an item; a report of particulars.
Detailed, dē-tāld', *p.a.* Related in particulars; exact.
Detain, dē-tān', *vt.* To keep back or from; to withhold; to arrest; to check; to retard.
Detainer, dē-tān'ėr, *n.* One who detains; a holding of what belongs to another.
Detainment, dē-tān'ment, *n.* Detention.
Detect, dē-tekt', *vt.* To discover; to bring to light.
Detection, dē-tek'shon, *n.* Act of detecting; discovery of a person or thing.
Detective, dē-tek'tiv, *a.* Skilled or employed in detecting.—*n.* A police officer whose duty is to detect criminals; one who investigates cases for hire.
Detent, dē-tent', *n.* A pin, stud, or lever forming a check in a clock, watch, &c.
Detention, dē-ten'shon, *n.* Act of detaining; confinement; delay.
Deter, dē-tėr', *vt.* (deterring, deterred). To prevent by prohibition or danger; to discourage.
Deterge, dē-tėrj', *vt.* To cleanse, purge.
Detergent, dē-tėrj'ent, *a.* Cleansing; purging.—*n.* That which cleanses.
Deteriorate, dē-tē'ri-ō-rāt, *vi.* (deteriorating, deteriorated). To grow worse; to degenerate.—*vt.* To reduce in quality.
Deterioration, dē-tē'ri-o-rā"shon, *n.* The state or process of deteriorating.
Determent, dē-tėr'ment, *n.* Act of deterring; that which deters.
Determinable, dē-tėr'min-a-bl, *a.* That may be decided or determined.
Determinate, dē-tėr'min-āt, *a.* Fixed; positive; decisive.
Determinately, dē-tėr'min-āt-li, *adv.* With certainty; resolutely.
Determination, dē-tėr'min-ā"shon, *n.* Act of determining; firm resolution; judgment; strong direction to a given point; end.
Determine, dē-tėr'min, *vt.* (determining, determined). To bound; to fix permanently; to decide; to establish; to give a direction to; to resolve on; to bring to an end.—*vi.* To resolve; to conclude.
Determined, dē-tėr'mind, *a.* Resolute.
Deterrent, dē-tėr'ent, *a.* Tending or able to deter.—*n.* That which deters.
Detest, dē-test', *vt.* To abhor; to loathe.
Detestable, dē-test'a-bl, *a.* Extremely hateful; abominable; odious.
Detestably, dē-test'a-bli, *adv.* Abominably.
Detestation, dē-test-ā'shon, *n.* Extreme hatred; abhorrence; loathing.
Dethrone, dē-thrōn', *vt.* (dethroning, dethroned). To divest of royal authority and dignity; to depose.
Dethronement, dē-thrōn'ment, *n.* Removal from a throne; deposition.
Detonate, de'tō-nāt, *vt.* (detonating, detonated). To cause to explode; to cause to burn with a sudden report.—*vi.* To explode.
Detonation, de-tō-nā'shon, *n.* An explosion made by the inflammation of certain combustible bodies.
Detonator, det'ō-nā-tėr, *n.* The device by which fulminate of mercury is made to explode the charge in a torpedo, submarine mine, &c.
Detract, dē-trakt', *vt.* To draw away; to disparage.—*vi.* To take away from (especially reputation).
Detraction, dē-trak'shon, *n.* Act of detracting; depreciation; slander.
Detractor, dē-trakt'ėr, *n.* One who detracts; a slanderer; a muscle which detracts.

Detriment, de'tri-ment, *n.* Loss; damage; injury; prejudice; mischief; harm.
Detrimental, de-tri-ment'al, *a.* Causing detriment; injurious; hurtful.
Detritus, dē-trīt'us, *n.* A mass of matter worn off from solid bodies by attrition; disintegrated materials of rocks.
Detruncate, dē-trung'kāt, *vt.* To cut off; to lop; to shorten by cutting.
Detruncation, dē-trung-kā'shon, *n.* Act of cutting off.
Deuce, dūs, *n.* A card or die with two spots; the devil; perdition.
Deuterogamist, dū-tėr-og'a-mist, *n.* One who marries the second time.
Deuterogamy, dū-tėr-og'a-mi, *n.* A second marriage.
Deuteronomy, dū-tėr-on'o-mi, *n.* The second law, or second giving of the law by Moses; the fifth book of the Pentateuch.
Devastate, de'vas-tāt, *vt.* (devastating, devastated). To lay waste; to ravage.
Devastation, de-vas-tā'shon, *n.* Act of devastating; state of being devastated; havoc.
Develop, dē-vel'up, *vt.* To unfold; to lay open to view; to make to grow.—*vi.* To be unfolded; to become manifest; to grow or expand; to be evolved.
Development, dē-vel'up-ment, *n.* Act or process of developing; expansion; growth.
Deviate, dē'vi-āt, *vi.* (deviating, deviated). To stray; to wander; to swerve; to err.
Deviation, dē-vi-ā'shon, *n.* A turning aside from the right way, course, or line.
Device, dē-vīs', *n.* That which is devised; contrivance; scheme; an emblem.
Devil, de'vil, *n.* An evil spirit; Satan; a very wicked person; a machine for cutting, tearing, &c.—*vt.* (devilling, devilled). To pepper excessively and broil; to tease or cut up.
Devilish, de'vil-ish, *a.* Partaking of the qualities of the devil; diabolical; infernal.
Devil-may-care, de'vil-mā-kãr, *a.* Rollicking; reckless.
Devilment, de'vil-ment, *n.* Roguery.
Devilry, de'vil-ri, *n.* Extreme wickedness; wicked mischief.
Devious, dē'vi-us, *a.* Out of the common way or track; erring; rambling.
Devisable, dē-vīz'a-bl, *a.* That may be devised; that may be bequeathed.
Devise, dē-vīz', *vt.* (devising, devised). To form in the mind; to contrive; to invent; to give or bequeath by will.—*n.* Act of bequeathing by will; a will; a share of estate bequeathed.
Deviser, de-vīz'ėr, *n.* A contriver; inventor.
Devisor, de-vīz'ėr, *n.* One who bequeaths.
Devoid, dē-void', *a.* Destitute; not possessing; free from.
Devoir, de-vwär', *n.* Service or duty; act of civility or respect.
Devolution, de-vō-lū'shon, *n.* Act of rolling down; transference; a passing or falling upon a successor.
Devolve, dē-volv', *vt.* (devolving, devolved). To roll down; to deliver over; to transfer.—*vi.* To fall by succession.
Devote, dē-vōt', *vt.* (devoting, devoted). To set apart by vow; to consecrate; to addict (oneself); to apply closely to; to consign.
Devoted, dē-vōt'ed, *a.* Ardent; zealous; strongly attached.
Devotee, dev-o-tē', *n.* One wholly devoted, particularly to religion; a votary.
Devotion, dē-vō'shon, *n.* Act of devoting or state of being devoted; prayer; devoutness; ardent love or affection; attachment; earnestness.
Devotional, dē-vō'shon-al, *a.* Pertaining to devotion; used in devotion.
Devour, dē-vour', *vt.* To eat ravenously; to swallow up; to waste; to look on with keen delight.
Devout, dē-vout', *a.* Pious; expressing devotion; earnest; solemn.
Devoutly, dē-vout'li, *adv.* Piously.
Dew, dū, *n.* Moisture from the atmosphere condensed into drops on the surface of cold bodies, as grass, &c.; damp.—*vt.* To wet with dew; to moisten; to damp.
Dewiness, dū'i-nes, *n.* State of being dewy.
Dew-lap, dū'lap, *n.* The fold of skin that hangs from the throat of oxen, &c.
Dew-point, dū'point, *n.* The temperature at which dew begins to form.
Dewy, dū'i, *a.* Pertaining to dew; like dew; moist with dew.
Dexter, deks'tėr, *a.* Right, as opposed to left.
Dexterity, deks-te'ri-ti, *n.* Right-handedness; adroitness; expertness; skill.
Dexterous, deks'tėr-us, *a.* Expert in manual acts; adroit; done with dexterity.
Dexterously, deks'tėr-us-li, *adv.* With dexterity; expertly; skilfully; artfully.
Dextrine, deks'trin, *n.* A gummy matter prepared from starch.
Dextrose, deks'tros, *n.* Grape-sugar.
Dhow, dou, *n.* An Arab trading vessel.
Dhurra, dụr'ra, *n.* A kind of millet cultivated in Africa and elsewhere.
Diabetes, dī-a-bē'tēz, *n.* Disease characterized by a morbid discharge of urine.
Diabolic, Diabolical, dī-a-bol'ik, dī-a-bol'ik-al, *a.* Devilish; atrocious.
Diabolically, dī-a-bol'ik-al-li, *adv.* In a diabolical manner; very wickedly.
Diaconal, dī-ak'on-al, *a.* Pertaining to a deacon.
Diaconate, dī-ak'on-āt, *n.* Office of a deacon; body of deacons.
Diacoustics, dī-a-kous'tiks, *n.* The science of refracted sound.
Diacritical, dī-a-krit'ik-al, *a.* Separating; distinctive: applied to a mark used to distinguish letters similar in form.
Diadem, dī'a-dem, *n.* A badge of royalty worn on the head; a crown; a coronet.
Diæresis, dī-ē're-sis, *n.* Separation of one syllable into two; a mark signifying such a division, as in *aërial.*
Diagnose, dī-ag-nōs', *vt.* To ascertain from symptoms the true nature of.
Diagnosis, dī-ag-nō'sis, *n.* The ascertaining from symptoms the true nature of diseases.
Diagnostic, dī-ag-nōs'tik, *a.* Pertaining to diagnosis.—*n.* A symptom.
Diagonal, dī-ag'on-al, *a.* Extending from one angle to another of a quadrilateral figure; lying in an oblique direction.—*n.* A straight line drawn between opposite angles of a quadrilateral figure.
Diagonally, dī-ag'on-al-li, *adv.* In a diagonal direction.
Diagram, dī'a-gram, *n.* A drawing to demonstrate the properties of any figure; an illustrative figure in outline.

Dial, dī'al, *n.* An instrument for showing the hour by the sun's shadow; face of a clock, &c.
Dialect, dī'a-lekt, *n.* The idiom of a language peculiar to a province; language; manner of speaking.
Dialectal, dī-a-lek'tal, *a.* Pertaining to a dialect.
Dialectic, Dialectical, dī-a-lek'tik, dī-a-lek'-tik-al, *a.* Relating to dialectics; pertaining to a dialect or dialects.
Dialectician, dī'a-lek-ti''shan, *n.* One skilled in dialectics; a logician; a reasoner.
Dialectics, dī-a-lek'tiks, *n.sing.* The art of reasoning; that branch of logic which teaches the rules and modes of reasoning; word-fence. Also **Dialectic** in same sense.
Dialling, dī'al-ing, *n.* The science which explains the principles of measuring time by dials; the art of constructing dials.
Dialogue, dī'a-log, *n.* A conversation between two or more persons.
Dial-plate, dī'al-plāt, *n.* The plate or face of a dial, clock, or watch.
Diamagnetic, dī-a-mag-net''ik, *a.* Applied to substances which, when under the influence of magnetism, point east and west.
Diameter, dī-am'et-ėr, *n.* A straight line passing through the centre of a circle, and terminated by the circumference; the distance through the centre of any object.
Diametric, Diametrical, dī-a-met'rik, dī-a-met'rik-al, *a.* Of or pertaining to a diameter.
Diametrically, dī-a-met'rik-al-li, *adv.* In a diametrical direction; directly.
Diamond, dī'a-mond, *n.* A valuable gem, remarkable for its hardness and transparency; a rhombus; a card of the suit marked with such figures in red; a very small printing type.—*a.* Resembling a diamond; set with diamonds.
Diapason, dī-a-pā'zon, *n.* The entire compass of a voice or instrument; an organ stop.
Diaper, dī'a-pėr, *n.* A figured linen or cotton cloth.—*vt.* To variegate or diversify with figures.—*vi.* To draw flowers or figures on.
Diaphanous, dī-af'an-us, *a.* Having power to transmit rays of light; transparent.
Diaphragm, dī'a-fram, *n.* The midriff, a muscular partition separating the thorax from the abdomen.
Diarrhœa, dī-a-rē'a, *n.* A morbidly frequent evacuation of the intestines.
Diary, dī'a-ri, *n.* A register of daily events or transactions; a journal.
Diastole, dī-as'to-lē, *n.* Dilatation of the heart in beating.
Diathermal, Diathermous, dī-a-thėr'mal, dī-a-thėr'mus, *a.* Freely permeable by heat.
Diathesis, dī-ath'e-sis, *n.* Predisposition.
Diatomic, dī-a-tom'ik, *a.* Consisting of two atoms.
Diatonic, dī-a-ton'ik, *a.* In *music*, applied to the major or minor scales.
Diatribe, dī'a-trīb, *n.* A continued disputation; a lengthy invective.
Dibble, dib'bl, *n.* A pointed instrument to make holes for planting seeds, &c.—*vt.* (dibbling, dibbled). To make holes for planting seeds, &c.
Dice, dīs, *n.*; pl. of **Die,** for gaming.—*vi.* (dicing, diced). To play with dice.
Dichotomous, dī-kot'o-mus, *a.* In *botany*, regularly divided by pairs from top to bottom.
Dickey, Dicky, dik'i, *n.* A false shirt-front; the driver's seat in a carriage.
Dicotyledon, dī'kot-i-lē''don, *n.* A plant whose seeds contain a pair of cotyledons.
Dictaphone, dik'ta-fōn, *n.* Trade name for an instrument into which correspondence is dictated, to be transcribed afterwards.
Dictate, dik'tāt, *vt.* (dictating, dictated). To deliver, as an order or direction; to prescribe; to tell what to say or write; to instigate.—*n.* An order delivered; an authoritative precept or maxim; an impulse.
Dictation, dik-tā'shon, *n.* Act of dictating; the art or practice of speaking that another may write down what is spoken.
Dictator, dik-tāt'ėr, *n.* One invested with absolute authority.
Dictatorial, dik-ta-tō'ri-al, *a.* Pertaining to a dictator; absolute; overbearing.
Dictatorship, dik-tāt'ėr-ship, *n.* The office of a dictator.
Diction, dik'shon, *n.* Choice of words; mode of expression; style.
Dictionary, dik'shon-a-ri, *n.* A book containing the words of a language arranged alphabetically, with their meanings, &c.; a work explaining the terms, &c., of any subject under heads alphabetically arranged.
Dictum, dik'tum, *n.*; pl. **Dicta.** An authoritative saying or assertion.
Did, did, *pret.* of *do*.
Didactic, Didactical, di-dak'tik, di-dak'tik-al, *a.* Adapted to teach; instructive.
Didactics, di-dak'tiks, *n.* The art or science of teaching.
Diddle, did'l, *vt.* To cheat or trick.
Die, dī, *vi.* (dying, died). To cease to live; to expire; to sink gradually; to vanish.
Die, dī, *n.*; pl. **Dice,** dīs, in first sense, in the others **Dies,** dīz. A small cube with numbered faces; any cubic body; the dado of a pedestal; a stamp used in coining money; an implement for turning out things of a regular shape.
Dielectric, dī-ē-lek'trik, *n.* Any medium through or across which electric induction takes place between two conductors.
Diesel, dēs'el, *n.* An oil-burning internal-combustion engine.
Diet, dī'et, *n.* A person's regular food; food prescribed medically; a meeting of dignitaries or delegates for legislative or other purposes.—*vt.* To furnish provisions for.—*vi.* To eat according to rules prescribed.
Dietary, dī'et-a-ri, *a.* Pertaining to diet.—*n.* A system of diet; allowance of food.
Dietetic, Dietetical, dī-et-et'ik, dī-et-et'ikal, *a.* Pertaining to diet.
Dietetics, dī-et-et'iks, *n.* Principles for regulating the diet.
Differ, dif'ėr, *vi.* To be unlike or distinct; to disagree; to be at variance.
Difference, dif'ėr-ens, *n.* State of being different; dissimilarity; that which distinguishes; dispute; point in dispute; remainder after a sum is subtracted.
Different, dif'ėr-ent, *a.* Distinct; dissimilar. (With *from*.)
Differential, dif-ėr-en'shi-al, *a.* Creating a difference; discriminating.—*n.* An infinitesimal difference between two states of a variable quantity; a differential gear.
Differentiate, dif-ėr-en'shi-āt, *vt.* To mark or distinguish by a difference.—*vi.* To acquire a distinct character.

Differently, dif-ėr-ent-li, *adv.* In a different manner; variously.
Difficult, dif'fi-kult, *a.* Not easy to be done, &c.; perplexed; hard to please; unyielding.
Difficulty, dif'fi-kul-ti, *n.* Hardness to be done; obstacle; perplexity; objection.
Diffidence, dif'fi-dens, *n.* Want of confidence; modest reserve; bashfulness.
Diffident, dif'fi-dent, *a.* Wanting confidence; bashful.
Diffidently, dif'fi-dent-li, *adv.* In a diffident manner; modestly.
Diffract, dif-frakt', *vt.* To bend from a straight line; to deflect.
Diffraction, dif-frak'shon, *n.* The modifications which light undergoes when it passes by the edge of an opaque body; deflection.
Diffuse, dif-fūz', *vt.* (diffusing, diffused). To pour out and spread; to circulate; to proclaim.—*a.* dif-fūs'. Widely spread; prolix; verbose.
Diffusely, dif-fūs'li, *adv.* In a diffuse manner; copiously; with too many words.
Diffusible, dif-fūz'i bl, *a.* That may be diffused or dispersed.
Diffusion, dif-fū'zhon, *n.* A spreading or scattering; dispersion; circulation.
Diffusive, dif-fūs'iv, *a.* Having the quality of diffusing; spread widely; verbose.
Diffusively, dif-fūs'iv-li, *adv.* Widely.
Dig, dig, *vt.* (digging, digged or dug). To open and turn up with a spade; to excavate.—*vi.* To work with a spade.
Digest, di-jest', *vt.* To arrange under proper heads; to think out; to dissolve in the stomach; to soften by a heated liquid; to bear with patience.—*vi.* To undergo digestion, as food.—*n.* dī'jest. A collection of laws; systematic summary.
Digester, di-jest'ėr, *n.* That which assists the digestion of food.
Digestible, di-jest'i-bl, *a.* Capable of being digested.
Digestion, di-jest'yon, *n.* Act of digesting; process of dissolving aliment in the stomach; operation of heating with some solvent.
Digestive, di-jest'iv, *a.* Having the power to cause digestion in the stomach.—*n.* A medicine which aids digestion.
Digging, dig'ing, *n.* The act of one who digs; *pl.* localities where gold is mined.
Dight, dīt, *vt.* To put in order; to array.
Digit, di'jit, *n.* A finger; three-fourths of an inch; the twelfth part of the diameter of the sun or moon; any integer under 10.
Digital, di'jit-al, *a.* Pertaining to the fingers or to digits.
Digitate, Digitated, di'jit-āt, di'jit-āt-ed, *a.* Branching into divisions like fingers.
Dignified, dig'ni-fīd, *a.* Marked with dignity; stately; grave.
Dignify, dig'ni-fī, *vt.* (dignifying, dignified). To invest with dignity; to exalt in rank or office; to make illustrious.
Dignitary, dig'ni-ta-ri, *n.* One of exalted rank or office; an ecclesiastic who has pre-eminence over priests and canons.
Dignity, dig'ni-ti, *n.* Nobleness or elevation of mind; honourable place; degree of excellence; grandeur of mien; an elevated office; one who holds high rank.
Digress, di-gres' or dī'gres, *vi.* To depart from the main subject; to deviate.
Digression, di-gre'shon or dī-, *n.* Act of digressing; departure from the main subject; the part of a discourse which digresses.
Digressional, Digressive, di-gre'shon-al, di-gres'iv, *a.* Pertaining to or consisting in digression.
Dike, Dyke, dīk, *n.* A ditch; an embankment; a wall; a vein of igneous rock.—*vt.* (diking, diked). To surround with a dike; to secure by a bank; to drain by ditches.
Dilacerate, dī-la'sė-rāt, *vt.* To rend asunder; to separate by force.
Dilapidate, di-la'pi-dāt, *vt.* To make ruinous; to squander.—*vi.* To go to ruin; to fall by decay.
Dilapidated, di-la'pi-dāt-ed, *p.a.* In a ruinous condition.
Dilapidation, di-la'pi-dā"shon, *n.* Decay; ruin; destruction; ruining or suffering to decay of a church building.
Dilatability, dī-lāt'a-bil"i-ti, *n.* Quality of being dilatable.
Dilatable, dī-lāt'a-bl, *a.* Capable of expansion; possessing elasticity; elastic.
Dilatation, Dilation, dil-at-ā'shon, dī-lā'-shon, *n.* Act of dilating; expansion; state of being expanded or distended.
Dilate, dī-lāt', *vt.* (dilating, dilated). To expand; to distend.—*vi.* To swell or extend in all directions; to speak copiously; to dwell on in narration (with *on* or *upon*).
Dilatorily, di'la-to-ri-li, *adv.* With delay.
Dilatory, di'la-tō-ri, *a.* Tardy; given to procrastination; making delay; sluggish.
Dilemma, di-lem'ma, *n.* An argument with two alternatives, each conclusive against an opponent; a difficult or doubtful choice.
Dilettante, dil-e-tan'tā, *n.*; pl. **Dilettanti,** dil-e-tan'tē. An amateur or trifler in art.
Diligence, di'li-jens, *n.* Steady application; assiduity; a four-wheeled stage-coach.
Diligent, di'li-jent, *a.* Steady in application; industrious; persevering; prosecuted with care and constant effort.
Dilly-Dally, dil'i-dal-i, *vi.* To loiter, trifle.
Diluent, dil'ū-ent, *a.* Diluting.—*n.* That which dilutes; a substance which increases the proportion of fluid in the blood.
Dilute, di-lūt', *vt.* (diluting, diluted). To render liquid or more liquid; to weaken by admixture of water.—*vi.* To become attenuated or diluted.—*a.* Thin; reduced in strength.
Dilution, di-lū'shon, *n.* Act of diluting.
Diluvial, Diluvian, di-lū'vi-al, di-lū'vi-an, *a.* Pertaining to a flood or deluge; effected or produced by a deluge.
Diluvium, di-lū'vi-um, *n.* A deluge or inundation; a deposit of sand, gravel, &c., caused by a flood.
Dim, dim, *a.* Not seeing clearly; not clearly seen; mysterious; tarnished.—*vt.* (dimming, dimmed). To dull; to obscure; to sully.
Dime, dīm, *n.* A silver coin the tenth of a dollar, or about 5*d.*
Dimension, di-men'shon, *n.* Extension in a single direction; measure of a thing, its size, extent, capacity (usually in *pl.*).
Diminish, di-min'ish, *vt.* To reduce; to abate; to degrade.—*vi.* To become less.
Diminution, di-min-ū'shon, *n.* Act of diminishing; state of becoming less.
Diminutive, di-min'ūt-iv, *a.* Small; little.—

n. A word formed from another word to express a little thing of the kind.
Dimissory, di-mis'so-ri, *a.* Dismissing to another jurisdiction; granting leave to depart.
Dimity, di'mi-ti, *n.* A stout cotton fabric woven with raised stripes or figures.
Dimly, dim'li, *adv.* Obscurely.
Dimmish, dim'ish, *a.* Somewhat dim.
Dimple, dim'pl, *n.* A small natural depression in the cheek or chin.—*vi.* (dimpling, dimpled). To form dimples.
Dimpled, dim'pld, *a.* Set with dimples.
Din, din, *n.* A loud sound long continued.—*vt.* (dinning, dinned). To stun with noise; to harass with clamour.
Dine, dīn, *vi.* (dining, dined). To eat a dinner.—*vt.* To give a dinner to.
Ding, ding, *vt.* (pret. and pp. dung or dinged). To strike; to drive; to thrust or dash.
Dingdong, ding'dong. The sound of bells, &c.
Dinghy, ding'gi, *n.* A small boat used by a ship.
Dingle, ding'gl, *n.* A small secluded valley.
Dingy, din'ji, *a.* Of a dusky colour; soiled.
Dinner, din'nėr, *n.* The principal meal of the day.
Dinner-jacket, din'nėr jak'et, *n.* A man's black evening-dress jacket without tails, worn on informal occasions.
Dint, dint, *n.* The mark made by a blow; dent; power exerted.—*vt.* To make a mark on by a blow or by pressure.
Diocesan, dī-os'es-an, *a.* Pertaining to a diocese.—*n.* A bishop; one in possession of a diocese.
Diocese, dī'ō-sēs, *n.* An ecclesiastical division of a state, subject to a bishop.
Dioptric, Dioptrical, dī-op'trik, dī-op'trik-al, *a.* Pertaining to refracted light.
Dioptrics, dī-op'triks, *n.* The science of the refractions of light passing through mediums, as air, water, or lenses.
Diorama, dī-ō-rä'ma, *n.* A contrivance for giving a high degree of optical illusion to painted scenes.
Dioramic, dī-ō-ram'ik, *a.* Pertaining to a diorama.
Dip, dip, *vt.* (dipping, dipped or dipt). To plunge in a liquid; to baptize by immersion.—*vi.* To dive into a liquid and emerge; to engage in a desultory way; to look cursorily; to choose by chance; to incline.—*n.* Act of dipping; a bath; candle; downward slope.
Diphtheria, dif-thē'ri-a, *n.* An epidemic inflammatory disease of the throat.
Diphthong, dif'thong, *n.* A union of two vowels pronounced in one syllable.
Diploma, di-plō'ma, *n.* A document conferring some power, privilege, or honour.
Diplomacy, di-plō'ma-si, *n.* The art or practice of conducting international negotiations; skill in securing advantages.
Diplomat, dip'lō-mat, *n.* A diplomatist.
Diplomatic, Diplomatical, dip-lō-mat'ik, dip-lō-mat'ik-al, *a.* Pertaining to diplomacy; skilful in gaining one's ends by tact; relating to diplomatics.
Diplomatics, dip-lō-mat'iks, *n.* The science of deciphering ancient writings, and of ascertaining their authenticity, date, &c.
Diplomatist, di-plō'mat-ist, *n.* One skilled or engaged in diplomacy.
Dipper, dip'ėr, *n.* He or that which dips; a ladle; a bird, the water-ousel.
Dipsomania, dip-sō-mā'ni-a, *n.* An uncontrollable craving for stimulants.
Dire, dīr, *a.* Dreadful; dismal; terrible.
Direct, di-rekt', *a.* Straight; right; in the line of father and son; not ambiguous; express.—*vt.* To point or aim at; to show the right course to; to conduct; to order; to instruct.
Direction, di-rek'shon, *n.* Act of directing; a pointing toward; course; guidance; command; address on a letter; a body of directors.
Directive, di-rekt'iv, *a.* Giving direction.
Directly, di-rekt'li, *adv.* In a direct manner; without delay; expressly.
Director, di-rekt'ėr, *n.* One who or that which directs; a superintendent; an instructor; a counsellor; one appointed to transact the affairs of a company.
Directorate, di-rek'tėr-āt, *n.* Office of a director; body of directors.
Directorship, di-rek'tėr-ship, *n.* The condition or office of a director.
Directory, di-rek'to-ri, *n.* A rule to direct; a book containing directions for public worship; a book containing a list of the inhabitants of a place, with their addresses; a board of directors.
Directress, Directrix, di-rekt'res, di-rekt'riks, *n.* A female who directs.
Direful, dīr'ful, *a.* Dire; dreadful; calamitous.
Direfully, dīr'ful-li, *adv.* Dreadfully.
Dirge, dėrj, *n.* A song or tune intended to express grief, sorrow, and mourning.
Dirk, dėrk, *n.* A kind of dagger or poniard.
Dirt, dėrt, *n.* Any foul or filthy substance.—*vt.* To make foul; to defile.
Dirtily, dėrt'i-li, *adv.* In a dirty manner; foully; meanly.
Dirty, dėrt'i, *a.* Soiled with dirt; mean; despicable; rainy; squally, &c.—*vt.* (dirtying, dirtied). To soil; to sully.
Disability, dis-a-bil'i-ti, *n.* Want of ability; incompetence; want of legal qualification.
Disable, dis-ā'bl, *vt.* (disabling, disabled). To deprive of power; to disqualify; to incapacitate.
Disabuse, dis-a-būz', *vt.* To undeceive.
Disadvantage, dis-ad-van'tāj, *n.* Want of advantage; unfavourable state; detriment.
Disadvantageous, dis-ad'van-tāj"us, *p.a.* Unfavourable to success or prosperity.
Disaffect, dis-af-fekt', *vt.* To make less faithful or friendly; to make discontented.
Disaffected, dis-af-fek'ted, *a.* Indisposed to favour or support; unfriendly.
Disaffection, dis-af-fek'shon, *n.* Alienation of affection; disloyalty; hostility.
Disaffirm, dis-af-fėrm', *vt.* To deny; to annul.
Disagree, dis-a-grē', *vi.* To be of a different opinion; to dissent; to be unfriendly; to be unsuitable.
Disagreeable, dis-a-grē'a-bl, *a.* Not agreeable; offensive; displeasing.
Disagreeably, dis-a-grē'a-bli, *adv.* Unpleasantly.
Disagreement, dis-a-grē'ment, *n.* Difference; unsuitableness; discrepancy; discord.
Disallow, dis-al-lou', *vt.* To refuse to allow; to disapprove of; to reject.
Disallowable, dis-al-lou'a-bl, *a.* Not allowable.

Disallowance, dis-al-lou'ans, *n.* Refusal to allow; disapprobation; rejection.
Disannul, dis-an-nul', *vt.* To annul.
Disappear, dis-ap-pēr', *vi.* To vanish from sight; to cease, or seem to cease, to be.
Disappearance, dis-ap-pēr'ans, *n.* Act of disappearing; removal from sight.
Disappoint, dis-ap-point', *vt.* To defeat of expectation or intention; to frustrate.
Disappointed, dis-ap-point'ed, *a.* Balked; soured in life.
Disappointment, dis-ap-point'ment, *n.* Failure of expectation or intention.
Disapprobation, dis-ap'prō-bā"shon, *n.* Disapproval; censure, expressed or unexpressed.
Disapproval, dis-ap-pröv'al, *n.* The act of disapproving; dislike.
Disapprove, dis-ap-pröv', *vt.* To censure as wrong; to regard with dislike; to reject.
Disapprovingly, dis-ap-pröv'ing-li, *adv.* By disapprobation.
Disarm, dis-ärm', *vt.* To take the arms or weapons from; to render harmless.—*vi.* To lay down arms; to disband.
Disarmament, dis-ärm'a-ment, *n.* Act of disarming.
Disarrange, dis-a-rānj', *vt.* To put out of arrangement or order; to derange.
Disarrangement, dis-a-rānj'ment, *n.* Act of disturbing order; disorder.
Disarray, dis-a-rā', *vt.* To undress; to throw into disorder.—*n.* Disorder; undress.
Disaster, diz-as'tėr, *n.* An unfortunate event; mishap; catastrophe; reverse.
Disastrous, diz-as'trus, *a.* Occasioning, accompanied by, or threatening disaster; calamitous; dismal.
Disavouch, dis-a-vouch', *vt.* To disavow.
Disavow, dis-a-vou', *vt.* To deny to be true; to reject; to dissent from.
Disavowal, dis-a-vou'al, *n.* Denial; repudiation.
Disband, dis-band', *vt.* To dismiss from military service; to disperse.—*vi.* To retire from military service; to dissolve connection.
Disbar, dis-bär', *vt.* To expel from being a member of the bar.
Disbelief, dis-bē-lēf', *n.* Refusal of credit or faith; distrust.
Disbelieve, dis-bē-lēv', *vt.* To refuse to credit.
Disburden, dis-bėr'dn, *vt.* To remove a burden from; to relieve.
Disburse, dis-bėrs', *vt.* (disbursing, disbursed). To pay out, as money; to expend.
Disbursement, dis-bėrs'ment, *n.* Act of disbursing; the sum paid out.
Disburthen, dis-bėr'ᴛʜen, *vt.* and *i.* A different orthography of *disburden*.
Disc, Disk, disk, *n.* A flat circular plate; the face of the sun, or a planet; the central part of a composite flower.
Discard, dis-kärd', *vt.* To throw away; to cast off; to dismiss; to discharge.
Discern, dis-sėrn' or di-zėrn', *vt.* To distinguish; to discriminate; to descry.—*vi.* To see or understand differences; to have clearness of mental sight.
Discerner, dis-sėrn'ėr, *n.* One who discerns; a clear-sighted observer.
Discernible, dis-sėrn'i-bl, *a.* That may be discerned; perceptible.
Discerning, dis-sėrn'ing, *p.a.* Having power to discern; sharp-sighted; acute.
Discerningly, dis-sėrn'ing-li, *adv.* With discernment; acutely; with judgment.
Discernment, dis-sėrn'ment, *n.* Act or power of discerning; judgment; sagacity.
Discharge, dis-chärj', *vt.* To unload; to let fly or go, as a missile; to fire off; to give vent to; to clear off by payment; to perform; to acquit; to dismiss; to release.—*vi.* To get rid of or let out a charge or contents.—*n.* Act of discharging; unloading; a firing off; emission; dismissal; release from obligation, debt, or penalty; absolution from a crime; ransom; performance; release; payment, as of a debt.
Disciple, dis-sī'pl, *n.* A learner; a pupil; an adherent to the doctrines of another.
Discipleship, dis-sī'pl-ship, *n.* The state or position of a disciple.
Disciplinable, dis'si-plin-a-bl, *a.* Capable of discipline, or of instruction.
Disciplinarian, dis'si-plin-ā"ri-an, *a.* Pertaining to discipline.—*n.* One who enforces discipline; a martinet.
Disciplinary, dis'si-plin-a-ri, *a.* Pertaining to discipline; intended for discipline.
Discipline, dis'si-plin, *n.* Training; method of government; order; subjection to laws; punishment; correction; execution of ecclesiastical laws.—*vt.* (disciplining, disciplined). To subject to discipline; to train up well; to chastise.
Disclaim, dis-klām', *vt.* To deny all claim to; to reject; to disown.
Disclaimer, dis-klām'ėr, *n.* One who disclaims; formal disavowal; renunciation.
Disclose, dis-klōz', *vt.* To open; to uncover; to reveal; to divulge.
Disclosure, dis-klō'zhūr, *n.* Act of disclosing; utterance of what was secret; that which is disclosed.
Discoloration, dis-kul'ėr-ā"shon, *n.* Act of discolouring; alteration of colour; stain.
Discolour, dis-kul'ėr, *vt.* To alter the colour of; to stain; to tinge.
Discomfit, dis-kom'fit, *vt.* To rout; to defeat.—*n.* Rout; overthrow.
Discomfiture, dis-kom'fit-ūr, *n.* Rout; overthrow; frustration; disappointment.
Discomfort, dis-kum'fėrt, *n.* Want of comfort; uneasiness; inquietude.—*vt.* To deprive of comfort; to grieve.
Discommend, dis-kom-mend', *vt.* To blame; to censure; to mention with disapprobation.
Discompose, dis-kom-pōz', *vt.* To disturb.
Discomposure, dis-kom-pō'zhūr, *n.* Disorder; agitation; disturbance; perturbation.
Disconcert, dis-kon-sėrt', *vt.* To disturb; to unsettle; to confuse; to ruffle.
Disconnect, dis-kon-nekt', *vt.* To separate; to disunite.
Disconnection, dis-kon-nek'shon, *n.* Separation; want of union.
Disconsolate, dis-kon'sō-lāt, *a.* Comfortless; hopeless; gloomy; cheerless.
Discontent, dis-kon-tent', *n.* Want of content; uneasiness of mind; dissatisfaction.
Discontented, dis-kon-tent'ed, *a.* Dissatisfied; given to grumble.
Discontentment, dis-kon-tent'ment, *n.* Discontent; uneasiness; inquietude.
Discontinuance, dis-kon-tin'ū-ans, *n.* A breaking off; cessation.
Discontinuation, dis-kon-tin'ū-ā"shon, *n.* Act of discontinuing; discontinuance.

Discontinue, dis-kon-tin'ū, *vt.* To leave off; to cause to cease; to cease to take or receive.—*vi.* To cease.
Discontinuity, dis-kon'tin-ū"i-ti, *n.* State of being discontinuous.
Discontinuous, dis-kon-tin'ū-us, *a.* Not continuous; broken off; interrupted.
Discord, dis'kord, *n.* Want of concord; disagreement; disagreement of sounds.
Discordance, Discordancy, dis-kord'ans, dis-kord'an-si, *n.* Want of concord; disagreement; inconsistency; discord.
Discordant, dis-kord'ant, *a.* Wanting agreement; incongruous; dissonant; jarring.
Discount, dis'kount, *n.* A sum deducted for prompt or advanced payment.—*vt.* dis-kount'. To advance the amount of, as of a bill, deducting a certain rate per cent; to make an allowance for supposed exaggeration; to disregard.
Discountable, dis-kount'a-bl, *a.* That may be discounted.
Discountenance, dis-koun'ten-ans, *vt.* To restrain by censure, cold treatment, &c.
Discounter, dis'kount-ėr, *n.* One who discounts bills and financial documents.
Discourage, dis-ku'rāj, *vt.* (discouraging, discouraged). To dishearten; to dissuade.
Discouragement, dis-ku'rāj-ment, *n.* Act of discouraging; that which discourages.
Discouraging, dis-ku'rāj-ing, *a.* Tending to discourage.
Discourse, dis-kōrs', *n.* A speech; treatise; sermon; conversation.—*vi.* (discoursing, discoursed). To talk; to converse; to treat of formally; to expatiate.—*vt.* To utter.
Discourteous, dis-kōr'tē-us, *a.* Void of courtesy; rude.
Discourtesy, dis-kōr'te-si, *n.* Incivility; rudeness; act of disrespect.
Discover, dis-kuv'ėr, *vt.* To lay open to view; to reveal; to have the first sight of; to find out; to detect.
Discoverable, dis-kuv'ėr-a-bl, *a.* That may be discovered.
Discoverer, dis-kuv'ėr-ėr, *n.* One who discovers; an explorer.
Discovery, dis-kuv'ė-ri, *n.* Act of discovering; disclosure; that which is discovered.
Discredit, dis-kred'it, *n.* Want of credit; disrepute; disbelief; distrust.—*vt.* To give no credit to; to deprive of credit; to make less reputable; to bring into disesteem.
Discreditable, dis-kred'it-a-bl, *a.* Tending to discredit; injurious to reputation.
Discreet, dis-krēt', *a.* Prudent; wary; judicious.
Discrepance, Discrepancy, dis-krep'ans, dis-krep'an-si, *n.* Discordance; disagreement.
Discrete, dis'krēt, *a.* Separate; distinct.
Discretion, dis-kre'shon, *n.* Quality of being discreet; prudence; discernment; judgment; freedom of choice or action.
Discretionarily, Discretionally, dis-kre'-shon-a-ri-li, dis-kre'shon-al-li, *adv.* At discretion; according to discretion.
Discretionary, dis-kre'shon-a-ri, *a.* Unrestrained except by discretion.
Discretive, dis-krēt'iv, *a.* Disjunctive; implying opposition or distinction.
Discriminate, dis-krim'in-āt, *vt.* (discriminating, discriminated). To distinguish; to select from.—*vi.* To make a distinction.—*a.* Having the difference marked; distinct.
Discriminately, dis-krim'in-āt-li, *adv.* In a discriminate manner.
Discriminating, dis-krim'in-āt-ing, *p.a.* Distinguishing; able to make nice distinctions.
Discrimination, dis-krim'in-ā"shon, *n.* Discernment; judgment; distinction.
Discriminative, dis-krim'in-āt-iv, *a.* That discriminates or distinguishes.
Discriminator, dis-krim'in-āt-ėr, *n.* One who discriminates.
Discursive, dis-kėrs'iv, *a.* Passing from one subject to another, desultory; rambling.
Discus, dis'kus, *n.* A round, flat piece of iron, &c., thrown in play; a quoit.
Discuss, dis-kus', *vt.* To drive away or dissolve (a tumour, &c.); to debate; to examine by disputation; to make a trial of, as food; to consume.
Discussion, dis-ku'shon, *n.* Dispersion; debate; examination.
Disdain, dis-dān', *vt.* To think unworthy; to deem worthless; to scorn; to contemn.—*n.* Contempt; scorn; haughtiness; pride.
Disdainful, dis-dān'fu̧l, *a.* Contemptuous; scornful; haughty; indignant.
Disdainfully, dis-dān'fu̧l-li, *adv.* With scorn.
Disease, diz-ēz', *n.* Any state of a living body in which the natural functions are disturbed; illness; disorder.—*vt.* (diseasing, diseased). To afflict with disease; to infect; to derange.
Disembark, dis-em-bärk', *vt.* To remove from a vessel to the land.—*vi.* To go ashore.
Disembarkation, Disembarkment, dis-em'-bärk-ā"shon, dis-em-bärk'ment, *n.* Act of disembarking.
Disembarrass, dis-em-ba'ras, *vt.* To free from perplexity; to clear; to extricate.
Disembody, dis-em-bo'di, *vt.* To divest of body; to free from connection with the human body; to disband (troops).
Disembogue, dis-em-bōg', *vt.* (disemboguing, disembogued). To pour out at the mouth, as a stream; to discharge into the ocean, a lake, &c.—*vi.* To flow out at the mouth.
Disembowel, dis-em-bou'el, *vt.* (disembowelling, disembowelled). To take out the bowels of.
Disembroil, dis-em-broil', *vt.* To disentangle; to free from perplexity.
Disenchant, dis-en-chant', *vt.* To free from enchantment.
Disencumber, dis-en-kum'bėr, *vt.* To free from encumbrance or obstruction.
Disencumbrance, dis-en-kum'brans, *n.* The act of disencumbering.
Disendow, dis-en-dou', *vt.* To deprive of endowment, as a church.
Disendowment, dis-en-dou'ment, *n.* The act of disendowing.
Disengage, dis-en-gāj', *vt.* To free from engagement; to detach; to release; to extricate.
Disengaged, dis-en-gājd', *p.a.* At leisure; not particularly occupied.
Disengagement, dis-en-gāj'ment, *n.* Release from engagement; separation; extrication; leisure.
Disennoble, dis-en-nō'bl, *vt.* To deprive of that which ennobles; to deprive of title.
Disentail, dis-en-tāl', *vt.* To free from being entailed.—*n.* The act of breaking the entail of an estate.
Disentangle, dis-en-tang'gl, *vt.* To free from entanglement; to clear.

Disenthrall, dis-en-thral′, *vt.* To give freedom to.
Disentitle, dis-en-tī′tl, *vt.* To deprive of title.
Disestablish, dis-es-tab′lish, *vt.* To cause to cease to be established; to withdraw (a church) from connection with the state.
Disestablishment, dis-es-tab′lish-ment, *n.* The act of disestablishing.
Disesteem, dis-es-tēm′, *n.* Want of esteem.—*vt.* To dislike moderately; to slight.
Disfavour, dis-fā′vėr, *n.* Want of favour; unfavourable regard.—*vt.* To withhold favour from; to discountenance.
Disfiguration, dis-fi′gūr-ā″shon, *n.* Act of disfiguring; some degree of deformity.
Disfigure, dis-fi′gūr, *vt.* (disfiguring, disfigured). To mar the figure of; to impair the beauty, symmetry, or excellence of.
Disfigurement, dis-fi′gūr-ment, *n.* Act of disfiguring, that which disfigures.
Disfranchise, dis-fran′chīz, *vt.* To deprive of the rights of a free citizen.
Disfranchisement, dis-fran′chiz-ment, *n.* Act of disfranchising.
Disgorge, dis-gorj′, *vt.* To vomit; to discharge violently; to surrender.
Disgrace, dis-grās′, *n.* State of being deprived of grace or favour; cause of shame; dishonour.—*vt.* (disgracing, disgraced). To bring to shame; to degrade; to dishonour.
Disgraceful, dis-grās′fųl, *a.* Shameful; causing shame; sinking reputation.
Disguise, dis-gīz′, *vt.* (disguising, disguised). To conceal by an unusual habit or mask; to dissemble; to give an unusual appearance to.—*n.* A dress intended to conceal; an assumed appearance, intended to deceive.
Disgust, dis-gust′, *n.* Distaste; loathing; repugnance.—*vt.* To cause distaste in; to offend the mind or moral taste of.
Disgustful, dis-gust′fųl, *a.* Exciting aversion in the natural or moral taste.
Disgusting, dis-gust′ing, *a.* Provoking disgust; loathsome; nasty.
Dish, dish, *n.* A broad open vessel for serving up meat at table; the meat served; any particular kind of food.—*vt.* To put in a dish; to make (a wheel) hollow or concave.
Dishabille, dis′a-bil, *n.* *See* DESHABILLE.
Dishearten, dis-härt′n, *vt.* To discourage; to depress.
Dishevel, di-she′vel, *vt.* (dishevelling, dishevelled). To put out of order, or spread loosely, as the hair.
Dishonest, dis-on′est, *a.* Void of honesty; fraudulent; knavish; perfidious.
Dishonesty, dis-on′est-i, *n.* Want of honesty or integrity.
Dishonour, dis-on′ėr, *n.* Want of honour; disgrace; ignominy.—*vt.* To deprive of honour; to treat with indignity; to violate the chastity of; to decline to accept or pay, as a draft.
Dishonourable, dis-on′ėr-a-bl, *a.* Destitute of honour; base; vile.
Disillusionize, dis-il-lū′zhon-īz, *vt.* To free from illusion.
Disinclination, dis-in′klin-ā″shon, *n.* Want of propensity, desire, or affection.
Disincline, dis-in-klīn′, *vt.* To take away inclination from; to make disaffected.
Disinfect, dis-in-fekt′, *vt.* To cleanse from infection.
Disinfectant, dis-in-fek′tant, *n.* An agent for removing the causes of infection.
Disinfection, dis-in-fek′shon, *n.* Purification from infecting matter.
Disingenuous, dis-in-jen′ū-us, *a.* Not open, frank, and candid; crafty; cunning.
Disingenuously, dis-in-jen′ū-us-li, *adv.* In a disingenuous manner; artfully.
Disinherit, dis-in-he′rit, *vt.* To cut off from hereditary right.
Disinheritance, dis-in-he′rit-ans, *n:* Act of disinheriting.
Disintegrable, dis-in′tē-gra-bl, *a.* That may be disintegrated.
Disintegrate, dis-in′tē-grāt, *vt.* To separate, as the integral parts of a body.
Disintegration, dis-in′tē-grā″shon, *n.* Act of separating integral parts of a substance.
Disinter, dis-in-tėr′, *vt.* To take out of a grave; to bring into view.
Disinterested, dis-in′tėr-est-ed, *a.* Not interested; free from self-interest; not dictated by private advantage; impartial.
Disinterment, dis-in-tėr′ment, *n.* Act of disinterring or taking out of the earth.
Disinthrall, dis-in-thral′, *vt.* *See* DISENTHRALL.
Disjoin, dis-join′, *vt.* To part asunder; to sever.—*vi.* To part.
Disjoint, dis-joint′, *vt.* To separate, as parts united by joints; to put out of joint; to make incoherent.
Disjointed, dis-joint′ed, *p.a.* Unconnected; incoherent; out of joint.
Disjunct, dis-jungkt′, *a.* Disjoined.
Disjunction, dis-jungk′shon, *n.* Act of disjoining; disunion.
Disjunctive, dis-jungk′tiv, *a.* Separating; uniting words or sentences in construction, but disjoining the sense.—*n.* A word that disjoins, as *or*, *nor*.
Disk, disk, *n.* *See* DISC.
Dislike, dis-līk′, *n.* A feeling the opposite of liking; a moderate degree of hatred; aversion; antipathy.—*vt.* To regard with some aversion or displeasure.
Dislocate, dis′lō-kāt, *vt.* To displace; to put out of joint.
Dislocation, dis-lō-kā′shon, *n.* Act of dislocating; displacement.
Dislodge, dis-loj′, *vt.* To remove or drive from a place of rest or a station.—*vi.* To go from a place of rest.
Dislodgment, dis-loj′ment, *n.* Act of dislodging; displacement.
Disloyal, dis-loi′al, *a.* Void of loyalty; false to a sovereign; faithless.
Disloyally, dis-loi′al-li, *adv.* In a disloyal manner; perfidiously.
Disloyalty, dis-loi′al-ti, *n.* Want of loyalty or fidelity; violation of allegiance.
Dismal, diz′mal, *a.* Dark; gloomy; doleful; calamitous; sorrowful.
Dismally, diz′mal-li, *adv.* Gloomily.
Dismantle, dis-man′tl, *vt.* To strip; to divest; to unrig; to deprive or strip, as of military equipment or defences; to break down.
Dismask, dis-mask′, *vt.* To strip off a mask from; to uncover.
Dismast, dis-mast′, *vt.* To break and carry away the masts from.
Dismay, dis-mā′, *vt.* To produce terror in; to appal; to dishearten.—*n.* Loss of courage; consternation; fright.

Dismember, dis-mem'bėr, *vt.* To sever limb from limb; to separate; to mutilate.
Dismemberment, dis-mem'bėr-ment, *n.* The act of dismembering.
Dismiss, dis-mis', *vt.* To send away; to permit to depart; to discharge.
Dismissal, dis-mis'al, *n.* Dismission.
Dismission, dis-mi'shon, *n.* Act of sending away; leave to depart; discharge.
Dismount, dis-mount', *vi.* To descend from a horse, &c.—*vt.* To unhorse; to throw cannon from their carriages or fixed positions.
Disobedience, dis-ō-bē'di-ens, *n.* Neglect or refusal to obey.
Disobedient, dis-ō-bē'di-ent, *a.* Neglecting or refusing to obey; refractory.
Disobey, dis-ō-bā', *vt.* To neglect or refuse to obey; to violate an order.
Disoblige, dis-ō-blij', *vt.* To fail to oblige; to be unaccommodating to.
Disobligement, dis-ō-blij'ment, *n.* Act of disobliging.
Disobliging, dis ō-blij'ing, *p.a.* Not disposed to gratify the wishes of another; unaccommodating.
Disorder, dis-or'dėr, *n.* Want of order; confusion; disease.—*vt.* To put out of order; to disturb; to produce indisposition; to craze.
Disordered, dis-or'dėrd, *p.a.* Deranged.
Disorderly, dis-or'dėr-li, *a.* Being without proper order; confusedly; unruly.
Disorganization, dis-or'gan-īz-ā"shon, *n.* Act of disorganizing; state of being disorganized.
Disorganize, dis-or'gan-īz, *vt.* To destroy organic structure or connected system in; to throw into confusion.
Disown, dis-ōn', *vt.* To refuse to acknowledge; to renounce; to repudiate.
Disparage, dis-pa'rāj, *vt.* (disparaging, disparaged). To dishonour by comparison with something inferior; to derogate from; to decry.
Disparagement, dis-pa'rāj-ment, *n.* Injury by union or comparison with something inferior; indignity; detraction.
Disparagingly, dis-pa'rāj-ing-li, *adv.* In a manner to disparage.
Disparate, dis'pa-rāt, *a.* Unequal; unlike.
Disparity, dis-pa'ri-ti, *n.* Inequality; difference in degree, age, rank, &c.
Dispark, dis-pärk', *vt.* To cause to be no longer a park; to throw open.
Dispart, dis-pärt', *vt.* and *i.* To separate.
Dispassionate, dis-pa'shon-āt, *a.* Free from passion; cool; impartial.
Dispassionately, dis-pa'shon-āt-li, *adv.* Without passion; calmly; coolly.
Dispatch, dis-pach'. *See* DESPATCH.
Dispeace, dis-pēs', *n.* Want of peace or quiet; dissension; quarrelling.
Dispel, dis-pel', *vt.* (dispelling, dispelled). To scatter; to banish.—*vi.* To fly different ways; to disappear.
Dispensable, dis-pens'a-bl, *a.* That may be dispensed with.
Dispensary, dis-pens'a-ri, *n.* A place where medicines are dispensed to the poor, and medical advice is given gratis; a place where medicines are compounded.
Dispensation, dis-pens-ā'shon, *n.* Act of dispensing; distribution; good or evil dealt out by providence; exemption.
Dispensatory, dis-pens'a-to-ri, *a.* Having power to grant dispensations.—*n.* A book containing the method of preparing the various kinds of medicines.
Dispense, dis-pens', *vt.* (dispensing, dispensed). To deal out in portions; to administer; to apply; to exempt; to grant dispensation for.—*vi.* To do without (with *with*).
Dispenser, dis-pens'ėr, *n.* One who dispenses, distributes, or administers.
Dispensing, dis-pens'ing, *p.a.* Granting dispensation or exemption.
Dispeople, dis-pē'pl, *vt.* To depopulate.
Disperse, dis-pėrs', *vt.* To scatter; to dispel; to diffuse; to distribute.—*vi.* To be scattered; to vanish.
Dispersion, dis-pėr'shon, *n.* Act of dispersing; diffusion; dissipation.
Dispirit, dis-pi'rit, *vt.* To deprive of spirit; to discourage; to daunt.
Dispirited, dis-pi'rit-ed, *p.a.* Dejected; tame.
Dispiriting, dis-pi'rit-ing, *p.a.* Discouraging.
Displace, dis-plās', *vt.* To remove from its place; to derange; to dismiss.
Displacement, dis-plās'ment, *n.* Act of displacing; quantity of water displaced by a floating body.
Displant, dis-plant', *vt.* To pluck up from the spot where planted; to remove from the usual place of residence; to depopulate.
Display, dis-plā', *vt.* To unfold; to spread before the eyes or mind; to show; to parade.—*vi.* To make a show; to talk without restraint.—*n.* An opening or unfolding; exhibition; parade.
Displease, dis-plēz', *vt.* To offend; to dissatisfy; to provoke.—*vi.* To disgust.
Displeased, dis-plēzd', *p.a.* Annoyed.
Displeasing, dis-plēz'ing, *p.a.* Disgusting; disagreeable.
Displeasure, dis-ple'zhūr, *n.* Dissatisfaction; resentment.
Displume, dis-plūm', *vt.* To strip of plumes or badges of honour.
Disport, dis-pōrt', *n.* Sport; pastime.—*vi.* To sport; to play; to wanton.
Disposable, dis-pōz'a-bl, *a.* Subject to disposal; free to be used or employed.
Disposal, dis-pōz'al, *n.* Act or power of disposing; disposition; control.
Dispose, dis-pōz', *vt.* (disposing, disposed). To arrange; to apply to a particular purpose; to incline.—*vi.* To regulate; (with *of*) to part with, to employ.
Disposed, dis-pōzd', *p.a.* Inclined.
Disposer, dis-pōz'ėr, *n.* One who disposes.
Disposition, dis-pō-zi'shon, *n.* Act of disposing; state of being disposed; arrangement; natural fitness; frame of mind; inclination.
Dispossess, dis-poz-zes', *vt.* To deprive of possession.
Dispossession, dis-poz-ze'shon, *n.* Act of putting out of possession.
Dispraise, dis-prāz', *n.* The opposite of praise; blame; censure.—*vt.* To blame; to mention with disapprobation.
Disproof, dis-prōf', *n.* Refutation.
Disproportion, dis-prō-pōr'shon, *n.* Want of proportion or symmetry.—*vt.* To violate proportion; to join unfitly.
Disproportional, dis-prō-pōr'shon-al, *a.* Showing disproportion; inadequate.
Disproportionate, dis-prō-pōr'shon-āt, *a.*

Not proportioned; unsymmetrical; inadequate.
Disproval, dis-pröv'al, *n.* Act of disproving; disproof.
Disprove, dis-pröv', *vt.* To prove to be false; to confute.
Disputable, dis-pūt'a-bl or dis'pūt-a-bl, *a.* That may be disputed; controvertible.
Disputant, dis'pūt-ant, *n.* One who argues in opposition to another.
Disputation, dis-pūt-ā'shon, *n.* Act of disputing; controversy in words; debate.
Disputatious, dis-pūt-ā'shus, *a.* Inclined to dispute; apt to controvert.
Disputative, dis-pūt'at-iv, *a.* Disputatious.
Dispute, dis-pūt', *vi.* (disputing, disputed). To contend in argument; to debate; to strive with.—*vt.* To attempt to prove to be false; to impugn; to contest; to strive to maintain. —*n.* Controversy in words; strife.
Disputer, dis-pūt'ėr, *n.* One who disputes or who is given to disputes.
Disqualification, dis-kwo'li-fi-kā"shon, *n.* Act of disqualifying; that which disqualifies.
Disqualify, dis-kwo'li-fī, *vt.* To divest of qualifications; to incapacitate.
Disquiet, dis-kwī'et, *n.* Uneasiness; anxiety. —*vt.* To make uneasy or restless.
Disquieting, dis-kwī'et-ing, *p.a.* Tending to disturb the mind.
Disquietude, dis-kwī'et-ūd, *n.* Uneasiness; anxiety.
Disquisition, dis-kwi-zi'shon, *n.* A systematic inquiry into any subject, by arguments; a treatise or dissertation.
Disregard, dis-rē-gärd', *n.* Neglect; slight. —*vt.* To omit to take notice of; to slight.
Disregardful, dis-rē-gärd'fụl, *a.* Neglectful; negligent; heedless.
Disrelish, dis-rel'ish, *n.* Distaste; dislike.—*vt.* To dislike the taste of; to feel some disgust at.
Disrepair, dis-rē-pār', *n.* A state of being not in repair.
Disreputable, dis-re'pūt-a-bl, *a.* Discreditable; low; mean.
Disrepute, dis-rē-pūt', *n.* Loss or want of reputation; disesteem; disgrace.
Disrespect, dis-rē-spekt', *n.* Want of respect; incivility.—*vt.* To show disrespect to.
Disrespectful, dis-rē-spekt'fụl, *a.* Irreverent; discourteous; rude.
Disrobe, dis-rōb', *vt.* To undress; to uncover; to divest of any surrounding appendage.
Disroot, dis-röt', *vt.* To tear up the roots.
Disruption, dis-rup'shon, *n.* Act of rending asunder; breach; rent; rupture.
Disruptive, dis-rupt'iv, *a.* Causing, or produced by, disruption.
Dissatisfaction, dis-sa'tis-fak"shon, *n.* Want of satisfaction; discontent.
Dissatisfied, dis-sa'tis-fīd, *p.a.* Discontented; offended.
Dissatisfy, dis-sa'tis-fī, *vt.* To fail to satisfy; to render discontented.
Dissect, dis-sekt', *vt.* To cut up; to anatomize; to divide and examine minutely.
Dissecting, dis-sekt'ing, *p.a.* Used in dissection.
Dissection, dis-sek'shon, *n.* Act of cutting up anatomically; act of separating into parts for the purpose of critical examination.
Dissector, dis-sekt'ėr, *n.* An anatomist.
Disseize, dis-sēz', *vt.* To deprive of possession; to dispossess wrongfully.
Disseizin, dis-sēz'in, *n.* Act of disseizing.
Dissemble, dis-sem'bl, *vt.* and *i.* (dissembling, dissembled). To hide under a false appearance; to conceal under some pretence.
Dissembler, dis-sem'bl-ėr, *n.* One who dissembles.
Disseminate, dis-se'min-āt, *vt.* (disseminating, disseminated). To scatter; to spread.
Dissemination, dis-se'min-ā"shon, *n.* Act of disseminating; propagation.
Disseminator, dis-se'min-āt-ėr, *n.* One who disseminates.
Dissension, dis-sen'shon, *n.* Disagreement in opinion; discord; strife.
Dissent, dis-sent', *vi.* To disagree in opinion; to separate from an established church, in doctrines, rites, or government.—*n.* Disagreement; separation from an established church.
Dissenter, dis-sent'ėr, *n.* One who withdraws from an established church; a nonconformist.
Dissentient, dis-sen'shi-ent, *a.* Declaring dissent; disagreeing.—*n.* One who declares his dissent.
Dissenting, dis-sent'ing, *p.a.* Disagreeing; connected with a body of dissenters.
Dissertation, dis-sėr-tā'shon, *n.* A formal discourse; treatise; disquisition.
Disserve, dis-sėrv', *vt.* To do an ill service to; to harm.
Disservice, dis-sėr'vis, *n.* An ill-service; injury; harm; mischief.
Dissever, dis-sev'ėr, *vt.* To part in two; to disunite.
Dissident, dis'si-dent, *a.* Dissenting.—*n.* A dissenter.
Dissilient, dis-si'li-ent, *a.* Starting asunder; opening with an elastic force.
Dissimilar, dis-si'mi-lėr, *a.* Unlike.
Dissimilarity, dis-si'mi-la"ri-ti, *n.* Unlikeness; want of resemblance.
Dissimilitude, dis-si-mil'i-tūd, *n.* Unlikeness; want of resemblance.
Dissimulate, dis-sim'ū-lāt, *vt.* and *i.* To dissemble.
Dissimulation, dis-si'mū-lā"shon, *n.* Act of dissembling; false pretension; hypocrisy.
Dissipate, dis'si-pāt, *vt.* (dissipating, dissipated). To scatter; to spend; to squander. —*vi.* To scatter; to disperse; to vanish.
Dissipated, dis'si-pāt'ed, *p.a.* Dissolute; devoted to pleasure and vice.
Dissipation, dis-si-pā'shon, *n.* Dispersion; waste; dissolute conduct; diversion.
Dissociate, dis-sō'shi-āt, *vt.* (dissociating, dissociated). To separate, as from society; to disunite; to part.
Dissociation, dis-sō'shi-ā"shon, *n.* Act of dissociating; state of separation; disunion.
Dissolubility, dis-so'lū-bil"i-ti, *n.* State of being dissoluble.
Dissoluble, dis'so-lū-bl, *a.* Capable of being dissolved.
Dissolute, dis'sō-lūt, *a.* Loose in behaviour and morals; licentious; debauched.
Dissolution, dis-sō-lū'shon, *n.* Act of dissolving; a melting or liquefaction; separation of parts; decomposition; death; destruction; the breaking up of an assembly.
Dissolvable, diz-zolv'a-bl, *a.* That may be dissolved, melted, or converted into fluid.

Dissolve, diz-zolv′, *vt.* To melt; to break up; to put an end to; to cause to vanish.—*vi.* To be melted; to become soft or languid; to waste away; to perish; to break up.
Dissolvent, diz-zolv′ent, *a.* Having power to dissolve.—*n.* That which has the power of melting; a solvent.
Dissolver, diz-zolv′ėr, *n.* One who or that which dissolves.
Dissonance, dis′sō-nans, *n.* Disagreement in sound; discord.
Dissonant, dis′sō-nant, *a.* Discordant in sound; harsh; jarring; incongruous.
Dissuade, dis-swād′, *vt.* (dissuading, dissuaded). To exhort against; to turn from a purpose by argument.
Dissuasion, dis-swā′zhon, *n.* Act of dissuading; advice in opposition to something.
Dissuasive, dis-swā′siv, *a.* Tending to dissuade.—*n.* Argument or motive that deters.
Dissuasively, dis-swā′siv-li, *adv.*. In a way to dissuade.
Dissyllabic, dis-sil-lab′ik, *a.* Consisting of two syllables only.
Dissyllable, dis′sil-la-bl, *n.* A word of two syllables only.
Distaff, dis′taf, *n.* The staff to which a bunch of flax or tow is tied, and from which the thread is drawn in spinning.
Distain, dis-tān′, *vt.* To discolour; to stain.
Distance, dis′tans, *n.* Remoteness in place or time; extent of interval between two things; the remoteness which respect requires; reserve; coldness.—*vt.* (distancing, distanced). To leave behind in a race; to outdo or excel.
Distant, dis′tant, *a.* Remote in place, time, relationship, &c.; implying haughtiness, indifference, &c.; cool; shy.
Distantly, dis′tant-li, *adv.* Remotely; at a distance; with reserve.
Distaste, dis-tāst′, *n.* Aversion of the taste or mind; dislike.—*vt.* To dislike.
Distasteful, dis-tāst′fụl, *a.* Unpleasant to the taste; nauseous; displeasing.
Distemper, dis-tem′pėr, *n.* Any morbid state of the body; disorder; a disease of young dogs; bad constitution of the mind; a kind of painting in which the pigments are mixed with size; a pigment so mixed.—*vt.* To disease; to derange; to ruffle.
Distemperature, dis-tem′pėr-ā-tūr, *n.* Tumult; perturbation of mind.
Distempered, dis-tem′pėrd, *p.a.* Diseased in body, or disordered in mind; biassed.
Distend, dis-tend′, *vt.* To stretch by force from within; to swell.—*vi.* To swell; to dilate.
Distensible, dis-tens′i-bl, *a.* Capable of being distended or dilated.
Distention, dis-ten′shon, *n.* Act of distending; state of being distended.
Distich, dis′tik, *n.* A couple of poetic lines.
Distil, dis-til′, *vi.* (distilling, distilled). To fall in drops; to practise distillation.—*vt.* To let fall in drops; to extract spirit from, by evaporation and condensation.
Distillation, dis-til-ā′shon, *n.* Act or process of distilling.
Distillatory, dis-til′ā-to-ri, *a.* Belonging to distillation.—*n.* A still.
Distiller, dis-til′ėr, *n.* One who distils.
Distillery, dis-til′ė-ri, *n.* The building where distilling is carried on.
Distinct, dis-tingkt′, *a.* Separated by some mark; not the same in number or kind; separate in place; clear; definite.
Distinction, dis-tingk′shon, *n.* Act of distinguishing; that which distinguishes; difference; elevation of rank in society; eminence; a title or honour.
Distinctive, dis-tingkt′iv, *a.* Marking distinction; having power to distinguish.
Distinctively, dis-tingkt′iv-li, *adv.* In a distinctive manner; with distinction; plainly.
Distinctly, dis-tingkt′li, *adv.* In a distinct manner; clearly; plainly; obviously.
Distinctness, dis-tingkt′nes, *n.* Quality or state of being distinct; clearness; precision.
Distinguish, dis-ting′gwish, *vt.* To mark out by some peculiarity; to perceive; to make eminent; to signalize.—*vi.* To make a distinction; to find or show the difference.
Distinguishable, dis-ting′gwish-a-bl, *a.* Capable of being distinguished; worthy of note.
Distinguished, dis-ting′gwisht, *p.a.* Eminent.
Distinguishing, dis-ting′gwish-ing, *p.a.* Constituting distinction; characteristic.
Distort, dis-tort′, *vt.* To twist; to pervert.
Distortion, dis-tor′shon, *n.* Act of distorting; a writhing motion; deformity; perversion of the true meaning of words.
Distract, dis-trakt′, *vt.* To draw towards different objects; to perplex; to disorder the reason of; to render furious.
Distracted, dis-trakt′ed, *p.a.* Disordered in intellect; crazy; frantic; insane.
Distractedly, dis-trakt′ed-li, *adv.* Madly; furiously; wildly.
Distracting, dis-trakt′ing, *p.a.* Perplexing.
Distraction, dis-trak′shon, *n.* Derangement; frenzy; diversion.
Distrain, dis-trān′, *vt.* To seize, as goods, for debt.—*vi.* To make seizure of goods.
Distrainable, dis-trān′a-bl, *a.* Liable to be distrained.
Distrainer, Distrainor, dis-trān′ėr, *n.* One who seizes goods for debt.
Distraint, dis-trānt′, *n.* A distraining of goods.
Distraught, dis-trạt′, *a.* Distracted.
Distress, dis-tres′, *n.* Anguish of body or mind; affliction; state of danger or destitution; act of distraining.—*vt.* To afflict with pain or anguish; to perplex.
Distressed, dis-trest′, *p.a.* Afflicted; oppressed with calamity or misfortune.
Distressful, dis-tres′fụl, *a.* Full of distress; proceeding from pain or anguish; calamitous; indicating distress.
Distressfully, dis-tres′fụl-li, *adv.* In a distressful or painful manner.
Distressing, dis-tres′ing, *p.a.* Afflicting; grievous.
Distributable, dis-tri′būt-a-bl, *a.* That may be distributed.
Distribute, dis-tri′būt, *vt.* (distributing, distributed). To divide among two or more; to apportion; to administer, as justice; to classify.
Distributer, dis-tri′būt′ėr, *n.* One who distributes.
Distribution, dis-tri-bū′shon, *n.* Act of distributing; apportionment.
Distributive, dis-tri′būt-iv, *a.* That distributes; expressing separation or division.—*n.* A word that divides or distributes, as *each*, *every*, *either*.

Distributively, dis-tri'būt-iv-li, *adv.* Singly; not collectively.
District, dis'trikt, *n.* A limited extent of country; a circuit; a region.
Distrust, dis-trust', *vt.* To have no trust in; to doubt; to suspect.—*n.* Want of trust; doubt; suspicion; discredit.
Distrustful, dis-trust'fụl, *a.* Apt to distrust; suspicious; not confident.
Disturb, dis-tėrb', *vt.* To throw into disorder; to agitate; to hinder; to move.
Disturbance, dis-tėrb'ans, *n.* State of being disturbed; commotion; excitement; interruption of a right.
Disturber, dis-tėrb'ėr, *n.* One who or that which disturbs.
Disunion, dis-ū'ni-un, *n.* A severing of union; disjunction; breach of concord.
Disunite, dis-ū-nīt', *vt.* To separate.—*vi.* To part; to become separate.
Disuse, dis-ūs', *n.* Cessation of use; desuetude.—*vt.* dis-ūz'. To cease to use; to neglect or omit to practise; to disaccustom.
Ditch, dich, *n.* A trench in the earth for drainage or defence.—*vi.* To dig a ditch.—*vt.* To dig a ditch in; to drain by a ditch; to surround with a ditch.
Ditcher, dich'ėr, *n.* One who digs ditches.
Dithyramb, di'thi-ramb, *n.* An ancient hymn in honour of Bacchus; a poem of impetuous and irregular character.
Ditto, dit'tō, *n.* A word used in lists, &c., meaning same as above; often written *Do.*
Ditty, dit'ti, *n.* A song; a poem to be sung.
Diuretic, dī-ū-ret'ik, *a.* Tending to produce discharges of urine.—*n.* A medicine that has this effect.
Diurnal, dī-ėrn'al, *a.* Relating to day; daily.—*n.* In the Roman Catholic Church, a book containing the office of each day.
Diurnally, dī-ėrn'al-li, *adv.* Daily.
Divagation, dī-va-gā'shon, *n.* Deviation.
Divan, di-van', *n.* Among the Turks, a court of justice; a council or council-chamber; a cushioned seat standing against the wall of a room.
Divaricate, dī-va'ri-kāt, *vi.* To branch off; to fork.
Divarication, dī-va'ri-kā"shon, *n.* A parting into two branches; a crossing of fibres at different angles.
Dive, dīv, *vi.* (diving, dived). To plunge into water head-foremost; to go under water to execute some work; to go deep.
Dive-bomber, dīv-bom'ėr, *n.* An aeroplane specially designed for diving low in order to drop its bombs.
Diver, dīv'ėr, *n.* One who dives; one who works under water; a bird which dives.
Diverge, di-vėrj', *vi.* (diverging, diverged). To proceed from a point in different directions; to deviate; to vary.
Divergence, Divergency, di-vėrj'ens, di-vėr'jen-si, *n.* Act of diverging; a receding from each other.
Divergent, di-vėrj'ent, *a.* Diverging; receding from each other.
Divers, dī'vėrz, *a.* Different; various; sundry; more than one, but not many.
Diverse, di-vėrs', *a.* Different; unlike; various.
Diversely, di-vėrs'li, *adv.* In a diverse manner; variously.
Diversifiable, di-vėrs'i-fī-a-bl, *a.* Capable of being diversified.
Diversification, di-vėrs'i-fi-kā"shon, *n.* Act of diversifying; variation; variegation.
Diversified, di-vėrs'i-fīd, *p.a.* Distinguished by various forms; variegated.
Diversify, di-vėrs'i-fī, *vt.* (diversifying, diversified). To make diverse in form or qualities; to variegate; to give diversity to.
Diversion, di-vėr'shon, *n.* Act of diverting; that which diverts; amusement; a feigned attack.
Diversity, di-vėrs'i-ti, *n.* State of being diverse; contrariety; variety.
Divert, di-vėrt', *vt.* To turn aside; to amuse.
Diverting, di-vėrt'ing, *p.a.* Amusing.
Divest, di-vest', *vt.* To strip of clothes; to deprive.
Dividable, di-vīd'a-bl, *a.* Divisible.
Divide, di-vīd', *vt.* (dividing, divided). To part asunder; to separate; to keep apart; to distribute, allot; to set at variance.—*vi.* To part; to be of different opinions; to vote by the division of a legislative house into parties.
Dividend, di'vi-dend, *n.* A number which is to be divided; share of profit; share divided to creditors.
Divider, di-vīd'ėr, *n.* One who or that which divides; a distributor; *pl.* compasses.
Divination, di-vin-ā'shon, *n.* Act of divining; a foretelling future events, or discovering things secret, by magical means.
Divine, di-vīn', *a.* Of or belonging to God; excellent in the highest degree.—*n.* One versed in divinity; a clergyman.—*vt.* (divining, divined). To foretell; to presage; to guess.—*vi.* To practise divination; to have or utter presages; to guess.
Diviner, di-vīn'ėr, *n.* One who divines; one who professes divination; a soothsayer.
Diving-bell, dīv'ing-bel, *n.* An apparatus by means of which persons may descend below water to execute various operations.
Divining-rod, di-vīn'ing-rod, *n.* A hazel rod, which is said to point downwards over a spot where water or treasure is to be found.
Divinity, di-vin'i-ti, *n.* The state of being divine; God; a deity; the science of divine things; theology.
Divisibility, di-viz'i-bil"i-ti, *n.* Quality of being divisible.
Divisible, di-viz'i-bl, *a.* Capable of division; separable.
Division, di-vi'zhon, *n.* Act of dividing; state of being divided; separation; partition; portion; a separate body of men; a process or rule in arithmetic; part of an army, comprising all arms and services in due proportion, and numbering (in the British army) from 18,000 to 20,000 men.
Divisional, di-vizh'on-al, *a.* Pertaining to division; belonging to a division or district.
Divisive, di-vīz'iv, *a.* Creating division or discord.
Divisor, di-vīz'or, *n.* In *arithmetic*, the number by which the dividend is divided.
Divorce, di-vōrs', *n.* A legal dissolution of marriage; disunion of things closely united.—*vt.* (divorcing, divorced). To dissolve the marriage contract between; to separate.
Divorcement, di-vōrs'ment, *n.* The act of divorcing.
Divot, div'ot, *n.* A piece of turf cut out by a golfer when striking the ball.

Divulge, di-vulj′, *vt.* (divulging, divulged). To make public; to disclose.
Divulsion, di-vul′shon, *n.* A pulling, tearing, or rending asunder, or separating.
Dizen, diz′n, *vt.* To dress; to bedizen.
Dizziness, diz′zi-nes, *n.* Giddiness; vertigo.
Dizzy, diz′zi, *a.* Having a sensation of whirling in the head; giddy; causing giddiness.—*vt.* (dizzying, dizzied). To make giddy.
Djereed, Djerid, je-rēd′, *n.* A blunt javelin used in oriental military sports.
Do, dö, *vt.* or *auxiliary* (doing, pret. did, pp. done). To perform; to bring about; to pay (as honour, &c.); to transact; to finish; to prepare; to cook.—*vi.* To act or behave; to fare in health; to succeed; to suffice; to avail.
Docile, dō′sīl, *a.* Easily taught; ready to learn; tractable; pliant.
Docility, dō-si′li-ti, *n.* Quality of being docile.
Dock, dok, *n.* A troublesome weed; the tail of a beast cut short; the stump of a tail; an inclosed area on the side of a harbour or bank of a river for ships; the place where the accused stands in court.—*vt.* To cut off; to curtail; to deduct from; to put a ship in dock.
Dockage, dok′āj, *n.* Pay for using a dock.
Docket, dok′et, *n.* A summary; a bill tied to goods; a list of cases in a court.—*vt.* To make an abstract of; to mark the contents of papers on the back; to attach a docket to.
Dockyard, dok′yärd, *n.* A yard near a dock for naval stores.
Doctor, dok′tėr, *n.* A person who has received the highest degree in a university faculty; one licensed to practise medicine; a physician.—*vt.* To treat medically; to adulterate.
Doctorate, dok′tėr-āt, *n.* The degree of a doctor.
Doctrinaire, dok-tri-nār′, *n.* A political theorist.
Doctrinal, dok′trin-al, *a.* Pertaining to doctrine; containing a doctrine.
Doctrine, dok′trin, *n.* Instruction; whatever is taught; a principle in any science; dogma; a truth of the gospel.
Document, do′kū-ment, *n.* Written evidence or proof; any authoritative paper containing instructions or proof.—*vt.* To furnish with documents.
Documentary, do-kū-ment′a-ri, *a.* Pertaining to or consisting in documents.
Dodecagon, dō-de′ka-gon, *n.* A figure with twelve sides.
Dodge, doj, *vt.* (dodging, dodged). To start aside; to quibble.—*vt.* To evade by a sudden shift of place.—*n.* An artifice; an evasion.
Dodo, dō′dō, *n.* An extinct bird of Mauritius, having a massive, clumsy body, short strong legs, and wings useless for flight.
Doe, dō, *n.* A female deer.
Doer, dö′ėr, *n.* One who does; actor; agent.
Does, duz. The third sing. present of *do*.
Doeskin, dō′skin, *n.* The skin of a doe; a compact twilled woollen cloth.
Doff, dof, *vt.* To put off.
Dog, dog, *n.* A domestic quadruped of many varieties; a mean fellow; a gay young man.—*vt.* (dogging, dogged). To follow insidiously; to worry with importunity.
Dog-cart, dog′kärt, *n.* A carriage with a box for holding sportsmen's dogs; a sort of double-seated gig.
Dog-cheap, dog′chēp, *a.* Very cheap.
Dog-day, dog′dā, *n.* One of the days when Sirius, the Dog-star, rises and sets with the sun.
Doge, dōj, *n.* The chief magistrate in republican Venice.
Dog-eared, dog′ērd, *a.* Having the corners of the leaves turned down (said of a book).
Dog-fish, dog′fish, *n.* A species of shark.
Dogged, dog′ed, *a.* Determined; pertinacious.
Doggedly, dog′ed-li, *adv.* With obstinate resolution.
Dogger, dog′ėr, *n.* A two-masted Dutch fishing-boat.
Doggerel, dog′ė-rel, *n.* A loose irregular kind of versification; wretched verse.
Doggish, dog′ish, *a.* Churlish; snappish.
Dogma, dog′ma, *n.* A settled opinion or belief; tenet; a doctrinal point.
Dogmatic, Dogmatical, dog-mat′ik, dog-mat′ik-al, *a.* Pertaining to a dogma; asserting, or asserted, with authority or arrogance; positive.
Dogmatics, dog-mat′iks, *n.* Doctrinal theology; essential doctrines of Christianity.
Dogmatism, dog′mat-izm, *n.* Positiveness in assertion; arrogance in opinion.
Dogmatist, dog′mat-ist, *n.* A dogmatic asserter; an arrogant advancer of principles.
Dogmatize, dog′mat-īz, *vi.* (dogmatizing, dogmatized). To assert with undue confidence; to advance principles with arrogance.
Dog-star, dog′stär, *n.* Sirius, a star of the first magnitude.
Dog-tooth, dog′töth, *n.* An eye-tooth.
Doily, doi′li, *n.* A small ornamental mat for glasses, &c.
Doings, dö′ingz, *n.pl.* Things done; transactions; conduct; bustle.
Doit, doit, *n.* A small Dutch copper coin worth about half a farthing; any small piece of money; a trifle.
Doldrums, dol′drumz, *n.pl.* The dumps.
Dole, dōl, *n.* That which is dealt out; share; gratuity; grief; sorrow.—*vt.* (doling, doled). To deal out; to distribute.
Doleful, dōl′fụl, *a.* Full of pain, grief, &c.; expressing or causing grief; gloomy.
Dolefully, dōl′fụl-li, *adv.* In a doleful manner; sorrowfully; dismally; sadly.
Dolichocephalic, Dolichocephalous, dol′-i-kō-se-fal″ik, dol′i-kō-sef″a-lus, *a.* Long-skulled: used to denote skulls in which the diameter from side to side is small in proportion to the diameter from front to back.
Doll, dol, *n.* A child's puppet in human form.
Dollar, dol′lėr, *n.* A coin of the United States and Canada (= 100 cents).
Dolman, dol′man, *n.* A lady's mantle.
Dolmen, dol′men, *n.* An ancient structure consisting of one large unhewn stone resting on others; a cromlech.
Dolomite, dol′o-mīt, *n.* A granular crystalline or schistose rock compounded of carbonate of magnesia and carbonate of lime.
Dolorous, dō′lėr-us, *a.* Sorrowful; doleful.
Dolorously, dō′lėr-us-li, *adv.* Sorrowfully.
Dolour, dō′lėr, *n.* Sorrow; lamentation.
Dolphin, dol′fin, *n.* A small species of whale remarkable for gambolling in the water; a fish celebrated for its changes of colour when dying.

Dolt, dōlt, *n.* A blockhead.
Doltish, dōlt′ish, *a.* Dull in intellect.
Domain, dō-mān′, *n.* Territory governed; estate; a demesne.
Dome, dōm, *n.* A hemispherical roof of a building; a large cupola.
Domestic, dō-mes′tik, *a.* Belonging to the house or home; tame; not foreign.—*n.* A household servant.
Domesticate, dō-mes′tik-āt, *vt.* To accustom to remain much at home; to tame.
Domestication, dō-mes′tik-ā″shon, *n.* Act of domesticating; state of being domesticated.
Domicile, do′mi-sīl, *n.* A habitation; family residence.—*vt.* (domiciling, domiciled). To establish in a residence.
Domiciliary, do-mi-si′li-a-ri, *a.* Pertaining to a domicile.
Dominant, dom′in-ant, *a.* Governing; predominant; ascendant.
Dominate, dom′in-āt, *vt.* (dominating, dominated). To rule; to predominate over.
Domination, dom-in-ā′shon, *n.* Rule; tyranny.
Domineer, dom-in-ēr′, *vi.* To rule tyrannically or with insolence (with *over*).
Domineering, dom-in-ēr′ing, *p.a.* Overbearing; insolent.
Dominical, dō-min′ik-al, *a.* Noting Sunday; relating to God.
Dominican, dō-min′ik-an, *n.* A Black-friar.
Dominie, dom′i-ni, *n.* A pedagogue.
Dominion, dō-min′i-on, *n.* Sovereign authority; district governed; region.
Domino, do′mi-nō, *n.* A masquerade dress; a half-mask; a person wearing a domino; *pl.* **(Dominoes),** a game played with pieces of ivory or bone dotted like dice.
Don, don, *n.* A Spanish title, corresponding to Eng. Mr.; an important personage; a resident Fellow of a college at Oxford or Cambridge.—*vt.* (donning, donned). To put on; to invest with.
Donate, dō′nāt, *vt.* To bestow.
Donation, dō-nā′shon, *n.* Act of giving; that which is given; a gift; a present.
Donative, don′at-iv, *n.* A gift; a largess; a benefice given by the patron, without presentation, institution, or introduction by the ordinary.—*a.* Vested or vesting by donation.
Donee, dō-nē′, *n.* One to whom a gift is made.
Donjon, don′jon, *n.* The principal tower of a castle; the keep.
Donkey, dong′ki, *n.* An ass.
Donna, don′na, *n.* A lady; as, *prima donna*, the first female singer in an opera, &c.
Donor, dō′nėr, *n.* One who gives.
Dooly, dö′li, *n.* A light palanquin or litter.
Doom, döm, *n.* Judicial sentence; fate; ruin.—*vt.* To condemn to punishment; to destine.
Doomed, dömd, *p.a.* Having the doom or fate settled; destined to speedy destruction.
Doomsday, dömz′dā, *n.* The day of judgment.
Door, dōr, *n.* The entrance of a house or room; the frame of boards that shuts such an entrance; avenue; means of approach.
Dor, Dorr, dor, *n.* A common British beetle.
Dorian, dō′ri-an, *n.* Pertaining to Doris in Greece.—*n.* A Greek of Doris.
Doric, dor′ik, *a.* Pertaining to Doris in Greece; denoting the earliest and plainest of the Grecian orders of architecture.
Dormancy, dor′man-si, *n.* State of being dormant; quiescence; sleep; abeyance.
Dormant, dor′mant, *a.* Sleeping; not used; inactive.
Dormer, Dormer-window, dor′mėr, dor′mėr-win-dō, *n.* A window in a sloping roof, the frame being placed vertically.
Dormitory, dor′mi-to-ri, *n.* A place to sleep in; a room in which a number sleep.
Dormouse, dor′mous, *n.*; pl. **Dormice,** dor′mīs. A small rodent which passes the winter in a lethargic or torpid state.
Dormy, dor′mi, *a.* In golf, applied to a player leading by as many holes as still remain to be played.
Dorsal, dor′sal, *a.* Pertaining to the back.
Dory, dō′ri, *n.* A European yellow fish, with a protrusible mouth; a small boat.
Dose, dōs, *n.* The quantity of medicine given at one time; something given to be swallowed. *vt.* (dosing, dosed). To give in doses; to give medicine to.
Dossier, dos′ē-ā, *n.* A collection of documents of information about a person or incident.
Dost, dust. The second sing. present of *do.*
Dot, dot, *n.* A small point, as made with a pen, &c.; a speck.—*vt.* (dotting, dotted). To mark with a dot; to diversify with small objects.—*vi.* To make dots.
Dotage, dōt′āj, *n.* Feebleness of mind, particularly in old age; excessive fondness.
Dotal, dōt′al, *a.* Pertaining to dower.
Dotard, dōt′ėrd, *n.* One whose mind is impaired by age; one foolishly fond.
Dotation, dō-tā′shon, *n.* Act of bestowing a marriage portion on a woman; endowment.
Dote, dōt, *vi.* (doting, doted). To have the intellect impaired by age; to be foolishly fond.
Doth, duth. The third sing. present of *do.*
Doting, dōt′ing, *p.a.* Having the mind impaired by age; foolishly fond.
Dotterel, Dottrel, dot′tėr-el, dot′trel, *n.* A species of plover; a booby; a dupe.
Double, du′bl, *a.* Twofold; forming a pair; of extra size, quality, &c.; deceitful.—*vt.* (doubling, doubled). To make twofold; to fold; to increase by adding an equal amount to; to sail round (a cape, &c.).—*vi.* To increase twofold; to turn or wind in running; to use sleights.—*n.* Twice as much; a turn in running; a shift; a duplicate; a wraith.
Double-bass, du′bl-bās, *n.* The lowest-toned instrument of the violin class.
Double-dealing, du′bl-dēl-ing, *n.* Deceitful practice; duplicity.
Double-entry, du′bl-en-tri, *n.* A mode of book-keeping in which every transaction is entered on the debit side of one account and the credit side of another.
Double-star, du′bl-stär, *n.* A star which in the telescope is resolved into two stars.
Doublet, du′blet, *n.* A close-fitting body garment; one of a pair; one of two words really the same but different in form.
Doubling, du′bl-ing, *n.* Act of making double; a fold; a lining.
Doubloon, dub-lön′, *n.* A Spanish gold coin, worth about 21*s.* sterling.
Doubly, du′bli, *adv.* In twice the quantity; to twice the degree.
Doubt, dout, *vi.* To waver in opinion or judgment; to question; to suspect.—*vt.* To deem uncertain; to distrust.—*n.* A wavering in opinion; uncertainty; suspicion.
Doubter, dout′ėr, *n.* One who doubts.

Doubtful, dout'ful, *a.* Full of doubt or doubts; hesitating; ambiguous; precarious; suspicious.
Doubtfully, dout'ful-li, *adv.* In a doubtful manner; dubiously.
Doubtless, dout'les, *adv.* Without doubt; unquestionably.
Doubtlessly, dout'les-li, *adv.* Doubtless.
Douceur, dö-sėr', *n.* A gift; bribe; gratuity.
Douche, dösh, *n.* A jet of water directed upon some part of the body.
Dough, dō, *n.* Flour or meal moistened and kneaded, but not baked; paste of bread.
Doughtily, dou'ti-li, *adv.* In a doughty manner.
Doughty, dou'ti, *a.* Noble; brave; valiant.
Doughy, dō'i, *a.* Like dough; soft; pale.
Douse, Dowse, dous, *vt.* and *i.* To plunge into water; to drench.
Dove, duv, *n.* A pigeon; a word of endearment.
Dove-cot, Dove-cote, duv'kot, duv'kōt, *n.* A place for pigeons.
Dovetail, duv'tāl, *n.* A mode of joining boards by letting one piece into another in the form of a dove's tail spread, or wedge reversed.—*vt.* and *i.* To unite by the above method; to fit exactly.
Dowager, dou'ā-jėr, *n.* A title given to the widow of a person of title, provided that she is mother, grandmother, or stepmother of the successor.
Dowdy, dou'di, *n.* An awkward, ill-dressed woman.—*a.* Ill-dressed; vulgar-looking.
Dowel, dou'el, *n.* A pin of wood or iron to join boards, &c.—*vt.* (dowelling, dowelled). To fasten by dowels.
Dower, dou'ėr, *n.* That portion of the property of a man which his widow enjoys during her life; the property which a woman brings to her husband in marriage; dowry.
Dowered, dou'ėrd, *p.a.* Furnished with dower, or a portion.
Dowerless, dou'ėr-les, *a.* Destitute of dower.
Dowlas, dou'las, *n.* A coarse linen cloth.
Down, doun, *n.* The fine soft feathers of birds; fine hair; the pubescence of plants; a hill; a dune; a tract of naked, hilly land.—*adv.* In a descending direction; on the ground; into less bulk; paid in ready money.—*prep.* Along in descent; toward the mouth of.—*a.* Downcast; dejected.
Downcast, doun'kast, *a.* Cast downward; dejected.
Down-come, doun'kum, *n.* A sudden or heavy fall; ruin; destruction.
Downfall, doun'fal, *n.* A falling down; loss of wealth or high position; ruin.
Downhill, doun'hil, *a.* Descending; easy.—*adv.* Down a hill or slope.
Downpour, doun'pōr, *n.* A pouring down; especially, a heavy or continuous shower.
Downright, doun'rīt, *adv.* Right down; in plain terms; utterly.—*a.* Directly to the point; plain; blunt; utter.
Downstairs, doun'stārz, *a.* or *adv.* Descending the stairs; on a lower flat.
Downthrow, doun'thrō, *n.* A throwing down; a falling or sinking of strata.
Downtrodden, doun'trod-n, *a.* Trodden down; oppressed.
Downward, Downwards, doun'wėrd, doun'wėrdz, *adv.* From a higher place or state to a lower; in direction from a head or source.
Downward, *a.* Sloping down; descending.
Downy, doun'i, *a.* Covered with, or pertaining to, down, soft; soothing.
Dowry, dou'ri, *n.* The property which a woman brings to her husband in marriage; a dower; a gift.
Doxology, doks-ol'o-ji, *n.* A hymn or form of giving glory to God.
Doze, dōz, *vi.* (dozing, dozed). To sleep lightly; to be half asleep.—*vt.* To pass or spend in drowsiness.—*n.* A slight sleep; a slumber.
Dozen, du'zn, *n.* Twelve things regarded collectively.
Dozy, dōz'i, *a.* Drowsy; sleepy; sluggish.
Drab, drab, *n.* A sluttish woman; a strumpet; a thick woollen cloth of a dun colour; a dull brownish colour.—*a.* Of a dull brown colour.
Drachm, dram, *n.* Same as *Drachma*, *Dram*.
Drachma, drak'ma, *n.* A Greek silver coin value one franc; a Greek weight of about 2 dwts. 7 grains troy.
Draconic, Draconian, drā-kon'ik, drā-kō'ni-an, *a.* Relating to Draco, the Athenian lawgiver; extremely severe.
Draff, draf, *n.* Refuse; dregs; waste matter.
Draft, dräft, *n.* A detachment of men or things; an order for money; the first sketch of any writing; a sketch.—*vt.* To make a draft of; to sketch; to select.
Draftsman, dräfts'man, *n.* *See* DRAUGHTSMAN.
Drag, drag, *vt.* (dragging, dragged). To draw along the ground by main force; to haul; to explore with a drag.—*vi.* To hang so as to trail on the ground; to move slowly.—*n.* A net drawn along the bottom of the water; an instrument to catch hold of things under water; a machine for dredging; a low cart; a long coach; a contrivance to stop a wheel of a carriage; whatever serves to retard.
Draggle, drag'gl, *vt.* (draggling, draggled). To dirty by drawing on the ground.—*vi.* To become dirty by being drawn on the ground.
Drag-net, drag'net, *n.* A net to be drawn along the bottom of a river or pond.
Dragoman, drag'ō-man, *n.*; pl. **Dragomans.** An interpreter and traveller's guide or agent in eastern countries.
Dragon, dra'gon, *n.* A fabulous winged monster; a fierce person; a kind of small lizard.
Dragonet, dra'gon-et, *n.* A little dragon; a small fish of the goby family.
Dragon-fly, dra'gon-flī, *n.* A fly that preys upon other insects.
Dragonish, dra'gon-ish, *a.* In the form of a dragon; dragon-like.
Dragon's-blood, dra'gonz-blud, *n.* The red juice of certain tropical plants, used for colouring varnishes, staining marble, &c.
Dragoon, dra-gön', *n.* A heavy cavalry soldier.—*vt.* To harass; to compel by force.
Drain, drān, *vt.* To draw off; to filter; to make dry; to exhaust.—*vi.* To flow off gradually.—*n.* A channel for liquid; a sewer; gradual or continuous withdrawal.
Drainage, drān'āj, *n.* The act or art of draining; the system of drains; that which flows out of drains.
Drainer, drān'ėr, *n.* A utensil on which articles are placed to drain; one who or that which drains.
Drake, drāk, *n.* The male of ducks.

Dram, dram, *n.* The eighth part of an ounce, or sixty grains apothecaries' measure; the sixteenth part of an ounce avoirdupois; as much spirituous liquor as is drunk at once.
Drama, drä'ma, *n.* A representation on a stage; a play; dramatic literature.
Dramatic, Dramatical, dra-mat'ik, dra-mat'-ik-al, *a.* Pertaining to the drama; represented by action; theatrical.
Dramatist, dră'mat-ist, *n.* The author of a dramatic composition.
Dramatize, dră'mat-iz, *vt.* To compose in the form of the drama.
Dramaturgy, drăm'a-tėr-ji, *n.* The science of dramatic composition and representation.
Drape, drāp, *vt.* (draping, draped). To cover with cloth or drapery.
Draper, drāp'ėr, *n.* One who sells cloths.
Drapery, drāp'ė-ri, *n.* The occupation of a draper; fabrics of wool or linen; clothes or hangings.
Drastic, dras'tik, *a.* Acting with strength or violence.—*n.* A strong purgative.
Draught, drăft, *n.* The act of drawing; quantity drunk at once; a sketch or outline; the depth a ship sinks in water; a current of air; *pl.* a game played on a checkered board.—*vt.* To draw out; to draft.—*a.* Used for drawing; drawn from the barrel, &c.
Draughtsman, drăfts'man, *n.* One who draws plans or designs; one of the pieces in the game of draughts.
Draughty, drăf'ti, *a.* Of or pertaining to draughts of air; exposed to draughts.
Dravidian, dra-vid'yan, *a.* Pertaining to Dravida, an old province of S. India: applied to a distinct family of tongues spoken in S. India, Ceylon, &c.
Draw, dra̤, *vt.* (drawing, pret. drew, pp. drawn). To pull along or towards; to cause to come; to unsheathe; to suck; to attract; to inhale; to stretch; to lead, as a motive; to represent by lines drawn on a surface; to describe; to infer; to derive; to draft; to require a certain depth of water; to bend (a bow); to end indecisively.—*vi.* To pull; to shrink; to advance; to practise drawing; to make a written demand for money.—*n.* Act of drawing; the lot or chance drawn; a drawn game.
Drawback, dra̤'bak, *n.* What detracts from profit or pleasure; duties on goods paid back when exported.
Drawbridge, dra̤'brij, *n.* A bridge which may be raised or drawn aside.
Drawer, dra̤'ėr, *n.* One who or that which draws; he who draws a bill; a sliding box in a case, &c.; *pl.* an under-garment for the lower limbs.
Drawing, dra̤'ing, *n.* Act of one who draws; representation of objects by lines and shades; delineation.
Drawing-room, dra̤'ing-röm, *n.* A room for receiving company in; formal reception of company at a court.
Drawl, dra̤l, *vi.* To speak with slow, prolonged utterance.—*vt.* To utter in a slow tone.—*n.* A lengthened utterance.
Draw-well, dra̤'wel, *n.* A deep well from which water is drawn by a long cord or pole.
Dray, drā, *n.* A low cart or carriage on wheels, drawn by a horse.
Dread, dred, *n.* Fear, united with respect; terror; the person or the thing dreaded.—*a.* Exciting great fear; terrible; venerable.—*vt.* and *i.* To fear in a great degree.
Dreadful, dred'fu̧l, *a.* Awful; terrible.
Dreadfully, dred'fu̧l-li, *adv.* Terribly.
Dreadless, dred'les, *a.* Fearless; intrepid.
Dreadnought, dred'na̤t, *n.* A person that fears nothing; a thick cloth with a long pile; a garment made of such cloth; a general term for a battleship.
Dream, drēm, *n.* The thought of a person in sleep; a vain fancy.—*vi.* To have images in the mind, in sleep; to imagine; to think idly.—*vt.* To see in a dream; to spend idly.
Dreamer, drēm'ėr, *n.* One who dreams; a fanciful man; a visionary.
Dreamless, drēm'les, *a.* Free from dreams.
Dreamy, drēm'i, *a.* Full of dreams; visionary.
Drear, drēr, *a.* Dismal; gloomy.
Drearily, drē'ri-li, *adv.* Gloomily.
Dreary, drē'ri, *a.* Dismal; gloomy; oppressively monotonous.
Dredge, drej, *n.* An oyster net; a dredging-machine.—*vt.* (dredging, dredged). To take with a dredge; to deepen with a dredging-machine; to powder; to sprinkle flour on meat while roasting.
Dredger, drej'ėr, *n.* One who uses a dredge; a utensil for scattering flour on meat while roasting; a dredging-machine.
Dredging-machine, drej'ing-ma-shēn, *n.* A machine to take up mud, &c., from the bottom of rivers or docks.
Dreggy, dreg'i, *a.* Containing dregs; foul.
Dregs, dregz, *n.pl.* Lees; grounds; the most vile and despicable part.
Drench, drensh, *vt.* To wet thoroughly; to soak; to purge violently.—*n.* A draught; a large dose of liquid medicine for an animal.
Dress, dres, *vt.* To make straight; to put in good order; to cleanse and cover a wound; to prepare; to curry, rub, and comb; to clothe; to array; to trim.—*vi.* To arrange in a line; to put on clothes; to pay regard to dress.—*n.* Apparel; attire; a lady's gown.
Dresser, dres'ėr, *n.* One who dresses; a table on which food is dressed; a low cupboard for dishes.
Dressing, dres'ing, *n.* Act of one who dresses; manure; application to a sore; stuffing of fowls, pigs, &c.; starch, &c., used in finishing silk, linen, &c.; moulding round doors, windows, &c.
Dressing-case, dres'ing-kās, *n.* A box containing toilet requisites.
Dressing-room, dres'ing-röm, *n.* A room for dressing in.
Dressy, dres'i, *a.* Showy in dress.
Dribble, drib'l, *vi.* (dribbling, dribbled). To fall in a quick succession of drops; to trickle; to take a football up the field by means of a series of short kicks, keeping the ball near to the foot and under control.—*vt.* To throw down in drops.
Driblet, drib'let, *n.* A small drop; a small sum, as one of a series.
Drift, drift, *n.* That which is driven by wind or water; impulse; tendency; aim; velocity of a current; the distance a vessel is driven by a current; rocks conveyed by glaciers and deposited over a country while submerged; in S. Africa, a ford.—*vi.* To move along like anything driven; to accumulate in heaps; to

float or be driven by a current.—*vt.* To drive into heaps.—*a.* Drifted by wind or currents.
Driftless, drift'les, *a.* Aimless.
Drill, dril, *vt.* To pierce with a drill; to teach soldiers their proper movements, &c.; to teach by repeated exercise; to sow in rows; to furrow.—*vi.* To sow in drills; to muster for exercise.—*n.* A pointed instrument for boring holes; act of training soldiers; a row of seeds; a furrow.
Drill, dril, *n.* A kind of coarse linen or cotton cloth.
Drink, dringk, *vi.* (drinking, pret. drank, pp. drunk or drunken). To swallow liquor; to take spirituous liquors to excess.—*vt.* To swallow, as liquids; to absorb.—*n.* Liquor to be swallowed; any beverage; potion.
Drinkable, dringk'a-bl, *a.* That may be drunk; fit or suitable for drink.
Drinker, dringk'ėr, *n.* One who drinks; a tippler.
Drip, drip, *vi.* (dripping, dripped). To fall in drops.—*vt.* To let fall in drops.—*n.* A falling in drops; the eaves; a projecting moulding.
Dripping, drip'ing, *n.* A falling in drops; the fat which falls from meat in roasting.
Drive, drīv, *vt.* (driving, pret. drove, pp. driven). To impel; to hurry on; to impel and guide; to convey in a carriage; to carry on.—*vi.* To be impelled along; to aim at; to strike with force.—*n.* A journey in a vehicle; a road for driving on; a sweeping blow.
Drivel, dri'vel, *vi.* (drivelling, drivelled). To slaver; to dote; to talk rubbish.—*n.* Slaver; senseless twaddle.
Driveller, dri'vel-ėr, *n.* An idiot, twaddler.
Driver, drīv'ėr, *n.* One who or that which drives; a large quadrilateral sail; a main wheel; a golf club for long strokes.
Drizzle, driz'l, *vi.* (drizzling, drizzled). To rain in small drops.—*vt.* To shed in small drops or particles.—*n.* A small or fine rain.
Drizzly, driz'li, *a.* Shedding small rain.
Droll, drōl, *a.* Comic; queer; facetious.—*n.* A jester; a farce.
Drollery, drōl'ė-ri, *n.* Buffoonery; comical stories.
Dromedary, drom'ē-da-ri, *n.* A swift camel, usually the Arabian, with one hump, in distinction from the Bactrian, which has two.
Drone, drōn, *n.* The male or non-working bee; an idler; a low humming sound; a large tube of the bagpipe.—*vi.* (droning, droned). To give a low dull sound; to hum.
Dronish, drōn'ish, *a.* Idle; sluggish.
Droop, dröp, *vi.* To hang down; to languish; to fail; to be dispirited.—*vt.* To let sink or hang down.—*n.* A drooping position or state.
Drop, drop, *n.* A globule of any liquid; an earring; a small quantity; part of a gallows; a distance to fall.—*vt.* (dropping, dropped). To pour or let fall in drops; to let fall; to let down; to quit; to utter casually.—*vi.* To fall in drops; to fall; to cease; to come unexpectedly.
Dropping, drop'ing, *n.* A falling in drops; that which drops; *pl.* the dung of animals.
Drop-scene, drop'sēn, *n.* A scenic picture, which descends in front of the stage.
Dropsical, drop'sik-al, *a.* Diseased with, or inclined to, dropsy; of the nature of dropsy.
Dropsy, drop'si, *n.* An unnatural collection of water in any part of the body.
Drosky, dros'ki, *n.* A light four-wheeled open carriage.
Dross, dros, *n.* The scum of metals; waste matter; refuse.
Drossy, dros'i, *a.* Like or pertaining to dross; full of dross; foul.
Drought, drout, *n.* Dry weather; want of rain; aridness; thirst; lack.
Droughty, drout'i, *a.* Dry; wanting rain.
Drove, drōv, *n.* A collection of cattle driven; a crowd of people in motion.
Drover, drōv'ėr, *n.* One who drives cattle or sheep to market.
Drown, droun, *vt.* To deprive of life by immersion in water, &c.; to inundate; to overwhelm.—*vi.* To be suffocated in water, &c.
Drowse, drouz, *vi.* (drowsing, drowsed). To nod in slumber; to doze; to look heavy.—*vt.* To make heavy with sleep, or stupid.
Drowsily, drou'zi-li, *adv.* Sleepily.
Drowsy, drou'zi, *a.* Inclined to sleep; dull; sluggish; lulling.
Drub, drub, *vt.* (drubbing, drubbed). To cudgel; to thrash.—*n.* A blow; a thump.
Drubbing, drub'ing, *n.* A sound beating.
Drudge, druj, *vi.* (drudging, drudged). To labour at mean work.—*n.* One who labours hard in servile employments; a slave.
Drudgery, druj'ė-ri, *n.* Hard labour; toilsome work; ignoble toil.
Drug, drug, *n.* Any substance used in medicine; an article of slow sale.—*vt.* (drugging, drugged). To mix with drugs; to introduce a narcotic into; to dose to excess with drugs.
Drugget, drug'et, *n.* A coarse woollen cloth or felted stuff.
Druggist, drug'ist, *n.* One who deals in drugs.
Druid, drū'id, *n.* A priest and judge among the ancient Celtic nations.
Druidic, Druidical, drū-id'ik, drū-id'ik-al, *a.* Pertaining to the Druids.
Druidism, drū'id-izm, *n.* The doctrines, rites, and ceremonies of the Druids.
Drum, drum, *n.* A hollow cylindrical instrument of music beaten with sticks; something in the form of a drum; the tympanum of the ear.—*vi.* (drumming, drummed). To beat a drum; to beat with the fingers, as with drumsticks; to beat rapidly.—*vt.* To expel or summon by beat of drum.
Drumhead, drum'hed, *n.* The head of a drum; the top part of a capstan.
Drum-major, drum'mā-jėr, *n.* The chief drummer of a regiment.
Drummer, drum'ėr, *n.* One whose office is to beat the drum in military exercises.
Drunk, drungk, *a.* Overcome with alcoholic liquor; intoxicated.
Drunkard, drungk'ėrd, *n.* A person who is habitually or frequently drunk.
Drunken, drungk'en, *p.a.* Inebriated; given to drunkenness; proceeding from intoxication.
Drunkenness, drungk'en-nes, *n.* Intoxication; inebriety.
Drupe, dröp, *n.* A stone fruit, as the plum.
Dry, drī, *a.* Destitute of moisture; arid; free from juice; thirsty; uninteresting; sarcastic; harsh; cold.—*vt.* (drying, dried). To free from moisture; to deprive of natural juice;

to drain.—*vi*. To lose moisture; to evaporate wholly.
Dryad, drī'ad, *n*. A nymph of the woods.
Dryer, Drier, drī'ėr, *n*. One who or that which dries; that which exhausts moisture.
Dryly, Drily, drī'li, *adv*. In a dry manner; coldly; sarcastically.
Dryness, drī'nes, *n*. State or quality of being dry; jejuneness; causticity.
Dry-nurse, drī'nėrs, *n*. A nurse who attends but does not suckle a child.
Dry-rot, drī'rot, *n*. A decay of timber, occasioned by various species of fungi.
Drysalter, drī'sạlt-ėr, *n*. A dealer in dye-stuffs, chemicals, &c.
Drysaltery, drī'sạlt-ė-ri, *n*. The articles kept by, or the business of, a drysalter.
Dual, dū'al, *a*. Expressing the number two; existing as two; twofold.
Dualism, dū'al-izm, *n*. A twofold division; the belief in two gods, the one good, the other evil; the doctrine of the existence of spirit and matter as distinct entities.
Dualist, dū'al-ist, *n*. One who holds the doctrine of dualism.
Duality, dū-al'i-ti, *n*. The state of being dual or twofold.
Dub, dub, *vt*. (dubbing, dubbed). To tap with a sword and make a knight; to speak of as; to smooth; to trim.
Dubiety, dū-bī'e-ti, *n*. Doubtfulness.
Dubious, dū'bi-us, *a*. Wavering in opinion; doubtful; uncertain.
Dubiously, dū'bi-us-li, *adv*. Doubtfully.
Ducal, dūk'al, *a*. Pertaining to a duke.
Ducally, dūk'al-li, *adv*. In a ducal manner.
Ducat, duk'at, *n*. A coin formerly common in Europe, either of silver (value 3*s*. to 4*s*.) or gold (value about 9*s*. 4*d*.).
Duchess, duch'es, *n*. The wife of a duke; a lady who has the sovereignty of a duchy.
Duchy, duch'i, *n*. The dominion of a duke.
Duck, duk, *vt*. and *i* . To plunge in water; to bow, stoop, or nod.—*n*. A water-fowl; a term of endearment; an inclination of the head; a canvas or coarse cloth.
Duckling, duk'ling, *n*. A young duck.
Duct, dukt, *n*. A canal or tube, especially in animal bodies and plants.
Ductile, duk'til, *a*. That may be drawn out; docile; tractable; flexible.
Ductility, duk-til'i-ti, *n*. The property of metals which renders them capable of being drawn out without breaking; obsequiousness; ready compliance.
Dud, dud, *n*. A shell which fails to explode; hence an incompetent person or a defective thing.
Dude, dūd, *n*. A dandy of the first water; a brainless exquisite.
Dudgeon, du'jon, *n*. A small dagger, or the handle of a dagger; ill-will; sullenness.
Due, dū, *a*. Owed; owing; suitable; proper; attributable; that ought to have arrived by the time specified.—*adv*. Directly.—*n*. That which law, office, rank, &c., require to be paid or done; fee; right; just title.
Duel, dū'el, *n*. A premeditated combat between two persons; single combat; contest.
Duellist, dū'el-ist, *n*. One who fights duels.
Duello, dū-el'lō, *n*. The art of duelling; the code of laws which regulate it.
Duenna, dö-en'na, *n*. Formerly, the chief lady in waiting on the Queen of Spain; an elderly woman in charge of a younger; a governess.
Duet, dū'et, *n*. A piece of music for two performers, vocal or instrumental.
Duffer, duf'ėr, *n*. A useless fellow.
Dug, dug, *n*. The pap or nipple: now applied only to beasts, unless in contempt.
Dug-out, dug out, *n*. A rudely hollowed-out canoe from trunk of tree; an underground shelter from shells; an elderly officer recalled to duty from retirement.
Duke, dūk, *n*. One of the highest order of nobility; a sovereign prince.
Dukedom, dūk'dum, *n*. The jurisdiction, possessions, title, or quality of a duke.
Dulcet, dul'set, *a*. Sweet; harmonious.
Dulcimer, dul'si-mėr, *n*. A stringed instrument of music, played on by two sticks.
Dull, dul, *a*. Stupid; slow; blunt; drowsy; cheerless; not bright or clear; tarnished; uninteresting.—*vt*. To make dull; to stupefy; to blunt; to make sad; to sully.—*vi*. To become dull, blunt, or stupid.
Dullard, dul'ėrd, *n*. A stupid person; dolt.
Dully, dul'li, *adv*. Stupidly; sluggishly.
Dulness, Dullness, dul'nes, *n*. Stupidity; heaviness; slowness; dimness.
Dulse, duls, *n*. An edible sea-weed.
Duly, dū'li, *adv*. Properly; fitly.
Dumb, dum, *a*. Incapable of speech; mute; silent; not accompanied with speech.
Dumb-bell, dum'bel, *n*. One of a pair of weights used for exercise.
Dumbly, dum'li, *adv*. Mutely.
Dumdum, dum-dum, *n*. A soft-nosed bullet which expands and lacerates on striking.
Dumfound, Dumbfound, dum-found', *vt*. To strike dumb; to confuse. Also *Dumfounder*.
Dummy, dum'i, *n*. One who is dumb; the exposed hand when three persons play at whist; a sham article.
Dump, dump, *n*. A dull state of the mind; sadness; a thud; a clumsy piece; *pl*. low spirits; gloom.
Dump, dump, *n*. A heap of refuse; a place where refuse is deposited; a large concentration of military stores, especially of ammunition.
Dumpish, dump'ish, *a*. Melancholy; depressed in spirits.
Dumpling, dump'ling, *n*. A pudding of boiled suet paste, with or without fruit.
Dumpy, dump'i, *a*. Short and thick.
Dun, dun, *a*. Of a dark dull colour; swarthy.—*vt*. (dunning, dunned). To demand a debt from; to urge importunately.—*n*. An importunate creditor; urgent demand for payment.
Dunce, duns, *n*. One slow at learning; a dullard; a dolt.
Dunderhead, dun'dėr-hed, *n*. A dolt.
Dune, dūn, *n*. A sand-hill on the sea-coast.
Dung, dung, *n*. The excrement of animals.—*vt*. To manure; to immerse (calico) in cow-dung and water.—*vi*. To void excrement.
Dungeon, dun'jon, *n*. A strong tower in the middle of a castle; a deep, dark place of confinement.
Dunghill, dung'hil, *n*. A heap of dung.—*a*. Sprung from the dunghill; mean; low.
Dunlin, dun'lin, *n*. A species of sandpiper.
Dunnage, dun'āj, *n*. Branches or brushwood, &c., used as a support for cargo.

Dunnish, dun'ish, *a.* Inclined to a dun colour; somewhat dun.
Duodecimal, dū-ō-de'si-mal, *a.* Proceeding in computation by twelves; twelfth.
Duodecimo, dū-ō-de'si-mō, *a.* Consisting of twelve leaves to a sheet.—*n.* A book in which a sheet is folded into twelve leaves.
Duodenum, dū-ō-dē'num, *n.* The first portion of the small intestines.
Dupe, dūp, *n.* One who is cheated; one easily deceived.—*vt.* (duping, duped). To impose on.
Duplex, dū'pleks, *a.* Double; twofold.
Duplicate, dū'pli-kāt, *a.* Double; twofold. —*n.* A copy; a transcript.—*vt.* To double.
Duplication, dū-pli-kā'shon, *n.* Act of doubling; a fold; multiplication by 2.
Duplicity, dū-pli'si-ti, *n.* Doubleness of heart or speech; guile; deception.
Durability, dūr-a-bil'i-ti, *n.* Quality of being durable.
Durable, dūr'a-bl, *a.* Having the quality of lasting long; permanent; firm.
Durably, dūr'a-bli, *adv.* In a durable manner.
Dura-mater, dū'ra-mā-tėr, *n.* The outer membrane of the brain.
Duramen, dū-rā'men, *n.* The heart-wood of an exogenous tree.
Durance, dūr'ans, *n.* Imprisonment; custody.
Duration, dūr-ā'shon, *n.* Continuance in time; power of continuance; permanency.
Durbar, dėr'bär, *n.* An Indian state levee or audience.
Duress, dūr'es, *n.* Constraint; imprisonment.
During, dūr'ing, *prep.* For the time of the continuance of.
Durst, dėrst, pret. of *dare.*
Dusk, dusk, *a.* Tending to darkness; moderately black.—*n.* A middle degree between light and darkness; twilight.
Duskish, dusk'ish, *a.* Moderately dusky.
Dusky, dusk'i, *a.* Partially dark; dark coloured; not bright.
Dust, dust, *n.* Fine dry particles of earth, &c.; powder; earth as symbolic of mortality; a low condition.—*vt.* To free from dust; to sprinkle, as with dust.
Duster, dust'ėr, *n.* A cloth, &c., for removing dust; a sieve.
Dusty, dust'i, *a.* Covered with dust; like dust.
Dutch, duch, *a.* Pertaining to Holland, or to its inhabitants.—*n.pl.* The people of Holland; *sing.* their language.
Duteous, dū'tē-us, *a.* Pertaining to duty; dutiful.
Dutiful, dū'ti-fụl, *a.* Regularly performing duties required toward superiors; respectful.
Duty, dū'ti, *n.* That which a person is bound to perform; obligation; act of reverence or respect; business, service, or office; tax, impost or customs.
Dux, duks, *n.* The head of a class in a school.
Dwarf, dwạrf, *n.* A person or plant much below the ordinary size.—*vt.* To stunt; to make or keep small; to cause to appear small by comparison.—*a.* Below the common size; stunted.
Dwarfish, dwạrf'ish, *a.* Like a dwarf; very small; petty.
Dwell, dwel, *vi.* (pret. and pp. dwelled or dwelt). To live in a place; to reside; to hang on with fondness; to continue.
Dweller, dwel'ėr, *n.* An inhabitant.
Dwelling, dwel'ing, *n.* Habitation; abode.
Dwindle, dwin'dl, *vi.* (dwindling, dwindled). To diminish gradually; to shrink; to sink.
Dye, dī, *vt.* (dyeing, dyed). To stain; to give a new and permanent colour to.—*n.* A colouring liquid or matter; tinge.
Dyer, dī'ėr, *n.* One whose occupation is to dye cloth and the like.
Dying, dī'ing, *a.* Mortal; destined to death; uttered, given, &c., just before death; pertaining to death; fading away.
Dyke, dīk. *See* Dike.
Dynamic, Dynamical, dī-nam'ik, dī-nam'ik-al, *a.* Pertaining to strength, or to dynamics.
Dynamics, dī-nam'iks, *n.* The science which investigates the action of force.
Dynamitard, Dynamiter, din'a-mīt-ärd, din'-a-mīt-ėr, *n.* One who uses dynamite for criminal purposes.
Dynamite, din'a-mīt, *n.* An explosive substance consisting of some powdery matter impregnated with nitro-glycerine.
Dynamo, dī'na-mō, *n.* A machine for producing an electric current by mechanical power.
Dynasty, di'nas-ti, *n.* A race of kings of the same family.
Dyne, dīn, *n.* A unit of force, being that force which, acting on a gramme for one second, generates a velocity of a centimetre per second.
Dysentery, dis'en-te-ri, *n.* A disorder of the intestines; a flux in which the stools consist chiefly of blood and mucus.
Dyspepsia, Dyspepsy, dis-pep'si-a, dis-pep'-si, *n.* Indigestion; difficulty of digestion.
Dyspeptic, dis-pep'tik, *a.* Afflicted with dyspepsia; pertaining to dyspepsia.—*n.* A person afflicted with bad digestion.

E

Each, ēch, *a.* and *pron.* Every one of any number considered individually.
Eager, ē'gėr, *a.* Sharp; ardent; keenly desirous; impetuous; earnest; intense.
Eagerly, ē-gėr-li, *adv.* With great ardour of desire; ardently; earnestly.
Eagerness, ē'gėr-nes, *n.* Ardent desire; vehemence; fervour; avidity.
Eagle, ē'gl, *n.* A large bird of prey, of great powers of flight and vision; a military standard.
Eaglet, ē'gl-et, *n.* A young eagle.
Eagle-wood, ē'gl-wụd, *n.* A fragrant wood, burned by Asiatics as incense.
Eagre, Eager, ā'gėr, ē'gėr, *n.* A tidal wave; a bore.
Ear, ēr, *n.* The organ of hearing; power of distinguishing musical sounds; heed; regard; anything resembling an ear or ears; a spike, as of corn.—*vi.* To form ears, as corn.—*vt.* To plough or till.
Ear-ache, ēr'āk, *n.* Pain in the ear.
Ear-drum, ēr'drum, *n.* The tympanum or middle ear.
Earl, ėrl, *n.* A British title of nobility, below a marquis and above a viscount.
Earldom, ėrl'dum, *n.* The domain, title, or dignity of an earl.
Earless, ēr'les, *a.* Without ears.

Earl-marshal, ėrl-mär'shal, *n.* An officer of state in England, who takes cognizance of matters relating to honour, pedigree, and state solemnities.
Early, ėr'li, *adv.* and *a.* In good time or season; before the usual time; prior in time.
Earn, ėrn, *vt.* To gain by labour; to deserve.
Earnest, ėrn'est, *a.* Ardent in the pursuit of an object; eager; zealous; serious.—*n.* Seriousness; a reality; first-fruits; a part given beforehand as a pledge for the whole; indication; token.
Earnestly, ėrn'est-li, *adv.* Warmly; zealously; importunately; eagerly.
Earnest-money, ėrn'est-mun-i, *n.* Money paid as earnest, to bind a bargain, &c.
Earnings, ėrn'ingz, *n.pl.* That which is gained or merited by labour or performance; wages; reward.
Ear-ring, ēr'ring, *n.* A jewel or ornament worn in the ear; a pendant.
Ear-shot, ēr'shot, *n.* The distance at which words may be heard.
Earth, ėrth, *n.* The globe we inhabit; the world; the fine mould on the surface of the globe; dry land; the ground; the hiding hole of a fox, &c.—*vt.* To cover with earth. —*vi.* To retire underground; to burrow.
Earthen, ėrth'en, *a.* Made of earth.
Earthenware, ėrth'en-wār, *n.* Ware made of clay; crockery; pottery.
Earthling, ėrth'ling, *n.* An inhabitant of the earth; a mortal; a frail creature.
Earthly, ėrth'li, *a.* Pertaining to the earth; sordid; worldly; sensual; conceivable.
Earthquake, ėrth'kwāk, *n.* A shaking, trembling, or concussion of the earth.
Earthward, ėrth'wėrd, *adv.* Toward the earth.
Earth-work, ėrth'wėrk, *n.* A rampart or fortification of earth.
Earth-worm, ėrth'wėrm, *n.* The common worm; a mean, sordid wretch.
Earthy, ėrth'i, *a.* Consisting of or resembling earth; gross; not refined.
Ear-trumpet, ēr'trum-pet, *n.* An instrument in form of a tube, to aid in hearing.
Earwig, ēr'wig, *n.* A well-known insect, erroneously supposed to creep into the human brain through the ear.
Ear-witness, ēr'wit-nes, *n.* One who can testify to a fact from his own hearing.
Ease, ēz, *n.* Freedom from toil, pain, anxiety, &c.; freedom from difficulty; freedom from stiffness or formality; unaffectedness.—*vt.* (easing, eased). To give ease to; to relieve; to calm; to alleviate; to shift a little.
Easel, ēz'el, *n.* The frame on which pictures are placed while being painted.
Easement, ēz'ment, *n.* That which gives ease; accommodation; privilege.
Easily, ēz'i-li, *adv.* In an easy manner.
East, ēst, *n.* That part of the heavens where the sun rises; the countries east of Europe.—*a.* In or toward the east; easterly.—*adv.* Eastwards.
Easter, ēs'tėr, *n.* A festival of the Christian church in March or April, in commemoration of Christ's resurrection.
Easterling, ēst'ėr-ling, *n.* A native of some country east of Britain; a Baltic trader.
Easterly, ēst'ėr-li, *a.* Coming from the east, as wind; situated or moving toward the east. —*adv.* On the east; in the direction of east.
Eastern, ēst'ėrn, *a.* Belonging to the east; toward the east; oriental.
Eastertide, ēst'ėr-tīd, *n.* The time at which Easter is celebrated.
Eastward, ēst'wėrd, *adv.* and *a.* Toward the east.
Easy, ēz'i, *a.* Being at ease; free from pain or anxiety; not difficult; gentle; complying; affluent; not stiff or formal.
Easy-chair, ēz'i-chār, *n.* A large, padded arm-chair.
Eat, ēt, *vt.* (pret. ate, pp, eaten or eat). To chew and swallow, as food; to wear away; to gnaw; to consume.—*vi.* To take food; to taste or relish; to corrode.
Eatable, ēt'a-bl, *a.* That may be eaten; proper for food.—*n.* That which is fit for, or used as food.
Eating, ēt'ing, *n.* The act of chewing and swallowing food; what is eaten.
Eau de Cologne, ō dė ko-lōn, *n.* A perfumed spirit.—**Eau de vie,** ō dė vē, *n.* Brandy.
Eaves, ēvz, *n.pl.* That part of the roof of a building which overhangs the walls.
Eavesdrop, ēvz'drop, *n.* The water which drops from the eaves.—*vi.* To listen to what is said within doors; to watch for opportunities of hearing private conversation.
Eavesdropper, ēvz'drop-ėr, *n.* One who tries to hear private conversation.
Ebb, eb, *n.* The flowing back of the tide; decline; decay.—*vi.* To flow back; to decay; to decline.
E-boat, ē-bōt, *n.* A German motor torpedo-boat.
Ebon, eb'on, *a.* Consisting of ebony; like ebony; black.
Ebonite, eb'o-nīt, *n.* Vulcanite.
Ebonize, eb'o-nīz, *vt.* To make black or like ebony.
Ebony, eb'on-i, *n.* A hard, heavy, dark wood admitting of a fine polish.
Ebriety, ē-brī'e-ti, *n.* Drunkenness.
Ebullient, ē-bul'yent, *a.* Boiling over, as a liquor; over enthusiastic.
Ebullition, ē-bul-li'shon, *n.* The operation of boiling; a sudden burst, as of passion; an overflowing; outbreak.
Eburnean, Eburnine, ē-bėr'nē-an, ē-bėr'nīn, *a.* Relating to or made of ivory.
Ecarté, ā-kär-tā, *n.* A game of cards for two persons with thirty-two cards.
Eccentric, ek-sen'trik, *a.* Not having its axis in the centre; not having the same centre; deviating from usual practice, &c.; anomalous; whimsical.—*n.* An eccentric person; mechanical contrivance for converting circular into reciprocating rectilinear motion.
Eccentrically, ek-sen'trik-al-li, *adv.* In an eccentric manner.
Eccentricity, ek-sen-tris'i-ti, *n.* State or quality of being eccentric; distance of the centre of a planet's orbit from the centre of the sun; singularity; oddness.
Ecclesiastes, ek-klē'zi-as"tēz, *n.* A canonical book of the Old Testament.
Ecclesiastic, ek-klē'zi-as-tik, *a.* Ecclesiastical. —*n.* A priest; a clergyman.
Ecclesiastical, ek-klē'zi-as"tik-al, *a.* Pertaining to the church; not civil or secular.
Ecclesiology, ek-klē'zi-ol"o-ji, *n.* The science of ecclesiastical antiquities.
Echelon, esh'e-lon, *n.* The position of troops

or ships in parallel lines, each line being a little to the right or left of the preceding one.
Echinus, ē-kī'nus, *n.* The sea-urchin; a form of moulding.
Echo, e'kō, *n.* A sound repeated or reverberated.—*vi.* To give out an echo.—*vt.* To reverberate or send back, as sound; to repeat with assent.
Eclat, e-klä', *n.* A burst of applause; renown; splendour.
Eclectic, ek-lek'tik, *a.* Proceeding by the method of selection; applied to certain philosophers who selected from the principles of various schools what they thought sound.—*n.* One who follows an eclectic method in philosophy, &c.
Eclecticism, ek-lek'ti-sizm, *n.* The doctrine or practice of an eclectic.
Eclipse, ē-klips', *n.* An interception of the light of the sun, moon, &c., by some other body; darkness; obscuration.—*vt.* (eclipsing, eclipsed). To cause an eclipse of; to excel.
Ecliptic, ē-klip'tik, *n.* The apparent path of the sun round the earth.—*a.* Pertaining to the ecliptic or an eclipse; suffering an eclipse.
Eclogue, ek'log, *n.* A pastoral poem.
Economic, Economical, ē-kon-om'ik, ē-kon-om'ik-al, *a.* Pertaining to economy or economics; frugal; careful.
Economically, ē-kon-om'ik-al-li, *adv.* With economy.
Economics, ē-kon-om'iks, *n.* The science of the application of wealth; political economy.
Economist, ē-kon'om-ist, *n.* One who practises economy; one versed in economics.
Economize, ē-kon'om-īz, *vt.* and *i.* (economizing, economized). To manage with prudence or frugality.
Economy, ē-kon'o-mi, *n.* Frugal use of money; the regular operations of nature; due order of things; judicious management.
Ecstasy, ek'sta-si, *n.* A trance; excessive joy; rapture; enthusiasm.
Ecstatic, Ecstatical, ek-stat'ik, ek-stat'ik-al, *a.* Causing or pertaining to ecstasy; entrancing; delightful beyond measure.
Ecumenic, Ecumenical, ek-ū-men'ik, ek-ū-men'i-kal, *a.* General; universal: applied to church councils.
Eczema, ek'ze-ma, *n.* A skin disease.
Edacious, ē-dā'shus, *a.* Voracious.
Eddish, ed'ish, *n.* The pasture or grass that comes after mowing or reaping.
Eddy, ed'i, *n.* A circular current of water or air.—*a.* Whirling.—*vi.* (eddying, eddied). To move circularly, or as an eddy.
Edelweiss, ā'dl-vīs, *n.* An Alpine plant.
Eden, ē'den, *n.* The garden of Adam and Eve; a delightful region or residence.
Edentata, ē-den-tā'ta, *n.pl.* An order of mammals with no, or rudimentary, teeth.
Edge, ej, *n.* The cutting side of an instrument; an abrupt border or margin; sharpness; keenness.—*vt.* (edging, edged). To bring to an edge; to sharpen; to fringe; to exasperate; to move by little and little.—*vi.* To move sideways or gradually.
Edged, ejd, *a.* Sharp; keen.
Edge-tool, ej'tōl, *n.* An instrument with a sharp edge.
Edgeways, Edgewise, ej'wāz, ej'wīz, *adv.* With the edge forward or towards; sideways.
Edging, ej'ing, *n.* A border; fringe.
Edible, ed'i-bl, *a.* Eatable.
Edict, ē'dikt, *n.* An order issued by a prince; a decree; manifesto.
Edification, ed'i-fi-kā"shon, *n.* A building up; improvement in knowledge, morals, &c.; instruction.
Edifice, ed'i-fis, *n.* A structure; a fabric; a large or splendid building.
Edify, ed'i-fī, *vt.* (edifying, edified). To build up, in a moral sense; to instruct or improve generally.
Edifying, ed'i-fī-ing, *p.a.* Improving; adapted to instruct.
Edile, ē'dīl, *n.* Same as *Ædile.*
Edit, ed'it, *vt.* To prepare for publication; to conduct, as regards literary contents.
Edition, ē-di'shon, *n.* A published book as characterized by form or editorial labours; the whole number of copies of a work published at once.
Editor, ed'it-ėr, *n.* One who prepares or superintends for publication.
Editorial, ed-i-tō'ri-al, *a.* Pertaining to or written by an editor.—*n.* A leading article in a newspaper.
Editorship, ed'it-ėr-ship, *n.* The office or business of an editor.
Educate, ed'ū-kāt, *vt.* (educating, educated). To teach; to cultivate and train; to enlighten.
Education, ed-ū-kā'shon, *n.* Act of educating; instruction and discipline; schooling.
Educational, ed'ū-kā'shon-al, *a.* Pertaining to education.
Educationist, ed-ū-kā'shon-ist, *n.* One who is versed in or promotes education.
Educative, ed'ū-kāt-iv, *a.* Tending or able to educate; imparting education.
Educator, ed'ū-kāt-ėr, *n.* One who educates.
Educe, ē-dūs', *vt.* (educing, educed). To draw out; to elicit; to extract.
Educible, ē-dūs'i-bl, *a.* That may be educed.
Eduction, ē-duk'shon, *n.* Act of drawing out or bringing into view.
Eel, ēl, *n.* A slimy serpent-like fish.
E'en, ēn. A contraction for *even.*
E'er, ār. A contraction for *ever.*
Eerie, ē'ri, *a.* Inspiring superstitious fear; weird.
Efface, ef-fās', *vt.* To remove from the face or surface of anything; to render illegible; to blot out; to wear away.
Effacement, ef-fās'ment, *n.* Act of effacing.
Effect, ef-fekt', *n.* That which is produced; result; purpose; validity; striking appearance; impression produced by a work of art, &c.; *pl.* goods; movables; personal estate. —*vt.* To produce; to cause; to fulfil; to execute.
Effective, ef-fekt'iv, *a.* Having the power to produce; efficacious; efficient; effectual; fit for duty or service.
Effectively, ef-fekt'iv-li, *adv.* Vith effect.
Effectual, ef-fek'tū-al, *a.* Producing the effect desired or intended; valid.
Effectuate, ef-fek'tū-āt, *vt.* To carry into effect; to bring to pass; to fulfil.
Effeminacy, ef-fem'in-a-si, *n.* State or character of being effeminate.
Effeminate, ef-fem'in-āt, *a.* Womanish; unmanly; weak; voluptuous.—*vt.* To unman; to weaken.—*vi.* To grow womanish or weak.
Effeminately, ef-fem'in-āt-li, *adv.* In an effeminate manner; womanishly; weakly.

Effendi, ef-fen'di, *n.* A Turkish title of respect.
Effervesce, ef-fėr-ves', *vi.* To bubble or sparkle, as any fluid when part escapes in gas; to exhibit signs of excitement.
Effervescence, ef-fėr-ves'ens, *n.* Act of effervescing; strong excitement.
Effervescent, ef-fėr-ves'ent, *a.* Boiling or bubbling, by means of the disengagement of gas.
Effete, ef-fēt', *a.* Worn out; exhausted; barren.
Efficacious, ef-fi-kā'shus, *a.* Producing the effect intended; having adequate power.
Efficacy, ef'fi-ka-si, *n.* Power to produce effects; production of the effect intended; virtue; force; energy.
Efficiency, ef-fi'shen-si, *n.* The state or character of being efficient; effectual agency.
Efficient, ef-fi'shent, *a.* Effecting; capable; qualified for duty.
Effigy, ef'fi-ji, *n.* The image or likeness of a person; portrait; figure.
Effloresce, ef-flo-res', *vi.* To bloom; to show a powdery substance on the surface.
Efflorescence, ef-flo-res'ens, *n.* The time, act, or process of flowering; a redness of the skin; mealy powder or minute crystals forming on a surface.
Efflorescent, ef-flo-res'ent, *a.* Showing efflorescence; liable to effloresce.
Effluence, ef'flu̧-ens, *n.* A flowing out; that which issues from any body or substance.
Effluent, ef'flu̧-ent, *a.* Flowing out.—*n.* A stream that flows out of another, or out of a lake.
Effluvial, ef-flū'vi-al, *a.* Pertaining to effluvia; containing effluvia.
Effluvium, ef-flū'vi-um, *n.*; pl. **-via.** Something flowing out invisibly; a disagreeable odour; a noxious exhalation.
Efflux, ef'fluks, *n.* Act or state of flowing out in a stream; flow; emanation.
Effluxion, ef-fluk'shon, *n.* Act of flowing out; that which flows out; emanation.
Effort, ef'fōrt, *n.* An exertion of strength; strenuous endeavour; struggle.
Effrontery, ef-frun'te-ri, *n.* Audacious impudence; shameless boldness.
Effulgence, ef-fulj'ens, *n.* A flood of light; great lustre; splendour.
Effulgent, ef-fulj'ent, *a.* Sending out a flood of light; gleaming; splendid.
Effuse, ef-fūz', *vt.* (effusing, effused). To pour out; to shed.—*vi.* To emanate.
Effusion, ef-fū'zhon, *n.* Act of pouring out; that which is poured out; in *pathology*, the escape of fluid out of its proper vessel into another part; cordiality of manner; a literary production.
Effusive, ef-fūs'iv, *a.* Pouring out; showing overflowing kindness.
Eft, eft, *n.* A newt.
Egg, eg, *n.* A roundish body produced by many female animals besides birds, from which their young is produced; something resembling an egg.—*vt.* To urge on; to instigate.
Eglantine, eg'lan-tin, *n.* The sweet-brier.
Egoism, eg'ō-izm or ē', *n.* The doctrine which refers all knowledge to the phenomena of personal existence; egotism.
Egoist, eg'ō-ist or ē', *n.* An egotist; one holding the doctrine of egoism.
Egotism, eg'ot-izm or ē', *n.* The practice of too frequently using the word *I*; an exaggerated love of self; self-exaltation.
Egotist, eg'ot-ist or ē', *n.* One always talking of himself; one who magnifies his own achievements.
Egotistic, Egotistical, eg-ot-is'tik, eg-ot-is'tik-al, or ē-, *a.* Addicted to egotism; vain.
Egotize, eg'ot-īz or ē', *vi.* (egotizing, egotized). To talk or write much of oneself.
Egregious, e-grē'jus, *a.* Remarkable; extraordinary; enormous.
Egress, ē'gres, *n.* Act of going out; power of departing from any confined place; exit.—*vi.* To go out.
Egret, eg'ret or ē'gret, *n.* A species of heron; an aigret.
Egyptian, ē-jip'shun, *a.* Pertaining to Egypt.—*n.* A native of Egypt; a gipsy.
Egyptology, ē-jip-tol'o-ji, *n.* The science of Egyptian antiquities.
Eh, eh, *exclam.* Denoting inquiry or slight surprise.
Eider, Eider-duck, ī'dėr, ī'dėr-duk, *n.* A species of sea-duck, producing down of the finest and softest kind.
Eider-down, ī'dėr-doun, *n.* Down or soft feathers of the eider-duck.
Eight, āt, *a.* One more than seven and less than nine.—*n.* This number; the symbol representing this number; an eight-oared racing boat or its crew.
Eighteen, āt'ēn, *a.* and *n.* Eight and ten united.
Eighteenth, āt'ēnth, *a.* and *n.* Next in order after the seventeenth; one of eighteen parts.
Eightfold, āt'fōld, *a.* Eight times the number or quantity.
Eighth, ātth, *a.* and *n.* Next after the seventh; one of eight parts; an octave.
Eighthly, ātth'li, *adv.* In the eighth place.
Eightieth, āt'i-eth, *a.* and *n.* The ordinal of eighty.
Eighty, āt'i, *a.* Eight times ten.
Eikon, ī'kōn, *n.* A likeness; an image.
Eirenicon, ī-rē'ni-kon, *n.* A proposal for the making of peace.
Eisteddfod, is-teᴛʜ-vōd', *n.* A meeting of Welsh bards and minstrels; a periodical Welsh festival for the recitation of poems, &c.
Either, ē'ᴛʜėr or ī'ᴛʜėr, *a.* or *pron.* One or the other; one of two; each.—*conj.* or *adv.* Used disjunctively as correlative to *or*.
Ejaculate, ē-jak'ū-lāt, *vt.* To exclaim; to utter suddenly and briefly.
Ejaculation, ē-jak'ū-lā''shon, *n.* Exclamation; a short prayer.
Ejaculatory, ē-jak'ū-la-to-ri, *a.* Of the nature of an ejaculation.
Eject, ē'jekt, *vt.* To throw out; to dismiss; to dispossess of land or estate; to expel.
Ejection, ē-jek'shon, *n.* Act of casting out; expulsion; dismission.
Ejectment, ē-jekt'ment, *n.* Act or process of ejecting; removal of a person from the wrongful possession of land or tenements.
Ejector, ē-jekt'or, *n.* One who or that which ejects.
Eke, ēk, *vt.* (eking, eked). To add to; to lengthen; to prolong.—*n.* An addition.—*adv.* Also; in addition.
Elaborate, ē-lab'o-rāt, *vt.* (elaborating, elaborated). To produce with labour; to refine by successive operations.—*a.* Wrought with labour; studied; high-wrought.

Elaborately, ē-lab'o-rāt-li, *adv.* In an elaborate manner.
Elaboration, ē-lab'o-rā''shon, *n.* Refinement by successive operations; the process in animal and vegetable organs by which something is produced.
Eland, ē'land, *n.* An African species of antelope.
Elapse, ē-laps', *vi.* (elapsing, elapsed). To slip or glide away.
Elastic, ē-las'tik, *a.* Having the power of returning to the form from which it is bent or distorted; rebounding.—*n.* Cord or ribbon made of cotton or silk, &c., with strands of rubber.
Elastically, ē-las'tik-al-li, *adv.* In an elastic manner; with a spring.
Elasticity, ē-las-tis'i-ti, *n.* State or property of being elastic.
Elate, ē-lāt', *a.* Elevated in mind; flushed, as with success.—*vt.* (elating, elated). To exalt; to puff up; to make proud.
Elated, ē-lāt'ed, *p.a.* Elate.
Elation, ē-lā'shon, *n.* Elevation of mind or spirits; buoyancy.
Elbow, el'bō, *n.* The bend or joint of the arm; an angle.—*vt.* To push with the elbow; to push, as through a crowd.—*vi.* To project; to push one's way.
Eld, eld, *n.* Old age; old time.
Elder, eld'ėr, *a.* Older; having lived a longer time; senior.—*n.* One who is older; an office-bearer in the Presbyterian Church; a small tree with a spongy pith and dark purple or red berries.
Elderly, eld'ėr-li, *a.* Somewhat old; beyond middle age.
Eldership, eld'ėr-ship, *n.* Seniority; office of an elder; order of elders.
Eldest, eld'est, *a.* Oldest; most aged.
Elect, ē-lekt', *vt.* To pick or choose; to select for an office.—*a.* Chosen; chosen to an office, but not yet in office.—*n. sing.* or *pl.* One or several chosen; those favoured by God.
Election, ē-lek'shon, *n.* Act of choosing; choice; voluntary preference; divine choice; predestination.
Electioneer, ē-lek'shon-ēr'', *vi.* To work for a candidate at an election.
Electioneering, ē-lek'shon-ēr''ing, *n.* The arts used to secure the election of a candidate.
Elective, ē-lekt'iv, *a.* Pertaining to or consisting in choice; exerting the power of choice.
Elector, ē-lekt'ėr, *n.* One who elects or has the right of voting.
Electoral, ē-lekt'ėr-al, *a.* Pertaining to election or electors.
Electorate, ē-lekt'ėr-āt, *n.* A body of electors.
Electric, Electrical, ē-lek'trik, ē-lek'tri-kal, *a.* Containing, conveying, or produced by electricity; full of fire or spirit, and capable of communicating it.
Electrically, ē-lek'tri-kal-li, *adv.* In the manner of electricity; by electricity.
Electrician, ē-lek-trish'an, *n.* One versed in the science of electricity.
Electricity, ē-lek-tris'i-ti, *n.* The force that manifests itself in lightning and in many other phenomena; the science which deals with these phenomena.
Electrifiable, ē-lek'tri-fī-a-bl, *a.* Capable of being electrified.
Electrify, ē-lek'tri-fī, *vt.* (electrifying, electrified). To communicate electricity to; to thrill.—*vi.* To become electric.
Electro, ē-lek'trō, *n.* An electrotype.
Electro-biology, ē-lec'trō-bī-ol''o-ji, *n.* The science of electric currents in living organisms; mesmerism or animal magnetism.
Electrocute, ē-lek'trō-kūt, *vt.* To execute a criminal by means of electricity.
Electrode, ē-lek'trōd, *n.* One of the terminals or poles of the voltaic circle.
Electro-dynamics, ē-lek'trō-di-nam''iks, *n.* The science of mechanical actions exerted on one another by electric currents.
Electro-gilt, ē-lek'trō-gilt, *a.* Gilded by means of the electric current.
Electrolysis, ē-lek-trol'i-sis, *n.* Decomposition by means of electricity.
Electrolyte, ē-lek'trō-līt, *n.* A compound decomposable by electricity.
Electrometer, ē-lek-trom'e-tėr, *n.* An instrument for measuring electricity.
Electron, ē-lek'tron, *n.* One of extremely small particles of negative electricity, which form essential constituents of atoms, and by which, according to the electron theory, heat and electricity are conducted.
Electroplate, ē-lek'trō-plāt, *vt.* To give a coating of silver or other metal by means of electricity.—*n.* Articles so coated.
Electrotype, ē-lek'trō-tīp, *n.* The art of producing copies of types, wood-cuts, &c., by the electric deposition of copper on a cast from the original; a copy thus produced.
Electuary, ē-lek'tū-a-ri, *n.* A medicine incorporated with some conserve or syrup.
Eleemosynary, el-ē-mos'i-na-ri, *a.* Given in or relating to charity; founded to dispense some gratuity.—*n.* One who subsists on charity.
Elegance, Elegancy, el'ē-gans, el'ē-gan-si, *n.* Quality of being elegant; beauty resulting from propriety; refinement.
Elegant, el'ē-gant, *a.* Pleasing to good taste; graceful; polished; refined; symmetrical.
Elegiac, el-ē-jī'ak, *a.* Belonging to elegy; plaintive.—*n.* Elegiac verse.
Elegiast, Elegist, e-lē'jī-ast, el'ē-jist, *n.* A writer of elegies.
Elegy, el'ē-ji, *n.* A poem or a song expressive of sorrow and lamentation.
Element, el'ē-ment, *n.* A fundamental part or principle; an ingredient; proper sphere; suitable state of things; *pl.* first principles of an art or science; data employed in a calculation; the bread and wine used in the Lord's supper.
Elemental, el-ē-ment'al, *a.* Pertaining to or produced by elements.
Elementary, el-ē-ment'ar-i, *a.* Primary; uncompounded; teaching first principles or rudiments.
Elephant, el'ē-fant, *n.* A huge quadruped, having a long trunk and tusks.
Elephantine, el'ē-fant'īn, *a.* Pertaining to the elephant; huge; clumsy.
Elevate, el'ē-vāt, *vt.* (elevating, elevated). To raise; to refine or dignify; to elate; to cheer.
Elevation, el-ē-vā'shon, *n.* Act of elevating; state of being elevated; an elevated station; a hill; representation of a building in vertical section.
Elevator, el'ē-vāt-ėr, *n.* One who or that which elevates; a hoist.

Eleven, ē-lev'n, *a.* Ten and one added.—*n.* The sum of ten and one; the symbol representing this number; a side of players in association football, cricket, &c.
Eleventh, ē-lev'nth, *a.* and *n.* Next after the tenth; one of eleven parts.
Elf, elf, *n.*; pl. **Elves,** elvz. A fairy; a goblin; a mischievous person.
Elfin, elf'in, *a.* Relating to elves.—*n.* An elf; a little urchin.
Elfish, elf'ish, *a.* Resembling or pertaining to elves.
Elicit, ē-lis'it, *vt.* To draw out by reasoning, discussion, &c.; to educe.
Elide, ē-līd', *vt.* (eliding, elided). To strike out; to cut off or suppress (a syllable).
Eligibility, el'i-ji-bil"i-ti, *n.* Worthiness or fitness to be chosen.
Eligible, el'i-ji-bl, *a.* Fit to be chosen; suitable; legally qualified.
Eligibly, el'i-ji-bli, *adv.* In a manner to be worthy of choice; suitably.
Eliminate, ē-lim'in-āt, *vt.* (eliminating, eliminated). To throw off; to cancel; to leave out of consideration.
Elimination, ē-lim'in-ā"shon, *n.* Act of eliminating.
Elision, ē-li'zhon, *n.* Act of eliding; suppression of a vowel or syllable.
Elite, ā-lēt', *n.pl.* A select body; the best.
Elixir, ē-lik'sėr, *n.* A liquor sought by the alchemists to transmute metals into gold or to prolong life; quintessence; a cordial.
Elizabethan, ē-liz'a-bēth"an, *a.* Pertaining to Queen Elizabeth or her times.
Elk, elk, *n.* The largest species of deer.
Ell, el, *n.* A measure of different lengths in different countries, the English ell being 45 inches.
Ellipse, el-lips', *n.* An oval figure.
Ellipsis, el-lips'is, *n.*; pl. **-ses.** A figure of syntax by which words are omitted; suppression of letters or words in printing.
Elliptic, Elliptical, el-lip'tik, el-lip'tik-al, *a.* Pertaining to an ellipse or ellipsis; having a part omitted.
Ellipticity, el-lip-tis'i-ti, *n.* Amount of divergence from a circle.
Elm, elm, *n.* A tree valuable for its timber.
Elocution, e-lō-kū'shon, *n.* Management of the voice and gesture in speaking; pronunciation; delivery.
Elocutionary, e-lō-kū'shon-a-ri, *a.* Pertaining to elocution.
Elocutionist, e-lō-kū'shon-ist, *n.* One who is versed in, or teaches, elocution.
Elogium, ē-lō'ji-um, *n.* A panegyric.
Elongate, ē-long'gāt, *vt.* (elongating, elongated). To lengthen.—*vi.* To recede apparently from the sun.—*a.* Long and slender.
Elongation, ē-long-gā'shon, *n.* Act of lengthening; state of being extended; continuation; apparent distance of a planet from the sun.
Elope, ē-lōp', *vi.* (eloping, eloped). To escape privately; to run away with a lover.
Elopement, ē-lōp'ment, *n.* Act of eloping; running away of a woman with a lover.
Eloquence, e'lō-kwens, *n.* The quality or faculty of being eloquent; oratory.
Eloquent, e'lō-kwent, *a.* Having the power of fluent, elegant, or forcible speech; characterized by eloquence.
Eloquently, e'lō-kwent-li, *adv.* With eloquence; in an eloquent manner.
Else, els, *a.* or *adv.* Other; besides; in addition.—*conj.* Otherwise; in the other case.
Elsewhere, els'whār, *adv.* In any other place; in some other place.
Elucidate, ē-lū'sid-āt, *vt.* To make clear; to free from obscurity; to explain.
Elucidation, ē-lū'sid-ā"shon, *n.* Act of elucidating; illustration; explanation.
Elucidative, ē-lū'sid-āt-iv, *a.* Tending to elucidate; explanatory.
Elucidator, ē-lū'sid-āt-ėr, *n.* One who explains; an expositor.
Elude, ē-lūd', *vt.* (eluding, eluded). To avoid by artifice or dexterity; to baffle; to evade.
Elusion, ē-lū'zhon, *n.* Act of eluding; evasion.
Elusive, ē-lū'siv, *a.* Practising elusion; evasive.
Elusory, ē-lū'so-ri, *a.* Tending to elude; evasive; fallacious.
Elvan, el'van, *n.* A granitic and felspar porphyritic rock.
Elvish, elv'ish, *a.* Elfish.
Elysian, ē-li'zhi-an, *a.* Pertaining to Elysium; exceedingly delightful.
Elysium, ē-li'zhi-um, *n.* The place of future happiness; any delightful place.
Elytron, Elytrum, el'i-tron, el'i-trum, *n.*; pl. **Elytra,** el'i-tra. The wing-sheath which covers the true wing in beetles.
Emaciate, ē-mā'shi-āt, *vi.* and *t.* (emaciating, emaciated). To become or make lean.
Emaciation, ē-mā'shi-ā"shon, *n.* Act of emaciating; leanness.
Emanant, em'a-nant, *a.* Emanating.
Emanate, em'a-nāt, *vi.* (emanating, emanated). To flow out; to issue; to spring.
Emanation, em-a-nā-shon, *n.* Act of emanating; that which issues from any source or substance; effluvium.
Emancipate, ē-man'si-pāt, *vt.* (emancipating, emancipated). To set free from slavery; to liberate.
Emancipation, ē-man'si-pā"shon, *n.* Liberation; freedom; enfranchisement.
Emancipator, ē-man'si-pāt-ėr, *n.* One who emancipates from bondage or restraint.
Emasculate, ē-mas'kū-lāt, *vt.* To castrate; to render effeminate; to expurgate.
Emasculation, ē-mas'kū-lā"shon, *n.* Castration; effeminacy.
Embalm, em-bām', *vt.* To preserve a dead body by aromatics; to cherish the memory of.
Embank, em-bangk', *vt.* To inclose or defend with a bank, mounds, or dikes.
Embankment, em-bangk'ment, *n.* Act of embanking; a bank raised for protecting against inundation, or for a railway, &c.
Embargo, em-bär'gō, *n.* Prohibition on ships from sailing; restraint or hindrance.—*vt.* To put an embargo on.
Embark, em-bärk', *vt.* To put on board a ship; to engage in.—*vi.* To go on board of a ship; to engage in; to take a share.
Embarkation, em-bärk-ā'shon, *n.* Act of embarking; that which is embarked.
Embarrass, em-ba'ras, *vt.* To involve in difficulties; to entangle; to disconcert.
Embarrassed, em-ba'rast, *p.a.* Entangled; confused; disconcerted; unable to pay.
Embarrassment, em-ba'ras-ment, *n.* Entanglement; trouble; abashment.
Embassy, em'bas-si, *n.* The mission, charge

or residence of an ambassador; an important message.
Embattle, em-bat'l, *vt.* To arrange in order of battle; to furnish with battlements.—*vi.* To be ranged in order of battle.
Embay, em-bā', *vt.* To inclose in a bay; to landlock.
Embellish, em-bel'lish, *vt.* To make beautiful; to adorn.
Embellishment, em-bel'lish-ment, *n.* Act of embellishing; that which embellishes.
Ember, em'bėr, *n.* A glowing cinder: chiefly in *pl.*
Ember-days, em'bėr-dāz, *n.pl.* Days appointed for fasting, being a Wednesday, Friday, and Saturday in each of the four seasons.
Ember-week, em'bėr-wēk, *n.* A week in which ember-days fall.
Embezzle, em-bez'l, *vt.* (embezzling, embezzled). To appropriate by breach of trust.
Embezzlement, em-bez'l-ment, *n.* Act of fraudulently appropriating money, &c., intrusted to one's care.
Embezzler, em-bez'l-ėr, *n.* One who embezzles.
Embitter, em-bit'ėr, *vt.* To make bitter or more bitter; to exasperate.
Emblaze, em-blāz', *vt.* To kindle; to blazon.
Emblazon, em-blā'zon, *vt.* To adorn with figures of heraldry; to sing the praises of.
Emblazoner, em-blā'zon-ėr, *n.* A blazoner.
Emblazonment, em-blā'zn-ment, *n.* Act of emblazoning; that which is emblazoned.
Emblazonry, em-blā'zn-ri, *n.* Blazonry; heraldic decoration.
Emblem, em'blem, *n.* A picture representing one thing and suggesting another; a symbol; type; device.
Emblematic, Emblematical, em-ble-mat'ik, em-ble-mat'ik-al, *a.* Pertaining to or comprising an emblem; symbolic.
Embodiment, em-bo'di-ment, *n.* Act of embodying; state of being embodied; that in which something is embodied; incarnation.
Embody, em-bo'di, *vt.* (embodying, embodied). To invest with a body; to form into a body (as troops), or into a system; to collect.
Embogue, em-bōg', *vi.* To discharge itself, as a river.
Embolden, em-bōld'en, *vt.* To give boldness to; to encourage.
Embolism, em'bol-izm, *n.* Obstruction of a blood-vessel by a clot of blood.
Emboss, em-bos', *vt.* To form bosses on; to fashion in relievo or raised work.
Embossment, em-bos'ment, *n.* Act of embossing; figures in relievo; raised work.
Embouchure, em'bö-shör, *n.* A mouth or aperture, as of a river, cannon, &c.
Embowel, em-bou'el, *vt.* To take out the bowels of; to eviscerate; to imbed.
Embower, em-bou'ėr, *vt.* To inclose in or cover with a bower; to shade.
Embrace, em-brās', *vt.* (embracing, embraced). To take within the arms; to press to the bosom; to seize ardently; to include; to accept.—*vi.* To join in an embrace.—*n.* Clasp with the arms; a hug; conjugal endearment.
Embraceor, Embrasor, em-brā'sėr, *n.* One who attempts to influence a jury illegally.
Embrasure, em-brā'zhūr, *n.* An opening in a wall or parapet through which cannon are fired.
Embrocate, em'brō-kāt, *vt.* To moisten and rub, as a diseased part of the body.
Embrocation, em-brō-kā'shon, *n.* Act of embrocating; the liquid used in embrocating.
Embroider, em-broi'dėr, *vt.* To adorn with ornamental needlework or figures.
Embroidery, em-broi'de-ri, *n.* Embroidered work; variegated needlework.
Embroil, em-broil', *vt.* To confuse; to disorder; to involve in troubles; to disturb.
Embroilment, em-broil'ment, *n.* The act of embroiling; state of contention, perplexity, or confusion; disturbance.
Embryo, em'bri-ō, *n.* The first rudiments of an animal in the womb or of a plant in the seed; the first state of anything.—*a.* Pertaining to anything in its first rudiments.
Embryology, em-bri-ol'o-ji, *n.* The doctrine of the development of embryos.
Embryonic, em-bri-on'ik, *a.* Pertaining to an embryo, or the embryo stage.
Emend, ē-mend', *vt.* To remove faults from; to improve the text or reading of.
Emendation, ē-mend-ā'shon, *n.* Correction in a text, writing, &c.; alteration for the better.
Emendator, ē-mend'āt-ėr, *n.* One who emends.
Emendatory, ē-mend'a-to-ri, *a.* Contributing to emendation.
Emerald, e'me-rald, *n.* A precious stone, akin to the beryl, usually green; a small printing type.—*a.* Of a bright-green colour.
Emerge, ē-mėrj', *vi.* (emerging, emerged). To rise out of a fluid or other substance; to issue; to rise into view; to reappear.
Emergence, ē-mėrj'ens, *n.* Act of emerging.
Emergency, ē-mėrj'en-si, *n.* Act of emerging; unforeseen occurrence; pressing necessity.
Emergent, ē-mėrj'ent, *a.* Rising out of; issuing from; sudden; casual; pressing.
Emeritus, ē-mer'i-tus, *a.* Discharged from duty with honour on account of infirmity, age, or long service.
Emerods, ē'me-rodz, *n.pl.* Hemorrhoids.
Emersion, ē-mėr'shon, *n.* Act of rising out of a fluid or other substance; reappearance of a heavenly body after eclipse, &c.
Emery, e'me-ri, *n.* A hard mineral used in cutting gems and for polishing.
Emetic, ē-met'ik, *a.* Causing vomiting.—*n.* A medicine that provokes vomiting.
Emeute, ā-möt', *n.* A seditious commotion; a riot; a tumult.
Emigrant, em'i-grant, *a.* Emigrating; pertaining to emigration or emigrants.—*n.* One who emigrates.
Emigrate, em'i-grāt, *vi.* (emigrating, emigrated). To remove from one country or state to another for the purpose of residence.
Emigration, em-i-grā'shon, *n.* Act of emigrating; a body of emigrants.
Eminence, em'in-ens, *n.* A rising ground; elevation; top; distinction; fame; a title of honour given to cardinals, &c.
Eminent, em'in-ent, *a.* Exalted; high in office; distinguished; illustrious.
Eminently, em'in-ent-li, *adv.* In an eminent manner or position.
Emir, em'ėr, *n.* An independent Mohammedan chief; a descendant of Mohammed; the head of certain departments in Mohammedan countries.

Emissary, em'is-sa-ri, *n.* One sent on private business; a secret agent; a spy.
Emission, ē-mi'shon, *n.* Act of emitting; that which is emitted.
Emissive, ē-mis'iv, *a.* Sending out; emitting.
Emissory, ē-mis'o-ri, *a.* Sending out; excretory.
Emit, ē-mit', *vt.* (emitting, emitted). To send out; to discharge; to vent.
Emmet, em'met, *n.* An ant.
Emollient, ē-mol'li-ent, *a.* Softening; making supple.—*n.* A substance which softens or allays irritation.
Emolument, ē-mol'ū-ment, *n.* Profit arising from office or employment; salary; gain.
Emotion, ē-mō'shon, *n.* Any agitation of mind; feeling.
Emotional, ē-mō'shon-al, *a.* Pertaining to or characterized by emotion.
Empale, em-pāl', *vt.* (empaling, empaled). To put to death by fixing on a stake.
Emperor, em'pėr-ėr, *n.* The sovereign of an empire.
Emphasis, em'fa-sis, *n.* A stress laid on a word or clause to enforce a meaning; impressiveness; weight.
Emphasize, em'fa-sīz, *vt.* (emphasizing, emphasized). To place emphasis on.
Emphatic, Emphatical, em-fat'ik, em-fat'ik-al, *a.* Characterized by emphasis; expressive; strong; energetic.
Emphatically, em-fat'ik-al-li, *adv.* With emphasis; strongly; forcibly.
Empire, em'pīr, *n.* Supreme power in governing; sway; dominion of an emperor; region over which dominion is extended.
Empiric, em-pi'rik, *n.* One whose knowledge is founded exclusively on experience; a quack; a charlatan.
Empirical, em-pi'rik-al, *a.* Pertaining to or derived from experience; relying on experience without due regard to theory.
Empiricism, em-pi'ri-sizm, *n.* The methods or practice of an empiric; quackery; the doctrine that knowledge comes solely from experience.
Employ, em-ploi', *vt.* To occupy; to engage in one's service; to keep at work; to make use of.—*n.* Business; occupation; engagement.
Employee, em-ploi'ē, *n.* One who works for an employer.
Employer, em-ploi'ėr, *n.* One who employs; one who keeps men in service.
Employment, em-ploi'ment, *n.* Act of employing; office; trade; profession; function.
Empoison, em-poi'zn, *vt.* To poison.
Emporium, em-pō'ri-um, *n.*; pl. **-ia** or **-iums.** A commercial centre; a warehouse or shop.
Empower, em-pou'ėr, *vt.* To give legal or moral power to; to authorize.
Empress, em'pres, *n.* The consort of an emperor; a female invested with imperial power.
Emprise, Emprize, em-prīz', *n.* Enterprise.
Empty, em'ti, *a.* Containing nothing, or nothing but air; void; unsatisfactory; unburdened; hungry; vacant of head.—*vt.* (emptying, emptied). To make empty.—*vi.* To become empty.—*n.* An empty packing-case, &c.
Empurple, em-pėr'pl, *vt.* To dye of a purple colour; to discolour with purple.
Empyreal, em-pi-rē'al or em-pi'rē-al, *a.* Formed of pure fire or light; pertaining to the highest region of heaven.
Empyrean, em-pi-rē'an, em-pi'rē-an, *a.* The highest heaven.
Emu, Emeu, ē-mū', *n.* A large Australian bird, allied to the ostrich and cassowary.
Emulate, em'ū-lāt, *vt.* (emulating, emulated). To strive to equal or excel; to vie with.
Emulation, em-ū-lā'shon, *n.* Act of emulating; rivalry; envy.
Emulative, em'ū-lāt-iv, *a.* Inclined to emulation; rivalling.
Emulator, em'ū-lāt-ėr, *n.* A rival; competitor.
Emulous, em'ū-lus, *a.* Eager to emulate; rivalling; engaged in competition.
Emulsion, ē-mul'shon, *n.* A soft liquid remedy resembling milk; any milk-like mixture.
Emulsive, ē-muls'iv, *a.* Milk-like; softening; yielding a milk-like substance.
Enable, en-ā'bl, *vt.* (enabling, enabled). To make able; to empower; to authorize.
Enact, en-akt', *vt.* To establish by law; to decree; to perform; to act.
Enactive, en-akt'iv, *a.* Having power to enact or establish as a law.
Enactment, en-akt'ment, *n.* The passing of a bill into a law; a decree; an act.
Enactor, en-akt'ėr, *n.* One who enacts.
Enamel, en-am'el, *n.* A substance of the nature of glass, used as a coating; that which is enamelled; a smooth glossy surface of various colours; the smooth substance on a tooth.—*vt.* (enamelling, enamelled). To lay enamel on; to paint in enamel; to form a surface like enamel; to adorn with different colours. —*vi.* To practise the art of enamelling.
Enameller, Enamellist, en-am'el-ėr, en-am'-el-ist, *n.* One who enamels.
Enamour, en-am'ėr, *vt.* To inspire with love; to charm; to fill with delight.
Encage, en-kāj', *vt.* To put into or confine in a cage.
Encamp, en-kamp', *vi.* To take up position in a camp; to make a camp.—*vt.* To form into or place in a camp.
Encampment, en-kamp'ment, *n.* Act of encamping; a camp.
Encaustic, en-kas'tik, *a.* Pertaining to the art of enamelling and to painting in colours that are fixed by burning.
Encave, en-kāv', *vt.* To put into a cave; to hide in a cave or recess.
Enceinte, ang-sangt, *n.* The rampart which surrounds a fortress; the area thus surrounded. —*a.* Pregnant; with child.
Encenia, en-sē'ni-a, *n.pl.* A commemorative ceremonial.
Encephalic, en-sē-fal'ik, *a.* Belonging to the encephalon or brain.
Encephalon, en-sef'a-lon, *n.* The contents of the skull; the brain.
Enchain, en-chān', *vt.* To fasten with a chain; to hold in bondage; to confine.
Enchant, en-chant', *vt.* To practise sorcery on; to charm; to enrapture; to fascinate.
Enchanted, en-chant'ed, *p.a.* Affected by sorcery; delighted beyond measure.
Enchanter, en-chant'ėr, *n.* A sorcerer; one who charms or delights.
Enchanting, en-chant'ing, *p.a.* Charming; delighting; ravishing.

Enchantment, en-chant'ment, *n.* Act of enchanting; incantation; magic; overpowering influence of delight; fascination.
Enchantress, en-chant'res, *n.* A female enchanter; a sorceress.
Enchase, en-chās', *vt.* To inclose in a border; to surround with an ornamental setting; to adorn by embossed work.
Enchorial, en-kō'ri-al, *a.* Belonging to or used in a country; native; demotic.
Encircle, en-sėr'kl, *vt.* To inclose with a circle; to encompass; to embrace.
Enclasp, en-klasp', *vt.* To clasp; to fasten with a clasp.
Enclave, en'klāv or äng-kläv, *n.* A place surrounded entirely by the territories of another power.
Enclitic, Enclitical, en-klit'ik, en-klit'ik-al, *a.* Said of a particle or word so united to the preceding word as to seem a part of it; throwing back the accent on the foregoing syllable.—*n.* An enclitic word.
Enclose, en-klōz', *vt.* To inclose.
Enclosure, en-klō'zhūr, *n.* Inclosure.
Encomiast, en-kō'mi-ast, *n.* One who praises another; a panegyrist.
Encomiastic, Encomiastical, en-kō'mi-as"-tik, en-kō'mi-ast"ik-al, *a.* Containing encomium; bestowing praise; laudatory.
Encomium, en-kō'mi-um, *n.*; pl. **-iums.** Panegyric; eulogy; praise.
Encompass, en-kum'pas, *vt.* To encircle; to hem in; to go or sail round.
Encore, äng-kōr'. Again; once more; a call for a repetition of a performance.—*vt.* (encoring, encored). To call for a repetition of.
Encounter, en-koun'tėr, *n.* A meeting in contest; a conflict; a meeting; controversy; debate.—*vt.* To meet face to face; to meet suddenly; to strive against.—*vi.* To meet unexpectedly; to conflict.
Encourage, en-ku'rāj, *vt.* (encouraging, encouraged). To give courage to; to stimulate; to embolden; to countenance.
Encouragement, en-ku'rāj-ment, *n.* Act of encouraging; incentive; favour.
Encourager, en-ku'rāj-ėr, *n.* One who encourages.
Encouraging, en-ku'rāj-ing, *p.a.* Furnishing ground to hope for success.
Encrimson, en-krim'zn, *vt.* To cover with a crimson colour.
Encroach, en-krōch', *vi.* To trespass on the rights and possessions of another; to intrude; to infringe: with *on* or *upon.*
Encroacher, en-krōch'ėr, *n.* One who encroaches.
Encroachment, en-krōch-ment, *n.* Act of encroaching; invasion; inroad; that which is taken by encroaching.
Encrust, en-krust', *vt.* To cover with a crust.
Encumber, en-kum'bėr, *vt.* To impede the motion of with a load; to embarrass; to load with debts or legal claims.
Encumbrance, en-kum'brans, *n.* That which encumbers; burden; hindrance; legal claims or liabilities; mortgage.
Encyclic, Encyclical, en-sī'klik, en-sī'kli-kal, *a.* Sent to many persons or places; circular.—*n.* A letter on some important occasion sent by the pope to the bishops.
Encyclopædia, Encyclopedia, en-sī'klō-pē"di-a, *n.* A collection, usually alphabetical, of articles on one or more branches of knowledge.
Encyclopædic, Encyclopedic, en-sī'klō-pē"-dik, *a.* Pertaining to an encyclopædia; universal as regards information.
Encyclopædist, Encyclopedist, en-sī'klō-pēd"ist, *n.* The compiler of an encyclopædia; one whose knowledge is very wide.
End, end, *n.* The extreme point; the last part; final state; completion; close of life; death; issue; result; aim; drift.—*vt.* To bring to an end; to conclude; to destroy.—*vi.* To come to an end; to close; to cease.
Endanger, en-dān'jėr, *vt.* To bring into danger; to expose to loss or injury.
Endear, en-dēr', *vt.* To make dear; to make more beloved.
Endearing, en-dēr'ing, *p.a.* Making dear or more beloved; exciting affection.
Endearment, en-dēr'ment, *n.* The act of endearing; tender affection; a caress.
Endeavour, en-dev'ėr, *n.* Effort; attempt; exertion; essay; aim.—*vi.* To try; to strive; to aim.—*vt.* To try to effect; to strive after.
Endemic, Endemical, en-dem'ik, endem'ik-al, *a.* Peculiar to a people or region, as a disease.—*n.* A disease of endemic nature.
Ending, end'ing, *n.* Termination.
Endive, en'div, *n.* A plant allied to chicory; garden succory.
Endless, end'les, *a.* Without end; everlasting; infinite; incessant.
Endlessly, end'les-li, *adv.* Incessantly.
Endlong, end'long, *adv.* With the end forward; lengthwise.
Endogen, en'dō-jen, *n.* A plant whose stem grows by additions developed from the inside, as palms and grasses.
Endogenous, en-doj'e-nus, *a.* Pertaining to endogens; developing from within.
Endorse, en-dors', *vt.* (endorsing, endorsed). To write on the back of, as one's name on a bill; to assign by endorsement; to ratify.
Endorsement, en-dors'ment, *n.* The act of endorsing; a docket; signature of one who endorses; sanction or approval.
Endoskeleton, en'dō-skel-e-ton, *n.* The internal bony structure of animals.
Endosmose, en'dos-mōs, *n.* The transmission of fluids or gases through porous partitions from the exterior to the interior.
Endow, en-dou', *vt.* To settle a dower on; to enrich or furnish, as with any gift, quality, or faculty; to indue; to invest.
Endowment, en-dou'ment, *n.* Act of endowing; revenue permanently appropriated to any object; natural capacity.
Endurable, en-dūr'a-bl, *a.* That can be endured.
Endurance, en-dūr'ans, *n.* State of enduring; continuance; patience; fortitude.
Endure, en-dūr', *vi.* (enduring, endured). To continue in the same state; to last; to abide; to submit.—*vt.* To sustain; to bear; to undergo; to tolerate.
Enduring, en-dūr'ing, *p.a.* Lasting long; permanent.
Endwise, end'wīz, *adv.* In an upright position; with the end forward.
Enema, en'e-ma, *n.* A liquid or gaseous medicine injected into the rectum; a clyster.
Enemy, en'e-mi, *n.* One who is unfriendly; an antagonist; a hostile army.

Energetic, Energetical, en-ėr-jet'ik, en-ėr-jet'ik-al, *a.* Acting with energy; forcible; potent; active; vigorous.
Energetically, en-ėr-jet'ik-al-li, *adv.* With energy and effect.
Energize, en'ėr-jīz, *vi.* (energizing, energized). To act with energy.—*vt.* To give energy to.
Energy, en'ėr-ji, *n.* Inherent power to operate or act; power exerted; force; vigour; strength of expression; emphasis; in physics, power to do work; it may be mechanical, electrical, thermal, chemical, &c.
Enervate, en'ėr-vāt or ē-nėrv'āt, *vt.* (enervating, enervated). To deprive of strength or force; to unnerve; to debilitate.
Enervation, en-ėr-vā'shon, *n.* Act of enervating; state of being enervated; effeminacy.
Enfeeble, en-fē'bl, *vt.* (enfeebling, enfeebled). To make feeble; to weaken.
Enfeeblement, en-fē'bl-ment, *n.* The act of weakening; enervation.
Enfeoff, en-fef', *vt.* To invest with the fee of an estate.
Enfeoffment, en-fef'ment, *n.* Act of enfeoffing; the instrument or deed by which one is enfeoffed; the property or estate thus given.
Enfilade, en-fi-lād, *vt.* (enfilading, enfiladed). To rake with shot through the whole length of a line or work; to fire in the flank of.—*n.* A firing in such a manner; the line of fire.
Enforce, en-fōrs', *vt.* To urge with energy; to impress on the mind; to compel; to put in execution.
Enforceable, Enforcible, en-fōrs'a-bl, en-fōrs'i-bl, *a.* Capable of being enforced.
Enforcement, en-fōrs'ment, *n.* Act of enforcing; compulsion; a giving of force or effect to; a putting in execution, as law.
Enfranchise, en-fran'chīz, *vt.* (enfranchising, enfranchised). To set free; to admit to the privileges of a citizen; to endow with the franchise.
Enfranchisement, en-fran'chīz-ment, *n.* Act of enfranchising; state of being enfranchised.
Engage, en-gāj', *vt.* (engaging, engaged). To bind by pledge or contract; to attach; to attract; to attack.—*vi.* To bind oneself; to embark on any business; to begin to fight.
Engaged, en-gājd', *p.a.* Pledged; affianced; attached to a wall (said of a column).
Engagement, en-gāj'ment, *n.* Act of engaging; obligation; betrothal; avocation; business; conflict; battle.
Engaging, en-gāj'ing, *p.a.* Winning; attractive; pleasing.
Engender, en-jen'dėr, *vt.* To breed; to beget; to occasion.—*vi.* To be caused or produced.
Engine, en'jin, *n.* Any instrument in some degree complicated; a machine to drive machinery, to propel vessels, railway trains, &c. —*vt.* (engining, engined). To furnish with an engine or engines.
Engineer, en-ji-nēr', *n.* One who constructs or manages engines; one who plans works for offence or defence; one who constructs roads, railways, &c.—*vt.* To direct the making of in the capacity of engineer.
Engineering, en-ji-nēr'ing, *n.* The art or business of an engineer.
Engird, en-gėrd', *vt.* To gird round; to encircle.
English, ing'glish, *a.* Belonging to England, or to its inhabitants.—*n.* The people or language of England.—*vt.* To translate into English.
Englishry, ing'glish-ri, *n.* A population of English descent; the persons of English descent in Ireland.
Engraft, en-grăft', *vt.* To ingraft.
Engrail, en-grāl', *vt.* To notch; to indent; to jag at the edges.
Engrain, en-grān', *vt.* To dye with grain; to dye deep; to paint in imitation of wood.
Engrave, en-grāv', *vt.* (engraving, engraved). To cut figures on with a burin; to represent by incisions; to imprint; to impress deeply.
Engraver, en-grāv'ėr, *n.* One who engraves; a cutter of figures on metal, wood, &c.
Engraving, en-grāv'ing, *n.* Act or art of engraving; an engraved plate; an impression from an engraved plate.
Engross, en-grōs', *vt.* To take up the whole of; to occupy, engage; to write a correct copy in legible characters; to take in undue quantities or degrees.—*vi.* To be employed in making fair copies of writings.
Engrosser, en-grōs'ėr, *n.* One who engrosses.
Engrossment, en-grōs'ment, *n.* Act of engrossing; state of being engrossed; exorbitant acquisition; copy of a deed in clear writing.
Engulf, en-gulf', *vt.* To ingulf; to swallow up.
Enhance, en-hans', *vt.* (enhancing, enhanced). To raise to a higher point; to increase; to aggravate.—*vi.* To grow larger.
Enhancement, en-hans'ment, *n.* Act of enhancing; rise; augmentation.
Enigma, ē-nig'ma, *n.* An obscure statement or question; riddle; anything inexplicable.
Enigmatic, Enigmatical, ē-nig-mat'ik, ē-nig-mat'ik-al, *a.* Relating to or containing an enigma; obscure; ambiguous.
Enigmatist, ē-nig'mat-ist, *n.* A maker of or dealer in enigmas.
Enjoin, en-join', *vt.* To order with urgency; to admonish; to prescribe.
Enjoy, en-joi', *vt.* To feel gladness in; to have, use, or perceive with pleasure.
Enjoyable, en-joi'a-bl, *a.* Capable of being enjoyed.
Enjoyment, en-joi'ment, *n.* State of enjoying; pleasure; satisfaction; fruition.
Enkindle, en-kin'dl, *vt.* To kindle.
Enlarge, en-lärj', *vt.* (enlarging, enlarged). To make large or larger; to set free.—*vi.* To grow large or larger; to expatiate.
Enlarged, en-lärjd', *p.a.* Not narrow nor confined; broad; comprehensive; liberal.
Enlargement, en-lärj'ment, *n.* Act of enlarging; state of being enlarged; expansion; release; addition.
Enlighten, en-līt'en, *vt.* To make clear; to enable to see more clearly; to instruct.
Enlightened, en-līt'end, *p.a.* Instructed; informed; unprejudiced.
Enlightener, en-līt'en-ėr, *n.* One who or that which enlightens or illuminates.
Enlightenment, en-līt'en-ment, *n.* Act of enlightening; state of being enlightened.
Enlist, en-list', *vt.* To enter on a list; to engage in public service, especially military; to engage the services of.—*vi.* To engage voluntarily in public service; to enter heartily into a cause.

Enlistment, en-list'ment, *n.* Act of enlisting; voluntary engagement to serve as a soldier, sailor or airman.
Enliven, en-līv'en, *vt.* To give life or vivacity to; to gladden; to invigorate.
Enlivener, en-līv'en-ėr, *n.* One who or that which enlivens or animates.
Enmity, en'mi-ti, *n.* Quality of being an enemy; hostility; ill-will; opposition.
Ennoble, en-nō'bl, *vt.* (ennobling, ennobled). To make noble; to exalt; to dignify.
Ennui, än-nwē, *n.* Dulness of spirit; weariness; listlessness; tedium.
Enormity, ē-nor'mi-ti, *n.* State or quality of being enormous; depravity; atrocity.
Enormous, ė-nor'mus, *a.* Great beyond the common measure; huge; outrageous.
Enormously, ē-nor'mus-li, *adv.* Excessively.
Enough, ē-nuf', *a.* That satisfies desire; that may answer the purpose.—*n.* A sufficiency; that which is equal to the powers or abilities. —*adv.* Sufficiently; tolerably.
Enounce, ē-nouns', *vt.* To declare; to state.
Enow, ē-nou'. An old form of *enough.*
Enrage, en-rāj', *vt.* To excite rage in; to incense.
Enrapture, en-rap'tūr, *vt.* To transport with rapture; to delight beyond measure.
Enrich, en-rich', *vt.* To make rich; to fertilize; to supply with an abundance of anything desirable; to adorn.
Enrichment, en-rich'ment, *n.* Act of enriching; something that enriches.
Enrobe, en-rōb', *vt.* To attire.
Enroll, Enrol, en-rōl', *vt.* To write in a roll or register; to record.
Enrolment, en-rōl'ment, *n.* Act of enrolling; a register; a record.
Ens, enz, *n.*; pl. **Entia,** en'shi-a. Entity.
Ensample, en-sam'pl, *n.* An example.
Ensanguine, en-sang'gwin, *vt.* To stain or cover with blood; to smear with gore.
Ensconce, en-skons', *vt.* To cover, as with a sconce; to protect; to hide.
Ensemble, ong-säm-bl, *n.* All parts of a thing considered together; general effect.
Enshrine, en-shrīn', *vt.* To inclose in a shrine or chest; to cherish.
Enshroud, en-shroud', *vt.* To cover with a shroud; to envelop.
Ensiform, en'si-form, *a.* Sword-shaped.
Ensign, en'sīn, *n.* A mark of distinction; the flag of a company of soldiers or a vessel; formerly the lowest rank of commissioned officer in the infantry.
Ensigncy, Ensignship, en'sīn-si, en'sīn-ship, *n.* Rank or commission of an ensign.
Ensilage, en'sil-āj, *n.* A mode of storing green fodder, vegetables, &c., by burying in pits or silos.
Enslave, en-slāv', *vt.* (enslaving, enslaved). To reduce to slavery; to overpower.
Enslavement, en-slāv'ment, *n.* Act of enslaving; slavery; servitude.
Enslaver, en-slāv'ėr, *n.* One who enslaves.
Ensnare, en-snār', *vt.* To entrap; to insnare.
Ensue, en-sū', *vi.* (ensuing, ensued). To follow as a consequence; to succeed.
Ensure, en-shör', *vt.* To make sure.
Entablature, en-tab'la-tūr, *n.* That part of a structure which lies upon the capitals of columns.
Entail, en-tāl', *vt.* To cut off an estate from the heirs general; to settle, as the descent of lands by gift to a man and to certain heirs; to devolve as a consequence or of necessity.—*n.* The act of entailing; an estate entailed; rule of descent settled for an estate.
Entailment, en-tāl'ment, *n.* Act of entailing; state of being entailed.
Entangle, en-tang'gl, *vt.* To knit or interweave confusedly; to involve; to hamper.
Entanglement, en-tang'gl-ment, *n.* Act of entangling; state of being entangled.
Enter, en'tėr, *vt.* To go or come into; to begin; to set down in writing; to register; to take possession of.—*vi.* To go or come in; begin; engage in; be an ingredient in.
Enteric, en-ter'ik, *a.* Belonging to the intestines.—*Enteric fever,* same as *Typhoid fever.*
Enterprise, en'tėr-prīz, *n.* That which is undertaken; a bold or hazardous attempt; adventurous spirit; hardihood.—*vt.* To undertake.
Enterprising, en'tėr-prīz-ing, *a.* Bold or prompt to attempt; venturesome.
Entertain, en-tėr-tān', *vt.* To receive as a guest; to cherish; to treat with conversation; to please; to admit, with a view to consider. —*vi.* To give entertainments.
Entertaining, en-tėr-tān'ing, *p.a.* Pleasing; amusing; diverting.
Entertainment, en-tėr-tān'ment, *n.* Act of entertaining; hospitable treatment; a festival; amusement.
Enthrall, Enthral, en-thral', *vt.* To reduce to the condition of a thrall; to enslave.
Enthrone, en-thrōn', *vt.* (enthroning, enthroned). To place on a throne.
Enthusiasm, en-thū'zi-azm, *n.* An ecstasy of mind, as if from divine or spiritual influence; ardent zeal; elevation of fancy.
Enthusiast, en-thū'zi-ast, *n.* One possessed of enthusiasm; a person of ardent zeal; one of elevated fancy.
Enthusiastic, en-thū'zi-as"tik, *a.* Filled with enthusiasm; ardent; devoted; visionary.
Enthusiastically, en-thū'zi-as"tik-al-li, *adv.* With enthusiasm.
Entice, en-tīs', *vt.* (enticing, enticed). To draw on, by exciting hope or desire; to allure.
Enticement, en-tīs'ment, *n.* Act or means of enticing; blandishment; wile.
Enticing, en-tīs'ing, *p.a.* Having the qualities that entice; fascinating.
Enticingly, en-tīs'ing-li, *adv.* Charmingly.
Entire, en-tīr', *a.* Whole; unshared; complete; sincere; hearty; in full strength.
Entirely, en-tīr'li, *adv.* Wholly; fully.
Entitle, en-tī'tl, *vt.* (entitling, entitled). To give a title to; to style; to characterize; to give a claim to; to qualify.
Entity, en'ti-ti, *n.* Being; essence; existence.
Entomb, en-töm', *vt.* To deposit in a tomb; to bury; to inter.
Entombment, en-töm'ment, *n.* Burial.
Entomologist, en-to-mol'o-jist, *n.* One versed in the science of insects.
Entomology, en-to-mol'o-ji, *n.* That branch of zoology which treats of the structure, habits, and classification of insects.
Entozoon, en-to-zō'on, *n.*; pl. **-zoa.** An intestinal worm; an animal living in some part of another animal.
Entrail, en'trāl, *n.* One of the intestines; generally in *pl.*; the bowels.

Entrain, en-trān′, *vt.* To put on board a railway train.—*vi.* To take places in a train.
Entrance, en′trans, *n.* Act or power of entering into a place; the door or avenue by which a place may be entered; beginning; act of taking possession.
Entrance, en-trans′, *vt.* To put in a trance or ecstasy; to enrapture; to transport.
Entrant, en′trant, *n.* One who enters.
Entrap, en-trap′, *vt.* To catch in a trap; to inveigle; to decoy.
Entreat, en-trēt′, *vt.* To beg earnestly; to beseech; to supplicate.—*vi.* To make an earnest request; to pray.
Entreaty, en-trēt′i, *n.* Urgent prayer; earnest petition; solicitation.
Entrée, äng-trā, *n.* Freedom of access; a dish served at table.
Entremets, äng-tr-mā, *n.* A side-dish or minor dish at table, as an omelet, a jelly, &c.
Entrench, en-trensh′, *vt.* Same as *Intrench.*
Entresol, en′tėr-sol or äng-tr-sol, *n.* A low story between the ground story and one of greater height above.
Entry, en′tri, *n.* Act of entering; entrance; the passage by which persons enter a house; act of taking possession of lands, &c.; act of committing to writing.
Entwine, en-twīn′, *vt.* To twine; to twist round; to intwine.
Entwist, en-twist′, *vt.* To twist round.
Enumerate, ē-nū′me-rāt, *vt.* (enumerating, enumerated). To count number by number; to reckon or mention a number of things, each separately.
Enumeration, ē-nū′me-rā″shon, *n.* Act of enumerating; detailed account; a summing up.
Enunciate, ē-nun′si-āt, *vt.* (enunciating, enunciated). To utter; to pronounce; to proclaim.
Enunciation, ē-nun′si-ā″shon, *n.* Act or manner of enunciating; expression; declaration; public attestation.
Enunciatory, ē-nun′si-a-to-ri, *a.* Containing enunciation; declarative.
Envelop, en-vel′op, *vt.* To cover by wrapping or folding; to lie around and conceal.
Envelope, en′vel-ōp, *n.* That which infolds; a wrapper; a covering for a letter, &c.; an investing integument.
Envelopment, en-vel′op-ment, *n.* The act of enveloping; that which envelops.
Envenom, en-ven′om, *vt.* To poison; to taint with malice; to exasperate.
Enviable, en′vi-a-bl, *a.* Exciting or capable of exciting envy.
Envious, en′vi-us, *a.* Feeling or harbouring envy; tinctured with or excited by envy.
Environ, en-vī′ron, *vt.* To encompass; to encircle; to besiege; to invest.
Environment, en-vī′ron-ment, *n.* Act of environing; state of being environed; that which environs; conditions under which one lives.
Environs, en-vī′rons, *n.pl.* Neighbourhood; vicinity.
Envisage, en-viz′āj, *vt.* To look in the face of; to apprehend directly or by intuition.
Envoy, en′voi, *n.* One sent on a mission; a person next in rank to an ambassador, deputed to transact business with a foreign power.
Envy, en′vi, *n.* Pain or discontent excited by another's superiority or success; malice; object of envy.—*vt.* (envying, envied). To feel envy towards or on account of; to begrudge.—*vi.* To be affected with envy.
Enwrap, en-rap′, *vt.* To envelop; to inwrap.
Eocene, ē′ō-sēn, *a.* and *n.* A term applied to the series of strata at the base of the tertiary formations.
Eolithic, ē-ō-lith′ik, *a.* Pertaining to the early part of the palæolithic period.
Eozoic, ē-ō-zō′ik, *a.* Pertaining to the oldest fossiliferous rocks.
Epact, ē′pakt, *n.* Days forming the excess of the solar over the lunar year; the moon's age at the end of the year.
Epaulet, Epaulette, e′pal-et, *n.* A shoulder knot; a badge worn on the shoulder by military men or naval officers.
Epergne, e-pärn′, *n.* An ornamental stand for the centre of a table.
Ephemera, e-fem′e-ra, *n.*; pl. **-ræ.** A fly that lives one day only; a short-lived insect.
Ephemeral, e-fē′me-ral, *a.* Continuing one day only; short-lived; fleeting.
Ephemeris, e-fem′e-ris, *n.*; pl. **Ephemerides,** e-fe-me′ri-dēz. A diary; an astronomical almanac; periodical literature.
Ephod, e′fod, *n.* A vestment worn by the Jewish high-priest.
Epic, ep′ik, *a.* Composed in a lofty narrative style; heroic.—*n.* A poem of elevated character, describing the exploits of heroes.
Epicarp, ep′i-kärp, *n.* The outer skin of fruits.
Epicure, ep′i-kūr, *n.* One devoted to sensual enjoyments; a voluptuary.
Epicurean, ep′i-kū-rē″an, *a.* Luxurious; given to luxury.—*n.* A follower of Epicurus; a luxurious eater; an epicure.
Epicurism, ep′i-kūr-izm, *n.* The doctrines or practices of an epicure.
Epicycle, ep′i-sī-kl, *n.* A little circle whose centre moves round in the circumference of a greater circle.
Epideictic, Epideictical, ep-i-dīk′tik, ep-i-dīk′ti-kal, *a.* Serving to display; having a rhetorical character; demonstrative.
Epidemic, Epidemical, ep-i-dem′ik, ep-i-dem′ik-al, *a.* Affecting a whole community, as a disease; prevalent.—**Epidemic,** ep-i-dem′ik, *n.* A disease which attacks many people at the same period.
Epidermis, ep-i-dėr′mis, *n.* The cuticle or scarf-skin of the body; the exterior coating of the leaf or stem of a plant.
Epiglottis, ep-i-glot′is, *n.* The cartilage at the root of the tongue that covers the glottis during the act of swallowing.
Epigram, ep′i-gram, *n.* A short poem, usually keenly satirical; a pointed or antithetical saying.
Epigrammatic, Epigrammatical, ep′i-gram-mat″ik, ep′i-gram-mat″ik-al, *a.* Pertaining to epigrams; like an epigram; pointed.
Epigrammatist, ep-i-gram′mat-ist, *n.* One who composes or deals in epigrams.
Epigraph, ep′i-graf, *n.* An inscription; quotation; motto.
Epilepsy, ep′i-lep-si, *n.* The falling-sickness; a disease characterized by spasms and loss of sense.
Epileptic, ep-i-lep′tik, *a.* Pertaining to epilepsy.—*n.* One affected with epilepsy.
Epilogue, ep′i-log, *n.* A speech or short poem spoken by an actor at the end of a play.

Epiphany, ē-pif'a-ni, *n.* A church festival on 6th January, celebrating the manifestation of Christ to the wise men of the East.
Epiphyte, ep'i-fīt, *n.* A plant growing upon another plant, but not nourished by it.
Episcopacy, ē-pis'kō-pa-si, *n.* Ecclesiastical government by bishops; the collective body of bishops.
Episcopal, ē-pis'kō-pal, *a.* Belonging to or vested in bishops.
Episcopalian, ē-pis'kō-pā''li-an, *a.* Pertaining to bishops, or government by bishops.—*n.* One who belongs to an episcopal church.
Episcopalianism, ē-pis'kō-pā''li-an-izm, *n.* The system of episcopal government.
Episcopate, ē-pis'kō-pāt, *n.* A bishopric; the collective body of bishops.
Episode, ep'i-sōd, *n.* A separate story introduced to give greater variety to the events related in a poem, &c.; an incident.
Episodic, Episodical, ep-i-sod'ik, ep-i-sod'-ik-al, *a.* Pertaining to an episode; contained in an episode.
Epistle, ē-pis'l, *n.* A writing communicating intelligence to a distant person; a letter.
Epistolary, ē-pis'tō-la-ri, *a.* Pertaining to epistles; suitable to correspondence.
Epitaph, ep'i-taf, *n.* That which is written on a tomb; an inscription, or a composition, in honour of the dead.
Epithalamium, ep'i-tha-lā'mi-um, *n.*; pl. **-iums** or **-ia.** A nuptial song or poem.
Epithet, ep'i-thet, *n.* Any word implying a quality attached to a person or thing.
Epitome, e-pit'o-mi, *n.* A brief summary; abridgment; compendium.
Epitomist, Epitomizer, e-pit'o-mist, e-pit'o-mī-zėr, *n.* The writer of an epitome.
Epitomize, e-pit'om-īz, *vt.* To make an epitome of; to abstract; to condense.
Epoch, ē'pok, *n.* A fixed point of time from which years are numbered; period; era; date.
Epode, ep'ōd, *n.* The third and last part of an ode, succeeding the antistrophe; a lyric in which a verse is followed by a shorter verse.
Eponym, ep'o-nim, *n.* A name of a place or people derived from that of a person.
Epopee, e-po-pē', *n.* An epic poem; the subject of an epic poem.
Epsom-salt, ep'sum-sąlt, *n.* The sulphate of magnesia, a cathartic.
Equability, ē-kwa-bil'i-ti, *n.* State or quality of being equable.
Equable, ē-kwa-bl, *a.* Uniform; even; steady.
Equably, ē'kwa-bli, *adv.* In an equable or uniform manner.
Equal, ē'kwal, *a.* The same in extent, number, degree, rank, &c.; same in qualities; uniform; proportionate; adequate; just.—*n.* One not inferior or superior to another.—*vt.* (equalling, equalled). To make equal to; to become or be equal to.
Equality, ē-kwal'i-ti, *n.* State or quality of being equal; likeness; evenness; plainness.
Equalization, ē'kwal-īz-ā''shon, *n.* Act of equalizing; state of being equalized.
Equalize, ē'kwal-īz, *vt.* (equalizing, equalized). To make equal, even, or uniform.
Equally, ē'kwal-li, *adv.* In an equal manner; alike; impartially.
Equanimity, ē-kwa-nim'i-ti or ek-, *n.* Evenness of mind; steadiness of temper.
Equate, ē-kwāt', *vt.* (equating, equated). To make equal; to reduce to an equation; to reduce to mean time or motion.
Equation, ē-kwā'shon, *n.* The act of equating; an expression asserting the equality of two quantities; a quantity to be taken into account in order to give a true result.
Equator, ē-kwā'tėr, *n.* The great circle of our globe which divides it into the northern and southern hemispheres; a circle in the heavens coinciding with the plane of the earth's equator.
Equatorial, ē-kwa-tō'ri-al, *a.* Pertaining to the equator.—*n.* An astronomical instrument.
Equerry, e'kwe-ri or ē-kwe'ri, *n.* An officer of princes or nobles who has the care of their horses.
Equestrian, ē-kwes'tri-an, *a.* Pertaining to horses or horsemanship; on horseback; skilled in horsemanship.—*n.* A horseman.
Equiangular, ē-kwi-ang'gū-lėr or ek-, *a.* Consisting of or having equal angles.
Equidistant, ē-kwi-dis'tant or ek-, *a.* Being at an equal distance from.
Equilateral, ē-kwi-lat'ėr-al or ek-, *a.* Having all the sides equal.
Equilibrist, ē-kwil'i-brist or ek-, *n.* One who keeps his balance in unnatural positions.
Equilibrium, ē-kwi-li'bri-um or ek-, *n.* State of rest produced by the counteraction of forces; balance.
Equimultiple, ē-kwi-mul'ti-pl or ek-, *a.* Multiplied by the same number or quantity.—*n.* Any number or quantity multiplied by the same number or quantity as another.
Equine, ē-kwīn', *a.* Pertaining to a horse; denoting the horse kind.
Equinoctial, ē-kwi-nok'shal, or ek-, *a.* Pertaining to the equinoxes.—*n.* The celestial equator: when the sun is on it, the days and nights are of equal length.
Equinox, ē'kwi-noks or ek', *n.* The time when the day and night are of equal length, about 21st March and 23rd September.
Equip, ē-kwip', *vt.* (equipping, equipped). To fit out or furnish, as for war; to dress; to array.
Equipage, ek'wi-pāj, *n.* An equipment; retinue; carriage of state and attendants; accoutrements.
Equipment, ē-kwip'ment, *n.* Act of equipping; habiliments; warlike apparatus; necessary adjuncts.
Equipose, ē'kwi-poiz or ek', *n.* Equality of weight or force; equilibrium.
Equipollence, Equipollency, ē-kwi-pol'-lens, ē-kwi-pol'len-si or ek-, *n.* Equality of power or force.
Equipollent, ē-kwi-pol'lent or ek-, *a.* Having equal power; equivalent.
Equiponderance, ē-kwi-pon'dėr-ans or ek-, *n.* Equality of weight; equipoise.
Equiponderant, ē-kwi-pon'dėr-ant or ek-, *a.* Being of the same weight.
Equitable, ek'wit-a-bl, *a.* Distributing equal justice; just; upright; impartial.
Equitably, ek'wit-a-bl, *adv.* In an equitable manner; justly; impartially.
Equity, ek'wi-ti, *n.* The giving to each man his due; impartiality; uprightness; a system of supplementary law founded upon precedents and established principles.
Equivalence, ē-kwiv'a-lens or ek-, *n.* State of being equivalent; equality of value.

Equivalent, ē-kwiv'a-lent or ek-, *a.* Equal in excellence, worth, or weight; of the same import or meaning.—*n.* That which is equal in value, &c.; compensation.
Equivocal, ē-kwiv'ō-kal, *a.* Capable of a double interpretation; doubtful.
Equivocate, ē-kwiv'ō-kāt, *vi.* To use ambiguous expressions to mislead; to quibble.
Equivocation, ē-kwiv'ō-kā"shon, *n.* Act of equivocating; ambiguity.
Equivocator, ē-kwiv'ō-kāt-ėr, *n.* One who equivocates.
Equivoke, Equivoque, ē'kwi-vōk, *n.* An ambiguous term; equivocation.
Era, ē'ra, *n.* A fixed point of time, from which years are counted; epoch; age.
Eradicate, ē-rad'i-kāt, *vt.* To root out; to destroy; to exterminate.
Eradication, ē-rad'i-kā"shon, *n.* Act of eradicating; total destruction.
Erase, ē-rās', *vt.* (erasing, erased). To scrape out; to efface; to expunge.
Erasement, ē-rās'ment, *n.* A rubbing out; obliteration.
Eraser, ē-rās'ėr, *n.* One who erases; an appliance to erase writing, &c.
Erastian, ē-ras'ti-an, *n.* A follower of Thomas Erastus, a 16th-century German, who maintained that the church is dependent on the state for its government and discipline.—*a.* Relating to the Erastians or their principles.
Erastianism, ē-ras'ti-an-izm, *n.* The principles of the Erastians.
Erasure, ē-rā'zhūr, *n.* Act of erasing; obliteration.
Ere, ār, *adv.*, *conj.*, and *prep.* Before; sooner than.
Erect, ē-rekt', *a.* Upright; bold; undismayed.—*vt.* To raise and set upright; to build; to found; to cheer.
Erecter, Erector, ē-rekt'ėr, *n.* One who erects.
Erectile, ē-rekt'īl, *a.* That may be erected.
Erection, ē-rek'shon, *a.* Act of erecting; formation; anything erected; structure.
Erelong, ār'long, *adv.* Before long.
Eremite, e'rē-mit, *n.* One who lives in a desert or wilderness; a hermit.
Erenow, ār'nou, *adv.* Before this time.
Ergo, ėr'gō, *adv.* Therefore.
Ergot, ėr'got, *n.* A disease of rye and other grasses; this diseased growth, used in medicine.
Ermine, ėr'min, *n.* An animal of the weasel kind, a native of N. Europe and America, valued for its white fur; the fur of the ermine.
Erode, ē-rōd', *vt.* (eroding, eroded). To gnaw off or away; to corrode.
Erosion, ē-rō'zhon, *n.* Act of eroding; state of being eaten away; corrosion.
Erotic, ē-rot'ik, *a.* Pertaining to or prompted by love; treating of love.
Err, er, *vi.* To wander; to stray; to depart from rectitude; to blunder.
Errand, e'rand, *n.* A message; mandate; business to be transacted by a messenger.
Errant, e'rant, *a.* Roving; wandering about in search of adventures.
Errantry, e'rant-ri, *n.* A wandering state; a roving or rambling; the employment of a knight-errant.
Erratic, e-rat'ik, *a.* Wandering; irregular; eccentric.
Erratum, e-rā'tum, *n.*; pl. **-ata.** An error or mistake in writing or printing.
Erroneous, e-rō'nē-us, *a.* Characterized by or containing error; wrong; mistaken.
Error, e'rėr, *n.* A deviation from truth or what is right; a mistake; a blunder; fault; offence.
Erse, ėrs, *n.* The Celtic language of the Highlands of Scotland; Gaelic; also the language spoken in parts of Ireland.
Erst, ėrst, *adv.* At first; long ago; hitherto.
Erubescence, e-rū-bes'ens, *n.* A becoming red; redness; a blushing.
Erubescent, e-rū-bes'ent, *a.* Red; blushing.
Eructate, ē-rukt'āt, *vt.* To belch up; to eject from the stomach, as wind. Also **Eruct.**
Eructation, ē-ruk-tā'shon, *n.* Act of belching; a belch; a violent bursting forth or ejection of matter from the earth.
Erudite, e'rū-dit, *a.* Fully instructed; deeply read; learned.
Erudition, e-rū-di'shon, *n.* Learning; knowledge gained by study; scholarship.
Erupt, ē-rupt', *vt.* To throw out by volcanic action.
Eruption, ē-rup'shon, *n.* A breaking forth; a violent emission; a sudden hostile excursion; a breaking out of pimples, pustules, &c.
Eruptive, ē-rup'tiv, *a.* Bursting out or forth; produced by eruption.
Erysipelas, e-ri-si'pe-las, *n.* A disease accompanied by fever and an eruption of a fiery acrid humour, chiefly on the face.
Escalade, es-ka-lād', *n.* The assault of a fortress by scaling the walls.—*vt.* To scale; to mount and pass or enter by means of ladders.
Escalator, es'ka-lā-tėr, *n.* A mechanism consisting of a series of steps which are carried up and down by means of a continuous chain; a moving stairway.
Escallop, es-kol'op, *n.* A bivalve shell; a scallop.
Escapade, es-ka-pād', *n.* A runaway adventure; a freak; a mad prank.
Escape, es-kāp', *vt.* (escaping, escaped). To get out of the way of; to pass without harm; to pass unobserved; to avoid.—*vi.* To be free; to avoid; to regain one's liberty.—*n.* Flight; to shun danger; an evasion of legal retraint or custody.
Escapement, es-kāp'ment, *n.* Means of escaping; that part of a time-piece by which the circular motion of the wheels is converted into a vibrating one.
Escarp, es-kärp', *vt.* To form into a scarp; to make to slope suddenly.—*n.* A sudden slope.
Escarpment, es-kärp'ment, *n.* A steep declivity; ground cut away nearly vertically.
Eschatology, es-ka-tol'o-ji, *n.* The doctrine of the last or final things, as death.
Escheat, es-chēt', *n.* The reversion of property to the original proprietor, or to the state, through failure of heirs or by forfeiture; the property itself.—*vi.* To revert, as land.—*vt.* To cause to be an escheat; to forfeit.
Eschew, es-chö', *vt.* To shun; to avoid.
Escort, es'kort, *n.* A guard attending an officer or baggage, &c.; persons attending as a mark of honour.—*vt.* es-kort'. To attend and guard.
Escritoire, es-kri-twär', *n.* A chest of drawers with appliances for writing; a writing-desk.
Esculent, es'kū-lent, *a.* Eatable; that may be used by man for food.—*n.* An edible.

Escutcheon, es-kuch'on, *n.* A shield; the shield on which a coat of arms is represented.
Esophagus, ē-sof'a-gus, *n.* Œsophagus.
Esoteric, es-ō-te'rik, *a.* Taught to a select few; private; select.
Espalier, es-pa'li-ėr, *n.* A trellis-work or lattice-work on which to train fruit-trees and shrubs; a tree or row of trees so trained.
Esparto, es-pär'tō, *n.* A grass found in S. Spain and N. Africa, extensively exported for the manufacture of paper, matting, &c.
Especial, es-pe'shal, *a.* Distinct; chief; special.
Especially, es-pe'shal-li, *adv.* In an uncommon degree; specially.
Esperanto, es-pėr-ant'ō, *n.* A language invented by Dr. Zamenhof (about 1887) for the purpose of enabling the inhabitants of all countries to converse with each other.
Espial, es-pī'al, *n.* Act of espying.
Espionage, es'pi-on-āj, *n.* Practice or employment of spies; practice of watching others without being suspected.
Esplanade, es-pla-nād', *n.* An open space between the glacis of a citadel and the houses of the town; any level space near a town for walks or drives; a terrace by the sea-side.
Espousal, es-pouz'al, *n.* Betrothal; nuptials: in this sense generally in *pl.*; the adopting of a cause.
Espouse, es-pouz', *vt.* (espousing, espoused). To give or take in marriage; to betroth; to wed; to embrace or adopt; to uphold.
Espouser, es-pouz'ėr, *n.* One who espouses.
Esprit, es-prē, *n.* Soul; spirit; mind; wit.
Espy, es-pī', *vt.* (espying, espied). To see at a distance; to descry; to discover.
Esquire, es-kwīr', *n.* A shield-bearer; a title of dignity next to a knight; a title of courtesy.
Essay, es-sā', *vt.* To try; to make experiment of.—*n.* es'sā. An endeavour or experiment; a literary composition to prove or illustrate a particular subject; a short treatise.
Essayist, es'sā-ist, *n.* A writer of an essay or essays.
Essence, es'sens, *n.* The nature, substance, or being of anything; predominant qualities of a plant or drug; an extract; perfume; fundamental doctrines, facts, &c., of a statement, &c.—*vt.* To perfume; to scent.
Essential, es-sen'shal, *a.* Relating to or containing the essence; necessary to the existence of; indispensable; highly rectified; volatile; diffusible (oils).—*n.* Something necessary; the chief point; constituent principle.
Essentiality, es-sen'shi-al"i-ti, *n.* The quality of being essential.
Establish, es-tab'lish, *vt.* To make stable; to found permanently; to institute; to enact; to sanction; to confirm; to make good.
Established, es-tab'lisht, *p.a.* Ratified; confirmed; set up and supported by the state.
Establishment, es-tab'lish-ment, *n.* Act of establishing; state of being established; confirmation; sanction; that which is established; a civil or military force or organization; form of doctrine and church government established under state control; place of residence or business; the number of men in a regiment, &c.
Estate, es-tāt', *n.* State; condition; rank; landed property; possessions; an order or class of men in the body politic.
Esteem, es-tēm', *vt.* To set a value on; to regard with respect; to prize.—*n.* Judgment of merit or demerit; estimation; great regard.
Estimable, es'tim-a-bl, *a.* Capable of being estimated; worthy of esteem or respect.
Estimate, es'tim-āt, *vt.* (estimating, estimated). To form an opinion regarding; to calculate; to appraise; to esteem.—*n.* Valuation; calculation of probable cost.
Estimation, es-tim-ā'shon, *n.* Act of estimating; valuation; opinion; esteem.
Estop, es-top', *vt.* To bar or debar; in *law*, to impede or bar by one's own act.
Estoppel, es-top'el, *n.* In *law*, a stop; a plea in bar, grounded on a man's own act.
Estovers, es-tō'vėrz, *n.pl.* The right of taking wood from an estate for fuel, fences, &c.
Estrange, es-trānj', *vt.* (estranging, estranged). To alienate, as the affections.
Estrangement, es-trānj'ment, *n.* Alienation of affection or friendship.
Estray, es-trā', *n.* A domestic animal found straying.
Estreat, es-trēt', *n.* In *law*, a true copy of a writing under which fines are to be levied.—*vt.* To levy (fines) under an estreat.
Estuary, es'tū-a-ri, *n.* The mouth of a river where the tide meets the current; a firth.
Etch, ech, *vt.* To produce designs on a copper or other plate by lines drawn through a thin coating, and then eaten into the plate by a strong acid; to draw finely in ink.—*vi.* To practise etching.
Etcher, ech'ėr, *n.* One who etches.
Etching, ech'ing, *n.* The act or art of the etcher; a mode of engraving; the impression taken from an etched plate.
Eternal, ē-tėrn'al, *a.* Everlasting; without beginning or end of existence; unchangeable. —*n.* An appellation of God.
Eternally, ē-tėrn'al-li, *adv.* For ever; unchangeably; without intermission.
Eternity, ē-tėrn'i-ti, *n.* Continuance without beginning or end; duration without end; the state or time after death.
Eternize, ē-tėrn'īz, *vt.* To make eternal or endless; to immortalize.
Etesian, e-tē'zi-an, *a.* Yearly; periodical.
Ether, ē'thėr, *n.* The clear upper air; refined air; a hypothetical medium of extreme tenuity universally diffused, and the medium of the transmission of light, heat, &c.; a very light, volatile, and inflammable fluid obtained from alcohol, used as a stimulant and anæsthetic.
Ethereal, ē-thē'rē-al, *a.* Formed of ether; heavenly; aerial; intangible.
Etherealize, ē-thē'rē-al-īz, *vt.* To convert into ether; to render ethereal.
Etherize, ē'thėr-īz, *vt.* To convert into ether; to treat with ether; to stupefy with ether.
Ethic, Ethical, eth'ik, eth'ik-al, *a.* Relating to morals; treating of morality; delivering precepts of morality.
Ethically, eth'ik-al-li, *adv.* In an ethical manner; according to morality.
Ethics, eth'iks, *n.* The doctrine of morals; moral philosophy; a system of moral principles.
Ethiop, Ethiopian, ē'thi-ōp, ē-thi-ō'pi-an, *n.* A native of Ethiopia.
Ethiopic, ē-thi-op'ik, *n.* The language of Ethiopia.—*a.* Relating to Ethiopia.

Ethnic, Ethnical, eth'nik, eth'nik-al, *a.* Pertaining to the gentiles; pagan; ethnological.
Ethnography, eth-nog'ra-fi, *n.* That branch of science which treats of the manners, customs, &c., peculiar to different nations.
Ethnologic, Ethnological, eth-no-loj'ik, eth-no-loj'ik-al, *a.* Relating to ethnology.
Ethnologist, eth-nol'o-jist, *n.* One skilled in ethnology; a student of ethnology.
Ethnology, eth-nol'o-ji, *n.* That branch of science which treats of the different races of men.
Ethology, eth-ol'o-ji, *n.* The science of ethics; the doctrine of the formation of character.
Etiolate, ē'ti-ō-lāt, *vi.* To be whitened by exclusion of sunlight.—*vt.* To whiten.
Etiquette, et-i-ket', *n.* Forms of ceremony or decorum; social observances.
Etruscan, ē-trus'kan, *a.* Relating to Etruria, an ancient country in Italy.—*n.* A native of ancient Etruria.
Etui, et-wē', *n.* A pocket-case for small articles.
Etymologic, Etymological, et'i-mo-loj"ik, et'i-mo-loj"ik-al, *a.* Pertaining to etymology.
Etymologist, et-i-mol'o-jist, *n.* One versed in etymology.
Etymology, et-i-mol'o-ji, *n.* That part of philology which traces the origin of words; the derivation or history of any word.
Etymon, e'ti-mon, *n.* An original root or primitive word.
Eucalyptus, ū-ka-lip'tus, *n.*; pl. **-tuses** or **-ti.** The generic name of some Australian trees of the myrtle order, usually called gum-trees.
Eucharist, ū'ka-rist, *n.* The sacrament of the Lord's Supper.
Eucharistic, Eucharistical, ū-ka-rist'ik, ū-ka-rist'ik-al, *a.* Pertaining to the Lord's Supper.
Euchre, ū'kėr, *n.* A game of cards played by two, three, or four players.
Eugenics, ū-jen'iks, *n.* The theory dealing with the production or treatment of a fine, healthy race.
Eulogist, ū'lo-jist, *n.* One who eulogizes.
Eulogistic, ū-lo-jis'tik, *a.* Commendatory; full of praise.
Eulogium, ū-lō'ji-um, *n.* Eulogy; encomium.
Eulogize, ū'lo-jīz, *vt.* (eulogizing, eulogized). To praise; to extol.
Eulogy, ū'lo-ji, *n.* A speech or writing in commendation; praise; panegyric.
Eunuch, ū'nuk, *n.* A castrated man.
Eupepsia, Eupepsy, ū-pep'si-a, ū-pep'si, *n.* Good digestion.
Eupeptic, ū-pep'tik, *a.* Having good digestion; easy of digestion.
Euphemism, ū'fem-izm, *n.* A mode of speaking by which a delicate word or expression is substituted for one which is offensive; a word or expression so substituted.
Euphemistic, ū-fem-is'tik, *a.* Rendering more decent or delicate in expression.
Euphonic, Euphonious, ū-fon'ik, ū-fō'ni-us, *a.* Having euphony; agreeable in sound.
Euphony, ū'fo-ni, *n.* An easy, smooth enunciation of sounds; harmony of sound.
Euphuism, ū'fū-izm, *n.* Excessive elegance and refinement of language.
Eurasian, ū-rā'shi-an, *n.* One born in India of a native mother and European father.
European, ū-rō-pē'an, *a.* Pertaining to Europe.—*n.* A native of Europe.
Euthanasia, ū-tha-nā'zi-a, *n.* An easy death; a putting to death by painless means.
Evacuate, ē-vak'ū-āt, *vt.* (evacuating, evacuated). To make empty; to quit; to withdraw from; to discharge.
Evacuation, ē-vak'ū-ā"shon, *n.* Act of evacuating; that which is discharged.
Evacuee, ē-vak'ū-ē, *n.* A person transferred from a vulnerable to a safe area on account of air-raids, &c.
Evade, ē-vād', *vt.* (evading, evaded). To avoid by dexterity; to slip away from; to elude; to baffle.—*vi.* To practise evasion.
Evaluate, ē-val'ū-āt, *vt.* To value carefully; to ascertain the amount of.
Evanesce, ev-a-nes', *vi.* To vanish.
Evanescence, ev-an-es'ens, *n.* A vanishing away; state of being liable to vanish.
Evanescent, ev-an-es'ent, *a.* Vanishing; fleeting; passing away.
Evangel, ē-van'jel, *n.* The gospel.
Evangelic, Evangelical, ē-van-jel'ik, ē-van-jel'ik-al, *a.* Pertaining to or according to the gospel; sound in the doctrines of the gospel; fervent and devout.
Evangelicism, ē-van-jel'i-sizm, *n.* Evangelical principles.
Evangelist, ē-van'jel-ist, *n.* One of the four writers of the history of Jesus Christ; a preacher of the gospel; a missionary.
Evangelize, ē-van'jel-īz, *vt.* and *i.* (evangelizing, evangelized). To preach the gospel to and convert.
Evanish, ē-van'ish, *vi.* To vanish away.
Evaporable, ē-va'pėr-a-bl, *a.* That may evaporate or be evaporated.
Evaporate, ē-va'pėr-āt, *vi.* (evaporating, evaporated). To pass off in vapour; to exhale; to be wasted.—*vt.* To convert into vapour; to disperse in vapours.
Evaporation, ē-va'pėr-ā"shon, *n.* Act of evaporating; conversion of a fluid or solid into vapour.
Evasion, ē-vā'zhon, *n.* Act of evading; artifice to elude; shift; equivocation.
Evasive, ē-vā'siv, *a.* That evades; shuffling; equivocating.
Eve, ēv, *n.* Evening; the evening before a church festival; the period just preceding some event.
Even, ē'vn, *a.* Level; smooth; equable; on an equality; just; settled; balanced; capable of being divided by 2 without a remainder.—*vt.* To make even or level; to equalize; to balance.—*adv.* Just; exactly; likewise; moreover.—*n.* The evening.
Even-handed, ē'vn-hand-ed, *a.* Impartial.
Evening, ē'vn-ing, *n.* The close of the day; the decline of anything.—*a.* Being at the close of day.
Event, ē'vent', *n.* That which happens; an incident; the consequence of anything; issue; result; conclusion.
Eventful, ē-vent'fụl, *a.* Full of incidents; producing numerous or great changes.
Eventide, ē'vn-tīd, *n.* The time of evening.
Eventual, ē-vent'ū-al, *a.* Pertaining to a final issue; happening as a consequence; final; ultimate.
Eventuality, ē-vent'ū-al"i-ti, *n.* That which happens; a contingent result.
Eventuate, ē-vent'ū-āt, *vi.* To come to pass.

Ever, ev'ėr, *adv.* At all times; at any time; continually; in any degree.
Evergreen, ev'ėr-grēn, *n.* A plant that always retains its greenness.—*a.* Always green.
Everlasting, ev-ėr-last'ing, *a.* Enduring for ever; eternal.—*n.* Eternity; the Eternal Being; a plant whose flowers endure for many months after being plucked.
Everlastingly, ev-ėr-last'ing-li, *adv.* Eternally; perpetually; continually.
Evermore, ev'ėr-mōr, *adv.* At all times; eternally.
Eversion, ē-vėr'shon, *n.* An overthrowing; destruction; subversion.
Every, ev'ri, *a.* Each one; all taken separately.
Everybody, ev'ri-bod-i, *n.* Every person.
Everyday, ev'ri-dā, *a.* Common; usual.
Everyone, ev'ri-wun, *n.* Every person.
Everywhere, ev'ri-whār, *adv.* In every place; in all places.
Evict, ē-vikt', *vt.* To dispossess by judicial process; to expel from lands, &c., by law.
Eviction, ē-vik'shon, *n.* Act of evicting; expulsion of a tenant.
Evidence, ev'i-dens, *n.* That which demonstrates that a fact is so; testimony; proof; witness.—*vt.* To make evident; to prove.
Evident, ev'i-dent, *a.* Clear; obvious; plain.
Evidential, ev-i-den'shal, *a.* Pertaining to evidence; affording evidence.
Evil, ē'vil, *a.* Not good; bad; wrong; unhappy; calamitious.—*n.* That which is not good; anything which produces pain, calamity, &c.; wrong; malady.—*adv.* Not well; ill.
Evince, ē-vins', *vt.* (evincing, evinced). To show in a clear manner; to manifest.
Eviscerate, ē-vis'sė-rāt, *vt.* To take out the entrails of; to disembowel.
Evisceration, ē-vis'sė-rā"shon, *n.* Act of eviscerating.
Evocation, ev-ō-kā'shon, *n.* A calling forth.
Evoke, ē-vōk', *vt.* (evoking, evoked). To call forth or out; to summon forth.
Evolution, ev-o-lū'shon, *n.* An unfolding; development; extraction of roots in arithmetic and algebra; systematic movement of troops or ships in changing their position; that theory which sees in the history of all things a gradual advance from a rudimentary condition to one more complex and of higher character.
Evolutional, Evolutionary, ev-o-lū'shon-al, ev-ō-lū'shon-a-ri, *a.* Pertaining to evolution; produced by or due to evolution.
Evolutionist, ev-o lū'shon-ist, *n.* and *a.* A believer in the doctrine of evolution.
Evolve, ē-volv', *vt.* (evolving, evolved). To unfold; to develop; to open and expand.—*vi.* To open or disclose itself.
Evulsion, ē-vul'shon, *n.* Act of plucking out.
Ewe, ū, *n.* A female sheep.
Ewer, ū'ėr, *n.* A kind of pitcher or vessel for holding water.
Exacerbate, eks-as'ėr-bāt, *vt.* To exasperate; to increase the violence of.
Exacerbation, eks-as'ėr-bā"shon, *n.* Increase of malignity; periodical increase of violence in a disease.
Exact, egz-akt', *a.* Strictly accurate; methodical; precise; true.—*vt.* To extort by means of authority; to demand of right; to compel.—*vi.* To practise extortion.
Exacting, egz-akt'ing, *p.a.* Disposed to exact or claim too much.
Exaction, egz-ak'shon, *n.* Act of exacting; extortion; that which is exacted.
Exactitude, egz-ak'ti-tūd, *n.* Accuracy.
Exactly, egs-akt'li, *adv.* In an exact manner; precisely; nicely; accurately.
Exactor, egz-akt'ėr, *n.* One who exacts; one unreasonably severe in his demands.
Exaggerate, egz-aj'ė-rāt, *vt.* (exaggerating, exaggerated). To increase beyond due limits; to depict extravagantly.
Exaggeration, egz-aj'ė-rā"shon, *n.* Representation of things beyond the truth.
Exalt, egz-ạlt', *vt.* To raise high; to raise to power or dignity; to extol.
Exaltation, egz-ạlt-ā'shon, *n.* Elevation to power, office, &c.; elevated estate.
Examination, egz-am'in-ā"shon, *n.* Act of examining; inquiry into facts, &c., by interrogation; scrutiny by study.
Examine, egz-am'in, *vt.* (examining, examined). To inspect carefully; to inquire into; to interrogate, as a witness, a student, &c.; to discuss.
Examiner, egz-am'in-ėr, *n.* One who examines.
Examining, egz-am'in-ing, *p.a.* Having power to examine; appointed to examine.
Example, egz-am'pl, *n.* A sample; pattern; model; precedent; instance.
Exasperate, egz-as'pė-rāt, *vt.* (exasperating, exasperated). To irritate; to enrage; to make worse; to aggravate.
Exasperation, egz-as'pė-rā"shon, *n.* Irritation; rage; fury.
Excamb, eks-kamb', *vt.* To exchange (land).
Excavate, eks'ka-vāt, *vt.* (excavating, excavated). To hollow out.
Excavation, eks-ka-vā'shon, *n.* Act of hollowing out; a cavity.
Excavator, eks'ka-vāt-ėr, *n.* One who excavates; a machine for excavating.
Exceed, ek-sēd', *vt.* To go beyond, as any limit; to surpass; to outdo.—*vi.* To go too far; to bear the greater proportion.
Exceeding, ek-sēd'ing, *a.* Great in extent, quantity, or duration.—*adv.* In a very great degree.
Exceedingly, ek-sēd'ing-li, *adv.* Greatly; very much.
Excel, ek-sel', *vt.* (excelling, excelled). To surpass; to transcend; to outdo.—*vi.* To be eminent or distinguished.
Excellence, Excellency, ek'sel-lens, ek'sel-len-si, *n.* Superiority; pre-eminence; any valuable quality; an official title of honour.
Excellent, ek'sel-lent, *a.* Of great value; distinguished in attainments; exquisite.
Except, ek-sept', *vt.* To take or leave out of any number specified; to exclude.—*vi.* To object; to make objection.—*prep.* Exclusively of; without.—*conj.* Unless.
Excepting, ek-sept'ing, *prep.* and *conj.* With exception of; excluding; except.
Exception, ek-sep'shon, *n.* Act of excepting; state of being excepted; that which is excepted; an objection; offence.
Exceptionable, ek-sep'shon-a-bl, *a.* Liable to objection; objectionable.
Exceptional, ek-sep'shon-al, *a.* Forming or making an exception.
Exceptious, ek-sep'shus, *a.* Disposed to make objections; captious.
Excerpt, ek-sėrpt', *n.* An extract; a passage

selected from an author.—*vt.* To pick out from a book, &c.; to cite.
Excess, ek-ses', *n.* That which exceeds; superabundance; intemperate conduct; that by which one thing exceeds another.
Excessive, ek-ses'iv, *a.* Beyond any given degree or limit; intemperate; extreme.
Excessively, ek-ses'iv-li, *adv.* Exceedingly.
Exchange, eks-chānj', *vt.* To change one thing for another; to commute; to bargain.—*n.* Act of exchanging; interchange; barter; the thing interchanged; place where merchants, &c., of a city meet to transact business; a method of finding the equivalent to a given sum in the money of another country.
Exchangeability, eks-chānj'a-bil"i-ti, *n.* Quality of being exchangeable.
Exchangeable, eks-chānj'a-bl, *a.* Capable, fit, or proper to be exchanged.
Exchanger, eks-chānj-ėr, *n.* One who exchanges; one who practises exchange.
Exchequer, eks-chek'ėr, *n.* An ancient English court for the care of the royal revenues, now a division of the High Court of Justice; a state treasury; pecuniary property.
Excisable, ek-sīz'a-bl, *a.* Liable or subject to excise.
Excise, ek-sīz', *n.* A tax on certain commodities of home production and consumption, as beer, &c.; also for licenses to deal in certain commodities.—*vt.* (excising, excised). To impose a duty on articles produced and consumed at home; to cut out.
Exciseman, ek-sīz'man, *n.* One who collects excise duties, or prevents the evasion of them.
Excision, ek-si'zhon, *n.* A cutting out or off; amputation; extirpation.
Excitability, ek-sīt'a-bil"i-ti, *n.* The state or quality of being excitable.
Excitable, ek-sīt'a-bl, *a.* Capable of being excited; prone to excitement.
Excite, ek-sīt', *vt.* (exciting, excited). To call into action; to rouse; to stimulate.
Excitement, ek-sīt'ment, *n.* Act of exciting; stimulation; agitation.
Exciting, ek-sīt'ing, *p.a.* Producing excitement; deeply interesting; thrilling.
Exclaim, eks-klām', *vi.* To call out; to shout.—*vt.* To declare with loud vociferation.
Exclamation, eks-klam-ā'shon, *n.* A loud outcry; a passionate sentence; a note by which emphatical utterance is marked, thus, !; an interjection.
Exclamatory, eks-klam'a-to-ri, *a.* Containing or expressing exclamation.
Exclude, eks-klūd', *vt.* (excluding, excluded). To shut out; to thrust out; to debar; to prohibit; to except.
Exclusion, eks-klū'zhon, *n.* Act of excluding; state of being excluded; prohibition; ejection.
Exclusionist, eks-klū'zhon-ist, *n.* One who would preclude another from a privilege.
Exclusive, eks-klū'siv, *a.* Excluding; not including; debarring from fellowship; illiberal.
Excogitate, eks-ko'jit-āt, *vt.* To invent or devise by thinking; to think out.
Excommunicate, eks-kom-mū'ni-kāt, *vt.* To eject from the communion of the church; to expel from fellowship.
Excommunication, eks-kom-mū'ni-kā"shon, *n.* Expulsion from the communion of a church.
Excoriate, eks-kō'ri-āt, *vt.* To break or wear off the cuticle of.
Excorticate, eks-kor'ti-kāt, *vt.* To strip of the bark or rind.
Excrement, eks'krē-ment, *n.* That which is separated from the nutriment by digestion, and discharged from the body; ordure; dung.
Excremental, Excrementitial, Excrementitious, eks-krē-men'tal, eks'krē-men-tish"al, eks'krē-men-tish"us, *a.* Pertaining to or consisting of excrement.
Excrescence, eks-kres'ens, *n.* Anything which grows out of something else and is useless or disfiguring; a troublesome superfluity.
Excrescent, eks-kres'ent, *a.* Growing out of something else abnormally; superfluous.
Excrete, eks-krēt', *vt.* (excreting, excreted). To separate and discharge from the body by vital action.
Excretion, eks-krē'shon, *n.* Act or process of excreting; that which is excreted.
Excretive, eks-krēt'iv, *a.* Having the power of excreting; excretory.
Excretory, eks'krē-to-ri, *a.* Having the quality of throwing off excrementitious matter by the glands.—*n.* A duct or vessel to receive secreted fluids, and to excrete them.
Excruciate, eks-krö'shi-āt, *vt.* To torture; to rack.
Excruciating, eks-krö'shi-āt-ing, *p.a.* Extremely painful; agonizing; distressing.
Excruciation, eks-krö'shi-ā"shon, *n.* Act of excruciating; agony; torture.
Exculpate, eks-kul'pāt, *vt.* To clear from a charge of fault or guilt; to absolve.
Exculpation, eks-kul-pā'shon, *n.* Act of exculpating; excuse.
Exculpatory, eks-kul'pa-to-ri, *a.* Serving to exculpate; clearing from blame.
Excursion, eks-kėr'shon, *n.* A journey for pleasure or health; a ramble; a trip.
Excursionist, eks-kėr'shon-ist, *n.* One who joins in an excursion for pleasure.
Excursive, eks-kėr'siv, *a.* Rambling; wandering; deviating.
Excursus, eks-kėr'sus, *n.*; pl. **-suses.** A dissertation appended to a book; digression.
Excusable, eks-kūz'a-bl, *a.* Admitting of excuse or justification; pardonable.
Excuse, eks-kūz', *vt.* (excusing, excused). To acquit of guilt; to pardon; to free from a duty.—*n.* eks-kūs'. A plea in extenuation of a fault; apology; that which excuses.
Excuser, eks-kūz'ėr, *n.* One who offers excuses, or pleads for another.
Execrable, ek'sē-kra-bl, *a.* Deserving to be execrated or cursed; hateful; detestable.
Execrate, ek'sē-krāt, *vt.* (execrating, execrated). To curse; to abominate.
Execration, ek-sē-krā'shon, *n.* Act of execrating; a curse; imprecation.
Executant, eks-ek'ū-tant, *n.* A performer.
Execute, ek'sē-kūt, *vt.* (executing, executed). To effect; to achieve; to inflict capital punishment on; to make valid, as by signing and sealing; to perform.—*vi.* To perform.
Execution, ek-sē-kū'shon, *n.* Act of executing; act of signing and sealing a legal instrument; capital punishment; mode of performing a work of art; facility of voice or finger in music.
Executioner, ek-sē-kū'shon-ėr, *n.* One who puts to death by law.

Executive, egz-ek'ūt-iv, *a.* That executes; carrying laws into effect, or superintending their enforcement.—*n.* The person or persons who administer the government.
Executor, egs-ek'ūt-ėr, *n.* One who executes or performs; the person appointed by a testator to execute his will.
Executorship, egz-ek'ūt-ėr-ship, *n.* The office of an executor.
Executory, egz-ek'ū-to-ri, *a.* That executes; performing official duties.
Executrix, egz-ek'ū-triks, *n.* A female executor.
Exegesis, eks-ē-jē'sis, *n.* An exposition; the science or art of literary interpretation, particularly of the Bible.
Exegetic, Exegetical, eks-ē-jet'ik, eks-ē-jet'ik-al, *a.* Explanatory; expository.
Exegetics, eks-ē-jet'iks, *n.pl.* A branch of theology dealing with scriptural interpretation.
Exemplar, egz-em'plėr, *n.* A pattern; copy.
Exemplarily, egz'em-pla-ri-li, *adv.* In an exemplary manner.
Exemplary, egz'em-pla-ri, *a.* Serving as a pattern; worthy of imitation; explanatory.
Exemplification, egz-em'pli-fi-kā''shon, *n.* A showing by example; instance.
Exemplify, egz-em'pli-fī, *vt.* (exemplifying, exemplified). To show by example; to serve as an instance of.
Exempt, egz-emt', *vt.* To free from; to privilege; to grant immunity from.—*a.* Free by privilege; not liable.
Exemption, egz-em'shon, *n.* Act of exempting; state of being exempt; immunity.
Exequatur, ek-sē-kwā'tėr, *n.* A warrant.
Exequies, eks'ē-kwiz, *n.pl.* Funeral rites.
Exercise, eks'ėr-sīz, *n.* Practice; use; drill; act of divine worship; application; a lesson or example for practice.—*vt.* (exercising, exercised). To employ; to practise; to train; to give anxiety to; to afflict.—*vi.* To take exercise.
Exert, egz-ėrt', *vt.* To put forth, as strength; to put in action; (*refl.*) to use efforts; to strive.
Exertion, egz-ėr'shon, *n.* Act of exerting.
Exfoliate, eks-fō'li-āt, *vt.* and *i.* To scale off.
Exhalation, egz-hāl-ā'shon, *n.* Act of exhaling; that which is exhaled; vapour; effluvia.
Exhale, egz-hāl', *vt.* (exhaling, exhaled). To breathe out; to cause to be emitted in vapour or minute particles; to evaporate.—*vi.* To fly off as vapour.
Exhaust, egz-ąst', *vt.* To drain of contents; to expend entirely; to treat thoroughly; to tire.
Exhausted, egz-ąst'ed, *p.a.* Wholly expended; fatigued.
Exhaustible, egz-ąst'i-bl, *a.* That may be exhausted.
Exhausting, egz-ąst'ing, *p.a.* Tending to exhaust.
Exhaustion, egz-ąst'shon, *n.* Act of exhausting; state of being exhausted.
Exhaustive, egz-ąst'iv, *a.* Causing exhaustion; thorough.
Exhaustless, egz-ąst'les, *a.* Inexhaustible.
Exhibit, egz-ib'it, *vt.* To show; to display; to administer by way of remedy.—*n.* Anything exhibited.
Exhibiter, Exhibitor, egz-ib'it-ėr, *n.* One who exhibits.
Exhibition, eks-i-bi'shon, *n.* Act of exhibiting; display; any public show; a benefaction for students in English universities.
Exhibitioner, eks-i-bi'shon-ėr, *n.* One maintained at an English university by an exhibition.
Exhibitory, egz-ib'i-to-ri, *a.* Exhibiting; showing; displaying.
Exhilarate, egz-il'a-rāt, *vt.* (exhilarating, exhilarated). To make cheerful; to inspirit.
Exhilaration, egz-il'a-rā''shon, *n.* Act of exhilarating; cheerfulness; gaiety.
Exhort, egz-hort', *vt.* To urge to a good deed; to encourage; to warn.
Exhortation, egz-hor-tā'shon, *n.* Act of exhorting; a persuasive discourse.
Exhortatory, egz-hor'ta-to-ri, *a.* Tending to exhort; serving for exhortation.
Exhorter, egz-hort'ėr, *n.* One who exhorts.
Exhumation, eks-hūm-ā'shon, *n.* Act of exhuming; disinterring of a corpse.
Exhume, eks'hūm, *vt.* (exhuming, exhumed). To unbury; to disinter.
Exigence, Exigency, eks'i-jens, eks'i-jen-si, *n.* Pressing necessity; urgency.
Exigent, eks'i-jent, *a.* Urgent; pressing.
Exigible, eks'i-ji-bl, *a.* That may be exacted.
Exiguous, ek-sig'ū-us, *a.* Slender.
Exile, eks'īl or egz'īl, *n.* State of being expelled from one's native country; banishment; the person banished.—*vt.* (exiling, exiled). To banish from one's country.
Exist, egz-ist', *vi.* To be; to live; to endure.
Existence, egz-ist'ens, *n.* State of being; life; continuation; anything that exists.
Existent, egz-ist'ent, *a.* Being; existing.
Exit, eks'it, *n.* A going out; the departure of a player from the stage; death; a way out.
Exodus, eks'ō-dus, *n.* Way out; departure; the second book of the Old Testament.
Exogen, eks'o-jen, *n.* A plant whose stem grows by additions to the outside of the wood.
Exogenous, eks-oj'en-us, *a.* Pertaining to the exogens or their mode of growth.
Exonerate, egz-on'ė-rāt, *vt.* To exculpate; to acquit; to justify.
Exonerative, egz-on'ė-rāt-iv, *a.* That exonerates; freeing from an obligation.
Exorable, eks'ōr-a-bl, *a.* That can be persuaded; placable.
Exorbitance, Exorbitancy, egz-or'bit-ans, egz-or'bit-an-si, *n.* A going beyond fair or usual limits; enormity; extravagance.
Exorbitant, egz-or'bit-ant, *a.* Excessive; extravagant.
Exorbitantly, egz-or'bit-ant-li, *adv.* Enormously; excessively.
Exorcise, eks'or-sīz, *vi.* (exorcising, exorcised). To purify from evil spirits by adjurations.
Exorcism, eks'or-sism, *n.* The act or ceremony of exorcising.
Exorcist, eks'or-sist, *n.* One who exorcises.
Exordium, egz-or'di-um, *n.* The introductory part of a discourse.
Exoskeleton, ek'sō-skel-e-ton, *n.* The external skeleton, as the shell of a crustacean; the dermoskeleton.
Exosmose, ek'sos-mōs, *n.* The passage of gases or liquids through membrane or porous media, from within outward.
Exoteric, Exoterical, eks-ō-te'rik, eks-ō-te'rik-al, *a.* Suitable to be imparted to the public; public: opposed to *esoteric* or secret.

Exotic, egz-ot'ik, *a.* Introduced from a foreign country; not native.—*n.* Anything introduced from a foreign country.
Expand, ek-spand', *vt.* and *i.* To spread out; to enlarge; to distend; to dilate.
Expanse, ek-spans', *n.* A surface widely extended; a wide extent of space or body.
Expansibility, ek-spans'i-bil"i-ti, *n.* The capacity of being expanded.
Expansible, ek-spans'i-bl, *a.* Capable of being expanded.
Expansile, ek-spans'īl, *a.* Expansible; producing expansion.
Expansion, ek-span'shon, *n.* Act of expanding; state of being expanded; dilatation; distension; enlargement.
Expansive, ek-spans'iv, *a.* Having the power to expand; widely extended or extending.
Ex-parte, eks-pär'te, *a.* One-sided; partial.
Expatiate, ek-spā'shi-āt, *vi.* (expatiating, expatiated). To move at large; to enlarge in discourse or writing.
Expatriate, eks-pā'tri-āt, *vt.* (expatriating, expatriated). To exile.
Expatriation, eks-pā'tri-ā"shon, *n.* Exile; the forsaking of one's own country.
Expect, ek-spekt', *vt.* To wait for; to look for to happen; to anticipate.
Expectance, Expectancy, ek-spekt'ans, ek-spekt'an-si, *n.* Act or state of expecting; expectation; hope.
Expectant, ek-spekt'ant, *a.* Expecting; awaiting.—*n.* One who expects; one who waits in expectation.
Expectation, ek-spekt-ā'shon, *n.* Act or state of expecting; prospect of good to come; prospect of reaching a certain age.
Expectorant, eks-pek'tō-rant, *a.* Having the quality of promoting discharges from the lungs.—*n.* A medicine which promotes expectoration.
Expectorate, eks-pek'tō-rāt, *vt.* (expectorating, expectorated). To expel, as phlegm, by coughing; to spit out.
Expectoration, eks-pek'tō-rā"shon, *n.* Act of expectorating; matter expectorated.
Expedience, Expediency, eks-pē'di-ens, eks-pē'di-en-si, *n.* Quality of being expedient; propriety; advisability.
Expedient, eks-pē'di-ent, *a.* Tending to promote the object proposed; proper under the circumstances; advantageous.—*n.* Means to an end; shift; plan.
Expediently, eks-pē'di-ent-li, *adv.* Fitly; suitably.
Expedite, eks'pē-dīt, *vt.* (expediting, expedited). To free from hindrance; to accelerate; to hasten by making easier.
Expedition, eks-pē-di'shon, *n.* State of being unimpeded; despatch; a march or voyage for hostile purposes; journey by a body of men for some valuable end; such body of men.
Expeditionary, eks-pē-di'shon-a-ri, *n.* Consisting in or forming an expedition.
Expeditious, eks-pē-di'shus, *a.* Speedy; prompt; nimble; active.
Expel, eks-pel', *vt.* (expelling, expelled). To drive out; to eject; to banish.
Expend, ek-spend', *vt.* To spend; to use or consume; to waste.
Expenditure, ek-spend'i-tūr, *n.* Act of expending; a laying out, as of money; money expended; expense.
Expense, ek-spens', *n.* That which is expended; cost; charge; price.
Expensive, ek-spens'iv, *a.* Requiring much expense; dear; lavish.
Expensively, ek-spens'iv-li, *adv.* In an expensive manner; at great cost or charge.
Experience, eks-pē'ri-ens, *n.* Personal trial; continued observation; knowledge gained by trial or observation; trial and knowledge from suffering or enjoyment; suffering itself.—*vt.* (experiencing, experienced). To try; to know by trial; to have happen; to undergo.
Experienced, eks-pē'ri-enst, *p.a.* Taught by experience; skilful by use or observation.
Experiment, eks-pe'ri-ment, *n.* A trial; an operation designed to discover something unknown, or to establish it when discovered.—*vi.* To make trial or experiment.
Experimental, eks-pe'ri-men"tal, *a.* Pertaining to, known by, or derived from experiment; having personal experience.
Experimentalist, eks-pe'ri-men"tal-ist, *n.* One who makes experiments.
Experimentally, eks-pe'ri-men"tal-li, *adv.* In an experimental way; by trial.
Experimenter, eks-pe'ri-men-tėr, *n.* One who makes experiments.
Expert, eks-pėrt', *a.* Skilful; dexterous; adroit.—*n.* eks'pėrt. An expert person; a scientific witness.
Expertly, eks-pėrt'li, *adv.* In a skilful or dexterous manner; adroitly.
Expiable, eks'pi-a-bl, *a.* That may be expiated or atoned for.
Expiate, eks'pi-āt, *vt.* (expiating, expiated). To atone for; to make reparation for.
Expiation, eks-pi-ā'shon, *n.* Act of expiating; atonement; reparation.
Expiator, eks'pi-āt-ėr, *n.* One who expiates.
Expiatory, eks'pi-a-to-ri, *a.* Able to make atonement.
Expiration, eks-pīr-ā'shon, *n.* Act of breathing out; death; end; expiry.
Expiratory, eks-pīr'a-to-ri, *a.* Pertaining to the expiration of breath.
Expire, eks-pīr', *vt.* (expiring, expired). To breathe out; to exhale.—*vi.* To emit the last breath; to die; to terminate.
Expiry, eks'pi-ri, *n.* Termination.
Explain, eks-plān', *vt.* To make plain or intelligible; to expound; to elucidate.—*vi.* To give explanations.
Explanation, eks-plan-ā'shon, *n.* Act of explaining; interpretation; clearing up of matters between parties at variance.
Explanatory, eks-plan'a-to-ri, *a.* Serving to explain.
Expletive, eks'plēt-iv, *a.* Serving to fill out; superfluous.—*n.* A word or syllable inserted to fill a vacancy or for ornament; an oath or interjection.
Expletory, eks'ple-to-ri, *a.* Expletive.
Explicable, eks'pli-ka bl, *a.* Capable of being explained.
Explicate, eks'pli-kāt, *vt.* To unfold the meaning of; to explain.
Explication, eks-pli-kā'shon, *n.* Explanation.
Explicit, eks-plis'it, *a.* Plain in language; express, not merely implied; open.
Explicitly eks-plis'it-li, *adv.* In an explicit manner; plainly; expressly.
Explode, eks-plōd', *vt.* (exploding, exploded). To drive out of use or belief; to cause to burst

with violence and noise.—*vi.* To burst with noise; to burst into activity or passion.
Exploit, eks-ploit', *n.* A deed; a heroic act; a deed of renown.—*vt.* To make use of; to work.
Exploitation, eks-ploi-tā'shon, *n.* Successful application of industry on any object, as land, mines, &c.
Exploration, eks-plōr-ā'shon, *n.* Act of exploring; strict or careful examination.
Explore, eks-plōr', *vt.* (exploring, explored). To travel with the view of making discovery; to search; to examine closely.
Explorer, eks-plōr'ėr, *n.* One who explores; a traveller in unknown regions.
Explosion, eks-plō'zhon, *n.* Act of exploding; a bursting with noise; a violent outburst of feeling.
Explosive, eks-plō'siv, *a.* Causing explosion; readily exploding.—*n.* Anything liable to explode, as gunpowder; a mute or non-continuous consonant, as *k*, *t*, *b*.
Exponent, eks-pō'nent, *n.* One who explains or illustrates; that which indicates; the index of a power in algebra.
Export, eks-pōrt', *vt.* To convey, in traffic, to another country.—*n.* eks'pōrt. Act of exporting; quantity of goods exported; a commodity exported.
Exportable, eks-pōrt'a-bl, *a.* That may be exported.
Exportation, eks-pōrt-ā'shon, *n.* Act of conveying goods to another country.
Exporter, eks-pōrt'ėr, *n.* One who exports.
Expose, eks-pōz', *vt.* (exposing, exposed). To put or set out; to disclose; to lay open to attack, censure, &c.; to make liable; to exhibit.
Exposé, eks-po-zā, *n.* Exposure; statement.
Exposed, eks-pōzd', *p.a.* In danger; liable; unsheltered.
Exposition, eks-pō-zi'shon, *n.* Act of exposing; explanation; exhibition.
Expositor, eks-poz'it-ėr, *n.* One who expounds; an interpreter.
Expository, eks-poz'i-to-ri, *a.* Containing exposition; explanatory.
Ex-post-facto, eks-pōst-fak'tō, *a.* After the deed is done; retrospective.
Expostulate, eks-pos'tū-lāt, *vi.* To remonstrate; to reason earnestly with a person on some impropriety.
Expostulation, eks-pos'tū-lā''shon, *n.* Act of expostulating; remonstrance.
Expostulatory, eks-pos'tū-la-to-ri, *a.* Containing expostulation.
Exposure, eks pō'zhūr, *n.* Act of exposing; state of being exposed; situation.
Expound, eks-pound', *vt.* To explain; to interpret; to unfold.
Expounder, eks-pound'ėr, *n.* One who expounds; an explainer; an interpreter.
Express, eks-pres', *vt.* To press out; to set forth in words; to declare; to make known by any means; (*refl.*) to say what one has got to say.—*a.* Clearly exhibited; given in direct terms; intended or sent for a particular purpose; travelling with special speed.—*n.* A messenger or vehicle sent on a particular occasion; a message specially sent; a specially fast railway train.—*adv.* For a particular purpose; with special haste.
Expressible, eks-pres'i-bl, *a.* That may be expressed.
Expression, eks-pre'shon, *n.* Act of expressing; a phrase or mode of speech; manner of utterance; a natural and lively representation in painting and sculpture; musical tone, grace, or modulation; play of features; representation of a quantity in algebra.
Expressionless, eks-pre'shon-les, *a.* Destitute of expression.
Expressive, eks-près'iv, *a.* Serving to express; representing with force; emphatical.
Expressively, eks-pres'iv-li, *adv.* In an expressive manner; with expression.
Expressly, eks-pres'li, *adv.* In direct terms; of set purpose.
Expropriate, eks-prō'pri-āt, *vt.* To take for public use; to dispossess.
Expropriation, eks-prō'pri-ā''shon, *n.* Act of dispossessing of proprietary rights.
Expulsion, eks-pul'shon, *n.* A driving away by violence; state of being driven away.
Expulsive, eks-puls'iv, *a.* Having the power of expelling; serving to expel.
Expunge, ek spunj', *vt.* (expunging, expunged). To blot out, as with a pen; to erase; to obliterate.
Expurgate, eks-pėr'gāt or eks'pėr-gāt, *vt.* (expurgating, expurgated). To render pure; to strike offensive passages out of (a book).
Expurgation, eks-pėr-gā'shon, *n.* Act of purging or cleansing; purification.
Expurgatory, eks-pėr'ga-to-ri, *a.* Serving to expurgate.
Exquisite, eks'kwi-zit, *a.* Select; highly finished; excellent; extreme; matchless, as pain or pleasure keenly felt.—*n.* A fop; a dandy.
Exscind, ek-sind', *vt.* To cut out or off.
Exsiccate, ek-sik'kāt, *vt.* To dry up completely.
Extant, eks'tant, *a.* Still existing; in being.
Extemporaneous, eks-tem'pō-rā''nē-us, *a.* Arising out of the time or occasion; on the spur of the moment; unpremeditated.
Extemporary, eks-tem'pō-ra-ri, *a.* Arising out of the time or occasion; extemporaneous.
Extempore, eks-tem'po-rē, *adv.* and *a.* Without study or preparation; extemporary.
Extemporize, eks-tem'pō-rīz, *vi.* To speak without preparation.—*vt.* To make without forethought; to prepare in haste.
Extend, eks-tend', *vt.* To stretch out; to spread; to prolong; to bestow on.—*vi.* To stretch; to reach; to become larger.
Extensibility, eks-tens'i-bil''i-ti, *n.* The capacity of suffering extension.
Extensible, eks-tens'i-bl, *a.* That may be extended; susceptible of enlargement.
Extensile, eks-tens'īl, *a.* Extensible.
Extension, eks-ten'shon, *n.* Act of extending; state of being extended; that property of a body by which it occupies a portion of space; enlargement; in *logic*, the objects to which a term may be applied.
Extensive, eks-ten'siv, *a.* Having great extent; large; comprehensive.
Extensor, eks-ten'sėr, *n.* A muscle which serves to extend or straighten.
Extent, eks-tent', *n.* Space or degree to which a thing is extended; compass; size.
Extenuate, eks-ten'ū-āt, *vt.* To lessen; to weaken the force of; to palliate.
Extenuation, eks-ten'ū-ā''shon, *n.* Act of extenuating; palliation; mitigation.
Exterior, eks-tē'ri-ėr, *a.* External; on the

outside; foreign.—*n*. The outward surface; that which is external.
Exterminate, eks-tėr'min-āt, *vt*. To destroy utterly; to extirpate; to root out.
Extermination, eks-tėr'min-ā"shon, *n*. Act of exterminating; eradication; extirpation.
Exterminative, eks-tėr'min-āt-iv, *a*. That exterminates or destroys.
Extern, eks-tėrn', *a*. External. [Poetic.]
External, eks-tėr'nal, *a*. On the outside; exterior; not being within, as causes or effects visible; foreign.
Externals, eks-tėr'nalz, *n.pl*. Outward parts; exterior form; outward ceremonies.
Exterritorial, eks-ter'i-tō"ri-al, *a*. Beyond the jurisdiction of the country in which one resides.
Extinct, ek-stingkt', *a*. Extinguished; abolished; having died out.
Extinction, ek-stingk'shon, *n*. Act of extinguishing; state of being extinguished; destruction; extermination.
Extinguish, ek-sting'gwish, *vt*. To put out; to quench; to destroy; to eclipse.
Extinguishable, ek-sting'gwish-a-bl, *a*. That may be quenched or destroyed.
Extinguisher, ek-sting'gwish-ėr, *n*. One who or that which extinguishes; a hollow, conical utensil to extinguish a candle.
Extinguishment, ek-sting'gwish-ment, *n*. Act of extinguishing; extinction.
Extirpate, eks-tėrp'āt or eks'terp-āt, *vt*. To root out; to eradicate; to destroy totally.
Extirpation, eks-tėrp-ā'shon, *n*. Act of rooting out; eradication; total destruction.
Extirpator, eks-tėrp'āt-ėr or eks'terp-āt-ėr, *n*. One who extirpates.
Extol, eks-tol', *vt*. (extolling, extolled). To exalt in eulogy; to magnify; to glorify.
Extort, eks-tort', *vt*. To exact by force; to wrest or wring.
Extortion, eks-tor'shon, *n*. Act of extorting; illegal or oppressive exaction.
Extortionate, eks-tor'shon-āt, *a*. Excessive in amount; oppressive in exacting money.
Extortioner, Extortionist, eks-tor'shon-ėr, eks-tor'shon-ist, *n*. One who practises extortion.
Extra, eks'tra, *a*. and *adv*. Additional; beyond what is usual, due, &c.—*n*. Something in addition.
Extract, eks-trakt', *vt*. To draw out or forth; to select; to draw or copy out; to find the root of a number.—*n*. eks'trakt. That which is extracted; a quotation; an essence, tincture, &c.
Extraction, eks-trak'shon, *n*. Act of extracting; lineage; operation of drawing essences, tinctures, &c.; operation of finding the roots of numbers.
Extractive, eks-trakt'iv, *a*. Capable of being extracted; serving to extract.—*n*. A base supposed to exist in all vegetable extracts.
Extractor, eks-trakt'ėr, *n*. One who extracts; an instrument for extracting teeth, &c.
Extradite, eks'tra-dīt, *vt*. To deliver up (a criminal) to the authorities of the country from which he has come.
Extradition, eks-tra-di'shon, *n*. The delivery, under a treaty, of a fugitive from justice by one government to another.
Extrados, eks-trā'dos, *n*. The exterior curve of an arch.
Extrajudicial, eks'tra-jū-di"shal, *a*. Out of the ordinary course of legal procedure; out of the proper court.
Extramundane, eks-tra-mun'dān, *a*. Beyond the limit of the material world.
Extramural, eks-tra-mūr'al, *a*. Outside the walls, as of a fortified city or university.
Extraneous, eks-trā'nē-us, *a*. That is without; foreign; not intrinsic; irrelevant.
Extraordinarily, eks-tra-or'din-a-ri-li, *adv*. In an extraordinary manner; unusually.
Extraordinary, eks-tra-or'din-a-ri, *a*. Beyond that which is ordinary; unusual; remarkable; special.
Extravagance, Extravagancy, eks-trav'a-gans, eks-trav'a-gan-si, *n*. A going beyond due bounds; excess; wastefulness.
Extravagant, eks-trav'a-gant, *a*. Exceeding due bounds; fantastic; wasteful; lavish.
Extravagantly, eks-trav'a-gant-li, *adv*. Unreasonably; excessively; wastefully.
Extravaganza, eks-trav'a-gan"za, *n*. A wild literary or musical composition.
Extravasate, eks-trav'a-sāt, *vt*. To force or let out of the proper vessels, as the blood.
Extreme, eks-trēm', *a*. Outermost; furthest; most violent; last; worst or best; most pressing.—*n*. The utmost point or verge of a thing; end; furthest or highest degree; (*pl*.) points at the greatest distance from each other.
Extremely, eks-trēm'li, *adv*. In the utmost degree; to the utmost point.
Extremist, eks-trēm'ist, *n*. A supporter of extreme doctrines or practice.
Extremity, eks-trem'i-ti, *n*. That which is extreme; utmost point, part, or degree; utmost distress or violence.
Extricable, eks'tri-ka-bl, *a*. That can be extricated.
Extricate, eks'tri-kāt, *vt*. (extricating, extricated). To disentangle; to set free.
Extrication, eks-tri-kā'shon, *n*. Act of extricating.
Extrinsic, Extrinsical, eks-trin'sik, eks-trin'sik-al, *a*. Being on the outside; extraneous; accessory.
Extrude, eks-tröd', *vt*. (extruding, extruded). To thrust out; to expel.
Extrusion, eks-trö'zhon, *n*. Act of extruding; a driving out; expulsion.
Exuberance, Exuberancy, eks-ū'bė-rans, eks-ū'bė-ran-si, *n*. Superabundance; overflowing fullness; rankness; luxuriance.
Exuberant, eks-ū'bė-rant, *a*. Superabundant; overflowing; luxuriant.
Exudation, eks-ūd-ā'shon, *n*. Act or process of exuding; something exuded.
Exude, eks-ūd', *vt*. (exuding, exuded). To discharge through the pores; to let ooze out.—*vi*. To flow through pores; to ooze out like sweat.
Exulcerate, eg-zul'sėr-āt, *vt*. To produce an ulcer on; to exasperate.
Exult, egz-ult', *vi*. To rejoice exceedingly; to triumph.
Exultant, egz-ult'ant, *a*. Rejoicing triumphantly.
Exultation, egz-ult-ā'shon, *n*. Lively joy; triumph; rapture; ecstasy.
Exuviæ, egz-ū'vi-ē, *n.pl*. Any parts of animals which are shed or cast off, as the skins of serpents, &c.
Exuviate, egz-ū'vi-āt, *vi*. To cast or throw off exuviæ.

Eyalet, ī'a-let, *n.* A Turkish province administered by a vizier or pacha.
Eyas, ī'as, *n.* A nestling; a young hawk still unable to prey for itself.
Eye, ī, *n.* The organ of vision; sight or view; power of perception; something resembling an eye in form; a small hole; a loop or ring for fastening.—*vt.* (eyeing, eyed). To fix the eye on; to observe or watch narrowly.
Eyeball, ī'bąl, *n.* The ball of the eye.
Eyebrow, ī'brou, *n.* The brow or hairy arch about the eye.
Eyed, īd, *a.* Having eyes.
Eye-glass, ī'glas, *n.* A glass to assist the sight.
Eyelash, ī'lash, *n.* The line of hair that edges the eyelid.
Eyeless, ī'les, *a.* Wanting eyes; blind.
Eyelet, Eyelet-hole, ī'let, ī'let-hōl, *n.* A small eye or hole to receive a lace.
Eyelid, ī'lid, *n.* The cover of the eye; the movable skin with which an animal covers or uncovers the eyeball.
Eye-service, ī'sėr-vis, *n.* Service performed only under the eye of an employer.
Eyeshot, ī'shot, *n.* Range of vision; view.
Eyesight, ī'sīt, *n.* The sight of the eye; view; observation; the sense of seeing.
Eyesore, ī'sōr, *h.* Something ugly to look at.
Eye-tooth, ī'töth, *n.* A tooth under the eye; a canine tooth; a fang.
Eye-witness, ī'wit-nes, *n.* One who sees a thing done.
Eyot, īot, *n.* A small river islet.
Eyre, ār, *n.* A circuit of a court of justice; a court of itinerant justices.
Eyrie, Eyry, ī'ri, *n.* An aerie; nest of a bird of prey.

F

Fabaceous, fā-ba'shus, *a.* Having the nature of the bean.
Fabian, fā'bi-an, *a.* Delaying; lingering.
Fable, fā'bl, *n.* A fictitious narrative to instruct or amuse, often to enforce a precept; falsehood; an idle story; the plot in a poem or drama.—*vi.* (fabling, fabled). To tell fables or falsehoods.—*vt.* To feign; to invent.
Fabled, fā'bld, *p.a.* Told in fables.
Fabliau, fab-lē-ō, *n.*; pl. **-iaux.** A kind of metrical tale common in early French literature.
Fabric, fab'rik, *n.* Frame or structure of anything; a building; texture; cloth.
Fabricate, fab'rik-āt, *vt.* (fabricating, fabricated). To make or fashion; to form by art or labour; to devise falsely.
Fabrication, fab-rik-ā'shon, *n.* Act of fabricating; that which is fabricated; fiction.
Fabricator, fab'rik-āt-ėr, *n.* One who fabricates.
Fabulist, fa'bū-list, *n.* An inventor or writer of fables.
Fabulous, fa'bū-lus, *a.* Containing or abounding in fable; feigned; mythical; incredible.
Façade, Facade, fa-säd', fa-säd', *n.* Front view or elevation of an edifice.
Face, fās, *n.* The front part of an animal's head, particularly of the human head; the visage; front; effrontery; assurance; dial of a watch, &c.—*vt.* (facing, faced). To meet in front; to stand opposite to; to oppose with firmness; to finish or protect with a thin external covering; to dress the face of (a stone, &c.).—*vi.* To turn the face; to look.
Facet, Facette, fas'et, fa-set', *n.* A small flat portion of a surface.
Facetiæ, fa-sē'shi-ē, *n.pl.* Jests; witticisms.
Facetious, fa-sē'shus, *a.* Witty; humorous; jocose; sprightly.
Facial, fā'shi-al, *a.* Pertaining to the face.
Facile, fa'sil, *a.* Easy; easily persuaded; yielding; dexterous.
Facilitate, fa-sil'it-āt, *vt.* To make easy; to lessen the labour of.
Facility, fa-sil'i-ti, *n.* Easiness to be performed; dexterity; readiness of compliance; *pl.* means to render easy; convenient advantages.
Facing, fās'ing, *n.* A covering in front for ornament or defence; a mode of adulterating tea; the movement of soldiers in turning round to the left, right, &c.; *pl.* trimmings on regimental garments.
Facsimile, fak-sim'i-lē, *n.* An exact copy or likeness.
Fact, fakt, *n.* Anything done; a deed; event; circumstance; reality; truth.
Faction, fak'shon, *n.* A party in political society in opposition to the ruling power; a party unscrupulously promoting its private ends; discord; dissension.
Factionary, fak'shon-a-ri, *n.* A party man; one of a faction.
Factionist, fak'shon-ist, *n.* One who takes part in or promotes faction.
Factious, fak'shus, *a.* Given to faction; prone to clamour against public measures or men; pertaining to faction.
Factitious, fak-ti'shus, *a.* Made by art; artificial.
Factitive, fak'ti-tiv, *a.* Causative: applied to verbs expressing an action that produces a new condition in the object.
Factor, fak'tėr, *n.* An agent, particularly a mercantile agent; in Scotland, one appointed to manage an estate; one of two or more numbers or quantities, which, when multiplied together, form a product; one of several elements which contribute to a result.
Factorage, fak'tėr-āj, *n.* Agency of a factor; commission paid to a factor.
Factorship, fak'tėr-ship, *n.* The business of a factor.
Factory, fak'to-ri, *n.* An establishment where factors in foreign countries reside to transact business for their employers; buildings appropriated to the manufacture of goods; a manufactory.
Factotum, fak-tō'tum, *n.* A person employed to do all kinds of work; confidential agent.
Faculæ, fak'ū-lē, *n.pl.* Spots sometimes seen on the sun's disc, which appear brighter than the rest of the surface.
Facultative, fak'ul-tāt-iv, *a.* Optional.
Faculty, fak'ul-ti, *n.* Any mental or bodily power; capacity; special power or authority; the body of individuals constituting one of the learned professions; a department of a university, or its professors.
Fad, fad, *n.* A favourite theory; crotchet; hobby.
Faddist, fad'ist, *n.* One who deals in fads.
Fade, fād, *vi.* (fading, faded). To lose colour,

strength, or freshness; to wither; to perish; to become indistinct.—*vt.* To cause to wither.

Fading, fād'ing, *p.a.* Liable to fade; transient.

Fæces, fē'sēz, *n.pl.* Grounds; dregs; excrement.

Fag, fag, *vi.* (fagging, fagged). To become weary; to drudge.—*vt.* To use as a drudge; to tire by labour.—*n.* A laborious drudge; a public schoolboy in England who performs certain tasks for a senior.

Fag-end, fag'end, *n.* The end of a web of cloth; the untwisted end of a rope; the refuse or meaner part of anything.

Faggot, Fagot, fag'ot, *n.* A bundle of sticks or twigs; a bundle of pieces of iron or steel for remanufacture; one hired to take the place of another at the muster of a military company; a shrivelled old woman.—*vt.* To tie up; to collect promiscuously.

Faggot-vote, fag'ot-vōt, *n.* A vote procured by the purchase of property, which is divided among a number so as to constitute a nominal voting qualification for each.

Fahrenheit, fä'ren-hīt, *a.* The name of the thermometer in which the freezing point is 32° and the boiling 212°.

Faience, fä-yängs, *n.* A sort of fine glazed pottery painted in various designs.

Fail, fāl, *vi.* To become deficient; to decline; to become extinct; not to produce the effect; to be unsuccessful; to be guilty of omission or neglect; to become bankrupt.—*vt.* To cease or omit to afford aid, supply, or strength to; to forsake.—*n.* Omission; failure; want.

Failing, fāl'ing, *n.* A natural weakness; foible; fault in character or disposition.

Failure, fāl'ūr, *n.* A failing; cessation of supply or total defect; non-performance; want of success; a becoming bankrupt.

Fain, fān, *a.* Glad; pleased; inclined; content to accept.—*adv.* Gladly.

Faint, fānt, *vi.* To become feeble; to become senseless and motionless; to swoon; to lose spirit; to vanish.—*a.* Enfeebled so as to be inclined to swoon; weak; indistinct; depressed.—*n.* A fainting fit; a swoon.

Faint-hearted, fānt'härt-ed, *a.* Cowardly; timorous; dejected.

Faintly, fānt'li, *adv.* Feebly; languidly; without vigour, vividness, or distinctness.

Fair, fār, *a.* Pleasing to the eye; beautiful; white or light in respect of complexion; not stormy or wet; favourable; reasonable; impartial; honourable; plain; unspotted; moderately good; middling.—*adv.* Openly; frankly; honestly; on good terms.—*n.* A fair woman; *the fair*, the female sex; a stated market.

Fairing, fār'ing, *n.* A present given at a fair.

Fairish, fār'ish, *a.* Moderately fair.

Fairly, fār'li, *adv.* Honestly, justly, equitably, reasonably, tolerably, &c.

Fair-spoken, fār'spōk-en, *a.* Using fair speech; courteous; plausible; bland.

Fairy, fā'ri, *n.* An imaginary being of human form, supposed to play a variety of pranks.—*a.* Belonging to fairies; given by fairies.

Faith, fāth, *n.* Belief; trust; confidence; conviction in regard to religion; system of religious beliefs; strict adherence to duty and promises; word or honour pledged.

Faithful, fāth'fu̧l, *a.* Full of faith; firm in adherence to duty; loyal; trusty; observant of compacts, vows, &c.

Faithfully, fāth'fu̧l-li, *adv.* In a faithful manner; loyally; sincerely.

Faithless, fāth'les, *a.* Destitute of faith; false; not observant of promises; deceptive.

Fake, fāk, *vt.* To lay (a rope) in coils.—*n.* Single coil of a rope.

Fakir, Fakeer, fä-kēr', *n.* An oriental ascetic or begging monk.

Falange, fal-an'gi, *n.* The Spanish fascist party.

Falcate, Falcated, fal'kāt, fal'kāt-ed, *a.* Bent like a sickle or scythe; hooked; curved.

Falchion, fa̧l'shon, *n.* A short, broad, curved sword; a scimitar.

Falcon, fa̧'kn or fa̧l'kon, *n.* The name of various small or medium-sized raptorial birds; a hawk of any kind trained to sport.

Falconer, fa̧'kn-ėr, *n.* A person who breeds and trains hawks, or sports with hawks.

Falconry, fa̧'kn-ri, *n.* The art of training hawks; hawking.

Faldstool, fa̧ld'stöl, *n.* A folding stool; desk at which litany is said.

Fall, fa̧l, *vi.* (pret. fell, pp. fallen). To sink to a lower position; to drop down; to empty or disembogue; to sink into sin, weakness, or disgrace; to come to an end suddenly; to decrease; to assume an expression of dejection, &c.; to happen; to pass or be transferred; to belong or appertain; to be uttered carelessly.—*n.* Descent; tumble; death; ruin; cadence; a cascade or cataract; extent of descent; declivity; autumn; that which falls; a kind of ladies' veil; lapse or declension from innocence or goodness; *naut.* the part of a tackle to which the power is applied in hoisting.

Fallacious, fal-lā'shus, *a.* Deceitful; misleading; sophistical; delusive.

Fallacy, fal'la-si, *n.* Deception; deceitfulness; a misleading or mistaken argument.

Fallibility, fal-i-bil'i-ti, *n.* Quality or state of being fallible.

Fallible, fal'i-bl, *a.* Liable to mistake or be deceived.

Falling-sickness, fa̧l'ing-sik-nes, *n.* Epilepsy.

Fallow, fal'ō, *a.* Pale red or pale yellow; ploughed, but not sowed; uncultivated.—*n.* Land left unsown after being ploughed.—*vt.* To plough and harrow land without seeding it.

Fallow-deer, fal'ō-dēr, *n.* A kind of deer smaller than the stag, and common in England in parks.

False, fa̧ls, *a.* Not true; forged; feigned; fraudulent; treacherous; inconstant; constructed for show or a subsidiary purpose.

False-hearted, fa̧ls'härt-ed, *a.* Deceitful; treacherous; perfidious.

Falsehood, fa̧ls'hōd, *n.* Quality of being false; untruth; fiction; a lie.

Falsely, fa̧ls'li, *adv.* In a false manner.

Falsetto, fa̧l-set'tō, *n.* A false or artificial voice; the tones above the natural compass of the voice.

Falsification, fa̧ls'i-fi-kā"shon, *n.* Act of falsifying; wilful misrepresentation.

Falsifier, fa̧ls'i-fī-ėr, *n.* One who falsifies.

Falsify, fa̧ls'i-fī, *vt.* (falsifying, falsified). To make false; to garble; to prove to be false; to break by falsehood.—*vi.* To violate the truth.

Falsity, fa̧ls'i-ti, *n.* The quality of being false; that which is false; a falsehood.

Falter, fa̧l'tėr, *vi.* To hesitate in speech; to

fail in exertion; to fail in the regular exercise of the understanding.
Faltering, fal'tėr-ing, *p.a.* Hesitating.
Fama, fā'ma, *n.* A widely prevailing rumour affecting the moral character of any one.
Fame, fām, *n.* A public report or rumour; favourable report; celebrity; reputation.
Famed, fāmd, *a.* Renowned; celebrated.
Fameless, fām'les, *a.* Without renown.
Familiar, fa-mil'i-ėr, *a.* Well acquainted; intimate; affable; well known; free; unconstrained.—*n.* An intimate; one long acquainted; a demon supposed to attend at call.
Familiarity, fa-mil'i-a''ri-ti, *n.* State of being familiar; affability; freedom from ceremony; intimacy.
Familiarize, fa-mil'i-ėr-īz, *vt.* To make familiar; to accustom.
Family, fam'i-li, *n.* Household; the parents and children alone; the children as distinguished from the parents; kindred; line of ancestors; honourable descent; a group or class of animals or plants.
Famine, fam'in, *n.* Scarcity of food; dearth.
Famish, fam'ish, *vt.* To kill or exhaust with hunger; to starve; to kill by denial of anything necessary.—*vi.* To die of hunger; to suffer extreme hunger or thirst.
Famous, fām'us, *a.* Much talked of and praised; renowned; distinguished; admirable.
Famously, fām'us-li, *adv.* In a famous manner; capitally.
Fan, fan, *n.* An instrument for winnowing grain; an instrument to agitate the air and cool the face; something by which the air is moved; a wing.—*vt.* (fanning, fanned). To cool and refresh by moving the air with a fan; to winnow; to stimulate.
Fanatic, Fanatical, fa-nat'ik, fa-nat'ik-al, *a.* Wild in opinions, particularly in religious opinions; excessively enthusiastic.—**Fanatic,** fa-nat'ik, *n.* A person affected by excessive enthusiasm, particularly on religious subjects; an enthusiast; a visionary.
Fanatically, fa-nat'ik-al-li, *adv.* With wild enthusiasm.
Fanaticism, fa-nat'i-sizm, *n.* Excessive enthusiasm; religious frenzy.
Fancied, fan'sid, *p.a.* Imagined; fanciful.
Fancier, fan'si-ėr, *n.* One who fancies; one who has a hobby for certain things.
Fanciful, fan'si-ful, *a.* Full of fancy; dictated by fancy; visionary; whimsical.
Fancy, fan'si, *n.* A phase of the intellect of a lighter cast than the imagination; thought due to this faculty; embodiment of such in words; opinion or notion; liking; caprice; false notion.—*vi.* (fancying, fancied). To imagine; to suppose without proof.—*vt.* To imagine; to like; to be pleased with.—*a.* Fine; ornamental; adapted to please the fancy; beyond intrinsic value.
Fancy-free, fan'si-frē, *a.* Free from the power of love.
Fandango, fan-dang'gō, *n.* A lively Spanish dance by two persons, male and female.
Fane, fān, *n.* A temple; a church.
Fanfare, fan'fār, *n.* A flourish of trumpets; an ostentatious boast; a bravado.
Fanfaron, fan'fa-ron, *n.* A braggart; ostentation.
Fanfaronade, fan'fa-ron-ād, *n.* A swaggering; vain boasting; bluster.
Fang, fang, *n.* A long, pointed tooth; the tusk of an animal; the hollow poison tooth of a serpent; a prong; a claw or talon.
Fanged, fangd, *p.a.* Furnished with fangs.
Fan-light, fan'līt, *n.* A window over a door and forming part of the door-opening.
Fanner, fan'ėr, *n.* One who fans; a ventilator; *pl.* a machine for winnowing grain.
Fan-palm, fan'päm, *n.* A palm of the E. Indies with enormous leaves, the taliput-palm.
Fantail, fan'tāl, *n.* A variety of the domestic pigeon.
Fantasia, fan-tä'zē-a, *n.* A species of music ranging amidst various airs and movements.
Fantastic, Fantastical, fan-tas'tik, fan-tas'tik-al, *a.* Pertaining to fantasy or fancy; whimsical; fanciful; odd; grotesque.
Fantasy, fan'ta-si, *n.* Fancy; a vagary of the imagination; a fanciful artistic production.—*vt.* To picture in fancy.
Far, fär, *a.* Remote; distant.—*adv.* To a great extent or distance in space or in time; in great part; very much; to a certain point.
Farad, far'ad, *n.* The unit of quantity in the measurement of electricity.
Farce, färs, *n.* A play full of extravagant drollery; absurdity; mere show.—*vt.* To stuff with forcemeat or mingled ingredients.
Farcical, färs'ik-al, *a.* Belonging to a farce; droll; ludicrous; ridiculous.
Fardel, fär'del, *n.* A bundle or little pack; a burden.
Fare, fār, *vi.* (faring, fared). To go; to travel; to be in any state, good or bad; to be entertained with food; to happen well or ill.—*n.* Sum charged for conveying a person; person conveyed; food; provisions of the table.
Farewell, fār'wel, *interj.* May you fare or prosper well.—*n.* Good-bye; departure; final attention.—*a.* Leave-taking; valedictory.
Far-fetched, fär'fecht, *a.* Brought from afar; not naturally introduced; forced.
Farina, fa-rī'na, *n.* Meal; flour.
Farinaceous, fa-rin-ā'shus, *a.* Made of farina; yielding farina; mealy.
Farm, färm, *n.* A portion of land under cultivation; ground let to a tenant for tillage, pasture, &c.—*vt.* To let out or take on lease, as lands; to cultivate; to lease, as taxes, imposts, &c.—*vi.* To cultivate the soil.
Farmer, färm'ėr, *n.* One who cultivates a farm; one who collects taxes, &c., for a certain rate per cent.
Farming, färm'ing, *a.* Pertaining to agriculture.—*n.* The business of a farmer; agriculture; husbandry; tillage of land.
Farmost, fär'mōst, *a.* Most distant or remote.
Farrago, fa-rā'gō, *n.* A mass composed of various materials; a medley.
Farrier, fa'ri-ėr, *n.* A smith who shoes horses; one who combines horse-shoeing with veterinary surgery.
Farriery, fa'ri-ė-ri, *n.* The art of the farrier; the veterinary art.
Farrow, fa'rō, *n.* A ig; a litter of pigs.—*vt.* or *i.* To bring forth pigs.
Farther, fär'THėr, *a. comp.* More remote.—*adv.* At or to a greater distance; beyond; moreover; in addition.
Farthermore, fär'THėr-mōr, *adv.* Furthermore; moreover; besides.
Farthermost, fär'THėr-mōst, *a. superl.* Being at the greatest distance.

Farthest, fär'ᴛʜest, *a. superl.* Most distant.—*adv.* At or to the greatest distance.
Farthing, fär'ᴛʜing, *n.* The fourth of a penny.
Farthingale, fär'ᴛʜing-gāl, *n.* A hoop-petticoat; circles of hoops used to extend the petticoat.
Fascia, fash'i-a, *n.*; pl. **-iæ.** A band or fillet, or something resembling this in shape.
Fascicle, fas'si-kl, *n.* A small bundle; a collection.
Fascicule, Fasciculus, fas'si-kūl, fas-sik'ū-lus, *n.* A fascicle; one of the separate divisions in which a book is published.
Fascinate, fas'si-nāt, *vt.* (fascinating, fascinated). To bewitch; to charm; to captivate.
Fascinating, fas'si-nāt-ing, *p.a.* Bewitching; enchanting; charming.
Fascination, fas-si-nā'shon, *n.* Act of bewitching; enchantment; charm; spell.
Fascine, fas-sēn', *n.* A faggot or bundle of sticks used in military defence.
Fascist, fash'ist, *n.* A member of an Italian organization formed to oppose Bolshevism, Communism, and Socialism in all their forms.
Fashion, fa'shon, *n.* The make or form of anything; external appearance; form of a garment; prevailing mode; custom; genteel life.—*vt.* To give shape to; to mould; to adapt.
Fashionable, fa'shon-a-bl, *a.* According to the prevailing mode; established by custom; prevailing at a particular time; observant of the fashion; stylish.
Fast, fäst, *a.* Firmly fixed; closely adhering; steadfast; durable; swift; dissipated.—*adv.* Firmly; rapidly; durably; near; with dissipation.—*vi.* To abstain from eating and drinking, or from particular kinds of food.—*n.* Abstinence from food; a religious mortification by abstinence; the time of fasting.
Fasten, fäs'n, *vt.* To fix firmly, closely, or tightly; to hold together; to affix.—*vi.* To become fixed; to seize and hold on.
Fastener, fäs'n-ėr, *n.* One who or that which fastens.
Fastening, fäs'n-ing, *n.* Anything that binds and makes fast.
Fastidious, fas-tid'i-us, *a.* Squeamish; delicate to a fault; difficult to please.
Fastness, fäst'nes, *n.* State of being fast; a stronghold; a fortress or fort.
Fat, fat, *a.* Fleshy; plump; unctuous; heavy; stupid; rich; fertile.—*n.* A solid oily substance found in parts of animal bodies; the best or richest part of a thing.—*vt.* (fatting, fatted). To make fat.
Fatal, fāt'al, *a.* Proceeding from fate; causing death; deadly; calamitous.
Fatalism, fāt'al-izm, *n.* The doctrine that all things take place by inevitable necessity.
Fatalist, fāt'al-ist, *n.* One who maintains that all things happen by inevitable necessity.
Fatality, fat-al'i-ti, *n.* State of being fatal; invincible necessity; fatalism; fatal occurrence; calamitous accident.
Fatally, fāt'al-li, *adv.* In a fatal manner; by decree of destiny; mortally.
Fate, fāt, *n.* Destiny; inevitable necessity; death; doom; lot; *pl.* the three goddesses supposed to preside over the birth and life of men.
Fated, fāt'ed, *a.* Decreed by fate; destined.
Fateful, fāt'fụl, *a.* Producing fatal events.
Father, fä'ᴛʜėr, *n.* A male parent; the first ancestor; the oldest member of a society or profession; the first to practise any art; a creator; a name given to God; a dignitary of the church; one of the early expounders of Christianity.—*vt.* To become a father to; to adopt; to profess to be the author of; to ascribe to one as his offspring or production.
Fatherhood, fä'ᴛʜėr-hụd, *n.* State of being a father; character or authority of a father.
Father-in-law, fä'ᴛʜėr-in-lạ, *n.* The father of one's husband or wife.
Fatherland, fä'ᴛʜėr-land, *n.* One's native country.
Fatherless, fä'ᴛʜėr-les, *a.* Destitute of a living father; without a known author.
Fatherly, fä'ᴛʜėr-li, *a.* Like a father, in affection and care; tender; paternal.
Fathom, faᴛʜ'um, *n.* A measure of length containing six feet.—*vt.* To try the depth of; to sound; to master; to comprehend.
Fathomable, faᴛʜ'um-a-bl, *a.* Capable of being fathomed.
Fathomless, faᴛʜ'um-les, *a.* That cannot be fathomed; bottomless; incomprehensible.
Fatigue, fa-tēg', *vt.* (fatiguing, fatigued). To employ to weariness; to tire; to harass with toil or labour.—*n.* Weariness from bodily or mental exertion; exhaustion; toil; labours of soldiers distinct from the use of arms.
Fatling, fat'ling, *n.* A young animal fattened for slaughter; a fat animal.
Fatness, fat'nes, *n.* Quality or state of being fat; greasy matter; richness; fertility.
Fatten, fat'n, *vt.* To make fat; to feed for slaughter; to make fertile.—*vi.* To grow fat.
Fatty, fat'i, *a.* Having the qualities of fat; greasy.
Fatuity, fa-tū'i-ti, *n.* State or quality of being fatuous; foolishness; imbecility.
Fatuous, fa'tū-us, *a.* Foolish; silly; feeble in mind; imbecile.
Fauces, fạ'sēz, *n.pl.* The back part of the mouth.
Faucet, fạ'set, *n.* A pipe to be inserted in a cask, for drawing liquor.
Faugh, fạ, *interj.* An exclamation of contempt or abhorrence.
Fault, fạlt, *n.* A slight offence; a defect; a flaw; a break or dislocation of strata.
Faultily, fạlt'i-li, *adv.* In a faulty manner; defectively.
Faultless, fạlt'les, *a.* Without fault; free from blemish; perfect.
Faulty, fạlt'i, *a.* Marked by faults; defective; imperfect; blamable; bad.
Faun, fạn, *n.* Among the Romans, a rural deity, the protector of agriculture and of shepherds; a sylvan deity.
Fauna, fạ'na, *n.* A collective term for the animals peculiar to a region or epoch.
Fauteuil, fō-tė-yė, *n.* An arm-chair.
Faux-pas, fō-pä, *n.* A false step; a breach of manners or moral conduct.
Faveolate, fa-vē'o-lāt, *a.* Formed like a honey-comb; alveolate.
Favonian, fa-vō'ni-an, *a.* Pertaining to the west wind.
Favose, fa-vōs', *a.* Resembling a honey-comb.
Favour, fā'vėr, *n.* Good-will; kindness; a kind act; leave; a yielding to another; a token of good-will; a knot of ribbons; advantage; prejudice.—*vt.* To regard with

good-will or kindness; to befriend; to show partiality to; to facilitate; to resemble in features.

Favourable, fā'vėr-a-bl, *a.* Kindly disposed; propitious; conducive; advantageous.

Favoured, fā'vėrd, *p.a.* Regarded with favour; having special facilities; featured.

Favourer, fā'vėr-ėr, *n.* One who favours.

Favourite, fā'vėr-it, *n.* A person or thing regarded with peculiar favour; a darling; a minion; one unduly favoured.—*a.* Regarded with particular favour.

Favouritism, fā'vėr-it-izm, *n.* Disposition to favour one or more persons or classes, to the neglect of others having equal claims; exercise of power by favourites.

Fawn, fąn, *n.* A young deer; a buck or doe of the first year; a light-brown colour; a servile cringe or bow; mean flattery.—*vi.* To bring forth a fawn; to show a servile attachment; to cringe to gain favour.—*a.* Light brown.

Fawningly, fąn'ing-li, *adv.* In a cringing servile way; with mean flattery.

Fay, fā, *n.* A fairy; an elf.—*vt.* To fit pieces of timber together.

Fealty, fē'al-ti, *n.* Fidelity to a superior; loyalty.

Fear, fēr, *n.* Painful emotion excited by apprehension of impending danger; dread; the object of fear; filial regard mingled with awe; reverence.—*vt.* To feel fear; to apprehend; to dread; to reverence.—*vi.* To be in apprehension of evil; to be afraid.

Fearful, fēr'fųl, *a.* Filled with fear; apprehensive; timid; impressing fear; dreadful.

Fearless, fēr'les, *a.* Free from fear; undaunted; courageous; bold; intrepid.

Feasibility, fēz-i-bil'i-ti, *n.* Quality of being feasible; practicability.

Feasible, fēz'i-bl, *a.* That may be done; practicable.

Feasibly, fēz'i-bli, *adv.* Practicably.

Feast, fēst, *n.* A festal day; a sumptuous entertainment; a banquet; a festival; that which delights and entertains.—*vi.* To partake of a feast; to eat sumptuously; to be highly gratified.—*vt.* To entertain sumptuously.

Feat, fēt, *n.* An exploit; an extraordinary act of strength, skill, or cunning.

Feather, feᴛʜ'ėr, *n.* One of the growths which form the covering of birds; a plume; projection on a board to fit into another board; kind of nature; birds collectively; a trifle.—*vt.* To cover or fit with feathers; to turn (an oar) horizontally over the water.

Feathery, feᴛʜ'ėr-i, *a.* Clothed or covered with feathers; resembling feathers.

Feature, fē'tūr, *n.* The make or cast of any part of the face; any single lineament; a prominent part or characteristic.

Featured, fē'tūrd, *a.* Having features of a certain cast.

Featureless, fē'tūr-les, *a.* Having no distinct features.

Feaze, fēz, *vt.* To untwist the end of anything made of threads or fibres.

Febrifuge, fe'bri-fūj, *n.* Any medicine that drives away or mitigates fever.—*a.* Dispelling or mitigating fever.

Febrile, fē'bril, *a.* Pertaining to fever; indicating fever, or derived from it.

February, feb'rū-a-ri, *n.* The second month in the year.

Feculence, fe'kū-lens, *n.* State or quality of being feculent; foulness; dregs.

Feculent, fe'kū-lent, *a.* Abounding with sediment; foul or filthy; impure.

Fecund, fē'kund, *a.* Fruitful in progeny; prolific; fertile; productive.

Fecundate, fē'kund-āt, *vt.* To make fruitful or prolific; to impregnate.

Fecundation, fē-kund-ā'shon, *n.* Act of fecundating; impregnation.

Fecundity, fē-kund'i-ti, *n.* State or quality of being fecund; fertility; richness of invention.

Federal, fed'ėr-al, *a.* Pertaining to a league or contract; confederated; founded on alliance between states which unite for national purposes.—*n.* One who upholds federal government.

Federalism, fed'ėr-al-izm, *n.* The principles of federal government.

Federalist, fed'ėr-al-ist, *n.* A federal.

Federalize, fed'ėr-al-īz, *vt.* or *i.* To unite in a federal compact.

Federate, fed'ėr-āt, *a.* Joined in confederacy.

Federation, fed-ėr-ā'shon, *n.* Act of uniting in a league; confederacy.

Federative, fed'ėr-āt-iv, *a.* Uniting in a confederacy.

Fee, fē, *n.* A reward for services; recompense for professional services; a fief; a freehold estate held by one who is absolute owner.—*vt.* (feeing, feed). To pay a fee to; to engage in one's service by advancing a fee to.

Feeble, fē'bl, *a.* Weak; impotent; deficient in vigour, as mental powers, sound, light, &c.

Feebly, fē'bli, *adv.* Weakly; without strength.

Feed, fēd, *vt.* (feeding, fed). To give food to; to furnish with anything of which there is constant consumption; to fatten.—*vi.* To take food; to eat; to prey; to graze; to grow fat.—*n.* That which is eaten; fodder; portion of provender given to a horse, cow, &c.

Feeder, fēd'ėr, *n.* One who or that which feeds; an encourager; an affluent; a branch railway; napkin tied round a child's neck at meal-times.

Feeding, fēd'ing, *n.* Act of giving food; act of eating; that which is eaten; provender.

Feel, fēl, *vt.* (feeling, felt). To perceive by the touch; to have the sense of; to be affected by; to examine by touching.—*vi.* To have perception by the touch; to have the sensibility moved; to have perception mentally.—*n.* Act of feeling; perception caused by the touch.

Feeler, fēl'ėr, *n.* One who feels; an observation, &c., put forth to ascertain the views of others; an organ of touch in the lower animals.

Feeling, fēl'ing, *a.* Possessing great sensibility; sensitive; sympathetic.—*n.* The sense of touch; sensation; sensibility; emotion; sympathy.

Feelingly, fēl'ing-li, *adv.* In a feeling manner; tenderly.

Feet, fēt, *n.pl.* of *foot.*

Feign, fān, *vt.* To pretend; to counterfeit; to simulate.—*vi.* To represent falsely; to pretend.

Feigned, fānd, *p.a.* Simulated; assumed.

Feignedly, fān'ed-li, *adv.* In pretence.

Feint, fānt, *n.* A pretence; an appearance of aiming at one part when another is intended to be struck.—*vi.* To make a feigned blow or thrust.

Feldspar. *See* FELSPAR.

Felicitate, fē-lis'it-āt, *vt.* To congratulate.

Felicitation, fē-lis'it-ā"shon, *n.* Congratulation.

Felicitous, fē-lis'it-us, *a.* Happy; extremely appropriate; managed with skill.

Felicity, fē-lis'i-ti, *n.* State of being in extreme enjoyment; bliss; the joys of heaven; skilfulness; appropriateness.

Feline, fē'līn, *a.* Pertaining to cats; like a cat.

Fell, fel, *a.* Cruel; fierce; savage.—*n.* A skin or hide of an animal; a seam sewed down level with the cloth; a stony or barren hill.—*vt.* To cause to fall; to hew down; to sew down a seam level with the cloth.

Fellah, fel'lā, *n.* An Egyptian peasant.

Felloe, fel'ō. Same as *Felly*.

Fellow, fel'ō, *n.* A partner; a companion; one of the same kind; an appellation of contempt; a member of a college or incorporated society.

Fellowship, fel'ō-ship, *n.* Companionship; joint interest; an association; an establishment in colleges for maintaining a fellow.

Felly, fel'i, *n.* One of the curved pieces which form the circular rim of a wheel.

Felon, fe'lon, *n.* One who has committed felony; a culprit; a whitlow.—*a.* Fierce; malignant; malicious.

Felonious, fe-lō'ni-us, *a.* Villainous; done with purpose to commit a crime.

Felony, fe'lon-i, *n.* Any crime which incurs the forfeiture of lands or goods; a heinous crime.

Felspar, fel'spär, *n.* A mineral consisting of silica and alumina, with potash, soda, or lime, a principal constituent in granite, porphyry, &c. Called also *Feldspar, Felspath*.

Felt, felt, *n.* A fabric made of wool, or wool and fur, wrought into a compact substance by rolling, beating, &c.; an article made of felt.—*vt.* To make into felt; to cover with felt.

Felting, felt'ing, *n.* Process of making felt; materials of which felt is made; felt.

Felucca, fe-luk'ka, *n.* A narrow Mediterranean vessel with lateen sails.

Female, fē'māl, *n.* One of that sex which conceives and brings forth young.—*a.* Belonging to the sex which produces young; feminine; weak.

Feminine, fem'in-in, *a.* Pertaining to females; womanly; effeminate; denoting the gender of words which signify females.

Femme-de-chambre, fam-dė-shăm-br, *n.* A lady's-maid; a chamber-maid.

Femoral, fem'o-ral, *a.* Belonging to the thigh.

Femur, fē'mėr, *n.* The thigh-bone.

Fen, fen, *n.* A marsh; bog; swamp where water stagnates.

Fence, fens, *n.* That which defends or guards; a wall, railing, &c., forming a boundary, &c.; defence; fencing; skill in fencing or argument; a purchaser or receiver of stolen goods.—*vt.* (fencing, fenced). To defend; to secure by an inclosure; to ward off by argument or reasoning.—*vi.* To practise the swordsman's art; to parry arguments; to prevaricate.

Fencer, fens'ėr, *n.* One who fences; one who teaches or practises the art of fencing.

Fencible, fen'si-bl, *n.* A soldier for defence of the country, not liable to serve abroad.

Fencing, fens'ing, *n.* The art of using a sword or foil in attack or defence; material used in making fences; that which fences.

Fend, fend, *vt.* To keep or ward off.—*vi.* To act on the defensive; to provide a livelihood.

Fender, fend'ėr, *n.* That which defends; a utensil to confine coals to the fireplace; something to protect the side of a vessel from injury.

Fenestration, fen-es-trā'shon, *n.* The arrangement of windows in a building.

Fenian, fē'ni-an, *n.* A member of a secret society, the object of which was the erection of an independent Irish republic.

Fennel, fen'el, *n.* A plant cultivated for the aromatic flavour of its seeds and for its leaves.

Fenny, fen'i, *a.* Growing in fens; marshy.

Fent, fent, *n.* A placket of a dress.

Feoff, fef, *n.* A fief or fee.

Feoffment, fef'ment, *n.* The gift or grant of a fee; the instrument or deed conveying it.

Feracious, fē-rā'shus, *a.* Fruitful.

Feral, fē'ral, *a.* Having become wild after a state of domestication or cultivation.

Feretory, fe'rē-to-ri, *n.* A movable shrine containing the relics of saints.

Ferial, fē'ri-al, *a.* Pertaining to holidays.

Ferine, fē'rīn, *a.* Pertaining to wild beasts.

Ferment, fėr'ment, *n.* That which causes fermentation, as yeast, &c.; intestine motion; agitation.—*vt.* fėr-ment'. To produce fermentation in; to set in agitation.—*vi.* To undergo fermentation; to be in agitation.

Fermentation, fėr-ment-ā'shon, *n.* Decomposition or conversion of an organic substance into new compounds by a ferment, indicated by the development of heat, bubbles, &c.; process by which grape juice is converted into wine; agitation; excitement.

Fermentative, fėr-ment'a-tiv, *a.* Causing fermentation; consisting in fermentation.

Fern, fėrn, *n.* The name of many cryptogams producing leaves called fronds.

Fernery, fėr'nėr-i, *n.* A place where ferns are artificially grown.

Ferny, fėrn'i, *a.* Abounding with fern.

Ferocious, fē-rō'shus, *a.* Fierce; savage; cruel.

Ferocity, fē-ros'i-ti, *n.* Savage wildness; fury; fierceness.

Ferreous, fe'rē-us, *a.* Partaking of or pertaining to iron.

Ferret, fe'ret, *n.* An animal allied to the weasel, employed in unearthing rabbits; a narrow tape made of woollen thread, cotton, or silk.—*vt.* To hunt with ferrets; to search out cunningly.

Ferriferous, fe-rif'ėr-us, *a.* Producing or yielding iron.

Ferruginous, fe-rū'jin-us, *a.* Of the colour of the rust or oxide of iron; partaking of or containing iron.

Ferrule, fe'rūl, *n.* A ring of metal round the end of a stick to strengthen it.

Ferry, fe'ri, *vt.* (ferrying, ferried). To carry over a river or other water in a boat.—*n.* Place where boats pass over to convey passengers; regular conveyance provided at such a place; a boat that plies at a ferry.

Ferryman, fe'ri-man, *n.* One who keeps a ferry.
Fertile, fėr'til, *a.* Fruitful; prolific; inventive; able to produce abundantly.
Fertility, fėr-til'i-ti, *n.* Fruitfulness; richness; fertile invention.
Fertilize, fėr'til-īz, *vt.* To make fertile or fruitful; to enrich; to impregnate.
Ferule, fe'rūl, *n.* A flat piece of wood, or rod, used to punish children.—*vt.* To punish with a ferule.
Fervency, fėr'ven-si, *n.* Eagerness; ardour; warmth of devotion.
Fervent, fėr'vent, *a.* Burning; vehement; ardent; earnest.
Fervid, fėr'vid, *a.* Burning; zealous; eager; earnest.
Fervour, Fervor, fėr'vėr, *n.* Heat or warmth; ardour; intensity of feeling; zeal.
Fescue, fes'kū, *n.* A straw, wire, &c., to point out letters to children; a kind of grass.
Festal, fest'al, *a.* Pertaining to a feast; joyous; gay; mirthful.
Fester, fes'tėr, *vi.* To suppurate; to rankle; to putrefy; to grow virulent.—*n.* A small inflammatory tumour.
Festival, fes'tiv-al, *a.* Festive; joyous.—*n.* The time of feasting; a feast; an anniversary day of joy, civil or religious.
Festive, fes'tiv, *a.* Pertaining to or becoming a feast; mirthful.
Festivity, fes-tiv'i-ti, *n.* Festive gaiety; social joy or mirth at an entertainment.
Festoon, fes-tön', *n.* A string of flowers, foliage, &c., suspended in a curve or curves; carved work in the form of a wreath of flowers, &c.—*vt.* To form in festoons; to adorn with festoons.
Fetch, fech, *vt.* To bring or draw; to make; to heave, as a sigh; to obtain as its price.—*vi.* To move or turn; to bring things.—*n.* A stratagem or trick; a wraith.
Fête, fāt, *n.* A feast or festival; a holiday.—*vt.* To honour with a feast.
Fetid, fē'tid, *a.* Stinking; having a strong or rancid scent.
Fetish, Fetich, fē'tish, *n.* An object regarded by some savage races as having mysterious powers, or as being the representative or habitation of a deity; any object of exclusive devotion.
Fetlock, fet'lok, *n.* The tuft of hair that grows behind on a horse's feet; the joint on which this hair grows; an instrument fixed to a horse's leg to prevent him from running off.
Fetor, fē'tėr, *n.* Offensive smell; stench.
Fetter, fet'ėr, *n.* A chain for the feet; anything that confines or restrains from motion: generally in *pl.*—*vt.* To put fetters upon; to restrain.
Fettle, fet'l, *vt.* (fettling, fettled). To put in right order.—*n.* Good trim, order, or condition.
Fetus, Fœtus, fē'tus, *n.*; pl. **-uses.** The young of an animal in the womb, or in the egg, after being perfectly formed.
Feu, fū, *n.* In Scotland, a piece of ground granted in perpetuity in consideration of an annual payment called feu-duty.
Feud, fūd, *n.* Hostility; a hereditary quarrel; a fief.
Feudal, fūd'al, *a.* Pertaining to feuds or fiefs; pertaining to the system of holding lands by military services.
Feudalism, fūd'al-izm, *n.* The system by which land was held in return for military service; the feudal system.
Feudalist, fūd'al-ist, *n.* One versed in feudal law; a supporter of the feudal system.
Feudatory, Feudatary, fūd'a-to-ri, fūd'a-ta-ri, *n.* The tenant of a feud or fief.—*a.* Holding from another on conditional tenure.
Feu-de-joie, fu̱-dė-zhwä. A bonfire, or a firing of guns in token of joy.
Fever, fē'vėr, *n.* A disease characterized by an accelerated pulse, heat, thirst, and diminished strength; agitation; excitement.—*vt.* To put in a fever.—*vi.* To be seized with fever.
Feverish, fē'vėr-ish, *a.* Having a slight fever; pertaining to fever; agitated; inconstant.
Few, fū, *a.* Not many; small in number.
Fewness, fū'nes, *n.* Quality of being few; smallness of number; paucity.
Fey, fā, *a.* On the verge of a sudden or violent death; fated soon to die and often showing this by unnatural gaiety.
Fez, fez, *n.* A close-fitting red cap with a tassel, worn in Turkey, Egypt, &c.
Fiancé, Fiancée, fē-äng-sā, *n.*, *masc.* and *fem.* An affianced or betrothed person.
Fiasco, fē-as'kō, *n.* An ignominious failure.
Fiat, fī'at, *n.* A decree; a command.
Fib, fib, *n.* A falsehood (a softer expression than *lie*).—*vi.* (fibbing, fibbed). To tell fibs.
Fibre, fī'bėr, *n.* A thread; a fine, slender body which constitutes a part of animals, plants, or minerals.
Fibril, fī'bril, *n.* A small fibre.
Fibrin, Fibrine, fī'brin, *n.* An organic substance found in animals and vegetables.
Fibrositis, fī-brō-sī'tis, *n.* Non-articular rheumatism; rheumatic inflammation of fibrous tissue.
Fibrous, fī'brus, *a.* Composed or consisting of fibres; containing fibres.
Fichu, fi-shö', *n.* A light ornamental piece of dress worn by ladies at the neck.
Fickle, fik'l, *a.* Of a changeable mind; vacillating; capricious.
Fickleness, fik'l-nes, *n.* Inconstancy.
Fictile, fik'til, *a.* Moulded by art; made of clay; manufactured by the potter.
Fiction, fik'shon, *n.* A feigned story; literature in the form of novels, tales, &c.; a falsehood; fabrication.
Fictitious, fik-ti'shus, *a.* Containing fiction; imaginary; counterfeit.
Fid, fid, *n.* A bar of wood or metal; a pin for various purposes on board ship.
Fiddle, fid'l, *n.* A stringed instrument of music; a violin; the wooden framework fixed on tables on board ship in rough weather, to keep the crockery from sliding off.—*vi.* (fiddling, fiddled). To play on a fiddle; to trifle; to trifle with the hands.—*vt.* To play on a fiddle.
Fiddler, fid'l-ėr, *n.* One who plays a fiddle.
Fidelity, fi-del'i-ti, *n.* Faithfulness; trustiness; loyalty; integrity.
Fidget, fij'et, *vi.* To move uneasily or in fits and starts.—*n.* An uneasy restless motion.
Fidgety, fij'et-i, *a.* Restless; uneasy.
Fiduciary, fi-dū'shi-a-ri, *a.* Held in trust; having the nature of a trust.—*n.* One who holds a thing in trust; a trustee.
Fie, fī. An exclamation denoting contempt or dislike.
Fief, fēf, *n.* An estate held of a superior on condition of military service.

Field, fēld, *n.* A piece of land suitable for tillage or pasture; piece of inclosed land; place of battle; battle; open space for action; sphere; blank space on which figures are drawn; those taking part in a hunt or race.—*vi.* and *t.* To watch and catch the ball, as in cricket.
Field-book, fēld'bu̇k, *n.* A book used in surveying.
Field-day, fēld'dā, *n.* A day when troops are drawn out for instruction in field exercises and evolutions.
Fieldfare, fēld'fār, *n.* A species of thrush found in Great Britain during the winter.
Field-glass, fēld'gläs, *n.* A kind of binocular telescope.
Field-marshal, fēld-mär'shal, *n.* A military officer of the highest rank.
Field-officer, fēld'of-fis-ėr, *n.* A major, lieutenant-colonel, or colonel.
Field-train, fēld-trān, *n.* A department of artillery that supplies ammunition on the field.
Fiend, fēnd, *n.* A demon; the devil; a wicked or cruel person.
Fiendish, fēnd'ish, *a.* Like a fiend; diabolic.
Fierce, fērs, *a.* Wild; savage; outrageous; violent.
Fiercely, fērs'li, *adv.* Violently; with rage.
Fierily, fī'ė-ri-li, *adv.* In a fiery manner.
Fiery, fī'ė-ri, *a.* Consisting of fire; like fire; impetuous; irritable; fierce.
Fife, fīf, *n.* A small wind-instrument used chiefly in martial music.—*vi.* (fifing, fifed). To play on a fife.
Fifer, fīf'ėr, *n.* One who plays on a fife.
Fifteen, fif'tēn, *a.* and *n.* Five and ten; a Rugby football team.
Fifteenth, fif'tēnth, *a.* The ordinal of fifteen.—*n.* A fifteenth part.
Fifth, fifth, *a.* The ordinal of five.—*n.* A fifth part.
Fifth column, fifth ko'lum, *n.* The individuals and organizations in a country which are prepared to give help to an enemy.
Fifthly, fifth'li, *adv.* In the fifth place.
Fiftieth, fif'ti-eth, *a.* The ordinal of fifty.—*n.* A fiftieth part.
Fifty, fif'ti, *a.* and *n.* Five tens; five times ten.
Fig, fig, *n.* The fruit of a tree of the mulberry family; the tree itself; a mere trifle; dress.
Fight, fīt, *vi.* (fighting, fought). To strive for victory; to contend in arms.—*vt.* To war against; to contend with in battle; to win by struggle.—*n.* A struggle for victory; a battle; an encounter.
Fighter, fīt'ėr, *n.* One who fights; a combatant; a warrior; an aeroplane designed for aerial combat.
Fighting, fīt'ing, *a.* Qualified for war; fit for battle; occupied in war.
Figment, fig'ment, *n.* A fiction; fabrication.
Figurant, fig'ūr-ant, *n.* A character on the stage who has nothing to say.
Figurate, fig'ūr-āt, *a.* Of a certain determinate form.
Figuration, fig-ūr-ā'shon, *n.* Act of giving figure; configuration; form.
Figurative, fig'ūr-āt-iv, *a.* Containing a figure or figures; representing by resemblance; typical; metaphoric; abounding in figures of speech.
Figure, fig'ūr, *n.* The form of anything as expressed by the outline; appearance; representation; a statue; a character denoting a number; a diagram; type; mode of expression in which words are turned from their ordinary signification; price.—*vt.* (figuring, figured). To make a likeness of; to represent by drawing, &c.; to cover or mark with figures; to image in the mind.—*vi.* To make a figure; to be distinguished.
Figured, fig'ūrd, *a.* Adorned with figures; free and florid.
Figure-head, fig'ūr-hed, *n.* The ornamental figure on a ship under the bowsprit.
Figuring, fig'ūr-ing, *n.* Act of making figures; figures collectively.
Filaceous, fil-ā'shus, *a.* Composed of threads.
Filament, fil'a-ment, *n.* A slender thread; a fine fibre.
Filamentary, Filamentose, Filamentous, fil-a-men'ta-ri, fil-a-men'tōs, fil-a-men'tus, *a.* Consisting of filaments.
Filatory, fil'a-to-ri, *n.* A machine which spins threads.
Filature, fil'a-tūr, *n.* The reeling off silk from cocoons; an establishment for reeling silk; a filatory.
Filbert, fil'bėrt, *n.* The fruit of the cultivated hazel.
Filch, filsh or filch, *vt.* To pilfer; to steal.
Filcher, filsh'ėr, *n.* A petty thief.
File, fīl, *n.* A line or wire on which papers are strung; the papers so strung; a row of soldiers one behind another; a steel instrument for cutting and smoothing iron, wood, &c.—*vt.* (filing, filed). To arrange or place on or in a file; to bring before a court by presenting the proper papers; to rub or cut with a file; to polish.—*vi.* To march in a line one after the other.
Filial, fil'i-al, *a.* Pertaining to or becoming a son or daughter.
Filiate, fil'i-āt, *vt.* To affiliate.
Filiation, fil-i-ā'shon, *n.* Affiliation.
Filibuster, fil'i-bus-tėr, *n.* A buccaneer; one of those lawless adventurers who in the present century have invaded a foreign country.—*vi.* To act as a filibuster.
Filiform, fil'i-form, *a.* Having the form of a thread or filament; slender.
Filigree, fil'i-grē, *n.* Ornamental open work in fine gold or silver wire.
Filings, fīl'ingz, *n.pl.* Fragments or particles rubbed off by the act of filing.
Fill, fil, *vt.* To make full; to occupy; to pervade; to satisfy; to surfeit; to supply with an occupant; to hold; to possess and perform the duties of.—*vi.* To grow or become full.—*n.* As much as fills or supplies want.
Filler, fil'ėr, *n.* One who fills; a tube for filling bottles, &c.
Fillet, fil'et, *n.* A little band to tie about the hair; the fleshy part of the thigh in veal; meat rolled together and tied round; something resembling a fillet or band.—*vt.* (filleting, filleted). To bind with a little band.
Fillibeg, fil'i-beg, *n.* The kilt worn by the Highlanders of Scotland.
Filling, fil'ing, *n.* A making full; materials for making full; woof of a fabric.
Fillip, fil'ip, *vt.* To strike with the nail of the finger, forced from the thumb with a sudden spring.—*n.* A jerk of the finger; something which tends to stimulate at once.

Filly, fil'i, *n.* A female colt; a wanton girl.
Film, film, *n.* A thin skin; a pellicle; (*pl.*) a cinema-show; the pictures.—*vt.* To cover with a thin skin.
Filmy, film'i, *a.* Like a film; composed of thin membranes or pellicles.
Filter, fil'tėr, *n.* A strainer; any substance through which liquors are passed.—*vt.* To purify by passing through a filter.—*vi.* To percolate; to pass through a filter.
Filth, filth, *n.* That which defiles; dirt; pollution.
Filthily, filth'i-li, *adv.* In a filthy manner.
Filthy, filth'i, *a.* Abounding in filth; dirty; foul; nasty; obscene.
Filtrate, fil'trāt, *vt.* To filter.
Filtration, fil-trā'shon, *n.* Act or process of filtering.
Fimbriate, fim'bri-āt, *a.* Fringed. Also *Fimbriated.*
Fin, fin, *n.* One of the organs which enable fishes to balance themselves and regulate their movements; anything resembling a fin.
Finable, fīn'a-bl, *a.* Liable to a fine.
Final, fīn'al, *a.* Pertaining to the end; last; ultimate; conclusive; decisive.
Finale, fē-nä'lā, *n.* The last part of a piece of music; the last piece or scene in a performance.
Finality, fī-nal'i-ti, *n.* Final state; state of being final; the doctrine that nothing exists except for a determinate end.
Finally, fīn'al-li, *adv.* Ultimately; lastly; completely; beyond recovery.
Finance, fi-nans', *n.* The science of public revenue and expenditure; management of money matters; *pl.* public funds or resources of money; private income.—*vi.* (financing, financed). To conduct financial operations.—*vt.* To manage the financial affairs of.
Financial, fi-nan'shal, *a.* Pertaining to finance.
Financier, fi-nan'sēr, *n.* One skilled in matters of finance.
Finch, finsh, *n.* A small singing bird.
Find, fīnd, *vt.* (finding, found). To come upon; to discover; to recover; to get; to perceive; to supply; to declare by verdict.—*n.* A discovery; the thing found.
Finding, fīnd'ing, *n.* Discovery; act of discovering; that which is found; a verdict.
Fine, fīn, *a.* Slender; minute; keen; delicate; refined; elegant; amiable; noble; splendid.—*n.* Payment of money imposed as a punishment; conclusion (*in fine*).—*vt.* (fining, fined). To make fine; to purify; to impose a pecuniary penalty on.
Finedraw, fīn'dra̤, *vt.* To sew up (a rent) neatly.
Finedrawn, fīn'dra̤n, *p.a.* Drawn out to too great fineness, or with too much subtlety.
Finely, fīn'li, *adv.* In a fine manner; gaily; handsomely; delicately.
Finer, fīn'ėr, *n.* One who refines or purifies.
Finery, fīn'ė-ri, *n.* Fine things; showy articles of dress; a furnace where cast-iron is converted into malleable iron.
Finespun, fīn'spun, *a.* Drawn to a fine thread; minute; over-elaborated.
Finesse, fi-nes', *n.* Artifice; stratagem.—*vi.* To use finesse or artifice.
Fin-footed, fin'fu̥t-ed, *a.* Having feet with toes connected by a membrane.
Finger, fing'gėr, *n.* One of the five members of the hand; something resembling a finger; skill in playing on a keyed instrument.—*vt.* To handle with the fingers; to touch lightly; to pilfer.—*vi.* To dispose the fingers aptly in playing on an instrument.
Fingered, fing'gėrd, *a.* Having fingers, or parts like fingers.
Fingering, fing'gėr-ing, *n.* Act of touching lightly; manner of touching an instrument of music; a loose worsted for stockings, &c.
Finger-post, fing'gėr-pōst, *n.* A post for the direction of travellers.
Finger-stall, fing'gėr-sta̤l, *n.* A cover for protection of a finger when injured.
Finical, fin'i-kal, *a.* Unduly particular about trifles; idly busy. Also *finicking* and *finikin.*
Fining, fīn'ing, *n.* The process of refining; that which is used to fine liquors.
Finis, fī'nis, *n.* An end; conclusion.
Finish, fin'ish, *vt.* To bring to an end; to perfect; to polish to a high degree.—*vi.* To come to an end; to expire.—*n.* Completion; the last touch to a work; polish.
Finite, fī'nīt, *a.* Limited; bounded; circumscribed; not infinite.
Finitely, fī'nīt-li, *adv.* In a finite manner or degree.
Finless, fin'les, *a.* Destitute of fins.
Finn, fin, *n.* A native of Finland.
Finnish, fin'ish, *a.* Relating to the Finns.—*n.* Their language.
Finny, fin'i, *a.* Furnished with fins.
Fiord, Fjord, fyord, *n.* An inlet of the sea, such as are common in Norway.
Fir, fėr, *n.* A resinous coniferous tree.
Fire, fīr, *n.* Heat and light emanating from a body; fuel burning; a conflagration; discharge of firearms; splendour; violence of passion; vigour of fancy; animation; ardent affection; affliction.—*vt.* (firing, fired). To set on fire; to irritate; to animate; to bake; to cause to explode; to discharge (firearms).—*vi.* To take fire; to be inflamed with passion; to discharge firearms.
Firearm, fīr'ärm, *n.* A weapon which expels its projectile by the combustion of powder.
Fire-brand, fīr'brand, *n.* A piece of wood kindled; an incendiary; one who inflames factions.
Fire-brigade, fīr'bri-gād, *n.* A body of men organized to extinguish fires.
Fire-damp, fīr'damp, *n.* The explosive carburetted hydrogen of coal-mines.
Fire-engine, fīr'en-jin, *n.* An engine for throwing water to extinguish fire.
Fire-escape, fīr'es-kāp, *n.* A machine to facilitate escape from a building on fire.
Fire-fly, fīr'flī, *n.* A winged insect which emits a brilliant light at night.
Fire-irons, fīr'ī-ėrnz, *n.pl.* A shovel, tongs, poker, &c.
Fireman, fīr'man, *n.* A man who extinguishes fires, or tends the fires of an engine.
Fire-new, fīr'nū, *a.* Brand-new.
Fire-proof, fīr'prōf, *a.* Incombustible.
Fire-ship, fīr'ship, *n.* A vessel filled with combustibles and furnished with grappling-irons, to hook and set fire to an enemy's ships.
Fire-side, fīr'sīd, *n.* A place near the fire or hearth; home; domestic life.
Fire-watcher, fīr-woch'ėr, *n.* Person detailed to keep watch in a building or street in case of

an outbreak of fire caused by incendiary bombs.
Firework, fīr'wėrk, *n.* Preparation of gunpowder, sulphur, &c., used for making a show, a signal, &c.
Fire-worship, fīr'wėr-ship, *n.* The worship of fire, which prevailed chiefly in Persia.
Firing, fīr'ing, *n.* Act of one who fires; act of discharging firearms; application of fire; fuel; process of treating articles with fire.
Firkin, fėr'kin, *n.* An old measure equal to 7½ gallons; a small cask for butter.
Firm, fėrm, *a.* Steady; stable; strong; dense; hard; not fluid; fixed; resolute.—*n.* A partnership or commercial house.—*vt.* To make firm or solid.—*vi.* To become firm.
Firmament, fėrm'a-ment, *n.* The sky or heavens; region of the air; an expanse.
Firmamental, fėrm-a-ment'al, *a.* Pertaining to the firmament.
Firman, fėr'man or fėr-män', *n.* A Turkish decree, order, or grant.
Firmly, fėrm'li, *adv.* In a firm manner; steadfastly; resolutely.
First, fėrst, *a.* Foremost in time, place, rank, value, &c.; chief; highest; the ordinal of *one.*—*adv.* Before all others in time, place, &c.
First-born, fėrst'born, *a.* Eldest.
First-class, fėrst'klas, *a.* First-rate.
First-fruit, fėrst'fröt, *n.* The fruit or produce first collected; first profits; first or earliest effect, in good or bad sense.
First-hand, fėrst'hand, *a.* Obtained direct from the first source, producer, maker, &c.
Firstling, fėrst'ling, *n.* The first produce or offspring, as of sheep or cattle.
Firstly, fėrst'li, *adv.* In the first place; first.
First-rate, fėrst'rāt, *a.* Of highest excellence; pre-eminent; of largest size.
Firth, fėrth, *n.* An arm of the sea into which a river discharges; a channel. Also *Frith.*
Fiscal, fis'kal, *a.* Pertaining to the public treasury.—*n.* A treasurer; a public prosecutor, as in Scotland.
Fish, fish, *n.* An animal that lives in water; the flesh of such animals used as food.—*vi.* To attempt to catch fish; to attempt to obtain by artifice.—*vt.* To catch or try to catch fish in; to draw out or up when in water.
Fisher, fish'ėr, *n.* One employed in fishing.
Fisherman, fish'ėr-man, *n.* One whose occupation is to catch fish.
Fishery, fish'ė-ri, *n.* The business of catching fish; a place for catching fish.
Fishing, fish'ing, *a.* Used in catching fish.—*n.* Art or practice of catching fish; place to fish in.
Fishmonger, fish'mung-gėr, *n.* A dealer in fish.
Fishwife, Fishwoman, fish'wīf, fish-wụ'man, *n.* A woman who sells fish.
Fishy, fish'i, *a.* Consisting of fish; like fish; worn out; dubious; unsafe.
Fissile, fis'sil, *a.* That may be split in the direction of the grain, or of natural joints.
Fission, fi'shon, *n.* The act of splitting into parts; reproduction in animals of a low type through the body dividing into parts.
Fissure, fi'shūr, *n.* A cleft; a longitudinal opening.—*vt.* To cleave; to crack.
Fist, fist, *n.* The hand clenched; the hand with the fingers doubled into the palm.—*vt.* To strike with the fist.
Fistic, fis'tik, *a.* Pertaining to boxing.
Fisticuffs, fis'ti-kufs, *n.* A blow with the fist; commonly in *pl.* boxing.
Fistula, fis'tū-la, *n.* A shepherd's pipe; a deep, narrow, sinuous ulcer.
Fistular, fis'tū-lėr, *a.* Hollow like a pipe.
Fit, fit, *n.* A sudden activity followed by a relaxation; paroxysm; convulsion; due adjustment of dress to the body.—*a.* Conformable to a standard of right, duty, taste, &c.; suitable; proper; congruous; qualified; adequate.—*vt.* (fitting, fitted). To make fit or suitable; to furnish with anything; to adapt; to qualify for.—*vi.* To be proper or becoming; to suit; to be adapted.
Fitch, fich, *n.* A vetch; a chick-pea; a polecat; its fur.
Fitchet, Fitchew, fich'et, fich'ū, *n.* A polecat.
Fitful, fit'fụl, *a.* Full of fits; varied by sudden impulses; spasmodic; chequered.
Fitly, fit'li, *adv.* Suitably; properly.
Fitter, fit'ėr, *n.* One who fits; one who puts the parts of machinery together.
Fitting, fit'ing, *a.* Fit; appropriate.—*n.pl.* Things fixed on; permanent appendages.
Fittingly, fit'ing-li, *adv.* Suitably.
Five, fīv, *a.* and *n.* Four and one added; the half of ten.
Fivefold, fīv'fōld, *a.* In fives; consisting of five in one; five times repeated.
Fives, fīvz, *n.* A ball-game for two or four players, played in a court with four walls.
Fix, fiks, *vt.* To make fast or firm; to settle; to define; to appoint; to deprive of volatility.—*vi.* To settle or remain permanently; to cease to be fluid; to congeal.—*n.* A condition of difficulty; dilėmma.
Fixation, fiks-ā'shon, *n.* Act of fixing; state in which a body resists evaporation.
Fixative, fiks'a-tiv, *a.* Tending or causing to fix.—*n.* A substance that causes something to be stable or not fleeting.
Fixed, fikst, *p.a.* Firm; fast; settled; deprived of volatility.
Fixture, fiks'tūr, *n.* That which is fixed; that which is permanently attached; an appendage.
Fizz, Fizzle, fiz, fiz'l, *vi.* To make a hissing sound. Also used as a noun.
Flabbergast, flab'ėr-gast, *vt.* To strike with astonishment or dismay.
Flabby, flab'i, *a.* Soft; yielding to the touch; languid; feeble.
Flaccid, flak'sid, *a.* Flabby; soft and weak; drooping; limber.
Flaccidity, flak-sid'i-ti, *n.* State or quality of being flaccid; want of firmness.
Flag, flag, *n.* A cloth, usually attached to a pole, and bearing devices expressive of nationality, &c.; a banner; a flat stone for paving; an aquatic plant with sword-shaped leaves.—*vi.* (flagging, flagged). To hang loose; to droop; to languish; to slacken.—*vt.* To lay with broad flat stones.
Flagellant, fla'jel-lant, *n.* One who whips himself in religious discipline.
Flagellate, fla'jel-lāt, *vt.* To whip.
Flagellation, fla-jel-lā'shon, *n.* A flogging; the discipline of the scourge.
Flageolet, fla'jel-et, *n.* A small wind-instrument like a flute with a mouth-piece.
Flagging, flag'ing, *n.* Flag-stones; a pavement or side-walk of flag-stones.

Flaggy, flag'i, *a.* Flexible; abounding with the plant flag; resembling flag-stone.

Flagitious, fla-ji'shus, *a.* Deeply criminal; corrupt; profligate; heinous.

Flag-officer, flag of'is-ėr, *n.* An admiral, vice-admiral or rear-admiral. **Flag-ship,** *n.* Ship flying the flag of the admiral commanding the fleet.

Flagon, fla'gon, *n.* A vessel with a narrow mouth, used for liquors.

Flagrancy, flā'gran-si, *n.* Quality of being flagrant; enormity.

Flagrant, flā'grant, *a.* Flaming in notice; glaring; notorious; enormous.

Flagrantly, flā'grant-li, *adv.* Glaringly; notoriously.

Flail, flāl, *n.* A wooden instrument for thrashing or beating grain, &c.

Flak, flak, *n.* German anti-aircraft fire.

Flake, flāk, *n.* A loose, filmy mass of anything; a scale; a fleecy or feathery particle, as of snow; a flock, as of wool.—*vt.* (flaking, flaked). To form into flakes.—*vi.* To break in layers; to peel off.

Flaky, flāk'i, *a.* Consisting of flakes; lying in flakes; like flakes or scales.

Flambeau, flam'bō, *n.* A light made of thick wicks covered with wax; a torch.

Flamboyant, flam-boi'ant, *a.* Noting that style of Gothic architecture characterized by wavy tracery in the windows; florid.

Flame, flām, *n.* Light emitted from fire; a blaze; fire; heat of passion; ardour of temper or imagination; ardent love; rage; one beloved.—*vi.* (flaming, flamed). To blaze; to glow; to rage.

Flaming, flām'ing, *p.a.* Emitting a flame; violent; vehement.

Flamingly, flām'ing-li, *adv.* Most brightly; with great show or vehemence.

Flamingo, fla-ming'gō, *n.* A web-footed, long-necked bird about 5 to 6 feet high.

Flamy, flām'i, *a.* Having the nature or colour of flame.

Flange, flanj, *n.* A projecting rim or edge on any substance; a raised edge on a wheel, &c.—*vt.* (flanging, flanged). To furnish with a flange.

Flank, flangk, *n.* The part of the side of an animal, between the ribs and the hip; the side of an army; the extreme right or left; the side of any building.—*vt.* To be situated at the side of; to place troops so as to command or attack the flank; to pass round the side of.

Flannel, flan'el, *n.* A soft, nappy, woollen cloth of loose texture; garment made of flannel.

Flap, flap, *n.* Something broad and flexible that hangs loose; the motion or sound of anything broad and loose, or a stroke with it; tail of a coat, &c.—*vt.* (flapping, flapped). To beat with a flap; to move, as something broad.—*vi.* To move, as wings; to wave loosely.

Flap-dragon, flap'dra-gon, *n.* A game of snatching raisins out of burning brandy.

Flap-eared, flap'ērd, *a.* Having broad loose ears.

Flap-jack, flap'jak, *n.* A sort of broad pancake; an apple-puff; a flat powder-compact.

Flapper, flap'ėr, *n.* One who or that which flaps; a young wild duck; a young girl (*colloq.*).

Flare, flār, *vi.* (flaring, flared). To burn with an unsteady light; to glitter with transient lustre; to give out a dazzling light.—*n.* An unsteady strong light.

Flaring, flār'ing, *p.a.* Glittering; showy.

Flash, flash, *n.* A sudden burst of flame and light; a gleam.—*a.* Vulgarly showy; counterfeit.—*vi.* To burst or break forth with a flash; to dart.—*vt.* To throw out like a burst of light.

Flashily, flash'i-li, *adv.* Gaudily; showily.

Flash-point, Flashing-point, flash'point, flash'ing-point, *n.* The temperature at which the vapour of oils will ignite and flash.

Flashy, flash'i, *a.* Characterized by empty show; gaudy; impulsive.

Flask, flask, *n.* A kind of bottle; a bottle for the pocket; a vessel for powder.

Flat, flat, *a.* Having an even surface; level; fallen; tasteless; vapid; depressed; dull; absolute; below the true pitch, as a sound.—*n.* A level; a shallow; the broad side of something; a mark in music (♭) indicating lowering of pitch; a story or floor of a house; a simpleton.

Flatling, Flatlong, flat'ling, flat'long, *adv.* Flatwise; with the flat side.

Flatly, flat'li, *adv.* In a flat manner; horizontally; evenly; without spirit; positively.

Flatten, flat'n, *vt.* To make flat; to level; to render less acute or sharp, as a sound.—*vi.* To grow or become flat.

Flatter, flat'ėr, *vt.* To gratify by praise; to compliment; to praise falsely.

Flatterer, flat'ėr-ėr, *n.* One who flatters; a fawner; a wheedler.

Flattering, flat'ėr-ing, *a.* Bestowing flattery; agreeable to one's self-love; gratifying.

Flattery, flat'ė-ri, *n.* False praise; sycophancy; cajolery.

Flatting, flat'ing, *n.* A mode of house-painting in which the paint has no gloss.

Flattish, flat'ish, *a.* Somewhat flat.

Flatulence, Flatulency, flat'ū-lens, flat'ū-len-si, *n.* State of being flatulent.

Flatulent, flat'ū-lent, *a.* Affected with gases in the stomach and intestines; generating wind in the stomach; empty; puffy.

Flatwise, flat'wīz, *a.* or *adv.* With the flat side downward or next to another object.

Flaunt, fląnt, *vi.* and *t.* To display ostentatiously.—*n.* Bold or impudent parade.

Flaunty, Flaunting, fląnt'i, fląnt'ing, *a.* Apt to flaunt; ostentatious; gaudy.

Flavour, flā'vėr, *n.* The quality of a substance which affects the smell or taste; relish; zest.—*vt.* To give a flavour to.

Flavoured, flā'vėrd, *p.a.* Having flavour.

Flavourless, flā'vėr-les, *a.* Without flavour; tasteless.

Flaw, flą, *n.* A crack; a defect; a speck; a gust of wind.—*vt.* To make a flaw in.

Flawless, flą'les, *a.* Without defect; perfect.

Flawy, flą'i, *a.* Full of flaws or cracks.

Flax, flaks, *n.* A plant, the fibres of which are formed into linen threads; the fibres prepared for manufacture.

Flax-dresser, flaks'dres-ėr, *n.* One who combs and prepares flax for the spinner.

Flaxen, flaks'n, *a.* Made of or like flax; of the colour of flax; fair.

Flaxy, flaks'i, *a.* Like flax; flaxen.

Flay, flā, *vt.* To strip the skin off an animal.

Flea, flē, *n.* An insect that leaps with great agility, and whose bite causes itch.

Flea-bite, flē'bīt, *n.* The bite of a flea; a thing of no moment.
Fleam, flēm, *n.* An instrument for opening the veins of animals to let blood.
Fleck, flek, *n.* A spot; streak; dapple.—*vt.* To spot; to streak or stripe; to dapple.
Flection, flek'shon, *n.* Act of bending; state of being bent.
Fledge, flej, *vt.* (fledging, fledged). To supply with the feathers necessary for flight.
Fledgeling, flej'ling, *n.* A bird just fledged.
Flee, flē, *vi.* (fleeing, fled). To run away; to hasten from.—*vt.* To shun.
Fleece, flēs, *n.* The coat of wool that covers a sheep, or is shorn at one time.—*vt.* (fleecing, fleeced). To strip of the fleece; to rob or cheat heartlessly; to cover as with a fleece.
Fleecy, flēs'i, *a.* Resembling wool or a fleece; covered with wool; woolly.
Fleer, flēr, *vi.* To grin with an air of civility; to mock; to leer.—*n.* A leer; derision or mockery expressed by words or looks.
Fleet, flēt, *n.* A squadron or body of ships; navy.—*a.* Swift of pace; nimble.—*vi.* To fly swiftly; to be in a transient state.
Fleeting, flēt'ing, *a.* Not durable; transient; momentary.
Fleetly, flēt'li, *adv.* Rapidly; swiftly.
Fleming, flem'ing, *n.* A native of Flanders.
Flemish, flem'ish, *a.* Pertaining to Flanders. —*n.* The language of the Flemings.
Flesh, flesh, *n.* The muscular part of an animal; animal food; beasts and birds used as food; the body, as distinguished from the soul; mankind; corporeal appetites; kindred; family.—*vt.* To feed with flesh; to initiate to the taste of flesh.
Flesh-brush, flesh'brush, *n.* A brush for exciting action in the skin by friction.
Fleshed, flesht, *a.* Fat; fleshy; having flesh of a particular kind.
Flesher, flesh'ėr, *n.* A butcher.
Flesh-fly, flesh'flī, *n.* A fly that feeds on flesh, and deposits her eggs in it.
Fleshings, flesh'ingz, *n.pl.* Tight-fitting flesh-coloured garments.
Fleshly, flesh'li, *a.* Carnal; wordly; lascivious; human; not spiritual.
Flesh-wound, flesh'wönd, *n.* A wound which affects the flesh only.
Fleshy, flesh'i, *a.* Muscular; fat; corpulent; plump; pulpy.
Flex, fleks, *vt.* To bend.
Flexibility, fleks-i-bil'i-ti, *n.* Quality of being flexible; pliancy; readiness to comply.
Flexible, fleks'i-bl, *a.* That may be bent; pliant; supple; tractable; plastic.
Flexile, fleks'īl, *a.* Pliant.
Flexion, flek'shon, *n.* Act of bending; a bend; part bent.
Flexor, fleks'ėr, *n.* A muscle which produces flexion.
Flexuous, Flexuose, fleks'ū-us, fleks'ū-ōs, *a.* Winding; bending.
Flexure, fleks'ūr, *n.* A bending; form of bending; part bent.
Flick, flik, *n.* A sharp sudden stroke, as with a whip; a flip.—*vt.* To strike with a flick; to flip.
Flicker, flik'ėr, *vi.* To flutter; to waver, as an unsteady flame.—*n.* A wavering gleam.
Flier, Flyer, flī'ėr, *n.* One who flies or flees; a part of a machine which moves rapidly.
Flight, flīt, *n.* Act of fleeing or flying; power or manner of flying; a flock of birds; a volley, as of arrows; space passed by flying; a soaring; lofty elevation, as of fancy; extravagant sally; a series of steps or stairs.
Flight-lieutenant, flīt-lef-ten'ant, *n.* Officer in the Royal Air Force, ranking with a captain in the army.
Flighty, flīt'i, *a.* Full of flights or sallies of imagination, caprice, &c.; volatile; giddy.
Flimsy, flim'zi, *a.* Thin; slight; weak; without force; shallow.
Flinch, flinsh, *vi.* To shrink; to withdraw; to wince; to fail.
Fling, fling, *vt.* (flinging, flung). To cause to fly from the hand; to hurl; to scatter; to throw to the ground.—*vi.* To fly into violent and irregular motions; to flounce; to rush away angrily.—*n.* A throw; a gibe; a lively Scottish dance.
Flint, flint, *n.* A very hard siliceous stone, which strikes fire with steel; anything proverbially hard.
Flint-lock, flint'lok, *n.* A musket-lock in which fire is produced by a flint.
Flinty, flint'i, *a.* Consisting of or like flint; very hard; cruel; inexorable.
Flip, flip, *n.* A flick; a drink consisting of beer and spirit sweetened, and heated by a hot iron.—*vt.* To flick.
Flippancy, flip'an-si, *n.* Quality of being flippant; heedless pertness; undue levity.
Flippant, flip'ant, *a.* Speaking confidently, without knowledge; heedlessly pert; shallow.
Flipper, flip'ėr, *n.* The paddle of a sea-turtle; the broad fin of a fish; the arm of a seal.
Flirt, flėrt, *vt.* To throw with a jerk; to make coquettish motions with (a fan).—*vi.* To run and dart about; to coquette; to play at courtship.—*n.* A sudden jerk; one who plays at courtship; a coquette.
Flirtation, flėrt-ā'shon, *n.* Playing at courtship; coquetry.
Flit, flit, *vi.* (flitting, flitted). To fly or dart along; to flutter; to change habitation (Scottish in this sense).
Flitch, flich, *n.* The side of a hog cured as bacon.
Flitter, flit'ėr, *vi.* To flutter.
Float, flōt, *n.* That which is borne on water or any fluid; a raft.—*vi.* To be borne on the surface of a fluid; to be buoyed up; to move with a light, irregular course.—*vt.* To cause to be conveyed on water; to flood; to get (a company, scheme, &c.) started.
Floatage, flōt'āj, *n.* Anything that floats on the water; floating capacity or buoyancy.
Floatation, flōt-ā'shon, *n.* *See* FLOTATION.
Float-board, flōt'bōrd, *n.* A board of an undershot water-wheel, on which the water strikes; board of a paddle-wheel.
Floating, flōt'ing, *p.a.* Circulating; fluctuating; not fixed or invested; unattached.
Flocculent, flok'ū-lent, *a.* Adhering in locks or flakes; fleecy.
Flock, flok, *n.* A lock of wool or hair; stuffing for mattresses, &c.; a company, as of sheep, birds, &c.; a Christian congregation in relation to their pastor.—*vi.* To gather in companies; to crowd; to move in crowds.
Flock-bed, flok'bed, *n.* A bed stuffed with flocks of wool, or cloth cut up fine.
Flock-paper, flok'pā-pėr, *n.* A wall-paper

having raised figures made of powdered wool attached by size and varnish.

Flocky, flok'i, *a.* Abounding with flocks or little tufts, like wool.

Floe, flō, *n.* A mass of ice floating in the ocean.

Flog, flog, *vt.* (flogging, flogged). To whip; to chastise with repeated blows.

Flogging, flog'ing, *n.* A whipping for punishment.

Flood, flud, *n.* A great flow of water; a deluge; a river; the flowing of the tide; a great quantity; abundance.—*vt.* To overflow; to deluge; to overwhelm.

Flood-gate, flud'gāt, *n.* A gate to stop or let out water.

Flood-mark, flud'märk, *n.* The line to which the tide rises; high-water mark.

Flood-tide, flud'tīd, *n.* The rising tide.

Floor, flōr, *n.* That part of a building on which we walk; bottom of a room; story in a building; a flat, hard surface of loam, lime, &c., used in some kinds of business, as in malting.—*vt.* To lay a floor upon; to strike down.

Flooring, flōr'ing, *n.* A floor; materials for floors.

Flop, flop, *vt.* and *i.* (flopping, flopped). To clap or flap; to let down suddenly; to plump down.—*n.* A sudden sinking to the ground.

Flora, flō'ra, *n.* The plants of a particular district or period; a work describing them.

Floral, flō'ral, *a.* Pertaining to or made of flowers.

Florescence, flō-res'ens, *n.* A flowering; season when plants expand their flowers.

Floret, flō'ret, *n.* A floweret; the separate little flower of an aggregate flower; a fencing foil; silk yarn or floss.

Floriculture, flō'ri-kul-tūr, *n.* The culture of flowers or flowering plants.

Floriculturist, flō'ri-kul-tūr-ist, *n.* One skilled in the cultivation of flowers.

Florid, flo'rid, *a.* Flowery; bright in colour; flushed with red; embellished with flowers of rhetoric; highly decorated.

Florin, flo'rin, *n.* A coin of different countries; a British silver coin, value 2*s.*

Florist, flo'rist, *n.* A cultivator of flowers; one who writes a flora.

Floscule, flos'kūl, *n.* A little flower; a floret.

Floss, flos, *n.* A downy or silky substance in plants; fine untwisted silk used in embroidery.

Flossy, flos'i, *a.* Composed of or like floss.

Flotation, flōt-ā'shon, *n.* Act of floating; the doctrine of floating bodies.

Flotilla, flō-til'la, *n.* A little fleet, or fleet of small vessels.

Flotsam, flot'sam, *n.* Portion of a wreck that continues floating.

Flounce, flouns, *vi.* (flouncing, flounced). To spring or turn with sudden effort; to start away in anger.—*vt.* To deck with a flounce or flounces.—*n.* A strip of cloth sewed round a gown with the lower border loose and spreading.

Flounder, floun'dėr, *n.* A flat fish found in the sea near the mouths of rivers.—*vi.* To struggle, as in mire; to roll, toss, and tumble.

Flour, flour, *n.* Finely ground meal of wheat or other grain; fine powder of any substance.—*vt.* To convert into flour; to sprinkle with flour.

Flourish, flu'rish, *vi.* To grow luxuriantly; to thrive; to live; to use florid language; to make ornamental strokes in writing, &c.; to move in bold and irregular figures.—*vt.* To adorn with flowers or figures; to ornament with anything showy; to brandish.—*n.* Showy splendour; parade of words and figures; fanciful stroke of the pen; decorative notes in music; brandishing.

Flourishing, flu'rish-ing, *p.a.* Prosperous; growing luxuriantly.

Floury, flour'i, *a.* Resembling flour.

Flout, flout, *vt.* To mock or insult; to jeer at.—*n.* A mock; an insult.

Flow, flō, *vi.* To move, as water; to issue; to abound; to glide smoothly; to hang loose and waving; to rise, as the tide; to circulate, as blood.—*vt.* To flow over; to flood.—*n.* A moving along, as of water; stream; current; rise of water; fulness; free expression; feeling.

Flowage, flō'āj, *n.* Act of flowing; state of being overflowed.

Flower, flou'ėr, *n.* The delicate and gaily-coloured leaves or petals on a plant; a bloom or blossom; youth; the prime; the best part; one most distinguished; an ornamental expression; *pl.* a powdery substance.—*vi.* To blossom; to bloom.—*vt.* To embellish with figures of flowers.

Floweret, flou'ėr-et, *n.* A small flower.

Flowering, flou'ėr-ing, *p.a.* Having flowers; blossoming.

Flowery, flou'ėr-i, *a.* Full of flowers; embellished with figurative language; florid.

Flowing, flō'ing, *p.a.* Moving as a stream; abounding; fluent; undulating.

Flown, flōn, pp. of *fly*.

Fluctuate, fluk'tū-āt, *vi.* To move as a wave; to waver; to hesitate; to experience vicissitudes.

Fluctuating, fluk'tū-āt-ing, *p.a.* Unsteady; wavering.

Fluctuation, fluk-tū-ā'shon, *n.* A rising and falling; change; vicissitude.

Flue, flö, *n.* A passage for smoke or heated air; a pipe for conveying heat; light downy matter; fluff.

Fluency, flų'en-si, *n.* Quality of being fluent; facility of words; volubility.

Fluent, flų'ent, *a.* Flowing; ready in the use of words; voluble; smooth.

Fluently, flų'ent-li, *adv.* In a fluent manner; with ready flow of words.

Fluff, fluf, *n.* Light down or nap such as rises from beds, cotton, &c.

Fluid, flų'id, *a.* Capable of flowing; liquid or gaseous.—*n.* Any substance whose parts easily move and change their relative position without separation; a liquid.

Fluidity, flų-id'i-ti, *n.* Quality or state of being fluid.

Fluke, flök, *n.* That part of an anchor which fastens in the ground; an accidental success; a flat-fish; a parasitic worm.

Flume, flöm, *n.* A channel for the water that drives a mill-wheel; an artificial channel for gold-washing.

Flummery, flum'mė-ri, *n.* A sort of jelly made of flour or meal; flattery; nonsense.

Flunkey, flung'ki, *n.* A male servant in livery; a cringing flatterer; a toady.

Fluor, flö'or, *n.* Fluor-spar.

Fluoric, flö-or'ik, *a.* Pertaining to fluor.

Fluor-spar, flö'or-spär, *n.* A mineral exhibiting yellow, green, blue, and red tints.
Flurry, flu'ri, *n.* Bustle; hurry; a gust of wind; light things carried by the wind.—*vt.* (flurrying, flurried). To agitate or alarm.
Flush, flush, *vi.* To become suddenly red, to blush.—*vt.* To cause to redden suddenly; to elate; to excite; to wash out by copious supplies of water; to cause to start up.—*n.* A sudden flow of blood to the face; sudden thrill; vigour; flow of water; run of cards of the same suit.—*a.* Fresh; full of vigour; affluent; even with the adjacent surface.
Fluster, flus'tėr, *vt.* To agitate; to make hot with drink.—*n.* Agitation; confusion; heat.
Flute, flöt, *n.* A small wind-instrument with holes and keys; a channel cut along the shaft of a column; a similar channel.—*vi.* (fluting, fluted). To play on a flute.—*vt.* To play or sing in notes like those of a flute; to form flutes or channels in.
Fluted, flöt'ed, *p.a.* Channelled; furrowed.
Fluting, flöt'ing, *n.* A channel or furrow; fluted work; sound like that of a flute.
Flutist, flöt'ist, *n.* A performer on the flute.
Flutter, flut'ėr, *vi.* To move or flap the wings rapidly; to be in agitation; to fluctuate.—*vt.* To agitate; to throw into confusion.—*n.* Quick, confused motion; agitation; disorder.
Fluty, flöt'i, *a.* Having the sound of a flute.
Fluvial, flö'vi-al, *a.* Belonging to rivers.
Fluviatile, flö'vi-a-til, *a.* Belonging to rivers; produced by river action.
Flux, fluks, *n.* Act of flowing, any flow of matter; dysentery; flow of the tide; anything used to promote fusion; fusion; liquid state from the operation of heat.—*vt.* To melt; to fuse.
Fluxion, fluk'shon, *n.* Act of flowing; flux; a flow of blood or other fluid; an infinitely small quantity; *pl.* the analysis of infinitely small variable quantities.
Fluxional, Fluxionary, fluk'shon-al, fluk'-shon-a-ri, *a.* Pertaining to mathematical fluxions.
Fly, flī, *vi.* (flying, pret. flew, pp. flown). To move through air by wings; to move in air by the force of wind, &c.; to rise in air; to move rapidly; to pass away; to depart suddenly; to spring; to flutter.—*vt.* To flee from; to cause to float in the air.—*n.* A winged insect; a revolving mechanism to regulate the motion of machinery; a light carriage; a cab.
Fly-blow, flī'blō, *vt.* To taint with eggs which produce maggots.—*n.* The egg of a fly.
Fly-fishing, flī'fish-ing, *n.* Angling for fish with flies, natural or artificial.
Flying-bomb, flī'ing-bom, *n.* A large self-propelled projectile, first used by the Germans in 1944.
Flying-fish, flī'ing-fish, *n.* A fish which can sustain itself in the air for a time by means of its long pectoral fins.
Flying-officer, flī'ing of'is-ėr, *n.* Officer in the Royal Air Force, ranking with a lieutenant in the army.
Fly-leaf, flī'lēf, *n.* A leaf of blank paper at the beginning and end of a book.
Fly-paper, flī'pā-pėr, *n.* A paper for destroying flies.
Fly-wheel, flī'whēl, *n.* A wheel to equalize the motive power of a machine.
Foal, fōl, *n.* The young of a mare, she-ass, &c.; a colt or filly.—*vt.* To bring forth, as a colt or filly.—*vi.* To bring forth a foal.
Foam, fōm, *n.* Froth; spume.—*vi.* To froth; to show froth at the mouth; to rage.—*vt.* To cause to give out foam; to throw out with rage or violence.
Foamy, fōm'i, *a.* Covered with foam; frothy.
Fob, fob, *n.* A little pocket for a watch in the waistband of the breeches.
Focal, fō'kal, *a.* Belonging to a focus.
Focus, fō'kus, *n.*; pl. **-cuses** or **-ci.** A point in which rays of light meet after being reflected or refracted; point of concentration.—*vt.* To bring to a focus.
Fodder, fod'ėr, *n.* Food for cattle, &c.—*vt.* To furnish with fodder.
Foe, fō, *n.* An enemy; an opposing army; one who opposes anything.
Foeman, fō'man, *n.* A personal antagonist.
Fœtus, fē'tus. *See* FETUS.
Fog, fog, *n.* A dense vapour near the surface of the land or water; mental confusion; dimness; second growth of grass; long grass that remains in pastures till winter.
Fogey, Fogy, fō'gi, *n.*; pl. **-eys, -ies.** A stupid fellow; an old-fashioned person.
Foggage, fog'āj, *n.* Rank or coarse grass not eaten down.
Foggy, fog'i, *a.* Filled with fog; cloudy; misty; producing fogs; stupid.
Foh, fo. An exclamation of disgust or contempt.
Foible, foi'bl, *n.* A weak point in character; a failing; the weak part of a sword.
Foil, foil, *vt.* To frustrate; to baffle; to balk.—*n.* Defeat; frustration; a sword used in fencing; a thin leaf of metal; anything which serves to set off a thing to advantage; something resembling a leaf; a curve in the tracery of Gothic windows, &c.
Foiler, foil'ėr, *n.* One who foils.
Foist, foist, *vt.* To introduce or insert surreptitiously or without warrant; to palm off.
Fold, fōld, *n.* The doubling or doubled part of any flexible substance; a plait; an inclosure for sheep; a flock of sheep; the Church.—*vt.* To double; to lay in plaits; to embrace; to confine, as sheep in a fold.—*vi.* To close together; to become folded.
Folder, fōld'ėr, *n.* One who folds; an instrument used in folding paper.
Foliaceous, fō-li-ā'shus, *a.* Leafy; of the nature or form of a leaf.
Foliage, fō'li-āj, *n.* Leaves collectively; ornamental representation of leaves.
Foliate, fō'li-āt, *vt.* To beat into a leaf or thin plate or lamina.
Foliated, fō'li-āt-ed, *p.a.* Covered with a thin plate; being in laminæ; having leaf-shaped ornaments.
Foliation, fō-li-ā'shon, *n.* The leafing of plants; operation of spreading foil over a surface; property in certain rocks of dividing into laminæ; tracery of Gothic windows.
Folio, fō'li-ō, *n.* A book of the largest size, formed by sheets of paper once doubled; a page; number appended to each page; a written page of a certain number of words.
Folk, fōk, *n.* People in general; certain people discriminated from others, as old *folks*.
Folk-lore, fōk'lōr, *n.* Rural superstitions, tales, traditions, or legends.
Follicle, fol'li-kl, *n.* A little bag or vesicle in animals or plants.

Follow, fol'ō, *vt.* To go or come after; to chase; to accompany; to succeed; to result from; to understand; to copy; to practise; to be occupied with; to be guided by.—*vi.* To come after another; to ensue; to result.
Follower, fol'ō-ėr, *n.* An adherent; disciple; imitator; attendant; dependant.
Following, fol'ō-ing, *n.* A body of followers. —*p.a.* Being next after; succeeding.
Folly, fol'i, *n.* Foolishness; imbecility; a weak or foolish act; criminal weakness.
Foment, fō-ment', *vt.* To apply warm lotions to; to abet; to stir up (in a bad sense).
Fomentation, fō-ment-ā'shon, *n.* Act of fomenting; lotion applied; instigation; encouragement.
Fomenter, fō-ment'ėr, *n.* One who foments; one who encourages or instigates.
Fond, fond, *a.* Foolish; foolishly tender and loving; doting; loving; relishing.
Fondle, fon'dl, *vt.* (fondling, fondled). To treat with fondness; to caress.
Fondly, fond'li, *adv.* Foolishly; lovingly.
Fondness, fond'nes, *n.* Affection; great liking.
Font, font, *n.* A large basin in which water is contained for baptizing; a complete assortment of printing types of one size.
Food, föd, *n.* Whatever supplies nourishment to animals or plants; nutriment; provisions; whatever feeds or augments.
Fool, föl, *n.* One destitute of reason; a simpleton; a silly person; a buffoon.—*vi.* To play the fool; to trifle.—*vt.* To make a fool of; to deceive.
Foolery, föl'ė-ri, *n.* Habitual folly; act of folly; absurdity.
Foolhardy, föl'här-di, *a.* Daring without judgment; foolishly bold; venturesome.
Foolish, föl'ish, *a.* Void of understanding; acting without judgment or discretion; silly; ridiculous; unwise.
Foolishly, föl'ish-li, *adv.* Unwisely; absurdly.
Foolscap, fölz'kap, *n.* Paper of the smallest regular size but one, about 17 inches by 14.
Foot, fụt, *n.*; pl. **feet,** fēt. The lower extremity of the leg; that on which a thing stands; the base; infantry; a measure of twelve inches; a measure of syllables in a verse.—*vi.* To dance; to tread to measure or music; to skip; to walk.—*vt.* To tread; to dance; to trip; to add a foot to, as to a stocking.
Football, fụt'bạl, *n.* An inflated leather ball to be driven by the foot; a game played with such a ball.
Foot-boy, fụt'boi, *n.* An attendant in livery.
Foot-cloth, fụt'kloth, *n.* The covering of a horse, reaching down to his heels.
Footfall, fụt'fạl, *n.* A footstep; a stumble.
Foothold, fụt'hōld, *n.* That on which one may tread or rest securely; firm standing.
Footing, fụt'ing, *n.* Ground for the foot; established place; basis; tread.
Foot-lights, fụt'lits, *n.pl.* A row of lights in a theatre on the front of the stage.
Footman, fụt'man, *n.* A menial servant; a runner; a servant in livery.
Footmark, fụt'märk, *n.* Mark of a foot.
Footpad, fụt'pad, *n.* A highwayman or robber on foot.
Footpath, fụt'path, *n.* A narrow path for foot passengers only.
Foot-pound, fụt'pound, *n.* The unit of work done by a mechanical force, representing one pound weight raised through a height of one foot.
Footprint, fụt'print, *n.* The impression of the foot.
Foot-sore, fụt'sōr, *a.* Having the feet sore or tender, as by much walking.
Foot-stalk, fụt'stạk, *n.* The stalk of a leaf.
Footstep, fụt'step, *n.* A track; the mark of the foot; vestige; *pl.* example; course.
Footstool, fụt'stöl, *n.* A stool for the feet.
Fop, fop, *n.* A coxcomb; a dandy.
Fopling, fop'ling, *n.* A petty fop.
Foppery, fop'ė-ri, *n.* Showy folly; idle affectation.
Foppish, fop'ish, *a.* Dressing in the extreme of fashion; affected in manners.
For, for, *prep.* In the place of; because of; in favour of; toward; during; in quest of; according to; as far as; notwithstanding; in proportion to.—*conj.* Because.
Forage, fo'rāj, *n.* Food for horses and cattle; act of providing forage.—*vi.* (foraging, foraged). To collect forage; to rove in search of food.—*vt.* To strip of provisions for horses, &c.; to supply with forage. **Forage cap,** *n.* Undress cap worn by soldiers of all branches of the army.
Forager, fo'rāj-ėr, *n.* One who forages.
Foramen, fō-rā'men, *n.*; pl. **Foramina,** fō-ram'in-a. A small natural opening in animals or plants.
Foraminifera, fō-ram'i-nif''ėr-a, *n.pl.* An order of minute animals furnished with a shell perforated by pores.
Foraminous, fō-ram'in-us, *a.* Full of minute holes; porous.
Forasmuch, for-az-much', *conj.* In consideration of; because that.
Foray, fo'rā, *vt.* To ravage; to pillage.—*n.* A predatory excursion; a raid.
Forbear, for-bār', *vi.* To keep away; to cease; to delay; to refrain.—*vt.* To abstain from; to avoid doing.
Forbearance, for-bār'ans, *n.* Act of forbearing; restraint of passion; long-suffering; mildness.
Forbearing, for-bār'ing, *p.a.* Patient; long-suffering.
Forbid, for-bid', *vt.* To prohibit; to oppose; to obstruct.—*vi.* To utter a prohibition.
Forbidden, for-bid'n, *p.a.* Prohibited.
Forbidding, for-bid'ing, *p.a.* Repelling approach; disagreeable; repulsive.
Force, fōrs, *n.* Strength; active power; might; violence; coercion; cogency; efficacy; power for war; troops; a waterfall.—*vt.* (forcing, forced). To compel; to impel; to take by violence; to ravish; to twist o overstrain; to ripen by artificial means; to stuff; to farce.—*vi.* To use force or violence.
Forced, fōrst, *p.a.* Affected; overstrained; unnatural.
Forceful, fōrs'fụl, *a.* Possessing force; acting with power; impetuous.
Forceless, fōrs'les, *a.* Feeble; impotent.
Forcemeat, fōrs'mēt, *n.* Meat chopped and seasoned, served up alone or as stuffing.
Forceps, for'seps, *n.* A surgical instrument on the principle of pincers for holding anything difficult to be held by the hand.
Forcible, fōrs'i-bl, *a.* Efficacious; potent; cogent; done by force; suffered by force.

Forcing, fōrs'ing, *n.* Art of raising plants or fruits, at an earlier season than the natural one, by artificial heat.
Forclose, Forclosure, *See* FORECLOSE.
Ford, fōrd, *n.* A shallow place in a river or other water, where it may be passed on foot. —*vt.* To cross by walking; to wade through.
Fordable, fōrd'a-bl, *a.* That may be forded.
Fordo, fōr-dö', *vt.* To destroy; to undo; to ruin; to exhaust.
Fore, fōr, *a.* In front of; anterior; coming first in time; prior.—*adv.* In the part that precedes or goes first.
Fore-and-aft, fōr'and-äft, *a.* In a direction from stem to stern.
Fore-arm, fōr'ärm, *n.* The part of the arm between the elbow and the wrist.
Forearm, fōr-ärm', *vt.* To arm for attack or resistance before the time of need.
Forebode, fōr-bōd', *vt.* To foretell; to prognosticate; to be prescient of.
Forecast, fōr-käst', *vt.* To foresee; to scheme beforehand.—*vi.* To foresee.—*n.* fōr'käst. Contrivance beforehand; foresight; estimate of what will happen.
Forecastle, fōr'kas-l, *n.* That part of the upper deck of a vessel forward of the foremast; the forward part of a merchant vessel.
Foreclose, fōr-klōz', *vt.* To preclude; to stop.
Foreclosure, fōr-klōz'ūr, *n.* Prevention.
Foredoom, fōr-döm', *vt.* To doom beforehand.
Forefather, fōr'fä-THėr, *n.* A progenitor; an ancestor.
Forefend, fōr-fend', *vt.* *See* FORFEND.
Forefinger, fōr'fing-gėr, *n.* The finger next to the thumb.
Fore-foot, fōr'fųt, *n.* One of the anterior feet of a quadruped.
Forefront, fōr'frunt, *n.* The foremost part.
Forego, fōr-gō', *vt.* To go before; to precede. *See* FORGO.
Foregoing, fōr-gō'ing, *p.a.* Preceding; antecedent.
Foregone, fōr-gon', or fōr'gon, *p.a.* Past; preceding; predetermined.
Foreground, fōr'ground, *n.* The part of a scene or picture represented as nearest the observer.
Forehand, fōr'hand, *a.* Done sooner than is regular or necessary; anticipative.
Forehanded, fōr'hand-ed, *a.* Early; timely; seasonable; prosperous.
Forehead, fōr'hed or fo'red, *n.* The part of the face above the eyes; the brow.
Foreign, fo'rin, *a.* Belonging to another nation or country; alien; not to the purpose; irrelevant.
Foreigner, fo'rin-ėr, *n.* A person born in a foreign country; an alien.
Forejudge, fōr-juj', *vt.* To judge beforehand, or before hearing the facts and proof.
Forejudgment, fōr-juj'ment, *n.* Judgment previously formed.
Foreknow, fōr-nō', *vt.* To know beforehand; to foresee.
Foreknowledge, fōr-nol'ej, *n.* Knowledge of a thing before it happens.
Foreland, fōr'land, *n.* Headland; cape.
Foreleg, fōr'leg, *n.* One of the anterior legs of an animal, chair, &c.
Forelock, fōr'lok, *n.* The lock of hair that grows from the fore part of the head.
Foreman, fōr'man, *n.* The first or chief man; chief man of a jury; chief workman.
Foremast, fōr'mast, *n.* The forward mast in any vessel.
Foremost, fōr'mōst, *a.* First in place, time, rank, or dignity; most advanced.
Forenoon, fōr'nön, *n.* The part of the day before noon, or from morning to noon.
Forensic, fō-ren'sik, *a.* Belonging to courts of justice, or to public debate; used in courts or legal proceedings.
Foreordain, fōr-or-dān', *vt.* To ordain beforehand.
Forepart, fōr'pärt, *n.* The anterior part; part first in time; part most advanced in place; beginning.
Forerun, fōr-run', *vt.* To run before; to usher in; to prognosticate.
Forerunner, fōr'run-ėr, *n.* One who runs before; harbinger; precursor; prognostic.
Foresaid, fōr'sed, *p.a.* Aforesaid.
Foresail, fōr'sāl, *n.* The lowermost square sail set on the foremast; a large fore-and-aft sail on a schooner's foremast.
Foresee, fōr-sē', *vt.* To see beforehand; to foreknow.
Foreshadow, fōr-sha'dō, *vt.* To shadow or typify beforehand.
Foreshore, fōr'shōr, *n.* The sloping part of a shore between high and low water-mark.
Foreshorten, fōr-short'n, *vt.* To shorten, in drawing and painting, the parts of figures that stand forward.
Foreshow, fōr-shō', *vt.* To show beforehand; to foretell.
Foresight, fōr'sit, *n.* Foreknowledge; provident care; forethought; sight on muzzle of gun or rifle.
Forest, fo'rest, *n.* An extensive wood; a district devoted to the purposes of the chase; a tract once a royal forest.—*a.* Relating to a forest; sylvan; rustic.—*vt.* To convert into a forest.
Forestall, fōr-stąl', *vt.* To anticipate; to hinder by preoccupation.
Forester, fo'rest-ėr, *n.* One who watches a forest and preserves the game; one who manages the timber on an estate; an inhabitant of a forest.
Forestry, fo'rest-ri, *n.* Art of cultivating forests, or of managing growing timber.
Foretaste, fōr'tāst, *n.* A taste beforehand; anticipation.—*vt.* To taste before possession; to anticipate.
Foretell, fōr-tel', *vt.* To tell beforehand; to predict.—*vi.* To utter prophecy.
Forethought, fōr'thąt, *n.* A thinking beforehand; foresight; provident care.
Foretoken, fōr-tō'kn, *vt.* To betoken beforehand.—*n.* A previous sign; prognostic.
Foretop, fōr'top, *n.* Hair on the forepart of the head; platform at the head of a foremast.
Forever, for-ev'ėr, *adv.* At all times; through endless ages; eternally.
Fore-vouched, fōr-voucht', *a.* Affirmed before.
Forewarn, fōr-warn', *vt.* To warn beforehand; to give previous notice to.
Foreword, fōr'wėrd, *n.* A preface.
Forfeit, for'fit, *vt.* To lose by a misdeed.—*n.* That which is forfeited; fine; penalty.
Forfeitable, for'fit-a-bl, *a.* Liable to be forfeited.

Forfeiture, for'fit-ūr, *n.* Act of forfeiting; loss of some right, estate, honour, &c., by a crime or fault; fine; penalty.
Forfend, for-fend', *vt.* To ward off; to avert.
Forgather, for-gaᴛʜ'ėr, *vi.* To meet.
Forge, fōrj, *n.* A furnace in which iron is heated and wrought; a smithy.—*vt.* (forging, forged). To frame or fabricate; to form by heating and hammering; to counterfeit.—*vi.* To commit forgery; to move on slowly and laboriously; to work one's way.
Forger, fōrj'ėr, *n.* One who forges; one who counterfeits.
Forgery, fōrj'ė-ri, *n.* The crime of counterfeiting; that which is forged or counterfeited.
Forget, for-get', *vt.* (forgetting, pret. forgot, pp. forgot, forgotten). To lose the remembrance of; to slight; to neglect.
Forgetful, for-get'ful, *a.* Apt to forget; neglectful; oblivious.
Forgetfulness, for-get'ful-nes, *n.* Oblivion; obliviousness; inattention.
Forget-me-not, for-get'mē-not, *n.* A small, bright blue flower.
Forging, fōrj'ing, *n.* The act of one who forges; an article of metal forged.
Forgive, for-giv', *vt.* (forgiving, pret. forgave, pp. forgiven). To pardon; to remit; to overlook.
Forgiveness, for-giv'nes, *n.* Act of forgiving; pardon; disposition to pardon; remission.
Forgiving, for-giv'ing, *p.a.* Disposed to forgive; merciful; compassionate.
Forgo, for-gō', *vt.* To forbear to enjoy or possess; to renounce; to resign.
Forisfamiliate, fō'ris-fa-mil"i-āt, *vt.* To free from parental authority; to put in possession of property in his father's lifetime.
Fork, fork, *n.* An instrument with two or more prongs, used for lifting or pitching anything; a branch or division; a prong.—*vi.* To shoot into branches; to divide into two.—*vt.* To raise or pitch with a fork, as hay, &c.
Forked, forkt, *a.* Opening into two or more prongs or shoots.
Forky, fork'i, *a.* Forked.
Forlorn, for-lorn', *a.* Deserted; abandoned; miserable.—**Forlorn hope,** a body of men appointed to perform some specially perilous service.
Form, form, *n.* Shape; manner; pattern; order; empty show; prescribed mode; ceremony; schedule; a long seat; a bench; a class; the seat or bed of a hare.—*vt.* To shape or mould; to arrange; to invent; to make up.—*vi.* To take a form.
Formal, form'al, *a.* Relating to outward form; according to form; precise; ceremonious; having mere appearance.
Formalism, form'al-izm, *n.* Quality of being addicted to mere forms; ceremonial religion.
Formalist, form'al-ist, *n.* One who observes forms.
Formality, form-al'i-ti, *n.* Quality of being formal; ceremony; a mere form.
Formally, form'al-li, *adv.* In a formal manner; precisely.
Format, for'mā, *n.* Size of a book as regards length and breadth; get-up.
Formation, form-ā'shon, *n.* Act of forming; production; manner in which a thing is formed; any assemblage of rocks or strata, referred to a common origin; arrangement.
Formative, form'at-iv, *a.* Giving form; plastic; derivative.—*n.* That which serves to give form to a word, and is no part of the root.
Former, form'ėr, *n.* He who forms.—*a. comp. deg.* Before in time; long past; mentioned before another.
Formerly, form'ėr-li, *adv.* In time past; of old; in days of yore.
Formic, for'mik, *a.* Pertaining to ants.
Formicary, for'mi-ka-ri, *n.* A colony of ants; an ant-hill.
Formidable, for'mid-a-bl, *a.* Exciting fear or apprehension; difficult to deal with or undertake.
Formless, form'les, *a.* Without a determinate form; shapeless.
Formula, form'ū-la, *n.*; pl. **-læ.** A prescribed form; a confession of faith; expression for resolving certain problems in mathematics; expression of chemical composition.
Formulary, form'ū-la-ri, *n.* A book containing prescribed forms, as of oaths, declarations, prayers; a book of precedents.—*a.* Prescribed; ritual.
Formulate, for'mū-lāt, *vt.* To express in a formula; to put into a precise and comprehensive statement.
Fornicate, for'ni-kāt, *vi.* To have unlawful sexual intercourse.
Fornication, for-ni-kā'shon, *n.* Incontinence of unmarried persons.
Fornicator, for'ni-kāt-ėr, *n.* One guilty of fornication.
Forsake, for-sāk', *vt.* (forsaking, pret. forsook, pp. forsaken). To abandon; to renounce; to withdraw from.
Forsooth, for-söth', *adv.* In very truth; in fact. (Chiefly used in irony.)
Forswear, for-swār', *vt.* To renounce upon oath; to abjure; to swear falsely; to perjure oneself.—*vi.* To swear falsely.
Fort, fōrt, *n.* A fortified place; a fortress.
Fortalice, fōr'ta-lis, *n.* A small fort; outwork of a fortification.
Forte, fōr'tā, *adv.* A direction to sing or play with force.
Forte, fōrt, *n.* The strong portion of a sword-blade; peculiar talent; strong point; chief excellence.
Forth, fōrth, *adv.* Forward in place or order; out into public view; abroad; onward in time.
Forthcoming, fōrth-kum'ing, *a.* Coming forth; making appearance; ready to appear.
Forthright, fōrth'rīt, *adv.* Straight forward; straightway.—*a.* Straightforward; direct.
Forthwith, fōrth-with', *adv.* Without delay.
Fortieth, for'ti-eth, *a.* The ordinal of forty.—*n.* One of forty equal parts.
Fortification, for'ti-fi-kā"shon, *n.* The art or science of fortifying places; the works erected in defence; a fortified place; additional strength.
Fortify, for'ti-fī, *vt.* (fortifying, fortified). To make strong; to strengthen by forts, batteries, &c.; to invigorate; to increase the strength of.
Fortissimo, for-tis'sē-mō, *adv.* Direction to sing or play with the utmost loudness.
Fortitude, for'ti-tūd, *n.* Firmness of mind to encounter danger, or to bear pain or adversity; resolute endurance.
Fortnight, fort'nīt, *n.* The space of fourteen days; two weeks.

Fortnightly, fort'nīt-li, *adv.* and *a.* Once a fortnight; every fortnight.

Fortress, fort'res, *n.* A fortified place; stronghold; place of security.

Fortuitous, for-tū'it-us, *a.* Happening by chance; accidental; incidental.

Fortunate, for'tū-nāt, *a.* Having good fortune; successful; coming by good luck.

Fortunately, for'tū-nāt-li, *adv.* By good fortune; happily.

Fortune, for'tūn, *n.* Chance; luck; the good or ill that befalls man; means of living; estate; great wealth; destiny; the power regarded as determining the lots of life.

Fortune-hunter, for'tūn-hunt-ėr, *n.* A man who seeks to marry a rich woman.

Fortune-teller, for'tūn-tel-ėr, *n.* One who pretends to foretell the events of one's life.

Forty, for'ti, *a.* and *n.* Four times ten.

Forum, fō'rum, *n.* A public place in ancient Rome, where causes were tried; a tribunal; jurisdiction.

Forward, for'wėrd, *adv.* Toward a place in front; onward.—*a.* Near or towards the forepart; in advance of something; ready; bold; pert; advanced beyond the usual degree; too ready.—*vt.* To help onward; to hasten; to send forward; to transmit.—*n.* In football, hockey, &c., one of the players in the front line.

Forwardly, for'wėrd-li, *adv.* Eagerly; hastily; pertly; saucily.

Forwardness, for'wėrd-nes, *n.* Promptness; eagerness; want of due reserve or modesty; pertness; earliness.

Forwards, for'wėrdz, *adv.* Same as *Forward.*

Fosse, fos, *n.* A ditch or moat; a trench; a kind of cavity in a bone.

Fossick, fos'ik, *vi.* To search for waste gold in relinquished workings, &c.

Fossil, fos'sil, *a.* Dug out of the earth; petrified and preserved in rocks.—*n.* Petrified remains of plants and animals found in the strata composing the surface of our globe.

Fossiliferous, fos-sil-if'ėr-us, *a.* Containing fossils.

Fossilize, fos'sil-īz, *vt.* To convert into a fossil state.—*vi.* To be changed into a fossil state; to become antiquated.

Fossorial, fos-sō'ri-al, *a.* Digging; burrowing.

Foster, fos'tėr, *vt.* To nourish; to bring up; to encourage; to promote.

Foster-child, fos'tėr-child, *n.* A child nursed by a woman not the mother, or bred by a man not the father. (Also *foster-brother*, *-mother*, *-parent*, &c.)

Fosterling, fos'tėr-ling, *n.* A foster-child.

Fother, foᴛʜ'ėr, *n.* A weight for lead = 19½ cwts.—*vt.* To stop a leak by letting down a sail over it.

Foul, foul, *a.* Covered with or containing extraneous matter which is offensive; turbid; obscene; rainy or tempestuous; unfair; loathsome; entangled or in collision.—*vt.* To defile; to dirty.—*vi.* To become dirty; to come into collision; to become clogged.—*n.* A colliding, or impeding due motion; an unfair piece of play.

Foulard, fō-lärd', *n.* A thin silk fabric, without twill; a silk handkerchief.

Foully, foul'li, *adv.* Filthily; unfairly.

Foul-mouthed, foul'mouᴛʜd, *a.* Using scurrilous or abusive language.

Foumart, fō'märt, *n.* The pole-cat.

Found, found, *vt.* To lay the base of; to establish; to institute; to form by melting metal and pouring it into a mould; to cast.—*vi.* To rest or rely (with *on* or *upon*). Pret. and pp. of *find*.

Foundation, found-ā'shon, *n.* Act of founding; base of an edifice; base; endowment; endowed institution.

Foundationer, found-ā'shon-ėr, *n.* One who derives support from the funds or foundation of a college or endowed school.

Founder, found'ėr, *n.* One who lays a foundation; an originator; an endower; one who casts metal.—*vi.* To fill with water and sink; to miscarry; to go lame, as a horse.

Foundery, found'ė-ri, *n.* The art of founding or casting; a foundry.

Foundling, found'ling, *n.* A child found without anyone to care for it.

Foundry, found'ri, *n.* An establishment for casting metals.

Fount, fount, *n.* A fountain (*poetical*); a complete stock of printing type; a font.

Fountain, fount'ān, *n.* A spring or source of water; an artificial jet or shower; head of a river; original; source.

Fountainhead, fount'ān-hed, *n.* The head of a stream; primary source; origin.

Fountain-pen, fount'ān-pen, *n.* A pen with a reservoir for ink.

Four, fōr, *a.* and *n.* Twice two; three and one.

Fourfold, fōr'fōld, *a.* and *adv.* Quadruple; four times told.—*n.* Four times as much.

Four-in-hand, fōr'in-hand, *n.* A vehicle drawn by four horses guided by one driver.

Fourscore, fōr'skōr, *a.* and *n.* Eighty.

Foursquare, fōr-skwār, *a.* Having four sides and four angles equal; quadrangular.

Fourteen, fōr'tēn, *a.* and *n.* Four and ten.

Fourteenth, fōr'tēnth, *a.* The ordinal of fourteen.—*n.* One of fourteen equal parts.

Fourth, fōrth, *a.* The ordinal of four.—*n.* One of four equal parts.

Fourthly, fōrth'li, *adv.* In the fourth place.

Foveate, Foveolate, fō'vē-āt, fō'vē-ō-lāt, *a.* Marked by little depressions or pits.

Fowl, foul, *n.* A bird; a domestic or barn-door bird.—*vi.* To catch wild fowls for game or food.

Fowler, foul'ėr, *n.* A sportsman who pursues wild fowls.

Fowling-piece, foul'ing-pēs, *n.* A light gun for shooting wild fowl.

Fox, foks, *n.* A carnivorous animal, remarkable for cunning; a sly cunning fellow.—*vt.* and *i.* To turn sour; to become marked with brown spots, as paper.

Foxglove, foks'gluv, *n.* A British plant yielding a powerful medicine, both sedative and diuretic; digitalis.

Fox-hound, foks'hound, *n.* A hound for chasing foxes.

Fox-trot, foks-trot, *n.* A dance of American origin.

Foxy, foks'i, *a.* Pertaining to foxes; wily; cunning; stained with reddish marks; sour.

Fracas, fra-kä', *n.* An uproar; a brawl.

Fraction, frak'shon, *n.* A fragment; a very small part; one or more of the equal parts into which a unit or number is divided.

Fractional, frak'shon-al, *a.* Belonging to a fraction; pertaining to a method of distilla-

tion by which products of different kinds are successively got from the substance treated.
Fractionize, Fractionate, frak'shon-īz, frak'-shon-āt, *vt.* To subject to the process of fractional distillation.
Fractious, frak'shus, *a.* Snappish; peevish; cross.
Fracture, frak'tūr, *n.* A breach or break; breaking of a bone; manner in which a mineral breaks.—*vt.* (fracturing, fractured). To break.
Fragile, fra'jil, *a.* Easily broken; frail; weak.
Fragility, fra-jil'i-ti, *n.* Quality of being fragile; delicacy of substance.
Fragment, frag'ment, *n.* A part broken off; an imperfect thing.
Fragmentary, frag'ment-a-ri, *a.* Composed of fragments; not complete; disconnected.
Fragrance, Fragrancy, frā'grans, frā'gran-si, *n.* Quality of being fragrant; sweetness of smell; perfume.
Fragrant, frā'grant, *a.* Sweet-smelling; spicy; balmy; aromatic.
Frail, frāl, *a.* Easily broken; weak; liable to fail and decay.—*n.* A kind of basket.
Frailty, frāl'ti, *n.* State or quality of being frail; infirmity; liableness to be deceived or seduced; failing; foible.
Frame, frām, *vt.* (framing, framed). To make; to construct; to devise; to adjust; to shape; to place in a frame.—*n.* Anything composed of parts fitted together; structure; bodily structure; framework; particular state, as of the mind; mood or disposition.
Framework, frām'wėrk, *n.* A structure or fabric for supporting anything; a frame.
Framing, frām'ing, *n.* Act of constructing a frame; frame thus constructed; rough timber-work of a house.
Franc, frangk, *n.* A silver coin of France, formerly of the value of 9½*d.*
Franchise, fran'chīz, *n.* Right granted by a sovereign or government; right of voting for a member of parliament.
Franciscan, fran-sis'kan, *n.* A mendicant friar of the order of St. Francis; a Gray Friar.
Francolin, frang'ko-lin, *n.* A bird allied to the partridge.
Frangibility, fran-ji-bil'i-ti, *n.* The state or quality of being frangible.
Frangible, fran'ji-bl, *a.* That may be broken; brittle; fragile.
Frank, frangk', *n.* One of the ancient German race of the Franks; a name given by Orientals to inhabitants of W. Europe.
Frank, frangk, *a.* Free in uttering real sentiments; candid; outspoken.—*n.* Signature of a privileged person formerly securing free transmission of a letter.—*vt.* To exempt from postage.
Frankincense, frangk'in-sens, *n.* An odoriferous gum-resin used as a perfume.
Franklin, frangk'lin, *n.* Formerly an English freeholder; a yeoman.
Frankly, frangk'li, *adv.* In a frank manner; openly; freely; unreservedly.
Frantic, fran'tik, *a.* Mad; raving; furious; outrageous; distracted.
Franticly, Frantically, fran'tik-li, fran'tik-al-li, *adv.* Madly; outrageously.
Fraternal, fra-tėr'nal, *a.* Brotherly; pertaining to brethren; becoming brothers.
Fraternity, fra-tėr'ni-ti, *n.* State or relationship of a brother; brotherhood; society, class, or profession.
Fraternize, fra'tėr-nīz, *vi.* (fraternizing, fraternized). To associate as brothers, or as men of like occupation or disposition.
Fratricidal, fra-tri-sīd'al, *a.* Pertaining to fratricide.
Fratricide, fra'tri-sīd, *n.* Murder of a brother; one who murders a brother.
Frau, frou, *n.* German married woman or widow; title equivalent to *Mrs.*
Fraud, fra̤d, *n.* Artifice by which the right or interest of another is injured; deception.
Fraudful, fra̤d'fu̇l, *a.* Full of fraud; deceitful.
Fraudfully, fra̤d'fu̇l-li, *adv.* In a fraudful or fraudulent manner.
Fraudulence, Fraudulency, fra̤d'ū-lens, fra̤d'ū-len-si, *n.* Quality of being fradulent.
Fraudulent, fra̤d'ū-lent, *a.* Using fraud in bargains, &c.; founded on fraud; dishonest.
Fraudulently, fra̤d'ū-lent-li, *adv.* By fraud, artifice, or imposition.
Fraught, fra̤t, *a.* Freighted; stored; abounding; pregnant.
Fräulein, froi'līn, *n.* German unmarried woman; title equivalent to *Miss.*
Fray, frā, *n.* An affray; a broil; a fight; a frayed place in cloth.—*vt.* To rub; to fret, as cloth, by wearing.—*vi.* To become worn by rubbing.
Freak, frēk, *n.* A sudden causeless turn of the mind; a caprice; a sport.—*vt.* To variegate.
Freakish, frēk'ish, *a.* Capricious; grotesque.
Freckle, frek'l, *n.* A yellowish spot in the skin; any small spot or discoloration.—*vt.* or *i.* (freckling, freckled). To give or acquire freckles.
Freckly, frek'l-i, *a.* Sprinkled with freckles.
Free, frē, *a.* Being at liberty; instituted by a free people; not arbitrary or despotic; open; clear; disjoined; licentious; candid; generous; gratuitous; guiltless.—*vt.* (freeing, freed). To set free; to liberate; to disentangle; to exempt; to absolve from some charge.
Freebooter, frē'böt-ėr, *n.* A robber; a pillager; a plunderer.
Freebooting, frē'böt-ing, *a.* Pertaining to or like freebooters.
Freeborn, frē'born, *a.* Born free; inheriting liberty.
Freedman, frēd'man, *n.* A man who has been a slave and is set free.
Freedom, frē'dum, *n.* State of being free; liberty; particular privilege; facility of doing anything; frankness; undue familiarity.
Freehand, frē'hand, *a.* Applied to drawing in which the hand is not assisted by any guiding or measuring instruments.
Freehanded, frē'hand-ed, *a.* Open-handed; liberal.
Freehold, frē'hōld, *n.* An estate for which the owner owes no service except to the crown; tenure by which such an estate is held.
Freeholder, frē'hōld-ėr, *n.* The possessor of a freehold.
Free-lance, frē'lans, *n.* A mercenary soldier of the middle ages; one unattached to any party.
Freely, frē'li, *adv.* In a free manner; readily; liberally.
Freeman, frē'man, *n.* One who is free; one who enjoys or is entitled to a franchise.

Freemason, frē'mā-sn, *n.* A member of a secret friendly society or organization.
Freemasonry, frē'mā-sn-ri, *n.* The mysteries in which freemasons are initiated.
Freeness, frē'nes, *n.* State or quality of being free; openness; frankness; liberality.
Free-spoken, frē'spōk-n, *a.* Accustomed to speak without reserve.
Freestone, frē'stōn, *n.* Any stone composed of sand or grit, easily cut.
Free-thinker, frē'thingk-ėr, *n.* One who is free from the common modes of thinking in religious matters; a deist; a sceptic.
Free-trade, frē'trād, *n.* Commerce free from customs on foreign commodities.
Free-will, frē'wil, *n.* The power of directing our own actions, without restraint by necessity or fate.—*a.* Spontaneous.
Freeze, frēz, *vi.* (freezing, pret. froze, pp. frozen or froze). To be congealed by cold; to be hardened into ice; to be of that degree of cold at which water congeals; to stagnate; to shiver or stiffen with cold.—*vt.* To congeal; to chill; to make credits, &c., temporarily unrealizable.
Freezing, frēz'ing, *a.* Such as to freeze; chilling.
Freight, frāt, *n.* The cargo of a ship; lading; hire of a ship; charge for the transportation of goods.—*vt.* To load with goods; to hire for carrying goods.
Freightage, frāt'āj, *n.* Act of freighting; money paid for freight.
Freighter, frāt'ėr, *n.* One who charters and loads a ship.
French, frensh, *a.* Pertaining to France or its inhabitants.—*n.* The language spoken by the people of France; the people of France.
Frenetic, Frenetical, fre-net'ik, fre-net'ik-al, *a.* Frenzied; frantic.
Frenzied, fren'zid, *a.* Affected with frenzy; proceeding from frenzy.
Frenzy, fren'zi, *n.* Madness; distraction; violent agitation of the mind.
Frequency, frē'kwen-si, *n.* State or character of being frequent; repetition.
Frequent, frē'kwent, *a.* That takes place repeatedly; often seen or done; doing a thing often.—*vt.* frē-kwent'. To visit often; to resort to habitually.
Frequentative, frē-kwent'at-iv, *a.* Denoting frequent repetition of an action.—*n.* A verb denoting frequent repetition.
Frequently, frē'kwent-li, *adv.* Often; many times at short intervals; commonly.
Fresco, fres'kō, *n.* A method of painting with mineral and earthy pigments on walls of which the plaster is not quite dry.
Fresh, fresh, *a.* Full of health and strength; vigorous; brisk; bright; not faded; in good condition; not stale; cool and agreeable; clearly remembered; new; not salt; unpractised; unused.
Freshen, fresh'n, *vt.* To make fresh; to revive.—*vi.* To grow fresh.
Freshet, fresh'et, *n.* A small stream of fresh water; flood of a river.
Freshly, fresh'li, *adv.* In a fresh manner; with freshness; newly; recently; anew.
Freshman, fresh'man, *n.* A novice; a first year's student at an English university.
Freshness, fresh'nes, *n.* State or quality of being fresh, in all senses.
Fret, fret, *vt.* (fretting, fretted). To eat into; to corrode; to wear away; to chafe; to vex; to ornament or furnish with frets; to variegate.—*vi.* To be vexed; to utter peevish expressions; to rankle. — *n.* Irritation; peevishness; an ornament of bands or fillets; a piece of perforated work; one of the crossbars on the finger-board of some stringed instruments.
Fretful, fret'fụl, *a.* Disposed to fret; peevish; irritable; petulant; angry.
Fretwork, fret'wėrk, *n.* Ornamental work consisting of a series or combination of frets.
Friability, Friableness, frī-a-bil'i-ti, frī'a-bl-nes, *n.* Quality of being friable.
Friable, frī'a-bl, *a.* Easily rubbed down, crumbled, or pulverized.
Friar, frī'ėr, *n.* A monk; a male member of a monastery.
Fribble, frib'bl, *n.* A frivolous, trifling fellow. —*vi.* (fribbling, fribbled). To trifle.
Fribbler, frib'bl-ėr, *n.* A trifler.
Fricassee, fri-kas-sē', *n.* A dish made by cutting chickens or rabbits, &c., into pieces, and dressing them in a frying-pan, &c., with strong sauces.
Fricasseed, fri-kas-sēd', *a.* Dressed in fricassee.
Friction, frik'shon, *n.* A rubbing; effect of rubbing; resistance which a moving body meets with from the surface on which it moves.
Friday, frī'dā, *n.* The sixth day of the week.— **Good Friday,** the Friday preceding Easter, sacred as the day of Christ's crucifixion.
Friend, frend, *n.* One attached to another by affection; a favourer; one who is propitious; a favourite; a Quaker.
Friendless, frend'les, *a.* Destitute of friends; wanting support; forlorn.
Friendliness, frend'li-nes, *n.* Friendly disposition.
Friendly, frend'li, *a.* Like or becoming a friend; kind; favourable; disposed to peace.
Friendship, frend'ship, *n.* Intimacy resting on mutual esteem; kindness; aid.
Frieze, frēz, *n.* A coarse woollen cloth with a nap on one side; that part of the entablature of a column between the architrave and the cornice; upper part of the wall of a room and its decoration.—*vt.* (friezing, friezed). To form a nap on cloth; to frizzle; to curl.
Friezed, frēzd, *p.a.* Shaggy with nap or frieze.
Frigate, fri'gāt, *n.* A large fast sailing-ship which performed the functions of the modern cruiser.
Fright, frīt, *n.* Sudden and violent fear; terror; consternation; an ugly or ill-dressed person.—*vt.* To frighten.
Frighten, frīt'n, *vt.* To strike with fright or fear; to terrify; to scare; to alarm.
Frightful, frīt'fụl, *a.* Causing fright; terrible; dreadful; fearful.
Frightfully, frīt'fụl-li, *adv.* In a frightful manner; dreadfully; terribly.
Frigid, fri'jid, *a.* Cold; wanting spirit or zeal; stiff; formal; lifeless.
Frigidity, fri-jid'i-ti, *n.* Coldness; coldness of affection; dulness.
Frigidly, frij'id-li, *adv.* Coldly; dully.
Frigorific, fri-go-rif'ik, *a.* Causing cold; cooling.
Frill, fril, *n.* A crisp or plaited edging on an

article of dress; a ruffle.—*vt.* To decorate with frills.
Frilling, fril'ing, *n.* Frills collectively; ruffles; gathers, &c.
Fringe, frinj, *n.* An ornamental appendage to furniture or dress, consisting of loose threads; margin; extremity.—*vt.* (fringing, fringed). To border with fringe or a loose edging.
Fringed, frinjd, *p.a.* Bordered with fringe; having a certain kind of border or margin.
Frippery, frip'è-ri, *n.* Old worn-out clothes; waste matter; trifles; trumpery.—*a.* Trifling; contemptible.
Frisian, friz'i-an, *a.* Belonging to Friesland.—*n.* A native or the language of Friesland.
Frisk, frisk, *vi.* To dance, skip, and gambol in frolic and gaiety.—*n.* A frolic; a fit of wanton gaiety.
Frisket, fris'ket, *n.* A frame to keep paper in position when printing.
Frisky, fris'ki, *a.* Jumping with gaiety; gay; frolicsome; lively.
Frit, frit, *n.* The matter of which glass is made after it has been calcined.
Frith, frith, *n.* Same as *Firth*.
Fritillary, frit'il-la-ri, *n.* A genus of herbaceous bulbous plants, natives of north temperate regions; also a British butterfly.
Fritter, frit'èr, *n.* A kind of small cake fried; a small piece of meat fried; a small piece.—*vt.* To cut into small pieces to be fried; to break into small pieces; to waste by degrees (with *away*).
Frivolity, fri-vol'i-ti, *n.* Acts or habit of trifling; unbecoming levity.
Frivolous, fri'vol-us, *a.* Trivial; trifling; petty.
Frizz, friz, *vt.* To curl; to crisp; to form the nap of cloth into little burs.
Frizzle, friz'l, *vi.* (frizzling, frizzled). To curl; to crisp, as hair; to make crisp by cooking.—*n.* A curl; a lock of hair crisped.
Fro, frō, *adv.* From; away; back or backward.
Frock, frok, *n.* An ecclesiastical garment; a lady's gown; a child's dress; a blouse for men.
Frock-coat, frok'kōt, *n.* A coat with full skirts of the same length before and behind.
Frog, frog, *n.* An amphibious animal, remarkable for its activity in swimming and leaping; a kind of button or tassel on a coat or vestment; a loop used to support a sword or bayonet; horny growth on sole of horse's hoof.
Frolic, fro'lik, *a.* Joyous; merry; frisky; *poetic.*—*n.* A merry prank; merry-making.—*vi.* To play merry pranks; to gambol.
Frolicsome, fro'lik-sum, *a.* Full of frolics; given to pranks.
From, from, *prep.* Out of the neighbourhood or presence of; by reason of; denoting source, distance, absence, departure, &c.
Frond, frond, *n.* The leaf of a fern or other cryptogamic plant.
Frondescence, frond-es'ens, *n.* The time, act, or state of unfolding leaves.
Front, frunt, *n.* The forehead; the whole face; the fore part; boldness; impudence; the area of military operations.—*a.* Relating to the front or face.—*vt.* To stand with the front opposed to; to oppose; to face; to supply with a front.—*vi.* To face; to look.
Frontage, frunt'āj, *n.* The front part of an edifice, quay, &c.
Frontal, frunt'al, *a.* Belonging to the forehead.—*n.* An ornament for the forehead; a frontlet; a small pediment.
Fronted, frunt'ed, *p.a.* Formed with a front.
Frontier, fron'tēr, *n.* That part of a country which fronts another country; extreme part of a country.—*a.* Bordering; conterminous.
Frontispiece, fron'tis-pēs, *n.* The principal face of a building; an illustration facing the title-page of a book.
Frontless, frunt'les, *a.* Wanting shame or modesty; not diffident.
Frontlet, frunt'let, *n.* A fillet or band worn on the forehead.
Frore, frōr, *a.* Frozen; frosty: *poetical.*
Frost, frost, *n.* That temperature of the air which causes freezing; frozen dew; rime; coldness or severity of manner.—*vt.* To injure by frost; to ornament with anything resembling hoar-frost; to furnish with frost-nails.
Frost-bite, frost'bīt, *n.* Insensibility or deadness in any part of the body caused by exposure to frost.—*vt.* To affect with frost-bite.
Frostily, frost'i-li, *adv.* With frost or excessive cold; coldly.
Frosting, frost'ing, *n.* The composition, resembling hoar-frost, used to cover cake, &c.
Frost-nail, frost'nāl, *n.* A nail driven into a horse-shoe to prevent slipping on ice.
Frosty, frost'i, *a.* Producing or characterized by frost; chill in affection; resembling hoar-frost; gray-haired.
Froth, froth. *n.* Bubbles caused by fermentation or agitation; spume; empty talk; light unsubstantial matter.—*vt.* To cause to foam.—*vi.* To foam; to throw up spume.
Frothy, froth'i, *a.* Full or consisting of froth; not firm or solid.
Frounce, frouns, *n.* Old form of *flounce.*
Frouzy, Frowzy, frou'zi, *a.* Fetid; musty; dingy; in disorder; slatternly.
Froward, frō'wėrd, *a.* Perverse; ungovernable; disobedient; peevish.
Frown, froun, *vi.* To express displeasure by contracting the brow; to look stern; to scowl.—*n.* A wrinkling of the brow; a sour or stern look; any expression of displeasure.
Frozen, frōz'en, *p.a.* Congealed by cold; frosty; chill.
Fructescence, fruk-tes'ens, *n.* The fruiting season.
Fructiferous, fruk-tif'èr-us, *a.* Bearing fruit.
Fructification, fruk'ti-fi-kā"shon, *n.* Act of fructifying; the bearing of fruit; arrangement of the organs of reproduction in plants.
Fructify, fruk'ti-fī, *vt.* (fructifying, fructified). To make fruitful; to fertilize.—*vi.* To bear fruit.
Frugal, frö'gal, *a.* Economical; careful; thrifty.
Frugality, frö-gal'i-ti, *n.* Prudent economy; thrift.
Frugally, frö'gal-li, *adv.* In a frugal manner; with economy.
Frugiferous, frö-jif'èr-us, *a.* Producing fruit or crops; fruitful.
Frugivorous, frö-jiv-èr-us, *a.* Feeding on fruits, seeds, or corn, as birds.
Fruit, fröt, *n.* Whatever of a vegetable nature is of use to man or animals; the reproductive produce of a plant; such products collectively; the seed or matured ovary; that which is produced; offspring; effect; outcome.—*vi.* To produce fruit.

Fruitage, fröt'āj, *n.* Fruit collectively.
Fruiterer, fröt'ėr-ėr, *n.* One who deals in fruit.
Fruitery, fröt'ė-ri, *n.* A repository for fruit.
Fruitful, fröt'fụl, *a.* Very productive; fertile; plenteous; prolific.
Fruitfully, fröt'fụl-li, *adv.* In a fruitful manner; plenteously; abundantly.
Fruition, frö-i'shon, *n.* A using or enjoying; enjoyment; gratification; pleasure derived from use or possession.
Fruitless, fröt'les, *a.* Destitute of fruit; unprofitable; abortive; ineffectual.
Fruity, frö'ti, *a.* Resembling fruit; having the taste or flavour of fruit.
Frumentaceous, frö-men-tā'shus, *a.* Having the character of or resembling wheat or other cereal.
Frump, frump, *n.* A cross-tempered, old-fashioned female.
Frustrate, frus'trāt, *vt.* (frustrating, frustrated). To balk; to foil; to bring to nothing; to render of no effect.
Frustration, frus-trā'shon, *n.* Disappointment; defeat.
Frustum, frus'tum, *n.*; pl. **-tums** or **-ta.** A piece; the part which remains of a cone, pyramid, &c., when the top is cut off by a plane parallel to the base.
Frutescent, Fruticose, Fruticous, frö-tes'ent, frö'tik-ōs, frö'tik-us, *a.* Shrub-like; shrubby.
Fry, frī, *vt.* (frying, fried). To cook by roasting over a fire.—*vi.* To be cooked as above; to simmer; to be in agitation.—*n.* A dish of anything fried; state of mental ferment; young fishes at an early stage; swarm of small fishes, &c.; insignificant objects.
Fuchsia, fū'shi-a, *n.* A beautiful flowering shrub.
Fuddle, fud'l, *vt.* (fuddling, fuddled). To make stupid by drink; to spend in drinking. —*vi.* To drink to excess.
Fudge, fuj, *n.* or *interj.* Stuff; nonsense.
Fuel, fū'el, *n.* That which serves to feed fire, or to increase excitement. &c.—*vt.* To feed or furnish with fuel.
Fugacious, fū-gā'shus, *a.* Flying or fleeing away; volatile; soon shed or dropped.
Fugacity, fū-gas'i-ti, *n.* Quality of flying away; volatility; instability.
Fugitive, fū'jit-iv, *a.* Apt to flee away; volatile; fleeting; vagabond; temporary.—*n.* One who flees from duty or danger; refugee.
Fugleman, fū'gl-man, *n.* One who stands in front of soldiers at drill, and whose movements they copy; an example.
Fugue, fūg, *n.* A musical composition in which the parts seem to chase each other.
Fulcrum, ful'krum, *n.*; pl. **-ra** or **-rums.** A support; that by which a lever is sustained, or the point about which it moves.
Fulfil, fụl-fil', *vt.* To carry into effect, as a prophecy, promise, &c.; to answer in execution or event; to perform; to complete.
Fulfilment, fụl-fil'ment, *n.* Accomplishment; execution; performance.
Fulgency, ful'jen-si, *n.* Splendour; glitter.
Fulgent, ful'jent, *a.* Glittering; shining.
Fuliginous, fū-lij'in-us, *a.* Sooty.
Full, fụl, *a.* Having all it can contain; abounding; crowded; entire; strong; loud; clear; mature; perfect; ample.—*n.* Complete measure; the highest state or degree (usually with *the*).—*adv.* Quite; altogether; exactly; directly.—*vt.* To scour and thicken, as woollen cloth, in a mill.
Full-blown, fụl'blōn, *a.* Fully expanded, as a blossom.
Fuller, fụl'ėr, *n.* One who fulls cloth.
Fuller's-earth, fụl'ėrz-ėrth, *n.* A soft friable clay, which absorbs grease, and is much used in fulling cloth.
Fulling, fụl'ing, *n.* The art or practice of fulling cloth, and making it compact and firm.
Fully, fụl'li, *adv.* With fulness; amply; perfectly.
Fulmar, ful'mär, *n.* A kind of petrel of the northern seas.
Fulminate, ful'min-āt, *vi.* (fulminating, fulminated). To lighten and thunder; to detonate; to issue threats, denunciations, &c. —*vt.* To utter or send out, as a denunciation or censure; to cause to explode.—*n.* A compound substance which explodes by percussion, friction, or heat.
Fulmination, ful-min-ā'shon, *n.* Act of fulminating; that which is fulminated; censure, anathema; chemical explosion.
Fulness, Fullness, fụl'nes, *n.* State of being full; abundance; extent; loudness.
Fulsome, ful'sum, *a.* Offensive from excess of praise; gross; nauseous.
Fulvous, ful'vus, *a.* Tawny; dull yellow.
Fumble, fum'bl, *vi.* (fumbling, fumbled). To grope about awkwardly; to attempt or handle something bunglingly.
Fume, fūm, *n.* Smoke; vapour; exhalation from the stomach, as of liquor; heat of passion. —*vi.* (fuming, fumed). To yield vapour or visible exhalations; to be hot with anger.—*vt.* To smoke; to perfume; to disperse in vapours.
Fumigate, fūm'i-gāt, *vt.* (fumigating, fumigated). To smoke; to purify from infection, &c.
Fumigation, fūm-i-gā'shon, *n.* Act of fumigating, to purify from infection.
Fumy, fūm'i, *a.* Producing fume or smoke; full of vapour.
Fun, fun, *n.* Sportive acts or words; merriment.
Funambulist, fū-nam'bū-list, *n.* A rope walker or dancer.
Function, fungk'shon, *n.* Performance; office; duty; proper office of any organ in animals or vegetables; a ceremonial; a mathematical quantity connected with and varying with another.
Functional, fungk'shon-al, *a.* Pertaining to functions, or to some office or function.
Functionary, fungk'shon-a-ri, *n.* One who holds an office or trust.
Fund, fund, *n.* A stock or capital; money set apart for any object more or less permanent; store; supply.—*vt.* To provide and appropriate a fund for paying the interest of, as a debt; to place in a fund, as money.
Fundament, fun'da-ment, *n.* The part of the body on which one sits; the anus.
Fundamental, fun-da-ment'al, *a.* Pertaining to the foundation; essential; primary.—*n.* A leading principle which serves as the groundwork of a system; an essential.
Fundamentalist, fun-da-ment'al-ist, *n.* One who believes in the literal interpretation and the infallibility of the Bible.
Funeral, fū'nė-ral, *n.* Burial; ceremony of

burying a dead body.—*a.* Used at the interment of the dead.
Funereal, fū-nē'rē-al, *a.* Suiting a funeral; dark; dismal; mournful.
Fungous, fung'gus, *a.* Like a mushroom or fungus; excrescent; growing suddenly, but not substantial or durable.
Fungus, fung'gus, *n.*; pl. **Fungi** or **Funguses,** fun'jī, fung'gus-es. A mushroom; a toadstool; spongy excrescence in animal bodies, as proud flesh formed in wounds.
Funicle, fū'ni-kl, *n.* A small cord or ligament.
Funicular, fū-nik'ū-lėr, *a.* Consisting of a small cord; dependent on the tension of a cord.
Funnel, fun'el, *n.* A utensil for conveying liquids into close vessels; the shaft of a chimney through which smoke ascends.
Funnily, fun'i-li, *adv.* In a droll manner.
Funny, fun'i, *a.* Making fun; droll; comical.
Fur, fėr, *n.* The short, fine, soft hair of certain animals, growing thick on the skin; furred animals collectively; something resembling fur.—*a.* Pertaining to or made of fur.—*vt.* (furring, furred). To line or cover with fur.
Furbelow, fėr'bē-lō, *n.* A kind of flounce; plaited border of a petticoat or gown.
Furbish, fėr'bish, *vt.* To rub or scour to brightness; to burnish.
Furbisher, fėr'bish-ėr, *n.* One who or that which furbishes.
Furcate, Furcated, fėr'kāt, fėr'kāt-ed, *a.* Forked; branching like the prongs of a fork.
Furfur, fėr'fėr, *n.* Dandruff; scales like bran.
Furious, fū'ri-us, *a.* Full of rage; violent; impetuous; frantic.
Furiously, fū'ri-us-li, *adv.* With fury; vehemently; violently.
Furl, fėrl, *vt.* To wrap a sail close to a yard, &c., and fasten by a cord.
Furlong, fėr'long, *n.* The eighth of a mile.
Furlough, fėr'lō, *n.* Leave of absence to a soldier for a limited time.—*vt.* To grant leave of absence from military service.
Furnace, fėr'nās, *n.* A structure in which a vehement fire may be maintained for melting ores, heating water, &c.; place or occasion of torture or trial.
Furnish, fėr'nish, *vt.* To supply; to equip; to yield; to provide.
Furniture, fėr'ni-tūr, *n.* That with which anything is furnished; equipment; outfit; movable wooden articles in a house.
Furor, fū'ror, *n.* Fury; rage.
Furore, fū-rō'rā, *n.* Great enthusiasm or excitement; commotion; mania; rage.
Furrier, fu'ri-ėr, *n.* A dealer in furs; one who dresses furs.
Furriery, fu'ri-ė-ri, *n.* Furs in general; the trade in furs; dressing of furs.
Furrow, fu'rō, *n.* A trench made by a plough; a groove; a wrinkle.—*vt.* To make furrows in; to groove; to wrinkle.
Furrowy, fu'rō-i, *a.* Full of furrows.
Furry, fėr'i, *a.* Covered or coated with fur; resembling fur.
Further, fėr'ᴛʜėr, *adv.* More in advance; besides; farther.—*a.* More distant; farther.—*vt.* To help forward; to advance.
Furtherance, fėr'ᴛʜėr-ans, *n.* A helping forward; promotion; advancement.
Furtherer, fėr'ᴛʜėr-ėr, *n.* A promoter.
Furthermore, fėr'ᴛʜėr-mōr, *adv.* More in addition; moreover; besides.
Furthermost, fėr'ᴛʜėr-mōst, *a.* Most remote.
Furthest, fėr'ᴛʜest, *a.* and *adv.* Most advanced; farthest.
Furtive, fėr'tiv, *a.* Stolen; sly; stealthy.
Furtively, fėr'tiv-li, *adv.* By stealth.
Fury, fū'ri, *n.* Rage; a violent rushing; frenzy; a goddess of vengeance, in mythology; a violent woman.
Furze, fėrz, *n.* A prickly evergreen shrub; whin; gorse.
Fuscous, fus'kus, *a.* Dark; swarthy; dusky.
Fuse, fūz, *n.* A length of easily melted metal inserted in an electrical circuit as a safety device.—*vt.* (fusing, fused). To liquefy by heat; to dissolve; to blend or unite.—*vi.* To be melted; to become blended.
Fuse, Fuze, fūz, *n.* A tube or case filled with combustible matter, used in blasting or in discharging a shell, &c.
Fusee, fū-zē', *n.* The conical part of a watch or clock, round which is wound the chain or cord; a fusil; a match used by smokers.
Fuselage, fū'sel-āj, *n.* The long, narrow, somewhat spindle-shaped body of an aeroplane.
Fusel-oil, fū'zel-oil, *n.* A colourless oily spirit separated in the rectification of ordinary distilled spirits.
Fusible, fūz'i-bl, *a.* That may be fused.
Fusil, fū'sil, *n.* A light musket or firelock.
Fusilier, fū-sil-ēr', *n.* An infantry soldier of a regiment formerly armed with fusils.
Fusillade, fū'zi-lād, *n.* A simultaneous discharge of musketry.
Fusion, fū'zhon, *n.* Act or operation of fusing; state of being melted or blended; complete union.
Fuss, fus, *n.* Bustle; much ado about trifles.—*vi.* To make a fuss or bustle.
Fussily, fus'i-li, *adv.* In a bustling manner.
Fussy, fus'i, *a.* Making a fuss; bustling.
Fusted, fus'ted, *a.* Mouldy; ill-smelling.
Fustian, fus'tyan, *n.* A coarse cotton stuff, with a pile like velvet; mere stuff; bombast; an inflated style.—*a.* Made of fustian; bombastic.
Fustic, fus'tik, *n.* The wood of a West Indian tree, used in dyeing yellow.
Fustigate, fus'ti-gāt, *vt.* To cudgel.
Fusty, fus'ti, *n.* Tasting or smelling of a foul or mouldy cask; mouldy; ill-smelling.
Futile, fū'til, *a.* Serving no useful end; trivial; worthless.
Futility, fū-til'i-ti, *n.* Quality of being futile; worthlessness; unimportance.
Future, fū'tūr, *a.* That is to be; pertaining to time to come.—*n.* The time to come; all that is to happen; the future tense.
Futurity, fū-tūr'i-ti, *n.* State of being future; time to come; after-ages.
Fuzz, fuz, *vi.* To fly off in minute particles.—*n.* Fine particles; loose, volatile matter.
Fuzzy, fuz'i, *a.* Like, or covered with, fuzz.
Fy, fī, *interj.* Same as *Fie.*

G

Gab, gab, *vi.* (gabbling, gabbed). To talk much; to chatter.—*n.* Idle talk.
Gabardine, Gaberdine, gab'ar-dēn, gab'ėr-dēn, *n.* A coarse upper garment.
Gabble, gab'l, *vi.* (gabbling, gabbled). To

talk fast, or without meaning.—*n.* Rapid talk without meaning; inarticulate sounds rapidly uttėred.

Gabel, Gabelle, ga-bel′, *n.* A tax or impost in some continental countries.

Gabion, gā′bi-on, *n.* A cylindrical wicker-basket filled with earth, used in fortifications.

Gable, gā′bl, *n.* The pointed end of a house; the triangular part of the end of a house.

Gaby, gā′bi, *n.* A silly person; a simpleton.

Gad, gad, *n.* A spike; a wedge or ingot of steel or iron.—*vi.* (gadding, gadded). To rove or ramble idly.

Gadabout, gad′a-bout, *n.* One who roves about idly.

Gadder, gad′ėr, *n.* A gadabout.

Gadfly, gad′fli, *n.* A fly which bites cattle.

Gadget, gad′jet, *n.* A tool, appliance, or contrivance.

Gadhelic, gad′e-lik, *a.* Pertaining to the branch of the Celtic race comprising the Erse of Ireland, the Gaels of Scotland, and the Manx.—*n.* Their language.

Gadwall, gad′wąl, *n.* A species of duck.

Gael, gāl, *n.* A Scottish Highlander.

Gaelic, gāl′ik, *a.* Pertaining to the Celtic inhabitants of Scotland.—*n.* Their language.

Gaff, gaf, *n.* A hook used by anglers in landing large fish; a spar to extend the upper edge of some fore-and-aft sails.—*vt.* To strike or secure (a salmon) by means of a gaff.

Gaffer, gaf′ėr, *n.* An old rustic; a foreman.

Gag, gag, *vt.* (gagging, gagged). To prevent from speaking by fixing something in the mouth; to silence by authority or force.—*n.* Something thrust into the mouth to hinder speaking; interpolations in an actor's part.

Gage, gāj, *n.* A pledge; a security; a kind of plum.—*vt.* (gaging, gaged). To pledge; to bind by pledge or security; to engage. *See* GAUGE.

Gaiety, gā′e-ti, *n.* State or quality of being gay; mirth; entertainment; showiness.

Gaily, gā′li, *adv.* In a gay manner; joyfully; merrily; with finery or showiness.

Gain, gān, *vt.* To obtain; to get, as profit or advantage; to receive, as honour; to win to one's side; to conciliate; to reach, arrive at. —*vi.* To reap advantage or profit; to make progress.—*n.* Something obtained as an advantage; profit; benefit.

Gainful, gān′fųl, *a.* Full of gain; profitable; advantageous; lucrative.

Gaining, gān′ing, *n.* That which one gains: usually in the *pl.* earnings.

Gainless, gān′les, *a.* Not producing gain; unprofitable.

Gainsay, gān′sā, *vt.* To contradict; to oppose in words; to dispute.

Gainsayer, gān′sā-ėr, *n.* One who gainsays.

'Gainst, genst. *See* AGAINST.

Gait, gāt, *n.* Walk; manner of walking or stepping; carriage.

Gaiter, gā′tėr, *n.* A covering for the leg fitting over the shoe.—*vt.* To dress with gaiters.

Gala, gal′a, *n.* An occasion of public festivity.

Galantine, gal-an-tēn′, *n.* A dish of veal or chicken, without bones, served cold.

Galaxy, ga′lak-si, *n.* The Milky Way; that long, luminous track in the heavens, formed by a multitude of stars; an assemblage of splendid persons or things.

Gale, gāl, *n.* A strong wind; a storm; a small shrub found in bogs.

Galena, ga-lē′na, *n.* The principal ore of lead.

Galiot, Galliot, gal′i-ot, *n.* A two-masted Dutch cargo vessel, with rounded ribs and flattish bottom.

Gall, gąl, *n.* A bitter fluid secreted in the liver; bile; rancour; malignity; an excrescence produced by the egg of an insect on a plant, especially the oak; a sore place in the skin from rubbing.—*vt.* To make a sore in the skin of by rubbing; to fret; to vex; to harass.

Gallant, gal′ant, *a.* Gay in attire; handsome; brave; showing politeness and attention to ladies (in this sense also pron. ga-lant′).—*n.* A gay sprightly man; a daring spirit; (pron. also ga-lant′) a man attentive to ladies; suitor; paramour.—*vt.* ga-lant′. To act the gallant towards; to be very attentive to (a lady).

Gallantly, gal′ant-li, *adv.* Gaily; bravely; nobly; in the manner of a wooer.

Gallantry, gal′ant-ri, *n.* Show; bravery; intrepidity; polite attentions to ladies; vicious love or pretensions to love.

Galleon, gal′ē-un, *n.* A large ship formerly used by the Spaniards.

Gallery, gal′ė-ri, *n.* A long apartment serving as a passage of communication, or for the reception of pictures, &c.; upper floor of a church, theatre, &c.; a covered passage; frame like a balcony projecting from a ship.

Galley, gal′i, *n.* A low, flat-built vessel navigated with sails and oars; the cook-room of a large ship; a frame used in printing.

Galley-slave, gal′i-slāv, *n.* A person condemned to work on board a galley.

Gallic, gal′ik, *a.* Pertaining to Gaul, or France.

Gallic, gąl′ik, *a.* Belonging to or derived from galls, or oak-apples.

Gallicism, gal′i-sizm, *n.* A French idiom.

Galligaskins, gal-li-gas′kinz, *n.pl.* Large open hose; leather guards for the legs.

Gallimaufry, gal-i-mą′fri, *n.* A hash; medley.

Gallinaceous, gal-li-nā′shus, *a.* Pertaining to that order of birds which includes the domestic fowl, pheasant, turkey, &c.

Galling, gąl′ing, *p.a.* Adapted to gall or chagrin; keenly annoying.

Gallipot, gal′li-pot, *n.* A small pot painted and glazed, used for holding medicines.

Gallon, gal′lun, *n.* A liquid measure of four quarts or eight pints.

Galloon, gal-lön′, *n.* A narrow close lace.

Gallop, gal′up, *vi.* To move or run with leaps; to ride at this pace; to move very fast.—*n.* The pace of a horse, by springs or leaps.

Gallopade, gal-up-ād′, *n.* A sidelong or curvetting kind of gallop; a kind of dance.—*vi.* To gallop; to dance a gallopade.

Galloper, gal′up-ėr, *n.* A horse or man that gallops.

Gallows, gal′ōz, *n. sing.* or *pl.*; also **Gallowses,** gal′ōz-ez, in *pl.* A structure for the hanging of criminals; one of a pair of braces for the trousers.

Galoche, Galosh, ga-losh′, *n.* A shoe worn over another shoe to keep the foot dry.

Galop, ga-lop′, *n.* A quick lively dance somewhat resembling a waltz.

Galore, ga-lōr′, *n.* Abundance; plenty.

Galvanic, gal-van′ik, *a.* Pertaining to galvanism; containing or exhibiting it.

Galvanism, gal'van-izm, *n.* A species of electricity developed by the action of various metals and chemicals upon each other.
Galvanist, gal'van-ist, *n.* One versed in galvanism.
Galvanize, gal'van-īz, *vt.* (galvanizing, galvanized). To affect with galvanism; to electroplate; to coat with tin or zinc; to restore to consciousness; to give spurious life to.
Galvanometer, gal-van-om'et-ėr, *n.* An instrument for detecting the existence and determining the strength and direction of an electric current.
Gambadoes, gam-bā'dōz, *n.pl.* Leather coverings for the legs in riding.
Gambit, gam'bit, *n.* An opening in chess incurring the sacrifice of a pawn.
Gamble, gam'bl, *vi.* (gambling, gambled). To play for money.
Gambler, gam'bl-ėr, *n.* One who plays for money or other stake.
Gambling, gam'bl-ing, *n.* The act or practice of gaming for money or anything valuable.
Gamboge, gam-bōj', *n.* A concrete vegetable juice, used as a pigment and cathartic.
Gambol, gam'bol, *vi.* (gambolling, gambolled). To skip about in sport; to frisk; to frolic.—*n.* A skipping about in frolic; a prank.
Gambrel, gam'brel, *n.* The prominent bend of a horse's hind leg.
Game, gām, *n.* Sport of any kind; exercise for amusement, testing skill, &c.; scheme pursued; field-sports; animals hunted.—*vi.* (gaming, gamed). To play at any sport; to play for a stake or prize; to practise gaming. **To die game,** to maintain a bold spirit to the last.
Game-cock, gām'kok, *n.* A cock bred or used to fight.
Gamekeeper, gām'kēp-ėr, *n.* One who has the care of game on an estate.
Gamesome, gām'sum, *a.* Sportive; playful.
Gamester, gām'stėr, *n.* A person addicted to gaming; a gambler.
Gamin, gam'in, *n.* A street arab; a neglected street-boy.
Gaming, gām'ing, *n.* The act or practice of gambling.
Gammer, gam'ėr, *n.* An old woman in humble life.
Gammon, gam'un, *n.* The thigh of a hog, pickled and smoked or dried; a smoked ham; an imposition or hoax.—*vt.* To pickle and dry in smoke; to hoax or humbug.
Gamut, gam'ut, *n.* A scale on which notes in music are written, consisting of lines and spaces; range or compass.
Gamy, Gamey, gām'i, *a.* Having the flavour of game; courageous.
Gander, gan'dėr, *n.* The male of the goose.
Gang, gang, *n.* A crew or band; a squad; a vein in mining; a gangue.
Gangliated, gang'gli-āt-ed, *a.* Having ganglions; forming a ganglion.
Ganglion, gang'gli-on, *n.*; pl. **-ia** or **-ions.** An enlargement in the course of a nerve; a mass of nervous matter giving origin to nerve-fibres; a tumour on a tendon.
Ganglionic, gang-gli-on'ik, *a.* Pertaining to a ganglion.
Gangrene, gang'grēn, *n.* An eating away of the flesh; first stage of mortification.—*vt.* (gangrening, gangrened). To mortify.—*vi.* To become mortified.
Gangrenous, gang'grēn-us, *a.* Mortified; attacked by gangrene.
Gangster, gang'stėr, *n.* A member of a criminal organization.
Gangue, gang, *n.* The mineral substance which incloses any metallic ore in the vein.
Gangway, gang'wā, *n.* A means of access formed of planks or boards; a passage across the House of Commons.
Gannet, gan'et, *n.* The solan-goose, an aquatic bird of the pelican tribe.
Ganoid, gan'oid, *a.* Applied to an order of fishes with scales of horny or bony plates covered with glossy enamel.
Gantlet, gänt'let, *n.* *See* GAUNTLET.
Gantlet, Gantlope, gant'let, gant'lōp, *n.* A punishment, in which the culprit was compelled to run between two ranks of men and receive a blow from each man.
Gaol, jāl, *n.* *See* JAIL.
Gap, gap, *n.* An opening; breach; hiatus; chasm.
Gape, gāp, *vi.* (gaping, gaped). To open the mouth wide; to yawn; to open in fissures; to stand open.—*n.* A gaping; the width of the mouth when opened, as of a bird, fish, &c.
Garage, gar'aj, *n.* A place for housing or repairing motor-cars.
Garb, gärb, *n.* Dress; clothes; mode of dress. —*vt.* To dress.
Garbage, gärb'āj, *n.* Waste matter; offal; vegetable refuse.
Garble, gär'bl, *vt.* (garbling, garbled). To pick out such parts as may serve a purpose; to falsify by leaving out parts; to corrupt.
Garden, gär'dn, *n.* A piece of ground appropriated to the cultivation of plants; a rich, well-cultivated tract; a delightful spot.—*a.* Pertaining to or produced in a garden.—*vi.* To lay out and to cultivate a garden.
Gardener, gär'dn-ėr, *n.* One whose occupation is to tend or keep a garden.
Gardening, gär'dn-ing, *n.* The act or art of cultivating gardens; horticulture.
Gargle, gär'gl, *vt.* (gargling, gargled). To wash, as the throat.—*n.* Any liquid preparation for washing the throat.
Gargoyle, gär'goil, *n.* A projecting water-spout on a building, often grotesque.
Garish, gār'ish, *a.* Gaudy; showy; dazzling.
Garland, gär'land, *n.* A wreath or chaplet of flowers, leaves, &c.; a collection of pieces of prose or verse.—*vt.* To deck with a garland.
Garlic, gär'lik, *n.* A plant allied to the onion, with a pungent taste and strong odour.
Garment, gär'ment, *n.* Any article of clothing, as a coat, a gown, &c.
Garner, gär'nėr, *n.* A granary; a store.—*vt.* To store in a granary; to store up.
Garnet, gär'net, *n.* A precious stone, generally of a red colour.
Garnish, gär'nish, *vt.* To adorn; to embellish (a dish) with something laid round.—*n.* Ornament; an embellishment round a dish.
Garnishing, Garnishment, gär'nish-ing, gär'nish-ment, *n.* That which garnishes.
Garniture, gär'ni-tūr, *n.* Ornamental appendages; furniture; dress.
Garret, ga'ret, *n.* A room in a house on the uppermost floor, immediately under the roof.
Garreteer, ga-ret-ēr', *n.* An inhabitant of a garret.

Garrison, ga'ri-sn, *n.* A body of troops stationed in a fort or town.—*vt.* To place a garrison in.
Garrotte, ga-rot', *vt.* To rob by seizing a person and compressing his windpipe till he become helpless.
Garrotter, ga-rot'ėr, *n.* One who commits the act of garrotting.
Garrulity, ga-rū'li-ti, *n.* Loquacity; practice or habit of talking much.
Garrulous, ga'rū-lus, *a.* Talkative; loquacious; characterized by long prosy talk.
Garter, gär'tėr, *n.* A band to hold up a stocking; the badge of the highest order of knighthood in Great Britain; the order itself.—*vt.* To bind with a garter.
Garth, gärth, *n.* A yard; a small inclosed place.
Gas, gas, *n.* An elastic aeriform fluid; coal-gas, used for giving light; any similar substance.
Gasalier, Gaselier, gas-a-lēr', gas'e-lēr, *n.* A hanging apparatus with branches for burning gas.
Gascon, gas'kon, *n.* A native of Gascony in France.
Gasconade, gas-kon-ād', *n.* A boast or boasting; a bravado.—*vi.* To boast; to brag.
Gaseous, gā'sē-us, *a.* In the form of gas.
Gas-fitter, gas'fit-ėr, *n.* One who fits up the pipes, brackets, &c., for gas-lighting.
Gash, gash, *vt.* To make a long deep incision in; to cut; to slash.—*n.* A deep and long cut, particularly in flesh.
Gasholder, gas'hōld-ėr, *n.* A large vessel for storing ordinary coal-gas.
Gasification, gas'i-fi-kā''shon, *n.* Act or process of converting into gas.
Gasify, gas'i-fī, *vt.* To convert into gas by heat.
Gasket, gas'ket, *n.* A cord on the yard of a ship to tie the sail to it; material used for packing joints, &c.
Gas-mask, gas-mask, *n.* A covering for the face used to give protection against poisonous gases in warfare.
Gasogene, Gazogene, gas'o-jēn, gaz'o-jēn, *n.* An apparatus for manufacturing aerated waters for domestic use.
Gasometer, gaz-om'et-ėr, *n.* An instrument to measure, mix, or store gases.
Gasp, gasp, *vi.* To open the mouth wide to catch breath; to labour for breath; to pant.—*vt.* To emit with a gasp.—*n.* Short painful catching of the breath.
Gasteropod, Gastropod, gas'tėr-o-pod, gas'-trō-pod, *n.* A mollusc such as snails, having a broad muscular foot attached to the ventral surface.
Gastric, gas'trik, *a.* Belonging to the stomach.
Gastronomy, gas-tron'o-mi, *n.* The art or science of good eating; epicurism.
Gate, gāt, *n.* A large door or entrance; a frame of timber, iron, &c., closing an entrance, &c.; a way or passage; the frame which stops the passage of water through a dam, lock, &c.
Gate-crasher, gāt-krash'ėr, *n.* An uninvited guest; one who obtains admission to a public entertainment without a ticket.
Gateway, gāt'wā, *n.* A way through the gate of some inclosure; the gate itself.
Gather, gaтн'ėr, *vt.* To bring together; to collect; to acquire; to pucker; to deduce by inference.—*vi.* To assemble; to increase.—*n.* A fold in cloth, made by drawing; a pucker.
Gatherer, gaтн'ėr-ėr. One who gathers.
Gathering, gaтн'ėr-ing, *n.* The act of collecting or assembling; an assembly; a collection of pus; an abscess.
Gatling-gun, gat'ling-gun, *n.* A type of machine-gun.
Gaucherie, gōsh-rē, *n.* Awkwardness.
Gaucho, gou'chō, *n.* A native of the S. American Pampas, of Spanish descent.
Gaud, gąd, *n.* A piece of showy finery.
Gaudily, gąd'i-li, *adv.* Showily; with ostentation of fine dress.
Gaudy, gąd'i, *a.* Showy; ostentatiously fine; tastelessly or glaringly adorned.
Gauge, gāj, *vt.* (gauging, gauged). To ascertain the contents of; to measure.—*n.* A measuring-rod; a measure; distance between the rails in a railway; calibre; size or dimensions.
Gauger, gāj'ėr, *n.* One who gauges; an official who ascertains the contents of casks.
Gaul, gąl, *n.* An inhabitant of Gaul, or ancient France.
Gaunt, gąnt, *a.* Emaciated; lean; thin; famished.
Gauntlet, gąnt'let, *n.* A large iron glove formerly worn as armour; a long glove covering the hand and wrist.
Gauze, gąz, *n.* A very thin, slight, transparent stuff.
Gauzy, gąz'i, *a.* Like gauze; thin as gauze.
Gavelkind, gā'vel-kīnd, *n.* An old English land-tenure by which land descends to all the sons in equal shares.
Gavotte, ga-vot', *n.* A sprightly dance; music for the dance.
Gawk, gąk, *n.* A simpleton; a booby.
Gawky, gąk'i, *a.* Awkward; clumsy; foolish.—*n.* A stupid clumsy fellow.
Gay, gā, *a.* Merry; frolicsome; showy; dressed out; dissipated.
Gaze, gāz, *vi.* (gazing, gazed). To fix the eyes and look earnestly; to stare.—*n.* A fixed look; a look of eagerness, wonder or admiration.
Gazelle, ga-zel', *n.* A small, elegant species of antelope, with soft, lustrous eyes.
Gazette, ga-zet', *n.* A newspaper, especially an official newspaper.—*vt.* (gazetting, gazetted). To insert in a gazette; to announce or publish officially.
Gazetteer, ga-zet-tēr', *n.* A writer or publisher of news; a dictionary of geographical information.
Gazing-stock, gāz'ing-stok, *n.* A person gazed at; an object of curiosity or contempt.
Gean, gēn, *n.* The wild cherry of Britain.
Gear, gēr, *n.* Dress; ornaments; apparatus; harness; tackle; a train of toothed wheels.—*vt.* To put gear on; to harness.
Gearing, gēr'ing, *n.* Harness; a train of toothed wheels working into each other.
Geese, gēs, *n.pl* of *goose.*
Gelatine, jel'a-tin, *n.* A concrete transparent substance obtained by boiling from certain parts of animals; the principle of jelly; glue.
Gelatinous, je-lat'in-us, *a.* Of the nature of gelatine; containing jelly.
Geld, geld, *vt.* To castrate; to emasculate.
Gelding, geld'ing, *n.* Act of castrating; a castrated animal, but chiefly a horse.
Gelid, je'lid, *a.* Icy cold; frosty or icy.
Gem, jem, *n.* A precious stone of any kind; a jewel; anything remarkable for beauty or

rarity.—*vt.* (gemming, gemmed). To adorn, as with gems; to bespangle; to embellish.

Geminate, jem'i-nāt, *vt.* To double.—*a.* Twin; combined in pairs.

Gemini, jem'i-nī, *n.pl.* The Twins, a sign of the zodiac, containing the two stars Castor and Pollux.

Gemma, jem'a, *n.*; pl. **-ae.** A bud; a leaf-bud.

Gemmation, jem-ā'shon, *n.* A budding; arrangement of parts in the bud.

Gemmeous, jem'ē-us, *a.* Pertaining to or resembling gems.

Gemmy, jem'i, *a.* Full of gems; glittering.

Gendarme, zhäng-därm, *n.* A private in the armed police of France.

Gender, jen'dėr, *n.* Sex, male or female; difference in words to express distinction of sex.—*vt.* To beget.—*vi.* To copulate; to breed.

Genealogical, jen'ē-a-loj''ik-al, *a.* Pertaining to genealogy.

Genealogist, jen-ē-al'o-jist, *n.* One who traces genealogies or writes on genealogy.

Genealogy, jen-ē-al'o-ji, *n.* An account of the descent of a person or family from an ancestor; pedigree; lineage.

Genera, jen'ė-ra, *n.pl.* *See* GENUS.

Generable, jen'ė-ra-bl, *a.* That may be generated.

General, jen'ė-ral, *a.* Of or belonging to a genus; not special; public; common; extensive, though not universal; usual; taken as a whole.—*n.* The whole; a comprehensive notion; a military officer of the highest rank.

Generalissimo, jen'ė-ral-is''si-mō, *n.* The supreme commander of an army.

Generality, jen-ė-ral'i-ti, *n.* State of being general; the bulk; the greatest part.

Generalization, jen'ė-ral-īz-ā''shon, *n.* Act of generalizing; general inference.

Generalize, jen'ė-ral-īz, *vt.* To make general; to bring under a general law or statement.—*vi.* To classify under general heads; to reason by induction.

Generally, jen'ė-ral-li, *adv.* In general; commonly; without detail.

Generalship, jen'ė-ral-ship, *n.* The office, skill, or conduct of a general officer.

Generate, jen'ė-rāt, *vt.* (generating, generated). To beget; to produce; to cause to be.

Generation, jen-ė-rā'shon, *n.* Act of generating; single succession in natural descent; people living at the same time; race.

Generative, jen'ė-rāt-iv, *a.* Having the power of generating; belonging to generation.

Generator, jen'ė-rāt-ėr, *n.* One who or that which generates.

Generic, Generical, jē-ne'rik, jē-ne'rik-al, *a.* Pertaining to a genus.

Generically, jē-ne'rik-al-li, *adv.* With regard to a genus.

Generosity, jen-ė-ros'i-ti, *n.* Nobleness of soul; liberality; munificence.

Generous, jen'ė-rus, *a.* Noble; bountiful; liberal; full of spirit, as wine; courageous, as a steed.

Generously, jen'ė-rus-li, *adv.* Nobly; magnanimously; liberally.

Genesis, jen'e-sis, *n.* Act of producing; origin; first book of the Old Testament.

Genetic, Genetical, je-net'ik, je-net'ik-al, *a.* Relating to origin or production.

Geneva, je-nē'va, *n.* A spirit distilled from grain or malt, with the addition of juniper-berries; gin.

Genial, jē'ni-al, *a.* Cordial; kindly; contributing to life and cheerfulness.

Geniality, jē-ni-al'i-ti, *n.* Sympathetic cheerfulness or cordiality.

Genially, jē'ni-al-li, *adv.* Cordially; cheerfully.

Geniculated, Geniculate, je-nik'ū-lāt-ed, je-nik'ū-lāt, *a.* Kneed; knotted; having joints like the knee, a little bent.

Genital, jen'it-al, *a.* Pertaining to generation or birth.

Genitals, jen'it-alz, *n.pl.* The parts of generation; sexual organs.

Genitive, jen'it-iv, *a.* and *n.* Applied to a case of nouns, pronouns, &c., in English called the possessive.

Genius, jē'ni-us, *n.*; pl. **Geniuses,** jē'ni-us-ez: in first sense **Genii,** jē'ni-ī. A tutelary deity; aptitude of mind for a particular study or course of life; uncommon powers of intellect; a man with uncommon intellectual faculties; nature; peculiar character.

Genre, zhäng-r, *n.* A term applied to the department of painting which depicts scenes of ordinary life.

Genteel, jen-tēl', *a.* Having the manners of well-bred people; refined; elegant.

Genteelly, jen-tēl'li, *adv.* In a genteel manner; politely; fashionably.

Gentian, jen'shan, *n.* A bitter herbaceous plant, valued medicinally as a tonic.

Gentile, jen'tīl, *a.* Pertaining to a family, race, or nation; pertaining to pagans.—*n.* Any person not a Jew or a Christian; a heathen.

Gentility, jen-til'i-ti, *n.* Politeness of manners; fashionable style or circumstances.

Gentle, jen'tl, *a.* Well-born; refined in manners; mild; placid; not rough, violent, or wild; soothing.—*n.* A person of good birth.

Gentlefolk, jen'tl-fōk, *n.* Persons of good breeding and family: more generally in *pl.* *gentlefolks*.

Gentleman, jen'tl-man, *n.* A man of good social position; technically any man above the rank of yeoman, comprehending noblemen; a man of good breeding or of high honour; a polite equivalent for 'man'.

Gentlemanlike, Gentlemanly, jen'tl-man-līk, jen'tl-man-li, *a.* Pertaining to or becoming a gentleman.

Gentleness, jen'tl-nes, *n.* Quality of being gentle; tenderness; mild treatment.

Gentlewoman, jen'tl-wu̧-man, *n.* A woman of good family or of good breeding.

Gently, jen'tli, *adv.* Softly; meekly; mildly; with tenderness.

Gentry, jen'tri, *n.* Wealthy or well-born people; people of a rank below the nobility.

Genuflection, Genuflexion, jen-ū-flek'shon, *n.* The act of bending the knee, particularly in worship.

Genuine, jen'ū-in, *a.* Belonging to the original stock; real; pure; true.

Genus, jē'nus, *n.*; pl. **Genera,** jen'ė-ra. A kind, class, or sort; an assemblage of species having distinctive characteristics in common.

Geocentric, Geocentrical, jē-o-sen'trik, jē-o-sen'trik-al, *a.* Having reference to the earth as a centre, applied to the position of a celestial object.

Geodesic, Geodetic, jē-o-des'ik, jē-o-det'ik, *a.* Pertaining to geodesy.

Geodesy, jē-od'e-si, *n.* The geometry of the earth.

Geognosy, jē-og'no-si, *n.* The science of the structure of the earth.

Geographer, jē-og'ra-fėr, *n.* One versed in geography or who writes on it.

Geographic, Geographical, jē-o-graf'ik, jē-o-graf'ik-al, *a.* Pertaining to geography; containing information regarding geography.

Geography, jē-og'ra-fi, *n.* The science of the external features of the world; a book describing the earth or part of it.

Geological, jē-o-loj'ik-al, *a.* Pertaining to geology.

Geologist, jē-ol'o-jist, *n.* One versed in the science of geology.

Geology, jē-ol'o-ji, *n.* The science of the structure of the earth as to its rocks, strata, soil, minerals, organic remains, and changes.

Geomancy, jē'o-man-si, *n.* A kind of divination by figures made on the ground or paper.

Geometer, jē-om'et-ėr, *n.* One skilled in geometry; a geometrician.

Geometric, Geometrical, jē-o-met'rik, jē-o-met'rik-al, *a.* Pertaining to geometry; according to the principles of geometry.

Geometrician, jē-om'e-tri''shan, *n.* One skilled in geometry.

Geometry, jē-om'e-tri, *n.* The science of magnitude; that branch of mathematics which treats of the properties and relations of lines, angles, surfaces, and solids.

George, jorj, *n.* A figure of St. George on horseback, worn by knights of the Garter.

Georgian, jorj'i-an, *a.* Relating to the reigns of the four Georges, kings of Great Britain.

Georgic, jorj'ik, *n.* A rural poem; a poetical composition on husbandry, &c.

Geothermic, jē-o-thėr'mik, *a.* Pertaining to the internal heat of the earth.

Geranium, jė-rā'ni-um, *n.* A plant cultivated for its beautiful flowers; the crane's-bill genus of plants.

Germ, jėrm, *n.* The earliest form of any animal or plant; origin; microbe; bacillus.

German, jėr'man, *a.* Come of the same parents. Cousins *german* are the sons or daughters of brothers or sisters, first cousins.

German, jėr'man, *a.* Belonging to Germany. —*n.* A native of Germany; the German language.

Germane, jėr'mān, *a.* Closely allied; relevant; pertinent.

Germanic, jėr-man'ik, *a.* Pertaining to Germany; Teutonic.

Germinal, jėrm'in-al, *a.* Pertaining to a germ.

Germinate, jėrm'in-āt, *vi.* (germinating, germinated). To sprout; to bud; to begin to vegetate or grow, as seeds.

Germination, jėrm-in-ā'shon, *n.* Act of germinating; first beginning of vegetation in a seed or plant.

Gerrymander, ge'ri-man-dėr, *vt.* To arrange so as to get an unfair result from the distribution of voters in political elections.

Gerund, je'rund, *n.* A kind of verbal noun in Latin; a verbal noun, such as 'teaching' in 'fit for teaching boys'.

Gerundial, je-run'di-al, *a.* Pertaining to or like a gerund.

Gestapo, ges-ta'pō, *n.* The German secret police, a terrorist organization.

Gestation, jest-ā'shon, *n.* The carrying of young in the womb from conception to delivery; pregnancy.

Gesticulate, jes-tik'ū-lāt, *vi.* To make gestures or motions, as in speaking.—*vt.* To represent by gesture; to act.

Gesticulation, jes-tik'ū-lā''shon, *n.* Act of gesticulating; a gesture.

Gesticulator, jes-tik'ū-lāt-ėr, *n.* One who gesticulates.

Gesticulatory, jes-tik'ū-lā-to-ri, *a.* Pertaining to gesticulation.

Gesture, jes'tūr, *n.* A posture or motion of the body or limbs; action intended to express an idea or feeling, or to enforce an argument.

Get, get, *vt.* (getting, pret. got, pp. got, gotten). To obtain; to gain; to reach; to beget; to learn; to induce.—*vi.* To arrive at any place or state by degrees; to become; to make gain.

Get-up, get'up, *n.* Equipment; dress.

Gewgaw, gū'ga, *n.* A showy trifle: a toy; a splendid plaything.

Geyser, gī'zėr, *n.* A hot-water spring, the water rising in a column.

Ghastly, gast'li, *a.* Deathlike in looks; hideous; frightful, as wounds.

Ghat, Ghaut, gät, gat, *n.* In India, a mountain pass; a chain of hills; a river landing-place.

Ghee, gē, *n.* In India, the butter made from buffalo milk converted into a kind of oil.

Gherkin, gėr'kin, *n.* A small-fruited variety of cucumber used for pickling.

Ghetto, get'to, *n.* Jewish pen or quarter, a Jewry; the quarters closed and locked at night, in Italian and Rhine-valley towns, in which Jews lived.

Ghost, gōst, *n.* The soul of man; a disembodied spirit; apparition; shadow.

Ghostly, gōst'li, *a.* Relating to the soul; spiritual; not carnal or secular; pertaining to apparitions.

Ghoul, göl, *n.* An imaginary evil being which preys upon human bodies.

Giant, jī'ant, *n.* A man of extraordinary stature; a person of extraordinary powers, bodily or intellectual.—*a.* Like a giant; extraordinary in size.

Giantess, jī'ant-es, *n.* A female giant.

Giaour, jour, *n.* A Turkish name for a non-Mohammedan; a Christian.

Gibberish, gib'bėr-ish, *n.* Rapid and inarticulate talk; unmeaning words.

Gibbet, jib'bet, *n.* A gallows; the projecting beam of a crane, on which the pulley is fixed. —*vt.* To hang on a gibbet; to expose to scorn, infamy, &c.

Gibbon, gib'on, *n.* A long-armed ape of the Indian Archipelago.

Gibbosity, gib-os'i-ti, *n.* A round or swelling prominence; convexity.

Gibbous, gib'us, *a.* Protuberant; convex.

Gibe, jīb, *vi.* (gibing, gibed). To utter taunting, sarcastic words; to flout; to sneer.—*vt.* To scoff at; to mock.—*n.* A scoff; taunt; reproach.

Giber, jīb'ėr, *n.* One who gibes.

Gibingly, jīb'ing-li, *adv.* With gibes; scornfully.

Giblet, jib'let, *n.* One of those parts of poultry usually excluded in roasting, as the head, gizzard, liver, &c.: usually in *pl.*

Gibus, zhē-bus, *n.* A crush-hat; opera-hat.

Giddy, gid'i, *a.* Having in the head a sensation of whirling or swimming; dizzy; fickle; heedless; rendered wild by excitement.
Gier-eagle, jēr'ē-gl, *n.* A kind of eagle.
Gift, gift, *n.* Anything given; act of giving; power of giving; talent or faculty.—*vt.* To endow with any power or faculty.
Gifted, gift'ed, *p.a.* Furnished with any particular talent; talented.
Gig, gig, *n.* A light one-horse carriage with one pair of wheels; a ship's light boat; a long narrow rowing-boat, adapted for racing.
Gigantic, jī-gan'tik, *a.* Like a giant; huge; colossal; immense.
Giggle, gig'l, *n.* A kind of laugh, with short catches of the voice or breath.—*vi.* (giggling, giggled). To laugh with short catches of the breath; to titter.
Giglet, Giglot, gig'let, gig'lot, *n.* A giggler; a giddy-girl.—*a.* Giddy; wanton.
Gigot, jig'ot, *n.* A leg of mutton.
Gilbertian, gil-bėr'shan, *a.* Whimsically topsy-turvy; resembling the humour of Sir W. S. Gilbert (1836-1911), author of the Savoy Operas and the *Bab Ballads.*
Gild, gild, *vt.* (pret. and pp. gilded or gilt). To overlay with gold in leaf or powder; to illuminate; to give a fair and agreeable appearance to.
Gild, gild, *n.* Same as *Guild.*
Gilder, gild'ėr, *n.* One who gilds; one whose occupation is to overlay things with gold.
Gilding, gild'ing, *n.* The art or practice of overlaying things with gold; a thin coating of gold; fair superficial show.
Gill, gil, *n.* The organ of respiration in fishes; the flap below the beak of a fowl; the flesh on the lower part of the cheeks.
Gill, jil, *n.* The fourth part of a pint; a sweetheart; a wanton girl.
Gillie, gil'i, *n.* A Highland male servant who attends on sportsmen.
Gillyflower, jil'li-flou-ėr, *n.* A name for the pink or carnation, the wallflower, &c.
Gilt, gilt, pp. of *gild.* Overlaid with gold; brightly adorned.—*n.* Gold laid on the surface of a thing; gilding.
Gimbals, jim'balz, *n.pl.* A contrivance of two movable hoops, used to keep the mariner's compass, &c., always horizontal.
Gimcrack, jim'krak, *n.* A trivial mechanism; a device; a toy.—*a.* Trivial; worthless.
Gimlet, gim'let, *n.* A small borer with a pointed screw at the end.
Gimp, gimp, *n.* A kind of silk twist or edging.
Gin, jin, *n.* A distilled spirit flavoured with juniper berries; a machine for driving piles, raising great weights, &c.; a machine for separating the seeds from cotton; a trap, snare.—*vt.* (ginning, ginned). To clear of seeds by a cotton-gin; to catch in a trap.
Ginger, jin'jėr, *n.* A tropical plant, the root of which has a hot, spicy quality.
Gingerly, jin'jėr-li, *adv.* Cautiously; timidly; delicately; gently.
Gingham, ging'am, *n.* A kind of striped cotton cloth.
Ginseng, jin'seng, *n.* The name of two plants, the roots of which are a favourite Chinese medicine.
Gipsy, jip'si, *n.* One of an oriental vagabond race scattered over Europe, &c., believed to have come originally from India; the language of the Gipsies; a name of slight reproach to a woman, implying roguishness.—*a.* Pertaining to or resembling the Gipsies.
Giraffe, ji-raf', *n.* The camelopard, the tallest of animals.
Gird, gėrd, *vt.* (pp. girded or girt). To bind; to make fast by binding; to invest; to encompass.—*vi.* To gibe; to sneer.—*n.* A stroke with a whip; a twitch; a sneer.
Girder, gėrd'ėr, *n.* One who girds; a main beam supporting a superstructure.
Girdle, gėr'dl, *n.* That which girds; a band or belt; something drawn round the waist and tied or buckled.—*vt.* (girdling, girdled). To bind with a girdle, belt, or sash; to gird.
Girl, gėrl, *n.* A female child; young woman.
Girl Guide, gėrl gīd, *n.* Member of an organization for young girls analogous to the Boy Scout organization, and also founded by Lord Baden-Powell.
Girlhood, gėrl'hųd, *n.* The state of a girl.
Girlish, gėrl'ish, *a.* Like a girl; befitting a girl.
Girt, gėrt, pret. and pp. of *gird.*
Girt, gėrt, *vt.* To gird; to surround.
Girth, gėrth, *n.* That which girds; band fastening a saddle on a horse's back; measure round a person's body or anything cylindrical.
Gist, jist, *n.* The main point of a question; substance or pith of a matter.
Give, giv, *vt.* (giving, pret. gave, pp. given). To bestow; to deliver; to impart; to yield; to afford; to utter; to show; to send forth; to devote (oneself); to pledge; to allow; to ascribe.—*vi.* To make gifts; to yield to pressure; to recede.
Giver, giv'ėr, *n.* One who gives; a donor.
Gizzard, giz'ėrd, *n.* The muscular stomach of a bird.
Glacial, glā'shi-al, *a.* Icy; frozen; relating to glaciers.
Glacier, glā'shi-ėr, *n.* An immense mass of ice formed in valleys above the snow-line, and having a slow movement downwards.
Glacis, glā'sis, *n.* The outer slope of a fortification.
Glad, glad, *a.* Affected with pleasure; pleased; cheerful; imparting pleasure.—*vt.* (gladding, gladded). To make glad; to gladden.
Gladden, glad'n, *vt.* To make glad.—*vi.* To become glad; to rejoice.
Glade, glād, *n.* A green clear space or opening in a wood.
Gladiator, glad'i-ā-tėr, *n.* Among the Romans, one who fought with swords, &c., for the entertainment of the people; a prize-fighter.
Gladiatorial, glad'i-a-tō"ri-al, *a.* Pertaining to gladiators.
Gladiolus, gla-dī-ō'lus, *n.*; pl. -li. A beautiful genus of bulbous-rooted plants, abundant in S. Africa; sword-lily.
Gladly, glad'li, *adv.* With pleasure; joyfully.
Gladsome, glad'sum, *a.* Joyful; cheerful; pleasing.
Glair, glār, *n.* The white of an egg, used as a varnish for paintings; any substance resembling the white of an egg.
Glaive, glāv, *n.* A sword.
Glamour, glam'ėr, *n.* Magic influence causing a person to see objects differently from what they really are; witchery.
Glance, glans, *n.* A sudden shoot of light or splendour; a glimpse or sudden look.—*vi.* (glancing, glanced). To shine; to gleam; to

dart aside; to look with a sudden rapid cast of the eye; to move quickly; to hint.—*vt.* To shoot or dart suddenly or obliquely; to cast for a moment.
Glancingly, glăns'ing-li, *adv.* By glancing; in a glancing manner; transiently.
Gland, gland, *n.* An acorn; any acorn-shaped fruit; a roundish organ in many parts of the body secreting some fluid; a secreting organ in plants.
Glanders, glan'dėrz, *n.* A disease of the mucous membrane about the mouth in horses.
Glandular, gland'ū-lėr, *a.* Having the character of a gland; consisting of glands.
Glandule, gland'ūl, *n.* A small gland.
Glare, glār, *n.* A bright dazzling light; a fierce piercing look.—*vi.* (glaring, glared). To shine with excessive lustre; to look with fierce piercing eyes.
Glaring, glār'ing, *p.a.* Excessively bright; vulgarly splendid; notorious; barefaced.
Glaringly, glār'ing-li, *adv.* Openly; notoriously.
Glass, gläs, *n.* A hard transparent substance; a small drinking vessel of glass; a mirror; quantity of liquor that a glass vessel contains; a lens; a telescope; a barometer; *pl.* spectacles.—*a.* Made of glass; vitreous.
Glass-blower, gläs'blō-ėr, *n.* One who blows and fashions glass vessels.
Glass-house, gläs'hous, *n.* A house where glass is made; a house made of glass.
Glass-paper, gläs'pā-pėr, *n.* A polishing paper covered with finely-pounded glass.
Glass-work, gläs'wėrk, *n.* The manufacture of glass; a place where glass is made.
Glassy, gläs'i, *a.* Made of glass; vitreous; resembling glass in its properties.
Glauber-salt, gla̤'bėr-sa̤lt, *n.* Sulphate of soda, a well-known cathartic.
Glaucoma, Glaucosis, gla̤-kō'ma, gla̤-kō'sis, *n.* An opacity of the vitreous humour of the eye, giving it a bluish-green tint.
Glaucous, gla̤'kus, *a.* Of a sea-green colour; covered with a fine bluish or greenish bloom or powder.
Glaze, glāz, *vt.* (glazing, glazed). To furnish with glass; to incrust with a vitreous substance; to make smooth and glossy.—*n.* A vitreous or transparent coating.
Glazer, glā'zėr, *n.* One who or that which glazes.
Glazier, glā'zhėr, *n.* One whose business is to set window-glass.
Glazing, glāz'ing, *n.* Act or art of one who glazes; enamel; glaze.
Gleam, glēm, *n.* A small stream of light; brightness.—*vi.* To shoot or dart, as rays of light; to shine; to flash.
Gleamy, glēm'i, *a.* Darting beams of light; casting light in rays.
Glean, glēn, *vt.* and *i.* To gather stalks and ears of grain left behind by reapers; to pick up here and there; to gather slowly and assiduously.
Gleaner, glēn'ėr, *n.* One who gleans.
Glebe, glēb, *n.* Soil; ground; land belonging to a parish church or ecclesiastical benefice.
Gleby, glēb'i, *a.* Turfy; cloddy.
Glede, glēd, *n.* A bird of prey, the common kite of Europe.
Glee, glē, *n.* Joy; mirth; a composition for voices in three or more parts.
Gleeful, Gleesome, glē'fu̇l, glē'sum, *a.* Full of glee; merry; gay; joyous.
Gleet, glēt, *n.* A transparent mucous discharge from the urethra; a thin ichor.
Glen, glen, *n.* A narrow valley; a dale; a depression or space between hills.
Glib, glib, *a.* Smooth; slippery; having plausible words always ready.
Glide, glīd, *vi.* (gliding, glided). To flow gently; to move or slip along with ease.—*n.* Act of moving smoothly.
Glider, glīd'ėr, *n.* A modification of the aeroplane, which can travel through the air for a certain time without engine power.
Glimmer, glim'ėr, *vi.* To shine faintly, and with frequent intermissions; to flicker.—*n.* A faint light; a twinkle.
Glimmering, glim'ėr-ing, *p.a.* Shining faintly.—*n.* A glimmer; faint view; glimpse.
Glimpse, glimps, *n.* A gleam or flash of light; short transitory view; faint resemblance; slight tinge.—*vi.* To appear by glimpses.
Glint, glint, *vi.* To glance; to give a flash of light.—*n.* A glance, flash, gleam.
Glisten, glis'n, *vi.* To glitter; to sparkle.
Glister, glis'tėr, *vi.* To glisten; to be bright; to sparkle.—*n.* Glitter; lustre.
Glitter, glit'ėr, *vi.* To sparkle with light; to be showy, specious, or striking.—*n.* Brightness; lustre.
Gloaming, glōm'ing, *n.* Fall of the evening; the twilight; decline.
Gloat, glōt, *vi.* To gaze earnestly; to feast the eyes; to contemplate with evil satisfaction.
Globate, Globated, glōb'āt, glōb'āt-ed, *a.* Having the form of a globe; spherical.
Globe, glōb, *n.* A round solid body; a sphere; the earth; an artificial sphere on whose surface is drawn a map of the earth or heavens.—*vt.* To gather into a round mass.
Globular, glob'ū-lėr, *a.* Having the form of a ball or sphere; spherical.
Globule, glob'ūl, *n.* A little globe; a small spherical particle; one of the red particles of the blood.
Globulin, glob'ū-lin, *n.* The main ingredient of blood globules and resembling albumen.
Glomerate, glom'ė-rāt, *vt.* To gather or wind into a ball.
Glomeration, glom-ė-rā'shon, *n.* Act of glomerating; body formed into a ball.
Gloom, glöm, *n.* Obscurity; thick shade; sadness; aspect of sorrow; darkness of prospect or aspect.—*vi.* To shine obscurely; to be cloudy or dark; to be sullen or sad.
Gloomily, glöm'i-li, *adv.* Darkly; dismally; sullenly.
Gloomy, glöm'i, *a.* Dark; dismal; downcast; sad.
Glorification, glō'ri-fi-kā"shon, *n.* Act of glorifying; laudation.
Glorify, glō'ri-fī, *vt.* (glorifying, glorified). To make glorious; to ascribe glory or honour to; to extol.
Gloriole, glō'ri-ōl, *n.* A circle, as of rays, in paintings, surrounding the heads of saints.
Glorious, glō'ri-us, *a.* Full of glory; renowned; celebrated; grand; brilliant.
Gloriously, glō'ri-us-li, *adv.* In a glorious manner; splendidly; illustriously.
Glory, glō'ri, *n.* Praise, honour, admiration,

or distinction; renown; magnificence; celestial bliss; the divine presence; the divine perfections; that of which one may be proud.—*vi.* (glorying, gloried). To boast; to rejoice; to be proud with regard to something.

Gloss, glos, *n.* Brightness from a smooth surface; sheen; specious appearance; an interpretation; comment.—*vt.* To give superficial lustre to; to give a specious appearance to; to render plausible; to comment; to annotate.

Glossarial, glos-sā'ri-al, *a.* Containing explanation.

Glossary, glos'a-ri, *n.* A vocabulary explaining antiquated or difficult words or phrases.

Glosser, glos'ėr, *n.* A writer of glosses.

Glossographer, glos-og'ra-fėr, *n.* A writer of glosses; a scholiast.

Glossology, Glottology, glos-ol'o-ji, glot-ol'o-ji, *n.* The science of language; comparative philology.

Glossy, glos'i, *a.* Smooth and shining; highly polished.

Glottal, glot'al, *a.* Pertaining to the glottis.

Glottis, glot'is, *n.* The narrow opening at the upper part of the windpipe.

Glove, gluv, *n.* A cover for the hand.—*vt.* (gloving, gloved). To cover with a glove.

Glover, gluv'ėr, *n.* One who makes or sells gloves.

Glow, glō, *vi.* To burn with intense heat, especially without flame; to feel great heat of body; to be flushed; to be ardent; to rage. —*n.* White heat; brightness of colour; animation.

Glowing, glō'ing, *p.a.* Exhibiting a bright colour; vehement; inflamed; fervent.

Glowworm, glō'wėrm, *n.* A wingless female beetle which emits a greenish light.

Gloze, glōz, *vi.* (glozing, glozed). To use plausible words; to flatter.—*vt.* To palliate by specious exposition.—*n.* Flattery; specious words.

Glucose, glö'kōs, *n.* Grape-sugar, a sugar produced from grapes, starch, &c.

Glue, glö, *n.* A tenacious, viscid matter which serves as a cement.—*vt.* (gluing, glued). To join with glue; to unite.

Gluey, glö'i, *a.* Viscous; glutinous.

Glum, glum, *a.* Sullen; moody; dejected.

Glume, glöm, *n.* The husk or chaff of grain; a bract of plants.

Glut, glut, *vt.* (glutting, glutted). To swallow greedily; to cloy; to satiate; to furnish beyond sufficiency.—*n.* Plenty, even to loathing; supply of an article beyond the demand.

Gluten, glö'ten, *n.* A tough, elastic, nitrogenous substance in the flour of wheat, &c.

Glutinate, glö'tin-āt, *vt.* To unite with glue.

Glutinous, glö'tin-us, *a.* Gluey; viscous; viscid; tenacious; resembling glue.

Glutton, glut'n, *n.* One who eats to excess; one eager of anything to excess; a carnivorous quadruped.

Gluttonize, glut'n-īz, *vi.* To indulge in gluttony.

Gluttonous, glut'n-us, *a.* Given to excessive eating; insatiable.

Gluttony, glut'n-i, *n.* Excess in eating; voracity of appetite.

Glycerine, glis'ėr-in, *n.* A transparent, colourless, sweet liquid obtained from fats.

Glyphic, glif'ik, *a.* Of or pertaining to carving or sculpture.

Glyptic, glip'tik, *a.* Pertaining to the art of engraving on precious stones.

Glyptography, glip-tog'ra-fi, *n.* The art of engraving on gems.

Gnarl, närl, *n.* A protuberance on the outside of a tree; a knot.

Gnarled, närld, *a.* Knotty; perverse.

Gnarr, Gnarl, när, närl, *vi.* To growl; to murmur; to snarl.

Gnash, nash, *vt.* To strike together, as the teeth.—*vi.* To strike or dash the teeth together, as in rage or pain.

Gnat, nat, *n.* A small two-winged fly, the female of which bites.

Gnaw, nạ, *vt.* To bite by little and little; to bite in agony or rage; to fret; to corrode.—*vi.* To use the teeth in biting; to cause steady annoying pain.

Gneiss, nīs, *n.* A species of rock composed of quartz, feldspar, and mica, and having a slaty structure.

Gnome, nōm, *n.* A sprite supposed to inhabit the inner parts of the earth; a dwarf; a maxim, aphorism.

Gnomic, Gnomical, nō'mik, nō'mik-al, *a.* Containing or dealing in maxims.

Gnomon, nō'mon, *n.* The style or pin of a dial; a geometrical figure.

Gnostic, nos'tik, *n.* One of an early religious sect whose doctrines were based partly on Christianity and partly on Greek and Oriental philosophy.

Gnosticism, nos'ti-sizm, *n.* The doctrines of the Gnostics.

Gnu, nū, *n.* A large South African antelope.

Go, gō, *vi.* (going, pret. went, pp. gone). To move; to proceed; to depart; to be about to do; to circulate; to tend; to be guided; to be alienated or sold; to reach; to avail; to conduce; to die; to fare; to become.

Goad, gōd, *n.* A pointed instrument to make a beast move faster; anything that stirs to action. —*vt.* To drive with a goad; to instigate.

Goal, gōl, *n.* The point set to bound a race; a mark that players in some outdoor sport must attain; a success scored by reaching this; final purpose; end.

Goat, gōt, *n.* A ruminant quadruped with long hair and horns.

Goatherd, gōt'hėrd, *n.* One whose occupation is to tend goats.

Goatish, gōt'ish, *a.* Resembling a goat; of a rank smell.

Goat-skin, gōt'skin, *n.* Leather made from the skin of goats.

Goat-sucker, gōt'suk-ėr, *n.* A bird that preys on nocturnal insects: the night-jar.

Gobbet, gob'et, *n.* A mouthful; a lump.

Gobble, gob'l, *vt.* (gobbling, gobbled). To swallow in large pieces or hastily.—*vi.* To make a noise in the throat, as a turkey.

Gobbler, gob'lėr, *n.* One who gobbles; a greedy eater; a gormandizer; a turkey-cock.

Go-between, gō'bē-twēn, *n.* Intermediary.

Goblet, gob'let, *n.* A kind of cup or drinking-vessel without a handle.

Goblin, gob'lin, *n.* A mischievous sprite; an elf.

Goby, gō'bi, *n.* A name of various small fishes.

Go-by, gō-bī', *n.* A passing without notice; intentional disregard or avoidance.

God, god, *n.* The Supreme Being; a divinity; a deity; *pl.* the audience in the gallery of a theatre.
Goddess, god'es, *n.* A female deity; a woman of superior charms.
Godfather, god'fä-THėr, *n.* A man who becomes sponsor for a child at baptism. (Also *godmother*, *-son*, *-daughter*, and *-child.*)
Godhead, god'hed, *n.* Godship; divinity; divine nature or essence.
Godless, god'les, *a.* Having or acknowledging no God; ungodly; atheistical.
Godlike, god'lik, *a.* Resembling God; divine; resembling a deity; of superior excellence.
Godliness, god'li-nes, *n.* Quality of being godly; piety; reverence for God.
Godly, god'li, *a.* Reverencing God; pious; devout; holy; religious; righteous.
Godsend, god'send, *n.* An unexpected acquisition or good fortune.
Godship, god'ship, *n.* Deity; rank of a god.
God-speed, god'spēd, *n.* Success; prosperity.
Godwit, god'wit, *n.* A bird resembling a curlew.
Goer, gō'ėr, *n.* One who or that which goes; a runner or walker.
Goffer, gof'ėr, *vt.* To plait or flute.
Goggle, gog'l, *vi.* (goggling, goggled). To roll or strain the eyes.—*a.* Prominent, rolling, or staring (eyes).—*n.* A strained or affected rolling of the eye; *pl.* a kind of spectacles to protect the eyes or cure squinting.
Goggle-eyed, gog'l-id, *a.* Having prominent, distorted, or rolling eyes.
Going, gō'ing, *n.* Act of one who goes; departure; way; state of roads.—**Goings-on,** actions; behaviour.
Goitre, goi'tėr, *n.* A morbid enlargement of the thyroid gland, forming a mass on the front of the neck.
Gold, gōld, *n.* A precious metal of a bright yellow colour; money; something pleasing or valuable; a bright yellow colour.—*a.* Made or consisting of gold.
Gold-beater, gōld'bēt-ėr, *n.* One who beats gold into thin leaves for gilding.
Gold-crest, gōld-krest, *n.* The smallest British bird; the golden-crested wren.
Golden, gōld'n, *a.* Made of gold; like gold; splendid; most valuable; auspicious.
Gold-field, gōld'fēld, *n.* District or region where gold is found.
Goldfinch, gōld'finsh, *n.* A beautiful singing bird.
Gold-fish, gōld'fish, *n.* A fresh-water fish of the carp family, of a bright orange colour.
Gold-leaf, gōld'lēf, *n.* Gold beaten into a thin leaf.
Goldsmith, gōld'smith, *n.* One who manufactures articles of gold and silver.
Goldylocks, gōld'i-loks, *n.* A plant with yellow flowers; a ranunculus.
Golf, golf, *n.* A game played over links with a small ball driven by clubs.—*vi.* To play golf.
Golfer, gol'fėr, *n.* One who plays golf.
Golfing, golf'ing, *n.* Act of playing golf.
Gondola, gon'dō-la, *n.* A long narrow pleasure-boat, used in Venice.
Gondolier, gon-dō-lēr', *n.* A man who rows a gondola.
Gong, gong, *n.* A kind of metallic drum; a similar article used instead of a bell.
Gonidium, go-nid'i-um, *n.*; pl. **-dia.** A secondary reproductive cell in the thallus of lichens.
Goniometer, gō-ni-om'et-ėr, *n.* An instrument for measuring solid angles.
Good, gụd, *a.* The opposite of bad; wholesome; useful; fit; virtuous; valuable; benevolent; clever; adequate; valid; able to fulfil engagements; considerable; full or complete; immaculate.—*n.* What is good or desirable; advantage; welfare; virtue; *pl.* commodities, chattels, movables.—**For good,** to close the whole business; finally.—*interj.* Well; right.
Good-bye, gụd-bī, *n.* or *interj.* A salutation at parting; farewell.
Good-day, gụd-dā', *n.* or *interj.* A salutation at meeting or parting; farewell.
Good-for-nothing, gụd'for-nu-thing, *n.* An idle, worthless person.—*a.* Worthless.
Good-humour, gụd-hū'mėr, *n.* A cheerful temper or state of mind.
Good-humoured, gụd-hū'mėrd, *a.* Being of a cheerful temper.
Goodly, gụd'li, *a.* Good-looking; handsome; graceful; desirable.
Good-man, gụd-man', *n.* A familiar appellation of civility; a rustic term of compliment; a husband.
Good-morning, gụd-morn'ing, *n.* or *interj.* A form of morning salutation.
Good-nature, gụd-nā'tūr, *n.* Natural mildness and kindness of disposition.
Good-natured, gụd-nā'tūrd, *a.* Naturally mild in temper; not easily provoked.
Goodness, gụd'nes, *n.* State or quality of being good; excellence, virtue, &c.; a euphemism for God.
Good-night, gụd-nīt', *n.* or *interj.* A form of salutation in parting for the night.
Good-sense, gụd-sens', *n.* Sound judgment.
Good-tempered, gụd-tem'pėrd, *a.* Having a good temper; good-natured.
Good-Templar, gụd-tem'plėr, *n.* A member of a society of total abstainers.
Good-wife, gụd-wīf', *n.* The mistress of a family in rural life.
Good-will, gụd-wil', *n.* Benevolence; business connection of some established business.
Goody, Goody-good, Goody-goody, gụd'i, gụd'i-gụd, gụd'i-gụd-i, *a.* Affected with mawkish morality; squeamish in morals.
Googly, gö-gli, *n.* At cricket, a ball which breaks in from the off while delivered with a leg-break action.
Goosander, gös'an-dėr, *n.* A swimming bird allied to the ducks and divers.
Goose, gös, *n.*; pl. **Geese,** gēs. A swimming bird larger than the duck; a tailor's smoothing-iron; a silly person.
Gooseberry, gös'be-ri, *n.* The fruit of a prickly shrub, and the shrub itself.
Goose-quill, gös'kwil, *n.* The large feather or quill of a goose, or a pen made with it.
Goosery, gös'ė-ri, *n.* A place for geese; qualities of a goose; folly.
Goose-step, gös-step, *n.* Act of marking time by raising the feet alternately without advancing.
Gopher, gō'fėr, *n.* The name given in America to several burrowing animals.
Gor-cock, gor'kok, *n.* The moor-cock or red grouse.
Gordian knot, gor'di-an not. An inextricable

difficulty; *to cut the Gordian knot*, to remove a difficulty by bold measures.

Gore, gōr, *n.* Blood that is shed; thick or clotted blood; a wedge-shaped piece of land or cloth; a gusset.—*vt.* (goring, gored). To cut in a triangular form; to pierce with a pointed instrument, or an animal's horns.

Gorge, gorj, *n.* The throat; the gullet; a narrow passage between hills or mountains; entrance into a bastion.—*vt.* and *i.* (gorging, gorged). To swallow with greediness; to glut; to satiate.

Gorgeous, gor'jus, *a.* Showy; splendid; magnificent.

Gorget, gor'jet, *n.* A piece of armour for defending the neck; a pendent ornament formerly worn by officers when on duty.

Gorgon, gor'gon, *n.* A monster of Greek mythology, one of three sisters.—*a.* Like a gorgon; very ugly or terrific.

Gorgonzola, gor-gon-zō'la, *n.* A kind of Italian ewe-milk cheese.

Gorilla, gor-il'la, *n.* The largest animal of the ape kind.

Gormand, gor'mand, *n.* A glutton.

Gormandize, gor'mand-īz, *vi.* To eat greedily or to excess.

Gormandizer, gor'mand-īz-ėr, *n.* A glutton.

Gorse, gors, *n.* A shrubby plant; furze; whin.

Gorsy, gors'i, *a.* Abounding in gorse.

Gory, gō'ri, *a.* Covered with gore; bloody; murderous.

Goshawk, gos'hąk, *n.* A large bird of the hawk family.

Gosling, goz'ling, *n.* A young goose.

Gospel, gos'pel, *n.* The history of Jesus Christ; any of the four records of Christ's life by his apostles; scheme of salvation as taught by Christ; any general doctrine.—*a.* Relating to the gospel; accordant with the gospel.

Gospeller, gos'pel-ėr, *n.* An evangelist; he who reads the gospel in the church service.

Gossamer, gos'a-mėr, *n.* A fine, filmy substance, like cobwebs, floating in the air in calm, sunny weather; a thin fabric.

Gossip, gos'ip, *n.* An idle tattler; idle talk.—*vi.* To prate; to run about and tattle.

Gossipry, gos'ip-ri, *n.* Relationship by baptismal rites; idle talk or gossip.

Gossipy, gos'ip-i, *a.* Full of gossip.

Goth, goth, *n.* One of an ancient Teutonic race; a barbarian; one defective in taste.

Gothic, goth'ik, *a.* Pertaining to the Goths; rude; barbarous; denoting the style of architecture characterized by the pointed arch.—*n.* The language of the Goths; the Gothic order of architecture.

Gothicism, goth'i-sizm, *n.* Rudeness of manners; conformity to the Gothic style of architecture.

Gouda, gou'da, *n.* A kind of cheese from *Gouda*, a town in Holland.

Gouge, gouj, göj, *n.* A chisel with a hollow or grooved blade.—*vt.* (gouging, gouged). To scoop out with, or as with, a gouge.

Gourd, gōrd, *n.* The popular name of the family of plants represented by the melon, cucumber, &c.; a cup made from the rind of a gourd.

Gourmand, gör'mänd, *n.* A glutton; a gourmet.

Gourmandize, gör'mand-īz, *vi.* To gormandize.

Gourmet, gör-mā or gör'met, *n.* A connoisseur in wines and meats; a nice feeder.

Gout, gout, *n.* A painful disease, affecting generally the small joints; a drop; a clot or coagulation.

Gout, gö, *n.* Taste; relish.

Gouty, gout'i, *a.* Diseased with or subject to gout; pertaining to gout.

Govern, gu'vėrn, *vt.* To direct and control; to regulate; to steer; to affect so as to determine the case, &c., in grammar.—*vi.* To exercise authority; to administer the laws.

Governable, gu'vėrn-a-bl, *a.* That may be governed.

Governance, gu'vėrn-ans, *n.* Exercise of authority; control.

Governess, gu'vėrn-es, *n.* A female who governs or instructs.

Government, gu'vėrn-ment, *n.* Rule; control; administration of public affairs; system of polity in a state; territory ruled by a governor; executive power; the influence of a word in grammar in regard to construction.

Governmental, gu-vėrn-ment'al, *a.* Pertaining to or sanctioned by government.

Governor, gu'vėrn-ėr, *n.* One who governs; one invested with supreme authority; a tutor; a contrivance in machinery for maintaining a uniform velocity.

Governorship, gu'vėrn-ėr-ship, *n.* The office of a governor.

Gowan, gou'an, *n.* The common daisy.

Gown, goun, *n.* A woman's outer garment; a long, loose garment worn by professional men, as divines.—*vt.* To put on a gown.

Gownsman, gounz'man, *n.* One whose professional habit is a gown, particularly a member of an English university.

Grab, grab, *vt.* (grabbing, grabbed). To seize; to snatch.—*n.* A sudden grasp; implement for clutching objects.

Grace, grās, *n.* Favour; kindness; love and favour of God; state of reconciliation to God; pardon; license or privilege; expression of thanks before or after meals; title of a duke or archbishop; elegance with appropriate dignity; an embellishment; one of three ancient goddesses in whose gift were grace and beauty; in *music*, a trill, shake, &c.—*vt.* (gracing, graced). To lend grace to; to adorn; to favour.

Graceful, grās'fụl, *a.* Full of grace; beautiful with dignity; elegant.

Gracefully, grās'fụl-li, *adv.* In a graceful manner; elegantly.

Graceless, grās'les, *a.* Void of grace; unregenerate; unsanctified; profligate.

Gracile, gras'īl, *a.* Slight and elegant.

Gracious, grā'shus, *a.* Full of grace; favourable; disposed to forgive offences and impart blessings; benignant; condescending.

Graciously, grā'shus-li, *adv.* Kindly; favourably; with kind condescension.

Gradation, gra-dā'shon, *n.* Arrangement by grades; regular advance step by step; rank; series; regular process by degrees.

Gradatory, grā'da-to-ri, *a.* Proceeding step by step; marking gradation.—*n.* Steps from the cloisters into the church.

Grade, grād, *n.* A step; degree; rank; gradient.—*vt.* (grading, graded). To arrange in order of rank, &c.; to reduce to a suitable slope.

Gradient, grā'di-ent, *a.* Moving by steps; rising or descending by regular degrees.—*n.* The degree of ascent or descent in a road, &c.; part of a road which slopes.
Gradual, grad'ū-al, *a.* Advancing step by step; regular and slow.—*n.* An order of steps.
Gradually, grad'ū-al-li, *adv.* By degrees; step by step; regularly; slowly.
Graduate, grad'ū-āt, *vt.* (graduating, graduated). To divide into regular intervals or degrees; to mark with such; to arrange by grades; to confer a university degree on; to reduce to a certain consistency by evaporation. —*vi.* To receive a university degree; to change gradually.—*n.* One who has received a degree of a university, &c.
Graduation, grad-ū-ā'shon, *n.* Marks to indicate degrees, &c.; regular progression; act of conferring or receiving academical degrees.
Graft, graft, *n.* A small scion of a tree inserted in another tree which is to support and nourish the scion; corrupt gains or practices in politics.—*vt.* To insert a graft on; to propagate by a graft; to join on as if organically a part.
Grail, Graal, grāl, *n.* The holy vessel containing the last drops of Christ's blood, brought to England by Joseph of Arimathea, and, being afterwards lost, eagerly sought for by King Arthur's knights.
Grain, grān, *n.* A single seed of a plant; corn in general; a minute particle; a small weight; fibres of wood with regard to their arrangement; substance of a thing with respect to the size, form, or direction of the constituent particles; texture; dye.—*vt.* To paint in imitation of fibres; to granulate.
Grained, grānd, *p.a.* Having a certain grain or texture; having a granular surface.
Graining, grān'ing, *n.* A kind of painting in imitation of the grain of wood.
Graip, grāp, *n.* A fork for digging potatoes, &c.
Grallatorial gral-a-tō'ri-al, *a.* Pertaining to the Grallatores, an order of birds including cranes, snipes, &c., called also the *waders*.
Gramineal, Gramineous, gra-min'ē-al, gra-min'ē-us, *a.* Grassy; pertaining to grass.
Graminivorous, gra-min-iv'ō-rus, *a.* Feeding on grass.
Grammar, gram'ėr, *n.* A system of principles and rules for speaking or writing a language; propriety of speech; an outline of any subject.
Grammarian, gram-mā'ri-an, *n.* One who is versed in or who teaches grammar.
Grammatical, Grammatic, gram-mat'ik-al, gram-mat'ik, *a.* Belonging to grammar; according to the rules of grammar.
Grammatically, gram-mat'ik-al-li, *adv.* According to grammar.
Grammaticize, gram-mat'i-sīz, *vt.* To render grammatical.
Gramme, gram, *n.* The French unit of weight, equal to 15·43 grains troy.
Gramophone, gram'o-fōn, *n.* An instrument for recording and reproducing speech and music by purely mechanical means.
Grampus, gram'pus, *n.* A large marine mammal.
Granary, gra'na-ri, *n.* A storehouse for grain after it is thrashed.
Grand, grand, *a.* Great, figuratively; majestic; magnificent; noble.
Grandam, gran'dam, *n.* An old woman; a grandmother.
Grandchild, grand'child, *n.* A son's or daughter's child.
Grand-daughter, grand'da-tėr, *n.* The daughter of a son or daughter.
Grandee, gran-dē', *n.* A man of elevated rank; a nobleman.
Grandeur, grand'yūr, *n.* Greatness; sublimity; splendour; magnificence.
Grandfather, grand'fä-ᴛʜėr, *n.* A father's or mother's father.
Grandiloquence, grand-il'ō-kwens, *n.* Lofty speaking; pompous language.
Grandiose, gran'di-ōs, *a.* Impressive from grandeur; bombastic; turgid.
Grandly, grand'li, *adv.* In a grand or lofty manner; splendidly; sublimely.
Grandmother, grand'muᴛʜ-ėr, *n.* The mother of one's father or mother.
Grandsire, grand'sīr, *n.* A grandfather; any ancestor.
Grandson, grand'sun, *n.* The son of a son or daughter.
Grand-stand, grand'stand, *n.* An erection on a race-course, &c., affording a good view.
Grange, grānj, *n.* A farm, with the buildings, stables, &c.
Grangerism, grān'jėr-izm, *n.* The practice of illustrating books by prints from various sources; mutilation of books for this object. Similarly *grangerize*.
Granite, gran'it, *n.* A rock composed of quartz, feldspar, and mica, or at least of two of them, confusedly crystallized.
Granitic, gran-it'ik, *a.* Like granite; pertaining to or consisting of granite.
Granivorous, grān-iv'ō-rus, *a.* Feeding on grain or seeds.
Grant, grant, *vt.* To bestow; to confer on; to admit as true; to convey by deed or writing; to cede.—*n.* A bestowing; a gift; a conveyance in writing; the thing conveyed.
Grantor, grant'or, *n.* The person who grants or conveys lands, &c.
Granular, gran'ū-lėr, *a.* Consisting of or resembling grains.
Granulate, gran'ū-lāt, *vt.* and *i.* (granulating, granulated). To form into grains; to make or become rough on the surface.
Granulation, gran-ū-lā'shon, *n.* Act of forming into grains; a process by which minute fleshy bodies are formed on wounds during healing; the fleshy grains themselves.
Granule, gran'ūl, *n.* A little grain.
Granulous, Granulose, gran'ūl-us, gran'ūl-ōs, *a.* Full of granules.
Grape, grāp, *n.* A single berry of the vine; grape-shot.
Grape-fruit, grāp'frōt, *n.* A pale-yellow fruit akin to the orange, but larger and sourer.
Grape-shot, grāp'shot, *n.* A cluster of small balls, confined in a canvas bag, to be fired from ordnance.
Graph, graf, *n.* A diagram representing the relation between two varying magnitudes by means of a curve or series of lines.
Graphic, Graphical, graf'ik, graf'ik-al, *a.* Pertaining to the art of writing or delineating; pictorial; vivid.
Graphically, graf'ik-al-li, *adv.* In a vivid and forcible way.

Graphite, graf'īt, *n.* A form of carbon, made into pencils; plumbago; black-lead.
Grapnel, grap'nel, *n.* A small anchor with four or five claws.
Grapple, grap'l, *vt.* (grappling, grappled). To lay fast hold on, with hands or hooks.—*vi.* To contend in close fight, as wrestlers.—*n.* A seizing; close hug in contest; grappling-iron.
Grappling-iron, grap'ling-ī-ėrn, *n.* An instrument of four or more iron claws for grappling and holding fast; a grapnel.
Grapy, grāp'i, *a.* Like grapes; full of grapes; made of grapes.
Grasp, gräsp, *vt.* To seize and hold by the fingers or arms; to take possession of; to comprehend.—*vi.* To make a clutch or catch. —*n.* Gripe of the hand; reach of the arms; power of seizing or comprehending.
Grasping, gräsp'ing, *p.a.* Avaricious; greedy.
Grass, gräs, *n.* Herbage; any plant of the family to which belong the grain-yielding and pasture plants.—*vt.* To cover with grass; to bleach on the grass.
Grasshopper, gräs'hop-ėr, *n.* An insect that hops among grass, allied to the locusts.
Grass-widow, gräs'wid-ō, *n.* A wife living temporarily apart from her husband.
Grassy, gräs'i, *a.* Abounding with grass; resembling grass; green.
Grate, grāt, *n.* A frame composed of parallel or cross-bars; grating; iron frame for holding coals used as fuel.—*vt.* (grating, grated). To furnish or make fast with cross-bars; to wear away in small particles by rubbing; to offend, as by a discordant sound.—*vi.* To rub roughly on; to have an annoying effect; to sound harshly.
Grateful, grāt'ful, *a.* Pleasing; gratifying; feeling or expressing gratitude.
Grater, grāt'ėr, *n.* An instrument for rubbing off small particles of a body.
Gratification, grat'i-fi-kā''shon, *n.* Act of gratifying; that which affords pleasure; satisfaction; recompense.
Gratify, grat'i-fī, *vt.* (gratifying, gratified). To please; to indulge, delight, humour.
Gratifying, grat'i-fī-ing, *p.a.* Giving pleasure; affording satisfaction.
Grating, grāt'ing, *n.* A frame or partition of bars or lattice-work.
Gratis, grā'tis, *adv.* Without recompense; freely.—*a.* Given or done for nothing.
Gratitude, grat'i-tūd, *n.* Quality of being grateful; an emotion of the heart, excited by a favour received; thankfulness.
Gratuitous, gra-tū'it-us, *a.* That is done out of favour; free; voluntary; asserted or taken without proof.
Gratuitously, gra-tū'it-us-li, *adv.* Freely; voluntarily.
Gratuity, gra-tū'i-ti, *n.* A free gift; donation; something given in return for a favour.
Gratulate, grat'ū-lāt, *vt.* To congratulate.
Gratulation, grat-ū-lā'shon, *n.* Congratulation.
Gratulatory, grat'ū-la-to-ri, *a.* Congratulatory.
Gravamen, gra-vā'men, *n.* Ground or burden of complaint.
Grave, grāv, *vt.* (graving, pret. graved, pp. graven, graved). To make incisions on; to engrave; to impress deeply, as on the mind; to clean, as a ship's bottom, and cover with pitch.—*n.* A pit for the dead; a tomb.—*a.* Weighty; serious; staid; thoughtful; not gay; not tawdry; in *music*, low.
Grave-digger, grāv'dig-ėr, *n.* One whose occupation is to dig graves.
Gravel, gra'vel, *n.* Small pebbles; a disease produced by small concretions in the kidneys and bladder.—*vt.* (gravelling, gravelled). To cover with gravel; to cause to stick in the sand or gravel; to puzzle.
Gravelly, gra'vel-i, *a.* Abounding with gravel; consisting of gravel.
Gravely, grāv'li, *adv.* In a grave, solemn manner; soberly; seriously.
Graver, grāv'ėr, *n.* One who engraves; an engraving tool; a burin.
Gravid, grav'id, *a.* Being with young; pregnant.
Graving-dock, grāv'ing-dok, *n.* A dock in which a ship's bottom may be graved or cleaned; a dry-dock.
Gravitate, grav'i-tāt, *vt.* To be affected by gravitation; to tend towards the centre.
Gravitation, grav-i-tā'shon, *n.* The force by which bodies are drawn towards the centre of the earth; tendency of all matter toward all other matter.
Gravity, grav'i-ti, *n.* The tendency of matter toward some attracting body, particularly toward the centre of the earth; state or character of being grave; weight; enormity.
Gravy, grā'vi, *n.* The juice that comes from flesh in cooking.
Gray, grā, *a.* Of the colour of hair whitened by age; white with a mixture of black; having gray hairs.—*n.* A gray colour; a gray animal, as a horse; early morning twilight.
Gray-beard, grā'bērd, *n.* An old man; an earthen jar for holding liquor.
Grayish, grā'ish, *a.* Somewhat gray.
Grayling, grā'ling, *n.* A fish of the salmon tribe.
Graywacke, Grauwacke, grā-wak'e, grou-wak'e, *n.* A sandstone in which fragments of minerals or rocks are embedded.
Gray-wether, grā'weᴛʜ-ėr, *n.* A large boulder of siliceous sandstone.
Graze, grāz, *vt.* (grazing, grazed). To rub or touch lightly in passing; to feed with growing grass, as cattle; to feed on.—*vi.* To pass so as to rub lightly; to eat grass; to supply grass.—*n.* A slight rub or brush.
Grazier, grā'zhėr, *n.* One who pastures cattle, and who rears them for market.
Grazing, grāz'ing, *n.* The act of feeding on grass; pasture.
Grease, grēs, *n.* Animal fat in a soft state; oily matter.—*vt.*(greasing, greased). To smear with grease.
Greasy, grēz'i, *a.* Smeared with grease; fatty; unctuous; like grease.
Great, grāt, *a.* Large in bulk or number; long-continued; of vast power and excellence; eminent; majestic; pregnant; distant by one more generation, as *great*-grandfather, &c.
Greatcoat, grāt'kōt, *n.* An overcoat.
Great-hearted, grāt'härt-ed, *a.* High-spirited; magnanimous; noble.
Greatly, grāt'li, *adv.* In a great degree; much; nobly; illustriously; bravely.
Greatness, grāt'nes, *n.* Quality of being great; magnitude; nobleness; grandeur.
Greave, grēv, *n.* Armour worn on the front of the lower part of the leg: generally in *pl.*

Grecian, grē′shan, *a.* Pertaining to Greece.—*n.* A Greek; one well versed in the Greek language.
Greed, grēd, *n.* Eager desire; avarice.
Greedily, grēd′i-li, *adv.* Ravenously; eagerly.
Greedy, grēd′i, *a.* Having a keen appetite for food or drink; covetous; avaricious.
Greek, grēk, *a.* Pertaining to Greece.—*n.* A native of Greece; the language of Greece.
Green, grēn, *a.* Having the colour of growing plants; verdant; fresh; containing its natural juices; unripe; young; easily imposed upon. —*n.* A green colour; a grassy plain or plot; *pl.* leaves and stems of young plants used in cookery.—*vt.* and *i.* To make or grow green.
Green-gage, grēn′gāj, *n.* A species of plum.
Greengrocer, grēn′grō-sėr, *n.* A retailer of fresh vegetables or fruit.
Greenhorn, grēn′horn, *n.* One easily imposed upon; a raw inexperienced person.
Greenhouse, grēn′hous, *n.* A building in which tender plants are cultivated.
Greenish, grēn′ish, *a.* Somewhat green.
Greenness, grēn′nes, *n.* Viridity; unripeness; freshness; vigour.
Green-room, grēn′röm, *n.* A retiring-room for actors in a theatre.
Green-sward, grēn′sward, *n.* Turf green with grass.
Greet, grēt, *vt.* To salute; to meet and address with kindness.—*vi.* To meet and salute.
Greeting, grēt′ing, *n.* Salutation at meeting; compliment from one absent.
Gregarious, grē-gā′ri-us, *a.* Assembling or living in a flock; not habitually solitary.
Gregorian, gre-gō′ri-an, *a.* Pertaining to persons named Gregory.
Grenade, gre-nād′, *n.* A small bomb, thrown by hand or fired from a rifle.
Grenadier, gren-a-dēr′, *n.* A tall foot-soldier, one of a regiment of British guards.
Grey, grā. *See* Gray.
Greyhound, grā′hound, *n.* A tall, slender, fleet dog kept for the chase.
Grice, grīs, *n.* A little pig.
Grid, grid, *n.* A grating; a gridiron.
Griddle, grid′l, *n.* A circular plate of iron, or a shallow pan, for baking cakes.
Gride, grīd, *vt.* and *i.* (griding, grided). To pierce; to wound; to cause to grate; to scrape or graze along.
Gridiron, grid′ī-ėrn, *n.* A grated utensil for broiling flesh and fish; a frame upon which a ship rests, for inspection or repair.
Grief, grēf, *n.* Pain of mind produced by loss, misfortune, &c.; sorrow; cause of sorrow; trouble.
Grievance, grēv′ans, *n.* A wrong suffered; cause of complaint; trouble.
Grieve, grēv, *vt.* (grieving, grieved). To cause grief to; to deplore.—*vi.* To feel grief; to sorrow; to lament.
Grievous, grēv′us, *a.* Causing grief; hard to be borne; atrocious.
Griffin, Griffon, grif′in, grif′on, *n.* A fabled monster, in the fore part an eagle, in the hinder a lion.
Grill, gril, *vt.* To broil on a gridiron; to torment, as if by broiling.—*vi.* To suffer, as if from grilling.—*n.* A grated utensil for broiling meat, &c.
Grilse, grils, *n.* A young salmon on its first return to fresh water.
Grim, grim, *a.* Of a forbidding or fear-inspiring aspect; stern; sullen; surly; ugly.
Grimace, gri-mās′, *n.* A distortion of the countenance; air of affectation.—*vi.* To make grimaces.
Grimalkin, gri-mal′kin, *n.* An old cat.
Grime, grīm, *n.* Foul matter.—*vt.* (griming, grimed). To sully or soil deeply.
Grimly, grim′li, *adv.* Fiercely; sullenly.
Grimy, grīm′i, *a.* Full of grime; foul.
Grin, grin, *vi.* (grinning, grinned). To show the teeth, as in laughter, scorn, or anguish.—*n.* Act of showing the teeth; a forced smile or restrained laugh.
Grind, grīnd, *vt.* (grinding, ground). To reduce to fine particles; to sharpen or polish by friction; to rub together; to oppress; to crush in pieces.—*vi.* To turn a mill; to be moved or rubbed together; to be pulverized by friction; to study hard.—*n.* Act of one who grinds; a laborious spell of work.
Grinder, grīnd′ėr, *n.* One who or that which grinds; a molar tooth.
Grindstone, grīnd′stōn, *n.* A circular stone, made to revolve, to sharpen tools.
Grip, grip, *n.* The act of grasping; grasp; a fast hold; a hilt or handle.—*vt.* and *i.* (gripping, gripped). To grasp by the hand; to clutch; to hold fast.
Gripe, grīp, *vt.* and *i.* (griping, griped). To grasp by the hand; to hold fast; to pinch; to give pain to the bowels.—*n.* Grasp; grip; something which grasps; *pl.* pinching pain in the bowels.
Griping, grīp′ing, *p.a.* Grasping; extortionate; oppressing; distressing the bowels.
Grisette, gri-zet′, *n.* A young French woman of the working-class, especially a dress-maker.
Grisly, griz′li, *a.* Dreadful; fearful; ghastly.
Grist, grist, *n.* Corn ground, or for grinding.
Gristle, gris′l, *n.* Cartilage.
Gristly, gris′li, *a.* Consisting of gristle; cartilaginous.
Grit, grit, *n.* Sand or gravel; a hard sandstone; texture of a stone; firmness of mind; coarse part of meal.
Gritty, grit′i, *a.* Containing sand or grit; consisting of grit; sandy.
Grizzle, griz′l, *n.* Gray; a gray colour.
Grizzled, griz′ld, *a.* Gray; of a mixed colour.
Grizzly, griz′li, *a.* Somewhat gray; gray with age.
Groan, grōn, *vi.* To utter a mournful voice, as in pain or sorrow; to moan.—*n.* A deep, mournful sound, uttered in pain, sorrow, or disapprobation; any low rumbling sound.
Groat, grōt, *n.* A former English coin and money of account, equal to fourpence; a small sum.
Groats, grōts, *n.pl.* Oats or wheat with the husks taken off.
Grocer, grō′sėr, *n.* A merchant who deals in tea, sugar, spices, &c.
Grocery, grō′sė-ri, *n.* A grocer's shop; the commodities sold by grocers.
Grog, grog, *n.* A mixture of spirit and water not sweetened.
Groggy, grog′i, *a.* Overcome with grog; tipsy; moving in an uneasy, hobbling manner.
Grogram, Grogran, grog′ram, grog′ran, *n.* A kind of coarse stuff made of silk and mohair, or silk and wool.
Groin, groin, *n.* The part of the human body

between the belly and thigh in front; the angular projecting curve made by the intersection of simple vaults at any angle.
Groined, groind, *a.* Having a groin or groins; formed of groins meeting in a point.
Groom, gröm, *n.* A man or boy who has the charge of horses; a bridegroom.—*vt.* To feed and take care of, as a groom does horses.
Groom's-man, Groomsman, grömz'man, *n.* One who acts as attendant on a bridegroom at his marriage.
Groove, gröv, *n.* A channel or long hollow cut by a tool; fixed routine of life.—*vt.* (grooving, grooved). To cut a groove in; to furrow.
Grope, grōp, *vi.* (groping, groped). To search in the dark by feeling; to feel one's way.—*vt.* To search out by feeling in the dark.
Gropingly, grōp'ing-li, *adv.* In a groping manner.
Gross, grōs, *a.* Thick; coarse; obscene; palpable; dense; shameful; dull; whole.—*n.* Main body; bulk; the number of twelve dozen.
Grossbeak, Grosbeak, grōs'bēk, *n.* A finch with a thick and strong bill.
Grossly, grōs'li, *adv.* Greatly; shamefully.
Grot, grot, *n.* A grotto: *poetical*.
Grotesque, grō-tesk', *a.* Wildly formed; extravagant; fantastic.—*n.* Whimsical figures or scenery.
Grotto, grot'tō, *n.* A natural cave; an artificial ornamented cave.
Ground, ground, *n.* Surface of the earth; soil; land; basis; reason; foil or background; predominating colour; *pl.* dregs, sediment; ornamental land about a mansion.—*vt.* To set on the ground; to found; to fix firmly; to instruct in first principles.—*vi.* To strike the bottom and remain fixed, as a ship.
Ground-floor, ground'flōr, *n.* Floor of a house on a level with the exterior ground.
Groundless, ground'les, *a.* Wanting foundation or reason; baseless; false.
Groundling, ground'ling, *n.* A fish that keeps at the bottom of the water.
Ground-rent, ground'rent, *n.* Rent for the privilege of building.
Groundsel, Groundsill, ground'sel, ground'sil, *n.* The timber of a building which lies on the ground; a sill.
Groundsel, ground'sel, *n.* A common annual weed, used as food for caged birds.
Ground staff, ground stäf, *n.* Mechanics and other non-flying members of aerodrome staff.
Ground-swell, ground'swel, *n.* Heaving of the sea caused by a distant storm.
Groundwork, ground'wėrk, *n.* Basis; fundamentals.
Group, gröp, *n.* A cluster; an assemblage; an artistic combination of figures; a class.—*vt.* To form into a group or groups.
Group Captain, gröp kap'tin, *n.* Officer in the Royal Air Force, ranking with a colonel in the army.
Grouping, gröp'ing, *n.* The art of arranging or mode of arrangement in a picture or work of art.
Grouse, grous, *n.* The name of several wild rasorial birds, more particularly the moorfowl or red grouse of Britain.
Grout, grout, *n.* Coarse meal; a thin mortar; dregs.—*vt.* To fill up with grout or mortar.
Grove, grōv, *n.* A shady cluster of trees; a small wood.
Grovel, gro'vel, *vi.* (grovelling, grovelled). To lie prone, or creep on the earth; to be low or mean.
Groveller, gro'vel-ėr, *n.* One who grovels; an abject wretch.
Grovelling, gro'vel-ing, *p.a.* Apt to grovel; abject; base.
Grow, grō, *vi.* (pret. grew, pp. grown). To be augmented by natural process; to increase; to make progress; to become; to accrue; to swell.—*vt.* To raise from the soil; to produce.
Grower, grō'ėr, *n.* One who grows.
Growl, groul, *vi.* To murmur or snarl, as a dog; to utter an angry, grumbling sound.—*vt.* To express by growling.—*n.* Angry sound of a dog; grumbling murmur.
Growler, groul'ėr, *n.* One that growls; a grumbler; a four-wheeled cab (*slang*).
Grown, grōn, *p.a.* Increased in growth; having arrived at full size or stature.
Grown-up, grōn'up, *a.* Adult.
Growth, grōth, *n.* Act or process of growing; product; increase; advancement.
Groyne, groin, *n.* A kind of small breakwater.
Grub, grub, *vi.* (grubbing, grubbed). To dig; to be employed meanly.—*vt.* To dig; to root out by digging.—*n.* The larva of an insect; caterpillar; maggot.
Grubber, grub'ėr, *n.* One who grubs; an instrument for digging up roots, weeds, &c.
Grudge, gruj, *vi.* (grudging, grudged). To cherish ill-will; to be envious.—*vt.* To permit or grant with reluctance; to envy.—*n.* Reluctance in giving; secret enmity.
Grudgingly, gruj'ing-li, *adv.* In a grudging, unwilling, or envious manner.
Gruel, grū'el, *n.* A light food made by boiling meal in water.
Gruesome, grö'sum, *a.* Causing one to shudder; frightful; horrible; repulsive.
Gruff, gruf, *a.* Of a rough or stern manner or voice; surly; harsh.
Gruffly, gruf'li, *adv.* Roughly; harshly.
Grum, grum, *a.* Morose; surly; glum.
Grumble, grum'bl, *vi.* (grumbling, grumbled). To murmur with discontent.
Grumbler, grum'bl-ėr, *n.* One who grumbles; a discontented man.
Grume, gröm, *n.* A fluid of a thick, viscid consistence; a clot, as of blood.
Grumpy, Grumpish, grum'pi, grum'pish, *a.* Surly; angry; gruff: *colloq.*
Grunt, grunt, *vi.* To make a noise like a hog; to utter a deep guttural sound.—*n.* A deep guttural sound, as of a hog.
Grunter, grunt'ėr, *n.* One who grunts; a pig.
Gruyère, grü-yār, *n.* Cheese made from a mixture of goats' and ewes' milk.
Guano, gwä'nō, *n.* A rich manure composed chiefly of the excrements of sea-fowls, and brought from S. America and the Pacific.
Guarantee, ga-ran-tē', *n.* An undertaking by a third person that a covenant shall be observed by the contracting parties or by one of them; one who binds himself to see the stipulations of another performed.—*vt.* (guaranteeing, guaranteed). To warrant; to pledge oneself for.
Guarantor, gar-an-tor', *n.* One who gives a guarantee.
Guard, gärd, *vt.* To keep watch over; to secure against injury, loss, or attack.—*vi.* To

watch, by way of caution or defence; to be in a state of caution or defence.—*n.* Defence; protector; sentinel; escort; one who has charge of a railway train, &c.; attention; caution; posture of defence.
Guarded, gärd′ed, *p.a.* Circumspect; framed or uttered with caution.
Guardedly, gärd′ed-li, *adv.* With circumspection.
Guard-house, Guard-room, gärd′hous, gärd′röm, *n.* A house or room for the accommodation of a guard of soldiers, and where military defaulters are confined.
Guardian, gärd′i-an, *n.* One who guards; one appointed to take charge of an orphan or ward.—*a.* Protecting.
Guardianship, gärd′i-an-ship, *n.* The office of a guardian; protection; care.
Guardsman, gärdz′man, *n.* An officer or a private in a body of guards.
Guava, gwä′va, *n.* A small tropical tree of the myrtle family.
Gudgeon, gu′jon, *n.* A metallic piece let into the end of a wooden shaft; a small freshwater fish; a person easily cheated.
Guerdon, gėr′don, *n.* A reward; requital; recompense.—*vt.* To reward.
Guerrilla, Guerilla, ge-ril′la, *n.* An irregular petty war; one engaged in such.
Guess, ges, *vt.* To conjecture; to form an opinion without certain means of knowledge; to surmise.—*vi.* To conjecture; to judge at random.—*n.* Conjecture; surmise.
Guess-work, ges′wėrk, *n.* Work performed at hazard or by mere conjecture.
Guest, gest, *n.* A visitor or friend entertained in the house or at the table of another.
Guffaw, guf-fa̧′, *n.* A loud burst of laughter.—*vi.* To burst into a loud laugh.
Guggle, gug′l, *vi.* To gurgle.
Guidance, gīd′ans, *n.* The act of guiding; direction; government; a leading.
Guide, gīd, *vt.* (guiding, guided). To lead; to direct; to influence; to regulate.—*n.* A person who guides; a director; a regulator; a guide-book.
Guide-book, gīd′bu̧k, *n.* A book for the guidance of travellers.
Guide-post, gīd′pōst, *n.* A post for directing travellers the way; a finger-post.
Guild, Gild, gild, *n.* A corporation of craftsmen, &c., for mutual aid and protection.
Guilder, gil′dėr, *n.* A Dutch coin normally equal to 1*s.* 8*d.* English.
Guildhall, gild-ha̧l′, *n.* Hall where a guild assembles; a town or corporation hall.
Guile, gīl, *n.* Wile; fraud; duplicity.
Guileful, gīl′fu̧l, *a.* Cunning; fraudulent.
Guileless, gīl′les, *a.* Artless; sincere; honest.
Guillemot, gil′e-mot, *n.* A marine swimming bird allied to the auks and divers.
Guillotine, gil-ō-tēn′, *n.* A machine for beheading persons; a machine for cutting paper.—*vt.* To behead by the guillotine.
Guilt, gilt, *n.* Criminality; sin; wickedness.
Guiltily, gilt′i-li, *adv.* In a guilty manner.
Guiltless, gilt′les, *a.* Free from guilt.
Guilty, gilt′i, *a.* Justly chargeable with guilt; criminal; pertaining to or indicating guilt.
Guinea, gin′ē, *n.* A former British gold coin, or a sum of money, worth 21 shillings sterling.
Guinea-fowl, gin′ē-foul, *n.* A fowl allied to the peacocks and pheasants.
Guinea-pig, gin′ē-pig, *n.* A tailless rodent about 7 inches in length.
Guipure, gē-pūr′, *n.* An imitation of antique lace.
Guise, gīz, *n.* External appearance; dress; mien; cast of behaviour.
Guiser, gīz′ėr, *n.* A person in disguise; a Christmas masker or mummer.
Guitar, gi-tär′, *n.* A musical instrument having six strings.
Gulch, gulch, *n.* A gully; dry bed of a torrent.
Gules, gūlz, *n.* Red (in *heraldry*).
Gulf, gulf, *n.* An arm of the sea extending into the land; bay; chasm; whirlpool; anything insatiable; a wide interval.
Gull, gul, *vt.* To cheat.—*n.* One easily cheated; a simpleton; a marine swimming bird.
Gullet, gul′et, *n.* The passage in the neck of an animal by which food and liquor are taken into the stomach.
Gullible, gul′i-bl, *a.* Easily gulled or cheated.
Gully, gul′i, *n.* A channel worn by water; a ravine.—*vt.* To wear into a gully.
Gulp, gulp, *vt.* To swallow eagerly.—*n.* Act of taking a large swallow.
Gum, gum, *n.* The fleshy substance of the jaws round the teeth; a juice which exudes from trees, &c., and thickens; a viscous substance.—*vt.* (gumming, gummed). To smear with or unite by a viscous substance.
Gum-boil, gum′boil, *n.* A boil on the gum.
Gummy, gum′i, *a.* Of the nature of gum; productive of gum; covered with gum.
Gumption, gum′shon, *n.* Understanding; capacity; shrewdness: *colloq.*
Gun, gun, *n.* Any species of firearm.
Gun-boat, gun′bōt, *n.* A small vessel of light draught, fitted for carrying one or more guns.
Gun-cotton, gun′kot-n, *n.* An explosive produced by soaking cotton, &c., in nitric and sulphuric acids, and leaving it to dry.
Gunman, gun′man, *n.* An armed bandit.
Gun-metal, gun′met-l, *n.* An alloy of copper and tin used for cannon, &c.
Gunner, gun′ėr, *n.* One who has the charge of ordnance.
Gunnery, gun′ė-ri, *n.* The art of firing cannon; the science of artillery.
Gunpowder, gun′pou-dėr, *n.* An explosive mixture of saltpetre, sulphur, and charcoal.
Gunshot, gun′shot, *n.* Range of a cannon-shot; firing of a gun.—*a.* Made by the shot of a gun.
Gunwale, Gunnel, gun′wāl, gun′el, *n.* The upper edge of a ship's side.
Gurgle, gėr′gl, *vi.* (gurgling, gurgled). To run or flow in a broken noisy current.—*n.* Sound produced by a liquid flowing from or through a narrow opening.
Gurnard, Gurnet, gėr′närd, gėr′net, *n.* A marine fish with an angular bony head.
Gush, gush, *vi.* To issue with violence and rapidity, as a fluid; to be effusively sentimental.—*n.* A sudden and violent issue of a fluid; the fluid thus emitted; effusive display of sentiment.
Gushing, gush′ing, *p.a.* Rushing forth with a gush; demonstratively affectionate.
Gusset, gus′et, *n.* A piece of cloth inserted in a garment.
Gust, gust, *n.* Taste; relish; a sudden blast of wind; a violent burst of passion.

Gustatory, gust'a-to-ri, *a.* Pertaining to taste.
Gusto, gust'ō, *n.* Relish; zest; taste.
Gusty, gust'i, *a.* Subject to sudden blasts of wind; stormy.
Gut, gut, *n.* The intestinal canal of an animal; *pl.* the entrails; a preparation of the intestines for various purposes; a channel.—*vt.* (gutting, gutted). To take out the entrails of; to plunder of contents; to destroy the interior of.
Gutta-percha, gut'ta-pėr'cha, *n.* The hardened milky juice of a tree of E. Asia, resembling caoutchouc.
Gutter, gut'ėr, *n.* A channel at the side of a road, &c., for water.—*vt.* To cut or form gutters in.—*vi.* To become channelled.
Guttle, gut'l, *vi.* and *t.* To guzzle.
Guttural, gut'tėr-al, *a.* Pertaining to the throat; formed in the throat.—*n.* A letter pronounced in the throat; any guttural sound.
Guy, gī, *n.* A rope to steady anything; a person of queer looks or dress.—*vt.* To steady or direct by means of a guy.
Guzzle, guz'l, *vi.* and *t.* (guzzling, guzzled). To swallow greedily or frequently.—*n.* A debauch.
Guzzler, guz'l-ėr, *n.* One who guzzles.
Gymnasium, jim-nā'zi-um, *n.*; pl. **-ia** or **-iums.** A place for athletic exercises; a school for the higher branches of education.
Gymnast, jim'nast, *n.* One who teaches or practises gymnastic exercises.
Gymnastic, jim-nast'ik, *a.* Pertaining to athletic exercises.
Gymnastics, jim-nast'iks, *n.pl.* The art of performing athletic exercises.
Gynæcocracy, Gynecocracy, jīn- or jin-ē-kok'ra-si, *n.* Female rule.
Gynæcology, Gynecology, jīn- or jin-ē-kol'o-ji, *n.* The medical science of the functions and diseases peculiar to women.
Gynæolatry, jīn- or jin-ē-ol'a-tri, *n.* The extravagant admiration of woman.
Gyp, jip, *n.* A college servant at Cambridge University.
Gypseous, jip'sē-us, *a.* Like gypsum.
Gypsum, jip'sum, *n.* A mineral found as alabaster or as plaster of Paris.
Gypsy, jip'si, *n.* *See* GIPSY.
Gyrate, jī'rāt, *vi.* (gyrating, gyrated). To move in a circle or spirally.—*a.* Moving in a circle.
Gyration, jī-rā'shon, *n.* A turning or whirling round.
Gyratory, jī'ra-to-ri, *a.* Moving in a circle.
Gyre, jīr, *n.* A circular motion, or a circle described by a moving body; a turn.
Gyrfalcon, jėr'fa-kn, *n.* A species of falcon.
Gyroscope, Gyrostat, jī'rō-skōp, jī'rō-stat, *n.* An apparatus for illustrating peculiarities of rotation.
Gyve, jīv, *n.* A fetter or shackle.—*vt.* (gyving, gyved). To fetter; to shackle.

H

Ha, hä. An exclamation denoting surprise, joy, grief, &c.
Haberdasher, ha'bėr-dash-ėr, *n.* A dealer in drapery goods, as woollens, silks, ribbons, &c.
Haberdashery, ha'bėr-dash-ė-ri, *n.* The wares sold by a haberdasher.
Habergeon, ha'bėr-jon or ha-bėr'jon, *n.* A coat of mail consisting of a jacket without sleeves.
Habiliment, ha-bil'i-ment, *n.* A garment: usually in *pl.*
Habilitate, ha-bil'i-tāt, *vi.* To qualify.
Habit, ha'bit, *n.* State of body, natural or acquired; mode of growth of a plant; aptitude acquired by practice; custom; manner; dress; outer dress worn by ladies on horse-back.—*vt.* To dress; to clothe; to array.
Habitable, ha'bit-a-bl, *a.* That may be inhabited.
Habitat, ha'bit-at, *n.* The natural abode or locality of a plant or animal.
Habitation, ha-bit-ā'shon, *n.* Occupancy; abode; residence.
Habited, ha'bit-ed, *p.a.* Clothed; dressed.
Habitual, ha-bit'ū-al, *a.* Formed or acquired by habit; customary; usual.
Habitually, ha-bit'ū-al-li, *adv.* By habit; constantly.
Habituate, ha-bit'ū-āt, *vt.* (habituating, habituated). To train to a habit; to make familiar by frequent use; to inure.
Habitude, ha'bit-ūd, *n.* Customary manner of life; long custom; habit.
Habitué, a-bē-tu-ā, *n.* A habitual frequenter of any place.
Hachure, hach'ūr or ä-shụr, *n.* Short lines marking half-tints and shadows in engraving, &c.
Hack, hak, *n.* A notch; cut; kick at football; a horse kept for hire; a worn-out horse; a literary drudge; frame for drying fish, &c.; rack for cattle.—*vt.* To cut irregularly; to notch; to mangle; to let out for hire.—*a.* Hired; much used or worn.
Hackery, hak'ėr-i, *n.* A rude two-wheeled cart of India drawn by oxen.
Hacking, hak'ing, *p.a.* Short and interrupted: as, a *hacking* cough.
Hackle, hak'l, *n.* A comb for dressing flax; raw silk; any flimsy substance unspun; a long pointed feather; a fly for angling.—*vt.* (hackling, hackled). To comb (flax or hemp).
Hackney, hak'ni, *n.* A horse kept for hire; a coach kept for hire; nag; drudge.—*a.* Let out for hire; much used; trite.—*vt.* To use much; to make trite.
Hackneyed, hak'nid, *p.a.* Much used; trite.
Haddock, had'ok, *n.* A sea-fish allied to the cod.
Hades, hā'dēz, *n.* The abode of the dead; state of departed souls.
Hadji, Hadjee, haj'ē, *n.* A Mohammedan who has performed the pilgrimage to Mecca.
Hæmal, hē'mal, *a.* Pertaining to the blood.
Hæmorrhage, hē'mor-āj, *n.* HEMORRHAGE.
Haft, haft, *n.* A handle; that part of an instrument which is taken into the hand.—*vt.* To set in a haft.
Hag, hag, *n.* An ugly old woman; a witch; an eel-shaped fish that eats into other fishes.
Haggard, hag'ärd, *a.* Wild; intractable; having the face worn and pale; gaunt.—*n.* An untrained or refractory hawk.
Haggis, hag'is, *n.* A Scottish dish, commonly made of a sheep's stomach, with the heart, lungs, and liver minced, and mixed with suet, onions, oatmeal, salt, &c., inside.
Haggish, hag'ish, *a.* Of the nature of a hag; deformed; ugly.

Haggle, hag'l, *vt.* (haggling, haggled). To cut into small pieces; to mangle.—*vi.* To be difficult in bargaining; to stick at small matters; to chaffer.
Hagiology, hā-ji-ol'o-ji, *n.* That branch of literature which has to do with the lives and legends of the saints.
Hah, häh. Same as *Ha.*
Ha-ha, hä'hä, *n.* A sunk fence or ditch.
Hail, hāl, *n.* Frozen drops of rain; a wish of health; a call.—*vi.* To pour down hail; to have as one's residence, or belong to (with *from*).—*vt.* To pour down in the manner of hail; to salute; to call to; to designate as.—*interj.* A salutation expressive of well-wishing.
Hailstone, hāl'stōn, *n.* A single pellet of hail falling from a cloud.
Hair, hãr, *n.* A small filament issuing from the skin of an animal; the mass of filaments growing from the skin of an animal; anything similar; a very small distance.
Hair-breadth, Hair's-breadth, hãr'bredth, hãrz'bredth, *n.* The diameter of a hair; a very small distance.—*a.* Of the breadth of a hair; very narrow.
Hair-cloth, hãr'kloth, *n.* A cloth made of hair or in part of hair.
Hair-dresser, hãr'dres-ėr, *n.* A barber.
Hairless, hãr'les, *a.* Destitute of hair; bald.
Hair-splitting, hãr'split-ing, *n.* The making minute distinctions in reasoning.
Hairy, hãr'i, *a.* Overgrown with hair; consisting of hair; resembling hair.
Hake, hāk, *n.* A fish of the cod family.
Halberd, hal'bėrd, *n.* An ancient weapon consisting of a long pole ending with an axe and sharp head.
Halberdier, hal-bėrd-ēr', *n.* One who is armed with a halberd.
Halcyon, hal'si-on, *n.* The kingfisher, fabled to have the power of producing calm weather during the period of incubation.—*a.* Calm; peaceful.
Hale, hāl, *a.* Sound; healthy; robust.—*n.* A violent pull.—*vt.* (haling, haled). To take, pull, or drag by force.
Half, häf, *n.*; pl. **Halves,** hävz. One part of a thing divided into two equal parts.—*a.* Consisting of a half.—*adv.* In part, or in an equal part or degree.
Half-back, häf-bak, *n.* Player in football or hockey who plays between the forwards and the backs.
Half-brother, häf'bruтн-ėr, *n.* A brother by one parent, but not by both.
Half-caste, häf'kast, *n.* One born of a Hindu and a European.
Half-crown, häf'kroun, *n.* A British silver coin, value 2*s.* 6*d.*
Half-dead, häf-ded', *a.* Almost dead.
Half-hearted, häf-härt'ed, *a.* Far from enthusiastic; lukewarm.
Half-length, häf'length, *a.* Containing one-half of the length.—*n.* Portrait showing only the upper half of the body.
Half-pay, häf'pā, *n.* Reduced allowance to an officer on retirement or when not in actual service.—*a.* Receiving half-pay.
Halfpenny, hā'pen-i, *n.*; pl. **Halfpence,** häf'pens or hā'pens. A copper coin, value half a penny.
Half-sister, häf'sis-tėr, *n.* A sister by one parent, but not by both.
Half-sovereign, häf'sov-ėr-in, *n.* A British gold coin, value 10*s.*
Half-witted, häf-wit'ed, *a.* Weak in intellect.
Halibut, ha'li-but, *n.* A large flat-fish allied to the turbot.
Halidom, hal'i-dom, *n.* Holiness; sacred word of honour.
Hall, hal, *n.* A large room, especially a large public room; a large room at the entrance of a house; a manor-house; the name of certain colleges at Oxford and Cambridge.
Halleluiah, Hallelujah, hal-lē-lu'ya, *n.* and *interj.* A word used in sacred songs of praise, signifying *praise ye Jehovah.*
Halliard. *See* HALYARD.
Hall-mark, hal'märk, *n.* The official stamp affixed to articles of gold and silver, as a mark of their legal quality.
Hallo, ha-lō', *interj.* Nearly equal to *halloo.*
Halloo, ha-lö', *interj.* and *n.* An exclamation to invite attention; hunting cry to a dog.—*vi.* (hallooing, hallooed). To cry out.—*vt.* To encourage with shouts; to call or shout to.
Hallow, hal'ō, *vt.* To make holy; to set apart for religious use; to treat as sacred.
Hallow-e'en, Hallow-even, hal'ō-ēn, hal'ō-ē-vn, *n.* The eve or vigil of All-Hallows' or All-Saints' Day.
Hallowmas, hal'ō-mas, *n.* The feast of All-Saints or the time at which it is held.
Hallucination, hal-lū'si-nā"shon, *n.* A mistaken notion; mere dream or fancy; morbid condition in which objects are believed to be seen and sensations experienced; object or sensation thus erroneously perceived.
Halo, hā'lō, *n.* A luminous ring round the sun or moon; any circle of light, as the glory round the head of saints; an ideal glory investing an object.—*vi.* To form itself into a halo.—*vt.* To surround with a halo.
Halt, halt, *vi.* To limp; to be lame; to hesitate; to cease marching.—*vt.* To stop; to cause to cease marching.—*a.* Lame; limping.—*n.* A limp; a stopping; stoppage on march.
Halter, hal'tėr, *n.* A rope or strap and head-stall for leading or confining a horse; a rope for hanging.—*vt.* To put a halter on.
Halve, häv, *vt.* (halving, halved). To divide into two equal parts.
Halyard, hal'yärd, *n.* Rope or tackle for raising and lowering the yards.
Ham, ham, *n.* The hind part of the knee; the back of the thigh; the thigh of an animal, particularly of a hog, salted and dried in smoke.
Hamadryad, ham'a-drī-ad, *n.* A wood-nymph, believed to die with the tree to which she was attached; the king cobra of India; the sacred baboon of ancient Egypt.
Hamlet, ham'let, *n.* A small village.
Hammer, ham'ėr, *n.* An instrument for driving nails, beating metals, and the like.—*vt.* To beat or forge with a hammer; to contrive by intellectual labour.—*vi.* To work with a hammer; to labour in contrivance.
Hammock, ham'ok, *n.* A kind of hanging bed.
Hamper, ham'pėr, *n.* A large basket for conveying things to market, &c.; something that encumbers; a clog.—*vt.* To put into a hamper; to hinder or impede; to embarrass.
Hamstring, ham'string, *n.* One of the tendons of the ham.—*vt.* (pp. hamstrung or hamstringed). To cut the tendons of the ham, and thus to lame or disable.

Hand, hand, *n.* The extremity of the arm, consisting of the palm and fingers; a measure of four inches; side or direction; skill; manner of acting; power; cards held at a game; a game; an index; a male or female in relation to an employer; person with some special faculty; style of penmanship.—*vt.* To give with the hand; to lead with the hand; to conduct; to handle.—*a.* Belonging to, or used by the hand.

Handbill, hand'bil, *n.* A loose printed sheet, &c., to be circulated.

Handbook, hand'bųk, *n.* A book for the hand; a manual; a guide-book.

Handbreadth, hand'bredth, *n.* A space equal to the breadth of the hand.

Handcuff, hand'kuf, *n.* A fetter for the hands or wrists.—*vt.* To manacle with handcuffs.

Handed, hand'ed, *a.* Having hands of this or that character: especially in compounds.

Handful, hand'fųl, *n.* As much as the hand will grasp or hold; a small quantity or number.

Hand-gallop, hand-gal'up, *n.* A slow and easy gallop.

Handicap, hand'i-kap, *n.* In racing, games, &c., an allowance to bring superior competitors to an equality with the others; a race or contest so arranged.—*vt.* To put a handicap on; to equalize by a handicap.

Handicraft, hand'i-kraft, *n.* Work performed by the hand; manual occupation.

Handicraftsman, hand'i-krafts-man, *n.* A man skilled in a handicraft; an artisan.

Handily, hand'i-li, *adv.* In a handy manner.

Handiwork, hand'i-wėrk, *n.* Product of manual labour; work or deed of any person.

Handkerchief, hand'kėr-chif, *n.* A cloth carried about the person for wiping the mouth, nose, &c.; a cloth worn about the neck.

Handle, han'dl, *vt.* (handling, handled). To feel, use, or hold with the hand; to discuss; to deal with; to treat or use well or ill.—*n.* That part of an instrument, &c., held in the hand; instrument for effecting a purpose.

Handline, hand'līn, *n.* A small line used in fishing from boats at sea.

Handmaid, Handmaiden, hand'mād, hand'-mād-n, *n.* Female servant or attendant.

Hand-mill, hand'mil, *n.* A mill worked by the hand.

Handrail, hand'rāl, *n.* A rail for the hand, supported by balusters, &c., as in staircases.

Handsel, hand'sel, *n.* An earnest; a new-year's gift; the first act of using anything.—*vt.* (handseling, handseled). To give a handsel to; to use or do for the first time.

Handsome, hand'sum, *a.* Well formed; having a certain share of beauty along with dignity; ample; generous.

Handsomely, hand'sum-li, *adv.* In a handsome manner; amply; generously.

Handwriting, hand-rīt'ing, *n.* The writing peculiar to each person; any writing.

Handy, hand'i, *a.* Skilled in using the hands; dexterous; ready; convenient for use.

Hang, hang, *vt.* (pret. and pp. hung and hanged). To suspend; to furnish with anything suspended; to cause to droop; to fit so as to allow of free motion; to put to death by suspending by the neck.—*vi.* To be suspended; to dangle; to adhere; to linger; to lean; to have a steep declivity; to be executed.

Hangar, hang'ar, *n.* A shed for housing aeroplanes.

Hang-dog, hang'dog, *n.* A degraded character.—*a.* Having a low or blackguard-like appearance.

Hanger, hang'ėr, *n.* One who or that which hangs; a short broad sword; that from which something is hung.

Hanger-on, hang-ėr-on', *n.*; pl. **Hangers-on.** A servile dependant; a parasite.

Hanging, hang'ing, *n.* Act of suspending; death by the halter; *pl.* linings for rooms, of tapestry, paper, &c.

Hangman, hang'man, *n.* A public executioner.

Hank, hangk, *n.* A skein of silk, yarn, &c.; a coil.—*vt.* To form into hanks.

Hanker, hang'kėr, *vi.* To desire eagerly; to think of something longingly (with *after*).

Hansom, Hansom-cab, han'sum, han'sum-kab, *n.* A two-wheeled cab.

Hap, hap, *n.* Chance; luck; fortune.—*vi.* To happen; to befall.

Haphazard, hap-ha'zėrd, *n.* Chance; accident.

Hapless, hap'les, *a.* Unlucky; unhappy.

Haply, hap'li, *adv.* By hap or chance; perhaps.

Happen, hap'n, *vi.* To come by chance; to occur.

Happily, hap'i-li, *adv.* In a happy manner; fortunately; gracefully.

Happiness, hap'i-nes, *n.* State of being happy; enjoyment of pleasure; good luck.

Happy, hap'i, *a.* Being in the enjoyment of agreeable sensations from the possession of good; fortunate; propitious; well suited; apt.

Harangue, ha-rang', *n.* A noisy or pompous address; a declamatory public address; a tirade.—*vi.* (haranguing, harangued). To make a harangue.—*vt.* To address by a harangue.

Harass, ha'ras, *vt.* To vex; to tire with labour; to fatigue with importunity.

Harassing, ha'ras-ing, *p.a.* Fatiguing; tending to wear with care or anxiety.

Harbinger, här'bin-jėr, *n.* A forerunner; that which precedes and gives notice of something else.—*vt.* To precede as harbinger.

Harbour, här'bėr, *n.* A shelter; a haven for ships; an asylum.—*vt.* To shelter; to entertain in the mind.—*vi.* To take shelter; to lodge or abide for a time.

Harbourage, här'bėr-āj, *n.* Shelter; lodgment.

Harbourless, här'bėr-les, *a.* Without a harbour; destitute of shelter.

Hard, härd, *a.* Not easily penetrated or separated; firm; difficult to understand; arduous; unfeeling; severe; unjust; harsh; stiff; grasping: applied to certain sounds, as sibilants contrasted with gutturals: applied to water not suitable for washing, from holding minerals.—*adv.* Close; diligently; with difficulty; fast; copiously; with force.

Harden, härd'n, *vt.* To make hard or more hard; to confirm in effrontery, obstinacy, wickedness, &c.; to make unfeeling; to inure; to render less liable to injury by exposure or use.—*vi.* To become hard or more hard; to become unfeeling; to become inured.

Hardened, härd'nd, *p.a.* Made hard or more hard; obstinate; confirmed; callous.

Hard-fisted, härd'fist-ed, *a.* Having hard or strong hands; covetous.

Hard-headed, härd'hed-ed, *a.* Shrewd; intelligent.
Hard-hearted, härd'härt-ed, *a.* Having an unfeeling heart; pitiless.
Hardihood, härd'i-hụd, *n.* Quality of being hardy; boldness; intrepidity; audacity; effrontery.
Hardily, härd'i-li, *adv.* In a hardy manner; boldly; stoutly; with endurance.
Hardish, härd'ish, *a.* Somewhat hard.
Hardly, härd'li, *adv.* With difficulty; scarcely; harshly.
Hardness, härd'nes, *n.* State or quality of being hard in all its senses; firmness; difficulty; obduracy; rigour; niggardliness, &c.
Hards, härdz, *n.pl.* The refuse or coarse part of flax or wool.
Hardship, härd'ship, *n.* Privation; affliction; oppression; injustice; grievance.
Hardware, härd'wār, *n.* Wares made of iron or other metal, as pots, knives, &c.
Hardy, härd'i, *a.* Bold; intrepid; full of assurance; inured to fatigue; capable of bearing exposure.
Hare, hār, *n.* A rodent animal allied to the rabbit, but not making burrows.
Harebell, hār'bel, *n.* A plant with a slender stem and pale-blue bell-shaped flowers.
Hare-brained, hār'brānd, *a.* Wild as a hare; giddy; volatile; heedless.
Harelip, hār'lip, *n.* A perpendicular division of one or both lips, but commonly the upper one, like that of a hare.
Harem, hā'rem, *n.* The apartments of the female members of a Mohammedan family; the occupants.
Haricot, ha'ri-kō, *n.* A ragout of meat and roots; the kidney-bean or French bean.
Hark, härk, *vi.* To listen; to lend the ear.
Harlequin, här'le-kwin, *n.* A performer in a pantomime, masked, dressed in tight spangled clothes, and armed with a magic wand; a buffoon in general.
Harlequinade, här'le-kwin-ād", *n.* Portion of a pantomime in which the harlequin appears; buffoonery.
Harlot, här'lot, *n.* A prostitute.
Harlotry, här'lot-ri, *n.* The trade or practice of prostitution.
Harm, härm, *n.* Injury; hurt; evil.—*vt.* To hurt; to damage; to impair.
Harmful, härm'fụl, *a.* Hurtful; injurious; noxious; mischievous.
Harmless, härm'les, *a.* Free from harm; not causing harm; inoffensive; uninjured.
Harmlessly, härm'les-li, *adv.* Without causing or receiving harm.
Harmonic, Harmonical, här-mon'ik, här-mon'ik-al, *a.* Pertaining to harmony; concordant; musical.—**Harmonic,** här-mon'ik, *n.* A less distinct tone accompanying a principal tone.
Harmonica, här-mon'i-ka, *n.* A musical toy played by striking rods or plates of glass or metal with small hammers.
Harmonicon, här-mon'i-kon, *n.* A kind of large and complicated barrel-organ.
Harmonics, här-mon'iks, *n.* The doctrine of harmony or of musical sounds.
Harmonious, här-mō'ni-us, *a.* Having harmony; having the parts adapted to each other; concordant; friendly.
Harmonist, här'mon-ist, *n.* One skilled in harmony; a musician; one who harmonizes.
Harmonium, här-mō'ni-um, *n.* A musical wind-instrument resembling a small organ.
Harmonize, här'mon-īz, *vi.* To be in harmony; to agree in sound or sense; to be in friendship.—*vt.* To bring into harmony; to set accompanying parts to.
Harmony, här'mo-ni, *n.* The just adaptation of parts to each other; musical concord; agreement; peace and friendship.
Harness, här'nes, *n.* Armour; furniture of a carriage or draught horse.—*vt.* To dress in armour; to put harness on.
Harp, härp, *n.* A stringed musical instrument of triangular form played with the fingers.—*vi.* To play on the harp; to dwell on tediously.
Harper, Harpist, härp'ėr, härp'ist, *n.* A player on the harp.
Harpoon, här-pön', *n.* A spear or javelin, used to strike whales, &c.—*vt.* To strike, catch, or kill with a harpoon.
Harpooner, här-pön'ėr, *n.* One who uses a harpoon.
Harpsichord, härp'si-kord, *n.* An obsolete stringed musical instrument something like a horizontal grand pianoforte.
Harpy, här'pi, *n.* A fabulous winged monster with the face of a woman; any rapacious animal; an extortioner.
Harquebuse, Harquebuss, här'kwē-bus, *n.* See ARQUEBUSE.
Harridan, ha'ri-dan, *n.* A hag; an odious old woman; a vixenish woman; a trollop.
Harrier, ha'ri-ėr, *n.* A small kind of hound for hunting hares; a kind of hawk.
Harrow, ha'rō, *n.* A frame set with spikes, to prepare ploughed land for seed or to cover the seed.—*vt.* To draw a harrow over; to lacerate; to torment.
Harrowing, ha'rō-ing, *p.a.* Causing acute distress to the mind.
Harry, ha'ri, *vt.* (harrying, harried). To pillage; to plunder; to ravage.
Harsh, härsh, *a.* Grating to the touch, taste, or ear; jarring; rough; severe.
Harshly, härsh'li, *adv.* In a harsh manner; severely; rudely.
Hart, härt, *n.* A stag or male of the red-deer.
Hart's-horn, härts'horn, *n.* Horn of the hart; ammoniacal preparation obtained from the horn; solution of ammonia.
Hart's-tongue, härts'tung, *n.* A common British fern.
Harum-scarum, hā'rum-skā'rum, *a.* Hare-brained; unsettled; giddy; rash.
Harvest, här'vest, *n.* The season of gathering a crop, especially corn; the crop gathered; the product of labour; fruit or fruits; effects; consequences.—*vt.* To reap or gather.
Harvester, här'vest-ėr, *n.* A reaper; labourer in gathering grain; reaping-machine.
Harvest-home, hät'vest-hōm, *n.* The bringing home of the harvest; the feast celebrating it.
Hash, hash, *vt.* To hack; to chop; to mince and mix.—*n.* That which is chopped; cooked meat chopped up and served again; a repetition; bungle.
Hashish, hash'ēsh, *n.* Bhang.
Hasp, hasp, *n.* A clasp that passes over a staple to be fastened by a padlock.—*vt.* To fasten with a hasp.
Hassock, has'ok, *n.* A thick mat or cushion used for kneeling on, &c.

Haste, hāst, *n.* Speed; hurry; sudden excitement of passion; precipitance.—*vt.* (hasting, hasted). To drive or urge forward; to hurry. —*vi.* To move with celerity; to be speedy.
Hasten, hās'n, *vt.* and *i.* To haste.
Hastily, hāst'i-li, *adv.* In a hasty manner; speedily; rashly; precipitately; passionately.
Hasty, hāst'i, *a.* Speedy; precipitate; rash; irritable; irascible; early ripe.
Hat, hat, *n.* A covering for the head.
Hatch, hach, *vt.* To produce from eggs; to contrive; to shade by crossing lines in drawing, &c.—*vi.* To produce young; to bring the young to maturity.—*n.* A brood; act of exclusion from the egg; frame of cross-bars over the opening in a ship's deck; the opening itself; hatchway; trap-door.
Hatchel, hach'el, *n.* A hackle or heckle.—*vt.* To hackle or heckle.
Hatchet, hach'et, *n.* A small axe with a short handle, used with one hand.
Hatchment, hach'ment, *n.* The coat of arms of a deceased person, set in a prominent position.
Hatchway, hach'wā, *n.* An opening in a ship's deck for communication with the interior.
Hate, hāt, *vt.* (hating, hated). To detest; to loathe; to abhor.—*n.* Great dislike; hatred.
Hateful, hāt'fụl, *a.* Exciting hate; odious; loathsome; malignant.
Hatefully, hāt'fụl-li, *adv.* Odiously; malignantly; maliciously.
Hater, hāt'ėr, *n.* One who hates.
Hatred, hāt'red, *n.* Great dislike or aversion; ill-will; rancour; abhorrence.
Hatter, hat'ėr, *n.* A maker or seller of hats.
Hauberk, hạ'bėrk, *n.* A coat of mail.
Haugh, hạh, *n.* In Scotland, a low-lying meadow beside a stream; a holm.
Haughty, hạt'i, *a.* Proud and disdainful; lofty and arrogant.
Haul, hạl, *vt.* To pull or draw with force; to drag; to compel to go.—*n.* A violent pull; draught of fish in a net; that which is taken or gained at once.
Haulage, hạl'āj, *n.* A hauling; length hauled; charge for hauling.
Haulm, Haum, hạlm, hạm, *n.* The stem or stalk of a plant, especially when dry.
Haunch, hạnsh, *n.* The hip; the thigh; part of an arch between the springing and the crown; the flank.
Haunt, hạnt, *vt.* To frequent; to resort to often; to appear in or about, as a spectre.—*vi.* To be much about; to visit often.—*n.* A place much frequented; a favourite resort.
Haunted, hạnt'ed, *p.a.* Frequently visited by apparitions; troubled by spectral visitants.
Hautboy, Hautbois, hō'boi, *n.*; pl. **Hautboys, Hautbois,** hō'boiz. An oboe; a wind-instrument of wood, sounded through a double-reed.
Hauteur, ō-tėr', *n.* Haughty manner or spirit; pride.
Have, hav, *vt.* (having, had). To possess; to accept; to enjoy; to hold in opinion; to be under necessity, or impelled by duty; to procure; to bring forth.
Haven, hā'vn, *n.* A harbour; port; shelter.
Haversack, hav'ėr-sak, *n.* A soldier's bag for provisions on the march.
Having, hav'ing, *n.* What one has; possession; goods.
Havoc, Havock, hav'ok, *n.* Devastation; wide and general destruction; slaughter.
Haw, hạ, *n.* A hedge or fence; the berry and seed of the hawthorn; hesitation of speech.—*vi.* To speak with hesitation.
Hawhaw, hạ'hạ, *n.* Same as *Ha-ha*.
Hawk, hạk, *n.* A rapacious bird of the falcon family.—*vi.* To catch birds by means of hawks; to practise falconry; to take prėy on the wing; to force up phlegm with noise.—*vt.* To carry about for sale from place to place.
Hawker, hạk'ėr, *n.* One who goes about selling wares; a pedlar.
Hawking, hạk'ing, *n.* Sport of taking wild fowls by means of hawks; falconry.
Hawse, hạs, *n.* That part of a vessel's bow where the holes for the cables are cut; the hole in the vessel's bow.
Hawser, hạ'sėr, *n.* A small cable.
Hawthorn, hạ'thorn, *n.* The hedge-thorn; the white-thorn, much used for hedges.
Hay, hā, *n.* Grass cut and dried for fodder.—*vt.* To make into hay.
Haymaker, hā'māk-ėr, *n.* One who cuts and dries grass for fodder.
Haymaking, hā'māk-ing, *n.* The business of cutting grass and preparing it for hay.
Hazard, ha'zėrd, *n.* A game at dice, &c.; risk; venture; chance; fortuitous event.—*vt.* To risk; to put in danger of loss or injury.
Hazardous, ha'zėrd-us, *a.* Perilous; risky.
Haze, hāz, *n.* Vapour which renders the air thick, though not so damp as in foggy weather; dimness; mental fog.
Hazel, hā'zl, *n.* A small tree of the oak family that bears edible nuts.—*a.* Pertaining to the hazel; of a light-brown colour.
Hazy, hāz'i, *a.* Thick with haze; mentally obscure or confused.
He, hē, *pron.* of the third person, nominative. A substitute for the third person masculine, representing the man or male named before; prefixed to names of animals to specify the male.
Head, hed, *n.* The anterior part of animals; uppermost part of the human body; seat of the brain, &c.; intellect; an individual; a chief; first place; top; chief part; principal source; crisis; height; promontory; division of discourse; headway.—*vt.* To form a head to; to behead; to lead; to go in front of in order to stop; to oppose.—*vi.* To form a head; to be directed, as a ship.
Headache, hed'āk, *n.* Pain in the head.
Head-dress, hed'dres, *n.* The covering or ornaments of a woman's head.
Head-gear, hed'gēr, *n.* Covering or ornaments of the head.
Headily, hed'i-li, *adv.* Hastily; rashly.
Heading, hed'ing, *n.* That which stands at the head; title of a section; passage excavated in the line of an intended tunnel.
Headland, hed'land, *n.* A cape; a promontory; a ridge or strip of unploughed land at the ends of furrows.
Headless, hed'les, *a.* Having no head.
Headlong, hed'long, *adv.* With the head foremost; precipitately.—*a.* Steep; precipitous; precipitate.
Head-mark, hed'märk, *n.* Distinctive mark or characteristic.
Head-money, hed'mu-ni, *n.* A tax levied on each individual; money paid for the heads of enemies or for prisoners caught.

Headmost, hed'mōst, *a.* Most advanced.
Head-piece, hed'pēs, *n.* Armour for the head; a helmet.
Head-quarters, hed-kwąr'tėrz, *n.pl.* The quarters of a commander; place where one chiefly resides or carries on business.
Headship, hed'ship, *n.* Office of a head or principal; authority; chief place.
Headsman, hedz'man, *n.* An executioner.
Head-stone, hed'stōn, *n.* The chief or corner stone; stone at the head of a grave.
Headstrong, hed'strong, *a.* Resolute; obstinate; violent.
Headway, hed'wā, *n.* Progress made by a ship in motion; progress or success.
Head-wind, hed'wind, *n.* A wind that blows right against a ship, &c.
Head-work, hed'wėrk, *n.* Mental or intellectual labour.
Heady, hed'i, *a.* Rash; hasty; headstrong; intoxicating.
Heal, hēl, *vt.* To make hale or sound; to cure; to reconcile.—*vi.* To grow whole or sound; to recover.
Healing, hēl'ing, *p.a.* Tending to cure; mild; mollifying.—*n.* Act or process by which a cure is effected.
Health, helth, *n.* A sound state of body or mind; freedom from disease; bodily conditions; wish of health and happiness (used in drinking).
Healthful, helth'fųl, *a.* Full of health; healthy; wholesome; salubrious.
Healthily, helth'i-li, *adv.* Without disease; soundly.
Healthy, helth'i, *a.* Being in health; sound; hale; salubrious; wholesome.
Heap, hēp, *n.* A mass; large quantity; pile.—*vt.* To raise in a heap; to amass; to pile.
Hear, hēr, *vt.* (hearing, heard). To perceive by the ear; to give audience to; to listen; to obey; to regard; to attend favourably; to try in a court of law; to learn; to approve.—*vi.* To enjoy the faculty of perceiving sound; to listen; to be told; to receive by report.
Hearer, hēr'ėr, *n.* One who hears; an auditor.
Hearing, hēr'ing, *n.* The faculty or sense by which sound is perceived; audience; opportunity to be heard; judicial trial; reach of the ear.
Hearken, härk'n, *vi.* To lend the ear; to listen: to give heed.
Hearsay, hēr'sā, *n.* Report; rumour.—*a.* Given at second hand.
Hearse, hėrs, *n.* A carriage for conveying the dead to the grave; bier.
Heart, härt, *n.* The primary organ of the blood's motion; the inner, vital, or most essential part; seat of the affections, will, &c.; disposition of mind; conscience; courage; spirit; what represents a heart; one of a suit of playing cards marked with such a figure.
Heartache, härt'āk, *n.* Sorrow; anguish.
Heart-breaking, härt'brāk-ing, *a.* Overpowering with grief or sorrow.
Heart-broken, härt'brōk-n, *a.* Deeply afflicted or grieved.
Heartburn, härt'bėrn, *n.* A burning sensation in the stomach from indigestion.
Heart-burning, härt'bėrn-ing, *n.* Discontent; secret enmity.
Hearten, härt'n, *vt.* To give heart or courage to; to encourage; to animate.
Heartfelt, härt'felt, *a.* Deeply felt; deeply affecting, either as joy or sorrow.
Hearth, härth, *n.* The part of a floor on which a fire is made; the house and its inmates; the fireside.
Hearthstone, härth'stōn, *n.* Stone forming the hearth; fireside.
Heartily, härt'i-li, *adv.* From the heart; sincerely; warmly; with keen relish.
Heartless, härt'les, *a.* Without heart; spiritless; without feeling or affection.
Heart-rending, härt'rend-ing, *a.* Overpowering with anguish; deeply afflictive.
Heart's-ease, härts'ēz, *n.* A plant, a species of violet; the pansy.
Heart-sick, härt'sik, *a.* Sick at heart; pained in mind; deeply depressed.
Heart-whole, härt'hōl, *a.* Whole at heart; not affected with love; of good courage.
Hearty, härt'i, *a.* Warm; cordial; healthy; having a keen appetite; large to satisfaction.
Heat, hēt, *n.* The sensation produced by bodies that are hot; hot air; hot weather; high temperature; degree of temperature; a single effort; a course at a race; animal excitement; rage; ardour; animation in thought or discourse; fermentation.—*vt.* To make hot; to warm with passion or desire; to rouse into action.—*vi.* To grow warm or hot.
Heater, hēt'ėr, *n.* One who or that which heats; metal for heating a smoothing-iron.
Heath, hēth, *n.* A small flowering shrub growing on waste or wild places; a place overgrown with heath; waste tract.
Heath-bell, hēth'bel, *n.* The flower of a species of heath.
Heath-cock, hēth'kok, *n.* The black-cock, a species of grouse.
Heathen, hē'THen, *n.* A pagan; one who worships idols; a barbarous person.—*a.* Gentile; pagan.
Heathendom, hē'THen-dum, *n.* That part of the world where heathenism prevails.
Heathenish, hē'THen-ish, *a.* Belonging to pagans; idolatrous; barbarous.
Heathenism, hē'THen-izm, *n.* Paganism; idolatry.
Heather, heTH'ėr, *n.* Common heath, a low shrub with clusters of rose-coloured flowers.
Heating, hēt'ing, *p.a.* Exciting action; stimulating.
Heave, hēv, *vt.* (heaving, pret. and pp. heaved, hove). To lift; to move upward; to cause to swell; to raise or force from the breast, as a groan; to throw; to turn in some direction.—*vi.* To rise; to swell, as the sea; to pant; to retch; *to heave in sight*, to appear, as a ship.—*n.* A rising or swell; an effort upward; a throw; a swelling, as of the breast.
Heaven, hev'n, *n.* The blue expanse surrounding the earth; the sky; the abode of God and of his angels; God or Providence; supreme felicity; bliss.
Heavenly, hev'n-li, *a.* Pertaining to heaven; divine; inhabiting heaven; enchanting.—*adv.* In a heavenly manner.
Heavenward, Heavenwards, hev'n-wėrd, hev'n-wėrdz, *adv.* Toward heaven.
Heave-offering, hēv'of-fėr-ing, *n.* Among the Jews, an offering to God.
Heaver, hēv'ėr, *n.* One who heaves; one who unloads coals from vessels.

Heavily, he'vi-li, *adv.* In a heavy manner; dully; gloomily; laboriously; densely.
Heaviness, he'vi-nes, *n.* Weight; gloom; dullness; oppressiveness.
Heavy, he'vi, *a.* That is heaved or lifted with difficulty; weighty; sad; grievous; burdensome; drowsy; wearisome; not easily digested; soft and miry; difficult; large in amount; dense; abundant; forcible.
Hebdomadal, heb-dom'ad-al, *a.* Consisting of seven days, or occurring every seven days; weekly.
Hebetate, heb'ē-tāt, *vt.* To dull; to blunt; to stupefy.
Hebetude, heb'ē-tūd, *n.* Dullness; stupidity.
Hebraic, Hebraical, hē-brā'ik, hē-brā'ik-al, *a.* Pertaining to the Hebrews or their language; Jewish.
Hebraist, hē'brā-ist, *n.* One versed in the Hebrew language.
Hebrew, hē'brö, *n.* An Israelite; a Jew; the Hebrew language.—*a.* Pertaining to the Hebrews.
Hebridean, Hebridian, heb-ri-dē'an, hē-brid'i-an, *a.* Pertaining to the Hebrides of Scotland.—*n.* A native of the Hebrides.
Hecatomb, he'ka-tom or -töm, *n.* A sacrifice of a hundred oxen; a great sacrifice of victims; great slaughter.
Heckle, hek'l, *n.* A sort of comb for flax or hemp; a hackle or hatchel.—*vt.* (heckling, heckled). To dress with a heckle; to question or catechize severely.
Hectare, hek'tãr, *n.* A French measure equal to 2·47 acres.
Hectic, hek'tik, *a.* A term applied to the fever which accompanies consumption; consumptive; feverish.—*n.* A hectic fever; a flush.
Hector, hek'tėr, *n.* A bully.—*vt.* To bully; to treat with insolence.—*vi.* To play the bully.
Hedge, hej, *n.* A fence consisting of thorns or shrubs.—*vt.* (hedging, hedged). To inclose with a hedge; to surround or restrain.—*vi.* To hide oneself; to bet on both sides; to skulk; to dodge or trim.—*a.* Pertaining to a hedge; mean; rustic.
Hedgehog, hej'hog, *n.* A small insectivorous quadruped covered with prickly spines.
Hedger, hej'ėr, *n.* One who makes or trims hedges.
Hedgerow, hej'rō, *n.* A row of shrubs forming a hedge.
Hedonic, hē-don'ik, *a.* Pertaining to pleasure.
Hedonism, hē'don-izm, *n.* The doctrine that the chief good of man lies in pursuit of pleasure.
Hedonist, hē'don-ist, *n.* One who professes hedonism.
Heed, hēd, *vt.* To look to or after; to regard with care; to notice.—*vi.* To mind; to consider.—*n.* Care; attention; regard.
Heedful, hēd'fụl, *a.* Giving heed; attentive; watchful; cautious; wary.
Heedless, hēd'les, *a.* Inattentive; careless; remiss; negligent.
Heel, hēl, *n.* The hind part of the foot; a cant.—*vt.* To add a heel to; to furnish with heels, as shoes.—*vi.* To cant over from a vertical position.
Heelball, hēl'bạl, *n.* A composition for blackening the heels of shoes, &c.
Heel-tap, hēl'tap, *n.* A piece of leather for the heel of a shoe; a small portion of liquor left in a glass.
Heft, heft, *n.* The act of heaving; effort; weight; gist.
Hegelian, he-gē'li-an, *a.* Pertaining to Hegel (hā'gl) or his system of philosophy.—*n.* A follower of Hegel.
Hegelianism, he-gē'li-an-izm, *n.* The system of philosophy of Hegel.
Hegemony, hē-jem'o-ni (or with g hard), *n.* Leadership; preponderance of one state among others.
Hegira, hej'i-ra, *n.* The flight of Mohammed from Mecca (16th July, 622); the beginning of the Mohammedan era.
Heifer, hef'ėr, *n.* A young cow.
Heigh-ho, hī'hō. An exclamation expressing some degree of languor or uneasiness.
Height, hīt, *n.* The condition of being high; distance of anything above its base or above the earth; eminence; any elevated ground; extent; degree; utmost degree.
Heighten, hīt'n, *vt.* To raise higher; to improve; to increase.
Heinous, hān'us, *a.* Hateful; characterized by great wickedness; flagrant.
Heir, ãr, *n.* One who succeeds or is to succeed another in the possession of property.
Heiress, ãr'es, *n.* A female heir.
Heirloom, ãr'löm, *n.* Any personal chattel which, by law, descends to the heir or has belonged to a family for a long time.
Heirship, ãr'ship, *n.* The state, character, or privileges of an heir; right of inheriting.
Heliacal, hē-lī'ak-al, *a.* Coincident with the rising or setting of the sun.
Helicopter, hel-i-kop'tėr, hel'i-kop-tėr, *n.* A type of aircraft supported in flight by a propeller rotating about a vertical axis. It can rise and descend vertically.
Heliocentric, hē'li-o-sen"trik, *a.* Relating to the sun as a centre; appearing as if seen from the sun's centre.
Heliograph, Heliostat, hē'li-o-graf, hē'li-o-stat, *n.* A sun telegraph; apparatus for reflecting the sun's light to a distance.
Heliotrope, hē'li-o-trōp, *n.* Blood-stone; a heliostat; a fragrant garden plant.
Heliotype, hē'li-o-tīp, *n.* A surface-printed picture direct from a photograph.
Helium, hē'li-um, *n.* An inert gas present in the air in small quantities, the lightest element next to hydrogen.
Helix, hē'liks, *n.*; pl. **Helices,** hel'i-sēz. A spiral line, as of wire in a coil; something that is spiral.
Hell, hel, *n.* The place or state of punishmeut for the wicked after death; the abode of tbe devil and his angels; the infernal powers; a gambling-house.
Hellebore, hel'e-bōr, *n.* A plant used by the ancients as a remedy for mental diseases, epilepsy, &c.
Hellenic, hel-len'ik or hel-lēn'ik, *a.* Pertaining to the inhabitants of Greece; Greek.
Hellenism, hel'len-izm, *n.* A Greek idiom; type of character peculiar to the Greeks.
Hellenist, hel'len-ist, *n.* A Grecian Jew; one skilled in the Greek language.
Hellish, hel'ish, *a.* Pertaining to hell; infernal; malignant; detestable.
Helm, helm, *n.* A helmet; instrument by which a ship is steered; the rudder, tiller, &c.; place or post of management.—*vt.* To cover or furnish with a helmet.

Helmet, hel'met, *n.* A covering for the head in war; head armour; a head-piece.
Helmsman, helmz'man, *n.* The man at the helm of a ship.
Helot, he'lot or hē'lot, *n.* A slave, originally a serf in ancient Sparta.
Help, help, *vt.* To lend strength or means towards effecting a purpose; to aid; to relieve; to remedy; to prevent; to avoid.—*vi.* To lend aid.—*n.* Aid; remedy; an assistant.
Helper, help'ėr, *n.* One who helps; an assistant; an auxiliary.
Helpful, help'ful, *a.* That gives help, aid, or assistance; useful.
Helpless, help'les, *a.* Without help in oneself; needing help; affording no help; beyond help.
Helpmate, help'māt, *n.* A companion who helps; an assistant; a wife.
Helter-skelter, hel'tėr-skel'tėr, *adv.* A word suggestive of hurry and confusion.
Helve, helv, *n.* The handle of an axe or hatchet.—*vt.* (helving, helved). To furnish with a helve, as an axe.
Helvetian, Helvetic, hel-vē'shan, hel-vet'ik, *a.* Of or pertaining to Switzerland.
Hem, hem, *n.* The border of a garment, doubled and sewed to strengthen it; edge; border.—*interj.* and *n.* A sort of half cough, suggested by some feeling.—*vt.* (hemming, hemmed). To form a hem or border on; to inclose and confine; to make the sound expressed by the word *hem*.
Hematite, he'ma-tit, *n.* A name of two ores of iron, red hematite and brown hematite.
Hemisphere, he'mi-sfēr, *n.* One half of a sphere; half the celestial or terrestrial sphere.
Hemispheric, Hemispherical, he-mi-sfe'rik, he-mi-sfe'rik-al, *a.* Pertaining to or forming a hemisphere.
Hemistich, he'mi-stik, *n.* Half a poetic line or verse, or a verse not completed.
Hemlock, hem'lok, *n.* An umbelliferous plant whose leaves and root are poisonous.
Hemorrhage, he'mor-āj, *n.* A bursting forth of blood; any discharge of blood from the blood-vessels.
Hemorrhoids, he'mor-oidz, *n.pl.* Piles.
Hemp, hemp, *n.* An annual herbaceous plant of the nettle family, the fibre of which, also called hemp, is made into sail-cloth, ropes, &c.
Hempen, hemp'n, *a.* Made of hemp.
Hemp-seed, hemp'sēd, *n.* The seed of hemp, used as food for fowls, and yielding an oil.
Hen, hen, *n.* The female of the domestic fowl; any female bird.
Henbane, hen'bān, *n.* A poisonous herb of the potato family used in medicine.
Hence, hens, *adv.* From this place, time, source, reason, &c.
Henceforth, hens-fōrth', *adv.* From this time forward.
Henceforward, hens-for'wėrd, *adv.* From this time forward; henceforth.
Henchman, hensh'man, *n.* A servant; a male attendant.
Hennery, hen'ėr-i, *n.* An inclosed place for hens.
Henpeck, hen'pek, *vt.* To rule: said of a wife who has the upper hand of her husband.
Henpecked, hen'pekt, *a.* Governed by his wife, as a husband.
Hepatic, hē-pat'ik, *a.* Pertaining to the liver.
Heptagon, hep'ta-gon, *n.* A plane figure having seven angles and seven sides.
Heptamerous, hep-tam'ėr-us, *a.* Consisting of seven parts.
Heptangular, hep-tang'gū-lėr, *a.* Having seven angles.
Heptarchy, hep'tär-ki, *n.* A government by seven persons, or the country governed by seven persons.
Heptateuch, hep'ta-tūk, *n.* The first seven books of the Old Testament.
Her, hėr, *pron.* The possessive and objective case of *she*: when the possessive is used without a noun it becomes *hers*.
Herald, he'rald, *n.* An officer whose business was to proclaim war or peace, bear messages, &c.; a forerunner; an officer who regulates matters relating to public ceremonies; one who records and blazons arms, &c.—*vt.* To introduce, as by a herald; to proclaim.
Heraldic, he-rald'ik, *a.* Pertaining to heralds or heraldry.
Heraldry, he'rald-ri, *n.* Art or office of a herald; art of recording genealogies and blazoning arms; heraldic figures or symbols.
Herb, hėrb, *n.* Any plant with a succulent stem which dies to the root every year.
Herbaceous, hėrb-ā'shus, *a.* Pertaining to herbs; having the nature of a herb.
Herbage, hėrb'āj, *n.* Herbs collectively; grass; pasture.
Herbal, hėrb'al, *n.* A book that contains descriptions of herbs or plants.
Herbalist, hėrb'al-ist, *n.* One skilled in herbs, or who makes collections of them.
Herbarium, hėr-bā'ri-um, *n.*; pl. **-iums** and **-ia.** A collection of herbs or plants dried and preserved.
Herbivorous, hėrb-iv'or-us, *a.* Eating herbs; subsisting on herbaceous plants.
Herb-Robert, hėrb'ro-bėrt, *n.* A very common British species of wild geranium.
Herculean, hėr-kū'lē-an, *a.* Belonging to or resembling Hercules; of extraordinary strength; very great or difficult.
Herd, hėrd, *n.* A number of animals feeding or driven together; flock; crowd; rabble; a keeper of cattle or sheep.—*vi.* and *t.* To unite into a herd, as beasts; to congregate.
Herdsman, hėrdz'man, *n.* One employed in tending herds of cattle.
Here, hēr, *adv.* In this place; at this point; hither.
Hereabout, Hereabouts, hēr'a-bout, hēr'a-bouts, *adv.* About this place.
Hereafter, hēr-af'tėr, *adv.* After this time; in a future state.—*n.* The time after this; a future state.
Hereby, hēr-bī', *adv.* By this; close by; near.
Hereditable, he-red'i-ta-bl, *a.* Heritable.
Hereditament, he-re-dit'a-ment, *n.* Any species of property that may be inherited.
Hereditarily, he-red'it-a-ri-li, *adv.* By inheritance.
Hereditary, he-red'it-a-ri, *a.* Relating to an inheritance; descending to an heir; that is or may be transmitted from a parent to a child.
Heredity, he-red'i-ti, *n.* Hereditary transmission of qualities; the doctrine that the offspring inherits parental characteristics.
Herein, hēr-in', *adv.* In this.
Hereinafter, hēr-in-äf'tėr, *adv.* In this writing or document afterwards.

Hereof, hēr-of′, *adv.* Of this; from this.
Hereon, hēr-on′, *adv.* On this.
Heresy, he′re-si, *n.* A fundamental error in religion; error in doctrine; heterodoxy.
Heretic, he′re-tik, *n.* One guilty of heresy.
Heretical, he-ret′ik-al, *a.* Containing heresy; contrary to the established faith.
Heretically, he-ret′ik-al-li, *adv.* In a heretical manner; with heresy.
Hereto, hēr-tö′, *adv.* To this.
Heretofore, hēr-tö-fōr′, *adv.* Before or up to the present; formerly.
Hereunto, hēr-un′tö, *adv.* To this.
Hereupon, hēr-up-on′, *adv.* On this; hereon.
Herewith, hēr-with′, *adv.* With this.
Heritable, he′rit-a-bl, *a.* Capable of being inherited; that may inherit.
Heritage, he′rit-āj, *n.* Inheritance; lot or portion by birth.
Heritor, he′rit-or, *n.* One who inherits; an heir; *Scots law,* a proprietor liable to pay public burdens.
Hermaphrodite, hėr-maf′rod-īt, *n.* An animal in which the characteristics of both sexes are really or apparently combined; a flower that contains both the stamen and the pistil.—*a.* Including or being of both sexes.
Hermaphroditic, hėr-maf′rod-it″ik, *a.* Partaking of both sexes.
Hermeneutic, Hermeneutical, hėr-mē-nū′-tik, hėr-mē-nū′tik-al, *a.* Interpreting; explaining.
Hermeneutics, hėr-mē-nū′tiks, *n.* The science of interpretation, particularly of interpreting the Scriptures.
Hermetic, Hermetical, hėr-met′ik, hėr-met′ik-al, *a.* Pertaining to alchemy or to occult science; effected by fusing together the edges of the aperture, as of a bottle; perfectly close and air-tight.
Hermetically, hėr-met′ik-al-li, *adv.* Chemically; by fusing the edges together.
Hermit, hėr′mit, *n.* One who lives in solitude; a recluse.
Hermitage, hėr′mit-āj, *n.* The habitation of a hermit.
Hernia, hėr′ni-a, *n.* A protrusion of some organ of the abdomen through an interstice; a rupture.
Hero, hē′rō, *n.*; pl. **Heroes,** hē′rōz. A man of distinguished valour; the person who has the principal share in some exploit, or in a play, novel, &c.
Heroic, he-rō′ik, *a.* Pertaining to a hero or heroes; intrepid and noble; reciting achievements of heroes; epic.
Heroically, he-rō′ik-al-li, *adv.* In a heroic manner; like a hero.
Heroin, her′o-in, *n.* A narcotic drug derived from morphia.
Heroine, he′rō-in, *n.* A female hero.
Heroism, he′rō-izm, *n.* The qualities of a hero; intrepidity; magnanimity.
Heron, her′un, *n.* A wading bird with a long bill, long slender legs and neck.
Heronry, he′run-ri, *n.* A place where herons breed.
Heronshaw, her′un-shą, *n.* A young heron.
Hero-worship, hē′rō-wėr-ship, *n.* Extravagant admiration of great men.
Herpes, hėr′pēz, *n.* A skin disease characterized by eruption of inflamed vesicles.
Herpetology, hėr-pe-tol′o-ji, *n.* The natural history of reptiles.
Herr, hãr, *n.* The German equivalent of the English Mr.
Herring, he′ring, *n.* One of those small food fishes which go in shoals in northern seas.
Herring-bone, he′ring-bōn, *a.* Applied to masonry, sewing, &c., which bears resemblance to the backbone of a herring.
Hers, hėrz, *pron. possessive. See* HER.
Herse, hėrs, *n.* A frame in form of a harrow; frame carrying candles in funerals, &c.
Herself, hėr-self′, *pron.* The emphatic and reflexive form of *she* and *her.*
Hesitancy, he′zi-tan-si, *n.* A hesitating; vacillation.
Hesitate, he′zi-tāt, *vi.* (hesitating, hesitated). To pause respecting decision or action; to stop in speaking; to stammer.
Hesitation, he-zi-tā′shon, *n.* Act of hesitating; doubt; a stopping in speech.
Hesperian, hes-pē′ri-an, *a.* Western; situated at the west.
Hest, hest, *n.* Command.
Hetarism, Hetairism, het′a-rizm, he-tī′rizm, *n.* That primitive state of society in which the women are held in common.
Heteroclite, he′te-rō-klīt, *n.* A word irregular in declension or conjugation; something abnormal or anomalous.
Heterodox, he′te-rō-doks, *a.* Holding opinions different from those established or prevalent; not orthodox; heretical.
Heterodoxy, he′te-rō-dok-si, *n.* The holding of heterodox opinions; heresy.
Heterogeneous, he′te-rō-jē″nē-us, *a.* Of a different kind or nature; composed of dissimilar parts.
Hew, hū, *vt.* (pret. hewed, pp. hewed or hewn). To cut with an axe, &c.; to cut; to hack; to make smooth, as stone; to shape.
Hewer, hū′ėr, *n.* One who hews wood or stone.
Hexagon, heks′a-gon, *n.* A plane figure of six angles and six sides.
Hexagonal, heks-ag′on-al, *a.* Having six angles and six sides.
Hexahedron, heks-a-hē′dron, *n.* A regular solid body of six sides; a cube.
Hexameter, heks-am′et-ėr, *n.* A verse of six metrical feet.—*a.* Having six metrical feet.
Hexangular, heks-ang′gū-lėr, *a.* Having six angles or corners.
Hey, hā, *interj.* An exclamation of joy or to call attention.
Heyday, hā′dā, *interj.* An exclamation of cheerfulness.—*n.* The bloom or height; the wildness or frolicsome period of youth.
Hiatus, hī-ā′tus, *n.*; pl. **Hiatuses.** A gap; break; lacuna; meeting of vowel sounds.
Hibernal, hī-bėr′nal, *a.* Belonging to winter; wintry.
Hibernate, hī-bėr′nāt, *vt.* To pass the winter in sleep or seclusion; to winter.
Hibernation, hī-bėr-nā′shon, *n.* Act of hibernating.
Hibernian, hī-bėr′ni-an, *a.* Pertaining to Ireland; Irish.—*n.* A native of Ireland.
Hiccup, Hiccough, hik′up, *n.* A spasmodic affection of the diaphragm and glottis; a convulsive catch of the respiratory muscles.—*vt.* and *i.* To have a hiccup; to utter with hiccups.
Hickory, hik′ō-ri, *n.* An American tree of the walnut family, valuable for timber.
Hid, Hidden, hid, hid′n, *p.a.* Unseen; unknown; abstruse; profound.

Hide, hīd, *vt.* (hiding, pret. hid, pp. hid, hidden). To withhold or withdraw from sight or knowledge; to screen; to secrete—*vi.* To be or to lie concealed; to keep oneself out of view.—*n.* The skin of an animal, either raw or dressed; the human skin; an old measure of land of about 80 acres.
Hide-bound, hīd'bound, *a.* Having the hide abnormally tight; having the bark so close or firm as to hinder growth.
Hideous, hid'ē-us, *a.* Frightful; shocking to the eye or ear.
Hideously, hid'ē-us-li, *adv.* Dreadfully; shockingly.
Hiding, hīd'ing, *n.* Concealment; state of being hidden.
Hie, hī, *vi.* (hying, hied). To hasten; to speed.
Hiemal, hī-em'al, *a.* Wintry; pertaining to winter.
Hiemation, hī-e-mā'shon, *n.* The spending or passing of winter.
Hierarch, hī'ėr-ärk, *n.* One who has authority in sacred things.
Hierarchical, Hierarchal, hī-ėr-ärk'ik-al, hī-ėr-är'kal, *a.* Pertaining to a hierarchy.
Hierarchy, hī'ėr-är-ki, *n.* Authority in sacred things; clergy in whom is confided the direction of sacred things; ecclesiastical or clerical rule.
Hieratic, hī-ėr-at'ik, *a.* Sacred; pertaining to priests: applied to a kind of developed hieroglyphics used by the ancient Egyptian priests.
Hieroglyph, Hieroglyphic, hī'ėr-o-glif, hī'-ėr-o-glif''ik, *n.* A figure of an animal, plant, &c., implying a word, idea, or sound, such as those in use among the ancient Egyptians; a character difficult to decipher.
Hieroglyphic, Hieroglyphical, hī'ėr-o-glif''ik, hī'ėr-o-glif''ik-al, *a.* Forming a hieroglyph; relating to hieroglyphics; emblematic.
Hierology, hī-ėr-ol'o-ji, *n.* Sacred lore; knowledge of hieroglyphics or sacred writing.
Hierophant, hī'ėr-o-fant, *n.* A priest; one who teaches the mysteries of religion.
Higgle, hig'l, *vi.* (higgling, higgled). To chaffer; to haggle; to carry wares about for sale.
Higgledy-piggledy, hig'l-di-pig'l-di, *adv.* In confusion; topsy-turvy.
High, hī, *a.* Having a great extent from base to summit; elevated; lofty; far above the earth; elevated in rank or office; dignified; proud; violent; solemn; strong; vivid; dear; remote; sharp; far advanced; committed against the sovereign or state; tending towards putrefaction; strong-scented.—*adv.* In a high manner; to a great altitude or degree; eminently; greatly.
High-born, hī'born, *a.* Being of noble birth or extraction.
High-bred, hī'bred, *a.* Bred in high life.
Highbrow, hī'brou, *n.* A person who pretends to be of a superior culture to the majority.
High-church, hī'chėrch, *a.* Belonging to that section of the Episcopal Church that maintains the highest notions respecting episcopacy, the priesthood, sacraments, &c.
High-flown, hī'flōn, *a.* Elevated; turgid; extravagant.
High-flying, hī'flī-ing, *a.* Extravagant in claims or opinions.
High-handed, hī'hand-ed, *a.* Violent; overbearing; oppressive.
Highland, hī'land, *n.* A mountainous region: often in pl.—*a.* Pertaining to mountainous regions, or to the Highlands of Scotland.
Highlander, hī'land-ėr, *n.* An inhabitant of the mountains; a native of the Highlands of Scotland.
Highly, hī'li, *adv.* In a high manner; in a great degree; decidedly; markedly.
High-minded, hī'mind-ed, *a.* Proud; arrogant; having honourable pride.
Highness, hī'nes, *n.* State or quality of being high; height; title of honour given to princes, &c.: used with poss. prons. *his, her,* &c.
High-pressure, hī'pre-shūr, *a.* Having or involving a pressure exceeding that of the atmosphere, or having a pressure greater than 50 lbs. to the square inch.
High-priest, hī'prēst, *n.* A chief priest.
Highroad, hī'rōd, *n.* A highway or much-frequented road.
High-souled, hī'sōld, *a.* Having a high or lofty spirit; highly honourable.
High-sounding, hī'sound-ing, *a.* Making a loud sound; bombastic; ostentatious.
High-spirited, hī'spi-rit-ed, *a.* Full of spirit; bold; daring.
High-strung, hī'strung, *a.* Strung to a high pitch; high-spirited; sensitive.
High-toned, hī'tōnd, *a.* High in tone or pitch; noble; elevated.
Highway, hī'wā, *n.* A public road; direct course; train of action.
Highwayman, hī'wā-man, *n.* One who robs on the public road or highway.
High-wrought, hī'rąt, *a.* Wrought with exquisite art or skill; inflamed to a high degree; keenly felt; intense.
Hike, hīk, *vi.* To tramp; to go on a long or fairly long walking expedition.
Hilarious, hi-lā'ri-us, *a.* Full of hilarity; gay; mirthful; merry.
Hilarity, hi-la'ri-ti, *n.* Cheerfulness; merriment; good humour; jollity.
Hill, hil, *n.* A natural elevation of less size than a mountain; an eminence.
Hillock, hil'ok, *n.* A small hill.
Hilly, hil'i, *a.* Abounding with hills.
Hilt, hilt, *n.* A handle, particularly of a sword.
Him, him, *pron.* The objective case of *he.*
Himself, him-self', *pron.* The emphatic and reflexive form of *he* and *him.*
Hind, hīnd, *n.* The female of the red-deer or stag; a farm servant; a rustic.—*a.* Backward; back; pertaining to the backward part.
Hinder, hīnd'ėr, *a.* Posterior; in the rear; latter; after.
Hinder, hin'dėr, *vt.* To prevent from moving or acting; to obstruct; to thwart; to check. —*vi.* To interpose obstacles or impediments.
Hindmost, Hindermost, hīnd'mōst, hīnd'-ėr-mōst, *a.* Farthest behind; last.
Hindrance, hin'drans, *n.* Act of hindering; impediment; obstruction.
Hindu, Hindoo, hin-dö' or hin'dö, *n.* and *a.* A person of Aryan race native to Hindustan; pertaining to such.
Hindustani, Hindoostanee, hin-dö-stan'ē, *n.* The chief language of Hindustan.
Hinge, hinj, *n.* The hook or joint on which a door, &c., hangs and turns; that on which anything depends or turns.—*vt.* (hinging, hinged). To furnish with hinges.—*vi.* To stand or turn, as on a hinge.

Hinny, hin'i, *n.* A mule; the produce of a stallion and a she-ass.
Hint, hint, *vt.* To suggest indirectly; to insinuate.—*vi.* To make an indirect allusion.—*n.* A distant allusion; a suggestion.
Hip, hip, *n.* The fleshy projecting part of the thigh; the haunch; the joint of the thigh; the fruit of the dog-rose or wild brier.—*interj.* Exclamation expressive of a call to anyone. *Hip, hip, hurrah!* the signal to cheer.
Hippocras, hip'ō-kras, *n.* A medicinal drink of wine and spices, &c.
Hippodrome, hip'ō-drōm, *n.* A racecourse for horses and chariots; a circus.
Hippophagy, hip-pof'a-ji, *n.* The act or practice of feeding on horse-flesh.
Hippopotamus, hip-ō-pot'a-mus, *n.*; pl. **-amuses** or **-ami.** A large, hoofed, pachydermatous animal, inhabiting the Nile and other rivers in Africa.
Hip-shot, hip'shot, *a.* Having the hip dislocated.
Hircine, hėr'sīn, *a.* Pertaining to or resembling a goat.
Hire, hīr, *vt.* (hiring, hired). To procure for temporary use, at a certain price; to engage in service for a stipulated reward; to let; to lease (with *out*).—*n.* Price paid for temporary use of anything; recompense for personal service; wages; pay.
Hireling, hīr'ling, *n.* One who is hired; a mercenary.—*a.* Serving for wages; venal; mercenary.
Hirer, hīr'ėr, *n.* One who hires.
Hirsute, hėr-sūt', *a.* Hairy; shaggy.
His, hiz, *pron.* The possessive case of *he.*
Hispid, his'pid, *a.* Rough with bristles; bristly.
Hiss, his, *vi.* To make a sound like that of the letter *s*, in contempt or disapprobation; to emit a similar sound; to whizz.—*vt.* To condemn by hissing.—*n.* The sound expressed by the verb.
Hist, hist, *interj.* A word commanding silence, equivalent to hush, whist, be silent.
Histology, his-tol'o-ji, *n.* The doctrine of animal or vegetable tissues.
Historian, his-tō'ri-an, *n.* A writer or compiler of history.
Historic, Historical, his-to'rik, his-to'rik-al, *a.* Pertaining to, connected with, contained in, or deduced from history.
Historically, his-to'rik-al-li, *adv.* In a historical manner; according to history.
Historiette, his-tō'ri-et", *n.* A short history or story; a tale; a novel.
Historiographer, his'tō-ri-og"ra-fėr, *n.* A writer of history; an official historian.
History, his'to-ri, *n.* An account of facts, particularly respecting nations or states; that branch of knowledge which deals with past events; narration; a story; an account of existing things, as animals or plants.
Histrionic, Histrionical, his-tri-on'ik, his-tri-on'ik-al, *a.* Pertaining to an actor or stage-playing; theatrical.
Histrionics, his-tri-on'iks, *n.* The art of theatrical representation.
Hit, hit, *vt.* (hitting, hit). To strike or touch with some force; to give a blow to; not to miss; to reach; to light upon; to suit.—*vi.* To strike; to come in contact; to reach the intended point; to succeed.—*n.* A stroke; a blow; a lucky chance; happy thought or expression.
Hitch, hich, *vi.* To move by jerks; to be entangled, hooked, or yoked.—*vt.* To fasten; to hook; to raise by jerks.—*n.* A catch; act of catching, as on a hook, &c.; knot or noose in a rope; a jerk; a temporary obstruction.
Hither, hiᴛʜ'ėr, *adv.* To this place.—*a.* Nearer; toward the person speaking.
Hithermost, hiᴛʜ'ėr-mōst, *a.* Nearest on this side.
Hitherto, hiᴛʜ'ėr-tö, *adv.* To this time; till now; to this place or limit.
Hitherward, hiᴛʜ'ėr-wėrd, *adv.* This way; toward this place.
Hitter, hit'ėr, *n.* One that hits.
Hive, hīv, *n.* A box or receptacle for honey-bees; the bees inhabiting a hive; a place swarming with busy occupants.—*vt.* (hiving, hived). To collect into a hive; to lay up in store.—*vi.* To take shelter together; to reside in a collective body.
Ho, hō, *interj.* A cry to excite attention, give notice, &c.
Hoar, hōr, *a.* White or whitish; hoary.—*vi.* To become mouldy or musty.
Hoard, hōrd, *n.* A store, stock, or large quantity of anything; a hidden stock.—*vt.* To collect; to store secretly.—*vi.* To form a hoard; to lay up in store.
Hoarding, hōrd'ing, *n.* A timber inclosure round a building, &c.
Hoar-frost, hōr'frost, *n.* The white particles of frozen dew; rime.
Hoarhound, hōr'hound, *n.* A labiate plant with hoary foliage: a popular remedy for colds.
Hoarse, hōrs, *a.* Having a grating voice, as when affected with a cold; discordant; rough; grating.
Hoarsely, hōrs'li, *adv.* With a rough, harsh, grating voice or sound.
Hoary, hōr'i, *a.* White or whitish; white or gray with age.
Hoax, hōks, *n.* Something done for deception or mockery; a practical joke.—*vt.* To deceive; to play a trick upon without malice.
Hob, hob, *n.* The part of a grate on which things are placed to be kept warm.
Hobble, hob'l, *vi.* (hobbling, hobbled). To walk lamely or awkwardly; to limp; to halt.—*vt.* To hopple.—*n.* An unequal, halting gait; perplexity.
Hobbledehoy, hob'l-dē-hoi, *n.* A raw gawky youth approaching manhood.
Hobby, hob'i, *n.* A small but strong British falcon; an active, ambling nag; a hobby-horse; any favourite object or pursuit.
Hobby-horse, hob'i-hors, *n.* A wooden horse for children; a favourite object of pursuit.
Hobgoblin, hob-gob'lin, *n.* A goblin; an imp; something that causes terror.
Hobnail, hob'nāl, *n.* A nail with a thick, strong head.
Hobnob, hob'nob, *vi.* (hobnobbing, hobnobbed). To drink familiarly; to be boon companions.
Hock, Hough, hok, *n.* The joint between the knee and fetlock; in man, the posterior part of the knee-joint.—*vt.* To hamstring.
Hock, hok, *n.* A light Rhenish wine.
Hockey, hok'i, *n.* A game at ball played with a club curved at the lower end.

Hocus, hō'kus, *vt.* (hocussing, hocussed). To impose upon; to cheat; to drug.
Hocus-pocus, hō'kus-pō'kus, *n.* A juggler's trick; trickery used by conjurers.
Hod, hod, *n.* A kind of trough for carrying mortar and brick on the shoulder.
Hodge, hoj, *n.* A rustic or clown.
Hodge-podge, hoj'poj, *n.* A mixed mass; a medley of ingredients; a hotch-potch.
Hodiernal, ho-di-ėrn'al, *a.* Modern.
Hodman, hod'man, *n.* A man who carries a hod.
Hodometer, ho-dom'et-ėr, *n.* An instrument for measuring the distance travelled by any vehicle.
Hoe, hō, *n.* An instrument to cut up weeds and loosen the earth.—*vt.* (hoeing, hoed). To dig or clean with a hoe.—*vi.* To use a hoe.
Hog, hog, *n.* A swine; a castrated boar; a sheep of a year old; a brutal or mean fellow. —*vi.* To bend, as a ship's bottom.
Hoggish, hog'ish, *a.* Brutish; filthy.
Hogshead, hogz'hed, *n.* A large cask; an old measure of capacity, containing about 52½ imperial gallons.
Hog-skin, hog'skin, *n.* Leather made of the skin of swine.
Hog-wash, hog'wosh, *n.* Refuse of a kitchen, brewery, &c., given to swine; swill.
Hoiden, hoi'den, *n.* A rude, bold girl; a romp.—*a.* Rude; bold; inelegant; rustic. —*vi.* To romp rudely or wildly.
Hoist, hoist, *vt.* To heave up; to lift upward by means of tackle.—*n.* Act of raising; apparatus for raising goods, &c.; an elevator.
Hoity-toity, hoi ti-toi'ti, *a.* Frolicsome; haughty.—*interj.* An exclamation denoting surprise, with some degree of contempt.
Hold, hōld, *vt.* (pret. held, pp. held, holden). To have in the grasp; to keep fast; to confine; to maintain; to consider; to contain; to possess; to withhold; to continue; to celebrate. —*vi.* To take or keep a thing in one's grasp; to stand as a fact or truth; not to give way or part; to refrain; to adhere; to derive title (with *of*).—*n.* A grasp; something which may be seized for support; power of keeping, seizing, or directing; influence; place of confinement; stronghold; interior cavity of a ship.
Holder, hōld'ėr, *n.* One who or that which holds; something by which a thing is held; one who possesses.
Holdfast, hōld'fast, *n.* That which holds fast; a catch, hook, &c.
Holding, hōld'ing, *n.* Act of keeping hold; tenure; a farm held of a superior.
Hole, hōl, *n.* A hollow place in any solid body; a perforation, crevice, &c.; a den; a subterfuge.—*vt.* (holing, holed). To make a hole or holes in; to drive into a hole.
Hole-and-corner, hōl'and-kor-nėr, *a.* Clandestine; underhand.
Holiday, ho'li-dā, *n.* A holy or sacred day; a festival; day of exemption from labour.—*a.* Pertaining to a festival.
Holiness, hō'li-nes, *n.* State or quality of being holy; moral goodness; sanctity.—**His Holiness,** a title of the pope.
Holism, hol'izm, *n.* A philosophical theory according to which a fundamental feature of nature is the existence of ' wholes ', which are more than assemblages of parts, and which are always tending to become more highly developed and comprehensive.
Holla, Hollo, Holloa, hol-lä', hol-lō'. An exclamation to someone at a distance, in order to call attention or in answer.
Holland, hol'land, *n.* Fine linen.
Hollands, hol'landz, *n.* Gin manufactured in Holland.
Hollow, hol'lō, *a.* Containing an empty space; not solid; deep; false; deceitful.—*n.* A depression or excavation; a cavity.—*vt.* To make a hole in; to excavate.
Hollow-ware, hol'ō-wār, *n.* A trade name for such iron articles as cauldrons, kettles, &c.
Holly, hol'i, *n.* An evergreen tree or shrub, with thorny leaves and scarlet berries.
Hollyhock, hol'i-hok, *n.* A tall biennial plant of the mallow family.
Holm, hōm or hōlm, *n.* A river isle; tract of rich land on the banks of a river.
Holm-oak, hōm'ōk or hōlm'ōk, *n.* The evergreen oak.
Holocaust, hol'o-kast, *n.* A burnt-sacrifice, of which the whole was consumed by fire; a great slaughter.
Holograph, hol'o-graf, *n.* A deed or document written wholly by the person from whom it proceeds.
Holometabolic, hol'o-met-a-bol"ik, *a.* Applied to insects which undergo a complete metamorphosis.
Holster, hōl'stėr, *n.* A leathern case for a pistol.
Holt, hōlt, *n.* A wood or woodland; a grove.
Holy, hō'li, *a.* Free from sin; immaculate; consecrated; sacred.
Holy-day, hō'li-dā. *See* HOLIDAY.
Holy-stone, hō'li-stōn, *n.* A soft sandstone used for cleaning the decks of ships.—*vt.* To scrub with holy-stone.
Homage, hom'āj, *n.* An act of fealty on the part of a vassal to his lord; obeisance; reverential worship.
Home, hōm, *n.* One's own abode; the abode of one's family; residence; one's own country; an establishment affording the comforts of a home.—*a.* Domestic; close; severe; poignant.—*adv.* To one's own habitation or country; to the point; effectively.
Home-bred, hōm'bred, *a.* Native; domestic; not polished by travel.
Homefelt, hōm'felt, *a.* Felt in one's own breast; inward; private.
Home Guard, hōm gärd, *n.* A voluntary unpaid force raised in 1940 for local defence.
Homeless, hōm'les, *a.* Destitute of a home.
Homely, hōm'li, *a.* Belonging to home; of plain features; plain; coarse.
Homeopathy, hō-mē-op'a-thi, *n.* *See* HOMŒOPATHY.
Homer, hō'mėr, *n.* A Hebrew measure of about 75 gallons or 11 bushels.
Homeric, hō-me'rik, *a.* Pertaining to or like Homer or his poetry.
Home-rule, hom'röl, *n.* Self-government for a detached part of a country.
Home-sick, hōm'sik, *a.* Affected with home-sickness.
Home-sickness, hōm'sik-nes, *n.* Depression of spirits occasioned by absence from one's home or country; nostalgia.
Homespun, hōm'spun, *a.* Spun or wrought at home; plain; coarse; homely.
Homestead, hōm'sted, *n.* A house with the

grounds and buildings contiguous; a home; native seat.
Homeward, hōm'wėrd, *adv.* Toward one's habitation or country.—*a.* Being in the direction of home.
Homewards, hōm'wėrdz, *adv.* Homeward.
Homicidal, ho-mi-sīd'al, *a.* Pertaining to homicide; murderous.
Homicide, ho'mi-sīd, *n.* Manslaughter; a person who kills another.
Homiletic, ho-mi-let'ik, *a.* Pertaining to homilies or homiletics.
Homiletics, ho-mi-let'iks, *n.* The art of preaching.
Homilist, ho'mi-list, *n.* One who writes or preaches homilies.
Homily, ho'mi-li, *n.* A sermon; a familiar religious discourse; a serious discourse or admonition.
Homing, hōm'ing, *a.* Coming home: applied to birds such as the carrier-pigeons.
Hominy, hom'i-ni, *n.* Maize hulled or coarsely ground, prepared for food by being boiled.
Homœopathic, hō'mē-o-path''ik, *a.* Pertaining to homœopathy.
Homœopathy, hō-mē-op'a-thi, *n.* A system of curing diseases by drugs (usually in very small doses) which produce in healthy persons symptoms like those of the disease.
Homogeneous, ho-mō-jē'nē-us, *a.* Of the same kind or nature; consisting of similar parts or elements.
Homogenesis, ho-mō-jen'e-sis, *n.* Sameness of origin; reproduction of offspring similar to their parents.
Homologate, hō-mol'o-gāt, *vt.* To approve; to ratify.
Homologous, hō-mol'o-gus, *a.* Having the same relative position, proportion, or structure; corresponding.
Homonym, ho'mō-nim, *n.* A word which agrees with another in sound, and perhaps in spelling, but differs in signification.
Homuncule, Homunculus, hō-mung'kūl, hō-mung'kūl-us, *n.* A manikin; dwarf.
Hone, hōn, *n.* A stone of a fine grit, used for sharpening instruments.—*vt.* (honing, honed). To sharpen on a hone.
Honest, on'est, *a.* Free from fraud; upright; just; sincere; candid; virtuous.
Honestly, on'est-li, *adv.* In an honest manner; with integrity; frankly.
Honesty, on'est-i, *n.* State or quality of being honest; integrity; candour; truth.
Honey, hun'i, *n.* A sweet viscous juice collected by bees from flowers; sweetness; a word of tenderness.—*vt.* To sweeten.
Honey-comb, hun'i-kōm, *n.* The waxy structure formed by bees for honey; anything having cells like a honey-comb.
Honey-combed, hun'i-kōmd, *p.a.* Having little cells resembling honey-combs.
Honey-dew, hun'i-dū, *n.* A sweet substance found on certain plants in small drops.
Honeyed, hun'id, *a.* Covered with honey; sweet.
Honeymoon, hun'i-mön, *n.* The first month after marriage; interval spent by a newly-married pair before settling down at home.
Honeysuckle, hun'i-suk-l, *n.* A beautiful flowering and climbing shrub; woodbine.
Honorarium, on-ėr-ā'ri-um, *n.* A fee for professional services.
Honorary, on'ėr-a-ri, *a.* Relating to honour; conferring honour; possessing a title or place without performing services or without receiving a reward.
Honour, on'ėr, *n.* Respect; esteem; testimony of esteem; dignity; good name; a nice sense of what is right; scorn of meanness; a a title of respect or distinction; one of the highest trump cards; *pl.* civilities paid; public marks of respect; academic and university distinction.—*vt.* To regard or treat with honour; to bestow honour upon; to exalt; to accept and pay when due, as a bill.
Honourable, on'ėr-a-bl, *a.* Worthy of honour; actuated by principles of honour; conferring honour; consistent with honour; performed with marks of honour; not base; honest; fair; a title of distinction.
Honourably, on'ėr-a-bli, *adv.* In an honourable manner.
Hood, hụd, *n.* A soft covering for the head; a cowl; a garment worn as part of academic dress, which indicates by its colours, material and shape the degree and University of its wearer; anything resembling a hood.—*vt.* To dress in a hood; to cover; to blind.
Hooded, hụd'ed, *a.* Covered with a hood.
Hooded crow, a grayish crow with a black head.
Hoodwink, hụd'wingk, *vt.* To blind by covering the eyes of; to impose on.
Hoof, höf, *n.*; pl. **Hoofs,** rarely **Hooves.** The horny substance that covers the feet of certain animals, as the horse.
Hoofed, höft, *a.* Furnished with hoofs.
Hoof-mark, höf'märk, *n.* The mark of an animal's hoof on the ground.
Hook, hök, *n.* A bent piece of iron or other metal for catching; that which catches; a sickle.—*vt.* To catch with a hook; to ensnare.—*vi.* To bend; to be curving.
Hookah, hö'kä, *n.* A tobacco-pipe with a large bowl and long pliable tube, so constructed that the smoke passes through water.
Hooked, hökt, *a.* Curved; bent; aquiline.
Hooligan, hö'li-gan, *n.* One of a gang of street roughs.
Hoop, höp, *n.* A band of wood or metal confining the staves of casks, tubs, &c.; a crinoline; a ring; a loud shout.—*vt.* To bind with hoops; to encircle.—*vi.* To shout; to whoop.
Hooping-cough, höp'ing-kof, *n.* A contagious ailment common in childhood, characterized by a convulsive cough.
Hoopoe, Hoopoo, hö'pō, hö'pö, *n.* A beautiful bird with a crest.
Hoot, höt, *vi.* To shout in contempt; to cry as an owl.—*vt.* To utter contemptuous cries at.—*n.* A cry or shout in contempt.
Hop, hop, *n.* A leap on one leg; a spring; a bitter plant of the hemp family used to flavour malt liquors.—*vi.* To leap or spring on one leg; to skip; to limp; to pick hops.—*vt.* To impregnate with hops.
Hope, hōp, *n.* A desire of some good, accompanied with a belief that it is attainable; trust; one in whom trust or confidence is placed; the object of hope.—*vi.* (hoping, hoped). To entertain hope; to trust.—*vt.* To desire with some expectation of attainment.
Hopeful, hōp'ful, *a* Full of hope; having qualities which excite hope; promising.

Hopeless, hōp'les, *a.* Destitute of hope; desponding; promising nothing desirable.
Hopper, hop'ėr, *n.* One who hops; a wooden trough through which grain passes into a mill; a boat to convey dredged matter.
Hopple, hop'l, *vt.* (hoppling, hoppled). To tie the feet of (a horse) to prevent leaping or running.—*n.* A fetter for the legs of horses, &c.
Hop-yard, Hop-garden, hop'yärd, hop'gär-dn, *n.* A field where hops are raised.
Horal, hōr'al, *a.* Relating to an hour.
Horary, hōr'a-ri, *a.* Hourly; noting the hours; continuing an hour.
Horatian, ho-rā'shan, *a.* Relating to or resembling Horace or his poetry.
Horde, hōrd, *n.* A tribe or race of nomads; a gang; a migratory crew; rabble.—*vi.* (hording, horded). To live together like migratory tribes.
Horehound, hōr'hound, *n.* *See* HOARHOUND.
Horizon, ho-rī'zon, *n.* The circle which bounds that part of the earth's surface visible from a given point; the apparent junction of the earth and sky.
Horizontal, ho-ri-zon'tal, *a.* Parallel to the horizon; level; near the horizon.
Hormones, hor'mōnz, *n.pl.* Products of the ductless glands, affecting other organs by way of the blood stream.
Horn, horn, *n.* A hard projection on the heads of certain animals; the material of such horns; wind-instrument of music; extremity of the moon; drinking-cup; powder-horn; something resembling a horn; the feeler of a snail, &c.
Hornblende, horn'blend, *n.* A dark green or black lustrous mineral, an important constituent of several rocks.
Horned, hornd, *a.* Furnished with horns, or projections resembling horns; having two tufts of feathers on the head, as owls.
Hornet, horn'et, *n.* A large stinging species of wasp.
Hornpipe, horn'pīp, *n.* An old Welsh instrument of music; a lively air or tune, of triple time; a dance to the tune.
Hornwork, horn'wėrk, *n.* An outwork in fortification, having angular points or horns.
Horny, horn'i, *a.* Consisting of horn; resembling horn; hardened by labour; callous.
Horologe, ho'ro-lōj, *n.* A time-piece of any kind.
Horological, ho-ro-loj'ik-al, *a.* Pertaining to horology.
Horology, ho-rol'o-ji, *n.* The science of measuring time; art of constructing machines for measuring time, as clocks, dials.
Horoscope, hor'os-kōp, *n.* In *astrology*, a figure or scheme of the heavens from which to cast nativities and foretell events.
Horrible, hor'ri-bl, *a.* Exciting horror; dreadful; frightful; awful; hideous.
Horribly, hor'ri-bli, *adv.* In a manner to excite horror; dreadfullly; terribly.
Horrid, hor'rid, *a.* That does or may excite horror; horrible; shocking.
Horridly, hor'rid-li, *adv.* In a horrid manner; dreadfully; shockingly.
Horrific, hor'rif-ik, *a.* Causing horror.
Horrify, hor'ri-fi, *vt.* (horrifying, horrified). To strike or impress with horror.
Horror, hor'rėr, *n.* A powerful feeling of fear and abhorrence; that which may excite terror; something frightful or shocking.
Horse, hors, *n.* A well-known quadruped, used for draft and carriage and in war; the male animal; cavalry; a name of various things resembling or analogous to a horse.—*vt.* (horsing, horsed). To supply with a horse; to carry on the back; to bestride.
Horseback, hors'bak, *n.* The back of a horse.
Horse-chestnut, hors'ches-nut, *n.* A flowering tree, the nuts of which have been used as food for animals.
Horse-cloth, hors'kloth, *n.* A cloth to cover a horse.
Horse Guards, hors'gärdz, *n.pl.* A body of cavalry for guards.
Horse-leech, hors'lēch, *n.* A large leech; one who cures horses.
Horseman, hors'man, *n.* A rider on horseback; a man skilled in riding; a soldier who serves on horseback.
Horsemanship, hors'man-ship, *n.* Act of riding, and of training and managing horses.
Horse-play, hors'plā, *n.* Rough or rude practical jokes or the like; rude pranks.
Horse-power, hors'pou-ėr, *n.* The power of a horse, or its equivalent, estimated as a power which will raise 32,000 lbs. avoirdupois one foot per minute: the standard for estimating the power of a steam-engine or motor, &c.
Horse-radish, hors'rad-ish, *n.* A perennial plant, having a root of a pungent taste.
Horseshoe, hors'shö, *n.* A shoe for horses, commonly of iron shaped like the letter U; anything shaped like a horse-shoe.—*a.* Having the form of a horse-shoe.
Horsewhip, hors'whip, *n.* A whip for driving horses.—*vt.* To lash.
Horsy, Horsey, hor'si, *a.* Connected with, fond of, or much taken up with horses.
Hortation, hor-tā'shon, *n.* Exhortation.
Hortative, hort'at-iv, *a.* Giving exhortation.
Hortatory, hort'a-to-ri, *a.* Giving exhortation or advice; encouraging.
Horticultural, hor-ti-kul'tūr-al, *a.* Pertaining to horticulture.
Horticulture, hor'ti-kul-tūr, *n.* The art of cultivating gardens.
Horticulturist, hor-tik-ul'tūr-ist, *n.* One skilled in horticulture.
Hosanna, hō-zan'na, *n.* An exclamation of praise to God, or an invocation of blessings.
Hose, hōz, *n. sing.* or *pl.* A covering for the thighs, legs, or feet; close-fitting breeches; stockings: in these senses plural; a flexible pipe used for conveying water.
Hosier, hō'zhi-ėr, *n.* One who deals in stockings, &c., or underclothing generally.
Hosiery, hō'zhi-ė-ri, *n.* The goods of a hosier; underclothing in general.
Hospice, hos'pis, *n.* A place of refuge and entertainment for travellers, as among the Alps.
Hospitable, hos'pit-a-bl, *a.* Kind to strangers and guests.
Hospitably, hos'pit-a-bli, *adv.* In a hospitable manner.
Hospital, hos'pit-al, *n.* A building for the sick, wounded, &c., or for any class of persons requiring public help.
Hospitality, hos-pit-al'i-ti, *n.* Quality of being hospitable.
Hospitaller, hos'pit-al-ėr, *n.* One of a religious community, whose office it was to re-

lieve the poor, the stranger, and the sick; one of the Knights of Malta.
Host, hōst, *n.* One who entertains a stranger or guest; an innkeeper; an army; any great number or multitude; the consecrated bread in the R. Catholic sacrament of the mass.
Hostage, host'āj, *n.* A person delivered to an enemy, as a pledge to secure the performance of conditions.
Hostel, Hostelry, hos'tel, hos'tel-ri, *n.* An inn; a lodging-house.
Hostess, hōst'es, *n.* A female host; a woman who keeps an inn.
Hostile, hos'til, *a.* Belonging to an enemy; unfriendly; antagonistic; adverse.
Hostility, hos-til'i-ti, *n.* State or quality of being hostile; state of war between nations or states; the actions of an open enemy (in *pl.*); animosity; enmity; opposition.
Hostler, os'lėr, *n.* The person who has the care of horses at an inn.
Hot, hot, *a.* Having sensible heat; burning; glowing; easily exasperated; vehement; eager; lustful; biting; pungent in taste.
Hot-bed, hot'bed, *n.* A bed of earth heated by fermenting substances, and covered with glass, used for early or exotic plants; a place which favours rapid growth.
Hot-blast, hot'blast, *n.* A current of heated air injected into a smelting furnace by means of a blowing-engine.
Hot-blooded, hot'blud-ed, *a.* High-spirited; irritable.
Hotchpot, hoch'pot, *n.* A hodge-podge or mixture; a commixture of property for equality of division.
Hotch-potch, hoch'poch, *n.* A mixture of miscellaneous things; jumble; in Scotland, a thick soup of vegetables boiled with meat.
Hotel, hō-tel', *n.* A superior house for strangers or travellers; an inn; in France, a large mansion in a town.
Hot-headed, hot'hed-ed, *a.* Of ardent passions; vehement; violent; rash.
Hot-house, hot'hous, *n.* A house kept warm to shelter tender plants; a conservatory.
Hotly, hot'li, *adv.* With heat; ardently.
Hot-press, hot'pres, *vt.* To press paper, &c., between hot plates to produce a glossy surface.
Hotspur, hot'spėr, *n.* A fiery, violent, or rash man.
Hot-tempered, hot'tem-pėrd, *a.* Of a fiery wrathful temper.
Hottentot, hot'n-tot, *n.* A member of a native race of S. Africa; their language.
Houdah, hou'da, *n.* *See* HOWDAH.
Hough, hok, *n.* The hock of an animal.—*vt.* To hamstring.
Hound, hound, *n.* A dog; a dog used in the chase; a dog-fish.—*vt.* To set on in chase; to hunt; to urge on.
Hour, our, *n.* The twenty-fourth part of a day, consisting of sixty minutes; the particular time of the day; an appointed time; *pl.* certain prayers in the R. Catholic Church.
Hour-glass, our'glas, *n.* A glass for measuring time by the running of sand from one compartment to the other.
Houri, hou'ri or hö'ri, *n.* Among Mohammedans, a nymph of Paradise.
Hourly, our'li, *a.* Happening or done every hour; often repeated; continual.—*adv.* Every hour; frequently.
House, hous, *n.*; pl. **Houses,** hou'zez. A building or erection for the habitation or use of man; any building or edifice; a dwelling; a household; a family; a legislative body of men; audience or attendance; a commercial establishment.—*vt.* (housing, housed). To put or receive into a house; to shelter.—*vi.* To take shelter; to take up abode.
House-boat, hous'bōt, *n.* A river boat supporting a wooden house.
Housebreaker, hous'brāk-ėr, *n.* One who breaks into a house; a burglar.
Housebreaking, hous'brāk-ing, *n.* Burglary.
Household, hous'hōld, *n.* Those who dwell under the same roof and compose a family.—*a.* Domestic.
Householder, hous'hōld-ėr, *n.* The chief of a household; one who keeps house with his family.
Housekeeper, hous'kēp-ėr, *n.* A householder; a female servant who has the chief care of the house or family.
Housekeeping, hous'kēp-ing, *n.* The care or management of domestic concerns.
Housel, hou'zel, *n.* The eucharist.
Houseless, hous'les, *a.* Destitute of a house, habitation, or shelter.
Housemaid, hous'mād, *n.* A female servant in a house.
House-surgeon, hous'sėr-jon, *n.* The resident medical officer in a hospital.
House-warming, hous'warm-ing, *n.* A feast on a family's entrance into a new house.
Housewife, hous'wif, *n.* The mistress of a family; a female manager of domestic affairs; a hussif (pronounced huz'if).
Housewifery, hous'wif-ri, *n.* The business of a housewife.
Housing, houz'ing, *n.* A horse-cloth; *pl.* the trappings of a horse.—*p.n.* Placing in houses; sheltering.
Hovel, ho'vel, *n.* A mean house; an open shed for cattle, &c.—*vt.* To put in a hovel.
Hover, ho'vėr, *vi.* To hang fluttering in the air; to be in doubt; to linger near.
How, hou, *adv.* In what manner; to what extent; for what reason; by what means; in what state.
Howbeit, hou-bē'it, *adv.* Be it as it may; nevertheless.
Howdah, hou'da, *n.* A seat on an elephant's back, usually covered overhead.
However, hou-ev'ėr, *adv.* In whatever manner or degree; in whatever state.—*conj.* Nevertheless; yet; still; though.
Howitzer, hou'its-ėr, *n.* A short piece of ordnance, designed for firing shells at a high angle.
Howl, houl, *vi.* To cry as a dog or wolf; to utter a loud mournful sound; to roar, as the wind.—*vt.* To utter or speak with outcry.—*n.* A loud protracted wail; cry of a wolf, &c.
Howlet, hou'let, *n.* An owl; an owlet.
Howling, houl'ing, *a.* Filled with howls or howling beasts; dreary.
Howsoever, hou-sō-ev'ėr, *adv.* In what manner soever; although.
Hoy, hoi. An exclamation, of no definite meaning.—*n.* A small coasting vessel.
Hoyden, hoi'dn, *n.* and *a.* *See* HOIDEN.
Hub, hub, *n.* The central cylindrical part of a wheel in which the spokes are set.
Hubbub, hub'bub, *n.* A great noise of many confused voices; tumult; uproar.

Huckaback, huk'a-bak, *n.* A coarse linen cloth, used principally for towels.
Huckle, huk'l, *n.* A hunch; a hump; the hip.
Hucklebone, huk'l-bōn, *n.* The hip-bone; the ankle-bone.
Huckster, huk'stėr, *n.* A retailer of small articles; a hawker.—*vi.* To deal in small articles; to higgle.—*vt.* To hawk.
Huddle, hud'l, *vi.* (huddling, huddled). To crowd or press together promiscuously.—*vt.* To throw or crowd together in confusion; to put on in haste and disorder.—*n.* A confused mass; confusion.
Hue, hū, *n.* Colour; tint; dye; a shouting; outcry; alarm.
Huff, huf, *n.* A fit of peevishness or petulance; anger.—*vt.* To treat with insolence; to bully; to make angry.—*vi.* To swell up; to bluster; to take offence.
Huffy, huf'I, *a.* Petulant; angry.
Hug, hug, *vt.* (hugging, hugged). To press close in an embrace; to hold fast; to cherish; to keep close to.—*n.* A close embrace; a particular grip in wrestling.
Huge, hūj, *a.* Of immense bulk; enormous; prodigious.
Hugely, hūj'li, *adv.* Very greatly; vastly.
Hugger-mugger, hug'ėr-mug'ėr, *n.* Concealment; confusion.—*a.* Secret; confused; makeshift.
Huguenot, hū'ge-not, *n.* A French Protestant of the period of the religious wars in France in the 16th century.
Hulk, hulk, *n.* The body of an old vessel; anything bulky or unwieldy.
Hulking, Hulky, hul'king, hul'ki, *a.* Large and clumsy of body; loutish.
Hull, hul, *n.* The outer covering of anything, particularly of a nut or of grain; husk; frame or body of a ship.—*vt.* To strip off the hull or hulls; to pierce the hull of a ship with a cannon-ball.
Hum, hum, *vi.* (humming, hummed). To utter the sound of bees; to make an inarticulate, buzzing sound.—*vt.* To sing in a low voice; to sing or utter inarticulately.—*n.* The noise of bees or insects; a low, confused noise; a low, inarticulate sound.—*interj.* A sound with a pause, implying doubt and deliberation.
Human, hū'man, *a.* Belonging to man or mankind; having the qualities of a man.
Humane, hū-mān', *a.* Having the feelings and dispositions proper to man; compassionate; merciful; tending to refine.
Humanism, hū'man-izm, *n.* Human nature or disposition; polite learning.
Humanist, hū'man-ist, *n.* One who pursues the study of polite literature; one versed in the knowledge of human nature.
Humanitarian, hū-man'i-tā''ri-an, *n.* A philanthropist; one who believes Christ to have been but a mere man; one who maintains the perfectibility of human nature without the aid of grace.
Humanity, hū-man'i-ti, *n.* The quality of being human or humane; mankind collectively; kindness; benevolence; classical and polite literature: generally plural, '*the humanities*'.
Humanize, hū'man-īz, *vt.* To render human or humane; to civilize; to soften.
Human-kind, hū'man-kīnd, *n.* The race of man; mankind.
Humanly, hū'man-li, *adv.* After the manner of men.
Humble, hum'bl, *a.* Of a low, mean, or unpretending character; lowly; modest; meek.—*vt.* (humbling, humbled). To make humble; to abase; to lower.
Humble-bee, hum'bl-bē, *n.* The common name of various large wild bees.
Humble-pie, hum'bl-pī, *n.* A pie made of the humbles.—**To eat humble-pie,** to have to take a humble tone; to apologize.
Humbles, hum'blz, *n.pl.* The heart, liver, kidneys, &c., of a deer.
Humbling, hum'bl-ing, *a.* Adapted to abase pride and self-dependence.
Humbly, hum'bli, *adv.* In an humble manner; meekly; submissively.
Humbug, hum'bug, *n.* A hoax; a cheat; a trickish fellow.—*vt.* (humbugging, humbugged). To impose on.
Humdrum, hum'drum, *a.* Commonplace; dull.—*n.* A droning tone; dull monotony.
Humectate, hū-mek'tāt, *vt.* To moisten.
Humeral, hū'mėr-al, *a.* Belonging to the shoulder.
Humid, hū'mid, *a.* Moist; damp.
Humidity, hū-mid'i-ti, *n.* State of being humid; moisture.
Humiliate, hū-mil'i-āt, *vt.* To humble; to depress; to mortify.
Humiliating, hū-mil'i-āt-ing, *a.* Tending to humiliate; mortifying.
Humiliation, hū-mil'l-ā''shon, *n.* Act of humbling; state of being humbled; cause of being humbled.
Humility, hū-mil'i-ti, *n.* Humbleness of mind; modesty; sense of insignificance.
Humming-bird, hum'ing-bėrd, *n.* A family of minute but richly-coloured birds that make a humming sound with their wings.
Hummock, hum'ok, *n.* A rounded knoll.
Humorist, Humourist, hū'mėr-ist or ū', *n.* One that makes use of a humorous style in speaking or writing; a wag.
Humorous, hū'mėr-us or ū', *a.* Containing humour; jocular; adapted to excite laughter.
Humorously, hū'mėr-us-li or ū', *adv.* In a humorous manner.
Humorsome, Humoursome, hū'mėr-sum or ū', *a.* Peevish; petulant; humorous.
Humour, hū'mėr or ū'mėr, *n.* Moisture or moist matter; fluid matter in an animal body, not blood; disposition; mood; a caprice; jocularity; a quality akin to wit, but depending for its effect less on point or brilliancy of expression.—*vt.* To comply with the inclination of; to soothe by compliance; to indulge.
Hump, hump, *n.* A protuberance, especially that formed by a crooked back; a hunch.
Humpback, hump'bak, *n.* A back with a hump; a humpbacked person; a kind of whale.
Humpbacked, hump'bakt, *a.* Having a crooked back.
Humus, hū'mus, *n.* Vegetable mould.
Hunch, hunsh, *n.* A hump; a protuberance; a thick piece; a push or jerk with the fist or elbow.—*vt.* To bend so as to form a hump; to push with the elbow.
Hunchback, hunsh'bak, *n.* A humpbacked person.

Hunchbacked, hunsh'bakt, *a.* Having a crooked back.
Hundred, hun'dred, *a.* Ten times ten.—*n.* The sum of ten times ten; the number 100; a division or part of a county in England.
Hundred-fold, hun'dred-fōld, *n.* A hundred times as much.
Hundredth, hun'dredth, *a.* The ordinal of a hundred.—*n.* One of a hundred equal parts.
Hundredweight, hun'dred-wāt, *n.* A weight of a hundred and twelve pounds avoirdupois, twenty of which make a ton.
Hungarian, hung-gā'ri-an, *n.* A native of Hungary; the language of the Hungarians; Magyar.—*a.* Pertaining to Hungary.
Hunger, hung'gėr, *n.* An uneasy sensation occasioned by the want of food; a craving of food; a strong or eager desire.—*vi.* To feel the uneasiness occasioned by want of food; to desire with great eagerness.
Hungry, hung'gri, *a.* Feeling uneasiness from want of food; having an eager desire; lean; barren.
Hunk, hungk, *n.* A large lump; a hunch.
Hunks, hungks, *n.* A miser; a niggard.
Hunt, hunt, *vt.* To chase or search for, for the purpose of catching or killing; to follow closely; to use or manage, as hounds; to pursue animals over.—*vi.* To follow the chase; to search.—*n.* The chase of wild animals for catching them; pursuit; an association of huntsmen; a pack of hounds.
Hunter, hunt'ėr, *n.* One who hunts; a horse used in the chase; a kind of watch with a hinged case which protects the glass.
Hunting, hunt'ing, *n.* The act or practice of pursuing wild animals; the chase.
Huntress, hunt'res, *n.* A female that hunts or follows the chase.
Huntsman, hunts'man, *n.* One who practises hunting; the person whose office it is to manage the chase.
Hurdle, hėr'dl, *n.* A movable frame made of twigs or sticks, or of bars or rods.—*vt.* (hurdling, hurdled). To make up, cover, or close with hurdles.
Hurdy-gurdy, hėr'di-gėr-di, *n.* A stringed instrument of music, whose sounds are produced by the friction of a wheel; a barrel-organ.
Hurl, hėrl, *vt.* To send whirling through the air; to throw with violence; to utter with vehemence.—*n.* Act of throwing with violence.
Hurly-burly, hėr'li-bėr'li, *n.* Tumult; bustle; confusion.
Hurricane, hu'ri-kān, *n.* A violent storm of wind travelling over 75 miles per hour.
Hurried, hu'rid, *p.a.* Characterized by hurry; done in a hurry; evidencing hurry.
Hurriedly, hu'rid-li, *adv.* In a hurried manner.
Hurry, hu'ri, *vt.* (hurrying, hurried). To drive or press forward with more rapidity; to urge to act with more celerity; to quicken.—*vi.* To move or act with haste; to hasten.—*n.* Act of hurrying; urgency; bustle.
Hurry-skurry, hu'ri-sku-ri, *adv.* Confusedly; in a bustle.—*n.* bustle.
Hurst, hėrst, *n.* A wood or grove.
Hurt, hėrt, *n.* A wound; bruise; injury; harm.—*vt.* (pret. and pp. hurt). To cause physical pain to; to bruise; to harm; to impair; to injure; to wound the feelings of.
Hurtful, hėrt'fụl, *a.* Causing hurt; tending to impair; detrimental; injurious.
Hurtle, hėr'tl, *vi.* (hurtling, hurtled). To meet in shock; to clash; to fly with threatening noise; to resound.
Husband, huz'band, *n.* A married man: the correlative of wife; a good manager; a steward.—*vt.* To manage with frugality; to use with economy.
Husbandman, huz'band-man, *n.* A tiller of the ground; a farmer.
Husbandry, huz'band-ri, *n.* Farming; care of domestic affairs; thrift.
Hush, hush, *a.* Silent; still; quiet.—*n.* Stillness; quiet.—*vt.* To make quiet; to repress, as noise.—*vi.* To be still; to be silent.
Hush-money, hush'mu-ni, *n.* Money paid to hinder disclosure of facts.
Husk, husk, *n.* The covering of certain fruits or seeds.—*vt.* To strip the husk from.
Husky, husk'i, *a.* Abounding with husks; consisting of husks; resembling husks; rough, as sound; harsh; hoarse.
Hussar, hụ-zär', *n.* A light-armed horse-soldier.
Hussif, huz'if, *n.* A case for holding such things as needles, thimble, thread, &c.
Hussy, huz'i, *n.* A worthless woman; a jade; a pert, frolicsome wench; a quean.
Hustings, hus'tingz, *n.pl.* An old court or meeting held in cities; the platform on which candidates for parliament used to stand when addressing the electors.
Hustle, hus'l, *vt.* and *i.* (hustling, hustled). To shake or shuffle together; to push or crowd; to jostle.
Huswife, huz'if, *n.* A housewife.
Hut, hut, *n.* A small house, hovel, or cabin; a temporary building to lodge soldiers.—*vt.* (hutting, hutted). To place in huts, as troops. —*vi.* To take lodgings in huts.
Hutch, huch, *n.* A chest or box; a corn bin; a box for rabbits; a low wagon used in coal-pits; a measure of 2 bushels.
Huzza, hụz-zä', *n.* A shout of joy.—*vi.* To utter a loud shout of joy.
Hyacinth, hī'a-sinth, *n.* A flowering, bulbous plant, of many varieties; a red variety of zircon, tinged with yellow or brown: also applied to varieties of garnet, sapphire, and topaz.
Hyacinthine, hī-a-sinth'īn, *a.* Pertaining to, made of, or like hyacinth.
Hyaline, hī'al-in, *a.* Glassy; transparent.
Hyalography, hī-al-og'ra-fi, *n.* The art of engraving on glass.
Hybrid, hīb'rid, *n.* A mongrel; an animal or plant produced from the mixture of two species.—*a.* Mongrel.
Hydatid, hid'a-tid, *n.* A larval form of tape-worm.
Hydra, hī'dra, *n.* A many-headed monster of Greek mythology.
Hydrangea, hī-dran'jē-a, *n.* An Asiatic shrub with beautiful flowers, cultivated in gardens.
Hydrant, hī'drant, *n.* A pipe with valves, &c., by which water is drawn from a main pipe.
Hydrate, hī'drāt, *n.* A chemical compound in which water or hydrogen is a characteristic ingredient.
Hydraulic, hī-drąl'ik, *a.* Pertaining to fluids in motion, or the action of water utilized for mechanical purposes.

Hydraulics, hī-dral'iks, *n.* The science of fluids in motion, and the application of water in machinery.
Hydrocarbon, hī-drō-kär'bon, *n.* A chemical compound of hydrogen and carbon.
Hydrocephalus, hī-drō-sef'a-lus, *n.* Water in the head.
Hydrodynamic, hī'drō-dī-nam"ik, *a.* Pertaining to the force or pressure of water.
Hydrodynamics, hī'drō-dī-nam"iks, *n.* The dynamics of water or similar fluids.
Hydrogen, hī'drō-jen, *n.* The gaseous elementary substance which combines with oxygen to form water.
Hydrogenous, hī-dro'jen-us, *a.* Pertaining to hydrogen.
Hydrographer, hī-drog'ra-fėr, *n.* One proficient in hydrography.
Hydrographic, Hydrographical, hī-drō-graf'ik, hī-drō-graf'ik-al, *a.* Treating of or pertaining to hydrography.
Hydrography, hī-drog'ra-fi, *n.* The science of the measurements and representation by charts of seas, rivers, &c.
Hydrology, hī-drol'o-ji, *n.* The science of water, its properties and laws.
Hydromel, hī'drō-mel, *n.* A liquor of honey diluted in water; mead.
Hydrometer, hī-drom'et-ėr, *n.* An instrument for measuring the specific gravities of liquids, and the strength of spirituous liquors.
Hydropathic, hī-drō-path'ik, *a.* Pertaining to hydropathy.—*n.* A hydropathic establishment.
Hydropathy, hī-dro'pa-thi, *n.* A mode of treating diseases by the copious use of pure water, internally and externally.
Hydrophobia, hī-drō-fō'bi-a, *n.* A morbid dread of water; a disease produced by the bite of a mad animal, especially a dog.
Hydrophyte, hī'drō-fīt, *n.* A plant which lives and grows in water.
Hydropic, hī-drop'ik, *a.* Dropsical.
Hydroponics, hī drō-pon'iks, *n.* The cultivation of plants in chemical solutions without soil.
Hydrostatic, hī-drō-stat'ik, *a.* Relating to hydrostatics.
Hydrostatics, hī-drō-stat'iks, *n.* The science which treats of the weight, pressure, and equilibrium of fluids, particularly water, when in a state of rest.
Hydrous, hī'drus, *a.* Watery.
Hydrozoon, hī-drō-zō'on, *n.*; pl. **-zoa,** A class of animals, mostly marine, including the jelly-fishes, &c.
Hyena, hī-ē'na, *n.* A carnivorous quadruped of Asia and Africa, feeding chiefly on carrion.
Hygeian, hī-jē'an, *a.* Relating to health, or the mode of preserving health.
Hygiene, hī'ji-ēn, *n.* A system of principles designed for the promotion of health; sanitary science.
Hygienic, hī-ji-en'ik, *a.* Relating to hygiene.
Hygrometer, hī-grom'et-ėr, *n.* An instrument for measuring the moisture of the atmosphere.
Hygroscope, hī'grō-skōp, *n.* An instrument for indicating the presence of moisture in the atmosphere.
Hymen, hī'men, *n.* The god of marriage.
Hymeneal, Hymenean, hī-men-ē'al, hī-men-ē'an, *a.* Pertaining to marriage.
Hymn, him, *n.* A song of praise; a song or ode in honour of God.—*vt.* To praise or celebrate in song.—*vi.* To sing in praise.
Hymnal, him'nal, *n.* A collection of hymns, generally for use in public worship.
Hymnology, him-nol'o-ji, *n.* The science or doctrine of hymns; hymns collectively.
Hyoid, hī'oid, *a.* Applied to a movable U-shaped bone between the root of the tongue and the larynx.
Hyperbola, hī-pėr'bō-la, *n.* A conic section, a curve formed by a section of a cone, when the cutting plane makes a greater angle with the base than the side of the cone makes.
Hyperbole, hī-pėr'bō-lē, *n.* Exaggeration; a figure of speech exceeding the truth.
Hyperbolic, Hyperbolical, hī-pėr-bol'ik, hī-pėr-bol'ik-al, *a.* Belonging to the hyperbola; containing hyperbole; exceeding the truth.
Hyperborean, hī-pėr-bō'rē-an, *a.* Being in the extreme north; arctic; frigid.—*n.* An inhabitant of the most northern regions.
Hypercritic, hī-pėr-krit'ik, *n.* One critical beyond measure; a captious censor.
Hypercritical, hī-pėr-krit'ik-al, *a.* Over-critical; excessively nice or exact.
Hypercriticism, hī-pėr-krit'i-sizm, *n.* Excessive rigour or nicety of criticism.
Hyphen, hī'fen, *n.* A character, thus (-), implying that two words or syllables are to be connected.
Hypnotic, hip-not'ik, *a.* Producing sleep.
Hypnotism, hip'no-tizm, *n.* A sleep-like condition caused by artificial means.
Hypnotize, hip'no-tīz, *vt.* To affect with hypnotism.
Hypochondria, hī-pō-kon'dri-a, *n.* An ailment characterized by exaggerated anxiety, mainly as to the health; low spirits.
Hypochondriac, hī-pō-kon'dri-ak, *a.* Pertaining to or affected with hypochondria.—*a.* One affected with hypochondria.
Hypocrisy, hi-pok'ri-si, *n.* A feigning to be what one is not; insincerity; a counterfeiting of religion.
Hypocrite, hi'pō-krit, *n.* One who feigns to be what he is not; a dissembler.
Hypocritical, hi-pō-krit'ik-al, *a.* Pertaining to or characterized by hypocrisy; insincere.
Hypodermal, Hypodermic, hī-pō-dėr'mal, hī-pō-dėr'mik, *a.* Pertaining to parts under the skin, or to the introduction of medicines under the skin.
Hypostasis, hī-pos'ta-sis, *n.*; pl. **-ses,** -sēz. The reality underlying or assumed to underlie a phenomenon; the distinct subsistence of the Father, Son, and Holy Ghost in the Godhead.
Hypotenuse, hī-pot'ē-nūs, *n.* The side of a right-angled triangle opposite the right angle.
Hypothec, hī-poth'ek, *n.* In *Scots law*, a lien such as a landlord has over a tenant's furniture or crops.
Hypothecate, hī-poth'e-kāt, *vt.* To pledge in security for a debt, but without transfer; to mortgage.
Hypothesis, hī-poth'e-sis, *n.*; pl. **-ses,** -sēz. A supposition; something assumed for the purpose of argument; a theory assumed to account for what is not understood.
Hypothetic, Hypothetical, hī-po-thet'ik, hī-po-thet'ik-al, *a.* Relating to or characterized by hypothesis; conjectural.

Hypsometer, hip-som'et-ėr, *n.* An apparatus for measuring altitudes.
Hyson, his'on, *n.* A Chinese green tea.
Hyssop, his'sop, *n.* An aromatic plant possessing stimulating, stomachic, and carminative properties.
Hysteria, Hysterics, his-tē'ri-a, his-ter'iks, *n.* A nervous affection chiefly attacking women, characterized by laughing and crying, convulsive struggling, sense of suffocation, &c.
Hysteric, Hysterical, his-te'rik, his-te'rik-al, *a.* Pertaining to hysterics or hysteria; affected by or subject to hysterics.

I

I, I, *pron.* The pronoun of the first person in the nominative case; the word by which a speaker or writer denotes himself.
Iamb, ī-amb', *n.* An iambus.
Iambic, ī-am'bik, *a.* Pertaining to the iambus; consisting of an iambus or of iambi.—*n.* An iambic foot; a verse of iambi.
Iambus, ī-am'bus, *n.*; pl. **-buses** or **-bi.** A poetic foot of two syllables, the first short and the last long, as in *delight*.
Iatric, Iatrical, ī-at'rik, ī-at'rik-al, *a.* Relating to medicine or physicians.
Iberian, ī-bē'ri-an, *a.* Spanish.—*n.* One of the primitive inhabitants of Spain, or their language.
Ibex, ī'beks, *n.* An animal of the goat family.
Ibis, ī'bis, *n.*; pl. **Ibises,** ī'bis-ez. A grallatorial bird allied to the stork.
Ice, īs, *n.* Water or other fluid congealed; ice-cream.—*vt.* (icing, iced). To cover with ice; to convert into ice; to cover with concreted sugar; to freeze.
Iceberg, īs'bėrg, *n.* A vast body of ice floating in the ocean.
Ice-bound, īs'bound, *a.* Totally surrounded with ice, as a ship.
Ice-cream, īs'krēm, *n.* A confection of cream, sugar, &c., frozen.
Iced, īst, *a.* Covered with ice; covered with concreted sugar.
Ice-house, īs-hous, *n.* A house for the preservation of ice during warm weather.
Ice-plant, īs'plant, *n.* A plant whose leaves appear as if covered with frost.
Ichneumon, ik-nū'mon, *n.* A carnivorous Egyptian animal resembling a weasel, which hunts out crocodiles' eggs.
Ichor, ī'kor, *n.* In *mythology*, the ethereal juice that flowed in the veins of the gods; in *medicine*, a watery, acrid humour or discharge.
Ichorous, ī-kor'us, *a.* Like ichor; serous.
Ichthyology, ik-thi-ol'o-ji, *n.* That part of zoology which treats of fishes.
Ichthyosaurus, ik'thi-ō-sa''rus, *n.* A fish-like lizard; an immense fossil marine reptile.
Icicle, īs'i-kl, *n.* A pendent, conical mass of ice.
Iconoclast, ī-kon'o-klast, *n.* A breaker of images; one who attacks cherished beliefs.
Iconography, ī-ko-nog'ra-fi, *n.* The knowledge of ancient statues, paintings, gems, &c.
Icy, īs'i, *a.* Abounding with ice; made of ice; resembling ice; chilling; frigid; destitute of affection or passion.
Idea, ī-dē'a, *n.* That which is seen by the mind's eye; an image in the mind; object of thought; notion; conception; abstract principle; ideal view.
Ideal, ī-dē'al, *a.* Existing in idea or fancy; visionary; imaginary; perfect.—*n.* An imaginary model of perfection.
Idealism, ī-dē'al-izm, *n.* The system that makes everything to consist in ideas, and denies the existence of material bodies, or which denies any ground for believing in the reality of anything but percipient minds and ideas.
Idealist, ī-dē'al-ist, *n.* One who holds the doctrine of idealism; a visionary.
Ideality, ī-dē-al'i-ti, *n.* Quality of being ideal; capacity to form ideals of beauty.
Idealize, ī-dē'al-īz, *vt.* To make ideal; to embody in an ideal form.
Ideally, ī-dē'al-li, *adv.* In an ideal manner; an idea; intellectually; mentally.
Ideation, ī-dē-ā'shon, *n.* The faculty for forming ideas; establishment of a distinct mental representation of an object.
Identical, ī-den'tik-al, *a.* The same.
Identifiable, ī-den'ti-fī-a-bl, *a.* That may be identified.
Identification, ī-den'ti-fi-kā''shon, *n.* Act of identifying.
Identify, ī-den'ti-fī, *vt.* To make to be the same; to consider as the same in effect; to ascertain or prove to be the same.
Identity, ī-den'ti-ti, *n.* Sameness, as distinguished from similitude and diversity; sameness in every possible circumstance.
Ideograph, Ideogram, id'ē-ō-graf, id'ē-ō-gram, *n.* A character, symbol, or figure which suggests the idea of an object; a hieroglyphic.
Ideology, ī-dē-ol'o-ji, *n.* The doctrine of ideas, or operations of the understanding.
Ides, īdz, *n.pl.* In the ancient Roman calendar the 15th day of March, May, July, and October, and the 13th day of the other months.
Idiocy, id'i-ō-si, *n.* State of being an idiot; hopeless insanity or madness.
Idiograph, id'i-ō-graf, *n.* A private or trade mark.
Idiom, id'i-om, *n.* A mode of expression peculiar to a language; the genius or peculiar cast of a language; dialect.
Idiomatic, id'i-om-at''ik, *a.* Pertaining to the particular genius or modes of expression of a language.
Idiomatically, id'i-om-at''ik-al-li, *adv.* According to the idiom of a language.
Idiopathic, id'i-o-path''ik, *a.* Pertaining to idiopathy.
Idiopathy, id-i-op'a-thi, *n.* A morbid state not produced by any preceding disease.
Idiosyncrasy, id'i-o-sin''kra-si, *n.* Peculiarity of temperament or constitution; mental or moral characteristic distinguishing an individual.
Idiosyncratic, id'i-o-sin-krat''ik, *a.* Of peculiar temper or disposition.
Idiot, i'di-ot, *n.* One void of understanding; one hopelessly insane.
Idiotic, Idiotical, id-i-ot'ik, id-i-ot'ik-al, *a.* Relating to or like an idiot; absurd.
Idiotism, id'i-ot-izm, *n.* An idiom; a peculiar or abnormal idiom.
Idle, ī'dl, *a.* Not engaged in any occupation; inactive; lazy; futile; affording leisure; trifling; trivial.—*vi.* (idling, idled). To be

idle; to lose or spend time in inaction.—*vt.* To spend in idleness.
Idleness, ī'dl-nes, *n.* Inaction; sloth; triviality; uselessness.
Idler, ī'dl-ėr, *n.* One who idles; a lazy person; sluggard.
Idly, īd'li, *adv.* Lazily; carelessly; ineffectually; unprofitably.
Idol, ī'dol, *n.* An image or symbol of a deity consecrated as an object of worship; a person honoured to adoration; anything on which we set our affections inordinately.
Idolater, ī-dol'at-ėr, *n.* A worshipper of idols; a pagan; a great admirer.
Idolatress, ī-dol'at-res, *n.* A female idolater.
Idolatrous, ī-dol'at-rus, *a.* Pertaining to idolatry; consisting in or partaking of an excessive attachment or reverence.
Idolatry, ī-dol'at-ri, *n.* The worship of idols; excessive attachment to or veneration for any person or thing.
Idolize, ī'dol-īz, *vt.* To worship as an idol; to love or reverence to adoration.
Idyl, id'il or ī'dil, *n.* A short highly wrought descriptive poem; a short pastoral poem.
Idyllic, ī-dil'ik, *a.* Belonging to idylls; pastoral.
If, if, *conj.* Granting or supposing that; on condition that; whether; although.
Igloo, ig'lö, *n.* An Eskimo winter-hut, made of blocks of frozen snow.
Igneous, ig'nē-us, *a.* Pertaining to or consisting of fire; resembling fire; proceeding from the action of fire.
Ignis-fatuus, ig'nis-fat'ū-us, *n.*; pl. **Ignes-fatui,** ig'nēz-fat'ū-ī. A light that flits about over marshy grounds; called also *Will-o'-the-wisp*, *Jack-a-lantern*, &c.
Ignite, ig-nīt', *vt.* (igniting, ignited). To set on fire.—*vi.* To take fire.
Ignition, ig-ni'shon, *n.* Act of setting on fire; act of catching fire; state of burning.
Ignoble, ig-nō'bl, *a.* Not noble; of low birth or family; base; dishonourable.
Ignobly, ig-nō'bli, *adv.* Meanly; basely.
Ignominious, ig-nō-mi'ni-us, *a.* Shameful; dishonourable; infamous; despicable.
Ignominy, ig'nō-mi-ni, *n.* Public disgrace; loss of character or reputation; infamy; shame; contempt.
Ignoramus, ig-nō-rā'mus, *n.*; pl. **-muses.** An ignorant person.
Ignorance, ig'nō-rans, *n.* State of being illiterate, uninformed, or uneducated; want of knowledge.
Ignorant, ig'nō-rant, *a.* Wanting knowledge or information.
Ignore, ig-nōr', *vt.* (ignoring, ignored). To pass over or overlook as if ignorant of; to disregard.
Iguana, ig-wä'na, *n.* An American reptile of the lizard family.
Iliac, il'i-ak, *a.* Pertaining to the lower bowels.
Ill, il, *a.* Bad or evil; producing evil; unfortunate; cross; crabbed; sick or indisposed; impaired; ugly; unfavourable; rude.—*n.* Evil; misfortune; calamity; disease; pain.—*adv.* Not well; badly; with pain or difficulty.
Illapse, il-laps', *vi.* To pass or glide into.—*n.* A sliding into; an immission or entrance of one thing into another.
Illation, il-lā'shon, *n.* An inference from premises; a deduction.
Illative, il-lā'tiv, *a.* Relating to illation; that denotes an inference.
Ill-blood, il'blud, *n.* Bad feeling; enmity.
Ill-bred, il-bred', *a.* Unpolite; rude.
Ill-breeding, il-brēd'ing, *n.* Want of good breeding; impoliteness; rudeness.
Ill-conditioned, il-kon-di'shond, *a.* Having bad qualities; of a surly temper.
Illegal, il-lē'gal, *a.* Not legal; contrary to law; prohibited; illicit.
Illegality, il-lē-gal'i-ti, *n.* State or quality of being illegal; unlawfulness.
Illegally, il-lē'gal-li, *adv.* In an illegal or unlawful manner; unlawfully.
Illegible, il-le'ji-bl, *a.* Not legible; that cannot be read.
Illegibly, il-le'ji-bli, *adv.* In an illegible manner.
Illegitimacy, il-lē-jit'i-ma-si, *n.* State of being illegitimate; bastardy.
Illegitimate, il-lē-jit'i-māt, *a.* Not legitimate; born out of wedlock; illogical; not authorized.—*vt.* To render illegitimate.
Ill-favoured, il'fā-vėrd, *a.* Not well-favoured or good-looking; plain; ugly.
Illiberal, il-lib'ėr-al, *a.* Not liberal; not generous; narrow in scope; uncharitable.
Illiberality, il-lib'ėr-al"i-ti, *n.* Quality of being illiberal; narrowness of mind.
Illicit, il-lis'it, *a.* Not permitted; unlawful; lawless.
Illimitable, il-lim'it-a-bl, *a.* That cannot be limited; boundless; infinite; vast.
Illiteracy, il-lit'ėr-a-si, *n.* State of being illiterate; want of education; ignorance.
Illiterate, il-lit'ėr-āt, *a.* Unlettered; ignorant of letters or books; not educated.
Ill-judged, il'jujd, *a.* Injudicious; unwise.
Ill-mannered, il-man'ėrd, *a.* Having bad manners; rude; boorish; impolite.
Ill-nature, il'nā-tūr, *n.* Bad temper; crossness; crabbedness.
Ill-natured, il'nā-tūrd, *a.* Cross; surly.
Illness, il'nes, *n.* State or quality of being ill; ailment; malady; sickness.
Illogical, il-lo'jik-al, *a.* Not logical; contrary to logic or sound reasoning.
Ill-starred, il'stärd, *a.* Influenced by unlucky stars; fated to be unfortunate.
Ill-tempered, il'tem-pėrd, *a.* Of bad temper; morose; crabbed; sour.
Ill-timed, il'tīmd, *a.* Done or said at an unsuitable time.
Illude, il-lūd', *vt.* (illuding, illuded). To deceive; to mock; to make sport of.
Illume, il-lūm', *vt.* To illuminate.
Illuminate, il-lūm'in-āt, *vt.* (illuminating, illuminated). To light up; to adorn with festal lamps or bonfires; to enlighten intellectually; to adorn with coloured pictures, &c., as manuscripts.
Illuminati, il-lū'mi-nā"tī, *n.pl.* A term applied to persons who affect to possess extraordinary knowledge.
Illumination, il-lūm'in-ā"shon, *n.* Act of illuminating; festive display of lights, &c.; splendour; infusion of intellectual or spiritual light; the adorning of manuscripts and books by hand with ornamental designs; such ornaments themselves.
Illuminative, il-lūm'in-āt-iv, *a.* Having the power of illuminating or giving light.
Illuminator, il-lūm'in-āt-ėr, *n.* One who or

that which gives light; one who decorates manuscripts, &c.
Illumine, il-lūm'in, *vt.* To illuminate.
Illusion, il-lū'zhon, *n.* Deception; deceptive appearance; hallucination.
Illusionist, il-lū'zhon-ist, *n.* One given to illusion, or one who produces illusions, as by sleight of hand.
Illusive, il-lū'siv, *a.* Tending to cause illusion; deceptive; deceitful.
Illusory, il-lū'so-ri, *a.* Deceiving by false appearances; fallacious.
Illustrate, il-lus'trāt or il'lus-trāt, *vt.* (illustrating, illustrated). To make clear or obvious; to explain; to explain and adorn by means of pictures, drawings, &c.
Illustration, il-lus-trā'shon, *n.* Act of illustrating; that which illustrates; an example; design to illustrate the text of a book.
Illustrative, il-lus'trāt-iv or il'lus-trāt-iv, *a.* Having the qualityof illustrating or elucidating.
Illustrator, il-lus'trāt-ėr or il'lus-trāt-ėr, *n.* One who illustrates; one who makes pictures for books.
Illustrious, il-lus'tri-us, *a.* Renowned; celebrated; noble; conferring honour or renown; glorious.
Illustriously, il-lus'tri-us-li, *adv.* Conspicuously; eminently; gloriously.
Illwill, il'wil, *n.* Unkind or hostile feeling; hatred; malevolence; malice.
Image, im'āj, *n.* A representation of any person or thing; a statue; an idol; embodiment; a picture drawn by fancy; the appearance of any object formed by the reflection or refraction of the rays of light.—*vt.* (imaging, imaged). To represent by an image; to mirror; to form a likeness of in the mind.
Imagery, im'āj-e-ri, *n.* Images in general; forms of the fancy; rhetorical figures.
Imaginable, im-aj'in-a-bl, *a.* That may or can be imagined.
Imaginary, im-aj'in-a-ri, *a.* Existing only in imagination; ideal; visionary.
Imagination, im-aj'in-ā"shon, *n.* The act of imagining; the faculty by which we form a mental image, or new combinations of ideas; mental image; a mere fancy; notion.
Imaginative, im-aj'in-āt-iv, *a.* That forms imaginations; owing existence to, or characterized by imagination.
Imagine, im-aj'in, *vt.* (imagining, imagined). To picture to oneself; to fancy; to contrive; to think; to deem.—*vi.* To conceive; to have a notion or idea.
Imago, im-ā'go, *n.* The last or perfect state of an insect.
Imam, Imaum, Iman, i-mäm', i-mam', i-män', *n.* A successor of Mohammed; the priest of a mosque.
Imbecile, im'be-sil, *a.* Destitute of strength; mentally feeble; fatuous; extremely foolish. —*n.* A poor, fatuous, or weak-minded creature.
Imbecility, im-be-sil'i-ti, *n.* Fatuity; silliness; helpless mental weakness.
Imbed, im-bed', *vt.* To lay in a bed; to lay in surrounding matter. Also *Embed.*
Imbibe, im-bib', *vt.* (imbibing, imbibed). To drink in; to absorb; to admit into the mind.
Imbitter, Imblazon, Imbody, Imbolden, Imbowel, Imbower. *See* EMBITTER, &c.
Imbricate, Imbricated, im'bri-kāt, im'bri-kāt-ed, *a.* Bent and hollowed, like a roof tile; lapping over each other, like tiles.
Imbrication, im-bri-kā'shon, *n.* State of being imbricate; a hollow like that of a roof tile.
Imbroglio, im-brō'lyō, *n.* An intricate and perplexing state of affairs; a misunderstanding of a complicated nature.
Imbrown, im-broun', *vt.* To make brown. Also *Embrown.*
Imbrue, im-brö', *vt.* (imbruing, imbrued). To soak; to drench in a fluid, chiefly in blood.
Imbue, im-bū', *vt.* (imbuing, imbued). To tinge deeply; to dye; to inspire or impregnate (the mind).
Imitable, im'i-ta-bl, *a.* That may be imitated; worthy of imitation.
Imitate, im'i-tāt, *vt.* (imitating, imitated). To follow as a model or example; to copy; to mimic; to counterfeit.
Imitation, im-i-tā'shon, *n.* Act of imitating; that which is made or produced as a copy; resemblance; a counterfeit.
Imitative, im'i-tāt-iv, *a.* That imitates; inclined to imitate; exhibiting an imitation.
Imitator, im'i-tāt-ėr, *n.* One who imitates; one who takes another as pattern or model.
Immaculate, im-ma'kū-lāt, *a.* Without spot; undefiled; pure.
Immanate, im'ma-nāt, *vi.* To flow or issue in: said of something intangible.
Immanent, im'ma-nent, *a.* Remaining in or within; inherent and indwelling.
Immaterial, im-ma-tē'ri-al, *a.* Not consisting of matter; unimportant.
Immaterialism, im-ma-tē'ri-al-izm, *n.* The doctrine that all being may be reduced to mind and ideas in the mind.
Immateriality, im-ma-tē'ri-al"i-ti, *n.* Quality of being immaterial.
Immature, im-ma-tūr', *a.* Not mature; not perfect or completed; premature.
Immaturity, im-ma-tūr'i-ti, *n.* State or quality of being immature; crudity.
Immeasurable, im-me'zhūr-a-bl, *a.* That cannot be measured; immense.
Immediate, im-mē'di-āt, *a.* Without anything intervening; acting without a medium; direct; not acting by secondary causes; present; without intervention of time.
Immediately, im-mē'di-āt-li, *adv.* Without the intervention of anything; directly; without delay; instantly; forthwith.
Immemorial, im-me-mō'ri-al, *a.* Beyond memory; extending beyond the reach of record or tradition.
Immemorially, im-me-mō'ri-al-li, *adv.* Beyond memory; from time out of mind.
Immense, im-mens', *a.* Immeasurable; huge; prodigious; enormous.
Immensely, im-mens'li, *adv.* To an immense extent; hugely; vastly.
Immensity, im-mens'i-ti, *n.* Condition or quality of being immense; that which is immense; infinity.
Immerge, im-mėrj', *vt.* (immerging, immerged). To dip or plunge; to immerse.—*vi.* To disappear by entering into any medium.
Immerse, im-mėrs', *vt.* (immersing, immersed). To plunge into water or other fluid; to overwhelm; to engage deeply.
Immersion, im-mėr'shon, *n.* Act of immersing; state of being overwhelmed or deeply

engaged; disappearance of a celestial body behind another or into its shadow.

Immesh, im-mesh', *vt.* To entangle in the meshes of a net, &c.

Immethodical, im-me-thod'ik-al, *a.* Not methodical; without systematic arrangement; disorderly.

Immigrant, im'mi-grant, *n.* A person who immigrates into a country.

Immigrate, im'mi-grāt, *vi.* To come into a country for permanent residence.

Immigration, im-mi-grā'shon, *n.* Act of removing into a country for settlement.

Imminence, im'mi-nens, *n.* Quality or condition of being imminent.

Imminent, im'mi-nent, *a.* Hanging over; impending; threatening; near at hand.

Imminently, im'mi-nent-li, *adv.* In an imminent manner or degree.

Immobile, im-mōb'il, *a.* Not mobile; immovable; fixed; stable.

Immobility, im-mō-bil'i-ti, *n.* State or quality of being immobile; resistance to motion.

Immoderate, im-mo'dėr-āt, *a.* Exceeding just or usual bounds; excessive; intemperate.

Immoderately, im-mo'dėr-āt-li, *adv.* Excessively; unreasonably.

Immodest, im-mo'dest, *a.* Not modest; indelicate; indecent; lewd.

Immodesty, im-mo'des-ti, *n.* Want of modesty.

Immolate, im'mō-lāt, *vt.* (immolating, immolated). To sacrifice; to kill, as a victim offered in sacrifice; to offer in sacrifice.

Immolation, im-mō-lā'shon, *n.* Act of immolating; a sacrifice offered.

Immoral, im-mo'ral, *a.* Not moral; wicked; depraved; licentious.

Immorality, im-mō-ral'i-ti, *n.* Quality of being immoral; any immoral act or practice; vice; licentiousness; depravity.

Immorally, im-mo'ral-li, *adv.* Wickedly; in violation of law or duty.

Immortal, im-mor'tal, *a.* Not mortal; everlasting; imperishable; not liable to fall into oblivion.—*n.* One who is exempt from death.

Immortality, im-mor-tal'i-ti, *n.* Condition or quality of being immortal; life destined to endure without end.

Immortalize, im-mor'tal-īz, *vt.* To render immortal; to make famous for ever.

Immortally, im-mor'tal-li, *adv.* With endless existence; eternally.

Immortelle, im-mor-tel', *n.* A flower of the sort called *everlasting.*

Immovability, im-möv'a-bil"i-ti, *n.* State or quality of being immovable.

Immovable, im-möv'a-bl, *a.* That cannot be moved from its place; not to be moved from a purpose; fixed; unchangeable; unfeeling.

Immovably, im-möv'a-bli, *adv.* Unalterably; unchangeably.

Immunity, im-mū'ni-ti, *n.* Freedom from service or obligation; particular privilege or prerogative; state of not being liable.

Immure, im-mūr', *vt.* (immuring, immured). To inclose within walls; to imprison.

Immutable, im-mū'ta-bl, *a.* Unchangeable; unalterable; invariable.

Immutably, im-mu'ta-bli, *adv.* Unchangeably; unalterably.

Imp, imp, *n.* A young or little devil; a mischievous child.—*vt.* (imping, imped). To graft; to mend a deficient wing by the insertion of a feather; to strengthen.

Impact, im'pakt, *n.* A forcible touch; a blow; the shock of a moving body that strikes against another.

Impair, im-pār', *vt.* To make worse; to lessen in quantity, value, excellence, or strength.

Impale, im-pāl', *vt.* (impaling, impaled). To put to death by fixing on a stake; to join, as two coats of arms on one shield, with an upright line between.

Impalpable, im-pal'pa-bl, *a.* Not to be felt; so fine as not to be perceived by the touch; not easily or readily apprehended by the mind.

Impanate, im-pā'nāt or im'pa-nāt, *a.* Embodied in the bread used in the eucharist.

Impanation, im-pa-nā'shon, *n.* The supposed real presence in the eucharist; consubstantiation.

Impanel, im-pan'el, *vt.* (impanelling, impanelled). To form or enrol the list of jurors in a court of justice.

Imparity, im-pa'ri-ti, *n.* Inequality.

Impark, im-pärk', *vt.* To inclose for a park; to sever from a common.

Impart, im-pärt', *vt.* To give, grant, or communicate; to bestow on another; to confer; to reveal; to disclose.

Impartial, im-pär'shal, *a.* Not partial; not biassed; equitable; just.

Impartiality, im-pär'shi-al"i-ti, *n.* State or quality of being impartial; freedom from bias; equity.

Impartially, im-pär'shal-li, *adv.* Without bias of judgment; justly.

Impartible, im-pärt'i-bl, *a.* Not subject to partition; that may be imparted.

Impassable, im-pas'a-bl, *a.* That cannot be passed or travelled over.

Impassibility, im-pas'i-bil"i-ti, *n.* State or quality of being impassible.

Impassible, im-pas'i-bl, *a.* Incapable of passion or suffering; not to be moved to passion or sympathy; unmoved.

Impassion, im-pa'shon, *vt.* To move or affect strongly with passion.

Impassionable, im-pash'on-a-bl, *a.* Easily excited; susceptible of strong emotion.

Impassioned, im-pa'shond, *p.a.* Actuated by passion; having the feelings warmed, as a speaker; expressive of passion, as a harangue.

Impassive, im-pas'iv, *a.* Not susceptible of pain or suffering; impassible; unmoved.

Impatience, im-pā'shens, *n.* Condition or quality of being impatient; uneasiness under pain, suffering, &c.

Impatient, im-pā'shent, *a.* Not patient; uneasy under given conditions and eager for change; not suffering quietly; not enduring delay.

Impatiently, im-pā'shent-li, *adv.* In an impatient manner.

Impawn, im-pạn', *vt.* To pawn; to pledge; to deposit as security.

Impeach, im-pēch', *vt.* To charge with a crime; to bring charges of maladministration against a minister of state, &c.; to call in question; to disparage.

Impeachable, im-pēch'a-bl, *a.* Liable to be impeached.

Impeachment, im-pēch'ment, *n.* Act of impeaching; a calling in question; accusation brought by the House of Commons against some high official before the House of Lords, who act as judges.
Impearl, im-pėrl', *vt.* To decorate with pearls or things resembling pearls.
Impeccability, im-pek'a-bil''i-ti, *n.* Quality of being impeccable.
Impeccable, im-pek'a-bl, *a.* Not peccable, or liable to sin.
Impecunious, im-pē-kū'ni-us, *a.* Not having money; without funds.
Impede, im-pēd', *vt.* (impeding, impeded). To entangle or hamper; to obstruct.
Impediment, im-ped'i-ment, *n.* That by which one is impeded; obstruction.
Impel, im-pel', *vt.* (impelling, impelled). To drive or urge forward; to press on; to instigate; to incite; to actuate
Impellent, im-pel'ent, *a.* Having the quality of impelling.—*n.* A power that impels.
Impend, im-pend', *vi.* To hang over; to threaten; to be imminent.
Impenetrability, im-pe'ne-tra-bil''i-ti, *n.* Quality of being impenetrable; that quality of matter by which it excludes all other matter from the space it occupies.
Impenetrable, im-pe'ne-tra-bl, *a.* That cannot be penetrated; not admitting the entrance or passage of other bodies; impervious; obtuse or unsympathetic.
Impenitence, im-pe'ni-tens, *n.* Obduracy; hardness of heart.
Impenitent, im-pe'ni-tent, *a.* Not penitent; not repenting of sin; obdurate.
Imperative, im-pe'rat-iv, *a.* Expressive of command; obligatory; designating a mood of the verb which expresses command, &c.
Imperatively, im-pe'rat-iv-li, *adv.* In an imperative manner; authoritatively.
Imperceptible, im-pėr-sep'ti-bl, *a.* Not perceptible; not easily apprehended by the senses; fine or minute.
Imperfect, im-pėr'fekt, *a.* Not perfect; not complete; not perfect in a moral view; faulty; *imperfect tense*, a tense expressing an uncompleted action or state, especially in time past.
Imperfection, im-pėr-fek'shon, *n.* Want of perfection; defect; fault; failing.
Imperfectly, im-pėr'fekt-li, *adv.* In an imperfect manner; not fully.
Imperforate, im-pėr'fo-rāt, *a.* Not perforated or pierced; having no opening or pores.
Imperial, im-pē'ri-al, *a.* Pertaining to an empire or emperor; supreme; suitable for an emperor; of superior excellence.—*n.* A tuft of hair beneath a man's lower lip; a size of paper measuring 30 by 22 inches.
Imperialism, im-pē'ri-al-izm, *n.* State of being imperial; imperial power or authority.
Imperialist, im-pē'ri-al-ist, *n.* A subject or soldier of an emperor; one favourable to empire or imperial government.
Imperil, im-pe'ril, *vt.* (imperilling, imperilled). To bring into peril; to endanger.
Imperious, im-pē'ri-us, *a.* Commanding; haughty; domineering; arrogant; urgent; authoritative.
Imperishable, im-pe'rish-a-bl, *a.* Not perishable; indestructible; everlasting.
Impermeable, im-pėr'mē-a-bl, *a.* Not permeable; not permitting fluids to pass through; impervious.
Impersonal, im-pėr'son-al, *a.* Not having personal existence; not endued with personality; not referring to any particular person; *impersonal verb*, a verb (such as *it rains*) used only with an impersonal nominative.—*n.* That which wants personality; an impersonal verb.
Impersonality, im-pėr'son-al''i-ti, *n.* Condition of being impersonal.
Impersonally, im pėr'son-al-li, *adv.* In an impersonal manner; as an impersonal verb.
Impersonate, im-pėr'son-āt, *vt.* To invest with personality; to assume the character of; to represent in character, as on the stage.
Impertinence, im-pėr'ti-nens, *n.* The quality of being impertinent; irrelevance; that which is impertinent; rudeness.
Impertinent, im-pėr'ti-nent, *a.* Not pertinent; irrelevant; petulant and rude; pert; intrusive.
Impertinently, im-pėr'ti-nent-li, *adv.* Irrelevantly; intrusively; rudely.
Imperturbability, im-pėr-tėrb'a-bil''i-ti, *n.* Quality of being imperturbable.
Imperturbable, im-pėr-tėrb'a-bl, *a.* That cannot be agitated; unmoved; calm.
Impervious, im-pėr'vi-us, *a.* Not pervious; impassable; impenetrable.
Impetigo, im-pe-ti'gō, *n.* An eruption of itching pustules in clusters on the skin.
Impetrate, im'pe-trāt, *vt.* To obtain by prayer or petition.
Impetuosity, im-pe'tū-os''i-ti, *n.* Quality of being impetuous; violence; vehemence; ardour and hurry of feelings.
Impetuous, im-pe'tū-us, *a.* Rushing with great force; forcible; precipitate; vehement of mind; hasty; passionate.
Impetuously, im-pe'tū-us-li, *adv.* Violently; with haste and force.
Impetus, im'pe-tus, *n.* The force with which any body is driven or impelled; momentum.
Impi, im'pi, *n.* A body of Kaffir soldiers.
Impiety, im-pi'e-ti, *n.* Want of piety; irreverence toward the Supreme Being; ungodliness; an act of wickedness.
Impinge, im-pinj', *vi.* (impinging, impinged). To dash against; to clash.
Impious, im'pi-us, *a.* Destitute of piety; irreverent toward the Supreme Being; profane; tending to dishonour God or his laws.
Impiously, im'pi-us-li, *adv.* Profanely; wickedly; blasphemously.
Impish, imp'ish, *a.* Having the qualities of an imp.
Implacability, im-plā'ka-bil''i-ti, *n.* Quality of being implacable; irreconcilable enmity or anger.
Implacable, im-plā'ka-bl, *a.* Not to be appeased; inexorable; unrelenting.
Implacably, im-plā'ka-bli, *adv.* In an implacable manner; inexorably.
Implant, im-plant', *vt.* To set, fix, or plant; to insert; to instil; to infuse.
Implead, im-plēd', *vt.* To institute and prosecute a suit against; to sue at law.
Impleader, im-plēd'ėr, *n.* One who impleads.
Implement, im'plē-ment, *n.* A tool, utensil, or instrument.—*vt.* To fulfil the conditions of; to perform.
Implex, im'pleks, *a.* Infolded; intricate.
Implicate, im'pli-kāt, *vt.* (implicating, im-

plicated). To involve or bring into connection with; to prove to be connected or concerned, as in an offence.
Implication, im-pli-kā'shon, *n.* Act of implicating; state of being implicated; entanglement; a tacit inference; something to be understood though not expressed.
Implicit, im-pli'sit, *a.* Implied; fairly to be understood, though not expressed in words; trusting to another; unquestioning.
Implicitly, im-pli'sit-li, *adv.* In an implicit manner; with unreserved confidence.
Implore, im-plōr, *vt.* and *i.* (imploring, implored). To call upon or for, in supplication; to beseech, entreat.
Imply, im-plī', *vt.* (implying, implied). To involve or contain in substance or by fair inference; to signify indirectly; to presuppose.
Impolicy, im-po'li-si, *n.* Bad policy; inexpediency.
Impolite, im-pō-līt', *a.* Not polite; not of polished manners; uncivil.
Impolitic, im-po'lit-ik, *a.* Not politic; wanting policy or prudence; inexpedient.
Imponderable, im-pon'dėr-a-bl, *a.* Not having weight that can be measured.
Import, im-pōrt', *vt.* To bring into a place from abroad; to bear or convey, as the meaning; to signify; to imply; to be of moment or consequence to; to concern.—*n.* im'pōrt. That which is brought into a country from abroad; signification; purport; drift; importance.
Importable, im-pōrt'a-bl, *a.* That may be imported.
Importance, im-pōrt'ans, *n.* Quality of being important; weight; moment; rank or standing; weight in self-estimation.
Important, im-pōrt'ant, *a.* Full of import; momentous; influential; grave; consequential.
Importantly, im-pōr'tant-li, *adv.* In an important manner; weightily; forcibly.
Importation, im-pōrt-ā'shon, *n.* Act or practice of importing; a quantity imported.
Importer, im-pōrt'ėr, *n.* One who imports; a merchant who brings goods from abroad.
Importunate, im-por'tū-nāt, *a.* Given to importune; troublesome by importuning; urgent in request or demand; persistent.
Importunately, im-por'tū-nāt-li, *adv.* With pressing solicitation.
Importune, im-por-tūn', *vt.* (importuning, importuned). To press with solicitation; to urge with frequent application.—*vi.* To solicit earnestly and repeatedly.
Importunity, im-por-tūn'i-ti, *n.* Pressing or frequent solicitation; application urged with troublesome frequency.
Impose, im-pōz', *vt.* (imposing, imposed). To place, set, or lay on; to lay on, as a tax, penalty, duty, &c.; to lay on, as hands; to obtrude fallaciously; to palm or pass off.—*vi.* Used in phrase *to impose on* or *upon*, to deceive; to victimize.
Imposing, im-pōz'ing, *p.a.* Impressive in appearance; commanding; stately; majestic.
Imposition, im-pō-zi'shon, *n.* Act of imposing; act of laying on hands in the ceremony of ordination; that which is imposed; a tax, toll, duty, &c.; burden; imposture.
Impossibility, im-pos'i-bil"i-ti, *n.* State or character of being impossible; that which cannot be, or cannot be done.
Impossible, im-pos'i-bl, *a.* Not possible; that cannot be or be done.
Impost, im'pōst, *n.* That which is imposed by authority; tax or duty; point where an arch rests on a wall or column.
Imposthume, im-pos'tūm, *n.* An abscess.
Imposter, im-pos'tėr, *n.* One who imposes on others; a deceiver under a false character.
Imposture, im-pos'tūr, *n.* Imposition; fraud; deception.
Impotence, Impotency, im'pō-tens, im'pō-ten-si, *n.* State or quality of being impotent; want of ability or power; want of the power of procreation.
Impotent, im'pō-tent, *a.* Entirely wanting vigour of body or mind; feeble; destitute of the power of begetting children.
Impotently, im'pō-tent-li, *adv.* In an impotent manner; feebly; weakly.
Impound, im-pound', *vt.* To confine in a pound or close pen; to confine; to take possession of for use when necessary.
Impoverish, im-po'vėr-ish, *vt.* To make poor; to reduce to indigence; to exhaust the strength or fertility of, as of soil.
Impoverishment, im-po'vėr-ish-ment, *n.* Act of impoverishing.
Impracticability, im-prak'ti-ka-bil"i-ti, *n.* State or quality of being impracticable.
Impracticable, im-prak'ti-ka-bl, *a.* Not practicable; unmanageable; stubborn; incapable of being passed.
Imprecate, im'prē-kāt, *vt.* (imprecating, imprecated). To invoke, as a curse or some evil.
Imprecation, im-prē-kā'shon, *n.* Act of imprecating; prayer that a curse or calamity may fall on anyone; malediction.
Impregnability, im-preg'na-bil"i-ti, *n.* State of being impregnable.
Impregnable, im-preg'na-bl, *a.* That cannot be taken by force; able to resist attack; invincible, as affection.
Impregnably, im-preg'na-bli, *adv.* In an impregnable manner or position.
Impregnate, im-preg'nāt, *vt.* To make pregnant; to imbue; to saturate.
Impregnation, im-preg-nā'shon, *n.* The act of impregnating: fecundation; infusion.
Impress, im-pres', *vt.* To press into; to imprint; to stamp on the mind; to inculcate; to compel to enter into public service, as seamen; to take for public use.—*n.* im'press. That which is impressed; mark made by pressure; impression; character; act of compelling to enter into public service.
Impressible, im-pres'i-bl, *a.* That may be impressed; susceptible of impression; readily or easily affected.
Impression, im-pre'shon, *n.* Act of impressing; that which is impressed; mark; effect produced on the mind; an indistinct notion; idea; copy taken by pressure from type, &c.; edition; copies forming one issue of a book.
Impressionable, im-pre'shon-a-bl, *a.* Susceptible of impression.
Impressionism, im-pre'shon-izm, *n.* Views or practice of an impressionist.
Impressionist, im-pre'shon-ist, *n.* One who lays stress on impressions; an artist who depicts scenes by their most striking characteristics as they first impress the spectator.
Impressive, im-pres'iv, *a.* Making an impression; solemn; awe-inspiring.

Impressively, im-pres'iv-li, *adv.* In an impressive manner.
Impressment, im-pres'ment, *n.* Act of impressing men into the public service.
Imprimatur, im-pri-mā'tėr, *n.* A license to print a book, &c.; mark of approval in general.
Imprimis, im-pri'mis, *adv.* In the first place.
Imprint, im-print', *vt.* To impress; to stamp; to fix on the mind or memory.—*n.* im'print. The name of the printer or publisher of a book, &c., with place and time of publication.
Imprison, im-pri'zn, *vt.* To put into a prison; to confine; to deprive of liberty.
Imprisonment, im-pri'zn-ment, *n.* Act of imprisoning; state of being imprisoned.
Improbability, im-pro'ba-bil"i-ti, *n.* Quality of being improbable; unlikelihood.
Improbable, im-pro'ba-bl, *a.* Not probable; not likely to be true; unlikely.
Improbably, im-pro'ba-bli, *adv.* In an improbable manner; without probability.
Improbity, im-prō'bi-ti, *n.* Dishonesty.
Impromptu, im-promp'tū, *n.* A saying, poem, &c., made off-hand; an extemporaneous composition.—*a.* Off-hand; extempore.—*adv.* Off-hand.
Improper, im-pro'pėr, *a.* Not proper; unfit; not decent; erroneous; wrong.
Improperly, im-pro'pėr-li, *adv.* In an improper manner; unsuitably; erroneously.
Impropriety, im-prō-prī'e-ti, *n.* Quality of being improper; that which is improper; an unsuitable act, expression, &c.
Improvability, im-pröv'a-bil"i-ti, *n.* State or quality of being improvable.
Improvable, im-pröv'a-bl, *a.* That may be improved; susceptible of improvement.
Improve, im-pröv', *vt.* (improving, improved). To better; to ameliorate; to mend; to rectify; to use to good purpose; to apply to practical purposes.—*vi.* To grow better.
Improvement, im-pröv'ment, *n.* Act of improving; state of being improved; a change for the better; that which improves; a beneficial or valuable addition or alteration.
Improvidence, im-pro'vi-dens, *n.* Want of providence or foresight; wastefulness.
Improvident, im-pro'vi-dent, *a.* Not provident; wanting foresight or forethought; careless.
Improving, im-pröv'ing, *p.a.* Tending to improve; edifying; instructive.
Improvise, im-pro-vīz', *vt.* To form on the spur of the moment; to compose and recite, &c., without previous preparation.
Improvvisatore, im-prov-vis'a-tō-rā, *n.*; pl. **-tori,** -tō-rē. An extempore versifier.
Improvvisatrice, im-prov-vis'a-trē-chā, *n.* A female improvvisatore.
Imprudence, im-prö'dens, *n.* Want of prudence; indiscretion; a rash act.
Imprudent, im-prö'dent, *a.* Not prudent; indiscreet; heedless; rash.
Imprudently, im-prö'dent-li, *adv.* In an imprudent manner; indiscreetly.
Impudence, im'pū-dens, *n.* The quality of being impudent; impudent language or behaviour; effrontery; impertinence.
Impudent, im'pū-dent, *a.* Offensively forward in behaviour; bold-faced; impertinent.
Impudently, im'pū-dent-li, *adv.* In an impudent manner; impertinently.
Impugn, im-pūn', *vt.* To attack by words or arguments; to contradict; to call in question.
Impulse, im'puls, *n.* Force communicated instantaneously; effect of a sudden communication of motion; influence acting on the mind; motive; sudden determination.
Impulsion, im-pul'shon, *n.* Act of impelling; impelling force; impulse.
Impulsive, im-puls'iv, *a.* Having the power of impelling; actuated or governed by impulse.
Impulsively, im-puls'iv-li, *adv.* In an impulsive manner; by impulse.
Impunity, im-pū'ni-ti, *n.* Freedom from punishment or injury, loss, &c.
Impure, im-pūr', *a.* Not pure; mixed with extraneous substance; obscene; unchaste; lewd; defiled by sin or guilt; unholy.
Impurely, im-pūr'li, *adv.* In an impure manner; with impurity.
Impurity, im-pūr'i-ti, *n.* State or quality of being impure; foul matter; obscenity.
Imputable, im-pūt'a-bl, *a.* That may be imputed or charged to a person; chargeable.
Imputation, im-pū-tā'shon, *n.* The act of imputing; attribution; censure; reproach.
Impute, im-pūt', *vt.* (imputing, imputed). To set to the account of; to ascribe.
In, in, *prep.* Within; inside of; surrounded by; indicating presence or situation within limits, whether of place, time, circumstances, &c.—*adv.* In or within some place, state, circumstances, &c.; not out.
Inability, in-a-bil'i-ti, *n.* Want of ability; want of adequate means.
Inaccessible, in-ak-ses'i-bl, *a.* Not accessible; not to be obtained; forbidden access.
Inaccuracy, in-ak'kū-ra-si, *n.* The state of being inaccurate; an inaccurate statement; a mistake in a statement; an error.
Inaccurate, in-ak'kū-rāt, *a.* Not accurate; not exact or correct; erroneous.
Inaccurately, in-ak'kū-rāt-li, *adv.* In an inaccurate manner; incorrectly; erroneously.
Inaction, in-ak'shon, *n.* Want of action; forbearance of labour; idleness; rest.
Inactive, in-ak'tiv, *a.* Not active; not engaged in action; idle; indolent.
Inactivity, in-ak-tiv'i-ti, *n.* State or quality of being inactive.
Inadequacy, in-ad'ē-kwā-si, *n.* Quality of being inadequate; insufficiency.
Inadequate, in-ad'ē-kwāt, *a.* Not equal to the purpose; disproportionate; defective.
Inadequately, in-ad'ē-kwāt-li, *adv.* In an inadequate manner; not sufficiently.
Inadmissibility, in-ad-mis'i-bil"i-ti, *n.* Quality of being inadmissible.
Inadmissible, in-ad-mis'i-bl, *a.* Not admissible; not proper to be admitted, allowed, or received.
Inadvertence, Inadvertency, in-ad-vėrt'ens, in-ad-vėrt'en-si, *n.* Quality of being inadvertent; any oversight or fault which proceeds from negligence or want of attention.
Inadvertent, in-ad-vėrt'ent, *a.* Not paying strict attention; heedless; unwary; negligent.
Inadvertently, in-ad-vėrt'ent-li, *adv.* In an inadvertent manner; from want of attention.
Inalienable, in-āl'yen-a-bl, *a.* Incapable of being alienated or transferred to another.
Inalterable, in-al'tėr-a-bl, *a.* Unalterable.
Inamorata, in-ä'mō-rä"tä, *n.* A female in love; a mistress.

Inamorato, in-ä'mō-rä''tō, *n.* A male lover.
Inane, in-ān', *a.* Empty; void; void of sense or intelligence.—*n.* Infinite void space.
Inanimate, in-an'i-māt, *a.* Not animate; destitute of animation or life; inactive; dull; spiritless.
Inanition, in-a-nis'hon, *n.* Vacuity; exhaustion from want of food.
Inanity, in-an'i-ti, *n.* The quality of being inane; vacuity; mental vacuity; silliness.
Inapplicable, in-ap'pli-ka-bl, *a.* Not applicable; not suitable; inappropriate.
Inapposite, in-ap'pō-zit, *a.* Not apposite; not fit or suitable; not pertinent.
Inappreciable, in-ap-prē'shi-a-bl, *a.* Not appreciable; so small as hardly to be noticed.
Inapproachable, in-ap-prōch'a-bl, *a.* Not approachable; unapproachable.
Inappropriate, in-ap-prō'pri-āt, *a.* Not appropriate; unsuited; not proper.
Inapt, in-apt', *a.* Unapt; unsuitable; unfit.
Inaptitude, in-apt'i-ti-tūd, *n.* Want of aptitude; unsuitableness.
Inarch, in-ärch', *vt.* To graft without separating (for a time) the scion from its parent tree.
Inarticulate, in-är-tik'ū-lāt, *a.* Not articulate; not jointed or articulated; not uttered distinctly.
Inarticulately, in-är-tik'ū-lāt-li, *adv.* Not with distinct syllables; indistinctly.
Inartificial, in-är'ti-fi''shal, *a.* Not artificial; simple; artless.
Inartificially, in-är'ti-fi''shal-li, *adv.* In an inartificial or artless manner.
Inasmuch, in-az-much', *adv.* Seeing; seeing that; this being the fact.
Inattention, in-at-ten'shon, *n.* Want of attention; heedlessness; neglect.
Inattentive, in-at-tent'iv, *a.* Not attentive; regardless; thoughtless.
Inattentively, in-at-tent'iv-li, *adv.* Without attention; heedlessly.
Inaudibility, in-ą'di-bil''i-ti, *n.* State or quality of being inaudible.
Inaudible, in-ą'di-bl, *a.* Not audible; that cannot be heard.
Inaudibly, in-ą'di-bli, *adv.* In a manner not to be heard.
Inaugural, in-ą'gū-ral, *a.* Pertaining to inauguration.
Inaugurate, in-ą'gū-rāt, *vt.* To induct into an office with suitable ceremonies; to perform initiatory ceremonies in connection with.
Inauguration, in-ą'gū-rā''shon, *n.* Act of inaugurating; ceremonies connected with such an act.
Inauspicious, in-ą-spi'shus, *a.* Not auspicious; ill-omened; unfavourable.
Inauthoritative, in-ą-thor'i-tā-tiv, *a.* Having no authority.
Inboard, in'bōrd, *a.* Within a ship or other vessel.—*adv.* On board of a vessel.
Inborn, in'born, *a.* Born in; innate; implanted by nature; natural; inherent.
Inbreathe, in-brēᴛʜ', *vt.* To breathe in, or infuse by breathing.
Inbred, in'bred, *a.* Bred within; innate.
Inca, in'ka, *n.* A king or prince of Peru before its conquest by the Spaniards.
Incage, in-kāj', *vt.* To encage.
Incalculable, in-kal'kū-la-bl, *a.* Not calculable; very great.
Incalculably, in-kal'kū-la-bli, *adv.* In a degree beyond calculation.
Incandescence, in-kan-des'ens, *n.* Condition of being incandescent.
Incandescent, in-kan-des'ent, *a.* White or glowing with heat.—**Incandescent light,** a form of gas light; a form of electric light given forth from a filament of carbon inclosed in an airless glass globe.
Incantation, in-kan-tā'shon, *n.* The act of using certain words and ceremonies to raise spirits, &c.; the form of words so used; a magical charm or ceremony.
Incapability, in-kā'pa-bil''i-ti, *n.* Quality of being incapable.
Incapable, in-kā'pa-bl, *a.* Not capable; possessing inadequate power or capacity; not susceptible; incompetent; unqualified or disqualified.—*n.* One physically or mentally weak.
Incapably, in-kā'pa-bli, *adv.* In an incapable manner.
Incapacitate, in-ka-pa'si-tāt, *vt.* To render incapable; to deprive of competent power or ability; to disqualify.
Incapacity, in-ka-pa'si-ti, *n.* Want of capacity; incompetency; disqualification.
Incarcerate, in-kär'sė-rāt, *vt.* To imprison; to shut up or inclose.
Incarceration, in-kär'sė-rā''shon, *n.* Act of incarcerating; imprisonment.
Incarnadine, in-kär'na-dīn, *vt.* To tinge with the colour of flesh; to dye red.
Incarnate, in-kär'nāt, *vt.* To clothe with flesh; to embody in flesh.—*a.* Invested with flesh; embodied in flesh.
Incarnation, in-kär-nā'shon, *n.* Act of taking on a human body and the nature of man; the state of being incarnated; a vivid exemplification in person or act.
Incase, in-kās', *vt.* To inclose in a case.
Incaution, in-ką'shon, *n.* Want of caution.
Incautious, in-ką'shus, *a.* Not cautious; unwary; heedless; imprudent.
Incautiously, in-ką'shus-li, *adv.* In an incautious manner; unwarily; heedlessly.
Incendiarism, in-sen'di-a-rizm, *n.* Act or practice of maliciously setting fire to buildings.
Incendiary, in-sen'di-a-ri, *n.* A person who maliciously sets fire to property; one guilty of arson; one who inflames factions; a firebrand; small bomb dropped from an aeroplane and intended to cause a fire.—*a.* Relating to arson; tending to excite sedition or quarrels.
Incense, in'sens, *n.* Aromatic substance burned in religious rites; odours of spices and gums, burned in religious rites; flattery or agreeable homage.—*vt.* (incensing, incensed). To perfume with incense.
Incense, in-sens', *vt.* (incensing, incensed). To inflame to violent anger; to exasperate.
Incentive, in-sen'tiv, *a.* Inciting; encouraging,—*n.* That which incites; that which prompts to good or ill; motive; spur.
Inception, in-sep'shon, *n.* The act of beginning; first or initial stage.
Inceptive, in-sep'tiv, *a.* Pertaining to inception; beginning; applied to a verb which expresses the beginning of an action.—*n.* An inceptive verb.
Inceptor, in-sep'tėr, *n.* A beginner; one who is on the point of taking the degree of M.A. at an English university.

Incertitude, in-sėr'ti-tūd, *n.* Uncertainty.
Incessant, in-ses'ant, *a.* Unceasing; unintermitted; continual; constant.
Incessantly, in-ses'ant-li, *adv.* Without ceasing; continually.
Incest, in'sest, *n.* Sexual commerce between near blood relations.
Incestuous, in-sest'ū-us, *a.* Guilty of incest; involving the crime of incest.
Inch, insh, *n.* The twelfth part of a foot in length; a small quantity or degree.—*vt.* To drive or force by inches.
Inch-meal, insh'mēl, *adv.* By inches; by little and little.
Inchoate, in'kō-āt, *a.* Recently begun; incipient; rudimentary.
Inchoative, in'kō-āt-iv or in-kō'at-iv, *a.* Expressing or indicating beginning; inceptive.
Incidence, in'si-dens, *n.* A falling or occurring; manner or direction of falling.
Incident, in'si-dent, *a.* Falling or striking; happening; liable to happen; appertaining to or following another thing.—*n.* That which happens; event; an appertaining fact.
Incidental, in-si-dent'al, *a.* Casual; occasional; appertaining and subsidiary.
Incidentally, in-si-dent'al-li, *adv.* Casually; beside the main design.
Incinerate, in-sin'ė-rāt, *vt.* To burn to ashes.
Incipient, in-si'pi-ent, *a.* Beginning.
Incise, in-sīz', *vt.* (incising, incised). To cut in or into; to carve; to engrave.
Incision, in-si'zhon, *n.* Act of cutting into; cut; gash; sharpness; trenchancy.
Incisive, in-sī'siv, *a.* Having the quality of cutting into anything; sharply and clearly expressive; trenchant.
Incisor, in-sīz'ėr, *n.* A front tooth which cuts or separates.
Incite, in-sīt', *vt.* (inciting, incited). To move to action by impulse or influence; to instigate; to encourage.
Incitement, in-sīt'ment, *n.* Act of inciting; that which incites; motive; impulse.
Incivil, in-si'vil, *a.* Not civil; impolite.
Incivility, in-si-vil'i-ti, *n.* Want of civility; rudeness; rude act.
Inclemency, in-kle'men-si, *n.* Want of clemency; harshness; severity of weather.
Inclement, in-kle'ment, *a.* Not clement; harsh; stormy; rigorously cold.
Inclemently, in-kle'ment-li, *adv.* In an inclement manner.
Inclination, in-klin-ā'shon, *n.* The act of inclining; deviation from a normal direction; a leaning of the mind or will; tendency; bent; bias; predilection; liking.
Incline, in-klīn', *vi.* (inclining, inclined). To deviate from a direction regarded as normal; to slope; to be disposed; to have some wish or desire.—*vt.* To cause to lean or bend towards or away from; to give a leaning to; to dispose.—*n.* An ascent or descent; a slope.
Inclined, in-klīnd', *p.a.* Having a leaning or inclination; disposed.
Inclose, in-klōz', *vt.* (inclosing, inclosed). To shut up or confine on all sides; to environ; to cover with a wrapper or envelope.
Inclosure, in-klō'zhūr, *n.* Act of inclosing; what is inclosed; a space inclosed or fenced; something inclosed with a letter, &c.
Include, in-klöd', *vt.* (including, included). To hold or contain; to comprise; to comprehend.
Inclusion, in-klö'zhon, *n.* Act of including.
Inclusive, in-klö'siv, *a.* Inclosing; comprehended in the number or sum; comprehending the stated limit.
Inclusively, in-klö'siv-li, *adv.* In an inclusive manner; so as to include something mentioned.
Incog, in-kog', *adv.* or *pred.a.* An abbreviation of *incognito.*
Incognito, in-kog'ni-tō, *pred.a.* or *adv.* In disguise.—*n.* (fem. being **Incognita**). One passing under an assumed name; assumption of a feigned character.
Incognizable, in-kog'ni-za-bl or in-kon'i-za-bl, *a.* Not cognizable.
Incognizance, in-kog'ni-zans or in-kon'i-zans, *n.* Failure to recognize or apprehend.
Incognizant, in-kog'ni-zant or in-kon'i-zant, *a.* Not cognizant.
Incoherence, Incoherency, in-kō-hēr'ens, in-kō-hēr'en-si, *n.* Quality of being incoherent; want of connection or agreement.
Incoherent, in-kō-hēr'ent, *a.* Not coherent; wanting rational connection, as ideas, language, &c.; rambling and unintelligible.
Incoherently, in-kō-hēr'ent-li, *adv.* In an incoherent manner.
Incombustibility, in-kom-bust'i-bil"i-ti, *n.* Quality of being incombustible.
Incombustible, in-kom-bust'i-bl, *a.* Not combustible; that cannot be burned.
Income, in'kum, *n.* Receipts or emoluments regularly coming in from property or employment; annual receipts; revenue.
Income-tax, in'kum-taks, *n.* A tax levied on incomes according to their amount.
Incoming, in'kum-ing, *p.a.* Coming in.
Incommensurability, in-kom-men'sūr-a-bil"-i-ti, *n.* Quality or state of being incommensurable.
Incommensurable, in-kom-men'sūr-a-bl, *a.* Not commensurable; having no common measure.
Incommensurably, in-kom-men'sūr-a-bli, *adv.* So as not to admit of a common measure.
Incommensurate, in-kom-men'sūr-āt, *a.* Not commensurate; incommensurable; inadequate; insufficient.
Incommode, in-kom-mōd', *vt.* (incommoding, incommoded). To give trouble to; to inconvenience; to embarrass.
Incommodious, in-kom-mō'di-us, *a.* Not commodious; inconvenient.
Incommunicable, in-kom-mū'ni-ka-bl, *a.* Not communicable; not to be communicated.
Incommunicative, in-kom-mū'ni-kāt-ive, *a.* Not communicative; not inclined to impart information.
Incomparable, in-kom'pa-ra-bl, *a.* Not comparable; that admits of no comparison with others; matchless.
Incomparably, in-kom'pa-ra-bli, *adv.* Beyond comparison.
Incompatibility, in-kom-pat'i-bil"i-ti, *n.* State or quality of being incompatible; inconsistency; disposition or temper entirely out of harmony.
Incompatible, in-kom-pat'i-bl, *a.* Not compatible; inconsistent; irreconcilably different; that cannot be made to accord.
Incompetence, Incompetency, in-kom'pē-tens, in-kom'pē-ten-si, *n.* State or quality of

being incompetent; want of suitable faculties, adequate means, or proper qualifications.

Incompetent, in-kom'pē-tent, *a.* Not competent; incapable; wanting legal qualifications; not admissible.

Incomplete, in-kom-plēt', *a.* Not complete; imperfect; defective.

Incompletely, in-kom-plēt'li, *adv.* Imperfectly.

Incomprehensibility, in-kom'prē-hens'i-bil"i-ti, *n.* Quality of being incomprehensible.

Incomprehensible, in-kom'prē-hens"i-bl, *a.* Not comprehensible; beyond the reach of the human intellect.

Incompressibility, in-kom-pres'i-bil"i-ti, *n.* State or quality of being incompressible.

Incompressible, in-kom-pres'i-bl, *a.* Not compressible; resisting compression.

Inconceivable, in-kon-sēv'a-bl, *a.* Incapable of being conceived or thought of.

Inconceivably, in-kon-sēv'a-bli, *adv.* In a manner beyond conception.

Inconclusive, in-kon-klös'iv, *a.* Not conclusive; not settling a point in debate.

Inconclusively, in-kon-klös'iv-li, *adv.* In an inconclusive manner.

Incondensable, in-kon-dens'a-bl, *a.* Not condensable; incapable of being condensed.

Incondite, in-kon'dit, *a.* Rude; unpolished; said of literary compositions.

Incongruent, in-kong'grụ-ent, *a.* Incongruous.

Incongruity, in-kong-grụ'i-ti, *n.* Want of congruity; inconsistency; absurdity.

Incongruous, in-kong'grụ-us, *a.* Not congruous; not such as to mingle well or unite in harmony; inconsistent.

Inconsequence, in-kon'sē-kwens, *n.* The condition or quality of being inconsequent; want of logical consequence.

Inconsequent, in-kon'sē-kwent, *a.* Not consequent; not having due relevance; not following from the logical premises.

Inconsequential, in-kon'sē-kwen"shal, *a.* Not consequential; not of importance.

Inconsiderable, in-kon-sid'ėr-a-bl, *a.* Not considerable; unimportant; insignificant.

Inconsiderably, in-kon-sid'ėr-a-bli, *adv.* In an inconsiderable degree; very little.

Inconsiderate, in-kon-sid'ėr-āt, *a.* Not considerate; hasty; thoughtless; injudicious.

Inconsiderately, in-kon-sid'ėr-āt-li, *adv.* Heedlessly; imprudently.

Inconsistence, Inconsistency, in-kon-sist'-ens, in-kon-sist'en-si, *n.* The condition or quality of being inconsistent; opposition or disagreement of particulars; self-contradiction; incongruity; discrepancy.

Inconsistent, in-kon-sist'ent, *a.* Not consistent; incompatible; discrepant; not exhibiting consistent sentiments or conduct.

Inconsistently, in-kon-sist'ent-li, *adv.* Incongruously; with self-contradiction.

Inconsolable, in-kon-sōl'a-bl, *a.* Not to be consoled; grieved beyond consolation.

Inconspicuous, in-kon-spik'ū-us, *a.* Not conspicuous; unobtrusive.

Inconstancy, in-kon'stan-si, *n.* The quality of being inconstant; instability of temper or affection; fickleness.

Inconstant, in-kon'stant, *a.* Not constant; subject to change of opinion or purpose; not firm in resolution; fickle.

Inconstantly, in-kon'stant-li, *adv.* In an inconstant manner.

Incontestable, in-kon-test'a-bl, *a.* Not contestable; not to be disputed; unquestionable.

Incontestably, in-kon-test'a-bli, *adv.* In a manner to preclude debate.

Incontinence, Incontinency, in-kon'ti-nens, in-kon'ti-nen-si, *n.* State or quality of being incontinent; indulgence of lust; inability of organs to restrain discharges.

Incontinent, in-kon'ti-nent, *a.* Not continent; not restraining the passions or appetites; unchaste; unable to restrain discharges.

Incontinently, in-kon'ti-nent-li, *adv.* In an incontinent manner; unchastely; at once.

Incontrovertible, in-kon'trō-vėrt"i-bl, *a.* Not controvertible; too clear to admit of dispute.

Inconvenience, in-kon-vē'ni-ens, *n.* The quality of being inconvenient; annoyance; molestation; trouble; disadvantage.—*vt.* To put to inconvenience; to trouble.

Inconvenient, in-kon-vē'ni-ent, *a.* Not convenient; wanting due facilities; causing embarrassment; inopportune.

Inconveniently, in-kon-vē'ni-ent-li, *adv.* Unsuitably; unseasonably.

Inconvertible, in-kon-vėrt'i-bl, *a.* Not convertible; that cannot be changed into or exchanged for something else.

Incorporate, in-kor'pō-rāt, *vt.* To form into one body; to unite; to blend; to associate with another whole, as with a government; to form into a legal body or corporation.—*vi.* To unite; to grow into or coalesce.—*a.* Incorporated; united in one body.

Incorporation, in-kor'pō-rā"shon, *n.* Act of incorporating; state of being incorporated; union of different things; a body of individuals authorized to act as a single person.

Incorporeal, in-kor-pō'rē-al, *a.* Not corporeal; not consisting of matter; spiritual.

Incorrect, in-ko-rekt', *a.* Not correct; inaccurate; erroneous; faulty; untrue.

Incorrectly, in-ko-rekt'li, *adv.* Not in accordance with fact; inaccurately.

Incorrigible, in-ko'ri-ji-bl, *a.* That cannot be corrected; bad beyond correction or reform.

Incorrigibly, in-ko'ri-ji-bli, *adv.* In an incorrigible manner.

Incorrodible, in-ko-rōd'i-bl, *a.* That cannot be corroded.

Incorrupt, in-ko-rupt', *a.* Not corrupt; not marred by corruption or decay; pure; untainted; above the power of bribes.

Incorruptibility, in-ko-rupt'i-bil"i-ti, *n.* Quality of being incorruptible.

Incorruptible, in-ko-rupt'i-bl, *a.* Not corruptible; that cannot corrupt or decay; inflexibly just and upright.

Incorruption, in-ko-rup'shon, *n.* Exemption from corruption or decay.

Incrassate, in-kras'āt, *vt.* To thicken; to inspissate.—*vi.* To become thick or thicker.

Increase, in-krēs', *vi.* (increasing, increased). To become greater; to augment; to advance in any quality, good or bad; to multiply by the production of young.—*vt.* To make greater or larger; to add to.—*n.* in'krēs. A growing larger in size, quantity, &c.; augmentation; addition; increment; profit; interest; offspring.

Increasingly, in-krēs'ing-li, *adv.* In the way of increasing; by continual increase.
Incredibility, in-kred'i-bil"i-ti, *n.* Quality of being incredible; that which is incredible.
Incredible, in-kred'i-bl, *a.* Not credible; too improbable to admit of belief.
Incredibly, in-kred'i-bli, *adv.* In a manner to preclude belief.
Incredulity, in-krē-dū'li-ti, *n.* Quality of being incredulous; scepticism.
Incredulous, in-kred'ū-lus, *a.* Not credulous; refusing or withholding belief.
Increment, in'krē-ment, *n.* Act or process of increasing; increase; increase in the value of real property from adventitious causes.
Incriminate, in-krim'in-āt, *vt.* To bring an accusation against; to charge with a crime or fault.
Incrust, in-krust', *vt.* To cover with a crust or hard coat; to form a crust on.
Incrustation, in-krust-ā'shon, *n.* Act of incrusting; a crust or hard coat on the surface of a body; a covering or inlaying of marble or mosaic, &c.
Incubate, in'kū-bāt, *vi.* To brood or sit on eggs for hatching.
Incubation, in-kū-bā'shon, *n.* The act of incubating; the maturation of a contagious poison in the animal system.
Incubator, in'kū-bāt-ėr, *n.* One who or that which incubates; an apparatus for hatching eggs by artificial heat.
Incubus, in'kū-bus, *n.*; pl. **-buses** or **-bi.** A name of nightmare; something that weighs heavily on a person; burden or incumbrance; dead weight.
Inculcate, in-kul'kāt, *vt.* To press or urge forcibly and repeatedly; to teach.
Inculcation, in-kul-kā'shon, *n.* The act of inculcating.
Inculpate, in-kul'pāt, *vt.* To show to be in fault; to impute guilt to; to incriminate.
Incumbency, in-kum'ben-si, *n.* State of being incumbent; state of holding a benefice or office.
Incumbent, in-kum'bent, *a.* Lying on; resting on a person, as duty or obligation.—*n.* One in possession of an ecclesiastical benefice or other office.
Incumbrance, in-kum'brans, *n.* *See* EN-.
Incunable, Incunabulum, in-kū'na-bl, in-kū-nab'ū-lum, *n.*; pl. **-ula.** A book printed before the year 1500.
Incur, in-kėr', *vt.* (incurring, incurred). To expose oneself to; to become liable to; to bring on or contract, as expense.
Incurable, in-kūr'a-bl, *a.* That cannot be cured; not admitting remedy; irremediable. —*n.* A person diseased beyond cure.
Incurious, in-kū'ri-us, *a.* Not curious.
Incursion, in-kėr'shon, *n.* An entering into a territory with hostile intention; inroad.
Incursive, in-kėr'siv, *a.* Of the nature of an incursion; hostile; making an incursion.
Incurvate, Incurve, in-kėrv'āt, in-kėrv', *vt.* To bend or curve.
Incurvate, in-kėrv'āt, *a.* Curved inward or upward.
Incurvature, in-kėrv'a-tūr, *n.* An incurving or bending.
Incuse, in-kūz', *vt.* To impress by stamping.—*a.* Impressed by stamping.
Indebted, in-det'ed, *a.* Being in debt; obliged by something received.
Indebtedness, in-det'ed-nes, *n.* State of being indebted; amount of debt owed.
Indecency, in-dē'sen-si, *n.* The quality of being indecent; what is indecent in language, actions, &c.; indecorum; immodesty.
Indecent, in-dē'sent, *a.* Not decent; unseemly; immodest; obscene; filthy.
Indecently, in-dē'sent-li, *adv.* In an indecent manner.
Indecipherable, in-dē-sī'fėr-a-bl, *a.* Incapable of being deciphered.
Indecision, in-dē-si'zhon, *n.* Want of decision; irresolution; hesitation.
Indecisive, in-dē-sīs'iv, *a.* Not decisive; wavering; vacillating.
Indecisively, in-dē-sīs'iv-li, *adv.* In an indecisive manner; without decision.
Indeclinable, in-dē-klīn'a-bl, *a.* Not declinable; not varied by terminations of case, &c.
Indecomposable, in-dē'kom-pōz"a-bl, *a.* Incapable of decomposition.
Indecorous, in-dē-kō'rus or in-de'kō-rus, *a.* Not decorous; unseemly; indecent; unbecoming.
Indecorum, in-dē-kō'rum, *n.* Want of decorum; unseemly conduct.
Indeed, in-dēd', *adv.* In reality; in fact; really; truly.
Indefatigable, in-dē-fat'ig-a-bl, *a.* That cannot be wearied; untiring; unremitting.
Indefeasibility, in-dē-fēz'i-bil"i-ti, *n.* Quality of being indefeasible.
Indefeasible, in-dē-fēz'i-bl, *a.* Not defeasible; not to be made void, as a right, &c., claim, or title.
Indefensible, in-dē-fens'i-bl, *a.* Not defensible; untenable.
Indefinable, in-dē-fīn'a-bl, *a.* Incapable of being defined; not to be clearly explained.
Indefinite, in-def'i-nit, *a.* Not definite; not limited; not precise; uncertain; vague.
Indefinitely, in-def'i-nit-li, *adv.* In an indefinite manner; not precisely.
Indelible, in-de'li-bl, *a.* Not to be deleted or blotted out; that cannot be obliterated.
Indelibly, in-de'li-bli, *adv.* In an indelible manner; too deeply imprinted to be effaced.
Indelicacy, in-de'li-ka-si, *n.* Condition or quality of being indelicate.
Indelicate, in-de'li-kāt, *a.* Wanting delicacy; offensive to modesty or nice sense of propriety; somewhat immodest.
Indemnification, in-dem'ni-fi-kā"shon, *n.* Act of indemnifying; reparation; reimbursement of loss or damage.
Indemnify, in-dem'ni-fī, *vt.* To make safe from loss or harm; to reimburse or compensate.
Indemnity, in-dem'ni-ti, *n.* Security given against loss, damage, or punishment; compensation for loss or injury sustained.
Indent, in-dent', *vt.* To notch; to cut into points or inequalities; to bind by indenture. —*n.* A cut or notch; an indentation.
Indentation, in-dent-ā'shon, *n.* Act of indenting; a cut in the margin of something; an angular depression in any border.
Indented, in-dent'ed, *p.a.* Notched; bound by indenture.
Indenture, in-den'tūr, *n.* That which is indented; a deed under seal between two or more parties, each having a duplicate.—*vt.* To indent; to bind by indenture.

Independence, in-dē-pend'ens, *n.* State of being independent; complete exemption from control; self-reliance; political freedom.

Independent, in-dē-pend'ent, *a.* Not dependent; not subject to control; moderately wealthy; not subject to bias or influence; free; bold; separate from; irrespective.—*n.* One who is independent; (with *cap.*) one who maintains that every congregation is an independent church.

Independently, in-dē-pend'ent-li, *adv.* In an independent manner; leaving out of consideration; without bias or influence.

Indescribable, in-dē-skrib'a-bl, *a.* That cannot be described.

Indestructible, in-dē-strukt'i-bl, *a.* That cannot be destroyed; imperishable.

Indeterminable, in-dē-tėr'min-a-bl, *a.* That cannot be determined, ascertained, or fixed.

Indeterminate, in-dē-tėr'min-āt, *a.* Not determinate; not settled or fixed; uncertain.

Indetermination, in-dē-tėr'min-ā"shon, *n.* Want of determination; vacillation.

Index, in'deks, *n.*; pl. **Indexes** or **Indices,** in'dek-sez, in'di-sēz. Something that points out; the hand ☞ used by printers, &c.; a table of contents; list of books disapproved of by R. Catholic authorities; the forefinger; the figure denoting to what power any mathematical quantity is involved.—*vt.* To provide with an index; to place in an index.

Indexer, in'deks-ėr, *n.* One who makes an index.

Indiaman, in'di-a-man, *n.* A large ship employed in the India trade.

Indian, in'di-an, *a.* Pertaining to India, or to the Indies, East or West; pertaining to the aborigines of America; made of maize, or Indian corn.—*n.* A native of the Indies; an aboriginal native of America.

India-paper, in'di-a-pā-pėr, *n.* A delicate paper used for first proofs of engravings.

India-rubber, in'di-a-rub-ėr, *n.* Caoutchouc, used to rub out pencil marks, &c.

Indicate, in'di-kāt, *vt.* To point out; to show; to intimate; to suggest.

Indication, in-di-kā'shon, *n.* Act of indicating; what points out; mark; token; sign.

Indicative, in-dik'a-tiv, *a.* That serves to point out; serving as an indication; designating a mood of the verb that declares directly or asks questions.—*n.* The indicative mood.

Indicator, in'di-kāt-ėr, *n.* One who or that which indicates; a recording instrument of various kinds.

Indicatory, in'di-ka-to-ri, *a.* Serving to indicate or make known.

Indict, in-dīt', *vt.* To charge with a crime or misdemeanour in due form of law.

Indictable, in-dīt'a-bl, *a.* That may be indicted; subject to indictment.

Indiction, in-dik'shon, *n.* A cycle of fifteen fiscal or financial years.

Indictment, in-dīt'ment, *n.* The act of indicting; a formal charge; a written accusation of a crime or a misdemeanour.

Indifference, in-dif'ėr-ens, *n.* The state or quality of being indifferent; impartiality; unconcern; apathy; mediocrity.

Indifferent, in-dif'ėr-ent, *a.* Impartial; unconcerned; apathetic; immaterial or of little moment; middling; tolerable.

Indifferentism, in-dif'ėr-ent-izm, *n.* Systematic indifference; want of zeal.

Indifferently, in-dif'ėr-ent-li, *adv.* Impartially; without concern; tolerably.

Indigence, in'di-jens, *n.* State of being indigent; want; penury.

Indigene, in'di-jēn, *n.* A native.

Indigenous, in-di'jen-us, *a.* Native, as persons; not foreign or exotic, as plants.

Indigent, in'di-jent, *a.* Destitute of means of comfortable subsistence; needy.

Indigested, in-di-jest'ed, *a.* Not digested; not reduced to due form; crude.

Indigestible, in-di-jest'i-bl, *a.* Not digestible; digested with difficulty.

Indigestion, in-di-jest'yon, *n.* Incapability of or difficulty in digesting; dyspepsia.

Indignant, in-dig'nant, *a.* Affected with indignation; feeling the mingled emotions of wrath and scorn or contempt.

Indignantly, in-dig'nant-li, *adv.* In an indignant manner; without indignation.

Indignation, in-dig-nā'shon, *n.* A feeling of displeasure at what is unworthy or base; anger, mingled with contempt, disgust, or abhorrence; violent displeasure.

Indignity, in-dig'ni-ti, *n.* An insult; an affront; an outrage.

Indigo, in'di-go, *n.* A blue vegetable dye, from India and other places; the leguminous plant that produces the dye.

Indirect, in-di-rekt', *a.* Not direct; circuitous; not tending directly to a purpose or end; not straightforward; not resulting directly.

Indirectly, in-di-rekt'li, *adv.* In an indirect manner; not by direct means.

Indiscreet, in-dis-krēt', *a.* Not discreet; injudicious; inconsiderate.

Indiscreetly, in-dis-krēt'il, *adv.* In an indiscreet manner.

Indiscretion, in-dis-kre'shon, *n.* The condition or quality of being indiscreet; imprudence; an indiscreet act.

Indiscriminate, in-dis-krim'in-āt, *a.* Without discrimination; confused.

Indispensable, in-dis-pens'a-bl, *a.* Not to be dispensed with; necessary or requisite.

Indispensably, in-dis-pens'a-bli, *adv.* In an indispensable manner; unavoidably.

Indispose, in-dis-pōz', *vt.* To disincline; to disqualify; to affect with indisposition.

Indisposed, in-dis-pōzd', *p.a.* Not disposed; disinclined; averse; somewhat ill.

Indisposition, in-dis'pō-zi"shon, *n.* The state of being indisposed; slight ailment.

Indisputable, in-dis'pūt-a-bl, *a.* Not to be disputed; unquestionable; certain.

Indissoluble, in-dis'sō-lū-bl, *a.* Not capable of being dissolved; perpetually binding or obligatory; not to be broken.

Indissolvable, in-diz-zolv'a-bl, *a.* That cannot be dissolved; indissoluble.

Indistinct, in-dis-tingkt', *a.* Not distinct; faint; confused; imperfect or dim.

Indistinctly, in-dis-tingkt'li, *adv.* In an indistinct manner; dimly or obscurely.

Indistinguishable, in-dis-ting'gwish-a-bl, *a.* Incapable of being distinguished.

Indite, in-dīt', *vt.* and *i.* (inditing, indited). To compose or write; to direct or dictate.

Inditement, in-dīt'ment, *n.* Act of inditing.

Inditer, in-dīt'ėr, *n.* One who indites.

Indium, in'di-um, *n.* A soft lead-coloured metallic element.

Individual, in-di-vid'ū-al, *a.* Subsisting as

one indivisible entity; pertaining to one only; peculiar to a single person or thing.—*n.* A being or thing forming one of its kind; a person.
Individualism, in-di-vid'ū-al-izm, *n.* The quality of being individual; self-interest; a system or condition in which each individual works for his own ends.
Individuality, in-di-vid'ū-al''i-ti, *n.* Quality or condition of being individual; separate existence; the sum of the traits peculiar to an individual.
Individualize, in-di-vid'ū-al-īz, *vt.* To single out; to distinguish by distinctive characters.
Individually, in-di-vid'ū-al-li, *adv.* In an individual manner; separately.
Individuate, in-di-vid'ū-āt, *vt.* To give the character of individuality to; to individualize; —*vi.* To become individual.
Indivisibility, in-di-viz'i-bil''i-ti, *n.* State or quality of being indivisible.
Indivisible, in-di-viz'i-bl, *a.* Not divisible; not separable into parts.—*n.* An elementary part or particle.
Indocile, in-dō'sīl or in-dos'il, *a.* Not docile or teachable; intractable.
Indoctrinate, in-dok'trin-āt, *vt.* To imbue with any doctrine; to teach; to instruct.
Indo-European, Indo-Germanic, in'dō-ū-rō-pē''an, in'dō-jėr-man''ik, *a.* and *n.* Same as *Aryan.*
Indolence, in'dō-lens, *n.* Habitual love of ease; laziness; idleness.
Indolent, in'dō-lent, *a.* Habitually idle or lazy; slothful; idle; causing little or no pain.
Indomitable, in-dom'it-a-bl, *a.* Not to be tamed or subdued; irrepressible.
Indoor, in'dōr, *a.* Being within doors; being within the house.—**Indoors,** in'dōrz, *adv.* Within doors; inside a house.
Indorse, &c. *See* ENDORSE, &c.
Indubitable, in-dū'bit-a-bl, *a.* Not to be doubted; too plain to admit of doubt; evident.
Induce, in-dūs', *vt.* (inducing, induced). To lead by persuasion or argument; to prevail on; to actuate; to produce or cause.
Inducement, in-dūs'ment, *n.* Act of inducing; that which induces; motive; incentive.
Inducible, in-dūs'i-bl, *a.* That may be inferred by induction.
Induct, in-dukt', *vt.* To lead or bring into; to put in possession of an ecclesiastical living or office, with customary ceremonies.
Inductile, in-duk'tīl, *a.* Not ductile.
Induction, in-duk'shon, *n.* The act of inducting; introduction of a clergyman into a benefice, &c.; a prologue or prelude; method of reasoning from particulars to generals; the conclusion thus arrived at; process by which one body, having electrical or magnetic properties, causes like properties in another body without direct contact.
Inductive, in-dukt'iv, *a.* Relating to induction; proceeding by induction; employed in drawing conclusions by induction.
Inductively, in-dukt'iv-li, *adv.* In an inductive manner; by induction.
Indue, in-dū', *vt.* (induing, indued). To put on; to invest; to supply with.
Indulge, in-dulj', *vt.* (indulging, indulged). To give free course to; to gratify by compliance; to humour to excess.—*vi.* To indulge oneself; to practise indulgence.
Indulgence, in-dulj'ens, *n.* The act or practice of indulging; a favour; intemperance; gratification of desire; tolerance; remission of the penance attached to certain sins.
Indulgent, in-dulj'ent, *a.* Prone to indulge; disposed to leniency or forbearance.
Indulgently, in-dulj'ent-li, *adv.* In an indulgent manner.
Indurate, in'dū-rāt, *vi.* To grow hard.—*vt.* To make hard; to deprive of sensibility.
Induration, in-dū-rā'shon, *n.* Act of hardening; process of growing hard; obduracy.
Industrial, in-dus'tri-al, *a.* Pertaining to industry, or to the products of industry, art, or manufacture.
Industrious, in-dus'tri-us, *a.* Given to or characterized by industry; diligent; active.
Industriously, in-dus'tri-us-li, *adv.* In an industrious manner; diligently.
Industry, in'dus-tri, *n.* Habitual diligence; steady attention to business; the industrial arts generally, or any one of them; manufacture; trade.
Indwell, in'dwel, *vi.* To dwell or exist inwardly or within some place.
Inebriant, in-ē'bri-ant, *a.* Intoxicating.—*n.* Anything that intoxicates.
Inebriate, in-ē'bri-āt, *vt.* To make drunk; to intoxicate.—*n.* An habitual drunkard.
Inebriation, in'ē-bri-ā''shon, *n.* Act of inebriating; state of being inebriated.
Inebriety, in-ē-brī'e-ti, *n.* Drunkenness.
Inedited, in-ed'it-ed, *a.* Not edited; unpublished.
Ineffable, in-ef'fa-bl, *a.* Incapable of being expressed in words; indescribable.
Ineffably, in-ef'fa-bli, *adv.* In an ineffable manner; unutterably; unspeakably.
Ineffaceable, in-ef-fās'a-bl, *a.* Incapable of being effaced.
Ineffective, in-ef-fekt'iv, *a.* Not effective; inefficient; useless; impotent.
Ineffectual, in-ef-fek'tū-al, *a.* Not effectual; inefficient; impotent; fruitless.
Inefficacious, in-ef'fi-kā''shus, *a.* Not producing the effect desired.
Inefficacy, in-ef'fi-ka-si, *n.* Want of efficacy; failure of effect.
Inefficiency, in-ef-fi'shen-si, *n.* Condition or quality of being inefficient; inefficacy.
Inefficient, in-ef-fi'shent, *a.* Not efficient; inefficacious; effecting nothing.
Inelastic, in-ē-las'tik, *a.* Not elastic.
Inelasticity, in-ē'las-tis''i-ti, *n.* Absence of elasticity; quality of being inelastic.
Inelegance, Inelegancy, in-el'ē-gans, in-el'ē-gan-si, *n.* Condition or quality of being inelegant; inelegant point or feature.
Inelegant, in-el'ē-gant, *a.* Not elegant; wanting elegance, beauty, polish, or refinement.
Ineligibility, in-el'i-ji-bil''i-ti, *n.* State or quality of being ineligible.
Ineligible, in-el'i-ji-bl, *a.* Not capable of being elected; not worthy to be chosen.
Ineloquent, in-el'ō-kwent, *a.* Not eloquent.
Inept, in-ept', *a.* Unsuitable; improper; foolish; silly; nonsensical.
Ineptitude, in-ept'i-tūd, *n.* Condition or quality of being inept; unfitness; silliness.
Inequable, in-ē'kwa-bl, *a.* Not equable.
Inequality, in-ē-kwol'i-ti, *n.* Condition of being unequal; want of equality; an elevation or depression in a surface; diversity.

Inequitable, in-ek'wit-a-bl, *a.* Not equitable.
Ineradicable, in-ē-rad'i-ka-bl, *a.* Incapable of being eradicated.
Inert, in-ėrt', *a.* Destitute of the power of moving itself, or of active resistance to motion impressed; lifeless; sluggish; inactive.
Inertia, in-ėr'shi-a, *n.* Passiveness; inactivity; the property of matter by which it tends to retain its state of rest or of uniform rectilinear motion.
Inertly, in-ėrt'li, *adv.* In an inert manner; sluggishly.
Inessential, in-es-sen'shal, *a.* Not essential.
Inestimable, in-es'tim-a-bl, *a.* That cannot be estimated; invaluable; priceless.
Inestimably, in-es'tim-a-bli, *adv.* In a manner not to be estimated.
Inevitable, in-ev'it-a-bl, *a.* Not to be avoided; unavoidable; certain to befall.
Inevitably, in-ev'it-a-bli, *adv.* Unavoidably.
Inexact, in-egz-akt', *a.* Not exact; not precisely correct or true.
Inexcusable, in-eks-kūz'a-bl, *a.* Not to be excused; unjustifiable; indefensible.
Inexcusably, in-eks-kūz'a-bli, *adv.* In an inexcusable manner; beyond excuse.
Inexhaustible, in-egz-ạst'i-bl, *a.* Incapable of being exhausted; unfailing.
Inexorable, in-eks'ōr-a-bl, *a.* Not to be persuaded by entreaty or prayer; unbending; unrelenting; implacable.
Inexorably, in-eks'ōr-a-bli, *adv.* In an inexorable manner.
Inexpedience, Inexpediency, in-eks-pē'di-ens, in-eks-pē'di-en-si, *n.* The condition or quality of being inexpedient.
Inexpedient, in-eks-pē'di-ent, *a.* Not expedient; not advisable or judicious.
Inexpensive, in-eks-pen'siv, *a.* Not expensive.
Inexperience, in-eks-pē'ri-ens, *n.* Want of experience.
Inexperienced, in-eks-pē'ri-enst, *a.* Not having experience; unskilled.
Inexpert, in-eks-pėrt', *a.* Not skilled.
Inexpiable, in-eks'pi-a-bl, *a.* That cannot be expiated; that admits of no atonement.
Inexplicable, in-eks'pli-ka-bl, *a.* That cannot be explained or interpreted; unaccountable; mysterious.
Inexplicably, in-eks'pli-ka-bli, *adv.* In an inexplicable manner; unaccountably.
Inexplicit, in-eks-plis'it, *a.* Not explicit; not clear in statement.
Inexplosive, in-eks-plō'siv, *a.* Not liable to explode.—*n.* A substance not liable to explode.
Inexpressible, in-eks-pres'i-bl, *a.* Not to be expressed; unspeakable; indescribable.
Inexpressibly, in-eks-pres'i-bli, *adv.* In an inexpressible manner.
Inexpressive, in-eks-pres'iv, *a.* Not expressive; wanting in expression; inexpressible.
Inextinguishable, in-eks-ting'gwish-a-bl, *a.* That cannot be extinguished.
Inextricable, in-eks'tri-ka-bl, *a.* Not to be extricated or disentangled.
Infallibility, in-fal'i-bil''i-ti, *n.* Quality of being infallible; exemption from liability to error.
Infallible, in-fal'i-bl, *a.* Not fallible; not liable to fail; certain.
Infallibly, in-fal'i-bli, *adv.* In an infallible manner; to a certainty.
Infamous, in'fa-mus, *a.* Notoriously vile; detestable; branded with infamy.
Infamously, in'fa-mus-li, *adv.* In an infamous manner; scandalously.
Infamy, in'fa-mi, *n.* Total loss of reputation; public disgrace; qualities detested and despised; extreme vileness.
Infancy, in'fan-si, *n.* State of being an infant; early childhood; period from birth to the age of twenty-one; first age of anything.
Infant, in'fant, *n.* A very young child; one under twenty-one years of age.—*a.* Pertaining to infants.
Infanta, in-fan'ta, *n.* Formerly, in Spain and Portugal, any princess of the royal blood except the eldest.—**Infante,** in-fan'tā, *n.* Any son of the king except the eldest.
Infanticide, in-fant'i-sid, *n.* Child murder; a slayer of infants.
Infantile, Infantine, in'fant-il, in'fant-in, *a.* Pertaining to infancy or an infant.
Infantry, in'fant-ri, *n.* The soldiers or troops that serve on foot.
Infatuate, in-fa'tū-āt, *vt.* To make foolish; to inspire with an extravagant passion.
Infatuated, in-fa'tū-āt-ed, *p.a.* Besotted; inspired with foolish passion.
Infatuation, in-fa'tū-ā''shon, *n.* Act of infatuating; state of being infatuated; foolish passion.
Infect, in-fekt', *vt.* To taint with disease; to communicate bad qualities to; to corrupt.
Infection, in-fek'shon, *n.* Act or process of infecting; communication of disease; contagion; the thing which infects.
Infectious, Infective, in-fek'shus, in-fek'tiv, *a.* Capable of infecting; contagious; easily diffused from person to person.
Infectiously, in-fek'shus-li, *adv.* By infection; in an infectious manner.
Infecund, in-fē'kund, *a.* Not fecund.
Infeftment, in-feft'ment, *n.* The Scottish equivalent of *enfeoffment.*
Infelicitous, in-fē-lis'it-us, *a.* Not felicitous; unhappy; unfortunate.
Infelicity, in-fē-lis'i-ti, *n.* Unhappiness.
Infelt, in'felt, *a.* Felt within or deeply.
Infeoff, in-fef', *vt.* To enfeoff.
Infer, in-fėr', *vt.* (inferring, inferred). To gather by induction or deduction; to deduce.
Inferable, in-fėr'a-bl, *a.* That may be inferred from premises; deducible; derivable.
Inference, in'fėr-ens, *n.* The act of inferring; that which is inferred; deduction.
Inferential, in-fėr-en'shal, *a.* Of or pertaining to an inference.
Inferior, in-fē'ri-ėr, *a.* Lower in place, station, age, value, &c.; subordinate.—*n.* A person lower in rank, importance, &c.
Inferiority, in-fē'ri-or''i-ti, *n.* State or quality of being inferior.
Infernal, in-fėr'nal, *a.* Pertaining to the lower regions or hell; very wicked and detestable; diabolical.—**Infernal machine,** an explosive apparatus contrived for assassination or other mischief.
Infernally, in-fėr'nal-li, *adv.* In an infernal way; detestably.
Infertile, in-fėr'tīl, *a.* Not fertile; barren.
Infertility, in-fėr-til'i-ti, *n.* Barrenness.
Infest, in-fest', *vt.* To attack; to molest; to annoy continually.
Infidel, in'fi-del, *n.* A disbeliever; a sceptic;

one who does not believe in God or in Christianity.—*a.* Unbelieving; sceptical.

Infidelity, in-fi-del'i-ti, *n.* Want of faith or belief; scepticism; unfaithfulness in married persons; dishonesty; treachery.

Infiltrate, in-fil'trāt, *vi.* To enter by the pores or interstices; to percolate.

Infiltration, in-fil-trā'shon, *n.* Act or process of infiltrating; that which infiltrates.

Infinite, in'fi-nit, *a.* Not finite; without limits; not circumscribed in any way; vast.—*n.* The Infinite Being; infinite space.

Infinitely, in'fi-nit-li, *adv.* In an infinite manner; beyond all comparison.

Infinitesimal, in'fi-ni-tes"i-mal, *a.* Infinitely or indefinitely small.—*n.* An infinitely small quantity.

Infinitive, in-fin'it-iv, *a.* Designating a mood of the verb which expresses action without limitation of person or number, as, *to love.*—*n.* The infinitive mood.

Infinitude, in-fin'i-tūd, *n.* Infinity.

Infinity, in-fin'i-ti, *n.* State or quality of being infinite; unlimited extent of time, space, quantity, &c.; immensity.

Infirm, in-fėrm', *a.* Not firm; weak; sickly; enfeebled; irresolute.

Infirmary, in-fėrm'a-ri, *n.* A place where the sick and injured are nursed; a hospital.

Infirmity, in-fėrm'i-ti, *n.* State of being infirm; unsound state of the body; weakness of mind or resolution; failing; malady.

Infix, in-fiks', *vt.* To fix or fasten in; to implant, as principles, &c.

Inflame, in-flām', *vt.* To set on fire; to kindle; to excite or increase; to incense; to make morbidly red and swollen.—*vi.* To grow hot, angry, and painful; to take fire.

Inflammability, in-flam'a-bil"i-ti, *n.* State or quality of being inflammable.

Inflammable, in-flam'a-bl, *a.* That may be inflamed; easily kindled; combustible.

Inflammation, in-flam-ā'shon, *n.* Act of inflaming; state of being inflamed; a redness and swelling attended with heat, pain, and feverish symptoms.

Inflammatory, in-flam'a-to-ri, *a.* Pertaining to inflammation; tending to excite anger, animosity, tumult, or sedition.

Inflate, in-flāt', *vt.* (inflating, inflated). To distend by injecting air; to puff up; to elate; to raise above the real or normal value.

Inflated, in-flāt'ed, *p.a.* Puffed up; turgid; bombastic; unduly raised in price.

Inflation, in-flā'shon, *n.* Act of inflating; state of being distended with air; state of being puffed up, as with vanity; over-issue of currency, tending to cause a general rise in prices.

Inflatus, in-flā'tus, *n.* A blowing or breathing in; inspiration.

Inflect, in-flekt', *vt.* To bend; to decline or conjugate; to modulate, as the voice.

Inflection, in-flek'shon, *n.* Act of inflecting; state of being inflected; grammatical variation of nouns, verbs, &c.; modulation of the voice; deflection or diffraction.

Inflective, in-flekt'iv, *a.* Having the power of inflecting; having grammatical inflection.

Inflexed, in-flekst', *a.* Curved; bent inward.

Inflexibility, in-fleks'i-bil"i-ti, *n.* Firmness of purpose; unbending pertinacity or obstinacy.

Inflexible, in-fleks'i-bl, *a.* That cannot be bent; firm in purpose; pertinacious; inexorable.

Inflexibly, in-fleks'i-bli, *adv.* In an inflexible manner; firmly; inexorably.

Inflexion, in-flek'shon. *See* INFLECTION.

Inflict, in-flikt', *vt.* To cause to bear or suffer from; to impose, as pain, punishment, &c.

Infliction, in-flik'shon, *n.* Act of inflicting; punishment inflicted; calamity.

Inflorescence, in-flō-res'ens, *n.* A flowering; the manner in which blossoms are supported.

Inflow, in'flō, *n.* The act of flowing in or into; that which flows in; influx.

Influence, in'flu̧-ens, *n.* Agency or power serving to affect, modify, &c.; sway; effect; acknowledged ascendency with people in power.—*vt.* To exercise influence on; to bias; to sway.

Influent, in'flu̧-ent, *a.* Flowing in.

Influential, in-flu̧-en'shal, *a.* Exerting influence, physical or other; possessing power.

Influenza, in-flu̧-en'za, *n.* An epidemic catarrh or cold of an aggravated kind.

Influx, in'fluks, *n.* Act of flowing in; a coming in; importation in abundance; point at which one stream runs into another or into the sea.

Infold, in-fōld', *vi.* To fold in; to involve; to wrap up; to inclose; to embrace.

Inform, in-form', *vt.* To give form to; to give life to; to communicate knowledge to; to instruct, &c.—*vi.* To give information.

Informal, in-form'al, *a.* Not in the usual form or mode; not with the official or customary forms; without ceremony.

Informality, in-form-al'i-ti, *n.* Quality of being informal; want of regular form or order.

Informally, in-form'al-li, *adv.* In an informal manner; without the usual forms.

Informant, in-form'ant, *n.* One who informs.

Information, in-form-ā'shon, *n.* The act of informing; intelligence communicated or gathered; a charge or accusation before a magistrate.

Informatory, Informative, in-form'a-to-ri, in-form'a-tiv, *a.* Affording knowledge or information; instructive.

Informer, in-form'ėr, *n.* One who informs; one who makes a practice of informing against others for the sake of gain.

Infraction, in-frak'shon, *n.* Act of infringing; breach; violation; infringement.

Infrangible, in-fran'ji-bl, *a.* Not to be broken; not to be violated.

Infra-red, in'fra-red, *a.* Of the part of the spectrum beyond the red end of the visible spectrum.

Infrequency, in-frē'kwen-si, *n.* State of being infrequent; rareness.

Infrequent, in-frē'kwent, *a.* Not frequent; seldom happening; rare.

Infrequently, in-frē'kwent-li, *adv.* Not frequently; seldom; rarely.

Infringe, in-frinj', *vt.* (infringing, infringed). To break, as laws, agreements, &c.; to violate; to contravene.—*vi.* To encroach (with *on* or *upon*).

Infringement, in-frinj'ment, *n.* Breach; violation; encroachment.

Infuriate, in-fū'ri-āt, *vt.* To madden; to enrage.—*a.* Enraged; mad; raging.

Infuse, in-fūz', *vt.* (infusing, infused). To

pour in, as a liquid; to instil, as principles; to steep in liquor without boiling, in order to extract solutions, &c.
Infusible, in-fūz'i-bl, *a.* Not fusible.
Infusible, in-fūz'i-bl, *a.* That may be infused.
Infusion, in-fū'zhon, *n.* Act or process of infusing; that which is infused; liquor obtained by infusing or steeping.
Infusoria, in-fū-sō'ri-a, *n.pl.* A class of minute, mostly microscopic, animals, developed in organic infusions.
Infusorial, Infusory, in-fū-sō'ri-al, in-fū'so-ri, *a.* Pertaining to the Infusoria.
Ingathering, in'gaᴛʜ-ėr-ing, *n.* A gathering in; harvest.
Ingeminate, in-jem'i-nāt, *vt.* To double or repeat.—*a.* Redoubled; repeated.
Ingenerate, in-jen'ėr-āt, *a.* Inborn; innate.
Ingenious, in-jē'ni-us, *a.* Possessed of cleverness or ability; apt in contriving; contrived with ingenuity; witty or well conceived.
Ingeniously, in-jē'ni-us-li, *adv.* In an ingenious manner; with ingenuity.
Ingenuity, in-jen-ū'i-ti, *n.* Quality of being ingenious; ready invention; skill in contrivance.
Ingenuous, in-jen'ū-us, *a.* Open, frank, or candid; free from reserve or dissimulation.
Ingenuously, in-jen'ū-us-li, *adv.* Frankly; openly; candidly.
Ingest, in-jest', *vt.* To throw into the stomach.
Ingesta, in-jest'a, *n.pl.* Substances absorbed by or taken into an animal body.
Inglorious, in-glō'ri-us, *a.* Not glorious; not bringing honour or glory; disgraceful.
Ingluvies, in-glū'vi-ēz, *n.* The crop or craw of birds; the stomach of ruminants.
Ingoing, in'gō-ing, *n.* A going in; entrance. —*a.* Entering in.
Ingot, in'got, *n.* A mass of gold or silver cast in a mould; a mass of unwrought metal.
Ingraft, in-graft', *vt.* To graft; to attach by grafting; to insert.
Ingrail, in-grāl', *vt.* To engrail.
Ingrain, in-grān', *vt.* To engrain.
Ingrate, in'grāt, *n.* An ungrateful person.
Ingratiate, in-grā'shi-āt, *vt.* To get into another's good-will or confidence; to recommend; to insinuate; always *refl.*
Ingratitude, in-grat'i-tūd, *n.* Want of gratitude; unthankfulness.
Ingredient, in-grē'di-ent, *n.* That which is a component part of any mixture; an element, component, or constituent.
Ingress, in'gres, *n.* Entrance; power of entrance; means of entering.
Inguinal, in'gwin-al, *a.* Pertaining to the groin.
Ingulf, in-gulf', *vt.* To swallow up; to absorb; to overwhelm by swallowing.
Ingurgitate, in-gėr'jit-āt, *vt.* To ingulf; to swallow up.—*vi.* To drink largely; to swill.
Inhabit, in-ha'bit, *vt.* To live or dwell in; to occupy as a place of settled residence.—*vi.* To dwell; to live; to abide.
Inhabitable, in-ha'bit-a-bl, *a.* That may be inhabited; habitable.
Inhabitant, Inhabiter, in-hab'it-ant, in-ha'bit-ėr, *n.* One who inhabits; one who resides permanently in a place.
Inhabitation, in-ha'bi-tā"shon, *n.* The act of inhabiting; an abode.
Inhalation, in-ha-lā'shon, *n.* Act of inhaling; that which is inhaled.
Inhale, in-hāl', *vt.* (inhaling, inhaled). To draw into the lungs; to suck in.
Inhaler, in-hāl'ėr, *n.* One who or that which inhales; an apparatus for inhaling vapours and volatile substances, as steam, vapour of chloroform, &c.; a respirator.
Inharmonious, in-här-mō'ni-us, *a.* Not harmonious; unmusical; discordant.
Inhere, in-hēr', *vi.* To exist or be fixed in; to belong, as attributes or qualities, to a subject.
Inherence, Inherency, in-hēr'ens, in-hēr'en-si, *n.* State of inhering; existence in something.
Inherent, in-hēr'ent, *a.* Inhering; naturally pertaining; innate.
Inherently, in-hēr'ent-li, *adv.* In an inherent manner; by inherence.
Inherit, in-he'rit, *vt.* To come into possession of as an heir; to receive by nature from a progenitor; to hold as belonging to one's lot.—*vi.* To take or have possession of property.
Inheritable, in-he'rit-a-bl, *a.* Capable of being inherited.
Inheritance, in-he'rit-ans, *n.* Act of inheriting; that which is or may be inherited; what falls to one's lot; possession.
Inheritor, in-he'rit-ėr, *n.* One who inherits; an heir.
Inheritress, Inheritrix, in-he'rit-res, in-he'-rit-riks, *n.* A female who inherits.
Inhesion, in-hē'zhon, *n.* Act of inhering; inherence.
Inhibit, in-hib'it, *vt.* To hold in or back; to restrain; to forbid; to interdict.
Inhibition, in-hi-bis'hon, *n.* Act of inhibiting; a legal writ inhibiting a judge from further proceeding in a cause.
Inhibitory, in-hib'i-to-ri, *a.* Conveying an inhibition; prohibitory.
Inhospitable, in-hos'pit-a-bl, *a.* Not hospitable; wanting in hospitality; affording no entertainment to strangers.
Inhospitality, in-hos'pit-al"i-ti, *n.* Want of hospitality.
Inhuman, in-hū'man, *a.* Destitute of the kindness and tenderness that belong to a human being; cruel; merciless.
Inhumanity, in-hū-man'i-ti, *n.* Quality of being inhuman; cruelty.
Inhumanly, in-hū'man-li, *adv.* In an inhuman manner; cruelly; barbarously.
Inhumation, in-hūm-ā'shon, *n.* Interment.
Inhume, in-hūm', *vt.* (inhuming, inhumed). To bury; to inter (a dead body).
Inimical, in-im'ik-al, *a.* Unfriendly; hostile; adverse; hurtful; prejudicial.
Inimitable, in-im'it-a-bl, *a.* That cannot be imitated or copied; surpassing imitation.
Inimitably, in-im'it-a-bli, *adv.* To a degree beyond imitation.
Iniquitous, in-ik'wit-us, *a.* Characterized by iniquity; wicked; criminal.
Iniquity, in-ik'wi-ti, *n.* Want of equity; injustice; a sin or crime; wickedness.
Initial, in-i'shal, *a.* Placed at the beginning; pertaining to the beginning; beginning.—*n.* The first letter of a word; *pl.* the first letter in order of the words composing a name.—*vt.* (initialling, initialled). To put one's initials to; to mark by initials.
Initiate, in-i'shi-āt, *vt.* To begin; to be the first to practise or bring in; to instruct in rudiments; to introduce into any society or set; to let into secrets; to indoctrinate.

Initiation, in-i'shi-ā"shon, *n.* Act or process of initiating; beginning; formal introduction.

Initiative, in-i'shi-āt-iv, *a.* Serving to initiate. —*n.* An introductory step; first active procedure in any enterprise; power of taking the lead.

Initiatory, in-i'shi-a-to-ri, *a.* Serving to initiate; initiating; introductory.

Inject, in-jekt', *vt.* To throw, cast, or put in or into; to dart in; to cast or throw in.

Injection, in-jek'shon, *n.* Act of injecting; the throwing of a liquid medicine into the body by a syringe or pipe; that which is injected.

Injector, in-jekt'ėr, *n.* One who or that which injects; an apparatus for supplying the boilers of steam-engines with water.

Injudicial, in-jū-di'shal, *a.* Not judicial.

Injudicious, in-jū-di'shus, *a.* Not judicious; acting without judgment; indiscreet.

Injudiciously, in-jū-di'shus-li, *adv.* In an injudicious manner; indiscreetly.

Injunction, in-jungk'shon, *n.* Act of enjoining; a command; precept; urgent advice; admonition.

Injure, in'jėr, *vt.* (injuring, injured). To do harm to; to hurt; to damage.

Injurer, in'jėr-ėr, *n.* One who or that which injures.

Injurious, in-jū'ri-us, *a.* Causing injury; tending to injure; hurtful; harmful.

Injuriously, in-jū'ri-us-li, *adv.* In an injurious or hurtful manner.

Injury, in'jū-ri, *n.* The doing of harm; harm or damage; mischief; detriment.

Injustice, in-just'is, *n.* Want of justice or equity; iniquity; wrong.

Ink, ingk, *n.* A coloured liquid, usually black, for writing, printing, &c.—*vt.* To black or daub with ink.

Ink-bag, Ink-sac, ingk'bag, ingk'sak, *n.* A sac in some cuttle-fishes, containing a black viscid fluid.

Inkhorn, ingk'horn, *n.* A small vessel used to hold ink.—*a.* Pedantic; bookish.

Inkling, ingk'ling, *n.* A hint or whisper; a slight notion or idea.

Inkstand, ingk'stand, *n.* A vessel for holding ink.

Inky, ingk'i, *a.* Consisting of or like ink; black; tarnished or blackened with ink.

Inland, in'land, *a.* Interior; remote from the sea; domestic, not foreign; confined to a country.—*adv.* In or towards the interior of a country.—*n.* The interior part of a country.

Inlander, in'land-ėr, *n.* One who lives inland.

Inlay, in-lā', *vt.* (inlaying, inlaid). To lay in; to ornament by laying in thin slices of fine wood, ivory, &c., on some other surface.

Inlaying, in-lā'ing, *n.* Act or art of one who inlays; inlaid work.

Inlet, in'let, *n.* A passage for entrance; place of ingress; a narrow recess in a shore.

Inly, in'li, *adv.* Internally; inwardly; in the heart; mentally; secretly.

Inmate, in'māt, *n.* One who dwells in the same house with another; one of the occupants of hospitals, asylums, prisons, &c.

Inmost, in'mōst, *a.* Furthest within; remotest from the surface or external parts.

Inn, in, *n.* A house for the lodging and entertainment of travellers; college of law professors and students.

Innate, in-nāt', *a.* Inborn; natural; native; inherent.

Innately, in-nāt'li, *adv.* In an innate manner; naturally.

Innavigable, in-na'vig-a-bl, *a.* That cannot be navigated.

Inner, in'ėr, *a.* Interior; further inward than something else; internal.—*n.* A shot which strikes the target between the bull's-eye and the innermost ring.

Innermost, in'ėr-mōst, *a.* Furthest inward; most remote from the outward part.

Innervate, in-nėr'vāt, *vt.* To supply with nervous strength or stimulus.

Innervation, in-nėr-vā'shon, *n.* Act of innerving; nervous stimulation.

Inning, in'ing, *n.* The ingathering of grain; *pl.* turn for using the bat in cricket, &c.

Innkeeper, in'kēp-ėr, *n.* One who keeps an inn or tavern.

Innocence, Innocency, in'nō-sens, in'nō-sen-si, *n.* Quality of being innocent; freedom from crime or guilt; simplicity of heart.

Innocent, in'nō-sent, *a.* Not noxious or hurtful; free from guilt; simple-hearted; guileless.—*n.* One free from guilt or harm: a natural or simpleton.

Innocently, in'nō-sent-li, *adv.* In an innocent manner.

Innocuous, in-nok'ū-us, *a.* Harmless; not injurious; producing no ill effect.

Innominate, in-nom'i-nāt, *a.* Having no name.

Innovate, in'nō-vāt, *vi.* To introduce novelties or changes.

Innovation, in-nō-vā'shon, *n.* The act of innovating; change made in anything established.—**Innovator,** in'nō-vāt-ėr, *n.* One who innovates.

Innoxious, in-nok'shus, *a.* Free from mischievous qualities; innocent; harmless.

Innuendo, in-nū-en'dō, *n.*; pl. **Innuendos** or **-does,** -dōz. An oblique hint; insinuation.

Innumerable, in-nū'mėr-a-bl, *a.* Incapable of being numbered for multitude; extremely numerous; countless.

Innumerably, in-nū'mėr-a-bli, *adv.* Without number.

Innutrition, in-nū-tri'shon, *n.* Want of nutrition; failure of nourishment.

Innutritious, in-nū-tri'shus, *a.* Not nutritious.

Inobservant, in-ob-zėrv'ant, *a.* Not observant; not keen in observation; heedless.

Inobtrusive, in-ob-trö'siv, *a.* Unobtrusive.

Inoculate, in-ok'ū-lāt, *vt.* To graft by inserting a bud; to communicate a disease to by morbid matter introduced into the blood; to infect; to contaminate.

Inoculation, in-ok'ū-lā"shon, *n.* The act or practice of inoculating; communication of a disease by matter introduced into the blood.

Inodorous, in-ō'dėr-us, *a.* Wanting odour or scent; having no smell.

Inoffensive, in-of-fens'iv, *a.* Giving no offence or annoyance; harmless.

Inoffensively, in-of-fens'iv-li, *adv.* In an inoffensive manner.

Inofficial, in-of-fi'shal, *a.* Not official; not clothed with the usual forms of authority.

Inoperative, in-o'pe-rāt-iv, *a.* Not operative; not active; producing no effect.

Inopportune, in-op'por-tūn, *a.* Not opportune; inconvenient; unseasonable.
Inopportunely, in-op'por-tūn-li, *adv.* In an inopportune manner; unseasonably.
Inordinacy, in-or'din-a-si, *n.* The state or quality of being inordinate.
Inordinate, in-or'din-āt, *a.* Excessive; immoderate.
Inordinately, in-or'din-āt-li, *adv.* In an inordinate manner; excessively.
Inorganic, in-or-gan'ik, *a.* Not organic; devoid of the structure of a living being; pertaining to substances without carbon.
Inosculate, in-os'kū-lāt, *vi.* and *t.* To unite by apposition or contact, as arteries, nerves, &c.
Inosculation, in-os'kū-lā"shon, *n.* The act of inosculating; union by contact.
In-patient, in'pā-shent, *n.* A patient who is lodged as well as treated in a hospital.
Inquest, in'kwest, *n.* Inquiry; a judicial inquiry before a jury; the jury itself.
Inquietude, in-kwī'et-ūd, *n.* Want of quiet; uneasiness, either of body or mind.
Inquire, in-kwīr', *vi.* (inquiring, inquired). Often **enquire.** To ask a question; to seek for truth by discussion or investigation.—*vt.* To ask about; to seek by asking.
Inquirer, in-kwīr'ėr, *n.* One who inquires; one who seeks for knowledge or information.
Inquiring, in-kwīr'ing, *p.a.* Given to inquiry; disposed to investigation.
Inquiry, in-kwī'ri, *n.* Often **enquiry.** The act of inquiring; a question; research; investigation; examination.
Inquisition, in-kwi-zi'shon, *n.* The act of inquiring; inquiry; inquest; a R. Catholic court for the examination and punishment of heretics.
Inquisitional, Inquisitionary, in-kwi-zi'-shon-al, in-kwi-zi'shon-a-ri, *a.* Pertaining to inquisition, or to the Inquisition.
Inquisitive, in-kwiz'i-tiv, *a.* Addicted to inquiry; given to pry; troublesomely curious.
Inquisitively, in-kwiz'i-tiv-li, *adv.* In an inquisitive manner.
Inquisitor, in-kwiz'i-tėr, *n.* One whose duty it is to inquire and examine; a member of the Inquisition.
Inquisitorial, in-kwiz'i-tō"ri-al, *a.* Pertaining to an inquisitor; making searching inquiry.
Inroad, in'rōd, *n.* A hostile incursion; an invasion; attack; encroachment.
Insalubrious, in-sa-lū'bri-us, *a.* Not salubrious; unfavourable to health.
Insalubrity, in-sa-lū'bri-ti, *n.* State or quality of being insalubrious.
Insalutary, in-sal'ū-ta-ri, *a.* Not salutary; unhealthy; productive of evil.
Insane, in-sān', *a.* Not sane; deranged in mind or intellect; intended for insane persons; senseless.
Insanely, in-sān'li, *adv.* In an insane manner; foolishly; without reason.
Insanity, in-san'i-ti, *n.* The state of being insane; derangement of intellect; lunacy.
Insatiability, in-sā'shi-a-bil"i-ti, *n.* The quality of being insatiable.
Insatiable, in-sā'shi-a-bl, *a.* Not satiable; incapable of being satisfied or appeased.
Insatiate, in-sā'shi-āt, *a.* Not satisfied; insatiable.
Inscribe, in-skrīb', *vt.* (inscribing, inscribed). To write down; to imprint on, as on the memory; to address or dedicate; to mark with letters or words; to draw a figure within another.
Inscription, in-skrip'shon, *n.* The act of inscribing; words engraved; address of a book, &c., to a person.
Inscriptive, in-skript'iv, *a.* Written as an inscription; bearing inscription.
Inscrutability, in-skrö'ta-bil"i-ti, *n.* Quality of being inscrutable.
Inscrutable, in-skrö'ta-bl, *a.* Unsearchable; that cannot be penetrated or understood by human reason.
Insect, in'sekt, *n.* One of those small animals that have three divisions of the body—head, thorax, and abdomen—and usually three pairs of legs and two pairs of wings, as flies, &c.; a puny, contemptible person.—*a.* Pertaining to insects; like an insect; mean.
Insecticide, in-sek'ti-sīd, *n.* One who or that which kills insects; the killing of insects.
Insectivora, in-sek-tiv'ō-ra, *n.pl.* An order of mammals, as the hedgehog, &c., which live mainly on insects.
Insectivore, in-sek'ti-vōr, *n.* An animal that eats insects.
Insectivorous, in-sek-tiv'ō-rus, *a.* Feeding on insects; belonging to the Insectivora.
Insecure, in-sē-kūr', *a.* Not secure; not confident of safety; unsafe.
Insecurely, in-sē-kūr'li, *adv.* In an insecure manner.
Insecurity, in-sē-kū'ri-ti, *n.* The state of being insecure; want of security.
Insensate, in-sens'āt, *a.* Destitute of sense or sensation; stupid; irrational.
Insensibility, in-sens'i-bil"i-ti, *n.* State or quality of being insensible; want of sensation; callousness; apathy.
Insensible, in-sens'i-bl, *a.* Not perceived or perceptible by the senses; void of feeling; unfeeling; callous; indifferent.
Insensibly, in-sens'i-bli, *adv.* In an insensible manner; by slow degrees.
Insensitive, in-sens'i-tiv, *a.* Not sensitive.
Insentient, in-sen'shi-ent, *a.* Not sentient.
Inseparable, in-sep'a-ra-bl, *a.* Not separable; not to be parted; always together.
Insert, in-sėrt', *vt.* To put, bring, or set in; to thrust in; to set in or among.
Insertion, in-sėr'shon, *n.* Act of inserting; thing inserted; place or mode of attachment of a part or organ to its support.
Insessores, in-ses-sō'rēz, *n.pl.* The order of passerine or perching birds.
Insessorial, in-ses-sō'ri-al, *a.* Belonging to the Insessores or perching birds.
Inset, in-set', *vt.* To set in; to implant.—*n.* in'set. That which is set in; insertion.
Inshore, in'shōr, *a.* or *adv.* Near the shore.
Inside, in'sīd, *n.* The interior side or part of a thing.—*a.* Interior; internal.—*prep.* In the interior of; within.
Insidious, in-sid'i-us, *a.* Treacherous; guileful; working evil secretly.
Insight, in'sīt, *n.* Sight into; thorough knowledge; discernment; penetration.
Insignia, in-sig'ni-a, *n.pl.* Badges or distinguishing marks of office or honour.
Insignificance, Insignificancy, in-sig-ni'fi-kans, in-sig-ni'fi-kan-si, *n.* Quality or state of being insignificant; triviality.

Insignificant, in-sig-ni'fi-kant, *a.* Not significant; void of signification; trivial or trifling; mean; contemptible.
Insincere, in-sin-sēr', *a.* Not sincere; wanting sincerity; hypocritical; deceitful.
Insincerely, in-sin-sēr'li, *adv.* In an insincere manner; without sincerity.
Insincerity, in-sin-ser'i-ti, *n.* Quality of being insincere; deceitfulness.
Insinuate, in-sin'ū-āt, *vt.* To introduce by windings or gently; to work gradually into favour; to introduce by gentle or artful means; to hint.—*vi.* To creep or wind; to make an insinuation; to wheedle.
Insinuating, in-sin'ū-āt-ing, *p.a.* Given to or characterized by insinuation; insensibly winning favour and confidence.
Insinuation, in-sin'ū-ā"shon, *n.* Act of insinuating; wheedling manner; hint or innuendo.
Insipid, in-sip'id, *a.* Destitute of taste; vapid; flat; dull; heavy; spiritless.
Insipidity, in-si-pid'i-ti, *n.* Quality of being insipid; want of life or spirit.
Insist, in-sist', *vi.* To rest or dilate on; to be urgent or peremptory.
Insistence, in-sis'tens, *n.* Act of insisting; persistency; urgency.
Insnare, in-snār', *vt.* To catch in a snare; to entrap; to entangle; to involve.
Insobriety, in-sō-brī'e-ti, *n.* Want of sobriety; intemperance; drunkenness.
Insolate, in'so-lāt, *vt.* To dry or prepare in the sun's rays.
Insolation, in-so-lā'shon, *n.* Exposure to the rays of the sun; sunstroke.
Insolence, in'sō-lens, *n.* State or quality of being insolent; insolent language or behaviour.
Insolent, in'sō-lent, *a.* Showing haughty disregard of others; impudent; insulting.
Insolently, in'sō-lent-li, *adv.* In an insolent manner; haughty; rudely; saucily.
Insolubility, in-sol'ū-bil"i-ti, *n.* Quality of being insoluble.
Insoluble, in-sol'ū-bl, *a.* Incapable of being dissolved; not to be solved or explained.
Insolvable, in-sol'va-bl, *a.* Not solvable; not to be solved or explained.
Insolvency, in-sol'ven-si, *n.* State of being insolvent; inability to pay all debts.
Insolvent, in-sol'vent, *a.* Not solvent; not having money, &c., sufficient to pay debts.—*n.* One unable to pay his debts.
Insomnia, in-som'ni-a, *n.* Want of sleep; morbid or unnatural sleeplessness.
Insomuch, in-sō-much', *adv.* To such a degree; in such wise.
Inspan, in-span', *vt.* To yoke, as oxen.
Inspect, in-spekt', *vt.* To view or examine to ascertain the quality or condition, &c.
Inspection, in-spek'shon, *n.* Act of inspecting; careful survey; official examination.
Inspector, in-spekt'ėr, *n.* One who inspects; a superintendent; an overseer.
Inspectorate, in-spekt'ėr-āt, *n.* A body of inspectors or overseers; inspectorship.
Inspectorship, in-spekt'ėr-ship, *n.* The office of an inspector.
Inspirable, in-spīr'a-bl, *a.* That may be inspired or drawn into the lungs; inhalable.
Inspiration, in-spi-rā'shon, *n.* The act of inspiring; the drawing in of breath; the divine influence by which the sacred writers were instructed; influence emanating from any object; the state of being inspired; something conveyed to the mind when under extraordinary influence.
Inspiratory, in-spīr'a-to-ri, *a.* Pertaining to inspiration, or inhalation of air.
Inspire, in-spīr', *vt.* (inspiring, inspired). To breathe in; to breathe into; to communicate divine instructions to; to infuse ideas or poetic spirit into; to animate in general.—*vi.* To draw in breath; to inhale air into the lungs.
Inspired, in-spīrd', *p.a.* Having received inspiration; produced under the influence or direction of inspiration.
Inspirer, in-spīr'ėr, *n.* One who inspires.
Inspirit, in-spi'rit, *vt.* To infuse or excite spirit in; to cheer or encourage.
Inspissate, in-spis'āt, *vt.* To thicken by boiling or evaporating the thinner parts, &c.
Instability, in-sta-bil'i-ti, *n.* Want of stability; inconstancy; fickleness.
Install, in-stąl', *vt.* To place in a seat; to invest with any office with due ceremony.
Installation, in-stąl-ā'shon, *n.* The act of installing.
Instalment, in-stąl'ment, *n.* Act of installing; a part of a whole produced or paid at various times; part payment of a debt.
Instance, in'stans, *n.* Act or state of being instant or urgent; urgency; an example; an occurrence.—*vt.* To mention as an instance, example, or case.
Instant, in'stant, *a.*. Pressing or urgent; immediate; making no delay; present or current.—*n.* A moment.
Instantaneous, in-stant-ā'nē-us, *a.* Done or occurring in an instant.
Instantaneously, in-stant-ā'nē-us-li, *adv.* In an instant; in a moment.
Instantly, in'stant-li, *adv.* In an instant; immediately; with urgent importunity.
Instate, in-stāt', *vt.* (instating, instated). To set or place; to install.
Instead, in-sted', *adv.* In the place or room of; in place of that.
Instep, in'step, *n.* The fore part of the upper side of the foot, near its junction with the leg.
Instigate, in'sti-gāt, *vt.* To spur on; to urge; to incite; to impel.
Instigation, in-sti-gā'shon, *n.* Act of instigating; incitement; temptation.
Instigator, in'sti-gāt-ėr, *n.* One who instigates or incites another.
Instil, in-stil', *vt.* (instilling, instilled). To pour in, as by drops; to infuse by degrees; to insinuate imperceptibly.
Instillation, in-stil-ā'shon, *n.* Act of instilling.
Instilment, in-stil'ment, *n.* Instillation.
Instinct, in'stingkt, *n.* Spontaneous or natural impulse; the knowledge and skill which animals have without experience; intuitive feeling.—*a.* in-stingkt'. Animated or stimulated from within; inspired.
Instinctive, in-stingk'tiv, *a.* Prompted by instinct; spontaneous.
Instinctively, in-stingkt'iv-li, *adv.* In an instinctive manner; by force of instinct.
Institute, in'sti-tūt, *vt.* To set up or establish; to found; to begin; to appoint to an office; to invest with a benefice.—*n.* That which is instituted; established law; principle; a literary or scientific body; an institution; *pl.* a book of elements or principles.

Institution, in-sti-tū'shon, *n.* Act of instituting; something instituted; custom; a society for promoting any object; act of investing a clergyman with the care of souls.
Institutional, in-sti-tū'shon-al, *a.* Relating to institutions; instituted by authority; relating to elementary knowledge.
Institutionary, in-sti-tū'shon-a-ri, *a.* Relating to an institution or to institutions.
Instruct, in-strukt', *vt.* To impart knowledge to; to teach; to advise or give notice to.
Instruction, in-struk'shon, *n.* Act of instructing; information; education; authoritative direction; command.
Instructive, in-struk'tiv, *a.* Conveying instruction or a useful lesson.
Instructor, in-strukt'ėr, *n.* One who instructs; a teacher.
Instructress, in-strukt'res, *n.* A female who instructs.
Instrument, in'strų-ment, *n.* A tool; implement; one subservient to the execution of a plan; means used; any contrivance from which music is produced; a writing instructing one in regard to something agreed upon.
Instrumental, in-strų-ment'al, *a.* Conducive to some end; pertaining to or produced by instruments, as music.
Instrumentalist, in-strų-ment'al-ist, *n.* One who plays on a musical instrument.
Instrumentality, in'strų-men-tal'i-ti, *n.* State of being instrumental; agency.
Instrumentation, in'strų-men-tā"shon, *n.* The use of instruments; music for a number of instruments; art of arranging such music.
Insubordinate, in-sub-or'din-āt, *a.* Not submitting to authority; riotous.
Insubordination, in-sub-or'din-ā"shon, *n.* Quality or state of being insubordinate; resistance to lawful authority.
Insuetude, in'swē-tūd, *n.* State or quality of not being in use.
Insufferable, in-suf'ėr-a-bl, *a.* Not to be suffered; intolerable.
Insufferably, in-suf'ėr-a-bli, *adv.* Intolerably.
Insufficiency, in-suf-fi'shen-si, *n.* State of being insufficient; deficiency; inadequacy.
Insufficient, in-suf-fi'shent, *a.* Not sufficient; deficient; inadequate.
Insufficiently, in-suf-fi'shent-li, *adv.* In an insufficient manner; inadequately.
Insular, in'sū-lėr, *a.* Pertaining to an island; forming an island; narrow-minded.
Insularity, in-sū-la'ri-ti, *n.* State of being insular.
Insulate, in'sū-lāt, *vt.* To make into an island; to detach; to separate, as an electrified body, by interposition of non-conductors.
Insulation, in-sū-lā'shon, *n.* Act of insulating; state of being insulated.
Insulator, in'sū-lāt-ėr, *n.* One who or that which insulates; a body that interrupts the communication of electricity; non-conductor.
Insulin, ins'ū-lin, *n.* A substance extracted from the pancreas of animals, and found beneficial in diabetes.
Insult, in'sult, *n.* Any gross affront or indignity; act or speech of insolence or contempt.—*vt.* in-sult'. To treat with insult or insolence.—*vi.* To behave with insolent triumph.
Insulting, in-sult'ing, *p.a.* Containing or conveying insult.
Insuperability, in-sū'pėr-a-bil"i-ti, *n.* Quality of being insuperable.
Insuperable, in-sū'pėr-a-bl, *a.* That cannot be overcome; insurmountable.
Insuperably, in-sū'pėr-a-bli, *adv.* In an insuperable manner; insurmountably.
Insupportable, in-sup-pōrt'a-bl, *a.* That cannot be supported or borne; intolerable.
Insuppressible, in-sup-pres'i-bl, *a.* Not to be suppressed.
Insurable, in-shör'a-bl, *a.* That may be insured against loss or damage.
Insurance, in-shör'ans, *n.* Act of insuring against loss, &c.; a system of securing, by making certain payments, a certain sum of money at death, &c.
Insure, in-shör', *vt.* (insuring, insured). To make sure; to contract for the receipt of a certain sum in the event of loss, death, &c.
Insurer, in-shör'ėr, *n.* One who insures.
Insurgent, in-sėr'jent, *a.* Rising in opposition to lawful authority; rebellious.—*n.* One who rises in opposition to authority.
Insurmountable, in-sėr-mount'a-bl, *a.* That cannot be surmounted; insuperable.
Insurrection, in-sėr-rek'shon, *n.* A rising against authority; rebellion.
Insurrectional, Insurrectionary, in-sėr-rek'shon-al, in-sėr-rek'shon-a-ri, *a.* Pertaining to insurrection.
Insusceptibility, in-sus-sept'i-bil"i-ti, *n.* The quality of being insusceptible.
Insusceptible, in-sus-sept'i-bl, *a.* Not susceptible; not capable of being affected.
Intact, in-takt', *a.* Untouched; unimpaired.
Intaglio, in-tal'yō, *n.* Any figure engraved or cut into a substance; a gem with a figure or device sunk below the surface.
Intangible, in-tan'ji-bl, *a.* That cannot be touched; not perceptible to the touch.
Integer, in'ti-jėr, *n.* A whole; whole number, in contradistinction to a fraction.
Integral, in'ti-gral, *a.* Whole; forming a necessary part of a whole; not fractional.—*n.* A whole; an entire thing.
Integrant, in'ti-grant, *a.* Integral.
Integrate, in'ti-grāt, *vt.* To make or form into one whole; to give the sum or total of.
Integration, in-ti-grā'shon, *n.* The act of integrating.
Integrity, in-teg'ri-ti, *n.* State of being entire; an unimpaired state; honesty; probity.
Integument, in-teg'ū-ment, *n.* A covering, especially a skin, membrane, or shell.
Integumentary, Integumental, in-teg'ū-ment"a-ri, in-teg'ū-ment"al, *a.* Belonging to or composed of integument.
Intellect, in'tel-lekt, *n.* That mental faculty which receives ideas; the understanding; mental power; mind.
Intellection, in-tel-lek'shon, *n.* Act of understanding; simple apprehension of ideas.
Intellectual, in-tel-lek'tū-al, *a.* Relating or appealing to the intellect; having intellect.
Intellectualism, in-tel-lek'tū-al-izm, *n.* Intellectuality; the doctrine that knowledge is derived from pure reason.
Intellectuality, in-tel-lek'tū-al"i-ti, *n.* State of being intellectual; intellectual power.
Intelligence, in-tel'i-jens, *n.* The capacity to know; knowledge imparted or acquired; notice; an intelligent or spiritual being.

Intelligencer, in-tel'i-jens-ėr, *n.* One who conveys intelligence; a messenger or spy.
Intelligent, in-tel'i-jent, *a.* Endowed with the faculty of understanding or reason; endowed with a good intellect; well informed.
Intelligently, in-tel'i-jent-li, *adv.* In an intelligent manner.
Intelligibility, in-tel'i-ji-bil"i-ti, *n.* Quality or state of being intelligible.
Intelligible, in-tel'i-ji-bl, *a.* Capable of being understood; comprehensible; clear.
Intelligibly, in-tel'i-ji-bli, *adv.* In an intelligible manner.
Intemperance, in-tem'pėr-ans, *n.* Want of temperance; excess of any kind; habitual indulgence in alcoholic liquors.
Intemperate, in-tem'pėr-āt, *a.* Not temperate; addicted to an excessive use of alcoholic liquors; excessive or immoderate.—*n.* One not temperate.
Intemperately, in-tem'pėr-āt-li, *adv.* In an intemperate manner.
Intend, in-tend', *vt.* To design; to purpose; to mean.
Intendancy, in-tend'an-si, *n.* The office or district of an intendant.
Intendant, in-tend'ant, *n.* A manager; a steward; a local governor.
Intended, in-tend'ed, *p.a.* Purposed; betrothed.—*n.* An affianced lover.
Intense, in-tens', *a.* Closely strained; strict; extreme in degree; violent; severe.
Intensely, in-tens'li, *adv.* In an intense manner or degree.
Intensify, in-ten'si-fī, *vt.* To render intense or more intense; to aggravate.—*vi.* To become intense.
Intension, in-ten'shon, *n.* Act of intensifying; state of being strained; in *logic*, the qualities necessarily possessed by objects in virtue of their name.
Intensity, in-ten'si-ti, *n.* State of being intense; keenness; extreme degree; amount of energy.
Intensive, in-ten'siv, *a.* Serving to give emphasis.—*n.* Something giving emphasis.
Intent, in-tent', *a.* Having the mind bent on an object; sedulously applied.—*n.* Design or purpose; meaning; drift.
Intention, in-ten'shon, *n.* Act of intending; purpose; design; intension; method of treatment in surgery; a general concept.
Intentional, in-ten'shon-al, *a.* Done with design or purpose; intended.
Intentionally, in-ten'shon-al-li, *adv.* In an intentional manner; on purpose.
Intently, in-tent'li, *adv.* In an intent manner.
Inter, in-tėr', *vt.* (interring, interred). To bury; to inhume.
Interact, in'tėr-akt, *n.* Interval between two acts of a drama; any intermediate employment of time.—*vi.* To act reciprocally.
Interaction, in-tėr-ak'shon, *n.* Mutual or reciprocal action.
Intercalary, in-tėr'ka-la-ri, *a.* Inserted or introduced among others, as the odd day in leap-year; intermediate.
Intercalate, in-tėr'ka-lāt, *vt.* To insert between others, as a day, &c.
Intercede, in-tėr-sēd', *vi.* (interceding, interceded). To mediate; to plead in favour of one; to make intercession.
Intercept, in-tėr-sept', *vt.* To take or seize on by the way; to stop on its passage; to obstruct the progress of; to cut or shut off.
Interception, in-tėr-sep'shon, *n.* Act of intercepting.
Intercession, in-tėr-se'shon, *n.* Act of interceding; mediation; prayer or solicitation to one party in favour of another.
Intercessor, in'tėr-ses-ėr, *n.* One who intercedes; a mediator.
Intercessory, in-tėr-ses'so-ri, *a.* Containing intercession; mediatorial.
Interchain, in-tėr-chān', *vt.* To chain or link together.
Interchange, in-tėr-chānj', *vt.* To change, as one with the other; to exchange; to reciprocate.—*n.* in'tėr-chānj. Mutual change; exchange; alternate succession.
Interchangeable, in-tėr-chānj'a-bl, *a.* That may be interchanged.
Interchangeably, in-tėr-chānj'a-bli, *adv.* By way of interchange; alternately.
Intercolonial, in'tėr-ko-lō"ni-al, *a.* Subsisting between different colonies.
Intercommunicate, in'tėr-kom-mū"ni-kāt, *vi.* To communicate mutually.
Intercommunication, in'tėr-kom-mū'ni-kā"-shon, *n.* Reciprocal communication.
Intercommunion, in'tėr-kom-mūn"yon, *n.* Mutual communion or intercourse.
Intercourse, in'tėr-kōrs, *n.* Reciprocal dealings between persons or nations; fellowship; familiarity; sexual connection.
Interdict, in-tėr-dikt', *vt.* To forbid; to place under an interdict or prohibition.—*n.* in'tėr-dikt. A prohibition; a papal prohibition of the administration of religious rites.
Interdiction, in-tėr-dik'shon, *n.* Act of interdicting; prohibition.
Interdictory, in-tėr-dik'to-ri, *a.* Having power to interdict or prohibit.
Interest, in'tėr-est, *vt.* To concern; to engage the attention of.—*n.* Concern or regard; advantage; profit; profit per cent from money lent or invested; influence with a person.
Interested, in'tėr-est-ed, *p.a.* Having an interest; liable to be affected; chiefly concerned for one's private advantage.
Interesting, in'tėr-est-ing, *p.a.* Engaging the attention or curiosity.
Interfere, in-ter-fēr', *vi.* (interfering, interfered). To clash; to interpose; to take a part in the concerns of others.
Interference, in-tėr-fēr'ens, *n.* Act of interfering; clashing or collision.
Interim, in'tėr-im, *n.* The meantime; time intervening.—*a.* Belonging to an intervening time; temporary.
Interior, in-tē'ri-ėr, *a.* Internal; being within; inland.—*n.* The inner part of a thing; the inside; the inland part of a country, &c.
Interjacent, in-tėr-jā'sent, *a.* Lying or being between; intervening.
Interject, in-tėr-jekt', *vt.* To throw in between; to insert.
Interjection, in-tėr-jek'shon, *n.* Act of throwing between; a word thrown in between words to express some emotion; an exclamation.
Interjectional, in-tėr-jek'shon-al, *a.* Forming or being like an interjection.
Interlace, in-tėr-lās', *vt.* To weave together.—*vi.* To have parts intercrossing.
Interlard, in-tėr-lärd', *vt.* To mix; to diversify by mixture.

Interleave, in-tėr-lēv', *vt.* To insert, as blank leaves in a book between other leaves.
Interline, in-tėr-līn', *vt.* To put a line or lines between; to write or print in alternate lines or between lines.
Interlinear, Interlineal, in-tėr-lin'ē-ėr, in-tėr-lin'ē-al, *a.* Written or printed between lines; placed between lines; interlined.
Interlineation, in-tėr-lin'ē-ā"shon, *n.* Act of interlining; that which is interlined.
Interlock, in-tėr-lok', *vi.* and *t.* To unite or lock together by a series of connections.
Interlocution, in'tėr-lō-kū"shon, *n.* Dialogue; interchange of speech; an intermediate act or decree before final decision.
Interlocutor, in-tėr-lo'kūt-ėr, *n.* One who speaks in dialogue; *Scots law*, a judgment or order of any court of record.
Interlocutory, in-tėr-lo'kū-to-ri, *a.* Consisting of dialogue; not final or definitive.
Interlope, in-tėr-lōp', *vi.* To traffic without proper license; to intrude.
Interloper, in-tėr-lōp'ėr, *n.* An intruder.
Interlude, in'tėr-lūd, *n.* A short entertainment between the acts of a play, or between the play and the afterpiece; a piece of music between certain more important passages.
Interlunar, in-tėr-lū'nėr, *a.* Belonging to the time when the moon is invisible.
Intermarriage, in-tėr-ma'rij, *n.* Marriage between two families, tribes, &c.
Intermarry, in-tėr-ma'ri, *vi.* To become connected by marriage, as families.
Intermeddle, in-tėr-med'l, *vi.* To meddle in the affairs of others; to interfere.
Intermeddler, in-tėr-med'lėr, *n.* One who intermeddles.
Intermediary, in-tėr-mē'di-a-ri, *a.* Intermediate.—*n.* An intermediate agent.
Intermediate, in-tėr-mē'di-āt, *a.* Being between two extremes; intervening.
Intermedium, in-tėr-mē'di-um, *n.* Intervening agent, instrument, or space.
Interment, in-tėr'ment, *n.* Burial.
Intermezzo, in-tėr-met'zō, *n.* A short musical composition, generally of a light sparkling character; an interlude.
Interminable, in-tėr'min-a-bl, *a.* Admitting no limit; boundless; endless.
Interminate, in-tėr'min-āt, *a.* Unbounded; unlimited; endless.
Intermingle, in-tėr-ming'gl, *vt.* To mingle together.—*vi.* To be mixed or incorporated.
Intermission, in-tėr-mi'shon, *n.* Act or state of intermitting; pause; rest.
Intermit, in-tėr-mit', *vt.* (intermitting, intermitted). To cause to cease for a time; to suspend.—*vi.* To cease for a time.
Intermittent, in-tėr-mit'ent, *a.* Ceasing at intervals; ceasing and then returning, as certain fevers.—*n.* A fever which intermits.
Intermix, in-tėr-miks', *vt.* To mix together.—*vi.* To be mixed together.
Intermixture, in-tėr-miks'tūr, *n.* A mass formed by mixture; an admixture.
Intern, in-tėrn', *vt.* To send to and cause to remain in the interior of a country; to disarm and quarter in some place, as defeated troops.
Internal, in-tėrn'al, *a.* Inward; not external; domestic; not foreign.
Internally, in-tėrn'al-li, *adv.* Inwardly; mentally; spiritually.
International, in-tėr-na'shon-al, *a.* Relating to or mutually affecting nations; regulating the mutual intercourse between nations.
Internecine, in-tėr-nē'sīn, *a.* Marked by destructive hostilities; causing great slaughter.
Internuncio, in-tėr-nun'si-ō, *n.* A messenger; title of the pope's representative at republics and small courts.
Interpellate, in-tėr'pel-lāt, *vt.* To question; to interrupt by a question.
Interpellation, in'tėr-pel-lā"shon, *n.* Act of interpellating; question put in a legislative assembly to a member of the government.
Interpolate, in-tėr'pō-lāt, *vt.* To foist in; to add a spurious word or passage to.
Interpolation, in-tėr'pō-lā"shon, *n.* Act of interpolating; spurious word or passage inserted.
Interpolator, in-tėr'pō-lāt-ėr, *n.* One who interpolates.
Interposal, in-tėr-pōs'al, *n.* Act of interposing; interposition.
Interpose, in-tėr-pōz', *vt.* (interposing, interposed). To place between.—*vi.* To mediate; to put in or make a remark.
Interposition, in-tėr'pō-zi"shon, *n.* Act of interposing; intervention; mediation.
Interpret, in-tėr'pret, *vt.* To explain the meaning of; to expound; to construe; to represent artistically (as an actor).
Interpretable, in-tėr'pret-a-bl, *a.* That may be interpreted.
Interpretation, in-tėr'pret-ā"shon, *n.* Act of interpreting; explanation; representation of a character on the stage.
Interpretative, in-tėr'pret-āt-iv, *a.* Serving to interpret; containing explanation.
Interpreter, in-tėr'pret-ėr, *n.* One who interprets; a translator.
Interregnum, in-tėr-reg'num, *n.* The time between reigns; intermission or break in succession.
Interrelation, in'tėr-rē-lā"shon, *n.* Mutual or corresponding relation; correlation.
Interrogate, in-te'rō-gāt, *vt.* To question; to examine by asking questions.
Interrogation, in-te'rō-gā"shon, *n.* Act of interrogating; question put; a sign that marks a question, thus (?).
Interrogative, in-te-rog'at-iv, *a.* Denoting a question; expressed in the form of a question.—*n.* A word used in asking questions, as *who? what?*
Interrogator, in-te'rō-gāt'ėr, *n.* One who interrogates or asks questions.
Interrogatory, in-te-rog'a-to-ri, *n.* A question.—*a.* Containing or expressing a question.
Interrupt, in-tėr-rupt', *vt.* To break in upon the progress of; to cause to stop in speaking.
Interrupted, in-tėr-rupt'ed, *p.a.* Having interruptions; broken; intermitted.
Interruption, in-tėr-rup'shon, *n.* Act of interrupting; a break or breach; obstruction or hindrance; cause of stoppage.
Intersect, in-tėr-sekt', *vt.* To cut in between; to divide; to cut or cross mutually.—*vi.* To meet and cut or cross each other.
Intersection, in-tėr-sek'shon, *n.* Act or state of intersecting; the point or line in which two lines or two planes cut each other.
Intersperse, in-tėr-spėrs', *vt.* To scatter or set here and there among other things.
Interspersion, in-tėr-spėr'shon, *n.* Act of interspersing.

Interstellar, Interstellary, in-tėr-stel'lėr, in-tėr-stel'la-ri, *a.* Intervening between the stars; situated beyond the solar system.
Interstice, in-tėrs'tis, *n.* A narrow space between things closely set; a chink.
Interstitial, in-tėr-sti'shal, *a.* Pertaining to or containing interstices.
Interstratify, in-tėr-strat'i-fī, *vt.* and *i.* To place or be placed between other strata.
Intertexture, in-tėr-teks'tūr, *n.* Act of interweaving; state of things interwoven; what is interwoven.
Intertropical, in-tėr-tro'pik-al, *a.* Situated between the tropics.
Intertwine, in-tėr-twīn', *vt.* To unite by twining or twisting.—*vi.* To be interwoven.
Intertwist, in-tėr-twist', *vt.* To twist, as one with another.
Interval, in'tėr-val, *n.* A space between things; amount of separation between ranks, degrees, &c.; difference in gravity or acuteness between sounds.
Intervene, in-tėr-vēn', *vi.* (intervening, intervened). To come or be between; to interpose or interfere.
Intervention, in-tėr-ven'shon, *n.* Act of intervening; interposition; agency of persons between persons.
Interview, in'tėr-vū, *n.* A meeting between persons; a conference.—*vt.* To have an interview with to get information for publication.
Interviewer, in-tėr-vū'ėr, *n.* One who interrogates some person of position or notoriety to obtain matter for publication.
Interweave, in-tėr-wēv', *vt.* To weave together; to unite intimately; to interlace.
Intestable, in-test'a-bl, *a.* Legally unqualified to make a will.
Intestacy, in-test'a-si, *n.* State of being intestate.
Intestate, in-test'āt, *a.* Dying without having made a will; not disposed of by will.—*n.* A person who dies without making a will.
Intestinal, in-tes'tin-al, *a.* Pertaining to the intestines.
Intestine, in-tes'tin, *a.* Internal; domestic; not foreign. *n.* The canal extending from the stomach to the anus; *pl.* entrails or viscera in general.
Inthrall, in-thral', *vt.* *See* ENTHRALL.
Intimacy, in'ti-ma-si, *n.* State of being intimate; close friendship.
Intimate, in'ti-māt, *a.* Inward or internal; close in friendship; familiar; close.—*n.* An intimate or familiar friend.—*vt.* (intimating, intimated). To hint or indicate; to announce.
Intimately, in'ti-māt-li, *adv.* In an intimate manner; familiarly.
Intimation, in-ti-mā'shon, *n.* Act of intimating; a hint; announcement.
Intimidate, in-tim'id-āt, *vt.* To put in fear or dread; to cow; to deter with threats.
Intimidation, in-tim'id-ā"shon, *n.* Act of intimidating.
Intitle, in-tī'tl. *See* ENTITLE.
Into, in'tö, *prep.* In and to: expressing motion or direction towards the inside of, or a change of condition.
Intolerable, in-tol'ėr-a-bl, *a.* That cannot be borne; unendurable; insufferable.
Intolerably, in-tol'ėr-a-bli, *adv.* To a degree beyond endurance.
Intolerance, in-tol'ėr-ans, *n.* Quality of being intolerant; want of toleration.
Intolerant, in-tol'ėr-ant, *a.* That cannot bear; not enduring difference of opinion or worship; refusing to tolerate others.
Intolerantly, in-tol'ėr-ant-li, *adv.* In an intolerant manner.
Intonate, in'tōn-āt, *vi.* To sound the notes of the musical scale; to modulate the voice.—*vt.* To pronounce with a certain modulation.
Intonation, in-tōn-ā'shon, *n.* Act or manner of intonating; modulation of the voice; utterance with a special tone.
Intone, in-tōn', *vi.* To use a musical monotone in pronouncing.—*vt.* To pronounce with a musical tone; to chant.
Intoxicant, in-toks'i-kant, *n.* That which intoxicates; an intoxicating liquor.
Intoxicate, in-toks'i-kāt, *vt.* To make drunk; to elate to enthusiasm or madness.—*vi.* To cause intoxication.
Intoxicating, in-toks'i-kāt-ing, *p.a.* Causing intoxication.
Intoxication, in-toks'i-kā"shon, *n.* Act of intoxicating; state of being drunk; delirious excitement; frenzy.
Intractable, in-trakt'a-bl, *a.* Not tractable; not to be governed or managed; refractory.
Intrados, in-trā'dos, *n.* The interior and lower line or curve of an arch.
Intramural, in-tra-mū'ral, *a.* Being within the walls, as of a town or university.
Intransigent, in-tran'si-jent, *a.* Irreconcilable.—*n.* An irreconcilable person.
Intransitive, in-trans'it-iv, *a.* Designating a verb which expresses an action or state limited to the subject.
Intransmutable, in-trans-mūt'a-bl, *a.* That cannot be transmuted.
Intrant, in'trant, *n.* An entrant.
Intrench, in-trensh', *vt.* To dig a trench around, as in fortification; to fortify with a ditch and parapet; to lodge within an intrenchment.—*vi.* To invade; to encroach.
Intrenchment, in-trensh'ment, *n.* Act of intrenching; a trench; any protection; encroachment.
Intrepid, in-tre'pid, *a.* Undaunted; fearless; bold; daring; courageous.
Intrepidity, in-tre-pid'i-ti, *n.* Quality of being intrepid; undaunted courage.
Intricacy, in'tri-ka-si, *n.* State of being intricate; complication; complexity.
Intricate, in'tri-kāt, *a.* Involved; complicated.
Intrigue, in-trēg', *n.* An underhand plot or scheme; plot of a play, &c.; an illicit intimacy between a man and woman.—*vi.* (intriguing, intrigued). To engage in an intrigue; to carry on forbidden love.
Intriguing, in-trēg'ing, *p.a.* Addicted to intrigue; given to secret machinations.
Intrinsic, Intrinsical, in-trin'sik, in-trin'sik-al, *a.* Being within; inherent; essential.
Intrinsically, in-trin'sik-al-li, *adv.* In its nature; essentially; inherently.
Introduce, in-trō-dūs', *vt.* To lead or bring in; to insert; to bring to be acquainted; to present; to make known; to import; to bring before the public.
Introduction, in-trō-duk'shon, *n.* Act of introducing; act of making persons known to each other; act of bringing something into notice; a preliminary discourse.
Introductive, in-trō-duk'tiv, *a.* Introductory.

Introductory, in-trō-duk'to-ri, *a.* Serving to introduce; prefatory; preliminary.
Intromission, in-trō-mish'on, *n.* The act of intromitting.
Intromit, in-trō-mit', *vt.* To send in; to admit.—*vi. Scots law,* to intermeddle with the effects of another.
Introrse, in-trors', *a.* Turned or facing inwards.
Introspect, in-trō-spekt', *vt.* To look into or within.
Introspection, in-trō-spek'shon, *n.* The act of looking inwardly; examination of one's own thoughts or feelings.
Introvert, in-trō-vėrt', *vt.* To turn inward.
Intrude, in-tröd', *vi.* (intruding, intruded). To thrust oneself in; to force an entry or way in without permission, right, or invitation; to encroach.—*vt.* To thrust in.
Intrusion, in-trö'zhon, *n.* Action of intruding; encroachment.
Intrusive, in-trö'siv, *a.* Apt to intrude; characterized by intrusion.
Intrust, in-trust', *vt.* To deliver in trust; to confide to the care of. Also *entrust.*
Intuition, in-tū-i'shon, *n.* A looking on; direct apprehension of a truth without reasoning.
Intuitive, in-tū'it-iv, *a.* Perceived by the mind immediately without reasoning; based on intuition; self-evident.
Intuitively, in-tū'it-iv-li, *adv.* In an intuitive manner; by intuition.
Intumesce, in-tū-mes', *vi.* To enlarge or expand with heat; to swell out in bulk.
Intussuscept, in'tus-sus-sept, *vt.* To receive by intussusception.
Intussusception, in'tus-sus-sep"shon, *n.* Reception of one part within another; the doubling in of a part of the intestines into a lower part; process by which nutriment is absorbed.
Intwine, Intwist. *See* En-.
Inundate, in-un'dāt or in'-, *vt.* To spread or flow over; to flood; to overwhelm.
Inundation, in-un-dā'shon, *n.* Act of inundating; a flood.
Inure, in-ūr', *vt.* (inuring, inured). To accustom; to harden by use.—*vi.* To be applied.
Inurn, in-ėrn', *vt.* To put in an urn; to bury.
Inutility, in-ū-til'i-ti, *n.* Uselessness.
Invade, in-vād', *vt.* (invading, invaded). To enter with hostile intentions; to make an inroad on; to encroach on; to violate.
Invader, in-vād'ėr, *n.* One who invades; an assailant; an encroacher.
Invalid, in-va'lid, *a.* Not valid; having no force or effect; void; null.
Invalid, in'va-lēd, *n.* One weak or infirm; a person disabled for active service.—*a.* In ill health; infirm; disabled.—*vt.* To render an invalid; to enrol on the list of invalids.
Invalidate, in-va'li-dāt, *vt.* To render of no force or effect.
Invalidation, in-va'li-dā"shon, *n.* Act of invalidating.
Invalidity, in-va-lid'i-ti, *n.* State or quality of being invalid; want of force or efficacy.
Invaluable, in-va'lū-a-bl, *a.* Precious above estimation; inestimable; priceless.
Invaluably, in-va'lū-a-bli, *adv.* Inestimably.
Invar, in'var, *n.* An alloy of nickel and steel which is practically unaffected by extremes of temperature.
Invariable, in-vā'ri-a-bl, *a.* Not variable; unchangeable; always uniform.
Invariably, in-vā'ri-a-bli, *adv.* Uniformly.
Invasion, in-vā'zhon, *n.* Act of invading; hostile entrance; infringement; violation.
Invasive, in-vā'siv, *a.* Making invasion; aggressive.
Invective, in-vek'tiv, *n.* Violent utterance of censure; railing language; vituperation.—*a.* Containing invectives; abusive.
Inveigh, in-vā', *vi.* To attack with invectives; to rail against; to reproach; to upbraid.
Inveigle, in-vē'gl, *vt.* To persuade to something evil; to entice; to seduce.
Inveiglement, in-vē'gl-ment, *n.* Act of inveigling; seduction to evil; enticement.
Invent, in-vent', *vt.* To devise or produce, as something new; to fabricate; to concoct.
Invention, in-ven'shon, *n.* Act of inventing; contrivance of that which did not before exist; device; power of inventing; ingenuity; faculty by which an author produces plots, &c.
Inventive, in-vent'iv, *a.* Able to invent; quick at contrivance; ready at expedients.
Inventor, in-vent'ėr, *n.* One who invents; a contriver.
Inventorial, in-ven-tō'ri-al, *a.* Relating to an inventory.
Inventory, in'ven-to-ri, *n.* An account or catalogue of the goods and chattels of a deceased person; a catalogue of particular things.—*vt.* To make an inventory of.
Inventress, in-vent'res, *n.* A female who invents.
Inverse, in'vėrs or in-vėrs', *a.* Opposite in order or relation; inverted.
Inversely, in-vėrs'li, *adv.* In an inverse order or manner; in inverse proportion.
Inversion, in-vėr'shon, *n.* Act of inverting; state of being inverted; change of order so that the last becomes first, and the first last; a turning backward.
Invert, in-vėrt', *vt.* To turn upside down; to place in a contrary position; to reverse.
Invertebrate, in-vėr'tē-brāt, *a.* Destitute of a backbone or vertebral column.—*n.* An animal (one of the Invertebrata) in which there is no backbone.
Inverted, in-vėrt'ed, *p.a.* Turned upside down; changed in order.
Invest, in-vest', *vt.* To clothe; to array; to clothe with office or authority; to endow; to besiege; to lay out as money in some species of property.—*vi.* To make an investment.
Investigate, in-ves'ti-gāt, *vt.* To search into; to make careful examination of.
Investigation, in-ves'ti-gā"shon, *n.* Act of investigating; examination; search; scrutiny.
Investigator, in-ves'ti-gāt-ėr, *n.* One who investigates.
Investiture, in-ves'ti-tūr, *n.* Act of investing or giving possession of any manor, office, or benefice; clothing; covering.
Investment, in-vest'ment, *n.* Act of investing; act of besieging; money laid out for profit; that in which money is invested.
Investor, in-vest'ėr, *n.* One who invests.
Inveteracy, in-vet'ėr-a-si, *n.* State or quality of being inveterate; obstinacy of any quality or state acquired by time.

Inveterate, in-vet'ėr-āt, *a.* Long established; deep-rooted; obstinate; confirmed.
Invidious, in-vid'i-us, *a.* Envious; malignant; likely to incur hatred or to provoke envy.
Invidiously, in-vid'i-us-li, *adv.* In an invidious manner; malignantly.
Invigorate, in-vi'gor-āt, *vt.* To give vigour to; to give life and energy to.
Invigoration, in-vi'gor-ā"shon, *n.* Act of invigorating; state of being invigorated.
Invincible, in-vin'si-bl, *a.* Not to be conquered or overcome; insurmountable.—*n.* One who is invincible.
Invincibly, in-vin'si-bli, *adv.* Unconquerably.
Inviolability, in-vī'ō-la-bil"i-ti, *n.* Quality or state of being inviolable.
Inviolable, in-vī'ō-la-bl, *a.* Not to be violated; that ought not to be injured or treated irreverently; not susceptible of hurt.
Inviolably, in-vī'ō-la-bli, *adv.* In an inviolable manner; without profanation.
Inviolate, in-vī'ō-lāt, *a.* Not violated; uninjured; unprofaned; unbroken.
Invisibility, in-vi'zi-bil"i-ti, *n.* State of being invisible.
Invisible, in-vi'zi-bl, *a.* Not visible; that cannot be seen; imperceptible.
Invisibly, in-vi'zi-bli, *adv.* In an invisible manner; imperceptible to the eye.
Invitation, in-vi-tā'shon, *n.* Act of inviting; bidding to an entertainment, &c.
Invite, in-vīt', *vt.* (inviting, invited). To ask to do something; to ask to an entertainment, &c.; to allure or attract.—*vi.* To give invitation; to allure.
Inviting, in-vīt'ing, *p.a.* Attractive.
Invitingly, in-vīt'ing-li, *adv.* Attractively.
Invocate, in'vō-kāt, *vt.* To invoke.
Invocation, in-vō-kā'shon, *n.* Act of invoking; the form or act of calling for the assistance of any being, particularly a divinity.
Invoice, in'vois, *n.* A written account of the merchandise sent to a person, with the prices annexed.—*vt.* (invoicing, invoiced). To make an invoice of; to enter in an invoice.
Invoke, in-vōk', *vt.* (invoking, invoked). To call upon; to address in prayer; to call on for assistance and protection.
Involucre, in-vō-lū'kėr, *n.* Any collection of bracts round a cluster of flowers.
Involuntarily, in-vo'lun-ta-ri-li, *adv.* In an involuntary manner.
Involuntary, in-vo'lun-ta-ri, *a.* Not voluntary; independent of will or choice.
Involute, in'vō-lūt, *n.* A curve traced by any point of a tense string when it is unwound from a given curve.—*a.* Involved; rolled inward from the edges.
Involution, in-vō-lū'shon, *n.* Act of involving; state of being involved; complication; the raising of a quantity to any power assigned.
Involve, in-volv', *vt.* (involving, involved). To roll up; to envelop; to imply; to include; to implicate; to complicate; in algebra, &c., to raise a quantity to any assigned power.
Invulnerable, in-vul'nėr-a-bl, *a.* That cannot be wounded; incapable of receiving injury.
Inward, in'wėrd, *a.* Internal; being within; intimate; in the mind, soul, or feelings.—*adv.* Toward the inside; into the mind.—*n.pl.* The inner parts of an animal; the viscera.
Inwardly, in'wėrd-li, *adv.* In the inner parts; internally; privately.
Inwards, in'wėrdz, *adv.* Same as *Inward.*
Inweave, in-wēv', *vt.* To weave together.
Inworn, in-wōrn', *a.* Worn within or wrought within.
Inwrap, in-rap', *vt.* To wrap round; to involve; to perplex.
Inwrought, in-rąt', *p.a.* Wrought in or among other things; adorned with figures.
Iodide, ī'ō-dīd, *n.* A compound of iodine and a metal.
Iodine, ī'ō-dīn, ī'ō-dēn, *n.* A non-metallic element chiefly extracted from the ashes of sea-weeds, and much used in medicine.
Iodoform, ī-od'ō-form, *n.* A compound of carbon, hydrogen, and iodine, an antiseptic.
Ion, ī'on, *n.* An electrified particle formed by the transfer of electrons when molecules of gas are broken up.
Ionian, ī-ō'ni-an, *a.* Pertaining to Ionia; Ionic.—*n.* One of an ancient Greek race.
Ionic, ī-on'ik, *a.* Relating to Ionia, or to the Ionian Greeks; denoting an order of architecture distinguished by the volutes of its capital.
Iota, ī-ō'ta, *n.* The name of the Greek letter *i*; a tittle; a jot.
I O U, ī' ō ū, *n.* A signed paper having on it these letters and a sum of money borrowed, serving as an acknowledgment of a debt.
Ipecacuanha, i-pē-kak'ū-an"ha, *n.* A bitter emetic and tonic obtained from the root of a Brazilian plant.
Irade, i-rä'dā, *n.* A Turkish decree or proclamation.
Iranian, ī-rā'ni-an, *a.* Pertaining to *Iran*, the native name of Persia: applied to the Persian Zend, and cognate tongues.
Irascibility, ī-ras'i-bil"i-ti, *n.* Quality of being irascible.
Irascible, ī-ras'i-bl, *a.* Readily made angry; easily provoked; irritable.
Irascibly, ī-ras'i-bli, *adv.* In an irascible manner.
Irate, ī-rāt', *a.* Angry; enraged; incensed.
Ire, īr, *n.* Anger; wrath; rage.
Ireful, īr'fųl, *a.* Full of ire; angry; wroth.
Iricism, ī'ri-sizm, *n.* An Irish mode of expression; any Irish peculiarity.
Iridescence, ī-rid-es'ens, *n.* Property of being iridescent; exhibition of colours like those of the rainbow.
Iridescent, ī-rid-es'ent, *a.* Exhibiting colours like the rainbow; shimmering with rainbow colours.
Iris, ī'ris, *n.*; pl. **Irises,** ī'ris-ez. The rainbow; an appearance resembling the rainbow; the coloured circle round the pupil of the eye; the flag-flower.
Irish, ī'rish, *a.* Pertaining to Ireland or its inhabitants.—*n.* Natives of Ireland; the Celtic language of the natives of Ireland.
Irishism, ī'rish-izm, *n.* An Iricism.
Irk, ėrk, *vt.* To weary; to annoy; to vex. (Used impersonally.)
Irksome, ėrk'sum, *a.* Wearisome; vexatious.
Irksomely, ėrk'sum-li, *adv.* Tediously.
Iron, ī'ėrn, *n.* The most common and useful metal; an instrument made of iron; a utensil for smoothing cloth; *pl.* fetters; chains; handcuffs.—*a.* Made of iron; consisting of or like iron; harsh; severe; binding fast;

vigorous; inflexible.—*vt.* To smooth with an iron; to fetter; to furnish or arm with iron.

Iron-bound, ī'ėrn-bound, *a.* Bound with iron; surrounded with rocks; rugged.

Iron-clad, ī'ėrn-klad, *a.* Covered with iron plates; armour-plated.—*n.* A war-ship covered with thick iron plates.

Iron-gray, ī'ėrn-grā, *n.* A colour resembling freshly fractured iron.

Ironical, ī-ron'ik-al, *a.* Containing irony; given to irony; expressing one thing and meaning the opposite.

Ironically, ī-ron'ik-al-li, *adv.* By way of irony; by the use of irony.

Iron-master, ī'ėrn-mas-tėr, *n.* An owner of blast-furnaces, &c.

Ironmonger, ī'ėrn-mung-gėr, *n.* A dealer in iron-wares or hardware.

Ironmongery, ī'ėrn-mung-gė-ri, *n.* A general name for all articles made of iron.

Iron-mould, ī'ėrn-mōld, *n.* A spot on cloth occasioned by iron rust.

Iron ration, ī'ėrn rash'un, *n.* A soldier's emergency ration of beef, biscuit, tea, &c.

Iron-stone, ī'ėrn-stōn, *n.* An ore of iron having a stony character.

Ironware, ī'ėrn-wār, *n.* Iron worked up into utensils, tools, &c.

Irony, ī'ėrn-i, *a.* Made of or like iron; hard.

Irony, ī'ron-i, *n.* A mode of speech which expresses a sense contrary to that conveyed by the words; a subtle kind of sarcasm.

Irradiance, Irradiancy, ir-rā'di-ans, ir-rā'di-an-si, *n.* Lustre; splendour.

Irradiant, ir-rā'di-ant, *a.* Emitting rays of light.

Irradiate, ir-rā'di-āt, *vt.* To send forth rays of light upon; to enlighten.—*vi.* To emit rays.

Irradiation, ir-rā'di-ā"shon, *n.* Act of irradiating; illumination; apparent enlargement of an object strongly illuminated.

Irrational, ir-ra'shon-al, *a.* Not rational; void of reason or understanding; foolish; in *mathematics*, surd.

Irrationally, ir-ra'shon-al-li, *adv.* In an irrational manner; without reason; absurdly.

Irreclaimable, ir-rē-klām'a-bl, *a.* Not reclaimable; incorrigible.

Irreconcilable, ir-re'kon-sil"a-bl, *a.* Not reconcilable; inconsistent; incompatible.—*n.* One who is not to be reconciled; one who will not work in harmony with associates.

Irrecoverable, ir-rē-ku'vėr-a-bl, *a.* Not to be recovered or regained.

Irredeemable, ir-rē-dēm'a-bl, *a.* Not redeemable; not subject to be paid at its nominal value.

Irreducible, ir-rē-dūs'i-bl, *a.* Not reducible; that cannot be reduced.

Irreflective, ir-rē-flekt'iv, *a.* Not reflective.

Irrefragable, ir-ref'ra-ga-bl, *a.* That cannot be refuted; indisputable; undeniable.

Irrefutable, ir-rē-fūt'a-bl or ir-ref'ūt-a-bl, *a.* That cannot be refuted; unanswerable.

Irregular, ir-re'gū-lėr, *a.* Not regular; not according to rule or custom; anomalous; vicious; crooked; variable; deviating from the common rules in its inflections.—*n.* A soldier not in regular service.

Irregularity, ir-re'gū-la"ri-ti, *n.* State or character of being irregular; want of regularity; that which is irregular; immoral action or behaviour.

Irregularly, ir-re'gū-lėr-li, *adv.* In an irregular manner.

Irrelevance, Irrelevancy, ir-re'lē-vans, ir-re'lē-van-si, *n.* State or quality of being irrelevant.

Irrelevant, ir-re'lē-vant, *a.* Not relevant; not applicable; not to the purpose.

Irreligion, ir-rē-li'jon, *n.* Want of religion, or contempt of it; impiety.

Irreligious, ir-rē-li'jus, *a.* Not religious; contrary to religion; impious; ungodly; profane.

Irremediable, ir-rē-mē'di-a-bl, *a.* Not to be remedied; incurable; irreparable.

Irremissible, ir-rē-mis'i-bl, *a.* Not to be remitted or pardoned; unpardonable.

Irremovable, ir-rē-mōv'a-bl, *a.* Not removable; firmly fixed.

Irreparable, ir-re'pa-ra-bl, *a.* Not reparable; irretrievable; irremediable.

Irrepealable, ir-rē-pēl'a-bl, *a.* Not repealable; incapable of being repealed.

Irreprehensible, ir-rep'rē-hen"si-bl, *a.* Not reprehensible; blameless.

Irrepressible, ir-rē-pres'i-bl, *a.* Not repressible; incapable of being repressed.

Irreproachable, ir-rē-prōch'a-bl, *a.* Incapable of being reproached; upright; faultless.

Irreprovable, ir-rē-prōv'a-bl, *a.* Not reprovable; blameless; upright; unblamable.

Irresistance, ir-rē-zis'tans, *n.* Non-resistance; passive submission.

Irresistible, ir-rē-zist'i-bl, *a.* Not resistible; that cannot be resisted; resistless.

Irresolute, ir-re'zō-lūt, *a.* Not resolute; not firm in purpose; undecided; wavering.

Irresolution, ir-re'zō-lū"shon, *n.* Want of resolution or decision; vacillation.

Irresolvable, ir-rē-zolv'a-bl, *a.* Not resolvable; that cannot be resolved.

Irrespective, ir-rē-spekt'iv, *a.* Having no respect to particular circumstances (with *of*).

Irrespectively, ir-rē-spekt'iv-li, *adv.* Without regard to (with *of*).

Irrespirable, ir-rē-spīr'a-bl, *a.* Not respirable; unfit for respiration.

Irresponsible, ir-rē-spons'i-bl, *a.* Not responsible; not liable to answer for consequences.

Irresponsive, ir-rēspons'iv, *a.* Not responsive.

Irretrievable, ir-rē-trēv'a-bl, *a.* That cannot be retrieved; irreparable.

Irreverence, ir-rev'er-ens, *n.* Want of reverence; want of veneration for the deity or for things sacred; want of due regard to a superior; irreverent conduct or action.

Irreverent, ir-rev'er-ent, *a.* Exhibiting or marked by irreverence; wanting in respect.

Irreversible, ir-rē-vėr'si-bl, *a.* Not reversible; not to be annulled.

Irrevocable, ir-re'vōk-a-bl, *a.* Not to be recalled, revoked, or annulled; irreversible.

Irrigate, ir'ri-gāt, *vt.* To bedew or sprinkle; to water by means of channels or streams.

Irrigation, ir-ri-gā'shon, *n.* Act or operation of irrigating.

Irriguous, ir-ri'gū-us, *a.* Well watered; watery.

Irritability, ir'rit-a-bil"i-ti, *n.* Quality or state of being irritable.

Irritable, ir'rit-a-bl, *a.* Susceptible of irritation; very liable to anger; easily provoked.

Irritant, ir'rit-ant, *a.* Irritating; producing inflammation.—*n.* That which irritates; a medical application that causes pain or heat.

Irritate, ir'rit-āt, *vt.* To rouse to anger; to provoke; to inflame.
Irritating, ir'rit-āt-ing, *p.a.* Causing irritation; annoying.
Irritation, ir-rit-ā'shon, *n.* Act of irritating; exasperation; annoyance; vital action in muscles or organs caused by some stimulus.
Irruption, ir-rup'shon, *n.* A bursting in; a sudden invasion or incursion.
Irruptive, ir-rup'tiv, *a.* Rushing in or upon.
Is, iz. The third pers. sing. of the verb *to be.*
Ishmaelite, ish'ma-el-īt, *n.* A descendant of Ishmael; one at war with society.
Isinglass, ī'zing-glas, *n.* Fish-glue, a gelatinous substance prepared from the air-bladders of certain fishes.
Islam, is'lam, *n.* The religion of Mohammed; the whole body of those who profess it.
Islamism, is'lam-izm, *n.* Mohammedanism.
Islamite, is'lam-īt, *n.* A Mohammedan.
Island, ī'land, *n.* A piece of land surrounded by water; anything resembling an island.—*vt.* To cause to become or appear like an island; to dot, as with islands.
Islander, ī'land-ėr, *n.* An inhabitant of an island.
Isle, īl, *n.* An island.—*vt.* To island.
Islet, īl'et, *n.* A little isle.
Isobar, ī'sō-bär, *n.* A line on a map connecting places at which the mean height of the barometer at sea-level is the same.
Isochronal, Isochronous, ī-sok'ron-al, ī-sok'ron-us, *n.* Uniform in time; of equal time; performed in equal times.
Isoclinal, Isoclinic, ī-sō-klī'nal, ī-sō-klin'ik, *a.* Of equal inclination or dip; applied to lines connecting places at which the dip of the magnetic needle is equal.
Isolate, ī'sō-lāt, *vt.* To place in or as in an island; to place by itself; to insulate.
Isolation, is-ō-lā'shon, *n.* State of being isolated; insulation.
Isolationist, is-ō-lā'shon-ist, *n.* One who favours keeping aloof from other countries politically.
Isometric, Isometrical, ī-sō-met'rik, ī-sō-met'rik-al, *a.* Pertaining to or characterized by equality of measure.
Isosceles, ī-sos'e-lēz, *a.* Having two legs or sides only that are equal (an *isosceles* triangle).
Isotherm, ī'sō-thėrm, *n.* A line on a map connecting places with a like temperature.
Isothermal, ī-sō-thėrm'al, *a.* Pertaining to isotherms.
Israelite, iz'ra-el-īt, *n.* A descendant of *Israel* or Jacob; a Jew.
Issuable, ish'ū-a-bl, *a.* That may be issued.
Issue, ish'ū, *n.* The act of passing or flowing out; delivery; quantity issued at one time; event; consequence; progeny; offspring; an artificial ulcer to promote a secretion of pus; matter depending in a lawsuit.—*vi.* (issuing, issued). To pass or flow out; to proceed; to spring; to grow or accrue; to come to an issue in law; to terminate.—*vt.* To send out; to put into circulation; to deliver for use.
Issueless, ish'ū-les, *a.* Having no issue.
Isthmus, ist'mus or is'mus, *n.* A neck of land connecting two much larger portions.
It, it, *pron.* A pronoun of the neuter gender, third person, nominative or objective case.
Italian, i-ta'li-an, *a.* Pertaining to Italy.—*n.* A native of Italy; the language of Italy.
Italic, i-ta'lik, *a.* Pertaining to Italy; the name of a printing type sloping towards the right.—*n.* An italic letter or type.
Italicize, i-ta'li-sīz, *vt.* To print in italics.
Itch, ich, *n.* A sensation in the skin causing a desire to scratch; a constant teasing desire. —*vi.* To feel an itch; to have a teasing sensation impelling to something.
Itchy, ich'i, *a.* Affected with itch.
Item, ī'tem, *adv.* Also.—*n.* A separate particular; a scrap of news.—*vt.* To make a note of.
Iterate, it'ėr-āt, *vt.* To repeat; to utter or do a second time.
Iteration, it-ėr-ā'shon, *n.* Act of repeating; recital or performance a second time.
Iterative, it'ėr-āt-iv, *a.* Iterating; repeating.
Itinerancy, i- or ī-tin'ėr-an-si, *n.* A journeying; a passing from place to place.
Itinerant, i- or ī-tin'ėr-ant, *a.* Passing or travelling from place to place; not settled.—*n.* One who travels from place to place.
Itinerary, i- or ī-tin'ėr-a-ri, *n.* A work containing notices of places on a particular line of road; a travel route; plan of a tour.—*a.* Travelling; pertaining to a journey.
Itinerate, i- or ī-tin'ėr-āt, *vi.* To travel from place to place.
Its, its, *pron.* The possessive case singular of *it.*
Itself, it-self', *pron.* The neuter reflexive pronoun corresponding to *himself.*
Ivied, ī'vid, *a.* Covered with ivy.
Ivory, ī'vo-ri, *n.* The substance composing the tusks of the elephants, &c.; something made of ivory.—*a.* Consisting or made of ivory.
Ivy, ī'vi, *n.* A plant which creeps along the ground, or climbs walls, trees, &c.

J

Jabber, jab'ėr, *vi.* To gabble; to talk rapidly or indistinctly; to chatter.—*vt.* To utter rapidly with confused sounds.—*n.* Rapid and indistinct talk.
Jacinth, jā'sinth, *n.* The gem also called hyacinth.
Jack, jak, *n.* A name of various implements; a boot-jack; a contrivance for raising great weights by the action of screws; a contrivance for turning a spit; a coat serving as mail; a pitcher of waxed leather; a ball used for a mark in bowls; a flag on a bowsprit; the union flag; the male of certain animals; a young pike; the knave in a pack of cards.
Jackal, jak'al, *n.* An animal resembling a fox, and closely akin to the dog.
Jackanapes, jak'a-nāps, *n.* A monkey; an ape; a coxcomb; an impertinent fellow.
Jackass, jak'as, *n.* The male of the ass; a dolt; a blockhead.
Jack-boot, jak'bōt, *n.* A kind of large boot reaching up over the knee.
Jackdaw, jak'da, *n.* A small species of crow.
Jacket, jak'et, *n.* A short outer garment; a casing of cloth, felt, wood, &c.
Jack-pudding, jak'pud-ing, *n.* A merry-andrew; a buffoon; a zany.
Jacobean, ja-kō-bē'an, *a.* Pertaining to the time of James I. of England.

Jacobin, ja'kō-bin, *n.* One of a society of violent revolutionists in France during the first revolution; a politician of similar character.
Jacobite, ja'kō-bīt, *n.* A partisan of James II., king of England, after he abdicated the throne, and of his descendants.—*a.* Pertaining to the partisans of James II.
Jactation, Jactitation, jak-tā'shon, jak-ti-tā'shon, *n.* A restless tossing of the body; bragging; boastful display.
Jade, jād, *n.* A mean or poor horse; a low woman; a huzzy; a hard tenacious green stone of a resinous aspect when polished.—*vt.* (jading, jaded). To ride or drive severely; to weary or fatigue.—*vi.* To become weary; to sink.
Jag, jag, *vt.* (jagging, jagged). To cut into notches or teeth; to notch.—*n.* A notch; a ragged protuberance.
Jagged, jag'ed, *p.a.* Having notches or teeth; cleft; divided.
Jaggery, Jagghery, jag'ėr-i, *n.* Imperfectly granulated sugar; the inspissated juice of the palmyra-tree.
Jaggy, jag'i, *a.* Set with teeth; denticulated; uneven.
Jaguar, ja-gwär', *n.* The American tiger, a spotted carnivorous animal, the most formidable feline quadruped of the New World.
Jail, jāl, *n.* A prison; place of confinement.
Jailer, Jailor, jāl'ėr, *n.* The keeper of a jail.
Jain, Jaina, jān, jā'na, *n.* A Hindu religious sect believing doctrines similar to those of Buddhism.
Jalap, jal'ap, *n.* A purgative medicine, from the roots of a Mexican climbing plant.
Jam, jam, *n.* A conserve of fruits boiled with sugar and water.—*vt.* (jamming, jammed). To crowd; to squeeze tight; to wedge in.
Jamb, jam, *n.* The side-post or vertical side-piece of a door, window, &c.
Jangle, jang'gl, *vi.* (jangling, jangled). To sound harshly; to wrangle; to bicker.—*vt.* To cause to sound discordantly.—*n.* Prate; discordant sound.
Janitor, ja'ni-tor, *n.* A doorkeeper; one who looks after a public building.
Janizary, jan'i-za-ri, *n.* One of a body of Turkish foot-guards, suppressed in 1826.
January, ja'nū-a-ri, *n.* The first month of the year.
Japan, ja-pan', *n.* Work varnished and figured.—*vt.* (japanning, japanned). To cover with hard brilliant varnish, and embellish with figures; to varnish.
Japanner, ja-pan'ėr, *n.* One who japans.
Jape, jāp, *n.* A jest; a jibe.—*vi.* (japing, japed). To jest or joke.
Jar, jär, *vi.* (jarring, jarred). To strike together discordantly; to clash; to interfere; to be inconsistent.—*vt.* To shake; to cause a short tremulous motion in.—*n.* A rattling vibration of sound; a harsh sound; contention; clash of interests or opinions; a vessel of earthenware or glass.
Jardinière, zhär-dēn-yār, *n.* An ornamental stand for plants and flowers.
Jargon, jär'gon, *n.* Confused, unintelligible talk; gibberish; phraseology peculiar to a sect, profession, &c.; a variety of zircon.
Jargonelle, jär-gon-el', *n.* A variety of pear.
Jarrah, jar'ra, *n.* A timber-tree of W. Australia, a species of eucalyptus.
Jasmine, jas'min, *n.* A fragrant shrub, bearing white or yellow flowers.
Jasper, jas'pėr, *n.* A variety of quartz, of red, yellow, and some dull colours.
Jaundice, jan'dis, *n.* A disease characterized by yellowness of the eyes and skin, loss of appetite, and general lassitude.—*vt.* To affect with jaundice, or with prejudice, envy, &c.
Jaunt, jänt, *vi.* To ramble here and there; to make an excursion.—*n.* A trip; a tour; an excursion; a ramble.
Jauntily, jän'ti-li, *adv.* Briskly; gaily.
Jaunting-car, jänt'ing-kär, *n.* A light Irish car in which the passengers ride back to back on seats at right angles to the axle.
Jaunty, jän'ti, *a.* Gay and easy in manner or actions; airy; sprightly; showy.
Javelin, jav'lin, *n.* A light spear thrown from the hand.
Jaw, ja, *n.* The bones of the mouth in which the teeth are fixed.
Jay, jā, *n.* A bird allied to the crows.
Jazz, jaz, *n.* Syncopated or rag-time music, originally of negro origin.
Jealous, je'lus, *a.* Uneasy through fear of, or on account of, preference given to another; suspicious in love; apprehensive of rivalry; anxiously fearful or careful.
Jealously, je'lus-li, *adv.* In a jealous manner; with jealousy; emulously.
Jealousy, je'lus-i, *n.* Quality of being jealous; painful suspicion of rivalry; suspicious fear or apprehension; solicitude for others.
Jean, jān, *n.* A twilled cotton cloth.
Jeep, jēp, *n.* Small American car for carrying army personnel.
Jeer, jēr, *vi.* To flout; to mock; to utter severe, sarcastic reflections.—*vt.* To treat with scoffs or derision.—*n.* A scoff; biting jest; jibe.
Jeeringly, jēr'ing-li, *adv.* With raillery; scornfully; contemptuously.
Jehovah, jē-hō'va, *n.* An old Hebrew name of the Supreme Being.
Jejune, jē-jūn', *a.* Devoid of interesting matter; meagre; barren.
Jelly, je'li, *n.* Matter in a glutinous state; the thickened juice of fruit boiled with sugar; transparent matter obtained from animal substances by boiling.—*vi.* To become a jelly.
Jelly-fish, jel'i-fish, *n.* A gelatinous marine animal.
Jemmy, jem'i, *n.* A short crowbar used by burglars.
Jennet, jen'net, *n.* A small Spanish horse.
Jenny, jen'i, *n.* A machine for spinning, moved by water or steam.
Jeopard, je'pėrd, *vt.* To put in danger; to hazard.
Jeopardize, je'pėrd-īz, *vt.* To jeopard.
Jeopardous, je'pėrd-us, *a.* Hazardous.
Jeopardy, je'pėrd-i, *n.* Hazard; risk; exposure to death, loss, or injury.
Jerboa, jėr-bō'a, *n.* A small rodent resembling a mouse, but with long hind-limbs.
Jeremiad, jer-ē-mī'ad, *n.* A lamentation; a complaint: used in ridicule.
Jerk, jėrk, *vt.* To give a sudden pull, thrust, or push to; to throw with a quick motion.—*vi.* To make a sudden motion.—*n.* A sudden thrust, push, or twitch; a sudden spring; a spasmodic movement.
Jerked, jėrkt, *p.a.* Cut into thin slices, and dried, as beef.

Jerkin, jėr'kin, *n.* A jacket; a short coat; a close waistcoat.
Jerky, jėrk'i, *a.* Moving by jerks.
Jerry, jer'i, *n.* A German soldier.
Jersey, jėr'zi, *n.* A kind of close-fitting knitted woollen shirt.
Jess, jes, *n.* A short strap of leather tied round the legs of a hawk.
Jessamine, jes'a-min, *n.* *See* JASMINE.
Jest, jest, *n.* A joke; pleasantry; object of laughter; a laughing-stock.—*vi.* To make merriment; to joke.
Jester, jest'ėr, *n.* One who jests; a buffoon; a merry-andrew.
Jestingly, jest'ing-li, *adv.* In a jesting manner; not in earnest.
Jesuit, je'zū-it, *n.* One of the Society of Jesus, so called, founded by Ignatius Loyola, in 1534; a crafty person; an intriguer.
Jesuitic, Jesuitical, je-zū-it'ik, je-zū-it'ik-al, *a.* Pertaining to the Jesuits; crafty.
Jesuitism, je'zū-it-izm, *n.* The principles and practices of the Jesuits; cunning.
Jesus, jē'zus, *n.* The Saviour of men; Christ.
Jet, jet, *n.* A shooting forth or spouting; what issues from an orifice, as water, gas, &c.; a compact and very black species of coal, used for ornaments.—*vt.* (jetting, jetted). To emit in a jet.—*vi.* To issue in a jet.
Jet-black, jet'blak, *a.* Black as jet.
Jet-propulsion, jet-prō-pul'shon, *n.* Propulsion by the reaction to a jet of gas expelled from an engine.
Jetsam, Jetson, jet'sam, jet'sun, *n.* The throwing of goods overboard to lighten a ship in distress; goods so thrown away.
Jettison, jet'i-son, *n.* Jetsam.—*vt.* To throw overboard.
Jetty, jet'i, *n.* A kind of pier.—*a.* Made of jet, or black as jet.
Jew, jū, *n.* A Hebrew or Israelite.
Jewel, jū'el, *n.* A personal ornament of precious stones; a precious stone.—*vt.* (jewelling, jewelled). To adorn with jewels.
Jeweller, jū'el-ėr, *n.* One who makes or deals in jewels and other ornaments.
Jewellery, Jewelry, jū-el-ėr-i, jū'el-ri, *n.* Jewels in general.
Jewess, jū'es, *n.* A Hebrew woman.
Jewish, jū'ish, *a.* Pertaining to the Jews.
Jewry, jū'ri, *n.* The land of the Jews.
Jew's-harp, jūz'härp, *n.* A small musical instrument held between the teeth, sounding by the vibration of a steel tongue.
Jib, jib, *n.* The triangular foremost sail of a ship; the projecting arm of a crane.
Jib, Jibe, jib, jīb, *vt.* and *i.* (jibbed, jibed, jibd, jībd; jibbing, jibing, jib'ing, jīb'ing). To shift (as a fore-and-aft sail) from one side to the other; to pull against the bit, as a horse; to move restively.
Jib-boom, jib'böm, *n.* A spar which serves as a continuation of a bowsprit.
Jibe, jīb, *vt.* *See* GIBE.
Jiffy, jif'i, *n.* A moment; an instant. (Colloq.)
Jig, jig, *n.* A quick tune; a light lively dance; a mechanical contrivance of various kinds.—*vi.* (jigging, jigged). To dance a jig; to jolt.—*vt.* To jerk; to jolt.
Jilt, jilt, *n.* A woman who gives her lover hopes, and capriciously disappoints him.—*vt.* To deceive in love.—*vi.* To play the jilt.
Jingle, jing'gl, *vi.* and *t.* (jingling, jingled). To sound with a tinkling metallic sound; to clink.—*n.* A rattling or clinking sound.
Jingo, jing'go, *n.* An expletive used as a mild oath; a bellicose patriot; a Chauvinist.
Jinricksha, Jinrikisha, jin-rik'sha, jin-rik'i-sha, *n.* A small two-wheeled carriage drawn by one or more men, used in Japan, &c.
Job, job, *n.* A piece of work undertaken; a public transaction done for private profit.—*vt.* (jobbing, jobbed). To let out in separate portions or jobs; to let out for hire, as horses; to engage for hire; to peck or stab with something sharp.—*vi.* To work at chance jobs; to buy and sell as a broker; to let or hire horses.
Jobber, job'ėr, *n.* One who jobs or works at jobs; one who lets or hires out carriages or horses; one who deals or dabbles in stocks.
Jobbery, job'ėr-i, *n.* Act or practice of jobbing; underhand means used to procure some private end at public expense.
Job-master, job'mäs-tėr, *n.* One who hires or lets out carriages, horses, &c.
Jockey, jok'i, *n.* A man who rides horses in a race; a dealer in horses; one who takes undue advantage in trade.—*vt.* To play the jockey to; to ride in a race; to jostle by riding against; to cheat.
Jocose, jōk-ōs', *a.* Given to jokes and jesting; facetious; merry; waggish.
Jocular, jok'ū-lėr, *a.* Given to jesting; jocose; humorous; sportive.
Jocularity, jok-ū-la'ri-ti, *n.* Quality of being jocular; merriment; jesting.
Jocund, jōk' or jok'und, *a.* Blithe; merry.
Jog, jog, *vt.* (jogging, jogged). To push with the elbow or hand; to excite attention by a slight push.—*vi.* To move at a slow trot; to walk or travel idly or slowly.—*n.* A push; a shake or push to awaken attention.
Joggle, jog'l, *vt.* (joggling, joggled). To shake slightly.—*vi.* To shake; to totter.—*n.* A kind of joint in masonry and carpentry.
Jog-trot, jog'trot, *n.* A slow easy trot; a slow routine.—*a.* Monotonous; humdrum.
Join, join, *vt.* To bind, unite, or connect; to unite in league or marriage; to associate; to add; to couple.—*vi.* To unite; to be close, or in contact; to unite with in marriage, league, &c.—*n.* Place, act, &c., of joining.
Joiner, join'ėr, *n.* A mechanic who does the wood-work of houses; a carpenter.
Joinery, join'ėr-i, *n.* Carpentry.
Joining, join'ing, *n.* A joint, junction.
Joint, joint, *n.* A joining; joining of two or more bones; articulation; a fissure in strata; part of an animal cut off by a butcher.—*a.* Joined; united; shared; acting in concert.—*vt.* To form with joints; to fit together; to divide into joints or pieces.—*vi.* To coalesce as by joints, or as parts fitted to each other.
Jointed, joint'ed, *p.a.* Having joints or articulations; formed with knots or nodes.
Jointly, joint'li, *adv.* In a joint manner; together; unitedly; in concert.
Joint-stock, joint'stok, *a.* Pertaining to stock or shares held in company.
Jointure, joint'ūr, *n.* Property settled on a woman at marriage to be used after her husband's decease.—*vt.* To settle a jointure upon.
Joist, joist, *n.* One of the pieces of timber to which the boards of a floor or the laths of a ceiling are nailed.—*vt.* To fit with joists.
Joke, jōk, *n.* A jest; something said to excite

a laugh; raillery; what is not in earnest.—*vi.* (joking, joked). To jest; to sport.—*vt.* To cast jokes at; to rally.
Joker, jōk'ėr, *n.* One who jokes; a merry fellow; odd card in pack, used in some games as highest trump.
Jokingly, jōk'ing-li, *adv.* In a joking way.
Jole, Joll, jōl, *n.* Same as *Jowl.*
Jollification, jol'i-fi-kā"shon, *n.* A scene of merriment or festivity; merry-making.
Jollity, jol'i-ti, *n.* Quality of being jolly; mirth; merriment; gaiety; joviality.
Jolly, jol'i, *a.* Merry; gay; mirthful; jovial; festive; plump and agreeable in appearance.
Jolly-boat, jol'i-bōt, *n.* A ship's boat, about 12 feet in length with a bluff bow.
Jolt, jōlt, *vi.* and *t.* To shake with sudden jerks.—*n.* A shake by a sudden jerk.
Jonquil, jon'kwil, *a.* A species of narcissus or daffodil.
Jorum, jō'rum, *n.* A term for a drinking vessel with liquor in it.
Joss, jos, *n.* A Chinese idol.
Joss-stick, jos'stik, *n.* In China, a small reed covered with the dust of odoriferous woods, and burned before an idol.
Jostle, jos'l, *vt.* (jostling, jostled). To push or knock against.—*vi.* To hustle.
Jot, jot, *n.* An iota; a tittle.—*vt.* (jotting, jotted). To set down in writing.
Jotting, jot'ing, *n.* A memorandum.
Journal, jėr'nal, *n.* A diary; an account of daily transactions, or the book containing such; a daily or periodical paper; a narrative of the transactions of a society, &c.; that part of an axle which moves in the bearings.
Journalism, jėr'nal-izm, *n.* Occupation of writing in, or conducting a journal.
Journalist, jėr'nal-ist, *n.* The writer of a journal; a newspaper editor or contributor.
Journalistic, jėr-nal-is'tik, *a.* Pertaining to journalists or journalism.
Journalize, jėr'nal-iz, *vt.* To enter in a journal; to give the form of a journal to.
Journey, jėr'ni, *n.* A travelling from one place to another; tour; excursion; distance travelled.—*vi.* To travel from place to place.
Journeyman, jėr'ni-man, *n.* A workman who has fully learned his trade.
Joust, jöst, *n.* A fight on horseback man to man with lances.—*vi.* To engage in fight with lances on horseback; to tilt.
Jovial, jō'vi-al, *a.* Gay; merry; jolly.
Joviality, jō-vi-al'i-ti, *n.* Festivity; merriment.
Jovially, jō'vi-al-li, *adv.* In a jovial manner.
Jowl, jōl, *n.* The cheek.—**Cheek by jowl,** with heads close together; side by side.
Joy, joi, *n.* Pleasure caused by the acquisition or expectation of good; delight; exultation; cause of joy or happiness.—*vi.* To rejoice; to be glad.—*vt.* To gladden.
Joyful, joi'fụl, *a.* Full of joy; blithe; gleeful; joyous; happy; blissful; exulting.
Joyfully, joi'fụl-li, *adv.* In a joyful manner; gladly.
Joyless, joi'les, *a.* Destitute of joy; giving no joy or pleasure.
Joylessly, joi'les-li, *adv.* In a joyless manner.
Joyous, joi'us, *a.* Experiencing joy; causing joy; glad; gay; happy; delightful.
Joyously, joi'us-li, *adv.* In a joyous manner.
Jubilant, jū'bi-lant, *a.* Uttering songs of triumph; rejoicing; shouting with joy.
Jubilate, jū'bi-lāt, *vi.* To rejoice; to exult.
Jubilation, jū-bi-lā'shon, *n.* A rejoicing; exultation; feeling of triumph.
Jubilee, jū'bi-lē, *n.* Among the Jews, every fiftieth year; a season of great public joy; a celebration of a reign, marriage, &c., after it has lasted fifty years.
Judaic, Judaical, jū-dā'ik, jū-dā'ik-al, *a.* Pertaining to the Jews.
Judaism, jū'dā-izm, *n.* The religious doctrines and rites of the Jews; conformity to the Jewish rites and ceremonies.
Judaize, jū'dā-iz, *vi.* and *t.* To conform to the religious doctrines and rites of the Jews.
Judas, jū'das, *n.* A treacherous person.
Judge, juj, *n.* A civil officer who hears and determines causes in courts; one who has skill to decide on anything; a critic; a connoisseur.—*vi.* (judging, judged). To act as a judge; to pass sentence; to form an opinion; to estimate.—*vt.* To hear and determine; to examine into and decide; to try; to esteem.
Judgeship, juj'ship, *n.* Office of a judge.
Judgment, juj'ment, *n.* Act of judging; good sense; discernment; opinion or estimate; mental faculty by which man ascertains the relations between ideas; sentence pronounced; a calamity regarded as a punishment of sin; final trial of the human race.
Judgment-seat, juj'ment-sēt, *n.* The seat on which judges sit; court; tribunal.
Judicative, jū'di-kā-tiv, *a.* Having power to judge.
Judicatory, jū'di-kā-to-ri, *a.* Pertaining to the passing of judgment; dispensing justice. *n.* A court of justice; administration of justice.
Judicature, jū'di-kā-tūr, *n.* Power of distributing justice; a court of justice; extent of jurisdiction of a judge or court.
Judicial, jū-di'shal, *a.* Pertaining to courts of justice; inflicted as a penalty or in judgment; enacted by law or statute.
Judicially, jū-di'shal-li, *adv.* In a judicial manner; by a court of justice.
Judiciary, jū-di'shi-a-ri, *a.* Relating to courts of justice.—*n.* The system of courts of justice in a government; the judges taken collectively.
Judicious, jū-di'shus, *a.* Prudent; sagacious.
Judiciously, jū-di'shus-li, *adv.* Discreetly.
Jug, jug, *n.* A vessel for liquors, generally with a handle; a mug; a pitcher.—*vt.* (jugging, jugged). To put in a jug; to cook by putting into a jug, and this into boiling water (*jugged* hare).
Jugate, jū'gāt, *a.* Coupled together, as leaflets in compound leaves.
Juggernaut, jug'ėr-nạt, *n.* Any idea, custom, &c., to which one devotes himself or is ruthlessly sacrificed.
Juggle, jug'l, *vi.* (juggling, juggled). To play tricks by sleight of hand; to practise imposture.—*vt.* To deceive by artifice.—*n.* A trick by legerdemain; an imposture.
Juggler, jug'lėr, *n.* One who juggles.
Jugglery, jug'lėr-i, *n.* The art or the feats of a juggler; legerdemain; imposture.
Jugular, jụ'gū-lėr, *a.* Pertaining to the throat or neck.
Juice, jūs, *n.* Sap of vegetables, especially fruit; fluid part of animal substances.
Juicy, jūs'i, *a.* Abounding with juice.

Jujitsu, jö-jit'sö, *n.* A style of Japanese wrestling based on a knowledge of muscular action.
Jujube, jū'jūb, *n.* The fruit of a spiny shrub or small tree; the tree itself; a confection made with gum-arabic or gelatine.
Julep, jū'lep, *n.* A sweet drink.
Julian, jū'li-an, *a.* Pertaining to or derived from Julius Cæsar.
July, jū-lī', *n.* The seventh month of the year.
Jumble, jum'bl, *vt.* (jumbling, jumbled). To mix in a confused mass.—*vi.* To meet, mix, or unite in a confused manner.—*n.* Confused mass; disorder; confusion.
Jump, jump, *vi.* To leap; to skip; to spring; to agree, tally, coincide.—*vt.* To pass over by a leap; to pass over hastily.—*n.* Act of jumping; leap; spring; bound.
Jumper, jump'ėr, *n.* One who or that which jumps; a long iron chisel; a loose blouse or jersey worn by women.
Junction, jungk'shon, *n.* Act or operation of joining; state of being joined; point of union; place where railways meet.
Juncture, jungk'tūr, *n.* A joining or uniting; line or point of joining; point of time; point rendered critical by circumstances.
June, jūn, *n.* The sixth month of the year.
Jungle, jung'gl, *n.* Land covered with trees, brushwood, &c., or coarse, reedy vegetation.
Jungly, jung'gli, *a.* Consisting of jungles; abounding with jungles.
Junior, jū'ni-ėr, *a.* Younger; later or lower in office or rank.—*n.* A person younger than another or lower in standing.
Juniority, jū-ni-o'ri-ti, *n.* State of being junior.
Juniper, jū'ni-pėr, *n.* A coniferous shrub, the berries of which are used to flavour gin.
Junk, jungk, *n.* Pieces of old rope; salt beef supplied to vessels; a large flat-bottomed sea-going vessel used in China, a chunk.
Junket, jung'ket, *n.* Curds mixed with cream, sweetened and flavoured; a sweetmeat; a feast.—*vi.* and *t.* To feast.
Junta, jun'ta, *n.* A meeting; a junto; a grand Spanish council of state.
Junto, jun'tō, *n.* A select council which deliberates in secret on any affair of government; a faction; a cabal.
Jupiter, jū'pi-tėr, *n.* The chief deity of the Romans; the largest and brightest planet.
Jurassic, jū-ras'ik, *a.* Of or belonging to the formation of the *Jura* Mountains; Oolitic.
Juridical, jū-rid'ik-al, *a.* Relating to the administration of justice or to a judge.
Jurisconsult, jū'ris-kon-sult, *n.* Anyone learned in jurisprudence; a jurist.
Jurisdiction, jū-ris-dik'shon, *n.* Judicial power; right of exercising authority; district within which power may be exercised.
Jurisprudence, jū-ris-prö'dens, *n.* The science of law; the knowledge of the laws, customs, and rights of men necessary for the due administration of justice.
Jurist, jū'rist, *n.* A man who professes the science of law; one versed in the law, or more particularly, in the civil law.
Juror, jū'rėr, *n.* One who serves on a jury.
Jury, jū'ri, *n.* A number of men selected according to law and sworn to declare the truth on the evidence; a body who jointly decides as to prizes.—*a.* In *ships*, applied to a temporary substitute, as a *jury*-mast.
Juryman, jū'ri-man, *n.* A juror.
Just, just, *a.* Right; acting rightly; upright; impartial; fair; due; merited; exact.—*adv.* Exactly; precisely; near or nearly; almost; merely; barely.
Justice, jus'tis, *n.* Quality of being just; rectitude; propriety; impartiality; fairness; just treatment; merited reward or punishment; a judge holding a special office.
Justiceship, jus'tis-ship, *n.* Office or dignity of a justice.
Justiciary, Justiciar, jus-ti'shi-a-ri, jus-ti'-shi-ėr, *n.* An administrator of justice; a lord chief-justice.
Justifiable, just'i-fī-a-bl, *a.* That may be justified; warrantable; excusable.
Justifiably, just'i-fī-a-bli, *adv.* In a justifiable manner; rightly.
Justification, just'i-fi-kā"shon, *n.* Act of justifying; state of being justified; vindication; defence; remission of sin.
Justificatory, just-if'i-kā-to-ri, *a.* Tending to justify; vindicatory; defensory.
Justifier, just'i-fī-ėr, *n.* One who justifies.
Justify, just'i-fī, *vt.* (justifying, justified). To prove or show to be just; to defend or maintain; to excuse; to judge rightly of; to adjust.
Justle, jus'l, *vt.* Same as *Jostle.*
Justly, just'li, *adv.* Rightly; fairly; properly.
Justness, just'nes, *n.* Quality of being just; uprightness; equity.
Jut, jut, *vi.* (jutting, jutted). To project beyond the main body.—*n.* A projection.
Jute, jūt, *n.* A fibrous substance from an Indian plant of the linden family, used for carpets, bagging, &c.; the plant itself.
Jutty, jut'i, *n.* A jetty.
Juvenescent, jū-ve-nes'ent, *a.* Becoming young.
Juvenile, jū've-nīl, *a.* Young; youthful; pertaining to youth.—*n.* A young person.
Juvenility, jū-ve-nil'i-ti, *n.* Youthfulness; youthful age; light and careless manner.
Juxtapose, juks-ta-pōz', *vt.* To place near or next. Also **Juxtaposit,** jux-ta-poz'it.
Juxtaposition, juks'ta-pō-si"shon, *n.* A placing or being placed near.

K

Kafir, Kaffir, kaf'ėr, *n.* A member of the most important dark race in S. Africa.
Kaftan, kaf'tan, *n.* A kind of long vest with long hanging sleeves, tied at the waist with a girdle, worn in the East.
Kail, Kale, kāl, *n.* A kind of cabbage; colewort; cabbage or greens in general.
Kaiser, kī'zėr, *n.* An emperor.
Kaleidoscope, ka-lī'dos-kōp, *n.* An optical instrument which exhibits an endless variety of coloured figures.
Kalendar. *See* CALENDAR.
Kali, kā'li, *n.* Glasswort.
Kalif. *See* CALIF.
Kalmuk, Kalmuck, *n.* Calmuck.
Kangaroo, kang'ga-rö, *n.* An Australian marsupial quadruped that moves forward by leaps.
Karoo, Karroo, ka-rö', *n.* An arid tract of clayey table-lands in S. Africa.
Kedge, kej, *n.* A small anchor.—*vt.* To warp (a ship) by a rope attached to a kedge.

Keel, kēl, *n.* The principal timber in a ship, extending from stem to stern at the bottom; the corresponding part in iron vessels; the whole ship; something resembling a keel; a coal-barge.—*vi.* To capsize.
Keelhaul, kēl'hal, *vt.* To punish by dropping into the sea on one side of a ship and hauling up on the other.
Keelson, kēl'sun or kel'sun, *n.* An internal keel over the external keel.
Keen, kēn, *a.* Acute of mind; shrewd; sharp; eager; piercing; severe; bitter.
Keenly, kēn'li, *adv.* In a keen manner; eagerly; acutely; sharply; severely; bitterly.
Keep, kēp, *vt.* (keeping, kept). To hold; to preserve; to guard; to detain; to attend to; to continue any state, course, or action; to obey; to perform; to observe or solemnize; to confine to one's own knowledge; not to betray; to have in pay.—*vi.* To endure; not to perish or be impaired.—*n.* Care; guard; sustenance; a donjon or strong tower.
Keeper, kēp'ėr, *n.* One who has the care or custody of persons or things; a gamekeeper; a ring which keeps another on the finger.
Keeping, kēp'ing, *n.* A holding; custody; support; conformity; harmony.
Keepsake, kēp'sāk, *a.* Anything kept or given to be kept for the sake of the giver.
Keeve, kēv, *n.* A large vessel to ferment liquors in; a mashing-tub.
Keg, keg, *n.* A small cask or barrel.
Kelp, kelp, *n.* Large sea-weeds; alkaline substance yielded by sea-weeds when burned.
Kelson, kel'sun, *n.* Same as *Keelson*.
Kelt, Keltic, kelt, kel'tik. *See* CELT, CELTIC.
Kelt, kelt, *n.* A salmon in its spent state after spawning; a foul fish.
Ken, ken, *vt.* To know; to descry.—*n.* View; reach of sight; cognizance.
Kennel, ken'el, *n.* A house or cot for dogs; a pack of hounds; hole of a fox, &c.; a haunt; a gutter.—*vi.* and *t.* (kennelling, kennelled). To lodge in a kennel.
Kerb-stone. Same as *Curb-stone*.
Kerchief, kėr'chif, *n.* A cloth to cover the head; any loose cloth used in dress.
Kermes, kėr'mēz, *n.* A scarlet dye-stuff consisting of the bodies of certain insects found on oak-trees round the Mediterranean.
Kernel, kėr'nel, *n.* The edible substance contained in the shell of a nut; the core; the gist.—*vi.* (kernelling, kernelled). To harden or ripen into kernels, as the seeds of plants.
Kerosene, ke'ro-sēn, *n.* A lamp-oil from petroleum, extensively used in America.
Kersey, kėr'zi, *n.* A species of coarse woollen cloth, usually ribbed.—*a.* Homespun; homely.
Kerseymere, kėr'zi-mēr, *n.* Cassimere.
Kestrel, kes'trel, *n.* A small British falcon.
Ketch, kech, *n.* A strongly built vessel, usually two-masted.
Ketchup, kech'up, *n.* A sauce generally made from mushrooms.
Kettle, ket'l, *n.* A vessel of iron or other metal, used for heating and boiling water, &c.
Kettle-drum, ket'l-drum, *n.* A drum made of a copper vessel covered with parchment.
Key, kē, *n.* An instrument for shutting or opening a lock; a little lever by which certain musical instruments are played on by the fingers; fundamental tone in a piece of music; that which serves to explain a cipher, &c.—*vt.* To furnish or fasten with a key.
Key-board, kē'bōrd, *n.* The series of levers in a keyed musical instrument upon which the fingers press.
Keyed, kēd, *a.* Furnished with keys; set to a key, as a tune.
Keystone, kē'stōn, *n.* The top stone of an arch, which, being the last put in, enters like a wedge, and fastens the work together.
Khaki, kä'ki, *a.* Of a brownish-yellow earthy colour.—*n.* A brownish-yellow earthy colour; cloth of this colour worn by soldiers.
Khan, kan, *n.* In Asia, a governor; a prince; a chief; an eastern inn; a caravansary.
Khedive, ke-dīv', *n.* The governor or viceroy of Egypt.
Kibble, kib'l, *n.* A large bucket used in mining.
Kibe, kīb, *n.* A chilblain.
Kick, kik, *vt.* To strike with the foot; to strike in recoiling, as a gun.—*vi.* To strike with the foot or feet; to manifest opposition to restraint; to recoil.—*n.* A blow with the foot or feet; recoil of a firearm.
Kickshaw, kik'sha, *n.* Something fantastical; a light unsubstantial dish.
Kid, kid, *n.* A young goat; leather made from its skin; a small wooden tub.—*vt.* (kidding, kidded). To bring forth a kid.
Kidnap, kid'nap, *vt.* (kidnapping, kidnapped). To steal or forcibly abduct a human being.
Kidney, kid'ni, *n.* Either of the two glands which secrete the urine; sort or character.
Kilderkin, kil'dėr-kin, *n.* A small barrel; the eighth part of a hogshead.
Kill, kil, *vt.* To deprive of life; to slay; to slaughter for food; to deaden (pain); to overpower.
Killing, kil'ing, *p.a.* Depriving of life; overpowering; dangerous.
Kiln, kil, *n.* A fabric of brick or stone, which may be heated to harden or dry anything.
Kilogram, Kilogramme, kil'ō-gram, *n.* A French measure of weight, being 1000 grammes or 2.2 lbs. avoir.
Kilolitre, kil'ō-lē-tr, *n.* A French measure, 1000 litres or 220.09 gallons.
Kilometre, kil'ō-mā-tr, *n.* A French measure, 1000 metres, about ⅝ of a mile or 1093.633 yards.
Kilostere, kil'ō-stār, *n.* A French solid measure equal to 35317.41 cubic feet.
Kilt, kilt, *n.* A kind of short petticoat worn by the Highlanders of Scotland in lieu of trousers.—*vt.* To tuck up or plait like a kilt.
Kilted, kilt'ed, *a.* Wearing a kilt.
Kimono, kim-ō'nō, *n.* A loose robe with short wide sleeves, worn by both sexes in Japan; a type of dressing-gown.
Kin, kin, *n.* Race; family; consanguinity or affinity; kindred.—*a.* Kindred; congenial.
Kind, kīnd, *n.* Race; genus; variety; nature; character.—**In kind,** to pay with produce or commodities.—*a.* Humane; having tenderness or goodness of nature; benevolent; friendly.
Kindergarten, kin'dėr-gär-tn, *n.* An infants' school in which amusements are systematically combined with instruction.
Kindle, kin'dl, *vt.* (kindling, kindled). To set on fire; to light; to rouse; to excite to action.—*vi.* To take fire; to be roused or exasperated.

Kindly, kind'li, *a.* Of a kind disposition; congenial; benevolent; mild.—*adv.* In a kind manner; favourably.
Kindness, kind'nes, *n.* Quality or state of being kind; benevolence; a kind act.
Kindred, kin'dred, *n.* Relationship by birth; affinity; relatives by blood.—*a.* Related; of like nature; cognate.
Kine, kin, old *pl.* of *cow*.
Kinematic, ki-nē-mat'ik, *a.* Pertaining to kinematics. Also *Kinematical*.
Kinematics, ki-nē-mat'iks, *n.* That branch of mechanics which treats of motion without reference to the forces producing it.
Kinetic, ki-net'ik, *a.* Causing motion: applied to force actually exerted.
Kinetics, ki-net'iks, *n.* That branch of dynamics which treats of forces causing or changing motion in bodies.
King, king, *n.* The sovereign of a nation; monarch; a playing card having the picture of a king; chief piece in the game of chess; in draughts, a piece which has reached the opponent's base, and which can move backwards as well as forwards.
King-at-arms, king'at-ärmz, *n.* The name of the chief heralds in Britain.
Kingdom, king'dum, *n.* The dominion of a king; realm; a primary division of natural objects (*e.g.* the mineral kingdom); place where anything prevails and holds sway.
Kingfisher, king'fish-ėr, *n.* A bird having splendid plumage which preys on fish.
Kinglike, king'lik, *a.* Like a king.
Kingly, king'li, *a.* Like a king; belonging to a king; royal; regal; splendid.
King's-evil, kingz'ē-vl, *n.* Scrofula.
Kingship, king'ship, *n.* The state, office, or dignity of a king; royalty.
Kink, kingk, *n.* A twist in a rope or thread; a crotchet.—*vi.* To twist or run into knots.
Kinsfolk, kinz'fōlk, *n.* People of the same kin; kindred; relations.
Kinsman, kinz'man, *n.* A man of the same kin; a relative.
Kiosk, ki-osk', *n.* A Turkish word signifying a kind of open pavilion or summer-house; a small roofed stall or booth.
Kipper, kip'ėr, *n.* A salmon at the spawning season; a fish split open, salted, and dried or smoked.—*vt.* To cure (fish) by splitting open, salting, and drying.
Kirk, kėrk, *n.* A church (Scot.).
Kirtle, kėr'tl, *n.* A short skirt.
Kismet, kis'met, *n.* Fate or destiny.
Kiss, kis, *vi.* To touch with the lips; to caress by joining lips; to touch gently.—*vi.* To join lips; to come in slight contact.—*n.* A salute given with the lips.
Kit, kit, *n.* A wooden tub for fish, butter, &c.; an outfit.
Kit-cat, kit'kat, *a.* and *n.* A term applied to any portrait about half-length in which the hands are shown.
Kitchen, ki'chen, *n.* The room of a house appropriated to cooking.
Kitchen-garden, ki'chen-gär-dn, *n.* A garden for raising vegetables for the table.
Kitchen-range, ki'chen-rānj, *n.* A kitchen-grate.
Kite, kit, *n.* A bird of the falcon family; a light frame of wood and paper constructed for flying in the air.
Kith, kith, *n.* Relatives or friends collectively.
Kitten, kit'n, *n.* A young cat.—*vi.* To bring forth young, as a cat.
Kleptomania, klep-tō-mā'ni-a, *n.* An irresistible mania for pilfering.
Knack, nak, *n.* Facility of performance; dexterity.
Knag, nag, *n.* A knot in wood; a wart; the shoot of a deer's horn.
Knaggy, nag'i, *a.* Knotty; full of knots.
Knap, nap, *vt.* (knapping, knapped). To break short (as flints); to snap; to bite off.—*n.* A short sharp noise; a snap.
Knapsack, nap'sak, *n.* A bag for necessaries borne on the back by soldiers, &c.
Knar, Knarl, när, närl, *n.* A knot in wood.
Knarred, Knarled, närd, närld, *a.* Gnarled.
Knave, nāv, *n.* A petty rascal; a dishonest man; a card with a soldier or servant on it.
Knavery, nāv'ė-ri, *n.* The practices of a knave; dishonesty; roguery.
Knavish, nāv'ish, *a.* Partaking of knavery; dishonest; roguish.
Knead, nēd, *vt.* To work into a mass or suitable consistency for bread, &c.
Kneading-trough, nēd'ing-trof, *n.* A trough in which dough is kneaded.
Knee, nē, *n.* The joint connecting the two principal parts of the leg; a similar joint; piece of bent timber or iron used in a ship, &c.
Knee-breeches, nē'brēch-ez, *n.pl.* Breeches that reach only to the knee.
Knee-cap, nē'kap, *n.* The movable bone covering the knee-joint in front.
Kneed, nēd, *a.* Having knees; having a bend like a knee.
Kneel, nēl, *vi.* (pret. and pp. kneeled or knelt). To bend the knee; to rest on the bended knees.
Knee-pan, nē'pan, *n.* The knee-cap.
Knell, nel, *n.* The sound of a bell rung at a funeral; a death signal.—*vi.* To sound, as a funeral bell; to toll; to sound as a bad omen.
Knickerbockers, nik'ėr-bok-ėrz, *n.pl.* A kind of loosely fitting knee-breeches. Also **Knickers.**
Knick-knack, nik'nak, *n.* A trinket.
Knife, nīf, *n.*; pl. **Knives,** nivz. A cutting instrument consisting of a blade attached to a handle; cutting part of a machine.
Knight, nīt, *n.* Formerly one admitted to a certain military rank; now one who holds a dignity entitling him to have *Sir* prefixed to his name, but not hereditary; a champion; a piece in chess.—*vt.* To dub or create a knight.
Knight-errant, nīt-e'rant, *n.* A knight who travelled in search of adventures.
Knight-errantry, nīt-e'rant-ri, *n.* The character or practice of a knight-errant.
Knighthood, nīt'hud, *n.* The character, rank, or dignity of a knight; knightage.
Knightly, nīt'li, *a.* Pertaining to a knight.—*adv.* In a manner becoming a knight.
Knit, nit, *vt.* (knitting, knitted or knit). To tie in a knot; to form in a fabric by looping a continuous thread; to unite closely; to draw together; to contract.—*vi.* To interweave a continuous thread; to grow together.
Knitting, nit'ing, *n.* Formation of a fabric by knitting-needles; fabric thus formed.
Knob, nob, *n.* A hard protuberance; a boss; a round ball at the end of anything.
Knobbed, nobd, *p.a.* Containing knobs.
Knobby, nob'i, *a.* Full of knobs; hard.

Knobkerrie, nob'ker-i, *n.* A kind of bludgeon used by the Kafirs.
Knock, nok, *vt.* To strike with something thick or heavy; to strike against; to clash.—*vi.* To strike.—*n.* A stroke; a blow; a rap.
Knocker, nok'ėr, *n.* One who knocks; something on a door for knocking.
Knoll, nōl, *n.* A little round hill; ringing of a bell; knell.—*vt.* and *i.* To sound, as a bell.
Knot, not, *n.* A complication of threads or cords; a tie; ornamental bunch of ribbon, &c.; hard protuberant joint of a plant; a knob; bunch; group; a difficult question; a nautical mile (= 1.151 ordinary mile).—*vt.* (knotting, knotted). To tie in a knot; to unite closely.—*vi.* To become knotted; to knit knots.
Knotted, not'ed, *p.a.* Full of knots.
Knotty, not'i, *a.* Full of knots; difficult; intricate.
Knout, nout, *n.* A powerful whip formerly used as an instrument of punishment in Russia.
Know, nō, *vt.* (pret. knew, pp. known). To perceive with certainty; to understand; to be aware of; to distinguish; to be acquainted with; to have experience of.—*vi.* To have knowledge; not to be doubtful.
Knowable, nō'a-bl, *a.* That may be known.
Knowing, nō'ing, *p.a.* Well informed; intelligent; significant; cunning.
Knowingly, nō'ing-li, *adv.* In a knowing manner; with knowledge; intentionally.
Knowledge, nol'ej, *n.* The result or condition of knowing; clear perception; learning; information; skill; acquaintance.
Known, nōn, *p.a* Understood; familiar.
Knuckle, nuk'l, *n.* The joint of a finger, particularly at its base; knee-joint of a calf or pig.—*vt.* (knuckling, knuckled). To strike with the knuckles.—**To knuckle down,** or **under,** to yield.
Kola-nut. *See* COLA-NUT.
Koran, kō'ran, *n.* The book regulating the faith and practice of Mohammedans, written by Mohammed.
Kosmos. *See* COSMOS.
Kow-tow, kou-tou', *n.* Formerly the mode of saluting the Emperor of China by prostrating oneself and touching the ground with the forehead nine times.—*vi.* To perform the kow-tow.
Kraal, kräl, *n.* A S. African native village.
Kriegspiel, krēg'spēl, *n.* A game played with pieces representing troops.
Kudos, kū'dos, *n.* Glory; fame; renown.
Kyanize, kī'an-īz, *vt.* To preserve (timber) from dry-rot by steeping in a solution of corrosive sublimate.

L

La, lạ, *exclam.* Lo! look! see! behold!
Laager, lä'ger, *n.* In S. Africa, an encampment; a temporary defensive inclosure formed of wagons.—*vi.* To encamp.
Labefaction, lab-e-fak'shon, *n.* Decay.
Label, lā'bel, *n.* A slip of paper, &c., affixed to something and stating name, contents, &c.; a slip affixed to deeds to hold the seal.—*vt.* (labelling, labelled). To affix a label to.
Labial, lā'bi-al, *a.* Pertaining to the lips.—*n.* A vowel or consonant formed chiefly by the lips, as *b, m, p, o.*
Labium, lā'bi-um, *n.* A lip, especially the lower lip of insects.
Laboratory, lab-or'a-to-ri, *n.* A building or room for experiment in chemistry, physics, &c.; a chemist's work-room.
Laborious, la-bō'ri-us, *a.* Full of labour; arduous; diligent; assiduous.
Laboriously, la-bō'ri-us-li, *adv.* In a laborious manner; with toil or difficulty.
Labour, lā'bėr, *n.* Exertion, physical or mental; toil; work done or to be done; labourers in the aggregate; the pangs and efforts of childbirth.—*vi.* To engage in labour; to work; to proceed with difficulty; to be burdened.—*vt.* To cultivate; to prosecute with effort.
Laboured, lā'bėrd, *p.a.* Produced with labour; bearing the marks of effort.
Labourer, lā'bėr-ėr, *n.* One who labours; a man who does work that requires little skill, as distinguished from an artisan.
Labrum, lā'brum, *n.* An upper or outer lip.
Laburnum, la-bėr'num, *n.* A leguminous tree, with clusters of yellow flowers.
Labyrinth, lab'i-rinth, *n.* A place full of intricacies; a maze; an inexplicable difficulty; a part of the internal ear.
Labyrinthian, Labyrinthine, lab-i-rinth'i-an, lab-i-rinth'in, *a.* Pertaining to a labyrinth; winding; intricate; mazy.
Lac, lak, *n.* A resinous substance produced by insects on trees in Asia; in the East Indies, 100,000 (a *lac* of rupees).
Lace, lās, *n.* A cord used for fastening boots, &c.; ornamental cord or braid; a delicate fabric of interlacing threads.—*vt.* (lacing, laced). To fasten with a lace; to adorn with lace; to interlace; to mingle in small quantity.
Lacerable, la'sėr-a-bl, *a.* That may be lacerated or torn.
Lacerate, la'sėr-āt, *vt.* To tear; to rend; to torture; to harrow.
Laceration, la-sėr-ā'shon, *n.* Act of lacerating; the breach made by rending.
Laches, lach'es or lash'ez, *n.* Neglect; negligence; remissness; inexcusable delay.
Lachrymal, lak'rim-al, *a.* Generating or secreting tears; pertaining to tears.
Lachrymary, lak'rim-a-ri, *a.* Containing tears.
Lachrymatory, lak'rim-a-to-ri, *n.* A small vessel found in ancient sepulchres, for holding the tears of a deceased person's friends.
Lachrymose, lak'rim-ōs, *a.* Full of tears; tearful in a sentimental way; lugubrious.
Lacing, lās'ing, *n.* A fastening with a lace or cord; a cord used in fastening.
Lack, lak, *vt.* To want; to be without; to need; to require.—*vi.* To be in want.—*n.* Want; deficiency; need; failure.
Lackadaisical, lak-a-dā'zik-al, *a.* Affectedly pensive; weakly sentimental.
Lack-a-day, lak-a-dā'. Exclamation of sorrow or regret; alas!—alas! the day.
Lacker. *See* LACQUER.
Lackey, lak'i, *n.* A footboy or footman.—*vt.* and *i.* To attend as a lackey, or servilely.
Lack-lustre, lak'lus-tėr, *a.* Wanting lustre.
Laconic, Laconical, la-kon'ik, la-kon'ik-al, *a.* Expressing much in a few words; brief; sententious; pithy.

Laconism, Laconicism, la'kon-izm, la-kon'i-sizm, *n.* A concise style; a sententious expression.
Lacquer, lak'ėr, *n.* A varnish containing lac, &c.; ware coated with lacquer.—*vt.* To varnish or coat with lacquer.
Lacrosse, la-kros', *n.* A game at ball, played with a large battledore or *crosse*.
Lactation, lak-tā'shon, *n.* Act or time of giving suck; function of secreting milk.
Lacteal, lak'tē-al, *a.* Pertaining to milk; conveying chyle.—*n.* A vessel in animal bodies for conveying the chyle from the alimentary canal.
Lactescent, lak-tes'ent, *a.* Becoming milky; having a milky appearance or consistence.
Lactic, lak'tik, *a.* Procured from milk.
Lactine, Lactose, lak'tin, lak'tōs, *n.* Sugar of milk.
Lactometer, lak-tom'et-ėr, *n.* An instrument for ascertaining the quality of milk.
Lacuna, la-kū'na, *n.*; pl. **-næ.** A small depression; a blank space; gap; hiatus.
Lacustrine, Lacustral, la-kus'trin, la-kus'tral, *a.* Pertaining to a lake.
Lacy, lās'i, *a.* Resembling lace.
Lad, lad, *n.* A stripling; a young man.
Ladanum, lad'a-num, *n.* The resinous juice which exudes from several species of cistus in Spain, Portugal, Crete, Syria, &c.
Ladder, lad'ėr, *n.* An article of wood, rope, &c., consisting of two long side-pieces connected by cross-pieces forming steps; means of rising to eminence; vertical flaw in stocking, &c.
Lade, lād, *vt.* (lading, pret. laded, pp. laded, laden). To load; to throw in or out (a fluid) with some utensil.
Laden, lād'n, *p.a.* Loaded; burdened.
Lading, lād'ing, *n.* That which constitutes a load or cargo; freight; burden.
Ladle, lā'dl, *n.* A utensil with a long handle for serving out liquor from a vessel.—*vt.* (ladling, ladled). To serve with a ladle.
Lady, lā'di, *n.* A woman of rank or distinction, or of good breeding; a title given to a woman whose husband is not of lower rank than a knight, or whose father was not lower than an earl; the mistress of an estate.
Lady-bird, lā'di-bėrd, *n.* A small British beetle, the larva of which feeds on plant-lice.
Lady-day, lā'di-dā, *n.* The day of the annunciation of the Virgin Mary, March 25th.
Lady-like, lā'di-līk, *a.* Like a lady in manners.
Ladyship, lā'di-ship, *n.* Condition or rank of a lady: used as a title.
Lag, lag, *a.* Coming behind; sluggish; tardy.—*n.* Quantity of retardation of some movement.—*vi.* (lagging, lagged). To loiter, tarry.
Lager-beer, lä'gėr-bēr, *n.* A German beer stored for some months before use.
Laggard, lag'ärd, *a.* Slow; sluggish; backward.—*n.* One who lags; a loiterer.
Lagoon, Lagune, la-gön', *n.* A shallow lake connected with the sea or a river.
Laic, lā'ik, *a.* Belonging to the laity.—*n.* A layman.
Laicize, lā'i-sīz, *vt.* To make lay or laic; to deprive of clerical character.
Lair, lãr, *n.* A place to lie or rest; the resting-place of a wild beast, &c.
Laird, lārd, *n.* In Scotland, a land-owner or house-proprietor.
Laisser-faire, lā-sā-fār', *n.* A letting alone; non-interference.
Laity, lā'i-ti, *n.* The people, as distinguished from the clergy; non-professional people.
Lake, lāk, *n.* A body of water wholly surrounded by land; a pigment of earthy substance with red (or other) colouring matter.
Lama, lä'mä, *n.* A priest of the variety of Buddhism in Tibet and Mongolia.
Lamb, lam, *n.* The young of the sheep; one as gentle or innocent as a lamb.—*vi.* To bring forth young, as sheep.
Lambent, lam'bent, *a.* Touching lightly, as with the lips or tongue; playing about; gliding over; twinkling.
Lambkin, lam'kin, *n.* A little lamb.
Lame, lām, *a.* Crippled in a limb or limbs; disabled; limping; defective; not satisfactory; not smooth.—*vt.* (laming, lamed). To make lame; to render imperfect and unsound.
Lamella, la-mel'la, *n.*; pl. **Lamellæ.** A thin plate or scale.
Lamellar, la-mel'lėr, *a.* Composed of thin plates.
Lamellibranchiate, la-mel'li-brang"ki-āt, *a.* Having lamellar gills and bivalve shells, as mussels, oysters, &c.
Lamely, lām'li, *adv.* In a lame manner; poorly; feebly.
Lament, la-ment', *vi.* To express sorrow; to weep; to grieve.—*vt.* To bewail; to deplore.—*n.* A lamentation; an elegy or mournful ballad.
Lamentable, la'ment-a-bl, *a.* To be lamented; doleful; miserable; wretched.
Lamentably, la'ment-a-bli, *adv.* In a lamentable manner.
Lamentation, la-ment-ā'shon, *n.* Act of lamenting; expression of sorrow; complaint.
Lamina, la'mi-na, *n.*; pl. **-næ.** A thin plate or scale; a layer lying over another; the blade of a leaf.
Laminar, la'mi-när, *a.* In thin plates.
Lamination, la-mi-nā'shon, *n.* State of being laminated; arrangement in laminæ.
Lammas, lam'mas, *n.* The first day of August.
Lamp, lamp, *n.* A vessel for containing oil to be burned by means of a wick; any contrivance for supplying artificial light.
Lampblack, lamp'blak, *n.* A pigment made from the fine soot of gas, oil, &c.
Lampoon, lam-pön', *n.* A scurrilous or personal satire in writing; a satiric attack.—*vt.* To write a lampoon against.
Lamprey, lam'prā, *n.* The name of eel-like, scaleless fishes with suctorial mouths, inhabiting fresh and salt waters.
Lanate, lā'nāt, *a.* Woolly.
Lance, lans, *n.* A weapon consisting of a long shaft with a sharp-pointed head; a long spear.—*vt.* (lancing, lanced). To pierce with a lance; to open with a lancet.
Lance-corporal, lans kor'po-ral, *n.* The lowest rank of non-commissioned officer.
Lanceolate, lan'sē-o-lāt, *a.* Shaped like a lance-head.
Lancer, lans'ėr, *n.* One who lances; a cavalry soldier armed with a lance.
Lancet, lans'et, *n.* A sharp-pointed and two-edged instrument used in letting blood, &c.
Lancet-window, lans'et-win-dō, *n.* A high and narrow window pointed like a lancet.
Lancinating, lan'si-nāt-ing, *a.* Piercing: applied to a sharp shooting pain.

Land, land, *n.* The solid matter which constitutes the fixed part of the surface of the globe; soil; estate; country; people of a country or region.—*vt.* and *i.* To set or go on the land; to disembark.

Landau, lan-dạ', *n.* A kind of coach whose top may be opened and thrown back.

Land-breeze, land'brēz, *n.* A breeze setting from the land toward the sea.

Landed, land'ed, *p.a.* Having an estate in land; consisting in real estate or land.

Landgrave, land'grāv, *n.* Formerly a title of certain princes of the German empire.

Landholder, land'hōld-ėr, *n.* A holder or proprietor of land.

Landing, land'ing, *n.* Act of or place for going or setting on shore; level part of a staircase between the flights.

Landlady, land'lā-di, *n.* A woman who has property in land, and tenants holding from her; mistress of an inn, &c.

Landlocked, land'lokt, *a.* Inclosed by land, or nearly so, as a part of the sea.

Landloper, land'lōp-ėr, *n.* A vagrant.

Landlord, land'lord, *n.* The lord of land; owner of land or houses who has tenants under him; master of an inn, &c.

Landlubber, land'lub-ėr, *n.* A seaman's term of contempt for one not a sailor.

Landmark, land'märk, *n.* A mark to designate the boundary of land; an object on land that serves as a guide to seamen.

Land-mine, land'mīn, *n.* A bomb dropped by means of a parachute.

Land-owner, land'ōn-ėr, *n.* The owner or proprietor of land.

Land-rail, land'rāl, *n.* The corn-crake.

Landscape, land'skāp, *n.* A portion of land which the eye can comprehend in a single view; a country scene; picture representing a piece of country.

Landslip, Landslide, land'slip, land'slīd, *n.* A portion of a hill which slips down; the sliding down of a piece of land.

Landsman, landz'man, *n.* One who lives on the land; a raw inexperienced sailor.

Land-steward, land'stū-ėrd, *n.* A person who has the care of a landed estate.

Land-surveying, land'sėr-vā-ing, *n.* Act of surveying land; art of determining the boundaries and extent of land.

Landward, land'wėrd, *adv.* Toward the land. —*a.* Inland.

Lane, lān, *n.* A narrow way or street; a passage between lines of men.

Language, lang'gwāj, *n.* Human speech; speech peculiar to a nation; words especially used in any branch of knowledge; general style of expression; expression of thought or feeling in any way.

Languid, lang'gwid, *a.* Wanting energy; listless; dull or heavy; sluggish.

Languidly, lang'gwid·li, *adv.* Weakly; feebly.

Languish, lang'gwish, *vi.* To be or become faint, feeble, or spiritless; to fade; to sink under sorrow or any continued passion; to look with tenderness.

Languishing, lang'gwish-ing, *p.a.* Looking softly and tenderly; pining.

Languishment, lang'gwish-ment, *n.* State of languishing.

Languor, lang'gėr, lang'gwėr, *n.* Languidness; lassitude; a listless or dreamy state.

Languorous, lang'gwėr-us, *a.* Characterized by languor.

Lank, langk, *a.* Loose or lax; not plump; gaunt.

Lanky, lang'ki, *a.* Somewhat lank; lean.

Lanoline, lan'ō-lin, *n.* A greasy substance obtained from unwashed wool, used as an ointment.

Lantern, lan'tėrn, *n.* A case in which a light is carried; part of a lighthouse in which is the light; erection on the top of a dome, &c., to give light; a tower with the interior open to view.—*vt.* To provide with a lantern.

Lanyard, lan'yärd, *n.* A short piece of rope or line, used in ships.

Lap, lap, *n.* The loose lower part of a garment; the clothes on the knees of a person when sitting; the knees in this position; part of a thing that covers another; single round of a course in races; a lick, as with the tongue; sound as of water rippling on the beach.—*vt.* (lapping, lapped). To lap; to infold; to lick up; to wash gently against.—*vi.* To lie or be turned over; to lick up food; to ripple gently.

Lapel, Lapelle, la-pel', *n.* That part of the coat which laps over the facing, &c.

Lapidary, lap'i-da-ri, *n.* One who cuts and engraves precious stones.—*a.* Pertaining to the art of cutting stones.

Lappet, lap'et, *n.* A little lap or flap on a dress, especially on a head-dress.

Lapse, laps, *n.* A slipping or gradual falling; unnoticed passing; a slip; a failing in duty; deviation from rectitude. — *vi.* (lapsing, lapsed). To pass slowly; to glide; to slip in moral conduct; to fail in duty; to pass from one to another by some omission.

Lapwing, lap'wing, *n.* The peewit or green plover.

Larboard, lär'bōrd, *n.* The left-hand side of a ship; port (Obsolescent).—*a.* Pertaining to the left-hand side of a ship.

Larceny, lär'se-ni, *n.* Theft of goods or personal property.

Larch, lärch, *n.* A tall cone-bearing tree.

Lard, lärd, *n.* The fat of swine, after being melted and separated from the flesh.—*vt.* To apply lard to; to fatten; to stuff with bacon; to interlard.

Larder, lärd'ėr, *n.* A room, box, &c., where meat is kept before eating.

Large, lärj, *a.* Great in size, number, &c.; not small; copious; big; bulky; wide.—**At large,** without restraint; with all details.

Large-hearted, lärj'härt-ed, *a.* Liberal; munificent; generous.

Largely, lärj'li, *adv.* Widely; copiously; amply.

Largess, lärj-es', *n.* A present; a bounty bestowed.

Larghetto, lär-get'tō, *a.* and *adv.* In *music*, somewhat slow, but not so slow as *largo.*

Largo, lär'go, *a.* and *adv.* Slow; quicker than *adagio.*

Lariat, lä'ri-at, *n.* The lasso; a long cord or thong of leather with a noose used in catching wild horses, &c.

Lark, lärk, *n.* A small song-bird; a frolic.

Larum, la'rum, *n.* Alarm.

Larva, lär'va, *n.*; pl. **Larvæ.** An insect in the caterpillar or grub state.

Larval, lär'val, *a.* Belonging to a larva.

Laryngeal, Laryngean, la-rin-jē′al, la-rin-jē′an, *a.* Pertaining to the larynx.
Larynx, la′ringks, *n.*; pl. **Larynxes, Larynges,** la′ringks-ez, la-rin′jēz. The upper part of the windpipe, a cartilaginous cavity serving to modulate the sound of the voice.
Lascar, las′kär, *n.* An East Indian sailor.
Lascivious, las-si′vi-us, *a.* Wanton; lewd; lustful.
Lash, lash, *n.* The thong of a whip; a whip; a stroke with a whip; a stroke of satire; a cutting remark.—*vt.* To strike with a lash; to satirize; to dash against, as waves; to tie with a rope or cord.—*vi.* To ply the whip; to strike at.
Lass, las, *n.* A young woman; a girl.
Lassitude, las′i-tūd, *n.* Faintness; languor of body or mind.
Lasso, las′sō, *n.* A rope with a running noose, used for catching wild horses, &c.—*vt.* To catch with a lasso.
Last, läst, *a.* That comes after all the others; latest; final; next before the present; utmost.—*adv.* The last time; in conclusion.—*vi.* To continue in time; to endure; not to decay or perish.—*vt.* To form on or by a last.—*n.* A mould of the foot on which boots are formed; a weight of 4000 lbs.
Lasting, läst′ing, *p.a.* Durable; permanent.—*n.* A species of stiff woollen stuff.
Lastingly, läst′ing-li, *adv.* Durably.
Lastly, läst′li, *adv.* In the last place; finally.
Latch, lach, *n.* A catch for fastening a door.—*vt.* To fasten with a latch.
Latchet, lach′et, *n.* The string that fastens a shoe (Archaic).
Late, lāt, *a.* Coming after the usual time; slow; not early; existing not long ago, but not now; deceased; recent; modern; last or recently in any place, office, &c.—*adv.* At a late time or period; recently.
Lateen, la-tēn′, *a.* Said of a triangular sail having its fore edge fastened to an oblique yard.
Lately, lāt′li, *adv.* Not long ago; recently.
Latency, lā′ten-si, *n.* State of being latent.
Latent, lā′tent, *a.* Not apparent; under the surface.
Lateral, lat′ėr-al, *a.* Pertaining to or on the side; proceeding from the side.
Lath, läth, *n.* A long piece of wood nailed to the rafters to support tiles or plaster.—*vt.* To cover or line with laths.
Lathe, lāᴛʜ, *n.* A machine by which articles of wood, &c., are turned and cut into a smooth round form.
Lather, laᴛʜ′ėr, *n.* Foam or froth made by soap and water; foam or froth from profuse sweat, as of a horse.—*vt.* To spread over with the foam of soap.—*vi.* To become frothy.
Lathing, läth′ing, *n.* A covering made of laths; laths collectively.
Lathy, läth′i, *a.* Thin as a lath.
Latin, la′tin, *a.* Pertaining to the Latins, a people of Latium, in Italy; Roman.—*n.* The language of the ancient Romans.
Latinism, la′tin-izm, *n.* A Latin idiom.
Latinist, la′tin-ist, *n.* One skilled in Latin.
Latinity, la-tin′i-ti, *n.* Latin style or idiom; style of writing Latin.
Latinize, la′tin-īz, *vt.* To give Latin terminations or forms to.—*vi.* To use words or phrases borrowed from the Latin.
Latish, lāt′ish, *a.* Somewhat late.
Latitude, la′ti-tūd, *n.* Breadth; width; extent from side to side; scope; laxity; distance north or south of the equator, measured on a meridian; distance of a star north or south of the ecliptic.
Latitudinarian, la′ti-tūd-in-ā″ri-an, *a.* Indulging in latitude of opinion; lax in religious views.—*n.* One who indulges in latitude of opinion; one not strictly orthodox.
Latitudinarianism, la′ti-tūd-in-ā″ri-an-izm, *n.* Freedom of opinion, particularly in theology.
Latrine, la-trēn′, *n.* A privy, especially one in an institution or camp.
Latter, lat′ėr, *a.* Later; opposed to former; mentioned the last of two; modern; lately done or past.
Latterly, lat′ėr-li, *adv.* Lately.
Lattice, lat′is, *n.* A structure of crossed laths or bars forming small openings like network; a window made of laths crossing like network.—*a.* Furnished with a lattice.—*vt.* To form with cross bars and open work.
Laud, ląd, *n.* Praise; a hymn of praise; *pl.* a service of the church comprising psalms of praise.—*vt.* To praise; to celebrate.
Laudable, ląd′a-bl, *a.* Deserving praise; praiseworthy; commendable.
Laudably, ląd′a-bli, *adv.* In a laudable manner.
Laudanum, lą′da-num, *n.* Opium prepared in spirit of wine; tincture of opium.
Laudation, lą-dā′shon, *n.* Act of lauding; praise.
Laudatory, ląd′a-to-ri, *a.* Containing praise; tending to praise.—*n.* That which contains praise.
Laugh, läf, *vi.* To make the involuntary noise which sudden merriment excites; to treat with some contempt; to appear gay, bright, or brilliant.—*vt.* To express by laughing; to affect or effect by laughter.—*n.* The act of laughing; short fit of laughing.
Laughable, läf′a-bl, *a.* That may justly excite laughter; ridiculous; comical.
Laughably, läf′a-bli, *adv.* In a laughable manner; ludicrously.
Laugher, läft′ėr *n.* One who laughs.
Laughingly, läf′ing-li, *adv.* In a merry way; with laughter.
Laughing-stock, läf′ing-stok, *n.* An object of ridicule.
Laughter, läf′tėr, *n.* Act or sound of laughing, expression of mirth peculiar to man.
Launch, länsh or ląnsh, *vt.* To throw; to cause to slide into the water; to put out into another sphere of duty, &c.—*vi.* To glide, as a ship into the water; to enter on a new field of activity; to expatiate in language.—*n.* Act of launching; the largest boat carried by a man-of-war.
Laundress, län′dres or ląn′dres, *n.* A female who washes and dresses linen, &c.; a caretaker of chambers in the Inns of Court.
Laundry, län′dri or ląn′dri, *n.* Place where clothes are washed and dressed.
Laureate, lą′rē-āt, *a.* Decked or invested with laurel.—**Poet laureate,** in Great Britain, a poet specially appointed as the poet of the sovereign.—*n.* One crowned with laurel; a poet laureate.—*vt.* To crown with laurel; to honour with a degree, &c.
Laureateship, lą′rē-āt-ship, *n.* Office of a laureate.

Laureation, ļa-rē-ā'shon, *n.* Act of laureating.

Laurel, ļa'rel, *n.* The bay-tree, a fragrant tree or shrub used in ancient times in making wreaths for victors, &c.; *pl.* a crown of laurel; honour; distinction.

Laurelled, ļa'reld, *a.* Crowned with laurel, or with laurel wreath; laureate.

Lava, la'va, *n.* Rock-matter that flows in a molten state from volcanoes.

Lavatory, lav'a-to-ri, *n.* A room or place for personal ablutions.

Lave, lāv, *vt.* (laving, laved). To wash; to bathe; to throw out, as water; to bale.—*vi.* To bathe; to wash oneself; to wash, as the sea on the beach.

Lavender, lav'en-dėr, *n.* An aromatic plant of the mint family, which yields an essential oil and a perfume; a pale blue colour with a slight mixture of gray.

Laver, lā'vėr, *n.* A large basin.

Lavish, lav'ish, *a.* Profuse; liberal to a fault; extravagant; superabundant.—*vt.* To expend with profusion; to squander.

Lavishly, lav'ish-li, *adv.* Profusely; wastefully.

Law, ļa, *n.* A rule prescribed by authority; a statute; a precept; such rules or statutes collectively; legal procedure; litigation; a principle deduced from practice or observation; a formal statement of facts observed in natural phenomena.

Lawful, ļa'fųl, *a.* Agreeable to law; allowed by law; legal; rightful.

Lawfully, ļa'fųl-li, *adv.* In a lawful manner; legally.

Lawgiver, ļa'giv-ėr, *n.* One who makes or enacts a law; a legislator.

Lawless, ļa'les, *a.* Not subject to law; contrary to law; illegal; capricious.

Lawn, ļan, *n.* An open space between woods; a space of smooth level ground covered with grass; a fine linen or cambric.

Lawn-tennis, ļan'ten-is, *n.* A game played with balls and rackets on a lawn.

Lawsuit, ļa'sūt, *n.* A suit in law for the recovery of a supposed right.

Lawyer, ļa'yėr, *n.* One versed in the laws, or a practitioner of law.

Lax, laks, *a.* Loose; flabby; soft; slack; vague; equivocal; not strict; remiss; having too frequent discharges from the bowels.

Laxative, laks'at-iv, *a.* Having the power of relieving from constipation.—*n.* A gentle purgative.

Laxity, laks'i-ti, *n.* State or quality of being lax; want of strictness; looseness.

Lay, lā, *vt.* (pret. and pp. laid). To place in a lying position; to set or place in general; to impose; to bring into a certain state; to settle; to allay; to place at hazard; to wager; to contrive.—*vi.* To bring forth eggs; to wager.—*n.* A stratum; a layer; one rank in a series reckoned upward; a song; a narrative poem.—*a.* Not clerical; not professional.

Layer, lā'ėr, *n.* One who or that which lays; a stratum; a coat, as of paint; a row of masonry, &c.; a shoot of a plant, not detached from the stalk, partly laid underground for growth.—*vt.* To propagate by bending a shoot into the soil.

Lay-figure, lā'fig-ūr, *n.* A jointed wooden figure used by artists to hold draperies, &c.

Layman, lā'man, *n.* One not a clergyman.

Lazar, lā'zär, *n.* A leper, or a person infected with any nauseous disease.

Lazaretto, la-za-ret'tō, *n.* A hospital for diseased persons; a hospital for quarantine.

Lazar-house, lā'zär-hous, *n.* A lazaretto.

Lazily, lā'zi-li, *adv.* Sluggishly.

Laziness, lā'zi-nes, *n.* State or quality of being lazy; indolence; sloth.

Lazy, lā'zi, *a.* Disinclined to exertion; slothful; indolent; slow.

Lea, lē, *n.* A meadow; land under grass.

Lead, led, *n.* A soft and heavy metal; a plummet; a thin plate of type-metal, used to separate lines in printing; plumbago in pencils; *pl.* the leaden covering of a roof.—*a.* Made of lead; produced by lead.—*vt.* To cover with lead; to fit with lead.

Lead, lēd, *vt.* (pret. and pp. led). To guide or conduct; to direct and govern; to precede; to entice; to influence; to spend; to begin.—*vi.* To go before and show the way; to be chief or commander; to draw; to have a tendency.—*n.* Guidance; precedence.

Leaded, led'ed, *a.* Fitted with lead; set in lead; separated by leads.

Leaden, led'n, *a.* Made of lead; like lead; heavy; inert; dull.

Leader, lēd'ėr, *n.* One who leads; a guide; captain; head of a party; editorial article in a newspaper.

Leaderette, lē-dėr-et', *n.* A short leading article in a newspaper.

Leadership, lēd'ėr-ship, *n.* State or condition of a leader.

Leading, lēd'ing, *p.a.* Chief; principal.—**Leading question,** a question which suggests an answer that the questioner desires.

Leaf, lēf, *n.*; pl. **Leaves,** lēvz. One of the thin, expanded, deciduous growths of a plant; a part of a book containing two pages; a very thin plate; the movable side of a table; one side of a double door.—*vi.* To shoot out leaves; to produce leaves.

Leafage, lēf'āj, *n.* Leaves collectively; abundance of leaves.

Leafless, lēf'les, *a.* Destitute of leaves.

Leaflet, lēf'let, *n.* A little leaf.

Leafy, lēf'i, *a.* Full of leaves.

League, lēg, *n.* A combination between states for their mutual aid; an alliance; a compact; a measure of three miles or knots.—*vi.* (leaguing, leagued). To form a league; to confederate.

Leagued, lēgd, *p.a.* United in a league or mutual compact.

Leaguer, lēg'ėr, *n.* One who unites in a league; the camp of a besieging army; a siege.

Leak, lēk, *n.* A fissure in a vessel that admits water, or permits it to escape; the passing of fluid through an aperture.—*vi.* To let water in or out of a vessel through a crevice.

Leakage, lēk'āj, *n.* A leaking; quantity of a liquid that enters or issues by leaking; an allowance for the leaking of casks.

Leaky, lēk'i, *a.* Having a leak.

Leal, lēl, *a.* Loyal; true; faithful.

Lean, lēn, *vi.* (pret. and pp. leaned, leant). To slope or slant; to incline; to tend; to bend so as to rest on something; to depend.—*vt.* To cause to lean; to support or rest.

Lean, lēn, *a.* Wanting flesh or fat on the body; meagre; not fat; barren.—*n.* That part of flesh which consists of muscle without fat.

Leanly, lēn'li, *adv.* In a lean manner; meagrely; without fat or plumpness.
Leap, lēp, *vi.* (pret. and pp. leaped, leapt). To spring from the ground; to jump; to rush with violence; to bound.—*vt.* To pass over by leaping.—*n.* A jump; a spring; space passed by leaping; a sudden transition.
Leap-frog, lēp'frog, *n.* A game in which one stoops down and others leap over him.
Leap-year, lēp'yēr, *n.* A year containing 366 days: every fourth year.
Learn, lėrn, *vt.* (pret. and pp. learned, learnt). To gain knowledge of or skill in; to acquire by study.—*vi.* To gain knowledge; to receive instruction.
Learned, lėrn'ed, *a.* Having much knowledge; erudite; scholarly.
Learnedly, lėrn'ed-li, *adv.* In a learned manner; with much knowledge or erudition.
Learner, lėrn'ėr, *n.* One who learns; a pupil.
Learning, lėrn'ing, *n.* Acquired knowledge; erudition; scholarship; education.
Lease, lēs, *n.* A letting of lands, &c., for a rent; written contract for such letting; any tenure by grant or permission.—*vt.* (leasing, leased). To let; to grant by lease.
Leasehold, lēs'hōld, *a.* Held by lease.—*n.* Tenure by lease; land held in lease.
Leaseholder, lēs'hōld-ėr, *n.* A tenant under a lease.
Leash, lēsh, *n.* A thong or line by which a dog or hawk is held; three creatures of any kind.—*vt.* To bind by a leash.
Leasing, lēz'ing, *n.* Falsehood; lies.
Least, lēst, *a.* Smallest.—*adv.* In the smallest or lowest degree.—**At least, at the least,** to say no more; at the lowest degree.
Leather, leᴛʜ'ėr, *n.* The skin of an animal prepared for use; tanned hides in general.—*a.* Leathern.
Leathern, leᴛʜ'ėrn, *a.* Made of leather; consisting of leather.
Leathery, leᴛʜ'ėr-i, *a.* Like leather; tough.
Leave, lēv, *n.* Permission; liberty granted; a formal parting of friends.—*vt.* (leaving, left). To let remain; to have remaining at death; to bequeath; to quit; to abandon; to refer.—*vi.* To depart; to desist.
Leave, lēv, *vi.* (leaving, leaved). To leaf.
Leaved, lēvd, *a.* Furnished with leaves or foliage; made with leaves or folds.
Leaven, lev'n, *n.* A substance that produces fermentation, as in dough; yeast; barm.—*vt.* To mix with leaven; to excite fermentation in; to imbue.
Leavings, lēv'ingz, *n.pl.* Things left; relics; refuse; offal.
Leavy, lēv'i, *a.* Full of leaves.
Lecher, lech'ėr, *n.* A man given to lewdness.—*vi.* To practise lewdness; to indulge lust.
Lecherous, lech'ėr-us, *a.* Addicted to lewdness or lust; lustful; lewd.
Lechery, lech'ėr-i, *n.* Free indulgence of lust.
Lectern, lek'tėrn, *n.* A reading-desk in a church.
Lection, lek'shon, *n.* A reading; a difference or variety in a text.
Lecture, lek'tūr, *n.* A discourse on any subject; a reprimand; a formal reproof.—*vi.* (lecturing, lectured). To deliver a lecture or lectures.—*vt.* To reprimand; to reprove.
Lecturer, lek'tūr-ėr, *n.* One who lectures; one who delivers discourses to students.
Lectureship, lek'tūr-ship, *n.* The office of a lecturer.
Ledge, lej, *n.* A narrow shelf; a ridge or shelf of rocks.
Ledger, lej'ėr, *n.* The principal book of accounts among merchants and others.
Lee, lē, *n.* The quarter toward which the wind blows; shelter caused by an object keeping off the wind.—*a.* Pertaining to the side towards which the wind blows.
Leech, lēch, *n.* A physician or doctor; a blood-sucking wormlike animal.—*vt.* To treat or heal; to bleed by the use of leeches.
Leek, lēk, *n.* A culinary vegetable allied to the onion.—**To eat the leek,** to have to retract one's words.
Leer, lēr, *n.* A side glance; an arch or affected glance.—*vi.* To give a leer; to look meaningly.—*vt.* To turn with a leer; to affect with a leer.
Lees, lēz, *n.pl.* The slime of liquor; dregs; sediment.
Leet, lēt, *n.* A list of candidates for office.
Leeward, lö'wėrd, *a.* Pertaining to the lee.—*adv.* Toward the lee.
Leeway, lē'wā, *n.* The drifting of a ship to the leeward.—**To make up leeway,** to overtake work in arrear.
Left, left, *a.* Denoting the part opposed to the right of the body.—*n.* The side opposite to the right.
Left-hand, left'hand, *a.* Relating to the left hand; on the left side.
Left-handed, left'hand-ed, *a.* Using the left hand and arm with more dexterity than the right; sinister; insincere; awkward.
Left-off, left'of, *a.* Laid aside; no longer worn.
Leg, leg, *n.* The limb of an animal; a lower or posterior limb; the long or slender support of anything.
Legacy, leg'a-si, *n.* A bequest; a particular thing given by last will.
Legal, lē'gal, *a.* According to, pertaining to, or permitted by law; lawful; judicial.
Legality, lē-gal'i-ti, *n.* Condition or character of being legal; conformity to law.
Legalize, lē'gal-īz, *vt.* To make legal or lawful; to authorize; to sanction.
Legally, lē'gal-li, *adv.* In a legal manner; lawfully; according to law.
Legate, le'gāt, *n.* An ambassador; the pope's ambassador to a foreign state.
Legatee, leg-a-tē', *n.* One to whom a legacy is bequeathed.
Legatine, le'gāt-īn, *a.* Pertaining to a legate.
Legation, lē-gā'shon, *n.* An embassy; a diplomatic minister and his suite.
Legato, le-gā'tō, *a.* and *adv.* Played or sung in an even, smooth, gliding manner.
Legend, le'jend or lē'jend, *n.* A marvellous story handed down from early times; a non-historical narrative; an inscription.
Legendary, lej'end-a-ri or lē'jend-a-ri, *a.* Fabulous; traditional; mythical.
Legerdemain, lej'ėr-dē-mān", *n.* Sleight of hand; an adroit trick.
Legging, leg'ing, *n.* A covering for the leg; a long gaiter: generally in *pl.*
Leghorn, leg'horn, *n.* A kind of straw plait imported from Leghorn; a hat made of it.
Legibility, le-ji-bil'i-ti, *n.* Quality or state of being legible.
Legible, le'ji-bl, *a.* That may be read.

Legibly, le'ji-bli, *adv.* So as to be read.
Legion, lē'jon, *n.* A Roman body of infantry soldiers, in number from 3000 to above 6000; a military force; a great number.
Legionary, lē'jon-a-ri, *a.* Relating to, or consisting of, a legion.—*n.* A Roman soldier belonging to a legion.
Legislate, le'jis-lāt, *vi.* To make or enact a law or laws.
Legislation, le-jis-lā'shon, *n.* Act of making a law or laws; laws or statutes enacted.
Legislative, le'jis-lāt-iv, *a.* Capable of or pertaining to the enacting of laws.
Legislator, le'jis-lāt-ėr, *n.* A lawgiver; one who makes laws.
Legislature, le'jis-lāt-ūr, *n.* The body of men invested with power to make laws.
Legist, lē'jist, *n.* One skilled in the laws.
Legitim, le'ji-tim, *n.* In *Scots law*, the share of a father's movable property to which on his death his children are entitled by law.
Legitimacy, lē-jit'i-ma-si, *n.* State or quality of being legitimate; legality.
Legitimate, lē-jit'i-māt, *a.* Accordant with law; born in wedlock; genuine; following by logical or natural sequence; allowable; valid.—*vt.* To make legitimate.
Legitimation, lē-jit'i-mā-shon, *n.* Act of legitimating or rendering legitimate.
Legitimist, lē-jit'i-mist, *n.* One who believes in the sacredness of hereditary monarchies.
Legitimize, lē-jit'i-mīz, *vt.* To legitimate.
Legume, leg'ūm, le-gūm', *n.* A seed-vessel of two valves; a pod; *pl.* pulse, pease, beans, &c.
Leguminous, le-gū'min-us, *a.* Pertaining to legumes; consisting of pulse.
Leisure, lē'zhūr or lezh'ūr, *n.* Freedom from occupation; vacant time.—*a.* Not spent in labour; vacant.
Leisured, lē'zhūrd, *a.* Not requiring to work.
Leisurely, lē'zhūr-li, *a.* Done at leisure; deliberate; slow.—*adv.* Slowly; at leisure.
Lemma, lem'ma, *n.* A subsidiary proposition in mathematics.
Lemming, lem'ing, *n.* A small rodent mammal.
Lemon, le'mon, *n.* An acid fruit of the orange kind; the tree that produces this fruit.
Lemonade, le-mon-ād', *n.* A beverage, usually aerated, consisting of lemon-juice mixed with water and sweetened.
Lemur, lē'mėr, *n.* A quadrumanous mammal, allied to monkeys and rodents.
Lend, lend, *vt.* (lending, lent). To furnish on condition of the thing being returned; to afford or grant; *refl.* to accommodate.
Lender, lend'ėr, *n.* One who lends.
Length, length, *n.* State or quality of being long; extent from end to end; extension; long duration; extent or degree.—**At length**, at full extent; at last.
Lengthen, length'n, *vt.* To make long or longer; to extend.—*vi.* To grow longer.
Lengthily, length'i-li, *adv.* In a lengthy manner.
Lengthwise, length'wīz, *adv.* In the direction of the length; longitudinally.
Lengthy, length'i, *a.* Somewhat long.
Lenience, Leniency, lē'ni-ens, lē'ni-en-si, *n.* Quality of being lenient; lenity; mildness.
Lenient, lē'ni-ent, *a.* Acting without rigour; gentle; clement.
Leniently, lē'ni-ent-li, *adv.* In a lenient manner; mercifully; mildly.
Lenitive, le'nit-iv, *a.* Softening; assuasive; emollient.—*n.* A medicine or application that eases pain.
Lenity, le'ni-ti, *n.* Gentleness; mildness; mercy.
Leno, lē'nō, *n.* A kind of cotton gauze.
Lens, lenz, *n.*; pl. **Lenses**, len'zes. A transparent substance, usually glass, by which objects appear magnified or diminished; one of the glasses of a telescope, &c.
Lent, lent, *n.* A fast of forty days, from Ash-Wednesday till Easter.
Lenten, lent'en, *a.* Pertaining to Lent; used in Lent; sparing; plain.
Lentil, len'til, *n.* A pea-like plant, having seeds forming a very nutritious diet.
Lento, len'tō, *a.* and *adv.* A direction that music is to be performed slowly.
Leo, lē'ō, *n.* The Lion, the fifth sign of the zodiac.
Leonine, lē'ō-nīn, *a.* Belonging to a lion; resembling a lion; applied to a rhyming Latin measure of hexameter and pentameter verses.
Leopard, lep'ärd, *n.* A large carnivorous animal of the cat genus, with a spotted skin.
Leper, lep'ėr, *n.* One affected with leprosy.
Lepidopterous, lep-i-dop'tėr-us, *a.* Belonging to the order of insects called Lepidoptera, comprising butterflies and moths.
Leporine, lep'or-in, *a.* Pertaining to or resembling the hare.
Leprosy, lep'rō-si, *n.* A foul cutaneous disease, characterized by dusky red or livid tubercles on the face or extremities.
Leprous, lep'rus, *a.* Infected with leprosy.
Lesion, lē'zhon, *n.* Injury; wound; derangement.
Less, les, *a.* Smaller; not so large or great.—*adv.* In a smaller or lower degree.—*n.* A smaller quantity.
Lessee, les-sē', *n.* The person to whom a lease is given.
Lessen, les'n, *vt.* To make less; to lower; to depreciate.—*vi.* To become less; to abate.
Lesser, les'ėr, *a.* Less; smaller.
Lesson, les'n, *n.* Portion which a pupil learns at one time; portion of Scripture read in divine service; something to be learned; severe lecture; truth taught by experience.
Lest, lest, *conj.* For fear that; in case.
Let, let, *vt.* (letting, let). To permit; to allow; to lease.—*vi.* To be leased or let.
Let, let, *vt.* To hinder; to impede.—*n.* A hindrance; impediment.
Lethal, lēth'al, *a.* Deadly; mortal; fatal.
Lethargic, le-thär'jik, *a.* Drowsy; morbidly inclined to sleep; dull.
Lethargy, le'thär-ji, *n.* Morbid drowsiness; profound sleep; dulness.
Lethe, lē'thē, *n.* Oblivion.
Letter, let'ėr, *n.* A mark used as the representative of a sound; a written message; an epistle; the literal meaning; in *printing*, a single type; *pl.* learning; erudition.—*vt.* To impress or form letters on.
Lettered, let'ėrd, *a.* Versed in literature or science; belonging to learning.
Lettering, let'ėr-ing, *n.* The act of impressing letters; the letters impressed.
Letter-press, let'ėr-pres, *n.* Letters printed by types; print.

Lettuce, let'is, *n.* An annual composite plant, used in salads.
Leucoma, lū-kō'ma, *n.* A white opacity of the cornea of the eye.
Leucopathy, lū-kop'a-thi, *n.* The condition of an albino.
Levant, le-vant', *n.* The eastern coasts of the Mediterranean.—*vi.* To run away without paying debts.
Levanter, lē-vant'ėr, *n.* A strong east wind in the Mediterranean; one who levants.
Levantine, lē-vant'in, *a.* Pertaining to the Levant; designating a kind of silk cloth.
Levee, lev'ā or lev'ē, *n.* A morning reception of visitors held by a prince; in America, a river embankment.
Level, le'vel, *n.* An instrument for detecting variation from a horizontal surface; an instrument by which to find a horizontal line; a horizontal line or plane; a surface without inequalities; usual elevation; equal elevation with something else; horizontal gallery in a mine.—*a.* Horizontal; even; flat; having no degree of superiority.—*vt.* (levelling, levelled). To make level; to lay flat on the ground; to reduce to equality; to point, in taking aim.—*vi.* To point a gun, &c.; to aim.
Leveller, le'vel-ėr, *n.* One who levels; one who would destroy social distinctions.
Levelling, le'vel-ing, *n.* Act of one who levels; the art or practice of ascertaining the different elevations of objects.
Lever, lē'vėr, *n.* A bar used for raising weights, &c.; a kind of watch.
Leverage, lē'vėr-āj, *n.* Action or power of a lever; mechanical advantage gained by using a lever.
Leveret, lev'ėr-et, *n.* A hare in its first year.
Leviable, le'vi-a-bl, *a.* That may be levied.
Leviathan, lē-vī'a-than, *n.* An immense sea-monster.
Levigate, le'vi-gāt, *vt.* To grind to a fine impalpable powder; to make smooth.
Levin, le'vin, *n.* Lightning: *poetical.*
Levite, lē'vīt, *n.* One of the tribe of Levi; a priest; a cleric.
Levitical, lē-vit'ik-al, *a.* Belonging to the Levites; priestly.
Levity, le'vi-ti, *n.* Lightness; inconstancy; giddiness; want of seriousness.
Levy, le'vi, *vt.* (levying, levied). To raise (troops); to collect (taxes); to begin (war).—*n.* Act of raising troops or taxes; the troops or taxes raised.
Lewd, lūd, *a.* Lustful; sensual; vile.
Lewdly, lūd'li, *adv.* In a lewd manner.
Lewis gun, lö'is gun, *n.* An automatic rifle, gas-operated and air-cooled, capable of firing forty-seven rounds without reloading.
Lewisite, lö'is-īt, *n.* A poison gas.
Lexicographer, leks-i-kog'ra-fėr, *n.* The author or compiler of a dictionary.
Lexicographic, Lexicographical, leks'i-kō-graf"ik, leks'i-kō-graf"ik-al, *a.* Pertaining to lexicography.
Lexicography, leks-i-kog'ra-fi, *n.* The act or art of compiling a dictionary.
Lexicon, leks'i-kon, *n.* A word-book; a dictionary; a vocabulary containing an alphabetical arrangement of the words in a language, with the definition of each.
Leze-majesty, lēz'maj-es-ti, *n.* Any crime against the sovereign power in a state.
Liability, lī-a-bil'i-ti, *n.* State of being liable; that for which one is liable; *pl.* debts.
Liable, lī'a-bl, *a.* Answerable for consequences; responsible; subject; exposed: with *to.*
Liaison, lē-ā-zōng, *n.* A bond of union; an illicit intimacy between a man and woman.
Liar, lī'ėr, *n.* One who utters falsehood.
Lias, lī'as, *n.* A series of strata in England, lying at the basis of the oolitic series.
Libation, lī-bā'shon, *n.* Act of pouring a liquor, usually wine, on the ground or on a victim in sacrifice, in honour of some deity; the wine or other liquor so poured.
Libel, lī'bel, *n.* A defamatory writing; a malicious publication; the written statement of a plaintiff's ground of complaint against a defendant.—*vt.* (libelling, libelled). To frame a libel against; to lampoon; to exhibit a charge against in court.
Libeller, lī'bel-ėr, *n.* One who libels.
Libellous, lī'bel-us, *a.* Containing a libel; defamatory.
Liber, lī'bėr, *n.* The inner lining of the bark of exogenous trees; bast.
Liberal, li'bėr-al, *a.* Generous; ample; profuse; favourable to reform or progress; not too literal or strict; free.—*n.* One who advocates greater political freedom.
Liberalism, li'bėr-al-izm, *n.* Liberal principles; the principles or practice of liberals.
Liberality, li-bėr-al'i-ti, *n.* Largeness of mind; width of sympathy; generosity.
Liberalize, li'bėr-al-īz, *vt.* To render liberal; to free from narrow views.
Liberally, li'bėr-al-li, *adv.* In a liberal manner; bountifully; freely; not strictly.
Liberate, li'bėr-āt, *vt.* To free; to deliver; to set at liberty; to disengage.
Liberation, li-bėr-ā'shon, *n.* Act of liberating.
Liberator, li'bėr-āt-ėr, *n.* One who liberates.
Libertine, li'bėr-tin, *n.* A freedman; one who indulges his lust without restraint; a debauchee.—*a.* Licentious; dissolute.
Libertinism, li'bėr-tin-izm, *n.* The conduct of a libertine or rake.
Liberty, li'bėr-ti, *n.* State or condition of one who is free; privilege; immunity; license; district within which certain exclusive privileges may be exercised; freedom of action or speech beyond civility or decorum; state of being disengaged.
Libidinous, li-bid'i-nus, *a.* Characterized by lust; lascivious; lewd.
Libra, lī'bra, *n.* The Balance, the seventh sign in the zodiac.
Librarian, lī-brā'ri-an, *n.* The keeper of a library or collection of books.
Librarianship, lī-brā'ri-an-ship, *n.* The office or post of a librarian.
Library, lī'bra-ri, *n.* A collection of books; edifice or apartment for holding books.
Librate, lī'brāt, *vt.* To poise; to balance.—*vi.* To move, as a balance; to be poised.
Libration, lī-brā'shon, *n.* Act of librating; state of being balanced.
Libretto, li-bret'ō, *n.* The book of words of an opera, &c.
Lice, līs, *n.pl.* of *louse.*
License, Licence, lī'sens, *n.* Authority or liberty given to do any act; a certificate giving permission; excess of liberty; deviation from an artistic standard.—**License**, *vt.* (licensing,

licensed). To grant a license to; to authorize to act in a particular character.

Licensee, lī-sens-ē′, *n.* One to whom a license is granted.

Licenser, lī′sens-ėr, *n.* One who grants a license.

Licentiate, lī-sen′shi-āt, *n.* One who has a license to practise any art or to exercise a profession, as medicine or theology.

Licentious, lī-sen′shus, *a.* Characterized by license; profligate; libidinous.

Licentiously, lī-sen′shus-li, *adv.* In a licentious manner; dissolutely.

Lichen, lī′ken or lich′en, *n.* A plant without stem and leaves, growing on the bark of trees, on rocks, &c.; an eruption of small red or white pimples.

Lich-gate, lich′gāt, *n.* A churchyard gate, with a porch under which a bier might stand.

Licit, li′sit, *a.* Lawful; legal; legitimate.

Lick, lik, *vt.* To draw the tongue over the surface of; to lap; to take in by the tongue; to beat.—*n.* A drawing of the tongue over anything; a slight smear or coat; a blow.

Lickerish, lik′ėr-ish, *a.* Nice in the choice of food; dainty; having keen relish.

Lickspittle, lik′spit-l, *n.* A flatterer or parasite of the most abject character.

Licorice, lik′or-is, *n.* Liquorice.

Lictor, lik′tėr, *n.* An officer who attended the Roman magistrates, bearing an axe and rods.

Lid, lid, *n.* A movable cover of a vessel or box; eyelid.

Lie, lī, *vi.* (lying, lied). To utter falsehood with deceitful intention.—*n.* A falsehood; an intentional violation of truth.

Lie, lī, *vi.* (lying, pret. lay, pp. lain). To occupy a horizontal position; to rest on anything lengthwise; to be situated; to remain; to be incumbent; to exist; to depend; to be sustainable in law.—**To lie in,** to be in childbed. —**To lie to,** to stop and remain stationary.—*n.* Relative position of objects; general bearing or direction.

Lief, lēf, *a.* Beloved; agreeable; *poetical.*—*adv.* Gladly; willingly; readily.

Liege, lēj, *a.* Bound by a feudal tenure; subject; loyal; faithful.—*n.* A vassal; a lord or superior; a sovereign; a citizen in general: generally in *pl.*

Lien, lī′en, *n.* A legal claim; a right over the property of another until some claim or due is satisfied.

Lieu, lū, *n.* Place; stead: preceded by *in.*

Lieutenancy, lef-ten′an-si, *n.* Office or commission of a lieutenant; the collective body of lieutenants.

Lieutenant, lef-ten′ant, *n.* An officer who supplies the place of a superior in his absence; a commissioned army officer next in rank below a captain; commissioned naval officer below a lieutenant-commander.—**Lieutenant-colonel,** *n.* An army officer next in rank below a colonel.—**Lieutenant-commander,** *n.* A naval officer immediately below the rank of commander, and corresponding in rank to a major in the army.—**Lieutenant-general,** *n.* An army officer next in rank below a general.

Life, līf, *n.*; pl. **Lives,** līvz. State of animals and plants in which the natural functions are performed; vitality; present state of existence; time from birth to death; manner of living; animal being; spirit; vivacity; the living form; exact resemblance; rank in society; human affairs; a person; narrative of a life; eternal felicity.

Life-belt, līf′belt, *n.* A buoyant belt used to support the body in the water.

Life-blood, līf′blud, *n.* The blood necessary to life; vital blood.

Life-boat, līf′bōt, *n.* A boat for saving men in cases of shipwreck.

Life-buoy, līf′boi, *n.* A buoy to be thrown to a person in danger of drowning.

Life-giving, līf′giv-ing, *a.* Giving life; inspiriting; invigorating.

Life-guard, līf′gärd, *n.* A soldier that attends the person of a prince, &c.

Lifeless, līf′les, *a.* Deprived of life; dead; inanimate; dull; heavy; inactive.

Lifelike, līf′līk, *a.* Like a living person; true to the life.

Lifelong, līf′long, *a.* Lasting through life.

Life-rent, līf′rent, *n.* A right which entitles a person to use and enjoy property during life.

Life-size, līf′sīz, *a.* Of the size of the person or object represented.

Lifetime, līf′tīm, *n.* The time that life continues; duration of life.

Lift, lift, *vt.* To raise to a higher position; to hoist; to elevate; to raise in spirit; to collect when due.—*vi.* To raise; to rise.—*n.* Act of lifting; assistance; that which is to be raised; an elevator or hoist.

Ligament, li′ga-ment, *n.* That which unites one thing to another; a band; a substance serving to bind one bone to another.

Ligan, lī′gan, *n.* Goods sunk in the sea, but having something buoyant attached to mark their position.

Ligation, lī-gā′shon, *n.* Act of binding; ligature.

Ligature, li′ga-tūr, *n.* Anything that binds; a band or bandage.

Light, līt, *n.* That by which objects are rendered visible; day; that which gives or admits light; illumination of mind; knowledge; open view; explanation; point of view; situation; spiritual illumination.—*a.* Bright; clear; not deep, as colour; not heavy; not difficult; easy to be digested; active; not laden; slight; moderate; unsteady; gay; trifling; wanton; sandy; having a sensation of giddiness; employed in light work.—*adv.* Lightly; cheaply.—*vt.* (pret. and pp. lighted or lit). To give light to; to enlighten; to ignite.—*vi.* To brighten; to descend, as from a horse, &c.; to alight; to come by chance.

Lighten, līt′n, *vi.* To become brighter; to shine; to flash, as lightning.—*vt.* To illuminate; to enlighten; to flash forth; to make less heavy; to alleviate; to cheer; to gladden.

Lighter, līt′ėr, *n.* One who or that which lights or kindles; a large flat-bottomed boat used in loading and unloading ships.

Light-fingered, līt′fing-gėrd, *a.* Thievish; addicted to petty thefts.

Light-footed, līt′fụt-ed, *a.* Nimble; active.

Light-headed, līt′hed-ed, *a.* Thoughtless; unsteady; delirious; dizzy.

Light-hearted, līt′härt-ed, *a.* Free from grief or anxiety; gay; cheerful; merry.

Light-horse, līt′hors, *n.* Light-armed cavalry.

Light-horseman, līt′hors-man, *n.* A light-armed cavalry soldier.

Lighthouse, līt'hous, *n.* A tower with a light on the top to direct seamen at night.
Light-infantry, līt'in-fant-ri, *n.* Infantry trained for rapid movement.
Lightly, līt'li, *adv.* With little weight; easily; cheerfully; nimbly; airily.
Lightning, līt'ning, *n.* The sudden and vivid flash that precedes thunder, produced by a discharge of atmospheric electricity.
Lightning-rod, līt'ning-rod, *n.* A metallic rod to protect buildings or vessels from lightning. Also **Lightning-conductor.**
Lights, līts, *n.pl.* The lungs of animals.
Lightsome, līt'sum, *a.* Bright; gay; cheering.
Ligneous, lig'nē-us, *a.* Woody; wooden.
Lignify, lig'ni-fī, *vi.* and *t.* To turn into wood.
Lignite, lig'nīt, *n.* Fossil wood or brown-coal.
Lignum-vitæ, lig-num-vī'tē, *n.* A tropical tree having wood of extreme hardness.
Like, līk, *a.* Equal; similar; resembling; likely; feeling disposed.—*adv.* or *prep.* In the same manner; similarly; likely.—*vt.* (liking, liked). To be pleased with; to approve.—*vi.* To be pleased; to choose.—*n.* Some person or thing resembling another; a counterpart; a liking; a fancy.
Likeable, līk'a-bl, *a.* Such as to attract liking; lovable.
Likelihood, līk'li-hụd, *n.* Probability; appearance of truth or reality.
Likely, līk'li, *a.* Probable; credible; suitable. —*adv.* Probably.
Liken, līk'n, *vt.* To compare; to represent as resembling or similar.
Likeness, līk'nes, *n.* Quality or state of being like; resemblance; similarity; one who resembles another; a portrait.
Likewise, līk'wīz, *adv.* In like manner; also; moreover; too.
Liking, līk'ing, *n.* Inclination; desire; preference; satisfaction.
Lilac, lī'lak, *n.* A shrub with flowers generally bluish or white.
Lilliputian, lil-i-pū'shan, *n.* A person of very small size.—*a.* Very small.
Lilt, lilt, *vt.* and *i.* To sing cheerfully; to give musical utterance.—*n.* A song; a tune.
Lily, lil'i, *n.* A bulbous plant with showy and fragrant flowers.
Limb, lim, *n.* The arm or leg, especially the latter; a branch of a tree; graduated edge of a quadrant, &c.; border of the disc of the sun, moon, &c.—*vt.* To supply with limbs; to tear off the limbs of.
Limber, lim'bėr, *a.* Flexible; pliant.—*n.* A carriage with ammunition boxes attached to the gun-carriage.—*vt.* and *i.* To attach the limber to the gun-carriage.
Limbo, lim'bo, *n.* A supposed region beyond this world for souls of innocent persons ignorant of Christianity; any similar region; a prison of confinement.
Lime, līm, *n.* Any viscous substance; calcareous earth used in cement; mortar made with lime; the linden-tree; a tree producing an inferior sort of lemon.—*vt.* (liming, limed). To smear or manure with lime; to ensnare; to cement.
Lime-juice, līm'jūs, *n.* The juice of the lime-fruit, a specific against scurvy.
Lime-kiln, līm'kil, *n.* A furnace in which limestone is reduced to lime.
Limerick, lim'er-ik, *n.* A nonsense verse form of five lines, popularized by Edward Lear (1812-88) in his *Book of Nonsense* (1840).
Limestone, līm'stōn, *n.* A kind of stone consisting of varieties of carbonate of lime.
Limit, lim'it, *n.* Boundary; border; utmost extent; restraint; restriction.—*vt.* To bound; to circumscribe; to restrain; to restrict.
Limitable, lim'it-a-bl, *a.* That may be limited.
Limitation, lim-it-ā'shon, *n.* Act of limiting; state of being limited; restriction.
Limited, lim'it-ed, *a.* Narrow; circumscribed; confined; restricted.
Limitless, lim'it-les, *a.* Having no limits, boundless; infinite; vast.
Limn, lim, *vt.* To draw or paint, especially a portrait.
Limner, lim'nėr, *n.* One who limns; a portrait-painter.
Limp, limp, *vi.* To halt; to walk lamely.—*n.* A halt; act of limping.—*a.* Easily bent; plaint; flaccid.
Limpet, lim'pet, *n.* A marine mollusc, adhering to rocks.
Limpid, lim'pid, *a.* Clear; crystal; pellucid.
Limpidity, lim-pid'i-ti, *n.* Clearness; purity; transparency.
Limy, līm'i, *a.* Containing lime; resemblin lime.
Lin, Linn, lin, *n.* A cataract or waterfall; the pool below a fall.
Linch-pin, linsh'pin, *n.* A pin to keep a wheel on the axle-tree.
Linden, lind'en, *n.* The lime-tree.
Line, līn, *n.* A small rope or cord; a thread-like marking; a stroke or score; a row of soldiers, ships, words, &c.; a verse; ar outline; a short written communication; course of procedure, &c.; connected series, as of descendants; series of public conveyances, as steamers; the twelfth part of an inch; the equator; the regular infantry of an army; *pl.* works covering extended positions and presenting a front in only one direction to the enemy.—*vt.* (lining, lined). To draw lines upon; to set with men or things in lines; to cover on the inside; to put in the inside of.
Lineage, lin'ē-āj, *n.* Descendants in a line from a common progenitor; race.
Lineal, lin'ē-al, *a.* Composed of or pertaining to lines; in a direct line from an ancestor; hereditary.
Lineament, lin'ē-a-ment, *n.* One of the lines which mark the features; feature; form.
Linear, lin'ē-ėr, *a.* Pertaining to a line; like a line; slender.
Lineate, Lineolate, lin'ē-āt, lin'ē-ō-lāt, *a.* In *botany*, marked longitudinally with lines.
Linen, lin'en, *n.* Cloth made of flax; under clothing.—*a.* Made of flax; resembling linen cloth.
Liner, līn'ėr, *n.* A vessel of a line of ocean going steamships.
Linesman, līnz'man, *n.* An infantryman.
Ling, ling, *n.* A fish of the cod family.
Linger, ling'gėr, *vi.* To delay; to loiter; to hesitate; to remain long.—*vt.* To spend wearily.
Lingerer, ling'gėr-ėr, *n.* One who lingers.
Lingering, ling'gėr-ing, *a.* Protracted; given to linger.
Lingo, ling'gō, *n.* Language; speech; contemptuous term for a peculiar language.

Lingual, ling'gwal, *a.* Pertaining to the tongue.—*n.* A sound pronounced with the tongue, as *l.*
Linguist, ling'gwist, *n.* A person skilled in languages.
Linguistic, ling-gwist'ik, *a.* Relating to language; philological.
Linguistics, ling-gwist'iks, *n.* The science of language; comparative philology.
Liniment, lin'i-ment, *n.* A species of soft ointment; an embrocation.
Lining, lin'ing, *n.* The covering of the inner surface of anything.
Link, lingk, *n.* A single ring of a chain; anything closed like a link; anything connecting; a measure of 7·92 inches; a torch.—*vi.* To be connected.—*vt.* To join or connect, as by links; to unite.
Links, lingks, *n.pl.* A stretch of uncultivated flat or undulating ground.
Linnet, lin'et, *n.* A small singing bird.
Linseed, lin'sēd, *n.* Flax-seed.
Linsey-woolsey, lin'si-wul-si, *n.* A fabric made of linen and wool.—*a.* Made of linen and wool; of different and unsuitable ingredients.
Linstock, lin'stok, *n.* A staff holding a lighted match, formerly used in firing cannon.
Lint, lint, *n.* Flax; linen scraped into a soft substance, and used for dressing wounds.
Lintel, lin'tel, *n.* The horizontal part of the door or window frame.
Lion, lī'on, *n.* A carnivorous animal of the cat family; a sign in the zodiac, Leo; an object of interest and curiosity.
Lioness, lī'on-es, *n.* The female of the lion.
Lion-hearted, lī'on-härt-ed, *a.* Having a lion's courage; brave and magnanimous.
Lionize, lī'on-īz, *vt.* To treat as an object of curiosity and interest.
Lip, lip, *n.* One of the two fleshy parts covering the front teeth in man, &c.; edge or border.—*vt.* (lipping, lipped). To touch as with the lip.
Lipogram, lī'pō-gram, *n.* A writing in which a particular letter is wholly omitted.
Lip-stick, lip-stik, *n.* A cosmetic used by women for heightening the colour of the lips.
Liquate, lī'kwāt, *vi.* and *t.* To melt; to separate by melting.
Liquefaction, lik-wē-fak'shon, *n.* Act or operation of melting; state of being melted.
Liquefier, lik'wē-fī-ėr, *n.* That which melts.
Liquefy, lik'wē-fī, *vt.* To melt; to dissolve by heat.—*vi.* To become liquid.
Liquescent, li-kwes'sent, *a.* Becoming liquid; melting.
Liqueur, li-kūr' or li-kŏr', *n.* An alcoholic beverage sweetened and containing some infusion of fruits or aromatic substances.
Liquid, lik'wid, *a.* Fluid; not solid; soft; smooth; devoid of harshness.—*n.* A fluid; a letter with a smooth flowing sound, as *l* and *r.*
Liquidate, lik'wid-āt, *vt.* To clear from obscurity; to adjust; to settle, adjust, and apportion, as a bankrupt's affairs.
Liquidation, lik-wid-ā'shon, *n.* Act of liquidating.
Liquidator, lik'wid-āt-ėr, *n.* One who liquidates; a person appointed to wind up the affairs of a firm or company.
Liquidity, lik-wid'i-ti, *n.* State or quality of being liquid.
Liquor, lik'ėr, *n.* A liquid; spirituous fluids; drink.
Liquorice, lik'ėr-is, *n.* A plant of the bean family, the roots of which supply a sweet juice.
Lira, lē'rä, *n.*; pl. **Lire,** lē'rā. An Italian silver coin, corresponding in value to the franc.
Lisp, lisp, *vi.* To pronounce the sibilant letters imperfectly, as in pronouncing *th* for *s*; to speak imperfectly, as a child.—*vt.* To pronounce with a lisp, or imperfectly.—*n.* The habit or act of lisping.
Lissom, lis'um, *a.* Supple; flexible; lithe; nimble; active.
List, list, *n.* The selvedge of cloth; a limit or border; a roll or catalogue; inclination to one side; *pl.* a field inclosed for a combat.—*vt.* To enroll; to enlist.—*vi.* To enlist, as in the army; to desire; to be disposed; to hearken.
Listen, lis'n, *vi.* To hearken; to give heed.—*vt.* To hear; to attend.
Listless, list'les, *a.* Having no wish; indifferent; uninterested; languid; weary.
Listlessly, list'les-li, *adv.* Without attention; heedlessly.
Litany, li'ta-ni, *n.* A solemn supplication; a collection of short supplications uttered by the priest and people alternately.
Literal, li'tėr-al, *a.* According to the exact meaning; not figurative; expressed by letters.
Literally, li'tėr-al-li, *adv.* In a literal manner; not figuratively; word by word.
Literary, li'tėr-a-ri, *a.* Pertaining to letters or literature; versed in letters.
Literate, li'tėr-āt, *a.* Learned; literary.
Literatim, li-tėr-ā'tim, *adv.* Letter for letter.
Literato, li-tėr-ä'tō, *n.*; pl. **Literati,** li-tėr-ä'tī. A literary man; a litterateur.
Literature, li'tėr-a-tūr, *n.* Learning; literary knowledge; collective writings of a country or period; belles-lettres; the literary profession.
Lith, lith, *n.* A limb; a joint; a member.
Litharge, lith'ärj, *n.* An oxide of lead used in the arts.
Lithe, līTH, *a.* Pliant; flexible; limber.
Lithesome, līTH'sum, *a.* Pliant; nimble.
Lithia, lith'i-a, *n.* An oxide of lithium.
Lithium, lith'i-um, *n.* The lightest of all known solids.
Lithoglyphics, Lithoglyptics, lith-ō-glif'iks, lith-ō-glip'tiks, *n.* The art of engraving on precious stones, &c.
Lithograph, lith'ō-graf, *vt.* To draw on stone, and transfer to paper, &c., by printing.—*n.* A print from a drawing on stone.
Lithographer, li-tho'graf-ėr, *n.* One who practises lithography.
Lithographic, lith-ō-graf'ik, *a.* Pertaining to lithography; printed from stone.
Lithography, li-tho'gra-fi, *n.* The art of drawing with special pigments on a peculiar kind of stone, and of producing impressions of the designs on paper.
Lithology, li-thol'o-ji, *n.* The knowledge of rocks; study of the mineral structure of rocks.
Lithotomy, li-thot'ō-mi, *n.* The operation of cutting for stone in the bladder.
Litigant, li'ti-gant, *a.* Disposed to litigate; engaged in a lawsuit.—*n.* One engaged in a lawsuit.
Litigate, li'ti-gāt, *vt.* To contest in law.—*vi.* To carry on a suit by judicial process.

Litigation, li-ti-gā'shon, *n.* Act or process of litigating; a lawsuit.
Litigious, li-tij'us, *a.* Apt to go to law; disputable; contentious.
Litmus, lit'mus, *n.* A colouring matter procured from certain lichens, used as a chemical test.
Litre, lē'tr, *n.* The French standard measure of capacity, equal to 61.028 cubic inches; the English imperial gallon being fully 4½ litres.
Litter, lit'ėr, *n.* A frame supporting a bed in which a person may be borne; straw used as a bed for animals; the young produced at a birth by a quadruped; scattered rubbish; a condition of disorder.—*vt.* To furnish with bedding; to scatter in a slovenly manner; to bring forth.—*vi.* To lie in litter; to give birth to a litter.
Litterateur, lit'ėr-a-tör, *n.* A literary man; one whose profession is literature.
Little, lit'l, *a.* Small in size or extent; short in duration; slight; mean.—*n.* A small quantity, space, &c.—**A little,** somewhat.—*adv.* In a small degree or quantity.
Little-go, lit'l gō, *n.* The first examination necessary for the B.A. degree at Cambridge University, officially known as the Previous Examination.
Littoral, lit'ō-ral, *a.* Pertaining to or inhabiting the shore.—*n.* A tract along a shore.
Liturgic, Liturgical, li-tėr'jik, li-tėr'jik-al, *a.* Pertaining to a liturgy.
Liturgist, li'tėr-jist, *n.* One who favours a liturgy, or is learned in liturgies.
Liturgy, li'tėr-ji, *n.* A ritual or established formulas for public worship.
Live, liv, *vi.* (living, lived). To exist; to be alive; to dwell; to conduct oneself in life; to feed or subsist; to acquire a livelihood; to be exempt from spiritual death.—*vt.* To lead, pass, or spend.
Live, līv, *a.* Having life; alive; not dead, ignited; vivid, as colour.
Lived, livd or līvd, *a.* Having a life; as, long-*lived*.
Livelihood, līv'li-hụd, *n.* Means of living; maintenance; sustenance.
Livelong, liv' or liv'long, *a.* That lives or endures long; lasting; tedious.
Lively, līv'li, *a.* Vivacious; active; gay; vivid.—*adv.* Briskly; vigorously.
Liver, liv'ėr, *n.* One who lives; the organ in animals which secretes the bile.
Livery, liv'ėr-i, *n.* State of a horse that is kept and fed at a certain rate; distinctive dress of male servants; distinctive garb worn by any body; the body or guild wearing such a garb.—*vt.* (liverying, liveried). To clothe in, or as in, livery.—*a.* Resembling the liver.
Liveryman, liv'ėr-i-man, *n.* One who wears a livery; a freeman of one of the guilds of the city of London.
Livid, liv'id, *a.* Black and blue; of a lead colour; discoloured, as flesh by contusion.
Living, liv'ing, *p.a.* Having life; existing; in action or use.—*n.* Means of subsistence; manner of life; the benefice of a clergyman.
Lixiviation, lik-siv'i-ā''shon, *n.* The extraction of alkaline salts from ashes by pouring water on them.
Lixivium, lik-siv'i-um, *n.* Lye.
Lizard, li'zėrd, *n.* A four-footed, tailed reptile.
Llama, lä'mä or lyä'mä, *n.* A S. American ruminating animal allied to the camel, but smaller and without a hump.
Llanos, lan'ōz or lyä'nōz, *n.pl.* Vast grassy plains in S. America.
Lloyd's, loidz, *n.* A society in London for the collection and diffusion of maritime intelligence, the insurance, classification, and certification of vessels, &c.
Lo, lō, *exclam.* Look; see; behold.
Loach, lōch, *n.* A small fish inhabiting clear swift streams in England.
Load, lōd, *vt.* To charge with a load; to burden; to encumber; to bestow in great abundance; to charge, as a gun.—*n.* A burden; cargo; a grievous weight; something that oppresses.
Loading, lōd'ing, *n.* A cargo; a burden; something added to give weight.
Load-line, lōd'līn, *n.* A line on the side of a vessel to show the depth to which she sinks when not overloaded.
Loadstar, Lodestar, lōd'stär, *n.* A star that serves to guide; the pole-star.
Loadstone, Lodestone, lōd'stōn, *n.* An ore of iron; the magnetic oxide of iron, which can attract iron; a magnet.
Loaf, lōf, *n.*; pl. **Loaves,** lōvz. A mass of bread formed by the baker; a conical lump of sugar.—*vi.* To lounge.—*vt.* To spend idly.
Loafer, lōf'ėr, *n.* A lounger; a low idler.
Loam, lōm, *n.* A rich species of earth or mould.—*vt.* To cover with loam.
Loamy, lōm'i, *a.* Consisting of or like loam.
Loan, lōn, *n.* Lending; that which is lent; a sum of money lent at interest.—*vt.* and *i.* To lend.
Loath, Loth, lōth, *a.* Disliking; unwilling; averse; not inclined; reluctant.
Loathe, lōᴛʜ, *vt.* (loathing, loathed). To feel disgust at; to abhor; to abominate.—*vi.* To feel nausea or abhorrence.
Loathing, lōᴛʜ'ing, *n.* Extreme disgust or aversion; abhorrence; detestation.
Loathly, lōᴛʜ'li, *a.* Loathsome.
Loathness, lōᴛʜ'nes, *n.* Reluctance.
Loathsome, lōᴛʜ'sum, *a.* Exciting disgust; disgusting; detestable; abhorrent.
Lob, lob, *n.* A dolt; a lout.—*vt.* (lobbing, lobbed). To throw or toss slowly.
Lobar, lō'bär, *a.* Pertaining to a lobe.
Lobby, lob'i, *n.* An apartment giving admission to others; an entrance-hall.
Lobe, lōb, *n.* A round projecting part of something; such a part of the liver, lungs, brain, &c.; the lower soft part of the ear.
Lobelia, lō-bē'li-a, *n.* A genus of plants with bell-shaped flowers.
Lobster, lob'stėr, *n.* A ten-footed crustacean with large claws, allied to the crab.
Lobular, lob'ū-lėr, *a.* Having the character of a lobule.
Lobule, lob'ūl, *n.* A small lobe.
Local, lō'kal, *a.* Pertaining to a particular place; confined to a spot or definite district. —*n.* A local item of news; a local railway train.
Locale, lō-käl', *n.* A locality.
Localism, lō'kal-izm, *n.* State of being local; word or phrase limited to a place.
Locality, lō-kal'i-ti, *n.* State of being local; position; situation; place.
Localize, lō'kal-īz, *vt.* To make local; to discover or detect the place of.

Locally, lō'kal-li, *adv.* In a local manner; with respect to place; in place.

Locate, lō'kāt, *vt.* (locating, located). To place; to settle.—*vi.* To reside.

Location, lō-kā'shon, *n.* Act of locating; situation with respect to place; place.

Loch, loch, *n.* A lake; a landlocked arm of the sea.

Lock, lok, *n.* An appliance for fastening doors, &c.; mechanism by which a firearm is discharged; a fastening together; inclosure in a canal, with gates at either end; a tuft or ringlet of hair.—*vt.* To fasten with a lock and key; to shut up or confine; to join firmly; to embrace closely.—*vi.* To become fast; to unite closely by mutual insertion.

Lockage, lok'āj, *n.* Works forming the locks on a canal; toll paid for passing the locks.

Locker, lok'ėr, *n.* A close receptable, as a drawer in a ship, closed with a lock.

Locket, lok'et, *n.* A little case worn as an ornament, often containing a lock of hair.

Lock-jaw, lok'ja, *n.* A spasmodic rigidity of the under jaw.

Locksmith, lok'smith, *n.* An artificer who makes or mends locks.

Lock-up, lok'up, *n.* A place in which persons under arrest are temporarily confined.

Locomotion, lō-kō-mō'shon, *n.* Act or power of moving from place to place.

Locomotive, lō-kō-mō'tiv, *a.* Moving from place to place.—*n.* A steam-engine placed on wheels, and employed in moving a train of carriages on a railway.

Locomotor, lō-kō-mō'tor, *n.* and *a.* That which has locomotion.—**Locomotor ataxy,** a sort of paralysis in which the movements of the limbs are so irregular as to make walking impossible.

Locum-tenens, lō'kum-tē'nenz, *n.* One who temporarily acts for another.

Locust, lō'kust, *n.* A large insect allied to the grasshopper; the locust-tree.

Locust-tree, lō'kust-trē, *n.* The carob; the name of certain American trees.

Locution, lō-kū'shon, *n.* A phrase; a mode of speech.

Lode, lōd, *n.* An open ditch; a metallic vein, or any regular mineral vein.

Lodestar, *n.* Same as *Loadstar.*

Lodestone, *n.* Same as *Loadstone.*

Lodge, loj, *n.* A small country house; a temporary abode; place where members of a society, as freemasons, meet; the society itself.—*vt.* (lodging, lodged). To furnish with temporary accommodation; to set or deposit for keeping; to beat down (growing crops). —*vi.* To have a temporary abode; to settle; to reside.

Lodger, loj'ėr, *n.* One who lodges; one who lives in a hired room or rooms.

Lodging, loj'ing, *n.* A temporary habitation; rooms let to another: usually in *pl.*

Lodgment, loj'ment, *n.* Act of lodging; state of being lodged; accumulation of something deposited; occupation of a position by the besieging party.

Loft, loft, *n.* The space below and between the rafters; a gallery raised within a larger apartment or in a church.

Loftily, loft'i-li, *adv.* In a lofty manner or position; proudly; haughtily.

Lofty, loft'i, *a.* Elevated in place; rising to a great height; proud; haughty; sublime; stately.

Log, log, *n.* A bulky piece of timber unhewed; a floating contrivance for measuring the rate of a ship's velocity; a log-book.

Logan, Loggan, log'an, *n.* A large stone so balanced as to be easily moved.

Logan-berry, lō'gan-be"ri, *n.* A cross between a blackberry and a raspberry.

Logarithm, log'a-rithm, *n.* In *mathematics,* the exponent of the power to which a given invariable number must be raised in order to produce another given number.

Logarithmic, Logarithmical, log-a-rith'mik, log-a-rith'mik-al, *a.* Pertaining to logarithms; consisting of logarithms.

Log-book, log'bųk, *n.* Register of a ship's way, and of the incidents of the voyage.

Log-cabin, Log-house, Log-hut, log'ka-bin, log'hous, log'hut, *n.* A house made of logs laid on each other.

Loggerhead, log'ėr-hed, *n.* A blockhead; a dunce.—**At loggerheads,** quarrelling.

Logic, lo'jik, *n.* The science or art of reasoning; mode of arguing.

Logical, lo'jik-al, *a.* Pertaining to logic; skilled in logic; according to reason.

Logically, lo'jik-al-li, *adv.* In a logical manner.

Logician, lō-ji'shan, *n.* One skilled in logic.

Logistic, lō-jis'tik, *a.* Pertaining to judging, estimating, or calculating.

Logogram, log'ō-gram, *n.* A single type or symbol that forms a word.

Log-rolling, log'rōl-ing, *n.* The joining of a number of persons to collect logs; union for mutual assistance or praise.

Logwood, log'wųd, *n.* A wood of a dark-red colour, used as a dye-wood.

Loin, loin, *n.* The part of an animal on either side between the ribs and the haunch-bone.

Loiter, loi'tėr, *vi.* To be slow in moving; to spend time idly; to hang about.—*vt.* To waste carelessly: with *away.*

Loiterer, loi'tėr-ėr, *n.* One who loiters; a lingerer; an idler.

Loll, lol, *vi.* (lolling, lolled). To lean idly; to lie at ease; to hang out, as the tongue of a dog.—*vt.* To suffer to hang out.

Lollipop, lol'i-pop, *n.* A sugar confection which dissolves easily in the mouth.

Lone, lōn, *a.* Solitary; unfrequented; single.

Lonely, lōn'li, *a.* Unfrequented by men; retired; solitary.

Lonesome, lōn'sum, *a.* Solitary; secluded from society; lonely.

Long, long, *a.* Drawn out in a line; drawn out in time; tedious; protracted; late; containing much verbal matter.—*n.* Something that is long.—*adv.* To a great extent in space or in time; at a point of duration far distant. —*vi.* To desire eagerly: with *for.*

Longeval, lon-jēv'al, *a.* Long-lived.

Longevity, lon-jev'i-ti, *n.* Great length of life.

Longevous, lon-jēv'us, *a.* Long-lived.

Longhand, long'hand, *n.* Ordinary written characters, as distinguished from shorthand, &c.

Longheaded, long'hed-ed, *a.* Having a long head; shrewd; far-sighted.

Longing, long'ing, *p.a.* Earnestly desiring; manifesting desire.—*n.* An eager desire.

Longingly, long'ing-li, *adv.* With longing; with eager wishes or appetite.

Longish, long'ish, *a.* Somewhat long.
Longitude, lon'ji-tūd, *n.* Length; distance on the surface of the globe east or west, measured by meridians.
Longitudinal, lon-ji-tūd'in-al, *a.* Pertaining to longitude; running lengthwise.
Long-lived, long'livd, *a.* Having a long life or existence; lasting long.
Long-primer, long'prim-ėr, *n.* A printing type between small-pica and bourgeois.
Long-sighted, long'sīt-ed, *a.* Able to see at a great distance; far-seeing; sagacious.
Longsome, long'sum, *a.* Tiresome on account of length; tedious.
Long-spun, long'spun, *a.* Spun or extended to a great length; tedious.
Long-suffering, long'suf-ėr-ing, *a.* Patient; not easily provoked.—*n.* Patience of offence.
Long-tongued, long'tungd, *a.* Loquacious.
Longways, Longwise, long'wāz, long'wīz, *adv.* In the direction of length; lengthwise.
Long-winded, long'wind-ed, *a.* Not easily exhausted of breath; tedious.
Loo, lö, *n.* A game of cards.
Looby, lö'bi, *n.* An awkward, clumsy fellow.
Loofah, lö'fa, *n.* The dried fibrous interior of a kind of gourd, used as a flesh-brush.
Look, luk, *vi.* To direct the eye so as to see; to gaze; to consider; to expect; to heed; to face; to appear.—*vt.* To see; to express by a look.—*n.* Act of looking; sight; gaze; glance; mien; aspect.
Looking-glass, luk'ing-gläs, *n.* A mirror.
Look-out, luk-out', *n.* A careful watching for any object; place from which such observation is made; person watching.
Loom, löm, *n.* A frame or machine by which thread is worked into cloth; that part of an oar within the boat in rowing.—*vi.* To appear larger than the real dimensions, and indistinctly; to appear to the mind faintly.
Loon, lön, *n.* A worthless fellow; a rogue; a bird, the great northern diver.
Loop, löp, *n.* A noose; a doubling of a string, &c.; a small narrow opening.—*vt.* To form into or fasten with a loop.
Loophole, löp'hōl, *n.* A small opening in a fortification through which small-arms are discharged; a hole that affords means of escape; underhand method of evasion.
Loose, lös, *a.* Not attached; untied; not dense or compact; vague; careless; having lax bowels; unchaste.—*vt.* (loosing, loosed). To untie or unbind; to detach; to set free; to relax; to loosen.
Loose-box, lös'boks, *n.* A roomy stall in a stable for a horse that is not tied.
Loosely, lös'li, *adv.* In a loose manner; laxly; slackly; carelessly; dissolutely.
Loosen, lös'n, *vt.* To make loose.—*vi.* To become loose.
Loot, löt, *n.* Booty; plunder, especially such as is taken in a sacked city.—*vt.* To plunder.
Lop, lop, *vt.* (lopping, lopped). To cut off; to trim by cutting.—*n.* That which is cut from trees.
Lopping, lop'ing, *n.* That which is lopped off; branches lopped.
Lop-sided, lop'sīd-ed, *a.* Heavier at one side than the other; inclining to one side.
Loquacious, lo-kwā'shus, *a.* Talkative; garrulous; babbling.
Loquacity, lo-kwas'i-ti, *n.* Quality of being loquacious; garrulity.
Lorcha, lōr'cha, *n.* A light Chinese sailing vessel, carrying guns.
Lord, lord, *n.* A master; a ruler; proprietor of a manor; a nobleman; a British title applied to peers, sons of dukes and marquises, and the eldest sons of earls; honorary title of certain high officials; (with *cap.*) the Supreme Being.—*vi.* To act as a lord; to rule with arbitrary or despotic sway.
Lordling, lord'ling, *n.* A petty lord.
Lordly, lord'li, *a.* Becoming a lord; large; ample; proud; haughty.
Lordship, lord'ship, *n.* State or quality of being a lord; a title given to a lord; dominion; sovereignty.
Lore, lōr, *n.* Learning; erudition; space between the bill and the eye of a bird.
Lorgnette, lor-nyet', *n.* An opera-glass.
Lorgnon, lor-nyōng, *n.* A double eye-glass fitting into a handle.
Lorica, lo-rī'ka, *n.* A cuirass or corselet.
Loricate, lo'ri-kāt, *a.* Covered as with plates of mail.
Lorn, lorn, *a.* Undone; forsaken; lonely.
Lorry, lo'ri, *n.* A long four-wheeled wagon without sides.
Lose, löz, *vt.* (losing, lost). To cease to possess, as through accident; to fail to keep; to forfeit; not to gain or win; to miss; to cease or fail to see or hear; to misuse.—*vi.* To suffer loss; not to win.
Losing, löz'ing, *p.a.* Bringing or causing loss.
Loss, los, *n.* Act of losing; failure to gain; that which is lost; failure to utilize.
Lost, lost, *p.a.* Gone from our hold, view, &c.; not to be found; ruined; wasted; forfeited; perplexed; alienated.
Lot, lot, *n.* A person's part or share; fate which falls to one; part in life allotted to a person; a distinct portion; a considerable quantity or number; something used to decide what is yet undecided.—*vt.* (lotting, lotted). To assign by lot; to sort; to portion.
Loth, lōth, *a.* *See* LOATH.
Lothario, lō-thā'ri-ō, *n.* A gay libertine.
Lotion, lō'shon, *n.* A wash for the complexion; a fluid applied externally in ailments.
Lottery, lot'ė-ri, *n.* A scheme for the distribution of prizes by lot or chance.
Lotus, lō'tus, *n.* A tree, the fruit of which was fabled to cause forgetfulness of the past; also the Egyptian water-lily and other plants.
Loud, loud, *a.* Having a great sound; noisy; showy.—*adv.* Loudly.
Loudly, loud'li, *adv.* Noisily; clamorously.
Loudspeaker, loud-spē'kėr, *n.* A device for converting electrical energy into sounds capable of being heard at a distance.
Lough, loch, *n.* Irish lake or arm of the sea.
Lounge, lounj, *vi.* (lounging, lounged). To loiter; to loll.—*n.* An idle gait or stroll; act of reclining at ease; a place for lounging.
Lounger, lounj'ėr, *n.* An idler.
Louse, lous, *n.*; pl. **Lice,** līs. A wingless insect, parasitic on man and other animals.
Lousy, louz'i, *a.* Infested with lice.
Lout, lout, *n.* A mean, awkward fellow.—*vt.* To bend or stoop down.
Loutish, lout'ish, *a.* Like a lout; clownish.
Lovable, luv'a-bl, *a.* Worthy of love; amiable.
Love, luv, *vt.* (loving, loved). To regard with

affection; to like; to delight in.—*vi.* To be in love; to be tenderly attached.—*n.* Warm affection; fond attachment; the passion between the sexes; the object beloved; a word of endearment; Cupid, the god of love; the score of nothing at tennis, &c.

Love-bird, luv'bėrd, *n.* A small species of parrot.

Loveless, luv'les, *a.* Void of love; void of tenderness.

Love-lorn, luv'lorn, *a.* Forsaken by one's love; pining from love.

Lovely, luv'li, *a.* That may excite love; beautiful; charming; delightful.

Lover, luv'ėr, *n.* One who loves; a suitor; a wooer; one who likes strongly.

Loving, luv'ing, *p.a.* Fond; kind; affectionate; expressing love or kindness.

Loving-kindness, luv-ing-kīnd'nes, *n.* Tender regard; mercy; favour.

Lovingly, luv'ing-li, *adv.* With love; affectionately.

Low, lō, *a.* Depressed below any given surface or place; not high; deep; below the usual rate; not loud; wanting strength; mean; dishonourable; not sublime; plain.—*adv.* Not aloft; under the usual price; near the ground; not loudly.

Low, lō, *vi.* To bellow, as an ox or cow.

Lower, lō'ėr, *vt.* To make lower; to let down; to abase; to reduce.

Lower, lou'ėr, *vi.* To frown; to look sullen; to threaten a storm.

Lowering, lou'ėr-ing, *p.a.* Threatening a storm; cloudy; overcast.

Lowermost, lō'ėr-most, *a.* Lowest.

Lowery, lou'ėr-i, *a.* Cloudy; gloomy.

Lowing, lō'ing, *n.* The bellowing of cattle.

Lowland, lō'land, *n.* Land which is low with respect to the neighbouring country; a low or level country.—**The Lowlands,** the southern or lower parts of Scotland.

Lowly, lō'li, *a.* Humble in position of life; meek; free from pride.—*adv.* In a low manner or condition.

Low-water, lō'wą-tėr, *n.* The lowest point of the ebb or receding tide.

Loyal, loi'al, *a.* Faithful to a government, plighted love, duty, &c.; constant to friends or associates.

Loyalist, loi'al-ist, *n.* One who adheres to his sovereign or constituted authority.

Loyally, loi'al-li, *adv.* In a loyal manner.

Loyalty, loi'al-ti, *n.* State or quality of being loyal; fidelity; constancy.

Lozenge, lo'zenj, *n.* A figure with four equal sides, having two acute and two obtuse angles; a small cake of sugar, &c.; a small diamond-shaped pane of glass.

Lubber, lub'ėr, *n.* A heavy, clumsy fellow.

Lubberly, lub'ėr-li, *a.* Like a lubber; clumsy.

Lubricant, lū'brik-ant, *n.* A substance for oiling or greasing.

Lubricate, lū-brik-āt, *vt.* To make smooth; to smear with oil, to diminish friction.

Lubrication, lū-brik-ā'shon, *n.* Act or process of lubricating.

Lubricator, lū'brik-āt-ėr, *n.* One who or that which lubricates; an oil-cup attached to a machine.

Lubricity, lū-bris'i-ti, *n.* Smoothness of surface; slipperiness; lasciviousness.

Lucarne, lū'kärn, *n.* A dormer window.

Luce, lūs, *n.* The fish called the pike.

Lucent, lū'sent, *a.* Shining; resplendent.

Lucerne, Lucern, lū'sėrn, *n.* A leguminous plant valuable as fodder.

Lucid, lū'sid, *a.* Full of light; shining; bright; clear; not darkened or confused by delirium; easily understood.

Lucidity, lū-sid'i-ti, *n.* The state or quality of being lucid; clearness; intelligibility.

Lucidly, lū'sid-li, *adv.* In a lucid manner.

Lucifer, lū'si-fėr, *n.* The morning-star; Satan; a match ignitible by friction.

Luck, luk, *n.* That which happens to a person; chance; hap; fortune; success.

Luckily, luk'i-li, *adv.* In a lucky manner; fortunately; by good fortune.

Luckless, luk'les, *a.* Without luck; unlucky; hapless; unfortunate; ill-fated.

Lucky, luk'i, *a.* Meeting with good luck or success; fortunate; auspicious.

Lucrative, lū'krat-iv, *a.* Pertaining to gain; gainful; profitable.

Lucre, lū'kėr, *n.* Gain in money or goods; profit; emolument; pelf.

Lucubrate, lū'kū-brāt, *vi.* To work by lamp-light; to study laboriously; to meditate.

Lucubration, lū-kū-brā'shon, *n.* Act of lucubrating; what is composed by night; a literary composition.

Luculent, lū'kū-lent, *a.* Full of light; clear.

Ludicrous, lū'di-krus, *a.* That serves for sport; laughable; droll; ridiculous.

Ludicrously, lū'di-krus-li, *adv.* In a ludicrous manner.

Luff, luf, *n.* The weather part of a fore-and-aft sail.—*vi.* To put the helm so as to turn the ship toward the wind.

Lug, lug, *vt.* (lugging, lugged). To haul; to drag.—*n.* The ear; object resembling the ear, as the handle of a vessel.

Luggage, lug'āj, *n.* Anything cumbersome and heavy; a traveller's baggage.

Lugger, lug'ėr, *n.* A small vessel of two or three masts with lug-sails.

Lug-sail, lug'sāl, *n.* A square sail bent on a yard that hangs obliquely to the mast.

Lugubrious, lū-gū'bri-us, *a.* Mournful; indicating sorrow; doleful.

Lugworm, lug'wėrm, *n.* A worm which burrows in the muddy sand of the shore.

Lukewarm, lūk'wąrm, *a.* Moderately warm; tepid; not zealous; indifferent.

Lull, lul, *vt.* To sing to, as to a child; to soothe.—*vi.* To subside; to become calm.—*n.* A season of quiet or cessation.

Lullaby, lul'a-bī, *n.* A song to lull or quiet babes; that which quiets.

Lumbago, lum-bā'gō, *n.* A rheumatic affection of the muscles about the loins.

Lumbar, lum'bar, *n.* Pertaining to or near the loins.

Lumber, lum'bėr, *n.* Anything useless and cumbersome; in America, timber sawed or split for use.—*vt.* To fill with lumber; to heap together in disorder.—*vi.* To move heavily, as a vehicle; in America, to cut and prepare timber.

Luminary, lū'min-a-ri, *n.* Any body that gives light.

Luminosity, lū-min-os'i-ti, *n.* The quality of being luminous; brightness; clearness.

Luminous, lū'min-us, *a.* Shining; bright; giving light; clear; lucid.

Lump, lump, *n.* A small mass of matter; a mass of things.—*vt.* To throw into a mass; to take in the gross.
Lumper, lump'ėr, *n.* A labourer employed to load and unload vessels when in harbour.
Lumping, lump'ing, *a.* Bulky; heavy; big.
Lumpish, lump'ish, *a.* Like a lump; heavy; dull; inactive.
Lump-sugar, lump'shu̥g-ėr, *n.* Loaf-sugar in small lumps or pieces.
Lumpy, lump'i, *a.* Full of lumps; showing small irregular waves.
Lunacy, lū'na-si, *n.* Mental derangement; madness; insanity; craziness; mania.
Lunar, lū'nar, *a.* Pertaining to the moon; measured by the revolutions of the moon.
Lunatic, lū'nat-ik, *a.* Affected with lunacy; mad; insane.—*n.* A madman.
Lunation, lū-nā'shon, *n.* A lunar month; time from one new moon to the next.
Lunch, Luncheon, lunsh, lunsh'on, *n.* A slight repast between breakfast and dinner.—*vi.* To take a lunch.
Lune, lūn, *n.* Anything in the shape of a half-moon or a crescent.
Lunette, lū-net', *n.* A small fortified work with an angular front; window in a concave ceiling; crescent-shaped ornament.
Lung, lung, *n.* Either of the two organs of respiration in air-breathing animals.
Lunge, lunj, *n.* A sudden thrust or pass, as with a sword.—*vi.* (lunging, lunged). To make a thrust.
Lunged, lungd, *a.* Having lungs.
Lunula, Lunule, lū'nū-la, lū'nūl, *n.* Something in the shape of a crescent.
Lunular, lū'nū-lėr, *a.* Having the form of a small crescent.
Lupine, lū'pin, *n.* A leguminous flowering plant.—*a.* lū'pīn. Like a wolf; wolfish.
Lupulin, Lupuline, lū'pū-lin, *n.* The bitter aromatic principle of the hop.
Lupus, lū'pus, *n.* A disease which eats away the flesh of the face.
Lurch, lėrch, *vi.* To lurk; to roll or sway to one side.—*n.* A sudden roll or stagger; a difficult or helpless position.
Lurcher, lėrch'ėr, *n.* One that lurches; one that lies in wait; a mongrel dog for hunting.
Lurdan, Lurdane, lėr'dan, lėr'dān, *a.* Lazy and useless.—*n.* A lazy, stupid fellow.
Lure, lūr, *n.* Something held out to call a trained hawk; a bait; any enticement.—*vt.* (luring, lured). To attract by a lure or bait; to entice.
Lurid, lū'rid, *a.* Pale yellow, as flame; ghastly pale; wan; gloomy; dismal.
Lurk, lėrk, *vi.* To lie hid; to lie in wait.
Luscious, lu'shus, *a.* Very sweet; delicious; sweet to excess.
Lush, lush, *a.* Fresh; succulent.
Lust, lust, *n.* Longing desire; carnal appetite; depraved affections.—*vi.* To desire eagerly; to have carnal desire.
Lustful, lust'fu̥l, *a.* Inspired by lust or the sexual appetite; lewd; libidinous.
Lustily, lust'i-li, *adv.* In a lusty manner; with vigour of body; stoutly.
Lustral, lus'tral, *a.* Used in purification; pertaining to purification.
Lustrate, lus'trāt, *vt.* To purify as by water.
Lustration, lus-trā'shon, *n.* A solemn ceremony of purifying; purification.
Lustre, lus'tėr, *n.* Brightness; brilliancy; renown; a branched chandelier ornamented with cut glass; a glossy fabric for dress.
Lustring, lūs'tring, *n.* A glossy silk cloth.
Lustrous, lus'trus, *a.* Full of lustre; bright; shining; luminous.
Lustrum, lus'trum, *n.*; pl. **-rums** or **-ra.** In ancient Rome, the quinquennial purification of the people; a period of five years.
Lusty, lust'i, *a.* Vigorous; robust; healthful; bulky; large; lustful.
Lute, lūt, *n.* A stringed instrument of the guitar kind; a composition of clay, &c.—*vt.* (luting, luted). To play on the lute; to close or coat with lute.
Lutheran, lū'thėr-an, *a.* Pertaining to Martin Luther, the reformer.—*n.* A follower of Luther.
Lutheranism, lū'thėr-an-izm, *n.* The doctrines of the Protestant church in Germany.
Luxate, luks'āt, *vt.* To put out of joint, as a limb; to dislocate.
Luxation, luks-ā'shon, *n.* The act of luxating; dislocation.
Luxuriance, luks-ū'ri-ans, *n.* State of being luxuriant; rank growth; exuberance.
Luxuriant, luks-ū'ri-ant, *a.* Exuberant in growth; abundant.
Luxuriate, luks-ū'ri-āt, *vi.* To grow exuberantly; to feed or live luxuriously; to indulge without restraint.
Luxurious, luks-ū'ri-us, *a.* Given to luxury; voluptuous; furnished with luxuries.
Luxuriously, luks-ū'ri-us-li, *adv.* In a luxurious manner; voluptuously.
Luxury, luks'ū-ri, *n.* Extravagant indulgence; that which gratifies a fastidious appetite; anything delightful to the senses.
Lycanthropy, lī-kan'thro-pi, *n.* A kind of insanity in which the patient supposes himself to be a wolf.
Lyceum, lī-sē'um, *n.* A literary institute; a higher school.
Lycopod, lī'kō-pod, *n.* A plant of an order between mosses and ferns.
Lyddite, lid'īt, *n.* A powerful explosive substance.
Lye, lī, *n.* Water impregnated with alkaline salt imbibed from the ashes of wood; solution of an alkali.
Lying-in, lī'ing-in, *n.* and *a.* Childbirth.
Lyingly, lī'ing-li, *adv.* Falsely; by telling lies.
Lymph, limf, *n.* Water; a watery fluid; a colourless fluid in animal bodies.
Lymphatic, lim-fat'ik, *a.* Pertaining to lymph; phlegmatic; sluggish.—*n.* A vessel in animal bodies which contains or conveys lymph.
Lynch, linsh, *vt.* To inflict punishment upon, without the forms of law, as by a mob.
Lynx, lingks, *n.* A carnivorous animal resembling the cat, noted for its keen sight.
Lyre, līr, *n.* A stringed instrument of the harp kind much used by the ancients.
Lyric, Lyrical, li'rik, li'rik-al, *a.* Pertaining to a lyre; designating that species of poetry which has reference to the individual emotions of the poet, such as songs.—**Lyric,** li'rik, *n.* A lyric poem; an author of lyric poems.
Lyrist, līr'ist, *n.* One who plays on the lyre; a writer of lyrics or lyric poetry.

M

Macabre, mak-a'br, *a.* Gruesome; terrible.
Macadamize, mak-ad'am-iz, *vt.* To cover, as a road, with small broken stones, which, when consolidated, form a firm surface.
Macaroni, ma-ka-rō'ni, *n.* A paste of fine wheat flour made into small tubes; a kind of dandy in fashion in London about 1760.
Macaronic, ma-ka-rō'nik, *a.* Pertaining to macaroni, or to a macaroni; applied to burlesque verse consisting of vernacular words Latinized or Latin words modernized.
Macaroon, ma-ka-rön', *n.* A small sweet-cake, containing almonds.
Macaw, ma-ka̤', *n.* A bird of the parrot tribe with long tail-feathers.
Mace, mās, *n.* A staff with a heavy metal head; an ensign of authority borne before magistrates; a spice, the dried covering of the seed of the nutmeg.
Macer, mās'ėr, *n.* A mace-bearer.
Macerate, ma'se-rāt, *vt.* To steep almost to solution; to make lean or cause to waste away.
Maceration, ma-se-rā'shon, *n.* Act or process of macerating.
Machiavelian, ma'ki-a-vēl"i-an, *a.* Pertaining to *Machiavelli*, or denoting his principles; cunning in political management.
Machinate, mak'i-nāt, *vt.* and *i.* To plot or plan; to form, as a plot or scheme.
Machination, mak'i-nā"shon, *n.* A plot; an artful design or scheme.
Machine, ma-shēn', *n.* Any contrivance which serves to regulate the effect of a given force or to produce or change motion; an organized system; a person who acts as the tool of another.—*vt.* To apply machinery to; to produce by machinery.
Machine-gun, ma-shēn'gun, *n.* A small-calibre fire-arm arranged to fire from a stand, carriage or tripod, and provided with mechanical devices to produce a very rapid rate of fire, *e.g.* the *Vickers-Maxim*, the *Hotchkiss* and the *Bren gun*.
Machinery, ma-shēn'e-ri, *n.* The component parts of a complex machine; machines in general.
Machinist, ma-shēn'ist, *n.* A constructor of machines; one who works a machine.
Mackerel, mak'ėr-el, *n.* An edible sea fish.
Mackintosh, Macintosh, mak'in-tosh, *n.* A waterproof overcoat.
Macrocosm, mak'ro-kozm, *n.* The great world; the universe, analogous to the *microcosm*.
Macula, ma'kū-la, *n.*; pl. **-læ.** A spot, as on the skin.
Maculate, ma'kū-lāt, *vt.* To spot; to stain.—*a.* Marked with spots; impure.
Mad, mad, *a.* Disordered in intellect; insane; crazy; frantic; furious; infatuated.—*vt.* (madding, madded). To make mad.
Madam, ma'dam, *n.* My lady; a complimentary title given to ladies.
Madcap, mad'kap, *n.* and *a.* A flighty or hare-brained person; one who indulges in frolics.
Madden, mad'n, *vt.* To make mad.—*vi.* To become mad; to act as if mad.
Madder, mad'ėr, *n.* A climbing perennial plant, the root of which furnishes dyes and pigments.
Madding, mad'ing, *a.* Acting madly; wild.
Made, mād, pret. and pp. of *make*.
Madeira, ma-dē'ra, *n.* A rich wine made on the isle of Madeira.
Mademoiselle, mad-mwä-zel, *n.* Miss; a title given to young unmarried ladies in France.
Mad-house, mad'hous, *n.* A house where mad or insane persons are confined.
Madly, mad'li, *adv.* In a mad manner; frantically; furiously; rashly; wildly.
Madman, mad'man, *n.* A man who is mad; a maniac; a lunatic.
Madness, mad'nes, *n.* Lunacy; frenzy; extreme folly.
Madonna, ma-don'na, *n.* The Virgin Mary; a picture representing the Virgin.
Madrepore, ma'dre-pōr, *n.* A common branching variety of coral.
Madrigal, mad'ri-gal, *n.* A pastoral song; vocal composition in five or six parts.
Maestoso, mä-es-tō'zō. In *music*, with dignity.
Maestro, mä-es'trō, *n.* A master of any art; a musical composer.
Magazine, mag'a-zēn, *n.* A storehouse; a repository for ammunition or provisions; a serial publication.
Magazine-rifle, mag'a-zēn-rī-fl, *n.* A rifle that can fire a number of shots in rapid succession without reloading.
Magdalen, Magdalene, mag'da-len, mag'da-lēn, *n.* A reformed prostitute.
Magenta, ma-jen'ta, *n.* A brilliant blue-red colour derived from coal-tar.
Maggot, ma'got, *n.* The larva of a fly or other insect; a grub; an odd fancy.
Maggoty, ma'got-i, *a.* Full of maggots; capricious.
Magi, mā'jī, *n.pl.* The caste of priests among the ancient Medes and Persians; holy men or sages of the East.
Magic, ma'jik, *n.* The art of producing effects by superhuman means; sorcery; enchantment; power similar to that of enchantment.—*a.* Pertaining to magic; working or worked by or as if by magic.
Magical, ma'jik-al, *a.* Magic.
Magically, ma'jik-al-li, *adv.* In a magical manner; by enchantment.
Magician, ma-ji'shan, *n.* One skilled in magic; an enchanter.
Magilp, Magilph, ma-gilp', ma-gilf', *n.* A mixture of linseed-oil and mastic varnish used by artists as a vehicle for colours.
Magisterial, ma-jis-tē'ri-al, *a.* Pertaining to a master or magistrate; imperious; haughty; authoritative.
Magistracy, ma'jis-tra-si, *n.* The office or dignity of a magistrate; the body of magistrates.
Magistrate, ma'jis-trāt, *n.* A public civil officer, with executive or judicial authority.
Magnanimity, mag-na-nim'i-ti, *n.* Quality of being magnanimous; greatness of soul or mind.
Magnanimous, mag-nan'im-us, *a.* Great of soul or mind; elevated in sentiment; liberal and honourable; not selfish.
Magnate, mag'nāt, *n.* A great man; a person of rank or wealth.
Magnesia, mag-nē'si-a, *n.* Oxide of magnesium, a white slightly alkaline powder.

Magnesian, mag-nē'si-an, *a.* Pertaining to, containing, or resembling magnesia.
Magnesium, mag-nē'si-um, *n.* Metallic base of magnesia, a white malleable metal.
Magnet, mag'net, *n.* The loadstone, which has the property of attracting iron; a bar of iron or steel to which the properties of the loadstone have been imparted.
Magnetic, mag-net'ik, *a.* Pertaining to the magnet; possessing the properties of the magnet; attractive.
Magnetically, mag-net'ik-al-li, *adv.* In a magnetic manner; by magnetism.
Magnetism, mag'net-izm, *n.* A property of certain bodies whereby they naturally attract or repel one another; that branch of science which treats of magnetic phenomena; power of attraction.
Magnetize, mag'net-īz, *vt.* To give magnetic properties to.—*vi.* To acquire magnetic properties.
Magneto-electricity, mag-net'ō-ē-lek-tris'i-ti, *n.* Electricity evolved by the action of magnets.
Magneto, mag-nēt'ō, *n.* The igniting apparatus of a petrol engine.
Magnific, Magnifical, mag-nif'ik, mag-nif'-ik-al, *a.* Grand; splendid; illustrious.
Magnificence, mag-nif'i-sens, *n.* Grandeur of appearance; splendour; pomp.
Magnificent, mag-nif'i-sent, *a.* Grand in appearance; splendid; showy.
Magnificently, mag-nif'i-sent-li, *adv.* In a magnificent manner.
Magnifier, mag'ni-fī-ėr, *n.* One who or that which magnifies.
Magnify, mag'ni-fī, *vt.* To make great or greater; to increase the apparent dimensions of; to extol; to exaggerate.—*vi.* To possess the quality of causing objects to appear larger.
Magniloquence, mag-nil'ō-kwens, *n.* Elevated language; pompous words or style.
Magniloquent, mag-nil'ō-kwent, *a.* Speaking loftily or pompously.
Magnitude, mag'ni-tūd, *n.* Greatness; size; bulk; importance; consequence.
Magnum, mag'num, *n.* A bottle holding two English quarts.
Magpie, mag'pī, *n.* A chattering bird of the crow tribe with black and white plumage; a shot on the target between an inner and an outer.
Magyar, mag'yär, *n.* A Hungarian; the language of Hungary.
Maharajah, mä-hä-rä'ja, *n.* The title assumed by some Indian princes ruling over a considerable extent of territory.
Maharani, Maharanee, mä-hä-rä'nē, *n.* A female Indian ruler.
Mahdi, mä'di, *n.* A name of some of the successors of Mohammed; one who is to spread Mohammedanism over the world.
Mahl-stick, mal'stik, *n.* A rod used by artists as a rest for the hand in painting.
Mahogany, ma-hog'a-ni, *n.* A tree of tropical America; its wood, reddish in colour, used for cabinet work.
Mahomedan, Mahometan, &c. *See* MOHAMMEDAN, &c.
Mahout, ma-hout', *n.* An E. Indian elephant driver or keeper.
Maid, mād, *n.* A young unmarried woman; a girl; a virgin; a female servant.
Maiden, mād'n, *n.* A maid or virgin; an old Scottish instrument of capital punishment resembling the guillotine.—*a.* Pertaining to maidens; unpolluted; unused; first.
Maidenhair, mād'n-hār, *n.* An elegant fern found growing on rocks and walls.
Maidenhead, mād'n-hed, *n.* Virginity; the hymen.
Maidenhood, mād'n-hud, *n.* The state of being a maid; virginity.
Maidenly, mād'n-li, *a.* Like a maid; gentle; modest.
Maid-servant, mād'sėr-vant, *n.* A female servant.
Maigre, mā'gr, *a.* A term applied to a preparation cooked merely with butter.
Mail, māl, *n.* A bag for conveying letters, &c.; letters conveyed; person or conveyance carrying the mail; armour of chain-work, &c.—*vt.* (mailing, mailed). To send by mail; to post; to arm with mail.
Maim, mām, *vt.* To mutilate; to disable.—*n.* An injury by which a person is maimed.
Main, mān, *a.* Chief, or most important; mighty, vast; directly applied; used with all one's might.—*n.* Strength; great effort; chief or main portion; the ocean; a principal gas or water pipe in a street; a hand at dice; a match at cock-fighting.
Mainland, mān'land, *n.* The principal land, as opposed to an isle; the continent.
Mainly, mān'li, *adv.* In the main; chiefly.
Main-spring, mān'spring, *n.* The principal spring of any piece of mechanism; the main cause of any action.
Main-stay, mān'stā, *n.* The stay extending from the top of a vessel's main-mast to the deck; chief support.
Maintain, mān-tān', *vt.* To hold or keep in any particular state; to sustain; to continue; to uphold; to vindicate; to assert.—*vi.* To affirm a position; to assert.
Maintainable, mān-tān'a-bl, *a.* That may be maintained; sustainable; defensible.
Maintenance, mān'ten-ans, *n.* Act of maintaining; means of support or livelihood; continuance.
Maize, māz, *n.* Indian corn.
Majestic, ma-jes'tik, *a.* Having majesty; august; sublime; lofty; stately.
Majestically, ma-jes'tik-al-li, *adv.* In a majestic manner.
Majesty, ma'jes-ti, *n.* Grandeur or dignity; a title of emperors, kings, and queens.
Majolica, ma-jol'i-ka, *n.* A kind of pottery richly coloured and enamelled.
Major, mā'jėr, *a.* The greater in number, quantity, or extent; the more important.—*n.* A military officer next above a captain; a person aged twenty-one years complete.
Major-domo, mā-jėr-dō'mo, *n.* A man who takes charge of a large household; a great officer of a palace.
Major-general, mā'jėr-jen'ėr-al, *n.* An army officer next in rank below a lieutenant-general.
Majority, ma-jo'ri-ti, *n.* The greater number; excess of one number over another; full age; rank or commission of a major.
Majuscule, ma-jus'kūl, *n.* A capital letter.
Make, māk, *vt.* (making, made). To produce or effect; to cause to be; to compose; to constitute; to perform; to cause to have any quality; to force; to gain; to complete; to

arrive at; to have within sight.—*vi.* To act or do; to tend; to contribute; to flow toward land.—*n.* Form; structure; texture.
Make-believe, māk'bē-lēv, *n.* Pretence; sham.—*a.* Unreal; sham.
Maker, māk'ėr, *n.* One who makes; the Creator.
Make-shift, māk'shift, *n.* An expedient to serve a present purpose.
Make-up, māk'up, *n.* The manner in which one is dressed for a part in a play.
Making, māk'ing, *n.* Workmanship; what is made at one time; material; means of bringing success in life; state of being made.
Malachite, mal'a-kīt, *n.* Green carbonate of copper, used for many ornamental purposes.
Malacology, mal-a-kol'o-ji, *n.* The branch of zoology that treats of the mollusca.
Maladjustment, mal-ad-just'ment, *n.* A bad or wrong adjustment.
Maladministration, mal-ad-min'is-trā"shon, *n.* Bad management of affairs.
Maladroit, mal-a-droit', *a.* Awkward.
Malady, mal'a-di, *n.* Any disease of the human body; moral or mental disorder.
Malapert, mal'a-pėrt, *a.* Pert; saucy; impudent.—*n.* A pert, saucy person.
Malapropos, mal-ap'rō-pō", *a.* and *adv.* The opposite of apropos; ill to the purpose.
Malar, mā'lėr, *a.* Pertaining to the cheek or cheek-bone.
Malaria, ma-lā'ri-a, *n.* Noxious exhalations causing fever; fever produced by this cause.
Malarial, Malarious, ma-lā'ri-al, ma-lā'ri-us, *a.* Infected by malaria.
Malay, Malayan, ma-lā', ma-lā'yan, *n.* A native of the Malay Peninsula; their language.—*a.* Belonging to the Malays.
Malcontent, mal'kon-tent, *n.* A discontented person.—*a.* Discontented with the rule under which one lives.
Male, māl, *a.* Pertaining to the sex that begets young; masculine.—*n.* One of the sex that begets young; a plant which has stamens only.
Malediction, mal-e-dik'shon, *n.* Evil speaking; a curse; execration.
Malefactor, mal-e-fak'tėr, *n.* A criminal; a culprit; a felon.
Malevolence, ma-lev'ō-lens, *n.* Ill-will; personal hatred.
Malevolent, ma-lev'ō-lent, *a.* Having ill-will; evil-minded; spiteful; malicious.
Malformation, mal-form-ā'shon, *n.* Ill or wrong formation; deformity.
Malic, mā'lik, *a.* Pertaining to apples.
Malice, mal'is, *n.* A disposition to injure others; spite; ill-will; rancour.
Malicious, ma-li'shus, *a.* Evil-disposed; evil-minded; spiteful; rancorous.
Malign, ma-līn', *a.* Of an evil nature or disposition; malicious; pernicious.—*vt.* To defame; to vilify.
Malignance, Malignancy, ma-lig'nans, ma-lig'nan-si, *n.* Extreme malevolence; virulence.
Malignant, ma-lig'nant, *a.* Having extreme malevolence; unpropitious; virulent; dangerous to life; extremely heinous.—*n.* A man of extreme enmity.
Malignity, ma-lig'ni-ti, *n.* Evil disposition of heart; rancour; virulence.
Malinger, ma-ling'gėr, *vi.* To feign illness in order to avoid military duty.
Malingerer, ma-ling'gėr-ėr, *n.* One who feigns himself ill.
Malison, mal'i-zn, *n.* A malediction; curse.
Mall, mal, *n.* A heavy wooden beetle or hammer; a public walk; a level shaded walk.
Mallard, mal'ard, *n.* The common wild duck.
Malleability, mal'lē-a-bil"i-ti, *n.* Quality of being malleable.
Malleable, mal'lē-a-bl, *a.* Capable of being beaten out with a hammer; easily persuaded.
Mallet, mal'et, *n.* A wooden hammer; a long-handled mallet is used in polo, croquet, &c.
Mallow, mal'ō, *n.* A plant with downy leaves.
Malmsey, mäm'zi, *n.* A kind of grape; a strong sweet white wine.
Malnutrition, mal-nū-tri'shon, *n.* Faulty feeding.
Malpractice, mal-prak'tis, *n.* Evil practice.
Malt, mạlt, *n.* Barley or other grain steeped in water till it germinates, then dried in a kiln and used in brewing.—*vt.* To make into malt.—*vi.* To become malt.
Maltese, mạl-tēz', *n. sing.* and *pl.* A native or natives of Malta.—*a.* Belonging to Malta.
Malting, mạlt'ing, *n.* The act or process of making malt; a work where malt is made.
Malt-liquor, mạlt'lik-ėr, *n.* A liquor prepared from malt by fermentation, as beer.
Maltman, Maltster, mạlt'man, mạlt'stėr, *n.* A man who makes malt.
Maltreat, mal-trēt', *vt.* To treat ill or roughly; to abuse.
Maltreatment, mal-trēt'ment, *n.* Ill-usage.
Malversation, mal-vėr-sā'shon, *n.* Fraudulent tricks; corruption in office.
Mama, Mamma, ma-mä', *n.* Mother.
Mamma, mam'ma, *n.* pl. **mæ.** The breast; the organ that secretes the milk.
Mammal, mam'mal, *n.* An animal of the class Mammalia.
Mammalia, mam-mā'li-a, *n.pl.* The highest class in the animal kingdom, whose distinctive characteristic is that the female suckles the young.
Mammalian, mam-mā'li-an, *a.* Pertaining to the mammalia.
Mammilla, mam-mil'la, *n.* A nipple, or something of this form.
Mammillary, mam'mil-a-ri, *a.* Pertaining to or resembling a nipple.
Mammon, mam'on, *n.* A Syrian god of riches; riches; wealth.
Mammoth, mam'oth, *n.* An extinct species of elephant.—*a.* Very large; gigantic.
Man, man, *n.*; pl. **Men,** men. A human being; a male adult of the human race; mankind; the male sex; a male servant; a piece in a game, as chess, &c.—*vt.* (manning, manned). To furnish with men; to guard with men; *refl.* to infuse courage into.
Manacle, man'a-kl, *n.* An instrument of iron for fastening the hands; a handcuff: used chiefly in the *plural*.—*vt.* (manacling, manacled). To put manacles on; to fetter.
Manage, man'āj, *vt.* (managing, managed). To wield; to direct in riding; to conduct or administer; to have under command; to treat with judgment.—*vi.* To conduct affairs.
Manageable, man'āj-a-bl, *a.* That may be managed; tractable.
Management, man'āj-ment, *n.* Act of managing; administration; manner of treating; body directing a business, &c.

Manager, man'āj-ėr, *n.* One who manages; one at the head of a business; a good economist.

Manakin, man'a-kin, *n.* A manikin; a small tropical American bird.

Manatee, man-a-tē', *n.* The sea-cow, an aquatic herbivorous mammal.

Manchet, man'shet, *n.* A small loaf of fine bread.—*a.* Fine and white.

Manciple, man'si-pl, *n.* A steward; a purveyor of a college or inn of court.

Mandamus, man-dā'mus, *n.* A writ requiring a person, corporation, or inferior court to do some specified act.

Mandarin, man-da-rēn', *n.* A Chinese public official; the court-language of China.

Mandatary, Mandatory, man'da-ta-ri, man'-da-to-ri, *n.* One to whom a mandate is given.

Mandate, man'dāt, *n.* A command; written authority to act for a person.

Mandatory, man'da-to-ri, *a.* Containing a command; preceptive; directory.

Mandible, man'di-bl, *n.* An animal's jaw.

Mandibular, man-dib'ū-lėr, *a.* Belonging to the mandible or jaw.

Mandoline, Mandolin, man'dō-lin, *n.* A musical instrument of the guitar kind.

Mandrake, man'drāk, *n.* A narcotic plant with large thick roots.

Mandrel, Mandril, man'drel, man'dril, *n.* A bar or spindle, used variously.

Mandrill, man'dril, *n.* The great blue-faced or rib-nosed baboon.

Manducate, man'dūk-āt, *vt.* To chew.

Manducation, man-dūk-ā'shon, *n.* The act of chewing or eating.

Mane, mān, *n.* The long hair on the neck of a horse, lion, &c.

Manège, ma-nāzh', *n.* Horsemanship; a school for horsemanship.

Manequin, Manikin, man'i-kin, *n.* An artist's model of wood or wax.

Manes, mā'nēz, *n.pl.* Among the Romans the souls or shades of the dead.

Manful, man'fụl, *a.* Having the spirit of a man; bold; honourable; energetic.

Manfully, man'fụl-li, *adv.* Courageously.

Manganese, man-gan-ēz'; *n.* A metal resembling iron.

Manganite, man'gan-īt, *n.* An ore of manganese, used in the manufacture of glass.

Mange, mānj, *n.* A skin disease of horses, cattle, dogs, &c.

Mangel-wurzel, mang'gl-wėr'zl, *n.* A variety of beet.

Manger, mān'jėr, *n.* A trough in which food is placed for cattle and horses.

Mangle, mang'gl, *vt.* (mangling, mangled). To mutilate; to lacerate; to smooth, as linen.—*n.* A rolling press, or small calender, for smoothing cotton or linen.

Mango, mang'gō, *n.* The fruit of the mango-tree, a native of Asia.

Mangosteen, mang'gō-stēn, *n.* An E. Indian tree, with a delicious fruit.

Mangrove, man'grōv, *n.* A tropical tree growing on shores.

Mangy, mān'ji, *a.* Infected with the mange; scabby.

Manhole, man'hōl, *n.* A hole for admitting a man into a drain, steam-boiler, &c.

Manhood, man'hụd, *a.* State of one who is a man; humanity; virility; manliness.

Mania, mā'ni-a, *n.* Insanity; madness; eager desire for anything; morbid craving.

Maniac, mā'ni-ak, *a.* Affected with mania; mad.—*n.* A madman.

Maniacal, ma-nī'ak-al, *a.* Affected with mania.

Manicure, man'i-kūr, *n.* One whose occupation is to trim the nails, &c., of the hand.

Manifest, man'i-fest, *a.* Clearly visible; evident; obvious.—*vt.* To make manifest; to display or exhibit.—*n.* A document stating a ship's cargo, destination, &c.

Manifestation, man'i-fest-ā"shon, *n.* Act of manifesting; exhibition; revelation; what serves to make manifest.

Manifestly, man'i-fest-li, *adv.* Evidently.

Manifesto, man-i-fest'ō, *n.* A public declaration; a proclamation.

Manifold, man'i-fōld, *a.* Numerous and various; of divers kinds.—*vt.* To multiply impressions of, as by a copying apparatus.

Manikin, man'i-kin, *n.* A little man; a dwarf; model of the human body.

Manilla, Manila, ma-nil'a, *n.* A kind of cheroot manufactured in *Manila.*

Manipulate, ma-nip'ū-lāt, *vt.* To treat with the hands; to handle; to operate upon so as to disguise.

Manipulation, ma-nip'ū-lā"shon, *n.* Act, art, or mode of manipulating.

Manipulator, ma-nip'ū-lāt-ėr, *n.* One who manipulates.

Manis, mā'nis, *n.* The pangolin or scaly ant-eater.

Mankind, man-kind', *n.* The species of human beings; the males of the human race.

Manlike, man'līk, *a.* Like a man; masculine; manly.

Manliness, man'li-nes, *n.* The best qualities of a man; manhood; bravery.

Manly, man'li, *a.* Having the qualities that best become a man; brave, resolute, &c.

Manna, man'na, *n.* A substance furnished as food for the Israelites in the wilderness; the sweet juice of a species of ash.

Mannequin, man'ē-kin, *n.* Person employed by dressmakers, &c., to wear and display costumes.

Manner, man'ėr, *n.* The mode in which anything is done; method; bearing or conduct; *pl.* carriage or behaviour; civility in society; sort or kind.

Mannered, man'ėrd, *a.* Having manners of this or that kind.

Mannerism, man'ėr-izm, *n.* Adherence to the same manner; tasteless uniformity of style; peculiarity of personal manner.

Mannerly, man'ėr-li, *a.* Showing good manners; polite; respectful.

Mannish, man'ish, *a.* Characteristic of or resembling a man; bold or masculine.

Manœuvre, ma-nū'vėr or ma-nö'vėr, *n.* A regulated movement, particularly of troops or ships; management with address; stratagem.—*vi.* (manœuvring, manœuvred). To perform military or naval manœuvres; to employ stratagem; to manage with address.—*vt.* To cause to perform manœuvres.

Man-of-war, man'ov-wạr, *n.*; pl. **Men-of-war.** A war-vessel.

Manometer, ma-nom'et-ėr, *n.* An instrument to measure the elastic force of gases.

Manor, ma'nor, *n.* The land belonging to a lord; a lordship.

Manor-house, ma'nor-hous, *n.* The mansion belonging to a manor.
Manorial, ma-nō'ri-al, *a.* Pertaining to a manor.
Manse, mans, *n.* In Scotland, the dwelling-house of a Presbyterian minister.
Mansion, man'shon, *n.* A large dwelling-house; abode; house of the lord of a manor.
Manslaughter, man'slą-tėr, *n.* Murder; the unlawful killing of a man without malice.
Mansuete, man'swēt, *a.* Tame, gentle.
Mantel, Mantel-piece, man'tel, man'tel-pēs, *n.* The ornamental work above a fireplace; a narrow shelf or slab there.
Mantelet, Mantlet, man'tel-et, mant'let, *n.* A small mantle.
Mantilla, man-til'la, *n.* A mantle or hood; a Spanish lady's veil.
Mantle, man'tl, *n.* A kind of cloak worn over other garments; something that covers and conceals; incandescent hood for gas jet.—*vt.* (mantling, mantled). To cloak; to cover as with a mantle.—*vi.* To become covered with a coating; to cream; to display superficial changes of hue.
Mantle-piece, *n.* *See* MANTEL.
Mantua, man'tū-a, *n.* A lady's gown or mantle.
Manual, man'ū-al, *a.* Performed by the hand; used or made by the hand.—*n.* A small book; a compendium; the service-book of the R. Catholic Church; keyboard of an organ.
Manufactory, man-ū-fak'to-ri, *n.* A building in which goods are manufactured.
Manufacture, man-ū-fak'tūr, *n.* The process of making anything by hand or machinery; something made from raw materials.—*vt.* (manufacturing, manufactured). To fabricate from raw materials; to fabricate without real grounds.—*vi.* To be occupied in manufactures.
Manufacturer, man-ū-fak'tūr-ėr, *n.* One who manufactures; owner of a manufactory.
Manufacturing, man-ū-fak'tūr-ing, *p.a.* Pertaining to or occupied in manufactures.
Manumission, man-ū-mi'shon, *n.* Emancipation.
Manumit, man-ū-mit', *vt.* (manumitting, manumitted). To release from slavery.
Manure, man-ūr', *vt.* (manuring, manured). To fertilize with nutritive substances.—*n.* Any substance added to soil to accelerate or increase the production of the crops.
Manuscript, man'ū-skript, *n.* A paper written with the hand: often contracted to *MS.*, pl. *MSS.*—*a.* Written with the hand.
Manx, mangks, *n.* The native language of the Isle of Man; *pl.* the natives of Man.—*a.* Belonging to the Isle of Man.
Many, me'ni, *a.* Forming or comprising a number; numerous.—**The many,** the great majority of people; the crowd.—**So many,** the same number of; a certain number indefinitely.
Maori, mä'o-ri, *n.* One of the native inhabitants of New Zealand.
Map, map, *n.* A representation of the surface of the earth or of any part of it.—*vt.* (mapping, mapped). To draw in a map; to plan.
Maple, mā'pl, *n.* A tree of the sycamore kind.
Mar, mär, *vt.* (marring, marred). To injure in any manner; to hurt, impair, disfigure, &c.
Marabou, ma'ra-bö, *n.* A large stork yielding valuable white feathers.
Marasmus, ma-ras'mus, *n.* A wasting of flesh without apparent disease; atrophy.
Maraud, ma-rąd', *vi.* To rove in quest of plunder; to make an excursion for booty.
Marauder, ma-rąd'ėr, *n.* A plunderer.
Marble, mär'bl, *n.* A calcareous stone of compact texture; a little hard ball used by boys in play; an inscribed or sculptured marble stone.—*a.* Made of or like marble.—*vt.* (marbling, marbled). To stain like marble.
Marbling, mär'bl-ing, *n.* Imitation of marble; veined colouring on the edges of a book.
Marcescent, mär-ses'ent, *a.* Withering.
March, märch, *vi.* To move by steps and in order, as soldiers; to walk in a stately manner; to progress; to be situated next.—*vt.* To cause to march.—*n.* The measured walk of a body of men; a stately walk; distance passed over; a musical composition to regulate the march of troops, &c.; a frontier or boundary (usually in *pl.*); the third month of the year.
Marchioness, mär'shon-es, *n.* The wife of a marquis; a lady of the rank of a marquis.
Marchpane, märch'pān, *n.* A kind of sweet bread or biscuit.
Marcid, mär'sid, *a.* Withering; pining.
Mare, mãr, *n.* The female of the horse.
Margarine, mär'ga-rin, *n.* An imitation of butter, made from animal fat.
Marge, märj, *n.* Margin; *poet.*
Margin, mär'jin, *n.* An edge, border, brink; edge of a page left blank; difference between the cost and selling price.—*vt.* To furnish with a margin; to enter in the margin.
Marginal, mär'jin-al, *a.* Pertaining to a margin; written or printed in the margin.
Margrave, mär'grāv, *n.* A title of nobility in Germany, &c.
Margravine, mär'grā-vīn, *n.* The wife of a margrave.
Marigold, ma'ri-gōld, *n.* A composite plant bearing golden-yellow flowers.
Marine, ma-rēn', *a.* Pertaining to the sea; found in the sea; used at sea; naval; maritime.—*n.* A soldier who serves on board of a man-of-war; collective shipping of a country; whole economy of naval affairs.
Mariner, ma'rin-ėr, *n.* A seaman; sailor.
Mariolatry, mā-ri-ol'a-tri, *n.* The adoration of the Virgin Mary.
Marionette, ma'ri-o-net", *n.* A puppet moved by strings.
Marish, ma'rish, *n.* A marsh: *poet.*
Marital, ma'ri-tal, *a.* Pertaining to a husband.
Maritime, ma'ri-tīm, *a.* Relating to the sea; naval; bordering on the sea; having a navy and commerce by sea.
Marjoram, mär'jō-ram, *n.* A plant of the mint family.
Mark, märk, *n.* A visible sign or impression on something; a distinguishing sign; indication or evidence; pre-eminence or importance; a characteristic; heed or regard; object aimed at; proper standard; extreme estimate; a German silver coin formerly worth about one shilling.—*vt.* To make a mark or marks on; to denote (often with *out*); to regard, observe, heed.—*vi.* To note; to observe critically; to remark.
Marked, märkt, *p.a.* Pre-eminent; outstanding; prominent; remarkable.
Marker, märk'ėr, *n.* One who marks; a counter used in card-playing.

Market, mär'ket, *n.* An occasion on which goods are publicly exposed for sale; place in which goods are exposed for sale; rate of purchase and sale; demand for commodities; privilege of keeping a public market.—*vi.* To deal in a market.—*vt.* To offer for sale in a market.
Marketable, mär'ket-a-bl, *a.* Fit for the market; that may be sold.
Market-garden, mär'ket-gär-dn, *n.* A garden growing vegetables, &c., for market.
Marketing, mär'ket-ing, *n.* Attendance upon a market; commodities purchased.
Market-town, mär'ket-toun, *n.* A town with the privilege of a stated public market.
Marking-ink, märk'ing-ingk, *n.* Indelible ink, used for marking linen, &c.
Marksman, märks'man, *n.* One who is skilful to hit a mark; one who shoots well.
Marl, märl, *n.* A rich calcareous earth much used for manure.—*vt.* To manure with marl.
Marlaceous, märl-ā'shus, *a.* Resembling marl; partaking of the qualities of marl.
Marline, mär'lin, *n.* A small line of two strands, used for winding round ships' ropes. —*vt.* To wind marline round.
Marlinespike, mär'lin-spīk, *n.* An iron tool for opening the strands of rope.
Marly, märl'i, *a.* Consisting in or partaking of marl; resembling marl.
Marmalade, mär'ma-lād, *n.* A preserve made from various fruits, especially acid fruits, such as the orange.
Marmorate, mär'mo-rāt, *a.* Covered with marble; variegated like marble.
Marmoreal, mär-mō'rē-al, *a.* Pertaining to marble; made of marble.
Marmot, mär'mot, *n.* A hibernating rodent animal of northern latitudes.
Maroon, ma-rön', *n.* A fugitive slave in the W. Indies; a brownish crimson or claret colour.—*vt.* To land and leave on a desolate island.
Marque, märk, *n.* Used in phrase *letter* or *letters of marque*, meaning a license to a private vessel to attack the ships, &c., of a public enemy.
Marquee, mär-kē', *n.* A large tent erected for a temporary purpose; an officer's field tent.
Marquetry, mär'ket-ri, *n.* Inlaid work.
Marquis, Marquess, mär'kwis, mär'kwes, *n.* A title of honour next below that of duke.
Marquisate, mär'kwis-āt, *n.* The dignity or lordship of a marquis.
Marriage, ma'rij, *n.* The act or ceremony of marrying; matrimony; wedlock.
Marriageable, ma'rij-a-bl, *a.* Of an age suitable for marriage; fit to be married.
Married, ma'rid, *p.a.* Joined in marriage; conjugal; connubial.
Marrow, ma'rō, *n.* A soft substance in the cavities of bones; the best part; a kind of gourd, also called *vegetable marrow*.
Marrow-bone, ma'rō-bōn, *n.* A bone containing marrow.
Marry, ma'ri, *vt.* (marrying, married). To unite in wedlock; to dispose of in wedlock; to take for husband or wife.—*vi.* To take a husband or a wife.—*interj.* Indeed; forsooth.
Mars, märz, *n.* The god of war; a planet.
Marsh, märsh, *n.* A swamp; a tract of low wet land.—*a.* Pertaining to boggy places.
Marshal, mär'shal, *n.* One who regulates rank and order at a feast, procession, &c.; a military officer of the highest rank, generally called *field-marshal*.—*vt.* (marshalling, marshalled). To dispose in order; to array.
Marshaller, mär'shal-ėr, *n.* One who marshals or disposes in due order.
Marshalling, mär'shal-ing, *n.* Act of arranging in due order; arrangement of coats of arms on a shield.
Marsh-mallow, märsh'mal-ō, *n.* A plant of the hollyhock genus.
Marsh-marigold, märsh'ma-ri-gōld, *n.* A marsh plant of the ranunculus family.
Marshy, märsh'i, *a.* Abounding in marshes; boggy; fenny; produced in marshes.
Marsupial, mär-sū'pi-al, *n.* and *a.* One of a large group of mammalians whose young are born in an imperfect condition and nourished in an external abdominal pouch.
Mart, märt, *n.* A market.
Martello-tower, mär-tel'ō-tou-ėr, *n.* A small round fort defending the sea-board.
Marten, mär'ten, *n.* A fierce kind of weasel, valued for its fur.
Martial, mär'shal, *a.* Pertaining to war; warlike.
Martin, mär'tin, *n.* A species of swallow.
Martinet, mär'ti-net, *n.* A precise, punctilious, or strict disciplinarian.
Martingale, mär'tin-gāl, *n.* A strap to prevent a horse from rearing; a short spar under the bowsprit.
Martinmas, mär'tin-mas, *n.* The feast of St. Martin of Tours, the 11th of November.
Martyr, mär'tėr, *n.* One who suffers death or persecution on account of his belief; one greatly afflicted.—*vt.* To put to death for adhering to one's belief.
Martyrdom, mär'tėr-dom, *n.* The doom or death of a martyr.
Martyrize, mär'tėr-īz, *vt.* To devote to martyrdom.
Martyrology, mär-tėr-ol'o-ji, *n.* A history or account of martyrs.
Marvel, mär'vel, *n.* A wonder; something very astonishing.—*vi.* (marvelling, marvelled). To feel admiration or astonishment.
Marvellous, mär'vel-us, *a.* Exciting wonder or surprise; wonderful; astonishing.
Marvellously, mär'vel-us-li, *adv.* In a marvellous manner; wonderfully.
Mascot, mas'kot, *n.* A thing supposed to bring good luck to its owner.
Masculine, mas'kū-lin, *a.* Male; manly; robust; bold or unwomanly; designating nouns which are the names of male animals, &c.
Mash, mash, *n.* A mixture of ingredients beaten or blended together; a mixture of ground malt and warm water yielding wort.—*vt.* To mix; to beat into a confused mass.
Masher, mash'ėr, *n.* One who or that which mashes; a silly fop.
Mask, mask, *n.* A cover for the face; a masquerade; a sort of play common in the 16th and 17th centuries; pretence.—*vt.* To cover with a mask; to disguise; to hide.
Masked, maskt, *a.* Having the face covered; wearing a mask; concealed; disguised.
Masochism, mas'ō-kism, *n.* Pathological sexual condition in which pleasure is derived from cruel treatment by the associate.
Mason, mā'sn, *n.* One who prepares stone, and constructs buildings; a freemason.

Masonic, ma-son'ik, *a.* Pertaining to the craft or mysteries of freemasons.
Masonry, mā'sn-ri, *n.* The art or occupation of a mason; stonework; the doctrines and practices of freemasons.
Masque, mask, *n. See* MASK.
Masquerade, mas-kėr-ād', *n.* An assembly of persons wearing masks; a disguise.—*vi.* To assemble in masks; to go in disguise.
Masquerader, mas-kėr-ā'dėr, *n.* One who masquerades; one disguised.
Mass, mas, *n.* A body of matter; a lump; magnitude; an assemblage; collection; the generality; the communion service in the R. Catholic Church.—**The Masses,** the populace.—*vt.* and *i.* To form into a mass; to assemble in crowds.
Massacre, mas'sa-kėr, *n.* Ruthless, unnecessary, or indiscriminate slaughter.—*vt.* (massacring, massacred). To kill with indiscriminate violence; to slaughter.
Massage, ma-säzh' or mas'āj, *n.* A process of kneading, rubbing, pressing, &c., parts of a person's body to effect a cure.—*vt.* (massaging, massaged). To treat by this process.
Masseuse, mas'ŏz, *n.* A female who practises massage.
Masseur, mas-ŏr, *n.* One who practises massage.
Masseter, mas-sē'tėr, *n.* Either of the pair of muscles which raise the under jaw.
Massive, mas'iv, *a.* Bulky and heavy; ponderous; pertaining to a mass; not local or special.
Massy, mas'i, *a.* Having the nature of a mass; massive.
Mast, mäst, *n.* A long upright timber in a vessel, supporting the yards, sails, and rigging; the fruit of the oak, beech, &c. (no *pl.*).—*vt.* To supply with a mast or masts.
Masted, mäst'ed, *a.* Furnished with a mast or masts.
Master, mäs'tėr, *n.* One who rules or directs; an employer; owner; captain of a merchant ship; teacher in a school; a man eminently skilled in some art; a word of address for men (written *Mr.* and pron. mis'tėr) and boys (written in full); a vessel having masts.—*vt.* To bring under control; to make oneself master of.—*a.* Belonging to a master; chief.
Masterful, mäs'tėr-fụl, *a.* Inclined to exercise mastery; imperious; headstrong.
Master-hand, mäs'tėr-hand, *n.* The hand of a person extremely skilful; a person eminently skilful.
Master-key, mäs'tėr-kē, *n.* The key that opens many locks.
Masterly, mäs'tėr-li, *a.* Suitable to a master; most excellent; skilful.
Masterpiece, mäs'tėr-pēs, *n.* Chief performance; anything done with superior skill.
Mastership, mäs'tėr-ship, *n.* Office of a master; dominion; rule; mastery.
Master-stroke, mäs'tėr-strōk, *n.* A masterly act or achievement.
Mastery, mäs'tė-ri, *n.* Command; pre-eminence; victory; superior dexterity.
Mast-head, mäst'hed, *vt.* To send to the top of a mast and cause to remain there by way of punishment.
Mastic, Mastich, mas'tik, *n.* A resin from a tree of S. Europe, &c.; a kind of mortar.
Masticate, mas'ti-kāt, *vt.* To chew and prepare for swallowing.
Mastication, mas-ti-kā'shon, *n.* Act of masticating.
Masticatory, mas'ti-kā-to-ri, *a.* Adapted to masticate.—*n.* A substance to be chewed to increase the saliva.
Mastiff, mas'tif, *n.* A large heavy dog with deep and pendulous lips.
Mastodon, mas'to-don, *n.* An extinct quadruped like the elephant, but larger.
Mat, mat, *n.* An article of interwoven rushes, twine, &c., used for cleaning or protecting; anything growing thickly or closely interwoven.—*vt.* (matting, matted). To cover with mats; to entangle.—*vi.* To grow thickly together.
Matador, ma-ta-dōr', *n.* The man appointed to kill the bull in bull-fights; a card in ombre and quadrille.
Match, mach, *n.* A person or thing equal to another; union by marriage; one to be married; a contest; a small body that catches fire readily or ignites by friction.—*vt.* To equal; to show an equal to; to set against as equal in contest; to suit; to marry.—*vi.* To be united in marriage; to suit; to tally.
Matchless, mach'les, *a.* That cannot be matched; having no equal; unrivalled.
Matchlock, mach'lok, *n.* Formerly the lock of a musket; containing a match for firing; the musket itself.
Mate, māt, *n.* A companion; a match; a husband or wife; second officer in a ship.—*vt.* (mating, mated). To equal; to match; to marry; to checkmate.
Maté, mä'tā, *n.* Paraguay tea; the leaves of the Brazilian holly used in S. America as a substitute for tea.
Material, ma-tē'ri-al, *a.* Consisting of matter; not spiritual; important; essential; substantial.—*n.* Anything composed of matter; substance of which anything is made.
Materialism, ma-tē'ri-al-izm, *n.* The doctrine of materialists.
Materialist, ma-tē'ri-al-ist, *n.* One who asserts that all existence is material.
Materialistic, ma-tē'ri-al-ist''ik, *a.* Relating to or partaking of materialism.
Materialize, ma-tē'ri-al-īz, *vt.* To reduce to a state of matter; to regard as matter.
Materially, ma-tē'ri-al-li, *adv.* In a material manner; in the state of matter; not formally; substantially; essentially.
Maternal, ma-tėr'nal, *a.* Motherly; pertaining to a mother; becoming a mother.
Maternity, ma-tėr'ni-ti, *n.* The state, character, or relation of a mother.
Math, math, *n.* A mowing: as in after-*math*.
Mathematical, Mathematic, ma-thē-mat'ik-al, ma-thē-mat'ik, *a.* Pertaining to mathematics.
Mathematician, ma'thē-ma-ti''shan, *n.* One versed in mathematics.
Mathematics, ma-thē-ma'tiks, *n.* The science of magnitude and number, comprising arithmetic, geometry, algebra, &c.
Matin, ma'tin, *n.* Morning; *pl.* morning prayers or songs; time of morning service.
Matinée, mat'i-nā, *n.* An entertainment or reception held early in the day.
Matrass, mat'ras, *n.* A chemical vessel with a tapering neck used for evaporation, &c.
Matricide, mat'ri-sīd, *n.* The killing of a mother; the murderer of his or her mother.
Matriculate, ma-trik'ū-lāt, *vt.* To enroll;

to admit to membership, particularly in a university.—*vi.* To be entered as a member.
Matriculation, ma-trik'ū-lā''shon, *n.* Act of matriculating.
Matrimonial, mat-ri-mō'ni-al, *a.* Pertaining to matrimony; nuptial.
Matrimony, mat'ri-mō-ni, *n.* Marriage; wedlock; the married or nuptial state.
Matrix, mā'triks, *n.*; pl. **Matrices** (mā'tri-sēz). The womb; a mould; substance in which a mineral, &c., is embedded.
Matron, mā'tron, *n.* An elderly married woman, or an elderly lady; head nurse or superintendent of a hospital, &c.
Matronly, mā'tron-li, *a.* Like or becoming a matron; elderly; sedate.
Matte, Matt, mat, *n.* Metal imperfectly smelted or purified.
Matted, mat'ed, *p.a.* Laid with mats; entangled.
Matter, mat'ėr, *n.* Not mind; body; that of which anything is made; substance as distinct from form; subject; business; circumstance; import; moment; pus.—*vi.* To be of importance; to signify; to form pus.
Matter-of-fact, mat'ėr-ov-fakt, *a.* Treating of facts; precise; prosaic.
Mattery, mat'ėr-i, *a.* Purulent.
Matting, mat'ing, *n.* Material for mats; mats collectively; coarse fabric for packing.
Mattock, mat'ok, *n.* A pick-axe with one or both of its ends broad.
Mattress, mat'res, *n.* A bed stuffed with hair, or other soft material, and quilted.
Maturation, ma-tūr-ā'shon, *n.* Process of maturing; ripeness; suppuration.
Maturative, ma-tū'ra-tiv, *a.* Ripening; conducing to suppuration.
Mature, ma-tūr', *a.* Ripe; perfect; completed; ready; having become payable.—*vt.* (maturing, matured). To make mature; to advance toward perfection.—*vi.* To become ripe or perfect; to become payable.
Maturely, ma-tūr'li, *adv.* In a mature manner; completely; with full deliberation.
Maturity, ma-tūr'i-ti, *n.* State of being mature; ripeness; time when a bill of exchange becomes due.
Matutinal, ma-tū tin'al, *a.* Pertaining to the morning.
Maud, mạd, *n.* A woollen plaid or wrap.
Maudlin, mạd'lin, *a.* Over-emotional; sickly sentimental; approaching to intoxication.
Maugre, mạ'gėr, *adv.* In spite of; in opposition to; notwithstanding.
Maul, mạl, *n.* A large hammer or mallet.—*vt.* To beat with a maul; to maltreat severely.
Maul-stick, mạl'stik, *n.* *See* MAHL-STICK.
Maunder, mạn'dėr, *vi.* To speak with a beggar's whine; to drivel.
Mausoleum, mạ-sō-lē'um, *n.* A magnificent tomb or sepulchral monument.
Mauve, mōv, *n.* A purple dye obtained from aniline.
Mavis, mā'vis, *n.* The throstle or song-thrush.
Maw, mạ, *n.* The stomach, especially of animals; paunch; crop of fowls.
Mawkish, mạk'ish, *a.* Apt to cause satiety or loathing; insipid; sickly.
Maxilla, mak-sil'la, *n.*; pl. æ. A jaw-bone; a jaw.
Maxillar, Maxillary, mak-sil'lar, maks'il-la-ri, *a.* Pertaining to the jaw or jaw-bone.
Maxim, mak'sim, *n.* An established principle; axiom; aphorism; a light machine-gun.
Maximum, mak'sim-um, *n.* The greatest degree or quantity.—*a.* Greatest.
May, mā, *n.* The fifth month of the year; hawthorn blossom.—*vi.* To celebrate the festivities of May-day.—*v. aux.* (pret. might, mīt). Used to imply possibility, opportunity, permission, desire, &c.
May-day, mā'dā, *n.* The first day of May.
May-dew, mā'dū, *n.* The dew gathered on the first day of May.
Mayhap, mā'hap, *adv.* Perhaps.
Maying, mā'ing, *n.* The gathering of flowers on May-day.
Mayonnaise, Mayonaise, mā-on-āz, *n.* A sauce of yolks of eggs, oil, &c.
Mayor, mā'ėr, *n.* The chief magistrate of a city or borough.
Mayoral, mā'ėr-al, *a.* Pertaining to a mayor.
Mayoralty, mā'ėr-al-ti, *n.* Office of a mayor.
Mayoress, mā'ėr-es, *n.* Wife of a mayor.
May-pole, mā'pōl, *n.* A pole to dance round on May-day.
Mazarine, maz-a-rēn', *n.* A deep blue colour.
Maze, māz, *vt.* (mazing, mazed). To bewilder; to amaze.—*n.* Perplexed state of things; bewilderment; a labyrinth; a confusing network of paths or passages.
Mazurka, Mazourka, ma-zụr'ka, *n.* A lively Polish dance; music written for it.
Mazy, mā'zi, *a.* Winding; intricate.
Me, mē, *pron. pers.* The objective of *I.*
Mead, mēd, *n.* A fermented liquor made from honey and water; a meadow: *poet.*
Meadow, me'dō, *n.* A low level tract of land under grass.—*a.* Belonging to a meadow.
Meadow-sweet, me'dō-swēt, *n.* A common British herbaceous plant with corymbs of white flowers.
Meadowy, me'dō-i, *a.* Pertaining to a meadow; resembling a meadow.
Meagre, mē'gėr, *a.* Thin; lean; poor; scanty.
Meagrely, mē'gėr-li, *adv.* Poorly; thinly; scantily.
Meal, mēl, *n.* Portion of food taken at one time; a repast; ground grain; flour.
Mealies, mē-lēz, *n.pl.* A name given in South Africa to maize or Indian corn.
Mealy, mēl'i, *a.* Having the qualities of meal; powdery; farinaceous.
Mealy-mouthed, mēl'i-mouŦHd, *a.* Unwilling to tell the truth in plain language; soft-spoken; inclined to hypocrisy.
Mean, mēn, *a.* Low in rank or birth; humble; base; contemptible; occupying a middle position; middle; intermediate.—*n.* What is intermediate; average rate or degree; medium; *pl.* measure or measures adopted; agency (generally used as *sing.*); income or resources.—*vt.* (pret. and pp. *meant*). To have in the mind; to intend; to signify; to import.—*vi.* To have thought or ideas, or to have meaning.
Meander, mē-an'dėr, *n.* A winding course; a bend in a course; a labyrinth.—*vi.* To wind about; to be intricate.
Meaning, mēn'ing, *p.a.* Significant.—*n.* Design; signification; purport; force.
Meaningless, mēn'ing-les, *a.* Having no meaning.
Meaningly, mēn'ing-li, *adv.* Significantly.

Meanly, mēn'li, *adv.* In a mean manner; poorly; basely; shabbily.
Meantime, mēn'tīm, *adv.* During the interval; in the intervening time.—*n.* The interval between one period and another.
Meanwhile, mēn'whīl, *adv.* and *n.* Meantime.
Measles, mē'zlz, *n.* A contagious disease in man, characterized by a crimson rash.
Measly, Measled, mēz'li, mē'zld, *a.* Infected with measles or eruptions like measles.
Measurable, me'zhūr-a-bl, *a.* That may be measured; not very great; moderate.
Measure, me'zhūr, *n.* The extent or magnitude of a thing; a standard of size; a measuring rod or line; that which is allotted; moderation; just degree; course of action; legislative proposal; musical time; metre; a grave solemn dance; pl. beds or strata.—*vt.* (measuring, measured). To ascertain the extent or capacity of; to estimate; to value; to pass through or over; to proportion; to allot.—*vi.* To have a certain extent.
Measured, me'zhūrd, *p.a.* Deliberate and uniform; stately; restricted; moderate.
Measureless, me'zhūr-les, *a.* Without measure; boundless; vast; infinite.
Measurement, me'zhūr-ment, *n.* Act of measuring; amount ascertained.
Meat, mēt, *n.* Food in general; the flesh of animals used as food; the edible portion of something (the *meat* of an egg).
Meatus, mē-ā'tus, *n.* A passage; a duct or passage of the body.
Mechanic, me-kan'ik, *a.* Mechanical.—*n.* An artisan; an artisan employed in making and repairing machinery.
Mechanical, me-kan'ik-al, *a.* Pertaining to mechanism or machinery; resembling a machine; done by the mere force of habit; pertaining to material forces; physical.
Mechanically, me-kan'ik-al-li, *adv.* In a mechanical manner; by the mere force of habit; by physical force or power.
Mechanician, me-kan-i'shan, *n.* One skilled in mechanics; a machine-maker.
Mechanics, me-kan'iks, *n.* The science which treats of motion and force.
Mechanism, mek'an-izm, *n.* A mechanical contrivance; structure of a machine.
Mechanist, mek'an-ist, *n.* Mechanician.
Mechlin, mek'lin, *n.* A kind of fine lace.
Medal, med'al, *n.* A piece of metal in the form of a coin, stamped with some figure or device, as a memento or reward.
Medallion, me-dal'yon, *n.* A large antique medal; a circular or oval tablet.
Medallist, Medalist, med'al-ist, *n.* An engraver or stamper of medals; one skilled in medals; one who has gained a medal.
Meddle, med'l, *vi.* (meddling, meddled). To interfere; to intervene officiously.
Meddler, med'lėr, *n.* One who meddles; an officious person; a busy-body.
Meddlesome, med'l-sum, *a.* Given to interfering; meddling; officiously intrusive.
Meddling, med'ling, *p.a.* Given to meddle; officious; busy in other men's affairs.
Mediæval. *See* MEDIEVAL.
Medial, mē'di-al, *a.* Middle; mean; pertaining to a mean or average.
Median, mē'di-an, *a.* Situated in the middle; passing through or along the middle.
Mediate, mē'di-āt, *a.* Middle; intervening; acting as a means; not direct.—*vi.* (mediating, mediated). To negotiate between contending parties, with a view to reconciliation; to intercede.
Mediately, mē'di-āt-li, *adv.* Indirectly.
Mediation, mē-di-ā'shon, *n.* Act of mediating; intercession; entreaty for another.
Mediative, mē'di-āt-iv, *a.* Of or belonging to a mediator.
Mediator, mē'di-āt-ėr, *n.* One who mediates; an intercessor; an advocate.
Mediatorial, mē'di-a-tō"ri-al, *a.* Mediative.
Medic, Medick, mē'dik, *n.* A leguminous plant yielding fodder and allied to clover.
Medicable, med'ik-a-bl, *a.* That may be cured.
Medical, med'i-kal, *a.* Pertaining to the art of curing diseases; tending to cure.
Medically, med'i-kal-li, *adv.* According to the rules of medicine.
Medicament, me-dik'a-ment, *n.* Anything used for healing; a medicine.
Medicate, med'i-kāt, *vt.* (medicating, medicated). To treat with medicine; to impregnate with anything medicinal.
Medicative, med'i-kā-tiv, *a.* Tending to cure or heal.
Medicinal, me-dis'in-al, *a.* Pertaining to medicine; containing healing ingredients.
Medicinally, me-dis'in-al-li, *adv.* In a medicinal manner; with medicinal qualities.
Medicine, med'sin, *n.* Any substance used as a remedy for disease; a drug; the science and art of curing diseases.
Medieval, Mediæval, mē-di-ēv'al, *a.* Pertaining to the middle ages.
Medievalism, mē-di-ēv'al-izm, *n.* Medieval principles or practices.
Mediocre, mē'di-ō-kėr, *a.* Of moderate degree; middling.
Mediocrity, mē-di-ok'ri-ti, *n.* State of being mediocre; a moderate degree or rate; a person of mediocre talents or abilities.
Meditate, med'i-tāt, *vi.* (meditating, meditated). To dwell on anything in thought; to cogitate.—*vt.* To think on; to scheme; to intend.
Meditation, med-i-tā'shon, *n.* Act of meditating; serious contemplation.
Meditative, med'i-tāt-iv, *a.* Addicted to meditation; expressing meditation.
Mediterranean, med'i-te-rā'nē-an, *a.* Surrounded by land: now applied exclusively to the *Mediterranean* Sea.
Medium, mē'di-um, *n.*; pl. **-ia, -iums.** Something holding a middle position; a mean; means of motion or action; agency of transmission; instrumentality.—*a.* Middle; middling.
Medlar, med'lėr, *n.* A tree and its fruit, which resembles a small apple.
Medley, med'li, *n.* A mingled mass of ingredients; a miscellany; a jumble.
Medoc, me-dok', *n.* A kind of claret.
Medulla, me-dul'la, *n.* Marrow.
Medullary, Medullar, me-dul'la-ri, me-dul'lėr, *a.* Pertaining to, consisting of, or resembling marrow.
Medusa, me-dū'sa, *n.*; pl. **-æ.** A general name for the jelly-fishes or sea-nettles.
Meed, mēd, *n.* Reward; recompense.
Meek, mēk, *a.* Soft, gentle, or mild of temper; forbearing; humble; submissive.

Meekly, mēk'li, *adv.* Gently; humbly.
Meerschaum, mēr'shum, *n.* A silicate of magnesium, used for tobacco-pipes; a tobacco-pipe made of this.
Meet, mēt, *vt.* (meeting, met). To come face to face with; to come in contact with; to encounter; to light on; to receive; to satisfy.—*vi.* To come together; to encounter; to assemble.—*n.* A meeting, as of huntsmen. —*a.* Fit; suitable; proper.
Meeting, mēt'ing, *n.* A coming together; an interview; an assembly; encounter.
Meeting-house, mēt'ing-hous, *n.* A house of public worship for dissenters.
Meetly, mēt'li, *adv.* Fitly; suitably.
Megalithic, meg-a-lith'ik, *a.* Consisting of large stones.
Megalosaurus, meg'a-lō-sa''rus, *n.* A fossil carnivorous reptile 40 to 50 feet long.
Megaphone, meg'a-fōn, *n.* A cone-shaped speaking-trumpet.
Megrim, mē'grim, *n.* A neuralgic pain in the side of the head; *pl.* low spirits; whims or fancies.
Melancholia, mel-an-kō'li-a, *n.* Morbid melancholy.
Melancholic, mel'an-kol-ik, *a.* Disordered by melancholy; hypochondriac; gloomy.
Melancholy, mel'an-ko-li, *n.* Mental alienation characterized by gloom and depression; hypochondria; dejection; sadness. — *a.* Gloomy; dejected; calamitous; sombre.
Melanic, me-lan'ik, *a.* Black; belonging to a black type or class.
Melanochroic, mel'an-ō-krō''ik, *a.* A term applied to the dark-skinned white races of man.
Mêlée, mā-lā', *n.* A confused fight; an affray.
Meliorate, mē'lyor-āt, *vt.* To make better; to improve.—*vi.* To grow better.
Melioration, mē'lyor-ā''shon, *n.* Improvement.
Mellifluence, mel-if'lu-ens, *n.* A flow of honey or sweetness; a sweet smooth flow.
Mellifluent, Mellifluous, mel-if'lu-ent, mel-if'lu-us, *a.* Flowing with honey or sweetness; smooth; sweetly flowing.
Mellow, mel'ō, *a.* Soft with ripeness; soft to the ear, eye, or taste; toned down by time; half-tipsy.—*vt.* To make mellow; to soften.—*vi.* To become mellow.
Melodeon, me-lō'de-on, *n.* A wind-instrument of the accordion kind.
Melodic, me-lod'ik, *a.* Of the nature of melody; relating to melody.
Melodics, me-lod'iks, *n.* That branch of music which investigates the laws of melody.
Melodious, me-lō'di-us, *a.* Containing melody; musical; agreeable to the ear.
Melodiously, me-lō'di us-li, *adv.* In a melodious manner; musically; sweetly.
Melodist, me'lō-dist, *n.* A composer or singer of melodies.
Melodrama, me-lō-dra'ma, *n.* Properly a musical drama; a serious play, with startling incidents, exaggerated sentiment, and splendid decoration.
Melodramatic, me'lō-dra-mat''ik, *a.* Pertaining to melodrama; sensational.
Melodrame, me'lō-dram, *n.* A melodrama.
Melody, me'lō-di, *n.* An agreeable succession of sounds; sweetness of sound; the particular air or tune of a musical piece.
Melon, me'lon, *n.* A kind of cucumber and its large, fleshy fruit.
Melt, melt, *vt.* To reduce from a solid to a liquid state by heat; to soften; to overcome with tender emotion.—*vi.* To become liquid; to dissolve; to be softened to love, pity, &c.; to pass by imperceptible degrees.
Melting, melt'ing, *p.a.* Tending to soften; affecting; feeling or showing tenderness.
Member, mem'bėr, *n.* An organ or limb of an animal body; part of an aggregate; one of the persons composing a society, &c.; a representative in a legislative body.
Membership, mem'bėr-ship, *n.* State of being a member; the members of a body.
Membrane, mem'brān, *n.* A thin flexible texture in animal bodies; a similar texture in plants.
Membranous, mem'bra-nus, *a.* Belonging to or like a membrane; consisting of membranes.
Memento, mē-men'tō, *n.* That which reminds; a souvenir; a keepsake.
Memoir, mem'oir, mem'wär, *n.* A written account of events or transactions; a biographical notice; recollections of one's life (usually in the *pl.*).
Memorabilia, mem'or-a-bil''i-a, *n.pl.* Things worthy of remembrance or record.
Memorable, mem'or-a-bl, *a.* Worthy to be remembered; signal; remarkable; famous.
Memorably, mem'or-a-bli, *adv.* In a memorable manner.
Memorandum, mem-or-an'dum, *n.*; pl. **-dums** or **-da.** A note to help the memory; brief entry in a diary; formal statement.
Memorial, mē-mō'ri-al, *a.* Pertaining to memory or remembrance; serving to commemorate.—*n.* That which preserves the memory of something; a monument; memorandum; a written representation of facts, made as the ground of a petition.
Memorialist, mē-mō'ri-al-ist, *n.* One who writes, signs, or presents a memorial.
Memorialize, mē-mō'ri-al-īz, *vt.* To present a memorial to; to petition by memorial.
Memorize, mem'or-īz, *vt.* To cause to be remembered; to record.
Memory, mem'ō-ri, *n.* The faculty of the mind by which it retains knowledge or ideas; remembrance; recollection; the time within which a person may remember what is past; something remembered.
Menace, men'ās, *n.* A threat; indication of probable evil.—*vt.* (menacing, menaced). To threaten.
Menacingly, men'ās-ing-li, *adv.* In a menacing or threatening manner.
Menage, men-äzh', *n.* A household; housekeeping; household management.
Menagerie, me-naj'ėr-i, *n.* A collection of wild animals kept for exhibition.
Mend, mend, *vt.* To repair; to restore to a sound state; to amend.—*vi.* To advance to a better state; to improve.
Mendacious, men-dā'shus, *a.* Lying; false; given to telling untruths.
Mendacity, men-das'i-ti, *n.* Quality of being mendacious; deceit; untruth.
Mender, mend'ėr, *n.* One who mends.
Mendicancy, men'di-kan-si, *n.* State of being a mendicant; beggary.
Mendicant, men'di-kant, *a.* Begging.—*n.*

A beggar; one who makes it his business to beg alms; a begging friar.
Mendicity, men-dis'i-ti, *n.* State of being a mendicant; the life of a beggar.
Menhaden, men-hā'den, *n.* A fish of the herring type.
Menial, mē'ni-al, *a.* Belonging to household servants; low with regard to employment.—*n.* A domestic servant (used mostly disparagingly).
Meningitis, men-in-jī'tis, *n.* Inflammation of the membranes of the brain or spinal cord.
Menses, men'sēz, *n.pl.* The monthly discharge of a woman.
Menstrual, men'stry-al, *a.* Monthly; pertaining to the menses of females.
Menstruate, men'stry-āt, *vi.* To discharge the menses.
Menstruation, men-stry-ā'shon, *n.* Act of menstruating; period of menstruating.
Menstruum, men'stry-um, *n.*; pl. **-uums** or **-ua.** Any fluid which dissolves a solid.
Mensurable, men'sūr-a-bl, *a.* Measurable.
Mensuration, men-sūr-ā'shon, *n.* The act, process, or art of measuring.
Mental, men'tal, *a.* Pertaining to the mind; performed by the mind; intellectual.
Mentally, men'tal-li, *adv.* In a mental manner; intellectually; in thought.
Menthol, men'thol, *n.* A white crystalline substance obtained from oil of peppermint.
Mention, men'shon, *n.* A brief notice or remark about something.—*vt.* To make mention of; to name.
Mentionable, men'shon-a-bl, *a.* That can or may be mentioned.
Mentor, men'tor, *n.* A friend and sage adviser.
Menu, mėn'ö, *n.* A list of dishes to be served at a dinner, &c.; a bill of fare.
Mephitis, me-fī'tis, *n.* Noxious exhalations.
Mercantile, mėr'kan-til, *a.* Pertaining to merchandise; trading; commercial.
Mercenary, mėr'se-na-ri, *a.* Hired; venal; that may be hired; greedy of gain; sordid.—*n.* One who is hired; a soldier hired into foreign service.
Mercer, mėr'sėr, *n.* One who has a shop for silks, woollens, linens, cottons, &c.
Mercery, mėr'sė-ri, *n.* The goods in which a mercer deals.
Merchandise, mėr'chand-īz, *n.* The goods of a merchant; objects of commerce; trade.
Merchant, mėr'chant, *n.* One who carries on trade on a large scale; a man who exports and imports goods.—*a.* Relating to trade; commercial.
Merchantman, mėr'chant-man, *n.* A ship engaged in commerce; a trading vessel.
Merciful, mėr'si-fyl, *a.* Full of mercy; compassionate; tender; clement; mild.
Mercifully, mėr'si-fyl-li, *adv.* In a merciful manner; tenderly; mildly.
Merciless, mėr'si-les, *a.* Destitute of mercy; pitiless; cruel; hard-hearted.
Mercilessly, mėr'si-les-li, *adv.* In a merciless manner.
Mercurial, mėr-kū'ri-al, *a.* Like the god Mercury; flighty; fickle; pertaining to or containing quicksilver.
Mercurialize, mėr-kū'ri-al-īz, *vt.* To affect or treat with mercury.
Mercury, mėr'kū-ri, *n.* Quicksilver, a heavy metal, liquid at all ordinary temperatures; the planet nearest the sun.
Mercy, mėr'si, *n.* Willingness to spare or forgive; clemency; pity; a blessing; benevolence; unrestrained exercise of authority.
Mere, mēr, *a.* This or that and nothing else; simple, absolute, entire, utter.—*n.* A pool or small lake; a boundary.
Merely, mēr'li, *adv.* For this and no other purpose; solely; simply; only.
Meretricious, me-rē-tri'shus, *a.* Pertaining to prostitutes; alluring by false show; gaudy.
Merganser, mėr-gan'sėr, *n.* The goosander.
Merge, mėrj, *vt.* (merging, merged). To cause to be swallowed up or incorporated.—*vi.* To be sunk, swallowed, or lost.
Meridian, mē-rid'i-an, *n.* Pertaining to midday or noon; pertaining to the acme or culmination.—*n.* Mid-day; point of greatest splendour; any imaginary circle passing through both poles, used in marking longitude; a similar imaginary line in the heavens passing through the zenith of any place.
Meridional, mē-rid'i-on-al, *a.* Pertaining to the meridian; southern; southerly.
Meringue, mer-ang', *n.* A mixture of white of egg and pounded sugar; a light cake of this material with whipped cream in the centre.
Merino, me-rē'no, *a.* Belonging to a Spanish variety of sheep with long and fine wool; made of the wool of the merino sheep.—*n.* A merino sheep; a woollen stuff twilled on both sides.
Merit, me'rit, *n.* What one deserves; desert; value; good quality.—*vt.* To deserve; to have a just title to; to incur.
Meritorious, me-rit-ō'ri-us, *a.* Having merit; praiseworthy.
Merk, mėrk, *n.* An old Scottish silver coin, value thirteen pence and one-third of a penny sterling.
Merle, mėrl, *n.* The blackbird.
Merlin, mėr'lin, *n.* A courageous species of hawk about the size of a blackbird.
Mermaid, mėr'mād, *n.* A fabled marine creature, having the upper part like a woman and the lower like a fish.
Merrily, me'ri-li, *adv.* In a merry manner; with mirth; with gaiety and laughter.
Merriment, me'ri-ment, *n.* Mirth; noisy gaiety; hilarity.
Merry, me'ri, *a.* Joyous; jovial; hilarious; gay and noisy; mirthful; sportive.
Merry-andrew, me-ri-an'drö, *n.* A buffoon; one whose business is to make sport for others.
Merry-thought, me'ri-that, *n.* The furcula or forked bone of a fowl's breast.
Mersion, mėr'shon, *n.* Immersion.
Mésalliance, mā-zal-yängs, *n.* A misalliance; an unequal marriage.
Meseems, mē-sēmz', *v. impers.* (pret. meseemed). It seems to me.
Mesentery, me'sen-te-ri, *a.* A membrane retaining the intestines in a proper position.
Mesh, mesh, *n.* The space between the threads of a net; something that entangles; implement for making nets.—*vt.* To catch in a net.
Meshy, mesh'i, *a.* Formed like net-work.
Mesmeric, mez-me'rik, *a.* Pertaining to mesmerism; hypnotic.
Mesmerism, mez'mėr-izm, *n.* The doctrine that some persons can exercise influence over the will and nervous system of others; animal magnetism; hypnotism.

Mesmerist, mez'mėr-ist, *n.* One who practises or believes in mesmerism.
Mesmerize, mez'mėr-īz, *vt.* To bring into a state of mesmeric or hypnotic sleep.
Mesne, mēn, *a.* In *law*, middle; intervening.
Mesocephalic, Mesocephalous, mes'o-se-fal''ik, mes-o-sef'a-lus, *a.* Applied to the human skull when of medium breadth.
Mesozoic, mes-o-zō'ik, *a.* In *geology*, pertaining to the secondary age, between the palæozoic and cainozoic.
Mess, mes, *n.* A dish of food; food for a person at one meal; a number of persons who eat together, especially in the army or navy; a disorderly mixture; muddle.—*vi.* To take meals in common with others.
Message, mes'āj, *n.* A communication, written or verbal; an official written communication.
Messenger, mes'en-jėr, *n.* One who bears a message; a harbinger.
Messiah, mes-si'a, *n.* The Anointed One; Christ, the Anointed.
Messieurs, mes'yėrz, *n.* Sirs; gentlemen; the plural of *Mr.*, generally contracted into *Messrs.* (mes'ėrz).
Messmate, mes'māt, *n.* An associate in a company who regularly eat together.
Messuage, mes'wāj, *n.* A dwelling-house, with the adjacent buildings.
Metabolic, me-ta-bol'ik, *a.* Pertaining to change or metamorphosis.
Metabolism, me-tab'ol-izm, *n.* Change or metamorphosis; chemical change of nutriment taken into the body.
Metacentre, me-ta-sen'tėr, *n.* That point in a floating body on the position of which its stability depends.
Metal, me'tal, *n.* An elementary substance, such as gold, iron, &c., having a peculiar lustre and generally fusible by heat; the broken stone for covering roads.
Metallic, me-tal'ik, *a.* Pertaining to, consisting of, or resembling metal.
Metalline, me'tal-in, *a.* Pertaining to, consisting of, or impregnated with metal.
Metallist, me'tal-ist, *n.* A worker in metals, or one skilled in metals.
Metallurgic, me-tal-ėr'jik, *a.* Pertaining to metallurgy.
Metallurgy, me'tal-ėr-ji, *n.* Art of working metals; art or operation of separating metals from their ores by smelting.
Metamorphic, me-ta-mor'fik, *a.* Pertaining to metamorphosis or metamorphism.
Metamorphose, me-ta-mor'fōs, *vt.* To change into a different form; to transform.
Metamorphosis, me-ta-mor'fos-is, *n.*; pl. **-ses.** Change of form or shape; transformation.
Metaphor, me'ta-for, *n.* A figure of speech founded on resemblance, as 'that man is a fox'.
Metaphoric, Metaphorical, me-ta-fo'rik, me-ta-fo'rik-al, *a.* Pertaining to metaphor; not literal; figurative.
Metaphrase, me'ta-frāz, *n.* A verbal translation from one language into another.
Metaphrastic, me-ta-frast'ik, *a.* Close or literal in translation.
Metaphysic, me-ta-fi'zik, *a.* Metaphysical.—*n.* Metaphysics.
Metaphysical, me-ta-fi'zik-al, *a.* Pertaining to metaphysics; according to rules or principles of metaphysics.
Metaphysician, me'ta-fi-zi''shan, *n.* One who is versed in metaphysics.
Metaphysics, me-ta-fi'ziks, *n.* The science of the principles and causes of all things existing; the philosophy of mind as distinguished from that of matter.
Metathesis, me-ta'the-sis, *n.* Transposition, as of the letters or syllables of a word.
Mete, mēt, *vt.* (meting, meted). To measure; to measure out; to dole.
Metempsychosis, me-temp'si-kō''sis, *n.* Transmigration of souls; passing of the soul after death into some other animal body.
Meteor, mē'tē-ėr, *n.* An atmospheric phenomenon; a transient luminous body; something that transiently dazzles.
Meteoric, mē-tē-or'ik, *a.* Pertaining to or consisting of meteors; proceeding from a meteor; transiently or irregularly brilliant.
Meteorite, mē'tē-ėr-īt, *n.* A meteorolite.
Meteorolite, mē'tē-ėr-ō-līt, *n.* A meteoric stone; an aerolite.
Meteorological, mē'tē-ėr-ol-oj''ik-al, *a.* Pertaining to meteorology.
Meteorologist, mē'tē-ėr-ol''o-jist, *n.* One versed or skilled in meteorology.
Meteorology, mē'tē-ėr-ol''o-ji, *n.* The science of atmospheric phenomena.
Meter, mē'tėr, *n.* One who or that which measures.
Methinks, mē-thingks', *v. impers.* (pret. methought). It seems to me; I think.
Method, me'thod, *n.* Mode or manner of procedure; system; classification.
Methodic, Methodical, me-thod'ik, me-thod'ik-al, *a.* Systematic; orderly.
Methodism, me'thod-izm, *n.* Observance of method or system; (with *cap.*) the doctrines and worship of the Methodists.
Methodist, me'thod-ist, *n.* One who observes method; (with *cap.*) one of a sect of Christians founded by John Wesley.
Methodize, me'thod-īz, *vt.* To reduce to method; to dispose in due order.
Methought, mē-that', pret. of *methinks*.
Methyl, meth'il, *n.* The hypothetical radical of wood-spirit and its combinations.
Methylated, meth'i-lāt-ed, *a.* Impregnated or mixed with methyl; containing wood-naphtha.
Metonymy, me-ton'i-mi, *n.* A figure of speech in which one word is put for another, as when we say, 'We read *Virgil*', meaning his *poetry*.
Metre, mē'tėr, *n.* Rhythmical arrangement of syllables into verses, &c.; rhythm; verse.
Metre, Mètre, mē'tėr, mā-tr, *n.* The French standard measure of length, equal to 39·37 English inches.
Metric, met'rik, *a.* Pertaining to the decimal system.
Metric, Metrical, met'rik, met'rik-al, *a.* Pertaining to rhythm; consisting of verse.
Metropolis, me-tro'po-lis, *n.* The capital of a country; see of a metropolitan bishop.
Metropolitan, met-rō-po'li-tan, *a.* Belonging to a metropolis, or to a mother-church.—*n.* An archbishop.
Mettle, met'l, *n.* Moral or physical constitution; spirit; courage; fire.
Mettled, met'ld, *a.* High-spirited; ardent.
Mettlesome, met'l-sum, *a.* Full of spirit; brisk; fiery.

Mew, mū, *n.* A sea-mew; a gull; moulting of a hawk; a coop for fowls; a place of confinement; the cry of a cat.—*vt.* To moult; to shut up, as in a cage.—*vi.* To moult; to cry as a cat.
Mewl, mūl, *vi.* To cry as a child; to squall.
Mews, mūz, *n.* Place where carriage-horses are kept in large towns; a lane in which stables are situated.
Mezzo, med'zō, *a.* In *music*, middle; mean.
Mezzo soprano, a treble voice between soprano and contralto.
Mezzotint, mez'ō-tint or med'zō-tint, *n.* A manner of engraving on copper or steel in imitation of drawing in Indian ink.
Miasma, mī-az'ma, *n.*; pl. **Miasmata,** mī-az'ma-ta. The effluvia of any putrefying bodies; noxious emanation; malaria.
Miasmatic, mī-az-mat'ik, *a.* Producing, caused by, affected by miasma.
Miaul, myąl, *vi.* To cry as a cat or kitten; to mew.
Mica, mī'ka, *n.* A mineral cleavable into thin shining elastic plates.
Micaceous, mī-kā'shus, *a.* Pertaining to, containing, like, or consisting of mica.
Mice, mīs, *n.pl.* of *mouse.*
Michaelmas, mi'kel-mas, *n.* The feast of St. *Michael*, the 29th of September.
Microbe, mī'krōb, *n.* A microscopic organism such as a bacillus or bacterium.
Microcosm, mī'krō-kozm, *n.* The little world: used for man, according to an old view an epitome of the *macrocosm.*
Micrography, mī-krog'ra-fi, *n.* The description of microscopic objects.
Micrology, mī-krol'o-ji, *n.* Attention to small or minute points.
Micrometer, mī-krom'et-ėr, *n.* An instrument for measuring small objects, spaces, or angles.
Microphone, mī'krō-fōn, *n.* An instrument to augment small sounds by means of electricity.
Microphyte, mī'krō-fīt, *n.* A microscopic plant, especially one that is parasitic.
Microscope, mī'krō-skōp, *n.* An optical instrument for magnifying.
Microscopic, Microscopical, mī-krō-skop'ik, mī-krō-skop'ik-al, *a.* Pertaining to a microscope; visible only by the aid of a microscope; very minute.
Micturate, mik'tūr-āt, *vi.* To pass urine.
Mid, mid, *a.*; no compar.; superl. midmost. Middle; intervening.
Mid-air, mid'ār, *n.* The middle of the sky; a lofty position in the air.
Mid-day, mid'dā, *n.* The middle of the day; noon.—*a.* Pertaining to noon.
Midden, mid'n, *n.* A dunghill.
Middle, mid'l, *a.*; no compar.; superl. middlemost. Equally distant from the extremes; intermediate; intervening.—**Middle ages,** the period from the fall of the Roman Empire to about 1450.—*n.* Point or part equally distant from the extremities; something intermediate.
Middle-aged, mid'l-ājd, *a.* Being about the middle of the ordinary age of man.
Middle-class, mid'l-kläs, *n.* The class of people holding a social position between the working-classes and the aristocracy.—*a.* Of or relating to the middle-classes.
Middleman, mid'l-man, *n.* An intermediary between two parties; an agent between producers and consumers.
Middlemost, mid'l-mōst, *a.* Being in the middle, or nearest the middle.
Middling, mid'ling, *a.* Of middle rank, state, size, or quality; medium; mediocre.
Midge, mij, *n.* A small gnat or fly.
Midland, mid'land, *a.* Being in the interior country: inland.
Midmost, mid'mōst, *a.* Middlemost.
Midnight, mid'nīt, *n.* The middle of the night; twelve o'clock at night.—*a.* Pertaining to midnight; dark as midnight.
Midriff, mid'rif, *n.* The diaphragm.
Midshipman, mid'ship-man, *n.* A young officer in the navy, below a sub-lieutenant.
Midst, midst, *n.* The middle.—*prep.* Amidst: *poet.*
Midsummer, mid'sum-ėr, *n.* The middle of summer; the summer solstice, about June 21.
Midway, mid'wā, *n.* The middle of the way or distance.—*a.* and *adv.* In the middle of the way; half-way.
Midwife, mid'wīf, *n.* A woman that assists other women in childbirth.
Midwifery, mid'wif-ri, *n.* Obstetrics.
Midwinter, mid'win-tėr, *n.* The middle of winter; the winter solstice, December 21.
Mien, mēn, *n.* Look; bearing; carriage.
Miff, mif, *n.* A slight quarrel.
Might, mīt, *n.* Great power or ability to act; strength; force.—*v. aux.* Pret. of *may.*
Mightily, mīt'i-li, *adv.* In a mighty manner; with might; powerful; greatly.
Mighty, mīt'i, *a.* Having might; strong; powerful; potent; very great; vast.
Mignonette, min-yon-et', *n.* A fragrant annual plant.
Migrant, mī'grant, *n.* One who migrates; a migratory bird or other animal.
Migrate, mī'grāt, *vi.* (migrating, migrated). To remove to a distant place or country.
Migration, mī'grā-shon, *n.* Act of migrating; removal from one place to another.
Migratory, mī'grā-to-ri, *a.* Disposed to migrate; roving; passing from one climate to another, as birds.
Mikado, mi-kä'dō, *n.* The emperor of Japan.
Milch, milsh, *a.* Giving milk, as cows.
Mild, mīld, *a.* Gentle in temper or disposition. merciful; soft; bland; mellow.
Mildew, mil'dū, *n.* A minute parasitic fungus that causes decay in vegetable matter; condition so caused.—*vt.* and *i.* To taint with mildew.
Mildly, mīld'li, *adv.* In a mild manner; softly; gently; tenderly.
Mildness, mīld'nes, *n.* State or quality of being mild; gentleness; clemency.
Mile, mīl, *n.* A measure of length or distance equal to 1760 yards.
Mileage, mīl'āj, *n.* Fees paid for travel by the mile; aggregate of miles travelled, &c.
Milestone, mīl'stōn, *n.* A stone or block set up to mark the miles on a road.
Milfoil, mil'foil, *n.* A common plant with finely divided leaves, and small, white or rose-coloured flowers; yarrow.
Miliary, mil'i-a-ri, *a.* Resembling millet-seeds; accompanied with an eruption like millet-seeds.
Militancy, mil'i-tan-si, *n.* Warfare; combativeness.

Militant, mil'i-tant, *a.* Serving as a soldier; fighting; combative.
Militarism, mil'i-ta-rizm, *n.* The system that leads a nation to pay excessive attention to military affairs.
Military, mil'i-ta-ri, *a.* Pertaining to soldiers or war; martial; soldierly; belligerent.—*n.* The whole body of soldiers; the army.
Militate, mil'i-tāt, *vi.* (militating, militated). To stand arrayed; to have weight or influence.
Militia, mi-li'sha, *n.* A body of soldiers not permanently organized in time of peace.
Militiaman, mi-li'sha-man, *n.* One who belongs to the militia.
Milk, milk, *n.* A whitish fluid secreted in female animals, serving as nourishment for their young; what resembles milk; white juice of plants.—*vt.* To draw milk from.
Milker, milk'ėr, *n.* One who milks; a cow giving milk.
Milkmaid, milk'mād, *n.* A woman who milks or is employed in the dairy.
Milkman, milk'man, *n.* A man that sells milk or carries milk to market.
Milksop, milk'sop, *n.* A piece of bread sopped in milk; one devoid of manliness.
Milky, milk'i, *a.* Pertaining to, resembling, yielding, or containing milk.
Mill, mil, *n.* A machine for making meal or flour; a machine for grinding, &c.; building that contains the machinery for grinding, &c. —*vt.* To pass through a mill; to stamp in a coining press; to throw, as silk; to full, as cloth.
Mill-dam, mil'dam, *n.* A mill-pond.
Milled, mild, *p.a.* Passed through a mill; having the edge transversely grooved, as a coin.
Millenarian, mil-le-nā'ri-an, *a.* Consisting of a thousand years; millennial.—*n.* One who believes in the millennium.
Millenary, mil'le-na-ri, *a.* Pertaining to a thousand.—*n.* Period of a thousand years; commemoration of an event that happened a thousand years ago.
Millennial, mil-len'i-al, *a.* Pertaining to the millennium, or to a thousand years.
Millennium, mil-len'i-um, *n.* An aggregate of a thousand years; the thousand years of Christ's reign on earth.
Milleped, Milliped, mil'le-ped, mil'li-ped, *n.* A worm-like animal with many feet; a wood-louse.
Miller, mil'ėr, *n.* One who keeps or attends a mill for grinding grain.
Millesimal, mil-les'im-al, *a.* Thousandth; consisting of thousandth parts.
Millet, mil'et, *n.* A kind of small grain of various species used for food.
Milliard, mil-yärd', *n.* A thousand millions.
Milligramme, mil'i-gram, *n.* The thousandth part of a gramme.
Millimètre, mil-i-mā'tr, *n.* The thousandth part of a metre.
Milliner, mil'in-ėr, *n.* One who makes head-dresses, hats, &c., for females.
Millinery, mil'in-ė-ri, *n.* Articles made or sold by milliners; occupation of a milliner.
Milling, mil'ing, *n.* The process of grinding or passing through a mill; the transverse grooves on the edge of a coin.
Million, mil'yon, *n.* A thousand thousands; a very great number, indefinitely.
Millionaire, mil'yon-ār, *n.* One worth a million of pounds, &c.; a very rich person.
Millionth, mil'yonth, *a.* The ten hundred thousandth.
Mill-pond, mil'pond, *n.* A pond furnishing water for driving a mill-wheel.
Mill-race, mil'rās, *n.* The stream of water driving a mill-wheel; channel in which it runs.
Millstone, mil'stōn, *n.* One of the stones used in a mill for grinding grain.
Mill-wheel, mil'whēl, *n.* A wheel used to drive a mill; a water-wheel.
Mill-wright, mil'rīt, *n.* A mechanic who constructs the machinery of mills.
Milt, milt, *n.* The spleen of an animal; the soft roe of fishes, or the spermatic organ of the males.
Milter, milt'ėr, *n.* A male fish.
Mime, mīm, *n.* A species of ancient drama in which gestures predominated; an actor in such performances.
Mimetic, Mimetical, mī-met'ik, mī-met'ik-al, *a.* Apt to imitate; given to aping or mimicry; characterized by mimicry.
Mimic, mim'ik, *a.* Imitative; consisting of imitation.—*n.* One who imitates or mimics. —*vt.* (mimicking, mimicked). To imitate, especially for sport; to ridicule by imitation.
Mimicry, mim'ik-ri, *n.* Imitation, often for sport or ridicule.
Mimosa, mi-mō'sa, *n.* A leguminous plant.
Minaret, min'a-ret, *n.* A slender lofty turret on Mohammedan mosques, with one or more balconies; a small spire.
Minatory, min'a-to-ri, *a.* Threatening; menacing.
Mince, mins, *vt.* (mincing, minced). To cut or chop into very small pieces; to extenuate or palliate; to utter with affected softness; to clip, as words.—*vi.* To walk with short steps; to speak with affected nicety.—*n.* Mince-meat.
Mince-meat, mins'mēt, *n.* A mixture of raisins and currants with chopped candied peel, suet, apples, &c.
Mince-pie, mins'pī, *n.* A pie made with mince-meat and other ingredients.
Mincing, mins'ing, *p.a.* Speaking or walking affectedly; affectedly elegant.
Mind, mīnd, *n.* The intellectual power in man; understanding; cast of thought and feeling; inclination; opinion; memory.—*vt.* To attend to; to observe; to regard.
Minded, mīnd'ed, *a.* Disposed; inclined.
Mindful, mīnd'fụl, *a.* Bearing in mind; attentive; regarding with care; heedful.
Mindless, mīnd'les, *a.* Destitute of mind; unthinking; stupid; negligent; careless.
Mine, mīn, *adj. pron.* My; belonging to me.—*n.* A pit from which coal, ores, &c., are taken; an underground passage in which explosives may be lodged for destructive purposes; a contrivance floating on or near the surface of the sea, to destroy ships by explosion; a rich source or store of wealth.—*vi.* (mining, mined). To dig a mine; to dig for ores, &c.; to burrow.—*vt.* To undermine; to sap.
Miner, mīn'ėr, *n.* One who works in a mine.
Mineral, mi'ne-ral, *n.* An inorganic body existing on or in the earth.—*a.* Pertaining to or consisting of minerals; impregnated with mineral matter.
Mineralize, mi'ne-ral-īz, *vt.* To convert into a mineral; to impregnate with mineral substance.—*vi.* To engage in collecting minerals.

Mineralogic, Mineralogical, mi'ne-ral-oj''-ik, mi'ne-ral-oj''ik-al, *a.* Pertaining to mineralogy.

Mineralogist, mi-ne-ral'o-jist, *n.* One who is versed in the science of minerals.

Mineralogy, mi-ne-ral'o-ji, *n.* The science of the properties of mineral substances.

Mingle, ming'gl, *vt.* (mingling, mingled). To mix up together; to blend; to debase by mixture.—*vi.* To be mixed; to join.

Miniature, min'i-a-tūr, *n.* A painting of very small dimensions, usually in water-colours, on ivory, vellum, &c.; anything represented on a greatly reduced scale; a small scale.—*a.* On a small scale; diminutive.

Minify, min'i-fī, *vt.* To make little or less: opposite of *magnify*.

Minikin, min'i-kin, *n.* A darling; a favourite. —*a.* Small; diminutive.

Minim, min'im, *n.* Something exceedingly small; a dwarf; a note in music equal to two crochets; the smallest liquid measure; a single drop.

Minimize, min'i-mīz, *vt.* (minimizing, minimized). To reduce to a minimum; to represent as of little moment; to depreciate.

Minimum, min'i-mum, *n.* The least quantity assignable; the smallest amount or degree.

Mining, mīn'ing, *a.* Pertaining to mines.—*n.* The art or employment of digging mines.

Minion, min'yon, *n.* An unworthy favourite; a servile dependant; a minx; a small kind of printing type.

Minish, min'ish, *vt.* To diminish.

Minister, min'is-tėr, *n.* A servant; attendant; agent; a member of a government; a political representative or ambassador; the pastor of a church.—*vt.* To give; to supply.—*vi.* To perform service; to afford supplies; to contribute.

Ministerial, min-is-tē'ri-al, *a.* Pertaining to ministry, ministers of state, or ministers of the gospel.

Ministerialist, min-is-tē'ri-al-ist, *n.* A political supporter of the ministry.

Ministering, min'is-tėr-ing, *p.a.* Attending and serving as a subordinate agent.

Ministrant, min'is-trant, *a.* Performing service; acting as minister or attendant.

Ministration, min-is-trā'shon, *n.* Act of ministering; service; ecclesiastical function.

Ministrative, min'is-trāt-iv, *a.* Ministering; affording service.

Ministry, min'is-tri, *n.* The act of ministering; service; instrumentality; state of being a minister; profession of a minister of the gospel; the clergy; the administration.

Minium, min'i-um, *n.* Red oxide of lead; red-lead.

Miniver, min'i-ver, *n.* The fur of the Siberian squirrel; a fine white fur.

Mink, mingk, *n.* A quadruped allied to the polecat and weasel.

Minnesinger, min'ne-sing-ėr, *n.* One of a class of German lyric poets of the twelfth and thirteenth centuries.

Minnow, min'ō, *n.* A very small British fish inhabiting fresh-water streams.

Minor, mī'nor, *a.* Lesser; smaller; of little importance; petty; in *music*, less by a lesser semitone.—*n.* A person not yet 21 years of age.

Minorite, mī'nor-īt, *n.* A Franciscan friar.

Minority, mi-no'ri-ti, *n.* State of being a minor; period from birth until 21 years of age; the smaller number or a number less than half; the party that has the fewest votes.

Minster, min'stėr, *n.* A monastery; the church of a monastery; a cathedral church.

Minstrel, min'strel, *n.* A musician; a bard; a singer.

Minstrelsy, min'strel-si, *n.* The art or occupation of a minstrel; instrumental music; music; song; a body of songs or ballads.

Mint, mint, *n.* The place where money is coined; a source of abundant supply; a herbaceous aromatic plant.—*vt.* To coin; to invent; to forge; to fabricate.

Mintage, mint'āj, *n.* That which is coined or stamped; duty paid for coining.

Minter, mint'ėr, *n.* One who mints.

Minuend, mī'nū-end, *n.* The number from which another is to be subtracted.

Minuet, mi'nū-et, *n.* A slow graceful dance; the tune or air for it.

Minus, mī'nus, *a.* Less; less by so much; wanting; the sign (—).

Minuscule, mi-nus'kūl, *n.* A small sort of letter used in MSS. in the middle ages.

Minute, mi-nūt', *a.* Very small; precise; particular; exact.

Minute, mi'nit, *a.* The sixtieth part of an hour or degree; short sketch of an agreement, &c., in writing; a note to preserve the memory of anything.—*vt.* (minuting, minuted). To write down a concise statement or note of.

Minute-book, mi'nit-bụk, *n.* A book containing minutes or short notes.

Minutely, mi-nūt'li, *adv.* With minuteness; exactly; nicely.

Minutiæ, mi-nū'shi-ē, *n.pl.* Small or minute things; minor or unimportant details.

Minx, mingks, *n.* A pert, forward girl.

Miocene, mī'ō-sēn, *a.* and *n.* The middle subdivision of the tertiary strata.

Miracle, mi'ra-kl, *n.* A marvel; a supernatural event; a miracle-play.

Miracle-play, mi'ra-kl-plā, *n.* Formerly a dramatic representation exhibiting the lives of the saints, or other sacred subjects.

Miraculous, mi-ra'kū-lus, *a.* Performed supernaturally; wonderful; extraordinary.

Miraculously, mi-ra'kū-lus-li, *adv.* By miracle; supernaturally; wonderfully.

Mirage, mi-räzh', *n.* An optical illusion, causing remote objects to be seen double, or to appear as if suspended in the air.

Mire, mīr, *n.* Wet, muddy soil; mud.—*vt.* and *i.* (miring, mired). To sink in mire; to soil with mud.

Mirror, mi'rėr, *n.* A looking-glass; any polished substance that reflects images; an exemplar.—*vt.* To reflect, as in a mirror.

Mirth, mėrth, *n.* The feeling of being merry; merriment; glee; hilarity.

Mirthful, mėrth'fụl, *a.* Full of mirth; merry; jovial; amusing.

Mirthless, mėrth'les, *a.* Without mirth; joyless.

Miry, mīr'i, *a.* Full of mire; abounding with deep mud; consisting of mire.

Misadventure, mis-ad-ven'tūr, *n.* An unlucky accident; misfortune; ill-luck.

Misadvised, mis-ad-vīzd', *a.* Ill-advised.

Misalliance, mis-al-lī'ans, *n.* Improper association; an unequal marriage.

Misanthrope, Misanthropist, mis'an-thrōp,

mis-an'thrō-ist, *n.* A hater of mankind.
Misanthropic, Misanthropical, mis-an-throp'ik, mis-an-throp'ik-al, *a.* Pertaining to a misanthrope; hating mankind.
Misanthropy, mis-an'thrō-pi, *n.* Hatred or dislike to mankind.
Misapplication, mis-ap'pli-kā"shon, *n.* The act of misapplying; a wrong application.
Misapply, mis-ap-plī', *vt.* To apply amiss; to apply to a wrong purpose.
Misapprehend, mis-ap'prē-hend", *vt.* To misunderstand; to take in a wrong sense.
Misapprehension, mis-ap'prē-hen"shon, *n.* Act of misapprehending; mistake.
Misappropriate, mis-ap-prō'pri-āt, *vt.* To appropriate wrongly.
Misarrange, mis-a-rānj', *vt.* To arrange improperly.
Misbecome, mis-bē-kum', *vt.* Not to become; to suit ill.
Misbecoming, mis-bē-kum'ing, *p.* and *a.* Unbecoming.
Misbegotten, mis-bē-got'n, *p.a.* Unlawfully or irregularly begotten.
Misbehave, mis-bē-hāv', *vi.* To behave ill; to conduct oneself improperly.
Misbehaviour, mis-bē-hāv'yėr, *n.* Ill behaviour; misconduct.
Misbelief, mis-bē-lēf', *n.* Erroneous belief; false religion.
Misbelieve, mis-bē-lēv', *vt.* To believe erroneously.
Miscalculate, mis-kal'kū-lāt, *vt.* To calculate erroneously.
Miscalculation, mis-kal'kū-lā"shon, *n.* Erroneous calculation.
Miscall, mis-kąl', *vt.* To call by a wrong name; to revile or abuse.
Miscarriage, mis-ka'rij, *n.* Act of miscarrying; failure; act of bringing forth young before the time; abortion.
Miscarry, mis-ka'ri, *vi.* To fail to reach its destination; to fail of the intended effect; to bring forth young before the proper time.
Miscellaneous, mis-sel-lā'nē-us, *a.* Consisting of several kinds; promiscuous; producing written compositions of various sorts.
Miscellany, mis'sel-la-ni, *n.* A mixture of various kinds; a collection of various literary productions.
Mischance, mis-chans', *n.* Ill-luck; misfortune; mishap; disaster.
Mischief, mis'chif, *n.* Harm; injury; damage; vexatious affair; annoying conduct.
Mischievous, mis'chiv-us, *a.* Causing mischief; harmful; fond of mischief; troublesome in conduct.
Mischievously, mis'chiv-us-li, *adv.* In a mischievous manner.
Miscible, mis'i-bl, *a.* That may be mixed.
Misconceive, mis-kon-sēv', *vt.* and *i.* To conceive erroneously; to misapprehend.
Misconception, mis-kon-sep'shon, *n.* An erroneous conception; misapprehension.
Misconduct, mis-kon'dukt, *n.* Misbehaviour; mismanagement.—*vt.* mis-kon-dukt'. To conduct amiss; *refl.* to misbehave.
Misconstruction, mis-kon-struk'shon, *n.* Wrong construction or interpretation.
Misconstrue, mis-kon'strö, *vt.* To construe or interpret erroneously.
Miscount, mis-kount', *vt.* and *i.* To mistake in counting.—*n.* An erroneous counting.
Miscreant, mis'krē-ant, *n.* A vile wretch; an unprincipled scoundrel.
Misdate, mis-dāt', *vt.* To date erroneously.—*n.* A wrong date.
Misdeed, mis-dēd', *n.* An evil action; transgression.
Misdeem, mis-dēm', *vt.* To misjudge.
Misdemean, mis-dē-mēn', *vt.* To behave ill: used *refl.*
Misdemeanant, mis-dē-mēn'ant, *n.* One who commits a misdemeanour.
Misdemeanour, mis-dē-mēn'ėr, *n.* Ill behaviour; an offence inferior to felony.
Misdirect, mis-di-rekt', *vt.* To direct to a wrong person or place.
Misdirection, mis-di-rek'shon, *n.* Act of misdirecting; wrong direction; error of a judge in charging a jury, in matters of law or of fact.
Misdo, mis-dö', *vt.* To do amiss.
Misdoer, mis-dö'ėr, *n.* One who commits a fault or crime.
Misdoubt, mis-dout', *n.* Suspicion of crime or danger.—*vt.* To suspect of deceit or danger.
Misemploy, mis-em-ploi', *vt.* To employ amiss or to no purpose; to misuse.
Miser, mī'zėr, *n.* A niggard; one who in wealth acts as if suffering from poverty.
Miserable, miz'ėr-a-bl, *a.* Very unhappy; wretched; worthless; despicable.
Miserably, miz'ėr-a-bli, *adv.* In a miserable manner.
Miserly, mī'zėr-li, *a.* Like a miser in habits; penurious; sordid; niggardly.
Misery, miz'ėr-i, *n.* Great unhappiness; extreme distress; wretchedness.
Misfeasance, mis-fē'zans, *n.* In *law*, a wrong done; wrong-doing in office.
Misfit, mis-fit', *n.* A bad fit.—*vt.* To make (a garment, &c.) of a wrong size; to supply with something not suitable.
Misfortune, mis-for'tūn, *n.* Ill fortune; calamity; mishap.
Misgive, mis-giv', *vt.* To fill with doubt; to deprive of confidence; to fail.
Misgiving, mis-giv'ing, *n.* A failing of confidence; doubt; distrust.
Misgovern, mis-guv'ėrn, *vt.* To govern ill.
Misgovernment, mis-guv'ėrn-ment, *n.* Act of misgoverning; bad administration.
Misguide, mis-gīd', *vt.* To guide into error; to direct to a wrong purpose or end.
Mishap, mis-hap', *n.* A mischance; an unfortunate accident.
Misinform, mis-in-form', *vt.* To give erroneous information to.
Misinterpret, mis-in-tėr'pret, *vt.* To interpret erroneously.
Misinterpretation, mis-in-tėr'pre-tā"shon, *n.* Act of interpreting erroneously.
Misjudge, mis-juj', *vt.* To judge erroneously.—*vi.* To err in judgment.
Mislay, mis-lā', *vt.* To lay in a wrong place; to lay in a place not recollected.
Mislead, mis-lēd', *vt.* To lead astray; to cause to mistake; to deceive.
Mislike, mis-līk', *vt.* To dislike; to disapprove; to have aversion to.
Mismanage, mis-man'āj, *vt.* To manage ill; to administer improperly.
Mismanagement, mis-man'āj-ment, *n.* Bad management.
Misname, mis-nām', *vt.* To call by the wrong name.

Misnomer, mis-nō'mėr, *n.* A mistaken or inapplicable name or designation.
Misogamist, mi-sog'am-ist, *n.* A hater of marriage.
Misogamy, mi-sog'a-mi, *n.* Hatred of marriage.
Misogynist, mi-soj'in-ist, *n.* A woman-hater.
Misogyny, mi-soj'i-ni, *n.* Hatred of the female sex.
Misplace, mis-plās', *vt.* To put in a wrong place; to set on an improper object.
Misplacement, mis-plās'ment, *n.* Act of misplacing.
Misprint, mis-print', *vt.* To print wrongly.—*n.* A mistake in printing.
Misprision, mis-prizh'on, *n.* Neglect or oversight; neglect to make known a crime.
Misprize, Misprise, mis-prīz', *vt.* To slight or undervalue.
Mispronounce, mis-prō-nouns', *vt.* or *i.* To pronounce erroneously.
Mispronunciation, mis-prō-nun'si-ā"shon, *n.* Wrong pronunciation.
Misquotation, mis-kwōt-ā'shon, *n.* An erroneous quotation; act of quoting wrongly.
Misquote, mis-kwōt', *vt.* To quote erroneously; to cite incorrectly.
Misrelate, mis-rē-lāt', *vt.* To relate wrongly.
Misreport, mis-rē-pōrt', *vt.* To give an incorrect account of.—*n.* An erroneous report.
Misrepresent, mis-rep'rē-zent", *vt.* To represent falsely.
Misrepresentation, mis-rep'rē-zent-ā"shon, *n.* False or incorrect account.
Misrule, mis-röl', *n.* Bad rule; misgovernment.—*vt.* To govern badly or oppressively.
Miss, mis, *vt.* To fail in hitting, obtaining, finding, &c.; to feel the loss of; to omit; to let slip.—*vi.* To fail to strike what is aimed at; to miscarry.—*n.* A failure to hit, obtain, &c.; loss; want; an unmarried woman.
Missal, mis'al, *n.* The R. Catholic mass-book.
Missel-thrush, mis'el-thrush, *n.* A British thrush, larger than the common thrush.
Misshape, mis-shāp', *n.* A bad or incorrect form.—*vt.* To shape ill.
Misshapen, mis-shāp'n, *a.* Ill-formed; ugly.
Missile, mis'il, *a.* Capable of being thrown.—*n.* A weapon or projectile thrown with hostile intention, as an arrow, a bullet.
Missing, mis'ing, *p.a.* Not to be found; wanting; lost.
Mission, mi'shon, *n.* A sending or delegating; duty on which one is sent; destined end or function; persons sent on some political business or to propagate religion; a station of missionaries.
Missionary, mi'shon-a-ri, *n.* One sent to propagate religion.—*a.* Pertaining to missions.
Missive, mis'iv, *a.* Such as is sent; proceeding from some authoritative source.—*n.* A message; a letter or writing sent.
Misspell, mis-spel', *vt.* To spell wrongly.
Misspelling, mis-spel'ing, *n.* A wrong spelling.
Misspend, mis-spend', *vt.* To spend amiss; to waste.
Misspent, mis-spent', *p.a.* Ill-spent; wasted.
Misstate, mis-stāt', *vt.* To state wrongly; to misrepresent.
Misstatement, mis-stāt'ment, *n.* A wrong statement.
Mist, mist, *n* Visible watery vapour; aqueous vapour falling in numerous but almost imperceptible drops; something which dims or darkens.
Mistakable, mis-tāk'a-bl, *a.* That may be mistaken.
Mistake, mis-tāk', *vt.* To misunderstand or misapprehend; to regard as one when really another.—*vi.* To err in opinion or judgment.—*n.* An error in opinion or judgment; blunder; fault.
Mistaken, mis-tāk'n, *p.a.* Erroneous; incorrect.
Mister, mis'tėr, *n.* *See* MASTER.
Mistily, mist'i-li, *adv.* In a misty manner; vaguely; darkly; obscurely.
Mistime, mis-tīm', *vt.* To time wrongly.
Mistletoe, mis'l-tō or miz'l-tō, *n.* A plant that grows parasitically on various trees, and was held in veneration by the Druids.
Mistranslate, mis-trans-lāt', *vt.* To translate erroneously.
Mistranslation, mis-trans-lā'shon, *n.* An erroneous translation or version.
Mistress, mis'tres, *n.* The female appellation corresponding to *master*; a woman who has authority, ownership, &c.; a female teacher; a concubine; a title of address applied to married women (written *Mrs.* and pronounced mis'iz).
Mistrust, mis-trust', *n.* Want of confidence or trust; suspicion.—*vt.* To distrust; to suspect; to doubt.
Mistrustful, mis-trust'fụl, *a.* Full of mistrust; suspicious; wanting confidence.
Misty, mist'i, *a.* Overspread with mist; dim; obscure; clouded; hazy.
Misunderstand, mis-un'dėr-stand", *vt.* To understand wrongly; to mistake.
Misunderstanding, mis-un'dėr-stand"ing, *n.* Misconception; difference; dissension.
Misuse, mis-ūz', *vt.* To use to a bad purpose; to abuse.—*n.* mis-ūs'. Improper use; misapplication.
Mite, mīt, *n.* A minute animal of the class Arachnida (cheese-*mite*, &c.); a very small coin formerly current; a very little creature.
Mitigant, mi'ti-gant, *a.* Softening; soothing.
Mitigate, mi'ti-gāt, *vt.* To make soft or mild; to assuage, lessen, abate, moderate.
Mitigation, mi-ti-gā'shon, *n.* Act of mitigating; alleviation.
Mitrailleuse, mē-trā-yėz, *n.* A primitive type of French breech-loading machine-gun with a number of barrels.
Mitre, mī'tėr, *n.* A high pointed cap worn by bishops.—*vt.* (mitring, mitred). To adorn with a mitre.
Mitred, mī'tėrd, *p.a.* Wearing a mitre; having the privilege of wearing a mitre.
Mitre-wheel, mī'tr-whēl, *n.* A bevel wheel at right angles to another.
Mitt, mit, *n.* A mitten.
Mitten, mit'n, *n.* A covering for the hand without fingers, or without a separate cover for each finger.
Mittimus, mit'i-mus, *n.* A warrant of commitment to prison; a writ for removing records from one court to another.
Mix, miks, *vt.* (mixing, mixed or mixt). To unite or blend promiscuously; to mingle; to associate.—*vi.* To become united or blended; to join; to associate.
Mixable, miks'a-bl, *a.* Miscible.

Mixed, mikst, *p.a.* Promiscuous; indiscriminate; miscellaneous.
Mixen, mik'sn, *n.* A dunghill.
Mixture, miks'tūr, *n.* Act of mixing; state of being mixed; a compound; a liquid medicine of different ingredients.
Mizzen, Mizen, miz'n, *n.* A fore-and-aft sail on the aftermost mast of a ship, called the mizzen-mast.—*a.* Belonging to the mizzen.
Mizzle, miz'l, *vi.* (mizzling, mizzled). To rain in very fine drops.—*n.* Small rain.
Mnemonic, Mnemonical, nē-mon'ik, nē-mon'ik-al, *a.* Pertaining to mnemonics.
Mnemonics, nē-mon'iks, *n.* The art of memory; rules for assisting the memory.
Moan, mōn, *vi.* To utter a low dull sound through grief or pain.—*vt.* To bewail or deplore.—*n.* A low dull sound due to grief or pain; a sound resembling this.
Moanful, mōn'ful, *a.* Expressing sorrow.
Moat, mōt, *n.* A deep trench round a castle or other fortified place.—*vt.* To surround with a ditch for defence.
Mob, mob, *n.* A crowd; disorderly assembly; rabble.—*vt.* (mobbing, mobbed). To attack in a disorderly crowd; to crowd round and annoy.
Mobile, mō'bil, *a.* Capable of being easily moved; changeable; fickle.
Mobility, mō-bil'i-ti, *n.* State of being mobile; susceptibility of motion; inconstancy.
Mobilization, mōb' or mob'il-i-zā"shon, *n.* The act of mobilizing.
Mobilize, mōb' or mob'il-īz, *vt.* To put (troops, &c.) in a state of readiness for active service.
Moccasin, mok'a-sin, *n.* A shoe of deer-skin or soft leather, worn by N. American Indians; a venomous serpent of the U. States.
Mock, mok, *vt.* To mimic in contempt or derision; to flout; to ridicule; to set at naught; to defy.—*vi.* To use ridicule; to gibe or jeer.—*n.* A derisive word or gesture; ridicule; derision.—*a.* Counterfeit; assumed.
Mocker, mok'ėr, *n.* A scorner; a scoffer.
Mockery, mok'ė-ri, *n.* Derision; sportive insult; counterfeit appearance; vain effort.
Mock-heroic, mok-he-rō-ik, *a.* Burlesquing the heroic in poetry, action, &c.
Mocking-bird, mok'ing-bėrd, *n.* An American bird of the thrush family.
Mockingly, mok'ing-li, *adv.* By way of mockery or derision.
Modal, mōd'al, *a.* Pertaining to mode or mood, not to essence.
Modality, mō-dal'i-ti, *n.* The quality of being modal.
Mode, mōd, *n.* Manner; method; fashion; custom.
Model, mo'del, *n.* A pattern; an image, copy, facsimile; standard, plan, or type; a person from whom an artist studies his proportions, postures, &c.—*vt.* (modelling, modelled). To plan after some model; to form in order to serve as a model; to mould.—*vi.* To make a model.
Modeller, mo'del-ėr, *n.* One who models; one who makes figures in clay, &c.
Modelling, mo'del-ing, *n.* The making of a model; appearance of relief in painted figures.
Moderate, mo'de-rāt, *vt.* To restrain from excess; to temper, lessen, allay.—*vi.* To become less violent or intense; to preside as a moderator.—*a.* Not going to extremes; temperate; medium; mediocre.—*n.* One not extreme in opinions.
Moderately, mo'de-rāt-li, *adv.* In a moderate manner or degree; not very.
Moderation, mo-de-rā'shon, *n.* Act of moderating; state or quality of being moderate; act of presiding as a moderator.
Moderatism, mo'de-rāt-izm, *n.* Adherence to moderate views or doctrines.
Moderator, mo'de-rāt-ėr, *n.* One who or that which moderates; a president, especially of courts in Presbyterian churches.
Moderatorship, mo'de-rāt-ėr-ship, *n.* The office of a moderator.
Modern, mod'ėrn, *a.* Pertaining to the present time; of recent origin; late; recent.—*n.* A person of modern times.
Modernism, mod'ėrn-izm, *n.* Modern practice, character, phrase, or mode of expression.
Modernize, mod'ėrn-īz, *vt.* To adapt to modern ideas, style, or language.
Modest, mod'est, *a.* Restrained by a sense of propriety; bashful; diffident; chaste; moderate; not excessive.
Modestly, mod'est-li, *adv.* With modesty; diffidently; not excessively.
Modesty, mod'es-ti, *n.* Quality of being modest; bashful reserve; chastity; freedom from excess.
Modicum, mod'i-kum, *n.* A little; a small quantity; small allowance or share.
Modification, mod'i-fi-kā"shon, *n.* Act of modifying; state of being modified; change.
Modify, mod'i-fī, *vt.* (modifying, modified). To qualify; to change or alter; to vary.
Modillion, mō-dil'yon, *n.* A carved bracket used in cornices of buildings.
Modish, mōd'ish, *a.* According to the mode or fashion; affectedly fashionable.
Modiste, mō-dēst', *n.* A woman who deals in articles of ladies' dress; dressmaker.
Modulate, mod'ū-lāt, *vt.* To proportion; to adjust; to vary (the voice) in tone; to transfer from one key to another.—*vi.* To pass from one key into another.
Modulation, mod-ū-lā'shon, *n.* Act of modulating; act of inflecting the voice; melodious sound; change from one scale to another.
Modulator, mod'ū-lāt-ėr, *n.* One who or that which modulates.
Module, mod'ūl, *n.* In *architecture*, a measure to regulate the proportions of a building.
Modulus, mod'ū-lus, *n.* In *mathematics*, &c., a constant quantity used in connection with some variable quantity.
Modus, mō'dus, *n.* A way, manner, or mode.
Mogul, mō-gul', *n.* A Mongolian.—**The Great Mogul,** the sovereign of the Mongolian empire in Hindustan.
Mohair, mō'hār, *n.* The hair of the Angora goat; cloth made of this hair; an imitation wool and cotton cloth.
Mohammedan, mō-ham'med-an, *a.* Pertaining to Mohammed, or the religion founded by him.—*n.* A follower of Mohammed.
Mohammedanism, mō-ham'med-an-izm, *n.* The religion of Mohammed.
Moidore, moi'dōr, *n.* An old gold coin of Portugal, valued at £1, 7*s.* sterling.
Moiety, moi'e-ti, *n.* The half; a portion.

Moil, moil, *vi.* To labour; to toil.
Moire, mwär, *n.* A watered appearance on metals or cloths; watered silk.
Moist, moist, *a.* Moderately wet; damp.
Moisten, mois'n, *vt.* To make moist or damp; to wet in a small degree.
Moisture, mois'tūr, *n.* A moderate degree of wetness; humidity.
Molar, mō'lėr, *a.* Serving to grind the food in eating.—*n.* A grinding or double tooth.
Molasses, mō-las'ez, *n.sing.* A syrup from sugar in the process of making; treacle.
Mold. Same as *Mould.*
Mole, mōl, *n.* A small discoloured protuberance on the human body; a mound or breakwater to protect a harbour from the waves; a small burrowing insectivorous animal.
Molecular, mō-lek'ū-lėr, *a.* Belonging to or consisting of molecules.
Molecule, mo'le-kūl, *n.* A very minute particle of matter.
Mole-hill, mōl'hil, *n.* A little hillock of earth thrown up by moles; a very small hill.
Moleskin, mōl'skin, *n.* A strong twilled fustian or cotton cloth.
Molest, mō-lest', *vt.* To annoy; to disturb; to harass; to vex.
Molestation, mō-lest-ā'shon, *n.* Act of molesting; disturbance; annoyance.
Mollification, mol'i-fi-kā''shon, *n.* Act of mollifying, mitigating, or appeasing.
Mollifier, mol'i-fi-ėr, *n.* One who or that which mollifies.
Mollify, mol'i-fī, *vt.* (mollifying, mollified). To soften; to assuage; to appease; to reduce in harshness; to tone down.
Mollusc, Mollusk, mol'usk, *n.* An animal whose body is soft, as mussels, snails, cuttle-fish, &c.: one of the *Mollusca.*
Molluscous, mol-lus'kus, *a.* Pertaining to the mollusca; soft and flabby.
Molten, mōlt'n, old pp. of *melt.* Melted; made of melted metal.
Moment, mō'ment, *n.* A minute portion of time; a second; momentum; importance; gravity.
Momentarily, mō'ment-a-ri-li, *adv.* Every moment; for a moment.
Momentary, mō-ment-a-ri, *a.* Done in a moment; continuing only a moment.
Momentous, mō-ment'us, *a.* Of moment; important; weighty.
Momentum, mō-ment'um, *n.*; pl. **-ta.** The force possessed by a body in motion; impetus.
Monachal, mon'ak-al, *a.* Monastic.
Monachism, mon'ak-izm, *n.* The monastic life or system.
Monad, mon'ad, *n.* An ultimate atom.
Monadic, mon-ad'ik, *a.* Having the nature or character of a monad.
Monarch, mon'ärk, *n.* A supreme governor of a state; a sovereign; one who or that which is chief of its kind.—*a.* Supreme; ruling.
Monarchal, mon-ärk'al, *a.* Pertaining to a monarch; suiting a monarch; sovereign.
Monarchic, Monarchical, mon-ärk'ik, mon-ärk'ik-al, *a.* Pertaining to monarchy; vested in a single ruler.
Monarchist, mon'ärk-ist, *n.* An advocate of monarchy.
Monarchy, mon'är-ki, *n.* Government in which the supreme power is lodged in a single person, actually or nominally; a kingdom.
Monastery, mon'as-te-ri, *n.* A house for monks, sometimes for nuns; abbey; priory; convent.
Monastic, mon-as'tik, *a.* Pertaining to monasteries or monks; recluse.—*n.* A monk.
Monasticism, mon-as'ti-sizm, *n.* Monastic life; the monastic system or condition.
Monatomic, mon-a-tom'ik, *a.* Said of an element one atom of which will combine with only one atom of another element.
Monday, mun'dā, *n.* The second day of the week.
Monetary, mo'ne-ta-ri, *a.* Relating to money; consisting in money.
Monetize, mon-et-īz', *vt.* To form into coin or money.
Money, mun'i, *n.* Coin; pieces of gold, silver, or other metal, stamped by public authority and used as the medium of exchange; a circulating medium; wealth; affluence.
Moneyed, mun'id, *a.* Having money; rich.
Monger, mung'gėr, *n.* A trader: now only in composition, as in iron*monger.*
Mongol, Mongolian, mon'gol, mon-gō'li-an, *n.* A native of Mongolia.—*a.* Belonging to Mongolia.
Mongoose, mong' or mung'gös, *n.* A common ichneumon of India.
Mongrel, mung'grel, *a.* Of a mixed breed; hybrid.—*n.* An animal of a mixed breed.
Monied, mun'id, *a.* *See* MONEYED.
Monism, mon'izm, *n.* The doctrine that there is only a single principle from which everything is developed, this principle being either mind (*idealistic monism*) or matter (*materialistic monism*).
Monition, mō-ni'shon, *n.* Admonition; warning; intimation.
Monitor, mo'ni-tėr, *n.* One who admonishes; one who warns of faults or informs of duty; a senior pupil in a school appointed to instruct and look after juniors; a lizard.
Monitorial mo-ni-tō'ri-al, *a.* Relating to a monitor; conducted by monitors; admonitory.
Monitory, mo'ni-to-ri, *a.* Giving admonition.
Monitress, Monitrix, mon'i-tres, mon'i-triks, *n.* A female monitor.
Monk, mungk, *n.* A male inhabitant of a monastery, bound to celibacy.
Monkey, mung'ki, *n.* A long-tailed quadrumanous animal; a playful or mischievous youngster.
Monkey-jacket, mung'ki-jak-et, *n.* A close-fitting jacket, generally of stout material.
Monkish, mungk'ish, *a.* Like a monk, or pertaining to monks; monastic.
Monk's-hood, mungks'hụd, *n.* The plant aconite.
Monocarp, mon'ō-kärp, *n.* A plant that perishes after having once borne fruit.
Monochord, mon'ō-kord, *n.* An instrument of one string, used in musical acoustics.
Monochrome, mon'ō-krōm, *n.* A painting in one colour, but with light and shade.
Monocotyledon, mon'ō-kot-i-lē''don, *n.* A plant with one cotyledon only.
Monodist, mon'od-ist, *n.* One who writes monodies.
Monodrama, mon'ō-dra-ma, *n.* A dramatic performance by a single person.
Monody, mon'ō-di, *n.* A poem in which a single mourner gives vent to his grief.

Monogamist, mon-og'a-mist, *n.* One who practises or upholds monogamy.
Monogamous, mon-og'a-mus, *a.* Upholding or practising monogamy.
Monogamy, mon-og'a-mi, *n.* The practice or principle of marrying only once; the marrying of only one at a time.
Monogram, mon'ō-gram, *n.* A cipher composed of several letters interwoven.
Monograph, mon'ō-graf, *n.* An account of a single person, thing, or class of things.
Monolith, mon'ō-lith, *n.* A pillar, column, &c., consisting of a single stone.
Monologue, mon'ō-log, *n.* A speech uttered by one person alone; a soliloquy.
Monomania, mon-ō-mā'ni-a, *n.* Insanity in regard to a single subject or class of subjects; a craze.
Monomaniac, mon-ō-mā'ni-ak, *a.* Affected with monomania.—*n.* A person affected by monomania.
Monometallism, mon-ō-met'al-izm, *n.* The having only one metal as the standard of coinage; the theory of a single metallic standard.
Monopolist, mo-nop'o-list, *n.* One that monopolizes or possesses a monopoly.
Monopolize, mo-nop'o-līz, *vt.* To obtain a monopoly of; to engross entirely.
Monopoly, mo-nop'o-li, *n.* An exclusive trading privilege; assumption of anything to the exclusion of others.
Monosyllabic, mon'ō-sil-lab"ik, *a.* Consisting of one syllable, or of words of one syllable.
Monosyllable, mon'ō-sil-la-bl, *n.* A word of one syllable.
Monotheism, mon'ō-thē-izm, *n.* The doctrine of the existence of one God only.
Monotone, mon'ō-tōn, *n.* A single tone; unvaried pitch of the voice.
Monotonous, mon-ot'on-us, *a.* Exhibiting monotony; wanting variety; unvaried.
Monotony, mon-ot'o-ni, *n.* Uniformity of sound; a dull uniformity; an irksome sameness or want of variety.
Monsignore, Monsignor, mon-sē-nyō'rā, mon-sēn'yor, *n.* A title of a bishop or high dignitary of the R. Catholic Church.
Monsoon, mon-sön', *n.* The trade-wind of the Indian seas, blowing from N.E. from November to March, and S.W. from April to October.
Monster, mon'stėr, *n.* An animal of unnatural form or of great size; one unnaturally wicked or evil.—*a.* Of inordinate size.
Monstrance, mon'strans, *n.* In the R. Catholic Church, a glass-faced shrine in which the consecrated host is presented for the adoration of the people.
Monstrosity, mon-stros'i-ti, *n.* State or quality of being monstrous; that which is monstrous.
Monstrous, mon'strus, *a.* Unnatural in form; enormous; huge; horrible.—*adv.* Exceedingly.
Monstrously, mon'strus-li, *adv.* In a monstrous manner; shockingly; terribly.
Month, munth, *n.* The period measured by the moon's revolution (the lunar month, about 29½ days); one of the twelve parts of the year (the calendar month, 30 or 31 days).
Monthly, munth'li, *a.* Done or happening once a month, or every month.—*n.* A publication appearing once a month.—*adv.* Once a month; in every month.
Monument, mon'ū-ment, *n.* Anything by which the memory of a person or of an event is preserved; a memorial; a singular or notable instance.
Monumental, mon-ū-ment'al, *a.* Pertaining to or serving as a monument; preserving memory; great and conspicuous.
Moo, mö, *vi.* (mooing, mooed). To low, as a cow.—*n.* The low of a cow.
Mood, möd, *n.* Temper of mind; disposition; a fit of sullenness; a form of verbs expressive of certainty, contingency, &c.; a form of syllogism.
Moody, möd'i, *a.* Subject to moods or humours; out of humour; gloomy; sullen.
Moon, mön, *n.* The changing luminary of the night; the heavenly body next to the earth, revolving round it in about 29½ days; a satellite of any planet; a month.
Moonbeam, mön'bēm, *n.* A ray of light from the moon.
Moon-calf, mön'käf, *n.* A monster; a deformed creature; a dolt; a stupid fellow.
Moonlight, mön'līt, *n.* The light afforded by the moon.—*a.* Illuminated by the moon; occurring during moonlight.—**Moon-lit,** mön'lit, *a.* Illuminated by the moon.
Moonlighter, mön'līt-ėr, *n.* One of those who in Ireland commit agrarian outrages by night.
Moonlighting, mön'līt-ing, *n.* The practices of moonlighters.
Moonshine, mön'shīn, *n.* The light of the moon; show without substance; pretence.
Moonstone, mön'stōn, *n.* A translucent variety of felspar used in trinkets, &c.
Moonstruck, mön'struk, *a.* Affected by the influence of the moon; lunatic.
Moony, mön'i, *a.* Pertaining to or like the moon or moonlight; bewildered or silly.
Moor, mör, *n.* A tract of waste land, or of hilly ground on which game is preserved; a native of the northern coast of Africa.—*vt.* To secure a ship in a particular station, as by cables and anchors.—*vi.* To be confined by cables.
Moorage, mör'āj, *n.* A place for mooring.
Moor-cock, Moor-fowl, mör'kok, mör'foul, *n.* The red-grouse.
Mooring, mör'ing, *n.* Act of one who moors; *pl.* the anchor, &c., by which a ship is moored; the place where a ship is moored.
Moorish, mör'ish, *a.* Pertaining to the Moors.
Moorish, Moory, mör'ish, mör'i, *a.* Having the character of a moor; moorland.
Moorland, mör'land, *n.* A waste, barren district; a moor.—Used also adjectively.
Moose, mös, *n.* The American variety of the elk.
Moot, möt, *vt.* To debate; to discuss.—*a.* Debatable; subject to discussion.
Moot-point, möt'point, *n.* A point debated or liable to be debated.
Mop, mop, *n.* A cloth or collection of yarns fastened to a handle, and used for cleaning; a grimace.—*vt.* (mopping, mopped). To rub with a mop; to wipe.—*vi.* To grimace.
Mope, mōp, *vi.* (moping, moped). To show a downcast air; to be spiritless or gloomy.—*n.* One who mopes.
Mopet, Mopsey, mop'et, mop'sē, *n.* A puppet made of cloth; a pet name of a little girl; a woolly variety of dog.

Mopish, mōp'ish, *a.* Inclined to mope; dull; spiritless; dejected.
Moraine, mō-rān', *n.* An accumulation of debris on glaciers or in the valleys at their foot.
Moral, mo'ral, *a.* Relating to morality or morals; ethical; virtuous; supported by reason and probability.—*n.* The practical lesson inculcated by any story; *pl.* general conduct as right or wrong; mode of life; ethics.
Morale, mō-räl', *n.* Mental condition of soldiers, &c., as regards courage, zeal, hope.
Moralist, mo'ral-ist, *n.* One who teaches morals; a writer or lecturer on ethics; one who inculcates or practises moral duties.
Morality, mō-ral'i-ti, *n.* The doctrine of moral duties; ethics; moral character or quality; quality of an action in regard to right and wrong; an old form of drama in which the personages were allegorical representations of virtues, vices, &c.
Moralize, mo'ral-īz, *vt.* To apply to a moral purpose; to draw a moral from.—*vi.* To make moral reflections; to draw practical lessons from the facts of life.
Morally, mo'ral-li, *adv.* In a moral or ethical sense; virtuously; virtually.
Morass, mō-ras', *n.* A tract of low, soft, wet ground; a marsh; a swamp; a fen.
Morbid, mor'bid, *a.* Diseased; sickly; not sound and healthful.
Morbidly, mor'bid-li, *adv.* In a morbid or diseased manner.
Morbific, mor-bif'ik, *a.* Causing disease.
Mordacious, mor-dā'shus, *a.* Biting; pungent; sarcastic.
Mordacity, mor-das'i-ti, *n.* Quality of being mordacious; pungency.
Mordant, mor'dant, *n.* A substance, such as alum, which fixes colours; matter by which gold-leaf is made to adhere.—*a.* Biting; severe.
More, mōr, *a. comp.* of *much* and *many.* Greater in amount, extent, degree, &c.; greater in number.—*adv.* In a greater degree, extent, or quantity; in addition.—*n.* A greater quantity or number; something further.
Moreen, mō-rēn', *n.* A woollen, or woollen and cotton, fabric used for curtains, &c.
Moreover, mōr-ō'vėr, *adv.* Further; besides; likewise.
Moresque, mō-resk', *a.* After the manner of the Moors.—*n.* Decoration in the Moorish manner; arabesque.
Morganatic, mor-ga-nat'ik, *a.* Applied to a kind of marriage with a female of lower rank, the offspring of which do not inherit the father's rank, though otherwise legitimate.
Moribund, mo'ri-bund, *a.* In a dying state.
Morion, mo'ri-on, *n.* A helmet without visor or beaver.
Mormon, mor'mon, *n.* A member of a sect founded in the United States in 1830, who practise polygamy; a Latter-day Saint. Also **Mormonite, Mormonist.**
Morn, morn, *n.* The morning: *poetic.*
Morning, morn'ing, *n.* The first part of the day; the time between dawn and the middle of the forenoon; the first or early part. Often used as an *adj.*
Morning-star, morn'ing-stär, *n.* The planet Venus when it rises before the sun.
Morning-tide, morn'ing-tīd, *n.* Morning time; morning.
Morocco, mō-rok'ō, *n.* A fine kind of leather prepared from goat skin.
Moron, mo'ron, *n.* A feeble-minded or degenerate person.
Morose, mō-rōs', *a.* Of a sour or sullen temper; gloomy; churlish; surly.
Morosely, mō-rōs'li, *adv.* In a morose manner; with sullenness.
Morphia, Morphine, mor'fi-a, mor'fīn, *n.* The narcotic principle of opium, a powerful anodyne.
Morphologist, mor-fol'o-jist, *n.* One versed in morphology.
Morphology, mor-fol'o-ji, *n.* The science which treats of the form and arrangement of the structures of plants and animals.
Morris, Morrice, mo'ris, *n.* A dance borrowed from the Moors; a fantastic dance formerly practised in England.
Morrow, mo'rō, *n.* The day next after the present, or a specified day.
Morse, mors, *n.* The walrus.
Morsel, mor'sel, *n.* A bite; a mouthful; a fragment; a little piece in general.
Mortal, mor'tal, *a.* Subject to death; deadly; fatal; human.—*n.* A being subject to death; a human being.
Mortality, mor-tal'i-ti, *n.* State of being mortal; actual death of great numbers of men or beasts; death-rate.
Mortally, mor'tal-li, *adv.* In a manner that must cause death; in the manner of a mortal.
Mortar, mor'tär, *n.* A vessel, in which substances are pounded with a pestle; a short piece of ordnance, thick and wide, for throwing shells, &c.; a mixture of lime and sand with water, used as a cement for building.
Mortgage, mor'gāj, *n.* A conveyance of land or house property as security for a debt; the deed effecting this conveyance.—*vt.* (mortgaging, mortgaged). To grant or assign on mortgage; to pledge.
Mortgagee, mor-ga-jē', *n.* The person to whom an estate is mortgaged.
Mortgager, mor'gāj-ėr, *n.* The person who mortgages.
Mortification, mor'ti-fi-kā"shon, *n.* Act of mortifying; condition of being mortified; death of a part of an animal body while the rest is alive; the subduing of the passions by penance, abstinence, &c.; chagrin.
Mortify, mor'ti-fī, *vt.* (mortifying, mortified). To affect with gangrene or mortification; to subdue by abstinence or rigorous severities; to humiliate; to chagrin.—*vi.* To lose vitality while yet a portion of a living body.
Mortifying, mor'ti-fī-ing, *p.a.* Humiliating; tending to mortify or humiliate.
Mortise, mor'tis, *n.* A hole cut in one piece of material to receive the tenon of another piece.—*vt.* To cut a mortise in; to join by a tenon and mortise.
Mortmain, mort'mān, *n.* Possession of lands or tenements in hands that cannot alienate, such as ecclesiastical or other bodies.
Mortuary, mor'tū-a-ri, *n.* A place for the temporary reception of the dead.—*a.* Pertaining to the burial of the dead.
Mosaic, mō-zā'ik, *n.* Inlaid work of marble, precious stones, &c., disposed on a ground of

cement so as to form designs.—*a.* Pertaining to or composed of mosaic.

Mosaic, Mosaical, mō-zā'ik, mō-zā'ik-al, *a.* Pertaining to Moses.

Moselle, mō-zel', *n.* A species of white French and German wine.

Moslem, moz'lem, *n.* An orthodox Mohammedan.

Mosque, mosk, *n.* A Mohammedan place of worship.

Mosquito, mos-kē'tō, *n.* A stinging gnat or fly.

Moss, mos, *n.* A small plant with simple branching stems and numerous small leaves; a bog; a place where peat is found.—*vt.* To cover with moss by natural growth.

Moss-trooper, mos'tröp-ėr, *n.* One of the marauders on the borders of England and Scotland before the union of the crowns.

Mossy, mos'i, *a.* Overgrown or abounding with moss; covered or bordered with moss.

Most, mōst, *a.* superl. of *more.* Greatest in any way.—*adv.* In the greatest degree, quantity, or extent; mostly; chiefly.—*n.* The greatest number; the majority; greatest amount; utmost extent, degree, &c.

Mostly, mōst'li, *adv.* For the most part; mainly; chiefly; generally speaking.

Mote, mōt, *n.* A small particle; anything proverbially small.

Motet, Motett, mo-tet', *n.* A sacred cantata.

Moth, moth, *n.* The name of numerous nocturnal insects allied to the butterflies.

Mother, muᴛʜ'ėr, *n.* A female parent; a woman who has borne a child; source or origin; an abbess or other female at the head of a religious institution; a slimy substance that gathers in vinegar, &c.—*a.* Native; natural; inborn; vernacular.

Mother-church, muᴛʜ'ėr-chėrch, *n.* An original church; a metropolitan church.

Mother-country, muᴛʜ'ėr-kun-tri, *n.* A country which has sent out colonies; a country as the producer of anything.

Motherhood, muᴛʜ'ėr-hụd, *n.* State of being a mother.

Mother-in-law, muᴛʜ'ėr-in-lạ, *n.* The mother of one's husband or wife.

Motherly, muᴛʜ'ėr-li, *a.* Like or becoming a mother; maternal; affectionate.

Mother-of-pearl, muᴛʜ'ėr-ov-pėrl, *n.* The hard silvery brilliant internal layer of several kinds of shells.

Mother-wit, muᴛʜ'ėr-wit, *n.* Native wit; common-sense.

Mothery, muᴛʜ'ėr-i, *a.* Containing or like mother.

Mothy, moth'i, *a.* Full of moths.

Motile, mō'til, *a.* Having inherent power of motion.

Motion, mō'shon, *n.* Act or process of moving; power of moving; movement; internal impulse; proposal made; evacuation of the intestines.—*vi.* To make a significant gesture with the hand.

Motionless, mō'shon-les, *a.* Wanting motion; being at rest.

Motive, mō'tiv, *n.* That which incites to action; cause; inducement; purpose; theme in a piece of music; prevailing idea of an artist.—*a.* Causing motion.—*vt.* To supply a motive to or for; to prompt.

Motivity, mō-tiv'i-ti, *n.* Power of moving.

Motley, mot'li, *a.* Variegated in colour; parti-coloured; heterogeneous; diversified—*n.* A dress of various colours.

Motor, mō'tor, *n.* A moving power; force or agency that sets machinery in motion; a motor-car.—*a.* Imparting motion.

Motor-car, mō'tor-kär, *n.* A self-propelling conveyance for passengers.

Mottle, mot'l, *n.* A blotched or spotted character of surface.—*vt.* (mottling, mottled). To mark with spots or blothes as if mottled.

Mottled, mot'ld, *p.a.* Spotted; marked with spots of different colours.

Motto, mot'tō, *n.*; pl. **-oes,** or **-os.** A short sentence or phrase, or a single word, adopted as expressive of one's guiding idea.

Mould, mōld, *n.* Fine soft earth; mustiness or mildew; dust from incipient decay; form in which a thing is cast; model; shape; character.—*vt.* To cause to contract mould; to cover with mould or soil; to model; to shape; to fashion.—*vi.* To become mouldy.

Moulder, mōld'ėr, *n.* One who moulds or is employed making castings in a foundry.—*vi.* To turn to mould or dust by natural decay.—*vt.* To convert into mould or dust.

Moulding, mōld'ing, *n.* Anything cast in a mould; ornamental contour or form in wood or stone along an edge or a surface.

Mould-warp, mōld'wạrp, *n.* The animal otherwise called the mole.

Mouldy, mōld'i, *a.* Overgrown with mould; musty; decaying.

Moult, mōlt, *vi.* and *t.* To shed or cast the hair, feathers, skin, horns, &c., as birds and other animals.—*n.* Act or process of changing the feathers, &c.; time of moulting.

Mound, mound, *n.* An artificial elevation of earth; a bulwark; a rampart; the globe which forms part of the regalia.

Mount, mount, *n.* A hill; a mountain; that with which something is fitted; a setting, frame, &c.; opportunity or means of riding on horseback; a horse.—*vi.* To rise; to get on horseback or upon any animal; to amount.—*vt.* To raise aloft; to climb; to place oneself upon, as on horseback; to furnish with horses; to set in or cover with something; to set off to advantage.

Mountain, moun'tin, *n.* An elevated mass larger than a hill; anything very large.—*a.* Pertaining to a mountain; found on mountains.

Mountain-ash, moun'tin-ash, *n.* A British tree with scarlet berries; the rowan.

Mountaineer, moun-tin-ēr', *n.* An inhabitant of a mountainous district; a climber of mountains.—*vi.* To practise the climbing of mountains.

Mountainous, moun'tin-us, *a.* Full of mountains; large, as a mountain; huge.

Mountebank, moun'ti-bangk, *n.* One who mounts a bench or stage in a public place, and vends medicines or nostrums; a quack; any boastful and false pretender.

Mounting, mount'ing, *n.* Act of one who mounts; that with which an article is mounted or set off; trimming, setting, &c.

Mourn, mōrn, *vi.* To sorrow; to lament; to wear the customary habit of sorrow.—*vt.* To grieve for; to deplore.

Mourner, mōrn'ėr, *n.* One who mourns; one who attends a funeral.

Mournful, mōrn'fụl, *a.* Expressing sorrow; sad; calamitous; sorrowful.
Mournfully, mōrn'fụl-li, *adv.* In a mournful manner; with sorrow.
Mourning, mōrn'ing, *n.* Lamentation; dress worn by mourners.—*a.* Employed to express grief.
Mouse, mous, *n.*; pl. **Mice,** mīs. A small rodent quadruped that infests houses, fields, &c.—*vi.* mouz (mousing, moused). To hunt for or catch mice.
Mouser, mouz'ėr, *n.* A cat good at catching mice.
Moustache, mụs-tash', *n.* The long hair on the upper lip.
Mouth, mouth, *n.*; pl. **Mouths,** mouTHz. The opening in the head of an animal into which food is received, and from which voice is uttered; opening of anything hollow, as of a pitcher, or of a cave, pit, &c.; the part of a river, &c., by which it joins with the ocean. —*vt.* mouTH. To take into the mouth; to utter with a voice affectedly big.—*vi.* To speak with a loud, affected voice; to vociferate.
Mouther, mouTH'ėr, *n.* One who mouths.
Mouthful, mouth'fụl, *n.* As much as the mouth contains at once; a small quantity.
Mouth-organ, mouth-or'gan, *n.* A small popular wind-instrument, flat in shape, with openings for the various notes, which are produced by inhalation and exhalation.
Mouth-piece, mouth'pēs, *n.* The part of a wind-instrument to which the mouth is applied; a tube by which a cigar, &c., is held in the mouth; one who delivers the opinions of others.
Movable, mөv'a-bl, *a.* Capable of being moved; changing from one time to another.—*n.* Any part of a man's goods capable of being moved; *pl.* goods, commodities, furniture.
Movably, mөv'a-bli, *adv.* In a movable manner or state.
Move, mөv, *vt.* (moving, moved). To cause to change place, posture, or position; to set in motion; to affect; to rouse; to prevail on; to propose, as a resolution.—*vi.* To change place or posture; to stir; to begin to act; to shake; to change residence; to make a proposal to a meeting —*n.* The act of moving; a movement; proceeding; action taken.
Movement, mөv'ment, *n.* Act of moving; motion; change of position; manner of moving; gesture; an agitation to bring about some result desired; wheel-work of a clock.
Mover, mөv'ėr, *n.* A person or thing that moves or gives motion; one who offers a motion in an assembly.
Moving, mөv'ing, *p.a.* Causing to move or act; pathetic; affecting.
Mow, mou or mō, *n.* A pile of hay or sheaves of grain deposited in a barn; part of a barn where they are packed; a wry face.—*vt.* To lay in a mow.—*vi.* To make mouths.
Mow, mō, *vt.* (pret. mowed, pp. mowed or mown). To cut down, as grass, &c.; to cut the grass from; to cut down in great numbers. —*vi.* To cut grass; to use the scythe.
Mower, mō'ėr, *n.* One who mows; a mowing-machine.
Mowing-machine, mō'ing-ma-shēn, *n.* A machine to cut down grass, grain, &c.
Much, much, *a.*; comp. *more,* superl. *most.* Great in quantity or amount; abundant.—*adv.* In a great degree; by far; greatly.—*n.* A great quantity; something strange or serious.
Mucilage, mū'si-lāj, *n.* A solution in water of gummy matter; a gummy substance found in certain plants.
Mucilaginous, mū-si-laj'in-us, *a.* Pertaining to or secreting mucilage; slimy.
Muck, muk, *n.* Dung in a moist state; something mean, vile, or filthy.—*vt.* To manure with muck; to remove muck from.
Muck-worm, muk'wėrm, *n.* A worm that lives in muck; a miser.
Mucky, muk'i, *a.* Filthy; nasty.
Mucous, Mucose, mū'kus, *a.* Pertaining to mucus, or resembling it; slimy.—**Mucous membrane,** a membrane that lines all the cavities of the body which open externally, and secretes mucus.
Mucus, mū'kus, *n.* A viscid fluid secreted by the mucous membrane.
Mud, mud, *n.* Moist and soft earth; sediment from turbid waters; mire.—*vt.* (mudding, mudded). To soil with mud; to make turbid.
Muddle, mud'l, *vt.* (muddling, muddled). To make muddy; to intoxicate partially; to confuse; to make a mess of.—*vi.* To become muddy; to act in a confused manner.—*n.* A mess; confusion; bewilderment.
Muddle-headed, mud'l-hed-ed, *a.* Stupidly confused or dull; doltish.
Muddy, mud'i, *a.* Abounding in mud; miry; stupid; obscure.—*vt.* (muddying, muddied). To soil with mud; to cloud.
Muezzin, Mueddin, mụ-ed'zin, mụ-ed'in, *n.* A Mohammedan crier who proclaims from a minaret the summons to prayers.
Muff, muf, *n.* A warm cover for receiving both hands; a soft, useless fellow.
Muffin, muf'in, *n.* A light spongy cake.
Muffle, muf'l, *vt.* (muffling, muffled). To cover close, particularly the neck and face; to conceal; to deaden the sound of by wrapping cloth, &c., round.—*n.* The tumid and naked portion of the upper lip and nose of ruminants and rodents.
Muffled, muf'ld, *p.a.* Wrapped up closely; dulled or deadened: applied to sound.
Muffler, muf'lėr, *n.* A cover for the face or neck; a stuffed glove for lunatics.
Mufti, Muftee, muf'ti, muf'tē, *n.* A doctor of Mohammedan law; civilian dress.
Mug, mug, *n.* A small vessel of earthenware or metal for containing liquor; a jug.
Muggy, Muggish, mug'i, mug'ish, *a.* Damp and close; moist; mouldy.
Mulatto, mū-lat'tō, *n.* A person who is the offspring of a white and a negro.
Mulberry, mul'be-ri, *n.* The berry of a tree, and the tree itself, cultivated to supply food for silk-worms; a prefabricated harbour, used in the military operations of 1944.
Mulch, mulsh, *n.* Dungy material protecting the roots of newly-planted shrubs, &c.
Mulct, mulkt, *n.* A fine.—*vt.* To fine; to deprive.
Mule, mūl, *n.* The offspring of an ass and mare, or a horse and she-ass; a hybrid animal.
Muleteer, mūl-et-ēr', *n.* One who drives mules.
Mulish, mūl'ish, *a.* Like a mule; stubborn.
Mull, mul, *vt.* To heat, sweeten, and flavour with spices, as ale or wine.

Mullet, mul'et, *n.* A name for fishes of two different families, the gray mullets and the red mullets.
Mulligatawny, mul'i-ga-tạ''ni, *n.* An E. Indian curry-soup.
Mullion, mul'yon, *n.* An upright division between the lights of windows, screens, &c., in Gothic architecture.
Mullioned, mul'yond, *a.* Having mullions.
Multangular, mul-tang'gū-lėr, *a.* Having many angles.
Multifarious, mul-ti-fā'ri-us, *a.* Having great diversity or variety.
Multiform, mul'ti-form, *a.* Having many forms, shapes, or appearances.
Multilateral, mul-ti-lat'ėr-al, *a.* Having many sides; many-sided.
Multilineal, mul-ti-lin'ē-al, *a.* Having many lines.
Multipartite, mul'ti-pär-tīt, *a.* Divided into several or many parts.
Multiped, mul'ti-ped, *n.* An animal that has many feet.
Multiple, mul'ti-pl, *a.* Manifold; having many parts or divisions.—*n.* A number which contains another an exact number of times.
Multiplex, mul'ti-pleks, *a.* Manifold; complex.
Multiplicand, mul'ti-pli-kand'', *n.* A number to be multiplied by another.
Multiplication, mul'ti-pli-kā''shon, *n.* Act or process of multiplying; state of being multiplied; reproduction of animals.
Multiplicative, mul'ti-pli-kāt-iv, *a.* Tending to multiply.
Multiplicator, mul'ti-pli-kāt-ėr, *n.* A multiplier.
Multiplicity, mul-ti-plis'i-ti, *n.* State of being multiplex or manifold; great number.
Multiplier, mul'ti-plī-ėr, *n.* One who or that which multiplies; the number by which another is multiplied.
Multiply, mul'ti-plī, *vt.* (multiplying, multiplied). To increase in number; to add to itself any given number of times.—*vi.* To increase in number, or to become more numerous by reproduction; to extend.
Multitude, mul'ti-tūd, *n.* State of being many; a great number, collectively or indefinitely; a crowd.—**The multitude,** the populace.
Multitudinous, mul-ti-tūd'in-us, *a.* Consisting of or pertaining to a multitude.
Multivalve, mul'ti-valv, *n.* An animal which has a shell of many valves or pieces.
Multure, mul'tūr, *n.* The grinding of grain.
Mum, mum, *a.* Silent.—*n.* A species of ale brewed from wheaten malt, &c.
Mumble, mum'bl, *vi.* (mumbling, mumbled). To mutter; to speak with mouth partly closed; to eat with the lips close.—*vt.* To utter with a low, inarticulate voice.
Mumbler, mum'blėr, *n.* One who mumbles or speaks with a low, inarticulate voice.
Mumm, mum, *vt.* To mask; to sport in a mask or disguise.
Mummer, mum'ėr, *n.* A masker; a masked buffoon; a play-actor.
Mummery, mum-ėr-i, *n.* A masquerade; buffoonery; hypocritical parade.
Mummify, mum'i-fī, *vt.* To make into a mummy; to embalm as a mummy.
Mummy, mum'i, *n.* A dead human body embalmed after the manner of the ancient Egyptians, with wax, balsams, &c.
Mump, mump, *vt.* or *i.* To mumble or mutter; to munch; to implore alms.
Mumpish, mump'ish, *a.* Dull; sullen; sour.
Mumps, mumps, *n.* Silent displeasure; sullenness; a disease consisting in an inflammation of the salivary glands.
Munch, munsh, *vt.* and *i.* To chew audibly.
Mundane, mun'dān, *a.* Belonging to this world; worldly; earthly.
Municipal, mū-ni'si-pal, *a.* Belonging to a corporation or city.
Municipality, mū-ni'si-pal''i-ti, *n.* A town possessed of local self-government; community under municipal jurisdiction.
Munificence, mū-ni'fi-sens, *n.* A bestowing liberally; liberality; generosity.
Munificent, mū-ni'fi-sent, *a.* Liberal in giving; bountiful; liberal; generous.
Munificently, mū-ni'fi-sent-li, *adv.* Liberally; generously.
Muniment, mū'ni-ment, *n.* Support; defence; a charter; a writing by which claims and rights are defended.
Munition, mū-ni'shon, *n.* Military stores; ammunition; material for any enterprise.
Mural, mū'ral, *a.* Pertaining to a wall; resembling a wall; perpendicular or steep.
Murder, mėr'dėr, *n.* Act of killing a human being with premeditated malice.—*vt.* To kill (a human being) with premeditated malice; to mar by bad execution.
Murderer, mėr'dėr-ėr, *n.* One who murders, or is guilty of murder.
Murderess, mėr'dėr-es, *n.* A female who commits murder.
Murderous, mėr'dėr-us, *a.* Pertaining to murder; guilty of murder; meditating murder; bloody.
Muriatic, mū-ri-at'ik, *a.* Pertaining to or obtained from brine or sea-salt; hydrochloric.
Muricate, Muricated, mū'ri-kāt, mū'ri-kāt-ed, *a.* Armed with sharp points or prickles.
Murk, mėrk, *n.* Darkness; gloom.
Murky, mėr'ki, *a.* Dark; obscure; gloomy.
Murmur, mėr'mėr, *n.* A low continued or repeated sound; a hum; a grumble or mutter. —*vi.* To utter a murmur or hum; to grumble. —*vt.* To utter indistinctly; to mutter.
Murmurer, mėr'mėr-ėr, *n.* One who murmurs.
Murmuring, mėr'mėr-ing, *n.* A continued murmur; a low confused noise.
Murrain, mu'rān, *n.* A deadly and infectious disease among cattle, &c.
Muscadel, Muscatel, Muscadine, mus'ka-del, mus'ka-tel, mus'ka-dīn, *a.* and *n.* A sweet and strong Italian or French wine; the grapes which produce this wine; a delicious pear.
Muscat, mus'kat, *n.* A kind of grape, and the wine made from it. *See* MUSCADEL.
Muscle, mus'l, *n.* A definite portion of an animal body consisting of fibres susceptible of contraction and relaxation, and thus effecting motion; a mussel.
Muscled, mus'ld, *a.* Having muscles.
Muscoid, mus'koid, *a.* Resembling moss.
Muscovado, mus-kō-vā'dō, *n.* or *a.* Unrefined sugar.
Muscovite, mus'kō-vīt, *n.* A native of Muscovy, or Russia; common mica.

Muscular, mus'kū-lėr, *a.* Pertaining to or consisting of muscle; performed by a muscle; strong; brawny; vigorous.
Muscularity, mus-kū-la'ri-ti, *n.* State of being muscular.
Muse, mūz, *n.* One of the nine sister goddesses of the Greeks and Romans presiding over the arts; poetic inspiration; a fit of abstraction. —*vi.* (musing, mused). To ponder; to meditate in silence; to be absent in mind.—*vt.* To meditate on.
Museum, mū-zē'um, *n.* A repository of interesting objects connected with literature, art, or science.
Mushroom, mush'röm, *n.* An edible fungus; an upstart.—*a.* Pertaining to mushrooms; resembling mushrooms in rapidity of growth.
Music, mū'zik, *n.* Melody of harmony; the science of harmonious sounds; the written or printed score of a composition.
Musical, mū'zik-al, *a.* Belonging to music; producing music; melodious; harmonious; fond of or skilled in music.
Musically, mū'zik-al-li, *adv.* In a musical, melodious, or harmonious manner.
Music-hall, mū'zik-hal, *n.* A place of public entertainment in which the spectators are treated to singing, dancing, &c.
Musician, mū-zi'shan, *n.* One skilled in music.
Musing, mūz'ing, *n.* Meditation.
Musk, musk, *n.* A strong-scented substance obtained from the musk-deer; the animal itself; a musky smell; a plant giving out such a smell.—*vt.* To perfume with musk.
Musk-deer, musk'dēr, *n.* A deer of Central Asia, the male of which yields the perfume musk.
Musket, mus'ket, *n.* Early form of military hand-gun, with a smooth bore; a sparrow-hawk or hawk of inferior kind.
Musketeer, mus-ket-ēr', *n.* A soldier armed with a musket.
Musketry, mus'ket-ri, *n.* The fire of muskets; troops armed with muskets; the art or science of firing small-arms.
Musky, musk'i, *a.* Having the odour of musk; fragrant.
Muslin, muz'lin, *n.* A fine thin cotton cloth. —*a.* Made of muslin.
Musquito, mus-kē'tō, *n.* *See* MOSQUITO.
Musrole, muz'rōl, *n.* The nose-band of a horse's bridle.
Mussel, mus'el, *n.* The common name of a genus of bivalve shell-fish.
Mussulman, mus'ul-man, *n.*; pl. **-mans.** A Mohammedan or follower of Mohammed.
Must, must, *vi.* without inflection, and present or past. A defective or auxiliary verb expressing obligation or necessity.—*n.* New wine unfermented.
Mustard, mus'tėrd, *n.* An annual plant cultivated for its pungent seeds; the condiment obtained from its seeds.
Mustard gas, mus'tėrd gas, *n.* A poisonous gas with a pungent smell resembling that of mustard.
Muster, mus'tėr, *vt.* To collect, as troops; to assemble or bring together.—*vi.* To assemble; to meet in one place.—*n.* An assembling of troops; register of troops mustered; an array.
Muster-roll, mus'tėr-rōl, *n.* A roll or register of troops, or of a ship's company.
Musty, mus'ti, *a.* Mouldy; sour; stale.
Mutability, mū-ta-bil'i-ti, *n.* Quality or state of being mutable; inconstancy.
Mutable, mū'ta-bl, *a.* Changeable; inconstant; unstable; variable; fickle.
Mutation, mū-tā'shon, *n.* Act or process of changing; change; alteration, either in form or qualities; modification.
Mutchkin, much'kin, *n.* A liquid measure in Scotland containing four gills.
Mute, mūt, *a.* Silent; incapable of speaking; dumb; not pronounced, or having its sound checked by a contact of the vocal organs, as certain consonants (*t*, *p*, *k*, &c.).—*n.* A dumb person; a hired attendant at a funeral; a mute consonant.—*vi.* (muting, muted). To eject the contents of the bowels, as birds.
Mutely, mūt'li, *adv.* In a mute manner; silently; without uttering words or sounds.
Mutilate, mū'ti-lāt, *vt.* To injure or disfigure by cutting a piece from; to maim; to render imperfect.
Mutilation, mū-ti-lā'shon, *n.* Act of mutilating; state of being mutilated; removal of some essential part.
Mutineer, mū-ti-nēr', *n.* One guilty of mutiny.
Mutinous, mū'ti-nus, *a.* Exciting or engaging in mutiny; seditious.
Mutiny, mū'ti-ni, *n.* An insurrection of soldiers or seamen; revolt against constituted authority.—*vi.* (mutinying, mutinied). To rise against lawful authority.
Mutter, mut'ėr, *vi.* To utter words with compressed lips; to mumble; to murmur.—*vt.* To utter with a low, murmuring voice.—*n.* Murmur; obscure utterance.
Mutterer, mut'ėr-ėr, *n.* One who mutters; a grumbler.
Muttering, mut'ėr-ing, *n.* The sound made by one who mutters.
Mutton, mut'n, *n.* The flesh of sheep, raw or dressed for food.
Mutton-chop, mut-n-chop', *n.* A rib of mutton for broiling.
Mutual, mū'tū-al, *a.* Reciprocal; interchanged; given and received on both sides.
Mutually, mū'tū-al-li, *adv.* In a mutual manner; reciprocally.
Muzzle, muz'l, *n.* The projecting mouth and nose of an animal; the open end of a gun or pistol, &c.; a cover for the mouth which hinders an animal from biting.—*vt.* (muzzling, muzzled). To cover the mouth of to prevent biting or eating; to gag.
Muzzy, muz'i, *a.* Bewildered; tipsy.
My, mī, *pron.* The possessive case sing. of *I*; belonging to me.
Myalgia, mī-al'ji-a, *n.* Cramp.
Mycelium, mī-sē'li-um, *n.*; pl. **-lia.** The cellular filamentous spawn of fungi.
Mycology, mī-kol'o-ji, *n.* That department of botany which investigates fungi.
Myology, mī-ol'o-ji, *n.* The science and description of the muscles.
Myopia, Myopy, mī-ō'pi-a, mī'o-pi, *n.* Short-sightedness; near-sightedness.
Myriad, mi'ri-ad, *n.* A countless number; the number of ten thousand collectively.—*a.* Innumerable.
Myrmidon, mėr'mi-don, *n.* A soldier of a rough character; a ruffian under an unscrupulous leader.
Myrrh, mėr, *n.* An aromatic gum resin exuded by a spiny Arabian shrub.

Myrtle, mėr'tl, *n.* An evergreen shrub.
Myself, mi-self', *compd. pron.*; pl. **Ourselves,** our-selvz'. As a nominative it is used, generally after I, to express emphasis—I, and not another; in the objective often used reflexively and without any emphasis.
Mysterious, mis-tē'ri-us, *a.* Containing mystery; beyond human comprehension; unintelligible; enigmatical.
Mysteriously, mis-tē'ri-us-li, *adv.* In a mysterious manner.
Mystery, mis'tėr-i, *n.* Something above human intelligence; a secret; an old form of drama in which the characters and events were drawn from sacred history; a trade, craft, or calling.
Mystic, Mystical, mis'tik, mis'tik-al, *a.* Obscure to human comprehension; involving some secret meaning or import; mysterious; pertaining to mysticism.
Mystic, *n.* One who holds the doctrines of mysticism.
Mysticism, mis'ti-sizm, *n.* Views in religion based on communication between man and God through spiritual perception; obscurity of doctrine.
Mystification, mis'ti-fi-kā"shon, *n.* The act of mystifying or state of being mystified.
Mystify, mis'ti-fī, *vt.* (mystifying, mystified). To perplex intentionally; to bewilder; to befog.
Myth, mith, *n.* A tradition or fable embodying the notions of a people as to their gods, origin, early history, &c.; an invented story.
Mythic, Mythical, mith ik, mith'ik-al, *a.* Relating to myths; described in a myth; fabulous; fabled.
Mythological, Mythologic, mith-o-loj'ik-al, mith-o-loj'ik, *a.* Relating to or proceeding from mythology; fabulous.
Mythologist, Mythologer, mi-thol'o-jist, mi-thol'o-jėr, *n.* One versed in mythology.
Mythology, mith-ol'o-ji, *n.* The science or doctrine of myths; the myths of a people collectively.
Mythopœic, Mythopoetic, mith-ō-pē'ik, mith'ō-pō-et"ik, *a.* Myth-making; producing or tending to produce myths.

N

Nab, nab, *vt.* (nabbing, nabbed). To catch or seize suddenly or unexpectedly.
Nabob, nā'bob, *n.* A provincial governor under a viceroy in the Mogul empire; a European who has enriched himself in the East.
Nacre, nā'kėr, *n.* Mother-of-pearl.
Nacreous, nā'krē-us, *a.* Consisting of or resembling nacre.
Nadir, nā'dėr, *n.* That point of the lower hemisphere of the heavens directly opposite to the zenith; the lowest point.
Nævus, nē'vus, *n.* A birth-mark.
Nag, nag, *n.* A small horse; a horse in general. —*vt.* and *i.* (nagging, nagged). To find fault constantly.
Naiad, nā'yad, *n.* A water-nymph; a female deity that presides over rivers and springs.
Naïf, nä-ēf, *a.* Ingenuous; having a natural lustre without being cut, as jewels.
Nail, nāl, *n.* The horny substance at the end of the human fingers and toes; a claw; a small pointed piece of metal, to be driven into timber, &c.; a stud or boss; a measure of 2¼ inches.—*vt.* To fasten or stud with nails; to hold fast or make secure.
Nailer, nāl'ėr, *n.* One who makes nails.
Nailery, nāl'ė-ri, *n.* A manufactory where nails are made.
Nainsook, nān'sųk, *n.* A kind of muslin.
Naïve, nä-ēv', *a.* Ingenuous; simple; artless.
Naïvely, nä-ēv'li, *adv.* In a naïve manner.
Naïveté, nä-ēv'tā, *n.* Native simplicity; unaffected ingenuousness.
Naked, nā'ked, *a.* Not having clothes on; bare; nude; open to view; mere, bare, simple; destitute; unassisted.
Nakedly, nā'ked-li, *adv.* In a naked manner; without covering.
Nakedness, nā'ked-nes, *n.* State of being naked; nudity; bareness.
Namable, Nameable, nām'a-bl, *a.* Capable or worthy of being named.
Namby-pamby, nam'bi-pam'bi, *a.* Affectedly pretty; insipid; vapid.
Name, nām, *n.* That by which a person or thing is designated; appellation; title; reputation; eminence; sound only; not reality; authority; behalf; a family.—*vt.* (naming, named). To give a name to; to designate; to style; to nominate; to speak of or mention as.
Nameless, nām'les, *a.* Without a name; not known to fame; inexpressible.
Namely, nām'li, *adv.* By name; particularly; that is to say.
Namer, nām'ėr, *n.* One who names or calls by name.
Namesake, nām'sāk, *n.* One whose name has been given to him for the sake of another; one of the same name as another.
Nankeen, Nankin, nan-kēn', *n.* A species of cotton cloth usually of a yellow colour; *pl.* breeches made of this material.
Nap, nap, *n.* The woolly substance on the surface of cloth, &c.; the downy substance on plants; a short sleep.—*vi.* (napping, napped). To have a short sleep; to drowse.
Nape, nāp, *n.* The prominent joint of the neck behind; the back part of the neck.
Napery, nā'pėr-i, *n.* A collective term for linen cloths used for domestic purposes.
Naphtha, naf'tha or nap', *n.* A volatile, limpid, bituminous liquid, of a strong peculiar odour and very inflammable.
Napkin, nap'kin, *n.* A sort of towel used at table; a handkerchief.
Nappy, nap'i, *a.* Having abundance of nap or down on the surface.
Narcissus, när-sis'us, *n.* An extensive genus of bulbous flowering plants.
Narcotic, när-kot'ik, *n.* A substance which relieves pain and produces sleep.—*a.* Having the properties of a narcotic.
Nard, närd, *n.* An aromatic plant, usually called spikenard; an unguent prepared from the plant.
Nardine, närd'in, *a.* Pertaining to nard; having the qualities of spikenard.
Narghile, Nargileh, när'gi-le, *n.* A hookah.
Narial, nā'ri-al, *a.* Pertaining to the nostrils; nasal.
Narrate, na-rāt' or nar', *vt.* (narrating, narrated). To tell or relate, orally or in writing.

Narration, na-rā'shon, *n.* Act of narrating; a narrative; relation; story.
Narrative, nar'a-tiv, *a.* Pertaining to narration.—*n.* That which is narrated or related; a relation orally or in writing.
Narrator, na-rāt'ėr or nar'rāt-ėr, *n.* One who narrates.
Narrow, na'rō, *a.* Of little breadth; not wide or broad; very limited; straitened; not liberal; bigoted; near; close; scrutinizing.—*n.* A narrow channel; a strait: usually in *pl.*—*vt.* To make narrow.—*vi.* To become narrow; to contract in breadth.
Narrowly, na'rō-li, *adv.* In a narrow manner; contractedly; closely; sparingly.
Narrow-minded, na'rō-mīnd-ed, *a.* Illiberal; of confined views or sentiments.
Nasal, nā'zal, *a.* Pertaining to the nose; formed or affected by the nose, as speech.—*n.* An elementary sound uttered partly through the nose.
Nascent, nas'ent, *a.* Arising; coming into being; springing up.
Nastily, nas'ti-li, *adv.* In a nasty manner.
Nasturtium, nas-tėr'shi-um, *n.* A genus of herbs, including the common water-cress.
Nasty, nas'ti, *a.* Filthy; dirty; indecent; disagreeable in taste or smell; troublesome.
Natal, nā'tal, *a.* Pertaining to birth; dating from one's birth; pertaining to the buttocks.
Natant, nā'tant, *a.* Floating; swimming.
Natation, na-tā'shon, *n.* Art or act of swimming.
Natatores, nā-ta-tō'rēz, *n.pl.* The order of swimming birds.
Natatorial, nā-ta-tō'ri-al, *a.* Swimming; adapted to swimming; belonging to the Natatores.
Natatory, nā'ta-to-ri, *a.* Enabling to swim; natatorial.
Natch, nach, *n.* The rump of an ox.
Nation, nā'shon, *n.* A body of people inhabiting the same country, or united under the same government; great number.
National, na'shon-al, *a.* Pertaining to a nation; public; attached to one's own country.
Nationality, na-shon-al'i-ti, *n.* Quality of being national; national character; strong attachment to one's own nation; a nation.
Nationalize, na'shon-al-īz, *vt.* To make the common property of the nation as a whole.
Nationally, na'shon-al-li, *adv.* In a national manner; as a whole nation.
Native, nā'tiv, *a.* Pertaining to the place or circumstances of one's birth; indigenous; inborn; occurring in nature pure or unmixed.—*n.* One born in a place or country; an indigenous animal or plant; an oyster raised in an artificial bed.
Natively, nā'tiv-li, *adv.* In a native manner; by birth; naturally; originally.
Nativity, na-tiv'i-ti, *n.* Birth; time, place, and manner of birth.
Natron, nā'tron, *n.* Native carbonate of soda, or mineral alkali.
Nattily, nat'i-li, *adv.* Sprucely; tidily.
Natty, nat'i, *a.* Neat; tidy; spruce.
Natural, na'tūr-al, *a.* Pertaining to nature; produced or effected by nature; consistent with nature; not artificial; according to the life; not revealed; bastard; unregenerated.—*n.* An idiot; a fool.
Naturalism, na'tūr-al-izm, *n.* The doctrine that there is no interference of any supernatural power in the universe; realism in art.
Naturalist, na'tūr-al-ist, *n.* One versed in natural science or natural history.
Naturalization, na'tūr-al-iz-ā"shon, *n.* Act of investing an alien with the privileges of a native citizen.
Naturalize, na'tūr-al-īz, *vt.* To make natural; to confer the privileges of a native subject upon; to acclimatize.
Naturally, na'tūr-al-li, *adv.* In a natural manner; according to nature; without affectation; according to life; spontaneously.
Nature, nā'tūr, *n.* The universe; the total of all agencies and forces in the creation; the inherent or essential qualities of anything; individual constitution; sort; natural human instincts; reality as distinct from that which is artificial.
Naught, nąt, *n.* Nought; nothing.—**To set at naught,** to slight or disregard.—*a.* Worthless.
Naughtily, ną'ti-li, *adv.* In a naughty manner; mischievously.
Naughty, ną'ti, *a.* Bad; mischievous.
Nausea, ną'shē-a, *n.* Sickness.
Nauseate, ną'shē-āt, *vi.* To feel nausea.—*vt.* To loathe; to affect with disgust.
Nauseous, ną'shus, *a.* Loathsome; disgusting.
Nautch-girl, nąch'gėrl, *n.* In India, a native professional dancing girl.
Nautical, ną'tik-al, *a.* Pertaining to ships, seamen, or navigation; naval; marine.
Nautilus, ną'ti-lus, *n.* A mollusc with a many-chambered shell in the form of a flat spiral.
Naval, nā'val, *a.* Pertaining to ships; pertaining to a navy; nautical; maritime.
Nave, nāv, *n.* The central block or hub of a wheel; middle part, lengthwise, of a church.
Navel, nā'vl, *n.* A depression in the centre of the abdomen, the end of the umbilical cord.
Navicert, na'vi-sėrt, *n.* A certificate that a ship's cargo does not contravene contraband regulations in war-time.
Navigable, na'vi-ga-bl, *a.* That may be navigated; affording passage to ships.
Navigate, na'vi-gāt, *vi.* To conduct or guide a ship; to sail.—*vt.* To manage in sailing, as a vessel; to sail or guide a ship over.
Navigation, na-vi-gā'shon, *n.* Act of navigating; science or art of managing ships.
Navigator, na'vi-gāt-ėr, *n.* One who directs the course of a ship.
Navvy, nav'i, *n.* A labourer engaged in the making of canals, railways, &c.
Navy, nā'vi, *n.* All the ships of a certain class belonging to a country; the whole of the ships of war belonging to a nation.
Nawab, na-wąb', *n.* A viceroy; a deputy.
Nay, nā, *adv.* No; not only so.—*n.* Denial; refusal.
Nazarean, Nazarene, naz'a-rē-an, naz-a-rēn', *n.* An inhabitant of Nazareth; a name given in contempt to Christ and the early Christians.
Nazarite, naz'a-rīt, *n.* A Jew who bound himself to extraordinary purity of life.
Nazi, nä'tsi, *n.* A member of the German National Socialist party.
Neap, nēp, *a.* Low, or not rising high: applied to the lowest tides.
Neaped, nēpt, *a.* Left aground by the falling of the tide, as a ship.

Neap-tide, nēp'tīd, *n.* A low tide.
Near, nēr, *a.* Not distant in place, time, or degree; intimate; affecting one's interest or feelings; parsimonious; narrow; on the left of a horse; not circuitous.—*prep.* Close to; nigh.—*adv.* Almost; within a little; close to the wind.—*vt.* and *i.* To approach; to come near.
Nearly, nēr'li, *adv.* Closely; intimately; almost.
Near-sighted, nēr'sīt-ed, *a.* Short-sighted.
Neat, nēt, *n.* Cattle of the bovine genus.—*a.* Pure; clean; trim; tidy; clever; smart; without water added.
Neatherd, nēt'hėrd, *n.* A person who has the care of cattle.
Neatly, nēt'li, *adv.* Tidily; smartly; cleverly.
Neb, neb, *n.* The nose; the beak of a fowl.
Nebula, neb'ū-la, *n.* pl. **-æ.** Celestial objects like white clouds, generally clusters of stars.
Nebular, neb'ū-lėr, *a.* Pertaining to nebulæ.
Nebulous, neb'ū-lus, *a.* Cloudy; hazy.
Necessarily, ne'ses-sa-ri-li, *adv.* In a necessary manner; by necessity; indispensably.
Necessary, ne'ses-sa-ri, *a.* Such as must be; inevitable; essential; acting from necessity.—*n.* Anything indispensably requisite.
Necessitate, nē-ses'si-tāt, *vt.* To make necessary; to render unavoidable; to compel.
Necessitous, nē-ses'sit-us, *a.* Wanting the necessaries of life; indigent; destitute.
Necessity, nē-ses'si-ti, *n.* Condition of being necessary; need; irresistible compulsion; what is absolutely requisite; extreme indigence.
Neck, nek, *n.* The part of an animal's body between the head and the trunk; a narrow tract of land; the slender part of a vessel, as a bottle.
Neckcloth, nek'kloth, *n.* A piece of linen or cotton cloth worn round the neck.
Neckerchief, nek'ėr-chif, *n.* A kerchief for the neck.
Necklace, nek'lās, *n.* A string of beads, precious stones, &c., worn round the neck.
Necklet, nek'let, *n.* A small chain worn round the neck for suspending a locket.
Neck-tie, nek'tī, *n.* A tie worn round the neck.
Necrolatry, nek-rol'a-tri, *n.* Excessive veneration for or worship of the dead.
Necrology, nek-rol'o-ji, *n.* A register of deaths; a collection of obituary notices.
Necromancer, nek'rō-man-sėr, *n.* One who practises necromancy; a sorcerer.
Necromancy, nek'rō-man-si, *n.* The revealing of future events through pretended communication with the dead; sorcery.
Necropolis, nek-ro'po-lis, *n.* A city of the dead; a cemetery.
Necrosis, nek-rō'sis, *n.* Death or mortification of a bone; a disease of plants.
Nectar, nek'tar, *n.* The fabled drink of the gods; any very sweet and pleasant drink; the honey of a flower.
Nectareal, Nectarean, Nectareous, nek-tā'rē-al, nek-tā'rē-an, nek-tā'rē-us, *a.* Resembling nectar; very sweet and pleasant.
Nectarine, nek'ta-rīn, *a.* Sweet as nectar.—*n.* A variety of the common peach.
Nectarous, nek'tar-us, *a.* Sweet as nectar.
Nectary, nek'ta-ri, *n.* The part of a flower that contains or secretes the nectar.
Née, nā, *pp.* Born: a term indicating a married woman's maiden name.
Need, nēd, *n.* A state that requires supply or relief; urgent want; necessity; poverty; destitution.—*vt.* To have necessity or need for; to lack, require.—*vi.* To be necessary: used impersonally.
Needful, nēd'fụl, *a.* Needy; necessary; requisite.
Needle, nē'dl, *n.* An instrument for interweaving thread; a small steel instrument for sewing; a magnetized piece of steel in a compass attracted to the pole; anything in the form of a needle.
Needless, nēd'les, *a.* Not needed or wanted; unnecessary; not requisite; useless.
Needlessly, nēd'les-li, *adv.* In a needless manner; without necessity.
Needle-work, nē'dl-wėrk, *n.* Work done with a needle; business of a seamstress.
Needly, nē'dl-i, *a.* Relating to or resembling a needle.
Needs, nēdz, *adv.* Of necessity; necessarily; indispensably: generally with *must*.
Needy, nēd'i, *a.* Being in need; necessitous; indigent; very poor.
Ne'er, nār. A contraction of *never*.
Nefarious, nē-fā'ri-us, *a.* Wicked in the extreme; infamous; atrocious.
Negation, nē-gā'shon, *n.* A denial; contradiction or contradictory condition.
Negative, neg'at-iv, *a.* That denies; implying denial or negation; implying absence; the opposite of positive.—*n.* A word which denies, as *not*, *no*; a proposition by which something is denied; a veto; a photographic picture on glass or celluloid, in which the lights and shades are the opposite of those in nature.—*vt.* To prove the contrary of; to reject by vote.
Negatively, neg'at-iv-li, *adv.* In a negative manner; with or by denial.
Neglect, neg-lekt', *vt.* To treat with no regard; to slight; to set at naught; to overlook.—*n.* Omission; slight; negligence.
Neglectful, neg-lekt'fụl, *a.* Showing neglect; heedless; careless; inattentive.
Negligé, neg'lē-zhā, *n.* Easy or unceremonious dress; a loose gown.—*a.* Carelessly arrayed; careless. Also *negligée*.
Negligence, neg'li-jens, *n.* Quality of being negligent; neglect; carelessness.
Negligent, neg'li-jent, *a.* Characterized by neglect; apt to neglect; careless; neglectful.
Negligently, neg'li-jent-li, *adv.* In a negligent manner; carelessly; heedlessly.
Negotiability, nē-gō'shi-a-bil"i-ti, *n.* Quality of being negotiable.
Negotiable, nē-gō'shi-a-bl, *a.* That may be negotiated; that may be transferred by assignment or indorsement.
Negotiate, nē-gō'shi-āt, *vi.* To treat with another respecting purchase and sale; to hold diplomatic intercourse; to conduct communications in general.—*vt.* To procure or bring about by negotiation; to pass into circulation (as a bill of exchange).
Negotiation, nē-gō'shi-ā"shon, *n.* A negotiating; the treating with another regarding sale or purchase; diplomatic bargaining.
Negotiator, nē-gō'shi-āt-ėr, *n.* One who negotiates.
Negress, nē'gres, *n.* A female negro.
Negro, nē'grō, *n.* A black man; a male of the African race.
Negus, nē'gus, *n.* A beverage of wine, hot

water, sugar, nutmeg, and lemon-juice, or of wine, water, and sugar.

Negus, nē'gus, *n.* The Emperor of Abyssinia.

Neigh, nā, *vi.* To utter the cry of a horse; to whinny.—*n.* The voice of a horse.

Neighbour, nā'bėr, *n.* One who lives or dwells near, or on friendly terms with another; a fellow-being.—*vt.* To be near to; to adjoin.

Neighbourhood, nā'bėr-hụd, *n.* Condition of being neighbours; neighbours collectively; vicinity; locality.

Neighbouring, nā'bėr-ing, *p.a.* Living or being near; adjoining.

Neighbourly, nā'bėr-li, *a.* Like or becoming a neighbour; friendly; social.

Neither, nē'THėr or nī'THėr, *pron.* and *pron. adj.* Not either; not the one or the other.—*conj.* Not either; nor.

Nelumbo, nē-lum'bō, *n.* The Hindu and Chinese lotus.

Nematoid, nem'a-toid, *n.* A round-worm; one of an order of entozoa or intestinal worms.—*a.* Pertaining to or resembling the nematoids.

Nemesis, nem'e-sis, *n.* A female Greek divinity personifying retributive justice; just retribution or punishment.

Neo-Latin, nē'ō-lat-in, *a.* and *n.* Applied to the Romance languages.

Neolithic, nē-ō-lith'ik, *a.* Belonging to a period in which implements of polished stone were used, the more recent of the two stone periods.

Neologism, nē-ol'o-jizm, *n.* A new word or phrase, or new use of a word.

Neologist, nē-ol'o-jist, *n.* One who is given to neology; an introducer of new words; an innovator in theology.

Neology, nē-ol'o-ji, *n.* The introduction of a new word or of new words; novel doctrines; rationalistic views in theology.

Neon, nē'on, *n.* An inert gas present in small amount in the air.

Neophyte, nē'ō-fīt, *n.* One newly implanted in the church; proselyte; novice; tyro.—*a.* Newly entered on some state.

Neoteric, nē-ō-te'rik, *a.* New; recent; modern.

Nepenthe, Nepenthes, nē-pen'thē, nē-pen'thēz, *n.* A potion supposed to make persons forget their sorrows; any draught or drug capable of removing pain or care.

Nephew, ne'vū, *n.* The son of a brother or sister.

Nephritic, ne-frit'ik, *a.* Pertaining to the kidneys.

Nephritis, nē-frī'tis, *n.* Inflammation of the kidneys.

Nepotism, nē'pot-izm, *n.* Undue patronage of relations; favouritism shown to nephews and other relatives.

Neptune, nep'tūn, *n.* The god of the sea; a planet, the remotest from the sun except Pluto.

Neptunian, nep-tū'ni-an, *a.* Pertaining to the ocean or sea; formed by water.

Nereid, nē'rē-id, *n.* A sea nymph; a marine annelid; a sea-centipede.

Nerve, nėrv, *n.* One of the fibrous threads in animal bodies whose function is to convey sensation and originate motion; fortitude; courage; energy; something resembling a nerve.—*vt.* (nerving, nerved). To give strength or vigour to; to steel.

Nerveless, nėrv'les, *a.* Destitute of nerve or strength; weak; wanting strength of will.

Nervous, nėrv'us, *a.* Pertaining to the nerves; affecting the nerves; having the nerves easily affected; easily agitated; having nerve or bodily strength; vigorous; sinewy.

Nervously, nėrv'us-li, *adv.* In a nervous manner.

Nervousness, nėrv'us-nes, *n.* State or quality of being nervous.

Nescience, nē'shi-ens, *n.* Want of knowledge; ignorance.

Ness, nes, *n.* A promontory or cape.

Nest, nest, *n.* The place or bed formed by a bird for laying and hatching her eggs; a number of persons frequenting the same haunt; a snug abode.—*vi.* To build a nest; to nestle.

Nestle, nes'l, *vi.* (nestling, nestled). To make or occupy a nest; to lie close and snug.—*vt.* To shelter, as in a nest; to cherish.

Nestling, nes'ling, *n.* A young bird in the nest, or just taken from the nest.

Net, net, *n.* A texture of twine, &c., with meshes, commonly used to catch fish, birds, &c.; a snare.—*vt.* (netting, netted). To make into a net; to take in a net; to capture by wile.

Net, Nett, net, *a.* Being clear of all deductions; estimated apart from all expenses.—*vt.* (netting, netted). To gain as clear profit.

Nether, ne'THėr, *a.* Lower.

Nethermost, ne'THėr-mōst, *a.* Lowest.

Netting, net'ing, *n.* A piece of net-work.

Nettle, net'l, *n.* A weed with stinging hairs.—*vt.* (nettling, nettled). To irritate or annoy somewhat; to pique.

Nettle-rash, net'l-rash, *n.* An eruption upon the skin.

Netty, net'i, *a.* Like a net; netted.

Net-work, net'wėrk, *n.* Work formed like a net; an interlacement.

Neural, nū'ral, *a.* Pertaining to the nerves or nervous system.

Neuralgia, nū-ral'ji-a, *n.* Pain in a nerve.

Neuralgic, nū-ral'jik, *a.* Pertaining to neuralgia.

Neurology, nū-rol'o-ji, *n.* That branch of science which treats of the nerves.

Neuropter, Neuropteran, nū-rop'tėr, nū-rop'tėr-an, *n.* An insect (order Neuroptera) having naked wings, reticulated with veins, as the dragon-flies.

Neurotic, nū-rot'ik, *a.* Relating to the nerves; liable to nervous diseases; hysterical.

Neuter, nū'tėr, *a.* Neutral; neither masculine nor feminine; neither active nor passive, as a verb.—*n.* An animal of neither sex; a plant with neither stamens nor pistils; a noun of the neuter gender.

Neutral, nū'tral, *a.* Not siding with any party in a dispute; indifferent; neither acid nor alkaline.—*n.* A person or nation that takes no part in a contest between others.

Neutrality, nū-tral'i-ti, *n.* State of being neutral.

Neutralization, nū-tral-īz-ā''shon, *n.* Act of neutralizing.

Neutralize, nū'tral-īz, *vt.* To render neutral or inoperative; to counteract.

Neutron, nū'tron, *n.* An uncharged particle of the same mass as a proton.

Never, nev'ėr, *adv.* Not ever; at no time; in no degree; not at all.

Nevermore, nev'ėr-mōr, *adv.* Never again; at no future time.
Nevertheless, nev'ėr-ᴛʜē-les", *adv.* Not the less; notwithstanding; yet; however.
New, nū, *a.* Recent in origin; novel; not before known; different; unaccustomed; fresh after any event; not second-hand.—*adv.* Newly; recently.
Newel, nū'el, *n.* The upright structure in a winding staircase supporting the steps.
New-fangled, nū-fang'gld, *a.* Fond of novelty; of new and unfamiliar fashion.
New-fashioned, nū'fa-shond, *a.* Made in a new fashion; lately come into fashion.
Newfoundland, nū-found'land or nū'found-land, *n.* A large dog, remarkable for sagacity and swimming powers.
Newish, nū'ish, *a.* Somewhat new.
Newly, nū'li, *adv.* Lately; freshly; recently; in a new and different manner; anew.
New-made, nū-mād', *n.* Newly made.
Newness, nū'nes, *n.* State or quality of being new; novelty; unfamiliarity.
News, nūz, *n.* Recent intelligence or information; tidings; a newspaper.
Newsmonger, nūz'mung-gėr, *n.* One who deals in news.
Newspaper, nūz'pā-pėr, *n.* A sheet of paper printed periodically for circulating news.
Newt, nūt, *n.* A small amphibian of lizard-like appearance.
Next, nekst, *a.* superl. of *nigh.* Nearest in place, time, rank, or degree.—*adv.* At the time or turn nearest.
Nexus, nek'sus, *n.* Tie; connection.
Nib, nib, *n.* The bill or beak of a bird; the point of anything, particularly of a pen.—*vt.* (nibbing, nibbed). To furnish with a nib; to mend the nib of, as a pen.
Nibble, nib'l, *vt.* and *i.* (nibbling, nibbled). To bite by little at a time; to bite at; to carp at.—*n.* A little bite.
Nibbler, nib'lėr, *n.* One who nibbles; a carper.
Niblick, nib'lik, *n.* A golf-club with a small heavy iron head.
Nice, nīs, *a.* Fastidious; punctilious; accurate; pleasant; delicate; dainty.
Nicely, nīs'li, *adv.* Fastidiously; exactly; finely; becomingly; pleasantly; satisfactorily.
Nicety, nīs'e-ti, *n.* State or quality of being nice; precision; a minute difference; *pl.* delicacies or dainties.
Niche, nich, *n.* A recess in a wall for a statue, a vase, &c.
Nick, nik, *n.* The exact point of time; the critical time; a notch; a score.—*vt.* To hit upon exactly; to make a nick in; to mark with nicks.
Nickel, nik'el, *n.* A valuable metal of a white colour and great hardness, magnetic, and when pure malleable and ductile.
Nickel-silver, nik'el-sil-vėr, *n.* An alloy composed of copper, zinc, and nickel.
Nick-nack, nik'nak, *n.* A trinket; gimcrack; trifle. Also **Nick-knack, Knick-knack.**
Nickname, nik'nām, *n.* A name given in contempt or jest.—*vt.* To give a nickname to.
Nicotine, nik'ō-tin, *n.* A volatile alkaloid from tobacco, highly poisonous.
Nictate, Nictitate, nik'tāt, nik'ti-tāt, *vi.* To wink.
Nidificate, Nidify, nid'i-fi-kāt, nid'i-fī, *vi.* To make a nest and bring out young.
Nidor, nī'dor, *n.* Scent; smell of cooked food.
Nidus, nī'dus, *n.* Any part of a living organism where a parasite finds nourishment; bodily seat of a zymotic disease.
Niece, nēs, *n.* The daughter of one's brother or sister.
Niggard, nig'ėrd, *n.* A miser; a stingy person; a sordid, parsimonious wretch.—*a.* Miserly; stingy; sordidly parsimonious.
Niggardly, nig'ėrd-li, *a.* Niggard.—*adv.* In a niggard manner.
Nigger, nig'ėr, *n.* A familiar or contemptuous name for a negro.
Nigh, nī, *a.* Near; ready to aid.—*adv.* Near; almost.—*prep.* Near to.
Night, nīt, *n.* The daily period of darkness; the time from sunset to sunrise; a state or time of darkness, depression, &c.; ignorance; obscurity; death.
Night-cap, nīt'kap, *n.* A cap worn in bed; liquor taken before going to bed.
Nightfall, nīt'fąl, *n.* The close of the day; evening.
Nightingale, nīt'in-gāl, *n.* A small insectivorous migratory bird that sings at night.
Night-jar, nīt'jär, *n.* The goat-sucker.
Nightly, nīt'li, *a.* Done by night or every night; nocturnal.—*adv.* By night; every night.
Nightmare, nīt'mār, *n.* A feeling of suffocation during sleep, accompanied by intense anxiety or horror; some oppressive or stupefying influence.
Nightshade, nīt'shād, *n.* A plant of the potato genus, &c., which possesses narcotic or poisonous properties.
Night-walker, nīt'wąk-ėr, *n.* One who walks at night; a somnambulist.
Nightward, nīt'wėrd, *a.* Approaching toward night.
Night-watch, nīt'woch, *n.* A guard in the night; a distinct period in the night.
Nigrescent, nī-gres'ent, *a.* Approaching to blackness.
Nihilism, nī'hil-izm, *n.* Nothingness; the doctrine that nothing can be known; principles of a Russian secret society of communists.
Nihilist, nī'hil-ist, *n.* One who holds the doctrine or principles of nihilism.
Nil, nil, *n.* Nothing.
Nimble, nim'bl, *a.* Quick in motion; moving with ease and celerity; agile; prompt.
Nimbly, nim'bli, *adv.* With agility.
Nimbus, nim'bus, *n.* A rain-cloud; a halo surrounding the head in representations of divine or sacred personages.
Nincompoop, nin'kom-pöp, *n.* A fool; a blockhead; a simpleton.
Nine, nīn, *a.* and *n.* One more than eight.
Nine-fold, nīn'fōld, *a.* Nine times.
Ninepins, nīn'pinz, *n.pl.* A game with nine pins of wood at which a bowl is rolled.
Nineteen, nīn'tēn, *a.* and *n.* Nine and ten.
Nineteenth, nīn'tēnth, *a.* The ordinal of nineteen.—*n.* A nineteenth part.
Ninetieth, nīn'ti-eth, *a.* The ordinal of ninety.—*n.* A ninetieth part.
Ninety, nīn'ti, *a.* and *n.* Nine times ten.
Ninny, nin'i, *n.* A fool; a simpleton.
Ninth, nīnth, *a.* The ordinal of nine.—*n.* A ninth part.
Ninthly, nīnth'li, *adv.* In the ninth place.

Nip, nip, *vt.* (nipping, nipped). To catch and compress sharply; to pinch; to snip or bite off; to blast, as by frost; to benumb.—*n.* A pinch, as with the fingers; a blast by frost; a small drink.
Nippers, nip'ėrz, *n.pl.* Small pincers.
Nipple, nip'l, *n.* A teat; pap; something like a nipple; nozzle.
Nit, nit, *n.* The egg of a louse, &c.
Nitrate, nī'trāt, *n.* A salt of nitric acid.
Nitre, nī'tėr, *n.* Nitrate of potassium or saltpetre, used for making gunpowder, in dyeing, medicine, &c.
Nitric, nī'trik, *a.* Pertaining to nitre; containing nitrogen and oxygen.
Nitrify, nī'tri-fī, *vt.* To convert into nitre.
Nitrogen, nī'tro-jen, *n.* The elementary uninflammable gas constituting about four-fifths of the atmospheric air.
Nitrogenous, nī-troj'e-nus, *a.* Pertaining to or containing nitrogen.
Nitro-glycerine, nī-trō-glis'ėr-in, *n.* A powerful explosive produced by the action of nitric and sulphuric acids on glycerine.
Nitrous, nī'trus, *a.* Pertaining to nitre; applied to compounds containing less oxygen than those called *nitric.*
Nitry, nī'tri, *a.* Pertaining to or producing nitre.
Nitwit, nit'wit, *n.* A person of little intelligence.
Nival, nī'val, *a.* Snowy; growing among snow, or flowering during winter.
No, nō, *adv.* A word of denial or refusal; not in any degree; not.—*n.* A denial; a negative vote.—*a.* Not any; none.
Nobility, nō-bil'i-ti, *n.* State or quality of being noble; the peerage.
Noble, nō'bl, *a.* Of lofty lineage; belonging to the peerage; illustrious; lofty in character; magnanimous; magnificent; stately.—*n.* A person of rank; a peer; an old English gold coin, value 6*s.* 8*d.* sterling.
Nobleman, nō'bl-man, *n.* A noble; a peer.
Noblesse, nō-bles', *n.* The nobility.
Nobly, nō'bli, *adv.* In a noble manner; heroically; with magnanimity; splendidly.
Nobody, nō'bo-di, *n.* No person; no one; a person of no standing or position.
Noctambulist, nok-tam'bū-list, *n.* A night-walker or somnambulist.
Nocturn, nok'tėrn, *n.* A religious service formerly used in the R. Catholic Church at midnight, now a part of matins.
Nocturnal, nok-tėrn'al, *a.* Done or happening at night; nightly.
Nocturne, nok'tėrn, *n.* A painting or piece of music expressing some of the characteristic effects of night.
Nod, nod, *vi.* (nodding, nodded). To make a slight bow; to let the head sink from sleep; to incline the head, as in assent or salutation, &c.—*vt.* To incline; to signify by a nod.—*n.* A quick inclination of the head.
Nodal, nōd'al, *a.* Pertaining to a node.
Nodated, nōd'āt-ed, *a.* Knotted.
Noddle, nod'l, *n.* The head.
Noddy, nod'i, *n.* A simpleton; a fool; a sea-fowl of the tern kind.
Node, nōd, *n.* A knot; a protuberance; a sort of knot on a stem where leaves arise; one of the two points in which two great circles of the celestial sphere intersect.
Nodose, nōd'ōs, *a.* Knotted; jointed.
Nodosity, nō-dos'i-ti, *n.* State or quality of being nodose; a knotty protuberance.
Nodular, nod'ū-lėr, *a.* Pertaining to or in the form of a nodule.
Nodule, nod'ūl, *n.* A little knot or lump.
Noetic, nō-et'ik, *a.* Relating to the mind.
Nog, nog, *n.* A wooden pin.
Noggin, nog'in, *n.* A small wooden cup.
Noise, noiz, *n.* A sound of any kind; a din; clamour; frequent talk.—*vt.* (noising, noised). To spread by rumour or report.
Noiseless, noiz'les, *a.* Making no noise; silent.
Noisily, noiz'i-li, *adv.* In a noisy manner.
Noisome, noi'sum, *a.* Noxious to health; offensive; disgusting; fetid.
Noisy, noiz'i, *a.* Making a loud noise; turbulent; obstreperous.
Nomad, nō'mad, *n.* One who leads a wandering or pastoral life.
Nomadic, nō-mad'ik, *a.* Pertaining to nomads; wandering for pasturage; pastoral.
No Man's Land, nō-manz-land, *n.* The ground between hostile trenches.
Nomenclature, no'men-kla-tūr, *n* A system of names; vocabulary of terms appropriated to any branch of science.
Nominal, no'mi-nal, *a.* Pertaining to a name; titular; not real; merely so called.
Nominalist, no'mi-nal-ist, *n.* One of a sect of philosophers who maintained that general notions (such as the notion of a tree) have no existence but as names: opposed to *realist.*
Nominally, no'mi-nal-li, *adv.* In a nominal manner; by name or in name only.
Nominate, no'mi-nāt, *vt.* To name; to designate or propose for an office.
Nomination, no-mi-nā'shon, *n.* Act of nominating; power of appointing to office; state of being nominated.
Nominative, no'mi-nāt-iv, *a.* A term applied to the case of a noun or pronoun when subject of a sentence.—*n.* The nominative case; a nominative word.
Nominator, no'mi-nāt-ėr, *n.* One who nominates.
Nominee, no-mi-nē', *n.* A person nominated; one proposed to fill a place or office.
Nonage, non'āj, *n.* Minority in age.
Nonagenarian, non'a-je-nā''ri-an, *n.* One between ninety and a hundred years old.
Nonagon, non'a-gon, *n.* A plane figure having nine sides and nine angles.
Nonce, nons, *adv.* Present occasion or purpose.
Nonchalance, non'sha-lans, *n.* Indifference.
Nonchalant, non'sha-lant, *a.* Indifferent; careless; cool.
Non-commissioned, non-kom-mi'shond, *a.* Not having a commission; holding the rank of lance-corporal, corporal, or sergeant.
Non-conductor, non-kon-dukt'ėr, *n.* A substance which does not conduct, or transmits with difficulty, heat, electricity, &c.
Nonconforming, non-kon-form'ing, *a.* Not conforming to the established church.
Nonconformist, non-kon-form'ist, *n.* One who does not conform to the established church.
Nonconformity, non-kon-form'i-ti, *n.* Neglect or failure of conformity; refusal to unite with an established church.
Non-content, non-kon-tent', *n.* In the House of Lords, one who gives a negative vote.

Nondescript, non'dē-skript, *a.* That has not been described; abnormal; odd; indescribable.—*n.* A person or thing not easily described or classed.
None, nun, *n.* or *pron.* Not one; not any; not a part; not the least portion.
Nonentity, non-en'ti-ti, *n.* Non-existence; a thing not existing; a person utterly without consequence or importance.
Nones, nōnz, *n.pl.* The seventh day of March, May, July, and October, and the fifth of the other months.
Nonesuch, nun'such, *n.* A person or thing that has not its equal or parallel.
Non-juring, non-jūr'ing, *a.* Not swearing allegiance; pertaining to non-jurors.
Non-juror, non-jūr'ėr, *n.* One who refused to take the oath of allegiance to the crown of England at the Revolution of 1688.
Nonpareil, non-pa-rel', *n.* A person or thing having no equal; a nonesuch; a sort of apple; a very small printing type.
Nonplus, non'plus, *n.* A state in which one can say or do no more.—*vt.* (nonplussing, nonplussed). To bring to a stand; to puzzle.
Non-residence, non-re'zi-dens, *n.* Failure to reside where official duties require one to reside, or on one's own lands; residence by clergymen away from their cures.
Nonsense, non'sens, *n.* Words without meaning; absurdity; things of no importance.
Nonsensical, non-sens'ik-al, *a.* Destitute of sense; unmeaning; absurd; foolish.
Non-sequitur, non-sek'wi-tėr, *n.* An inference which does not follow from the premises.
Nonsuit, non'sūt, *n.* Stoppage of a suit at law by the plaintiff failing to make out a cause of action.—*vt.* To subject to a nonsuit.
Noodle, nö'dl, *n.* A simpleton.
Nook, nök, *n.* A corner; a secluded retreat.
Noology, nō-ol'o-ji, *n.* The science of intellectual facts or phenomena.
Noon, nön, *n.* The middle of the day; twelve o'clock; the prime.
Noonday, nön'dā, *n.* Mid-day; noon.—*a.* Pertaining to mid-day; meridional.
Noontide, nön'tīd, *n.* The time of noon; mid-day.—*a.* Pertaining to noon.
Noose, nös or nöz, *n.* A running knot, which binds the closer the more it is drawn.—*vt.* (noosing, noosed). To tie or catch in a noose; to entrap.
Nor, nor, *conj.* A word used to render negative a subsequent member of a clause or sentence; correlative to *neither* or other negative; also equivalent to *and not.*
Nordic, nor'dik, *a.* Of or belonging to those peoples of Northern Europe who are long-headed, tall, blue-eyed and fair-haired.
Norm, norm, *n.* A rule; a pattern; a type.
Normal, nor'mal, *a.* According to a rule; conforming with a certain type or standard; regular; perpendicular.—**Normal school,** a training-college for teachers.—*n.* A perpendicular.
Norman, nor'man, *n.* A native of Normandy.—*a.* Pertaining to Normandy or the Normans; denoting the round-arched style of architecture.
Norse, nors, *n.* The language of Norway and Iceland.—*a.* Belonging to ancient Scandinavia.
Norseman, nors'man, *n.* A native of ancient Scandinavia.
North, north, *n.* One of the cardinal points, the opposite of *south*; a region opposite to the south.—*a.* Being in the north.
North-east, north-ēst', *n.* The point midway between the north and east.—*a.* North-eastern.—*adv.* North-eastward.
North-easter, north-ēst'ėr, *n.* A wind from the north-east.
North-easterly, north-ēst'ėr-li, *a.* Toward or from the north-east.
North-eastern, north-ēst'ėrn, *a.* Pertaining to, from, toward, or in the north-east.
North-eastward, north-ēst'wėrd, *adv.* Toward the north-east.
Northerly, norᴛʜ'ėr-li, *a.* Pertaining to the north; northern; proceeding from the north.—*adv.* Toward the north.
Northern, norᴛʜ'ėrn, *a.* Being in the north; toward the north; proceeding from the north.—*n.* An inhabitant of the north.
Northerner, norᴛʜ'ėr-nėr, *n.* A native or inhabitant of a northern part.
Northernmost, norᴛʜ'ėrn-mōst, *a.* Situated at the point farthest north.
Northward, Northwards, north'wėrd, north'wėrdz, *adv.* and *a.* Toward the north.
Northwardly, north'wėrd-li, *adv.* In a northern direction.
North-west, north-west', *n.* The point mid-way between the north and west.—*a.* North-western.—*adv.* North-westward.
North-westerly, north-west'ėr-li, *a.* Toward or from the north-west.
North-western, north-west'ėrn, *a.* Pertaining to, from, toward, or in the north-west.
North-westward, north-west'wėrd, *adv.* Towards the north-west.
Norwegian, nor-wē'jan, *a.* Belonging to Norway.—*n.* A native of Norway.
Nose, nōz, *n.* The organ of smell, employed also in respiration and speech; the power of smelling; scent; sagacity; a nozzle.—*vt.* and *i.* (nosing, nosed). To smell; to twang through the nose; to pry officiously.
Nosegay, nōz'gā, *n.* A bunch of flowers used to regale the sense of smell; a bouquet.
Nosology, no-sol'o-ji, *n.* Arrangement or classification of diseases.
Nostalgia, nos-tal'ji-a, *n.* Vehement desire to revisit one's native country; home-sickness.
Nostril, nos'tril, *n.* One of the two apertures of the nose.
Nostrum, nos'trum, *n.* A quack medicine, the ingredients of which are kept secret.
Not, not, *adv.* A word that expresses negation, denial, or refusal.
Notability, nōt-a-bil'i-ti, *n.* Notableness; a notable person or thing; a person of note.
Notable, nōt'a-bl, *a.* Worthy of note; remarkable; conspicuous.—*n.* A person or thing of note or distinction.
Notably, nōt'a-bli, *adv.* In a notable manner; remarkably; especially.
Notarial, nōt-ā'ri-al, *a.* Pertaining to a notary.
Notary, nōt'a-ri, *n.* An officer authorized to attest documents, to protest bills of exchange, &c.: called also *Notary Public.*
Notation, nōt-ā'shon, *n.* Act of recording anything by marks, or the marks employed, as in algebra, music, &c.
Notch, noch, *n.* An incision; nick; indentation.—*vt.* To cut a notch in; to indent.
Note, nōt, *n.* A mark, sign, or token; an ex-

planatory or critical comment; a memorandum; a bill, account; a paper promising payment; a communication in writing; notice; reputation; distinction; a character representing a musical sound, or the sound itself.—*vt.* (noting, noted). To observe carefully; to mark; to set down in writing.

Note-book, nōt'bųk, *n.* A book in which notes or memoranda are written.

Noted, nōt'ed, *p.a.* Celebrated; famous.

Noteworthy, nōt'wėr-ᴛʜi, *a.* Deserving notice; worthy of observation or notice.

Nothing, nu'thing, *n.* Not anything; non-existence; a trifle; a cipher.—*adv.* In no degree.

Notice, nōt'is, *n.* Act of noting; regard; information; order; intimation; civility; a brief critical review.—*vt.* (noticing, noticed). To take note of; to perceive; to make observations on; to treat with attention.

Noticeable, nōt'is-a-bl, *a.* That may be noticed; worthy of observation.

Notification, nōt'i-fi-kā''shon, *n.* Act of notifying; intimation; the writing which communicates information.

Notify, nōt'i-fī, *vt.* To make known; to declare; to give notice to; to inform.

Notion, nō'shon, *n.* A mental conception; idea; opinion; slight feeling or inclination.

Notional, nō'shon-al, *a.* Partaking of the nature of a notion; visionary; fanciful.

Notoriety, nō-tō-rī'e-ti, *n.* State of being notorious; discreditable publicity; one who is notorious.

Notorious, nō-tō'ri-us, *a.* Publicly known and spoken of; known to disadvantage.

Notoriously, nō-tō'ri-us-li, *adv.* In a notorious manner; publicly; openly.

Notwithstanding, not-wiᴛʜ-stand'ing, *prep.* and *conj.* In spite of; nevertheless.

Nought, nạt, *n.* Not anything; nothing; a cipher.

Noumenon, nou'men-on, *n.* An object conceived by the understanding, as opposed to *phenomenon*.

Noun, noun, *n.* A word that denotes any object of which we speak.

Nourish, nu'rish, *vt.* To feed; to supply with nutriment; to encourage; to foster.

Nourisher, nu'rish-ėr, *n.* A person or thing that nourishes.

Nourishing, nu'rish-ing, *p.a.* Helping to nourish; promoting growth; nutritious.

Nourishment, nu'rish-ment, *n.* Act of nourishing; nutrition; food; nutriment.

Nous, nous, *n.* Intellect; mind; talent.

Novel, no'vel, *a.* Of recent origin or introduction; new and striking; unusual.—*n.* A fictitious prose narrative picturing real life.

Novelist, no'vel-ist, *n.* A writer of novels.

Novelty, no'vel-ti, *n.* Quality of being novel; a new or strange thing.

November, nō-vem'bėr, *n.* The eleventh month of the year.

Novice, no'vis, *n.* One who is new in any business; a beginner; a tyro; a probationer.

Novitiate, nō-vi'shi-āt, *n.* State of being a novice; time of probation of a novice.

Now, nou, *adv.* and *conj.* At the present time; at that time; after this; things being so.—*n.* The present time.

Nowadays, nou'a-dāz, *adv.* In these days; in this age.

Noway. Noways, nō'wā, nō'wāz, *adv.* In no manner or degree; nowise.

Nowhere, nō'whār, *adv.* Not in any place or state.

Nowise, nō'wīz, *adv.* Not in any manner or degree.

Noxious, nok'shus, *a.* Hurtful; pernicious; unwholesome; corrupting to morals.

Nozzle, noz'l, *n.* The projecting spout of something; terminal part of a pipe.

Nuance, nų-ängs, *n.* A gradation of colour; delicate degree in transitions.

Nubile, nū'bīl, *a.* Marriageable (used only of a woman).

Nuciferous, nū-sif'ėr-us, *a.* Bearing or producing nuts.

Nucleus, nū'klē-us, *n.*; pl. **-lei.** A kernel or something similar; a mass about which matter is collected; body of a comet.

Nude, nūd, *a.* Naked; bare; undraped.

Nudge, nuj, *n.* A jog with the elbow.—*vt.* (nudging, nudged). To give a jog with the elbow.

Nudity, nūd'i-ti, *n.* State of being nude.

Nugatory, nū'ga-to-ri, *a.* Trifling; futile; worthless.

Nugget, nug'et, *n.* A lump, as of gold.

Nuisance, nū'sans, *n.* That which annoys or is offensive; a plague or pest; a bore.

Null, nul, *a.* Of no force or validity; of no importance or account.—*n.* A cipher.

Nullify, nul'i-fī, *vt.* (nullifying, nullified). To render null; to deprive of force.

Nullity, nul'i-ti, *n.* State or quality of being null; what is of no force or efficacy.

Numb, num, *a.* Benumbed; without sensation and motion; torpid.—*vt.* To make numb or torpid; to deaden.

Number, num'bėr, *n.* An aggregate of units, or a single unit; a numeral; many; one of a numbered series of things; part of a periodical; metrical arrangement of syllables; difference of form in a word to express unity or plurality.—*vt.* To reckon; to enumerate; to put a number on; to reach the number of.

Numberless, num'bėr-les, *a.* That cannot be numbered; countless; innumerable.

Numbles, num'blz, *n.pl.* The entrails of a deer; the humbles.

Numerable, nū'mėr-a-bl, *a.* That may be numbered.

Numeral, nū'mėr-al, *a.* Pertaining to number; consisting of or representing number.—*n.* A figure used to express a number.

Numerary, nū'mėr-a-ri, *a.* Belonging to number; numerical.

Numerate, nū'mėr-āt, *vt.* (numerating, numerated). To count; to enumerate.

Numeration, nū-mėr-ā'shon, *n.* Act or art of numbering.

Numerator, nū'mėr-āt-ėr, *n.* One who numbers; the number (above the line) in vulgar fractions which shows how many parts of a unit are taken.

Numerical, nū-me'rik-al, *a.* Belonging to number; consisting in numbers.

Numerically, nū-me'rik-al-li. *adv.* In numbers; with respect to number.

Numerous, nū'mėr-us, *a.* Consisting of a great number of individuals; many.

Numismatic, nū-mis-mat'ik, *a.* Pertaining to coins or medals.

Numismatics, nū-mis-mat'iks, *n.* The science or knowledge of coins and medals.

Numismatist, nū-mis'mat-ist, *n.* One versed in numismatics.
Numskull, num'skul, *n.* A blockhead; a dunce; a dolt; a stupid fellow.
Nun, nun, *n.* A woman devoted to religion who lives in a convent; a female monk.
Nuncio, nun'shi-o, *n.* An ambassador of the pope at the court of a sovereign.
Nuncupative, Nuncupatory, nun-kū'pat-iv, nun-kū'pa-to-ri, *a.* Orally pronounced; not written, as a will.
Nunnery, nun'ė-ri, *n.* A house in which nuns reside.
Nuptials, nup'shalz, *n.pl.* Marriage.
Nuptial, nup'shal, *a.* Pertaining to marriage.
Nurse, nėrs, *n.* One who suckles or nourishes a child; one who tends the young, sick, or infirm; an attendant in a hospital; one who or that which nurtures or protects.—*vt.* (nursing, nursed). To act as nurse to; to suckle; to rear; to tend in sickness or infirmity; to foment; to foster.
Nursery, nėr'sė-ri, *n.* The place in which children are nursed and taken care of; a place where trees, plants, &c., are propagated.
Nurseryman, nėr'sė-ri-man, *n.* One who has a nursery of plants, or is employed in one.
Nursling, nėrs'ling, *n.* An infant.
Nurture, nėr'tūr, *n.* Upbringing; education; nourishment.—*vt.* (nurturing, nurtured). To nourish; to educate; to bring or train up.
Nut, nut, *n.* A fruit containing a seed or kernel within a hard covering; a small block of metal or wood with a grooved hole, to be screwed on the end of a bolt.—*vi.* (nutting, nutted). To gather nuts.
Nutant, nū'tant, *a.* Drooping or nodding.
Nutation, nū-tā'shon, *n.* A nodding; a slight gyratory movement of the earth's axis.
Nut-brown, nut'broun, *a.* Brown as a nut long kept and dried.
Nut-cracker, nut'krak-ėr, *n.* An instrument for cracking nuts: also pl. *Nut-crackers.*
Nutmeg, nut'meg, *n.* The aromatic kernel of the fruit of a tree of the Malay Archipelago.
Nutrient, nū'tri-ent, *a.* Nutritious.—*n.* Any substance which nourishes.
Nutriment, nū'tri-ment, *n.* That which nourishes; nourishment; food; aliment.
Nutrition, nū-tri'shon, *n.* Act or process of nourishing; that which nourishes; nutriment.
Nutritious, nū-tri'shus, *a.* Serving to nourish; containing or supplying nutriment.
Nutritive, nū'tri-tiv, *a.* Pertaining to nutrition; nutritious.
Nut-shell, nut'shel, *n.* The hard shell inclosing the kernel of a nut.
Nutty, nut'i, *a.* Abounding in nuts; flavoured like a nut; resembling a nut.
Nux-vomica, nuks-vom'i-ka, *n.* The fruit of an E. Indian tree, containing strychnine; a drug containing strychnine.
Nuzzle, nuz'l, *vi.* and *t.* (nuzzling, nuzzled). To rub or work with the nose; to put a ring into the nose of; to lie snug; to nestle.
Nylon, nī'lon, *n.* A strong, synthetic textile material, used as a substitute for silk, &c.
Nymph, nimf, *n.* A goddess of the mountains, forests, meadows, or waters; a young and attractive woman; a maiden; the chrysalis of an insect.
Nymphomania, nim-fō-mā'ni-a, *n.* Morbid or unnatural sexual desire in women.

O

O, ō. An exclamation used in earnest or solemn address; often distinguished from *Oh*, which is more strictly expressive of emotion.
Oaf, ōf, *n.* A fairy changeling; a dolt.
Oafish, ōf'ish, *a.* Stupid; dull; doltish.
Oak, ōk, *n.* A valuable tree of many species.
Oaken, ōk'n, *a.* Made or consisting of oak.
Oakling, ōk'ling, *n.* A young oak.
Oakum, ōk'um, *n.* Old ropes untwisted into loose fibres, employed for calking, &c.
Oaky, ōk'i, *a.* Like oak; firm; strong.
Oar, ōr, *n.* A long piece of timber used to propel a boat.—*vt.* To impel by rowing.
Oared, ōrd, *a.* Furnished with oars.
Oarsman, ōrz'man, *n.* One who rows at the oar.
Oasis, ō-ā'sis, *n.*; pl. **-ses.** A fertile spot where there is water in a desert.
Oast, ōst, *n.* A kiln to dry hops or malt.
Oat, ōt, *n.* A cereal plant valuable for its grain.
Oat-cake, ōt'kāk, *n.* A cake made of oatmeal.
Oaten, ōt'n, *a.* Made of or pertaining to oats.
Oath, ōth, *n.* An appeal to God for the truth of what is affirmed; an imprecation.
Oat-meal, ōt'mēl, *n.* Meal of oats produced by grinding or pounding.
Obduracy, ob'dū-ra-si, *n.* State or quality of being obdurate; impenitence; obstinacy.
Obdurate, ob'dū-rāt, *a.* Hardened in heart; hardened against good; stubborn; inflexible.
Obdurately, ob'dū-rāt-li, *adv.* In an obdurate manner; stubbornly; inflexibly.
Obedience, ō-bē'di-ens, *n.* Act of obeying; quality of being obedient; submission to authority.
Obedient, ō-bē'di-ent, *a.* Submissive to authority; dutiful; compliant.
Obediently, ō-bē'di-ent-li, *adv.* In an obedient manner; dutifully; submissively.
Obeisance, ō-bā'sans, *n.* A bow or curtsy; act of reverence, deference, or respect.
Obelisk, o'be-lisk, *n.* A tall four-sided pillar, tapering as it rises, and terminating in a small pyramid; a mark (†) used in printing.
Obese, ō-bēs', *a.* Excessively corpulent; fat.
Obesity, ō-bēs'i-ti, *n.* State or quality of being obese; excessive corpulency.
Obey, ō-bā', *vt.* To comply with, as commands or requirements; to be ruled by; to yield to. —*vi.* To submit to authority.
Obfuscate, ob-fus'kāt, *vt.* To darken; to confuse.
Obit, ō'bit, *n.* A person's decease; a funeral ceremony or office for the dead.
Obituary, ō-bit'ū-a-ri, *n.* An account of a person or persons deceased; list of the dead. —*a.* Relating to the decease of a person.
Object, ob'jekt, *n.* That about which any faculty of the mind is employed; end; purpose; a concrete reality; the word, clause, &c., governed by a transitive verb or by a preposition.—*vt.* ob-jekt'. To oppose; to offer as an objection.—*vi.* To oppose in words or arguments.
Objection, ob-jek'shon, *n.* Act of objecting; adverse reason; fault found.
Objectionable, ob-jek'shon-a-bl, *a.* Justly liable to objections; reprehensible.

Objective, ob-jek'tiv, *a.* Pertaining to an object; relating to whatever is exterior to the mind (also pron. ob'jek-tiv); belonging to the case which follows a transitive verb or preposition.—*n.* The objective case; object, place, &c., aimed at.
Objectivity, ob-jek-tiv'i-ti, *n.* State or quality of being objective.
Object-lesson, ob'jekt-les-n, *n.* A lesson from actual examples.
Objector, ob-jekt'ėr, *n.* One who objects.
Objuration, ob-jū-rā'shon, *n.* Act of binding by oath.
Objurgate, ob-jėr'gāt, *vt.* and *i.* To chide, reprove, or reprehend.
Objurgation, ob-jėr-gā'shon, *n.* Act of objurgating; reproof.
Oblate, ob-lāt', *a.* Flattened or depressed at the poles, as a sphere or globe.
Oblation, ob-lā'shon, *n.* Anything offered in sacred worship; a sacrifice.
Obligate, ob'li-gāt, *vt.* To bring under some obligation; to oblige.
Obligation, ob-li-gā'shon, *n.* That which morally obliges; binding power of a promise, contract, or law; a favour bestowed and binding to gratitude; a bond with a condition annexed, and a penalty for non-fulfilment.
Obligatory, ob'li-ga-to-ri, *a.* Imposing an obligation; binding; requiring performance.
Oblige, ō-blij', *vt.* (obliging, obliged). To constrain; to bind by any restraint; to lay under obligation of gratitude; to render service or kindness to.
Obliging, ō-blij'ing, *p.a.* Having the disposition to oblige; civil; courteous; kind.
Obligingly, ō-blij'ing-li, *adv.* In an obliging manner; kindly; complaisantly.
Oblique, ob-lēk', *a.* Neither perpendicular nor parallel; slanting; indirect; sinister.
Obliquely, ob-lēk'li, *adv.* In an oblique manner; indirectly.
Obliquity, ob-lik'wi-ti, *n.* State of being oblique; deviation from a perpendicular or parallel; deviation from moral rectitude; a mental or moral twist.
Obliterate, ob-lit'ė-rāt, *vt.* To blot out; to efface; to cause to be forgotten.
Obliteration, ob-lit'ė-rā"shon, *n.* Act of obliterating; effacement; extinction.
Oblivion, ob-li'vi-on, *n.* State of being forgotten; forgetfulness; act of forgetting.
Oblivious, ob-li'vi-us, *a.* That easily forgets; forgetful; causing forgetfulness.
Oblong, ob'long, *a.* Rectangular, and longer than broad.—*n.* An oblong figure.
Obloquy, ob'lō-kwi, *n.* Censorious speech; contumely; odium; infamy.
Obnoxious, ob-nok'shus, *a.* Odious; offensive; hateful; unpopular.
Oboe, ō'bō, *n.* A musical wind-instrument made of wood; a hautboy.
Obscene, ob-sēn', *a.* Indecent; offensive to chastity and delicacy; inauspicious.
Obscenely, ob-sēn'li, *adv.* In an obscene manner; impurely; unchastely.
Obscenity, ob-sen'i-ti, *n.* State or quality of being obscene; ribaldry; lewdness.
Obscurant, Obscurantist, ob-skū'rant, ob-skū'rant-ist, *n.* One who labours to prevent enlightenment, inquiry, or reform.
Obscurantism, ob-skū'rant-izm, *n.* The system or principles of an obscurant.
Obscuration, ob-skūr-ā'shon, *n.* Act of obscuring; state of being obscured.
Obscure, ob-skūr', *a.* Darkened; dim; not easily understood; abstruse; unknown to fame; indistinct.—*vt.* (obscuring, obscured). To darken; to make less visible, legible, or intelligible; to tarnish.
Obscurely, ob-skūr'li, *adv.* In an obscure manner; not clearly; indirectly.
Obscurity, ob-skū'ri-ti, *n.* State or quality of being obscure; darkness.
Obsecrate, ob'sē-krāt, *vt.* To beseech; to entreat; to supplicate.
Obsecration, ob-sē-krā'shon, *n.* Entreaty.
Obsequies, ob'se-kwiz, *n.pl.* Funeral rites and solemnities.
Obsequious, ob-sē'kwi-us, *a.* Promptly obedient or submissive; compliant; fawning.
Observable, ob-zėrv'a-bl, *a.* That may be observed; worthy of notice; remarkable.
Observably, ob-zėrv'a-bli, *adv.* In a manner worthy of observation.
Observance, ob-zėrv'ans, *n.* Act of observing; respect; performance of rites, &c.; rule of practice; thing to be observed.
Observant, ob-zėrv'ant, *a.* Observing; regardful; carefully attentive.
Observantly, ob-zėrv'ant-li, *adv.* In an observant manner.
Observation, ob-zėr-vā'shon, *n.* The act, power, or habit of observing; information or notion gained by observing; a remark; due performance.
Observatory, ob-zėr'va-to-ri, *n.* A place for astronomical observations; place of outlook.
Observe, ob-zėrv', *vt.* (observing, observed). To take notice of; to behold with attention; to remark; to keep religiously; to celebrate; to comply with; to practise.—*vi.* To remark; to be attentive.
Observer, ob-zėrv'er, *n.* One who observes; a spectator; one who observes phenomena for scientific purposes.
Observing, ob-zėrv'ing, *p.a.* Given to observation; attentive.
Observingly, ob-zėrv'ing-li, *adv.* With observation; attentively; carefully.
Obsession, ob-sesh'on, *n.* Act of besieging; persistent attack; state of being beset.
Obsolescent, ob-sō-les'ent, *a.* Becoming obsolete; passing into desuetude.
Obsolete, ob'sō-lēt, *a.* Antiquated; out of date; rudimentary.
Obstacle, ob'sta-kl, *n.* A stoppage; hindrance; obstruction; impediment.
Obstetric, Obstetrical, ob-stet'rik, ob-stet'rik-al, *a.* Pertaining to midwifery.
Obstetrician, ob-stet-rish'an, *n.* One skilled in obstetrics; an accoucheur.
Obstetrics, ob-stet'riks, *n.* The science or art of midwifery.
Obstinacy, ob'sti-na-si, *n.* State or quality of being obstinate; inflexibility; pertinacity.
Obstinate, ob'sti-nāt, *a.* Inflexible; stubborn; fixed firmly in opinion or resolution.
Obstinately, ob'sti-nāt-li, *adv.* In an obstinate manner; stubbornly; pertinaciously.
Obstreperous, ob-strep'ėr-us, *a.* Making a tumultuous noise; loud; noisy; clamorous.
Obstruct, ob-strukt', *vt.* To block up, as a way or passage; to impede; to hinder in passing; to retard; to interrupt.
Obstruction, ob-struk'shon, *n.* Act of ob-

structing; that which impedes progress; obstacle; impediment; check.
Obstructionist, ob-struk'shon-ist, *n.* One who practises obstruction; an obstructive.
Obstructive, ob-strukt'iv, *a.* Hindering; causing impediment.—*n.* One who hinders the transaction of business.
Obstruent, ob'stry-ent, *a.* Obstructing.—*n.* Anything that obstructs the natural passages in the body.
Obtain, ob-tān', *vt.* To get possession of; to acquire; to earn.—*vi.* To be received in common use; to prevail; to hold good.
Obtainable, ob-tān'a-bl, *a.* That may be obtained, procured, or gained.
Obtest, ob-test', *vt.* To call upon earnestly; to implore; to supplicate.
Obtestation, ob-test'ā-shon, *n.* Entreaty.
Obtrude, ob-tröd', *vt.* (obtruding, obtruded). To thrust prominently forward; to offer with unreasonable importunity.—*vi.* To enter when not desired.
Obtruder, ob-tröd'ėr, *n.* One who obtrudes.
Obtrusion, ob-trö'zhon, *n.* Act of obtruding; a thrusting upon others by force or unsolicited.
Obtrusive, ob-trö'siv, *a.* Disposed to obtrude; forward.
Obtrusively, ob-trö'siv-li, *adv.* In an obtrusive manner.
Obturate, ob'tū-rāt, *vt.* To block or plug up, as a passage.
Obtuse, ob-tūs', *a.* Not pointed or acute; greater than a right angle; dull; stupid.
Obverse, ob'vėrs, *n.* and *a.* That side of a coin or medal which has the face or head or principal device on it.
Obviate, ob'vi-āt, *vt.* (obviating, obviated). To meet, as difficulties or objections; to get over; to remove.
Obvious, ob'vi-us, *a.* Easily discovered, seen, or understood; evident; manifest.
Obviously, ob'vi-us-li, *adv.* In an obvious manner; quite clearly; evidently.
Obvolute, ob'vo-lūt, *a.* Rolled or turned in.
Ocarina, ō-ka-rē'na, *n.* A small musical wind-instrument of terra cotta, &c.
Occasion, ok-kā'zhon, *n.* Occurrence; incident; opportunity; cause; need; juncture.—*vt.* To cause; to produce.
Occasional, ok-kā'zhon-al, *a.* Occurring at times; made as opportunity admits; incidental.
Occasionally, ok-kā'zhon-al-li, *adv.* At times; sometimes but not often; not regularly.
Occident, ok'si-dent, *n.* The west.
Occidental, ok-si-dent'al, *a.* Western.
Occipital, ok'si'pit-al, *a.* Pertaining to the occiput, or back part of the head.
Occiput, ok'si-put, *n.* That part of the skull which forms the hind part of the head.
Occult, ok-kult', *a.* Hidden; invisible and mysterious.—*vt.* To conceal by way of eclipse.
Occultation, ok-kult-ā'shon, *n.* A hiding or concealing; eclipse of a heavenly body.
Occupancy, ok'kū-pan-si, *n.* Act of occupying; a holding in possession; term during which one is occupant.
Occupant, ok'kū-pant, *n.* An occupier.
Occupation, ok-kū-pā'shon, *n.* Act of occupying; act of taking possession; tenure; business; employment; vocation.
Occupier, ok'kū-pī-ėr, *n.* One who occupies; one who holds possession; an occupant.
Occupy, ok'kū-pī, *vt.* (occupying, occupied). To take possession of; to hold and use; to cover or fill; to employ; to engage: often *refl.*—*vi.* To be an occupant.
Occur, ok-kėr', *vi.* (occurring, occurred). To come to the mind; to happen; to be met with; to be found here and there.
Occurrence, ok-ku'rens, *n.* The act of occurring or taking place; any incident or accidental event; an observed instance.
Ocean, ō'shan, *n.* The vast body of water which covers more than three-fifths of the globe; the sea; one of the great areas into which the sea is divided; any immense expanse.—*a.* Pertaining to the great sea.
Oceanic, ō-shē-an'ik, *a.* Pertaining to the ocean; found or formed in the ocean.
Ocellate, Ocellated, ō-sel'lāt, ō-sel'lāt-ed, *a.* Resembling an eye; studded with little eyes.
Ocellus, ō-sel'lus, *n.*; pl. **-li.** One of the minute simple eyes of insects, spiders, &c.
Ochlocracy, ok-lok'ra-si, *n.* The rule of the mob or multitude.
Ochre, ō'kėr, *n.* A clay used as a pigment, of a pale-yellow or brownish-red colour.
Ochry, Ochreous, ō'kėr-i, ō'krē-us, *a.* Consisting of, resembling, or containing ochre.
Octagon, ok'ta-gon, *n.* A plane figure having eight angles and sides.
Octagonal, ok-tag'on-al, *a.* Having eight angles and eight sides.
Octahedral, ok-ta-hed'ral, *a.* Having eight equal faces or sides.
Octahedron, ok-ta-hed'ron, *n.* A solid figure having eight faces or sides.
Octangular, ok-tang'gū-lėr, *a.* Having eight angles.
Octave, ok'tāv, *a.* Eighth; denoting eight.—*n.* An eighth; the eighth day or the eight days after a church festival; a stanza of eight lines; in *music*, an interval of seven degrees or twelve semitones.
Octavo, ok-tā'vō, *n.* A book in which the sheets are folded into eight leaves.—*a.* Having eight leaves to the sheet: written 8*vo*.
Octennial, ok-ten'i-al, *a.* Happening every eighth year; lasting eight years.
October, ok-tō'bėr, *n.* The tenth month of the year.
Octogenarian, ok'tō-je-nā"ri-an, *n.* One between eighty and ninety years of age.
Octopus, ok'tō-pus, *n.*; pl. **-puses.** A two-gilled cuttle-fish, having eight arms furnished with suckers.
Octoroon, ok-tō-rön', *n.* The offspring of a quadroon and a white person.
Octosyllabic, ok'tō-sil-lab"ik, *a.* Consisting of eight syllables.
Octroi, ok-trwä, *n.* A duty levied at the gates of French cities on goods brought in.
Ocular, ok'ū-lėr, *a.* Pertaining to or depending on the eye; received by actual sight.
Ocularly, ok'ū-lėr-li, *adv.* In an ocular manner; by the eye, sight, or actual view.
Oculist, ok'ū-list, *n.* One skilled in diseases of the eyes.
Odalisk, Odalisque, ō'da-lisk, *n.* A female slave or concubine in a seraglio.
Odd, od, *a.* Not even; not exactly divisible by 2; not included with others; incidental; casual; belonging to a broken set; queer.
Oddfellow, od'fel-ō, *n.* A member of a friendly society, modelled on freemasonry.

Oddity, od'i-ti, *n.* Singularity; a singular person or thing.
Oddly, od'li, *adv.* In an odd manner; not evenly; strangely; unusually; uncouthly.
Oddment, od'ment, *n.* A remnant.
Odds, odz, *n. sing.* or *pl.* Inequality; excess; difference in favour of one; advantage; amount by which one bet exceeds another.
Ode, ōd, *n.* A song; a short poem; a lyric poem of a lofty cast.
Odious, ō'di-us, *a.* Hateful; offensive; disgusting.
Odiously, ō'di-us-li, *adv.* Hatefully.
Odium, ō'di-um, *n.* Hatred; dislike; the quality that provokes hatred, blame, &c.
Odontoid, ō-don'toid, *a.* Tooth-like.
Odontology, ō-don-tol'o-ji, *n.* The science which treats of the teeth.
Odoriferous, ō-dor-if'ėr-us, *a.* Diffusing smell; perfumed; fragrant.
Odorous, ō'dor-us, *a.* Emitting a scent or odour; sweet of scent; fragrant.
Odour, Odor, ō'dor, *n.* Any scent or smell; fragrance; reputation.
Odourless, ō'dor-les, *a.* Free from odour.
Œcumenic. *See* ECUMENIC.
O'er, ō'ėr, contracted from *over.*
Œsophagus, ē-sof'a-gus, *n.* The gullet; the canal through which food and drink pass to the stomach.
Of, ov, *prep.* Denoting source, cause, motive, possession, quality, condition, material; concerning, relating to, about.
Off, of, *adv.* Away; distant; not on; from; not toward.—**Well off, ill off,** in good or bad circumstances.—*a.* Distant; farther away; as applied to horses; right hand.—*prep.* Not on; away from; to seaward from. —*interj.* Begone!
Offal, of'al, *n.* The parts of an animal butchered which are unfit for use; refuse.
Offence, of-fens', *n.* Injury; an affront, insult, or wrong; displeasure; transgression of law; misdemeanour.
Offend, of-fend', *vt.* To displease; to shock; to cause to sin or neglect duty.—*vi.* To sin; to commit a fault; to cause dislike or anger.
Offender, of-fend'ėr, *n.* One who offends; a transgressor; a delinquent; a trespasser.
Offensive, of-fens'iv, *a.* Causing offence; causing displeasure or annoyance; disgusting; impertinent; used in attack; aggressive.—*n.* Act or posture of attack.
Offensively, of-fens'iv-li, *adv.* In an offensive manner; disagreeably; aggressively.
Offer, of'ėr, *vt.* To present for acceptance or rejection; to tender; to bid, as a price or wages.—*vi.* To present itself; to declare a willingness; to make an attempt.—*n.* Act of offering; act of bidding a price; the sum bid.
Offerer, of'ėr-ėr, *n.* One who offers.
Offering, of'ėr-ing, *n.* Act of one who offers; that which is offered; a gift; oblation.
Offertory, of'ėr-to-ri, *n.* Sentences read or repeated in church while the alms or gifts are collecting; the alms collected.
Off-hand, of'hand, *a.* Done without thinking or hesitation; unpremeditated.—*adv.* On the spur of the moment; promptly.
Office, of'is, *n.* Special duty or business; high employment or position under government; function; service; a formulary of devotion; a place where official or professional business is done; persons intrusted with certain duties; persons who transact business in an office; *pl.* kitchens, outhouses, &c., of a mansion or farm.
Office-bearer, of'is-bār-ėr, *n.* One who holds office.
Officer, of'is-ėr, *n.* A person invested with an office; one who holds a commission in the army or navy.—*vt.* To furnish with officers.
Official, of-fi'shal, *a.* Pertaining to an office or public duty; made by virtue of authority. —*n.* One invested with an office of a public nature.
Officialism, of-fi'shal-izm, *n.* Excessive official routine.
Officially, of-fi'shal-li, *adv.* In an official manner or capacity; by authority.
Officiate, of-fi'shi-āt, *vi.* To perform official duties; to act in an official capacity.
Officinal, of-fi'si-nal, *a.* Used in a shop, or belonging to it; used in the preparation of recognized medicines sold by apothecaries.
Officious, of-fi'shus, *a.* Troublesome in trying to serve; intermeddling.
Officiously, of-fi'shus-li, *adv.* In an officious manner; with forward zeal; meddlesomely.
Offing, of'ing, *n.* That part of the sea nearer to the horizon than to the shore.
Offscouring, of-skour'ing, *n.* Refuse.
Offset, of'set, *n.* A shoot or scion; a sum or amount set off against another as an equivalent; a contrast or foil.—*vt.* To set off, as one account against another.
Offshoot, of'shöt, *n.* A shoot of a plant; anything growing out of another.
Offspring, of'spring, *n. sing.* or *pl.* That which springs from a stock or parent; a child or children; progeny; issue.
Oft, oft, *adv.* Often: *poet.*
Often, of'n, *adv.* Frequently; many times.
Oftentimes, of'n-tīmz, *adv.* Often.
Ofttimes, oft'tīmz, *adv.* Frequently; often.
Ogee, ō-jē', *n.* An architectural moulding, with an outline like the letter *s.*
Ogham, og'am, *n.* A kind of writing practised by the ancient Irish.
Ogle, ō'gl, *vt.* (ogling, ogled). To view with side glances.—*n.* A side glance or look.
Ogler, ō'glėr, *n.* One who ogles.
Ogre, ō'gėr, *n.* A monster in fairy tales, who lived on human flesh; one like an ogre.
Ogress, ō'gres, *n.* A female ogre.
Oh, ō, *exclam.* (*See* O.) Denoting surprise, pain, sorrow, or anxiety.
Ohm, ōm, *n.* The unit of electric resistance.
Oil, oil, *n.* An unctuous inflammable liquid drawn from various animal and vegetable substances; a similar substance of mineral origin; an oil-colour.—*vi.* To smear or rub over with oil.
Oil-cake, oil'kāk, *n.* A cake of compressed linseed, rape, or other seed from which oil has been extracted.
Oil-cloth, oil'kloth, *n.* Painted canvas for floor-covering, &c.; floor-cloth.
Oil-colour, oil'kul-ėr, *n.* A pigment made by grinding a colouring substance in oil.
Oiler, oil'ėr, *n.* One who oils; something used for oiling machinery.
Oil-painting, oil'pānt-ing, *n.* Art of painting with oil-colours; picture painted in oil-colours.
Oil-skin, oil'skin, *n.* Waterproof cloth.
Oily, oil'i, *a.* Consisting of, containing, or resembling oil; unctuous; hypocritically pious.

Ointment, oint'ment, *n.* Any soft, unctuous substance used for smearing the body or a diseased part; an unguent.
Old, ōld, *a.* Grown up to maturity and strength; aged; of some particular age; long made or used; not new or fresh; ancient; antiquated. —**Of old,** long ago; in ancient times.
Olden, ōld'n, *a.* Old; ancient.
Old-fashioned, ōld-fa'shond, *a.* Characterized by antiquated fashion; aping old people.
Oldish, ōld'ish, *a.* Somewhat old.
Oleaginous, ō-lē-a'jin-us, *a.* Oily; unctuous.
Oleander, ō-lē-an'dėr, *n.* An evergreen flowering shrub.
Oleograph, ō'lē-ō-graf, *n.* A picture produced in oils by a process analogous to lithographic printing.
Olfactory, ol-fak'to-ri, *a.* Pertaining to smelling; having the sense of smelling.—*n.* An organ of smelling.
Oligarch, o'li-gärk, *n.* One of a few persons in power; an aristocrat.
Oligarchic, Oligarchical, o-li-gärk'ik, o-li-gärk'ik-al, *a.* Pertaining to oligarchy.
Oligarchy, o'li-gär-ki, *n.* Government in which the supreme power is in a few hands; those who form such a class or body.
Olio, ō'li-o, *n.* A dish of meat boiled or stewed; medley; miscellany.
Olive, o'liv, *n.* An evergreen tree; its fruit, from which a valuable oil is expressed; the colour of the olive; the emblem of peace.—*a.* Relating to, or of the colour of the olive.
Olympiad, ō-lim'pi-ad, *n.* A period of four years reckoned from one celebration of the Olympic games to another, the first Olympiad beginning 776 B.C.
Olympian, Olympic, ō-lim'pi-an, ō-lim'pik, *a.* Pertaining to Olympus, or to Olympia, in Greece; relating to the Greek games celebrated at Olympia.
Ombre, om'bėr, *n.* An old game at cards, usually played by three persons.
Omega, ō'me-ga or ō-me'ga, *n.* The last letter of the Greek alphabet, long *o*; the last, or the ending.
Omelet, o'me-let, *n.* A kind of pancake or fritter made with eggs, &c.
Omen, ō'men, *n.* An event thought to portend good or evil; an augury; presage.—*vi.* To augur; to betoken.—*vt.* To predict.
Omened, ō'mend, *p.a.* Containing an omen.
Ominous, o'min-us, *a.* Containing an omen, and especially an ill omen; inauspicious.
Ominously, o'min-us-li, *adv.* In an ominous manner; with ill omen.
Omissible, ō-mis'i-bl, *a.* Capable of being omitted.
Omission, ō-mi'shon, *n.* Act of omitting; neglect or failure to do something required; failure to insert or mention; something omitted.
Omissive, ō-mis'iv, *a.* Omitting; neglecting.
Omit, ō-mit', *vt.* (omitting, omitted). To pass over or neglect; not to insert or mention.
Omnibus, om'ni-bus, *n.* A large vehicle for conveying passengers; a book which contains a variety of items.
Omnifarious, om-ni-fā'ri-us, *a.* Of all varieties, forms, or kinds.
Omnipotence, om-nip'ō-tens, *n.* Almighty or unlimited power; an attribute of God.
Omnipotent, om-nip'ō-tent, *a.* All-powerful; almighty; possessing unlimited power.
Omnipotently, om-nip'ō-tent-li, *adv.* In an omnipotent manner.
Omnipresence, om-ni-prez'ens, *n.* Presence in every place at the same time.
Omnipresent, om-ni-prez'ent, *a.* Present in all places at the same time; ubiquitous.
Omniscience, Omnisciency, om-ni'shi-ens, om-ni'shi-en-si, *n.* The faculty of knowing all things; universal knowledge.
Omniscient, om-ni'shi-ent, *a.* Knowing all things; having universal knowledge.
Omnisciently, om-ni'shi-ent-li, *adv.* By omniscience.
Omnium-gatherum, om'ni-um-gaᴛʜ''ėr-um, *n.* A miscellaneous collection.
Omnivorous, om-niv'or-us, *a.* All-devouring; eating food of every kind.
Omphalic, om-fal'ik, *a.* Pertaining to the navel.
On, on, *prep.* Above and touching; by contact with the surface or upper part; in addition to; at or near; immediately after and as a result; in reference or relation to; toward or so as to affect; at the peril of; among the staff of; pointing to a state, occupation, &c.—*adv.* Onward; in continuance; adhering; not off.
Once, wuns, *adv.* One time; formerly; immediately after; as soon as.—**At once,** all together; suddenly; forthwith.
Oncoming, on'kum-ing, *a.* Approaching; nearing.—*n.* Approach.
One, wun, *a.* Being but a single thing or a unit; closely united; forming a whole; single. —*n.* The first of the simple units; the symbol representing this (= 1).—**At one,** in union or concord.—*pron.* Any single person; any man; any person; a thing; particular thing.
Oneness, wun'nes, *n.* State or quality of being one; singleness; individuality; unity.
Onerary, on'e-ra-ri, *a.* Fitted for the carriage of burdens; comprising a burden.
Onerous, on'ė-rus, *a.* Burdensome; heavy.
Onerously, on'ė-rus-li, *adv.* So as to burden or oppress.
Oneself, wun-self', *pron.* Oneself; one's own person.
One-sided, wun-sīd'ed, *a.* Having one side only; limited to one side; partial; unfair.
Ongoing, on'gō-ing, *n.* A going on; conduct; behaviour; generally in *pl.*
Onion, un'yun, *n.* A plant with a bulbous root, used as an article of food.
Onlooker, on'luk-ėr, *n.* A spectator.
Only, ōn'li, *a.* Single; sole; alone.—*adv.* For one purpose alone; simply; merely; solely.—*conj.* But; excepting that.
Onomatopœia, on'o-ma-tō-pē''a, *n.* The formation of words by imitation of sounds.
Onomatopoetic, Onomatopœic, on'o-ma-tō-pō-et''ik, on'o-ma-tō-pē''ik, *a.* Pertaining to or formed by onomatopœia.
Onrush, on'rush, *n.* A rapid onset.
Onset, on'set, *n.* A violent attack; assault.
Onslaught, on'slat, *n.* An attack; onset.
Ontology, on-tol'o-ji, *n.* The doctrine of being; that part of metaphysics which treats of things or existences.
Onus, ō'nus, *n.* A burden.
Onward, Onwards, on'wėrd, on'wėrdz, *adv.* Forward; on; in advance.
Onward, *a.* Advanced or advancing; progressive; improved.
Onyx, o'niks, *n.* A semi-pellucid gem with

variously-coloured veins, a variety of quartz; an agate with layers of chalcedony.

Oolite, ō'ol-it, *n.* A species of limestone; a series of strata, comprehending limestones, &c., which underlie the chalk formation.

Oolitic, ō-o-lit'ik, *a.* Pertaining to oolite; composed of oölite; resembling oolite.

Oology, ō-ol'o-ji, *n.* The study of birds' eggs.

Ooze, öz, *n.* A soft flow, as of water; soft mud or slime; liquor of a tan-vat.—*vi.* (oozing, oozed). To flow or issue forth gently; to percolate.—*vt.* To emit in the shape of moisture.

Oozy, öz'i, *a.* Miry; containing soft mud.

Opacity, ō-pas'i-ti, *n.* State or quality of being opaque.

Opal, ō'pal, *n.* A precious stone, which exhibits changeable reflections of green, blue, yellow, and red.

Opalescent, ō-pal-es'ent, *a.* Resembling opal; having the iridescent tints of opal.

Opaline, ō'pal-in, *a.* Pertaining to or like opal.—*n.* A semi-translucent glass.

Opaque, ō-pāk', *a.* Not transparent.

Ope, ōp, *vt.* and *i.* To open: *poet.*

Open, ō'pn, *a.* Not shut, covered, or blocked; not restricted; accessible; public; spread out; free, liberal, bounteous; candid; clear; exposed; fully prepared; attentive; amenable; not settled; enunciated with a full utterance.—*n.* An open or clear space.—*vt.* To make open; to unclose; to cut into; to spread out; to begin; to make public; to declare open; to reveal.—*vi.* To unclose itself; to be parted; to begin.

Opener, ō'pn-ėr, *n.* One who or that which opens.

Open-handed, ō'pn-hand-ed, *a.* Having an open hand; generous; liberal.

Open-hearted, ō'pn-härt-ed, *a.* Candid; frank; generous.

Opening, ō'pn-ing, *a.* First in order; beginning.—*n.* Act of one who or that which opens; an open place; aperture; beginning; vacancy; opportunity of commencing a business, &c.

Openly, ō'pn-li, *adv.* In an open manner; publicly; candidly; plainly; evidently.

Opera, o'pe-ra, *n.* A dramatic composition set to music and sung and acted on the stage; a theatre where operas are performed.

Opera-glass, o'pe-ra-gläs, *n.* A small binocular telescope used in theatres, &c.

Operate, o'pe-rāt, *vi.* (operating, operated). To work; to act; to produce effect; to exert moral power or influence.—*vt.* To act; to effect; to drive, as a machine.

Operatic, o-pe-rat'ik, *a.* Pertaining to the opera; resembling the opera.

Operation, o-pe-rā'shon, *n.* Act or process of operating; agency; action; process; surgical proceeding to which the human body is subjected; movements of troops or war-ships.

Operative, o'pe-rāt-iv, *a.* That operates; producing the effect; having to do with manual or other operations.—*n.* One who works or labours; an artisan.

Operator, o'pe-rāt-ėr, *n.* One who operates.

Operculum, ō-pėr'kū-lum, *n.* A little lid or cover, especially applied in zoology and botany.

Operetta, op-e-ret'ta, *n.* A short musical drama of a light character.

Operose, o'pe-rōs, *a.* Tedious; troublesome.

Ophicleide, o'fi-klīd, *n.* A large brass wind-instrument.

Ophidian, ō-fid'i-an, *a.* Pertaining to serpents.

Ophiology, of-i-ol'o-ji, *n.* That branch of zoology which treats of serpents.

Ophthalmia, of-thal'mi-a, *n.* Inflammation of the eye or its appendages.

Ophthalmic, of-thal'mik, *a.* Pertaining to the eye or to ophthalmia.

Ophthalmist, of-thal'mist, *n.* An oculist.

Opiate, ō'pi-āt, *n.* Any medicine that contains opium; a narcotic.

Opine, ō-pīn', *vi.* and *t.* To think; to suppose.

Opinion, ō-pin'yon, *n.* A judgment or belief; notion; persuasion; estimation.

Opinionated, ō-pin'yon-āt-ed, *a.* Stiff or obstinate in opinion; conceited.

Opinionative, ō-pin'yon-āt-iv, *a.* Unduly attached to one's own opinions; opinionated.

Opium, ō'pi-um, *n.* The inspissated juice of a kind of poppy, one of the most energetic of narcotics.

Opodeldoc, op-ō-del'dok, *n.* A solution of soap in alcohol, with the addition of camphor and essential oils, used as a liniment.

Opossum, ō-pos'um, *n.* The name of several marsupial mammals of America.

Opponent, op-pō'nent, *a.* Opposing; antagonistic; opposite.—*n.* One who opposes; an adversary; an antagonist.

Opportune, op-or-tūn', *a.* Seasonable; timely; well-timed; convenient.

Opportunely, op-or-tūn'li, *adv.* In an opportune manner; seasonably.

Opportunist, op-or-tūn'ist, *n.* One who waits upon favourable opportunities; a politician more influenced by place and power than principle.

Opportunity, op-or-tūn'i-ti, *n.* A fit or convenient time; favourable conjuncture.

Oppose, op-pōz', *vt.* (opposing, opposed). To place over against; to place as an obstacle; to act against; to resist; to check.—*vi.* To make objections; to act obstructively.

Opposed, op-pōzd', *p.a.* Adverse; hostile.

Opposer, op-pōz'ėr, *n.* One who opposes.

Opposite, op'pō-zit, *a.* Facing; adverse; contrary; inconsistent.—*n.* An adversary.

Oppositely, op'pō-zit-li, *adv.* So as to be opposite; adversely; against each other.

Opposition, op-pō-zi'shon, *n.* Act of opposing; attempt to check or defeat; contradiction; inconsistency; the collective body of opponents of a ministry.

Oppositionist, op-pō-zi'shon-ist, *n.* One who belongs to an opposition.

Oppress, op-pres', *vt.* To press or weigh down unduly; to harass; to overpower; to overburden.

Oppression, op-pres'shon, *n.* Act of oppressing; severity; hardship; dulness of spirits.

Oppressive, op-pres'iv, *a.* Burdensome; unjustly severe; tyrannical.

Oppressor, op-pres'ėr, *n.* One who oppresses; a cruel governor or taskmaster.

Opprobrious, op-prō'bri-us, *a.* Containing opprobrium; scurrilous; abusive.

Opprobrium, op-prō'bri-um, *n.* Scurrilous language; disgrace; scurrility; infamy.

Oppugn, op-pūn', *vt.* To attack by arguments or the like; to oppose or resist.

Oppugnant, op-pug'nant, *a.* Resisting; opposing; hostile.

Optative, op'tā-tiv, *a.* Expressing a desire; designating that mood of the verb in which desire is expressed.—*n.* The optative mood of a verb.

Optic, op'tik, *a.* Pertaining to sight; relating to the science of optics.—*n.* An organ of sight; an eye.

Optical, op'tik-al, *a.* Relating to the science of optics; optic.

Optician, op-ti'shan, *n.* A person skilled in optics; one who makes or sells optical instruments.

Optics, op'tiks, *n.* The science which treats of the nature and properties of light and vision, optical instruments, &c.

Optimism, op'tim-izm, *n.* The opinion or doctrine that everything is for the best; tendency to take the most hopeful view.

Optimist, op'tim-ist, *n.* One who believes in optimism.

Optimistic, op-tim-ist'ik, *a.* Relating to or characterized by optimism.

Option, op'shon, *n.* Choice; free choice; power of choosing.

Optional, op'shon-al, *a.* Left to one's own option or choice; depending on choice.

Opulence, op'ū-lens, *n.* Wealth; riches.

Opulent, op'ū-lent, *a.* Wealthy; rich.

Opulently, op'ū-lent-li, *adv.* In an opulent manner; richly.

Opuscule, Opuscle, ō-pus'kūl, ō-pus'l, *n.* A small work; a little book.

Or, or, *conj.* A particle that marks an alternative, and frequently corresponds with *either* and *whether*.—*adv.* Ere; before.—*n.* Heraldic name for gold.

Oracle, o'ra-kl, *n.* Among the Greeks and Romans, the answer of a god to an inquiry respecting some future event; place where the answers were given; the sanctuary of the ancient Jews; any person reputed uncommonly wise; a wise or authoritative utterance.

Oracular, ō-rak'ū-lėr, *a.* Pertaining to or like an oracle; uttering oracles; authoritative; sententious; ambiguous.

Oracularly, ō-rak'ū-lėr-li, *adv.* In an oracular manner; authoritatively.

Oral, ō'ral, *a.* Pertaining to the mouth; spoken, not written.

Orally, ō'ral-li, *adv.* In an oral manner; by word of mouth; verbally.

Orange, o'ranj, *n.* An evergreen fruit-tree, and also its fruit; the colour of this fruit, a reddish yellow.—*a.* Belonging to an orange; coloured as an orange.

Orangeman, o'ranj-man, *n.* A member of a society of Irish Protestants.

Orange-peel, o'ranj-pēl, *n.* The rind of an orange separated from the fruit; the peel of the bitter orange dried and candied.

Orangery, o'ranj-e-ri, *n.* A place for raising oranges; a house for orange-trees.

Orang-utan, Orang-outang, o-rang'ö-tan, o-rang'ö-tang, *n.* One of the largest of the anthropoid or manlike apes.

Orate, ō'rāt, *vi.* (orating, orated). To make an oration; to talk loftily; to harangue.

Oration, ō-rā'shon, *n.* A formal public speech; an eloquent speech or address.

Orator, o'ra-tėr, *n.* A public speaker; a skilled or eloquent speaker.

Oratorical, o-ra-to'rik-al, *a.* Pertaining to an orator or to oratory; rhetorical.

Oratorio, o-ra-tō'ri-ō, *n.* A sacred musical composition.

Oratory, o'ra-to-ri, *n.* A small chapel; the art of public speaking; eloquence.

Orb, orb, *n.* A sphere; a heavenly body; a circular disc; a hollow globe.—*vt.* To encircle.

Orbed, orbd, *p.a.* Round; circular.

Orbicular, or-bik'ū-lėr, *a.* In the form of an orb; circular; spherical.

Orbit, or'bit, *n.* The path of a planet or comet; cavity in which the eye is situated.

Orbital, or'bit-al, *a.* Pertaining to an orbit.

Orchard, or'chėrd, *n.* An inclosure devoted to the culture of fruit-trees.

Orchestra, or'kes-tra, *n.* That part of the Greek theatre allotted to the chorus; that part of a theatre, &c., appropriated to the musicians; a body of musicians.

Orchestral, or-kes'tral, *a.* Pertaining to an orchestra; suitable for or performed in the orchestra.

Orchestration, or-kes-trā'shon, *n.* Arrangement of music for an orchestra; instrumentation.

Orchid, Orchis, or'kid, or'kis, *n.* A perennial plant with tuberous fleshy root and beautiful flowers.

Ordain, or-dān', *vt.* To establish authoritatively; to decree; to invest with ministerial or sacerdotal functions.

Ordainment, or-dān'ment, *n.* The act of ordaining; appointment.

Ordeal, or'dē-al, *n.* A trial by fire and water; severe trial or strict test.

Order, or'dėr, *n.* Regular disposition; proper state; established method; public tranquillity; command; instruction to supply goods or to pay money; rank, class, division, or dignity; a religious fraternity; division of natural objects; *pl.* clerical character, specially called holy orders.—**In order,** for the purpose.—*vt.* To place in order; to direct; to command; to give an order or commission for.—*vi.* To give command.

Orderly, or'dėr-li, *a.* In accordance with good order; well ordered; regular; on duty.—*n.* A private soldier or non-commissioned officer, who attends on a superior officer.—*adv.* According to due order.

Ordinal, or'din-al, *a.* Expressing order or succession.—*n.* A number denoting order (as *first*); a book containing an ordination service.

Ordinance, or'din-ans, *n.* That which is ordained; law, statute, edict, decree.

Ordinarily, or'din-a-ri-li, *adv.* In an ordinary manner; usually; generally.

Ordinary, or'din-a-ri, *a.* Conformable to order; regular; customary; common; of little merit.—*n.* An ecclesiastical judge; a judge who takes cognizance of causes in his own right; an eating-house where the prices are settled.—**In ordinary,** in actual and constant service; statedly attending, as a physician; but a ship *in ordinary* is one laid up.

Ordinate, or'din-āt, *a.* Regular; methodical.—*n.* In *geometry*, a line of reference determining the position of a point.

Ordination, or-din-ā'shon, *n.* Act of ordaining; act of conferring sacerdotal power; act of settling a Presbyterian clergyman in a charge.

Ordnance, ord'nans, *n.* Cannon or great guns collectively; artillery.—**Ordnance survey,** the detailed survey of Britain.

Ordure, or'dūr, *n.* Dung; excrement.
Ore, ōr, *n.* A mineral substance from which metals are obtained by smelting; metal.
Organ, or'gan, *n.* An instrument or means; a part of an animal or vegetable by which some function is carried on; a medium of conveying certain opinions; a newspaper; the largest wind-instrument of music.
Organic, or-gan'ik, *a.* Pertaining to or acting as an organ; pertaining to the animal and vegetable worlds; organized; systematized.
Organically, or-gan'ik-al-li, *adv.* In an organic manner; by or with organs.
Organism, or'gan-izm, *n.* Organic structure; a body exhibiting organic life.
Organist, or'gan-ist, *n.* One who plays on the organ.
Organization, or'gan-i-zā"shon, *n.* Act or process of organizing; suitable disposition of parts for performance of vital functions.
Organize, or'gan-īz, *vt.* To give an organic structure to; to establish and systematize; to arrange so as to be ready for service.
Organizer, or'gan-iz-ėr, *n.* One who organizes, establishes, or systematizes.
Organon, Organum, or'ga-non, or'ga-num, *n.* A body of rules and canons for the direction of the scientific faculty.
Orgasm, or'gazm, *n.* Immoderate excitement or action.
Orgy, or'ji, *n.* A wild or frantic revel; a drunken party.
Oriel, ō'ri-el, *n.* A large projecting bay-window supported on brackets or corbels.
Orient, ō'ri-ent, *a.* Rising, as the sun; eastern; oriental; bright.—*n.* The East; lustre as that of a pearl.—*vt.* To define the position of; to cause to lie from east to west.
Oriental, ō-ri-ent'al, *a.* Eastern; from the east.—*n.* A native of some eastern country.
Orientalism, ō-ri-ent'al-izm, *n.* An eastern mode of thought or expression; erudition in oriental languages or literature.
Orientalist, ō-ri-ent'al-ist, *n.* One versed in the eastern languages and literature.
Orientate, ō-ri-ent'āt, *vt.* To orient.
Orientation, ōr'i-en-tā"shon, *n.* A turning towards the east; position east and west.
Orifice, o'ri-fis, *n.* The mouth or aperture of a tube, pipe, &c.; an opening; a vent.
Oriflamme, o'ri-flam, *n.* The ancient flag or royal standard of France.
Origin, o'ri-jin, *n.* Source; beginning; derivation; cause; root; foundation.
Original, ō-ri'jin-al, *a.* Pertaining to origin; primitive; first in order; having the power to originate; not copied.—*n.* Origin; source; first copy; model; that from which anything is translated or copied; a person of marked individuality.
Originality, ō-ri'jin-al"i-ti, *n.* Quality or state of being original; power of producing new thoughts, &c.
Originally, ō-ri'jin-al-li, *adv.* In an original manner; primarily; at first.
Originate, ō-ri'jin-āt, *vt.* (originating, originated). To give origin to; to produce.—*vi.* To have origin; to be begun.
Origination, ō-ri'jin-ā"shon, *n.* Act or mode of originating; first production.
Originator, ō-ri'jin-āt-ėr, *n.* One who or that which originates.
Oriole, ō'ri-ōl, *n.* A bird with golden plumage.
Orion, ō-rī'on, *n.* A constellation near the equator.
Orison, o'ri-zon, *n.* A prayer.
Orlop, or'lop, *n.* The lowest deck in a three-decker; sometimes a temporary deck.
Ormolu, or'mō-lū, *n.* A fine kind of brass made to imitate gold; gilt bronze.
Ornament, or'na-ment, *n.* That which adorns or embellishes; decoration.—*vt.* To decorate; to adorn.
Ornamental, or-na-ment'al, *a.* Serving to ornament; pertaining to ornament.
Ornamentation, or'na-men-tā"shon, *n.* Act of ornamenting; ornaments or decorations.
Ornate, or'nāt, *a.* Richly ornamented; adorned; of a florid character.
Ornately, or'nāt-li, *adv.* In an ornate manner.
Ornithological, or'ni-tho-loj"ik-al, *a.* Pertaining to ornithology.
Ornithologist, or-ni-thol'o-jist, *n.* A person who is skilled in ornithology.
Ornithology, or-ni-thol'o-ji, *n.* The science which treats of birds.
Orographic, Orographical, or-ō-graf'ik, or-ō-graf'ik-al, *a.* Relating to orography.
Orography, ō-rog'ra-fi, *n.* The scientific treatment of mountains; orology.
Orology, ō-rol'o-ji, *n.* Orography.
Orotund, ō'rō-tund, *a.* Characterized by fulness and clearness; rich and musical.
Orphan, or'fan, *n.* A child bereaved of father or mother, or of both.—*a.* Bereaved of parents.—*vt.* To reduce to being an orphan.
Orphanage, or'fan-āj, *n.* The state of an orphan; a home for orphans.
Orphanhood, or'fan-hụd, *n.* The state of being an orphan.
Orphean, or-fē'an, *a.* Pertaining to Orpheus; melodious.
Orpiment, or'pi-ment, *n.* A yellow mineral consisting of sulphur and arsenic.
Orrery, o're-ri, *n.* A machine exhibiting the motions, relative magnitudes, and distances of the bodies composing the solar system.
Orris, o'ris, *n.* A sort of gold or silver lace; a kind of iris.
Ort, ort, *n.* A scrap of food left; a fragment; a piece of refuse; commonly in *pl.*
Orthodox, or'thō-doks, *a.* Sound in opinion or doctrine; sound in religious doctrines; in accordance with sound doctrine.
Orthodoxly, or'thō-doks-li, *adv.* In an orthodox way; with soundness of faith.
Orthodoxy, or'thō-doks-i, *n.* Character or state of being orthodox; soundness of faith.
Orthoepic, Orthoepical, or-thō-ep'ik, or-thō-ep'ik-al, *a.* Pertaining to orthoepy.
Orthoepist, or'thō-ep-ist, *n.* One well skilled in pronunciation.
Orthoepy, or'thō-e-pi or or-thō'e-pi, *n.* Correct pronunciation of words.
Orthographer, or-thog'ra-fėr, *n.* One versed in orthography.
Orthographic, Orthographical, or-thō-graf'ik, or-thō-graf'ik-al, *a.* Pertaining to orthography.
Orthography, or-thog'ra-fi, *n.* The art of writing words with the proper letters; spelling.
Orthopter, Orthopteran, or-thop'tėr, or-thop'tėr-an, *n.* One of an order of insects including cockroaches, grasshoppers, and locusts.
Ortolan, or'tō-lan, *n.* A European bird of

the bunting family, esteemed for the delicacy of its flesh.
Oscillate, os'sil-lāt, *vi.* To swing; to vibrate; to vary or fluctuate.
Oscillation, os-sil-lā'shon, *n.* Act or state of oscillating; vibration.
Oscillatory, os'sil-la-to-ri, *a.* Oscillating; swinging; vibrating.
Oscitant, os'si-tant, *a.* Yawning; gaping; drowsy; sluggish.
Osculate, os'kū-lāt, *vt.* and *i.* To kiss; to touch, as curves.
Osculation, o-skū-lā'shon, *n.* Act of kissing; a kiss; a coming in contact.
Osier, ō'zhi-ėr, *n.* The name of various species of willow, employed in basket-making.—*a.* Made of osier or twigs; like osier.
Osmose, os'mōs, *n.* The tendency of fluids to pass through porous partitions and mix.
Osprey, os'prā, *n.* A kind of hawk or eagle which feeds on fish; one of its feathers.
Osseous, os'ē-us, *a.* Bony; like bone.
Ossicle, os'i-kl, *n.* A small bone.
Ossification, os'i-fi-kā"shon, *n.* The process of changing into a bony substance.
Ossifrage, os'i-frāj, *n.* The sea-eagle or osprey.
Ossify, os'i-fī, *vt.* and *i.* To change into bone, or into a substance of the hardness of bone.
Ostensible, os-ten'si-bl, *a.* Put forth as having a certain character, apparent and not real; pretended; professed.
Ostensibly, os-ten'si-bli, *adv.* In an ostensible manner; professedly.
Ostensive, os-ten'siv, *a.* Showing; exhibiting.
Ostentation, os-ten-tā'shon, *n.* Ambitious display; vain show; parade; pomp.
Ostentatious, os-ten-tā'shus, *a.* Characterized by ostentation; showy.
Osteology, os-tē-ol'o-ji, *n.* The science which treats of the bones and bone-tissue.
Osteopathy, os-tē-op'a-thi, *n.* A system of medical treatment, based on the view that the proper adjustment of the vital mechanism is a more important factor than chemical intake in the maintenance of health.
Ostracism, os'tra-sizm, *n.* A mode of political banishment in ancient Athens effected by public vote; expulsion.
Ostracize, os'tra-sīz, *vt.* To banish by ostracism; to expel; to banish from society.
Ostreaculture, os'trē-a-kul"tūr, *n.* The artificial cultivation of oysters.
Ostrich, os'trich, *n.* A large running bird of Africa, Arabia, and S. America, the largest of existing birds.
Other, uᴛʜ'ėr, *a.* and *pron.* Not the same; second of two; not this; opposite: often used reciprocally with *each.*
Otherwise, uᴛʜ'ėr-wīz, *adv.* In a different manner; not so; by other causes; in other respects.—*conj.* Else; but for this.
Otiose, ō'shi-ōs, *a.* Being at rest or ease; idle; unemployed; careless.
Otiosity, ō-shi-os'i-ti, *n.* The state or quality of being otiose; idleness or leisure.
Otology, ō-tol'o-ji, *n.* Knowledge of the ear and its diseases.
Ottava-rima, ot-tä'vä-rē-mä, *n.* A stanza of eight lines, the first six rhyming alternatively, the last two forming a couplet.
Otter, ot'ėr, *n.* An aquatic carnivorous animal resembling the weasel, but larger.
Otto, ot'tō. *See* Attar.
Ottoman, ot'tō-man, *a.* Pertaining to or derived from the Turks.—*n.* A Turk; a kind of couch introduced from Turkey.
Oubliette, ö'blē-et, *n.* A dungeon with an opening only at the top.
Ouch, ouch, *n.* The socket in which a precious stone is set; a brooch.
Ought, at, *n.* Aught.—*v.* To be held or bound in duty or moral obligation.
Ounce, ouns, *n.* The twelfth part of a pound troy, and the sixteenth of a pound avoirdupois; an Asiatic animal like a small leopard.
Our, our, *a.* or *pron.* Pertaining or belonging to us. **Ours** is used when no noun follows.
Ourself, our-self', *pron.* Used for *myself*, as a more dignified word, in the regal style.
Ourselves, our-selvz', *pron. pl.* We or us, not others: added to *we* by way of emphasis, but in the objective often without emphasis and reflexively.
Ousel, Ouzel, ö'zl, *n.* A blackbird; also other birds of the thrush family.
Oust, oust, *vt.* To eject; to turn out.
Out, out, *adv.* On or towards the outside; not in or within; forth; beyond usual limits; not in proper place; public; exhausted; deficient; not in employment; loudly; in error; at a loss; having taken her place as a woman in society.—*n.* One who is out; a nook or corner.—*vt.* To put out.—*interj.* Away! begone!
Out-and-out, out'and-out, *a.* Thorough; thorough-paced; absolute; complete.
Outbid, out-bid', *vt.* To bid more than another.
Outbreak, out'brāk, *n.* A breaking forth; eruption; sudden manifestation as of anger, disease, &c.
Outburst, out'bėrst, *n.* A bursting or breaking out; an outbreak.
Outcast, out'käst, *p.a.* Cast out; rejected.—*n.* An exile; one driven from home or country.
Outcome, out'kum, *n.* The issue; result; consequence.
Outcrop, out'krop, *n.* Exposure of strata at the surface of the ground.
Outcry, out'krī, *n.* A loud cry; exclamation; clamour; noisy opposition.
Outdistance, out-dis'tans, *vt.* To excel or leave behind in any competition.
Outdo, out-dö', *vt.* To excel; to surpass.
Outdoor, out'dōr, *a.* In the open air; being without the house.
Outdoors, out'dōrz, *adv.* Abroad; in the open air.
Outer, out'ėr, *a.* Being on the outside; external.—*n.* That part of a target beyond the circles surrounding the bull's-eye; a shot which hits this part.
Outermost, out'ėr-mōst, *a.* Being farthest out; being on the extreme external part.
Outfall, out'fal, *n.* Mouth of a river, drain, &c.
Outfit, out'fit, *n.* A fitting out, as for a voyage; equipment of one going abroad.
Outfitter, out'fit-ėr, *n.* One who makes an outfit; clothier, &c.
Outflank, out-flangk', *vt.* To manœuvre so as to attack in the flank; to get the better of.
Outflow, out'flō, *n.* Act of flowing out; efflux.
Outgeneral, out-jen'ė-ral, *vt.* To gain advantage over by superior military skill.

Outgo, out-gō′, *vt.* To go beyond; to excel. —*n.* out′gō. Expenditure.
Outgoing, out-gō′ing, *n.* Act of going out; expenditure; outlay.—*a.* Going out.
Outgrow, out-grō′, *vt.* To surpass in growth; to grow too great or old for anything.
Outgrowth, out′grōth, *n.* Excrescence; result.
Out-herod, out-her′od, *vt.* To excel in evil or enormity.
Out-house, out′hous, *n.* A small house or building near the main one.
Outing, out′ing, *n.* A short excursion; an airing; short time spent out-of-doors.
Outlandish, out-land′ish, *a.* Foreign; strange; uncouth; bizarre.
Outlast, out-läst′, *vt.* To last longer than.
Outlaw, out′la̧, *n.* A person excluded from the benefit of the law.—*vt.* To deprive of the benefit and protection of law; to proscribe.
Outlawry, out′la̧-ri, *n.* The putting of a man out of the protection of law.
Outlay, out′lā, *n.* Expenditure.
Outlet, out′let, *n.* Place by which anything is discharged; exit; a vent.
Outline, out′līn, *n.* The line by which a figure is defined; contour; general scheme. —*vt.* To draw the exterior line of; to sketch.
Outlive, out-liv′, *vt.* To survive.
Outlook, out′lu̧k, *n.* A looking out; vigilant watch; place of watch; prospect.
Outlying, out′lī-ing, *a.* Lying at a distance from the main body; being on the frontier.
Outmanœuvre, out-ma-nö′vėr, or -nū′vėr, *vt.* To surpass in manœuvring.
Outmarch, out-märch′, *vt.* To march so as to leave behind.
Outmost, out′mōst, *a.* Farthest outward.
Outnumber, out-num′bėr, *vt.* To exceed in number.
Out-of-door, out′ov-dōr, *a.* Open-air.
Out-of-doors, out′ov-dōrz, *adv.* Out of the house.
Out-of-the-way, out-ov-the-wā, *a.* Secluded; unusual; uncommon.
Out-patient, out′pā-shent, *n.* A patient not residing in a hospital, but who receives medical advice, &c., from the institution.
Outpost, out′pōst, *n.* A station at a distance from the main body of an army; troops placed at such a station.
Outpour, out-pōr′, *vt.* To pour out.
Output, out′pu̧t, *n.* Quantity of material produced within a specified time.
Outrage, out′rāj, *vt.* (outraging, outraged). To do extreme violence or injury to; to abuse; to commit a rape upon.—*n.* Excessive abuse; injurious violence.
Outrageous, out-rā′jus, *a.* Characterized by outrage; furious; exorbitant; atrocious.
Outrageously, out-rā′jus-li, *adv.* In an outrageous manner; furiously; excessively.
Outre, ö-trā, *a.* Extravagant; bizarre.
Outreach, out-rēch′, *vt.* To go or extend beyond.
Outride, out-rīd′, *vt.* To pass by riding.
Outrider, out′rīd-ėr, *n.* A servant on horseback who attends a carriage.
Outrigger, out′rig-ėr, *n.* A structure of spars, &c., rigged out from the side of a sailing-boat; a projecting bracket on a boat, with the rowlock at the extremity; a light boat provided with such apparatus.
Outright, out′rīt, *adv.* Completely; utterly.
Outrun, out-run′, *vt.* To exceed in running; to leave behind; to go beyond.
Outset, out′set, *n.* Beginning.
Outshine, out-shīn′, *vi.* To shine out or forth.—*vt.* To excel in lustre.
Outside, out′sīd, *n.* The external surface or superficies; exterior; the utmost; extreme estimate.—*a.* Exterior; superficial.—*prep.* On the outside of.
Outsider, out′sīd-ėr, *n.* One not belonging to a party, association or set; a horse which is not considered to have a chance of winning a race.
Outskirt, out′skėrt, *n.* Parts near the edge of an area; border; purlieu: generally in *pl.*
Outspan, out-span′, *vt.* and *i.* To unyoke (a team of oxen) from a wagon.
Outspoken, out′spō-kn, *a.* Free or bold of speech; candid; frank.
Outspread, out-spred′, *vt.* To spread out; to diffuse.—*a.* Extended; expanded.
Outstanding, out-stand′ing, *a.* Projecting outward; prominent; unpaid; undelivered.
Outstrip, out-strip′, *vt.* To outgo; to outrun; to advance beyond; to exceed.
Outvie, out-vī′, *vt.* To exceed; to surpass.
Outvote, out-vōt′, *vt.* To exceed in the number of votes; to defeat by plurality of votes.
Outwalk, out-wa̧k′, *vt.* To walk farther, or faster than; to leave behind in walking.
Outward, out′wėrd, *a.* External; exterior; visible; adventitious.—*adv.* Tending toward the exterior; from a port or country.
Outward-bound, out′wėrd-bound, *a.* Bound to some foreign port; going seaward.
Outwardly, out′wėrd-li, *adv.* Externally; in appearance; not sincerely.
Outwards, out′wėrdz, *adv.* Outward.
Outwear, out-wār′, *vt.* To wear out; to last longer than.
Outweigh, out-wā′, *vt.* To exceed in weight, value, &c.; to overbalance.
Outwit, out-wit′, *vt.* (outwitting, outwitted). To overreach; to defeat by superior ingenuity.
Outwork, out′wėrk, *n.* Part of a fortification distant from the main fortress.
Ouzel, *n.* *See* Ousel.
Ova, ō′va, *n.*; plural of *ovum.*
Oval, ō′val, *a.* Shaped like an egg; elliptical. —*n.* A figure shaped like an egg or ellipse.
Ovarian, ō-vā′ri-an, *a.* Belonging to the ovary.
Ovariotomy, ō-vā′ri-ot″o-mi, *n.* The operation of removing a tumour in the ovary.
Ovary, ō′va-ri, *n.* The female organ in which ova are formed.
Ovate, ō′vāt, *a.* Egg-shaped; oval.
Ovation, ō-vā′shon, *n.* A lesser triumph among the ancient Romans; triumphal reception; public marks of respect.
Oven, uv′n, *n.* A place built in closely for baking, heating, or drying.
Over, ō′vėr, *prep.* Above; denoting motive, occasion, or superiority; across; throughout; upwards of.—*adv.* From side to side; in width; on all the surface; above the top or edge; in excess; completely; too.—*a.* Upper; covering.—*n.* (*cricket*) The number of balls (six or eight) which the bowler delivers in succession from one end of the pitch, before a change is made to the other end.
Overact, ō-vėr-akt′, *vt.* To perform to excess.

Overalls, ō'vėr-ạlz, *n.pl.* Loose trousers worn over others to protect them.
Overarch, ō-vėr-ärch', *vt.* and *i.* To arch over; to cover with an arch.
Overawe, ō-vėr-ạ', *vt.* To restrain by awe.
Overbalance, ō-vėr-bal'ans, *vt.* To weigh down; to exceed in importance; to destroy the equilibrium of.—*n.* Excess.
Overbear, ō-vėr-bār', *vt.* To bear down; to overpower; to domineer over.
Overbearing, ō-vėr-bār'ing, *a.* Haughty and dogmatical; imperious; domineering.
Overboard, ō'vėr-bōrd, *adv.* Over the side of a ship; out of a ship.
Overburden, ō-vėr-ber'dn, *vt.* To load with too great weight; to overload.
Overcast, ō-vėr-käst', *vt.* To cloud; to darken; to sew coarsely over a rough edge.
Overcharge, ō-vėr-chärj', *vt.* To charge or burden to excess; to fill too numerously.—*n.* ō'vėr-chärj. An excessive charge.
Overcloud, ō-vėr-kloud', *vt.* To cover or overspread with clouds.
Overcoat, ō'vėr-kōt, *n.* An upper coat; top-coat.
Overcome, ō-vėr-kum', *vt.* To be victorious over; to master; to get the better of.—*vi.* To gain the superiority.
Overcrowd, ō-vėr-kroud', *vt.* To crowd to excess, especially with human beings.
Overdo, ō-vėr-dö', *vt.* To do to excess; to fatigue; to boil, bake, or roast too much.
Overdose, ō'vėr-dōs, *n.* Too great a dose.—*vt.* ō-vėr-dōs'. To dose excessively.
Overdraw, ō-vėr-drạ', *vt.* To draw upon for a larger sum than is standing at one's credit; to exaggerate.
Overdue, ō'vėr-dū, *a.* Past the time of payment or arrival.
Overflow, ō-vėr-flō', *vt.* (pp. overflowed and overflown). To flow or spread over; to flood; to overwhelm.—*vi.* To be so full that the contents run over; to abound.—*n.* ō'vėr-flō. An inundation; superabundance.
Overflowing, ō-vėr-flō'ing, *p.a.* Abundant; copious; exuberant.
Overgrow, ō-vėr-grō', *vt.* To grow beyond; to cover with growth or herbage.—*vi.* To grow beyond the fit or natural size.
Overgrowth, ō'vėr-grōth, *n.* Exuberant or excessive growth.
Overhand, ō'vėr-hand, *a.* and *adv.* With the hand over the object.
Overhang, ō-vėr-hang', *vt.* and *i.* To hang, impend, jut, or project over.
Overhaul, ō-vėr-hạl', *vt.* To examine thoroughly with a view to repairs; to re-examine; to gain upon or overtake.—*n.* ō'vėr-hạl. Examination; inspection; repair.
Overhead, ō-vėr-hed', *adv.* Above; aloft.
Overhear, ō-vėr-hēr', *vt.* To hear by accident or stratagem.
Overheat, ō-vėr-hēt', *vt.* To heat to excess.
Overhung, ō-vėr-hung', *p.a.* Hung or covered over; adorned with hangings.
Overissue, ō'vėr-ish-ū, *n.* An excessive issue, as of coin or notes.—*vt.* To issue in excess.
Overjoy, ō-vėr-joi', *vt.* To give excessive joy to.—*n.* ō'vėr-joi. Joy to excess.
Over-king, ō'vėr-king, *n.* A king holding sway over several petty kings or princes.
Overland, ō'vėr-land, *a.* Passing by land; made upon or across the land.
Overlap, ō-vėr-lap', *vt.* To lap or fold over.—*n.* ō'vėr-lap. The lapping of one thing over another.
Overlay, ō-vėr-lā', *vt.* To lay over; to coat or cover; to smother.
Overleap, ō-vėr-lēp', *vt.* To leap over; to pass by leaping.
Overlie, ō-vėr-lī', *vt.* To lie over or upon; to smother by lying on.
Overload, ō-vėr-lōd', *vt.* To load too much; to overburden.
Overlook, ō-vėr-lụk', *vt.* To oversee; to superintend; to view from a higher place; to pass by indulgently.
Overlord, ō'vėr-lord, *n.* One who is lord over another; a feudal superior.
Overmaster, ō-vėr-mäs'tėr, *vt.* To gain the mastery over; to subdue.
Overmatch, ō-vėr mach', *vt.* To be more than a match for.—*n.* ō'vėr-mach. One superior in power.
Overmuch, ō'vėr-much, *a.* and *adv.* Too much.—*n.* More than sufficient.
Overnice, ō'vėr-nīs, *a.* Fastidious; too scrupulous.
Overnight, ō'vėr-nīt, *adv.* Through or during the night; in the night before.
Overpass, ō-vėr-päs', *vt.* To pass over; to overlook; to omit; to surpass.
Overpay, ō-vėr-pā', *vt.* To pay too highly.
Overpeople, ō-vėr-pē'pl, *vt.* To overstock with inhabitants.
Overplus, ō'vėr-plus, *n.* That which is over and above; surplus.
Overpower, ō-vėr-pou'ėr, *vt.* To be too powerful for; to bear down by force; to overcome; to subdue; to crush.
Overpowering, ō-vėr-pou'ėr-ing, *p.a.* Excessive in degree or amount; irresistible.
Over-production, ō'vėr-prō-duk-shon, *n.* Production in excess of demand.
Overrate, ō-vėr-rāt', *vt.* To rate at too much; to regard too highly.
Overreach, ō-vėr-rēch', *vt.* To reach over or beyond; to deceive by artifice; to outwit.
Override, ō-vėr-rīd', *vt.* To ride over; to supersede; to set at naught.
Overrule, ō-vėr-röl', *vt.* To control; to govern with high authority; to disallow.
Overrun, ō-vėr-run', *vt.* To run or spread over; to ravage; to outrun.—*vi.* To overflow; to run over.
Oversea, ō'vėr-sē, *a.* Foreign; from beyond sea.—**Overseas**, ō-vėr-sēz, *adv.* Abroad.
Oversee, ō-vėr-sē', *vt.* To see or look over; to overlook; to superintend.
Overseer, ō-vėr-sēr', *n.* One who oversees or overlooks; a superintendent; an inspector.
Overset, ō-vėr-set', *vt.* To set over; to upset or capsize; to overthrow.—*vi.* To capsize.
Overshadow, ō-vėr-sha'dō, *vt.* To throw a shadow over; to shelter.
Overshoe, ō'vėr-shö, *n.* A shoe worn over another; an outer waterproof shoe.
Overshoot, ō-vėr-shöt', *vt.* To shoot over; to shoot beyond.
Overshot, ō-vėr-shot', *p.a.* Shot beyond; having the water flowing on to the top, as a water-wheel.
Oversight, ō'vėr-sīt, *n.* Superintendence; a mistake, error, omission, neglect.
Oversman, ō'vėrz-man, *n.* An overseer; a superintendent; an umpire.

Overspread, ō-vėr-spred', *vt.* To spread over; to cover over; to scatter over.
Overstate, ō-vėr-stāt', *vt.* To state in too strong terms; to exaggerate in statement.
Overstep, ō-vėr-step', *vt.* To step over or beyond; to exceed.
Overstock, ō-vėr-stok', *vt.* To stock to excess; to fill too full.
Overstrain, ō-vėr-strān', *vt.* To strain or stretch too much; to exaggerate.—*vi.* To make too violent efforts.—*n.* ō'vėr-strān. Excessive strain; injurious effort.
Overt, ō'vėrt, *a.* Open to view; manifest; not hidden; public; apparent.
Overtake, ō-vėr-tāk', *vt.* To come up with; to catch; to take by surprise.
Overtask, ō-vėr-täsk', *vt.* To impose too heavy a task or duty on.
Overtax, ō-vėr-taks', *vt.* To tax too heavily; to make too severe demands upon.
Overthrow, ō-vėr-thrō', *vt.* To throw or turn over; to overset; to defeat; to destroy.—*n.* ō'vėr-thrō. Ruin; defeat.
Overthwart, ō-vėr-thwart', *prep.* Athwart.—*vt.* To cross; to lie or be across.
Overtime, ō'vėr-tīm, *n.* Time during which one works beyond the regular hours.
Overtly, ō'vėrt-li, *adv.* Openly; publicly.
Overtop, ō-vėr-top', *vt.* To rise above the top of; to excel; to surpass.
Overture, ō'vėr-tūr, *n.* A proposal; offer; a musical introduction to oratorios, operas, &c.
Overturn, ō-vėr-tėrn', *vt.* To overset or overthrow; to capsize; to subvert; to ruin.
Overvalue, ō-vėr-val'ū, *vt.* To value too highly; to rate at too high a price.
Overweening, ō-vėr-wēn'ing, *a.* Haughty; arrogant; proud; conceited.
Overweigh, ō-vėr-wā', *vt.* To outweigh.
Overweight, ō-vėr-wāt', *vt.* To overburden. —*n.* Excess of weight; preponderance.
Overwhelm, ō vėr-whelm', *vt.* To whelm entirely; to swallow up; to submerge; to crush.
Overwise, ō'vėr-wīz, *a.* Wise to affectation.
Overwork, ō-vėr-wėrk', *vt.* To work beyond strength; to tire with labour.—*n.* ō'vėr-wėrk. Work done beyond one's strength or beyond the amount required.
Overworn, ō'vėr-wōrn, *a.* Worn to excess; worn out; trite; threadbare.
Overwrought, ō-vėr-rat', *p.a.* Wrought to excess; excited to excess; tasked beyond strength.
Oviform, ō'vi-form, *a.* Egg-shaped.
Ovine, ō'vīn, *a.* Pertaining to sheep; consisting of sheep.
Oviparous, ō-vip'a-rus, *a.* Bringing forth eggs; producing young from eggs.
Ovoid, ō'void *a.* Egg-shaped.
Ovoviviparous, ō'vō-vi-vip"a-rus, *a.* Producing eggs which are hatched within the body (as is the case with vipers): opposed to *oviparous*.
Ovule, ō'vūl, *n.* A small ovum; a germinal vesicle of animals; a rudimentary seed.
Ovum, ō'vum, *n.*; pl. **ova.** A small vesicle within the ovary of a female, when impregnated becoming the embryo.
Owe, ō, *vt.* (owing, owed). To be indebted in; to be obliged or bound to pay; to be obliged for.
Owing, ō'ing, *ppr.* Required by obligation to be paid; ascribable; due.
Owl, oul, *n.* A nocturnal bird of prey.
Owlet, oul'et, *n.* An owl; a young owl.
Owlish, oul'ish, *a.* Resembling an owl.
Own, ōn, *a.* Belonging to: used, distinctively and emphatically, after a possessive pronoun, or a noun in the possessive.—*vt.* To hold or possess by right; to acknowledge or avow; to concede.
Owner, ōn'ėr, *n.* One who owns; the rightful possessor or proprietor.
Ownership, ōn'ėr-ship, *n.* State of being an owner; legal or just claim or title.
Ox, oks, *n.*; *pl.* **Oxen,** oks'en. Any animal of the bovine genus; a male of the bovine genus castrated.
Oxalic, ok-sal'ik, *a.* Pertaining to sorrel.
Ox-eye, oks'ī, *n.* A name of several plants, especially a species of chrysanthemum.
Oxidate, oks'id-āt, *vt.* To oxidize.
Oxidation, oks-id-ā'shon, *n.* The operation or process of converting into an oxide.
Oxide, oks'īd, *n.* A compound of oxygen with another element.
Oxidize, oks'id-īz, *vt.* To convert into an oxide; to cause to combine with oxygen.—*vi.* To change into an oxide.
Oxlip, oks'lip, *n.* A species of primrose.
Oxonian, ok-sō'ni-an, *a.* Pertaining to Oxford.—*n.* A native of Oxford; a member of the University of Oxford.
Oxygen, oks'i-jen, *n.* A gaseous element, a component of atmospheric air and water, and essential to animal and vegetable life and combustion.
Oxygenate, oks'i-jen-āt, *vt.* To unite or cause to combine with oxygen.
Oxygenize, oks'i-jen-īz, *vt.* To oxygenate.
Oxygenous, oks-ij'en-us, *a.* Pertaining to, obtained from, or containing oxygen.
Oyer, ō'yėr, *n.* A hearing or trial of causes in law.—*Court of oyer and terminer*, an English court for determining felonies and misdemeanours.
Oyez, ō'yes. The introduction to a proclamation by a public crier, repeated three times.
Oyster, ois'tėr, *n.* A bivalve shell-fish or mollusc.
Oyster-bed, ois'tėr-bed, *n.* A bed or breeding-place of oysters.
Ozocerite, Ozokerite, ō-zō-sē'rīt, ō-zō-kē'-rīt, *n.* A mineral wax or paraffin of a brown or brownish-yellow colour.
Ozone, ō'zōn, *n.* A kind of gas with a peculiar odour, a modification of oxygen existing in the atmosphere.

P

Pabular, pab'ū-lėr, *a.* Pertaining to food.
Pabulum, pab'ū-lum, *n.* Food; that which feeds either mind or body.
Pace, pās, *n.* A step; space between the two feet in walking; distance of 2½ feet or 5 feet; gait; rate of progress.—*vi.* (pacing, paced). To step; to walk slowly; to move by lifting the legs on the same side together, as a horse. —*vt.* To measure by steps; to accompany and set a proper rate of motion; to race.
Pacer, pās'ėr, *n.* One who paces; a horse trained to pace.
Pacha. *See* PASHA.

Pachydermatous, pak-i-dėr'ma-tus, *a.* Thick-skinned; not sensitive to ridicule, sarcasm, &c.

Pacific, pa-sif'ik, *a.* Suited to make peace; pacifying; calm.—**The Pacific Ocean,** the ocean between America, Asia, and Australia.

Pacification, pa'si-fi-kā''shon, *n.* Act of making peace; appeasement.

Pacificator, pa-sif'i-kāt-ėr, *n.* One who pacifies; a peacemaker.

Pacificatory, pa-sif'i-ka-to-ri, *a.* Tending to make peace; conciliatory.

Pacifier, pa'si-fī-ėr, *n.* One who pacifies.

Pacify, pa'si-fī, *vt.* (pacifying, pacified). To give peace to; to appease; to allay.

Pack, pak, *n.* A bundle; a bale; a set of playing-cards; a set of hounds or dogs; a gang.—*vt.* To make up into a bundle; to fill methodically with contents; to manipulate with fraudulent design; to dismiss without ceremony; to stuff.—*vi.* To make up bundles; to depart in haste (with *off* or *away*).

Package, pak'āj, *n.* A bundle or bale; a packet; charge for packing goods.

Packer, pak'ėr, *n.* One who packs or prepares merchandise for transit.

Packet, pak'et, *n.* A small pack; a parcel; a vessel employed regularly, in carrying mails, goods and passengers.

Pack-horse, pak'hors, *n.* A horse employed in carrying goods and baggage on its back.

Pack-ice, pak'īs, *n.* An assemblage of large floating pieces of ice.

Packing, pak'ing, *n.* Act of one who packs; material used in packing; stuffing.

Pack-man, pak'man, *n.* One who carries a pack on his back; a pedlar.

Pack-saddle, pak'sad-l, *n.* The saddle of a pack-horse, made for bearing burdens.

Packsheet, pak'shēt, *n.* A strong coarse cloth for covering goods in bales.—Also *Packing-sheet.*

Pact, pakt, *n.* A contract; an agreement or covenant.

Pad, pad, *n.* An easy-paced horse; a robber who infests the road on foot; a soft saddle; a cushion; a quantity of blotting-paper.—*vi.* (padding, padded). To walk or go on foot; to rob on foot.—*vt.* To furnish with padding.

Padding, pad'ing, *n.* Act of stuffing; material used in stuffing; literary matter inserted in a book, &c., merely to increase the bulk.

Paddle, pad'l, *vi.* (paddling, paddled). To play in water with hands or feet; to row.—*vt.* To propel by an oar or paddle.—*n.* A broad short oar; a float-board of a paddle-wheel.

Paddle-box, pad'l-boks, *n.* The wooden covering of the paddle-wheel of a steamer.

Paddler, pad'l-ėr, *n.* One who paddles.

Paddle-wheel, pad'l-whēl, *n.* A wheel with boards on its circumference, propelling a steamship.

Paddock, pad'ok, *n.* A toad or frog; an inclosure under pasture, usually adjoining a house.

Paddy, pad'i, *n.* Rice in the husk, whether in the field or gathered.

Padlock, pad'lok, *n.* A lock with a link to be fastened through a staple.—*vt.* To fasten or provide with a padlock.

Padre, päd'rā, *n.* A chaplain.

Pæan, pē'an, *n.* A war-song; song of triumph.

Pædagogics, Pædagogy, pē-da-goj'iks, pē'-da-goj-i, *n.* *See* PEDAGOGICS, PEDAGOGY.

Pagan, pā'gan, *n.* A heathen.—*a.* Heathenish; idolatrous.

Paganism, pā'gan-izm, *n.* Religious worship of pagans; heathenism.

Paganize, pā'gan-īz, *vt.* To convert to heathenism.

Page, pāj, *n.* A young male attendant on persons of distinction; one side of a leaf of a book; a written record.—*vt.* (paging, paged). To number the pages of.

Pageant, pa'jent, *n.* Something intended for pomp; a show, as at a public rejoicing.—*a.* Showy; pompous.

Pageantry, pa'jent-ri, *n.* Pageants collectively; show; pompous spectacle.

Pagination, pa-jin-ā'shon, *n.* Act of paging; figures indicating the number of pages.

Pagoda, pa-gō'da, *n.* A Hindu or Buddhist temple; an Indian coin worth 8*s.* to 9*s.*

Pah, pä, *interj.* An exclamation expressing contempt or disgust.

Paideutics, pā-dū'tiks, *n.* The science of teaching.

Paigle, pā'gl, *n.* The cowslip or primrose.

Pail, pāl, *n.* An open vessel for carrying liquids.

Pailful, pāl'fụl, *n.* The quantity that a pail will hold.

Paillasse, pal-yas', *n.* An under bed of straw.

Pain, pān, *n.* A penalty; bodily suffering; distress; anguish; *pl.* The throes of childbirth; labour; diligent effort.—*vt.* To cause pain to; to afflict; to distress.

Painful, pān'fụl, *a.* Full of pain; distressing; grievous; difficult.

Painless, pān'les, *a.* Free from pain.

Painstaking, pānz'tāk-ing, *a.* Giving close application; laborious and careful.—*n.* The taking of pains; careful labour.

Paint, pānt, *vt.* To represent by colours and figures; to cover with colour; to portray; to delineate.—*vi.* To practise painting.—*n.* A substance used in painting; a pigment; rouge.

Painter, pānt'ėr, *n.* One whose occupation is to paint; one skilled in representing things in colours; a rope to fasten a boat.

Painting, pānt'ing, *n.* Art or employment of laying on colours; art of representing objects by colours; a picture; colours laid on.

Pair, pār, *n.* Two things of like kind, suited, or used together; a couple; a man and his wife; two members on opposite sides in parliament, &c., who agree not to vote for a time.—*vi.* To join in pairs; to mate.—*vt.* To unite in pairs.

Palace, pa'lās, *n.* The house in which an emperor, king, bishop, &c., resides; a splendid residence.

Paladin, pal'a-din, *n.* A knight attached to a sovereign's court; a knight-errant; a heroic champion; a hero.

Palæography, pal-ē-og'ra-fi, *n.* The art of deciphering ancient writing.

Palæolith, pal'ē-ō-lith, *n.* An unpolished stone implement of the earlier stone age.

Palæolithic, pal'ē-ō-lith''ik, *a.* Belonging to the earlier stone period, when rude unpolished stone implements were used.

Palæontology, pal'ē-on-tol''o-ji, *n.* The science of fossil organic remains.

Palæozoic, pal'ē-ō-zō''ik, *a.* In *geology*, applied to the lowest division of stratified groups.

Palanquin, Palankeen, pa-lan-kēn′, *n.* A covered conveyance used in India, China, &c., borne on the shoulders of men.

Palatable, pa′lat-a-bl, *a.* Agreeable to the palate or taste; savoury.

Palatal, pa′lat-al, *a.* Pertaining to the palate; uttered by the aid of the palate.—*n.* A sound pronounced by the aid of the palate, as that of *j*.

Palate, pa′lāt, *n.* The roof of the mouth; taste; relish; intellectual taste.

Palatial, pa-lā′shal, *a.* Pertaining to a palace; becoming a palace; magnificent.

Palatinate, pa-lat′i-nāt, *n.* The province or seignory of a palatine.

Palatine, pa′la-tīn, *a.* Pertaining to a palace; possessing royal privileges.—*County palatine*, a county over which an earl, bishop, or duke ruled with royal powers.—*n.* One invested with royal privileges and rights.

Palaver, pa-la′vėr, *n.* A long or serious conference; idle talk.—*vt.* To flatter or humbug. —*vi.* To talk idly; to engage in a palaver.

Pale, pāl, *n.* A pointed stake; an inclosure; sphere or scope.—*vt.* (paling, paled). To inclose with pales; to fence in.—*vi.* To turn pale.—*a.* Whitish; wan; deficient in colour; not bright; dim.

Palea, pā′lē-a, *n.*; pl. **-eæ.** A bract between the florets of composite plants; an interior bract of the flowers of grasses.

Paleography, &c. *See* PALÆ-.

Palestra, pa-les′tra, *n.* A place of wrestling; wrestling or other athletic exercises.

Paletot, pal′e-tō, *n.* A loose overcoat.

Palette, pa′let, *n.* A thin oval board on which a painter lays his pigments.

Palfrey, pa̤l′fri, *n.* A riding horse; a small horse fit for ladies.

Pali, pä′lē, *n.* The sacred language of the Buddhists, not now spoken.

Palimpsest, pal′imp-sest, *n.* A parchment from which writing has been erased to make room for other writing, the first remaining faintly visible.

Paling, pāl′ing, *n.* A fence formed with pales, or vertical stakes or posts.

Palingenesis, pal-in-jen′e-sis, *n.* A transformation; a great geological change.

Palinode, pal′i-nōd, *n.* A recantation.

Palisade, pa-li-sād′, *n.* A fence or fortification of pales or posts.—*vt.* (palisading, palisaded). To surround or fortify with stakes.

Palish, pāl′ish, *a.* Somewhat pale or wan.

Pall, pa̤l, *n.* An outer mantle of dignity; a cloth thrown over a coffin at a funeral; a linen cloth to cover a chalice; a covering.—*vt.* To cover with a pall; to shroud; to make vapid; to cloy.—*vi.* To become vapid or cloying.

Palladium, pal-lā′di-um, *n.* A statue of the goddess Pallas; bulwark; safeguard; a grayish-white hard malleable metal.

Pallet, pal′et, *n.* A palette; a tool used by potters, &c.; a small rude bed.

Palliate, pal′i-āt, *vt.* To extenuate; to mitigate; to lessen, abate, alleviate.

Palliation, pal-i-ā′shon, *n.* Act of palliating; what serves to palliate.

Palliative, pal′i-āt-iv, *a.* Serving to palliate. —*n.* That which palliates.

Pallid, pal′id, *a.* Pale; wan.

Pallium, pal′i-um, *n.*; pl. **-ia.** A kind of ancient cloak; a vestment sent by the pope to metropolitans, &c.; the mantle of a mollusc.

Pallor, pal′or, *n.* Paleness.

Palm, päm, *n.* The inner part of the hand; a measure of 3 or 4 inches; a name of plants constituting an order of endogens; a branch or leaf of such a plant; victory; triumph.—*vt.* To conceal in the palm of the hand; to impose by fraud.

Palmaceous, pal-mā′shus, *a.* Belonging to the palm tribe.

Palmate, pal′māt, *a.* Having the shape of a hand; entirely webbed, as feet.

Palmer, päm′ėr, *n.* A pilgrim who returned from the Holy Land with a branch of palm; one who palms or cheats.

Palmiped, pä′mi-ped, *a.* Web-footed.

Palmist, päm′ist, *n.* One who deals in palmistry.

Palmistry, pam′is-tri, *n.* The art of telling fortunes by the hand.

Palm-oil, päm′oil, *n.* A fatty substance resembling butter, obtained from palms.

Palm-Sunday, päm′sun-dā, *n.* The Sunday next before Easter.

Palmy, päm′i, *a.* Abounding in palms; flourishing; prosperous; victorious.

Palpable, pal′pa-bl, *a.* Perceptible by the touch; plain; obvious.

Palpably, pal′pa-bli, *adv.* Plainly; obviously.

Palpitate, pal′pi-tāt, *vi.* (palpitating, palpitated). To pulsate rapidly; to throb; to tremble.

Palpitation, pal-pi-tā′shon, *n.* Act of palpitating; violent pulsation of the heart.

Palsy, pa̤l′zi, *n.* Paralysis, especially of a minor kind.—*vt.* (palsying, palsied). To affect with palsy; to paralyse.

Palter, pa̤l′tėr, *vi.* To act insincerely; to shift; to dodge.

Paltry, pa̤l′tri, *a.* Mean and trivial; trifling; worthless; contemptible.

Paludal, pal′ū-dal, *a.* Pertaining to marshes. Also *paludine*, *palustral*, *palustrine*.

Pampas, pam′pas, *n.pl.* The immense grassy treeless plains of South America.

Pamper, pam′pėr, *vt.* To gratify to the full; to furnish with that which delights.

Pamphlet, pam′flet, *n.* A small book, stitched but not bound; a short treatise.

Pamphleteer, pam-flet-ēr′, *n.* A writer of pamphlets; a scribbler.

Pan, pan, *n.* A broad and shallow vessel, of metal or eathenware; a pond for evaporating salt water to make salt; part of a gun-lock holding the priming; the skull; the Greek and Roman god of flocks and herds.

Panacea, pan-a-sē′a, *n.* A remedy for all diseases; a universal medicine.

Pancake, pan′kāk, *n.* A thin cake fried in a pan or baked on an iron plate.

Pancreas, pan′krē-as, *n.* A fleshy gland or organ between the bottom of the stomach and the vertebræ; the sweet-bread in cattle.

Pancreatic, pan-krē-at′ik, *a.* Pertaining to the pancreas.

Pandean, pan-dē′an, *a.* Pertaining to Pan. *Pandean pipes*, *Pan's pipes*, a musical wind-instrument composed of pipes of different lengths tied together; a syrinx.

Pandect, pan′dekt, *n.* A treatise containing the whole of a science; *pl.* the digest of

Roman civil law made by order of Justinian.

Pandemonium, pan-dē-mō'ni-um, *n.* The abode of the evil spirits; any lawless, disorderly place or assemblage.

Pander, pan'dėr, *n.* A pimp; a male bawd.—*vi.* To act as agent for the lusts of others; to be subservient to lust or desire. Also *Pandar.*

Pane, pān, *n.* A plate of glass inserted in a window, door, &c.; a panel.

Panegyric, pa-ne-ji'rik, *n.* A laudatory speech; eulogy; encomium; laudation.

Panegyric, Panegyrical, pa-ne-ji'rik, pa-ne-ji'rik-al, *a.* Containing panegyric, praise, or eulogy; encomiastic.

Panegyrist, pa-ne-ji'rist, *n.* One who makes a panegyric; eulogist; encomiast.

Panegyrize, pa'ne-ji-rīz, *vt.* To make a panegyric on; to eulogize.

Panel, pa'nel, *n.* A surface distinct from others adjoining in a piece of work; a sunk portion in a door, &c.; a piece of wood on which a picture is painted; list of Health Insurance doctors for a district; a doctor's list of insured persons; list of those summoned to serve on a jury; in Scotland, the accused.—*vt.* (panelling, panelled). To form with panels.

Panelling, pa'nel-ing, *n.* Panelled work.

Pang, pang, *n.* A sharp and sudden pain; painful spasm; throe.

Pangolin, pan'gō-lin, *n.* The scaly ant-eater or manis.

Panic, pan'ik, *n.* A sudden fright; terror inspired by a trifling cause.—*a.* Extreme, sudden, or causeless: said of fright.

Panicle, pan'i-kl, *n.* A branching form of inflorescence, as in the lilac.

Pannier, pa'ni-ėr, *n.* A wicker-basket; a basket for a person's or beast's back.

Panoplied, pa'nō-plid, *a.* Wearing a panoply.

Panoply, pa'nō-pli, *n.* Complete armour of defence; a full suit of armour.

Panorama, pan-ō-rä'ma, *n.* A picture presenting from a central point a view of objects in every direction.

Panoramic, pan-ō-ram'ik, *a.* Belonging to or like a panorama.

Pansy, pan'zi, *n.* A garden variety of violet; heart's-ease.

Pant, pant, *vi.* To breathe quickly; to gasp; to desire ardently.—*n.* A gasp; a throb.

Pantaloon, pan'ta-lön, *n.* A character in the old Italian comedy; in harlequinades, a fatuous old man, the butt of the clown.

Pantaloons, pan'ta-lönz, *n.pl.* Tightly fitting trousers; trousers in general.

Pantheism, pan'thē-izm, *n.* The doctrine that the universe is God, or that all things are manifestations of God.

Pantheist, pan'thē-ist, *n.* One who believes in pantheism.

Pantheistic, pan-thē-ist'ik, *a.* Pertaining to pantheism.

Pantheon, pan'thē-on, *n.* A temple dedicated to all the gods; all the divinities collectively worshipped by a people.

Panther, pan'thėr, *n.* A spotted carnivorous animal, otherwise called the leopard.

Pantograph, pan'tō-graf, *n.* An instrument for copying maps, plans, &c., on any scale.

Pantomime, pan'tō-mīm, *n.* A representation in dumb-show; a Christmas stage entertainment of the burlesque kind.

Pantomimic, pan-tō-mim'ik, *a.* Pertaining to pantomime or dumb-show.

Pantry, pan'tri, *n.* An apartment in which provisions are kept, or where plate and knives, &c., are cleaned.

Panzer division, pant'zėr di-vi'zhon, *n.* A German armoured division, consisting of tanks, &c.

Pap, pap, *n.* A kind of soft food for infants; the pulp of fruit; a teat; a round hill.

Papa, pa-pä', *n.* A childish name for father.

Papacy, pā'pa-si, *n.* The office and dignity of the pope; the popes collectively; papal authority or jurisdiction; popedom.

Papal, pā'pal, *a.* Belonging to the pope.

Papaveraceous, pa-pā'vėr-ā"shus, *a.* Pertaining to the poppy family.

Papaw, pa-pä', *n.* A tropical tree and its fruit, whose juice makes tough meat tender.

Paper, pā'pėr, *n.* A substance formed into thin sheets used for writing, printing, &c.; a leaf, or sheet of this; a journal; an essay or article; promissory notes, bills of exchange, &c.—*a.* Made or consisting of paper; appearing merely in documents without really existing; slight.—*vt.* To cover with paper; to inclose in paper.

Paper-hanger, pā'pėr-hang-ėr, *n.* One who lines walls with paper-hangings.

Paper-hangings, pā'pėr-hang-ingz, *n.pl.* Paper for covering the walls of rooms, &c.

Paper-money, pā'pėr-mun-i, *n.* Bank-notes or the like circulated instead of coin.

Papery, pā'pėr-i, *a.* Like paper.

Papier-mâché, pap-yā-mä-shā, *n.* A material prepared by pulping different kinds of paper into a mass, which is moulded into various articles, dried, and japanned.

Papillary, pap'il-la-ri, *a.* Pertaining to or resembling the nipple. Also *papillose.*

Papist, pā'pist, *n.* A Roman Catholic.

Papistic, Papistical, pā-pis'tik, pā-pis'tik-al, *a.* Popish; pertaining to Popery.

Papistry, pā'pist-ri, *n.* Popery.

Pappus, pap'us, *n.* A downy substance on seeds.

Pappy, pap'i, *a.* Like pap; succulent.

Papular, pap'ū-lėr, *a.* Covered with pimples. Also *papulose, papulous.*

Papyrus, pa-pī'rus, *n.*; pl. **-ri.** An Egyptian sedge, the stems of which afforded an ancient writing material; a written scroll of papyrus.

Par, pär, *n.* State of equality; equality in condition or value; state of shares or stocks when they may be purchased at the original price.

Parable, pa'ra-bl, *n.* An allegorical representation of something real in life or nature, embodying a moral.

Parabola, pa-ra'bō-la, *n.* A conic section, shown when a cone is cut by a plane parallel to one of its sides; the curve described theoretically by a projectile.

Parabolic, Parabolical, pa-ra-bol'ik, pa-ra-bol'ik-al, *a.* Expressed by or pertaining to parable; belonging to a parabola.

Parachute, pa'ra-shöt, *n.* An apparatus like a large umbrella, enabling an aëronaut to drop to the ground without injury.

Paraclete, pa'ra-klēt, *n.* One called to aid or support; the Holy Spirit.

Parade, pa-rād', *n.* Ostentation; show; military display; place where such display is held.

—*vt.* (parading, paraded). To exhibit in ostentatious manner; to marshal in military order. —*vi.* To walk about for show; to go about in military procession.
Paradigm, pa'ra-dim, *n.* A pattern, model, or example.
Paradise, pa'ra-dīs, *n.* The garden of Eden; a place of bliss; heaven.
Paradox, pa'ra-doks, *n.* An assertion or proposition seemingly absurd, yet true in fact; a seeming contradiction.
Paradoxical, pa-ra-doks'ik-al, *a.* Having the nature of a paradox; inclined to paradox.
Paraffin, pa'ra-fin, *n.* A solid white substance obtained from the distillation of wood, bituminous coal or shale, &c.
Paraffin-oil, pa'ra-fin-oil, *n.* The oil obtained in the distillation of bituminous shale, used for illuminating and lubricating.
Paragon, pa'ra-gon, *n.* A model; a perfect example of excellence.
Paragraph, pa'ra-graf, *n.* The character ¶ used as a reference, &c.; a distinct section of a writing, distinguished by a break in the lines; a brief notice.
Parakeet, pa'ra-kēt, *n.* *See* PARRAKEET.
Parallactic, pa-ral-lak'tik, *a.* Pertaining to the parallax of a heavenly body.
Parallax, pa'ral-laks, *n.* The apparent change of position of an object when viewed from different points; the difference between the place of a heavenly body as seen from the earth's surface and its centre at the same time.
Parallel, pa'ral-lel, *a.* Extended in the same direction, and in all parts equally distant, as lines or surfaces; running in accordance with something; equal in all essential parts.—*n.* A line which throughout its whole length is equidistant from another line; conformity in all essentials; likeness; comparison; counterpart.—*vt.* To place so as to be parallel; to correspond to; to compare.
Parallelepiped, pa-ral-lel'e-pip"ed, *n.* A regular solid comprehended under six parallelograms, the opposite ones being parallel and equal.
Parallelism, pa'ral-lel-izm, *n.* State of being parallel; resemblance; comparison.
Parallelogram, pa-ral-lel'ō-gram, *n.* A quadrilateral, whose opposite sides are parallel and equal.
Paralogism, pa-ral'o-jism, *n.* A fallacious argument; an illogical conclusion.
Paralyse, pa'ra-līz, *vt.* (paralysing, paralysed). To affect with paralysis; to reduce to a helpless state.
Paralysis, pa-ral'i-sis, *n.* A diseased state of nerves by which the power of action or sensation is lost.
Paralytic, pa-ra-lit'ik, *a.* Pertaining to or affected with paralysis.—*n.* A person affected with palsy.
Paramatta, pa-ra-mat'ta, *n.* A light twilled dress fabric of wool and cotton.
Paramount, pa'ra-mount, *a.* Chief; superior to all others.
Paramour, pa'ra-mör, *n.* A lover; one who wrongfully holds the place of a spouse.
Parapet, pa'ra-pet, *n.* A wall or rampart breast-high; a wall on the edge of a bridge, quay, &c.
Paraphernalia, pa'ra-fėr-nā"li-a, *n.pl.* That which a bride brings besides her dowry, as clothing, jewels, &c.; personal attire; trappings.
Paraphrase, pa'ra-frāz, *n.* A statement giving the meaning of another statement; a loose or free translation; a sacred song based on a portion of Scripture.—*vt.* To make a paraphrase of; to explain or translate with latitude.
Paraphrast, pa'ra-frast, *n.* One who paraphrases.
Paraphrastic, Paraphrastical, pa-ra-frast'ik, pa-ra-frast'ik-al, *a.* Pertaining to or resembling a paraphrase; not literal.
Paraselene, pa'ra-se-lē"nē, *n.*; pl. **-lenæ.** A mock moon; a luminous ring round the moon.
Parashot, pa'ra-shot, *n.* Marksman trained to deal with paratroops.
Parasite, pa'ra-sīt, *n.* One who frequents the rich, and earns his welcome by flattery; a sycophant; an animal that lives upon or in another; a plant which grows on another.
Parasitic, Parasitical, pa-ra-sit'ik, pa-ra-sit'ik-al, *a.* Belonging to a parasite; living on some other body.
Parasol, pa'ra-sol, *n.* A small umbrella used to keep off the sun's rays.
Paratroops, pa'ra-tröps, *n.* Troops landed by means of parachutes.
Paravane, pa'ra-vān, *n.* A torpedo-shaped machine fitted with an apparatus for severing the moorings of sea-mines.
Parboil, pär'boil, *vt.* To boil partly.
Parbuckle, pär'buk-l, *n.* A purchase formed by a single rope round an object (as a barrel) for moving on an inclined plane.
Parcel, pär'sel, *n.* A portion of anything; a small bundle or package; a collection.—*vt.* (parcelling, parcelled). To divide into portions; to make up into packages.
Parcel-post, pär'sel-pōst, *n.* Department of a post-office by which parcels are sent.
Parcener, pär'sen-ėr, *n.* A coheir.
Parch, pärch, *vt.* To dry to extremity; to scorch.—*vi.* To become very dry; to be scorched.
Parchment, pärch'ment, *n.* The skin of a sheep or goat dressed for writing on; a document written on this substance.
Pard, pärd, *n.* The leopard or panther.
Pardon, pär'dn, *vt.* To forgive; to forbear to exact a penalty for; to overlook; to excuse. —*n.* Forgiveness; remission of a penalty.
Pardonable, pär'dn-a-bl, *a.* That may be pardoned; venial; excusable.
Pardoner, pär'dn-ėr, *n.* One who pardons; formerly a seller of the pope's indulgences.
Pare, pār, *vt.* (paring, pared). To trim by cutting; to dress; to cut away by little and little; to diminish.
Paregoric, pa-re-go'rik, *a.* Encouraging; soothing; assuaging pain.—*n.* An anodyne.
Parent, pā'rent, *n.* One who brings forth or begets; a father or mother; a progenitor; cause; origin.
Parentage, pā'rent-āj, *n.* Extraction; birth.
Parental, pa-rent'al, *a.* Pertaining to or becoming parents; tender; affectionate.
Parenthesis, pa-ren'the-sis, *n.*; pl. **-theses.** A sentence or words inserted in another sentence, usually in brackets, thus, ( ).
Parenthetic, Parenthetical, pa-ren-thet'ik, pa-ren-thet'ik-al, *a.* Pertaining to or of the nature of a parenthesis.

Parer, păr'ėr, *n.* One who or that which pares; an instrument for paring.
Parergon, par-ėr'gon, *n.* Something done incidentally; something subsidiary.
Parget, pär'jet, *n.* Plaster laid on roofs or walls, especially if ornamental.—*vt.* To cover with parget.
Pargeting, Parge-work, pär'jet-ing, pärj'-wėrk, *n.* Ornamental plaster-work.
Parhelion, pär-hē'li-on, *n.*; pl. **-lia.** A mock sun or meteor, appearing as a bright light near the sun.
Pariah, pā'ri-a, *n.* One of the lowest class of people in Hindustan; an outcast.
Parian, pā'ri-an, *a.* Pertaining to *Paros*, an isle in the Ægean Sea producing a fine marble. —*n.* A fine porcelain clay.
Parietal, pa-rī'et-al, *a.* Pertaining to a wall.
Paring, pār'ing, *n.* That which is pared off; rind; act of slicing off and burning the surface of grass-land.
Parish, pa'rish, *n.* An ecclesiastical division under the care of a priest or parson; a subdivision of a county for civil purposes.—*a.* Belonging to a parish; parochial.
Parishioner, pa-rish'on-ėr, *n.* One who belongs to a parish; a member of the parish church.
Parisian, pa-riz'i-an, *a.* Pertaining to *Paris*. —*n.* A native or resident of Paris.
Parity, pa'ri-ti, *n.* Equality; likeness; like state or degree; analogy.
Park, pärk, *n.* A piece of ground inclosed; ornamental ground adjoining a house; ground in a town for recreation; an assemblage of heavy ordnance.—*vt.* To inclose in a park; to bring together, as artillery; to draw up motor-cars and leave them for a time in an inclosed space, or at the side of the road.
Parka, pär'ka, *n.* Hooded skin jacket of Eskimos.
Parlance, pär'lans, *n.* Conversation; talk; idiom.
Parley, pär'li, *vi.* To confer; to discuss orally. —*n.* Mutual discourse; conference with an enemy in war.
Parliament, pär'li-ment, *n.* An assembly of persons for deliberation, &c.; the legislature of Great Britain and Northern Ireland; any similar legislative assembly.
Parliamentarian, pär'li-ment-ā"ri-an, *n.* An adherent of parliament; one of those who adhered to the parliament in the time of Charles I.
Parliamentary, pär'li-ment"a-ri, *a.* Pertaining to, done by, or according to the rules and usages of parliament.
Parlour, pär'lėr, *n.* The sitting-room in a house which the family usually occupy.
Parnassian, pär-nas'i-an, *a.* Pertaining to *Parnassus*, the mountain in Greece sacred to Apollo and the Muses.
Parochial, pa-rō'ki-al, *a.* Belonging to a parish; narrow in views; provincial.
Parodist, pa'rod-ist, *n.* One who makes parodies.
Parody, pa'rod-i, *n.* An adaptation of the words of an author, &c., to a different purpose; a burlesque imitation.—*vt.* (parodying, parodied). To imitate in parody.
Parole, pa-rōl', *n.* Words or oral declarations; word of honour; a promise by a prisoner of war not to bear arms against his captors for a certain period, or the like; a military countersign.
Paronomasia, Paronomasy, pa-ron'om-ā"-zi-a, pa-ron-om'a-si, *n.* A pun.
Paroxysm, pa'roks-izm, *n.* A violent access of feeling (as of rage); convulsion; spasm.
Parquetry, pär'ket-ri, *n.* Inlaid wood-work, principally used for floors.
Parr, pär, *n.* A young salmon.
Parrakeet, pa'ra-kēt, *n.* A small parrot of the eastern hemisphere.
Parricide, pa'ri-sīd, *n.* A person who murders his father or mother; the murder of a parent.
Parrot, pa'rot, *n.* A family of birds, including parrakeets, macaws, cockatoos, &c.; a bird which can imitate the human voice.
Parry, pa'ri, *vt.* and *i.* (parrying, parried). To ward off.
Parse, pärs, *vt.* (parsing, parsed). To tell the relation of the parts of speech in a sentence.
Parsee, pär-sē', *n.* An adherent of the Zoroastrian religion in India; a fire-worshipper.
Parsimonious, pär-si-mō'ni-us, *a.* Niggardly; miserly; penurious.
Parsimony, pär'si-mō-ni, *n.* The habit of being sparing in expenditure of money; excessive frugality; miserliness; closeness.
Parsley, pärs'li, *n.* A garden vegetable, used for flavouring in cooking.
Parsnip, pärs'nip, *n.* An umbelliferous plant with a fleshy esculent root.
Parson, pär'sn, *n.* The priest or incumbent of a parish; a clergyman.
Parsonage, pär'sn-āj, *n.* The official dwelling-house of a parson.
Part, pärt, *n.* A portion or piece of a whole; a section; a constituent or organic portion; share; lot; party; duty; business; character assigned to an actor in a play; *pl.* faculties; superior endowments; regions; locality.—*vt.* To divide; to sever; to share; to distribute; to separate; to intervene.—*vi.* To become separated, broken, or detached; to quit each other; to depart.
Partake, pär-tāk', *vi.* (partaking, pret. partook, pp. partaken). To take or have a part with others; to share; to have something of the nature, claim, or right.—*vt.* To share.
Partaker, pär-tāk'ėr, *n.* One who partakes; a sharer; accomplice; associate.
Parterre, pär-tār', *n.* A piece of ground with flower-beds; the pit of a theatre.
Parthenogenesis, pär'the-nō-jen"e-sis, *n.* Propagation of a plant or animal without the intervention of a male.
Partial, pär'shal, *a.* Belonging to or affecting a part only; not general; biased to one party; having a fondness.
Partiality, pär'shi-al"i-ti, *n.* Unfair bias; undue favour shown; a liking or fondness.
Partially, pär'shal-li, *adv.* With undue bias; in part; to some extent.
Partible, pärt'i-bl, *a.* Divisible.
Participate, pär-tis'i-pāt, *vi.* and *t.* To partake, share.
Participation, pär-tis'i-pā"shon, *n.* Act of participating; a sharing with others.
Participator, pär-tis'i-pāt-or, *n.* One who participates or partakes; a partaker.
Participial, pär-ti-sip'i-al, *a.* Of the nature of, or formed from, a participle.—*n.* A word having the nature of a participle.

Participle, pär'ti-si-pl, *n.* A word having the properties of both an adjective and verb.
Particle, pär'ti-kl, *n.* An atom; a jot; a very small portion; a word not inflected.
Particular, pär-tik'ū-lėr, *a.* Pertaining to a single person or thing; private; special; exact; precise; circumstantial; notable; fastidious.—*n.* A single instance; detail; distinct circumstance.
Particularity, pär-tik'ū-la"ri-ti, *n.* State or quality of being particular; minuteness of detail; that which is particular.
Particularize, pär-tik'ū-lėr-īz, *vt.* To make particular mention of; to specify in detail.—*vi.* To be particular to details.
Particularly, pär-tik'ū-lėr-li, *adv.* In a particular manner; distinctly; specially.
Parting, pärt'ing, *p.a.* Serving to part or divide; given at separation; departing.—*n.* Division; separation; leave-tàking.
Partisan, Partizan, pär'ti-zan, *n.* An adherent of a party or faction; a party man.—*a.* Adhering to a faction.
Partition, pär-ti'shon, *n.* Act of parting or dividing; division; a division-wall; part where separation is made.—*vt.* To divide by partitions; to divide into shares.
Partitive, pär'ti-tiv, *a.* Denoting a part; referring to a part; distributive.
Partlet, pärt'let, *n.* A name for a hen.
Partly, pärt'li, *adv.* In part; in some measure.
Partner, pärt'nėr, *n.* One who shares with another; an associate in business; a husband or wife.
Partnership, pärt'nėr-ship, *n.* Fellowship; the association of two or more persons in any business; joint interest or property.
Partridge, pär'trij, *n.* A game bird of the grouse family.
Parturient, pär-tū'ri-ent, *a.* Bringing forth or about to bring forth young.
Parturition, pär-tū-ri'shon, *n.* The act of bringing forth young.
Party, pär'ti, *n.* A body of individuals; one of two litigants; a company made up for an occasion; a single person; a detachment of troops.—*a.* Of or pertaining to a party.
Party-coloured, pär'ti-kul-ėrd, *a.* Coloured differently in different parts; motley.
Party-wall, pär'ti-wąl, *n.* A wall that separates one house from the next.
Parvenu, pär've-nū, *n.* An upstart; a person who has newly risen to eminence.
Parvis, Parvise, pär'vis, *n.* Area round a church; a room above the church porch.
Pas, pä, *n.* A step; precedence.
Paschal, pas'kal, *a.* Pertaining to the passover or to Easter.
Pasha, pash'ä or pa-shä', *n.* A Turkish governor of a province, or military commander.
Pasquil, pas'kwil, *n.* A pasquin.
Pasquin, Pasquinade, pas'kwin, pas-kwin-ād', *n.* A lampoon; a satirical publication.—*vt.* To lampoon.
Pass, päs, *vi.* (pret. and pp. passed or past). To go by or past; to change; to die; to elapse; to be enacted; to be current; to thrust in fencing or fighting; to go successfully through an examination.—*vt.* To go past, beyond, or over; to cross; to live through; to undergo with success (as an examination); to circulate; to utter; to take no notice of; to enact; to thrust; to void, as fæces.—*n.* A passage; a defile; a license to pass; a thrust; manipulation; condition; extremity.
Passable, pas'a-bl, *a.* That may be passed, travelled, or navigated; current; tolerable; allowable; pretty fair.
Passably, pas'a-bli, *adv.* Tolerably.
Passage, pas'āj, *n.* Act of passing; transit; a journey, especially by a ship; road; channel; a gallery or corridor; access; episode; part of a book, &c., referred to; enactment; an encounter.
Passant, pas'ant, *a.* In *heraldry*, said of an animal which appears to walk with head directed forward.
Pass-book, päs'bök, *n.* A book in which to enter articles bought on credit; bank-book.
Passé, Passée, pas-ā, *a.* Past; faded; past the heyday of life.
Passenger, pas'en-jėr, *n.* A traveller; one who travels in a public conveyance; one who does not pull his weight in a crew or team.
Passeres, pas'ėr-ēz, *n.pl.* An extensive order of birds, also called insessorial or perching birds.
Passerine, pas'ėr-in, *a.* Pertaining to the order Passeres.
Passible, pas'i-bl, *a.* Capable of feeling; susceptible of impressions.
Passim, pas'im, *adv.* Here and there.
Passing, päs'ing, *p.a.* Current; cursory; fleeting.—*adv.* Exceedingly; very.
Passing-bell, päs'ing-bel, *n.* A bell rung at the time of, or just after, a person's death.
Passion, pa'shon, *n.* A suffering or enduring; the last suffering of Christ; a strong feeling or emotion; violent anger; ardour; vehement desire; love.
Passionate, pa'shon-āt, *a.* Moved by passion; vehement; animated; irascible; hasty.
Passionately, pa'shon-āt-li, *adv.* In a passionate manner; vehemently; angrily.
Passionless, pa'shon-les, *a.* Void of passion; calm of temper.
Passion-play, pa'shon-plā, *n.* A play representing scenes in the passion of Christ.
Passion-Sunday, pa'shon-sun-dā, *n.* The fifth Sunday in Lent.
Passion-week, pa'shon-wēk, *n.* The week immediately preceding Easter.
Passive, pas'iv, *a.* Capable of feeling; suffering; not acting; unresisting; inert; in *grammar*, expressing that the nominative is the object of some action or feeling.
Passively, pas'iv-li, *adv.* In a passive manner; without action; unresistingly.
Pass-key, päs'kē, *n.* A key for several locks; a master-key; a latch-key.
Passover, päs'ō-vėr, *n.* A feast of the Jews commemorative of the deliverance in Egypt, when the destroying angel passed over the houses of the Israelites; the sacrifice offered.
Passport, päs'pōrt, *n.* A license empowering a person to travel; that which enables one to reach some desired object.
Pass-word, päs'wėrd, *n.* A secret word to distinguish a friend from a stranger.
Past, päst, *p.a.* Gone by or beyond; belonging to an earlier period; spent; ended.—*n.* Former time.—*prep.* Beyond; out of reach of; after.—*adv.* By; so as to pass.
Paste, pāst, *n.* A mass in a semi-fluid state; a mixture of flour, &c., used in cookery, or to cause substances to adhere; a mixture of clay

for pottery; a brilliant glassy substance, used in making imitations of gems.—*vt.* (pasting, pasted). To unite or fasten with paste.
Pasteboard, pāst-bōrd, *n.* A thick paper formed of sheets pasted together; cardboard.
Pastel, pas'tel, *n.* A coloured crayon; a drawing made with coloured crayons; the art of drawing with coloured crayons.
Pastern, pas'tėrn, *n.* The part of a horse's leg between the joint next the foot and the hoof.
Pasteurization, past'ūr-ī-zā"shun, *n.* Checking the activity of bacteria in milk, &c., by heating it to 60° or 70° C.
Pastil, Pastille, pas'til, pas-tēl', *n.* A mass of resins, spices, &c., burned to disinfect or scent a room; a kind of sugar confectionery.
Pastime, pas'tīm, *n.* Recreation; diversion; sport; play.
Pastor, pas'tor, *n.* A minister of a church.
Pastoral, pas'tor-al, *a.* Pertaining to shepherds; rustic; rural; relating to the care of souls, or to a pastor.—*n.* A poem dealing with shepherds; a poem of rural life; a letter addressed by a bishop to the clergy and people of his diocese.
Pastorate, pas'tor-āt, *n.* Office or jurisdiction of a pastor; the body of pastors.
Pastry, pās'tri, *n.* Eatables made of paste; crust of pies, tarts, &c.
Pasturage, pas'tūr-āj, *n.* Grazing ground; growing grass for cattle.
Pasture, pas'tūr, *n.* Grass for the food of cattle; grazing ground; grass land.—*vt.* (pasturing, pastured). To feed on growing grass. —*vi.* To graze.
Pasty, pās'ti, *a.* Like paste.—*n.* A meat pie covered with paste.
Pat, pat, *n.* A light stroke with the fingers or hand; a tap; a small lump of butter beaten into shape.—*vt.* (patting, patted). To strike gently; to tap.—*a.* Hitting the mark; apt; convenient.—*adv.* Fitly; just in the nick.
Patch, pach, *n.* A piece of cloth sewn on a garment to repair it; a small piece of silk stuck on the face for adornment; a small piece of ground.—*vt.* To mend by sewing on a patch; to repair clumsily; to make hastily without regard to forms (with *up*).
Patchwork, pach'wėrk, *n.* Work composed of varied pieces sewn together; work composed of pieces clumsily put together.
Patchy, pach'i, *a.* Full of patches.
Pate, pāt, *n.* The head, or rather the top of the head.
Patella, pa-tel'la, *n.* A small pan, vase, or dish; the knee-pan.
Paten, pa'ten, *n.* A metallic flat dish; the plate on which the consecrated bread in the eucharist is placed.
Patent, pā'tent or pa'tent, *n.* A writing (called *letters patent*) granting a privilege, as a title of nobility; a similar writing, securing exclusive right to an invention or discovery.—*a.* Open; manifest; secured by patent; lacquered (leather).—*vt.* To secure, as the exclusive right of a thing to a person.
Patentee, pā'ten-tē or pa'ten-tē, *n.* One to whom a patent is granted.
Paterfamilias, pā'tėr-fa-mil"i-as, *n.* The head or father of a family.
Paternal, pa-tėr'nal, *a.* Fatherly; derived from the father; hereditary.
Paternity, pa-tėr'ni-ti, *n.* Fathership; relation of a father to his offspring; origin; authorship.
Paternoster, pa'tėr-nos-tėr, *n.* The Lord's prayer; a rosary; every tenth bead in a rosary.
Path, päth, *n.* A way beaten by the feet of man or beast; a footway; course or track; way or passage; course of life.
Pathetic, pa-thet'ik, *a.* Full of pathos; affecting; exciting pity, sorrow, &c.
Pathetically, pa-thet'ik-al-li, *adv.* In a pathetic manner; touchingly.
Pathologic, Pathological, path-o-loj'ik, path-o-loj'ik-al, *a.* Pertaining to pathology.
Pathologist, pa-thol'o-jist, *n.* One who is versed in or who treats of pathology.
Pathology, pa-thol'o-ji, *n.* That part of medicine which explains the nature of diseases, their causes and symptoms.
Pathos, pā'thos, *n.* Expression of strong or deep feeling; that quality which excites tender emotions, as pity, sympathy, &c.
Pathway, päth'wā, *n.* A path; course of life.
Patience, pā'shens, *n.* Quality of being patient; endurance; composure; forbearance; a card game for one.
Patient, pā'shent, *a.* Enduring without murmuring; not easily provoked; persevering; not hasty.—*n.* A person or thing passively affected; a person under medical treatment.
Patiently, pā'shent-li, *adv.* In a patient manner; with patience; submissively.
Patin, pa'tin. *See* PATEN.
Patina, pat'i-na, *n.* The fine green rust on ancient bronzes, copper coins, &c.
Patois, pat-wä, *n.* A rustic or provincial form of speech.
Patriarch, pā'tri-ärk, *n.* The chief of a race, tribe, or family; a dignitary above an archbishop in the Greek Church.
Patriarchal, pā-tri-ärk'al, *a.* Belonging to a patriarch; subject to a patriarch.
Patrician, pa-tri'shan, *a.* Belonging to the senators of ancient Rome; of noble birth.—*n.* A person of noble birth.
Patrimonial, pat-ri-mō'ni-al, *a.* Pertaining to a patrimony; inherited.
Patrimony, pat'ri-mo-ni, *n.* A paternal inheritance; a church estate or revenue.
Patriot, pā'tri-ot or pat', *n.* A person who loves his country, and zealously defends its interests.—*a.* Patriotic.
Patriotic, pā-tri-ot'ik or pat-, *a.* Actuated or inspired by the love of one's country; directed to the public welfare.
Patriotism, pā'tri-ot-izm or pat', *n.* The qualities of a patriot; love of one's country.
Patristic, pa-tris'tik, *a.* Pertaining to the fathers of the Christian church.
Patristics, pa-tris'tiks, *n.* That branch of theology which treats of the doctrines of the Christian fathers.
Patrol, pa-trōl', *n.* The marching round by a guard at night to secure the safety of a camp; the guard who go such rounds; on active service, a small party sent out to harass the enemy (fighting patrol), or to get information (reconnaissance patrol).—*vi.* (patrolling, patrolled). To go the rounds as a patrol. —*vt.* To pass round, as a guard.
Patron, pā'tron, *n.* A protector; one who supports or protects a person or a work; one

who has the disposition of a church-living, professorship, or other appointment; a guardian saint.

Patronage, pat'ron-āj or pā', *n.* Act of patronizing; special support; guardianship, as of a saint; right of presentation to an ecclesiastical benefice.

Patroness, pā'tron-es, *n.* A female patron.

Patronize, pat'ron-īz or pā', *vt.* To act as patron of; to countenance or favour; to assume the air of a superior to.

Patronizing, pat'ron-īz-ing or pā', *p.a.* Assuming the airs of a patron; acting like one who condescends to patronize or favour.

Patronymic, pat-rō-nim'ik, *n.* A name derived from that of parents or ancestors.

Patten, pat'en, *n.* A raised wooden shoe or sole.

Patter, pat'ėr, *vi.* To make a sound like that of falling drops; to move with quick steps; to mumble; to talk in a glib way.—*n.* A quick succession of small sounds; chatter; prattle.

Pattern, pat'ėrn, *n.* A model proposed for imitation; a sample; an ornamental design.

Patty, pat'i, *n.* A little pie; a pasty.

Paucity, pa̤'si-ti, *n.* Fewness; scarcity; smallness of quantity.

Paul, pa̤l, *n.* Same as *Pawl.*

Pauline, pa̤l'īn, *a.* Pertaining to St. *Paul,* or to his writings.

Paunch, pa̤nsh, *n.* The belly, and its contents; the abdomen.

Paunchy, pa̤nsh'i, *a.* Big-bellied.

Pauper, pa̤'pėr, *n.* A poor person; one dependent on the public for maintenance.

Pauperism, pa̤'pėr-izm, *n.* State of indigent persons requiring public support.

Pauperize, pa̤'pėr-īz, *vt.* To reduce to pauperism.

Pause, pa̤z, *n.* A temporary cessation; cessation proceeding from doubt; suspense.—*vi.* (pausing, paused). To make a short stop; to delay; to deliberate; to hesitate.

Pave, pāv, *vt.* (paving, paved). To cover with stone, brick, &c., so as to make a level and solid surface for carriages or foot-passengers.

Pavement, pāv'ment, *n.* The solid floor of a street, courtyard, &c.; paved part of a road used by foot-passengers; material with which anything is paved.

Pavid, pav'id, *a.* Timid; fearful.

Pavilion, pa-vil'yon, *n.* A tent; a small building having a tent-formed roof; a building of ornamental character for entertainments; the outer ear.—*vt.* To furnish with pavilions; to shelter with a tent.

Paving, pā'ving, *n.* Pavement.—*a.* Used for pavements.

Pavior, Paviour, pāv'i-ėr, *n.* A person whose occupation is to pave.

Pavonine, pav'ō-nīn, *a.* Belonging to or like a peacock; iridescent.

Paw, pa̤, *n.* The foot of animals having claws.—*vi.* To draw the fore-foot along the ground.—*vt.* To scrape with the fore-foot; to handle roughly.

Pawl, pa̤l, *n.* A short bar preventing a capstan, &c., from rolling back.

Pawn, pan, *n.* Something given as security for money borrowed; a pledge; state of being pledged; a pawnshop; a man of the lowest rank in chess.—*vt.* To give in pledge; to pledge with a pawnbroker.

Pawnbroker, pa̤n'brōk-ėr, *n.* A person licensed to lend money at a legally fixed rate of interest on goods deposited with him.

Pay, pā, *vt.* (paying, paid). To give money, &c., for goods received or service rendered; to reward; to discharge, as a debt; to give; to cover with tar or pitch.—*vi.* To make a payment; to be profitable or remunerative.—*n.* An equivalent for money due, goods, or services; salary; wages; reward.

Payable, pā'a-bl, *a.* That may or ought to be paid; justly due.

Pay-bill, pā'bil, *n.* A statement of the amount of money to be paid.

Payee, pā-ē', *n.* One to whom money is to be paid.

Paymaster, pā'mäs-tėr, *n.* An officer whose duty is to pay the men their wages.

Payment, pā'ment, *n.* Act of paying; what is given for service done; reward.

Paynim, pā'nim, *n.* A pagan; heathen.

Pea, pē, *n.*; pl. **Peas, Pease.** A well-known flowering plant cultivated for its seeds; one of the seeds of the plant.

Peace, pēs, *n.* A state of quiet; calm; repose; public tranquillity; freedom from war; concord.

Peaceable, pēs'a-bl, *a.* Disposed to peace; peaceful; pacific; calm.

Peaceably, pēs'a-bli, *adv.* In a peaceable manner; quietly.

Peaceful, pēs'fṳl, *a.* Free from war, noise, or disturbance; quiet; mild.

Peacefully, pēs'fṳl-li, *adv.* Quietly; calmly.

Peace-maker, pēs'māk-ėr, *n.* One who reconciles parties at variance.

Peace-offering, pēs'of-ėr-ing, *n.* Something offered to procure reconciliation.

Peach, pēch, *n.* A well-known tree and its fruit, allied to the almond.—*vi.* To betray one's accomplice.

Peacock, pē'kok, *n.* A large gallinaceous bird with rich plumage: properly the male bird.

Peahen, pē'hen, *n.* The female of the peacock.

Pea-jacket, pē'jak-et, *n.* A thick woollen jacket worn by seamen, fishermen, &c.

Peak, pēk, *n.* A projecting point; the top of a mountain ending in a point; the upper corner of a sail extended by a yard; also, the extremity of the yard or gaff.—*vi.* To look sickly; to be emaciated.

Peaked, pēkt, *a.* Ending in a peak or point.

Peal, pēl, *n.* A series of loud sounds, as of bells, thunder, &c.; a set of bells tuned to each other; chime.—*vi.* To give out a peal.—*vt.* To cause to ring or sound.

Pear, pār, *n.* A well-known fruit-tree; one of the fruits of the tree.

Pearl, pėrl, *n.* A smooth lustrous whitish gem produced by certain molluscs; something resembling a pearl; a small printing type; what is choicest and best.—*a.* Relating to or made of pearl or mother-of-pearl.—*vt.* To set or adorn with pearls.

Pearlash, pėr'lash, *n.* Commercial carbonate of potash.

Pearly, pėrl'i, *a.* Containing pearls; like a pearl or mother-of-pearl; clear; pure.

Peasant, pe'zant, *n.* A rustic; one whose business is rural labour.—*a.* Rustic.

Peasantry, pe'zant-ri, *n.* Peasants; rustics; the body of country people.

Peascod, Peasecod, pēz'kod, *n.* The pod of a pea.

Pease, pēz, *n.pl.* of *Pea.*
Peat, pēt, *n.* A kind of turf used as fuel; a small block of this cut and dried for fuel.
Peaty, pēt'i, *a.* Composed of peat; resembling peat; abounding in peat.
Pebble, peb'l, *n.* A stone rounded by the action of water; agate and rock-crystal used for glass in spectacles.
Pebbly, peb'li, *a.* Full of pebbles.
Pecan, Pecan-nut, pē-kan', pē-kan'nut, *n.* A species of hickory and its fruit.
Peccable, pek'a-bl, *a.* Liable to sin; apt to transgress the divine law.
Peccadillo, pek-a-dil'lō, *n.* A slight trespass or offence; a petty crime or fault.
Peccant, pek'ant, *a.* Sinning; criminal; morbid; bad; not healthy.
Peccary, pek'a-ri, *n.* A quadruped of America, allied to the swine.
Peck, pek, *n.* A dry measure of eight quarts. —*vt.* and *i.* To strike with the beak, or something pointed; to pick up, as food, with the beak.
Pecker, pek'ėr, *n.* One who or that which pecks; a woodpecker.
Peckish, pek'ish, *a.* Hungry.
Pecten, pek'ten, *n.* A marine bivalve mollusc having a shell with diverging furrows.
Pectic, pek'tik, *a.* Having the property of forming a jelly.
Pectinal, pek'tin-al, *a.* Pertaining to or resembling a comb.
Pectinate, pek'tin-āt, *a.* Toothed like a comb.
Pectoral, pek'to-ral, *a.* Pertaining to the breast.—*n.* A breastplate; a medicine for the chest and lungs.
Peculate, pe'kū-lāt, *vi.* To appropriate money or goods intrusted to one's care.
Peculation, pe-kū-lā'shon, *n.* Act of peculating; embezzlement.
Peculator, pe'kū-lāt-ėr, *n.* One who peculates.
Peculiar, pē-kū'li-ėr, *a.* One's own; characteristic; particular; unusual; odd.
Peculiarity, pē-kū'li-a"ri-ti, *n.* Quality of being peculiar; something peculiar to a person or thing.
Peculiarly, pē-kū'li-ėr-li, *adv.* In a peculiar manner; especially; singularly.
Pecuniary, pē-kū'ni-a-ri, *a.* Relating to or connected with money; consisting of money.
Pedagogic, ped-a-goj'ik, *a.* Resembling or belonging to a pedagogue.
Pedagogics, ped-a-goj'iks, *n.* The science or art of teaching.
Pedagogue, ped'a-gog, *n.* A teacher of children; a schoolmaster.
Pedagogy, ped'a-go-ji, *n.* The art or office of a pedagogue; the teaching profession.
Pedal, pēd'al, *a.* Pertaining to a foot or to a pedal.—*n.* pe'dal. A lever to be pressed by the foot; a part of a musical instrument acted on by the feet.
Pedant, pe'dant, *n.* One who makes a vain display of his learning; a narrow-minded scholar.
Pedantic, pe-dant'ik, *a.* Pertaining to or characteristic of a pedant.
Pedantically, pe-dant'ik-al-li, *adv.* In a pedantic manner.
Pedantry, pe'dant-ri, *n.* The qualities or character of a pedant; boastful display of learning; obstinate adherence to rules.
Peddle, ped'l, *vi.* and *t.* (peddling, peddled). To travel and sell small-wares; to trifle.
Peddler, ped'lėr, *n.* One who peddles; a pedlar.
Pedestal, pe'des-tal, *n.* The base or support of a column, pillar, statue, vase, &c.
Pedestrian, pe-des'tri-an, *a.* Going on foot; performed on foot.—*n.* One who journeys on foot; a remarkable walker.
Pedestrianism, pe-des'tri-an-izm, *n.* Practice of walking; art of a professional walker.
Pedicel, pe'di-sel, *n.* A small short foot-stalk of a leaf, flower, or fruit.
Pedigree, pe'di-grē, *n.* Lineage; line of ancestors; genealogy.
Pediment, pe'di-ment, *n.* The triangular mass resembling a gable at the end of buildings in the Greek style; a triangular decoration over a window, a door, &c.
Pedlar, Pedler, ped'lėr, *n.* A petty dealer who carries his wares with him.
Pedometer, pe-dom'et-ėr, *n.* An instrument which measures how far a person walks.
Peduncle, pē'dung-kl, *n.* The stem that supports the flower and fruit of a plant.
Peel, Peel-tower, pēl, pēl'tou-ėr, *n.* An old strong square fortress.
Peel, pēl, *vt.* To strip off, as bark or rind; to flay; to pare; to pillage.—*vi.* To lose the skin, bark or rind; to fall off, as bark or skin. —*n.* The skin or rind; a baker's wooden shovel.
Peep, pēp, *vi.* To chirp as a chicken; to begin to appear; to look through a crevice.—*n.* A chirp; a look through a small opening; first appearance.
Peer, pēr, *n.* One of the same rank; an equal; an associate; a nobleman (duke, marquis, earl, viscount, or baron).—*vi.* To appear; to peep out; to look narrowly.
Peerage, pēr'āj, *n.* The rank or dignity of a peer; the body of peers.
Peeress, pēr'es, *n.* A woman ennobled by descent, by creation, or by marriage.
Peerless, pēr'les, *a.* Matchless.
Peevish, pē'vish, *a.* Fretful; querulous; hard to please; froward.
Peewit, pē'wit, *n.* The lapwing.
Peg, peg, *n.* A piece of wood used in fastening things together; the pin of a musical instrument; a pin on which to hang anything.—*vt.* (pegging, pegged). To fasten with pegs.—*vi.* To work diligently.
Pekoe, pē'kō, *n.* A fine black tea.
Pelagian, pe-lā'ji-an, *n.* One who denies original sin, and asserts the doctrine of free-will and the merit of good works.—*a.* Pertaining to these doctrines or to Pelagius, their founder.
Pelagic, pe-laj'ik, *a.* Belonging to the ocean; inhabiting the open ocean.
Pelargonium, pel-är-gō'ni-um, *n.* A genus of ornamental plants, usually called *Geraniums.*
Pelasgian, Pelasgic, pe-las'ji-an, pe-las'jik, *a.* Pertaining to the Pelasgi, prehistoric inhabitants of Greece.
Pelerine, pel'ėr-in, *a.* A lady's long cape.
Pelf, pelf, *n.* Money; riches; filthy lucre.
Pelican, pel'i-kan, *n.* A large web-footed bird with a very large bill.
Pelisse, pe-lēs', *n.* A coat for ladies or children.
Pell, pel, *n.* A skin; a roll of parchment.

Pellet, pel'et, *n.* A little ball; one of the globules of small shot.
Pellicle, pel'i-kl, *n.* A thin skin or film.
Pell-mell, pel'mel, *adv.* With confused violence; in utter confusion.
Pellucid, pel-lū'sid, *a.* Transparent; not opaque; translucent.
Pelt, pelt, *n.* A raw hide; a blow; a heavy shower.—*vt.* To strike with something thrown. —*vi.* To throw missiles; to fall in a heavy shower.
Peltate, pel'tāt, *a.* In *botany*, fixed to the stalk by some point within the margin.
Peltry, pelt'ri, *n.* Undressed skins; furs in general.
Pelvic, pel'vik, *a.* Pertaining to the pelvis.
Pelvis, pel'vis, *n.* The bony cavity forming the framework of the lower part of the abdomen.
Pen, pen, *n.* An instrument for writing with ink; style or quality of writing; a small inclosure for cows, &c.; a fold.—*vt.* (penning, penned). To write; to compose; to coop or shut up.
Penal, pē'nal, *a.* Relating to, enacting, or incurring punishment.
Penalty, pen'al-ti, *n.* Punishment for a crime or offence; forfeit for non-fulfilment of conditions; sum to be forefeited; a fine.
Penance, pen'ans, *n.* An ecclesiastical punishment imposed for sin; voluntary suffering as an expression of penitence.
Penates, pē-nā'tēz, *n.pl.* Household gods.
Pence, pens, *n.* The plural of *penny*.
Penchant, päng'shäng, *n.* Strong inclination; bias.
Pencil, pen'sil, *n.* A small brush used by painters; an instrument of black-lead, &c., for writing and drawing; a converging or diverging aggregate of rays of light.—*vt.* (pencilling, pencilled). To write or mark with a pencil.
Pend, pend, *vi.* To impend; to wait for settlement.
Pendant, pen'dant, *n.* Anything hanging down by way of ornament; a hanging apparatus for giving light, &c.; an appendix or addition; a flag borne at the mast-head.
Pendent, pen'dent, *a.* Hanging; pendulous; projecting.—*n.* Something hanging.
Pending, pend'ing, *p.a.* Hanging in suspense; undecided.—*pret.* During.
Pendulate, pen'dū-lāt, *vi.* To swing freely like a pendulum; to swing.
Pendulous, pen'dū-lus, *a.* Hanging; hanging so as to swing; swinging.
Pendulum, pen'dū-lum, *n.* A body suspended and swinging; the swinging piece in a clock which regulates its motion.
Penetrable, pen'e-tra-bl, *a.* That may be entered or pierced; susceptible of moral or intellectual impression.
Penetrably, pen'e-tra-bli, *adv.* In a penetrable manner; so as to be penetrable.
Penetralia, pen'e-trā''li-a, *n.pl.* The inner parts of a building; a sanctuary; hidden things.
Penetrate, pen'e-trāt, *vt.* and *i.* To enter or pierce, as into another body; to affect, as the mind; to cause to feel; to understand.
Penetrating, pen'e-trāt-ing, *p.a.* Sharp; subtle; acute; discerning.
Penetration, pen-e-trā'shon, *n.* Act of penetrating; sagacity; discernment.
Penetrative, pe'ne-trāt-iv, *a.* Piercing; sharp; subtle; acute; discerning.
Penguin, pen'gwin, *n.* A web-footed, flightless sea bird.
Penicillin, pen-i-sil'in, *n.* A bacteria-destroying substance derived from a mould.
Peninsula, pen-in'sū-la, *n.* A portion of land almost surrounded by water.
Peninsular, pen-in'sū-lėr, *a.* In the form of, pertaining to, or inhabiting a peninsula.
Penis, pē'nis, *n.* The male organ of generation.
Penitence, pe'ni-tens, *n.* State of being penitent; repentance; contrition.
Penitent, pe'ni-tent, *a.* Suffering sorrow on account of one's own sins; contrite.—*n.* One who repents of sin.
Penitential, pe-ni-ten'shal, *a.* Pertaining to or expressing penitence.—*n.* A Roman Catholic book of rules for penitents.
Penitentiary, pe-ni-ten'sha-ri, *a.* Relating to penance.—*n.* One who does penance; an office or official of the R. Catholic church connected with the granting of dispensations, &c.; a house of correction.
Penknife, pen'nif, *n.* A small pocket-knife.
Penman, pen'man, *n.*; pl. **-men.** A writer.
Penmanship, pen'man-ship, *n.* The use of the pen; art or manner of writing.
Pennant, pen'ant, *n.* A small flag; a pennon; a pendant.
Penniless, pen'i-les, *a.* Without money.
Pennon, pen'on, *n.* A small pointed flag carried on spears or lances.
Penny, pen'i, *n.*; pl. **Pennies** or **Pence,** pen'iz, pens. (*Pennies* denotes the number of coins; *pence* the value.) A bronze coin, the twelfth of a shilling; money.
Pennyweight, pen'i-wāt, *n.* A troy weight containing twenty-four grains.
Penny-wise, pen'i-wīz, *a.* Wise in saving small sums at the hazard of larger.
Pennyworth, pen'i-wėrth, *n.* As much as is bought for a penny; any purchase.
Pensil, pen'sil, *a.* Hanging; suspended.
Pension, pen'shon, *n.* A stated yearly allowance in consideration of past services; a boarding-house on the Continent (pronounced päng-syong).—*vt.* To grant a pension to.
Pensionary, pen'shon-a-ri, *a.* Receiving a pension; consisting in a pension.—*n.* A pensioner.
Pensioner, pen'shon-ėr, *n.* One in receipt of a pension; a student at Cambridge, who pays for his board and other charges, as contrasted with a scholar, exhibitioner, or sizar.
Pensive, pen'siv, *a.* Thoughtful; expressing thoughtfulness with sadness.
Pent, pent, *p.a.* Shut up; confined (often with *up*).
Pentagon, pen'ta-gon, *n.* A plane figure having five angles and five sides.
Pentagonal, pen-tag'on-al, *a.* Having five corners or angles.
Pentahedron, pen-ta-hē'dron, *n.* A solid figure having five equal faces.
Pentameter, pen-tam'et-ėr, *n.* A poetic verse of five feet.
Pentateuch, pen'ta-tūk, *n.* The first five books of the Old Testament.
Pentecost, pen'tē-kost, *n.* A festival of the Jews on the fiftieth day after the Passover; Whitsuntide.
Penthouse, pent'hous, *n.* A shed standing

aslope from the main wall or building; a roof sloping up against a wall.
Pent-roof, pent'röf, *n.* A sloping roof all of whose slope is on one side.
Penult, pēn'ult or pen'ult, *n.* The last syllable of a word except one.
Penultimate, pen-ul'ti-māt, *a.* The last but one.—*n.* The last syllable but one; penult.
Penumbra, pen-um'bra, *n.* The partial shadow on the margin of the total shadow in an eclipse; the point of a picture where the shade blends with the light.
Penurious, pe-nū'ri-us, *a.* Pertaining to penury; parsimonious; niggardly.
Penury, pe'nū-ri, *n.* Poverty; indigence; want of the necessaries of life.
Peon, pē'on, *n.* An attendant; a native constable; a day-labourer; a kind of serf.
Peony, pē'o-ni, *n.* A genus of plants of the ranunculus family, with large flowers.
People, pē'pl, *n.* The body of persons who compose a community, race, or nation; persons indefinitely.—*vt.* (peopling, peopled). To stock with inhabitants; to populate.
Pepper, pep'ėr, *n.* A plant and its aromatic pungent seed, much used in seasoning, &c.—*vt.* To sprinkle with pepper; to pelt with shot or missiles; to drub thoroughly.
Pepper-box, pep'ėr-boks, *n.* A box with a perforated lid, for sprinkling pepper.
Pepper-corn, pep'ėr-korn, *n.* The berry or fruit of the pepper plant.
Peppermint, pep'ėr-mint, *n.* A plant of the mint genus having a penetrating aromatic smell and a strong pungent taste.
Peppery, pep'ėr-i, *a.* Having the qualities of pepper; choleric; irascible.
Pepsin, Pepsine, pep'sin, *n.* The active principle of gastric juice.
Peptic, pep'tik, *a.* Promoting digestion; relating to digestion; digestive.
Per, pėr, *prep.* A Latin preposition used in the sense of *by* or *for*, chiefly in certain Latin phrases, as *per annum*, by or for the year.
Peradventure, pėr-ad-ven'tūr, *adv.* Perhaps.
Perambulate, pėr-am'bū-lāt, *vt.* To walk through or over; to traverse; to survey.
Perambulation, pėr-am'bū-lā"shon, *n.* Act of perambulating; survey or inspection.
Perambulator, pėr-am'bū-lāt-ėr, *n.* One who perambulates; a child's carriage propelled by hand from behind.
Perceivable, pėr-sēv'a-bl, *a.* That may be perceived; perceptible.
Perceive, pėr-sēv', *vt.* (perceiving, perceived). To apprehend by the organs of sense or by the mind; to observe; to discern.
Percentage, pėr-sent'āj, *n.* The allowance, duty, rate of interest, proportion, &c., reckoned on each hundred.
Perceptible, pėr-sep'ti-bl, *a.* Perceivable.
Perceptibly, pėr-sep'ti-bli, *adv.* In a perceptible manner.
Perception, pėr-sep'shon, *n.* Act, process, or faculty of perceiving; discernment.
Perceptive, pėr-sep'tiv, *a.* Relating to perception; having the faculty of perceiving.
Perch, pėrch, *n.* A spiny fresh-water fish; a roost for fowls; an elevated place or position; 5½ yards, also called a rod or pole; 30¼ square yards, a square rod.—*vi.* To sit on a perch; to light, as a bird.—*vt.* To place on a perch.
Perchance, pėr-chans', *adv.* Perhaps.
Percipient, pėr-sip'i-ent, *a.* Perceiving; having the faculty of perception.
Percolate, pėr'kō-lāt, *vt.* and *i.* To strain through; to filter.
Percolation, pėr-kō-lā'shon, *n.* Act of percolating; passing of liquid through a porous body.
Percolator, pėr'kō-lāt-ėr, *n.* One who or that which filters.
Percuss, pėr-kus', *vt.* To strike against; to tap or strike in medical practice.
Percussion, pėr-ku'shon, *n.* Collision; impact; the act of striking the surface of the body to determine by sound the condition of the organs subjacent.
Percussive, pėr-kus'iv, *a.* Acting by percussion; striking against.
Perdition, pėr-di'shon, *n.* Entire ruin; utter destruction; eternal death.
Perdu, Perdue, pėr'dū or pėr-dū', *a.* Hid; in concealment; out of sight.
Peregrinate, pe're-grin-āt, *vi.* To travel from place to place; to wander.
Peregrination, pe're-grin-ā"shon, *n.* A travelling; a wandering.
Peregrine, pe're-grin, *n.* A kind of falcon.
Peremptorily, pe'remp-to-ri-li, *adv.* In a peremptory manner; absolutely; positively.
Peremptory, pe'remp-to-ri, *a.* Such as to preclude debate; decisive; absolute.
Perennial, pe-ren'i-al, *a.* Lasting through the year; perpetual; unceasing.—*n.* A plant whose root remains alive more years than two.
Perennially, pe-ren'i-al-li, *adv.* In a perennial manner; continually.
Perfect, pėr'fekt, *a.* Finished; complete; fully informed; completely skilled; faultless; in *grammar*, denoting a tense which expresses an act completed.—*vt.* To accomplish; to make perfect; to make fully skilful.
Perfectibility, pėr-fek'ti-bil"i-ti, *n.* The quality of being perfectible.
Perfectible, pėr-fek'ti-bl, *a.* Capable of becoming or being made perfect.
Perfection, pėr-fek'shon, *n.* State of being perfect; an excellence perfect in its kind.
Perfective, pėr-fek'tiv, *a.* Conducing to perfection.
Perfectly, pėr'fekt-li, *adv.* In a perfect manner; consummately; completely; exactly.
Perfervid, pėr-fėr'vid, *a.* Very fervid.
Perfidious, pėr-fi'di-us, *a.* Guilty of or involving perfidy; treacherous; faithless.
Perfidy, pėr'fi-di, *n.* Act of breaking faith or allegiance; the violation of a trust reposed; treachery; disloyalty.
Perforate, pėr'fo-rāt, *vt.* To bore or penetrate through; to pierce with a pointed instrument.
Perforation, pėr-fo-rā'shon, *n.* Act of perforating; a hole bored.
Perforator, pėr'fo-rāt-ėr, *n.* One who or that which perforates.
Perforce, pėr-fōrs', *adv.* By force or violence; of necessity.
Perform, pėr-form', *vt.* To accomplish; to effect; to do; to act.—*vi.* To act a part; to play on a musical instrument, &c.
Performable, pėr-form'a-bl, *a.* That may be performed.
Performance, pėr-form'ans, *n.* Act of performing; deed; achievement; a literary work; exhibition on the stage; entertainment at a place of amusement.

Performer, pėr-form'ėr, *n.* One who performs, as an actor, musician, &c.
Performing, pėr-form'ing, *p.a.* Exhibiting performances or tricks.
Perfume, pėr'fūm or pėr-fūm', *n.* A pleasant scent or smell; fragrance.—*vt.* (perfuming, perfumed). To scent with perfume; to impregnate with a grateful odour.
Perfumer, pėr-fūm'ėr, *n.* One who or that which perfumes; one who sells perfumes.
Perfumery, pėr-fūm'ėr-i, *n.* Perfumes in general; the art of preparing perfumes.
Perfunctory, pėr-fungk'to-ri, *a.* Done carelessly or in a half-hearted manner; negligent.
Perhaps, pėr-haps', *adv.* It may be; peradventure; perchance; possibly.
Peri, pē'ri, *n.* In Persian belief, a fairy or spiritual being excluded from paradise till penance is accomplished.
Pericardium, pe-ri-kär'di-um, *n.* The membranous sac that incloses the heart.
Peridot, pe'ri-dot, *n.* A variety of the precious stone, chrysolite.
Perigee, pe'ri-jē, *n.* That point in the moon's orbit nearest the earth.
Perihelion, pe-ri-hēl'i-on, *n.* That point of the orbit of a planet or comet nearest the sun.
Peril, pe'ril, *n.* Risk; hazard; danger.—*vt.* (perilling, perilled). To hazard; to expose to danger.
Perilous, pe'ril-us, *a.* Dangerous; hazardous; full of risk.
Perilously, pe'ril-us-li, *adv.* Dangerously.
Perimeter, pe-rim'et-ėr, *n.* The outer boundary of a body or figure.
Period, pē'ri-od, *n.* The time taken up by a heavenly body in revolving round the sun; the time at which anything ends; end; an indefinite portion of any continued state or existence; a complete sentence; the point that marks the end of a sentence, thus (.).
Periodic, pē-ri-od'ik, *a.* Pertaining to period or revolution; happening by recurrence, at a stated time.
Periodical, pē-ri-od'ik-al, *n.* A magazine, newspaper, &c., published at regular periods. —*a.* Periodic.
Periodically, pē-ri-od'ik-al-li, *adv.* In a periodical manner; at stated periods.
Periosteum, pe-ri-os'tē-um, *n.* A membrane investing the bones of animals.
Peripatetic, pe'ri-pa-tet"ik, *a.* Walking about; itinerant; pertaining to Aristotle's system of philosophy, taught while walking.— *n.* One who walks; a follower of Aristotle.
Periphery, pe-rif'ėr-i, *n.* The boundary line of a figure.
Periphrasis, pe-rif'ra-sis, *n.* A roundabout form of expression; circumlocution.
Periphrastic, pe-ri-fras'tik, *a.* Characterized by periphrasis; circumlocutory.
Peripteral, pe-rip'tėr-al, *a.* Surrounded by a single row of columns, as a temple.
Periscope, pe'ri-skōp, *n.* An apparatus or structure rising above the deck of a submarine vessel, giving by means of mirrors, &c., a view of outside surroundings, though the vessel itself remains submerged; a similar device used in trenches.
Periscopic, pe-ri-skop'ik, *a.* Viewing on all sides: applied to spectacles having concavo-convex lenses.
Perish, pe'rish, *vi.* To die; to wither and decay; to be destroyed; to come to nothing.
Perishable, pe'rish-a-bl, *a.* Liable to perish; subject to decay or destruction.
Peristyle, pe'ri-stil, *n.* A range of surrounding columns.
Peritoneum, Peritonæum, pe'ri-tō-nē"um, *n.* A membrane investing the internal surface of the abdomen, and the viscera contained in it.
Peritonitis, per'i-tō-nī"tis, *n.* Inflammation of the peritoneum.
Periwig, pe'ri-wig, *n.* A small wig; a peruke.
Periwinkle, pe-ri-wing'kl, *n.* A univalve mollusc found abundantly on British rocks; a British under-shrub.
Perjure, pėr'jūr, *vt.* (perjuring, perjured). To forswear; wilfully to make a false oath when administered legally.
Perjurer, pėr'jūr-ėr, *n.* One who perjures himself.
Perjury, pėr'jū-ri, *n.* Act or crime of forswearing; act of violating an oath or solemn promise.
Perk, pėrk, *a.* Trim; spruce; pert.—*vi.* To hold up the head pertly.—*vt.* To make trim; to prank; to hold up (the head) pertly.
Permanence, Permanency, pėr'ma-nens, pėr'ma-nen-si, *n.* State or quality of being permanent; duration; fixedness.
Permanent, pėr'ma-nent, *a.* Lasting; durable; not decaying; abiding; fixed.
Permeable, pėr'mē-a-bl, *a.* That may be permeated or passed through, as solid matter.
Permeate, pėr'mē-āt, *vt.* (permeating, permeated). To pass through the pores or interstices of; to penetrate without rupture or displacement of parts.
Permeation, pėr-mē-ā'shon, *n.* Act of permeating.
Permian, pėr'mi-an, *a.* In *geology*, a term applied to a system of rocks lying beneath the trias and immediately above the carboniferous system.
Permissible, pėr-mis'i-bl, *a.* Allowable.
Permission, pėr-mi'shon, *n.* Act of permitting; allowance; authorization.
Permissive, pėr-mis'iv, *a.* That permits; granting permission or liberty; allowing.
Permit, pėr-mit', *vt.* and *i.* (permitting, permitted). To allow; to grant; to suffer; to concede.—*n.* per'mit. A written permission or licence given by competent authority.
Permutation, pėr-mū-tā'shon, *n.* Interchange; in *mathematics*, any of the ways in which a set of quantities can be arranged.
Permute, pėr-mūt', *vt.* To interchange.
Pernicious, pėr-ni'shus, *a.* Having the quality of destroying or injuring; destructive; deadly; noxious.
Perorate, pe'rō-rāt, *vi.* To make a peroration; to speechify; to spout.
Peroration, pe-rō-rā'shon, *n.* A rhetorical passage at the conclusion of a speech.
Peroxide, pėr-ok'sid, *n.* The oxide of a given base which contains the greatest quantity of oxygen.
Perpend, per-pend', *vt.* To weigh in the mind; to consider; to ponder.
Perpendicular, pėr-pen-di'kū-lėr, *a.* Perfectly upright or vertical; being at right angles to a given line or surface.—*n.* A line at right angles to the plane of the horizon or to another line.

Perpendicularly, pėr-pen-di'kū-lėr-li, *adv.* Vertically; at right angles.

Perpetrate, pėr'pe-trāt, *vt.* To do in a bad sense; to be guilty of; to commit.

Perpetration, pėr'pe-trā'shon, *n.* The act of perpetrating; commission.

Perpetrator, pėr'pe-trāt-ėr, *n.* One that perpetrates.

Perpetual, pėr-pe'tū-al, *a.* Continuing without end; permanent; everlasting.

Perpetually, pėr-pe'tū-al-li, *adv.* Constantly; continually.

Perpetuate, pėr-pe'tū-āt, *vt.* To make perpetual; to preserve from oblivion.

Perpetuation, pėr-pe'tū-ā"shon, *n.* Act of perpetuating or making perpetual.

Perpetuity, pėr-pe-tū'i-ti, *n.* State or quality of being perpetual; endless duration; something of which there will be no end.

Perplex, pėr-pleks', *vt.* To entangle or involve; to embarrass; to distract.

Perplexing, pėr-pleks'ing, *p.a.* Troublesome; embarrassing; difficult; intricate.

Perplexity, pėr-pleks'i-ti, *n.* State of being puzzled, or at a loss; bewilderment; state of being intricate or involved.

Perquisite, pėr'kwi-zit, *n.* Something in addition to regular wages or salary.

Perruque, pe-rök', *n.* A peruke.

Perry, pe'ri, *n.* The fermented juice of pears, prepared in the same way as cider.

Persecute, pėr'se-kūt, *vt.* (persecuting, persecuted). To harass with unjust punishment; to afflict for adherence to a particular creed.

Persecution, pėr-se-kū'shon, *n.* Act or practice of persecuting; state of being persecuted; continued annoyance.

Persecutor, pėr'se-kūt-ėr, *n.* One who persecutes.

Perseverance, pėr-se-vē'rans, *n.* Act or habit of persevering; continued diligence.

Persevere, pėr-se-vēr', *vi.* (persevering, persevered). To continue steadfastly in any business; to pursue steadily any design.

Persevering, pėr-se-vēr'ing, *p.a.* Given to persevere; constant in purpose.

Persian, pėr'shi-an, *a.* Pertaining to Persia, the Persians or their language.—*n.* A native of Persia; language spoken in Persia; a thin silk formerly used for lining.

Persiflage, pėr'sē-fläzh, *n.* Idle bantering talk.

Persist, pėr-sist', *vi.* To continue steadily in any business or course; to persevere; to continue in a certain state.

Persistence, Persistency, pėr-sist'ens, pėr-sist'en-si, *n.* Act or state of persisting; perseverance; continuance; obstinacy.

Persistent, pėr-sist'ent, *a.* Persisting; steady; tenacious.

Persistently, pėr-sist'ent-li, *adv.* In a persistent manner.

Person, pėr'son, *n.* An individual human being; each of the three beings of the Godhead; bodily form; one of the three inflections of a verb.—**In person,** by oneself; not by representatives.

Personable, pėr'son-a-bl, *a.* Having a well-formed body; of good appearance.

Personage, pėr'son-āj, *n.* A person of importance; a man or woman of distinction.

Personal, pėr'son-al, *a.* Pertaining to a person; peculiar or proper to him or her; belonging to face and figure; denoting the person in a grammatical sense.

Personality, pėr-son-al'i-ti, *n.* State of being personal; that which constitutes an individual a distinct person; disparaging remark on one's conduct and character; in *law*, personal estate.

Personally, pėr'son-al-li, *adv.* In person; with respect to an individual; particularly.

Personalty, pėr'son-al-ti, *n.* Personal property, in distinction from real property.

Personate, pėr'son-āt, *vt.* To assume the character or appearance of; to act the part of.

Personation, pėr-son-ā'shon, *n.* The act of personating.

Personification, pėr-son'i-fi-kā"shon, *n.* Act of personifying; embodiment; a metaphor which represents inanimate objects as possessing the attributes of persons.

Personify, pėr-son'i-fī, *vt.* To represent with the attributes of a person; to impersonate.

Personnel, pėr-son-el', *n.* The body of persons employed in any occupation.

Perspective, pėr-spek'tiv, *n.* The art of representing objects on a flat surface so that they appear to have their natural dimensions and relations; a representation of objects in perspective; view.—*a.* Pertaining to the art of perspective.

Perspicacious, pėr-spi-kā'shus, *a.* Quick-sighted; of acute discernment.

Perspicacity, pėr-spi-kas'i-ti, *n.* Acuteness of discernment; penetration; sagacity.

Perspicuity, pėr-spi-kū'i-ti, *n.* The quality of being perspicuous; easiness to be understood; plainness; distinctness.

Perspicuous, pėr-spi'kū-us, *a.* Clear to the understanding; lucid.

Perspiration, pėr-spi-rā'shon, *n.* Act of perspiring; exudation of sweat; sweat.

Perspiratory, pėr-spir'a-to-ri, *a.* Pertaining to perspiration.

Perspire, pėr-spīr', *vi.* (perspiring, perspired). To emit the moisture of the body through the skin; to sweat; to exude.—*vt.* To emit through pores.

Persuade, pėr-swād', *vt.* (persuading, persuaded). To influence by argument, advice, &c.; to induce; to prevail on.

Persuasion, pėr-swā'zhon, *n.* Act of persuading; settled opinion or conviction; a creed or belief; a sect or party.

Persuasive, pėr-swā'siv, *a.* Having the power of persuading; calculated to persuade.—*n.* That which persuades; an incitement.

Pert, pėrt, *a.* Lively; brisk; saucy; bold.

Pertain, pėr-tān', *vi.* To belong; to relate; to concern; to regard.

Pertinacious, pėr-ti-nā'shus, *a.* Obstinate; inflexible; determined; persistent.

Pertinacity, pėr-ti-nas'i-ti, *n.* Obstinacy; resolution; constancy.

Pertinence, Pertinency, pėr'ti-nens, pėr'ti-nen-si, *n.* Quality or state of being pertinent; fitness; appositeness.

Pertinent, pėr'ti-nent, *a.* Related to the subject or matter in hand; apposite; fit.

Pertinently, pėr'ti-nent-li, *adv.* In a pertinent manner; appositely; to the purpose.

Pertly, pėrt'li, *adv.* Smartly; saucily.

Perturb, pėr-tėrb', *vt.* To disturb; to agitate; to disquiet; to confuse.

Perturbation, pėr-tėrb-ā'shon, *n.* Act of

perturbing; disorder; uneasiness; cause of disquiet.

Peruke, pe-rök' or pe-rūk', *n.* A wig or periwig.

Perusal, pe-rūz'al, *n.* Act of perusing or reading.

Peruse, pe-rūz', *vt.* (perusing, perused). To read through; to read with attention; to examine carefully.

Peruvian, pe-rū'vi-an, *a.* Pertaining to Peru. —*n.* A native of Peru.

Pervade, pėr-vād', *vt.* (pervading, pervaded). To pass or flow through; to permeate; to be diffused through.

Pervasion, pėr-vā'zhon, *n.* Act of pervading.

Pervasive, pėr-vā'siv, *a.* Tending or having power to pervade.

Perverse, pėr-vėrs', *a.* Obstinate in the wrong; stubborn; untractable; petulant.

Perversely, pėr-vėrs'li, *adv.* Stubbornly; obstinately in the wrong.

Perversion, pėr-vėr'shon, *n.* A diverting from the true intent or object; misapplication.

Perversity, pėr-vėr'si-ti, *n.* State or quality of being perverse; disposition to thwart.

Perversive, pėr-ver'siv, *a.* Tending to pervert.

Pervert, pėr-vert', *vt.* To turn from truth or proper purpose; to corrupt; to misinterpret; to misapply.—*n.* pėr'vėrt. One who has been perverted.

Pervious, pėr'vi-us, *a.* That may be penetrated; permeable.

Peseta, pe-sē'ta, *n.* A Spanish silver coin corresponding to a franc.

Pessimism, pes'im-izm, *n.* The doctrine that the present state of things tends only to evil; the tendency always to look at the dark side of things.

Pessimist, pes'im-ist, *n.* One who believes in pessimism, or takes an unfavourable view of affairs.

Pessimistic, pes-im-is'tik, *a.* Pertaining to pessimism.

Pest, pest, *n.* A deadly epidemic disease; plague; pestilence; a mischievous person.

Pester, pes'tėr, *vt.* To plague; to trouble; to annoy with little vexations.

Pest-house, pest'hous, *n.* A hospital for contagious and deadly diseases.

Pestiferous, pes-tif'ėr-us, *a.* Pestilential; noxious; infectious; contagious.

Pestilence, pes'ti-lens, *n.* Any contagious disease that is epidemic and fatal; something morally evil or destructive.

Pestilent, pes'ti-lent, *a.* Pestilential; mischievous; pernicious; troublesome.

Pestilential, pes-ti-len'shal, *a.* Partaking of the nature of a pestilence or the plague; destructive; pernicious.

Pestle, pes'l, *n.* An instrument for pounding substances in a mortar.—*vt.* and *i.* (pestling, pestled). To pound with a pestle.

Pet, pet, *n.* A darling; any little animal fondled and indulged; fit of peevishness.—*vt.* (petting, petted). To fondle; to indulge.

Petal, pe'tal, *n.* A flower leaf.

Petard, pe-tärd', *n.* An engine of war fixed on gates, barricades, &c., to destroy them by explosion.

Peter-pence, Peter's-pence, pē'tėr-pens, pē'tėrz-pens, *n.pl.* Money contributed annually to the popes.

Petiole, pe'ti-ol, *n.* The foot-stalk of a leaf.

Petite, pė-tēt', *a.* Small in figure; tiny.

Petition, pē-ti'shon, *n.* An entreaty, supplication, or prayer; a written application in legal proceedings.—*vt.* To supplicate; to solicit.

Petitionary, pē-ti'shon-a-ri, *a.* Supplicatory; containing a petition.

Petitioner, pē-ti'shon-ėr, *n.* One who petitions or presents a petition.

Petrel, pet'rel, *n.* A web-footed sea-bird often found far from land.

Petrifaction, pet-ri-fak'shon, *n.* The process of changing into stone; a fossil.

Petrifactive, pet-ri-fak'tiv, *a.* Having power to convert into stone.

Petrify, pet-ri-fī, *vt.* To turn into stone or a fossil; to paralyse or stupefy.—*vi.* To become stone, or of a stony hardness.

Petrol, pet'rol, *n.* Petroleum spirit; refined petroleum used as the source of power for the internal-combustion engines of motor-cars, aeroplanes, &c.

Petroleum, pe-trō'lē-um, *n.* Rock-oil; an inflammable liquid found in the earth.

Petrology, pe-trol'o-ji, *n.* The study of rocks.

Petrous, pet'rus, *a.* Like stone; stony.

Petticoat, pet'i-kōt, *n.* A loose under-garment worn by women.

Pettifog, pet'i-fog, *vi.* (pettifogging, pettifogged). To act in petty cases, as a lawyer.

Pettifogger, pet'i-fog'ėr, *n.* A lawyer employed in small or mean business.

Pettifoggery, pet-i-fog'ė-ri, *n.* The practice of a pettifogger; tricks; quibbles.

Pettish, pet'ish, *a.* In a pet; peevish.

Pettitoes, pet'i-tōz, *n.pl.* The toes or feet of a pig; sometimes used for the human feet.

Petto, pet'tō, *n.* The breast; hence, ***in petto,*** in secrecy.

Petty, pet'i, *a.* Small; little; trifling; trivial.

Petulance, Petulancy, pe'tū-lans, pe'tū-lan-si, *n.* Quality of being petulant; peevishness; pettishness; frowardness.

Petulant, pe'tū-lant, *a.* Irritable; peevish; fretful; saucy; pert; capricious.

Pew, pū, *n.* An inclosed seat in a church.

Pewit, pē'wit, *n.* The lapwing or peewit.

Pewter, pū'tėr, *n.* An alloy mainly of tin and lead; a vessel made of pewter.—*a.* Relating to or made of pewter.

Pewterer, pū'tėr-ėr, *n.* One who makes vessels and utensils of pewter.

Pewtery, pū'tė-ri, *a.* Belonging to or resembling pewter.

Phaeton, fā'ton, *n.* An open carriage on four wheels.

Phalange, fa-lanj', *n.* One of the small bones of the fingers and toes.

Phalanx, fal'angks, *n.*; pl. **-anges, anxes.** The heavy-armed infantry of an ancient Greek army; a body of troops in close array; a small bone of the fingers or toes.

Phallic, fal'lik, *a.* Pertaining to the phallus.

Phallus, fal'lus, *n.* The emblem of the generative power in nature, especially in certain religious usages.

Phantasm, fan'tazm, *n.* An apparition; a phantom; an idea, notion, or fancy.

Phantasmagoria, fan-tas'ma-gō"ri-a, *n.* An exhibition of figures by shadows, as by the magic lantern; illusive images.

Phantasmal, fan-taz'mal, *a.* Spectral; illusive.

Phantasy, fan'ta-si, *n.* *See* FANTASY.

Phantom, fan'tom, *n.* An apparition; a spectre; a fancied vision; a phantasm.
Pharisaic, Pharisaical, fa-ri-sā'ik, fa-ri-sā'ik-al, *a.* Pertaining to or resembling the Pharisees; hypocritical.
Pharisaism, fa'ri-sā-izm, *n.* The notions, doctrines, and conduct of the Pharisees; formality and hypocrisy in religion.
Pharisee, fa'ri-sē, *n.* A Jew strict in religious observances; a hypocrite.
Pharmaceutic, Pharmaceutical, fär-ma-sū'tik, fär-ma-sū'tik-al, *a.* Pertaining to the knowledge or art of pharmacy.
Pharmaceutics, fär-ma-sū'tiks, *n.* Pharmacy.
Pharmacology, fär-ma-kol'o-ji, *n.* The science of drugs; the art of preparing medicines.
Pharmacopœia, fär'ma-kō-pē"a, *n.* A book describing the preparation of medicines.
Pharmacy, fär'ma-si, *n.* The art or practice of preparing medicines.
Pharos, fā'ros, *n.* A lighthouse.
Pharynx, fa'ringks, *n.* The muscular sac between the mouth and the œsophagus.
Phase, fāz, *n.* A particular stage of the moon or a planet in respect to illumination; state of a varying phenomenon; one of the various aspects of a question.
Phasis, fā'siz, *n.*; pl. **phases,** fā'sēz. A phase: used in astronomy.
Pheasant, fe'zant, *n.* A bird commonly reared and preserved for sport and food.
Pheasantry, fe'zant-ri, *n.* A place for breeding, rearing, and keeping pheasants.
Phenomenal, fē-no'men-al, *a.* Pertaining to or constituted by a phenomenon; extremely remarkable; astounding.
Phenomenon, fē-no'me-non, *n.*; pl. **-mena.** An appearance; anything visible; an appearance whose cause is not immediately obvious; something extraordinary.
Phial, fī'al, *n.* A small glass bottle.
Philabeg, Philibeg, fil'a-beg, fil'i-beg, *n.* *See* FILLIBEG.
Philander, fi-lan'dėr, *vi.* To make love sentimentally to a lady; to flirt.
Philanthropic, Philanthropical, fī-lan-throp'ik, fi-lan-throp'ik-al, *a.* Relating to philanthropy; entertaining good-will towards all men; benevolent.
Philanthropist, fi-lan'throp-ist, *n.* One devoted to philanthropy; one who exerts himself in doing good to his fellowmen.
Philanthropy, fi-lan'thro-pi, *n.* The love of man or of mankind; benevolence towards the whole human family.
Philatelist, fi-lat'e-list, *n.* One who collects postage-stamps.
Philately, fi-lat'e-li, *n.* The practice of collecting postage-stamps.
Philharmonic, fil-här-mon'ik, *a.* Loving harmony; musical.
Philippic, fi-lip'ik, *n.* A discourse or declamation full of acrimonious invective.
Philistine, fi-lis'tīn or fil'is-tin, *n.* A person deficient in culture, and wanting in taste; a person of narrow views.
Philistinism, fil'is-tin-izm, *n.* Manner or modes of thinking of Philistines.
Philological, Philologic, fil-ō-loj'ik-al, fil-ō-loj'ik, *a.* Pertaining to philology.
Philologist, Philologer, fi-lol'o-jist, fi-lol'o-jėr, *n.* One versed in philology.
Philology, fi-lol'o-ji, *n.* The study of language; linguistic science.
Philomel, Philomela, fil'ō-mel, fil-ō-mē'la, *n.* The nightingale.
Philosopher, fi-los'o-fėr, *n.* A person versed in philosophy; one who studies moral or mental science.
Philosophic, Philosophical, fi-lō-sof'ik, fi-lō-sof'ik-al, *a.* Pertaining or according to philosophy; given to philosophy; calm; cool; temperate; rational.
Philosophically, fi-lō-sof'ik-al-li, *adv.* Calmly; wisely; rationally.
Philosophize, fi-los'o-fīz', *vi.* To act the philosopher; to reason like a philosopher; to formulate a philosophical theory.
Philosophy, fi-los'o-fi, *n.* The science which tries to account for the phenomena of the universe; metaphysics; the general principles underlying some branch of knowledge; practical wisdom.
Philtre, Philter, fil'tėr, *n.* A love-charm; a potion supposed to excite love.
Phlebitis, flē-bī'tis, *n.* Inflammation of a vein.
Phlebotomy, flē-bot'o-mi, *n.* The act or practice of opening a vein; blood-letting.
Phlegm, flem, *n.* The viscid matter of the digestive and respiratory passages; bronchial mucus; coldness; indifference.
Phlegmatic, fleg-mat'ik, *a.* Abounding in or generating phlegm; cold; sluggish.
Phlogistic, flo-jis'tik, *a.* Pertaining to phlogiston; inflammatory.
Phlogiston, flo-jis'ton, *n.* A hypothetical element formerly thought to exist and to be pure fire or the principle of combustion.
Phœnix, fē'niks, *n.* A bird of ancient legend, said to live 500 years, when it burnt itself, and rose again from its ashes; an emblem of immortality; a paragon.
Pholas, fō'las, *n.* A marine mollusc which pierces rocks, wood, &c.
Phonetic, fō-net'ik, *a.* Pertaining to the voice; representing sounds.
Phonetics, fō-net'iks, *n.pl.* The doctrine or science of sounds, especially of the human voice; the representation of sounds.
Phonograph, fō'nō-graf, *n.* An instrument for registering and reproducing sounds; a predecessor of the gramophone.
Phonography, fō-nog'ra-fi, *n.* The description of sounds; the representation of sounds by characters; phonetic shorthand.
Phonology, fō-nol'o-ji, *n.* The science of elementary vocal sounds.
Phonometer, fō-nom'et-ėr, *n.* An instrument for numbering the vibrations of sounds.
Phonotypy, fō-not'i-pi, *n.* Phonetic printing.
Phosgene, fos'jēn, *n.* A poison gas, carbon oxychloride.
Phosphate, fos'fāt, *n.* A salt of phosphoric acid.
Phosphorate, fos'for-āt, *vt.* To combine or impregnate with phosphorus.
Phosphoresce, fos-for-es', *vi.* To give out a phosphoric light.
Phosphorescence, fos-for-es'ens, *n.* State or quality of being phosphorescent.
Phosphorescent, fos-for-es'ent, *a.* Shining with a faint light like that of phosphorus; luminous without sensible heat.
Phosphoric, fos-fo'rik, *a.* Pertaining to, or obtained from, or resembling phosphorus.

Phosphorize, fos'for-īz, *vt.* To phosphorate.
Phosphorous, fos'for-us, *a.* Pertaining to or obtained from phosphorus.
Phosphorus, fos'for-us, *n.* An elementary substance which undergoes slow combustion at common temperatures.
Phosphuretted, fos'fū-ret-ed, *a.* Combined with phosphorus.
Photograph, fō'tō-graf, *n.* A picture obtained by photography.—*vt.* To produce a representation of by photographic means.
Photographer, fō-tog'raf-ėr, *n.* One who takes pictures by means of photography.
Photographic, Photographical, fō-tō-graf'ik, fō-tō-graf'ik-al, *a.* Pertaining to photography.
Photography, fō-tog'ra-fi, *n.* The art or practice of producing representations of scenes and objects by the action of light on chemically prepared surfaces.
Photogravure, fō'tō-grav-ūr, *n.* A process by which an engraving is produced on a metal plate by light acting on a sensitive surface.
Photology, fō-tol'o-ji, *n.* The doctrine or science of light.
Photometer, fō-tom'et-ėr, *n.* An instrument for measuring the intensity of lights.
Phrase, frāz, *n.* A short sentence or expression; an idiom; style; diction.—*vt.* and *i.* (phrasing, phrased). To style; to express.
Phraseology, frā-zē-ol'o-ji, *n.* Manner of expression; peculiar words used in a sentence; diction; style.
Phrenetic, fre-net'ik, *a.* Having the mind disordered; frantic.—*n.* A frenzied person.
Phrenic, fren'ik, *a.* Belonging to the diaphragm.
Phrenologist, fre-nol'o-jist, *n.* One versed in phrenology.
Phrenology, fre-nol'o-ji, *n.* The doctrine that a person's endowments may be discovered by the configuration of the skull.
Phthisical, tiz'ik-al, *a.* Having or belonging to phthisis; consumptive.
Phthisis, thī'sis, *n.* A wasting disease of the lungs, commonly called consumption.
Phylactery, fi-lak'tėr-i, *n.* An amulet worn by the Jews, containing a strip of parchment inscribed with Old Testament texts.
Phylloxera, fil-ok-sē'ra, *n.* An insect which infests and destroys oaks, vines, &c.
Physic, fi'zik, *n.* The science of medicine; the art of healing; a medicine; a cathartic.—*vt.* (physicking, physicked). To treat with physic; to remedy.
Physical, fi'zik-al, *a.* Pertaining to nature or natural productions; bodily, as opposed to mental or moral; material; pertaining to physics.
Physically, fi'zik-al-li, *adv.* In a physical manner; as regards the material world; bodily.
Physician, fi-zi'shan, *n.* A person skilled in the art of healing; a doctor.
Physicist, fi'zi-sist, *n.* One skilled in physics; a natural philosopher.
Physics, fi'ziks, *n.* That branch of science which deals with mechanics, dynamics, light, heat, sound, electricity, and magnetism; natural philosophy.
Physiognomist, fi-zi-og'nō-mist, *n.* One who is skilled in physiognomy.
Physiognomy, fi-zi-og'no-mi, *n.* The art of perceiving a person's character by his countenance; particular cast or expression of countenance.
Physiography, fi-zi-og'ra-fi, *n.* The science of the earth's physical features and phenomena; physical geography.
Physiologic, Physiological, fi'zi-ō-loj"ik, fi'zi-ō-loj"ik-al, *a.* Pertaining to physiology.
Physiologist, fi-zi-ol'o-jist, *n.* One who is versed in physiology.
Physiology, fi-zi-ol'o-ji, *n.* The science of the phenomena of life; the study of the functions of living beings.
Physique, fi-zēk', *n.* A person's physical or bodily structure or constitution.
Phytoid, fī'toid, *a.* Plant-like.
Phytology, fī-tol'o-ji, *n.* The science of plants; botany.
Piacular, pī-ak'ū-lär, *a.* Expiatory; having power to atone; requiring expiation.
Pia-mater, pī'a-mā-tėr, *n.* A membrane investing the surface of the brain.
Pianist, pi'an-ist, *n.* A performer on the pianoforte.
Piano, pi-ä'nō, *a.* In *music*, soft.
Piano, pi-an'ō, *n.* A pianoforte.
Pianoforte, pi-an'ō-fōr-tā, *n.* A musical metal-stringed instrument with a key-board, sounded by hammers acting on the strings.
Piazza, pi-az'za, *n.* A rectangular open space surrounded by colonnades.
Pibroch, pē'broch, *n.* A species of music for the bagpipe.
Pica, pī'ka, *n.* A printing type having six lines in an inch, used as the standard size.
Picador, pik-a-dōr', *n.* A horseman with a lance who excites the bull in a bull-fight.
Picaresque, pik-a-resk', *a.* Pertaining to rogues; describing the fortunes of adventurers.
Picaroon, pik-a-rön', *n.* A rogue or cheat; one who lives by his wits.
Piccolo, pik'ko-lō, *n.* A small flute with shrill tones; an octave flute.
Piceous, pis'ē-us, *a.* Pitchy.
Pick, pik, *vt.* To strike at with something pointed; to peck at; to clean by the teeth, fingers, &c.; to select; to pluck; to gather.—*vi.* To eat slowly; to nibble; to pilfer.—*n.* A pointed tool; a pick-axe; choice; selection.
Pickaxe, pik'aks, *n.* A sharp-pointed iron tool used in digging, mining, &c.
Picked, pikt, *p.a.* Select; choice.
Picker, pik'ėr, *n.* One who picks; a name of tools or apparatus of many various shapes.
Pickerel, pik'ėr-el, *n.* A fresh-water fish of the pike family.
Picket, pik'et, *n.* A pointed stake used in fortification; a pale; an advanced guard or outpost; a game at cards.—*vt.* To fortify with pickets; to post as a guard of observation.
Picking, pik'ing, *n.* Act of one who picks; *pl.* perquisites not always honestly obtained.
Pickle, pik'l, *n.* Brine; a solution of salt and water for preserving flesh, fish, &c.; vegetables preserved in vinegar; a state of difficulty or disorder; a troublesome child.—*vt.* (pickling, pickled). To preserve in or treat with pickle.
Pickpocket, pik'pok-et, *n.* One who steals from the pocket of another.
Picnic, pik'nik, *n.* and *a.* A pleasure-party the members of which carry provisions with them.—*vi.* (picnicking, picnicked). To take part in a picnic party.

Picquet, pik'et, *n.* *See* PIQUET.
Picric, pik'rik, *a.* An acid used in dyeing.
Pictorial, pik-tō'ri-al, *a.* Pertaining to or forming pictures; illustrated by pictures.
Pictorially, pik-tō'ri-al-li, *adv.* In a pictorial manner; with pictures or engravings.
Picture, pik'tūr, *n.* A painting, drawing, &c., exhibiting the resemblance of anything; any resemblance or representation; *pl.* the moving photographs shown in cinematography; the cinema.—*vt.* To represent pictorially; to present an ideal likeness of; to describe in a vivid manner.
Picturesque, pik-tūr-esk', *a.* Forming, or fitted to form, a pleasing picture; abounding with vivid imagery; graphic.
Piddle, pid'l, *vi.* (piddling, piddled). To deal in trifles; to peddle.
Piddock, pid'ok, *n.* The pholas.
Pie, pī, *n.* A paste baked with something in or under it; a mass of types unsorted; the magpie.
Piebald, pī'bąld, *a.* Having spots or patches of various colours; pied; mongrel.
Piece, pēs, *n.* A portion of anything; a distinct part; a composition or writing of no great length; a separate performance; a picture; a coin; a single firearm.—*vt.* (piecing, pieced). To patch; to join.—*vi.* To unite or join on.
Piecemeal, pēs'mēl, *adv.* In or by pieces; in fragments; by little and little.
Piecer, pēs'ėr, *n.* One who pieces; one employed in a spinning factory to join threads.
Piece-work, pēs'wėrk, *n.* Work done by the piece or job; work paid by quantity.
Pied, pīd, *a.* Party-coloured; spotted.
Pier, pēr, *n.* A mass of solid stonework for supporting an arch, bridge, &c.; a projecting wharf or landing-place.
Pierce, pērs, *vt.* (piercing, pierced). To stab or perforate with a pointed instrument; to penetrate; to move deeply.—*vi.* To enter; to penetrate.
Piercer, pērs'ėr, *n.* One who or that which pierces; an instrument that bores; that organ of an insect with which it pierces.
Piercing, pērs'ing, *p. a.* Penetrating; cutting; keen; sharp; severe.
Pietism, pī'et-izm, *n.* The principles of the pietists.
Pietist, pī'et-ist, *n.* One of a party in Germany who proposed to revive declining piety in the Reformed Churches; one who displays strong religious feelings.
Piety, pī'e-ti, *n.* Reverence or veneration towards God; godliness; devotion; religion.
Pig, pig, *n.* A young swine; a swine in general; an oblong mass of unforged metal.—*vt.* or *i.* (pigging, pigged). To bring forth pigs; to act like pigs.
Pigeon, pi'jon, *n.* A well-known bird of many varieties; a dove; a simpleton; a gull.
Pigeon-hearted, pi'jon-härt-ed, *a.* Timid.
Pigeon-hole, pi'jon-hōl, *n.* A hole for pigeons to enter their dwelling; a division in a desk or case for holding papers.
Pigeon-livered, pi'jon-li-vėrd, *a.* Mild in temper; soft; gentle; cowardly.
Pig-headed, pig'hed-ed, *a.* Having a head like a pig; stupidly obstinate.
Pig-iron, pig'ī-ėrn, *n.* Iron in pigs, as it comes from the blast-furnace.
Pigment, pig'ment, *n.* Paint; any preparation used by painters, dyers, &c., to impart colours to bodies; colouring matter.
Pigmy. *See* PYGMY.
Pig-skin, pig'skin, *n.* The skin of a pig, especially when prepared for saddlery, &c.
Pig-tail, pig'tāl, *n.* The tail of a pig; the hair of the head tied behind in a tail.
Pike, pīk, *n.* A spike or pointed piece; a fork used in husbandry; a fresh-water fish with a pointed snout; a toll-bar.
Pikeman, pīk'man, *n.* A soldier armed with a pike.
Pilaster, pi-las'tėr, *n.* A square pillar, slightly projecting from a wall.
Pilch, pilch, *n.* A flannel cloth for an infant.
Pilchard, pil'shärd, *n.* A fish resembling the herring, but smaller.
Pile, pīl, *n.* A heap; a large mass of buildings; a galvanic or voltaic battery; hair; nap on cloth; a beam driven into the ground to support some superstructure; a heraldic figure like a wedge.—*vt.* (piling, piled). To heap; to amass; to drive piles into; to support with piles.
Piles, pīlz, *n.pl.* A disease of the rectum near the anus; hemorrhoids.
Pilfer, pil'fėr, *vi.* To steal in small quantities; to practise petty theft.—*vt.* To filch.
Pilferer, pil'fėr-ėr, *n.* One who pilfers.
Pilgrim, pil'grim, *n.* A wanderer; one who travels to visit a holy place or relics.
Pilgrimage, pil'grim-āj, *n.* A journey to some holy place; the journey of human life.
Pill, pil, *n.* A medicine in the form of a little ball; anything nauseous to be accepted.—*vt.* To dose with pills; to form into pills; to rob; to plunder.
Pillage, pil'āj, *n.* Act of plundering; plunder; spoil.—*vt.* (pillaging, pillaged). To rob by open violence; to plunder.
Pillager, pil'āj-ėr, *n.* One who pillages.
Pillar, pil'ėr, *n.* A column; a perpendicular support; a supporter.
Pill-box, pil-boks, *n.* A small concrete blockhouse, used as a machine-gun emplacement.
Pillion, pil'yon, *n.* A cushion for a woman to ride on behind a person on horseback; the pad of a saddle.
Pillory, pil'o-ri, *n.* A frame of wood with movable boards and holes, through which were put the head and hands of an offender.—*vt.* (pillorying, pilloried). To punish with the pillory; to expose to ridicule, abuse, &c.
Pillow, pil'ō, *n.* A long soft cushion; something that bears or supports.—*vt.* To rest or lay on for support.
Pillow-case, Pillow-slip, pil'ō-kās, pil'ō-slip, *n.* The movable case or sack which is drawn over a pillow.
Pillowy, pil'ō-i, *a.* Like a pillow; soft.
Pillworm, pil'wėrm, *n.* The millipede, which can roll itself into a ball.
Pilose, pī'lōs, *a.* Hairy.
Pilot, pī'lot, *n.* One whose occupation is to steer ships; a guide; a director of one's course.—*vt.* To act as pilot of; to guide through dangers or difficulties.
Pilotage, pī'lot-āj, *n.* The pay, duty, or office of a pilot.
Pilot-engine, pī'lot-en-jin, *n.* A locomotive sent before a train to see that the way is clear.
Pilot Officer, pī'lot of'is-er, *n.* Officer in the

Royal Air Force ranking with a second-lieutenant in the Army.
Pilule, pil'ūl, *n.* A little pill.
Pimp, pimp, *n.* A man who provides gratifications for others' lusts; a procurer.—*vi.* To pander; to procure women for others.
Pimpernel, pim'pėr-nel, *n.* A little red-flowered annual found in British cornfields.
Pimple, pim'pl, *n.* A small elevation of the skin, with an inflamed base.
Pimpled, pim'pld, *a.* Having pimples; full of pimples.
Pimply, pim'pli, *a.* Pimpled.
Pin, pin, *n.* A longish piece of metal, wood, &c., used for a fastening, or as a support; a peg; a bolt.—*vt.* (pinning, pinned). To fasten with a pin or pins; to hold fast.—*vt.* To inclose; to pen or pound.
Pinafore, pin'a-fōr, *n.* A little apron.
Pincers, pin'sėrz, *n.pl.* An instrument for gripping anything; nippers; prehensile claws.
Pinch, pinsh, *vt.* To press hard or squeeze; to nip; to afflict.—*vi.* To press painfully; to be sparing.—*n.* A close compression, as with the fingers; a nip; a pang; straits; a strong iron lever; as much as is taken by the finger and thumb; a small quantity.
Pinchbeck, pinsh'bek, *n.* An alloy of copper and zinc resembling gold.—*a.* Sham; not genuine.
Pincher, pinsh'ėr, *n.* One who or that which pinches; *pl.* pincers.
Pin-cushion, pin'kụ-shon, *n.* A small cushion in which pins are kept.
Pindaric, pin-da'rik, *a.* After the manner of Pindar, the Greek lyric poet.—*n.* An ode in imitation of Pindar; an irregular ode.
Pine, pīn, *n.* A valuable evergreen coniferous tree, furnishing timber, turpentine, pitch, and resin; the pine-apple.—*vi.* (pining, pined). To languish; to grow weakly with pain, grief, &c.
Pineal, pin'ē-al, *a.* Resembling a pine-cone in shape.
Pine-apple, pīn'ap-l, *n.* A fruit like the cone of a pine-tree but different in character; the plant itself.
Pinery, pīn'ėr-i, *n.* A hot-house for pine-apples; a place where pine-trees grow.
Piney, Piny, pīn'i, *a.* Pertaining to pines; abounding with pines.
Pinfold, pin'fōld, *n.* A place in which cattle are temporarily confined; a pound.
Ping, ping, *n.* The sound made by a flying bullet.
Pinion, pin'yon, *n.* A bird's wing; the joint of a wing remotest from the body; a large wing-feather; a small toothed wheel; a fetter for the arms.—*vt.* To bind the wings of; to cut off, as the first joint of the wing; to fetter.
Pink, pingk, *n.* A garden flower; a light rose-colour or pigment; the flower or something supremely excellent.—*a.* Of a fine light rose-colour.—*vt.* To work in eyelet-holes; to scallop; to stab.—*vi.* To wink or blink.
Pink-eye, pingk'ī, *n.* A disease attacking horses, a kind of influenza.
Pink-eyed, pingk'īd, *a.* Having small eyes.
Pin-money, pin'mun-i, *n.* A sum of money settled on a wife for her private expenses.
Pinnace, pin'ās, *n.* A small vessel navigated with oars and sails, usually with two masts; a boat with eight oars.
Pinnacle, pin'a-kl, *n.* A rocky peak; the summit; a minor structure or turret above a building.
Pinnate, pin'āt, *a.* Shaped or branching like a feather.
Pint, pīnt, *n.* The eighth part of a gallon.
Pioneer, pī-on-ēr', *n.* One whose business is to prepare the road for an army, make entrenchments, &c.; one who leads the way.—*vt.* To prepare a way for.—*vi.* To act as pioneer.
Pious, pī'us, *a.* Devout; godly; holy; proceeding from piety.
Pip, pip, *n.* The kernel or seed of fruit; a spot on cards; a disease of fowls.
Pipe, pīp, *n.* A wind-instrument of music; a long tube; a tube with a bowl at one end for tobacco; the windpipe; a call of a bird; a wine measure containing about 105 imperial gallons.—*vi.* (piping, piped). To play on a pipe; to whistle.—*vt.* To utter in a high tone; to call by a pipe or whistle.
Pipe-clay, pīp'kla, *n.* The purest kind of potter's-clay.—*vt.* To whiten with pipe-clay.
Piper, pīp'ėr, *n.* One who plays on a pipe; a bagpiper; a sea-urchin.
Piping, pīp'ing, *p.a.* Giving out a whistling sound; accompanied by the music of the pipe; boiling.—*n.* Pipes, as for water, &c.; a jointed stem for propagating plants.
Pippin, pip'in, *n.* An apple of various kinds.
Pipy, pīp'i, *a.* Resembling a pipe; tubular.
Piquancy, pē'kan-si, *n.* Quality of being piquant; sharpness; pungency.
Piquant, pē'kant, *a.* Making a lively impression; sharp; lively; interesting; pungent.
Pique, pēk, *n.* Irritation; offence taken; slight anger.—*vt.* (piquing, piqued). To nettle; to touch with envy, jealousy, &c.; to pride or value (oneself).—*vi.* To cause irritation.
Piquet, pik'et, *n.* A picket; a game at cards for two, with thirty-two cards.
Piracy, pī'ra-si, *n.* The act or practice of robbing on the high seas; infringement of the law of copyright.
Pirate, pī'rāt, *n.* A robber on the high seas; a ship engaged in piracy; one who publishes others' writings without permission.—*vi.* (pirating, pirated). To rob on the high-seas.—*vt.* To take without right, as writings.
Piratical, pī-rat'ik-al, *a.* Having the character of a pirate: pertaining to piracy.
Piratically, pī-rat'ik-al-li, *adv.* In a piratical manner; by piracy.
Pirogue, pi-rōg', *n.* A canoe made from a trunk of a tree hollowed out.
Pirouette, pi'rö-et, *n.* A turning about on the toes in dancing.—*vi.* To make a pirouette; to whirl about on the toes.
Piscatorial, Piscatory, pis-kā-tō'ri-al, pis'ka-to-ri, *a.* Relating to fishing.
Pisces, pis'sēz, *n.pl.* The Fishes, a sign in the zodiac; the vertebrate animals of the class fishes.
Pisciculture, pis-i-kul'tūr, *n.* Fish culture.
Piscina, pis-sī'na, *n.* A niche in churches, with a small basin and water drain, into which the priest empties any water used.
Piscine, pis'sīn, *a.* Pertaining to fish.
Pish, pish, *exclam.* A word expressing contempt.—*vi.* To express contempt by uttering *pish!*
Pismire, pis'mīr, *n.* The ant or emmet.

Piss, pis, *vi.* To discharge urine.—*vt.* To eject, as urine.
Pistachio, pis-tā'shi-ō, *n.* The nut of a small tree cultivated in S. Europe for its fruit; the tree itself, also called *pistacia.*
Pistil, pis'til, *n.* The seed-bearing organ of a flower.
Pistillate, pis'til-lāt, *a.* Having a pistil.
Pistol, pis'tol, *n.* A small firearm fired with one hand.—*vt.* (pistolling, pistolled). To shoot with a pistol.
Pistole, pis-tōl', *n.* An old gold coin of Spain, France, &c., worth about 16*s.* sterling.
Piston, pis'ton, *n.* A cylindrical piece of metal which fits exactly into a hollow cylinder, and works alternately in two directions.
Piston-rod, pis'ton-rod, *n.* A rod which connects a piston to some other piece, and either moved by the piston or moving it.
Pit, pit, *n.* A hollow in the earth; the shaft of a mine; a vat in tanning, dyeing, &c.; a concealed hole for catching wild beasts; a small cavity or depression; part of the floor of a theatre.—*vt.* (pitting, pitted). To lay in a pit or hole; to mark with little hollows; to set in competition.
Pit-a-pat, pit'a-pat, *adv.* In a flutter; with palpitation or quick succession of beats.
Pitch, pich, *vt.* To thrust, as a pointed object; to fix; to set; to throw; to set the key-note of; to set in array; to smear or cover with pitch.—*vi.* To settle; to fall headlong; to fix choice; to encamp; to rise and fall, as a ship. —*n.* A throw; degree of elevation; highest rise; descent; elevation of a note; (cricket) prepared ground between wickets; a thick dark resinous substance obtained from tar.
Pitch-dark, pich'därk, *a.* Dark as pitch; very dark.
Pitcher, pich'ėr, *n.* A vessel with a spout, for holding liquors.
Pitchfork, pich'fork, *n.* A fork used in throwing hay, &c.; a tuning-fork.—*vt.* To lift or throw with a pitchfork; to put suddenly into any position.
Pitch-pine, pich'pīn, *n.* A pine abounding in resinous matter which yields pitch.
Pitch-pipe, pich'pīp, *n.* A small pipe used in finding or regulating the pitch of a tune.
Pitchy, pich'i, *a.* Like pitch; smeared with pitch; black; dark; dismal.
Piteous, pi'tē-us, *a.* That may excite pity; sorrowful; sad; miserable; pitiful.
Pitfall, pit'fąl, *n.* A pit slightly covered over, forming a kind of trap.
Pith, pith, *n.* The spongy substance in the centre of exogenous plants; the spinal cord or marrow of an animal; strength or force; energy; cogency; essence.
Pithily, pith'i-li, *adv.* In a pithy manner; cogently; with energy.
Pithy, pith'i, *a.* Consisting of pith; terse and forcible; energetic; sententious.
Pitiable, pi'ti-a-bl, *a.* Deserving pity or compassion; lamentable; miserable.
Pitiably, pi'ti-a-bli, *adv.* Woefully.
Pitiful, pi'ti-fụl, *a.* Full of pity; compassionate; woeful; to be pitied; paltry; despicable.
Pitiless, pi'ti-les, *a.* Feeling no pity; hard-hearted; merciless; relentless; unmerciful.
Pitman, pit'man, *n.* One who works in a pit; a miner.
Pit-saw, pit'są, *n.* A large saw worked by two men, one of whom stands in a pit below.
Pittance, pit'ans, *n.* A very small portion allowed or assigned; a charity gift.
Pity, pi'ti, *n.* Sympathy or compassion; ground of pity; thing to be regretted.—*vt.* (pitying, pitied). To feel pain or grief for; to sympathize with.—*vi.* To be compassionate.
Pivot, pi'vot, *n.* A pin on which something turns; a turning-point; that on which important results depend.—*vt.* To place on or furnish with a pivot.
Pix, piks, *n.* *See* Pyx.
Pixy, Pixie, pik'si, *n.* A sort of English fairy.
Placable, pla'ka-bl, *a.* Readily appeased or pacified; willing to forgive.
Placard, plak'ėrd or pla-kärd', *n.* A written or printed bill posted in a public place; a poster.—*vt.* To post placards.
Place, plās, *n.* An open space in a town; a locality, spot, or site; position; room; an edifice; quarters; a passage in a book; rank; office; calling; ground or occasion; stead.—*vt.* (placing, placed). To put or set; to locate; to appoint or set in an office, rank, or condition; to invest; to lend.
Placeman, plās'man, *n.* One who has an office, especially under a government.
Placenta, pla-sen'ta, *n.* The after-birth; an organ developed in mammals during pregnancy, connecting the mother and fœtus; the part of the seed-vessel to which the seeds are attached.
Placid, pla'sid, *a.* Gentle; quiet; mild; unruffled; calm.
Placidity, pla-sid'i-ti, *n.* State or quality of being placid.
Placidly, pla'sid-li, *adv.* Mildly; calmly.
Placket, plak'et, *n.* A petticoat; the opening or split in a petticoat or skirt.
Plagiarism, plā'ji-a-rizm, *n.* The act of plagiarizing; literary theft.
Plagiarist, plā'ji-a-rist, *n.* One who plagiarizes the writings of another.
Plagiarize, plā'ji-a-rīz, *vt.* To purloin the published thoughts or words of another.
Plagiary, plā'ji-a-ri, *n.* One who purloins another's writings; a literary thief; plagiarism.
Plague, plāg, *n.* A stroke or calamity; severe trouble; a pestilential disease; a person who annoys or troubles.—*vt.* (plaguing, plagued). To vex; to scourge as with disease or any evil.
Plaguily, plāg'i-li, *adv.* Vexatiously; in a manner so as to plague or embarrass.
Plaguy, plāg'i, *a.* Vexatious; troublesome.
Plaice, plās, *n.* A flat-fish, allied to the flounder, but larger.
Plaid, plād, *n.* A large woollen cloth, frequently of tartan, worn as a wrap.
Plain, plān, *a.* Without elevations and depressions; smooth; level; clear; undisguised; artless; sincere; simple; mere; bare; evident; obvious.—*n.* A piece of level land.—*adv.* Distinctly.
Plain-dealing, plān'dēl-ing, *n.* Conduct free from stratagem or disguise; sincerity.—*a.* Dealing with sincerity.
Plainly, plān'li, *adv.* Distinctly; sincerely; clearly; bluntly.
Plain-speaking, plān-spēk-ing, *n.* Plainness or bluntness of speech; candour.
Plain-spoken, plān'spōk-n, *a.* Speaking plainly or with bluntness.
Plaint, plānt, *n.* A complaint or lamentation; representation made of injury or wrong done.

Plaintiff, plānt'if, *n.* In *law*, the person who commences a suit before a tribunal for the recovery of a claim: opposed to *defendant*.

Plaintive, plānt'iv, *a.* Expressive of sorrow or grief; repining; mournful; sad.

Plait, plāt, *n.* A fold; a doubling of cloth, &c.; a braid, as of hair, &c.—*vt.* To fold; to double in narrow strips; to braid.

Plaited, plāt'ed, *p.a.* Folded; braided.

Plan, plan, *n.* The representation of anything on a flat surface; sketch; scheme; project; method; process.—*vt.* (planning, planned). To form a plan or representation of; to scheme.—*vi.* To form a scheme.

Plane, plān, *a.* Without elevations or depressions; perfectly level; even; flat.—*n.* A smooth or perfectly level surface; a joiner's tool, used in paring or smoothing wood.—*vt.* To make level or smooth; to smooth by the use of a plane.

Plane, Plane-tree, plān, plān'trē, *n.* A forest tree with a straight smooth stem and palmate leaves; a kind of maple.

Planet, pla'net, *n.* A celestial body which revolves about the sun or other centre.

Planetary, pla'net-a-ri, *a.* Pertaining to or produced by planets.

Plangent, plan'gent, *a.* Beating; dashing, as a wave; noisy; resonant.

Planish, pla'nish, *vt.* To make smooth, as wood; to smooth and toughen, as a metallic surface, by blows of a hammer; to polish.

Planisphere, pla'ni-sfēr, *n.* A sphere projected on a plane; a map exhibiting the circles of a sphere.

Plank, plangk, *n* A flat broad piece of sawed timber.—*vt.* To cover or lay with planks.

Plant, plant, *n.* One of the living organisms of the vegetable kingdom; a herb; a shoot or slip; the machinery, &c., necessary to carry on a business.—*vt.* To set in the ground for growth; to set firmly; to establish; to furnish with plants; to set and direct, as cannon.—*vi.* To set plants in the ground.

Plantain, plan'tān, *n.* A species of herbs found in temperate regions, represented in Britain by rib-grass and others.

Plantain, Plantain-tree, plan'tān, plan'tān-trē, *n.* A tropical plant of the same genus as the banana.

Plantar, plan'tar, *a.* Pertaining to the sole of the foot.

Plantation, plan-tā'shon, *n.* The act of planting; the place planted; a wood or grove; a colony; an estate cultivated by non-European labourers.

Planter, plant'ėr, *n.* One who plants; one who owns a plantation abroad.

Plantigrade, plan'ti-grād, *a.* Walking on the sole of the foot and not on the toes.

Plaque, plak, *n.* An ornamental plate; a flat plate on which enamels are painted; a brooch; the plate of a clasp.

Plash, plash, *n.* A puddle; a pool; a splash.—*vi.* To make a noise in water; to splash.—*vt.* To bend down and interweave the branches or twigs of.

Plasma, plas'ma or plaz'ma, *n.* Formless matter; the simplest form of organized matter in the vegetable and animal body.

Plasmic, Plasmatic, plaz'mik, plaz-mat'ik, *a.* Pertaining to a plasma.

Plaster, pläs'tėr, *n.* An adhesive substance used in medical practice; a mixture of lime, water, sand, &c., for coating walls; calcined gypsum, used with water for finishing walls, for casts, cement, &c.—*vt.* To overlay with plaster; to lay on coarsely.

Plasterer, pläs'tėr-ėr, *n.* One who overlays with plaster.

Plastering, pläs'tėr-ing, *n.* The act of putting on plaster; a covering of plaster.

Plastic, plas'tik, *a.* Having the power to give form to matter; capable of being moulded; applied to sculpture, as distingu shed from painting, &c.—**Plastics,** plas'tiks, *n.* The science or craft of converting various resins into durable materials; the articles so made.

Plasticity, plas-tis'i-ti, *n.* The state or quality of being plastic.

Plastron, plas'tron, *n.* A breastplate; a protection for the chest used by fencers.

Plat, plat, *vt.* (platting, platted). To plait; to weave; to make a ground-plan of.—*n.* A plot of ground devoted to some special purpose.

Platan, Platane, plat'an, plat'ān, *n.* The plane-tree.

Plate, plāt, *n.* A flat piece of metal; gold and silver wrought into utensils; a shallow flattish dish for eatables; an engraved piece of metal for printing; a page of stereotype for printing.—*vt.* (plating, plated). To cover with a thin coating of metal, as of silver.

Plate-armour, plāt'är-mėr, *n.* Defensive armour consisting of plates of metal.

Plateau, pla-tō', *n.*; pl. **-teaux** or **-teaus** (-tōz). An elevated, broad, flat area of land; a table-land.

Plate-glass, plāt'gläs, *n.* A superior kind of thick glass used for mirrors, windows, &c.

Plate-layer, plāt'lā-ėr, *n.* A workman on railways whose occupation is to lay rails.

Plate-mark, plāt'märk, *n.* A mark on gold and silver articles to indicate their quality.

Platform, plat'form, *n.* A raised structure with a flat surface; the place where guns are mounted on a battery; the raised walk at a railway-station; a structure for speakers at public meetings; a declared system of policy.

Plating, plāt'ing, *n.* The art of covering articles with gold or silver; the coating itself.

Platinotype, pla'tin-ō-tīp, *n.* A permanent photographic print produced by a process in which platinum is used.

Platinum, pla'tin-um, *n.* The heaviest of all metals, hard, ductile, malleable, and of a silvery colour.

Platinum-steel, pla'tin-um-stēl, *n.* Steel alloyed with about 1-110th of platinum.

Platitude, pla'ti-tūd, *n.* A trite or stupid remark; a truism.

Platitudinous, pla-ti-tūd'i-nus, *a.* Of the nature of platitude.

Platonic, plā-ton'ik, *a.* Pertaining to Plato, or his philosophy, school, or opinions.

Platonist, plā'ton-ist, *n.* One who adheres to the philosophy of Plato.

Platoon, pla-tön', *n.* A quarter of a company of infantry, usually 30 to 40 men, commanded by a subaltern.

Platter, plat'ėr, *n.* A large flat dish.

Platting, plat'ing, *n.* Slips of cane, straw, &c., platted or plaited, for hats, &c.

Plaudit, pla̧'dit, *n.* Applause; acclamation: usually in *pl.*

Plauditory, pla̤'di-to-ri, *a.* Applauding; commending.
Plausibility, pla̤z-i-bil'i-ti, *n.* Quality of being plausible; speciousness.
Plausible, pla̤z'i-bl, *a.* Apparently worthy of praise; apparently right; specious; fair-spoken.
Plausibly, pla̤z'i-bli, *adv.* In a plausible manner; speciously.
Play, plā, *vi.* To do something for amusement; to sport; to gamble; to perform on an instrument of music; to act with free motion; to personate a character.—*vt.* To put in action or motion; to use, as an instrument of music; to act; to contend against; to perform.—*n.* Any exercise for diversion; sport; gaming; action; use; practice; a drama; motion; scope; swing.
Play-bill, plā'bil, *n.* A bill exhibited as an advertisement of a play.
Play-book, plā'bu̥k, *n.* A book of dramatic compositions.
Player, plā'ėr, *n.* An actor; musician; gamester.
Play-fellow, plā'fel-ō, *n.* A companion in amusements or sports.
Playful, plā'fu̥l, *a.* Full of play; sportive; given to levity; indulging a sportive fancy.
Playground, plā'ground, *n.* A piece of ground set apart for open-air recreation.
Play-house, plā'hous, *n.* A theatre.
Playmate, plā'māt, *n.* A play-fellow.
Plaything, plā'thing, *n.* A toy.
Playwright, plā'rīt, *n.* A maker of plays.
Plea, plē, *n.* A suit or action at law; that which is alleged in support, justification, or defence; an excuse; a pleading.
Pleach, plēch, *vt.* To plash; to interweave.
Plead, plēd, *vi.* (pleading, pleaded or pled). To argue in support of or against a claim; to present an answer to the declaration of a plaintiff; to supplicate with earnestness; to urge.—*vt.* To discuss and defend; to argue; to offer in excuse; to allege in a legal defence.
Pleader, plēd'ėr, *n.* One who pleads; a lawyer who argues in a court of justice.
Pleading, plēd'ing, *n.* The act of one who pleads; one of the written statements in a litigant's demand or defence.
Pleasance, ple'zans, *n.* Pleasure; part of a garden secluded by trees or hedges.
Pleasant, ple'zant, *a.* Pleasing; agreeable; grateful; humorous; sportive.
Pleasantly, ple'zant-li, *adv.* In a pleasant manner; pleasingly; agreeably; gaily.
Pleasantry, ple'zant-ri, *n.* Gaiety; humour; raillery; a jest; a frolic.
Please, plēz, *vt.* (pleasing, pleased). To excite agreeable sensations or emotions in; to delight; to gratify; to seem good to.—*vi.* To give pleasure; to be kind enough.
Pleasing, plēz'ing, *p.a.* Giving pleasure or gratification; agreeable; pleasant.
Pleasurable, ple'zhūr-a-bl, *a.* Pleasing; giving pleasure; affording gratification.
Pleasurably, ple'zhūr-a-bli, *adv.* In a pleasurable manner; with pleasure.
Pleasure, ple'zhūr, *n.* The gratification of the senses or of the mind; agreeable emotion; delight; joy; approbation; choice; will; purpose; command; arbitrary will or choice.
Pleasure-ground, ple'zhūr-ground, *n.* Ground laid out in an ornamental manner for recreation or amusement.
Plebeian, ple-bē'an, *a.* Pertaining to the common people; vulgar; common.—*n.* One of the lower ranks of men; one of the common people of ancient Rome.
Plebiscite, pleb'i-sit or pleb'i-sīt, *n.* A vote of a whole people or community.
Plectrum, plek'trum, *n.* A small instrument for striking the strings of a lyre, &c.
Pledge, plej, *n.* Personal property given in security of a debt; a pawn; a surety; a hostage; the drinking of another's health.—*vt.* (pledging, pledged). To deposit as a security; to engage solemnly; to drink a health to.
Pledget, plej'et, *n.* A compress or small flat mass of lint laid over a wound.
Pleiad, plī'ad, *n.*; pl. **Pleiads, Pleiades,** plī'adz, plī'ā-dēz. Any one of the cluster of seven stars situated in the neck of the constellation Taurus.
Pleiocene, plī'ō-sēn. *See* PLIOCENE.
Plenary, plē'na-ri, *a.* Full; complete.
Plenipotence, Plenipotency, ple-nip'o-tens, ple-nip'o-ten-si, *n.* Fulness or completeness of power.
Plenipotent, ple-nip'o-tent, *a.* Possessing full power.
Plenipotentiary, ple'ni-pō-ten"shi-a-ri, *n.* A person with full power to act for another; an ambassador with full power.—*a.* Containing or invested with full power.
Plenish, ple'nish, *vt.* To replenish.
Plenitude, ple'ni-tūd, *n.* The state of being full or complete; plenty; abundance.
Plenteous, plen'tē-us, *a.* Abundant; copious; ample.
Plentiful, plen'ti-fu̥l, *a.* Being in plenty or abundance; copious; ample; abundant.
Plentifully, plen'ti-fu̥l-li, *adv.* Copiously; abundantly.
Plenty, plen'ti, *n.* Abundance; copiousness; sufficiency.—*a.* Plentiful; abundant.
Pleonasm, plē'on-azm, *n.* A redundancy of words; use of more words than necessary.
Pleonastic, plē-on-as'tik, *a.* Pertaining to pleonasm; redundant.
Plethora, pleth'o-ra, *n.* Excess of blood; repletion; superabundance; a glut.
Plethoric, ple-thor'ik, *a.* Characterized by plethora; having a full habit of body.
Pleura, plū'ra, *n.*; pl. **-æ.** A thin membrane which covers the inside of the thorax, and invests either lung.
Pleural, plū'ral, *a.* Pertaining to the pleura.
Pleurisy, Pleuritis, plū'ri-si, plū-rī'tis, *n.* An inflammation of the pleura.
Pleuritic, plū-rit'ik, *a.* Pertaining to pleurisy.
Pleuro-pneumonia, plū'rō-nū-mō"ni-a, *n.* A disease of cattle, consisting in an inflammation of the pleura and lungs.
Plexus, plek'sus, *n.* A net-work of vessels, nerves, or fibres.
Pliability, plī-a-bil'i-ti, *n.* Pliancy.
Pliable, plī'a-bl, *a.* Easy to be bent; flexible; supple; pliant; easily persuaded.
Pliancy, plī'an-si, *n.* The state or quality of being pliant or pliable.
Pliant, plī'ant, *a.* Pliable; readily yielding to force or pressure without breaking; flexible; plastic; limber.
Plicate, plī'kāt, *a.* Plaited; folded.
Pliers, plī'ėrz, *n.pl.* A small pair of pincers for bending wire, &c.

Plight, plīt, *vt.* To pledge, as one's word or honour; to give as a security: never applied to property or goods.—*n.* A pledge; a solemn promise; predicament; risky or dangerous state.
Plighter, plīt'ėr, *n.* One who plights.
Plimsoll line, plim'sol lin, *n.* Statutory loading line on British ships.
Plinth, plinth, *n.* A flat square slab, serving as the foundation of a column or pedestal.
Pliocene, plī'ō-sēn, *a.* and *n.* A term applied to the most modern division of the tertiary strata.
Plod, plod, *vi.* (plodding, plodded). To trudge or walk heavily; to toil; to drudge. —*vt.* To accomplish by toilsome exertion.
Plodder, plod'ėr, *n.* One who plods; a dull, heavy, laborious person.
Plodding, plod'ing, *p.a.* Given to plod; diligent, but slow and laborious in execution.
Plot, plot, *n.* A small piece of ground; a plan, as of a field, &c., on paper; a scheme; a conspiracy; the story of a play, novel, &c.—*vt.* (plotting, plotted). To make a plan of; to devise.—*vi.* To conspire; to contrive a plan.
Plotter, plot'ėr, *n.* One who plots; a conspirator.
Plough, plou, *n.* An instrument for turning up the soil.—*vt.* To turn up with the plough; to make grooves in; to run through, as in sailing.—*vi.* To turn up the soil with a plough; to use a plough.
Ploughboy, plou'boi, *n.* A boy who guides a team in ploughing.
Plough-land, plou'land, *n.* Land suitable for tillage.
Ploughman, plou'man, *n.* One who holds a plough; a farm labourer.
Ploughshare, plou'shār, *n.* The part of a plough which cuts the ground at the bottom of the furrow.
Plover, pluv'ėr, *n.* A grallatorial bird, as the golden plover, lapwing, &c.
Pluck, pluk, *vt.* To pick or gather; to pull sharply; to twitch; to strip by plucking; to reject as failing in an examination.—*n.* The heart, liver, and lights of a sheep, ox, &c.; courage or spirit.
Pluckily, pluk'i-li, *adv.* In a plucky manner; spiritedly.
Plucky, pluk'i, *a.* Spirited; courageous.
Plug, plug, *n.* A stopple or stopper; a bung; a peg; a quid of tobacco.—*vt.* (plugging, plugged). To stop with a plug; to make tight by stopping a hole.
Plum, plum, *n.* A fleshy fruit containing a kernel; the tree producing it; a raisin; a handsome sum or fortune generally; £100,000.
Plumage, plöm'āj, *n.* The feathers of a bird.
Plumb, plum, *n.* A plummet; a perpendicular position.—*a.* Perpendicular.—*adv.* In a perpendicular direction.—*vt.* To set perpendicularly; to sound with a plummet; to ascertain the capacity of; to sound.
Plumbago, plum-bā'gō, *n.* Graphite or black-lead.
Plumber, plum'ėr, *n.* One who works in lead.
Plumbery, Plummery, plum'ė-ri, *n.* Manufactures in lead; place where plumbing is carried on; business of a plumber.
Plumbing, plum'ing, *n.* The art of casting and working in lead; plumber's work.
Plumb-line, plum'lin, *n.* A line with a weight attached, used to determine a perpendicular; a plummet.
Plume, plöm, *n.* The feather of a bird; a feather or feathers worn as an ornament; an ostrich's feather.—*vt.* (pluming, plumed). To pick and adjust, as feathers; to strip of feathers; to adorn with feathers; *refl.* to pride.
Plummet, plum'et, *n.* A piece of lead, &c., attached to a line, used in sounding the depths of water; a plumb-line.
Plumose, Plumous, plöm'ōs, plöm'us, *a.* Feathery; resembling feathers.
Plump, plump, *a.* Fat; stout; chubby.—*vt.* To make plump; to dilate.—*vi.* To plunge or fall like a heavy mass; to fall suddenly; to vote for only one candidate.—*adv.* Suddenly; at once; flatly.
Plumply, plump'li, *adv.* Fully; roundly.
Plumpy, plump'i, *a.* Plump; fat; jolly.
Plumy, plöm'i, *a.* Feathered; adorned with plumes.
Plunder, plun'dėr, *vt.* To deprive of goods or valuables; to pillage; to spoil.—*n.* Robbery; pillage; spoil; booty.
Plunderer, plun'dėr-ėr, *n.* One who plunders.
Plunge, plunj, *vt.* (plunging, plunged). To thrust into water or other fluid; to immerse; to thrust or push; to cast or involve.—*vi.* To dive or rush into water, &c.; to pitch or throw oneself headlong; to throw the body forward and the hind-legs up, as a horse.—*n.* Act of plunging into water, &c.; act of throwing oneself headlong, like an unruly horse.
Plunger, plunj'ėr, *n.* One who or that which plunges; a diver; a solid cylinder used as a piston in pumps.
Pluperfect, plö'pėr-fekt, *a.* Applied to that tense of a verb which denotes that an action was finished at a certain period, to which the speaker refers.
Plural, plö'ral, *a.* Relating to, containing, or expressing more than one.—*n.* The number which designates more than one.
Pluralist, plö'ral-ist, *n.* A clergyman who holds more benefices than one.
Plurality, plö-ral'i-ti, *n.* State of being plural; two or more; majority; more than one benefice held by the same clergyman.
Plurally, plö'ral-li, *adv.* In a plural manner; in a sense implying more than one.
Plus, plus, *n.* A character (+) noting addition. —**Plus-fours,** *n.* Wide knickerbockers, with 4 in. overlap below the knee.
Plush, plush, *n.* A textile fabric with a velvet nap on one side.
Plutocracy, plö-tok'ra-si, *n.* The power or rule of wealth.
Plutocrat, plö'to-krat, *n.* A person possessing power on account of his riches.
Plutonic, plö-ton'ik, *a.* Pertaining to Pluto or to the regions of fire; volcanic; subterranean; dark.
Plutonium, plö-tōn'i-um, *n.* An element got from uranium by bombarding it with neutrons.
Pluvial, plö'vi-al, *a.* Relating to rain; rainy.
Pluviometer, plö-vi-om'et-ėr, *n.* A rain-gauge.
Ply, plī, *vt.* (plying, plied). To employ with diligence; to work at; to assail briskly; to beset; to press.—*vi.* To work steadily; to go in haste; to run regularly between any two ports, as a vessel.—*n.* A fold; a plait.

Plyer, plī'ėr, *n.* One who or that which plies; pl. same as *Pliers.*
Pneumatic, nū-mat'ik, *a.* Pertaining to air; moved or played by means of air; filled with or fitted to contain air.
Pneumatically, nū-mat'ik-al-li, *adv.* By pneumatic force; according to pneumatics.
Pneumatics, nū-mat'iks, *n.* That branch of physics which treats of the mechanical properties of elastic fluids and particularly of air.
Pneumatology, nū-ma-tol'o-ji, *n.* The branch of philosophy which treats of the mind or spirit; psychology.
Pneumonia, nū-mō'ni-a, *n.* An inflammation of the lungs.
Poach, pōch, *vt.* To cook (eggs) by breaking and pouring among boiling water; to pierce; to tread or stamp.—*vi.* To encroach on another's ground to steal game; to kill game contrary to law; to be or become swampy.
Poacher, pōch'ėr, *n.* One who steals game; one who kills game unlawfully.
Poachy, pōch'i, *a.* Wet and soft; easily penetrated by the feet of cattle, as land.
Pock, pok, *n.* A pustule raised on the skin in disease, especially in small-pox.
Pocket, pok'et, *n.* A small bag or pouch in a garment, &c.; a certain quantity, from 1½ to 2 cwt., as of hops; a mass of rich ore.—*vt.* To put in the pocket; to take clandestinely.
Pocket-book, pok'et-bụk, *n.* A small book for carrying papers in the pocket.
Pocket-money, pok'et-mun-i, *n.* Money for the pocket or for occasional expenses.
Pocky, pok'i, *a.* Having pocks or pustules.
Pococurante, pō'kō-kö-ran"tā, *n.* An apathetic, careless, indifferent person.
Pod, pod, *n.* The seed-vessel of certain plants, as peas, &c.—*vi.* (podding, podded). To produce pods; to swell and appear like a pod.
Podagra, pod-ag'ra, *n.* Gout in the foot.
Podgy, poj'i, *a.* Fat and short.
Poem, pō'em, *n.* A piece of poetry; a composition in verse.
Poesy, pō'e-si, *n.* The art of making or composing poems; poetry.
Poet, pō'et, *n.* The author of a poem; a person distinguished for poetic talents.
Poetaster, pō'et-as-tėr, *n.* A petty poet; a pitiful rhymer or writer of verses.
Poetess, pō'et-es, *n.* A female poet.
Poetic, poetical, pō-et'ik, pō-et'ik-al, *a.* Pertaining or suitable to poetry; expressed in poetry or measure; possessing the peculiar beauties of poetry.
Poetically, pō-et'ik-al-li, *adv.* In a poetical manner.
Poetics, pō-et'iks, *n.* That branch of criticism which treats of the nature of poetry.
Poetry, pō'et-ri, *n.* The language of the imagination or emotions expressed rhythmically; the artistic expression of thought in emotional language; whatever appeals to the sense of ideal beauty; verse; poems.
Poh, pō, *interj.* Exclamation of contempt.
Poignancy, poin'an-si, *n.* Quality of being poignant; severity; acuteness.
Poignant, poin'ant, *a.* Sharp to the taste; pointed; keen; bitter; severe; piercing.
Poilu, pwa-lü, *n.* A soldier in the French army.
Point, point, *n.* The sharp end of anything; a small headland; sting of an epigram; telling force of expression; exact spot; verge; stage; degree; a mark of punctuation; a mark or dot; end or purpose; characteristic; argument; (cricket) fielder square with wicket on off side; *pl.* The movable guiding rails at junctions on railways.—*vt.* To make pointed; to aim; to indicate; to punctuate; to fill the joints of with mortar.—*vi.* To direct the finger to an object; to indicate the presence of game, as dogs do; to show distinctly.
Point-blank, point-blangk, *a.* and *adv.* Having a horizontal direction; direct; express.
Pointed, point'ed, *p.a.* Having a sharp point; sharp; personal; epigrammatic.
Pointedly, point'ed-li, *adv.* In a pointed manner; with explicitness.
Pointer, point'ėr, *n.* One who or that which points; a kind of dog trained to point out game.
Point-lace, point'lās, *n.* A fine kind of lace.
Pointless, point'les, *a.* Having no point; blunt; without wit or application.
Pointsman, points'man, *n.* A man who has charge of the points on a railway.
Poise, poiz, *n.* Weight; balance; that which balances.—*vt.* (poising, poised). To balance in weight; to hold in equilibrium.—*vi.* To be balanced or suspended; to depend.
Poison, poi'zn, *n.* Any agent capable of producing a morbid effect on anything endowed with life.—*vt.* To infect with poison; to taint, impair, or corrupt.
Poisonous, poi'zn-us, *a.* Having the qualities of poison; venomous; deadly.
Poke, pōk, *n.* A bag or sack; a pouch; a gentle thrust.—*vt.* (poking, poked). To thrust or push against with something pointed; to stir; to jog.—*vi.* To grope; to search.
Poker, pōk'ėr, *n.* One who or that which pokes; an iron bar used in poking a fire; a game at cards.
Polar, pō'lėr, *a.* Pertaining to the pole or poles; situated near or proceeding from one of the poles; pertaining to the magnetic pole.
Polarity, pō-la'ri-ti, *n.* State of being polar; property of pointing towards the poles.
Polarization, pō'lėr-iz-ā"shon, *n.* Act of polarizing; state of having polarity.
Polarize, pō-lėr-iz, *vt.* To communicate polarity or polarization to.
Pole, pōl, *n.* A long piece of wood; a measure of 5½ yards or 30¼ square yards; one of the extremities of the axis of the celestial sphere or the earth; the pole-star; one of the two points in a magnet in which the power seems concentrated; (with cap.) a native of Poland.—*vt.* (poling, poled). To furnish with poles; to impel by poles.
Pole-axe, pōl'aks, *n.* A battle-axe; an axe used in killing cattle.
Pole-cat, pōl'kat, *n.* A carnivorous animal, nearly allied to the weasel, distinguished by its offensive smell.
Polemic, pō-lem'ik, *a.* Pertaining to controversy; disputative.—*n.* A disputant.
Polemical, pō-lem'ik-al, *a.* Polemic.
Polemics, pō-lem'iks, *n.* Disputation; controversial writings.
Pole-star, pōl'stär, *n.* A star situated close to the North Pole; a lode-star.
Police, pō-lēs', *n.* The internal government of a community; a body of civil officers for enforcing order, cleanliness, &c.—*vt.* (policing, policed). To guard or regulate by police.

Policeman, pō-lēs'man, *n.* An ordinary member of a body of police.
Policy, po'li-si, *n.* The governing a city, state, or nation; line of conduct with respect to foreign or internal affairs; dexterity of management; pleasure-grounds around a mansion; contract of insurance.
Poliomyelitis, pol'i-ō-mī-el-it"is, *n.* Inflammation of the grey matter of the spinal cord; infantile paralysis.
Polish, po'lish, *vt.* To make smooth and glossy; to refine.—*vi.* To become smooth or glossy.—*n.* Gloss; elegance of manners.
Polished, po'lisht, *p.a.* Smooth and glossy; refined; polite.
Polite, pō-līt', *a.* Polished in manners; refined; urbane; elegant; well-bred.
Politely, pō-līt'li, *adv.* In a polite manner; courteously.
Politic, po'li-tik, *a.* Showing policy; adapted to the public prosperity; sagacious; subtle; well devised.—**Body politic,** the citizens of a state.
Political, pō-lit'ik-al, *a.* Belonging or pertaining to a nation or state; public; derived from connection with government; politic; treating of politics.
Politically, pō-lit'ik-al-li, *adv.* In a political manner; with reference to politics.
Politician, po-li-ti'shan, *n.* One versed in or occupying himself with politics.
Politics, po'li-tiks, *n.* The science of government; political affairs, or the contests of parties for power.
Polity, po'li-ti, *n.* The form or system of civil government; method of government.
Polka, pōl'ka, *n.* A dance of Bohemian origin; the air played to the dance.
Poll, pōl, *n.* The head or the back part of the head; register of persons; the voting of electors; an election.—*vt.* To lop or clip; to enrol or register; to receive or give, as votes.
Pollard, pol'ėrd, *n.* A tree with its top cut off that it may throw out branches; a stag that has cast its horns; a coarse product of wheat.—*vt.* To make a pollard of.
Polled, pōld, *p.a.* Lopped, cropped, or clipped; having no horns or antlers.
Pollen, pol'en, *n.* The fecundating dust or male element of flowers.
Pollenize, pol'en-īz, *vt.* To supply or impregnate with pollen.
Pollinate, pol'i-nāt, *vt.* To pollenize.
Poll-tax, pōl'taks, *n.* A tax levied by the poll or head; a capitation-tax.
Pollute, pol-lūt', *vt.* (polluting, polluted). To defile; to profane; to taint morally; to debauch.
Pollution, pol-ū'shon, *n.* Act of polluting; defilement; uncleanness.
Polo, pō'lō, *n.* A game at ball resembling hockey, played on horseback.
Polonaise, pol-o-nāz', *n.* A dress worn by ladies; a melody in imitation of Polish dance tunes.
Polony, po-lō'ni, *n.* A kind of high-dried sausage made of partly-cooked pork.
Poltroon, pol-trön' or pol', *n.* An arrant coward; a dastard.—*a.* Base; vile.
Polyandry, po-li-an'dri, *n.* The practice of having more husbands than one at the same time.
Polyanthus, po-li-an'thus, *n.*; pl. **-thuses.** A garden variety of the primrose.
Polygamist, po-lig'a-mist, *n.* A person who practises polygamy.
Polygamy, po-lig'a-mi, *n.* The practice of having more wives or husbands than one at the same time.
Polyglot, po'li-glot, *a.* Many-tongued; containing, speaking, or knowing several languages.—*n.* A book (as a Bible) printed in several languages in parallel columns.
Polygon, po'li-gon, *n.* A plane figure of many angles and sides.
Polygraph, po'li-graf, *n.* An instrument for multiplying copies of a writing.
Polygraphy, po-lig'ra-fi, *n.* The art of writing in various ciphers.
Polygyny, po-lij'i-ni, *n.* The practice of having more wives than one at the same time.
Polyhedron, po-li-hē'dron, *n.* A body or solid contained by many sides or planes.
Polyp, Polype, po'lip, *n.* The sea-anemone, or some allied animal.
Polypetalous, po-li-pe'tal-us, *a.* Having many petals, as a flower.
Polypous, po'li-pus, *a.* Pertaining to a polypus.
Polypus, po'li-pus, *n.*; pl. **Polypi,** po'li-pī. A polyp; a kind of tumour.
Polysyllabic, po'li-sil-lab"ik, *a.* Consisting of many syllables.
Polysyllable, po-li-sil'la-bl, *n.* A word of more syllables than three.
Polysynthesis, po-li-sin'the-sis, *n.* A compounding of several elements.
Polysynthetic, po'li-sin-thet"ik, *a.* Compounded of several elements, as words.
Polytechnic, po-li-tek'nik, *a.* Comprehending many arts; designating a school teaching many branches of art or science.—*n.* A school of instruction in arts.
Polytheism, po'li-thē-izm, *n.* The doctrine of a plurality of gods.
Polytheist, po'li-thē-ist, *n.* A person who believes in a plurality of gods.
Pomace, pom'ās, *n.* The substance of apples, &c., crushed by grinding.
Pomaceous, pō-mā'shus, *a.* Pertaining to or consisting of apples.
Pomade, pō-mäd', *n.* Perfumed ointment; pomatum.
Pomander, pom'an-dėr, *n.* A perfume ball.
Pomatum, pō-mā'tum, *n.* A perfumed unguent for the hair.
Pome, pōm, *n.* A fruit of the character of the apple, pear, &c.
Pomegranate, pōm'gran-āt, *n.* A fruit of the size of an orange, containing numerous seeds; the tree producing the fruit.
Pommel, pum'el, *n.* A knob or ball; the knob on the hilt of a sword; the protuberant part of a saddle-bow.—*vt.* (pommelling, pommelled). To beat; to belabour.
Pomology, pō-mol'o-ji, *n.* The science of fruits; the cultivation of fruit-trees.
Pomp, pomp, *n.* A showy procession; display; pageantry; splendour; parade.
Pomposity, pom-pos'i-ti, *n.* Ostentation; vainglorious show.
Pompous, pomp'us, *a.* Displaying pomp; showy; ostentatious; high-flown.
Pompously, pomp'us-li, *adv.* In a pompous manner; ostentatiously.

Pond, pond, *n.* A body of water less than a lake, artificial or natural.
Ponder, pon'dėr, *vt.* To weigh in the mind; to consider.—*vi.* To deliberate.
Ponderable, pon'dėr-a-bl, *a.* That may be weighed.
Ponderous, pon'dėr-us, *a.* Heavy; weighty; massive.
Pongee, pon'jē, *n.* A soft unbleached silk.
Poniard, pon'yärd, *n.* A small dagger.—*vt.* To pierce with a poniard; to stab.
Pontiff, pon'tif, *n.* A high-priest; applied particularly to the pope.
Pontifical, pon-tif'ik-al, *a.* Belonging to a high-priest or to the pope.—*n.* A book containing rites performable by a bishop; *pl.* the dress of a priest or bishop.
Pontificate, pon-tif'i-kāt, *n.* The dignity of a high-priest; papacy.
Pontonier, Pontonnier, pon-to-nēr', *n.* One who constructs pontoon-bridges.
Pontoon, pon-tön, *n.* A kind of boat for supporting temporary bridges; a water-tight structure to assist in raising submerged vessels.
Pony, pō'ni, *n.* A small horse.
Poodle, pö'dl, *n.* A small dog with long silky curling hair.
Pooh, pö, *interj.* An exclamation of contempt or disdain; poh.
Pooh-pooh, pö-pö', *vt.* To sneer at.
Pool, pöl, *n.* A small pond; a puddle; a hole in the course of a stream; the stakes at cards, &c.; a variety of play at billiards.
Poop, pöp, *vt.* The stern of a ship; the highest and aftmost deck of a ship.
Poor, pör, *a.* Needy; indigent; destitute of value or merit; infertile; mean; paltry; lean; weak; impotent; unhappy; wretched.
Poorly, pör'li, *adv.* In a poor manner or state; in poverty or indigence; insufficiently.—*a.* Somewhat ill; not in health.
Pop, pop, *n.* A small, smart sound.—*vi.* (popping, popped). To make a small, smart sound; to enter or issue forth suddenly.—*vt.* To offer with a quick sudden motion; to thrust or push suddenly.—*adv.* Suddenly.
Pop-corn, pop'korn, *n.* Parched maize.
Pope, pōp, *n.* The head of the Roman Catholic church.
Popedom, pōp'dum, *n.* The jurisdiction, office, or dignity of the pope; papal dignity.
Popery, pōp'ė-ri, *n.* The doctrines and practices of the Roman Catholic church (a Protestant term).
Popinjay, pop'in-jā, *n.* A parrot; the green woodpecker; a fop.
Popish, pōp'ish, *a.* Pertaining to the pope, or to the Roman Catholic church.
Poplar, pop'lėr, *n.* A tree of numerous species.
Poplin, pop'lin, *n.* A fabric made of silk and wool, of many varieties.
Poppy, pop'i, *n.* A plant with showy flowers and yielding opium.
Populace, po'pū-lās, *n.* The common people; the multitude; the mob.
Popular, po'pū-lėr, *a.* Pertaining to the common people; familiar; plain; liked by people in general; prevalent.
Popularity, po-pū-la'ri-ti, *n.* State or quality of being popular; favour of the people.
Popularize, po'pū-lėr-īz, *vi.* To make popular or suitable to the common mind; to spread among the people.
Popularly, po'pū-lėr-li, *adv.* In a popular manner; currently; commonly.
Populate, po'pū-lāt, *vt.* To people; to furnish with inhabitants.
Population, po-pū-lā'shon, *n.* Act or process of populating; number of people in a country, &c.; the inhabitants.
Populous, po'pū-lus, *a.* Abounding in people; full of inhabitants.
Porbeagle, por'bē'gl, *n.* A kind of shark.
Porcelain, pōr'se-lān, *n.* The finest species of pottery ware.
Porch, pōrch, *n.* A portico; covered approach at the entrance of buildings.
Porcine, pōr'sīn, *a.* Pertaining to swine; like a swine; hog-like.
Porcupine, por'kū-pīn, *n.* A rodent animal, about 2 feet long, with erectile spines.
Pore, pōr, *n.* A minute opening in the skin, through which the perspirable matter passes; a small interstice.—*vi.* (poring, pored). To look with steady attention; to read or examine with perseverance.
Porgie, Porgy, por'gi, *n.* A kind of fish.
Pork, pōrk, *n.* The flesh of swine, fresh or salted, used for food.
Porker, pōrk'ėr, *n.* A hog; a young pig for roasting.
Pornography, por-nog'ra-fi, *n.* Literature in which prostitutes figure.
Porosity, pōr-os'i-ti, *n.* Quality or state of being porous.
Porous, pōr'us, *a.* Having pores.
Porphyry, por'fi-ri, *n.* A reddish Egyptian stone like granite; a hard igneous rock containing crystals of felspar, &c.
Porpoise, por'pus, *n.* A small cetaceous mammal of the Northern Seas.
Porridge, po'rij, *n.* A kind of soup or broth; a dish of oatmeal boiled in water till thickened.
Porringer, po'rin-jėr, *n.* A small dish for porridge.
Port, pōrt, *n.* A harbour or haven; a gate; an opening in the side of a ship; a port-hole; the left side of a ship; mien; demeanour.—*vt.* To carry (as a rifle) slanting upwards towards the left; to turn to the left, as the helm.
Port, Port-wine, pōrt, pōrt'wīn, *n.* A kind of wine made in Portugal.
Portable, pōrt'a-bl, *a.* That may be carried; not bulky or heavy.
Portage, pōrt'āj, *n.* Act of carrying; carriage; freight.
Portal, pōrt'al, *n.* A door or gate; the main entrance of a cathedral, &c.—*a.* Belonging to a vein connected with the liver.
Portcullis, pōrt-kul'is, *n.* A sliding or falling grating of timber or iron at the gateway of a fortified place.
Porte, pōrt, *n.* The government of the Turkish empire.
Portend, por-tend', *vt.* To foretoken; to presage; to threaten.
Portent, pōr'tent, *n.* That which foretokens; an omen of ill.
Portentous, por-tent'us, *a.* Ominous; foreshowing ill; monstrous; wonderful.
Porter, pōr'tėr, *n.* A doorkeeper; a carrier; a dark brown malt liquor.
Porterage, pōr'tėr-āj, *n.* Charge for the carriage of burdens by a porter; carriage.
Portfolio, pōrt-fō'li-ō, *n.* A case for drawings,

papers, &c.; office and functions of a minister of state.
Port-hole, pōrt'hōl, *n.* The embrasure of a ship of war.
Portico, pōr'ti-kō, *n.* A colonnade or covered walk; a porch.
Portion, pōr'shon, *n.* A part; a share or allotment; fate; final state.—*vt.* To parcel; to divide.
Portioner, pōr'shon-ėr, *n.* One who portions; in Scotland, the proprietor of a small feu.
Portly, pōrt'li, *a.* Of noble carriage or bearing; stately; rather tall, and inclining to stoutness.
Portmanteau, pōrt-man'tō, *n.* A bag for carrying clothes, &c., in travelling.
Portrait, pōr'trāt, *n.* A picture of a person; a vivid description.
Portraiture, pōr'trā-tūr, *n.* A portrait; the art or practice of making portraits, or describing vividly in words.
Portray, pōr-trā', *vt.* To delineate; to depict; to describe in words.
Portrayal, pōr-trā'al, *n.* The act of portraying; delineation; representation.
Portuguese, por'tū-gēz, *a.* Pertaining to Portugal.—*n.* The language of Portugal; the people of Portugal.
Pory, pō'ri, *a.* Porous; having pores.
Pose, pōz, *n.* Attitude or position; an artistic posture.—*vi.* (posing, posed). To attitudinize; to assume characteristic airs.—*vt.* To cause to assume a certain posture; to state or lay down; to perplex or puzzle.
Poser, pōz'ėr, *n.* One who poses; something that poses, puzzles, or puts to silence.
Posit, poz'it, *vt.* To lay down as a proposition or principle; to present as a fact.
Position, pō-zi'shon, *n.* State of being placed; place; posture; rank; state; principle laid down; thesis.
Positive, poz'it-iv, *a.* Definitely laid down; explicit; absolute; actual; confident; dogmatic; affirmative; noting the simple state of an adjective; applied to the philosophical system of Auguste Comte, which limits itself to human experience; applied to electricity produced by rubbing a vitreous substance.—*n.* That which is positive; the positive degree.
Positively, poz'it-iv-li, *adv.* Absolutely; not negatively; really; dogmatically.
Positivism, poz'it-iv-izm, *n.* The positive philosophy.
Positivist, poz'it-iv-ist, *n.* A believer in the doctrines of the positive philosophy.
Posse, pos'se, *n.* A small body of men; possibility.
Possess, po-zes', *vt.* To have and hold; to own; to affect by some power or influence; to pervade; to put in possession; to furnish or fill.
Possession, po-ze'shon, *n.* Act or state of possessing; ownership; occupancy; land, estate, or goods owned.
Possessive, po-zes'iv, *a.* Pertaining to possession; expressing or denoting possession.—*n.* The possessive case; a pronoun or other word denoting possession.
Possessor, po-zes'ėr, *n.* One who possesses; owner; master; occupant.
Posset, pos'et, *n.* A drink of hot milk curdled by wine or other liquor.
Possibility, pos-i-bil'i-ti, *n.* State or condition of being possible.
Possible, pos'i-bl, *a.* That may be or exist; that may be done; practicable; not impossible, though improbable.
Possibly, pos'i-bli, *adv.* In a possible manner; perhaps; perchance.
Post, pōst, *n.* A piece of timber, &c., set upright; a place assigned; a military or other station; office or employment; a carrier of letters, messages, &c.; a system for the public conveyance of letters, &c.; a post-office; a size of paper, about 18 or 19 inches by 15.—*vi.* To travel with post-horses; to hasten on.—*vt.* to place; to place in the post-office; to transfer (accounts or items) to the ledger; to make master of full details; to fix up in some public place.—*a.* Used in travelling quickly.—*adv.* Travelling as a post; swiftly.
Postage, pōst'āj, *n.* The charge for conveying letters or other articles by post.
Postal, pōst'al, *a.* Relating to posts, or the carrying of mails.
Postboy, pōst'boi, *n.* A boy who rides post; a courier.
Post-card, pōst'kārd, *n.* A card sent by post as a means of correspondence.
Post-chaise, pōst-shāz', *n.* A chaise for travellers who travel with post-horses.
Post-date, pōst-dāt', *vt.* To inscribe with a later date than the real one.
Poster, pōst'ėr, *n.* One who posts; a courier; a large printed bill for advertising.
Posterior, pos-tē'ri-or, *a.* Later or subsequent; hinder.—*n.* A hinder part; *pl.* the hinder parts of an animal.
Posterity, pos-te'ri-ti, *n.* Descendants; succeeding generations.
Postern, post'ern, *n.* A back door; a private entrance; a covered passage under a rampart.
Post-haste, pōst-hāst', *n.* Haste or speed.—*adv.* With speed or expedition.
Post-horse, pōst'hors, *n.* A horse for the rapid conveyance of passengers, &c.
Posthumous, post'ū-mus, *a.* Born after the death of the father; published after the death of the author; existing after one's decease.
Postilion (or **-ll-**), pos-til'yon, *n.* One who rides the near leading horse of a carriage and four, or the near horse of a pair.
Postman, pōst'man, *n.* A post or courier; a letter-carrier.
Postmaster, pōst'mäs-tėr, *n.* The officer who superintends a post-office.
Postmeridian, pōst-me-rid'i-an, *a.* After the meridian; being in the afternoon.
Post-mortem, pōst-mor'tem, *a.* After death.
Post-obit, pōst-ob'it, *n.* A bond which secures to a lender money on the death of some specified person.
Post-office, pōst'of-is, *n.* An office where letters are received for transmission; a government department that has the duty of conveying letters, &c.
Postpone, pōst-pōn', *vt.* (postponing, postponed). To put off to a later time; to set below something else in value.
Postponement, pōst-pōn'ment, *n.* Act of postponing.
Post-prandial, pōst-pran'di-al, *a.* Happening after dinner.
Postscript, pōst'skript, *n.* A paragraph added to a letter after it is signed; something added on to a book, &c., by way of supplement.

Postulate, pos'tū-lāt, *n.* Something assumed for the purpose of future reasoning; enunciation of a self-evident problem.—*vt.* To assume or take for granted.
Posture, pos'tūr, *n.* Attitude; relative position of parts; situation; condition.
Posy, pō'zi, *n.* A verse or motto inscribed on a ring, &c., or sent with a nosegay; a bouquet.
Pot, pot, *n.* A metallic or earthenware vessel more deep than broad; the quantity contained in a pot; a sort of paper of small-sized sheets.—*vt.* (potting, potted). To put in a pot; to preserve in pots; to plant in a pot of earth.
Potable, pō'ta-bl, *a.* Drinkable.
Potash, pot'ash, *n.* Vegetable alkali in an impure state, procured from the ashes of plants.—**Potash water,** an aerated drink of carbonic acid water with bicarbonate of potash superadded.
Potassic, pō-tas'ik, *a.* Relating to or containing potassium.
Potassium, pō-tas'si-um, *n.* The metallic basis of potash, a soft, white, light metal.
Potation, pō-tā'shon, *n.* A drinking or drinking bout; a draught.
Potato, pō-tā'tō, *n.*; pl. **-oes.** A well-known plant and its esculent tuber.
Pot-boiler, pot'boil-ėr, *n.* A work of art executed merely to earn money.
Poteen, po-tēn', *n.* Irish whisky, especially illicitly distilled whisky.
Potency, pō'ten-si, *n.* State or quality of being potent; might; force.
Potent, pō'tent, *a.* Mighty; strong; powerful; efficacious.
Potentate, pō'ten-tāt, *n.* One who possesses great power or sway; a monarch.
Potential, pō-ten'shal, *a.* Possible; latent; that may be manifested.
Potentiality, pō-ten'shi-al"i-ti, *n.* Quality of being potential; possibility; not actuality.
Potentially, pō-ten'shal-li, *adv.* In a potential manner; in possibility; not in act.
Potently, pō'tent-li, *adv.* Powerfully.
Pother, poᴛʜ'ėr, *n.* Bustle; confusion; flutter.—*vi.* To make a pother or stir.—*vt.* To harass; to puzzle.
Pot-house, pot'hous, *n.* A low drinking house.
Potion, pō'shon, *n.* A draught; a liquid medicine; a dose to be drunk.
Pot-luck, pot'luk, *n.* What may be for a meal without special preparation.
Pot-pourri, pō-pö-rē, *n.* A mixed dish of meat and vegetables; a medley.
Potsherd, pot'shėrd, *n.* A piece or fragment of an earthenware pot.
Pottage, pot'āj, *n.* A food of meat boiled to softness in water; porridge.
Potter, pot'ėr, *n.* One who makes earthenware vessels or crockery.—*vi.* To busy oneself about trifles; to move slowly.
Pottery, pot'ė-ri, *n.* The ware made by potters; place where earthen vessels are made.
Pottle, pot'l, *n.* A measure of four pints; a large tankard; a small basket for fruit.
Pouch, pouch, *n.* A pocket; a small bag.—*vt.* To put into a pouch; to pocket.
Poult, pōlt, *n.* A young chicken, grouse, &c.
Poulterer, pōl'tėr-ėr, *n.* A dealer in poultry.
Poultice, pōl'tis, *n.* A soft composition applied to sores.—*vt.* (poulticing, poulticed). To apply a poultice to.
Poultry, pōl'tri, *n.* Domestic fowls.
Pounce, pouns, *n.* A fine powder to prevent ink from spreading on paper; the claw or talon of a bird.—*vt.* (pouncing, pounced). To sprinkle or rub with pounce.—*vi.* To fall on and seize with the pounces or talons; to fall on suddenly.
Pound, pound, *n.* A standard weight of 12 ounces troy or 16 ounces avoirdupois; a money of account, consisting of twenty shillings; an inclosure for cattle.—*vt.* To confine in a public pound; to beat; to pulverize.
Poundage, pound'āj, *n.* A rate per pound; payment rated by the weight of a commodity; confinement of cattle in a pound.
Pounder, pound'ėr, *n.* One who or that which pounds; a thing denominated from a certain number of pounds, as a cannon, or a fish.
Pour, pōr, *vi.* To flow or issue forth in a stream.—*vt.* To let flow out or in; to emit; to throw in profusion.
Pourparler, pör-pär-lā, *n.* A preliminary conference.
Poussette, pö-set', *vi.* To swing round in couples, as in a country-dance.
Pout, pout, *vi.* To thrust out the lips; to look sullen; to be prominent.—*n.* Protrusion of the lips.
Pouter, pout'ėr, *n.* One who pouts; a kind of pigeon with a prominent breast.
Poverty, po'vėr-ti, *n.* State of being poor; indigence; want; defect; insufficiency.
Powder, pou'dėr, *n.* A dry substance of minute particles; dust; gunpowder.—*vt.* To reduce to fine particles; to sprinkle with powder; to corn, as meat.—*vi.* To fall to dust; to use powder for the hair or face.
Powdery, pou'dėr-i, *a.* Dusty; friable.
Power, pou'ėr, *n.* Ability to act or do; strength; influence; talent; command; authority; one who exercises authority; a state or government; warrant; a mechanical advantage or effect; product of the multiplication of a number by itself.
Powerful, pou'ėr-fụl, *a.* Having great power; strong; potent; cogent; influential.
Powerfully, pou'ėr-fụ-li, *adv.* In a powerful manner; with great force or energy.
Powerless, pou'ėr-les, *a.* Destitute of power; weak; impotent.
Pox, poks, *n.* A disease characterized by pocks or pustules.
Practicability, prak'ti-ka-bil"i-ti, *n.* Quality or state of being practicable.
Practicable, prak'ti-ka-bl, *a.* That may be done or effected; feasible; passable.
Practicably, prak'ti-ka-bli, *adv.* In a practicable manner.
Practical, prak'ti-kal, *a.* Pertaining to practice, action, or use; not merely theoretical; skilled in actual work.
Practically, prak'ti-kal-li, *adv.* In a practical manner; by experience; in effect.
Practice, prak'tis, *n.* A doing or effecting; custom; habit; actual performance; exercise of any profession; medical treatment; training; drill; dexterity.
Practise, prak'tis, *vt.* (practising, practised). To put in practice; to do or perform frequently or habitually; to exercise, as any profession; to commit; to teach by practice.—*vi.* To perform certain acts frequently for instruction or amusement; to exercise some profession.

Practitioner, prak-ti'shon-ėr, *n.* One engaged in some profession, particularly law or medicine.
Prætor, prē'tor, *n.* A title of certain ancient Roman magistrates.
Prætorian, prē-tō'ri-an, *a.* Belonging to a prætor.—*n.* A soldier of the Prætorian guard.
Pragmatic, Pragmatical, prag-mat'ik, prag-mat'ik-al, *a.* Meddling; impertinently busy or officious.
Prairie, prā'ri, *n.* An extensive tract of grassy land, generally destitute of trees.
Praise, prāz, *n.* Approbation or admiration expressed; eulogy; honour; gratitude or homage to God, often in song; the object, ground, or reason of praise.—*vt.* (praising, praised). To extol; to commend; to honour.
Praiseworthy, prāz'wėr-ᴛʜi, *a.* Deserving of praise; commendable; laudable.
Prance, prans, *vi.* (prancing, pranced). To spring, leap, or caper, as a horse; to strut about ostentatiously.
Prandial, pran'di-al, *a.* Relating to a dinner, or meal in general.
Prank, prangk, *vt.* To adorn in a showy manner; to dress up.—*vi.* To have a showy appearance.—*n.* A merry trick; a caper.
Prate, prāt, *vi.* (prating, prated). To babble, chatter, tattle.—*vt.* To utter foolishly.—*n.* Trifling talk; unmeaning loquacity.
Prating, prāt'ing, *p.a.* Given to prate; loquacious.
Pratique, prat'ēk, *n.* A licence to a ship to trade after quarantine.
Prattle, prat'l, *vi.* (prattling, prattled). To talk much and idly, like a child; to prate.—*n.* Trifling or puerile talk.
Prawn, pran, *n.* A small crustaceous animal of the shrimp family.
Praxis, praks'is, *n.* Use; practice; discipline.
Pray, prā, *vi.* and *t.* To beg, supplicate, or implore; to address God.
Prayer, prā'ėr, *n.* One who prays; the act of praying; a petition; a solemn petition to God; a formula of worship, public or private; that part of a written petition which specifies the thing desired to be granted.
Prayer-book, prā'ėr-bųk, *n.* A book containing prayers or forms of devotion.
Prayerful, prā'ėr-fųl, *a.* Given to prayer; devotional; using much prayer.
Praying, prā'ing, *p.a.* Given to prayer.
Preach, prēch, *vi.* To deliver a sermon; to give earnest advice.—*vt.* To proclaim; to publish in religious discourses; to deliver in public, as a discourse.
Preacher, prēch'ėr, *n.* One who preaches; a person who delivers a sermon.
Preaching, prēch'ing, *n.* The act or profession of a preacher; a sermon.
Preachment, prēch'ment, *n.* A sermon; a discourse affectedly solemn (in contempt).
Preamble, prē-am'bl or prē', *n.* An introduction; introductory part of a statute.
Prebend, preb'end, *n.* The stipend of a canon of a cathedral or collegiate church.
Prebendary, preb'end-a-ri, *n.* An ecclesiastic who enjoys a prebend; a canon.
Precarious, prē-kā'ri-us, *a.* Depending on the will of another; uncertain; insecure.
Precaution, prē-ką'shon, *n.* Previous care; caution to prevent evil or secure good.—*vt.* To caution beforehand.
Precede, prē-sēd', *vt.* (preceding, preceded). To go before in time, rank, or importance; to preface.
Precedence, Precedency, prē-sed'ens, prē-sēd'en-si, *n.* Act or state of preceding; priority; order according to rank; superior importance.
Precedent, prē-sēd'ent, *a.* Preceding; going before in time; anterior.
Precedent, prē' or pre'sē-dent, *n.* Something done or said, serving as an example or rule.
Precedented, prē' or pre'sē-dent-ed, *a.* Authorized by or according with a precedent.
Precentor, prē-sen'tor, *n.* The leader of a choir in a cathedral or of the singing to a congregation.
Precept, prē'sept, *n.* Anything enjoined as an authoritative rule of action; injunction; doctrine; maxim.
Preceptive, prē-sep'tiv, *a.* Containing precepts; didactic.
Preceptor, prē-sep'tor, *n.* A teacher; an instructor; the teacher of a school.
Preceptress, prē-sep'tres, *n.* A female preceptor or teacher.
Precession, prē-se'shon, *n.* Act of going before; advance.
Precinct, prē'singt, *n.* A bounding line; a part near a border; a minor territorial division.
Precious, pre'shus, *a.* Of great worth or value; costly; cherished; affected.
Preciously, pre'shus-li, *adv.* In a precious manner; valuably; exceedingly.
Preciousness, pre'shus-nes, *n.* Quality of being precious; literary affectation.
Precipice, pre'si-pis, *n.* A headlong declivity; a steep or overhanging cliff.
Precipitance, Precipitancy, prē-si'pi-tans, prē-si'pi-tan-si, *n.* Headlong hurry; rash or excessive haste.
Precipitant, prē-si'pi-tant, *a.* Falling or rushing headlong; precipitate.
Precipitate, prē-si'pi-tāt, *vt.* and *i.* To throw or hurl headlong; to hasten excessively; to cause to sink or to fall to the bottom of a vessel, as a substance in solution.—*a.* Headlong; overhasty.—*n.* A substance deposited from a liquid in which it has been dissolved.
Precipitately, prē-si'pi-tāt-li, *adv.* Headlong; too hastily; with rash haste.
Precipitation, prē-si'pi-tā"shon, *n.* Act or process of precipitating; state of being precipitated; rash, tumultuous haste.
Precipitous, prē-si'pi-tus, *a.* Very steep; headlong in descent.
Précis, prā-sē', *n.* A concise or abridged statement; a summary; an abstract.
Precise, prē-sis', *a.* Sharply or exactly defined; exact; strictly accurate or correct; particular; formal; punctilious.
Precisely, prē-sīs'li, *adv.* In a precise manner; definitely; strictly; accurately.
Precisian, prē-si'zhan, *n.* One rigidly exact in the observance of rules.
Precision, prē-si'zhon, *n.* State of being precise; exactness; accuracy.
Preclude, prē-klöd', *vt.* (precluding, precluded). To shut out; to hinder; to render inoperative by anticipative action.
Preclusive, prē-klö'siv, *a.* Tending to preclude; hindering by previous obstacles.
Precocious, prē-kō'shus, *a.* Ripe before the

natural time; acting like an adult though not grown up.
Precocity, prē-kos'i-ti, *n.* State or quality of being precocious; early development of the mental powers.
Precognition, prē-kog-ni'shon, *n.* Previous knowledge; preliminary examination, as of a witness before a trial (*Scots law*).
Precognosce, prē'kog-nos, *vt.* To take the precognition of (*Scots law*).
Preconceive, prē-kon-sēv', *vt.* To form a conception or opinion of beforehand.
Preconception, prē-kon-sep'shon, *n.* Act of preconceiving; conception previously formed.
Preconcert, prē-kon-sėrt', *vt.* To arrange by previous agreement.—*n.* prē-kon'sėrt. A previous arrangement.
Precursive, prē-kėr'siv, *a.* Precursory.
Precursor, prē-kėr'sėr, *n.* A forerunner; a harbinger.
Precursory, prē-kėr'so-ri, *a.* Forerunning.
Predaceous, prę-dā'shus, *a.* Living by prey; given to prey on other animals.
Predatory, pred'a-to-ri, *a.* Plundering; pillaging; practising rapine.
Predecease, prē-dē-sēs', *vt.* To die before.—*n.* The decease of one before another.
Predecessor, prē-dė-ses'ėr, *n.* One who has preceded another in any state, office, &c.
Predestinarian, prē-des'ti-nā"ri-an, *a.* Belonging to predestination.—*n.* One who believes in the doctrine of predestination.
Predestinate, prē-des'ti-nāt, *vt.* To foreordain.—*a.* Foreordained.
Predestination, prē-des'ti-nā"shon, *n.* The act of foredaining events; the doctrine that God has from eternity determined whatever comes to pass, and has preordained men to everlasting happiness or misery.
Predestine, prē-des'tin, *vt.* To decree beforehand; to foreordain.
Predeterminate, prē-dē-tėr'mi-nāt, *a.* Determined beforehand.
Predetermination, prē-dē-tėr'mi-nā"shon, *n.* Purpose formed beforehand.
Predetermine, prē-dē-tėr'min, *vt.* and *i.* To determine beforehand.
Predial, prē'di-al, *a.* Consisting of land or farms; landed; attached to land.
Predicable, pre'di-ka-bl, *a.* That may be attributed to something.—*n.* Anything that may be affirmed of another.
Predicament, prē-dik'a-ment, *n.* Class or kind; condition; dangerous or trying state.
Predicant, pre'di-kant, *n.* One that affirms anything; a preaching friar; a Dominican.—*a.* Predicating; preaching.
Predicate, pre'di-kāt, *vt.* and *i.* To affirm one thing of another; to assert.—*n.* In *logic*, that which is affirmed or denied of the subject; in *grammar*, the word or words which express what is affirmed or denied of the subject.
Predication, pre-di'kā'shon, *n.* The act of predicating; affirmation; assertion.
Predicative, pre'di-kāt-iv, *a.* Expressing predication.
Predict, prē-dikt', *vt.* To foretell; to prophesy.
Prediction, prē-dik'shon, *n.* The act of predicting; a prophecy.
Predictive, prē-dik'tiv, *a.* Foretelling.
Predictor, prē-dik'tor, *n.* One who predicts.
Predilection, prē-di-lek'shon, *n.* A previous liking or preference; a prepossession of mind in favour of a person or thing.
Predispose, prē-dis-pōz', *vt.* To dispose beforehand; to fit or adapt previously.
Predisposition, prē-dis'pō-zi"shon, *n.* State of being predisposed; susceptibility from antecedent causes.
Predominance, Predominancy, prē-dom'i-nans, prē-dom'i-nan-si, *n.* Prevalence over others; superiority; ascendency.
Predominant, prē-dom'i-nant, *a.* Predominating; prevalent; ruling; controlling.
Predominate, prē-dom'i-nāt, *vi.* and *t.* To have surpassing power or authority; to rule.
Pre-eminence, prē-em'i-nens, *n.* State of being pre-eminent; superiority.
Pre-eminent, prē-em'i-nent, *a.* Eminent above others; surpassing or distinguished.
Pre-emption, prē-em'shon, *n.* The act or right of purchasing before others.
Preen, prēn, *vt.* To trim with the beak: said of birds dressing their feathers.
Pre-engage, prē-en-gāj', *vt.* To engage by previous agreement or influence.
Pre-establish, prē-es-tab'lish, *vt.* To establish beforehand.
Pre-exist, prē-egz-ist', *vi.* To exist beforehand, or before something else.
Pre-existence, prē-egz-ist'ens, *n.* Previous existence.
Prefabricate, prē-fab'ri-kāt, *vt.* To manufacture separately parts, of a building, &c., designed to be easily fitted together afterwards.
Preface, pre'fās, *n.* Introduction to a discourse or book, &c.—*vt.* (prefacing, prefaced). To introduce by preliminary remarks.
Prefatory, pre'fā-to-ri, *a.* Pertaining to or having the nature of a preface.
Prefect, prē'fekt, *n.* One placed over others; a governor, chief magistrate; a senior pupil entrusted with the maintenance of discipline.
Prefecture, prē'fekt-ūr, *n.* Office, jurisdiction, or official residence of a prefect.
Prefer, prē-fėr', *vt.* (preferring, preferred). To bring or lay before; to present, as a petition, &c.; to exalt; to set higher in estimation; to choose rather.
Preferable, pre'fėr-a-bl, *a.* Worthy to be preferred; more desirable.
Preferably, pre'fėr-a-bli, *adv.* Rather.
Preference, pre'fėr-ens, *n.* Act of preferring: state of being preferred; choice.
Preferential, pre-fėr-en'shal, *a.* Implying preference.
Preferment, prē-fėr'ment, *n.* Act of preferring; promotion; a superior office.
Prefiguration, prē-fig'ūr-ā"shon, *n.* Antecedent representation by similitude.
Prefigure, prē-fig'ūr, *vt.* To exhibit by antecedent representation; to foreshow.
Prefix, prē-fiks', *vt.* To put before or at the beginning of something.—*n.* prē'fiks. A letter, syllable, or word added at the beginning of a word.
Pregnancy, preg'nan-si, *n.* State of being pregnant; time of going with child.
Pregnant, preg'nant, *a.* Being with young; full of meaning or consequence.
Prehensible, prē-hen'si-bl, *a.* That may be seized.
Prehensile, prē-hen'sīl, *a.* Fitted for seizing or laying hold; grasping.

Prehension, prē-hen'shon, *n.* A taking hold of; apprehension.
Prehistoric, prē-his-tor'ik, *a.* Relating to a time anterior to written records.
Prejudge, prē-juj', *vt.* To judge beforehand; to condemn unheard.
Prejudgment, prē-juj'ment, *n.* Judgment without full examination.
Prejudicate, prē-jū'di-kāt, *vt.* and *i.* To prejudge; to judge with prejudice.
Prejudice, pre'jū-dis, *n.* An unwarranted bias; prepossession; detriment; injury.—*vt.* To bias the mind of; to do harm to.
Prejudicial, pre-jū-di'shal, *a.* Causing prejudice; hurtful; detrimental.
Prelacy, pre'la-si, *n.* The office of a prelate; episcopacy; bishops, collectively.
Prelate, pre'lat, *n.* An ecclesiastic of high rank, as an archbishop, bishop, &c.
Prelatic, Prelatical, pre-lat'ik, pre-lat'ik-al, *a.* Pertaining to prelates or prelacy.
Prelatist, pre'lat-ist, *n.* An advocate for prelacy; a high-churchman.
Prelect, prē-lekt', *vi.* To read or deliver a lecture or public discourse.
Prelection, prē-lek'shon, *n.* A lecture.
Prelector, prē-lek'tor, *n.* A lecturer.
Prelibation, prē-lī-bā'shon, *n.* A foretaste.
Preliminary, prē-lim'in-a-ri, *a.* Introductory; preparatory; prefatory.—*n.* Something introductory; preface; prelude.
Prelude, prel'ūd or prē-lūd', *vt.* (preluding, preluded). To introduce; to preface.—*vi.* To form a prelude.—*n.* prel'ūd or prē'lūd. Something preparatory; a musical introduction.
Prelusive, prē-lū'siv, *a.* Partaking of the nature of a prelude; introductory.
Premature, pre'ma-tūr, *a.* Happening, performed, &c., too early; untimely.
Premeditate, prē-me'di-tāt, *vt.* and *i.* To meditate upon beforehand; to contrive previously; to deliberate.
Premeditation, prē-me'di-tā''shon, *n.* Act of premeditating; previous deliberation.
Premier, pre'mi-ėr, *a.* First; chief.—*n.* The first minister of state; prime minister.
Premise, prē-mīz', *vt.* (premising, premised). To put forward by way of preface; to lay down, as antecedent to another statement.—*vi.* To make an introductory statement.
Premise, Premiss, pre'mis, *n.* A proposition laid down as a base of argument; *pl.* the portion of a legal document where articles of property to be transferred are described; a house and its adjuncts.
Premium, prē'mi-um, *n.* A reward or prize; a bonus; a bounty; sum paid for insurance; increase in value.
Premonish, prē-mon'ish, *vt.* To forewarn.
Premonition, prē-mō-ni'shon, *n.* Previous warning, notice, or information.
Premonitory, prē-mon'i-to-ri, *a.* Giving previous warning or notice.
Prentice, pren'tis. Apprentice.
Preoccupancy, prē-ok'kū-pan-si, *n.* Preoccupation; previous occupancy.
Preoccupation, prē-ok'kū-pā''shon, *n.* Act of preoccupying; prior possession; state of being preoccupied.
Preoccupied, prē-ok'kū-pīd, *p.a.* Occupied beforehand; absorbed; abstracted.
Preoccupy, prē-ok'kū-pī, *vt.* To occupy before another; to engross before another; to engross beforehand.
Preordain, prē-or-dān', *vt.* To appoint beforehand; to foreordain.
Preparation, pre-pa-rā'shon, *n.* Act or operation of preparing; that which is prepared; state of being prepared.
Preparative, prē-pa'rat-iv, *a.* Tending to prepare; preparatory.—*n.* That which serves to prepare; preparation.
Preparatory, prē-pa'ra-to-ri, *a.* Serving to prepare; introductory; preliminary.
Prepare, prē-pār', *vt.* and *i.* (preparing, prepared). To make ready; to adjust; to provide; to procure as suitable.
Prepay, prē-pā', *vt.* To pay in advance.
Prepayment, prē-pā'ment, *n.* Act of prepaying; payment in advance.
Prepense, prē-pens', *a.* Premeditated.
Preponderance, prē-pon'dėr-ans, *n.* State of being preponderant.
Preponderant, prē-pon'dėr-ant, *a.* Superior in power, influence, or the like.
Preponderate, prē-pon'dėr-āt, *vi.* To outweigh; to exceed in influence or power.
Preposition, pre-pō-zi'shon, *n.* A word governing a noun, pronoun, or clause.
Prepositional, pre-pō-zi'shon-al, *a.* Pertaining to a preposition.
Prepossess, prē-po-zes', *vt.* To take possession of beforehand; to preoccupy; to prejudice.
Prepossessing, prē-po-zes'ing, *p.a.* Creating a favourable impression; attractive.
Prepossession, prē-po-ze'shon, *n.* Preconceived opinion; prejudice; bias.
Preposterous, prē-pos'tėr-us, *a.* Absurd; irrational; monstrous; utterly ridiculous.
Prepuce, prē'pūs, *n.* The foreskin.
Pre-Raphaelite, prē-raf'a-el-īt, *n.* A supporter of the style of painting before Raphael, or the modern revival of that style.
Prerogative, prē-ro'ga-tiv, *n.* A prior claim or title; an exclusive privilege; an official and hereditary right.
Presage, prē'sāj or pres'āj, *n.* A presentiment; a prognostic, omen, or sign.—*vt.* and *i.* prē-sāj', (presaging, presaged). To betoken; to forebode; to predict.
Presbyter, pres'bi-tėr, *n.* An elder; a priest; a parson.
Presbyterian, pres-bi-tē'ri-an, *a.* Pertaining to presbyters; pertaining to ecclesiastical government by presbyteries.—*n.* A member of one of the Christian churches who vest church governments in presbyteries.
Presbyterianism, pres-bi-tē'ri-an-izm, *n.* The doctrines, principles, and ecclesiastical government of presbyterians.
Presbytery, pres'bi-te-ri, *n.* A body of presbyters; a church court consisting of the presbyterian pastors within a district, and one elder from each church.
Prescience, prē'shi-ens, *n.* Foreknowledge.
Prescient, prē'shi-ent, *a.* Foreknowing.
Prescind, prē-sind', *vt.* To consider apart from other ideas or notions.
Prescribe, prē-skrīb', *vt.* (prescribing, prescribed). To lay down authoritatively for direction; to appoint; to direct to be used as a remedy.—*vi.* To give directions; to give medical directions; to become of no validity through lapse of time.
Prescription, prē-skrip'shon, *n.* Act of

prescribing; that which is prescribed; a claim or title based on long use; the loss of a legal right by lapse of time.
Prescriptive, prē-skrip'tiv, *a.* Consisting in or acquired by long use.
Presence, pre'zens, *n.* State of being present; existence in a certain place; company; sight; port; mien; the person of a great personage; an appearance or apparition; readiness.
Present, pre'zent, *a.* Being at hand, in view, or in a certain place; now existing; ready at hand; quick in emergency.—*n.* Present time; *pl.* term used in a legal document for the document itself.
Present, prē-zent', *vt.* To introduce to or bring before a superior; to show; to give or bestow; to nominate to an ecclesiastical benefice; to lay before a public body for consideration; to point or aim, as a weapon.—*n.* pre'-zent. A donation; a gift.
Presentable, prē-zent'a-bl, *a.* That may be presented; in such trim as to be able to present oneself.
Presentation, pre-zent-ā'shon, *n.* Act of presenting; thing presented; the act or right of presenting a clergyman to a parish.
Presentee, pre-zent-ē', *n.* One presented to a benefice.
Presentiment, prē-sen'ti-ment, *n.* Previous apprehension; anticipation of impending evil; foreboding.
Presently, pre'zent-li, *adv.* Immediately; forthwith; speedily; soon.
Presentment, prē-zent'ment, *n.* Act of presenting; appearance; representation.
Preservation, pre-zėr-vā'shon, *n.* Act of preserving; state of being preserved; safety.
Preservative, prē-zėrv'at-iv, *a.* Tending to preserve.—*n.* That which preserves; a preventive of injury or decay.
Preserve, prē-zėrv', *vt.* (preserving, preserved). To save from injury; to keep in a sound state; to maintain; to restrict the hunting of, as game.—*n.* Something that is preserved, as fruit, vegetables, &c.; ground set apart for animals intended for sport or food.
Preside, prē-zīd', *vi.* (presiding, presided). To exercise authority or superintendence; to have the post of chairman.
Presidency, pre'zi-den-si, *n.* Act of presiding; the office, jurisdiction, or term of office of a president.
President, pre'zi-dent, *n.* One who presides; the head of a province or state; the highest officer of state in a republic.
Presidential, pre-zi-den'shal, *a.* Pertaining to a president.
Presidentship, pre'zi-dent-ship, *n.* The office of president.
Press, pres, *vt.* To bear or weigh heavily upon; to squeeze; to urge; to enforce; to emphasize; to solicit earnestly; to force into service.—*vi.* To bear heavily or with force; to crowd; to push with force.—*n.* A pressing; a crowd; an instrument for squeezing or crushing; a machine for printing; the art or business of printing; periodical literature; an upright cupboard; urgency.
Press-gang, pres'gang, *n.* A detachment of seamen empowered to impress men.
Pressing, pres'ing, *p.a.* Urgent.
Pressman, pres'man, *n.* One who attends to a printing press; a journalist.
Pressure, pre'shūr, *n.* The act of pressing; the force of one body acting on another; moral force; distress or difficulty; urgency.
Prestidigitation, pres'ti-di'ji-tā"shon, *n.* Skill in legerdemain; juggling.
Prestidigitator, pres-ti-di'ji-tā-tėr, *n.* A juggler.
Prestige, pres'tij or pres-tēzh', *n.* Influence based on high character or conduct.
Presto, pres'tō, *adv.* Quickly; in a trice.
Presumable, prē-zūm'a-bl, *a.* That may be presumed.
Presumably, prē-zūm'a-bli, *adv.* As may be presumed.
Presume, prē-zūm', *vt.* (presuming, presumed). To take for granted; to take the liberty; to make bold.—*vi.* To infer; to act in a forward way.
Presumption, prē-zum'shon, *n.* Act of presuming; supposition; forwardness; arrogance.
Presumptive, prē-zum'tiv, *a.* Based on presumption or probability.
Presumptuous, prē-zum'tū-us, *a.* Taking undue liberties; arrogant; overweening.
Presuppose, prē-sup-pōz', *vt.* To suppose or imply as previous; to take for granted.
Pretence, prē-tens', *n.* Act of pretending; simulation; feint; pretext.
Pretend, prē-tend', *vt.* To feign; to simulate; to assume or profess to feel; use as a pretext.—*vi.* To assume a false character; to sham; to put in a claim.
Pretended, prē-tend'ed, *p.a.* Ostensible; feigned; assumed; hypocritical.
Pretender, prē-tend'ėr, *n.* One who pretends; one who lays claim to anything.
Pretension, prē-ten'shon, *n.* Claim true or false; an assumed right.
Pretentious, prē-ten'shus, *a.* Full of pretension; showy.
Preterit, Preterite, pre'tėr-it, *a.* Past.—*n.* The past tense.
Pretermit, prē-tėr-mit', *vt.* To omit; to overlook.
Preternatural, prē-tėr-na'tūr-al, *a.* Beyond what is natural; abnormal; anomalous.
Pretext, prē'tekst or prē-tekst', *n.* An ostensible reason or motive; a pretence.
Prettily, prit'i-li, *adv.* In a pretty manner.
Pretty, prit'i, *a.* Having diminutive beauty; of a pleasing form without dignity; comely; neatly arranged; affectedly nice; foppish.—*adv.* Moderately.
Prevail, prē-vāl', *vi.* To gain the victory or superiority; to be in force; to succeed; to gain over by persuasion.
Prevailing, prē-vāl'ing, *p.a.* Predominant; having superior influence; prevalent.
Prevalence, Prevalency, pre'va-lens, pre'va-len-si, *n.* State or quality of being prevalent; superiority.
Prevalent, pre'va-lent, *a.* Prevailing; predominant; extensively existing.
Prevaricate, prē-va'ri-kāt, *vi.* To act or speak evasively; to shuffle; to quibble.
Prevarication, prē-va'ri-kā"shon, *n.* Act of prevaricating; a shuffling or quibbling; misrepresentation by giving evasive evidence.
Prevaricator, prē-va'ri-kāt-or, *n.* One who prevaricates.
Prevenient, prē-vē'ni-ent, *a.* Going before; preventing; preventive.
Prevent, prē-vent', *vt.* To stop or intercept; to impede; to thwart.

Prevention, prē-ven'shon, *n.* The act of preventing; a hindering by previous action; measure of precaution.
Preventive, prē-vent'iv, *a.* Tending to prevent.—*n.* That which prevents; an antidote previously taken. Also *Preventitive.*
Previous, prē'vi-us, *a.* Antecedent; prior.
Previously, prē'vi-us-li, *adv.* In time previous; before; beforehand.
Prevision, prē-vi'zhon, *n.* Foresight.
Prey, prā, *n.* Property taken from an enemy; spoil; booty; a victim.—*vi.* To take prey or booty; to get food by rapine; to cause to pine away: with *on.*
Price, prīs, *n.* The value which a seller sets on his goods; cost; value; worth.—*vt.* (pricing, priced). To set a price on; to ask the price of.
Priceless, prīs'les, *a.* Too valuable to admit of a price; invaluable; inestimable.
Prick, prik, *n.* A slender pointed thing that can pierce; a thorn; a puncture by a prick; a sting; tormenting thought.—*vt.* To pierce with a prick; to erect, as ears; to spur; to sting with remorse; to trace by puncturing.—*vi.* To spur on; to ride rapidly; to feel a prickly sensation.
Pricking, prik'ing, *n.* Act of piercing with a sharp point; a sensation of sharp pain, as if being pricked.
Prickle, prik'l, *n.* A small sharp-pointed shoot; a thorn; a small spine.—*vt.* To prick; to cause a prickly feeling in.
Prickly, prik'li, *a.* Full of small sharp points or prickles; pricking or stinging.
Pride, prīd, *n.* State or quality of being proud; inordinate self-esteem; a cause of pride; glory or delight; highest pitch; splendid show.—*vt.* To indulge pride; to value (oneself).
Priest, prēst, *n.* A man who officiates in sacred offices; a clergyman above a deacon and below a bishop.
Priestcraft, prēst'kraft, *n.* The craft or stratagems of priests.
Priestess, prēst'es, *n.* A female priest.
Priesthood, prēst'hụd, *n.* The office or character of a priest; the order of priests.
Priestlike, prēst'līk, *a.* Resembling a priest or that which belongs to priests.
Priestly, prēst'li, *a.* Resembling a priest; pertaining to a priest; sacerdotal.
Priest-ridden, prēst'rid-n, *a.* Entirely swayed or governed by priests.
Prig, prig, *n.* A conceited, narrow-minded fellow; one who affects superiority; a thief.—*vt.* (prigging, prigged). To steal.
Priggish, prig'ish, *a.* Conceited; affected.
Prim, prim, *a.* Formal; affectedly nice; demure.—*vt.* (primming, primmed). To deck with nicety.
Primacy, prī'ma-si, *n.* Position of chief rank; the office or dignity of primate or archbishop.
Prima donna, prē'ma don'na. The first or chief female singer in an opera.
Prima facie, prī'ma fā'shi-ē. At first view or appearance.
Primage, prim'āj, *n.* Money paid to the master of a ship for looking after goods; priming in steam-engines.
Primal, prī'mal, *a.* Primary; primitive.
Primarily, prī'ma-ri-li, *adv.* In a primary manner; originally; in the first place.
Primary, prī'ma-ri, *a.* First; chief; first in time; original; elementary; radical.—*n.* That which stands first or highest in importance; a large feather of a bird's wing.
Primate, prī'māt, *n.* A chief ecclesiastic; an archbishop.
Primatial, prī-mā'shal, *a.* Pertaining to a primate.
Prime, prīm, *a.* Foremost; first; original; first in rank, excellence, or importance; not divisible by any smaller number.—*n.* The earliest stage; full health, strength, or beauty; the best part.—*vt.* (priming, primed). To make ready for action; to supply with powder for communicating fire to a charge; to instruct or prepare beforehand; to lay on the first colour in painting.
Primer, prim'ėr, *n.* An elementary educational book; a size of printing-type.
Primeval, prīm-ē'val, *a.* Being of the earliest age or time; original; primitive.
Priming, prīm'ing, *n.* The powder used to ignite a charge; a first layer of paint; water carried over with the steam into the cylinder.
Primitive, prim'it-iv, *a.* Being the first or earliest of its kind; original; antiquated; primary; radical; not derived.—*n.* That which is original; an original word.
Primitively, prim'it-iv-li, *adv.* In a primitive manner; primarily; in antique style.
Primly, prim'li, *adv.* In a prim manner.
Primogenital, prī-mō-jen'it-al, *a.* Pertaining to primogeniture.
Primogeniture, prī-mō-jen'it-ūr, *n.* Seniority among children; right by which the eldest son succeeds to his father's real estate.
Primordial, prīm-or'di-al, *a.* First of all; first in order; original; earliest formed.—*n.* First principle or element.
Primrose, prim'rōz, *n.* An early flowering plant.—*a.* Resembling a yellow primrose in colour; abounding with primroses.
Prince, prins, *n.* A chief ruler; the son of a king or emperor; the chief of any body of men.
Princedom, prins'dum, *n.* The jurisdiction, rank, or state of a prince.
Princely, prins'li, *a.* Pertaining to a prince; noble; august; magnificent.
Princess, prin'ses, *n.* A female of the rank of a prince; the consort of a prince.
Principal, prin'si-pal, *a.* First; chief; most important or considerable.—*n.* A chief or head; the president, governor, or chief in authority; one primarily engaged; a capital sum lent on interest.
Principality, prin-si-pal'i-ti, *n.* Sovereignty; territory of a prince; a prince.
Principally, prin'si-pal-li, *adv.* Chiefly; mainly.
Principia, prin-sip'i-a, *n.pl.* First principles; elements.
Principle, prin'si-pl, *n.* Cause or origin; a general truth; a fundamental law; a rule of action; uprightness; an element.
Principled, prin'si-pld, *a.* Holding certain principles; fixed in certain principles.
Prink, pringk, *vt.* To deck.—*vi.* To dress for show; to strut.
Print, print, *vt.* To mark by pressure; to stamp; to form or copy by pressure, as from types, &c.—*vi.* To use or practise typography; to publish.—*n.* A mark made by pressure; an engraving, &c.; state of being printed; a newspaper; printed calico.

Printer, print'ėr, *n.* One who prints; more especially, the printer of letterpress.
Printing, print'ing, *n.* The act, art, or practice of impressing letters or figures on paper, cloth, &c.; typography.
Printing-office, print'ing-of-is, *n.* An office where letterpress printing is executed.
Printing-press, print'ing-pres, *n.* A press for the printing of books, &c.
Print-work, print'wėrk, *n.* A place for printing calicoes.
Prior, prī'or, *a.* Preceding; earlier.—*adv.* Previously.—*n.* A monk next in dignity to an abbot.
Prioress, prī'or-es, *n.* A female prior.
Priority, prī-or'i-ti, *n.* State of being prior; pre-eminence; preference.
Priory, prī'o-ri, *n.* A convent of which a prior is the superior.
Prise, prīz, *vt.* (prising, prised). To raise as by means of a lever; to force up.
Prism, prizm, *n.* A solid whose ends are any similar, equal, and parallel plane figures, and whose sides are parallelograms.
Prismatic, priz-mat'ik, *a.* Pertaining to a prism; formed or exhibited by a prism.
Prismoid, priz'moid, *n.* A body that approaches to the form of a prism.
Prison, pri'zn, *n.* A place of confinement; a jail.—*vt.* To imprison.
Prisoner, pri'zn-ėr, *n.* One shut up in a prison; a captive.
Pristine, pris'tīn, *a.* Original; first; earliest.
Prithee, pri'THē. A colloquial corruption of pray thee, I pray thee.
Privacy, priv'a-si, *n.* A state of being private; seclusion; secrecy.
Private, prī'vat, *a.* Separate from others; solitary; personal; secret; not having a public or official character.—**In private,** secretly.—*n.* A common soldier.
Privateer, prī-va-tēr', *n.* A private vessel licensed to seize or plunder the ships of an enemy.—*vi.* To engage in privateering.
Privately, prī'vat-li, *adv.* In a private or secret manner; not openly; personally.
Privation, prīvā'shon, *n.* Act of depriving; state of being deprived; destitution; want; hardship.
Privative, pri'va-tiv, *a.* Causing deprivation.—*n.* A prefix to a word which gives it a contrary sense.
Privet, priv'et, *n.* A shrub much used for ornamental hedges.
Privilege, pri'vi-lej, *n.* A separate and personal advantage; a prerogative, immunity, or exemption.—*vt.* To grant some right or exemption to; to authorize.
Privily, pri'vi-li, *adv.* Privately; secretly.
Privity, pri'vi-ti, *n.* Privacy; joint knowledge of a private concern.
Privy, pri'vi, *a.* Private; assigned to private uses; secret; privately knowing (with *to*).—*n.* A water-closet or necessary house.
Privy-council, pri'vi-koun-sil, *n.* The council of state of the British sovereign.
Prize, prīz, *n.* That which is seized; that which is deemed a valuable acquisition; a reward.—*vt.* (prizing, prized). To value highly.
Prize-fight, prīz'fīt, *n.* A boxing-match for a prize.
Prize-ring, prīz'ring, *n.* An inclosed place for prize-fights; boxers collectively.
Probability, pro-ba-bil'i-ti, *n.* Likelihood; appearance of truth.
Probable, pro'bab-l, *a.* Likely; credible.
Probably, pro'ba-bli, *adv.* In a probable manner; as is probable; likely.
Probate, prō'bāt, *n.* The proceeding by which a person's will is established and registered; official proof of a will.
Probation, prō-bā'shon, *n.* Act of proving; proof; trial; period of trial; novitiate.
Probationary, prō-bā'shon-a-ri, *a.* Serving for probation or trial.
Probationer, prō-bā'shon-ėr, *n.* One who is on probation; a novice; in Scotland, a student in divinity licensed to preach.
Probative, Probatory, prō'bat-iv, prō'ba-to-ri, *a.* Serving for trial or proof.
Probe, prōb, *n.* A surgeon's instrument for examining a wound, ulcer, or cavity.—*vt.* (probing, probed). To apply a probe to; to examine thoroughly.
Probity, prō'bi-ti, *n.* Uprightness; honesty; rectitude; integrity.
Problem, prob'lem, *n.* A question proposed for solution; a knotty point to be cleared up.
Problematic, Problematical, prob-lem-at'-ik, prob-lem-at'ik-al, *a.* Of the nature of a problem; questionable; doubtful.
Proboscis, prō-bos'is, *n.*; pl. **Proboscides,** prō-bos'i-dēz. The snout or trunk of an elephant, &c.; the sucking-tube of insects.
Procedure, prō-sēd'ūr, *n.* Act or manner of proceeding; conduct; management.
Proceed, prō-sēd', *vi.* To go forth or forward; to issue, arise, emanate; to prosecute any design; to carry on a legal action; to take a university degree.
Proceeding, prō-sēd'ing, *n.* A going forward; transaction; procedure.
Proceeds, prō'sēdz, *n.pl.* Money brought in by some piece of business.
Process, prō'ses, *n.* A proceeding or moving forward; gradual progress; course; method of manipulation; lapse; course of legal proceedings; a projecting portion.
Procession, prō-se'shon, *n.* A marching forward; a train of persons moving with ceremonious solemnity.
Processional, prō-se'shon-al, *a.* Pertaining to a procession.—*n.* A service-book containing prayers, hymns, &c.
Proclaim, prō-klām', *vt.* To announce publicly; to promulgate; to publish.
Proclamation, pro-kla-mā'shon, *n.* Act of claiming; an official public announcement.
Proclivity, prō-kliv'i-ti, *n.* Inclination; propensity; tendency.
Proclivous, prō-kliv'us, *a.* Inclining forward; tending by nature.
Proconsul, prō-kon'sul, *n.* A Roman officer who acted in the place of a consul; the governor of a province.
Procrastinate, prō-kras'ti-nāt, *vt.* and *i.* To put off from day to day; to postpone.
Procrastination, prō-kras'ti-nā''shon, *n.* Act or habit of procrastinating; dilatoriness.
Procreate, prō'krē-āt, *vt.* To beget; to generate; to engender.
Procreation, prō-krē-ā'shon, *n.* Act of procreating or begetting.
Proctor, prok'tor, *n.* A legal practitioner in a civil or ecclesiastical court; an official in a university who sees that good order is kept.

Procumbent, prō-kum′bent, *a.* Lying down; prone; trailing on the ground.
Procurable, prō-kūr′a-bl, *a.* Obtainable.
Procuration, pro-kūr-ā′shon, *n.* Service rendered as procurator; agency.
Procurator, pro-kūr′āt-or, *n.* The manager of another's affairs as his representative; legal agent or prosecutor.
Procure, prō-kūr′, *vt.* (procuring, procured). To obtain; to cause, effect, contrive.—*vi.* To pimp.
Procurement, prō-kūr′ment, *n.* The act of procuring or obtaining.
Procurer, prō-kūr′ėr, *n.* A pimp.
Procuress, prō-kū′res or prok′ū-res, *n.* A female pimp; a bawd.
Prod, prod, *n.* A pointed instrument, as a goad; a stab.—*vt.* (prodding, prodded). To prick with a pointed instrument; to goad.
Prodigal, prod′i-gal, *a.* Lavish; wasteful.—*n.* A waster; a spendthrift.
Prodigality, prod-i-gal′i-ti, *n.* Extravagance in expenditure; profusion; waste.
Prodigally, prod′i-gal-li, *adv.* Lavishly.
Prodigious, prō-dij′us, *a.* Portentous; extraordinary; huge; enormous.
Prodigiously, prō-dij′us-li, *adv.* Enormously; astonishingly; excessively.
Prodigy, prod′i-ji, *n.* A portent; a wonder or miracle; a monster.
Produce, prō-dūs′, *vt.* (producing, produced). To bring forward; to exhibit; to bring forth, bear, yield; to supply; to cause; to extend, as a line.—*n.* prō′dūs. What is produced; outcome; yield; agricultural products.
Producer, prō-dūs′ėr, *n.* One who produces.
Producible, prō-dūs′i-bl, *a.* That may be produced.
Product, pro′dukt, *n.* That which is produced; result; effect; number resulting from multiplication.
Production, prō-duk′shon, *n.* Act or process of producing; product; performance; literary composition.
Productive, prō-duk′tiv, *a.* Having the power of producing; fertile; causing to exist; producing commodities of value.
Productivity, prō-duk-tiv′i-ti, *n.* Power of producing.
Proem, prō′em, *n.* A prelude or preface; introduction.
Profanation, pro-fan-ā′shon, *n.* Act of violating sacred things; desecration.
Profane, prō-fān′, *a.* Not sacred; secular; irreverent; blasphemous; impure.—*vt.* (profaning, profaned). To treat with irreverence; to desecrate.
Profanely, prō-fān′li, *adv.* In a profane manner; impiously; blasphemously.
Profanity, prō-fan′i-ti, *n.* Quality of being profane; profane language or conduct.
Profess, prō-fes′, *vt.* To avow; to acknowledge; to declare belief in; to pretend; to declare oneself versed in.—*vi.* To declare openly.
Professedly, prō-fes′ed-li, *adv.* By profession or avowal; avowedly.
Profession, prō-fe′shon, *n.* Act of professing; declaration; vocation, such as medicine, law, &c.; the body of persons engaged in such calling.
Professional, prō-fe′shon-al, *a.* Pertaining to a profession.—*n.* A member of any profession; one who makes a living by arts, sports, &c., in which amateurs engage.
Professor, prō-fes′or, *n.* One who professes; a teacher of the highest rank in a university, &c.
Professorial, prō-fes′sō′ri-al, *a.* Pertaining to a professor.
Professoriate, prō-fes-sō′ri-āt, *n.* A body of professors; the teaching staff of professors.
Professorship, prō-fes′or-ship, *n.* The office or post of a professor.
Proffer, prof′ėr, *vt.* (proffering, proffered). To offer for acceptance.—*n.* An offer made.
Proficiency, Proficience, prō-fi′shen-si, prō-fi′shens, *n.* State of being proficient; skill and knowledge acquired.
Proficient, prō-fi′shent, *a.* Fully versed; competent.—*n.* An adept or expert.
Proficiently, prō-fi′shent-li, *adv.* In a proficient manner.
Profile, prō′fīl, *n.* An outline; an outline of the human face seen sideways; the side face.—*vt.* To draw in profile.
Profit, pro′fit, *n.* Any advantage, benefit, or gain; pecuniary gain.—*vt.* To benefit; to advance.—*vi.* To derive profit; to improve; to be made better or wiser.
Profitable, pro′fit-a-bl, *a.* Bringing profit or gain; lucrative; beneficial; useful.
Profitably, pro′fit-a-bli, *adv.* In a profitable manner; gainfully; advantageously.
Profitless, pro′fit-les, *a.* Void of profit, gain, or advantage.
Profligacy, pro′fli-ga-si, *n.* A profligate course of life; depravity; debauchery.
Profligate, pro′fli-gāt, *a.* Abandoned to vice; utterly dissolute.—*n.* A depraved man.
Profound, prō-found′, *a.* Deep; deep in skill or knowledge; far-reaching; bending low; humble.—*n.* The ocean; the abyss.
Profoundly, prō-found′li, *adv.* In a profound manner; deeply; extremely.
Profundity, prō-fund′i-ti, *n.* State or quality of being profound; depth.
Profuse, prō-fūs′, *a.* Lavish; exuberant.
Profusely, prō-fūs′li, *adv.* Lavishly.
Profusion, prō-fū′zhon, *n.* State or quality of being profuse; exuberant plenty.
Progenitor, prō-jen′i-tor, *n.* A forefather.
Progeny, pro′je-ni, *n.* Offspring; descendants.
Prognathic, Prognathous, prog-nath′ik, prog-nā′thus, *a.* Having projecting jaws.
Prognosis, prog-nō′sis, *n.* A forecast of the course of a disease.
Prognostic, prog-nos′tik, *a.* Foreshowing.—*n.* Omen; presage; token.
Prognosticate, prog-nos′tik-āt, *vt.* To foretell; to predict; to foreshow.—*vi.* To judge or pronounce from prognostics.
Prognostication, prog-nos′tik-ā″shon, *n.* Act of prognosticating; presage.
Programme, prō′gram, *n.* A plan of proceedings; statement of the order of proceedings in any entertainment.
Progress, prō′gres, *n.* A going forward; a journey of state; a circuit; advance; development.—*vi.* prō-gres′. To advance; to improve.
Progression, prō-gre′shon, *n.* Act of progressing; progress; regular or proportional advance.
Progressive, prō-gres′iv, *a.* Making steady progress; advancing; advocating progress.

Prohibit, prō-hib'it, *vt.* To forbid; to interdict by authority; to prevent.
Prohibition, prō-hi-bi'shon, *n.* Act of prohibiting; an interdict; inhibition; the forbidding by law of the manufacture, importation, or sale of alcoholic liquors for ordinary use.
Prohibitive, Prohibitory, prō-hib'it-iv, prō-hib'i-to-ri, *a.* Implying prohibition; forbidding.
Project, prō-jekt', *vt.* To throw out or forth; to scheme; to delineate.—*vi.* To shoot forward; to jut.—*n.* pro'jekt. A scheme, plan.
Projectile, prō-jek'til, *a.* Throwing forward. —*n.* A body impelled forward; a missile from a gun.
Projection, prō-jek'shon, *n.* Act of projecting; a prominence; representation of something by lines, &c., drawn on a surface.
Projector, prō-jek'tor, *n.* One who plans; that which casts something forward.
Prolapse, Prolapsus, prōlaps', prō-lap'sus, *n.* A falling down of some internal organ from its proper position.
Prolate, prō'lat, *a.* Applied to a sphere projecting too much at the poles.
Prolegomenon, prō-le-gom'e-non, *n.*; pl. **-mena.** A preliminary observation; *pl.* an introduction.
Prolepsis, prō-lep'sis, *n.* Something of the nature of an anticipation; a rhetorical figure.
Proleptic, Proleptical, prō-lep'tik, prō-lep'-tik-al, *a.* Pertaining to anticipation.
Proletarian, prō-le-tā'ri-an, *n.* and *a.* Applied to a member of the poorest class.
Proletariat, Proletariate, prō-le-tā'ri-āt, *n.* Proletarians collectively; the lower classes.
Prolific, prō-lif'ik, *a.* Fruitful; productive.
Prolix, prō'liks, *a.* Long and wordy; diffuse.
Prolixity, prō-liks'i-ti, *n.* State or quality of being prolix.
Prologue, prō'log, *n.* A preface or introduction; address spoken before a dramatic performance.—*vt.* To preface.
Prolong, prō-long,' *vt.* To lengthen out; to protract; to postpone.
Prolongation, prō-long-gā'shon, *n.* Act of prolonging; part prolonged; extension.
Prolusion, prō-lū'zhon, *n.* A prelude; a preliminary trial.
Promenade, pro-me-näd', *n.* A walk for pleasure; a place set apart for walking.—*vi.* (promenading, promenaded). To walk for pleasure.
Prominence, pro'mi-nens, *n.* State of being prominent; projection; protuberance.
Prominent, pro'mi-nent, *a.* Jutting out; protuberant; eminent.
Prominently, pro'mi-nent-li, *adv.* Eminently; conspicuously.
Promiscuous, prō-mis'kū-us, *a.* Confused; indiscriminate; miscellaneous.
Promise, pro'mis, *n.* A statement binding the person who makes it; ground or basis of expectation; pledge.—*vt.* (promising, promised). To make a promise of; to afford reason to expect.—*vi.* To make a promise; to afford expectations.
Promising, pro'mis-ing, *p.a.* Giving promise or grounds for good hopes.
Promissory, pro'mis-o-ri, *a.* Containing a promise or binding declaration.
Promontory, pro'mon-to-ri, *n.* A headland; a cape.
Promote, prō-mōt', *vt.* (promoting, promoted). To forward or further; to advance; to encourage; to exalt; to form (a company).
Promoter, prō-mōt'ėr, *n.* One who or that which promotes; an encourager; one engaged in getting up a joint-stock company.
Promotion, prō-mō'shon, *n.* Act of promoting; advancement; encouragement.
Prompt, promt, *a.* Ready; unhesitating; done without delay.—*vt.* To incite to action; to tell a speaker words he forgets; to suggest.
Prompter, promt'ėr, *n.* One who prompts; anyone who suggests words to a speaker.
Promptitude, promt'i-tūd, *n.* State or quality of being prompt; cheerful alacrity.
Promptly, promt'li, *adv.* Readily.
Promulgate, prō-mul'gāt, *vt.* (promulgating, promulgated). To publish; to proclaim.
Promulgation, prō-mul-gā'shon, *n.* Act or promulgating; publication.
Promulgator, prō'mul-gāt-or, *n.* One who promulgates.
Prone, prōn, *a.* Bending forward; lying with the face downward; sloping; apt.
Pronely, prōn'li, *adv.* In a prone manner or position.
Prong, prong, *n.* A spike, as of a fork.
Pronominal, prō-nom'in-al, *a.* Belonging to or of the nature of a pronoun.
Pronoun, prō'noun, *n.* A word used instead of a noun.
Pronounce, prō-nouns', *vt.* and *i.* (pronouncing, pronounced). To articulate by the organs of speech; to utter formally; to declare or affirm.
Pronounceable, prō-nouns'a-bl, *a.* That may be pronounced or uttered.
Pronounced, prō-nounst', *p.a.* Strongly marked or defined; decided; glaring.
Pronunciation, prō-nun'si-ā"shon, *n.* Act or mode of pronouncing; utterance.
Proof, pröf, *n.* Something which tests; trial; what serves to convince; evidence; firmness; a certain standard of strength in spirit; an impression in printing for correction; early impression of an engraving.—*a.* Impenetrable; able to resist.
Prop, prop, *n.* A body that supports a weight; a support.—*vt.* (propping, propped). To support by a prop; to sustain generally.
Propaganda, pro-pa-gan'da, *n.* An institution or system for propagating any doctrine.
Propagandism, prop-a-gan'dizm, *n.* The system or practice of propagating tenets.
Propagandist, prop-a-gan'dist, *n.* One who labours in spreading any doctrines.
Propagate, pro'pa-gāt, *vt.* To multiply by generation or reproduction; to diffuse; to increase.—*vi.* To have young or issue; to be multiplied by generation, &c.
Propagation, pro-pa-gā'shon, *n.* Act of propagating; diffusion.
Propagator, pro'pa-gāt-or, *n.* One who propagates.
Propel, prō-pel', *vt.* (propelling, propelled). To drive, push, or thrust forward.
Propeller, prō-pel'ėr, *n.* One who or that which propels; a screw for propelling steamboats.
Propense, prō-pens', *a.* Naturally inclined; disposed; prone.
Propensity, prō-pens'i-ti, *n.* Bent of mind; natural tendency; disposition.
Proper, pro'pėr, *a.* One's own; peculiar;

used as the name of a particular person or thing; adapted; correct; real.
Properly, pro'pėr-li, *adv.* In a proper manner; fitly; rightly; strictly.
Property, pro'pėr-ti, *n.* A peculiar quality or attribute; characteristic; ownership; the thing owned; estate; a stage requisite.
Prophecy, pro'fe-si, *n.* A foretelling; a prediction; inspired prediction or utterance.
Prophesy, pro'fe-sī, *vt.* To foretell; to predict.—*vi.* To utter prophecies.
Prophet, pro'fet, *n.* One who foretells future events.
Prophetess, pro'fet-es, *n.* A female prophet.
Prophetic, Prophetical, prō-fet'ik, prō-fet'-ik-al, *a.* Pertaining to a prophet or prophecy; unfolding future events.
Prophylactic, prō-fi-lak'tik, *a.* Preventive of disease.—*n.* A medicine which preserves against disease.
Propinquity, prō-pin'kwi-ti, *n.* Nearness; vicinity; kindred.
Propitiate, prō-pi'shi-āt, *vt.* To make propitious; to appease.
Propitiation, prō-pi'shi-ā"shon, *n.* Act of propitiating or what propitiates; atonement.
Propitiatory, prō-pi'shi-a-to-ri, *a.* Having the power to make propitious; conciliatory.—*n.* Among the Jews, the mercy-seat.
Propitious, prō-pi'shus, *a.* Favourable; disposed to be gracious or merciful.
Propitiously, prō-pi'shus-li, *adv.* Favourably.
Proportion, pro-pōr'shon, *n.* Comparative relation; relative size and arrangement; symmetry; just or equal share; lot; that rule which enables us to find a fourth proportional to three numbers.—*vt.* To adjust in due proportion; to form with symmetry.
Proportionable, pro-pōr'shon-a-bl, *a.* That may be proportioned; in proportion; corresponding; symmetrical.
Proportional, pro-pōr'shon-al, *a.* Having a due proportion; relating to proportion.—*n.* A number or quantity proportioned.
Proportionally, pro-pōr'shon-al-li, *adv.* In proportion; in due degree.
Proportionate, pro-pōr'shon-āt, *a.* Proportional.—*vt.* To make proportional.
Proportionately, pro-pōr'shon-āt-li, *adv.* With due proportion.
Proposal, prō-pōz'al, *n.* That which is proposed; offer; proposition.
Propose, prō-pōz', *vt.* (proposing, proposed). To offer for consideration.—*vi.* To make a proposal; to purpose; to offer oneself in marriage.
Proposer, prō-pōz'ėr, *n.* One who proposes.
Proposition, pro-pō-zi'shon, *n.* That which is proposed; a proposal; offer of terms; a form of speech in which something is affirmed or denied.
Propound, prō-pound', *vt.* To propose; to offer for consideration; to put, as a question.
Proprietary, prō-prī'e-ta-ri, *a.* Belonging to a proprietor.—*n.* A proprietor; a body of proprietors.
Proprietor, pro-prī'e-tor, *n.* An owner; one who has legal right to anything.
Proprietress, Proprietrix, prō-prī'e-tres, prō-prī'e-triks, *n.* A female proprietor.
Propriety, prō-prī'e-ti, *n.* State of being proper; fitness; consonance with established principles or customs; justness.
Propulsion, prō-pul'shon, *n.* Act of propelling or of driving forward.
Prorogate, prō'ro-gāt, *vt.* To prorogue.
Prorogation, prō-ro-gā'shon, *n.* Act of proroguing; interruption of a session and continuance of parliament to another session.
Prorogue, prō-rōg', *vt.* (proroguing, prorogued). To defer, to adjourn to an indefinite period, as parliament.
Prosaic, prō-zā'ik, *a.* Pertaining to prose; dull; commonplace.
Proscribe, prō-skrīb', *vt.* To outlaw; to condemn as dangerous; to interdict.
Proscription, prō-skrip'shon, *n.* Act of proscribing; outlawry; utter rejection.
Proscriptive, prō-skrip'tiv, *a.* Pertaining to or consisting in proscription; proscribing.
Prose, prōz, *n.* Speech or language not in verse.—*vi.* (prosing, prosed). To write or speak in a dull, tedious, style.—*a.* Relating to prose; prosaic.
Prosecute, pro'se-kūt, *vt.* and *i.* (prosecuting, prosecuted). To persist in; to carry on; to pursue at law.
Prosecution, pro-sekū'shon, *n.* Act of prosecuting; the carrying on of a suit at law; the party by whom criminal proceedings are instituted.
Prosecutor, pro'se-kūt-or, *n.* One who prosecutes, especially in a criminal suit.
Prosecutrix, pro'sē-kūt-riks, *n.* A female who prosecutes.
Proselyte, pro'se-līt, *n.* A convert to the Jewish faith; a new convert.—*vt.* To make a convert of.
Proselytism, pro'se-līt-izm, *n.* The making of proselytes; conversion.
Proselytize, pro'se-lit-īz, *vt.* To make a proselyte of.—*vi.* To engage in making proselytes.
Prosodic, pro-sod'ik, *a.* Pertaining to prosody.
Prosodist, pro'so-dist, *n.* One versed in prosody.
Prosody, pro'so-di, *n.* The rules of metre or versification.
Prosopopeia, Prosopopœia, pro'so-pō-pē"-ya, *n.* A figure of rhetoric by which inanimate things are spoken of as living; personification.
Prospect, pros'pekt, *n.* A distant view; sight; scene; outlook; exposure; expectation.—*vt.* and *i.* pros-pekt'. To make search for precious stones or metals.
Prospective, pros-pek'tiv, *a.* Looking forward; regarding the future.
Prospectus, pros-pek'tus, *n.* A statement of some enterprise proposed, as a literary work, a new company, &c.
Prosper, pros'pėr, *vi.* To increase in wealth or any good; to thrive.—*vt.* To make to succeed.
Prosperity, pros-pe'ri-ti, *n.* Flourishing state; satisfactory progress; success.
Prosperous, pros'pėr-us, *a.* Successful; flourishing; fortunate; thriving.
Prosperously, pros'pėr-us-li, *adv.* Successfully.
Prostitute, pros'ti-tūt, *vt.* (prostituting, prostituted). To offer publicly for lewd purposes for hire; to devote to anything base.—*a.* Openly devoted to lewdness.—*n.* A female given to indiscriminate lewdness.
Prostitution, pros-ti-tū'shon, *n.* Practice of offering the body to indiscriminate intercourse with men; debasement.

Prostrate, pros'trāt, *a.* Lying with the body flat; lying at mercy.—*vt.* (prostrating, prostrated). To lay flat or prostrate; to bow in reverence; to overthrow; to ruin.

Prostration, pros-trā'shon, *n.* Act of prostrating; great depression of strength or spirits.

Prostyle, pros'tīl, *a.* Having pillars in front.

Prosy, prōz'i, *a.* Like prose; dull and tedious in discourse or writing.

Protean, prō'tē-an, *a.* Assuming different shapes; variable; changeable.

Protect, prō-tekt', *vt.* To shield from danger, injury, &c.; to guard against foreign competition by tariff regulations.

Protection, prō-tek'shon, *n.* Act of protecting; shelter; defence; the system of favouring articles of home production by duties on foreign articles.

Protectionist, prō-tek'shon-ist, *n.* One who favours the protection of some branch of industry; one opposed to free-trade.

Protective, prō-tekt'iv, *a.* Affording protection; sheltering; defensive.

Protector, prō-tekt'or, *n.* One who protects; a defender; a guardian; a preserver.

Protectorate, prō-tekt'or-āt, *n.* Government by a protector; a country protected by another.

Protectress, Protectrix, prō-tekt'res, prō-tekt'riks, *n.* A woman who protects.

Protégé, pro-tā-zhā; fem. **Protégée,** pro-tā-zhā, *n.* One under the care of another.

Proteid, prō'tē-id, *n.* A name of certain nitrogenous substances forming the soft tissues of the body, and found also in plants.

Protest, prō-test', *vi.* To affirm with solemnity; to make a formal declaration of opposition.—*vt.* To assert; to mark for non-payment, as a bill.—*n.* prō'test. A formal declaration of dissent; a declaration that payment of a bill has been refused.

Protestant, pro'test-ant, *n.* One of the party who adhered to Luther at the Reformation; a member of a reformed church.—*a.* Belonging to the religion of the Protestants.

Protestantism, pro'test-an-tizm, *n.* The principles or religion of Protestants.

Protestation, prō-test-ā'shon, *n.* The act of protesting; a protest.

Protocol, prō'tō-kol, *n.* A diplomatic document serving as a preliminary to diplomatic transactions.

Proton, prō'ton, *n.* A positively charged particle, the nucleus of a hydrogen atom.

Protoplasm, prō'tō-plazm, *n.* A substance constituting the basis of living matter in animals and plants.

Prototype, prō'tō-tīp, *n.* An original type or model; a pattern.

Protract, prō-trakt', *vt.* To prolong; to delay; to defer; to draw to a scale.

Protraction, prō-trak'shon, *n.* Act of protracting; act of laying down on paper the dimensions of a field, &c.

Protractive, prō-trakt'iv, *a.* Protracting.

Protractor, prō-trakt'or, *n.* One who or that which protracts; an instrument for surveying; a muscle which draws forward a part.

Protrude, prō-tröd', *vt.* and *i.* (protruding, protruded). To thrust forward; to project.

Protrusion, prō-trö'zhon, *n.* State of being protruded; a thrusting forth.

Protrusive, prō-trö'siv, *a.* Protruding; prominent.

Protuberance, prō-tū'bėr-ans, *n.* A swelling or tumour; a prominence; a knob.

Protuberant, prō-tū'bėr-ant, *a.* Swelling; bulging out.

Protuberate, prō-tū'bėr-āt, *vi.* To bulge out.

Proud, proud, *a.* Having a high opinion of oneself; haughty; of fearless spirit; ostentatious; magnificent.—**Proud flesh,** an excessive granulation in wounds or ulcers.

Proudly, proud'li, *adv.* In a proud manner; haughtily; with lofty airs or mien.

Provable, pröv'a-bl, *a.* That may be proved.

Prove, pröv, *vt.* (proving, proved). To try by experiment; to test; to establish the truth or reality of; to demonstrate; to obtain probate of.—*vi.* To be found by experience or trial; to turn out to be.

Proven, prö'vn, *pp.* Proved.

Provenance, prov'e-nans, *n.* Origin.

Provender, prov'en-dėr, *n.* Dry food or fodder for beasts; provisions; food.

Proverb, pro'vėrb, *n.* A popular saying, expressing a truth or common fact; an adage; a maxim; a by-word; a dark saying.

Proverbial, prō-vėrb'i-al, *a.* Pertaining to or like a proverb; commonly spoken of.

Proverbially, prō-vėrb'i-al-li, *adv.* In a proverbial style; by way of proverb.

Provide, prō-vīd', *vt.* and *i.* (providing, provided). To procure beforehand; to prepare; to supply; to stipulate previously.

Provided, prō-vīd'ed, *conj.* On condition.

Providence, pro'vi-dens, *n.* Foresight; the care which God exercises over his creatures; God; a providential circumstance.

Provident, pro'vi-dent, *a.* Foreseeing and providing for wants; prudent; frugal.

Providential, pro-vi-den'shal, *a.* Effected by providence.

Providentially, pro-vi-den'shal-li, *adv.* By the intervention of providence.

Providently, pro'vi-dent-li, *adv.* In a provident manner; with prudent foresight.

Province, pro'vins, *n.* A territory at some distance from the metropolis; a large political division; sphere of action; department.

Provincial, prō-vin'shal, *a.* Pertaining to or forming a province; characteristic of the people of a province; rustic.—*n.* A person belonging to a province.

Provincialism, prō-vin'shal-izm, *n.* A rustic idiom or word.

Provision, prō-vi'zhon, *n.* Act of providing; preparation; stores provided; victuals; stipulation; proviso.—*vt.* To supply with provisions.

Provisional, prō-vi'zhon-al, *a.* Provided for present need; temporary.

Provisionally, prō-vi'zhon-al-li, *adv.* In a provisional manner; temporarily.

Proviso, prō-vī'zō, *n.* An article or clause in any statute or contract; stipulation.

Provisory, prō-vi'zo-ri, *a.* Making temporary provision; temporary; conditional.

Provocation, pro-vō-kā'shon, *n.* Act of provoking; cause of resentment; incitement.

Provocative, prō-vok'a-tiv, *a.* Serving to provoke; exciting.—*n.* A stimulant.

Provoke, prō-vōk', *vt.* (provoking, provoked). To incite; to stimulate; to incense; to irritate.—*vi.* To produce anger.

Provoking, prō-vōk'ing, *p.a.* Exciting resentment; annoying; vexatious.
Provost, pro'vost, *n.* The head of certain bodies, as colleges; chief dignitary of a cathedral; chief magistrate of a Scottish burgh.
Provost-marshal, pro'vo-mär-shal, *n.* A military officer who attends to offences against discipline.
Prow, prou, *n.* The forepart of a ship.
Prowess, prou'es, *n.* Bravery; boldness and dexterity in war; gallantry.
Prowl, proul, *vi.* and *t.* To roam or wander stealthily.—*n.* Act of one who prowls.
Proximate, proks'i-māt, *a.* Nearest; next; in closest relationship; immediate.
Proximity, proks-im'i-ti, *n.* State of being proximate; immediate nearness.
Proximo, proks'i-mō, *a.* The next (month); usually contracted to *prox.*
Proxy, proks'i, *n.* Agency of a substitute; a deputy; a writing by which one authorizes another to vote in his stead.
Prude, pröd, *n.* A woman affecting great reserve and excessive delicacy.
Prudence, prö'dens, *n.* Quality of being prudent; caution; discretion.
Prudent, prö'dent, *a.* Provident; careful; discreet; judicious.
Prudential, prö-den'shal, *a.* Proceeding from or dictated by prudence; politic.
Prudery, pröd'ė-ri, *n.* The conduct of a prude; affected delicacy of feeling.
Prudish, pröd'ish, *a.* Like a prude; affecting excessive modesty or virtue.
Prune, prön, *vt.* (pruning, pruned). To trim; to cut or lop off; to clear from superfluities. —*n.* A plum, particularly a dried plum.
Prunella, prụ-nel'a, *n.* A smooth woollen stuff used for the uppers of ladies' shoes.
Prurience, Pruriency, prö'ri-ens, prö'ri-en-si, *n.* An itching desire for anything; tendency to lascivious thoughts.
Prurient, prö'ri-ent, *a.* Itching after something; inclined to lascivious thoughts.
Prussic-acid, prus' or prụs'ik-a-sid, *a.* The common name for *Hydrocyanic Acid.*
Pry, prī, *vi.* (prying, pried). To peep narrowly; to look closely; to peer.—*n.* A keen glance.
Prying, prī'ing, *p.a.* Apt to pry; inspecting closely; looking into with curiosity.
Psalm, säm, *n.* A sacred song or hymn.
Psalmist, säm'ist or sal'mist, *n.* A writer or composer of psalms.
Psalmodist, säm'od-ist or sal'mod-ist, *n.* One who writes or sings psalms.
Psalmody, säm'od-i or sal'mo-di, *n.* Act or art of singing psalms; psalms collectively.
Psalter, sạl'tėr, *n.* The Book of Psalms; a book containing the Psalms separately.
Psaltery, sạl'te-ri, *n.* A Hebrew stringed instrument of music; a kind of dulcimer.
Pseudo-, sū'dō. A prefix signifying false or spurious.
Pseudonym, sū'dō-nim, *n.* A false or feigned name; a name assumed by a writer.
Pshaw, shạ, *interj.* An expression of contempt, disdain, or impatience.
Psychiatry, sī'ki-at-ri, *n.* Medical treatment of diseases of the mind.
Psychic, Psychical, sī'kik, sī'kik-al, *a.* Belonging to the soul; psychological; pertaining to that force by which spiritualists aver they produce "spiritual" phenomena.
Psychologic, Psychological, sī-ko-loj'ik, sī-ko-loj'ik-al, *a.* Pertaining to psychology or science of mind.
Psychologist, sī-kol'o-jist, *n.* One who is conversant with psychology.
Psychology, sī-kol'o-ji, *n.* That branch of knowledge which deals with the mind; mental science.
Ptarmigan, tär'mi-gan, *n.* The white grouse.
Ptolemaic, to-lē-mā'ik, *a.* Pertaining to Ptolemy, or to his system of the universe, in which the sun revolved round the earth.
Ptomaine, tō'mān, *n.* A name of certain substances generated during putrefaction or morbid conditions prior to death.
Ptyalism, tī'al-izm, *n.* Salivation.
Puberty, pū'bėr-ti, *n.* The age at which persons can beget or bear children.
Pubescence, pū-bes'ens, *n.* Puberty; the downy substance on plants.
Pubescent, pū-bes'ent, *a.* Arriving at puberty; covered with fine soft hairs.
Public, pub'lik, *a.* Not private; pertaining to a whole community; open or free to all; common; notorious.—*n.* The people, indefinitely.—**In public,** in open view.
Publican, pub'li-kan, *n.* A collector of public revenues; keeper of a public-house.
Publication, pub-li-kā'shon, *n.* Act of publishing; announcement; promulgation; act of offering a book, &c., to the public by sale; any book, &c., published.
Public-house, pub'lik-hous, *n.* An inn or shop for the retail of spirituous liquors.
Publicist, pub'li-sist, *n.* A writer on current political topics.
Publicity, pub-lis'i-ti, *n.* State of being made public; notoriety; currency.
Publicly, pub'lik-li, *adv.* In a public manner; openly; without concealment.
Publish, pub'lish, *vt.* To make public; to proclaim, promulgate; to cause to be printed and offered for sale.
Publisher, pub'lish-ėr, *n.* One who publishes, especially books.
Pucker, puk'ėr, *vt.* and *i.* To gather into small folds; to wrinkle.—*n.* A fold or wrinkle, or a collection of folds.
Pudder, pud'ėr, *n.* Bustle; pother.
Pudding, pụd'ing, *n.* An intestine; a sausage; a dish variously compounded, of flour, milk, eggs, fruit, &c.
Puddle, pud'l, *n.* A small pool of dirty water; clay worked into a mass impervious to water. —*vt.* (puddling, puddled). To make muddy; to make water-tight with clay; to convert pig-iron into wrought-iron.
Puddling, pud'ling, *n.* The operation of working clay so as to resist water; clay thus used; process of converting cast-iron into malleable iron.
Pudenda, pū-dẹn'da, *n.pl.* The parts of generation.
Pudgy, puj'i, *a.* Fat and short.
Puerile, pū'ėr-īl, *a.* Boyish; childish.
Puerility, pū-ėr-il'i-ti, *n.* State of being puerile; boyishness; that which is puerile.
Puerperal, pū-ėr'pėr-al, *a.* Pertaining to childbirth.
Puff, puf, *n.* A sudden emission of breath; a whiff; a short blast of wind; a puff-ball; piece of light pastry; a consciously exaggerated commendation.—*vi.* To give a quick

blast with the mouth; to breathe hard after exertion.—*vt.* To drive with a blast; to inflate; to praise extravagantly.
Puff-adder, puf'ad-ėr, *n.* A venomous snake which swells out the upper part of its body.
Puff-ball, puf'bal, *n.* A ball-shaped fungus which when ripe discharges a fine powder.
Puffin, puf'in, *n.* A diving bird of the auk family.
Puffy, puf'i, *a.* Puffed out; turgid.
Pug, pug, *n.* A monkey; a dwarf variety of dog.
Pugilism, pū'jil-izm, *n.* The practice of boxing or fighting with the fist.
Pugilist, pū'jil-ist, *n.* One who fights with his fists.
Pugilistic, pū-jil-ist'ik, *a.* Pertaining to pugilism.
Pugnacious, pug-nā'shus, *a.* Disposed to fight; quarrelsome.
Pugnacity, pug-nas'i-ti, *n.* Quality of being pugnacious; inclination to fight.
Pug-nose, pug'nōz, *n.* A nose turned up at the end; a snub-nose.
Puisne, pū'ni, *a.* Younger or inferior in rank.
Puissance, pū'is-ans, *n.* Power; might.
Puissant, pū'is-ant, *a.* Powerful; strong; mighty; forcible.
Puke, pūk, *vi.* and *t.* (puking, puked). To vomit.
Pulchritude, pul'kri-tūd, *n.* Beauty; comeliness.
Pule, pūl, *vi.* (puling, puled). To cry like a chicken; to whine; to whimper.
Pulkha, pul'ka, *n.* A Laplander's travelling sledge.
Pull, pul, *vt.* To draw towards one; to tug; to rend; to pluck; to gather.—*vi.* To draw; to tug.—*n.* Act of pulling; a twitch; act of rowing a boat; a drink; a struggle.
Pullet, pul'et, *n.* A young hen.
Pulley, pul'i, *n.* A small wheel in a block, used in raising weights.
Pullman-car, pul'man-kär, *n.* A luxuriously fitted up railway-carriage.
Pull-over, pul'ō-vėr, *n.* A knitted jersey without buttons, pulled over the head when put on.
Pull-through, pul'thrō, *n.* A cord with a weight at one end and a loop for a piece of oiled rag at the other, used for cleaning the barrel of a rifle.
Pulmonary, pul'mon-a-ri, *a.* Pertaining to or affecting the lungs.
Pulp, pulp, *n.* Moist, soft animal or vegetable matter.—*vt.* To make into pulp; to deprive of the pulp.
Pulpit, pul'pit, *n.* An elevated place for a preacher; preachers generally.
Pulpy, pul'pi, *a.* Like pulp; soft; fleshy.
Pulsate, pul'sāt, *vi.* To beat or throb.
Pulsation, pul-sā'shon, *n.* The beating of the heart or an artery; a throb.
Pulse, puls, *n.* The beating of the heart or an artery; vibration; leguminous plants or their seeds, as beans, &c.—*vi.* (pulsing, pulsed). To beat or throb.
Pulverize, pul'vėr-īz, *vt.* To reduce to dust or fine powder.
Pulverulent, pul-ver'ū-lent, *a.* Powdery.
Puma, pū'ma, *n.* A carnivorous quadruped of the cat kind; the cougar.
Pumice, pū'mis or pum'is, *n.* A light and spongy stone, used for polishing.
Pumiceous, pū-mi'shus, *a.* Pertaining to, consisting of or like pumice.
Pump, pump, *n.* A machine for raising water or extracting air; a shoe used in dancing.—*vi.* To work a pump.—*vt.* To raise with a pump; to free from liquid by a pump; to put artful questions to extract information.
Pumpkin, pump'kin, *n.* A plant and its fruit; a kind of gourd or vegetable marrow.
Pun, pun, *n.* A play on words like in sound, but different in meaning; a kind of quibble.—*vi.* (punning, punned) To make a pun or puns.
Punch, punsh, *n.* An instrument for driving holes in metal, &c.; a blow or thrust; a beverage of spirits, lemon-juice, water, &c.; a buffoon; a short-legged, barrel-bodied horse; a short fat fellow.—*vt.* To stamp or perforate with a punch; to hit with the fist.
Puncheon, pun'shon, *n.* A perforating or stamping tool; a punch; a cask containing from 84 to 120 gallons.
Punchy, punsh'i, *a.* Short and fat; squat.
Punctilio, pungk-til'i-ō, *n.* A nice point of exactness in conduct or ceremony.
Punctilious, pungk-til'i-us, *a.* Very exact in forms of behaviour or ceremony.
Punctual, pungk'tū-al, *a.* Exact; made or done at the exact time.
Punctuality, pungk-tū-al'i-ti, *n.* Quality of being punctual; scrupulous exactness.
Punctuate, pungk'tū-āt, *vt.* To mark with the points necessary in writings.
Punctuation, pungk-tū-ā'shon, *n.* The act, art, or system of punctuating a writing.
Puncture, pungk'tūr, *n.* The act of pricking; a small hole thus made.—*vt.* (puncturing, punctured). To pierce with a small point.
Pundit, pun'dit, *n.* A learned Brahman; an Indian scholar; any learned man.
Pungency, pun'jen-si, *n.* State or quality of being pungent; sharpness; keenness.
Pungent, pun'jent, *a.* Biting; acrid; caustic; keen; stinging.
Punic, pū'nik, *a.* Pertaining to the Carthaginians; faithless.—*n.* The language of the Carthaginians; Phœnician.
Punish, pun'ish, *vt.* To inflict pain or any evil on, as a penalty; to chastise; to hurt.
Punishable, pun'ish-a-bl, *a.* Liable to punishment; capable of being punished.
Punishment, pun'ish-ment, *n.* Act of punishing; penalty.
Punitive, pū-ni-tiv, *a.* Pertaining to, awarding, or involving punishment.
Punitory, pū'ni-to-ri, *a.* Punitive.
Punka, Punkah, pung'ka, *n.* A large fan slung from the ceilings of rooms in India to produce a current of air.
Punning, pun'ing, *p.a.* Given to make puns; containing a pun or puns.
Punster, pun'stėr, *n.* One skilled in punning.
Punt, punt, *n.* A square-ended flat-bottomed boat.—*vt.* To convey in a punt; to propel (a boat) with a pole.
Puny, pū'ni, *a.* Small and weak; petty.
Pup, pup, *n.* A puppy.—*vi.* (pupping, pupped). To bring forth whelps.
Pupa, pū'pa, *n.*; pl. **-æ.** The chrysalis form of an insect.
Pupil, pū'pil, *n.* A young person under the care of a tutor; the aperture in the iris through which the rays of light pass.
Pupilage (or **-il-**), pū'pil-āj, *n.* State of being

a pupil or ward; wardship; a person's minority.
Pupilary (or **-ll-**), pū'pil-a-ri, *a.* Pertaining to a pupil or ward, or to the pupil of the eye.
Puppet, pup'et, *n.* A small figure in the human form mechanically worked; a person who is a mere tool.
Puppy, pup'i, *n.* A whelp; a young dog; a conceited, foppish fellow.
Puppyism, pup'i-izm, *n.* Extreme affectation or conceit; silly foppery.
Purblind, pėr'blind, *a.* Dim-sighted.
Purchasable, pėr'chās-a-bl, *a.* That may be purchased or bought.
Purchase, pėr'chās, *vt.* (purchasing, purchased). To buy; to obtain by labour, danger, &c.—*n.* Acquisition of anything by money; what is bought; mechanical advantage.
Purchaser, pėr'chās-ėr, *n.* A buyer.
Pure, pūr, *a.* Clean; clear; unmixed; spotless; chaste; genuine; sincere; absolute.
Purely, pūr'li, *adv.* Innocently; stainlessly; chastely; wholly; absolutely.
Purgation, pėr-gā'shon, *n.* Act or operation of purging.
Purgative, pėr'ga-tiv, *a.* Having the power of purging.—*n.* A medicine that purges.
Purgatory, pėr'ga-to-ri, *a.* Tending to purge or cleanse.—*n.* In the R. Catholic religion, a place in which souls after death are purified from sins; any place or state of temporary suffering.
Purge, pėrj, *vt.* and *i.* (purging, purged). To make pure or clean; to clear from accusation; to evacuate the bowels of.—*n.* The act of purging; a cathartic medicine.
Purification, pū'ri-fi-kā"shon, *n.* Act of purifying; a cleansing from guilt or sin.
Purifier, pū'ri-fi-ėr, *n.* One who or that which purifies or cleanses.
Purify, pū'ri-fi, *vt.* (purifying, purified). To make pure or clear; to free from admixture; to free from guilt.—*vi.* To become pure or clear.
Purism, pūr'izm, *n.* Practice of rigid purity; fastidious niceness in the use of words.
Purist, pūr'ist, *n.* One excessively nice in the use of words, &c.
Puritan, pūr'i-tan, *n.* One very strict in religious matters or in conduct; an early Protestant dissenter from the Church of England.—*a.* Pertaining to the Puritans.
Puritanic, Puritanical, pūr-i-tan'ik, pūr-i-tan'ik-al, *a.* Puritan; over rigid in religion.
Purity, pūr'i-ti, *n.* State or quality of being pure; cleanness; innocence; chastity.
Purl, pėrl, *n.* Spiced malt liquor; gentle murmur of a stream.—*vi.* To murmur, as a stream; to reverse a stitch in knitting.
Purlieu, pėr'lū, *n.* Part lying adjacent; outskirts: generally in *pl.*
Purloin, pėr-loin', *vt.* To steal or pilfer; to filch; to take by theft or plagiarism.
Purple, pėr'pl, *n.* A colour produced by mixing red and blue; a purple robe, the badge of the Roman emperors; regal power.—*a.* Of a colour made of red and blue; dyed with blood.—*vt.* (purpling, purpled). To make purple.
Purport, pėr'pōrt, *n.* Meaning; import.—*vt.* To signify; to profess.
Purpose, pėr'pos, *n.* End or aim; design; intention; matter in question.—*vt.* and *i.* (purposing, purposed). To propose; to intend.
Purposeless, pėr'pos-les, *a.* Having no purpose or effect.
Purposely, pėr'pos-li, *adv.* By purpose or design; intentionally.
Purr, pėr, *vi.* To murmur, as a cat when pleased.—*n.* The sound of a cat when pleased.
Purse, pėrs, *n.* A small bag or receptacle for money; money collected as a prize or a present; finances.—*vt.* (pursing, pursed). To put in a purse; to pucker.
Purse-proud, pėrs'proud, *a.* Proud of wealth.
Purser, pėrs'ėr, *n.* A person belonging to a ship, who keeps accounts.
Purslane, pėrs'lān, *n.* A succulent plant, used as a pot-herb, and for salads, &c.
Pursuance, pėr-sū'ans, *n.* The pursuing or carrying out (of a design).
Pursuant, pėr-sū'ant, *a.* Done in prosecution of anything; conformable.
Pursue, pėr-sū', *vt.* (pursuing, pursued). To follow with a view to overtake; to chase; to use measures to obtain; to carry on.—*vi.* To go in pursuit; to act as prosecutor.
Pursuer, pėr-sū'ėr, *n.* One who pursues; the plaintiff.
Pursuit, pėr-sūt', *n.* Act of pursuing; chase; quest; business occupation.
Pursuivant, pėr'swi-vant, *n.* A state messenger; an attendant on heralds.
Pursy, pėr'si, *a.* Fat and short-winded.
Purtenance, pėr'te-nans, *n.* Appurtenance; the pluck of an animal.
Purulence, Purulency, pū'ru̥-lens, pū'ru̥-len-si, *n.* State of being purulent; pus.
Purulent, pū'ru̥-lent, *a.* Consisting or of the nature of pus.
Purvey, pėr-vā', *vt.* To provide.—*vi.* To supply provisions, especially for a number.
Purveyance, pėr-vā'ans, *n.* Act of purveying; the former royal prerogative of obtaining necessaries on easy terms.
Purveyor, pėr-vā'or, *n.* One who purveys; a caterer.
Purview, pėr'vū, *n.* The body of a statute; the scope of a statute; limit; sphere.
Pus, pus, *n.* The soft yellowish substance formed in suppuration; matter of a sore.
Puseyism, pū'zi-izm, *n.* The doctrines promulgated by Dr. *Pusey* and other divines; tractarianism.
Push, pu̥sh, *vt.* To press against with force; to thrust or shove; to enforce; to urge; to prosecute energetically.—*vi.* To make a thrust or effort; to force one's way.—*n.* Act of pushing; vigorous effort; emergency; enterprise.
Pushing, pu̥sh'ing, *p.a.* Pressing forward in business; enterprising; energetic.
Pushto, Pushtoo, push'tō, push'tö, *n.* The language of the Afghans.
Pusillanimity, pū'sil-la-nim"i-ti, *n.* Weakness of spirit; cowardice; timidity.
Pusillanimous, pū-sil-lan'im-us, *a.* Without strength of mind; timid; cowardly.
Puss, pu̥s, *n.* A cat; a hare.
Pussy, pu̥s'i, *n.* A diminutive of puss.
Pustular, pus'tū-lėr, *a.* Having the character of or proceeding from a pustule.
Pustulate, pus'tū-lāt, *vi.* To form into pustules.—*a.* Covered with pustule-like prominences.

Pustule, pus'tūl, *n.* A small blister; small elevation of the cuticle, containing pus.
Put, put, *vt.* (putting, put). To place in any position or situation; to apply; to propose or propound; to state in words.
Put, Putt, put, *vt.* (putting, putted). To throw (a heavy stone) from the shoulder; in golf, to play the ball into the hole.—*n.* A rustic; a silly fellow.
Putative, pū'ta-tiv, *a.* Supposed; reputed.
Putid, pū'tid, *a.* Disgusting; vile; nasty.
Putrefaction, pū-trē-fak'shon, *n.* Process or state of putrefying; decomposition.
Putrefactive, pū-trē-fak'tiv, *a.* Pertaining to or causing putrefaction.
Putrefy, pū'trē-fī, *vt.* (putrefying, putrefied). To render putrid.—*vi.* To decay; to rot.
Putrescence, pū-tres'ens, *n.* State of becoming rotten; a putrid state.
Putrescent, pū-tres'ent, *a.* Growing putrid.
Putrid, pū'trid, *a.* In a state of decay; rotten; corrupt.
Putridity, pū-trid'i-ti, *n.* State of being putrid; corruption.
Putt, put, *n.* An odd person; a put.
Putter, put'ėr, *n.* One who puts, sets, or places; a kind of golfing club (pron. put'ėr).
Putting-green, put'ing-grēn, *n.* A smooth piece of sward round a hole in a golf course.
Puttock, put'ok, *n.* The common kite.
Putty, put'i, *n.* A paste made of whiting and linseed-oil.—*vt.* To cement or fill with putty.
Puzzle, puz'l, *vt.* (puzzling, puzzled). To perplex; to entangle.—*vi.* To be bewildered.—*n.* Perplexity; something to try ingenuity.
Puzzle-headed, puz'l-hed-ed, *a.* Having a head easily puzzled; bungling.
Puzzlement, puz'l-ment, *n.* The state of being puzzled; bewilderment.
Puzzler, puz'l-ėr, *n.* One who or that which puzzles.
Puzzling, puz'ling, *p.a.* Such as to puzzle; perplexing; embarrassing; bewildering.
Pyæmia, pī-ē'mi-a, *n.* Blood-poisoning.
Pygmy, pig'mi, *n.* A dwarf; anything little.—*a.* Dwarfish; little.
Pyjamas, pī-jäm'az, *n.pl.* A sleeping-suit.
Pylorus, pī-lō'rus, *n.* The lower orifice of the stomach.
Pyramid, pi'ra-mid, *n.* A solid body having triangular sides meeting in a point at the top.
Pyramidal, pi-ram'id-al, *a.* Formed like a pyramid; relating to a pyramid.
Pyramidic, Pyramidical, pi-ra-mid'ik, pi-ra-mid'ik-al, *a.* Having the form of a pyramid; relating to a pyramid.
Pyre, pīr, *n.* A heap of combustibles for burning a dead body; a funeral pile.
Pyrethrum, pi-reth'rum, *n.* A plant akin to the chrysanthemum.
Pyretic, pī-ret'ik, *n.* A medicine for fever.—*a.* Pertaining to fever; feverish.
Pyrites, pi-rī'tēz, *n.* A mineral combining sulphur with iron, copper, cobalt, &c.
Pyrolatry, pī-rol'a-tri, *n.* Fire-worship.
Pyroligneous, pī-rō-lig'nē-us, *a.* Generated by the distillation of wood.
Pyrology, pī-rol'o-ji, *n.* The science of heat.
Pyrometer, pī-rom'et-ėr, *n.* An instrument for measuring high degrees of heat.
Pyrotechnic, pī-rō-tek'nik, *a.* Pertaining to pyrotechny or fireworks. Also *Pyrotechnical.*
Pyrotechnics, Pyrotechny, pī-rō-tek'niks, pī-rō-tek'ni, *n.* The art of making fireworks; the use of fireworks.
Pyrotechnist, pī-rō-tek'nist, *n.* One skilled in pyrotechny.
Pyrrhic, pi'rik, *n.* and *a.* An ancient Grecian warlike dance; a metrical foot of two short syllables.—**Pyrrhic victory,** a victory like those of Pyrrhus of Epirus over the Romans, costing more to the victor than to the vanquished.
Pyrrhonism, pi'ron-izm, *n.* Scepticism; universal doubt.
Pythagorean, pi-tha'gō-rē''an, *a.* Pertaining to Pythagoras or his philosophy, which taught the transmigration of souls.
Python, pī'thon, *n.* A large non-venomous serpent.
Pythoness, pī'thon-es, *n.* The priestess who gave oracular answers at Delphi; a female with a spirit of divination.
Pyx, piks, *n.* A vessel used in the R. Catholic Church for holding the host; a box or chest for specimen coins at the British Mint; the metallic box containing the nautical compass-card.—**Trial of the Pyx,** the trial by weight and assay of the gold and silver coins of the United Kingdom.—*vt.* To test by weight and assay.

Q

Qua, kwā, *adv.* In the quality or character of; as being; as.
Quack, kwak, *vi.* To cry like a duck; to boast; to practise quackery.—*n.* The cry of a duck; a pretender to skill or knowledge, especially medical.—*a.* Pertaining to quackery.
Quackery, kwak'ė-ri, *n.* Practice or boastful pretences of a quack, particularly in medicine.
Quackish, kwak'ish, *a.* Like a quack.
Quacksalver, kwak'sal-vėr, *n.* A quack who deals in salves and ointments.
Quad, kwod, *n.* A quadrangle or court.
Quadragesima, kwod-ra-je'si-ma, *n.* Lent.
Quadragesimal, kwod-ra-je'si-mal, *a.* Belonging to Lent; used in Lent.
Quadrangle, kwod-rang-gl, *n.* A plane figure, have four angles and sides; an inner square of a building.
Quadrangular, kwod-rang'gū-lėr, *a.* Having four angles and four sides.
Quadrant, kwod'rant, *n.* The fourth part of a circle or its circumference; an old instrument for taking altitudes and angles; an old form of sextant.
Quadrat, kwod'rat, *n.* A piece of type-metal for leaving a blank in printing.
Quadrate, kwod'rāt, *a.* Square.—*n.* A square surface or figure.—*vi.* To square with; to agree or suit.
Quadratic, kwod-rat'ik, *a.* In *algebra*, involving the square of an unknown quantity.
Quadrature, kwod'ra-tūr, *n.* Act of squaring; position of one heavenly body in respect to another when distant from it 90°.
Quadrennial, kwod-ren'ni-al, *a.* Comprising four years; occurring once in four years.
Quadrilateral, kwod-ri-lat'ėr-al, *a.* Having four sides and four angles.—*n.* A plane figure having four sides and angles.

Quadrille, kwo-dril′ or ka-dril′, *n.* A game at cards for four; a dance for four couples, each forming the side of a square; music for such a dance.
Quadrillion, kwod-ril′yon, *n.* The fourth power of a million; a number represented by a unit and 24 ciphers.
Quadripartite, kwod-ri-pär′tīt, *a.* Divided into or having four parts.
Quadrisyllable, kwod-ri-sil′la-bl, *n.* A word consisting of four syllables.
Quadroon, kwod-rön′, *n.* The offspring of a mulatto by a white person.
Quadrumana, kwod-ru̥′ma-na, *n.pl.* An order of mammals comprising the monkey tribe, characterized by the four limbs terminating in prehensile hands.
Quadrumanous, kwod-ru̥′ma-nus, *a.* Pertaining to the Quadrumana; four-handed.
Quadruped, kwod′ru̥-ped, *n.* An animal with four legs or feet.
Quadruple, kwod′ru̥-pl, *a.* Fourfold.—*n.* Four times the sum or number.—*vt.* To make fourfold.—*vi.* To become fourfold.
Quadruplicate, kwod-ru̥′pli-kāt, *a.* Fourfold.—*vt.* To make fourfold.
Quadruplication, kwod-ru̥′pli-kā″shon, *n.* Act of quadruplicating.
Quaff, kwäf, *vt.* and *i.* To drain to the bottom; to drink copiously.
Quag, kwag, *n.* A quagmire.
Quagga, kwag′a, *n.* An animal of S. Africa closely allied to the zebra.
Quaggy, kwag′i, *a.* Boggy.
Quagmire, kwag′mīr, *n.* A piece of soft, wet, boggy land; a bog; a fen.
Quail, kwāl, *vi.* To shrink; to flinch; to cower.—*n.* A small bird allied to the partridge.
Quaint, kwānt, *a.* Fanciful; curious; odd and antique; singular; whimsical.
Quaintly, kwānt′li, *adv.* In a quaint manner; oddly; fancifully; whimsically.
Quake, kwāk, *vi.* (quaking, quaked). To shake; to tremble; to quiver.—*n.* A shake; tremulous agitation.
Quaker, kwāk′ėr, *n.* One who quakes; one of the religious sect called the *Society of Friends*.
Quakeress, kwāk′ėr-es, *n.* A female Quaker.
Quakerism, kwāk′ėr-izm, *n.* The manners, tenets, or worship of the Quakers.
Quaky, kwāk′i, *a.* Shaky.
Qualification, kwo′li-fi-kā″shon, *n.* Act of qualifying; state of being qualified; suitable quality or characteristic; legal power; ability; modification; restriction.
Qualified, kwo′li-fīd, *p.a.* Having qualification; competent; limited; modified.
Qualify, kwo′li-fī, *vt.* (qualifying, qualified). To give proper or suitable qualities to; to furnish with the knowledge, skill, &c., necessary; to modify or limit; to soften or moderate; to dilute.—*vi.* To become qualified or fit.
Qualitative, kwo′li-tā-tiv, *a.* Relating to quality; estimable according to quality.
Quality, kwo′li-ti, *n.* Sort, kind, or character; a distinguishing property or characteristic; degree of excellence; high rank.
Qualm, kwäm, *n.* A sudden fit of nausea; a twinge of conscience; compunction.
Quandary, kwon-dā′ri or kwon′da-ri, *n.* A state of perplexity; a predicament.
Quantify, kwon′ti-fī, *vt.* To determine the quantity of; to modify with regard to quantity.
Quantitative, kwon′ti-tā-tiv, *a.* Relating to or having regard to quantity.
Quantity, kwon′ti-ti, *n.* That property in virtue of which a thing is measurable; bulk; measure; amount; metrical value of syllables.
Quantum, kwan′tum, *n.* A quantity; an amount; a sufficient amount.
Quaquaversal, kwā-kwa-vėr′sal, *a.* Inclined towards every side.
Quarantine, kwo′ran-tīn, *n.* The period during which a ship suspected of being infected is obliged to forbear all intercourse with a port.—*vt.* To cause to perform quarantine.
Quarrel, kwo′rel, *n.* An angry dispute; a brawl; cause of dispute; a dart for a crossbow; a glazier's diamond.—*vi.* (quarrelling, quarelled). To dispute violently; to disagree.
Quarrelsome, kwo′rel-sum, *a.* Apt to quarrel; contentious; irascible; choleric.
Quarrier, kwo′ri-ėr, *n.* A worker at a quarry.
Quarry, kwo′ri, *n.* A place where stones are dug from the earth; any animal pursued for prey; game killed.—*vt.* (quarrying, quarried). To dig or take from a quarry.
Quarryman, kwo′ri-man, *n.* A quarrier.
Quart, kwąrt, *n.* The fourth part of a gallon; two pints.
Quartan, kwąr′tan, *a.* Recurring every fourth day.
Quarter, kwąr′tėr, *n.* The fourth part of anything; 28 lbs.; 8 bushels; any direction or point of the compass; a district; locality; division of a heraldic shield; proper position; mercy to a beaten foe; *pl.* shelter or lodging; encampment.—*vt.* To divide into four equal parts; to cut to pieces; to furnish with lodgings or shelter; to add to other arms on an heraldic shield.—*vi.* To lodge.
Quarter-day, kwąr′tėr-dā, *n.* A day when quarterly payments are made.
Quarter-deck, kwąr′tėr-dek, *n.* The upper deck of a ship abaft the main-mast.
Quartering, kwąr′tėr-ing, *n.* The conjoining of coats of arms in one shield; a compartment on a shield.
Quarterly, kwąr′tėr-li, *a.* Recurring each quarter of the year.—*adv.* Once in a quarter of a year.—*n.* A periodical published quarterly.
Quarter-master, kwąr′tėr-mäs-tėr, *n.* An officer who has charge of the barracks, tents, stores, &c., of a regiment; a petty officer in the navy, who steers, signals, &c.
Quartern, kwąr′tėrn, *n.* The fourth part of a pint, peck, stone, &c.
Quartern-loaf, kwąr′tėrn-lōf, *n.* A loaf of bread weighing about 4 lbs.
Quarter-sessions, kwąr′tėr-se-shonz, *n.pl.* In England, a criminal court held quarterly for petty offences.
Quartette, Quartet, kwąr-tet′, *n.* A musical composition in four parts; the performers of such a composition.
Quarto, kwąr′tō, *n.* A book in which the sheets are folded into four leaves.—*a.* Having four leaves to the sheet.
Quartz, kwąrtz, *n.* A pure variety of silica, a constituent of granite and other rocks.
Quash, kwosh, *vt.* To subdue or quell; to suppress; to annul or make void.
Quantification, kwon′ti-fi-kā″shon, *n.* The act or process of quantifying.

Quasi, kwā'sī. A prefix implying appearance without reality; sort of; sham.
Quassia, kwas'i-a, *n.* A bitter S. American plant, yielding a tonic used in medicine.
Quatercentenary, kwa-tėr-sen'te-na-ri, *n.* A four hundredth anniversary.
Quaternary, kwa-tėr'na-ri, *a.* Consisting of four; arranged in fours: applied to the strata above the tertiary.
Quaternion, kwa-tėr'ni-on, *n.* A set of four; a quantity employed in mathematics.
Quatorzain, kwa'tor-zān, *n.* A stanza or poem of fourteen lines.
Quatrain, kwot'rān, *n.* A stanza of four lines rhyming alternately.
Quaver, kwā'vėr, *vi.* To have a tremulous motion; to vibrate.—*vt.* To utter with a tremulous sound.—*n.* A shake or rapid vibration of the voice, or on a musical instrument; a musical note equal to half a crotchet.
Quay, kē, *n.* A built landing-place for vessels; a wharf.
Quayage, kē'āj, *n.* Money paid for the use of a quay.
Quean, kwēn, *n.* A worthless woman.
Queasy, kwē'zi, *a.* Sick at the stomach; inclined to vomit; fastidious; squeamish.
Queen, kwēn, *n.* The wife of a king; a female sovereign; a pre-eminent woman; the sovereign of a swarm of bees; a playing-card; a piece at chess.
Queenhood, kwēn'hụd, *n.* The rank, quality, or character of a queen.
Queenly, kwēn'li, *a.* Like a queen; becoming a queen; suitable to a queen.
Queer, kwēr, *a.* Odd; droll; peculiar.
Queerly, kwēr'li, *adv.* In a queer manner.
Quell, kwel, *vt.* To subdue; to allay.
Quench, kwensh, *vt.* To put out, as fire; to allay or slake, as thirst; to repress.
Quenchable, kwensh'a-bl, *a.* That may be quenched or extinguished.
Quenchless, kwensh'les, *a.* That cannot be quenched; inextinguishable; irrepressible.
Quercitron, kwėr'sit-ron, *n.* The dyer's-oak, a tree of N. America; the dye-stuff itself.
Querimonious, kwe-ri-mō'ni-us, *a.* Apt to complain; complaining; querulous.
Quern, kwėrn, *n.* A stone hand-mill for grinding grain.
Querulous, kwe'rū-lus, *a.* Complaining; murmuring; peevish.
Query, kwē'ri, *n.* A question; the mark of interrogation (?).—*vi.* (querying, queried). To ask a question or questions.—*vt.* To question; to mark with a query.
Quest, kwest, *n.* Act of seeking; search; pursuit; inquiry; solicitation.
Question, kwest'yon, *n.* Act of asking; an interrogation; inquiry; discussion; subject of discussion.—*vi.* To ask a question; to doubt. —*vt.* To interrogate; to doubt; to challenge.
Questionable, kwest'yon-a-bl, *a.* That may be questioned; doubtful.
Questionnaire, kwest'yon-ār, kest-ē-on-ār', *n.* A list or series of questions designed to elicit information on a specific subject.
Queue, kū, *n.* The tail of a wig; a pigtail; a file of persons waiting, in the order of their arrival, to be served in a shop or admitted to a theatre, &c.—*vi.* To join or wait in a queue.
Quibble, kwib'l, *n.* A turn of language to evade the point in question; a pun.—*vi.* (quibbling, quibbled). To evade the question or truth by artifice; to prevaricate; to pun.
Quick, kwik, *a.* Alive; brisk; swift; keen; sensitive; irritable.—*n.* A growing plant, usually hawthorn, for hedges; the living flesh; sensitiveness.—*adv.* Quickly; soon.
Quicken, kwik'n, *vt.* To revive or resuscitate; to cheer; to increase the speed of; to sharpen; to stimulate.—*vi.* To become alive; to move quickly or more quickly.
Quick-hedge, kwik'hej, *n.* A fence or hedge of growing plants.
Quicklime, kwik'līm, *n.* Lime burned but not yet slaked with water.
Quickly, kwik'li, *adv.* In a quick manner; speedily; rapidly; soon; without delay.
Quicksand, kwik'sand, *n.* A movable sandbank under water; sand yielding under the feet; something treacherous.
Quickset, kwik'set, *n.* A plant set to grow, particularly for a hedge, as hawthorn.—*vt.* To plant with shrubs for a hedge.—*a.* Composed of living plants, as a hedge.
Quicksilver, kwik'sil-vėr, *n.* Mercury.
Quid, kwid, *n.* A piece of tobacco chewed and rolled about in the mouth.
Quiddity, kwid'i-ti, *n.* Essence or nature; a trifling nicety; quirk or quibble.
Quidnunc, kwid'nungk, *n.* One curious to know everything that passes; a newsmonger.
Quiescence, kwī-es'ens, *n.* Rest; repose.
Quiescent, kwī-es'ent, *a.* Resting; still; tranquil; silent.—*n.* A silent letter.
Quiet, kwī'et, *a.* At rest; calm; still; peaceful; patient; secluded; not glaring or showy. —*n.* Rest; repose; peace; security.—*vt.* To make quiet; to calm; to lull; to allay.
Quietism, kwī'et-izm, *n.* The practice of resigning oneself to mental inactivity to bring the soul into direct union with God.
Quietly, kwī'et-li, *adv.* In a quiet manner; calmly; so as not to attract attention.
Quietude, kwī'et-ūd, *n.* Rest; quiet.
Quietus, kwī-ē'tus, *n.* A final discharge of an account; a finishing stroke.
Quill, kwil, *n.* The strong feather of a goose, &c.; a feather made into a pen; the spine of a porcupine; a piece of reed used by weavers; a plait of a ruffle.—*vt.* To plait.
Quilt, kwilt, *n.* A padded bed-cover.—*vt.* To form into a quilt; to sew pieces of cloth with soft substance between.
Quilting, kwilt'ing, *n.* The act of making a quilt; the material used for quilts.
Quinary, kwī'na-ri, *a.* Consisting of five; arranged by fives.
Quince, kwins, *n.* The fruit of a tree allied to the pear and apple; the tree itself.
Quincentenary, kwin-sen'te-na-ri, *n.* A five hundredth anniversary.
Quincunx, kwin'kungks, *n.* An arrangement of five objects in a square, one at each corner and one in the middle.
Quinine, kwin'ēn or kwin-īn', *n.* An alkaline substance obtained from the bark of trees of the cinchona genus.
Quinquagesima, kwin-kwa-je'si-ma, *n.* Shrove Sunday; fiftieth day before Easter.
Quinquennial, kwin-kwen'ni-al, *a.* Occurring once in five years; lasting five years.
Quinquennium, kwin-kwen'ni-um, *n.* The space of five years.

Quinsy, kwin'zi, *n.* An inflammation of the tonsils or throat.
Quintain, kwin'tān, *n.* A figure to be tilted at in old English sports.
Quintal, kwin'tal, *n.* A weight of 220 lbs.
Quintan, kwin'tan, *a.* Recurring every fifth day.
Quintessence, kwint-es'ens, *n.* The fifth or highest essence of a natural body; the purest or most essential part of a thing.
Quintette, Quintet, kwin-tet', *n.* A musical composition in five parts; the performers of such a composition.
Quintuple, kwin'tu̧-pl, *a.* Fivefold.—*vt.* To make fivefold.
Quip, kwip, *n.* A sharp sarcastic turn; a severe retort; a gibe.
Quire, kwīr, *n.* A chorus; a choir; part of a church where the singers sit; twenty-four sheets of paper.
Quirk, kwėrk, *n.* An artful turn for evasion; a shift; a quibble.
Quisling, kwiz'ling, *n.* A traitor to his country who is prepared to act as head or member of a puppet government.
Quit, kwit, *a.* Discharged; released; free; clear.—*vt.* (quitting, quitted). To discharge; to rid; to acquit; to leave; to abandon.
Quite, kwīt, *adv.* Completely; wholly; entirely; altogether; very.
Quittance, kwit'ans, *n.* Acquittance; recompense; return; repayment.
Quiver, kwi'vėr, *n.* A case or sheath for arrows.—*vi.* To shake with small rapid movements; to tremble; to shiver.
Quixotic, kwiks-ot'ik, *a.* Chivalrous to extravagance; aiming at visionary ends.
Quiz, kwiz, *n.* A hoax; a jest; one who quizzes; one liable to be quizzed; a game or test in which two or more persons or teams compete in answering questions.—*vt.* (quizzing, quizzed). To make fun of, as by obscure questions; to look at inquisitively; to tease; to test by questioning.
Quizzical, kwiz'i-kal, *a.* Addicted to quizzing or teasing; comical; humorously critical.
Quoad sacra, kwō'ad sā'kra, *a.* So far as regards sacred matters.
Quodlibet, kwod'li-bet, *n.* A nice point in theological discussion; a subtlety.
Quoin, koin, *n.* An external solid angle, as of a building; a wedge.
Quoit, koit, *n.* A flattish ring of iron, thrown at a mark.—*vi.* To throw or play at quoits.
Quondam, kwon'dam, *a.* Former.
Quorum, kwō'rum, *n.* A number of the members of any body competent to transact business.
Quota, kwō'ta, *n.* A share or proportion assigned to each.
Quotable, kwōt'a-bl, *a.* That may be quoted.
Quotation, kwōt-a'shon, *n.* Act of quoting; passage quoted; the naming of the price of commodities, or the price specified.
Quote, kwōt, *vt.* (quoting, quoted). To adduce or cite, as from some author; to name as the price of an article.
Quoth, kwōth, *vt.* Said; used only in the 1st and 3rd persons preterite, before its subject.
Quotidian, kwō-ti'di-an, *a.* Daily.—*n.* A fever whose paroxysms return every day.
Quotient, kwō'shent, *n.* The number obtained by dividing one number by another.

R

Rabbet, rab'et, *vt.* To cut so as to make a joint along an edge.—*n.* The cut so made on an edge to form a joint.
Rabbi, rab'bī, *n.* A Jewish teacher or expounder of the law.
Rabbinic, Rabbinical, rab-bin'ik, rab-bin'ik-al, *a.* Pertaining to the Hebrew learning and teachers after Christ.
Rabbit, rab'it, *n.* A burrowing rodent allied to the hare.
Rabble, rab'l, *n.* A crowd of vulgar, noisy people; the mob; the lower class of people.
Rabblement, rab'l-ment, *n.* A rabble.
Rabid, ra'bid, *a.* Raving; furious; mad.
Rabidly, ra'bid-li, *adv.* Madly; furiously.
Rabies, rā'bi-ēs, *n.* A disease affecting certain animals, especially dogs, from which hydrophobia is communicated.
Raccoon, Racoon, ra-kön', *n.* An American carnivorous animal.
Race, rās, *n.* A body of individuals sprung from a common stock; a breed or stock; a running; a contest in speed; a course or career; a rapid current or channel.—*vi.* (racing, raced). To run swiftly; to contend in running.—*vt.* To cause to contend in speed.
Race-course, rās'kōrs, *n.* The ground or path on which races are run.
Race-horse, rās'hors, *n.* A horse bred or kept for racing.
Raceme, ras'ēm, *n.* A species of inflorescence, in which a number of flowers with short pedicels stand on a common stem.
Rachis, rā'kis, *n.* The spine of animals; shaft of a feather; stalk of the frond in ferns.
Racial, rā'si-al, *a.* Pertaining to race or lineage; pertaining to the races of man.
Racily, rā'si-li, *adv.* In a racy manner.
Racing, rās'ing, *n.* Act of running in a race; the business of joining in horse-races.
Rack, rak, *vt.* To stretch unduly; to distort; to punish on the rack; to torture; to strain.—*n.* Something used for stretching; an instrument of torture; torment; anguish; a frame for fodder, &c.; a bar with teeth on one of its edges; flying broken clouds; wreck.
Racket, rak'et, *n.* A confused din; clamour; the bat used in tennis, &c.; *pl.* a game like tennis.—*vi.* To make a racket; to frolic.
Rack-rent, rak'rent, *n.* An exorbitant rent.—*vt.* To subject to paying a full or exorbitant rent.
Racy, rā'si, *a.* Strong and well-flavoured; spirited; piquant.
Radar, rā'där, *n.* A method of finding the position of an object (ship, aircraft, &c.) by reflection of radio waves.
Raddle, rad'l, *n.* A red pigment; rouge.
Radial, rā'di-al, *a.* Relating to a radius; grouped or appearing like radii or rays.
Radiance, rā'di-ans, *n.* Brightness shooting in rays; lustre; brilliancy; splendour.
Radiant, rā'di-ant, *a.* Emitting rays of light or heat; issuing in rays; beaming.
Radiate, rā'di-āt, *vi.* To emit rays of light; to shine; to spread abroad as in rays.—*vt.* To emit in divergent lines; to enlighten.—*a.* Having rays or lines resembling radii.
Radiation, rā-di-ā'shon, *n.* Act of radiating; emission of rays; beamy brightness.

Radical, ra'di-kal, *a.* Pertaining to the root; original; thorough-going; native; underived; relating to radicals in politics.—*n.* A root; a simple, underived word; one who advocates extreme political reform.

Radicalism, ra'di-kal-izm, *n.* The principles of radicals in politics.

Radically, ra'di-kal-li, *adv.* In a radical manner; fundamentally; essentially.

Radicle, ra'di-kl, *n.* A small root; that part of the seed which becomes the root.

Radio, rā'di-ō, *n.* A combining form used in compound words as equivalent to *wireless*; also used as a noun for the wireless system of transmission.

Radiolocation, rā'di-o-lō-kā"shon, *n.* Method of detecting the approach of aircraft by radio devices; radar.

Radish, ra'dish, *n.* A plant, the young root of which is eaten raw, as a salad.

Radium, rā'di-um, *n.* An intensely radio-active element extracted from pitchblende, and used in medicine.

Radius, rā'di-us, *n.*; pl. **-ii, -iuses.** A straight line from the centre of a circle to the circumference; a bone of the forearm.

Radix, rā'diks, *n.* A root, as of a plant or a word; source; origin.

Raff, raf, *n.* Refuse; a worthless person; the rabble.

Raffle, raf'l, *n.* A kind of lottery.—*vi.* (raffling, raffled). To engage in a raffle.—*vt.* To dispose of by raffle.

Raft, räft, *n.* Logs fastened together and floated; a floating structure.

Rafter, räf'tėr, *n.* A large sloping piece of timber supporting a roof.

Rag, rag, *n.* A rough separate fragment; a tattered cloth; a shred; a tatter.

Ragamuffin, rag-a-muf'in, *n.* A paltry fellow; a mean wretch.

Rage, rāj, *n.* Violent anger; fury; enthusiasm; rapture.—*vi.* (raging, raged). To be furious with anger; to be violently agitated.

Ragged, rag'ed, *a.* Rent or worn into rags; tattered; rugged; wearing tattered clothes.

Ragout, ra-gö', *n.* A dish of stewed and highly seasoned meat and vegetables.

Ragwort, rag'wėrt, *n.* A British weed of the same genus as the groundsel.

Raid, rād, *n.* A hostile incursion; a foray.—*vi.* To engage in a raid.—*vt.* To make a raid on.

Raider, rād'ėr, *n.* One who makes a raid.

Rail, rāl, *n.* A horizontal bar of wood or metal; a connected series of posts; a railing; one of the parallel iron bars forming a track for locomotives, &c.; a railway; a grallatorial bird.—*vt.* To inclose with rails; to furnish with rails.—*vi.* To use abusive language; to scold; to inveigh.

Railing, rāl'ing, *n.* A fence; rails in general.

Raillery, rāl'ė-ri, *n.* Light ridicule or satire; banter; jesting language.

Railroad, rāl'rōd, *n.* A railway.

Railway, rāl'wā, *n.* A road having iron rails laid in parallel lines, on which carriages run; all the land, buildings, and machinery required for traffic on such a road.

Raiment, rā'ment, *n.* Clothing; vestments.

Rain, rān, *n.* The moisture of the atmosphere falling in drops; a shower of anything.—*vi.* To fall in drops from the clouds; to fall like rain.—*vt.* To pour or shower down.

Rainbow, rān'bō, *n.* An arc of a circle, consisting of all the prismatic colours, appearing in the heavens opposite the sun.

Rainfall, rān'fąl, *n.* A fall of rain; the amount of water that falls as rain.

Rain-gauge, rān'gāj, *n.* An instrument for measuring the rainfall.

Rainy, rān'i, *a.* Wet; showery.

Raise, rāz, *vt.* (raising, raised). To cause to rise; to lift upward; to excite; to recall from death; to stir up; to construct; to levy; to breed; to originate; to give vent to; to inflate; to cause to be relinquished (a siege).

Raisin, rā'zn, *n.* A dried grape.

Raisonné, rā-zon-nā', *a.* Arranged and digested systematically.

Rajah, rä'jä, *n.* A Hindu king or ruler; a title of Hindus of rank.

Rake, rāk, *n.* An implement for collecting hay or straw, smoothing earth, &c.; a dissolute, lewd man; slope.—*vt.* (raking, raked). To apply a rake to; to gather with a rake; to ransack; to enfilade.—*vi.* To use a rake; to search minutely; to incline; to slope aft, as masts.

Raking, rāk'ing, *n.* Act of using a rake; what is collected by a rake; severe scrutiny.

Rakish, rāk'ish, *a.* Like a rake; dissolute; debauched; sloping, as masts.

Rally, ral'i, *vt.* (rallying, rallied). To reunite, as disordered troops; to collect, as things scattered; to attack with raillery; to banter.—*vi.* To recover strength or vigour.—*n.* A stand made by retreating troops; recovery of strength.

Ram, ram, *n.* The male of the sheep; a battering-ram; the loose hammer of a pile-driving machine; a heavy steel beak of a war-vessel; an iron-clad ship with such a beak; one of the signs of the zodiac.—*vt.* (ramming, rammed). To strike with a ram; to batter; to cram.

Ramble, ram'bl, *vi.* (rambling, rambled). To roam carelessly about; to talk incoherently: to have parts stretching irregularly.—*n.* An irregular excursion.

Rambler, ram'blėr, *n.* One who rambles; an irregular wanderer; a rover.

Rambling, ram'bling, *p.a.* Roving; unsettled; straggling; irregularly formed.

Ramification, ra'mi-fi-kā"shon, *n.* The act or process of ramifying; a branch or set of branches; an offshoot.

Ramify, ra'mi-fī, *vt.* To divide into branches.—*vi.* To be divided; to branch out.

Rammer, ram'ėr, *n.* An instrument for driving down anything; a ramrod.

Ramose, Ramous, rā'mōs, rā'mus, *a.* Branched; branchy; full of branches.

Ramp, ramp, *vi.* To climb, as a plant; to rear on the hind-legs; to spring.—*n.* A spring or leap; a slope; a swindle; an attempt to get money under false pretences.

Rampage, ram'pāj or ram-pāj', *vi.* To prance about; to rage and storm.—*n.* Violent conduct.

Rampant, ram'pant, *a.* Rank in growth; exuberant; unrestrained; in *heraldry*, standing up on the hind-legs.

Rampart, ram'pärt, *n.* A mound of earth round a place, capable of resisting cannon-shot; a bulwark; a defence.

Ramrod, ram'rod, *n.* A rod formerly used in ramming down the charge in a gun, pistol, &c.
Ramson, Ramsons, ram'zon, ram'zonz, *n.* A British species of wild garlic.
Ranch, ranch, *n.* In North America, a farming establishment for rearing cattle and horses.
Rancid, ran'sid, *a.* Having a rank or stinking smell; strong-scented; sour; musty.
Rancidity, ran-sid'i-ti, *n.* Quality of being rancid.
Rancorous, rang'kor-us, *a.* Characterized by rancour; malignant; malicious; virulent.
Rancour, rang'kor, *n.* Deep-seated enmity; malice; malignity.
Random, ran'dum, *n.* Action without definite object; chance; caprice.—**At random,** in a haphazard manner.—*a.* Left to chance; done without previous calculation.
Ranee, Rani, ran'ē, *n.* The wife of a rajah; a female Indian ruler.
Range, rānj, *vt.* (ranging, ranged). To set in a row; to dispose systematically; to wander through or scour.—*vi.* To rank; to rove about; to fluctuate.—*n.* A row; a rank; compass or extent; a kitchen grate; distance to which a projectile is carried; a place for gun practice.
Ranger, rānj'ėr, *n.* One who ranges; an official connected with a forest or park.
Rank, rangk, *n.* A row; a line; a social class; comparative station; titled dignity.—*vt.* To place in a line; to classify.—*vi.* To belong to a class; to put in a claim against a bankrupt.—*a.* Luxuriant in growth; strong-scented; utter; coarse; disgusting.
Rankle, rang'kl, *vi.* (rankling, rankled). To fester painfully; to continue to irritate.—*vt.* To irritate; to inflame.
Rankly, rangk'li, *adv.* In a rank manner; with vigorous growth; coarsely; grossly.
Ransack, ran'sak, *vt.* To plunder; to search thoroughly.
Ransom, ran'sum, *n.* Release from captivity by payment; price paid for redemption or pardon.—*vt.* To pay a ransom for; to buy off; to deliver.
Rant, rant, *vi.* To speak in extravagant language.—*n.* Boisterous, empty declamation; bombast.
Ranter, rant'ėr, *n.* One who rants; a boisterous preacher.
Ranunculus, ra-nun'kū-lus, *n.* A genus of flowering plants, the buttercup or crowfoot.
Rap, rap, *n.* A quick smart blow; a knock.—*vi.* (rapping, rapped). To strike a quick, sharp blow.—*vt.* To strike with a quick blow.
Rapacious, ra-pā'shus, *a.* Greedy of plunder; subsisting on prey; extortionate.
Rapacity, ra-pa'si-ti, *n.* Exorbitant greediness; extortionate practices.
Rape, rāp, *n.* A seizing by violence; carnal knowledge of a woman against her will; a plant of the cabbage kind, whose seeds yield an oil.—*vt.* (raping, raped). To carry off violently; to ravish.
Rapid, ra'pid, *a.* Very swift; speedy; hurried.—*n.* A swift current in a river.
Rapidity, ra-pid'i-ti, *n.* State or quality of being rapid; celerity; velocity.
Rapidly, ra'pid-li, *adv.* In a rapid manner; with great speed; swiftly.
Rapier, rā'pi-ėr, *n.* A long narrow sword; a sword used only in thrusting.
Rapine, ra'pin, *n.* Act of plundering; violent seizure of goods; pillage.
Rapparee, Raparee, rap-a-rē', *n.* An armed Irish plunderer.
Rappee, rap-pē', *n.* A coarse kind of snuff.
Rapt, rapt, *a.* Transported; enraptured.
Raptorial, rap-tō'ri-al, *a.* Pertaining to the birds of prey (Raptores).
Rapture, rap'tūr, *n.* Extreme joy or pleasure; ecstasy; transport; enthusiasm.
Rapturous, rap'tūr-us, *a.* Marked with rapture; ecstatic; ravishing.
Rare, rār, *a.* Not dense or compact; sparse; not frequent; uncommon; very valuable; underdone, as meat.
Rarefaction, rā-rē-fak'shon, *n.* Act or process of rarefying; state of being rarefied.
Rarefy, rā'rē-fī, *vt.* and *i.* (rarefying, rarefied). To make or become less dense.
Rarely, rār'li, *adv.* In a rare degree or manner; seldom; not often.
Rarity, ra'ri-ti, *n.* State of being rare; a thing valued for its scarcity; tenuity.
Rascal, ras'kal, *n.* A scoundrel; a rogue.—*a.* Worthless; mean; low; base.
Rascality, ras-kal'i-ti, *n.* Act of a rascal; mean dishonesty; base fraud.
Rascallion, ras-kal'yun, *n.* A low mean person; a rascally wretch. Also *Rapscallion.*
Rascally, ras'kal-li, *a.* Like a rascal; dishonest; base; worthless.
Rase, rāz, *vt.* (rasing, rased). To graze; to erase; to raze.
Rash, rash, *a.* Precipitate; hasty; overbold; incautious.—*n.* An eruption on the skin.
Rasher, rash'ėr, *n.* A thin slice of bacon.
Rashly, rash'li, *adv.* In a rash manner; hastily; without due deliberation.
Rasorial, ra-sō'ri-al, *a.* Pertaining to the gallinaceous or scratching birds (Rasores).
Rasp, räsp, *vt.* To rub with something rough; to grate; to utter harshly.—*vi.* To rub or grate.—*n.* A coarse file; a raspberry.
Raspberry, räz'be-ri, *n.* The fruit of a plant allied to the bramble; the plant itself.
Raspy, räsp'i, *a.* Grating; harsh; rough.
Rasure, rā'zhūr, *n.* Erasure.
Rat, rat, *n.* A small rodent; one who deserts his party.—*vi.* (ratting, ratted). To catch or kill rats; to desert one's party.
Ratable, rāt'a-bl, *a.* That may be rated or set at a certain value; liable to taxation.
Ratafia, rat-a-fē'a, *n.* A spirituous liquor flavoured with the kernels of cherries, &c.
Ratchet, rach'et, *n.* A catch which abuts against the teeth of a wheel to prevent it running back.
Ratchet-wheel, rach'et-whēl, *n.* A wheel having teeth, into which a ratchet drops.
Rate, rāt, *n.* Proportion; standard; degree; degree of speed; price; a tax; assessment.—*vt.* (rating, rated). To fix the value, rank, or degree of; to appraise; to reprove; to scold.—*vi.* To be classed in a certain order.
Ratel, ra-tel', *n.* A carnivorous quadruped of the badger family.
Rate-payer, rāt'pā-ėr, *n.* One who is assessed and pays a rate or tax.
Rath, Rathe, räth, rāthe, *a.* Early.—*adv.* Soon; early.
Rather, räᴛʜ'ėr, *adv.* More readily; preferably; more properly; somewhat.
Ratification, ra'ti-fi-kā"shon, *n.* Act of

ratifying; confirmation; act of giving sanction.
Ratify, ra'ti-fī, *vt.* (ratifying, ratified). To confirm; to approve and sanction.
Ratio, rā'shi-ō, *n.* Relation or proportion; rate.
Ratiocination, ra-shi-os'i-nā"shon, *n.* The act or process of reasoning.
Ration, ra'shon, *n.* A daily allowance of provisions; allowance.—*vt.* To supply with rations.
Rational, ra'shon-al, *a.* Endowed with reason; agreeable to reason; judicious.
Rationale, ra-shon-ā'lē, *n.* Exposition of the principles of some process, action, &c.
Rationalism, ra'shon-al-izm, *n.* A system of opinions deduced from reason, as distinct from inspiration or opposed to it.
Rationalist, ra'shon-al-ist, *n.* An adherent of rationalism; one who rejects the supernatural element in Scripture.
Rationality, ra-shon-al'i-ti, *n.* The quality of being rational; the power of reasoning.
Rationally, ra'shon-al-li, *adv.* In a rational manner; reasonably.
Ratline, Ratlin, rat'lin, *n.* One of the ropes forming ladders on a ship's shrouds.
Ratsbane, rats'bān, *n.* Poison for rats.
Rattan, rat'an or rat-tan', *n.* An Asiatic palm; a walking-stick made from this.
Ratter, rat'ėr, *n.* One who rats; one who catches rats; a dog employed to catch rats.
Rattle, rat'l, *vi.* and *t.* (rattling, rattled). To clatter; to chatter fluently.—*n.* A rapid succession of clattering sounds; an instrument or toy which makes a clattering sound; one who talks much and rapidly.
Rattlesnake, rat'l-snāk, *n.* A venomous American snake, with horny pieces at the point of the tail which rattle.
Raucous, ra̤'kus, *a.* Hoarse; harsh.
Ravage, ra'vāj, *n.* Devastation; havoc.—*vt.* (ravaging, ravaged). To lay waste; to pillage.
Rave, rāv, *vi.* (raving, raved). To be delirious; to speak enthusiastically; to dote.
Ravel, ra'vel, *vt.* (ravelling, ravelled). To disentangle; to make intricate; to involve.
Ravelin, rav'lin, *n.* A detached triangular work in fortification.
Raven, rā'vn, *n.* A bird of prey of the crow kind, of a black colour.
Raven, Ravin, rav'en, rav'in, *n.* Prey; plunder.—*vi.* To prey with rapacity.—*vt.* To devour.
Ravenous, rav'en-us, *a.* Furiously voracious; hungry even to rage.
Ravenously, rav'en-us-li, *adv.* With raging voracity.
Ravine, ra-vēn', *n.* A long hollow formed by a torrent; a gorge or pass.
Raving, rāv'ing, *n.* Irrational, incoherent talk; delirious utterances.
Ravish, ra'vish, *vt.* To carry away by violence; to enrapture; to commit a rape upon.
Ravishing, ra'vish-ing, *p.a.* Delighting to rapture; transporting.
Ravishment, ra'vish-ment, *n.* Act of ravishing; rapture; transport; ecstasy.
Raw, ra̤, *a.* Not cooked or dressed; not manufactured; unfinished; not diluted; bare, as flesh; galled; sensitive; inexperienced; cold and damp.
Ray, rā, *n.* A line of light; a gleam of intellectual light; one of a number of diverging radii; a flat-fish.—*vt.* and *i.* (raying, rayed). To shine forth; to radiate; to streak.
Rayon, rā'on, *n.* Artificial silk, made from cellulose.
Raze, rāz, *vt.* (razing, razed). To graze; to lay level with the ground; to efface.
Razor, rā'zor, *n.* A knife for shaving off hair.
Reach, rēch, *vt.* To extend; to hand; to extend or stretch from a distance; to arrive at; to gain.—*vi.* To extend; to stretch out the hand in order to touch; to make efforts at attainment.—*n.* Act or power of extending to; straight course of a river; scope.
React, rē-akt', *vi.* To act in return; to return an impulse; to act reciprocally upon each other.—*vt.* To perform anew.
Reaction, rē-ak'shon, *n.* A reacting; reciprocal action; tendency to revert to a previous condition; exhaustion consequent on activity, and *vice versa.*
Reactionary, rē-ak'shon-a-ri, *a.* Pertaining to or favouring reaction.—*n.* One who attempts to reverse political progress.
Reactive, rē-ak'tiv, *a.* Having power to react; tending to reaction.
Read, rēd, *vt.* (reading, read). To peruse; to utter aloud, following something written or printed; to explain.—*vi.* To peruse; to study; to stand written or printed; to make sense.—*a.* red. Instructed by reading; learned.
Readable, rēd'a-bl, *a.* That may be read; legible; fit or deserving to be read.
Reader, rēd'ėr, *n.* One who reads; one who reads aloud prayers, lectures, &c.; one who corrects for the press; a reading-book.
Readily, re'di-li, *adv.* In a ready manner; quickly; promptly; easily; cheerfully.
Readiness, re'di-nes, *n.* Quickness; promptitude; facility; aptitude; alacrity.
Reading, rēd'ing, *a.* Addicted to reading; studious.—*n.* Perusal; study of books; public or formal recital; form of a word or passage in a manuscript, &c.; rendering.
Readmit, rē-ad-mit', *vt.* To admit again.
Ready, re'di, *a.* Prepared; in order; prompt; willing; inclined; at hand; opportune.
Ready-made, re'di-mād, *a.* Made beforehand; kept in stock ready for use or sale.
Reaffirm, rē-af-fėrm', *vt.* To affirm again.
Reagent, rē-ā'jent, *n.* Anything that produces reaction; a substance employed chemically to detect the presence of other bodies.
Real, rē'al, *a.* Actual; true; genuine; in *law,* pertaining to things fixed or immovable, as lands and houses.
Realism, rē'al-izm, *n.* The endeavour in art or literature to reproduce nature or describe life as it actually appears.
Realist, rē'al-ist, *n.* One who practises or believes in realism.
Realistic, rē-al-ist'ik, *a.* Pertaining to realism; representing scenes vividly.
Reality, rē-al'i-ti, *n.* State or quality of being real; actuality; fact; truth.
Realize, rē'al-īz, *vt.* (realizing, realized). To make real; to convert into money; to impress on the mind as a reality; to render tangible or effective; to acquire; to gain.
Really, rē'al-li, *adv.* Actually; in truth; in fact; indeed.
Realm, relm, *n.* The dominions of a sovereign; a region, sphere, or domain.

Realty, rē'al-ti, *n.* The fixed nature of property termed *real*; real property.
Ream, rēm, *n.* A package of paper, consisting generally of 20 quires, or 480 sheets.
Reanimate, rē-an'i-māt, *vt.* To animate again; to revive; to infuse new life into.
Reap, rēp, *vt.* and *i.* To cut with a scythe, &c., as grain; to gather; to clear of a grain crop; to receive as a reward of labour, &c.
Reaper, rēp'ėr, *n.* One who reaps; a machine for reaping.
Reappear, rē-ap-pēr', *vi.* To appear a second time or anew.
Reappoint, rē-ap-point', *vt.* To appoint again.
Rear, rēr, *n.* The part behind; the part of an army behind the rest; the background.—*vt.* To raise; to bring up, as young; to breed, as cattle; to build up.—*vi.* To rise on the hind-legs, as horse; to become erect.
Rear-guard, rēr'gärd, *n.* The part of an army that marches in the rear.
Rearmost, rēr'mōst, *a.* Farthest in the rear; last of all.
Rear-mouse, rēr'mous, *n.* A bat.
Rearrange, rē'a-rānj, *vt.* To arrange again; to put in different order.
Rearward, rēr'wąrd, *n.* The rear-guard; the end.—*a.* At or towards the rear.
Reason, rē'zn, *n.* A motive or cause; explanation; faculty for logical operations; justice; equity; moderate demands.—*vi.* To exercise the faculty of reason; to argue; to discuss.—*vt.* To examine or discuss by arguments; to persuade by reasoning.
Reasonable, rē'zn-a-bl, *a.* Having the faculty of reason; rational; conformable to reason; moderate; fair; tolerable.
Reasonably, rē'zn-a-bli, *adv.* In a reasonable manner; moderately; tolerably.
Reasoning, rē'zn-ing, *n.* The act or process of exercising the faculty of reason; arguments employed.
Reassemble, rē-as-sem'bl, *vt.* and *i.* To assemble again.
Reassert, rē-as-sėrt', *vt.* To assert again.
Reassurance, rē-a-shör'ans, *n.* Act of reassuring; a second assurance against loss.
Reassure, rē-a-shör', *vt.* To assure anew; to free from fear or terror; to reinsure.
Reave, rēv, *vt.* (reaving, reaved or reft). To take away by violence; to bereave.
Reaver, rēv'ėr, *n.* One who reaves; a robber.
Rebate, rē-bāt', *vt.* (rebating, rebated). To blunt; to diminish; to make a discount from.
Rebate, Rebatement, rē-bāt', rē-bāt'ment, *n.* Abatement in price; deduction.
Rebel, re'bel, *n.* One who makes war against or opposes constituted authorities.—*a.* Rebellious; acting in revolt.—*vi.* rē-bel' (rebelling, rebelled). To oppose lawful authority; to revolt; to conceive a loathing.
Rebellion, rē-bel'yon, *n.* Act of rebelling; an armed rising against a government.
Rebellious, rē-bel'yus, *a.* Pertaining to rebellion; mutinous; insubordinate.
Rebound, rē-bound', *vi.* To spring or bound back; to recoil.—*n.* The act of flying back on collision; resilience.
Rebuff, rē-buf', *n.* A sudden check; a repulse; refusal.—*vt.* To beat back; to check; to repel the advances of.
Rebuild, rē-bild', *vt.* To build again.
Rebuke, rē-būk', *vt.* (rebuking, rebuked). To reprimand; to reprove sharply.—*n.* A direct and severe reprimand; reproof.
Rebukingly, rē-būk'ing-li, *adv.* In a rebuking manner; by way of rebuke.
Rebus, rē'bus, *n.* A set of words represented by pictures of objects; a kind of puzzle made up of such pictures.
Rebut, rē-but', *vt.* (rebutting, rebutted). To repel; to refute; in *law*, to oppose by argument, plea, or countervailing proof.
Rebuttal, rē-but'al, *n.* Refutation.
Rebutter, rē-but'ėr, *n.* One who rebuts; answer of a defendant to a plaintiff.
Recalcitrant, rē-kal'si-trant, *a.* Not submissive; refractory.
Recalcitrate, rē-kal'si-trāt, *vi.* To show resistance; to be refractory.
Recall, rē-kąl', *vt.* To call or bring back; to revive in memory.—*n.* A calling back.
Recant, rē-kant', *vt.* To retract, as a declaration.—*vi.* To retract one's words.
Recantation, rē-kant-ā'shon, *n.* Act of recanting; retraction.
Recapitulate, rē-ka-pit'ū-lāt, *vt.* To give a summary of.—*vi.* To repeat briefly.
Recapitulation, rē-ka-pit'ū-lā''shon, *n.* Act of recapitulating; summary.
Recapture, rē-kap'tūr, *n.* Act of retaking; a prize retaken.—*vt.* To retake.
Recast, rē-kast', *vt.* To throw again; to mould anew.
Recede, rē-sēd', *vi.* (receding, receded). To go back; to withdraw.—*vt.* To cede back.
Receipt, rē-sēt', *n.* Act of receiving; that which is received; a written acknowledgment of something received; a recipe.—*vt.* To give a receipt for; to discharge, as an account.
Receivable, rē-sēv'a-bl, *a.* That may be received.
Receive, rē-sēv', *vt.* (receiving, received). To take, as a thing offered; to admit; to entertain; to contain; to be the object of; to take stolen goods.
Receiver, rē-sēv'ėr, *n.* One who receives; one who takes stolen goods from a thief.
Recency, rē'sen-si, *n.* Newness; freshness.
Recension, rē-sen'shon, *n.* A revision of the text of an author; an edited version.
Recent, rē'sent, *a.* New; late; fresh.
Recently, rē'sent-li, *adv.* Lately.
Receptacle, rē-sep'ta-kl, *n.* A place or vessel in which anything is received; repository.
Reception, rē-sep'shon, *n.* Act or manner of receiving; welcome; a formal receiving of guests; admission or acceptance.
Receptionist, rē-sep'shon-ist, *n.* One who in a hotel, at a doctor's, &c., receives guests or patients.
Receptive, rē-sep'tiv, *a.* Such as to receive readily; able to take in or contain.
Receptivity, rē-sep-tiv'i-ti, *n.* The state or quality of being receptive.
Recess, rē-ses', *n.* A withdrawing; place or period of retirement; time during which business is suspended; a niche in a wall; an alcove.
Recession, rē-se'shon, *n.* Act of receding; withdrawal; a granting back.
Rechauffé, rā-shō-fā, *n.* A warmed-up dish; a concoction of old materials.
Recherché, rė-sher'shā, *a.* Much sought after; out of the common; exquisite.
Recipe, re'si-pē, *n.* A medical prescription; a statement of ingredients for a mixture.

Recipient, rē-si'pi-ent, *n.* One who or that which receives; a receiver.
Reciprocal, rē-sip'rō-kal, *a.* Reciprocating; alternate; done by each to the other; mutual; interchangeable.
Reciprocally, rē-sip'rō-kal-li, *adv.* In a reciprocal manner; mutually.
Reciprocate, rē-sip'rō-kāt, *vi.* To move backward and forward; to alternate.—*vt.* To exchange; to give in requital.
Reciprocation, rē-sip'rō-kā"shon, *n.* Act of reciprocating; a mutual giving.
Reciprocity, re-si-pros'i-ti, *n.* Reciprocation; interchange; reciprocal obligation; equal commercial rights mutually enjoyed.
Recital, rē-sīt'al, *n.* Act of reciting; narration; a musical entertainment.
Recitation, re-si-tā'shon, *n.* Recital; the delivery before an audience of the compositions of others.
Recitative, re'si-ta-tēv, *n.* A species of singing approaching ordinary speaking.
Recite, rē-sīt', *vt.* and *i.* (reciting, recited). To repeat aloud, as a writing committed to memory; to relate; to recapitulate.
Reciter, rē-sīt'ėr, *n.* One who recites; a book containing passages for recitation.
Reck, rek, *vt.* To heed; to regard.
Reckless, rek'les, *a.* Heedless; careless; rash.
Recklessly, rek'les-li, *adv.* Carelessly.
Reckon, rek'n, *vt.* and *i.* To count; to estimate; to account, consider.
Reckoner, rek'n-ėr, *n.* One who or that which reckons or computes.
Reckoning, rek'n-ing, *n.* Calculation; a statement of accounts with another; landlord's bill; calculation of a ship's position.
Reclaim, rē-klām', *vt.* To claim back; to reform; to tame; to recover; to reduce to a state fit for cultivation.
Reclaimable, rē-klām'a-bl, *a.* That may be reclaimed, reformed, or tamed.
Reclamation, re-kla-mā'shon, *n.* Act of reclaiming; a claim made.
Recline, rē-klīn', *vt.* and *i.* (reclining, reclined). To lean; to rest or repose.
Recluse, rē-klös', *a.* Retired; solitary.—*n.* A person who lives in seclusion; a hermit.
Reclusion, rē-klö'zhon, *n.* Seclusion.
Recognition, re-kog-ni'shon, *n.* Act of recognizing; avowal; acknowledgment.
Recognizable, re'kog-nīz-a-bl, *a.* That may be recognized.
Recognizance, rē-kog'niz-ans or rē-kon'i-zans, *n.* Recognition; an obligation, as to appear at the assizes, keep the peace, &c.
Recognize, re'kog-nīz, *vt.* (recognizing, recognized). To know again; to admit a knowledge of; to acknowledge formally; to indicate one's notice by a bow, &c.; to indicate appreciation of.
Recoil, rē-koil', *vi.* To move or start back; to retreat; to shrink; to rebound.—*n.* A starting or falling back; rebound, as of a gun.
Recollect, re'kol-lekt, *vt.* To remember; to recover composure of mind (with refl. pron.).
Recollect, rē-kol-lekt', *vt.* To collect again.
Recollection, re-kol-lek'shon, *n.* Act of recollecting; remembrance; something recalled to mind.
Recommence, rē-kom-mens', *vt.* To begin anew.
Recommend, re-kom-mend', *vt.* To praise to another; to make acceptable; to commit with prayers; to advise.
Recommendation, re'kom-mend-ā"shon, *n.* The act of recommending; a favourable representation; that which procures favour.
Recommit, rē-kom-mit', *vt.* To commit again; to refer again to a committee.
Recommitment, Recommittal, rē-kom-mit'-ment, rē-kom-mit'al, *n.* Act of recommitting; a further commitment or reference.
Recompense, re'kom-pens, *vt.* (recompensing, recompensed). To compensate; to requite; to make amends for.—*n.* Compensation; reward; amends.
Reconcilable, re'kon-sil-a-bl, *a.* Capable of being reconciled.
Reconcile, re'kon-sīl, *vt.* (reconciling, reconciled). To make friendly again; to adjust or settle; to harmonize.
Reconcilement, re-kon-sīl'ment, *n.* Reconciliation; renewal of friendship.
Reconciliation, re'kon-si-li-ā"shon, *n.* Act of reconciling; renewal of friendship.
Recondite, rē-kon'dīt or re'kon-dīt, *a.* Abstruse; profound.
Reconnaissance, re-kon'nā-sans, *n.* The act or operation of reconnoitring.
Reconnoitre, re-kon-noi'tėr, *vt.* and *i.* (reconnoitring, reconnoitred). To make a preliminary survey of; to survey for military purposes.
Reconquer, rē-kong'kėr, *vt.* To conquer again; to recover by conquest.
Reconquest, rē-kong'kwest, *n.* A conquest again or anew.
Reconsider, rē-kon-si'dėr, *vt.* To consider again.
Reconsideration, rē-kon-si'dėr-ā"shon, *n.* Act of reconsidering; renewed consideration.
Reconstruct, rē-kon-strukt', *vt.* To construct again; to rebuild.
Record, rē-kord', *vt.* To preserve in writing; to register; to chronicle.—*n.* rek'ord. A written memorial; a register; a public document; memory; one's personal history; best result in contests.
Recorder, rē-kord'ėr, *n.* One who records; an official registrar; magistrate presiding over court of quarter sessions of borough; a kind of straight flute or flageolet; a registering apparatus.
Recount, rē-kount', *vt.* To relate in detail; to count again.—*n.* A second counting.
Recoup, rē-köp', *vt.* To recompense or compensate; to indemnify.
Recourse, rē-kōrs', *n.* A going to with a request, as for aid; resort in perplexity.
Recover, rē-kuv'ėr, *vt.* To get back; to regain; to revive; to rescue; to obtain in return for injury or debt.—*vi.* To grow well; to regain a former condition.
Recoverable, rē-kuv'ėr-a-bl, *a.* That may be recovered or regained.
Recovery, rē-kuv'ėr-i, *n.* Act of recovering; restoration from sickness, &c.; the obtaining of something by legal procedure.
Recreant, re'krē-ant, *a.* Craven; cowardly; apostate.—*n.* One who basely yields in combat; a cowardly wretch.
Recreate, re'krē-āt, *vt.* To revive; to enliven; to amuse.—*vi.* To take recreation.
Re-create, rē-krē-āt', *vt.* To create anew.
Recreation, re-krē-ā'shon, *n.* Refreshment

of the strength and spirits after toil; amusement; entertainment.
Recreative, re'krē-āt-iv, *a.* Serving to re-create; refreshing; diverting.
Recrement, re'krē-ment, *n.* Refuse; dross.
Recriminate, rē-krim'in-āt, *vi.* To return one accusation with another.—*vt.* To accuse in return.
Recrimination, rē-krim'in-ā"shon, *n.* Act of recriminating; a counter-accusation.
Recriminative, Recriminatory, rē-krim'in-āt-iv, rē-krim'in-ā-to-ri, *a.* Recriminating or retorting accusation.
Recrudesce, re-krö-des', *vi.* To revive or show renewed activity.
Recrudescence, rē-krö-des'ens, *n.* Renewed outbreak; increased severity after remission.
Recruit, rē-kröt', *vt.* To repair; to supply with new soldiers.—*vi.* To gain new supplies of anything; to raise new soldiers.—*n.* A soldier newly enlisted.
Rectangle, rek'tang-gl, *n.* A quadrilateral having all its angles right angles.
Rectangular, rek-tang'gū-lėr, *a.* Right-angled.
Rectification, rek'ti-fi-kā"shon, *n.* Act or operation of rectifying; process of refining by repeated distillation.
Rectifier, rek'ti-fī-ėr, *n.* One who or that which rectifies; a refiner of alcohol.
Rectify, rek'ti-fī, *vt.* (rectifying, rectified). To correct; to refine by repeated distillation.
Rectilineal, Rectilinear, rek-ti-lin'ē-al, rek-ti-lin'ē-ėr, *a.* Consisting of straight lines.
Rectitude, rek'ti-tūd, *n.* Integrity; probity; uprightness; honesty.
Rector, rek'tor, *n.* A ruler; an Episcopal clergyman who has the cure of a parish; a head of certain institutions, chiefly academical.
Rectorial, rek-tō'ri-al, *a.* Pertaining to a rector or rectory.
Rectorship, Rectorate, rek'tor-ship, rek'-tor-āt, *n.* Office or rank of a rector.
Rectory, rek'to-ri, *n.* A church or living held by a rector; a rector's house.
Rectum, rek'tum, *n.* The lowest part of the large intestine opening at the anus.
Recumbent, rē-kum'bent, *a.* Leaning; reclining; reposing; inactive.
Recuperate, rē-kū'pėr-āt, *vt.* and *i.* (recuperating, recuperated). To recover.
Recuperation, rē-kū'pėr-ā"shon, *n.* Recovery.
Recuperative, rē-kū'pėr-ā-tiv, *a.* Tending or pertaining to recovery.
Recur, rē-kėr', *vi.* (recurring, recurred). To return; to be repeated at a stated interval.
Recurrence, rē-ku'rens, *n.* Act of recurring; return; recourse.
Recurrent, rē-ku'rent, *a.* Recurring from time to time.
Recusancy, Recusance, re'kū-zan-si, re'kū-zans, *n.* Nonconformity.
Recusant, re'kū-zant, *a.* Obstinate in refusal; refusing to conform to the established church. —*n.* A nonconformist.
Red, red, *a.* Of a colour resembling that of arterial blood.—*n.* A colour resembling that of arterial blood; a red pigment.
Redact, rē-dakt', *vt.* To edit; to give a presentable literary form to.
Redaction, rē-dak'shon, *n.* Act of preparing for publication; the work thus prepared.
Redactor, rē-dakt'ėr, *n.* An editor.
Redan, rē-dan', *n.* A field fortification of two faces, forming an angle towards the enemy.
Redargue, red'är-gū, *vt.* To put down by argument; to refute.
Redbreast, red'brest, *n.* A British bird; the robin.
Redcoat, red'kōt, *n.* A familiar name for a British soldier.
Red-deer, red'dēr, *n.* The common stag.
Redden, red'n, *vt.* To make red.—*vi.* To become red; to blush.
Reddish, red'ish, *a.* Somewhat red.
Reddition, red-di'shon, *n.* A giving back; restitution.
Reddle, red'l, *n.* Red chalk; raddle.
Redeem, rē-dēm', *vt.* To buy back; to ransom; to rescue; to save; to atone for; to employ to the best purpose; to perform, as what has been promised.
Redeemable, rē-dēm'a-bl, *a.* That may be redeemed.
Redeemer, rē-dēm'ėr, *n.* One who redeems; Jesus Christ.
Redeliver, rē-dē-liv'ėr, *vt.* To deliver back or again.
Redemption, rē-dem'shon, *n.* The act of redeeming; state of being redeemed; ransom; release; deliverance.
Red-handed, red'hand-ed, *a.* With red or bloody hands; in the act.
Red-hot, red'hot, *a.* Red with heat; very hot.
Redintegrate, re-din'ti-grāt, *vt.* To make whole again.
Red-lead, red'led, *n.* An oxide of lead of a fine red colour, used in painting, &c.; minium.
Red-letter, red'let-ėr, *a.* Having red letters; fortunate or auspicious.
Redolence, re'dō-lens, *n.* Quality of being redolent; fragrance; perfume; scent.
Redolent, re'dō-lent, *a.* Emitting an odour; having or diffusing a sweet scent.
Redouble, rē-du'bl, *vt.* To double again.—*vi.* To become twice as much.
Redoubt, rē-dout', *n.* *See* REDOUT.
Redoubtable, rē-dout'a-bl, *a.* Such as to cause dread; formidable; valiant.
Redoubted, rē-dout'ed, *a.* Redoubtable.
Redound, rē-dound', *vi.* To conduce; to contribute; to have effect.
Redout, Redoubt, rē-dout', *n.* A small inclosed fortification.
Redpoll, red'pōl, *n.* A name for several species of linnets.
Redraft, rē-dräft', *vt.* To draft anew.—*n.* A second draft; a second order for money.
Redraw, rē-dra̹', *vt.* To draw again.—*vi.* To draw a new bill of exchange.
Redress, rē-dres', *vt.* To set right; to adjust; to repair; to relieve.—*n.* Relief; deliverance; reparation.
Redshank, red'shangk, *n.* A bird allied to the snipes, with red legs.
Redskin, red'skin, *n.* A Red Indian, or Indian of North America.
Redstart, Redtail, red'stärt, red'tāl, *n.* A bird with a red tail; a small singing bird.
Red-tape, red'tāp, *n.* Excessive official routine and formality.—*a.* Characterized by excessive routine or formality.
Reduce, rē-dūs', *vt.* (reducing, reduced). To bring down; to decrease; to degrade; to

subdue; to bring under rules or within categories; to restore to its proper place.
Reducible, rē-dūs'i-bl, *a.* That may be reduced.
Reduction, rē-duk'shon, *n.* Act of reducing; diminution; conversion into another state or form; subjugation.
Redundancy, Redundance, rē-dun'dan-si, rē-dun'dans, *n.* Superfluity.
Redundant, rē-dun'dant, *a.* Superfluous; having more words than necessary.
Reduplicate, rē-dū'pli-kāt, *vt.* and *i.* To double again; to repeat.
Reduplication, rē-dū'pli-kā"shon, *n.* Act of reduplicating; the repetition of a root or initial syllable.
Redwing, red'wing, *n.* A species of thrush.
Redwood, red'wụd, *n.* A name of various reddish timbers.
Re-echo, rē-e'kō, *vt.* and *i.* To echo back; to reverberate.—*n.* The echo of an echo.
Reed, rēd, *n.* A tall broad-leaved grass growing in marshy places, or its hollow stems; a musical instrument; a rustic pipe.
Reed-pipe, rēd'pīp, *n.* A musical pipe made of reed.
Reedy, rēd'i, *a.* Abounding with reeds; harsh and thin, as a voice.
Reef, rēf, *n.* The part of a sail which can be drawn together to expose a smaller area; a range of rocks in the sea near the surface; a vein containing gold.—*vt.* To take in a reef in; to reduce the extent of a sail.
Reefer, rēf'ėr, *n.* One who reefs; a midshipman.
Reef-point, rēf'point, *n.* One of the small pieces of line for tying up a sail when reefed.
Reefy, rēf'i, *a.* Full of reefs or rocks.
Reek, rēk, *n.* Vapour; steam; exhalation; smoke.—*vi.* To smoke; to exhale.
Reel, rēl, *n.* A bobbin for thread; a revolving appliance for winding a fishing-line; a staggering motion; a lively Scottish dance.—*vt.* To wind upon a reel; to stagger.
Re-elect, rē-ē-lekt', *vt.* To elect again.
Re-embark, rē-em-bärk', *vt.* and *i.* To embark again.
Re-enact, rē-en-akt', *vt.* To enact again.
Re-enforce, rē-en-fōrs', *vt.* and *i.* To reinforce.
Re-engage, rē-en-gāj', *vt.* and *i.* To engage a second time.
Re-enter, rē-en'tėr, *vt.* and *i.* To enter again or anew.
Re-entry, rē-en'tri, *n.* An entering again; the resuming possession of lands lately lost.
Re-establish, rē-es-tab'lish, *vt.* To establish anew; to fix or confirm again.
Reeve, rēv, *n.* A bailiff; a steward; a peace officer.—*vt.* and *i.* (reeving, reeved). To pass a rope through any hole in a block, &c.; to pass through such hole.
Re-examine, rē-eg-zam'in, *vt.* To examine anew.
Re-export, rē-eks-pōrt', *vt.* To export after having been imported.—*n.* rē-eks'pōrt. Any commodity re-exported.
Re-fashion, rē-fa'shon, *vt.* To fashion or form into shape a second time.
Refection, rē-fek'shon, *n.* Refreshment after hunger or fatigue; a repast.
Refectory, rē-fek'to-ri, *n.* A room for refreshment or meals.
Refer, rē-fėr', *vt.* (referring, referred). To trace or carry back; to attribute; to appeal; to assign.—*vi.* To respect or have relation; to appeal; to apply; to allude.
Referable, ref'ėr-a-bl, *a.* That may be referred, assigned, attributed, &c.
Referee, ref-ėr-ē', *n.* One to whom a matter in dispute is referred for decision; an umpire.
Reference, re'fėr-ens, *n.* Act of referring; allusion; relation; one of whom inquiries may be made.
Referendum, ref-ėr-en'dum, *n.* The referring of a measure passed by a legislature to the people for final approval.
Refill, rē-fil', *vt.* To fill again.
Refine, rē-fīn', *vt.* (refining, refined). To increase the fineness of; to purify; to make elegant; to give culture to.—*vi.* To become purer; to indulge in hair-splitting.
Refined, rē-fīnd', *p.a.* Free from what is coarse, rude, &c.; polished; polite.
Refinement, rē-fīn'ment, *n.* Act of refining; elegance; culture; nicety.
Refiner, rē-fīn'ėr, *n.* One who refines, specially metals, liquors, sugars, &c.
Refinery, rē-fīn'ėr-i, *n.* A place and apparatus for refining sugar, metals, &c.
Refit, rē-fit', *vt.* and *i.* (refitting, refitted). To fit anew; to repair.—*n.* Repair.
Reflect, rē-flekt', *vt.* To cast back; to throw off, as light or heat, after striking the surface; to mirror.—*vi.* To throw back light or heat; to meditate; to bring reproach.
Reflecting, rē-flekt'ing, *p.a.* Serving to reflect; thoughtful; meditative.
Reflection, rē-flek'shon, *n.* Act of reflecting; that which is produced by being reflected; meditation; a censorious remark; reproach.
Reflective, rē-flekt'iv, *a.* Throwing back rays; meditating.
Reflector, rē-flekt'or, *n.* One who reflects; a polished surface for reflecting light, &c.
Reflex, rē'fleks, *a.* Bent or directed back; done involuntarily or unconsciously.—*n.* A reflection.
Reflexible, rē-fleks'i-bl, *a.* Capable of being reflected or thrown back.
Reflexion, rē-flek'shon. *See* REFLECTION.
Reflexive, rē-flek'siv, *a.* Reflective; having respect to something past; in *grammar*, having for its object a pronoun which stands for the subject: also applied to such pronouns.
Refluent, ref'lụ-ent, *a.* Flowing back.
Reflux, rē'fluks, *n.* A flowing back; ebb.
Refold, rē-fōld, *vt.* To fold again.
Reform, rē-form', *vt.* and *i.* To change from worse to better; to amend; to form anew.—*n.* A beneficial change; amendment; a change in the regulations of parliamentary representation.
Reformation, re-for-mā'shon, *n.* Act of reforming; amendment; the Protestant revolution of the sixteenth century.
Re-formation, rē-for-mā'shon, *n.* The act of forming anew; a second forming.
Reformatory, rē-for'ma-to-ri, *n.* An institution for reclaiming young criminals.
Reformed, rē-formd', *a.* Restored to a good state; amended; having accepted the principles of the Reformation.
Reformer, rē-form'ėr, *n.* One who reforms; one who took a part in the Reformation; one who promotes political reform.

Refract, rē-frakt′, *vt.* To bend back sharply; to deflect (a ray of light) on passing from one medium into another.
Refracting, rē-frakt′ing, *p.a.* Serving or tending to refract.
Refraction, rē-frak′shon, *n.* Act of refracting; a change of direction in rays on passing from one medium into another.
Refractive, rē-frakt′iv, *a.* Pertaining to refraction; having power to refract.
Refractor, rē-frakt′ėr, *n.* That which refracts; a refracting telescope.
Refractory, rē-frak′to-ri, *a.* Sullen in disobedience; stubborn; unmanageable; resisting ordinary treatment.
Refragable, re′fra-ga-bl, *a.* That may be opposed, gainsaid, or refuted.
Refrain, rē-frān′, *vt.* To restrain; to keep (oneself) from action.—*vi.* To forbear; to abstain.—*n.* The burden of a song; part repeated at the end of every stanza.
Refrangible, rē-fran′ji-bl, *a.* Capable of being refracted; subject to refraction.
Refresh, rē-fresh′, *vt.* To revive; to reanimate; to freshen.
Refresher, rē-fresh′ėr, *n.* One who or that which refreshes; additional fee paid to counsel in a long case.
Refreshing, rē-fresh′ing, *a.* Invigorating; reanimating; enlivening.
Refreshment, rē-fresh′ment, *n.* Act of refreshing; that which refreshes; *pl.* food and drink.
Refrigerant, rē-fri′jė-rant, *a.* Cooling.—*n.* A medicine which abates heat.
Refrigerate, rē-fri′jė-rāt, *vt.* To cool.
Refrigeration, rē-fri′jė-rā″shon, *n.* Act of refrigerating; abatement of heat.
Refrigerator, rē-frij′ė-rāt-ėr, *n.* That which refrigerates; an apparatus for cooling or for making ice; a refrigerant.
Refrigeratory, rē-fri′jė-ra-to-ri, *a.* Cooling. —*n.* A refrigerator.
Refringent, rē-frin′jent, *a.* Refractive; refracting.
Refuge, re′fūj, *n.* Protection from danger or distress; a retreat; a shelter; a device; contrivance; shift.—*vt.* and *i.* To shelter.
Refugee, re-fū-jē′, *n.* One who flees for refuge; one who flees to another country or place for safety.
Refulgence, Refulgency, rē-ful′jens, rē-ful′-jen-si, *n.* Splendour; brilliancy.
Refulgent, rē-ful′jent, *a.* Casting a bright light; shining; splendid.
Refund, rē-fund′, *vt.* To pay back; to repay; to reimburse.
Refurnish, rē-fėr′nish, *vt.* To furnish anew.
Refusal, rē-fūz′al, *n.* Act of refusing; choice of taking or refusing.
Refuse, rē-fūz′, *vt.* (refusing, refused). To deny, as a request or demand; to decline; to reject.—*vi.* To decline a request or offer.
Refuse, re′fūz, *a.* Rejected; worthless.—*n.* Waste matter; dregs.
Refutable, rē-fūt′a-bl or ref′, *a.* That may be refuted or disproved.
Refutation, re-fūt-ā′shon, *n.* Act or process of refuting; disproof.
Refute, rē-fūt′, *vt.* (refuting, refuted). To disprove; to overthrow by argument.
Regain, rē-gān′, *vt.* To gain anew; to recover; to retrieve; to reach again.
Regal, rē′gal, *a.* Kingly; royal.
Regale, rē-gāl′, *vt.* and *i.* (regaling, regaled). To refresh sumptuously; to feast.—*n.* A splendid feast; a treat.
Regalia, rē-gā′li-a, *n.pl.* Ensigns of royalty, as the crown, sceptre, &c.
Regality, rē-gal′i-ti, *n.* Royalty; kingship.
Regally, rē′gal-li, *adv.* In a regal manner.
Regard, rē-gärd′, *vt.* To notice carefully; to observe; to respect; to heed; to view in the light of; to relate to.—*n.* Look or gaze; respect; notice; heed; esteem; deference; *pl.* good wishes.
Regardant, rē-gärd′ant, *a.* Regarding; in *heraldry*, with the face turned backwards in an attitude of vigilance.
Regardful, rē-gärd′ful, *a.* Having or paying regard.
Regarding, rē-gärd′ing, *prep.* Respecting; concerning; relating to.
Regardless, rē-gärd′les, *a.* Without regard or heed; heedless; negligent; careless.
Regatta, rē-gat′a, *n.* A race in which yachts or boats contend for prizes.
Regelation, rē-je-lā′shon, *n.* The freezing together of pieces of moist ice.
Regency, rē′jen-si, *n.* Government of a regent; men intrusted with the power of a regent.
Regeneracy, rē-jen′ė-ra-si, *n.* State of being regenerated.
Regenerate, rē-jen′ė-rāt, *vt.* To generate anew; to bring into a better state.—*n.* Born anew; changed to a spiritual state.
Regeneration, rē-jen′ė-rā″shon, *n.* Act of regenerating; that change by which love to God is implanted in the heart.
Regent, rē′jent, *a.* Ruling.—*n.* A ruler; one who governs during the minority or disability of the king.
Regicide, re′ji-sīd, *n.* One who kills a king; the murder of a king.
Regime, rā-zhēm′, *n.* Mode of management; administration; rule.
Regimen, re′ji-men, *n.* Orderly government; regulation of diet, exercise, &c.
Regiment, re′ji-ment, *n.* A body of troops under the command of a colonel.
Regimental, re-ji-ment′al, *a.* Belonging to a regiment.
Regimentals, re-ji-ment′alz, *n.pl.* Uniform of a regiment; articles of military dress.
Region, rē′jun, *n.* A tract of land; country; territory; portion of the body.
Register, re′jis-tėr, *n.* An official record; a roll; a book for special entries of facts; device for indicating work done by machinery; musical compass; a stop in an organ.—*vt.* To record; to insure (a letter).—*vi.* To enter one's name.
Registered, re′jis-tėrd, *p.a.* Enrolled; protected by enrolment; insured.
Register-office, re′jis-tėr-of-is, *n.* An office where registers or records are kept.
Registrar, re′jis-trär, *n.* An officer who keeps a public register or record.
Registration, re-jis-trā′shon, *n.* Act of registering; enrolment.
Registry, re′jis-tri, *n.* Registration; place where a register is kept; an entry.
Regius, rē′ji-us, *a.* Occupying a university chair founded by the crown.
Regnant, reg′nant, *a.* Reigning.

Regress, rē'gres, *n.* Return; power of returning.—*vi.* rē-gres'. To go back.
Regression, rē-gre'shon, *n.* The act of passing back or returning; retrogression.
Regret, rē-gret', *n.* Grief at something done or undone; remorse; penitence.—*vt.* (regretting, regretted). To be sorry for; to lament.
Regretful, rē-gret'fụl, *a.* Full of regret.
Regrettable, rē-gret'a-bl, *a.* Admitting of or calling for regret.
Regular, re'gū-lėr, *a.* Conformed to a rule, law, or principle; normal; methodical; uniform; having the parts symmetrical; thorough.—*n.* A monk who has taken the vows in some order; a soldier of a permanent army.
Regularity, re-gū-la'ri-ti, *n.* State or character of being regular; steadiness or uniformity.
Regularly, re'gū-lėr-li, *adv.* In uniform order; at fixed periods; methodically.
Regulate, re'gū-lāt, *vt.* (regulating, regulated). To adjust by rule; to put or keep in good order; to direct.
Regulation, re-gū-lā'shon, *n.* Act of regulating; a rule; a precept.
Regulator, re'gū-lāt-ėr, *n.* One who or that which regulates.
Regurgitate, rē-gėr'jit-tāt, *vt.* and *i.* To pour or cause to surge back.
Rehabilitate, rē-ha-bil'i-tāt, *vt.* To restore to a former capacity or position; to re-establish in esteem.
Rehearsal, rē-hėrs'al, *n.* Act of rehearsing; recital; a trial performance.
Rehearse, rē-hėrs', *vt.* (rehearsing, rehearsed). To repeat; to recite; to relate; to repeat in private for trial.
Reign, rān, *vi.* To be sovereign; to rule; to prevail.—*n.* Royal authority; supremacy; time of a sovereign's supreme authority.
Reimburse, rē-im-bėrs', *vt.* To refund; to pay back.
Reimbursement, rē-im-bėrs'ment, *n.* Act of reimbursing; repayment.
Reimport, rē-im-pōrt', *vt.* To carry back to the country of exportation.—*n.* rē-im'pōrt. Something reimported.
Reimpose, rē-im-pōz', *vt.* To impose anew.
Rein, rān, *n.* The strap of a bridle, by which a horse is governed; an instrument for restraining; restraint.—*vt.* To govern by a bridle; to restrain.—*vi.* To obey the reins.
Reindeer, rān'dēr, *n.* A deer of northern parts, with broad branched antlers.
Reinforce, rē-in-fōrs', *vt.* To strengthen by new assistance, as troops.—*n.* An additional thickness given to an object to strengthen it.
Reinforcement, rē-in-fōrs'ment, *n.* Act of reinforcing; additional troops or ships.
Reins, rānz, *n.pl.* The kidneys; lower part of the back; seat of the affections and passions.
Reinsert, rē-in-sėrt', *vt.* To insert a second time.
Reinstate, rē-in-stāt', *vt.* To instate anew; to restore to a former position.
Reinsurance, rē-in-shör'ans, *n.* A renewed insurance; a contract by which an insurer devolves to another the risks he had undertaken himself; act of reinsuring.
Reinsure, rē-in-shör', *vt.* To insure again.
Reinvest, rē-in-vest', *vt.* To invest anew.
Reinvestment, rē-in-vest'ment, *n.* A second or repeated investment.
Reissue, rē-ish'ū, *vt.* To issue a second time.—*n.* A second or repeated issue.
Reiterate, rē-it'ėr-āt, *vt.* To repeat again and again; to do or say repeatedly.
Reiteration, rē-it'ėr-ā"shon, *n.* Repetition.
Reject, rē-jekt', *vt.* To cast off; to discard; to repel; to forsake; to decline.
Rejection, rē-jek'shon, *n.* Act of rejecting; refusal to accept or grant.
Rejoice, rē-jois', *vi.* (rejoicing, rejoiced). To be glad; to exult.—*vt.* To gladden; to cheer.
Rejoicing, rē-jois'ing, *n.* Act of expressing joy; festivity.
Rejoin, rē-join', *vt.* To join again; to answer.—*vi.* To answer to a reply.
Rejoinder, rē-join'dėr, *n.* An answer to a reply.
Rejudge, re-juj', *vt.* To judge again.
Rejuvenate, rē-jū'ven-āt, *vt.* To restore to youth; to make young again.
Rejuvenescence, rē-jū'ven-es"ens, *n.* A renewing of youth.
Relapse, rē-laps', *vi.* (relapsing, relapsed). To slip back; to return to a former state.—*n.* A falling back, either in health or morals.
Relate, rē-lāt', *vt.* (relating, related). To tell; to narrate; to ally by kindred.—*vi.* To refer; to stand in some relation.
Related, rē-lāt'ed, *p.a.* Connected by blood; standing in some relation.
Relation, rē-lā'shon, *n.* Act of relating; account; reference; connection; kindred; a relative; proportion.
Relationship, rē-lā'shon-ship, *n.* The state of being related; kinship.
Relative, re'lat-iv, *a.* Having relation or reference; not absolute or existing by itself; relevant.—*n.* Something considered in its relation to something else; one allied by blood; a word which relates to or represents another word or sentence.
Relatively, re'lat-iv-li, *adv.* In a relative manner; not absolutely; comparatively.
Relator, rē-lāt'ėr, *n.* One who relates.
Relax, rē-laks', *vt.* To slacken; to loosen or weaken; to unbend.—*vi.* To become loose, feeble, or languid; to abate in severity.
Relaxation, re-laks-ā'shon, *n.* Act of relaxing; abatement of rigour; recreation.
Relay, rē-lā', *n.* A supply of horses placed on the road to relieve others; a squad of men to relieve others; a supply stored up.—*vt.* To lay again; to lay a second time.
Release, rē-lēs', *vt.* (releasing, released). To liberate; to disengage; to acquit.—*n.* Liberation; discharge; acquittance.
Re-lease, rē-lēs', *vt.* To lease again.
Relegate, re'lē-gāt, *vt.* To consign to some remote destination; to banish.
Relent, rē-lent', *vi.* To soften in temper; to yield or become less severe.
Relentless, rē-lent'les, *a.* Unmerciful; implacable; pitiless.
Relet, rē-let', *vt.* To let anew, as a house.
Relevance, Relevancy, re'le-vans, re'le-van-si, *n.* State or quality of being relevant; pertinence.
Relevant, re'le-vant, *a.* Applicable; pertinent; to the purpose.
Reliable, rē-lī'a-bl, *a.* That may be relied on; trustworthy.

Reliably, rē-lī′a-bli, *adv.* In a reliable manner; so as to be relied on.
Reliance, rē-lī′ans, *n.* Act of relying; trust; confidence; dependence.
Reliant, rē-lī′ant, *a.* Confident; self-reliant.
Relic, re′lik, *n.* A remaining fragment; the body of a deceased person (usually in *pl.*); a memento or keepsake.
Relict, re′likt, *n.* A widow.
Relief, rē-lēf′, *n.* Ease or mitigation of pain; succour; remedy; redress; assistance given to a pauper; one who relieves another by taking duty; prominence of figures above a plane surface in sculpture, carving, &c.; prominence or distinctness.
Relieve, rē-lēv′, *vt.* (relieving, relieved). To remove or lessen, as anything that pains; to ease; to succour; to release from duty; to give variety to; to set off by contrast; to give the appearance of projection to.
Relievo, rē-lē′vō or rel-ē-ā′vō, *n.* Rilievo.
Religion, rē-li′jon, *n.* An acknowledgment of our obligation to God; practical piety; devotion; any system of faith and worship.
Religionist, rē-li′jon-ist, *n.* A religious bigot; a formalist.
Religiosity, rē-li′ji-os″i-ti, *n.* A natural tendency of mind towards religion; weak superficial religious sentiment.
Religious, rē-li′jus, *a.* Pertaining to religion; teaching religion; used in worship; devout; scrupulously faithful.
Religiously, rē-li′jus-li, *adv.* Piously; reverently; strictly; conscientiously.
Relinquish, rē-ling′kwish, *vt.* To give up; to leave; to resign; to renounce.
Reliquary, re′li-kwa-ri, *n.* A depository for relics; a shrine.
Reliquiæ, re-lik′wi-ē, *n.pl.* Relics; fossil remains.
Relish, re′lish, *vt.* To enjoy the taste of; to have a taste for; to give an agreeable taste to. —*vi.* To have a pleasing taste.—*n.* Taste, usually pleasing; fondness; flavour; something to increase the pleasure of eating.
Relive, rē-liv′, *vi.* To live again.
Reluctance, Reluctancy, rē-luk′tans, rē-luk′tan-si, *n.* Aversion; unwillingness.
Reluctant, rē-luk′tant, *a.* Loath; averse; acting with slight repugnance.
Relume, Relumine, rē-lūm′, rē-lū′min, *vt.* To illuminate again.
Rely, rē-lī′, *vt.* (relying, relied). To rest with confidence; to trust: with *on* or *upon*.
Remain, rē-mān′, *vi.* To continue in a place or condition; to abide; to be left; to last.—*n.* That which is left; *pl.* a dead body; literary works of one who is dead.
Remainder, rē-mān′dėr, *n.* That which remains; residue; remnant; an estate limited so as to be enjoyed after the death of the present possessor or otherwise.—*a.* Left over.
Remake, rē-māk′, *vt.* To make anew.
Remand, rē-mand′, *vt.* To call or send back; to send back to jail.
Remanent, rem′a-nent, *a.* Remaining.
Remark, rē-märk′, *n.* Notice; an observation in words; a comment.—*vt.* To observe; to utter by way of comment.
Re-mark, rē-märk′, *vt.* To mark anew.
Remarkable, rē-märk′a-bl, *a.* Worthy of remark; conspicuous; unusual; extraordinary.
Remarkably, rē-märk′a-bli, *adv.* Strikingly; singularly; surprisingly.
Remarry, rē-ma′ri, *vt.* and *i.* To marry again.
Remediable, re-mē′di-a-bl, *a.* Curable.
Remedial, re-mē′di-al, *a.* Affording a remedy; healing; intended for a remedy.
Remedy, re′me-di, *n.* That which cures a disease; that which counteracts an evil; redress.—*vt.* (remedying, remedied). To cure; to repair; to redress; to counteract.
Remember, rē-mem′bėr, *vt.* To have in the memory; to think of; to observe; to give a gratuity for service done.—*vi.* To have something in remembrance.
Remembrance, rē-mem′brans, *n.* The keeping of a thing in mind; memory; what is remembered; a memorial; a keepsake.
Remembrancer, rē-mem′brans-ėr, *n.* An officer in the exchequer; a recorder.
Remind, rē-mīnd′, *vt.* To put in mind; to cause to remember.
Reminder, rē-mīnd′ėr, *n.* One who reminds; a hint that awakens remembrance.
Reminiscence, re-mi-nis′ens, *n.* Recollection; what is recalled to mind; account of past incidents within one's knowledge.
Reminiscent, re-mi-nis′ent, *a.* Having remembrance; calling to mind.
Remiss, rē-mis′, *a.* Careless; negligent; heedless; slack.
Remission, rē-mi′shon, *n.* Act of remitting; relinquishment; abatement; pardon.
Remissly, rē-mis′li, *adv.* Carelessly; negligently; slackly.
Remit, rē-mit′, *vt.* (remitting, remitted). To relax; to abate; to relinquish; to forgive; to transmit or send.—*vi.* To slacken; to abate in violence for a time.
Remittance, rē-mit′ans, *n.* Act of remitting; the sum or thing remitted.
Remittent, rē-mit′ent, *a.* Temporarily ceasing.—*n.* A remittent fever.
Remnant, rem′nant, *n.* That which is left; a scrap, fragment.—*a.* Remaining.
Remodel, rē-mo′del, *vt.* To model anew.
Remonetize, rē-mon′et-īz, *vt.* To make again a legal or standard money of account.
Remonstrance, rē-mon′strans, *n.* Act of remonstrating; expostulation; strong representation against something.
Remonstrant, rē-mon′strant, *a.* Remonstrating.
Remonstrate, rē-mon′strāt, *vi.* To present strong reasons against an act; to expostulate.
Remora, rem′o-ra, *n.* The sucking-fish.
Remorse, rē-mors′, *n.* Reproach of conscience; compunction for wrong committed.
Remorseful, rē-mors′fụl, *a.* Full of remorse; impressed with a sense of guilt.
Remorseless, rē-mors′les, *a.* Without remorse; ruthless; relentless; merciless.
Remote, rē-mōt′, *a.* Distant in place or time; not immediate or direct; slight; inconsiderable.
Remotely, rē-mōt′li, *adv.* In a remote manner; distantly; slightly.
Remould, rē-mōld′, *vt.* To mould anew.
Remount, rē-mount′, *vt.* and *i.* To mount again.—*n.* A fresh horse to mount.
Removable, rē-mö̈v′a-bl, *a.* That may be removed.
Removal, rē-mö̈v′al, *n.* Act of removing; a moving to another place.

Remove, rē-möv′, *vt.* (removing, removed). To move from its place; to take away; to displace from an office; to banish or destroy.—*vi.* To be moved from its place; to change the place of residence.—*n.* A removal; departure.
Removed, rē-mövd′, *p.a.* Remote.
Remunerate, rē-mū′nė-rāt, *vt.* To reward for service; to recompense.
Remuneration, rē-mū′nė-rā″shon, *n.* Act of remunerating; reward; compensation.
Remunerative, rē-mū′nė-rāt-iv, *a.* Affording remuneration; profitable.
Renaissance, re-nā′sans, *n.* Revival; the revival of letters and arts in the fifteenth century.
Renal, rē′nal, *a.* Pertaining to the kidneys.
Renard, re′närd, *n.* A fox.
Renascence, rē-nas′ens, *n.* The state of being renascent; also same as *Renaissance.*
Renascent, rē-nas′ent, *a.* Springing into being again; reappearing; rejuvenated.
Rencounter, Rencontre, ren-koun′tėr, ren-kon′tėr, *n.* An abrupt meeting of persons; a casual combat; encounter.—*vi.* To meet an enemy unexpectedly.
Rend, rend, *vt.* (rending, rent). To force asunder; to tear away; to sever.—*vi.* To be or become torn; to split.
Render, ren′dėr, *vt.* To give in return; to give back; to present; to afford; to invest with qualities; to translate; to interpret; to clarify, as tallow.
Rendering, ren′dėr-ing, *n.* Version; translation; interpretation.
Rendezvous, ren′de-vö, *n.* A place of meeting.—*vi.* To meet at a particular place.
Rendible, rend′i-bl, *a.* Capable of being rent.
Rendition, ren-di′shon, *n.* A rendering; interpretation; translation; surrender.
Renegade, re′nė-gād, *n.* An apostate; a deserter.
Renew, rē-nū′, *vt.* To make new again; to repair; to repeat; to grant anew; to transform.—*vi.* To grow or begin again.
Renewal, rē-nū′al, *n.* Act of renewing; a new loan on a new bill or note.
Reniform, rē′ni-form, *a.* Having the shape of the kidneys.
Renitent, rē-nī′tent, *a.* Resisting pressure; persistently opposed.
Rennet, ren′et, *n.* The prepared inner membrane of the calf's stomach, which coagulates milk; a kind of apple.
Renounce, rē-nouns′, *vt.* (renouncing, renounced). To disown; to reject; to forsake.—*vi.* To revoke.
Renovate, re′nō-vāt, *vt.* To renew; to restore to freshness.
Renovater, Renovator, re′nō-vāt-ėr, *n.* One who or that which renovates.
Renovation, re-nō-vā′shon, *n.* Act of renovating; renewal.
Renown, rē-noun′, *n.* Fame; glory; reputation.—*vt.* To make famous.
Renowned, rē-nound′, *a.* Famous; celebrated; eminent; remarkable.
Rent, rent, *n.* Money, &c., payable yearly for the use of lands or tenements; a tear; a schism.—*vt.* To let on lease; to hold on condition of paying rent.—*vi.* To be leased or let for rent.
Rental, rent′al, *n.* A roll or account of rents; gross amount of rents from an estate.
Renter, rent′ėr, *n.* The lessee or tenant who pays rent.—*vt.* To sew together finely; to fine-draw.
Rent-roll, rent′rōl, *n.* A list of rents falling to be paid.
Renunciation, rē-nun′si-ā″shon, *n.* Act of renouncing; disavowal; abandonment.
Reoccupy, rē-ok′kū-pī, *vt.* To occupy anew.
Reopen, rē-ō′pen, *vt.* and *i.* To open again.
Reorganize, rē-or′gan-īz, *vt.* To organize anew.
Rep, Repp, rep, *n.* A dress fabric with a corded surface, the ribs being transverse.
Repair, rē-pār′, *vt.* To restore; to refit; to mend; to retrieve.—*vi.* To betake oneself; to resort.—*n.* Restoration; supply of loss; state as regards repairing; a resorting; abode.
Reparable, re′pa-ra-bl, *a.* That may be repaired.
Reparation, re-pa-rā′shon, *n.* Act of repairing; restoration; satisfaction for injury; amends.
Reparative, re-pa′ra-tiv, *a.* Repairing; tending to amend.—*n.* That which repairs or makes amends.
Repartee, re-pär-tē′, *n.* A smart, ready, and witty reply.
Repass, rē-pas′, *vt.* and *i.* To pass again or back.
Repast, rē-past′, *n.* Act of taking food; food taken; a meal.—*vt.* and *i.* To feed.
Repatriate, rē-pā′tri-āt, *vt.* To restore to one's own country.
Repay, rē-pā′, *vt.* To pay back or again; to refund; to requite.
Repayable, rē-pā′a-bl, *a.* That is to be or may be repaid.
Repayment, rē-pā′ment, *n.* Act of repaying; money repaid.
Repeal, rē-pēl′, *vt.* To recall; to revoke; to abrogate, as a law.—*n.* Act of repealing; abrogation.
Repeat, rē-pēt′, *vt.* To do or utter again; to recite; to recapitulate.—*n.* Repetition.
Repeatedly, rē-pēt′ed-li, *adv.* With repetition; again and again; indefinitely.
Repeater, rē-pēt′ėr, *n.* One who repeats; a watch that strikes the hours; an indeterminate decimal.
Repeating, rē-pēt′ing, *a.* Producing a like result several times in succession.
Repel, rē-pel′, *vt.* (repelling, repelled). To drive back; to resist successfully.—*vi.* To cause repugnance; to shock.
Repellence, Repellency, rē-pel′ens, rē-pel′-en-si, *n.* Quality of being repellent.
Repellent, rē-pel′ent, *a.* Having the effect of repelling; repulsive; deterring.
Repent, rē-pent′, *vi.* To feel regret for something done or left undone; to be penitent.—*vt.* To remember with self-reproach or sorrow.
Repent, rē′pent, *a.* Creeping.
Repentance, rē-pent′ans, *n.* Act of repenting; sorrow for sin; penitence; contrition.
Repentant, rē-pent′ant, *a.* Repenting.
Repercuss, rē-pėr-kus′, *vt.* To drive back (as sound or air); to make rebound.
Repercussion, rē-pėr-ku′shon, *n.* Act of driving back; reverberation.
Repercussive, rē-pėr-kus′iv, *a.* Having power of repercussion; causing to reverberate.
Repertoire, rep′ėr-twär, *n.* The aggregate of pieces that an actor or company performs.

Repertory, re'pėr-to-ri, *n.* A treasury; a magazine; a repository.
Repetition, re-pē-ti'shon, *n.* Act of repeating; recital; that which is repeated.
Repine, rē-pīn', *vi.* (repining, repined). To fret oneself; to complain discontentedly; to murmur.
Replace, rē-plās', *vt.* (replacing, replaced). To put again in the former place; to put in the place of another; to take the place of.
Replenish, rē-plen'ish, *vt.* To fill again; to fill completely; to stock abundantly.
Replete, rē-plēt', *a.* Filled up; full; abounding; thoroughly imbued.
Repletion, rē-plē'shon, *n.* State of being replete; superabundant fulness; surfeit.
Replevin, Replevy, rē-plev'in, rē-plev'i, *n.* A personal action to recover goods.
Replevy, rē-plev'i, *vt.* (replevying, replevied). To reclaim (as goods wrongfully seized) upon giving security to try the cause in court.
Replica, rep'li-ka, *n.* A copy of a picture or a piece of sculpture made by the hand that executed the original; facsimile.
Replication, re-pli-kā'shon, *n.* An answer; a copy; a replica.
Reply, rē-plī', *vi.* and *t.* (replying, replied). To answer; to respond; to do something in return.—*n.* An answer; a response; a rejoinder.
Report, rē-pōrt', *vt.* and *i.* To bring back, as an answer; to relate; to give an official statement of; to take down from the lips of a speaker, &c.; to lay a charge against.—*n.* An account; rumour; repute; noise of explosion; official statement; account of proceedings.
Reporter, rē-pōrt'ėr, *n.* One who reports; one of a newspaper staff who gives accounts of public meetings, events, &c.
Reposal, rē-pōz'al, *n.* The act of reposing or resting with reliance.
Repose, rē-pōz', *vt.* (reposing, reposed). To lay at rest.—*vi.* To lie at rest; to rely.—*n.* A lying at rest; tranquillity; composure; absence of show of feeling.
Reposeful, rē-pōz'ful, *a.* Full of repose; affording repose or rest; trustful.
Reposit, rē-poz'it, *vt.* To lay up; to lodge, as for safety.
Repository, rē-poz'i-to-ri, *n.* A place where things are stored; warehouse.
Repoussé, rė-pös'sā, *a.* Embossed.
Reprehend, re-prē-hend', *vt.* To charge with a fault; to reprove; to censure.
Reprehensible, re-prē-hen'si-bl, *a.* Deserving reprehension; blamable.
Reprehension, re-prē-hen'shon, *n.* Act of reprehending; reproof; censure; blame.
Reprehensive, re-prē-hen'siv, *a.* Containing reprehension or reproof.
Represent, re-prē-zent', *vt.* To exhibit by a likeness of; to typify; to act the part of; to describe; to be a substitute for; to exemplify.
Representable, re-prē-zent'a-bl, *a.* That may be represented.
Representation, re'prē-zen-tā"shon, *n.* The act of representing; an image or likeness; dramatic performance; a remonstrance; the representing of a constituency.
Representative, re-prē-zent'a-tiv, *a.* Fitted or serving to represent; conducted by the agency of delegates; typical.—*n.* One who or that which represents; a person elected to represent a constituency.
Repress, rē-pres', *vt.* To press back; to check; to quell.
Repressible, rē-pres'i-bl, *a.* Capable of being repressed.
Repression, rē-pre'shon, *n.* Act of repressing or subduing; check; restraint.
Repressive, rē-pres'iv, *a.* Having power or tending to repress.
Reprieve, rē-prēv', *vt.* (reprieving, reprieved). To grant a respite to; to relieve temporarily.—*n.* Suspension of the execution of a criminal's sentence; respite.
Reprimand, rep'ri-mand, *n.* A severe reproof for a fault.—*vt.* rep-ri-mand'. To administer a sharp rebuke to.
Reprint, rē-print', *vt.* To print again.—*n.* rē'print. A second or new edition.
Reprisal, rē-prīz'al, *n.* Seizure from an enemy by way of retaliation; retaliation.
Reproach, rē-prōch', *vt.* To charge severely with a fault; to censure.—*n.* Censure; blame; source of blame; disgrace.
Reproachable, rē-prōch'a-bl, *a.* Deserving reproach.
Reproachably, rē-prōch'a-bli, *adv.* In a reproachable manner.
Reproachful, rē-prōch'ful, *a.* Containing or expressing reproach; opprobrious.
Reprobate, re'prō-bāt, *a.* Morally abandoned; profligate.—*n.* A wicked, depraved wretch. —*vt.* To disapprove strongly; to reject.
Reprobation, re-prō-bā'shon, *n.* Strong disapproval; condemnation; rejection.
Reproduce, rē-prō-dūs', *vt.* To produce again; to generate, as offspring; to portray or represent.
Reproduction, rē-prō-duk'shon, *n.* Act or process of reproducing; that which is produced anew; an accurate copy.
Reproductive, rē-prō-duk'tiv, *a.* Pertaining to or used in reproduction.
Reproof, rē-pröf', *n.* Words intended to reprove; rebuke.
Reprovable, rē-pröv'a-bl, *a.* Worthy of being reproved; blamable.
Reproval, rē-pröv'al, *n.* Reproof.
Reprove, rē-pröv', *vt.* (reproving, reproved). To charge with a fault orally; to chide; to rebuke.
Reptile, rep'tīl, *a.* Creeping; grovelling.—*n.* An animal that moves on its belly, or by means of small short legs.
Reptilian, rep-til'i-an, *a.* Belonging to the class of reptiles.—*n.* A reptile.
Republic, rē-pub'lik, *n.* A commonwealth; a state in which the supreme power is vested in elected representatives.
Republican, rē-pub'lik-an, *a.* Pertaining to or consisting of a republic.—*n.* One who favours republican government.
Republicanism, rē-pub'lik-an-izm, *n.* A republican form of government; republican principles.
Republication, rē-pub'li-kā"shon, *n.* A second or new publication.
Republish, rē-pub'lish, *vt.* To publish a second time or anew.
Repudiate, rē-pū'di-āt, *vt.* (repudiating, repudiated). To divorce; to reject; to disavow.
Repudiation, rē-pū'di-ā"shon, *n.* Act of repudiating; rejection; disavowal.

Repugnance, rē-pug′nans, *n.* Aversion; reluctance; dislike; inconsistency.
Repugnant, rē-pug′nant, *a.* Opposed; inconsistent; inimical; offensive.
Repulse, rē-puls′, *n.* Act of repelling; a check or defeat; refusal; denial.—*vt.* (repulsing, repulsed). To repel.
Repulsion, rē-pul′shon, *n.* Act of repelling; feeling of aversion.
Repulsive, rē-puls′iv, *a.* That repulses or repels; repellent; forbidding.
Repurchase, rē-pėr′chās, *vt.* To buy back.—*n.* Purchase again of what has been sold.
Reputable, re′pūt-a-bl, *a.* Held in esteem; estimable.
Reputation, re-pūt-ā′shon, *n.* Character derived from public opinion; repute; good name; honour; fame.
Repute, rē-pūt′, *vt.* (reputing, reputed). To estimate; to deem.—*n.* Reputation; character; good character.
Reputedly, rē-pūt′ed-li, *adv.* In common repute.
Request, rē-kwest′, *n.* An expressed desire; a petition; thing asked for; a state of being asked for.—*vt.* To ask; to beg.
Requiem, rē′kwi-em, *n.* A mass for the dead in the R. Catholic Church; music for this mass.
Require, rē-kwīr′, *vt.* (requiring, required). To ask as of right; to demand; to have need for; to find it necessary.
Requirement, rē-kwīr′ment, *n.* Act of requiring; demand; an essential condition; something necessary.
Requisite, re′kwi-zit, *a.* Necessary; essential.—*n.* Something indispensable.
Requisition, re-kwi-zi′shon, *n.* Act of requiring; demand; a written call or invitation.—*vt.* To make a demand upon or for.
Requital, rē-kwīt′al, *n.* Act of requiting; reward; recompense; retribution.
Requite, rē-kwīt′, *vt.* (requiting, requited). To repay; to reward; to retaliate on.
Reredos, rēr′dos, *n.* The decorated wall behind the altar in a church.
Rere-mouse, rēr′mous, *n.* Rear-mouse.
Rereward, rēr′wạrd, *n.* Rearward.
Rescind, rē-sind′, *vt.* To abrogate; to annul; to repeal; to revoke.
Rescission, rē-si′zhon, *n.* Act of rescinding.
Rescript, rē′skript, *n.* Official decision; an edict or decree.
Rescue, res′kū, *vt.* (rescuing, rescued). To deliver from confinement, danger, or evil.—*n.* Act of rescuing; deliverance.
Rescuer, res′kū-ėr, *n.* One that rescues.
Research, rē-sėrch′, *n.* A diligent seeking of facts or principles; investigation.—*vt.* To search again.
Reseat, rē-sēt′, *vt.* To seat again; to furnish with a new seat.
Reseize, rē-sēz′, *vt.* To seize again; to reinstate.
Resemblance, rē-zem′blans, *n.* Likeness; similarity; something similar; similitude.
Resemble, rē-zem′bl, *vt.* (resembling, resembled). To be like; to liken; to compare.
Resent, rē-zent′, *vt.* To take ill; to consider as an affront; to be angry at.—*vi.* To feel resentment.
Resentful, rē-zent′fụl, *a.* Full of resentment; of a vindictive temper.
Resentment, rē-zent′ment, *n.* Deep sense of injury; indignation; revengeful feeling.
Reservation, re-zėrv-ā′shon, *n.* Act of reserving; reserve; concealment; state of being treasured up; proviso.
Reserve, rē-zėrv′, *vt.* (reserving, reserved). To keep in store; to retain.—*n.* Act of reserving; that which is retained; retention; habit of restraining the feelings; coldness towards others; shyness; troops kept for an exigency.
Reserved, rē-zėrvd′, *a.* Showing reserve; not free or frank; restrained; cautious.
Reservoir, re′zėr-vwạr, *n.* A place where anything is kept in store; an artificial lake to supply a town with water.
Reset, rē-set′, *n.* The receiving of stolen goods.—*vt.* (resetting, resetted). To receive stolen goods (Scots).
Reset, rē-set′, *vt.* To set again.
Resetter, rē-set′ėr, *n.* A receiver of stolen goods.
Reside, rē-zīd′, *vi.* (residing, resided). To have one's abode; to dwell; to inhere.
Residence, re′zi-dens, *n.* Act or state of residing; abode; home; dwelling.
Residency, re′zi-den-si, *n.* Residence; official residence of a British resident in India.
Resident, re′zi-dent, *a.* Residing.—*n.* One who resides; a dweller; a public minister at a foreign court.
Residenter, re′zi-dent-ėr, *n.* A resident.
Residential, re-zi-den′shal, *a.* Pertaining to or suitable for residence.
Residual, rē-zid′ū-al, *a.* Left after a part is taken.
Residuary, rē-zid′ū-a-ri, *a.* Pertaining to the residue.
Residue, re′zi-dū, *n.* That which remains after a part is taken; remainder.
Residuum, rē-zid′ū-um, *n.* Residue.
Resign, rē-zīn′, *vt.* To give up; to renounce; to submit, as to Providence.
Resignation, re-zig-nā′shon, *n.* Act of resigning; state of being resigned; habitual submission to Providence.
Resigned, rē-zīnd′, *a.* Submissive; patient.
Resile, rē-zīl′, *vi.* (resiling, resiled). To withdraw from a purpose or agreement.
Resilience, Resiliency, rē-si′li-ens, rē-si′li-en-si, *n.* Act of resiling or rebounding; rebound from being elastic.
Resilient, rē-si′li-ent, *a.* Inclined to resile; rebounding.
Resin, re′zin, *n.* An inflammable vegetable substance; the hardened juice of pines.
Resinous, re′zin-us, *a.* Pertaining to, like, or obtained from resin.
Resist, rē-zist′, *vt.* and *i.* To withstand; to oppose; to struggle against.
Resistance, rē-zist′ans, *n.* Act of resisting; check; quality of not yielding to force.
Resistant, Resistent, rē-zis′tent, *a.* Making resistance.—*n.* One who or that which resists.
Resistible, rē-zist′i-bl, *a.* That may be resisted.
Resistless, rē-zist′les, *a.* That cannot be resisted; that cannot resist.
Resolute, re′zō-lūt, *a.* Having fixedness of purpose; determined; steadfast.
Resolutely, re′zō-lūt-li, *adv.* In a resolute manner; steadily; determinedly.
Resolution, re-zō-lū′shon, *n.* Character of

being resolute; determination; a formal decision; operation of separating the component parts; solution.
Resolvable, rē-zolv'a-bl, *a.* That may be resolved.
Resolve, rē-zolv', *vt.* (resolving, resolved). To separate the component parts of; to analyse; to solve; to determine; to decide.—*vi.* To separate into component parts; to melt; to determine; to decide.—*n.* Fixed purpose of mind; resolution.
Resolvent, rē-zolv'ent, *a.* Having power to resolve or to dissolve; causing solution.
Resolver, rē-zolv'ėr, *n.* One who or that which resolves; one who determines.
Resonance, re'zo-nans, *n.* State or quality of being resonant; act of resounding.
Resonant, re'zo-nant, *a.* Resounding; full of sounds.
Resort, rē-zort', *vi.* To have recourse; to go; to repair frequently.—*n.* Recourse; concourse; a haunt.
Resound, rē-zound', *vt.* To give back the sound of; to echo; to praise.—*vi.* To sound again; to echo; to be much praised.
Resource, rē-sōrs', *n.* Any source of aid or support; expedient; *pl.* funds; means.
Respect, rē-spekt', *vt.* To regard; to relate to; to honour; to have consideration for.—*n.* Regard; attention; due deference; bias; a point or particular; reference.
Respectability, rē-spekt'a-bil"i-ti, *n.* State or quality of being respectable.
Respectable, rē-spekt'a-bl, *a.* Worthy of respect; held in good repute; moderately good.
Respectably, rē-spekt'a-bli, *adv.* In a respectable manner; moderately; pretty well.
Respectful, rē-spekt'fụl, *a.* Marked by respect; civil; dutiful; courteous.
Respecting, rē-spekt'ing, *prep.* In regard to; regarding; concerning.
Respective, rē-spekt'iv, *a.* Relating severally each to each; relative.
Respectively, rē-spekt'iv-li, *adv.* In their respective relations; as each belongs to each.
Respirable, rē-spīr'a-bl, *a.* That may be respired or breathed; fit for respiration.
Respiration, re-spi-rā'shon, *n.* Act of respiring or breathing.
Respirator, re'spi-rāt-ėr, *n.* An appliance covering the mouth, and serving to exclude cold air, dust, &c.; a device to prevent the breathing in of poison-gas.
Respiratory, re'spī-ra"to-ri, *a.* Serving for respiration; pertaining to respiration.
Respire, rē-spīr', *vi.* and *t.* (respiring, respired). To breathe; to recover one's breath.
Respite, res'pit, *n.* Temporary intermission; interval; a reprieve.—*vt.* (respiting, respited). To grant a respite to; to reprieve.
Resplendence, rē-splen'dens, *n.* Brilliant lustre.
Resplendent, rē-splen'dent, *a.* Very bright; shining with brilliant lustre.
Respond, rē-spond', *vi.* To answer; to suit.—*n.* A short anthem; response.
Respondent, rē-spond'ent, *a.* Answering; corresponding.—*n.* One who responds; one who answers in a lawsuit.
Response, rē-spons', *n.* An answer; reply.
Responsibility, rē-spons'i-bil"i-ti, *n.* State of being responsible; that for which one is responsible; ability to answer in payment.
Responsible, rē-spons'i-bl, *a.* Answerable; accountable; important.
Responsive, rē-spons'iv, *a.* Making reply; answering; correspondent; suited.
Responsory, rē-spon'so-ri, *a.* Containing response or answer.—*n.* A response.
Rest, rest, *n.* Cessation of action; peace; sleep; an appliance for support; a pause; remainder; the others.—*vi.* To cease from action; to lie for repose; to be supported; to be in a certain state; remain; to be left.—*vt.* To lay at rest; to place, as on a support.
Restaurant, res'tō-rong, *n.* An establishment for the sale of refreshments.
Restaurateur, res-tō'ra-tėr, *n.* The keeper of a restaurant.
Restful, rest'fụl, *a.* Giving rest; quiet.
Restitution, res-ti-tū'shon, *n.* Act of restoring; reparation; amends.
Restive, res'tiv, *a.* Stubborn; fidgeting; impatient under restraint or opposition.
Restless, rest'les, *a.* Without rest; disturbed; uneasy; anxious.
Restorable, rē-stor'a-bl, *a.* Capable of being restored.
Restoration, re-stō-rā'shon, *n.* Act of restoring; replacement; recovery; the re-establishment of the English monarchy in 1660.
Restorative, rē-stōr'at-iv, *a.* Having power to renew strength.—*n.* A medicine which restores strength.
Restore, rē-stōr', *vt.* (restoring, restored). To make strong again; to repair; to cure; to re-establish; to give back.
Restrain, rē-strān', *vt.* To hold back; to curb; to check; to repress; to restrict.
Restraint, rē-strānt', *n.* Act of restraining; hindrance; curb; limitation.
Restrict, rē-strikt', *vt.* To limit; to curb.
Restriction, rē-strik'shon, *n.* Act of restricting; limitation; a reservation.
Restrictive, rē-strikt'iv, *a.* Having the quality of restricting; imposing restraint.
Result, rē-zult', *vi.* To rise as a consequence; to issue; to ensue; to end.—*n.* Consequence; effect; issue; outcome.
Resultant, rē-zult'ant, *a.* Following as a result or consequence.
Resumable, rē-zūm'a-bl, *a.* That may be resumed.
Resume, rē-zūm', *vt.* (resuming, resumed). To take up again; to begin again.
Résumé, rā'zö-mā, *n.* A recapitulation; a summary.
Resumption, rē-zum'shon, *n.* Act of resuming.
Resumptive, rē-zum'tiv, *a.* Resuming.
Resurgent, rē-sėr'jent, *a.* Rising again.
Resurrection, re-zėr-rek'shon, *n.* A rising again; the rising of the dead at the general judgment.
Resuscitate, rē-sus'i-tāt, *vt.* and *i.* To revive.
Resuscitation, rē-sus'i-tā"shon, *n.* Act of resuscitating; restoration to life.
Retail, rē-tāl', *vt.* To sell in small quantities: to tell to many.—*n.* rē'tāl. The sale of commodities in small quantities: used also as *adj.*
Retailer, rē-tāl'ėr, *n.* One who retails.
Retain, rē-tān', *vt.* To hold back; to keep in possession; to detain; to hire; to engage.
Retainer, rẹ-tān'ėr, *n.* One who retains; an adherent or dependent; a fee to engage a counsel.

Retake, rē-tāk', *vt.* To take again or back.
Retaliate, rē-ta'li-āt, *vi.* and *t.* To return like for like; to repay; to take revenge.
Retaliation, rē-ta'li-ā"shon, *n.* The return of like for like; requital; reprisal.
Retaliative, Retaliatory, rē-ta'li-ā-tiv, rē-tal'i-ā-to-ri, *a.* Returning like for like.
Retard, rē-tärd', *vt.* To render slower; to impede; to delay; to postpone.
Retardation, rē-tärd-ā'shon, *n.* Act of retarding; diminution in speed; obstruction.
Retch, rech, *vi.* To make an effort to vomit; to strain, as in vomiting.
Retention, rē-ten'shon, *n.* Act or power of retaining; maintenance; memory.
Retentive, rē-ten'tiv, *a.* Characterized by retention; having power to retain ideas.
Reticence, re'ti-sens, *n.* Act or character of keeping silence; keeping of one's own counsel.
Reticent, re'ti-sent, *a.* Having a disposition to be silent; reserved.
Reticular, re-tik'ū-lėr, *a.* Having the form or character of a net.
Reticulate, Reticulated, re-tik'ū-lāt, re-tik'ū-lāt-ed, *a.* Resembling net-work.
Reticulation, re-tik'ū-lā"shon, *n.* Net-work.
Reticule, re'ti-kūl, *n.* A net-work bag.
Retiform, re'ti-form, *a.* Reticular.
Retina, re'ti-na, *n.* One of the coats of the eye, where visual impressions are received.
Retinue, re'ti-nū, *n.* A train of attendants; a suite.
Retiral, rē-tīr'al, *n.* Act of retiring.
Retire, rē-tīr' *vi.* (retiring, retired). To go back; to withdraw from business or active life; to go to bed.—*vt.* To remove from service; to pay when due, as a bill of exchange.
Retired, rē-tīrd', *a.* Secluded; private; having given up business.
Retirement, rē-tīr'ment, *n.* Act of retiring; retired life; seclusion.
Retiring, rē-tīr'ing, *a.* Reserved; unobtrusive; granted to one who retires from service.
Retort, rē-tort', *vt.* To retaliate; to throw back.—*vi.* To return an argument or charge.—*n.* A severe reply; a repartee; a chemical vessel for distilling.
Retouch, rē-tuch', *vt.* To improve by new touches, as a picture, &c.
Retrace, rē-trās', *vt.* To trace back; to trace over again.
Retract, rē-trakt', *vt.* To draw back; to recall.—*vi.* To unsay one's words.
Retractable, rē-trakt'a-bl, *a.* Capable of being retracted.
Retractation, rē-trak-tā'shon, *n.* Retraction.
Retractile, rē-trakt'il, *a.* Capable of being drawn back, as claws.
Retraction, rē-trak'shon, *n.* Act of drawing back; recantation; retractation.
Retractive, rē-trakt'iv, *a.* Tending to retract.
Retractor, rē-trakt'ėr, *n.* One who retracts; a muscle that draws back some part.
Retranslate, rē-trans-lāt', *vt.* To translate back into the original tongue.
Retreat, rē-trēt', *n.* Act of retiring; seclusion; a shelter; the retiring of an army from an enemy.—*vi.* To draw back; to retire from an enemy.
Retrench, rē-trensh', *vt.* To lessen; to limit or restrict.—*vi.* To economize.
Retrenchment, rē-trensh'ment, *n.* Act of curtailing; economy; an interior rampart.
Retribution, re-tri-bū'shon, *n.* Act of rewarding; a requital for evil done.
Retributive, Retributory, rē-tri'būt-iv, rē-tri'bū-to-ri, *a.* Making retribution; entailing justly deserved punishment.
Retrievable, rē-trēv'a-bl, *a.* That may be retrieved or recovered.
Retrieval, rē-trēv'al, *n.* Act of retrieving.
Retrieve, rē-trēv', *vt.* (retrieving, retrieved). To recover; to regain; to repair.
Retriever, rē-trēv'ėr, *n.* A dog that brings in game which a sportsman has shot.
Retroact, rē-trō-akt' or ret'rō-akt, *vi.* To act backward, in opposition, or in return.
Retrocede, rē-trō-sēd' or ret', *vi.* To go back; to retire.—*vt.* To cede back.
Retrocession, rē-trō-se'shon or ret-, *n.* Act of going or of ceding back.
Retrograde, ret'rō-grād or re', *a.* Going backward; appearing to move from east to west in the sky.—*vi.* To go backward.
Retrogression, rē-trō-gre'shon or ret-, *n.* Act of going backward.
Retrogressive, rē-trō-gres'iv or ret-, *a.* Going or moving backward; declining.
Retrorse, rē-trors', *a.* Turned or directed backwards, as a part of a plant.
Retrospect, ret'rō-spekt or rē', *n.* A view of things past; backward survey.
Retrospection, ret-rō-spek'shon or rē-, *n.* Act or faculty of looking on things past.
Retrospective, ret-rō-spekt'iv or rē-, *a.* Looking back; affecting things past.
Retroussé, rė-trö'sā, *a.* Turned up at the end, as a nose.
Return, rē-tėrn', *vi.* To come or go back; to recur.—*vt.* To send back; to repay; to report officially; to elect; to yield.—*n.* Act of returning; repayment; election of a representative; profit; an official statement; *pl.* tabulated statistics; a light tobacco.
Returning-officer, rē-tėrn'ing-of-is-ėr, *n.* The presiding officer at an election who declares the persons duly elected.
Return-ticket, rē-tėrn'ti-ket, *n.* A ticket for a journey to a place and back.
Retuse, rē-tūs', *a.* Having a rounded end, with a slight hollow or indentation, as a leaf.
Reunion, rē-ūn'yon, *n.* Union after separation; a meeting for social purposes.
Reunite, rē-ū-nīt', *vt.* and *i.* To unite again; to reconcile after variance.
Reveal, rē-vēl', *vt.* To disclose; to divulge; to make known by divine means.
Reveille, re-vel'ye, *n.* A bugle-call sounded at sun-rise.
Revel, re'vel, *n.* A feast with noisy jollity.—*vi.* (revelling, revelled). To carouse; to delight.
Revelation, re-ve-lā'shon, *n.* Act of revealing; that which is revealed; divine communication; the Apocalypse.
Reveller, re'vel-ėr, *n.* One who revels.
Revelry, re'vel-ri, *n.* Noisy festivity; jollity.
Revenge, rē-venj', *vt.* and *i.* (revenging, revenged). To take vengeance for; to avenge.—*n.* Act of revenging; retaliation; deliberate infliction of injury in return for injury; vindictive feeling.
Revengeful, rē-venj'ful, *a.* Full of revenge; vindictive; resentful.

Revenue, re've-nū, *n.* Income; the annual income of a state.
Reverberate, rē-vėr'bė-rāt, *vt.* and *i.* To return, as sound; to echo; to reflect, as heat or light.
Reverberation, rē-vėr'bė-rā"shon, *n.* Act of reverberating; an echo.
Reverberatory, rē-vėr'bė-ra-to-ri, *a.* Producing reverberation; reverberating.
Revere, rē-vēr', *vt.* (revering, revered). To regard with awe and respect; to venerate.
Reverence, rev'er-ens, *n.* Awe combined with respect; veneration; an obeisance; a reverend personage; a title of the clergy.—*vt.* To revere; to pay reverence to.
Reverend, rev'er-end, *a.* Worthy of reverence; a title given to clergymen.
Reverent, rev'er-ent, *a.* Expressing reverence; humble; impressed with reverence.
Reverential, re-ver-en'shal, *a.* Proceeding from reverence, or expressing it.
Reverie, re'ver-i, *n.* A loose train of thoughts; a day-dream; a visionary project.
Reversal, rē-vėrs'al, *n.* Act of reversing; a change or overthrowing.
Reverse, rē-vėrs', *vt.* (reversing, reversed). To alter to the opposite; to annul.—*n.* A reversal; a complete change or turn; a check; a defeat; the contrary; the back or undersurface.—*a.* Turned backward; opposite.
Reversible, rē-vėrs'i-bl, *a.* That may be reversed, turned outside in, or the like.
Reversion, rē-vėr'shon, *n.* A reverting or returning; succession to an office after the present holder's term; a return towards some ancestral type; return of an estate to the grantor or his heirs.
Reversioner, rē-vėr'shon-ėr, *n.* One who has the reversion of an estate.
Revert, rē-vėrt', *vt.* To reverse.—*vi.* To return to a former position, habit, statement, &c.; to return to the donor.
Revertible, rē-vėrt'i-bl, *a.* That may revert, as an estate.
Revet, rē-vet', *vt.* (revetting, revetted). To face (an embankment) with mason-work, &c.
Revetment, rē-vet'ment, *n.* A facing to a wall or bank; a retaining wall.
Review, rē-vū', *vt.* To view again; to reconsider; to write a critical notice of; to inspect.—*vi.* To write reviews.—*n.* A re-examination; a criticism; a periodical containing criticisms; official inspection of troops.
Reviewer, rē-vū'ėr, *n.* One who writes reviews.
Revile, rē-vīl', *vt.* (reviling, reviled). To vilify; to upbraid; to abuse.
Revisal, rē-vīz'al, *n.* Revision.
Revise, rē-vīz', *vt.* (revising, revised). To go over with care for correction.—*n.* A revision; a second proof-sheet in printing.
Reviser, rē-vīz'ėr, *n.* One who revises.
Revision, rē-vi'zhon, *n.* Act of revising; revisal; what is revised.
Revisit, rē-vi'zit, *vt.* To visit again.
Revival, rē-vīv'al, *n.* Act of reviving; restoration from neglect or depression; religious awakening.
Revive, rē-vīv', *vi.* (reviving, revived). To return to life; to recover new vigour.—*vt.* To bring again to life; to refresh; to bring again into use or notice.
Revivify, rē-viv'i-fī, *vt.* To recall to life.
Revocable, re'vōk-a-bl, *a.* That may be revoked.
Revocation, re-vōk-ā'shon, *n.* Act of revoking; annulment; repeal.
Revoke, rē-vōk', *vt.* (revoking, revoked). To repeal; to annul.—*vi.* In *card playing*, to neglect to follow suit.
Revolt, rē-vōlt', *vi.* To renounce allegiance; to rebel; to be disgusted: with *at.*—*vt.* To shock.—*n.* Rebellion; mutiny.
Revolting, rē-vōlt'ing, *a.* Exciting extreme disgust; shocking.
Revolution, re-vō-lū'shon, *n.* Act of revolving; rotation; a turn; circuit; a cycle of time; a radical change; overthrow of existing political institutions.
Revolutionary, re-vō-lū'shon-a-ri, *a.* Pertaining to or tending to produce a revolution.—*n.* A revolutionist.
Revolutionist, re-vō-lū'shon-ist, *n.* The favourer of revolution.
Revolutionize, re-vō-lū'shon-īz, *vt.* To bring about a complete change in.
Revolve, rē-volv', *vi.* (revolving, revolved). To turn round an axis or centre.—*vt.* To cause to turn round; to consider attentively.
Revolver, rē-volv'ėr, *n.* A pistol having a revolving set of cartridge chambers, so constructed as to discharge several shots in quick succession without being reloaded.
Revue, rē-vū', *n.* A loosely-constructed and spectacular theatrical exhibition, depending on music and scenic and staging effects.
Revulsion, rē-vul'shon, *n.* A violent drawing away; a violent change, especially of feeling.
Reward, rē-ward', *n.* What is given in return for good done; recompense; punishment.—*vt.* To repay; to requite.
Rewrite, rē-rīt', *vt.* To write over again.
Reynard, rē'närd. *See* RENARD.
Rhabdomancy, rab'dō-man-si, *n.* Divination by a rod or wand.
Rhadamanthine, Rhadamantine, rad-a-man'thin, rad-a-man'tin, *a.* Severely or rigorously just.
Rhapsodic, Rhapsodical, rap-sod'ik, rap-sod'ik-al, *a.* Pertaining to rhapsody.
Rhapsodist, rap'sod-ist, *n.* One who writes or sings rhapsodies or extravagant matter.
Rhapsody, rap'so-di, *n.* A short epic poem, or portion of an epic; a confused series of extravagantly enthusiastic statements.
Rhea, rē'a, *n.* A valuable East India fibre used for textile purposes, the produce of a species of nettle.
Rhenish, ren'ish, *a.* Pertaining to the river Rhine.
Rhetoric, re'to-rik, *n.* The art of using language effectively; the art which teaches oratory; eloquence; flashy oratory; declamation.
Rhetorical, re-to'rik-al, *a.* Pertaining to, exhibiting, or involving rhetoric.
Rhetorician, re-to-ri'shan, *n.* One who teaches or is versed in rhetoric; a declaimer.
Rheum, rūm, *n.* A thin serous fluid secreted by the mucous glands, &c.
Rheumatic, rū-mat'ik, *a.* Pertaining to or like rheumatism; subject to rheumatism.
Rheumatism, rū'mat-izm, *n.* A painful disease of the muscles and joints.
Rheumy, rūm'i, *a.* Pertaining to, like, or affected with rheum.
Rhinal, rī'nal, *a.* Pertaining to the nose.

Rhinoceros, ri-nos'e-ros, *n.* A large hoofed animal, allied to the hippopotamus, with one or two horns on the nose.
Rhizome, rī'zōm or riz'om, *n.* A prostrate stem which throws out rootlets.
Rhododendron, rō-dō-den'dron, *n.* An evergreen shrub with large brilliant flowers.
Rhomb, Rhombus, rom, rom'bus, *n.* A quadrilateral whose sides are equal, but the angles not right angles.
Rhombic, rom'bik, *a.* Having the figure of a rhomb.
Rhomboid, rom'boid, *n.* A quadrilateral whose opposite sides only are equal, and whose angles are not right angles.
Rhomboidal, rom-boid'al, *a.* Having the shape of a rhomboid.
Rhubarb, rō'bärb, *n.* A plant of which the leaf-stalks are used in cookery, and the roots of some species in medicine.
Rhyme, Rime, rīm, *n.* A correspondence of sound in the ends of words or verses; a short poem; a word rhyming with another.—*vi.* (rhyming, rhymed). To make verses; to accord in sound.—*vt.* To put into rhyme.
Rhymer, Rhymster, rīm'ėr, rīm'stėr, *n.* One who makes rhymes; a poor poet.
Rhythm, rithm, *n.* Periodical emphasis in verse or music; metrical movement; harmony; rhyme; metre; verse.
Rhythmic, Rhythmical, rith'mik, rith'mik-al, *a.* Pertaining to or having rhythm.
Rib, rib, *n.* One of the curved bones springing from the backbone; something resembling a rib; a long ridge on cloth.—*vt.* (ribbing, ribbed). To furnish with ribs; to inclose with ribs.
Ribald, ri'bald, *n.* A low, lewd fellow.—*a.* Low; obscene.
Ribaldry, ri'bald-ri, *n.* Obscene language; indecency.
Riband, ri'band, *a.* *See* RIBBON.
Ribbon, ri'bon, *n.* A narrow band of silk, satin, &c.
Rice, rīs, *n.* A cereal plant, whose seed forms a light nutritious food.
Rich, rich, *a.* Having abundant possessions; wealthy; costly; valuable; fertile; plentiful; bright; mellow; highly flavoured; highly provocative of amusement.
Riches, rich'ez, *n.* Wealth; opulence; affluence.
Richly, rich'li, *adv.* In a rich manner; abundantly; splendidly; amply.
Richness, rich'nes, *n.* Wealth; fertility; brilliancy; sweetness.
Rick, rik, *n.* A stack or pile of grain or hay.—*vt.* To pile up in ricks, as hay.
Rickets, rik'ets, *n.pl.* A disease of children in which there is usually some distortion of the bones.
Rickety, rik'et-i, *a.* Affected with rickets; feeble; shaky.
Ricochet, rik'o-shet, *n.* A rebounding from a flat, horizontal surface.—*vt.* and *i.* rik-o-shet'. To operate upon by ricochet firing; to rebound.
Rid, rid, *vt.* (ridding, rid). To make free; to clear; to disencumber.—*a.* Free; clear.
Riddance, rid'ans, *n.* Act of ridding; disencumbrance.
Riddle, rid'l, *n.* A puzzling question; an enigma; a coarse sieve.—*vt.* (riddling, riddled). To solve; to sift; to make many holes in.
Riddlings, rid'lingz, *n.pl.* That which is separated out by riddling.
Ride, rīd, *vi.* (riding, pret. rode, pp. ridden). To be borne on horseback, in a vehicle, &c.; to have ability as an equestrian; to be at anchor.—*vt.* To sit on, so as to be carried; to go over in riding; to domineer over.—*n.* An excursion on horseback, or in a vehicle; a road for the amusement of riding.
Rider, rīd'ėr, *n.* One who rides; one who manages a horse; a supplement or amendment; subsidiary problem.
Ridge rij, *n.* A long narrow prominence; strip thrown up by a plough; a long crest of hills; upper angle of a roof.—*vt.* (ridging, ridged). To form into ridges.
Ridicule, ri'di-kūl, *n.* Laughter with contempt; mockery; satire.—*vt.* To treat with ridicule; to make sport of.
Ridiculous, ri-dik'ū-lus, *a.* Worthy of or fitted to excite ridicule; droll; absurd.
Riding, rī'ding, *n.* One of the three great divisions of Yorkshire.
Riding, rīd'ing, *p.a.* Used in riding; pertaining to riding.
Riding-habit, rīd'ing-ha-bit, *n.* A garment worn by ladies on horseback.
Rifacimento, rē-fä'chē-men''tō, *n.*; pl. **-ti.** A recasting of a literary work.
Rife, rīf, *a.* Abundant; prevalent; replete.
Riffraff, rif'raf, *n.* Refuse; the rabble.
Rifle, rī'fl, *n.* A gun the inside of whose barrel is grooved; *pl.* a body of troops with rifles.—*vt.* (rifling, rifled). To groove spirally the bore of; to rob; to plunder.
Rifleman, rī'fl-man, *n.* One of a body of troops armed with rifles.
Rift, rift, *n.* An opening; a cleft; a fissure.—*vt.* and *i.* To cleave; to split.
Rig, rig, *vt.* (rigging, rigged). To clothe; to accoutre; to fit with tackling.—*n.* Dress; style of the sails and masts of a ship.
Rigadoon, rig-a-dön', *n.* A gay brisk dance performed by one couple.
Rigger, rig'ėr, *n.* One whose occupation is to fit up the rigging of a ship.
Rigging, rig'ing, *n.* The ropes which support the masts, extend the sails, &c., of a ship.
Right, rīt, *a.* Straight; upright; just; suitable; proper; real; correct; belonging to that side of the body farther from the heart; to be worn outward; perpendicular; formed by one line perpendicular to another.—*adv.* Justly; correctly; very; directly; to the right hand.—*n.* What is right; rectitude; a just claim; authority; side opposite to the left.—*vt.* To put right; to do justice to; to restore to an upright position.—*vi.* To resume a vertical position.
Righteous, rīt'yus, *a.* Upright; pious; just; honest; virtuous; equitable.
Righteously, rīt'yus-li, *a.* Uprightly.
Righteousness, rīt'yus-nes, *n.* Integrity; purity of heart and rectitude of life; justice.
Rightful, rīt'fụl, *a.* Having a just or legal claim; just; lawful.
Right-hand, rīt'hand, *a.* Belonging to or on the side next the right hand; essentially needful or serviceable.
Right-handed, rīt'hand-ed, *a.* Using the right hand more easily than the left.
Rightly, rīt'li, *adv.* In a right manner; properly; fitly; justly; correctly.

Rigid, ri'jid, *a.* Stiff; unyielding; not pliant; strict; stern; rigorous.
Rigidity, ri-jid'i-ti, *n.* State or quality of being rigid; stiffness; severity; harshness.
Rigidly, ri'jid-li, *adv.* Stiffly; strictly.
Rigmarole, rig'ma-rōl, *n.* A succession of confused statements.
Rigor, rī'gor, *n.* A sudden coldness attended by shivering.
Rigorous, rig'or-us, *a.* Characterized by rigour; severe; stringent.
Rigorously, rig'or-us-li, *adv.* Strictly; rigidly.
Rigour, rig'or, *n.* Stiffness; strictness; austerity; severity; intense cold.
Rilievo, rē-lē-ā'vō, *n.* Relief, in *carving*, &c.
Rill, ril, *n.* A small brook.
Rim, rim, *n.* The border or edge of a thing; brim.—*vt.* (rimming, rimmed). To put a rim round.
Rime, rīm, *n.* White or hoar frost; a chink; rhyme.
Rimose, Rimous, rī'mōs, rī'mus, *a.* Full of chinks and fissures.
Rimple, rim'pl, *n.* Rumple.
Rimy, rīm'i, *a.* Abounding with rime; frosty.
Rind, rīnd, *n.* The outward coat of trees, fruits, &c.; bark; peel.
Rinderpest, rin'dėr-pest, *n.* A virulent contagious disease affecting cattle.
Ring, ring, *n.* Anything in the form of a circle; a circle of gold, &c., worn on the finger; an area in which games, &c., are performed; a group of persons; sound of a bell; a metallic sound.—*vt.* To encircle; to cause to sound; to repeat often or loudly.—*vi.* To sound; to resound; to tingle.
Ringleader, ring'lēd-ėr, *n.* The leader of a circle of persons engaged in any evil course.
Ringlet, ring'let, *n.* A small ring; a curl.
Ringworm, ring'wėrm, *n.* A contagious skin disease forming discoloured rings.
Rink, ringk, *n.* A portion of a sheet of ice marked off for curling; a smooth flooring for skating on with roller-skates.
Rinse, rins, *vt.* (rinsing, rinsed). To wash by laving water over; to cleanse the interior by the introduction of any liquid.
Riot, rī'ot, *n.* An uproar; a tumult; wild and loose festivity; revelry.—*vi.* To engage in a riot; to revel.
Rioter, rī'ot-ėr, *n.* One who engages in a riot.
Riotous, rī'ot-us, *a.* Indulging in riot or revelry; tumultuous; seditious; excessive.
Rip, rip, *vt.* (ripping, ripped). To tear or cut open; to take out by cutting or tearing.—*n.* A rent; a scamp.
Riparian, rī-pā'ri-an, *a.* Pertaining to the bank of a river.
Ripe, rīp, *a.* Brought to perfection in growth; mature; complete; ready for action or effect. —*vt.* and *i.* (riping, riped). To mature.
Ripen, rīp'n, *vi.* To grow or become ripe; to become ready.—*vt.* To mature.
Ripple, rip'l, *vi.* (rippling, rippled). To show a ruffled surface, as water; to make a gentle sound, as running water.—*vt.* To clean the seeds from, as flax.—*n.* A ruffle of the surface of water; a comb for separating the seeds from flax.
Rise, rīz, *vi.* (rising, pret. rose, pp. risen). To pass to a higher position; to stand up; to bring a session to an end; to arise; to swell by fermentation; to slope upwards; to become apparent; to come into existence; to rebel.—*n.* Act of rising; ascent; elevation; origin; beginning; appearance above the horizon; increase; advance.
Risible, ri'zi-bl, *a.* Having the faculty of laughing; ludicrous; ridiculous.
Rising, rīz'ing, *p.a.* Increasing in power, &c.; advancing to adult years.—*n.* Act of one who or that which rises; appearance above the horizon; resurrection; an insurrection; a prominence.
Risk, risk, *n.* Hazard; peril; jeopardy.—*vt.* To hazard; to dare to undertake.
Risky, risk'i, *a.* Dangerous; full of risk.
Rissole, ris'ōl, *n.* A dish of minced meat or fish covered with a paste and fried.
Rite, rīt, *n.* A formal act of religion, &c.; form; ceremony; observance; usage.
Ritual, rit'ū-al, *a.* Pertaining to rites.—*n.* A book containing the rites of a church; a system of rights; ceremonial.
Ritualism, rit'ū-al-izm, *n.* Observance of prescribed forms in religion.
Ritualist, rit'ū-al-ist, *n.* One skilled in ritual; one who favours an elaborate ritual.
Rivage, riv'āj, *n.* A bank, shore.
Rival, rī'val, *n.* One who pursues the same object as another; a competitor.—*a.* Having the same pretensions or claims; competing.—*vt.* (rivalling, rivalled). To strive to excel; to compete with.
Rivalry, rī'val-ri, *n.* Act of rivalling; competition; emulation.
Rive, rīv, *vt.* and *i.* (riving, rived, pp. rived and riven). To tear or rend; to split; to cleave.
Rivel, riv'l, *vt.* and *i.* (rivelling, rivelled). To wrinkle; to corrugate.
River, ri'vėr, *n.* A large stream of water on land; a copious flow; abundance.
Rivet, ri'vet, *n.* A metallic bolt whose end is hammered broad after insertion.—*vt.* (riveting, riveted). To fasten with rivets; to clinch; to make firm.
Riveter, ri'vet-ėr, *n.* One who rivets; a workman employed in fixing rivets.
Rivulet, ri'vū-let, *n.* A small stream.
Roach, rōch, *n.* A fresh-water fish of the carp family.
Road, rōd, *n.* An open way or public passage; a highway; a means of approach; a roadstead (usually in *plural*).
Road-book, rōd'bu̇k, *n.* A traveller's guide-book of towns, distances, &c.
Road-metal, rōd'me-tal, *n.* Broken stones used for macadamizing.
Roadstead, rōd'sted, *n.* A place where ships may ride at anchor off a shore.
Roadster, rōd'stėr, *n.* A horse well fitted for the road or employed in travelling.
Roadway, rōd'wā, *n.* The part of a road travelled by horses and carriages; highway.
Roam, rōm, *vi.* To wander; to rove; to ramble.
Roan, rōn, *a.* Of a mixed colour with a shade of red predominant.—*n.* A roan colour, or horse of this colour; a leather prepared from sheep-skin.
Roar, rōr, *vi.* To cry with a full, loud sound; to bellow; to bawl or squall.—*vt.* To cry out aloud.—*n.* A full, loud sound of some continuance; cry of a beast.
Roaring, rōr'ing, *n.* Loud, continued sound;

a bronchial disease in horses.—*a.* Characterized by noise; disorderly; very brisk.
Roast, rōst, *vt.* To cook by exposure to a fire; to parch by heat; to banter severely.—*vi.* To become roasted.—*n.* Roasted meat; part selected for roasting.—*a.* Roasted.
Roasting-jack, rōst'ing-jak, *n.* An apparatus for turning meat roasting before a fire.
Rob, rob, *vt.* (robbing, robbed). To strip unlawfully and by force; to deprive by stealing; to deprive.
Robber, rob'ėr, *n.* One who robs.
Robbery, rob'ėr-i, *n.* Act or practice of robbing; theft.
Robe, rōb, *n.* A gown, or long, loose garment, worn over other dress; an elegant dress.—*vt.* (robing, robed). To put a robe upon; to invest.
Robin, rob'in, *n.* The European bird called also redbreast.
Roborant, rob'o-rant, *a.* Strengthening.—*n.* A tonic.
Robot, rōb'ot, *n.* Any mechanical contrivance designed to perform work normally requiring the exercise of human intelligence.
Robust, rō-bust', *a.* Sturdy; vigorous; muscular.
Rocambole, rok'am-bōl, *n.* A kind of garlic.
Rochet, roch'et, *n.* A sort of short surplice, with tight sleeves, worn by bishops.
Rock, rok, *vt.* To move backwards and forwards without displacing; to swing.—*vi.* To sway; to reel.—*n.* A large mass of stone; defence; source of peril or disaster; a kind of solid sweetmeat.
Rock-crystal, rok'kris-tal, *n.* Crystallized quartz.
Rocker, rok'ėr, *n.* One who rocks; a curving piece on which a cradle, &c., rocks; a trough for washing ore by agitation.
Rockery, rok'ėr-i, *n.* An ornamented mound formed of fragments of rock, for ferns, &c.
Rocket, rok'et, *n.* A projectile firework; a similar device used as a lethal weapon; a garden plant.
Rocking-horse, rok'ing-hors, *n.* A wooden horse mounted on rockers; a hobby-horse.
Rocking-stone, rok'ing-stōn, *n.* A large stone so poised as to oscillate readily.
Rock-oil, rok'oil, *n.* Petroleum.
Rock-salt, rok'sạlt, *n.* Mineral salt; common salt found in masses in the earth.
Rocky, rok'i, *a.* Full of rocks; resembling a rock; stony; obdurate.
Rococo, ro-kō'kō, *n.* and *a.* A meaninglessly decorative style of ornamentation of the time of Louis XIV and XV.
Rod, rod, *n.* A straight slender stick; a badge of office; an enchanter's wand; a fishing-rod; a measure of 5½ lineal yards.
Rodent, rō'dent, *a.* Gnawing; belonging to the gnawing animals (Rodentia).—*n.* An animal that gnaws, as the squirrel.
Rodeo, rōd-ā'o, *n.* A public exhibition of horse-breaking, lariat-throwing, &c.
Rodomontade, rod'ō-mon-tād", *n.* Vain boasting; empty bluster; rant.
Roe, rō, *n.* The spawn of fishes; female of the hart.
Roebuck, Roe-deer, rō'buk, rō'dēr, *n.* A small species of European deer of elegant shape and remarkably nimble.
Rogation, rō-gā'shon, *n.* A supplication; the litany.
Rogue, rōg, *n.* A knave; a wag; a sly fellow.
Roguery, rōg'ėr-i, *n.* Knavish tricks; fraud; waggery; mischievousness.
Roguish, rōg'ish, *a.* Pertaining to or like a rogue; knavish; waggish.
Roil, roil, *vt.* To render turbid by stirring.
Roister, rois'tėr, *vi.* To bluster; to swagger.
Roisterer, rois'tėr-ėr, *n.* A blustering or turbulent fellow.
Rôle, rōl, *n.* A part represented by an actor; any conspicuous part or function.
Roll, rōl, *vt.* To turn on its surface; to wrap on itself by turning; to involve in a bandage or the like; to press with a roller.—*vi.* To turn over and over; to run on wheels; to be tossed about; to sound with a deep prolonged sound.—*n.* Act of rolling; something rolled up; an official document; a catalogue; a cake of bread; a roller; a prolonged deep sound.
Roll-call, rōl'kạl, *n.* The calling over a list of names, as of soldiers.
Roller, rōl'ėr, *n.* One who or that which rolls; a cylinder for smoothing, crushing, &c.; that on which something may be rolled up; a long, heavy, swelling wave.
Roller-skate, rōl'ėr-skāt, *n.* A skate mounted on small wheels or rollers.
Rollick, rol'ik, *vi.* To move with a careless swagger; to be jovial.
Rolling, rōl'ing, *p.a.* Revolving; making a continuous noise; undulating.
Rolling-pin, rōl'ing-pin, *n.* A round piece of wood with which dough is rolled out.
Rolling-stock, rōl'ing-stok, *n.* The carriages, vans, engines, &c., of a railway.
Rollock, rol'ok, *n.* Same as *Rowlock*.
Roly-poly, rō'li-pō-li, *n.* Paste spread with jam and rolled into a pudding.
Romaic, rō-mā'ik, *n.* and *a.* The vernacular language of modern Greece.
Roman, rō'man, *a.* Pertaining to Rome or its people and to the Roman Catholic religion; applied to the common upright letter in printing.
Romance, rō-mans', *n.* A tale in verse in a Romance dialect; a popular epic or tale in prose or verse of some length; a tale of extraordinary adventures; tendency to the wonderful or mysterious; a fiction.—*a.* (with *cap.*). A term applied to the languages sprung from the Latin.—*vi.* To tell fictitious stories.
Romancer, rō-mans'ėr, *n.* One who romances; a writer of romance.
Romancist, rō-mans'ist, *n.* A romancer.
Romanesque, rō-man-esk', *a.* and *n.* Applied to the debased style of architecture that prevailed in later Roman Empire.
Romanism, rō'man-izm, *n.* The tenets of the Church of Rome.
Romanist, rō'man-ist, *n.* A Roman Catholic.
Romantic, rō-man'tik, *a.* Pertaining to romance; fanciful; extravagant; wildly picturesque.
Romanticism, rō-man'ti-sizm, *n.* State or quality of being romantic; a reaction in literature or art from classical to mediæval or modern qualities; romantic feeling.
Romanticist, rō-man'ti-sist, *n.* One imbued with romanticism.
Romany, Rommany, rom'a-ni, *n.* A Gipsy; the language spoken by the Gipsies.
Romish, rōm'ish, *a.* Belonging to the Roman Catholic Church (used somewhat slightingly).

Romp, romp, *n.* Rude play or frolic; a boisterous girl.—*vi.* To play boisterously; to frisk about.
Rompish, romp'ish, *a.* Inclined to romp.
Rondeau, ron'dō, *n.* A poem of thirteen lines, with two rhymes, and a refrain occurring twice; a piece of three strains.
Rondel, ron'del, *n.* A poem like the rondeau.
Ronion, Ronyon, ron'yon, *n.* A mangy, scabby animal; a drab.
Rood, röd, *n.* A cross or crucifix; the fourth part of an acre; a measure of 5½ lineal yards.
Roof, röf, *n.* The cover of any building; a canopy; the palate; a house.—*vi.* To cover with a roof; to shelter.
Roofing, röf'ing, *n.* Act of covering with a roof; materials of a roof; the roof itself.
Roof-spotter, röf-spot'ėr, *n.* Person stationed on the roof of a building to watch local developments in an air-raid.
Roof-tree, röf'trē, *n.* A main beam in a roof.
Rook, ruk, *n.* A kind of crow; a cheat; a piece in chess.—*vi.* and *t.* To cheat; to rob.
Rookery, ruk'ėr-i, *n.* A grove used for nesting-places by rooks; a resort of thieves, &c.
Rooky, ruk'i, *a.* Inhabited by rooks.
Room, röm, *n.* Space; scope; opportunity; stead; apartment in a house; chamber.
Roomy, röm'i, *a.* Spacious; wide; large.
Roost, röst, *n.* The pole on which birds rest at night; a collection of fowls resting together.—*vi.* To occupy a roost; to settle.
Rooster, röst'ėr, *n.* The male of the domestic fowl; a cock: used in America.
Root, röt, *n.* That part of a plant which fixes itself in the earth; lower part of anything; origin; a form from which words are derived. —*vi.* To fix the root; to be firmly fixed.—*vt.* To plant deeply; to impress durably; to tear up or out; to eradicate.
Rooted, röt'ed, *a.* Fixed; deep; radical.
Rootlet, röt'let, *n.* A little root.
Rooty, röt'i, *a.* Full of roots.
Rope, rōp, *n.* A cord or line of some thickness; a row or string of things united.—*vi.* (roping, roped). To draw out in threads.—*vt.* To pull by a rope; to fasten or inclose with a rope.
Ropery, rōp'ėr-i, *n.* A place where ropes are made.
Ropy, rōp'i, *a.* Stringy; viscous; glutinous.
Rorqual, ror'kwal, *n.* A large whale of several species.
Rosaceous, rōz-ā'shus, *a.* Rose-like; relating to roses.
Rosary, rōz'a-ri, *n.* A garland of roses; an anthology; a string of beads on which R. Catholics number their prayers.
Rose, rōz, *n.* A plant and its flower, of many species; an ornamental knot of ribbon; a perforated nozzle of a spout, &c.—*a.* Of a purplish-red colour.
Roseate, rōz'ē-āt, *a.* Rosy; blooming.
Rosemary, rōz'ma-ri, *n.* An evergreen shrub, yielding a fragrant essential oil.
Rosery, rōz'ėr-i, *n.* A place where roses grow; a nursery of rose bushes.
Rosette, rō-zet', *n.* An ornamental knot of ribbons; an architectural ornament.
Rose-water, rōz'wa-tėr, *n.* Water tinctured with roses by distillation.
Rosewood, rōz'wud, *n.* The wood of a tree used in cabinet-work, when freshly cut having a faint smell of roses.
Rosin, ro'zin, *n.* The resin left after distilling off the volatile oil from turpentine; resin in a solid state.—*vt.* To rub with rosin.
Roster, ros'tėr, *n.* A list showing the rotation in which individuals, regiments, &c., are called on to serve.
Rostral, ros'tral, *a.* Resembling the beak of a ship; pertaining to the beak.
Rostrate, ros'trāt, *a.* Beaked.
Rostrum, ros'trum, *n.*; pl. **-tra.** The beak or bill of a bird; the ram of an ancient ship; *pl.* a platform or pulpit.
Rosy, rōz'i, *a.* Like a red rose in colour; blooming; blushing; cheering; hopeful.
Rot, rot, *vi.* (rotting, rotted). To become rotten; to decay.—*vt.* To make rotten.—*n.* Putrid decay; a fatal distemper of sheep; a disease injurious to plants; nonsense.
Rotary, rō'ta-ri, *a.* Turning, as a wheel on its axis.
Rotate, rō'tāt, *vi.* (rotating, rotated). To revolve round a centre or axis, like a wheel; to act in turn.—*vt.* To cause to turn like a wheel.
Rotation, rō-tā'shon, *n.* Act of rotating; the turning of a wheel or solid body on its axis; succession in a series.
Rotatory, rō'ta-to-ri, *a.* Pertaining to, exhibiting, or producing rotation; rotary.
Rote, rōt, *n.* Repetition of words by memory; mere effort of memory.
Rotten, rot'n, *a.* Decomposed; decaying; putrid; unsound; corrupt; fetid.
Rotund, rō-tund', *a.* Round; spherical.
Rotunda, rō-tun'da, *n.* A round building.
Rotundity, rō-tund'i-ti, *n.* Roundness.
Rouble, rö'bl, *n.* The unit of the Russian money system.
Roué, rö-ā, *n.* A man devoted to pleasure and sensuality; a licentious man; a rake.
Rouge, rözh, *n.* A cosmetic to impart ruddiness to the complexion.—*vt.* and *i.* (rouging, rouged). To paint with rouge.
Rouge-et-noir, rözh-e-nwär, *n.* A game at cards.
Rough, ruf, *a.* Not smooth; rugged; boisterous; harsh; rude; cruel; vague; hasty.—*vt.* To make rough; to rough-hew.—**To rough it,** to submit to hardships.—*n.* State of being rough or unfinished; a rowdy.
Rough-cast, ruf'kast, *vt.* To form roughly; to cover with a coarse plaster.—*n.* A first plan or model; a coarse plastering.
Roughen, ruf'n, *vt.* To make rough.—*vi.* To become rough.
Rough-hew, ruf'hū, *vt.* To hew without smoothing; to give the first form to a thing.
Roughly, ruf'li, *adv.* Coarsely; without finish; harshly; approximately.
Rough-rider, ruf'rīd-ėr, *n.* One who breaks horses.
Rough-shod, ruf'shod, *a.* Shod with shoes armed with points.
Roulade, rö-läd, *n.* In *music*, a rapid run of notes, introduced as an embellishment.
Rouleau, rö-lō', *n.*; pl. **-leaus** (-lōz) or **-leaux** (-lōz). A little roll; a roll of coin in paper.
Roulette, rö-let', *n.* A game of chance; an engraver's tool with a toothed wheel.
Round, round, *a.* Circular; spherical; large; open; candid; brisk, as a trot; not minutely accurate, as a number.—*n.* That which is round; rung of a ladder; a circular course or

series; circuit made by one on duty; a vocal composition in parts; ammunition for firing once; a turn or bout.—*vt.* To make round; to encircle; to make full and flowing; to pass round.—*vi.* To become round or full; to make a circuit.—*adv.* In a circle; around; not directly.—*prep.* About; around.

Roundabout, round'a-bout, *a.* Indirect; circuitous.—*n.* A revolving structure on which children ride.

Roundel, roun'del, *n.* Anything round; a rondel or roundelay.

Roundelay, round'ē-lā, *n.* A poem of thirteen verses, eight in one rhyme and five in another; a short and lively rural strain; a rural dance.

Rounder, roun'dėr, *n.* One who rounds; *pl.* a game played with a bat and ball by two sides.

Roundhead, round'hed, *n.* A member of the Puritan or parliamentary party in the English Civil War.

Roundish, round'ish, *a.* Somewhat round.

Roundly, round'li, *adv.* In a round manner; openly; plainly; vigorously.

Round-robin, round-rob'in, *n.* A written petition signed by names in a circle.

Rouse, rouz, *vt.* (rousing, roused). To arouse; to awaken; to stir up.—*vi.* To awake; to arise.—*n.* A carousal; a drinking frolic.

Rousing, rouz'ing, *a.* Having power to rouse or excite; very active or busy.

Rout, rout, *n.* A crowd; a rabble; a fashionable evening assembly; total defeat of troops; confusion of troops defeated.—*vt.* To defeat and throw into confusion; to overthrow; to rouse or drive out.

Route, röt, *n.* A course or way.

Routine, rö-tēn', *n.* A round of business or pleasure; regular course.

Rove, rōv, *vi.* (roving, roved). To move about aimlessly; to roam; to ramble.—*vt.* To wander over; to card into flakes, as wool.

Rover, rōv'ėr, *n.* One who roves; a pirate.

Row, rō, *n.* A series in a line; a rank; a line of houses; an excursion in a boat with oars.—*vt.* To impel by oars, as a boat; to transport by rowing.—*vi.* To work with the oar.

Row, rou, *n.* A noisy disturbance; a riot.—*vt.* To scold.

Rowan, rou'an, *n.* The mountain-ash.

Rowdy, rou'di, *n.* A turbulent fellow; a rough.—*a.* Disreputable; blackguardly.

Rowdyism, rou'di-izm, *n.* The conduct of a rowdy; turbulent blackguardism.

Rowel, rou'el, *n.* The little wheel of a spur, formed with sharp points.

Rowlock, rō'lok, *n.* A contrivance on a boat's gunwale to support the oar.

Royal, roi'al, *a.* Pertaining to a king; regal; kingly; august.—*n.* A large kind of paper; a shoot of a stag's antlers.

Royalist, roi'al-ist, *n.* An adherent to a king or kingly government.

Royally, roi'al-li, *adv.* In a royal or kingly manner; like a king; as becomes a king.

Royalty, roi'al-ti, *n.* State or character of being royal; a royal personage; share paid to a superior, inventor, or author.

Rub, rub, *vt.* (rubbing, rubbed). To move something along the surface of with pressure; to scour; to remove by friction; to chafe.—*vi.* To move along with pressure; to fret.—*n.* Act of rubbing; friction; obstruction; difficulty; a gibe.

Rubber, rub'ėr, *n.* One who rubs; thing used in polishing or cleaning; india-rubber; obstruction or difficulty; contest of three games in whist.

Rubbish, rub'ish, *n.* Refuse; debris; trash.

Rubbishy, rub'ish-i, *a.* Trashy; paltry.

Rubble, rub'l, *n.* Broken stones of irregular shapes; masonry of such stones.

Rubescent, rö-bes'ent, *a.* Becoming red; blushing.

Rubicund, rö'bi-kund, *a.* Red or highly coloured, as the face; ruddy.

Rubigo, rö-bi'gō, *n.* Mildew.

Rubric, rö'brik, *n.* Important words in a manuscript, &c., coloured red; a heading or title; direction in a prayer-book.

Ruby, rö'bi, *n.* A very valuable gem or precious stone of various shades of red; a fine red colour; a blotch on the face; a small printing type.—*vt.* To make red.—*a.* Red.

Ruche, Ruching, rösh, rösh'ing, *n.* Quilled or goffered trimming.

Ruck, ruk, *vt.* To wrinkle; to crease.—*n.* A wrinkle; an undistinguished crowd; those of no special merit.

Rucksack, ruk'sak, *n.* A bag made to strap on the shoulders, and used by walkers, climbers, &c.

Rud, Rudd, rud, *n.* Red ochre.

Rudd, rud, *n.* A fresh-water fish.

Rudder, rud'ėr, *n.* The instrument by which a ship is steered.

Ruddle, rud'l, *n.* A species of red earth, used for marking sheep.—*vt.* (ruddling, ruddled). To mark with ruddle.

Ruddoc, Ruddock, rud'ok, *n.* The robin-redbreast.

Ruddy, rud'i, *a.* Of a red colour; reddish; of a lively flesh colour.—*vt.* (ruddying, ruddied). To make red or ruddy.

Rude, röd, *a.* Unformed by art or skill; rough; uncivilized; uncivil; impudent; violent.

Rudely, röd'li, *adv.* In a rude manner; violently; coarsely; unskilfully.

Rudiment, rö'di-ment, *n.* The original of anything; a first principle; an undeveloped organ; *pl.* first elements of a science or art.

Rudimentary, rö-di-ment'a-ri, *a.* Pertaining to rudiments; consisting in first principles; initial; in an undeveloped state.

Rue, rö, *vt.* (ruing, rued). To repent of; to regret.—*vi.* To become sorrowful or repentant.—*n.* An acrid ill-smelling plant.

Rueful, rö'ful, *a.* Woeful; mournful; piteous; expressing or suggesting sorrow.

Ruff, ruf, *n.* A plaited collar or frill; a ruffle; act of trumping at cards.—*vt.* To trump instead of following suit at cards.

Ruffian, ruf'i-an, *n.* A boisterous brutal fellow.—*a.* Like a ruffian; brutal.

Ruffianism, ruf'i-an-izm, *n.* The character or conduct of a ruffian.

Ruffianly, ruf'i-an-li, *a.* Like a ruffian: violent.

Ruffle, ruf'l, *vt.* (ruffling, ruffled). To rumple; to derange; to disturb.—*vi.* To bluster.—*n.* A plaited cambric, &c., attached to one's dress; frill; state of being agitated; low vibrating beat of a drum.

Rufous, rö'fus, *a.* Reddish; of a dull or brownish red.

Rug, rug, *n.* A heavy fabric used to cover a bed, protect a carpet, &c.; a mat.

Ruga, rö'ga, *n.*; pl. -æ. A wrinkle.
Rugby, rug'bi, *n.* One of the two principal varieties of football, played by fifteen men a side, with an oval ball, handling being permitted.
Rugged, rug'ed, *a.* Full of rough projections; rough; harsh; crabbed.
Rugose, Rugous, rö'gōs, rö'gus, *a.* Wrinkled.
Ruin, rö'in, *n.* Destruction; fall; overthrow; anything in a state of decay; that which destroys; *pl.* remains of a city, house, &c.; state of being destroyed.—*vt.* To bring to ruin; to destroy; to impoverish.
Ruinate, rö'i-nāt, *vt.* To ruin.—*a.* In ruins.
Ruination, rö-i-nā'shon, *n.* Act of ruinating; overthrow; demolition.
Ruinous, rö'in-us, *a.* Fallen to ruin; dilapidated; destructive; baneful.
Rule, röl, *n.* A ruler or measure; a guiding principle or formula; a precept, law, maxim; government; control; regulation; order; method.—*vt.* (ruling, ruled). To govern; to manage; to decide; to mark with lines by a ruler.—*vi.* To exercise supreme authority; to maintain a level, as the market price; to settle, as a rule of court.
Ruler, röl'ėr, *n.* One who rules or governs; an instrument by which lines are drawn.
Ruling, röl'ing, *a.* Having control; reigning; predominant.—*n.* A point settled by a judge, chairman, &c.
Rum, rum, *n.* Spirit distilled from cane-juice or molasses.—*a.* Odd; queer.
Rumble, rum'bl, *vi.* (rumbling, rumbled). To make a dull, continued sound.—*n.* A low, heavy, continued sound; a seat for servants behind a carriage.
Ruminant, rö'min-ant, *a.* Chewing the cud. —*n.* An animal that chews the cud; a hoofed ruminating animal.
Ruminate, rö'min-āt, *vi.* To chew the cud; to meditate.—*vt.* To meditate on.
Rumination, rö-min-ā'shon, *n.* Act of ruminating; meditation or reflection.
Rummage, rum'āj, *vt.* (rummaging, rummaged). To search narrowly but roughly; to ransack.—*n.* A careful search; turning about of things.
Rummer, rum'ėr, *n.* A large drinking-glass.
Rummy, rum'i, *a.* Pertaining to rum.
Rumour, rö'mėr, *n.* A current story; a mere report.—*vt.* To report; to spread abroad.
Rump, rump, *n.* End of an animal's backbone; buttocks; fag-end of something.
Rumple, rum'pl, *vt.* (rumpling, rumpled). To wrinkle; to ruffle.—*n.* A fold or plait.
Rumpus, rum'pus, *n.* A great noise; disturbance.
Run, run, *vi.* (running, pret. ran, pp. run). To move by using the legs more quickly than in walking; to take part in a race; to flee; to spread; to ply; to move or pass; to become fluid; to continue in operation; to have a certain direction; to have a certain purport; to be current; to continue in time.—*vt.* To cause to run; to pursue, as a course; to incur; to break through (a blockade); to smuggle; to pierce; to melt; to carry on.—*n.* Act of running; course or distance run; a trip; course, tenor, &c.; general demand, as on a bank; place where animals may run; generality.
Runagate, run'a-gāt, *n.* A fugitive; vagabond; renegade.
Runaway, run'a-wā, *n.* One who flies from danger or restraint; deserter; fugitive.—*a.* Effected by running away or eloping.
Rune, rön, *n.* One of a set of alphabetic characters peculiar to the ancient northern nations of Europe.
Rung, rung, *n.* A heavy staff; the round or step of a ladder.
Runic, rön'ik, *a.* Pertaining to runes.
Runlet, Rundlet, run'let, rund'let, *n.* A small barrel of no certain capacity.
Runnel, run'l, *n.* A rivulet or small brook.
Runner, run'ėr, *n.* One who runs; a messenger; a bird of the order Cursores; a stem running along the ground and taking root; that on which something runs or slides.
Running, run'ing, *a.* Kept for the race; continuous; in succession; discharging pus.
Runt, runt, *n.* A dwarfed animal; a variety of pigeon; stalk of a cabbage.
Rupee, rö-pē', *n.* A silver coin, the unit of value in India: nominally worth 1*s.* 4*d.*
Rupture, rup'tūr, *n.* Act of breaking or bursting; fracture; breach; open hostility; hernia. —*vt.* (rupturing, ruptured). To cause a rupture in; to break.
Rural, rö'ral, *a.* Pertaining to the country; rustic.
Ruse, röz, *n.* Artifice; trick; deceit.
Rush, rush, *vi.* To move with great speed; to enter over-hastily.—*n.* A violent motion or course; an eager demand; a plant found in damp places; a reed.
Rushen, rush'n, *a.* Made of rushes.
Rushy, rush'i, *a.* Abounding with rushes; made of rushes.
Rusk, rusk, *n.* A light hard cake browned in the oven.
Russet, rus'et, *a.* Of a reddish-brown colour; coarse; homespun; rustic.—*n.* A reddish-brown colour; coarse country cloth; a kind of winter apple.
Russian, ru'shi-an, *a.* Pertaining to Russia.—*n.* A native of Russia; the language of Russia.
Rust, rust, *n.* The red coating formed on iron exposed to moisture; a parasitic fungus; loss of power by inactivity.—*vi.* To contract rust; to degenerate in idleness.—*vt.* To make rusty.
Rustic, rus'tik, *a.* Pertaining to the country; rural; homely; unpolished.—*n.* A countryman, a peasant; a clown.
Rusticate, rus'ti-kāt, *vi.* To dwell in the country.—*vt.* To banish from a university for a time.
Rustication, rus-ti-kā'shon, *n.* Act of rusticating; state of being rusticated.
Rusticity, rus-tis'i-ti, *n.* State or quality of being rustic; simplicity; artlessness.
Rustle, rus'l, *vi.* and *t.* (rustling, rustled). To make the noise of things agitated, as straw, leaves, &c.—*n.* The noise of things that rustle; a slight sibilant sound.
Rusty, rust'i, *a.* Covered with rust; impaired by inaction; rough; grating.
Rut, rut, *n.* The track of a wheel; a line cut with a spade; line of routine; time during which certain animals are under sexual excitement.—*vt.* (rutting, rutted). To cut in ruts. —*vi.* To be in heat, as deer.
Ruth, röth, *n.* Mercy; pity: *poetical.*
Ruthenium, rö-thē'ni-um, *n.* A rare metal occurring in platinum ore.
Ruthful, röth'ful, *a.* Rueful; merciful.

Ruthless, röth'les, *a.* Cruel; pitiless.
Ruttish, rut'ish, *a.* Lustful.
Rutty, rut'i, *a.* Full of ruts.
Rye, rī, *n.* A cereal plant and its seed.
Rye-grass, rī'gräs, *n.* A kind of grass much cultivated for cattle and horses.
Ryot, rī'ot, *n.* A Hindu cultivator of the soil.

S

Sabaism, sa-bā'izm, *n.* The worship of the heavenly bodies.
Sabaoth, sa-bā'oth, *n.* Armies; hosts.
Sabbatarian, sa-ba-tā'ri-an, *n.* A strict observer of the Sabbath.—*a.* Pertaining to the Sabbath.
Sabbath, sa'bath, *n.* The day of rest; Sunday.
Sabbatic, Sabbatical, sa-bat'ik, sa-bat'ik-al, *a.* Pertaining to the Sabbath; pertaining to a recurrence by sevens.
Sable, sā'bl, *n.* A small animal of the weasel family; the fur of the sable; black.—*a.* Black; dark.
Sabot, sä-bō', *n.* A wooden shoe worn by continental peasants.
Sabotage, sä-bō-täzh, *n.* Malicious destruction of employers' property or national plant by employees on strike or during war-time.
Sabre, sā'bėr, *n.* A sword with one edge; a cavalry sword.—*vt.* (sabring, sabred). To strike or kill with a sabre.
Sabretache, Sabretash, sā'bėr-tash, *n.* A leathern pocket worn by cavalry, suspended from the sword-belt.
Sac, sak, *n.* A bag; receptacle for a liquid.
Saccharin, sak'a-rin, *n.* A substance of great sweetness obtained from coal-tar.
Saccharine, sak'ka-rīn, *a.* Pertaining to or of the nature of sugar; sugary.
Saccharose, sak'a-rōs, *n.* A chemical name for pure or crystalline sugar.
Sacerdotal, sa-sėr-dōt'al, *a.* Pertaining to priests or the priesthood; priestly.
Sachem, sā'chem, *n.* A chief among some of the American Indian tribes.
Sachet, sä-shā, *n.* A small bag for odorous substances.
Sack, sak, *n.* A bag for flour, wool, &c.; that which a sack holds; a sort of jacket; a dry wine; pillage of a town.—*vt.* To put in sacks; to pillage, as a town.
Sackbut, sak'but, *n.* A musical instrument of the trumpet or trombone kind.
Sackcloth, sak'kloth, *n.* Cloth of which sacks are made.
Sacking, sak'ing, *n.* The material of which sacks are made, a cloth of flax or hemp.
Sacque, sak, *n.* A loose gown.
Sacral, sā'kral, *a.* Pertaining to the sacrum.
Sacrament, sa'kra-ment, *n.* A solemn religious ordinance observed by Christians, as baptism or the Lord's Supper.
Sacramental, sa-kra-ment'al, *a.* Constituting or pertaining to a sacrament.
Sacred, sā'kred, *a.* Set apart for a holy purpose; consecrated; religious; set apart to some one in honour; venerable.
Sacredly, sā'kred-li, *adv.* In a sacred manner; religiously; inviolably; strictly.
Sacrifice, sa'kri-fis, *n.* The offering of anything to God; anything offered to a divinity; surrender made in order to gain something else.—*vt.* (sacrificing, sacrificed). To make an offering or sacrifice of.—*vi.* To offer up a sacrifice to some deity.
Sacrificial, sa-kri-fi'shal, *a.* Pertaining to sacrifice; performing sacrifices.
Sacrilege, sa'kri-lej, *n.* Violation of sacred things.
Sacrilegious, sa-kri-lē'jus, *a.* Relating to or implying sacrilege; profane; impious.
Sacring, sā'kring, *n.* Consecration.
Sacrist, sā'krist, *n.* A sacristan.
Sacristan, sa'krist-an, *n.* A church officer who has the care of the sacred utensils.
Sacristy, sa'krist-i, *n.* An apartment in a church where the sacred utensils, vestments, &c., are kept; the vestry.
Sacrosanct, sa'krō-sangt, *a.* Sacred and inviolable; holy and venerable.
Sacrum, sā'krum, *n.* The bone forming the lower extremity of the vertebral column.
Sad, sad, *a.* Sorrowful; affected with grief; gloomy; distressing; calamitous.
Sadden, sad'n, *vt.* To make sad.—*vi.* To become sad.
Saddle, sad'l, *n.* A seat for a rider on a horse's back; something like a saddle in shape or use.—*vt.* (saddling, saddled). To put a saddle on; to burden.
Saddle-bow, sad'l-bō, *n.* The upper front part of a saddle; a pommel.
Saddle-cloth, sad'l-kloth, *n.* A cloth to be placed under a saddle; a housing.
Saddler, sad'lėr, *n.* One whose occupation is to make saddles or harness in general.
Saddlery, sad'lėr-i, *n.* The articles sold by a saddler; the trade of a saddler.
Sadducee, sad'ū-sē, *n.* One of a sect among the Jews who denied the resurrection and the existence of angels or spirits.
Sadism, säd'ism, *n.* A form of sexual perversion, in which pleasure is taken in the cruel treatment of the companion.
Safe, sāf, *a.* Secure; free from danger; unharmed; no longer dangerous; trustworthy.—*n.* A strong box or chamber for securing valuables; a cool receptacle for meat.
Safeguard, sāf'gärd, *n.* One who or that which guards; a defence; protection; a passport.—*vt.* To guard.
Safely, sāf'li, *adv.* In a safe manner; without injury; securely.
Safety, sāf'ti, *n.* State of being safe; freedom from danger, hurt, or loss.
Safety-lamp, sāf'ti-lamp, *n.* A miner's lamp which will not set fire to inflammable gases.
Safety-match, sāf'ti-mach, *n.* A match which lights only on a special substance.
Safety-valve, sāf'ti-valv, *n.* A valve on a boiler, which lets the steam escape when the pressure becomes too great.
Saffron, saf'ron, *n.* A bulbous plant allied to the crocus, with flowers of a rich orange colour.—*a.* Of a deep yellow.
Sag, sag, *vi.* (sagging, sagged). To sink in the middle; to yield under care, difficulties, &c.
Saga, sä'ga, *n.* An ancient Scandinavian legend of some length.
Sagacious, sa-gā'shus, *a.* Quick of perception; shrewd; sage.
Sagaciously, sa-gā'shus-li, *adv.* With discernment or penetration.

Sagacity, sa-gas'i-ti, *n.* Quickness of discernment; shrewdness; high intelligence.
Sage, sāj, *a.* Wise; sagacious; well-judged; grave.—*n.* A wise man; a man venerable for years, and of sound judgment; a labiate plant.
Sagely, sāj'li, *adv.* Wisely; sapiently.
Sagittal, sa'ji-tal, *a.* Pertaining to an arrow; resembling an arrow.
Sagittarius, sa-ji-tā'ri-us, *n.* The archer, a sign of the zodiac.
Sagittate, sa'ji-tāt, *a.* Shaped like the head of an arrow.
Sago, sā'gō, *n.* A starchy substance much used as food, prepared from the pith of several species of palms.
Sahib, sä'ib, *n.* An Eastern term of respect, much the same as " Sir " or " Mr."
Sail, sāl, *n.* A piece of cloth to catch the wind and so move a ship; a ship; a passage in a ship.—*vi.* To be carried over the water by sails or steam, &c.; to begin a voyage; to glide.—*vt.* To pass over by means of sails; to navigate.
Sail-cloth, sāl'kloth, *n.* Canvas used in making sails for ships.
Sailer, sāl'ėr, *n.* One who sails; a ship, with reference to her speed.
Sailing, sāl'ing, *p.a.* Moved by sails and not by steam.—*n.* Act of setting sail; art or rules of navigation.
Sailor, sāl'or, *n.* A seaman; a mariner.
Sainfoin, Saintfoin, sān'foin, sānt'foin, *n.* A leguminous plant used as fodder.
Saint, sānt, *n.* One eminent for piety and virtue; one of the blessed; a person canonized —*vt.* To canonize.
Sainted, sānt'ed, *a.* Holy; sacred; canonized; gone to heaven; dead.
Saintly, sānt'li, *a.* Like a saint.
Sake, sāk, *n.* Cause; purpose; regard.
Saker, sā'kėr, *n.* A species of hawk or falcon; an ancient small piece of artillery.
Sal, sal, *n.* Salt.
Sal, säl, *n.* A valuable timber tree of India.
Salaam, sa-läm', *n.* A ceremonious salutation or obeisance among orientals.—*vt.* and *i.* To salute with a salaam.
Salacious, sa-lā'shus, *a.* Lustful.
Salacity, sa-las'i-ti, *n.* Lust; lecherousness.
Salad, sa'lad, *n.* A dish of certain vegetables, as lettuce, cress, &c., dressed and eaten raw.
Salamander, sa-la-man'dėr, *n.* A small harmless amphibian; a kind of lizard formerly believed able to live in fire.
Salamandrine, sa-la-man'drīn, *a.* Pertaining to or resembling a salamander.
Salaried, sa'la-rid, *p.a.* Having a salary.
Salary, sa'la-ri, *n.* A stipulated recompense for services; stipend; wages.
Sale, sāl, *n.* Act of selling; power or opportunity of selling; market; auction; state of being to be sold.
Saleable, sāl'a-bl, *a.* That may be sold; being in demand.
Salesman, sālz'man, *n.* One employed to sell goods.
Salic, sal'ik, *a.* Belonging to the Salian Franks; usually applied to a clause in their code of laws which excluded females from the throne.
Salicin, Salicine, sal'i-sin, sal'i-sēn, *n.* A bitter crystallizable substance extracted from willow and poplar bark, a valuable tonic.
Salicylic, sal-i-sil'ik, *n.* An acid used as an antiseptic, &c.
Salience, sā'li-ens, *n.* Projection; protrusion.
Salient, sā'li-ent, *a.* Springing; darting; projecting; conspicuous.
Salina, sa-lī'na, *n.* A salt marsh; a salt-work.
Saline, sa-līn', *a.* Consisting of salt; salt.—*n.* A salt spring.
Saliva, sa-lī'va, *n.* The fluid secreted by certain glands, which moistens the mouth and assists digestion.
Salivant, sa'li-vant, *a.* Exciting salivation.—*n.* That which produces salivation.
Salivary, sa'li-va-ri, *a.* Pertaining to the saliva; secreting or conveying saliva.
Salivate, sa'li-vāt, *vt.* To produce an unusual secretion and discharge of saliva.
Salivation, sa-li-vā'shon, *n.* Act of salivating; excessive secretion of saliva.
Sallow, sal'ō, *a.* Having a pale, sickly, yellowish colour.—*n.* A kind of willow.
Sally, sal'i, *n.* A leaping forth; a rush of troops from a besieged place; a dart of intellect, fancy, &c.; frolic.—*vi.* (sallying, sallied). To leap forth; to issue suddenly.
Salmagundi, Salmagundy, sal-ma-gun'di, *n.* A dish of chopped meat, eggs, anchovies, cabbage, &c.; a miscellany.
Salmi, Salmis, säl'mē, *n.* A ragout of woodcocks, larks, thrushes, &c.
Salmon, sa'mun, *n.* A large fish highly valued as food.
Salmon-trout, sa'mun-trout, *n.* The sea-trout, like the salmon in form and colour.
Salon, sä-long, *n.* An apartment for the reception of company; a saloon.
Saloon, sa-lön', *n.* A spacious apartment; a large public room; main cabin of a steamer.
Salse, säls, *n.* A mud volcano.
Salsify, sal'si-fi, *n.* A plant cultivated for its edible root.
Salt, sạlt, *n.* A substance for seasoning and preserving food; a compound produced by the combination of a base with an acid; taste; savour; piquancy; an old sailor.—*a.* Impregnated with salt; pungent.—*vt.* To sprinkle or season with salt.
Saltant, sal'tant, *a.* Leaping; dancing.
Saltation, sal-tā'shon, *n.* A leaping; beating or palpitation.
Saltatory, sal'ta-to-ri, *a.* Leaping; used in leaping.
Salt-cellar, sạlt'sel-lėr, *n.* A small vessel used at table for holding salt.
Salter, sạlt'ėr, *n.* One who salts; drysalter.
Saltern, sạlt'ėrn, *n.* A salt-work.
Saltire, Saltier, sal'tėr, *n.* A heraldic figure formed by the crossing of two diagonal bands.
Saltish, sạlt'ish, *a.* Somewhat salt.
Salt-mine, sạlt'mīn, *n.* A mine where rock-salt is obtained.
Salt-pan, Salt-pit, sạlt'pan, sạlt'pit, *n.* A place where salt is obtained by evaporation.
Saltpetre, sạlt'pē-tėr, *n.* Nitre.
Salts, sạlts, *n.pl.* Salt used as a medicine.
Salt-water, sạlt'wạ-tėr, *n.* Water impregnated with salt; sea-water.
Salt-work, sạlt'wėrk, *n.* A place where salt is made.
Salubrious, sa-lū'bri-us, *a.* Healthful.
Salubrity, sa-lū'bri-ti, *n.* Healthfulness.
Salutary, sa'lū-ta-ri, *a.* Healthful; wholesome; beneficial; profitable.

Salutation, sa-lū-tā'shon, *n.* Act of saluting; a greeting; a salute.
Salute, sa-lūt', *vt.* (saluting, saluted). To greet; to greet by a bow, &c.; to kiss; to honour.—*vi.* To perform a salutation; to greet each other.—*n.* Act of saluting; greeting; a kiss; a bow; discharge of artillery, &c.
Salvable, sal'va-bl, *a.* That may be saved; admitting of salvation.
Salvage, sal'vāj, *n.* Act of saving a ship or goods from shipwreck, fire, &c.; an allowance for the saving of property; goods thus saved.
Salvation, sal-vā'shon, *n.* Act of saving; redemption of man from sin; that which saves.
Salve, salv, *vt.* (salving, salved). To save a ship or goods from wreck, fire, &c.
Salve, salv or säv, *n.* A healing ointment; remedy.—*vt.* (salving, salved). To apply salve to; to remedy.
Salver, sal'vėr, *n.* A tray on which articles are presented.
Salvo, sal'vō, *n.* A reservation; excuse; salute of guns; a shouting or cheering.
Salvor, sal'vor, *n.* One who saves a ship or goods from wreck or destruction.
Sambo, sam'bō, *n.* The offspring of a black person and a mulatto.
Same, sām, *a.* Identical; not different or other; of like kind; just mentioned.—**All the same,** nevertheless.
Sameness, sām'nes, *n.* Similarity; identity; monotony.
Samite, sā'mīt, *n.* An old rich silk stuff interwoven with gold or embroidered.
Samlet, sam'let, *n.* A little salmon.
Samphire, sam'fīr, *n.* Saint Peter's wort; sea-fennel.
Sample, sam'pl, *n.* A specimen; a part presented as typical of the whole.—*vt.* (sampling, sampled). To take a sample of.
Sampler, sam'plėr, *n.* One who samples; one who exhibits samples of goods; a piece of fancy sewed or embroidered work.
Sanable, san'a-bl, *a.* Curable.
Sanative, san'a-tiv, *a.* Healing.
Sanatorium, san-a-tō'ri-um, *n.* A place to which people go for the sake of health.
Sanatory, san'a-to-ri, *a.* Conducive to health; healing.
Sanctification, sangk'ti-fi-kā"shon, *n.* Act of sanctifying; consecration.
Sanctified, sangk'ti-fīd, *p.a.* Made holy; consecrated; sanctimonious.
Sanctify, sangk'ti-fī, *vt.* (sanctifying, sanctified). To make holy; to hallow; to make pure from sin.
Sanctimonious, sangk-ti-mō'ni-us, *a.* Making a show of sanctity; hypocritical.
Sanction, sangk'shon, *n.* Confirmation; ratification; authority.—*vt.* To ratify; to authorize; to countenance.
Sanctity, sangk'ti-ti, *n.* State of being sacred; holiness; inviolability.
Sanctuary, sangk'tū-a-ri, *n.* A sacred place; a place of worship; part of a church where the altar is placed; a place of protection to criminals, debtors, &c.; shelter.
Sanctum, sangk'tum, *n.* A sacred place; a private room.
Sand, sand, *n.* Fine particles of stone; *pl.* tracts of sand on the sea-shore, &c.—*vt.* To sprinkle or cover with sand.
Sandal, san'dal, *n.* A kind of shoe consisting of a sole fastened to the foot.
Sandal-wood, san'dal-wu̧d, *n.* The fragrant wood of certain E. Indian trees.
Sand-blast, sand'blast, *n.* Sand driven by a blast of steam or air, and used in engraving and cutting glass, &c.
Sand-blind, sand'blīnd, *a.* Having imperfect sight; dim-sighted.
Sand-crack, sand'krak, *n.* A crack in the hoof of a horse.
Sanderling, san'dėr-ling, *n.* A small wading bird found on sandy shores.
Sand-glass, sand'gläs, *n.* A glass that measures time by the running of sand.
Sandiver, san'di-vėr, *n.* The scum of glass in fusion, used, when pulverized, as a polishing substance.
Sandix, Sandyx, san'diks, *n.* A kind of red-lead used as a pigment.
Sand-martin, sand'mär-tin, *n.* A British swallow which nests in sandy banks.
Sand-paper, sand'pā-pėr, *n.* Paper coated with fine sand, used to smooth and polish.
Sandpiper, sand'pī-pėr, *n.* A grallatorial bird allied to the snipe, plover, &c.
Sandstone, sand'stōn, *n.* A stone composed of agglutinated grains of sand.
Sandwich, sand'wich, *n.* Slices of bread, with meat or something savoury between.—*vt.* To insert like the meat in a sandwich; to fit between two other pieces.
Sandwich-man, sand'wich-man, *n.* A man carrying two advertising boards, one before and one behind.
Sandy, sand'i, *a.* Abounding with sand; like sand; yellowish red; arid or dry.
Sane, sān, *a.* Sound in mind; discreet.
Sangaree, sang'ga-rē, *n.* Wine and water sweetened and spiced.
Sang-froid, sang'frwä, *n.* Coolness; imperturbable calmness.
Sanguinary, sang'gwin-a-ri, *a.* Bloody; murderous; savage; cruel.
Sanguine, sang'gwin, *a.* Consisting of blood; full of blood; of the colour of blood; cheerful; confident.
Sanguineous, sang-gwin'ē-us, *a.* Bloody; abounding with blood; sanguine.
Sanicle, san'i-kl, *n.* An umbelliferous plant of several species.
Sanies, sā'ni-ēz, *n.* A thin reddish discharge from wounds or sores.
Sanitary, san'i-ta-ri, *a.* Pertaining to or designed to secure health; hygienic.
Sanitation, san-i-tā'shon, *n.* The adoption of sanitary measures for the health of a community.
Sanity, san'i-ti, *n.* State of being sane; soundness of mind.
Sans, sanz, *prep.* Without; deprived of.
Sans-culotte, Sans-culottist, sanz-ku̧-lot', sanz-ku̧-lot'ist, *n.* A rabid republican.
Sanskrit, Sanscrit, san'skrit, *n.* and *a.* The ancient language of the Hindus.
Sap, sap, *vt.* (sapping, sapped). To undermine; to destroy by some invisible process.—*vi.* To proceed by undermining.—*n.* A trench; vital juice of plants.
Sapajou, Sajou, sap'a-jö, sä'jö, *n.* A South American prehensile-tailed monkey.
Sapid, sa'pid, *a.* Savoury.
Sapidity, sa-pid'i-ti, *n.* Savour; relish.

Sapience, sā'pi-ens, *n.* Wisdom: often used ironically.
Sapient, sā'pi-ent, *a.* Wise; sage; discerning: now generally ironic.
Sapless, sap'les, *a.* Withered; dry.
Sapling, sap'ling, *n.* A young tree.
Saponaceous, sa-pon-ā'shus, *a.* Soapy.
Saponify, sa-pon'i-fī, *vt.* To convert into soap by combination with an alkali.
Sapor, sā'por, *n.* Taste; savour; relish.
Sapper, sap'ėr, *n.* One who saps; a soldier employed to dig saps or trenches; a member of the Royal Engineers (applied to all ranks).
Sapphic, saf'fik, *a.* Pertaining to *Sappho,* a Grecian poetess, or to a kind of verse invented by her.—*n.* A Sapphic verse.
Sapphire, saf'fīr, *n.* A precious stone of very great hardness, and of various shades of blue; a rich blue colour; blue.
Sappy, sap'i, *a.* Abounding with sap; juicy; succulent; young and soft.
Saraband, sa'ra-band, *n.* A slow Spanish dance; a piece of music for the dance.
Saracen, sa'ra-sen, *n.* A Mussulman of the early and proselytizing period.
Sarcasm, sär'kazm, *n.* A bitter cutting jest; a severe gibe; keen irony.
Sarcastic, sär-kas'tik, *a.* Containing sarcasm; scornfully severe; taunting.
Sarcastically, sär-kas'tik-al-li, *adv.* In a sarcastic manner; with sarcasm.
Sarcenet, Sarsenet, särs'nėt, *n.* A fine thin silk used for linings, &c.
Sarcode, sär'kōd, *n.* Structureless gelatinous matter forming the bodies of animals belonging to the protozoa.
Sarcoid, sär'koid, *a.* Resembling flesh.
Sarcophagous, sär-kof'a-gus, *a.* Flesh-eating; feeding on flesh.
Sarcophagus, sär-kof'a-gus, *n.*; pl. **-gi** and **-guses.** A coffin of stone.
Sard, Sardine, särd, sär'dīn, *n.* A variety of carnelian of a deep blood-red colour.
Sardine, sär'dēn, *n.* Pilchards and other small fish preserved in olive oil and tinned.
Sardius, sär'di-us, *n.* Sard.
Sardonic, sär-don'ik, *a.* Forced, as a laugh; bitterly ironical; sarcastic.
Sardonyx, sär'dō-niks, *n.* A precious stone, a variety of onyx, with layers of sard.
Sark, särk, *n.* A shirt.
Sarmentum, sär-men'tum, *n.*; pl. **-ta.** A running stem giving off leaves or roots at intervals.
Sarsaparilla, sär'sa-pa-ril"la, *n.* The rhizome of several tropical plants yielding a demulcent medicine.
Sartorial, sär-tō'ri-al, *a.* Pertaining to a tailor.
Sash, sash, *n.* A long band or scarf worn for ornament; the frame of a window; a frame for a saw.—*vt.* To furnish with sashes or sash windows.
Sasin, sā'sin, *n.* An Indian antelope, remarkable for swiftness and beauty.
Sasine, sā'sin, *n.* In *Scots law,* the act of giving possession of feudal property, or the instrument by which the fact is proved.
Sassafras, sas'a-fras, *n.* A kind of laurel, the root of which has medicinal virtues.
Sassenach, sas'en-ach, *n.* A name applied by British Celts to Saxons.
Satan, sā'tan, *n.* The devil or prince of darkness; the chief of the fallen angels.
Satanic, sā-tan'ik, *a.* Having the qualities of Satan; devilish; infernal.
Satchel, sa'chel, *n.* A little sack or bag; a bag for a school-boy's books.
Sate, sāt, *vt.* (sating, sated). To satiate; to satisfy the appetite of; to glut.
Sateen, sa-tēn', *n.* A glossy fabric like satin, but with a woollen or cotton face.
Satellite, sa'tel-līt, *n.* An attendant; an obsequious dependant; a small planet revolving round another.
Satiable, sā'shi-a-bl, *a.* That may be satiated.
Satiate, sā'shi-āt, *vt.* (satiating, satiated). To fully satisfy the desire of; to surfeit; to glut. —*a.* Filled to satiety.
Satiety, sa-tī'e-ti, *n.* State of being satiated; repletion; surfeit.
Satin, sa'tin, *n.* A glossy close-woven silk cloth.—*a.* Belonging to or made of satin.
Satinet, sa'ti-net, *n.* A thin species of satin; a cloth made in imitation of satin, having a cotton warp and woollen filling.
Satin-wood, sa'tin-wụd, *n.* The wood of an Indian tree, heavy and durable.
Satiny, sa'tin-i, *a.* Resembling satin.
Satire, sa'tīr, *n.* A writing ridiculing vice or folly; an invective poem; sarcastic or contemptuous ridicule.
Satiric, Satirical, sa-ti'rik, sa-ti'rik-al, *a.* Belonging to satire; given to satire; sarcastic.
Satirist, sa'ti-rist, *n.* One who satirizes.
Satirize, sa'ti-rīz, *vt.* To expose by satire; to censure in a satiric manner.
Satisfaction, sa-tis-fak'shon, *n.* Act of satisfying; gratification of desire; contentment; payment; compensation.
Satisfactorily, sa-tis-fak'to-ri-li, *adv.* So as to give satisfaction.
Satisfactory, sa-tis-fak'to-ri, *a.* Giving satisfaction; making amends.
Satisfy, sa'tis-fī, *vt.* and *i.* (satisfying, satisfied). To gratify fully; to content; to fulfil the claims of; to answer; to free from doubt.
Satrap, sā'trap or sat'rap, *n.* A governor of a province of ancient Persia; a viceroy.
Saturable, sa'tūr-a-bl, *a.* That may be saturated.
Saturate, sa'tūr-āt, *vt.* To imbue till no more can be received; to soak thoroughly.
Saturation, sa-tūr-ā'shon, *n.* Act of saturating; complete impregnation.
Saturday, sa'tėr-dā, *n.* The seventh day of the week.
Saturn, sa'tėrn, *n.* An ancient Roman deity; a planet.
Saturnalia, sa-tėr-na'li-a, *n.pl.* The Roman festival of Saturn; noisy revelry.
Saturnalian, sa-tėr-na'li-an, *a.* Loose; dissolute.
Saturnine, sa'tėrn-īn, *a.* Morose; gloomy; phlegmatic.
Satyr, sa'tėr, *n.* A sylvan deity of the ancient Greeks and Romans, part man and part goat, and extremely wanton.
Sauce, sạs, *n.* A liquid to be eaten with food to give it relish; pertness.—*vt.* To make savoury with sauce; to be pert to.
Sauce-boat, sạs'bōt, *n.* A dish for holding sauce at table.
Sauce-pan, sạs'pan, *n.* A small metallic vessel for boiling or stewing.
Saucer, sạ'sėr, *n.* A piece of china, &c., in which a cup is set.

Saucily, sạs'i-li, *adv.* Pertly; petulantly.
Saucy, sạs'i, *a.* Showing impertinent boldness; pert; impudent; rude.
Saunter, sạn'tėr, *vi.* To stroll about idly; to loiter.—*n.* A stroll; a leisurely pace.
Saurian, sạ'ri-an, *a.* Pertaining to the lizards.—*n.* A scaly reptile, as the lizard.
Sausage, sạ'sāj, *n.* The prepared intestine of an ox, &c., stuffed with minced meat.
Savage, sa'vāj, *a.* Wild; uncultivated; barbarous; brutal.—*n.* One who is uncivilized; a barbarian.
Savagely, sa'vāj-li, *adv.* Barbarously.
Savagery, sa'vāj-ri, *n.* State of being savage; cruelty; barbarity.
Savant, sä-väng', *n.* A man of learning; a man eminent for his scientific acquirements.
Save, sāv, *vt.* (saving, saved). To preserve; to protect; to rescue; to spare; to keep from doing or suffering; to reserve; to obviate.—*vi.* To be economical.—*prep.* Except.
Saveloy, sav'e-loi, *n.* A highly seasoned dried sausage, made of young salted pork.
Savin, Savine, sav'in, *n.* A tree or shrub of the juniper kind.
Saving, sāv'ing, *a.* Thrifty; that secures from evil; containing some reservation.—*n.* What is saved; sums accumulated by economy: generally *pl.*—*prep.* Excepting.
Saviour, sāv'yėr, *n.* One who saves from evil, destruction, or danger; Christ.
Savory, sā'vėr-i, *n.* A labiate plant used to flavour dishes, &c.
Savour, sā'vor, *n.* Taste; flavour; odour; distinctive quality.—*vi.* To have a particular taste; to partake of some characteristic of something else.—*vt.* To taste or smell with pleasure; to like.
Savoury, sā'vo-ri, *a.* Having a good savour; palatable; agreeable.
Savoy, sav'oi, *n.* A variety of cabbage with crisp leaves for winter use.
Saw, sạ, *n.* A cutting instrument consisting of a thin blade of steel with a toothed edge; a saying or maxim.—*vt.* and *i.* To cut with a saw.
Sawdust, sạ'dust, *n.* Small fragments of wood produced by the action of a saw.
Saw-fish, sạ'fish, *n.* A fish allied to the sharks, with a long serrated bony snout.
Saw-fly, sạ'flī, *n.* The name of various insects allied to ants and bees.
Saw-mill, sạ'mil, *n.* A mill for sawing timber, driven by water, steam, &c.
Sawyer, sạ'yėr, *n.* One who saws timber.
Sax-horn, saks'horn, *n.* A brass wind-instrument.
Saxifrage, sak'si-frāj, *n.* A plant which grows among rocks.
Saxon, saks'on, *n.* An Anglo-Saxon; one of English race; a native of modern Saxony.—*a.* Pertaining to the Saxons or to modern Saxony; Anglo-Saxon.
Saxophone, saks'ō-fōn, *n.* A wind-instrument similar to the sax-horn, with a clarinet mouthpiece.
Say, sā, *vt.* (saying, said). To utter in words; to speak; to declare; to assume.—*vi.* To speak; to relate.—*n.* A speech; statement.
Saying, sā'ing, *n.* Something said; speech; an adage; a maxim; a proverb.
Scab, skab, *n.* An incrusted substance over a sore in healing; a disease of sheep; the mange in horses.
Scabbard, skab'ard, *n.* The sheath of a sword.
Scabbed, skabd or skab'ed, *a.* Abounding with scabs; scabby.
Scabby, skab'i, *a.* Affected with scab or scabs; mangy; mean; worthless.
Scabies, skā'bi-ez, *n.* Scab; mange; itch.
Scabious, skā'bi-us, *a.* Consisting of scabs; rough; itchy; leprous.
Scabrid, skab'rid, *a.* Slightly scabrous.
Scabrous, skab'rus or skā'brus, *a.* Rough.
Scaffold, skaf'old, *n.* A temporary platform for workmen; an elevated platform for the execution of a criminal.—*vt.* To furnish with a scaffold.
Scaffolding, skaf'old-ing, *n.* A structure for support of workmen in building.
Scagliola, skal-yō'la, *n.* A composition of gypsum, splinters of marble, &c., imitative of marble, and used in decoration.
Scald, skạld, *vt.* To burn or injure with hot liquor; to expose to a boiling or violent heat.—*n.* An injury caused by a hot liquid.—*a.* Covered with scurf; scabby; paltry.
Scald, skald or skạld, *n.* An ancient Scandinavian bard.
Scaldic, skald'ik or skạld'ik, *a.* Pertaining to the scalds.
Scale, skāl, *n.* A thin flake on the skin of an animal; dish of a balance; balance itself (generally *pl.*); anything graduated used as a measure; series of steps or ranks; relative dimensions; succession of notes; gamut.—*vt.* (scaling, scaled). To weigh, as in scales; to strip of scales; to clean; to climb, as by a ladder.—*vi.* To come off in thin layers.
Scalene, skā'lēn, *a.* A term applied to a triangle of which the three sides are unequal.
Scall, skạl, *n.* Scab, scabbiness.
Scalled, skạld, *a.* Scurvy; scabby.
Scallion, skal'yun, *n.* A shallot.
Scallop, skal'op or skol'op, *n.* An edible bivalve of the oyster family; a curving on the edge of anything.—*vt.* To cut the edge of into scallops or segments of circles.
Scalloped, skal'opt, *p.a.* Cut at the edge into segments of circles.
Scalp, skalp, *n.* The skin of the top of the head, with the hair on it.—*vt.* To deprive of the scalp.
Scalpel, skal'pel, *n.* A knife used in anatomical dissections.
Scaly, skāl'i, *a.* Covered with scales; resembling scales, laminæ, or layers.
Scammony, skam'o-ni, *n.* A gum-resin obtained from a species of convolvulus, used as a drastic purge; the plant itself.
Scamp, skamp, *n.* A knave; swindler; rogue.—*vt.* To do in a perfunctory manner.
Scamper, skam'pėr, *vi.* To run with speed; to scurry.—*n.* A hurried run.
Scan, skan, *vt.* (scanning, scanned). To measure by the metrical feet, as a verse; to scrutinize; to eye.
Scandal, skan'dal, *n.* Public reproach; shame; defamatory talk; slander.
Scandalize, skan'dal-īz, *vt.* To offend by some action deemed disgraceful; to shock.
Scandal-monger, skan'dal-mung-gėr, *n.* One who deals in or retails scandals.
Scandalous, skan'dal-us, *a.* Causing scandal; shameful; defamatory; slanderous.
Scandalously, skan'dal-us-li, *adv.* In a scandalous manner; disgracefully.

Scandent, skan'dent, *a.* Climbing.
Scansion, skan'shon, *n.* The act of scanning; metrical structure of verse.
Scansorial, skan-sō'ri-al, *a.* Adapted to climbing; belonging to the climbing birds (Scansores).
Scant, skant, *a.* Not full; scarcely sufficient; scarce.—*vt.* To limit; to stint; to grudge.—*adv.* Scarcely; hardly.
Scantily, Scantly, skant'i-li, skant'li, *adv.* In a scant or scanty manner.
Scantling, skant'ling, *n.* A small quantity; a sample; timber cut into pieces less than five inches square; the dimensions of timber, stones, &c.; a trestle for supporting a cask.
Scanty, skant'i, *a.* Scant; insufficient.
Scape, skāp, *n.* A stem rising directly from a root and bearing the fructification without leaves; the shaft of a feather or column.—*vt.* and *i.* To escape.
Scape-goat, skāp'gōt, *n.* One made to bear the blame of others.
Scapegrace, skāp'grās, *n.* A graceless fellow; a careless, hare-brained fellow.
Scapula, skap'ū-la, *n.* The shoulder-blade.
Scapular, skap'ū-lėr, *a.* Pertaining to the shoulder, or to the shoulder-blade.
Scapular, Scapulary, skap'ū-lėr, skap'ū-la-ri, *n.* A monastic garment resting on the shoulders, with a flap hanging down in front and another behind.
Scapus, skā'pus, *n.*; pl. **-pi.** The shaft of a column.
Scar, skär, *n.* The mark of a wound or ulcer; a cicatrix; a cliff; a bare place on the side of a hill.—*vt.* (scarring, scarred). To mark with a scar; to wound.
Scarab, Scarabee, ska'rab, ska'ra-bē, *n.* The sacred beetle of the Egyptians.
Scaramouch, ska'ra-mouch, *n.* A buffoon; a poltroon or braggadocio.
Scarce, skārs, *n.* Not plentiful; deficient; uncommon.
Scarce, Scarcely, skārs, skārs'li, *adv.* Hardly; scantly; barely; with difficulty.
Scarcity, skārs'i-ti, *n.* State or condition of being scarce; deficiency; dearth.
Scare, skār, *vt.* (scaring, scared). To strike with sudden terror; to frighten.—*n.* A sudden fright; a causeless alarm.
Scarecrow, skār'krō, *n.* Anything set up to scare birds from crops; anything terrifying without danger; a ragged or very odd-looking person.
Scarf, skärf, *n.*; pl. **Scarfs,** skärfs, and **Scarves,** skärvz. A light article of dress worn round the neck, &c.; a joint in timber.—*vt.* To unite (timber) by means of a scarf.
Scarf-skin, skärf'skin, *n.* The outer human skin; the cuticle; the epidermis.
Scarify, ska'ri-fī, *vt.* (scarifying, scarified). To make small superficial incisions in the skin; to remove the flesh about a tooth.
Scarlatina, skar-la-tē'na, *n.* A malady characterized by fever and a red rash.
Scarlet, skär'let, *n.* A bright-red colour.—*a.* Of a bright-red colour.
Scarlet-fever, skär'let-fē-vėr, *n.* Same as *Scarlatina.*
Scarp, skärp, *n.* The interior slope of a ditch.—*vt.* To cut down like a scarp.
Scathe, skāth, *n.* Damage; injury.—*vt.* (scathing, scathed). To injure; to harm.
Scatheful, skāth'fųl, *a.* Harmful.
Scatheless, skāth'les, *a.* Without harm.
Scathing, skāth'ing, *p.a.* Injuring; harming; blasting.
Scatter, skat'ėr, *vt.* To disperse; to spread; to strew; to disunite.—*vi.* To be dispersed; to straggle apart.
Scatter-brain, skat'ėr-brān, *n.* A thoughtless person.
Scatter-brained, skat'ėr-brānd, *a.* Giddy; thoughtless.
Scattered, skat'ėrd, *p.a.* Thinly spread; loose and irregular in arrangement.
Scaup, skąp, *n.* A bed of shell-fish; a species of duck which feeds on molluscs, &c.
Scaur, skąr, *n.* A scar or cliff.
Scavenger, ska'ven-jėr, *n.* One employed to clean the streets.
Scene, sēn, *n.* A stage; a distinct part of a play; a painted device on the stage; place of action or exhibition; general appearance of any action; a view; display of emotion.
Scenery, sēn'ė-ri, *n.* The painted representations on the stage; pictorial features; landscape characteristics.
Scenic, Scenical, sēn'ik, sēn'ik-al, *a.* Pertaining to the stage; dramatic; theatrical.
Scenographic, sēn-o-graf'ik, *a.* Pertaining to scenography.
Scenography, sē-nog'ra-fi, *n.* Representation or drawing according to perspective.
Scent, sent, *n.* That which causes the sensation of smell; odour; fragrance; power of smelling; chase followed by the scent; track.—*vt.* To perceive by the sense of smell; to imbue with odour.
Scentless, sent'les, *a.* Having no scent; inodorous; destitute of smell.
Sceptic, skep'tik, *n.* One who doubts or disbelieves.—*a.* Sceptical.
Sceptical, skep'tik-al, *a.* Doubting; doubting the truth of revelation.
Scepticism, skep'ti-sizm, *n.* Doubt; incredulity.
Sceptre, sep'tėr, *n.* A staff or baton carried by a ruler as a symbol of authority.
Sceptred, sep'tėrd, *a.* Invested with a sceptre; having royal power; regal.
Schedule, shed'ūl, sed'ūl, *n.* A paper containing a list, and annexed to a larger writing, as to a will, deed, &c.; an inventory.—*vt.* (scheduling, scheduled). To place in a schedule.
Scheme, skēm, *n.* A combination of things adjusted by design; a system; project; diagram.—*vt.* and *i.* (scheming, schemed). To plan, contrive, project.
Schemer, skēm'ėr, *n.* A contriver; plotter.
Scheming, skēm'ing, *a.* Intriguing.
Scherzo, skert'so, *n.* A passage of a sportive character in musical pieces.
Schiedam, skē-dam', *n.* Holland gin.
Schism, sizm, *n.* A separation; breach among people of the same religious faith.
Schismatic, Schismatical, siz-mat'ik, siz-mat'ik-al, *a.* Pertaining to schism; implying schism; tending to schism.
Schismatic, siz-mat'ik, *n.* One who practises or promotes schism.
Schist, shist, *n.* A rock of a slaty structure.
Schistose, Schistous, shis'tōz, shis'tus, *a.* Having the character of schist.
Scholar, skol'ėr, *n.* One who attends a school;

a pupil; a learned person; a junior member of an English university who is aided by college revenues.

Scholarly, skol'ėr-li, *a.* Like a scholar; becoming a scholar or man of learning.

Scholarship, skol'ėr-ship, *n.* Erudition; a foundation for the support of a student.

Scholastic, skō-las'tik, *a.* Pertaining to a scholar or school; pertaining to the schoolmen; pedantic; needlessly subtle.

Scholasticism, skō-las'ti-sizm, *n.* The philosophy of the schoolmen.

Scholiast, skō'li-ast, *n.* A writer of scholia; a grammarian who annotated the classics.

Scholium, skō'li-um, *n.*; pl. **-ia** or **-iums.** A marginal note; comment.

School, sköl, *n.* A place of instruction; a body of pupils; disciples; sect or body; a system or custom; a shoal (of fishes).—*a.* Relating to a school; scholastic.—*vt.* To instruct; to reprove.

School-house, sköl'hous, *n.* A house used as a school; a schoolmaster's house.

Schooling, sköl'ing, *n.* Instruction in school; tuition; reproof; reprimand.

Schoolman, sköl'man, *n.* A philosopher or divine of the middle ages, who adopted the system of Aristotle.

Schoolmaster, sköl'mäs-tėr, *n.* He who teaches a school, or in a school.

Schoolmistress, sköl'mis-tres, *n.* The mistress of or in a school; a lady teacher.

Schooner, skön'ėr, *n.* A vessel with two or more masts, her chief sails fore-and-aft.

Schottische, shot-tish', *n.* A dance resembling a polka; the music for such a dance.

Sciagraphy, sī-ag'ra-fi, *n.* The art of representing or delineating shadows.

Sciatic, Sciatical, sī-at'ik, sī-at'ik-al, *a.* Pertaining to the hip or to sciatica.

Sciatica, sī-at'i-ka, *n.* Neuralgia or inflammation of the sciatic nerve or great nerve of the thigh.

Science, sī'ens, *n.* Knowledge; knowledge reduced to a system; the facts pertaining to any department of mind or matter in their due connections; skill resulting from training.

Sciential, sī-en'shal, *a.* Pertaining to science.

Scientific, sī-en-tif'ik, *a.* Pertaining to science; versed in science; according to the rules or principles of science.

Scientifically, sī-en-tif'ik-al-li, *adv.* In a scientific manner.

Scientist, sī'ent-ist, *n.* One versed in science; a scientific man.

Scilicet, sī'li-set. To wit; namely; abbreviated to *Scil.* or *Sc.*

Scimitar, si'mi-tėr, *n.* A short curved sword.

Scintilla, sin-til'la, *n.* A spark; glimmer; trace.

Scintillate, sin'til-lāt, *vi.* To emit sparks; to sparkle, as the fixed stars.

Scintillation, sin-til-lā'shon, *n.* Twinkling; coruscation.

Sciography, sī-og'ra-fi, *n.* *See* SCIAGRAPHY.

Sciolism, sī'ol-izm, *n.* Superficial knowledge.

Sciolist, sī'ol-ist, *n.* One who knows things superficially; a smatterer.

Sciomachy, Sciamachy, sī-om'ak-i, sī-am'ak-i, *n.* A fighting with a shadow.

Scion, sī'on, *n.* A cutting or twig; a young shoot; a descendant; an heir.

Scirrhosity, Scirrosity, ski-ros'i-ti, si-ros'i-ti, *n.* State of being scirrhous; a scirrhus.

Scirrhous, ski'rus or si'rus, *a.* Pertaining to or proceeding from a scirrhus.

Scirrhus, Scirrhosis, ski'rus or si'rus, ski-rō'sis or si-rō'sis, *n.* A hard tumour.

Scissel, Scissil, sis'sel, sis'sil, *n.* Clippings or shreds of metal, as in coining.

Scission, si'zhon, *n.* Act of cutting; state of being cut; division.

Scissors, siz'ėrz, *n.pl.* A cutting instrument consisting of two blades.

Sclav, Sclavonic. *See* SLAV.

Scleroma, Sclerosis, sklē-rō'ma, sklē-rō'sis, *n.* Induration of the cellular tissue.

Scoff, skof, *n.* An expression of derision or scorn; a gibe.—*vi.* To utter contemptuous language; to jeer; to mock.—*vt.* To mock at.

Scoffer, skof'ėr, *n.* One who scoffs.

Scoffingly, skof'ing-li, *adv.* In a scoffing manner; by way of derision.

Scold, skōld, *vi.* To find fault with rude clamour; to utter harsh, rude rebuke.—*vt.* To reprimand loudly; to chide.—*n.* A clamorous, foul-mouthed woman.

Scolding, skōld'ing, *n.* Act of one who scolds; railing language; a rating.

Scolecida, skō-lē'si-da, *n.pl.* The tape-worms and allied animals.

Scollop, skol'op, *n.* A scallop.

Sconce, skons, *n.* A case or socket for a candle; a projecting candlestick; a detached fort; a head-piece; the skull.—*vt.* To ensconce.

Scoop, sköp, *n.* An implement for lifting things; an instrument for hollowing out; the act of scooping.—*vt.* To take out with a scoop; to lade out; to hollow out.

Scope, skōp, *n.* An aim or end; intention; amplitude of range; space; sweep.

Scorbutic, skor-būt'ik, *a.* Pertaining to or diseased with scurvy.

Scorch, skorch, *vt.* To burn superficially; to singe; to parch.—*vi.* To be so hot as to burn a surface; to be dried up; to ride a cycle at excessive speed.

Score, skōr, *n.* A notch; a long scratch or mark; an account or reckoning; the number twenty; a debt; the number of points made in certain games; motive; ground; draught of a musical composition.—*vt.* (scoring, scored). To make scores or scratches on; to record; to get for oneself, as points, &c., in games.

Scorer, skōr'ėr, *n.* One who keeps the scores of competitors, or the like; an instrument to mark numbers, &c., on trees.

Scoria, skō'ri-a, *n.*; pl. **-iæ.** Dross; cinder; the cellular, slaggy lavas of a volcano.

Scorify, skō'ri-fī, *vt.* To reduce to dross; to separate the dross from the valuable metal.

Scorn, skorn, *n.* Extreme contempt; subject of contempt.—*vt.* To hold in extreme contempt; to despise.—*vi.* To feel or show scorn.

Scorner, skorn'ėr, *n.* One who scorns; a scoffer.

Scornful, skorn'ful, *a.* Filled with or expressing scorn; contemptuous.

Scornfully, skorn'ful-li, *adv.* In a scornful manner.

Scorpion, skor'pi-on, *n.* An animal of the class Arachnida, with a jointed tail terminating with a venomous sting; a sign of the zodiac.

Scot, skot, *n.* A native of Scotland; a tax or contribution.

Scotch, skoch, *a.* Pertaining to Scotland or its inhabitants; Scottish.—*n.* The dialect of Scotland; the people of Scotland.

Scotch, skoch, *vt.* To cut with shallow incisions; to notch.—*n.* A slight cut.

Scotchman, skoch'man, *n.* A native of Scotland.

Scot-free, skot'frē, *a.* Free from payment of scot; untaxed; unhurt; clear; safe.

Scotia, skō'ti-a, *n.* A hollow moulding in the base of a column.

Scots, skots, *a.* Scottish.—*n.* The Scottish language.

Scotsman, skots'man, *n.* A native of Scotland.

Scottice, skot'ti-sē, *adv.* In the Scottish manner or language.

Scotticism, skot'i-sizm, *n.* An idiom or expression peculiar to Scots.

Scottish, skot'ish, *a.* Pertaining to Scotland, its inhabitants, or language.

Scoundrel, skoun'drel, *n.* A mean, worthless fellow; a rascal.—*a.* Base; unprincipled.

Scoundrelism, skoun'drel-izm, *n.* The practices of a scoundrel; rascality.

Scoundrelly, skoun'drel-li, *a.* Base; mean.

Scour, skour, *vt.* and *i.* To clean by rubbing; to purge violently; to range for the purpose of finding something; to pass swiftly over.

Scourer, skour'ėr, *n.* One who or that which scours.

Scourge, skėrj, *n.* A lash; a whip; an affliction sent for punishment; one who harasses. —*vt.* (scourging, scourged). To lash; to chastise; to harass.

Scout, skout, *n.* A person sent to obtain intelligence regarding an enemy; a college servant.—*vi.* To act as a scout.—*vt.* To watch closely; to treat with disdain.

Scout-master, skout-mäs'tėr, *n.* The leader of a troop of Boy Scouts.

Scow, skou, *n.* A flat-bottomed boat.

Scowl, skoul, *vi.* To wrinkle the brows, as in displeasure; to frown.—*n.* A deep angry frown; gloom.

Scrabble, skrab'l, *vi.* and *t.* To scrawl; to scribble.—*n.* A scribble.

Scrag, skrag, *n.* Something dry, or lean with roughness.

Scragged, skrag'ed, *a.* Like a scrag; scraggy.

Scraggy, skrag'i, *a.* Rough or rugged; scragged; lean and bony.

Scramble, skram'bl, *vi.* (scrambling, scrambled). To move or climb on all-fours; to push rudely in eagerness for something.—*n.* Act of scrambling; eager contest.

Scrambling, skram'bling,' *a.* Irregular; straggling.

Scrannel, skran'el, *a.* Slight; slender.

Scrap, skrap, *n.* A small piece; a fragment; a little picture for ornamenting screens, &c.

Scrap-book, skrap'bụk, *n.* A book for preserving extracts, drawings, prints, &c.

Scrape, skrāp, *vt.* (scraping, scraped). To rub with something hard; to clean by a sharp edge; to act on with a grating noise; to erase; to collect laboriously.—*vi.* To roughen or remove a surface by rubbing; to make a grating noise.—*n.* Act of scraping; an awkward bow; an awkward predicament.

Scraper, skrāp'ėr, *n.* One who or that which scrapes; an instrument for scraping or cleaning.

Scraping, skrāp'ing, *n.* What is scraped from a substance, or is collected by scraping.

Scrappy, skrap'i, *a.* Consisting of scraps; incomplete; disjointed.

Scratch, skrach, *vt.* and *i.* To mark or wound with something sharp; to tear with the nails; to withdraw from the list of competitors.—*n.* A score in a surface; a slight wound; a line from which runners start, &c.; one most heavily handicapped in a contest.—*a.* Taken at random; hastily collected.

Scratcher, skrach'ėr, *n.* One who or that which scratches; a gallinaceous bird.

Scratch-wig, skrach'wig, *n.* A wig that covers only a portion of the head.

Scrawl, skrạl, *vt.* and *i.* To write or draw carelessly or awkwardly.—*n.* Inelegant or hasty writing.

Screak, skrēk, *vi.* To screech; to creak.

Scream, skrēm, *vi.* To shriek; to utter a shrill cry.—*n.* A sharp, shrill cry.

Screamer, skrēm'ėr, *n.* One that screams; a name of certain birds.

Screaming, skrēm'ing, *a.* Crying out with a scream; causing screams of laughter.

Screech, skrēch, *vi.* To scream; to shriek.—*n.* A sharp, shrill cry.

Screech-owl, skrēch-oul, *n.* An owl that screeches, in opposition to one that hoots.

Screed, skrēd, *n.* A strip of cloth; a lengthy statement; a harangue.

Screen, skrēn, *n.* An article to intercept heat, cold, &c.; a shelter; a kind of sieve; an ornamental partition in a church.—*vt.* To shelter; to conceal; to sift.

Screenings, skren'ingz, *n.pl.* The refuse matter left after sifting coal, &c.

Screes, skrēz, *n.pl.* Debris of rocks; shingle.

Screw, skrö, *n.* A cylinder with a spiral ridge which enables it when turned to enter another body; a screw-propeller; a twist or turn; a niggard.—*vt.* To fasten by a screw; to twist; to oppress.

Screw-driver, skrö'drīv-ėr, *n.* An instrument for turning screw-nails.

Screw-key, skrö'kē, *n.* An instrument for turning large screws or their nuts.

Screw-nail, skrö'nāl, *n.* A nail grooved like a screw.

Screw-propeller, skrö'prō-pel-ėr, *n.* An apparatus on the principle of the common screw, for propelling steam-vessels.

Screw-steamer, skrö'stēm-ėr, *n.* A steamer propelled by a screw-propeller.

Scribble, skrib'l, *vt.* and *i.* (scribbling, scribbled). To write with haste or without care; to tease coarsely, as cotton or wool.—*n.* Careless writing; a scrawl.

Scribbler, skrib'lėr, *n.* One who writes carelessly or badly; a machine which teases cotton or wool.

Scribe, skrīb, *n.* A writer; notary; copyist; doctor of the law among the Jews.

Scrimmage, skrim'āj, *n.* A tussle; a confused, close struggle in football.

Scrimp, skrimp, *vt.* To make too small or short; to scant; to limit.—*a.* Scanty.

Scrip, skrip, *n.* A small bag; a wallet; a small writing; a certificate of stock.

Script, skript, *n.* Handwriting; printing type resembling handwriting.

Scriptorium, skrip-tō'ri-um, *n.* A room set apart for writing or copying.

Scriptural, skrip'tūr-al, *a.* Contained in or according to the Scriptures; biblical.
Scripturally, skrip'tūr-al-li, *adv.* In a scriptural manner.
Scripture, skrip'tūr, *n.* The Old and New Testaments; the Bible: often *pl.*—*a.* Scriptural.
Scrivener, skri'ven-ėr, *n.* An old name for a notary; a money-broker; a writer; a poor author.
Scrofula, skro'fū-la, *n.* A disease, a variety of consumption, often showing itself by glandular tumours in the neck which suppurate.
Scrofulous, skro'fū-lus, *a.* Pertaining to scrofula; diseased or affected with scrofula.
Scroll, skrōl, *n.* A roll of paper or parchment; a draft or first copy; a spiral ornament; a flourish added to a person's name.
Scrotum, skrō'tum, *n.* The bag which contains the testicles.
Scrub, skrub, *vt.* (scrubbing, scrubbed). To rub hard with something rough, to make clean or bright.—*vi.* To be diligent and penurious. —*n.* One who labours hard and lives sparingly; a mean fellow; a worn-out brush; low underwood.—*a.* Mean.
Scrubby, skrub'i, *a.* Small and mean; stunted in growth; niggardly; shabby.
Scrunsh, skrunsh, *vt.* To crunch.
Scruple, skrö'pl, *n.* A weight of 20 grains; doubt; hesitation; backwardness.—*vi.* (scrupling, scrupled). To doubt; to hesitate.
Scrupulosity, skrö-pū-los'i-ti, *n.* Quality or state of being scrupulous; preciseness.
Scrupulous, skrö'pū-lus, *a.* Having scruples; cautious; conscientious; exact.
Scrupulously, skrö'pū-lus-li, *adv.* In a scrupulous manner; carefully; exactly.
Scrutineer, skrö'ti-nēr, *n.* One who scrutinizes, as votes at an election.
Scrutinize, skrö'ti-nīz, *vt.* and *i.* To examine closely; to investigate.
Scrutinous, skrö'tin-us, *a.* Given to scrutiny; closely inquiring or examining.
Scrutiny, skrö'ti-ni, *n.* Close search; careful investigation; an authoritative examination of votes given at an election.
Scud, skud, *vi.* (scudding, scudded). To run quickly; to run before a strong wind with little or no sail.—*vt.* To pass over quickly.—*n.* Act of scudding; loose, vapoury clouds.
Scuffle, skuf'l, *n.* A confused struggle.—*vi.* (scuffling, scuffled). To strive confusedly at close quarters.
Scull, skul, *n.* A short oar, used in pairs.—*vt.* To propel by sculls, or by moving an oar at the stern.
Sculler, skul'ėr, *n.* One who rows with a scull or sculls; a boat rowed by sculls.
Scullery, skul'ė-ri, *n.* A place where culinary utensils are cleaned and kept.
Scullion, skul'yon, *n.* A servant of the scullery; a low, worthless fellow.
Sculptor, skulp'tor, *n.* One who works in sculpture; an artist who carves or models figures.
Sculptural, skulp'tūr-al, *a.* Pertaining to sculpture.
Sculpture, skulp'tūr, *n.* The art of carving wood or stone into images; an image in stone, &c.—*vt.* (sculpturing, sculptured). To carve; to form, as images on stone, &c.
Scum, skum, *n.* Impurities which rise to the surface of liquors; refuse.—*vt.* (scumming, scummed). To take the scum from.—*vi.* To throw up scum.
Scumble, skum'bl, *vt.* To cover thinly with opaque colours to modify the effect.
Scummer, skum'ėr, *n.* A skimmer.
Scummings, skum'ingz, *n.pl.* The matter skimmed from boiling liquors.
Scummy, skum'i, *a.* Covered with scum.
Scupper, skup'ėr, *n.* A hole for carrying off water from the deck of a ship.
Scurf, skėrf, *n.* Dry scales or flakes on the skin; matter adhering to a surface.
Scurfy, skėrf'i, *a.* Having scurf; covered with scurf; resembling scurf.
Scurrility, sku-ril'i-ti, *n.* Scurrilous language; low abuse; insolence.
Scurrilous, sku'ril-us, *a.* Foul-mouthed; abusive; obscenely jocular.
Scurry, sku'ri, *vt.* (scurrying, scurried). To run rapidly; to hurry.—*n.* Hurry; haste.
Scurvily, skėr'vi-li, *adv.* In a scurvy manner; basely; meanly; shabbily.
Scurvy, skėr'vi, *n.* A disease caused by insufficiency of vegetable food.—*a.* Vile; mean; malicious.
Scutage, skū'tāj, *n.* A tax on feudal tenants.
Scutch, skuch, *vt.* To dress by beating, as flax.
Scutcheon, skuch'on, *a.* A shield for armorial bearings; an escutcheon.
Scute, skūt, *n.* A scale, as of a reptile.
Scuttle, skut'l, *n.* A broad basket; a pail for coals; a hatchway in a ship's deck; a short run; a quick pace.—*vt.* (scuttling, scuttled). To sink by making holes in (a ship).—*vi.* To scurry.
Scye, sī, *n.* The curve in a piece of a garment to receive the sleeve.
Scythe, sīᴛʜ, *n.* An implement for mowing grass, &c.—*vt.* To cut with a scythe.
Sea, sē, *n.* The mass of salt water covering most of the earth; some portion of this; a name of certain lakes; a large wave; a surge; a flood.
Sea-anemone, sē'a-nem'o-nē, *n.* A beautiful sea-shore plant-like animal.
Sea-board, sē'bōrd, *n.* The sea-coast or sea-shore.—*a.* Bordering on the sea.
Sea-born, sē'born, *a.* Produced by the sea; born at sea.
Sea-breeze, sē'brēz, *n.* A wind or current of air blowing from the sea upon land.
Sea-calf, sē'käf, *n.* The common seal.
Sea-coast, sē'kōst, *n.* The land adjacent to the sea or ocean.
Sea-dog, sē'dog, *n.* The dog-fish; the common seal; a sailor who has been long afloat.
Seafarer, sē'fār-ėr, *n.* One who fares or travels by sea; a mariner; a seaman.
Seafaring, sē'fār-ing, *a.* Going to sea; employed in seamanship.
Sea-fight, sē'fīt, *n.* A naval action.
Sea-fish, sē'fish, *n.* Any fish that lives usually in salt-water.
Sea-girt, sē'gėrt, *a.* Surrounded by the sea.
Sea-going, sē'gō-ing, *a.* Travelling by sea, as a vessel which trades with foreign ports.
Sea-green, sē'grēn, *a.* Having the greenish colour of sea-water.
Sea-horse, sē'hors, *n.* The walrus; a small fish with head shaped like a horse's.
Seal, sēl, *n.* A hard substance bearing some

device, used to make impressions; the wax stamped with a seal; assurance; that which makes fast; a carnivorous marine mammal.—*vt.* To set a seal to; to confirm; to fasten; to shut or keep close.
Sea-legs, sē'legz, *n.pl.* The ability to walk on a ship's deck when pitching or rolling.
Sealer, sēl'ėr, *n.* One who seals; an officer in Chancery who seals writs, &c.; one engaged in the seal-fishery.
Sea-level, sē'le-vel, *n.* The level of the surface of the sea.
Sealing, sēl'ing, *n.* The operation of taking seals and curing their skins.
Sealing-wax, sēl'ing-waks, *n.* A resinous compound used for sealing letters, &c.
Sea-lion, sē'li-on, *n.* The name of several large seals.
Seam, sēm, *n.* The joining of two edges of cloth; a line of juncture; a vein of metal, coal, &c.; a scar.—*vt.* To unite by a seam; to scar.
Seaman, sē'man, *n.* A sailor; a mariner.
Seamanship, sē'man-ship, *n.* The art or skill of a seaman; art of managing a ship.
Sea-mark, sē'märk, *n.* An object on land which directs mariners; a beacon.
Sea-mew, sē'mū, *n.* A gull; a sea-gull.
Seamstress, sēm'stres, *n.* A woman whose occupation is sewing; a sempstress.
Seamy, sēm'i, *a.* Having a seam; showing seams; showing the worst side; disagreeable.
Séance, sā-ạngs, *n.* A session, as of some public body; a sitting with the view of evoking spiritual manifestations.
Sea-piece, sē'pēs, *n.* A picture of a scene at sea.
Seaplane, sē'plān, *n.* An aeroplane fitted with floats to enable it to take off from and light on water.
Sea-port, sē'pōrt, *n.* A harbour on the sea-coast; a town on or near the sea.
Sear, sēr, *vt.* To wither; to dry; to cauterize; to deaden.—*a.* Dry; withered.
Sear, sēr, *n.* A catch in the mechanism of a rifle which holds back the cocking-piece.
Search, sėrch, *vt.* To look through to find something; to examine.—*vi.* To seek diligently; to inquire.—*n.* Act of searching; examination; inquiry.
Searchable, sėrch'a-bl, *a.* That may be searched or explored.
Searcher, sėrch'ėr, *n.* One who or that which searches; an investigator.
Searching, sėrch'ing, *a.* Penetrating; trying; closely scrutinizing.
Searchless, sėrch'les, *a.* Inscrutable.
Sea-room, sē'röm, *n.* Ample distance from land, shoals, or rocks, for a vessel.
Sea-rover, sē'rōv-ėr, *n.* A pirate.
Sea-scape, sē'skāp, *n.* A picture representing a scene at sea; a sea-piece.
Sea-serpent, sē'sėr-pent, *n.* An enormous marine animal resembling a serpent, the existence of which is doubtful.
Sea-shore, sē'shōr, *n.* The shore of the sea; ground between high and low water mark.
Sea-sick, sē'sik, *a.* Affected with sickness caused by the motion of a vessel at sea.
Sea-sickness, sē'sik-nes, *n.* Sickness produced by the motion of a vessel at sea.
Sea-side, sē'sīd, *n.* The sea-coast.
Season, sē'zn, *n.* A division of the year; a suitable time; a time; time of the year marked by special activity; seasoning.—*vt.* To accustom; to acclimatize; to flavour.—*vi.* To become suitable by time.
Seasonable, sē'zn-a-bl, *a.* Natural to the season; opportune; timely.
Seasoning, sē'zn-ing, *n.* Something added to food to give it relish; relish; condiment.
Seat, sēt, *n.* That on which one sits; a chair; stool, &c.; place of sitting; a right to sit; residence; station.—*vt.* To place on a seat; to settle; to locate; to assign seats to; to fit up with seats.
Seaward, sē'wėrd, *a.* and *adv.* Toward the sea.
Sea-weed, sē'wēd, *n.* A marine plant.
Sea-worthy, sē'wėr-ꟸHi, *a.* Fit to go to sea; fit for a voyage.
Sebaceous, sē-bā'shus, *a.* Made of, containing, or secreting fatty matter.
Sebiferous, sē-bif'ėr-us, *a.* Producing fat.
Secant, sē'kant, *a.* Cutting.—*n.* A straight line that cuts a curve or figure.
Secede, sē-sēd', *vi.* (seceding, seceded). To withdraw from fellowship or association.
Seceder, sē-sēd'ėr, *n.* One who secedes.
Secern, sē-sėrn', *vt.* To separate; to distinguish; to secrete.
Secernent, sē-sėr'nent, *n.* That which promotes secretion; a secreting vessel.—*a.* Secreting.
Secession, sē-se'shon, *n.* Act of seceding.
Secessionist, sē-se'shon-ist, *n.* One who advocates or engages in a secession.
Seclude, sē-klöd', *vt.* (secluding, secluded). To shut up apart; to separate; *refl.* to withdraw into solitude.
Secluded, sē-klöd'ed, *a.* Separated from others; retired; sequestered.
Seclusion, sē-klö'zhon, *n.* Act of secluding; retired mode of life; privacy.
Seclusive, sē-klö'siv, *a.* Tending to seclude or keep in retirement.
Second, se'kund, *a.* Next after the first; repeated again; inferior; other.—*n.* One who or that which comes next a first; one who supports another; attendant in a duel; sixtieth part of a minute; a lower part in music; *pl.* a coarse kind of flour.—*vt.* To follow in the next place; to support; to join with in proposing some measure.
Secondarily, se'kun-da-ri-li, *adv.* In a secondary manner; secondly.
Secondary, se'kun-da-ri, *a.* Of second place; subordinate; not elementary.
Second-cousin, se'kund-ku-zn, *n.* The child of a parent's first-cousin.
Seconder, se'kund-ėr, *n.* One who supports what another attempts, affirms, or proposes.
Second-hand, se'kund-hand, *a.* Received not from the original possessor; not new.
Secondly, se'kund-li, *adv.* In the second place.
Second-rate, se'kund-rāt, *n.* The second order in size, dignity, or value.
Second-sight, se'kund-sīt, *n.* The power of seeing things future; prophetic vision.
Secrecy, sē'kre-si, *n.* State or character of being secret; seclusion; fidelity to a secret.
Secret, sē'kret, *a.* Hidden; concealed; private; unseen.—*n.* Something hidden or not to be revealed; a mystery.
Secretarial, se-krē-tā'ri-al, *a.* Pertaining to a secretary.
Secretariate, se-krē-tā'ri-āt, *n.* The position or business of a secretary.

Secretary, se'krē-ta-ri, *n.* A person employed to write orders, letters, &c.; an escritoire; one who manages the affairs of a department of government.
Secretaryship, se'krē-ta-ri-ship, *n.* The office or employment of a secretary.
Secrete, sē-krēt', *vt.* (secreting, secreted). To hide; to separate from the blood in animals, or from the sap in vegetables.
Secretion, sē-krē'shon, *n.* Act or process of secreting; matter secreted, as bile, &c.
Secretive, sē-krēt'iv, *a.* Causing secretion; secretory; given to secrecy; reticent.
Secretly, sē'kret-li, *adv.* In a secret manner; privately; privily; not openly.
Secretory, sē-krē'to-ri, *a.* Performing the office of secretion; secreting.
Sect, sekt, *n.* A body of persons united in tenets, chiefly in religion or philosophy; a school; a denomination.
Sectarian, sek-tā'ri-an, *a.* Pertaining to a sect or sectary.—*n.* One of a sect.
Sectarianism, sek-tā'ri-an-izm, *n.* State or quality of being sectarian; rigid devotion to a party, chiefly in religion.
Sectary, sek'ta-ri, *n.* One that belongs to a sect; a schismatic; a sectarian.
Sectile, sek'til, *a.* Capable of being cut in slices with a knife.
Section, sek'shon, *n.* Act of cutting; a distinct part; subdivision of a chapter, &c.; representation of an object as if cut asunder by an intersecting plane; a quarter of a platoon of infantry, the normal fire-unit.
Sectional, sek'shon-al, *a.* Pertaining to a section; composed of independent sections.
Sector, sek'tor, *n.* A part of a circle between two radii; a mathematical instrument useful in making diagrams.
Secular, se'kū-lėr, *a.* Pertaining to things not spiritual or sacred; worldly; temporal; coming once in a century.
Secularism, sek'ū-lėr-izm, *n.* The elimination of the religious element from life.
Secularist, sek'ū-lėr-ist, *n.* An upholder of secularism; one who theoretically rejects every form of religious faith.
Secularize, se'kū-lėr-īz, *vt.* To make secular; to convert from sacred to secular use.
Securable, sē-kūr'a-bl, *a.* That may be secured.
Secure, sē-kūr', *a.* Free from care or danger; heedless; undisturbed; safe; confident.—*vt.* (securing, secured). To make safe or certain; to seize and confine; to guarantee; to fasten.
Securely, sē-kūr'li, *adv.* In a secure manner; in security; safely.
Security, sē-kū'ri-ti, *n.* Safety; confidence; protection; a guarantee; a surety; an evidence of property, as a bond, a certificate of stock, &c.
Sedan, sē-dan', *n.* A kind of covered chair for a single person, borne on poles by two men.
Sedate, sē-dāt', *a.* Composed in manner; staid; placid; sober; serious.
Sedately, sē-dāt'li, *adv.* In a sedate manner; calmly; tranquilly.
Sedative, se'da-tiv, *a.* Tending to soothe; assuaging pain.—*n.* A medicine which assuages pain, &c.
Sedentary, se'den-ta-ri, *a.* Accustomed to sit much; requiring much sitting.
Sederunt, se-dē'runt, *n.* A sitting of a court or the like; a formal meeting.
Sedge, sej, *n.* A coarse grass-like plant growing mostly in marshes and swamps.
Sedgy, sej'i, *a.* Abounding in sedge.
Sediment, se'di-ment, *n.* That which settles at the bottom of liquor; lees.
Sedimentary, se-di-ment'a-ri, *a.* Pertaining to sediment; formed of sediment.
Sedition, sē-di'shon, *n.* A commotion in a state; insurrection; civic discord.
Seditious, sē-di'shus, *a.* Pertaining to sedition; stirring up sedition; inflammatory.
Seduce, sē-dūs', *vt.* (seducing, seduced). To lead astray; to corrupt; to entice to a surrender of chastity.
Seducer, sē-dūs'ėr, *n.* One who seduces.
Seducible, sē-dūs'i-bl, *a.* Capable of being seduced.
Seduction, sē-duk'shon, *n.* Act of seducing; allurement; the persuading of a female to surrender her chastity.
Seductive, sē-duk'tiv, *a.* Tending to seduce; enticing; alluring.
Sedulity, se-dū'li-ti, *n.* Unremitting industry; diligence; assiduity.
Sedulous, se'dū-lus, *a.* Assiduous; diligent; industrious.
See, sē, *vt.* (seeing, pret. saw, pp. seen). To perceive by the eye; to notice; to discover; to understand; to receive; to experience; to attend.—*vi.* To have the power of sight; to understand; to consider.—*interj.* Lo! look!—*n.* A seat of episcopal power; a diocese.
Seed, sēd, *n.* That product of a plant which may produce a similar plant; seeds collectively; the semen; first principle; offspring.—*vi.* To produce seed; to shed the seed.—*vt.* To sow; to supply with seed.
Seeded, sēd'ed, *a.* Sown; sprinkled or covered with seed; bearing seed.
Seedling, sēd'ling, *n.* A plant reared from the seed.
Seedsman, sēdz'man, *n.* A person who deals in seeds; a sower.
Seed-time, sēd'tīm, *n.* The season proper for sowing.
Seedy, sēd'i, *a.* Abounding with seeds; run to seed; shabby; feeling or appearing wretched.
Seeing, sē'ing, *conj.* Since; inasmuch as.
Seek, sēk, *vt.* and *i.* (seeking, sought). To search for; to solicit; to have recourse to.
Seem, sēm, *vi.* To appear; to look as if; to imagine; to feel as if.
Seeming, sēm'ing, *p.a.* Appearing; specious.—*n.* Appearance; semblance.
Seemingly, sēm'ing-li, *adv.* Apparently.
Seemly, sēm'li, *a.* Becoming; suitable; decorous.—*adv.* In a suitable manner.
Seer, sēr, *n.* One who sees into futurity; a prophet.
See-saw, sē'sa̤, *n.* A swinging movement up and down; a game in which children swing up and down on the two ends of a balanced piece of timber.—*vi.* and *t.* To move up and down or to and fro.
Seethe, sēᴛʜ, *vt.* (seething, seethed). To boil; to soak.—*vi.* To be in a state of ebullition; to be hot.
Seggar, seg'är, *n.* A case of fire-clay in which fine stoneware is inclosed while baked in the kiln.
Segment, seg'ment, *n.* A part cut off; a

section; a natural division of a body (as an orange).
Segregate, se'grē-gāt, *vt.* To set apart or separate.
Segregation, se-grē-gā'shon, *n.* Act of segregating; separation.
Seignior, Seigneur, sēn'yėr, *n.* A lord or great man; a feudal superior.
Seigniorage, Seignorage, sēn'yėr-āj, *n.* Something claimed by the sovereign or a superior as a prerogative; a royalty.
Seigniorial, Seigneurial, sēn-yō'ri-al, sēn-yō'ri-al, *a.* Pertaining to a seignior.
Seigniory, Seignory, sēn'yėr-i, *n.* A lordship; authority as sovereign lord.
Seine, Sein, sēn or sān, *n.* A large fishing net.—*vt.* (seining, seined). To catch with a seine.
Seismic, Seismal, sīs'mik, sīs'mal, *a.* Pertaining to earthquakes.
Seismograph, sīs'mō-graf, *n.* An instrument to register shocks of earthquakes.
Seismology, sīs-mol'o-ji, *n.* The science of earthquakes.
Seizable, sēz'a-bl, *a.* Liable to be taken.
Seize, sēz, *vt.* (seizing, seized). To lay hold of suddenly; to take by force or legal authority; to attack, as a disease, fear, &c.; to comprehend; to put in possession.—*vi.* To take hold or possession.
Seizin, sēz'in, *n.* A taking possession; possession; thing possessed.
Seizure, sēz'ūr, *n.* Act of seizing; thing taken or seized; a sudden attack.
Sejant, Sejeant, sē'jant, *a.* Sitting.
Seldom, sel'dom, *adv.* Rarely; not often.
Select, sē-lekt', *vt.* To choose; to pick out; to cull.—*a.* Chosen; choice; exclusive.
Selection, sē-lek'shon, *n.* Act of selecting; a collection of things selected.
Selective, sē-lek'tiv, *a.* Pertaining to selection; selecting; tending to select.
Selenite, sel'en-īt, *n.* Foliated or crystallized sulphate of lime, somewhat resembling mica.
Selenium, se-lē'ni-um, *n.* A non-metallic element akin to sulphur and tellurium.
Selenology, sel-ē-nol'o-ji, *n.* That branch of astronomy which treats of the moon.
Self, self, *n.*; pl. **Selves,** selvz. One's individual person; personal interest; a blossom of a uniform colour (with *pl.* **Selfs**).—*a.* or *pron.* Same. Affixed to pronouns and adjectives to express emphasis or distinction, or reflexive usage.
Self-acting, self'akt-ing, *a.* Acting of itself; automatic.
Self-command, self-kom-mand', *a.* Command of one's powers or feelings; coolness.
Self-conceit, self-kon-sēt', *n.* A high opinion of oneself; vanity; self-sufficiency.
Self-confident, self-kon'fi-dent, *a.* Confident of one's own strength or abilities.
Self-conscious, self-kon'shus, *a.* Conscious of one's personal states or acts; apt to think of how oneself appears.
Self-contained, self-kon-tānd', *a.* Wrapped up in oneself; reserved.
Self-control, self-kon-trōl', *n.* Control exercised over oneself; self-command.
Self-denial, self-dē-nī'al, *n.* The forbearing to gratify one's own desires.
Self-denying, self-dē-nī'ing, *a.* Denying oneself; forbearing to indulge one's own desires.
Self-educated, self-ed'ū-kāt-ed, *a.* Educated by one's own efforts.
Self-esteem, self-es-tēm', *n.* The esteem or good opinion of oneself; vanity.
Self-evident, self-ev'i-dent, *a.* Evident in its own nature; evident without proof.
Self-government, self-gu'vėrn-ment, *n.* The government of oneself; government by rulers appointed by the people.
Self-important, self-im-pōrt'ant, *a.* Important in one's own esteem; pompous.
Self-imposed, self'im-pōzd, *a.* Imposed or voluntarily taken on oneself.
Selfish, self'ish, *a.* Devoted unduly to self; influenced by a view to private advantage.
Self-made, self'mād, *a.* Made by oneself; risen in the world by one's exertions.
Self-possessed, self-po-zest', *a.* Cool and composed; not excited or flustered.
Self-possession, self-po-ze'shon, *n.* The possession of one's faculties; self-command.
Self-respect, self'rē-spekt, *n.* Respect for oneself; proper pride.
Self-righteous, self-rīt'yus, *a.* Righteous in one's own esteem; sanctimonious.
Self-same, self'sām, *a.* Exactly the same; the very same; identical.
Self-satisfied, self-sa'tis-fīd, *a.* Satisfied with oneself; showing complacency.
Self-seeking, self'sēk-ing, *a.* Selfish.
Self-styled, self'stīld, *a.* Called by a title assumed without warrant.
Self-sufficient, self-suf-fi'shent, *a.* Having too much confidence in oneself; conceited; assuming; overbearing.
Self-will, self'wil, *n.* One's own will; wilfulness; obstinacy.
Self-willed, self'wild, *a.* Wilful, obstinate.
Sell, sel, *vt.* (selling, sold). To give in exchange for money, &c.; to betray.—*vi.* To practise selling; to be sold.
Seller, sel'ėr, *n.* The person who sells.
Selvedge, Selvage, sel'vej, sel'vāj, *n.* The edge of cloth; border of close work.
Selvedged, Selvaged, sel'vejd, sel'vājd, *a.* Having a selvedge.
Semaphore, se'ma-fōr, *n.* An apparatus for signalling at a distance, usually a pole supporting a movable arm.
Semblance, sem'blans, *n.* Similarity; resemblance; image; appearance.
Semeiology, sē-mi-ol'o-ji, *n.* The doctrine of signs; semeiotics.
Semeiotics, sē-mī-ot'iks, *n.* The science of signs; the doctrine of symptoms of disease.
Semen, sē'men, *n.* The seed or fecundating fluid of male animals; sperm.
Semibreve, se'mi-brēv, *n.* A note in music equivalent to two minims.
Semicircle, se'mi-sėr-kl, *n.* The half of a circle.
Semicircular, se-mi-sėr'kū-lėr, *a.* Forming a semicircle.
Semicolon, se'mi-kō-lon, *n.* The point (;), marking a greater break than a comma.
Semi-detached, se'mi-dē-tacht", *a.* Partly separated; joined on to another house, but the two detached from other buildings.
Seminal, se'min-al, *a.* Pertaining to seed; germinal; rudimental.
Seminary, se'min-a-ri, *n.* A school or academy; a place for educating for the priesthood.

Semination, se-min-ā'shon, *n.* Act of sowing; the natural dispersion of seeds.
Semiquaver, se'mi-kwā-vėr, *n.* Half a quaver in music.
Semite, sem'īt, *n.* A descendant of Shem; one of the Semitic race; a Shemite.
Semitic, sem-it'ik, *a.* Pertaining to the Semites; Hebrew.
Semitone, se'mi-tōn, *n.* Half a tone in music.
Semi-vowel, se'mi-vou-el, *n.* A sound partaking of the nature of both a vowel and a consonant, as *l*, *m*, *r*.
Semolina, se-mō-lī'na, *n.* The large hard grains of flour, separated from the fine flour.
Sempiternal, sem-pi-tėrn'al, *a.* Everlasting.
Sempstress, semp'stres, *n.* A woman who lives by needlework; a seamstress.
Senary, sē'na-ri, *a.* Of six; belonging to six; containing six.
Senate, se'nāt, *n.* The legislative body in ancient Rome; the upper branch of a legislature; the governing body of a university, &c.
Senator, se'nat-or, *n.* A member of a senate.
Senatorial, se-na-tō'ri-al, *a.* Pertaining to a senate.
Senatus, se-nā'tus, *n.* A senate; the governing body in certain universities.
Send, send, *vt.* (sending, sent). To cause to go or be carried; to transmit; to direct to go and act; to make befall.—*vi.* To despatch an agent or message.
Sendal, sen'dal, *n.* A thin silk stuff.
Senescence, sē-nes'ens, *n.* State of growing old.
Senescent, sē-nes'ent, *a.* Growing old.
Seneschal, se'ne-shal, *n.* A kind of steward in the houses of princes, &c.
Senile, sē'nīl, *a.* Pertaining to old age; characterized by the failings of old age.
Senility, sē-nil'i-ti, *n.* State of being old; dotage.
Senior, sē'ni-or, sēn'yor, *a.* Older; older or more advanced in office.—*n.* One older in age or office.
Seniority, sē-ni-or'i-ti, *n.* State of being senior; superiority in office.
Senna, sen'na, *n.* The dried leaves of certain plants used as a purgative; the plant itself.
Se'nnight, sen'nit, *n.* A week.
Sennit, sen'it, *n.* A sort of flat braided cordage used on ships.
Señor, sen-yōr, *n.* A Spanish form of address, corresponding to Mr. or Sir; a gentleman.
Señora, sen-yō'ra, *n.* Madame or Mrs.; a lady.
Señorita, sen-yō-rē'tă, *n.* Miss; a young lady.
Sensation, sen-sā'shon, *n.* Impression made through the senses; feeling; power of feeling; what produces excited interest.
Sensational, sen-sā'shon-al, *a.* Relating to sensation; producing excited interest.
Sensationalism, sen-sā'shon-al-izm, *n.* The doctrine that all ideas are derived through our senses; sensational writing.
Sense, sens, *n.* The faculty of receiving impressions; a separate faculty of perception; sight, hearing, taste, smell, or touch; consciousness; discernment; understanding; good judgment; meaning.
Senseless, sens'les, *a.* Wanting sense; unfeeling; unreasonable; foolish.
Senselessly, sens'les-li, *adv.* Stupidly.
Sensibility, sens-i-bil'i-ti, *n.* State or quality of being sensible; acuteness of perception; delicacy of feeling.
Sensible, sens'i-bl, *a.* That may be perceived by the senses; perceptible; sensitive; easily affected; cognizant; reasonable.
Sensibly, sens'i-bli, *adv.* In a sensible manner; appreciably; judiciously.
Sensitive, sens'i-tiv, *a.* Having the capacity of receiving impressions; easily affected; having the feelings easily hurt.
Sensitively, sens'i-tiv-li, *adv.* In a sensitive manner.
Sensitize, sens'i-tīz, *vt.* To render sensitive; to make capable of being acted on by the rays of the sun.
Sensorial, sen-sō'ri-al, *a.* Sensory.
Sensorium, sen-sō'ri-um, *n.* The common centre at which all the impressions of sense are received; the brain.
Sensory, sen'so-ri, *a.* Relating to the sensorium; conveying sensation.
Sensual, sens'ū-al, *a.* Pertaining to the senses, as distinct from the mind; carnal; voluptuous; indulging in lust.
Sensualism, sens'ū-al-izm, *n.* Sensuality; sensationalism.
Sensualist, sens'ū-al-ist, *n.* A person given to sensuality; a voluptuary.
Sensuality, sens-ū-al'i-ti, *n.* Quality of being sensual; indulgence in lust.
Sensualize, sens'ū-al-īz, *vt.* To make sensual; to debase by carnal gratifications.
Sensuous, sens'ū-us, *a.* Pertaining to the senses; readily affected through the senses.
Sentence, sen'tens, *n.* Opinion; a maxim; a judgment; a number of words containing complete sense.—*vt.* (sentencing, sentenced). To pass sentence upon; to condemn.
Sentential, sen-ten'shal, *a.* Comprising sentences; pertaining to a sentence.
Sententious, sen-ten'shus, *a.* Abounding in maxims; terse; gravely judicial.
Sentient, sen'shi-ent, *a.* Having the capacity of sensation; perceptive; sensible.
Sentiment, sen'ti-ment, *n.* Thought prompted by emotion; tenderness of feeling; sensibility; a thought or opinion.
Sentimental, sen-ti-men'tal, *a.* Having sentiment; apt to be swayed by emotional feelings; mawkishly-tender.
Sentimentalist, sen-ti-men'tal-ist, *n.* One who affects sentiment.
Sentimentality, sen'ti-men-tal"i-ti, *n.* State or quality of being sentimental.
Sentinel, sen'ti-nel, *n.* One who is set to keep watch; a sentry (now archaic or poetical).
Sentry, sen'tri, *n.* A soldier placed on guard; guard; watch; sentinel's duty.
Sentry-box, sen'tri-boks, *n.* A box or small shed to shelter a sentinel at his post.
Sepal, sē'pal or sep'al, *n.* The leaf of a calyx.
Separable, se'pa-ra-bl, *a.* That may be separated; capable of separation.
Separate, se'pa-rāt, *vt.* (separating, separated). To put or set apart; to disjoin.—*vi.* To go apart; to cleave or split.—*a.* Detached; distinct; individual.
Separately, se'pa-rāt-li, *adv.* In a separate state; apart; distinct; singly.
Separation, se-pa-rā'shon, *n.* Act of separating; disunion; incomplete divorce.
Separatist, se'pa-rāt-ist, *n.* One who advocates separation; a seceder.

Separator, se'pa-rāt-ėr, *n.* One who or that which separates.
Separatory, Separative, se'pa-ra-to-ri, se'-pa-ra-tiv, *a.* Tending to separate; causing or used in separation.
Sepia, sē'pi-a, *n.* The cuttle-fish; a brown pigment obtained from the cuttle-fish.
Sepoy, sē'poi, *n.* A native Indian soldier in the British service.
Sept, sept, *n.* A clan; a race or family.
September, sep-tem'bėr, *n.* The ninth month of the year.
Septenary, sep'ten-a-ri, *a.* Consisting of or proceeding by sevens; lasting seven years.
Septennial, sep-ten'ni-al, *a.* Lasting seven years; happening every seven years.
Septet, Septette, sep-tet', *n.* A musical composition for seven voices or instruments.
Septic, sep'tik, *a.* Promoting or causing putrefaction.—*n.* A substance causing putrefaction.
Septicæmia, sep-ti-sē'mi-a, *n.* Blood-poisoning by absorption of putrid matter.
Septuagenarian, sep'tū-a-jen-ā"ri-an, *n.* A person seventy years of age.
Septuagesima, sep'tū-a-jes"i-ma, *n.* The third Sunday before Lent.
Septuagint, sep'tū-a-jint, *n.* A Greek version of the Old Testament, finished about 200 B.C.
Septum, sep'tum, *n.*; pl. **-ta.** A wall separating cavities, as in animals or plants.
Sepulchral, sē-pul'kral, *a.* Pertaining to a sepulchre; grave; hollow, as a voice.
Sepulchre, se'pul-kėr, *n.* A tomb.—*vt.* To bury.
Sepulture, se'pul-tūr, *n.* Burial.
Sequacious, sē-kwā'shus, *a.* Following; logically consistent; consecutive.
Sequel, sē'kwel, *n.* That which follows; a succeeding part; result; issue.
Sequence, sē'kwens, *n.* A coming after; succession; arrangement; series.
Sequent, Sequential, sē'kwent, sē-kwen'-shal, *a.* Following; succeeding.
Sequester, se-kwes'tėr, *vt.* To set apart; *refl.* to retire into seclusion; in *law*, to separate from the owner until the claims of creditors be satisfied; to appropriate.
Sequestered, se-kwes'tėrd, *a.* Secluded.
Sequestrate, se-kwes'trāt, *vt.* To set apart; to divide among creditors.
Sequestration, se-kwes-trā'shon, *n.* Act of sequestering; separation.
Sequestrator, se-kwes'trāt-or, *n.* One who sequesters or sequestrates.
Seraglio, se-räl'yō, *n.* Originally the old palace of the Turkish sultan at Constantinople; so a harem.
Serai, se-rī', *n.* In Eastern countries, a place for the accommodation of travellers.
Seraph, se'raf, *n.*; pl. **-phs** or **-phim.** An angel of the highest rank or order.
Seraphic, se-raf'ik, *a.* Pertaining to a seraph; celestial; pure.
Serenade, se-rē-nād', *n.* Music played at night under the windows of ladies.—*vt.* (serenading, serenaded). To entertain with a serenade.—*vi.* To perform a serenade.
Serene, sē-rēn', *a.* Clear; bright; calm; unruffled; formerly a form of address for princes, &c., in Germany and Austria.—*n.* Serenity; what is serene.
Serenely, sē-rēn'li, *adv.* In a serene manner; calmly; quietly; coolly.
Serenity, sē-ren'i-ti, *n.* State of being serene; peace; calmness; coolness.
Serf, sėrf, *n.* A villein; a forced labourer attached to an estate; a bondman.
Serfdom, sėrf'dom, *n.* The state or condition of serfs.
Serge, sėrj, *n.* A tough twilled worsted cloth; a twilled silken fabric.
Sergeant, Serjeant, sär'jant, *n.* A non-commissioned officer above corporal; a police-officer; one of an order of barristers abolished in 1873.
Sergeantcy, Serjeantcy, sär'jant-si, *n.* The office of a sergeant.
Sergeantship, sär'jant-ship, *n.* The office of a sergeant.
Serial, sē'ri-al, *a.* Pertaining to a series; forming a series.—*n.* A written composition issued in numbers.
Seriatim, sē-ri-ā'tim, *adv.* In regular order; one after the other.
Sericeous, sē-ri'shus, *a.* Pertaining to silk silky.
Sericulture, sē'ri-kul-tūr, *n.* The breeding and treatment of silk-worms.
Series, sē'ri-ēz or sē'rēz, *n.*; pl. the same. A succession of things; sequence; course.
Serio-comic, sē'ri-ō-kom"ik, *a.* Having a mixture of seriousness and comicality.
Serious, sē'ri-us, *a.* Grave; earnest; momentous; attended with danger.
Seriously, sē'ri-us-li, *adv.* Gravely; earnestly; in an important degree.
Serjeant, sär'jant, *n.* *See* SERGEANT.
Sermon, sėr'mon, *n.* A religious discourse by a clergyman; a homily.—*vt.* To tutor; to lecture.
Sermonize, sėr'mon-īz, *vi.* To preach; to inculcate rigid rules; to harangue.
Seroon, se-rön', *n.* A hamper of certain kinds of goods, as raisins or almonds.
Serosity, sē-ros'i ti, *n.* State of being serous.
Serous, sēr'us, *a.* Pertaining to serum; thin; watery; like whey; secreting serum.
Serpent, sėr'pent, *n.* A scaly reptile without feet; a bass musical instrument of wood; a firework.—*a.* Pertaining to a serpent.
Serpentine, sėr'pent-īn, *a.* Resembling or pertaining to a serpent; spiral.—*n.* A rock resembling a serpent's skin in appearance, used for decoration.—*vi.* To wind like a serpent.
Serpigo, sėr-pī'go, *n.* Ring-worm.
Serrate, Serrated, ser'rāt, ser'rāt-ed, *a.* Notched on the edge like a saw; toothed.
Serration, ser-rā'shon, *n.* Formation in the shape of a saw.
Serrature, ser'ra-tūr, *n.* A notching in the edge of anything, like a saw; serration.
Serried, se'rid, *a.* Crowded; in close order.
Serum, sē'rum, *n.* The watery part of curdled milk; whey; the thin part of the blood, &c.
Serval, sėr'val, *n.* A small S. African leopard.
Servant, sėrv'ant, *n.* One who serves; an attendant in a household; a drudge.
Serve, sėrv, *vt.* (serving, served). To work for and obey; to minister to; to set on a table for a meal; to conduce to; to be sufficient for; to manage or work; to deliver or transmit to; to perform the conditions of.—*vi.* To perform offices for another; to perform duties; to suffice; to suit.
Server, sėrv'ėr, *n.* One who or that which serves; a salver.

Service, sėrv'is, *n.* Act of one who serves; employment; kind office; military or naval duty; period of such duty; usefulness; public religious worship; liturgy; set of dishes for the table; supply of things regularly provided.
Serviceable, sėrv'is-a-bl, *a.* That renders service; useful; beneficial.
Service-book, sėrv'is-bųk, *n.* A book used in church service; a prayer-book.
Service-tree, sėrv'is-trē, *n.* A European tree of the pear family.
Serviette, sėr-vi-et', *n.* A table-napkin.
Servile, sėr'vīl, *a.* Slavish; mean; dependent; fawning; meanly submissive.
Servilely, sėr'vīl-li, *adv.* In a servile manner; slavishly; meanly.
Servility, sėr-vil'i-ti, *n.* State of being servile; mean submission.
Servitor, sėrv'i-tor, *n.* A male servant.
Servitude, sėrv'i-tūd, *n.* State of a slave; slavery; compulsory labour.
Sesame, ses'a-mē, *n.* An annual herbaceous plant, the seeds of which yield a fine oil.
Sesquipedalian, Sesquipedal, ses'kwi-pē-dā''li-an, ses'kwi-pē-dal, *a.* Containing a foot and a half: applied to long words; using long words.
Sessile, ses'il, *a.* Attached without any sensible projecting support; having no stalk.
Session, se'shon, *n.* The sitting of a court, &c., for business; time or term of sitting.—**Court of Session,** the highest civil court of Scotland.
Sessional, se'shon-al, *a.* Relating to sessions.
Sestet, Sestette, ses'tet, ses-tet', *n.* A musical composition for six voices or six instruments; the last six lines of a sonnet.
Set, set, *vt.* (setting, set). To put or dispose in a certain place or position; to fix; to appoint; to estimate; to regulate or adjust; to fit to music; to adorn; to intersperse; to incite.—*vi.* To disappear below the horizon; to solidify; to tend; to point out game; to apply oneself.—*p.a.* Placed, fixed, &c.; determined; established.—*n.* The descent of the sun, &c.; attitude, position; turn or bent; number of things combining to form a whole; a complete assortment; a clique.
Seta, sē'ta, *n.*; pl. **-æ.** A bristle or sharp hair.
Setaceous, se-tā'shus, *a.* Bristly.
Set-off, set'of, *n.* Any counterbalance; an equivalent; a counter claim.
Seton, sē'ton, *n.* A twist of silk or cotton drawn under the skin to keep up an issue.
Setose, sē'tōs, *a.* Bristly.
Settee, set-tē', *n.* A long seat with a back to it; a kind of sofa.
Setter, set'ėr, *n.* One who or that which sets; a sporting dog.
Setting, set'ing, *n.* Act of sinking below the horizon; that in which something, as a jewel, is set; music set for certain words.
Settle, set'l, *n.* A bench with a high back and arms.—*vt.* (settling, settled). To place in a more or less permanent position; to establish; to quiet; to determine; to reconcile; to pay; to square or adjust; to colonize.—*vi.* To become fixed; to fix one's abode; to subside; to become calm; to adjust differences or accounts.
Settled, set'ld, *p.a.* Established; steadfast; stable; methodical.
Settlement, set'l-ment, *n.* Act of settling; establishment in life; colonization; a colony; adjustment; liquidation; arrangement; settling of property on a wife.
Settler, set'lėr, *n.* One who settles; a colonist; that which decides anything.
Settling, set'ling, *n.* Act of one who settles; payment, as of an account; *pl.* dregs.
Set-to, set-tö', *n.* A sharp contest.
Seven, se'ven, *a.* and *n.* One more than six.
Sevenfold, se'ven-fōld, *a.* Repeated seven times.—*adv.* Seven times as much or often.
Seventeen, se'ven-tēn, *a.* and *n.* Seven and ten.
Seventeenth, se'ven-tēnth, *a.* and *n.* The next in order after the sixteenth; one of seventeen equal parts.
Seventh, se'venth, *a.* Next after the sixth; containing or being one part in seven.—*n.* One part in seven.
Seventhly, se'venth-li, *adv.* In the seventh place.
Seventieth, se'ven-ti-eth, *a.* and *n.* The next after sixty-ninth; one of seventy equal parts.
Seventy, se'ven-ti, *a.* and *n.* Seven times ten.
Sever, se'vėr, *vt.* To separate by violence; to keep distinct.—*vi.* To separate.
Severable, se'vėr-a-bl, *a.* Capable of being severed.
Several, se'vėr-al, *a.* Separate; distinct; more than two, but not very many.
Severally, se'vėr-al-li, *adv.* Separately.
Severalty, se'vėr-al-ti, *n.* A state of separation from the rest, or from all others.
Severance, se'vėr-ans, *n.* Act of severing; separation.
Severe, sē-vēr', *a.* Serious; grave; harsh; stern; austere; rigidly exact; keen.
Severely, sē-vēr'li, *adv.* Harshly; strictly.
Severity, sē-ve'ri-ti, *n.* State or quality of being severe; rigour; intensity; austerity.
Sèvres, sā-vr, *n.* A kind of beautiful porcelain, made at *Sèvres*, near Paris.
Sew, sō, *vt.* and *i.* To unite or make by needle and thread.
Sewage, sū'āj, *n.* The filthy matter which passes through sewers.
Sewer, sū'ėr, *n.* A subterranean drain, as in a city, to carry off water, filth, &c.
Sewer, sō'ėr, *n.* One who sews.
Sewerage, sū'ėr-āj, *n.* The system of sewers as in a city; sewage.
Sewing, sō'ing, *n.* Act of using a needle; that which is sewed; stitches made.
Sex, seks, *n.* That character by which an animal is male or female.
Sexagenarian, seks-a'jen-ā''ri-an, *n.* A person sixty years of age.—*a.* Sixty years old.
Sexagenary, seks-a'jen-a-ri, *a.* Pertaining to the number sixty.—*n.* A person sixty years old.
Sexagesima, seks-a-jes'i-ma, *n.* The second Sunday before Lent.
Sexennial, seks-en'ni-al, *a.* Lasting six years, or happening once in six years.
Sextain, seks'tān, *n.* A stanza of six lines.
Sextant, seks'tant, *n.* The sixth part of a circle; an instrument for measuring the angular distances of objects by reflection.
Sexto-decimo, seks-tō-des'i-mō, *n.* The size of a book when each sheet makes sixteen leaves: usually written 16mo (*sixteenmo*).
Sexton, seks'ton, *n.* An under officer of a church who takes care of the sacred vessels, acts as janitor, &c.
Sextuple, seks'tū-pl, *a.* Sixfold.

Sexual, seks'ū-al, *a.* Pertaining to, proceeding from, characterized by sex.
Sexuality, seks'ū-al'i-ti, *n.* State of being sexual.
Sexually, seks'ū-al-li, *adv.* In a sexual manner.
Sforzando, sfor-tsän'dō. A musical term marking notes that are to be emphasized, contracted *sf.*
Shabbily, shab'i-li, *adv.* In a shabby manner; with shabby clothes; meanly.
Shabby, shab'i, *a.* Poor in appearance; threadbare; mean; paltry; stingy.
Shabby-genteel, shab'i-jen-tēl, *a.* Shabby but having some appearance of gentility.
Shabrack, shab'rak, *n.* The saddle-cloth of a cavalry-officer.
Shackle, shak'l, *n.* A fetter; a manacle; that which obstructs free action.—*vt.* (shackling, shackled). To bind with shackles; to hamper.
Shad, shad, *n. sing.* and *pl.* A fish of the herring family.
Shade, shād, *n.* Obscurity caused by the interception of light; obscure retreat; twilight dimness; a screen; darker part of a picture; gradation of light; a scarcely perceptible degree or amount; a ghost.—*vt.* (shading, shaded). To screen from light; to obscure; to protect; to darken; to mark with gradations of colour.
Shading, shād'ing, *n.* Act of making shade; light and shade in a picture.
Shadoof, sha-döf', *n.* An oriental contrivance for raising water, consisting of a long pole working on a post and weighted at one end, the other end having a bucket attached.
Shadow, sha'dō, *n.* A figure projected by the interception of light; shade; an inseparable companion; an imperfect representation; a spirit; protection.—*vt.* To shade; to cloud; to screen; to represent faintly; to follow closely.
Shadowy, sha'dō-i, *a.* Full of shadow; shady; dark; dim; unsubstantial.
Shady, shād'i, *a.* Abounding in shade; affording shade; of dubious morality.
Shaft, shäft, *n.* The long part of a spear or arrow; body of a column; spire of a steeple, &c.; pole of a carriage; a kind of large axle; a narrow passage, as into a mine.
Shafting, shäft'ing, *n.* A system of shafts communicating motion in machinery.
Shag, shag, *n.* Coarse hair or nap; cloth with a coarse nap; tobacco leaves shredded for smoking.—*vt.* (shagging, shagged). To make shaggy.
Shaggy, shag'i, *a.* Covered with shag; rough; rugged.
Shagreen, sha-grēn', *n.* A leather with a granulated surface prepared without tanning from the skins of horses, sharks, &c.
Shah, shä, *n.* A title given by Europeans to the monarch of Persia.
Shake, shāk, *vt.* (shaking, pret. shook, pp. shaken). To cause to move with quick vibrations; to agitate; to move from firmness; to cause to waver; to trill.—*vi.* To tremble; to shiver; to quake.—*n.* A wavering or rapid motion; tremor; shock; a trill in music; a crack in timber.
Shake-down, shāk'doun, *n.* A temporary substitute for a bed, formed on the floor.
Shaker, shāk'ėr, *n.* A person or thing that shakes; a member of a religious sect.
Shako, shak'ō, *n.* A stiff military cap with a peak in front.
Shaky, shāk'i, *a.* Apt to shake or tremble; unsteady; feeble.
Shale, shāl, *n.* A fine-grained rock; a clay rock having a slaty structure.
Shall, shal, *verb auxiliary*; pret. *should*, shụd. In the first person it forms part of the future tense; in the second and third persons it implies authority.
Shalli, shal'i, *n.* A kind of twilled cloth made from Angora goat's hair.
Shalloon, sha-lön', *n.* A slight woollen stuff.
Shallop, shal'op, *n.* A small light boat.
Shallot, sha-lot', *n.* A species of onion.
Shallow, shal'ō, *a.* Not deep; superficial; simple; silly.—*n.* A place where the water is not deep; a shoal.
Shallowly, shal'ō-li, *adv.* In a shallow manner; superficially.
Shaly, shāl'i, *a.* Pertaining to shale; partaking of the qualities of shale.
Sham, sham, *n.* That which appears to be what it is not; imposture; humbug.—*a.* False; counterfeit.—*vt.* and *i.* (shamming, shammed). To feign, pretend.
Shamanism, shä'man-izm, *n.* An idolatrous religion of Northern Asia, &c., characterized by a belief in sorcery and in demons who require to be propitiated.
Shamble, sham'bl, *vi.* (shambling, shambled). To walk awkwardly, as if the knees were weak.—*n.* The gait of one who shambles.
Shambles, sham'blz, *n.pl.* A flesh-market; a slaughter-house; a place of butchery.
Shambling, sham'bling, *p.a.* Walking with an irregular, clumsy pace.
Shame, shām, *n.* A painful sensation excited by guilt, disgrace, &c.; reproach; disgrace. —*vt.* (shaming, shamed). To make ashamed; to disgrace.
Shamefaced, shām'fāst, *a.* Easily put out of countenance; modest; bashful.
Shameful, shām'fụl, *a.* Full of shame; disgraceful; scandalous; infamous.
Shameless, shām'les, *a.* Destitute of shame; immodest; unblushing.
Shammy, Shamoy, sham'i, sham'oi, *n.* A soft leather for polishing, prepared originally from the skin of the chamois.
Shampoo, sham-pö', *vt.* (shampooing, shampooed). To press and rub the body after a hot bath; to wash and rub thoroughly the head.
Shamrock, sham'rok, *n.* A trefoil plant, the national emblem of Ireland.
Shandry, Shandrydan, shan'dri, shan'dri-dan, *n.* A one-horse Irish conveyance.
Shandygaff, shan'di-gaf, *n.* A mixture of beer and ginger-beer or lemonade.
Shank, shangk, *n.* The leg; the shin-bone; the part of a tool connecting the acting part with a handle; the stem of an anchor.
Shanked, shangkt, *a.* Having a shank.
Sha'n't, shänt. A colloquial contraction of *shall not.*
Shanty, shan'ti, *n.* A hut or mean dwelling; song sung by sailors working together.
Shape, shāp, *vt.* (shaping, shaped). To form; to mould; to adjust.—*vi.* To suit.—*n.* Form or figure; make; a model; a dish of blancmange, &c.
Shapeless, shāp'les, *a.* Destitute of any regular form; deformed.

Shapely, shāp'li, *a.* Well-formed; symmetrical; handsome.
Shard, shärd, *n.* A fragment of an earthen vessel; the wing-case of a beetle.
Share, shār, *n.* A part bestowed or contributed; lot or portion; a plough-share.—*vt.* (sharing, shared). To part among two or more; to participate in.—*vi.* To have part.
Share-broker, shār'brōk-ėr, *n.* A dealer in the shares and securities of joint-stock companies and the like.
Shareholder, shār'hōld-ėr, *n.* One who holds shares in a joint property.
Share-list, shār'list, *n.* A list giving the prices of shares of banks, railways, &c.
Sharer, shār'ėr, *n.* One who shares.
Shark, shärk, *n.* A voracious sea-fish; an unscrupulous person; a sharper.
Sharp, shärp, *a.* Having a very thin edge or fine point; keen; abrupt; not blurred; shrewd; acid; shrill; fierce; short and rapid; biting; barely honest; in *music*, raised a semitone.—*n.* A note raised a semitone, marked by the sign (♯); the sign itself; *pl.* the hard parts of wheat.—*vt.* To sharpen.—*adv.* Sharply; exactly; rapidly.
Sharp-cut, shärp'kut, *a.* Cut sharply and clearly; well-defined; clear.
Sharpen, shärp'n, *vt.* To make sharp or sharper; to whet.—*vi.* To become sharp.
Sharpener, shärp'nėr, *n.* One who or that which sharpens; a tool for sharpening.
Sharper, shärp'ėr, *n.* One who lives by sharp practices; a tricky fellow; a cheat; a sharpener.
Sharply, shärp'li, *adv.* In a sharp manner; severely; keenly; acutely; abruptly.
Sharpness, shärp'nes, *n.* Keenness; pungency; acuteness.
Sharp-shooter, shärp'shöt-ėr, *n.* A soldier skilled in shooting with exactness.
Sharp-sighted, shärp'sīt-ed, *a.* Having quick sight; having acute discernment.
Shaster, Shastra, shäs'tėr, shäs'tra, *n.* A book of laws or precepts among the Hindus.
Shatter, shat'ėr, *vt.* To break into many pieces; to overthrow, destroy.—*vt.* To be broken into fragments.—*n.* A fragment.
Shattery, shat'ėr-i, *a.* Easily shattered; brittle; loose of texture.
Shave, shāv, *vt.* (shaving, shaved). To cut off the hair from the skin with a razor; to cut off thin slices from; to skim along; to fleece.—*vi.* To cut off the beard with a razor.—*n.* A cutting off of the beard; a thin slice; an exceedingly narrow escape.
Shave-grass, shāv'gräs, *n.* One of the plants called horsetail, used for polishing.
Shaveling, shāv'ling, *n.* A man shaved; a monk or friar, in contempt.
Shaver, shāv'ėr, *n.* A barber; one who fleeces; a fellow; a wag.
Shaving, shāv'ing, *n.* Act of one who shaves; a thin slice pared off.
Shaw, shạ, *n.* A grove or thicket.
Shawl, shạl, *n.* An article of dress, used mostly as a loose covering for the shoulders.
She, shē, *pron. nominative.* The feminine pronoun of the third person.
Shea, shē'a, *n.* A tree of tropical Asia and Africa, called also *butter-tree*.
Sheaf, shēf, *n.*; pl. **Sheaves,** shēvz. A bundle of the stalks of wheat, oats, &c.; any similar bundle.—*vt.* To make into sheaves.—*vi.* To make sheaves.
Sheafy, shēf'i, *a.* Pertaining to or consisting of sheaves.
Shealing, Sheal, shēl'ing, shēl, *n.* A hut or shed. Also *Sheiling, Shieling.*
Shear, shēr, *vt.* and *i.* (pret. sheared or shore, pp. sheared or shorn). To cut with shears; to clip the wool from; to cut from a surface; to fleece.
Shearer, shēr-ėr, *n.* One who shears.
Shearing, shēr'ing, *n.* Act of shearing; the result of the operation of clipping.
Shearling, shēr'ling, *n.* A sheep sheared only once.
Shears, shērz, *n.pl.* An instrument of two blades for cutting.
Shear-steel, shēr'stēl, *n.* Steel prepared from bars of common steel, heated, beaten together, and drawn out.
Shear-water, shēr'wạ-tėr, *n.* A marine bird of the petrel family.
Sheath, shēth, *n.* A case for a sword, &c.; a scabbard; wing-case of an insect.
Sheathe, shēᴛʜ, *vt.* (sheathing, sheathed). To put into a sheath; to protect by a casing.
Sheathed, shēᴛʜd, *p.a.* Put in or having a sheath; covered with sheathing.
Sheathing, shēᴛʜ'ing, *n.* Act of one who sheathes; that which sheathes; covering of metal to protect a ship's bottom.
Sheave, shēv, *n.* A small grooved wheel on which a rope works; the wheel of a pulley.
Shebeen, shē-bēn', *n.* An unlicensed house where excisable liquors are sold.
Shed, shed, *vt.* (shedding, shed). To cast or throw off; to emit or diffuse; to let fall in drops; to spill.—*vi.* To let fall seed, a covering, &c.—*n.* A watershed; the opening between the threads in a loom through which the shuttle passes; a penthouse; a hut; a large open structure.
Sheen, shēn, *n.* Brightness; splendour.—*a.* Bright; shining: *poetical.*
Sheeny, shēn'i, *a.* Bright; shining; fair.
Sheep, shēp, *sing.* and *pl.* A ruminant animal valued for its wool and flesh; a silly or timid fellow.—**Sheep's eye,** a loving or wistful glance.
Sheep-cot, Sheep-cote, shēp'kot, shēp'kōt, *n.* A small inclosure for sheep; a pen.
Sheepfold, shēp'fōld, *n.* A fold or pen in which sheep are collected or confined.
Sheepish, shēp'ish, *a.* Like a sheep; foolish; bashful; over-modest or diffident.
Sheep-run, shēp'run, *n.* A large tract of grazing country for pasturing sheep.
Sheep-skin, shēp'skin, *n.* The skin of a sheep prepared with the wool on; leather prepared from it.
Sheep-walk, shēp'wạk, *n.* A tract of some extent where sheep pasture.
Sheer, shēr, *a.* Mere; downright; precipitous.—*vi.* To deviate from the proper course.—*n.* The upward bend of a ship at stem or stern.
Sheers, shērz, *n.pl.* A hoisting apparatus of two or more poles fastened near the top, from which depends the necessary tackle.
Sheet, shēt, *n.* A broad, thin piece of anything; broad expanse; piece of linen or cotton spread on a bed; piece of paper; a rope fastened to the lower corner of a sail.—*vt.* To furnish with sheets; to shroud.

Sheet-anchor, shēt'ang-kėr, *n.* A large anchor used only in danger; last refuge.
Sheeting, shēt'ing, *n.* Linen or cotton cloth for making bed-sheets.
Sheet-iron, shēt'ī-ėrn, *n.* Iron in broad plates.
Sheet-lightning, shēt'līt-ning, *n.* Lightning appearing in wide expanded flashes.
Sheikh, shēk, *n.* An Arab chief; a title of dignity among the Arabs.
Sheil, Sheiling, shēl, shēl'ing, *n.* *See* SHEALING.
Shekel, she'kel, *n.* An ancient Jewish weight of about half an ounce, and silver coin formerly worth about *2s. 7d.* sterling.
Shelf, shelf, *n.*; pl. **Shelves,** shelvz. A board fixed along a wall to support articles; a ledge; a ledge of rocks in the sea.
Shelfy, shelf'i, *a.* Full of rocky shelves.
Shell, shel, *n.* A hard outside covering; an outside crust; framework; any slight hollow structure; a projectile containing a bursting charge.—*vt.* To strip off the shell of; to throw bomb-shells into or among.—*vi.* To cast the exterior covering.
Shellac, shel-lak', *n.* Lac melted and formed into thin cakes.
Shell-fish, shel'fish, *n. sing.* and *pl.* A mollusc or a crustacean whose external covering consists of a shell.
Shell-shock, shel'shok, *n.* Neurosis caused by shell-fire.
Shelly, shel'i, *a.* Abounding with shells; consisting of shells.
Shelter, shel'tėr, *n.* A protection; asylum; refuge; security.—*vt.* To protect; to screen. —*vi.* To take shelter.
Shelve, shelv, *vt.* (shelving, shelved). To place on a shelf; to dismiss from use or attention; to furnish with shelves.—*vi.* To slope.
Shelving, shelv'ing, *n.* The operation of fixing up shelves; shelves collectively.
Shelvy, shelv'i, *a.* Full of shelves of rock.
Shepherd, shep'ėrd, *n.* One who tends sheep.
Shepherdess, shep'ėrd-es, *n.* A woman who tends sheep; a rural lass.
Sherbet, sher'bet, *n.* An Eastern drink of water, the juice of fruits, and sugar.
Sherd, shėrd, *n.* A fragment; a shard.
Shereef, Sheriff, Sherif, she-rēf', *n.* A descendant of Mohammed through his daughter Fatima; chief magistrate of Mecca.
Sheriff, she'rif, *n.* An officer in each county to whom is entrusted the administration of the law; in Scotland, the chief judge of a county.
Sherry, she'ri, *n.* A wine of southern Spain.
Shew, shō. *See* SHOW.
Shibboleth, shib'bō-leth, *n.* The watchword of a party; a cry or motto.
Shield, shēld, *n.* A broad piece of armour carried on the arm; protection; an escutcheon with a coat of arms.—*vt.* To cover, as with a shield; to protect.
Shieling, shēl'ing, *n.* *See* SHEALING.
Shift, shift, *vi.* To change; to change place or direction; to manage; to practise indirect methods.—*vt.* To remove; to alter; to dress in fresh clothes.—*n.* A change; expedient; evasion; an under garment; a squad of workmen; the working time of a relay of men; the spell of work.
Shifter, shift'ėr. *n.* One who or that which shifts; a trickster.
Shiftless, shift'les, *a.* Destitute of expedients; wanting in energy or effort.
Shifty, shift'i, *a.* Full of shifts; fertile in expedients or evasions; tricky.
Shillelah, shil-lel'a, *n.* An Irish name for an oaken or blackthorn sapling used as a cudgel.
Shilling, shil'ing, *n.* An English silver coin equal to twelve pence.
Shilly-shally, shil'i-shal-i, *vi.* To hesitate.—*n.* Foolish trifling; irresolution.
Shimmer, shim'ėr, *vi.* To emit a faint or tremulous light; to glisten.—*n.* A glistening.
Shin, shin, *n.* The fore-part of the leg, between the ankle and the knee.
Shine, shīn, *vi.* (shining, shone). To give out a steady brilliant light; to be lively, bright, or conspicuous.—*vt.* To cause to shine.—*n.* Brightness; fair weather.
Shingle, shing'gl, *n.* A thin piece of wood used in covering roofs; loose gravel and pebbles.—*vt.* To cover with shingles; to hammer so as to expel slag or scoriæ from in puddling iron.
Shingles, shing'glz, *n.* An eruptive disease which spreads around the body.
Shingling, shing'gling, *n.* A covering of shingles; a process in reducing iron from the cast to the malleable state.
Shingly, shing'gli, *a.* Abounding with shingle or gravel.
Shining, shīn'ing, *a.* Bright; illustrious.
Shinto, Shintoism, shin'to, shin'to-izm, *n.* The ancient religion of Japan.
Shinty, shin'ti, *n.* Hockey.
Shiny, shīn'i, *a.* Bright; brilliant; clear.
Ship, ship, *n.* A vessel of some size adapted to navigation; a three-masted, square-rigged vessel.—*vt.* (shipping, shipped). To put on board of a ship; to transport in a ship; to hire for service in a ship; to fix in its place.—*vi.* To engage for service on a ship; to embark.
Shipboard, ship'bōrd, *n.* The deck or interior of a ship: used in *on shipboard.*
Ship-broker, ship'brō-kėr, *n.* A broker who procures insurance, &c., for ships.
Ship-builder, ship'bild-ėr, *n.* One who builds ships; a naval architect; a shipwright.
Ship-building, ship'bild-ing, *n.* The art of constructing vessels for navigation.
Ship-chandler, ship'chand-lėr, *n.* One who deals in cordage, canvas, &c., for ships.
Ship-letter, ship'let-ėr, *n.* A letter sent by a common ship, and not by mail.
Ship-master, ship'mas-tėr, *n.* The master, captain, or commander of a ship.
Shipmate, ship'māt, *n.* One who serves in the same ship; a fellow-sailor.
Shipment, ship'ment, *n.* Act of putting goods on board of a ship; goods shipped.
Ship-owner, ship'ōn-ėr, *n.* A person who owns a ship or ships, or any share therein.
Shippen, Shippon, ship'n, *n.* A house or shed for cattle or sheep.
Shipper, ship'ėr, *n.* One who sends goods on board a ship for transportation.
Shipping, ship'ing, *n.* Ships in general; aggregate tonnage.
Ship-shape, ship'shāp, *a.* Having a seaman-like trim; well arranged.
Ship's-husband, ships'huz-band, *n.* A person appointed to look after the repairs, stores, &c., of a ship while in port.
Shipwreck, ship'rek, *n.* The wreck or loss

of a ship; destruction; ruin.—*vt.* To wreck; to cast away; to ruin.
Shipwright, ship'rīt, *n.* A builder of ships or other vessels; a ship-carpenter.
Ship-yard, ship'yärd, *n.* A yard or place in which ships are constructed.
Shire, shīr (but shir in county names), *n.* A county.
Shirk, shėrk, *vt.* and *i.* To avoid unfairly; to seek to avoid duty.
Shirt, shėrt, *n.* A man's loose under garment of linen, &c.; a lady's blouse.—*vt.* To clothe with a shirt.
Shirting, shėrt'ing, *n.* Cloth for shirts.
Shittah-tree, shit'ta-trē, *n.* A species of acacia.
Shittim-wood, shit'tim-wụd, *n.* The hard and durable wood of the shittah-tree.
Shive, shīv, *n.* A slice; a fragment.
Shiver, shi'vėr, *vt.* To shatter.—*vi.* To fall into many small pieces; to tremble, as from cold; to shudder.—*n.* A small fragment; a shaking fit; shudder.
Shivery, shi'vėr-i, *a.* Pertaining to shivering; characterized by shivering.
Shoal, shōl, *n.* A multitude; a crowd; a sand-bank or bar; a shallow.—*vi.* To become more shallow.—*a.* Shallow.
Shoaly, shōl'i, *a.* Full of shoals.
Shock, shok, *n.* A violent striking against; violent onset; a sudden disturbing emotion; a stook; a thick mass of hair.—*vt.* To give a shock to; to encounter violently; to disgust; to make up into shocks or stooks.
Shocking, shok'ing, *a.* Serving to shock; dreadful; disgusting; offensive.
Shock troops, shok trōps, *n.* Picked soldiers specially trained for offensive action.
Shod, shod, pret. and pp. of *shoe.*
Shoddy, shod'i, *n.* Fibre obtained from old woollen fabrics mixed with fresh wool and manufactured anew; inferior cloth made from this.—*a.* Made of shoddy; trashy.
Shoe, shö, *n.* A covering for the foot; a plate of iron nailed to the hoof of a horse, &c.—*vt.* (shoeing, shoed). To furnish with shoes.
Shoeblack, shö'blak, *n.* A person that cleans shoes.
Shoe-horn, Shoeing-horn, shö'horn, shö'-ing-horn, *n.* A curved implement used to aid in putting on shoes.
Shoemaker, shö'māk-ėr, *n.* One who makes shoes.
Shog, shog, *n.* A sudden shake; a shock; a jog.
Shone, shon, pret. and pp. of *shine.*
Shook, shụk, pret. and pp. of *shake.*—*n.* The staves for a single barrel made into a package.
Shoot, shöt, *vt.* (shooting, shot). To cause to fly forth; to discharge; to hit or kill with a missile; to empty out suddenly; to thrust forward; to pass rapidly under, over, &c.—*vi.* To charge a missile; to dart along; to sprout; to project.—*n.* A shooting; a young branch; a sloping trough; a place for shooting rubbish.
Shooting, shöt'ing, *n.* Sport of killing game with firearms; tract over which game is shot; sensation of a darting pain.—*a.* Pertaining to one who shoots.
Shooting-box, shöt'ing-boks, *n.* A lodge used by sportsmen in the shooting season.
Shop, shop, *n.* A place where goods are sold by retail; a building in which mechanics work; one's special business.—*vi.* (shopping, shopped). To visit shops for purchasing goods.
Shopkeeper, shop'kēp-ėr, *n.* One who keeps a shop; one who sells goods by retail.
Shop-lifter, shop'lift-ėr, *n.* One who steals in a shop on pretence of buying.
Shopman, shop'man, *n.* A petty trader; one who serves in a shop.
Shoppy, shop'i, *a.* Pertaining to a shop; given to talk only of one's own calling.
Shop-walker, shop'wąk-ėr, *n.* An attendant in a shop who directs customers, sees that they are served, &c.
Shop-woman, shop'wụ-man, *n.* A woman who serves in a shop.
Shore, shōr, *n.* Land along the edge of the sea; the coast; a prop.—*vt.* To support by props: pret. of *shear.*
Shorn, shōrn, pp. of *shear.*
Short, short, *a.* Not long or tall; scanty; deficient; concise; snappish; severe; brittle.—*adv.* Abruptly; insufficiently.—*n.* Something short; *pl.* garments resembling trousers, but ending above the knee.—**In short,** in few words; briefly.
Shortage, short'āj, *n.* Amount short or deficient; deficit.
Shortcoming, short'kum-ing, *n.* A failing of the usual quantity; a delinquency.
Short-dated, short'dāt-ed, *a.* Having little time to run.
Shorten, short'n, *vt.* To make short or shorter; to deprive.—*vi.* To contract.
Shorthand, short'hand, *n.* A shorter mode of writing than is usually employed.
Short-handed, short'hand-ed, *a.* Not having the usual number of assistants.
Short-horn, short horn, *n.* One of a breed of cattle with very short horns.
Short-lived, short'līvd, *a.* Not living or lasting long; of short continuance.
Shortly, short'li, *adv.* Quickly; soon; briefly.
Short-sighted, short'sīt-ed, *n.* Unable to see far; myopic; wanting foresight.
Short-winded, short'wind-ed, *a.* Affected with shortness of breath.
Shot, shot, *n.* Act of shooting; a projectile; a bullet; bullets collectively; range or reach; a marksman; the number of fish caught in one haul; a reckoning.—*vt.* (shotting, shotted). To load with shot.—*a.* Having a changeable colour, as silk; interwoven.
Should, shụd, the pret. of *shall,* denoting present or past duty or obligation, or expressing a hypothetical case.
Shoulder, shōl'dėr, *n.* The joint by which the arm or the fore-leg is connected with the body; a projection; support.—*vt.* To push with the shoulder; to put upon the shoulder.—*vi.* To push forward.
Shoulder-blade, shōl'dėr-blād, *n.* The bone of the shoulder; scapula.
Shoulder-knot, shōl'dėr-not, *n.* An ornamental knot of ribbon or lace on the shoulder.
Shoulder-strap, shōl'dėr-strap, *n.* A strap worn on the shoulder, either to support dress, or as a badge of distinction.
Shout, shout, *vi.* To utter a loud and sudden cry.—*vt.* To utter with a shout.—*n.* A loud sudden cry.
Shove, shuv, *vt.* and *i.* (shoving, shoved). To push forward; to press against; to jostle.—*n.* Act of shoving; a push.

Shovel, shu'vel, *n.* An instrument with a broad shallow blade, for lifting earth, &c.—*vt.* (shovelling, shovelled). To throw with a shovel.
Shovelful, shu'vel-fụl, *n.* As much as a shovel will hold.
Shovel-hat, shu'vel-hat, *n.* A clergyman's hat with a broad brim, turned up at the sides.
Show, shō, *vt.* (pret. showed, pp. shown or showed). To display to the view of others; to let be seen; to make known; to prove; to bestow, afford.—*vi.* To appear.—*n.* Act of showing; exhibition; appearance; pretence; pageant; things exhibited for money.
Shower, shō'ėr, *n.* One who shows.
Shower, shou'ėr, *n.* A fall of rain, &c.; a copious supply.—*vt.* To water with a shower; to bestow liberally.—*vi.* To rain in showers.
Showery, shou'ėr-i, *a.* Raining in showers; abounding with frequent falls of rain.
Showily, shō'i-li, *adv.* In a showy manner.
Showman, shō'man, *n.* One who exhibits a show; the owner of a travelling show.
Show-room, shō'röm, *n.* A room in which a show is exhibited; an apartment where goods are displayed.
Showy, shō'i, *a.* Making a great show; ostentatious; gorgeous; gaudy.
Shrapnel, shrap'nel, *n.* A shell filled with bullets, timed to burst at any given point.
Shred, shred, *vt.* (shredding, shred or shredded). To tear into small pieces.—*n.* A long, narrow piece cut off; a tatter.
Shreddy, shred'i, *a.* Consisting of shreds.
Shrew, shrö, *n.* A peevish, ill-tempered woman; a scold; a shrew-mouse.
Shrewd, shröd, *a.* Astute; sagacious; discerning; sharp.
Shrewdly, shröd'li, *adv.* Astutely.
Shrewish, shrö'ish, *a.* Having the qualities of a shrew; peevish; vixenish.
Shrew-mouse, shrö'mous, *n.* A small insectivorous animal resembling a mouse.
Shriek, shrēk, *vi.* To cry out shrilly; to scream.—*n.* A shrill cry; a scream.
Shrievalty, shrēv'al-ti, *n.* The office or jurisdiction of a sheriff.
Shrift, shrift, *n.* The act of shriving or being shriven; confession to a priest; absolution.
Shrike, shrīk, *n.* An insessorial bird which feeds on insects, small birds, &c.; a butcher-bird.
Shrill, shril, *a.* Sharp or piercing in sound; uttering an acute sound.—*vi.* and *t.* To utter an acute piercing sound.
Shrilly, shril'li, *adv.* In a shrill manner; acutely.—*a.* shril'i. Somewhat shrill.
Shrimp, shrimp, *n.* A small crustacean allied to the lobster; a mannikin.
Shrimper, shrimp'ėr, *n.* A fisherman who catches shrimps.
Shrine, shrīn, *n.* A case, as for sacred relics; a tomb; altar; a place hallowed from its associations.—*vt.* (shrining, shrined). To enshrine.
Shrink, shringk, *vi.* (pret. shrank or shrunk, pp. shrunk or shrunken). To contract spontaneously; to shrivel; to withdraw, as from danger; to flinch.—*vt.* To cause to contract. —*n.* Contraction.
Shrinkage, shringk'āj, *n.* A shrinking; diminution in bulk or quantity; reduction.
Shrinkingly, shringk'ing-li, *adv.* With shrinking.
Shrive, shrīv, *vt.* (shriving, pret. shrove or shrived, pp. shriven or shrived). To hear the confession of; to confess and absolve.
Shrivel, shri'vel, *vi.* and *t.* (shrivelling, shrivelled). To shrink into wrinkles; to shrink and form corrugations.
Shroud, shroud, *n.* That which clothes or covers; a winding-sheet; one of the large ropes in a ship supporting the mast.—*vt.* To cover; to dress for the grave; to screen.
Shrove-tide, shrōv'tīd, *n.* Confession time before Lent.
Shrove-Tuesday, shrōv'tūz-dā, *n.* The Tuesday before the first day of Lent.
Shrub, shrub, *n.* A woody plant less than a tree; a plant with several woody stems from the same root; a beverage containing the juice of fruit, &c.
Shrubbery, shrub'ėr-i, *n.* An ornamental plantation of shrubs; shrubs collectively.
Shrubby, shrub'i, *a.* Full of shrubs; resembling a shrub; consisting of brushwood.
Shrug, shrug, *vt.* and *i.* (shrugging, shrugged). To draw up or to contract, as the shoulders.—*n.* A drawing up of the shoulders.
Shrunken, shrungk'n, *p.a.* Having shrunk; shrivelled; contracted.
Shuck, shuk, *n.* A shell or husk.
Shudder, shud'ėr, *vi.* To tremble with fear, horror, &c.; to quake.—*n.* A tremor.
Shuffle, shuf'l, *vt.* (shuffling, shuffled). To shove one way and the other; to confuse; to change the position of cards.—*vi.* To change position; to quibble; to move with a dragging gait; to scrape the floor in dancing.—*n.* An evasion; mixing of cards; scraping movement in dancing.
Shuffler, shuf'lėr, *n.* One who shuffles; one who prevaricates; one who plays tricks.
Shuffling, shuf'ling, *a.* Moving with irregular gait; evasive; prevaricating.
Shun, shun, *vt.* (shunning, shunned). To avoid; to refrain from; to neglect.
Shunt, shunt, *vi.* and *t.* In railways, to turn from one line of rails into another; to free oneself of.
Shut, shut, *vt.* (shutting, shut). To close or stop up; to bar; to preclude; to exclude; to confine.—*vi.* To close itself; to be closed.—*a.* Made close; closed; not resonant.
Shutter, shut'ėr, *n.* One who shuts; a movable covering for a window or aperture.
Shuttle, shut'l, *n.* An instrument used by weavers for shooting the thread of the woof between the threads of the warp.
Shuttle-cock, shut'l-kok, *n.* A cork stuck with feathers, and struck by a battledore.—*vt.* To throw backwards and forwards.
Shy, shī, *a.* Timid; retiring; reserved; coy; cautious; wary.—*vi.* (shying, shied). To start suddenly aside, as a horse.—*vt.* To throw.—*n.* The starting suddenly aside of a horse.
Shyly, shī'li, *adv.* In a shy or timid manner; not familiarly; diffidently.
Shyness, shī'nes, *n.* Quality or state of being shy; reserve; coyness.
Siamese, sī-a-mēz', *n. sing.* and *pl.* A native of Siam; the language of Siam.
Sibilant, si'bi-lant, *a.* Hissing.—*n.* A letter uttered with a hissing, as *s* and *z*.
Sibilate, si'bi-lāt, *vt.* To pronounce with a hissing sound.
Sibilation, si-bi-lā'shon, *n.* The act of sibilating; a hiss.

Sibyl, si'bil, *n.* A prophetess; sorceress.
Sibylline, si'bil-lin, *a.* Pertaining to the sibyls; like the productions of the sibyls; prophetical.
Sic, sik, *adv.* Thus; it is so: often used within brackets in quoting, to note that a peculiarity in the quotation is literally exact.
Siccate, sik'āt, *vt.* To dry.
Siccative, sik'a-tiv, *a.* Drying; causing to dry.
Siccity, sik'si-ti, *n.* Dryness; aridity.
Sice, sīs, *n.* The number six at dice.
Sick, sik, *a.* Affected with disease of any kind; ill; inclined to vomit; disgusted or weary; pertaining to those who are sick.
Sick-bay, sik'bā, *n.* A place in a ship partitioned off for invalids.
Sicken, sik'n, *vt.* To make sick; to disgust.—*vi.* To become sick; to be disgusted; to languish.
Sickening, sik'n-ing, *a.* Making sick; disgusting.
Sickish, sik'ish, *a.* Somewhat sick.
Sickle, sik'l, *n.* An instrument for cutting grain, used with one hand; a reaping-hook.
Sickly, sik'li, *a.* Affected with sickness; not healthy; ailing; languid; faint.—*adv.* In a sick manner or condition.
Sickness, sik'nes, *n.* Disease; ill-health; illness; nausea.
Sick-room, sik'röm, *n.* The apartment where one lies ill.
Side, sīd, *n.* The broad or long surface of a body; edge, border; right or left half of the body; part between the top and bottom; any party or interest opposed to another.—*a.* Being on, from, or toward the side; indirect.—*vi.* (siding, sided). To embrace the opinions of one party.
Side-arms, sīd'ärmz, *n.pl.* Arms carried by the side, as sword, bayonet, &c.
Sideboard, sīd'bōrd, *n.* A piece of furniture used to hold dining utensils, &c.
Sided, sīd'ed, *p.a.* Having a side or sides; used in composition.
Side-light, sīd'līt, *n.* A light at a side; information thrown indirectly on a subject.
Sidelong, sīd'long, *adv.* Laterally; obliquely.—*a.* Lateral; oblique.
Sidereal, sī-dē'rē-al, *a.* Pertaining to stars; measured by the motion of the stars.
Siderite, sid'ėr-īt, *n.* Magnetic iron ore or loadstone.
Siderography, sid-ėr-og'ra-fi, *n.* The art or practice of engraving on steel.
Siderolite, sid'ėr-ō-līt, *n.* A meteoric stone chiefly consisting of iron.
Side-saddle, sīd'sad-l, *n.* A saddle for a woman.
Sidesman, sīdz'man, *n.* An assistant to the churchwardens.
Sidewalk, sīd'wąk, *n.* A raised walk for foot-passengers by the side of a street or road.
Sideways, sīd'wāz, *adv.* See SIDEWISE.
Sidewise, sīd'wīz, *adv.* Toward one side; laterally; on one side.
Siding, sīd'ing, *n.* A short additional line of rails laid for the purpose of shunting.
Sidle, sīd'l, *vi.* (sidling, sidled). To go or move side foremost; to move to one side.
Siege, sēj, *n.* A regular attack on a fortified place; continued endeavour to gain possession.
Siege-train, sēj'trān, *n.* The artillery, carriages, ammunition, &c., carried with an army for attacking fortified places.
Sienna, sē-en'na, *n.* An earth of a fine yellow colour, used as a pigment.
Siesta, sē-es'ta, *n.* A sleep or rest in the hottest part of the day.
Sieve, siv, *n.* A utensil for separating the smaller particles of a loose substance.
Sift, sift, *vt.* To separate by a sieve; to examine minutely.—*vi.* To pass as if through a sieve.
Sifter, sift'ėr, *n.* One who sifts; a sieve.
Sigh, sī, *vi.* To make a long breath audibly, as from grief; to make a melancholy sound.—*n.* A long breath made audibly, as in grief.
Sight, sīt, *n.* Act or power of seeing; view; vision; visibility; estimation; a show; an appliance for guiding the eye.—*vt.* To see; to descry; to give the proper elevation and direction to, as a piece of ordnance.
Sighted, sīt'ed, *a.* Having sight; seeing in a particular manner; having sights, as a rifle.
Sightless, sīt'les, *a.* Wanting sight; blind.
Sightly, sīt'li, *a.* Pleasing to the sight or eye; agreeable to look on.
Sight-seeing, sīt'sē-ing, *n.* The act of seeing sights or visiting scenes of interest.
Sight-seer, sīt'sē-ėr, *n.* One who goes to see sights or curiosities.
Sigillaria, sij-il-lā'ri-a, *n.* A large fossil plant of the coal formation.
Sign, sīn, *n.* A mark or stamp indicative of something; a token; indication; emblem; a symbol or character.—*vt.* To express by a sign; to affix a signature to.—*vi.* To make a sign or signal.
Signal, sig'nal, *n.* A sign to communicate intelligence, orders, &c., at a distance.—*a.* Worthy of note; remarkable.—*vt.* or *i.* (signalling, signalled). To communicate by signals.
Signal-box, sig'nal-boks, *n.* A small house from which railway signals are worked.
Signalize, sig'nal-īz, *vt.* To make remarkable; to distinguish by some fact or exploit.
Signally, sig'nal-li, *adv.* In a signal manner; eminently; remarkably; memorably.
Signal-man, sig'nal-man, *n.* A man who works signals.
Signatory, Signatary, sig'na-to-ri, sig'na-ta-ri, *a.* Relating to the signing of documents.—*n.* One who signs; a state representative who signs a public document.
Signature, sig'na-tūr, *n.* A mark impressed; the name of a person written by himself; in *printing*, a distinctive letter or mark at the bottom of the first page of each sheet.
Sign-board, sīn'bōrd, *n.* A board on which one sets a notice of his occupation or of articles for sale.
Signer, sīn'ėr, *n.* One who signs.
Signet, sig'net, *n.* A seal; seal used by the sovereign in sealing private letters.
Signet-ring, sig'net-ring, *n.* A ring containing a signet or private seal.
Signifiable, sig-ni-fī'a-bl, *a.* That may be signified.
Significance, Significancy, sig-ni'fi-kans, sig-ni'fi-kan-si, *n.* Meaning; import.
Significant, sig-ni'fi-kant, *a.* Signifying something; indicative; important.
Significantly, sig-ni'fi-kant-li, *adv.* In a significant manner; meaningly; expressively.

Signification, sig'ni-fi-kā"shon, *n.* Act of signifying; meaning; import; sense.
Significative, sig-ni'fi-kāt-iv, *a.* Signifying; expressive of a certain idea or thing.
Significatory, sig-ni'fi-ka-to-ri, *a.* Having signification or meaning.
Signify, sig'ni-fī, *vt.* (signifying, signified). To make known either by signs or words; to betoken; to mean; to imply; to import.
Signitary, sig'ni-ta-ri, *a.* *See* SIGNATORY.
Sign-manual, sīn-man'ū-al, *n.* One's own name written by oneself; signature.
Signor, Signior, sēn'yor, *n.* An English form of Italian *Signore*, Spanish *Señor*, equivalent to *Sir* or *Mr.*; a gentleman.
Signora, sēn-yō'ra, *n.* *Madam* or *Mrs.*; a lady.
Signorina, sēn-yō-rē'na, *n.* *Miss*; a young lady.
Sign-post, sīn'pōst, *n.* A post on which a sign hangs; a finger-post.
Silence, sī'lens, *n.* State of being silent; quiet; secrecy; absence of mention.—*vt.* To put to silence; to quiet; to cause to cease firing.
Silent, sī'lent, *a.* Not speaking; mute; dumb; taciturn; making no noise.
Silently, sī'lent-li, *adv.* In a silent manner.
Silhouette, sil'ö-et, *n.* A profile portrait filled in with a dark colour.
Silica, Silex, sil'i-ka, sī'leks, *n.* Oxide of silicon, the chief constituent of quartz, flint, &c.
Silicate, sil'i-kāt, *n.* A compound of silica with certain bases.
Siliceous, Silicious, si-lish'us, *a.* Pertaining to, containing, or like silica.
Silicon, Silicium, sil'i-kon, si-lis'i-um, *n.* The non-metallic element of which silica is the oxide.
Silicosis, si-li-kō'sis, *n.* A disease of the lungs caused by inhaling small particles of silica.
Siliqua, sil'i-kwa, *n.*; pl. **-quæ,** The long pod of such cruciferous plants as wallflower; a weight for gold or gems; a carat.
Silk, silk, *n.* The fine thread produced by various caterpillars, particularly the silk-worm; cloth made of silk; garment made of this cloth.—*a.* Pertaining to silk; silken.
Silken, silk'n, *a.* Made of silk; silky.
Silk-worm, silk'wėrm, *n.* A worm which produces silk; the larva of various moths which spin a silken cocoon for the chrysalis.
Silky, silk'i. *a.* Made of silk; like silk; soft and smooth to the touch.
Sill, sil *n.* The timber or stone at the foot of a door or window; the threshold; the floor of a gallery in a mine.
Sillabub, sil'la-bub, *n.* A liquor made by mixing wine or cider with milk.
Silly, sil'li, *a.* Weak in intellect; foolish; unwise.
Silo, sī'lō, *n.* The pit in which green fodder is preserved in the method of ensilage.
Silt, silt, *n.* A deposit of fine earth from running or standing water.—*vt.* To fill with silt.
Silurian, sī-lū'ri-an, *a.* Applied to the lowest division of the palæozoic strata.
Silva, Silvan, sil'va, sil'van, *a.* *See* SYLVA.
Silver, sil'vėr, *n.* A precious metal of a white colour; money; plate made of silver.—*a.* Made of silver; silvery.—*vt.* and *i.* To cover with a coat of silver; to tinge with gray.
Silver-glance, sil'vėr-glans, *n.* A mineral, a native sulphuret of silver.
Silvering, sil'vėr-ing, *n.* Art or operation of covering anything with silver; the silver thus laid on.
Silverize, sil'vėr-īz, *vt.* To coat or cover with silver.
Silvern, sil'vėrn, *a.* Made of silver; silver.
Silverside, sil'vėr-sīd, *n.* A cut of beef from the underside of the rump, often salted.
Silversmith, sil'vėr-smith, *n.* One whose occupation is to work in silver.
Silver-tongued, sil'vėr-tungd, *a.* Having a smooth tongue or speech.
Silvery, sil'vėr-i, *a.* Like silver; covered with silver; clear as the sound of a silver bell.
Simian, Simious, si'mi-an, si'mi-us, *a.* Pertaining to apes or monkeys; ape-like.
Similar, si'mi-lėr, *a.* Like; resembling; having like parts and relations but not of the same magnitude.
Similarity, si-mi-la'ri-ti, *n.* State of being similar; likeness; resemblance.
Similarly, si'mi-lėr-li, *a.* In a similar or like manner; with resemblance.
Simile, si'mi-lė, *n.* A figure of speech consisting in likening one thing to another.
Similitude, si-mil'i-tūd, *n.* Likeness; resemblance; comparison.
Simmer, si'mėr, *vi.* To boil gently.
Simoniac, si-mō'ni-ak, *n.* One guilty of simony.
Simoniacal, si-mō-nī'ak-al, *a.* Pertaining to or guilty of simony.
Simony, si'mon-i, *n.* The crime of buying or selling ecclesiastical preferment.
Simoom, si-möm', *n.* A hot suffocating wind in Africa and Arabia.
Simous, sī'mus, *a.* Having a snub-nose.
Simper, sim'pėr, *vi.* To smile in a silly manner.—*n.* A silly or affected smile.
Simple, sim'pl, *a.* Not complex; single; not involved; clear; artless; mere; plain; sincere; silly.—*n.* Something not mixed; a medicinal herb.
Simpleton, sim'pl-ton, *n.* A simple or silly person; one easily deceived.
Simplicity, sim-plis'i-ti, *n.* State or quality of being simple; singleness; artlessness; sincerity; plainness; foolishness.
Simplify, sim'pli-fī, *vt.* To make simple; to make plain or easy.
Simply, sim'pli, *adv.* In a simple manner; artlessly; plainly; merely; foolishly.
Simulacrum, sim-ū-lā'krum, *n.*; pl. **-cra.** An image or likeness; a phantom.
Simulate, sim'ū-lāt, *vt.* To counterfeit; to feign.
Simulation, sim-ū-lā'shon, *n.* Act of simulating; pretence.
Simulator, sim'ū-lāt-or, *n.* One who feigns.
Simultaneous, si-mul-tā'nē-us, *a.* Taking place or done at the same time.
Sin, sin, *n.* A transgression of the divine law; moral depravity; an offence in general.—*vi.* (sinning, sinned). To violate the divine law or any rule of duty.
Sinapism, sin'a-pizm, *n.* A mustard poultice.
Since, sins, *adv.* From that time; from then till now; ago.—*prep.* Ever from the time of; after.—*conj.* From the time when; because that.
Sincere, sin-sēr', *a.* Pure; unmixed; real; genuine; guileless; frank; true.
Sincerely, sin-sēr'li, *adv.* In a sincere manner; unfeignedly; genuinely; really.
Sincerity, sin-se'ri-ti, *n.* Honesty of mind or intention; freedom from hypocrisy.

Sinciput, sin'si-put, *n.* The fore part of the skull.
Sine, sin, *n.* A geometrical line drawn from one end of an arc perpendicular to the diameter through the other end.
Sinecure, sī'nē-kūr, *n.* An ecclesiastical benefice without cure of souls; a paid office without employment.
Sinew, si'nū, *n.* The fibrous cord which unites a muscle to a bone; a tendon; strength.—*vt.* To bind, as by sinews; to strengthen.
Sinewy, si'nū-i, *a.* Consisting of a sinew or sinews; brawny; vigorous; firm.
Sinful, sin'ful, *a.* Full of sin; wicked; iniquitous; wrong.
Sing, sing, *vi.* (pret. sang, sung, pp. sung). To utter sounds with melodious modulations of voice; to have a ringing sensation.—*vt.* To utter with musical modulations of voice; to celebrate in song; to tell.
Singe, sinj, *vt.* (singeing, singed). To burn slightly; to burn the surface of.—*n.* A burning of the surface.
Singer, sing'ėr, *n.* One who sings; a bird that sings.
Single, sing'gl, *a.* Being one or a unit; individual; unmarried; performed by one person; simple; sincere.—*vt.* (singling, singled). To select individually: with *out.*
Single-entry, sing'gl-en-tri, *n.* A system of book-keeping in which each entry appears only once on one side or other of an account.
Single-handed, sing'gl-hand-ed, *a.* Unassisted; by one's own efforts.
Single-minded, sing'gl-mind-ed, *a.* Free from guile; honest; straightforward.
Single-stick, sing'gl-stik, *n.* A stick for fencing with; fencing with such sticks.
Singly, sing'gli, *adv.* In a single manner; individually; separately; sincerely.
Sing-song, sing'song, *n.* A drawling tone; repetition of similar words or tones.
Singular, sing'gū-lėr, *a.* That is single; expressing one person or thing; remarkable; rare; odd.—*n.* The singular number.
Singularity, sing-gū-la'ri-ti, *n.* Peculiarity; eccentricity.
Singularly, sing'gū-lėr-li, *adv.* Peculiarly; remarkably; oddly; so as to express one.
Sinister, si'nis-tėr, *a.* Left; evil; baneful; malign; unlucky.
Sinistral, si'nis-tral, *a.* Belonging to the left hand or side; sinistrous.
Sinistrorse, si'nis-trors, *a.* Directed to the left.
Sinistrous, si'nis-trus, *a.* Sinister; being on or inclined to the left.
Sink, singk, *vi.* (pret. sank or sunk, pp. sunk). To descend in a liquid; to subside; to enter; to decline in worth, strength, &c.—*vt.* To immerse; to submerge; to make by digging; to depress; to degrade.—*n.* A receptacle for liquid filth; a sewer; place where iniquity is gathered.
Sinker, singk'ėr, *n.* One who sinks; a weight on some body to sink it.
Sinking, singk'ing, *a.* Causing to sink; depressing; set apart for the reduction of a debt.
Sinless, sin'les, *a.* Free from sin; innocent.
Sinner, sin'ėr, *n.* One who sins; a transgressor; offender; criminal.
Sinn Fein, shin fān, *n.* An Irish republican party, aiming at complete independence and separation, with the restoration of the old Irish tongue.
Sinologue, sin'o-log, *n.* A student of the Chinese language, literature, history, &c.
Sinology, si-nol'o-ji, *n.* The knowledge of the Chinese language, &c.
Sinter, sin'tėr, *n.* Stony matter precipitated by springs.
Sinuate, sin'ū-āt, *a.* Winding.
Sinuosity, sin-ū-os'i-ti, *n.* Quality of being sinuous; a curving; a wavy line.
Sinuous, sin'ū-us, *a.* Bending or curving in and out; crooked.
Sinus, sī'nus, *n.* A curved opening; a bay; a cavity containing pus; a fistula.
Sinusitis, si-nū-zī'tis, *n.* Inflammation of one of the air-cavities of the skull connecting with the nose.
Sip, sip, *vt.* (sipping, sipped). To drink in small quantities; to drink out of.—*vi.* To take a fluid with the lips.—*n.* A small quantity of liquid taken with the lips.
Siphon, sī'fon, *n.* A bent tube used for drawing off liquids, as from a cask, &c.
Siphon-bottle, sī'fon-bot-l, *n.* A bottle for aerated waters, discharged through a bent tube by the pressure of the gas within.
Sippet, sip'et, *n.* A small sip; a small piece of bread served with soup, &c.
Sir, sėr, *n.* A word of respect used to men; title distinctive of knights and baronets.
Sirdar, sėr'där, *n.* A chieftain or head-man in Hindustan; the head of the Egyptian army.
Sire, sīr, *n.* A respectful word of address to a king; a father; male parent of a horse, &c.
Siren, sī'ren, *n.* A sea-nymph who enticed seamen by songs, and then slew them; a woman dangerous from her fascinations; a fog-signal; a signal used as an air-raid warning.—*a.* Bewitching.
Sirius, si'ri-us, *n.* The Dog-star.
Sirloin, sėr'loin, *n.* The upper part of a loin of beef; a loin of beef.
Sirocco, si-rok'kō, *n.* An oppressive south or south-east wind in Italy.
Sirrah, si'ra, *n.* A word of address like 'sir', with an angry force added.
Sirup, si'rup, *n.* *See* SYRUP.
Siskin, sis'kin, *n.* A greenish European song-bird of the finch family.
Sist, sist, *vt.* In *Scots law,* to stop; to cite or summon.
Sister, sis'tėr, *n.* A female born of the same parents; a female of the same kind, society, &c.; a senior hospital nurse.
Sisterhood, sis'tėr-hud, *n.* State or condition of a sister; a society of females.
Sister-in-law, sis'tėr-in-la, *n.* A husband or wife's sister.
Sisterly, sis'tėr-li, *a.* Becoming a sister; affectionate.
Sistrum, sis'trum, *n.* A jingling metallic instrument used by the ancient Egyptians in the religious ceremonies.
Sit, sit, *vi.* (sitting, sat). To rest on the lower extremity of the body; to incubate; to remain; to be placed; to suit; to have a seat in Parliament, &c.; to hold a session.—*vt.* To keep the seat upon (a horse, &c.).
Site, sīt, *n.* Situation; a plot of ground for building on.
Sitology, sī-tol'o-ji, *n.* Dietetics.
Sitter, sit'ėr, *n.* One who sits; one who sits for his portrait; a bird that incubates.
Sitting, sit'ing, *n.* Act of one who sits; occasion

on which one sits for a portrait; session; seat in a church pew.
Sitting-room, sit'ing-röm, *n.* An apartment for sitting in; sufficient space for sitting in.
Situate, sit'ū-āt, *a.* Placed with respect to any other object.
Situated, sit'ū-āt-ed, *a.* Having a site or position; situate; circumstanced.
Situation, sit-ū-ā'shon, *n.* Position; station; plight; post or engagement.
Sitz-bath, sits-bäth, *n.* A bath in which one can bathe sitting; a bath taken in a sitting posture.
Six, siks, *a.* and *n.* One more than five.
Sixfold, siks'fōld, *a.* and *adv.* Six times.
Sixpence, siks'pens, *n.* An English silver coin worth six pennies; value of six pennies.
Sixpenny, siks'pen-i, *a.* Worth sixpence.
Sixteen, siks'tēn, *a.* and *n.* Six and ten.
Sixteenmo, siks'tēn-mō, *n.* Sexto-decimo.
Sixteenth, siks'tēnth, *a.* The sixth after the tenth.—*n.* One of sixteen equal parts.
Sixth, siksth, *a.* Next after the fifth.—*n.* One part in six.
Sixthly, siksth'li, *adv.* In the sixth place.
Sixtieth, siks'ti-eth, *a.* and *n.* The next after fifty-ninth; one of sixty equal parts.
Sixty, siks'ti, *a.* and *n.* Six times ten.
Sizable, Sizeable, sīz'a-bl, *a.* Of considerable bulk; of reasonable size.
Sizar, sī'zär, *n.* At Cambridge and Dublin Universities, an undergraduate who is assisted financially by the college, but who has not the standing of a scholar or exhibitioner.
Size, sīz, *n.* Comparative magnitude; bigness; bulk; a glutinous substance used by painters, &c.—*vt.* (sizing, sized). To arrange according to size; to take the size of; to cover with size.
Sized, sīzd, *a.* Having a particular size.
Sizer, sīz'ėr, *n.* One who or that which sizes; a kind of gauge.
Sizing, sīz'ing, *n.* Size or weak glue; act of covering with size.
Sizy, sīz'i, *a.* Glutinous; ropy.
Skain, skān, *n.* A skein.
Skate, skāt, *n.* A narrow steel bar fastened under the foot, for moving rapidly on ice; a flat fish.—*vi.* (skating, skated). To slide on skates.
Skater, skāt'ėr, *n.* One who skates on ice.
Skating-rink, skāt'ing-ringk, *n.* A rink or prepared area for skating.
Skein, skān, *n.* A small hank of thread.
Skeleton, ske'le-ton, *n.* The bony framework of an animal; general structure or frame; outline.—*a.* Resembling a skeleton.
Skeleton-key, ske'le-ton-kē, *n.* A thin light key that opens various locks.
Skerry, ske'ri, *n.* A rocky isle; a rock.
Sketch, skech, *n.* An outline or general delineation; a first rough draught.—*vt.* To draw a sketch of; to give the chief points of; to plan.—*vi.* To practise sketching.
Sketcher, skech'ėr, *n.* One who sketches.
Sketchy, skech'i, *a.* Having the nature of a sketch; unfinished; incomplete.
Skew, skū, *a.* Oblique.—*adv.* Awry; obliquely.—*vt.* To put askew.
Skew-bridge, skū'brij, *n.* A bridge set obliquely over a road, &c.
Skewer, skū'ėr, *n.* A pin for fastening meat.—*vt.* To fasten with skewers.
Ski, skē, *n.* A long, narrow snow-shoe for running or travelling over snow.
Skid, skid, *n.* A drag for the wheels of a vehicle.—*vt.* (skidding, skidded). To check with a skid.—*vi.* To slip sideways on mud, ice, &c., as a cycle.
Skiff, skif, *n.* A small light boat.
Skilful, skil'fụl, *a.* Skilled; dexterous; expert; clever.
Skilfully, skil'fụl-li, *adv.* In a skilful manner; dexterously.
Skill, skil, *n.* Ability; knowledge united with dexterity; aptitude.
Skilled, skild, *a.* Having skill; expert.
Skillet, skil'et, *n.* A small vessel of metal, with a long handle, for heating water, &c.
Skilligalee, Skilligolee, skil'i-ga-lē", skil'i-gō-lē", *n.* A thin soup, such as is served to prisoners or paupers.
Skim, skim, *vt.* (skimming, skimmed). To remove the scum from; to take off from a surface; to pass lightly over; to glance over superficially.—*vi.* To glide along.
Skimmer, skim'ėr, *n.* A utensil for skimming liquors; an aquatic swimming bird.
Skim-milk, skim'milk, *n.* Milk from which the cream has been taken.
Skimming, skim'ing, *n.* Act of one who skims a liquid; scum removed.
Skin, skin, *n.* The natural outer coating of animals; a hide; bark; rind.—*vt.* (skinning, skinned). To strip the skin from; to cover superficially.—*vi.* To be covered with skin.
Skin-deep, skin'dēp, *a.* Superficial; slight.
Skinflint, skin'flint, *n.* A niggard.
Skink, skingk, *n.* A small lizard of Egypt, &c.
Skinner, skin'ėr, *n.* One who skins; one who deals in skins, pelts, or hides; a furrier.
Skinny, skin'i, *a.* Consisting of skin or nearly so; wanting flesh.
Skip, skip, *vi.* (skipping, skipped). To leap lightly; to bound; to spring.—*vt.* To pass with a bound; to omit.—*n.* A light leap; a large basket on wheels, used in mines.
Skipper, skip'ėr, *n.* The master of a merchant vessel; a sea-captain; the cheese maggot.
Skipping, skip'ing, *a.* Frisky; bounding.
Skipping-rope, skip'ing-rōp, *n.* A small rope swung by young persons under their feet and over their heads in play.
Skirmish, skėr'mish, *n.* A slight battle; a brief contest.—*vi.* To fight in short contests or in small parties.
Skirt, skėrt, *n.* The lower and loose part of a garment; border; a woman's garment like a petticoat.—*vt.* To border.—*vi.* To be on the border.
Skirting-board, skėrt'ing-bōrd, *n.* The board round the bottom of a wall.
Skit, skit, *n.* A satirical or sarcastic attack; a pasquinade; a squib.
Skittish, skit'ish, *a.* Timorous; wanton; frisky; hasty; fickle.
Skittles, skit'lz, *n.pl.* A game with nine pins set upright, to be knocked down with as few throws as possible of a ball.
Skiver, ski'vėr, *n.* An inferior leather made of split sheep-skin.
Skulk, skulk, *vi.* To lurk; to sneak out of the way; to shun doing one's duty.
Skulk, Skulker, skulk, skulk'ėr, *n.* A person who skulks or avoids duties.
Skull, skul, *n.* The bony case which contains the brain.

Skull-cap, skul'kap, *n.* A cap fitting closely to the head.
Skunk, skungk, *n.* An animal of the weasel family, with glands that emit a fetid fluid.
Skurry, sku'ri, *n.* and *v.* *See* SCURRY.
Sky, skī, *n.* The apparent arch of the heavens; the region of clouds; climate.
Skyey, skī'i, *a.* Like or pertaining to the sky.
Skylark, skī'lärk, *n.* The common lark that mounts and sings as it flies.
Skylarking, skī'lärk-ing, *n.* Gambols in the rigging of a ship; frolicking of any kind.
Sky-light, skī'līt, *n.* A window in the roof of a building.
Skyward, skī'wėrd, *a.* and *adv.* Toward the sky.
Slab, slab, *n.* A thin flat piece of anything, as marble.—*a.* Thick and slimy.
Slabber, slab'ėr, *vi.* To slaver; to drivel.—*vt.* To sup up hastily; to besmear.—*n.* Slaver.
Slabby, slab'i, *a.* Viscous; slimy.
Slack, slak, *a.* Not tight or tense; loose; remiss; backward; not busy.—*adv.* In a slack manner; partially; insufficiently.—*n.* The part of a rope that hangs loose; small broken coal.—*vt.* and *i.* To slacken; to slake.
Slacken, slak'n, *vi.* To become slack; to abate; to flag.—*vt.* To lessen the tension of; to relax.
Slackly, slak'li, *adv.* In a slack manner; loosely; negligently; remissly.
Slag, slag, *n.* The scoria from a smelting furnace or volcano; fused dross of metal.
Slaggy, slag'i, *a.* Pertaining to or like slag.
Slake, slāk, *vt.* (slaking, slaked). To quench, as thirst or rage; to extinguish.—*vi.* To abate; to become extinct.—*n.* A muddy tract adjoining the sea.
Slam, slam, *vt.* and *i.* (slamming, slammed). To shut with violence; to bang.—*n.* A violent shutting of a door.
Slander, slan'dėr, *n.* A false report maliciously uttered; defamation.—*vt.* To defame; to calumniate.
Slanderer, slan'dėr-ėr, *n.* One who slanders; a defamer; a calumniator.
Slanderous, slan'dėr-us, *a.* Containing slander; that utters slander; defamatory.
Slang, slang, *n.* and *a.* A class of expressions not generally approved of, as being inelegant or undignified.—*vt.* To address with slang; to abuse vulgarly.
Slangey, Slangy, slang'i, *a.* Of the nature of slang; addicted to the use of slang.
Slant, slant, *a.* Sloping.—*vt.* and *i.* To turn from a direct line; to slope; to incline.—*n.* A slope.
Slantly, Slantwise, slant'li, slant'wīz, *adv.* So as to slant; obliquely.
Slap, slap, *n.* A blow with the open hand, or something broad.—*vt.* (slapping, slapped). To strike with the open hand.—*adv.* With a sudden and violent blow.
Slap-dash, slap'dash, *adv.* All at once; off-hand; at random.
Slash, slash, *vt.* To cut by striking violently and at random.—*vi.* To strike violently and at random with a cutting instrument.—*n.* A long cut; a cut made at random.
Slashed, slasht', *p.a.* Cut with a slash; having long narrow openings, as a sleeve.
Slat, slat, *n.* A narrow strip of wood.
Slate, slāt, *n.* Rock which splits into thin layers; a slab of smooth stone for covering buildings; a tablet for writing upon.—*vt.* (slating, slated). To cover with slates; to criticise severely.
Slate-pencil, slāt'pen-sil, *n.* A pencil of soft slate, used for writing on slates.
Slater, slāt'ėr, *n.* One who slates buildings; a small crustaceous animal.
Slating, slāt'ing, *n.* Act of covering with slates; the cover thus put on; severe criticism.
Slattern, slat'ėrn, *n.* A female who is not tidy; a slut.—*a.* Slatternly.
Slatternly, slat'ėrn-li, *a.* Like a slattern; slovenly; sluttish.
Slaty, slāt'i, *a.* Resembling slate.
Slaughter, sla̧'tėr, *n.* A slaying; carnage; massacre; a killing of beasts for market.—*vt.* To slay; to kill for the market.
Slaughter-house, sla̧'tėr-hous, *n.* A place where beasts are killed for the market.
Slaughterous, sla̧'tėr-us, *a.* Murderous.
Slav, Slavonian, släv, sla-vō'ni-an, *n.* One of a race of Eastern Europe, comprising the Russians, Poles, Bohemians, Bulgarians, &c.
Slave, slāv, *n.* A person wholly subject to another; a bondman; drudge.—*vi.* (slaving, slaved). To labour as a slave.
Slave-driver, slāv'drīv-ėr, *n.* An overseer of slaves; a severe or cruel master.
Slaver, slā'vėr, *n.* A person or vessel engaged in the slave-trade.
Slaver, sla'vėr, *n.* Saliva drivelling from the mouth; drivel.—*vi.* To suffer the saliva to issue from the mouth.—*vt.* To smear with saliva.
Slaverer, sla'vėr-ėr, *n.* One who slavers; a driveller.
Slavery, slāv'ė-ri, *n.* State of a slave; bondage; servitude; drudgery.
Slave-trade, slāv'trād, *n.* The business of purchasing or kidnapping men and women, and selling them for slaves.
Slavic, Slavonic, Slavonian, slav'ik, sla-von'ik, sla-vō'ni-an, *a.* Pertaining to the Slavs, or to their language.
Slavish, slāv'ish, *a.* Pertaining to slaves; servile; mean; oppressively laborious.
Slavishly, slāv'ish-li, *adv.* In a slavish manner; servilely; meanly.
Slay, slā, *vt.* (pret. slew, pp. slain). To kill by violence; to murder; to destroy.
Slayer, slā'ėr, *n.* One who slays; murderer.
Sleazy, slē'zi, *a.* Thin; flimsy; wanting firmness of texture, as silk. Also *Sleezy*.
Sled, sled, *n.* A sledge.—*vt.* (sledding, sledded). To convey on a sled.
Sledge, Sledge-hammer, slej, slej'ham-ėr, *n.* A large, heavy hammer, used by iron-workers.
Sledge, slej, *n.* A vehicle on runners used over snow or ice; a sleigh.—*vt.* and *i.* To convey or travel in a sledge.
Sleek, slēk, *a.* Smooth and glossy.—*vt.* To make smooth and glossy.
Sleeky, slēk'i, *a.* Of a sleek appearance.
Sleep, slēp, *vi.* (sleeping, slept). To take rest by a suspension of voluntary exercise of the powers of body and mind; to be dormant or inactive.—*vt.* To pass in sleeping; to get rid of by sleeping: with *off*.—*n.* That state in which volition is suspended; slumber; death; dormant state.
Sleeper, slēp'ėr, *n.* One that sleeps; a timber

supporting a weight; in railways, a beam of wood supporting the rails.
Sleeping, slēp'ing, *a.* Reposing in sleep; pertaining to sleep; causing sleep.—**Sleeping sickness,** *n.* A tropical African disease due to microscopic animals introduced into the blood by the bites of tsetse flies.
Sleepless, slēp'les, *a.* Without sleep; wakeful; having no rest; perpetually agitated.
Sleeplessness, slēp'les-nes, *n.* State of being sleepless; persistent inability to sleep.
Sleepy, slēp'i, *a.* Inclined to sleep; drowsy; lazy; sluggish.
Sleet, slēt, *n.* Hail or snow mingled with rain. —*vi.* To snow or hail with rain.
Sleety, slēt'i, *a.* Consisting of or like sleet.
Sleeve, slēv, *n.* That part of a garment covering the arm.—*vt.* (sleeving, sleeved). To furnish with sleeves.
Sleeveless, slēv'les, *a.* Having no sleeves; wanting a pretext; bootless.
Sleigh, slā, *n.* A vehicle on runners for transporting persons on snow or ice.
Sleight, slīt, *n.* A sly artifice; an artful trick; dexterity.
Slender, slen'dėr, *a.* Thin; slim; slight; feeble; meagre; scanty.
Slenderly, slen'dėr-li, *adv.* In a slender manner; slightly; scantily; insufficiently.
Sleuth-hound, slöth'hound, *n.* A bloodhound; a hound employed in tracking.
Slew, slö, *vt.* To slue. Pret. of *slay*.
Sley, slā, *n.* A weaver's reed.
Slice, slīs, *vt.* (slicing, sliced). To cut into thin pieces; to divide.—*n.* A thin, broad piece cut off; a broad flat utensil.
Slide, slīd, *vi.* (sliding, pret. slid, pp. slid, slidden). To move along a surface by slipping; to pass smoothly or gradually.—*vt.* To thrust smoothly along a surface.—*n.* A smooth and easy passage; that part of an apparatus which slides into place.
Slider, slīd'ėr, *n.* One who slides; part of an instrument that slides.
Sliding, slīd'ing, *a.* Made so as to slide freely; fitted for sliding.—*n.* The act of one who slides; lapse; backsliding.
Sliding-scale, slīd'ing-skāl, *n.* A sliding-rule; a varying rate of payment.
Slight, slīt, *a.* Small; trifling; not thorough; slender; frail.—*n.* Intentional disregard.—*vt.* To disregard; to treat with disrespect.
Slightly, slīt'li, *adv.* In a slight manner or measure; but little; somewhat; slenderly.
Slim, slim, *a.* Slight; slender; thin; flimsy; cunning.—*vi.* To reduce weight by means of dieting.
Slime, slīm, *n.* A soft or glutinous substance; moist earth or mud; viscous substance exuded by certain animals.—*vt.* (sliming, slimed). To cover with slime; to make slimy.
Slimy, slīm'i, *a.* Abounding with slime; consisting of slime; viscous; glutinous.
Sling, sling, *vt.* (slinging, slung). To throw; to hang so as to swing; to place in a sling.—*n.* An instrument for throwing stones; a bandage to support a wounded limb; a rope for raising heavy articles.
Slinger, sling'ėr, *n.* One who uses the sling.
Slink, slingk, *vi.* (slinking, slunk). To sneak; to steal away.—*vt.* To cast prematurely.—*n.* A premature calf.
Slip, slip, *vi.* (slipping, slipped). To move smoothly along; to glide; to depart secretly; to have the feet slide; to err; to escape insensibly.—*vt.* To put or thrust secretly; to omit; to disengage oneself from; to make a slip of for planting.—*n.* A sliding of the feet; an unintentional error; a twig cut for planting or grafting; a long narrow piece; a leash by which a dog is held; a long strip of printed matter; a loose covering; an inclined plane upon which a ship is built.
Slipper, slip'ėr, *n.* One who slips or lets slip; a loose light shoe for household wear.
Slippery, slip'ėr-i, *a.* So smooth as to cause slipping; untrustworthy; uncertain.
Slipshod, slip'shod, *a.* Shod with slippers; having shoes down at heel; slovenly.
Slipslop, slip'slop, *n.* Bad liquor; feeble composition.—*a.* Feeble; poor; jejune.
Slit, slit, *vi.* (slitting, slit or slitted). To cut lengthwise; to cut into long strips.—*n.* A long cut or opening.
Slitter, slit'ėr, *n.* One who or that which slits.
Sliver, sli'vėr or slī'vėr, *vt.* To cleave; to cut into long thin pieces.—*n.* A long piece cut off; a splinter.
Slobber, slob'ėr, *vi.* and *t.* To slaver; to slabber.—*n.* Slaver; liquor spilled.
Slobbery, slob'ėr-i, *a.* Moist; sloppy.
Sloe, slō, *n.* A British shrub of the plum genus, the blackthorn; also its fruit.
Slogan, slō'gan, *n.* A war-cry; a watchword.
Sloop, slöp, *n.* A vessel with one mast, hardly different from a cutter.
Slop, slop, *vt.* (slopping, slopped). To soil by liquid; to spill.—*n.* Water carelessly thrown about; a smock-frock; *pl.* mean liquid food; waste dirty water; wide breeches; ready-made clothing.
Slope, slōp, *n.* An oblique direction; a declivity.—*vt.* and *i.* (sloping, sloped). To form with a slope; to incline.
Sloppy, slop'i, *a.* Muddy; plashy; slovenly.
Slopy, slōp'i, *a.* Sloping.
Slot, slot, *n.* A bolt or bar; an oblong hole; track of a deer.—*vt.* (slotting, slotted). To make a slot in.
Sloth, slōth or sloth, *n.* Indolence; laziness; idleness; a South American mammal.
Slothful, slōth'ful or sloth', *a.* Addicted to sloth; sluggish; lazy; indolent.
Slouch, slouch, *n.* A stoop in walking; an ungainly gait; a droop.—*vi.* To hang down; to have a drooping gait.—*vt.* To cause to hang down.
Slouch-hat, slouch'hat, *n.* A hat with a hanging brim; a soft hat.
Slouching, slouch'ing, *a.* Drooping downward; walking heavily and awkwardly.
Slough, slou, *n.* A place of deep mud; a hole full of mire.
Slough, sluf, *n.* The cast-off skin of a serpent, &c.; the dead flesh that separates from living parts in a wound, &c.—*vi.* To come off as a slough from the living parts.
Sloughy, slou'i, *a.* Full of sloughs; miry.
Sloughy, sluf'i, *a.* Resembling dead matter separating from a wound.
Sloven, slu'ven, *n.* A man habitually negligent of neatness and order.
Slovenly, slu'ven-li, *a.* Disorderly; not neat or tidy.—*adv.* In a negligent manner.
Slow, slō, *a.* Moving little in a long time;

not rapid; dilatory; heavy in wit; dull; behind in time.—*vt.* and *i.* To delay; to slacken in speed.
Slowly, slō'li, *adv.* In a slow manner; tardily; gradually.
Slow-worm, slō'wėrm, *n.* The blind-worm.
Sloyd, sloid, *n.* A system of manual training for schools, originating in Sweden.
Slub, slub, *n.* A roll of wool drawn out and slightly twisted by spinning machinery.
Slubber, slub'ėr, *vt.* To slobber; to soil; to do lazily or carelessly.
Sludge, sluj, *n.* Mire; soft mud.
Sludgy, sluj'i, *a.* Miry; slushy.
Slue, slö, *vt.* (sluing, slued). To turn or swing round (as the yard of a ship).
Slug, slug, *n.* A sluggard; a shell-less snail injurious to plants; a piece of metal used for the charge of a gun.
Sluggard, slug'ärd, *n.* A person habitually lazy; a drone.—*a.* Sluggish.
Sluggish, slug'ish, *a.* Lazy; slothful; inert; not quick.
Sluice, slös, *n.* A contrivance to control the flow of water in a river, dam, &c.; a trough to separate gold from sand, &c.; flood-gate.—*vt.* (sluicing, sluiced). To wet abundantly; to cleanse by means of sluices.
Slum, slum, *n.* A low, dirty street of a city.—*vi.* (slumming, slummed). To visit slums from benevolent motives.
Slumber, slum'bėr, *vi.* To sleep; to be inert or inactive.—*n.* Light sleep; repose.
Slumberous, Slumbrous, slum'bėr-us, slum'-brus, *a.* Inviting or causing sleep.
Slump, slump, *n.* The whole number taken in one lot; a sudden fall in prices or values.—*vt.* To throw into one lot.—*vi.* To sink in walking, as in snow.
Slung, slung, pret. & pp. of *sling.*
Slunk, slungk, pret. & pp. of *slink.*
Slur, slėr, *vt.* (slurring, slurred). To soil; to traduce; to pass lightly over; to pronounce in a careless indistinct manner.—*n.* A slight reproach; a stain or stigma.
Slush, slush, *n.* Sludge or soft mud; wet, half-melted snow.
Slushy, slush'i, *a.* Consisting of slush; resembling slush.
Slut, slut, *n.* A woman negligent of tidiness and dress; a slattern.
Sluttish, slut'ish, *a.* Not neat or cleanly.
Sly, slī, *a.* Cunning; crafty; wily; shrewd.
Slyly, slī'li, *adv.* Cunningly; craftily.
Slyness, slī'nes, *n.* Artful secrecy; cunning; craftiness.
Smack, smak, *vi.* To make a sharp noise with the lips; to taste; to savour.—*vt.* To make a sharp noise with; to slap.—*n.* A loud kiss; a sharp noise; a smart blow; a slap; a slight taste; a smattering; a fishing-vessel.
Small, smal, *a.* Little; petty; short; weak; gentle; not loud; narrow-minded; mean.—*n.* The small part of a thing; *pl.* small-clothes.
Smallage, smal'āj, *n.* Celery.
Small-arms, smal'ärmz, *n.pl.* A general name for rifles, pistols, &c., as distinguished from cannon.
Small-beer, smal'bēr, *n.* A species of weak beer; poor stuff.
Small-clothes, smal'klōтнz, *n.pl.* Breeches or trousers.
Small-hand, smal'hand, *n.* The style of writing commonly used, as distinguished from text or large-hand.
Smallish, smal'ish, *a.* Somewhat small.
Small-pox, smal'poks, *n.* A contagious eruptive disease.
Smalt, smalt, *n.* Common glass tinged to a fine deep-blue by cobalt.
Smart, smärt, *n.* A quick, keen pain; pungent grief.—*a.* Keen; quick; sharp; brisk; witty; spruce; well dressed.—*vi.* To feel a sharp pain; to be acutely painful; to be punished.
Smarten, smärt'n, *vt.* To make smart.
Smartly, smärt'li, *adv.* Keenly; briskly; sharply; wittily; sprucely.
Smash, smash, *vt.* To dash to pieces.—*vi.* To go to pieces.—*n.* A breaking to pieces; ruin; bankruptcy.
Smatter, smat'ėr, *vi.* To have a slight knowledge; to talk superficially.—*n.* A superficial knowledge.
Smatterer, smat'ėr-ėr, *n.* One who has only a superficial knowledge.
Smattering, smat'ėr-ing, *n.* A superficial knowledge.
Smear, smēr, *vt.* To overspread with anything adhesive; to daub; to soil.
Smell, smel, *vt.* (smelling, smelled or smelt). To perceive by the nose; to perceive the scent of; to detect.—*vi.* To give out an odour.—*n.* The faculty by which odours are perceived; scent; perfume.
Smelling, smel'ing, *n.* The sense of smell.
Smelling-salts, smel'ing-saltz, *n.pl.* Volatile salts used as a stimulant.
Smelt, smelt, *vt.* To melt, as ore, to separate the metal.—*n.* A small fish allied to the salmon.
Smelter, smelt'ėr, *n.* One who smelts ore.
Smeltery, smelt'ė-ri, *n.* A place for smelting ores.
Smew, smū, *n.* A swimming bird of the merganser family.
Smile, smīl, *vi.* (smiling, smiled). To show pleasure, sarcasm, pity, &c., by a look; to appear propitious.—*vt.* To express by a smile; to affect by smiling.—*n.* A set of the features expressing pleasure, scorn, &c.; favour.
Smiling, smīl'ing, *p.a.* Wearing a smile; gay in aspect.
Smirch, smėrch, *vt.* To stain; to smudge.
Smirk, smėrk, *vi.* To smile affectedly or pertly.—*n.* An affected smile.
Smite, smīt, *vt.* (smiting, pret. smote, pp. smit, smitten). To strike; to slay; to blast; to afflict; to affect with love, &c.—*vi.* To strike; to clash together.
Smith, smith, *n.* One who works in metals.
Smithery, smith'ė-ri, *n.* The workshop of a smith; a smithy; work done by a smith.
Smithy, smith'i, *n.* The shop of a smith.
Smock, smok, *n.* A chemise; a smock-frock.—*vt.* To clothe with a smock; to pucker diagonally.
Smock-frock, smok'frok, *n.* A loose outer garment worn by farm labourers.
Smocking, smok'ing, *n.* An ornamental diagonal puckering, in form of a honey-comb, and capable of being expanded.
Smoke, smōk, *n.* The exhalation from a burning substance; vapour; idle talk; nothingness; a drawing in and puffing out of tobacco fumes.—*vi.* (smoking, smoked). To emit smoke; to use tobacco.—*vt.* To apply

smoke to; to befoul by smoke; to fumigate; to use in smoking.
Smokeless, smōk'les, *a.* Having no smoke.
Smoker, smōk'ėr, *n.* One who smokes; one who uses tobacco.
Smoking, smōk'ing, *n.* Act of one who or that which smokes; the use of tobacco.—*a.* Pertaining to smoking.
Smoky, smōk'i, *a.* Emitting smoke; filled or tarnished with smoke; like smoke.
Smolt, smōlt, *n.* A salmon a year or two old, when it has acquired its silvery scales.
Smooth, smōTH, *a.* Even on the surface; glossy; moving equably; not harsh; bland.—*n.* Smooth part of anything.—*vt.* To make smooth; to level; to make easy; to palliate; to soothe.
Smoothen, smōTH'n, *vt.* To make smooth.
Smoothly, smōTH'li, *adv.* Evenly; not roughly; blandly; with insinuating language.
Smote, smōt, pret. of *smite.*
Smother, smuTH'ėr, *n.* Stifling smoke; suffocating dust.—*vt.* To stifle; to suffocate; to suppress.—*vi.* To be suffocated or suppressed; to smoulder.
Smothery, smuTH'ėr-i, *a.* Tending to smother; stifling; full of smother or dust.
Smoulder, smōl'dėr, *vi.* To burn and smoke without flame; to exist in a suppressed state.
Smudge, smuj, *vt.* (smudging, smudged). To stain with dirt or filth; to smear.—*n.* A stain; a smear.
Smug, smug, *a.* Neat; spruce; affectedly nice.—*vt.* (smugging, smugged). To make smug.
Smuggle, smug'l, *vt.* (smuggling, smuggled). To import or export secretly and in defiance of law; to convey clandestinely.
Smuggler, smug'lėr, *n.* One who smuggles; a vessel employed in smuggling goods.
Smuggling, smug'ling, *n.* The importing or exporting secretly goods subject to duty.
Smut, smut, *n.* A spot or stain; a spot of soot, &c.; a disease in grain; obscene language.—*vt.* and *i.* (smutting, smutted). To stain with smut; to tarnish.
Smutch, smuch, *vt.* To smudge.—*n.* A foul spot; a smudge.
Smutty, smut'i, *a.* Soiled with smut; affected with mildew; obscene.
Snack, snak, *n.* A small portion of food; a hasty repast; a bite; a share.
Snaffle, snaf'l, *n.* A bridle consisting of a slender bitmouth without a curb.—*vt.* To bridle; to manage with a snaffle.
Snag, snag, *n.* A short projecting stump; a shoot; the tine of a deer's antler; a tree in a river dangerous to vessels.
Snail, snāl, *n.* A slimy, slow-creeping mollusc; a slug; a sluggard.
Snake, snāk, *n.* A serpent.
Snaky, snāk'i, *a.* Pertaining to a snake; cunning; insinuating; infested with snakes.
Snap, snap, *vt.* (snapping, snapped). To bite or seize suddenly; to break with a sharp sound; to break short.—*vi.* To try to seize with the teeth; to break suddenly or without bending.—*n.* A quick eager bite; a sudden breaking; a sharp noise; a kind of biscuit.
Snappish, snap'ish, *a.* Apt to snap; peevish; tart; crabbed.
Snap-shot, snap'shot, *n.* A hasty shot at a moving animal; a photograph taken hastily with a hand camera.
Snare, snār, *n.* A line with a noose for catching animals; anything that entraps.—*vt.* (snaring, snared). To catch with a snare; to ensnare.
Snarl, snärl, *vi.* To growl, as an angry dog; to talk in rude murmuring terms.—*vt.* To entangle.—*n.* A sharp angry growl; a knot; embarrassment.
Snarling, snärl'ing, *a.* Given to snarl; growling; snappish; peevish.
Snary, snār'i, *a.* Tending to ensnare.
Snatch, snach, *vt.* To seize hastily or abruptly.—*vi.* To make a grasp.—*n.* A hasty catch; a short fit or turn; a small portion; a snack.
Sneak, snēk, *vt.* To creep privately; to go furtively; to crouch.—*n.* A mean fellow; one guilty of underhand work.
Sneaking, snēk'ing, *p.a.* Pertaining to a sneak; mean; servile; underhand.
Sneaky, snēk'i, *a.* Mean; underhand.
Sneer, snēr, *vi.* To show contempt by a look; to jeer; to speak derisively.—*n.* A look or grin of contempt; a scoff; a jeer.
Sneeze, snēz, *vi.* (sneezing, sneezed). To emit air through the nose, &c., by a kind of involuntary convulsive effort.—*n.* A single act of sneezing.
Snick, snik, *vt.* To cut; to clip; to snip.
Sniff, snif, *vi.* To draw air audibly up the nose; to snuff.—*n.* A slight smell; snuff.
Snigger, snig'ėr, *vi.* To laugh in a suppressed manner.—*n.* A suppressed laugh; a giggle.
Snip, snip, *vt.* (snipping, snipped). To cut off at a stroke with shears; to clip.—*n.* A single cut with shears; a bit cut off.
Snipe, snīp, *n.* A grallatorial bird with a long bill; a simpleton.—*vi.* To shoot singly at the enemy, generally from specially constructed cover and with a specially sighted rifle.
Snippet, snip'et, *n.* A small part or share.
Snivel, sni'vel, *vi.* (snivelling, snivelled). To run at the nose; to whimper.—*n.* Whimpering; maudlin sentiment.
Snivelling, sni'vel-ing, *p.a.* Apt to snivel or whine; tearful; weakly sentimental.
Snivelly, sni'vel-i, *a.* Running at the nose; pitiful; whining.
Snob, snob, *n.* A shoemaker; one who apes gentility; a would-be aristocrat.
Snobbery, snob'ėr-i, *n.* The quality of being snobbish.
Snobbish, Snobby, snob'ish, snob'i, *a.* Like a snob; pretending to gentility.
Snobbism, snob'izm, *n.* The manners of a snob; state or habit of being snobbish.
Snood, snöd, *n.* A fillet or ribbon for the hair.
Snooze, snöz, *n.* A nap or short sleep.—*vi.* (snoozing, snoozed). To take a short nap.
Snore, snōr, *vi.* (snoring, snored). To breathe with a rough, hoarse noise in sleep.—*n.* A breathing with a hoarse noise in sleep.
Snort, snort, *vi.* To force air with violence through the nose.—*n.* A loud sound produced by forcing the air through the nostrils.
Snot, snot, *n.* The mucus of the nose.
Snout, snout, *n.* The projecting nose of a beast; muzzle; nozzle.
Snow, snō, *n.* Watery particles congealed in the air, and falling in flakes.—*vi.* To fall in snow; used impersonally.—*vt.* To scatter like snow.
Snow-ball, snō'bal, *n.* A ball of snow.—*vt.* To pelt with snow-balls.—*vi.* To throw snow-balls.

Snowberry, snō'be-ri, *n.* A shrub bearing fruits of snow-white berries.
Snow-boot, snō'bȫt, *n.* A boot to be worn when walking in snow.
Snowdrop, snō'drop, *n.* An early plant with white drooping flowers.
Snow-plough, snō'plou, *n.* An implement for clearing away the snow from roads, &c.
Snow-shoe, shō'shȫ, *n.* A light frame worn on each foot to keep the wearer from sinking in snow; a snow-boot.
Snow-slip, snō'slip, *n.* A large mass of snow which slips down a mountain.
Snow-white, snō'whīt, *a.* White as snow.
Snowy, snō'i, *a.* White like snow; abounding with snow; pure white.
Snub, snub, *vt.* (snubbing, snubbed). To stop or rebuke with a tart, sarcastic remark; to slight designedly.—*n.* A check; a rebuke.
Snub-nose, snub'nōz, *n.* A flat nose.
Snuff, snuf, *vt.* To draw up through the nose; to smell; to crop, as the snuff of a candle.—*vi.* To draw up air or tobacco through the nose; to take offence.—*n.* A drawing up through the nose; resentment; burned wick of a candle; pulverized tobacco.
Snuffer, snuf'ėr, *n.* One who snuffs; *pl.* instrument for removing the snuff of a candle.
Snuffle, snuf'l, *vi.* (snuffling, snuffled). To speak through the nose; to breathe hard through the nose.—*n.* A sound made by air drawn through the nostrils; nasal twang; *pl.* an ailment accompanied by snuffling with the nose.
Snuffy, snuf'i, *a.* Pertaining to or like snuff; soiled with snuff.
Snug, snug, *a.* Neat; trim; cozy.
Snuggery, snug'ė-ri, *n.* A snug place.
Snuggle, snug'l, *vi.* (snuggling, snuggled). To lie close for convenience or warmth; to nestle.
Snugly, snug'li, *adv.* Comfortably; safely.
So, sō, *adv.* In this or that manner; to that degree; thus; extremely; very; the case being such; thereby.—*conj.* Provided that; in case that; therefore; accordingly.
Soak, sōk, *vt.* To let lie in a fluid till the substance has imbibed all that it can; to steep; to wet thoroughly.—*vi.* To steep; to enter by pores; to tipple.
Soaker, sōk'ėr, *n.* One who soaks; a hard drinker.
Soaking, sōk'ing, *p.a.* Such as to soak; that wets thoroughly; drenching.
Soaky, sōk'i, *a.* Moist on the surface; steeped in or drenched with water.
So-and-so, sō'and-sō, *n.* A certain person not named; an indefinite person or thing.
Soap, sōp, *n.* A compound of oil or fat with an alkali, used in washing.—*vt.* To rub or cover with soap.
Soapy, sōp'i, *a.* Resembling soap; smeared with soap; unctuous.
Soar, sōr, *vi.* To mount upon the wing; to rise high; to tower.—*n.* A towering flight; a lofty ascent.
Sob, sob, *vi.* (sobbing, sobbed). To sigh or weep convulsively; to make a similar sound.—*n.* A convulsive catching of the breath in weeping or sorrow.
Sober, sō'bėr, *a.* Temperate; not drunk; calm; cool; staid; grave; dull-looking.—*vt.* To make sober.—*vi.* To become sober.
Soberly, sō'bėr-li, *adv.* Temperately; coolly; gravely.
Sobriety, sō-brī'e-ti, *n.* Temperance; abstemiousness; moderation; saneness; sedateness; gravity.
Sobriquet, so-brē-kā, *n.* A nickname.
Sociability, sō'shi-a-bil"i-ti, *n.* Quality of being sociable.
Sociable, sō'shi-a-bl, *a.* Fond of companions; inclined to mix in society; social.
Sociably, sō'shi-a-bli, *adv.* In a sociable manner; conversably; familiarly.
Social, sō'shal, *a.* Pertaining to society; sociable; consisting in union or mutual converse; living in communities.
Socialism, sō'shal-izm, *n.* A theory of social organization aiming at co-operative action and community of property.
Socialist, sō'shal-ist, *n.* One who advocates socialism; a collectivist.
Socialistic, sō-shal-is'tik, *a.* Pertaining to socialism.
Sociality, sō-shal'i-ti, *n.* Sociability.
Socialize, sō'shal-īz, *vt.* To render social; to regulate according to socialism.
Socially, sō'shal-li, *adv.* In a social manner or way; in regard to social position.
Society, sō-sī'e-ti, *n.* Fellowship; company; a body of persons united for some object; persons living in the same circle; those who take the lead in social life.
Socinian, sō-sin'i-an, *n.* One who rejects the doctrine of the Trinity, the deity of Christ, and the atonement, &c.
Sociologist, sō-shi-ol'o-jist, *n.* One versed in sociology.
Sociology, sō-shi-ol'o-ji, *n.* The science which treats of society, its development, the progress of civilization, &c.
Sock, sok, *n.* The shoe of the ancient actors of comedy; a short woven covering for the foot.
Socket, sok'et, *n.* A cavity into which anything is fitted.
Socle, so'kl, *n.* A plain, low pedestal; a plain face or plinth at the lower part of a wall.
Sod, sod, *n.* That layer of earth which is covered with grass; piece of turf.
Soda, sō'da, *n.* The alkali carbonate of sodium used in washing, glass-making, &c., and extensively made from salt.
Sodality, sō-dal'i-ti, *n.* A fellowship or fraternity.
Soda-water, sō'da-wa̤'tėr, *n.* An effervescent drink generally consisting of water into which carbonic acid has been forced.
Sodden, sod'n, *a.* Seethed; saturated; soaked and soft; not well baked; doughy.
Soddy, sod'i, *a.* Turfy; covered with sod.
Sodium, sō'di-um, *n.* A soft light silvery metal.
Sodomite, sod'om-īt, *n.* One guilty of sodomy.
Sodomy, sod'om-i, *n.* A carnal copulation against nature.
Sofa, sō'fa, *n.* A long seat with a stuffed bottom, back, and ends.
Soffit, sof'it, *n.* The lower surface of an arch, architrave, or overhanging cornice, &c.
Soft, soft, *a.* Easily yielding to pressure; delicate; mild; effeminate; not loud or harsh; not strong or glaring.—*adv.* Softly.—*interj.* Be soft; stop; not so fast.
Soften, sof'n, *vt.* To make soft or more soft; to mollify; to alleviate; to tone down.—*vi.*

To become soft; to relent; to become milder.
Softening, sof'n-ing, *n.* Act of making or becoming more soft or softer.
Softish, soft'ish, *a.* Somewhat soft.
Softly, soft'li, *adv.* In a soft manner; gently; quietly; mildly; tenderly.
Soft-spoken, soft'spō-kn, *a.* Speaking softly; mild; affable.
Soho, sō-hō', *interj.* A word used in calling; a sportsman's halloo.
Soi-disant, swa-dē-zäng, *a.* Self-styled; pretended; would-be.
Soil, soil, *vt.* To sully; to tarnish; to manure; to feed (cattle) indoors with green fodder.—*vi.* To tarnish.—*n.* Dirt; ordure; tarnish; the upper stratum of the earth; mould; loam; earth; land; country.
Soil-pipe, soil'pīp, *n.* A pipe for conveying foul or waste water from a house.
Soiree, swa̧'rā, *n.* A meeting of some body at which there are tea and other refreshments, with music, speeches, &c.
Sojourn, sō'jėrn, *vi.* To reside for a time.—*n.* A temporary residence or stay.
Sojourner, sō'jėrn-ėr, *n.* One who sojourns; a temporary resident.
Solace, so'lās, *vt.* (solacing, solaced). To cheer or console; to allay.—*n.* Consolation; comfort; relief; recreation.
Solan-goose, sō'lan-gös, *n.* The gannet.
Solar, sō'lėr, *a.* Pertaining to the sun, or proceeding from it; sunny; measured by the progress of the sun.
Solatium, sō-lā'shi-um, *n.* A compensation in money.
Solder, sol'dėr, *vt.* To unite metals by a fused metallic substance; to patch up.—*n.* A metallic cement.
Soldier, sōl'jėr, *n.* A man in military service; a man of distinguished valour.
Soldiering, sōl'jėr-ing, *n.* The occupation of a soldier.
Soldier-like, Soldierly, sōl'jėr-līk, sōl'jėr-li, *a.* Like or becoming a soldier; brave.
Soldiery, sōl'jė-ri, *n.* Soldiers collectively; the body of military men.
Sole, sōl, *n.* The under side of the foot; the bottom of a shoe; a marine fish allied to the flounder.—*vt.* (soling, soled). To furnish with a sole, as a shoe.—*a.* Single; individual; only; alone.
Solecism, so'le-sizm, *n.* A grammatical error; deviation from correct idiom.
Solecize, so'le-sīz, *vi.* To commit solecism.
Solely, sōl'li, *adv.* Singly; alone; only.
Solemn, so'lem, *a.* Marked with religious gravity or sanctity; impressive; earnest; affectedly grave.
Solemnity, so-lem'ni-ti, *n.* Gravity; impressiveness; a solemn ceremony.
Solemnize, so'lem-nīz, *vt.* To honour by solemn ceremonies; to celebrate; to make grave.
Solemnly, so'lem-li, *adv.* With solemnity; religiously; with formal gravity.
Sol-fa, sol'fä, *vi.* and *t.* (sol-faing, sol-faed). To sing the notes of the scale, using the syllables *do* (or *ut*), *re*, *mi*, *fa*, *sol*, *la*, *si*.
Solfeggio, sol-fej'i-ō, *n.* and *a.* In *music*, a system of arranging the scale by the names *do* (or *ut*), *re*, *mi*, *fa*, *sol*, *la*, *si*.
Solicit, sō-lis'it, *vt.* and *i.* To ask earnestly; to beg; to invite; to disquiet; to incite.
Solicitant, sō-lis'it-ant, *n.* One who solicits.
Solicitation, sō-lis'it-ā"shon, *n.* Earnest request; supplication; entreaty.
Solicitor, sōlis'it-ėr, *n.* One who solicits; an attorney; a law-agent.
Solicitor-general, sō-lis'it-ėr-jen-ė-ral, *n.* An officer of the British crown next in rank to the attorney-general, or in Scotland to the lord-advocate.
Solicitous, sō-lis'it-us, *a.* Anxious; very desirous; concerned; apprehensive.
Solicitude, sō-lis'i-tūd, *n.* State of being solicitous; carefulness; concern; anxiety.
Solid, so'lid, *a.* Resisting pressure; not liquid or gaseous; not hollow; cubic; sound; not frivolous.—*n.* A body that naturally retains the same shape.
Solidarity, so-li-dar'i-ti, *n.* Unity or communion of interests and responsibilities.
Solidification, so-lid'i-fi-kā"shon, *n.* Act or process of solidifying.
Solidify, so-lid'i-fī, *vt.* (solidifying, solidified). To make solid.—*vi.* To become solid.
Solidity, so-lid'i-ti, *n.* State or quality of being solid; density; firmness; soundness.
Solidly, so'lid-li, *adv.* In a solid manner; firmly; compactly; on firm grounds.
Soliloquize, sō-lil'ō-kwīz, *vi.* To utter a soliloquy.
Soliloquy, sō-lil'ō-kwi, *n.* A speaking to oneself; discourse of a person alone.
Solitaire, so'li-tār, *n.* A solitary; an article of jewelry in which a single gem is set; a game for a single person.
Solitarily, so'li-ta-ri-li, *adv.* In a solitary manner; in solitude; alone.
Solitary, so'li-ta-ri, *a.* Being alone; lonely; retired; not much frequented; shared by no companions; single; sole.—*n.* A hermit; a recluse.
Solitude, so'li-tūd, *n.* State of being alone; a lonely life; a lonely place.
Solmization, Solmisation, sol-mī-zā'shon, *n.* Solfeggio; act of sol-faing.
Solo, sō'lō, *n.* A tune or air for a single instrument or voice.
Soloist, sō'lō-ist, *n.* A solo singer or performer.
Solstice, sol'stis, *n.* The time when the sun arrives at the point farthest north or south of the equator, namely 21st June and 22nd Dec.; either of the two points in the ecliptic where the sun then appears to be.
Solstitial, sol-sti'shal, *a.* Pertaining to a solstice; happening at a solstice.
Solubility, so-lū-bil'i-ti, *n.* Quality of being soluble.
Soluble, so'lū-bl, *a.* Susceptible of being dissolved in a fluid; capable of being solved, as a problem.
Solution, sō-lū'shon, *n.* A dissolving; preparation made by dissolving a solid in a liquid; act of solving; explanation; termination or crisis of a disease.
Solvable, solv'a-bl, *a.* Soluble.
Solve, solv, *vt.* (solving, solved). To explain; to make clear; to unravel; to work out.
Solvency, sol'ven-si, *n.* Ability to pay debts.
Solvent, sol'vent, *a.* Having the power of dissolving; able to pay all debts.—*n.* A fluid that dissolves any substance.
Somatic, sō-mat'ik, *a.* Corporeal; bodily.
Somatology, sō-ma-tol'o-ji, *n.* The doctrine of living bodies; the science of matter.
Sombre, som'bėr, *a.* Dark; gloomy; dismal.

—*vt.* (sombring, sombred). To make sombre.
Sombrero, som-brār'ō, *n.* A broad-brimmed hat.
Sombrous, som'brus, *a.* Sombre; gloomy.
Some, sum, *a.* A certain; a; a little; indefinite and perhaps considerable; about or near.—*pron.* An indefinite part, quantity, or number; certain individuals.
Somebody, sum'bo-di, *n.* A person indeterminate; a person of consideration.
Somehow, sum'hou, *adv.* In some way not yet known; one way or another.
Somersault, Somerset, sum'ėr-sạlt, sum'ėr-set, *n.* A leap in which the heels turn over the head; a turn of the body in the air.
Something, sum'thing, *n.* A thing, quantity, or degree indefinitely; a person or thing of importance.—*adv.* Somewhat.
Sometime, sum'tīm, *adv.* Once; formerly; by and by.—*a.* Former; whilom.
Sometimes, sum'tīmz, *adv.* At some or certain times; not always; now and then.
Somewhat, sum'whot, *n.* Something; more or less.—*adv.* In some degree; a little.
Somewhere, sum'whăr, *adv.* In some place; to some place.
Somite, sō'mīt, *n.* A single segment in the body of an articulated animal.
Somnambulate, som-nam'bū-lāt, *vi.* and *t.* To walk or walk over in sleep.
Somnambulism, som-nam'bū-lizm, *n.* The act or practice of walking in sleep.
Somnambulist, som-nam'bū-list, *n.* One who walks in his sleep.
Somniferous, som-nif'ėr-us, *a.* Bringing or causing sleep; soporific.
Somnific, som-nif'ik, *a.* Causing sleep.
Somniloquence, Somniloquism, som-nil'ō-kwens, som-nil'ō-kwizm, *n.* The act of talking in sleep.
Somnolence, som'nō-lens, *n.* Sleepiness.
Somnolent, som'nō-lent, *a.* Sleepy; drowsy.
Son, sun, *n.* A male child.
Sonant, sō'nant, *a.* Sounding; uttered with voice and not breath merely.—*n.* A sonant letter.
Sonata, sō-nä'tä, *n.* A musical composition of several movements for a solo instrument.
Song, song, *n.* That which is sung; vocal music or melody; a poem to be sung; a lyric; poetry; a trifle.
Song-bird, song'bėrd, *n.* A bird that sings.
Songster, song'stėr, *n.* A singer.
Songstress, song'stres, *n.* A female singer.
Son-in-law, sun'in-lạ, *n.* A man married to one's daughter.
Sonnet, son'et, *n.* A poem of fourteen pentameter lines.
Sonneteer, son-et-ēr', *n.* A composer of sonnets; a petty poet.
Sonorous, sō-nō'rus, *a.* Giving sound when struck; resonant; high-sounding.
Sonship, sun'ship, *n.* State of being a son; filiation; the character of a son.
Soon, sön, *adv.* In a short time; shortly; early; quickly; promptly; readily; gladly.
Soot, söt, *n.* A black substance formed from burning matter.—*vt.* To cover or foul with soot.
Sooth, söth, *a.* True.—*n.* Truth; reality.
Soothe, söᴛʜ, *vt.* (soothing, soothed). To please with soft words; to flatter; to pacify; to assuage; to soften.
Soothing, söᴛʜ'ing, *p.a.* Serving to soothe, calm, or assuage; mollifying.
Soothsayer, söth'sā-ėr, *n.* One who foretells or predicts; a prophet.
Soothsaying, söth'sā-ing, *n.* A foretelling; a prediction; divination.
Sooty, söt'i, *a.* Producing soot; consisting of soot; foul with soot; dusky; dark.
Sop, sop, *n.* Something dipped in broth or liquid food; anything given to pacify.—*vt.* (sopping, sopped). To steep in liquor.
Sophism, sof'izm, *n.* A specious but fallacious argument; a subtlety in reasoning.
Sophist, sof'ist, *n.* A captious or fallacious reasoner.
Sophistic, Sophistical, sō-fist'ik, sō-fist'ik-al, *a.* Pertaining to sophistry; fallaciously subtle; not sound in reasoning.
Sophisticate, sō-fist'ik-āt, *vt.* To pervert by sophistry; to adulterate.
Sophistication, sō-fis'ti-kā''shon, *n.* Adulteration; act or art of quibbling; a quibble.
Sophistry, sof'ist-ri, *n.* Fallacious reasoning.
Soporiferous, sō-pō-rif'ėr-us, *a.* Soporific.
Soporific, sō-pō-rif'ik, *a.* Causing sleep.—*n.* A drug or anything that induces sleep.
Soppy, sop'i, *a.* Soaked; wet.
Soprano, sō-prä'nō, *n.* The highest female voice; a singer with such a voice.
Sorb, sorb, *n.* The service-tree or its fruit.
Sorcerer, sōr'sėr-ėr, *n.* A wizard; an enchanter; a magician.
Sorceress, sōr'sėr-es, *n.* A female sorcerer.
Sorcery, sōr'sėr-i, *n.* Magic; enchantment; witchcraft.
Sordid, sor'did, *a.* Dirty; foul; vile; base; niggardly; covetous.
Sordidly, sor'did-li, *adv.* Basely; covetously.
Sore, sōr, *a.* Painful; severe; distressing; tender; galled.—*n.* An ulcer, wound, &c.—*adv.* Severely; sorely.
Sorely, sōr'li, *adv.* In a sore manner; grievously; greatly; violently; severely.
Sorghum, sor'gum, *n.* A kind of millet.
Sororal, sō-rō'ral, *a.* Sisterly.
Sorrel, so'rel, *n.* A plant allied to the docks; a reddish or yellow-brown colour.—*a.* Of a reddish colour.
Sorrily, so'ri-li, *adv.* In a sorry manner; meanly; pitiably; wretchedly.
Sorrow, so'rō, *n.* Affliction or distress of mind; grief; regret.—*vi.* To feel sorrow; to grieve.
Sorrowful, so'rō-fụl, *a.* Full of sorrow; sad; mournful; dejected.
Sorry, so'ri, *a.* Feeling sorrow; grieved; sorrowful; wretched; pitiful.
Sort, sort, *n.* Nature or character; kind; species; manner; a set.—*vt.* To assort; to arrange; to reduce to order.—*vi.* To consort; to agree.
Sorter, sort'ėr, *n.* One who sorts; one who separates and arranges.
Sortie, sor'tē, *n.* The issuing of troops from a besieged place; a sally.
Sortilege, sor'ti-lej, *n.* Act or practice of drawing lots; divination by lots.
Sortment, sort'ment, *n.* Act of sorting; assortment.
So-so, sō'sō, *a.* Middling.
Sot, sot, *n.* A dolt or blockhead; an habitual drunkard.
Sottish, sot'ish, *a.* Like a sot; foolish; given to drunkenness.

Sou, sö, *n.* A French copper coin, worth about a halfpenny.
Soubrette, sö-bret', *n.* An intriguing servant-girl in a comedy.
Soufflé, söf-lā, *n.* A light dish, partly composed of white of eggs.
Sough, suf, *vi.* To emit a rushing or roaring sound like wind; to sound like the sea.—*n.* A rushing sound; a deep sigh.
Soul, sōl, *n.* The spiritual principle in man; the moral and emotional part of man's nature; elevation of mind; fervour; essence; an inspirer or leader; a person.
Souled, sōld, *a.* Instinct with soul or feeling.
Soulless, sōl'les, *a.* Without a soul; without nobleness of mind; mean; spiritless.
Sound, sound, *a.* Not in any way defective; healthy; valid; free from error; orthodox; just; heavy.—*n.* A narrow channel of water; a strait; air-bladder of a fish; that which is heard; noise.—*vt.* To measure the depth of; to examine medically; to try to discover the opinion, &c., of; to cause to give out a sound; to pronounce.—*vi.* To give out a sound; to appear on narration; to be spread or published.
Sounding, sound'ing, *a.* Causing sound; sonorous; having a lofty sound; bombastic.
Sounding-board, sound'ing-bōrd, *n.* A canopy over a platform, &c., to direct the sound of a speaker's voice to the audience.
Sounding-line, sound'ing-līn, *n.* A line for ascertaining the depth of water.
Soundings, sound'ingz, *n.pl.* The depths of water in rivers, harbours, &c.
Soundless, sound'les, *a.* That cannot be fathomed; noiseless.
Soundly, sound'li, *adv.* Healthily; validly; thoroughly; with heavy blows.
Soundness, sound'nes, *n.* Healthiness; solidity; validity; orthodoxy.
Soup, söp, *n.* A liquid food made generally from flesh and vegetables.
Soup-kitchen, söp'ki-chen, *n.* An establishment for supplying soup to the poor.
Sour, sour, *a.* Acid or sharp to the taste; tart; peevish; morose.—*vt.* To make sour; to make cross or discontented; to embitter. —*vi.* To become sour or peevish.
Source, sōrs, *n.* That from which anything rises; the spring, &c., from which a stream proceeds; first cause; origin.
Sourish, sour'ish, *a.* Somewhat sour.
Sourly, sour'li, *adv.* Acidly; peevishly.
Souse, sous, *n.* Pickle; the ears, feet, &c., of swine pickled; a swoop.—*vt.* (sousing, soused). To steep in pickle; to plunge into water.—*vi.* To swoop.—*adv.* With sudden descent or plunge.
Soutane, sö'tän, *n.* A cassock.
South, south, *n.* The region in which the sun is at mid-day.—*a.* Being in or toward the south; pertaining to or from the south.—*adv.* Toward the south.
South-east, south'ēst, *n.* The point midway between the south and east.—*a.* Pertaining to or from the south-east.—*adv.* Toward the south-east.
South-easter, south-ēst'ėr, *n.* A wind from the south-east.
South-easterly, south-ēst'ėr-li, *a.* In the direction of south-east; from the south-east.
South-eastern, south-ēst'ėrn, *a.* Pertaining to or toward the south-east.
Southerly, suᴛʜ'ėr-li, *a.* Lying at or toward the south; coming from the south.
Southern, suᴛʜ'ėrn, *a.* Belonging to the south; southerly.
Southerner, suᴛʜ'ėr-nėr, *n.* An inhabitant or native of the south.
Southernmost, suᴛʜ'ėrn-mōst, *a.* Farthest toward the south.
Southing, souᴛʜ'ing, *n.* Motion to the south; difference of latitude in sailing southward.
Southmost, south'mōst, *a.* Farthest toward the south.
Southward, south'wėrd, *adv.* and *a.* Toward the south.
South-west, south'west, *n.* The point midway between the south and west.—*a.* Pertaining to or from the south-west.—*adv.* Toward the south-west.
South-wester, south-west'ėr, *n.* A strong south-west wind; a waterproof hat with a flap hanging over the neck, often *Sou'wester.*
South-westerly, south-west'ėr-li, *a.* In the direction of south-west; from the south-west.
South-western, south-west'ėrn, *a.* Pertaining to or toward the south-west.
Souvenir, sö-ve-nēr', *n.* A keepsake.
Sovereign, so've-rin, *a.* Supreme in power; chief.—*n.* A monarch; the standard British gold coin, value 20*s.*, or £1 sterling.
Sovereignty, so've-rin-ti, *n.* Supreme power; dominion.
Soviet, sov'i-et, *n.* The method of government in Russia since the Revolution, local soviets (elected councils) sending delegates to larger bodies, and these, in their turn, to the Supreme Congress, which elects the Supreme Council.
Sovran, sov'ran, *n.* and *a.* Sovereign.
Sow, sou, *n.* The female of the swine.
Sow, sō, *vt.* (pret. sowed, pp. sowed or sown). To scatter seed over; to spread abroad.—*vi.* To scatter seed for growth.
Sowar, sou'ar, *n.* An Indian cavalry soldier.
Sower, sō'ėr, *n.* One who sows.
Soy, soi, *n.* A sauce prepared in China and Japan from a bean; the plant producing the bean.
Spa, spą, *n.* A place to which people go on account of a spring of mineral water.
Space, spās, *n.* Extension; room; interval between points or objects; quantity of time; a while.—*vt.* (spacing, spaced). To arrange at proper intervals; to arrange the spaces in.
Spacial, Same as *Spatial.*
Spacious, spā'shus, *a.* Roomy; widely extended; ample; capacious.
Spade, spād, *n.* An instrument for digging; a playing card of a black suit.—*vt.* (spading, spaded). To dig with a spade; to use a spade on.
Spadeful, spād'fųl, *n.* As much as a spade will hold.
Spake, spāk. A preterit of *speak.*
Span, span, *n.* Reach or extent in general; space between the thumb and little finger; nine inches; a short space of time; the stretch of an arch; a yoke of animals.—*vt.* (spanning, spanned). To extend across; to measure with the hand with the fingers extended.
Spandrel, span'drel, *n.* The triangular space between the curve of an arch and the rectangular part inclosing it.
Spangle, spang'gl, *n.* A small glittering metal

ornament; a small sparkling object.—*vt.* (spangling, spangled). To adorn with spangles.
Spangly, spang'gli, *a.* Like a spangle or spangles; glittering; glistening.
Spaniard, Span'yėrd, *n.* A native of Spain.
Spaniel, span'yel, *n.* A dog of several breeds; a cringing, fawning person.
Spanish, span'ish, *a.* Pertaining to Spain.—*n.* The language of Spain.
Spank, spangk, *vi.* To move or run along quickly.—*vt.* To slap or smack.
Spanker, spangk'ėr, *n.* One that spanks; a large fore-and-aft sail on the mizzen-mast.
Spanking, spangk'ing, *a.* Moving quickly; dashing; free-going.
Spanner, span'ėr, *n.* A screw-key.
Span-new, span'nū, *a.* Quite new.
Spar, spär, *n.* A long piece of timber; a pole; a crystalline mineral; boxing-match; flourish of the fists.—*vi.* (sparring, sparred). To fight in show; to box; to bandy words.
Sparable, spar'a-bl, *n.* A nail driven into the soles of shoes and boots.
Spare, spâr, *a.* Scanty; thin; sparing or chary; superfluous; held in reserve.—*vt.* (sparing, spared). To use frugally; to dispense with; to omit; to use tenderly; to withhold from.—*vi.* To be frugal; to use mercy or forbearance.
Sparely, spār'li, *adv.* Sparingly.
Sparing, spār'ing, *a.* Saving; economical.
Sparingly, spār'ing-li, *adv.* Frugally; not lavishly; seldom; not frequently.
Spark, spärk, *n.* A particle of ignited substance, which flies off from burning bodies; a small transient light; a gay man; a lover.—*vi.* To emit particles of fire; to sparkle.
Sparkish, spärk'ish, *a.* Gay; gallant.
Sparkle, spär'kl, *n.* A little spark; lustre.—*vi.* (sparkling, sparkled). To emit sparks; to glitter; to be animated.
Sparkling, spärk'ling, *a.* Emitting sparks; glittering; lively.
Sparrow, spa'rō, *n.* A bird of the finch family.
Sparse, spärs, *a.* Thinly scattered; not thick or close together.
Sparsely, spärs'li, *adv.* Thinly.
Spartan, spär'tan, *a.* Pertaining to ancient Sparta; hardy; undaunted; enduring.
Spasm, spazm, *n.* A violent contraction of a muscle; a convulsive fit.
Spasmodic, spaz-mod'ik, *a.* Relating to spasm; convulsive; overstrained in expression or style.
Spastic, spas'tik, *a.* Spasmodic.
Spat, spat, *n.* The spawn of shell-fish.—*vi.* (spatting, spatted). To emit spawn or spat.
Spatch-cock, spach'kok, *n.* A fowl killed and broiled for some immediate occasion.
Spate, Spait, spāt, *n.* A sudden heavy flood, especially in mountain streams.
Spatial, spā'shal, *a.* Pertaining to space; existing in space.
Spatter, spat'ėr, *vt.* To scatter a liquid substance on; to sprinkle; to asperse.—*n.* Act of spattering; something sprinkled.
Spatula, spat'ū-la, *n.* A broad thin flexible blade, used by painters, apothecaries, &c.
Spavin, spa'vin, *n.* A disease of horses affecting the joint of the hind-leg between the knee and the fetlock, and causing lameness.
Spawn, spạn, *n.* The eggs or ova of fish, frogs, &c., when ejected; offspring, in contempt.—*vt.* and *i.* To eject or deposit as spawn.
Spawner, spạn'ėr, *n.* A female fish.
Spay, spā, *vt.* To destroy the ovaries of, as is done to female animals.
Speak, spēk, *vi.* (pret. spoke, spake, pp. spoken). To utter words; to talk; to deliver a speech; to argue; to plead; to be expressive.—*vt.* To utter with the mouth; to pronounce; to accost; to express.
Speakable, spēk'a-bl, *n.* That can be spoken.
Speaker, spēk'ėr, *n.* One who speaks; the person who presides in a deliberative assembly, as the House of Commons.
Speaking, spēk'ing, *p.a.* Used to convey speech; forcibly expressive; vivid in resemblance; extending to phrases of civility.
Spear, spēr, *n.* A long, pointed weapon; a lance.—*vt.* To pierce or kill with a spear.
Spearman, spēr'man, *n.* One armed with a spear.
Special, spe'shal, *a.* Pertaining to a species; particular; distinctive; having a particular purpose or scope.
Specialism, spe'shal-izm, *n.* Devotion to a particular branch of knowledge.
Specialist, spe'shal-ist, *n.* One who devotes himself to some particular subject.
Speciality, spe-shi-al'i-ti, *n.* Special characteristic; that in which a person is specially versed.
Specialize, spe'shal-īz, *vt.* To assign a specific use to.—*vi.* To apply oneself to a particular subject.
Specially, spe'shal-li, *adv.* Especially; for a particular purpose or occasion.
Specialty, spe'shal-ti, *n.* Special characteristic; a special pursuit; a special product.
Specie, spē'shi, *n.* Metallic money; coin.
Species, spē'shēz, *n. sing.* and *pl.* Outward appearance; a kind, sort, or variety; a class.
Specific, spe-sif'ik, *a.* Pertaining to, designating or constituting a species; definite; precise.—*n.* A remedy which exerts a special action in the cure of a disease; an infallible remedy.
Specifically, spe-sif'ik-al-li, *adv.* In a specific manner; definitely; particularly.
Specification, spe'si-fi-kā"shon, *n.* The act of specifying; details of particulars; particular mention; statement.
Specify, spe'si-fī, *vt.* (specifying, specified). To make specific; to state in detail.
Specimen, spe'si-men, *n.* A sample; a part intended to typify the whole.
Specious, spē'shus, *a.* Superficially correct; appearing well at first view; plausible.
Speciously, spē'shus-li, *adv.* Plausibly.
Speck, spek, *n.* A small spot; a stain; a flaw; an atom.—*vt.* To spot.
Speckle, spek'l, *n.* A speck; a small coloured marking.—*vt.* (speckling, speckled). To mark with small specks.
Speckled, spek'ld, *p.a.* Marked with specks; spotted.
Spectacle, spek'ta-kl, *n.* A show; a sight; an exhibition; a pageant; *pl.* glasses to assist or correct defective vision.
Spectacular, spek-tak'ū-lėr, *a.* Pertaining to or of the nature of a show.
Spectator, spek-tā'tor, *n.* A looker-on; a beholder; an eye-witness.
Spectral, spek'tral, *a.* Pertaining to a spectre; ghostly; pertaining to spectra.
Spectre, spek'tėr, *n.* An apparition; a ghost; a phantom.
Spectroscope, spek'trō-skōp, *n.* The instrument employed in spectrum analysis.

Spectrum, spek'trum, *n.*: pl. **-tra.** An image seen after the eyes are closed; the coloured band of light, showing prismatic colours, produced when a beam of light is subjected to analysis by a spectroscope.

Specular, spek'ū-lăr, *a.* Having a smooth reflecting surface.

Speculate, spek'ū-lāt, *vi.* (speculating, speculated). To meditate; to engage in risky financial transactions with a view to profit.

Speculation, spek-ū-lā'shon, *n.* Contemplation; theory; hazardous financial transactions.

Speculative, spek'ū-lāt-iv, *a.* Given to speculation; theoretical; adventurous in business.

Speculator, spek'ū-lāt-or, *n.* A theorizer; one who speculates in business.

Speculum, spek'ū-lum, *n.*; pl. **-la** or **-lums.** A mirror; a metallic reflector.

Speech, spēch, *n.* The faculty of speaking; language; talk; a formal discourse; oration.

Speechify, spēch'i-fī, *vi.* To make a speech; to harangue.

Speechless, spēch'les, *a.* Destitute of the faculty of speech; dumb; mute; silent.

Speed, spēd, *n.* Success; velocity; haste.—*vi.* (speeding, sped). To make haste; to prosper.—*vt.* To despatch in haste; to help forward; to dismiss with good wishes.

Speedily, spēd'i-li, *adv.* In a speedy manner; quickly; with haste; soon.

Speedometer, spēd-om'et-ėr, *n.* A speed-indicator.

Speedway, spēd'wā, *n.* The track on which motor-cycle races are run.

Speedwell, spēd'wel, *n.* A common herbaceous plant with blue flowers.

Speedy, spēd'i, *a.* Having speed; quick.

Spell, spel, *n.* An incantation; a charm; fascination; a turn of work; a period.—*vt.* (pret. and pp. spelled or spelt). To give the letters of in order; to read; to import.—*vi.* To form words with the proper letters.

Spelling, spel'ing, *n.* Act of one who spells; orthography; letters that form a word.

Spelling-book, spel'ing-buk, *n.* A book for teaching children to spell and read.

Spelt, spelt, *n.* An inferior wheat.

Spelter, spel'tėr, *n.* Zinc, commonly impure.

Spence, spens, *n.* A buttery.

Spencer, spen'sėr, *n.* A man's or woman's outer coat or jacket.

Spend, spend, *vt.* (spending, spent). To lay out, as money; to squander; to pass, as time; to exhaust of force.—*vi.* To spend money; to be dissipated.

Spendthrift, spend'thrift, *n.* and *a.* One who spends improvidently; a prodigal.

Spent, spent, *p.a.* Wearied; exhausted; having deposited spawn.

Sperm, spėrm, *n.* The seminal fluid of animals.

Spermaceti, spėr-ma-se'ti, *n.* A fatty material obtained from a species of whale.

Spermatic, spėr-mat'ik, *a.* Seminal.

Spermatozoon, spėr'ma-to-zō"on, *n.*; pl. **-oa.** One of the microscopic bodies in the semen of animals essential to impregnation.

Sperm-whale, spėrm'whāl, *n.* The spermaceti whale or cachalot.

Spew, spū, *vt.* To vomit; to cast out with abhorrence.—*vi.* To vomit.

Sphene, sfēn, *n.* A yellowish or greenish mineral.

Sphenoid, sfē'noid, *a.* Resembling a wedge.—*n.* A wedge-shaped body.

Spheral, sfēr'al, *a.* Pertaining to the spheres; rounded like a sphere.

Sphere, sfēr, *n.* An orb; a ball; a globe; a sun, star, or planet; circuit of motion, action, &c.; range; province; rank.—*vt.* (sphering, sphered). To place in a sphere or among the spheres.

Spheric, Spherical, sfe'rik, sfe'rik-al, *a.* Pertaining to a sphere; globular.

Spherically, sfe'rik-al-li, *adv.* In the form of a sphere.

Sphericity, sfe-ris'i-ti, *n.* Roundness.

Spherics, sfer'iks, *n.* In *geometry*, the doctrine of the properties of the sphere.

Spheroid, sfēr'oid, *n.* A body like a sphere, but not perfectly spherical.

Spheroidal, sfēr-oid'al, *a.* Having the form of a spheroid.

Spherule, sfe'rūl, *n.* A little sphere.

Sphincter, sfingk'tėr, *n.* A ring-like muscle closing the external orifices of organs, as the mouth or anus.

Sphinx, sfingks, *n.* A monster or figure with the bust of a woman on the body of a lioness, said to have proposed a riddle; a person who puts puzzling questions.

Sphragistics, sfra-jis'tiks, *n.* The science of seals.

Sphygmograph, sfig'mō-graf, *n.* An instrument to indicate the nature of the pulse.

Spicate, spī'kāt, *a.* Eared like corn.

Spice, spīs, *n.* A vegetable production, aromatic to the smell and pungent to the taste; something piquant; flavour; smack.—*vt.* (spicing, spiced). To season with spice; to flavour.

Spicery, spīs'ė-ri, *n.* Spices in general; a repository of spices; spiciness.

Spicily, spīs'i-li, *adv.* In a spicy manner; pungently; with flavour.

Spick-and-span, spik'and-span, *a.* Trim; flawless.—*adv.* Quite (with *new*).

Spicule, spik'ūl, *n.* A little spike; a little sharp needle-shaped body.

Spicy, spīs'i, *a.* Producing or abounding with spice; pungent; piquant; racy.

Spider, spī'dėr, *n.* An animal that spins webs for taking its prey.

Spigot, spi'got, *n.* A peg to stop a faucet or cask.

Spike, spīk, *n.* A piece of pointed iron; an ear of corn. &c.—*vt.* (spiking, spiked). To fasten or set with spikes; to stop the vent of a cannon with a nail, &c.; to fix upon a spike.

Spikelet, spik'let, *n.* A small spike.

Spikenard, spīk'närd, *n.* An aromatic plant of the East Indies; a fragrant essential oil; an ancient unguent.

Spiky, spīk'i, *a.* Set with spikes; like a spike; having a sharp point.

Spile, spīl, *n.* A spigot.—*vt.* To supply with a spile or spigot.

Spill, spil, *vt.* (pret. and pp. spilled or spilt). To suffer to fall, flow over, &c.; to shed.—*vi.* To be shed; to be suffered to fall, be lost, or wasted.—*n.* A spigot; piece of wood or paper used to light a lamp, &c.; a fall.

Spilth, spilth, *n.* That which is spilled or wasted lavishly.

Spin, spin, *vt.* (spinning, spun). To draw out and twist into threads; to protract; to whirl; to make threads, as a spider.—*vi.* To work at drawing and twisting threads; to rotate; to

go quickly.—*n.* Act of spinning; a rapid run.
Spinach, Spinage, spin'āj, *n.* A culinary vegetable.
Spinal, spīn'al, *a.* Pertaining to the spine.
Spindle, spin'dl, *n.* A pin carrying a bobbin in a spinning machine; a small axis; a long, slender stalk; a measure of yarn.—*vi.* To grow in a long slender stalk.
Spindle-legs, Spindle-shanks, spin'dl-legz, spin'dl-shangks, *n.* Long slender legs, or a person having such.
Spine, spīn, *n.* A prickle; a thorn; a thin, pointed spike in animals; the backbone or spinal column.
Spined, spīnd, *a.* Having spines.
Spinel, Spinelle, spi-nel', *n.* A kind of gem or hard stone.
Spinet, spin'et, *n.* An old instrument of music resembling a harpsichord.
Spinnaker, spin'a-kėr, *n.* A triangular sail carried by yachts on the opposite side to the main-sail in running before the wind.
Spinner, spin'ėr, *n.* One who spins; a contrivance for spinning; a spider.
Spinney, Spinny, spin'i, *n.* A small wood; a clump of trees.
Spinose, Spinous, spīn'ōs, spīn'us, *a.* Full of spines; thorny.
Spinster, spin'stėr, *n.* A woman who spins; an unmarried woman; an old maid.
Spiny, spīn'i, *a.* Thorny; difficult.
Spiracle, spi'ra-kl or spī'ra-kl, *n.* Any aperture in animals for breathing.
Spiræa, spī-rē'a, *n.* A genus of flowering plants.
Spiral, spī'ral, *a.* Pertaining to a spire; winding like a screw.—*n.* A curve winding like a screw.
Spirally, spī'ral-li, *adv.* In a spiral form or direction; in the manner of a screw.
Spire, spīr, *n.* A winding line like a screw; a spiral; a wreath; a convolution; a steeple; a stalk or blade of grass, &c.—*vi.* (spiring, spired). To taper up.
Spirit, spi'rit, *n.* The breath of life; the soul; a spectre; vivacity; courage; mood; essence; real meaning; intent; a liquid obtained by distillation; *pl.* alcoholic liquor.—*vt.* To infuse spirit into; to encourage.
Spirited, spi'rit-ed, *p.a.* Showing spirit; animated; lively; bold; courageous.
Spiritless, spi'rit-les, *a.* Destitute of life or spirit; dejected; depressed.
Spirit-level, spi'rit-le-vel, *n.* A glass tube nearly filled with spirit, for determining when a thing is horizontal by the central position of an air-bubble.
Spiritual, spi'rit-ū-al, *a.* Pertaining to spirit; not material; mental; intellectual; divine; pure; ecclesiastical.
Spiritualism, spi'rit-ū-al-izm, *n.* State of being spiritual; doctrine of the existence of spirit distinct from matter; belief that communication can be held with departed spirits.
Spiritualist, spi'rit-ū-al-ist, *n.* One who professes a regard for spiritual things only; one who believes in spiritualism.
Spiritualistic, spi'rit-ū-a-lis"tik, *a.* Relating to spiritualism.
Spirituality, spi'rit-ū-al"i-ti, *n.* Quality or state of being spiritual; spiritual nature or character.
Spiritualize, spi'rit-ū-al-īz, *vt.* To render spiritual; to convert to a spiritual meaning.
Spiritually, spi'rit-ū-al-li, *adv.* In a spiritual manner.
Spirituous, spi'rit-ū-us, *a.* Alcoholic; ardent.
Spirt, spėrt, *vt.* To force out in a jet; to squirt.—*vi.* To gush out in a jet.—*n.* A jet of fluid.
Spiry, spīr'i, *a.* Of a spiral form; tapering to a point; abounding in steeples.
Spissitude, spis'i-tūd, *n.* Density of soft or liquid substances; thickness; viscosity.
Spit, spit, *n.* A prong on which meat is roasted; low land running into the sea.—*vt.* (spitting, spitted). To put on a spit; to pierce.
Spit, spit, *vt.* and *i.* (spitting, spat). To eject from the mouth, as saliva.—*n.* What is ejected from the mouth; spittle.
Spitchcock, spich'kok, *n.* An eel split and broiled.—*vt.* To split (an eel) and broil it.
Spite, spīt, *n.* A feeling of ill-will; malice; rancour.—**In spite of,** notwithstanding.—*vt.* (spiting, spited). To mortify or chagrin; to thwart.
Spiteful, spīt'ful, *a.* Having a desire to annoy or injure; malignant; malicious.
Spitfire, spit'fīr, *n.* A violent or passionate person; one who is irascible or fiery.
Spittle, spit'l, *n.* Saliva; the moist matter ejected from the mouth.
Spittoon, spit-tōn', *n.* A vessel to receive discharges of spittle.
Splanchnic, splangk'nik, *a.* Belonging to the viscera or entrails.
Splash, splash, *vt.* and *i.* To bespatter with liquid matter.—*n.* A quantity of wet matter thrown on anything; a noise from water dashed about; a spot of dirt.
Splash-board, splash'bōrd, *n.* A board in front of a vehicle to ward off dirt thrown by the horses' heels.
Splashy, splash'i, *a.* Full of dirty water; wet; wet and muddy.
Splay, splā, *vt.* To slope or form with an angle.—*n.* A sloped surface.—*a.* Turned outward, as a person's feet.
Splay-footed, splā'fut-ed, *a.* Having the feet turned outward; having flat feet.
Spleen, splēn, *n.* The milt, an organ in the abdomen connected with digestion; spite; ill-humour; low spirits.
Spleeny, splēn'i, *a.* Affected with or characterized by spleen; splenetic.
Splendent, splen'dent, *a.* Shining; gleaming; illustrious.
Splendid, splen'did, *a.* Brilliant; magnificent; famous; celebrated.
Splendidly, splen'did-li, *adv.* Brilliantly; magnificently; richly.
Splendour, splen'dėr, *n.* Brilliancy; magnificence; display; pomp; grandeur.
Splenetic, sple-net'ik or splen'e-tik, *a.* Affected with spleen; morose; sullen; spiteful.—*n.* One affected with spleen.
Splenic, splēn'ik, *a.* Belonging to the spleen.
Splice, splīs, *vt.* (splicing, spliced). To unite, as two ropes, by interweaving the strands; to unite by overlapping, as timber.—*n.* Union of ropes by interweaving; piece added by splicing.
Splint, splint, *n.* A splinter; piece of wood to confine a broken bone when set.
Splinter, splint'ėr, *n.* A piece of wood, or other solid substance, split off.—*vt.* To split into splinters; to shiver.

Splintery, splint'ėr-i, *a.* Liable to splinter; consisting of splinters.
Split, split, *vt.* (splitting, split). To divide lengthwise; to cleave; to rend; to burst.—*vi.* To part asunder; to burst; to crack; to differ in opinion.—*n.* A rent; fissure; breach or separation.—*a.* Divided; rent; deeply cleft.
Splotch, sploch, *n.* A spot; smear.
Splotchy, sploch'i, *a.* Marked with splotches.
Splutter, splut'ėr, *n.* A bustle; a stir.—*vi.* To speak confusedly; to sputter.
Spode, spōd, *n.* A material composed of calcined ivory, of which vases, &c., are made.
Spoil, spoil, *n.* Pillage; booty; plunder.—*vt.* To plunder; to impair; to ruin; to injure by over-indulgence.—*vi.* To grow useless; to decay.
Spoiler, spoil'ėr, *n.* One who spoils; a plunderer.
Spoke, spōk, *n.* A bar of a wheel; the round of a ladder; a bar.—*vt.* (spoking, spoked). To furnish with spokes. Pret. of *speak.*
Spoken, spōk'n, *p.a.* Oral; speaking (as in fair-spoken).
Spoke-shave, spōk'shāv, *n.* A small plane used by wheelwrights and others.
Spokesman, spōks'man, *n.* One who speaks for another.
Spoliate, spō'li-āt, *vt.* To spoil; to plunder.
Spoliation, spō-li-ā'shon, *n.* Pillage.
Spondaic, spon-dā'ik, *a.* Pertaining to a spondee; composed of spondees.
Spondee, spon'dē, *n.* A metrical foot of two long syllables.
Sponge, spunj, *n.* A soft porous marine substance which readily imbibes liquids; a mean parasite.—*vt.* (sponging, sponged). To wipe with a sponge; to wipe out completely; to harass by extortion; to get by mean arts.—*vi.* To imbibe; to act as a hanger-on.
Sponger, spunj'ėr, *n.* One who sponges.
Spongy, spunj'i, *a.* Soft and full of cavities; soaked and soft.
Sponsion, spon'shon, *n.* A solemn promise; act of becoming surety.
Sponsor, spon'sor, *n.* A surety or guarantor; a godfather or godmother.
Spontaneity, spon-ta-nē'i-ti, *n.* Self-originated activity; readiness.
Spontaneous, spon-tā'nē-us, *a.* Voluntary; self-originated; acting by its own impulse.
Spontaneously, spon-tā'nē-us-li, *adv.* Of one's own accord.
Spook, spök, *n.* A ghost; an apparition.
Spool, spöl, *n.* A reel to wind thread or yarn on.
Spoon, spön, *n.* A domestic utensil for taking up liquids, &c., at table.—*vt.* To take up with a spoon.
Spoonerism, spön'ėr-izm, *n.* An inadvertent and usually amusing transposition of sounds, e.g. *half-warmed fish* for *half-formed wish.*
Spoonful, spön'fu̧l, *n.* As much as a spoon contains.
Spoon-meat, spön'mēt, *n.* Food that is or must be taken with a spoon.
Spoony, Spooney, spön'i, *a.* Weak-minded; foolishly fond.—*n.* A silly fellow.
Spoor, spör, *n.* The track or trail of an animal.
Sporadic, spō-rad'ik, *a.* Scattered; occurring here and there in a scattered manner.
Spore, spōr, *n.* The reproductive germ of a cryptogamic plant; a germ of certain animal organisms.
Sporran, Sporan, spo'ran, *n.* The fur pouch worn in front of the kilt.
Sport, spōrt, *n.* A game; a merry-making; out-of-door recreation, as shooting, horse-racing, &c.; jest; object of mockery; a plant or animal that differs from the normal type.—*vt.* To divert (oneself); to wear in public.—*vi.* To play; to frolic; to practise the diversions of the field.
Sportful, spōrt'fu̧l, *a.* Sportive.
Sporting, spōrt'ing, *a.* Indulging in sport; belonging to sport.
Sportive, spōrt'iv, *a.* Full of sport; gay; playful; frolicsome; jocular.
Sportsman, spōrts'man, *n.* One who engages in shooting, fishing, &c.
Spot, spot, *n.* A place discoloured; a speck; a blemish; a flaw; a locality.—*vt.* (spotting, spotted). To make a spot on; to stain; to catch with the eye.—*vi.* To act as observer of enemy's position, of effect of gunfire, or of approach of hostile aircraft.
Spotless, spot'les, *a.* Free from spots; unblemished; pure; immaculate.
Spotted, spot'ed, *a.* Marked with spots; speckled.
Spotty, spot'i, *a.* Full of spots; spotted.
Spousal, spouz'al, *a.* Nuptial; connubial.
Spouse, spouz, *n.* A husband or wife.
Spout, spout, *n.* A nozzle, or projecting mouth of a vessel; a water-spout; a jet or gush of water.—*vt.* and *i.* To discharge in a jet and with some force; to mouth or utter pompously.
Spouter, spout'ėr, *n.* One who spouts; one who speaks in a pompous manner.
Sprain, sprān, *vt.* To overstrain, as the muscles or ligaments of a joint.—*n.* A violent strain of a joint without dislocation.
Sprat, sprat, *n.* A small fish of the herring family.
Sprawl, spra̧l, *vi.* To struggle or show convulsive motions; to lie or crawl with the limbs stretched.
Spray, sprā, *n.* A twig; collection of small branches; water or any liquid flying in small drops or particles.—*vt.* To cause to take the form of spray; to treat with spray.
Spread, spred, *vt.* (spreading, spread). To stretch or expand; to overspread; to disseminate; to emit; to diffuse.—*vi.* To stretch out; to be diffused.—*n.* Extent; diffusion; a meal or banquet.
Spread-eagle, spred'ē-gl, *n.* The figure of an eagle with the wings and legs extended.—*a.* Pretentious; defiantly bombastic.
Spree, sprē, *n.* A merry frolic; a carousal.
Sprig, sprig, *n.* A small shoot or twig; a spray; a scion; a small square brad.
Spriggy, sprig'i, *a.* Full of sprigs or small branches.
Sprightly, sprīt'li, *a.* Full of spirit; lively; brisk; gay; vivacious.
Spring, spring, *vi.* (pret. sprang or sprung, pp. sprung). To leap; to start up; to dart; to warp; to become cracked; to originate.—*vt.* To start or rouse; to propose on a sudden; to crack; to jump over.—*n.* A leap; resilience; an elastic body, made of various materials, especially steel; cause; an issue of water; source of supply; season of the

year when plants begin to grow; a crack in timber.
Spring-board, spring'bōrd, *n.* An elastic board used in vaulting, &c.
Springe, sprinj, *n.* A gin; a snare.—*vt.* (springeing, springed). To ensnare.
Springer, spring'ėr, *n.* One who springs; the bottom stone of an arch.
Spring-halt. *See* STRING-HALT.
Spring-tide, spring'tīd, *n.* The high tide which happens at the new and full moon.
Spring-time, spring'tīm, *n.* The spring.
Spring-water, spring'wa-tėr, *n.* Water issuing from a spring.
Springy, spring'i, *a.* Elastic; light of foot; abounding with springs; wet; spongy.
Sprinkle, spring'kl, *vt.* and *i.* (sprinkling, sprinkled). To scatter in small drops; to bedew.—*n.* A small quantity scattered in drops.
Sprinkling, spring'kling, *n.* Act of one who sprinkles; a sprinkle; a small quantity distributed in a scattered manner.
Sprint, sprint, *n.* A short swift foot-race; a spurt.
Sprit, sprit, *n.* A small spar which crosses a sail to extend and elevate it.
Sprite, sprit, *n.* A spirit; a kind of goblin.
Sprout, sprout, *vi.* To bud; to push out new shoots.—*n.* A shoot of a plant; *pl.* young coleworts; Brussels sprouts.
Spruce, sprös, *a.* Neat in dress; trim; smug. —*n.* A pine-tree yielding valuable timber.
Sprucely, sprös'li, *adv.* In a spruce manner; with extreme or affected neatness.
Spry, sprī, *a.* Nimble; active; lively.
Spud, spud, *n.* A small spade for cutting the roots of weeds.
Spue, spū, *vt.* and *i.* Same as *Spew.*
Spume, spūm, *n.* Froth; foam.—*vi.* To froth.
Spumescent, spūm-es'ent, *a.* Frothy.
Spumy, spūm'i, *a.* Consisting of spume; foamy.
Spun, spun, pret. & pp. of *spin.*
Spunge, spunj. Same as *Sponge.*
Spunk, spungk, *n.* Touchwood; tinder; mettle; pluck; courage.
Spur, spėr, *n.* An instrument with sharp points, worn on horsemen's heels; incitement; stimulus; a sharp outgrowth; a mountain mass that shoots from another.—*vt.* (spurring, spurred). To prick with a spur; to incite; to put spurs on.—*vi.* To travel with great expedition.
Spurgall, spėr'gal, *n.* A place galled by the spur.—*vt.* To gall with the spurs.
Spurge, spėrj, *n.* A plant with an acrid milky juice powerfully purgative.
Spurious, spū'ri-us, *a.* Bastard; not genuine; counterfeit; false.
Spurn, spėrn, *vt.* To drive away, as with the foot; to reject with disdain; to treat with contempt.—*vi.* To kick up the heels; to manifest disdain.
Spurred, spėrd, *a.* Wearing spurs.
Spurrier, spėr'i-ėr, *n.* One who makes spurs.
Spurt, spėrt, *vt.* and *i.* To spirt.—*n.* A gush of liquid; sudden effort for an emergency; sudden increase of speed.
Spur-wheel, spėr'whēl, *n.* A cog-wheel with teeth perpendicular to the axis.
Sputter, sput'ėr, *vi.* To emit saliva in speaking; to throw out moisture; to speak hastily and indistinctly.
Sputum, spū'tum, *n.* Spittle.
Spy, spī, *vt.* (spying, spied). To gain sight of; to gain knowledge of by artifice; to explore. —*vi.* To pry.—*n.* One who keeps watch on the actions of others; a secret emissary.
Spy-glass, spī'gläs, *n.* A small telescope.
Squab, skwob, *a.* Short and fat; plump; unfeathered.—*n.* A short, fat person; an unfledged bird; a kind of couch.
Squabble, skwob'l, *vi.* (squabbling, squabbled). To dispute noisily; to wrangle.—*n.* A scuffle; a brawl.
Squad, skwod, *n.* A small party of men assembled for drill; any small party.
Squadron, skwod'ron, *n.* The principal division of a regiment of cavalry, usually from 100 to 200 men; a division of a fleet; a group of some twelve or so military aeroplanes.—
Squadron leader, *n.* Officer in the Royal Air Force ranking with a major in the Army.
Squalid, skwo'lid, *a.* Foul; filthy.
Squall, skwal, *vi.* To cry out; to scream violently.—*n.* A loud scream; a violent gust of wind; a brief storm of wind.
Squally, skwal'i, *a.* Abounding with squalls.
Squalor, skwol'ėr, *n.* Foulness; filthiness.
Squama, skwā'ma, *n.*; pl. **-mæ.** A scale or scaly part of plants or animals.
Squamose, Squamous, skwa-mōs', skwā'mus, *a.* Covered with or consisting of scales.
Squander, skwon'dėr, *vt.* To spend lavishly; to fling away; to waste.
Square, skwār, *a.* Having four equal sides and four right angles; forming a right angle; just; honest; even; suitable.—*n.* A figure having four equal sides and right angles; any similar figure or area; an instrument having one edge at right angles to another; product of a number multiplied by itself; level; equality.—*vt.* (squaring, squared). To make square; to form to right angles; to adjust; to fit; to settle (accounts); to multiply a number by itself.—*vi.* To suit; to spar (colloq.).
Squarely, skwār'li, *adv.* In a square form; directly; fairly; honestly.
Squash, skwosh, *vt.* To crush; to beat or press into pulp or a flat mass.—*n.* Something easily crushed; sudden fall of a heavy soft body; a kind of gourd.
Squat, skwot, *vi.* (squatting, squatted). To sit upon the hams or heels; to cower; to settle on land without any title.—*a.* Cowering; short and thick.—*n.* The posture of one who squats.
Squatter, skwot'ėr, *n.* One that settles on unoccupied land without a title; in Australia, one who occupies a large area of pasturage.
Squaw, skwa, *n.* Among American Indians, a female or wife.
Squawk, skwak, *vi.* To cry with a harsh voice.
Squeak, skwēk, *vi.* To utter a sharp, shrill sound.—*n.* A sharp, shrill sound.
Squeal, skwēl, *vi.* To cry with a sharp, shrill voice.—*n.* A shrill, sharp cry.
Squeamish, skwēm'ish, *a.* Having a stomach easily turned; fastidious.
Squeezable, skwēz'a-bl, *a.* Capable of being squeezed.
Squeeze, skwēz, *vt.* (squeezing, squeezed). To subject to pressure; to harass by extortion;

to hug.—*vi.* To press; to crowd.—*n.* An application of pressure; compression.
Squelch, skwelch, *vt.* To crush; to destroy. —*vi.* To be crushed.—*n.* A flat heavy fall.
Squib, skwib, *n.* A small firework; a lampoon; a skit.—*vi.* (squibbing, squibbed). To throw squibs; to utter sarcastic reflections.
Squid, skwid, *n.* A cuttle-fish.
Squill, skwil, *n.* A plant allied to the onions, &c.; a species of shrimp.
Squinch, skwinsh, *n.* An arched structure formed across an angle to support the masonry above it.
Squint, skwint, *a.* Looking obliquely or different ways.—*n.* An oblique look; an affection in which the optic axes do not coincide. —*vi.* To look obliquely.
Squire, skwīr, *n.* A gentleman next in rank to a knight; a country gentleman; a beau.—*vt.* (squiring, squired). To attend as a squire or beau; to escort.
Squireling, skwīr'ling, *n.* A petty squire.
Squirm, skwėrm, *vi.* To wriggle; to writhe. —*n.* A wriggling motion.
Squirrel, skwi'rel, *n.* A rodent with a long bushy tail, living in trees.
Squirt, skwėrt, *vt.* To eject out of an orifice in a stream.—*vi.* To spirt.—*n.* An instrument which ejects a liquid in a stream; a syringe; a small jet; a spirt.
Stab, stab, *vt.* and *i.* (stabbing, stabbed). To pierce or kill with a pointed weapon; to wound figuratively; to injure secretly.—*n.* A thrust or wound with a pointed weapon; underhand injury; poignant pain.
Stability, sta-bil'i-ti, *n.* State or quality of being stable; steadfastness; firmness.
Stable, stā'bl, *a.* Firm; firmly established; steadfast.—*n.* A house for horses, &c.—*vt.* (stabling, stabled). To put or keep in a stable. —*vi.* To dwell in a stable.
Stabling, stā'bl-ing, *n.* Act of keeping in a stable; accommodation for horses.
Stablish, stab'lish, *vt.* To establish.
Stably, stā'bli, *adv.* Firmly; with stability.
Staccato, stak-kä'tō, *a.* In *music*, a direction to perform notes in a detached or pointed manner.
Stack, stak, *n.* A large, regularly built pile of hay, grain, &c.; a number of chimneys standing together; a single tall chimney; a high rock detached.—*vt.* To build into a stack; to pile together.
Stack-yard, stak'yärd, *n.* A yard for stacks of hay, corn, &c.
Staddle, stad'l, *n.* A frame supporting a stack; a tree left uncut when others are cut down.
Stade, stād, *n.* A stadium.
Stadium, stā'di-um, *n.* A Greek measure equal to 606 feet 9 inches; a large sports ground.
Staff, stäf, *n.*; pl. **Staves** or **Staffs,** stāvz, stäfs. A stick or rod; a prop or support; a baton; the five parallel lines on which musical characters are written; a body of officers attached to an army as a whole (pl. *staffs*); a body of persons assisting in any undertaking.
Staff-officer, stäf'of-is-ėr, *n.* An officer upon the staff of an army or regiment.
Stag, stag, *n.* A male animal, especially the male red-deer; a hart.
Stage, stāj, *n.* An elevated platform; the platform on which theatrical performances are exhibited; place of action; a halting-place; distance between two stopping-places; degree of progression; point reached.—*vt.* To put upon the theatrical stage.
Stage-coach, stāj'kōch, *n.* Formerly a coach running regularly for the conveyance of passengers.
Stager, stāj'ėr, *n.* One that has long acted on the stage of life; a person of experience.
Stage-struck, stāj'struk, *a.* Seized by a passionate desire to become an actor.
Stagey, Stagy, stāj'i, *a.* Pertaining to the stage; theatrical.
Stagger, stag'ėr, *vi.* To reel; to totter; to waver.—*vt.* To cause to waver; to amaze; to arrange working hours so that employees enter and leave their place of work at intervals in batches, instead of simultaneously.—*n.* A sudden swaying of the body; *pl.* a disease of cattle, &c., attended with giddiness.
Stag-hound, stag'hound, *n.* A large hound used in hunting the stag or red-deer.
Staging, stāj'ing, *n.* A temporary structure for support; scaffolding.
Stagnancy, stag'nan-si, *n.* Stagnation.
Stagnant, stag'nant, *a.* Not flowing; motionless; still; dull; not brisk.
Stagnate, stag'nāt, *vi.* (stagnating, stagnated). To cease to flow; to become motionless or dull.
Stagnation, stag-nā'shon, *n.* State of being or becoming stagnant.
Staid, stād, *a.* Sober; grave; sedate.
Staidly, stād'li, *adv.* Gravely; sedately.
Stain, stān, *vt.* To mark or spot; to discolour; to soil; to disgrace; to tinge with colour.—*vi.* To take stains; to become stained.—*n.* A discoloration; a spot; disgrace; a colour.
Stainless, stān'les, *a.* Free from stains; untarnished; unblemished.
Stair, stār, *n.* One of a set of steps to go up or down by; a series of connected steps.
Staircase, stār'kās, *n.* The part of a building which contains the stairs.
Staith, stāth, *n.* A kind of wharf for coal.
Stake, stāk, *n.* A sharpened piece of wood; a post; that which is pledged or wagered; hazard (preceded by *at*).—*vt.* (staking, staked). To support, defend, or mark with stakes; to pledge; to wager.
Stalactite, sta-lak'tīt, *n.* A mass of calcareous matter attached, like an icicle, to the roof of a cavern.
Stalactitic, sta-lak-tit'ik, *a.* Pertaining to, resembling, or containing stalactites.
Stalagmite, sta-lag'mīt, *n.* A deposit of stalactitic matter on the floor of a cavern.
Stale, stāl, *a.* Vapid; tasteless; not new; musty; trite.—*vt.* (staling, staled). To make stale.—*vi.* To discharge urine, as cattle.—*n.* Urine of horses and cattle.
Stalk, stạk, *n.* The stem of a plant; part that supports a flower, leaf, fruit, &c.; a stately step or walk.—*vi.* To walk in a dignified manner.—*vt.* To watch and follow warily, as game, for the purpose of killing.
Stalker, stạk'ėr, *n.* One who stalks; a kind of fishing-net.
Stalking-horse, stạk'ing-hors, *n.* A horse behind which a fowler conceals himself; a mask; a pretence.
Stalky, stạk'i, *a.* Resembling a stalk.
Stall, stạl, *n.* A place where a horse or ox is

kept and fed; division of a stable; a bench or shed where anything is exposed to sale, &c.; the seat of a clerical dignitary in the choir; a seat in a theatre.—*vt.* To put into a stall; to plunge into mire.

Stallage, stąl'āj, *n.* The right of erecting stalls in fairs; rent paid for a stall.

Stallion, stal'yun, *n.* A horse not castrated.

Stalwart, Stalworth, stal'wėrt, stal'wėrth, *a.* Stout-hearted; tall and strong.

Stamen, stā'men, *n.* The male organ of fructification in plants.

Stamina, sta'mi-na, *n.pl.* Whatever constitutes the principal strength; robustness; power of endurance.

Stammer, stam'ėr, *vi.* and *t.* To make involuntary breaks in utterance; to stutter.—*n.* Defective utterance; a stutter.

Stamp, stamp, *vt.* To strike by thrusting the foot down; to impress; to imprint; to affix a postage-stamp to; to coin; to form.—*vi.* To strike the foot forcibly downward.—*n.* Act of stamping; an instrument for crushing or for making impressions; mark imprinted; a postage-stamp; character; sort.

Stampede, stam-pēd', *n.* A sudden fright and flight, as of horses.—*vi.* (stampeding, stampeded). To take sudden flight.—*vt.* To cause to break off in a stampede.

Stamping-mill, Stamp-mill, stamp'ing-mil, stamp'mil, *n.* A machine by which ores are pounded.

Stanch, Staunch, stänsh, stąnsh, *vt.* To stop from running, as blood; to stop the flow of blood from.—*vi.* To cease to flow.—*a.* Strong and tight; constant and zealous; loyal.

Stanchion, stan'shon, *n.* A prop or support; a post of timber or iron.

Stand, stand, *vi.* (stånding, stood). To be upon the feet in an upright position; to be on end; to have locality; to stop; to endure; to persevere; to be as regards circumstances; to be equivalent; to become a candidate; to hold a certain course; to be valid.—*vt.* To set on end; to endure.—*n.* Act of standing; a stop; a halt; a station; a small table or frame; platform for spectators at gatherings.

Standard, stand'ärd, *n.* A flag of war; a banner; a rule or measure; criterion; test; a certain grade in schools; an upright support. —*a.* Serving as a standard; satisfying certain legal conditions; not trained on a wall, &c., but standing by itself.

Standard-bearer, stand'ärd-bār-ėr, *n.* An officer who bears a standard.

Stander-by, stand'ėr-bī, *n.* One who stands near; a by-stander.

Standing, stand'ing, *a.* Upright; erect; established; permanent; stagnant.—*n.* Act of one who stands; duration; place to stand in; power to stand; rank.

Standish, stan'dish, *n.* A case for pen and ink.

Stand-point, stand'point, *n.* A fixed point or station; point of view from which a matter is considered.

Stand-still, stand'stil, *n.* A stop.

Stand-up, stand'up, *a.* Erect; fought by combatants standing boldly up.

Stanhope, stan'hōp, *n.* A light two-wheeled carriage without a top.

Stannary, stan'a-ri, *n.* A tin mine.—*a.* Relating to the tin mines or works.

Stannic, stan'ik, *a.* Pertaining to tin.

Stanniferous, stan-if'ėr-us, *a.* Containing or affording tin.

Stanza, stan'za, *n.* A verse or connected number of lines of poetry.

Stanzaic, stan-zā'ik, *a.* Consisting of or relating to stanzas; arranged as a stanza.

Staple, stā'pl, *n.* An emporium; a principal commodity; chief constituent; thread or pile of wool, cotton, or flax; raw material; an iron loop with two points.—*a.* Chief; principal; established in commerce.—*vt.* (stapling, stapled). To adjust the staples of, as wool.

Stapler, stā'pl-ėr, *n.* A dealer in staple commodities; one who assorts wool.

Star, stär, *n.* Any celestial body except the sun and moon; a heavenly body similar to our sun; a figure with radiating points; a badge of honour; an asterisk, thus *; a brilliant theatrical performer.—*vt.* (starring, starred). To adorn with stars; to bespangle.—*vi.* To shine as a star; to appear as an eminent actor among inferior players.

Starboard, stär'bōrd, *n.* and *a.* The right-hand side of a ship.

Starch, stärch, *n.* A vegetable substance, employed for stiffening linen, &c.; stiffness of behaviour.—*vt.* To stiffen with starch.

Starched, stärcht, *p.a.* Stiffened with starch; precise; formal.

Starchy, stärch'i, *a.* Consisting of starch; resembling starch; stiff; precise.

Star-crossed, stär'krost, *a.* Not favoured by the stars; ill-fated.

Stare, stār, *vi.* (staring, stared). To look with fixed eyes wide open; to gaze; to stand out stiffly.—*vt.* To affect or abash by staring.—*n.* A fixed look with the eyes; a starling.

Star-fish, stär'fish, *n.* A marine animal like a star with five or more rays.

Star-gazer, stär'gāz-ėr, *n.* One who gazes at the stars; an astrologer.

Stark, stärk, *a.* Stiff; rigid; strong; mere; downright.—*adv.* Wholly.

Starless, stär'les, *a.* Having no stars visible.

Starlight, stär'līt, *n.* The light proceeding from the stars.

Starlike, stär'līk, *a.* Like a star; lustrous.

Starling, stär'ling, *n.* A bird allied to the crows, capable of being taught to whistle.

Starlit, stär'lit, *a.* Lighted by stars.

Starred, stärd, *p.a.* Adorned with stars; influenced in fortune by the stars.

Starry, stär'i, *a.* Abounding or adorned with stars; like stars.

Start, stärt, *vi.* To move with sudden quickness; to wince; to deviate; to set out; to begin; to move from its place.—*vt.* To rouse suddenly; to startle; to originate; to dislocate.—*n.* A sudden motion; a twitch; outset; a handicap.

Starter, stąrt'ėr, *n.* One who starts; one who sets persons or things in motion.

Startle, stärt'l, *vi.* (startling, startled). To move suddenly.—*vt.* To cause to start; to frighten.—*n.* A start, as from fear.

Startling, stärt'ling, *a.* Such as to startle; surprising; alarming.

Starvation, stärv-ā'shon, *n.* Act of starving; keen suffering from hunger or cold.

Starve, stärv, *vi.* (starving, starved). To perish with cold; to suffer from hunger; to be very indigent.—*vt.* To kill or distress with hunger or cold; to make inefficient through insufficient expenditure.

Starveling, stärv'ling, *n.* A person, animal, or plant weak through want of nutriment.—*a.* Pining with want.

State, stāt, *n.* Condition; situation; rank; pomp; grandeur; an estate (of the realm); a commonwealth; a nation; civil power.—*a.* National; public; governmental.—*vt.* (stating, stated). To express the particulars of; to narrate.

State-craft, stāt'kraft, *n.* The art of conducting state affairs; statesmanship.

Stated, stāt'ed, *p.a.* Established; regular.

State-house, stāt'hous, *n.* The building in which a state legislature meets.

Stately, stāt'li, *a.* Such as pertains to state; august; grand; lofty; dignified.

Statement, stāt'ment, *n.* Expression of a fact or opinion; narrative.

State-room, stāt'röm, *n.* A magnificent room; separate cabin in a steamer.

Statesman, stāts'man, *n.* A man versed in state affairs or in the arts of government.

Static, stat'ik, *a.* Statical.

Statical, stat'ik-al, *a.* Pertaining to bodies at rest or in equilibrium.

Statics, stat'iks, *n.* That branch of dynamics which treats of forces in equilibrium, the body on which they act being at rest.

Station, stā'shon, *n.* Place where anything stands; post assigned; situation; social position; a regular stopping-place, as on railways, &c.—*vt.* To assign a position to; to post.

Stationary, stā'shon-a-ri, *a.* Fixed; not moving; not appearing to move.

Stationer, stā'shon-ėr, *n.* One who sells paper, pens, ink, pencils, &c.

Stationery, stā'shon-ė-ri, *n.* and *a.* Articles sold by stationers, as paper, ink, &c.

Station-master, stā'shon-mās-tėr, *n.* The official in charge of a railway-station.

Statist, stat'ist, *n.* A statistician.

Statistical, Statistic, sta-tis'tik-al, sta-tis'tik, *a.* Pertaining to statistics.

Statistician, stat-is-ti'shan, *n.* One versed in statistics.

Statistics, sta-tist'iks, *n.* A collection of facts, tabulated numerically; the science of subjects as elucidated by facts.

Statuary, stat'ū-a-ri, *n.* One who carves statues; the art of carving statues; statues regarded collectively.

Statue, stat'ū, *n.* An image of a human figure or animal in marble, bronze, or other solid substance.

Statuesque, stat-ū-esk', *a.* Partaking of or having the character of a statue.

Statuette, stat-ū-et', *n.* A small statue.

Stature, stat'ūr, *n.* The height of anyone standing; bodily tallness.

Status, stā'tus, *n.* Social position; rank; condition; position of affairs.

Statutable, stat'ūt-a-bl, *a.* Made by or in conformity to statute.

Statute, stat'ūt, *n.* A law passed by the legislature of a state; an enactment; a fundamental or permanent rule or law.

Statute-book, stat'ūt-bųk, *n.* A book of statutes; the whole statutes of a country.

Statutory, stat'ū-to-ri, *n.* Enacted by statute.

Staunch, stąnsh. *See* STANCH.

Stave, stāv, *n.* A pole; one of the pieces of timber of casks, &c.; a stanza; in *music*, the staff.—*vt.* (staving, staved). To break in a stave of; to break a hole in (pret. & pp. also *stove*).—**To stave off,** to put off; to delay.

Stay, stā, *vt.* (pret. & pp. stayed or staid). To prop; to stop; to delay; to await.—*vi.* To remain; to reside; to delay; to forbear to act; to stop.—*n.* Sojourn; stop; obstacle; a prop; a rope to support a mast; *pl.* a stiffened bodice worn by females; a corset.—**To miss stays,** to fail in the attempt to tack about.

Stead, sted, *n.* Place or room which another had or might have; assistance: preceded by *in*.—*vt.* To be of use to.

Steadfast, sted'fäst, *a.* Firm; constant; resolute; steady.

Steadily, sted'i-li, *adv.* In a steady manner; without shaking or tottering; assiduously.

Steady, sted'i, *a.* Firm; stable; constant; regular; equable.—*vt.* (steadying, steadied). To make or keep firm.

Steady-going, sted'i-gō-ing, *a.* Of steady or regular habits.

Steak, stāk, *n.* A slice of beef, &c., broiled or cut for broiling.

Steal, stēl, *vt.* (pret. stole, pp. stolen). To take feloniously; to pilfer; to gain by address or imperceptibly; to perform secretly.—*vi.* To pass silently or privily; to practise theft.

Stealing, stēl'ing, *n.* Theft.

Stealth, stelth, *n.* A secret method of procedure; a proceeding by secrecy.

Stealthily, stel'thi-li, *adv.* By stealth.

Stealthy, stel'thi, *a.* Done by stealth; furtive; sly.

Steam, stēm, *n.* The vapour of water; aeriform fluid generated by the boiling of water.—*vi.* To give out steam; to rise in vaporous form; to sail by means of steam.—*vt.* To expose to steam; to apply steam to.

Steam-boat, Steam-vessel, stēm'bōt, stēm'-ves-el, *n.* A vessel propelled by steam.

Steam-engine, stēm'en-jin, *n.* An engine worked by steam.

Steamer, stēm'ėr, *n.* A steam-boat; a fire-engine with pumps worked by steam; a vessel in which articles are subjected to steam.

Steam-power, stēm'pou-ėr, *n.* The power of steam mechanically applied.

Steam-ship, stēm'ship, *n.* A steam-boat.

Steam-whistle, stēm'whis-l, *n.* A whistle sounded by steam passing through.

Steamy, stēm'i, *a.* Consisting of or abounding in steam; damp; misty.

Stearine, Stearin, stē'a-rin, *n.* The chief and harder ingredient of animal fats.

Steatite, stē'a-tīt, *n.* A mineral consisting of magnesia and alumina.

Stedfast, sted'fast. *See* STEADFAST.

Steed, stēd, *n.* A horse; a horse of high mettle, for state or war.

Steel, stēl, *n.* A very hard form of iron, produced by addition of carbon; weapons, swords &c.; a knife-sharpener; sternness; rigour.—*a.* Made of or like steel; unfeeling; rigorous.—*vt.* To furnish with steel; to harden.

Steely, stēl'i, *a.* Made of or like steel; hard.

Steelyard, stēl'yärd, *n.* A kind of balance for weighing, with unequal arms.

Steenbok, stēn'bok or stān'bok, *n.* A species of antelope of South Africa.

Steep, stēp, *a.* Sloping greatly; precipitous.

—*n.* A precipitous place; a cliff; process of steeping; liquid in which something is steeped.—*vt.* To soak; to imbue.
Steepen, stēp'n, *vi.* To become steep.
Steeple, stē'pl, *n.* A lofty erection attached to a church, &c.; spire.
Steeple-chase, stē'pl-chās, *n.* A horse-race across country and over obstacles.
Steeply, stēp'li, *adv.* Precipitously.
Steepy, stēp'i, *a.* Steep; precipitous.
Steer, stēr, *vt.* and *i.* To direct and govern, as a ship; to guide; to pursue a course in life. —*n.* A young ox; a bullock.
Steerage, stēr'āj, *n.* The steering of a ship; part of a ship allotted to inferior passengers, usually in the fore part.
Steersman, stērz'man, *n.* One who steers a ship.
Steeve, stēv, *vi.* To rise up from the bows at an angle: said of a bowsprit.
Stela, Stele, stē'la, stē'lē, *n.*; pl. **-læ.** A small column serving as a monument.
Stellar, Stellary, stel'ėr, stel'a-ri, *a.* Pertaining to stars; astral; starry.
Stellate, stel'lāt, *a.* Resembling a star; radiated.
Stelliform, stel'li-form, *a.* Radiated.
Stellular, Stellulate, stel'ū-lėr, stel'ū-lāt, *a.* Like stars; having marks like stars.
Stem, stem, *n.* The principal body of a tree, shrub, &c.; the stalk; stock or branch of a family; the prow of a vessel.—*vt.* (stemming, stemmed). To make way against; to press forward through; to dam up; to check.
Stench, stensh, *n.* An ill smell; stink.
Stencil, sten'sil, *n.* A thin plate with a pattern cut through it, brushed over with colour to mark a surface below.—*vt.* (stencilling, stencilled). To form by a stencil; to colour with stencils.
Sten gun, sten gun, *n.* A machine carbine suitable for use at short range (up to 200 yards) and capable of firing 96 rounds (three magazines) per minute. The name is derived from the initials of the two patentees, Saltoun and Thornton, and from Enfield, the place of patent.
Stenograph, sten'ō-graf, *n.* A writing in shorthand; a kind of typewriter.
Stenographer, Stenographist, ste-nog'ra-fėr, ste-nog'ra-fist, *n.* One who is skilled in stenography or shorthand.
Stenographic, Stenographical, sten-ō-graf'-ik, sten-ō-graf'ik-al, *a.* Pertaining to or expressed in shorthand.
Stenography, ste-nog'ra-fi, *n.* The art of writing in shorthand; shorthand.
Stentorian, sten-tō'ri-an, *a.* Extremely loud; able to utter a loud and deep sound.
Step, step, *vi.* (stepping, stepped). To move the leg and foot in walking; to walk.—*vt.* To set (the foot); to fix the foot of, as of a mast.—*n.* A pace; a small space; a grade; a rise; footprint; gait; footfall; action adopted; something to support the feet in ascending; round of a ladder; *pl.* a step-ladder.
Stepbrother, step'bruᴛʜ-ėr, *n.* A father's or mother's son by another marriage.—Also *stepsister.*
Stepfather, step'fä-ᴛʜėr, *n.* A mother's second or subsequent husband.—Also *stepmother.*
Step-ladder, step'lad-ėr, *n.* A portable self-supporting ladder.
Steppe, step, *n.* An extensive treeless plain in Russia and Siberia.
Stepping-stone, step'ing-stōn, *n.* A stone to raise the feet above a stream or mud; a means of progress or advancement.
Stepson, step'sun, *n.* The son of a husband or wife by a form r marriage.—Also *stepdaughter, stepchild.*
Stère, stār, *n.* The French unit for solid measure, equal to a cubic metre or 35·3156 cubic feet.
Stereographic, ste'rē-ō-graf''ik, *a.* Relating to stereography.
Stereography, ste-rō-og'ra-fi, *n.* The art of delineating solid bodies on a plane.
Stereoscope, ste'rē-ō-skōp, *n.* An optical instrument by which two pictures taken under a small difference of angular view and placed side by side appear as one, the objects seeming solid and real.
Stereoscopic, ste'rē-ō-skop''ik, *a.* Pertaining to the stereoscope.
Stereotype, ste'rē-ō-tīp, *n.* and *a.* A metal plate presenting a facsimile of a page of type; an electrotype plate.—*vt.* To make a stereotype of; to fix unchangeably.
Stereotyped, ste'rē-ō-tīpt, *p.a.* Made or printed from stereotype plates; fixed.
Stereotypic, ste'rē-ō-tip''ik, *a.* Pertaining to stereotype plates.
Sterile, ste'rīl, *a.* Barren; unfruitful; incapable of reproduction; barren of ideas.
Sterility, ste-ril'i-ti, *n.* Quality or state of being sterile; unproductiveness.
Sterilize, ste'ril-īz, *vt.* To make sterile; to render free from bacteria or germs.
Sterilizer, ste'ril-īz-ėr, *n.* One who sterilizes; an apparatus to destroy bacilli, &c.
Sterlet, stėr'let, *n.* A species of sturgeon.
Sterling, stėr'ling, *a.* An epithet distinctive of English money; genuine; of excellent quality.
Stern, stėrn, *a.* Austere; harsh; rigid; stringent.—*n.* The hind part of a ship.
Sternal, stėr'nal, *a.* Pertaining to the sternum.
Stern-chaser, stėrn'chās-ėr, *n.* A cannon placed in a ship's stern, pointed backward.
Sternly, stėrn'li, *adv.* In a stern manner.
Sternmost, stėrn'mōst, *a.* Furthest astern.
Stern-sheets, stėrn'shēts, *n.* The after-part of a boat, usually furnished with seats.
Sternum, stėr'num, *n.* The breast-bone.
Sternutation, stėr-nū-tā'shon, *n.* The act of sneezing.
Stertorous, stėr'to-rus, *a.* Characterized by deep snoring.
Stethoscope, ste'thō-skōp, *n.* An instrument for sounding the chest, lungs, &c.
Stevedore, stē've-dōr, *n.* One who loads or unloads vessels.
Stew, stū, *vt.* To boil slowly in a closed vessel.—*vi.* To be cooked slowly.—*n.* Meat stewed; a bathing house with hot baths; a brothel; a state of excitement.
Steward, stū'ėrd, *n.* One who manages affairs for another; one who helps to manage a public function; an officer on a vessel who attends to passengers, &c.
Stewardess, stū'ärd-es, *n.* A female steward.
Stewartry, stū'ėrt-ri, *n.* In Scotland, a division nearly equivalent to a county.
Sthenic, sthen'ik, *a.* Attended with morbid increase of vital energy.

Stibial, stib'i-al, *a.* Pertaining to antimony.
Stibnite, stib'nīt, *n.* An ore of antimony of a lead-gray colour.
Stich, stik, *n.* A line in poetry.
Stick, stik, *vt.* (sticking, stuck). To pierce or stab; to fasten by piercing, gluing, &c.; to fix; to set.—*vi.* To adhere; to abide firmly; to be brought to a stop; to scruple.—*n.* A rod or wand; a staff; a stiff, awkward person.
Sticking-plaster, stik'ing-pläs-tėr, *n.* An adhesive plaster for closing wounds.
Stickle, stik'l, *vi.* (stickling, stickled). To stick up pertinaciously for something; to scruple.
Stickleback, stik'l-bak, *n.* A small British fish found in ponds and streams, and remarkable for building nests.
Stickler, stik'lėr, *n.* One who stickles; an obstinate contender about trifles.
Sticky, stik'i, *a.* Adhesive; gluey; viscid.
Stiff, stif, *a.* Rigid; tense; not moving easily; thick; not natural and easy; formal in manner; stubborn; difficult; strong.
Stiffen, stif'n, *vt.* To make stiff.—*vi.* To become stiff or stiffer.
Stiffening, stif'n-ing, *n.* Something used to make a substance more stiff; starch, &c.
Stiffly, stif'li, *adv.* In a stiff manner; firmly; rigidly; obstinately; formally.
Stiff-necked, stif'nekt, *a.* Stubborn; inflexibly obstinate; contumacious.
Stiffness, stif'nes, *n.* Want of pliancy; rigidity; viscidness; stubbornness; formality.
Stifle, stī'fl, *vt.* and *i.* (stifling, stifled). To suffocate; to smother; to suppress.—*n.* The joint of a horse next to the buttock.
Stigma, stig'ma, *n.*; pl. **-mas** or **-mata.** A brand made with a red-hot iron; any mark of infamy; part of a flower pistil which receives the pollen; *pl. stigmata*, bodily marks like Christ's wounds impressed supernaturally.
Stigmatic, stig-mat'ik, *a.* Pertaining to stigmas or stigmata.—*n.* A person marked with stigmata.
Stigmatize, stig'mat-īz, *vt.* To characterize by some opprobrious epithet.
Stile, stīl, *n.* A step or steps to aid persons in getting over a fence or wall.
Stiletto, sti-let'tō, *n.* A small strong dagger; a pointed instrument for making eyelet-holes.—*vt.* (stilettoing, stilettoed). To stab or pierce with a stiletto.
Still, stil, *a.* At rest; calm; silent; not loud; soft; not effervescing.—*vt.* To make still; to check; to appease or allay.—*adv.* To this time; always; nevertheless; yet.—*n.* A vessel or apparatus for distilling; a distillery.
Still-born, stil'born, *a.* Dead at the birth; abortive; produced unsuccessfully.
Still-life, stil'līf, *n.* Objects such as dead game, vegetables, &c., represented in painting.
Stillness, stil'nes, *n.* Calmness; quiet.
Still-room, stil'röm, *n.* An apartment for distilling; a store-room in a house.
Stilly, stil'i, *a.* Still; quiet: *poet.*—*adv.* stil'li. Silently; calmly; quietly.
Stilt, stilt, *n.* Either of a pair of poles, with a rest for the foot, used for raising the feet in walking.
Stilted, stilt'ed, *a.* Elevated as if on stilts; stiff and bombastic; jerky.
Stilton, stil'ton, *n.* A rich white cheese, named from *Stilton* in Huntingdonshire, but made chiefly in Leicestershire.
Stimulant, stim'ū-lant, *a.* Serving to stimulate.—*n.* An agent which produces an increase of vital energy; an intoxicant.
Stimulate, stim'ū-lāt, *vt.* To rouse up; to incite; to excite greater vitality in.
Stimulating, stim'ū-lāt-ing, *p.a.* Serving to stimulate or rouse; rousing; stirring.
Stimulation, stim-ū-lā'shon, *n.* Act of stimulating; incitement; use of a stimulus.
Stimulative, stim'ū-lāt-iv, *a.* Stimulating.
Stimulus, stim'ū-lus, *n.* pl. **-li.** Something that stimulates; an incitement.
Sting, sting, *vt.* (stinging, stung). To pierce, as wasps, &c.; to prick, as a nettle; to pain acutely.—*n.* A sharp-pointed defensive organ of certain animals; the thrust of a sting into the flesh; something that gives acute pain; the biting effect of words.
Stingily, stin'ji-li, *adv.* In a stingy or niggardly manner; meanly; shabbily.
Stinging, sting'ing, *p.a.* Furnished with a sting; goading; sharp; keen.
Stingo, sting'gō, *n.* Pungent ale; rare good liquor.
Stingy, stin'ji, *a.* Very niggardly; meanly avaricious; scanty.
Stink, stingk, *vi.* (stinking, stunk). To emit a strong offensive smell; to be in disrepute.—*n.* A strong offensive smell.
Stink-pot, stingk'pot, *n.* An earthen jar charged with stinking combustibles, formerly used in boarding an enemy's vessel.
Stint, stint, *vt.* To restrict; to make scanty.—*vi.* To cease; to desist from.—*n.* Limit; restraint; restriction.
Stipe, Stipes, stīp, stī'pēz, *n.* A stalk or stem.
Stipend, stī'pend, *n.* Yearly allowance; salary.
Stipendiary, sti-pend'i-a-ri, *a.* Receiving stipend.—*n.* A paid magistrate in a town; one who performs services for a stipend.
Stipple, stip'l, *vt.* (stippling, stippled). To engrave by means of dots.—*n.* A process of engraving by means of dots.
Stipulate, stip'ū-lāt, *vi.* (stipulating, stipulated). To make an agreement; to contract; to settle terms.
Stipulation, stip-ū-lā'shon, *n.* Act of stipulating; a contract; item in a contract.
Stipulator, stip'ū-lāt-or, *n.* One who stipulates.
Stipule, stip'ūl, *n.* A small leaf-like appendage to a leaf.
Stir, stėr, *vt.* (stirring, stirred). To put into motion; to agitate; to rouse; to provoke; to disturb.—*vi.* To move oneself; not to be still; to be awake or out of bed.—*n.* Commotion; bustle; disorder.
Stirrer, stėr'ėr, *n.* One who or that which stirs; an instigator; an inciter.
Stirring, stėr'ing, *p.a.* Active in business; bustling; rousing; exciting.
Stirrup, sti'rup, *n.* A metal loop, suspended by a strap, to support the foot in riding.
Stirrup-cup, sti'rup-kup, *n.* A cup of liquor presented to a rider on parting.
Stirrup-pump, sti'rup-pump, *n.* A small hand-pump used for extinguishing incendiary bombs and the fires caused by them.
Stitch, stich, *n.* A sharp pain; one complete movement of a needle in sewing; a complete

turn or link in knitting, netting, &c.—*vt.* and *i.* To sew by making stitches in; to unite by stitches.
Stitching, stich'ing, *n.* Act signified by the verb to stitch; work done by stitching.
Stithy, stiᴛʜ'i or stith'i, *n.* An anvil; a smithy.
Stiver, stī'vėr, *n.* An old Dutch coin, worth about 1*d.* sterling; something insignificant.
Stoa, stō'a, *n.* A porch or portico.
Stoat, stōt, *n.* The ermine in its summer fur.
Stock, stok, *a.* A post; a lifeless mass; stem of a tree; wooden piece of a rifle; a stiff cravat; an original progenitor; lineage; capital invested in any business; money funded in government securities; store; animals belonging to a farm; liquor used to form a foundation for soups and gravies; a sweet-smelling garden-plant; *pl.* an instrument of punishment confining the offender's ankles or wrists; timbers on which a ship is supported while building.—*vt.* To provide with a stock; to lay up in store.—*a.* Kept in stock; standing; permanent.
Stockade, stok-ād', *n.* A defence of strong posts stuck close to each other; an inclosure made with posts.—*vt.* (stockading, stockaded). To fortify with posts fixed in the ground.
Stockbroker, stok'brō-kėr, *n.* A broker who buys and sells stocks or shares for others.
Stockbroking, stok'brō-king, *n.* The business of a stockbroker.
Stock-exchange, stok'eks-chānj, *n.* The place where stocks or shares are bought and sold; an organized association of stockbrokers.
Stock-fish, stok'fish, *n.* Fish, as cod, &c., split open and dried in the sun without salting.
Stockholder, stok'hōld-ėr, *n.* A shareholder or proprietor of stock.
Stocking, stok'ing, *n.* A close-fitting knitted covering for the foot and leg.
Stock-jobber, stok'job-ėr, *n.* One who speculates in stocks.
Stock-list, stok'list, *n.* A list showing the price of stocks, the transactions in them, &c.
Stock-pot, stok'pot, *n.* A pot in which stock for soups or gravies is boiled.
Stock-still, stok'stil, *a.* Still as a stock or fixed post; perfectly still.
Stock-taking, stok'tāk-ing, *n.* A periodical examination and valuation of the goods in a shop, &c.
Stodge, stoj, *vt.* (stodging, stodged). To stuff or cram.—*n.* A jumbled mass.
Stodgy, stoj'i, *a.* Crammed together roughly; crude and indigestible.
Stoic, stō'ik, *n.* One of an Athenian sect of philosophers, who held that men should strive to be unmoved by joy or grief, regarding virtue alone as the highest good; an apathetic person; one indifferent to pleasure or pain.
Stoical, stō'ik-al, *a.* Like a stoic; manifesting indifference to pleasure or pain.
Stoicism, stō'i-sizm, *n.* Indifference to pleasure or pain.
Stoke, stōk, *vt.* (stoking, stoked). To keep supplied with fuel, as a fire.
Stoker, stōk'ėr, *n.* One who attends to a furnace or large fire.
Stole, stōl, *n.* A long and narrow scarf worn round the neck, with the ends hanging down, by clergymen of the Anglican and Roman Catholic churches.
Stolid, stol'id, *a.* Dull; foolish; stupid.
Stolidity, sto-lid'i-ti, *n.* Dullness of intellect; stupidity.
Stolon, stō'lon, *n.* In *botany*, a sucker.
Stoma, stō'ma, *n.*; pl. **-ata.** A minute orifice or pore in plants or animals.
Stomach, stum'ak, *n.* A membranous sac, the principal organ of digestion; appetite; inclination.—*vt.* To brook; to put up with.
Stomacher, stum'a-chėr, *n.* An ornamental article of dress worn by females on the breast.
Stomachic, stō-mak'ik, *a.* Pertaining to the stomach.—*n.* A medicine for the stomach.
Stone, stōn, *n.* A hard mass of earthy or mineral matter; a pebble; a precious stone; concretion in the kidneys or bladder; a testicle; the nut of a fruit; a measure of 14 lbs. avoirdupois.—*a.* Made of stone; like stone.—*vt.* (stoning, stoned). To pelt with stones; to free from stones; to provide with stones.
Stone-blind, stōn'blīnd, *a.* Totally blind.
Stone-chat, Stone-chatter, stōn'chat, stōn'-chat-ėr, *n.* A small insessorial bird of the warbler family.
Stone-cutter, stōn'kut-ėr, *n.* One whose occupation is to cut or hew stones.
Stone-dead, stōn'ded, *a.* As lifeless as a stone.
Stone-deaf, stōn'def, *a.* Totally deaf.
Stone-dresser, stōn'dres-ėr, *n.* One who smooths and shapes stone for building.
Stone-fruit, stōn'fröt, *n.* Fruit whose seeds are covered with a hard shell enveloped in the pulp, as peaches, plums, &c.
Stone's-cast, Stone's-throw, stōnz'kast, stōnz'thrō, *n.* The distance which a stone may be thrown by the hand.
Stone-ware, stōn'wăr, *n.* Common glazed pottery ware.
Stone-work, stōn'wėrk, *n.* Work consisting of stone; mason's work of stone.
Stony, stōn'i, *a.* Pertaining to, abounding in, or like stone; hard; pitiless; frigid.
Stony-hearted, stōn'i-härt-ed, *a.* Hard-hearted; cruel; pitiless; unfeeling.
Stook, stụk, *n.* A set of sheaves of corn, &c., set on end.—*vt.* To set up in stooks.
Stool, stöl, *n.* A portable seat without a back for one person; the seat used in evacuating the bowels; a discharge from the bowels.
Stoop, stöp, *vi.* To bend the body forward and downward; to yield; to deign; to pounce.—*n.* Act of stooping; bend of the back or shoulders; a condescension; swoop.
Stooping, stöp'ing, *p.a.* Having a stoop; in act to stoop; bowed, as the shoulders.
Stop, stop, *vt.* (stopping, stopped). To stuff up; to close; to arrest the progress of; to put an end to; to regulate the sounds of musical strings by the fingers, &c.—*vi.* To cease from any motion; to come to an end; to stay; to remain.—*n.* Obstruction; interruption; pause; a series of pipes in an organ giving distinctive sounds; a point in writing.
Stop-cock, stop'kok, *n.* A tap to stop or regulate the supply of water, gas, &c.
Stop-gap, stop'gap, *n.* That which fills up a gap; a temporary expedient.
Stoppage, stop'āj, *n.* Act of stopping; a halt.
Stopper, stop'ėr, *n.* One who or that which stops; a stopple.—*vt.* To close with a stopper.
Stopping, stop'ing, *n.* Act of one who stops; that which stops or fills up.
Stopple, stop'l, *n.* That which closes the

mouth of a vessel; a plug.—*vt.* (stoppling, stoppled). To close with a stopple.
Stop-watch, stop'woch, *n.* A watch one of the hands of which can be stopped instantaneously so as to mark with accuracy any point of time.
Storage, stōr'āj, *n.* Act of storing charge for keeping goods in a store.
Store, stōr, *n.* A large quantity for supply; abundance; a place where goods are kept; a shop; *pl.* necessary articles laid up for use.—*a.* Pertaining to a store; kept in store.—*vt.* (storing, stored). To amass; to supply; to reposit in a store for preservation.
Storehouse, stōr'hous, *n.* A place in which things are stored; a repository.
Store-keeper, stōr'kēp-ėr, *n.* One who has the care of a store or stores.
Store-room, stōr'röm, *n.* A room for the reception of stores.
Storey. Same as *Story.*
Storied, stō'rid, *a.* Having stories or tales associated with it; celebrated in story.
Stork, stork, *n.* A large grallatorial or wading bird resembling the heron.
Storm, storm, *n.* A violent disturbance of the atmosphere; a tempest; an outbreak; assault on a strong position.—*vt.* To take by assault; to attack.—*vi.* To be in violent agitation; to rage.
Storm-glass, storm'glăs, *n.* A weather-glass consisting of a tube containing a chemical solution sensible to atmospheric changes.
Storm-stayed, storm'stād, *a.* Stopped or interrupted on a journey by stormy weather.
Stormy, storm'i, *a.* Abounding with storms; boisterous; passionate; angry.
Story, stō'ri, *n.* A narrative; an account; a tale; a fiction; a falsehood.
Story, Storey, stō'ri, *n.* A stage or floor of a building.
Stoup, stöp or stoup, *n.* A basin for holy water in a R. Catholic church; a flagon.
Stout, stout, *a.* Bold; valiant; sturdy; bulky; corpulent.—*n.* A dark-brown malt liquor.
Stoutly, stout'li, *adv.* Boldly; lustily.
Stove, stōv, *n.* An apparatus for warming a room, cooking, &c.—*vt.* (stoving, stoved). To heat in a stove. Pret. of *stave.*
Stow, stō, *vt.* To put in a suitable place; to pack; to compactly arrange anything in.
Stowage, stō'āj, *n.* Act of stowing; room for things to be packed away; charge for stowing goods.
Stowaway, stō'a-wā, *n.* One who hides himself on a ship to obtain a free passage.
Strabismus, stra-biz'mus, *n.* A squint in a person's eyes.
Straddle, strad'l, *vi.* and *t.* (straddling, straddled). To spread the legs wide; to sit astride; to stride across; to drop bombs along or across a target so as to cover a large area.
Straggle, strag'l, *vi.* (straggling, straggled). To rove; to wander in a scattered way; to occur at intervals.
Straggler, strag'lėr, *n.* One who straggles; a vagabond.
Straight, strāt, *a.* Stretched tight; direct; correct; upright.—*n.* A straight part or piece; straight direction.—*adv.* Immediately; directly.—*vt.* To straighten.
Straight-edge, strāt'ej, *n.* An implement with a perfectly straight edge for testing surfaces or drawing straight lines.
Straighten, strāt'n, *vt.* To make straight.
Straightforward, strāt'for-wėrd, *a.* Proceeding in a straight course; candid; honest; frank; open.—*adv.* Directly forward.
Straightforwardly, strāt'for-wėrd-li, *adv.* In a straightforward manner.
Straightly, strāt'li, *adv.* In a straight line.
Straightway, strāt'wā, *adv.* Directly; immediately; forthwith; without delay.
Strain, strān, *vt.* To stretch tightly; to exert to the utmost; to overtask; to sprain; to carry too far; to wrest; to filter.—*vi.* To exert oneself; to filter.—*n.* Violent effort; excessive stretching or exertion; tenor; theme; a lay; tune; race; family blood; tendency.
Strained, strānd, *a.* Stretched to the utmost; forced or unnatural.
Strainer, strān'ėr, *n.* One who strains; an instrument for filtration.
Strait, strāt, *a.* Confined; narrow; close; strict.—*n.* A narrow passage; a narrow stretch of water (often *pl.*); a position of hardship or difficulty.
Straiten, strāt'n, *vt.* To make strait; to distress; to hamper.
Strait-laced, strāt'lāst, *a.* Laced tightly; excessively strict or scrupulous.
Straitly, strāt'li, *adv.* Narrowly; closely; strictly.
Strait-waistcoat, strāt'wāst-kōt, *n.* A strong garment used to restrain lunatics.
Strake, strāk, *n.* A continuous line of planking or plates on a ship's side.
Stramineous, stra-min'ē-us, *a.* Consisting of or like straw.
Stramonium, stra-mō'ni-um, *n.* The thorn-apple; a drug obtained from it.
Strand, strand, *n.* The shore of a sea or lake; one of the twists of a rope.—*vt.* and *i.* To drive or be driven ashore.
Strange, strānj, *a.* Foreign; wonderful; odd; not familiar.
Strangely, strānj'li, *adv.* In a strange manner; wonderfully; remarkably.
Stranger, strān'jėr, *n.* A foreigner; an alien; one unknown; a visitor.
Strangle, strang'gl, *vt.* (strangling, strangled). To choke; to throttle; to suppress or stifle.
Strangles, strang'glz, *n.pl.* An abscess in the lower jaw of horses.
Strangulate, strang'gū-lāt, *vt.* To strangle; to stop vital action in by compression.
Strangulation, strang-gū-lā'shon, *n.* Act of strangling; compression of the windpipe; constriction.
Strangury, strang'gū-ri, *n.* A disease in which there is pain in passing the urine, which is excreted in drops.
Strap, strap, *n.* A long narrow slip of leather, &c.; a plate or strip of metal.—*vt.* (strapping, strapped). To beat with a strap; to fasten with a strap.
Strapper, strap'ėr, *n.* One who uses a strap; a kind of groom or attendant on horses.
Strapping, strap'ing, *a.* Tall and well made; handsome.
Strass, stras, *n.* A variety of flint-glass or paste used to make artificial gems.
Stratagem, stra'ta-jem, *n.* A piece of generalship; an artifice in war; a wile.
Strategic, Strategical, stra-tej'ik, stra-tej'ik-al, *a.* Pertaining to strategy; effected by strategy.

Strategist, stra'te-jist, *n.* One skilled in strategy.
Strategy, stra'te-ji, *n.* The science of military operations; generalship.
Strath, strath, *n.* In Scotland, a valley of considerable size.
Strathspey, strath-spā', *n.* A Scottish dance and tune resembling a reel, but slower.
Stratification, stra'ti-fi-kā''shon, *n.* Arrangement in strata or layers.
Stratify, stra'ti-fī, *vt.* To form into a stratum or strata; to lay in strata.
Stratosphere, stra'tō-sfēr, *n.* The upper region of the earth's atmosphere.
Stratum, strā'tum, *n.*; pl. **-ta.** A layer of any substance, as sand, clay, &c., especially when one of a number.
Stratus, strā'tus, *n.* A low horizontal cloud.
Straw, stra, *n.* The dry stalk of grain, pulse, &c.—*a.* Made of straw.
Strawberry, stra'be-ri, *n.* A herbaceous plant and its succulent fruit.
Strawberry-tree, stra'be-ri-trē, *n.* Arbutus.
Strawy, stra'i, *a.* Made of straw; consisting of straw; like straw; light.
Stray, strā, *vi.* To go astray; to err; to roam. —*a.* Having gone astray; straggling.—*n.* Any domestic animal that wanders at large, or is lost.
Streak, strēk, *n.* A long mark; a stripe; appearance of a mineral when scratched.—*vt.* To form streaks in.
Streaky, strēk'i, *a.* Striped; variegated with streaks.
Stream, strēm, *n.* A river or brook; a current; drift.—*vi.* and *t.* To move in a stream; to stretch in a long line; to float at full length in the air.
Streamer, strēm'ėr, *n.* That which streams out; a long pennon; a luminous beam or column.
Streamlet, strēm'let, *n.* A small stream.
Streamline, strēm-līn', *vt.* To shape so as to reduce resistance to air or water.
Streamy, strēm'i, *a.* Abounding with streams; beaming.
Street, strēt, *n.* A road in a town or village; the roadway and houses together.
Strength, strength, *n.* Property of being strong; force or energy; power; support; vigour; intensity; amount or numbers of an army, fleet, or the like.—**On the strength of,** in reliance upon, on the faith of.
Strengthen, strength'en, *vt.* and *i.* To make or become strong or stronger.
Strenuous, stren'ū-us, *a.* Energetic; vigorous; zealous; ardent; earnest.
Stress, stres, *vt.* To put in difficulties; to subject to emphasis.—*n.* Constraint; pressure; weight; violence, as of weather; emphasis.
Stretch, strech, *vt.* To draw out tight; to extend; to straighten; to strain; to exaggerate.—*vi.* To reach or extend; to spread; to have elasticity.—*n.* Strain; extent; scope; expanse; a turn or spell.
Stretcher, strech'ėr, *n.* One who stretches; a contrivance for stretching things; a litter for carrying persons.
Strew, strö or strō, *vt.* (pp. strewed or strewn). To scatter or sprinkle; to cover by scattering; to besprinkle.
Stria, strī'a, *n.*; pl. **-iæ.** A term for fine streaks on surfaces of minerals, plants, &c.
Striate, Striated, strī'āt, strī'āt-ed, *a.* Marked with fine thread-like lines.
Striation, strī-ā'shon, *n.* State of being striate; striate markings.
Stricken, strik'n, pp. of *strike.* Struck; smitten; advanced in age.
Strickle, strik'l, *n.* An instrument to strike grain to a level with the measure; an instrument for whetting scythes.
Strict, strikt, *a.* Tight; tense; exact; severe; rigorous; not loose or vague.
Strictly, strikt'li, *adv.* In a strict manner; correctly; definitely; rigorously; severely.
Stricture, strik'tūr, *n.* A contraction of any canal of the body; a critical remark; censure.
Stride, strīd, *vi.* (striding, pret. strode, pp. stridden). To walk with long steps; to straddle.—*vt.* To pass over at a step.—*n.* A long step; a measured tread.
Strident, strī'dent, *a.* Harsh; grating.
Strife, strīf, *n.* Act of striving; struggle; contest; discord; conflict; quarrel or war.
Strike, strīk, *vi.* (striking, pret. struck, pp. struck, stricken). To move or turn aside rapidly; to light (upon); to make a blow; to hit; to be stranded; to yield; to quit work to compel better terms.—*vt.* To smite; to mint; to thrust in; to notify by sound; to occur to; to impress strongly; to effect at once; to lower, as the flag or sails of a vessel. —*n.* Act of workmen who quit work to force their employer to give better terms; a strickle.
Striker, strīk'ėr, *n.* One who or that which strikes; one who engages in a strike.
Striking, strīk'ing, *p.a.* Surprising; remarkable; notable; impressive.
String, string, *n.* A small cord; a piece of twine; a line with the things on it; chord of a musical instrument; a series.—*vt.* (stringing, strung). To furnish with string; to put on a string; to make tense.
Stringency, strin'jen-si, *n.* State of being stringent.
Stringent, strin'jent, *a.* Strict; rigorous; rigid.
String-halt, Spring-halt, string'halt, spring'-halt, *n.* A curious spasmodic catching of the hind-leg of a horse.
Stringy, string'i, *a.* Consisting of strings; fibrous; ropy; viscid; sinewy.
Strip, strip, *vt.* (stripping, stripped). To deprive of a covering; to skin; to deprive; to pillage.—*vi.* To take off the covering or clothes.—*n.* A long narrow piece.
Stripe, strīp, *n.* A long narrow division or marking; a streak; a strip; a stroke with a lash; a wale or weal.—*vt.* (striping, striped). To form or variegate with stripes.
Stripling, strip'ling, *n.* A tall slender youth; a lad.
Strive, strīv, *vi.* (striving, pret. strove, pp. striven). To endeavour; to make efforts; to struggle; to vie.
Stroke, strōk, *n.* A blow; calamity; attack; striking of a clock; touch; a masterly effort; a dash in writing or printing; a touch of the pen; a line; a gentle rub; the sweep of an oar; a stroke-oar.—*vt.* (stroking, stroked). To rub gently with the hand.
Stroke-oar, strōk'ōr, *n.* The aftmost oar of a boat; the man that uses it.
Stroll, strōl, *vi.* To ramble; to rove; to roam. —*n.* A short leisurely walk.

Stroller, strōl'ėr, *n.* One who strolls; a vagabond; a vagrant; an itinerant player.
Strong, strong, *a.* Having power or force; robust; not easily broken; firm; effectual; earnest; containing much alcohol; glaring; forcible; tending upwards in price; effecting inflection by internal vowel change.
Stronghold, strong'hōld, *n.* A place of strength or security; a fortified place.
Strongly, strong'li, *adv.* With strength or power; forcibly; firmly; greatly.
Strong-room, strong'röm, *n.* A room in which valuables are kept.
Strontia, stron'shi-a, *n.* An oxide of strontium.
Strontium, stron'shi-um, *n.* A metal of a yellow colour, somewhat harder than lead.
Strop, strop, *n.* A strip of leather, &c., for sharpening razors.—*vt.* (stropping, stropped). To sharpen on a strop.
Strophe, strō'fē, *n.* The former of two corresponding stanzas in an ode.
Strove, strōv, pret. of *strive.*
Strow, strō. *See* STREW.
Struck, struk, pret. and pp. of *strike.*
Structural, struk'tūr-al, *a.* Pertaining to structure.
Structure, struk'tūr, *n.* A building of any kind; manner of building; make; organization.
Struggle, strug'l, *vi.* (struggling, struggled). To make great efforts; to strive; to contend.—*n.* A violent effort of the body; forcible effort; contest; strife.
Strum, strum, *vi.* and *t.* (strumming, strummed). To play unskilfully on a stringed instrument; to thrum.
Struma, strö'ma, *n.*; pl. **-mæ.** A scrofulous swelling or tumour; scrofula.
Strumose, Strumous, strö'mōs, strö'mus, *a.* Scrofulous.
Strumpet, strum'pet, *n.* A prostitute.
Strut, strut, *vi.* (strutting, strutted). To walk with affected dignity.—*n.* A lofty, proud step or walk; a strengthening piece placed diagonally in a framework.
Strychnia, Strychnine, strik'ni-a, strik'nīn, *n.* A vegetable alkaloid poison obtained from the seeds of nux-vomica.
Stub, stub, *n.* The stump of a tree; a remaining part of anything.—*vt.* (stubbing, stubbed). To grub up by the roots.
Stubble, stub'l, *n.* The stumps of a grain crop left in the ground after reaping.
Stubbly, stub'li, *a.* Covered with stubble; resembling stubble; short and stiff.
Stubborn, stub'orn, *a.* Not to be moved or persuaded; obstinate; intractable.
Stubbornly, stub'orn-li, *adv.* Obstinately.
Stubby, stub'i, *a.* Abounding with stubs; short and thick.
Stucco, stuk'kō, *n.* A fine plaster; work made of stucco; plaster of Paris or gypsum.—*vt.* (stuccoing, stuccoed). To overlay with stucco.
Stuck-up, stuk'up, *a.* Giving oneself airs of importance; proud; pompous.
Stud, stud, *n.* A post; a prop; a nail with a large head; an ornamental button; a set of breeding horses; a person's horses collectively.—*vt.* (studding, studded). To adorn with studs; to set thickly, as with studs.
Stud-book, stud'bụk, *n.* A book containing a genealogy or register of horses, &c.
Studding-sail, stud'ing-sāl, *n.* A sail set on the outer edge of a principal sail during a light wind.
Student, stū'dent, *n.* One who studies; a scholar; a bookish person.
Stud-horse, stud'hors, *n.* A breeding horse.
Studied, stu'did, *a.* Made the object of study; qualified by study; premeditated.
Studio, stū'di-ō, *n.* The work-place of a painter or sculptor.
Studious, stū'di-us, *a.* Given to study; mindful; earnest; careful; deliberate.
Studiously, stū'di-us-li, *adv.* Diligently; carefully; deliberately.
Study, stu'di, *n.* Earnest endeavour; application to books, &c.; subject which one studies; apartment devoted to study; a reverie; a preparatory sketch.—*vt.* and *i.* (studying, studied). To apply the mind to; to investigate; to have careful regard to.
Stuff, stuf, *n.* Substance indefinitely; material; cloth; a light woollen fabric; goods; trash.—*vt.* To pack; to thrust in; to fill, as meat with seasoning; to fill, as an animal's skin to preserve the form.—*vi.* To cram; to feed gluttonously.
Stuffing, stuf'ing, *n.* That which is used to fill anything, as a cushion; substance put into a fowl for cooking.
Stuffy, stuf'i, *a.* Difficult to breathe in; close; stifling.
Stultify, stul'ti-fī, *vi.* To prove foolish; to cause to seem absurd; to make a fool of.
Stumble, stum'bl, *vi.* (stumbling, stumbled). To trip in moving; to walk unsteadily; to fall into error; to light by chance (with *on*).—*n.* A trip in walking or running; a blunder.
Stumbling-block, Stumbling-stone, stum'bling-blok, stum'bling-stōn, *n.* Any cause of stumbling or erring.
Stump, stump, *n.* The part of a tree, limb, &c., left after the rest is cut off or destroyed; a worn-down tooth; a wicket in cricket.—*vt.* To lop, as trees; to make a tour through, delivering speeches; to put out of play in cricket by knocking down a stump.—*vi.* To walk stiffly or noisily.
Stump-orator, stump'o-ra-tėr, *n.* A man who harangues the people; a frothy speaker.
Stump-speech, stump'spēch, *n.* A speech made from an improvised platform; a frothy harangue.
Stumpy, stump'i, *a.* Full of stumps; short and thick.
Stun, stun, *vt.* (stunning, stunned). To overpower the sense of hearing of; to stupefy; to make senseless with a blow; to surprise completely.
Stunner, stun'ėr, *n.* Something that stuns; a person or thing of showy appearance.
Stunning, stun'ing, *p.a.* Such as to stun; first-rate; excellent.
Stunt, stunt, *vt.* To stop the growth of; to dwarf.—*n.* A check in growth.
Stunted, stunt'ed, *a.* Hindered from growth; dwarfish in growth or size.
Stupe, stūp, *n.* Flannel, flax, &c., wrung out of hot water, applied to a sore.
Stupefaction, stū-pē-fak'shon, *n.* State of being stupefied; insensibility; stupidity.
Stupefy, stū'pē-fī, *vt.* (stupefying, stupefied). To deprive of sensibility.
Stupendous, stū-pen'dus, *a.* Of astonishing magnitude; grand or awe-inspiring.

Stupid, stū'pid, *a.* Struck senseless; foolish; dull in intellect; nonsensical.
Stupidity, stū-pid'i-ti, *n.* Extreme intellectual dullness; senselessness.
Stupidly, stū'pid-li, *adv.* In a stupid manner.
Stupor, stū'por, *n.* A condition in which the faculties are deadened; torpor; insensibility.
Stuprate, stū'prāt, *vt.* To ravish; to debauch.
Sturdily, stėr'di-li, *adv.* Hardily; stoutly; lustily.
Sturdy, stėr'di, *a.* Stout; strong; hardy; firm; robust; vigorous.
Sturgeon, stėr'jon, *n.* A genus of large fishes having flesh valuable as food.
Stutter, stut'ėr, *vi.* To stammer.—*n.* A stammer; broken utterance of words.
Sty, stī, *n.* An inclosure for swine; a pig-sty; any filthy hovel or place.—*vt.* (stying, stied). To shut up in a sty.
Sty, Stye, stī, *n.* A small inflammatory tumour on the edge of the eyelid.
Stygian, stij'i-an, *a.* Pertaining to Styx, a fabled river of hell over which the shades of the dead passed; dark and gloomy; infernal.
Style, stīl, *n.* A burin; pin of a sun-dial; manner of writing with regard to language; a characteristic mode in the fine arts; type; external manner, mode, or fashion; title; in *botany*, a slender prolongation of the ovary supporting the stigma.—*vt.* (styling, styled). To term; to designate.
Stylet, stil'et, *n.* In *surgery*, a probe.
Stylish, stil'ish, *a.* In the mode; fashionable.
Stylist, stīl'ist, *n.* A writer or speaker careful of his style; a master of style.
Stylite, stī'līt, *n.* An ascetic who lived on the top of high columns or pillars.
Stylobate, stī'lō-bāt, *n.* A continuous pedestal on which a row of columns stands.
Stylograph, stī'lo-graf, *n.* A pointed fountain-pen.
Stylus, stī'lus, *n.* A style or pointed instrument.
Styptic, stip'tik, *a.* Able to stop bleeding.—*n.* A substance which stops a flow of blood.
Suable, sū'a-bl, *a.* That may be sued at law.
Suasion, swā'zhon, *n.* Persuasion.
Suasive, swā'ziv, *a.* Having power to persuade.
Suave, swāv, *a.* Gracious in manner; blandly polite; pleasant.
Suavity, swa'vi-ti, *n.* Graciousness of manner; blandness; urbanity.
Sub, sub, *n.* A contraction for *subordinate.*
Subacid, sub-as'id, *a.* Acid in a small degree; moderately acid or sour.
Subaltern, sub-al'tėrn or sub'al-tėrn, *a.* Holding a subordinate position.—*n.* A commissioned military officer below the rank of captain.
Subaquatic, Subaqueous, sub-a-kwat'ik, sub-ak'wē-us, *a.* Being under water; in *geol.* formed or deposited under water.
Subclass, sub'klas, *n.* A subdivision of a class.
Subcommittee, sub-kom-mit'tē, *n.* An under committee; a division of a committee.
Subcutaneous, sub-kū-tā'nē-us, *a.* Situated immediately under the skin.
Subdivide, sub-di-vīd', *vt.* To divide part of into more parts.—*vi.* To be subdivided; to separate.
Subdivision, sub-di-vi'zhon, *n.* Act of subdividing; a part of a larger part.
Subdual, sub-dū'al, *n.* Act of subduing.
Subduce, Subduct, sub-dūs', sub-dukt', *vt.* To take away; to subtract.
Subdue, sub-dū', *vt.* (subduing, subdued). To subjugate; to overpower; to tame; to soften; to tone down.
Subdued, sub-dūd', *a.* Toned down; reduced in intensity; low in tone.
Sub-editor, sub-ed'it-ėr, *n.* An under or assistant editor.
Subjacent, sub-jā'sent, *a.* Lying under or below.
Subject, sub'jekt, *a.* Ruled by another; liable; prone; submissive.—*n.* One who owes allegiance to a ruler or government; matter dealt with; theme; topic; the nominative of a verb; the thinking agent or principle.—*vt.* sub-jekt'. To subdue; to make liable; to cause to undergo.
Subjection, sub-jek'shon, *n.* Act of subjecting; subjugation; enthralment.
Subjective, sub-jekt'iv or sub'jekt-iv, *a.* Relating to the subject; belonging to ourselves, the conscious subject; exhibiting strongly the personality of the author.
Subjectivity, sub-jek-tiv'i-ti, *n.* State or quality of being subjective; character of exhibiting the individuality of an author.
Subject-matter, sub'jekt-mat-ėr, *n.* The matter or theme presented for consideration.
Subjoin, sub-join', *vt.* To add at the end; to affix; to annex; to attach.
Subjoinder, sub-join'dėr, *n.* A rejoinder.
Subjugate, sub'jū-gāt, *vt.* To subdue; to conquer and compel to submit.
Subjugation, sub-jū-gā'shon, *n.* Act of subjugating or subduing; subdual; subjection.
Subjunctive, sub-jungk'tiv, *a.* and *n.* Applied to a mood of verbs that expresses condition, hypothesis, or contingency.
Sublease, sub'lēs, *n.* A lease granted to a subtenant.
Sublet, sub-let', *vt.* To let to another person, the party letting being himself a lessee.
Sublimate, sub'li-māt, *vt.* To raise by heat into vapour, as a solid, which, on cooling, returns again to the solid state; to refine; to elevate.—*n.* The product of sublimation.
Sublimation, sub-li-mā'shon, *n.* The process or operation of sublimating; exaltation; a highly refined product.
Sublimatory, sub'li-ma-to-ri, *n.* A vessel used in sublimation.—*a.* Used in sublimation.
Sublime, sub-līm', *a.* High in place or excellence; affecting the mind with a sense of grandeur; noble; majestic.—**The sublime,** the grand in the works of nature or of art; grandeur of style; highest degree.—*vt.* (subliming, sublimed). To render sublime; to sublimate.—*vi.* To be susceptible of sublimation.
Sublimely, sub-līm'li, *adv.* In a sublime manner; grandly; majestically; loftily.
Sublimity, sub-lim'i-ti, *n.* State or quality of being sublime; grandeur; majesty.
Sublunar, sub-lū'nėr, *a.* Being under or nearer than the moon.
Sublunary, sub'lū-na-ri, *a.* Under or beneath the moon; mundane; worldly.
Submarine, sub-ma-rēn', *a.* Being under the surface of the sea.—*n.* A vessel which can be submerged at will and which can travel under the water.
Submerge, sub-mėrj', *vt.* and *i.* (submerging,

submerged). To put under or cover with water; to drown; to sink.
Submerse, Submersed, sub-mėrs', sub-mėrst', *a.* Being or growing under water.
Submersion, sub-mėr'shon, *n.* Act of submerging; state of being under fluid; a dipping or plunging.
Submission, sub-mi'shon, *n.* Act of submitting; surrender; humble behaviour; obedience; resignation.
Submissive, sub-mis'iv, *a.* Yielding; obedient; compliant; humble; modest.
Submissively, sub-mis'iv-li, *adv.* In a submissive manner; obediently; humbly.
Submit, sub-mit', *vt.* (submitting, submitted). To yield or surrender; to refer; to state, as a claim.—*vi.* To surrender; to acquiesce; to suffer without complaint.
Suborder, sub-or'dėr, *n.* A subdivision of an order.
Subordinacy, Subordinance, sub-or'di-na-si, sub-or'di-nans, *n.* State of being subordinate.
Subordinate, sub-or'din-āt, *a.* Inferior; occupying a lower position.—*n.* One who stands in rank, power, &c., below another.—*vt.* To place in a lower order or rank.
Subordinately, sub-or'din-āt-li, *adv.* In a lower rank, dignity, &c.
Subordination, sub-or'din-ā"shon, *n.* The act of subordinating; inferiority of rank; subjection.
Suborn, sub-orn', *vt.* To bribe to commit perjury; to bribe to some wickedness.
Subornation, sub-orn-ā'shon, *n.* Act of suborning.
Suborner, sub-orn'ėr, *n.* One who suborns.
Subpœna, sub-pē'na, *n.* A writ summoning a witness under a penalty.—*vt.* (subpœnaing, subpœnaed). To serve with a writ of subpœna.
Subscribe, sub-skrīb', *vt.* and *i.* (subscribing, subscribed). To append one's own signature to; to promise to contribute (money) by writing one's name; to assent.
Subscriber, sub-skrīb'ėr, *n.* One who subscribes.
Subscript, sub'skript, *a.* Underwritten; written below something.
Subscription, sub-skrip'shon, *n.* Act of subscribing; signature; attestation; a sum subscribed.
Subsection, sub'sek-shon, *n.* The part or division of a section.
Subsequence, sub'sē-kwens, *n.* The state of being subsequent.
Subsequent, sub'sē-kwent, *a.* Following in time; succeeding; next.
Subsequently, sub'sē-kwent-li, *adv.* At a later time; after something else in order.
Subserve, sub-sėrv', *vt.* and *i.* (subserving, subserved). To serve; to be instrumental to; to promote.
Subservience, Subserviency, sub-sėr'vi-ens, sub-sėr'vi-en-si, *n.* State of being subservient.
Subservient, sub-sėr'vi-ent, *a.* Acting as a tool; serving to promote some end.
Subside, sub-sīd', *vi.* (subsiding, subsided). To sink or fall to the bottom; to settle down; to abate.
Subsidence, sub-sīd'ens or sub'si-dens, *n.* Act or process of subsiding.
Subsidiary, sub-si'di-a-ri, *a.* Pertaining to a subsidy; aiding; assistant; subordinate.—*n.* An assistant.
Subsidize, sub'si-dīz, *vt.* (subsidizing, subsidized). To furnish with a subsidy; to purchase the assistance of another by a subsidy.
Subsidy, sub'si-di, *n.* A sum of money granted for a purpose; a sum given by a government to meet expenses.
Subsist, sub-sist', *vi.* To have existence; to live; to inhere.
Subsistence, sub-sist'ens, *n.* Existence; real being; livelihood; sustenance.
Subsistent, sub-sist'ent, *a.* Having being or existence; inherent.
Subsoil, sub'soil, *n.* The bed or stratum of earth below the surface soil.
Subspecies, sub'spē-shēz, *n.* A subdivision of a species.
Substance, sub'stans, *n.* That of which a thing consists; material; a body; essence; purport; means and resources.
Substantial, sub-stan'shal, *a.* Actually existing; real; solid; strong; moderately wealthy.
Substantiality, sub-stan'shi-al"i-ti, *n.* State of being substantial.
Substantially, sub-stan'shal-li, *adv.* With reality of existence; strongly; in substance; in the main.
Substantiate, sub-stan'shi-āt, *vt.* To give substance to; to prove.
Substantiation, sub-stan'shi-ā"shon, *n.* Act of substantiating; evidence; proof.
Substantive, sub'stan-tiv, *a.* Expressing existence; independent; real; of the nature of a noun.—*n.* A noun.
Substitute, sub'sti-tūt, *vt.* (substituting, substituted). To put in the place of another; to exchange.—*n.* A person or thing in the place of another; a deputy.
Substitution, sub-sti-tū'shon, *n.* Act of substituting; state of being substituted.
Substratum, sub'strā-tum, *n.*; pl. **-ta.** A layer or stratum under another.
Substructure, sub'struk-tūr, *n.* An under structure; a foundation.
Subsume, sub-sūm', *vt.* (subsuming, subsumed). In *logic*, to include under a more general category.
Subtenant, sub-te'nant, *n.* One who rents land or houses from a tenant.
Subtend, sub-tend', *vt.* To stretch or extend under, or be opposite to.
Subterfuge, sub'tėr-fūj, *n.* An artifice to escape or justify; evasion; a dishonest shift.
Subterranean, Subterraneous, sub-te-rā'-nē-an, sub-te-rā'nē-us, *a.* Being under the surface of the earth.
Subtilize, sub'til-īz, *vt.* and *i.* To make subtle; to refine; to spin into niceties.
Subtle, sut'l, *a.* Thin or tenuous; acute; sly; cunning; artful.
Subtlety, sut'l-ti, *n.* Quality of being subtle; delicacy; craft; cunning; acuteness; nicety of distinction; something subtle.
Subtly, sut'li, *adv.* Artfully; cunningly; nicely.
Subtract, sub-trakt', *vt.* To withdraw or take from; to deduct.
Subtraction, sub-trak'shon, *n.* The taking of a number or quantity from a greater.
Subtractive, sub-trakt'iv, *a.* Tending or having power to subtract.
Subtrahend, sub'tra-hend, *n.* A sum or number to be subtracted.

Subulate, sū'bū-lāt, *a.* Slender and gradually tapering toward the point.
Suburb, sub'ėrb, *n.* An outlying part of a city or town.
Suburban, sub-ėrb'an, *a.* Relating to the suburbs; being in the suburbs of a city.
Subvene, sub-vēn', *vi.* (subvening, subvened). To arrive or happen so as to obviate something.
Subvention, sub-ven'shon, *n.* Act of coming to aid; a government grant in aid; subsidy.
Subversion, sub-vėr'shon, *n.* Act of subverting; overthrow; destruction; ruin.
Subversive, sub-vėrs'iv, *a.* Tending to subvert, overthrow, or ruin: with *of.*
Subvert, sub-vėrt', *vt.* To ruin utterly; to overturn; to pervert.
Subway, sub'wā, *n.* An underground passage.
Succedaneous, suk-sē-dā'nē-us, *a.* Supplying the place of something else.
Succedaneum, suk-sē-dā'nē-um, *n.*; pl. **-nea.** A substitute.
Succeed, suk-sēd', *vt.* To follow in order; to take the place of; to come after.—*vi.* To follow in order; to ensue; to become heir; to obtain the end or object desired; to prosper.
Success, suk-ses', *n.* Issue; favourable result; good fortune; prosperity; something that succeeds.
Successful, suk-ses'fu̇l, *a.* Accompanied by or attaining success; having the desired effect; prosperous: fortunate.
Successfully, suk-ses'fu̇l-li, *adv.* Prosperously; fortunately; favourably.
Succession, suk-se'shon, *n.* A following of things in order; series of things; lineage; right of inheriting; act or right of succeeding to an office, rank, &c.
Successional, suk-se'shon-al, *a.* Pertaining to succession; consecutive.
Successive, suk-ses'iv, *a.* Coming in succession; consecutive.
Successively, suk-ses'iv-li, *adv.* In succession; in a series or order.
Successor, suk-ses'or, *n.* One who succeeds or follows another.
Succinct, suk-singkt', *a.* Compressed into few words; brief; concise.
Succinctly, suk-singkt'li, *adv.* Concisely.
Succinic, suk-sin'ik, *a.* Pertaining to amber; obtained from amber.
Succory, suk'ko-ri, *n.* Chicory.
Succour, suk'ėr, *vt.* To help when in difficulty; to aid; to relieve.—*n.* Aid; help; assistance given in distress; the person or thing that brings relief.
Succourer, suk'ėr-ėr, *n.* One who succours.
Succulence, Succulency, suk'kū-lens, suk'-kū-len-si, *n.* Juiciness.
Succulent, suk'kū-lent, *a.* Full of sap or juice; sappy; juicy.
Succumb, suk-kum', *vi.* To yield; to submit; to sink unresistingly.
Succursal, suk-kėr'sal, *a.* Serving as a chapel of ease: said of a church attached to a parish church.—*n.* A chapel of ease; a branch establishment.
Succussion, suk-ku'shon, *n.* Act of shaking; a shock.
Such, such, *a.* Of like kind or degree; similar; like; the same as mentioned.
Suchwise, such'wīz, *adv.* In such a manner.
Suck, suk, *vt.* and *i.* To draw with the mouth; to draw milk from with the mouth; to imbibe; to absorb.—*n.* Act of sucking; milk drawn from the breast.
Sucker, suk'ėr, *n.* One who or that which sucks; an organ in animals for sucking; piston of a pump; shoot of a plant; the sucking-fish.
Sucking-fish, suk'ing-fish, *n.* The remora.
Suckle, suk'l, *vt.* (suckling, suckled). To give suck to; to nurse at the breast.
Suckling, suk'ling, *n.* A young child or animal nursed by the mother's milk.
Sucrose, sū'krōs, *n.* A name for the sugars identical with cane-sugar.
Suction, suk'shon, *n.* Act of sucking; the sucking up of a fluid by the pressure of the external air.
Suctorial, suk'tō-ri-al, *a.* Adapted for sucking; living by sucking; adhering by sucking.
Sudatorium, sū-da-tō'ri-um, *n.* A hot-air bath for producing perspiration.
Sudatory, sū'da-to-ri, *n.* A sudatorium.—*a.* Sweating; perspiring; sudorific.
Sudden, sud'en, *a.* Happening without warning; abrupt; quick; hasty; violent.
Suddenly, sud'en-li, *adv.* Unexpectedly; hastily; without preparation; all at once.
Sudoriferous, sū-do-rif'ėr-us, *a.* Producing sweat; secreting perspiration.
Sudorific, sū-do-rif'ik, *a.* Causing sweat.—*n.* A medicine that produces sweat.
Suds, sudz, *n.pl.* Water impregnated with soap and forming a frothy mass.
Sue, sū, *vt.* (suing, sued). To seek justice from by legal process; to seek in marriage.—*vi.* To woo; to prosecute a suit at law; to petition.
Suet, sū'et, *n.* The harder fat of an animal about the kidneys and loins.
Suety, sū'et-i, *a.* Containing or like suet.
Suffer, suf'ėr, *vt.* To endure; to undergo; to be affected by; to permit.—*vi.* To undergo pain; to be injured.
Sufferable, suf'ėr-a-bl, *a.* That may be tolerated, permitted, endured, or borne.
Sufferance, suf'ėr-ans, *n.* Endurance; pain endured; passive consent; allowance.
Sufferer, suf'ėr-ėr, *n.* One who endures pain; one who permits or allows.
Suffering, suf'ėr-ing, *n.* The bearing of pain; pain endured; distress.
Suffice, suf'fīs, *vi.* (sufficing, sufficed). To be sufficient.—*vt.* To satisfy; to content.
Sufficiency, suf-fi'shen-si, *n.* State of being sufficient; competence; ability; conceit.
Sufficient, suf-fi'shent, *a.* Adequate; enough; competent; fit; able.
Sufficiently, suf-fi'shent-li, *adv.* To a sufficient degree; enough.
Suffix, suf'fiks, *n.* A letter or syllable added to the end of a word.—*vt.* To add a letter or syllable to a word.
Suffocate, suf'fō-kāt, *vi.* (suffocating, suffocated). To stifle; to choke by stopping respiration; to kill by depriving of oxygen.
Suffocation, suf-fō-kā'shon, *n.* Act of suffocating; condition of being suffocated.
Suffocative, suf'fō-kāt-iv, *a.* Tending or able to suffocate, choke, or stifle.
Suffragan, suf'ra-gan, *a.* Assisting in ecclesiastical duties.—*n.* An assisting bishop; any bishop in relation to his archbishop.
Suffrage, suf'frāj, *n.* A vote; assent; right of voting for a representative.
Suffuse, suf-fūz', *vt.* (suffusing, suffused). To overspread, as with a fluid or a colour.

Suffusion, suf-fū'zhon, *n.* Act of suffusing; state of being suffused; that which is suffused.
Sugar, shu̦'gėr, *n.* A sweet granular substance, manufactured from sugar-cane, maple, beet, &c.; something sweet like sugar.—*a.* Belonging to or made of sugar.—*vt.* To season, mix, &c., with sugar; to sweeten.
Sugar-candy, shu̦'gėr-kan-di, *n.* Sugar clarified and crystallized.
Sugar-cane, shu̦'gėr-kān, *n.* The cane or plant from whose juice much sugar is obtained.
Sugar-loaf, shu̦'gėr-lōf, *n.* A conical mass of refined sugar; something of like shape.
Sugar-plum, shu̦'gėr-plum, *n.* A comfit made of boiled sugar; a bon-bon.
Sugary, shu̦'gėr-i, *a.* Like sugar; containing sugar; sweet; flattering.
Suggest, su-jest' or sug-jest', *vt.* To hint; to insinuate; to propose; to intimate.
Suggestion, su-jest'yon, *n.* A hint; a tentative proposal; insinuation; intimation.
Suggestive, su-jest'iv, *a.* Containing a suggestion; suggesting what does not appear on the surface.
Suggestively, su-jest'iv-li, *adv.* In a suggestive manner; by way of suggestion.
Suicidal, sū-i-sīd'al, *a.* Pertaining to or partaking of the crime of suicide.
Suicide, sū'i-sīd, *n.* Self-murder; one guilty of self-murder.
Suint, swint, *n.* The natural grease of wool.
Suit, sūt, *n.* Act of suing; a request; courtship; a suing at law; a set of things.—*vt.* and *i.* To adapt; to fit; to be agreeable to; to agree.
Suitability, sūt-a-bil'i-ti, *n.* State or quality of being suitable; fitness.
Suitable, sūt'a-bl, *a.* That suits; fitting; proper; appropriate; becoming.
Suitably, sūt'a-bli, *adv.* In a suitable manner; fitly; agreeably; with propriety.
Suite, swēt, *n.* A company of attendants; a retinue; a connected series, as of apartments.
Suitor, sūt'or, *n.* One who sues; one who prosecutes a suit at law; a wooer.
Sulcate, Sulcated, sul'kāt, sul'kāt-ed, *a.* Furrowed; grooved; channelled.
Sulcus, sul'kus, *n.*; pl. **-ci.** A furrow; groove.
Sulk, sulk, *vi.* To indulge in a sulky or sullen fit or mood.
Sulkily, sulk'i-li, *adv.* In a sulky manner.
Sulks, sulks, *n.pl.* Sulky fit or mood.
Sulky, sulk'i, *a.* Sullen; morose.—*n.* A light two-wheeled carriage for one person.
Sullen, sul'en, *a.* Gloomily angry and silent; morose; sour; dismal; sombre.
Sullenly, sul'en-li, *adv.* In a sullen manner; gloomily; with sulky moroseness.
Sullens, sul'enz, *n.pl.* The sulks.
Sully, sul'i, *vt.* (sullying, sullied). To soil; to tarnish; to stain or pollute.—*vi.* To be soiled.—*n.* Soil; tarnish; spot.
Sulphate, sul'fāt, *n.* A salt of sulphuric acid.
Sulphide, sul'fīd, *n.* A combination of sulphur with another element.
Sulphite, sul'fīt, *n.* A salt composed of sulphurous acid with a base.
Sulphur, sul'fėr, *n.* Brimstone; a simple mineral substance of a yellow colour which burns with a pale-blue flame.
Sulphurate, sul'fū-rāt, *vt.* To combine with sulphur; to subject to the action of sulphur.
Sulphureous, sul-fū'rē-us, *a.* Sulphurous.
Sulphuret, sul'fū-ret, *n.* A sulphide.
Sulphuretted, sul'fū-ret-ed, *a.* Having sulphur in combination.
Sulphuric, sul-fū'rik, *a.* Pertaining to sulphur.
Sulphurous, sul'fėr-us, *a.* Impregnated with or containing sulphur; like sulphur.
Sulphury, sul'fėr-i, *a.* Partaking of sulphur; sulphureous.
Sultan, sul'tan, *n.* A Mohammedan sovereign; formerly, the ruler of Turkey.
Sultana, sul-tä'na, *n.* The queen of a sultan; a kind of raisin.
Sultanic, sul-tan'ik, *a.* Belonging to a sultan.
Sultry, sul'tri, *a.* Very hot; oppressive; close and heavy.
Sum, sum, *n.* The whole; aggregate; essence or substance; a quantity of money; an arithmetical problem.—*vt.* (summing, summed). To add into one whole; to reckon up; to recapitulate.
Sumac, Sumach, sū'mak, *n.* A shrub the leaves of which are used for tanning.
Summarily, sum'a-ri-li, *adv.* In a summary manner; briefly; promptly.
Summarist, sum'a-rist, *n.* A writer of a summary or summaries.
Summarize, sum'a-rīz, *vt.* To make a summary, abstract, or abridgment of.
Summary, sum'a-ri, *a.* Concise; brief; intended to facilitate despatch.—*n.* An abridged account; an abstract.
Summation, sum-ā'shon, *n.* Act or process of summing; addition; aggregate.
Summer, sum'ėr, *n.* The warmest season of the year; a lintel; a girder.—*a.* Relating to summer.—*vi.* To pass the summer.—*vt.* To keep or carry through the summer.
Summersault, Summerset, sum'ėr-sa̦lt, sum'ėr-set, *n.* Same as *Somersault.*
Summer time, sum'ėr tīm, *n.* A system of reckoning time in which clocks are kept one hour in advance of Greenwich mean time during the summer months.
Summit, sum'it, *n.* The top; highest point; highest degree; acme.
Summon, sum'un, *vt.* To call by authority to appear at a place, especially a court of justice; to send for; to call up.
Summoner, sum'un-ėr, *n.* One who summons or cites by authority.
Summons, sum'unz, *n.* A call by authority to appear; a citation; document containing such citation; an earnest call.
Sump, sump, *n.* A pond of water for use in salt-works; a reservoir.
Sumpter, sump'tėr, *n.* A horse or mule that carries baggage; a pack-horse.
Sumptuary, sump'tū-a-ri, *a.* Relating to expense; regulating expenditure.
Sumptuous, sump'tū-us, *a.* Very expensive or costly; splendid; magnificent.
Sumptuously, sump'tū-us-li, *adv.* In a sumptuous manner; splendidly.
Sun, sun, *n.* The self-luminous orb which gives light and heat to all the planets; sunshine or sunlight; sunny position; chief source of light, glory, &c.; a year.—*vt.* (sunning, sunned). To expose to the sun's rays.
Sunbeam, sun'bēm, *n.* A ray of the sun.
Sun-bonnet, sun'bon-et, *n.* A bonnet for protecting the face and neck from the sun.
Sun-burn, sun'bėrn, *vt.* To discolour or scorch by the sun; to tan.
Sunday, sun'dā, *n.* The Christian Sabbath;

the first day of the week.—*a.* Belonging to the Christian Sabbath.
Sunder, sun′dėr, *vt.* To part; to separate; to disunite in any manner.
Sun-dial, sun′dī-al, *n.* An instrument to show the time by a shadow cast by the sun.
Sundown, sun′doun, *n.* Sunset.
Sundry, sun′dri, *a.* Several; divers; various; a few.
Sunflower, sun′flou-ėr, *n.* A plant with a large yellow flower.
Sunken, sungk′en, *p.a.* Sunk; covered with water; below the general surface.
Sunless, sun′les, *a.* Destitute of the sun; shaded.
Sunlight, sun′līt, *n.* The light of the sun.
Sunlit, sun′lit, *a.* Lit by the sun.
Sunnite, sun′īt, *n.* An orthodox Mohammedan who receives the *sunna* or traditionary law as of equal importance with the Koran.
Sunny, sun′i, *a.* Like the sun; brilliant; exposed to the sun; having much sunshine; bright or cheerful.
Sunrise, Sunrising, sun′rīz, sun′rīz-ing, *n.* The first appearance of the sun in the morning; time of such appearance; the east.
Sunset, Sunsetting, sun′set, sun′set-ing, *n.* The descent of the sun below the horizon; evening; close or decline; the west.
Sun-shade, sun′shād, *n.* A shade from the rays of the sun; a small umbrella.
Sunshine, sun′shīn, *n.* The light of the sun; warmth; brightness; cheerfulness.
Sunshiny, sun′shīn-i, *a.* Sunny.
Sunstroke, sun′strōk, *n.* A bodily affection produced by exposure to the sun.
Sup, sup, *vt.* (supping, supped). To take into the mouth with the lips, as a liquid.—*vi.* To take supper.—*n.* A sip; a small mouthful.
Superable, sū′pėr-a-bl, *a.* That may be overcome or surmounted.
Superabound, sū′pėr-a-bound″, *vi.* To abound to excess; to be superabundant.
Superabundance, sū′pėr-a-bun″dans, *n.* Excessive abundance; more than enough.
Superabundant, sū′pėr-a-bun″dant, *a.* Abounding to excess; more than sufficient.
Superadd, sū-pėr-ad′, *vt.* To add over and above; to add something extrinsic.
Superannuate, sū-pėr-an′nū-āt, *vt.* To pension off on account of old age.—*vi.* To retire on a pension.
Superannuated, sū-pėr-an′nū-āt-ed, *a.* Impaired or disabled by old age; having received a retiring allowance for long service.
Superannuation, sū-pėr-an′nū-ā″shon, *n.* Act of superannuating; a senile state.
Superb, sū-pėrb′, *a.* Magnificent; sumptuous; splendid; august; grand.
Superbly, sū-pėrb′li, *adv.* In a superb, magnificent, or splendid manner.
Supercargo, sū-pėr-kär′gō, *n.* A person in a merchant ship who superintends the commercial concerns of the voyage.
Superciliary, sū-pėr-sil′i-a-ri, *a.* Pertaining to the eyebrow; being above the eyelid.
Supercilious, sū-pėr-sil′i-us, *a.* Lofty with pride; haughty; overbearing.
Supereminent, sū-pėr-em′in-ent, *a.* Eminent in a superior degree.
Supererogation, sū-pėr-e′rō-gā″shon, *n.* Giving more than enough; performance of more than duty requires.
Supererogatory, sū′pėr-e-rog″a-to-ri, *a.* Partaking of supererogation.
Superexcellent, sū-pėr-ek′sel-lent, *a.* Excellent in an uncommon degree.
Superficial, sū-pėr-fi′shal, *a.* Being on the surface; shallow; not thorough.
Superficiality, sū-pėr-fish′i-al″i-ti, *n.* Quality of being superficial; shallowness.
Superficially, sū-pėr-fi′shal-li, *adv.* Without going deep; slightly; not thoroughly.
Superficies, sū-pėr-fi′shēz, *n.* Surface; the exterior part.
Superfine, sū-pėr-fīn′, *a.* Very fine; excessively subtle.
Superfluity, sū-pėr-flu′i-ti, *n.* Superabundance; something beyond what is necessary.
Superfluous, sū-pėr′flu-us, *a.* Being more than is wanted; redundant; unnecessary.
Superheat, sū′pėr-hēt, *vt.* To heat to an extreme degree; to heat steam apart from water, until it resembles a perfect gas.
Superhuman, sū-pėr-hū′man, *a.* Above or beyond what is human; divine.
Superimpose, sū′pėr-im-pōz″, *vt.* To lay or impose on something else.
Superincumbent, sū′pėr-in-kum″bent, *a.* Lying or pressing on something else.
Superinduce, sū′pėr-in-dūs″, *vt.* To bring in or on as an addition to something.
Superintend, sū′pėr-in-tend″, *vt.* To have the charge and oversight of; to direct or manage; to take care of with authority.
Superintendence, sū′pėr-in-tend″ens, *n.* Oversight; direction; management.
Superintendent, sū′pėr-in-tend″ent, *n.* One who manages and directs; an overseer.—*a.* Overlooking others with authority.
Superior, sū-pē′ri-or, *a.* Higher; higher in rank or dignity; greater in excellence.—*n.* One who is superior to another; chief of a monastery, convent, or abbey.
Superioress, sū-pē′ri-or-es, *n.* A lady superior.
Superiority, sū-pē′ri-o″ri-ti, *n.* Quality of being superior; pre-eminence; advantage.
Superlative, sū-pėr′lat-iv, *a.* Highest in degree; supreme.—*n.* That which is superlative; the highest degree of adjectives or adverbs.
Superlatively, sū-pėr′lat-iv-li, *adv.* In a superlative manner; in the highest degree.
Superlunar, Superlunary, sū-pėr-lū′nėr, sū-pėr-lū′na-ri, *a.* Being above the moon; not sublunary or of this world.
Supermundane, sū-pėr-mun′dān, *a.* Being above the world or mundane affairs.
Supernacular, sū-pėr-nak′ū-lėr, *a.* Of the first quality; exquisite: said of liquor.
Supernaculum, sū-pėr-nak′ū-lum, *n.* Wine or other liquor of great excellence.
Supernal, sū-pėr′nal, *a.* Relating to things above; celestial; heavenly.
Supernatant, sū-pėr-nā′tant, *a.* Swimming above; floating on the surface.
Supernatural, sū-pėr-na′tūr-al, *a.* Being above or beyond nature; miraculous.
Supernaturalism, sū-pėr-na′tūr-al-izm, *n.* State of being supernatural; the doctrine that the universe is under divine or supernatural government.
Supernumerary, sū-pėr-nū′me-ra-ri, *a.* Exceeding the number stated, necessary, or usual.—*n.* A person or thing beyond a

number stated, but required on an emergency.
Superpose, sū-pėr-pōz′, *vt.* To put or place over or above.
Superposition, sū′pėr-pō-zi″shon, *n.* Act of superposing; position of strata over other strata.
Superscribe, sū-pėr-skrīb′, *vt.* To write upon or over; to put an inscription on.
Superscription, sū-pėr-skrip′shon, *n.* Act of superscribing; that which is written or engraved above or on the outside; address on a letter, &c.
Supersede, sū-pėr-sēd′, *vt.* (superseding, superseded). To set aside; to take the place of; to supplant.
Supersensitive, sū-pėr-sens′i-tiv, *a.* Excessively sensitive.
Supersession, sū-pėr-se′shon, *n.* Act of superseding.
Supersonic, sū-pėr-son′ik, *a.* Faster than sound; above the audible limit.
Superstition, sū-pėr-sti′shon, *n.* Groundless belief in supernatural agencies; a popular belief held without reason.
Superstitious, sū-pėr-sti′shus, *a.* Addicted to superstition; proceeding from or manifesting superstition.
Superstructure, sū-pėr-struk′tūr, *n.* Any structure raised on something else.
Supervene, sū-pėr-vēn′, *vi.* (supervening, supervened). To come, as something extraneous; to happen.
Supervention, sū-pėr-ven′shon, *n.* Act of supervening.
Supervisal, sū-pėr-vīz′al, *n.* Supervision.
Supervise, sū-pėr-vīz′, *vt.* (supervising, supervised). To oversee and direct; to superintend; to inspect.
Supervision, sū-pėr-vi′zhon, *n.* Act of supervising; superintendence; direction.
Supervisor, sū-pėr-vī′zor, *n.* One who supervises; a superintendent; an overseer.
Supervisory, sū-pėr-vī′zo-ri, *a.* Pertaining to or having supervision.
Supine, sū-pīn′, *a.* Lying on the back; indolent; careless.—*n.* sū′pīn. A part of the Latin verb.
Supinely, sū-pīn′li, *adv.* In a supine manner; carelessly; indolently; listlessly.
Supper, sup′ėr, *n.* The last meal of the day; the evening meal.
Supperless, sup′ėr-les, *a.* Wanting supper.
Supplant, sup-plant′, *vt.* To take the place of, usually by stratagem.
Supple, sup′l, *a.* Pliant; flexible; yielding.—*vt.* (suppling, suppled). To make supple.—*vi.* To become supple.
Supplement, sup′lē-ment, *n.* An addition; an appendix.—*vt.* sup-lē-ment′. To increase or complete by a supplement.
Supplemental, Supplementary, sup-lē-ment′al, sup-lē-ment′a-ri, *a.* Of the nature of a supplement; serving to supplement.
Suppletory, sup′lē-to-ri, *a.* Supplying deficiencies; supplemental.
Suppliance, sup′li-ans, *n.* The act of supplicating; supplication; entreaty.
Suppliant, sup′li-ant, *a.* Supplicating; entreating earnestly; beseeching.—*n.* A supplicant; a humble petitioner.
Supplicant, sup′li-kant, *a.* Suppliant.—*n.* One who supplicates; a suppliant.
Supplicate, sup′li-kāt, *vt.* (supplicating, supplicated). To beg humbly for; to entreat; to address in prayer.—*vi.* To beg; to petition; to beseech.
Supplication, sup-li-kā′shon, *n.* Humble and earnest prayer; entreaty.
Supplicatory, sup′li-kā-to-ri, *a.* Containing supplication; suppliant.
Supply, sup-plī′, *vt.* (supplying, supplied). To furnish; to provide; to satisfy.—*n.* Act of supplying; quantity supplied; store; *pl.* stores or articles necessary; money provided for government expenses.
Support, sup-pōrt′, *vt.* To rest under and bear; to prop; to endure; to assist; to second; to maintain; to provide for.—*n.* Act of supporting; a prop; help; sustenance; maintenance.
Supportable, sup-pōrt′a-bl, *a.* That may be supported; endurable; bearable.
Supporter, sup-pōrt′ėr, *n.* One who or that which supports; a defender; adherent; prop; figure on each side of a heraldic shield.
Supposable, sup-pōz′a-bl, *a.* That may be supposed or imagined to be or exist.
Supposal, sup-pōz′al, *n.* A supposition.
Suppose, sup-pōz′, *vt.* (supposing, supposed). To lay down or regard as matter of fact; to take for granted; to imagine; to imply.—*vi.* To think; to imagine.
Supposition, sup-po-zi′shon, *n.* Act of supposing; hypothesis; assumption; surmise.
Suppositional, sup-po-zi′shon-al, *a.* Based on supposition; hypothetical.
Supposititious, sup-po′zi-ti″shus, *a.* Substituted; not genuine; spurious.
Suppress, sup-pres′, *vt.* To put down; to crush; to quell; to check; to conceal.
Suppression, sup-pre′shon, *n.* Act of suppressing; concealment; morbid retention of discharges; ellipsis.
Suppressive, sup-pres′iv, *a.* Suppressing or tending to suppress.
Suppressor, sup-pres′or, *n.* One who suppresses.
Suppurate, sup′pū-rāt, *vi.* (suppurating, suppurated). To form or generate pus; to fester.
Suppuration, sup-pū-rā′shon, *n.* Process or state of suppurating.
Suppurative, sup′pū-rāt-iv, *a.* Promoting suppuration.
Supramundane, sū-pra-mun′dān, *a.* Being above the world; celestial.
Supremacy, sū-prem′a-si, *n.* State or character of being supreme; supreme authority.
Supreme, sū-prēm′, *a.* Highest in authority; utmost; greatest possible.
Supremely, sū-prēm′li, *adv.* In a supreme manner or degree; to the utmost extent.
Sural, sū′ral, *n.* Pertaining to the calf of the leg.
Surcease, sėr-sēs′, *vi.* To cease; to leave off.—*n.* Cessation; stop: *poetical.*
Surcharge, sėr-chärj′, *vt.* To overload.—*n.* An excessive load; an overcharge.
Surcingle, sėr′sing-gl, *n.* A belt, band, or girth for a horse.
Surcoat, sėr′kōt, *n.* An outer garment; a loose garment worn over mail.
Surd, sėrd, *n.* A non-sonant consonant sound; a quantity that cannot be expressed in finite terms, as the square root of 2.—*a.* Uttered with breath only and not with voice; not capable of expression in rational numbers.

Sure, shör, *a.* Certain; positive; unfailing; stable; secure.—*adv.* Certainly.

Surely, shör'li, *adv.* In a sure manner; firmly; stably; certainly; presumably.

Surety, shör'ti, *n.* State of being sure; certainty; security; one who gives security; a bail.

Surf, sėrf, *n.* The swell of the sea which breaks on the shore, rocks, &c.

Surface, sėr'fās, *n.* The exterior part of anything that has length and breadth; outside; external appearance.—*a.* Pertaining to the surface; superficial.

Surfaceman, sėr'fās-man, *n.* One who keeps the permanent way of a railway in order.

Surfeit, sėr'fit, *n.* An overloading of the stomach; disgust caused by excess; satiety.—*vt.* and *i.* To feed to excess; to nauseate; to cloy.

Surfy, sėrf'i, *a.* Abounding with surf.

Surge, sėrj, *n.* The swelling of a wave; a large wave; a rolling swell of water.—*vi.* (surging, surged). To swell; to rise high and roll, as waves.

Surgeon, sėr'jon, *n.* A medical man who treats diseases or injuries of the body by manual operation.

Surgeoncy, sėr'jon-si, *n.* Office of surgeon.

Surgery, sėr'je-ri, *n.* The operative branch of medical practice; a doctor's consulting room and dispensary.

Surgical, sėr'ji-kal, *a.* Pertaining to surgeons or surgery.

Surgy, sėrj'i, *a.* Full of surges; rising in surges.

Surloin, sėr-loin', *n.* A sirloin.

Surly, sėr'li, *a.* Gloomily sour or morose; churlish; boisterous; dismal.

Surmise, sėr-mīz', *n.* A supposition; conjecture; speculation.—*vt.* (surmising, surmised). To guess; to imagine; to suspect.

Surmount, sėr-mount', *vt.* To mount or rise above; to overcome.

Surname, sėr'nām, *n.* The family name of an individual.—*vt.* To give a surname to.

Surpass, sėr-päs', *vt.* To go beyond; to excel; to outdo.

Surpassable, sėr-päs'a-bl, *a.* Capable of being surpassed.

Surpassing, sėr-päs'ing, *a.* Excellent in an eminent degree; exceeding others.

Surplice, sėr'plis, *n.* A loose white garment worn by clergy and choristers.

Surplus, sėr'plus, *n.* and *a.* Excess beyond what is required; balance.

Surplusage, sėr'plus-āj, *n.* Surplus matter.

Surprisal, sėr-prīz'al, *n.* Act of surprising; a taking unawares; a surprise.

Surprise, sėr-prīz', *n.* Act of coming upon unawares, or of taking suddenly; emotion excited by something unexpected; astonishment.—*vt.* (surprising, surprised). To fall upon unexpectedly; to take unawares; to astonish.

Surprising, sėr-prīz'ing, *a.* Exciting surprise; wonderful; extraordinary.

Surprisingly, sėr-prīz'ing-li, *adv.* In a surprising manner; astonishingly; remarkably.

Surrealism, sėr-ē'al-izm, *n.* A form of art which claims to express the unconscious mind.

Surrebutter, sėr-rē-but'ėr, *n.* The plaintiff's reply in pleading to a defendant's rebutter.

Surrejoinder, sėr-rē-join'dėr, *n.* The plaintiff's reply to a defendant's rejoinder.

Surrender, sėr-ren'dėr, *vt.* To deliver up; to yield to another; to resign; to relinquish.—*vi.* To yield.—*n.* Act of surrendering; a yielding or giving up.

Surreptitious, sėr-rep-ti'shus, *a.* Done by stealth; clandestine; underhand.

Surrogate, su'rō-gāt, *n.* The deputy of a bishop or his chancellor.

Surround, sėr-round', *vt.* To be round about; to encompass; to invest.

Surrounding, sėr-round'ing, *n.* An environment: generally in *pl.*

Surtax, sėr'taks, *n.* A tax heightened for a particular purpose; an extra tax.

Surtout, sėr-tö', *n.* An upper coat with long wide skirts; a frock-coat.

Surveillance, sėr-vāl'yans, *n.* A keeping watch over; superintendence; oversight.

Survey, sėr-vā', *vt.* To oversee; to examine; to measure and value, as land, &c.; to determine the boundaries, natural features, &c., of.—*n.* sėr'vā or sėr-vā'. A general view; examination; determination or account of topographical particulars.

Surveying, sėr-vā'ing, *n.* The art or practice of measuring and delineating portions of the earth's surface.

Surveyor, sėr-vā'or, *n.* One who surveys; an overseer; inspector.

Survival, sėr-vīv'al, *n.* A living beyond the life of another person, thing, or event; old habit, belief, &c., existing merely from custom.

Survive, sėr-vīv', *vt.* (surviving, survived). To outlive; to live beyond the life of; to outlast.—*vi.* To live after another or after anything else.

Survivor, sėr-vīv'or, *n.* One who survives; the longer liver of two persons.

Susceptibility, sus-sep'ti-bil''i-ti, *n.* Quality of being susceptible.

Susceptible, sus-sep'ti-bl, *a.* Capable of admitting any change or influence; impressible; sensitive.

Susceptive, sus-sep'tiv, *a.* Susceptible.

Suspect, sus-pekt', *vt.* To imagine as existing; to mistrust; to imagine to be guilty; to doubt.—*vi.* To have suspicion.—*n.* sus'pekt. A suspected person.

Suspend, sus-pend', *vt.* To hang; to cause to cease for a time; to debar temporarily; to stay.

Suspender, sus-pend'ėr, *n.* One who suspends; *pl.* braces.

Suspense, sus-pens', *n.* State of being uncertain; indecision; cessation for a time.

Suspensible, sus-pen'si-bl, *a.* Capable of being suspended or held from sinking.

Suspension, sus-pen'shon, *n.* Act of suspending; intermission; abeyance; deprivation of office or privileges for a time.

Suspension-bridge, sus-pen'shon-brij, *n.* A bridge of chains, wire-ropes, or the like.

Suspensive, sus-pen'siv, *a.* Suspensory.

Suspensory, sus-pen'so-ri, *a.* Serving to suspend; suspending.

Suspicion, sus-pi'shon, *n.* Act of suspecting; fear of something wrong; mistrust.

Suspicious, sus-pi'shus, *a.* Mistrustful; inclined to suspect; apt to raise suspicion; doubtful.

Suspiciously, sus-pi'shus-li, *adv.* With suspicion; so as to excite suspicion.

Sustain, sus-tān′, *vt.* To rest under and bear up; to support; to aid effectually; to undergo; to endure; to hold valid; to confirm; to continue.
Sustenance, sus′ten-ans, *n.* Act of sustaining; support; maintenance; food.
Sustentation, sus-ten-tā′shon, *n.* Act of sustaining; support; maintenance.
Sutile, sū′tīl, *a.* Done by sewing or stitching.
Sutler, sut′lėr, *n.* One who follows an army and sells provisions to the troops.
Sutling, Suttling, sut′ling, *n.* The occupation of a sutler.
Suttee, sut-tē′, *n.* A Hindu widow burnt on the funeral pile of her husband; self-immolation of Hindu widows.
Suture, sū′tūr, *n.* A sewing together; a seam; the uniting of the parts of a wound by stitching; seam or joint of the skull.
Suzerain, sụ′ze-rān, *n.* A feudal lord or baron; a lord paramount.
Suzerainty, sụ′ze-rān-ti, *n.* The office or dignity of a suzerain.
Swab, swob, *n.* A mop for cleaning floors, decks, &c.—*vt.* (swabbing, swabbed). To clean with a swab.
Swaddle, swod′l, *vt.* (swaddling, swaddled). To swathe; to bind tight with clothes.—*n.* A swaddling-band.
Swaddling-band, swod′ling-band, *n.* A band of cloth to swaddle an infant.
Swag, swag, *vi.* (swagging, swagged). To sway, as something heavy and pendent; to sag.
Swagger, swag′ėr, *vt.* To strut; to bluster.—*n.* Pretentious strut; bluster.
Swaggering, swag′ėr-ing, *p.a.* Apt to swagger; exhibiting an insolent bearing.
Swain, swān, *n.* A peasant or rustic; a hind; a country gallant; a wooer.
Swallow, swol′ō, *vt.* To receive through the gullet into the stomach; to ingulf; to absorb; to believe readily; to put up with.—*n.* The gullet; voracity; capacity of swallowing; a small migratory bird.
Swamp, swomp, *n.* A piece of wet spongy land; a fen; a bog.—*vt.* To sink in a swamp; to overwhelm; to overset or fill, as a boat in water.
Swampy, swomp′i, *a.* Low, wet, and spongy; marshy.
Swan, swon, *n.* A long-necked web-footed bird of the duck family.
Swannery, swon′ėr-i, *n.* A place where swans are bred and reared.
Swan's-down, swonz′doun, *n.* The down of the swan; a kind of soft thick cloth.
Swap, swop, *vt.* (swapping, swapped). To barter; to exchange.—*n.* An exchange.
Sward, swạrd, *n.* The grassy surface of land; turf; sod.—*vt.* To cover with sward.
Swardy, swạrd′i, *a.* Covered with sward.
Swarm, swạrm, *n.* A large body of small insects; a multitude.—*vi.* To depart from a hive in a body; to crowd; to abound; to climb a tree, pole, &c., by clasping it with the arms and legs.
Swart, Swarth, swạrt, swạrth, *a.* Swarthy.
Swarthy, swạrth′i, *a.* Being of a dark hue or dusky complexion; tawny; black.
Swash, swosh, *vi.* To splash or dash, as water; to bluster.
Swash-buckler, swosh-buk-lėr, *n.* A swaggering fellow; a bravo; a bully.
Swastika, swas′tik-a, *n.* An ancient Aryan symbol adopted by Nazi Germany. It consists of a cross with arms of equal length, each arm having a prolongation at right angles. It was intended to represent the sun.
Swath, swạth or swäth, *n.* A line of mown grass or grain; track formed by mowing; sweep of a scythe in mowing.
Swathe, swāᴛʜ, *vt.* (swathing, swathed). To bind with a bandage; to swaddle.—*n.* A bandage.
Sway, swā, *vi.* To swing or vibrate; to incline; to govern.—*vt.* To swing; to wield; to bias; to influence; to rule.—*n.* Swing or sweep; preponderance; power; rule; ascendency.
Swear, swār, *vi.* and *t.* (swearing, pret. swore, pp. sworn). To make a solemn declaration, with an appeal to God for its truth; to make promise upon oath; to cause to take an oath; to curse.
Swearer, swār′ėr, *n.* One who swears.
Sweat, swet, *n.* The moisture which comes out upon the skin; labour; moisture resembling sweat.—*vi.* (pret. and pp. sweated or sweat). To emit sweat or moisture; to toil.—*vt.* To exude; to cause to perspire; to employ at starvation wages.
Sweater, swet′ėr, *n.* One who sweats; a grinding employer; a heavy woollen jersey worn by athletes.
Sweating-system, swet′ing-sis-tem, *n.* The practice of employing poor people at starvation wages.
Sweaty, swet′i, *a.* Moist with sweat; consisting of sweat; laborious.
Swede, swēd, *n.* A native of Sweden; a Swedish turnip.
Swedish, swēd′ish, *a.* Pertaining to Sweden.—*n.* The language used in Sweden.
Sweep, swēp, *vt.* (sweeping, swept). To rub over with a brush; to carry with a long swinging motion; to drive off in numbers at a stroke.—*vi.* To pass with swiftness and violence; to pass with pomp; to move with a long reach.—*n.* Reach of a stroke, &c.; range; rapid survey; a curve; one who sweeps chimneys.
Sweeping, swēp′ing, *a.* Wide and comprehensive in scope.
Sweepings, swēp′ingz, *n.pl.* Things collected by sweeping; rubbish.
Sweepstake, Sweepstakes, swēp′stāk, swēp′stāks, *n.* A prize made up of several stakes.
Sweepy, swēp′i, *a.* Swaying; wavy.
Sweet, swēt, *a.* Agreeable to the taste or senses; having the taste of honey or sugar; fragrant; melodious; beautiful; not salt or sour; gentle.—*n.* A sweet substance; a bonbon; a word of endearment.
Sweetbread, swēt′bred, *n.* The pancreas of an animal used as food.
Sweet-brier, swēt′brī-ėr, *n.* A shrubby plant cultivated for its fragrant smell.
Sweeten, swēt′n, *vt.* To make sweet.—*vi.* To become sweet.
Sweetening, swēt′n-ing, *n.* Act of making sweet; that which sweetens.
Sweetheart, swēt′härt, *n.* A lover, male or female.
Sweetish, swēt′ish, *a.* Somewhat sweet.
Sweetly, swēt′li, *adv.* In a sweet manner; gratefully; harmoniously.

Sweetmeat, swēt'mēt, *n.* A confection made of sugar; fruit preserved with sugar.
Sweet-pea, swēt'pē, *n.* A pea-like plant with showy sweet-scented flowers.
Sweet-william, swēt-wil'yam, *n.* A plant, a species of pink.
Swell, swel, *vi.* (pp. swelled or swollen). To grow larger; to heave; to bulge out; to increase.—*vt.* To expand or increase; to puff up.—*n.* Act of swelling; gradual increase; a rise of ground; a wave or surge; an arrangement in an organ for regulating the intensity of the sound; an important person; a dandy.
Swelling, swel'ing, *a.* Tumid; turgid.—*n.* A tumour; a protuberance.
Swelter, swel'tėr, *vi.* To be overcome with heat; to perspire.—*vt.* To oppress with heat.
Sweltry, swel'tri, *a.* Sultry.
Swerve, swėrv, *vi.* (swerving, swerved). To deviate; to turn aside; to waver.
Swift, swift, *a.* Speedy; rapid; fleet; ready; prompt.—*n.* A bird like the swallow.
Swiftly, swift'li, *adv.* Speedily; fleetly.
Swig, swig, *vt.* and *i.* (swigging, swigged). To drink in large gulps.—*n.* A large draught.
Swill, swil, *vi.* To swallow large draughts; to drink greedily.—*n.* Drink taken in large quantities; liquid food given to swine.
Swim, swim, *vi.* (swimming, pret. swam, swum, pp. swum). To float; to move through water by the motion of the limbs or fins; to be flooded; to be dizzy.—*vt.* To pass by swimming.—*n.* Act of swimming; distance swum; air-bladder of fishes.
Swimmer, swim'ėr, *n.* One who swims; a bird or other animal that swims.
Swimming, swim'ing, *n.* The act or art of moving on the water by means of the limbs; a dizziness or giddiness in the head.
Swimmingly, swim'ing-li, *adv.* Smoothly; without obstruction; with great success.
Swindle, swin'dl, *vt.* (swindling, swindled). To cheat; to defraud deliberately.—*n.* A scheme to dupe people out of money; fraud.
Swindler, swin'dlėr, *n.* One who swindles; a cheat; one who defrauds people grossly.
Swine, swīn, *n. sing.* and *pl.* A hog; a pig; a sow or boar; *pl.* hogs collectively.
Swineherd, swīn'hėrd, *n.* A keeper of swine.
Swing, swing, *vi.* (swinging, swung). To move to and fro, as a body suspended; to turn round at anchor; to be hanged.—*vt.* To make to oscillate; to brandish.—*n.* Sweep of a body; swinging gait; apparatus for persons to swing in; free course.
Swinge, swinj, *vt.* (swingeing, swinged). To beat soundly; to whip; to chastise.
Swingeing, swinj'ing, *a.* Great; large; excessive.
Swingle, swing'gl, *vt.* To scutch flax.—*n.* An instrument for scutching flax.
Swingle-tree, Swing-tree, swing'gl-trē, swing'trē, *n.* A cross-bar by which a horse is yoked to a carriage, plough, &c.
Swinish, swīn'ish, *a.* Like swine; gross.
Swink, swingk, *vi.* To labour; to toil.
Swipe, swīp, *vt.* and *i.* (swiping, swiped). To strike with a sweeping blow.—*n.* A sweeping blow.
Swipes, swīps, *n.pl.* Poor washy beer.
Swirl, swėrl, *vi.* To form eddies; to whirl in eddies.—*n.* An eddy.
Swish, swish, *vt.* To swing or brandish; to lash.—*n.* A sound as of a switch in the air, a scythe in cutting grass, &c.
Swiss, swis, *n. sing.* or *pl.* A native of Switzerland.—*a.* Belonging to the Swiss.
Switch, swich, *n.* A small flexible twig or rod; a movable rail at junctions; a device for changing the course of an electric current.—*vt.* To strike with a switch; to shunt.
Switzer, swit'zėr, *n.* A Swiss.
Swivel, swi'vel, *n.* A link in a chain partly consisting of a pivot turning in a hole in the next link; a fastening that allows the thing fastened to turn round freely.—*vi.* (swivelling, swivelled). To turn on a swivel.
Swollen, Swoln, swōln, *p.* and *a.* Swelled.
Swoon, swön, *vi.* To faint.—*n.* A fainting fit; a faint; syncope.
Swoop, swöp, *vi.* To dart upon prey suddenly; to stoop.—*vt.* To take with a swoop.—*n.* The pouncing of a bird on its prey; a falling on and seizing.
Swop, swop, *vt.* *See* SWAP.
Sword, sōrd, *n.* A military weapon consisting of a long steel blade and a hilt, used for thrusting or cutting; the emblem of justice, authority, war, or destruction; the military profession.
Sword-arm, sōrd'ärm, *n.* The right arm.
Sword-fish, sōrd'fish, *n.* A large fish allied to the mackerel having the upper jaw elongated so as to somewhat resemble a sword.
Sword-play, sōrd'plā, *n.* Fencing or fighting with swords.
Swordsman, sōrdz'man, *n.* A man who carries a sword; a man skilled in the sword.
Sworn, swōrn, *p.a.* Bound by oath; having taken an oath; closely bound.
Sybarite, sib'a-rīt, *n.* A person devoted to luxury and pleasure.
Sycamine, sik'a-mīn, *n.* The mulberry.
Sycamore, si'ka-mōr, *n.* A fruit-tree of the fig family; a maple naturalized in Britain; the plane-tree of America.
Sycophancy, si'kō-fan-si, *n.* Obsequious flattery; servility.
Sycophant, si'kō-fant, *n.* A servile hanger-on of great people; a parasite; mean flatterer.
Sycophantic, si-kō-fant'ik, *a.* Obsequiously flattering; meanly parasitic.
Syenite, si'en-īt, *n.* A granitic rock composed of quartz, hornblende, and felspar.
Syllabary, sil'a-ba-ri, *n.* A catalogue of the primitive syllables of a language.
Syllabic, Syllabical, sil-lab'ik, sil-lab'ik-al, *a.* Pertaining to a syllable or syllables.
Syllabicate, Syllabify, sil-lab'i-kāt, sil-lab'i-fī, *vt.* To form into syllables.
Syllable, sil'la-bl, *n.* A sound or combination of sounds uttered with one effort; the smallest expressive element of language.—*vt.* To articulate.
Syllabus, sil'la-bus, *n.* An abstract; compendium; a summary statement proceeding from a pope.
Syllogism, sil'lō-jizm, *n.* A form of reasoning or argument, consisting of two premisses and a conclusion.
Syllogistic, Syllogistical, sil-lō-jis'tik, sil-lō-jis'tik-al, *a.* Pertaining to a syllogism; consisting of a syllogism.
Syllogize, sil'lō-jīz, *vi.* To reason by syllogisms.
Sylph, silf, *n.* A fabulous aerial spirit; a woman of graceful and slender proportions.

Sylphid, silf'id, *n.* A diminutive sylph.
Sylphine, silf'in, *a.* Like or relating to a sylph.
Sylva, Silva, sil'va, *n.* The forest trees of any region or country collectively.
Sylvan, sil'van, *a.* Pertaining to a wood; wooded; rural.
Sylviculture, sil-vi-kul'tūr, *n.* The culture of forest trees; arboriculture.
Symbol, sim'bol, *n.* A sign; an emblem; a type; a figure; an attribute; a creed or summary of articles of religion.
Symbolic, Symbolical, sim-bol'ik, sim-bol'-ik-al, *a.* Serving as a symbol; representative; figurative; typical.
Symbolism, sim'bol-izm, *n.* The attributing to things a symbolic meaning; meaning expressed by symbols; use of symbols.
Symbolist, sim'bol-ist, *n.* One who symbolizes; one addicted to using symbols.
Symbolize, sim'bol-īz, *vt.* To represent by a symbol; to typify; to treat as symbolic.—*vi.* To express or represent in symbols.
Symbology, Symbolology, sim-bol'o-ji, sim-bol-ol'o-ji, *n.* The doctrine of symbols; symbols collectively.
Symmetrical, sim-met'rik-al, *a.* Having symmetry; proportional in all its parts; finely or regularly made.
Symmetrize, sim'me-trīz, *vt.* To make symmetrical; to reduce to symmetry.
Symmetry, sim'me-tri, *n.* Due proportion of parts or elements; harmony; correspondence of arrangement.
Sympathetic, Sympathetical, sim-pa-thet'ik, sim-pa-thet'ik-al, *a.* Able to participate in the sorrows and joys of others; compassionate.
Sympathize, sim'pa-thīz, *vi.* (sympathizing, sympathized). To have sympathy; to feel in consequence of what another feels; to condole; to harmonize.
Sympathy, sim'pa-thi, *n.* Fellow-feeling; compassion; agreement of inclinations; correspondence of sensations or affections.
Symphonic, sim-fon'ik, *a.* Pertaining to a symphony.
Symphonious, sim-fō'ni-us, *a.* Agreeing in sound; harmonious.
Symphonist, sim-fō'nist, *n.* A composer of symphonies.
Symphony, sim'fō-ni, *n.* Unison of sound; a musical composition for a full orchestra.
Symposium, sim-pō'zi-um, *n.*; pl. **-ia.** A merry feast; a convivial party; a discussion by different writers in a periodical.
Symptom, sim'tom, *n.* That which indicates the existence and character of something else; a mark, sign, or token.
Symptomatic, sim-tom-at'ik, *a.* Pertaining to symptoms; serving as a symptom.
Synæresis, si-nē're-sis, *n.* The contraction of two syllables into one.
Synagogue, sin'a-gog, *n.* A congregation of Jews met for worship; a Jewish place of worship.
Synchronal, sin'kron-al, *a.* Synchronous.
Synchronism, sin'kron-izm, *n.* Concurrence of events in time; tabular arrangement of history according to dates.
Synchronize, sin'kron-īz, *vi.* To agree in time.—*vt.* To make to agree in time.
Synchronous, sin'kron-us, *a.* Happening at the same time; simultaneous.
Synchrony, sin'kron-i, *a.* Synchronism.
Synclinal, sin-klī'nal, *a.* In *geology*, dipping in opposite directions toward a common line or plane.
Syncopate, sin'ko-pāt, *vt.* To contract by omission of letters from the middle; to prolong a note in music.
Syncopation, sin-ko-pā'shon, *n.* Act of syncopating; contraction of a word; interruption of the regular measure in music.
Syncope, sin'ko-pē, *n.* A contraction of a word by elision in the middle; a sudden pause; suspension; a fainting or swooning.
Syncopize, sin'ko-pīz, *n.* To contract by syncope.
Syncretism, sin'krēt-izm, *n.* The attempted blending of irreconcilable principles, as in philosophy or religion.
Syndesmology, sin-des-mol'o-ji, *n.* The department of anatomy that deals with the ligaments.
Syndic, sin'dik, *n.* A magistrate; one chosen to transact business for others.
Syndicalism, sin'dik-al-izm, *n.* A policy involving ownership of the means of production in each trade by a union of the workers in that trade, such policy to be brought about by means of the general strike and other violent methods.
Syndicate, sin'di-kāt, *n.* A body of syndics; office of a syndic; body of persons associated to promote some enterprise.—*vt.* To form a syndicate or body for the use of.
Synecdoche, sin-ek'do-kē, *n.* A rhetorical figure by which the whole of a thing is put for a part, or a part for the whole.
Synod, sin'od, *n.* A council or meeting of ecclesiastics; an ecclesiastical court; a meeting or council in general.
Synodic, Synodical, sin-od'ik, sin-od'ik-al, *a.* Pertaining to a synod; pertaining to conjunction of heavenly bodies.
Synonym, sin'ō-nim, *n.* A word having the same signification as another.
Synonymous, sin-on'im-us, *a.* Having the same meaning.
Synonymy, sin-on'im-i, *n.* Quality of being synonymous; synonyms collectively.
Synopsis, sin-op'sis, *n.*; pl. **-ses.** A summary; brief statement of topics; conspectus.
Synoptic, Synoptical, sin-op'tik, sin-op'tik-al, *a.* Affording a synopsis or general view.
Syntactic, Syntactical, sin-tak'tik, sin-tak'-tik-al, *a.* Pertaining to syntax.
Syntax, sin'taks, *n.* The construction of sentences in grammar; due arrangement of words in sentences.
Synthesis, sin'the-sis, *n.*; pl. **-ses.** The putting of things together to form a whole; composition or combination.
Synthetic, Synthetical, sin-thet'ik, sin-thet'-ik-al, *a.* Pertaining to synthesis; consisting in synthesis.
Syphilis, sif'i-lis, *n.* A contagious and hereditary venereal disease.
Syphilitic, sif-i-lit'ik, *a.* Pertaining to or infected with syphilis.
Syphon, sī'fon, *a.* *See* SIPHON.
Syriac, si'ri-ak, *a.* Pertaining to Syria.—*n.* The ancient language of Syria.
Syrian, si'ri-an, *a.* Pertaining to Syria.—*n.* A native of Syria.
Syringe, si'rinj, *n.* A tube and piston serving

to draw in and expel fluid.—*vt.* (syringing, syringed). To inject by a syringe; to cleanse by injections from a syringe.

Syrinx, sī'ringks, *n.* The Pandean pipes; the organ of voice in birds.

Syrup, si'rup, *n.* A strong solution of sugar in water; any sweet thick fluid; the uncrystallizable fluid separated from crystallized sugar in refining.

Syrupy, si'rup-i, *a.* Like syrup.

System, sis'tem, *n.* An assemblage of things forming a connected whole; a complex but ordered whole; the body as a functional unity; a plan or scheme; method.

Systematic, Systematical, sis-tem-at'ik, sis-tem-at'ik-al, *a.* Pertaining to system; methodical.

Systematize, sis'tem-at-īz, *vt.* To reduce to a system or regular method.

Systemic, sis-tem'ik, *a.* Pertaining to a system, or to the body as a whole.

Systemize, sis'tem-īz, *vt.* *See* SYSTEMATIZE.

Systole, sis'to-lē, *n.* The contraction of the heart and arteries for driving onwards the blood and carrying on the circulation.

Systolic, sis-tol'ik, *a.* Relating to systole.

Sythe, sīTH, *n.* A scythe.

Syzygy, siz'i-ji, *n.* The conjunction or opposition of any two heavenly bodies.

T

Tab, tab, *n.* A small flap or projecting piece.

Tabard, tab'ärd, *n.* A sort of short cloak; a herald's coat.

Tabaret, tab'a-ret, *n.* A satin-striped silk used for furniture.

Tabbinet, tab'i-net, *n.* *See* TABINET.

Tabby, tab'i, *n.* A rich watered silk or other stuff; a cat of a brindled colour; a female cat.—*vt.* To water or cause to look wavy.

Tabby-cat, tab'i-kat, *n.* A tabby.

Tabefaction, tā-bē-fak'shon, *n.* A wasting away; gradual loss of flesh by disease.

Tabernacle, tab'ėr-na-kl, *n.* A booth; a temporary habitation; a place of worship; a repository for holy things.—*vi.* To sojourn.

Tabes, tā'bēz, *n.* A wasting disease.

Tabid, ta'bid, *a.* Relating to tabes; wasted by disease; emaciated.

Tabinet, tab'i-net, *n.* A fabric of silk and wool used for curtains.

Table, tā'bl, *n.* A thing with a flat surface; an article of furniture having a flat surface; fare or eatables; persons sitting at a table; a syllabus; index; list.—*vt.* (tabling, tabled). To tabulate; to lay on a table.—*a.* Appertaining to a table.

Tableau, tab-lō', *n.*; pl. **Tableaux,** tab-loz'. A picture; a striking group or dramatic scene.

Table-cloth, tā'bl-kloth, *n.* A cloth for covering a table, particularly at meals.

Table-cover, tā'bl-kuv-ėr, *n.* A cloth laid on a table between meal times.

Table d'hôte, tä'bl-dōt, *n.* A common table for guests at a hotel.

Table-land, tā'bl-land, *n.* A distinct area or region of elevated flat land; a plateau.

Tablet, tab'let, *n.* A small slab for writing on; a slab bearing an inscription; a small flattish cake, as of soap, &c.

Table-talk, tā'bl-tąk, *n.* Talk or conversation at table; familiar conversation.

Taboo, ta-bö', *n.* The setting of something apart from human contact; prohibition of contact or intercourse.—*vt.* (tabooing, tabooed). To interdict approach to or contact with.

Tabor, Tabour, tā'bor, *n.* A small drum.—*vt.* To play on a tabor.

Taboret, Tabouret, tā'bor-et, *n.* A small tabor; a frame for embroidery.

Tabret, tā'bret, *n.* A small tabor.

Tabular, ta'bū-lėr, *a.* In form of a table; having a flat surface; set in columns.

Tabulate, ta'bū-lāt, *vt.* (tabulating, tabulated). To set down in a table of items.—*a.* Tabular.

Tacit, ta'sit, *a.* Implied, but not expressed in words; silent; unspoken.

Tacitly, ta'sit-li, *adv.* In a tacit manner; silently; by implication; without words.

Taciturn, ta'si-tėrn, *a.* Habitually silent; not apt to talk or speak.

Taciturnity, ta-si-tėrn'i-ti, *n.* Habitual silence or reserve in speaking.

Tack, tak, *n.* A small nail; a slight fastening; a rope for certain sails; course of a ship as regards the wind; in *Scots law*, a lease.—*vt.* To fasten by tacks; to attach slightly; to append.—*vi.* To change the course of a ship so as to have the wind acting from the other side.

Tackle, tak'l, *n.* Gear or apparatus; pulleys and ropes for moving weights; ropes and rigging, &c., of a ship.—*vt.* (tackling, tackled). To supply with tackle; to set vigorously to work upon; to seize.

Tackling, tak'ling, *n.* Tackle; gear; rigging; harness, or the like.

Tact, takt, *n.* Touch; nice perception or discernment; adroitness in words or actions.

Tactic, Tactical, tak'tik, tak'tik-al, *a.* Pertaining to tactics.

Tactician, tak-ti'shan, *n.* One versed in tactics.

Tactics, tak'tiks, *n.pl.* The science and art of disposing forces in order for battle, and performing evolutions.

Tactile, tak'tīl, *a.* Capable of being touched or felt; pertaining to the sense of touch.

Taction, tak'shon, *n.* Act of touching; touch; contact.

Tactless, takt'les, *a.* Destitute of tact.

Tactual, tak'tu-al, *a.* Pertaining to touch.

Tadpole, tad'pōl, *n.* The young of the frog in its first state from the spawn.

Tael, tāl, *n.* A Chinese money of account equal to about 3*s.* sterling; a weight of 1⅓ oz.

Tænia, tē'ni-a, *n.* The tape-worm; a fillet or band; a ligature.

Taffeta, Taffety, taf'e-ta, taf'e-ti, *n.* A silk fabric, or a mixed fabric of silk and wool.

Taffrail, Tafferel, taf'rāl, taf'e-rel, *n.* The rail at the stern of a ship.

Tag, tag, *n.* A metallic point to the end of a string; an appendage; catch-word of an actor's speech.—*vt.* (tagging, tagged). To fit with a tag; to tack or join.

Tag-rag, tag'rag, *n.* The rabble.

Tail, tāl, *n.* The projecting termination of an animal behind; the hinder or inferior part; the reverse of a coin; limited ownership.

Tail-end, tāl'end, *n.* The latter end.

Tailor, tā'lor, *n.* One who makes men's outer

garments.—*vi.* To practise making men's clothes.
Tail-piece, tāl'pēs, *n.* A piece forming a tail; ornamental design at the end of a chapter in a book.
Tail-race, tāl'rās, *n.* The water which runs from the mill after acting on the wheel.
Taint, tānt, *vt.* To defile; to infect; to vitiate. —*vi.* To be infected or corrupted.—*n.* Infection; corruption; a stain; a blemish on reputation.
Take, tāk, *vt.* (taking, pret. took, pp. taken). To receive or accept; to capture; to captivate; to understand; to feel concerning; to employ; to need; to form or adopt; to assume; to note down; to be infected or seized with; to bear; to conduct, carry; to leap over.—*vi.* To direct one's course; to please; to have the intended effect; to admit of being made a portrait of.
Taking, tāk'ing, *a.* Alluring; attracting.—*n.* A seizing; apprehension; agitation.
Talc, talk, *n.* A magnesian mineral, unctuous to the touch.—*vt.* To rub with talc.
Talcky, Talcose, Talcous, talk'i, talk'ōs, talk'us, *a.* Like talc; consisting of talc.
Tale, tāl, *n.* Number counted; reckoning; a story; a narrative.
Talent, ta'lent, *n.* An ancient weight and denomination of money; a special faculty; general mental power; people of high abilities collectively.
Talented, ta'lent-ed, *a.* Furnished with talents or great intellectual power.
Talion, tā'li-on, *n.* The law of retaliation or punishment of like for like.
Talisman, ta'lis-man, *n.* A charm; a magical figure cut or engraved on stone or metal; something producing extraordinary effects.
Talismanic, ta-lis-man'ik, *a.* Having the properties of a talisman; magical.
Talk, tak, *vi.* To utter words; to converse.—*vt.* To speak; to gain over by persuasion; to discuss.—*n.* Familiar conversation; report; rumour; subject of discourse; discussion.
Talkative, tak'a-tiv, *a.* Given to much talking; loquacious; garrulous; prating.
Talker, tak'ėr, *n.* One who talks; a loquacious person; a prattler.
Tall, tal, *a.* High in stature; lofty; remarkable; extravagant.
Tallow, tal'ō, *n.* The fat of oxen, sheep, &c., melted and separated from the fibrous matter. —*vt.* To smear with tallow.
Tallow-chandler, tal'ō-chand-lėr, *n.* One who makes tallow candles.
Tallowy, tal'ō-i, *a.* Greasy.
Tally, tal'i, *n.* A piece of wood on which notches are cut to keep accounts; anything made to suit another.—*vt.* (tallying, tallied). To record on a tally; to make to correspond. —*vi.* To correspond or agree exactly.
Tally-ho, tal'i-hō'', *interj.* and *n.* A huntsman's cry to urge on his hounds.
Talmud, tal'mud, *n.* The Hebrew civil and canonical laws, traditions, &c.
Talon, ta'lon, *n.* The claw of a bird of prey.
Talus, tā'lus, *n.* The ankle; slope; a sloping heap of broken rocks.
Tamable, Tameable, tām'a-bl, *a.* That may be tamed.
Tamarind, tam'a-rind, *n.* A tropical leguminous tree and its fruit.
Tamarisk, tam'a-risk, *n.* A shrub or small tree of S. Europe and Asia.
Tambour, tam'bör, *n.* A drum; a cylindrical stone, as in a column; a circular frame for embroidery.—*vt.* and *i.* To embroider with a tambour; to work on a tambour frame.
Tambourine, tam-bö-rēn', *n.* A musical instrument of the drum species played on with the hand, and having jingles attached.
Tame, tām, *a.* Having lost its natural wildness; domesticated; spiritless; insipid.—*vt.* (taming, tamed). To make tame; to subdue; to depress.
Tameless, tām'les, *a.* Untamable.
Tamely, tām'li, *adv.* In a tame manner; submissively; meanly; without spirit.
Tamil, tam'il, *n.* One of a Dravidian race of S. India; their language.
Tamine, Taminy, tam'in, tam'i-ni, *n.* A glazed woollen or worsted stuff; a strainer of hair or cloth.
Tamis, Tammy, tam'i, *n.* A sieve.
Tamp, tamp, *vt.* To ram tight with clay, &c.; to stamp or make firm.
Tamper, tam'pėr, *vi.* To meddle or interfere; to influence secretly.
Tampion, Tompion, tam'pi-on, tom'pi-on, *n.* The stopper of a cannon; a plug.
Tan, tan, *vt.* (tanning, tanned). To convert into leather, as skins; to make sunburnt; to flog.—*vi.* To become tanned.—*n.* Bark used for tanning; a yellowish-brown colour.—*a.* Like tan in colour; tawny.
Tandem, tan'dem, *adv.* With two horses harnessed singly one before the other.—*n.* A wheeled carriage so drawn; a cycle for two persons, one behind the other.
Tang, tang, *n.* A taste; characteristic flavour or property; part of a tool which fits into the handle; tongue of a buckle.
Tangency, Tangence, tan'jen-si, tan'jens, *n.* State of being tangent; a contact.
Tangent, tan'jent, *n.* A straight line which touches a circle or curve, but which, when produced, does not cut it.
Tangential, tan-jen'shal, *a.* Pertaining to a tangent; in the direction of a tangent.
Tangibility, tan-ji-bil'i-ti, *n.* Quality of being tangible or perceptible by touch.
Tangible, tan'ji-bl, *a.* That may be touched; real; actual; evident.
Tangle, tang'gl, *vt.* (tangling, tangled). To unite confusedly; to involve; to complicate. —*n.* A confused knot of threads, &c.; an embarrassment; a species of sea-weed.
Tangly, tang'gli, *a.* Knotted; intricate; covered with sea-weed.
Tanist, tan'ist, *n.* An elective prince among the ancient Irish.
Tanistry, tan'ist-ri, *n.* An Irish custom, according to which the prince was elected by the family to which he belonged.
Tank, tangk, *n.* A storage vessel to contain liquids or gas; a reservoir; an armoured car with caterpillar wheels, protected by guns fired from inside.
Tankard, tang'kärd, *n.* A large drinking vessel, often with a cover.
Tanner, tan'ėr, *n.* One who tans hides, or converts them into leather by the use of tan.
Tannery, tan'ėr-i, *n.* A place where tanning is carried on; art or process of tanning.
Tannic, tan'ik, *a.* Applied to an acid in oak,

gall-nuts, &c., the efficient substance in tanning.
Tannin, tan'in, *n.* Tannic acid.
Tanning, tan'ing, *n.* The converting of hides into leather by the use of tan or other substances; leather manufacture.
Tansy, tan'zi, *n.* An aromatic and bitter herb with yellow flowers; a dish made of eggs, cream, sugar, the juice of tansy, &c.
Tantalize, tan'ta-līz, *vt.* (tantalizing, tantalized). To torment by presenting something desirable which cannot be attained; to excite by hopes that are never realized.
Tantamount, tan'ta-mount, *a.* Equal; equivalent in value, force, or effect.
Tantivy, tan-ti'vi, *n.* A violent gallop in the hunting-field; a hunting-cry inciting to speed. —*a.* Swift; hasty.—*adv.* Swiftly; at full speed.
Tantrum, tan'trum, *n.* A fit of ill-humour; display of temper: chiefly in *pl.*
Tap, tap, *n.* A plug to stop a hole in a cask; a spigot; a faucet; a gentle blow; a pat.—*vt.* (tapping, tapped). To broach, as a cask; to draw liquid from; to strike gently.—*vi.* To strike a gentle blow.
Tape, tāp, *n.* A narrow strip of woven work, used for strings and the like.
Tape-line, Tape-measure, tāp'līn, tāp'mezhūr, *n.* A tape marked with feet, inches, &c., used in measuring.
Taper, tā'pėr, *n.* A long wick coated with wax; a small light; tapering form; gradual diminution of thickness.—*vi.* To become gradually smaller.—*vt.* To cause to taper.
Tapestry, ta'pes-tri, *n.* A kind of rich woven hangings of wool and silk, with pictorial representations.—*vt.* To adorn with tapestry.
Tape-worm, tāp'wėrm, *n.* A parasitic worm found in the intestines of animals.
Tapioca, tap-i-ō'ka, *n.* A farinaceous substance prepared from cassava meal.
Tapir, tā'pir, *n.* A hoofed animal allied to the rhinoceros, with a nose resembling a small proboscis.
Tapis, tä-pē', *n.* Table-cover; carpet; hence, *on the tapis*, under consideration.
Tapping, tap'ing, *n.* The surgical operation of letting out fluid, as in dropsy.
Tap-room, tap'röm, *n.* A room in which beer is served from the tap.
Tap-root, tap'röt, *n.* Main root of a plant.
Tapster, tap'stėr, *n.* One whose business is to tap or draw liquor in a tavern.
Tar, tär, *n.* A thick, dark, viscid substance obtained from pine or fir, coal, shale, &c.; a sailor.—*vt.* (tarring, tarred). To smear with tar.
Tarantella, tar-an-tel'la, *n.* A whirling Italian dance; music for the dance.
Tarantula, ta-ran'tū-la, *n.* A kind of spider found in S. Italy; the dance tarantella.
Taraxacum, ta-rak'sa-kum, *a.* Dandelion or its roots as used medicinally.
Tarboosh, Tarbouche, tär'bösh, *n.* A fez.
Tardigrade, tär'di-grād, *a.* Slow-paced; pertaining to the tardigrades.—*n.* One of a family of mammals comprising the sloths.
Tardily, tär'di-li, *adv.* Slowly.
Tardy, tär'di, *a.* Slow; dilatory; late; backward; reluctant.
Tare, tär, *n.* A leguminous plant; vetch; allowance for the weight of the package of a commodity.
Targe, tärj, *n.* A target or shield.
Target, tär'get, *n.* A small circular shield; a mark shot at in rifle practice, &c.
Targeteer, Targetier, tär-get-ēr', *n.* One armed with a target.
Targum, tär'gum, *n.* A Chaldee version of the Hebrew Scriptures.
Tariff, ta'rif, *n.* A list of goods with the duties to be paid; a list of charges generally.
Tarlatan, tär'la-tan, *n.* A thin cotton stuff resembling gauze.
Tarn, tärn, *n.* A small mountain lake.
Tarnish, tär'nish, *vt.* To sully; to dim.—*vi.* To lose lustre.—*n.* A spot; soiled state.
Tarpan, tär'pan, *n.* The wild horse of Tartary.
Tarpaulin, Tarpauling, tär-pa̤'lin, tär-pa̤'ling, *n.* Canvas covered with tar.
Tarpon, Tarpum, tär'pon, tär'pum, *n.* A large, edible American sea-fish.
Tarry, ta'ri, *vi.* (tarrying, tarried). To stay; to delay.—*vt.* To wait for.
Tarry, tär'i, *a.* Consisting of tar, or like tar; covered or smeared with tar.
Tarsia, tär'si-a, *n.* A kind of Italian marquetry, representing landscapes, flowers, &c.
Tarsus, tär'sus, *n.*; pl. **-si.** The ankle or ankle-joint.
Tart, tärt, *a.* Sharp to the taste; sour; acid; severe; snappish.—*n.* A species of pastry, consisting of fruit baked in paste.
Tartan, tär'tan, *n.* Cloth woven in colours in a checkered pattern; a Mediterranean vessel somewhat resembling a sloop.—*a.* Consisting of or resembling tartan.
Tartar, tär'tar, *n.* A native of Tartary; a very irascible or rigorous person; a shrew; a reddish crust deposited by wine on casks; a concretion formed on the teeth.
Tartarean, Tartareous, tär-tā'rē-an, tär-tā'rē-us, *a.* Pertaining to Tartarus or the infernal regions; hellish.
Tartareous, tär-tā'rē-us, *a.* Consisting of tartar; resembling tartar.
Tartaric, tär-tar'ik, *a.* Pertaining to or obtained from tartar.
Tartarize, tär'tar-īz, *vt.* To impregnate with tartar; to refine by the salt of tartar.
Tartarous, tär'tar-us, *a.* Containing or consisting of tartar.
Tartish, tärt'ish, *a.* Somewhat tart.
Tartly, tärt'li, *adv.* In a tart manner; sharply; severely; with sourness of aspect.
Tar-water, tär'wa̤-tėr, *n.* A cold infusion of tar in water.
Task, täsk, *n.* A piece of work imposed by another or requiring to be done; burdensome employment; toil.—*vt.* To impose a task upon.
Task-master, täsk'mäs-tėr, *n.* One who imposes a task, or burdens with labour.
Task-work, täsk-wėrk, *n.* Work imposed or performed as a task.
Tassel, tas'el, *n.* An ornament consisting of a knob with hanging threads.—*vi.* (tasselling, tasselled). To put forth a tassel or flower, as maize.—*vt.* To adorn with tassels.
Taste, tāst, *vt.* (tasting, tasted). To test by the tongue and palate; to perceive the flavour of; to experience; to partake of.—*vi.* To make trial by the tongue and palate; to have a flavour; to have experience.—*n.* Act of tasting; sense of tasting; flavour; intellectual relish or discernment; manner or style.

Tasteful, tāst'fụl, *a.* Having a high taste or relish; having good taste.
Tasteless, tāst'les, *a.* Having no taste; insipid; stale; flat; void of good taste.
Taster, tāst'ėr, *n.* One who tests provisions or liquors by tasting samples.
Tastily, tāst'i-li, *adv.* With good taste.
Tasty, tāst'i, *a.* Having or showing good taste; tasteful; palatable; nice; fine.
Ta-ta, ta'ta, *n.* and *interj.* A familiar form of salutation at parting; good-bye.
Tatter, tat'ėr, *n.* A rag or part torn and hanging to the thing.
Tatterdemalion, tat'ėr-dē-mā''li-on, *n.* A ragged fellow.
Tattered, tat'ėrd, *p.a.* Showing tatters; torn; hanging in rags.
Tatting, tat'ing, *n.* A kind of crochet, made with a shuttle-shaped needle.
Tattle, tat'l, *vi.* (tàttling, tattled). To talk idly; to gossip.—*n.* Prate; idle talk.
Tattler, tat'lėr, *n.* One who tattles; an idle talker; one who spreads idle gossip.
Tattling, tat'ling, *a.* Given to idle talk.
Tattoo, tat-tö', *n.* A beat of drum and bugle-call at night, calling soldiers to their quarters. —*vt.* and *i.* To prick the skin and stain the punctured spot with colours.
Taunt, tạnt, *vt.* To reproach with severe or sarcastic words; to upbraid.—*n.* A bitter or sarcastic reproach.
Taurine, tạ'rīn, *a.* Relating to or like a bull.
Taurus, tạ'rus, *n.* The Bull, one of the twelve signs of the zodiac.
Taut, tạt, *a.* Tight; not slack.
Tautologic, Tautological, tạ-to-loj'ik, tạ-to-loj'ik-al, *a.* Relating to or containing tautology; repeating the same thing.
Tautology, tạ-tol'o-ji, *n.* Needless repetition of the same meaning in different words.
Tavern, ta'vėrn, *n.* A house where liquors are sold; an inn.
Taw, tạ, *vt.* To make into white leather for gloves, &c., by treating skins with alum, salt, and other matters.—*n.* A marble to be played with; a game at marbles.
Tawdry, tạ'dri, *a.* Tastelessly ornamental; cheap and showy.
Tawery, tạ'ė-ri, *n.* A place where skins are tawed or treated with alum, &c.
Tawny, tạ'ni, *a.* Of a yellowish-brown colour, like things tanned.
Tax, taks, *n.* A contribution levied by authority; a rate, duty, or impost charged on income or property; a burdensome duty; an exaction. —*vt.* To impose a tax on; to put to a certain effort; to accuse.
Taxable, taks'a-bl, *a.* That may be taxed; liable by law to the assessment of taxes.
Taxation, taks-ā'shon, *n.* Act of levying taxes; the aggregate of taxes.
Taxicab, Taxi, tak'si-kab, tak'si, *n.* A motor hackney vehicle provided with a meter which shows distance run and fare due.
Taxidermy, tak'si-dėr-mi, *n.* The art of stuffing animals, or of preserving the skins.
Taxology, tak-sol'o-ji, *n.* *See* TAXONOMY.
Taxonomy, tak-son'o-mi, *n.* That department of natural history which treats of the laws and principles of classification.
Tea, tē, *n.* The dried leaves of plants cultivated in China, Assam, Ceylon, &c.; the plant itself; a decoction of tea leaves in boiling water; any decoction of vegetables.—*vi.* (tea-ing, teaed). To take tea.
Teach, tēch, *vt.* (teaching, taught). To instruct; to inform; to make familiar with.—*vi.* To practise giving instruction.
Teachable, tēch'a-bl, *a.* That may be taught; apt to learn; docile.
Teacher, tēch'ėr, *n.* One who teaches; an instructor; a preceptor; a schoolmaster.
Teaching, tēch'ing, *n.* Act or business of instructing; instruction.
Tea-cup, tē'kup, *n.* A small cup for drinking tea from.
Teak, tēk, *n.* An E. Indian tree which furnishes hard and valuable timber.
Teal, tēl, *n.* A small British duck found about fresh-water lakes.
Team, tēm, *n.* A brood; horses or other beasts harnessed together; a side in a game, match, &c.
Teamster, tēm'stėr, *n.* One who drives a team.
Tea-pot, tē'pot, *n.* A vessel in which tea is infused.
Tear, tēr, *n.* A drop of the watery fluid appearing in the eyes; any transparent drop.
Tear, tār, *vt.* (pret. tore, pp. torn). To pull in pieces; to rend; to wound; to drag; to pull with violence; to make by rending.—*vi.* To be rent or torn; to rage.—*n.* A rent.
Tear-drop, tēr'drop, *n.* A tear.
Tearful, tēr'fụl, *a.* Abounding with tears; weeping; shedding tears.
Tearless, tēr'les, *a.* Shedding no tears; without tears; unfeeling.
Tease, tēz, *vt.* (teasing, teased). To pull apart the fibres of; to annoy; to torment.
Teasel, tē'zl, *n.* The fuller's thistle, used to raise the nap on woollen cloths.—*vt.* To raise a nap, as on cloth, by teasels.
Tea-service, tē'sėr-vis, *n.* A complete set of dishes or utensils for the tea-table.
Tea-set, tē'set, *n.* A tea-service.
Teat, tēt, *n.* The projecting part of the female breast; pap; nipple.
Tea-things, tē'thingz, *n.pl.* Tea-service.
Techily, Tetchily, tech'i-li, *adv.* In a techy manner; peevishly; fretfully.
Technic, tek'nik, *a.* Technical.
Technical, tek'ni-kal, *a.* Pertaining to an art, science, profession, handicraft, &c.
Technicality, tek-ni-kal'i-ti, *n.* Quality or state of being technical.
Technics, tek'niks, *n.* The arts in general (used as a sing.); technical objects or terms.
Technique, tek-nēk', *n.* Method of manipulation in an art; artistic execution.
Technological, tek-no-loj'ik-al, *a.* Pertaining to technology.
Technology, tek-nol'o-ji, *n.* The science of the industrial arts.
Techy, Tetchy, tech'i, *a.* Peevish; fretful.
Tectonic, tek-ton'ik, *a.* Pertaining to building or construction.
Tectonics, tek-ton'iks, *n.* The art of building or construction.
Ted, ted, *vt.* (tedding, tedded). To spread or turn, as new-mowed grass or hay.
Tedious, tē'di-us, *a.* Tiresome; wearisome; irksome; fatiguing; dilatory; tardy.
Tediously, tē'di-us-li, *adv.* Wearisomely.
Tedium, tē'di-um, *n.* Irksomeness.
Tee, tē, *n.* A point of aim or starting-point in

certain games, as quoits and golf; a small cone of sand, rubber, &c., on which golfer places his ball when driving off.—*vt.* To place (ball) on tee.
Teem, tēm, *vi.* To bring forth young; to be prolific.—*vt.* To bring forth.
Teeming, tēm'ing, *a.* Producing young; prolific; overflowing; exceedingly abundant.
Teens, tēnz, *n.pl.* The years of one's age having the termination *-teen.*
Teeth, tēth, *n.pl.* of *tooth.*
Teethe, tēᴛʜ, *vi.* (teething, teethed). To have the teeth growing or cutting the gums.
Teething, tēᴛʜ'ing, *n.* Operation, process, or period of the first growth of teeth.
Teetotal, tē'tō-tal, *a.* Totally abstaining from intoxicants.
Teetotaler, Teetotaller, tē'tō-tal-ėr, *n.* A total abstainer from intoxicants.
Teetotalism, tē'tō-tal-izm, *n.* The principles or practice of teetotalers.
Tee-totum, tē-tō'tum, *n.* A small four-sided toy of the top kind.
Tegular, teg'ū-lėr, *a.* Resembling a tile; consisting of tiles.
Tegument, teg'ū-ment, *n.* A cover or covering; an integument.
Tegumentary, teg-ū-ment'a-ri, *a.* Pertaining to teguments.
Teil, tēl, *n.* The lime-tree or linden.
Teind, tēnd, *n.* In Scotland, a tithe.
Telegram, tel'e-gram, *n.* A communication sent by telegraph.
Telegraph, tel'e-graf, *n.* Any apparatus for transmitting messages to a distance; an apparatus for transmitting messages along a wire by electricity, but now also wireless.—*vt.* To convey or announce by telegraph.
Telegraphic, Telegraphical, tel-e-graf'ik, tel-e-graf'ik-al, *a.* Pertaining to the telegraph; communicated by a telegraph.
Telegraphist, tel'e-graf-ist or te-leg'ra-fist, *n.* One who works a telegraph.
Telegraphy, te-leg'ra-fi, *n.* The art or practice of communicating by a telegraph.
Telemeter, te-lem'et-ėr, *n.* A range-finder or similar instrument; an instrument to transmit variations marked by some physical instrument.
Teleology, tel-ē-ol'o-ji, *n.* The science or doctrine of final causes.
Teleostean, tel-ē-os'tē-an, *n.* One of an order of fishes having a well-ossified skeleton, and including most familiar food-fishes.
Telepathic, tel-e-path'ik, *a.* Pertaining to telepathy.
Telepathy, te-lep'a-thi or tel'e-path-i, *n.* Occult communication between persons at some distance.
Telephone, tel'e-fōn, *n.* An instrument transmitting sound to a distance by means of electricity and telegraph wires.—*vt.* (telephoning, telephoned). To transmit by means of the telephone.
Telephonic, tel-e-fon'ik, *a.* Relating to the telephone; communicated by the telephone.
Telescope, tel'e-skōp, *n.* An optical instrument for viewing distant objects.—*vt.* (telescoping, telescoped). To drive the parts of into each other, like the joints of a telescope.
Telescopic, tel-e-skop'ik, *a.* Pertaining to a telescope; seen only by a telescope.
Television, tel'e-vizh''un, *n.* Radio transmission of scenes or pictures so that they can be received at a distance (on a cathode ray tube screen).
Telic, tel'ik, *a.* Denoting end or purpose.
Tell, tel, *vt.* (telling, told). To number; to relate; to disclose; to explain; to distinguish; to inform;. to bid.—*vi.* To give an account; to take effect.
Teller, tel'ėr, *n.* One who tells; an officer of a bank who receives and pays money; one appointed to count votes.
Telling, tel'ing, *p.a.* Having great effect.
Tell-tale, tel'tāl, *a.* Telling tales; blabbing; serving to betray; informative.—*n.* One who discloses private concerns, or what he should suppress.
Tellurian, tel-ū'ri-an, *a.* Pertaining to the earth.—*n.* An inhabitant of the earth.
Telluric, tel-ū'rik, *a.* Pertaining to the earth or to tellurium.
Tellurium, tel-ū'ri-um, *n.* A non-metallic element of a tin-white crystalline appearance.
Telpherage, tel'fėr-āj, *n.* A system of transporting goods on a kind of elevated railway by means of electricity.
Temerarious, tem-ē-rā'ri-us, *a.* Reckless.
Temerity, tē-me'ri-ti, *n.* Contempt of danger; extreme boldness; rashness.
Temper, tem'pėr, *vt.* To proportion duly; to moderate; to form to a proper hardness.—*n.* Due mixture; disposition of the mind; temperament; irritation; state of a metal as to its hardness; medium.
Tempera, tem'pe-ra, *n.* Distemper, in *painting.*
Temperament, tem'pėr-a-ment, *n.* Due mixture of qualities; combined mental and physical constitution; disposition.
Temperance, tem'pėr-ans, *n.* Moderation in indulgence of the natural appetites; sobriety; abstinence from intoxicants.
Temperate, tem'pėr-āt, *a.* Moderate; abstemious; free from ardent passion; calm; cool; measured; sober.
Temperately, tem'pėr-āt-li, *adv.* Moderately; calmly.
Temperature, tem'pėr-a-tūr, *n.* State with regard to heat or cold; climatic heat.
Tempered, tem'pėrd, *a.* Having a certain disposition or temper; disposed.
Tempest, tem'pest, *n.* A violent storm; hurricane; violent tumult or commotion.
Tempestuous, tem-pest'ū-us, *a.* Very stormy; turbulent; subject to storms of passion.
Templar, tem'plėr, *n.* One of a religious military order established to protect pilgrims to the Holy Land; a lawyer or student living in the Temple in London.—**Good Templars,** a modern teetotal society.
Temple, tem'pl, *n.* A place of worship; a church; part of the head between the forehead and the ear.
Templet, Template, tem'plet, tem'plāt, *n.* A board whose edge is shaped so as to serve as a guide in making an article with a corresponding contour.
Tempo, tem'pō, *n.* The time of a piece of music; musical time.
Temporal, tem'pō-ral, *a.* Pertaining to time; pertaining to this life; not spiritual or ecclesiastical; secular; pertaining to the temples of the head.—*n.* Anything temporal or secular; a temporality.
Temporality, tem-pō-ral'i-ti, *n.* State or

quality of being temporal; a secular possession; *pl.* revenues of an ecclesiastic from lands, tithes, &c.
Temporally, tem'pō-ral-li, *adv.* In a temporal manner; with respect to this life.
Temporalty, tem'pō-ral-ti, *n.* The laity; a secular possession; a temporality.
Temporarily, tem'pō-ra-ri-li, *adv.* For a time only; provisionally.
Temporary, tem'pō-ra-ri, *a.* Lasting but for a time; transient; provisional.
Temporize, tem'pō-rīz, *vi.* To comply with the time or occasion; to trim.
Temporizer, tem'pō-rīz-ėr, *n.* A time-server.
Tempt, temt, *vt.* To incite to an evil act; to provoke; to entice; to put to a test.
Temptation, tem-tā'shon, *n.* Act of tempting; state of being tempted; enticement to evil; an allurement.
Tempter, temt'ėr, *n.* One who tempts; the devil.
Tempting, temt'ing, *p.a.* Adapted to tempt; attractive; seductive.
Temptress, temt'res, *n.* A female who tempts.
Temse, Tems, tems, *n.* A sieve; a bolter.
Temulence, tem'ū-lens, *n.* Drunkenness.
Temulent, tem'ū-lent, *a.* Drunken.
Ten, ten, *a.* and *n.* Twice five; nine and one.
Tenable, te'na-bl, *a.* That may be held or maintained.
Tenacious, te-nā'shus, *a.* Holding fast; retentive; adhesive; stubborn.
Tenaciously, te-nā'shus-li, *adv.* Obstinately; with firm adherence; toughly.
Tenacity, te-nas'i-ti, *n.* State or quality of being tenacious; adhesiveness; glutinousness; toughness; cohesiveness.
Tenancy, te'nan-si, *n.* A holding lands or tenements as a tenant; tenure.
Tenant, te'nant, *n.* One who occupies lands or houses for which he pays rent.—*vt.* To hold as a tenant.—*vi.* To live as a tenant; to dwell.
Tenantable, te'nant-a-bl, *a.* In a state suitable for a tenant; fit to be rented.
Tenantless, te'nant-les, *a.* Having no tenant.
Tenantry, te'nant-ri, *n.* The body of tenants.
Tench, tensh, *n.* A European fresh-water fish of the carp family.
Tend, tend, *vi.* To move in or have a certain direction; to conduce; to attend.—*vt.* To attend; to guard; to take care of.
Tendance, ten'dans, *n.* Act of tending or attending; attendance.
Tendency, ten'den-si, *n.* Inclination; leaning; bent; proneness.
Tender, ten'dėr, *n.* One who attends; a small vessel employed to attend on a larger one; a carriage with fuel, &c., attached to a locomotive; an offer of money or service; an estimate; thing offered.—*vt.* To present for acceptance.—*a.* Fragile; delicate; compassionate; kind.
Tenderly, ten'dėr-li, *adv.* In a tender manner; with tenderness; mildly; fondly.
Tendinous, ten'din-us, *a.* Pertaining to a tendon; full of tendons; sinewy.
Tendon, ten'don, *n.* A sinew; a hard, insensible cord or bundle of fibres by which a muscle is attached to a bone.
Tendril, ten'dril, *n.* A slender, twining growth, by which a plant adheres to something.
Tenebrosity, te-nē-bros'i-ti, *n.* Darkness.
Tenebrous, Tenebrose, te'nē-brus, te'nē-brōs, *a.* Dark; gloomy.
Tenement, te'nē-ment, *n.* An abode; a habitation; a block of buildings divided into separate houses.
Tenemental, Tenementary, te-nē-ment'al, te-nē-ment'a-ri, *a.* Pertaining to a tenement; capable of being leased; held by tenants.
Tenet, te'net, *n.* A doctrine, opinion, principle, or dogma.
Tenfold, ten'fōld, *a.* Ten times more.
Tennis, ten'is, *n.* A game in which a ball is driven against a wall, and caused to rebound; in ordinary use, lawn-tennis.
Tenon, ten'on, *n.* The specially shaped end of a piece of wood, &c., to be inserted into the mortise to form a joint.
Tenor, ten'or, *n.* A prevailing course or direction; purport; substance, as of a discourse; the highest of the male adult chest voices; one who sings a tenor part.—*a.* Adapted for singing or playing the tenor.
Tense, tens, *n.* Inflection of a verb to express time.—*a.* Stretched; tight; strained to stiffness; rigid; not lax.
Tensile, tens'īl, *a.* Pertaining to tension; capable of tension.
Tension, ten'shon, *n.* Act of stretching; state of being stretched; tightness; strain; intensity; elastic force.
Tensity, tens'i-ti, *n.* State of being tense.
Tensor, ten'sor, *n.* A muscle that extends or stretches the part to which it is fixed.
Tent, tent, *n.* A portable shelter consisting of some flexible covering; a roll of lint, &c., to dilate a sore.—*vi.* To lodge in a tent.—*vt.* To supply with tents; to probe; to keep open with a tent, as a sore.
Tentacle, ten'ta-kl, *n. sing.* and *pl.* A filiform organ of various animals, used for prehension or as a feeler.
Tentative, ten'ta-tiv, *a.* Experimental; empirical.—*n.* An essay; a trial.
Tentatively, ten'ta-tiv-li, *adv.* By way of experiment or trial.
Tenter, ten'tėr, *n.* A machine for stretching cloth; a tenter-hook; a person in a manufactory who looks after machines.—*vt.* To hang or stretch on tenters.
Tenter-hook, ten'tėr-hu̧k, *n.* A hook for stretching cloth on a tenter; anything that painfully strains, racks, or tortures.
Tenth, tenth, *a.* Next after the ninth.—*n.* One of ten equal parts.
Tenthly, tenth'li, *adv.* In the tenth place.
Tenuity, ten-ū'i-ti, *n.* State of being thin or fine; thinness; slenderness; rarity.
Tenuous, ten'ū-us, *a.* Thin; slender.
Tenure, ten'ūr, *n.* A holding or manner of holding real estate; condition of occupancy; manner of possessing in general.
Tepefaction, te-pē-fak'shon, *n.* Act of making tepid; state of being made tepid.
Tepefy, te'pē-fī, *vt.* (tepefying, tepefied). To make tepid.—*vi.* To become tepid.
Tepid, te'pid, *a.* Moderately warm; lukewarm.
Tepidity, te-pid'i-ti, *n.* State of being tepid; moderate warmth.
Teraph, te'raf, *n.*; pl. **-phim.** A household deity or image.
Teratology, ter-a-tol'o-ji, *n.* The science of monsters or malformations.

Terce, tėrs, *n.* A tierce; in *Scots law*, the right of a widow to a liferent of one-third of her deceased husband's heritage.

Tercentenary, tėr-sen'ten-a-ri, *a.* Comprising three hundred years.—*n.* The three-hundredth anniversary.

Terebene, ter'ē-bēn, *n.* A liquid hydrocarbon produced by treating oil of turpentine with sulphuric acid.

Terebinth, te'rē-binth, *n.* The turpentine-tree.

Teredo, te-rē'dō, *n.* A worm-like molluscous animal, the ship-worm, which perforates submerged wood.

Terete, te-rēt', *a.* Cylindrical and smooth; long and round.

Tergal, tėr'gal, *a.* Pertaining to the back.

Tergiversate, tėr'ji-vėr-sāt, *vi.* To make use of shifts or subterfuges.

Tergiversation, tėr'ji-vėr-sā"shon, *n.* A shift; subterfuge; evasion; fickleness.

Term, tėrm, *n.* A limit; boundary; time for which anything lasts; period of session, &c.; day on which rent or interest is paid; a word; a word having a technical meaning; *pl.* conditions; relative position or footing.—*vt.* To name; to call.

Termagant, tėr'ma-gant, *n.* A brawling woman; a shrew; a scold.—*a.* Quarrelsome; shrewish.

Terminable, tėr'min-a-bl, *a.* That may be terminated or bounded; limitable.

Terminal, tėr'min-al, *a.* Pertaining to or forming the end; terminating.—*n.* An extremity; the clamping screw at each end of a voltaic battery.

Terminate, tėr'min-āt, *vt.* and *i.* (terminating, terminated). To bound; to limit; to end.—*a.* Limited.

Termination, tėr-min-ā'shon, *n.* Act of terminating; close; extremity; ending of a word; conclusion; result.

Terminology, tėr-min-ol'o-ji, *n.* The science or theory of technical or other terms; terms used in any art, science, &c.

Terminus, tėr'mi-nus, *n.*; pl. **-ni.** A boundary; a limit; station at the end of a railway, &c.

Termite, tėr'mīt, *n.* A neuropterous insect commonly called the white ant.

Termless, tėrm'les, *a.* Boundless; nameless.

Termly, tėrm'li, *a.* and *adv.* At every term.

Tern, tėrn, *n.* A long-winged bird of the gull family.—*a.* Consisting of three.

Ternary, tėr'na-ri, *a.* Proceeding by threes; consisting of three.

Ternate, tėr'nāt, *a.* Arranged in threes.

Terpsichorean, tėrp'si-kō-rē"an, *a.* Relating to Terpsichore, the goddess of dancing.

Terra, ter'ra, *n.* Earth; the earth.—**Terra firma,** dry land.

Terrace, te'rās, *n.* A raised level bank of earth; a raised flat area; a row of houses; flat roof of a house.—*vt.* (terracing, terraced). To form into or furnish with a terrace.

Terra-cotta, ter'ra-kot-a, *n.* A kind of pottery, commonly of a reddish colour; a work of art in terra-cotta.

Terrapin, te'ra-pin, *n.* A fresh-water tortoise.

Terraqueous, te-rak'wē-us, *a.* Consisting of land and water, as the globe or earth.

Terrene, te-rēn', *a.* Earthly; terrestrial.

Terrestrial, te-res'tri-al, *a.* Pertaining to the earth; mundane; pertaining to land.—*n.* An inhabitant of the earth.

Terrible, te'ri-bl, *a.* Adapted to arouse terror; dreadful; fearful; extraordinary.

Terribly, te'ri-bli, *adv.* In a terrible manner; dreadfully; excessively; very greatly.

Terrier, te'ri-ėr, *n.* A small variety of dog that creeps into holes in the earth, after animals that burrow.

Terrific, te-rif'ik, *a.* Terrifying; dreadful.

Terrifically, te-rif'ik-al-li, *adv.* In a terrific manner; terribly; frightfully.

Terrify, te'ri-fī, *vt.* (terrifying, terrified). To cause or produce terror in; to alarm.

Terrigenous, te-rij'en-us, *a.* Earth-born.

Territorial, te-ri-tō'ri-al, *a.* Pertaining to a territory; concerned with a certain district. **Territorial Army,** a force raised by voluntary enlistment, primarily for home defence, and serving as a second line to the regular British Army.

Territory, te'ri-to-ri, *n.* A definite piece of land under any distinct administration; a dominion; region; country.

Terror, te'ror, *n.* Such fear as agitates body and mind; dread; alarm; cause of fear.

Terrorism, te'ror-izm, *n.* A system of government by terror; intimidation.

Terrorize, te'ror-īz, *vt.* To impress with terror; to domineer over by means of terror.

Terse, tėrs, *a.* Free from superfluities of language; concise; forcible; pithy.

Tersely, tėrs'li, *adv.* Pithily; concisely.

Tertian, tėr'shan, *a.* Occurring or having its paroxysms every third day, as a fever.

Tertiary, tėr'shi-a-ri, *a.* Third; applied to the third great division of stratified rocks, resting on the chalk.—*n.* The tertiary system of rocks.

Tessellar, tes'se-lār, *a.* Formed in tesseræ.

Tessellate, tes'se-lāt, *vt.* To form with tesseræ; to lay with checkered work.

Tessellation, tes-se-lā'shon, *n.* Tessellated work, or the operation of making it.

Tessera, tes'e-ra, *n.*; pl. **-ræ.** A small cube of marble, ivory, &c., used for mosaic work.

Test, test, *n.* A vessel used in trying or refining gold, &c.; a cupel; examination; means of trial; a standard; oath taken before admission to privileges; a hard outer covering.—*vt.* To put to a trial; to refine; to examine; to prove; to attest.

Testacean, tes-tā'shē-an, *n.* A testaceous animal; a mollusc with a shell.

Testaceous, tes-tā'shus, *a.* Having a molluscous shell; pertaining to shell-fish.

Testacy, tes'ta-si, *n.* The state of being testate.

Testament, tes'ta-ment, *n.* In *law*, a person's will; (with cap.) one of the two general divisions of the Scriptures.

Testamental, tes-ta-ment'al, *a.* Testamentary.

Testamentary, tes-ta-ment'a-ri, *a.* Pertaining to a will; bequeathed or done by will.

Testate, tes'tāt, *a.* Having left a will.

Testator, tes-tāt'or, *n.* A man who leaves a will or testament at death.

Testatrix, tes-tāt'riks, *n.* A woman who leaves a will at death.

Tester, tes'tėr, *n.* One who tests; a flat canopy over a bed, pulpit, &c.; an old silver sixpence.

Testicle, tes'ti-kl, *n.* One of the two glands which secrete the seminal fluid in males.

Testify, tes'ti-fī, *vi.* (testifying, testified). To bear witness; to give evidence.—*vt.* To bear witness to.
Testily, tes'ti-li, *adv.* Irritably; peevishly.
Testimonial, tes-ti-mō'ni-al, *n.* A certificate of qualifications; a gift in token of appreciation or esteem.
Testimony, tes'ti-mo-ni, *n.* Witness; evidence; affirmation; attestation; profession; divine revelation; law of God.
Testy, tes'ti, *a.* Fretful; peevish; petulant.
Tetanus, tet'a-nus, *n.* Spasm with rigidity; lock-jaw.
Tetchy, tech'i. *See* TECHY.
Tête-à-tête, tāt-ä-tāt, *adv.* Face to face; in private.—*n.* A private interview or talk.
Tether, teTH'ėr, *n.* A rope confining a grazing animal within certain limits; scope allowed. —*vt.* To confine with a tether.
Tetragon, tet'ra-gon, *n.* A plane figure having four angles; a quadrilateral.
Tetrahedron, te-tra-hē'dron, *n.* A solid body having four equal triangles as its faces.
Tetralogy, te-tral'o-ji, *n.* A group of four connected dramatic compositions.
Tetrameter, te-tram'et-ėr, *n.* A metrical verse of four feet.
Tetrarch, tet'rärk, *n.* A Roman governor of the fourth part of a province; a petty king.
Tetrarchate, Tetrarchy, tet'rärk-āt, tet'rärk-i, *n.* Office or jurisdiction of a tetrarch.
Tetrasyllable, tet'ra-si-la-bl, *n.* A word consisting of four syllables.
Tetter, tet'ėr, *n.* A cutaneous disease.
Teuton, tū'ton, *n.* A person of Germanic race in the widest sense of the term.
Teutonic, tū-ton'ik, *a.* Belonging to the Teutons and to the languages spoken by them. —*n.* The languages collectively of the Teutons.
Text, tekst, *n.* An author's own work as distinct from annotations; a passage of Scripture selected as the subject of a discourse; a topic; a large kind of handwriting; particular kind of lettering.
Text-book, tekst'bụk, *n.* A book containing the leading principles of a science, &c., arranged for the use of students.
Textile, teks'til, *a.* Woven; capable of being woven.—*n.* A fabric made by weaving.
Textorial, teks-tō'ri-al, *a.* Pertaining to weaving.
Textual, teks'tū-al, *a.* Contained in the text; pertaining to the text.
Textualist, teks'tū-al-ist, *n.* One who adheres to the text; one who can quote texts.
Texture, teks'tūr, *n.* A web; that which is woven; a fabric; manner in which constituent parts are connected; the grain or peculiar character of a solid.
Thalamus, thal'ạ-mus, *n.*; pl. **-mi.** A large ganglion in the brain; the receptacle of a flower, or part on which the carpels are placed.
Thaler, tä'lėr, *n.* A German coin, formerly worth about 3*s*.
Thallogen, Thallophyte, thal'ō-jen, thal'ō-fīt, *n.* A stemless plant consisting only of expansions of cellular tissue.
Thallus, thal'us, *n.* A solid mass of cells, forming the substance of the thallogens.
Than, THan, *conj.* A particle used after certain adjectives and adverbs expressing comparison or diversity, as *more*, *other*, &c.
Thane, thān, *n.* Among the Anglo-Saxons, a man of similar rank to a baron.
Thanedom, thān'dum, *n.* The district, office, or jurisdiction of a thane.
Thank, thangk, *n.* Expression of gratitude; an acknowledgment of favour or kindness: almost always in *pl.*—*vt.* To give thanks to; to express gratitude to for a favour.
Thankful, thangk'fụl, *a.* Grateful; impressed with a sense of kindness received, and ready to acknowledge it.
Thankfully, thangk'fụl-li, *adv.* In a thankful manner; gratefully.
Thankless, thangk'les, *a.* Ungrateful; not obtaining or likely to gain thanks.
Thank-offering, thangk'of-ėr-ing, *n.* An offering made with a sense of gratitude.
Thanksgiving, thangks'giv-ing, *n.* Act of giving thanks; public celebration of divine goodness.
That, THat, *a.* and *pron.*; pl. **Those,** THōz. A pronominal adjective pointing to a person or thing mentioned or understood; a demonstrative pronoun; a relative pronoun equivalent to *who* or *which*.—*conj.* Introducing a reason, purpose, or result, a noun clause, or a wish.
Thatch, thach, *n.* Straw or rushes used to cover a building or stacks.—*vt.* To put thatch on.
Thatcher, thach'ėr, *n.* One who thatches.
Thatching, thach'ing, *n.* Act or art of covering buildings with thatch; material so used.
Thaumaturgy, thạ'ma-tėr-ji, *n.* Miracle-working; magic; legerdemain.
Thaw, thạ, *vi.* To melt, as ice or snow; to cease to freeze; to become genial.—*vt.* To melt; to make less cold or reserved.—*n.* The melting of ice or snow; warmth after frost.
The, THē or THi, *def. art.* Used before nouns with a specifying or limiting effect; used before adjectives and adverbs in the comparative degree it means by so much.
Theanthropism, thē-an'thro-pizm, *n.* The state of being God and man.
Thearchy, thē'är-ki, *n.* Government by God; theocracy.
Theatre, thē'a-tėr, *n.* A house for the exhibition of dramatic performances; a place of action; a room for anatomical demonstrations, &c.
Theatric, Theatrical, thē-at'rik, thē-at'rik-al, *a.* Pertaining to a theatre; calculated for display; artificial; false.
Theatricals, thē-at'rik-alz, *n.pl.* Dramatic performances, especially by amateurs.
Theca, thē'ka, *n.*; pl. **-cæ.** The spore-case of ferns, mosses, and other cryptogams.
Thee, THē, *pron.* The objective and dative case of *thou*.
Theft, theft, *n.* Act of stealing; unlawful taking of another's goods; thing stolen.
Theine, Thein, thē'in, *a.* A bitter principle found in tea, coffee, &c.
Their, THār, *pronominal* or *possessive adj.* Pertaining or belonging to them.—**Theirs,** possessive case of *they*, used without a noun.
Theism, thē'izm, *n.* Acknowledgment of the existence of a God; belief in gods.
Theist, thē'ist, *n.* One who believes in the existence of a God.
Theistic, Theistical, thē-ist'ik, thē-ist'ik-al, *a.* Pertaining to theism or to a theist.

Them, THem, *pron.* The dative and objective case of *they*; those persons or things.
Thematic, thē-mat'ik, *n.* Pertaining to a theme.
Theme, thēm, *n.* A subject or topic; short dissertation by a student; leading subject in a musical composition.
Themselves, THem-selvz', *pron.* Pl. of *himself*, *herself*, *itself*.
Then, THen, *adv.* At that time, past or future; soon afterwards.—*conj.* In that case; therefore.
Thence, THens, *adv.* From that place or time; for that reason; elsewhere.
Thenceforth, THens'fōrth, *adv.* From that time forward.
Thenceforward, THens'for-wėrd, *adv.* From that time or place onward.
Theocracy, thē-ok'ra-si, *n.* Government by the immediate direction of God; the state thus governed.
Theocrasy, thē-ok'ra-si, *n.* Intimate union of the soul with God in contemplation.
Theocratic, Theocratical, thē-o-krat'ik, thē-o-krat'ik-al, *a.* Pertaining to a theocracy.
Theodicy, thē-od'i-si, *n.* A vindication of the ways of God in creation; a doctrine as to the providential government of God.
Theodolite, thē-od'o-līt, *n.* An instrument for measuring horizontal and vertical angles, used by surveyors.
Theogony, thē-og'o-ni, *n.* Doctrine as to the genealogy of pagan deities.
Theologian, thē-o-lō'ji-an, *n.* A person well versed in theology; a divine.
Theologic, Theological, thē-o-loj'ik, thē-o-loj'ik-al, *a.* Pertaining to theology.
Theologist, thē-ol'o-jist, *n.* A theologian.
Theologize, thē-ol'o-jīz, *vi.* To theorize on theological subjects.
Theology, thē-ol'o-ji, *n.* The science of God and divine things; divinity.
Theomancy, thē-om'an-si, *n.* Divination from the responses of oracles.
Theophany, thē-of'an-i, *n.* The actual appearing of God to man.
Theorbo, thē-or'bō, *n.* A musical instrument somewhat like a large lute.
Theorem, thē'ō-rem, *n.* A proposition to be proved by reasoning; a speculative truth.
Theoretic, Theoretical, thē-ō-ret'ik, thē-ō-ret'ik-al, *a.* Pertaining to theory; speculative; not practical.
Theoretically, thē-ō-ret'ik-al-li, *adv.* In or by theory; not practically.
Theoretics, thē-ō-ret'iks, *n.pl.* The theoretical parts of a science; speculation.
Theorist, Theorizer, thē'ō-rist, thē'ō-rīz-ėr, *n.* One who forms theories.
Theorize, thē'ō-rīz, *vi.* (theorizing, theorized). To form a theory or theories; to speculate.
Theory, thē'ō-ri, *n.* Speculation; hypothesis to explain something; rules or knowledge of an art as distinguished from practice.
Theosophy, thē-os'o-fi, *n.* Knowledge of the deity obtained by spiritual ecstasy; direct intuition or divine illumination.
Therapeutic, the-ra-pūt'ik, *a.* Pertaining to the healing art; curative.
Therapeutics, the-ra-pūt'iks, *n.* That part of medicine which deals with the application and operation of remedies.
There, THār, *adv.* In or at that place; at that point; thither.
Thereabout, Thereabouts, THār-a-bout', THār-a-bouts', *adv.* About that; near that place; nearly.
Thereafter, THār-aft'ėr, *adv.* After that; accordingly; afterward.
Thereat, THār-at', *adv.* At that place; at that thing or event; on that account.
Thereby, THār-bī', *adv.* By that; in consequence of that; near that place; nearly.
Therefor, THār-for', *adv.* For that or this.
Therefore, THār'for, *adv.* or *conj.* For that or this reason; consequently.
Therefrom, THār-from', *adv.* From this or that.
Therein, THār-in', *adv.* In that or this place, time, thing, or respect.
Thereof, THār-ov', *adv.* Of that or this.
Thereon, THār-on', *adv.* On that or this.
Thereto, Thereunto, THār-tö', THār-un-tö', *adv.* To that or this.
Thereunder, THār-un'dėr, *adv.* Under that or this.
Thereupon, THār-up-on', *adv.* Upon that or this; in consequence of that; immediately.
Therewith, THar-with', *adv.* With that or this.
Therewithal, THār-with-ạl', *adv.* Therewith.
Theriotomy, thē-ri-ot'o-mi, *n.* The anatomy of animals.
Thermæ, thėr'mē, *n.pl.* Hot springs or hot baths.
Thermal, Thermic, thėr'mal, thėr'mik, *a.* Pertaining to heat; warm; hot.
Thermograph, Thermometrograph, thėr'-mō-graf, thėr'mō-met-ro-graf, *n.* An instrument for recording variations of temperature.
Thermometer, thėr-mom'et-ėr, *n.* An instrument for measuring temperature.
Thermometric, Thermometrical, thėr'mō-met-rik, thėr'mō-met-rik-al, *a.* Pertaining to a thermometer.
Thermotic, thėr-mot'ik, *a.* Relating to heat; dependent on heat.
Thermotics, thėr-mot'iks, *n.* The science of heat.
Thesaurus, the-sạ'rus, *n.* A treasury; a lexicon.
These, THēz, *pronominal adj.* Pl. of this.
Thesis, thē'sis, *n.*; pl. **-ses.** A proposition which a person advances; a theme; an essay written by a candidate for a degree.
Thespian, thes'pi-an, *a.* Relating to dramatic acting.
Theurgy, thē'ėr-ji, *n.* The working of a divine agency in human affairs.
Thewed, thūd, *a.* Having thews or muscle.
Thews, thūz, *n.pl.* Muscles, sinews, strength.
They, THā, *pron. pl.* The plural of *he*, *she*, or *it*; sometimes used indefinitely.
Thick, thik, *a.* Having extent measured through; dense; foggy; crowded; close; stupid; gross.—*n.* The thickest part.—*adv.* In close succession; fast or close together.
Thicken, thik'n, *vt.* To make thick or thicker. —*vi.* To become thick.
Thickening, thik'n-ing, *n.* Something put into a liquid or mass to make it more thick.
Thicket, thik'et, *n.* A wood or collection of trees or shrubs closely set.
Thick-head, thik'hed, *n.* A stupid fellow.
Thick-headed, thik'hed-ed, *a.* Stupid.
Thickish, thik'ish, *a.* Somewhat thick.
Thickly, thik'li, *adv.* Densely; closely; in quick succession.

Thickness, thik'nes, *n.* Measure through and through; thick part; denseness.
Thickset, thik'set, *a.* Thickly planted; stout; stumpy.—*n.* A close hedge; dense underwood.
Thick-skinned, thik'skind, *a.* Having a thick skin or rind; callous; insensible.
Thief, thēf, *n.*; pl. **Thieves,** thēvz. A person who steals or is guilty of theft.
Thieve, thēv, *vi.* and *t.* (thieving, thieved). To practise theft; to steal.
Thievish, thēv'ish, *a.* Given to stealing.
Thigh, thī, *n.* The thick part of the leg above the knee; the femur.
Thill, thil, *n.* The shaft of a cart, gig, &c.
Thiller, Thill-horse, thil'ėr, thil'hors, *n.* The horse which goes between the thills.
Thimble, thim'bl, *n.* A metal cover for the finger in sewing.
Thimble-rig, thim'bl-rig, *n.* A sleight-of-hand trick with three thimbles and a pea.
Thin, thin, *a.* Not thick; rare; sparse; slim; lean; meagre; faint or feeble.—*vt.* (thinning, thinned). To make thin.—*vi.* To become thin.
Thine, ᴛʜīn, *pronominal adj., poss.* of *thou.* Thy; belonging to thee.
Thing, thing, *n.* Whatever may be thought of or spoken of; any separate entity; a creature; matter, circumstance, event; *pl.* clothes, personal belongings, &c.
Think, thingk, *vi.* (thinking, thought). To have the mind occupied on some subject; to judge; to intend; to imagine; to consider.—*vt.* To imagine; to believe; to consider.
Thinker, thingk'ėr, *n.* One who thinks; one who writes on speculative subjects.
Thinking, thingk'ing, *p.a.* Having the faculty of thought; cogitative.—*n.* Act or state of one who thinks; thought.
Thinly, thin'li, *adv.* In a thin manner or condition; not thickly; slightly.
Thinnish, thin'ish, *a.* Somewhat thin.
Thin-skinned, thin'skind, *a.* Having a thin skin; unduly sensitive; irritable.
Third, thėrd, *a.* The next after the second; being one of three equal parts.—*n.* The third part of anything.
Thirdly, thėrd'li, *adv.* In the third place.
Thirst, thėrst, *n.* The desire or distress occasioned by want of water; eager desire after anything.—*vi.* To feel thirst; to desire vehemently.
Thirsty, thėrst'i, *a.* Feeling thirst; having a vehement desire; dry; parched.
Thirteen, thėr'tēn, *a.* and *n.* Ten and three.
Thirteenth, thėr'tēnth, *a.* The third after the tenth.—One of thirteen equal parts.
Thirtieth, thėr'ti-eth, *a.* The next after the twenty-ninth.—*n.* One of thirty equal parts.
Thirty, thėr'ti, *a.* and *n.* Thrice ten.
This, ᴛʜis, *a.* and *pron.*; pl. **These,** ᴛʜēz. A demonstrative, used with or without a noun, referring to something present, near, or just ended.
Thistle, this'l, *n.* A prickly composite plant, the national emblem of Scotland.
Thistle-down, this'l-doun, *n.* The fine down attached to the seeds of thistles.
Thistly, this'li, *a.* Overgrown with thistles; like a thistle; prickly.
Thither, ᴛʜiᴛʜ'ėr, *adv.* To that place: opposed to *hither*; to that end or point.
Thitherward, Thitherwards, ᴛʜiᴛʜ'ėr-wėrd, ᴛʜiᴛʜ'ėr-wėrdz, *adv.* Toward that place.
Tho', ᴛʜō. A short spelling of *though.*
Thole, Thole-pin, thōl, thōl'pin, *n.* A pin in the gunwale of a boat to support an oar: also written *thowl.*
Thong, thong, *n.* A strap of leather, used for fastening anything.
Thorax, thō'raks, *n.*; pl. **-races.** That part of the human body which contains the lungs, heart, &c.; the chest.
Thorn, thorn, *n.* A tree or shrub armed with spines or prickles; a prickle; anything troublesome.
Thorny, thorn'i, *a.* Full of thorns or spines; prickly; troublesome; vexatious.
Thorough, thu'rō, *a.* Passing through or to the end; complete; perfect.
Thorough-bred, thu'rō-bred, *a.* Bred from pure and unmixed blood, as horses; completely bred or accomplished; high-spirited.—*n.* An animal of pure blood.
Thoroughfare, thu'rō-fār, *n.* A passage through; unobstructed way; power of passing.
Thorough-going, thu'rō-gō-ing, *a.* Going, or ready to go, all lengths; extreme.
Thoroughly, thu'rō-li, *adv.* In a thorough manner; fully; entirely; completely.
Thorough-paced, thu'rō-pāst, *a.* Trained in all the paces of a horse; complete; downright.
Thorp, Thorpe, thorp, *n.* A group of houses in the country; a hamlet; a village.
Those, ᴛʜōz, *a.* and *pron.* Pl. of *that.*
Thou, ᴛʜou, *pron.* The second personal pronoun singular: in ordinary language supplanted by the plural form *you.*
Though, ᴛʜō, *conj.* Granting it to be the fact that; notwithstanding that; if.—*adv.* However.
Thought, that, *n.* The power or act of thinking; idea; opinion; judgment; notion; purpose; contemplation; care; concern.
Thoughtful, that'ful, *a.* Full of thought; meditative; careful; considerate; anxious.
Thoughtfully, that'ful-li, *adv.* In a thoughtful manner; considerately.
Thoughtless, that'les, *a.* Free from thought or care; light-minded; heedless; careless.
Thought-reading, that'rēd-ing, *n.* A power by which it is claimed some persons are able to read the thoughts of others.
Thousand, thou'zand, *a.* and *n.* Ten hundred; a great number indefinitely.
Thousandth, thou'zandth, *a.* Completing the number a thousand.—*n.* One of a thousand equal parts.
Thowel, Thowl, thōl, *n.* Thole.
Thraldom, thral'dom, *n.* Bondage.
Thrall, thral, *n.* A slave; a bondsman.
Thrash, Thresh, thrash, thresh, *vt.* To beat out the grain or seeds from; to beat soundly; to drub.
Thrasher, Thresher, thrash'ėr, thresh'ėr, *n.* One who thrashes grain; a species of shark.
Thrashing, Threshing, thrash'ing, thresh'ing, *n.* Act of beating out grain; a sound drubbing.
Thrasonical, thra-son'ik-al, *a.* Given to bragging; boastful.
Thread, thred, *n.* A fine cord; any fine filament; prominent spiral part of a screw; continued course or tenor; general purpose.—*vt.* To pass a thread through; to pass or pierce through.
Threadbare, thred'bār, *a.* Having the nap worn off; worn out; trite; hackneyed.

Thready, thred'i, *a.* Like thread; consisting of or containing thread.
Threat, thret, *n.* A menace; declaration of intention to punish or hurt.
Threaten, thret'n, *vt.* To use threats towards; to menace; to show to be impending.—*vi.* To use threats.
Threatening, thret'n-ing, *a.* Indicating a threat, or something impending.
Three, thrē, *a.* and *n.* Two and one.
Threefold, thrē'fōld, *a.* Consisting of three in one; triple.—*adv.* Trebly.
Threepence, thrē'pens, thrip'ens, *n.* A silver coin of the value of three pennies.
Threepenny, thrē'pen-i, thrip'en-i, *a.* Worth threepence; of little value; mean.—*n.* A threepence.
Three-ply, thrē'plī, *a.* Threefold; consisting of three strands, as cord, yarn, &c.
Threescore, thrē'skōr, *a.* Three times a score; sixty.
Threne, thrēn, *n.* A lamentation.
Threnetic, thren-et'ik, *a.* Mournful.
Threnodist, thren'o-dist, *n.* A writer of threnodies.
Threnody, thren'o-di, *n.* A song of lamentation; a dirge.
Thresh, thresh, *vt.* *See* THRASH.
Threshold, thresh'ōld, *n.* The stone or piece of timber which lies under a door; a door-sill; entrance; outset.
Thrice, thrīs, *adv.* Three times.
Thrid, thrid, *vt.* To thread; to slip through.
Thrift, thrift, *n.* Frugality; economy; sea-pink.
Thriftily, thrift'i-li, *adv.* In a thrifty manner; frugally.
Thriftless, thrift'les, *a.* Having no thrift; wasteful; profuse; extravagant.
Thrifty, thrift'i, *a.* Characterized by thrift; frugal; economical.
Thrill, thril, *vt.* To send a quiver through; to affect with a keen tingling.—*vi.* To quiver; to move tremulously.—*n.* A warbling; thrilling sensation.
Thrilling, thril'ing, *p.a.* Serving to thrill; exciting.
Thrips, thrips, *n.* A minute insect, destructive to wheat.
Thrive, thrīv, *vi.* (thriving, pret. throve, pp. thriven). To prosper; to grow vigorously; to flourish.
Thriving, thrīv'ing, *p.a.* Prosperous; successful; growing; flourishing.
Thro', thrö. A short spelling of *through.*
Throat, thrōt, *n.* The fore part of the neck of an animal; the opening downward at the back of the mouth.
Throb, throb, *vi.* (throbbing, throbbed). To beat, as the heart, with unusual force or rapidity; to palpitate.—*n.* A beat or strong pulsation.
Throe, thrō, *n.* Extreme pain; anguish of travail in childbirth.—*vi.* (throeing, throed). To struggle in extreme pain.
Thrombosis, throm'bō-sis, *n.* The obstruction of a blood-vessel by a clot of blood.
Thrombus, throm'bus, *n.* A clot of blood.
Throne, thrōn, *n.* The seat of a king or ruler; sovereign power and dignity.—*vt.* (throning, throned). To place on a royal seat; to enthrone; to exalt.
Throng, throng, *n.* A crowd; a great number.—*vi.* and *t.* To crowd or press together.
Throstle, thros'l, *n.* The song-thrush or mavis; a machine for spinning.
Throttle, throt'l, *n.* The windpipe or trachea; the throat; the gullet.—*vt.* (throttling, throttled). To choke; to strangle.
Through, thrö, *prep.* From end to end of; by means of; on account of; throughout.—*adv.* From end to end; to completion.—*a.* Going with little or no interruption from one place to another.
Throughout, thrö-out', *prep.* Quite through; in every part of.—*adv.* In every part.
Throw, thrō, *vt.* (pret. threw, pp. thrown). To fling or cast; to propel; to twist filaments of together; to venture at dice; to shed; to utter; to overturn.—*vi.* To cast; to cast dice.—*n.* Act of one who throws; a cast; distance to which a thing is thrown; venture.
Throw-back, thrō'bak, *n.* Reversion to an ancestral or earlier type; atavism.
Throwster, thrō'stėr, *n.* One who throws or twists silk.
Thrum, thrum, *n.* The end of weavers' threads cut off; any coarse yarn.—*vt.* (thrumming, thrummed). To make of or cover with thrums; to drum; to tap.—*vi.* To make a drumming noise.
Thrummy, thrum'i, *a.* Containing or resembling thrums.
Thrush, thrush, *n.* A singing bird; a disease affecting the lips and mouth; also a disease in the feet of the horse.
Thrust, thrust, *vt.* (pret. and pp. thrust). To push or drive with force; to shove; to stab; to obtrude (oneself).—*vi.* To make a push; to make a lunge with a weapon; to intrude.—*n.* A violent push; a stab; a horizontal outward pressure.
Thud, thud, *n.* The dull sound of a blow; a blow causing a dull sound.
Thumb, thum, *n.* The short thick finger of the hand.—*vt.* To soil or handle awkwardly with the fingers.
Thumbkins, thum'kinz, *n.* An instrument of torture for compressing the thumb.
Thumbless, thum'les, *a.* Having no thumb; clumsy.
Thumb-screw, thum'skrö, *n.* A screw to be turned by the fingers; the thumbkins.
Thump, thump, *n.* A dull, heavy blow; sound made by such a blow.—*vt.* and *i.* To strike with something thick or heavy.
Thumper, thump'ėr, *n.* A person or thing that thumps; something strikingly large or extraordinary.
Thumping, thump'ing, *a.* Heavy; strikingly large.
Thunder, thun'dėr, *n.* The sound which follows lightning; any loud noise.—*vi.* To emit the sound of thunder; to make a loud noise.—*vt.* To emit with noise and terror; to publish, as any denunciation.
Thunderbolt, thun'dėr-bōlt, *n.* A shaft of lightning; a daring hero; a fulmination.
Thunder-clap, thun'dėr-klap, *n.* A clap or sudden loud burst of thunder.
Thunder-cloud, thun'dėr-kloud, *n.* A cloud that produces lightning and thunder.
Thundering, thun'dėr-ing, *a.* Producing or accompanied by a noise like thunder; extraordinary or excessive.
Thunderous, thun'dėr-us, *a.* Producing thunder; thundery.

Thunder-storm, thun′dėr-storm, *n.* A storm accompanied with thunder.
Thunder-struck, thun′dėr-struk, *a.* Struck or blasted by lightning; amazed.
Thundery, thun′dėr-i, *a.* Accompanied with thunder.
Thurible, thū′ri-bl, *n.* A kind of censer for incense.
Thurifer, thū′ri-fėr, *n.* An attendant who carries a thurible.
Thursday, thėrz′dā, *n.* The fifth day of the week.
Thus, THus, *adv.* In this manner; to this degree or extent; accordingly.
Thwack, thwak, *vt.* To strike, bang, beat.—*n.* A heavy blow; a bang.
Thwart, thwart, *a.* Transverse; being across.—*vt.* To cross; to frustrate or defeat.—*n.* The bench on which the rowers sit, athwart the boat.
Thy, THī, *pron. poss.* of *thou.* Belonging or pertaining to thee.
Thyme, tīm, *n.* A small aromatic shrub.
Thymol, tīm′ol, *n.* A crystalline substance obtained from oil of thyme, an antiseptic and disinfectant.
Thymy, tīm′i, *a.* Abounding with thyme; fragrant.
Thyrsus, thėr′sus, *n.*; pl. **-si.** A staff wreathed with ivy and vine branches.
Thyself, THī-self′, *pron.* Used after *thou*, to express distinction with emphasis; also used without *thou*.
Tiara, ti-a′ra, *n.* An ornament worn on the head; the pope's triple crown.
Tibia, tib′i-a, *n.* A kind of ancient musical pipe; the shin-bone.
Tibial, tib′i-al, *a.* Pertaining to the tibia.
Tic, tik, *n.* Facial neuralgia.
Tick, tik, *vi.* To make a small noise by beating, &c.—*vt.* To mark with a tick or dot.—*n.* A small distinct noise; a small dot; a small parasitical mite; cover containing the feathers, &c., of a bed; credit.
Ticket, tik′et, *n.* A label; a card or paper enabling one to enter a place, travel in a railway, &c.—*vt.* To put a ticket on; to label.
Ticking, tik′ing, *n.* A striped closely-woven cloth containing the feathers, &c., of beds.
Tickle, tik′l, *vt.* (tickling, tickled). To touch and cause a peculiar thrilling sensation in; to please; to flatter; to puzzle.
Tickler, tik′lėr, *n.* One who tickles or pleases; something that puzzles or perplexes.
Ticklish, tik′lish, *a.* Easily tickled; touchy; liable to be overthrown; difficult; critical.
Tidal, tīd′al, *a.* Pertaining to tides.
Tide, tīd, *n.* Time; season; the rising and falling of the sea; flow; current.—*vt.* or *i.* (tiding, tided). To drive with the tide.—**To tide over,** to surmount.
Tideless, tīd′les, *a.* Having no tide.
Tide-table, tīd′tā-bl, *n.* A table showing the time of high-water.
Tide-waiter, tīd′wāt-ėr, *n.* An officer who watches the landing of goods, to secure the payment of customs duties.
Tide-way, tīd′wā, *n.* The channel in which the tide sets.
Tidily, tī′di-li, *adv.* Neatly.
Tidings, tī′dingz, *n.pl.* News; intelligence.
Tidy, tī′di, *a.* Clean and orderly; neat; trim; moderately large.—*vt.* (tidying, tidied). To make tidy.—*n.* A piece of fancy work to throw over a chair, &c.
Tie, tī, *vt.* (tying, tied). To bind; to fasten; to oblige; to constrain.—*n.* That which binds or fastens together; a fastening; a neck-tie; bond; obligation; an equality in numbers.
Tie-beam, tī′bēm, *n.* The beam which connects the bottom of a pair of rafters.
Tier, tēr, *n.* A row; a rank.
Tierce, tērs, *n.* A measure equal to one-third of a pipe, or 35 imperial gallons; a cask; in *fencing*, a position in which the wrists and nails are turned downwards.
Tiercel, Tiercelet, tēr′sel, tērs′let, *n.* A male hawk or falcon.
Tie-wig, tī′wig, *n.* A wig having a queue tied with a ribbon.
Tiff, tif, *n.* A fit of peevishness; a slight quarrel; small draught of liquor.—*vi.* To be in a pet.—*vt.* To sip.
Tiffany, tif′a-ni, *n.* A gauze or very thin silk.
Tiffin, tif′in, *n.* In India, a lunch.
Tiger, tī′gėr, *n.* An Asiatic carnivorous striped mammal of the cat family as large as the lion; a boy in livery.
Tigerish, tī′gėr-ish, *a.* Like a tiger.
Tight, tīt, *a.* Compact; well-knit; stanch not loose; fitting close or too close; taut; slightly intoxicated; difficult to obtain, as money.
Tighten, tīt′n, *vt.* To make tight or tighter.—*vi.* To become tight.
Tightly, tīt′li, *adv.* In a tight manner; closely. compactly.
Tights, tīts, *n.pl.* A tight-fitting covering for the legs or whole body.
Tigress, tī′gres, *n.* A female tiger.
Tigrine, tī′grin, *a.* Like a tiger.
Tigrish, tī′grish, *a.* Tigerish.
Tike, tīk, *n.* A dog; a boor; a clown.
Tile, tīl, *n.* A slab of baked clay for covering roofs, floors, walls, &c.—*vt.* (tiling, tiled). To cover with tiles; to guard against the entrance of the unitiated.
Tiler, tīl′ėr, *n.* One who makes or lays tiles; the doorkeeper of a masonic lodge.
Tilery, tīl′ėr-i, *n.* A tile work.
Tiling, tīl′ing, *n.* The laying of tiles; tiles collectively.
Till, til, *n.* A money box or drawer for money in a shop, &c.—*prep.* To the time of; until.—*vt.* To cultivate; to plough and prepare for seed.
Tillage, til′āj, *n.* Act or operation of tilling; cultivation; agriculture.
Tiller, til′ėr, *n.* One who tills; the handle of a rudder; shoot of a plant springing from the root.—*vi.* To put forth shoots from the root.
Tilt, tilt, *vi.* To run or ride and thrust with a lance; to joust; to lean or slope; to heel over.—*vt.* To set in a sloping position; to cover with an awning.—*n.* Inclination forward; a military contest with lances on horseback; a tilt-hammer; an awning.
Tilth, tilth, *n.* Tillage; state of the soil in respect to ploughing, &c.
Tilt-hammer, tilt′ham-ėr, *n.* A large hammer raised by machinery and allowed to fall by its weight.
Timber, tim′bėr, *n.* Wood suitable for building purposes; trees yielding such wood; one of the main beams of a fabric.—*vt.* To furnish with timber.

Timbering, tim'bėr-ing, *n.* Timber materials; the timber in a structure.
Timbre, tim'br or tam'br, *n.* Characteristic quality of sound.
Timbrel, tim'brel, *n.* A kind of drum or tabor; a tambourine.
Time, tīm, *n.* The measure of duration; a particular part or point of duration; occasion; season; epoch; present life; leisure; rhythm; rate of movement.—*vt.* (timing, timed). To adapt to the time or occasion; to regulate or measure as to time.
Time-bill, tīm'bil, *n.* A bill of the times of starting and arrival of railway trains, &c.
Time-fuse, tīm'fūz, *n.* A fuse arranged so as to explode a charge at a certain time.
Time-honoured, tīm'on-ėrd, *a.* Honoured for a long time.
Time-keeper, tīm'kēp-ėr, *n.* A clock; one appointed to keep the workmen's time.
Timeless, tīm'les, *a.* Untimely; eternal.
Timely, tīm'li, *a.* Being in good time; opportune.—*adv.* Early; in good season.
Timeous, Timous, tīm'us, *a.* Timely.
Time-piece, tīm'pēs, *n.* A clock or watch.
Time-server, tīm'sėrv-ėr, *n.* One who adapts his opinions, &c., to the times.
Time-serving, tīm'sėrv-ing, *n.* Obsequious compliance; sycophancy.
Time-table, tīm'tā-bl, *n.* A table of the times of school classes, starting of trains, &c.
Timid, ti'mid, *a.* Fearful; timorous; wanting courage; faint-hearted; shy.
Timidity, ti-mid'i-ti, *n.* State or quality of being timid; habitual cowardice.
Timidly, ti'mid-li, *adv.* Weakly; without courage.
Timorous, ti'mor-us, *a.* Fearful of danger; timid.
Timorously, ti'mor-us-li, *adv.* Timidly.
Timothy-grass, tim'o-thi-gräs, *n.* A hard coarse pasture grass extensively cultivated.
Tin, tin, *n.* A malleable metal of a white colour tinged with gray; a dish made of tin.—*vt.* (tinning, tinned). To cover with tin; to put in a tin.
Tincal, ting'kal, *n.* Crude or unrefined borax.
Tinctorial, tingk-tō'ri-al, *a.* Relating to tinctures or dyes; colouring.
Tincture, tingk'tūr, *n.* A tinge, tint, or shade; slight quality added to anything; flavour; extract or solution of the active principles of some substance.—*vt.* (tincturing, tinctured). To tinge; to imbue.
Tinder, tin'dėr, *n.* An inflammable substance used for obtaining fire from a spark.
Tindery, tin'dėr-i, *a.* Like tinder.
Tine, tīn, *n.* The tooth of a fork or harrow; a prong; point of a deer's horn.
Tin-foil, tin'foil, *n.* Tin, alloyed with a little lead, reduced to a thin leaf.
Tinge, tinj, *vt.* (tingeing, tinged). To give a certain hue or colour to; to tint; to imbue.—*n.* A slight colour; tint; tincture; smack.
Tingle, ting'gl, *vi.* (tingling, tingled). To feel a kind of thrilling sensation.—*vt.* To cause to give a sharp, ringing sound.
Tinker, ting'kėr, *n.* A mender of kettles, pans, &c.; a botcher.—*vt.* and *i.* To mend; to cobble; to botch.
Tinkle, ting'kl, *vi.* (tinkling, tinkled). To make small, sharp sounds; to tingle; to clink. —*vt.* To cause to clink.—*n.* A sharp, ringing noise.
Tinkling, ting'kling, *n.* A small, sharp, ringing sound.
Tinman, tin'man, *n.* A dealer in tinware.
Tinner, tin'ėr, *n.* One who works in tin.
Tinning, tin'ing, *n.* Act or process of covering with tin; covering of tin.
Tinplate, tin'plāt, *n.* Thin sheet-iron coated with tin.
Tinsel, tin'sel, *n.* Thin, glittering metallic sheets; cloth overlaid with foil; something superficially showy.—*a.* Consisting of tinsel; showy to excess.—*vt.* (tinselling, tinselled). To adorn with tinsel.
Tinsmith, tin'smith, *n.* A tinner.
Tint, tint, *n.* A tinge; a slight colouring; hue. —*vt.* To tinge.
Tinting, tint'ing, *n.* A forming of tints; a particular way of shading in engraving.
Tintinnabular, Tintinnabulary, tin-tin-nab'ū-lėr, tin-tin-nab'ū-la-ri, *a.* Relating to bells or their sound.
Tintinnabulation, tin'tin-nab-ū-lā"shon, *n.* A tinkling or ringing sound, as of bells.
Tinware, tin'wār, *n.* Articles made of tinned sheet-iron.
Tiny, tī'ni, *a.* Very small; little; puny.
Tip, tip, *n.* A small end or point; a tap; a small present in money.—*vt.* (tipping, tipped). To form the tip of; to cant up, as a cart; to give a small money-gift to.
Tip-cart, tip'kärt, *n.* A cart which can be canted up to empty its contents.
Tippet, tip'et, *n.* A cape or covering for the neck and shoulders.
Tipple, tip'l, *vi.* (tippling, tippled). To drink spirituous liquors habitually.—*vt.* To drink or imbibe often.—*n.* Liquor.
Tippler, tip'lėr, *n.* A toper; a soaker.
Tip-staff, tip'stäf, *n.* A staff tipped with metal; a constable; a sheriff's officer.
Tipsy, tip'si, *a.* Fuddled; affected with strong drink; intoxicated.
Tiptoe, tip'tō, *n.* The tip or end of the toe.
Tiptop, tip'top, *a.* Excellent; first-rate.
Tirade, ti-rād', *n.* A violent declamation; an invective; a harangue.
Tirailleur, ti-räl'yėr, *n.* A French sharp-shooter; a skirmisher.
Tire, tīr, *n.* A head-dress; a band or hoop round a wheel; attire.—*vt.* (tiring, tired). To fatigue; to weary; to adorn; to attire.—*vi.* To become weary.
Tiresome, tīr'sum, *a.* Wearisome; tedious.
Tire-woman, tīr'wu̧m-an, *n.* A lady's-maid; a dresser in a theatre.
Tiring-room, tīr'ing-röm, *n.* The room or place where players dress for the stage.
Tiro, tī'rō. *See* TYRO.
'Tis, tiz, a contraction of *it is*.
Tissue, ti'shū, *n.* Any woven stuff; a textile fabric; a primary layer of organic substance; a fabrication.
Tissue-paper, ti'shū-pā-pėr, *n.* A very thin paper, used for protecting or wrapping.
Tit, tit, *n.* A morsel; a small horse; a woman, in contempt; a titmouse or tomtit.
Titan, tī'tan, *n.* A giant deity in Greek mythology.
Titanic, tī-tan'ik, *a.* Pertaining to the Titans; gigantic; huge; pertaining to titanium.
Titanium, tī-tā'ni-um, *n.* A metallic element somewhat resembling tin.

Titbit, Tidbit, tit'bit, tid'bit, *n.* A small morsel; a particularly nice piece.
Tithe, tīTH, *n.* The tenth part of anything; tenth part allotted to the clergy; any small part.—*vt.* (tithing, tithed). To levy a tithe on. —*vi.* To pay tithes.
Tither, tīTH'ėr, *n.* One who collects tithes.
Tithing, tīTH'ing, *n.* Act of levying tithes; a tithe.
Tithing-man, tīTH'ing-man, *n.* A peace officer or constable.
Tithonic, tī-thon'ik, *a.* Pertaining to the chemical rays of light.
Titillate, ti'til-lāt, *vi.* To tickle.
Titillation, ti-til-lā'shon, *n.* Act of tickling; state of being tickled; any slight pleasure.
Titlark, tit'lärk, *n.* A common European bird somewhat resembling a lark.
Title, tī'tl, *n.* An inscription put over anything; heading; name; appellation of dignity; a right; document which is evidence of a right.—*vt.* (titling, titled). To entitle; to name.
Titled, tī'tld, *a.* Having a title of nobility.
Title-deed, tī'tl-dēd, *n.* The writing evidencing a man's right or title to property.
Title-page, tī'tl-pāj, *n.* The page of a book which contains its title.
Title-role, tī'tl-rōl, *n.* The part in a play which gives its name to it.
Titling, tit'ling, *n.* The titlark.
Titmouse, tit'mous, *n.*; pl. **-mice.** A small insessorial bird with shrill notes.
Titrate, tī'trāt, *vt.* (titrating, titrated). To submit to the process of titration.
Titration, tī-trā'shon, *n.* A process for ascertaining the quantity of a chemical constituent in a compound by means of a liquid of known strength.
Titter, tit'ėr, *vi.* To laugh with restraint.—*n.* A restrained laugh.
Tittle, tit'l, *n.* A small particle; a jot.
Tittlebat, tit'l-bat, *n.* The stickleback.
Tittle-tattle, tit'l-tat'l, *n.* Idle trifling talk; empty prattle.—*vi.* To prate.
Titular, tit'ū-lėr, *a.* Holding a position by title or name only; nominal.
Titularly, tit'ū-lėr-li, *adv.* Nominally.
Titulary, tit'ū-la-ri, *a.* Consisting in a title; pertaining to a title.
To, tu̧ or tö, *prep.* Denoting motion towards; indicating a point reached, destination, addition, ratio, opposition, or contrast; marking an object; the sign of the infinitive mood.—*adv.* Forward; on.
Toad, tōd, *n.* A reptile resembling the frog, but not adapted for leaping.
Toad-eater, tōd'ēt-ėr, *n.* A toady.
Toad-eating, tōd'ēt-ing, *n.* Parasitism; sycophancy.—*a.* Pertaining to a toad-eater or his ways.
Toad-stone, tōd'stōn, *n.* A sort of trap-rock, of a brownish-gray colour; a stone fabled to be formed within a toad.
Toad-stool, tōd'stöl, *n.* A fungus.
Toady, tō'di, *n.* A base sycophant; a flatterer. —*vt.* (toadying, toadied). To fawn upon.
Toadyism, tō'di-izm, *n.* Mean sycophancy; servile adulation.
To-and-fro, tö'and-frō', *a.* Backward and forward; reciprocal.
Toast, tōst, *vt.* To scorch by the heat of a fire; to warm thoroughly; to drink in honour of.—*n.* Bread scorched by the fire; anyone or anything honoured in drinking; a sentiment proposed in drinking.
Toaster, tōst'ėr, *n.* One who toasts; an instrument for toasting bread or cheese.
Tobacco, tō-bak'ō, *n.* A narcotic plant of the potato family; its leaves prepared for smoking.
Tobacconist, tō-bak'ō-nist, *n.* A dealer in tobacco.
Toboggan, Tobogan, tō-bog'an, *n.* A kind of sled used for sliding down snow-covered slopes.—*vi.* To use such a sled.
Tocsin, tok'sin, *n.* An alarm-bell.
Tod, tod, *n.* A mass of foliage; an old weight of 28 pounds for wool; a fox.
To-day, tu̧-dā', *n.* The present day; also, on this day, adverbially.
Toddle, tod'l, *vi.* (toddling, toddled). To walk with short, tottering steps.—*n.* A little toddling walk.
Toddy, tod'i, *n.* A sweet juice extracted from palm-trees; a mixture of spirit and hot water sweetened.
To-do, tu̧-dö', *n.* Ado; bustle; commotion.
Toe, tō, *n.* One of the small members forming the extremity of the foot.—*vt.* (toeing, toed). To touch or reach with the toes.
Toffy, Toffee, tof'i, *n.* A sweetmeat composed of boiled sugar with butter.
Toft, toft, *n.* A house and homestead.
Toga, tō'ga, *n.* A loose robe, the principal outer garment of the ancient Romans.
Together, tu̧-geTH'ėr, *adv.* In company; in concert; without intermission.
Toil, toil, *vi.* To labour; to work; to drudge. —*n.* Labour with fatigue; a string or wet for taking prey.
Toilet, toi'let, *n.* A cloth over a table in a dressing-room; a dressing-table; act or mode of dressing; attire.
Toilet-table, toi'let-tā-bl, *n.* A dressing-table.
Toilful, toil'fu̧l, *a.* Toilsome; wearisome.
Toilless, toil'les, *a.* Free from toil.
Toilsome, toil'sum, *a.* Attended with toil; laborious; wearisome; fatiguing.
Tokay, tō-kā', *n.* A rich highly-prized wine produced at Tokay in Northern Hungary, made from white grapes.
Token, tō'kn, *n.* A mark; sign; indication; souvenir; keepsake; a piece of money current by sufferance, not coined by authority.
Tolerable, tol'ė-ra-bl, *a.* That may be tolerated; passable; middling.
Tolerably, tol'ė-ra-bli, *adv.* In a tolerable manner; moderately well; passably.
Tolerance, tol'ė-rans, *n.* The quality of being tolerant; toleration; endurance.
Tolerant, tol'ė-rant, *a.* Ready to tolerate; enduring; indulgent; favouring toleration.
Tolerate, tol'ė-rāt, *vt.* (tolerating, tolerated). To allow or permit; to treat with forbearance; to put up with; to allow religious freedom to.
Toleration, tol'ė-rā'shon, *n.* Act of tolerating; allowance given to that which is not wholly approved; recognition of the right of private judgment in religion.
Toll, tōl, *n.* A tax on travellers or vehicles passing along public roads, &c.; stroke of a bell.—*vi.* To pay or take toll; to sound, as a bell, with slow, measured strokes.—*vt.* To take toll from; to sound (a bell); to ring on account of.

Tollage, tōl'āj, *n.* Toll; payment of toll.
Toll-bar, tōl'bär, *n.* A bar on a road, for stopping passengers till they pay toll.
Tollbooth, Tolbooth, tōl'böth, *n.* The old Scottish name for a burgh jail.
Toll-gate, tōl'gāt, *n.* A gate where toll is taken.
Toll-house, tōl'hous, *n.* A house where a man who takes the toll is stationed.
Toll-man, tōl'man, *n.* The keeper of a toll-bar.
Tomahawk, to'ma-hąk, *n.* A hatchet used in war by the N. American Indians.—*vt.* To cut or kill with a tomahawk.
Tomato, tō-mä'tō, *n.*; pl. **-toes.** A tropical plant and its fruit, now widely cultivated.
Tomb, töm, *n.* A grave; a sepulchral structure.—*vt.* To bury; to entomb.
Tombac, Tombak, tom'bak, *n.* A kind of brass, or alloy of copper and zinc, used as an imitation of gold.
Tombless, töm'les, *a.* Destitute of a tomb or sepulchral monument.
Tomboy, tom'boi, *n.* A wild, romping girl.
Tombstone, töm'stōn, *n.* A stone erected over a grave; a sepulchral monument.
Tom-cat, tom'kat, *n.* A full-grown male cat.
Tome, tōm, *n.* A volume; a large book.
Tomentose, Tomentous, tō-men'tōs, tō-men'tus, *a.* Downy; nappy.
Tomentum, tō-men'tum, *n.* Pubescence; downy matter.
Tomfool, tom'föl, *n.* A silly fellow.
Tomfoolery, tom-föl'ė-ri, *n.* Foolishness; trifling; absurd knick-knacks.
Tommy, tom'i, *n.* A private soldier in the British Army.
Tommy gun, tom'i gun, *n.* The Thompson self-loading rifle, a type of sub-machine-gun.
Tom-noddy, tom-nod'i, *n.* A sea-bird, the puffin; a blockhead; a dolt; a dunce.
To-morrow, tö-mo'rō, *n.* The day after the present; on the day after the present, adverbially.
Tompion, tom'pi-on, *n.* Tampion.
Tomtit, tom'tit, *n.* The titmouse.
Ton, ton, *n.* The fashion; high mode.
Ton, tun, *n.* A weight equal to 20 hundred-weight or 2240 pounds avoirdupois.
Tonal, tō'nal, *a.* Pertaining to tone.
Tone, tōn, *n.* Any sound in relation to its pitch, quality, or strength; sound as expressive of sentiment; timbre; healthy activity of animal organs; mood; tenor; prevailing character.—*vt.* (toning, toned). To give a certain tone to.—**To tone down,** to soften.
Tongs, tongz, *n.pl.* A metal instrument for taking hold of coals, heated metals, &c.
Tongue, tung, *n.* The fleshy movable organ in the mouth, of taste, speech, &c.; speech; a language; strip of land; a tapering flame; pin of a buckle.—*vt.* To utter; to scold; to modify with the tongue in playing, as in the flute.
Tonguester, tung'stėr, *n.* A babbler.
Tongue-tied, Tongue-tacked, tung'tīd, tung'takt, *a.* Having an impediment in the speech; unable to speak freely.
Tonic, ton'ik, *a.* Increasing strength; restoring healthy functions; relating to tones or sounds.—*n.* A medicine that gives tone to the system; the key-note in music.
Tonicity, to-nis'i-ti, *n.* The elasticity of living parts, as muscles.
To-night, tö-nīt', *n.* The present night; in the present or coming night, adverbially.
Tonite, tōn'īt, *n.* A powerful explosive prepared from pulverized gun-cotton.
Tonnage, tun'āj, *n.* The number of tons carried by a ship; a duty on ships; ships estimated by their carrying capacity.
Tonsil, ton'sil, *n.* One of the two oblong glands on each side of the throat.
Tonsilar, Tonsillar, Tonsillitic, ton'sil-ėr, ton-si-lit'ik, *a.* Pertaining to the tonsils.
Tonsile, ton'sil, *a.* That may be shorn.
Tonsor, ton'sor, *n.* A barber; one who shaves.
Tonsorial, ton-sō'ri-al, *a.* Pertaining to a barber or to shaving.
Tonsure, ton'sūr, *n.* The act of clipping the hair; the round bare place on the heads of the Roman Catholic priests.
Tonsured, ton'sūrd, *a.* Having a tonsure; clerical.
Tontine, ton'tīn, *n.* An annuity shared by subscribers to a loan, and going wholly to the last survivor.
Tony, tō'ni, *n.* A simpleton.
Too, tö, *adv.* Over; more than sufficiently; very; likewise; also; besides.
Tool, töl, *n.* Any instrument to be used by the hands; a person used as an instrument by another.—*vt.* To shape or mark with a tool.
Tooling, töl'ing, *n.* Skilled work with a tool; carving; ornamental marking.
Toot, töt, *vi.* To make a noise like that of a pipe or horn.—*vt.* To sound, as a horn.—*n.* A sound blown on a horn.
Tooth, töth, *n.*; pl. **Teeth,** tēth. A bony growth in the jaws for chewing; any projection resembling a tooth.—*vt.* To furnish with teeth; to indent.
Toothache, töth'āk, *n.* A pain in the teeth.
Toothed, tötht, *a.* Having teeth or cogs.
Toothless, töth'les, *a.* Having no teeth.
Toothpick, töth'pik, *n.* An instrument to pick out substances lodged among the teeth.
Toothsome, töth'sum, *a.* Grateful to the taste; palatable.
Top, top, *n.* The highest part of anything; highest rank; platform in ships surrounding the head of the lower masts; a whirling toy.—*a.* Being on the top; highest.—*vi.* (topping, topped). To rise aloft; to be eminent.—*vt.* To cap; to surmount; to rise to the top of.
Topaz, tō'paz, *n.* A transparent or translucent gem of various light colours.
Top-boots, top-böts, *n.pl.* Boots having tops of light-coloured leather, used chiefly for riding.
Top-coat, top'kōt, *n.* An upper or over coat.
Top-dress, top'dres, *vt.* To spread manure on the surface of.
Top-dressing, top'dres-ing, *n.* A dressing of manure laid on the surface of land.
Tope, tōp, *n.* A fish of the shark kind; a Buddhist monument containing relics, &c.—*vi.* (toping, toped). To drink spirituous liquors to excess.
Toper, tōp'ėr, *n.* One who topes; a tippler.
Topgallant, top'gal-ant, *a.* Being the third above the deck; above the topmast.
Top-heavy, top'he-vi, *a.* Having the top or upper part too heavy for the lower.
Topiary, tō'pi-a-ri, *a.* Shaped by clipping, pruning, or training.
Topic, to'pik, *n.* Subject of any discourse; matter treated of.

Topical, to'pik-al, *a.* Pertaining to a topic; local; pertaining to the topics of the day.
Topically, to'pik-al-li, *adv.* Locally; with application to a particular part.
Top-knot, top'not, *n.* A knot worn by females on the top of the head.
Topmast, top'mäst, *n.* The mast which is next above the lower mast.
Topmost, top'mōst, *a.* Highest; uppermost.
Topographer, Topographist, to-pog'raf-ėr, to-pog'raf-ist, *n.* One who deals with or is versed in topography.
Topographic, Topographical, to-po-graf'ik, to-po-graf'ik-al, *a.* Descriptive of a place.
Topography, to-pog'ra-fi, *n.* The description of a particular place, tract of land, &c.
Toponomy, to-pon'o-mi, *n.* The place-names of a country or district; a register of them.
Topping, top'ing, *p.a.* Rising aloft; pre-eminent; fine; gallant.
Topple, top'l, *vi.* (toppling, toppled). To fall, as with the top first.—*vt.* To throw forward.
Top-sail, top'sāl, *n.* The second sail above the deck on any mast.
Top-soiling, top'soil-ing, *n.* Removal of the topmost soil before a railway, &c., is begun.
Topsy-turvy, top'si-tėr-vi, *adv.* Upside down.
Toque, tōk, *n.* A kind of flattish hat.
Torch, torch, *n.* A light to be carried in the hand; a flambeau.
Torch-light, torch'līt, *n.* The light of a torch or of torches: also adjectively.
Toreador, tor'e-a-dor", *n.* A Spanish bull-fighter, especially one on horseback.
Toreutic, to-rū'tik, *a.* Pertaining to carved work.
Torment, tor'ment, *n.* Extreme pain; torture; that which gives pain.—*vt.* tor-ment'. To torture; to distress; to tease.
Tormenter, tor-ment'ėr, *n.* One who torments.
Tormentil, Tormentilla, tor'men-til, tor-men-til'a, *n.* A weed with small yellow flowers.
Tormenting, tor-ment'ing, *a.* Causing torment.
Tormentor, tor-ment'or, *n.* One who torments; a kind of harrow with wheels.
Tornado, tor-nā'dō, *n.*; pl. **-oes.** A violent whirling wind; a hurricane.
Torpedo, tor-pē'dō, *n.*; pl. **-oes.** A fish allied to the rays; an explosive engine propelled under water.
Torpedo-boat, tor-pē'dō-bōt, *n.* A small swift boat intended to discharge torpedoes.
Torpedo-catcher, tor-pē'dō-kach-ėr, *n.* A swift and powerful war-vessel intended to act against torpedo-boats.
Torpescence, tor-pes'ens, *n.* A becoming torpid.
Torpescent, tor-pes'ent, *a.* Becoming torpid.
Torpid, tor'pid, *a.* Numb; stupefied; stupid; sluggish; inactive.
Torpidity, tor-pid'i-ti, *n.* State of being torpid; numbness; dullness; inactivity.
Torpify, tor'pi-fī, *vt.* To make torpid.
Torpor, tor'por, *n.* State of being torpid; numbness; loss of motion; sluggishness.
Torrefaction, to-rē-fak'shon, *n.* Operation of drying or roasting by a fire.
Torrefy, to'rē-fī, *vt.* To dry, roast, or scorch by a fire; to dry or parch.
Torrent, to'rent, *n.* A violent rushing stream.
Torrential, Torrentine, to-ren'shal, to-ren'tin, *a.* Pertaining to a torrent.
Torrid, to'rid, *a.* Parched; violently hot; burning or parching.
Torridity, to-rid'i-ti, *n.* State of being torrid.
Torsion, tor'shon, *n.* The act of twisting; the force with which a body, such as a wire, resists a twist; the twisting of the cut end of an artery to stop the flow of blood.
Torsk, torsk, *n.* A fish of the cod tribe, caught and salted and dried as food.
Torso, tor'sō, *n.* The trunk of a statue deprived of its head and limbs.
Tort, tort, *n.* Wrong; injury.
Tortile, tor'til, *n.* Twisted; coiled.
Tortious, tor'shus, *a.* Of the nature of or implying tort or injury.
Tortive, tor'tiv, *a.* Twisted.
Tortoise, tor'tois or tor'tis, *n.* A reptile covered with a flattened shell; a turtle.
Tortoise-shell, tor'tois-shel, *n.* The shell of tortoises which inhabit tropical seas.
Tortuose, tor'tū-ōs, *a.* Tortuous.
Tortuosity, tor-tū-ōs'i-ti, *n.* State of being tortuous.
Tortuous, tor'tū-us, *a.* Twisted; circuitous and underhand; roundabout.
Torture, tor'tūr, *n.* Extreme pain; agony; torment.—*vt.* (torturing, tortured). To pain to extremity; to torment; to harass.
Tory, tō'ri, *n.* An ardent supporter of established institutions in politics; a Conservative. —*a.* Pertaining to Tories.
Toryism, tō'ri-izm, *n.* The principles or practices of the Tories.
Toss, tos, *vt.* To pitch; to fling; to jerk, as the head; to agitate.—*vi.* To roll and tumble; to be in violent commotion.—*n.* A throw; pitch; throw of the head.
Tosser, tos'ėr, *n.* One who tosses.
Toss-up, tos'up, *n.* The throwing up of a coin to decide something; an even chance.
Tot, tot, *n.* Anything small or insignificant.—*vt.* (totting, totted). To sum (with *up*).
Total, tō'tal, *a.* Pertaining to the whole; complete.—*n.* The whole; an aggregate.
Totalitarian, tō-tal'it-ār"i-an, *a.* Applied to states under a highly centralized government which suppresses all rival political parties.
Totality, tō-tal'i-ti, *n.* Total amount.
Totally, tō'tal-li, *adv.* Wholly; completely.
Totem, tō'tem, *n.* A figure, as of an animal, plant, &c., used as a badge of a tribe or family among rude races.
Tother, tuтн'ėr. Other; the other. [Colloq.]
Totter, tot'ėr, *vi.* To threaten to fall; to vacillate; to shake; to reel.
Tottery, tot'ėr-i, *a.* Unsteady; shaking.
Toucan, tö'kan, *n.* A scansorial bird of tropical America having an enormous beak.
Touch, tuch, *vt.* To perceive by the sense of feeling; to come in contact with; to taste; to reach or arrive at; to refer to; to affect. —*vi.* To be in contact; to take effect; to make mention; to call when on a voyage.—*n.* Act of touching; contact; sense of feeling; a trait; a little; a stroke; distinctive handling; in football, &c., part of the field beyond the flags.
Touch-hole, tuch'hōl, *n.* The vent of a fire-arm communicating fire to the charge.
Touching, tuch'ing, *a.* Affecting; moving; pathetic.—*prep.* Concerning; with respect to.

Touch-needle, tuch'nē-dl, *n.* A small bar of an alloy of gold or silver, used with the touchstone to test articles of gold and silver.
Touch-piece, tuch'pēs, *n.* A coin given by sovereigns of England to those whom they touched to cure scrofula or king's evil.
Touchstone, tuch'stōn, *n.* A compact, dark-coloured, siliceous stone used in testing gold and silver; a test or criterion.
Touchwood, tuch'wụd, *n.* Soft decayed wood, serving the purpose of tinder.
Touchy, tuch'i, *a.* Irritable; irascible; apt to take offence.
Tough, tuf, *a.* Flexible and not brittle; tenacious; durable; viscous; stiff; stubborn.
Toughen, tuf'n, *vi.* To grow tough.—*vt.* To make tough.
Toughish, tuf'ish, *a.* Somewhat tough.
Toupee, Toupet, tö-pē', tö'pā, *n.* A curl or artificial lock of hair; a small wig or upper part of a wig.
Tour, tör, *n.* A journey; a lengthy jaunt or excursion.—*vi.* To make a tour.
Tourist, tör'ist, *n.* One who makes a tour.
Tourmalin, Tourmaline, tör'ma-lin, *n.* A mineral of various colours, possessing strong electrical properties.
Tournament, tör'na-ment, *n.* A martial sport performed by knights on horseback; contest in which a number take part.
Tourney, tör'ni, *n.* A tournament.—*vi.* To tilt; to engage in a tournament.
Tourniquet, tör'ni-ket, *n.* A bandage tightened by a screw to check a flow of blood.
Touse, touz, *vt.* (tousing, toused). To pull or drag; to tousle.
Tousle, tou'zl, *vt.* (tousling, tousled). To dishevel.
Tout, tout, *vi.* To ply or seek for customers. —*n.* One who plies for customers.
Tout-ensemble, tö-tạng-sạng-bl, *n.* The whole taken together; general effect.
Touter, tout'ėr, *n.* A tout.
Tow, tō, *vt.* To drag, as a boat, by a rope.—*n.* Act of towing; state of being towed; coarse part of flax or hemp.
Towage, tō'āj, *n.* Act of towing; price for towing.
Toward, Towards, tō'ėrd, tō'ėrdz, *prep.* In the direction of; regarding; in aid of; for; about.—*adv.* At hand; going on.
Toward, tō'wėrd, *a.* Pliable; docile; apt.
Towardly, tō'wėrd-li, *a.* Docile; tractable.
Towel, tou'el, *n.* A cloth for drying the skin after washing, or for domestic purposes.
Towelling, tou'el-ling, *n.* Cloth for towels.
Tower, tou'ėr, *n.* A lofty narrow building; a citadel; a fortress.—*vi.* To soar; to be lofty; to stand sublime.
Towering, tou'ėr-ing, *a.* Very high; extreme; violent.
Towery, tou'ėr-i, *a.* Having towers.
Towing-path, tō'ing-path, *n.* A path used in towing boats along a canal, &c.
Tow-line, tō'līn, *n.* A rope used in towing.
Town, toun, *n.* Any collection of houses larger than a village; a city; borough; inhabitants of a town; the metropolis.—*a.* Pertaining to a town.
Town-clerk, toun'klärk, *n.* An officer who acts as clerk to the council of a town.
Town-council, toun'koun-sil, *n.* The elective governing body in a town.
Town-councillor, toun'koun-sil-ėr, *n.* A member of a town-council.
Town-hall, toun'hạl, *n.* A building belonging to a town in which the town-council ordinarily hold their meetings.
Townsfolk, tounz'fōk, *n.pl.* Townspeople.
Township, toun'ship, *n.* Territory of a town; division of certain parishes.
Townsman, tounz'man, *n.* An inhabitant of a town; one of the same town.
Townspeople, tounz'pē-pl, *n.pl.* The inhabitants of a town.
Town-talk, toun'tạk, *n.* The common talk of the town; general topic.
Tow-rope, tō'rōp, *n.* A rope used in towing.
Toxic, Toxical, tok'sik, tok'sik-al, *a.* Pertaining to poisons; poisonous.
Toxicant, tok'si-kant, *n.* A poison of a stimulating, narcotic, or anæsthetic nature.
Toxicology, toks-i-kol'o-ji, *n.* That branch of medicine which treats of poisons and their antidotes.
Toxin, toks'in, *n.* A poisonous substance generated in an animal body.
Toxophilite, tok-sof'i-līt, *n.* A lover of archery.—*a.* Pertaining to archery.
Toy, toi, *n.* A plaything; a bauble; a trifle.—*vi.* To dally; to trifle.
Toyshop, toi'shop, *n.* A shop where toys are sold.
Trace, trās, *n.* A mark left by anything; footstep; vestige; track; one of the straps by which a carriage, &c., is drawn.—*vt.* (tracing, traced). To track out; to follow by marks left; to draw or copy with lines or marks.
Traceable, trās'a-bl, *a.* That may be traced.
Tracer bullet, trās'ėr bụl'et, *n.* One that leaves a trail of light marking its course.
Tracery, trās'ė-ri, *n.* A species of rich open work, seen in Gothic windows, &c.
Trachea, trā'kē-a, *n.* The wind-pipe.
Tracheotomy, trā-kē-ot'o-mi, *n.* The operation of cutting into the trachea, as in suffocation.
Tracing, trās'ing, *n.* Act of one who traces; copy of a design made by following its lines through a transparent medium.
Tracing-paper, trās'ing-pā-pėr, *n.* Transparent paper for making tracings of designs.
Track, trak, *n.* A footprint; rut made by a wheel; trace; beaten path; course.—*vt.* To trace; to follow step by step; to tow by a line from the shore.
Tracker, trak'ėr, *n.* One who hunts by following the track.
Trackless, trak'les, *a.* Having no track; untrodden; pathless.
Track-road, trak'rōd, *n.* A towing-path.
Tract, trakt, *n.* A region of indefinite extent; a short dissertation.
Tractable, trakt'a-bl, *a.* That may be easily managed; docile; manageable.
Tractably, trakt'a-bli, *adv.* In a tractable manner; with ready compliance.
Tractarian, trak-tā'ri-an, *n.* Applied to the writers of the '*Tracts* for the Times', a series of high church papers published at Oxford between 1833 and 1841.
Tractarianism, trak-tā'ri-an-izm, *n.* The doctrines or teaching of the tractarians.
Tractate, trak'tāt, *n.* A treatise; tract.
Traction, trak'shon, *n.* The act of drawing a body along a surface of land or water.

Traction-engine, trak'shon-en-jin, *n.* A locomotive for dragging heavy loads on roads.
Trade, trād, *n.* Employment; commerce; traffic; those engaged in any trade.—*a.* Pertaining to trade.—*vi.* (trading, traded). To traffic; to carry on commerce; to have dealings.—*vt.* To sell or exchange in commerce.
Trade-mark, trād'märk, *n.* A distinctive mark put by a manufacturer on his goods.
Trader, trād'ėr, *n.* One engaged in trade.
Tradesfolk, trādz'fōk, *n.pl.* Tradesmen.
Tradesman, trādz'man, *n.* One who practises a trade; a shopkeeper; an artisan.
Trades-people, trādz'pē-pl, *n.* Tradesmen.
Trades-union, trādz-ūn'yon, *n.* A combination of workmen in a trade to secure conditions most favourable for labour.
Trades-unionism, trādz-ūn'yon-izm, *n.* The principles or practices of trades-unions.
Trades-unionist, trādz-ūn'yon-ist, *n.* A member of a trades-union.
Trade-wind, trād'wind, *n.* A periodic wind blowing for six months in one direction.
Trading, trād'ing, *p.a.* Carrying on commerce; engaged in trade; venal.
Tradition, tra-di'shon, *n.* The handing down of opinions, stories, &c., from father to son, by oral communication; a statement so handed down.
Traditional, Traditionary, tra-di'shon-al, tra-di'shon-a-ri, *a.* Relating to or derived from tradition.
Traditionalism, tra-di'shon-al-izm, *n.* Adherence to or importance placed on tradition.
Traditionally, tra-di'shon-al-li, *adv.* In a traditional manner; by tradition.
Traditive, tra'dit-iv, *a.* Transmitted by tradition.
Traduce, tra-dūs', *vt.* (traducing, traduced). To calumniate; to vilify; to defame.
Traducer, tra-dūs'ėr, *n.* One that traduces; a slanderer; a calumniator.
Traducianism, tra-dū'si-an-izm, *n.* The doctrine that the souls of children as well as their bodies are begotten.
Traducible, tra-dūs'i-bl, *n.* Capable of being traduced.
Traffic, traf'ik, *n.* An interchange of commodities; commerce; goods or persons passing along a road, railway, &c.; dealings.—*vi.* (trafficking, trafficked). To trade; to deal; to trade meanly or mercenarily).
Trafficker, traf'ik-ėr, *n.* One who traffics.
Trafficless, traf'ik-les, *a.* Destitute of traffic.
Tragacanth, trag'a-kanth, *n.* A leguminous plant yielding a mucilaginous substance called gum-dragon.
Tragedian, tra-jē'di-an, *n.* A writer of tragedy; an actor of tragedy.
Trágedienne, tra-jē'di-en, *n.* A female actor of tragedy.
Tragedy, tra'je-di, *n.* A drama representing an important event generally having a fatal issue; a fatal and mournful event; a murderous or bloody deed.
Tragic, Tragical, tra'jik, tra'jik-al, *a.* Pertaining to tragedy; murderous; calamitous.
Tragically, tra'jik-al-li, *adv.* In a tragic manner.
Tragi-comedy, tra-ji-ko'me-di, *n.* A drama in which tragedy and comic scenes are blended.
Tragopan, trag'ō-pan, *n.* An Asiatic bird of the pheasant family with two fleshy horns on the head.
Trail, trāl, *n.* Something dragged behind; a train; the end of a field gun-carriage that rests on the ground in firing; a path; track followed by a hunter; the position of a rifle when carried horizontally at the full extent of the right arm.—*vt.* To draw behind or along the ground; to drag.—*vi.* To be dragged along a surface; to hang down loosely; to grow along the ground.
Trailer, trāl'ėr, *n.* One who trails; a plant which cannot grow upward without support; a carriage dragged by a motor vehicle; a series of excerpts advertising coming attractions at the cinema.
Trail-net, trāl'net, *n.* A net trailed behind a boat; a trawl-net.
Train, trān, *vt.* To draw; to entice; to rear and instruct; to drill; to bring into proper bodily condition; to shape; to bring to bear, as a gun.—*vi.* To undergo special drill.—*n.* A trail; that part of a gown which trails; tail; a series; course; retinue; line of carriages and an engine on a railway; line to conduct fire to a charge or mine.
Train-band, trān'band, *n.* A band or company of militia.
Train-bearer, trān'bār-ėr, *n.* One who holds up a train, as of a robe or gown of state.
Trained, trānd, *p.a.* Formed by training; exercised; instructed; skilled by practice.
Trainer, trān'ėr, *n.* One who prepares men or horses for races, &c.
Training, trān'ing, *n.* Act of one who trains; education; drill.
Training-school, trān'ing-sköl, *n.* A normal school.
Training-ship, trān'ing-ship, *n.* A ship to train lads for the sea.
Train-oil, trān'oil, *n.* Oil from the blubber or fat of whales.
Traipse, trāps, *vi.* (traipsing, traipsed). To gad about in an idle way.
Trait, trāt or trā, *n.* A stroke; touch; feature; characteristic; peculiarity.
Traitor, trā'tor, *n.* One who betrays his trust or allegiance; one guilty of treason.
Traitorous, trā'tor-us, *a.* Guilty of treason; treacherous; treasonable.
Traitress, trā'tres, *n.* A female traitor.
Trajectory, tra-jek'to-ri, *n.* The path described by a body, as a planet, projectile, &c.
Tram, tram, *n.* One of the rails or tracks of a tramway; a tram-car; a tramway; a kind of silk thread.
Trammel, tram'el, *n.* A net for birds or fishes; shackles for regulating the motions of a horse; whatever hinders or confines; an iron hook.—*vt.* (trammelling, trammelled). To impede; to shackle.
Tramontane, tra-mon'tān, *a.* Being beyond the mountains; foreign; barbarous.
Tramp, tramp, *vt.* and *i.* To tread under foot; to travel on foot.—*n.* A tread; sound made by the feet in walking; journey on foot; a strolling beggar; a cargo steamer which makes irregular and usually short voyages.
Trample, tram'pl, *vt.* (trampling, trampled). To tread on heavily; to tread down; to treat with pride or insult.—*vi.* To treat in contempt; to tread with force.
Tramp-pick, tramp'pik, *n.* A kind of iron pick or lever which the foot helps to drive into the ground.

Tram-road, tram'rōd, *n.* A track for wheels, made of flat stones or iron plates.
Tramway, tram'wā, *n.* A railway for passenger cars laid along a road or street.
Trance, trans, *n.* A state of insensibility; ecstasy; catalepsy.—*vt.* (trancing, tranced). To entrance; to enchant.
Tranquil, tran'kwil, *a.* Quiet; calm; undisturbed; peaceful.
Tranquillity, tran-kwil'i-ti, *n.* State of being tranquil; quietness; calmness; peace.
Tranquillize, tran'kwil-īz, *vt.* To render tranquil; to quiet; to compose.
Tranquilly, tran'kwil-li, *adv.* Quietly.
Transact, trans-akt', *vt.* and *i.* To carry through; to perform; to manage.
Transaction, trans-ak'shon, *n.* The doing of any business; affair; proceeding; *pl.* reports of proceedings of societies.
Transactor, trans-ak'tor, *n.* One who transacts.
Transalpine, trans-al'pīn, *a.* Being beyond the Alps.
Transatlantic, trans-at-lan'tik, *a.* Being beyond or crossing the Atlantic.
Transcend, trans-send', *vt.* To rise above; to surpass; to outgo; to excel; to exceed.
Transcendence, Transcendency, trans-send'-ens, trans-send'en-si, *n.* Transcendent state; superior excellence.
Transcendent, trans-send'ent, *a.* Supreme in excellence; transcending human experience.
Transcendental, trans-send-ent'al, *a.* Transcendent; transcending knowledge acquired by experience; abstrusely speculative.
Transcendentalism, trans-send-ent'al-izm, *n.* A system of philosophy which claims to go deeper than experience can.
Transcendently, trans-send'ent-li, *adv.* In a transcendent manner; supereminently.
Transcribe, tran-skrīb', *vt.* (transcribing, transcribed). To write over again or in the same words; to copy.
Transcript, tran'skript, *n.* That which is transcribed; a copy; an imitation.
Transcription, tran-skrip'shon, *n.* Act of transcribing; a copy; transcript.
Transept, tran'sept, *n.* The transverse portion of a church built in form of a cross.
Transfer, trans-fėr', *vt.* (transferring, transferred). To convey from one place or person to another; to make over.—*n.* trans'fėr. Act of transferring; removal of a thing from one place or person to another; something transferred.
Transferable, trans-fėr'a-bl or trans'fėr-a-bl, *a.* Capable of being transferred.
Transferee, trans-fėr-ē', *n.* The person to whom a transfer is made.
Transference, trans'fėr-ens, *n.* Act of transferring; passage of anything from one place to another.
Transferrer, trans-fėr'ėr, *n.* One who makes a transfer or conveyance.
Transfiguration, trans-fig'ūr-ā"shon, *n.* A change of form or figure; the supernatural change in the appearance of Christ on the mount; a Church feast held on the 6th of August, in commemoration of this change.
Transfigure, trans-fig'ūr, *vt.* To change in form or shape; to idealize.
Transfix, trans-fiks', *vt.* To pierce through; to cause to be immovable.
Transfluent, trans'flu̧-ent, *a.* Flowing or running across or through.
Transform, trans-form', *vt.* To change the form of; to change, as the natural disposition of.—*vi.* To be changed in form.
Transformation, trans-for-mā'shon, *n.* Act of transforming; an entire change in form, disposition, &c.
Transfuse, trans-fūz', *vt.* (transfusing, transfused). To transfer by pouring; to cause to pass from one to another.
Transfusion, trans-fū'zhon, *n.* Act of transfusing, as the blood of one animal into another.
Transgress, trans-gres', *vt.* To break or violate; to infringe.—*vi.* To do wrong; to sin.
Transgression, trans-gre'shon, *n.* Act of transgressing; a trespass; offence; crime.
Transgressor, trans-gres'or, *n.* One who transgresses; an offender; a criminal.
Tranship, tran-ship', *vt.* To convey or transfer from one ship to another.
Transhipment, tran-ship'ment, *n.* The act of transhipping.
Transience, Transiency, tran'si-ens, tran'si-en-si, *n.* State or quality of being transient; evanescence.
Transient, tran'si-ent, *a.* Passing quickly; fleeting; momentary; fugitive.
Transiently, tran'si-ent-li, *adv.* In a transient manner; not with continuance.
Transit, tran'sit, *n.* Act of passing; passage; passage of a heavenly body over the disc of a larger one.
Transition, tran-zi'shon, *n.* Passage from one place, state, or topic to another.—*a.* Pertaining to passage from one state, &c., to another.
Transitional, Transitionary, tran-zi'shon-al, tran-zi'shon-a-ri, *a.* Containing or denoting transition.
Transitive, tran'sit-iv, *a.* In *grammar,* taking an object after it, as a verb.
Transitively, tran'sit-iv-li, *adv.* In a transitive manner; with a grammatical object.
Transitory, tran'si-to-ri, *a.* Passing away; fleeting; transient.
Transit-trade, tran'sit-trād, *n.* The trade arising from the passage of goods through one country or place to another.
Translatable, trans-lāt'a-bl, *a.* Capable of being translated.
Translate, trans-lāt', *vt.* (translating, translated). To remove from one place to another; to transfer; to render into another language.
Translation, trans-lā'shon, *n.* Act of translating; removal; act of turning into another language; interpretation; a version.
Translator, trans-lāt'or, *n.* One who renders one language into another.
Transliterate, trans-lit'ėr-āt, *vt.* To write or spell in different characters intended to express the same sound.
Translucence, Translucency, trans-lū'sens, trans-lū'sens-i, *n.* Quality of being translucent.
Translucent, trans-lū'sent, *a.* Transmitting rays of light, but not so as to render objects distinctly visible; transparent; clear.
Translucid, trans-lū'sid, *a.* Translucent.
Translunar, Translunary, trans-lū'nėr, trans'lū-na-ri, *a.* Being beyond the moon.
Transmarine, trans-ma-rēn', *a.* Lying or being beyond the sea.
Transmigrate, trans'mi-grāt, *vi.* To pass from one country or body to another.

Transmigration, trans-mi-grā'shon, *n.* Act of transmigrating; the passing of a soul into another body after death.
Transmigratory, trans-mī'gra-to-ri, *a.* Passing from one place or state to another.
Transmissible, Transmittible, trans-mis'i-bl, trans-mit'i-bl, *a.* That may be transmitted.
Transmission, trans-mi'shon, *n.* Act of transmitting; transference; a passing through any body, as of light through glass.
Transmissive, trans-mis'iv, *a.* Transmitted; transmitting.
Transmit, trans-mit', *vt.* (transmitting, transmitted). To send from one person or place to another; to hand down; to allow to pass through.
Transmittal, Transmittance, trans-mit'al, trans-mit'ans, *n.* Transmission.
Transmogrify, trans-mog'ri-fī, *vt.* To transform; to change the appearance of.
Transmutable, trans-mūt'a-bl, *a.* Capable of being transmuted.
Transmutation, trans-mū-tā'shon, *n.* Act of transmuting; conversion into something different.
Transmute, trans-mūt', *vt.* (transmuting, transmuted). To change from one nature or substance into another.
Transoceanic, trans'ō-shē-an"ik, *a.* Beyond the ocean; crossing the ocean.
Transom, tran'sum, *n.* A strengthening horizontal beam; a cross-bar.
Transparence, trans-pā'rens, *n.* Transparency.
Transparency, trans-pā'ren-si, *n.* State or quality of being transparent; something transparent; a picture painted on transparent materials.
Transparent, trans-pā'rent, *a.* That can be seen through distinctly; not sufficient to hide underlying feelings.
Transparently, trans-pā'rent-li, *adv.* Clearly; so as to be seen through.
Transpicuous, trans-pik'ū-us, *a.* Transparent; pervious to the sight.
Transpierce, trans-pērs', *vt.* To pierce through; to penetrate.
Transpirable, trans-pīr'a-bl, *a.* Capable of being transpired.
Transpiration, trans-pi-rā'shon, *n.* Act or process of transpiring; exhalation.
Transpiratory, trans-pīr'a-to-ri, *a.* Pertaining to transpiration; exhaling.
Transpire, trans-pīr', *vt.* (transpiring, transpired). To emit through the pores of the skin; to send off in vapour.—*vi.* To exhale; to escape from secrecy; to become public.
Transplant, trans-plant', *vt.* To remove and plant in another place.
Transplantation, trans-plant-ā'shon, *n.* Act of transplanting; removal.
Transpontine, trans-pon'tīn, *a.* Situated beyond the bridge; across the bridge.
Transport, trans-pōrt', *vt.* To carry from one place to another; to carry into banishment; to carry away by violence of passion; to ravish with pleasure.—*n.* trans'pōrt. Transportation; a ship employed to carry soldiers, warlike stores, &c.; passion; ecstasy.
Transportable, trans-pōrt'a-bl, *a.* That may be transported.
Transportation, trans-pōrt-ā'shon, *n.* Act of transporting; banishment to a penal settlement; transmission; conveyance.
Transposable, trans-pōz'a-bl, *a.* Capable of being transposed.
Transposal, trans-pōz'al, *n.* Act of transposing; transposition.
Transpose, trans-pōz', *vt.* (transposing, transposed). To change the order of things by putting each in the other's place; to cause to change places.
Transposition, trans-pō-zi'shon, *n.* Act of transposing; state of being transposed; change of the order of words for effect.
Trans-ship, trans-ship', *vt.* To tranship.
Transubstantiate, tran-sub-stan'shi-āt, *vt.* To change to another substance.
Transubstantiation, tran-sub-stan'shi-ā"shon, *n.* Change into another substance; conversion of the bread and wine in the eucharist into the body and blood of Christ.
Transude, tran-sūd', *vi.* (transuding, transuded). To pass or ooze through the pores of a substance.
Transumptive, tran-sump'tiv, *a.* Transferred; metaphorical.
Transverberate, trans-vėr'bėr-āt, *vt.* To beat or strike through.
Transversal, trans-vėrs'al, *a.* Transverse; running or lying across.
Transverse, trans'vėrs or trans-vėrs', *a.* Lying or being across or in a cross direction.
Transversely, trans'vėrs-li or trans-vėrs'li, *adv.* In a transverse manner or direction.
Trap, trap, *n.* A contrivance for catching unawares; an ambush; a contrivance in drains to prevent effluvia rising; a carriage of any kind, on springs; a kind of movable ladder; an igneous rock.—*vt.* (trapping, trapped). To catch in a trap; to insnare; to adorn.—*vi.* To set traps for game.
Trapan, tra-pan', *vt.* To insnare.
Trap-door, trap'dōr, *n.* A door in a floor or roof, with which when shut it is flush.
Trape, trāp, *vi.* (traping, traped). To traipse.
Trapes, Traipse, trāps, *n.* A slattern; an idle sluttish woman.—*vi.* To gad about in an idle way.
Trapeze, tra-pēz', *n.* A sort of swing, consisting of a cross-bar suspended by cords, for gymnastic exercises.
Trapezium tra-pē'zi-um, *n.*; pl. **-ia** or **-iums.** A plane figure contained by four straight lines, two of them parallel; a bone of the wrist.
Trapezoid, tra'pē-zoid, *n.* A plane four-sided figure having no two sides parallel.
Trappean, Trappy, trap-ē'an, trap'i, *a.* Pertaining to the rock known as trap.
Trapper, trap'ėr, *n.* One who traps animals for their furs.
Trappings, trap'ingz, *n.pl.* Ornaments; dress; decorations; finery.
Trappist, trap'ist, *n.* A member of an ascetic order of the Roman Catholic Church.
Traps, traps, *n.pl.* Personal luggage.
Trash, trash, *n.* Loppings of trees; broken pieces; rubbish; refuse.—*vt.* To lop.
Trashy, trash'i, *a.* Worthless; useless.
Trass, tras, *n.* A volcanic production found in the Rhine valley, and used as a cement.
Traumatic, tra̤-mat'ik, *a.* Pertaining to wounds.—*n.* A medicine useful in the cure of wounds.
Travail, tra'vāl, *vi.* To labour; to toil; to suffer the pangs of childbirth.—*n.* Labour; severe toil; childbirth.

Trave, Travis, trāv, tra'vis, *n.* A cross beam; frame to confine a horse while shoeing.

Travel, tra'vel, *n.* Act of journeying; journey to a distant country; *pl.* account of occurrences during a journey.—*vi.* (travelling, travelled). To journey; to go to a distant country; to pass; to move.

Travelled, tra'veld, *p.a.* Having made many journeys; experienced from travelling.

Traveller, tra'vel-ėr, *n.* One who travels; one who travels from place to place to solicit orders for goods, &c.

Travelling, tra'vel-ing, *p.a.* Pertaining to, used in, or incurred by travel.

Traverse, tra'vėrs, *a.* Transverse.—*n.* Something that is transverse; something that thwarts; a denial.—*vt.* (traversing, traversed). To cross; to thwart; to cross in travelling; to deny.—*adv.* Athwart; crosswise.

Traverse-table, tra'vėrs-tā-bl, *n.* A table by means of which the dead-reckoning in navigation is worked out; a movable platform for shifting carriages, &c., from one line of rails to another.

Traversing-platform, tra'vėrs-ing-plat-form, *n.* A platform to support a gun and carriage, which can easily be turned round.

Travertin, tra'vėr-tin, *n.* A white limestone deposited from the water of springs holding carbonate of lime in solution.

Travesty, tra'ves-ti, *vt.* (travestying, travestied). To transform so as to have a ludicrous effect; to burlesque.—*n.* A burlesque treatment; parody.

Trawl, tral, *vi.* To fish with a trawl-net; to drag, as a net.—*n.* A trawl-net.

Trawler, tral'ėr, *n.* One who trawls; a fishing vessel which fishes with a trawl-net.

Trawling, tral'ing, *n.* The act of one who trawls; fishing with a trawl-net.

Trawl-net, tral'net, *n.* A long purse-shaped net for deep-sea fishing, dragged behind a vessel.

Tray, trā, *n.* A sort of waiter or salver, of wood, metal, &c., on which dishes and the like are presented.

Treacherous, trech'ėr-us, *a.* Guilty of treachery; faithless; traitorous; perfidious.

Treacherously, trech'ėr-us-li, *adv.* Traitorously; faithlessly; perfidiously.

Treachery, trech'ė-ri, *n.* Violation of allegiance or of faith; perfidy; treason.

Treacle, trē'kl, *n.* The uncrystallizable part of sugar obtained in refineries; molasses.

Tread, tred, *vi.* (pret. trod, pp. trod, trodden). To set the foot on the ground; to step; to walk with a measured step; to copulate, as fowls.—*vt.* To plant the foot on; to trample; to dance; to walk on in a formal manner; to copulate with, as a bird.—*n.* A step; gait; horizontal part of the step of a stair.

Treadle, Treddle, tred'l, *n.* The part of a loom or other machine moved by the foot.

Treadmill, tred'mil, *n.* A mill worked by persons or animals treading on movable steps.

Treadwheel, tred'whēl, *n.* A wheel with steps on its exterior surface, by treading on which the wheel is turned.

Treason, trē'zon, *n.* A betrayal; breach of allegiance; treachery; disloyalty.

Treasonable, trē'zon-a-bl, *a.* Pertaining to, consisting of, or involving treason.

Treasure, tre'zhūr, *n.* Wealth accumulated; great abundance; something very much valued.—*vt.* (treasuring, treasured). To lay up or collect; to prize.

Treasurer, tre'zhūr-ėr, *n.* One who has the charge of a treasury or funds.

Treasure-trove, tre'zhūr-trōv, *n.* Money or bullion found hidden, the owner of which is not known.

Treasury, tre'zhū-ri, *n.* A place where treasure is laid up; department of government which controls the revenue; a book containing much valuable material.

Treat, trēt, *vt.* To handle; to act towards; to discourse on; to entertain; to manage.—*vi.* To handle; to discourse; to negotiate.—*n.* An entertainment given as a compliment; an unusual gratification.

Treating, trēt'ing, *n.* Act of one who treats; bribing voters with meat or drink.

Treatise, trē'tiz, *n.* A written composition on some particular subject; a dissertation.

Treatment, trēt'ment, *n.* Act or manner of treating; management; usage.

Treaty, trē'ti, *n.* Negotiation; agreement between two or more nations.

Treble, tre'bl, *a.* Threefold; triple; in *music*, pertaining to the highest sounds.—*n.* The highest part in a concerted piece of music; a soprano.—*vt.* and *i.* (trebling, trebled). To make or become thrice as much.

Trebly, tre'bli, *adv.* Triply.

Tree, trē, *n.* A perennial plant having a woody trunk and branches; something resembling a tree; a cross; a wooden piece in machines, &c.—*vt.* (treeing, treed). To cause to take refuge in a tree.—*vi.* To take refuge in a tree.

Treenail, Trenail, trē'nāl, *n.* A long wooden pin, used to secure the planks of a ship's side, &c.

Trefoil, trē'foil, *n.* A three-leaved plant, as clover; an architectural ornament, consisting of three cusps.

Trek, trek, *vi.* (trekking, trekked). To travel by wagon.

Trellis, trel'is, *n.* A structure of cross-barred work or lattice-work.—*vt.* To furnish with a trellis; to form like a trellis.

Trematode, Trematoid, trem'a-tōd, trem'a-toid, *a.* A parasitic worm living in the intestines of animals.

Tremble, trem'bl, *vi.* (trembling, trembled). To shake involuntarily; to quiver; to vibrate.—*n.* An involuntary shaking; a tremor.

Trembling, trem'bling, *n.* Act or state of shaking involuntarily; a tremor.

Tremendous, trē-men'dus, *a.* Such as may cause trembling; terrible; extraordinary.

Tremendously, trē-men'dus-li, *adv.* In a tremendous manner; astoundingly.

Tremor, tre'mor, *n.* An involuntary trembling; a shivering; vibration.

Tremulous, tre'mū-lus, *a.* Trembling; shaking; quivering; vibratory.

Trench, trensh, *vt.* To dig a ditch in; to turn over and mix, as soil.—*vi.* To cut a trench or trenches; to encroach (with *on* or *upon*).—*n.* A long narrow excavation; a deep ditch cut for defence.

Trenchant, tren'shant, *a.* Cutting; keen; severe.

Trencher, trensh'ėr, *n.* A wooden plate on which meat may be carved; food; pleasures of the table.

Trencher-cap, trensh'ėr-kap, *n.* A cap surmounted by a square flat piece.
Trencher-man, trensh'ėr-man, *n.* A great eater.
Trench mortar, trensh mor'tär, *n.* A small portable mortar used for throwing bombs for short distances.
Trend, trend, *vi.* To extend in a particular direction.—*n.* Direction; tendency.
Trental, tren'tal, *n.* An office for the dead in the Roman Catholic service, consisting of thirty masses said on thirty successive days.
Trepan, trē-pan', *n.* A surgical saw for removing a portion of the skull.—*vt.* (trepanning, trepanned). To perforate with a trepan; to insnare.
Trepang, Tripang, trē-pang', *n.* The sea-slug found in eastern seas, and used as a food in China.
Trephine, tre-fēn', *n.* An improved form of the trepan.—*vt.* (trephining, trephined). To perforate with a trephine.
Trepidation, tre-pid-ā'shon, *n.* Confused alarm; perturbation; involuntary trembling.
Trespass, tres'pas, *vi.* To enter unlawfully upon the land of another; to do wrong; to offend.—*n.* An offence; a sin; wrong done by entering on the land of another.
Trespasser, tres'pas-ėr, *n.* One who trespasses; a wrong-doer; a sinner.
Tress, tres, *n.* A braid, lock, or curl of hair.
Tressel, tres'l. Same as *Trestle.*
Trestle, tres'l, *n.* A frame for supporting things; a frame with three or four legs attached to a horizontal piece.
Trestle-bridge, tres'l-brij, *n.* A bridge supported on trestles.
Tret, tret, *n.* An allowance to purchasers for waste.
Trews, tröz, *n.pl.* The tartan trousers of soldiers in Highland regiments.
Triable, trī'a-bl, *a.* That may be tried.
Triad, trī'ad, *n.* A union of three; a trinity.
Trial, trī'al, *n.* Act of trying; examination by a test; experience; probation; temptation; judicial examination.
Triangle, trī-ang'gl, *n.* A figure having three sides and angles.
Triangular, trī-ang'gū-lėr, *a.* Having three angles; having the form of a triangle.
Triarchy, trī'ärk-i, *n.* Government by three persons.
Trias, trī'as, *n.* In *geology*, the upper new red sandstone.
Triassic, trī-as'ik, *a.* Pertaining to the trias.
Tribal, trī'bal, *a.* Belonging to a tribe.
Tribalism, trī'bal-izm, *n.* The state of existence in separate tribes; tribal feeling.
Tribe, trīb, *n.* A division or class of people; a family or race; a class of animals or plants.
Tribesman, trībz'man, *n.* A member of a tribe.
Tribrach, trī'brak, *n.* A metrical foot of three short syllables.
Tribulation, tri-bū-lā'shon, *n.* Severe trouble or affliction; distress; trial; suffering.
Tribunal, trī-bū'nal, *n.* The seat of a judge; a court of justice.
Tribune, trī'būn, *n.* Among the ancient Romans, a magistrate chosen by the people, to protect them from the patricians; a platform; tribunal; throne of a bishop.
Tribuneship, Tribunate, trī'būn-ship, trī'būn-āt, *n.* The office of a tribune.
Tribunician, Tribunitial, trī-būn-i'shan, trī-būn-i'shal, *a.* Pertaining to tribunes.
Tributary, tri'bū-ta-ri, *a.* Paying tribute to another; subject; contributing.—*n.* One that pays tribute; a stream which falls into another.
Tribute, tri'būt, *n.* A sum paid by one prince or nation to another; personal contribution.
Trice, trīs, *n.* A very short time; an instant.—*vt.* (tricing, triced). To hoist by a rope.
Tricennial, trī-sen'ni-al, *a.* Belonging to the period of thirty years, or occurring once in that period.
Tricentenary, trī-sen'ten-a-ri, *n.* A period of three hundred years; the three hundredth anniversary.
Trichina, tri-kī'na, *n.*; pl. **-næ.** A minute nematoid worm, the larva of which causes disease in the flesh of mammals.
Trichiniasis, Trichinosis, trik-i-nī'a-sis, trik-i-nō'sis, *n.* The disease produced by trichinæ.
Trichord, trī'kord, *n.* A musical instrument with three strings.—*a.* Having three strings; having three strings for each note, as a piano.
Trichotomy, trī-kot'o-mi, *n.* Division into three parts.
Trick, trik, *n.* An artifice; a crafty device; fraud; a knack or art; a personal practice or habit; a prank; all the cards played in one round.—*vt.* To deceive; to impose on; to cheat; to draw in outline; to dress; to adorn (often with *out*).
Trickery, trik'ė-ri, *n.* Artifice; imposture.
Tricking, trik'ing, *n.* Dress; ornament.
Trickish, trik'ish, *a.* Full of tricks; artful.
Trickle, trik'l, *vi.* (trickling, trickled). To fall in drops; to flow gently.
Tricksome, trik'sum, *a.* Full of tricks.
Trickster, trik'stėr, *n.* One who practises tricks.
Tricksy, Tricksey, trik'si, *a.* Full of tricks and devices; artful; given to pranks.
Tricky, trik'i, *a.* Trickish; mischievous.
Tricolour, Tricolor, trī'kul-ėr, *n.* The national French banner of blue, white, and red divided vertically.
Tricostate, trī-kos'tāt, *a.* Having three ribs or ridges.
Tricuspid, Tricuspidate, trī-kus'pid, trī-kus'pi-dāt, *a.* Having three cusps or points.
Tricycle, trī'si-kl, *n.* A cycle with three wheels.
Trident, trī'dent, *n.* Any instrument of the form of a fork with three prongs.
Tried, trīd, *p.a.* Tested by trial or experience; staunch; true.
Triennial, trī-en'ni-al, *a.* Continuing three years; happening every three years.
Trier, trī'ėr, *n.* One who or that which tries; one who tries judicially.
Trifarious, trī-fā'ri-us, *a.* Arranged in three rows; threefold.
Trifid, trī'fid, *a.* Divided into three parts.
Trifle, trī'fl, *n.* Something of no moment or value; a kind of fancy confection.—*vi.* (trifling, trifled). To act with levity; to play or toy; to finger lightly.—*vt.* To waste.
Trifler, trīf'lėr, *n.* One who trifles or acts with levity.
Trifling, trīf'ling, *a.* Apt to trifle; frivolous; trivial; insignificant.

Trifoliate, trī-fō'li-āt, *a.* Having three leaves.
Triforium, trī-fō'ri-um, *n.*; pl. **-ia.** A gallery above the arches of the nave of a church.
Triform, trī'form, *a.* Having a triple form or shape.
Trifurcate, trī-fėr'kāt, *a.* Having three branches or forks.
Trig, trig, *vt.* (trigging, trigged). To stop or fasten, as a wheel.—*a.* Trim; spruce; neat.
Trigamist, tri'ga-mist, *n.* One who has three husbands or wives at the same time.
Trigamous, tri'ga-mus, *a.* Pertaining to trigamy.
Trigamy, tri'ga-mi, *n.* The state of having three husbands or wives at the same time.
Trigger, trig'ėr, *n.* The catch which, on being pressed, liberates the striker of a gun.
Triglyph, trī'glif, *n.* A block in Doric friezes, repeated at equal intervals, with three perpendicular channels.
Trigonometric, Trigonometrical, tri'gon-o-met"rik, tri'gon-o-met"rik-al, *a.* Pertaining to trigonometry.
Trigonometry, tri-gon-om'et-ri, *n.* The science of determining the sides and angles of triangles; a geometrical method of calculation.
Trigyn, trī'jin, *n.* A plant having three styles or pistils.
Trihedron, trī-hē'dron, *n.* A solid figure having three equal sides.
Trilateral, trī-lat'ėr-al, *a.* Having three sides, as a triangle.
Trilinear, trī-lin'ē-ėr, *a.* Consisting of three lines.
Trilingual, trī-ling'gwal, *a.* Consisting of three languages.
Triliteral, trī-li'tėr-al, *a.* Consisting of three letters.
Trilith, Trilithon, trī'lith, trī'lith-on, *n.* Three large blocks of stone placed together like door-posts and a lintel, and standing by themselves, as in sundry ancient monuments.
Trill, tril, *n.* A shake of the voice in singing; a quavering sound.—*vt.* To sing with a quavering voice; to sing sweetly or clearly.—*vi.* To sound with tremulous vibrations; to pipe; to trickle.
Trillion, tril'yon, *n.* The product of a million multiplied twice by itself.
Trilobate, trī-lō'bāt, *n.* Having three lobes.
Trilocular, tri-lok'ū-lėr, *a.* Three-celled.
Trilogy, tril'o-ji, *n.* A series of three connected dramas, each complete in itself.
Trim, trim, *vt.* (trimming, trimmed). To put in order; to embellish; to clip or pare; to adjust.—*vi.* To hold a middle course between parties.—*a.* Set in good order; properly adjusted; neat; tidy.—*n.* Condition; order; mood; dress.
Trimester, trī-mes'tėr, *n.* A term or period of three months.
Trimeter, trim'et-ėr, *n.* and *a.* A line of poetry consisting of three measures.
Trimly, trim'li, *adv.* Neatly; smartly.
Trimmer, trim'ėr, *n.* One who trims; a labourer who arranges the cargo of coal on a ship; one who fluctuates between parties.
Trimming, trim'ing, *n.* Act of one who trims; behaviour of one who fluctuates between parties; ornamental appendages; *pl.* accessories.
Trinal, trīn'al, *a.* Threefold; triple.
Trine, trīn, *a.* Threefold.—*n.* Position of planets distant from each other 120 degrees.
Tringle, tring'gl, *n.* A curtain-rod, or similar rod on which rings run.
Trinitarian, tri-ni-tā'ri-an, *a.* Pertaining to the Trinity.—*n.* One who believes in the Trinity.
Trinity, tri'ni-ti, *n.* A union of three in one; the union in one Godhead of the Father, Son, and Holy Spirit.
Trinket, tring'ket, *n.* A small ornament; a trifle.—*vi.* To intrigue; to traffic.
Trinketer, tring'ket-ėr, *n.* One who traffics; an intriguer.
Trinketry, tring'ket-ri, *n.* Ornaments of dress; trinkets.
Trinomial, trī-nō'mi-al, *a.* Consisting of three terms connected by the signs + or —.
Trio, trī'ō or trē'ō, *n.* Three united; musical composition for three voices or instruments; performers of a trio.
Triolet, trī'o-let or trē'o-let, *n.* A stanza of eight lines, the first being repeated as the fourth and seventh, and the second as the eighth.
Trip, trip, *vi.* (tripping, tripped). To run or step lightly; to skip; to stumble; to err.—*vt.* To cause to fall or stumble; to loose an anchor.—*n.* A stumble; a light short step; an excursion or jaunt; a mistake.
Tripang. *See* TREPANG.
Tripartite, trip'ar-tīt or trī-pärt'īt, *a.* Divided into three parts; made between three parties.
Tripe, trīp, *n.* The stomach of ruminating animals prepared for food.
Tripedal, trī'ped-al, *a.* Having three feet.
Tripersonal, trī-pėr'son-al, *a.* Consisting of three persons.
Tripery, trī'pėr-i, *n.* A place where tripe is prepared or sold.
Tripetalous, trī-pe'tal-us, *a.* Having three petals.
Trip-hammer, trip'ham-ėr, *n.* A large hammer used in forges; a tilt-hammer.
Triphthong, trif'thong or trip'thong, *n.* A union of three vowels in one syllable, as in *adieu.*
Triple, tri'pl, *a.* Threefold; treble.—*vt.* (tripling, tripled). To treble.
Triplet, trip'let, *n.* Three of a kind; three lines of poetry rhyming together; one of three children born at a birth.
Triplicate, tri'pli-kāt, *a.* Threefold.—*n.* A third thing corresponding to two others.
Triplication, tri-pli-kā'shon, *n.* The act of trebling.
Triplicity, tri-pli'si-ti, *n.* State of being threefold.
Triply, tri'pli, *adv.* In a triple manner.
Tripod, trī'pod, *n.* A three-footed pot, seat, or stand.
Tripos, trī'pos, *n.* A tripod; in Cambridge University, an examination for the B.A. degree with honours.
Tripper, trip'ėr, *n.* One who trips, trips up, or walks nimbly; one who takes a jaunt.
Tripping, trip'ing, *p.a.* Nimble; quick.
Triptych, trip'tik, *n.* A picture or carving in three compartments side by side; a treatise in three sections.
Trireme, trī'rēm, *n.* A galley or vessel with three ranks of oars on a side.
Trisect, trī-sekt', *vt.* To cut into three equal parts.

Trisection, trī-sek'shon, *n.* Act of trisecting; division of a thing into three equal parts.
Tristichous, tri'stik-us, *a.* In *botany*, arranged in three vertical rows.
Trisulcate, trī-sul'kāt, *a.* Having three furrows or grooves.
Trisyllabic, Trisyllabical, tri-sil-lab'ik, tri-sil-lab'ik-al, *a.* Consisting of three syllables.
Trisyllable, tri-sil'la-bl, *n.* A word consisting of three syllables.
Trite, trīt, *a.* Hackneyed; threadbare; stale.
Tritheism, trī'thē-izm, *n.* The opinion that the Father, Son, and Holy Spirit are three beings or gods.
Triton, trī'ton, *n.* A sea deity with fish-like lower extremities.
Triturable, tri'tū-ra-bl, *a.* Capable of being triturated.
Triturate, tri'tū-rāt, *vt.* (triturating, triturated). To rub or grind to a very fine powder.
Trituration, tri-tū-rā'shon, *n.* Act of triturating; that which is triturated.
Triumph, trī'umf, *n.* A magnificent procession in honour of a victorious Roman general; victory; achievement; joy for success.—*vi.* To rejoice for victory; to obtain victory; to exult insolently.
Triumphal, trī-umf'al, *a.* Pertaining to or used in a triumph.
Triumphant, trī-umf'ant, *a.* Feeling triumph; victorious; celebrating victory; expressing joy for success.
Triumphantly, trī-umf'ant-li, *adv.* In a triumphant manner; exultantly.
Triumvir, trī-um'vėr, *n.* One of three men united in office.
Triumvirate, trī-um'vėr-āt, *n.* A coalition of three men in office or authority.
Triune, trī'ūn, *n.* Three in one.
Trivalve, trī'valv, *n.* A shell, &c., with three valves.
Trivet, tri'vet, *n.* Anything supported by three feet; an iron frame whereon to place vessels before or over a fire.
Trivial, tri'vi-al, *a.* Common; commonplace; trifling; insignificant.
Triviality, tri-vi-al'i-ti, *n.* State or quality of being trivial; a trifle.
Trivially, tri'vi-al-li, *adv.* In a trivial or trifling manner; lightly; insignificantly.
Trocar, trō'kar, *n.* An instrument used in dropsy, &c., for drawing off the fluid.
Trochaic, trō-kā'ik, *a.* Pertaining to or consisting of trochees.
Trochar, trō'kar, *n.* Same as *Trocar.*
Troche, trōch or trosh, *n.* A small circular lozenge containing a drug.
Trochee, trō'kē, *n.* A metrical foot of two syllables, the first long and the second short.
Trod, Trodden. *See* TREAD.
Troglodyte, trō'glod-īt, *n.* A cave-dweller; one living in seclusion.
Trogon, trō'gon, *n.* A tropical bird with gorgeous plumage.
Trojan, trō'jan, *a.* Pertaining to ancient Troy. —*n.* An inhabitant of ancient Troy; a jolly fellow; a plucky determined fellow.
Troll, trōl, *vt.* To roll; to pass round; to sing in a full, jovial voice.—*vi.* To go round; to fish for pike by trolling.—*n.* A going round; a part-song; a reel on a fishing-rod; a dwarfish being in Scandinavian mythology, dwelling in caves and mounds.
Trolley, Trolly, trol'i, *n.* A kind of small truck; a small narrow cart.
Trolling, trōl'ing, *n.* Act of one who trolls; a method of rod-fishing for pike with a dead bait; trawling.
Trollop, trol'lop, *n.* A woman loosely dressed; a slattern; a drab.
Trombone, trom'bōn, *n.* A deep-toned instrument of the trumpet kind.
Tromp, tromp, *n.* A blowing-machine used in a process of smelting iron.
Troop, tröp, *n.* A collection of people; a company; a body of soldiers; *pl.* soldiers in general; a troupe.—*vi.* To collect in numbers; to march in a body.
Trooper, tröp'ėr, *n.* A horse-soldier.
Troop-ship, tröp'ship, *n.* A transport.
Tropæolum, trō-pē'o-lum, *n.* A trailing or climbing plant of the geranium family.
Trope, trōp, *n.* A word used figuratively; a figure of speech.
Trophied, trō'fid, *a.* Adorned with trophies.
Trophy, trō'fi, *n.* A memorial of some victory; an architectural ornament representing the stem of a tree, hung with military weapons.
Tropic, tro'pik, *n.* Either of two circles on the celestial sphere, limiting the sun's apparent annual path; either of two corresponding parallels of latitude including the torrid zone; *pl.* the regions between or near these.—*a.* Pertaining to the tropics.
Tropical, tro'pik-al, *a.* Pertaining to the tropics or to a trope.
Tropology, tro-pol'o-ji, *n.* Doctrine of tropes; employment of tropes.
Trot, trot, *vi.* (trotting, trotted). To run with small steps; to move fast.—*vt.* To cause to trot.—*n.* Pace of a horse more rapid than a walk.
Troth, trōth or troth, *n.* Truth; faith.
Trotter, trot'ėr, *n.* One who trots; a trotting horse; foot of an animal.
Troubadour, trö'ba-dör, *n.* One of a class of poets who flourished in S. Europe, especially in Provence, from the eleventh to the end of the thirteenth century.
Trouble, tru'bl, *vt.* (troubling, troubled). To disturb; to distress; to busy.—*n.* Distress; agitation; affliction; labour.
Troublesome, tru'bl-sum, *a.* Annoying; vexatious; burdensome; tiresome.
Troublous, tru'blus, *a.* Full of trouble or disorder; agitated; disquieting.
Trough, trof, *n.* A long vessel for holding water or food for animals; a depression between two waves.
Trounce, trouns, *vt.* (trouncing, trounced). To punish or to beat severely.
Troupe, tröp, *n.* A troop; a company of performers, as acrobats.
Trousering, trou'zėr-ing, *n.* Cloth for making trousers.
Trousers, trou'zėrz, *n.pl.* A garment for men, covering the lower part of the trunk and each leg separately.
Trousseau, trö-sō, *n.* The clothes and general outfit of a bride.
Trout, trout, *n.* A fresh-water fish of the salmon tribe.
Troutlet, Troutling, trout'let, trout'ling, *n.* A small trout.
Trouvère, trö'vār, *n.* One of a class of ancient poets of Northern France, who produced chiefly narrative poetry.

Trover, trō'vėr, *n.* The gaining possession of goods by finding them, or otherwise than by purchase.
Trow, trou or trō, *vi.* To believe; to suppose.
Trowel, trou'el, *n.* A hand-tool for lifting and dressing mortar and plaster, &c.; a gardener's tool.—*vt.* (trowelling, trowelled). To dress or form with a trowel.
Trowsers, trou'zėrz. *See* TROUSERS.
Troy, Troy-weight, troi, troi'wāt, *n.* A weight used for gold and silver, divided into 12 ounces, each of 20 pennyweights, each of 24 grains, so that a pound troy = 5760 grains.
Truancy, trö'an-si, *n.* Act of playing truant.
Truant, trö'ant, *n.* One who shirks duty; one who stays from school without leave.—*a.* Idle; wilfully absenting oneself.
Truce, trös, *n.* A temporary cessation of hostilities; armistice; short quiet.
Truck, truk, *vi.* and *t.* To barter.—*n.* Exchange of commodities; barter; payment of workmen's wages partly in goods; a small wheel; a barrow with two low wheels; an open railway wagon for goods; the cap at the end of a flagstaff or topmast.
Truckage, truk'āj, *n.* The practice of bartering; price for conveyance of goods on a truck.
Truckle, truk'l, *n.* A small wheel or castor. —*vt.* (truckling, truckled). To move on rollers; to trundle.—*vi.* To yield obsequiously; to submit.
Truckle-bed, truk'l-bed, *n.* A low bed that runs on wheels and may be pushed under another.
Truculence, Truculency, tru'kū-lens, tru'kū-len-si, *n.* Ferocity; fierceness.
Truculent, tru'kū-lent, *a.* Terrible of aspect; fierce; wild; savage; fell.
Trudge, truj, *vi.* (trudging, trudged). To walk with labour or fatigue; to walk heavily.
True, trö, *a.* Conformable to fact; truthful; genuine; constant; faithful; loyal; honest; exact; correct; right.
Trueblue, trö'blö, *n.* A person of inflexible honesty or stanchness.—*a.* Stanch; inflexible.
Trueborn, trö'born, *a.* Of genuine birth; having a right by birth to any title.
Truebred, trö'bred, *a.* Of a genuine breed or education.
Truehearted, trö'härt-ed, *a.* Being of a true or faithful heart; honest; sincere.
Truelove, trö'luv, *n.* One truly loved or loving; a lover; a sweetheart.
Truepenny, trö'pen-i, *n.* A familiar phrase for an honest fellow.
Truffle, truf'l, *n.* An edible fungus growing beneath the surface of the ground.
Truism, trö'izm, *n.* A self-evident truth.
Trull, trul, *n.* A strumpet; a trollop.
Truly, trö'li, *adv.* In a true manner; according to the truth; honestly; justly.
Trump, trump, *n.* A winning card; one of a suit for the time being superior to the others; a person upon whom one can depend; a trumpet.—*vt.* To take with a trump card; to concoct or forge.
Trumpery, trum'pė-ri, *n.* Worthless finery; trifles; trash.—*a.* Worthless.
Trumpet, trum'pet, *n.* A metal wind-instrument of music; one who praises.—*vt.* To publish by sound of trumpet; to noise abroad; to sound the praises of.
Trumpeter, trum'pet-ėr, *n.* One who sounds a trumpet; one who proclaims; a variety of the domestic pigeon.
Trumpet-major, trum'pet-mā-jėr, *n.* A head trumpeter in a band or regiment.
Truncate, trung'kāt, *vt.* To cut off; to lop.—*a.* Truncated.
Truncated, trung'kāt-ed, *p.a.* Cut short abruptly.
Truncation, trung-kā'shon, *n.* Act of truncating; state of being truncated.
Truncheon, trun'shon, *n.* A short staff; a club; a baton of authority; a tree the branches of which have been lopped off to produce rapid growth.—*vt.* To beat; to cudgel.
Trundle, trun'dl, *vi.* (trundling, trundled). To roll, as on little wheels or as a bowl.—*vt.* To cause to roll.—*n.* A little wheel; a small truck.
Trundle-bed, trun'dl-bed, *n.* A truckle-bed.
Trunk, trungk, *n.* The woody stem of a tree; body of an animal without the limbs; main body; chest for containing clothes, &c.; proboscis of an elephant, &c.; a long wooden tube.
Trunk-hose, trungk'hōz, *n.* A kind of short wide breeches gathered in above the knees.
Trunk-line, trungk'līn, *n.* The main line of a railway, canal, &c.
Trunnion, trun'yon, *n.* A knob on each side of a gun, &c., serving to support it.
Truss, trus, *n.* A bundle, as of hay or straw; a bandage used in cases of rupture; a combination of timbers constituting an unyielding frame.—*vt.* To put in a bundle; to make tight or fast; to skewer.
Trussing, trus'ing, *n.* The timbers, &c., which form a truss.
Trust, trust, *n.* Reliance; confidence; hope; credit; that which is intrusted; safe-keeping; care; management.—*vt.* To rely on; to believe; to intrust; to sell to upon credit; to be confident.—*vi.* To have reliance; to confide readily.—*a.* Held in trust.
Trustee, trus-tē', *n.* One appointed to hold property for the benefit of those entitled to it.
Trusteeship, trus-tē'ship, *n.* The office or functions of a trustee.
Trust-estate, trust'es-tāt, *n.* An estate held by a trustee or trustees.
Trustful, trust'fu̧l, *a.* Full of trust; reliant.
Trustily, trust'i-li, *adv.* Faithfully; honestly.
Trustingly, trust'ing-li, *adv.* In a trusting manner.
Trustless, trust'les, *a.* Devoid of trust; unfaithful; unreliable.
Trustworthy, trust'wėr-ᴛʜi, *a.* Worthy of trust or confidence; faithful; reliable.
Trusty, trust'i, *a.* That may be trusted; trustworthy; that will not fail; strong.
Truth, tröth, *n.* Conformity to fact or reality; integrity; constancy; exactness; reality; verified fact.
Truthful, tröth'fu̧l, *a.* Closely adhering to truth; veracious; correct; true.
Truthfully, tröth'fu̧l-li, *adv.* In a truthful manner.
Truthless, tröth'les, *a.* Wanting truth; untrue; faithless.
Try, trī, *vt.* (trying, tried). To test; to make trial of; to afflict; to examine judicially; to attempt.—*vi.* To endeavour.—*n.* The act of trying; a trial; experiment; in *Rugby football*, the right of trying to kick a goal, obtained

by carrying the ball behind the opponents' goal-line and touching it down.
Tryable, Triable, trī'a-bl, *a.* Capable of being tried; fit to be tried or stand trial.
Trying, trī'ing, *a.* Severe; afflictive.
Tryst, trist, *n.* An appointment to meet; a rendezvous.—*vi.* To agree to meet at any particular time or place.
Tsar, tsär. Same as *Czar.*
Tsetse, tset'se, *n.* An African fly whose bite is often fatal to horses and cattle.
T-square, tē'skwār, *n.* A sort of ruler shaped like a T, used in drawing straight or perpendicular lines.
Tub, tub, *n.* An open wooden vessel; a small cask; a clumsy boat; a vessel used as a bath.—*vt.* (tubbing, tubbed). To set in a tub.—*vi.* To make use of a bathing-tub.
Tuba, tū'ba, *n.* A large musical instrument of brass, low in pitch.
Tubbing, tub'ing, *n.* The lining of the shaft of a mine, &c., to prevent falling in of the sides.
Tubby, tub'i, *a.* Like a tub; tub-shaped.
Tube, tūb, *n.* A pipe; a hollow cylinder; the underground electric railway system in London.—*vt.* (tubing, tubed). To furnish with a tube.
Tuber, tū'bėr, *n.* An underground fleshy stem or root; a knot or swelling in any part.
Tubercle, tū'bėr-kl, *n.* A small tuber; a little projecting knob; a small mass of morbid matter developed in different parts of the body.
Tubercular, tū-bėr'kū-lėr, *a.* Pertaining to or affected with tubercles; consumptive. Also *Tuberculate, Tuberculose, Tuberculous.*
Tuberculosis, tū-bėr'kū-lō"sis, *n.* A disease due to the formation of tubercles; consumption.
Tuberose, Tuberous, tū'bėr-ōs, tū'bėr-us, *a.* Knobbed; having tubers; resembling a tuber.
Tubful, tub'fụl, *n.* Quantity a tub holds.
Tubing, tūb'ing, *n.* Act of providing with tubes; a length of tube; series of tubes.
Tubular, tūb'ū-lėr, *a.* Having the form of a tube; consisting of tubes. Also *Tubulose, Tubulous.*
Tubule, tūb'ūl, *n.* A small tube or pipe.
Tuck, tuk, *vt.* To gather into a narrower compass; to fold in or under.—*n.* A horizontal fold in a garment to shorten it.
Tucker, tuk'ėr, *n.* One who tucks; a sort of frill round the top of a woman's dress.
Tucket, tuk'et, *n.* A flourish on a trumpet; a fanfare.
Tuesday, tūz'dā, *n.* The third day of the week.
Tufa, Tuff, tū'fa, tuf, *n.* A porous vesicular rock or stone.
Tuft, tuft, *n.* A cluster; clump; head of flowers.—*vt.* To adorn with tufts.
Tuft-hunter, tuft'hunt-ėr, *n.* A hanger-on in the society of titled persons.
Tufty, tuft'i, *a.* Abounding with tufts; bushy.
Tug, tug, *vt.* and *i.* (tugging, tugged). To pull with effort; to haul along; to drag by steam-tug.—*n.* A drawing or pulling with force; a tug-boat.
Tug-boat, tug'bōt, *n.* A powerful steam-boat used for towing other vessels.
Tug-of-war, tug'ov-wạr, *n.* A trial of strength between two parties of men tugging at opposite ends of a rope.
Tuition, tū-i'shon, *n.* Guardianship; instruction; business of teaching.
Tulip, tū'lip, *n.* A plant of the lily family with richly-coloured flowers.
Tulle, tụl, *n.* A thin silk fabric.
Tumble, tum'bl, *vi.* (tumbling, tumbled). To roll about; to lose footing and fall.—*vt.* To throw about; to rumple; to overturn.—*n.* A fall; a somersault.
Tumbler, tum'blėr, *n.* One who tumbles; an acrobat; a large drinking-glass; a variety of pigeon.
Tumbrel, Tumbril, tum'brel, tum'bril, *n.* A dung-cart; a covered military cart for tools, ammunition, &c.; a kind of ducking-stool for scolds.
Tumefaction, tū-me-fak'shon, *n.* Act of swelling; a tumour; a swelling.
Tumefy, tū'me-fī, *vt.* To cause to swell.—*vi.* To swell; to rise in a tumour.
Tumid, tū'mid, *a.* Swollen; distended; pompous; inflated; bombastic.
Tumidity, tū-mid'i-ti, *n.* A swelled state.
Tumour, tū'mor, *n.* A morbid swelling in some part of the body.
Tumular, tū'mū-lėr, *a.* Pertaining to a tumulus.
Tumult, tū'mult, *n.* A commotion or disturbance; uproar; high excitement.
Tumultuary, tū-mul'tū-a-ri, *a.* Tumultuous.
Tumultuous, tū-mul'tū-us, *a.* Full of tumult; disorderly; turbulent; violent.
Tumulus, tū'mū-lus, *n.*; pl. **-li.** A mound or large heap of earth; a barrow.
Tun, tun, *n.* Any large cask; a vat; a measure of 4 hogsheads or 252 gallons.—*vt.* (tunning, tunned). To put into a tun.
Tunable, tūn'a-bl, *a.* That may be tuned.
Tundra, tun'dra, *n.* An immense stretch of flat boggy country in the arctic parts of Siberia.
Tune, tūn, *n.* A short air or melody; harmony; correct intonation; state of an instrument when it can give the proper sounds; frame of mind; mood.—*vt.* (tuning, tuned). To put into tune; to adapt.
Tuneful, tūn'fụl, *a.* Full of tune; melodious.
Tuneless, tūn'les, *a.* Destitute of tune; unmusical.
Tuner, tūn'ėr, *n.* One who tunes musical instruments.
Tungsten, tung'sten, *n.* A heavy metal of a grayish-white colour.
Tunic, tū'nik, *n.* A garment of various kinds; an ecclesiastical vestment worn over the alb; a full-dress military coat; a covering membrane; an integument.
Tuning, tūn'ing, *n.* The art or operation of bringing musical instruments into tune.
Tuning-fork, tūn'ing-fork, *n.* A steel two-pronged instrument for regulating the pitch of voices or instruments.
Tunnage, tun'āj. *See* TONNAGE.
Tunnel, tun'el, *n.* A tubular opening; a funnel; a subterranean passage cut through a hill, &c.—*vt.* (tunnelling, tunnelled). To form a tunnel through or under.
Tunny, tun'i, *n.* A large fish of the mackerel tribe.
Tup, tup, *n.* A ram.
Turanian, tū-rā'ni-an, *a.* Applied to the family of languages which includes the Turkish, Mongolian, &c.
Turban, tėr'ban, *n.* A head-dress worn by the Orientals, consisting of a fez and a sash

wound round it; a kind of head-dress worn by ladies.
Turbid, tėr'bid, *a.* Muddy; having the sediment disturbed; not clear.
Turbidity, tėr-bid'i-ti, *n.* State of being turbid; muddiness.
Turbidly, tėr'bid-li, *adv.* Muddily.
Turbinate, tėr'bi-nāt, *a.* Shaped like a whipping-top; conical; spiral.
Turbine, tėr'bīn, *n.* A kind of water-wheel, usually horizontal, made to revolve under the influence of pressure derived from a fall of water; a similar contrivance driven by steam.
Turbot, tėr'bot, *n.* A species of large flatfish.
Turbulence, Turbulency, tėr'bū-lens, tėr'bū-len-si, *n.* State of being turbulent; tumult; confusion; riotous behaviour.
Turbulent, tėr'bū-lent, *a.* Being in violent commotion; refractory; disorderly.
Tureen, tu-rēn', *n.* A large and deep dish for holding soup at table.
Turf, tėrf, *n.* The grassy layer on the surface of the ground; a sod.—**The turf,** the racecourse; the business of horse-racing.—*vt.* To cover with turf or sod.
Turfen, tėrt'n, *a.* Made of turf; covered with turf.
Turfy, tėrf'i, *a.* Abounding with turf; like turf; formed of turf; pertaining to the turf.
Turgent, tėr'jent, *a.* Swelling; turgid.
Turgescence, tėr-jes'ens, *n.* State of becoming turgid; bombast.
Turgescent, tėr-jes'ent, *a.* Swelling.
Turgid, tėr'jid, *a.* Swelling; swollen; bloated; inflated; bombastic.
Turgidity, tėr-jid'i-ti, *n.* State of being turgid; bombast; inflation of style.
Turk, tėrk, *n.* A member of the ruling race of Turkey; a tyrannical man.
Turkey, tėr'ki, *n.* A large gallinaceous fowl.
Turkey-red, tėr'ki-red, *n.* A brilliant and durable red dye on cotton cloth.
Turkey-stone, Turkey-hone, tėr'ki-stōn, tėr'ki-hōn, *n.* A fine-grained siliceous stone used for sharpening instruments.
Turkish, tėr'kish, *a.* Pertaining to Turkey, or to the Turks, or to their language.—*n.* The language spoken by the Turks.—**Turkish bath,** *n.* A hot-air or steam bath, inducing copious perspiration, followed by shampooing and massage, &c.
Turmeric, tėr'mer-ik, *n.* An E. Indian plant of the ginger family yielding a condiment, a yellow dye, and a test for alkalies.
Turmoil, tėr'moil, *n.* Disturbance; trouble; disquiet.—*vt.* To harass.
Turn, tėrn, *vt.* To cause to move round; to shape by a lathe; to direct; to alter in course; to blunt; to reverse; to change.—*vi.* To revolve; to depend; to change position or course; to return; to have recourse; to become; to become sour; to reel; to become nauseated; to result.—*n.* Act of turning; a revolution; a bend; a short walk; an alteration of course; occasion; occasional act of kindness or malice; purpose; character; short spell, as of work; nervous shock.
Turn-coat, tėrn'kōt, *n.* One who meanly forsakes his party or principles.
Turn-cock, tėrn'kok, *n.* A man connected with a public water-supply who turns on water from the mains, regulates fire-plugs, &c.
Turner, tėrn'ėr, *n.* One who turns; one who forms things with a lathe.
Turnery, tėrn'ė-ri, *n.* The art of forming things by the lathe; things made in the lathe.
Turning, tėrn'ing, *n.* A turn; bend; place where a road diverges from another; art or operation of shaping articles in a lathe.
Turning-point, tėrn'ing-point, *n.* The point on which or where a thing turns; the point at which a deciding change takes place.
Turnip, tėr'nip, *n.* A plant of the cabbage genus, cultivated for its bulbous esculent root.
Turnkey, tėrn'kē, *n.* A person who has charge of the keys of a prison.
Turn-out, tėrn'out, *n.* A coming forth; persons who have come out on some particular occasion; an equipage; the net quantity of produce yielded.
Turn-over, tėrn'ō-vėr, *n.* The amount of money turned over or drawn in a business.
Turnpike, tėrnpīk, *n.* A turnstile; a toll-bar or toll-gate.
Turnsole, Turnsol, tėrn'sōl, *n.* A plant whose flower turns toward the sun.
Turnstile, tėrn'stīl, *n.* A post at some passage surmounted by horizontal arms which move as a person pushes through.
Turn-table, tėrn'tā-bl, *n.* A revolving platform for reversing engines on a railway, or for shifting them from one line of rails to another.
Turpentine, tėr'pen-tīn, *n.* A resinous substance flowing from trees, as the pine, larch, fir, &c.; the oil distilled from this.
Turpitude, tėr-pi-tūd, *n.* Inherent baseness or vileness; moral depravity.
Turps, tėrps, *n.* The oil distilled from the resinous substance of pine-trees, &c.; oil or spirit of turpentine.
Turquoise, tėr'koiz, *n.* A greenish-blue or blue opaque precious stone.
Turret, tu'ret, *n.* A little tower on a larger building; a strong cylindrical iron structure on an iron-clad.
Turreted, tu'ret-ed, *a.* Furnished with turrets; formed like a tower.
Turret-ship, tu'ret-ship, *n.* A man-of-war with one or more rotating armoured turrets containing heavy guns.
Turtle, tėr'tl, *n.* A species of small pigeon; the sea-tortoise.
Turtle-dove, tėr'tl-duv, *n.* The European turtle or pigeon.
Tuscan, tus'kan, *a.* Pertaining to Tuscany in Italy; designating the unornamented, unfluted order of architecture.—*n.* An inhabitant of Tuscany; the Tuscan order; the Tuscan dialect of Italian.
Tush, tush, an *exclamation* indicating impatience or contempt.—*n.* A tusk; the canine tooth of a horse.
Tusk, tusk, *n.* A long prominent tooth of certain animals, as the elephant.
Tusked, Tusky, tuskt, tusk'i, *a.* Furnished with tusks.
Tusker, tusk'ėr, *n.* An elephant that has its tusks developed.
Tussle, tus'l, *n.* A struggle; scuffle.
Tussock, tus'ok, *n.* A clump, tuft, or small hillock of growing grass.
Tut, tut, *exclam.* Synonymous with *tush.*
Tutelage, tū'tel-āj, *n.* Guardianship; protection; state of being under a guardian.

Tutelar, Tutelary, tū'tel-ėr, tū'tel-a-ri, *a.* Guardian; protecting.
Tutor, tū'tor, *n.* A guardian; a private instructor; a fellow of an English college who superintends the studies of undergraduates.—*vt.* To instruct.
Tutorage, tū'tor-āj, *n.* Guardianship.
Tutoress, tū'tor-es, *n.* A female tutor.
Tutorial, tū-tō'ri-al, *a.* Belonging to or exercised by a tutor or instructor.
Tuyere, twi-yār' or tu-yār', *n.* The nozzle or the pipe that introduces the blast into a blast-furnace.
Twaddle, twod'l, *vi.* (twaddling, twaddled). To prate; to chatter; to prose.—*n.* Empty, silly talk; gabble.
Twaddler, twod'lėr, *n.* One who twaddles.
Twaddly, twod'li, *a.* Consisting of twaddle.
Twain, twān, *a.* Two.—*n.* A pair.
Twang, twang, *vi.* To make the sound of a string which is stretched and suddenly pulled.—*vt.* To make to sound sharply.—*n.* A sharp vibrating sound; a nasal sound.
Twangle, twang'gl, *vi.* To twang lightly.
Twank, twangk, *n.* A sharp twanging sound.
'Twas, twoz, a contraction of *It was.*
Tweak, twēk, *vt.* To twitch; to pinch and pull suddenly.—*n.* A sharp pinch or jerk.
Tweed, twēd, *n.* A twilled woollen fabric made in mixed colours.
Tweezers, twē'zėrz, *n.pl.* Small pincers to pluck out hairs, &c.; small forceps.
Twelfth, twelfth, *a.* The second after the tenth.—*n.* One of twelve equal parts.
Twelfth-day, twelfth'dā, *n.* The twelfth day after Christmas; festival of the Epiphany.
Twelfth-night, twelfth'nīt, *n.* The evening of the festival of the Epiphany.
Twelve, twelv, *a.* and *n.* Ten and two.
Twelve-month, twelv'munth, *n.* A year.
Twelve-penny, twelv'pen-i, *a.* Sold for or costing a shilling.
Twentieth, twen'ti-eth, *a.* The ordinal of twenty.—*n.* One of twenty equal parts.
Twenty, twen'ti, *a.* and *n.* Two tens, or twice ten.
Twenty-fold, twen'ti-fōld, *a.* Twenty times as many.
Twibill, twī'bil, *n.* A kind of double axe or mattock.
Twice, twīs, *adv.* Two times; doubly.
Twiddle, twid'l, *vt.* and *i.* (twiddling, twiddled). To twirl in a small way; to fiddle with.
Twig, twig, *n.* A small shoot or branch.—*vt.* and *i.* (twigging, twigged). To observe; to understand.
Twiggy, twig'i, *a.* Abounding with twigs.
Twilight, twī'līt, *n.* The faint light of the sun reflected after sunset and before sunrise; dubious view or condition.—*a.* Faint; seen or done by twilight.
Twill, twil, *vt.* To weave so as to produce a kind of diagonal ribbed appearance.—*n.* A textile fabric with a kind of diagonal ribbed surface; surface of this kind.
Twin, twin, *n.* One of two born together; one of a pair or couple.—*a.* Being one of two born at a birth; very similar; two-fold.
Twine, twīn, *n.* A strong thread composed of two or three strands; a twist.—*vt.* and *i.* (twining, twined). To twist; to weave; to coil; to wrap closely about.
Twinge, twinj, *vt.* and *i.* (twinging, twinged). To affect with or have a sharp, sudden pain.—*n.* A sudden, sharp, darting pain.
Twinkle, twingk'l, *vi.* (twinkling, twinkled). To sparkle; to shine with a quivering light.—*n.* A gleam or sparkle.
Twinkling, twingk'ling, *n.* A quick movement of the eye; a wink; an instant; the scintillation of the stars.
Twinling, twin'ling, *n.* A twin lamb.
Twin-screw, twin'skrö, *n.* A steam-vessel fitted with two propellers on separate shafts.
Twirl, twėrl, *vt.* and *i.* To turn round with rapidity; to spin.—*n.* A rapid whirl.
Twist, twist, *n.* Something twined, as a thread, &c.; roll of tobacco; a spiral; contortion; mental or moral bent.—*vt.* and *i.* To form into a cord; to twine; to contort; to insinuate; to pervert.
Twit, twit, *vt.* (twitting, twitted). To reproach; to taunt; to upbraid.
Twitch, twich, *vt.* To pull with a sudden jerk; to tug.—*vi.* To be suddenly contracted.—*n.* A sudden pull; short spasmodic contraction of a muscle.
Twitter, twit'ėr, *vi.* To utter small, tremulous notes, as birds; to chirp.—*n.* A chirp or continued chirping.
'Twixt, twikst, a contraction of *betwixt.*
Two, tö, *a.* and *n.* One and one together.
Two-faced, tö'fāst, *a.* Having two faces; insincere; given to double-dealing.
Two-fold, tö'fōld, *a.* Double.—*adv.* Doubly; in a double degree.
Two-handed, tö'hand-ed, *a.* Having two hands; used or wielded by both hands.
Twopence, tup'ens, *n.* Two pennies; a small silver coin formerly current.
Twopenny, tup'en-i, *a.* Of the value of twopence; of little worth; insignificant.
Tymbal, tim'bal, *n.* A kettle-drum.
Tympanum, tim'pa-num, *n.*; pl. **-na.** The drum of the ear.
Type, tīp, *n.* A distinguishing mark; emblem; symbol; ideal representative; model; letter used in printing; such letters collectively.
Typescript, tīp'skript, *n.* Matter produced by a type-writer.
Type-setter, tīp'set-ėr, *n.* One who sets up type; a compositor; a type-setting machine.
Type-writer, tīp'rīt-ėr, *n.* A machine used as a substitute for the pen, producing letters by inked types.
Typhoid, tī'foid, *n.* A fever characterized by abdominal pains and diarrhœa; enteric fever.
Typhoon, tī-fön', *n.* A violent hurricane on the coasts of China and Japan.
Typhous, tī'fus, *a.* Relating to typhus.
Typhus, tī'fus, *n.* A contagious or epidemic fever characterized by a deep livid eruption.
Typical, tip'ik-al, *a.* Pertaining to a type; emblematic; symbolic; representative.
Typically, tip'ik-al-li, *adv.* In a typical manner; by way of image; symbolically.
Typify, tip'i-fī, *vt.* To serve as a type of; to represent; to exemplify.
Typographic, Typographical, tī-po-graf'ik, tī-po-graf'ik-al, *a.* Pertaining to typography or printing.
Typography, tī-pog'ra-fi, *n.* The art of printing; style of printing.
Typology, tī-pol'o-ji, *n.* A discourse on types; the doctrine of types in Scripture.

Tyrannic, Tyrannical, tī-ran'ik, tī-ran'ik-al, *a.* Pertaining to a tyrant; despotic; cruel.
Tyrannize, ti'ran-īz, *vi.* To act the tyrant; to rule with oppressive severity.
Tyrannous, ti'ran-us, *a.* Tyrannical; unjustly severe; oppressive.
Tyranny, ti'ran-i, *n.* Rule of a tyrant; despotic exercise of power; oppression.
Tyrant, tī'rant, *n.* A despot; a cruel sovereign or master; an oppressor.
Tyre, tīr, *n* A ring round the circumference of a wheel; a tire.
Tyrian, ti'ri-an, *a.* Pertaining to Tyre, the ancient Phœnician city; of a purple colour.
Tyro, Tiro, tī'rō, *n.*; pl. **-os.** A beginner; a raw hand; a novice.
Tyrolese, ti' or tī'rol-ēz, *a.* Belonging to the Tyrol.—*n.* A native or natives of the Tyrol.
Tzar, Tzarina, tsär, tsä-rē'na. Same as *Czar, Czarina.*

U

Ubiety, ū-bī'e-ti, *n.* The state of being somewhere.
Ubiquitous, ū-bi'kwi-tus, *a.* Existing or being everywhere; omnipresent.
Ubiquity, ū-bi'kwi-ti, *n.* Existence everywhere at the same time; omnipresence.
U-boat, ū'bōt, *n.* A German submarine.
Udder, ud'ėr, *n.* The glandular organ of cows, &c., in which the milk is produced.
Udometer, ū-dom'et-ėr, *n.* A rain-gauge.
Ugh, u̦, an *exclamation* expressing horror or recoil, usually accompanied by a shudder.
Ugly, ug'li, *a.* Repulsive; disagreeable in appearance; hateful; ill-omened.
Uhlan, Ulan, ö'lan, *n.* A light cavalry soldier.
Ukase, ū-kās', *n.* An edict of the Russian government.
Ukulele, ū'ku̦-lā''lē, *n.* A small Hawaiian guitar.
Ulcer, ul'sėr, *n.* A sore that discharges pus.
Ulcerate, ul'sėr-āt, *vt.* To affect with an ulcer.—*vi.* To become ulcerous.
Ulceration, ul-sėr-ā'shon, *n.* The process of ulcerating; an ulcer.
Ulcerous, ul'sėr-us, *a.* Having the nature of an ulcer; affected with ulcers.
Uliginous, ū-li'ji-nus, *a.* Oozy; slimy.
Ullage, ul'āj, *n.* The quantity that a cask wants of being full.
Ulna, ul'na, *n.* The larger of the two bones of the forearm.
Ulster, ul'stėr, *n.* A long loose overcoat.
Ulterior, ul-tē'ri-or, *a.* Being beyond or on the farther side; more remote; distant; not avowed; reserved.
Ultimate, ul'ti-māt, *a.* Farthest; last or final; extreme; arrived at as a final result.
Ultimately, ul'ti-māt-li, *adv.* As an ultimate result; finally; at last.
Ultimatum, ul-ti-mā'tum, *n.*; pl. **-ta** or **-tums.** The last offer; a final proposition which being rejected may be followed by war.
Ultimo, ul'ti-mō, *a.* The last (month): usually contracted to *ult.*
Ultra, ul'tra, *prefix, a.* Beyond due limit; extreme.—*n.* An ultraist.
Ultraist, ul'tra-ist, *n.* One who advocates extreme measures; an extremist.
Ultramarine, ul'tra-ma-rēn'', *a.* Being beyond the sea.—*n.* A beautiful and durable sky-blue.
Ultramontane, ul-tra-mon'tān, *a.* Beyond the mountains.—*n.* One who belongs to the Italian party in the Church of Rome.
Ultramontanism, ul-tra-mon'tān-izm, *n.* The views of that party (the Italian) who exalt the power and influence of the pope.
Ultramundane, ul-tra-mun'dān, *a.* Being beyond the world.
Ultra-violet, ul'tra-vī''ō-let, *a.* Of the part of the spectrum beyond the violet end of the visible spectrum.
Ultroneous, ul-trō'nē-us, *a.* Spontaneous.
Ululate, ul'ū-lāt, *vi.* To howl, as a dog.
Umbel, um'bel, *n.* That mode of inflorescence which consists of a number of flower-stalks spreading from a common centre, each bearing a single flower.
Umbellate, um'bel-āt, *a.* Bearing umbels; having the form of an umbel.
Umbellifer, um-bel'i-fėr, *n.* An umbelliferous plant.
Umbelliferous, um-bel-lif'ėr-us, *a.* Producing or bearing umbels.
Umber, um'bėr, *n.* A soft earthy pigment of an olive-brown colour in its raw state, but redder when burnt.
Umbilical, Umbilic, um-bil'ik-al, um-bil'ik, *a.* Pertaining to the navel.
Umbilicus, um-bi-lī'kus, *n.* The navel.
Umbles, um'blz, *n.pl.* The humbles of a deer.
Umbo, um'bō, *n.* The boss of a shield; a boss or knob.
Umbra, um'bra, *n.* The total shadow of the earth or moon in an eclipse.
Umbrage, um'brāj, *n.* Shade; obscurity; jealousy; offence; resentment.
Umbrageous, um-brā'jus, *a.* Shady.
Umbrella, um-brel'la, *n.* A portable shade which opens and folds, for sheltering the person from the sun or rain.
Umlaut, u̦m'lout, *n.* The change of a vowel in one syllable through the influence of a different vowel in the syllable immediately following.
Umpirage, um'pīr-āj, *n.* The post or action of an umpire; arbitration.
Umpire, um'pīr, *n.* A person to whose decision a dispute is referred; a judge, arbiter, or referee.
Unable, un-ā'bl, *a.* Not able; not having sufficient ability; not equal for some task.
Unacceptable, un-ak-sept'a-bl, *a.* Not acceptable or pleasing; unwelcome.
Unaccommodating, un-ak-kom'mō-dāt-ing, *a.* Not ready to oblige; uncompliant.
Unaccomplished, un-ak-kom'plisht, *a.* Not performed completely; not having accomplishments.
Unaccountable, un-ak-kount'a-bl, *a.* Not to be accounted for; not responsible.
Unaccustomed, un-ak-kus'tumd, *a.* Not accustomed; not habituated; unusual.
Unacknowledged, un-ak-nol'ejd, *a.* Not acknowledged; not recognized or owned.
Unacquainted, un-ak-kwānt'ed, *a.* Not acquainted; not having familiar knowledge.
Unadorned, un-a-dornd', *a.* Not adorned; not embellished.
Unadvisable, un-ad-vīz'a-bl, *a.* Not advisable; not expedient; not prudent.
Unadvised, un-ad-vīzd', *a.* Not advised; not prudent; not discreet; rash.

Unadvisedly, un-ad-vīz'ed-li, *adv.* Imprudently; indiscreetly; rashly.
Unaffected, un-af-fekt'ed, *a.* Not affected; natural; simple; sincere; not moved.
Unaided, un-ād'ed, *a.* Without aid.
Unalloyed, un-al-loid', *a.* Not alloyed; entire; perfect.
Unalterable, un-al'tėr-a-bl, *a.* Not alterable; unchangeable; immutable.
Unamiable, un-ā'mi-a-bl, *a.* Not amiable; not adapted to gain affection.
Unanimity, ū-na-ni'mi-ti, *n.* State of being unanimous; perfect concord.
Unanimous, ū-nan'i-mus, *a.* Being of one mind; agreeing in determination; formed by unanimity.
Unanswerable, un-an'sėr-a-bl, *a.* Not to be satisfactorily answered; irrefutable.
Unappealable, un-ap-pēl'a-bl, *a.* Not appealable; admitting no appeal; that cannot be carried to a higher court by appeal.
Unappeasable, un-ap-pēz'a-bl, *a.* Not to be appeased or pacified; not placable.
Unappreciated, un-ap-prē'shi-āt-ed, *a.* Not duly estimated or valued.
Unapproachable, un-ap-prōch'a-bl, *a.* That cannot be approached; inaccessible.
Unappropriate, un-ap-prō'pri-āt, *a.* Not appropriate; inappropriate.
Unappropriated, un-ap-prō'pri-āt-ed, *a.* Not appropriated; not applied to a specific object.
Unapt, un-apt', *a.* Not apt; dull; unfit.
Unarmed, un-ärmd', *a.* Not having arms or armour; not equipped.
Unasked, un-askt', *a.* Not asked; unsolicited.
Unaspiring, un-as-pīr'ing, *a.* Not ambitious.
Unassailable, un-as-sāl'a-bl, *a.* Not assailable; that cannot be assaulted.
Unassuming, un-as-sūm'ing, *a.* Not assuming; retiring; modest.
Unassured, un-a-shörd', *a.* Not confident; not to be trusted; not insured.
Unattended, un-at-tend'ed, *a.* Having no attendants; not medically attended.
Unattractive, un-at-trakt'iv, *a.* Not attractive.
Unauthorized, un-a'thor-īzd, *a.* Not authorized; not warranted.
Unavailable, un-a-vāl'a-bl, *a.* Not available; vain; useless.
Unavailing, un-a-vāl'ing, *a.* Of no avail; ineffectual; useless.
Unavoidable, un-a-void'a-bl, *a.* Not to be shunned; inevitable.
Unaware, un-a-wār', *pred.a.* or *adv.* Not aware; unconscious; inattentive.
Unawares, un-a-wārz', *adv.* Unexpectedly; inadvertently; unconsciously.
Unbar, un-bär', *vt.* To unfasten; to open.
Unbearable, un-bār'a-bl, *a.* Not to be endured; intolerable.
Unbecoming, un-bē-kum'ing, *a.* Not becoming; improper.
Unbefitting, un-bē-fit'ing, *a.* Unsuitable.
Unbegot, Unbegotten, un-bē-got', un-bē-got'n, *a.* Not begotten; not generated.
Unbelief, un-bē-lēf', *n.* Incredulity; infidelity; disbelief of the gospel.
Unbeliever, un-bē-lēv'ėr, *n.* One who does not believe; an infidel.
Unbelieving, un-bē-lēv'ing, *a.* Not believing; incredulous; infidel.
Unbend, un-bend', *vi.* To become relaxed or not bent; to give up stiffness of manner.—*vt.* To free from bend or flexure; to relax.
Unbiased, Unbiassed, un-bī'ast, *a.* Free from any bias or prejudice; impartial.
Unbid, Unbidden, un-bid', un-bid'n, *a.* Not bid; spontaneous; uninvited.
Unbind, un-bīnd', *vt.* To untie; to loose.
Unblushing, un-blush'ing, *a.* Not blushing; shameless; impudent.
Unbolt, un-bōlt', *vt.* To remove a bolt from; to unbar.
Unbolted, un-bōlt'ed, *a.* Unsifted; not having the bran separated by a bolter.
Unbosom, un-bö'zum, *vt.* To open the bosom of; to reveal in confidence.
Unbound, un-bound', *a.* Not bound; loose; not under obligation.
Unbounded, un-bound'ed, *a.* Having no bound or limit; infinite; unrestrained.
Unbridled, un-brī'dld, *a.* Unrestrained.
Unbroken, un-brōk'n, *a.* Not broken; not tamed; not interrupted.
Unburden, Unburthen, un-bėr'dn, un-bėr'THn, *vt.* To rid of a load or burden.
Unburned, Unburnt, un-bėrnd', un-bėrnt', *a.* Not burnt, scorched, or baked.
Unbutton, un-but'n, *vt.* To undo the buttons of.
Uncalled, un-kald', *a.* Not called; not summoned; not invited.
Uncanny, un-kan'i, *a.* Not canny; mysterious; of evil and supernatural character.
Uncanonical, un-ka-non'ik-al, *a.* Not canonical; not acknowledged as authentic.
Uncared, un-kārd', *a.* Not regarded; not heeded: often with *for.*
Unceasing, un-sēs'ing, *a.* Not ceasing; continual.
Uncertain, un-sėr'tān, *a.* Not certain; doubtful; inconstant.
Uncertainty, un-sėr'tin-ti, *n.* Want of certainty; dubiety.
Unchallenged, un-chal'lenjd, *a.* Not objected to; not called in question.
Unchangeable, un-chānj'a-bl, *a.* Not capable of change; immutable; unchanging.
Unchanging, un-chānj'ing, *a.* Not changing; suffering no change.
Uncharitable, un-cha'rit-a-bl, *a.* Not charitable; ready to think evil; harsh.
Unchaste, un-chāst', *a.* Not chaste; lewd.
Unchristian, un-kris'ti-an, *a.* Contrary to the spirit or laws of Christianity.
Unchurch, un-chėrch', *vt.* To expel from a church; to deprive of the character of a church.
Uncial, un'shi-al, *n.* A letter of large size used in ancient Greek and Latin manuscripts.
Unciform, un'si-form, *a.* Having a curved or hooked form.
Uncinate, un'si-nāt, *a.* Hooked at the end; unciform.
Uncivil, un-si'vil, *a.* Not civil; ill-mannered.
Uncivilized, un-si'vil-īzd, *a.* Not civilized.
Uncle, ung'kl, *n.* The brother of one's father or mother.
Unclean, un-klēn', *a.* Not clean; foul; dirty; morally impure; lewd.
Uncleanly, un-klen'li, *a.* Not cleanly; foul; dirty; indecent.
Uncloak, un-klōk', *vt.* and *i.* To deprive of the cloak; to unmask.
Unclose, un-klōz', *vt.* To open; to disclose; to lay open.

Unclothe, un-klōᴛʜ', *vt.* To strip the clothes from; to divest of covering.
Unclouded, un-kloud'ed, *a.* Free from clouds; clear; not obscured.
Uncomely, un-kum'li, *a.* Not comely.
Uncomfortable, un-kum'fort-a-bl, *a.* Not comfortable; uneasy; ill at ease.
Uncommon, un-kom'mon, *a.* Not common; rare; strange; remarkable.
Uncommunicative, un-kom-mū'ni-kāt-iv, *a.* Not apt to communicate; reserved.
Uncompromising, un-kom'prō-mīz-ing, *a.* Not agreeing to terms; unyielding.
Unconcern, un-kon-sėrn', *n.* Want of concern; apathy; indifference.
Unconcerned, un-kon-sėrnd', *a.* Not concerned; not anxious; feeling no solicitude.
Unconditional, un-kon-di'shon-al, *a.* Not limited by conditions; absolute.
Unconfined, un-kon-fīnd', *a.* Not confined; free from restraint or control.
Unconfirmed, un-kon-fėrmd', *a.* Not confirmed; not firmly established.
Unconformable, un-kon-for'ma-bl, *a.* Not conformable; not consistent; applied to strata not parallel with those above or below.
Unconnected, un-kon-nekt'ed, *a.* Not connected; separate; incoherent; loose.
Unconquerable, un-kong'kėr-a-bl, *a.* Not conquerable; insuperable.
Unconscionable, un-kon'shon-a-bl, *a.* Not conscionable; inordinate; unreasonable.
Unconscious, un-kon'shus, *a.* Not conscious; not perceiving; unaware.
Unconstitutional, un-kon'sti-tū"shon-al, *a.* Not agreeable to the constitution.
Uncontrollable, un-kon-trōl'a-bl, *a.* That cannot be controlled or restrained.
Uncontroverted, un-kon'trō-vėrt-ed, *a.* Not controverted; not called in question.
Unconverted, un-kon-vėrt'ed, *a.* Not converted; not regenerated.
Uncork, un-kork', *vt.* To draw the cork from.
Uncorrected, un-ko-rekt'ed, *a.* Not corrected; not revised; not reformed.
Uncorrupt, un-ko-rupt', *a.* Not corrupt.
Uncouple, un-ku'pl, *vt.* To loose, as dogs coupled together; to disjoin.
Uncourteous, un-kōrt'yus, *a.* Not courteous; uncivil.
Uncourtly, un-kōrt'li, *a.* Not courtly; blunt; uncivil; rude.
Uncouth, un-köth', *a.* Strange; odd in appearance; awkward.
Uncover, un-ku'vėr, *vt.* To divest of a cover; to disclose.—*vi.* To take off the hat.
Unction, ungk'shon, *n.* Act of anointing; an unguent; religious fervour; sham devotional fervour; oiliness.
Unctuous, ung'tū-us, *a.* Oily; greasy; nauseously emotional; oily; fawning.
Uncultivated, un-kul'ti-vāt-ed, *a.* Not cultivated; not tilled; boorish or rude.
Uncut, un-kut', *a.* Not cut.
Undated, un'dāt-ed, *a.* Wavy.
Undated, un-dāt'ed, *a.* Not dated.
Undaunted, un-dạnt'ed, *a.* Intrepid; fearless.
Undeceive, un-dē-sēv', *vt.* To free from deception or mistake.
Undecided, un-dē-sīd'ed, *a.* Not decided; hesitating; irresolute.
Undefinable, un-dē-fīn'a-bl, *a.* Not definable; indefinable.
Undefined, un-dē-fīnd', *a.* Not defined; lacking in clearness or definiteness.
Undemonstrative, un-dē-mon'stra-tiv, *a.* Not demonstrative; reserved.
Undeniable, un-dē-nī'a-bl, *a.* Incapable of being denied; indisputable.
Under, un'dėr, *prep.* Below; beneath; undergoing; affected by; subject to; inferior; during the time of; included in; in accordance with.—*adv.* In a lower condition or degree.—*a.* Lower; subject; subordinate.
Underbred, un'dėr-bred, *a.* Of inferior breeding or manners; ill-bred; vulgar.
Underbuy, un-dėr-bī', *vt.* To buy at a lower price than.
Undercarriage, un'dėr-kar-ij, *n.* The landing apparatus of an aircraft.
Undercharge, un-dėr-chärj', *vt.* To charge insufficiently.—*n.* un'dėr-chärj. Too low a charge or price.
Underclothes, Underclothing, un'dėr-klōᴛʜz, un'dėr-klōᴛʜ-ing, *n.* Clothes worn under others or next the skin.
Undercurrent, un'dėr-ku-rent, *n.* A current below another; some movement or influence not apparent.
Undergo, un-dėr-gō', *vt.* To bear; to experience; to suffer.
Undergraduate, un-dėr-grad'ū-āt, *n.* A student who has not taken his first degree.
Underground, un'dėr-ground, *a.* and *adv.* Below the surface of the ground.
Undergrowth, un'dėr-grōth, *n.* Shrubs or small trees growing among large ones.
Underhand, un'dėr-hand, *a.* Working by stealth; secret; deceitful.—*adv.* In a clandestine manner.
Underhung, un'dėr-hung, *a.* Projecting beyond the upper jaw: said of the under jaw.
Underlay, un-dėr-lā', *vt.* To lay beneath; to support by something laid under.
Underlie, un-dėr-lī', *vt.* To lie beneath; to be at the basis of.
Underline, un-dėr-līn', *vt.* To mark with a line below the words.
Underling, un'dėr-ling, *n.* An inferior person or agent; a mean sorry fellow.
Undermine, un-dėr-mīn', *vt.* To sap; to injure by underhand means.
Undermost, un'dėr-mōst, *a.* Lowest in place, state, or condition.
Underneath, un-dėr-nēth', *adv.* Beneath; below.—*prep.* Under; beneath.
Underplot, un'dėr-plot, *n.* A subordinate plot in a story; a clandestine scheme.
Underrate, un-dėr-rāt', *vt.* To rate too low; to undervalue.
Undersell, un-dėr-sel', *vt.* To sell at a lower price than.
Undershot, un-dėr-shot', *a.* Moved by water passing under, as a wheel.
Undershrub, un'dėr-shrub, *n.* A low shrub, the branches of which decay yearly.
Undersign, un-dėr-sīn', *vt.* To write one's name at the foot or end of; to subscribe.
Undersized, un'dėr-sīzd, *a.* Being of a size or stature less than common; dwarfish.
Understand, un-dėr-stand', *vt.* To comprehend; to see through; to suppose to mean; to infer; to assume; to recognize as implied although not expressed.—*vi.* To comprehend; to learn.

Understanding, un-dėr-stand′ing, *a.* Intelligent.—*n.* Comprehension; discernment; knowledge; intellect; agreement of minds; anything agreed upon.
Understate, un-dėr-stāt′, *vt.* To state too low or as less than actually.
Understrapper, un′dėr-strap-ėr, *n.* A petty fellow; an inferior agent.
Undertake, un′dėr-tāk, *vt.* To take in hand; to engage in; to attempt; to guarantee.—*vi.* To take upon oneself; to promise; to stand bound.
Undertaker, un′dėr-tāk-ėr, *n.* One who undertakes; one who manages funerals.
Undertaking, un′dėr-tāk-ing, *n.* That which is undertaken; enterprise; promise.
Undertone, un′dėr-tōn, *n.* A low tone.
Under-tow, un′dėr-tō, *n.* An undercurrent opposite to that at the surface; the backward flow of a wave breaking on a beach.
Undervalue, un-dėr-val′ū, *vt.* To value below the real worth; to esteem lightly.
Underwear, un′dėr-wār, *n.* Underclothes.
Underwood, un′dėr-wu̇d, *n.* Small trees that grow among large trees; coppice.
Underworld, un′dėr-wėrld, *n.* The lower world; this world; the antipodes; the place of departed souls; Hades.
Underwrite, un-dėr-rīt′, *vt.* To write under; to subscribe one's name and become answerable for a certain amount.
Underwriter, un′dėr-rīt-ėr, *n.* One who underwrites or insures; an insurer.
Underwriting, un′dėr-rīt-ing, *n.* The business of an underwriter.
Undesirable, un-dē-zīr′a-bl, *a.* Not desirable.
Undetermined, un-dē-tėr′mind, *a.* Not determined; not decided, fixed, or settled.
Undeterred, un-dē-tėrd′, *a.* Not restrained by fear or obstacles.
Undigested, un-di-jest′ed, *a.* Not digested; not properly prepared or arranged; crude.
Undignified, un-dig′ni-fīd, *a.* Not dignified; showing a want of dignity.
Undine, un′dīn, *n.* A water-spirit of the female sex.
Undisguised, un-dis-gīzd′, *a.* Not disguised; open; candid; artless.
Undisposed, un-dis-pōzd′, *a.* Not set apart; not allocated; not sold: with *of.*
Undisputed, un-dis-pūt′ed, *a.* Not disputed; not called in question; incontestable.
Undistinguished, un-dis-ting′gwisht, *a.* Not having any distinguishing mark; not famous; not possessing distinction.
Undisturbed, un-dis-tėrbd′, *a.* Free from disturbance; calm; tranquil; not agitated.
Undivided, un-di-vīd′ed, *a.* Not divided; whole; entire.
Undo, un-dö′, *vt.* To reverse what has been done; annul; to loose; to take to pieces; to ruin.
Undoer, un-dö′ėr, *n.* One who reverses what has been done; one who ruins.
Undoing, un-dö′ing, *n.* Reversal; ruin.
Undone, un′dun, *pp.* Not done.
Undone, un-dun′, *pp.* Untied or unfastened; reversed; ruined.
Undoubted, un-dout′ed, *a.* Not doubted; indubitable; indisputable.
Undoubtedly, un-dout′ed-li, *adv.* Without doubt; without question; indubitably.
Undress, un-dres′, *vt.* To divest of dress or clothes; to strip.—*n.* un′dres. A loose negligent dress; ordinary dress.
Undressed, un-drest′, *a.* Not dressed; not attired; not prepared; in a raw state.
Undue, un-dū′, *a.* Not due; not yet demandable by right; not right; inordinate.
Undulate, un′dū-lāt, *vi.* To have a wavy motion; to wave.—*vt.* To cause to wave.
Undulation, un-dū-lā′shon, *n.* Act of undulating; a waving motion; a wavy form; a gentle slope; a vibratory motion.
Undulatory, un′dū-la-to-ri, *a.* Having an undulating character; moving like waves.
Unduly, un-dū′li, *adv.* In an undue manner; unlawfully; unwarrantably; excessively.
Undutiful, un-dū′ti-fu̇l, *a.* Not dutiful; not obedient; rebellious; irreverent.
Undying, un-dī′ing, *a.* Not dying; imperishable.
Unearned, un-ėrnd′, *a.* Not merited by labour or services.—**Unearned increment,** the increase in the value of property not due to any expenditure on the part of the owner.
Unearth, un-ėrth′, *vt.* To drive or bring from the earth; to uncover; to discover.
Unearthly, un-ėrth′li, *a.* Not earthly; weird.
Uneasy, un-ēz′i, *a.* Restless; disturbed; somewhat anxious; unquiet; stiff; not graceful; unpleasing; irksome.
Uneducated, un-ed′ū-kāt-ed, *a.* Not educated; illiterate; ignorant.
Unemotional, un-ē-mō′shon-al, *a.* Not emotional; impassive.
Unemployed, un-em-ploid′, *a.* Not employed; having no work; not being in use.
Unending, un-end′ing, *a.* Not ending; perpetual; eternal.
Unendurable, un-en-dūr′a-bl, *a.* Intolerable.
Unengaged, un-en-gājd′, *a.* Not engaged.
Unenglish, un-ing′glish, *a.* Not English.
Unenlightened, un-en-līt′nd, *a.* Not enlightened; not illuminated, mentally or morally.
Unenterprising, un-en′tėr-prīz-ing, *a.* Wanting in enterprise; not adventurous.
Unenviable, un-en′vi-a-bl, *a.* Not enviable; not to be envied.
Unequable, un-ē′kwa-bl, *a.* Not equable; changeful; fitful.
Unequal, un-ē′kwal, *a.* Not equal; inadequate; insufficient; not equable.
Unequalled, un-ē′kwald, *a.* Not to be equalled; unrivalled.
Unequivocal, un-ē-kwiv′ō-kal, *a.* Not equivocal; not doubtful; clear; evident.
Unerring, un-er′ing, *a.* Not erring; incapable of error; certain.
Unessential, un-es-sen′shal, *a.* Not essential; not absolutely necessary.
Uneven, un-ē′vn, *a.* Not even or level; rough; crooked; not fair or just; odd.
Unexampled, un-egz-am′pld, *a.* Having no example or similar case; unprecedented.
Unexcelled, un-ek-seld′, *a.* Not excelled.
Unexceptionable, un-ek-sep′shon-a-bl, *a.* Not liable to any exception; excellent.
Unexpected, un-eks-pekt′ed, *a.* Not expected; not looked for; sudden.
Unexpired, un-eks-pīrd′, *a.* Not expired; not having come to the end of its term.
Unexplored, un-eks-plōrd′, *a.* Not explored; not visited by any traveller.
Unfading, un-fād′ing, *a.* Not fading; not liable to wither or decay; ever fresh.

Unfailing, un-fāl'ing, *a.* Not liable to fail; that does not fail; certain.
Unfair, un-fār', *a.* Not honest or impartial; not just; inequitable; disingenuous.
Unfaithful, un-fāth'fųl, *a.* Not faithful.
Unfamiliar, un-fa-mil'i-ėr, *a.* Not familiar; not accustomed; strange.
Unfashionable, un-fa'shon-a-bl, *a.* Not fashionable or according to the fashion.
Unfasten, un-fäs'n, *vt.* To loose; to unfix.
Unfathered, un-fä'THėrd, *a.* Fatherless; having no acknowledged father or author.
Unfatherly, un-fä'THėr-li, *a.* Not becoming a father; unkind.
Unfathomable, un-faTH'um-a-bl, *a.* That cannot be fathomed; incomprehensible.
Unfavourable, un-fā'vėr-a-bl, *a.* Not favourable; not propitious; discouraging.
Unfeeling, un-fēl'ing, *a.* Devoid of feeling; hard-hearted; harsh; brutal.
Unfeigned, un-fānd', *a.* Not feigned; sincere.
Unfermented, un-fer-ment'ed, *a.* Not having undergone fermentation.
Unfetter, un-fet'ėr, *vt.* To loose from fetters; to set at liberty.
Unfilial, un-fil'i-al, *a.* Not filial; undutiful.
Unfinished, un-fin'isht, *a.* Not finished.
Unfit, un-fit', *a.* Not fit; unsuitable; not competent.—*vt.* To make unfit.
Unfix, un-fiks', *vt.* To cause to be no longer fixed; to loosen; to unsettle.
Unflinching, un-flinsh'ing, *a.* Not flinching; not shrinking; resolute.
Unfold, un-fōld', *vt.* To open the folds of; to display.—*vi.* To open out.
Unforeseen, un-fōr-sēn', *a.* Not foreseen.
Unforgiving, un-for-giv'ing, *a.* Not forgiving; implacable.
Unformed, un-formd', *a.* Not formed or moulded into regular shape.
Unfortunate, un-for'tū-nāt, *a.* Not fortunate; unlucky; unhappy.—*n.* One who is unfortunate; a prostitute.
Unfortunately, un-for'tū-nāt-li, *adv.* In an unfortunate manner; by ill fortune.
Unfounded, un-found'ed, *a.* Having no real foundation; groundless; idle.
Unfrequent, un-frē'kwent, *a.* Not frequent.
Unfrequented, un-frē-kwent'ed, *a.* Not frequented; rarely visited; solitary.
Unfriended, un-frend'ed, *a.* Not having friends; not countenanced or supported.
Unfriendly, un-frend'li, *a.* Not friendly.
Unfrock, un-frok', *vt.* To divest of a frock; to deprive of the character of a priest.
Unfruitful, un-fröt'fųl, *a.* Not fruitful; barren.
Unfunded, un-fund'ed, *a.* Not funded; having no permanent fund for the payment of its interest: said of government debt when it exists in the form of exchequer bills or the like.
Unfurl, un-fėrl', *vt.* To loose from a furled state; to expand to catch the wind.
Unfurnished, un-fėr'nisht, *a.* Not furnished; unsupplied; unprovided.
Ungainly, un-gān'li, *a.* Not handsome; uncouth; clumsy; awkward; ill-shaped.
Ungallant, un-gal'ant, *a.* Not gallant; not polite, courtly, or attentive to ladies.
Ungenerous, un-jen'ėr-us, *a.* Not generous; illiberal; dishonourable; mean.
Ungentle, un-jen'tl, *a.* Not gentle; harsh.
Ungentlemanly, un-jen'tl-man-li, *a.* Not becoming a gentleman.
Ungird, un-gėrd', *vt.* To loose from a girdle or band; to unbind.
Unglazed, un-glāzd', *a.* Not glazed; not furnished with panes of glass.
Ungodly, un-god'li, *a.* Not godly; wicked.
Ungovernable, un-gu'vėrn-a-bl, *a.* That cannot be governed; wild; refractory.
Ungraceful, un-grās'fųl, *a.* Not graceful.
Ungracious, un-grā'shus, *a.* Not gracious; uncivil; rude; impolite.
Ungrammatical, un-gram-mat'ik-al, *a.* Not according to grammar.
Ungrateful, un-grāt'fųl, *a.* Not grateful; not thankful; unpleasing; harsh.
Ungrounded, un-ground'ed, *a.* Having no foundation or support; groundless.
Ungrudging, un-gruj'ing, *a.* Without a grudge; freely giving; hearty; liberal.
Ungual, ung'gwal, *a.* Pertaining to or having a nail, claw, or hoof.
Unguarded, un-gärd'ed, *a.* Not guarded; not cautious; negligent.
Unguent, un'gwent, *n.* An ointment.
Unguiculate, ung-gwik'ū-lāt, *a.* Having claws.
Unguiform, ung'gwi-form, *a.* Claw-shaped.
Ungulate, ung'gū-lāt, *n.* A hoofed quadruped. —*a.* Hoof-shaped; having hoofs.
Unhallowed, un-hal'ōd, *a.* Not hallowed or sanctified; profane; unholy.
Unhand, un-hand', *vt.* To loose from the hand or hands; to lose hold of.
Unhandsome, un-hand'sum, *a.* Not handsome; unfair; unbecoming; impolite.
Unhandy, un-hand'i, *a.* Not handy; awkward; not convenient.
Unhappily, un-hap'i-li, *adv.* In an unhappy manner; unfortunately.
Unhappy, un-hap'i, *a.* Not happy; sad; unfortunate; unlucky; evil; ill-omened.
Unharmed, un-härmd', *a.* Not harmed.
Unharness, un-här'nes, *vt.* To strip of harness; to loose from harness; to disarm.
Unhat, un-hat', *vt.* and *i.* To take off the hat, as in respect or reverence.
Unhealthy, un-helth'i, *a.* Not healthy; sickly; insalubrious; unwholesome.
Unheard, un-hėrd', *a.* Not heard; not admitted to audience; not known (with *of*).
Unheeded, un-hēd'ed, *a.* Not heeded; disregarded; neglected.
Unheeding, un-hēd'ing, *a.* Not heeding; careless.
Unhesitating, un-he'zi-tāt-ing, *a.* Not hesitating; not remaining in doubt; prompt.
Unhinge, un-hinj', *vt.* To take from the hinges; to unfix; to loosen; to derange.
Unholy, un-hō'li, *a.* Not holy; not sacred; unhallowed; profane; impious; wicked.
Unhoped, un-hōpt', *a.* Not hoped for; not expected: often followed by *for*.
Unhopeful, un-hōp'fųl, *a.* Not hopeful.
Unhorse, un-hors', *vt.* To throw from a horse; to cause to dismount.
Unhouse, un-houz', *vt.* To deprive of a house; to dislodge; to deprive of shelter.
Unhurt, un-hėrt', *a.* Not hurt; not harmed; free from wound or injury.
Unicorn, ū'ni-korn, *n.* A fabulous animal like a horse, with a long single horn on the forehead.

Unicostate, ū-ni-kos'tāt, *a.* Having one rib or ridge; in *botany*, having one large vein down the centre, called the midrib.
Unification, ū'ni-fi-kā"shon, *n.* The act of unifying or uniting into one.
Uniform, ū'ni-form, *a.* Having always one and the same form; equable; invariable; consistent.—*n.* A distinctive dress worn by the members of the same body.
Uniformity, ū-ni-for'mi-ti, *n.* State or character of being uniform; conformity to one type; agreement; consistency.
Uniformly, ū'ni-form-li, *adv.* In a uniform manner; invariably.
Unify, ū'ni-fī, *vt.* To form into one.
Unigenous, ū-ni'jen-us, *a.* Of one kind; of the same genus.
Unilluminated, un-il-lūm'in-āt-ed, *a.* Not illuminated; dark; ignorant.
Unimaginable, un-im-aj'in-a-bl, *a.* Not imaginable; inconceivable.
Unimpaired, un-im-pārd', *a.* Not impaired; not diminished; uninjured.
Unimpassioned, un-im-pa'shond, *a.* Not impassioned; tranquil; not violent.
Unimpeachable, un-im-pēch'a-bl, *a.* Not impeachable; blameless; irreproachable.
Unimportant, un-im-pōr'tant, *a.* Not important; not of great moment.
Unimproved, un-im-prövd', *a.* Not improved; not cultivated.
Uninhabited, un-in-ha'bit-ed, *a.* Not inhabited by men; having no inhabitants.
Uninjured, un-in'jėrd, *a.* Not injured.
Uninstructed, un-in-strukt'ed, *a.* Not instructed; not educated.
Unintelligent, un-in-tel'i-jent, *a.* Not intelligent; not showing intelligence; stupid.
Unintelligible, un-in-tel'i-ji-bl, *a.* Not intelligible; meaningless.
Unintentional, un-in-ten'shon-al, *a.* Not intentional; done without design.
Uninterested, un-in'tėr-est-ed, *a.* Not interested; having no interest or concern.
Uninteresting, un-in'tėr-est-ing, *n.* Not interesting; dull; tame.
Uninterrupted, un-in'tėr-rupt"ed, *a.* Not interrupted; unintermitted; incessant.
Uninviting, un-in-vīt'ing, *a.* Not inviting; unattractive; rather repellent.
Union, ūn'yon, *n.* Act of joining; combination; agreement; harmony; marriage; confederacy; a trades-union; a mixed fabric of cotton, flax, jute, silk, or wool, &c.; a certain kind of flag.
Unionist, ūn'yon-ist, *n.* One who advocates union; a trades-unionist; one who upholds the union of the three kingdoms of Great Britain and Ireland.
Union Jack, ūn'yon-jak, *n.* The national flag of Great Britain and Northern Ireland, formed by the union of the cross of St. George, the saltire of St. Andrew, and the saltire of St. Patrick.
Uniparous, ū-nip'a-rus, *a.* Producing one at a birth.
Unique, ū-nēk', *a.* Without a like or equal; unmatched; unequalled.
Unison, ū'ni-son, *n.* Accordance; agreement; harmony; concord.
Unisonant, Unisonous, ū-ni'sō-nant, ū-ni'sō-nus, *a.* Being in unison; concordant.
Unit, ū'nit, *n.* A single thing or person; an individual; the number 1; a dimension or quantity assumed as a standard.
Unitarian, ū-ni-tā'ri-an, *n.* One who ascribes divinity to God only, and denies the Trinity.—*a.* Pertaining to Unitarians.
Unitarianism, ū-ni-tā'ri-an-izm, *n.* The doctrines of Unitarians.
Unitary, ū'ni-ta-ri, *a.* Of or relating to a unit.
Unite, ū-nīt', *vt.* (uniting, united). To combine; to connect; to associate.—*vi.* To become one; to combine; to concur.
United, ū-nīt'ed, *a.* Joined; combined together; made one.
Unitedly, ū-nīt'ed-li, *adv.* In a united manner; jointly; in combination.
Unity, ū'ni-ti, *n.* State of being one; concord; agreement; harmony; artistic harmony and symmetry.
Univalve, ū'ni-valv, *n.* A shell having one valve only.
Universal, ū-ni-vėrs'al, *a.* Pertaining to all; total; whole.—*n.* A general notion or idea.
Universalist, ū-ni-vėrs'al-ist, *n.* One who holds that all men will be saved.
Universality, ū'ni-vėrs-al"i-ti, *n.* State of being universal.
Universally, ū-ni-vėrs'al-li, *adv.* With extension to the whole; without exception.
Universe, ū'ni-vėrs, *n.* The whole system of created things; the world.
University, ū-ni-vėrs'i-ti, *n.* An institution for instruction in science and literature, &c., and having the power of conferring degrees.
Univocal, ū-ni'vō-kal, *a.* Having one meaning only; having unison of sounds.—*n.* A word having only one meaning.
Unjust, un-just', *a.* Not just, upright, or equitable.
Unjustifiable, un-jus'ti-fī"a-bl, *a.* Not justifiable.
Unjustly, un-just'li, *adv.* Wrongfully.
Unkempt, un-kempt', *a.* Uncombed; rough.
Unkind, un-kīnd', *a.* Not kind; cruel.
Unkindly, un-kind'li, *a.* Unkind; ungracious.—*adv.* In an unkind manner.
Unknowingly, un-nō'ing-li, *adv.* Without knowledge or design; unwittingly.
Unknown, un-nōn', *a.* Not known; not discovered, found out, or ascertained.
Unlace, un-lās', *vt.* To loose the lacing or fastening of; to unfasten.
Unlade, un-lād', *vi.* To take out the lading or cargo of; to discharge.
Unlawful, un-la'ful, *a.* Not lawful; illegal.
Unlearn, un-lėrn', *vt.* To forget the knowledge of.
Unlearned, un-lėr'ned, *a.* Not learned or erudite; illiterate; (un-lėrnd') not known.
Unless, un-les', *conj.* If it be not that; if . . . not; except; excepting.
Unlettered, un-let'ėrd, *a.* Unlearned.
Unlicensed, un-li'senst, *a.* Not having a licence; done without due licence.
Unlike, un-līk', *a.* Not like; dissimilar; having no resemblance; diverse.
Unlikely, un-līk'li, *a.* Not likely; improbable; likely to fail; unpromising.
Unlimber, un-lim'bėr, *vt.* To take off or detach the limbers from.
Unlimited, un-lim'it-ed, *a.* Not limited; boundless; indefinite.
Unload, un-lōd', *vt.* To take the load from; to discharge; to empty out.

Unlock, un-lok′, *vt.* To unfasten; to open.
Unlooked-for, un-lökt′for, *a.* Not looked for; not expected; not foreseen.
Unloose, un-lös′, *vt.* To loose; to untie; to undo; to set at liberty.
Unlovely, un-luv′li, *a.* Not lovely; not attractive; repulsive or repellent.
Unlucky, un-luk′i, *a.* Not lucky; unfortunate; not successful; ill-omened.
Unmake, un-māk′, *vt.* To reverse the making of; to destroy.
Unman, un-man′, *vt.* To deprive of the character of a man; to unnerve.
Unmanageable, un-man′āj-a-bl, *a.* Not manageable; beyond control.
Unmanly, un-man′li, *a.* Not manly; effeminate; childish; cowardly.
Unmannerly, un-man′ėr-li, *a.* Not mannerly; rude; ill-bred.
Unmask, un-mask′, *vt.* To strip of a mask; to expose.—*vi.* To put off a mask.
Unmatched, un-macht′, *a.* Matchless.
Unmeaning, un-mēn′ing, *a.* Having no meaning; senseless; vacuous.
Unmeasured, un-me′zhūrd, *a.* Not measured; immense; infinite; excessive.
Unmeet, un-mēt′, *a.* Not meet or fit.
Unmentionable, un-men′shon-a-bl, *a.* Not mentionable.
Unmerciful, un-mėr′si-ful, *a.* Not merciful; cruel; merciless.
Unmerited, un-mer′it-ed, *a.* Not deserved.
Unmindful, un-mīnd′ful, *a.* Not mindful; regardless.
Unmistakable, Unmistakeable, un-mis-tāk′-a-bl, *a.* Not capable of being mistaken; clear; obvious.
Unmitigated, un-mi′ti-gāt-ed, *a.* Not mitigated; thorough-paced.
Unmixed, Unmixt, un-mikst′, *a.* Not mixed; pure; unadulterated; unalloyed.
Unmoor, un-mör′, *vt.* To loose from moorings.—*vi.* To weigh anchor.
Unmotherly, un-muᴛʜ′ėr-li, *a.* Not resembling or becoming a mother.
Unmoved, un-mövd′, *a.* Not moved; firm; calm; cool.
Unmusical, un-mū′zik-al, *a.* Not musical.
Unnameable, un-nām′a-bl, *a.* Incapable of being named; indescribable.
Unnamed, un-nāmd′, *a.* Not having received a name; not mentioned.
Unnatural, un-na′tūr-al, *a.* Not natural; contrary to nature; affected; artificial.
Unnavigable, un-na′vi-ga-bl, *a.* Not navigable; incapable of being navigated.
Unnecessary, un-ne′ses-sa-ri, *a.* Not necessary; needless.
Unneighbourly, un-nā′bėr-li, *a.* Not neighbourly; not kind and friendly.
Unnerve, un-nėrv′, *vt.* To deprive of nerve, strength, or composure; to enfeeble.
Unnoted, un-nōt′ed, *a.* Not noted; disregarded.
Unnoticed, un-nōt′ist, *a.* Not observed.
Unnumbered, un-num′bėrd, *a.* Not numbered; innumerable; indefinitely numerous.
Unobjectionable, un-ob-jek′shon-a-bl, *a.* Not liable to objection; unexceptionable.
Unobservant. Unobserving, un-ob-zėrv′ant, un-ob-zėrv′ing, *a.* Not observant.
Unobtrusive, un-ob-trö′siv, *a.* Not obtrusive; not forward; modest; retiring.
Unoccupied, un-ok′kū-pīd, *a.* Not occupied; not possessed; at leisure.
Unoffending, un-of-fend′ing, *a.* Not giving offence; harmless; innocent; inoffensive.
Unofficial, un-of-fi′shal, *a.* Not official.
Unopposed, un-op-pōzd′, *a.* Not opposed; not meeting with any obstruction.
Unorthodox, un-or′tho-doks, *a.* Not orthodox; heterodox.
Unostentatious, un-os′ten-tā″shus, *a.* Not ostentatious; not showy; modest.
Unpack, un-pak′, *vt.* To take from a package; to unload.
Unpaid, un-pād′, *a.* Not paid; remaining due; not receiving a salary.
Unpalatable, un-pa′lat-a-bl, *a.* Not palatable; disagreeable to the taste or feelings.
Unparalleled, un-pa′ral-eld, *a.* Having no parallel; unequalled; matchless.
Unpardonable, un-pär′dn-a-bl, *a.* Not to be forgiven; incapable of being pardoned.
Unparliamentary, un-pär′li-men″ta-ri, *a.* Contrary to the usages or rules of proceeding in parliament; unseemly, as language.
Unpatriotic, un-pā′tri-ot″ik, *a.* Not patriotic; wanting in patriotism.
Unperceivable, un-pėr-sēv′a-bl, *a.* Imperceptible.
Unpin, un-pin′, *vt.* To loose from pins; to unfasten.
Unpleasant, un-ple′zant, *a.* Not pleasant.
Unpleasing, un-plēz′ing, *a.* Unpleasant.
Unplumbed, un-plumd′, *a.* Not fathomed.
Unpoetic, Unpoetical, un-pō-et′ik, un-pō-et′ik-al, *a.* Not poetical.
Unpolished, un-po′lisht, *a.* Not polished; rude; plain.
Unpopular, un-po′pū-lėr, *a.* Not popular.
Unpractical, un-prak′ti-kal, *a.* Not practical.
Unpractised, un-prak′tist, *a.* Not having been taught by practice; raw; unskilful.
Unprecedented, un-pre′sē-dent-ed, *a.* Having no precedent; unexampled.
Unprejudiced, un-pre′jū-dist, *a.* Not prejudiced; free from bias; impartial.
Unpremeditated, un-prē-me′di-tāt-ed, *a.* Not previously meditated; spontaneous.
Unprepared, un-prē-pārd′, *a.* Not prepared.
Unpretending, un-prē-tend′ing, *a.* Not pretending to any distinction; unassuming.
Unprincipled, un-prin′si-pld, *a.* Not having settled principles; immoral.
Unproductive, un-prō-duk′tiv, *a.* Not productive; infertile; not returning a profit.
Unprofessional, un-prō-fe′shon-al, *a.* Contrary to the customs of a profession; not belonging to a profession.
Unprofitable, un-pro′fit-a-bl, *a.* Not profitable; useless; profitless.
Unpromising, un-pro′mis-ing, *a.* Not giving promise of success, &c.
Unproved, un-prövd′, *a.* Not proved; not established as true by proof.
Unpublished, un-pub′lisht, *a.* Not published.
Unpunctual, un-pungk′tū-al, *a.* Not punctual; not exact as to time.
Unqualified, un-kwo′li-fīd, *a.* Not qualified; not having the requisite qualifications; not modified by conditions.
Unquestionable, un-kwest′yon-a-bl, *a.* Not to be called in question; indubitable.
Unquiet, un-kwī′et, *a.* Not quiet; disturbed.

Unravel, un-ra'vel, *vt.* To disentangle; to disengage or separate; to solve.
Unread, un-red', *a.* Not perused; illiterate.
Unreadable, un-rēd'a-bl, *a.* Incapable of being read; illegible; not worth reading.
Unready, un-re'di, *a.* Not ready; not prompt to act.
Unreal, un-rē'al, *a.* Not real; not substantial.
Unreality, un-rē-al'i-ti, *n.* Want of real existence; that which has no reality.
Unreason, un-rē'zn, *n.* Want of reason; folly; absurdity.
Unreasonable, un-rē'zn-a-bl, *a.* Not reasonable; immoderate.
Unrecorded, un-rē-kord'ed, *a.* Not recorded or registered; not kept in remembrance by documents or monuments.
Unredeemed, un-rē-dēmd', *a.* Not redeemed; not fulfilled; unmitigated.
Unrefined, un-rē-fīnd', *a.* Not refined or purified; not polished in manners, taste, &c.
Unregenerate, un-rē-jen'ė-rāt, *a.* Not regenerated or renewed in heart.
Unregistered, un-re'jis-tėrd, *a.* Not registered or entered in a register.
Unrelated, un-rē-lāt'ed, *a.* Not connected by blood; having no connection.
Unrelenting, un-rē-lent'ing, *a.* Not relenting; relentless; hard; pitiless.
Unreliable, un-rē-lī'a-bl, *a.* Not reliable; untrustworthy.
Unrelieved, un-rē-lēvd', *a.* Not relieved; monotonous.
Unremitting, un-rē-mit'ing, *a.* Not remitting or abating; incessant; continued.
Unrepresented, un-re'prē-zent"ed, *a.* Not represented; not having a representative; not yet put on the stage.
Unrequited, un-rē-kwīt'ed, *a.* Not requited; not recompensed.
Unreserved, un-rē-zėrvd', *a.* Not reserved or restricted; full; free; open; frank.
Unreservedly, un-rē-zėrv'ed-li, *adv.* Without reservation; frankly.
Unrest, un-rest', *n.* Disquiet; uneasiness.
Unresting, un-rest'ing, *a.* Never resting.
Unrestrained, un-rē-strānd', *a.* Not restrained; licentious; loose.
Unriddle, un-rid'l, *vt.* To solve; to interpret.
Unrighteous, un-rīt'yus, *a.* Not righteous; not just; wicked.
Unripe, un-rīp', *a.* Not ripe; not mature; not fully prepared; not completed.
Unrivalled, un-rī'vald, *a.* Having no rival; incomparable.
Unrobe, un-rōb', *vt.* To strip of a robe; to undress.
Unroll, un-rōl', *vt.* and *i.* To open out from being in a roll; to unfold; to display.
Unromantic, un-rō-man'tik, *a.* Not romantic; not given to romantic fancies.
Unroof, un-röf', *vt.* To strip off the roof of.
Unruffled, un-ruf'ld, *a.* Not ruffled; calm; tranquil; not agitated; not disturbed.
Unruly, un-rö'li, *a.* Disregarding rule; turbulent; ungovernable; disorderly.
Unsafe, un-sāf', *a.* Not safe; perilous.
Unsaid, un-sed', *a.* Not spoken.
Unsatisfactory, un-sa'tis-fak"to-ri, *a.* Not satisfactory; not satisfying.
Unsavoury, un-sā'vo-ri, *a.* Not savoury; insipid; unpleasing; offensive.
Unsay, un-sā', *vt.* To recant; to retract.
Unscathed, un-skāᴛʜd', *a.* Not scathed; uninjured.
Unscrew, un-skrö', *vt.* To draw the screw from; to unfasten by screwing back.
Unscriptural, un-skrip'tūr-al, *a.* Not warranted by the Bible.
Unscrupulous, un-skrö'pū-lus, *a.* Having no scruples; regardless of principle.
Unseal, un-sēl', *vt.* To remove the seal from; to open after having been sealed.
Unseasonable, un-sē'zn-a-bl, *a.* Not seasonable; ill-timed; untimely.
Unseat, un-sēt', *vt.* To remove from a seat; to depose from a seat in a legislature.
Unseemly, un-sēm'li, *a.* Not seemly; indecorous; improper.—*adv.* Unbecomingly.
Unseen, un-sēn', *a.* Not seen; invisible.
Unselfish, un-sel'fish, *a.* Not selfish.
Unsentimental, un-sen'ti-men"tal, *a.* Not sentimental; matter-of-fact.
Unserviceable, un-sėr'vis-a-bl, *a.* Useless.
Unsettle, un-set'l, *vt.* To change from a settled state; to unhinge; to derange.
Unsettled, un-set'ld, *p.a.* Not settled; not calm or composed; having no fixed habitation; irregular; unpaid.
Unsex, un-seks', *vt.* To deprive of the qualities of sex; to deprive of the qualities of a woman.
Unshaken, un-shā'kn, *a.* Not shaken; resolute; firm.
Unshapely, un-shāp'li, *a.* Not shapely; ill formed.
Unshapen, un-shā'pn, *a.* Shapeless; deformed.
Unsheathe, un-shēᴛʜ', *vt.* To draw from the sheath or scabbard.
Unship, un-ship', *vt.* To take out of a ship.
Unshod, un-shod', *a.* Having no shoes.
Unshrinking, un-shringk'ing, *a.* Not shrinking; not recoiling; fearless.
Unsightly, un-sīt'li, *a.* Not sightly; repulsive; ugly; deformed.
Unsisterly, un-sis'tėr-li, *a.* Not like or becoming a sister.
Unsized, un-sīzd', *a.* Not sized or stiffened; not made with size.
Unskilful, un-skil'ful, *a.* Not skilful; having no or little skill; wanting dexterity.
Unsociable, un-sō'shi-a-bl, *a.* Not sociable.
Unsocial, un-sō'shal, *a.* Not social; not caring to mix with one's fellows.
Unsoiled, un-soild', *a.* Not soiled; pure.
Unsold, un-sōld', *a.* Not sold.
Unsolicited, un-sō-lis'it-ed, *a.* Not asked.
Unsophisticated, un-sō-fist'ik-āt-ed, *a.* Pure; natural; artless; simple.
Unsought, un-sat', *a.* Not sought for.
Unsound, un-sound', *a.* Not sound; erroneous; not orthodox.
Unsparing, un-spār'ing, *a.* Not sparing; profuse; severe; rigorous.
Unspeakable, un-spēk'a-bl, *a.* Incapable of being spoken or uttered; unutterable.
Unspoken, un-spō'kn, *a.* Not spoken.
Unspotted, un-spot'ed, *a.* Free from spots; free from moral stain; pure.
Unstable, un-stā'bl, *a.* Not stable; inconstant; irresolute; wavering.
Unstamped, un-stampt', *a.* Not having a stamp impressed or affixed.
Unsteady, un-sted'i, *a.* Not steady; shaking; fickle; varying.
Unstinted, un-stint'ed, *a.* Not stinted; profuse.

Unstop, un-stop′, *vt.* To free from a stopper, as a bottle; to free from obstruction.
Unstring, un-string′, *vt.* To deprive of strings; to relax; to loosen.
Unstrung, un-strung′, *a.* Deprived of strings; having the nerves shaken.
Unstudied, un-stud′id, *a.* Not studied; not premeditated; easy; natural; ignorant.
Unsubstantial, un-sub-stan′shal, *a.* Not substantial; not real; not nutritive.
Unsuccessful, un-suk-ses′fụl, *a.* Not successful; not fortunate in the result.
Unsuitable, un-sūt′a-bl, *a.* Not suitable; ill adapted; unfit.
Unsuited, un-sūt′ed, *a.* Not suited; unfit.
Unsullied, un-sul′id, *a.* Not sullied; pure.
Unsung, un-sung′, *a.* Not sung; not celebrated in song or poetry.
Unsurpassed, un-sėr-past′, *a.* Not surpassed, excelled, or outdone.
Unsusceptible, un-sus-sep′ti-bl, *a.* Not susceptible.
Unsuspecting, un-sus-pekt′ing, *a.* Not suspecting; free from suspicion.
Unsuspicious, un-sus-pi′shus, *a.* Not suspicious; unsuspecting.
Unswathe, un-swāᴛʜ′, *vt.* To take a swathe from; to relieve from a bandage.
Unswerving, un-swėrv′ing, *a.* Not swerving; unwavering; firm.
Unsworn, un-swōrn′, *a.* Not sworn; not bound by oath.
Untainted, un-tānt′ed, *a.* Not tainted.
Untamable, Untameable, un-tām′a-bl, *a.* Not capable of being tamed.
Untasted, un-tāst′ed, *a.* Not tasted; not experienced.
Untaught, un-tạt′, *a.* Not educated; unlettered; ignorant.
Untenable, un-ten′a-bl, *a.* Not to be maintained by argument; not defensible.
Unthanked, un-thangkt′, *a.* Not repaid by thanks.
Unthankful, un-thangk′fụl, *a.* Not thankful; ungrateful.
Unthinkable, un-thingk′a-bl, *a.* That cannot be made an object of thought.
Unthinking, un-thingk′ing, *a.* Not given to think; not heedful; inconsiderate.
Unthought, un-thạt′, *a.* Not thought or conceived: often followed by *of*.
Unthread, un-thred′, *vt.* To draw or take out a thread from.
Unthrift, un′thrift, *n.* Thriftlessness; a thriftless man; a prodigal.
Unthrifty, un-thrift′i, *a.* Not thrifty; prodigal; lavish; wasteful.
Untidy, un-tī′di, *a.* Not tidy; slovenly.
Untie, un-tī′, *vt.* (untying, untied). To loosen, as a knot; to undo; to unfasten.
Until, un-til′, *prep.* or *conj.* Till; to; till the time or point that.
Untimely, un-tīm′li, *a.* Not timely; ill-timed; inopportune.—*adv.* Unseasonably.
Untiring, un-tīr′ing, *a.* Not tiring; unwearied.
Untitled, un-tī′tld, *a.* Not titled; having no title of rank or dignity.
Unto, un′tö, *prep.* To.
Untold, un-tōld′. *a.* Not told; not revealed or counted.
Untouched, un-tucht′, *a.* Not touched; uninjured; not affected.
Untoward, un-tō′wėrd, *a.* Not toward; froward; awkward; vexatious.
Untowardly, un-tō′wėrd-li, *a.* Untoward.—*adv.* Perversely.
Untraceable, un-trās′a-bl, *a.* Incapable of being traced.
Untractable, un-trak′ta-bl, *a.* Not tractable; refractory.
Untravelled, un-tra′veld, *a.* Not trodden by passengers; not having travelled.
Untried, un-trīd′, *a.* Not tried; not attempted; not yet experienced; not determined in law.
Untrod, Untrodden, un-trod′, un-trod′n, *a.* Not having been trod; unfrequented.
Untroubled, un-tru′bld, *a.* Not troubled; not agitated or ruffled; not turbid.
Untrue, un-trö′, *a.* Not true; false.
Untrustworthy, un-trust′wėr-ᴛʜi, *a.* Not worthy of being trusted; unreliable.
Untruth, un-tröth′, *n.* Falsehood.
Untruthful, un-tröth′fụl, *a.* Not truthful.
Untune, un-tūn′, *vt.* To put out of tune; to make incapable of harmony; to disorder.
Untwine, un-twīn′, *vt.* To untwist; to disentangle; to separate.
Untwist, un-twist′, *vt.* and *i.* To separate, as threads twisted.
Unused, un-ūzd′, *a.* Not used; not put to use; not accustomed.
Unusual, un-ū′zhū-al, *a.* Not usual; rare.
Unutterable, un-ut′ėr-a-bl, *a.* That cannot be uttered; inexpressible.
Unvalued, un-va′lūd, *a.* Not valued; not prized; neglected; inestimable.
Unvaried, un-vā′rid, *a.* Not varied.
Unvarnished, un-vär′nisht, *a.* Not varnished; not artfully embellished; plain.
Unvarying, un-vā′ri-ing, *a.* Uniform.
Unveil, un-vāl′, *vt.* To remove a veil from; to uncover; to disclose to view.
Unvoiced, un-voist′, *a.* Not spoken; not uttered with voice as distinct from breath.
Unwarrantable, un-wo′rant-a-bl, *a.* Not warrantable; unjustifiable; illegal.
Unwarranted, un-wo′rant-ed, *a.* Not warranted; unjustifiable; not certain.
Unwary, un-wā′ri, *a.* Not cautious.
Unwashed, un-wosht′, *a.* Not washed; dirty.
Unwavering, un-wā′vėr-ing, *a.* Not wavering; steady; steadfast.
Unwearied, un-wē′rid, *a.* Not wearied or tired; indefatigable; assiduous.
Unweave, un-wēv′, *vt.* To undo what has been woven; to disentangle.
Unwed, un-wed′, *a.* Unmarried.
Unwelcome, un-wel′kum, *a.* Not welcome; not pleasing or grateful.
Unwell, un-wel′, *a.* Not well; indisposed.
Unwholesome, un-hōl′sum, *a.* Not wholesome; insalubrious; causing sickness.
Unwieldy, un-wēl′di, *n.* Movable with difficulty; unmanageable.
Unwilling, un-wil′ing, *a.* Not willing; loath; disinclined; reluctant.
Unwind, un-wīnd′, *vt.* To wind off.—*vi.* To admit of being unwound.
Unwisdom, un-wiz′dom, *n.* Want of wisdom; foolishness; folly.
Unwise, un-wīz′, *a.* Not wise; injudicious.
Unwitting, un-wit′ing, *a.* Not knowing; unconscious; unaware.
Unwomanly, un-wụ′man-li, *a.* Not womanly; unbecoming a woman.

Unwonted, un-wōnt′ed, *a.* Not wonted; not common; unusual; infrequent.
Unworldly, un-wėrld′li, *a.* Not worldly; not influenced by worldly or sordid motives.
Unworn, un-wōrn′, *a.* Not worn.
Unworthy, un-wėr′ᴛʜi, *a.* Not worthy; worthless; base; not becoming or suitable.
Unwrap, un-rap′, *vt.* To open or undo, as what is wrapped up.
Unwritten, un-rit′n, *a.* Not written; blank; understood though not expressed.
Unwrought, un-ra̤t′, *a.* Not manufactured; not worked up.
Unyielding, un-yēld′ing, *a.* Stiff; firm; obstinate.
Unyoke, un-yōk′, *vt.* To loose from a yoke.
Up, up, *adv.* Aloft; in or to a higher position; upright; above the horizon; out of bed; in a state of sedition; from the country to the metropolis; quite; to or at an end.—*prep.* To a higher place or point on; towards the interior of.
Upas, ū′pas, *n.* A poisonous tree of Java and the neighbouring islands.
Upbraid, up-brād′, *vt.* To reproach; to chide; to taunt.
Upbringing, up′bring-ing, *n.* Training; education; breeding.
Upcast, up′kast, *a.* Cast up.—*n.* The ventilating shaft of a mine.
Upheaval, up-hēv′al, *n.* Act of upheaving; lifting of a portion of the earth's crust.
Upheave, up-hēv′, *vt.* To heave or lift up from beneath.
Uphill, up′hil, *a.* Leading or going up a rising ground; difficult; fatiguing.
Uphold, up-hōld′, *vt.* To hold up; to keep erect; to support; to sustain.
Upholder, up-hōld′ėr, *n.* A supporter; defender.
Upholster, up-hōl′stėr, *vt.* To furnish with upholstery.
Upholsterer, up-hōl′stėr-ėr, *n.* One who furnishes houses with curtains, carpets, &c.
Upholstery, up-hōl′stė-ri, *n.* The articles supplied by upholsterers.
Upkeep, up′kēp, *n.* Maintenance.
Upland, up′land, *n.* Higher grounds; hill-slopes.—*a.* Pertaining to uplands.
Uplander, up′land-ėr, *n.* An inhabitant of the uplands.
Uplift, up-lift′, *vt.* To lift up.—*n.* up′lift. A raising; rise; exaltation.
Up-line, up′līn, *n.* A line of railway which leads to a main terminus from the provinces.
Upmost, up′mōst, *a.* Highest; uppermost.
Upon, up-on′, *prep.* Up and on; resting on; on.
Upper, up′ėr, *a.* Higher in place or rank.—*n.* The upper part of a shoe.
Upper-hand, up′ėr-hand, *n.* Superiority.
Uppermost, up′ėr-mōst, *a. superl.* Highest in place, rank, or power.
Uppish, up′ish, *a.* Assuming lofty airs; arrogant.
Upraise, up-rāz′, *vt.* To raise or lift up.
Uprear, up-rēr′, *vt.* To rear up; to raise.
Upright, up′rīt, *a.* Straight up; erect; honest; just.—*n.* A vertical piece.
Uprise, up-rīz′, *vi.* To rise up; to slope upwards.—*n.* up′rīz. Rise; elevation.
Uprising, up-rīz′ing, *n.* Rise; ascent or acclivity; a riot; a rebellion.
Uproar, up′rōr, *n.* A great tumult; violent disturbance; bustle and clamour.
Uproarious, up-rō′ri-us, *a.* Making an uproar or tumult; tumultuous.
Uproot, up-röt′, *vt.* To tear up by the roots.
Upset, up-set′, *vt.* To overturn; to discompose completely.—*n.* up′set. Act of upsetting.—*a.* Fixed; determined.—**Upset price,** the price at which anything is exposed to sale by auction.
Upshot, up′shot, *n.* Final issue; end.
Upside, up′sīd, *n.* The upper side.
Upstairs, up′stärz, *a.* or *adv.* Ascending the stairs; in or pertaining to the upper part of a house.
Upstart, up-stärt′, *vi.* To start up suddenly.—*n.* up′stärt. A parvenu.
Upthrow, up-thrō′, *vt.* To throw up.—*n.* up′thrō. A lifting up of a portion of the earth's crust; an upheaval.
Upward, up′wėrd, *a.* Directed to a higher place; ascending.—*adv.* Upwards.
Upwards, up′wėrdz, *adv.* To a higher place; above (with *of*).
Uranium, ū-rā′ni-um, *n.* A rare metal, coloured like nickel or iron.
Uranography, ū-ra-nog′ra-fi, *n.* The description of the heavenly bodies, &c.
Uranus, ū′ra-nus, *n.* The most distant of all the planets except Neptune and Pluto.
Urban, ėr′ban, *a.* Of or belonging to a city or town.
Urbane, ėr-bān′, *a.* Courteous; polite.
Urbanity, ėr-ban′i-ti, *n.* Politeness; courtesy.
Urchin, ėr′chin, *n.* A hedgehog; a sea-urchin; a child or small boy.
Urdu, u̧r′du̧, *n.* Hindustani.
Ureter, ū-rē′tėr, *n.* The duct that conveys the urine from the kidney to the bladder.
Urethra, ū-rē′thra, *n.* The duct by which the urine is discharged from the bladder.
Urge, ėrj, *vt.* (urging, urged). To press to do something; to incite; to solicit; to insist on.—*vi.* To press forward.
Urgency, ėrj′en-si, *n.* Pressure of difficulty or necessity; importunity.
Urgent, ėrj′ent, *a.* That urges; pressing; importunate; vehement; eager.
Urgently, ėrj′ent-li, *adv.* In an urgent manner; with importunity; vehemently.
Uric, ū′rik, *a.* Pertaining to or obtained from urine.
Urinal, ū′rin-al, *n.* A convenience for persons requiring to pass urine.
Urinary, ū′ri-na-ri, *a.* Pertaining to urine.
Urinate, ū′ri-nāt, *vi.* To discharge urine.
Urine, ū′rin, *n.* An animal fluid secreted by the kidneys and stored in the bladder before being discharged.
Urn, ėrn, *n.* A vase swelling in the middle; a vessel for water.
Ursine, ėr′sīn, *a.* Pertaining to or resembling a bear.
Urticate, ėr′ti-kāt, *vt.* and *i.* To sting like a nettle.
Urtication, ėr-ti-kā′shon, *n.* The stinging of nettles; whipping with nettles to restore feeling.
Us, us, *pron.* The objective case of *we.*
Usable, ūz′a-bl, *a.* That may be used.
Usage, ūz′āj, *n.* Act or manner of using; treatment; practice; custom; use.
Usance, ūz′ans, *n.* Usury; interest.

Use, ūs, *n.* Act of employing anything; employment; utility; need; practice; wont.—*vt.* ūz (using, used). To put to use; to employ; to accustom; to treat.—*vi.* To be accustomed.
Useful, ūs'ful, *a.* Valuable for use; serviceable; beneficial; advantageous.
Useless, ūs'les, *a.* Worthless; unavailing.
User, ūz'ėr, *n.* One who uses.
Usher, ush'ėr, *n.* A door-keeper; an officer who introduces strangers, &c.; a subordinate teacher.—*vt.* To give entrance to; to introduce.
Usual, ū'zhū-al, *a.* Customary; common; frequent; ordinary; general.
Usually, ū'zhū-al-li, *adv.* Customarily.
Usufruct, ū'zū-frukt, *n.* In *law*, the use and enjoyment of lands or tenements.
Usurer, ū'zhūr-ėr, *n.* One who takes exorbitant interest.
Usurious, ū-zhū'ri-us, *a.* Pertaining to usury.
Usurp, ū-zėrp', *vt.* To seize and hold without right; to appropriate wrongfully.
Usurpation, ū-zėrp-ā'zhon, *n.* Act of usurping; illegal seizure or possession.
Usurper, ū-zėrp'ėr, *n.* One who seizes power or possessions without right.
Usury, ū'zhū-ri, *n.* Extortionate interest for money; practice of taking exorbitant interest.
Utensil, ū-ten'sil, *n.* That which is used; an instrument; implement.
Uterine, ū'tėr-īn, *a.* Pertaining to the uterus.
Uterus, ū'tėr-us, *n.*; pl. **-ri.** The womb.
Utilitarian, ū-til'i-tā"ri-an, *a.* Pertaining to utility or utilitarianism.—*n.* One who holds the doctrine of utilitarianism.
Utilitarianism, ū-til'i-tā"ri-an-izm, *n.* The doctrine that utility is the sole standard of moral conduct; the doctrine of the greatest happiness of the greatest number.
Utility, ū-til'i-ti, *n.* State or quality of being useful; usefulness; a useful thing.
Utilize, ū'til-īz, *vt.* (utilizing, utilized). To render useful; to put to use; to make use of.
Utmost, ut'mōst, *a.* Being farthest out; uttermost; extreme.—*n.* The greatest power, degree, or effort.
Utopia, ū-tō'pi-a, *n.* A place or state of ideal perfection.
Utopian, ū-tō'pi-an, *a.* Ideally perfect.—*n.* An ardent but unpractical reformer.
Utricle, ū'tri-kl, *n.* A little sac, cell, or reservoir.
Utter, ut'ėr, *a.* Complete; total; absolute.—*vt.* To give vent to; to put into circulation; to declare; to speak.
Utterable, ut'ėr-a-bl, *a.* That may be uttered, pronounced, or expressed.
Utterance, ut'ėr-ans, *n.* Act of uttering; pronunciation; words uttered.
Utterly, ut'ėr-li, *adv.* Totally; absolutely.
Uttermost, ut'ėr-mōst, *a.* Being in the furthest or greatest degree; extreme.—*n.* The utmost power or degree.
Uvula, ū'vū-la, *n.* The small fleshy body which hangs over the root of the tongue.
Uxorial, ug-zō'ri-al, *a.* Pertaining to a wife; uxorious.
Uxorious, ug-zō'ri-us, *a.* Excessively or dotingly fond of one's wife.

V

Vacancy, vā'kan-si, *n.* Empty space; vacuity; an interval of leisure; listlessness; a place or office not occupied.
Vacant, vā'kant, *a.* Empty; void; unoccupied; leisure; thoughtless; inane.
Vacate, va-kāt', *vt.* (vacating, vacated). To make vacant; to leave unoccupied; to annul.
Vacation, va-kā'shon, *n.* Act of vacating; intermission; recess; holidays.
Vaccinate, vak'si-nāt, *vt.* To inoculate with the cow-pox, in order to ward off small-pox.
Vaccination, vak-si-nā'shon, *n.* The act, art, or practice of vaccinating.
Vaccine, vak'sīn, *a.* Pertaining to cows or to cow-pox.
Vacillate, va'sil-lāt, *vi.* To sway; to waver; to fluctuate.
Vacillating, va'sil-lāt-ing, *p.a.* Inclined to vacillate; apt to waver; inconstant.
Vacillation, va-sil-lā'shon, *n.* A wavering; fluctuation of mind; unsteadiness.
Vacuity, va-kū'i-ti, *n.* Emptiness; vacancy; inanity; vacant expression.
Vacuous, va'kū-us, *a.* Empty; void; vacant; inane; inexpressive.
Vacuum, va'kū-um, *n.* Empty space; a void; an inclosed space void of air.—**Vacuum cleaner,** *n.* An apparatus used for removing dust from carpets, &c., by means of suction.
Vade-mecum, vā-dē-mē'kum, *n.* A manual; a pocket companion.
Vagabond, va'ga-bond, *a.* Wandering to and fro; pertaining to a vagrant.—*n.* A wanderer; a vagrant; a rascal.
Vagabondage, va'ga-bond-āj, *n.* The state or condition of a vagabond.
Vagary, va-gā'ri, *n.* A wild freak; a whim.
Vagina, va-jī'na, *n.* A sheath; the canal in females leading inwards to the uterus.
Vaginal, va'ji-nal, *a.* Pertaining to or like a sheath; pertaining to the vagina.
Vagrancy, vā'gran-si, *n.* State or life of a vagrant.
Vagrant, vā'grant, *a.* Wandering; unsettled.—*n.* A wanderer; a vagabond; a sturdy beggar; a tramp.
Vague, vāg, *a.* Indefinite; hazy; uncertain.
Vaguely, vāg'li, *adv.* In a vague manner.
Vail, vāl, *vi.* To avail: *poetical.*—*n.* A tip or gratuity to a domestic; veil.
Vain, vān, *a.* Without real value; empty; worthless; ineffectual; light-minded; conceited.—**In vain,** to no purpose.
Vainglorious, vān-glō'ri-us, *a.* Feeling or marked by vainglory; boastful.
Vainglory, vān-glō'ri, *n.* Empty pride; undue elation.
Vainly, vān'li, *adv.* In a vain manner; without effect; with vanity; idly.
Vair, vār, *n.* In *heraldry*, one of the furs represented by little shield-shaped pieces.
Valance, Valence, val'ans, val'ens, *n.* The drapery hanging round a bed, couch, &c.
Vale, vāl, *n.* A valley.
Valediction, va-lē-dik'shon, *n.* A farewell.
Valedictory, va-lē-dik'to-ri, *a.* Bidding farewell; pertaining to a leave-taking.
Valence, Valency, vā'lens, vā'len-si, *n.* The force which determines with how many atoms

of an element an atom of another element will combine chemically.
Valentine, va'len-tīn, *n.* A sweetheart selected or got by lot on St. *Valentine's* Day, 14th February; a missive of an amatory or satirical kind, sent on this day.
Valet, va'let or va'lā, *n.* A man-servant.—*vt.* To attend on a gentleman's person.
Valetudinarian, va'le-tū-di-nā"ri-an, *a.* Infirm; sickly.—*n.* One of a sickly constitution.
Valetudinary, va-le-tū'di-na-ri, *n.* and *a.* Same as *Valetudinarian.*
Valiant, val'yant, *a.* Brave; courageous; intrepid; heroic.
Valiantly, val'yant-li, *adv.* Bravely; heroically.
Valid, va'lid, *a.* Well based or grounded; sound; just; good or sufficient in law.
Validate, va'lid-āt, *vt.* To make valid.
Validity, va-lid'i-ti, *n.* Justness; soundness; legal sufficiency.
Valise, va-lēs', *n.* A small travelling-bag.
Valley, val'i, *n.* A low tract of land between hills; a river-basin.
Valorous, va'lor-us, *a.* Brave; valiant.
Valour, va'lor, *n.* Bravery; courage; intrepidity; prowess in war.
Valuable, va'lū-a-bl, *a.* Of great worth; precious; worthy.—*n.* A thing of value; choice article of personal property: usually in *pl.*
Valuation, va-lū-ā'shon, *n.* Act or art of valuing; appraisement; estimated worth.
Valuator, va'lū-āt-or, *n.* One who sets a value; an appraiser.
Value, va'lū, *n.* Worth; utility; importance; import; precise signification.—*vt.* (valuing, valued). To rate at a certain price; to estimate; to esteem; to prize; to regard.
Valueless, va'lū-les, *a.* Worthless.
Valuer, va'lū-ėr, *n.* One who values; valuator.
Valvate, val'vāt, *a.* Having or like a valve.
Valve, valv, *n.* A leaf of a folding door; a lid for an orifice, opening only one way and regulating the passage of fluid or air; a separable portion of the shell of a mollusc.
Valved, valvd, *a.* Having a valve or valves.
Valvular, valv'ū-lėr, *a.* Containing valves; having the character of or acting as a valve.
Vamp, vamp, *n.* The upper leather of a boot; a piece added for appearance sake.—*vt.* To repair; to furbish up; to patch.
Vampire, vam'pīr, *n.* A dead person believed to have an unnatural life so as to be able to leave the grave at night and suck the blood of living persons; an extortioner; a blood-sucker; a vampire-bat.
Vampire-bat, vam'pīr-bat, *n.* A blood-sucking bat of South America with long sharp teeth.
Van, van, *n.* The front of an army or fleet; foremost portion; a winnowing fan; a covered vehicle for goods.
Vanadium, va-nā'di-um, *n.* A silvery brittle metal.
Vandal, van'dal, *n.* One who wilfully or ignorantly destroys any work of art or the like.
Vandalism, van'dal-izm, *n.* Conduct of a vandal; hostility to art or literature.
Vane, vān, *n.* A weathercock; the broad part of a feather on either side of the shaft; blade of a windmill, &c.
Vanguard, van'gärd, *n.* The troops who march in the van of an army.
Vanilla, va-nil'a, *n.* A tropical orchid; a fragrant substance obtained from it, used for seasoning.
Vanish, va'nish, *vi.* To disappear; to pass away.
Vanity, va'ni-ti, *n.* Quality or state of being vain; worthlessness; vain pursuit; desire of indiscriminate admiration; conceit; a trifle.
Vanquish, vang'kwish, *vt.* To conquer; to overcome; to confute.
Vanquisher, vang'kwish-ėr, *n.* A conqueror.
Vantage, van'tāj, *n.* Advantage; vantage-ground; in lawn tennis, being in a position to win the game by winning the next point.
Vantage-ground, van'tāj-ground, *n.* Place or state which gives one an advantage.
Vapid, va'pid, *a.* Spiritless; flat; dull.
Vapidity, va-pid'i-ti, *n.* Flatness; dulness; want of life or spirit.
Vaporable, vā-por-a-bl, *a.* Capable of being converted into vapour.
Vaporize, vā-por-īz, *vt.* To convert into vapour.—*vi.* To pass off in vapour.
Vaporous, vā'por-us, *a.* Like vapour; full of vapours; unreal; whimsical.
Vapour, vā'por, *n.* An exhalation or fume; visible moisture or steam; hazy matter; a vain imagination; *pl.* a nervous hysterical affection; the blues.—*vi.* To boast; to bully.
Vapourer, vā'por-ėr, *n.* A braggart; a bully.
Vapoury, vā'por-i, *a.* Vaporous; hypochondriac.
Variability, vā-ri-a-bil'i-ti, *n.* State of being variable; liability to vary.
Variable, vā'ri-a-bl, *a.* That may vary or alter; changeable; fickle; unsteady.
Variance, vā'ri-ans, *n.* Variation; disagreement; dissension; discord.
Variant, vā'ri-ant, *a.* Varying; different.—*n.* Something the same, but with another form; a different version.
Variation, vā-ri-ā'shon, *n.* Act or process of varying; alteration; amount or rate of change; inflection; deviation.
Varicose, va'ri-kōs, *a.* Exhibiting a morbid enlargement or dilation, as the veins.
Varied, vā'rid, *p.a.* Characterized by variety; diverse; various.
Variegate, vā'ri-e-gāt, *vt.* (variegating, variegated). To diversify in appearance; to mark with different colours.
Variegation, vā'ri-e-gā"shon, *n.* State of being variegated; diversity of colours.
Variety, va-rī'e-ti, *n.* State or quality of being varied or various; diversity; a varied assortment; a sort; a kind.
Variorum, vā-ri-ō'rum, *a.* Applied to an edition of a work containing the notes of various editors.
Various, vā'ri-us, *a.* Different; several; changeable; uncertain; diverse.
Varlet, vär'let, *n.* A footman; a rascal.
Varletry, vär'let-ri, *n.* The rabble.
Varnish, vär'nish, *n.* A clear solution of resinous matter, for coating surfaces and giving a gloss; outside show; gloss.—*vt.* To lay varnish on; to gloss over.
Vary, vā'ri, *vt.* (varying, varied). To change; to diversify.—*vi.* To alter; to change; to differ; to swerve; to disagree.
Vascular, vas'kū-lėr, *a.* Pertaining to those

vessels that have to do with conveying blood, chyle, &c.
Vasculum, vas'kū-lum, *n.*; pl. **-la.** A botanist's case for carrying specimens.
Vase, väz, *n.* A vessel of some size and of various materials and forms, generally ornamental rather than useful.
Vase-painting, väz-pānt'ing, *n.* The embellishment of vases with pigments.
Vassal, vas'al, *n.* A feudal tenant; a subject; a retainer; a bondman.
Vassalage, vas'al-āj, *n.* Servitude; dependence.
Vast, väst, *a.* Of great extent; immense; mighty; great in importance or degree.—*n.* A boundless space; immensity.
Vastly, väst'li, *adv.* Very greatly; exceedingly.
Vat, vat, *n.* A large vessel for holding liquors; a tun; a wooden tank or cistern.—*vt.* (vatting, vatted). To put in a vat.
Vatican, vat'i-kan, *n.* The palace of the Pope at Rome; the papal power or government.
Vaticinate, vā-tis'i-nāt, *vi.* and *t.* To prophesy; to foretell.
Vaudeville, vōd'vēl, *n.* A light, gay song; a ballad; a dramatic piece with light or comic songs.
Vault, vạlt, *n.* An arched roof; a subterranean chamber; a cellar; a leap; a leap with the hand resting on something.—*vt.* To arch.—*vi.* To leap; to bound.
Vaulted, vạlt'ed, *p.a.* Arched; concave.
Vaulting, vạlt'ing, *n.* Vaulted work; vaults collectively.—*p.a.* Leaping.
Vaunt, vạnt, *vi.* To brag; to exult.—*vt.* To boast of; to make a vain display of.—*n.* A boast.
Vauntingly, vạnt'ing-li, *adv.* With vaunting; boastfully.
Vaward, vä'wėrd, *n.* The van or vanguard.—*a.* Being in the van or front.
Veal, vēl, *n.* The flesh of a calf.
V-bomb, vē'bom, *n.* A self-propelled bomb or rocket employed by the Germans in 1944 and 1945.
Veda, vā'dä or vē'da, *n.* The body of ancient Sanskrithymns on which Brahmanism is based.
Vedette, Vidette, vē-det', *n.* A mounted sentry; a picket or outpost.
Veer, vēr, *vi.* To change direction; to turn round.—*vt.* To direct to a different course.
Vegetable, ve'je-ta-bl, *a.* Belonging to or like plants.—*n.* A plant; a plant for culinary purposes.
Vegetal, ve'je-tal, *a.* Vegetable; pertaining to the vital phenomena common to plants and animals.
Vegetarian, ve-je-tā'ri-an, *n.* One who abstains from animal food and lives on vegetables.
Vegetate, ve'je-tāt, *vi.* (vegetating, vegetated). To grow as plants; to live a monotonous, useless life; to have a mere existence.
Vegetation, ve-je-tā'shon, *n.* The process of growing, as plants; plants in general.
Vegetative, ve'je-tāt-iv, *a.* Having the power of growing, as plants; having the power to produce growth in plants.
Vehemence, vē'he-mens, *n.* Ardour; violence; force; impetuosity; fury.
Vehement, vē'he-ment, *a.* Very eager or urgent; ardent; violent; furious.
Vehemently, vē'he-ment-li, *adv.* With vehemence; passionately; violently.
Vehicle, vē'hi-kl, *n.* Any kind of carriage moving on land; conveyance; medium.
Vehicular, Vehiculary, vē-hik'ū-lėr, vē-hik'-ū-lėr-i, *a.* Pertaining to a vehicle.
Veil, vāl, *n.* A screen; an article of dress shading the face; a covering or disguise; the soft palate.—*vt.* To cover with a veil; to envelop; to disguise.
Vein, vān, *n.* A blood-vessel which returns impure blood to the heart and lungs; a blood-vessel; a sap tube in leaves; a crack in a rock, filled up by substances different from the rock; a streak; disposition; mood.—*vt.* To fill or variegate with veins.
Veining, vān'ing, *n.* Arrangement of veins; a streaked appearance as if from veins.
Veiny, vān'i, *a.* Full of veins.
Veldt, Veld, felt, *n.* A term in S. Africa for open uninclosed country.
Velleity, vel-lē'i-ti, *n.* Volition in the weakest form; mere inclination.
Vellicate, vel'i-kāt, *vt.* To twitch.
Vellum, vel'um, *n.* A fine parchment made of calf's skin.
Velocipede, vē-los'i-pēd, *n.* A light vehicle propelled by the rider; bicycle, &c.
Velocity, vē-los'i-ti, *n.* Rate of motion; speed; rapidity.
Velutinous, ve-lū'ti-nus, *a.* Velvety.
Velvet, vel'vet, *n.* A rich silk stuff with a close, fine, soft pile.—*a.* Made of or like velvet.
Velveteen, vel-vet-ēn', *n.* A cloth made of cotton in imitation of velvet; cotton velvet.
Velvety, vel'vet-i, *a.* Made of or resembling velvet.
Venal, vē'nal, *a.* Ready to accept a bribe; mercenary.
Venality, vē-nal'i-ti, *n.* State of being venal; prostitution of talents or services.
Venation, vē-nā'shon, *n.* The manner in which the veins of leaves are arranged.
Vend, vend, *vt.* To sell.
Vendace, ven'dās, *n.* A fish of the salmon family found only in a few British lakes and in Sweden.
Vender, ven'dėr, *n.* One who vends; a seller.
Vendetta, ven-det'ta, *n.* A blood-feud; the practice of the nearest of kin executing vengeance on a murderer.
Vendible, vend'i-bl, *a.* That may be vended or sold; saleable; marketable.
Vendor, ven'dor, *n.* A vender; a seller.
Veneer, ve-nēr', *n.* A thin facing of fine wood glued on a less valuable sort; any similar coating; fair outward show.—*vt.* To overlay with veneer; to put a fine superficial show on.
Venerable, ve'nė-ra-bl, *a.* Worthy of veneration; deserving respect from age, character, or associations.
Venerate, ve'nė-rāt, *vt.* (venerating, venerated). To reverence; to revere; to regard as sacred.
Veneration, ve-nė-rā'shon, *n.* The highest degree of respect and reverence; respect mingled with some degree of awe.
Venereal, ve-nē'rē-al, *a.* Pertaining to sexual intercourse.
Venery, ve'nė-ri, *n.* Hunting; sexual intercourse.
Venesection, ve-nē-sek'shon, *n.* Blood-letting; phlebotomy.
Venetian, vē-nē'shi-an, *a.* Belonging to

Venice; denoting a window blind made of thin slats of wood.
Vengeance, venj'ans, *n.* Punishment in return for an injury; penal retribution.
Vengeful, venj'ful, *a.* Full of vengeance; vindictive; retributive; revengeful.
Venial, vē'ni-al, *a.* That may be pardoned or forgiven; excusable.
Venison, ven'zn or ven'i-zn, *n.* The flesh of deer.
Venom, ve'nom, *n.* Poison; spite; malice; malignity; virulency.
Venomous, ve'nom-us, *a.* Full of venom; poisonous; noxious; spiteful.
Venose, vē'nōz, *n.* Having numerous branched veins, as leaves.
Venous, vē'nus, *a.* Pertaining to a vein; contained in veins, as blood; venose.
Vent, vent, *n.* A small opening; flue or funnel; an outlet; the anus; utterance; expression; sale; market.—*vt.* To let out; to publish.
Ventage, vent'āj, *n.* A small hole, as of a musical instrument.
Venter, ven'tėr, *n.* The abdomen; in *law*, the uterus.
Ventilate, ven'ti-lāt, *vt.* (ventilating, ventilated). To winnow; to expose to the air; to supply with fresh air; to let be freely discussed.
Ventilation, ven-ti-lā'shon, *n.* Act of ventilating; replacement of vitiated air by fresh air, a bringing forward for discussion.
Ventilator, ven'ti-lāt-ėr, *n.* A contrivance for keeping the air fresh in any close space.
Ventral, ven'tral, *a.* Belonging to the belly; abdominal.
Ventricle, ven'tri-kl, *n.* A small cavity in an animal body; either of two cavities of the heart which propel the blood into the arteries.
Ventricular, ven-trik'ū-lėr, *a.* Pertaining to a ventricle; distended in the middle.
Ventriloquism, Ventriloquy, ven-tri'lo-kwizm, ven-tri'lo-kwi, *n.* The art of uttering sounds so that the voice appears to come not from the actual speaker.
Ventriloquist, ven-tri'lo-kwist, *n.* One who practises or is skilled in ventriloquism.
Ventriloquize, ven-tri'lo-kwīz, *vi.* To practise ventriloquism.
Venture, ven'tūr, *n.* An undertaking which involves hazard or danger; a commercial speculation; thing put to hazard; chance.—*vi.* (venturing, ventured). To make a venture; to dare.—*vt.* To risk.
Venturesome, ven'tūr-sum, *a.* Apt or inclined to venture; bold; hazardous.
Venturous, ven'tūr-us, *a.* Venturesome.
Venue, ven'ū, *n.* A thrust; the place where an action is laid or the trial of a cause takes place.
Venus, vē'nus, *n.* The Roman goddess of beauty and love; a planet.
Veracious, ve-rā'shus, *a.* Observant of truth; truthful; true.
Veracity, ve-ras'i-ti, *n.* Truthfulness; truth; that which is true.
Veranda, Verandah, ve-ran'da, *n.* An open portico or light gallery along the front of a building.
Veratrin, Veratrine, ve-rā'trin, *n.* A poisonous drug obtained from plants of the hellebore genus.
Verb, vėrb, *n.* The part of speech which signifies to be, to do, or to suffer.
Verbal, vėrb'al, *a.* Relating to words; spoken; literal; derived from a verb.—*n.* A noun derived from a verb.
Verbalism, vėrb'al-izm, *n.* Something expressed orally.
Verbalist, vėrb'al-ist, *n.* One who deals in words merely; a minute critic of words.
Verbalize, vėrb'al-iz, *vt.* To convert into or employ as a verb.
Verbally, vėrb'al-li, *adv.* In a verbal manner; by words uttered; word for word.
Verbatim, vėr-bā'tim, *adv.* Word for word; in the same words.
Verbena, vėr-bē'na, *n.* A genus of plants (and type of an order), some of which are cultivated for the beauty of their flowers.
Verbiage, vėr'bi-āj, *n.* Verbosity.
Verbose, vėr-bōs', *a.* Wordy; prolix.
Verbosity, vėr-bos'i-ti, *n.* Superabundance of words; wordiness; prolixity.
Verdancy, vėr'dan-si, *n.* Greenness; inexperience.
Verdant, vėr'dant, *a.* Green with herbage or foliage; simple and inexperienced.
Verd-antique, vėrd-an-tēk', *n.* A stone consisting of an aggregate of serpentine and lighter-coloured stone having a greenish colour; a green porphyry used as marble.
Verderer, Verderor, vėr'dėr-ėr, vėr'dėr-or, *n.* An official having charge of the trees, &c., in a royal forest.
Verdict, vėr'dikt, *n.* The answer of a jury; decision in general; opinion.
Verdigris, Verdegris, vėr'di-gris, vėr'de-gris, *n.* The rust of copper; a substance obtained by exposing copper to the air in contact with acetic acid.
Verditer, vėr'di-tėr, *n.* A blue or bluish-green pigment.
Verdure, vėr'dūr, *n.* Greenness; freshness of vegetation; green vegetation.
Verdurous, vėr'dūr-us, *a.* Verdant.
Verge, vėrj, *n.* A rod of office; a mace; a wand; brink; margin; compass; scope.—*vi.* (verging, verged). To incline; to tend; to border.
Verger, vėrj'ėr, *n.* A mace-bearer; an official who takes care of the interior of a church.
Veridical, ve-rid'ik-al, *a.* Veracious.
Verifiable, ve'ri-fī-a-bl, *a.* That may be verified.
Verification, ve'ri-fi-kā"shon, *n.* Act of verifying; confirmation.
Verify, ve'ri-fī, *vt.* (verifying, verified). To prove to be true; to confirm; to fulfil.
Verily, ve'ri-li, *adv.* In truth; really; truly.
Verisimilar, ve-ri-si'mi-lėr, *a.* Having the appearance of truth; probable; likely.
Verisimilitude, ve'ri-si-mil"i-tūd, *n.* The appearance of truth; probability; likelihood.
Veritable, ve'ri-ta-bl, *a.* True; real; actual.
Verity, ve'ri-ti, *n.* Truth; reality; a truth.
Verjuice, vėr'jūs, *n.* An acid liquor expressed from fruit; sourness of temper, manner, &c.
Vermeil, vėr'mil, *n.* Vermilion; silver or bronze gilt.
Vermicelli, vėr-mi-chel'li, *n.* An Italian article of food made of flour, &c., in the form of long threads.
Vermicide, vėr'mi-sīd, *n.* A substance which destroys intestinal worms.
Vermicular, vėr-mik'ū-lėr, *a.* Pertaining to worms; like a worm; vermiculated.

Vermiculate, vėr-mik'ū-lāt, *vt.* To ornament so as to suggest worms or a worm-eaten surface.—*a.* Worm-like in appearance.
Vermiculation, vėr-mik'ū-lā''shon, *n.* A worm-like motion or ornamentation.
Vermiculose, Vermiculous, vėr-mik'ū-lōs, vėr-mik'ū-lus, *a.* Containing worms or grubs; like worms.
Vermifuge, vėr'mi-fūj, *n.* A medicine that expels intestinal worms.
Vermilion, vėr-mil'yon, *n.* Cinnabar or red sulphide of mercury; a beautiful red colour. —*vt.* To colour with vermilion.
Vermin, vėr'min, *n. sing.* and *pl.* A term for all sorts of small noxious mammals or insects.
Verminate, vėr'min-āt, *vi.* To breed vermin.
Verminous, vėr'min-us, *a.* Pertaining to vermin; like vermin; caused by vermin; infested by vermin.
Vermivorous, vėr-miv'o-rus, *a.* Devouring worms; feeding on worms.
Vernacular, vėr-nak'ū-lėr, *a.* Belonging to the country of one's birth or the everyday idiom of a place.—*n.* The native idiom of a place.
Vernacularism, vėr-nak'ū-lėr-izm, *n.* A vernacular idiom.
Vernal, vėr'nal, *a.* Pertaining to the spring; belonging to youth.
Vernation, vėr-nā'shon, *n.* The arrangement of the young leaves within the bud.
Vernier, vėr'ni-ėr, *n.* A small sliding scale, parallel to the fixed scale of a barometer, or other graduated instrument, and subdividing the divisions into more minute parts.
Verónica, ve-ron'i-ka, *n.* A genus of plants including the various species of speedwell.
Verrucose, Verrucous, ver'ū-kōs, ver'ū-kus, *a.* Warty.
Versant, vėr'sant, *n.* Part of a country sloping in one direction; slope of surface.
Versatile, vėrs'a-til, *a.* Readily turning; inconstant; having many accomplishments.
Versatility, vėrs-a-til'i-ti, *n.* Aptness to change; facility in taking up various intellectual pursuits.
Verse, vėrs, *n.* A line of poetry; metre; poetry; versification; a stanza; a short division of any composition.
Versed, vėrst, *a.* Conversant; practised; skilled: with *in.*
Versicle, vėrs'i-kl, *n.* A little verse; a short verse in a church service, spoken or chanted.
Versification, vėrs'i-fi-kā''shon, *n.* Act or art of versifying; metrical composition.
Versifier, vėrs'i-fī-ėr, *n.* One who versifies; one who makes verses.
Versify, vėrs'i-fī, *vi.* (versifying, versified). To make verses.—*vt.* To form or turn into verse.
Version, vėr'shon, *n.* Act of translating; a translation; rendering; account.
Verso, vėr'sō, *n.* A left-hand page.
Verst, verst, *n.* A Russian measure of length, about two-thirds of an English mile.
Versus, vėr'sus, *prep.* Against.
Vert, vėrt, *n.* In *law*, growing wood, or the right to cut it; the heraldic name of green.
Vertebra, vėr'te-bra, *n.*; pl. **-ræ.** One of the bones of the spine; *pl.* the spine.
Vertebral, vėr'te-bral, *a.* Pertaining to the vertebræ; consisting of vertebræ.
Vertebrata, vėr-te-brā'ta, *n.pl.* The highest division of animals, consisting of those which possess a backbone.
Vertebrate, vėr'te-brāt, *a.* Having a backbone.—*n.* One of the Vertebrata.
Vertex, vėr'teks, *n.*; pl. **-texes** or **-tices.** The highest point; top; apex; zenith.
Vertical, vėr'ti-kal, *a.* Pertaining to the vertex; directly over the head; perpendicular to the horizon; upright.
Vertiginous, vėr-ti'jin-us, *a.* Giddy or dizzy; affected with vertigo.
Vertigo, vėr-tī'gō or vėr'ti-gō, *n.* Dizziness or swimming of the head; giddiness.
Vertu, vėr'tu̧, *n.* Excellence in objects of art or curiosity; such objects collectively.
Vervain, vėr'vān, *n.* A plant once held in repute for its medicinal virtues.
Verve, verv, *n.* Spirit; energy.
Very, ve'ri, *a.* True; real; actual.—*adv.* Truly; in a great or high degree.
Vesical, ve'si-kal, *a.* Pertaining to the bladder.
Vesicant, ve'si-kant, *n.* A blistering application.
Vesicate, ve'si-kāt, *vt.* To blister.
Vesication, ve-si-kā'shon, *n.* The process of raising blisters on the skin.
Vesicle, ve'si-kl, *n.* A small bladder-like structure or cavity; a little sac or cyst.
Vesicular, ve-sik'ū-lėr, *a.* Pertaining to or consisting of or full of vesicles.
Vesiculose, Vesiculous, ve-sik'ū-lōs, ve-sik'-ū-lus, *a.* Vesicular.
Vesper, ves'pėr, *n.* The evening; the evening-star; *pl.* evening worship or service.—*a.* Relating to the evening or to vespers.
Vespiary, ves'pi-a-ri, *n.* A nest of wasps, hornets, &c.
Vessel, ves'el, *n.* A hollow utensil for holding liquids or solids; a ship; a tube or canal for blood or sap; a person.
Vest, vest, *n.* Undergarment for the upper part of the body; a waistcoat.—*vt.* To clothe; to endow; to invest.—*vi.* To descend to; to devolve; to take effect, as a title or right.
Vesta, ves'ta, *n.* The Roman goddess of hearth and home; a wax match.
Vestal, ves'tal, *a.* Pertaining to Vesta; virgin; chaste.—*n.* A virgin consecrated to Vesta; a woman of spotless chastity.
Vested, vest'ed, *a.* Clothed or habited; robed; well settled or established.
Vestibule, ves'ti-būl, *n.* A passage or hall inside the outer door of a house.
Vestige, ves'tij, *n.* Footprint; mark or trace of something; mark or remnant left.
Vestment, vest'ment, *n.* A garment; a special article of dress worn by clergymen when officiating.
Vestry, ves'tri, *n.* A room connected with a church, where the ecclesiastical vestments are kept; a body of ratepayers elected for the local government of a parish.
Vesture, ves'tūr, *n.* Dress; apparel; clothing.
Vesuvian, ve-sū'vi-an, *n.* A kind of match for lighting cigars, &c.
Vetch, vech, *n.* The popular name of plants allied to the bean, cultivated for fodder.
Vetchy, vech'i, *a.* Consisting of or abounding with vetches.
Veteran, ve'te-ran, *a.* Having been long exercised; long experienced in war.—*n.* An old soldier; a man of great experience.
Veterinary, ve'te-ri-na-ri, *a.* Pertaining to the art of healing the diseases of domestic animals.

Veto, vē'tō, *n.* The power or right of forbidding; any authoritative prohibition or refusal. —*vt.* (vetoing, vetoed). To forbid; to interdict.
Vex, veks, *vt.* To irritate; to torment; to annoy; to distress; to make sorrowful.
Vexation, veks-ā'shon, *n.* Irritation; annoyance; grief; affliction.
Vexatious, veks-ā'shus, *a.* Irritating; annoying; distressing; troublesome.
Vexed, vekst, *a.* Annoyed; troubled; much disputed or contested.
Vexillum, vek-sil'um, *n.*; pl. **-illa.** An ancient Roman military standard; an ecclesiastical banner.
Via, vī'a, *prep.* By way of.
Viable, vī'a-bl, *a.* Capable of living, applied to a new-born child.
Viaduct, vī'a-dukt, *n.* A long bridge for carrying a road or railway over a valley.
Vial, vī'al, *n.* A phial; a small glass bottle.
Viand, vī'and, *n.* Meat dressed; food; victuals: used chiefly in *pl.*
Viaticum, vī-at'i-kum, *n.* Provisions for a journey; the communion given to a dying person.
Vibrant, vī'brant, *a.* Vibrating; tremulous.
Vibrate, vī'brāt, *vi.* (vibrating, vibrated). To swing; to quiver; to be unstable.—*vt.* To wave to and fro; to cause to quiver.
Vibration, vī-brā'shon, *n.* Act of vibrating; a swing; a quivering motion.
Vibratory, vī'bra-to-ri, *a.* Causing to vibrate; vibrating.
Vicar, vi'kėr, *n.* A substitute in office; deputy; the priest of a parish in England who receives the smaller tithes, or a salary.
Vicarage, vi'kėr-āj, *n.* The benefice of a vicar; residence of a vicar.
Vicarial, vī-kā'ri-al, *a.* Pertaining to a vicar; delegated; vicarious.
Vicariate, vī-kā'ri-āt, *n.* Office of a vicar.—*a.* Vicarial.
Vicarious, vī-kā'ri-us, *a.* Pertaining to a substitute; deputed, substituted or suffered for or in the place of another.
Vice, vis, *n.* A blemish; fault; moral failing; profligacy; a fault or bad trick in a horse; an iron instrument which holds fast anything worked upon; a prefix denoting position second in rank.
Vice, vī'sē, *prep.* In place of.
Vice-admiral, vīs-ad'mi-ral, *n.* A naval officer, the next in rank to an Admiral.
Vice-chancellor, vīs-chan'sel-lor, *n.* An officer acting as deputy for a chancellor.
Vice-consul, vīs-kon'sul, *n.* One who acts for a consul; a consul of subordinate rank.
Vicegerent, vīs-jē'rent, *n.* One who acts in the place of a superior; a substitute.
Vicenary, vis'e-na-ri, *a.* Belonging to or consisting of twenty.
Vicennial, vi-sen'ni-al, *a.* Lasting twenty years.
Vice-president, vīs-pre'zi-dent, *n.* An office-bearer next in rank below a president.
Vice-regal, vīs-rē'gal, *a.* Pertaining to a viceroy or viceroyalty.
Viceroy, vīs'roi, *n.* One who governs in place of a king or queen.
Viceroyalty, Viceroyship, vīs-roi'al-ti, vīs'roi-ship, *n.* The dignity, office, or jurisdiction of a viceroy.
Vicinage, vi'sin-āj, *n.* Neighbourhood.
Vicinity, vi-sin'i-ti, *n.* Neighbourhood; proximity.
Vicious, vi'shus, *a.* Characterized by vice; faulty; depraved; immoral; spiteful.
Vicissitude, vi-sis'i-tūd, *n.* Change or alternation; one of the ups and downs of life.
Victim, vik'tim, *n.* A living being sacrificed; a person or thing destroyed; a person who suffers; a gull.
Victimize, vik'tim-īz, *vt.* To make a victim of; to cheat; to deceive.
Victor, vik'tor, *n.* One who conquers; one who proves the winner.—*a.* Victorious.
Victoria, vik-tō'ri-a, *n.* A four-wheeled carriage, with a collapsible top, seated for two persons.—**Victoria Cross,** a British decoration granted for valour in battle.
Victorious, vik-tō'ri-us, *a.* Having gained victory; conquering; indicating victory.
Victory, vik'to-ri, *n.* Conquest; a gaining of the superiority in any contest.
Victress, vik'tres, *n.* A female that conquers.
Victual, vit'l, *n.* Food provided; provisions: generally in *pl.*—*vt.* (victualling, victualled). To supply with victuals or stores.
Victualler, vit'l-ėr, *n.* One who furnishes victuals; a tavern-keeper; a ship carrying provisions for other ships.
Vicugna, Vicuña, vi-kön'ya, *n.* A South American animal yielding a wool used for delicate fabrics.
Vide, vī'dē, *vt.* See; refer to.
Videlicet, vī-del'i-set, *adv.* To wit; that is; namely: usually abbreviated to *viz.*
Vidette, vi-det', *n.* *See* VEDETTE.
Vidimus, vī'di-mus or vid', *n.* An examination, as of accounts; an abstract of contents.
Viduity, vi-dū'i-ti, *n.* Widowhood.
Vie, vī, *vi.* (vying, vied). To contend.
Viennese, vi-en-ēz', *n. sing.* and *pl.* A native of Vienna; natives of Vienna.
View, vū, *n.* A look; inspection; consideration; range of vision; power of perception; sight; scene; pictorial sketch; judgment; intention.—*vt.* To see; to survey; to consider.—*vi.* To look.
Viewer, vū'ėr, *n.* One who views, surveys, or examines; an inspector; an overseer.
Viewless, vū'les, *a.* Invisible.
Viewy, vū'i, *a.* Holding peculiar views; given to doctrinaire notions.
Vigesimal, vi-jes'i-mal, *a.* Twentieth.
Vigil, vi'jil, *n.* Act of keeping awake; a devotional watching; the eve or day preceding a church festival.
Vigilance, vi'ji-lans, *n.* Watchfulness.
Vigilant, vi'ji-lant, *a.* Watchful; circumspect; wary; on the outlook; alert.
Vignette, vin-yet' or vi-net', *n.* Flowers, head and tail pieces, &c., in books; a wood-cut without a definite border; a small photographic portrait; a small attractive picture.
Vigorous, vi'gor-us, *a.* Full of vigour; strong; lusty; powerful; energetic.
Vigour, vi'gor, *n.* Active force or strength; physical force; strength of mind.
Viking, vik'ing, *n.* An ancient Scandinavian rover or sea-robber.
Vile, vīl, *a.* Morally worthless; despicable; depraved; bad.
Vilely, vīl'li, *adv.* Basely; meanly.

Vilification, vi′li-fi-kā″shon, *n.* The act of vilifying or defaming.
Vilify, vi′li-fī, *vt.* (vilifying, vilified). To defame; to traduce; to slander.
Vilipend, vi′li-pend, *vt.* To slander.
Vill, vil, *n.* A hamlet; a district of a parish.
Villa, vil′a, *n.* A country seat; a suburban house.
Village, vil′āj, *n.* A collection of houses, smaller than a town and larger than a hamlet.
Villager, vil′āj-ėr, *n.* An inhabitant of a village.
Villain, vil′an or vil′ān, *n.* A feudal serf; a peasant; a knave or scoundrel.
Villainous, vil′an-us, *a.* Base; vile; wicked; depraved; mean.
Villainy, vil′an-i, *n.* Depravity; wickedness; a crime.
Villein, vil′en, *n.* A feudal serf.
Villeinage, Villenage, vil′en-āj, *n.* The feudal tenure of lands and tenements by a villein; tenure at the will of a lord.
Villi, vil′lī, *n.pl.* Fine small fibres; soft hairs on certain fruits, flowers, &c.
Villosity, vil-los′i-ti, *n.* The state of being villous.
Villous, Villose, vil′lus, vil′lōs, *a.* Having a velvety, shaggy, or woolly surface.
Vim, vim, *n.* Vigour; energy.
Vinaceous, vī-nā′shus, *a.* Belonging to wine or grapes; of the colour of wine.
Vinaigrette, vin-ā-gret′, *n.* A small box, with perforations on the top, for holding smelling-salts.
Vinaigrous, vin′āg-rus, *a.* Sour like vinegar; crabbed; peevish.
Vincible, vin′si-bl, *a.* Conquerable.
Vinculum, ving′kū-lum, *n.*; pl. **-la.** A bond of union; a bond or tie.
Vindicate, vin′di-kāt, *vt.* (vindicating, vindicated). To prove to be just or valid; to maintain the rights of; to defend; to justify.
Vindication, vin-di-kā′shon, *n.* Act of vindicating; a defence or justification.
Vindicative, vin′di-kāt-iv, *a.* Tending to vindicate.
Vindicator, vin′di-kāt-or, *n.* One who vindicates; one who defends.
Vindicatory, vin′di-ka-to-ri, *n.* Tending to vindicate; justificatory; punitory.
Vindictive, vin-dik′tiv, *a.* Revengeful.
Vine, vīn, *n.* A climbing plant producing grapes; the slender stem of any climbing plant.
Vinegar, vi′nē-gėr, *n.* Diluted and impure acetic acid, obtained from wine, beer, &c.; sourness of temper.
Vinegarette, vi′nē-gėr-et, *n.* A vinaigrette.
Vinery, vin′ė-ri, *n.* A hot-house for vines.
Vineyard, vin′yärd, *n.* A plantation of vines producing grapes.
Vinous, Vinose, vīn′us, vīn′ōs, *a.* Having the qualities of wine; pertaining to wine.
Vintage, vint′āj, *n.* The gathering of the grape crop; the crop itself; the wine produced by the grapes of one season.
Vintager, vint′āj-ėr, *n.* One that gathers the vintage.
Vintner, vint′nėr, *n.* One who deals in wine; a wine-seller; a licensed victualler.
Vintnery, vint′nėr-i, *n.* The trade or occupation of a vintner.
Viol, vī′ol, *n.* An ancient musical instrument like the violin.
Viola, vī′ō-la, *n.* The violet, an extensive genus of plants.
Viola, vē-o′la, *n.* The tenor violin.
Violable, vī′ō-la-bl, *a.* That may be violated.
Violate, vī′ō-lāt, *vt.* (violating, violated). To injure; to outrage; to desecrate; to profane; to transgress.
Violation, vī-ō-lā′shon, *n.* Infringement; transgression; desecration; rape.
Violator, vī′ō-lāt-or, *n.* One who violates.
Violence, vī′ō-lens, *n.* Quality of being violent; vehemence; outrage; injury.
Violent, vī′ō-lent, *a.* Impetuous; furious; outrageous; fierce; severe.
Violently, vī′ō-lent-li, *adv.* With violence.
Violet, vī′ō-let, *n.* A genus of plants that includes the pansy, &c.; a plant having a bluish purple flower with a delicious smell; a rich bluish-purple.—*a.* Of a bluish-purple colour.
Violin, vī-ō-lin′, *n.* A musical instrument with four strings, played with a bow; a fiddle.
Violinist, vī-ō-lin′ist, *n.* A player on the violin.
Violist, vī′ō-list, *n.* A player on the viola.
Violoncellist, vī′ō-lon-sel″ist, *n.* A player on the violoncello.
Violoncello, vī′ō-lon-sel″lō or vē′ō-lon-chel″lō, *n.* A large and powerful bow instrument of the violin kind.
Viper, vī′pėr, *n.* A venomous serpent.
Viperine, vī′pėr-īn, *a.* Pertaining to a viper or to vipers.
Viperish, vī′pėr-ish, *a.* Inclining to the character of a viper.
Viperous, vī′pėr-us, *a.* Having the qualities of a viper.
Virago, vi-rā′gō, *n.* A man-like woman; a termagant.
Virelay, vi′re-lā, *n.* A short poem, in short lines, with a refrain, and only two rhymes.
Virescent, vī-res′sent, *a.* Slightly green; beginning to be green.
Virgilian, vėr-jil′i-an, *a.* Pertaining to Virgil, or resembling his style.
Virgin, vėr′jin, *n.* A woman who has had no carnal knowledge of man; a maid; a sign of the zodiac.—*a.* Chaste; maidenly; unsullied.
Virginal, vėr′jin-al, *a.* Maidenly; virgin.—*n.* An ancient keyed musical instrument resembling the spinet.
Virginity, vėr-jin′i-ti, *n.* Maidenhood; perfect chastity.
Virgo, vėr′gō, *n.* The Virgin in the zodiac.
Viridity, vi-rid′i-ti, *n.* Greenness; verdure.
Virile, vi′rīl or vi′ril, *a.* Pertaining to a man; masculine; manly; strong.
Virility, vi-ril′i-ti, *n.* Manhood; the power of procreation; masculine action or vigour.
Virose, vī′rōs, *a.* Poisonous; emitting a fetid odour.
Virtu, vir-tö′, *n.* *See* Vertu.
Virtual, vėr′tū-al, *a.* Being in essence or effect, not in name or fact.
Virtually, vėr′tū-al-li, *adv.* In efficacy or effect, though not really.
Virtue, vėr′tū, *n.* Moral goodness; rectitude; morality; chastity; merit; efficacy.
Virtuoso, vėr-tū-ō′sō, *n.*; pl. **-osos** or **-osi.** A man skilled in the fine arts, or antiquities, curiosities, &c.

Virtuous, vėr'tū-us, *a.* Marked by virtue; morally good; pure or chaste.
Virtuously, vėr'tū-us-li, *adv.* In a virtuous manner.
Virulence, vi'rū-lens, *n.* Acrimony; malignity; rancour.
Virulent, vi'rū-lent, *a.* Very poisonous or noxious; bitter in enmity; malignant.
Virulently, vi'rū-lent-li, *adv.* In a virulent manner; with malignant activity.
Virus, vī'rus, *n.* Contagious poisonous matter; extreme acrimony; malignity.
Vis, vis, *n.* Force; power; energy.
Visage, vi'zāj, *n.* The face or countenance.
Visaged, vi'zājd, *a.* Having a visage of this or that sort.
Vis-à-vis, vē-zä-vē, *adv.* Face to face.—*n.* One placed face to face with another; a light carriage for two persons sitting face to face.
Viscera, vis'e-ra, *n. pl.* The entrails.
Visceral, vis'e-ral, *a.* Pertaining to the viscera.
Viscid, vis'id, *a.* Sticky or adhesive; glutinous; tenacious.
Viscidity, vis-id'i-ti, *n.* Glutinousness.
Viscosity, vis-kos'i-ti, *n.* Viscidity.
Viscount, vī'kount, *n.* A nobleman of rank between an earl and baron.
Viscountess, vī'kount-es, *n.* The wife of a viscount.
Viscous, vis'kus, *a.* Glutinous; viscid.
Visé, vē-zā, *n.* An indorsation upon a passport denoting that it has been examined and found correct.
Visibility, vi-zi-bil'i-ti, *n.* State or quality of being visible.
Visible, vi'zi-bl, *a.* Perceivable by the eye; apparent; open; conspicuous.
Visibly, vi'zi-bli, *adv.* In a visible manner; manifestly; conspicuously; obviously.
Vision, vi'zhon, *n.* Act of seeing; sight; that which is seen; an apparition; a fanciful view.
Visionary, vi'zhon-a-ri, *a.* Pertaining to visions; imaginative; imaginary; not real.—*n.* One who is visionary; one who upholds impracticable schemes.
Visit, vi'zit, *vt.* To go or come to see; to view officially; to afflict.—*vi.* To practise going to see others; to make calls.—*n.* Act of visiting; a call.
Visitant, vi'zit-ant, *n.* A visitor.
Visitation, vi-zit-ā'shon, *n.* Act of visiting; a formal or official visit; special dispensation of divine favour or retribution.
Visitor, vi'zit-or, *n.* One who visits; a caller; an inspector.
Visiting, vi'zit-ing, *a.* Pertaining to visits; authorized to visit and inspect.—*n.* The act or practice of paying visits.
Visiting-card, vi'zit-ing-kärd, *n.* A small card bearing one's name, &c., to be left in paying visits.
Visor, Vizor, vī'zor, *n.* The movable face-guard of a helmet; a mask.
Vista, vis'ta, *n.* A view through an avenue; trees, &c., that form the avenue; an extended view.
Visual, vi'zhū-al, *a.* Pertaining to sight or vision; used in seeing.
Vital, vī'tal, *a.* Pertaining to life; necessary to life; indispensable; essential.
Vitalism, vī'tal-izm, *a.* The doctrine that ascribes all organic functions to a vital principle distinct from chemical and other physical forces.
Vitality, vī-tal'i-ti, *n.* State or quality of having life; principle of life; animation.
Vitalize, vī'tal-īz, *vt.* To give life to; to furnish with the vital principle.
Vitally, vī'tal-li, *adv.* Essentially.
Vitals, vī'talz, *n.pl.* Parts essential to life.
Vitamin, vī'ta-min, *n.* One of several substances necessary for animal nutrition, and occurring in minute quantities in natural foods; numerous types have been distinguished, and designated by the letters of the alphabet.
Vitiate, vi'shi-āt, *vt.* (vitiating, vitiated). To make faulty; to impair; to corrupt; to invalidate.
Vitiation, vi-shi-ā'shon, *n.* Act of vitiating; depravation.
Viticulture, vit'i-kul-tūr, *n.* The culture of the vine.
Vitreous, vit'rē-us, *a.* Glassy; pertaining to glass; resembling glass.
Vitrescence, vi-tres'ens, *n.* Quality of being vitrescent; glassiness.
Vitrescent, vi-tres'ent, *a.* Tending to become glass or glassy.
Vitric, vit'rik, *a.* Vitreous.
Vitrifaction, Vitrification, vit-ri-fak'shon, vit'ri-fi-kā"shon, *n.* The act, process, or operation of converting into glass by heat.
Vitrifacture, vit-ri-fak'tūr, *n.* The manufacture of glass.
Vitrify, vit'ri-fī, *vt.* To convert into glass by heat.—*vi.* To become glass.
Vitriol, vit'ri-ol, *n.* Sulphuric acid or one of its compounds.
Vitriolic, vit'ri-ol'ik, *a.* Pertaining to vitriol; like vitriol; very biting or sarcastic.
Vitriolize, vit'ri-ol-īz, *vt.* To convert into vitriol; to treat with vitriol.
Vitta, vit'a, *n.*; pl. **-æ.** A head-band, fillet, or garland; a receptacle of oil in the fruits of umbelliferous plants.
Vituline, vit'ū-līn, *a.* Belonging to a calf, or to veal.
Vituperate, vī-tū'pe-rāt, *vt.* To abuse; to censure offensively; to rate.
Vituperation, vī-tū'pe-rā"shon, *n.* Act of vituperating; abuse; abusive language.
Vituperative, vī-tū'pe-rāt-iv, *a.* Containing vituperation; abusive; railing.
Vivacious, vī-vā'shus or vi-, *a.* Lively; brisk; sprightly; tenacious of life.
Vivacity, vī-vas'i-ti or vi-, *n.* Animation; spirit; liveliness; briskness.
Vivandière, vē-väng-di-ār, *n.* A female sutler.
Vivarium, vī-vā'ri-um, *n.*; pl. **-ia.** A place for keeping animals in their natural state.
Viva voce, vī'va vō'sē, *adv.* By word of mouth; orally: sometimes used adjectively.
Vivid, vi'vid, *a.* Bright, clear, or lively; forcible; striking; realistic.
Vividly, vi'vid-li, *adv.* In a vivid manner; with life; with striking truth.
Vivify, vi'vi-fī, *vt.* (vivifying, vivified). To make alive; to endue with life; to animate.
Viviparous, vī-vip'a-rus, *a.* Producing young in a living state.
Vivisection, vi-vi-sek'shon, *n.* Act of experimenting on a living animal.
Vivisector, vi'vi-sek-tėr, *n.* One who practises vivisection.

Vixen, viks'en, *n.* A she-fox; a snappish, bitter woman; a termagant.
Vixenish, viks'en-ish, *a.* Pertaining to a vixen.
Vizier, vi-zēr' or vi'zi-ėr, *n.* A high political officer in Turkey, &c.
Vizor, *n.* *See* VISOR.
Vley, Vlei, vlī or flī, *n.* In S. Africa, a swampy pool that dries up at certain seasons.
Vocable, vō'ka-bl, *n.* A word; a term.
Vocabulary, vō-kab'ū-la-ri, *n.* A list of words arranged alphabetically and explained briefly; range of expression.
Vocal, vō'kal, *a.* Pertaining to the voice; uttered by the voice; endowed with a voice; having a vowel character.
Vocalic, vō-kal'ik, *a.* Pertaining to vowel sound; having many vowels.
Vocalist, vō'kal-ist, *n.* A vocal musician; a public singer.
Vocalize, vō'kal-īz, *vt.* To form into voice; to make vocal.
Vocally, vō'kal-li, *adv.* With voice; with an audible sound; in words.
Vocation, vō-kā'shon, *n.* A calling; employment; profession; business.
Vocative, vo'ka-tiv, *a.* Relating to calling by name.—*n.* The vocative case.
Vociferate, vō-sif'ė-rāt, *vi.* and *t.* (vociferating, vociferated). To cry out with vehemence, to exclaim.
Vociferation, vō-sif'ė-rā"shon, *n.* A violent outcry; clamour.
Vociferous, vō-sif'ėr-us, *a.* Making a loud outcry; clamorous; noisy.
Vodka, vod'ka, *n.* An intoxicating spirit distilled from rye, much used in Russia.
Vogue, vōg, *n.* Temporary mode or fashion.
Voice, vois, *n.* The sound uttered by the mouth; articulate human utterance; state of vocal organs; speech; sound emitted; right of expressing an opinion; vote; a form of verb inflection.—*vt.* (voicing, voiced). To utter or express; to declare.
Voiceless, vois'les, *a.* Having no voice or vote.
Void, void, *a.* Empty; devoid; ineffectual; null.—*n.* An empty space.—*vt.* To make vacant; to quit; to nullify; to emit; to evacuate from the bowels.
Voidance, void'ans, *n.* Act of voiding; ejection from a benefice; vacancy.
Volant, vō'lant, *a.* Flying; nimble; rapid.
Volapuk, vō'la-puk, *n.* An artificial language devised in 1879 and intended as an international medium of communication.
Volatile, vo-la-tīl, *a.* Readily diffusible in the atmosphere; flighty; airy; fickle; fugitive.
Volatility, vo-la-til'i-ti, *n.* Quality of being volatile; capability of evaporating; flightiness; fickleness; levity.
Volatilize, vo'la-til-īz, *vt.* To cause to exhale or evaporate.—*vi.* To become vaporous.
Volcanic, vol-kan'ik, *a.* Pertaining to volcanoes; produced by a volcano.
Volcanism, vol'kan-izm, *n.* Volcanic character or phenomena.
Volcanist, vol'kan-ist, *n.* One versed in volcanoes.
Volcano, vol-kā'no, *n.*; pl. **-oes.** A mountain emitting clouds of vapour, gases, showers of ashes, lava, &c.
Vole, vōl, *n.* A rodent animal resembling a rat or mouse; a deal at cards that draws all the tricks.
Volition, vō-li'shon, *n.* Act or power of willing; will.
Volley, vol'i, *n.* A discharge of a number of missile weapons, as small-arms; emission of many things at once.—*vt.* and *i.* To discharge or be discharged in a volley; to sound like a volley; to strike and return a ball (in lawn-tennis, &c.) before it touches the ground.
Volt, vōlt, *n.* A sudden movement in fencing to avoid a thrust; the unit of electromotive force.
Voltage, vōlt'āj, *n.* Electromotive force as measured in volts.
Voltaic, vol-tā'ik, *a.* Pertaining to voltaism.
Voltaism, vol'ta-izm, *n.* Electricity produced by chemical action; galvanism.
Volubility, vo-lū'bil'i-ti, *n.* Great readiness or fluency of speech.
Voluble, vo'lū-bl, *a.* Rolling round or revolving; glib in speech; over fluent.
Volubly, vo'lū-bli, *adv.* In a voluble or fluent manner; with volubility.
Volume, vo'lūm, *n.* Something rolled up; a book; a coil; a convolution; mass or bulk; quantity or strength.
Volumeter, vo-lū'me-tėr, *n.* An instrument for measuring the volumes of gases.
Volumetric, vo-lū-met'rik, *a.* Pertaining to the measurement of volumes of substances.
Voluminous, vō-lū'min-us, *a.* Bulky; being in many volumes; having written much; copious.
Voluntarily, vo'lun-ta-ri-li, *adv.* Spontaneously; of one's own free will.
Voluntary, vo'lun-ta-ri, *a.* Willing; free to act; spontaneous; regulated by the will.—*n.* A volunteer; a supporter of voluntaryism; an organ solo during a church service.
Voluntaryism, vo'lun-ta-ri-izm, *n.* The principle of supporting anything, especially religion, entirely by voluntary effort.
Volunteer, vo-lun-tēr', *n.* A person who enters into military or other service of his own free will.—*a.* Pertaining to volunteers.—*vt.* To offer or bestow voluntarily.—*vi.* To enter into any service voluntarily.
Voluptuary, vō-lup'tū-a-ri, *n.* One addicted to luxury; a sensualist.
Voluptuous, vō-lup'tū-us, *a.* Pertaining to sensual pleasure; luxurious.
Voluptuously, vō-lup'tū-us-li, *adv.* Luxuriously; sensually.
Volute, vō-lūt', *n.* A spiral scroll characteristic of Ionic and Corinthian capitals.
Voluted, vō-lūt'ed, *a.* Having a volute or volutes.
Vomit, vo'mit, *vi.* To eject the contents of the stomach by the mouth.—*vt.* To eject from the stomach; to belch forth.—*n.* Matter ejected from the stomach; an emetic.
Vomitory, vo'mi-to-ri, *a.* Causing vomiting. —*n.* An emetic.
Voodoo, vö-dö, *n.* A person among the American negroes who professes to be a sorcerer; sorcery; an evil spirit.
Voracious, vō-rā'shus, *a.* Eating or swallowing greedily; ravenous; rapacious.
Voracity, vō-ras'i-ti, *n.* Quality of being voracious; greediness of appetite.
Vortex, vor'teks, *n.*; pl. **-tices** or **-texes.** A whirling motion in any fluid; a whirlpool or a whirlwind; an eddy.

Vortical, vor'tik-al, *a.* Pertaining to a vortex; whirling.
Vorticose, Vortiginal, vor'ti-kōs, vor-ti'jin-al, *a.* Vortical.
Votaress, vō'ta-res, *n.* A female votary.
Votary, vō'ta-ri, *n.* One who is bound by a vow; one devoted to some particular service, state of life, &c.
Vote, vōt, *n.* Act or power of expressing opinion or choice; a suffrage; thing conferred by vote; result of voting; votes collectively.—*vi.* (voting, voted). To give a vote.—*vt.* To choose or grant by vote.
Voter, vōt'ėr, *n.* One who votes; an elector.
Votive, vōt'iv, *a.* Pertaining to a vow; promised or given, in consequence of a vow.
Vouch, vouch, *vt.* To attest; to affirm; to answer for.—*vi.* To bear witness; to stand surety.
Voucher, vouch'ėr, *n.* One who vouches; a paper which serves to vouch the truth of accounts, or to confirm facts of any kind; a written evidence of the payment of money.
Vouchsafe, vouch-sāf', *vt.* (vouchsafing, vouchsafed). To condescend to grant; to concede.—*vi.* To deign.
Voussoir, vös'wạr, *n.* One of the wedge-shaped stones of an arch.
Vow, vou, *n.* A solemn promise; an oath; promise of fidelity.—*vt.* To promise solemnly; to dedicate, as to a divine power.—*vi.* To make vows.
Vowel, vou'el, *n.* A sound produced by opening the mouth and giving utterance to voice; the letter which represents such a sound.—*a.* Pertaining to a vowel; vocal.
Voyage, voi'āj, *n.* A journey by water to a distance.—*vi.* (voyaging, voyaged). To pass by water.
Voyager, voi'āj-ėr, *n.* One who voyages.
Vulcanic, vul-kan'ik, *a.* Volcanic.
Vulcanism, vul'kan-izm, *n.* The phenomena of volcanoes, hot springs, &c.
Vulcanite, vul'kan-īt, *n.* A superior vulcanized india-rubber; ebonite.
Vulcanize, vul'kan-īz, *vt.* To harden (india-rubber) by combining with sulphur, &c.
Vulgar, vul'gėr, *a.* Pertaining to the common people; vernacular; common; coarse.—**The vulgar,** the common people.
Vulgarian, vul-gā'ri-an, *n.* A vulgar person.
Vulgarism, vul'gėr-izm, *n.* A vulgar phrase or expression; vulgarity.
Vulgarity, vul-ga'ri-ti, *n.* Coarseness; an act of low manners.
Vulgarize, vul'gėr-īz, *vt.* To make vulgar.
Vulgarly, vul'gėr-li, *adv.* In a vulgar manner; commonly; coarsely.
Vulgate, vul'gāt, *n.* The Latin version of the Scriptures used by the R. Catholic church.
Vulnerable, vul'nėr-a-bl, *a.* That may be wounded; liable to injury.
Vulnerary, vul'nėr-a-ri, *a.* Useful in healing wounds.—*n.* A plant useful in the cure of wounds.
Vulpine, vul'pīn, *a.* Pertaining to the fox; cunning; crafty.
Vulpinite, vul'pin-īt, *n.* A variety of gypsum employed for small statues, &c.
Vulture, vul'tūr, *n.* A bird of prey which lives chiefly on carrion.
Vulturine, vul'tūr-īn, *a.* Belonging to or resembling the vulture.

W

Wabble, wob'l, *vi.* (wabbling, wabbled). To vacillate; to wobble.—*n.* A rocking motion.
Wacke, wak'ē, *n.* A soft and earthy volcanic rock usually containing crystals.
Wad, wod, *n.* A soft mass of fibrous material, used for stuffing; material for stopping the charge in a gun.—*vt.* (wadding, wadded). To furnish with a wad or wadding.
Wad, Wadd, wod, *n.* An earthy ore of manganese.
Wadding, wod'ing, *n.* A soft fibrous stuff used for stuffing articles of dress; wad.
Waddle, wod'l, *vi.* (waddling, waddled). To walk with a rolling gait; to toddle.
Waddy, wad'i, *n.* A wooden club used by the Australian aborigines.
Wade, wād, *vi.* (wading, waded). To walk through a substance that hinders the lower limbs, as water; to move or pass with labour.—*vt.* To ford.
Wader, wād'ėr, *n.* One that wades; a wading or grallatorial bird.
Wafer, wā'fėr, *n.* A thin cake, as of bread; a thin disc of paste for fastening letters.—*vt.* To seal with a wafer.
Waft, wäft, *vt.* To impel through water or air.—*vi.* To sail or float.—*n.* A sweep, as with the arm; a breath of wind.
Waftage, wäft'āj, *n.* The act of wafting; state of being wafted.
Wag, wag, *vt.* and *i.* (wagging, wagged). To swing or sway; to wave; to nod.—*n.* A wit; a joker.
Wage, wāj, *vt.* (waging, waged). To carry on; to engage in, as in a contest.—*n.* Payment for work done; hire; recompense: generally in *pl.*
Wager, wā'jėr, *n.* A bet; stake laid; subject on which bets are laid.—*vt.* and *i.* To bet; to stake.
Waggery, wag'ė-ri, *n.* Merriment; jocular talk; pleasantry.
Waggish, wag'ish, *a.* Roguish in merriment; jocular; sportive.
Waggle, wag'l, *vi.* and *t.* (waggling, waggled). To sway; to wag with short movements.
Wagon, Waggon, wag'on, *n.* A four-wheeled vehicle for heavy loads.
Wagonage, wag'on-āj, *n.* Money paid for conveyance by wagon.
Wagoner, wag'on-ėr, *n.* One who drives a wagon.
Wagonette, wag-on-et', *n.* A four-wheeled pleasure vehicle with longitudinal seats.
Wagtail, wag'tāl, *n.* A small bird of several species; a pert person.
Waif, wāf, *n.* A stray article; a neglected, homeless wretch.
Wail, wāl, *vt.* To lament; to bewail.—*vi.* To weep.—*n.* A mournful cry or sound.
Wailing, wāl'ing, *n.* Loud weeping.
Wain, wān, *n.* A wagon.
Wainscot, wān'skot, *n.* The timber-work that lines the walls of a room.—*vt.* (wainscotting, wainscotted). To line with wainscot.
Wainscotting, wān'skot-ing, *n.* Wainscot, or the material used for it.
Waist, wāst, *n.* That part of the human body between the ribs and hips; middle part of a ship.

Waistband, wāst'band, *n.* The band of trousers, &c., which encompasses the waist.
Waistcoat, wāst'kōt, *n.* A short sleeveless garment worn under the coat; a vest.
Wait, wāt, *vi.* To stay in expectation; to continue in patience; to attend; to serve at table.—*vt.* To await.—*n.* Act of waiting; ambush; a musician who promenades in the night about Christmas time.
Waiter, wāt'ėr, *n.* One who waits; a male attendant; a small tray or salver.
Waiting-maid, Waiting-woman, wāt'ing-mād, wāt'ing-wu̧-man, *n.* A maid-servant who attends a lady.
Waitress, wāt'res, *n.* A female waiter.
Waive, wāv, *vt.* (waiving, waived). To relinquish; to forgo.
Wake, wāk, *vi.* (waking, woke or waked). To be awake; to awake; to become active.—*vt.* To rouse from sleep; to arouse.—*n.* The feast of the dedication of a parish church; a vigil; the watching of a dead body prior to burial; track left by a ship; track in general.
Wakeful, wāk'fu̧l, *a.* Keeping awake in bed; indisposed to sleep; watchful; vigilant.
Waken, wāk'n, *vi.* To wake.—*vt.* To rouse from sleep; to rouse into action.
Waldenses, wa̧l-den'sēz, *n.* A sect of reforming Christians in Northern Italy.
Wale, wāl, *n.* A streak produced by a whip on an animal's skin; a weal; a plank along a ship a little above the water-line.—*vt.* (waling, waled). To mark with wales.
Walk, wa̧k, *vi.* To advance by steps without running; to go about; to behave.—*vt.* To pass over or through on foot; to lead about. —*n.* A short excursion on foot; gait; an avenue, promenade, &c.; sphere; way of living; tract of ground for grazing.
Walker, wa̧k'ėr, *n.* One who walks; a pedestrian.
Walking, wa̧k'ing, *n.* The act or practice of moving on the feet without running; practice of taking walks; pedestrianism.
Walking-stick, wa̧k'ing-stik, *n.* A staff or stick carried in the hand in walking.
Wall, wa̧l, *n.* A structure of stone or brick, inclosing a space, forming a division, supporting a weight, &c.; side of a building or room; means of protection.—*vt.* To inclose with a wall; to defend by walls.
Wallet, wol'et, *n.* A bag or knapsack; pack; bundle.
Wall-eye, wa̧l'ī, *n.* An eye in which the iris is of a very light grey or whitish colour.
Wall-flower, wa̧l'flou-ėr, *n.* A plant with fragrant yellowish flowers.
Walloon, wo-lön', *n.* A people inhabiting part of Belgium and north-eastern France; their language, a French dialect.
Wallop, wol'op, *vt.* To beat; to drub; to thrash.
Wallow, wol'ō, *vi.* To tumble and roll in water or mire; to live in filth or gross vice.
Walnut, wa̧l'nut, *n.* A valuable tree, a native of Persia; the edible nut of the tree.
Walrus, wol'rus, *n.* A huge marine carnivorous mammal inhabiting the arctic seas.
Waltz, wa̧lts, *n.* A kind of dance for two persons; music for the dance.—*vi.* To dance a waltz.
Waltzer, wa̧lts'ėr, *n.* A person who waltzes.
Wampum, wom'pum, *n.* Small beads made of shells, used by the American Indians as money or ornaments.
Wan, won, *a.* Dark or gloomy; languid of look; pale.
Wand, wond, *n.* A long flexible stick; a rod; a staff of authority; a baton.
Wander, won'dėr, *vi.* To ramble here and there; to roam; to rove; to err; to be delirious.—*vt.* To traverse.
Wanderer, won'dėr-ėr, *n.* One who wanders; a rambler; one that goes astray.
Wandering, won'dėr-ing, *a.* Given to wander; unsettled.—*n.* A travelling without a settled course; aberration.
Wane, wān, *vt.* (waning, waned). To diminish; to grow less, as the moon; to fail; to decline. —*n.* Decline; decrease.
Wannish, won'ish, *a.* Somewhat wan.
Want, wont, *n.* State of not having; deficiency; lack; need; indigence.—*vt.* To be without; to lack; to require; to desire.—*vi.* To be deficient; to be in want.
Wanton, won'ton, *a.* Not kept in due restraint; unprovoked; lustful; frolicsome; rank.—*n.* A lewd person; a trifler.—*vi.* To revel unrestrainedly; to sport lasciviously.
Wantonly, won'ton-li, *adv.* Without restraint or provocation; sportively; lasciviously.
Wapenshaw, Wapinshaw, wä'pn-sha̧, wä'-pin-sha̧, *n.* In Scotland, a review of persons under arms.
Wapentake, wä'pn-tāk, *n.* An old division of some of the northern shires of England.
Wapiti, wap'i-ti, *n.* The North American stag.
War, wa̧r, *n.* A contest between nations or parties carried on by force of arms; profession of arms; art of war; hostility; enmity. —*vi.* (warring, warred). To make or carry on war; to strive.
Warble, wa̧r'bl, *vt.* and *i.* (warbling, warbled). To utter musically in a quavering manner; to carol; to sing musically.—*n* A quavering melodious sound; a song.
Warbler, wa̧r'bl-ėr, *n.* A singer; a song-bird.
War-cry, wa̧r'krī, *n.* A word, cry, motto, or phrase used in common by troops in battle.
Ward, wa̧rd, *vt.* To guard; to fend off; to turn aside.—*n.* Guard; a defensive motion or position in fencing; custody; guardianship; a minor who is under guardianship; a division of a town or county; apartment of an hospital; a piece in a lock.
Warden, wa̧r'den, *n.* A guardian; a keeper; head of a college; superior of a conventual church; member of organization for assistance of civil population in air-raids.
Warder, wa̧rd'ėr, *n.* A guard; a keeper.
Wardrobe, wa̧rd'rōb, *n.* A piece of furniture in which wearing apparel is kept; a person's wearing apparel collectively.
Ward-room, wa̧rd'röm, *n.* A room in a warship where the senior officers mess.
Wardship, wa̧rd'ship, *n.* Guardianship; also pupilage.
Ware, wār, *n.* Articles of merchandise; goods: generally in *pl.*; sea-weeds, employed as a manure, &c.—*a.* On one's guard; aware: *poet.*—*vt.* To beware of: *poet.*
Warehouse, wār'hous, *n.* A storehouse for goods; a large shop.—*vt.* To deposit or secure in a warehouse.

Warehouseman, wãr'hous-man, *n.* One who keeps or is employed in a warehouse.
Warfare, wạr'fãr, *n.* Military service; war; contest; hostilities.
Warily, wā'ri-li, *adv.* Cautiously.
Warlike, wạr'līk, *a.* Pertaining to war; military; fit for war; disposed for war.
Warm, wạrm, *a.* Having moderate heat; flushed; zealous; excitable; brisk; rich.—*vt.* To make warm; to animate; to interest.—*vi.* To become warm or animated.
Warmer, wạrm'ėr, *n.* One who or that which warms.
Warm-hearted, wạrm'härt-ed, *a.* Having warmth of heart; cordial; sincere; hearty.
Warmly, wạrm'li, *adv.* In a warm manner; with heat; hotly; eagerly; earnestly.
Warmth, wạrmth, *n.* Gentle heat; cordiality; ardour; animation; enthusiasm; slight anger or irritation.
Warn, wạrn, *vt.* To caution against; to admonish; to advise; to inform previously.
Warning, wạrn'ing, *n.* Act of one who warns; caution against danger, &c.; admonition; previous notice.
War-office, wạr'of-is, *n.* A public office or department managing military affairs.
Warp, wạrp, *vt.* and *i.* To turn or twist out of shape; to contort; to pervert; to move, as a ship, by a rope attached to something.—*n.* The threads extended lengthwise in a loom; a rope used in moving a ship; deposit of rich mud; twist of wood in drying.
Warped, wạrpt, *a.* Twisted by shrinking; perverted.
Warrant, wo'rant, *vt.* To guarantee; to authorize; to justify.—*n.* An act or instrument investing one with authority; guarantee; document authorizing an officer to seize an offender; authority; a voucher; right.
Warrantable, wo'rant-a-bl, *a.* Authorized; justifiable; defensible; lawful.
Warranter, wo'rant-ėr, *n.* One who gives authority; one who guarantees.
Warrant-officer, wo'rant-of-is-ėr, *n.* An officer ranking below a commissioned officer.
Warrantor, wo'rant-or, *n.* One who warrants.
Warranty, wo'ran-ti, *n.* Warrant; guarantee; authority; a legal deed of security.
Warren, wo'ren, *n.* Ground appropriated for rabbits; a preserve in a river for fish.
Warrior, wạ'ri-or, *n.* A soldier; a brave or able soldier.
War-ship, wạr'ship, *n.* A ship constructed for engaging in warfare; a man-of-war.
Wart, wạrt, *n.* A hard dry growth on the skin.
Warty, wạrt'i, *a.* Full of or like warts; overgrown with warts.
Wary, wā'ri, *a.* Cautious; prudent.
Was, woz, *v.* The first and third person singular of the past tense of *to be.*
Wash, wosh, *vt.* To apply water, &c., to, to cleanse; to flow along or dash against; to remove by ablution; to tint lightly.—*vi.* To cleanse oneself by water; to stand the operation of washing; to stand the test.—*n.* Act of washing; clothes washed on one occasion; flow or dash of water; sound made by water; a shallow; swill; lotion; thin coat of colour or metal.
Wash-board, wosh'bōrd, *n.* A board with a ribbed surface for washing clothes on; a board to prevent the sea from breaking over the gunwale of a boat; a skirting-board.
Washer, wosh'ėr, *n.* One who or that which washes; a ring of iron, leather, &c., used under a nut that is screwed on a bolt.
Washerwoman, wosh'ėr-wụ-man, *n.* A woman that washes clothes for hire.
Washhand-basin, wosh'hand-bā-sn, *n.* A basin for washing the hands in.
Washhand-stand, wosh'hand-stand, *n.* A wash-stand.
Wash-house, Washing-house, wosh'hous, wosh'ing-hous, *n.* A building or an apartment for washing linen, &c.
Washing, wosh'ing, *n.* Act of cleansing with water; ablution; clothes washed.
Wash-out, wosh'out, *n.* A shot which misses the target, so a complete failure (used of persons and things).
Wash-stand, wosh'stand, *n.* A piece of bedroom furniture supporting a basin.
Wash-tub, wosh'tub, *n.* A tub in which clothes are washed.
Washy, wosh'i, *a.* Watery; highly diluted; thin; weak; feeble; worthless.
Wasp, wosp, *n.* An active, stinging, winged insect, resembling the bee.
Waspish, wosp'ish, *a.* Like a wasp; venomous; irritable; snappish.
Wassail, wos'el, *n.* A festive occasion with drinking of healths; a drinking bout; liquor used on such occasions.—*vi.* To hold a merry drinking meeting.
Wast, wost. The second person singular of *was.*
Wastage, wāst'āj, *n.* Loss by use, leakage, &c.
Waste, wāst, *vt.* (wasting, wasted). To make desolate; to ravage; to wear away gradually; to squander.—*vi.* To decrease gradually.—*a.* Desolate; spoiled; refuse.—*n.* Act of wasting; prodigality; refuse matter; gradual decrease; a desert region.
Wasteful, wāst'fụl, *a.* Causing waste; destructive; ruinous; lavish; prodigal.
Waste-pipe, wāst'pīp, *n.* A pipe for carrying off waste water, &c.
Waster, wāst'ėr, *n.* One who wastes; a prodigal; a squanderer.
Wasting, wāst'ing, *a.* Such as to waste; desolating; enfeebling.
Watch, woch, *n.* A keeping awake to guard, &c.; vigilance; a guard; time during which a person is on guard or duty; a small pocket time-piece.—*vi.* To keep awake; to give heed; to act as a guard, &c.; to wait.—*vt.* To look with close attention at or on; to tend; to guard.
Watch-dog, woch'dog, *n.* A dog kept to guard premises and property.
Watcher, woch'ėr, *n.* One who watches.
Watch-fire, woch'fīr, *n.* A fire kept up in the night as a signal, or for the use of a guard.
Watchful, woch'fụl, *a.* Keeping on the watch; vigilant; attentive; cautious.
Watch-house, woch'hous, *n.* A guard-house; a lock-up.
Watch-maker, woch'māk-ėr, *n.* One who makes or repairs watches.
Watchman, woch'man, *n.* A guard; a caretaker on duty at night.
Watch-tower, woch'tou-ėr, *n.* A tower on which a sentinel is placed to watch.
Watchword, woch'wėrd, *n.* A word by

which sentinels distinguish a friend from an enemy; a motto.

Water, wạ'tėr, *n.* A transparent fluid; a fluid consisting of hydrogen and oxygen; the sea; rain; saliva; urine; colour or lustre of a diamond, &c.—*vt.* To wet or supply with water; to give a wavy appearance to, as silk. —*vi.* To shed liquid matter; to take in water; to gather saliva; to have a longing desire.

Water-bailiff, wạ'tėr-bā-lif, *n.* A custom-house officer for searching ships; one who watches a river to prevent poaching.

Water-bed, wạ'tėr-bed, *n.* An india-rubber bed or mattress filled with water.

Water-cart, wạ'tėr-kärt, *n.* A cart carrying water for sale, watering streets, &c.

Water-closet, wạ'tėr-kloz-et, *n.* A privy in which the discharges are carried away by water.

Water-colour, wạ'tėr-kul-ėr, *n.* A pigment ground up with water and isinglass or other mucilage instead of oil.

Water-course, wạ'tėr-kōrs, *n.* A stream of water; a channel for water.

Watered, wạ'tėrd, *a.* Having a wavy and shiny appearance on the surface.

Waterfall, wạ'tėr-fạl, *n.* A fall or steep descent in a stream; a cascade.

Water-frame, wạ'tėr-frām, *n.* A frame for spinning cotton, at first driven by water.

Water-gas, wạ'tėr-gas, *n.* An illuminating gas obtained by decomposing water.

Watering, wạ'tėr-ing, *n.* Act of one who waters; ornamentation giving a wavy lustre.

Watering-place, wạ'tėr-ing-plās, *n.* A place to which people resort for mineral waters, or for bathing, &c.

Water-level, wạ'tėr-le-vel, *n.* The level at which water stands; a levelling instrument in which water is employed.

Water-line, wạ'tėr-līn, *n.* The line formed by the surface of water, as on ships.

Water-logged, wạ'tėr-logd, *a.* Floating but full of water, as a ship.

Waterman, wạ'tėr-man, *n.* A boatman.

Water-mark, wạ'tėr-märk, *n.* A mark indicating the rise and fall of water; a mark made in paper during manufacture.

Water-mill, wạ'tėr-mil, *n.* A mill whose machinery is driven by means of water.

Water-polo, wạ'tėr-pō"lō, *n.* A ball-game played by swimmers, who try to throw the ball into their opponents' goal.

Water-power, wạ'tėr-pou-ėr, *n.* The power of water employed to drive machinery.

Waterproof, wạ'tėr-pröf, *a.* So compact as not to admit water.—*n.* Cloth made waterproof; a garment of such cloth.—*vt.* To render impervious to water.

Watershed, wạ'tėr-shed, *n.* A rise of land from which rivers, &c., naturally flow in opposite directions.

Water-spout, wạ'tėr-spout, *n.* A column of spray or water drawn up from the sea or a lake by a violent whirlwind.

Water-tight, wạ'tėr-tīt, *a.* So tight as to retain or not to admit water; stanch.

Water-way, wạ'tėr-wā, *n.* That part of a river, the sea, &c., through which vessels sail.

Water-wheel, wạ'tėr-whēl, *n.* A wheel for raising water, or moved by water.

Water-works, wạ'tėr-wėrks, *n.pl.* The works and appliances for the distribution of water to communities; ornamental fountains.

Watery, wạ'tėr-i, *a.* Pertaining to or like water; thin; moist; tasteless; insipid.

Wattle, wot'l, *n.* A hurdle of interlaced rods. —*vt.* (wattling, wattled). To interlace (twigs or branches); to plat.

Watt, wot, *n.* The practical unit of power, or rate of conveying energy, used in electricity.

Waul, wạl, *vi.* To cry as a cat.

Wave, wāv, *vi.* and *t.* (waving, waved). To sway or play loosely; to undulate; to brandish; to beckon.—*n.* A swell or ridge on moving water; anything resembling a wave; an undulation; a signal made by waving the hand, a flag, &c.

Wave, wāv, *vt.* To waive. *See* WAIVE.

Waved, wāvd, *a.* Undulating; wavy.

Wavelet, wāv'let, *n.* A small wave.

Waver, wā'vėr, *vi.* To wave gently; to fluctuate; to be undetermined.

Waverer, wā'vėr-ėr, *n.* One who wavers.

Wavy, wāv'i, *a.* Rising or swelling in waves; full of waves; undulating.

Wax, waks, *n.* A tenacious substance excreted by bees or in the ear; any similar substance; sealing-wax.—*vt.* To smear or rub with wax. —*vi.* To increase; to grow; to become.

Wax-cloth, waks'kloth, *n.* Cloth covered with a waxy coating; floor-cloth.

Waxen, waks'en, *a.* Made of wax.

Wax-work, waks'wėrk, *n.* Work in wax; figures of persons in wax as near reality as possible.

Waxy, waks'i, *a.* Resembling wax; made of wax; abounding in wax.

Way, wā, *n.* A track, path, or road of any kind; distance traversed; progress; direction; line of business; condition; device; method; course; *pl.* the timbers on which a ship is launched.

Way-bill, wā'bil, *n.* A list of passengers or goods carried by a public conveyance.

Wayfarer, wā'fār-ėr, *n.* One who fares or travels; a traveller; a foot-passenger.

Wayfaring, wā'fār-ing, *a.* Travelling; passing; being on a journey.

Waylay, wā-lā', *vt.* To lay oneself in the way of; to beset in ambush.

Wayside, wā'sīd, *n.* The side of a road.—*a.* Growing, situated, &c., by sides of roads.

Wayward, wā'wėrd, *a.* Full of troublesome whims; froward; peevish; perverse.

Waywardly, wā'wėrd-li, *adv.* Perversely.

Wayworn, wā'wōrn, *a.* Worn or wearied by travelling.

We, wē, *pron.* Plural of I.

Weak, wēk, *a.* Not strong; feeble; infirm; frail; silly; vacillating; wanting resolution; wanting moral courage; ineffective; denoting verbs inflected by adding a letter or syllable.

Weaken, wēk'n, *vt.* To make weak or weaker. —*vi.* To become weak or weaker.

Weakling, wēk'ling, *n.* A weak creature.

Weakly, wēk'li, *adv.* Feebly; not forcibly; injudiciously.—*a.* Infirm.

Weakness, wēk'nes, *n.* The state or quality of being weak; irresolution; want of validity; a failing.

Weal, wēl, *n.* Welfare; prosperity; happiness; mark of a stripe; wale.

Weald, wēld, *n.* A piece of open forest land; a wold.

Wealth, welth, *n.* Riches; affluence; opulence; abundance.
Wealthy, welth'i, *a.* Possessing wealth; rich; opulent; abundant; ample.
Wean, wēn, *vt.* To accustom to do without the mother's milk; to alienate; to disengage from any habit.
Weanling, wēn'ling, *n.* A child or animal newly weaned.
Weapon, we'pon, *n.* Any instrument of offence or defence.
Wear, wār, *vt.* (pret. wore, pp. worn). To carry as belonging to dress; to have on; to waste by rubbing; to destroy by degrees; to produce by rubbing; to exhibit.—*vi.* To last well or ill; to waste gradually; to make gradual progress.—*n.* Act of wearing; diminution by friction, use, time, &c.; fashion.
Wear, wār, *vt.* (pret. & pp. wore). To bring on the other tack by turning the ship round, stern towards the wind.
Wearer, wār'ėr, *n.* One who wears.
Wearily, wē'ri-li, *adv.* In a weary manner; like one fatigued.
Wearing, wār'ing, *a.* Used by being worn; such as to wear; exhausting.
Wearisome, wē'ri-sum, *a.* Causing weariness; tiresome; fatiguing; monotonous.
Weary, wē'ri, *a.* Having the strength or patience exhausted; tired; disgusted; tiresome.—*vt.* (wearying, wearied). To make weary; to tire.—*vi.* To become weary.
Weasand, Weazand, wē'zand, *n.* The windpipe.
Weasel, wē'zl, *n.* A small carnivorous animal akin to the ferret, &c.
Weather, weᴛʜ'ėr, *n.* The general atmospheric conditions at any particular time. *a.* Turned towards the wind; windward.—*vt.* To affect by the weather; to sail to the windward of; to bear up against and overcome.
Weather-beaten, weᴛʜ'ėr-bēt-n, *a.* Beaten by the weather; hardened by exposure.
Weather-cock, weᴛʜ'ėr-kok, *n.* Something in the shape of a cock, &c., for showing the direction of the wind; a vane; a fickle person.
Weather-gage, weᴛʜ'ėr-gāj, *n.* Advantage of the wind obtained by a ship in manœuvring; advantage of position.
Weather-glass, weᴛʜ'ėr-gläs, *n.* A barometer.
Weatherly, weᴛʜ'ėr-li, *a.* Applied to a ship that makes very little leeway.
Weathermost, weᴛʜ'ėr-mōst, *a.* Being farthest to the windward.
Weather-wise, weᴛʜ'ėr-wīz, *a.* Wise or skilful in forecasting the weather.
Weather-worn, weᴛʜ'ėr-wōrn, *a.* Worn by the action of the weather.
Weave, wēv, *vt.* (weaving, pret. wove, pp. woven). To form by interlacing thread, yarn, &c.; to form a tissue with; to work up; to contrive.—*vi.* To practise weaving; to be woven.
Weaver, wēv'ėr, *n.* One who weaves; one whose occupation is to weave.
Weaving, wēv'ing, *n.* Act or art of producing cloth or other textile fabrics.
Weazen, wē'zn, *n.* Thin; lean; wizened.
Web, web, *n.* The whole piece of cloth woven in a loom; a large roll of paper; membrane which unites the toes of water-fowl; the threads which a spider spins; a cobweb; anything carefully contrived.
Webbed, webd, *a.* Having the toes united by a membrane or web.
Webbing, web'ing, *n.* A strong fabric of hemp, two or three inches wide.
Webby, web'i, *a.* Relating to or like a web.
Weber, vā'ber, *n.* The electric unit of magnetic quantity.
Web-foot, web'fụt, *n.* A foot whose toes are united by a membrane.
Web-footed, web'fụt-ed, *a.* Having the toes united by a membrane.
Wed, wed, *vt.* and *i.* (wedding, wedded and wed). To marry; to unite closely.
Wedded, wed'ed, *a.* Pertaining to matrimony; intimately united.
Wedding, wed'ing, *n.* Marriage; nuptials.
Wedge, wej, *n.* A body sloping to a thin edge at one end.—*vt.* (wedging, wedged). To drive as a wedge is driven; to crowd or compress; to fasten or split with a wedge.
Wedlock, wed'lok, *n.* The wedded state; marriage.
Wednesday, wenz'dā, *n.* The fourth day of the week.
Wee, wē, *a.* Small; little.
Weed, wēd, *n.* Any plant regarded as useless or troublesome; a sorry, worthless animal; a cigar; *pl.* mourning dress of a widow or female.—*vt.* To free from weeds or anything offensive.
Weeder, wēd'ėr, *n.* One that weeds; a tool for weeding.
Weedy, wēd'i, *a.* Consisting of weeds; abounding with weeds; worthless.
Week, wēk, *n.* The space of seven days; space from one Sunday to another.
Week-day, wēk'dā, *n.* Any day of the week except Sunday.
Weekly, wēk'li, *a.* Coming or done once a week; lasting for a week.—*n.* A periodical appearing once a week.—*adv.* Once a week.
Ween, wēn, *vi.* To think; to fancy.
Weep, wēp, *vi.* (pret. and pp. wept). To manifest grief, &c., by shedding tears; to drip; to droop.—*vt.* To lament; to shed or drop, as tears; to get rid of by weeping.
Weeper, wēp'ėr, *n.* One who weeps; a sort of white linen cuff on a mourning dress.
Weeping, wēp'ing, *n.* Lamenting; the shedding of tears.
Weever, wē'vėr, *n.* A spined edible fish.
Weevil, wē'vil, *n.* An insect of the beetle family, destructive to grain, fruit, &c.
Weft, weft, *n.* The woof of cloth.
Weigh, wā, *vt.* To raise; to find the heaviness of; to allot or take by weight; to consider; to balance; to burthen.—*vi.* To have weight; to amount to in weight; to bear heavily.
Weigh-bridge, wā'brij, *n.* A machine for weighing carts, wagons, &c., with their load.
Weigh-house, wā'hous, *n.* A public building at or in which goods are weighed.
Weight, wāt, *n.* Heaviness; gravity; the amount which anything weighs; a metal standard for weighing; a heavy mass; pressure; burden; importance; moment.—*vt.* To add to the heaviness of.
Weighty, wāt'i, *a.* Heavy; important; momentous; cogent.
Weir, wēr, *n.* A dam across a stream for supplying water to a mill, irrigation, &c.;

a fence of twigs in a stream for catching fish.

Weird, wērd, *n.* Destiny; fate.—*a.* Connected with fate; unearthly.

Welcome, wel'kum, *a.* Received with gladness; grateful; pleasing.—*n.* Greeting or kind reception.—*vt.* (welcoming, welcomed). To receive kindly and hospitably.

Weld, weld, *vt.* To melt together, as heated iron; to unite closely.—*n.* A junction by fusion of heated metals; a species of mignonette used as a yellow dye.

Welfare, wel'fār, *n.* Well-being; prosperity; happiness.

Welkin, wel'kin, *n.* The sky; the heavens; the firmament.

Well, wel, *n.* A spring; a pit sunk for water; perpendicular space in a building in which stairs or a hoist is placed.—*vi.* To bubble up; to issue forth.

Well, wel, *adv.* In a proper manner; rightly; commendably; considerably.—*a.* Being in health; comfortable; fortunate; convenient; proper.

Welladay, wel'a-dā, *interj.* Welaway! alas! lackaday!

Well-being, wel'bē-ing, *n.* State of being well; prosperity; happiness; welfare.

Well-born, wel'born, *a.* Born of a good family; of good descent.

Well-bred, wel'bred, *a.* Of good breeding; polite; refined.

Wellington, wel'ing-ton, *n.* A kind of long boot worn by men; a long-legged rubber boot made in one piece.

Wellingtonia, wel-ing-tō'ni-a, *n.* A genus of large coniferous trees.

Well-meaning, wel'mēn-ing, *a.* Having a good intention.

Well-spoken, wel'spōk-n, *a.* Spoken well; speaking well; civil; courteous.

Well-spring, wel'spring, *n.* A fountain; a source of continual supply.

Well-timed, wel'tīmd, *a.* Done at a proper time; opportune.

Well-to-do, wel'tö-dö, *a.* Being in easy circumstances; well off; prosperous.

Welsh, welsh, *a.* Pertaining to Wales or to its people.—*n.* The language of Wales; *pl.* the inhabitants of Wales.

Welt, welt, *n.* A border or edging; a strip of leather sewed round the upper of a boot to which the sole is fastened.—*vt.* To furnish with a welt; to beat severely.

Welter, welt'ėr, *vi.* To roll; to tumble about; to wallow.—*n.* A turmoil.—*a.* Said of a horse race in which extra heavy weights are laid on some horses.

Wen, wen, *n.* A harmless fatty tumour.

Wench, wensh, *n.* A young woman; a woman of loose character.—*vi.* To frequent the company of women of ill-fame.

Wend, wend, *vt.* To go; to direct.—*vi.* To go; to travel.

Went, went. Used as the pret. of *go*.

Were, wer, *v.* The past tense plural indicative and the past subjunctive of *be*.

Werewolf, wēr'wụlf, *n.* A werwolf.

Wert, wėrt, The second person singular of *was* or *were*.

Werwolf, wėr'wụlf, *n.* A man transformed into a wolf.

Wesleyan, wes'li-an, *a.* Pertaining to the religious body established by John Wesley.—*n.* A Methodist.

West, west, *n.* The point where the sun sets, opposite the east.—*a.* Being in or towards the west; coming from the west.—*adv.* To the west.

Westerly, west'ėr-li, *a.* Tending or being towards the west; coming from the west.—*adv.* Tending or moving towards the west.

Western, west'ėrn, *a.* Being in or moving toward the west; coming from the west.

Westernmost, west'ėrn-mōst, *a.* Farthest to the west.

Westing, west'ing, *n.* Space or distance westward.

Westmost, west'mōst, *a.* Farthest to the west.

Westward, west'wėrd, *adv.* Toward the west.

Westwardly, west'wėrd-li, *adv.* In a direction toward the west.

Westwards, west'wėrdz, *adv.* Westward.

Wet, wet, *a.* Covered or soaked with water; moist; rainy.—*n.* Water; moisture; rain.—*vt.* (wetting, wetted). To make wet; to soak in liquor.

Wether, weᴛʜ'ėr, *n.* A ram castrated.

Wet-nurse, wet'nėrs, *n.* A nurse engaged to suckle an infant.

Wettish, wet'ish, *a.* Somewhat wet.

Wey, wā, *n.* A certain weight or measure: of wool, 182 lbs.; of wheat, 5 quarters; of cheese, 224 lbs., &c.

Whack, whak, *vt.* and *i.* To thwack; to give a resounding blow to.—*n.* A resounding blow; a thwack.

Whale, whāl, *n.* The largest of sea animals, a mammal.

Whalebone, whāl'bōn, *n.* An elastic horny substance obtained from the upper jaw of certain whales; baleen.

Whaler, whāl'ėr, *n.* A person or ship employed in the whale-fishery.

Wharf, whạrf, *n.*; pl. **-fs** or **-ves.** A quay for loading or unloading ships.

Wharfage, whạrf'āj, *n.* The fee for using a wharf; accommodation at a wharf; wharfs collectively.

Wharfinger, whạrf'in-jėr, *n.* A person who owns or has the charge of a wharf.

What, whot, *pron.* An interrogative pronoun used chiefly of things; employed adjectively as equivalent to how great, remarkable, &c.; substantively as equivalent to the thing (or things) which.

Whatever, whot-ev'ėr, *pron.* Used as substantive, anything that; all that; used as an adj., of any kind.

What-not, whot'not, *n.* A piece of household furniture with shelves for books, &c.

Whatsoever, Whatsoe'er, whot-sō-ev'ėr, whot-sō-ār', *pron.* Whatever (emphatic).

Wheat, whēt, *n.* A cereal plant; its seeds, which yield a white nutritious flour.

Wheatear, whēt'ēr, *n.* A bird akin to the stone-chat.

Wheat-ear, whēt'ēr, *n.* An ear of wheat.

Wheaten, whēt'n, *a.* Pertaining to wheat; made of wheat.

Wheedle, whē'dl, *vt.* and *i.* (wheedling, wheedled). To flatter; to cajole; to coax.

Wheel, whēl, *n.* A circular frame turning on an axis; an old instrument of torture; a revolution; a cycle.—*vt.* To cause to turn round.—*vi.* To turn round; to revolve; to roll forward.

Wheel-barrow, whēl'ba-rō, *n.* A barrow with one wheel.

Wheeled, whēld, *a.* Having wheels.

Wheeler, whēl'ėr, *n.* One who wheels; a maker of wheels; horse next a carriage.

Wheel-wright, whēl'rīt, *n.* A wright whose occupation is to make wheels.

Wheeze, whēz, *vi.* (wheezing, wheezed). To breathe hard and audibly, as persons affected with asthma.

Wheezy, whēz'i, *a.* Affected with wheezing.

Whelk, whelk, *n.* A shell-fish, a species of periwinkle or mollusc; a pustule.

Whelm, whelm, *vt.* To engulf; to swallow up; to ruin or devastate.

Whelp, whelp, *n.* A puppy; a cub; a young man.—*vi.* To bring forth whelps.—*vt.* To bring forth; to originate.

When, when, *adv.* and *conj.* At what or which time; while; whereas: used substantively with *since* or *till.*

Whence, whens, *adv.* and *conj.* From what place, source, &c.; how.

Whencesoever, whens-sō-ev'ėr, *adv.* From whatever place, cause, or source.

Whene'er, Whenever, when-ār', when-ev'ėr, *adv.* At whatever time.

Whensoever, when-sō-ev'ėr, *adv.* At whatever time.

Where, whār, *adv.* and *conj.* At or in what place; at the place in which; whither.

Whereabout, whār'a-bout, *adv.* and *conj.* About what place; concerning which.

Whereabouts, whār'a-bouts, *adv.* and *conj.* Near what or which place; whereabout: often used substantively.

Whereas, whār-az', *conj.* Things being so; when really or in fact.

Whereat, whār-at', *adv.* and *conj.* At which or what.

Whereby, whār-bī', *adv.* and *conj.* By which or what.

Wherefore, whār'for, *adv.* and *conj.* For which reason; consequently; why.

Wherein, whār-in', *adv.* and *conj.* In which; in which thing, time, respect, &c.

Whereinto, whār-in-tö', *adv.* and *conj.* Into which or what.

Whereof, whār-ov', *adv.* and *conj.* Of which or what.

Whereon, whār-on', *adv.* and *conj.* On which or on what.

Wheresoever, Wheresoe'er, whār-sō-ev'ėr, whār'sō-ār, *adv.* In whatever place.

Whereto, whār-tö', *adv.* and *conj.* To which or what; to what end.

Whereupon, whār-up-on', *adv.* Upon which or what; in consequence of which.

Wherever, Where'er, whār-ev'ėr, whār-ār', *adv.* At whatever place.

Wherewith, Wherewithal, whār-with', whār-with-al', *adv.* and *conj.* With which or what.—*n.* Means or money.

Wherry, whe'ri, *n.* A light river boat for passengers.

Whet, whet, *vt.* (whetting, whetted or whet). To rub to sharpen; to edge; to excite; to stimulate.—*n.* Act of sharpening; something that stimulates the appetite.

Whether, wheᴛʜ'ėr, *pron.* Which of two.—*conj.* or *adv.* Which of two or more, introducing alternative clauses.

Whetstone, whet'stōn, *n.* A stone used for sharpening instruments by friction.

Whew, whū, *exclam.* A sound made with the lips, expressing astonishment or contempt.—*n.* The sound thus uttered.

Whey, whā, *n.* The thin part of milk, from which the curd, &c., have been separated.

Which, which, *pron.* An interrogative pronoun, used adjectively or substantively; a relative pronoun, the neuter of *who*; an indefinite pronoun, any one which.

Whichever, Whichsoever, which-ev'ėr, which-sō-ev'ėr, *pron.* No matter which; anyone.

Whiff, whif, *n.* A puff of air; a puff conveying a smell.—*vt.* and *i.* To puff; to throw out whiffs; to smoke.

Whiffle, whif'l, *vi.* (whiffling, whiffled). To veer about; to be fickle; to prevaricate.

Whig, whig, *n.* Formerly a member of the political party in Britain, opposed to the *Tories*; one of the more conservative section of the Liberal party, opposed to the *Radicals.*—*a.* Belonging to or composed of Whigs.

Whiggery, Whiggism, whig'ėr-i, whig'izm, *n.* The principles of the Whigs.

Whiggish, whig'ish, *a.* Pertaining to Whigs or their principles.

While, whīl, *n.* A time; short space of time.—*conj.* During the time that; though.—*vt.* (whiling, whiled). To cause to pass pleasantly: usually with *away.*

Whilom, whī'lom, *a.* Former; quondam.

Whilst, whīlst, *adv.* While.

Whim, *n.* A sudden fancy; a caprice.

Whimbrel, whim'brel, *n.* A British bird closely allied to the curlew.

Whimper, whim'pėr, *vi.* To express grief with a whining voice.—*vt.* To utter in a low, whining tone.—*n.* A peevish cry.

Whimsical, whim'zik-al, *a.* Full of whims; capricious; odd; fantastic.

Whimsy, Whimsey, whim'zi, *n.* A whim; a caprice; a capricious notion.

Whin, whin, *n.* Gorse; furze.

Whin-chat, whin'chat, *n.* A British chat commonly found among broom and furze.

Whine, whīn, *vi.* (whining, whined). To express distress by a plaintive drawling cry.—*n.* A drawling plaintive tone; mean or affected complaint.

Whinny, whin'i, *vi.* (whinnying, whinnied). To neigh, especially in a low tone.—*n.* Neigh of a horse.—*a.* Abounding in whins.

Whinstone, whin'ston, *n.* A hard or tough unstratified rock.

Whip, whip, *vt.* (whipping, whipped). To put or snatch with a sudden motion; to flog; to drive with lashes; to beat into a froth.—*vi.* To start suddenly and run.—*n.* A lash; the driver of a carriage; a member of parliament who looks after the attendance of his party; the summons he sends out.

Whip-hand, whip'hand, *n.* The hand that holds the whip; control.

Whipper-snapper, whip'ėr-snap-ėr, *n.* A diminutive, insignificant person.

Whipping, whip'ing, *n.* Act of striking with a whip; flagellation.

Whipster, whip'stėr, *n.* A nimble little fellow; a sharp shallow fellow.

Whir, whėr, *vi.* (whirring, whirred). To fly, revolve, &c., with a whizzing or buzzing sound; to whiz.—*n.* A buzzing sound.
Whirl, whėrl, *vt.* and *i.* To turn round rapidly; to move quickly.—*n.* A rapid turning.
Whirl-bone, whėrl'bōn, *n.* The knee-pan.
Whirligig, whėrl'i-gig, *n.* A toy which children spin or whirl round.
Whirlpool, whėrl'pöl, *n.* An eddy or gulf where the water moves round in a circle.
Whirlwig, whėrl'wig, *n.* A beetle which circles round rapidly on the surface of ponds, &c.
Whirlwind, whėrl'wind, *n.* A whirling wind; a violent wind moving as if round an axis, this axis at the same time progressing.
Whisk, whisk, *vt.* To sweep or agitate with a light rapid motion.—*vi.* To move nimbly.—*n.* A rapid, sweeping motion; a small besom; an instrument for frothing cream, eggs, &c.
Whisker, whis'kėr, *n.* Long hair growing on the cheek.
Whiskified, Whiskeyfied, whis'ki-fīd, *a.* Affected with whisky; intoxicated.
Whisky, Whiskey, whis'ki, *n.* An ardent spirit distilled generally from barley; a light one-horse chaise.
Whisper, whis'pėr, *vt.* To speak with a low sibilant voice; to converse secretly.—*vt.* To utter in a whisper.—*n.* A low soft sibilant voice; a faint utterance.
Whispering, whis'pėr-ing, *a.* Speaking in a whisper; having or giving a soft sibilant sound.—*n.* Act of one who whispers; tale-bearing.
Whist, whist, *interj.* Silence! hush!—*a.* Silent.—*n.* A game at cards, played by four persons.
Whistle, whis'l, *vi.* (whistling, whistled). To utter a clear shrill sound by forcing the breath through the lips; to warble; to sound shrilly.—*vt.* To utter or signal by whistling.—*n.* Sound produced by one who whistles; any similar sound; a small pipe blown with the breath; instrument sounded by steam.
Whit, whit, *n.* The smallest particle; tittle.
White, whīt, *a.* Being of the colour of pure snow; pale; pallid; pure and unsullied.—*n.* The colour of snow; a white pigment; white of an egg, eye, &c.—*vt.* (whiting, whited). To make white.
White-bait, whīt'bāt, *n.* The fry or young of the herring and sprat.
White-friar, whīt'frī-ėr, *n.* A friar of the Carmelite order, from their white cloaks.
White-iron, whīt'ī-ėrn, *n.* Thin sheet-iron covered with a coating of tin; tinplate.
White-lead, whīt'led, *n.* A carbonate of lead much used in painting; ceruse.
White-livered, whīt'liv-ėrd, *a.* Cowardly.
Whiten, whīt'n, *vt.* To make white; to bleach; to blanch.—*vi.* To grow white.
White-smith, whīt'smith, *n.* A tinsmith; a worker in iron who finishes or polishes.
Whitewash, whīt'wosh, *n.* A composition of lime or whiting and water, for whitening walls, &c.—*vt.* To cover with whitewash; to restore the reputation of.
Whither, whiᴛʜ'ėr, *adv.* To what or which place; where.
Whithersoever, whiᴛʜ'ėr-sō-ev-ėr, *adv.* To whatever place.
Whiting, whīt'ing, *n.* A small fish of the cod tribe; pulverized chalk used in whitewashing, for cleaning plate, &c.
Whitish, whīt'ish, *a.* Somewhat white.
Whitlow, whit'lō, *n.* A swelling about the small bones of the fingers, generally terminating in an abscess.
Whit-Monday, whit'mun-dā, *n.* The Monday following Whitsunday.
Whitsun, whit'sun, *a.* Pertaining to Whitsuntide.
Whitsunday, whit'sun-dā, *n.* The seventh Sunday after Easter.
Whitsuntide, whit'sun-tīd, *n.* The season of Pentecost.
Whittle, whit'l, *n.* A large knife.—*vt.* (whittling, whittled). To cut or pare with a knife.
Whiz, whiz, *vi.* (whizzing, whizzed). To make a humming or hissing sound.—*n.* A hissing and humming sound.
Who, hö, *pron.*; possessive **Whose,** höz; objective **Whom,** höm. A relative and interrogative pronoun always used substantively and with reference to persons.
Whoever, hö-ev'ėr, *pron.* Any one without exception; any person whatever.
Whole, hōl, *a.* Sound; healthy; healed; intact; entire.—*n.* An entire thing; total assemblage of parts.
Whole-length, hōl'length, *n.* A picture or statue exhibiting the whole figure.
Wholesale, hōl'sāl, *n.* Sale of goods by the entire piece or in large quantities.—*a.* Pertaining to trade in large quantities; extensive and indiscriminate.
Wholesome, hōl'sum, *a.* Tending to promote health; salubrious; useful; salutary.
Wholly, hōl'li, *adv.* As a whole; entirely.
Whoop, whöp or höp, *vi.* To shout loudly; to hoot.—*vt.* To shout at; to hoot; to insult with shouts.—*n.* A shout; a loud clear call.
Whooping-cough, *n.* *See* HOOPING-COUGH.
Whop, whop, *vt.* (whopping, whopped). To beat.
Whopper, whop'ėr, *n.* Anything uncommonly large; a manifest lie.
Whore, hōr, *n.* A prostitute; a harlot.—*vi.* (whoring, whored). To have to do with prostitutes.
Whoredom, hōr'dum, *n.* Lewdness; fornication; prostitution.
Whoremonger, hōr'mung-gėr, *n.* One who practises whoring; a fornicator.
Whoreson, hōr'sun, *n.* A bastard.
Whorl, whorl or whėrl, *n.* A ring of leaves, &c., of a plant all on the same plane.
Whortleberry, whort'l-be-ri, *n.* The bilberry and its fruit.
Whose, höz, *pron.* The possessive case of *who* or *which*.
Whoso, hö'sō, *pron.* Whosoever: whoever.
Whosoever, hö-sō-ev'ėr, *pron.* Any person whatever; any one.
Why, whī, *adv.* and *conj.* For what reason; wherefore.
Wick, wik, *n.* The loose spongy string or band in candles or lamps.
Wicked, wik'ed, *a.* Evil in principle or practice; sinful; immoral; bad; roguish.
Wickedly, wik'ed-li, *adv.* In a wicked manner; viciously; immorally.
Wickedness, wik'ed-nes, *n.* Immorality; depravity; sin; a wicked act.
Wicker, wik'ėr, *n.* A small pliable twig;

work made of such twigs.—*a.* Made of plaited twigs.

Wicket, wik'et, *n.* A small gate; in *cricket*, the three upright rods and the bails which rest on them at which the bowler aims.

Wide, wīd, *a.* Having a great extent each way; broad; extensive; liberal; remote from anything.—*adv.* At or to a distance; far from; astray.

Wide-awake, wīd'a-wāk, *a.* On the alert.—*n.* A soft felt hat with a broad brim.

Widely, wīd'li, *adv.* Extensively; far.

Widen, wīd'n, *vt.* To make wide or wider.—*vi.* To grow wide or wider.

Widgeon, Wigeon, wi'jon, *n.* A migratory water-fowl of the duck group.

Widow, wi'dō, *n.* A woman whose husband is dead.—*vt.* To bereave of a husband.

Widower, wi'dō-ėr, *n.* A man whose wife is dead.

Widowhood, wi'dō-hụd, *n.* The condition of being a widow or a widower.

Width, width, *n.* Breadth; extent from side to side.

Wield, wēld, *vt.* To manage freely in the hands; to sway; to exercise.

Wieldable, wēld'a-bl, *a.* Capable of being wielded.

Wielder, wēld'ėr, *n.* One who wields.

Wieldy, wēld'i, *a.* Manageable.

Wife, wīf, *n.*; pl. **Wives,** wīvz. A married woman.

Wifelike, wīf'līk, *a.* Resembling or pertaining to a wife or woman.

Wifely, wīf'li, *a.* Like or becoming a wife.

Wig, wig, *n.* An artificial covering of hair for the head.

Wigging, wig'ing, *n.* A rating; a scolding.

Wight, wīt, *n.* A human being; a person.—*a.* Strong and active; of warlike prowess.

Wigwam, wig'wam, *n.* A tent or hut of the North American Indians.

Wild, wīld, *a.* Living in a state of nature; not tame; not cultivated; desert; stormy; furious; frolicsome; rash; extravagant; excited.—*n.* An uncultivated tract.

Wilder, wil'dėr, *vt.* To bewilder.

Wilderness, wil'dėr-nes, *n.* A desert; waste; irregular collection of things.

Wildfire, wīld'fīr, *n.* A kind of lightning unaccompanied by thunder; erysipelas.

Wilding, wīld'ing, *n.* A young tree that grows without cultivation.

Wildish, wīld'ish, *a.* Somewhat wild.

Wildly, wīld'li, *adv.* In a wild state or manner; irrationally; savagely.

Wile, wīl, *n.* An artifice; stratagem; trick.—*vt.* (wiling, wiled). To entice; to while.

Wileful, wīl'fụl, *a.* Wily; tricky.

Wilful, wil'fụl, *a.* Under the influence of self-will; obstinate; wayward; intentional.

Wilfully, wil'fụl-li, *adv.* In a wilful manner; obstinately; with set purpose.

Wiliness, wī'li-nes, *n.* Cunning; guile.

Will, wil, *v. aux.* (past. would), expresses futurity in the second and third persons, and willingness, &c., or determination in the first.—*vt.* and *i.* To determine by choice; to wish; to bequeath.—*n.* Wish; choice; determination; purpose; legal declaration of a person as to what is to be done after his death with his property; faculty by which we determine to do or not to do something; volition.

Willing, wil'ing, *a.* Ready; desirous; spontaneous; voluntary; prompt.

Willingly, wil'ing-li, *adv.* In a willing manner; cheerfully; readily; gladly.

Will-o'-the-wisp, wil'o-ᴛʜi-wisp, *n.* The ignis-fatuus.

Willow, wil'ō, *n.* A tree or shrub, valuable for basket-making, &c.

Willowy, wil'o-i, *a.* Abounding with willows; slender and graceful.

Willy-nilly, wil'i-nil-i, *adv.* Willing or unwilling.

Wilt, wilt, *vi.* To fade; to wither or droop.

Wily, wī'li, *a.* Using wiles; cunning; sly.

Wimble, wim'bl, *n.* An instrument for boring holes.—*vt.* (wimbling, wimbled). To bore, as with a wimble.

Wimple, wim'pl, *n.* A female head-dress still worn by nuns.—*vt.* (wimpling, wimpled). To cover with a wimple; to hoodwink.—*vi.* To ripple; to undulate.

Win, win, *vt.* (winning, won). To gain; to be victorious in; to allure; to reach; to attain.—*vi.* To gain the victory.

Wince, wins, *vi.* (wincing, winced). To shrink, as from pain; to start back.—*n.* A start, as from pain.

Wincey, win'si, *n.* A strong cloth with a cotton warp and a woollen weft.

Winch, winsh, *n.* The bent handle for turning a wheel, &c.; a kind of windlass turned by a crank handle.

Wind, wind, in poetry often wīnd, *n.* Air in motion; a current of air; breath; power of respiration; empty words; flatulence.—*vt.* wīnd (pret. & pp. wound, sometimes winded). To blow, as a horn.—*vt.* wind (pret. & pp. winded). To follow by the scent; to render scant of wind; to let rest and recover wind.

Wind, wīnd, *vt.* (pret. & pp. wound). To bend or turn; to twist; to coil.—*vi.* To twine or twist; to crook; to bend; to meander.

Windage, wind'āj, *n.* The difference between the diameter of a gun and that of the shell; influence of the wind in deflecting a missile; extent of deflection.

Wind-bag, wind'bag, *n.* A bag filled with wind; a man of mere words; a noisy pretender.

Wind-bound, wind'bound, *a.* Prevented from sailing by a contrary wind.

Winder, wīnd'ėr, *n.* One who or that which winds; an instrument for winding yarn, &c.

Windfall, wind'fạl, *n.* Fruit blown down; an unexpected legacy or advantage.

Windgall, wind'gạl, *n.* A soft tumour on the fetlock-joints of a horse.

Winding, wīnd'ing, *a.* Bending; twisting; spiral.—*n.* A turn or turning; a bend.

Winding-sheet, wīnd'ing-shēt, *n.* A sheet in which a corpse is wrapped.

Wind-instrument, wind'in-stru-ment, *n.* An instrument of music played by wind or breath, as an organ, flute, &c.

Windlass, wind'las, *n.* A revolving cylinder on which a rope is wound, used for raising weights, &c., by hand or other power.

Windlestraw, win'dl-strạ, *n.* A kind of grass; a stalk of grass.

Windmill, wind'mil, *n.* A mill driven by the wind.

Window, win'dō, *n.* An opening in a wall

for the admission of light or air; the frame (usually fitted with glass) in this opening.
Window-sash, win'dō-sash, *n.* The light frame in which glass is set in windows.
Windpipe, wind'pīp, *n.* The cartilaginous pipe or passage for the breath; the trachea.
Wind-sail, wind'sāl, *n.* A wide tube or funnel of canvas, used to convey air into the lower apartments of a ship.
Wind-up, wīnd'up, *n.* The conclusion or final settlement of any matter; the close.
Windward, wind'wėrd, *n.* The point from which the wind blows.—*a.* and *adv.* Towards the wind.
Windy, wind'i, *a.* Boisterous; exposed to the wind; empty; flatulent.
Wine, wīn, *n.* An intoxicating liquor obtained from the fermented juice of grapes, &c.
Wine-cellar, wīn'sel-ėr, *n.* An apartment or cellar for storing wine.
Wine-fat, wīn'fat, *n.* The vat into which the liquor flows from the wine-press.
Wine-glass, wīn'gläs, *n.* A small glass in which wine is drunk.
Wine-press, wīn'pres, *n.* An apparatus in which the juice is pressed out of grapes.
Wine-taster, wīn'tāst-ėr, *n.* A person employed to judge of wine for purchasers.
Wing, wing, *n.* One of the anterior limbs in birds; organ of flight; flight; a lateral extension; side; side division of an army, &c.—*vt.* To furnish with wings; to fly; to traverse by flying; to wound in the wing.
Wing-case, wing'kās, *n.* The hard case which covers the wings of beetles, &c.
Wing-commander, wing-kom-mand'ėr, *n.* Officer in the Royal Air Force corresponding in rank to a commander in the navy or a lieutenant-colonel in the army.
Winged, wingd, *a.* Having wings; swift.
Winglet, wing'let, *n.* A little wing.
Wink, wingk, *vi.* To shut and open the eyelids; to give a hint by the eyelids; to connive; to be wilfully blind (with *at*).—*n.* Act of shutting and opening the eyelids rapidly; a twinkling; a hint given by means of the eye.
Winner, win'ėr, *n.* One who wins.
Winning, win'ing, *a.* Attractive; charming. —*n.* The sum won by success in competition; chiefly in *pl.*
Winnow, win'ō, *vt.* To separate the chaff from by wind; to fan; to sift; to scrutinize. —*vi.* To separate chaff from corn.
Winsey, win'si, *n.* Same as *Wincey.*
Winsome, win'sum, *a.* Attractive; winning.
Winter, win'tėr, *n.* The cold season of the year; a year; any cheerless situation.—*a.* Belonging to winter.—*vi.* To pass the winter. —*vt.* To keep or feed during winter.
Winterly, win'tėr-li, *a.* Wintry.
Wintry, Wintery, win'tri, win'tėr-i, *a.* Pertaining or suitable to winter; cold; stormy.
Winy, wīn'i, *a.* Like wine.
Winze, winz, *n.* A small shaft in a mine.
Wipe, wīp, *vt.* (wiping, wiped). To clean by gentle rubbing; to strike gently; to efface.—*n.* A rub for the purpose of cleaning; a gibe.
Wire, wīr, *n.* A thread of metal; a telegraph wire; the telegraph.—*vt.* (wiring, wired). To bind with wire; to put a wire on; to send by telegraph.—*vi.* To communicate by telegraph.
Wire-draw, wīr'dra̤, *vt.* To draw into wire; to spin out at length; to protract.
Wireless, wīr'les, *n.* Wireless telegraphy or telephony; communication between distant places by means of electromagnetic waves, without the use of wires.
Wire-puller, wīr'pu̧l-ėr, *n.* One who pulls the wires of puppets; one who secretly controls the actions of others; an intriguer.
Wire-pulling, wīr'pu̧l-ing, *n.* The procedure of a wire-puller.
Wire-worm, wīr'wėrm, *n.* A name for hard, wiry larvæ or grubs.
Wiry, wīr'i, *a.* Made of or like wire; tough; lean and sinewy.
Wisdom, wiz'dom, *n.* Sound judgment and sagacity; prudence; learning or erudition.
Wisdom-tooth, wiz'dom-töth, *n.* A large back double tooth, the last to come.
Wise, wīz, *a.* Having wisdom; sagacious; judicious; skilled; sage.—*n.* Manner; mode.
Wiseacre, wīz'ā-kėr, *n.* A pretender to wisdom; a dunce who poses as a wise man.
Wisely, wīz'li, *adv.* Sensibly; judiciously.
Wish, wish, *vi.* To have a desire; to long; with *for.*—*vt.* To desire; to long for; to invoke.—*n.* A desire; the thing desired.
Wishful, wish'fu̧l, *a.* Desirous; eager; earnest.
Wishy-washy, wish'i-wosh'i, *a.* Very thin and weak; diluted; feeble.
Wisp, wisp, *n.* A small bundle of straw, &c.
Wistful, wist'fu̧l, *a.* Thoughtful; attentive; earnest; pensive; longing.
Wistfully, wist'fu̧l-li, *adv.* In a wistful manner; attentively; pensively; longingly.
Wit, wit, *vt.* and *i.* (pres. tense, wot, pret. wist, pres. part. witting and wotting). To know; to be aware.—**To wit,** namely; that is to say.—*n.* Understanding; sense; wisdom; intelligence; faculty of associating ideas cleverly and in apt language; a person possessing this faculty; cleverness.
Witch, wich, *n.* A woman who practises sorcery.—*vt.* To bewitch.
Witchcraft, wich'kraft, *n.* Sorcery; enchantment; fascination.
Witch-elm. *See* WYCH-ELM.
Witchery, wich'ė-ri, *n.* Witchcraft; fascination.
Witch-hazel, *See* WYCH-HAZEL.
Witching, wich'ing, *a.* Bewitching.
Witenagemot, wit'en-a-ge-mot″, *n.* The Anglo-Saxon national council.
With, wiTH, *prep.* Against; in the company of; among; showing; marked by; immediately after; through; by.—*n.* With or wīth. A withe.
Withal, wiTH-a̤l', *adv.* Moreover; likewise; at the same time.—*prep.* With: used after relatives at the end of a clause.
Withdraw, wiTH-dra̤', *vt.* To draw back or away; to retract; to cause to retire.—*vi.* To retire; to secede.
Withdrawal, wiTH-dra̤'al, *n.* Act of withdrawing or taking back; a recalling.
Withe, with or wīth, *n.* A willow twig; any flexible twig used to bind something.
Wither, wiTH'ėr, *vi.* To fade or shrivel; to become dry and wrinkled; to decline.—*vt.* To cause to fade; to prove fatal to.
Withering, wiTH'ėr-ing, *a.* Such as to wither, blast, or fatally affect.
Withers, wiTH'ėrz, *n.pl.* The junction of the shoulder-bones of a horse, forming the highest part of the back.

Withhold, wiᴛʜ-hōld,′ *vt.* To hold back; to restrain; to retain; not to grant.
Within, wiᴛʜ-in′, *prep.* In the interior of; in the compass of.—*adv.* In the inner part; inwardly; indoors; at home.
Without, wiᴛʜ-out′, *prep.* On the outside of; out of; beyond; not having.—*adv.* On the outside; outwardly; out-of-doors.
Withstand, wiᴛʜ-stand′, *vt.* and *i.* To oppose; to resist.
Withy, wi′thi, *n.* A withe.
Witless, wit′les, *a.* Destitute of wit; thoughtless; indiscreet; silly.
Witness, wit′nes, *n.* Testimony; attestation of a fact or event; one who knows or sees anything; one who gives evidence in a trial.—*vt.* To attest; to see the execution of a legal instrument, and subscribe it.—*vi.* To bear testimony.
Witted, wit′ed, *a.* Having wit.
Witticism, wit′i-sizm, *n.* A witty remark.
Wittily, wit′i-li, *adv.* With wit.
Wittingly, wit′ing-li, *adv.* Knowingly; by design.
Witty, wit′i, *a.* Possessed of wit; full of wit; keenly or brilliantly humorous; facetious.
Wive, wīv, *vt.* and *i.* (wiving, wived). To provide with or take a wife.
Wivern. *See* WYVERN.
Wives, wīvz, pl. of *wife.*
Wizard, wiz′ard, *n.* A wise man or sage; a sorcerer; a magician; a conjurer.
Wizen, Wizened, wiz′n, wiz′nd, *a.* Hard, dry, and shrivelled; withered; weazen.
Woad, wōd, *n.* A plant, the leaves of which yield a blue dye.
Wobble, wob′l, *vi.* (wobbling, wobbled). To move unsteadily in rotating; to rock.
Woe, Wo, wō, *n.* Grief; misery; affliction.
Woebegone, wō′bē-gon, *a.* Overwhelmed with woe; sorrowful; melancholy.
Woeful, Woful, wō′fụl, *a.* Full of woe; sorrowful; afflicted; wretched; pitiful.
Woefully, Wofully, wō′fụl-li, *adv.* In a woeful manner; wretchedly; extremely.
Wold, wōld, *n.* A tract of open country; a low hill; a down.
Wolf, wụlf, *n.*; pl. **Wolves,** wụlvz. A carnivorous quadruped akin to the dog, crafty and rapacious; a cruel or cunning person.
Wolf Cub, wụlf kub, *n.* A junior Boy Scout, between the ages of 8 and 11.
Wolfish, wụlf′ish, *a.* Like a wolf.
Wolfram, wụl′fram, *n.* An ore of the metal tungsten; the metal itself.
Wolf's-bane, wụlfs′bān, *n.* The plant monk's-hood or aconite.
Woman, wụ′man, *n.*; pl. **Women,** wi′men. The female of the human race; the female sex; an adult female.
Womanhood, wụ′man-hụd, *n.* The state, character, or qualities of a woman.
Womanish, wụ′man-ish, *a.* Suitable to a woman; feminine; effeminate.
Womankind, wụ′man-kīnd, *n.* Women collectively; the female sex.
Womanlike, wụ′man-līk, *a.* Like a woman.
Womanly, wụ′man-li, *a.* Becoming a woman; feminine in a praiseworthy sense.
Womb, wöm, *n.* The uterus; place where anything is produced; any deep cavity.
Wombat, wom′bat, *n.* A marsupial mammal about the size of a badger.
Won, wun, pret. and pp. of *win.*
Wonder, wun′dėr, *n.* Something very strange; a prodigy or marvel; feeling excited by something strange.—*vi.* To be struck with wonder; to marvel; to entertain some doubt and curiosity.
Wonderful, wun′dėr-fụl, *a.* Marvellous; surprising; strange; astonishing.
Wonderfully, wun′dėr-fụl-li, *adv.* In a wonderful manner; surprisingly; very.
Wonderment, wun′dėr-ment, *n.* Wonder; surprise; astonishment.
Wondrous, wun′drus, *a.* Wonderful; strange.—*adv.* Remarkably.
Wondrously, wun′drus-li, *adv.* In a wondrous or wonderful manner or degree.
Won't, wōnt. A contraction for *will not.*
Wont, wōnt or wunt, *a.* Accustomed.—*n.* Custom; habit; use.—*vi.* (pret. & pp. wont, sometimes wonted). To be accustomed to use.
Wonted, wōnt′ed or wunt′ed, *a.* Accustomed; usual.
Woo, wö, *vt.* and *i.* (wooing, wooed). To make love to; to solicit in love; to court.
Wood, wụd, *n.* A large collection of growing trees; the hard or solid substance of trees; timber.—*vi.* To take in or get supplies of wood.—*vt.* To supply with wood.
Woodbine, Woodbind, wụd′bīn, wụd′bīnd, *n.* The wild honeysuckle.
Woodcock, wụd′kok, *n* A bird allied to the snipe, esteemed for the table.
Wood-cut, wụd′kut, *n.* An engraving on wood, or a print from such engraving.
Wood-cutting, wụd′kut-ing, *n.* Act of cutting wood; wood-engraving.
Wooded, wụd′ed, *a.* Abounding in or covered with wood or growing timber.
Wooden, wụd′n, *a.* Made of wood; clumsy; awkward; dull.
Wood-engraving, wụd′en-grāv-ing, *n.* The art of producing designs in relief on the surface of a block of wood; an impression from such a block.
Woodland, wụd′land, *n.* Land covered with wood.—*a.* Relating to woods; sylvan.
Woodman, wụd′man, *n.* A forester.
Woodpecker, wụd′pek-ėr, *n.* A climbing bird which feeds on insects and their larvæ on trees.
Wood-pigeon, wụd′pi-jon, *n.* The ring-dove or cushat.
Woodruff, Woodroof, wụd′ruf, wụd′rụf, *n.* A plant of the madder family.
Wood-sorrel, wụd′so-rel, *n.* A common British wild flower.
Wood-work, wụd′wėrk, *n.* The part of any structure that is made of wood.
Woody, wụd′i, *a.* Abounding with wood; wooded; consisting of wood; like wood.
Wooer, wö′ėr, *n.* One who woos.
Woof, wöf, *n.* The threads that cross the warp in weaving; the weft; texture in general.
Wool, wụl, *n.* That soft species of hair on sheep; any fleecy substance resembling wool.
Wool-gathering, wụl′gaᴛʜ-ėr-ing, *n.* Act of gathering wool; indulgence of idle fancies; a foolish or fruitless pursuit.
Wool-grower, wụl′grō-ėr, *n.* A person who raises sheep for the production of wool.
Woollen, wụl′en, *a.* Made of or pertaining to wool.—*n.* Cloth made of wool.

Woolly, wụl'i, *a.* Consisting of wool; resembling wool; clothed with wool.
Woolpack, wụl'pak, *n.* A bag of wool; a bundle or bale weighing 240 lbs.
Woolsack, wụl'sak, *n.* A sack of wool; seat of the lord-chancellor in House of Lords.
Wool-stapler, wụl'stā-pl-ėr, *n.* A dealer in wool; a sorter of wool.
Wootz, wụts, *n.* A very superior kind of steel imported from the East Indies.
Word, wėrd, *n.* An articulate sound expressing an idea; a term; information; a saying; motto; order; assertion or promise; in *pl.*, talk; wrangle.—*vi.* To express in words.
Word-book, wėrd'bụk, *n.* A vocabulary; a dictionary.
Wording, wėrd'ing, *n.* The mode of expressing in words; form of stating.
Wordy, wėrd'i, *a.* Using many words; verbose.
Wore, wōr, pret. of *wear.*
Work, wėrk, *n.* Effort; labour; employment; a task; achievement; a literary or artistic performance; some extensive structure; establishment where labour of some kind is carried on; result of force acting.—*vi.* (pret. and pp. worked or wrought). To put forth effort; to labour; to take effect; to tend or conduce; to seethe; to ferment.—*vt.* To bestow labour upon; to bring about; to keep at work; to influence; to achieve; to fashion; to embroider; to cause to ferment.
Workable, wėrk'a-bl, *a.* That can be worked, or that is worth working.
Workaday, wėrk'a-dā, *a.* Working-day; everyday; toiling.
Worker, wėrk'ėr, *n.* One that works; a toiler; a labourer; a working bee.
Workhouse, wėrk'hous, *n.* A house in which able-bodied paupers work; a pauper asylum.
Working, wėrk'ing, *a.* Engaged in bodily toil; industrious.—*n.* Act of labouring; movement; operation; fermentation; *pl.* portions of a mine, &c., worked.
Working-class, wėrk'ing-klas, *n.* Those who earn their bread by manual labour.
Working-day, wėrk'ing-dā, *n.* A day on which labour is performed.—*a.* Relating to such days; laborious.
Workman, wėrk'man, *n.* An artisan; mechanic; labourer; worker.
Workmanlike, wėrk'man-līk, *a.* Like a proper workman; skilful; well performed.
Workmanly, wėrk'man-li, *a.* Workmanlike.
Workmanship, wėrk'man-ship, *n.* Skill or art of a workman; style or character of execution; art; dexterity; handicraft.
Workshop, wėrk'shop, *n.* A shop or building where any craft or work is carried on.
World, wėrld, *n.* The whole creation; the earth; any celestial orb; a large portion of our globe; sphere of existence; a domain or realm; mankind; the public; great degree or quantity.
Worldling, wėrld'ling, *n.* One devoted exclusively to worldly pleasures.
Worldly, wėrld'li, *a.* Relating to this world or this life; secular; carnal; sordid.
World-wide, wėrld'wīd, *a.* Wide as the world; extending over all the world.
Worm, wėrm, *n.* A small creeping animal; an intestinal parasite; *pl.* the disease caused by such parasites; something vermicular or spiral.—*vi.* To wriggle; to work gradually and secretly.—*vt.* To effect by stealthy means; *refl.* to insinuate oneself; to extract cunningly.
Worm-eaten, wėrm'ēt-n, *a.* Gnawed by worms; having cavities made by worms.
Wormling, wėrm'ling, *n.* A minute worm.
Wormwood, wėrm'wụd, *n.* A plant with bitter, tonic, and stimulating qualities.
Wormy, wėrm'i, *a.* Abounding with worms; eaten by worms; grovelling; earthy.
Worn, wōrn, *pp.* of *wear.*
Worn-out, wōrn'out, *a.* Useless from being much worn; wearied; exhausted.
Worry, wu'ri, *vt.* (worrying, worried). To tear with the teeth, as dogs; to harass; to annoy.—*vi.* To trouble oneself; to fret.—*n.* Trouble; care; anxiety.
Worse, wėrs, *a.* Bad or ill in a greater degree; inferior; more unwell; more ill off.—**The worse,** defeat; disadvantage.—*adv.* In a manner or degree more evil or bad.
Worsen, wėr'sn, *vi.* and *t.* To grow or make worse.
Worser, wėrs'ėr, *a.* and *adv.* A redundant comparative of *worse.*
Worship, wėr'ship, *n.* Dignity; honour; a title of honour; religious service; adoration; reverence.—*vt.* (worshipping, worshipped). To adore; to pay divine honours to; to idolize.—*vi.* To perform religious service.
Worshipful, wėr'ship-fụl, *a.* Worthy of honour or high respect; honourable.
Worshipper, wėr'ship-ėr, *n.* One who worships.
Worst, wėrst, *a.* Bad or evil in the highest degree.—*n.* The most evil state or action.—*adv.* Most extremely.—*vt.* To defeat.
Worsted, wụst'ed, *n.* Yarn spun from wool, and used in knitting.—*a.* Made of worsted.
Wort, wėrt, *n.* The infusion of malt before it becomes beer by fermentation; an herb.
Worth, wėrth, *a.* Equal in value or price to; deserving of; possessing.—*n.* Value; price; merit; excellence.—*vi.* To be; to betide.
Worthily, wėr'THi-li, *adv.* In a worthy manner; suitably; deservedly; justly.
Worthless, wėrth'les, *a.* Having no worth; valueless; contemptible; not deserving.
Worthy, wėr'THi, *a.* Possessing worth; estimable; virtuous; deserving; fitting.—*n.* A man of eminent worth; a local celebrity.
Wot, wot. *See* Wit.
Would, wụd, Pret. of *will*, mainly used in subjunctive or conditional senses.
Would-be, wụd'bē, *a.* Wishing to be; vainly pretending to be.—*n.* A vain pretender.
Wound, wönd, *n.* A cut or stab, &c.; injury; hurt or pain to the feelings; damage.—*vt.* or *i.* To inflict a wound on; to pain.
Wove, wōv, pret. and sometimes pp. of *weave.*
Wrack, rak, *n.* Sea-weed generally; wreck; a thin flying cloud.
Wraith, rāth, *n.* An apparition of a person about to die or newly dead.
Wrangle, rang'gl, *vi.* (wrangling, wrangled). To dispute angrily; to argue.—*n.* A dispute.
Wrangler, rang'glėr, *n.* One who wrangles; in Cambridge University, one who attains a first class in the final examination for honours in mathematics.
Wrap, rap, *vt.* (wrapping, wrapped or wrapt). To fold or roll; to cover by something wound;

to envelop.—*n.* An outer article of dress for warmth.
Wrapper, rap'ėr, *n.* One that wraps; a cover; a loose upper garment.
Wrapping, rap'ing, *a.* Used or designed to wrap.—*n.* A cover; a wrapper.
Wrath, räth or rąth, *n.* Violent anger; rage; fury.
Wrathful, räth'fųl or rąth'fųl, *a.* Full of wrath; furious; wroth.
Wreak, rēk, *vt.* To revenge or avenge; to inflict; to gratify by punishment.
Wreath, rēth, *n.* Something twisted or curled; a garland; a chaplet; a snow-drift.
Wreathe, rēтн, *vt.* (wreathing, wreathed). To twist into a wreath; to entwine; to encircle; to dress in a garland.—*vi.* To be entwined.
Wreathy, rēth'i, *a.* Forming a wreath; spiral.
Wreck, rek, *n.* Ruin; overthrow; a ruin; destruction of a vessel at sea.—*vt.* To cause to become a wreck; to ruin.
Wreckage, rek'āj, *n.* Act of wrecking; remains of a ship or cargo that has been wrecked.
Wrecker, rek'ėr, *n.* One who causes shipwrecks or plunders wrecks; one who recovers goods from wrecked vessels.
Wren, ren, *n.* A name of various small birds; a small song-bird; a member of the Women's Royal Naval Service (W.R.N.S.).
Wrench, rensh, *n.* A violent twist; injury by twisting; an instrument for screwing a bolt or nut.—*vt.* To pull with a twist; to distort.
Wrest, rest, *vt.* To twist; to take or force by violence; to distort.—*n.* Act of wresting; a wrench; an implement to tune stringed instruments with.
Wrestle, res'l, *vi.* (wrestling, wrestled). To contend by grappling and trying to throw down; to struggle.—*vt.* To contend with in wrestling.—*n.* A bout at wrestling.
Wrestler, res'lėr, *a.* One who wrestles.
Wretch, rech, *n.* A miserable person; a mean, base, or vile creature.
Wretched, rech'ed, *a.* Very miserable; distressing; worthless; despicable.
Wretchedly, rech'ed-li, *adv.* In a wretched manner; most miserably; contemptibly.
Wriggle, rig'l, *vi.* and *t.* (wriggling, wriggled). To move with writhing or twisting.—*n.* A quick twisting motion.
Wright, rīt, *n.* An artisan or artificer; a worker in wood; a carpenter.
Wring, ring, *vt.* (wringing, wrung). To twist with the hands; to twist and compress; to torture; to extort.—*vi.* To writhe.
Wringer, ring'ėr, *n.* One who wrings; an apparatus for forcing water from clothes.
Wrinkle, ring'kl, *n.* A small ridge or furrow; a crease; a hint; a notion.—*vt.* and *i.* (wrinkling, wrinkled). To form into wrinkles; to contract into furrows; to crease.
Wrinkly, ring'kl-i, *a.* Somewhat wrinkled; puckered.
Wrist, rist, *n.* The joint by which the hand is united to the arm.
Wristband, rist'band, *n.* The band of a sleeve covering the wrist.
Wristlet, rist'let, *n.* Some small object worn round the wrist; a bracelet.
Writ, rit, *n.* That which is written; the Scriptures; a legal document commanding a person to do some act.
Write, rīt, *vt.* (writing, pret. wrote, pp. written). To form by a pen, &c.; to set down in letters or words; to cover with letters; to send in writing; to compose.—*vi.* To trace characters with a pen, &c.; to be engaged in literary work; to conduct correspondence.
Writer, rīt'ėr, *n.* One who writes; an author; a clerk; in Scotland, a law agent.
Writhe, rīтн, *vt.* (writhing, writhed). To twist or distort, as the body or limbs.—*vi.* To twist and turn; to be distorted, as from agony.
Writing, rīt'ing, *n.* Act of one who writes; a book, manuscript, or document; style.
Written, rit'n, *a.* Expressed in writing.
Wrong, rong, *a.* Not right; not fit; not what ought to be; erroneous.—*n.* What is not right; an injustice; injury.—*adv.* In a wrong manner.—*vt.* To do wrong to; to treat with injustice.
Wrong-doer, rong'dö-ėr, *n.* One who does wrong.
Wrongful, rong'fųl, *a.* Injurious; unjust.
Wrong-headed, rong'hed-ed, *a.* Obstinately or perversely wrong; stubborn.
Wrongly, rong'li, *adv.* In a wrong manner; mistakenly; erroneously; unjustly.
Wrongous, rong'us, *a.* In *Scots law*, unjust.
Wroth, roth, *a.* Very angry; indignant.
Wrought, rąt, pret. and pp. of *work.*
Wry, rī, *a.* Crooked; twisted; askew.
Wryneck, rī'nek, *n.* A twisted neck; a small European bird allied to the woodpeckers.
Wych-elm, wich'elm, *n.* An elm with large leaves and pendulous branches.
Wych-hazel, wich'hā-zel, *n.* An American shrub with yellow flowers.
Wynd, wīnd, *n.* A narrow alley; a lane.
Wyvern, wī'vėrn, *n.* An heraldic monster, a sort of dragon, with two wings, two eagle's legs, and a tapering body.

X

Xanthic, zan'thik, *a.* Yellowish.
Xanthin, Xanthine, zan'thin, *n.* A yellow colouring matter.
Xanthous, zan'thus, *a.* Fair-haired.
Xebec, zē'bek or ze-bek', *n.* A three-masted vessel used in the Mediterranean.
Xerotes, zē'ro-tēz, *n.* A dry habit of the body.
Xiphoid, zīf'oid, *a.* Shaped like a sword.
X-rays, eks'rāz, or **Röntgen rays, runt'gen,** *n.* Electromagnetic waves of high frequency, which penetrate most substances, except bones, metal, &c., and enable photographs to be taken of these in the living body.
Xylem, *n.* Woody vegetable tissue.
Xylograph, zī'lo-graf, *n.* A wood-engraving.
Xylography, zi-log'ra-fi, *n.* Wood-engraving; a process of decorative painting on wood.
Xyloid, zī'loid, *a.* Having the nature of wood: resembling wood.
Xylonite, zī'lō-nīt, *n.* Celluloid.
Xylophagous, zi-lof'a-gus, *a.* Wood-eating.
Xylophone, zī'lo-fōn, *n.* A musical instrument in which the notes are given by pieces of wood struck with hammers.
Xyst, Xystus, zist, zis'tus, *n.* A covered portico or open court for athletic exercises.
Xyster, zis'tėr, *n.* A surgeon's instrument for scraping bones.

Y

Yacht, yot, *n.* A light vessel used for racing, pleasure, &c.—*vi.* To sail in a yacht.
Yachter, yot'ėr, *n.* A yachtsman.
Yachting, yot'ing, *a.* Belonging to a yacht.—*n.* Act of sailing a yacht.
Yachtsman, yots'man, *n.* One who keeps or sails a yacht.
Yahoo, yä'hö, *n.* A rude, boorish person.
Yak, yak, *n.* A wild ox with long silky hair.
Yam, yam, *n.* A climbing plant, cultivated in tropical climates for its large roots.
Yankee, yang'kē, *n.* A citizen of New England; a native of the United States.
Yap, yap, *vi.* (yapping, yapped). To yelp; to bark.—*n.* Cry of a dog; yelp.
Yard, yärd, *n.* A standard measure of 3 feet; a long beam slung crosswise to a mast and supporting a sail; piece of enclosed ground.
Yard-arm, yärd'ärm, *n.* Either end of a ship's yard.
Yard-stick, yärd'stik, *n.* A stick 3 feet in length.
Yare, yãr, *a.* Ready; dexterous.
Yarn, yärn, *n.* Thread prepared from wool or flax for weaving; a story.
Yarrow, ya'rō, *n.* Milfoil.
Yataghan, yat'a-gan, *n.* A dagger-like sabre about 2 feet long.
Yaw, ya̤, *vi.* To swerve suddenly in sailing.—*n.* The sudden temporary deviation of a ship.
Yawl, ya̤l, *n.* A small ship's boat, usually rowed by four or six oars; a small two-masted yacht.—*vi.* To howl; to yell.
Yawn, ya̤n, *vi.* To have the mouth open involuntarily while a deep breath is taken; to gape.—*n.* A gaping; act of yawning; a chasm.
Ye, yē, *pron.* The nominative and objective plural of the second personal pronoun.
Yea, yā, *adv.* Yes: the opposite of *nay*.
Yean, yēn, *vt.* and *i.* To bring forth young, as a goat or sheep.
Yeanling, yēn'ling, *n.* A lamb.
Year, yēr, *n.* The period of time during which the earth makes one revolution in its orbit; twelve months; *pl.* old age; time of life.
Year-book, yēr-bu̧k, *n.* A book published every year giving fresh information regarding matters that change.
Yearling, yēr'ling, *n.* A young beast one year old.—*a.* Being a year old.
Yearly, yēr'li, *a.* Annual; happening every year.—*adv.* Once a year.
Yearn, yėrn, *vi.* To feel uneasiness of mind from longing or pity; to long.
Yearning, yėrn'ing, *a.* Longing.—*n.* A feeling of longing desire.
Yeast, yēst, *n.* A yellowish substance produced in alcoholic fermentation; barm.
Yeasty, yēst'i, *a.* Like or containing yeast.
Yell, yel, *vi.* To cry out with a loud piercing noise; to scream.—*n.* A loud, piercing outcry.
Yellow, yel'ō, *a.* Being of a bright golden colour.—*n.* A bright golden colour.
Yellow-fever, yel'ō-fē-vėr, *n.* A malignant fever of warm climates, attended with yellowness of the skin.
Yellow-hammer, Yellow-ammer, yel'ō-ham-ėr, yel'ō-am-ėr, *n.* A species of bunting, with much yellow in its plumage.
Yellowish, yel'ō-ish, *a.* Somewhat yellow.
Yelp, yelp, *vi.* To utter a sharp bark or cry, as a dog.—*n.* A sharp cry of a dog.
Yeoman, yō'man, *n.*; pl. **-men.** A man who owns a small estate in land; a gentleman farmer; one of the yeomanry.
Yeomanly, yō'man-li, *a.* Pertaining to a yeoman.—*adv.* Like a yeoman; bravely.
Yeomanry, yō'man-ri, *n.* The collective body of yeomen; a volunteer cavalry force.
Yes, yes, *adv.* Even so; expressing affirmation or consent: opposed to *no*.
Yester, yes'tėr, *a.* Pertaining to the day before the present; last.
Yesterday, yes'tėr-dā, *n.* The day before the present.—*adv.* On the day last past.
Yestereve, Yestereven, yes'tėr-ēv, yes'tėr-ē-vn, *n.* The evening last past.
Yestermorn, Yestermorning, yes'tėr-morn, yes-tėr-mor'ning, *n.* The morn or morning last past.
Yesternight, yes'tėr-nīt, *n.* The night last past.
Yet, yet, *adv.* In addition; still; hitherto; nevertheless.—*conj.* Nevertheless, however.
Yew, yū, *n.* An evergreen tree, with poisonous leaves, and yielding a hard durable timber.
Yield, yēld, *vt.* To produce in return for labour, &c.; to afford; to grant; to give up.—*vi.* To submit; to comply; to produce.—*n.* Amount yielded; product; return.
Yielding, yēld'ing, *a.* Inclined to yield; accommodating; compliant; facile.
Yodel, Yodle, yō'dl, *vt.* and *i.* (yodelling, yodling; yodelled, yodled). To sing like the Swiss and Tyrolese mountaineers by changing suddenly from the natural voice to the falsetto.
Yoke, yōk, *n.* Gear connecting draught animals by passing across their necks; a pair of draught animals; something resembling a yoke; shoulder-piece of a garment supporting the rest; servitude; burden; a bond; a tie.—*vt.* (yoking, yoked). To put a yoke on; to couple; to enslave.
Yoke-fellow, Yoke-mate, yōk'fel-ō, yōk'-māt, *n.* An associate; a partner.
Yokel, yō'kl, *n.* A rustic; an ignorant peasant; a country bumpkin.
Yolk, yōk, *n.* The yellow part of an egg.
Yon, yon, *a.* That; those; yonder.
Yonder, yon'dėr, *a.* That or those away there.—*adv.* At or in that place there.
Yore, yōr, *adv.* Long ago; in old time: now used only in the phrase *of yore*.
You, yö, *pron.* The nominative and objective plural of *thou*: commonly used when a single person is addressed.
Young, yung, *a.* Being in the early stage of life; youthful.—*n.* The offspring of an animal.
Youngish, yung'ish, *a.* Somewhat young.
Youngling, yung'ling, *n.* Any animal in the first part of life; a young person.
Youngster, yung'stėr, *n.* A young person.
Younker, yung'kėr, *n.* A youngster.
Your, yör, possessive corresponding to *ye, you*. Pertaining or belonging to you.
Yours, yörz, *poss. pron.* That or those which belong to you.
Yourself, yör-self', *pron.*; pl. **-selves.** You, used distinctively or reflexively.
Youth, yöth, *n.* State or quality of being

young; period during which one is young; a young man; young persons collectively.
Youthful, yöth'ful, *a.* Young; pertaining to youth; fresh or vigorous, as in youth.
Yowl, youl, *vi.* To give a long distressful or mournful cry, as a dog.—*n.* A mournful cry.
Yule, yöl, *n.* Christmas.

Z

Zaffre, zaf'ėr, *n.* A substance obtained from cobalt, used by enamellers as a blue colour.
Zany, zā'ni, *n.* A buffoon or merry-andrew.
Zareba. Same as *Zereba.*
Zax, zaks, *n.* An instrument used for cutting and dressing slates.
Zeal, zēl, *n.* Eagerness; passionate ardour; enthusiasm.
Zealot, ze'lot, *n.* One who is zealous; a fanatical partisan; a bigot.
Zealotry, ze'lot-ri, *n.* Behaviour of a zealot; excessive zeal; fanaticism.
Zealous, ze'lus, *a.* Inspired with zeal; fervent; eager; earnest.
Zealously, ze'lus-li, *adv.* In a zealous manner; ardently; eagerly; fervently.
Zebec, Zebeck, zē'bek, *n.* Same as *Xebec.*
Zebra, zē'bra, *n.* A striped South African animal allied to the horse and ass.
Zebu, zē'bū, *n.* The humped ox of India.
Zemindar, zem-in-där', *n.* In India, a landholder or landed proprietor.
Zenana, ze-nä'na, *n.* The portion of a Hindu's house devoted to females.
Zend, zend, *n.* An ancient Iranian or Persian language, closely allied to Sanskrit.
Zenith, zē'nith or zen'ith, *n.* The point of the heavens right above a spectator's head; highest point.
Zephyr, zef'ėr, *n.* The west wind; any soft, mild, gentle breeze.
Zeppelin, zep'el-in, *n.* A German air-ship.
Zereba, ze-rē'ba, *n.* In the Soudan, a temporary camp guarded by a fence of bushes, &c.
Zero, zē'rō, *n.* Number or quantity diminished to nothing; a cipher; lowest point.
Zest, zest, *n.* Orange or lemon peel, used to flavour liquor; relish; charm; gusto.
Zigzag, zig'zag, *n.* Something in the form of straight lines with sharp turns.—*a.* Having sharp turns or bends.—*vi.* (zigzagging, zigzagged). To move in a zigzag fashion; to form zigzags.
Zigzaggy, zig'zag-i, *a.* Zigzag.
Zinc, zingk, *n.* A metal of bluish-white colour, used for roofing, to form alloys, &c.
Zincky, Zinky, zingk'i, *a.* Pertaining to or like zinc; containing zinc.
Zincode, zingk'ōd, *n.* The positive pole of a galvanic battery.
Zincography, zing-kog'ra-fi, *n.* A mode of printing similar to lithography, a plate of zinc taking the place of the stone.
Zincoid, zingk'oid, *a.* Zincky.
Zip-fastener, zip-fas'n-ėr, *n.* A kind of fastener, pulled open or shut by a tag, and joining two edges together, used on purses, tobacco-pouches, golf-bags, &c.
Zircon, zėr'kon, *n.* A hard lustrous mineral, one of the gems called also jargon.
Zither, Zithern, zith'ėr, zith'ėrn, *n.* A flat musical instrument with from twenty-nine to forty-two strings, played with the fingers.
Zodiac, zō'di-ak, *n.* An imaginary belt or zone in the heavens, within which the apparent motions of the sun, moon, and principal planets are confined, divided into twelve equal parts or signs.
Zodiacal, zō-dī'ak-al, *a.* Pertaining to the zodiac.
Zoetrope, zō'ē-trōp, *n.* An optical contrivance by which, when the instrument revolves, certain painted figures inside appear to move in a lifelike manner.
Zone, zōn, *n.* A girdle or belt; one of the five great divisions of the earth, bounded by circles parallel to the equator; any well-defined belt.
Zonule, zōn'ūl, *n.* A little zone.
Zoogony, Zoogeny, zō-og'o-ni, zō-oj'e-ni, *n.* The doctrine of the origin of life.
Zoography, zō-og'ra-fi, *n.* The description of animals.
Zooid, zō'oid, *a.* Resembling or pertaining to an animal.—*n.* An organism, in some respects resembling a distinct animal.
Zoolite, zō'ol-īt, *n.* An animal substance petrified or fossil.
Zoological, zō-o-loj'ik-al, *a.* Pertaining to zoology.
Zoologist, zō-ol'o-jist, *n.* One who is versed in zoology.
Zoology, zō-ol'o-ji, *n.* The science of the natural history of animals.
Zoon, zō'on, *n.* An animal.
Zoonomy, zō-on'o-mi, *n.* The laws of animal life, or the science which treats of it.
Zoophagous, zō-of'a-gus, *a.* Feeding on animals; carnivorous.
Zoophyte, zō'o-fīt, *n.* A name applied to many plant-like animals, as sponges.
Zoroastrian, zor-o-as'tri-an, *a.* Pertaining to Zoroaster or Zoroastrianism.—*n.* A believer in this religion.
Zoroastrianism, zor-o-as'tri-an-izm, *n.* The ancient Persian religion founded by Zoroaster, one feature of which was a belief in a good and an evil power perpetually at strife; the religion of the Parsees; fire-worship.
Zouave, zwäv, *n.* A French infantry soldier dressed after the Turkish fashion.
Zulu, zö'lö, *n.* A member of a branch of the Kaffir race in South Africa.
Zymic, zim'ik, *a.* Pertaining to fermentation.
Zymology, zī-mol'o-ji, *n.* The doctrine of ferments and fermentation.
Zymotic, zī-mot'ik, *a.* Pertaining to fermentation; applied to epidemic and contagious diseases, supposed to be produced by germs acting like a ferment.

APPENDIX

I. Words, Phrases, and Noteworthy Sayings,

From the Latin, Greek, and Modern Languages, met with in Current English.

L. = Latin; Gr. = Greek; Fr. = French; O. Fr. = Old French; G. = German; It. = Italian; Sp. = Spanish.

à bas. [Fr.] Down, down with.
Ab extra. [L.] From without.
Ab initio. [L.] From the beginning.
Ab intra. [L.] From within.
à bon marché. [Fr.] Cheap; a good bargain.
Ab origine. [L.] From the origin.
Ab ovo. [L.] From the egg; from the beginning.
Ab ovo usque ad mala. [L.] From the egg to the apples (as in Roman banquets); from beginning to end.
Absente reo. [L.] The accused being absent.
Absit invidia. [L.] Let there be no ill-will; envy apart.
Absit omen. [L.] May this not prove ominous of evil!
Ab uno disce omnes. [L.] From one specimen judge of all the rest.
Ab urbe condita. [L.] From the building of the city (*i.e.* Rome).
à cheval. [Fr.] On horseback.
Ad aperturam (libri). [L.] At the opening of the book; wherever the book opens.
Ad calendas Græcas. [L.] At the Greek calends; *i.e.* never, as the Greeks had no calends in their mode of reckoning.
Ad captandum vulgus. [L.] To attract or please the rabble.
Addenda. [L.] Things to be added; list of additions.
Ad finem. [L.] To the end.
Ad hoc. [L.] To or with respect to this (object); said of a body elected or appointed for a definite work (as an education committee).
Ad hominem. [L.] To the man; to an individual's interests or passions; personal.
Ad infinitum. [L.] To infinity.
Ad interim. [L.] In the meanwhile.
Ad libitum. [L.] At pleasure; as much as one pleases.
Ad nauseam. [L.] To the point of disgust or satiety.
Ad referendum. [L.] For further consideration.
Ad rem. [L.] To the purpose; to the point.
Adscriptus glebæ. [L.] Attached to the soil.
Adsum. [L.] I am present; here!
Ad unguem. [L.] To the nail; to a nicety; exactly; perfectly.
Ad unum omnes. [L.] All to a man.
Ad utrumque paratus. [L.] Prepared for either event.
Ad valorem. [L.] According to the value.
Ad vitam aut culpam. [L.] For life or fault; *i.e.* till some misconduct be proved.
Advocatus diaboli. [L.] Devil's advocate; a person chosen to dispute before the papal court the claims of a candidate for canonization.
Æquo animo. [L.] With an equable mind; with equanimity.
Affaire d'amour. [Fr.] A love affair.
Affaire d'honneur. [Fr.] An affair of honour; a duel.
Affaire du cœur. [Fr.] An affair of the heart.
A fortiori. [L.] With stronger reason.
Agnus Dei. [L.] Lamb of God.
à grands frais. [Fr.] At great expense.
à haute voix. [Fr.] Aloud.
à la belle etoile. [Fr.] Under the stars; in the open air.
à la bonne heure. [Fr.] In good time; very well.
à l'abri. [Fr.] Under shelter.
à la carte. [Fr.] According to the bill of fare.
à la française. [Fr.] After the French mode.
à la mode. [Fr.] According to the custom or fashion.
Al fresco. [It.] In the open air; cool.
Allez-vous-en. [Fr.] Away with you.
Allons. [Fr.] Let us go; come on; come.
Alter ego. [L.] One's other self.
Alter idem. [L.] Another exactly similar.
Amende honorable. [Fr.] Satisfactory apology; reparation.
à merveille. [Fr.] To a wonder; marvellously.
Amor patriæ. [L.] Love of country.
Amour propre. [Fr.] Self-love; vanity.
Ancien régime. [Fr.] The former order of things.
Anguis in herba. [L.] A snake in the grass; an unsuspected danger.
Anno ætatis suæ. [L.] In the year of his or her age.
Anno Christi. [L.] In the year of Christ.
Anno Domini. [L.] In the year of our Lord.
Anno mundi. [L.] In the year of the world.
Anno urbis conditæ. [L.] In the year from the time when the city (Rome) was built.
Annus mirabilis. [L.] Wonderful year.
Ante meridiem. [L.] Before noon.
à outrance. [Fr.] To extremities.
Aperçu. [Fr.] A general sketch or survey.
à perte de vue. [Fr.] Till beyond one's view.
à peu près. [Fr.] Nearly.
à pied. [Fr.] On foot.
A posteriori. [L.] From effect to cause; empirical.
A priori. [L.] From cause to effect; independent of experience.
Arbiter elegantiarum. [L.] A judge or supreme authority in matters of taste.
Arcades ambo. [L.] Arcadians both; fellows of the same stamp.
Arcana imperii. [L.] State secrets.
Ardentia verba. [L.] Glowing language.
Argumentum ad hominem. [L.] An argument to the individual man; *i.e.* to his interests and prejudices.

Argumentum ad ignorantiam. [L.] An argument founded on the ignorance of the person addressed.
Arrière-pensée. [Fr.] Mental reservation.
Ars est celare artem. [L.] It is true art to conceal art.
Ars longa, vita brevis. [L.] Art is long, life is short.
Artium baccalaureus. [L.] Bachelor of Arts.
Artium magister. [L.] Master of Arts.
Au contraire. [Fr.] On the contrary.
Au courant. [Fr.] Fully acquainted with matters.
Au désespoir. [Fr.] In despair.
Audi alteram partem. [L.] Hear the other side.
Au fait. [Fr.] Well acquainted with; expert.
Au fond. [Fr.] At bottom.
Au reste. [Fr.] As for the rest.
Au revoir. [Fr.] Adieu until we meet again.
Aussitôt dit, aussitôt fait. [Fr.] No sooner said than done.
Autant d'hommes, autant d'avis. [Fr.] So many men, so many minds.
Aut Cæsar aut nullus. [L.] Either Cæsar or nobody.
Aut vincere aut mori. [L.] Either to conquer or to die; death or victory.
Aux armes; [Fr.] To arms!
Avant-propos. [Fr.] Preliminary matter; preface.
A vostra salute. [It.] } To your health.
à votre santé. [Fr.] }

Ballon d'essai. [Fr.] A trial balloon; a device to test opinion.
Bas-bleu. [Fr.] A blue-stocking; a literary woman.
Beatæ memoriæ. [L.] Of blessed memory.
Beau idéal. [Fr.] The ideal of perfection.
Beau monde. [Fr.] The world of fashion.
Beaux esprits. [Fr.] Men of wit.
Beaux yeux. [Fr.] Fine eyes; good looks.
Bel esprit. [Fr.] A person of wit or genius; a brilliant mind.
Ben trovato. [It.] Well invented.
Bête noir. [Fr.] A black beast; a bugbear.
Bis dat qui cito dat. [L.] He gives twice who gives quickly.
Bona fides (*bona fide*). [L.] Good faith (in good faith).
Bon ami. [Fr.] Good friend.
Bon gré, mal gré. [Fr.] With good or ill grace; willing or unwilling.
Bon jour. [Fr.] Good day; good morning.
Bon mot. [Fr.] A witty saying.
Bonne foi. [Fr.] Good faith.
Bon soir. [Fr.] Good evening.
Bon ton. [Fr.] Fashionable society.
Bon vivant. [Fr.] A good liver; a gourmand.
Bon voyage. [Fr.] A good voyáge or journey to you!
Bordereau. [Fr.] A memorandum.
Breveté. [Fr.] Patented.
Brutum fulmen. [L.] A harmless thunder-bolt.

Cadit quæstio. [L.] The question falls; there is no further discussion.
Cadre. [Fr.] Framework; the permanent organization in outline of a regiment or corps.
Cætera desunt. [L.] The rest is wanting.
Cæteris paribus. [L.] Other things being equal.
Campo santo. [It.] A burying-ground; lit., a holy field.
Canaille. [Fr.] Rabble.
Caput mortuum. [L.] Worthless residue.
Carpe diem. [L.] Enjoy the present day; improve the time.
Casus belli. [L.] That which causes or justifies war.
Catalogue raisonné. [Fr.] A catalogue arranged according to subjects.
Cause célèbre. [Fr.] A celebrated or notorious case (in law).
Caveat emptor. [L.] Let the buyer beware (or look after his own interest).
Cave canem. [L.] Beware of the dog.
Cedant arma togæ. [L.] Let arms yield to the gown; that is, military authority to the civil power.
Cela va sans dire. [Fr.] That goes without saying; that is a matter of course.
C'est à dire. [Fr.] That is to say.
C'est égal. [Fr.] It's all one.
C'est magnifique, mais ce n'est pas la guerre. [Fr.] It is magnificent, but it is not war.
C'est une autre chose. [Fr.] That's quite another thing.
Ceteris paribus. [L.] See *Cæteris.*
Chacun à son goût. [Fr.] Every one to his taste.
Chapeaux bas; [Fr.] Hats off!
Chef-d'œuvre. [Fr.] Masterpiece.
Chemin de fer. [Fr.] Iron road; a railway.
Cherchez la femme. [Fr.] Find out the woman (who is at the bottom of the affair).
Chère amie. [Fr.] A dear (female) friend.
Chevalier d'industrie. [Fr.] One who lives by his wits; a swindler.
Ci-gît. [Fr.] Here lies.
Cogito, ergo sum. [L.] I think, therefore I exist.
Coiffeur. [Fr.] A hair-dresser.
Comme il faut. [Fr.] As it should be.
Compagnon de voyage. [Fr.] A travelling companion.
Compte rendu. [Fr.] An account rendered; a report.
Con amore. [It.] With love; very earnestly.
Conseil d'état. [Fr.] A council of state; a privy-council.
Consensus facit legem. [L.] Consent makes the law.
Consilio et prudentia. [L.] By wisdom and prudence.
Constantia et virtute. [L.] By constancy and virtue (or bravery).
Contra bonos mores. [L.] Against good manners or morals; immoral.
Contretemps. [Fr.] An unexpected or untoward event; a hitch.
Coram nobis. [L.] Before us; in our presence.
Coram populo. [L.] In the presence of the people.
Corpus Christi. [L.] Body of Christ.
Corpus vile. [L.] A worthless body or subject.
Corrigenda. [L.] Things to be corrected; a list of errors.
Coup. [Fr.] A stroke.—*Coup d'essai*, a first attempt.—*Coup d'état*, a sudden decisive blow in politics; a stroke of policy.—*Coup de grâce*, a finishing stroke.—*Coup de main*, a sudden attack or enterprise.—*Coup de maître*, a master stroke.—*Coup d'œil*, a rapid glance of the eye.—*Coup de pied*, a kick.—*Coup de soleil*, sunstroke.—*Coup de théâtre*, a theatrical effect.
Coûte que coûte. [Fr.] Cost what it may.
Credat Judæus Apella. [L.] Let Apella, the superstitious Jew, believe it, I won't.
Credo quia absurdum. [L.] I believe because it is absurd, or contrary to reason.
Crux criticorum. [L.] The puzzle of critics.
Cucullus non facit monachum. [L.] The cowl does not make the monk.
Cui bono? [L.] For whose advantage? to what end?
Cul-de-sac. [Fr.] A blind alley; often used figuratively.
Cum grano salis. [L.] With a grain of salt; with some allowance.
Cum privilegio. [L.] With privilege.

Curiosa felicitas. [L.] Nice felicity of expression.
Currente calamo. [L.] With a running or rapid pen.

D'accord. [Fr.] In agreement.
Dame d'honneur. [Fr.] Maid of honour.
Débâcle. [Fr.] The break-up of ice in a river; hence, a general, confused rout.
De bon augure. [Fr.] Of good augury or omen.
De bonne grâce. [Fr.] With good grace; willingly.
De die in diem. [L.] From day to day.
De facto. [L.] In point of fact; actual or actually.
Dégagé. [Fr.] Free; easy; unconstrained.
De gustibus non est disputandum. [L.] There is no disputing about tastes.
Dei gratia. [L.] By the grace of God.
De jure. [L.] From the law; by right.
Delenda est Carthago. [L.] Carthage must be blotted out, or destroyed.
Demi-monde. [Fr.] Women of doubtful reputation and position, intermediate between courtesans and honourable women.
De mortuis nil nisi bonum. [L.] (Say) nothing but good of the dead.
Dénouement. [Fr.] The issue; the end of a plot.
De novo. [L.] Anew.
Deo adjuvante. [L.] God assisting.
Deo favente. [L.] God favouring.
Deo gratias. [L.] Thanks to God.
Deo juvante. [L.] With God's help.
Deo volente. [L.] God willing; by God's will.
De profundis. [L.] Out of the depths.
De rigueur. [Fr.] Indispensable; obligatory.
Dernier ressort. [Fr.] A last resource.
Désagrément. [Fr.] Something disagreeable.
Desunt cætera. [L.] The remainder is wanting.
De trop. [Fr.] Too much; more than is wanted; out of place.
Deus ex machina. [L.] Literally, a god from a machine; used in reference to forced or unlikely events introduced in a drama, novel, &c., to resolve a difficult or awkward situation; derived from the use of deities in the ancient dramas.
Dichtung und Wahrheit. [G.] Poetry and truth; fiction and fact.
Dies iræ, dies illa. [L.] 'Day of wrath, O dreadful day!' (Stanley's version), the first line of an old Latin hymn on the day of judgment.
Dies non. [L.] A day on which judges do not sit.
Dieu et mon droit. [Fr.] God and my right (British royal motto).
Dis aliter visum. [L.] The gods thought otherwise.
Disjecta membra. [L.] Scattered remains.
Distingué. [Fr.] Distinguished; of genteel or elegant appearance.
Divide et impera. [L.] Divide and rule.
Dolce far niente. [It.] Sweet doing-nothing; sweet idleness.
Dominus vobiscum. [L.] The Lord be with you.
Double entendre (or *entente*). [Fr.] A double meaning; a play on words.
Dramatis personæ. [L.] Characters of the drama or play.
Dulce et decorum est pro patria mori. [L.] It is sweet and glorious to die for one's country.
Dum spiro, spero. [L.] While I breathe I hope.
Dum vivimus, vivamus. [L.] While we live, let us live.

Eau-de-vie. [Fr. ' water of life '.] Brandy.
Ecce homo. [L.] Behold the man!
École. [Fr.] School.
Édition de luxe. [Fr.] A splendid and expensive edition of a book.
Editio princeps. [L.] The first printed edition of a book.
Ego et rex meus. [L.] I and my king.
Élite. [Fr.] The best part; the pick.
Emeritus. [L.] Retired or superannuated after long service.
Émeute. [Fr.] A riot.
En arrière. [Fr.] In the rear; behind; back.
En avant. [Fr.] Forward.
En déshabillé. [Fr.] In undress.
En effet. [Fr.] In effect; substantially; really.
En famille. [Fr.] With one's family; in a domestic state.
Enfant gâté. [Fr.] A spoiled child.
Enfants perdus. [Fr.] Lost children; a forlorn hope.
Enfant terrible. [Fr.] A terrible child, that is, one who makes disconcerting remarks.
Enfant trouvé. [Fr.] A foundling.
Enfin. [Fr.] In short; at last; finally.
En masse. [Fr.] In a mass or body.
En plein jour. [Fr.] In broad day.
En rapport. [Fr.] In harmony; in agreement.
En revanche. [Fr.] In requital; by way of retaliation.
En route. [Fr.] On the way.
En suite. [Fr.] In company; in a set.
Entente cordiale. [Fr.] Cordial understanding, especially between two states.
Entourage. [Fr.] Surroundings; friends, confidants, &c., closely associated with a person.
Entre nous. [Fr.] Between ourselves.
En vérité. [Fr.] In truth; verily.
Eo animo. [L.] With that design.
E pluribus unum. [L.] One out of many; one composed of many (motto of the United States).
Errata. [L.] Errors; list of errors.
Esprit de corps. [Fr.] The animating spirit of a collective body, as a regiment.
Esse quam videri. [L.] To be rather than to seem.
Est modus in rebus. [L.] There is a limit in all things.
Et cætera (or *Et cetera*). [L.] And the rest.
Et hoc (or *Et id*) *genus omne.* [L.] And everything of the sort.
Et sequentes, Et sequentia. [L.] And those that follow.
Et sic de cæteris. [L.] And so of the rest.
Et tu, Brute! [L.] And thou also, Brutus!
Eureka! [Gr.] I have found it!
Ewigkeit. [G.] Eternity.
Ex animo. [L.] Heartily; sincerely.
Ex cathedra. [L.] From the chair; with high authority.
Excelsior. [L.] Higher, that is, taller, loftier.
Exceptio probat regulam. [L.] The exception proves (or tests) the rule.
Exceptis excipiendis. [L.] The due exceptions being made.
Exempli gratia. [L.] By way of example.
Exeunt omnes. [L.] All go out or retire.
Ex hypothesi. [L.] From hypothesis or supposition.
Exit. [L.] He goes out.
Ex necessitate rei. [L.] From the necessity of the case.
Ex nihilo nihil fit. [L.] Out of nothing, nothing comes.
Ex officio. [L.] In virtue of (his) office.
Ex parte. [L.] From one party or side.
Ex pede Herculem. [L.] From the foot we recognize a Hercules; we judge of the whole from the specimen.
Experimentum crucis. [L.] A crucial, testing, or decisive experiment.
Experto crede. [L.] Trust one who has had experience.
Exposé. [Fr.] A statement; a recital.

Ex post facto. [L.] After the deed is done; retrospective.
Expressis verbis [L.] In express terms.
Extra muros. [L.] Beyond the walls.
Ex uno disce omnes. [L.] From one judge of the rest.

Facile princeps. [L.] Easily pre-eminent; indisputably the first.
Facilis est descensus Averni (or *Averno*). [L.] The descent to Avernus (or hell) is easy.
Faire bonne mine. [Fr.] To put a good face upon the matter.
Fait accompli. [Fr.] A thing already done.
Fama clamosa. [L.] A current scandal.
Fas est et ab hoste doceri. [L.] It is right to be taught even by an enemy.
Fata obstant. [L.] The Fates oppose it.
Faux pas. [Fr.] A false step; a slip in behaviour.
Favete linguis. [L.] Favour with your tongues; avoid words of ill omen; be silent.
Femme de chambre. [Fr.] A chamber-maid; lady's-maid.
Feræ naturæ. [L.] Of a wild nature; undomesticated (animals).
Festina lente. [L.] Hasten slowly.
Feu de joie. [Fr.] A discharge of firearms as a sign of rejoicing.
Feuilleton. [Fr.] A fly-sheet; a novel or story appearing in a newspaper.
Fiat justitia, ruat cœlum. [L.] Let justice be done though the heavens should fall.
Fiat lux. [L.] Let there be light.
Fide et amore. [L.] By faith and love.
Fide et fiducia. [L.] By fidelity and confidence.
Fidei defensor. [L.] Defender of the faith.
Fide non armis. [L.] By faith, not by arms.
Fides Punica. [L.] Punic or Carthaginian faith; treachery.
Fidus Achates. [L.] Faithful Achates; a true friend.
Fille de joie. [Fr.] A prostitute.
Fin de siècle. [Fr.] End of the (nineteenth) century.
Finis coronat opus. [L.] The end crowns the work.
Flagrante bello. [L.] During hostilities.
Flagrante delicto. [L.] In the commission of the crime; red-handed.
Fons et origo. [L.] The source and origin.
Force majeure. [Fr.] Greater force or strength; overwhelming force; compulsion.
Fortiter in re. [L.] With firmness in acting.
Fortuna favet fortibus. [L.] Fortune favours the bold.
Fuimus Troes. [L.] We were once Trojans.
Fuit Ilium. [L.] Troy has been; Troy is no more.
Furor loquendi. [L.] A rage for speaking.

Gallicè. [L.] In French.
Garçon. [Fr.] A boy; a waiter.
Garde du corps. [Fr.] A body-guard.
Garde mobile. [Fr.] A guard liable to general service.
Gardez bien. [Fr.] Take good care.
Gaucherie. [Fr.] An awkward, clumsy, or bungling action.
Gaudeamus igitur. [L.] So let us be joyful.
Genius loci. [L.] The genius or guardian spirit of a place.
Gens d'affaires. [Fr.] Men of business.
Gens d'armes. [Fr.] Men at arms.
Gens de guerre. [Fr.] Military men.
Gens de lettres. [Fr.] Literary men.
Gens de robe. [Fr.] Lawyers.
Gentilhomme. [Fr.] A gentleman.
Germanicè. [L.] In German.
Gloria in excelsis (Deo). [L.] Glory (to God) in the highest.
Gloria patri. [L.] Glory be to the Father.
Gnothi seauton. [Gr.] Know thyself.
Goût. [Fr.] Taste; relish.
Grâce à Dieu. [Fr.] Thanks to God.
Guerra al cuchillo. [Sp.] War to the knife.
Guerre à mort. [Fr.] War to the death.
Guerre à outrance. [Fr.] War to the uttermost.

Habitué. [Fr.] One in the habit of frequenting a place.
Haud longis intervallis. [L.] At brief intervals.
Haut goût. [Fr.] High flavour; elegant taste.
Hic et nunc. [L.] Here and now.
Hic et ubique. [L.] Here and everywhere.
Hic jacet. [L.] Here lies.
Hinc illæ lacrimæ. [L.] Hence these tears.
Hodie mihi, cras tibi. [L.] Mine to-day, yours to-morrow.
Hoi polloi. [Gr.] The many; the vulgar; the rabble.
Homme d'affaires. [Fr.] A business man.
Homme de lettres. [Fr.] A man of letters; a literary man.
Homme d'esprit. [Fr.] A man of wit or genius.
Homme d'état. [Fr.] A statesman.
Homo sum; humani nihil a me alienum puto. [L.] I am a man; I count nothing human indifferent to me.
Honi soit qui mal y pense. [O.Fr.] Evil to him who evil thinks (motto of the Order of the Garter).
Horæ subsecivæ. [L.] Leisure hours.
Horresco referens. [L.] I shudder as I relate.
Hors de combat. [Fr.] Out of condition to fight.
Hors de la loi. [Fr.] In the condition of an outlaw.
Hôtel de ville. [Fr.] A town-hall.
Hôtel-Dieu. [Fr.] A hospital.
Humanum est errare. [L.] To err is human.

Ibidem. [L.] At the same place (in a book).
Ich dien. [G.] I serve (motto of the Prince of Wales).
Ici on parle français. [Fr.] French is spoken here.
Id est. [L.] That is; often contracted *i.e.*
Id genus omne. [L.] All of that sort or description.
Ignoratio elenchi. [L.] An overlooking or misinterpretation of the question at issue.
Ignotum per ignotius. [L.] The unknown (explained) by the still more unknown.
Il n'y a pas de quoi. [Fr.] Don't mention it; it's not worth speaking of.
Il penseroso. [It.] The pensive man.
Impasse. [Fr.] A deadlock; an insurmountable difficulty.
Impedimenta. [L.] Luggage or baggage.
Imperium in imperio. [L.] A government or rule within another.
In æternum. [L.] For ever.
In articulo mortis. [L.] At the point of death; in the last struggle.
In capite. [L.] In chief.
In commendam. [L.] In trust; formerly used of livings held by bishops who did not discharge the duties.
In curia. [L.] In court.
Index expurgatorius. [L.] A list of books which Roman Catholics may read only in approved expurgated editions; also used as equivalent to the next term.
Index librorum prohibitorum. [L.] A list of books which Catholics are forbidden to read.
In dubio. [L.] In doubt.
In esse. [L.] In being; in actuality.
In extenso. [L.] At full length.
In extremis. [L.] At the point of death.
In forma pauperis. [L.] As a poor man.
Infra dignitatem. [L.] Below one's dignity.

In loco. [L.] In the place; in the natural or or proper place.
In loco parentis. [L.] In the place of a parent.
In medias res. [L.] Into the midst of things.
In memoriam. [L.] To the memory of; in memory.
In nomine. [L.] In the name of.
In nubibus. [L.] In the clouds.
In omnia paratus. [L.] Prepared for all things.
In partibus infidelium. [L.] In parts belonging to infidels, or countries not adhering to the Roman Catholic faith.
In petto. [It.] Within the breast; in reserve.
In posse. [L.] In possible existence; in possibility.
In præsenti. [L.] At the present moment.
In propria persona. [L.] In one's own person.
In puris naturalibus. [L.] Quite naked.
In re. [L.] In the matter of.
In rerum natura. [L.] In the nature of things.
In sæcula sæculorum. [L.] For ages on ages.
In situ. [L.] In its original situation.
In statu quo. [L.] In the former state.
Inter alia. [L.] Among other things.
Inter arma silent leges. [L.] Laws are silent in time of war (in the midst of arms).
Inter nos. [L.] Between ourselves.
In terrorem. [L.] As a means of terrifying; by way of warning.
Inter se. [L.] Among themselves.
In toto. [L.] In the whole; entirely.
Intra muros. [L.] Within the walls.
In transitu. [L.] On the passage; in course of transit.
In vacuo. [L.] In empty space; in a vacuum.
In vino veritas. [L.] There is truth in wine; truth is told under the influence of liquor.
Invita Minerva. [L.] Against the will of Minerva; without genius or natural abilities.
Ipse dixit. [L.] He himself said it; a dogmatic saying or assertion.
Ipsissima verba. [L.] The very words.
Ipso facto. [L.] By that very fact.
Ira furor brevis est. [L.] Anger is a short madness.
Italicè. [L.] In Italian.

Jacquerie. [Fr.] French peasantry; a revolt of peasants.
Jacta est alea. [L.] The die is cast.
Jardin des Plantes. [Fr.] Garden of Plants (the Botanical Garden at Paris).
Je ne sais quoi. [Fr.] I know not what; a something or other.
Jet d'eau. [Fr.] A jet of water; a fountain.
Jeu de main. [Fr.] Horse-play; a practical joke.
Jeu de mots. [Fr.] A play on words; a pun.
Jeu d'esprit. [Fr.] A display of wit; a witticism.
Jeunesse dorée. [Fr.] Gilded youth; rich and fashionable young men.
Jubilate Deo. [L.] Rejoice in God; be joyful in the Lord.
Jure divino. [L.] By divine law.
Jure humano. [L.] By human law.
Juris peritus. [L.] One learned in the law.
Juris utriusque doctor. [L.] Doctor of both the civil and canon law.
Jus canonicum. [L.] The canon law.
Jus civile. [L.] The civil law.
Jus divinum. [L.] The divine law.
Jus et norma loquendi. [L.] The law and rule of speech.
Jus gentium. [L.] The law of nations.
Jus gladii. [L.] The right of the sword.
Juste milieu. [Fr.] The golden mean.

Laborare est orare. [L.] To labour is to pray; work is worship.
Labor omnia vincit. [L.] Labour conquers everything.
Laisser-faire. [Fr.] Let alone; applied to a particular economic and political policy.
L'allegro. [It.] The merry man.
Lapsus calami. [L.] A slip of the pen.
Lapsus linguæ. [L.] A slip of the tongue.
Lapsus memoriæ. [L.] A slip of the memory.
Lares et penates. [L.] Household gods.
Lasciate ogni speranza voi ch'entrate. [It.] All hope abandon ye who enter here (inscription on the entrance to the hell of Dante's Inferno).
Latet anguis in herba. [L.] A snake lies hid in the grass.
Latine dictum. [L.] Spoken in Latin.
Laudator temporis acti. [L.] One who praises time past.
Laus Deo. [L.] Praise to God!
L'avenir. [Fr.] The future.
Le beau monde. [Fr.] The fashionable world.
Lebewohl. [G.] Farewell.
Legatus a latere. [L.] A papal ambassador.
Le grand monarque. [Fr.] The great monarch; Louis XIV of France.
Le pas. [Fr.] Precedence in place or rank.
Le roi est mort, vive le roi! [Fr.] The king is dead, long live the king (his successor)!
Le roy (or *la reyne*) *le veult.* [Norm. Fr.] The king (or the queen) wills it; the formula used by the sovereign in assenting to a bill.
Le roy (or *la reyne*) *s'avisera.* [Norm. Fr.] The king (or the queen) will consider; the formula formerly used by the sovereign in rejecting a bill.
Les absents ont toujours tort. [Fr.] The absent are always in the wrong.
Lèse-majesté. [Fr.] High treason.
L'état c'est moi. [Fr.] It is I who am the state.
Lettre de cachet. [Fr.] A sealed letter containing private orders; a royal warrant.
Lex loci. [L.] The law or custom of the place.
Lex non scripta. [L.] Unwritten law; common law.
Lex scripta. [L.] Statute law.
Lex talionis. [L.] The law of retaliation.
L'homme propose, et Dieu dispose. [Fr.] Man proposes, and God disposes.
L'inconnu. [Fr.] The unknown.
Lite pendente. [L.] During the trial.
Loco citato. [L.] In the place cited.
Locum tenens. [L.] One occupying the place of another; a substitute.
Locus classicus. [L.] A classical passage.
Locus standi. [L.] Place of standing; the right to appear and be heard before a court in a particular case.
Longo intervallo. [L.] By or at a long interval.
Lucus a non lucendo. [L.] Used as typical of an absurd derivation—*lucus*, a grove, having been derived by an old grammarian from *luceo*, to shine—' from not shining '.
Lusus naturæ. [L.] A sport or freak of nature.

Ma chère. [Fr.] My dear (fem.).
Ma foi. [Fr.] Upon my faith.
Magna est veritas, et prevalebit. [L.] Truth is mighty, and will prevail.
Magnum opus. [L.] A great work.
Maison de santé. [Fr.] A private asylum or hospital.
Maître d'hôtel. [Fr.] A house-steward.
Mala-fide. [L.] With bad faith; treacherously.
Mal-à-propos. [Fr.] Ill-timed; out of place.
Mal de dents. [Fr.] Toothache.
Mal de mer. [Fr.] Sea-sickness.
Mal de tête. [Fr.] Headache.
Mal entendu. [Fr.] A misunderstanding.
Malgré nous. [Fr.] In spite of us.
Malum in se. [L.] Evil or an evil in itself.

Manu propria. [L.] With one's own hand.
Mardi gras. [Fr.] Shrove-Tuesday.
Mare clausum. [L.] A closed sea; a sea belonging to a single nation.
Mariage de convenance. [Fr.] Marriage from motives of interest rather than of love.
Mariage de la main gauche. [Fr.] Left-handed marriage; morganatic marriage.
Materfamilias. [L.] Mother of a family.
Matériel. [Fr.] Baggage and munitions of an army; material equipment as opposed to men.
Mauvais goût. [Fr.] Bad taste.
Mauvais sujet. [Fr.] A bad subject; a worthless scamp.
Mea culpa. [L.] My fault; by my fault.
Me judice. [L.] I being judge; in my opinion.
Mêlée. [Fr.] A confused conflict.
Memento mori. [L.] Remember death.
Mens sana in corpore sano. [L.] A sound mind in a sound body.
Mens sibi conscia recti. [L.] A mind conscious of rectitude.
Meo periculo. [L.] At my own risk.
Meo voto. [L.] According to my wish.
Mésalliance. [Fr.] A bad match; marriage with one of a lower rank.
Meum et tuum. [L.] Mine and thine.
Mirabile dictu. [L.] Wonderful to relate.
Mirabile visu. [L.] Wonderful to see.
Mise en scène. [Fr.] The getting up for the stage, or the putting on the stage.
Modus operandi. [L.] Manner of working.
Modus vivendi. [L.] Manner of living; used of a temporary working agreement or compromise.
Mon ami. [Fr.] My friend (masc.).
Mon cher. [Fr.] My dear (masc.).
Mont-de-piété. [Fr.] A public or municipal pawnshop.
Monumentum œre perennius. [L.] A monument more lasting than brass.
More majorum. [L.] After the manner of our ancestors.
Mors janua vitœ. [L.] Death is the gate of life.
Mot d'ordre. [Fr.] Watchword.
Motu proprio. [L.] Of his own accord.
Multum in parvo. [L.] Much in little.
Mutatis mutandis. [L.] With the necessary changes.

Natura non facit saltum. [L.] Nature does not make a leap.
Necessitas non habet legem. [L.] Necessity has no law.
Née. [Fr.] Born; used in giving the maiden name of a married woman.
Négligé. [Fr.] Morning dress; an easy loose dress.
Nemine contradicente. [L.] No one speaking in opposition; without opposition.
Nemine dissentiente. [L.] No one dissenting; without a dissenting voice.
Nemo me impune lacessit. [L.] No one assails me with impunity (motto of Scotland).
Ne plus ultra. [L.] Nothing farther; the uttermost point; perfection.
N'est-ce pas? [Fr.] Isn't that so?
Ne sutor supra crepidam. [L.] Let not the shoemaker go beyond his shoe; let no one meddle with what lies beyond his range.
Nicht wahr? [G.] Isn't that so?
Nil admirari. [L.] To be astonished at nothing.
Nil desperandum. [L.] There is no reason for despair.
N'importe. [Fr.] It matters not.
Nisi Dominus, frustra. [L.] Except the Lord (keep the city the watchman waketh) in vain; Ps. cxxvii. 1 (motto of Edinburgh).
Noblesse oblige. [Fr.]Rank imposes obligations.
Nolens volens. [L.] Willing or unwilling.
Noli me tangere. [L.] Touch me not.
Nom de guerre. [Fr.] A war name; a pseudonym; a pen name.
Nom de plume. [Fr.] A pen name. [Incorrect for *Nom de guerre.*]
Non compos mentis. [L.] Not in sound mind.
Non est. [L.] He (or it) is not.
Non est inventus. [L.] He has not been found.
Non libet. [L.] It does not please (me).
Non liquet. [L.] The case is not clear.
Non multa, sed multum. [L.] Not many things, but much.
Non omnis moriar. [L.] I shall not wholly die.
Non sequitur. [L.] It does not follow.
Nosce teipsum. [L.] Know thyself.
Nota bene. [L.] Mark well.
Notre Dame. [Fr.] Our Lady.
Nous avons changé tout cela. [Fr.] We have changed all that.
Nous verrons. [Fr.] We shall see.
Novus homo. [L.] A new man; one who has raised himself from obscurity.
Nuance. [Fr.] Shade; tint.
Nudis verbis. [L.] In plain words.
Nulla dies sine linea. [L.] Not a day without a line; no day without something done.
Numquam. [L.] Never.

Obiit. [L.] He, or she, died.
Obiter dictum. [L.] A thing said by the way.
Obscurum per obscurius. [L.] An obscurity (explained) by something more obscure still.
Oderint dum metuant. [L.] Let them hate provided they fear.
Odi profanum vulgus. [L.] I loathe the profane rabble.
Odium theologicum. [L.] The hatred of theologians.
Œuvres. [Fr.] Works.
Omnia vincit amor. [L.] Love conquers all things.
Omnia vincit labor. [L.] Labour overcomes all things.
On dit. [Fr.] They say.
Onus probandi. [L.] The burden of proof.
Operœ pretium est. [L.] It is worth while.
Ora et labora. [L.] Pray and work.
Ora pro nobis. [L.] Pray for us.
Ore rotundo. [L.] With round full voice.
O! si sic omnia. [L.] O! if all things (were) so; O! if he had always so spoken or acted.
O tempora! O mores! [L.] Alas for the times! Alas for the manners (or morals)!
Otium cum dignitate. [L.] Ease with dignity.
Oui-dire. [Fr.] Hearsay.

Pace. [L.] By leave of; not to give offence to.—*Pace tua*, with your consent.
Palmam qui meruit ferat. [L.] Let him who has won the palm wear it.
Panem et circenses. [L.] Bread and the games of the circus.
Pardonnez-moi. [Fr.] Pardon me; I beg your pardon.
Parergon. [Gr.] An incidental or subsidiary work.
Par excellence. [Fr.] By way of eminence.
Par example. [Fr.] For example.
Pari passu. [L.] With equal pace; side by side.
Par nobile fratrum. [L.] A noble pair of brothers; two just alike.
Parole d'honneur. [Fr.] Word of honour.
Parti. [Fr.] A party; a person.
Particeps criminis. [L.] An accomplice in a crime.
Parvenu. [Fr.] A person of low origin who has risen suddenly to wealth or position; an upstart.
Pas. [Fr.] A step.

Passim. [L.] Everywhere; throughout; in all parts of the book, chapter, &c.
Pâté de foie gras. [Fr.] Goose-liver paste.
Paterfamilias. [L.] Father of a family; head of a household.
Pater patriæ. [L.] Father of his country.
Patres conscripti. [L.] Conscript fathers; Roman senators.
Pax vobiscum. [L.] Peacè be with you.
Peccavi. [L.] I have sinned or been to blame.
Peine forte et dure. [Fr.] Strong and severe punishment; a kind of judicial torture.
Penchant. [Fr.] A strong liking.
Pensée. [Fr.] A thought.
Per. [L.] For; through; by.—*Per contra.* Contrariwise.—*Per annum.* By the year; annually.—*Per capita.* By the head; per head.—*Per centum.* By the hundred.—*Per diem.* By the day; daily.—*Per saltum.* By a leap or jump.—*Per se.* By itself.
Perfervidum ingenium Scotorum. [L.] The intense earnestness of Scotsmen.
Persona grata. [L.] An acceptable person.
Petitio principii. [L.] A begging of the question.
Peu à peu. [Fr.] Little by little.
Pièce de résistance. [Fr.] A resistance piece; something substantial by way of entertainment, &c.
Pied-à-terre. [Fr.] A resting-place, a temporary lodging.
Pinxit. [L.] He (or she) painted (it).
Pis aller. [Fr.] The worst or last shift.
Plebs. [L.] The common people.
Poco à poco. [It.] Little by little.
Poeta nascitur, non fit. [L.] The poet is born, not made.
Point d'appui. [Fr.] Point of support.
Pons asinorum. [L.] The asses' bridge; a name for the fifth proposition of the first book in Euclid.
Poste restante. [Fr.] To remain in the post-office till called for.
Post hoc ergo propter hoc. [L.] After this, therefore on account of this; subsequent to, therefore due to this—an illogical way of reasoning.
Pour encourager les autres. [Fr.] To encourage the others.
Pour faire rire. [Fr.] To excite laughter.
Pour passer le temps. [Fr.] To pass the time.
Pour prendre congé. [Fr.] To take leave.
Preux chevalier. [Fr.] A brave knight.
Prima donna. [It.] First lady; the chief female singer in an opera, &c.
Prima facie. [L.] At first view or consideration.
Primo. [L.] In the first place.
Primum mobile. [L.] The source of motion; the mainspring.
Primus inter pares. [L.] First among his peers or equals.
Pro aris et focis. [L.] For our altars and our hearths; for civil and religious liberty.
Pro bono publico. [L.] For the good of the public.
Pro et contra. [L.] For and against.
Profanum vulgus. [L.] The profane herd.
Pro forma. [L.] For the sake of form.
Propaganda fide. [L.] For extending the faith.
Pro patria. [L.] For our country.
Pro rata. [L.] According to rate or proportion.
Pro rege, lege, et grege. [L.] For the king, the law, and the people.
Pro tanto. [L.] For so much; as far as it goes.
Protégé. [Fr.] One under the protection of another.
Pro tempore. [L.] For the time being.
Proxime accessit (or *accesserunt*). [L.] He (or they) came very near; applied to students in a prize-list below the very highest.
Punica fides. [L.] Punic or Carthaginian faith; treachery.

Quantum libet. [L.] As much as you please.
Quantum meruit. [L.] As much as he deserved.
Quantum sufficit. [L.] As much as suffices.
Quelque chose. [Fr.] Something; a trifle.
Quid pro quo. [L.] Something in return; an equivalent.
Qui s'excuse s'accuse. [Fr.] He who excuses himself accuses himself.
Qui va là? [Fr.] Who goes there?
Qui vive? [Fr.] Who lives? Who goes there? *To be on the qui vive* means to be alert or watchful.
Quoad hoc. [L.] To this extent.
Quoad sacra. [L.] As far as sacred things are concerned; for ecclesiastical purposes only.
Quod avertat Deus! [L.] Which may God avert!
Quod erat demonstrandum. [L.] Which was to be proved or demonstrated.
Quod erat faciendum. [L.] Which was to be done.
Quod vide. [L.] Which see.
Quorum pars magna fui. [L.] Of whom, or which, I was an important part.
Quos Deus vult perdere, prius dementat. [L.] Those whom God wishes to destroy, he first makes mad.
Quot homines, tot sententiæ. [L.] Many men, many minds.

Raconteur. [Fr.] A teller of stories.
Raison d'être. [Fr.] The reason for a thing's existence.
Rapprochement. [Fr.] The act of bringing or coming together.
Rara avis in terris, nigroque simillima cygno. [L.] A rare bird on earth, and very like a black swan (formerly believed to be non-existent).
Re. [L.] In the matter of.
Réchauffé. [Fr.] Lit., something warmed up; hence old literary material worked up into a new form.
Rédacteur. [Fr.] An editor.
Reductio ad absurdum. [L.] A reducing to the absurd; a method of proof in which a proposition is shown to be true by demonstrating the absurdity of its contradictions; indirect proof.
Rem acu tetigisti. [L.] You have touched the matter with a needle; you have hit the nail on the head.
Rencontre. [Fr.] An encounter; a hostile meeting.
Répondez s'il vous plaît. [Fr.] Please reply.
Requiescat in pace. [L.] May he (or she) rest in peace.
Res gestæ. [L.] Things done; exploits; history.
Res judicata. [L.] A case or suit already settled.
Res, non verba. [L.] Things, not words.
Respice finem. [L.] Look to the end.
Résumé. [Fr.] A summary or abstract.
Resurgam. [L.] I shall rise again.
Revenons à nos moutons. [Fr.] Let us return to our sheep; let us return to our subject.
Refacimento. [It.] Re-making or adaptation; the recasting of a literary work or musical composition.
Rôle. [Fr.] A character represented on the stage; also other similar meanings.
Roué. [Fr.] One devoted to licentious pleasure.
Rouge et noir. [Fr.] Red and black; a game of chance.
Rus in urbe. [L.] The country in town.

Sanctum sanctorum. [L.] Holy of holies.
Sang froid. [Fr.] Coolness; indifference.
Sans peur et sans reproche. [Fr.] Without fear and without reproach.
Sans souci. [Fr.] Without care.
Sartor resartus. [L.] The patcher repatched; the tailor patched or mended.

Satis superque. [L.] Enough, and more than enough.
Satis verborum. [L.] Enough of words; no more need be said.
Sauve qui peut. [Fr.] Let him save himself who can.
Savoir faire. [Fr.] The knowing how to act; tact.
Savoir vivre. [Fr.] Good-breeding; refined manners.
Schadenfreude. [G.] Pleasure in injury; mischievous joy.
Scripsit. [L.] Wrote (it).
Sculpsit. [L.] Engraved (it).
Semper idem. [L.] Always the same.
Seriatim. [L.] In a series; one by one.
Sic itur ad astra. [L.] Such is the way to the stars, or to immortality.
Sic passim. [L.] So here and there throughout; so everywhere.
Sic semper tyrannis. [L.] Ever so to tyrants.
Sic transit gloria mundi. [L.] Thus passes away the glory of this world.
Similia similibus curantur. [L.] Like things are cured by like.
Si monumentum quæris, circumspice. [L.] If you seek his monument, look around you.
Simplex munditiis. [L.] Elegant in simplicity.
Sine cura. [L.] Without charge or care.
Sine die. [L.] Without a day being appointed.
Sine dubio. [L.] Without doubt.
Sine mora. [L.] Without delay.
Sine qua non. [L.] Without which, not; something indispensable.
Siste, viator. [L.] Stop, traveller.
Sit tibi terra levis. [L.] Light lie the earth upon thee.
Si vis pacem, para bellum. [L.] If you wish for peace, prepare for war.
Soi-disant. [Fr.] Self-styled.
Sotto voce. [It.] In an undertone.
Spero meliora. [L.] I hope for better things.
Splendide mendax. [L.] Nobly untruthful; untrue for a good object.
Sponte sua. [L.] Of one's (or its) own accord.
Statu quo ante bellum. [L.] In the state in which things were before the war.
Status quo. [L.] The state in which.
Stet. [L.] Let it stand; do not delete.
Sturm und Drang. [G.] Storm and stress.
Suaviter in modo, fortiter in re. [L.] Gentle in manner, resolute in execution.
Sub judice. [L.] Under consideration.
Sub pœna. [L.] Under a penalty.
Sub silentio. [L.] In silence.
Sub voce. [L.] Under such or such a word.
Succès d'estime. [Fr.] A partial success, or one based on certain merits.
Suggestio falsi. [L.] The suggesting of what is false.
Sui generis. [L.] Of its own peculiar kind; in a class by itself.
Summum bonum. [L.] The chief good.
Summum jus, summa injuria. [L.] The rigour of the law is the height of oppression.
Sunt lacrimæ rerum. [L.] There are tears for things; misfortunes call for tears.
Suppressio veri. [L.] A suppression of the truth.
Sursum corda. [L.] Lift up your hearts.
Suum cuique. [L.] Let every one have his own.

Tableau vivant. [Fr.] A living picture; the representation of some scene by a group of persons.
Table d'hôte. [Fr.] A public dinner at an inn or hotel.
Tabula rasa. [L.] A smooth or blank tablet.
Tantæne animis cælestibus iræ? [L.] Can such anger dwell in heavenly minds?
Tant mieux. [Fr.] So much the better.
Tant pis. [Fr.] So much the worse.
Te Deum laudamus. [L.] We praise Thee, O God.
Te judice. [L.] You being the judge.
Tempora mutantur, nos et mutamur in illis. [L.] The times are changing and we with them.
Tempus fugit. [L.] Time flies.
Terminus ad quem. [L.] The term or limit to which.
Terminus a quo. [L.] The term or limit from which.
Terra firma. [L.] Solid earth; a secure foothold.
Terra incognita. [L.] An unknown country.
Tertium quid. [L.] A third something; a nondescript.
Tiers état. [Fr.] The third estate; the commons.
Timeo Danaos et dona ferentes. [L.] I fear the Greeks, even when they bring gifts.
To kalon. [Gr.] The beautiful; the chief good.
Tot homines, quot sententiæ. [L.] So many men, so many minds.
Toto cœlo. [L.] By the whole heavens; diametrically opposite.
Tour de force. [Fr.] A notable feat of strength or skill.
Tout-à-fait. [Fr.] Wholly; entirely.
Tout-à-l'heure. [Fr.] Instantly.
Tout au contraire. [Fr.] On the contrary.
Tout de même. [Fr.] All or quite the same.
Tout de suite. [Fr.] Immediately.
Tout ensemble. [Fr.] The whole taken together.
Tria juncta in uno. [L.] Three joined in one (motto of the Order of the Bath).
Tu quoque. [L.] You also; you're another.

Ubi bene, ibi patria. [L.] Where it is well with one, there is one's country.
Ubi supra. [L.] Where above mentioned.
Ultimus Romanorum. [L.] The last of the Romans.
Ultra vires. [L.] Beyond powers or rights conferred by law.
Una voce. [L.] With one voice; unanimously.
Uno animo. [L.] With one mind; unanimously.
Urbi et orbi. [L.] To the city (Rome) and the world.
Ut infra. [L.] As below.
Uti possidetis. [L.] As you hold in possession.
Ut supra. [L.] As above.

Væ victis. [L.] Woe to the vanquished.
Vale. [L.] Farewell.
Valet de chambre. [Fr.] A personal attendant; a body-servant.
Variæ lectiones. [L.] Various readings.
Variorum notæ. [L.] The notes of various commentators.
Varium et mutabile semper fœmina. [L.] Woman is ever a changeful and capricious thing.
Veni, vidi, vici. [L.] I came, I saw, I conquered. [Cæsar's message to the senate when he conquered Pharnaces, king of Pontus.]
Verbatim et literatim. [L.] Word for word and letter for letter.
Verbum sat sapienti. [L.] A word is enough for a wise man.
Vexata quæstio. [L.] A disputed question.
Via media. [L.] A middle course.
Via, veritas, vita. [L.] The way, the truth, the life.
Vice versa. [L.] The terms of the case being interchanged or reversed.
Videlicet. [L.] Namely (lit., one may see).
Video meliora proboque, deteriora sequor. [L.] I see and approve the better course, I follow the worse.
Vide ut supra. [L.] See what is stated above.
Vi et armis. [L.] By force and arms; by main force.

Vigilate et orate. [L.] Watch and pray.
Virginibus puerisque [L.] For maidens and boys.
Virtute et fide. [L.] By or with virtue and faith.
Virtute et labore. [L.] By virtue and labour.
Vis-à-vis. [Fr.] Opposite; face to face.
Vis inertiæ. [L.] The power of inertia; resistance to force applied.
Vis medicatrix naturæ. [L.] The healing power of nature.
Vis viva. [L.] Living force; energy.
Vita brevis, ars longa. [L.] Life is short, art is long.
Vivat rex (regina). [L.] Long live the king (queen)!
Viva voce. [L.] By the living voice; orally.
Vive la république. [Fr.] Long live the republic!
Vive l'empereur. [Fr.] Long live the emperor!
Vive le roi. [Fr.] Long live the king!
Voilà. [Fr.] Behold; there is; there are.
Voilà tout. [Fr.] That's all.
Voilà une autre chose. [Fr.] That's another thing; that is quite a different matter.
Vox et præterea nihil. [L.] A voice and nothing more; sound but no sense.
Vox populi, vox Dei. [L.] The voice of the people is the voice of God.
Vraisemblance. [Fr.]. Probability; apparent truth.
Vulgo. [L.] Commonly.

Wanderjahre. [G.] Journeymen-years.
Weltanschauung. [G.] World-view; theory or conception of life or of the world in all its aspects.
Weltschmerz. [G.] World-pain; pain or pessimism arising from the contemplation of the misery and suffering of the world.

Zeitgeist. [G.] Time-spirit; spirit of the age.
Zollverein. [G.] Customs union.

II. Abbreviations and Contractions commonly used in Writing and Printing

A. or *ans.* Answer.
a. or @ (L. *ad*). To or at.
A.A. Anti-aircraft; Automobile Association.
A.A.A. Amateur Athletic Association.
A.A.G. Assistant Adjutant-General.
A.B. (L. *Artium Baccalaureus*). Bachelor of Arts; able-bodied seaman.
Abp. Archbishop.
A.C. (L. *Ante Christum*). Before Christ.
a/c., Acct. Account.
A.C.A. Associate of the Institute of Chartered Accountants.
Acad. Academy.
A.C.P. Associate of the College of Preceptors.
A.D. (L. *Anno Domini*). In the year of our Lord.
A.D.C. Aide-de-camp.
ad inf. (L. *ad infinitum*). To infinity.
ad init. (L. *ad initium*). At the beginning.
Ad lib. or *Ad libit.* (L. *ad libitum*). At pleasure.
Advt. Advertisement.
Æ. or *æt.* (L. *ætatis*). Of age (so and so); aged.
A.F.C. Air Force Cross.
A.F.M. Air Force Medal.
A.F.S. Auxiliary Fire Service.
A.F.V. Armoured Fighting Vehicle.
A.G. Adjutant-General; Attorney-General.
A.H. (L. *Anno Hegiræ*). In the year of the Hegira.
A.I.C.E. Associate of the Institution of Civil Engineers.
A.K.C. Associate of King's College (London).
Ala. Alabama.
Alas. Alaska.
Am. or *Amer.* America or American.
A.M. (L. *Anno Mundi*). In the year of the world; (L. *Ante Meridiem*), before noon; (L. *Artium Magister*), Master of Arts.
Anon. Anonymous.
Ans. Answer.
A.O.F. Ancient Order of Foresters.
Ap. (L. *Apud*). According to; in the writings of.
A.P.M. Assistant Provost-Marshal.
App. Appendix.
Aq. (L. *aqua*). Water.
A.Q.M.G. Assistant Quarter-Master-General.
A.R.A. Associate of the Royal Academy.
A.R.A.M. Associate of the Royal Academy of Music.
A.R.C.A. Associate of the Royal College of Arts.
A.R.C.M. Associate of the Royal College of Music.
A.R.C.O. Associate of the Royal College of Organists.
A.R.C.S. Associate of the Royal College of Science.
A.R.H.A. Associate of the Royal Hibernian Academy.
A.R.I.B.A. Associate of the Royal Institute of British Architects.
Ariz. Arizona
Ark. Arkansas.
A.R.P. Air Raid Precautions.
A.R.R.C. Associate of the Royal Red Cross.
A.R.S.A. Associate of the Royal Scottish Academy.
A.R.S.M. Associate of the Royal School of Mines.
A.R.S.W. Associate of the Royal Society of Water-Colours.
A.S., A.-Sax. Anglo-Saxon.
A.S.E. Amalgamated Society of Engineers.
A.T.C. Air Training Corps.
A.T.S. Auxiliary Territorial Service.
At. Wt. Atomic Weight.
A.U.C. (L. *Anno Urbis Conditæ* or *Ab Urbe Conditâ*). In the year from the building of the city (= Rome).
A.V. Authorized Version (of the Bible).

b. Born.
B.A. Bachelor of Arts. British Association.
Bart. or *Bt.* Baronet.
Batt. Battalion.
B.B.C. British Broadcasting Corporation.
B.C. Before Christ; British Columbia.
B.C.L. Bachelor of Civil Law.
B.D. Bachelor of Divinity.
B.E.M. British Empire Medal.
b.l. Bill of lading.
B.L. Bachelor of Law.
B.Mus. Bachelor of Music.
Bp. Bishop.
B.R. British Railways.
Brit. Britain, British.
B.S. Bachelor in Surgery.
b.s. Bill of Sale.
B.Sc. Bachelor of Science.
B.Th. Bachelor of Theology.
B.V. Blessed Virgin.—*B.V.M.* Blessed Virgin Mary.

C. Centigrade; Conservative.
C. or *Cap.* (L. *caput*). Chapter.
c. or *ca.* (L. *circa*). About.
C.A. Chartered Accountant.
Cal. or *Calif.* California.
Cantab. (L. *Cantabrigiensis*). Of Cambridge.
Cantuar. (L. *Cantuariensis*). Of Canterbury.

Cap. (L. *caput*). Chapter.
C.B. Companion of the Bath.
C.B.E. Commander of the Order of the British Empire.
C.C. Cricket (or Cycling) Club; County Court (or Councillor).
C.C.C. Corpus Christi College.
C.D. Civil Defence.
C.E. Civil Engineer.
Cent. (L. *centum*). A hundred.
Cf. (L. *confer*). Compare.
C.F. Chaplain to the Forces.
C.G. Coast-guard; Centre of Gravity.
C.G.M. Conspicuous Gallantry Medal.
cg. Centigramme.
C.G.S. (used adjectively). Centimetre, Gramme, Second (as units of length, mass, and time).
Ch. Chapter; Church.
C.H. Companion of Honour.
Ch.B. Bachelor of Surgery.
C.I. Order of the Crown of India.
Cicestr. (*Cicestrensis*). Of Chichester.
C.I.D. Criminal Investigation Department.
C.I.E. Companion of the Order of the Indian Empire.
C.J. Chief Justice.
C.M. (L. *Chirurgiæ Magister*). Master in Surgery; Common Metre.
cm. Centimetre.
C.M.G. Companion of the Order of St. Michael and St. George.
C.M.S. Church Missionary Society.
Co. Company; County.
c/o. Care of.
C.O.D. Cash on delivery.
Colo. Colorado.
Conn. Connecticut.
Cp. Compare.
C.P. Clerk of the Peace.
C.P.C. Clerk of the Privy Council.
C.P.R. Canadian Pacific Railway.
C.P.S. (L. *Custos Privati Sigilli*). Keeper of the Privy Seal.
Cr. Credit or Creditor.
Cr. 8vo. Crown octavo.
C.S. Civil Service; Clerk to the Signet; Court of Session.
C.S.I. Companion of the Star of India.
C.S.M. Company sergeant-major.
C.T.C. Cyclists' Touring Club.
Curt. Current; this month.
C.V.O. Commander of the Royal Victorian Order.
Cwt. (L. *centum*, a hundred, and Eng. *weight*). A hundred-weight or hundred-weights.

d. (L. *denarius, denarii*). A penny or pence; died.
D.A.A.G. Deputy-Assistant Adjutant-General.
D.A.G. Deputy Adjutant-General.
Dak. Dakota.
D.A.Q.M.G. Deputy-Assistant Quarter-Master-General.
D.B.E. Dame Commander of the Order of the British Empire.
D.C. District of Columbia; (It. *Da Capo*), from the beginning again; Direct current.
D.C.L. Doctor of Civil Law.
D.C.M. Distinguished Conduct Medal.
D.C.V.O. Dame Commander of the Royal Victorian Order.
D.D. Doctor of Divinity.
D.D.S. Doctor of Dental Surgery.
Del. Delaware; (L. *delineavit*). he (or she) drew it.
D.F.C. Distinguished Flying Cross.
D.F.M. Distinguished Flying Medal.
D.G. (L. *Dei Gratia*). By the Grace of God; Dragoon Guards.
Dip. Diploma.
D.L. Deputy Lieutenant.
D.Lit. (or *Litt.*). Doctor of Literature.
D.Mus. Doctor of Music.
Do. (It. *ditto*). The same.
D.O.R.A. Defence of the Realm Act.
D.P.H. Diploma in Public Health.
Dr. Debtor; Doctor; Dram(s).
D.S. (It. *Dal Segno*). From the sign (musical term).
D.Sc. Doctor of Science.
D.S.C. Distinguished Service Cross.
D.S.M. Distinguished Service Medal.
D.S.O. Distinguished Service Order.
D.Th. (L. *Doctor Theologiæ*). Doctor of Theology.
Dunelm. (*Dunelmensis*). Of Durham.
D.V. (L. *Deo volente*). God willing.
Dwt. (L. *denarius*, penny, and Eng. *weight*). A pennyweight or pennyweights.

E. East or eastern; English.
Eblan. (L. *Eblanensis*). Of Dublin.
Ebor. (L. *Eboracensis*). Of York.
E.C. Eastern Central (postal district, London).
Ed. Edition or editor.
E.D.S. English Dialect Society.
E.E. Errors excepted; Early English.
E.E.T.S. Early English Text Society.
e.g. (L. *exempli gratia*). For example.
E.G.M. Empire Gallantry Medal.
E.M.F. Electromotive force.
E.N.E. East-north-east.
E.N.S.A. Entertainments National Service Association.
E.R. East Riding; (L. *Eduardus Rex*) King Edward; (L. *Elizabeth Regina*) Queen Elizabeth.
E.S.E. East-south-east.
Esq. Esquire.
et al. (L. *et alibi*, or *alii*). And elsewhere, or others.
Etc. (L. *et cæteri, cæteræ*, or *cætera*). And others; and so forth.
Et seq. or *et sqq.* (L. *et sequentes* or *sequentia*). And the following.
Exon. (L. *Exoniensis*). Of Exeter.
E. & O.E. Errors and omissions excepted.

F. Fahrenheit.
f. Feminine; (or *ff*) following (verse or verses, &c.).
F.A.A. Fleet Air Arm.
F.A.N.Y. First Aid Nursing Yeomanry.
F.B.A. Fellow of the British Academy.
F.C. Free Church (of Scotland).
F.C.A. Fellow of the Institute of Chartered Accountants.
F.C.P. Fellow of the College of Preceptors.
Fcp. Foolscap.
F.C.S. Fellow of the Chemical Society.
F.D. (L. *Fidei Defensor* or *Defensatrix*). Defender of the Faith.
F.E.I.S. Fellow of the Educational Institute of Scotland.
F.E.S. Fellow of the Entomological Society; Fellow of the Ethnological Society.
F.F.A. Fellow of the Faculty of Actuaries.
F.F.P.S. Fellow of the Faculty of Physicians and Surgeons (Glas.).
F.G.S. Fellow of the Geological Society.
F.I.A. Fellow of the Institute of Actuaries (or Auctioneers).
F.I.C. Fellow of the Institute of Chemistry.
F.I.Inst. Fellow of the Imperial Institute.
F.I.J. Fellow of the Institute of Journalists.
Fla. Florida.
F.L.S. Fellow of the Linnæan Society.
F.M. Field Marshal.
Fo. Folio.
F.O. Foreign Office.
f.o.b. Free on Board (goods delivered).
F.P. Fire-plug.
F.P.S. Fellow of the Philological Society.
F.R.A.M. Fellow of the Royal Academy of Music.
F.R.A.S. Fellow of the Royal Astronomical Society.
F.R.C.I. Fellow of the Royal Colonial Institute.
F.R.C.O. Fellow of the Royal College of Organists.
F.R.C.P. Fellow of the Royal College of Physicians.

F.R.C.P.E. Fellow of the Royal College of Physicians, Edinburgh.
F.R.C.S. Fellow of the Royal College of Surgeons.
F.R.C.S.E. Fellow of the Royal College of Surgeons, Edinburgh.
F.R.C.S.I. Fellow of the Royal College of Surgeons, Ireland.
F.R.C.V.S. Fellow of the Royal College of Veterinary Surgeons.
F.R.G.S. Fellow of the Royal Geographical Society.
F.R.H.S. Fellow of the Royal Horticultural Society.
F.R.Hist.S. Fellow of the Royal Historical Society.
F.R.I.B.A. Fellow of the Royal Institute of British Architects.
F.R.Met.S. Fellow of the Royal Meteorological Society.
F.R.S. Fellow of the Royal Society.
F.R.S.C. Fellow of the Royal Society, Canada.
F.R.S.E. Fellow of the Royal Society, Edinburgh.
F.R.S.L. Fellow of the Royal Society of Literature.
F.S.A. Fellow of the Society of Antiquaries.
F.S.A.Scot. Fellow of the Society of Antiquaries, Scotland.
F.S.I. Fellow of the Sanitary Institute.
F.S.S. Fellow of the Statistical Society.
Ft. Foot or feet.
F.T.C.D. Fellow of Trinity College, Dublin.
F.Z.S. Fellow of the Zoological Society.

G. German.
Ga. Georgia.
G.B.E. Knight or Dame Grand Cross of the Order of the British Empire.
G.C. George Cross.
G.C.B. Knight Grand Cross of the Bath.
G.C.H. Knight Grand Cross of Hanover.
G.C.I.E. Knight Grand Commander of the Indian Empire.
G.C.M. Greatest Common Measure.
G.C.M.G. Knight Grand Cross of St. Michael and St. George.
G.C.S.I. Knight Grand Commander of the Star of India.
G.C.V.O. Knight or Dame Grand Cross of the Royal Victorian Order.
G.I. General Issue. (American private soldier.)
gm. Grammes.
G.M. George Medal; Grand Master.
G.M.C. General Medical Council.
G.M.T. Greenwich Mean Time.
G.O.M. Grand Old Man (W. E. Gladstone).
G.P.O. General Post-office.
gr. Grain or Grains.
G.S.O. General Staff Officer.
G.R. Georgius Rex.
G.T.C. Girls' Training Corps.
G.W.R. Great Western Railway.

H.A.C. Honourable Artillery Company.
H.B.M. His (or Her) Britannic Majesty.
H.C.F. Highest Common Factor.
H.C.M. His (or Her) Catholic Majesty.
H.C.S. Home Civil Service.
H.E. His Excellency; High Explosive.
H.G. Home Guard.
H.H. His (or Her) Highness.
Hhd. Hogshead or Hogsheads.
H.I.H. His (or Her) Imperial Highness.
H.I.M. His (or Her) Imperial Majesty.
H.L.I. Highland Light Infantry.
H.M. His (or Her) Majesty.
H.M.I.S. His (or Her) Majesty's Inspector of Schools.
H.M.S. His (or Her) Majesty's Service; His (or Her) Majesty's Ship.
Hon. Honourable.
H.P. Horse-power.
H.Q. Head-quarters.
H.R.H. His (or Her) Royal Highness.

Ia. Iowa.
Ib. or *ibid.* (L. *ibidem*). In the same place.
I.C.S. Indian Civil Service.
Id. (L. *idem*). The same.
I.D.B. Illicit Diamond Buying.
i.e. (L. *id est*). That is.
I.H.S. Usually looked upon as the initials of *Iesus* (*Jesus*) *Hominum Salvator*, Jesus the Saviour of Men, but originally ΙΗΣ the first three letters of ΙΗΣΟΥΣ (*Iēsous*) the Greek form of *Jesus*.
Ill. Illinois.
I.L.P. Independent Labour Party.
Imp. (L. *imperator*). Emperor; Imperial.
I.M.S. Indian Medical Service.
In. Inch or inches.
Incog. (It. *incognito, incognita*). Unknown.
Ind. Indiana.
Ind. T. Indian Territory.
In loc. (L. *in loco*). In its place.
In loc. cit. (L. *in loco citato*). In the place cited.
I.N.R.I. (L. *Iesus Nazarenus Rex Iudæorum*). Jesus of Nazareth, King of the Jews.
Inst. Instant; the present month.
I.O.F. Independent Order of Foresters.
I.O.G.T. Independent Order of Good Templars.
I.O.M. Isle of Man.
I.O.O.F. Independent Order of Oddfellows.
I O U. I owe you—an acknowledgment for money.
I.R.A. Irish Republican Army.
I.S.C. Indian Staff Corps.
I.W. Isle of Wight.

J.C. Jesus Christ.
Jno. John.
J.P. Justice of the Peace.
J.T.C. Junior (Officers') Training Corps.
J.U.D. (L. *Juris Utriusque Doctor*). Doctor of both Laws (that is, civil and canon).

Kans. Kansas.
K.B. Knight of the Bath (prior to 1815); Knight Bachelor; King's Bench.
K.B.E. Knight Commander of the Order of the British Empire.
K.C. King's Counsel; King's College.
Kc. Kilocycle(s).
K.C.B. Knight Commander of the Bath.
K.C.I.E. Knight Commander of the Indian Empire.
K.C.M.G. Knight Commander of St. Michael and St. George.
K.C.S.I. Knight Commander of the Star of India.
K.C.V.O. Knight Commander of the Royal Victorian Order.
K.D.G. King's Dragoon Guards.
kg. Kilogram(s).
K.G. Knight of the Garter.
km. Kilometre(s).
K.M. Knight of Malta.
K.O. Knock-out.
K.P. Knight of St. Patrick.
Kt. Knight.
K.T. Knight of the Thistle.
Ky. Kentucky.

L., *l.*, or £ (L. *libra*). Pound or pounds (sterling).
L., *lb.*, or ℔. Pound or pounds (weight).
L. Latin; Liberal.
La. Louisiana.
L.A. Law Agent; Literate in Arts.
L.A.H. Licentiate Apothecaries' Hall (Ireland).
L.A.S. Licentiate of the Apothecaries' Society.
Lb. or ℔. Pound or pounds (weight).
l.b.w. Leg before wicket.
L.C. Lord Chamberlain; Lord Chancellor.
l.c. (L. *loco citato*). In the place quoted; also lower-case (in printing).
L.C.C. London County Council.
L.Ch. Licentiate in Surgery.
L.C.J. Lord Chief-justice.

L.C.M. Least (or lowest) common multiple.
L.C.P. Licentiate of the College of Preceptors.
L.Div. Licentiate in Divinity.
L.D.S. Licentiate of Dental Surgery.
L.D.V. Local Defence Volunteers.
L.F.P.S. Licentiate of the Faculty of Physicians and Surgeons.
L.H.D. (L. *Literarum humaniorum doctor*). Doctor of Literature.
Lib. (L. *liber*). Book.
Litt.D. Doctor of Literature.
Lit. Hum. (L. *literæ humaniores*). Classics.
L.L. or *L.Lat.* Low Latin.
L.L.A. Lady Literate in Arts.
LL.B. (L. *Legum Baccalaureus*). Bachelor of Laws. [LL. is written because the word is plural.]
LL.D. (L. *Legum Doctor*). Doctor of Laws. [See *LL.B.*]
LL.M. (L. *Legum Magister*). Master of Laws. [See *LL.B.*]
L.M. Long Metre; Licentiate in Midwifery.
L.M.S. London, Midland and Scottish Railway.
L.N.E.R. London and North-Eastern Railway.
loc. cit. (L. *loco citato*). In the place quoted.
Loq. (L. *loquitur*). Speaks.
L.R.A.M. Licentiate of the Royal Academy of Music.
L.R.C.M. Licentiate of the Royal College of Music.
L.R.C.P. Licentiate Royal College of Physicians.
L.R.C.P.E. Licentiate Royal College of Physicians, Edinburgh.
L.R.C.S. Licentiate Royal College of Surgeons.
L.R.C.S.E. Licentiate Royal College of Surgeons, Edinburgh.
L.R.C.V.S. Licentiate of the Royal College of Veterinary Surgeons.
L.S.D. (L. *Libræ, Solidi, Denarii*). Pounds, shillings, pence.
Lt. Lieutenant.
Ltd. Limited.
LXX. Septuagint.

M. (L. *mille*). Thousand; (L. *meridies*), noon; mile or miles; Monsieur
m. Minute or minutes; married; masculine.
M.A. Master of Arts. [See *A.M.*]
Mass. Massachusetts.
M.B. (L. *Medicinæ Baccalaureus*). Bachelor of Medicine.
M.B.E. Member of the Order of the British Empire.
M.C. Military Cross; Master of Ceremonies; Member of Congress; Master in Surgery. [See *C.M.*]
M.C.C. Marylebone Cricket Club.
M.D. (L. *Medicinæ Doctor*). Doctor of Medicine.
Md. Maryland.
M.E. Middle English.
Me. Maine.
M.E.C. Member of the Executive Council.
M.Eng. Master of Engineering.
Messrs. Messieurs, Gentlemen.
M.F.H. Master of Foxhounds.
M.G.C. Machine-gun Corps.
Mgr. Monsignor.
M.H.R. Member of the House of Representatives.
M.H.S. Member of the Historical Society.
M.Inst.C.E. Member of the Institution of Civil Engineers.
Mich. Michigan.
M.I.E.E. Member of the Institution of Electrical Engineers.
M.I.M.E. Member of the Institution of Mining Engineers.
M.I.Mech.E. Member of the Institution of Mechanical Engineers.
Minn. Minnesota.
Miss. Mississippi.
M.L.A. Member of the Legislative Assembly.
M.L.C. Member of the Legislative Council.
Mlle. Mademoiselle or Miss.
mm. Millimetres.
M.M. Military Medal.
MM. Messieurs.
Mme. Madame.
Mo. Missouri.
M.O. Medical Officer.
M.O.H. Medical Officer of Health.
Mont. Montana.
M.P. Member of Parliament.
M.P.S. Member of the Pharmaceutical Society; Member of the Philological Society.
Mr. Master (pron. *Mister*).
M.R. Master of the Rolls.
M.R.A.S. Member of the Royal Academy of Science; Member of the Royal Asiatic Society.
M.R.C.P. Member of the Royal College of Physicians.
M.R.C.P.E. Member of the Royal College of Physicians, Edinburgh.
M.R.C.S. Member of the Royal College of Surgeons.
M.R.C.S.E. Member of the Royal College of Surgeons, Edinburgh.
M.R.C.V.S. Member of the Royal College of Veterinary Surgeons.
M.R.I.A. Member of the Royal Irish Academy.
Mrs. Mistress.
M.R.S.L. Member of the Royal Society of Literature.
MS. Manuscript; *MSS.* Manuscripts.
M.Sc. Master of Science.
M.S.M. Meritorious Service Medal.
Mus. B. (L. *Musicæ Baccalaureus*). Bachelor of Music.
Mus.D. or *Mus.Doc.* (L. *Musicæ Doctor*). Doctor of Music.
Mus.M. Master of Music.
M.V.O. Member of the Royal Victorian Order.

N. Noon; North; Northern; Nationalist (Irish); Note.
N.A. North America or North American.
N.A.A.F.I. Navy, Army and Air Force Institutes.
N.A.T.O. North Atlantic Treaty Organization.
N.B. New Brunswick; North Britain (Scotland); (L. *Nota Bene*) Note well.
N.C. North Carolina.
N.C.B. National Coal Board.
N.C.O. Non-commissioned officer.
N.D. No Date.
N.Dak. North Dakota.
N.E. New England; North-east; North-eastern.
Nebr. Nebraska.
Nem. con. (L. *nemine contradicente*). No one contradicting; unanimously.
Nem. dis. (L. *nemine dissentiente*). No one dissenting.
Nev. Nevada.
N.F.S. National Fire Service.
N.H. New Hampshire.
N.J. New Jersey.
N.Mex. New Mexico.
N.N.E. North-north-east.
N.N.W. North-north-west.
No. (L. *numero*). Number.
Non obst. (L. *non obstante*). Notwithstanding.
Non seq. (L. *non sequitur*). It does not follow.
N.P. Notary-public.
N.R. North Riding.
N.R.A. National Rifle Association.
N.S. New Style; Nova Scotia.
N.S.P.C.C. National Society for the Prevention of Cruelty to Children.
N.S.W. New South Wales.
N.T. New Testament.
N.U.M. National Union of Mineworkers.
N.U.T. National Union of Teachers.
N.W. North-west; Northwestern.
N.Y. New York.
N.Z. New Zealand.

O. Ohio.
Ob. (L. *obiit*). Died.
O.B.E. Officer of the Order of the British Empire.
O.C.T.U. Officer Cadets' Training Unit.
O.E. Old English.
O.E.E.C. Organization for European Economic Cooperation.
O.F. Old French.
O.H.G. Old High German.
O.H.M.S. On His or Her Majesty's Service.
O.K. All correct.
Okla. Oklahoma.
O.M. Order of Merit.
op. (L. *opus*). Work.

O.P. Out of print; Order of Preachers (Dominicans); observation post.
Oreg. Oregon.
O.S. Old Style.
O.S.B. Order of St. Benedict.
O.T Old Testament.
O.T.C. Officers' Training Corps.
Oxon. (L. *Oxoniensis*). Of Oxford.
Oz. Ounce. [*Note.* The *z*, as in *viz.*, represents an old symbol for a terminal contraction.]

p. page; *pp.* pages.
Pa. Pennsylvania.
P. & O. Co. Peninsular and Oriental Steam Navigation Company.
P.C. Police Constable; Privy Council or Privy Councillor.
P.E.I. Prince Edward Island.
Per cent. or *per ct.* (L. *per centum*). By the hundred.
P.G.M. Past Grand Master.
Ph.D. (L. *Philosophiæ Doctor*). Doctor of Philosophy.
Pinx. or *Pxt.* (L. *Pinxit*). He (or she) painted it.
P.M. (L. *post meridiem*). Afternoon; Past Master; Postmaster; Prime Minister.
P.M.G. Postmaster-General.
P.O. Post-office; postal order.
P.O.W. Prisoner of war.
Pp. Pages.
P.P. Parish Priest.
P.P.C. (Fr. *pour prendre congé*). To take leave.
P.R.A. President of the Royal Academy.
Pro tem. (L. *pro tempore*). For the time being.
Prox. (L. *proximo*). Next or of the next month.
P.R.S. President of the Royal Society.
P.R.S.A. President of the Royal Scottish Academy.
P.R.S.E. President of the Royal Society of Edinburgh.
P.S. (L. *post scriptum*). Postscript.
P.S. Privy Seal.
P.T. Post Town; Pupil Teacher; physical training.
P.T.O. Please turn over.
P.W.D. Public Works Department.
Pxt. See *Pinx.*

Q. Query or question.
Q.B. Queen's Bench.
Q.C. Queen's College; Queen's Counsel.
Q.E.D. (L. *quod erat demonstrandum*). Which was to be demonstrated.
Q.E.F. (L. *quod erat faciendum*). Which was to be done.
Q.E.I. (L. *quod erat inveniendum*). Which was to be found out.
Q.M. Quarter-master.
Q.M.G. Quartermaster-general.
Q.S. Quarter-Sessions.
q.v. (L. *quod vide*). Which see.

R. (L. *Rex*). King. (*Regina*). Queen; Réaumur; Radical.
R.A. Royal Academician; Royal Artillery.
R.A.D.A.R. Radio detection and ranging.
R.A.F. Royal Air Force.
R.A.M. Royal Academy of Music.
R.A.M.C. Royal Army Medical Corps.
R.A.O.C. Royal Army Ordnance Corps.
R.A.S. Royal Asiatic Society; Royal Astronomical Society.
R.A.S.C. Royal Army Service Corps.
R.C. Roman Catholic.
R.C.A. Royal College of Art.
R.C.M. Royal College of Music.
R.C.P. Royal College of Physicians.
R.C.S. Royal College of Surgeons (or of Science).
R.C.V.S. Royal College of Veterinary Surgeons.
R.D. Rural Dean.
R.E. Royal Engineers.
R.E.M.E. Royal Electrical and Mechanical Engineers.
Rev. Reverend.
R.F.A. Royal Field Artillery.
R.G.A. Royal Garrison Artillery.
R.G.S. Royal Geographical Society.
R.H.A. Royal Horse Artillery; Royal Hibernian Academy.
R.H.G. Royal Horse Guards.
R.H.S. Royal Horticultural, Historical, or Humane Society.
R.I. Rhode Island; Royal Institute of Painters in Water-Colours.
R.I.B.A. Royal Institute of British Architects.
R.I.P. (L. *requiescat in pace*). May he (or she) rest in peace!
R.M. Royal Mail; Royal Marines; Resident Magistrate (Irel.).
R.M.A. Royal Military Academy; Royal Marine Artillery.
R.M.C. Royal Military College.
R.N. Royal Navy.
R.N.R. Royal Naval Reserve.
R.N.V.R. Royal Naval Volunteer Reserve.
Roffen. (*Roffensis*). Of Rochester.
R.R.C. Royal Red Cross.
R.S.A. Royal Scottish Academy.
R.S.M. Royal School of Mines; Regimental Sergeant-major.
R.S.P.C.A. Royal Society for the Prevention of Cruelty to Animals.
R.S.V.P. (Fr. *Répondez, s'il vous plait*). Answer, if you please.
R.S.W. Royal Scottish Water-Colour Society.
Rt. Hon. Right Honourable.
R.T.O. Rail. Transport Officer.
R.T.R. Royal Tank Regiment.
Rt. Rev. Right Reverend.
R.U. Rugby Union.
R.U.I. Royal University of Ireland.
R.V. Revised Version.
R.W. Right Worshipful or Right Worthy.
R.W.G.M. Right Worshipful Grand Master.
R.W.G.S. Right Worthy Grand Secretary.
R.W.G.T. Right Worthy Grand Treasurer; Right Worthy Grand Templar.
R.W.G.W Right Worshipful Grand Warden.
R.W.S.G.W. Right Worshipful Senior Grand Warden.
R.Y.S. Royal Yacht Squadron.

S. Saint; Signor; south; southern; Socialist.
s. Second or seconds; shillings.
S.A. South Africa, South Australia, or South America; Sturm Abteilung (Storm troops).
S.A.A.A. Scottish Amateur Athletic Association.
S.C. South Carolina.
Sc. (L. *scilicet*). To wit; namely; being understood; (L. *sculpsit*). He (or she) engraved it.
Sc.B. (L. *Scientiæ Baccalaureus*). Bachelor of Science.
Sc.D. (L. *Scientiæ Doctor*). Doctor of Science.
S.C.U. Scottish Cyclists' Union.
S.Dak. South Dakota.
S.D.F. Social Democratic Federation.
S.E. South east; south-eastern.
Seq. or *Sqq.* (L. *sequentes* or *sequentia*). The following or the next.
S.F.A. Scottish Football Association.
S.G. Solicitor-general.
S.J. Society of Jesus.
S.P.C.K. Society for the Promotion of Christian Knowledge.
S.P.G. Society for the Propagation of the Gospel.
S.P.Q.R. (L. *Senatus Populusque Romanus*) The Senate and People of Rome.
S.R. Southern Railway.
S.S. Schutz-Staffel (Nazi Special Guard).
S.S.C. Solicitor before the Supreme Courts (in Scotland).
S.S.E. South-south-east.
S.S.W. South-south-west.
S.T.D. (L. *Sacræ Theologiæ Doctor*). Doctor of Divinity.
Stg. Sterling.
S.T.P. (L. *Sacræ Theologiæ Professor*). Doctor of Divinity.
S.T.S. Scottish Text Society.
s.v. (L. *sub voce*). Under the word or title.
S.W. Senior Warden; south-west; south-western.

T.B. Torpedo-boat; tuberculosis.
T.C.D. Trinity College, Dublin.
T.D. Territorial Decoration.
Tenn. Tennessee.
Tex. Texas.
T.N.T. Trinitrotoluene (high explosive).
T.O. Turn over.
Toc. H. Talbot House.
T.R.H. Their Royal Highnesses.
T.T. Teetotaller.
T.T.L. To take leave.
T.U. Trade Union.
T.U.C. Trades Union Congress.
T.V. Television.

U.F. United Free (Church).
U.K. United Kingdom.
Ult. (L. *ultimo*). Last, or of the last month
U.N. United Nations.
U.N.O. United Nations Organization.
U.N.R.R.A. United Nations Relief and Rehabilitation Administration.
U.P. United Presbyterian.
U.S. United States.
U.S.A. United States of America; United States Army.
U.S.N. United States Navy.
U.S.S. United States Senate; United States ship or steamer.
U.S.S.R. Union of Socialist Soviet Republics.

V. (L. *versus*). Against; (L. *vide*). See; verse.
V.A. Vicar-Apostolic; Vice-Admiral; Royal Order of Victoria and Albert.
Va. Virginia.
V.A.D. Voluntary Aid Detachment.
V.C. Victoria Cross.
V.D. Various Dates; Volunteer Officers' Decoration.
V.G. Vicar-general.
Vid. (L. *vide*). See.
V.I.P. Very important person.
Viz. (L. *videlicit*). Namely; to wit. See note under *Oz.*
V.R. (L. *Victoria Regina*). Queen Victoria.
V.S. Veterinary Surgeon.
Vt. Vermont.

W. West; western.
W.A. West Africa; Western Australia.
W.A.A.F. Women's Auxiliary Air Force.
Wash. Washington (State).
W.C. Water-closet; Western Central (postal district, London).
w.f. Wrong fount (in printing).
W.I. West Indies.
Winton. (*Wintoniensis*). Of Winchester.
Wis. Wisconsin.
W.L.A. Women's Land Army.
W.M. Worshipful Master.
W.N.W. West-north-west.
W.R. West Riding.
W.R.A.C. Women's Royal Army Corps.
W.R.A.F. Women's Royal Air Force.
W.R.N.S. Women's Royal Naval Service.
W.S. Writer to the Signet.
W.S.W. West-south-west.
W.Va. West Virginia.
W.V.S. Women's Voluntary Services.
Wyo. Wyoming.

X. Christ. (*Note.* The *X* represents the Greek Χ (=CH) in ΧΡΙΣΤΟΣ (*Christos*).
Xmas. Christmas.
Xn. Christian.
Xnty. Christianity.
Xt. Christ.
Xtian. Christian.

Y. Year.
Ye. The. [The *Y* in this and similar instances is a substitute for or representative of the Anglo-Saxon þ (=th).]
Y.M.C.A. Young Men's Christian Association.
Y.W.C.A. Young Women's Christian Association.

Z.S. Zoological Society.

III. Forms of Address in Ceremonious Communications with Persons of Title or Official Position

Ambassador. The title 'Excellency' belongs specially to ambassadors, as well as to governors of colonies. Address letters 'His Excellency (with name or distinctive title following) His Britannic Majesty's Ambassador and Minister Plenipotentiary to the Court of ——'. Begin: 'Sir', 'My Lord', according as the ambassador possesses title or not. When personal reference is made say 'Your Excellency'. An envoy extraordinary or chargé d'affaires, though inferior to an ambassador strictly so called, also usually receives the title 'Excellency'; and the wives of ambassadors are generally addressed similarly during their husbands' tenure of office and while residing abroad.

Archbishop. Address: 'His Grace the Lord Archbishop of ——'. Begin: 'My Lord Archbishop'. Refer to as 'Your Grace'. The most formal method of addressing the Archbishop of Canterbury is as follows: 'The Most Reverend Father in God, Geoffrey (or whatever the Christian name is), by Divine Providence Lord Archbishop of Canterbury; Primate of All England and Metropolitan'. The Archbishop of York is addressed as 'The Most Reverend Father in God,——, by Divine Permission Lord Archbishop of York, Primate of England and Metropolitan'. An Irish archbishop is now addressed as 'The Most Reverend the Archbishop of ——'. In America the common form of address is 'The Most Reverend A— B—, D.D.' The wife of an Archbishop has no special title in right of her husband's dignity, being only plain Mrs.

Archdeacon. An archdeacon is styled 'Venerable': 'The Venerable the Archdeacon of——'. Begin: 'Venerable Sir', or 'Reverend Sir', or 'Mr. Archdeacon' (especially in speaking).

Baron. Address: 'The Right Hon. Lord ——'; less formally 'The Lord ——'. Begin: 'My Lord'. Refer to as 'Your Lordship'.

Baron's Daughter. Barons' daughters are all entitled to be called 'Honourable'. Unmarried they are addressed as 'The Hon. A— B—', with Christian and surname. They retain the title 'Hon.' after marriage, the wife of a commoner being 'The Hon. Mrs.' with husband's surname, the wife of a knight or baronet being 'The Hon. Lady', with husband's surname. Begin: 'Madam'. If a higher rank is conferred by the husband the title of course corresponds.

Baron's Son. All the sons are 'Honourable', with Christian name and surname. The eldest sons of barons and viscounts of Scotland (i.e. creations prior to 1707) are addressed as 'The Hon. the Master of' (peerage title), or 'The Hon. (John), Master of '. Begin: 'Sir'. The wife of a baron's son is 'The Hon. Mrs.', with husband's surname or both Christian name and surname. Begin: 'Madam'. If the daughter of an earl, marquis, or duke, she must be addressed accordingly.

Baroness. Address: 'The Right Hon. Lady ——', or 'Lady ——'. Begin: 'Madam'; refer to as 'Your Ladyship'.

Baronet. Address: 'Sir A— B—, Bt.', giving Christian name and surname. The Christian name *must* be given; it is quite wrong to speak, for instance, of 'Sir Vernon Harcourt' where 'Vernon' is merely one of the surnames. Begin: 'Sir'. A baronet's wife is addressed as 'Lady' with husband's surname (her Christian name would also be used if the daughter of a duke, marquis, or earl). Begin: 'Madam'; refer to as 'Your Ladyship'.

Bishop. Address: 'The Right Rev. the Lord Bishop of ——', or 'The Right Rev. A— B—, Lord Bishop of ——', or simply 'The Lord Bishop of ——'. Begin: 'My Lord Bishop'; refer to as 'Your Lordship'. In formal documents a bishop is styled 'The Right Reverend Father in God, John, by Divine Permission, Lord Bishop of ——'. A bishop suffragan is addressed as 'The Right Rev. the Bishop Suffragan of ——'. Begin: 'Right Rev. Sir'. Bishops' wives have no share in their husbands' titles.

In Ireland the bishops of the Protestant church are now most correctly addressed as 'The Right Reverend the Bishop of ——' (or in the case of Meath and Tuam 'The Most Reverend'). Begin: 'Right Rev. Sir'. In Scotland the usage is 'The Right Rev. Bishop (surname)'; or 'The Right Rev. A— B—, Bishop of '. Begin: 'Right Rev. Sir'. The Primus of the Scottish Episcopal Church is addressed as 'The Most Rev.'. Begin: 'Most Rev. Sir'. Neither Irish nor Scottish bishops can claim to be spoken of as 'Lord Bishop', 'Your Lordship', though this is sometimes done.

A retired bishop is still addressed as 'Right Reverend'; 'The Right Reverend Bishop ——', 'Right Rev. Sir'. In America the form of address to a bishop is generally 'The Right Rev. A— B—'.

[Roman Catholic bishops in Ireland are addressed as 'Right Reverend'.]

Canon. Address: 'The Rev. Canon ——'. Begin: 'Reverend Sir'.

Cardinal. The special title of a cardinal as such is 'His Eminence'. Begin: 'Your Eminence'.

Chargé d'Affaires. See *Ambassador*.

Clergy. The general form of address is 'The Reverend A— B—'. Begin: 'Rev. Sir' or simply 'Sir'. If a clergyman is the son of a duke or marquis he is to be addressed as 'The Rev. Lord A— B—'; if the son of an earl, viscount, or baron: 'The Rev. the Honourable A— B—'. If he is a baronet, 'The Rev. Sir A— B—, Bart.'

Congress, Members of (U.S.). Addressed generally 'The Honourable A— B—'.

Consul. There is no special form of address to a person as such. 'A— B—, Esq., H. B. M.'s Consul', 'Consul-general', or as the case may be. In the United States, however, a consul is commonly called 'Honourable'.

Countess. Address: 'The Right Honourable the Countess of ——'. Begin: 'Madam'; refer to as 'Your Ladyship'.

Dean. Address: 'The Very Reverend the Dean of ——'. Begin: 'Very Rev. Sir'; more familiarly 'Mr. Dean' (used in oral communications).

Doctor. The initials denoting the particular degree are placed after the usual form of address, whether D.D., LL.D., M.D., D.Litt., D.Sc., Mus.Doc., &c. 'The Rev. A— B—, D.D.'; 'A— B—, Esq., M.D.' Less formally: 'The Rev. Doctor B—'; 'Doctor A— B—'.

Dowager. When the holder of a title marries, the widow of a previous holder of the same title becomes 'dowager', provided she is the mother, grandmother or step-mother of the present holder. This word is often inserted in addressing her: 'The Right Hon. the Dowager Countess of ——'; 'The Dowager Lady ——'. Instead of 'Dowager', to which some ladies object, the Christian name may be used: 'The Right Hon. Mary Countess of ——'. Begin: 'Madam'; refer to as 'Your Ladyship'.

Duchess. Address: 'Her Grace the Duchess of ——'. Begin: 'Madam'; refer to as 'Your Grace'.

Duke. Address: 'His Grace the Duke of ——'. Begin: 'My Lord Duke'; refer to as 'Your Grace'. Royal dukes are different. See *Prince*.

Duke's Daughter. Address: 'Lady', with Christian name and surname. Begin: 'Madam'; refer to as 'Your Ladyship'. If married to a commoner or a peer by courtesy, the surname is derived from the husband's name or title; if to a peer, the wife takes a title corresponding to her husband's.

Duke's Son. A duke's eldest son takes by courtesy one of his father's secondary titles, and is thus usually a marquis or an earl, being addressed exactly as if really a peer with the respective rank. His wife receives the corresponding title, being thus a marchioness or countess, and their eldest son takes also a courtesy title belonging to the family, being thus either an earl, a viscount or a baron.

A duke's younger son is addressed similarly to his sisters: 'Lord A— B—'. Begin: 'My Lord'; refer to as 'Your Lordship'. Their wives are treated in a corresponding manner: 'Lady A— B—'; 'Madam', 'Your Ladyship'.

Earl. Address: 'The Right Honourable the Earl of ——', or 'The Earl of ——'. Begin: 'My Lord'; refer to as 'Your Lordship'. The wife of an earl is a countess. (See above.)

Earl's Children. The eldest son of an earl (like the eldest son of a duke) takes a courtesy title from his father and thus ranks either as a viscount or a baron, being treated as if really a peer and his wife as a peeress. The younger sons of an earl are all called 'Honourable'; 'The Hon. A— B—', the same as the sons of a baron. (See above.)

The daughters of an earl are addressed as the daughters of a duke. (See above.)

Envoy. See *Ambassador*.

Executive Council, Members of (in colonial governments). Generally addressed as 'The Honourable A— B—'.

Governor of Colony. Colonial governors have the title of 'Excellency' in virtue of their office. Address: 'His Excellency A— B—, Esq. (Sir A— B—, The Right Honourable the Earl of, &c.), Governor of ——'. Begin according to rank; refer to as 'Your Excellency'. A duke holding such a position would, however, be 'His Grace', 'Your Grace'. A governor's wife does not have any claim to be called 'Her Excellency'.

Governor of State (U.S.). Usually addressed as 'His Excellency'. 'His Excellency A— B—, Governor of ——', or 'His Excellency the Governor of ——'.

Judge. This in Britain has not a very distinctive meaning. In England and Ireland the judges of the supreme courts are called Lords Justices and Justices; in Scotland the judges are the Lords of Session. (See *Justice, Lord Justice, Lords of Session.*) In England the county court judges, however, are regularly called 'Judge'. 'His Honour Judge ——' (surname); on the bench referred to as 'Your Honour'.

In many British colonies the members of the higher courts are called judges and addressed as 'The Honourable A— B—'. In the United States the term judge is regularly applied to all such functionaries; and all are addressed in the same way.

Justice. Judges of the High Court of Justice in England, in the Chancery and other divisions, are called justices. Address: 'The Honourable Mr. Justice ——'; of if a knight, 'The Hon. Sir A— B—'. Begin in both cases 'Sir'. On the bench he is addressed as 'My Lord'; and referred to as 'Your Lordship'.

Justice of Peace. In England is formally addressed in documents as 'The Worshipful' and on the bench is referred to as 'Your Worship'.

King. To be addressed as 'The King's Most Excellent Majesty'. Begin: 'Sire', or 'May it please Your Majesty'; refer to as 'Your Majesty'.

King's Counsel. Ordinary address with the addition of K.C.

Knight Bachelor. Treated as a baronet, but 'Kt.' is not usually appended to the name in addressing a letter. As in the case of a baronet, carefully avoid using a surname instead of a Christian name.

Knight of the Bath, St. Michael and St. George, Star of India, Indian Empire. Address: 'Sir A— B—, G.C.B.', or K.C.B., K.C.M.G., K.C.S.I., K.C.I.E., as the case may be. Begin: 'Sir'.

Knight of the Garter, Thistle, St. Patrick. As above, with the initials K.G., K.T., K.P. respectively following the name.

Knight's Wife (of any class). As baronet's wife.

Legislative Council, Members of. These (who belong to colonial governments) are generally addressed as the 'Honourable A— B—'.

Lord Advocate of Scotland. Address: 'The Right Honourable the Lord Advocate'. Begin: 'My Lord'; refer to as 'Your Lordship'.

Lord Chancellor. Address: 'The Right Hon. the Lord High Chancellor'; or 'The Right Hon. Earl —— (or as the case may be), Lord High Chancellor'. Begin: 'My Lord'; refer to as 'Your Lordship'.

Lord Chief Justice (England). Address: 'The Right Honourable the Lord Chief Justice', or 'The Right Honourable Sir A— B—, Lord Chief Justice'. Begin: 'My Lord' or 'Sir', as the case may be.

Lord Justice (English Supreme Court of Appeal). Address: 'The Right Honourable the Lord Justice ——', or 'The Right Honourable Sir A— B—'. Begin: 'Sir'. When on the bench they are addressed 'My Lord', 'Your Lordship'.

Lord Mayor. Only London, York, and a few other cities have a Lord Mayor. Address: 'The Right Honourable the Lord Mayor of ——', or 'The Right Hon. A— B—, Lord Mayor of ——'. Begin: 'My Lord'; refer to as 'Your Lordship'.

The Lord Mayor's wife is addressed: 'The Right Honourable the Lady Mayoress of——'. Begin: 'My Lady'; refer to as 'Your Ladyship'.

Lord Provost. Address: 'The Right Hon. the Lord Provost of Edinburgh'; 'The Right Hon. the Lord Provost of Glasgow'; 'The Lord Provost of Aberdeen', 'Perth', or 'Dundee'. Begin: 'My Lord', or 'My Lord Provost'; refer to as 'Your Lordship'. The Lord Provost's wife has no share in the title.

Lords of Appeal (in Ordinary). These are judicial members of the House of Lords, who rank as barons and are so addressed. Their wives are baronesses; their children are addressed as if they were children of a baron.

Lords of Session. These are the judges of the supreme court of Scotland. Some of these lords decide to retain their surname when elevated to the bench ('LordYoung'), others substitute the name of an estate. Address: 'The Honourable Lord ——'. Begin: 'My Lord'; refer to as 'Your Lordship'.

Maid of Honour. Address: 'The Honourable Miss ——'. Begin: 'Madam'.

Marchioness. Address: 'The Most Honourable the Marchioness of ——'. Begin: 'Madam'; refer to as 'Your Ladyship'.

Marquis. Address: 'The Most Hon. the Marquis of——'. Begin: 'My Lord Marquis' refer to as 'Your Lordship'.

Marquis's Children. The eldest son takes a courtesy title like the eldest son of a duke, and is similarly addressed. Younger sons and daughters are like those of a duke.

Mayor. Address: 'The Mayor of ——', or in formal documents 'The Right Worshipful the Mayor of ——'. Address: 'Sir'; refer to as 'Your Worship'.

In the United States mayors are usually styled 'Honourable'; 'The Honourable A— B—, Mayor of'.

Member of Parliament. Not specially recognized except by adding 'M.P.' to ordinary address: 'A— B—, Esq., M.P.'; 'Sir A— B—, Bart., M.P.'

Moderator of General Assembly (Scotland). 'The Right Rev.'; ex-moderators are styled 'The Very Rev.'

Officers, Military, Naval and Air Force. Their professional rank is put before any title they may independently possess: 'General' or 'Admiral the Right Hon. the Earl of ——'; 'Colonel the Honourable A— B—'.

Premier. No special title or address as such.

President (U.S.). Address: 'His Excellency the President of the United States'; 'His Excellency A— B—, President of the United States'. The Vice-President and ex-presidents are 'Honourable'; 'The Honourable the Vice-President'; 'The Honourable A— B—'.

Prince. Address: 'His Royal Highness Prince A——' (Christian name). If a royal duke: 'His Royal Highness the Duke of ——'. Begin in any case: 'Sir'; refer to as 'Your Royal Highness'.

Princess. Address: 'Her Royal Highness the Princess A— (Christian name)'; or if a duchess: 'Her Royal Highness the Duchess of ——'. Begin: 'Madam'; refer to as 'Your Royal Highness'.

Privy-Councillor. All members of the privy-council are entitled to be addressed as 'Right Honourable'; 'The Right Honourable A— B—' (omit 'Esq.'). Otherwise according to rank.

Queen. Address: 'The Queen's Most Excellent Majesty'. Begin: 'Madam', or 'May it please Your Majesty'; refer to as 'Your Majesty'.

Recorder. Addressed as 'The Worshipful';

in London ' The Right Worshipful '. Begin: ' Sir '; refer to as ' Your Worship '.

Secretary of State. Address as ' His Majesty's Principal Secretary of State for the —— Department '.

Senators (Canada and United States). Addressed as ' The Honourable A— B—'.

Sheriff of London. As recorder of London.

Viscount. Address: ' The Right Hon. the Lord Viscount ——', or ' The Right Hon. Lord ——', or ' The Lord Viscount ——'. Begin: ' My Lord '; refer to as ' Your Lordship '.

Viscountess. Address: ' The Right Honourable the Viscountess ——', or ' The Viscountess ——'; ' The Right Hon. Lady——'. Begin: ' Madam '; refer to as ' Your Ladyship '.

Viscount's Children. Are addressed in the same way as those of a baron.

IV. Weights and Measures

BRITISH WEIGHTS AND MEASURES

Linear Measure

	1 inch	= 2·540 centimetres	
12 inches	= 1 foot	= 3·048 decimetres	
3 feet	= 1 yard	= 9·144 decimetres	
5½ yards	= 1 rod, pole or perch	= 5·0292 metres	
40 poles	= 1 furlong	= 2·0117 hektometres	
8 furlongs	= 1 mile	= 1·6093 kilometres	

Mile Measurements

Statute mile	= 1760 yards.	Russian verst	= 1168 yards
Scots mile	= 1984 yards.	Italian mile	= 1467 yards
Irish mile	= 2240 yards.	Spanish mile	= 5028 yards

Other Linear Measures

4 inches	= 1 hand	7·92 inches	= 1 link
9 inches	= 1 span	6 feet	= 1 fathom
22 yards	= 1 chain	10 chains	= 1 furlong

10 cables (6080 feet) = 1 nautical mile

1 knot = speed of 1 nautical m.p.h.

Square Measure

144 square inches	= 1 square foot
9 square feet	= 1 square yard
30¼ square yards	= 1 sq. rod, pole or perch
40 poles	= 1 rood
4 roods	= 1 acre
640 acres	= 1 square mile

Cubic or Solid Measure

1728 cubic inches	= 1 cubic foot
27 cubic feet	= 1 cubic yard
5 cubic feet	= 1 barrel bulk shipping
40 cubic feet	= 1 ton shipping
40 cu. ft. unhewn timber	= 1 load
50 cu. ft. hewn timber	= 1 load
108 cubic feet	= 1 stack of wood
128 cubic feet	= 1 cord of wood
165 cubic feet	= 1 standard
277¼ cu. inches of water	= 1 imperial gallon = 10 lbs

Liquid Measure

4 gills	= 1 pint	= ·568 litres
2 pints	= 1 quart	= 1·136 litres
4 quarts	= 1 gallon	= 4·54596 litres
9 gallons	= 1 firkin (ale or beer)	
36 gallons	= 1 barrel (ale or beer)	
42 gallons	= 1 tierce	
54 gallons	= 1 hogshead	(ale or beer)
72 gallons	= 1 puncheon	(ale or beer)
108 gallons	= 1 pipe or butt	(ale or beer)

Dry Measure

2 gallons	= 1 peck	= 9·0919 litres
4 pecks	= 1 bushel	= 3·637 dekalitres
8 bushels	= 1 quarter	= 2·909 hektolitres
5 quarters	= 1 load	= 1·454 kilolitres

Avoirdupois Weight

16 drams	= 1 ounce
16 ounces	= 1 pound
14 pounds	= 1 stone
28 pounds	= 1 quarter
4 quarters	= 1 hundredweight
20 hundredweights	= 1 ton

Troy Weight

24 grains	= 1 pennyweight
20 pennyweights	= 1 ounce
12 ounces	= 1 pound
25 pounds	= 1 quarter
100 pounds	= 1 hundredweight
20 hundredweights	= 1 ton of gold or silver
A carat	= 3·17 grains

Apothecaries' Weight

20 grains	= 1 scruple	= 1·296 grams
3 scruples	= 1 drachm	= 3·888 grams
8 drachms	= 1 ounce	= 31·1035 grams
12 ounces	= 1 pound	= 373·2420 grams

THE METRIC SYSTEM

Measures of Weight

10 milligrams	= 1 centigram	= 0·15432 grains
10 centigrams	= 1 decigram	= 1·54323 grains
10 decigrams	= 1 gramme	= 15·4323 grains
10 grammes	= 1 dekagram	= 5·6438 drams
10 dekagrams	= 1 hektogram	= 3·5274 ozs.
10 hektograms	= 1 kilogram	= 2·2046223 lbs.
10 kilograms	= 1 myriagram	= 22·046223 lbs.
10 myriagrams	= 1 quintal	= 1·968412 cwt.
10 quintals	= 1 tonne	= 0·984206 ton

Square Measure

100 sq. millimetres	= 1 sq. centimetre	= 0·1550 sq. in.
100 sq. centimetres	= 1 sq. decimetre	= 15·50 sq. ins.
100 sq. decimetres	= 1 sq. metre	= 10·7639 sq. ft.
100 sq. metres	= 1 sq. dekametre	= 119·60 sq. yds.
100 sq. dekametres	= 1 sq. hektometre.	= 2 acres 1 rood 35 poles
100 sq. hektometres	= 1 sq. kilometre	= 246 acres 3 roods 20 poles

The Are is the unit

10 milliare	= 1 centiare	= 10·7643 sq. ft.
10 centiares	= 1 deciare	= 11·96033 sq. yds.
10 deciares	= 1 are	= 119·6033 sq. yds.
10 ares	= 1 dekare	= ·247110 acres
10 dekares	= 1 hektare	= 2·471098 acres
100 hektares	= 1 sq. kilometre	= ·38611 sq. mile

Measures of Capacity

The unit is the Litre = 61·025387 cu. ins.

10 millilitres	= 1 centilitre	= ·0022 gallon
10 centilitres	= 1 decilitre	= ·0220 ,,
10 decilitres	= 1 litre	= ·2201 ,,
10 litres	= 1 dekalitre	= 2·2009 ,,
10 dekalitres	= 1 hektolitre	= 22·0091 ,,
10 hektolitres	= 1 kilolitre	= 220·0905 ,,

1 cubic cm. of water	= 1 gramme
1,000 cubic cms. of water = 1 litre	= 1 kilogram
1 cubic metre (1,000 litres)	= 1 metric ton

Time Measure

60 seconds	= 1 minute
60 min.	= 1 hour
24 hrs.	= 1 day
7 days	= 1 week
4 weeks	= 1 month
13 Lunar months	= 1 year
12 Calendar months	= 1 year
365 days	= 1 com. year
366 ,,	= 1 leap ,,
365¼ ,,	= 1 Julian year
365 d. 5 h. 48 m. 51 sec.	= 1 Solar ,,
100 years	= 1 century

Angular and Circular Measure (Sexagesimal)

60 seconds (″)	= 1 minute (′)
60 minutes	= 1 degree (°)
90 degrees	= 1 quadrant or right angle
360 ,,	= 1 circle

Miscellaneous

24 sheets	= 1 quire of paper
20 quires	= 1 ream ,,
4 inches	= 1 hand
4840 sq. yds.	= 1 English acre
6250 ,,	= 1 Scotch ,,
7840 ,,	= 1 Irish ,,
12 dozen	= 1 gross

V. Signs and Symbols used in Writing and Printing

MATHEMATICAL

+ Plus, the sign of addition or increase; as, $a+b+c$ (read *a* plus *b* plus *c*); also marks a positive as opposed to a negative quantity.

— Minus, the sign of subtraction, diminution, or decrease; as $-b-c$; also marks a negative as opposed to a positive quantity.

± ∓ Plus or minus, leaving it doubtful whether a quantity is to be added or subtracted; one or other as the case may be.

× The sign of multiplication; multiplied by or into; as $a\times b$, or 3×5; $a\times b$ is usually written *ab*, also *a.b*.

÷ The sign of division; divided by; as, $a\div b$, $24\div 6$. Division is also indicated by placing one quantity above another with a horizontal line between; as, $\frac{a}{b}$, $\frac{24}{6}$; also thus *a/b*.

∼ The difference between two quantities, leaving it doubtful which is the greater; as, $a\sim b$.

= The sign of equality; equal to, is equal or equivalent to; as, $a=b$, $10+2=12$.

> Is greater than; as $a>b$, *a* is greater than *b*.

< Is less than; as, $a<b$, *a* is less than *b*.

∝ Varies as, said of a quantity that increases or diminishes according as another quantity increases or diminishes, and in the same ratio; as, $a \propto b$.

: Is to, : : as; signs used to indicate ratio or proportion; thus, $a : b :: c : d$, that is, *a* is to *b* in the same ratio as *c* is to *d*; $3 : 5 :: 6 : 10$.

∵ Because or since, ∴ Therefore. {∵ $a=b$ and $c=d$ ∴ $a+c = b+d$; that is, because *a* is equal to *b*, and *c* is equal to *d*, therefore *a* plus *c* is equal to *b* plus *d*.

∞ Indefinitely great; infinity.

0 Indefinitely small; a quantity less than any assignable quantity; zero.

√ √‾ The radical or root sign. When used alone it indicates the square root; as, $\sqrt{b}$, $\sqrt{16}$.

Higher roots are indicated by small figures called indices, thus, $\sqrt[3]{a}$, $\sqrt[4]{a}$, $\sqrt[10]{a}$, $\sqrt[n]{a+b}$, that is, the cube root of *a*, the fourth root of *a*, the tenth root of *a*, the *n*th root of $a+b$. The same roots might also be indicated by small fractions, as, $a^{\frac{1}{3}}$, $a^{\frac{1}{4}}$, $a^{\frac{1}{10}}$, $(a+b)^{\frac{1}{n}}$, and so on.

So also the *powers* to which quantities are raised are indicated by similar small figures or indices, thus, a^3, a^5, a^n, a^{n-1}, &c.

( ), [ ], { } Indicate that the quantities inclosed are to be treated together as forming a single term or expression; as, $2(a+\frac{b}{2}+4)$.

∠ Angle, the angle; as, ∠ A B C, the angle A B C.

∟ Right angle, the right angle; as, ∟ A B C, the right angle A B C.

⊥ The perpendicular, perpendicular to; as, A B ⊥ C D, A B is perpendicular to C D.

∥ Parallel, parallel to; as, A B ∥ C D, A B is parallel to C D.

△ Triangle, the triangle; as, △ A B C, the triangle A B C.

□ Square, the square; as, □ A B C D, the square A B C D.

▭ Rectangle, the rectangle; as, ▭ A B C D, the rectangle A B C D.

○ Circle, the circle; circumference; 360°.

π The number 3·1415926... that is, the ratio of the circumference of a circle to its diameter, approximately equivalent to 3⅐ to 1, or 22 to 7.

° Degree or degrees, whether of a circle or of temperature; as, 32° the freezing point of water (Fahr.), 360° the whole circumference of a circle.

′ Minutes in circular measurement, as, 6° 20′, six degrees twenty minutes.

″ Seconds in circular measurement; as, 60″, sixty seconds.

′, ″, ‴, are used also to denote feet, inches, and lines.

ASTRONOMICAL

☉	The Sun.	♂	Mars.
●	New Moon.	♃	Jupiter.
☽	First Quarter.	♄	Saturn.
○	Full Moon.	♅ *or* ⛢	Uranus.
☾	Last Quarter.	♆	Neptune.
☿	Mercury.	☄	Comet.
♀	Venus.	*	Star.
⊕ *or* ♁	The Earth.		

The asteroids are designated by the numbers attached to them as indicating the order of their discovery, the particular number being inclosed within a small circle; thus (64) designates Angelina, the sixty-fourth asteroid.

Signs of the Zodiac

Aries, the Ram	♈
Taurus, the Bull	♉
Gemini, the Twins	♊
Cancer, the Crab	♋
Leo, the Lion	♌
Virgo, the Virgin	♍
Libra, the Scales	♎
Scorpio, the Scorpion	♏
Sagittarius, the Archer	♐
Capricornus, the Goat	♑
Aquarius, the Waterman	♒
Pisces, the Fishes	♓

MEDICAL

℈ Scruple; ℈i, one scruple; ℈ij, two scruples ℈ss, half a scruple; ℈iss, a scruple and a half.

ʒ Dram or drachm; ʒi, one dram; ʒij, two drams; ʒss, half a dram; ʒiss, a dram and a half.

℥ Ounce; ℥i, one ounce; ℥ij, two ounces; ℥ss, half an ounce; ℥iss, an ounce and a half.

♏ A minim; a drop.

āā (Gr. *ana*), of each a like quantity.

℞ (L. *recipe*), take.

ROMAN NOTATION

I=1, II=2, III=3, IV or IIII=4, V=5, VI=6, VII=7, VIII=8, IX=9, X=10, XI=11, XII=12, XIII=13, XIV=14, XV=15, XVI=16, XVII=17, XVIII=18, XIX=19, XX=20, XXI=21, XXX=30, XL=40, L=50, LX=60, LXX=70, LXXX=80, XC=90, C=100, CI=101, CXX=120, CC=200, CCC=300, CCCC=400, D=500, DC=600, DCC=700, DCCC=800, DCCCC or CM=900, M=1000; also IↃ=D=500, CIↃ=M=1000, IↃↃ=5000; MDCCCXCVIII=1898; MCMII=1902.

It will be noticed that if any letter be followed by one of equal or less value the total value is equal to the sum of the two taken together, but if a letter be preceded by one of less value the difference of their separate values is to be understood.

CHEMICAL

By means of chemical symbols, or formulas, the composition of the most complicated substances can be very easily expressed, and that, too, in a very small compass; and by using these symbols along with the algebraic signs + and = (more rarely —) the most complicated chemical reactions can be expressed with great conciseness and complete accuracy, both qualitatively and quantitatively. Abbreviated expressions or equations of this kind often give, in a single line, more information as to details than could be given in many lines of letterpress.

Elements	Symbols
Actinium	Ac
Aluminium	Al
Americium	Am
Antimony (Stibium)	Sb
Argon	A
Arsenic	As
Astatine	At
Barium	Ba
Beryllium	Be
Bismuth	Bi
Boron	B
Bromine	Br
Cadmium	Cd
Cæsium	Cs
Calcium	Ca
Carbon	C
Cerium	Ce
Chlorine	Cl
Chromium	Cr
Cobalt	Co
Copper (Cuprum)	Cu
Dysprosium	Dy
Erbium	Er
Europium	Eu
Fluorine	F
Francium	Fr
Gadolinium	Gd
Gallium	Ga
Germanium	Ge
Gold (Aurum)	Au
Hafnium	Hf
Helium	He
Holmium	Ho
Hydrogen	H
Illinium	Il
Indium	In
Iodine	I
Iridium	Ir
Iron (Ferrum)	Fe
Krypton	Kr
Lanthanium	La
Lead (Plumbum)	Pb
Lithium	L
Lucetium	Lu
Magnesium	Mg
Manganese	Mn
Masurium	Ma
Mercury (Hydrargyrum)	Hg
Molybdenum	Mo
Neon	Ne
Neodymium	Nd
Neptunium	Np
Nickel	Ni
Niobium	Nb
Nitrogen	N
Osmium	Os
Oxygen	O
Palladium	Pd
Phosphorus	P
Platinum	Pt
Plutonium	Pu
Polonium	Po
Potassium (Kalium)	K
Praseodymium	Pr
Protactinium	Pa
Radium	Ra
Radon	Rn
Rhenium	Re
Rhodium	R
Rubidium	Rb
Ruthenium	Ru
Samarium	Sm
Scandium	Sc
Selenium	Se
Silicon	Si
Silver (Argentum)	Ag
Sodium (Natrium)	Na
Strontium	Sr
Sulphur	S

Elements	Symbols	Elements	Symbols
Tantalum	Ta	Uranium	U
Tellurium	Te	Vanadium	V
Terbium	Tb	Xenon	Xe
Thallium	Tl	Ytterbium	Yb
Thorium	Th	Yttrium	Yt
Thulium	Tm	Zinc	Zn
Tin (Stannum)	Sn	Zirconium	Zr
Titanium	Ti		
Tungsten (Wolfram)	W		

When any of the above symbols stands by itself it indicates one atom of the element it represents. Thus H stands for one atom of hydrogen, O for one atom of oxygen, and Cl for one atom of chlorine.

When a symbol has a small figure or number underwritten, and to the right of it, such figure or number indicates the number of atoms of the element. Thus O_2 signifies two atoms of oxygen, S_5 five atoms of sulphur, and C_{10} ten atoms of carbon.

When two or more elements are united to form a chemical compound, their symbols are written one after the other, to indicate the compound. Thus H_2O means water, a compound of two atoms of hydrogen and one of oxygen; $C_{12}H_{22}O_{11}$ indicates cane-sugar, a compound of twelve atoms of carbon, twenty-two of hydrogen, and eleven of oxygen.

These two expressions as they stand denote respectively a molecule of the substance they represent, that is, the smallest possible quantity of it capable of existing in the free state. To express several molecules a large figure is prefixed; thus $2H_2O$ represents two molecules of water, $4(C_{12}H_{22}O_{11})$ four molecules of cane-sugar.

When a compound is formed of two or more compounds the symbolical expressions for the compound are usually connected together by a comma; thus, the crystallized magnesic sulphate is $MgSO_4,7H_2O$. The symbols may also be used to express the changes which occur during chemical action, and they are then written in the form of an equation, of which one side represents the substances as they exist before the change, the other the result of the reaction. Thus, $2H_2+O_2-2H_2O$ expresses the fact that two molecules of hydrogen, each containing two atoms, and one of oxygen, also containing two atoms, combine to give two molecules of water, each of them containing two atoms of hydrogen and one of oxygen.

COMMERCIAL

£ Pound or pounds sterling; as, £100.

/ Shilling or shillings; as, 2/6, two shillings and sixpence.

℔. Pound or pounds in weight; as, 60 ℔.

$ Dollar or dollars; as, $100.

@ At; as, 200 @ £1 each.

% Per cent; as, 5%.

a/c Account.

c/o Care of.

d/a Days after acceptance.

d/s Days after sight.

b/l Bill of Lading.

l/c Letter of Credit.

VI. A Key to Noted Names in Fiction, Mythology, Etc.

A Guide to Literary Allusions

Achates, a-kā′tēz. The faithful companion of Æneas in Virgil's *Æneid*, adopted as a type of staunch companionship.

Acheron, ak′e-ron. In classical fable, a river of the infernal regions.

Achilles, a-kil′lēz. The chief Greek hero in the siege of Troy as told in Homer's *Iliad*. He slew Hector, but according to later writers was himself slain by Paris, who wounded him in the right heel, where alone he was vulnerable. His bosom friend was Patroclus, who was killed by Hector.

Actæon, ak-tē′on. A huntsman who, having surprised Diana bathing, was turned by her into a stag and torn by his own dogs.

Adams, Parson. A country curate in Fielding's *Joseph Andrews*: poor, pious, learned, absent-minded, and extremely ignorant of the world.

Admetus, ad-mē′tus. A mythological king of Thessaly under whom, for a year, Apollo served as a shepherd. See *Alcestis*.

Adonis, a-dō′nis. In Greek mythol. a beautiful youth beloved by Venus and killed by a wild boar.

Æneas, ē-nē′as. The hero of Virgil's poem the *Æneid*, a Trojan warrior, who came to Italy after the fall of Troy, passing through various adventures by the way. He was said to be the son of Anchises and Venus, and was regarded as the remote founder of Rome. See also *Dido*.

Æolus, ē′o-lus. God of the winds among the Greeks and Romans. He kept the winds confined in a cave in the Æolian Islands.

Æsculapius, es-kų-lā′pi-us, or **Asklepios.** The god of medicine among the Greeks and Romans.

Agamemnon, ag-a-mem′non. Leader of the Greeks in the war against Troy, slain by his wife Clytemnestra and her paramour Ægisthus.

Aguecheek, Sir Andrew. A silly and ridiculous character in Shakespeare's *Twelfth Night*, a crony of Sir Toby Belch.

Ahriman, Ahrimanes. ä′ri-man, ä-ri-mā′nēz. The evil principle or deity in the religious system of Zoroaster.

Ajax, ā′jaks. A Greek hero of the war against Troy, who became frenzied and killed himself when the armour of Achilles was awarded to Ulysses. He is the hero of a tragedy by Sophocles.

Aladdin, a-lad′din. A well-known character in the *Arabian Nights*, son of a poor tailor in

China. He gains possession of a magic ring and lamp, and thus has at his beck and call the Genii who are attached to them as slaves.

Alcestis, al-ses'tis. The heroine of a drama of Euripides. She was the wife of Admetus, and gave herself up to death in his stead, but was brought back from the grave alive by Hercules.

Alcides, al-sī'dēz. A name of Hercules.

Alcinous, al-sin'o-us. In Homer's *Odyssey*, the king of the Phæacians and father of Nausicaa. He hospitably entertained Ulysses.

Alcmena, alk-mē'na. The mother of Hercules by Jupiter. See *Amphitryon*.

Ali Baba. The hero of the story of *The Forty Thieves* (in the *Arabian Nights*), whose treasure cave he is enabled to enter by overhearing their magic password "Open sesame".

Alice. The child heroine of Lewis Carroll's *Alice's Adventures in Wonderland* and *Through the Looking Glass*.

Allworthy, Mr. A country gentleman in Fielding's *Tom Jones*, distinguished for benevolence, charity, rectitude, and modesty. He brings up Jones, who turns out to be the natural son of his sister.

Amelia. The heroine of Fielding's novel of the same name, wife of the profligate Captain Booth, and a most perfect specimen of wifehood.

Amphion, am-fī'on. A son of Zeus or Jupiter, at the sound of whose lyre the stones moved into their places so as to form the walls of Thebes in Greece.

Amphitryon, am-fit'ri-on. In Greek myth. a king of Thebes who married Alcmena. Jupiter assumed Amphitryon's form and Alcmena became, by him, the mother of Hercules. There are comedies by Plautus and Molière on the incidents connected with this story.

Anchises, an-kī'sēz. The father of Æneas.

Andrews, Joseph. A novel by Fielding, written to ridicule Richardson's *Pamela*, the hero being a virtuous footman who overcame temptations.

Andromache, an-drom'a-kē. The wife of Hector, a beautiful and touching figure in Homer's *Iliad*.

Andromeda, an-drom'e-da. In Greek fable, the fair daughter of an Ethiopian queen, exposed to a sea monster at the command of an oracle, but rescued by Perseus.

Antæus, an-tē'us. A giant invincible so long as he touched the earth, but ultimately killed by Hercules, who held him up and crushed him.

Antigone, an-tig'o-nē. The heroine of Sophocles' tragedy of this name, daughter of Œdipus, put to death by the tyrant Creon of Thebes, for burying her brother contrary to his orders.

Antiph'olus. The name of the twin brothers, exactly resembling each other, who are the chief characters in Shakespeare's *Comedy of Errors*.

Anto'nio. The name of the merchant in Shakespeare's *Merchant of Venice*, who incurs the enmity of Shylock the jew.

Anubis, a-nū'bis. The dog-shaped divinity of ancient Egypt.

Aphrodite, af-rō-dī'tē. The Greek goddess identified by the Romans with Venus.

Apis, ā'pis. The sacred bull of ancient Egypt, worshipped as a symbol of the god Osiris.

Apollo. The Greek and Roman god of music and prophecy, the averter of disease and suffering, originally a sun-god (his epithet Phœbus meaning radiant or beaming). He was a son of Zeus and Latona, and brother of Artemis (Diana).

Apollyon. A demon in Bunyan's *Pilgrim's Progress*.

Arachne, a-rak'nē. In class. mythol. a maiden who, having surpassed Minerva in weaving, was changed by her into a spider.

Aramis. One of the Three Musketeers in Dumas' book of that name.

Ares, ā'rēz. The Greek god of war; same as Mars.

Argo. In Greek legend, the ship in which Jason and his companion heroes, the Argonauts, sailed to bring back the golden fleece from Colchis at the eastern extremity of the Euxine. Jason obtained the fleece by the aid of Medea, daughter of the King of Colchis. See *Jason*, *Medea*.

Argus. A creature of Greek mythol. who had a hundred eyes and was ever watchful.

Ariadne, a-ri-ad'nē. In Greek myth. the daughter of Minos, king of Crete. She gave Theseus a clue of thread to guide him out of the labyrinth after he had killed the Minotaur. Theseus deserted her in the isle of Naxos, and she was commonly said to have married Bacchus.

Arion, a-rī'on. An ancient Greek poet (ab. 625 B.C.), fabled to have been flung into the sea by sailors, who coveted the prizes he had won, but to have been carried safe to land by a dolphin.

Ar'temis. The Greek goddess identified by the Romans with Diana.

Arthur. A British king at the time of the settlement of the Anglo-Saxons in Britain. Nothing is really known of him, but he has become the centre of a vast upgrowth of legend or fable, especially in regard to the exploits of his Knights of the Round Table.

Asca'nius. In Virgil's *Æneid*, the son of Æneas and his wife Creusa.

As'gard. In Scand. mythol. the abode of the gods, rising above Midgard, that is, the earth.

Astræ'a. In class. mythol. the goddess of justice, the last of the deities to leave the earth at the close of the golden age.

Atalan'ta. A famous huntress of Greek myth. who agreed to marry anyone who could outstrip her in running. She was vanquished by a wooer (Hippomenes), who dropped successively three golden apples as he ran, and thus led her to stop and pick them up.

Ate, ā'tē. A Greek goddess of hatred, crime, and retribution.

Athelstane. A heavy-witted thane in Scott's *Ivanhoe*, betrothed to Rowena.

Athene, a-thē'nē. The Greek goddess of wisdom, usually identified with the Roman Minerva. She is also called Pallas or Pallas Athene.

Athos. One of the Three Musketeers in Dumas' book of that name.

Atlan'tis. A large island believed by the ancients to have existed in the Atlantic westward of the Straits of Gibraltar.

Atlas. In Greek mythol. a Titan compelled to support the vault of heaven.

Atreus, at'rūs. In Greek mythol. the father of

Agamemnon and Menelaus, who are hence called Atridæ (a-trī'dē).
At'ropos. One of the three fates among the Greeks; it was she who cut the thread of life. The others were Clotho and Lachesis.
Aurora, ą-rō'ra. In Roman mythol. the goddess of the dawn, in Greek called *Eōs*.
Av'alon. A sort of fairyland or elysium mentioned in connexion with the legends of King Arthur.

Baal. A deity of the Canaanites.
Bacchus, bak'us. The Greek and Roman God of wine, in Greek commonly called *Dionysus*.
Balder, Baldur. A Scand. deity, the son of Odin and Frigga, beautiful, wise, amiable, and beloved of all the gods; slain through the guile of the evil god Loki.
Bal'derstone, Caleb. A devoted but ridiculous old domestic in Scott's *Bride of Lammermoor*, who thinks it his duty by all shifts to uphold the dignity of the family in the direst scarcity of all external aids to assist him.
Balfour, David. The hero of R. L. Stevenson's *Kidnapped* and *Catriona*.
Banquo, bang'kwō. A thane in Shakespeare's *Macbeth*, whom Macbeth causes to be murdered, and whose ghost haunts him.
Bar'dolph. The red-nosed follower of Falstaff in Shakespeare's *Merry Wives*, *Henry IV*, and *Henry V*—a swaggering, drunken, but amusing rascal.
Barmecide, bär'mē-sīd. In the *Arabian Nights*, a prince of the Barmecide family, who pretended to treat a beggar named Shacabac to a sumptuous feast, pressing him to eat, though no dishes were on the table.
Bassa'nio. The lover of Portia in Shakespeare's *Merchant of Venice*. See *Portia*.
Bates, Miss. A character in Jane Austen's *Emma*, famous for her never-ending flow of trivial conversation.
Beatrice, bē'a-tris (It. bā-ā-trē'chā). A young lady beloved by Dante, and celebrated in his *Divine Comedy*; also the heroine of Shakespeare's *Much Ado About Nothing*.
Bede, Adam. The hero of a novel by George Eliot, a manly and straightforward artisan, in love with Hetty Sorrel, who is seduced by the young squire Arthur Donnithorne. He marries Dinah Morris.
Belch, Sir Toby. A jolly toper, the uncle of Olivia in Shakespeare's *Twelfth Night*. He plays on the folly of Sir Andrew Aguecheek.
Be'lial. A biblical word meaning worthlessness or wickedness, often treated as a proper name. Milton so calls the chief of the fallen angels.
Beller'ophon. A hero of Greek myth. who killed the Chimæra when mounted on the winged horse Pegasus. He tried to mount to heaven on Pegasus, but fell and wandered about blind till his death.
Bello'na. The goddess of war among the Romans.
Ben'edick. One of the chief characters in Shakespeare's *Much Ado About Nothing*, who has many an encounter of wit with Beatrice, whom he at last marries. His name (frequently spelled *Benedict*) is often used to denote a newly married man.
Bennet, Elizabeth. The heroine of Miss Austen's *Pride and Prejudice*.
Be'owulf. The hero of a celebrated Anglo-Saxon epic, who kills two man-eating semi-human monsters. He also slays a fiery dragon, but dies from its poisonous bite.
Bergerac, Cyrano de. French dramatist, romance-writer, and notorious duellist of the seventeenth century, hero of Edmond Rostand's play of the same name.
Bob'adil, Captain. A cowardly braggart in Ben Jonson's *Every Man in his Humour*. He proposes to annihilate a hostile army by selecting nineteen other warriors like himself, and challenging and killing the enemy by successive twenties.
Boniface. A landlord in Farquhar's *Beaux' Stratagem*.
Booby, Lady. A lady of loose morals in Fielding's *Joseph Andrews*. She tries to lead Joseph astray.
Booth, Captain. The dissipated but good-natured husband of Amelia, in Fielding's novel of that name.
Boreas, bō'rē-as. In Greek and Roman myth. a personification of the north wind.
Bottom, Nick. The Athenian weaver in Shakespeare's *Midsummer-Night's Dream*, upon whom the fairy queen Titania is made to dote, and whose head is changed by Puck into that of an ass.
Bountiful, Lady. A benevolent country lady in Farquhar's *Beaux' Stratagem*.
Bowling, Tom, bō'ling. A naval character in Smollett's *Roderick Random*, an excellent piece of portraiture.
Box and Cox. The chief characters in the farce which bears their names. This farce was written by John Maddison Morton, and was first produced in 1847.
Bradwardine, Baron, brad-wąr'din. A Scottish nobleman in Scott's *Waverley*, brave and pedantic, but a devoted adherent of the exiled Stuarts. His daughter Rose is in love with, and eventually married to Waverley.
Brahma, brä'mä. The supreme god of the Hindu trinity. He is the creator, as opposed to Vishnu the preserver, and Siva the destroyer.
Bramble, Matthew. An elderly gentleman in Smollett's *Humphry Clinker*, shrewd, cynical, and irascible, but generous and benevolent. His sister **Tabitha** is a niggardly, malicious, vain, and ridiculous old maid, who finally weds Lishmahago.
Breck, Alan. A Jacobite fugitive, companion of David Balfour, in Stevenson's *Kidnapped* and *Catriona*.
Briareus, brī'a-rūs. In Greek fable, a giant with a hundred arms and fifty heads.
Brobding'nag. The country of the giants in Swift's *Gulliver's Travels*.
Brunehild, brö'ne-hilt. A princess of extraordinary strength and prowess in the German epic the *Nibelungenlied*, who is overcome by the devices of Siegfried and married to Gunther, King of Burgundy. Her vengeance on Siegfried, when she discovers how she had been tricked, leads to many important incidents in the poem.
Bucephalus, bų-sef'a-lus. The famous horse of Alexander the Great.
Buddha, bųd'a. An Indian sage who lived in the 5th century B.C. He founded the religious cult which bears his name.
Bull, John. The English nation personified, originally used in Arbuthnot's political satire *The History of John Bull*.
Bumble. The celebrated pompous parish beadle in Dickens's *Oliver Twist*.

Burchell, Mr., ber'chel. A chief character in Goldsmith's *Vicar of Wakefield*, who appears as a plain man of abrupt manners and no position in life, but is really the baronet Sir William Thornhill.

Buzfuz, Serjeant. A bullying lawyer in the famous breach of promise trial in Dickens's *Pickwick*.

Ca'cus. A mythical robber and giant of ancient Italy, slain by Hercules for stealing his cattle.

Cade'nus. A name assumed by Swift, being an anagram of L. *decanus*, dean.

Cal'iban. A deformed, brutal, and malignant creature in Shakespeare's *Tempest*, offspring of the hag Sycorax, and servant of Prospero.

Calliope, kal-lī'ō-pē. The muse who presided over eloquence and heroic poetry.

Calypso, ka-lip'sō. An ocean nymph who lived in the island Ogygia, where she detained Ulysses for seven years when on his return from Troy.

Cap'ulets. The noble house in Verona to which Juliet belonged in Shakespeare's *Romeo and Juliet*.

Car'abas, Marquis of. A fanciful title standing for a great nobleman or grandee; most familiar from its occurrence in the story of *Puss in Boots*.

Carton, Sydney. In *A Tale of Two Cities*, the jackal to Mr. Stryver. He sacrifices his life to save Charles Darnay, and is one of the most dramatic figures in the book.

Casaubon, Mr. A pedant in George Eliot's *Middlemarch*.

Cassan'dra. Daughter of King Priam of Troy, gifted with the power of prophecy, but condemned by Apollo to be always disbelieved.

Cassio. Lieutenant of Othello, and dupe of Iago in Shakespeare's *Othello*.

Cassiopeia, -pē'ya. In Greek fable, a queen of Ethiopia, mother of Andromeda, made a constellation after her death.

Castor and Pollux. Twin deities among the Greeks and Romans, sons of Jupiter, eventually placed among the stars as *Gemini* or the Twins.

Ceres. The Roman goddess of corn.

Chadband, Rev. Mr. A hypocritical clergyman in Dickens's *Bleak House*.

Charon, kā'ron. The Greek and Roman god who ferried the souls of the dead across the Styx to Hades.

Charybdis, ka-rib'dis. See *Scylla*.

Chauvin. The principal character in several French plays, e.g. in Scribe's *Soldat Laboureur*. He is a type of absurd patriotism and exaggerated militarism.

Chiron, kī'ron. One of the Centaurs, famed for his knowledge of medicine, music, and other arts, the preceptor of Achilles and other heroes of ancient Greece.

Christian. The hero of Bunyan's *Pilgrim's Progress*, his wife being Christiana.

Chuzzlewit, Martin. The hero of Dickens's novel of the same name, a young man who goes to America with Mark Tapley, and meets with experiences that do much to improve his character.

Cimme'rians. A people fabled by Homer to live in a land of darkness.

Cinderella. The heroine of a well-known and widely-spread fairy tale.

Circe, sėr'se. A sorceress of Greek mythol.

Claudio. Brother of Isabella in Shakespeare's *Measure for Measure*.

Claudius. The name of Hamlet's uncle.

Clinker, Humphry. The hero of a novel by Smollett, brought up in the workhouse and employed as a servant by Matthew Bramble. He turns out to be a natural son of his employer, and marries his fellow-servant, Winifred Jenkins.

Clio, klī'o. The muse of history.

Clo'tho. One of the Fates or Parcæ among the Greeks and Romans, the other two being Atropos and Lachesis. Clotho spins the thread of life.

Clytemnestra, klī-tem-nes'tra. The wife of Agamemnon, whom she and her paramour Ægisthus murdered on his return from Troy. She was slain by her son Orestes.

Cocytus, kō-sī'tus. In classical myth. a river of the infernal regions.

Collins, Mr. A character in Jane Austen's *Pride and Prejudice*. A snobbish, self-centred English country parson.

Co'mus. A god of revelry among the ancients; in Milton's masque of the same name a lewd enchanter.

Cophet'ua. A legendary king of Africa, celebrated in a ballad as having loved and married a beggar maid.

Copperfield, David. The hero of Dickens's novel of the same name, in which are introduced also Mr. Micawber, David's aunt Betsy Trotwood, the Peggottys, Steerforth, Uriah Heep, Agnes Wickfield, Mr. Dick, &c. Experiences of Dickens's own early life are embodied in this novel.

Corde'lia. In Shakespeare's *King Lear*, the youngest and favourite daughter of the king, whose mind, however, is turned against her, so that he disinherits her, and gives over his kingdom to her two sisters.

Cov'erley, Sir Roger de. An old knight and country gentleman pictured by Steele and Addison in the pages of the *Spectator*, a delightful compound of simplicity, modesty, benevolence, harmless pomposity, eccentricity, and whim.

Crawley. The name of an aristocratic family in Thackeray's *Vanity Fair*.

Crawley, Rev. Josiah. Perpetual curate of Hogglestock in Trollope's novel *The Last Chronicle of Barset*. His memory had given way under his many misfortunes, and he was for long suspected of having stolen a cheque but was at last proved innocent.

Cronos. A Greek deity corresponding with the Italian Saturn.

Crusoe, Robinson, krö'sō. The hero of Defoe's famous story.

Cuttle, Captain. A retired sea captain in Dickens's *Dombey and Son*; simple, credulous, ignorant, warm-hearted, and generous. He has an iron hook in place of one of his hands, and a favourite saying of his is, "When found, make a note of."

Cymbeline, sim'be-līn. A semi-mythical king of Britain, standing for the historical Cunobelinus, whose name occurs on coins.

Cytherea, sith-e-rē'a. A name of Venus.

Dæ'dalus. A mythical Greek sculptor and artificer, who fled from Crete by means of wings fashioned by himself. His son Icarus accompanied him, but was drowned.

Dag'onet, Sir. The court fool of the famous King Arthur.

Dalgetty, Dugald, dal'get-i. A soldier of fortune in Scott's *Legend of Montrose*, brave and experienced, but vulgar, conceited, pedantic, and always with an eye to the main chance.

Damocles, dam'o-klēz. A courtier whom King Dionysius of Syracuse treated to a splendid feast, but over whose head he caused a naked sword to be suspended by a horse hair, as a lesson that danger may overhang greatness and outward felicity.

Da'mon and Phin'tias (or **Pyth'ias**). Two Greeks of Syracuse whose names have become proverbial for friendship. When Phintias was condemned to death, in order that he might be allowed to go home to settle his affairs, Damon took his place as surety that he would return — as he did — to meet his fate.

Danae, dan'a-ē. A Greek princess shut up in a brazen tower, to which Jove gained access in form of a golden shower, and thus became by her the father of Perseus.

Dantes, Edmond. The hero of Dumas' *Count of Monte Cristo*.

Daphne, daf'nē. A maiden who, when pursued by Apollo, escaped by being changed into a laurel.

Darby and Joan. A married couple, the type of simple domestic happiness. They are celebrated in ballad literature.

D'Artagnan. A Gascon soldier of fortune who appears in Dumas' *The Three Musketeers* and in several other of his books.

Deans, dēnz, **Jeanie** and **Effie.** The heroines of Scott's *Heart of Midlothian*.

Demeter, dē-mē'ter. The Greek goddess corresponding to the Roman Ceres.

Desdemo'na. The heroine of Shakespeare's *Othello*, killed by her husband Othello, who is led by the devilish malice of Iago to believe her unfaithful to him.

Deucalion and Pyrrha, dū-kā'li-on, pir'a. In Greek mythol. a man and wife who alone survived a deluge and became originators of a new race of men.

Diana, dī-an'a. The Roman goddess corresponding to the Greek Artemis, the sister of Apollo, a chaste virgin, goddess of hunting and of the moon.

Di'do. The mythical Queen of Carthage, described by Virgil in the *Æneid* as hospitably entertaining the shipwrecked Æneas. She fell in love with him, and put an end to her life when he deserted her.

Diomede, dī'o-mēd. A renowned Grecian chief at the siege of Troy.

Dionysus, dī-o-nī'sus. A Greek name of the god Bacchus.

Dobbin, Colonel. One of the chief characters in Thackeray's *Vanity Fair*, an excellent soldier and thorough gentleman, though somewhat shy and awkward. He is devoted to Amelia Sedley and also to her husband George Osborne.

Doe, John, dō. An imaginary person whose name used to appear in certain English actions at law, along with that of Richard Roe, an equally shadowy personage.

Dogberry and Verges. Two ridiculous constables in Shakespeare's *Much Ado about Nothing*.

Dombey, Mr. In Dickens's *Dombey and Son*, a wealthy London merchant full of pride and self-importance.

Don Ju'an. The hero of a Spanish legend which has been much employed for the dramatic and operatic stage, and has furnished the name to Byron's poem. The don is the type of a finished and reckless libertine who is at last dragged down alive to the infernal regions. Byron's unfinished poem borrows little or nothing but the name from the old legend.

Don Quix'ote (Spanish pron. kē-hō'tā). The hero of the great Spanish romance of Cervantes, a Castilian country gentleman so crazed by reading books of chivalry that he sallies forth as a knight-errant to succour the oppressed and redress wrongs. As his squire he takes along with him Sancho Panza, an ignorant, credulous, and vulgar peasant, pot-bellied, gluttonous, and selfish, yet faithful to his master, shrewd and amusing.

Doone, Lorna. Heroine of R. D. Blackmore's novel of that name.

Doubting Castle. The castle of giant Despair in *The Pilgrim's Progress*.

Dro'mio. The name of the twin slaves in Shakespeare's *Comedy of Errors*, attendants on the brothers Antipholus.

Dulcin'ea del Tobo'so. The country girl whom Don Quixote selected as the lady of his knightly devotion.

Durbeyfield, Tess. Heroine of Thomas Hardy's *Tess of the d'Urbervilles*.

Dur'ward, Quentin. The hero of Scott's novel of the same name, an archer in the Scottish Guard of Louis XI of France, who finally wins the hand of the young Countess Isabella De Croye.

Eb'lis. In Mohammedan mythology, the chief of the evil angels.

Egeria, ē-jē'ri-a. In Roman legend, a nymph from whom King Numa Pompilius is said to have received instructions in regard to religious institutions.

Eldora'do. The name of a country exceednigly rich in gold, once imagined to exist in the Orinoco region of S. America.

Elec'tra. The daughter of Agamemnon and Clytemnestra, and sister of Orestes, whom she abetted in the murder of their mother, to avenge the death of their father. Her story was treated by the Greek tragedians Sophocles and Euripides in still extant tragedies.

Elia. Pseudonym under which Charles Lamb wrote his famous series of essays.

Emily. "Little Em'ly", niece of Daniel Peggotty in Dickens's *David Copperfield*, betrothed to Ham Peggotty, but seduced by Steerforth.

Endymion, en-dim'i-on. A beautiful shepherd kissed by Diana as he lay asleep on Mount Latmus. Keats has a celebrated poem of this name.

E'os. The Greek name equivalent to *Aurora*.

Er'ato. One of the muses; she presided over lyric and especially amatory poetry.

Erebus. A gloomy region under the earth.

E'ris. A Greek goddess of strife or discord.

E'ros. The Greek name of the god of love; Cupid.

Esmond, Col. Henry. The hero of Thackeray's novel called *Esmond* (time, the reign of Queen Anne), a chivalrous soldier and man of taste.

Eumæus, ū-mē'us. In Homer's *Odyssey*, the faithful swine-herd of Ulysses, attached to and respected by his master.
Euphrosyne, ū-fros'i-nē. In Greek myth. one of the three graces, the others being Aglaia and Thalia.
Euro'pa. A nymph of Greek fable carried off by Jove in the form of a white bull.
Eurydice, ū-rid'i-sē. The wife of the poet Orpheus.
Euterpe, ū-tėr'pē. The muse of music.
Excal'ibur. The famous sword of King Arthur.
Eyre, Jane, ār. The heroine of a novel by Charlotte Brontë, governess to a gentleman called Rochester, to whom she is married after the death of his insane wife.

Fagin, fā'gin. An old Jew and receiver of stolen goods in Dickens's *Oliver Twist*, who trains boys to steal.
Fairservice, Andrew. In Scott's *Rob Roy*, the pragmatical, conceited, and not over honest Scottish gardener at Osbaldistone Hall.
Faith'ful. A companion of Christian in Bunyan's *Pilgrim's Progress*, burned alive at Vanity Fair.
Falstaff, Sir John, fal'staf. The "fat knight", the finest comic character of Shakespeare and of literature, appearing in *Henry IV* (both parts) and the *Merry Wives*. Gross, sensual, dishonest, and utterly unprincipled, he would be despicable were it not for his overflowing wit and humour, his gaiety and good sense.
Fat'ima. The last of Bluebeard's wives.
Faulconbridge, Philip. In Shakespeare's *King John*, a natural son of Richard I, an outspoken and daring soldier, true as steel to his friends.
Faust, foust. The chief character in Goethe's celebrated dramatic poem, in popular German legend known as Dr. Faustus, as also in Marlowe's tragedy of same name. Faustus was a magician and astrologer who sold himself to the devil on condition of obtaining for a period every kind of worldly enjoyment, at the end of which he realizes with horror and despair the penalty he has now to pay.
Fig'aro. A sharp-witted barber and valet, the hero of Beaumarchais' French comedies *The Barber of Seville* and *Marriage of Figaro*, on which are based operas by Rossini and Mozart.
Flor'izel. The Prince of Bohemia in Shakespeare's *Winter's Tale*, in love with Perdita.
Fluel'len. A brave but pedantic Welsh captain in Shakespeare's *Henry V*, whose parallel between Monmouth and Macedon is well known.
Flying Dutchman. A phantom ship seen in the neighbourhood of the Cape of Good Hope, said to be commanded by a Dutch captain (Vanderdecken) who for his impiety has to sail till the day of judgment.
Fortuna'tus. The hero of a popular tale who obtained an inexhaustible purse and a cap that would carry him wherever he pleased.
Fosco, Count. The arch-villain in W. W. Collins's *The Woman in White*.
Fra Diavolo, frä dē-äv'o-lō. A brigand chief of S. Italy who has given name to an opera by Auber, with words by Scribe.
Frank'enstein, -stin. A student of physiology in Mrs. Shelley's romance of the same name. He attains profound knowledge and constructs a hideous monster endued with the attributes of humanity. The monster, though craving sympathy and love, proves the curse and ruin of its creator.
Freischutz, frī'shüts. A marksman of German legend who obtains seven magic bullets, six of which hit whatever he aims at, but the seventh goes as the fiend directs.
Friar Tuck. The friar who is said to have been among Robin Hood's merry men.
Friday, Man. In Defoe, the friend and servant of Robinson Crusoe.

Gal'ahad, Sir. One of the knights of King Arthur's Round Table, celebrated for his chastity.
Galatea, gal-a-tē'a. A nymph of Greek fable beloved by and loving Acis, who was killed by the Cyclops Polyphemus from jealousy.
Gamp, Sarah. A monthly nurse in Dickens's *Martin Chuzzlewit*. She is extremely fond of liquor, carries a big baggy umbrella, and makes frequent references to a purely imaginary friend of hers named Mrs. Harris.
Gan'elon. One of Charlemagne's knights, celebrated for malevolence and treachery.
Ganymede, gan'i-mēd. A beautiful youth of Greek fable, carried to heaven from Mount Ida by an eagle, and made cup-bearer to the gods.
Gargan'tua. The hero of the humorous and fantastic romance of the same name by Rabelais. He was a giant of tremendous size who had a son equally wonderful named Pantagruel.
Gaw'ain. One of the knights of the Round Table, a nephew of King Arthur, renowned for strength as well as for courtesy.
Gelert, gel'ėrt. The faithful hound of Llewellyn, which kills a wolf that would have devoured its master's infant, and is rashly slain by him before he sees how matters really stand.
Geryon, jē'ri-on. In ancient classical legend, a monstrous king of Hesperia, who fed his oxen on human flesh and was slain by Hercules.
Giant Despair. A formidable giant in *The Pilgrim's Progress* who lived in Doubting Castle.
Gil Blas, zhēl bläs. The hero of a diverting novel by Le Sage. Though the book is written in French, the scene is laid in Spain, and some incidents are taken from Spanish writers.
Gilpin, John, gil'pin. A London linen-draper and train-band captain whose exploits on horseback are celebrated in Cowper's humorous poem of the same name.
Glubbdub'drib. In Swift's *Gulliver's Travels*, an island inhabited by sorcerers or magicians, who called up at Gulliver's desire the spirits of many personages of former times.
Glumdal'clitch. An amiable girl giantess (forty feet high) who had the care of Gulliver when he was in Brobdingnag.
Godi'va, Lady. The wife of Leofric, Earl of Mercia, who, according to legend, sought relief from taxation for the people of Coventry. Her husband promised to grant her request if she would ride naked through the town. This she did, first having forbidden the townspeople to look out of the windows. Only

one person, hence called "Peeping Tom", ventured to disobey, and he was immediately struck blind. The story has been versified by Tennyson.

Gon'eril. One of the two evil daughters of King Lear.

Goodfellow, Robin. A tricky imp or sprite of popular English tales, called also *Puck*.

Gran'dison, Sir Charles. The hero of Richardson's novel *The History of Sir Charles Grandison*, a somewhat tiresome character intended to exemplify the perfect Christian gentleman.

Greatheart. In *The Pilgrim's Progress*, the guide of Christiana and her children to the Celestial City.

Grisel'da. The heroine of one of Chaucer's *Canterbury Tales*, borrowed from the Italian. She was subjected to the cruellest trials by her husband in order to test her patience and obedience, but never complained or murmured.

Grub Street. The former name of a street in London which has become identified with hack writers and poor literature.

Grundy, Mrs. A farmer's wife frequently spoken of by Mrs. Ashfield, another farmer's wife, in Morton's comedy *Speed the Plough* (1798). Mrs. Ashfield is much given to speculating about "what Mrs. Grundy will say" in such and such circumstances.

Guinevere, gwin'e-vēr. The wife of King Arthur, notorious for her guilty attachment to Sir Lancelot.

Gulliver, Lemuel. The hero of Swift's *Gulliver's Travels*. He makes various voyages, and in one way or another visits some remarkable countries, especially Lilliput, Brobdingnag, Laputa, and the land of the Houyhnhnms.

Gyges, gi'jēz. A king of ancient Lydia fabled to have had a magic ring which rendered him invisible, and thus helped him to slay his predecessor Candaules.

Halcyone, hal-sī'o-nē. In Greek myth. daughter of Æolus and wife of Ceyx, at whose death she threw herself into the sea and became a kingfisher.

Hamlet. The prince of Denmark, hero of Shakespeare's tragedy, the substance of which is contained in old chronicles.

Har'lowe, Clarissa. The heroine of Richardson's novel *Clarissa*, a girl of great sweetness, purity, and moral dignity, who is overcome by drugs and betrayed by the man she loves, the libertine Lovelace. She scorns his offered reparation of marriage and dies of grief and shame.

Haroun Alraschid. The Caliph around whose nocturnal adventures part of the *Arabian Nights* centres.

Har'pagon. A miser, the hero of Molière's comedy *L'Avare* (The Miser).

Har'ris, Mrs. Mrs. Gamp's oft-quoted but imaginary friend. See *Gamp*.

Hatto. In German legend, an archbishop of Mainz who is devoured by an army of rats (or mice) as a judgment upon him for having, during a severe famine, shut up a number of poor people in a barn and burned them.

He'bē. The Greek goddess of youth and cup-bearer to the gods (before Ganymede). She is represented as a very beautiful young girl.

Hecate, hek'ā-tē. A Greek goddess whose powers were various. She was especially a goddess of the infernal regions and patroness of magicians and witches.

Hector. The son of Priam, King of Troy, and husband of Andromache, the most valiant among the Trojans, and the noblest hero described in the *Iliad*. He was slain by Achilles, and his body was dragged round the city walls in revenge for his having killed Patroclus.

Hecuba. The wife of King Priam of Troy, and mother of Hector, Paris, and Cassandra. After the fall of Troy she was given to Ulysses as a slave, and some say she drowned herself in despair.

Heep, Uriah. Clerk to Mr. Wickfield, the lawyer in Dickens's *David Copperfield*, a sneaking and malignant character, always proclaiming how "'umble" he is, but really trying to ruin his employer and marry his daughter Agnes.

Helen. The wife of Menelaus, King of Sparta, and daughter of Jupiter and Leda, the most beautiful woman of her time. She was carried off to Troy by Paris, and thus caused the Trojan war, the Greek princes having combined in a great expedition against Troy in order to recover her.

Hel'icon. A mountain of Greece anciently sacred to Apollo and the muses.

He'lios. The Greek name for the sun and the sun-god, in the latter sense identified with Phœbus or Apollo.

Hephæ'stus. Same as *Vulcan*.

Hera. Same as *Juno*.

Her'cules or **Her'acles.** In classical mythology, a hero or demi-god, son of Jupiter and Alcmena, renowned for his wonderful achievements, twelve of which are specially singled out as the *twelve labours of Hercules*.

Hermes, hėr'mēz. The Greek deity regarded as equivalent to the Roman Mercury, the messenger of the gods, the inventor of the lyre (which he resigned to Apollo), the god of commerce, and also of fraud and cunning. He is generally represented with small wings attached to his head and ankles, and with a winged rod—the *caduceus*.

He'ro. The beautiful priestess of Venus at Sestos, to visit whom Leander used to swim the Hellespont. On his death she drowned herself. Another Hero has an important part in Shakespeare's *Much Ado about Nothing*.

Hesperides, hes-per'i-dēz. In Greek myth. three nymphs who lived in pleasant gardens in an island of the western ocean, and had charge of a tree which produced golden apples. Hercules had to fetch apples from this tree, which was watched by a dragon.

Hes'perus. In classical literature, a personification of the evening star (the planet Venus).

Hes'tia. The Greek name of the goddess Vesta.

Hip'pocrene, -krē-nē or -krēn. A fountain of the muses in Ancient Greece near Mount Helicon.

Holmes, Sherlock. The greatest private detective of fiction and hero of four novels and 56 short stories by Conan Doyle.

Honeycomb, Will. One of the members of the club described in the *Spectator*, an oracle on matters of fashion.

Hood, Robin. The famous archer and outlaw of mediæval England, a creation of popular mythology.

Horatio. In Shakespeare's *Hamlet*, the friend of the Prince of Denmark.

Ho'rus. An ancient Egyptian deity personifying the sun.

Houyhnhnms, hö'inmz. In Swift's *Gulliver's Travels*, the race of wonderful horses among whom his hero is thrown.

Hu'dibras. The hero of the famous satire in verse by Samuel Butler directed against the Nonconformists. Hudibras is a ridiculous Presbyterian knight-errant with a squire named Ralph.

Hy'dra. A many-headed monster slain by Hercules.

Hyperion, hī-pē'ri-on, more strictly hī-pēr-i'on. In ancient myth. one of the Titans; sometimes a name equivalent to the sun.

Iago, ī-ä'gō. The "ancient" or ensign of Othello in Shakespeare's tragedy who, out of jealousy and devilish malignity, persuades Othello of Desdemona's unfaithfulness.

Ic'arus, the son of Dædalus. He fled with his father but soared so high that the sun melted the wax with which his artificial wings were fastened, causing him to fall into the sea and be drowned.

Il'ium or **Ilion.** A poetic name of Troy, whence the name of Homer's poem the *Iliad*.

Imogen, im'o-jen. The wife of Posthumus and heroine of Shakespeare's *Cymbeline*.

I'o. In classical myth. a princess beloved by Jupiter, and temporarily changed into a cow to avoid the enmity of Juno.

Iphigenia, if-i-je-ni'a. A daughter of Agamemnon and Clytemnestra, who was about to be sacrificed to avert the wrath of the gods, but was miraculously carried away from Aulis to the Crimea.

I'ris. The goddess of the rainbow, also a messenger of the gods, especially of Juno.

I'sis. An Egyptian goddess of the moon, wife of Osiris and mother of Horus, often represented as veiled.

Islands of the Blest or **Fortunate Islands.** Islands believed by the Greeks to lie far out in the Atlantic and to form a sort of Elysium.

Isolde, i-sold'. A heroine of mediæval romance belonging to the Arthurian cycle, the beloved of Sir Tristram.

Ixi'on. In classical mythology, a Thessalian king who for his wickedness was punished in the infernal regions by being bound to a perpetually-revolving fiery wheel.

Ja'nus. A Roman deity represented with two faces turning opposite ways, and whose temple was closed in time of peace.

Jaques, jak'wes or zhäk. A melancholy and contemplative lord in Shakespeare's *As You Like it*.

Jarley, Mrs. The proprietrix of a travelling waxwork in Dickens's *Old Curiosity Shop*.

Jarndyce, Mr. A kindly, upright old man in Dickens's *Bleak House*. A party in the renowned Chancery case, Jarndyce and Jarndyce.

Jarvie, Bailie Nicol. A Glasgow magistrate in Scott's *Rob Roy*, and an admirable humorous creation.

Ja'son. An ancient Greek hero, the leader of the Argonauts and husband of Medea.

Jellyby, Mrs., jel'i-bi. In Dickens's *Bleak House*, a lady so immersed in missionary matters, and so much concerned for the poor heathen in Africa, that she neglects her own household.

Jenkins, Winifred. In Smollett's *Humphry Clinker*, Miss Tabitha Bramble's maid. She writes letters amusing because of their blunders, and eventually marries the hero.

Jes'sica. The daughter of Shylock the Jew in Shakespeare's *Merchant of Venice*.

Jingle, Alfred. An amusing swindling stroller in Dickens's *Pickwick*, who talks in a peculiar elliptical style, and after cheating Mr. Pickwick is rescued by him from a debtor's prison. His henchman is Job Trotter.

Jocas'ta. See *Œdipus*.

Jones, Tom. The hero of a novel by Fielding, manly and good-hearted, but dissipated and wanting in self-respect. He marries Sophia, daughter of Squire Western.

Jourdain, M. The "nouveau riche" hero of Molière's comedy *Le Bourgeois Gentilhomme*.

Juan, Don. See *Don Juan*.

Ju'liet. The heroine of Shakespeare's famous tragedy *Romeo and Juliet*, a member of the Capulet family.

Ju'no. The supreme goddess among the Romans, identified with the Greek Hera.

Ju'piter. The supreme Roman deity, identified with the Greek Zeus.

Laertes, lā-ėr'tēz. In Greek story, the father of Ulysses; in Shakespeare's *Hamlet*, son of Polonius and brother of Ophelia.

Laga'do. In Swift's *Gulliver's Travels*, the capital of Balnibarbi, visited by Guliver in his Laputa journey. Lagado is celebrated for its academy of projectors, who try to perform numerous ridiculous scientific experiments.

Lammermoor, Bride of. Lucy Ashton, heroine of a tragic novel by Scott.

Lan'celot or **Launcelot.** The most famous of King Arthur's knights, paramour of Queen Guinevere.

Languish, Lydia. A very romantic young lady, the heroine of Sheridan's comedy *The Rivals*.

Laocoon, la-ok'o-on. In Greek legend, a Trojan priest who along with his two sons was killed by two enormous serpents—an incident represented in a very famous group of statuary.

Lapu'ta. A sort of flying island visited by Gulliver, raised above the earth by means of a huge load-stone, and inhabited by persons engaged in the most abstruse studies.

Lato'na. The mother of Apollo and Diana.

Lean'der. In Greek story, a young man of Abydos who used to swim the Hellespont to visit Hero of Sestos.

Lear, lēr. A mythical king of Britain, the subject of Shakespeare's tragedy *King Lear*.

Leatherstocking. A mighty hunter appearing in several of Fenimore Cooper's books.

Leda. In Greek myth. the wife of Tyndareus. Jupiter falling in love with her, and visiting her in the form of a swan, she produced two eggs, from one of which came forth Pollux and Helen, and from the other Castor and Clytemnestra.

Leigh, Amyas. The hero of Kingsley's *Westward Ho!*

Lenore, le-nōr'. A heroine of German ballads whose dead lover in spectral form carries her on horseback with him to the graveyard.

Lil'liput. The land of the Lilliputians, who were pygmies about six inches high, in Swift's *Gulliver's Travels.*

Lismaha'go. In Smollett's *Humphry Clinker*, a Scottish half-pay officer, gaunt and grim, pedantic, and disputatious, and full of national pride; he gets married to Tabitha Bramble and her £4000.

Little Dorrit. The heroine of a novel by Dickens, born and brought up in the Marshalsea Prison.

Lo'ki. In Scandinavian myth. the evil god who brought about the death of Balder.

Lorelei, lō'rē-lī. In German legend, a siren of the Rhine, who lures men to destruction.

Lovelace. The libertine hero of Richardson's novel *Clarissa.*

Lucre'tia. The heroine of a legendary tale of early Rome, who stabbed herself after being defiled by Sextus Tarquinius.

Lugg'nagg. An island in Swift's *Gulliver's Travels.*

Lycidas, lis'i-das. A poetic name under which Milton in a celebrated elegy laments his deceased friend Edward King.

Lyndon, Barry. The hero of Thackeray's *Memoirs of Barry Lyndon*, an Irishman who relates his own adventures as an audacious sharper and swindler.

Lyonnesse, lī-on-nes'. A tract in the south-west of England said to be now covered by the sea.

Mab. The queen of the fairies according to Shakespeare and other English poets.

Macbeth'. A historic personage who raised himself to be King of Scotland, and is celebrated, along with his wife Lady Macbeth, in Shakespeare's famous tragedy. The events of this are, however, almost entirely fictitious.

Macduff'. A Scottish thane who slays Macbeth. See preceding entry.

Mal'aprop, Mrs. A lady in Sheridan's comedy *The Rivals*, notorious for her amusing blunders in the use of words; aunt and guardian of Lydia Languish.

Malvo'lio. The pompous and conceited steward or major-domo of Olivia in Shakespeare's *Twelfth Night.*

Mammon, Sir Epicure. A sensualist of boundless imagination in Jonson's play *The Alchemist.*

Man of Feeling. The hero of a sentimental and lachrymose novel by Henry Mackenzie (1771).

Mantalini, man-ta-lē'nē. A dissipated fop in Dickens's *Nicholas Nickleby.* He is the husband of a fashionable milliner and is reduced to turning his wife's mangle.

Marchioness, The. A half-starved girl, maid of all work to Sampson Brass in Dickens's *Old Curiosity Shop.* She is eventually married to Dick Swiveller.

Mar'mion. A brave but profligate English lord, hero of Scott's poem of same name. He was slain at Flodden.

Marner, Silas. The character who gives name to a novel by George Eliot. He is a weaver who believes himself deserted by God, and has his small store of gold stolen, but is restored to heart and hope by a little foundling child who comes to him.

Mars. The Roman god of war.

Mede'a. The daughter of a king of Colchis, in Greek legend, and a famous sorceress, who helps Jason to carry off the golden fleece, and is married to him. Ultimately he deserts her, and in revenge she murders her two children.

Megæra, me-jē'ra. In classical myth. one of the three Furies.

Meleager, mel-ē-ā'ger. A Greek legendary hero, slayer of the formidable Calydonian boar and lover of Atalanta; his life depended on how long a firebrand remained unconsumed.

Melpomene, mel-pom'e-nē. The muse who presided over tragedy.

Melusine, mā-lü-sēn. A fairy of French legend, who is condemned to become every Saturday a serpent from the waist downward.

Menelaus, men-e-lā'us. A mythical king of Sparta, husband of Helen and brother of Agamemnon.

Mephistopheles, mef-is-tof'e-lēz. A fiend or spirit of evil who figures in the Faust story, and is made a striking personage by Goethe. See *Faust.*

Mercury. See *Hermes.*

Mercutio, mėr-kū'shi-ō. The witty and elegant friend of Romeo in Shakespeare's *Romeo and Juliet.*

Mer'lin. The famous enchanter in the legends connected with King Arthur.

Micaw'ber, Mr. Wilkins. A delightfully humorous character in Dickens's *David Copperfield*, given to high-flown language, fond of good living, and carelessly improvident; often, if one could believe him, in the deepest gloom, but generally hopeful and waiting "for something to turn up".

Mi'das. A legendary king of Phrygia, who, having obtained from the gods the gift of turning everything he touched into gold, found it a curse. Apollo gave him an ass's ears for deciding a musical contest against him.

Minerva. See *Athene.*

Mi'nos. A legendary king and law-giver of Crete, made after death one of the judges of the lower world.

Min'otaur. A monster of Greek fable, half man half bull, who lived in the Cretan labyrinth, and was slain by Theseus.

Miran'da. The daughter of Prospero in Shakespeare's *Tempest.*

Montague, mon'ta-gū. The noble house of Verona, to which Romeo belonged in Shakespeare's *Romeo and Juliet.*

Munchausen, mun-chạ'sn. The putative author of a book of amusing but fictitious adventures.

Narcis'sus. A youth of Greek fable, who, falling in love with his own image as reflected in a fountain, pined away and finally was changed into the flower which bears his name.

Nausicaa, nạ-sik'ā-a. A princess of the Phæacians in Homer's *Odyssey*, who takes compassion on Ulysses when shipwrecked.

Nestor. A legendary king in southern Greece, one of those who went to Troy. Because he lived to such a great age, his advice was deemed equal to that of the gods themselves.

Newcome, Colonel. One of the most prominent characters in Thackeray's novel *The Newcomes*, brave, simple, and good, though not over wise.

Nibelungen, nē'be-lụng-en. A race or family in German legend possessed of a great treasure. Their name is attached to the old German epic the Nibelungenlied or song of the Nibelungs.

Niobe, nī'o-bē. A queen of classic story, whose children were all slain by Apollo and Diana, and who was herself turned into stone.

Norns. The three fates of Scandinavian mythology.

Nym. A follower of Falstaff's in Shakespeare's *Merry Wives* and *Henry V*, an amusing rogue who eventually gets hanged.

Ob'eron. The king of the fairies, familiar to us from Shakespeare's *Midsummer-Night's Dream*, celebrated also in a poem by Wieland and in an opera by Weber.

Ochiltree, Ed'ie, *och'*il-trē. A blue-gown or licensed beggar, a shrewd and humorous character in Scott's *Antiquary*.

O'din. The supreme Scandinavian deity, king of gods and men.

Odysseus, ō-dis'ūs. The Greek form of Ulysses; hence the name of the great Homeric epic, the *Odyssey*, which narrates the wanderings and adventures of Ulysses on his way home from the Trojan war.

Œdipus, ē'di-pus. A legendary king of Thebes in Greece, son of Laius and Jocasta, celebrated in tragedy. Unaware of his parentage, he unwittingly killed his own father, and having answered the riddle of the Sphinx obtained the throne of Thebes and his own mother as his wife. When the real state of matters became known Jocasta hanged herself, and Œdipus put out his eyes and left Thebes as a poor wanderer, attended by his daughter Antigone.

Œnone, ē-nō'nē. A nymph of classic fable married to Paris, who deserted her for Helen.

Old'buck, Jonathan. An elderly gentleman of antiquarian tastes, from whom Scott's *Antiquary* takes its name, a confirmed bachelor and contemner of women, hasty, sarcastic, and whimsical, but shrewd and kind-hearted; an admirably humorous portrait.

Old Man of the Sea. In the *Arabian Nights*, a malignant old wretch who managed to get himself planted on the shoulders of Sindbad, who only got rid of him by intoxicating him.

Olym'pus. A mountain of northern Greece supposed to be the abode of the gods.

Ophe'lia. The daughter of Polonius in Shakespeare's *Hamlet*, loving and loved by Hamlet, but driven mad by his treatment of her and by her father's death.

Ores'tes. A hero of Greek tragedy, the son of Agamemnon and Clytemnestra. He killed his mother in punishment for his father's murder, and for this crime was pursued by the Furies. His friendship with Pylades, who married his sister Electra, was proverbial.

Orion, ō-rī'on. A giant and mighty hunter of Greek fable, who was blinded as a punishment, but recovered his sight by travelling eastwards and exposing his eyes to the rays of the rising sun. After death he became a constellation.

Orlan'do. One of the paladins of Charlemagne, a hero of romance and Italian epic. *Roland* is another form of the name. In Shakespeare's *As You Like It* Orlando is the name of Rosalind's lover.

Orpheus, or'fūs. A mythical musician of Greece, who could charm beasts and make rocks and woods move to his melody.

Osborne, Capt. George. In Thackeray's *Vanity Fair*, a dandified, selfish, and shallow-hearted young officer, who marries Amelia Sedley and is killed at Waterloo after proposing an elopement with Becky Sharp.

Osi'ris. The chief god of the ancient Egyptians.

Ossian. A warrior-bard of Gaelic and Irish tradition.

Othello. In Shakespeare's tragedy, a Moor or African who commands the Venetian forces, marries Desdemona, the daughter of a Venetian senator, kills her when deceived by the devilish Iago, and then kills himself.

O'Trigger, Sir Lucius. A fighting Irishman in Sheridan's comedy *The Rivals*. "A very pretty quarrel as it stands" is a phrase of Sir Lucius.

Overreach, Sir Giles. A proud and unscrupulous rascal in Massinger's comedy *A New Way to Pay Old Debts*.

Pallas. A name of Minerva.

Pamela, pa-mē'la or pam'ē-la. The heroine of a novel by Richardson, a servant who resists her master's attempts to seduce her, and ultimately becomes his wife.

Pan. Among the Greeks and Romans a god of flocks and herds, represented with two horns, pointed ears, and goat's legs.

Pan, Peter. The whimsical hero of Sir James Barrie's play of the same name. He is known as the boy who did not wish to grow up.

Pando'ra. In classical myth. a woman sent by the gods to bring evils upon men as a punishment for the theft of fire by Prometheus. Prometheus would not have anything to do with her, but his brother Epimetheus married her. Later accounts say she had a box of blessings, which was incautiously opened so that all the contents except hope escaped.

Pangloss, Dr. A ridiculous pedant in Colman's comedy *The Heir-at-law*.—Also the name of an optimistic character in Voltaire's *Candide*.

Pantag'ruel. An enormous giant, son of Gargantua in Rabelais' famous romance. See *Gargantua*.

Panurge, pan-ėrj. An important character in Rabelais' romance of *Gargantua and Pantagruel*, a great friend of the latter. In spite of his being a drunkard, rogue, and coward, he is remarkably clever and amusing.

Panza, Sancho, sän'chō pän'thä or san'kō pan'za. See *Don Quixote*.

Par'is. The son of Priam of Troy, celebrated for passing judgment as to the comparative beauty of the three goddesses, Hera, Aphrodite, and Athene (Juno, Venus, and Minerva); and for carrying off Helen, the wife of Menelaus, and thus causing the Trojan war.

Parolles, pa-rol'es. A braggart and coward in Shakespeare's *All's Well*.

Patroc'lus. The bosom friend of Achilles in Homer's *Iliad*. He was slain by Hector.

Patterne, Sir Willoughby. The hero of Meredith's book *The Egoist*.

Peck'sniff. In Dickens's *Martin Chuzzlewit*, a sleek, unctuous hypocrite, an architect by profession.

Penelope, pe-nel'o-pē. The wife who, during her husband's long absence from home, is pestered with wooers. She remains faithful, however, and puts them off by saying she will wed no one till the web she has in hand is finished. Every night she unravels what she has woven by day.

Penthesilea, pen-thes-i-lē'a. In Homer and Virgil, a queen of the Amazons.

Per'dita. The heroine of Shakespeare's *Winter's Tale*, daughter of Leontes, King of Sicily. She was exposed as a child and brought up as a shepherdess.

Perseus, per'sūs. The son of Zeus and Danaë. He slew the Gorgon Medusa and by means of her head turned a sea monster to stone and so rescued Andromeda.

Petruchio, pe-trö'çhi-ō. The hero of Shakespeare's *Taming of the Shrew*, husband of the shrew Katharina.

Phædra. Wife of Theseus, who fell in love with her stepson Hippolytus.

Philoctetes, fi-lok-tē'tēz. A Greek hero who had been a companion of Hercules and had some of this hero's arrows, without which Troy could not be taken; the subject of a tragedy by Sophocles.

Pickwick, Samuel. The hero of Dickens's *Pickwick Papers*, in which are narrated the diverting experiences of Mr. Pickwick and certain members of a club named after him, especially Messrs. Winkle, Tupman, and Snodgrass.

Pied Piper of Hamelin. A wonderful musician of German legend who pipes away all the rats from the town of Hamelin, but is defrauded of his promised reward, and thereupon pipes away the children of the town, who with him enter a neighbouring hill and are never more seen.

Pistol. A follower of Falstaff in Shakespeare's plays, a ranting, swaggering bully and coward.

Pla'giary, Sir Fretful. A character in Sheridan's comedy *The Critic*, a vain and irritable playwright.

Polo'nius. Lord Chamberlain of Denmark in Shakespeare's *Hamlet*, father of Laërtes and Ophelia, garrulous and not without worldly wisdom, but not so wise as he thinks.

Polyphe'mus. A Cyclops or one-eyed giant in Homer's *Odyssey*, who imprisoned Ulysses and his companions in his cave and devoured some of them. The rest, however, blinded him when in a drunken sleep and escaped.

Porthos. One of the Three Musketeers in Dumas' novel of that name. He is a man of great physical strength and of unswerving loyalty.

Portia, pōr'shi-a. A rich heiress in Shakespeare's *Merchant of Venice*, whose father has settled that the suitor whom she marries must first select from three sealed caskets the one which contains her picture. Fortunately her lover, Bassanio, chooses rightly. Disguised as a doctor of law, she afterwards gives judgment against Shylock the Jew. See *Shylock*.

Poseidon, po-sī'don. The Greek sea god corresponding to Neptune.

Poyser, Mrs. In George Eliot's *Adam Bede*, a farmer's wife remarkable for the sharpness of her tongue, and her pithy and epigrammatic sayings.

Pri'am. The King of Troy in the classical story of the Trojan war, father of Hector and Paris, and husband of Hecuba, slain by Pyrrhus.

Primrose, Dr. The vicar in Goldsmith's famous *Vicar of Wakefield*, a good and simple man with amiable weaknesses and vanities.

Prometheus, prō-mē'thūs. A divine personage of Greek mythology, who brought fire from heaven to man, and was punished by Zeus (Jupiter), who had him chained to a rock of Mount Caucasus, where an eagle or vulture fed constantly on his liver till he was delivered by Chiron.

Pro'serpine. The daughter of Ceres and wife of Pluto, who caught her while she was gathering flowers in Sicily and carried her off to the lower world.

Pros'pero. The magician and exiled Duke of Milan in Shakespeare's *Tempest*, father of Miranda, and master of Ariel and Caliban.

Proudie, Mrs. The nagging, domineering wife of the Bishop in Trollope's *Barchester Towers* and *Last Chronicle of Barset*.

Puck. Another name for Robin Goodfellow (q.v.).

Puff. A literary quack "a professor of the art of puffing," as he calls himself, in Sheridan's comedy *The Critic*.

Pylades, pil'a-dēz. The bosom friend of Orestes.

Pyramus and Thisbe, pir'a-mus, thiz'bē. In Ovid's *Metamorphoses*, two lovers of Babylon, whose parents were against their marriage. They conversed in secret and agreed to meet at the tomb of Ninus. Thisbe arrived first, but ran away at the sight of a lioness. Unfortunately she dropped her robe and this the wild beast proceeded to worry. When Pyramus arrived he saw the garment, stained with blood from the lioness's mouth, and, concluding that his lover was dead, he killed himself. Thisbe did likewise when she discovered the tragedy. The story is introduced in Shakespeare's *Midsummer-Night's Dream*.

Quixote, Don. See *Don Quixote*.

Ras'selas. A prince of Abyssinia in a moral tale by Dr. Johnson. He is detained in delightful captivity in a certain "happy valley". From this he escapes and travels through the world, but, finding no greater happiness there, returns to his old abode.

Re'gan. One of King Lear's unnatural daughters.

Rhadaman'thus. A legendary king of Lycia, who for his justice was made after death a judge in the other world.

Ridd, John. Hero of R. D. Blackmore's *Lorna Doone*.

Robin Hood. See *Hood*.

Rochester. The morose hero of Charlotte Brontë's *Jane Eyre*.

Roe, Richard. A fictitious character whose name formerly appeared in certain English legal proceedings along with that of John Doe.

Ro'land. A hero of tales connected with Charlemagne, whose nephew he was. He is said to have been killed in the rout of Charlemagne's rearguard at Roncesvalles.

Ro'meo. The hero of Shakespeare's tragedy *Romeo and Juliet*, one of the Montague family.

Rom'ola. The heroine of a novel of the same name, by George Eliot, the scene of which is Florence in the time of Savonarola and the revival of learning in Italy.

Romulus, rom'ū-lus. The legendary founder and first king of Rome, twin brother of Remus.

Rosalind, roz'a-lind. The sprightly and charming daughter of the banished duke in Shakespeare's *As You Like It.*

Rosinante, roz'i-nan-tā. Don Quixote's famous steed.

Round Table. The large circular table at which King Arthur and his knights used to sit, giving its name to an order of knighthood instituted by the king.

Rowland, rō'land. Same as *Roland*. Rowland and Oliver were two of the most renowned of Charlemagne's heroes, and their names became proverbial.

Scheherazade or Shahrazad, shā-ė-ra-zäd', shä-ra-zäd'. The bride of the Sultan Shariyar, and the narrator of the stories that form the *Arabian Nights.*

Schlemihl, Peter, shlā'mēl. The hero of a short German story by Chamisso. The book relates how he sold his shadow to a "man in gray", and the misfortunes that thereafter attend him.

Scrible'rus, Marti'nus. A fictitious character, a man of learning but no taste, the subject of humorous memoirs written by Dr. John Arbuthnot in conjunction with Pope.

Scrooge, skröj. In Dickens's *Christmas Carol,* a "grasping, covetous old hunks" of a London merchant, who is converted to an entirely different disposition by a series of visions or dream pictures he sees at Christmas.

Scylla, sil'a. In ancient geography a rock in the Strait of Messina which, with the adjacent whirlpool **Charybdis** (ka-rib'dis) was proverbial as a source of danger to mariners, since in trying to avoid the one they were liable to encounter the other. Scylla was also represented as a hideous monster.

Semele, sem'e-le. In ancient myth. the mother of Bacchus by Jupiter.

Shallow, Justice. A foolish justice in Shakespeare's *Merry Wives* and *Henry IV* (second part).

Shandy, Tristram. The titular hero of Sterne's *Life and Opinions of Tristram Shandy,* in which, however, his father and uncle, "Uncle Toby", take the chief place.

Sharp, Becky. One of the two chief female characters in Thackeray's *Vanity Fair*—clever, good-looking, heartless, ambitious, and utterly unscrupulous.

Shy'lock. The Jew in Shakespeare's *Merchant of Venice,* who lends money to Antonio, "the merchant", stipulating that if it is not paid at a certain date he may take a pound of his debtor's flesh.

Siegfried, zēg'frēt. A hero of Teutonic legend, who is celebrated in the German epic the *Nibelungenlied. Sigurd* is another form of the name.

Sikes, Bill. A brutal housebreaker in Dickens's *Oliver Twist,* who murders the girl Nancy who lives with him. He is accidentally hanged by a rope in trying to escape.

Silence. A country justice, friend of Justice Shallow, in Shakespeare's *Henry IV* (part two).

Sile'nus. In classical myth. the companion of Bacchus, represented as a jovial, drunken, sensual old man.

Sind'bad the Sailor. A merchant and mariner in the *Arabian Nights* who makes several wonderful voyages.

Sis'yphus. In Greek myth, a man condemned to roll a great stone up a hill in Hades. When it reached the top, it immediately rolled down again.

Sly, Christopher. A tinker in the "Induction" to Shakespeare's *Taming of the Shrew,* who, being dead drunk, is dressed up and made to fancy himself a lord.

Smike. An ill-used boy in Dickens's *Nicholas Nickleby,* befriended by Nicholas and discovered to be the son of his Uncle Ralph.

Squeers. In Dickens's *Nicholas Nickleby,* the ignorant and brutal schoolmaster of Dotheboys Hall.

Stella. A name given by Swift to Esther Johnson, with whom he was long on most intimate terms.

Steyne, Marquis of, stān. A great English nobleman who figures in Thackeray's *Vanity Fair,* and also appears in *Pendennis.*

Stre'phon. The name of a shepherd in Sir Philip Sidney's *Arcadia;* often used in a general sense for a rural swain.

Struld'brugs. Wretched beings described in Swift's *Gulliver's Travels,* living in Luggnagg. They cannot die, though they suffer all the infirmities of old age.

Surface, Charles. A spendthrift but good-hearted fellow in Sheridan's *School for Scandal.* His brother Joseph is a plausible hypocrite who professes much prudence and benevolence.

Svengali. The villain in Du Maurier's *Trilby.* While the heroine is in a hypnotic trance, he teaches her to sing.

Swiv'eller, Dick. The light-hearted and amusing shabby-genteel clerk to Sampson Brass in Dickens's *Old Curiosity Shop.* He eventually comes into a small annuity and marries "The Marchioness".

Syc'orax. A foul witch mentioned in Shakespeare's *Tempest,* mother of Caliban.

Tannhäuser, tän-hoi-zėr. In German legend, a knight who gains admission into a hill where Venus holds her court, and there remains for years sunk in sensual delights. Being at last allowed to go, he repairs to Rome to seek absolution from the pope, but is refused, and thereupon returns and is no more seen.

Tapley, Mark. In Dickens's *Martin Chuzzlewit,* the humble friend who accompanies young Martin to America, and whose pride in life it is to keep "jolly" in the most depressing circumstances.

Tartuffe, tär-töf'. A hypocritical priest in Molière's comedy of same name; hence anyone who uses religion as a cloak.

Tearsheet, Doll. A courtesan in Shakespeare's *King Henry IV* (part two).

Teazle, Lady. The heroine of Sheridan's *School for Scandal,* wife of Sir Peter Teazle, who is much her senior. She is ignorant of the world, thoughtless and imprudent, and thus gives rise to scandal though really fond of her husband.

Telemachus, te-lem'a-kus. Son of Ulysses. When his father had been long absent after the fall of Troy, Telemachus went in quest of him, accompanied by Athene in the form of Mentor.

Thalia. The Muse of Comedy.

The'mis. The Greek goddess of justice.

Thersites, thėr-sī'tēz. The ugliest and most scurrilous of the Greeks in the Trojan war.

Theseus, thē'sūs. A famous legendary king of Athens who overcame the Centaurs and slew the Minotaur with the assistance of Ariadne, whom he afterwards deserted.

The'tis. A sea-nymph of Greek myth., mother of Achilles by Peleus.

Thor. The Scandinavian god of thunder.

Tilburi'na. Daughter of the governor of Tilbury Fort, a character in the burlesque tragedy introduced in Sheridan's comedy *The Critic*.

Ti'mon. A misanthropical Athenian, the hero of Shakespeare's *Timon of Athens*.

Tire'sias. A celebrated blind soothsayer of Greek fable.

Tisiphone, ti-sif'o-nē. In classical myth. one of the three Furies.

Tita'nia. The queen of the fairies and wife of Oberon.

Ti'tans. A race of giant Greek deities who warred against Saturn and Jupiter, and were thrown into Tartarus.

Titho'nus. A young man of whom Aurora is fabled to have been enamoured and whom Jupiter made immortal, but as he was not also endowed with perpetual youth he withered away and was changed into a cicada.

Touchstone. A wise and witty clown in Shakespeare's *As You Like It*.

Trim, Corporal. An old soldier acting as servant to Uncle Toby in Sterne's *Tristram Shandy*, simple, ignorant, honest, and affectionate.

Trin'culo. A jester in Shakespeare's *Tempest*.

Triptol'emus. A Greek hero, the patron of agriculture and inventor of the plough, son of Demeter or Ceres.

Tro'ilus. A son of Priam of Troy, represented in post-classical times as in love with Cressida.

Troy. See *Ilium*.

Trulliber, Parson. A coarse, ignorant clergyman in Fielding's *Joseph Andrews*.

Trun'nion, Commodore. An old retired sea-dog in Smollett's *Peregrine Pickle*.

Twist, Oliver. Hero of Dickens's novel of the same name, a boy of good parentage brought up in a workhouse and thrown among thieves in London, but always gentle and innocent.

Tyb'alt. A fiery young Capulet in Shakespeare's *Romeo and Juliet*, who slays Mercutio and is slain by Romeo.

Tyr, tēr. In Scandinavian myth, the god of war, son of Odin and brother of Thor.

Ulysses, ū-lis'sēz, in Greek **Odysseus,** ō-dis'ūs. King of Ithaca, one of the heroes of the Trojan war, husband of Penelope and father of Telemachus; his wanderings after the war form the subject of the *Odyssey*.

Una. A lovely damsel in Spenser's *Faërie Queene*, a personification of truth. She is introduced as riding on a white ass and leading a lamb; and she comes to the court of the fairy queen Gloriana to get a champion to slay a destructive dragon, the Red Cross Knight being accordingly sent with her. When separated from the Red Cross Knight a lion fawns on her and becomes her attendant. Eventually she is married to the Red Cross Knight.

Uncle Toby. See *Shandy*.

Undine, un'dīn, Germ. ün-dē'nė. A water-nymph or sylph, heroine of a charming German story by de la Motte Fouqué.

Ura'nia. The muse who presided over astronomy.

Uranus, ū'ra-nus. A Greek deity, represented as the most ancient of the gods, the father of Cron'os or Saturn and grandfather of Zeus or Jupiter. The name means literally heaven.

Valentine and Orson. The heroes of an old romance, twin brothers born in a forest, and the one suckled and brought up by a bear, the other reared at the king's court. Orson became a wild man of the forest, but was ultimately reclaimed from savagery by his brother.

Valhalla. The banquet-hall of slain warriors.

Valkyrias. The fatal sisters of Odin, usually nine in number, the choosers of the slain.

Valjean, Jean. In Victor Hugo's *Les Misérables*, a released convict, sentenced for a venial offence.

Vanessa. A name given by Swift to Esther Vanhomrigh, who loved him, followed him to Ireland, and died of a broken heart.

Vath'ek. The hero of Beckford's powerful romance of the same name, an eastern monarch guilty of the greatest crimes, in league with demons, and eventually entombed in the abyss of Eblis or hell.

Vernon, Diana. The heroine of Scott's *Rob Roy*, perhaps the most charming of all his female characters—beautiful, well-read, and educated, fond of field-sports, spirited and self-reliant. We meet with her at Osbaldistone Hall and in the Highlands, and are told that she became the wife of Frank Osbaldistone.

Vicar of Wakefield. See *Primrose*.

Vulcan, Vulca'nus. The Roman deity who presided over fire and the working of metals, identified with the similar Greek deity Hephæstus.

Wadman, Widow. A buxom lady in Sterne's *Tristram Shandy*, whose wiles nearly captivate Uncle Toby.

Wandering Jew. A Jew who, according to a legend that arose in the middle ages, was condemned for harsh treatment of Christ to wander over the world till his second coming.

Wandering Willie (Willie Steenson). In Scott's *Redgauntlet*, a blind fiddler who relates what is probably one of the finest short stories in our literature.

Wa'verley. The first of Scott's great series of novels, to which it gives its name. The hero is Edward Waverley, a young English gentleman, and the scene is chiefly in Scotland, during the rebellion of 1745.

Weller, Sam. The valet or personal attendant of Mr. Pickwick in Dickens's *Pickwick Papers*, a genuine Londoner, ready-witted, uneducated, full of humour, and devoted to his master's interests.

Western, Squire. A jolly, ignorant, coarse, hot-tempered, and intensely prejudiced English squire in Fielding's *Tom Jones*. His charming daughter Sophia is in love with and marries Tom Jones.

Whiskeran'dos, Don. The lover of Tilburina in Puff's ridiculous tragedy which is introduced into Sheridan's comedy *The Critic*.

Wimble, Will. An amusing character in the *Spectator*, a member of the club to which Sir Roger de Coverley and others belong.

Winkle, Rip Van. An American Dutchman, hero of a story by Washington Irving, a good-humoured, indolent sort of fellow, who encounters a strange company playing at ninepins in the Kaatskill Mountains; and having tasted their liquor falls asleep and does not awake for twenty years.

Wooden Horse. A huge figure of a horse made of wood, and containing armed Greeks, which the Trojans were induced by the Greeks to admit into Troy, thus leading to the capture of the city.

Worldly Wiseman, Mr. A character in *The Pilgrim's Progress* who, by his talk, endeavours to prevent Christian from completing his journey.

Ygg'drasil. The tree of the universe, a huge ash which holds an important place in Scandinavian mythology and cosmogony.

Yor'ick. Jester to the king of Denmark in Shakespeare's *Hamlet*. Sterne has introduced a personage of this name into his *Tristram Shandy*—simple, light-hearted, and humorous—intended as a portrait of himself.

Zeph'yrus, Zephyr. In classical myth, a personification of the west wind.

Zeus. See *Jupiter*.

19.95

Margareta Fuchs/Veronika Krapf

Von wilden und weisen Frauen

lœwenzahn

tirol
Unser Land

AUTONOME PROVINZ BOZEN SÜDTIROL | PROVINCIA AUTONOMA DI BOLZANO ALTO ADIGE

Deutsche Kultur und Familie

Gefördert vom Land Tirol/Abteilung Kultur und der Südtiroler Landesregierung/Abteilung Deutsche Kultur und Familie.

E-Mail: loewenzahn@studienverlag.at
Internet: www.loewenzahn.at

Satz: loewenzahn/Manuela Weiß
Umschlaggestaltung: loewenzahn/Kurt Höretzeder, Büro für Grafische Gestaltung, Scheffau/Tirol
Alle Fotografien: Ursula Fuchs Hofer

Gedruckt auf umweltfreundlichem, chlor- und säurefrei gebleichtem Papier.

Bibliografische Information Der Deutschen Bibliothek
Die Deutsche Bibliothek verzeichnet diese Publikation in der Deutschen Nationalbibliografie; detaillierte bibliografische Daten sind im Internet über <http://dnb.ddb.de> abrufbar.

ISBN 978-3-7066-2443-5

Margareta Fuchs/Veronika Krapf

Von wilden und weisen Frauen

150 geheimnisvolle Frauen-Sagen aus Tirol

mit Fotografien von Ursula Fuchs Hofer

lœwenzahn

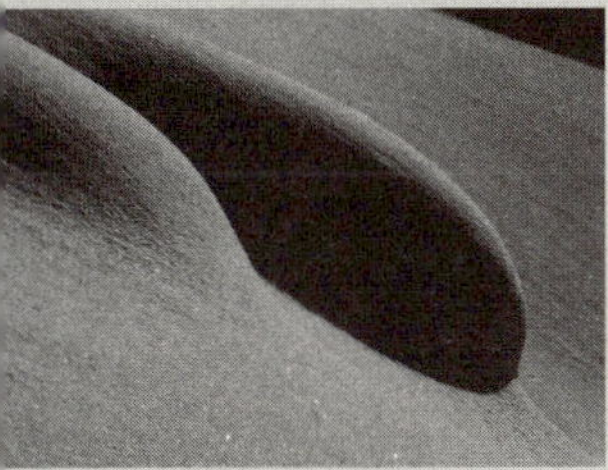
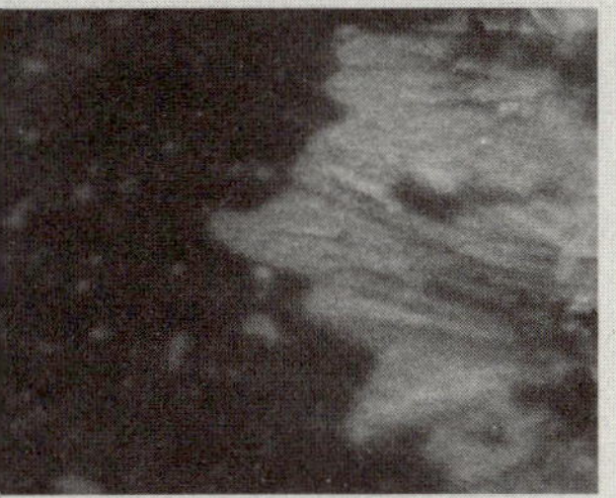

Inhalt

Inhalt

Inhalt

Vorwort

Als sich der bayrische Schriftsteller und Tirolforscher Ludwig Steub auf seiner Tirolreise im Jahre 1842 während einer Rast in einem Ötztaler Wirtshaus nach den örtlichen Sagen erkundigte, bekam er von seinem Gegenüber, einem älteren Herrn, die entrüstete Antwort: „Was? Sagen? Wir haben keine Sagen im Ötztale! ... Wir sind aufgeklärt im Ötztal, so aufgeklärt als anderswo! ...“ Ludwig Steub und seine Reisebegleiter benötigten einige Zeit, um den aufgebrachten Herrn wieder versöhnlich zu stimmen: seine Frage nach den Volkssagen hatte den Ötztaler regelrecht beleidigt, er fühlte sich und sein Tal dadurch ins Lächerliche gezogen. Allerdings war er nicht der Einzige, der damals so dachte: bereits knappe zwanzig Jahre vorher waren einige Sagen aus diesem Tal in einer Zeitung abgedruckt worden, was die Ötztaler dermaßen in Rage gebracht hatte, dass sie sich beim Landgericht in Silz im Bezirk Imst erkundigten, „wie sie den böswilligen Injurianten gerichtlich belangen könnten, welcher der Ehre ihres Landes so nahe getreten war und sie noch mit alten Geschichten höhnte ...“

In der Zwischenzeit hat sich die Einstellung zu dem über viele Generationen hinweg überlieferten Erzählgut gottlob geändert. Ähnlich der Wiederaufwertung alter Traditionen und Bräuche sind die Sagen heute wieder populär geworden.

Zahlreiche Sagen im Tiroler Raum sind erfasst und aufgeschrieben worden, die meisten davon in der zweiten Hälfte des 19. Jahrhunderts. Etliche dieser Sagen, welche durch unermüdliche Sammler wie Ignaz V. Zingerle, Adolf Heyl, Johann Nepomuk Mahl-Schedl (Ritter von Alpenburg), Christian Schneller, Karl Felix Wolff u.a. in mühsamer Forschungsarbeit zusammengetragen worden sind, haben wir in unser Buch aufgenommen. Die hier ausgewählten Sagen und Legenden stammen aus dem Gebiet des Alt-Tirols: neben Südtiroler Geschichten finden sich Nord- und Osttiroler Sagen sowie Geschichten und Legenden aus dem Trentino, aus den dortigen deutschen Sprachinseln und aus dem ampezzanischen Dolomitengebiet. Manche dieser Geschichten haben wir in ihrer ursprünglichen Sprache belassen, obwohl sie sich manchmal etwas mühsam lesen; doch auch der Wandel im sprachlichen Ausdruck stellt, so finden wir, ein interessantes Phänomen dar. Einige Sagen wurden von uns übersetzt und nacherzählt, manchmal umgeschrieben, gekürzt oder sprachlich angepasst, doch haben wir stets darauf geachtet, die Sagen so wenig wie möglich zu verändern.

Nicht aufgenommen wurden die sogenannten „Dolomitensagen" von Karl Felix Wolff u.a. Sie sind größtenteils bereits anderweitig publiziert und ausführlich analysiert worden, vor allem aber zwang uns ihre zumeist platzfüllende Erzähllänge zu dieser nicht leichten Entscheidung.

Der Begriff „Sage", so haben wir immer gelernt, hängt mit dem Wort „sagen" zusammen, also mit dem mündlichen Erzählen, mit dem „Gesagten". Laut der feministischen Forscherin Barbara Walker jedoch bedeutet das altnordische „Saga" wörtlich „Sie-die-spricht". Gemeint ist die skandinavische Orakelpriesterin, eine weibliche Weise im Besitz der heiligen Poesie. Diese Geschichten wurden laut Walker von den „Sagas", den „Sagerinnen" aufbewahrt und auch in Runenzeichen niedergeschrieben, zumal das Lesen und Schreiben/Legen von Runen in erster Linie eine Frauenangelegenheit war.

In unserem Buch wollen wir die verschiedenen Tiroler „Sagerinnen" zu Wort kommen lassen. Seltsame und geheimnisvolle Frauen begegnen uns in diesen teilweise uralten Sagen. Manche lassen die Zeiten erahnen, in denen das Wissen um die Bedeutung des Weiblich-Göttlichen noch allgegenwärtig und eine tiefe Verbundenheit zur Natur und allen ihr innewohnenden Wesen selbstverständlich waren.

Sie verdeutlichen aber auch, wie sich Rolle und Position der Frau in der Gesellschaft im Laufe der Zeit verändert haben; sie beschreiben die Geschichte ihres Machtverfalls, zeigen auf, wie aus der einstmals hochrespektierten Weisen Frau die gefährliche Hexe wurde, die es zu bekämpfen galt, so wie ihr Wissen schlussendlich ins Lächerliche gezogen wurde.

In den Tiroler Sagen haben wilde, unzähmbare Weiber, rätselhafte Seherinnen, unbekannte Königinnen überlebt. Diesen und allen anderen Frauenfiguren möchten wir unser Buch widmen, ihre zunehmend in Vergessenheit geratenen Geschichten wieder erzählen und mit neuem Leben füllen.

Sagen spiegeln aber auch die jeweiligen religiös-moralischen Wertevorgaben einer Gesellschaft wider. So berichten zahlreiche Tiroler Geschichten beispielsweise von Frauen, die für das Ausleben ihrer Sinnlichkeit und Lebensfreude teuer büßen müssen; sie schildern von ihrer Gefährdung durch den „Leibhaftigen", den Teufel. Oft gewannen wir den Eindruck, dass eine Sage im Laufe der Zeit „manipuliert" wurde, dass ein neues Sagenende, zumeist ein moralisierendes, bestrafendes, zu einem späteren Zeitpunkt hinzugefügt wurde. Frömmigkeit und Bescheidenheit, Sparsamkeit und Enthaltsamkeit sind nur einige der in vielen Sagen als erstrebenswert dargestellten weiblichen Tugenden. Sagen übermitteln somit oft auch eine gesellschaftspädagogische Botschaft, doch wer sich in dieses Erzählgut vertieft, entdeckt auch Geschichten, die von Mut, Authentizität und Solidarität, vor allem aber von der wunderbaren Kraft der Liebe erzählen.

Beim oberflächlichen Lesen einer Sage ist es vor allem der spannungsgeladene, manchmal geheimnisvoll-schaurige Inhalt, der uns beeindruckt. Doch eine Sage ist wie eine Zwiebel, in Besitz vieler Schalen. Es sind dies die „Schichten" der sich im Laufe der Zeit wandelnden gesellschaftlichen Wertevorgaben und religiösen Weltanschauungen. Die Sagen öffnen Fenster zu diesen weit zurückliegenden Zeiten, gewähren einen kleinen Einblick in die Gefühls-, Gedanken- und Vorstellungswelt unserer VorfahrInnen. Für sie bestand die Welt nicht nur aus einer materiellen Dimension; auch andere, unsichtbare Wirklichkeiten wurden wahr- und ernstgenommen, für die der heutige Mensch in seinem mechanistischen Naturverständnis oft nur mehr ein spöttisches Lächeln übrig hat. Diese ganzheitliche Wahrnehmung unserer Vorfahren, das Wissen um den Wirkungsbereich der Elemente Erde, Wasser, Feuer, Luft, hat sich in den Sagen in der Erscheinungsform der „Elementarwesen" wie Riesinnen, Fanggen usw. festgesetzt.

Viele Tiroler Sagen stehen mit einem klar benannten Ort, Berg, Gewässer, Schloss u.a. in Verbindung. Solche Sagen erweisen sich oft als Wegweiser zu außergewöhnlichen und geschichtsträchtigen Plätzen, zu christlichen und/oder vorchristlichen Kultorten.

Alte Völker und Kulturen haben aber nicht nur örtlich ihren Fußabdruck hinterlassen. Germanische, römische, keltische, etruskische, rätische und venetische Siedlungsspuren lassen sich auch in den Tiroler Sagen und ihren Figuren ausmachen wie beispielsweise in den „Venediger Manndlen" oder den in österreichischen Sagen überlieferten „Fenes-Leuten": solche und viele andere Bezeichnungen, vielleicht auch der Name „Fanis" des sagenhaften ladinischen Reiches, erinnern an die Veneter, laut manchen Forschern das älteste europäische Volk, das um ca. 1000 v. Chr. aus dem Osten auch in die Alpenregion und nach Tirol gekommen war und u.a. auf dem Gebiet des Bergbaus große Kenntnis hatte. Rätia oder Reit(h)ia, die große rätovenetische Mutter-Gottheit, deren Spuren wir beispielsweise im Nonstal und auf dem Ritten begegnen, gemahnt mit ihren Wesenszügen als Heilerin und Herrin der Tiere an die Gestalt der Seligen oder Saligen in der Tiroler Sagenwelt.

Da die Sagen trotz oder wegen ihrer Kürze sehr komplexe Überlieferungsträger sind, findet sich unter jeder in diesem Buch wiedergegebenen Sage ein kürzerer oder längerer informativer Anhang, den wir „Wissenswertes" genannt haben. Er ist für jene LeserInnen gedacht, die mehr über den spezifischen Sagenhintergrund, die symbolische Bedeutung der Sagenelemente und die kultur- und mythengeschichtlichen Zusammenhänge mit anderen Regionen und Ländern erfahren möchten.

Unser Buch ist in zehn Kapitel gegliedert, in welchen von den verschiedenen weiblichen Sagengestalten erzählt wird. Zum besseren Verständnis beginnt jedes Kapitel mit einer Beschreibung der jeweiligen Sagenfigur, da manche von ihnen laut unserer Erfahrung vor allem in der jüngeren Bevölkerung kaum mehr bekannt sind, wie beispielsweise die Stampe, die Fangga oder die Trute. Auch einige erklärende Hinweise zum Kontext, in welchen die Sagengestalt eingebettet ist, werden hier erwähnt.

Das letzte Kapitel erzählt einige Tiroler Legenden um Maria und andere weibliche Heilige. Da wir in unserem Buch, wie vorhin erwähnt, auch Mythenzusammenhänge und -hintergründe aufzeigen wollen, finden sich auch dort einige Bemerkungen zu den „Ahninnen“ der christlichen Heiligen, ohne dadurch das christlich-religiöse Empfinden einiger LeserInnen brüskieren zu wollen. Doch zahlreiche christliche Heilige sind ÜberlieferungsträgerInnen uralter Mythen und haben häufig den Platz vorchristlicher Gottheiten eingenommen.

Im Laufe der Jahrhunderte, und dabei spielte die Haltung der frühen christlichen Religion eine richtungsweisende Rolle, hat eine schrittweise Entheiligung der Natur stattgefunden. Auch musste das einstige magische, gefühlvollere Weltbild zunehmend einer starren „wissenschaftlichen“ Einsicht weichen, die menschliche Wahrnehmung auf eine rein materielle Ebene reduziert werden. Diese Entweihung der Natur und der Missbrauch des Naturraums als „politisches“, vorwiegend männliches Machtinstrument, haben zu einer dramatischen menschlichen Abgeschnittenheit von der Schöpfung geführt und das Wissen um die der Natur innewohnenden Kräfte, das für unsere Vorfahren noch selbstverständlich war und sich in vielen Sagen und Mythen niedergeschlagen hat, verdrängt.

Die „mythische“ Eingebundenheit in ein größeres Ganzes ist nicht nur bei unseren VorfahrInnen, sondern bei allen Völkern weltweit beleg- und nachvollziehbar; sie führt uns tief in die Geschichte der Religion, der Bedeutung der Mythen, ja in die Geschichte der Menschheit selbst sowie in den Bereich der Psychologie hinein, wir erfahren von archetypischen Bildern, von den menschlichen Ursymbolen, die seit Tausenden von Jahren auf der ganzen Welt in Geschichten, Bildern und Symbolen, in unseren Träumen und in der künstlerischen Darstellung immer wieder aus dem kollektiven Unbewussten auftauchen.

In der Sagenforschung spielt deshalb neben der Recherche laut unserer Erfahrung auch die Vertiefung der Sagenthemen auf emotionaler Ebene eine wichtige Rolle; nicht Alles ist mit Verstand und Logik erklärbar. Hierfür ist auch das Aufsuchen von „sagenhaften“ Plätzen aufschlussreich, denn oft können wir deren Energien erst dadurch wahrnehmen und viele Sagen auf einer tieferen und nachhaltigeren Weise erfahren und begreifen.

Mystische Naturfotografien der Sterzingerin Ursula Fuchs Hofer unterstreichen auf eindrucksvolle Weise das Eingebundensein der Sagenfiguren in das Reich der Natur und deren geheimnisvolle Ausstrahlung, die nur wahrnehmen kann, wer sich ausreichend Zeit und emotionale Offenheit für dieses „Sehen“ zugesteht.

Wir wünschen unserem Sagenbuch, dass es eine spannende und bereichernde Lektüre wird, sowohl für sageninteressierte Laien als auch für Sagen- und MärchenkennerInnen – für alle, die Freude an Sagen, Märchen und Mythen haben. Die Wiederentdeckung der in ihnen enthaltenen Weisheit geht Hand in Hand mit der Rückbesinnung auf die Weisheit der Natur, unser Aller Mutter, Terra Mater. Unser Wunsch ist es somit auch, mit dieser Sammlung einen kleinen Beitrag zu leisten gegen die fortschreitende Zerstörung der Natur und ihrer Wesen(heiten).

Margareta Fuchs und Veronika Krapf

Fangga und Riesin

Viele Völker der Welt besitzen mythische Geschichten von **Riesinnen** und Riesen (althochdeutsch „risi/riso“ oder „wrisil“ = „stark“), unter anderem die Eskimos, Indianer, Inder und afrikanische Völker. Jene der Griechen mit den Titanen, Giganten und Zyklopen und den Riesen der nordischen Sagen gehören wohl zu den bekanntesten. Oft sind Riesen die ersten Wesen überhaupt im Kosmos, die am Anfang der Zeit – noch vor den Göttern – über die Welt herrschten, wie beispielsweise der/die zwittrige Urriese/in Ymir bei den Germanen, aus dessen/deren Körper Erde, Himmel und Meer geschaffen wurden.

In der nordischen Mythologie gibt es viele Erzählungen über Riesinnen: Die Riesin Sol verkörperte die Sonne, die Riesin Nott fuhr nachts mit ihrem Pferd über den Himmel, zur Meerriesin Ran gelangten die Ertrunkenen, in die wunderschöne Riesin Gerda verliebte sich der Gott Freyr, die starke, auf einem Wolf reitende Riesin Hyrrokin schob das Schiff der Asen, das wie festgenagelt im Sand lag und auf dem sich Balders Leiche befand, ins Wasser.

Auch die mittelalterlichen Heldensagen sind reich an Riesen und Riesinnen. Als Beispiel sei nur das Ecke-Lied mit den Riesen Ecke und Fasold genannt.

RiesInnen werden mit ungebärdiger, wilder Naturkraft assoziiert. Man dachte sie sich auf Bergen und Felsen hausend, und Steine und Felsen waren auch ihre Waffen. So schleuderte die Riesin Runze laut dem alten Volksglauben und ebenso im Eckelied Steine und Lawinen ins Tal. Auch auf Jochgrimm hauste eine Riesin namens Runza mit ihrem Mann. Den beiden schmeckte der Wein sehr gut und die Weinbauern aus dem Etschland mussten für sie immer genügend Wein in einer großen Grube bereithalten. Mit einem Schritt gelangte diese Riesin von Jochgrimm auf das Vigiljoch bei Marling.

Runzen oder Runsen waren im Pitztal, einem Nebental des Inntals, auch die Bezeichnungen für die riesigen Waldweiber. Laut örtlichen Sagen wohnten sie in sehr abgelegenen Waldgegenden und unzugänglichen Felsen. Sie waren sehr hässlich, hatten struppiges, langes Haar und große, rötliche Augen. Sie ließen sich aber nur sehr selten blicken.

Oft werden Riesinnen als einäugig, am ganzen Körper behaart oder mit über die Schultern zurückgeworfenen Brüsten beschrieben. In Sagen und Märchen stillen sie mitunter ihre Kinder dreimal sieben Jahre, was dann oft als Grund für ihr übermenschliches Wachstum genannt wird.

RiesInnen werden oft als gutmütig, aber einfältig dargestellt. Häufig wurden sie von Menschen überlistet, enttäuscht und betrogen. Da sie Heiden waren, wurden sie in vielen Gegenden von den Christen vertrieben. Meistens fanden sie ein gewaltsames Ende oder zogen davon, weil sie sich in ihrer Existenz schwer bedroht sahen.

Auch in der Tiroler Sagenwelt und Überlieferung werden Geschichten von Riesinnen oder ähnlichen Gestalten erzählt.

Eine weitere beeindruckende Sagengestalt ist die **Fangga** (Mehrzahl: Fanggen, Fenken, Fänggen, Fenggen), bekannt auch als Wildfangg, ein böses Waldweib. Längst nicht so viele Sagen berichten von ihnen, wie vergleichsweise von Saligen und Hexen, aber sie erscheinen uns genau so wichtig und mit interessantem mythischem Hintergrund. Naturverbundenheit, Einklang mit der Natur und besonders auch der nachhaltige Umgang mit ihr, speziell mit Bäumen und Wäldern, spielen bei dieser Sagenfigur eine wichtige Rolle.

Von ihrer Gestalt her werden die Fanggen beschrieben als grauenerregende Riesenweiber mit einer tiefen Männerstimme, über und über borstig behaart, mit einem breitem Mund, der von einem Ohr bis zum anderen reicht. Manchmal glühen ihre schwarzen Augen und sprühen Blitze. Als Bekleidung nutzen sie Wildkatzenpelze, Baumrinden, Flechten und Ähnliches. Selbst ihr Haar ist über und über voll Baumbart.

Das Leben der Fanggen ist an Bäume bzw. an Wälder gebunden. Wird irgendwo ein Baum gefällt oder ein Wald gerodet, verschwinden mit diesem die Fanggen. Dieser Wesenszug erinnert an die Dryaden und Hamadryaden in der griechischen Mythologie. Dryaden sind Baumgeister, Baumnymphen. Die Hamadryaden waren ebenso langlebig und an das Leben von Bäumen gebunden wie diese; sie lebten in den Bäumen, waren Teil von ihnen. Kein Baum durfte gefällt werden, ohne zuvor die Nymphen anzurufen. Geschah dies doch, wurde der Frevler bestraft. In der römischen Mythologie entsprachen den Hamadryaden die „*Virae querquetulanae*".

Auch die Fangga-Sagen weisen in die Zeit des Beginns der Christianisierung zurück. Ihr heidnischer Zug kommt in einigen Sagen zum Ausdruck, wie z.B. bei der hier angeführten Sage „Stutz-Förche", in der die Magd von religiösen Dingen nichts hören wollte. Auch von ihrer Scheu vor Gebeten, der christlichen Lehre, Messen und dem Läuten der Kirchenglocken wird öfters berichtet.

Es wird auch erzählt, ihnen würde nach dem Fleisch der Menschen gelüsten, besonders nach dem von Kindern, die sie zuvor oft mästen würden. Kinder, v.a. die Buben, sollten demnach nach dem Betläuten nicht mehr außer Haus gehen, um vor der Fangga sicher zu sein. Die Sage „Die böse Fenkin", in welcher eine Fangga einen Buben mästet, erinnert an das bekannte Grimm-Märchen „Hänsel und Gretel". Somit wurde die Fangga im Laufe der Zeit zum Kinderschreck.

Die Fanggen Tirols sind vorwiegend weiblich. Oftmals werden sie als die Gemahlinnen der Waldriesen bezeichnet. Sie sind ihnen allerdings nicht untertan, sondern ihnen gleichgestellt. Mancherorts gaben die Fanggen ihre eigenen Töchter als Mägde zu den Bauern in Dienst, um sie vor den wilden Vätern zu schützen. Beeindruckend sind ihre ungeheure Kraft und Stärke, welche sie auch zum Nutzen für den Bauern einsetzen.

Im Laufe der mündlichen Überlieferung erhalten sie immer menschlichere Züge. Allerdings behalten sie eine Abneigung vor dem Kreuzzeichen bei. Sie bleiben jedoch nur eine beschränkte Zeit bei den Menschen, welchen sie treu und fleißig dienen, um dann wieder in den Wald zurückgerufen zu werden, weil beispielsweise einer ihrer Angehörigen gestorben ist.

In Vorarlberg finden wir anstatt der riesigen Fanggen kleine Waldleute. Vom Äußeren her gleichen sie den Menschen, besitzen aber einen etwas gedrungeneren Körperbau. Sie wohnen in Felsenklüften und Erdhöhlen, den sogenannten Fenggalöchern. Kleine Fanggen kommen mitunter auch in Tirol vor. Trotz ihres kleinen Wuchses besitzen sie große Kräfte, sie zähmen Gämsen und Wölfe und halten sie als Reittiere oder trinken ihre Milch. Hierin erinnern sie an die Saligen, welche sich ebenso Gämsen als Haustiere hielten. Beide Sagengestalten besitzen großes Wissen um die Heilkräfte von Pflanzen.

Hauptsächlich bewohnten diese „wilden Weiber" einen großen Urwald im Urgtal zwischen Landeck und Ladis und einen weiteren Wald, „Bannwald" genannt, am Pillerberg im Oberinntal. Von mancher Fangga leben noch Sagen, die sich mit jenen von den Riesenfrauen mischen.

1

Frau Hütt (Frau Hitt)

Zu den Zeiten der Riesen, von denen manche meinen, dass sie schon beim Leben Noahs im Lande Tirol gesessen, lebte hoch auf dem Gebirge, zu dessen Füßen zu späteren Zeiten die Stadt Innsbruck entstehen sollte, eine Riesenkönigin, die hieß Frau Hütt.

Ihr Felsenschloss war aus lauter Kristall gebaut, dessen Funkeln und Glänzen bis hinunter in die Talniederungen zu sehen war. Das Reich der Riesenkönigin war schöner als alle Rosengärten, voll herrlicher Wälder und Almwiesen und mit fruchtbarem Weideland.

Frau Hütt hatte einen einzigen kleinen Sohn, den sie über alles liebte. Eines Tages riss der Riesenknabe eine junge Tanne aus, um sich damit ein Steckenpferd zu machen, aber zufällig befand sich die Tanne am Rande eines sumpfigen Mooses, und da geschah es, dass das Erdreich unter seinen Füssen nachgab und er, mit dem Baum in seiner Hand, bis zum Haupt im tiefen Moder einsank. Zwar gelang es ihm, sich allein aus diesem unfreiwilligen Moorbad zu befreien, aber er war über und über voll schwarzem Schlamm, der auf dem Rückweg zur Mutter überall zu Boden tropfte.

Frau Hütt tröstete ihren kleinen, schmutzigen Sohn, sie versprach ihm ein neues schönes Röcklein und befahl ihrem Diener, ihn zu entkleiden und ihm mit weichen weißen Brosamen den schwarzen Schlamm wegzuputzen. Kaum aber hatte dieser begonnen, mit der heiligen Gottesgabe so sündlich umzugehen, verdunkelte sich der Himmel, ein schweres Gewitter zog auf, heftige Erdstöße erschütterten das Gebirge und der wunderschöne Palast der Königin Hütt stürzte in einem Trümmerhaufen zusammen. Von den höchsten Berggipfeln donnerten Lawinen und Muren zu Tal und begruben das fruchtbare Königreich unter riesigen Steinmassen. Im selben Augenblick wurde die Riesenkönigin, ihren kleinen Sohn im Arm haltend, zur Felsgestalt versteinert, und so wird sie stehen bis zum jüngsten Tage.

›› Wissenswertes ‹‹

In der Sagen- und Märchenwelt gibt es zahlreiche Versteinerungsgeschichten. Meistens erfolgt die Versteinerung als Strafe aufgrund eines Vergehens wie beispielsweise Mord, unsittliche Liebschaften, Sonntagsentheiligung, Hartherzigkeit oder wegen anderer Freveltaten. Viele dieser Sagen tragen christlichen Charakter und sie wurden und werden den Kindern häufig als abschreckendes Beispiel erzählt. In Tirol, besonders in der Gegend von Innsbruck, wurde diese Sage laut Alpenburg mutwilligen Kindern erzählt, wenn sie sich mit Brot bewarfen oder anderen Übermut trieben. „Spart eure Brosamen für die Armen“, so hieß es, „damit es euch nicht so geht wie der Frau Hütt.“

Schwedischen Sagen zufolge werden Riesen, die wie die Zwerge das Tageslicht scheuen, durch den Strahl der aufgehenden Sonne überrascht und versteinert. – Von existierenden Riesenvölkern berichtet bereits das Alte Testament. Zahlreiche Riesen lebten demnach bis zur Zeit Noahs auf der Erde. Doch da sie schlecht waren, wurden sie von der Sintflut vernichtet. Nur ein Einziger von ihnen, namens Og, überlebte die Sintflut. Er wurde ein mächtiger König. Die Bibel berichtet, dass sein eisernes Bett neun Ellen lang und vier Ellen breit war (4,05 x 1,80 m). An anderer Stelle wird das Land „Basan", über welches er herrschte, als „das Land der Riesen" bezeichnet. – In der Sprachforschung wird diskutiert, ob es einen Zusammenhang gibt zwischen „Frau Hütt" und dem Namen des Innsbrucker Stadtteils „Hötting". Eine „Frau Hitte" soll auch mit ihren Hunden im Tschannberg zwischen Gufidaun und Lajen wohnen; laut Sage lockt sie Kinder zu sich in den Berg. – Eine schlafende Riesenfrau, die „Frau Gant", ist auch am Fuße der Felswand des Gantkofels bei St Michael/Eppan zu erkennen. Ihr Kopf ist das unterste Drittel des Gantkofels, Stirne, Nase und Kinn sind im Profil deutlich zu sehen. Die Übergangsstelle der Felswand zum schräg abfallenden Waldesrücken bildet den Hals der Riesin.

Frau Gant ist nur von St. Michael aus zu sehen, und zwar am besten in der Umgebung des heutigen Pubs „Columbus", des ehemaligen Gasthofs „Zur Goldenen Traube".

2

Die Riesin Melka und ihre Freier

Zuhinterst im Kaunser- oder Kaunertal, am Fuße des Hohen Riß, lebte in uralter Zeit in einem aus rohen Steinen erbauten Turm eine junge Riesin. Sie hieß Melka, und sie war ein Weib von unbeschreiblicher Kraft und außerordentlicher Schönheit. Ihr Haar war gut drei Ellen lang und glänzte, zu Zöpfen geflochten, wie Gold. Melka hatte gelobt, nur denjenigen zum Manne zu nehmen, der es schaffte, sie zu besiegen und, sie an ihrem langen Haar ziehend, zu seinem Heim zu zwingen.

Nun wohnten zu jener Zeit im Kaunser Tal drei Brüder, alle drei von hünenhafter Gestalt und gewaltiger Körperkraft. Torbald, so hieß der Älteste, war so stark, dass er einen Ochsen mit einem einzigen Fausthieb zu Fall brachte. Sigrin, der Zweitgeborene, war imstande, einen mehrere Zentner wiegenden Stein fünfzig Meter weit zu schleudern. Der jüngste der drei Brüder hieß Hildung. Er hatte seine Kraft noch nie erprobt, denn er hatte ein sanftes, friedliches Gemüt, doch, wer weiß, vielleicht war er der Stärkste der drei Brüder?

Als Torbald von Melkas Gelöbnis erfuhr, trat er den Kampf gegen sie an, denn er wäre stolz und froh gewesen, sie zur Frau zu haben. Jedoch nach einem langen, verzweifelten Kampf unterlag er schlussendlich und musste das kühne Unternehmen mit seinem Leben bezahlen.

Da trat Sigrin den Kampf an. Doch all seine Kraft und sein Bemühen waren vergebens – er endete gleich wie sein älterer Bruder.

Als Hildung vom Tod seiner beiden Brüder erfuhr, wandelte sich seine Sanftmut in Trauer und Wut. Auch er machte sich nun auf, um gegen Melka zu kämpfen, aber nicht, weil er sie zur Frau wollte, sondern um seine Brüder zu rächen. Kaum aber erblickte die schöne Riesin den jungen Hildung, entbrannte ihr Herz in heißer Liebe zu ihm. Sie wollte nichts mehr von einem Zweikampf mit ihm wissen, ja sie bot ihm an, ihm freiwillig auf seinen Hof zu folgen. Hildung aber bestand auf einem Kampf. Doch Melka wollte oder konnte Hildung nicht in die Knie zwingen. Nach kurzem Kampf schleifte der unerbittliche Sieger Melka an ihren goldblonden Haarsträhnen fort, aber nicht seinem Heim zu, sondern bergauf und bergab, um den ganzen Nißler Ferner herum und wieder zurück zum Turm der Riesin, den er in immer noch ungestillter Wut auf die bereits leblose Melka warf.

Heute noch heißt man die dort herumliegenden Steintrümmer „Das Grab der Riesin" und weit hinten im Kaunertal steht am Bach ein Hof, der „der Riesenhof" genannt wird.

›› Wissenswertes ‹‹

Beim „Hohen Riff" (Rifenkarspitz oder Rifenferner im Kaunertal) scheint es sich um einen Schreibfehler zu handeln. Laut Karl Finsterwalder wurde er oft auch „Hohes Riff" genannt, daher die Verwechslung mit „Hohes Riss". Die Besiedlung dieses engen, nicht gerade siedlungsgünstigen Tales geht zum Teil auf die mittelalterliche „Siedlungsfreude" zurück. – Von der außergewöhnlichen Kraft einer Riesin namens Rome wird auch in der Wolfdietrich-Sage erzählt, die den Helden samt Pferd über viele Meilen in ihre Riesenklause zu den anderen Riesinnen trägt.

3

Die Langtüttin

Die Langtüttin, wegen ihrer langen Brüste so genannt, war ein hässliches Weib, das den Kindern nachlief und ihnen die Brüste bot. Aus einer Brust floss Milch, aus der anderen Eiter. Sie hatte ein kleines frisches Mädchen bei sich, das spitzige Schühlein trug, deren Spuren man heutzutage noch sieht. Einmal lockte sie ein Büblein von acht Jahren zu sich. Sie gab ihm die Brust, bereitete ihm ein Lager und fragte es: „Michele, willst du Nöcklen essen?" Als das Kind die Frage bejahte, nahm sie unter einem Steine den schönsten Teig hervor und kochte ihm damit die besten Nudel. Sie hatte auch ein gar wundersam ausgeschmücktes Kämmerlein und eine kleine Küche mit herrlichem Geräte. Das Kind musste einige Tage bei ihr bleiben. Als es sah, dass es nicht leicht weggelassen würde, stellte es sich, als ob es auf die Seite gehen müsste, und ging von der Langtüttin fort. Schnell hüpfte es über den Zaun, dort, wo die Spalten ein Kreuz bildeten. Da war sie auch schon hinter ihm, erwischte ihn beim Rockzipfel, den sie davon riss. Michele aber lief über Stock und Stein davon, denn sie konnte ihm wegen des Kreuzes nicht mehr folgen.

Die Langtüttin und der wilde Mann kamen oft im Pillerberg, Laner genannt, dort, wo jetzt noch der weiße Stein liegt, zusammen. Vom Ferner bis zu dieser Stelle machten sie nur drei Schritte. Oft saßen sie stundenlang beisammen und spielten. Einmal hatte sie neunundneunzig Mal gewonnen, doch das hundertste Mal verspielte sie. Deshalb musste sie zum hangenden Ferner wandern und ward seitdem nie mehr gesehen.

›› Wissenswertes ‹‹

Nocken aus Germteig nannte man früher „Nudeln". – Da Riesen aus uralter, heidnischer Zeit stammen, hassen sie christliche Symbole wie das Kreuz oder das Glockengeläute. Letztendlich werden sie in zahlreichen Sagen durch das Aufkommen des Christentums vertrieben.

Laut anderer Sage habe eine „Langtüttin" genannte Hexe mit dem ewig umgehenden Schuster gelost, wer von ihnen um die Welt ziehen oder ewig auf dem Ferner sitzen soll. Das Los verdammte die Langtüttin zur Fernerhut und so sitzt sie auf dem großen Ötztaler Ferner bis auf den Jüngsten Tag.

Auch in den feltrinischen Ausläufern der Dolomiten (Provinz Belluno/Venetien) erzählt man sich von den „Vane", riesenhafte Frauen mit großen Hinterteilen und lang hängenden Brüsten, die sich von wild wachsenden Früchten ernähren und in der Abenddämmerung an den Bächen ihre Wäsche besorgen.

4

Die Riesentochter

Zur Zeit, als auf dem Schlosse Tirol noch Riesen wohnten, ging einmal eine Riesenjungfrau gegen St. Peter hinüber. Da sah sie auf einer Wiese sechs Zwerglein miteinander spielen und es gefielen ihr die winzigen Männlein so, dass sie sich kein besseres Spielzeug wünschte, sie in die Schürze nahm und auf ihr Schloss trug. Als der alte Riese seine Tochter mit gehobener Schürze daherkommen sah, fragte er sie, was sie darin trage. „Sechs Mücken habe ich auf dem Felde gefangen“, antwortete das törichte Kind, zeigte dem alten Riesen den Fang und lächelte in kindischer Freude.

›› Wissenswertes ‹‹

Folgende Version wurde von J.N.Ritter von Alpenburg aufgezeichnet: Auf dem Berge über dem Schlosse Tirol lebte ein Ur-Riese mit seiner Familie. Einmal kam das Riesenmadl herab, und dem Kinde gefielen einige an der Erde herumkrabbelnde Käfer so wohl, dass sie sechs Stück derselben in ihr Schürzchen nahm, oder in ein Tüchlein band, und sie freudig dem Vater zeigte. „Dirndl! Dirndl! Was machst denn da? Wo gedenkst denn hin?“, sprach der alte Riese unter Kopfschütteln. „Das sind ja Algunder Bauern. Das sind gar nützliche Manndlen – pack's gleich wieder ein, und trag's sauber wieder abi!“

Laut Sagenforscher Hans Fink hausten diese Riesen auf dem Mutjoch. Diese Sage wird im ganzen deutschen mitteleuropäischen Sprachraum in verschiedenen Varianten erzählt. So berichtet Paul Zaunert in seinen „Deutsche Natursagen“ aus der Oberpfalz: „... Als der alte Riese zum Riesenfräulein sagte: ‚Das sind unsere Nachfolger, die werden uns vertreiben‘, da schrie das Fräulein ganz wild vor Zorn: ‚Nein, die will ich vertreiben‘, ging hinaus, fasste den Bauern mit seinem Gespann und zerdrückte alles in ihrer Schürze.“

In einer anderen Version endet die Sage mit den Worten der Mutter: „Tu's weg, mein Kind, wir müssen fort aus diesem Land, und sie werden hier wohnen.“

Das alte Riesengeschlecht, die Fleischesser, müssen den Acker bauenden und Korn säenden Menschen weichen.

5

Das Ende der Riesin Grostàna

Lange, sehr lange ist es her, es war damals, als Christus im Stall von Bethlehem geboren wurde. Zu jener Zeit gab es bei uns noch wenige Siedlungen und Dörfer. Rau war das Leben der Menschen in den Bergen, einfach und bescheiden. Kartoffeln gab es noch nicht und auch keine Polenta. Was es zum Abendessen gab? Eine Schüssel lauwarme Milch, frisch gemolken, und dazu ein Stück hartes Brot aus Roggenmehl, das einzige Getreide, das auf den mageren kleinen Feldern wuchs, welche die Menschen neben ein paar Viehweiden den großen wilden Wäldern abgetrotzt hatten.

Der kleine Bach am Rande der Siedlung versorgte die Dorfbewohner mit dem nötigen Trinkwasser, im Winter aber, und diese Geschichte spielt im Winter, da war der Bach oft zugefroren, und so musste zuerst eine dicke Eisschicht durchgehackt werden, um zum spärlichen Rinnsal darunter zu gelangen. Wie waren die Menschen an diesen eisig kalten Tagen froh über ihre Winterbekleidung aus Schaffell, denn der Winter biss zu, wo er nur konnte.

In den Behausungen gab es einen einzigen warmen Raum, der als Koch- und Schlafstelle gleichzeitig diente, und in der Mitte dieses Raumes brannte in einer Vertiefung aus gestampfter Erde den ganzen Tag über ein herrlich warmes Feuer: Denn an Holz fehlte es glücklicherweise nie. Mit Hilfe von Eseln wurde es aus den nahen Wäldern herbeigeschafft; stark und klug, wie sie waren, genügte ein Wort, und sie fanden den Weg zu den Behausungen allein zurück. Niemals erhob jemand eine Hand gegen sie oder schlug sie gar, denn alle, auch die Übelgelauntesten unter den Dorfbewohnern, wussten, ohne die Esel würde man sterben – vor Kälte oder vor Hunger.

An einem frostig kalten Winterabend verschwanden im Dorf ein Esel und ein Ochse. Ihr Verschwinden wurde erst am nächsten Morgen bemerkt, denn die Haustiere befanden sich hinter den Hütten in aus Steinen aufgeschichteten Stallungen oder Höhlen, deren einzige Öffnung nachtsüber dicht mit Fichtenzweigen abgedeckt wurde.

Des Nachts, vor allem zur Winterzeit, war es besser, im Haus zu bleiben, dies wusste ein jeder. Die Nachtwelt gehörte anderen Wesen, seltsamen und unberechenbaren, guten und weniger guten, bedrohlichen und gefährlichen. Und manchmal, und das war das Schlimmste, was geschehen konnte, tauchte die Grostàna auf. Wehe dem, der dann im Freien war! Der- oder diejenige war verloren! Denn die Grostàna war riesengroß, aus der Ferne schaute sie aus wie eine riesige sich bewegende Fichte, aber im nächsten Augenblick war sie auch schon da, und wen sie im Freien antraf, der wurde von ihr ausgelöscht, aufgesaugt in die riesige, tintige Masse ihres Körpers.

Wie eine enorme Wolke schwebte ihr großer Schatten Ausschau haltend über Dörfer und Wälder, und nur hinter verschlossenen Fensterläden und Türen war man in Sicherheit.

In jener Nacht – es war die Nacht, als Jesus geboren wurde, aber dies wusste niemand, denn damals beteten die Menschen auch bei uns zu anderen Gottheiten – richtete sich die Grostàna zwischen den Bergen auf und breitete sich mit ihrem tiefschwarzen, tintigen Gesicht mit den furchterregenden Augen, die alles sahen, über dem weiten Nachthimmel aus. Doch keine Menschenseele war zu sehen, und auch alle Schafe und Ziegen waren in ihren Ställen in Sicherheit. Da wurde die Grostàna vor Wut immer dunkler, mit ihren wilden, vor Zorn glitzernden Augen spähte sie aufmerksam durch die dunkle Nacht.

Da, mitten im Wald, sah sie plötzlich einen Esel und einen Ochsen, die unter größter Anstrengung auf dem tief verschneiten Weg vorsichtig talwärts stapften. Die Grostàna fing an, ihren furchtbaren Atem auf die beiden Tiere zu blasen, um sie dann in sich aufsaugen zu können

– aber in diesem Moment fiel aus dem höchsten Himmel ein herrlich glänzender blauer Stern auf sie nieder, durchbohrte ihren massigen Tintenleib mit einem Strahl, der so funkelte und blitzte, dass die beschneiten Wälder und Weiden und alle Siedlungen für kurze Zeit hell erleuchtet waren, und eine Stimme, laut und mächtig wie ein Donnergrollen, ertönte aus dem Stern: „Grostàna, die Zeit deiner Macht ist abgelaufen! Diese beiden Geschöpfe sind auf dem Weg nach Bethlehem, denn sie wollen mit ihrem warmen Atem das Jesuskind erwärmen, das heute Nacht geboren wird. Und jetzt werde ich sie auf meinem schnellen blauen Strahl dorthin bringen. Du aber wirst für alle Zeit im großen Nichts verschwinden." Dann war alles wieder wie vorher – eine sternenklare klirrend kalte Winternacht, da Jesus im Stall von Bethlehem geboren wurde.

Die Grostàna aber ward nie mehr gesehen.

›› Wissenswertes ‹‹

Die Herkunft dieser Legende ist unbekannt, doch im Fersental, eine deutsche Sprachinsel im Trentino, gibt es einen Berg, namens „Gronlàit", und andere Sagen, welche von der „Graonstana" (wildes Weib-Hexe) handeln und so kann vermutet werden, dass die Geschichte der Grostàna in dieser Gegend entstanden ist. – Ochs und Esel, alte Kulttiere, die in keiner Weihnachtskrippe fehlen dürfen, sind älter als alle anderen Krippenfiguren. Menschliche Darstellungen kamen erst später hinzu. Die beiden Tiere stehen in der christlichen Symbolik für die alten Welten: der Ochse als Sinnbild des Judentums und der Esel für das Heidentum.

6

Eine Riesin in Landeck

In Landeck kam zu einem Bauern ein baumstarkes Mädel und wollte in den Dienst treten. Die Dirne gefiel ihm, denn sie war schön und acht Schuh hoch. Er nahm sie an und sie arbeitete, wie ein Vieh. Einen großen Wasserzuber mit Wäsche trug sie allein zum Brunnen und wieder zurück. Wenn in einem Wirtshause Raufhändel waren, holte man die Dirne und sie stiftete Ordnung und Ruhe. Jeder Bursche fürchtete sich vor ihr, denn sie nahm mit einer Hand den Stärksten auf und trug ihn, wohin sie wollte. So diente sie viele Jahre bei dem Bauern, der ihr Arbeit und Haussegen zu verdanken hatte. Einmal hörte man sie nachts weinen und morgens war sie verschwunden. Niemand wusste wohin.

›› Wissenswertes ‹‹

Ein Fuß ist neben der Elle, der Handspanne u.a. eine der ältesten Längeneinheiten (ca. 30 cm lang). Es wird vermutet, dass diese Maße schon vor der Erfindung der Schrift gebräuchlich waren.

Diese Sagenfigur erinnert mit ihrer Größe an die „Ridnauner Riesin" Maria Fastnauer, ca. 2,30 m hoch gewachsen. Sie stammte aus einer armen Bergbauernfamilie und tingelte um 1900 mit einem Zirkus durch ganz Europa, um ihre Not leidenden Angehörigen finanziell zu unterstützen. Ständiges Heimweh war dabei ihr Begleiter.

7

Die wilde Bäuerin in der Girstenmühle

Vor uralten Zeiten hauste beim Girstner oder besser in der Girstenmühle bei Unterinn eine Bäuerin, welchen von einem wilden Mann herstammte und selber wild und unhold war. Kinder hatte sie keine, denn die Ehe zwischen wilden Heiden und Christen blieb gewöhnlich ungesegnet.

Es hatte sich nämlich zugetragen, dass ihre Mutter, eine Bauerntochter der dortigen Gegend, einen Sommer über auf der Bergwiese Sennerin machen musste. Einmal kehrte bei ihr ein wilder Mann ein, um sich beim Herdfeuer zu wärmen und Milch zu trinken, weil ihn Hunger und Durst plagten. Das eine Wort gab das andere, der junge Mensch, obwohl über und über zottelig wie ein Bär, gefiel der unerfahrenen Dirne und ihm wieder ihre Gefälligkeit. Es tat so einem wilden Heiden wohl, einmal wieder ein freundliches Menschenwort zu hören. Der Wilde ging, kam aber von Zeit zu Zeit wieder zu ihrer Hütte herab und pflog Umgang mit ihr, und das Mädel wies seine Begleitung nicht zurück. Sie bekam ein Mägdlein, stark und wohlgeformt von Angesicht, aber von zügelloser

Wildheit, und es wuchs dem Kinde alsbald ein Bart und Haar über den ganzen Leib. Als sie herangewachsen und zu ihren Jahren gekommen war, heiratete sie den Girstner, der trotz Behaarung und Wildheit die Dirne begehrte. Sie wurde zwar ein braves Bauernweib, allein stärker als andere zog es sie zeitlebens zum Walde hin; sie war gerne allein und verkehrte nicht viel mit Leuten.

›› Wissenswertes ‹‹

Girste = Gerste. – Wilde Männer werden oft als die Männer der Fanggen angesehen. In dieser Sage wird eine Fangga als Tochter aus der Ehe zwischen einem Wilden Mann und einer Menschenfrau geboren. Die tiefe Verbundenheit mit Baum und Wald, welche für die Fanggen kennzeichnend ist, kommt auch in dieser Sage deutlich hervor. Zwar ist die Sagenfigur der Fangga weitgehend in Vergessenheit geraten, doch erinnern Redewendungen heute noch an ihr charakteristisches Wesen: ein wildes, unbändiges Mädchen ist ein „Wildfang"; eine Frau, die sich nicht über den Tisch ziehen lässt, „hat Haare auf den Zähnen".

8

Saltthon

Ein Bauer von Arzl im Oberinntal ging einmal in den Wald, um Kienholz zu machen. Dort fand er aber einen so harten Zunderstock, dass es ihn viele Mühe kostete, ihn zu klieben. Als er mit dieser Arbeit beschäftigt war, kam eine Fangga daher und fragte den Bauern: „Wie heißest du?" Da antwortete der Bauer dem Waldweibe: „Saltthon." Da sprach die Fangga freudig: „Jetzt bekomm ich einmal Menschenfleisch, das soll mir schmecken." Darauf sagte der Bauer, der ein pfiffiger Kauz war: „Du wirst mich aber nicht roh essen. Wenn das Fleisch schmecken soll, muss es gebraten sein." Nun fragte die Fangga: „Wie geht denn das?" Da erwiderte der Bauer: „Du musst zuerst diesen Zunderstamm spalten, ihn dann anzünden, und dann kannst du mich am Feuer braten. Fahr nur mit deinen starken Händen hinein und reiß den Stock auseinander." Das tat das Waldweiblein und griff in die Spalte hinein. Der Bauer zog aber sogleich den hineingeschlagenen Keil heraus, und die Fangga war eingeklemmt. Wie sie sich so überlistet und gefangen sah, fing sie an zu schreien und um Hilfe zu rufen. Da kam der Waldmann so herab getümmelt, dass noch heutzutage der Ort Timmels heißt, und rief: „Wer hat dir ein Leides getan?" Antwortete die Fangga: „Saltthon." Als der Waldmann dies hörte, war er unwillig und rief: „Saltthon, saltg'litten!" Dann lief er davon und ließ die Fangga im Stiche. Der Bauer kam nun mit heiler Haut nach Hause, wagte sich aber nie mehr so spät in den Wald hinauf.

›› Wissenswertes ‹‹

Klieben = spalten, Saltthon = Selbergetan, saltg'litten= selbergelitten – Diese Sage enthält Motive aus antiken Überlieferungen, nämlich aus der Niemand-Episode in der „Odyssee“: Odysseus und seine Gefährten befanden sich auf der Rückkehr aus dem Trojanischen Krieg und landeten auf einer Insel, vermutlich auf Sizilien. Odysseus stellte sich dem Zyklopen Polyphem mit dem Namen Niemand vor. Er und seine Gefährten wurden eingesperrt, und Polyphem sprach die Drohung aus, dass er sie alle fressen wolle. Da blendete Odysseus Polyphem, indem er ihm mit einem glühenden Speer in dessen einziges Auge, das Zyklopenauge, stach. Polyphem rief die anderen Zyklopen zu Hilfe, aber als diese hörten, dass „Niemand“ es getan hätte, sorgten sie sich nicht weiter um ihn.

Dieses Sagenmotiv vom „Selbergetan“ findet man auch in anderen Tiroler Sagen wieder. In der ladinischen Sage ergeht es auch der Bregostana, einem behaarten, boshaften, raubgierigen, Kinder fressenden Weib, das in Wäldern, Höhlen und Felswänden lebt, ähnlich. Am besten schmeckten ihr laut Sage die menschlichen Gedärme. Sie vertauschte auch gerne ihre Kinder mit denen der Menschen.

9

Die böse Fenkin

Ein Junge hatte sich beim Klaubholzsammeln im Walde ziemlich weit verirrt und befand sich von ungefähr auf der Kuppe eines Felsen. Da trat urplötzlich aus dessen Höhlung ein altes, garstiges Weiblein hervor, blickte zum Jungen empor und sagte: „Was gibst du mir, wenn ich dich von diesem Felsen herunterlüpfe?“ Derselbe erwiderte: „Nichts.“ Das Weiblein stellte noch zweimal an den Jungen die gleiche Frage, erhielt aber immer dieselbe Antwort. Da hob die Alte den Jungen herunter, nahm ihn mit sich in die Höhle, sperrte ihn dort in eine Schweinekofe und fütterte ihn wie die Schweine mit Spülicht. Dem Jungen kam ein Rechenzahn, den er zufällig bei sich trug, sehr zustatten; denn jedes Mal beim Füttern sollte derselbe durch ein Astloch in der Türe den Finger heraus heben, in den die Alte ihn geschnitten hätte, um zu versuchen, ob er beim Schlachten bald fett genug wäre. Anstatt des Fingers aber reichte er jenen Rechenzahn der Fenkin, und diese schnitt darein und sagte dabei jedes Mal: „Hier ist alles hart wie Bein, da mag es das Mästen noch leiden.“

Leider aber verlor eines Tages der Junge seinen Rechenzahn, deshalb musste er der Alten den Finger zum Hineinschneiden hinhalten. Da versetzte dieselbe: „Junge, jetzt bist du fett genug.“ Bald darauf rief derselbe recht eindringlich: „Nali, Nali, lasse mich für kurze Zeit aus dem Ställchen heraus, ich will dir gern ein paar Läuse suchen!“ Die Alte folgte seiner Bitte. Als nun der Junge in der Stube der Alten Läuse suchte, schlief diese allmählich ein, während jener sich sofort aus dem Staube machte und eiligst nach Hause lief. Gleichzeitig musste für jene ein Mädchen einen Kessel voll Wasser in der Küche sieden, um in demselben den Jungen zu brühen. Wie die Fenkin, aus ihrem Schlafe erwacht, merkte, dass ihr der Junge entlaufen wäre, so ergriff sie in ihrem furchtbaren Zorne das Mädchen, weil dieses denselben hatte entwischen lassen, und stürzte es in das heiße Wasser im Kessel und brühte es.

›› Wissenswertes ‹‹

Spülicht (tirolerisch „Spuele") ist das Schweinefutter; auch die an Schweine verfütterte alte Molke wurde so bezeichnet. – Nali = Großmütterchen; beim erwähnten Mädchen handelt es sich möglicherweise um die Tochter der Fenkin. – Diese Sage aus dem Paznaun erinnert sehr stark an das Hänsel-und-Gretel-Motiv, welches auch in anderen Sagen zu finden ist (vgl. z.B. Kapitel Percht: „Die Stempa"). Auch hier überlistet der Bub die Fenkin, indem er ihr statt eines Knochens einen Rechenzahn hinhält. Hier wird die Gestalt der Fangga hexenhaft überzeichnet. Sie ist zu einer kinderfressenden alten Frau geworden. Mancherorts wird von den Fanggen erzählt, dass sie den Menschen aufgelauert haben, junge Buben an alten dürren Bäumen zu Staub zerrieben oder sie in ihre Nase aufgeschnupft haben.

Dieses Märchenmotiv zeigt die laut C.G.Jung wichtige helfende Funktion solcher Märchen im seelischen Ablösungs- und Selbstfindungsprozess auf.

10

Die Entführung der Wöchnerin

Eine Bäuerin hatte nach dem Wochenbette den Weg zur Kirche angetreten, um sich darin vorsegnen zu lassen. Weil dieselbe nichts Geweihtes an ihrem Leibe trug noch bei sich hatte, zudem gegen den bestehenden Brauch ohne alle Begleitung diesen Gang machen wollte, so wurde sie von einer „Fangga" aufgegriffen und entführt oder der vorherrschenden Volksmeinung zufolge zerrissen. Ein kleines Töchterlein der Wöchnerin, das während deren Abwesenheit in die Küche gegangen war, um Wasser zu trinken, kam hastig aus derselben in die Wohnstube gelaufen und rief voll Verwunderung: „Vater, komm doch in die Küche und sieh, welch großen Bart heute unsere Mutter hat!" Der Vater, darüber nicht wenig erstaunt, folgte seinem Kinde in die Küche und musste daselbst mit nicht geringer Bestürzung wahrnehmen, dass statt der lieben Mutter ein hässliches Weibsbild mit struppigem Barte – eine leibhaftige Fangga – beim Herde saß und ihn stier anblickte. Alsbald erhob sich diese von ihrem Sitze, schritt eilends durch den Hausgang bei der Tür hinaus und verschwand. Alles Suchen nach der Bäuerin war vergebens; von der unglücklichen Person war nie mehr eine Spur zu entdecken.

Beim Fürsegnen handelt es sich um den christlichen Brauch der Aussegnung. Noch bis in die 60er/70er Jahre des 20. Jh. war es mancherorts üblich, dass die Wöchnerin zum Pfarrer ging, um sich aussegnen zu lassen. Dies ist auf den Glauben zurückzuführen, dass Gebärende unrein geworden seien. Mancherorts war es üblich, denjenigen Geschenke zu überreichen, welche der Wöchnerin auf dem Weg zur Kirche begegneten. Nicht ausgesegnete Wöchnerinnen durften das Haus nicht verlassen, denn sonst bestand die Gefahr, vom Teufel oder vom Wilden Mann vertragen zu werden oder, wie in dieser Geschichte, von einer Fangga. Im Schutze der eigenen Dachtraufe – „nicht über den Tropfstall hinaus“ – waren sie jedoch in Sicherheit. Eine Sage aus dem Vinschgau erzählt von einer Wöchnerin, die sich ohne Gewei htes auf den Weg machte und vom Teufel überrascht wurde. Dieser konnte ihr allerdings nichts anhaben, da sie sich auf einem Karwendelstock, einer Quendelpflanze, ausruhte. Wurde eine Wöchnerin allerdings von einem Wilden Mann entführt, gab es kein Zurück mehr. In Sagen aus dem Sarntal und der Brunecker Gegend legte der Teufel den Frauen, die sich nicht rechtzeitig aussegnen ließen, ein fremdes Kind in die Wiege, einen sogenannten „Wechselbalg“.

11

Die Fangga und der Jäger

Ein Jäger, der den ganzen Tag gejagt hatte und sehr müde war, kam spät abends zu einer leeren Sennhütte. Es beschloss, darin zu übernachten, legte seine gemachte Beute, eine fette Gämse, aufs Dach hinauf und ging in die Hütte. Als er sich dort bei einem aufgemachten Feuer wärmte und die Abendkost bereitete, hörte er plötzlich ein Jammern vor dem Hause und vernahm deutlich die Worte: „Da liegt unsere schöne Kuh, sie ist tot, ja tot.“

Gleich darauf kam ein wunderschönes Weib in die Hütte und sprach: „Du hast uns eine Kuh getötet, deshalb will ich dich in Stücke zerreißen.“ Der Jäger erwiderte aber ohne sich lange zu besinnen: „Und ich erschieße dich.“ Da fürchtete sich die Fangga doch ein wenig und sprach: „Diesmal will ich dir nichts zu Leide tun, aber wenn du in Zukunft noch eine unserer Kühe tötest, dann wehe dir! Doch komme in unseren Stall, dann kannst du sehen, wo uns die Kuh abgeht.“ Der Schütze folgte den Worten der Fangga und ging mit ihr. Sie führte ihn in eine unterirdische Höhle, in welcher ringsum Krippen angebracht waren. An jeder hing eine Gämse, nur eine Stelle war leer. Auf diese wies die Fangga hin und sprach: „Siehst du, hier ist eine leere Krippe, hier hast du uns eine Kuh herausgeschossen. Jetzt geh nach Hause und tu’ unseren Kühen kein Leid mehr.“ Der Jäger ging aus der Höhle und schoss keine Gämse mehr.

›› Wissenswertes ‹‹

Die Fangga dieser Sage hat große Ähnlichkeit mit den Saligen, welche Gämsen als ihre Haustiere halten, sie pflegen und beschützen.

Auch Holda erscheint manchmal als Waldfrau, und an der Spitze ihrer Gämsenherde zieht sie mit dem Melkeimer in der Hand einher. Im Norden Deutschlands ist es „Frau Harke", die wie die Berchta in den Raunächten umgeht; auch sie hegt und schützt das Wild.

12

Das Kind der Fangga

Zu Flies war eine Dirn in Dienst, die täglich mehr arbeitete als zehn andere zusammen, und stark war sie wie ein Riese. Aber ihren Namen sagte sie niemandem; sie betete nie und wusste nichts vom Christentum, und obschon man sie belehren wollte, fasste sie nichts auf. Das schmerzte den Bauern und die Bäuerin wohl, aber weil sie sonst brav war, behielt man sie von Jahr zu Jahr im Dienst.

Zur Michaelizeit ging der Bauer mit der Dirn auf den Imster Markt, zwei Ochsen und ein Kalb musste sie treiben helfen, aber bei der Schönwieserbrücke schickte er sie wieder heim.

Da lief sie nun ohne zu rasten und etwas zu essen über den Kronburger Schlossberg, den Zammerberg und über Eichholz nach Haus, dass die Leute staunten, weil dazu andere Kräfte erfordert werden als bei gewöhnlichen Menschen.

Der Bauer verkaufte Ochsen und Kalb sehr gut und ging dann den Weg über den Pillerberg. Wie er nun durch den Bannwald stieg, das Ochsenjoch der verkauften Ochsen über der Schulter, und fast in der Mitte war, rief eine ungeheuer laute Stimme aus dem Walde heraus: „Jochtrager! Jochtrager! Sag der Stuza-Mutza, d'Hoachrinta sei toad!"

Darauf war wieder alles still. Das machte ihn nachdenken, und als er heimkam, saßen Weib und Dirn gerade beim Musessen. Er warf sein Joch ab, wischte sich den Schweiß von der Stirne und erzählte das im Bannwald erlebte Abenteuer. Wie ihm die Rede entfuhr: „Sag der Stuza-Mutza, d'Hoachrinta sei toad!", da sprang die Dirn mit dem hellen Geschrei: „D'Muota, d'Muota!" empor, ließ alles stehen und liegen und lief dem Bannwalde zu. Niemals wurde sie mehr gesehen.

Bald verbreitete sich die Nachricht, dass die Stuza-Mutza statt ihrer Mutter nun im Bannwald hause, und das Geschäft der Alten, Kinder zu stehlen und zu fressen und dergleichen, fleißig fortsetzte.

›› Wissenswertes ‹‹

Der Name Pillerberg, auch Bühlerberg genannt, bedeutet laut Alpenburg so viel wie „Heuschober".

Dass Fanggen auch eine Vorliebe für Menschenfleisch haben, speziell für das von Kindern, wird des Öfteren berichtet. Doch kann auch vermutet werden, dass sie, wie alle übernatürlichen Wesen, von der menschlichen Gemeinschaft als lästige Fremdkörper empfunden und deshalb ins Abseits, in die Isolation gedrängt wurden. Möglicherweise waren es aber auch die alteingesessenen Ureinwohnerinnen, derer man sich entledigen wollte.

13

Stutz-Förche

Zwischen Landeck und Ladis am rechten Ufer des Inns liegt der berüchtigte Fanggen-Urwald im Urgental. Ein Hirt von der Fitzeralm, im Weiler Urgen geboren, suchte in dem wilden Tale ein verlorenes Stück Vieh und fand ein ganz behaartes Kind, und zwar ein Madl. Er nahm es mit sich, erzog es und gebrauchte es dann später als Magd.

Es lernte zwar zu sprechen, von religiösen Dingen wollte es aber nie etwas hören, und war am liebsten im Walde. Einmal gingen zwei Männer von Urgen durch den Gebirgssteig an der Grenze des Urgenwaldes. Da tönte es aus dem Dickicht der Tannen rau und gebieterisch in ihre Ohren: „Saget der Stutz-Förche, die Rohrinde sei gefällt und tot." Die Männer staunten, wussten die Worte nicht zu deuten, eilten aber schnell durch den finsteren Waldgrund nach Hause. Einer davon, ein Freund vom Bauern, bei welchem das gefundene Mädchen diente, erzählte dieses so laut, dass es dies in der Nebenkammer hören konnte, wo es eben war. Da fing die Dirn an zu schreien und zu heulen und zu jammern und lief eilig der Urgenwildnis zu, und ward nie mehr gesehen.

Man hatte damals einige Urbäume für den Straßenbau gefällt und will den Tod der Rohrinde mit dem Baume in Verbindung bringen. Später wurde der Wald gänzlich niedergehauen, und alle Fangginnen waren verschwunden.

›› Wissenswertes ‹‹

Madl = Mädchen.

Die tiefe Verbundenheit der Fanggen mit Bäumen und dem Wald drückt sich bereits durch ihre Benennung mit Hilfe von Baumnamen aus: z.B. Stutzförche (von Föhre) oder Rohrinde/Raurinde (von Rinde). In dieser Sage sind die Fanggen unerkannte fleißige Mägde, bis sie eines Tages durch eine Todesbotschaft aufgefordert werden, nach Hause zurückzukehren. Auch in anderen Sagen finden wir solche dämonische Rufer, welche an Pan und seine Todesbotschaft in der griechischen Mythologie erinnern.

Nach dem Volksglauben gibt es Fanggen als kollektive wie auch als Einzelwesen. Ihre Existenz ist an einen bestimmten Wald gebunden; verschwindet dieser, so sterben auch die Fanggen aus. So war das Baumfällen für die Menschen ein Mittel, um sich der Fanggen zu entledigen.

14

Die wilde Fangga

Ihr Büblein bleibet fein im Haus,
Es hat schon „betgeläutet“,
Vom Wald zieht „d' wildö Fangga“ aus,
Und schleicht ums Dorf und beutet,
Gott schütz euch vor dem Riesenweib,
Sie schnupf, „mei Seal“, zum Zeitvertreib,
Oft einen ganzen Haufen
Von Buben, die verlaufen.

Hernach nimmt sie ein' alten Baum
Voll dürrer Äst und Spitzen,
Und krallt in ihren Nasenraum,
Und tut sie „z' Toad“ fast ritzen,
Wohl schrein die Buben ach! und weh!
Da nützt kein „Herr dein Will'n gescheh'.“;
Sie stoßt und dreht und rackelt,
Und lacht dazu, dass's nackelt.

Sie stemmt nach solcher Höllenqual
In d' Seiten beide Hände,
Und niest die Buben übers Tal,
Gleich patsch! an d' Felsenwände.
Dort kleppt wie Mörtel Bein und Fleisch
Mit Haut und Haar ein roter Meisch
Von Knödl, Kraut und Ruben –
Kein Mensch kennt mehr die Buben!

›› Wissenswertes ‹‹

Der Verfasser dieses Gedichtes, ein unermüdlicher Volksgut- und Sagensammler, hieß eigentlich Johann Nepomuk Mahl-Schedl. Zur Anerkennung für sein patriotisches Wirken erhielt er 1849 die Eiserne Krone und 1851 den Ritterstand mit dem Prädikat „von Alpenburg", wie er sein mit einem botanischen Garten verbundenes Schloss gerne nannte.

15

Die Waldfrauen

In einer Berghöhle ob Schluderns wohnten einst drei Fräulein, die waren ganz wild und vom Umgang mit Menschen durch einen großen Wald abgeschlossen. Ihre Nahrung bestand teils aus Kräutern, die sie im Wald suchten, teils aus Menschen, welche sie anpackten. Wenn es sich nämlich ereignete, dass sie einen Menschen erblickten, so fielen sie über ihn her und schleppten ihn mit sich in ihre Höhle. Hier wurde er angebunden und zur Arbeit gezwungen. War er fleißig, so fütterten sie ihn, bis er recht fett war, zeigte er sich faul und ungeschickt, so wurde ihm gleich auf einem Baumstamm der Kopf abgehauen. Daher wich ihnen jedermann fleißig aus und niemand wagte es, an ihrer Höhle vorbeizugehen. Nur ein Bauer hatte einmal den Mut dazu und kam wirklich ungeschoren davon. Die Sache ging aber so: Als er an der Höhle vorbeikam, gingen die Fräulein zwar auf ihn los, schleppten ihn aber nicht in die Höhle, sondern gaben ihm bloß einen Gürtel. Diesen, sagten sie, solle er nehmen und damit seinen Leib umgürten. Der Bauer war ein listiger Kerl, tat als ob alles recht wäre und ging mit dem Gürtel weiter. Nachdem er ein Stück gegangen war, versuchte er die Beschaffenheit des Gürtels, aber nicht an sich, sondern an einem Baume. Kaum hatte er den Gürtel um den Baum geschlungen, so brach dieser ab, und der Bauer freute sich über seine Klugheit. Er ging nun seinen Weg weiter und als er heimkam, fand er die Magd schwer krank. Sie aß nichts und trank nichts und lag da wie gestorben. Aber auf einmal sprang sie auf und lief unaufhaltsam dem Walde zu. Der Bauer rannte ihr nach und sie lief geraden Weges zur Höhle der Wilden Fräulein, denn sie selbst war auch eines von ihnen und sobald sie ihre Schwestern, die vor der Höhle warteten, erreicht hatte, verschwanden alle drei von der Stelle und wurden von da an nie mehr gesehen.

›› Wissenswertes ‹‹

In dieser Sage verquickt sich die Gestalt d er wilden, menschenfeindlichen Fangga mit jener der Saligen. – In der Mythologie ist der Gürtel ein ambivalentes Attribut, er verleiht Zauberkraft und Verwandlungsfähigkeit, Weisheit, Herrschergewalt und Tod, steht aber auch für Liebe, eheliche Treue, Keuschheit, Fruchtbarkeit. Auch der Tiroler Hexenmeister Kachler aus Tiers war in Besitz eines Gürtels, der ihm laut Sage Zwölfmännerkraft verlieh. – Der Bäume und Menschen zerreißende Gürtel ist in vielen mitteleuropäischen und nordischen Sagen bekannt. Fast immer sind es Geistwesen, die einen Menschen mit einem Zerreißgürtel beschenken, um sich an ihm zu rächen.

Der Gürtel wird als bäumeausreißender, zumeist weiblich definierter Wirbelsturm gedeutet. In Tirol ist es die Windsbraut oder die Hurl, ein böswilliges Wesen, stärker und gefährlicher als der „männliche" Wind. Um die Windin zu besänftigen, wurden noch im letzten Jahrhundert in Pfitsch und andernorts Windopfer in Form von Mehl dargebracht, d.h. ins Freie geworfen („weiße Gabe"). Auch das Werfen von eigenen Messern war früher weit verbreitet. Diese Messer wurden Truten- oder Hexenmesser genannt, hatten zumeist neun Kreuze und neun Halbmonde eingestanzt und wurden mit dem Ruf „Neun Kreuz und neun Mun (Monde) kimp koa Hexe net drun!" in die Luft geworfen.

Auch in Istrien stellte man sich den Karststurm, die Bora, als launische, uralte Hexe vor.

Perchta/Stampe

Die **Perchta** ist eine Sagengestalt Tirols, die sich in der europäischen Mythologie in unterschiedlicher Form und unter verschiedenen Namen wiederfindet: Berchta, Perhta, Berta, Königin Bert(h)a, Berachte, Perchte, Perchtha, aber auch **Stampe**, Gstampe, Stempa (von stampfen, treten). In benachbarten Ländern erscheint sie in der Gestalt der Befana, auch als Berchtl, Berchtli, Bechtli, Bechteli, als Diana oder Dyana, Babania, Redódesa, Donnazza, Boscignara usw.

In vielen Zügen gleicht sie der Frau Holle, Holda oder Hulda, deren Gestalt ebenso reich und wandelbar und v.a. in Mitteldeutschland zu finden ist. Das Adjektiv „hold" im Namen Holda weist nicht nur auf die milde Seite der Göttin hin, sondern erinnert auch an Hel, die Jenseitsgöttin. Sie hat somit eine helle und eine dunkle Seite. Bis zum 10. Jh. war die „halja" oder „hella" das Totenreich, die Unterwelt; erst später wurde die Hölle zu einem Qualort.

Perchta ist die glänzende, weiße Göttin, worauf auch bereits das althochdeutsche Wort „perahta" (leuchtend, glänzend) hinweist. Schon dem Sinn des Wortes nach treffen wir hier auf eine gütige, Freude bringende Person.

Ebenso wie die Holda führt Perchta Aufsicht über die Spinnerinnen. Fleißige Spinnerinnen werden belohnt: Sie haben volle Spulen oder einen in Gold verwandelten Flachsknoten; tüchtige Mägde finden Münzen im Eimer.

Manche Forscher sehen in der Gestalt der Percht urspünglich einen Seelendämon oder das Glied einer ganzen Dämonenhorde – wie wir dies z.B. in den Sagen finden, wo sie als Anführerin der Kinderseelen erscheint oder in der angeführten Sage aus Folgareit; zumeist tritt sie jedoch als Einzelgestalt auf. Sie wird oft auch als Königin der „Heimchen", der Seelen der ungetauften verstorbenen Kinder, bezeichnet, welche häufig einen zerbrochenen Pflug schleppen müssen. Dies zeichnet die Perchta als fruchtbarkeitsbringende Vorfrühlingsgöttin aus; ihre Liebe zu den Feldern und zur Landwirtschaft ist ein weiteres Merkmal.

Zum Totenheer würde die Namensableitung von „pergan" (verbergen) passen. Statt der einstigen Anführung des gespenstischen Totenheeres teilt man der Perchta in späteren Zeiten den Zug der Kinder vom Fest der Unschuldigen Kinder (28. Dezember) zu.

Im Laufe der Zeit wird sie allerdings immer mehr mit Zügen eines hexenhaften Wesens überzeichnet. So treffen wir oft auf Erzählungen, welche Perchta als grauenhaftes und Kinder abschreckendes

Wesen beschreiben. In manchen Sagen heißt es auch, dass Perchta die neugeborenen Kinder aus der Wiege raube. Im Heidentum aber gilt sie als Beschützerin der Mütter und der Kinder. Im Ahrntal nannte man früher die Hebamme „Stampe".

In den Tiroler Sagen hat die Perchtl eine mehrfache Rolle: einmal als die Seelenführerin der ungetauften Kinder, dann, wie die Hulda als Spinnefrau, und endlich noch als eine fast legendenhafte Gestalt des christlichen und geschichtlichen Mythos.

In vielen Beschreibungen hat Perchta Verunstaltungen und absonderliche Hässlichkeiten: Oft hat sie einen großen Fuß, häufig auch einen Gans- oder Schwanenfuß. Perchta taucht auch als Wilde, Eiserne Perchta auf, oft ganz aus Eisen, sonst auch mit Eisenhandschuh oder mit eiserner Nase. Der Name „Frau Eisen" wird manchmal auch mit dem Namen der großen Göttin Isis in Verbindung gebracht.

Die Perchtl der Tiroler Sagen erscheint zu „Gömachten" oder „Gömnachten", dem Vorabend des Heiligen Dreikönigstages. Er wird auch Perchtentag, Perchtnachten oder Stampennacht u.Ä. genannt. Mancherorts geht sie langsam, Schritt für Schritt mit ihrer Kinderschar um, andernorts fährt sie mit der „Wilden Fahrt".

Am Gömnachtabend war es lange Zeit Brauch, Essen für die Perchta und ihre Kinder bereit zu stellen, damit sie und ihre Kinderschar sich auf ihrem Weg stärken können. So wurden im Tiroler Raum Nudeln, eine sonntägliche Süßspeise in Krapfenform, auf die Hausdächer gegeben oder ein Perchtatisch, „tabula fortunae", gedeckt. Niemand durfte bei der Mahlzeit der Perchta und ihrer Kinder zusehen.

Am Tag der Perchta, so wie auch häufig in den restlichen Raunächten, herrschte Arbeitsverbot, man durfte nicht spinnen. In einem alten Sprichwort heißt es: „Die Perchtl nistet sich hinein", d.h. sie verwirrt den Flachs. Säumige, Faule, Eigennützige oder Vorwitzige bestraft Perchta hart, z.B. indem sie ihr Hackl, eine kleine Axt, einschlägt oder jemanden durch ihren Hauch blendet.

Im Tiroler Volksglauben ist Perchta mitunter die Gemahlin von Pontius Pilatus, nämlich Claudia Procula. Vergeblich bat sie einst ihren Mann, Christus nicht kreuzigen zu lassen. Nach dessen Tod und dem Selbstmord ihres Mannes ließ sie sich taufen. Sie gilt als Beschützerin der ungetauften Kinder und begleitet laut Legende am 6. Jänner, dem Tauftage Christi, die Kinderseelen auf der Suche nach der Quelle des urheiligen Taufflusses, des Jordans.

So steht der Perchtltag auch mit dem Dreikönigsfest der Katholischen Kirche in Zusammenhang, welche an diesem Tag ein mehrfaches Fest feiert, so die Erscheinung der Heiligen Drei Könige und die Taufe Jesu im Jordan.

In anderen Tiroler Sagen soll Perchta auch die Tochter des Herodes gewesen sein und ihm zum Mord der Unschuldigen Kinder geraten haben, weshalb sie in der Dreikönigsnacht die Welt durchwandern muss.

Laut einer deutschen Legende war Bertha die Gemahlin des Frankenkönigs Pipin (741-768) und Mutter Karls des Gro-

ßen, beschrieben als „Berthe mit dem fuoze". Ihr in der Legende beschriebener großer Fuß wird häufig mit der früheren weiblichen Haupttätigkeit, dem Spinnen, in Zusammenhang gebracht. Andere sehen in dieser Fußabnormität bzw. im Schwanenfuß den Restmythos der nordischen Walküre oder der Göttin Freyja, die sich beide in Schwäne verwandeln konnten und die Toten in die Walhalla begleiteten bzw. sie dort bewirteten. In einer Sibyllen-Weissagung aus dem 14. Jh. wird von der Seherin Sibylle erzählt, die dem König Salomon die Zukunft enthüllte und Gänsefüße hatte.

Die Gans besaß bei vielen Völkern der Antike kultisch-göttliche Bedeutung. So war die Nilgans bei den Ägyptern die Weltenschöpferin, denn sie hatte das Welten-Ei gelegt, aus welchem die Sonne geschlüpft ist. Heute ist die Gans Synonym einer dummen Frau.

Auch die zahlreichen Sagen von der „Weißen Frau" werden in der Sagenforschung in einen Zusammenhang mit der Bertha/Holda gestellt. Als Ahnfrau steht sie in verschiedenen Ländern für einstmalige glückliche Zeiten. In Italien und in Frankreich ist heute noch das Sprichwort bekannt: „Vorbei sind die Zeiten, als Bertha noch spann ..."

Ab dem 13. Jh. wird Berta oft mit der heidnischen Diana gleichgesetzt oder als Domina Perchta beschrieben, die, anstatt in die Kirche zu gehen und zu beten, lieber tanze, sich schminke und Jünglinge verführe.

Im Laufe der Zeit wurde so aus der einstigen machtvollen „doppelseitigen" Frauengestalt eine Schreckfigur.

16

Frau Berchta in Lajen

Berchta ist eine lange, tief verschleierte Frau gewesen mit aufgelöstem, langem, wallendem Kopfhaare. Sie ist meist im Abenddunkel nach dem Betläuten gesehen worden, wie sie an der Spitze einiger kleiner, kläffender Hunde durch den mit Gestrüppe bewachsenen Gebirgsbach zwischen Tschöffes und dem Grödnerbach niederstieg.

Ein alter Schneider erzählte mir, er habe selber die kleinen Hundlen der Frau Berchta gesehen, wie sie einmal im Hofe eines Bauernhauses daherkamen. Er versuchte die kleinen Köter zu erwischen, aber so oft er einen in den Händen zu haben glaubte, war er wieder entwischt.

›› Wissenswertes ‹‹

Tschöffes, heute Tschöfas, ist eine Fraktion von Lajen.

So wie die Berchta in dieser tief symbolischen Sage waren auch antike Göttinnen wie Hekate, Istar, Isis, Demeter verschleiert. Der Schleier steht für Unergründbarkeit und verborgenes, geheimes Wissen. Er versinnbildlicht das in der Dunkelheit verborgene Licht. Da die unverhüllte Wahrheit gefährlich sein könnte, schützt der Schleier sowohl die Wahrheit selbst als auch die, die sie ergründen wollen. In den Berchta-Sagen treten Hunde oftmals als ihre Begleittiere auf. Sie ist somit der großen rätischen Göttin Reitia ähnlich, die ebenfalls einen blauen Schleier trug und deren Begleittier der Wolf, das Stammtier des Hundes, war. Auch Wotan, der männliche Anführer der wilden Jagd, wurde von kläffenden Hunden begleitet. In der Mythologie findet man den Hund oft als Wächter der Grenze zur Unterwelt. Häufig ist er an der Seite von Muttergöttinnen und mythischen Jägerinnen zu finden. Auch unzählige andere Sagen erzählen von dämonischen Hunden mit glühenden Augen, die Schätze behüten. Oft sind sie riesengroß oder feurig. Arme, verwünschte Seelen erscheinen in Hundegestalt, und so erinnern Berchtas Hunde an ihre Rolle als Seelenführerin.

17

Die Berchtl bei der Brücke in Virgen

Es mag so manche Tanne im Virgental umgehauen und an ihrer Stelle eine andere groß gewachsen sein, seitdem ein Bauer einmal mit der Berchtl eine seltsame Geschichte erlebte. Er ging in der Nacht vor dem Heiligen Dreikönigstage von Windischmatrei heim und wie er weiter ins Tal hineinkam, war es schon tief in der Nacht und „stockdunkel wie in einem Sack". Er hätte die Finsternis mit den Händen greifen können, und durch das Tal pfiff ein eiskalter Wind. Es war dem guten Mann, der sonst eben nicht zu den furchtsamen Hennen gehörte und jede Stunde der Nacht schon mehr als zwanzig Mal auf „freier Weite" zugebracht hatte, heut' gerade nicht zu Mute wie etwa einem Robler, der es mit jedem aufnehmen möchte, und sagte deshalb fein andächtig: „Gott Lob und Dank!", als er die Brücke erreicht hatte, von der es zu seinem Haus nicht mehr weit war. Aber da hörte er auf der anderen Seite ein Gemurmel von vielen Stimmen, als käme die „Wilde Fahrt" daher, und um auf jeden Fall auszuweichen, möge es sein, was es wolle, stieg er unter die Brücke hinab, denn weit davon, dachte er, sei gut für den Schuss, und setzte sich auf einen Stein, wo das Schneegestöber nicht zugekommen war. Da hörte er zahlreiche Schritte auf der Brücke und als sie hinüber waren, sagte eine Stimme: „Wartet, Kinder! Da unten ist ein Stock, in den muss ich dieses Hackl hineinhauen", und in dem Augenblick stand die Berchtl vor ihm und schlug ein Hackl in sein Knie, dass es steckte, und verschwand dann, wie ein Nebel zergeht. Dem Bauer war jetzt noch weniger ums Lachen als zuvor, denn es war keine Möglichkeit mehr, das Hackl herauszubringen. Er ging nach Hause und suchte dann Hilfe bei allen Geistlichen und Doktoren weit und breit, das Hackl aber blieb, ohne ihm Schmerzen zu machen, in seinem Knie. So war nun ein Jahr bald herum, denn die Zeit vergeht, ohne dass man es merkt, und da kam ihm ein glücklicher Gedanke in den Sinn. Er ging in der Heiligen Dreikönigsnacht wieder hinaus zur Brücke und setzte sich auf den gleichen Stein. „Vielleicht kommt die Berchtl", dachte er, „und holt das Hackl ab." Und wirklich täuschte er sich nicht. Bald hörte er sie mit ihrem ganzen Gefolge über die Brücke gehen und als sie hinüber war, sagte sie: „Wartet! Voriges Jahr hab ich da unten in einen Stock ein Hackl eingehauen, ich muss es wieder mitnehmen!" Kaum gesagt, stand sie unten vor dem Bauer und zog ihm schnell das Hackl heraus, dass man nichts mehr spürte, wo es gesteckt hatte, und war dann weg wie der Wind. Dem Mann aber war besser zu Mute als einer Armen Seele, wenn sie aus dem Fegfeuer erlöst wird, und er ging, wie sich jeder leicht einbilden mag, freudiger heim zu als vor einem Jahr.

›› Wissenswertes ‹‹

vgl. „Frau Berchta bei Villanders" (S.46)
Windischmatrei = Matrei in Osttirol, Robeln = Rangeln, ein beliebter Tiroler Männer-Raufsport, Hackl = eine kleine Axt.

Die Wilde Fahrt oder Jagd oder Das Wilde Gejaid ist das in den winterlichen Raunächten umziehende, wütende, dämonische Heer und wird als das Seelenheer der Toten gedeutet. Es wird von Perchta oder vom Wilden Jäger (Wotan), manchmal auch von allen beiden gemeinsam, angeführt. Alles, was sich ihnen in den Weg stellt, wird niedergewälzt. Manche sehen in der Perchta oder Stampe auch eine Lichtgöttin, die nach der Wintersonnenwende mit ihrem Umzug das Zunehmen der Kraft der Sonne und des Lichtes unterstützt. Perchta duldet keine neugierigen Beobachter. Wer dieses Tabu nicht respektiert, den haucht sie an, so dass er erblindet oder hackt ihm ihr Beil ins Knie, und der Betroffene muss ein ganzes Jahr lang – bis zu ihrem neuerlichen Erscheinen – damit leben. Nur die Perchta kann das Beil wieder entfernen. Die Axt ist ein uraltes Kraftsymbol. Wegen ihrer Dreiecksform wird sie mit dem weiblichen Schamdreieck symbolisch in Verbindung gebracht. Vom Christentum wurde dieses Symbol in der Legende vom Hl. Wolfgang übernommen, der mit einem Holzbeil dargestellt wird.

18

Die Gömnacht-Perchtl zu Hechenblaiken

Ein Sohn des Hechenblaikner Hofbauern kam einst spät in der Gömnacht nach Hause und führte sein Ross zur Tränke; da sah er die Perchtl mit dem Kinderheere über den Hof und vorüberziehen. Alle Kinder trugen weiße Hemden, als ein Zeichen der Unschuld, und das Hemdchen des letzten Kindes war etwas zu lang, daher trat das Kind immer hinauf und war in seinem Gange gehemmt. Da rief der Knecht: „Huderwachl hintennach! Komm her, ich will dir das Hemd hinaufbinden!", und das Kind kam auch und der junge Bauer nahm ein Strumpfband und band dem Mädchen das Hemd hinauf. Da sprach das Kind: „Jetzt dank ich Dir schön, jetzt hab ich einen Namen!", und verschwand. Da drehte sich die alte Perchtl, die schon ein gutes Stück voraus war, auch um und rief: „Hab Dank Bub, dass du den armen Huderwachl durch Namengebung erlöst hast! Und dafür sollt ihr auf dem Hofe hier gesegnet sein bis ins neunte Glied und auf den neunten Stamm." Damit zog sie von hinnen. Das Wort der Perchtl aber wurde zu eitel Segen. Das Getreide trug schwerer, üppiger wurde der Wiesenwuchs, das Vieh mehrte sich in den Ställen, der Viehschelm konnte niemals Macht über dasselbe gewinnen, und das blieb lange Jahre so und der Segen erbte sich fort von einem Erbsohn auf den anderen. Beim neunten aber wendete sich das Glück. Dieser hieß Franz, und obschon er eine reiche Dirne geheiratet hatte, kam er in seinem Hauswesen doch merklich zurück. Da kam 1809 der Bauernkrieg gegen Österreich und Franz Hechenblaikner zog als Schütze mit aus gegen den Feind seines Vaterlandes und seines Kaisers. Es gedenkt seiner noch das Ahndl des Wirtes in Bruck, wo das Zillertal in das Inntal ausmündet, wie der Franz sich noch ein Glas Branntwein geben ließ und zu einigen Kameraden sagte: „Jetzt gehe ich und hol mir ein paar Feinde!" Und wie er über die Straße hinausging in das Zillertal, das aber die Bayern schon besetzt hielten und niemals lebend wiederkehrte. Wohl schoss der Franz auf die Bayern, aber diese schossen auch auf ihn, er wurde getroffen, verwundet, gefangen, niedergestoßen und in die Ziller geworfen. Lange blieb sein Leichnam an der Zillerbrücke hängen.

Die Witwe des letzten Hechenblaikners hatte nur Töchter. Ihr Hauswesen verfiel immer mehr und zuletzt ging der früher so stattliche Hof ganz in fremde Hände über.

Da haben die Leute lange gesagt: „Die Perchtl, ja die Perchtl, die hat's weit vorausgesehen."

Ahndl = Großmutter.

Hechenblaiken ist ein uralter, sagenumwobener Bauernhof in der Gemeinde Reith im Alpbachtal in Nordtirol. Huderwachtl bedeutet so viel wie „wehendes altes Tuch". – Durch das Mitleid mit dem Kind, vor allem aber, weil der Knecht ihm einen Namen gegeben hat, ist das Kind in seinem Fortkommen nun endlich nicht mehr beeinträchtigt. Dafür wird er von der Percht großzügig, neun Generationen lang, belohnt. Die Zahl neun ist in vielen Kulturen und Religionen von besonderer Bedeutung, vor allem aber in der nordischen Symbolik die heilige Zahl schlechthin. So hing auch Odin neun Tage und Nächte lang auf der Weltenesche und erlangte dadurch schamanisches Wissen. – 1809 erklärte Österreich den Krieg an Frankreich und seine Verbündeten. Auch viele Bauern Tirols erhoben sich, um das Vaterland zu verteidigen und den Feind zu vertreiben.

19

Der Unschuldigen-Gottesacker

Zu Reit, dem Pfarrorte der äußeren Talhöfe im Alpbachgrund, durch den der Alpbach vom Plakner-Joch herunterrollt, befand sich bis vor nicht allzu langer Zeit neben dem großen Friedhof noch ein kleiner, kaum von der Größe eines länglichen Saales, der wurde der „Unschuldigen"-Gottesacker genannt, weil auf ihm ausschließlich die ohne Taufe verstorbenen Neugeborenen begraben wurden. Solche Friedhöfe gab es auch in vielen anderen Dörfern. Den Einwohnern war es aber ein großer Schmerz, wenn sie ein Kindlein so schnell verloren, dass es nicht die Heilige Taufe oder doch mindestens die Nottaufe empfangen konnte. Daher wurde in der Regel alles aufgeboten, selbst einem schon halbtoten Kinde noch die Segnung der heiligen Taufe und einen Namen geben zu lassen, und Doktoren wie Hebammen wurden hoch gelobt und belohnt, wenn es ihnen gelang, dem fliehendem Leben eines solchen Kindes noch die kurze Frist zu geben, damit es nur auf dem großen Gottesacker begraben wurde.

Auf einem Bauernhofe wurde auch ein Kind geboren, das wenige Stunden nach der Geburt in Krämpfe fiel und dem Verscheiden nahe kam. Die Hebamme aber war bereits wieder nach Reit hinunter und ebenso weit wohnte der geistliche Herr. Wenig weiter war es nach Alpbach und dort hielt sich just damals ein Wunderdoktor auf, in der Absicht, den Haselwurm zu fangen. Selbiger Mann war weit und breit berühmt und so wurde ein Bote nach ihm gesendet. Bevor er aber kam, verschied jenes Kind. Die betrübten Eltern lebten jedoch des festen Glaubens, der Wunderdoktor vermöge durch seine Kunst dem Kinde dennoch auf so lange Lebensfähigkeit zu verleihen, bis die Nottaufe an Letzterem vollzogen sei, und dazu genügte es, wenn das verstorbene Kind nur ein Glied bewegte oder nur einige schwache Atemzüge tat.

Wie der Wunderdoktor kam, rühmte er sich auch gleich seiner großen Künste und zählte an den Fingern her, wie viele Kinder er schon dem „Unschuldigen"-Gottesacker entrissen und für den großen „gerettet" habe, darauf begann er seine Kunst an dem toten Kinde mit Anhauchen, Streichen, Kneippen und Murmeln von Zaubersprüchen, wobei er endlich die Eltern aus der Stube gehen hieß und ganz allein beim Kinde gelassen zu werden verlangte.

Als nun alle hinausgegangen waren, so sah der Doktor mit einem Male ein uraltes Mütterlein sich ihm gegenüber stehen, das hatte ein Gesicht wie Spinnweben so grau und aschenfarbig und schneeweißes Haar. Erst wurde der Doktor unwillig, dass seinem Befehle nicht vollständig Folge geleistet worden war, und gebot der Alten, sich aus der Stube hinaus zu den anderen zu scheren, denn er hielt sie für eine Urahndl. Aber die Alte wich nicht und wankte nicht und zuckte mit keiner Wimper und nun überkam den Doktor ein Grausen. Und da sprach die Alte: „Phraschtl, das Kind, der arme Wurm, ist mein, bekümmere du dich um deinem Wurm!", streckte die Hände aus, fasste das Kind und verschwand mit ihm. Und das ist die Perchtl gewesen, die hatte bereits des Kindes Seele und trug nun selbst den kleinen Leichnam zu Grabe hinunter nach Reit auf den Unschuldigen-Gottesacker. Der Wunderdoktor aber wanderte, von Verwünschungen begleitet, nach Alpbach hinauf, und rühmte sich niemals wieder, gestorbene Kinder lebendig machen zu können.

Philippus Theophrastus (Phraschtl) Aureolus Bombastus von Hohenheim, genannt Paracelsus (geb. 1493 in Einsiedeln, gestorben 1541 in Salzburg), war ein bereits zu seinen Lebzeiten berühmter Arzt, Alchemist, Astrologe und Philosoph. Er hielt sich auch in Tirol auf. Um seine Figur ranken sich viele Sagen, so auch jene des Haselwurms, eines halbmythischen Wesens der Tiroler Sagenwelt, das von der Paradiesschlange abstammen soll. Der Genuss seines Fleisches und der Gebrauch einiger seiner Körperteile versprachen außergewöhnliches Wissen, die Kenntnis aller Tiersprachen, das Heben von Schätzen, Heilung von vielen Krankheiten usw. Ihn zu finden, war äußerst kompliziert. – Paracelsus sagte von sich selbst, dass er sein Heilwissen von Weisen Frauen gelernt habe. Doch in dieser Sage muss er das Feld räumen, denn Perchta ist die Schützerin und Herrin der toten ungetauften Kinderseelen.

Totgeborene Kinder oder ohne Taufe verstorbene Neugeborene konnten früher aufgrund der Kirchenlehre (Augustinus) nicht in den Himmel kommen, da die Schuld der Erbsünde, die erst durch die Taufe getilgt wird, auf ihnen lastete. Demzufolge kamen diese Kinder in die Vorhölle, in den „limbus puerorum", und blieben für ewig von der göttlichen Erlösung ausgeschlossen. Sie durften auch nicht im Friedhof beerdigt werden und erhielten kein Grab. Für die Gläubigen, vor allem für die Mütter, war dies sehr schmerzhaft; sie konnten sich damit nur schwer abfinden. So unternahmen sie oft beschwerliche Wallfahrten mit ihren toten Kindern, in der Hoffnung, dass durch die Hilfe der Mutter Gottes das totgeborene Kind wenigstens für die Zeit der Nottaufe zu Leben erweckt würde und ihnen somit der Weg ins Paradies offen stünde. Auf den Mund des Kindes wurde ein Vogelfederchen gelegt. Wenn dieses sich in die Höhe bewegte, wurde dies als Atem gedeutet. In Wirklichkeit stieg mancherorts von einem glühenden Kohlebecken ein warmer Luftstrom auf und bewegte so die Feder. Solche Wallfahrtsorte waren in Nordtirol Maria Waldrast, in Südtirol Maria Trens und im heutigen Trentino die Muttergottes in Pellizzano im Val di Sole und in Spormaggiore am Eingang zum Nonstal. Erst im 20. Jh. rückte die katholische Kirche von dieser radikalen Haltung ab.

20

Die Stampe

Zu Heiligen-Dreikönigen-Raunachten ist ein alter Schatzer in Afers auf dem Schatzereck gestanden. Da hat er die Gstampe über die Goller Wiese draußen hereinfahren gespürt. Augenblicklich ist er ins Haus gerannt, und wie er die Tür zugeschlagen hat, ist sie schon vorüber mit schrecklichem Pfeifen und Winseln. Um ein Haar hätte sie ihn erwischt.

Wenn die Gstampe kommt, darf man keinen Laut hören lassen im Haus, und wer husten muss, tut es in den Mohnstampf hinein.

Ein alter Hofer in Afers hatte am Firstbaum des Stadels immer einen Kalbskopf hängen. Er hat den Ehehalten nie gesagt, warum, aber er wollte vor der Gstampe geschützt sein, deswegen durfte der Kopf nicht fort.

›› Wissenswertes ‹‹

Schatzereck = ein Bühel in Hausnähe des Bauern; Mohnstampf = ein hölzernes Gefäß, in welchem der Mohn kleingestampft wurde; die Ehehalten = die bäuerlichen Dienstboten.

Der Mohn spielt nicht nur in der Südtiroler Küche, sondern auch in den Südtiroler Totengeistersagen eine wichtige Rolle, denn diese Geister liebten Mohnkörner sehr. Ein Zusammenhang mit dem Tod aufgrund seiner einschläfernden Wirkung kann vermutet werden. Er zählt zu den „Hexenpflanzen" und war die heilige Pflanze der Großen Göttin Demeter/Hekate.

Das Kalb war in Sage und Volksglauben Tirols ein bedeutendes Tier. So war es früher Brauch, als Bauopfer – neben anderem Kleingetier – ein Kalb lebend einzumauern. Tierhörner, auch aus Holz geschnitzte, hängt/hängte man zum Schutz gegen Blitzschlag auf den Firstbaum oder an den Dachfirst.

21

Frau Berchta bei Villanders

Auf dem Villanderer Berge weiß man von der Wilden Fahrt und der Frau Berchta gar vieles zu erzählen. In den sogenannten Klöckelnächten durfte sich niemand mehr außer Haus aufhalten, denn Frau Berchta nahm jeden, den sie noch im Freien fand, mit sich fort. So sah sie einmal, als sie nach dem Betläuten mit einem Wagen voll Menschen vorbeifuhr, eine Bauerndirne beim Brunnen, warf sie auf den Wagen und fuhr mit ihr weg. Dies arme Mädel kam nie wieder zum Vorscheine.

Als Frau Berchta einmal an einem Bauernhause vorbeifuhr, riefen ihr die Bewohner desselben zu: „Lass meinen Teil auch! Lass meinen Teil auch!" Am Morgen fanden sie einen Mann an die Haustüre genagelt. Als in der folgenden Nacht Frau Berchta wieder vorüberfuhr, riefen sie ihr zu: „Nimm meinen Teil auch! Nimm meinen Teil auch", und sie nahm den Leichnam wieder fort.

Überhaupt hatte Frau Berchta gar sonderbare Sitten und neckte das Weibervolk und hielt es in strenger Zucht und Ordnung. Die Dirnen wussten aber auch gar wirksame Mittel dagegen wie das Atmen in eine Mohnstampfe und Ähnliches. Am schlimmsten zeigte sie sich aber um Weihnachten. Da musste das Werg abgesponnen und das Garn abgewunden, das Geschirre gescheuert und alles rein und geordnet sein, andernfalls sie das Vergehen schwer ahnden würde.

›› Wissenswertes ‹‹

Werg = Flachs- oder Hanffasern minderer Qualität, die sich zu groben Garnen verspinnen lassen.

Die dämonenhaften Züge der Frau Berchta kommen hier besonders zum Tragen. Das Zerreißmotiv ist in den Tiroler Sagen vor allem vom Wilden Jäger und vom Wilden Mann, der die Wilden Fräulein verfolgt, bekannt. Die Raunächte gehören der Berchta („Die Nacht ist mein!"), die Strafe bei Widersetzung gegen dieses Verbot ist in dieser Sage besonders grausam.

Das Spinnen war wie die restliche Textilarbeit eine Domäne der Frau. Frau Berchta vom Villanderer Berg erinnert als Aufseherin über das „Weibervolk" an die deutsche Frau Holle.

22

Berchtlsagen aus Alpbach I und II

I.

Ein Viertelstündchen inner der Kirche liegt gegen die Thalerkögel und das Hösl zu am erlenbeschatteten Bache ein Dörflein, von recht schönen Obstangern und Feldungen umgeben. Dort war einmal am Gömachtabend beim Lederer Bauern, derweil die Mutter kochte, ein Mädchen vor der Tür und spielte ganz allein und war recht zufrieden dabei, denn Kinder haben selten Langeweile. Da kam ein steinaltes Weiblein daher – es war die Berchtl – und ging zu dem Kind hinzu und gab ihm einen verrosteten Vierer. Das Kind lief geschwind in die Küche hinein und gab ihn der Mutter. Diese tat ihn zu ihrem übrigen Geld und wollte dann dem Weiblein ein Küchel dafür hinaustragen, aber es war nirgends mehr zu sehen oder zu erfragen, es war verschwunden mit Laub und Staub. Seit der Zeit schaute es bei diesem Bauern aus, als wenn ihm Zeug und Sach durch den Kamin und die Fenster hineinkämen, und auf seinem Gelde ruhte ein besonderer Segen.

›› Wissenswertes ‹‹

In dieser Sage steht der Segen spendende Zug der Perchtl im Vordergrund. Kinder, vor allem Mädchen, stehen besonders in ihrer Gunst.

II.

Am Gömachtabend war es vordem der Brauch, von allen Gerichten des Nachtmahls einen Löffel voll dem Feuer zu geben. In manchem Hause ließ man auch das Übergebliebene auf dem Tische stehen für die Berchtl und ihre Kinder. Wenn alles schlafen war, kam sie dann und aß. Da wollte sie einmal einer belauschen und legte sich in den großen Backtrog hinein, der unter der Bank stand, und guckte durch eine Spalte heraus. Die Berchtl kam wirklich. Sie war ein meeraltes Weiblein mit zerrütteten Haaren und trug ein so zerlumptes Gewand, dass zehn Katzen nicht im Stande gewesen wären, darin eine Maus zu fangen. Es waren auch viele Kinder bei ihr, Buben und Dirnlein, die hatten auch gerade so zaunzerrissene Kleider an. Da sagte die Alte zum Jüngsten: „Geh hin und verstreich dort die Spalte, wo der Wunderwitz außergafft." Das Kind ging zum Backtrog hin, fuhr mit dem Finger über die Spalte und der Mensch darin war augenblicklich stockblind. Das hatte er zum Lohn für die Neugierde, dass er Gespenster anschauen wollte, und niemand konnte ihm helfen. Auf den Rat eines erfahrenen Mannes setzte er sich am nächsten Gömachtsabend wieder in den Backtrog und klagte darin seine Not. Da kam wieder die Berchtl mit ihren Kindern, kostete von den Speisen auf dem Tisch, und bevor sie ging, sagte sie zum gleichen Buben: „Geh zum Trog und tu' die Spalte wieder auf." Das Kind ging hin, blies durch die Ritze und der Blinde war wieder sehend, wie früher.

›› Wissenswertes ‹‹

Der Gömacht- oder Gömnacht- oder Gebnachtabend ist der 5. Jänner. Der Brauch, in den Raunächten Haus und Hof zu räuchern und Speiseopfer (Kücheln, gekochte Eier, Brot, Knödel, Essensreste, Milch usw.) für die Perchta auf das Hausdach oder in der Küche bereitzustellen, war früher weit verbreitet. Man erwartete sich dadurch Segen für Haus und Hof. Später wurde die Tradition des Räucherns dem Schutz durch die Heiligen Drei Könige zugeordnet. – Bereits die Römer opferten in ihren Häusern auf dem Hausaltar ihren Herdgottheiten, den Laren. Speiseopfer für die Feen sind auch aus Slowenien, Frankreich u.a. Ländern bekannt. Doch auch der Perchta selbst schenkt man mancherorts, z.B. im Fränkischen, Dörrobst, Äpfel, Nüsse, Lebkuchen und Kekse. – In Niederösterreich und in der Steiermark wurde früher ein Löffel in das Milchopfer (Perchtenmilch) hineingesteckt. Er diente als Löffelorakel. – Neben dem Beil-Einhacken ist das Blenden ein typisches Perchta-Motiv. Sie bestraft jeden, der ihre Verbote nicht respektiert.

In Sage und Volksglauben spielt das Kind aufgrund seiner Unschuld eine bedeutende Rolle. Oft wird es als Helfer in Notsituationen eingesetzt; es bringt Glück. Auch in den Perchta-Sagen ist es oft ihr ausführender Arm.

Mancherorts, wie z.B. im Fersental, gingen die Kinder am Vormittag des 5. Jänner von Haus zu Haus und bekamen Geschenke.

23

Bertasage aus Folgareit

Einmal war in einer Höhle eine Frau, die hieß Berta. Sie hatte drei Mägde; die erste ringelte ihr die Locken, die zweite gniedete ihr die Haare und flocht ihr die Zöpfe, die dritte bereitete ihr das Essen.

Frau Berta war sehr edelmütig. Sie kam oft nach Folgareit herauf und ging zu allen Weibern, um ihnen arbeiten zu helfen. Am häufigsten kam sie zu den Alten und ließ sich Faden oder Garn geben, um Knäuel zu winden. Da wurde sie aber nie fertig, denn der Faden und das Garn gingen in ihrer Hand nie aus. Alle Weiber waren ihr gut und gaben ihr zu essen, was sie nur hatten. Einmal aber kam sie zu einer Alten und bat sie um zwei Eimer, Wasser zu holen. Diese aber gab ihr zwei Siebe. Frau Berta ging zum Brunnen, schöpfte mit den Sieben Wasser und nahm sie auf; bald aber war sie ganz nass und war alles Wasser über sie hinabgeronnen. Sie versuchte nochmals das Sieb zu füllen, aber vergebens. Da wurde sie sehr zornig, ging zur bösen Alten, die sie beim Bügeln antraf und stürzte sie in einen Kessel voll siedenden Wassers. Aber am nächsten Morgen ging der Mann der Alten in Frau Bertas Höhle und erschlug sie und ihre Mägde mit der Hacke. Mit der Zeit sollen die Leute auch gar manche Gerätschaften in jener Höhle gefunden haben.

›› Wissenswertes ‹‹

gnieden = glätten.

Folgareit, zimbrisch „Vielgereuth“, italienisch Folgaria, liegt auf einer großen Hochfläche ca. 20 km östlich von Rovereto an der Grenze zur Provinz Vicenza. Bereits im 12. Jh. hatten sich hier Zimbern angesiedelt.

Während sich im benachbarten Luserna die zimbrische Sprache bis auf heute erhalten hat, wird in Folgaria nur mehr Italienisch bzw. der Trentiner Dialekt gesprochen. – Interessant in dieser Geschichte ist die Konstellation der drei Frauen, die der Berta dienen müssen. Auch in dieser Sagenversion zeigt Frau Berta ihren hilfreichen und großzügigen Charakter: das Garn geht nie zu Ende. – Das Motiv des Wassertragens in einem durchlöcherten Gefäß ist in vielen Sagen und Mythen verbreitet. In der griechischen Mythologie müssen die 50 Danaiden, die Töchter von Danaos, die auf Befehl ihres Vaters in der Brautnacht ihre Ehemänner töteten, zur Strafe Wasser in ein durchlöchertes Fass schöpfen. Antike Mythen erzählen aber auch von Frauen, die mit Hilfe von Sieben Zauberei, auch Heilzauber betreiben. Auch bei den Germanen ist das Sieb ein Zauberattribut der Hexen, auf dem sie sich u.a. durch die Lüfte fortbewegten. In vielen europäischen Überlieferungen wurde das Sieb auch zum Orakeln verwendet: Das Siebdrehen benutzte man vor allem, um Diebe zu erkennen.

In dieser Geschichte wird der Frau Berta, wie es häufig in jüngeren Sagenvarianten von mächtigen Frauengestalten der Fall ist, ihr ursprüngliches Wissen um magische Hilfsmittel abgesprochen und von den Menschen gegen sie eingesetzt, um ihre Kraft zu brechen; Frau Berta wird als naiv und nicht besonders klug dargestellt. Auch wird die Hacke, Bertas Attribut, als Todeswaffe gegen sie verwendet. – In einer anderen Sage aus Folgaria wird Frau Berta als „Schutzfrau jeder braven Familie“ bezeichnet, als „wohlwollend gegen jene, die sie achten und ehren“. Doch wer sie beleidige, dem ergehe es schlecht: Die besten Kühe geben dann keine Milch mehr oder sie wird gleich sauer.

24

Bertasage aus Ronchi bei Ala

Es herrschte früher der Glaube, dass, wenn abends Weiber allein ohne einen Mann im „Filò" waren, ihnen leicht etwas Übles zustoßen konnte, besonders kamen die „Frauberte", und dann wehe! Eines Abends saßen zwölf Weiber in einem Filò und spannen und redeten von allerlei Dingen. Es war schon elf Uhr nachts, da bemerkte eine: „Wir sind heute ohne Männer, gehen wir, sonst begegnet uns ein Unglück." Kaum hatte sie es gesagt, so klopfte es schon an die Türe und herein trat eine Frau Berta.

„Seid gegrüßt, Frau Berta mit der langen Nase!" [„Padrona, Frauberta dal nas longh"], riefen die Weiber – denn so musste man sie immer anreden – und eine stand auf und räumte der Frau Berta ihren Stuhl ein. „Wird eine andere nach mir kommen, die eine noch längere Nase hat!", erwiderte die Frau Berta und setzte sich nieder. Bald klopfte es wieder an die Türe und herein trat die zweite Frau Berta mit einer noch längeren Nase.

„Seid gegrüßt, Frau Berta mit der langen Nase!", sagten die Weiber wieder und es stand die Zweite auf und räumte der Frau Berta ihren Stuhl ein. „Wird eine andere nach mir kommen, die eine noch längere Nase hat!", sagte dieselbe und setzte sich nieder. Und so ging es fort, bis auch die Zwölfte kam, die hatte die längste Nase und die Frauberte saßen auf den Stühlen, die Weiber aber standen und zitterten vor Angst.

Da sagte die erste Frau Berta: „Was wollen wir tun?" Und die Zweite: „Wir wollen Wäsche machen." Und die Erste sagte zu den Weibern: „Bringt uns die Wassereimer, wir müssen Wasser holen." Die Weiber zitterten, denn sie wussten, was das bedeutete – denn die Frauberte wollten sie sieden und brühen. Daher liefen sie und jede kam mit zwei Körben wieder zurück. Nun gingen die Frauberte fort zur Etsch hinab und wollten die Körbe füllen, aber das Wasser lief bald wieder aus und sie mühten sich lange vergeblich ab. Voll Wut kehrten sie wieder zum Filò zurück, aber da war es dunkel und die Türe gesperrt und jedes der Weiber lag beim Manne im Bette. Da ging eine Frau Berta an das Fenster der Schlafkammer eines von den Weibern und schrie hinein: „Dank' es der Hose, bei der du liegst, sonst weh dir!"

Am nächsten Tag sagten die Weiber: „Heute Nacht kommen die Frauberte gewiss wieder und wir müssen uns vorsehen." Auf ihre Bitten versteckte sich ein Mann neben dem Filò in der Heukrippe eines Ochsen. Um elf Uhr kamen die Frauberte wieder ganz so, wie in der vorigen Nacht. Als sich aber die zwölfte niedergesetzt hat, sprang der Mann aus seinem Versteck hervor und erschlug alle zwölf. So wurden die Weiber wieder gerettet.

Das „Filò“ ist sowohl die Spinnstube als auch die Spinnstubentätigkeit (filare = spinnen). Ala, eine Kleinstadt römischen Ursprungs, liegt im Süden der Region Trentino/Südtirol an der Grenze zur Provinz Verona. – Wie in anderen außertirolischen Perchta-Geschichten tritt die Berta in dieser Sage in der Mehrzahl auf, wiederum ist sie böse und nun nur für Frauen bedrohlich. Frauen bedürfen hier der Hilfe des Mannes, um gegen die Berta geschützt zu sein. Ein Charakteristikum ist ihre lange Nase, die auch in anderen Sagen beschrieben wird. Bereits in mittelalterlichen Handschriften wird sie als Frau Perchta mit der langen oder eisernen Nase beschrieben. Auch der Bozner Hans Vintler, Verfasser der Schrift „Die pluemen der tugent“ (1411), ein Werk, in welchem 18 Tugenden und Laster sowie allerlei Aberglauben des Volkes anschaulich geschildert werden, schreibt hier u.a.: „... und etleich gelauben an die fraun, die da haisset Percht mit der eisnen nas ...“ Die Perchtenforscherin Marianne Rumpf stellt die Hypothese auf, dass die Anspielung auf die eiserne Nase oder das Tragen des eisernen Handschuhs mit dem früher häufig von der Lepra verursachten Verlust von Gliedern oder auch der Nase erklärt werden könnte. Almosen bettelnde Kranke hätten demzufolge ihre verunstalteten Körperteile hinter Masken o.Ä. versteckt, um nicht erkannt zu werden. Geschwüre seien im Elsässischen „Eissen“ genannt worden.

Am letzten Faschingsabend war früher in vielen Gegenden das Perchtenlaufen, eine Art Maskenumzug, üblich. Es war ein Fruchtbarkeitsbrauch in der Vorfrühlingszeit und hat sich bis heute u.a. im Salzburgischen erhalten. Maskierte Burschen stellen „schöne und schiache“ Perchten dar. Wenn sie früher durch die Gassen sprangen und in die Häuser kamen, wurden sie von den Bäuerinnen aufgrund der Förderung von Fruchtbarkeit, vor allem was den Flachswuchs anging, gern gesehen und gut bewirtet. Sagen erzählen auch, dass sich die „echte“ Perchta manchmal daruntermischte und mitsprang. Dies war ein Omen für eine gute Flachsernte. Wer jedoch ihre Echtheit bezweifelte, der musste laut Sage sterben.

In den heutigen Umzügen wird die einstige winterliche Fruchtbarkeitsgöttin dämonisiert und ins Lächerliche gezogen, doch weist die Tatsache, dass mancherorts eine weiße, eine rote und eine schwarze Percht dargestellt werden, immer noch auf ihre einstmals wichtige Position hin.

25

Der eiserne Handschuh

Auf Leibnig fand eine Bäuerin am Dreikönigstage morgens einen eisernen Handschuh auf dem Herde liegen. Sie zeigte ihren Fund dem Bauern und dieser sagte, dass derselbe vermutlich der „Wilden Berchta“ gehöre. Man erzählte die Sache dem Pfarrer, welcher den Rat gab, den Handschuh in einem Kasten sorgfältig aufzubewahren, das ganze Jahr ihn nicht anzusehen und ihn in der Dreikönigsnacht wieder auf den Herd zu legen. Der Rat wurde befolgt, und als am folgenden Morgen die Bäuerin in die Küche ging, um Suppe zu kochen, fand sie an der Stelle des Handschuhes ein Häuflein Gold.

›› Wissenswertes ‹‹

Leibnig befindet sich in Osttirol, ca. 14 km von Lienz entfernt. – Wer Berchtas Besitz mit Respekt behandelt, der wird dafür belohnt. In dieser Sage zeigt sich, wie lange sich im Volk christliche Elemente, Heidentum und Aberglauben parallel gehalten und vermischt haben. Wie in anderen Sagen ist der Pfarrer, Vertreter des Christentums, der Ratgeber für richtiges Handeln auch gegenüber unchristlichen Gestalten.

Laut den Forschungen von Marianne Rumpf könnten die eisernen Handschuhe ein Hinweis sein, dass es sich um Klauenhandschuhe, wie sie im Mittelalter zur Grundausstattung von Aussätzigen gehörten, handeln könnte. In einer Illustration der Handschrift „Die pluemen der tugent" in der Wiener Nationalbibliothek fehlt die linke Hand der Perchta, was Marianne Rumpf mit dem durch Lepra verursachten Verlust von Gliedern deutet.

26

Die Stempa

Vor dem Konzil lebte am Kiesereck die Stempa. Sie stahl kleine Kinder und sperrte sie in Vogelkäfige. Hin und wieder ging sie zu einem der Käfige und sagte: „Zeig deinen Finger her", den steckte sie sich dann zum Probieren in den Mund. War er dick, öffnete sie die Tür des Vogelkäfigs, fuhr mit der Hand hinein, packte das Kind und schwupps, welch guter Bissen! War der Finger mager, dann hagelte es Ohrfeigen.

Einmal fing sie einen kleinen Buben, der war so hübsch und anmutig, dass sich in der Stempa mütterliche Gefühle zu regen begannen; sie sperrte ihn nicht ein und behandelte ihn auch nicht schlecht. Eines Tages befahl sie ihm, vom Dachboden einen Besen zu holen. Der Kleine suchte im Finstern herum, und da hörte er auf einmal eine weinende Stimme. Ganz leise näherte er sich einem der Käfige, stellte sich auf die Zehenspitzen, um etwas zu sehen, und da erblickte er im Käfig ein wunderschönes Mädchen, das weinte und weinte und weinte. „Warum weinst du?", fragte er sie voller Mitleid. „Weil mich die Stempa von meiner Mutter geraubt und in diesen Käfig eingesperrt hat." „Warum?" „Um mich zu mästen. Dann will sie mich essen." Der Bub versuchte den Käfig zu öffnen, doch es gelang ihm nicht, denn die Tür war mit einem dicken eisernen Draht verschlossen. Da rief auch schon die Stempa: „Hübscher Bub, hast du den Besen gefunden?" Schnell nahm er den Besen, versprach dem Mädchen, bald wiederzukommen und kehrte mit klopfendem Herzen in die Küche zurück. „Endlich", murmelte die Stempa, „Geh jetzt schlafen, denn ich habe zu tun." Vor Angst zitternd verkroch sich der Bub unter der Bettdecke, aber so, dass er mit einem Auge hervorspähen konnte. Die Stempa schaute sich um, dann eilte sie ins Freie. Mit einem Stock zog sie einen Kreis, setzte sich auf den Besen und rief: „Drei Sicheln rundherum!" Da begann der Besen zu zittern, erhob sich in die Luft und dann ab Richtung Maso dei Corn.

Der Bub hatte alles mitangesehen, schnell sprang er aus dem Bett und kehrte auf den Dachboden zurück. Erneut versuchte er, den Draht zu entwinden, doch es gelang ihm nicht. Da zählte er die Käfige. Es waren derer zehn, und in allen war ein Kind eingesperrt, aber keines konnte weder sprechen noch weinen, so fett waren sie.

Plötzlich fing die Luft an zu beben, der Bub versteckte sich voller Furcht, und da kam auch schon durch einen Spalt zwischen den Wandbrettern die Stempa auf ihrem Besen daher. Sie lehnte ihn an die Wand und zog dann aus einem mitgebrachten Käfig vorsichtig ein Kind heraus, nicht größer als eine Fingerlänge. Voller Freude betrachtete sie es, dann sperrte sie es in einen leeren Käfig. Nun begab sie sich zu einem anderen: „Steck deinen Finger heraus." Das Kind steckte den Finger heraus; die Stempa nahm ihn vorsichtig zwischen die Zähne. Sie versuchte einen anderen Finger und noch einen andern, nickte zufrieden mit dem Kopf und rief: „Drei Sicheln rundherum!" Wie durch Zauberhand öffnete sich die Käfigtür. Sie griff hinein, packte das Kind, steckte es sich in den Mund, und mit einem Bissen war es verschluckt.

In der Zwischenzeit war es dem Buben gelungen, sich leise, leise davonzuschleichen, und unten in der Küche verkroch er sich, vor Angst bebend, unter der Bettdecke.

Am nächsten Morgen – die Stempa hatte sich gerade zum Brunnen begeben, um ihre Wäsche mit Hilfe von Zauberei zu waschen – kehrte der Bub auf den Dachboden zurück. Er eilte zu den Käfigen und flüsterte: „Drei Sicheln rundherum!" Alle Käfigtüren öffneten sich. Er half den Kindern heraus. Dann zog er einen Kreis auf dem Boden und mit Mühe setzte er den Besen hinein. Er schob die Kinder hin, denn die waren so dick, dass sie sich kaum bewegen konnten. Auch dem Mädchen half er aus dem Käfig. Er half allen auf den Besen und befahl ihnen, sich am vorderen Kind festzuhalten. „Drei Sicheln rundherum!", flüsterte er. Der Besen stieg zitternd in die Luft, doch ohne davonzufliegen. Das Herz schlug dem Buben vor Angst bis zum Hals. „Wär' ich doch jetzt bei meiner Mama!", dachte er verzweifelt. Und da, schnell wie ein Blitz, flog der Besen aus dem Dachboden heraus, pfeifend vor Geschwindigkeit überflogen sie die Wiesen. Die Stempa schaute hoch und sah ihren Besen voller Kinder. Mit drei Sätzen eilte sie auf den Dachboden, ergriff einen anderen Besen und war auch schon in der Luft, um sie zu verfolgen. Aber in der Zwischenzeit waren die Kinder schon zu Hause, beim „Jop". Sie hörten das wütende Heulen der Stempa, der Jop-Vater ging vor die Tür und zog einen Kreis ums ganze Haus. Er setzte zwei schwarze Katzen hinein, nahm den Besen und sagte: „Besen, gesegneter Besen, kehr heim zu deiner Stempa." Mit der rechten Hand machte er das Kreuzzeichen darüber und als die Stempa ganz nah bei ihm vorbeiflog, schleuderte er ihr den Besen entgegen. Blitzschnell zischte der Besen durch die Luft. Er durchbohrte die Stempa, die stürzte vom Himmel und landete im Brunnen der Màrcheli-Bauern. Diese traten mit einem Bild vom Hl. Lorenz und von der Hl. Barbara vor die Tür. Und da löste sich die Stempa in Nichts auf.

Das „Konzil“ fand zwischen 1545 und 1563 in Trient statt. Es war ein bedeutendes Ereignis, denn es ging um die katholische Antwort auf die Reformation von Martin Luther. In zahlreichen Sagen wird das Konzil als Moment genannt, ab welchem herkömmliche Energien/Fähigkeiten, wie die magisch-intensive Verbundenheit mit der Natur, an Kraft und Lebendigkeit verloren und das Christliche über das heidnische Element, den Teufel, siegte. – Durch ein christliches Ritual, das Kreuzzeichen, gelingt es auch hier, die mächtige heidnische Kraft der Stempa auszulöschen. In dieser Sage ist aus der hilfreichen Berchta eine böse, zaubermächtige Hexe geworden. Ihre „Schwäche“ für Kinder ist zwar geblieben, hat nun aber völlig andere Züge angenommen. Waren die Kinder in älteren Perchta-Sagen in deren unterirdischem Reich und in ihrer Obhut nie einer Gefahr ausgesetzt, so geht es ihnen nun wie „Hänsel und Gretel“ im Märchen der Gebrüder Grimm.

Der Kreis ist ein universelles Symbol, er bedeutet Ewigkeit und Zeitlosigkeit. Seine Magie ist in vielen Kulturen und bei vielen Völkern bekannt. Durch das Ziehen eines Kreises erfolgt eine Zweiteilung zwischen „drinnen“ und „draußen“, es entsteht ein Mikrokosmos im Makrokosmos. Das Kreisziehen symbolisiert das In-Verbindung-Treten mit dem Göttlichen, so dass sich die benötigte Kraft entfalten kann, ob als Zauberkreis oder, wie in dieser Geschichte, als Schutzkreis, wo christliche Menschen sich der Kreismagie bedienen, um „das Böse“ zu eliminieren. Der Zauberkreis ist auch in anderen Sagen als Schutzmittel gegen die Wilde Fahrt bekannt. – Die schwarze Katze gilt als ein Hexenbegleittier und Teufelswesen. Einer schwarzen Katze zu begegnen, bedeutet das Herannahen bzw. Heraufbeschwören eines Unglücks. In vielen Erzählungen wird die schwarze Katze auch als Schutz gegen böse Mächte verwendet. Durch das Hineinsetzen zweier schwarzer Katzen in den Kreis verstärkt sich dessen Schutzkraft noch zusätzlich, die Anwesenheit zweier Unheil bringender Tiere macht es der Stempa unmöglich, an ihre Opfer heranzukommen.

Die Sichel als uraltes Hilfsgerät des Menschen wurde zu rituellen und abergläubischen Handlungen genützt. Inner- und außerhalb Tirols wurden zu diesen Zwecken Sicheln gezeichnet, geschnitzt oder eingekerbt, um beispielsweise Wind- und Heuhexen, Truten, Dämonen usw. zu vertreiben. Die Tatsache, dass sie ursprünglich ein bedeutendes matriarchales Symbol war (Symbol für Mond oder Schüssel), ist im Laufe der Zeit ganz in Vergessenheit geraten. – Der Hl. Lorenz und die Hl. Barbara sind wichtige Schutzheilige der Bergknappen.

27

Die Stampe

Vom Zischtler in Olang wird erzählt, dass die Wilde Fahrt immer durch den Hof gefahren sei. Um diese Durchfahrt zu unterbinden, wurde ein Tor zugemauert. Einmal zur Weihnachtszeit saß man beisammen und spielte Karten. „Oh, i muaß scheißn giahn“, meinte einer mitten im Spiel. Die anderen wollten ihn aufhalten: „Heute geht die Stampe um, besser du gehst heute Nacht nicht ins Freie!“ „Stampe hin, Stampe her, scheißen muaß i!“, war seine Antwort und noch bevor ihn einer zurückhalten konnte, war er schon bei der Tür hinaus. Und es geschah, wie es die anderen vorausgesagt hatten: Die Stampe kam, nahm ihn mit und fuhr mit ihm dahin. Erst am Tag darauf kam er wieder zurück, geschmückt mit einer Mohnblüte auf dem Hut. So weit war er gekommen. Zum Glück hat er noch gesagt, „Stampe hin, Stampe her“, wer weiß, ob er sonst überhaupt wieder zurückgekommen wäre.

Viele Stampe-Sagen erzählen von ihrer Fahrt durch Haus und Hof, was auf dämonenhafte Züge hinweist. Um sich vor diesen wilden Durchzügen oder vor anderen „bösen“ Besuchern zu schützen, wurden früher an den steinernen Haustürschwellen Kreuze oder Grübchen eingekerbt, die dies verhindern sollten. Eine solche Stufe mit Schalensteinen ist beispielsweise in einem alten Brixner Stadthaus heute noch ersichtlich.

Um ihren „Besuch“ zu verhindern, brachte man am letzten Rauchabend drei Kreuzlein an den Fensterstockrahmen an. Am 5. Jänner, dem Vorabend des Hl.-Drei-Königsfests, wurde die Stampenvesper oder das Stampenamt abgehalten. Auch wenn heute die Perchta oder Stampe in Vergessenheit geraten ist, so gab es im Tauferertal noch im 18. Jh. eine Perchtwiese und einen Stampacker. In jedem Hause, das einen Kreuzgang hat, d.h. drei Haustüren, Vorder-, Hinter- und Seitentür (oder wenigstens zwei, nämlich eine vordere und eine Hintertür), musste in der Heiligen Nacht „geratscht“ werden, damit die Berchte oder Stampe keinen Schaden verursache. In einem Hause der Gemeinde Kematen wurde lt. Adolf Heyl noch in den dreißiger Jahren des 19. Jh. „geratscht“. Die Ratsche ist ein hölzernes Instrument, das in katholischen Gegenden unter anderem zwischen Gründonnerstag und Ostersonntag anstelle des Glockengeläutes verwendet wird, da, wie man sagt, die Glocken an diesen Tagen nach Rom geflogen sind.

Das Motiv der blühenden Blumen am Hut oder zwischen den Zehen bei zurückgekehrten Entführten ist typisch für Wilde-Jagd-Sagen.

28

Das Kindsmädchen mit dem Kind

Einmal ging ein Kindsmädchen mit einem Kinde auf dem Arm beim Regenstein vorüber und sah dort eine weißgekleidete Jungfrau, welche auf das Mädchen zuschritt, ihr das Kind aus dem Arm nahm und durch die bekannte Tür in das Innere des Felsens eilte. Das Mädchen wollte nach, fand aber zu seinem Schrecken keinen Eingang mehr. Bestürzt eilte es nach Hause und erzählte dort, was ihm passiert war. Die Eltern des Kindes gingen zum Pfarrer von Margreid und erzählten den Vorfall. Dieser gab ihnen den Bescheid, dass sie übers Jahr zur selben Stunde die Tür wieder erblicken werden und ihnen das Kind unversehrt aus derselben entgegenkommen werde.

Es lässt sich denken, mit welchem Bangen die guten Eltern den verhängnisvollen Tag erwarteten. Der Herr Pfarrer hatte aber wahr gesprochen. Im nächsten Jahre am selben Tage und zur selben Stunde fand man das Kind lachend und unversehrt am bezeichneten Orte. Sogar die Blumen, welche es unmittelbar vor seinem Verschwinden gepflückt, hielt es noch in der Hand und sie waren noch ganz frisch.

Der Regenstein ist ein sagenumwobener wassertriefender Felskopf mit Tuff- und Sinterformationen bei Kurtatsch im Südtiroler Unterland. Eine andere örtliche Sage erzählt beispielsweise von einer Prinzessin, die hier alle hundert Jahre in Gestalt einer Schlange und mit einem goldenen Schlüssel im Maul erscheint und auf Erlösung wartet.

Bei St.Georgen/Bruneck steht das sogenannte „Stöckl", eine um 1837 renovierte Marienkapelle auf dem Fundament einer viel älteren Vorgängerin. Laut Sage soll sich früher anstelle dieses Kirchleins der Eingang zu einer Höhle befunden haben, in welcher eine wunderschöne Frau mit vielen Kindern lebte, die sie den Menschen des Tales geraubt hatte. Tatsächlich befinden sich in der Nähe dieser Kapelle der Eingang zu einem nicht mehr genützten Bergwerksstollen und die „große und die kleine Pipe", welche die Reste zweier vorgeschichtlicher Wallburgen tragen. Auch bei Luserna lebte Frau Berchta mit lauter kleinen Kindern in einer Höhle.

Desgleichen erzählen weitere Südtiroler Sagen und Frau-Holle-Sagen im restlichen deutschen Sprachraum von Kindern, die genau ein Jahr in Höhlen zubrachten und dann völlig unversehrt wieder zu ihren Eltern zurückkehrten (vgl. „Das vergessene Kind beim Schatze", Kapitel Bäuerin und Magd).

Seherin und Prophetin

Eine der faszinierendsten Sagengestalten Tirols ist die **Seherin** bzw. **Prophetin**, im Trentino als Sibilla, im restlichen Tirol vor allem unter dem Namen Willeweis/Willeweiß bekannt. Uralt und geheimnisvoll, von den Menschen geachtet und gefürchtet, so wird sie beschrieben; sie konnte in die Vergangenheit zurückblicken und in die Zukunft vorausschauen.

Zur Herkunft und Namensdeutung dieser Figur gibt es in der Sagenforschung unterschiedliche Auslegungen. Manche bringen die Willeweis mit dem Sibyllen-Volksbuch „Zwölf Sibyllen-Weissagungen“ aus dem 16. Jh. in Verbindung, die Anfang des 19. Jh. von einem tschechischen Dichter bearbeitet und auch ins Deutsche übersetzt wurden. Dieses deutsche Volksbuch erfuhr im Alpengebiet weite Verbreitung und erfreute sich großer Beliebtheit. Doch wurde es von der Kirche, da „schädlich und den Aberglauben nährend“, nicht gut geheißen. Die meisten dieser Schriften landeten im Feuer. Der Lanaer Richard Staffler fand vor ca. 50 Jahren eine solche Abschrift als Anhang in einem alten Kochbuch. In solchen Sagen ist häufig von Endschlachten und Weltuntergang die Rede.

Andere Willeweis-Sagen, wie beispielsweise jene der Welschnofener Willeweis, erinnern an die germanischen Seherinnen. Es waren vor allem antike römische Geschichtsschreiber, die von diesen berichteten. Ihnen zufolge besaßen germanische Frauen prophetische Gaben und manche unter ihnen wurden ausdrücklich als Seherinnen und Wahrsagerinnen verehrt. Alte, weiß gekleidete Frauen sollen mit den Heeren mitgezogen sein, aus dem Blut und dem Eingeweide der Gefangenen, aus der Bewegung des Wassers u.a. geweissagt haben. Auch die Römer sollen sich nicht gescheut haben, die Dienste germanischer Seherinnen in Anspruch zu nehmen.

Die Seherin „Veleda“ aus dem Stamm der Brukterer im 1. Jh. n. Chr. beispielsweise genoss laut Tacitus beinahe göttliche Verehrung. Sie wohnte in einem hohen Turm, und ein von ihr dazu ausgewählter Verwandter überbrachte Fragen und Antworten. Angeblich schlichtete sie auch Geschäftszwiste; Verträge sollen in ihrer Gegenwart geheiligt worden sein. Später wurde sie von den Römern gefangengenommen und nach Italien deportiert.

Auf einer ägyptischen Insel fand man eine Tonscherbe aus dem 2. Jh. n. Chr., die von „Waluburg“, einer Seherin aus dem Stamme der Semnonen, berichtet. Auch sie wurde vermutlich von den Römern deportiert und höchstwahrscheinlich nach Ägypten verschleppt. „Walu“ ist wahrscheinlich auf das germanische „walus“

= Stab, altnordisch „völr" oder „vol", zurückzuführen. Die Völva oder Vala war die Stabträgerin; der Zauberstab war das Zeichen ihres Berufes. Auf ihm reitend konnte ihre Seele in andere, unsichtbare Welten gelangen. Sie war also auch Schamanin.

Spuren der germanischen Seherin sind in einigen Märchen der Gebrüder Grimm zu finden, wie beispielsweise im Märchen „Rapunzel", in welchem die Zauberin das Mädchen Rapunzel in ihren hohen Turm einschließt, sowie im Märchen „Die Gänsemagd", das von einem sprechenden toten Pferdekopf namens Falada erzählt (weiße Pferde wurden als Orakeltiere bei den Germanen auf heiligen Hainen gehalten; abgeschlagene Tier- und Menschenhäupter konnten nach nordischem und antikem Glauben weissagen; der Name des Pferdes erinnert an die Veleda).

Die Willeweis wird auch mit einer anderen rätselhaften Figur, der/dem Bilwiz oder Bilwis, in Verbindung gebracht. Bis heute konnte keine endgültige Erklärung zu dieser Sagengestalt gefunden werden. Vielleicht hängt sie mit der nordischen Bil, einer alten Mondgöttin, zusammen. In ihrer/seiner Urgestalt ist dies ein menschenfeindlicher weiblicher oder männlicher Naturdämon, der in Bergen oder in bzw. unter Bäumen lebt. Angeblich hat man ihm, zur Abwehr oder um die Zukunft zu erforschen, einst Kleider oder gar Kinder geopfert. Bei Wolfram von Eschenbach kann diese dämonische Gestalt die Menschen mit einem magischen Pfeil, dem „Bilwizschuss" lähmen. Der Begriff „Hexenschuss" stammt fast sicher von diesem Sagenzug. Die frühesten Belege stammen aus Österreich und Bayern. Die Erzählung von der Willeweis am Pirchboden bei Lengstein/Ritten erinnert an diese Sagengestalt.

Im Laufe der Jahrhunderte und unter dem immer stärker werdenden christlichen Einfluss veränderten sich Charakter und Namen dieses Wesens (Pilweis, Bilbis). Oft wurde dieser Begriff als Schimpfwort für böse Weiber verwendet. Möglicherweise hängt auch der tirolerische Dialektausdruck „Bisgur" für eine bösartige Frau damit zusammen. So wurde Bilwis ausschließlich weiblich dar- und häufig der Hexe, der Perchta oder der Trute gleichgestellt.

Ab dem 16. Jh. überlappt sich die Bilwiz mit den Eigenschaften eines Haus- oder Korngeistes, der sich mit sichelförmigen Scheren an den Füßen fremdes Korn aneignet. Zahlreiche Abwehrbräuche und Schutzmittel sind bekannt. Bis in die 60er Jahre des 20. Jh. hinein wurde in vielen Gegenden Tirols als „Opfer" eine Korngarbe auf dem Feld stehen gelassen oder es wurde Korn in die Ackerraine geworfen.

Bei den alten Griechen und Römern waren die Sibyllen weithin bekannte Prophetinnen. Meist wurde die Sibylle als ältere Frau dargestellt, die im Zustand der Ekstase drohendes Unheil ankündigte. So soll eine Sibylle den Trojanischen Krieg vorausgesagt haben. Früheste griechische Quellen berichten von nur einer Sibylle, später erhöhte sich ihre Zahl. In der römischen Mythologie spielt vor allem die Sibylle von Cumae in Kampanien eine große Rolle. Der Überlieferung zufolge

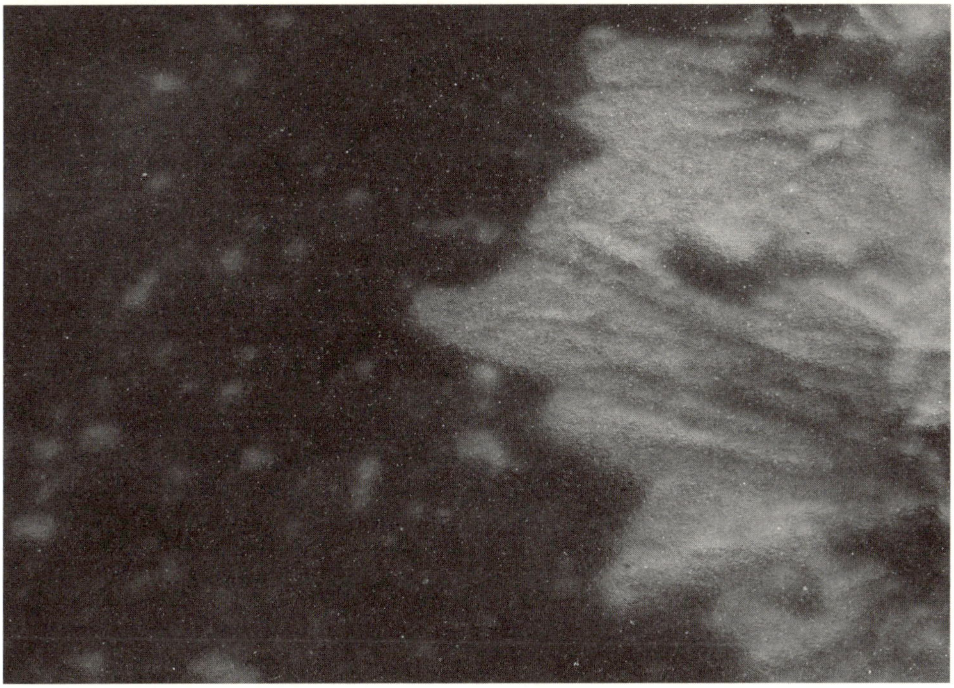

erschien sie dem letzten König von Rom, Lucius Tarquinius Superbus, und bot ihm zu einem hohen Preis ihre rätselhaften Weissagungen in neun prophetischen Schriften an. Als er ihr Angebot ablehnte, verbrannte sie vor seinen Augen drei Bücher und bot ihm die restlichen sechs Bücher nochmals um denselben Preis an. Nach seiner neuerlichen Ablehnung vernichtete sie weitere drei Bücher. Zuletzt kaufte er ihr die restlichen drei Bücher um denselben Preis ab. Sie wurden in einem römischen Tempel aufbewahrt und bei Notzeiten von einem besonderen Kollegium um Rat befragt. Die Bücher fielen im Jahre 83 v.Chr. einem Brand zum Opfer. Eine neue Sammlung wurde verfasst, doch ca. 400 Jahre später wurden diese Schriften definitiv vernichtet.

Sibyllinische Orakel sind auch aus der jüdisch-christlichen Religionsgeschichte bekannt. Sie sind in vierzehn Büchern zusammengefasst. Darin geht es u.a. um apokalyptische Texte, Beschreibungen von der Zerstörung der Welt, den Tag des Gerichts, um Weissagungen gegen verschiedene Völker. Auch Götzendienst, Geldgier und sexuelle Ausschweifungen werden darin verurteilt. Mitunter beziehen sich die Orakel auf biblische Personen und Ereignisse, wie beispielsweise die Sintflut als Sinnbild der globalen Zerstörung. Auf die Zeit der Sintflut wird in den Tiroler Sagen sehr oft Bezug genommen.

Sibyllinische Prophezeiungen wurden von christlichen Theologen im Nachhinein oft als Andeutung des Erscheinens Christi interpretiert, deshalb findet man ihre Darstellungen auch in verschiedenen Kirchen, beispielsweise in Brixen in der Frauenkirche und in Cortina d'Ampezzo, wo bei Restaurierungsarbeiten eines alten Gebäudes, heute Sitz einer Bank, Fragmente von fünf Sibyllen freigelegt wurden. Sie stammen vermutlich aus dem 14. Jh. und stellen ein einzigartiges Kunstobjekt ihrer Art im Alttiroler Gebiet dar.

Auch in der christlichen Sterbeliturgie wird im Gebet des Franziskaners Thomas von Celano (13. Jh.) auf die sibyllinischen Weissagungen hinsichtlich des Jüngsten Gerichtes hingewiesen: „Dies irae, dies illa, solvet saeculum in favilla, teste David cum Sibylla" (Tag des Zornes, jener Tag, der das All in Staub auflöst, wie bezeugt von David und der Sibylla).

29

Die Jocher Fräulein

Ober dem Jocher in Wälschnoven, auf dem Joch unter dem Rosengarten, hausten vorzeiten drei Willeweis. Dies waren Zauberjungfrauen, die da oben seit der Sintflut ferne von den Menschen ein kümmerliches Dasein fristeten. Doch weil ihnen die Zukunft offen war, standen sie bei den Leuten in hohem Ansehen. Eine von ihnen pflegte stets ein blaues Gewand zu tragen, und manche Leute wissen von ihr zu sagen, dass es ein Geist sei, der da oben auf der kalten Höhe büßen müsse, weil er im Leben geglaubt habe, die Nadel, mit welcher die Totenhemden genäht werden, dürfe man nicht weiterverwenden.

Alle drei kamen sie öfters zum Jocher herab, taten aber keinem Menschen etwas zuleide. Allein das Ingesinde des Jocherbauern fürchtete sich dennoch vor den gespenstigen Jungfrauen, insbesondere vor der mit dem blauen Gewande, weil sie die größte von allen dreien war, und auch der hervorstechenden Farbe des Gewandes wegen. Daher, als sie wieder einmal dem Bauernhofe einen Besuch abstatteten, lief die Dirne geschwind zum Geistlichen ins Dorf hinab und meldete ihm den Besuch oben auf dem Hofe. Der Geistliche machte sich alsbald auf den Weg, den Geist fortzubannen.

Nun ist aber beim Jocher in der „Bàlt“ seit undenklicher Zeit ein stehendes Wässerlein, das der Sammler dieser Geschichten selber in Augenschein genommen, um sich davon zu überzeugen; das hat keinen sichtbaren Einfluss, und doch schwindet es nicht. Dieses Wässerlein war der Lieblingsplatz der drei Jungfrauen. Auch diesmal waren sie wieder dort, sich zu baden und zu zwagen und zu kämmen, denn es hatten die drei ein wunderbar langes und schönes Haar, das sie indes nicht in Zöpfe zu binden pflegten, sondern frei fliegen ließen, wie's auch recht ist. Und wie der geistliche Herr ankommt und fragt, wo denn der Geist wäre, sagten ihm die Leute: „In der Bàlt beim Wasser. Aber“, sagten sie weiter, „sehen kann sie nur das Kind, für uns Erwachsene bleiben sie meist unsichtbar.“ Und der Geistliche zeigte dem kleinen Mädchen ein schönes Bild und versprach es ihm, wenn es mit ihm hinabgehe. Das Kind fürchtete sich nun wohl und wollte nicht gehen, aber der freundliche Herr nahm es bei der Hand und sprach ihm Mut ein, und es könne ihm nichts geschehen, weil er bei ihm sei.

Als sie in die Bàlt gelangten, rief das Kind: „Dort ist der Geist!“ und zeigte zum Wasser hin. Der Herr sagte zum Kinde: „Jetzt darfst du wieder hinaufgehen“, und das Mädchen lief fort. Nun fing der Geistliche zu segnen an, aber nach einiger Zeit sahen die Leute von oben, die unterdessen Eier für ihn gesotten und warme Milch bereitgestellt hatten, wie der Herr rasch vom Hofe weg und talab eilte. Sie riefen ihm wohl nach, dass sie die Eier für ihn gerichtet hätten, allein vergeblich, der Herr hörte nichts. Es war nämlich der Geist mit dem blauen Gewande hinter ihm her, und der Geistliche, der nicht das rechte Buch mitgenommen hatte, rannte den Weg hinab. Bei jedem Bildstöcklein am Wege streifte er den Geist wohl von sich ab, der ihm auf den Fersen war, und gewann wieder einen kleinen Vorsprung. Aber es half nicht viel.

Beim Schmiedsackerer verlor er noch gar die Schuhe, der Geist hatte sie ihm abgetreten. Und der Schmiedsackerer, sein Freund, der natürlich auch vom Gespenste nichts sah, rief: „Herr Pfarrer, wohin lauft Ihr so eilig? Ihr habt die Schuhe verloren! Wartet ein wenig, ich bringe sie nach.“ Der Geistliche sagte nichts und lief und lief. Endlich gelangte er zum Widum, flog hinein und der Geist ihm nach, und wie er auf seinem Zimmer eben das rechte Buch aufschlägt, stürmt schon die mit dem blauen Gewande herein. Er spricht nun den rechten Bannspruch, und der half ihm aus der Not. Der Geist war festgebannt und konnte dem geistlichen Herrn nichts mehr anhaben. Dieser zwang die Gebannte, ihm alle ihre Nadeln herauszugeben, mit denen sie im Leben Totenhemden genäht und von denen sie keine mehr als einmal in Gebrauch genommen hatte. Darauf verschwand der Geist.

›› Wissenswertes ‹‹

Wälschnoven = Welschnofen, zwagen = sich (die Haare) waschen. – Die Bàlt ist ein im Keller gelegener Raum, wo landwirtschaftliche Geräte aufbewahrt werden.

Oberhalb von Welschnofen liegen in aussichtsreicher Lage nebeneinander der Ober- und der Unterjocher, Letzterer heute eine Jausenstation. Im uralten Keller des Oberjocherhofes konnten wir uns selbst vom Vorhandensein dieser geheimnisvollen, ca. 1 Quadratmeter großen und bei unserer Anwesenheit ca. 35 cm tief mit Wasser gefüllten Wasserstelle überzeugen.

Diese drei Willeweis erinnern in ihrer Dreier-Konstellation an die Nornen, die in der germanischen Mythologie einen hohen Rang einnahmen, denn sie spannen die Schicksalsfäden der Menschen.

Im Mittelalter und auch noch in späterer Zeit war es üblich, die Leichen in ein Leintuch einzunähen oder einzuwickeln. Dies vermutlich nicht aus Gründen der Sparsamkeit, sondern um eine Wiederkehr der Toten zu verhindern. Das Tuch musste an der Leiche selbst genäht werden. Sagen abgelegener piemontesischer Bergtäler (bei Biella) erzählen, dass die Armen Seelen Vorübergehende, sofern sie derer habhaft werden konnten, baten, den Faden aus ihrem Laken zu ziehen, um sie von ihrem Totenmantel zu befreien. Durch die Berührung mit dem Toten wird der Totennadel Zauberkraft verliehen, ähnlich wie Totenschädeln, -knochen oder -zähnen. Als Zauberhilfsmittel ist sie auch in anderen Sagen und bei anderen Sagengestalten bekannt, so wurde sie vom Tiroler Zauberer Pfeifer Huisele für seinen Wetterzauber verwendet.

Ein blaues Gewand ist charakteristisch für ZauberInnen und Hexen. In einer nordischen Sage wird die auf einem erhöhten Zaubergestell sitzende Seherin Thorbjörg beschrieben. Sie trug eine Haube aus schwarzem Lammfell, Handschuhe aus Katzenfell und einen blauen Mantel, der bis zum Saum mit kostbaren Edelsteinen geschmückt war. Auch zahlreiche Himmelsgottheiten, christliche und vorchristliche, tragen einen blauen Mantel.

Die blaue Farbe fand im Schutzzauber (blauer Wollfaden, blaues Tuch, blaue Steine) häufig Verwendung. Blau blühende Blumen galten in der Volksmedizin als Zauberkräuter (Gundermann, Wegwarte, Ehrenpreis, Vergissmeinnicht, usw.). Dem Kämmen kommt in der Mythologie vieler Völker, aber auch in der Volksmedizin und im Aberglauben, eine wichtige Bedeutung zu. Zauberinnen trugen ihr Haar offen, denn bei Zauberhandlungen mussten alle Knoten und bindenden Bänder, so auch im Haar, vermieden werden. Aufgrund seiner Unschuld glaubte man das Kind noch mit besonderen Kräften begabt und mit den überirdischen Mächten besonders eng verknüpft. So verwundert es nicht, dass nur das kleine Mädchen die drei Willeweis sehen konnte.

30

Die Willeweis in Wälschnoven

Die Willeweis stellen sich die Leute als ein altes Weiblein vor, dessen Gebaren etwas Geheimnisvolles hat. Das Weiblein ist einsam und verschwiegen, hat mit allerlei seltsamem Kräuterwerk zu tun und ist besser vertraut mit den Tieren des Waldes und den verwitterten Steinen als mit den Menschen. Ihre Gedanken haften nicht an der Gegenwart, sie schaut im Geiste Vergangenes und Werdendes. Unter alten Tannen oder breitästigen Buchen ist ihr liebster Sitz, eine menschliche Wohnstatt hat sie nicht. Hie und da summt sie ein längst vergessenes Lied oder einen Zauberspruch. Das Weiblein ist meeralt; die Knochen derer, so mit ihr gelebt, sind längst weiß gebleicht, aber sie wird nicht erdrückt davon, kein Blitzstrahl kann sie treffen, Feuer und Wasser können ihr nichts anhaben, das Weiblein kann nicht sterben.

Der Klang der Glocke trifft ihr Ohr unsanft, daher meidet sie die Nähe der Kirche. Dann und wann sucht sie einen Bauernhof auf, wenn es sie arg friert, und „pfestert" dann wohl die ganze Nacht durch auf dem warmen Herde in einer Ecke oder hinter dem wärmenden Stubenofen. Dann ereignet es sich wohl auch, dass sie etwa das eine- oder das andere Mal mit dem Gesinde den Nachtrosenkranz betet; sonst gewahrte man an ihr kein christliches Zeichen. ie kommt und geht, und niemand weiß, woher und wohin. Unversehens betritt sie einen vom Mittelpunkte des Dorfes möglichst weit entfernten Bauernhof, grüßt nicht und dankt nicht auf den Gruß und öffnet nur dann und wann unaufgefordert ihren Mund, um von der Vergangenheit und Zukunft zu reden, aber stets nur kurz und in spruchartiger Rede. Am öftesten hält sie sich in der Gegend hinter dem Dorfe auf, im sogenannten Loch oder auf dem Joch, auf Gstalt, auf dem Zischgl, häufig auf Kar oben.

In einem Bauernhofe im Loch prophezeite sie einst: „Das Klöanlhaus ban Bach aus, das Unterwirtshaus in Rach auf und das Plankenhaus der Lahn aus." Die beiden ersten Weissagungen sind eingetroffen, die Erfüllung der dritten steht bevor.

Beim Reiter auf Kar sah eine Zeitlang die Bäuerin des Morgens, wenn sie in die Küche ging, die Willeweis auf dem Herde kauern. Es war ein uraltes Weiblein, Gesicht und Hände über und über mit Runzeln bedeckt. Dann und wann tat sie den Mund auf und Vergangenes und Zukünftiges kund. Ein alter Bauer riet dem Reiter, Eierschalen auf den Herd zu stellen. Sie steckten also ringsum auf den Herd halbe Eierschalen in die Asche, und am folgenden Morgen, als die Bäuerin wieder in die Küche kam, rief die Willeweis:

„I bin die Willeweis, an alter Greis,
Woaß in Karerwall neunmal Wies' und neunmal Wall,
In Schlearn an Nusskarn, die Gepleng a Mösserkling',
Die Roatwond a Kinderhond, ober an Heard voll weißer Hafen woaß i nia." →

Darauf verschwand das Weiblein und ließ sich beim Reiter nie mehr sehen.

Vom Kafmannhof erzählen die Leute, dass diesen Hof vor alter Zeit nicht rechte Christenleute, sondern ein „verwunschenes" Geschlecht besessen hätten. Dieses Geschlecht sei von den Christen aus dem Hofe verdrängt worden, und nur eine Person von den „Verwunschenen" sei zurückgeblieben, die Willeweis nämlich. Sie sah den Kafmannhof noch immer als ihren rechten, angestammten Sitz an, und erst nach geraumer Zeit habe man sie endlich vom Hofe weggebracht. Einer der „Verwunschenen", der Gletschmann, ein riesengroßer, wilder Mensch, der nach der Einwanderung der Christen nur mehr so herumirrte und oft beim Kafmannhof vorüberkam, pflegte gewöhnlich dort Einkehr zu halten, um nach der Willeweis zu sehen.

›› Wissenswertes ‹‹

pfestern = fröstelnd am Ofen kauern. – Gepleng = eine sagenumwobene steinige Gegend im Latemargebirge, ehemaliges Alm- und Bergbaugebiet.

In dieser Sage erinnert die Willeweis sowohl an einen Hausgeist, der sich das selbstverständliche Recht herausnimmt, sich in Häusern aufzuhalten, als auch an eine Naturdämonin, die mit den Kräften der Natur aufs Engste verbunden ist. Das hohe Alter dieser Sage wird durch den Hinweis auf die vorchristlichen Ureinwohner des Kafmannhofes bestätigt.

Die Willeweis wird zumeist als uralt geschildert. Sie erinnert hierin an die Sibylle von Cumae in der römischen Mythologie, von der erzählt wird, dass sie sich von Apollon wünschen konnte, was sie wollte, wenn sie seine Geliebte würde. Laut Mythos wünschte sie sich so viele Lebensjahre, wie ein Haufen Sandkörner enthielte, sie vergaß aber, gleichzeitig auch um ewige Jugend zu bitten. So alterte sie immer weiter, bis sie schließlich so stark geschrumpft war, dass sie in eine von der Höhlendecke herabhängende Flasche passte, ohne je vom Tod erlöst zu werden.

31

Von der Willeweis auf dem Birchboden

Mitten im Walde ober Lengstein findet sich ein freier Plan, mit duftigem Rasen belegt und nur von ein paar Lärchen bestanden. Es ist der Birchboden. Fast inmitten desselben steht ein buschig umkränzter Lärchenbaum. Wenn einer bei Nachtszeit da vorüber muss, läuft's ihm allemal kalt über den Rücken, und so einer vom Husten geplagt wird, wirft er sich auf den Boden und hustet in den Wasen, auf dass er von den Unholden nicht verspürt werde. Da oben wohnte vorzeiten ein unheimliches Weiblein. Die gespenstige Frau saß auf dem Rasen und las in einem altmodischen Buche. Es war die Willeweis. Wandte sich jemand in der Not an sie, dann brauchte er bloß am Waldesrand stehen zu bleiben und auf den Plan hinauszurufen: „Die Wile tut die Wele begraben"; alsdann kam die Willeweis herbei, nahm den nächtlichen Gast freundlich auf und sprach weise Worte zu ihm.

Eines Abends zündete sich nun ein alter Reinpalter von Lengstein am Herdfeuer seinen Kentel an und zog aus, bei der weltweisen Frau da oben die Meisterschaft in den Zauberkünsten und die Weltweisheit zu lernen. Er hatte manches Jahr in des Winters langen Nächten gesessen, Zauberbücher aufgeschlagen und vergeblich über die Weltordnung gegrübelt. Er stieg also auf sein Ross und rief mit mächtiger Stimme: „Der Reinpalter reitet auf krumpem Ross. Wia tuat die Wile die Wele bagrobn?“ Alsbald erhob sich das greise Mütterlein mit einem Stabe in der Hand und begann freundlich mit ihm zu reden. Der Reinpalter aber begab sich mit ihr zu dem bezeichneten Baum und fragte sie, wie es um die Welt stehe, und nach dem Sinne des Spruches, mit dem sie von den Leuten gerufen werde. Und das Weiblein schlug ihr meeraltes Buch auf und teilte ihm mit, wie der Wele Bestattung vor sich gegangen und noch vieles andere. Doch was der Reinpalter da oben erfahren, und was im Zauberbuch gestanden, ist weder mir noch dir kund geworden. So viel aber ist bekannt, dass der Mann gesund und ohne Schaden wieder heimgekommen ist, und dass ihn der Zuspruch der Willeweis befriedigt hat. Von da an ging er fleißig seiner Arbeit nach; aber was er auf dem Birchboden erfahren hatte, sagte er niemandem.

›› Wissenswertes ‹‹

Wasen = Rasen/Gras. – Kentel/Kentl/Kienspan = ein besonders harzreiches Holzscheit, das früher als Fackel oder als Wandleuchte benützt wurde.

Die Willeweis erinnert hier, wie in der Einleitung dieses Kapitels erwähnt, an den Bilwis, einen elbischen Naturgeist, der in oder unter Bäumen wohnt. Die enge Verbundenheit der Willeweis mit der Baumseele dieses heiligen Baumes ermöglicht es ihr, geheimes Wissen zu erspüren. – Der Mythenzug des hinkenden Pferdes ist uralt. Er wird sowohl mit dem Pferd des Odin in der nordischen Sage in Verbindung gebracht als auch als Erscheinungsform des Teufels (ein Wesen der Anderswelt) gedeutet. Eine andere Interpretation bringt es in Zusammenhang mit dem uralten Vegetationskult bzw. dem lähmenden Vegetationsdämon, als Sinnbild für das Absterben, das Wachstum und das Gedeihen der Natur. Ihm zu Ehren und um ihm zur Heilung bzw. zu neuem Leben zu verhelfen, haben früher in zahlreichen Ländern kultische Feiern verschiedener Art stattgefunden.

Die Namen Wile und Wele tauchen in Tiroler Sagen auch als Saligen-Namen auf; eine ladinische Sage (K.F. Wolff) erzählt von der Kristána Wellia, einer wilden Felsbewohnerin. Velia Carinei ist auch als Name einer vornehmen Etruskerin dokumentiert. Auch die Vilen, weibliche elbische Wesen in den osteuropäischen Sagen, leben in Wäldern und Bergen.

Wile und We sind laut der germanischen Mythologie die Brüder von Odin, der zentralen nordischen Göttergestalt. Somit gehören sie zu den ältesten Göttern. Als die drei einmal zusammen am Strand spazieren gingen, fanden sie zwei große Hölzer, die die Flut an Land getrieben hatte. Odin hauchte ihnen Leben ein, so dass sie atmen konnten, Wile gab ihnen Vernunft und Verstand, und We verlieh ihnen die Gabe des Gehörs, des Gesichtes und der Rede. Sie wurden die ersten Menschen, genannt Asch und Embla, und von ihnen stammt laut der germanischen Mythologie die ganze Menschheit ab. Mit dem Namen und der Gestalt der Willeweis haben sie aber höchstwahrscheinlich nichts zu tun.

32

Willeweis

So hieß ein altes Weiblein in Welschnofen, dem man nachsagte, dass es schon einige hundert Jahre auf dem Buckel habe. Tagelang saß es den Bauern in der Hütte herum, bald hier, bald dort. Am liebsten hockte es in der Küche neben dem Herdfeuer, sprach fast nichts, deutete nichts und zitterte im heißesten Sommer vor Kälte und innerem Schauder. Gab man ihm zu essen, so flüsterte es ganz leise und zaghaft: „Dank recht schian, I wear schun gian."

Überhaupt redete die Willeweis, wenn sie schon einmal redete, immer in Reimen. Das Versprechen aber, bald zu gehen, vergaß sie immer wieder und blieb oft so lange an dem Herde sitzen, dass es den Leuten schon recht lästig wurde.

Wohl gäbe es ein Mittel, hieß es, die Willeweis auf immer loszuwerden. Man müsse dem Weiblein irgend etwas zeigen, vormachen oder sagen, wodurch es in Erstaunen gerate, dann gehe sie und komme nimmer. Doch das war eine schwere Sache, die Willeweis schaute ja fast nie auf und schien alles schon gesehen und gehört zu haben, was es Wunderliches und Seltsames auf dieser Welt gibt.

Beim Pircher hängten sich der Bauer, die Bäuerin, die Knechte, Mägde und Kinder die großen Kuhschellen um den Hals, schrien „muh-muh" und zogen so im Hause herum, in die Küche und aus der Küche. Doch die Willeweis sagte nur:

„De Plog, de Müah! I kenn Enk decht längst schun als Ochsn und als Küah!"

Beim Strobele-Strutzer kam der Bauer, der einen langen Bart trug, im Gewand der Bäuerin zum Herd und kochte, die Bäuerin stapfte in den Hosen ihres Mannes in die Küche, setzte sich dort auf den Hackstock und rauchte aus der Pfeife, dass ihr fast übel wurde. Die Buben liefen als Mädlein ein und aus, die Mädlein als Buben. Die Willeweis machte nur:

„Hm, hm! Die Hos als Kittel, der Hias als Grittel, die Lies als Luis – ist mir nicht nuis."

Beim Fötsch tranken sie die Suppe aus Krügen, aßen die Knödel mit der Hand, das Mus abends mit der Gabel und sprachen dazu in einer ganz neuen, selbst erfundenen Sprache. Die Willeweis machte es geradeso mit Suppe, Knödel und Mus und sprach in demselben närrischen Kauderwelsch: „Faringalorum, Fötscheber quutal, Laarin madorum plötsch geber zutal."

Beim Geiger auf Kar spielten die Kinder mit den Eierschalen, die von der Bäuerin schon lange Zeit her aufgehoben worden waren, „Kochelets". Sie streuten die Asche über den ganzen Herd aus und setzten die halben Eierschalen als Häflein auf, gossen Wasser ein und sotten Kaffee und Milch, Gramillentee und alle Gattungen von Suppen.

Als das die Willeweis sah, schlug sie die Hände über dem Kopf zusammen und konnte sich nicht genugsam darüber verwundern. Dann sprach sie: →

„Ich bin ein alter Narr, gedenk den Wald im Kar.
Neunmal als Wies, neunmal als Wald, den Schlern als Nusskern.
Die Rotwand als Kinderhand, die Gepleng als Messerkling,
das Tschagerjoch als Knospenbloch. – Aber von so vielen Hafelen auf einem Herd hab ich mein Lebtag noch nicht g'hört".

Mit diesen Worten machte sie sich auf und davon, man hat sie seit der Zeit nie mehr gesehen.

›› Wissenswertes ‹‹

Gramillentee = Kamillentee.

Diese von F.S. Weber bearbeitete und 1914 erschienene Sage ist eine humorvolle Nacherzählung einer älteren Willeweis-Sage aus Welschnofen.

Das Motiv der Eierschalen taucht in vielen europäischen Sagen auf. Sie sind ein wirksames, wenn nicht das einzige Mittel, um Naturwesen wie den Wilden Mann, die Willeweis, den Zwerg usw. zu veranlassen, die menschliche Wohnstätte zu verlassen.

Nicht immer gelingt es den Menschen mit Hilfe christlicher Bannflüche, diese manchmal unheimlich oder lästig erscheinenden Wesen zu vertreiben und sie beispielsweise in eine Felsenwand oder in einen See zu verbannen. So greift der Mensch in den Sagen oft zu einer List, denn es ist nicht ratsam, ein dämonisches Wesen zu beleidigen. Schweigsamkeit und hohes Alter sind typisch für das „entrische", dämonische Wesen. Gelingt es dem Menschen aber, es zu verblüffen, so dass es selbst sein Schweigen bricht, sozusagen sein „Rätsel" verrät, indem es sein Alter oder auch seinen Namen nennt, ist seine Macht gebrochen und es muss fort, so formuliert es der Volkskundler Siegfried De Rachewiltz. Zwar nennt die Willeweis keine Jahres- oder Alterszahl, aber es werden Vergleiche angestellt, z.B. „so alt wie der Karer Wald". Sie war bereits, wie in manchen Sagen wörtlich erwähnt, vor der Sintflut da, ist gewissermaßen so alt wie die Erde selbst. Laut dem Volkskundler Siegfried De Rachewiltz könnte auch ein Zusammenhang zwischen dem Aufstellen der Eierschalen und dem Totenkult bestehen, so wie Schalen generell (Schalensteine, Schalen als Wohnort von Toten, Töpfe für Totenspeisen ...) häufig damit zusammenhängen. Auch der Brauch des Beschenkens zu Allerseelen (stellvertretend an die Kinder anstelle der Armen Seelen) erfährt eine ähnliche Deutung. – In der Mythologie steht der Herd sowohl als Schwelle zum Jenseits als auch als Kernstück der menschlichen Behausung; bei archäologischen Ausgrabungen werden häufig Tierknochen unter der Feuerstelle gefunden (Tieropfer). – Jacob Grimm berichtet, dass laut dem Volksglauben der Friesen die Seelen in Eierschalen ins Totenreich hinüberschifften.

33

Fürweilung

Einige Tage vor dem 17. August 1891 kam in Kollmann ein altes Weiblein zum Geistlichen und legte ihm einen Fünfguldenzettel hin mit der Bitte, er möge ja schnell Messen für die Armen Seelen lesen, sie fühle sich so beklommen, es sei ihr, als ob die ganze Luft voll Teufel wäre, es müsse etwas Schreckliches geschehen. Am 17. August brach die Gandermuhr los, verschüttete einen großen Teil des Dorfes, und viele Menschenleben wurden vernichtet.

›› Wissenswertes ‹‹

Der Ganderbach ist ein sagenumwobener Wildbach zwischen Barbian und Kollmann an der orografisch rechten Seite des Eisacktals.

Fürweilung ist der tirolerische Ausdruck für Vorahnung. Zu allen Zeiten hat es Menschen mit einer außergewöhnlichen Sensibilität gegeben, die ein nahendes Unglück stimmungsmäßig vorerleben und geahnt haben. Es ist ein der Depression ähnlicher Zustand, begleitet von Unruhe, Angst und großer Sorge. Die „Gabe" der Fürweilung scheint manchmal in Familien generationsübergreifend vorhanden zu sein. Man könnte sie als eine Art Vorstufe der Prophetie bezeichnen.

34

Der Sandwirt

Als im Jahre 1848 Nachrichten von Siegen der Italiener über die österreichischen Truppen verbreitet wurden, bemerkte ein Aberstückler: „Es geht halt so, wie die Willeweiß prophezeit hat. In Wälschland wird es unsern Leuten so schlecht gehen, dass die meisten zugrunde gehen. Wenn es aber so weit gekommen ist, dass der Kaiser mit seinen zwei letzten Soldaten durch den Kuntersweg hereinzieht, wird der Sandwirt erscheinen und die Leute aufbieten. Dann gibt es einen so großen Landsturm, wie er noch nie da gewesen ist, und die wälschen Rebeller werden für immer geschlagen sein. Viele Leute glauben zwar, dass der Sandwirt zu Mantua erschossen worden sei. Dies ist aber erlogen. Er hat sich nur versteckt und lebt in der Sarner Scharte oder im Ifinger, kurz in einem oder dem andern von den beiden Bergen."

Wissenswertes

Im Jahre 1848 hatten sich verschiedene norditalienische Städte gegen die österreichische Herrschaft erhoben. Auch im heutigen Trentino, dem damals südlichsten Teil Tirols, früher Welschtirol oder Welschsüdtirol genannt, stieg der Wunsch nach einer Vereinigung mit Italien, denn ein großer Teil dieser Bevölkerung war italienischsprachig. Viele Tiroler waren zu jener Zeit bereit, ihre Heimat „gegen die Wälschen" auch mit den Waffen zu verteidigen. Der Begriff „welsch/walsch/Wallische" wird auch heute noch von deutschsprachigen Südtirolern für die italienische Sprache und für Italiener verwendet. – Diese Sage um den Tiroler Freiheitshelden Andreas Hofer wurde von Zingerle im Sarntal aufgezeichnet. Wie große Helden in anderen Mythen, lebt Andreas Hofer in dieser Sage, in das Innere des Berges entrückt, weiter.

35

Von der Willeweis aus Niederlana

In Niederlana lebte einst eine Willeweis. Sie war im Besitz eines Buches voller Weissagungen. Dieses hielt sie in einem gezwieselten Baum aufbewahrt. Als zwischen Mitter- und Niederlana eine Kirche gebaut wurde, brach sie in Wehklagen aus. Sie weissagte auch, dass diese Kirche dereinst ganz vereinsamen werde.

Wissenswertes

gezwieselt = doppelspitzig, gegabelt.

Auch in dieser Sage gibt es einen Zusammenhang zwischen der Willeweis und einem Baum. Bei der Kirche handelt es sich um die bereits 1215 erwähnte Kirche St. Margareth. Die Gegend dahinter hieß früher „Hexenkuchl". Lange Zeit führte diese Kirche mit schönen Fresken wirklich ein Schattendasein, sie wurde erst in den letzten Jahrzehnten aufgewertet. Es handelt sich hier vermutlich um eine heidnische Kultstätte, die durch eine christliche Kirche überbaut und bezeichnenderweise der Hl. Margareta geweiht wurde. Sie erinnert somit an die rätoromanische „Sontga Margriata": Beide sind vorchristliche Heilige Frauen, die in die Zukunft sehen und deren Reich in der Natur liegt. Margareta, die „Heilige mit dem Wurm" wird in Tirol sehr verehrt.

Laut Heiligenforschung hat sie die Stelle einer vorchristlichen Göttin eingenommen (siehe Kapitel Heilige und Maria).

In vielen Mythen steht der Drache für die Urkraft und die Fruchtbarkeit der Erde. Mit der Durchsetzung der patriarchalen Kultur zum einen und der Christianisierung zum anderen wurde der Drache, wie die Schlange, zum Symbol des Bösen und in vielen Legenden und Mythen getötet.

36

Von der Willeweiß

Von der Willeweiß hat man früher allerhand erzählt. Sie hat gesagt, einmal werden Wagen kommen ohne Ross, und in der Luft werden sie gehen wie Vögel. Das hat man früher aber nicht geglaubt, und derweil ist es jetzt so. Die Willeweiß hat auch gesagt, wenn der Obstbaum da oben so gewachsen ist, dass man ein Füllen dranhängen kann, dann wird auf der Malser Heide eine Schlacht stattfinden, dass ein Füllen bis an die die Füße im Blut stehen wird. Aber das ist nicht wahr gewesen.

Von der Willeweiß ist auch ein Buch gedruckt worden, und da hat's immer geheißen, in der Willeweiß steht das geschrieben.

›› Wissenswertes ‹‹

Diese Sage geht vermutlich auf das Sibyllen-Volksbuch aus dem 19. Jh. zurück. Ähnliche Prophezeiungen sind auch vom Untersberg bei Salzburg bekannt.

37

Die Sibilla von Comano

An der Stelle, wo sich heute das bekannte Thermalbad von Comano befindet, lebte einst in einer Höhle eine Sibylle. Niemand wusste, wie alt sie war und woher sie kam – sie war immer schon da gewesen. Der Ruf ihrer Hellsichtigkeit war weitum bekannt, und so kamen aus nah und fern viele Menschen, um sie um Rat zu fragen. Jedes Mal aber orakelte sie inmitten ihrer Weissagungen: „Der Tag wird kommen, an dem unzählige Menschen in diesem Tal nach dem Schatz suchen, den sie verloren haben. Ohne Pickel und ohne Hammer werden sie suchen, Arme und Reiche, alle wie Brüder, Menschen aus vielen Ländern, Menschen mit unterschiedlichem Glauben, und jeder – der Erste und der Letzte – wird seinen Teil erhalten."

Niemand konnte sich indes die geheimnisvollen Worte der Sibylle erklären, niemand hatte eine Ahnung, welcher Schatz wohl in den Felsen verborgen sein könnte. Die Seherin jedoch gab außer diesen Worten nichts von ihrem Geheimnis preis. →

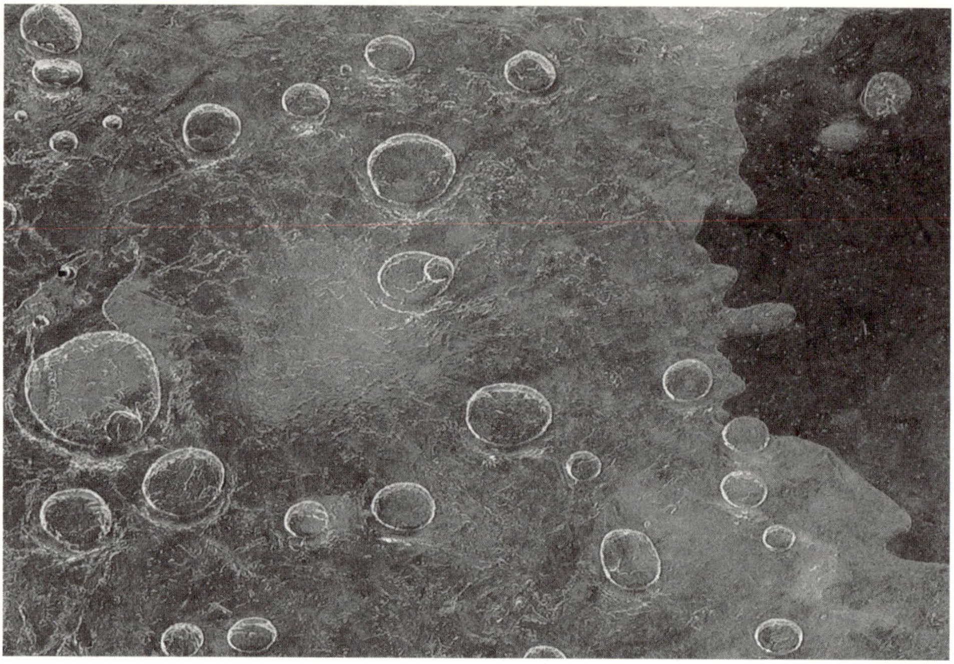

Eines Tages beschloss ein Ritter, sich hier ein großes Schloss zu erbauen. Skrupellos und schwer bewaffnet machte er sich daran, die Seherin aus ihrer Höhle zu verjagen. Er hatte jedoch nicht mit dem jungen Baron von Castel Spine gerechnet, der sich zum Schutz der weitum verehrten Sibilla dem Ritter in den Weg stellte. Ein erbitterter Kampf folgte, bei dem der rücksichtslose Ritter tödlich verletzt wurde. Doch der Baron konnte sich seines Sieges nicht erfreuen, denn zu Tode ermattet sank er selbst zu Boden, ein hohes Fieber befiel ihn und am ganzen Körper überzog sich seine Haut plötzlich mit roten Flecken. Er spürte, dass sein Ende nahe war.

Da stand plötzlich die trotz ihres Alters strahlende Sibilla vor ihm, die zu ihm sprach: „Sorge dich nicht, du wirst nicht sterben! Folge mir in meine Höhle." Sie nahm ihn bei der Hand und führte ihn in ihre Behausung. Dort, mitten in der Höhle, sprudelte ein kristallklares Quellwasser aus dem Felsen, und die Sibilla befahl ihm, sich damit zu waschen und davon zu trinken. Wenige Augenblicke später fühlte er bereits seine wundersame Heilung durch das Wasser der Sibilla. Jedem, dem er auf dem Nachhauseritt begegnete, erzählte er von seinem Abenteuer und von seiner Genesung. So ergab es sich, dass eine große Menge Neugieriger und Schaulustiger sich vor der Höhle der Sibilla einfand, aber sowohl sie als auch die wunderbare Quelle waren nun plötzlich verschwunden.

Die Zeit verging. Der Baron von Castel Spine vermählte sich mit seiner Verlobten Lauretta und wurde Vater von vielen Kindern. Die Sage erzählt, dass er fast hundert Jahre alt wurde, vielfacher Großvater. Schwert und Rüstung interessierten ihn nicht mehr, viel lieber beschäftigte er sich nun mit seinen Enkelkindern. Umso mehr traf es ihn, als einer seiner Enkelsöhne eines Tages schwer erkrankte. Kein Arzt und keine Medizin konnten helfen. Sein Zustand verschlechterte sich von Tag zu Tag. Verzweifelt dachte der Baron von Castel Spine an den fernen Tag zurück, als das Wasser der Sibylle ihm einst das Leben gerettet hatte. „Ich muss die Quelle der Sibilla finden", dachte er sich. Mit Hilfe einiger Diener begab sich der alte Baron in die verlassene, düstere Höhle, wo die alte Seherin einst ihre Prophezeiungen ausgesprochen hatte. Er begann zu suchen, mit seinen Händen zu graben, Steine wegzuklauben ... und plötzlich sprudelte aus dem felsigen Untergrund kristallklares Wasser hervor! Schnell füllte der Baron einen Krug damit, eilte nach Hause und wusch damit sein todkrankes Enkelkind. Und auch dieses Mal rettete das Wasser der Sibilla ein Menschenleben.

Da verstanden die Menschen endlich den Sinn der Prophezeiung der Sibilla und was es mit dem verborgenen Schatz im Felsen auf sich hatte.

Für den Baron von Castel Spine aber war dies ein Wink der göttlichen Vorsehung. Aus Dankbarkeit machte er sich noch in seinen alten Jahren als Pilger auf den Weg. In Caravaggio, fern seiner Heimat, soll er gestorben sein.

›› Wissenswertes ‹‹

Während in den meisten Tiroler Legenden die Muttergottes oder Heilige mit der Entstehung von heilkräftigen bzw. heiligen Quellen in Verbindung gebracht werden, ist es in dieser Sage eine heidnische, vorchristliche Gestalt. Der Baron von Castel Spine repräsentiert das christliche Element. Wie schon der Name „Sibilla von Comano" verrät, ist hier der Zusammenhang mit der Sibylle der römischen Mythologie offensichtlich. Am Eingang des Judikarien (Val Giudicarie) gelegen, sind die Thermen von Comano europaweit für ihr heilkräftiges Wasser, vor allem bei Hauterkrankungen, bekannt. Die Quelle war bereits von den Römern und bis ins Mittelalter genutzt worden. Später wurde das Heilbad verschüttet, zeitgleich soll laut Legende auch die Sibilla verschwunden sein. Das heilkräftige Wasser wurde laut Überlieferung erst im 18. Jh. wiederentdeckt. Zuerst fand es vor allem in der Bleichung von Hanf Verwendung, dann entdeckten die Bauern der Umgebung die Heilkraft dieses Wassers bei Krätze und anderen Hautkrankheiten. Die Sage wurde 1845 vom Trentiner Dichter Giovanni Prati neu erzählt.

In einem Manuskript des Hl. Trientner Konzils wird von einem Besuch von Monsignor Francesco di Montepulciano, einem der Prälaten des Trientner Konzils, bei dieser Sibilla berichtet. Demzufolge sei er über enge, dunkle Wege tief in eine Grotte hinein- bzw. hinabgestiegen, die aus verborgenen Felsspalten Tageslicht erhielt. Zwei junge, grün gekleidete Mädchen, einen Efeukranz mit fünf Blättern auf dem Kopf, die im Dienste der Sibilla standen, fragten ihn, was er wolle. Er musste dann vier Stunden warten, bis die Sibilla, ebenfalls grün und mit einem schneeweißen Überwurf gekleidet, einen Efeukranz aus sieben Blättern auf dem Haar, erschien. Sie sei von sechs grün gekleideten Frauen begleitet gewesen und habe in der Hand ein Buch gehalten. Der Bericht endet damit, dass er erklärt, ohne Schaden die Grotte auf dem gleichen Wege wieder verlassen und viele Geheimnisse von der Sibilla erfahren zu haben.

38

Die Gannaruna

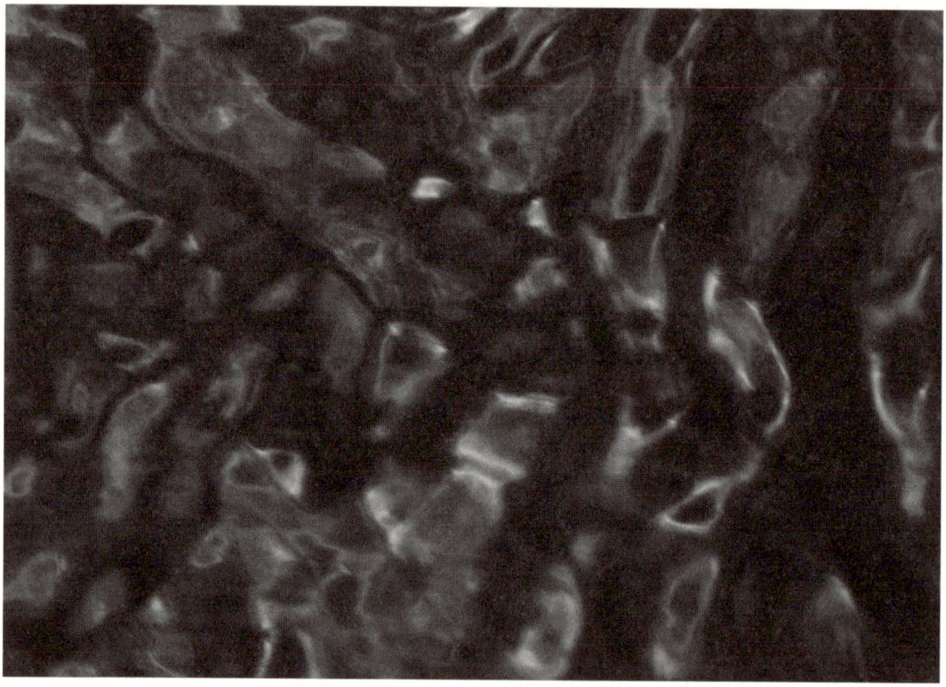

Unweit Ehrenburg im Pustertal entspringt am Fuße des Getzenberges in tiefem Waldesdunkel an einsamer Stelle ein sagenhaftes Brünnlein mit dem uralten Namen Gannaruna. Hier lebte einst eine weise alte Frau. Früher war sie eine Königin gewesen, deren Reich vom Getzenberg über die Rodenecker und Lüsner Alm bis nach Untermoi im Gadertal reichte. Ihr Palast stand auf dem Berg Col dla Vödla oberhalb Alfarei bei Untermoi. Später hat sie sich in eine Höhle im Getzenberger Wald zurückgezogen und in größter Einfachheit gelebt. Man sagte von ihr, dass sie nicht nur die Menschen, sondern auch sämtliche Geister des Waldes und der Nacht kenne. Sie wusste jedem einen Rat zu geben; niemand konnte sie betrügen, und gegen Anmaßende und Rücksichtslose war sie sehr streng. Auch auf die Heilung vieler Krankheiten verstand sie sich. Einfache Leute wie Edelmänner kamen zu ihr, um sie um Rat zu fragen, und auch den Jungfrauen brachte ihr Erscheinen Glück. Besonders hilfreich zeigte sie sich am frühen Morgen nach der Walpurgisnacht, wenn es einem Burschen gelang, von der hüllenlos dastehenden Frau beim Anschlag der ersten Morgensonne einen Schluck Wasser aus der Quelle dargeboten zu bekommen. Wissen die ältesten Berichte noch von Nacktheit, so trug sie nach jüngeren Meinungen nur ein weißes leinenes Hemd.

Auch der ewige Jude, der über den Getzenberg herkam und vom Brünnlein trank, sagte, dass das Wasser der Ganna so köstlich zu trinken sei, wie das des Jordanflusses.

›› Wissenswertes ‹‹

Der Col dla Vödla, dessen ladinischer Name bezeichnenderweise „Berg der Alten" bedeutet, ist eine einsame, stimmungs- und geheimnisvolle Bergdoppelkuppe, ein „weiblicher" Berg zwischen der Lüsner Alm und Untermoi. Die Quelle Gannaruna ist heute nicht mehr eindeutig auffindbar. Bereits K.F. Wolff erfuhr bei seinen Nachforschungen, dass mehrere Quellen im Getzenberger Wald so bezeichnet wurden. Zur Worterklärung des Namens Gannaruna sei Folgendes angemerkt: Ganna (Mehrzahl Gannes) wurde im ladinischen Enneberg auch die Waldfrau genannt, die häufig an Quellen oder Gewässern lebte (siehe Kapitel Salige). Ganna war auch der Name einer germanischen Seherin aus dem Stamm der Semnonen gegen Ende des 1. Jh. n. Chr. Sie war politisch so einflussreich, dass sie im Gefolge des semnonischen Königs mit nach Rom reiste, wo ihr der römische Kaiser Domitian seinen Respekt erwies. Der Name Ganna wird meist mit altnord. „gandr" = Zauberstab zusammenhängend gedeutet. Das althochdeutsche „Runa" bedeutet raunen, geheimes Flüstern. Die germanische Seherin redete in Worten, die dem gemeinen Volk oft unverständlich waren. – Der ewige Jude Ashaver ist ein laut christlicher Legende ewig umgehender jüdischer Schuster; er soll Christus auf seinem Kreuzweg die Rast vor seiner Haustür verweigert haben. Darauf soll Jesus ihn angesehen und zu ihm gesagt haben: „Ich will stehen und ruhen, du aber sollst gehen!" Seither ist Ahasver zur ewigen Wanderschaft verdammt, ohne sterben zu können.

Salige

Selige oder **Salige**, Wildes Fräulein oder Antrische Dirn, Schneefräulein, Holde, Hohle oder Heidnische (Hoadnische), Bergfrau, Fai oder Gana, Guana oder Anguana, Salvària, Vivana oder Diale ... Wohl kaum eine andere weibliche Gestalt der Tiroler Sagen ist so namensreich, und ebenso vielschichtig ist auch ihr Wesen.

In jedem Tal Tirols gibt es Steine, Felsen oder Höhlen, wo früher laut Sage solche Saligen gelebt haben. Ihr „verwandte" Sagengestalten sind im gesamten Alpenraum und darüber hinaus zu finden. Züge aus der germanischen, römischen und keltischen Mythologie lassen sich in den Seligen-Sagen erkennen.

Mythologisch reichen viele dieser Geschichten in früh- und vorchristliche Zeit zurück, dies wird durch den Sagenzug untermauert, dass sie, die Hoadnischen (Heidnischen), nicht beten und nicht zur Messe gehen.

Hinsichtlich ihrer äußeren Erscheinung werden die Seligen in den Sagen unterschiedlich beschrieben: dunkelhaarig, klein, gekleidet mit Stoffen, welche die Natur zur Verfügung stellt, wie Moos, Baumbart, Tierfelle und dergleichen oder als wunderschöne, weiß gekleidete Frauen mit langem blonden Haar. Mancherorts (im Fersental) sind sie ewig jung und schön, andernorts auch alte und runzlige weibliche Wesen. Während sie außerhalb Tirols manchmal der Königin Hulda unterstellt sind, leben sie in der Tiroler Sage zumeist frei von jeglicher Herrschaft.

Übereinstimmend in allen Sagen in und außerhalb von Tirol sind die Saligen und die ihnen verwandten Wesen in der unberührten Natur zu Hause und leben in völligem Einklang mit ihr. Sie halten sich im tiefen Wald auf, in Höhlen, Löchern, Felsen oder Steinen, hoch oben am Gletscher oder aber auch in Wassernähe oder im Wasser. Oft leben sie in Frauengemeinschaften, häufig erscheinen sie als Frauendreiheit. Sie wissen um die Geheimnisse der Natur und ihrer Zyklen und geben ihr Wissen bereitwillig den Menschen weiter. Diesen haben sie die Flachswirtschaft gelehrt; sie bringen den Kranken heilende Kräuter, sagen dem Bauern, wann eine günstige Zeit zum Säen oder zum Ernten ist, beschenken die Menschen mit lebensnotwendigen Gaben. Sie dienen freiwillig als Magd, helfen dort, wo sie gebraucht werden, ohne einen Lohn hierfür zu wollen; im Gegenteil: Werden sie belohnt, fühlen sie sich gekränkt und verlassen den Menschen. Sie lieben die Milch und belohnen mitunter den Spender dafür mit Gold oder kostbaren Steinen. Eines ihrer Merkmale ist ihr wunderschöner Gesang, dem Männer zumeist nicht widerstehen können.

Sie entscheiden völlig frei, ob und wen sie zum Mann nehmen wollen, dieser muss aber bestimmte Bedingungen einhalten oder ein Tabu respektieren, andernfalls verlässt die Selige ihn auf der Stelle. Wenn sie bei den Menschen leben, werden die Wilden Fräulein nach mehreren Jahren wieder abberufen. Mancherorts können die Seligen fliegen oder, wie die Vivànes im Fassatal, sich unsichtbar machen.

Ihre Fertigkeiten sind Gepflogenheiten weit zurückliegender Zeiten: Manchmal zerklopfen sie Korn mit einem Stein oder schlagen Feuer mit Hilfe von Baumschwamm und Stein.

Die Wilden Fräulein sind Beschützerinnen der Vegetation und der Tiere; als solche erscheinen sie frevelhaften Menschen, ermahnen und bestrafen diese, falls sie Tieren etwas zuleide tun; sie pflegen kranke oder verletzte Tiere wieder gesund und erwecken ihre Schutztiere, die Gämsen, wieder zu neuem Leben.

So freundlich sie sind, so furchtbar können die Folgen ihrer Verwünschungen sein, meistens über neun Generationen hin. Mancherorts ist ihre Macht so groß, dass ihnen Opfer dargebracht werden müssen.

Sagen erzählen auch, dass diese Antrischen die „ungleichen" Kinder Evas seien, die sie, da sie derer so viele gehabt hätten, dem Herrgott verschwiegen habe, oder dass sie von Adam schon vor der Zeit des Sündenfalls gezeugt worden seien.

In den verschiedenen Gebieten Alt-Tirols haben sie unterschiedliche Namen, zumeist aber eine ähnliche, wenn nicht identische Rolle.

Für den Begriff „salig" gibt es unterschiedliche Deutungen: die dialektale Gepflogenheit des Oberinntales, derzufolge anstelle des Vokals „e" ein „a" verwendet wird („Walt" statt „Welt", „Fald" statt „Feld", „salig" statt „selig", usw.). Im Althochdeutschen bedeutet „salig" soviel wie gut, gesegnet, glücklich, selig. Ob der Begriff auch mit „Seele" in Zusammenhang steht, ist nicht restlos geklärt, auch wenn vieles dafür spricht – so wurden die Saligen in Latzfons früher beispielsweise als „Selige Seelen" bezeichnet. „Antrisch" erinnert an das lateinische „antrum" (Höhle) und „entrisch" wird mit der Bedeutung „unheimlich" und „uralt" verknüpft. „Hohle" weist auf die dämonischen Züge dieser Sagengestalt hin, denn mancherorts wird sie mit einem hohlen Rücken beschrieben so wie der mittelalterliche Teufel.

Im ladinischen Gadertal wird die Selige zur Gana, im Fassatal zur Kristàna und zur Vivàna oder Vivèna, im Ampezzanischen und im Trentino zur Anguàna, Guana oder Enguàna. Im Fersental und in den zimbrischen Sprachinseln ist sie die Salinghe, die hailige Frau oder das seeleghe baible.

Die ampezzanische Anguàna oder Longana lebt zumeist in Wassernähe, oft hat sie lange hängende Brüste und, ähnlich wie manchmal die Diàles im Engadin, Ziegenfüße. Die Salvària (Wilde) im Buchensteinischen kann sich auch in Tiere, z.B. in einen Fischotter, verwandeln. Die Vivàne aus dem Fassatal sind duftige, fast durchsichtige, schöne Frauen, die bis zum Ende der Welt leben, sie haben auch die Gabe, die Zukunft zu deuten, und die Eulen, welche jede Sprache verstehen, bringen ihnen Nachrichten aus der ganzen Welt zu.

Die Anguana in den Lessinischen Bergen an der Grenze zwischen dem Trentino und der Provinz Verona zeigt sich halb als Frau und halb als Schlange.

Jüngere Sagen machen die Selige mitunter zur menschenfeindlichen bösen Hexe.

Die Tatsache, dass Salige zumeist in Verbindung mit Steinen, Felsen oder Steinhaufen vorkommen, deutet darauf hin, dass der Sagenkern uralt ist und in die Zeit des Steinkultes und der Steinverehrung zurückreicht.

In der Sagenforschung erfahren die Wilden Fräulein unterschiedliche Deutungen: Sie werden als verdrängte Ureinwohnerinnen der Alpen angesehen (sie haben möglicherweise den „neuen" Besiedlern beispielsweise das Käsen gelernt oder Fundstellen von Mineralien gezeigt); sie sind göttliche, d.h. Leben erhaltende, bestrafende und vernichtende Wesen und mit überirdischen Kräften ausgestattet oder sie werden als mythisch-dämonologische Wesenheiten aus einer Zeit angesehen, in der die Geschehnisse der Natur als Taten persönlicher Wesen und nicht auf der Grundlage physikalischer Kräfte verstanden wurden; sie gebieten über die Kräfte der Natur, sind Schutzgeister von Gletschern, Bergen, Wäldern, Quellen usw.

Beeindruckende Forschungsergebnisse präsentiert die berühmte Archäologin Marija Gimbutas: denen zufolge haben die lange verehrten Göttinnen des Alten Europa über viele christliche Jahrhunderte hinweg in Volkssagen und -glauben überlebt. Zu ihren Begleittieren und Symbolen zählten u.a. die Eule und Geier/Habicht (Todesvorboten und -symbole), der Kuckuck (im Tiroler Volksglauben bezeichnenderweise ein Teufelstier), die Taube (wie der Kuckuck Symboltier für Frühling/Neubeginn sowie Seelentier) und die Schlange, die mit ihrem jährlichen Rückzug ins Erdinnere und ihrer Häutung für Lebenserneuerung und Wiedergeburt steht.

Die ebenfalls mit diesen Tieren in Erscheinung tretende Salige, welche Glück, Reichtum, Gesundheit, Leben und Tod zuweisen kann, wäre demnach die in die Tiefen der Wälder oder die auf Bergesgipfel zurückgedrängte Göttin, welche auch in den Tiroler Sagen bis heute überlebt hat.

In der psychoanalytischen Deutung ist die Salige, ähnlich anderen Gestalten der Sagenwelt sowie der Mythologie anderer Kulturkreise, ein mächtiges archetypisches Urbild aus archaischer Zeit. Sie ist die „Anima", welche nach C.G. Jung alle weiblichen Seelenanteile im Manne verkörpert, z.B. die Beziehung zu seinem Unbewussten, dem Natursinn, der Gefühlsebene usw. Die Auseinandersetzung mit diesen archetypischen Leitbildern ist laut Jung für die seelische Entwicklung des einzelnen Menschen eine wichtige und wertvolle Erfahrung.

Aus unserer Sicht (dies wurde bereits vom Sagenforscher Wilhelm Mannhardt, 1831-1880, ähnlich formuliert) sind Wesen und Wirken der Seligen, so wie anderer dämonischer Sagengestalten, neben den anderen Deutungen auch als eine Art mythisch-religiöse Naturerfahrung erklärbar. Man muss sich vorstellen, was es für unsere Vorfahren bedeutet haben mag, den Kräften und Mächten der Natur, der Begegnung mit dem Numinosen und dem Unheimlichen, der Angst vor dem Unbekannten, der Wald- und Bergeinsamkeit, sehr oft ganz allein und über viele Monate hinweg ausgesetzt und ausgeliefert gewesen zu sein.

39

Die Gämse

Der Großvater des Jenner-Bauern auf Hütte in Platt kehrte einst von Seba, einer Alm, die von Pill gegen das Ötztal liegt, zurück. Der Weg führte ihn über die Großwand, eine schauerliche Felswand, die oberhalb von Moos hervorragt. Zu seinem nicht geringen Erstaunen sah er in dieser einsamen Gegend ein Feuer. In der Meinung, es könnte von Mähern angezündet sein und er könnte dabei Bekannte aus dem Tale finden, ging er darauf los. Wie war er aber überrascht, als er in die Nähe kam und bei einem Kinde ein Mädchen von etwa sechzehn Jahren, zwei ältere Fräulein und eine Frau erblickte. Alle fünf waren gar wunderschön, besonders die drei Fräulein. Das Kind weinte und die alte Frau tröstete es damit, dass sie ihm Milch versprach. Da ging alsbald ein Fräulein weg und brachte eine Schüssel voll Milch. Als der Bauer dieses sah, trat er beherzt näher hinzu und ward freundlich aufgenommen. Er zog nun sein schwarzes Brot aus der Tasche, um es da zu verzehren. Die Frauen luden ihn aber ein, mit ihnen zu essen, und er nahm den Antrag von Herzen gerne an. Es ward eine herrliche Suppe gebracht und dann wurde eine ganze gebratene Gämse aufgetischt. Die Alte sprach ihm zu, er solle sich den Braten schmecken lassen, nur solle er sich hüten, ein Beinlein zu verrücken. Er folgte ihrem Geheiß, schlug in den Braten tapfer ein und suchte kein Beinlein aus dem Geleise zu bringen. Doch siehe, trotz aller Sorgfalt entschlüpfte doch ein Beinlein am linken Fuße und kam aus seinen Fugen. Als er dies bemerkte, gestand er dieses offen den Frauen. Diese beruhigten ihn aber und sagten, das mache nicht so viel, es werde deswegen eine Gämse nur ein wenig am linken Fuße hinken. Nur solle er recht behutsam sein, auf dass er kein anderes Beinchen verrücke. Er folgte ihrem Rate, aß sich kugelsatt, sagte dann sein „Vergelts Gott“ und kehrte gestärkt und munter nach Hause. Die Frauen gingen ihm aber im Kopfe um, und er dachte nur mehr an die Wilden Fräulein. Nach einiger Zeit ging er in jener Gegend auf die Jagd und sah dort eine ganz abgemagerte Gämse, welche am linken Fuße sehr hinkte. Weil sie so hager war, schoss er sie nicht, sondern dachte: Ich lasse dich fetter werden und dann werde ich dich holen. Gedacht, getan. Er wartete drei Jahre lang, bis die Gämse voll und fett war. Dann schoss er sie und schickte sie dem damaligen Seelsorger in Platt, dem Pater Ignazi. Als dieser die Gämse zerlegte, fand sich, dass eben jenes Beinlein am linken Fuße fehlte, welches der Jäger aus seinen Fugen herausgerückt hatte.

Der wohlwollende und hilfsbereite Charakterzug der Saligen kommt in dieser Geschichte deutlich zum Ausdruck. Diese Sage beinhaltet schamanische Bruchstücke: Sie erinnert an den Jagdzauber der Naturvölker steinzeitlicher Kultur, die sich beim erlegten Tier entschuldigen, es würdigen und sich bei ihm bedanken. Die Knochen dürfen aufgrund der Überzeugung, dass sich in ihnen die Kraft und die Seele des Tieres befinden, nicht beschädigt werden. Nach dem Verzehr werden sie wieder in ihrer ursprünglichen Anordnung zusammengestellt, auf dass sie sich wieder mit Fleisch bedecken und zu neuem Leben erwachen können und somit auch in Zukunft Nahrung bieten. – Auch in der christlichen Tradition schlägt sich diese Einstellung in der Reliquienverehrung nieder, der zufolge den Knochen von Heiligen eine besondere Kraft innewohne. In der Tiroler Volksmedizin fanden in den letzten Jahrhunderten sowohl Tier- als auch Menschenknochen häufig Anwendung.

40

Die Salgfräulein

Bei Graun im Obervinschgau steht ein Mittelgebirge, die „Salge" genannt. Hier sollen in alter Zeit die Salgfräulein gehaust haben. Sie wohnten unter diesen Steinblöcken in weiten, prachtvollen Räumen und waren den Menschen hold und freundlich. Sie waren gewöhnlich guter Dinge, nur hie und da und besonders bei schlechtem Wetter, ging ihnen die gute Laune aus. Oft saßen sie abends, weißgekleidet auf dem „Großen Stein" unter dem alten Lärchenbaume und sangen allerlei Lieder. Als sie eines Abends wieder so sangen, ging ein Hirte vorüber, der von dem schönen Gesange so bezaubert wurde, dass er stille stand, sich auf einen Stein setzte und tief in die Nacht hinein den Salgfräulein zuhorchte, bis sie mit dem untergehenden Monde verschwunden waren. Da kam er erst wieder zu sich, dachte an sein junges Weib und an seine Herde und kehrte nach Hause zurück. Seitdem er aber die Salgfräulein gesehen hatte, blieb er einsilbig und schwermütig, denn die schönen Fräulein gingen ihm stets im Kopfe um. Ohne seinem Weibe je ein Wort davon zu sagen, ging er oft auf die Salg, um dem Gesange zu horchen. Endlich wurden die schönen Fräulein mit ihm vertrauter, führten ihn in ihre prächtigen Kammern und zeigten ihm ganze Herden von Gämsen, die sie als ihre Haustiere hegten. Seitdem kam der Bauer öfters auf die Salg in Heimgart und blieb oft länger aus. Dies bemerkte sein Weib bald und allerlei eifersüchtige Gedanken erwachten in ihr. Sie machte ihm über sein häufiges Wegbleiben die bittersten Vorwürfe und beschloss, der Ursache seiner nächtlichen Gänge auf die Spur zu kommen.

Als er eines Abends wieder weggehen wollte, um, wie er sagte, eine verlorene Geiß zu suchen, tat das Weib gar zärtlich und bat ihn inständig, ja bald wieder zu kommen. Währenddem hatte sie aber, ohne dass er es bemerkte, einen Faden an einem seiner Jackenknöpfe befestigt, behielt aber den daran hangenden Knäuel zurück. Als der Bauer eine Strecke gegangen war und schon ein gutes Stück Faden vom Knäuel abgewickelt hatte, verließ auch sie das Haus und folgte dem leitenden Faden, der sie zur Salg führte. Dort traf sie ihren

Mann mitten unter den Salgfräulein an, die ihm Lieder vorsangen. Wie sie dies sah, fing sie an zu weinen und zu klagen, verwünschte den Tag ihrer Hochzeit und die Salgfräulein. Da verschwanden die Salgfräulein unter den Steinen und wurden seitdem nie wieder gesehen. Der Bauer lebte auch nicht mehr lange.

›› Wissenswertes ‹‹

Wie in vielen anderen Sagen leben auch die Salgfräulein im Vinschgau unter Steinblöcken, welche hier sogar deren Namen tragen. Sie erscheinen als freundlich, hold und männerverführend. Auch andere Tiroler Erzählungen (z.B. aus der Wildschönau bei Kufstein) bestätigen die Freiheit in der Beziehungsgestaltung dieser Frauen; die vom Christentum vorgeschriebene Keuschheit liegt ihnen völlig fern. Sie sind zwar „Fräulein" oder „Jungfrauen", aber wie bei der jungfräulichen griechischen Artemis bedeutet dies nur, dass sie keinem Mann angehören. Auch in mythologischen Erzählungen um die in der Natur beheimateten griechisch/römischen Nymphen steht häufig die Sexualität im Mittelpunkt; daher auch die Ableitung des Begriffs „Nymphomanie" für sexuelle Besessenheit.

Bei Stilfs im Vinschgau befindet sich ein großer Felsen, genannt „Opferknott", dessen unterer Teil den Namen „Thialknott" trägt. „Dialen" werden die Wilden Frauen im benachbarten Engadin genannt, ihr Name hängt mit dem romanischen Begriff „Gottheit" zusammen. Laut Volksüberlieferung holte die örtliche Hebamme aus diesem Felsen die neugeborenen Kinder. Zahlreiche Gegenstände sollen hier über lange Zeit geopfert worden sein (Beeren, Schwämme, Geld usw.), angeblich auch Tieropfer, vor oder nach der Jagd.

In anderen Sagen werden die Seligen Fräulein aber auch als lebensbedrohlich und mächtig beschrieben: Auf dem Weg zur Zerzeralm im Vinschgau heißt ein Platz „Zu den Wilden Fräulein". Es war dies ein Steinhaufen, der mittlerweile aufgrund der Errichtung eines Fahrweges zerstört wurde, und unter ihm ruhten laut Volksmeinung die Wilden Fräulein. Kinder, die zum ersten Mal auf die Alm gingen, mussten hier Steine aufheben, sie anspucken und sie mit den Worten „Ich opfere, ich opfere den Wilden Fräulein" auf den Steinhaufen werfen. Auch Erwachsene unterließen laut Zingerle diesen uralten Brauch nicht, denn wer diese Opferung nicht befolgte, setzte sich großer Gefahr aus. Eine Frau aus dem Zerzertal ging in Begleitung ihrer Magd nach Burgeis, um sich nach dem Wochenbett aussegnen zu lassen. Als sie an diesem Steinhaufen vorbeikamen, fiel ihr ein, dass sie den geweihten Wachsstock zu Hause vergessen hatte, und so schickte sie die Magd zurück, um ihn zu holen. Als diese aber zurückkehrte, war die Bäuerin verschwunden und wurde nie mehr gefunden. – Das christlich-katholische Ritual der Aussegnung der Wöchnerin war in Tirol bis ins 20. Jh. üblich. Vor der erfolgten Aussegnung durch den Priester, zu welcher sie eine eigens geweihte Kerze mitnahm, durfte die Frau die Messe nicht besuchen. In diesen Tagen war sie, so wie auch das neugeborene Kind, den Gefahren von Dämonen, Geistern und auch den Wilden Fräulein besondes ausgesetzt, sie durfte sich deshalb nicht außerhalb der Dachrinne des Hauses (dämonischer „Grenzbereich") begeben. Während dieser Zeit war sie aber auch von allen schweren Arbeiten befreit.

Auf einem anderen gepflasterten Wegstück musste ein Kind, welches das erste Mal auf die Zerzeralm ging, eine Platte, auf die ein Kreuz eingehauen war, küssen, ansonsten würde es sich auf dem Rückwege den Fuß brechen. – Die Sitte des Werfens von Steinen auf einen Haufen ist in vielen Ländern bezeugt, häufig hängt dies mit einem an einem solchen Ort geschehenen Todesfall, auch Mord, zusammen. Forscher sehen im Werfen von Steinen eine Art Opfer als Furcht vor dem Toten oder vor Dämonen. Steine waren aber auch Sitz weiblicher Gottheiten.

Der wunderschöne, verführerische Gesang der Wilden Fräulein wird auch in anderen Feensagen Europas beschrieben. Auch die auf einem Felsen am Rhein sitzende Loreley lockt mit ihrem betörenden Gesang die Schiffer in die gefährliche Strömung, so dass sie mit ihren Booten an den Felsenriffen zerschellen. Im griechischen Epos der Odyssee waren es die Sirenen, vogelähnliche Mischwesen mit Mädchenköpfen, die von einer Klippe aus die vorüberfahrenden Seeleute durch ihre Gesänge betörten und in den Tod lockten. Odysseus entging ihnen, indem er die Ohren seiner Gefährten mit Wachs verstopfte und sich selbst an den Mast seines Schiffes binden ließ.

Die Assoziation weiblicher Sagengestalten mit Steinen, Felsen oder Höhlen geht weit über den Alpenraum hinaus. So befinden sich auch in Sardinien zahlreiche „Domus de Janas", zu Deutsch „Wohnungen der Feen". Es sind in Gruppen errichtete, in Felsen gehauene Gräber, die der Ozieri-Kultur aus der Jungsteinzeit (ca. 3300-2700 v. Chr.) zugeschrieben werden. Dass in diesen uralten Grabstätten die Feen zu Hause sind, unterstreicht auch hier die Charakterzüge eines Jenseitswesens.

41

Die Heilige Frau

Zwischen den Höfen „Slompi" und „Màrcheli" verläuft ein schmaler Weg, und dort befand sich einst neben einer Scheune ein Brunnen aus einem ausgehöhlten Baumstamm. Wer in alten Zeiten dort vorbeiging, sah auf der Wiese immer lange Frauenkleider zum Trocknen ausgebreitet. Und je mehr die Sonne sie trocknete, desto weißer und glänzender wurden sie. Doch wehe, wenn jemand sie an sich nehmen wollte! Denn diese Kleider waren heiß wie Feuer. Wenn dann die Sonne unterging, verbreiteten sie ringsum Licht wie aus einer Lampe, und dann mieden die Menschen diesen Ort, voller Furcht.

Ein Mann, von dem man sagte, dass er sich vor nichts und niemandem fürchte, wollte es genauer wissen. Eines Abends versteckte er sich in der Scheune.

Als die Kirchturmglocke von San Lorenzo zur Mitternacht schlug, öffnete sich der Berg und eine Strahlende Frau trat hervor, in den Armen hielt sie einen Korb mit schmutziger Wäsche. Sie ging hin zum Brunnen und zog einen Kreis um ihn. Sie flüsterte: „Einen Kreis um den Brunnen ziehen, die Kleider hineinwerfen und warten ..." Und da fing das Brunnenwasser an, ihre Kleider zu waschen, auszuspülen und auszudrücken, geradeso als ob tausend Hände am Werk wären. Dann nahm sie die Kleider aus dem Wasser und breitete sie auf der Wiese aus. Sie zog erneut einen Kreis: „Einen Kreis um die Kleider ziehen und warten, bis die Sonne sie mit Licht bemalt", sagte sie. Anschließend sammelte sie die anderen im Gras liegenden Kleider ein und ging in den Berg zurück, der sich hinter ihr wieder verschloss.

Der Mann blieb den ganzen Tag in der Scheune, von dort aus konnte er beobachten, wie diese Kleider immer mehr zu leuchten begannen. Er vergaß sogar auf sein Essen; Mitternacht kam erneut und alles begann wieder von vorne. Dann, als die Frau wieder im Berg verschwand, verließ er sein Versteck, er zog sich sein Hemd aus, zog einen Kreis um den Brunnen, warf das Hemd hinein und wiederholte die Worte, die er gehört hatte. Das Wasser wusch sein Hemd. Er breitete es auf der Wiese aus, zog einen zweiten Kreis und wartete. Als die ersten Sonnenstrahlen kamen, fing sein Hemd an wie Licht zu leuchten. Zur Mittagsstunde wollte er es zu sich nehmen, aber da verbrannte er sich eine Hand daran. Voller Angst ging er nach Hause, aber bereits vor Mitternacht trieb ihn die Neugier erneut in die Scheune zurück. Der Berg öffnete sich, die Strahlende Frau erschien und ging zum Brunnen. Da erblickte sie zwischen ihren zum Trocknen ausgebreiteten Kleidern das Hemd des Mannes. Sie zog einen Kreis und flüsterte: „Einen Kreis um das Hemd ziehen und warten." Und nun wurde der Mann plötzlich von einer unsichtbaren Kraft ergriffen, die ihn zwang, sein Versteck zu verlassen, zu seinem Hemd hinzugehen und hineinzuschlüpfen. Da spürte er, wie er in einen Raben verwandelt wurde.

Von diesem Tag an sahen die Leute aus Fierozzo nie mehr die leuchtenden Kleider auf der Wiese ausgebreitet. Wohl aber begegneten sie immer wieder und für lange Zeit einem Raben mit einem verbrannten Flügel. Er lief ihnen schnarrend entgegen, so als ob er ihnen etwas sagen wollte.

›› Wissenswertes ‹‹

Die Heilige oder Strahlende Frau trägt Züge sowohl der Saligen als auch der strahlenden Berta. Oft ist die Unterscheidung zwischen zwei Sagenfiguren nicht klar zu ziehen, die Grenzen sind fließend. Die Heilige Frau zeigt sich hier als Göttin des Lichtes. Eine Wilde-Fräulein-Sage aus Ridnaun bei Sterzing, in welcher der Ehemann niemals sagen darf „die Sonne geht unter", andernfalls verlasse sie ihn, erinnert ebenfalls an diesen überirdischen Machtbereich. Das Sich-in-Verbindung-Setzen mit göttlichen Energien ist für Nicht-Eingeweihte ein Tabu. Es zu überschreiten, wird hart bestraft. – In dieser Sage bedient sich die Strahlende Frau des magischen Kreises als Hilfsmittel. Ihr Wohnort ist das Berginnere, das sie nur bei Nacht verlässt. Das Fersental oder Valle dei Mòcheni, eine zimbrisch-deutsche Sprachinsel im Trentino („des mòchen i" = das mache ich) war über lange Zeit Bergwerksgebiet (Gold, Silber, Kupfer und Blei). Erste Bergbauspuren sind bereits aus der Bronzezeit bekannt. Ab dem 13. Jh. setzte die Zuwanderung von Bergleuten aus dem deutschen Sprachraum ein. Der Höhepunkt der Einwanderung war im 16. und 17. Jh. Der Mineralienabbau hat Kultur, Sagen- und Vorstellungswelt dieser Talbewohner sehr stark beeinflusst. Der unermüdliche Volkstumsforscher und Begründer des Volkskundemuseums von S.Michele all'Adige, Giuseppe Sebesta, sieht diese Heilige Frau als Symbol für den Mineralienreichtum und -abbau. Das Waschen und Ausbreiten ihrer Kleider steht demzufolge für das Waschen und Trocknen der Mineralien. Der Rabe wäre der Bergmann auf der Suche nach wertvollem Gestein, der bei dieser gefährlichen Arbeit zum Schluss den Tod findet. In der Mythologie steht der Rabe sowohl als solares Symbol als auch als Sinnbild der Dunkelheit, häufig ist er Begleiter von Todesgottheiten. Sebesta zieht auch Parallelen mit einigen weiblichen Sagengestalten der Dolomitensagen von K.F. Wolff: mit den Delibànen am Monte Pòre, einem vor- und frühgeschichtlichen Bergwerksgebiet im Buchensteinischen, der seinen Namen von der venetisch-römischen Übergangsgöttin Pora hat. Laut Sage mussten dort als Opfer bzw. als Gegenleistung für den Mineralienfund Frauen für sieben Jahre ins Berginnere hinabsteigen; oder die Geschichte der Bleichen Berge, in welcher die Mondprinzessin, die im Licht geboren ist, auch auf der Erde ohne Licht nicht überleben kann.

42

Der Ziegenhirt von Pregossi

Ein Ziegenhirt von Pregossi war einst am Abhange eines Berges, dort, wo heute der Ronco Cagnolo ist, als er bemerkte, wie seine ganze Herde unter einem Steine hineinging und dort verschwand. Er ging ihnen nach und kam zuerst in eine Höhle, dann in einen wunderschönen Garten voll Blumenduft. Da kam ein schönes Fräulein, eine Enguana und führte ihn zu vielen anderen schönen Fräulein, die luden ihn zum Essen ein und fragten ihn dann, ob er nicht als Gärtner bei ihnen bleiben wolle. Er sagte zu und blieb. Nach einigen Wochen aber kam ihm das Heimweh, er nahm Abschied und ging nach Hause. Da fand er alles verändert und kannte zu seinem großen Erstaunen keinen Menschen mehr. Endlich kam eine Alte, die sagte: „Aber wo bist du doch gewesen – ich suche dich schon seit zweihundert Jahren?" Da nahm sie ihn bei der Hand und er fiel tot um; denn die Alte, die ihn so lange gesucht hatte, war der Tod – la morte!

›› Wissenswertes ‹‹

Pregossi bei Torcegno ist ein kleiner Weiler in der parallel zum Fersental (Val di Mocheni) liegenden Valsugana im Trentino, ca. 40 km von der Landeshauptstadt Trient entfernt. – Trotz aller Herrlichkeit verlässt der heimwehgeplagte Mensch den Aufenthaltsort der Enguanes, das Land, wo man nicht stirbt; Zeit, Krankheit und Tod sind hier unbekannt. Zurückgekehrt in die irdische, von den Gesetzen der Zeit regierte Welt, erwartet ihn die Todin. Was ihm wie wenige Wochen erschien, waren in Wirklichkeit 200 Jahre. Die Wohnstätte der Enguanes ist paradiesisch schön. Dass der Hirte hier nicht, wie in den meisten Sagen, der Schönheit und Anmut der Enguanes verfällt, sondern von ihnen als Gärtner eine „aktive" Rolle erhält, ist eine interessante Sagenvariante.

Diese unter Steinen gelegene Wohnstätte der Enguana erinnert an das Land der Seligen, das Jenseits, das in vielen Märchen und Sagen von Wesen wie Seligen Fräulein, Feen, Zwergen, Geistern usw. bevölkert ist, von hellen und dunklen Kräften. Eine Vingscher Saligen-Sage erzählt auch von der Weißen und der Schwarzen Mahrt. Die Seele des Menschen gehört ebenso zur nichtstofflichen „Anderswelt".

Unzählige Mythen und Märchen weltweit erzählen von dem in dieser Sage enthaltenen archetypischen Thema, das als Jenseitserfahrung schamanischer Art gedeutet werden kann.

43

Die Sage vom Schlaraffenlande

Das Schlaraffenland liegt zwischen Brand bei Längenfeld und Burgstein. Einst sangen nicht weit von Brand sieben wilde Frauen ihr Lied; da wollte ein Bursche, der es hörte, sich ihnen nähern, allein alle waren im Nu verschwunden. Der Getäuschte schaute nach der Richtung, in der sie entflohen waren, und sah eine große Türe geöffnet, durch diese erblickte er eine weite, herrliche Landschaft. Da standen auf den üppigen Fluren die herrlichsten Bäume, an denen köstliche Früchte hingen; Tal und Hügel waren reich überwachsen, und zwischen Äckern lachten stattliche Dörfer und prächtige Städte. Der Bursche wollte das schöne Land betreten, allein die Frauen kämpften gegen ihn, und endlich wurde das Tor vor seinen Augen geschlossen. Später konnte er den Eingang nicht mehr finden. Diese herrliche Landschaft wurde von den Wanderern, die noch spät auf dem Wege waren, öfters gesehen.

›› Wissenswertes ‹‹

Niemand beschreitet das Jenseits gegen den Willen der Wilden Frauen. In den keltischen Mythen sind es die Feen (Herrinnen der Anderswelt), die den Eingang zu diesem paradiesähnlichen Aufenthaltsort hüten, und nur von ihnen Auserwählte werden in dieses Reich eingelassen. Solche Geschichten stammen laut der Schweizerin Ursula Welser-Biffiger vermutlich aus der Zeit der Christianisierung, in der mancherorts noch matriarchale Kulte gepflegt wurden („in den Venusbergen"). – Das Schlaraffenland steht für das „irdische" Paradies im Gegensatz zum christlich-himmlischen Paradies: Laut der christlichen Lehre der vergangenen Jahrhunderte wäre die Welt „ein Jammertal", erst im Jenseits würden dem Menschen Glück und Wonne zustehen, doch dies zu glauben, weigerte sich das Volk lange Zeit.

Allgemein wird die vor ca. 10.000 Jahren erfolgte Umstellung unserer Ahnen von der einstigen Jäger- und Sammlerkultur auf die Ackerbaukultur als riesiger Fortschritt in der Entwicklung der Menschheit betrachtet. Doch Forschungsergebnisse, wie z.B. jene der Tiefenökologin Dolores La Chapelle, beleuchten auch die Schattenseiten dieser Umstellung. Laut Beobachtung der heute noch lebenden einfachsten Jäger- und Sammlerkulturen würden diese durchschnittlich nur zwei Tage in der Woche für die Beschaffung der Nahrung arbeiten. Die restliche Zeit, und dies ist der Großteil der Zeit, steht für beliebtere Tätigkeiten wie Musik, Tanz, künstlerische Darstellung, Beschäftigung mit „sich selbst" oder dem „Nichtstun" zur Verfügung. Verglichen mit den von Stress und Hektik bestimmten heutigen Lebens- und Arbeitsverhältnissen sind dies „paradiesische" Zustände, versinnbildlicht in dieser Sage durch den Reichtum der herrlichen und üppigen Landschaft.

44

Die Kaiserfrau am Nachtberge

Nachtberg heißt der Berg, der die Täler Brantenberg und Thiersee voneinander scheidet. Seinen Namen hat er wahrscheinlich von den tiefen Schatten, die seine dichten Föhren- und Fichtenwälder über ihn ausbreiten. In diesen Forsten hielt sich einst viel Hoch- und Rotwild auf, und allbekannt war der Reichtum des edlen Wildes auf dem Nachtberge. Das war zu verlockend für Jäger und Wilderer. Der Nachtberg war ihr liebstes Jagdrevier, aber mancher Schütze verschwand auch spurlos und ward nie wieder gesehen. Da ereignete es sich auch einmal, dass der Senner der Alpe, die im Bereich des Nachtberges lag, Butter und Käse zu Tale trug. Wie er so für sich hinging, sah er plötzlich auf einem niedrigen Hügel, der beiläufig hundert Schritte von ihm entfernt lag, eine hohe Frau stehen, in deren ganzer Gestalt und Haltung hohe Würde ausgedrückt war. Sie trug einen grünen Hut und ein langes, dunkles Kleid, das an die alten, faltenreichen Jagdröcke mahnte. Als der Senner dies sah, blieb er verwundert stehen. Da winkte sie ihm freundlich und er folgte etwas zögernd diesem Zeichen. Wie er ihr nahe stand, überfiel ihn ein kalter Schauer, denn er hatte noch nie eine so schöne und so geisterhafte Frau gesehen. Sie sprach zu ihm: „Einstmals waren hier die herrlichsten Jagdreviere, und Grafen und Fürsten jagten in diesen Wäldern nach edlem Wilde, doch jetzt haben die bösen Menschen bald die unschuldigen Tiere hier oben ausgetilgt und mancher ehrliche Mann ist den Wilderern erlegen. Darum habe ich dich zum Beschützer meines Reiches und meiner Tiere erwählt und dich gerufen, auf dass du das Wild schützest und jeden Wilddieb tötest!" Da graute dem Senner vor diesem Vorschlage und er wollte nicht darauf eingehen. Als die Frau dies sah, drohte sie ihm mit erhobenem Finger und sprach: „Wehe dir, wenn du mir nicht folgest! Ich werde dann deine Alpenwirtschaft, die ich so lange beschützt habe, verderben und kein einziges Stück deiner Herde soll am Leben bleiben. Da schauderte es dem Senner und er versprach, der Mahnung zu folgen und jeden Wildschützen aus dem Wege zu räumen. Er hielt auch sein Wort und schonte keinen. Da begann das Wild wieder auf dem Nachtberge sich zu vermehren und der Berg war gescheut der Kaiserfrau wegen, der man das Verunglücken so vieler Wildschützen zuschrieb. Heutzutage zeigt man noch die Fußspuren am Steine, worauf sie damals gestanden war, und noch lebt ein alter Wildschütze, der sie einmal auf jenem Felsen stehend und ihm drohend gesehen haben will. Selbst dann, wenn man glaubte, die letzte Gämse sei dort geschossen worden, seien wieder neue Gämsenherden gekommen, ohne dass man wusste woher.

›› Wissenswertes ‹‹

Thiersee, bis ca. 1504 Teil des bayerischen Herzogtums, liegt in der Nähe von Kufstein. – Die würdevolle, grün gekleidete Frau in dieser Sage erinnert an die griechische Waldgöttin Artemis, welche als Mutter der wilden Tiere und Hüterin der Wildnis verehrt wurde, was einem sehr alten Göttinnenbild entspricht. Manchmal wird Artemis auch „die Bergmutter" genannt.

Auch die Vivènes in den Dolomitensagen sind grün gekleidet, ebenso geheimnisvolle Frauen in vielen Sagen anderer Länder. Auch andere naturdämonische Wesen sind grün, wie beispielsweise die Wassergeister; auch der Teufel trägt grüne Kleider. Die Farbe grün steht für die der Natur innewohnenden Kraft. – Auch in dieser Sage tritt die schöne und mächtige Frau auf einem Spurenstein in Erscheinung.

45

Die Wasserfräulein

Im Kalterer See war ein Mann ertrunken. Als sein Sohn später auf dem Wasser fuhr, sah er ein grünes Männlein, das ihm freundlich zurief: „Komm mit mir in mein Haus." Der Bursche wollte jedoch nicht, denn er fürchtete das Seemannl und noch mehr scheute er den Wassertod. Als der Grüne dies bemerkte, kam er auf ihn zu und gab im eine Floßfeder mit den Worten: „Nimm diese Feder und folge mir keck, denn so lange du sie bei dir trägst, kannst du nicht ertrinken." Er führte den Jüngling in die Tiefe des Sees, wo sie zu einem wunderschönen Kristallhause kamen. Der grüne Mann führte ihn hinein und zeigte ihm all die Pracht und Herrlichkeit. Wie sie so durch die schönen Zimmer gingen, sah der Bursche seinen Vater leibhaftig in einem kristallenen Kasten liegen. Er bat nun den Führer flehentlich um seinen Vater. „Du kannst ihn haben, wenn du die Leiche deines Vaters und seine Seele, die dort im Glase sich befindet, den bewachenden Fräulein entreißen kannst. Nimm diese Nebelkappe und versuche dein Glück." Der Bursche macht sich unsichtbar und singt in einer Ecke ein wunderschönes Lied. Als die Fräulein dies hören, eilen sie neugierig den lieblichen Tönen zu. Augenblicklich enteilt er, springt auf die Leiche seines Vaters zu, greift nach dem Glase, in dem die Seelen sich befinden, und eilt mit beiden von dannen. Wie staunte er aber, als er dem See mit seinem kostbaren Raube entstiegen war und ein Fräulein an der Leiche seines Vaters angeklammert fand! Sie war nun seine Gefangene und ging mit ihm und seinem geretteten Vater nach Hause, wo sie treu und redlich diente. Der Jüngling, der später das Seefräulein heiratete, besuchte noch oft den Wassermann in seiner kristallenen Burg.

In vor- und frühchristlicher Zeit war nach dem Tode des Menschen die Unterwelt der Aufenthaltsort der Seele. In der nordischen Sage war dies das Reich der Hel. Ertrank aber ein Mensch, empfing ihn die Meerriesin Ran. Auch in anderen Mythen und Sagen wurde der/die Ertrunkene von den Wassergeistern empfangen. Bei den Griechen wurde die Seele der Verstorbenen in den Flüssen der Unterwelt gereinigt.

Das Sagenmotiv des Wassermannes als Hüter der ertrunkenen Seelen in Flaschen, Gläsern oder Töpfen ist uralt und findet sich nicht nur in Tiroler, sondern in vielen Sagen Mitteleuropas. Manchmal wird erzählt, dass der Wassermann hofft, am Jüngsten Tage so viele Seelen zu haben wie der liebe Gott. Gelingt es einem lebenden Menschen, in das unterirdische Wasserreich zu gelangen, kann er die Seelen der Ertrunkenen befreien, indem er die Töpfe umwendet. Dadurch wird der Ertrunkene wieder zum Menschen oder die Seele fliegt als weiße Taube befreit davon. In dieser Tiroler Sage sind Wasserfräulein die strengen Hüterinnen der Seele.

46

Die Anguana vom Scin-See

Einstmals lebten im Scin-See in Ampezzo einige Anguane, die hatten Ziegenfüße. Wenn sie ihre Wäsche waschen mussten, wollten sie sich dabei keine große Mühe machen: Sie breiteten einfach ihre Kleider, lauter zerfetzte, schleimige Tücher und Lumpen aus grünen Algen, auf der Wiese neben dem See aus, und dann zog auch schon ein Gewitter auf und es regnete in Strömen.

So war die Wäsche leicht gemacht und trocknete duftend auf der Wiese. Aber die Leute im Tal hatten dann jedesmal einen großen Schaden, weil Hagel die Heuernte zunichte machte und Gerste und Bohnen zu Boden fielen.

Einmal stieg ein Mann von Alverà von den Almen herunter, wo er gemäht hatte. Dabei dachte er an seine fünf Kinder, es waren die schönsten Kinder im ganzen Dorf, und auch an ihre Mutter, die gut und sorgsam war. Auf seinen Schultern trug er sein Werkzeug. Da sah er beim Lago di Scin auf der Wiese die schmutzige Wäsche der Anguane und hinter der Tofana bereits die schwarzen Gewitterwolken. Erzürnt verfluchte er die faulen Frauen. Er nahm seine Harke und zog damit die schmutzigen Tücher der Anguane in den See. Dann ging er weiter, und noch bevor er in Alverà ankam, waren die Wolken verschwunden und der Himmel wieder hell und klar.

Aber als er über die Türschwelle trat, lag seine Frau krank im Bett. Am nächsten Tag ging es ihr noch schlechter, und nach ein paar Tagen war sie völlig schwach und abgemagert. Der Mann war verzweifelt. Am achten Tag vertraute er sich einer Nachbarin an, die ihm riet, sich an einen Hirten zu wenden, welcher oberhalb von Larièto seine Herde weidete.

Diesem erzählte er nun von seiner Frau und auch, dass er die gesamte Wäsche der Anguane in den See geworfen hatte.

„Sicher waren sie es, die dich verwunschen haben. Bringe ihnen eine schwarze Ziege, wie in den Zeiten des Silvanus und des Zan de Rame, in einer Gewitternacht, denn dort steigen sie aus dem Wasser. Versuche es, mehr kann ich dir nicht raten." Und er hatte Glück, denn genau an diesem Abend zogen Gewitterwolken auf, und erstes Donnergrollen war aus dem Fanestal zu hören. Ein großer Regenbogen verband den Monte Cristallo mit dem Monte Falòria. Schnell lief er nach Hause, holte seine einzige Ziege und machte sich auf den Weg zum See. Die Anguane waren gerade dabei, ihre gewaschenen Stoffe aufzusammeln. Als sie ihn sahen, blieben sie einen Augenblick am Ufer stehen.

Er legte die Ziege zu Füßen der Ältesten und bat sie, seine Frau wieder gesund zu machen. Aber da tauchten sie mit feindseligem und wildem Gelächter in das Wasser und waren verschwunden. Ihm blieb nichts anderes übrig, als wieder nach Hause zurückzukehren. Nur eine Anguana, die letzte in der Reihe, war nicht in das Wasser getaucht. Neugierig beobachtete sie den Mann, dann folgte sie ihm heimlich, sich immer hinter Lärchen versteckend, damit er sie nicht sehen konnte.

Als der Mann nach Hause kam, erwartete ihn ein trauriges Geschehnis: Seine Frau war verstorben, und die Kinder schrien lauthals. Sie waren schmutzig und zerzaust, denn seit Tagen hatte sie niemand mehr gekämmt. Aber er musste sich nun um die Tote kümmern, sie ankleiden und ihre Beerdigung vorbereiten.

Da trat die kleine Anguana in die Küche, wo die Kinder am offenen Herd, am Larìn, saßen, tränenüberströmt und ascheverschmiert, und die jüngeren der Geschwister schliefen auf den warmen Steinplatten des Larìns. Die zwei Älteren sahen sie erschrocken an, aber da nahm sie einen goldenen Kamm heraus und begann die Kleinen zu kämmen, langsam und vorsichtig, eine Locke nach der anderen, so dass sie nicht aufwachten. Da waren auch die beiden Älteren beruhigt, ließen sich auch von ihr kämmen und waschen, und dann schliefen sie ein.

Von dem Tag an blieb die Anguana im Haus, untertags jedoch immer versteckt unter dem Larìn. Jeden Morgen, nachdem der Bauer gegangen war, kam sie hervor, kämmte und wusch die Kinder und flocht der Ältesten ihre Zöpfe. Im Spiegel des Waschwassers aber sah sie ihr eigenes Gesicht, und unter ihrem Kleid schauten ihre erschreckenden Ziegenfüße hervor. Eine Anguana war sie, wild und hässlich, und so versteckte sie sich immer wieder schnell unter dem Larìn, nachdem sie das Mittagessen zubereitet und das Haus aufgeräumt hatte. Der ältesten Tochter trug sie auf, ihrem Vater zu sagen, sie selbst hätte alles erledigt. Würden die Kinder etwas verraten, so drohte sie, dann würde sie verschwinden, und so schwiegen sie. Die Anguana aber blieb verborgen unter dem Larìn, und der Bauer glaubte, seine Älteste hätte alle Hausarbeiten verrichtet. Von nun an hatten die Kinder wieder die schönsten Haare im ganzen Dorf. →

So vergingen die Jahre, und da merkte die Anguana, dass sie nicht mehr fort konnte, auch wenn sie es gewollt hätte. Sie verspürte nämlich etwas in ihrem Inneren, was die anderen Anguane nicht kannten – sie fühlte Liebe in ihrem Herzen, für die Kinder und auch für den Mann, von dem sie eigentlich nur seine schweren Schritte kannte. Und das war der Grund, warum sie nicht mehr wegkonnte.

Die Zeit verstrich, und das Mädchen war inzwischen zu einer jungen Frau herangewachsen, mit glänzenden Zöpfen, welche sie auf ihrem Kopf gewunden trug. Eines Tages verliebte sie sich, und der junge Mann kam sie öfters besuchen. Es war ein schöner und starker Bursche, die Anguana hatte ihn zwischen den Steinen des Ofens heraus beobachtet. Nun aber kam sie nicht mehr unter dem Larìn hervor, denn sie fürchtete, ihn zu erschrecken – bestimmt hätte er nie das Pflegekind einer Anguana geheiratet!

So blieb sie unter dem Herd.

Abends saßen der Bursche und das Mädchen oft zusammen und schmiedeten Zukunftspläne. Sie dachte zwar schon hin und wieder an die Anguana, doch lange hatten sie sie nicht mehr gesehen, bestimmt war sie fort gegangen.

Eines Abends brachte der junge Mann Maurerkelle und Mörtel mit – er wollte den Herd ausbessern. Er begann den Mörtel hinaufzustreichen, verschloss Fugen und Ritzen, doch die Anguana schwieg. Würde sie jetzt herausspringen, so wäre das Glück des Mädchens zerstört! So kauerte sie sich eng zusammen, hielt ihre Ziegenfüße umschlungen und bald schon konnte sie sich nicht mehr rühren unter dem Larìn. Sie verspürte große Schmerzen und verstand nicht, warum. Schlussendlich war sie eingemauert, ohne Wasser, unter dem heißen, trockenen Stein – sie, die doch immer im Wasser gelebt hatte.

Ein langsames, qualvolles Sterben begann. Manchmal, wenn ein besonders großes Feuer im Herd brannte, schmerzte sie die Hitze sehr und dann weinte sie wie ein Mensch, wie es Anguane eigentlich nicht können. Da sagte der junge Mann: „Dein Vater hat heute grünes Holz gebracht, hör nur das Geräusch wie es zischt." Doch das Mädchen hatte die Anguana ganz vergessen; sie dachte, dass das Holz noch feucht sei und legte es auf den Herd, um es zu trocknen.

Viele Jahre später, als die Kindeskinder den alten Larìn neu errichteten, fanden sie darunter eine grünliche Masse, vertrockneten Algen gleich und graues Pulver, wie Asche, und darin lag ein goldener Kamm.

Da erzählte ihnen die alte Großmutter mit dünner und zittriger Stimme eine merkwürdige Geschichte von der „Anguana vom Larìn", aber die Enkelkinder glaubten ihr nicht und meinten, sie wolle nur den Diebstahl eines goldenen Kammes vertuschen.

Der „Larìn“ ist ein offener Herd, wie er früher in den Bauernhäusern typisch war. – Der inmitten von Lärchen gelegene kleine Lago von Scin befindet sich in der Nähe von Cortina d'Ampezzo. Die cadorischen Anguane, im Trentino auch als Eguane, Guane oder Enguane bekannt, sind in den Sagen oft in Wassernähe zu Hause. Agno war in der griechischen Mythologie eine Quellnymphe, die bei lang andauernder Trockenheit vom Priester beschworen wurde, ausführliche Regenfälle zu schicken. Doch auch das lateinische „anguis“ (Schlange, Drachen, oder Echse) ist mit dem Wort „Anguana“ verwandt. Diese haben, wie andere weibliche Wasser- oder Waldwesen aus den Nachbarprovinzen, verunstaltete Füße. So tragen beispielsweise die Aganis in den Julischen Alpensagen einwärts gekehrte Füße, und im Friaul erzählt man sich von Hexen mit Hahnen- oder Löwenfüßen. In dieser Sage sind es Ziegenfüße, die dadurch an Pan/Silvanus, den griechisch/römisch/etruskischen fröhlichen Gott des Waldes und der Natur erinnern sowie an andere Waldgottheiten mit Ziegenfüßen, die Ägipanen. Wie Pan vor allem in der Mittagszeit nicht in seiner Ruhe gestört werden durfte, wollen auch die Anguanes nicht unnötig arbeiten; sie werden deshalb von den Menschen oft als faul oder träge beschrieben. Sie sind im Besitz magischer Kräfte, die ihnen die Arbeiten erleichtern. – Im Felsmassiv des Monte Falòria bei Cortina befindet sich in einer Felswand eine große viereckige Felsnische, welche als Tor des „Dio Silvano“ bezeichnet wird und als ein vorchristlicher Kultort gilt. Noch im vergangenen Jahrhundert sollen die Bauern ihren Hut gezogen haben, wenn sie hier vorbeigingen. Nicht weit davon entfernt liegt der Col Jana; Jana (= Diana) war laut einer örtlichen Sage die Lebensgefährtin des Dio Silvano. Heute trägt dieser Hügel einen kleinen Weiler namens Cojana.

Der mythische, in mehreren Dolomitensagen erwähnte Zan de Rame und seine Frau Dona Dindia haben laut Nachforschungen von Peppe Richebuono tatsächlich um 1400 bei Fraina bei Cortina gelebt, wie aus einem Pergament von 1632 hervorgeht, in welchem ein Pachtvertrag von 1450 zitiert wird und beide namentlich genannt werden.

Die Anguana dieser Sage erinnert an eine andere ladinische Sage: an Tanna, die große Königin der Crodères, die ihre Größe und Macht einbüßt, weil sie sich menschlichen Gefühlen hingibt. Erst als sie wieder darübersteht, wie alle überirdischen Wesen, nimmt sie ihren ursprünglichen göttlichen Sitz der Macht wieder ein.

Der Kamm ist ein Kraftsymbol der Alten Göttin. Das Kämmen mit einem goldenen Kamm spielt – oft in Verbindung mit Musik – in vielen Geschichten von Wasserfrauen (z.B. Loreley) aber auch in zahlreichen anderen Sagen eine große Rolle, wie beispielsweise in Percht-, Schatzhüterinnen-, verwünschten Frauen- und Geistersagen.

47

Die drei Seligen Fräulein ob der Morin im Ötztal

Einst raubte einer armen Hirtenfrau aus Längenfeld im Ötztale ein Lämmergeier ihr Kind, einen Knaben, als sie zur Alm emporstieg, auf welcher ihr Mann hütete, während sie an einer Wegkapelle kniend ihren Rosenkranz betete. Aber der Himmel fügte es, dass der Geier sich droben auf einem Felsstück mit seinem Raube niederließ, gar nicht weit von dem Hirten, der den Geier mit Steinwürfen verscheuchte, und so der Retter seines eigenen Kindes wurde, das er seit dem Frühling nicht gesehen hatte. Es waren aber die drei seligen Fräulein, welche in der Nähe des Ötztaler Ferners über und hinter einer, die „Morin“ geheißenen Felswand wohnten, schon bei der Rettung jenes Hirtenknaben unsichtbar tätig und hilfreich gewesen.

Der Knabe erwuchs und trug stets in seiner Seele den Zug nach den Höhen des Gebirges; er wurde ein kühner Bergsteiger und Bergschütze; als solchen zog ihn von jeher ein geheimnisvoller Trieb nach der Platte über der Morin, denn dort – so ging die Sage – sollte auch ein Tierparadies sein, da sollte es Gämsen in Scharen geben, ja sogar noch Steinböcke, aber kein Jäger könne dahin gelangen. Der junge kecke Knabe aber wollte das Wagestück bestehen und begann seine Wanderung, die damit endete, dass er unter Todesgefahren sich verstieg, endlich nicht mehr wusste, wo er war, und von der eisbedeckten Platte, die sich über zehntausend Fuß hoch in die Wolken erhebt, herab auf eine grüne Alpe rutschte, die er von droben kaum sehen konnte, dass ihm darüber hören und sehen verging.

Als der Jäger wieder zu Bewusstsein kam, lag er auf Speik und Edelweiß gebettet in der Kristallgrotte der drei seligen Fräulein, die ihn zum zweiten Male gerettet hatten. Sie umstanden ihn, strahlend vom himmlischen Liebreiz, und ihr Anblick weckte in ihm die süßeste Empfindung. Er blieb nun ein gut gepflegter Gast der seligen Fräulein, durfte ihre herrliche Wohnung, ihre Gärten, ihre Tiere sehen, aber es wurde ihm auch gesagt, dass seine lieblichen Wirtinnen die Schutzgöttinnen der Alpentiere seien, und ihm das Versprechen abgenommen, nie ein solches Tier zu töten, nicht Gämse, nicht Alpenhasen, nicht Schneehuhn, nicht einmal ein Murmeltier.

Drei Tage durfte der Bub bei den seligen Fräulein verbleiben, durfte sie küssen und anbeten, dann aber musste er dreierlei heilig und bei seiner Seele Seligkeit angeloben, wenn er jemals wiederkehren, oder wenn er auch für den Fall seiner Nichtwiederkehr, drunten glücklich sein wolle, zum Ersten Verschwiegenheit so tief wie das Grab, dass er je die seligen Fräulein gesehen und bei ihnen gewesen; zum andern niemals ein Alpentier weder zu töten, noch zu verfolgen; zum Dritten, nie einem Menschenauge den Weg gewahren zu lassen, der ihm gezeigt werden würde, um bequemer zu ihnen zurückzukehren. Ein viertes Versprechen, nämlich den Seligen die Liebe, die er gegen sie an Tag gelegt, zu bewahren, und mit keiner Dirne vertraut zu tun, keinen Handschlag oder Kuss zu geben, verstand sich, wie die Seligen meinten, schon von selbst ohne Schwur und Gelöbnis. Dann ward der Alpensohn nach einem zärtlichem Abschied in eine bergestiefe Kluft hinabgelassen, die sich tief unten im Tale der brausenden Achen unter bergenden Alpenrosenbüschen öffnete, nachdem ihm noch mitgeteilt worden war, dass er an jedem Vollmondabende auf drei Tage wieder zum Besuche kommen dürfe, und nur durch diese Kluft in den Berg eingehen und unten ein bestimmtes Zeichen geben könne.

Der Bub kam wie umgewandelt nach Hause. Ihm war, als habe ihm geträumt, und bald genug hieß er der Träumer, denn er nahm nie mehr einen Stutzen in die Hand, ging auf keine Jagd mehr mit, besuchte keinen Tanzplatz, aber in jeder Vollmondnacht schlich er zur Felskluft tief unter der Morin und trat in das Bergesinnere und war drei Tage lang glücklich mit den seligen Fräulein, deren wunderlieblichem Gesange er oft beseligt lauschte. Daheim aber verfiel seine Gestalt, er wurde bleich und matt, vergeblich indes war es, dass Eltern und Freunde in ihn drangen, doch zu sagen, was ihm fehle? Es fehle ihm ja nichts, sprach er auf solche Fragen, er habe ja Freude in Fülle.

Da Vater und Mutter seine heimlichen Weggänge in den Vollmondnächten wahrnahmen, so schlichen sie ihm einmal nach und hart am Eingange traf sein Ohr der Mutter Stimme, die ihn bei seinem Namen rief, und alsbald schoben sich die Felswände vor des Jünglings Augen zusammen, und im Berge stürzten mit Krach und Donnergepolter Steine auf Steine nieder. Des Jünglings Glück war ihm nun unwiederbringlich verloren. Trübsinnig und in sich gekehrt ging der Unglückliche in seinen Heimatort zurück – achtete weder der Mutter Tränen noch des Vaters Schelten über sein Wesen, blieb teilnahmslos für jeden aufmunternden Zuspruch und für jede Zerstreuung und siechte so kraftlos und tatenlos dahin, bis der Herbst kam, die Herden von den Almen in die Winterställe des Talortes getrieben wurden und das schöne Naturleben der Gebirgswelt erstarb und unter Schnee begraben wurde.

Da kamen ein paar alte Freunde in das Haus des Hirtensohnes, die sprachen von einem Jagdgange, den sie hinauf nach der Platte unternehmen wollten, und da funkelten zum ersten Male wieder die Augen des jungen bleichen Gebirgsschützen, die Jagdlust, die Wildererlust, die unüberwindliche, regte sich in ihm – vielleicht war es auch ein anderer Trieb. Er wollte noch einmal eindringen in das gefeite Gebiet der seligen Fräulein, und gehe es auf Tod und Leben. Am Leben lag ihm ohnehin nichts mehr – und der Tod war ihm Befreiung.

Der Jüngling brachte sein Jagdzeug in Ordnung, lieh sich einen Stutzen, denn der seinige war zerschellt und zerspellt in einer Felsschlucht ob der Morin liegen geblieben, und schloss sich dem frühen Weidgange der Wilderer an. Erst ging er mit ihnen, dann eilte er voraus, höher – immer höher – wie von einer unwiderstehlichen Macht gezogen – es war ihm so leicht ums Herz, allzu lange hatte die dumpfe Luft der Talenge ihm die Brust gedrückt. Er stieg so rasch, als ob er Arsenik gegessen habe, das tödliche Gift, das manche Älpler in kleinsten Gaben genießen, um sich luftiger zu machen, und endlich erblickte er eine Wächtergämse. Diese pfiff und entschwand hinter dem Grat, auf dem sie gestanden war. Der Alpenjäger erklomm den Grat, da sah er unter sich, aber außer der Schussweite, auf einer kleinen Matte, ein starkes Rudel Gämsen. Nur eine war ziemlich nahe, und diese eine verfolgte er unablässig, bis das geängstigte Tier nicht weiter konnte und an einem Abgrund stillstand, den vor eitel Jagdeifer der Schütze gar nicht sah. Er legte an – da klang es wie eine klagende Mädchenstimme, aber der Jäger horchte nicht hin – er zielte scharf, er schoss. Siehe, da umleuchtete ihn ein heller Glanz, die Gämse stand ungetroffen in dem Glanze, und vor ihr schwebten in blendender Helle, aber strengen und zürnenden Angesichts die drei seligen Fräulein und nahten ihm, und bei ihrem ersten Anblick ohne Liebe und ohne Lächeln überrieselte den Jüngling ein tiefes Grauen – er wankte zurück – noch einen Schritt und hinterrücks taumelte er in den tausend Fuß tiefen Schlund, von seinen Fußtritten löste sich bröckelndes Gestein, eine Mure schoss ihm polternd nach und begrub ihn unter ihrem Schutt und Gerölle.

›› Wissenswertes ‹‹

In dieser in romantisch-pathetischem Stil aufgeschriebenen Ötztaler Sage verbergen sich Spuren matriarchal-schamanischer Mythologie und jugendlich-männlicher Initiation. Es ist die Begegnung zwischen einem jungen Burschen, eigentlich noch einem Knaben, und drei göttlich/halbgöttlichen weiblichen (Geist-)Wesen, deren Aufenthaltsort in der unberührten Natur zu finden ist. – Bei vielen Schamanen wird bereits im Kindesalter ihr künftiger Lebensweg klar, manchmal sind dies schwache, kränkliche Kinder; oft lassen auch außergewöhnliche Ereignisse in ihrem Leben ihre zukünftige schamanische Bestimmung erahnen. So wird auch in dieser Sage das Kleinkind von einem Lämmergeier, Symboltier des Todes und der Lebenserneuerung, der den Wilden Fräulein zu gehorchen hat, in die Lüfte (zu „höheren" Bestimmungen) getragen. Doch der Vater holt den Sohn wieder zurück. Als Jugendlicher treibt ihn eine innere „geheimnisvolle Kraft" wieder hinauf in dieselben Berge. Die drei Frauen bergen den abgestürzten Burschen, sie pflegen und heilen ihn. Sie lassen ihn eintreten in die überirdische Welt (eine höhere Bewusstseinsebene), gewähren ihm Einblick in ihr Wissen und ihre Machtsphäre und führen ihn in die Liebe ein. Wie in Trance, also ist seine Initiationszeit noch nicht abgeschlossen, kehrt er wieder nach Hause zurück. Doch besteht er diese Probezeit, aus der er gereift und gefestigt hervorgehen sollte, nicht bzw. entscheidet er sich zur Rückkehr in ein „normales" oberflächliches Leben; nicht nur das, er sagt seinen Lehrerinnen den Kampf an, denn er schießt auf eine Gämse, ein heiliges Wesen und Manifestation des Wilden Fräuleins. Die Strafe bleibt nicht aus: Die Gämse ist unverwundbar, er hingegen muss sterben. – Aus Schamanenberichten weiß man, dass die Berufung zum Schamanen oder zur Schamanin für die Betroffenen zu Beginn oft nicht leicht akzeptiert wird, denn sie bringt ein Leben der Selbstaufgabe, Entsagung und Einsamkeit mit sich, gleichzeitig auch ein hohes soziales Ansehen. Eine Verweigerung scheint es nicht zu geben: Viele Erzählungen berichten, dass diese mit dem Tode enden würde.

Adler und andere Raubvögel sind in vielen Völkern der Welt schamanische Kraftwesen, die manchmal (im Traum oder in Wirklichkeit) erscheinen, um dem sich auf der Probe befindenden Menschen zu helfen, in eine höhere Bewusstseinsebene zu gelangen.

Einer stark vereinfachten psychoanalytischen Interpretation zufolge (nach C.G. Jung) könnte sich der Bursche auch auf der Suche nach seiner „Anima", seiner inneren weiblichen Seite befinden, die es für den Mann zu integrieren gilt so wie für die Frau den Animus, die männliche Seite.

Die in dieser Sage genannten Blumen Speik und Edelweiß sind uralte Tiroler Heil- und Zauberkräuter. In vielen anderen Sagen schützen sie vor den Übergriffen des Teufels. Als Speik werden in Tirol mehrere stark duftende Alpenblumen bezeichnet. Der „echte" Speik ist ein Baldriangewächs (sein Namen ist aus „spica celtica" entstanden, lat. Valeriana celtica), reich an ätherischem Öl. Er war früher ein Allheilmittel und wurde bis in den Orient exportiert. Fast ausgerottet steht er heute, wie auch das Edelweiß, unter strengem Naturschutz. Speikgräber war früher ein eigener Beruf. In vielen Gegenden gibt es Almwiesen mit dem Namen Speikboden (z.B. das heutige Skigebiet im Ahrntal), auf denen der Speik besonders reiche Ernte trug. Mit Speik wurden in Tirol auch die Ställe geräuchert, um die Hexen zu vertreiben. Der Edelweißtee wurde früher in Tirol wegen seiner schmerzlindernden Wirkung bei Magen- und Darmproblemen getrunken (Bauchwehblüml). Heute wird es in der Naturkosmetik gegen Hautalterung verwendet. – Eine Sage aus den Julischen Alpen erzählt von einer schönen Fee auf den höchsten Bergzacken, die den

Jäger zu sich lockt. Kaum aber streckt er die Arme nach ihr aus, lässt sie Felsgeröll auf ihn los, und er muss sterben. Die Fee aber weint vor Sehnsucht nach Liebe, und aus ihren Tränen entsteht das Edelweiß. Eine weitere heilkräftige Alpenblume ist die Moschus-Schafgarbe (Achillea moschata); sie wird auch Wildfräuleinkraut genannt. – Als Göttin-Heilerin galt auch Reitia.

Die dreitägige Besuchserlaubnis zur Vollmondzeit in die Höhle der Wilden Fräulein erinnert an die griechisch/römischen Mondgöttinnen Artemis/Diana und ihre „Vorgängerin" Selene und an den mit ihnen zusammenhängenden in ältester Zeit praktizierten Mondkultus. Diese Göttinnen zogen sich laut Mythos zur Neumondzeit drei Tage in eine Höhle zurück.

In zahlreichen Sagen und Mythen verschiedener Länder begegnet uns die Dreier-Konstellation der Frauen: die keltischen Matres, die nordischen Nornen, die östlichen Moiren, die römischen Parsen. Chione, die „Schneekönigin", war eine der drei Horen aus der griechischen Mythologie, eine unantastbare jungfräuliche Göttin der Berge.

Aus der ladinischen Sage ist die Bergkönigin Tanna mit der blauen Krone, die Königin der Crodères bekannt. Auch in den französischen Alpen trägt eine Fee denselben Namen, im Altfranzösischen bedeutet dieser Name „Höhle", „Loch".

Beliebter Aufenthaltsort der Wilden Fräulein ist neben Steinen, Felsen und Höhlen auch der Berg selbst. Zahlreiche Berge von außergewöhnlicher Ausstrahlung, heilige Berge also, und auch viele der höchsten Berge der Welt, waren/sind ursprünglich weiblich. So wird der Mount Everest, der erst 1865 von den Briten diesen Namen erhielt, im Tibet „Chomolungma" genannt, was „Große Mutter Erde" oder „Muttergöttin der Erde" bedeutet, im Nepal „Sagarmatha" = „Göttin/Kopf des Himmels". Annapurna heißt soviel wie „Nahrung spendende Göttin". Die Cho Oyu mit ihren riesigen Eis- und Felsmassen bedeutet „Göttin des Türkis". Aber auch Tiroler Berge mit einer außergewöhnlichen Ausstrahlung sind weiblich, wie beispielsweise die Marmolata, die Presanella und die Paganella („schöne Heidin") im Trentino, die Serles in Nordtirol und die Weißkugel in Südtirol. Aus dem „Wild-Fräule-Kopf" in den Stubaier Alpen (siehe Atlas Tirolensis von Peter Anich und Blasius Huber, 1774) wurde der „Wilde Freiger".

48

Die Saligen in Lüsen

Einst hielten sich auch in Lüsen die Saligen Fräulein auf, und in fast jedem Hause wohnte ein solches seltsames Wesen. Das war noch eine glückliche Zeit – denn überall, wo eine Salige hauste, war Segen und Überfluss.

Einmal ging ein Weiblein an einem Haus, vor dem eben eine Salige saß und die frischgebackenen Brotlaibe zählte, vorüber und bat um einen Laib. Die Salige gab dem Weiblein gern einen Brotlaib, setzte aber hinzu: „Frage nie nach dem Ende!"

Das Weiblein hielt sich an diese geheimnisvolle Mahnung und hatte zeit seines Lebens immer Brot. Denn der Laib wurde niemals kleiner, mochte es herabschneiden, wie viel es wollte. Als es starb und die Tochter den Brotlaib erbte, sagte diese einmal unwirsch: „Ja hat es denn mit diesem alten Wecken überhaupt nie ein Ende?"

Da war der Zauber vorbei, und das Brot nahm ab und war noch am gleichen Abend aufgebraucht wie ein gewöhnlicher Laib. Da hatte die Tochter nichts mehr zu essen und musste auch betteln gehen, wie weiland ihre Mutter.

In vielen Sagen wird die Zeit, in der sich die Seligen Fräulein zeigten, als Inbegriff für „die glückliche, gute Zeit" beschrieben. Die Selige war/ist Synonym für Fruchtbarkeit und Überfluss; wen sie beschenkt, der braucht sich nicht mehr um die Zukunft zu sorgen – im Gegenteil: Wer ihr Tun oder den „ewigen" Überfluss bezweifelt, führt dessen Ende herbei.

Eine von Hugo de Rossi im Fassatal aufgezeichnete Sage (hsg. von Ulrike Kindl) erzählt von einer Vivàna, die einem Bauern ihren Dienst anbot. Mit einer Gerstengarbe kehrte sie nicht nur alle Zimmer, sondern auch den Keller sauber. Dies konnte der Bauer nicht mitansehen, und er gab ihr stattdessen einen Bund Tannenreisig. Da verschwand sie spurlos, und der Keller war fingerdick mit Tannennadeln bedeckt. Hätte er ihr Handeln nicht angezweifelt, wäre der Boden mit Gerste bedeckt gewesen.

Sehr oft tritt das Salige Fräulein im Zusammenhang mit Getreide in Erscheinung. Umgekehrt hat sich bei den Bauern in verschiedenen Tiroler Gegenden bis zu Beginn der zweiten Hälfte des vorigen Jahrhunderts hinein der uralte Restglaube an eine Kornmutter (Fruchtbarkeitsgottheit) gehalten, die sich beim Kornschneiden in die in einer Ackerecke stehenden Garbe flüchte. Diese Überzeugungen erinnern laut dem Brixner Volkskundler H. Fink an den Kult der Reismutter in Indonesien, an die Kartoffelmutter in Peru und an die Maismutter bei den nordamerikanischen Indianern. Fink berichtet, dass man noch in der Mitte des vorigen Jahrhunderts in Rodeneck großen Wert darauf legte, die erste Garbe nur mit der Sichel (ein uraltes Göttinnensymbol) zu schneiden und niemals mit der harten Sense oder gar der groben Maschine abzumähen. In Toblach kniete sich der Schnitter vor den letzten Ähren nieder und betete. Bis in die vierziger Jahre wagte es in St. Andrä bei Brixen niemand, die letzten Halme des Roggenackers zu schneiden; sie wurden beim Umbauen des Ackers für den Buchweizen eingepflügt. Zahlreiche weitere kultische Bräuche waren in ganz Tirol beim Kornschnitt und beim Brotbacken üblich.

49

Von den seligen Leuten bei Brixen

Wo immer eine Selige im Dienste war, warf sie, bevor sie wieder aufstand, zum Abschiede einen Garnknäuel in die Stube, der nie gar wurde, bis sich einmal jemand verschwatzte und verwundert ausrief: „Weard denn dös Zuig nimmer gor?" Dann hatte der Knäuel auch sofort ein Ende.

Dasselbe erzählt man in St. Andrä bei Brixen, wo die seligen Leute hinten in den wälschen Köfeln hausten. Auch hier sind sie bei den Bauern in Dienst getreten und haben nach dem Pflügen die Weisung gegeben: „Baur, san, es geat der guate Wind!" – oder: „Baur, hear au mit San, es geat die rechte Luft öt!" Ebenso ist hier ein Bauer nachts heimgegangen und hört eine Stimme im Wald: „Sog deiner Dirn, die Tinzl-Tanzl isch g'storben!" Der Bauer erzählt daheim, was er gehört hat, und die Dirne geht weinend davon und lässt den nicht endenden Garnknäuel zurück.

Dasselbe wird vom Moarhof in Lüsen erzählt. Die Stimme im Walde rief hier: „Hoss! Hoss! Moarhofer afn weißn Ross, sog zi deiner Dirn, dö tuit Mittn riahrn, die Hirla Harla isch g'storben." Die Dirne springt auf, lässt den bekannten Knäuel zurück und segnet noch das Haus, in dem sie so gute Behandlung erfahren hat. Die Seligen wohnten hier unter dem Moarhof.

Mittn = Backzuber.

Das Motiv des nie endenden Garnknäuels ist im gesamten Tiroler Gebiet und auch in anderen europäischen Ländern bekannt. Die Seligen stehen in einer besonders innigen Beziehung zur Natur, sind sie selbst ja auch Teil von ihr, und so wissen sie genau Bescheid, wann die richtige Zeit ist für das Säen oder die Ernte. „Bauer, säe, es geht der gute Wind“, heißt es in dieser Sage, und „Bauer, hör auf mit dem Säen, es geht nicht die richtige Luft!“ Gerne geben sie ihr Wissen den Menschen weiter. Manchmal hält sich der Mensch nicht an ihre Ratschläge oder glaubt es besser zu wissen, was oft die Vernichtung der Ernte aufgrund unvorhergesehener Wetterverhältnisse, welche die Selige vorausgeahnt hat, zur Folge hat.

Ein anderes weitverbreitetes Sagenmotiv ist das der Abberufung aufgrund eines Todesfalles. Bereits Plutarch (50-120 n.Chr.) berichtet von einem derartigen Ereignis. Auf einem Schiff, das von Griechenland nach Italien fuhr, hörte man von einer nahen Insel her eine mächtige Stimme, die dem Steuermann auftrug: „Wenn du nach Palodes kommst, melde, dass der große Pan tot ist.“ In Palodes erhob sich laut Plutarch bei dieser Mitteilung ein großes Seufzen von vielen. – Laut Sagenforschern gehört diese Geschichte wie viele ähnliche Versionen anderer Länder in die Reihe vom Sterben der Vegetationsgötter. Auch das weiße Pferd (in manchen Ländern ein schwarzes) scheint ein archetypisches Symbol zu sein.

Die Seligen tragen oft seltsame Namen, die kaum zu deuten sind: Gira-Gingele, Hirla-Harla, Tinzl-Tanzl, Welle, Loade u.v.a., sehr häufig ist ihr Namen bis zu ihrer Abberufung geheim. In vielen Religionen sind Götternamen mit einem Namenstabu belegt. Uralten Überzeugungen zufolge hat man ein Wesen, wenn man seinen wahren Namen kennt, in seiner Gewalt bzw. wird dessen Macht gebrochen. Das „Rumpelstilzchen“ der Gebrüder Grimm ist ein ähnliches Beispiel. In anderen Sagen darf das Haar der Saligen nicht berührt und schon gar nicht geschnitten werden. Dass das Haar als Sitz der Lebenskraft und -macht angesehen wird, ist bereits aus dem Alten Testament in der Geschichte um den umbezwingbaren Samson oder Simson überliefert. Als seine Frau ihm die Haare abschnitt, konnte er von seinen Feinden überwältigt werden.

50

Die Saligen an der Rotwand

Das alte Badweib vom Naturnser Badhaus besaß zwar nur einen kleinen Acker und ein paar Ziegen, aber trotzdem, oder gerade deswegen, war sie stets zufrieden und frohen Sinnes. Diese Geißen trieb sie täglich zu den kargen Grasflecken an den öden Felshängen des Naturnser Sonnenbergs hinauf, dort wo einst das Riesenschloss stand, welches mit der Burg Juval durch eine lederne Luftbrücke verbunden war.

Diese weitum sichtbaren rötlichen Felsen, Rotwand genannt, sind seit undenklichen Zeiten das Reich der Saligen Fräulein, welche die Menschen manchmal zu sich locken, sie mitunter auch beschenken oder ihnen gar einen guten Rat erteilen.

Eines Tages war die Alte wieder einmal mit ihren Ziegen dort hinaufgestiegen, doch die pralle Sommerhitze hatte sie so geschwächt, dass sie sich auf einen Felsblock hinsetzen

musste, doch selbst der war heiß. Zwischen den Steinen wuchs nichts mehr außer verdorrten Disteln und dornigen Sträuchern, denn die schlimmen Wetterverhältnisse der letzten Monate hatten alles Gras und alle Feldfrüchte vernichtet. Wie würde es wohl in Zukunft weitergehen mit ihr und ihren Geißen, wenn es nichts mehr zu essen gab, weder für sie noch für ihre Tiere? Vor Hunger und Schwäche wurde sie so müde, dass ihr die Augen zufielen; sie erwachte erst, als sie im Schlaf spürte, nicht alleine zu sein. →

Wie erschrak sie, als sie sich von mehreren unbekannten, weißgekleideten Frauen mit langen Haaren umgeben sah! Es waren Salige Frauen, und eine von ihnen überreichte ihr lächelnd ein Zeggerle, gefüllt mit schwarzen Körnern, sagte ihr, sie solle diese sogleich in ihren Acker säen, dann könne sie für alle Zukunft ohne Sorge sein. Bereits nach wenigen Wochen würde aus diesen Samen eine hundertfache Frucht erwachsen und niemals mehr würde es ihr und ihren Mitmenschen an Nahrung mangeln.

Und so war es auch. Die Samenkörner im Zeggerle der Saligen waren so zahlreich, dass sie nicht nur für die Bestellung ihres Feldes reichten, sondern auch noch für jene aller anderen Bauern im Dorf. Schon wenige Wochen später grünten die Äcker von der neuen Saat, und als sie blühten, glich das Feld einem rosaroten Blütenmeer, das von vielen summenden Bienen aufgesucht wurde.

Bevor die Herbststürme über die Felder brausten, waren alle Getreidetruhen gefüllt mit der neuen, fremden Frucht, die in Tirol „Schwarzplenten" genannt wird.

Die fremden Frauen wurden nie mehr gesehen, doch wenn an der Rotwand die weißen Nebelschwaden hängen bleiben und dann langsam in Richtung Schnalstal davongleiten, sagen die Leute: „Heut tanzen die Saligen wieder."

›› Wissenswertes ‹‹

Zeggerle = kleines geflochtenes Körbchen.

Auch in dieser Sage ist die Salige die Leben Erhaltende, Fruchtbarkeit Spendende und Helferin in der Not: sie überbringt einer armen alten Frau ein bis dahin unbekanntes Lebensmittel: den Schwarzplenten (Buchweizen), ein aus Mittelasien stammendes äußerst mineralien- und vitaminreiches Knöterichgewächs, das wie Getreide zum Kochen und Backen verwendet wird und aus der Tiroler Küche nicht wegzudenken ist. Nicht umsonst lautet das Sprichwort: „Knödel, Nudel, Mues und Plenten, sein die vier Tiroler Elementen." Früher wurde der Schwarzplenten in Südtirol bezeichnenderweise auch „Heidenmehl" genannt.

Laut einer anderen Sage befand sich am Sonnenberg das Schloss eines Riesen. Er war so groß, dass der große Felsrücken von Schloss Juval ihm als Sitzgelegenheit diente, wenn er sein Land überblickte.

In vielen Mythen werden Nebelschwaden, Wolken und Tau mit Luft- und Wassergeistern in Verbindung gebracht; in den Tiroler Sagen werden diese Naturphänomene häufig mit den schwebenden Saligen assoziiert. In der griechisch/römischen Mythologie finden wir die Chariten/Grazien, die tanzenden Göttinnen der Anmut. „Sagenhafte" Erklärungen bzw. Ursachen für Naturphänomene sind auch aus anderen Sagenkreisen bekannt: Bei Görz z.B. tanzen die Vilen nachts in ihren mit Edelsteinen besetzten durchsichtigen Gewändern auf einem Wiesengrunde im Reigen. Bei Sonnenaufgang löst sich dieser Schmuck nach und nach und wird zu Reif auf der Wiese.

51

Die Ganna aus dem Mittagstal

In den ladinischen Ortschaften erzählte man sich früher viel von den Gannes und den Salvans. Es waren dies Wilde Leute, die in den Felsen hausten, dort wo manchmal Füchse oder andere Tiere Zuflucht finden. Sie ernährten sich von Wild und bekleideten sich mit Fellen von Wölfen, Bären oder auch wilden Stieren, die man damals noch zu sehen bekam. Reden aber konnten sie kaum, vor dem Donner fürchteten sie sich wie vor dem Teufel und oft litten sie entsetzlichen Hunger.

Oberhalb von Kolfuschg und in den Felsen des Puezstockes lebten einst sehr viele Salvans und Gannes, und heute noch trägt eine Quelle dort den Namen „Salvanbrunnen". Im Winter kamen sie oft voller Schnee und Eis vom Puez herab zu den Höfen, v.a. nach Longiarú und Pezzedì, und wenn man ihnen etwas zu essen gab, so nahmen sie dies gern an. Niemandem taten sie etwas zuleide; wenn man sie aber neckte oder gar beleidigte, dann rächten sie sich bitter – und noch dazu hatten sie Kräfte wie Riesen! Des Nachts liebten sie es auch, die Schafe aus den Ställen der Bauern auf die Weiden zu treiben und sie dort zu hüten.

Im Val de Mesdí, zu deutsch Mittagstal, oberhalb Kolfuschg lebte eine schöne junge Ganna, welche oft nach Pezzedì [Pecei] herunter kam, um sich zu wärmen. Dabei lernte sie auch die ladinische Sprache. Dem Bauern, der noch unverheiratet war, gefiel sie sehr, und so fragte er sie, ob sie ihn heiraten wolle. Sie war damit einverstanden, aber er hatte ihr versprechen müssen, niemals ihr Gesicht mit dem Handrücken zu berühren, sonst müsse sie ihn sogleich und für immer verlassen.

So ließ sie sich taufen, heiratete den Bauern und wurde Hofherrin von Pezzedì.

Lange Zeit ging alles gut. Die Ganna war eine tüchtige Bäuerin, eine gute Ehefrau und eine liebevolle Mutter. Aber eines Samstags, während sie ihre Kinder wusch, spürte sie etwas auf ihrer Stirn und da sagte sie zu ihrem Mann: „Schau, irgendetwas sitzt auf meiner Stirn, ich weiß nicht, was es ist." Der Mann, der gerade müde von der Arbeit nach Hause gekommen war, sah eine kleine Fliege auf ihrer Stirn sitzen; er wollte sie mit der Hand wegscheuchen und berührte dabei mit dem Handrücken die Stirn seiner Frau.

Da stieß sie einen lauten Schrei aus und vor Schrecken wurde sie ganz rot im Gesicht. Sie schaute Mann und Kinder ein letztes Mal mit einem Blick voller Liebe an, dann verschwand sie vom Hof – und wurde nie mehr wieder gesehen.

Manche Forscher zählen die Wilden Frauen und Männer zu den einstigen Tiroler Ureinwohnern/Innen, die im Laufe der aus Norden und Süden sich wiederholenden Einbrüche fremder Stämme und Völker gezwungen waren, Schutz und Sicherheit in den wilden Wäldern und Bergen zu suchen. Hier konnte sich auch das Heidentum viel länger halten als in den Talsiedlungen. Eine Sage aus Storo im trentinischen Judikarien erzählt von einer wunderschönen Heidin, die in einer Höhle wohnt. Sie bewacht die aus einem zerstörten Tempel geretteten heidnischen Kultgegenstände, u.a. ein goldenes Kalb. Eine Latzfonser Sage berichtet von der Heirat einer seligen Magd mit einem Bauern nach christlich-katholischem Ritus. Doch „ihre Leute" sind damit nicht einverstanden. Nach der Kommunion während der Hochzeitsmesse ist die Braut plötzlich und für immer verschwunden. Nur manchmal hört man ihr Weinen aus der Ferne. Aufzeichnungen aus dem Eisacktal (Jaufental, Stilfes) beschreiben die Saligen Fräulein als kleingestaltig oder als Trägerinnen uralter Gepflogenheiten: Sie zeigen den Bauern, wie man mit Steinen und Baumschwamm Feuer schlagen kann, sie tragen Kleider aus Wurzelwerk und schlafen auf einem Lager aus Moos und Laub im Wald; die für die Mithilfe auf dem Acker erhaltene Schüssel Milch schmeckt ihnen sehr. Die Wilden Fräulein verfügen, ähnlich dem Wilden Mann, über Kenntnisse, welche die „neuen" Einwohner noch nicht kennen: „Hättest du mich mehr gefragt, dann hätt ich auch mehr gesagt, dann hätt ich dir gesagt, wie man von Jutte (Käsewasser) Käse macht".

Viele Sagen von Saligen und ihr ähnlichen Figuren erzählen von Tabus. Dieses Wort stammt eigentlich aus den Ländern der Südsee und bedeutet so viel wie „heilig" und „verboten". Im ursprünglichen Sinn ist ein Tabu mit einer besonderen, heiligen Kraft erfüllt, die nicht der Allgemeinheit zugänglich ist. Vor allem Stammeshäuptlinge sind Tabuträger. Tabugebote und -verbote finden sich auch heute noch in jeder Religion und jeder Kultur. In den Tiroler Seligen-Sagen sind das Aussprechen bestimmter Worte, die Namensnennung und das Berühren bestimmter menschlicher Körperteile, oft auch des Haares, Tabuthemen. Ebenso typisch ist es, dass Salige nur für eine beschränkte Zeit unter den Menschen weilen. Ähnliches ist auch von den nordischen Walküren überliefert, die nur für eine bestimmte Zeit auf der Welt blieben und dann wieder in Gestalt von Schwänen, manchmal auch als Tauben, davonflogen. Auch sie durfte man nicht nach ihrem Namen fragen. – Der Berührung durch den Handrücken wohnt laut Überlieferung und Aberglauben eine besondere, zauberische Kraft inne, vor allem in Verbindung mit dem gleichzeitigen Deklamieren von bestimmten Zaubersprüchen.

Das in vielen Mythen beschriebene Motiv des Verlassens könnte auch mit dem an anderer Stelle beschriebenen Initations-Motiv des Mannes in Verbindung gebracht werden.

52

Die verjagte Vivana

Eines Abends saß ein Hirte auf der Alpe von Pozza am Herde und bereitete sich Rufiei zum Nachtmahl; plötzlich stand eine hungrige Vivana vor ihm und sagte: „Gib mir auch etwas zu essen, denn ich bin schrecklich hungrig." Der Hirte erwiderte, sie möge noch warten, bis die Rufiei gekocht wären. Aber während des Wartens fragte sie ihn, ob er einen Hund habe, und da glaubte er, sie sei eine Bregostana – er hatte nämlich noch nie eine gesehen – und antwortete ihr: „Kühe und Kälber habe ich wohl, aber Hund besitze ich keinen." Als die Rufiei gar gekocht waren, sagte er zur Vivana: „Ich hole noch schnell eine Schüssel für die Rufiei, bleib nur ruhig sitzen." Aber stattdessen ließ er seinen Hund auf sie los. Voller Verzweiflung fuhr diese sich in die Haare und rief: „Mich plagt so großer Hunger, und du vertreibst mich mit dem Hunde; aber merke dir eines: Hungrige ungesättigt zu entlassen, bringt kein Glück." Hierauf entfloh sie.

Sie ging auf einen nahe gelegenen Felsen, wohin der Hund nicht gelangen konnte, und stellte sich in Zauberhaltung mit den Händen vor der Brust, so dass die Daumen sich berührten und dem Hirten die Handfläche zugekehrt war, auf und sang mit klangvoller Stimme: „O belle krepe baite nose! Se la zent saesa ki noi sión, ke ton, aur, amor te man aón skasè kol cian no fosserón. Per Tello, que per duc flica e Mamo, che duc teisa, no plu pabol per te t aràs Zittene louva raskias." (O schöne Felsen und Alpen, die uns gehören. Wenn die Leute wüssten, wer wir sind, dass wir Glück, Gold und Liebe in Händen halten, würden wir nicht durch Hunde verjagt werden.Im Namen der Tello, die allen hilft, und des Mamo, der alle sättigt, für dich wird keine Speise mehr nützen, gehe hinweg, du Wehrwolf!").

Als der Bursche diesen Gesang hörte, tat es ihm leid, die Vivana verjagt zu haben. Er befürchtete nun, dass sie ihn verwünscht habe, und so bat er Leute von Pozza, sie mögen einen anderen Hirten heraufschicken. Und als am nächsten Abend der neue Hirte angelangt war, fiel er ohnmächtig hin, so dass er zu Tal gebracht werden musste. Von diesem Tag an aß er 7x7=49 (= Hexenformel), war aber dennoch stets hungrig und er wurde von Tag zu Tag schmäler und magerer. Eines Tages begegnete er einer alten Frau, die mehr wusste als andere und ihr erzählte er die ganze Geschichte. „Ich sehe wohl, das Weib war keine Bregostana, sondern eine Vivana, die Göttin der Felsen und Wälder. Sie beschützt die Almen und das Vieh vor Unglück, und du hast sie vertrieben. Es war schlecht von dir, ihr nichts zu Essen zu geben. Dem Mamo vom Berg musst du jederzeit, wenn du etwas isst, geben; täglich musst du von jetzt an 49 schwarzplentene Knödel essen und vier Krüge Wasser trinken, bis du nur mehr aus Haut und Knochen bestehst. Die Haare und der Bart werden dir so wachsen, dass du wie ein Waldmensch aussehen wirst. Geh auf die Alpe und bleibe dort „Jahr und Tag", zünde täglich in den Ecken der Alpenhütte ein Feuer an. Gib Kranebittbeeren und Sauerdorn hinein, bis die Hütte voller Rauch ist, dabei knie nieder und sprich: Mamo komm und erlöse mich! Ich will drei Jahre dafür räuchern!" Der Hirte befolgte den Rat und wirklich, nach „Jahr und Tag" erschien die Vivana und sprach zu ihm: „Bereite für drei Personen ein Mahl aus gelabter Milch, Krapfen mit einer Fülle von wildem Erdbeerspinat, Kranebittbeeren und Hagebutten." Während des Essens sagte die Vivana noch: „Im Namen Reza und ihrer Genossinnen, gib den Hungrigen stets zu Essen, dann wirst du Glück und Segen haben.", und sie verschwand noch bevor er sich bei ihr bedanken konnte, dass sie ihn von seinem Leiden erlöst hatte.

Die ladinischen „Rufiei" sind mit Sauerkraut gefüllte Teigtaschen.

Die Angst vor Hunden wird auch in anderen ladinischen Sagen beschrieben; dem Hund wird eine Dämonen abwehrende Macht zugeschrieben. Die Vivana formt ihre beiden Hände zu einem Dreieck – ein archaisches Symbol, das einst mit der weiblich-göttlichen Dreieinigkeit im Zusammenhang stand. Dieselbe Geste wurde in den sechziger/siebziger Jahren das Symbol der Feministinnen für sexuelle Selbstbestimmung. Die Vivana dieser Sage scheint den Hirten auf die Probe zu stellen. Da er ihr wahres Wesen nicht erkennt, wird er von ihr mit ewigem Hunger bestraft. Die in der Sage mehrmals erwähnte Zahl sieben ist eine universelle, heilige weibliche Zahl, der Großen Mutter zugeordnet, aber auch der Jungfräulichkeit. Sie spielt in allen Weltreligionen eine wichtige Rolle. – Auch in anderen Sagen haben die Verwünschungen zauberkundiger wilder Frauen ein unaufhaltbares Abmagern zur Folge. Bei der in der Sage genannten alten Frau handelt es sich um eine Weise Frau, die dem Hirten das wahre göttliche Wesen der fremden Frau erklärt und ihm sagt, was er zu tun habe: Nur eine schamanische Buße mit entsprechenden Ritualen kann ihm aus seiner großen inneren Not helfen. – Nach Beendigung seiner asketischen Rückzugszeit muss der Hirte der Vivana ein Kultmahl zubereiten. – Kranebitt (Wacholder) ist eine uralte Tiroler Räucher-, Heil- und Zauberpflanze, von Schamanen verschiedener Völker als heilige Pflanze verehrt. Auch der verdauungsfördernde Sauerdorn (Berberitze) war bereits in der Antike als Heilpflanze bekannt.

Der göttlichen Tello, Tellus Mater oder Terra Mater, die in den Mittelmeer-Religionen allen Wesen das Leben gegeben haben soll, wurde bei den Römern am 15. April gehuldigt; man opferte ihr an diesem Tag eine trächtige Kuh. Sie war auch die mütterliche Todesgöttin, in deren Schoß die Körper der Toten zurückkehrten. Ihre ständige Begleiterin war Ceres, die Korngöttin.

Mamo ist vermutlich der alte italische Vegetationsgott Mars, der später zum Kriegsgott wurde.

7x7=49 ist eine Hexenformel. – Bei der beim Abschied von ihr erwähnten Reza handelt es sich vermutlich um die rätisch/paleovenetische Göttin Reitia, Herrin der Natur, der Wälder und der Gewässer und heilende Göttin.

53

Von den letzten Saligen

Die letzten Saligen Fräulein im Vinschgau, so meldet die Sage, wurden noch im vergangenen Jahrhundert gesehen. Sie fanden sich als schneeweiße Tauben bei einem Getreideschnitt in den Grauner Feldern ein und trugen in ihren Schnäbeln die verbliebenen Körner zusammen. Ihr emsiges Treiben war aber nur von kurzer Dauer. Bald stieß der wilde Mann in Gestalt eines grimmigen Raubvogels unter sie, und sie zerstoben nach allen Windrichtungen.

›› Wissenswertes ‹‹

Viele Tiroler Sagen erzählen von der Verfolgung der Wilden Fräulein durch den Wilden Mann. Er lebt wie sie in der Wildnis und ist Heide. Gern lauert er den Seligen auf, um sie auf brutale Art in Stücke zu zerreißen. Gelingt es den Seligen jedoch rechtzeitig, sich auf einen Baumstrunk, auf welchen Holzarbeiter oder Bauern zu ihrem Schutz drei Kreuze eingehackt haben, zu setzen, ist der Wilde Mann machtlos. – In frühesten Vorstellungen der Menschen stellte man sich die Seele mit Flügeln oder auch als Vogel vor, häufig als Taube, eines der symbolträchtigsten Tiere. Sie war zahlreichen vorchristlichen großen Muttergottheiten geweiht, so Istar/Astarte, Isis, Venus/Aphrodite, Athene usw. Sie ist Sinnbild des Lebensgeistes, der Lebenserneuerung, des Friedens und der Liebe. Sie steht für den Übergang von einer Seinsart in die andere. Im Christentum wurde sie zum Symbol des heiligen Geistes, der Gott und Mensch in unendlicher Liebe verbindet; als weiße Taube versinnbildlicht sie auch die errettete Seele. So wie die Salige mit dem Jenseits in Verbindung gebracht werden kann, ist dies auch bei der Taube der Fall: Ein typisches Beispiel finden wir im Grimm'schen Märchen „Aschenputtel“, in welchem die verstorbene Mutter ihrer Tochter als weißer Vogel (Taube) zu Hilfe kommt. Auch nach dem früheren Glauben mancher slawischen Völker verwandeln sich die Seelen Verstorbener in Tauben. In einigen Tiroler Sagen fliegen Salige davon, wenn sie belästigt oder verfolgt werden (Lajen), dabei sehen sie manchmal einer schneeweißen Taube gleich.

Diese Sage erzählt vom definitiven Verschwinden der Saligen Fräulein aus der Vinschger Landschaft. Wer sich intensiver mit Sagen und Mythen auseinandersetzen will, kommt nicht umhin, sich mit Landschaftsbetrachtung und -mythologie zu beschäftigen, derzufolge die Seele der Landschaft an zahlreichen außergewöhnlichen, sprich heiligen Plätzen, oft in weiblich-göttlichen Gestalten personifiziert auftritt. Geschichten von Saligen, Hexen, Königinnen, verwunschenen Frauen, aber auch von Maria und anderen weiblichen Heiligen gewähren Einblick in eine Zeit, in welcher der Mensch noch aufs Innigste mit der Natur verbunden und die Kräfte der ihn umgebenden Landschaft noch wahrzunehmen imstande war.

Von verwunschenen Frauen und Truten

Immer wieder ist in den Tiroler Sagen von Frauen die Rede, die ruhe- und rastlos umherirrend auf eine Erlösung warten. So gibt es zahlreiche Erzählungen von Frauen, die nach ihrem Tode für ein lustvolles und ruchloses Leben büßen müssen, und unzählige Geschichten erzählen von weißen Schatzhüterinnen sowie von **Truten**, welche dazu verbannt sind, andere Menschen zu drücken. In diesem Kapitel erzählen wir von den beiden Letzteren.

Uralt und vielschichtig ist das Sagenmotiv der Schatzhüterinnen. Weiß gekleidete oder strahlende (Jung-)Frauen in Begleitung von Schlangen oder anderen Erdtieren, häufig mit einem Schlüssel winkend, treten plötzlich aus dem Innern der Erde oder aus verfallenen Schlossgemäuern hervor. Doch was erzählt uns die Sagenkunde hierzu?

So wie die Versetzung in den Himmel (Himmelfahrt) ist in der Mythologie auch die sogenannte „Entrückung" ins Erdinnere als Ort des ewigen Lebens bekannt. Viele griechische Sagenhelden führen ewiges Leben im Innern der Berge. Auch Heilige, wie beispielsweise die Hl. Thekla, leben im Felsinnern weiter. Die Entrückung in Berge war auch im germanischen Glauben bekannt. Zahlreiche Sagen in ganz Mitteleuropa erzählen vom Weiterleben von Helden, Heidenkönigen, Kaisern oder ganzer Heere in Bergestiefen. Auch Dörfer oder Klöster wurden Sagen zufolge samt ihrer Bewohner wegen ihres ruchlosen Verhaltens bestraft und ins Erd- oder Berginnere versenkt.

Auch Frau Holle und Frau Venus leben in der unterirdischen Welt. Nur einzelnen Menschen gelingt der Zutritt in ihr Reich. So wie Frau Holle (Holda oder Hel) oder die strahlende Bertha lebt auch die Weiße Frau im Berg. Im übertragenen Sinne könnte sie als göttliche Besitzerin der Schätze der Erde, der Fruchtbarkeit der Natur gedeutet werden.

Das Wort „weiß" hängt in seiner indogermanischen Wurzel mit „glänzen" und „Licht" zusammen. Weiß ist die Farbe der großen Lichtgottheiten, auch die Engel werden stets mit weißen Gewändern dargestellt. Die weiße Farbe wurde in vielen Kulturen für Heil-, Schutz- und Fruchtbarkeitszauber verwendet, in früheren Zeiten war sie auch die Farbe von Trauer, Tod und der Todesgöttin.

Da der Kontakt mit Göttern und Dämonen auch gefährlich sein konnte, trugen PriesterInnen und ZauberInnen ein Übel abwehrendes weißes Gewand. Auch neu-

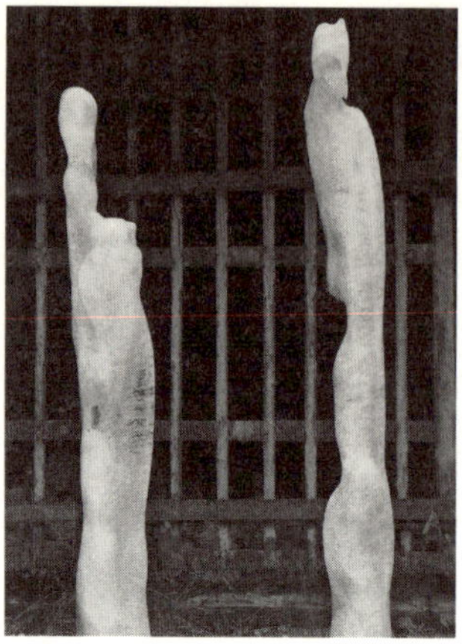

geborenen Kindern wurden und werden weiße Kleider angezogen. Mit weißen Gegenständen wurde die Trute abgewehrt (siehe „Trute"). Ebenso war die Farbe der Opfertiere häufig weiß.

Die Erscheinung der Weißen Frau und ihrer Begleittiere ist in den Sagen meistens eine entscheidende und folgenschwere Begegnung, die entweder den Tod oder ein Leben in Erfüllung und Erlösung zur Folge hat, nicht nur für die Weiße Frau, sondern auch für den „Sagenhelden".

Der in vielen Sagen mit einer Frau gemeinsam auftretende Drache hängt aus psychoanalytischer Sicht nach C.G.Jung mit dem „Mutter-Archetyp" zusammen; er steht demnach, neben der Vorstellung der Frau als Schutz gewährend und gebärend, für den Aspekt der zerstörenden und verschlingenden Mutter.

Die Schlange, Begleittier der Schatzhüterinnen, spielt in allen großen Religionen und Kulturen eine bedeutende Rolle.

Nach der tantrisch-hinduistischen Erkenntnislehre beispielsweise befindet sich am unteren Ende der Wirbelsäule eine besondere ätherische Kraft, die man sich als schlafende zusammengerollte Schlange, die Kundalini-Schlange, vorzustellen hat. Kann der Mensch diese Schlangenkraft erwecken und durch gezielte meditative Praktiken bis ins höchste Chakra aufsteigen lassen, erlangt der Mensch höchstes Glück, denn seine Seele kann sich mit der kosmischen Seele vereinigen.

In zahlreichen Sagen verschiedener Völker wird von Frauen erzählt, die in Begleitung von Schlangen auftreten oder sich in Schlangen verwandeln können.

In vorchristlichen Religionen war die Schlange eines jener Tiere, in welche sich die Große Göttin mit Vorliebe verwandelte. Sie wurde als heiliges Tier verehrt, denn sie wurde der kosmischen, sich immer wieder erneuernden Lebensenergie (Symbol der Spirale) gleichgesetzt. Viele Völker hielten sich Haus- und Tempelschlangen, sie wurden gepflegt und gefüttert, denn sie brachten Glück und Wohlstand.

Der Zusammenprall der indoeuropäischen Religion mit jener der alten Göttinnen hatte eine Entthronung und Dämonisierung des Weiblich-Göttlichen zur Folge. Im Alten Testament schließlich wurde die heilige Schlange dem Satan gleichgestellt und die Frau (Eva) zum Urmuster des Sündigen.

Der Glaube an die Segen bringende Hausschlange hielt sich jedoch trotzdem über viele Jahrhunderte weiter. Sie zu töten, würde Todesfall und Unglück in der Familie bewirken.

Auch alte Tiroler Bräuche bekunden ihre Verehrung: Noch um 1925 wurden Kettchen oder Rosenkränze aus sogenannten Beißwurmknöchelchen angefertigt.

Etliche Sagen erzählen auch von den **Truten** (Truden, Druden). Die Truten sind laut Volksglauben weibliche Nachtgeister, welche dazu verbannt sind, in der Nacht Menschen und auch Tiere im Schlaf zu drücken. Sie kommen in das Zimmer eines Schlafenden und „besitzen" diese, indem sie sich auf die Brust hocken und so lange drücken, bis dem Schlafenden die Luft wegbleibt. Hat jemand einen Alptraum, so schnürt sich die Brust eng zu, man bekommt kaum Luft, man möchte schreien, kann es aber nicht, dann heißt es: „Er wird von der Trute gedrückt".

Das Wort Trute stammt von dem mittelhochdeutschem Wort „trute" (trutt oder der alp, der die frauen reitt).

Hans Vintler, ein Bozner Dichter, schreibt 1411 in seinem Gedicht „Blume der Tugend" über die Truten Folgendes:

„Die trutte sei ain altes weib
Und chumme die leute saugen
Und etleich die glauben,
der alpe minne die leute."

Ursprünglich entsprach die Trute einer Jungfrau, aber im Umschwung der Religionsvorstellungen wurde sie zur „Unholden". Truten gehören zu den sogenannten Mahrtenwesen (sich „mahrende" Wesen, eine altgermanische Bezeichnung auch für den Alp). Auch eine Walküre trägt den Namen „Thrud".

Auch wenn sie oft mit Hexen in Verbindung gebracht und häufig mit ihnen im gleichen Atemzug genannt werden, unterscheiden sich die Truten dennoch wesentlich von ihnen, denn laut Volksmund können sie, wenn sie den guten Willen haben, dem bösen Trieb zu widerstehen, von ihrem Fluch befreit werden und doch noch in den Himmel kommen.

Truten, fast immer Frauen, erleben es als verhängnisvoll, wenn allnächtlich ihre Seele den Körper verlässt, um einen Menschen zu suchen, den sie „drücken" müssen, dass er ächzend den „Alptraum" erleidet. Der „Drücktrieb" ist angeboren und nicht eigene Schuld wie bei der Hexe, die sich dem Teufel verschreibt. Aus diesem Grunde haben viele Mitleid mit den Truten und versuchen, sie zu erlösen.

Laut Volksglauben gibt es mehrere Ursachen, warum ein Mädchen zur Trute wird: Sie hat in einem bösen Zeichen das Licht der Welt erblickt oder die Wehmutter hat sich eines Zaubermittels bedient oder die Mutter hat statt christlichen Ertragens der Wehen den Teufelsnamen angerufen.

Vom Aussehen her sind Truten junge oder ältere Frauen. Bezeichnend sind ihre buschigen Augenbrauen, welche gegen die Nase hin völlig zusammengewachsen und herausstehend sind. Der Blick ihrer Augen ist kalt und starr. Die Trutenschritte sind schleifend und leicht zu erkennen. Ihr Atem geht schwer. Bei der Arbeit untertags sind sie frisch und munter.

Zur Abwehr der Truten und sonstiger Hexenschäden setzte man neben dem Drudenfuß (Pentagramm) auch die Buchstaben I.N.R.I. (Jesus Nazarenus Rex Judaeorum), wie sie auf dem Kruzifix stehen, als Gegenmittel ein. Das schwarze Horn eines Steinbocks an der Stalltür hielt die Trute vom Vieh ab. Gerne trugen die Leute auch einen kleinen Wachsschuh als Amulett gegen die Trute auf der Brust. Der Schuh musste aus dem Wachs einer Kerze gegossen sein, die am Lichtmesstag (2. Februar) geweiht worden war.

Wenn man sich sonst nicht helfen kann, weil man weder aufspringen noch schreien kann, soll man die Daumen in die Hände einziehen. Auch ein Schuh, den man bei Tage getragen hat, umgekehrt hinzustellen, hilft als Abwehr gegen die Truten. Ddas erste Wasser aus der frisch geweihten Ostertaufe wurde ebenso als Gegenmittel eingesetzt.

Unter den Pflanzen hat der Bärlapp große Wirkung gegen jeden bösen Zauber. Aus seinen Sporen wird das sogenannte Hexenmehl gewonnen, das gegen Trutendruck Abhilfe schafft. Daher stammt auch der zweite Name Trutenkraut.

Wenn jemand der Trute den Tod anwünscht, so genügt es, sich ein Messer mit der Schneide nach oben oder eine Hechel (ein kammartiges, mit spitzen Drähten versehenes Gerät für die Flachsverarbeitung) auf die Brust zu legen – und die Trute wird sich tödlich verletzen.

Die Trute kann als dämonisierter Aspekt der Göttin angesehen werden. Die göttliche Diana/Artemis z.B. war für den Schutz und das Aufwachsen der Kinder zuständig.

Die Mondsichel war ihr Symbol, und die Sichel gehörte einst als Schutzzeichen zur Kindeswiege.

Auch der Aspekt der Todesgöttin hat sich in dieser Sagengestalt überliefert. In Primiero (Trentino) erzählte man sich von den „Smàre“, hohen, mageren, schwarz gekleideten Frauen, die des Nachts an den Betten schlafender Menschen erschienen, um sie zu ersticken.

Im nordspanischen Baskenland hatte die Todesgöttin einen ähnlichen Namen, nämlich Màri.

54

Vom Schatz auf Zwingenstein

Im Lanznasterhof zu Unterinn diente ein braves Mädchen, das im Sommer täglich auf dem Zwingensteiner Schlosshügel das Vieh hütete. Da kam eines Tages aus einem der jetzt verfallenen unterirdischen Gänge der alten Burg eine schöne Frau hervor, deren prächtiges Gewand um und um mit Gold und Edelsteinen geziert war. Sie nahm durch ihr freundliches Wesen dem Kinde alle Furcht, und es ließ sich sogar von der schönen Frau kämmen. Dies wiederholte sich nun alle Tage. Dadurch ward das Haar der Hirtin so fein und glänzend, dass sich die Leute darob verwunderten und sie nach der Ursache fragten. Aber das Mädchen verriet nichts, denn die Frau hatte ihm verboten, etwas zu sagen.

Als es Herbst war, kam die Frau zum letzten Male herauf und sagte zum Kinde: „Ich habe dich nun schon lange gekämmt, jetzt musst auch du mir einen Dienst leisten; du musst mich erlösen. Es wird dir schwer werden und du wirst viel Übles ausstehen, allein wenn du mutig aushältst, kannst du den Schatz gewinnen, den ich da unten hüten muss. Nun merke, was ich dir sage! Ein Wurm wird kommen und dich am Gehen hindern wollen; schreite nur herzhaft vorwärts, doch darfst du nicht auf den Wurm treten. Alsbald kommt sodann ein anderer von der Höhle herauf, der sich dir um die Füße windet, um dich nicht vorwärts zu lassen. Doch du geh nur mutig weiter und achte bloß, dass du den Wurm nicht trittst. Zuletzt kommt ein dritter, der sich in die Höhe windet und dreimal um deinen Hals ringelt. Jedoch erschrick nicht, denn keiner der Würmer darf dir ein Leid antun. Bestehst du diese dreifache Probe, dann gehört der Schatz dir, und mich hast du erlöst."

Das Mädchen versprach, alles so zu tun, wie es ihr aufgetragen worden, und die Frau verschwand. Jetzt betrat es den unterirdischen Gang, und als der erste Wurm ihr in den Weg kam, wich es sorgfältig aus und ging weiter. Auch der zweite Wurm war nicht imstande, ihre Schritte zu hemmen, obwohl das Kind ein Gruseln ankam, als das gräuliche Tier sich um seine Beine wand. Als aber der dritte Wurm so glatt und kalt sich ihr um den Hals legte, ward sie vom Schrecken erfasst, und, obwohl im Hintergrunde in einem weiten, wunderbar erleuchteten Gemache die schöne Frau sich zeigte und ihr zuwinkte und dahinter alles von Gold und Silber schimmerte, kehrte die Hirtin doch um und lief den Gang wieder hinaus und den Hügel hinab zum Lanznaster. Hinter sich hörte sie den Klang des Goldes, das wieder in die Tiefe des Berges hinabrollte.

Einige Tage darauf, als das Mädchen noch einmal die Schafe gegen die Burg hinauf hütete, kam die Frau aus dem Berge hervor, und Tränen perlten über ihre Wangen. „Du hast mir übel gelohnt", sagte sie, „nun muss ich wieder hundert Jahre im Berge wohnen. Bleib gut und fromm", sprach sie weiter, „und gedenke mein! Denn nur ein Mann aus deinem Stamme kann mich nunmehr erlösen. Sieh diesen Stein", – dabei setzte sie sich auf einen großen Felsblock – „aus dem wird ein Baum hervorwachsen. Ist er groß genug, so soll man ihn herausziehen, doch darf man ihn beileibe nicht umhauen. Aus seinem Holze wird eine Wiege gezimmert werden für jenes Kind, das, zum Manne herangewachsen, mich erlösen wird."

Nach diesen Worten verschwand die Frau und ließ sich nie wieder sehen.

›› Wissenswertes ‹‹

Uralte Vorstellungen der Göttin in ihren beiden Aspekten als Strahlende Frau des Lebens und als Herrin der Unterwelt lassen sich hier erahnen. In zahlreichen Sagen vermischen und überlappen sich Elemente aus christlicher und vorchristlicher Zeit. Die Formel vom „Erlöser in der Wiege" wird von manchen Forschern auf die christliche Legende vom Kreuzholz zurückgeführt: Ein Baum muss wachsen, und aus seinem Holz wird ein Kreuz, ein Sarg oder meistens eine Wiege gezimmert werden; das Kind, das in dieser Wiege gewiegt wird, kann die Weiße Frau erlösen.

Häufig erweisen sich die in Sagen erwähnten Örtlichkeiten als geschichtsträchtige Plätze, so werden auch auf dem Gelände der Burgruine Zwingenstein in Unterinn am Ritten seit einiger Zeit archäologische Ausgrabungen getätigt. Ein Kultplatz aus spätrömischer Zeit wird hier vermutet.

In einer ähnlichen Sagenversion muss das Mädchen mit dem Zweig eines Haselnussstrauchs dreimal auf eine Kranebittstaude (Wacholder) schlagen. Dieser ist wie die Eibe ein Todesbaum, und man glaubte früher, dass sich die Seelen der Verstorbenen in diesem Strauch verbergen und durch bestimmte Umstände wieder zum Leben zurückkehren könnten. Bei den Germanen durfte der Wacholder nicht zu profanen Zwecken gefällt werden; er galt als heiliges Holz, das bei der Verbrennung der Toten verwendet wurde. Mit dem Christentum wurde er zu einem antidämonischen Strauch, seine stechenden Nadeln sollten gegen Hexen, böse Geister, Truden und den Teufel selbst schützen. Nach anderen alten Sagen verdeckt die Kranebittstaude den Eingang zu Höhlen von Zwergen, Riesen, Kobolden, Geistern und Dämonen oder man findet unter ihr verborgen den Schlüssel zu einem unterirdischen Schatz: Wenn man mit einem Haselzweig an den Wacholder schlägt, öffnet sich das Versteck.

55

Die verwunschene Königstochter

Auf Säben bei Klausen herrschte einst ein mächtiger, aber sehr habgieriger König. Aus allen Flüssen der Umgebung ließ er das Gold waschen und sammelte so einen ungeheuren Schatz, den er in den tiefen Gewölben seiner Burg verschloss. Er hatte eine einzige Tochter, doch gönnte er sie keinem Mann. Da er auch ein mächtiger Zauberer war, so verwünschte er sie, mit seinem eigenen Ableben zur Hüterin seines Schatzes zu werden und gesellte ihr einen Wächterdrachen zu, der nur dann erlegt werden konnte, wenn ein völlig unschuldiger Jüngling ihm mit drei Haselstäben alle Schuppen vom Leibe schlüge. Dadurch wäre auch die Jungfrau erlöst und der Geldhort das Eigentum des Drachenbesiegers.

Viele Jünglinge hatten sich bereits auf den Drachenkampf eingelassen und viele mussten mit ihrem Leben bezahlen, teils weil sie ihre Unschuld bereits verloren hatten, teils weil sie sich gefürchtet hatten. Endlich kam wieder ein junger Mann, der dieses Abenteuer bestehen wollte.

Die Jungfrau erschien ihm in all ihrer Schönheit, besonders war ihr Oberleib reizend weiß und wie Milch und Blut, unterwärts aber war sie schwarz. Die oberteilige Schönheit der verwunschenen Königstochter entzückte und verblendete den Jüngling dermaßen, dass er ihren schwarzen Unterleib gar nicht wahrnahm, sondern die Jungfrau immer nur anstarrte. Da gab ihm der Drache mit der kralligen Vorderpfote einen ganz leisen Backenstreich, von dem ihm der Kopf anschwoll, so dick wie ein Melkstutzen, und nach einer Stunde war er hin – und die Jungfrau blieb verwünscht bis auf den heutigen Tag.

›› Wissenswertes ‹‹

Ein Melkstutzen ist ein eimerähnlicher runder Behälter aus Holz für die Milch. – Schwarzweiß ist die Göttin der Unterwelt infolge ihrer Doppelnatur als Leben spendende Erdgöttin und Herrin des Totenreichs. Auch die germanische Hel ist halb schwarz, halb menschenfarbig. – Dem Haselnussstrauch sprachen keltische und germanische PriesterInnen eine weissagende Kraft zu. Haselnüsse fanden sich in keltischen Fürstengräbern von Irland bis in den Alpenraum als Grabbeigaben. Christliche Legenden erzählen, wie der Haselnussstrauch Maria vor einer giftigen Schlange geschützt hat. So gilt die Haselnussstaude im Christentum als Marienstrauch.

Die elastischen Äste werden seit Tausenden von Jahren als Wünschelruten verwendet. Auch die Sage, dass silberne Schlüssel an der Haselstaude hängen, mit denen man Schatztruhen öffnen kann, zeugt von ihrer Fähigkeit, Energieströme zu leiten.

In Zusammenhang mit dieser Säbener Sage soll auch an die Sage von Arostoges, einem rätischen König, erinnert werden. Arostoges herrschte angeblich um das Jahr 220 v. Chr. auf dem „Felsennest" von Säben und hatte Besitz bis hinab nach Italien. Laut Sage hatte er eine Tochter und zwei Vettern, die seine Länder erben wollten. Sie verbündeten sich mit den Römern, zogen mit einem großen Kriegsvolk nach Säben, erschlugen den König und überließen die Tochter und die Burg den Römern. Den großen Schatz, laut Sage waren es 866 Saumladungen Gold, Silber und Edelsteine, verbargen die beiden Vettern in den Bergen um Säben.

Nach einer anderen Sage soll in der Umgebung des Schlosses Branzoll bei Klausen ein alter Bajuwaren-Herzog bei seiner Flucht vor den Feinden viel Gold vergraben haben. Bis vor wenigen Jahrzehnten hat es immer wieder goldgierige Schatzsucher gegeben, die im Thinnetal bei Klausen auf Suche gegangen sind. Dieser Namen erinnert an den höchsten etruskischen Gott Tinia oder Tin, der mit Hilfe der Blitze die Erde befruchtete und dadurch auch die Bodenschätze erzeugte. – Auf dem Felsberg des Klosters Säben (schon zur Jungsteinzeit besiedelt und ältester Wallfahrtsort Tirols), sind kostbare Funde der Vor- und Frühgeschichte, der Römer- und der frühchristlichen Zeit getätigt worden. Die Liebfrauenkirche steht auf einem uralten religiösen Kultplatz. Seit 300 Jahren besteht dort ein Frauenkloster der Benediktinerinnen.

Aus etymologischer Sicht bedeutet Säben so viel wie „großes Heiligtum".

56

Die drei Jungfrauen von Ehrenberg

Nicht weit vom alten Schlosse Ehrenberg ist ein Felsen, der eine Höhle hat. In dieser wohnen drei Jungfrauen, die kohlschwarz gekleidet sind. Sie spannen oft zur Nachtzeit ein langes Seil von ihrer Höhle aus bis zu einem einzeln stehenden Turme, und hängen daran Wäsche auf. Dies werden sie tun, bis sie erlöst werden. Wie sie erlöst werden können, hat noch niemand erfahren.

›› Wissenswertes ‹‹

Diese Sage aus dem Außerfern erinnert an die mythischen Nornen Urdr, Verdandi und Skuld. Laut Jacob Grimm, dem großen Forscher der Sagenkunde, war der Glaube an die Nornen ursprünglich in allen deutschen Völkern beheimatet. Grimm beschreibt, wie Nornen nachts in die Burg traten, dem Helden die Schicksalsfäden drehten und das goldene Seil mitten am Himmel ausbreiteten. Auch im trentinischen Fersental, das teilweise von deutschen Bergknappen besiedelt wurde, werden ähnliche Sagen im Kontext der Saligen Frauen erzählt.

In der Norngestsaga wird erzählt, dass die Nornen im Land herumfuhren und den Menschen ihr Geschick weissagten und dafür bewirtet und beschenkt wurden. Den ersten zwei Nornen wurde wohlwollende Gesinnung zugeschrieben, der dritten, Skuld, hingegen oft üble. Auch im Romanischen gibt es viele Geschichten von den „tre fate“, die ersten zwei „begaben“, die dritte verwünscht. Im bekannten Märchen Dornröschen treten 13 weise Frauen auf: zwölf gut gesinnte, die dreizehnte hingegen verwünschend.

57

Die weiße Frau

Als das Clarissenkloster zu Meran schon aufgehoben war, gingen einmal zwei Klosterfrauen abends von Schenna nach Meran. Wie sie in die Nähe des Schlosses Zenoburg kamen, sahen sie dort eine schneeweiße große Frau mit einem Schlüsselbunde, die ihnen winkte. Sie hatten aber nicht den Mut, ihr zu folgen. Da verschwand unter Seufzen die schöne Frau, und zugleich war es, als ob man viele, viele Münzen klingeln hörte.

Das Sagenmotiv der seufzenden strahlendweißen Frau mit einem Schlüsselbund ist in Tirol weit verbreitet. In der Symbolik bedeutet der Schlüssel Initiation, Wissen und Befreiung. Der Schlüsselbund versinnbildlicht die Möglichkeit und die Einladung, in den Besitz eines Schatzes, welcher Art auch immer, zu gelangen.

In der griechischen Mythologie war der Schlüsselbund ein Attribut von Hekate als Wächterin der Unterwelt. Auch die von den Rätern verehrte große Göttin Reitia wird mit einem Schlüssel in der Hand dargestellt, mit welchem sie nach ihrem Belieben die Tür ins Jenseits öffnet oder schließt. Der Schlüssel ist auch das Attribut des Hl. Petrus, ihm als Zeichen der Macht von Christus übertragen. So kann er binden und lösen; er ist auch der Wächter der Himmelspforte.

Der Zenoberghügel war als „Castrum Maiense" abwechselnd in romanischer, fränkischer, langobardischer und bayrischer Hand; er war bereits in der Jüngeren Eisenzeit besiedelt. Auch eine frühchristliche Kirche zum Hl. Valentin wird hier vermutet.

58

Der Träger

Als einmal ein Sarntaler Träger, der auf dem Wege nach Bozen sich verspätet hatte, beim Ravensteiner Schloss rastete, stand plötzlich eine wunderschöne Frau vor ihm. Sie grüßte ihn freundlich und sprach: „Du bist berufen, mein und dein Glück zu machen. Komm morgen um Mitternacht und ich werde als Drache erscheinen. Wenn du mich dann dreimal umarmst, gehört das Schloss mit allen Schätzen dir, und ich bin erlöst." Bald war sie verschwunden. Dem Träger ging die stolze Frau nicht wenig im Kopfe herum, und in aller Frühe begab er sich ins Kloster zu einem Pater, dem er die ganze Geschichte mitteilte. Dieser ermahnte ihn, zur bestimmten Stunde bei Ravenstein zu warten und das Schlossfräulein, so möglich, zu erlösen. Zum Abschiede gab er dem Burschen seinen Segen und ein geweihtes Kreuzlein. Der Träger besorgte alsdann seine Geschäfte und stieg, als es dunkelte, zum Schlosse hinauf, obwohl ein abscheuliches Wetter wütete. Schlag elf Uhr rastete er wieder auf dem Steine unter dem Nussbaume und wartete betend auf Mitternacht. Als es endlich zwölf Uhr war, ging im Schlosse ein Höllenlärm los und bald kam ein furchtbarer Drache daher. Seine Augen flammten wie feurige Teller und die Schuppen klapperten wie eine Windmühle. Da packte den Träger die Angst, allein er überwand sich und nahm den Drachen zweimal um den Hals. Schon wollte er ihn zum dritten Male umarmen, da überfiel ihn ein solches Grausen, dass er laut aufschrie – und das Untier war verschwunden. In den Ruinen jammerte es laut, und nebenbei klingelte und rollte es, als ob zahllose Taler in die Tiefe kollerten. Der Träger hatte keinen frohen Tag mehr und lebte nur noch ein Jahr.

Das Umarmen und Küssen von „Tabu"-Tieren findet sich bei allen Völkern als Entzauberungsmittel. An die Stelle der Schlange tritt häufig auch der Drache. Zahlreiche Mythen, Sagen und Legenden erzählen von Drachenkämpfen. Im Altertum war die Meinung verbreitet, dass Drachen auf Gold liegen, so hieß das Gold selbst dichterisch „Wurmbett".

Feuerspeien, gewaltige Kräfte und giftiges Blut erschweren die schicksalsträchtige Aufgabe. Doch ist es in erster Linie die Angst des „Helden", welcher den Sieg über den Drachen verhindert oder verunmöglicht. So könnte der Kampf mit dem Drachen und dessen Besiegen auch als Kampf gegen eigene innere Unsicherheiten und als Sieg über sich selbst gedeutet werden. Muss der „Sagenheld" einen Drachen besiegen, um beispielsweise eine schöne Jungfrau zu gewinnen, hat dies nach C.G. Jung mit dem Archetyp des „Schattens" zu tun: Die gefangene Jungfrau wäre demzufolge die gefangengehaltene personifizierte Anima des Mannes und der Drachenkampf die Auseinandersetzung zwischen seinen beiden Persönlichkeitsanteilen.

Oft wird der Sieg über den Drachen auch als Sieg des Christentums über die vorchristlichen Gottheiten/Göttinnen gedeutet (vgl. Legende vom Ritter Georg, der den Drachen besiegt).

59

Die Krönlnatter

In tiefer Nacht kam ein armer Reisender in die Nähe des Saubaches. Da stand auf einem Hügel eine alte Burg, die dem müden Wanderer nicht wenig in die Augen stach. „Ha, da find' ich vielleicht ein Nachtlager", dachte er bei sich und eilte dem grauen Gebäude zu. Als er zum Graben kam, ward die Zugbrücke niedergelassen. Er trat in den Schlosshof, sah jedoch weder einen Hund noch einen Menschen. Forschend ging er die Stiege hinauf und kam in den Rittersaal, wo eine alte mit Stroh gefüllte Himmelbettstätte zur Ruhe lud. Er legte sich hinein und begann bald zu schlafen. Um Mitternacht ward er jedoch durch ein Geräusch geweckt. Eine Natter, mit einem wunderschönen Krönlein auf dem Kopfe, schlüpfte zu ihm ins Bett und sah ihn flehend an. Er besann sich nicht lange und nahm ihr das funkelnde Krönlein ab. Husch war die Natter verschwunden und eine weiße Frau stand vor ihm, während ein mit Goldmünzen gefüllter Hafen aus der Oberdecke des Zimmers niederstürzte. Sie nahm den Schatz und reichte ihn dem Jüngling mit den Worten: „Empfang den Lohn für meine Erlösung. Ich war einst hier Burgwächterin und musste seit dreihundert Jahren bei dem Schatze umgehen, weil mir so lange niemand das Krönlein vom Haupte nahm." Alsogleich verschwand sie, doch der Fremde war nun ein reicher Herr und der Segen des Himmels ruhte auf dem Golde.

»» Wissenswertes ««

Im Bild der Gold gekrönten Schlange verbinden sich verschiedene symbolische Motive: Gold (Symbol für materiellen Reichtum und für einen geistigen Schatz; es steht für Erleuchtung, Weisheit und Harmonie), die Krone (Symbol für höchste Würde und Vollkommenheit) sowie die Schlange als mythologisches Tier des Totenreiches.

In dieser Sage aus Flaas/Jenesien ist der Mann imstande, seine Lebenschance wahrzunehmen und er besteht „die Probe". Dadurch werden beide „erlöst": sowohl die weiße Frau, die sich in jenseitiger Isolation befand, als auch der Mann, denn von nun an wandelt sich auch sein Leben schlagartig und nachhaltig zum Besseren.

60

Die Seeschlange

Vor uralter Zeit, als nur Wald in der Gegend von St. Ulrich war und ein wildes Volk darinnen wohnte, war an recht schönen Tagen eine Seeschlange am Ufer des Sees gesehen worden. Einstmals kamen nun Ritter zu diesem See und diese wollten nun im Mondschein auf dem See herumfahren. Aber die Bauern, welche sich vor der Schlange fürchteten, rieten den Rittern davon ab und erzählten ihnen von derselben. Da verlangten die Ritter diese Schlange zu sehen und ließen sich durch nichts abhalten, so dass sie wirklich auf den See hinausfuhren und dort die Schlange sahen, die so schön war, dass ein jeder sie besitzen wollte. Als sie ein andermal wieder zu dem See kamen, wollte der Kühnste von ihnen auf diese Schlange schießen, aber da schlug plötzlich sein Kahn um und er ertrank. Dem Zweiten war es ebenso gegangen; der Dritte jedoch wollte der Schlange nicht wehe tun, nahm ein Fischernetz und warf es aus, um so die Schlange zu fangen. Und als er sie so wirklich gefangen hatte, war er gar sehr erfreut darüber und trug sie nach Hause, wo sich die Bauern vor dem Tiere fürchteten. Er ließ eine große Wanne machen und pflegte darin die schöne Schlange. Als er aber wieder einmal nachsehen ging, fand er an ihrer statt eine wunderschöne Jungfrau. Diese dankte nun dem Ritter, dass er sie erlöst habe, denn sie war eine verwünschte Prinzessin. Nachdem die beiden geheiratet, lebten sie viele Jahre glücklich und fromm und bauten ein schönes Kloster. Heutzutage ist noch eine Stiftung, welche von der Seeschlange herstammt.

›› Wissenswertes ‹‹

Bei diesem See handelt es sich um den Pillersee, einen „brüllenden" See im Bezirk Kitzbühel. Der Name des Sees hat vermutlich mit dem Mundartbegriff „pillern" zu tun, einem Phänomen, das meist bei Unwettern oder im Frühjahr auftritt, wenn der See anfängt zu brausen, zu „pillern". Dieses Naturphänomen hat vermutlich zur Entstehung obiger Volkssage beigetragen. Am Pillersee sind viele weitere Sagen angesiedelt. So soll z.B. Pilatus zur Strafe, dass er Jesus den Juden zur Kreuzigung übergeben hat, seit seinem Tod in diesen See hineingebannt worden sein.

Die erste nachweisbare Besiedlung von St.Ulrich am Pillersee geht auf das 10. Jh. durch bajuwarische Stämme zurück. St.Ulrich war die Urpfarre des gesamten Tales. Im 12. Jh. siedelten sich auch Benediktinermönche des Klosters Rott am Inn (Bayern) an.

Statt im Berg- oder Erdinnern kann die Strahlende Frau auch als Seeschlange im Wasser leben.

Das Element „Wasser" steht für die Welt der Gefühle, der Emotionen und der Intuition. Diese Sage zeigt bei tieferer Betrachtung beispielhaft den tiefen Symbolgehalt von Mythen, Märchen und Sagen auf, der vor allem von C.G. Jung und seiner langjährigen Mitarbeiterin Aniela Jaffé erforscht und gedeutet worden ist.

61

Die Frau mit den goldenen Nüssen

Als vor etwa vierzig Jahren ein Wässerer um Mitternacht am Brugger Haus vorbeiging, sah er auf der Bank vor dem Hause eine alte Frau sitzen, die ihm winkte und drei goldene Nüsse vorhielt. Der Wässerer nahm die Goldfrüchte nicht und ging seiner Wege. Hätte er sie genommen, wäre er ein reicher Mann geworden.

›› Wissenswertes ‹‹

Wenn in Sagen wie in dieser aus Meran von Nüssen die Rede ist, ist nicht immer klar, ob die Hasel- oder Walnuss gemeint ist. Sowohl Hasel- als auch Walnüsse werden als Fruchtbarkeitssymbol gedeutet. In der spätlateinischen Zeit warfen Kinder den neu vermählten Eheleuten Walnüsse in den Weg. Im Glauben der Romanen, besonders der Italiener, war der Walnussbaum ein Hexenbaum. In der griechischen Mythologie war er der heilige Baum der Göttin Artemis und seine Nüsse eine Götterspeise.

Auch die Tiroler Stampe liebte die Walnüsse sehr.

62

Das Fräulein auf der Hochburg

Bei Lans liegt die längst zerfallene Hochburg, in der heutzutage noch ein Schatz liegt. Ein Fräulein mit einem Schlüsselbund erscheint bisweilen dort und winkt freundlich, wenn der Schatz blüht. Als in einer Christnacht ein Mädchen mit ihrer Nahnl in einem nahe gelegenen Hofe allein zu Hause wachte, löschte plötzlich das Licht aus. Da sie trotz allen Suchens das Feuerzeug nicht finden konnte und in der Asche auch kein Funke mehr glomm, sprach die Alte: „Geh' zum Nachbarn hinüber und hole in der Laterne Licht." Das Kind folgte, ging aufs Licht zu und kam ins Schloss, das wie neu gebaut dastand. Verdutzt stieg es die Treppe hinauf und fand im Saale ein schönes Fräulein, das am Kamine saß, in dem viele Kohlen glühten. Das Fräulein winkte freundlich, nahm eine Schaufel voll Kohlen und wollte sie dem Mädchen in die Schürze schütten. Da rief das Kind voll Schrecken: „Mein Gott, Sie verbrennen mir ja das Fürtuch!" Augenblicklich war das Schloss verschwunden und in der Tiefe jammerte und klingelte es. Das Mädchen ließ vor Schrecken die Kohlen fallen und lief atemlos nach Hause, wo sie alles der Nahnl erzählte. „O du ungeschicktes Madl!" rief sie aus, „hättest du die Kohlen genommen, wäre das Fräulein erlöst und der Schatz dein gewesen. Jetzt muss das arme Fräulein wieder hundert Jahre auf seine Erlösung warten und du bist keinen Kreuzer reicher!"

›› Wissenswertes ‹‹

Fürtuch = Schürze, Nahnl = Großmutter. – Lans liegt in der Nähe Innsbrucks.

Es ist ein häufig wiederkehrender Sagen- und Märchenzug, dass wertlose Gegenstände wie Laub, Stroh oder im Korb zurückgebliebene Reste in Gold umgewandelt werden, besonders oft geschieht dies bei Kohlen. Martin Luther erwähnt den Aberglauben, dass Frau Holle bei ihrem jährlichen Umgang als Gastgeschenk Kohlen zurücklässt, die sich dann in Gold verwandeln.

Kohlen, vor allem glühende, spielten im Volksglauben früher eine bedeutende Rolle. Sie wurden als Schutzmittel gegen Verhexung und Blitzschlag, aber auch als Heilmittel und Orakel verwendet und wurden besonders an bestimmten Tagen gesammelt oder verwendet wie beispielsweise zu Weihnachten, beim Johannisfeuer oder zu Allerheiligen.

63

Die Sage vom Burgstallegg

Einem Hirten, der in der Nähe dieser Burgruine seine Schafe weidete, begegnete des Öfteren eine wunderschöne Frau, mit der er manchmal ins Gespräch kam. Eines Tages enthüllte sie ihm ihr Geheimnis: „Ich bin das Fräulein aus der alten Burg. Ich kann dich zum reichsten Menschen weit und breit machen, wenn du mir im rechten Augenblick hilfreich beistehen willst, aber du darfst niemandem etwas davon erzählen."

An diesem Tag kehrte der Hirte erst spätabends nach Hause zurück, und der Bauer wies ihn deshalb böse zurecht. Der Hirte aber schwieg, wie es ihm die Jungfrau aufgetragen hatte. Jeden Nachmittag wiederholte sich nun dasselbe: Täglich erschien ihm nun die schöne Frau, sie plauderte mit ihm, und jeden Tag trieb er seine Herde erst beim Nachtwerden heim. Dies ärgerte den Bauern schließlich so sehr, dass er ihn eines Tages vom Dienst jagte.

Da wusste der Hirte keinen Ausweg mehr und er erzählte dem Bauern vom schönen Fräulein auf dem Burgstallegg. Als er am nächsten Tag seine Schafe wieder dort hinauftrieb, erschien ihm das schöne Fräulein mit Tränen in den Augen. Mit vor Traurigkeit zitternder Stimme sagte sie: „Deine Geschwätzigkeit hat uns beide unglücklich gemacht. Jetzt muss ich wieder hundert Jahre warten, bis ich von meinen Erdenqualen erlöst werden kann." Und sie verschwand vor seinen Augen. Tränenüberströmt ging er nach Hause. Das Burgfräulein aber wurde seit jenem Tag nie mehr gesehen.

›› Wissenswertes ‹‹

Das Burgstallegg, auch „Gschlößlwand" genannt, liegt in einsamer, aussichtsreicher Lage über dem Etschtal an der Abbruchkante der Aldeiner Hochfläche in der Nähe des sagenumwobenen Göller Sees, von dort aus auch erreichbar. Es ist eine urzeitliche Siedlung auf zwei Kuppelhälften, die durch eine 15 m tiefe und 4 m breite Felsspalte getrennt sind. Auf beiden spiegelbildlich angeordneten Anlagen befindet sich eine riesige Ansammlung von porphyrnen Steintrümmerresten mit einer Mauerdicke von einem bis zu vier Metern. Der Zweck dieser Anlage ist noch nicht restlos geklärt. In Frage kommt eine gut gesicherte Urzeitstätte mit einem Grottenheiligtum oder einer Kultstätte; neueren Forschungsergebnissen zufolge könnte es sich um einen Brandopferplatz handeln. Als mögliche Entstehungszeit vermutet der Archäologe Reimo Lunz die Spätphase der Eisenzeit. Bedauerlicherweise haben inkompetente „Schatzgräber" die Anlage aufgesucht.

Das Burgstallegg ist von verschiedenen Sagen umrankt. Als ein Hirte einmal vom Burgstallegg nach Hause ging, sahen die Leute, dass die Blumen auf seinem Hut, welche er dort gepflückt hatte, aus purem Gold waren. Am Heiligen Abend schweben lauter kleine Lichter über den Mauern, aus den Trümmern hört man verzweifelte und qualvolle Rufe. Doch wer es wagt, am Weihnachtsabend auf Burgstallegg zu gehen, muss sterben. Denn an diesem Abend gehen die Geister jener Menschen um, die in den Verliesen dieses Schlosses zugrunde gegangen sein sollen.

Wie so oft, sind Orte, an denen Sagen angesiedelt sind, auch uralte archäologisch bedeutsame Stätten.

64

Die Trude zu Unterholz

Auf einem Hofe zu Unterholz im Pfitschtale diente eine brave fleißige Magd bei einem reichen Bauern. Sie hatte aber die Gewohnheit, zur Nachtzeit gar zu gern fortzugehen. Das gefiel dem Bauern nicht und er wollte sie vom Dienst entlassen. Da bekannte ihm die Dirn, dass sie das Unglück habe, eine Trud zu sein; sie verabscheue aber diese dämonische Gewalt, daher gehe sie nachts in den Wald und drücke die Bäume.

Da erkundigte sich der Bauer, weil er Mitleid fühlte, bei einem Tierarzt in Mareit, der als Hexenmeister bekannt war, und bei einem Knappen auf dem Schneeberg, der mancherlei Bann verstand, und beide rieten ihm, er solle der Dirn seine beste Kuh opfern, d.h. ihr erlauben, dass sie in der Nacht dieselbe totdrücken dürfe, jedoch dürfe er nicht das geringste Leid darum verspüren.

Der Bauer, um die Seele der braven Magd zu retten, erlaubte es, und als die Trude die Kuh um die Mitte nahm und so heftig und so lange zusammendrückte, bis diese tot niederfiel, war sie für immer geheilt.

›› Wissenswertes ‹‹

Diese Sage zeigt, wie andere auch, dass eine Frau, die den Trutenfluch ausüben muss, dies den anderen Mitmenschen gegenüber verheimlicht. Sie drückt nicht aus Bosheit, im Gegenteil, sie verabscheut eigentlich diese dämonische Gewalt, kann aber nicht anders, als ihrem Trieb zu folgen. In Ranggen (westlich von Innsbruck gelegen) war man der Überzeugung, dass eine nicht ausgesegnete Frau zur Trude würde. Sie kann davon nur befreit werden, wenn ihr jemand ein sehr liebes und wichtiges Haustier, wie in diesem Falle die Kuh, zur Verfügung stellt, das sie dann „besitzen" kann, so dass es zu Tode kommt. Dadurch ist sie von ihrem Fluch befreit.

65

Hansl und Franzl

Wie der Salzburger, ein Wirtshauspächter, erst zehn Jahre alt war, diente er im Radlhof im Dorfe Ried bei Sterzing, und schlief mit dem ledigen Radlbauer in einer Stube. Sein Herr erzählte dem Buben oft, dass ihn eine Trud drücke. Er sehe sie als junges starkes Weibsbild mit starrem kalten Blick in die Stube treten, sie springe auf ihn los und drücke ihn so auf die Brust, dass er sich nicht regen und auch nicht schreien, nur „gihna" könne. Dann bat er auch, wenn er rufe: „Jetzt kommt sie!", so solle der Franzl rufen: „Hansel!", denn der Bauer hieß Johannes. Die Trud weicht nämlich, sobald ein Mensch, den sie drückt, beim

Namen gerufen wird. Und richtig, die Trud kam und der Hansl schrie: „Jetzt kommt's!" – Wer aber nicht „Hansl" rief, das war der Franzl, weil er sich fürchtete und unter die Bettdecke gekrochen war, und hat den Hansl in Gottesnamen stöhnen lassen.

Einmal ist die Trud wieder gekommen und ist von den Füßen der Bettstatt auf ihn draufgesprungen, wie er selbst erzählt hat. Da hat er seine rechte Hand ausgestreckt und Haare von ihrem Kopf erwischt. Er hat sie daran gehalten, sie aber hat sich losgerissen unter Verlust des Haares, und als der Hansl das Haar bei Licht besah, so waren es Strohhalme. Endlich wurde dem Hansl die Kunst geraten, wenn sie wieder komme, so solle er sie auf den folgenden Tag bestellen. Wenn sie sich dann einfinde, solle er ihr die „drei weißen Gaben" geben. Solches geschah, die Trud kam ganz allein in die Küche zum Hansl und er kannte sie recht wohl, es war eine Frau aus Sterzing. Sie nahm die drei oben genannten Gaben, aber er musste sie ihr mit der linken Hand geben, und legte ihm Stillschweigen auf. Darauf hatte der Hansl vor der Trud auf immer Ruhe. Der Franzl aber hat's verplauscht.

›› Wissenswertes ‹‹

gihna = stöhnen.

Die Truten kommen, wenn die Leute schlafen, durch das Fenster, durch die Türe oder durch Fugen und Spalten herein, auch wenn diese geschlossen sind, und legen sich auf den Schlafenden, um ihn furchtbar zu drücken. Wenn aber jemand den Gequälten beim Namen ruft, muss die Trute schnell fliehen. Auch darf sie keinen Menschen vollends erdrücken.

Wenn einer die Trute kommen hört und ihr zuruft: „Komm morgen um die weißen Gaben", dann geht sie gleich fort und kommt am anderen Tag. Dann kann man erkennen, wer sie ist. Man muss ihr weißes Salz, weißes Mehl und ein weißes Ei geben, diese drei Gaben wird sie nehmen und niemals wiederkommen. So befreit man sich am besten von ihr.

Interessant ist hier die Dreizahl, welche im Tiroler Volksleben neben anderen Zahlen wie vier, sieben, neun, zwölf, 13, 99, u.a., eine magische Bedeutung hat: Aller guten Dinge sind drei. Ein Neugieriger darf dreimal raten. Gewisse Dinge müssen dreimal wiederholt werden. Wer am Morgen dreimal niest, hat Glück. Wer unter Schluckauf leider, soll an drei glatzköpfige Junggesellen denken. Auch die drei weißen Gaben oder weißen Teile waren zauberkräftig: Eier, Mehl und Milch. Für die Beherrschung der Zauberkunst des Bannens, Stellens und Angefrierens wurden ebenso die drei weißen Gaben angewendet.

Bemerkenswert ist in dieser Sage auch die Fähigkeit des Sich-Verwandelns in Strohhalme. Wenn jemand Türen und Fenster so fest zuschließt, dass die Trute nicht eindringen kann, dann schlüpft sie durch das Schlüsselloch und durch Fensterklüfte oder Löchlein herein, und zwar in Strohhalmform. Schafft es der Gedrückte noch, die Trute fest zu packen, so hält er letztendlich nichts als ein paar Halme Stroh in seinen Händen. Um dies zu vermeiden, muss man geweihte Kräuter in Schlüssellöcher und Fugen stecken. In einigen Tiroler Bauernhäusern konnten wir dies selbst entdecken.

66

Die Trude

Es war einmal eine Trude, die konnte immer sehr wenig schlafen und blieb daher immer mager und hatte ein schlechtes Aussehen, dass jedermann glauben musste, es sei etwas nicht in Ordnung mit ihr. Der Bauer, bei dem sie im Dienst war, stellte sie einmal darüber zur Rede und fragte sie lange Zeit hin und her, wo es denn fehle und wie ihr zu helfen wäre. Sie wollte nicht recht heraus mit der Sprache, fragte aber endlich, ob sie den besten Stier im Stall erwürgen dürfe. Der Bauer gab ihr lachend die Erlaubnis dazu, denn er meinte, dazu werde das Mädchen wohl nicht die Kraft haben. Aber richtig, am nächsten Tag lag der schönste Stier erwürgt im Stall, und der Magd war für immer geholfen. Denn sie brauchte jetzt nicht mehr bei der Nacht beständig herumzufahren, sondern hatte Schlaf und Ruhe genug und schaute in kurzer Zeit so frisch und gesund aus, als ob ihr gar nie etwas gefehlt hätte.

›› Wissenswertes ‹‹

Die Truten drücken nicht nur Menschen, sondern, wie in dieser Ultner Sage, auch Kühe und Pferde. Sogar Bäume sind vor ihnen nicht sicher. So sind die Birken den Truden verhasst und deshalb lassen sie an ihnen den Zorn aus, so lange, bis kein Stamm mehr rund bleibt.

Auch Eschen weisen oft Spuren vom Drücken der Trute auf: Wenn eine Esche eine „Alprast" (Verknorpelung) aufweist, so stammt diese von der Trute her, die weder Tier noch Mensch gefunden hat und daher ihren Drang an diesem Baum auslässt.

67

Die angenagelte Trute

Die Trute kam einmal in der Nacht in den Stierlhof zu Unterinn und schlich sich in die Kammer, wo die Tochter des Bauern schlief. Wie aber diese so erst ein wenig eingedöst war, hörte sie die eintretende Hexe und erkannte sie sogleich an den schleifenden Tritten. Daher packte sie sogleich ihr Kopfkissen und warf es, wie ihr gesagt worden war, dass man tun müsse, gegen die Türe. Mit einem Satze war sie sodann aus dem Bett, sprang dem Kissen nach und hob es vorsichtig in die Höhe, und siehe, es lag ein Federchen darunter, das vom Kissen zu Boden geschlagen wurde. Also war die Trute gefangen. Da nahm die Dirne das Federchen auf, drückte es an die Tür und schlug einen Nagel hindurch. Und wie das Mädel so siegesfroh die Feder in besseren Augenschein nahm, da verwandelte sich diese allmählich in ein menschliches Gebilde, und nach einer Weile stand die leibhaftige Trute vor der Dirne, fest an die Tür genagelt, und der Nagel war ihr durch den Mund gefahren. Sie ächzte und stöhnte, dass sich ein Stein erbarmen musste. Das Mädel fühlte auch wirklich Mitleid mit der Armen und befreite die Trute. Diese verschwand im Nu und der Stierlhof blieb seitdem vor ihren nächtlichen Besuchen verschont.

›› Wissenswertes ‹‹

Die Trute, aber auch Alp, Mahrt, Schrättele, Schräzel, wie die einzelnen Bezeichnungen für den Druckgeist in anderen Gegenden lauten, können auch in Gestalt eines Rauchwölkleins, einer Hummel, eines Schmetterlings, einer Schlange, Kröte oder, wie in dieser Sage, einer Feder, erscheinen.

Ein anderes Truten-Abwehrmittel wird in dieser Sage beschrieben: Beim Eintreten der Trute soll man ihr eiligst einen Kopfpolster entgegenwerfen. Darauf muss sie während der ganzen Nacht sitzen bleiben und bei Morgengrauen gehen, ohne drücken zu können.

68

Die große Trude

Am südlichen Abhange des Matscher Tales, in gerader Richtung von der Pfarrkirche hinauf, befindet sich eine terrassenförmige Gebirgsabstufung, auf welcher ein großer Stein liegt. Dieser zeigt Eindrücke, als ob jemand auf ihm gesessen wäre und Spuren im weichen Fels zurückgelassen hätte. Etwa siebenzig Schritte davon entfernt ist in einer Steinplatte die Stapfe eines rechten Fußes anderthalb Zoll tief eingeprägt. Man nennt es dort „Beim Trudenfuß“ und die Stapfe soll jedem genau passen, der unbeschuht in diese tritt. Am jenseitigen Bergabhange befindet sich am Wege, der zum Remsbache führt, oberhalb der

Mühle und der Schmiede, der zweite Fußtritt, der linke, in einem Steine. Hieran knüpft sich folgende Sage:

Vor undenklichen Zeiten war einmal eine ungewöhnlich große Trude, welche sich bei Tag immer in Wäldern und tiefen Felsschluchten verbarg. Als sie sich einmal auf jenem Steine beim Trudenfuße niedersetzte, sank sie wegen ihrer Schwere mehr als schuhtief in jenen Stein ein, woher jener Abdruck rührt. Als sie sich erhob, setzte sie den rechten Fuß auf die Steinplatte und den linken auf den Fels oberhalb der Mühlen, so dass sie mit einem Schritte das ganze Tal quer übersetzte. Die Spuren dieser zwei Tritte sieht man, wie gesagt, heutzutage noch. Die Trude war so groß, dass sie höher war als die Remsspitze oder die Weißkugel. Sie konnte sich aber auch außerordentlich klein machen, weshalb es ihr möglich war, heimlich in die Häuser zu kommen und die Leute nachts zu quälen. Sie legte sich ihnen alsdann auf die Brust und presste sie dergestalt, dass sie beinahe den Atem verloren und in Angstschweiß beinahe gebadet wurden. Oft sog sie an den Brüsten von Knaben und Mädchen so, dass sie hoch aufschwollen und morgens Milch daraus floss. Um sich vor diesen Plagen zu schützen, durfte man nur einen hölzernen Stiefel über das Bett des Schlafenden hängen. Geschah dies, so hatte sie ihre Gewalt verloren und musste abziehen. Zur Abwechslung ging sie auch in die Ställe und drückte die armen Tiere, bis sie schnaubten, an den Ketten rissen und morgens voll Schweiß standen. Oft sog sie auch den Kühen die Milch bis auf den letzten Tropfen aus. Jetzt existiert die Trude nicht mehr, aber die Kinder treiben noch ihr Unwesen, drücken die Leute und saugen an den Brüsten, dass sie hoch aufschwellen.

›› Wissenswertes ‹‹

Ein Bauer von Pfitsch erzählte dem Sammler dieser Sage, dass Truten an den Füßen gar leicht zu erkennen sind, sie haben nämlich die Gestalt von Trudenkreuzen, welche in einem Zuge in fünf Linien gemacht und sorgsam im Schuh verborgen werden. Wenn die Truten älter werden und im Hexenbund sind, so drücken sie dieses Zeichen mit den Füßen in die Steine ein, wo sie sich auf ihren Hexenflügen niederlassen. Daher kommt es, dass man die „Trudensteine“ mit solchen und ähnlichen Zeichen bezeichnet findet, und da sollte man in nächtlicher Zeit ja nicht ausruhen. – Um den bösen Nachtgeist abzuwehren, zeichnete man in Tirol den sechseckigen Drudenfuß an die Schlafzimmertüren, auf die Betten und Kinderwiegen.

Das Pentagramm oder der Drudenfuß ist ein uraltes Symbol. Schon in Äpypten stand der fünfzackige Stern für den Schoß der Erde. Manche nannten das Pentagramm den Stern der Ishtar oder Isis oder der Nephthys, Isis' Zwillingsschwester in der Unterwelt.

In Babylon war es üblich, das Pentagramm als schützendes oder heilendes Amulett zu tragen, häufig war es dort auch auf Töpfe gezeichnet, um ihren Inhalt zu schützen. Auch die KeltInnen verehrten das Pentagramm wie die ÄgypterInnen als Zeichen der Erdgöttin.

Wie bei anderen Figuren, die aus einer fortlaufenden Linie konstruiert sind, glaubte man auch beim Pentagramm, dass es Schutz vor Geistern biete, da diese die Tore einer unterbrochenen Linie bräuchten. Daher fand das Pentagramm über Jahrhunderte hinweg Verwendung, um magische Orte abzugrenzen und auch zur Geisterbeschwörung.

Mittelalterliche Kleriker nannten es daher außer Drudenfuß auch Satanszeichen, Hexenkreuz, Zauberstern, Elfenkreuz oder Hexenfuß. Es bestand der Glaube, dass ein Vampir oder Werwolf auf Fußsohle oder Handfläche ein Pentagramm trage.

Natürlich durchlochte Steine werden Trutensteine (oder Krottensteine) genannt und man schreibt ihnen schützende und abwehrende Kraft zu. Alte Hebammen besaßen solche Steine und liehen sie Frauen zum Schutze ihrer Kinder und auch Wöchnerinnen, welche als besonders gefährdet galten.

69

Das Mädchen, das eine Trute gewesen ist

Einmal mussten zwei Mädchen von der Alm ins Tal hinuntersteigen, um von der Mühle Mehl zu holen. Anschließend traten sie wieder den Rückweg zur Alm an. Als sie die Hälfte des Wegs hinter sich hatten, beschlossen sie, eine Rastpause einzulegen. Eines der beiden schlief ein, und nach kurzer Zeit flog aus seinem Mund eine Hornisse hervor, das Mädchen selbst aber lag wie tot am Boden. Zu Tode erschrocken schüttelte es die Andere und rief es beim Namen, doch vergeblich. Einige Zeit später kehrte die Hornisse zurück, flog wieder in den Mund des Mädchens hinein, und da erwachte es wieder. Die Freundin bestürmte es so lange mit Fragen, bis es endlich anfing zu reden: „Nun gut, ich werde dir alles sagen, aber du darfst niemandem etwas davon erzählen. Ich bin eine Trute, und wie ich eingeschlafen bin, war ich bei einem Mann im Dorf, um sein Blut zu saugen." Das andere Mädchen versprach, niemandem etwas davon zu erzählen und dann kehrten sie auf die Alm zurück.

Einige Tage später gerieten die beiden in Anwesenheit vieler Personen in einen heftigen Streit. Da sagte die eine: „Hör auf, andere Leute zu beschimpfen und zu beleidigen, denn die Wahrheit ist: Du bist eine Trute!" Weinend ging die andere fort und von jenem Tag an stritt sie sich mit niemandem mehr.

›› Wissenswertes ‹‹

Die Sage von der wandernden Seele wird bereits vom langobardischen Geschichtsschreiber Paulus Diaconus in der Historia Langobardorum um ca. 790 erzählt: Der fränkische König Guntram hatte einmal auf der Jagd gerastet und war eingeschlafen. Ein ihn begleitender Diener sah nun, wie im Schlaf ein kleines, schlangenähnliches Tierlein aus seinem Mund kroch und versuchte, über ein vorbeifließendes Bächlein zu kommen. Der Diener legte sein Schwert über das Wasser, das Tierlein kroch hinüber und verschwand in einem Berg. Nach einiger Zeit kehrte es zurück und schlüpfte wieder in Guntrams Mund. Als der König erwachte, erzählte er, dass er geträumt hätte, über eine eiserne Brücke und einen Fluss in einen Berg gekommen zu sein, wo er wunderbare Schätze gesehen habe. Man suchte und fand eine Menge Goldes. – In Luserna, einer zimbrischen Sprachinsel im Trentino, war man der Meinung, dass die Seele eines Menschen, bei dessen Taufe das Glaubensbekenntnis nicht richtig gebetet worden sei, zeitlebens nachts umgehen und Blut aus richtig getauften Menschen saugen müsse. Auch hier gab es zahlreiche Gegenmittel; die entlarvte Trute wurde nicht verklagt, sondern mit ihr vereinbart, dass sie ihre Schuld durch Arbeit am Haus und Hof abdienen müsse.

Hexe und Weise Frau

„Krumme Nase, spitzes Kinn, sitzt der Teufel ganz darin.“ – Solche und weitere Merkmale beschreiben das Aussehen der **Hexe**, nach unserem heutigen Vorstellungsbild zumeist ein hässliches, altes, boshaftes Weib.

Den Hexen wurde so manch Schändliches vorgeworfen: Die Buhlschaft mit dem Leibhaftigen, dem Teufel; Ketzerei, also Kulthandlungen und Anbetung von nicht- bzw. vorchristlichen Gottheiten; Tierverwandlung und Flugzauber; Ausübung von schwarzer Magie, Schadenszauber. Sie benützt ihre besondere Kraft, um Menschen und Tiere zu manipulieren („der böse Blick“), doch auch kraft ihrer Hände ist sie imstande, Gegenstände, Menschen oder Tiere tanzen, springen, fliegen oder auch lahm werden zu lassen. Sie beschreit Kinder und Tiere, bringt Seuchen und Krankheiten. Mit Leib und Seele hat sie sich dem Teufel verschrieben, doch auch er hat Respekt vor ihr.

Zauberei und Hexenwesen waren jedoch keine Erfindung des ausgehenden Mittelalters, sondern wurden bereits vor dem Jahr 1000 von der christlichen Gesetzgebung bestraft. Selbst in der Bibel heißt es: „Eine Zauberin darfst du nicht am Leben lassen …“ (Exodus 22, 17).

Doch vor allem infolge des im Jahre 1487 vom Dominikanermönch Heinrich Kramer Institoris verfassten „Hexenhammers“ (malleus maleficarum) häufte sich die „Hexenkriminalität“ fast sprunghaft. Dieses Schriftwerk enthielt u.a. Richtlinien, wie man Hexen erkennen konnte, welche Verbrechen auf Zauberei zurückzuführen wären und wie ein Hexenprozess durchgeführt werden sollte. Die Lehren des Thomas von Aquin, die Hexenbulle von Papst Innozenz VIII., vor allem aber ein pathologischer Frauenhass des Verfassers bildeten die Grundlage dieses Werkes.

Auch vor Tirol machte die Woge der Hexenhysterie nicht halt; stellvertretend für dieses tragische Tiroler Kapitel wird an dieser Stelle Barbara Pachler, die „Bachler Zottl“ aus Windlahn im Sarntal genannt, einst als blühend schönes Weib beschrieben, welche als letzte Sarner Hexe 1540 an der Richtstätte am Öttenbach in Sarnthein lebend verbrannt wurde.

Erst mit Kaiserin Maria Theresia und ihrem Sohn Joseph II. wurde das Delikt der Hexerei im Jahre 1787 aus dem Strafkodex gestrichen.

Viele den Hexen vorgeworfene und von der christlichen Kirche als heidnisch erklärte kultische Zeremonien basierten auf einer engen Verbindung mit den Kräften und Zyklen der Natur (z.B. Jahreszeitenfeste), die mancherorts bis ins 16./17. Jh. überlebt haben.

Eine Art christlicher Meilenstein gegen alles Dämonische war das Trientner Konzil (1543-1563), welches u.a. Zauberei, Liebestränke und Wahrsagerei aufs Strengste verbot. Es wird in vielen Tiroler Sagen erwähnt: So hat es laut Sage beispielsweise allen Pflanzen und Tieren die Sprache genommen, Hexen und Dämonen ihrer bösen, heidnischen Kraft beraubt und in abgelegene Täler verbannt (z.B. in das unberührte Val di Genova im Naturpark Adamello-Brenta im Trentino).

Der Begriff „Hexe" ist erst ab dem 14. Jh. gebräuchlich. Manche Forscher führen ihn auf das althochdeutsche „hagazussa", „Zaunreiterin", zurück. Diese sitzt auf dem „hag", dem Zaun/der Hecke; der Wortteil „zussa" wird als „böser/guter Geist" gedeutet. Die Hexe sitzt dieser Deutung zufolge also zwischen der zivilisierten und der wilden Welt und ist imstande, nach Belieben hin und her zu wechseln. Hag hat laut Forschung in seiner Wortbedeutung ursprünglich aber auch mit „hagia" = „heilig" zu tun: Die göttliche Hag wurde von den Sachsen und Dänen in Form eines Steinidols verehrt.

In Volksglauben und Sagen ist von Brand- und Wetterhexen, von Wald- und Kräuterhexen die Rede. Daraus kann man schließen, dass sie mit den vier Elementen Erde, Wasser, Feuer, Luft aufs Engste verbunden sind/waren und zu der der ungezähmten Wildnis innewohnenden Kraft Zugang hatten. Auch ihr fundiertes Kräuterwissen zeigt ihre Kenntnis und ihr Wissen über die Kräfte der Natur.

Doch so wie die **Weise Frau** im Laufe der Jahrhunderte degradiert und ihr ganzheitliches Wissen abgewertet wurde, haben auch viele ihrer Heilkräuter an Bedeutung verloren oder sind ganz in Vergessenheit geraten oder wurden im Laufe der letzten Jahrhunderte gar als antidämonische Abwehrkräuter eingesetzt, also gegen sie gerichtet, oder in den Bereich des nicht ernstzunehmenden Aberglaubens abgeschoben.

Der Einsatz von sogenannten Berufs- und Beschrei-/Verschreipflanzen bewahrte vor der negativen Kraft hexenhafter Wesen. „Berufen" bedeutet so viel wie besessen sein, „Beschreiung" ist eine Art Verfluchung. Tiere oder Menschen, die von einem bösen Blick angeschaut wurden, galten als „vermeint", sie konnten dann weder essen noch trinken und wurden apathisch. Solche Kräuter sind beispielsweise der Quendel, das Johanniskraut, die Raute und der Beifuß. Die uralte germanische Heil- und Zauberpflanze Gundelrebe wurde nun gegen hexischen Milchzauber angewendet. Auch das Holz der Elze (Traubenkirsche) besitzt mehr Kraft als die Hexe.

Ebenso die beim Kräutersammeln von den Weisen Frauen verwendeten Rituale erfuhren später eine entgegengesetzte Bedeutung. So war es einst wichtig, die Heilpflanzen auf einem Schemel oder Holz aus neunerlei Aghenholz (Nadelholz) zu ernten, sie mussten mit der Hand abgerissen oder mit einem hölzernen Gerät, aber niemals einem aus Eisen, geerntet werden. In den letzten Jahrhunderten behauptete man hingegen, dass man eine Hexe erkennen könne, wenn man sich auf einen Stuhl aus neunerlei Aghenholz setze.

Der Hexenglauben war auch in Tirol weit verbreitet. Darauf weisen noch heute die vielen Plätze und Namen wie Hexenstein, Hexenbichl, Hexenbödele usw. hin, auf denen laut Volksüberlieferung Hexen ihre Versammlungen abhielten. Kreuzwege galten als besonders „hexengefährlich“. Dieser Aberglaube geht auf die griechische Hekate, Göttin der Schwellenübergänge, zurück, laut Mythe als Kind auf einer Wegkreuzung ausgesetzt und von Hirten aufgezogen. Kreuzwege/Wegkreuzungen galten daher der Hekate heilig. In späteren Zeiten wurde sie zur Schutzherrin der Hexen. Mittlerweile stehen an solchen Stellen oft Kruzifixe oder Heiligenbilder.

Hexen treten in Sagen und Märchen oft in Begleitung von bestimmten Tieren in Erscheinung: dem Hasen, dem Raben und dem Ziegenbock, der Kröte, der Eule, der Ratte, der Spinne, der Fledermaus und der Schlange; vor allem aber der Katze. Viele als hexisch verrufene Tiere, von denen hier nur einige angeführt werden, waren in alten Kulturen hochverehrt.

Der Hase galt als Symbol der Göttin, der Weiblichkeit, der Fruchtbarkeit, des Mondes. Auch der germanischen Freyja und der griechischen Aphrodite wird er zugeordnet. Weltweit gibt es zahlreiche Märchen, die den Hasen als heiliges Tier mit dem Mond assoziieren. Eine Vinschger Sage aus Malettes bei Mals erzählt vom Auftreten der Hexen in Hasengestalt. Dieser Ort ist als Hexenplatz bekannt; es scheint ein uralter Kultort gewesen zu sein, zumal man dort eine Art Altar aus Stein gefunden hat.

Der Frosch war bereits im alten Ägypten das Symboltier der Göttin der Geburt, auch der griechischen Hekate wurden Frosch bzw. Kröte zugeordnet. In den mitteleuropäischen und Tiroler Sagen sowie in der Volksüberlieferung spielt die Kröte eine ähnliche Rolle. Dem Krötenrumpf wird eine Ähnlichkeit mit der weiblichen Gebärmutter nachgesagt, der Krötenrücken soll der weiblichen Vulva ähnlich sehen. Als wächserne Votivgabe wurde deshalb die Kröte als Symbol für die weibliche Gebärmutter bei diversen Frauenleiden und Unfruchtbarkeit in Wallfahrtsorten geopfert (z.B. in Maria Waldrast).

Die Eule war die Begleiterin von Athene, der griechischen Göttin der Weisheit. In der christlich/jüdischen Religion war sie das Symboltier der Lilith, der ersten Frau Adams. In vielen Kulturen galt sie als Totenvogel, ähnlich wie der Kauz im Tiroler Volksglauben.

Der Ziegenbock wird dem griechischen Hirtengott Pan zugeordnet. Bekannt für Tanz, Fröhlichkeit, aber auch Wollust und Ekstase, wurde er im Laufe des sexualfeindlichen Mittelalters immer mehr zum Tier des Teufels, der in Sagen und Märchen häufig mit Ziegenfüßen und -schwanz beschrieben wird.

Den größten Wandel vom Gottes- zum Teufeltier musste wohl die Katze über sich ergehen lassen. Vor allem der schwarzen Katze wurden und werden noch außergewöhnliche dämonische

Eigenschaften nachgesagt (einer schwarzen Katze zu begegnen bringe Unglück), so dass sie während des Hexenwahns oft verbrannt wurde.

Weitere Hexenattribute sind der Hexenbesen und der Hexenkessel. Der in vielen Sagen beschriebene Hexenbesen ruft heute nur noch Belustigung hervor, doch der Besen als kultisches Relikt hat auch im Tiroler Volks- und Brauchtum überlebt. Als Beispiel seien hier die bei den Nikolausumzügen als Teufel mitziehenden maskierten Männer genannt, die mit Birkenruten am liebsten auf junge Mädchen losgehen. Der Birkenbesen war bei vielen Völkern ein uraltes Fruchtbarkeitssymbol; symbolisch wurden Mädchen früher deshalb mit Birkenruten geschlagen. Auch das Verbrennen der alten Besen als kultischer Feuerbrauch ist aus vielen Gegenden Europas, auch aus Tirol, überliefert.

Der Stabritt als schamanisches Ritual wird im Kapitel Seherin und Prophetin beschrieben.

Grausamkeit und Perversion werden Hexen nachgesagt; sie würden nicht davor zurückschrecken, bei ihren nächtlichen Feiern unschuldige Kinder zu schlachten, zu kochen und zu essen, dem Teufel zu opfern.

Im Kessel, so wird den Hexen nachgesagt, würde während des Sabbats die Hexensalbe gekocht, die sich aus tierischen, menschlichen und heiligen Bestandteilen zusammensetze.

Laut anderen Überlieferungen ist der Kessel allerdings ein von vielen Völkern verwendetes uraltes kultisches Gerät. Der griechische Geschichtsschreiber Strabo (gest. 23 n.Chr.) berichtet von grauhaarigen kimbrischen Priesterinnen, deren Aufgabe es war, den über einen großen Kessel gebeugten Kriegsgefangenen die Kehlen durchzuschneiden und sie den Göttern zu opfern. Das im Kessel aufgefangene Blut diente ihnen zur Weissagung.

In zahlreichen Mythen, Märchen und Sagen aus der ganzen Welt ist von einem Kessel oder seinem Diebstahl die Rede. In den ältesten Mythen ist er Symbol der Großen Göttin. Als Gral wurde dieses uralte Symbol in den christlichen Glauben aufgenommen. Laut christlicher Legende ist er der Abendmahlskelch, in welchem Josef von Arimathia das Blut Christi am Kreuz aufgefangen hat.

Die mythischen „Mütter" der Hexe sind die großen weiblichen Gottheiten, die allesamt Zauberinnen und Heil- und Kräuterkundige waren, wie Hekate, Medea, Ischtar, Isis, Freyja und Diana, sowie deren Priesterinnen.

Herbaria (Kräuterfrau), Maliarda (Übeltäterin), Lamia (Nachtungeheuer), Stria (von „Strix" = Schreieule) oder Herodias, Furia und Diana sind nur einige der im Lauf der Jahrhunderte entstandenen, zumeist aus der Mythologie übernommenen Benennungen der ehemals erfahrenen und gefürchteten alten weisen Frau, die in allen wichtigen Lebensmomenten, von der Geburt bis zum Tod, um Rat und Hilfe gebeten wurde.

Die römische Diana war vermutlich wegen ihres starken Bezuges zur Natur nach der Einführung des Christentums weiterhin noch lange Zeit bei den Menschen sehr beliebt. Zum Kult um diese „dea paganorum" (Göttin der Heiden) gehörten auch nächtliche Feiern in der Natur. Dass sich Verehrung und Kult der Diana/Artemis auch in unseren Regionen vermutlich lange Zeit parallel zum Christentum gehalten haben, zeigt eine Freske in der kleinen Nikolaus-Kirche aus dem 15. Jh. in Klerant bei Brixen: Der Hl. Nikolaus tötet die in einem Baum wohnende Diana/Artemis.

70

Die Hexe mit der hölzernen Rippe

Es lebte einmal eine Bäuerin in Enneberg, die eine Hexe war und in der Pfinztagnacht mit den Hexen ausfuhr. Hinter dem Kreuzkofel auf dem Hexenstein kamen sie zusammen und hielten ihr festliches Gelage mit Sang und Tanz. Und weil sie gern Braten schmausten, wurde abwechselnd die Reihe herum eine von ihnen geschlachtet, gebraten und wohl zugerichtet. Die andern setzten sich um den Stein und aßen den Braten auf. Darnach sammelten sie die Knochen der gebratenen Hexe wieder ein, und der Satan, der immer fleißig dabei war, rief sie mit Fleisch und Bein wieder ins Leben zurück, so dass sie war wie vorher. Da traf auch unsere Bäuerin einmal die Reihe, geschlachtet zu werden; weil sie aber noch nicht lange bei der Hexengilde war, wollte es sie ein wenig gruseln, und sie nahm am folgenden Pfinztag ihren Knecht mit auf den Hexenstein, um ihn an ihrer statt schlachten und braten zu lassen. Sie sagte ihm aber nichts davon. Um Mitternacht kamen sie beide auf den Berg, wo schon etliche Hexlein versammelt waren, und plauderten. Der Knecht ahnte nichts Gutes, und während seine Bäuerin sich mit den andern unterhielt, machte er sich heimlich davon und kletterte auf den nächsten Baum. Als nun alle beisammen waren, erschien auch Seine Höllische Hoheit, der Herr Satan, in noblem Zweigespann, und nun sollte der Schmaus hergerichtet werden. Die Bäuerin sah sich erschrocken nach ihrem Knecht um, aber der war verschwunden und alles Suchen nach ihm vergeblich. Daher musste sie nun selber herhalten und sich schlachten und zubereiten lassen. Nun wurde der Braten aufgetragen und die Hexen setzten sich in einen Kreis und schmausten, die abgenagten Knochen aber warfen sie auf die Erde. Der Knecht, der vom Baum herab zugesehen hatte, rutschte verstohlen auf der andern Seite herunter, hob eine Rippe der gebratenen Bäuerin vom Boden auf und steckte sie ein. Darauf kletterte er wieder auf den Baum, und die lärmenden und schmausenden Hexen hatten davon nichts gemerkt. Wie aber der Schmaus zu Ende war und die Knochen der Bäuerin gesammelt und dem Satan zugetragen wurden, fehlte eine Rippe. Sie suchten und suchten, fanden sie aber nicht. Daher machten sie eine Rippe aus Holz, und der Satan machte die Bäuerin wieder lebendig.

Am andern Tage waren die Bäuerin und der Knecht wieder auf dem Hofe, keines sagte aber ein Wort zum andern über das Geschehene. Der Knecht trug jedoch die Rippe immerfort in seiner Tasche.

Später begab es sich einmal, dass die Bäuerin den Knecht schalt und in Harnisch brachte. Da zog dieser die Rippe aus der Tasche und sprach: „Du willst maulen mit mir und hast doch nur eine hölzerne Rippe statt der da!" Nach diesen Worten fiel die Bäuerin zu Boden und war augenblicklich eine Leiche.

Der Pfinztag (bairisch-österreichische Bezeichnung für Donnerstag) ist allgemeiner Hexentag (siehe „Der Bocherhof").

Schamanisch ist der Sagenkern dieser in zahlreichen Varianten auftretenden Sage. Auch in den Schilderungen von sibirischen Schamanen und denen anderer Länder Zentralasiens der heutigen Zeit ist vom Zerstückeln, Kochen und Wiederbeleben die Rede. Der Begriff „Schamane" stammt aus dem Tungusischen „saman" und bedeutet „einer, der gestorben ist". Um Schamane zu werden, muss ein Mensch demnach von den Geistern seiner Vorfahren getötet werden, sein Kopf wird ihm abgeschnitten, denn er soll mit eigenen Augen seiner Zerstückelung zusehen. Dann wird der zukünftige Schamane in einem magischen Kessel gekocht, bis nur noch seine Knochen übrig sind. Diese umhüllen sich wieder mit neuem Fleisch; der Mensch wird wiedergeboren. In Wirklichkeit ist dieser Akt der Zerstückelung ein Prozess der Transformation und der Erneuerung. Er bedeutet die Auflösung des alten Ichs, die Aufgabe des bisherigen Lebens bzw. der Identifizierung mit dem gesellschaftlichen Weltbild. Um zwischen den Welten hin- und herwandeln zu können, muss das „alte" Leben für die/den Schamanen/in gestorben sein. Leiden, Krankheit und Krisen bleiben zukünftigen Schamanen selten erspart, doch auch aufgrund dieser Erfahrungen werden sie zu großen HeilerInnen. Unzählige Märchen aus aller Welt erzählen von der notwendigen Selbstverstümmelung, um in höhere (Bewusstseins-) Ebenen zu gelangen: Die Märchenheldinnen müssen sich beispielsweise einen Finger ab- oder ein Stück Fleisch aus dem Schenkel herausschneiden, um das Ziel zu erreichen.

71

Die Partschuner Hebamme

Wo zwischen Unterinn und Signat die Felswand sich auftut und etliche knorrige Eichen ihre Wipfel in die Höhlung hineinrecken, wo weiland der Riese mit dem Wurm gehaust, da ragt das verwitterte Strohdach des Partschunerhofes hervor. Daselbst saß vor Zeiten eine gar wunderliche Frau, welche in der nachbarlichen Gegend Hebammendienste versah, wenn man zu ihr gerade das Zutrauen hatte. Denn ein jeglicher mochte sie nicht rufen, weil die Alte unheimlich war und sich mit Schlangen und Würmern abgab, die in des Gehöftes Frieden ihr Heimwesen trieben. Darum hielten sie die Leute für eine Hexe.

Da fügte es sich einmal, dass einem Kleinhäusler in der Nachbarschaft die alte Esche vor dem Hause ein Kind in die Stube geschüttelt hat. Des Armen Hauswesen litt es nicht, sich weit umzuschauen, deshalb wandte er sich an die Partschunerin und nahm sie in Kundschaft. Weil es ihr Handwerk so mit sich brachte, begab sie sich des nächsten Morgens samt dem Kinde und dessen Gothel nach Unterinn zur Kindstaufe. Sie waren in die „dürchlen" Felswände gekommen, gedachten da eine Weile zu rasten und lagerten sich auf einer Steinplatte, die seit alters als Viertelsgemarkung an der Stelle stand. Die Hexe hatte über das Kind Gewalt, so lange dasselbe ungetauft war, daher stellte sie es nackt und barfuß auf den Stein und ließ die Hände von ihm. Und siehe da, das Kind stand fest auf den Füßen und hub auf dem Steine zu tanzen an, als wär's auf dem Kirchtag. Die Gothel, die das Wunder sah, erschrak heftig.

Nach einer Weile wickelte die Hebamme das Kind wieder ein; und sie trugen es dem Pfarrhofe zu, wo das Kind dann getauft wurde.

Auf dem Heimweg rasteten sie wieder in den Partschuner Wänden auf dem gleichen Stein. Da wollte die Hexe das Kind wieder zum Tanze aufstellen, aber weil dasselbe getauft war, hatte sie die Macht darüber verloren, und das Kind ließ die Füße zum Stehen nicht mehr an. Zornig packte es die Hebamme wieder ein und brachte es nach Hause.

›› Wissenswertes ‹‹

Gothel = Patin, dürchel = durchlöchert.

Von dem hier geschilderten Riesen erzählt eine andere Rittner Sage: Er war der letzte Wilde Mann dieser Gegend, ein bärenstarker Riese und Heide, der in einer Höhle in den Partschuner Felswänden gehaust haben soll. Ein Lindwurm, dick wie ein Baumstamm, bewachte laut Überlieferung den Zugang zur Höhle.

Im Glauben vieler Völker waren Steine Sitz einer außergewöhnlichen, geheimen Kraft. Bei dieser Steinplatte handelt es sich vermutlich um keinen gewöhnlichen Stein, da er laut Sage auch als Grenzstein galt.

Mancherorts war man überzeugt, dass Mütter ihren Kindern die Hexerei vererben könnten, indem sie ihre kleinen, noch ungetauften Kinder zum Tanzen anhielten.

Viele Hebammen waren Weise Frauen, die mit den Kräften der Natur aufs Engste verbunden waren. In dieser Sage zeigt sich dies auch durch den vertrauten Umgang mit Schlangen und Würmern. Die Schlange, in vielen Kulturen Symbol der Fruchtbarkeit und der Kindgeburt, gilt als eines der Hexenbegleittiere, mit welchem sie ihren Zauber ausübten. Mit Hilfe von Schlangen sollen sie demzufolge auch Geburtshemm- und Abtreibungszauber vorgenommen haben. Hebammen verstanden, ob ein Kind überlebensfähig war oder nicht, ob es „verdiente", aufgenommen zu werden oder nicht. Das Wort „Hebamme" leitet sich von „heben" ab, es bezieht sich auf das einst übliche Niederlegen auf den Erdboden und das In-die-Luft-Heben des Kindes. Ein Kind galt somit als dreifach geboren: von der leiblichen Mutter, von der Mutter Erde und von der Hebamme als deren Stellvertreterin, die das Kind nach genauer Untersuchung der Sippe bzw. der Familie übergab. Im germanischen Norden wurde das Kind nach der Geburt vor dem Kindesvater auf den Boden gelegt: Befahl er, dass ihm das Kind gereicht werde, bedeutete dies seine Entscheidung für die Kindesanerkennung.

Das Ritual der Erdanbindung des neugeborenen Kindes bzw. seiner Einbindung in die Schöpfung mittels des In-die-Luft-Hebens wurde oft als Opfer an teuflische Mächte interpretiert. Im „Hexenhammer" heißt es: „Niemand schadet dem katholischen Glauben mehr als die Hebammen. Denn wenn sie die Kinder nicht töten, dann tragen sie, gleich als wollten sie etwas besorgen, die Kinder aus der Kammer hinaus und opfern dieselben in die Luft hebend den Dämonen ..."

Von der Esche ist nicht nur in vielen großen Mythen die Rede, sondern auch in Aberglauben und Volksmedizin Tirols. An bestimmten Tagen im Jahr, z.B. zu Pfingsten und Johanni, wurde Eschenlaub an die Tiere verfüttert, da sie dadurch das ganze Jahr vor Krankheiten geschützt wären. In Kriegszeiten wurde mit Eschenlaub sogar das Mehl fürs Brotbacken gestreckt. Abgekochte Rinden, Blätter oder Wurzelteile wurden früher bei Schlangenbissen verwendet. Überhaupt war man überzeugt, dass Schlangen Eschenlaub meiden; so wurde Eschenlaub auch in Ställen ausgelegt. In Tirol war man aber auch der Meinung, dass die Verknorpelungen der Eschen von den Truten und Hexen, die gerne in den Astgabelungen sitzen, herrühren. Eschen stehen oft an früher als unheimlich geltenden Orten, wie z.B. dem Flaugenstöckl in St.Andrä bei Brixen. Aber auch als heiliger Baum ist sie in einer Legende aus dem Pustertal bekannt: Eine Esche verlor auch im Winter nicht ihr Laub, und als man genauer nachschaute, fand man in ihren Zweigen eine Marienstatue, die seitdem als „Unsere Liebe Frau" in Ehrenburg verehrt wird.

In der Nähe vieler alter Bauernhöfe befinden sich heute noch Eschen, aber die Bedeutung ihrer gesundheitlich-kultischen und bodensichernden Verwendung ist heute größtenteils in Vergessenheit geraten.

72

Von den Hexen auf dem Piperbühel

Der Piperbühel ist grad ober Riffian gelegen, ganz in der Nähe von Klobenstein, dort hat vor Zeiten der Galgen gestanden, welcher zum Gericht von Ritten gehörte. Dort in der Nähe findest du noch gar manches Stück von einer alten Mauer aus der Heidenzeit, und die Leute erzählen sich, dass sich hier einmal ein Heidentempel befunden habe. Auch der Name Siffian soll davon herrühren, so behaupten die studierten Herren. Das kann ich dir freilich nicht beweisen, unsereiner hat dieses gelernte Zeug nicht los. Aber eines weiß ich, nämlich dass es hier immer unheimlich ist; das hat mir meine Nahnl selig oft erzählt: „Wenn du dich nicht fürchtest, Hias, werd ich dir eine Räubergeschichte davon erzählen." →

Beim Staffler auf Siffian da ist einmal ein Knecht gewesen. Der geht nachts von Klobenstein nach Siffian. Wie er beim Piperbühel vorbeikommt, tanzen droben die Hexen, und eine Musik hört er, wie man sie nicht oft hören kann. In seinem Übermut ruft er auf den Bühel hinauf: „Hör Hatzes, spiel mir eins auf!" In diesem Moment ist auf der rechten Seite vor ihm eine schöne breite Straße, die nach Siffian hinunterführt. Und rechts und links hört er gar seltene Pfeiflein und eine Musik, sag ich dir, dass er Lust bekommt, mitzuhüpfen und zu tanzen. Aber da sind auch schon die Hexen über ihn her und haben ihn auf die breite Straße gezogen. Da hat er sich vielleicht gefürchtet, er hat sich losgerissen und geschrien: „Hilfe, zu Hilfe, die Hexen, die Hexen!" So weit hat er noch denken können, dass er nicht auf die Hexenstraße gegangen ist; er läuft und läuft, so schnell er nur kann, hinunter linkerhand über die richtige Straße. Die Hexen sind ihm hinterher, und wäre er nicht genug gesegnet gewesen, dann hätten sie ihn leicht bekommen. So aber ist er noch durchgekommen, aber der Schrecken ist ihm durch und durch gegangen, und lange Zeit hat er nachher liegen müssen.

›› Wissenswertes ‹‹

Nahnl = Großmutter, Hias = Abkürzung für Matthias, Hatzes = der Teufel.

Der Ritten ist außerordentlich reich an Hexensagen. Auch zahlreiche vorchristliche Fundorte befinden sich auf dieser Hochfläche. Diese Geschichte ist ein weiteres Beispiel dafür, dass Sagen oft an Plätzen angesiedelt sind, die auch aus archäologischer Sicht interessant sind. So wurden auf dem Piperbühel Funde aus der Späten Bronzezeit und der Eisenzeit getätigt. Eine Besonderheit stellen der Grabstein des Laséke und eine Birkenrute dar, beide mit eingravierten räto-etruskischen Schriftzeichen. Es wird vermutet, dass es sich bei diesem Birkenstab um einen Kultgegenstand zweier rätischer Priesterinnen/Heilerinnen handelt. Reitia, die paleovenetisch/rätische Göttin, deren Namen höchstwahrscheinlich aus religiösen Gründen nicht ausgesprochen werden durfte, galt als die Inhaberin der rätischen Schrift, die jener der etruskischen sehr ähnlich ist. Schriftzeichen wurden vor allem in Zusammenhang mit Kult und Magie gesetzt, denn die Schrift galt als magisch, und es wird vermutet, dass nur Priesterinnen und Priester schreiben konnten.

73

Die Hexen und der Schlichterknecht

Einmal ist der Oberschlichter Bauer in aller Finsternis durch den Wald ober Lengstein heimgeritten. Jetzt gelangte er auf den Birchboden, das ist ein alter und weitum gefürchteter Hexenplatz, dass mit ihm auf dem ganzen Ritten nur noch der „Rosswagen" um den Vorrang streitet. Richtig, da waren auch schon die Hexen versammelt. Unter einem alten Lärchbaum, der beinahe in der Mitte stand, lag ein gewaltiger Stein; darauf wurde gesotten und gebraten, dass dem Schlichter der Duft verlockend in die Nase stieg. Und um den

Stein herum tanzten alte und junge Hexen, dass es klapperte wie von Totenbeinen; dazu ward gesungen und eine feine Musik gemacht. Auf der Lärche tanzten allerlei Lichter auf und nieder. →

Wie die Hexen den Schlichter daherreiten sahen, machten sie sich um ihn her zu schaffen und lockten ihn in ihre Mitte. Da schallte eine Stimme vom Steine herüber: „Spiel auf, Hatzes!" Denn die Musik war für den Augenblick verstummt. Noch zweimal wiederholte sich dieser Ruf, und nun wurden die Hexen derart unverschämt, dass sie den Schlichter vom Rosse herabzogen, während die Spielleute ein neues Stücklein anhuben. Da war seinem Geduldfasse der Boden ausgeschlagen, er raffte einen knorrigen Prügel, der auf dem Boden lag, auf und schrie: „Ja, spiel nur auf, Hatzes, der Tanz kann losgeh'n!" Sodann sprang er auf den Stein zu und hieb fluchend und wetternd um sich, dass der ganze Spuk auseinanderstob, wie wenn der Sturm dreingefahren wäre. Im nächsten Augenblicke saß er wieder auf seinem Ross und sprengte sausend über den Boden und durch den Wald seinem unten liegenden Hofe zu. Ihm aber jagten mit wildem Geschrei wie ein Bienenschwarm die Hexen nach.

Zum Glücke hatte der Schlichter bis zu seinem Gehöfte nicht mehr weit, und eben erblickte er das Gemäuer, als der wütende Haufen den Armen schon vom Ross zu ziehen begann. Da schauderte es ihn und er rief, was er vermochte, gegen sein Haus: „Macht auf! Um Gottes willen macht auf!" Der wilde Schwarm ließ aber von der Verfolgung nicht eher ab, als bis der Schlichter unter die Dachtraufe seines Hauses gelangt war. Über die Traufe geht aber die Gewalt der Hexen nicht mehr. Die Haustür stand mittlerweile auch schon offen, und nun war er sicher.

Die Leute glauben zwar, dass er trotz der Schnelligkeit seines Rosses verloren gewesen wäre; weil er aber ein wenig beduselt war, hätten die Hexen nicht volle Macht über ihn gehabt. Da stand nun der Schlichter, dem's brühwarm im Kopfe lag, in seiner Stube und erzählte fluchend, was alles da oben sich zugetragen. Darauf schlug des Schlichters Knecht zornig auf den Tisch und rief: „Des war mer a G'spiel! De Tuifl wear i amol osoalbn!" [„Das wär' mir ein Spiel! Diesen Teufelinnen werd ich's zeigen!"] Damit entriss er dem Bauern den Knotenstock und lief auf den Birchboden hinauf.

Wie da der Knecht vor dem Hexenkreis stand und seinen Knüttel fluchend hob, da fielen auch schon die Hexen über ihn her, warfen ihn zu Boden und drückten ihn mit solcher Gewalt rücklings in die Erde hinein, dass das Mal im Boden noch heut zu sehen ist. Den Leichnam aber trugen sie fort; niemand weiß, wohin. Daher gehen die Leute nur mit großer Scheu da vorüber, und wer bei Nacht über den Birchboden muss, weicht dem unheimlichen Grabe aus.

Der Lärchbaum aber, der dem Grabmal zunächst stand, legte sich einen grünen Kranz um, und der ward so breit und buschig, dass man ihn von weitem sehen konnte. Vor dem erschraken aber die Leute und es hieb einer den Kranz vom Stamme los. Alsbald wuchs aber ein neuer an derselben Stelle. Da schickten sie die Holzleute aus, den Baum umzuhauen. Aber es wuchs an der Stelle der gefällten eine junge Lärche empor, und die trägt wieder einen Kranz. Merkwürdig an der Sache ist aber noch, dass die zweite Lärche nur an die dreißig bis vierzig Jahre Wachstum zeigte; seitdem ist trotz der gesunden Waldluft Stillstand eingetreten, und wohl hundert Jahre sind abgelaufen, ohne dass der Baum weiter in die Höhe oder Breite gewachsen wäre.

Dachtraufe = Dachrinne, Hatzes = der Teufel

Auf dem sagenhaften Birchboden, heute unter dem Namen „Hexenbödele" bekannt, lebte einst auch eine Willeweis. Er ist ein gern besuchtes Naherholungsgebiet, doch in den letzten Jahren hat er infolge menschlicher Eingriffe an Ausstrahlung verloren. Auf der Lärche wächst ein riesiger „Hexenbesen", eine Wuchsanomalie, deren Ursache manche durch den Einfluss hoher Strahlungsintensität erklären. Am Baumstamm hängt seit langer Zeit ein Kruzifix. Bis vor wenigen Jahren war im Waldboden ein Flecken zu sehen, in welchem man die Umrisse des in den Boden gedrückten Knechtes zu sehen glaubte. In einiger Entfernung befindet sich auch eine Felsrutsche, somit handelt es sich bei diesem Ort um einen alten Kultplatz, vermutlich um einen Frauenkultort. Die Tatsache, dass laut Sage dieser Platz ein Treffpunkt für Hexen und daher für Männer gefährlich war, erhärtet diese Vermutung. Ein anderes wichtiges Element dieser Sage ist das Feuer sowie das Kochen auf einem Stein. Feuerrituale fanden vor allem zu bestimmten Zeitpunkten im Jahr statt, wie beispielsweise der Tagundnachtgleiche und der Sommersonnwende. Das Braten und Kochen mit im Feuer erhitzten Steinen hat sich von der Steinzeit über Antike und Mittelalter bis in die Neuzeit erhalten. Diese Methode ist sogar älter als das Kochen über dem Feuer: Glutheiße Steine wurden in die Flüssigkeit gegeben, die dadurch erhitzt und gekocht wurde. Das Kochen und Zubereiten von Speisen war außerdem ein wichtiges gemeinschaftliches Ritual.

74

Die Hexenfahrt

Ähnliches, wie es eine Höttinger Sage kündet, wird auch im Paznauntale erzählt. Ein Weib im Hofe Moos, die Bäuerin selbst soll es gewesen sein, schlich nächtlicherweile von des Mannes Seite, den sie schlafend wähnte. Er aber war wach, schlich der Bäuerin nach und sah, wie sie mit der Hexensalbe sich bestrich, und hörte sie dann die bekannten Hexenfahrworte aussprechen: „Oben hinaus und nirgends an!", und flugs flog sie davon. Gleich tat der Mann es ihr nach, strich sich, sprach das Zauberwort und ward im Hui durch die Luft auf einen Hexenboden entrückt, den ein Palast voll Pracht und Glanz schmückte, den Tanz und Lustbarkeit erfüllte, in dem die Tische mit Wein und Speisen sich unter der Last der Geräte bogen. Der Kreis zahlreich versammelter Hexenweiber zog den Mann in seine Wirbel, an seine Tische, und er tanzte mit und sah sich köstlich bewirtet. Sein Weib bot ihm Kuchen dar, davon nahm und aß der Mann, aber er schmeckte wie Judenmatzen, war ohne Salz und Schmalz. Der Mann hatte etwas Salz in seiner Tasche, das streute er auf und aß und sagte: „Das Salz ist doch eine herrliche Gottesgabe!" Da krachte es um ihn, als berste der Berg, Lichter und Feuer erloschen, alles schwand, und der Mann saß allein auf einem Felsen in öder, finsterer Wildnis, und als es Tag wurde, kannte er sich doch nicht aus in der Gegend und konnte auch nicht vom Felsen herab. Er wartete bis zur nächsten Nacht, frierend, hungrig und durstig. Da erschien die Gesellschaft wieder, da war alles wie vorher, und der Mann bat seine Frau, ihn nicht abermals alleinzulassen. Als der Hexensabbat beendet war, nahm sie ihn mit, führte ihn daheim auf den Mist und wollte ihm einen Eid des Schweigens abnehmen, dafür ihn aber in das Hexenbündnis aufnehmen.

Er sollte sagen: „Ich trete auf diesen Mist und schwöre ab dem Herrn Jesu Christ."

Er aber sprach: „Ich trete auf diesen Mist, und dich hinein, Luder, das du bist!", nahm den ersten besten Knüttel, schlug die Hexe tot und trat sie, wie sie war, in den Düngerhaufen hinein.

›› Wissenswertes ‹‹

Dem Salz wird von vielen Völkern seit jeher sowohl erhaltende als auch reinigende Kraft zugeschrieben; es wurde als konservierendes und kraftspendendes Mittel verwendet und diente zur Abwehr gegen alles Böse. Auch in abergläubischen Handlungen werden Salz und Brot, beide kostbar und begehrt, oft zusammen genannt und verwendet.

Bereits die mythischen Riesinnen der Edda beherrschten das Mahlen von Gold und von Salz, dies weist auf den einstigen großen Stellenwert des Salzes hin. In vielen alten Kulturen hatte Salz eine große kultische Bedeutung, so als Opfer für die Götter, bei Feiern und beim Beschließen von Vereinbarungen und Verträgen. Vor allem die germanischen Volksstämme schrieben dem Salz eine wichtige Rolle bei ihren Kulthandlungen zu.

Die Salzgewinnung erfolgte bei ihnen u.a. auch durch das Auskochen von salzhaltigem Flusswasser in einem Salzkessel. Jakob Grimm schließt nicht aus, dass diese kultische Tätigkeit vermutlich eine Aufgabe von Frauen/Priesterinnen war und dadurch in späteren Zeiten zum Bild der kesselrührenden Hexe geführt hat. Auch in der christlichen Religion (z.B. Salzweihung, -opferung und -verbrennung) und in Volks- und Aberglauben wurde später die Heiligkeit des Salzes übernommen, wenn auch mit einer neuen Bedeutung: Nun wird es zur Abwehr von Hexen und Dämonen verwendet. Demzufolge schützte beispielsweise das Tragen von Salz in den Kleidern vor dem bösen Blick; Neugeborene wurden in Salzwasser gebadet; Salz in Milcheimer und in den Butterfässern schützt vor dem Verhexen, und um den Teufel zu vertreiben, muss man eine Prise davon über die linke Schulter werfen u.v.m.

In den Tiroler Sagen hat Salz eine ambivalente Bedeutung: In manchen Erzählungen unternehmen Hexen weite Flugreisen, um Salz zu bekommen; andere erzählen, dass dämonische Wesen, allen voran der Teufel, das den Menschen heilige Salz so sehr verachten, dass am Hexensabbat alle Speisen salzlos zubereitet und gegessen werden; dies ist auch aus dem sibirischen Schamanismus bekannt. Auch Brot fehlt bei den Hexengelagen.

75

Der Hexentanz auf den Gandellen

Auf den Gandellen liegt ein großer Stein, der im Munde der Talbewohner Hexenstein heißt. Er hat den Namen daher, weil seit undenklichen Zeiten auf ihm die Vorsteherin der Hexenzunft wohnt. Sie ist ein uraltes, hässliches Weib mit bösen Augen, blauen Lippen und struppigen Haaren. In der Hand führt sie einen stumpfgekehrten Besen und ein weißgrauer Kittel ist ihr Kleid.

Will sie ihren Sitz verlassen, so schmiert sie die Sohlen mit der Hexensalbe, was sie auch tut, wenn sie ihre Schwestern an Donnerstagen abends zusammenruft. Denn wenn

sie mit dieser Salbe bestrichen ist, leuchtet sie fernhin wie ein brennender Pechkranz, und auf dieses Zeichen kommen von allen Höhen und Bergen blaue Flämmlein herbei. Das sind ihre Schwestern und Gesellinnen, die von allen Seiten ihrer Meisterin zueilen. Ist es Mitternacht, so gibt die Alte das Hexenzeichen, und flugs ist das ganze Hexenvolk auf den Gandellen versammelt und harrt des Befehles. Da winkt sie und nun beginnt der Hexentanz, wozu Katzen aufgeigen. Pfeilschnell schießen die Unholdinnen hin und her.

Einmal sah eine Magd dieses Treiben, und es gefiel ihr derart, dass sie lange Zeit am Fenster stand und zuschaute. Da kam plötzlich ein bildschönes Fräulein herangeflogen und lud die Dirn zum Tanze ein. Dieser gefiel der Antrag so gut, dass sie gleich ihr schönstes Gewand anzog und auf Befehl der Fremden sich die Zöpfe löste. Dann nahm das Fräulein aus einem Büchslein, das sie an der Brust trug, eine Salbe und reichte sie der Dirn mit dem Bedeuten, sich alsogleich die Füße zu schmieren. Kaum hatte sie dieses getan, so fühlte sie sich federleicht, und lustig trug es sie durch den Kamin hinauf und durch die kalte Nachtluft zum tollen Feste. Munter tanzte die Dirn. In der Mitte des Platzes stand ein Tisch, worauf guter Wein und die herrlichsten Speisen standen.

So ging es toll und voll die ganze Nacht zu, bis der Morgen andämmerte. Dann wurden plötzlich die Gesichter blass und gelb, und Fieberfrost schüttelte die verzerrten Glieder. Die Hexenmeisterin gab das Zeichen mit ihrem Besen, und – husch, husch – waren alle blitzschnell von dannen gefahren! Sie hatten höchste Zeit gehabt, denn alsbald läutete die Aveglocke. Die Magd befand sich mutterseelenallein auf den Gandellen, und die köstlichen Speisen hatten sich in stinkenden Dünger verwandelt.

›› Wissenswertes ‹‹

Dieser „Hexenstein“ liegt immer noch inmitten einer großen, ebenen, teilweise als Viehweide genützten Wiese, „Gandellen“ genannt, unterhalb von St. Leonhard im Passeier und es erscheint schon etwas ungewöhnlich, dass er, trotz besserer Nutzung der Wiese, von den Grundbesitzern nicht entfernt wurde. – Mit der Hexen- oder Flugsalbe, auch unter dem Namen Buhlsalbe, Hexenschmiere, Schlafsalbe, Unguenti Sabbati und anderen Namen bekannt, sollen sich die Hexen eingerieben haben, um zum Hexensabbat zu fliegen. Ob ihre Verwendung wirklich so stark verbreitet war, ist nicht nachweisbar, zumal dies häufig von grausam gefolterten oder verängstigten Frauen erzählt wurde. In diesen Geständnissen berichten Frauen auch von der Verwendung gräulicher Zutaten wie dem Fett neugeborener oder ungetaufter Kinder, Fledermausflügeln, Krötenzungen, Regelblut u.a. – Bei den Inhaltsstoffen der Flugsalben handelt es sich um halluzinogene Wirkstoffe alkaloidhaltiger Pflanzen, v.a. von Nachtschattenpflanzen, von Schierling, Alraune (Mandragora), Stechapfel, Tollkirsche und anderen hochgiftigen Pflanzen. Für eine möglichst rasche Körperaufnahme wurde sie auf empfindliche Stellen wie Handflächen oder Fußsohlen, Innenflachen der Oberschenkel, Pulsstellen, Stirn usw. aufgetragen. Laut Aussagen komme es zu einem prickelnden Gefühl auf der Haut, es fühle sich an, als würde ein Federkleid wachsen. Auch Sehstörungen und Herzrasen sowie Halluzinationen und Erlebnisse sexueller Natur sind die Folge. Auf dem Höhepunkt fällt man in einen Schlaf und erlebt wilde Flüge. Dies führte zu der Vorstellung, auf einem Besenstiele o.ä. zu reiten, mit anderen Hexen zu feiern und wilde sexuelle Spiele zu treiben. Einen Selbstversuch soll der bekannte Volkskundler Will-Erich Peuckert 1960 nach einem Rezept aus dem Jahre 1568 aus der „Magia Naturalis“ des Italieners Giambattista Porta durchgeführt haben. Die Hexensalbe war keine neue Erfindung, sondern bereits aus antiken Überlieferungen bekannt: So soll sich die Göttin Hera mit Ambrosia, der Nahrung der Götter, eingesalbt haben, um zu Zeus auf den Idaberg zu fliegen. Salben waren früher aber auch häufig verwendete Heilmittel. Die Pappelsalbe beispielsweise galt als universelles Heilmittel, ähnlich dem heutigen Aspirin, und wird seit dem 15. Jh. in vielen Kräuterbüchern angeführt. Pappelknospen wurden oft als Ingredienz der Hexensalbe genannt.

Die Fähigkeit der Tierverwandlung wird allen Hexen zugesprochen. Die Katze ist das dabei am häufigsten zitierte Tier. Ihr wurde die Eigenschaft nachgesagt, geheime Kräfte zu kennen und Verbindungen zu dem Übersinnlichen zu haben. Dabei war sie bereits in der Antike Begleittier vieler Göttinnen bzw. ein heiliges Tier. Aus der Mythologie Ägyptens ist die katzenköpfige Göttin Bastet überliefert. Hier galten Katzen als heilig, sie wurden sogar einbalsamiert. Die nordische Freyja fuhr im Frühling auf einem Katzen- oder Luchsgespann durch die Luft; auch Diana wird oft in Begleitung von Katzen abgebildet, und Durga/Kali, die große indische Göttin und Hexenkönigin mit roten Augen und langer „Hexenzunge“ reitet auf einem Tiger. Man vermutet, dass durch die ab dem 9. Jh. eingesetzte Wanderung der aus Asien stammenden Zigeuner nach Europa, welche Kali als ihre große Göttin verehrten, auch Einiges vom Hexenmythos dieser großen Göttin nach Europa gebracht wurde. Den Zigeunerinnen wird auch heute noch die Kunst des Wahrsagens, früher von Hexen und Zauberinnen ausgeübt, zugeschrieben. Eine „Nachtfahrende“ auf einer Tigerkatze ist auch am Schleswiger Dom (um 1300) abgebildet.

76

Oh Mander, husch, husch!

Jährlich zieht von Schnals herüber Mitte Juni eine Herde von über tausend Schafen auf die große Alm zu Gurgl auf die Weide und kehrt im September wieder dahin zurück. Einmal sind Schnalser in Hemdärmeln nach Gurgl gekommen, um ihre Schafe wieder heimzuholen. In der Nähe von Obergurgl begegnete ihnen eine alte Hexe, die war im warmen Sonnenschein mit dickwollenem Wintergewand angetan und zitterte vor Kälte, dass ihr Mund nur so papperte. Als sie die Schnalser sah, hauchte sie in die dürren Hände und rief: „O Mander, husch, husch!“ Die Schnalser lachten. Am anderen Tage ging der Schaftrieb richtig über den Ferner, wurde aber von einem Schneesturm überfallen, und 1300 Schafe gingen zugrunde nebst den Schnalsern, die dabei waren, bis auf zwei der Letzteren.

›› Wissenswertes ‹‹

Bereits im 14. Jh. wurde zwischen den Bauern von Schnals im Vinschgau und Vent im Ötztal ein Weiderechtsvertrag abgeschlossen, demzufolge die Schnalser Bauern ihre Schafe in den Sommermonaten im Niedertal im Ötzal weiden lassen dürfen. Auch heute noch werden ca. 2000 Schafe Anfang Juni über das Hoch- und Niederjoch auf die jenseits der Grenze liegenden Sommerweiden getrieben und erst im September wieder zurückbegleitet. Diese Wanderung über Schnee und Eis ist für Tiere und Menschen lang und beschwerlich, bei Schlechtwetter auch gefährlich. Vor ca. 20 Jahren fielen an die 70 Schafe beim Übertrieb einem Schneesturm zum Opfer, eine weitere Tragödie mit 200 erfrorenen Schafen ist aus dem Jahre 1844 belegt. Ähnliche Vorfälle in noch früheren Zeiten sind nicht auszuschließen. Uralt ist der Übergang vom Schnals- ins Ötztal. An dem sich in der Nähe befindenden Hauslabjoch (Tisenjoch) wurde „Ötzi", der weltberühmte „Mann aus dem Eis", eine 5300 Jahre alte Gletschermumie, gefunden. Archäologische Fundstellen, uralte steinerne Pyramiden, Schalensteine und Menhire konnten in Jochnähe und entlang der Wegübergänge nachgewiesen werden.

Siehe hierzu das Buch „Wege der Schafe" von Hans Haid, erschienen bei Tyrolia/Athesia, 2008.

77

Die Romhottel

Vor ungefähr 200 Jahren lebte auf dem Ritten ein Weibermensch, das eine gewaltige Meisterin über die Hexen und ihren Zauber war und für die Hexerei wirksamen Gegenzauber verstand. Weil sie das wirksamste Zauberpulver in Rom zu holen pflegte, wo sie zwölfmal gewesen sein soll, nannten sie die Leute bloß „die Romhottel". Das römische Pulver aber gab ihr ein wälscher Einsiedler, der nicht weit von Rom in der Abgeschiedenheit hauste und den die Hottel besuchte. Mit diesem roten Rompulver konnte sie alle Krankheiten an Leuten und Tieren vertreiben und die Menschen vor Unglück schützen. Das Pulver half namentlich gegen Hexenzauber, gegen das „Vermeinböckl" bei Leuten und Vieh; man musste es einnehmen, niemand durfte es aber mit den Händen anrühren. Ihren Zauber hatte die Hottel in Rom gelernt, und dass er nicht mehr von ihr weichen konnte, musste sie stets schwarzes Wachs, St. Oswaldkügelchen, einen Benediktenpfennig, Blätter vom Ölzweig, ein Agnus Dei und zwei St. Oswaldbrötchen in ihrem Sacke haben. Sie hatte aus Rom auch geweihte Palmblätter mitgenommen, und während sie den von den Hexen Bezauberten das Pulver, gemischt mit geweihtem Salz, auf einem St. Oswaldbrot eingab, wurden diese Palmblätter verbrannt und damit die behexte Person oder das „vermeinte" Vieh geräuchert. Dazu gab das Weib in besonders hartnäckigen Fällen den Verhexten auch noch Johannissegen ein. Sie soll auf dem Ritten damit nach und nach alles Hexenwerk weggezaubert haben.

Wo einer Bäuerin das Butterschlägeln nicht gelingen wollte, und das kam bekanntlich sicher von den Hexereien, da holte man die Romhottel, und sie streute bloß ein wenig Rompulver auf den Rahm, dann war bald die schönste Butter vorhanden.

Wenn eine Kuh gestockte Milch gab, so half wieder die Hottel, und die Milch wurde den Hexenzauber los. Freilich, in solchen Fällen ging der böse Zauber vom Butterkübel oder von der Kuh auf sie selber über, aber das Pulver befreite sie bald wieder davon. Wenn der Hottel etwa das Pulver zu früh ausging, so war auch ein Mittel; sie schabte vom Altarstein des Hochaltars in der Sankt Andreaskirche zu Antlas mit einem Ochseneisen rotes Pulver ab, immer an Freitagen um neun Uhr vormittags und dort, wo der Kelch des Priesters stand, und dieses Pulver tat in weniger schwierigen Fällen auch seine Wirkung. Sie hatte auch noch ein drittes Zauberpulver, von weißer Farbe, das sie aus Maria Einsiedeln holte, welches auch zauber- und heilkräftig war. Dieses Pulver vertrieb zwar den Hexenzauber aus dem Butterkübel, dafür jedoch fuhr er in die Kühe, von denen der Rahm im Kübel herrührte. Nach neun Tagen aber vermochte das weiße Pulver auch das Vieh zu entzaubern. Wenn sich eines der vorgenannten Zauberpulver nicht bewähren wollte, so verbrannte die Romhottel das Vermeinkräutl und einige andere wie Johannis- und Eisenkraut, Hasel- und Wolfswurz, und mischte die Asche in das Pulver. Dann hielt ihm kein Hexenzauber mehr stand.

➤➤ Wissenswertes ➤➤

Laut Heyl soll es diese Frau tatsächlich in der Mitte des 18. Jh. gegeben und Gertraud Peintnerin, genannt Moserin, geheißen haben. Sie habe von Almosen gelebt und von dem, was sie durch ihre Mittel gegen angebliche Hexerei erworben habe. Einmal sei sie deshalb auch gefangen genommen worden, und nur durch die Intervention einer gewichtigen Persönlichkeit, die die alte Frau aufgrund ihrer Einfalt in Schutz nahm, sei sie nach drei Tagen Kerkerhaft wieder auf freien Fuß gesetzt worden.

In der Zeit der Hexenprozesse und in den darauf folgenden Jahrhunderten waren zahlreiche antidämonische Gegenmittel aus der Welt der christlichen Heiligen gebräuchlich. Besonders das Benediktuskreuz und der Benediktuspfennig spielten eine wichtige Rolle, denn der Hl. Benedikt galt u.a. als Schutzpatron gegen Zauberei und Vergiftung. Benediktskreuze wurden als Schutz vor Teufelswerk und Hexen, zum Schutze der Tiere, für gute, gesunde Milch und erfolgreiches Buttern eingesetzt. Der geweihte Benediktuspfennig wurde als Talisman bei Unfruchtbarkeit, zur Abwehr gegen Pest und Verzauberung getragen, oft auch an die Butterkübel gehängt. Auch der am Palmsonntag geweihte Palmwedel gilt als magisches Abwehrmittel gegen Gewitter (Wetterhexen) und Zauberei. Bereits in der Antike war der Ölzweig kultbehaftet (u.a. bei den Olympischen Spielen), und auch Christus wurde bei seinem Einzug in Jerusalem mit Ölzweigen begrüßt.

Der „Johannissegen" oder die „Johannisminne" ist der am Johannistag (27. Dezember) geweihte Wein. Er war früher in und außerhalb von Tirol eine Art Allheiltrank: Er wehrt Gefahren ab, erhält die eheliche Liebe (Brautsegen) und den häuslichen Frieden. Man trank ihn zur Abwehr vor Gefahren vor Reisen, vor allem aber bedeutete er Schutz vor Krankheit und Zauberei.

Brot galt früher als wirkungsvolles Abwehrmittel gegen alle Hexenmächte. Besonders den geweihten Gebildbroten wie dem Osterlamm (Agnus Dei) schrieb man eine besondere Kraft zu. Im gleichen Zusammenhang sind vermutlich die Oswaldkügelchen zu sehen. Der Hl. Oswald galt mancherorts als „Brotvater" und Patron der Kornschnitter und Mäher. Laut Volksglauben hatte er auch die Herrschaft über das Wetter. Man traute ihm sowohl die Vernichtung der Ernte durch Schlechtwetter als auch die Verhütung von Hagelschlag zu.

Schutz vor Hexenwerk boten auch die am Hochunserfrauentag (Maria Himmelfahrt, 15. August) geweihten Kräuter. Diese Weihe entstammt dem germanischen Göttinnenkult. Viele der im christlichen Strauß enthaltenen Kräuter waren einst den alten Göttinnen heilig. Neben verschiedenen bekannten Heilpflanzen waren mancherorts auch „Hexenkräuter" wie der Teufelsabbiß, die Weinraute, die Wolfsmilch, das Johannis- und das Eisenkraut u.a. enthalten.

Das Johanniskraut (Hypericum perforatum), auch Jageteufel oder Teufelsflucht genannt, wurde gegen Zauberei und gegen den Teufel verwendet. Hält man ein Blatt dieser Pflanze gegen das Licht, erscheint es voll kleiner Löcher, daher der lateinische Name. Laut Sage handelt es sich um die Nadelstiche des Teufels, der aus Wut über die Macht, die das Kraut über ihn besaß, die Pflanze vernichten wollte. Den deutschen Namen hat die Pflanze von ihrem blutroten Saft, denn laut Legende ist sie aus dem Blute des enthaupteten Johannes entstanden. Bereits bei den Germanen war das Johanniskraut eine wichtige Heil- und Ritualpflanze.

Auch das Eisenkraut (Verbena officinalis), Sagen-, Druiden- oder Wunschkraut genannt, ist eine alte Kult- und Heilpflanze. Es wurde von den Galliern zum Weissagen und von den Germanen vor Kriegsbeginn und bei Friedensabschlüssen geopfert. Die einst heilige Pflanze wurde, wie viele andere, in späteren Jahrhunderten zu einem „Anti-Hexenkraut".

Die giftige Haselwurz (Asarum europeum), auch Brechwurz, Hexenrauch, Teufelsklaue, u.a.m. genannt, ist bereits seit dem Altertum als Arzneipflanze und Abtreibungsmittel bekannt.

Der Gelbe (Wolfs-Eisenhut) und der Blaue Eisenhut (Sturmhut), lat. Aconitum, früher Wolfswurz genannt, ist die giftigste Pflanze Europas. Sie enthält Aconitin, eines der stärksten Pflanzengifte: Bereits die Einnahme von 1,5 mg können innerhalb kürzester Zeit durch Atemlähmung und Herzversagen zum Tode führen. Schon im Altertum wurde dieses Gift benutzt. So soll der römische Kaiser Claudius von seiner Frau Agrippina damit ermordert worden sein. In den Hexensalben wurde die Pflanze nur äußerlich verwendet, sie erzeugte angeblich das Gefühl, ein Feder- oder Fellkleid zu tragen.

Das Schaben und Auskratzen von Gesteinspulver von heiligen Mauern war früher weit verbreitet. Solchem Pulver schrieb man besondere Kraft und Schutz zu. Als Beispiel seien die Kirche von Meransen (hier wurde aus der großen Zehe des Hl. Christophorus an der Außenmauer geschabt) und der Dom von Trient (Arche des Hl. Vigilius) genannt. Auch Schalensteinen wird eine solche Verwendung zugesprochen. Ebenso scheint dies in der Kirche des Hl. Andreas zu Antlas bei Lengstein der Fall gewesen zu sein. Auf dem Altarstein ist linkerseits eine kleine Mulde sichtbar, und an zwei Stellen scheint eine nachträgliche Ausbesserung mit dunkler Farbe erfolgt zu sein, die sich deutlich vom rötlichen Altarstein abhebt. Auch ein darin eingekerbtes Kreuzzeichen ist deutlich zu sehen.

Kleine Schabfigürchen sind aus Maria Einsiedeln bekannt.

78

Die Schlechtwetterpfanne

Zwei Passeirer Bauern kehrten von einer Wallfahrt in ihre Heimat zurück. Der Weg führte sie an einer armseligen Hütte vorbei, und weil sie müde und hungrig waren, gingen sie hinein. Es war aber nur ein Mädchen in der Hütte. Sie fragten das Kind, ob die Mutter nicht daheim sei. „Nein", antwortete das Kind, „die Mutter ist auf dem Felde." Ja, ob sie dann nicht bald komme? „Nein, vor Abend nicht." Da sagten die Bauern zum Mädchen: „Wir sind müde und hungrig, könnten wir nicht ein wenig Milch bekommen und uns eine Milchsuppe kochen? Brot darein hast du wohl auch?" Das Mädchen gab ihnen gerne das Verlangte und sie gingen alle drei in die Küche, wo die Bauern eine Pfanne herabnahmen, die Milch darin zu sieden. „Nein", sagte das Kind, „diese Pfanne lasse ich nicht her; die braucht die Mutter, wenn sie schlechtes Wetter macht. Nehmt nur eine andere!" Die

Bauern aber verstanden es, das Mädchen auf gute Manier zur Küche hinauszubringen, und wollten die Schlechtwetterpfanne probieren. Sie nahmen selbige herunter, gossen die Milch hinein und stellten sie übers Feuer. Wie die Milch in der Pfanne sich rührte, stiegen schon schwarze Wetterwolken den Himmel herauf. Bald darauf fängt die Milch in der Pfanne zu wallen und zu brodeln an, draußen wird es ganz finster und unheimlich und es hebt zu blitzen an. Endlich als die Milch zischend aufkochte und über die Pfanne schlug, krachte draußen ein Donnerschlag nach dem andern ganz entsetzlich und rauschte der Schauer zur Erde, als wäre das Ende der Welt da. Das Mädchen lief in die Küche und schrie die Bauern an, sie hätten nun doch die Schlechtwetterpfanne genommen und sie sollten nur schauen, wie sie mit heiler Haut davonkämen. Wenn ihre Mutter sie antreffe, werde es ihnen nicht gut ergehen. Und wie sie erschrocken durch das Fenster schauten, gewahrten sie die Alte, die zornig mit geballten Fäusten der Hütte zulief. Die Bauern schauten, durch die Hintertür davonzukommen und liefen, was ihre Beine konnten, und fürchteten doch, im nächsten Augenblick die Hexenkralle im Genick zu spüren.

›› Wissenswertes ‹‹

Schadenszauber, unter anderem das Hexen von Schlechtwetter, war eine der Hauptanschuldigungen gegen verdächtigte Hexen. Sie bedienten sich dabei des Analogiezaubers: Bereits wenige Tropfen Wassers genügten ihnen demnach, um einen Wetterumsturz herbeizuführen. Mit dem Finger oder einer Rute wurde in einem Gefäß (Kessel, Pfanne, Glas), in einer Wasserpfütze oder einem Bach gerührt, der entsprechende Zauberspruch rezitiert, und innerhalb kürzester Zeit kam es zu Regen oder Gewitter.

Dasselbe Prinzip der Analogie wird auch im jamaikanischen Voodoozauber angewendet; es findet sich aber auch in Heilverfahren wie in der Homöopathie wieder („similia similibus curentur") oder in der Kräuterheilkunde, wenn Heilkräutern aufgrund ihrer Ähnlichkeit mit bestimmten Körperteilen eine entsprechende Heilwirkung zugeschrieben wird (Signaturenlehre), z.B. dem Augentrost. – Rituale der Regenbeschwörung sind auch von den Etruskern und den Mayas überliefert und werden heute noch bei den Aborigines und weiteren naturnahen Völkern praktiziert.

Dass Hexen ihre Kinder, vor allem Mädchen, oder auch Enkelkinder in ihre Künste einweihten, davon war man während der Inquisitionszeit überzeugt. Aus diesem Grunde fielen auch Kinder dem Hexenwahn zum Opfer und wurden mit ihren Müttern verbrannt. Andererseits ist die Weitergabe dieses Wissens von Mutter auf Kind durchaus denkbar, so wie Eltern auch heutzutage ihre Lebenserfahrungen und Kenntnisse ihren Kindern weitergeben.

79

Die Sage vom Wodansbrunnen

In alter Zeit lebte ein Bauer, der hatte drei Töchter, aber keinen Sohn. Die Töchter wollten alle drei den väterlichen Hof erben, der Vater aber konnte nach altem Recht nur einer den Hof ungeteilt überlassen. Darüber herrschte bei den Schwestern immer Zank und Streit. Um dem Streit ein Ende zu machen, kaufte der Vater noch zwei andere Höfe, übergab dann allen drei Schwestern einen Hof mit der Verpflichtung, dass alle drei heiraten müssten; sollte aber kein Sohn zur Welt kommen, müssten alle drei Schwestern die Höfe einem entfernten Verwandten überlassen.

Nun traf es sich, dass die Jüngste zwar Kinder hatte, aber alles nur Mädchen; die anderen zwei hatten überhaupt keine Kinder. Alle drei waren darüber untröstlich, sie machten verschiedene Gelübde und Wallfahrten, aber es war alles vergebens, es kam kein männlicher Erbe. Da entschlossen sie sich, zu einer alten Wahrsagerin zu gehen, die auch gleichzeitig als Hexe verschrien war. Dieser trugen sie nun ihr Anliegen vor, und die Alte gab ihnen folgenden Rat: Die Jüngste, die zwar Kinder hatte, aber keinen Buben, musste vom heiligen „Lerch", der oberhalb des Wodansbrunnens stand, einen Zweig abbrechen, denselben in das Wasser des Wodansbrunnens tauchen, den Zweig dann oberhalb der Bettstatt aufhängen, aber mit der Spitze nach oben, gleichzeitig sollte sie abends vor dem Schlafengehen einen Schluck von dem Wasser des Wodansbrunnens trinken. Die anderen beiden Schwestern, die kein Kind hatten, mussten sich täglich abends nach Sonnenuntergang im Wodansbrunnen baden und zwar vier Wochen lang. Dieser Rat wurde von allen drei Schwestern genau befolgt. Nach einem Jahr gebaren alle drei Schwestern drei gesunde Knaben, worüber natürlich große Freude herrrschte. Die Leute der damaligen Zeit glaubten bestimmt, dass die drei Schwestern mit dem Teufel einen Vertrag abgeschlossen hätten.

Um das Jahr 1712 soll der damalige Kurat vom Fuirer-Bauern verlangt haben, dass er den Wodansbrunnen umnenne, denn was die Leute von ihm glauben würden, sei Aberglaube. Dem soll sich die Schwester des Bauern, welche Hebamme war und das Wasser gegen Frauenleiden mit Erfolg gebrauchen ließ, energisch widersetzt haben.

Diese Sage wurde dem Brixner Arzt und Heimatforscher Ignaz Mader vom Fuirer-Bauern Josef Oberhofer aus Pfunders mitgeteilt. Demzufolge wäre der Wodansbrunnen in den Namen „Waldbrunnen" umgetauft worden, der sich auf seinem Grund befindet. Eine seiner Vorfahrinnen war eine berühmte Hebamme, die in Pfunders ein Bad betrieben hat, das nicht nur von leidenden Frauen aus Pfunders, sondern auch aus der Umgebung aufgesucht worden ist. In Pfunders gab es bis vor kurzem noch eine zweite, reichlich fließende Quelle, und zwar im Moserfeld beim Parthof, westlich der Kirche gelegen. Es könnte sein, das das von der Hebamme benötigte Wasser von dort zum Zuhaus des Fuirer, wo sie „praktizierte", geleitet wurde. Bedauerlicherweise gibt es diese Quelle nicht mehr, ein Unternehmen hat hier angeblich Abfallschlacken deponiert und darüber den Sportplatz des Dorfes errichten lassen. Franz Oberhofer (geboren 1934), Sohn des erzählenden Josef Oberhofer und selbst in Besitz zahlreicher Anekdoten und Geschichten, war so freundlich, der Buchautorin M.F. den Standort des mittlerweile abgerissenen Hebammenhäusls, in welchem er selbst noch eine Zeitlang gelebt hatte, und den „Waldbrunnen" zu zeigen. Diesen Brunnen hätten früher auch viele Geistliche und Klosterfrauen aufgesucht, die, wie er sagt, „wegen ihres viel zu guten Essens oft Probleme mit dem Scheißen hatten. Aber das Waldbrunnenwasser hat alles wieder in Ordnung gebracht."

Der Sagenforscher Zingerle ist der Auffassung, dass aus den Martinsbräuchen Wotan herausblickt, da beide mit Pferd und Mantel in Erscheinung treten; tatsächlich ist die Kirche von Pfunders dem Hl. Martin geweiht.

80

Die drei Schwestern

Im Pertschollhofe lebten drei Schwestern, bildhübsche Dirnen, deren jede aber mit einem Gebresten behaftet war. – Die Älteste war taub, die Zweitälteste stumm und die Jüngste blind. Das war für die Eltern ein großes Kreuz, denn trotz ihres Wohlstandes und der Schönheit ihrer mannbaren Töchter, wollte sich kein Freier für sie finden.
Da traf es sich, dass der Höfler ein Paar Ochsen auf den Markt nach Bozen trieb und ein schönes Stück Geld dafür erlöste, so dass sein Leibgurt von harten Talern strotzte.
Ehe er sich auf den Heimweg begab, wollte er für die Seinen noch einen Marktkram kaufen. Er schlenderte dem Platze zu, wo Bude an Bude sich reihte, und sah da ein mit bunten Tüchern behangenes Gerüste, worauf ein rotbefracktes Männchen mit mächtiger Perücke und zierlichem Degen an der Seite stand, das sich für einen Wunderdoktor ausgab und sich rühmte, jedes Gebresten, heiße es, wie es wolle, durch sein Geheimmittel heilen zu können.

Flugs kaufte er sich für einen blanken Taler ein Fläschchen von dem Wunderbalsam, der nach der ausdrücklichen Versicherung des gelehrten Doktors die Tauben hörend, die Blinden sehend und die Stummen redend machen könne. – Damit wanderte er getrost nach seinem Berghofe zurück.

Die beiden älteren Schwestern nahmen sofort von der wunderkräftigen Essenz, während die Jüngste, die klügste von ihnen, damit noch zögerte, weil sie erst den Erfolg bei den anderen abwarten wollte. – Nun zeigte sich, dass der fremde Doktor tatsächlich Wunder bewirkte, jedoch ein Schalk und boshafter Zauberer war, der den Teufel mit dem Luzifer austrieb: Die Taube war hörend, dafür aber stumm geworden, und die Stumme hatte die Sprache erlangt, war dafür aber stocktaub geworden, und so hatten die beiden eigentlich nur ihre Gebresten gewechselt. Die Jüngste ließ nun den Balsam erst recht unberührt, denn sie dachte sich: „Was nützt es mir, wenn ich sehend – und dafür vielleicht krumm oder gar lahm werde!"

Eines Tages sagte die Jüngste zu ihren Schwestern: „Heute ist Johann der Täufer – da schlagen die Buben den Mädlen ihre Scheiben! Wir wollen nach dem Burgstall hinaufgehen, wo die Almer das große Sonnwendfeuer aufmachen – vielleicht, dass für uns auch ein Scheibel fliegt!"

Da wanderten die drei Arm in Arm den Höhen des Burgstall zu.

Als sie in der Mitte des Waldes zu einer Stelle kamen, wo die Wege sich kreuzten, saß im Halbdunkel der Dämmerung ein altes Weib auf einem Steine da, dass ihnen die welke Hand entgegenstreckte und ein Almosen heischte.

Die beiden Älteren gaben nur je ein paar Pfennige und wollten mit einem kurzen Gruß vorüberschreiten, da ihnen die Begegnung unheimlich schien. Die Jüngste jedoch, die, wie gesagt, die Klügste war, reichte der Alten ein blankes Silberstück hin und scherzte: „Der Stimme nach ist das die Kräuter-Nanne, die hier in der Nähe ihre Hütte hat, und weil heute ihr Tag ist, so soll sie sich was Gutes antun, und uns damit, indem sie uns von unsern Gebresten heilt, obendrein zu rechtschaff'nen Freiern verhilft!"

„Du verlangst viel in einem Atem!", sagte die Alte, „Doch wir wollen sehen, was sich machen lässt." Drauf fragte sie, ob die Dirnen schon irgendwelche Mittel gebraucht hätten, um sich ihrer Gebrechen zu entledigen. Als die Blinde nun erzählte, wie es den beiden Schwestern mit dem Balsam des fremden Wunderdoktors ergangen war, schüttelte die Alte bedenklich den Kopf und sagte, zu den Letzteren sich wendend: „Da seid ihr schlimm beraten gewesen! Ich will nun schauen, dass die Sache wieder in die Gräde kommt, doch wie die Bezahlung, so die Arbeit!"

Darauf berührte sie dieselben mit ihrem Krückenstabe und murmelte zwischen den Zähnen: „Hock, hock, hock – im alten Stock!" worauf die Älteste wieder taub und die andere stumm war. – Zur Jüngsten aber sagte sie: „Wenn ein feines Herrlein dir begegnen und dich fragen sollt: ‚Wo hinaus?', so gib ihm eine rechte und gereimte Antwort, und es werden dir die Augen aufgehen und du wirst von deiner Blindheit geheilt sein!"

Als die drei Schwestern zum Almgatter kamen, standen drei junge, schöne und vornehm gekleidete Herren da, und der erste fragte die Älteste: „Erlaube, schönes Kind – wo hinaus?" Die hatte aber, weil sie taub war, nichts gehört und ging fürbass.

Der Zweite vertrat der andern den Weg und fragte noch dringender: „Sag mir doch – wo hinaus?" Die hätte ihm gerne geantwortet, allein sie vermochte es nicht, denn sie war ja stumm, und so eilte sie ihrer Schwester nach.

Da verschwanden die beiden Herren, als hätte sie der Wind davongetragen.

Der Dritte näherte sich alsdann der Jüngsten, und, den Arm traulich um sie schlingend, flüsterte er ihr ins Ohr: „Herzallerliebste! Du sagst mir doch – wo hinaus?“

Diese war mit der Antwort nicht verlegen und erwiderte kurz und bündig: „Ei wo sonst, als in dein Haus!“

In diesem Augenblicke hatte sich das feine Herrlein in einen stämmigen, bildsauberen Berglerburschen verwandelt, und die Dirne, die nun plötzlich sehend geworden war, schritt an seiner Seite froh und seelenvergnügt dem Burgstall zu, wo bereits lichterloh ein lustig Feuer brannte und ein munt'res Völklein versammelt war.

Die beiden gesellten sich zu den anderen, und er ließ ihr zu Ehren die erste Scheibe fliegen, wobei er einen hellen Juchzer ausstieß und das G'satzl anstimmte:

„Des Scheibl schlag i der Liebsten mein,
und steigen soll's bis in den Himmel hinein,
wem's epper nit recht ist, der soll's sagen,
dem will i ein and'res Scheibel schlagen!“

Wenige Monde darauf waren die beiden ein glückliches Hochzeitspaar.

Damit aber die Freude eine ungetrübte sei, ließ sich die Kräuter-Nanne bewegen, auch die Schwestern von ihren Gebresten zu heilen, die dann auch bald Männer nach ihrem Sinn und Herzen bekamen.

›› Wissenswertes ‹‹

In dieser märchenähnlichen Schlernsage wird auf humorvolle Weise auf die einst herumziehenden Quacksalber und Kurpfuscher hingewiesen, deren teuer erkaufte Mittel zumeist ohne die erwünschte Wirkung blieben. – Der Burgstall am Schlern ist eine uralte heilige Kult- und Brandopferstätte. Weiheopfer aus der Bronze- bis in die Römerzeit wurden hier gefunden. In der Sagenwelt ist der Schlern einer der berühmtesten Hexentanzplätze Südtirols. – Die Fähigkeiten der Hexe als Kräuterkundige, Heilerin und Beziehungsvermittlerin werden in dieser Sage von den Mädchen gerne in Anspruch genommen, auch wenn diese „Wertschätzung“ vermutlich nur der Feder des Autors entstammt. Der Johannistag (24. Juni) mit dem Brauch der Johannisfeuer ist an die Stelle der vorchristlichen Sonnwendfeuer getreten. Dieses Fest wurde von der Kirche lange bekämpft und schlussendlich in den Johannistag umgestaltet. Die Johannisfeuer werden meistens auf Höhen oder Bergen entzündet; früher erhoffte man sich davon Heil-, Segen- und Glückswirkung. Auch war es üblich, über das Feuer zu springen. Die Höhe des Sprunges sollte der Ernte, besonders dem Flachs, Glück bringen; aber auch Liebespaare hofften dadurch auf die Erfüllung ihrer Wünsche. Vielfach fand am Johannistag auch der Brauch des Scheibenschlagens statt, ein ebenfalls uralter Feuerkult, als analoges Zaubermittel für die Kraft der Sonne, ähnlich wie das Scheibenschlagen in der Fasnachtszeit den Winter verabschieden sollte. Glühend heiße Holzscheiben werden hierbei mit Hilfe von Stecken von Berg- oder Hügelhängen ins Tal geschleudert. Dieser Brauch wird ausschließlich von Männern ausgeübt. Damit hängt auch die zweite Bedeutung des Scheibenschlagens zusammen: eine uralte Form der Brautwerbung. Je höher die Scheibe fliegt, desto größer die Liebe des Werfenden.

Einigen AutorInnen zufolge wären die Scheiben symbolisch nicht der Sonne, sondern dem Vollmond zuzuordnen und würden demnach der dreigestaltigen Mondgöttin gelten (beispielsweise in der Gestalt der „Wilbeth“, eine der drei Hl. Jungfrauen, deren Namen manche von „wheel“ = Rad ableiten).

81

Mäusemachen

In Wälschnofen waren Knecht und Dirn im Walde bei der Holzarbeit. Sie musste die Schoten, die der Knecht beim Hacken machte, zusammenrechen. Da sagte der Knecht im Spaße: „Wären die Schoten Mäuse und liefen in die Küche, könntest du dir viel Arbeit ersparen." „Ei, das brauchst nicht zweimal zu sagen", erwiderte lachend die Dirne, murmelte allerlei dahin – und die Schoten wurden Mäuse, welche in die Küche liegen und dort wieder ihre eigentliche Gestalt annahmen. Selbst Schoten, die am Stamme hingen, wurden Mäuse und zappelten so lange, bis sie loswurden. Dem Knechte gefiel dieser Spaß, er lernte von ihr die Hexerei und brachte es so weit, dass er in den Kreis stehen sollte. Da kam er einmal zu einem frommen Pater und gestand ihm alles. Dieser machte ihn bald der Hölle abwendig und nahm ihm, was er gelernt hatte. Diese Geschichte hat sich vor 60 Jahren zugetragen.

›› Wissenswertes ‹‹

Eines der ersten und einfachsten zauberischen Kunststücke ist laut Geständnissen von Hexen das Mäusemachen. Bereits Hexenkinder würden dies von ihren Müttern lernen. In zahlreichen alten Mythen ist von der Maus die Rede; häufig wird sie als „Unwettertier" bezeichnet, sehr oft als verwandlungsfähiges Tier beschrieben. Daher verwundert es nicht, dass sie auch in den Tiroler Sagen in die Nähe von Hexen und Zauberinnen gerückt wird. Eine Vinschger Sage erzählt, dass die „Stoaner Geade", so der Name einer Hexe, sich u.a. von Mäusen ernährt habe. Sie hätte sie mit einem eigenen Sprüchlein gelockt und ihren „geheimen Namen" gekannt. Im Volksglauben ist die Maus als Seelentier bekannt. Mancherorts wird erzählt, wie die Seele als weiße Maus aus dem Mund geschlüpft sei. Im Christentum wird die Hl. Gertrud von Nivelles (626-659) mit an ihr emporkletternden Mäusen und einem Spinnrocken gezeigt (z.B. in Dreikirchen). Die Maus beißt den (Lebens-)Faden von der Spindel ab. Somit scheint diese Heilige der christliche Ersatz einer vorchristlichen Seelenführerin geworden zu sein, zumal laut christlicher Überlieferung die Seelen der Verstorbenen die erste Nacht bei ihr verbringen. Im Laufe der Jahrhunderte wurde aus diesem Seelentier und beschützenden Hausgeist jedoch ein Schädling, für dessen Vertreibung nun die Hl. Gertrud zuständig ist.

82

Eine Hexe verwandelt ihren Mann

Ein Bauer hatte Verdacht geschöpft, dass es mit seinem jungen Weibe nicht richtig sei. Er drang zu wiederholtem Male in sie, sie möge ihm die Geheimnisse offenbaren und ihn in ihre Künste einweihen. Lange widerstand sie und gab ihm nur ausweichende Antworten. Endlich gab sie aber doch nach und sagte, er solle ihr in den Stall folgen. Dort wies sie ihn an, auf einen Haufen Mist zu treten und den Reim herzusagen: „Ich tritt auf den Mist, sag' an, wer du bist?"

Da zog sie flugs einen Kreis um ihn und antwortete: „Tritt nur den Mist, ich will dir zeigen, wer du bist!", worauf sie ihn in einen richtigen, vierbeinigen Esel verwandelte, der zeitlebens Stroh fressen und Mist treten musste, während die Hexe einen jüngeren Mann heiratete, der ihr schon lange besser gefallen hatte.

›› Wissenswertes ‹‹

Der Mist spielte früher in Volksmedizin, Heilzauber (z.B. gegen Beschreiung und Behexung) und Schadenszauber (z.B. Fruchtbarkeits- oder Wohlstandsübertragung durch fremden Mist auf den eigenen) eine wichtige Rolle. Das Kreisziehen als magisches Hilfsmittel für Transformation ist in unzähligen Mythen und Sagen überliefert. – Das Motiv der Eselsverwandlung ist bereits aus der Antike bekannt und findet sich in Sagen verschiedener Länder wieder. Gründe für diese Verwandlung sind Neugierde, mangelnder Respekt oder indiskretes Verhalten vonseiten des Mannes. Manchmal gelingt ihm die Entzauberung: Sie erfolgt zumeist durch die Einnahme bestimmter Blumen oder indem er einer reinen, blumenbekränzten Jungfrau während eines kirchlichen Umgangs (z.B. Fronleichnam) den Kranz vom Kopf frisst.

83

Der Bocherhof

Unter Frassilongo stand einmal ein Haus, der Bocherhof. In diesem Haus lebten drei schöne Schwestern, wie es im ganzen Tal keine schöneren gab. Von überall her kamen die Burschen auf den Bocherhof. Und lustig ist es hier zugegangen: Musik und Tanz und Gesang hat es hier gegeben. Nur am Pfinztag war es den Burschen verboten gewesen zu kommen, und das vewunderte sie sehr. In einer Pfinztagnacht schaute deshalb ein Bursche einmal bei ihrem Schlüsselloch hinein, und da sah er, wie die drei Dirnen die Herdplatte aufhoben und einen Topf herausnahmen. Da war eine Salbe drinnen, mit der schmierten sie sich ein. Dann nahmen sie die eiserne Kette der Feuerstelle in die Hände und sagten: „Bei einem Ring hinein und beim andern heraus, nirgends drauf bis auf den Platz in Bozen." Und da ging's bei der Kette hinauf und hinaus beim Kamin, und fort waren sie. Der Bursche betrat nun die Küche, schloss die Tür hinter sich, schmierte sich mit der gleichen Salbe ein, nahm die Kette in die Hand und sagte: „Bei der Kette hinauf und beim Kamin hinaus und überall drauf!" Aber bei allen Bäumen, Häusern, Bergen und Hügeln stieß er an, doch zuletzt kam er doch auf dem Platz in Bozen an. Da sah er drei Raben, und er erkannte, dass es die drei Schwestern waren. Zwei von ihnen wollten ihn töten, aber die Jüngste schenkte ihm das Leben, weil er versprochen hatte, niemandem etwas zu erzählen.

Ein heiliger Mönch hat später die drei Hexen in den Venusberg gebannt; auf den alten Mauern hat einige Zeit später ein Ziegenbock getanzt, und auch einen weißen Mann hat man heraussteigen gesehen.

Das Haus, wo diese drei Hexen gelebt haben, ist mittlerweile eingestürzt, und jetzt ist alles wieder still.

›› Wissenswertes ‹‹

Der Pfinztag (bairisch-österreichische Bezeichnung für Donnerstag) ist allgemeiner Hexentag. Dieser nach dem germanischen Wetter- und Vegetationsgott Donar benannte Wochentag war in vorchristlicher Zeit ein heiliger Tag und dementsprechend reich an „heidnischen" Vorstellungen und Gepflogenheiten. Mit dem Christentum wurde er zum „Hexentag". Doch haben auch im Christentum Züge dieses heiligen Tages überlebt wie z.B. im Fronleichnamsfest, welches am zweiten Donnerstag nach Pfingsten mit Flurprozessionen und Wettersegen gefeiert wird.

Um Kamin und Rauchloch ranken sich zahlreiche Sagen sowie kultische, volksmedizinische und abergläubische Bräuche. Dämonen, Hexen, Haus- und Totengeister halten sich in diesem „Grenzbereich" zwischen Himmel und Erde, zwischen drinnen und draußen nahe des kultbehafteten Feuers gerne auf. – Der Rabe ist ein Hexen- und Teufelstier, ein Symbol der Sünde im Gegensatz zur weißen Taube. Zwei Raben saßen auf Wodans Schultern und raunten ihm Nachrichten aus aller Welt zu. In der nordischen und keltischen Mythologie ist der Rabe ein Tier der Todesgöttin, in der christlichen Heiligenlegende das Begleittier des Hl. Oswald. Auch der Ziegenbock, ein uraltes Kulttier, wird dem Teufel zugeordnet. In der nordischen Mythologie zogen Ziegenböcke das Gespann von Donar. – Venusberge als Aufenthaltsorte von Hexen, Seherinnen oder Göttinnen sind in verschiedenen Ländern Europas bekannt. Es ist nicht auszuschließen, dass es auch im Fersental einen derartigen Berg oder Hügel gegeben hat. Wie bereits aus dem Namen abzuleiten ist, handelt es sich beim Venusberg um einen „Frauenberg". Der „prominenteste" Venusberg ist jener aus dem Tannhäuser-Epos: Der Ritter und Minnesänger Tannhäuser findet den Zugang zum Venusberg, dem Aufenthaltsort der göttlichen Venus, und gibt sich hier nun ganz den Freuden der Liebe mit ihr hin. Doch die Sehnsucht nach der irdischen Welt zwingt ihn, diese paradiesische Welt zu verlassen. Er begibt sich nach Rom zu Papst Urban IV. (1261-1264), um von ihm Vergebung für sein sündiges Treiben mit Frau Venus zu erhalten. Da ihm dies nicht gewährt wird, kehrt er für immer in den Venusberg zurück. – Venusberge sind aber auch Kult- und Totenhöhlen und Sitz von Zauberschulen.

84

Hexengeschichte aus dem 20. Jahrhundert

(Ausschnitt aus einem Gespräch mit dem achtzigjährigen Pius Mair aus Meransen)

Frage an P.M:
„Was ist mit den Hexen? Gab es welche in Meransen?"
P.M. [fängt an zu lachen]:
„Ja, die alte L...nerin und die Lahner Ursche. Die alte L...nerin hatte zu Hause nur zwei magere Kühe. Trotzdem hat sie immer genug Milch gehabt, und andere mussten die Milch bei ihr kaufen.

Der Kircher hat mir dies alles erzählt. Das hat mich als Kind schon alles schwer beeindruckt, wenn abends solche Sachen erzählt wurden, noch dazu war es in der Stube fast finster, denn Strom gab es erst ab 1942. Da hab ich oft die Haxen unter der Bank eingezogen.

Der Kircher hat erzählt, dass sie bei der alten L...nerin nur zu einer bestimmten Zeit Milch holen durften. Einmal ist er früher dorthin gekommen. Und da sah er, wie die alte L...nerin ihre Strumpfbänder aufgehängt hatte und daran gemolken hat. Da wollte er aber keine Milch mehr. Das hat aber der L...nerin nicht gepasst, dass der Kircher dies gesehen hat.

Einmal ist meine Mutter auf dem Feld gewesen, Heu eintun. Da ist die Windspreize gekommen und hat das ganze Heu durcheinandergewirbelt. Überall rundum. Nur die L...ner drunten konnte ganz gemütlich ihr Heu eintun. Da hat der Felderbauer mit der Heugabel ins Heu hineingestochen, und am nächsten Tag hatte die L...nerin Löcher davon in den Haxen.

Einmal ist sie mit der Lahner Ursche ins Greiten-Eck hinauf. Es war ein herrliches Wetter. ‚Schau, wie heint a schians Wetter isch', sagten die Leute. Aber die Lahner Ursche sagte, ‚Na, na, heint kimmp nou gonz a schiachs Wetter', sie ist zu einer Tschugge gegangen und hat ganz fest daran genaggelt, und da sind auch schon aus Pfunders herüber die ersten schwarzen Wolken gekommen und dann ein ‚teiflisches Wetter'.

Meine Schwester, die Moidl, die war ein Sonntagskind, die hat deswegen allerhand gesehen und verstanden. Einmal ist sie ganz aufgeregt nach Hause gerannt gekommen, denn sie hat gesehen, wie die L...nerin auf dem Hausdach die Dachschindeln weggeklaubt hat. Ihr Mann hatte nämlich vorher das Dach mit neuen Schindeln gedeckt. Die L...nerin klaubte und klaubte die ganze Nacht Schindeln. Am Morgen hat sie fertig gehabt. Und weißt du was? Kein einziger Regentropfen ist durch dieses Dach je durchgetreten. Das hat sie mit ihren besonderen Kräften fertiggebracht.

Einmal musste meine Schwester Moidl nach Mühlbach gehen. Da sah sie, dass auch die L...nerin unterwegs war, da machte die Moidl schnell einen Umweg, d.h. eine Abkürzung, denn die L...nerin war ihr unheimlich. Aber weiter drunten dann – wer ist ihr plötzlich von der Mühlbacher Seite entgegengekommen? Die L...nerin!

Man hat dann dies alles einmal dem Pater Guardian erzählt, denn die Patern haben für solche Sachen mehr Kraft als ein Pfarrer. Der hat sie dann zur Rede gestellt. Und es war auch so, dass sie mittlerweile eine sehr alte Frau geworden war und ‚es nicht dersterben konnte'. Oft musste deswegen für sie gebetet werden. Oft drinnen beim Sagenkreuz [am Anfang des Altfasstals], vor allem die Kinder, auch meine Schwester war beim Beten dabei. Denn Kindergebete sind viel wirksamer als die von den Erwachsenen."

Frage:

„Wann ist das denn alles gewesen?"

Antwort:

„Das ist alles in den zwanziger Jahren gewesen, glaub' ich. Aber auch viel später noch hat es allerhand hexenhafte Erlebnisse gegeben. Da hat mir der Hueber einmal erzählt, dass die Hueberin, seine Frau, nie imstande war, den Butter zu kübeln. Da hab ich zu ihm gesagt, da könnte ja eine Hexe im Spiel sein. ‚Und was kann man dagegen tun?', hat mich der Hueber gefragt. Da hab ich ihm den Rat gegeben, eine Kette im Herd zu erhitzen und sie dann in den Butterkübel zu werfen.

Der Hueber hat das auch getan, und wirklich, die L...nerin war dann voller Brandflecken!

Einmal war die Gatscherin viel zu spät dran beim Kirchengehen und da hat sie sich nicht mehr in die Kirche hineingetraut. ‚Ich geh ins Beinhaus und bet einfach dort', dachte sie sich. Wie sie vor der Tür des Beinhauses gestanden ist, hat sie allerhand Stimmen gehört. Sie hat die Tür aufgemacht – da war die L...nerin drinnen, die hat ‚an sellan Hupf gemacht', denn sie war drinnen beim Hexen! ...

Wie gesagt, sie konnte nicht sterben. Denn es war nämlich so, dass sie in der Kirche beim Kommuniongehen die Kommunion immer heimlich aus dem Mund nahm [P.M. zeigt, wie sie das anstellte: Sie legte die Hände vor den Mund und tat so, als ob sie ganz andächtig beten würde, in Wirklichkeit ließ sie dabei die Hostie in ihre Hände gleiten]. Diese Hostien haben ihr eine außerordentliche Kraft verliehen.

Schlussendlich hat sie aber erzählt, dass drinnen beim Sagenkreuz im Buggl vom Herrgott ein Loch ist, und dort hat sie das Gebetbuch mit den ganzen Hostien versteckt gehabt.

Jemand ist nachschauen gegangen, und wirklich, da war das Buch mit den ganzen Hostien, und allerhand Sprüchen.

Das Buch ist verbrannt worden, so ist es angeordnet worden, und der Bischof Geisler ist selbst von Brixen nach Meransen heraufgekommen mit dem Pater Guardian, um die Hostien zu entweihen.

Alles hat müssen verschwinden, sie haben ihr die Beichte abgenommen, und dann ist sie's endlich derstorben.

Ich bin später selbst einmal nachschauen gegangen zum Sagenkreuz. Und da ist wirklich ein Loch drinnen gewesen im Buggl vom Herrgott, und was war drinnen? Ein Pronterle-Nest!"

Haxen = Beine; Windspreize = Wirbelwind, Tschugge = ein kleiner Nadelbaum mit vielen dichten Ästen, Buggl = Rücken, Pronterle = Rotschwänzchen.

Der Name der Bäuerin wurde nicht genannt, um engste noch lebende Angehörige nicht zu kränken.

Geweihten Gegenständen wohnt laut Volksglauben eine besondere magische Kraft inne. So wird in vielen Tiroler Sagen Hostienmissbrauch geschildert, wie beispielsweise in einer Pfunderer Sage, in der ein Bursche, der „Flatscher", die bei der Kommunion empfangene Hostie mit nach Hause nahm, sich die Hand aufschnitt, die Hostie in die Wunde legte und sie einwachsen ließ. Denn dadurch glaubte er, so stark zu werden, dass er beim Raufen gegen alle gewinnen würde.

Der achtzigjährige Pius Mair aus Meransen weiß viel Sagenhaftes aus seinem Heimatdorf zu erzählen. Natürlich trägt er dabei manchmal „etwas dick auf". Herr Mair kennt zwischen Meransen und Mühlbach jeden Stock und jeden Stein; er hat über 25 Jahre lang den alten Plattenweg zwischen den beiden Dörfern in Stand gehalten. Er pflegt auch die Jungfernrast. Als das Wasser dort aufgrund einer neugelegten Wasserableitung ausblieb, hat er für Abhilfe gesorgt. Herr Mair kennt auch den Weg zur schwer auffindbaren sagenumwobenen Felsenhöhle „Lange Kirche" und hat ihn der Buchautorin M.F. gezeigt.

Büßerin und Bestrafte

Was erwartet uns etwa nach dem Tod? Diese Frage war immer schon ein zentrales menschliches Thema und es gibt auf der ganzen Welt wohl kaum ein Volk, das sich nicht zutiefst mit den religiösen Lebensthemen Ursprung und Ende, dem Woher und Wohin, der menschlichen Seele sowie mit Fragen nach dem Eingebundensein in ein höheres Gefüge beschäftigte.

Unzählige Sagen und Mythen der ganzen Welt sind aufs Engste mit dem Göttlich-Religiösen verwoben. Letztere sind, wie Mircea Eliade sagt, „die einzigen für den profanen Menschen wichtigen Geschichten, denn sie erzählen heilige Geschichten, die Geschichte der Götter, unsere Vorbilder". So schlagen sich in diesen alten Erzählungen die menschlichen Vorstellungen und Erfahrungen von Sterben und Tod, von guten und bösen, menschlichen und übermenschlichen Kräften nieder, sie beschreiben existentielle menschliche Themen wie Schuld und Sühne, Gewissenskonflikte, Bestrafung, Gotteserfahrung und Erlösung.

Zahlreich und vielgestaltig sind auch die Tiroler Sagen zu diesen Themen: Sie erzählen von Verstorbenen, die den Seelenfrieden noch nicht gefunden haben, von Bestrafung und Buße, von den Armen Seelen, die ihre Frevel und Sünden noch abdienen müssen, von noch nicht ruhenden Geistern und von erlösten Seelen. In all diesen Motiven spiegeln sich unsere christlich-religiösen Wertvorstellungen stark wider, die durch die Lehre der christlich-katholischen Kirche und ihre moralisch-sittlichen Grundsätze vorgegeben sind. Doch schimmert hinter moralisierenden Sagen mitunter auch viel älteres Sagengut durch, dessen definitive Deutung noch nicht abgeschlossen ist wie beispielsweise bei den Verbannungssagen unverheirateter Frauen und jener um die Pfaffenköchin.

Wie intensiv sich unsere Vorfahren mit diesen Themen auseinandergesetzt haben, erfahren wir aus den unzähligen überlieferten Tiroler Bräuchen, Traditionen und abergläubischen Handlungen. Die bis in die sechziger Jahre noch üblichen Armen-Seelen-Gaben auf dem Küchentisch in der Allerseelen-Nacht (in Mauls, Lüsen, Pfeffersberg, Villnöß und in vielen anderen Orten), das Pfunderer Krapfenbetteln, das Ahrntaler Pitschelesingen, die Bräuche des Schenkens und Beschenktwerdens zu Allerseelen, die sogenannten „Seelstücke" – stellvertretend an die Kinder anstelle der Armen Seelen verteilt –, der Glaube an den Aufenthalt der Ahnenseelen unter der Haustür-schwelle (Latzfons), die Überzeugung, zu Allerseelen würden die Armen Seelen im Wind mitziehen (Unterinntal), die unzähligen Rituale der Geisterabwendung, alltägliche Handlungen, wie beispielsweise das Brot nie umgekehrt hinzulegen, damit die Armen Seelen nicht unnötig leiden müssten, sind nur einige der zahlreichen Beispiele des Eingebundenseins der Toten ins Alltagsleben.

Was aber ist nun der moralische Hintergrund der Tiroler Sagen?

Nach der Lehre der katholischen Kirche muss sich der Mensch nach seinem Tod vor Gott verantworten. Wer ein Leben in vollendeter Liebe geführt hat, wird gleich zu ihm in den Himmel, in den Zustand des höchsten und endgültigen Glücks, aufgenommen. Stirbt ein Mensch mit einer bewusst begangenen, nicht bereuten schweren Sünde, z.B. Mord, kommt er in die Hölle, einen Zustand des ewigen Getrenntseins vom Göttlichen. Stirbt jemand beladen mit leichten, lässlichen Sünden, die im Leben zwar noch nicht gebüßt wurden, aber doch in der „Freundschaft Gottes", muss er/sie nach dem Tod noch eine Zeit der Läuterung durchmachen. Dieser Reinigungsort ist das Fegefeuer und die in diesem Zustand sich befindenden Menschen sind die Armen Seelen. Wenn für die Armen Seelen gebetet wird, kann ihre Läuterungs- und Sühnezeit verkürzt werden. Auch eine materielle Begleichung (z.B. das Bezahlen von Messen) ist möglich. Im frühen Mittelalter waren auch Buß- und Bittwallfahrten zu Pilgerorten sehr häufig.

Rudolf Steiner (1861-1925), der in unterschiedlichen Lebensbereichen, u.a. auch auf dem Gebiet der Philosophie und der Religion, impulsgebend gewirkt hat, schildert, dass sich nach dem physischen Tod das Ich in den ersten drei Tagen und Nächten (mancherorts die Zeit der Totenwache) langsam von seinen Körper ablöse. Dabei erlebe es noch einmal einen erinnernden seelischen Lebensrückblick und erfahre dabei, was andere an ihm bzw.

durch ihn erlebt haben und wie sich sein Verhalten auf andere Menschen ausgewirkt hat. Es sei eine Zeit der Läuterung, denn das Ich erkenne nun seine Unzulänglichkeit und Selbstbezogenheit im vergangenen irdischen Leben, das ihm jetzt in einem anderen, objektiven Licht erscheine. Dieses „richtige Sehen" wird laut Steiner aus religiöser Sicht als „Gericht", dieser nachtodliche Lebensabschnitt als Fegefeuer verstanden.

Neben der „Heißen Pein", dem Fegfeuer, ist im ganzen Alpengebiet auch die „Kalte Pein" bekannt, ein Leiden in bitterer Kälte im ewigen Eis und Schnee, sowie die „Nasse Pein", die Verbannung in ein Gewässer.

Viele Sagen handeln von verstorbenen **Büßerinnen** oder Sünderinnen, die auf Erlösung durch eine mutige Person bzw. eine „gute Tat" warten, wodurch das begangene Unrecht wiedergutgemacht wird: So wird die Zeit der Strafe beendet, die Seele ist endlich frei und kann in den Himmel eingehen.

In den Sagen hängt die Buße oder die Sühne mit dem zu Lebzeiten begangenen Unrecht zusammen; sie spiegeln die moralischen Vorgaben wider, die aus kirchlicher Sicht in den Zehn Geboten und in den Sieben Hauptsünden, den menschlichen Hauptlastern, nämlich Stolz, Geiz, Neid, Zorn, Unkeuschheit, Unmäßigkeit und Trägheit, ausgedrückt sind. Die Tatsache, dass es so viele derartige Sagen gibt, zeigt, dass man es auch im „heiligen" Tirol in den vergangenen Jahrhunderten mit den kirchlichen Vorgaben nicht immer so genau nahm. Vor allem mit der Befolgung des 6. Gebotes hatte die Kirche ihre „liebe Not". Alle damit möglichen zusammenhängenden Tätigkeiten, wie Tanz und Unterhaltung, galten zeitweise als gefährlich und unmoralisch. Unsittliches Tanzen, zu enges „Umschlingen und Verdrehen" wurde von den geistlichen und auch den weltlichen Obrigkeiten zeitweise auch mittels Gesetzen verboten.

Im 18. Jh. erschien unter einem Pseudonym ein mehrmals aufgelegtes Buch über die „Erlebnisse einer Tirolerin", einer mit Gauklern und fahrenden Leuten umherziehenden Händlerin, die neben ihren Kurzwaren auch ihren Körper anbot. „Tirolerin" war also damals eine andere Bezeichnung für eine Prostituierte.

Auch Gottes- und Sonntagsentheiligung, Verschwendung, Hartherzigkeit, Übermut usw. werden in den Sagen bestraft: Verwandlung in Stein, Verschüttung oder Überflutung des Wohnortes oder Tatortes, Vergletscherung und Verschneiung zählen zu den Folgen.

In den Sagen zeigt sich, dass für die Einhaltungen der moralischen Vorgaben von der Frau mehr Verantwortungsgefühl, Sitte und Anstand gefordert wurden als vom Mann. Selbstbewusstheit, Sinnlichkeit, Körperlichkeit, Widerspruchsgeist, Frechheit und andere weibliche „Untugenden" passten nicht ins patriarchale und kirchliche Gesellschaftsbild. Entsprechend hart sind die Strafen für die Frau in den Sagen. Die in diesem Kapitel vorliegenden Sagen wollen einen Einblick in dieses Thema mit all dessen Facetten geben.

85

Die Entstehung der Marmolata

Zu Füßen der Marmolata liegt Gries, eine kleine Fraktion von Canazei im Fassatal, mit der Kirchenpatronin „Maria im Schnee". Seit vielen Jahrhunderten begaben sich die Menschen aus Gries, Penia und den anderen umliegenden Dörfern am 5. August in einer feierlichen Prozession zu dieser Kirche.

Dort, wo heute das ewige Eis der Marmolata liegt, breiteten sich einst, vor sehr langer Zeit, weite grüne Almwiesen aus.

Doch einmal, vor vielen Jahren, war eine alte Frau am Vorabend des Feiertages noch oben auf den Almwiesen fleißig damit beschäftigt, das Heu zusammenzurechen und sie dachte noch nicht daran, mit den anderen nach Gries abzusteigen, um an der abendlichen Andacht vor dem großen Festtag teilzunehmen. Als sie das ganze Heu in ihrem „Tobià" eingebracht hatte, begann es plötzlich zu schneien. Da sang sie ganz zufrieden in ihrem Ladiner Dialekt „Madonna im Schnee hier, Madonna im Schnee da, mein Heu ist in Sicherheit im Tobià!"

Immer größere und dichtere Schneeflocken fielen an diesem Augustabend vom Himmel, und so blieb der Alten nichts anderes übrig, als die Nacht im Tobià zu verbringen und sich zum Schlafen ins Heu zu legen. Doch es schneite die ganze Nacht weiter und auch den ganzen nächsten Tag und noch viele weitere Tage und Nächte. Die grünen Almwiesen der Marmolata, die Frau und der Heustadel wurden für immer unter einer dichten Schneedecke begraben.

Der Gletscher der Marmolata ist heute noch weitum zu sehen.

➤➤ Wissenswertes ◂◂

Tobià (fassanisch/ladinisch) = Heustadel.

Das Fest Maria im Schnee wird am 5. August gefeiert. – Die Marmolata ist 3.343 m hoch; ihr Name hat etymologisch vermutlich weniger mit Marmor als vielmehr mit „glänzen" zu tun, denn ihre kalkigen Felsen und das ewige Eis des Gletschers glänzen und funkeln wunderschön in der Sonne. Die Marmolata ist, wie andere Dolomitenberge, ein riesiges versteinertes Korallenriff. Sie wird auch „die Königin der Dolomiten" genannt. – Vergletscherungssagen als Bestrafungsausdruck vonseiten des Göttlichen aufgrund eines begangenen Frevels sind in anderen Gegenden Tirols sowie in den ganzen Alpen verbreitet. Eine von Karl Felix Wolff nacherzählte Dolomitensage berichtet von der Königin Tanna mit der blauen Krone, die im Innern der „Marmaròle" lebte. Sie herrschte über die Crodères, die Felsensöhne, und gebot über die Kräfte der Natur. Auch sie ließ Schnee und Eis entstehen. Auch dieses namensverwandte Bergmassiv südlich von Cortina war einst ein mächtiger Gletscher.

Der beeindruckende Gletscher „Mer de Glace" (Eismeer) im Mont-Blanc-Massiv war laut Sage einst ebenso ein blühendes Weidegebiet, das aufgrund der Habsucht der Einwohner von Chamonix in eine weite Eisfläche verwandelt wurde.

Gries (1452 m) ist eine Fraktion der Gemeinde Canazei im Fassatal. Die kleine Kirche „Madonna della Neve" (Maria im Schnee), auf welche hier Bezug genommen wird, wurde 1570 erbaut, 1861 durch einen Brand zerstört und später vollständig wiederhergestellt. Die Einwohner von Gries wurden früher von den Fassanern scherzhaft „Botaces" genannt, da sie das Wasser angeblich stets in großen Fässern vom Brunnen holten und so daheim aufbewahrten.

86

Die Mutter des Heiligen Petrus

Die Mutter des Heiligen Petrus war eine sehr böse Frau. Nie machte sie etwas Gutes und stritt mit allen wegen nichts und wieder nichts.

Eines Tages ging sie zum Fluss, um Zwiebeln zu waschen, da fiel ihr ein Stängel aus der Hand. Sie versuchte noch, den Stängel zu schnappen, aber es gelang ihr nicht. Da sprach sie: „So verschwinde, geh, ich opfere dich den Seelen der Verstorbenen!" Als sie starb, schickte Gott sie hinunter zum Teufel.

Nun, dem Heiligen Petrus gefiel dies gar nicht, dass seine Mutter in der Hölle schmorte, und er flehte Gott so lange an, sie in den Himmel zu holen, bis dieser schließlich sprach: „Hol diesen Zwiebelstängel und wenn du es damit schaffst, sie heraufzuziehen, dann soll sie mit dir in den Himmel kommen." →

Und Petrus ging. Er nahm den Zwiebelstängel und brachte diesen in die Hölle, zum Teufel. Seine Mutter lief sofort hin, griff nach dem Stängel und Petrus zog und zog. Aber als dies die anderen sahen, versuchten auch sie, sich daranzuhängen. Aber die Mutter des Petrus begann zu streiten und zu zanken, stieß um sich und schrie mit lauter Stimme: „Verschwindet, bleibt hier, ihr Verdammten, mein Petrus zieht nur mich hinauf und nicht euch."

Durch das Ziehen und die Stöße aber riss der Stängel der Zwiebel und sie fiel erneut zurück in die Hölle. „Siehst du", sprach da der Herr, „wer in den Himmel kommen will, der muss es sich auch verdienen."

➤➤ Wissenswertes ➤➤

Diese Sage ist in zahlreichen Varianten (Lauch, Salat, Zwiebelstängel, Strohhalm ...) inner- und außerhalb Europas bekannt. Manchmal ist es auch die Mutter eines anderen Heiligen, und nur sehr selten tritt an die Stelle der Mutter der Vater. Im Neuen Testament wird bei Matthäus, Markus und Lukas zwar die kranke Schwiegermutter des Petrus, die von Jesus geheilt wird, erwähnt, doch erst in der Neuzeit taucht Petrus' Mutter als ein böses, geiziges, streitsüchtiges Weib auf. Im Hintergrund dieses Sagenmotivs der sündigen Mutter steht wohl Eva als die aus patriarchaler Sicht „Schuldige" am biblischen Sündenfall.

87

Der Teufel als Tänzer I

Mei, wie die Sennerin auf der Eggeralm ins Tanzen vernarrt war; nichts hat sie lieber getan. Der Pfarrer hat oft gepredigt: „Auf dem Tanzplatz wird die Unschuld krank, und auf dem Heimweg stirbt sie", und sie sollten nur einmal in den Kalender für Zeit und Ewigkeit schauen, wie der Tod hinter den Tänzern steht und mit zwei Knochen geigt; aber es war alles in den Wind geredet. Das wussten die Senner weitum und kamen oft bei ihr zusammen und tanzten bis Mitternacht. Eines Abends war sie mit ihrer Kameradin mutterseelenallein in der Sennhütte; es wollte niemand kommen. „Wenn nur heut' einer käm'!" Aber es kam keiner. „Wenn ich heut' doch wenigstens einmal mit einem herumtanzen könnte", sagte sie in ihrer Langweile, „und möcht's der Teufel selber sein!" Der andern ging bei diesen Worten ein Schaudern zu, und sie mahnte die Sennerin, nicht so zu reden, sonst könnt' er kommen, der Unterländer.

Nach einer Zeit hörten sie über den Rain herauf lustig jodeln, dass es ihnen in die Ohren gellte. „Endlich kommt einer", rief sie freudig aus, „und noch dazu ein Lustiger; der jodelt ja, wie ich's noch nie gehört habe." Und herein trat ein flinker Jägersmann, bildschön, versteht sich, mit einem nobligen Schnauzbart. Wie er die Sennerin ums Tanzen fragte, hatte sie auch schon ja gesagt. Jetzt drehten sie sich herum und immer wieder und immer schneller, und während sie miteinander walzten und der Jäger lustig auf den Boden stampfte und mit der Zunge schnalzte, da stellten sich allmählich mehrere Burschen aus nachbarlichen Sennhütten ein.

Der Tanz wollte nimmer aufhören, und die Sennerin wurde allmählich windelweiß vor Anstrengung und konnte kaum mehr atmen; der Jäger ließ sie nimmer aus. Nach und nach wurde dieser größer und immer größer, und Feuer ging ihm aus den Augen und erleuchtete die Stube: Der Sennerin liefen dicke Schweißtropfen herab und nässten den Boden. Da kam es den Zuschauern ganz unheimlich vor, furchtsam drängten sie sich in einen Winkel zusammen, und einer rannte zur Tür hinaus und gestracks ins Dorf hinab und holte den Geistlichen. Dieser lief, was er konnte, bergauf und brachte endlich mit harter Mühe den Jäger zum Weichen. Kaum ließ er die Tänzerin aus, da fiel sie um wie ein Holzblock und lag lange wie tot. Endlich kam sie zu sich, aber die übermenschliche Anstrengung und der Schrecken warfen sie aufs Krankenbett, und erst nach Monaten stand sie wieder auf.

›› Wissenswertes ‹‹

gestracks = schnurstracks.

Alt wie die Geschichte der Menschheit ist auch jene des Tanzes. Neben der kultisch-religiösen Bedeutung war er stets auch Ausdruck menschlicher Gefühle wie Lebenslust und Lebensfreude. Der Tanz erfuhr allerdings im Laufe der Jahrhunderte immer wieder abwechselnd Verpönung oder Wertschätzung: „O Mensch lerne tanzen, sonst wissen die Engel im Himmel mit dir nichts anzufangen“, soll der Kirchenvater Augustinus gesagt haben. Doch außerhalb des liturgischen Rahmens bezeichnete die Kirche den Tanz zeitweilig als Ursprung aller großen Sünden, als Unkeuschheit. Diese Einstellung und die weiter unten beschriebene um sich greifende „Tanzwut“ trugen mit dazu bei, dass in der mittelalterlichen Kirche das Motiv des Totentanzes entstand: Dieser sollte den Menschen anmahnen, ein frommes und tugendhaftes Leben zu führen, nicht an weltliche Vergnügungen, sondern an das Jenseits zu denken. Abbildungen des Totentanzes wurden ein beliebtes Motiv an Kirchen und Friedhofskapellen, das aufzeigt, wie der triumphierende Tod Menschen aller Gesellschaftsschichten, den Papst wie den Bettler, tanzend und musizierend ins Jenseits führt. Beispiele solcher Abbildungen finden sich in Navis oder Breitenwang in Nordtiol und im Rendenatal im Trentino (Simone Baschenis); aber auch zeitgenössische Maler wie z.B. Albin Egger-Lienz oder Rudolf Stolz (Totentanz im Sextner Friedhof) befassten sich mit dem Motiv des Totenreigens.

Im bäuerlichen Leben bot die fernab der kirchlichen Kontrolle gelegene Alm Gelegenheit zu Tanz und Ausgelassenheit. Während die Galtvieh-Almen von Männern bewirtschaftet wurden, waren jene der Milchkühe Domäne der Sennerinnen (Galtvieh = Vieh, das noch nie geworfen hat und keine Milch gibt, also zumeist Jungvieh). Diese Almen waren deshalb beliebte Treffpunkte. – Die in dieser Sage beschriebene Unfähigkeit der Sennerin, den Tanz zu beenden, erinnert auch an die im Mittelalter und noch später grassierende „Tanzwut“: Menschen tanzten so lange, manchmal auch aus religiöser Überzeugung und vor allem in Pestzeiten (Tanz als Form des Abwehrzaubers gegen den Tod), bis sie in Ekstase gerieten. Während in vielen Kulturen das intensive, in die Ekstase führende Tanzen als Kultritual gepflegt wird, ist dieser Zustand in dieser Sage das Werk

des Dämonischen, des Bösen. Diese Einstellung sollte noch lange andauern: Auch moderne Tänze der Neuzeit galten bis vor nicht allzu langer Zeit als skandalös und unmoralisch. Im Zustand der Ekstase treten Phänomene wie Schmerzunempfindlichkeit, überschäumend-orgiastische Lebensfreude, übersteigerte Gefühle u.a. auf, aber im Nachhinein kann auch eine tiefe Depression entstehen, wie in dieser Sage beschrieben.
In diesem Zusammenhang soll auch an den Tarantismo, eine süditalienische Form der Tanzwut, erinnert werden. Laut Volksglauben wird er durch den Biss einer Spinne, der Tarantel, ausgelöst, der Erregungszustände, gefolgt von Gleichgültigkeit und Melancholie, hervorruft. Betroffene Frauen entblößen sich angeblich auch gerne. Um davon geheilt werden zu können, bedarf es des Tarantella-Rituals, eines unglaublich schnellen Drehtanzes, den die Gebissene durchführen muss. Sie tanzt, unterstützt von schneller rhythmischer Musik, so lange, bis sie in Trance gerät und vor Erschöpfung zusammenbricht. Durch diesen „rituellen Tod“ kommt es zur Heilung.

88

Der Teufel als Tänzer II

Es war einmal ein Mädchen überaus niedergeschlagen, als hätte es Glück und Seligkeit verloren. Die Ursache war, weil es bei einer Hochzeitfeier nicht zu Spiel und Tanz gehen konnte: Ihm war nämlich vor kurzem der Liebste untreu geworden und in die Welt gegangen. Nachdem schon die Nacht angebrochen, trat ein schön gewachsener Jüngling zu ihm in die Stube und fragte, ob es nicht mit ihm auf den Tanzboden gehen möchte. Dem Dirndl war natürlich nichts auf der Welt lieber, es putzte sich schnell mit seinen Festkleidern aufs Allerprächtigste heraus. Dann gingen sie Arm in Arm dem Wirtshaus zu. Unter den Tänzern war dieser Jäger weitaus der flinkste. Er sang auch die hellsten, lustigsten Lieder, in kühnen Sprüngen tat es ihm niemand gleich auf keine Nähe. Ein Wildschütz beteuerte oft und vielmals, er habe selbst keine Gämse so verwegene Sätze machen sehen. Aber jedermann fühlte sich, wenn er diesem Tänzer ins Gesicht schaute, so unheimlich beklommen, ohne recht zu wissen, wie. Auf dem Heimweg fragte jener die Dirne, ob er nicht in der folgenden Nacht zu ihr aufs Fenster kommen dürfe? Sie sagte voll Freude zu. In der andern Nacht klopfte er, grade wie es am Kirchturme daneben Zwölfuhr schlug, an die Scheiben des schmalen Fensterleins. Als die Maid geöffnet hatte, griff er nach ihr und riss sie durch die Eisenstäbe, dass das warme Blut über die Wand hinabströmte, und trug die Schreiende durch die Luft davon. Die roten Spuren vermochte man nicht wegzutilgen.

Das Tanzen war früher eine der beliebtesten Vergnügungen im harten bäuerlichen Leben. Beim Dorfwirtshaus gab es einen eigenen Tanzplatz, aber auch Bauernstuben oder der Almaufenthalt boten Gelegenheit zu Tanz und Beisammensein. Getanzt wurde vor allem mit dem „Schatz", wenn dies nicht eingehalten wurde, waren Eifersucht, Rauferei und Verdruss oft die Folgen. Wurde ein Mädchen vom Liebhaber „stehengelassen", musste es neben tiefer Scham und Niedergeschlagenheit nicht selten auch noch den Spott anderer junger Leute aushalten. Der ausgelassene Tanz war aber auch die Möglichkeit sinnlicher bis zügelloser Begegnung, er wurde deshalb vonseiten der Kirche stets „verteufelt", doch die Tiroler kümmerten sich eigentlich nicht sehr um diese moralischen Vorhaltungen, bis im 19. Jh. aufgrund gesetzlicher Vorschriften nur mehr bei Hochzeiten und Kirchtagen getanzt werden durfte. – Das „Fensterlen" war früher im bäuerlichen Milieu, aber nicht nur dort, weit verbreitet. Des Nachts, wenn scheinbar alles schlief, schlich der Bursche zum Haus, in welchem das auserkorene Mädchen wohnte, und stieg zu ihrem Fenster hinauf bzw. in die Kammer hinein. Zur Erleichterung und Auflockerung dieses Liebesabenteuers hatten die Mädchen zumeist eine Flasche Schnaps in der Kammer bereitstehen. Zahlreiche Tiroler Scherzreime und Lieder zeugen heute noch von diesem einst beliebten ländlich-erotischen Stelldichein zwischen Bursch und Mädchen. Der Bauer oder Dienstherr sah solche Zusammenkünfte nicht gerne, denn er befürchtete nachteilige Auswirkungen auf die Arbeits- und Leistungsfähigkeit seiner Dienstboten am darauf folgenden Tag; doch wie aus dem Buch „Bauernerotik in den Alpen" von P. Streng und G. Bakakay zu entnehmen ist, haben sich gar manche Knechte und Mägde bei ihrem Dienstantritt dieses Vergnügen ausdrücklich ausbedungen. Doch manchmal wurde es den Dienstherren doch zu bunt: So ist beispielsweise aus Pfunders überliefert, dass im Jahre 1887 ein Bursche, der zu einer Magd fensterlen ging, von der Bäuerin durch einen Schrotschuss schwer verletzt wurde. In einer im Stubaital vom Sagensammler Heyl aufgezeichneten Sage bittet der Vater eines Mädchens ein Litzenmannl, eine Art kleiner Hausgeist, um Hilfe gegen das Zustandekommen des Fensterlen.

Aber vor allem die Kirche war gegen diese Art Begegnung. Sexuelle Vereinigung sollte in erster Linie der Fortpflanzung dienen. Vor den Fenstern angebrachte Eisenstäbe sollten das Einsteigen in die Kammer verhindern, doch, wie auch in Tiroler Liedern scherzhaft besungen wird, war dies nicht immer ein Hindernis. – In dieser Sage tritt der Teufel buchstäblich als der „Leibhaftige" in Erscheinung; zuerst hat er den Part des Trösters inne, dann den des Verführers und schlussendlich den des Bestrafenden, wodurch sich die ihm zugeordnete Kehrseite des Göttlichen erkennen lässt.

89

Gottesgericht über einen verschwemmten Hof

Über Villanders liegt eine Anhöhe, die so unfruchtbar ist, dass sie kaum den Schafen spärliche Weide gewährt. Das war nicht immer so; vor alten Zeiten hatte über diesen Hügel der Segen Gottes sein reiches Füllhorn geleert. Ein Bauernhof stand auf dem Hügel, der weitum der schönste war. Da war Geld und Gut. Der Stadel war eine weite Bedachung, und kaum hatte darin des Sommers und Herbstes Überfluss Platz. Aus den vielen kleinen glänzenden Fenstern des geräumigen Wohnhauses schauten Zufriedenheit und Wohlstand und die schmuckgetäfelte und gemalte Stube. Steffl, der Bauer, hatte von seinem Vater die Wirtschaft und darüber noch dazu den Segen Gottes geerbt; denn er war wie sein Vater, ein Biedermann im wahren Sinne des Wortes; auf Ordnung im Hause, auf Redlichkeit und Christentum hielt er viel und gab mit der Rechten, ohne dass es die Linke wusste; sein Weib war ein wahres Muster von einer Hausmutter und verdiente das Lob des starken Weibes in den Sprüchen Salomons im 31. Kapitel ohne Übertreibung. Vom Wohlstand genährt, vom Segen Gottes getragen, vom Christentum geführt, waren Steffl und sein Weib mit Ehren alt geworden; fünf Töchter hatten sie, die heranwuchsen wie blühende Rosen. Demut war in ihrem Betragen, Sittsamkeit und Unschuld strahlten ihnen aus den Augen, gehorsam waren sie auf den Wink, Lust zum Gebete und zur Arbeit merkte man an ihnen; unter den flinksten und bravsten Burschen in der ganzen Umgebung hätten sie die Auswahl bekommen.

Jahre vergingen, die älteste Tochter war schon mannbar geworden, da kam auf einmal Unglück ins Haus in der Gestalt eines verstockten Bösewichts. Es verlor nämlich der Bauer unter dem Jahre den Knecht, einen sehr braven Diener, und war nun verlegen, woher einen Arbeiter bekommen. Da kam wenige Tage darauf am Abend ein unbekannter Bursche mit einer überaus hübschen Gesichtslarve und Honig auf den Lippen; der beste Menschenkenner hätte sich an ihm verschaut, so wusste er in seinem Betragen Sittsamkeit und Bescheidenheit zu heucheln. Aber leider! Es war ein Wolf in Schafskleidern, der schon öfters in anderen Gegenden als Verführer den Laufpass bekommen hatte. Bei der wenigen Lebenserfahrung der unschuldigen, nichts Arges ahnenden Töchter war es ihm leicht, sie in das Netz der Verführung zu bringen. Nach einem Jahr entließ Steffel zwar den Wolf im Schafskleid, durch manche Äußerungen des Verführers und der Verführten aufmerksam gemacht und durch das Betragen der Töchter erschreckt. Aber es war leider zu spät, das Werk der Verführung war bei den zwei ältesten Töchtern schon vollendet, und in den Herzen der jüngeren wucherte auch der Same des Unkrautes üppig heran. Der Hauch der Unschuld war von der Stirn verwischt und hatte einem frechen Betragen Platz gemacht, von der Sittsamkeit war keine Spur mehr zu finden in dem eitlen, fast sündhaften Anzüge, Unlust zum Gebet und zur Arbeit sah man ihnen deutlich an und bemerkte dafür desto größere Freude am Tanz und andern sündhaften Unterhaltungen, in ihrem Betragen zeigten sie wenig Achtung und Liebe mehr gegen ihre musterhaften Eltern. Alle Tränen der Mutter, alle Ermahnungen des Vaters und selbst Strenge fruchteten nichts mehr. Sooft sie konnten, stahlen sie sich an Sonn- und Feiertagen aus dem Vaterhaus fort und begaben sich in liederliche Winkelhäuser zum Tanz, wo ihr Verführer gewiss niemals fehlte. Schon konnte die älteste Tochter ihre Schande nicht mehr länger verbergen. Darob erkrankte der Vater, und die Mutter bekam ein langwieriges Siechtum. Nach dem Tode des Vaters fanden die Tänze in dem väterlichen Hause statt; um die Tränen der siechen Mutter bekümmerte sich niemand. Diese musste verlassen, ohne Pflege, in einem Winkel des Hauses ihren Schmerz und ihren Kummer abwarten. Gram, Verdruss und Mangel an guter Pflege brachten ihr Siechtum zu rascherem Ende, als man anfangs geglaubt hatte. Die Vorstellung der sterbenden Mutter und ihr Tod brachte zwar die Töchter für einige Wochen auf dem Wege des Verderbens zum Stillstehen, jedoch zur Umkehr kam es nicht, dazu waren sie zu grundverdorben. Nach den wenigen Wochen wurde des Lasterlebens Fortsetzung wieder aufgenommen, und zwar in vergrößertem Maßstabe, ja es kam so weit, dass das Haus eine wahre Mörderhöhle der Seelen wurde, so dass der Himmel in seiner unendlichen Langmut nicht länger mehr zusehen konnte. Je ärger das Sündenleben war, umso schwerer war auch die Strafe. Es kam auf einmal um Mitternacht ganz unerwartet ein schreckliches Gewitter. Eine schwarze Wolke, Unheil verkündend, lagerte sich über dem Hügel, und aus derselben heraus wetterleuchtete es in einem fort, und lange nachrollende Donner begleiteten das Himmelsleuchten; ein Blitzstrahl zündete nieder und legte die Behausung in wenigen Augenblicken in Asche. Ein Wolkenbruch entstand und schwemmte das Erdreich bis auf die nackten Felsen vom Hügel fort, so dass am andern Tage von Haus und Hof nichts mehr zu sehen war.

›› Wissenswertes ‹‹

Anzüge = Benehmen.

Hinter dieser in pathetischem Stil niedergeschriebenen Sage verbirgt sich in Wirklichkeit eine Geschichte sexueller Ungezwungenheit und Ungehorsams. „Winkelhäuser" waren Häuser, in welchen infolge des eingeführten Tanzverbotes heimlich getanzt wurde, sie boten selbstverständlich auch Gelegenheit für eine sinnliche Begegnung. In Tirol nahm man es in den vergangenen Jahrhunderten mit den kirchlichen Geboten nicht immer ganz wörtlich, so war auch vorehelicher Geschlechtsverkehr kein Tabu, im Gegenteil: Der Sagensammler Heyl berichtet aus Stilfes bei Sterzing (Ende 19. Jh.) vom dortigen Brauch der Brautleute, sich zuerst gegenseitig zu „erkennen"; dann erst könne eine Trauung gültig vor sich gehen. Voreehelicher Geschlechtsverkehr, geknüpft an ein Heiratsversprechen, war deshalb weit verbreitet. Sagen mit einem schlimmen Ausgang als erzieherische Botschaft geben deshalb indirekt Aufschluss über die Moralvorstellungen zum einen und der Realsituation früherer Zeit zum anderen. Eine amüsante Anbandeltechnik aus dem Zillertal schildert Ludwig von Hörmann im Buch „Tiroler Volksleben": Hier hatten die Burschen häufig, so auch während des Tanzes, ein Stück Kuipech (Kaupech, dem heutigen künstlichen Kaugummi ähnlich) im Mund und ließen ein Ende heraushängen. Wollte der Bursche nun erfahren, ob er bei seiner Tänzerin Chancen für eine Gegenliebe hätte, sagte er, sie solle ein Stück Kuipech abbeißen. Machte es das Mädchen, hatte dies den gleichen Wert wie ein Kuss. Ekelte ihr davor, so wusste er gleich, dass es mit der Liebe nicht weit her war, denn das Sprichwort sagt: „Magst du mei Mummla (Gekautes) nit, hast du mi a nit lieb."

Das in der Sage erwähnte 31. Kapitel bezieht sich auf die im Alten Testament enthaltene und größtenteils König Salomo (ca. 972-932 v.Chr.) zugeschriebene „erzieherische" Spruchsammlung, in welcher in 21 Sprüchen ein Hohelied auf die „tüchtige Frau" gesungen wird.

90

Noglroath

Überall ist die Meinung verbreitet, dass jene Dirnen, welche sich sogar an Tonsurierten vergangen haben, nach dem Tode keine Ruhe finden. Sie werden in wilde Stuten verwandelt und müssen alsogleich zu einem Schmiede kommen und sich glühende Rosseisen aufschlagen lassen. Sind sie nun beim Rechten, der es versteht, sie zu beschlagen, dann geht es ihnen gut, und sie sind nicht auf ewig verloren; kann es aber der Schmied nicht, dann fällt ihre Seele dem Teufel zu. Denn das Beschlagen solcher Stuten ist ein Mysterium der Schmiede; sie nennen diese Kunst „Nagelroath", und nicht der zehnte versteht sich darauf. Wer diese Kunst aber versteht, der ist durch kein Mittel dahin zu bringen, auch nur ein Sterbenswörtlein davon auszusagen, sonst wäre er selber des Satans. Schon viele haben sich bemüht, davon etwas Rechtes zu erfahren, aber es ist noch keinem gelungen.

Hie und da ereignet es sich, dass die eine oder andere dieser verzauberten Seelen ein Eisen verliert, und daher kommt es, dass man Hufeisen auf den höchsten Felszinnen findet, wo nie, seit die Welt steht, ein wirkliches Ross hingekommen sein kann, wo höchstens Gämsen umherklettern.

›› Wissenswertes ‹‹

Die Tonsur, seit 1972 abgeschafft, ist das Ausscheren des Haupthaares und gehörte früher zum Aufnahmeritus in den geistlichen Stand.

Ein weit verbreitetes gesellschaftliches Phänomen, das sich auch in den Tiroler Sagen wie dieser aus dem Unterinntal niederschlägt, ist, bei gesellschaftlich nicht toleriertem Verhalten die Schuld hierfür vor allem der Frau zuzuweisen. Im Besonderen, wenn Sinnlichkeit und Sexualität im Spiel sind, werden Frauen demnach zu Verführerinnen und Männer deren Opfer. Das in einer vorherigen Sagenanmerkung erwähnte Enthaltsamkeitsgelübde war von der kirchlichen Obrigkeit zu keiner Zeit leicht in die Tat umzusetzen, zeitweise nicht einmal von ihr selbst respektiert. Aus einem Visitationsbericht des 16. Jh. geht beispielsweise hervor, dass zu jener Zeit in der Diözese Brixen 61 Priester im Konkubinat lebten, 25 davon sollen eigene Nachkommen gehabt haben.

An dieser Stelle soll auch eine im Mittelalter entstandene heitere Geschichte über die Listen von Frauen angeführt werden: jene von Aristoteles und Phyllis. Der Philosoph Aristoteles (384-322 v. Chr.) war der Lehrer von Alexander dem Großen, welcher der schönen Phyllis, einer Zofe seiner Mutter, in Liebe zugetan war. Als Aristoteles dies entdeckte, berichtete er dies sogleich dem Vater seines Schülers, dem König. Auch Alexander warnte er vor ihr, denn seiner Meinung nach übten schöne Frauen und die körperliche Liebe zu ihnen einen negativen Einfluss auf die Männer aus. Die schöne Phyllis aber rächte sich mit einer List. Sie betörte und umgarnte den alten Lehrer mit ihren Liebreizen, der ihr daraufhin Geld für eine Liebesnacht mit ihr anbot. Sie war damit einverstanden, aber anstelle des Geldes wünschte sie sich von ihm, dass er sich von ihr Zaumzeug anlegen lasse und sie, die Peitsche schwingend, auf ihm durch den Garten reiten dürfe. Aristoteles war damit einverstanden; Phyllis richtete dies nun so ein, dass ihr Geliebter Zeuge dieses lächerlichen Schauspiels wurde. Alexander der Große soll darüber tief bestürzt gewesen sein, seinen Lehrer habe er allerdings nicht verachtet, sondern die Richtigkeit seiner Warnung erkannt. Aristoteles aber soll heimlich das Königsschloss verlassen und sich auf die Insel Galicia begeben haben, wo er ein Buch über die Listen der Weiber verfasst habe, wogegen es laut seiner Erkenntnis keine andere Hilfe gebe, als ihnen fernzubleiben.

91

Sage von der Pfaffenköchin

Die Pfaffenköchin ist eine Widumhäuserin, die wegen ihrer Schandtaten bis zum Jüngsten Tage herumgeistern muss. Man erkennt sie an einem großen Licht, das sich von Osten nach Westen oder von Westen nach Osten mit der Geschwindigkeit eines galoppierenden Pferdes weiterbewegt, oft nimmt man ein Geräusch wahr, als ob Eisen auf einem Stein gerieben würde.

Einmal im Jahr muss die Pfaffenköchin beschlagen werden und zwar am Karfreitag während des 9-Uhr-Ratschens. Dafür braucht es einen Schmied, der in der dritten Generation Franz heißt; der dritte Franz also muss sie beschlagen. Dafür erhält er keine Bezahlung, nur zwei Eisen der Pfaffenköchin, die aber haben eine derartige Wunderkraft, dass man damit alle Krankheiten heilen kann. Außerdem bringen diese Eisen dem Besitzer Glück und großen Reichtum. Früher waren solche Pfaffenköchin-Eisen besonders für Robler und Raufer sehr wertvoll, denn wer ein solches Eisen hatte, konnte sich daraus einen Ring machen, der unbesiegbar machte. Allerdings musste dieser während des 9-Uhr-Ratschens am Karfreitag in einer einzigen Hitze in ganz kurzer Zeit vom Schmied hergestellt werden. Der Schmied musste bei dieser Arbeit splitternackt sein und niemand durfte zuschauen.

In Pfunders traf es einmal zu, dass ein Schmied die Pfaffenköchin beschlagen sollte, es hatten nämlich drei Schmiede hintereinander Franz geheißen, und die Pfaffenköchin war zum Beschlagen schon angemeldet. Doch der Schmied wollte diese Arbeit nicht tun, und so verkaufte er seine Werkstatt seinem jüngsten Bruder, und die Pfaffenköchin musste sich einen anderen Schmied suchen.

Mancherorts heißt die Pfaffenköchin auch „Perchta“.

Die Geschichte der „Pfaffenkellerin" ist auch in anderen mitteleuropäischen Ländern seit dem 13. Jh. überliefert. Der schreibende Zisterziensermönch Caesarius von Heisterbach (ca. 1200), Verfasser des Buches „Dialogus miraculorum", in welchem er zahlreiche Teufels-, Geister- und Wundergeschichten erzählt, nennt sie „ains priesters kellerin und schlaffweib". Strafweise tritt sie oft auch im Gefolge der Wilden Jagd in Erscheinung. Als „Pfäffin" wird sie von Hans Vintler in den „Pluemen der Tugent" erwähnt. So kann ein Zusammenhang mit den katholischen Zölibatsvorschriften vermutet werden. Das priesterliche Enthaltsamkeitszölibat wurde erstmals um ca. 300 n. Chr. als Gesetz verfasst. Im Mittelalter wurde das Ehelosigkeitszölibat festgeschrieben und wurde unabdingbare Zugangsvoraussetzung zur Priesterweihe. Verheirateten Geistlichen wurden bei Nichteinhaltung des Zölibates oft Amt und Besitz entzogen.

Die Gestalt der Pfaffenköchin ist in Tirol vor allem in der Gegend zwischen Trens, Mauls, Vals und Pfunders bis nach Terenten, aber auch im Rosengartengebiet, im Sarntal und in der Gegend um Hall verbreitet. Es ist der Geist einer bösen Pfarrhäuserin, die zur Strafe nach ihrem Tod als brennendes Reisigbündel oder als Lichtkugel, oft mit einem besenartigen Schweif, durch die Luft fliegen muss. Manchmal wird sie vom Teufel verfolgt; mitunter drückt er sie in eine Felswand hinein, wodurch ein tiefes Loch darin entsteht. In einer Sage bei Fink wird auch ihre Erlösung geschildert: Ein mutiger Bursche erfasste sie, küsste und herzte sie die ganze Nacht bis zum Morgengebet. Als die morgendliche Betglocke erklang, hielt er in seinen Armen ein junges Mädchen fest, das sich für die Erlösung bei ihm bedankte und für immer verschwand.

Nachdem die Pfaffenköchin bis zum Jüngsten Tag umgehen muss, bedarf sie ständig neuer Schuhe bzw. Hufeisen, zumal auch der Teufel sie als Ross verwendet. Hufeisen und Schmied sind häufige Sagenmotive inner- und außerhalb Tirols. Die Gestalt des Schmiedes tritt in Sage und Mythen oft in der Metapher als Meister ritueller und mystischer Fähigkeiten in Erscheinung. Seit der Mensch das Metallgießen entdeckt hat, gibt es den Schmied, der im Besitz von technischem, heilzauberischem und medizinischem Wissen ist. In alten Mythen ist von einer Verbindung zwischen dem Schmiedehandwerk und der Verehrung der Göttin die Rede. Hephaistos soll einst der Schmiedgott der Amazonen gewesen sein, von denen gesagt wird, dass sie die für die Metall- und Schmiedearbeit benötigten Männer absichtlich verkrüppelten. Hephaistos und Athene, die manchmal als Lehrmeisterin der Schmiede beschrieben wird, hatten einen gemeinsamen Tempel. In vielen Tiroler Sagen ist der Schmied sogar imstande, den Teufel zu überlisten und zu besiegen. Manchmal werden ihm auch übermenschliche, oft teufelsähnliche Fähigkeiten zugeschrieben. Vermutlich ist dies auf die christliche Verteufelung alter Götter zurückzuführen.

Das Motiv der Hufbeschlagung erinnert auch an eine nordische Sage um 1200: Der heidnische Gott Odin, im Christentum oft dem Teufel gleichgestellt, kehrt mit seinem Ross, das zu Lande, zu Wasser und in der Luft dahingleitet, bei einem Schmied ein, um es beschlagen zu lassen. Dann begibt er sich in riesigen Sprüngen nach Schweden in den Krieg. So vermischt sich in diesem Sagenmotiv heidnisches und christliches Sagengut.

Laut Fink wurden bei Kiens und Terenten vor längerer Zeit manchmal auffallend kleine Hufeisen gefunden, Pfaffeneisen genannt. Er vermutet, dass diese Hufeisen von Pferderassen aus der Zeit der germanisch-bajuwarischen Landnahme stammen könnten, zumal ihre Form sich mit germanischen Funden in Bayern deckt.

92

Mädchengestalt am Kalmbach

An den Sonntagen in der Fastenzeit sieht man am Kalmbache, da wo er sich in die Passer ergießt, ein blasses Mädchen sitzen und traurig nach den letzten Streifen der Abendglut blicken. Wenn diese verschwinden, wäscht jener Geist sich hastig einen Blutflecken von den Wangen, der jedoch nicht vergeht, obgleich das abrinnende Wasser wie Blut gefärbt ist. Dann fängt die Gestalt zu seufzen und zu weinen an und steigt um Mitternacht in das höhere Tal hinauf. Die Volkssage sieht in dieser Erscheinung den Geist einer Kindesmörderin, welche ihr Kind im wahnsinnigen Schmerze erdrückt hatte, indem sie, verlassen vom Vater des Kindes und aus Furcht vor der öffentlichen Verachtung, zu solcher verzweiflungsvollen Tat hingetrieben wurde.

In der Nähe ist die gefürchtete Kellerlahn mit ihren Schlammrunsen, darüber Hofers Alpe gelegen.

›› Wissenswertes ‹‹

Laut einem Bericht von Beda Weber (überliefert von Ludwig Steub) war es angeblich üblich, dass „die schönen Meraner Mädchen, welche uneheliche Kinder geboren, diese gewöhnlich nach Passeier bringen, wo sie für dreißig Gulden des Jahres schlecht und recht, aber mit großer Liebe auferzogen werden, so dass sie blühend wieder herauskommen".

Doch „ledige Kinder" waren oft, besonders bei Mägden und armen Mädchen, eine Tragödie. Häufig wurde ihnen der Arbeitsplatz aufgekündigt, auch fehlte es ihnen zumeist am nötigen Geld, um ihr Kind irgendwo in Pflege geben zu können, und Findelhäuser gab es nur in den Städten. Manchmal, wenn beispielsweise der Bauer oder dessen Sohn der Kindesvater war, wuchs das Kind zwar am selben Bauernhof auf, aber ein arbeitsreiches Leben von klein auf stand ihm bevor. In manchen Gegenden Tirols war bis vor gar nicht so langer Zeit eine voreheliche Schwangerschaft eine so große Schande, dass das schwangere Mädchen ihren Bauch aufs Engste einband, um ihn zu verbergen, was nicht nur schmerzhaft, sondern auch gesundheitsgefährdend werden konnte. Abortiv wirkende Pflanzen, in Tirol u.a. die Triebspitzen des giftigen Sefenstrauchs, die Arnika oder die Weinraute, ein in den meisten Tiroler Bauerngärten angebautes Kraut, wurden eingenommen. Lebensgefährliche Eingriffe (z.B. mit Stricknadeln) wurden praktiziert, um das Kind während der Schwangerschaft zu verlieren, oft ergebnislos. Auch herausgekratztes Mörtel- und Holzpulver aus Teufelsdarstellungen in Kirchen wurde zu diesem Zwecke verwendet, z.B. aus der St.-Jakobs-Kirche in Gröden und vermutlich auch aus der Andreaskirche in Antlass bei Lengstein. Die Art der Einnahme ist heute allerdings nicht mehr bekannt. Heimlich, zumeist ohne Beistand, oft auf dem Abort oder an einem geheimen Ort, erfolgte die Geburt. Not und Verzweiflung verleiteten die ledige Mutter manchmal zum Kindesmord, wie in dieser Sage aus dem Passeiertal. Im Laufe der Jahrhunderte wurde der Kindesmord in verschiedenen Ländern unterschiedlich schwer bestraft, lange Zeit stand darauf die Todesstrafe, oft auf sehr grausame Art und Weise. In einer Sage aus dem Unterinntal wurde eine die Tat schwer bereuende Kindsmörderin zur Buße in eine Kröte verwandelt und musste sieben Jahre lang als solche umgehen, dann war sie erlöst. Doch auch wenn es der Kindsmörderin gelang, alles zu verheimlichen, litt sie zeitlebens aufgrund der begangenen Tat schwer unter dem eigenen schlechten Gewissen, und laut Kirche blieb ihr, wie in dieser Sage, die Tür ins Himmelreich für immer verschlossen.

93

Das Knuidlweibele

In einem sehr alten Haus in Auer, das ursprünglich ein Schloss gewesen sein soll, haust in den großen, tiefen Kellern eine unheimliche Erscheinung, das „Knuidlweibele". Es ist dies der Geist einer ehemaligen, sehr hartherzigen Schlossherrin. Zuweilen zeigt er sich als eine Frau mit schwermütigem Gesichtsausdrucke in weißen oder auch in Trauerkleidern, zuweilen aber als eine Kugel in Form eines Knäuels, an dem man deutlich zwei Augen bemerken kann. Vor Jahren sollen einmal mehrere beherzte Burschen diesen Geist mit Steinwürfen bis in das Schloss Leiter verfolgt haben.

Das Knuidlweibele ist besonders von den Kindern sehr gefürchtet, weshalb manche Mutter in Auer ihren widerspenstigen Kindern zu drohen pflegt: „Ich geh' ums Knuidlweibele."

›› Wissenswertes ‹‹

Knuidl = Knäuel.

Die geisterhafte Erscheinung eines Knäuels oder einer Kugel ist auch andernorts bekannt: in Prettau im Ahrntal wurde die Sage vom Wollenwickele (Wollknäuel) aufgezeichnet. Manchmal rollte das Wollenwickele vom Berg herunter in die Ställe der Almen, da fingen die Kühe in Panik abscheulich an zu brüllen, und der Schaum hing ihnen vom Maul bis zum Boden herab. Das Wollewickele erschien immer bei Vollmond. Mit geweihten Kerzen, Gebeten und einem großen Feuer wurde versucht, das dämonische Wollewickele zu vertreiben. In der schwedischen Volkssage verwandeln sich Riesen aus Furcht vor Thors Blitz in Knäuel und rollen vom Berg herab auf die Almwiesen, um bei den Mähern Schutz zu suchen. Auch der Teufel, ein dämonisches Wesen, zeigt sich mitunter als Knäuel. Als ähnliche, aber reale Erscheinung ist in Tirol auch der Kugelblitz bekannt, eine Blitzform, die sich rollend weiterbewegt und mitunter auch durch Haus und Stall rollt. Wer Zeuge eines Kugelblitzes wurde, ist zumeist zeitlebens davon beeindruckt.

Die in wildromantischer Gegend gelegene Leiterburg befindet sich oberhalb von Auer und ist in einer schönen Wanderung über die felsige „Katzenleiter" erreichbar. Von dieser bereits im 12. Jh. erwähnten Burg, auch „Karnol" genannt, sind nur mehr einige Ruinenmauern sichtbar. Schatz- und Rittersagen ranken sich um diese Burg, auch archäologische Funde wurden hier getätigt.

94

Von der eitlen Kellnerin mit der Schlange

In Brixen wird erzählt, es sei einmal eine Kellnerin ungemein eitel und gatzig gewesen und hätte sich auf ihre Schönheit ein gutes Stück eingebildet. Was sie an Lohn verdiente, hängte sie an den Putz. Da begegnete ihr einmal eine arme Frau mit ihren halbverhungerten Kindern und bat sie um etwas. Voll Verachtung tänzelte aber das Mädchen vorüber. Die arme Frau war ihr viel zu wenig. Aber, o Schrecken! In der folgenden Nacht kroch ein hässlicher Wurm von gewaltiger Länge in ihr Bett, legte sich um ihren Hals und war nicht mehr fortzubringen. Sie musste nun zu ihrer Schande den Wurm tragen. Ein Pater, der mehr konnte als andere, und zu dem sie ihre Zuflucht genommen hatte, bannte wohl die Schlange vom Hals weg, konnte sie aber nicht weiter als bis zur Hüfte bringen, wo das Tier um den Leib gewunden verblieb. Da wurde der Wurm wenigstens nicht von den Leuten gesehen und der größten Schande war das Mädchen ledig. Dieses ging nun wohl in sich, aber erst nachdem es sieben Jahre lang gebetet und gefastet und Almosen gegeben und die Eitelkeit ganz abgetan hatte, war der Wurm auf einmal wieder weg.

›› Wissenswertes ‹‹

gatzig = naseweis.

Der moralisch-sittliche Hintergrund dieser Geschichte geht auf die „sieben Hauptsünden", die sieben menschlichen Hauptlaster, nämlich Stolz, Geiz, Neid, Zorn, Unkeuschheit, Unmäßigkeit und Trägheit zurück. Auch in dieser Sage folgt die Strafe Gottes auf den Fuß und zeigt sich wieder einmal durch ein „hässliches" Tier. Um davon erlöst zu werden, muss das Mädchen sieben Jahre lang ein tugendhaftes Leben führen. Den Hauptsünden werden die Tugenden gegenübergestellt: In der abendländischen Kultur werden sieben Tugenden genannt, die sich der Mensch als Lebenshaltung aneignen sollte: Glaube, Hoffnung und Liebe als christliche Tugenden und die aus der antiken Philosophie stammenden Tugenden Besonnenheit, Gerechtigkeit, Tapferkeit und Weisheit.

95

Totenmesse in der Peterskirche

In Auer lebte vor vielen Jahren eine fromme Alte, die gewohnt war, frühmorgens beim ersten Glockenzeichen in die Kirche zu gehen. Einst hörte sie gar frühe läuten und ging alsbald zur Peterskirche, woher die Glocken klangen. Als sie hinkam, stand die Türe sperrangelweit offen und die Kirche war mit unzähligen Betern dicht angefüllt; darunter waren einige Anverwandte. Eine von diesen trat auf sie zu und sagte, sie solle den Gottesdienst der Toten nicht stören und beim Weggehen auf dem Friedhof ein Stück ihres Kleides zurücklassen. Dann gab sie ihr eine brennende Kerze in die Hand. Die alte Frau packte kalter Schauder und sie wünschte sich weit über Berg und Tal; bald ging sie deshalb aus der unheimlichen Kirche und ließ auf dem Friedhof den Unterrock fallen. Am folgenden Tage fand sie denselben in viele hundert kleine Stücke zerrissen, die auf den Gräbern herumlagen. Die Kerze, welche sie mit nach Hause genommen hatte, war ein Totenbein. Die alte Frau hatte der Schrecken so angegriffen, dass sie in den Tagen starb.

›› Wissenswertes ‹‹

Das Motiv der Geistermesse tritt in zahlreichen Sagen oder Märchen der meisten europäischen Länder auf und ist bereits aus dem 7.-8. Jh. überliefert. Häufig ist in solchen Geschichten von verstorbenen Verwandten die Rede, die lebende Menschen warnen und den Rat geben, den Geistern ein Kleidungsstück zurückzulassen. Dieses Kleidungsstück wird am nächsten Morgen vor der Kirche gefunden, von den Geistern in tausend Fetzen zerrissen. In der Regel lebt die Person, welche Zeugin einer Geistermesse wird, nicht mehr lange, sie wird von den Toten geholt. In dieser Art Sage zeigen sich die Toten von ihrer gefährlichen Seite: „Wir lassen Euch den Tag, so lasst uns die Nacht."

96

Trattla-Pfott

Trattla heißt ein Stück Weges neben dem Bache in Martell. Hier ließen sich oft zwei Geister sehen in Gestalt von schwarzen Katzen, erschreckten bald einen Wanderer, verscheuchten bald das vorüberziehende Vieh, liefen bald voraus, bald hinten nach und schienen untereinander stets uneinig zu sein. Warum aber dieser Spuk hier umgeht, damit hat es folgende Bewandtnis:

Es lebte einmal ein Ehepaar in grässlichem Unfrieden, und zuletzt kam es so weit, dass das Weib den Entschluss fasste, sich in dem Plimabach zu ertränken. Sie hatte aber doch nicht den rechten Mut, probierte es oft, kam aber immer wieder mit dem Leben davon.

Einmal riss sie sich das Skapulier vom Halse, warf es fort und der Versuch gelang nun zum ersten Mal. Sie ertrank in den Wassern der Plima und in Trattla wurde ihr Leichnam ans Land gezogen. Einige Zeit darauf starb auch ihr Mann unausgesühnt und ungebessert dahin, und seit dieser Zeit geisterten beide in oben besagter Weise.

›› Wissenswertes ‹‹

„Pfott" ist im Vinschgau die Mundartbezeichnung für „Frau".

Ein Skapulier ist ein kleines Stoffstück, das die Abbildung „Unserer Lieben Frau vom Berge Karmel" aufgestickt oder -gedruckt hat. Seine Geschichte hängt eng mit der Geschichte des um 1100 am Karmelgebirge im heutigen Israel gegründeten Karmelitenordens zusammen. Laut Legende erschien die Muttergottes im 13. Jh. einem englischen Einsiedler und überreichte ihm ein Skapulier, ein Schutzkleid gegen alle möglichen Gefahren. Die „Miniatur"-Skapuliere haben denselben Zweck. Sie waren in Tirol besonders im 18. und 19. Jh. sehr beliebt. – Das christliche Sakrament der Ehe stellt den moralischen Hintergrund dieser Sage dar. Laut katholischer Lehre wurden die sieben Sakramente oder „Mysterien" von Jesus selbst eingesetzt, demzufolge wäre die Ehe eine von Gott gestiftete Institution. Das Ehepaar dieser Sage macht sich demnach auch des Vergehens schuldig, dem Bund der Ehe nicht Genüge getan zu haben. Auch der Spruch „Bis dass der Tod euch scheidet", bewahrheitet sich hier nicht, denn sie müssen zur Strafe auch noch nach dem Tod gemeinsam umgehen.

Für die christliche Kirche war Selbstmord früher ein ähnlich schweres Vergehen wie Mord. Lange Zeit erhielten Suizidtote kein christliches Begräbnis; sie wurden auch nicht in der geweihten Erde begraben oder nur in einer Ecke des Friedhofes. Die heutige katholische Lehre hingegen verurteilt zwar die Tat des Suizids, nicht aber den Täter oder die Täterin. – Vor der Leiche eines Selbstmörders hatte man früher große Scheu, da er als Wiedergänger gefürchtet war. Jahrhundertelang wurden deshalb besondere Beerdigungs- und Abwehrrituale durchgeführt.

97

Nonnengespenst auf Wolfsthurn

In dem schönen und stattlichen Schlosse über Mareit, Wolfsthurn oder auch Mareitenschloss genannt, das jetzt dem Freiherrn von Sternbach gehört und von diesem mehr im Villen- als im Burgstile erneuert worden ist, wandelt, zuzeiten sichtbar werdend, der Geist einer Nonne umher. Ein Ritter von Straßberg hatte aus einem nahen Kloster die Nonne entführt und sie zu beiderseitiger Sicherheit nicht auf seine Feste bei Gossensaß, sondern auf Burg Wolfsthurn gebracht, wo sie seine Besuche empfing und lange sehr vertraut mit ihm lebte. Weshalb des Ritters Geliebte noch geistern muss, meldet die Sage nicht, doch wird es wohl deshalb sein, weil sie als Nonne ihr Gelübde gebrochen.

›› Wissenswertes ‹‹

Dass das von katholischen Priestern, Mönchen und Nonnen abgelegte Pflichtgelübde, sexuell enthaltsam zu leben, in den vergangenen Jahrhunderten nicht von allen Betroffenen wörtlich genommen wurde, ist auch aus Visitationsberichten belegt. Viele Seelsorger hielten sich eine Konkubine, doch dies scheint für das Volk damals kein allzu großes Problem gewesen zu sein. Das in dieser Sage beschriebene über lange Zeit andauernde Verhältnis zwischen einer Klosterfrau und einem Ritter endet mit der Bestrafung der Nonne: Nach dem Tod kann ihre Seele keine ewige Ruhe finden.

Das Schloss Wolfsthurn in Mareit, Gemeinde Ratschings, wird bereits in der ersten Hälfte des 13. Jh. als der Sitz der Wölfe von Mareit erwähnt. Im 18. Jh. errichteten die Freiherren von Sternbach hier das einzige Barockschloss Südtirols. Auch die Burgruine Straßberg bei Ried bei Gossensaß, ehemaliger Gerichtssitz der Tiroler Grafen, stammt aus derselben Zeit.

98

Die Geister der Leuchtenburg

Auf einem hohen Eichenhügel am Kalterer See ragen die Ruinen der Leuchtenburg, während auf einem niedrigen Bühel nicht weit vom Dörfchen Piglon einige spärliche Reste der einst stolzen Laimburg bemerkbar sind. Auf diesen Burgen saßen einst zwei so gute Freunde, dass sie sich wie Brüder liebten. Um sich zu jeder Zeit besuchen zu können, verbanden sie die Schlösser durch einen unterirdischen Gang. Das innige Verhältnis dauerte so lange, bis einmal der Leuchtenburger von einer großen Reise mit einer wunderschönen Frau zurückkam. Diese liebte aber ihren Herrn nicht treu und redlich, sondern fasste eine wilde Neigung zum Laimburger, den sie in ihre Schlingen zu locken wusste. Als der Leuchtenburger einst den Laimburger bei seiner losen Frau ertappte, durchbohrte er die

Buhlerin, verfolgte den treulosen Freund durch den unterirdischen Gang, wo sich bald ein Zweikampf entspann, der mit dem Leben beider endete. Seit dieser Zeit ist es auf dem Leuchtenburger Hügel unheimlich.

Vor etlichen Jahren kehrten zwei Mädchen dort Streu zusammen und verspäteten sich bei der Arbeit. Als sie nach Hause gehen wollten, war es schon dunkel und sie kamen immer an die alte Stelle zurück. Da setzten sie sich endlich unter einem überhängenden Felsen nieder, um zu übernachten. Wie sie miteinander plauderten, stand plötzlich ein hell beleuchtetes Schloss auf dem Hügel und in ihrer Nähre hörten sie deutlich ein Weinen. Von Neugierde getrieben gingen sie endlich Hand in Hand dem Tone zu. Da fanden sie eine schwarz gekleidete Frau, die auf einem Steine saß und bitterlich weinte. Mitleidig fragten die Mädchen, was ihr fehle, dass sie gar so traurig sei. Auf diese Frage stand sie auf und führte sie in das Schloss, wo es gar herrlich und glänzend aussah. Zuletzt ging sie mit ihnen in den Keller, wo ganze Fässer voll Geld lagen. Seufzend sprach sie dann: „All dieses gehört dem unschuldigen Kinde, das mich, meinen Herrn und Buhlen erlöst. Wenn eine von euch den Mut hat, sich von zwei Schlangen, die kein Leid zufügen, von Fuß bis zum Kopfe umwinden zu lassen, ohne einen Laut von sich zu geben, kann sie ihr Glück machen." „Das will ich wohl tun, wenn's nichts Weiteres ist", erwiderte ein Mädchen. Augenblicklich wälzten sich zwei große Schlangen durch den Schlosshof her und umwanden bald mit ihren kalten Leibern das Mädchen, dessen Zähne vor Angst und Kälte klapperten. Tapfer hielt sich das Kind, doch als die abscheulichen Tiere auf seinen Mund losfuhren, als ob sie küssen wollten, entfloh ihm ein Ach. Da sank die schwarz gekleidete Frau jammernd in die Erde, die Würmer waren verschwunden und in der Tiefe klingelten und rollten die Taler, als ob sie nie enden wollten.

›› Wissenswertes ‹‹

Das weit verbreitete Sagenmotiv des Ehebruchs kann jenem der ehelichen Treue („Die Frau von Hochgalsaun", Kapitel Königin und Fürstin) gegenübergesetzt werden. Ehebruch, lateinisch „adulterium" wird von „ad alterum se conferre" abgeleitet und bedeutet so viel wie „Eigentum auf einen anderen übertragen". In Zeiten der weiblichen Erbfolge konnte eine Frau mit Besitz ihren Reichtum (=„matrimonium") auf einen anderen übertragen, so dass ihr ehemaliger Ehemann u. U. arm wurde. Die sexuelle eheliche Treue der Frau war deshalb vor allem aus ökonomischer Sicht wichtig. Seit Beginn der patriarchalen Zeit wird weiblicher Ehebruch nicht nur als moralisch schwer verwerflich angesehen, in vielen Kulturen der Vergangenheit (Germanen, Römer, Juden, Islam) stand darauf sogar die Todesstrafe, beispielsweise durch Steinigung, Moorversenkung oder Enthauptung. Bei den alten Germanen war das Delikt dabei oft weniger der Ehebruch an sich, sondern der außereheliche Geschlechtsverkehr ohne Erlaubnis des Ehemannes. Auch laut Bibel, vor allem im Alten Testament, ist weiblicher Ehebruch um vieles schwerwiegender als der männliche. Aus der Sicht der katholischen Kirche ist Ehebruch, besonders der andauernde, eine schwere Sünde. Die in dieser Sage erfolgte Selbstjustiz durch den Ehemann verstärkt die über den Tod hinausführende seelische Verstrickung zwischen dem Betrogenen, der untreuen Ehefrau und dem Nebenbuhler. Nur eine außergewöhnlich mutige Tat eines unschuldigen Mädchens hätte die Erlösung ihrer Seelen bewirken können. – Die auf dem Rücken des Mitterberges zwischen Auer und Kaltern gelegene Burgruine Leuchtenburg ist vermutlich um 1200 entstanden. Sie war u.a. im Besitz der Herren von Rottenburg und der Trientner Fürstbischöfe. Nicht weit von ihr entfernt erhebt sich die aus dem 13. Jh. stammende Laimburg, heute nur mehr Ruine. Dieses Gebiet um Mitterberg/Piglon/Stadlhof/Pfatten war schon sehr früh besiedelt, wie zahlreiche vorgeschichtliche Funde belegen. Berühmt sind vor allem die hier entdeckte Siedlung aus dem 9.-7. Jh. v. Chr. und eine große Nekropole.

99

Das verlorene Mädel

Ein Bauer in Schenna, der von seinem ersten Weibe ein „recht flüchtiges“ Madl hatte, heiratete zum zweiten Male. Die Stiefmutter sah der Tochter auf die Finger und hielt sie in strenger Zucht. Das gefiel dieser aber nicht, sie verließ gegen den Willen ihrer Eltern die Heimat und verdingte sich bei einem Bauern in Verdins als Magd. Etliche Jahre diente sie dort brav und redlich und man hatte nur das an ihr auszusetzen, dass sie nie ihre Eltern besuchte. Selbst als die Stiefmutter schwer erkrankt war und sie rufen ließ, folgte sie nicht diesem Wunsche, sondern nahm lachend den Graskorb auf den Rücken und ging mit ihrer Gesellin in den Wald. Als sie dort schon längere Zeit Gras gemacht hatten, sagte plötzlich die ungehorsame Tochter: „Jetzt hab' ich die Stiefmutter rufen hören, aber die ist sicher, dass ich komme.“ So sagte sie dreimal zur Magd. Als diese später von ihrer Arbeit aufsah und ihre Gesellin mit den Augen suchte, sah sie wohl den Korb an einen Baum gelehnt und die Sichel am Boden – allein die ungehorsame Tochter war für immer entführt. Am Platze, wo sie zum letzten Male gesehen ward, steht nun eine kleine Kapelle.

›› Wissenswertes ‹‹

Das Stiefmutter- und Stiefkindmotiv ist Thema unzähliger Märchen und Sagen. Die hohe Geburtenanzahl und die damit zusammenhängende hohe Frauensterblichkeit bei der Geburt führten früher auch in Tirol sehr oft zu einer raschen Wiederverheiratung seitens des verwitweten Vaters und Bauern. Dabei spielte „die Liebe“ zumeist eine untergeordnete Rolle, es ging vielmehr um praktische Gründe: Die durch den Tod der Ehefrau und Mutter entstandene Lücke musste so rasch wie möglich geschlossen werden. In dieser Sage mit erzieherisch-moralischer Botschaft wagt die Stieftochter den Ausbruch aus der familiären/stiefmütterlichen Bevormundung. Doch auf diesen Bruch, der laut Geschichte in der höchst verwerflichen mangelnden Hilfeleistung vonseiten der Stieftochter ihrer erkrankten Stiefmutter gegenüber gipfelt, folgt eine harte Strafe: das Mädchen wird aus ihrem jungen Erdenleben herausgerissen.

100

Sterzinger Mooslied

Gehts los't und seid ruhig und fein,
Wia hoach iatz die Madler galsch sein:
Rosaure von Purzlbaamgschlecht,
Der war holt koan Mannsbild nia recht.

Der David ist ihr zu zart,
Der Ludwig hat gor koan Bart,
Der Jörg ischt tschergat und krump,
Der Hans, sagt sie, sell war a Lump.

Der Kosmas ischt ihr zu betrüabt,
Der Thomas zu wieni verliabt,
Der Rochus ischt ihr zu znicht,
Der Franzl hat Tupfn in Gsicht.

Der Wenzl hat an schelchen Blick,
Der Peter, der ischt ihr zu dick,
Der Martl, der ischt ihr zu faul,
Der Klaus hat a Hölzl in Maul.

Der Luis, der ischt ihr zu stolz,
Der Jaggl ischt wie a Stuck Holz,
Ban Toni hats Betn koa Ziel,
Der Wolfgang, der isst ihr zu viel.

Der Bartl, sagt sie, sei nix nutz,
Der Heinrich voll Schmier und voll Schmutz,
Der Benjamin sei wie a Kind,
Der Tobias ischt an zwoa Augn blind.

Der Simon ischt a bissl derrüahrt,
Der Korl zu wieni studiart,
Der Leonhard ischt viel zu verzagt,
Der Lipp ward von Wuecher geplagt.

Der Rupert hat zu wieni Geld,
Der Natz isch a durschtiger Held,
Der Moritz schnupft zuviel Tabak,
Der Paul hat an lochrigen Frack.

Der Rudl hat an verdrahnten Gang,
Der Adolf a Maul wia a Zang,
Der Blas tuet zu viel seggiarn,
Der Much will koan Geld spendiarn.

So hat sie lang gwählt und lang glauscht,
Derweil sein die Jahrlan verrauscht,
Wurmschnitzlig die Zähnd brechn los,
Iatz huckt sie in Störzinger Moos.

Und iatz, sagt er, schaut sie aus,
Ist a Spott, sagt er, ist a Graus,
Alls voll Kot, sagt er, alls voll Mist,
Iatz betracht sie, sagt er, liaber Christ.

hoach galsch = überheblich.

Vor der Trockenlegung um 1877 anlässlich des Baus der Brennereisenbahn war die Gegend zwischen Sterzing und Stilfes ein ausgedehntes Moorgebiet, bevölkert von zahlreichen Fröschen, Kröten und anderem Sumpfgetier. Dieser Sumpfboden war laut Volksüberlieferung das Sammelgebiet all jener verstorbenen Jungfrauen, die aus eigener Schuld unverheiratet geblieben waren. Zur Strafe sind sie nun auf alle Ewigkeit ins Sterzinger Moos verbannt. Wollte seinerzeit ein Fuhrmann nach Einbruch der Dunkelheit noch mit seinem Fuhrwerk durchs Moos Richtung Süden fahren, lief er große Gefahr, von den Jungfern ins Moor hinuntergezogen zu werden. Laut Sage müssen die Jungfern bis zum Jüngsten Tag das ganze Sterzinger Moos mit den Fingern nach Spannen ausmessen. Dabei beten sie gemeinsam eine herzzerreißende Litanei, wobei die Vorbeterin so anfängt: „Mi ruit's, dass i nit g'heirat' hon", und die anderen Jungfrauen antworten: „Mi aa, mi aa, mi aa" ... Andere lamentieren so: „Hätt' i's lei g'wagg, g'wagg, g'wagg, hätt' i längst ein' schun g'habb, g'habb, g'habb ..." Auch in anderen Gebieten Tirols gibt es Banngebiete für ledige Jungfrauen: Im Vinschgau ist es das Plauser Moos, in Kiens eine Felsenhöhle oberhalb des Dorfes, im Schlerngebiet der Tschafon-Berg und der Schlern selbst. In Welschnofnen kamen die Jungfrauen auf den Plun, im Süden des Dorfes, mussten dort büßen und „Jungfernplärrer" tun.

Doch auch die Hagestolze haben nicht leicht lachen, denn auch ihnen ist der Himmel versagt. Sie müssen nämlich auf dem Roßkopf, dem Sterzinger Hausberg, jahrein jahraus „Wolken schieben oder Fürze klieben" (spalten). Laut einer anderen Überlieferung landen sie auf dem in der Nähe des Sterzinger Mooses gelegenen Custozahügel (Kronbühel), von wo aus sie voller Sehnsucht zu ihren Leidensgenossinnen hinüberschielen. Aber auch andernorts ist das Leben nach dem Tod für unverheiratete Junggesellen nicht leicht: Sie müssen Steinböcke salzen, Felsen abreiben, Nebel schieben (in der Floite und in Stillup im Zillertal) oder schwarzen Gänsedreck so lange kauen bis er weiß wie Wachs ist; müssen Linsen klieben so wie Holzscheiter, aber auch diese Arbeit ist sehr schwierig, denn da die Linsen rund sind, rutschen sie immer wieder ab. Oder sie müssen Beer-Ameisen (die kleinste Ameisenart) ringeln, wie es bei Schweinen gemacht wird, wenn ihnen ein Drahtring durch den Rüssel geschoben wird, damit sie nicht in der Erde wühlen; oder aber sie müssen Kühe plattern (am Petereck bei St.Peter/Ellbögen im nördlichen Wipptal).

Bannplätze für unverheiratete Jungfrauen gibt es aber auch in zahlreichen anderen Gebieten außerhalb Tirols. Verbannungsorte sind neben Gletschern oder Bergen zumeist Sumpf- oder Wassergegenden. Bereits um 43 n. Chr. erwähnte der römische Geograf Pomponius Mela die Sumpfinsel Sena im Atlantischen Ozean, der Bretagne vorgelagert, wo neun Jungfrauen zur ewigen Jungfrauenschaft verdammt lebten.

Verbannungs-Sagen für Unverheiratete werden mit der gesellschaftlich als wichtig angesehenen Fähigkeit von Fruchtbarkeit und Fortpflanzung in Verbindung gebracht. Wer diesen gesellschaftlichen Normen nicht entspricht, muss mit Verachtung und Spott rechnen. Doch vielleicht hat die Sterzinger Moos-Sage auch einen älteren Hintergrund. Ein Vergleich mit der Insel Sena bietet sich an: Hier soll sich laut Mythos einst ein Heiligtum einer gallischen Gottheit oder der Göttin Diana befunden haben. Neun Priesterinnen, die lebenslängliche Jungfräulichkeit geschworen hatten und Seherinnen und Heilerinnen gewesen waren, sollen hier gelebt haben. Am Rande vom Sterzinger Moos befindet sich die Sterzinger Pfarrkirche „Maria im Moos", vermutlich über einem römischen Gräberfeld errichtet. Auch eine heute leider nicht mehr zugängliche Quelle befindet sich im Kirchenbezirk. Die römisch/griechische Diana/Artemis wurde u.a. in Sümpfen verehrt. Laut dem Sagenforscher K.F. Wolff könnte der alte Name Sterzings, „Vipitenum", „Vipitina", so viel wie „Frauenfeld" bedeuten. Die Sage von den Jungfern im Sterzinger Moos wäre demzufolge eine geschichtlich später erfolgte Verunglimpfung der möglicherweise einst an dieser heiliger Stätte lebenden und mit einer wichtigen Funktion, vielleicht derer der Priesterinnen, betrauten Jungfrauen. Der heutige Bau der Sterzinger Pfarrkirche „Maria im Moos“ ist mit über 32 m Firsthöhe der höchste zwischen München und Verona. Ihre außerordentliche Ausstrahlung ist aufgrund des in der Nähe gelegenen populären Wallfahrtortes Maria Trens ein wenig in den Hintergrund gerückt. Doch auch der Tiroler Hexenmeister Pfeifer Huisele soll im 17. Jh. einst gesagt haben: „Alle laufen sie nach Maria Trens, derweil wäre die Mooszussl viel die bessere.“

Eine andere Sage berichtet, dass sich zwischen Sterzing und Stilfes einst die Stadt „Grande“, die Hauptstadt von ganz Tirol, befunden habe. Aufgrund eines Seeausbruchs im Pfitscher Tal sei sie untergegangen. Das vom Sterzinger Moos übrig gebliebene nördlich von Stilfes gelegene Sumpfbiotop „Grantemoos“ erinnert mit seinem Namen heute noch an diese Sage.

101

Das Eschenloher Schlossfräulein

Auf den Ruinen des Schlosses Eschenloh in Ulten sieht man zur Nachtzeit am Fenster ein blaues (rotblaues) Lichtlein brennen, und in der Dämmerung erscheint oftmals eine schöne Jungfrau, die weinend an den Schlossabhängen wandelt und wehmütige Lieder singt. Sie muss nach ihrem Tode noch umgehen, weil sie zu Lebzeiten unehrbare Lieder gesungen, ein zu freies Leben geführt und mit ihren Reizen viele Herren verführt hat.

›› Wissenswertes ‹‹

Die Ruine der Burganlage von Eschenlohe (auch Eschenloch genannt) befindet sich in St. Pankraz in Ulten. Urkundlich wurde die Burg als Schloss Ulten im 12. Jh. erstmals erwähnt, seither hat sie mehrmals den Besitzer gewechselt. Seit 1492 ist die Familie Trapp im Besitz der Burganlage. Der Name Eschenlohe stammt vermutlich aus der Zeit der Herrschaft des Grafen von Eschenloch, einem Sohn Meinhards II. von Tirol, der sie 1319-1349 als Pflegschaft innehatte.

Das Licht ist ein Erscheinungsbild der Seele; daran erinnert auch das Lebenslicht. Das rotblaue Licht, welches in Eschenloh beobachtet wurde, deutet auf die harte Qual der Jungfrau, der Armen Seele, hin, während grünliches, die Farbe der Hoffnung, baldige Erlösung vermuten lässt. Je näher die Seele der Erlösung kommt, desto lichter, heller und weißer wird sie. Im Moment der Erlösung umstrahlt die Arme Seele ein wunderbarer Lichterglanz.

Zu den Lieblingsaufenthaltsorten der Seelen gehören auch geweihte Orte, Wegkreuze, Waldkapellen und Gottesäcker, auf denen sie als zarte Lichtlein umherirren.

102

Die glühende Sennin

Über dem Alperschontale liegt eine Landecker Gerichtsalpe; herkömmlich verteilt der Richter die Almtriften zur Hut an die berechtigten Gemeinden des Stanzertales und des Landecker Gerichtsbezirkes im Wechsel, auch ist bei dieser Hut den Sennern oder Sennerinnen von Alters her gestattet, einiges eigen Vieh, Kühe, Schweine oder Schafe, mit aufzutreiben, es droben mit an die Weide gehen zu lassen, und es dann im Herbst zu ihrem Benefiz zu verkaufen. Nun war auf der Alm Alper schon eine junge, leichtsinnige Sennin, die trieb einige Schweine mit auf, die ihr gehörten, und sorgte für dieselben gar zu mütterlich, denn sie fütterte diese vom Gute der Gemeinde mit Schotten und Zieger, dass sie fett und rund wurden, wie Murfl, die anderen Schweine aber bekamen speres Käswasser zu schlucken, welches nicht anlegt. Dabei war die Sennin stets wohlauf, munter, g'sapssig, sang die schönsten Liedlen, war von allen gern gesehen, und niemand dachte daran, dass sie eine Almdiebin sei. Häufig kamen ein paar Enziangräber aus Schnann, dem Heimatdorfe dieser Dirne, zur Almzeit herauf zur Alperschonalpe und blieben auch einmal länger droben, nachdem die Heimfahrt bereits erfolgt war. Sie brauchten die leere Thaie als Trockenplatz und Niederlage für ihre Wurzelbürden. Als die Männer nun herab ins Tal und nach Schnann kamen, vorerst nur mit einem Teile ihres Enzianvorrates, so vernahmen sie mit Verwunderung, dass die junge hübsche Sennerin jählings gestorben sei und sie just noch recht kämen, mit ihr zur Leiche zu gehen. Das taten sie denn auch mit aufrichtiger Betrübnis, und ein paar Tage später gingen sie wieder zur Alpe hinauf, den noch droben gelassenen Enzian herabzuholen. Fast war es schon Nacht, als die beiden Männer droben ankamen, da hörten sie, wie sie der Kaser sich nahten, Schweine zum Fresstroge locken, und zwar ganz mit der Stimme der verstorbenen jungen Sennin. Und wie sie näher kamen, erblickten sie dieselbe leibhaftig, einen Ember voll Käswasser in den Händen, aber dabei über und über glühend, in der Thaie herumfahren. Bestürzt standen die Männer und seufzten, da rief ihnen der Geist zu: „Ja, seufzt nur über mich! Ich muss glühen und brennen, bis mein unredlicher Frevel abgebüßt ist bis auf den letzten Heller!“, und verschwand vor den Augen mit Geheul und Brandgeruch.
In dieser Gegend ist die schaurige und weit berufene Schnannerklamm, die vom Dorfe Schnann den Namen hat, und in der es an Klammmännerspuk nicht mangelt.

Schotten = gestockte Milch, Zieger = kleiner, kegelförmiger, aus Sauermilch hergestellter Käse, sper = dürftig, Thaie = ein seit dem 14. Jh. dokumentierter Ausdruck für eine Sennhütte im Almgebiet, Ember = Eimer, Schaff.

Zwischen den Lechtaler Alpen und der Verwallgruppe zieht sich das Stanzertal vom Arlberg bis nach Landeck hin. Hier befindet sich, wenige Gehminuten von der Ortschaft Schnann entfernt, die sagenumwobene Schnanner Klamm, ein imposantes Naturdenkmal mit tosenden Wasserfällen, heute ein beliebtes Ausflugsziel für Naturfreunde.

Das Schwein ist in vielen alten Mythen ein Göttinnentier. So war es das heilige Begleittier der vermutlich aus der etruskischen Religion stammenden römischen Ceres (die griechische Demeter), Göttin der Ehe, des Todes und des Ackerbaus. Durch sein Wühlen in der Erde und das Aufreißen des Bodens wird das Schwein kultur- und mythengeschichtlich mit der Zeit des ersten Ackerbaus in Beziehung gesetzt. In der christlichen Religion wurde es zum Teufelstier, mit Begierde, Unkeuschheit und Unmäßigkeit in Verbindung gebracht. In zahlreichen Erzählungen aus dem ganzen Alpengebiet kommen Schwein, Sau, Eber oder Wildschwein vor. Aus Savoyen beispielsweise ist eine Sage überliefert, in welcher sich im Gebiet des Voirons ein Venustempel befand. Und auch als die Menschen der Ebene bereits zum neuen christlichen Glauben übergetreten waren, verehrten die dortigen Alpenbewohner immer noch die heidnische Venus. Da ließ der Bischof von Genf den Heidentempel und das Götzenbild niederreißen. Doch nun nahm Venus, laut Sage eine Erscheinungsform Satans, die Gestalt eines grässlichen Wildschweins an und stellte sich drohend den Menschen in den Weg und griff jeden an, der zum christlichen Glauben übertreten wollte. Das teuflische Schwein aber drang mit Gewalt in das Kapelleninnere ein und konnte hier niedergestreckt werden. Ein Edler namens Amadeus von Langin, der auch lebensgefährlich verwundet wurde, errichtete als Dank zur Wiedergenesung an der Stelle des abgerissenen Tempels eine Kapelle zu Ehren der Heiligen Jungfrau (vergleiche dazu das Märchen „Vom tapferen Schneiderlein" der Gebrüder Grimm).

Die Seele wird oftmals als leuchtende Flamme versinnbildlicht. Auch die Irrlichter werden als die Seelen Verstorbener umschrieben, welche noch auf Erden herumirren müssen. Das Glühen dieser Sennerin kann verglichen werden mit dem Glühen der Seelen im Fegfeuer. Ihre zu Lebzeiten begangenen Frevel muss sie in Form von Glut und Hitze abbüßen. Doch nicht nur durch die „warme Pein" müssen Seelen nach dem Tode büßen, sondern bekannt ist auch als Gegenstück die „kalte und die nasse Pein". So taucht z.B. aus dem Radelsee bei Brixen jeden Freitag aus den Wellen ein Priester auf, der gegen seine Pfarrkinder ausgesagt haben soll. Er trägt keinen Kopf und seine Haut ist weiß, was bedeutet, dass er bereits viel abgebüßt hat. Oftmals müssen die Armen Seelen ihre Vergehen an jenem Ort abdienen, wo sie zu Lebzeiten begangen wurden. Auch auf der Saubacher Alpe in Flaas muss in der Walpurgisnacht der feurige Geist einer Sennin umfahren, da sie zu Lebzeiten oft den Sonntag entheiligt hatte.

103

Die Wilde Jägerin

Auf der Alpe „Hochtennen", die das Inntal vom Lechtal scheidet, war es vor Jahren nicht geheuer. Wer droben über Nacht verweilen wollte, der sah gar bald schwarze Wolken zusammenziehen, hörte bald darauf wettern und wüten, und mitten im Wetter stand eine riesige, feurige Frauengestalt, eine lange Peitsche in der Hand. Bald sah man sie auch so gestaltet keuchend und schnaubend als Höllenfürstin dahinfliegen, gefolgt von einem Heere feuriger Stiere, und so ging es in den wogenden Nebeln herum, ein wahrer Höllenreigen, bis zum Morgengrauen. Dann ging's im brausenden Fluge einer Felsenwand zu, wo ein furchtbarer Schlund war, in welchem die feurige Riesin voraus, die Herde ihr nach, versank und Gebrüll und Gelächter weithin über die Höhen erschallte.

Wenn sich einer auf dem Wege verspätete und in diese Wetternacht geriet, so verirrte er sich, und wenn er meinte, an Ort und Stelle zu sein, so war er doch wieder am alten Fleck, oder er kam gar an die Felswand und fiel sich zu Tode. Daher scheute sich Jung und Alt, sowohl Hirten als auch Jäger, über die „Tennen" zu gehen, und musste es sein, so bekreuzigten sie sich und beteten um Schutz vor Gefahr. Die Wand mit ihrem Schlund ist wohl zu sehen, doch hütet man sich sogar bei Tag, in deren Bereich zu kommen. Dieses Schreckgespenst – sehr an die Holla mahnend – soll bei Lebzeiten eine saubere Dirn gewesen sein, schön wie Milch und Blut. Dessen war sie sich auch bewusst, sie brach manch unschuldiges Herz entzwei, und Hoffart und Stolz wohnten in ihrem Herzen, und daraus ging unbändiger Trotz in all ihr Tun und Lassen über. Sie war Sennin auf der Hochtennenalpe und trieb aus boshaftem Zeitvertreib das ihr anvertraute Vieh an die jähe Felsenwand und ergötzte sich, wenn die unglücklichen Tiere in den finstern Schlund des Abgrunds fielen und zerschellten. Sie lachte laut auf zum Gebrülle der armen Opfer.

So trieb sie es viele, viele Jahre. Doch ihre Stunde schlug früher als sie gedachte. Der gerechte Richter sandte den Tod – aber selbst das Grab wurde ihrem Leibe nicht vergönnt. Sobald die Aveglocke abends läutete, da stieg sie aus dem Grabe hinauf zu ihrem Sündenpfuhl und büßte als Wilde Jägerin ihren Frevel.

›› Wissenswertes ‹‹

In dieser Sage überlappen sich mehrere weibliche Sagengestalten. Zu Beginn ist von einer kraftvollen Riesin die Rede, sagengeschichtlich eine der ältesten Gestalten überhaupt. So wie die Perchta die Wilde Jagd anführt, jagt sie dann als „Höllenfürstin" durch die Luft und endet schließlich in einem tiefen Schlund (Schlünde, Höhlen, das Erdinnere sind Aufenthaltsorte der Göttin). Im Verlauf der Sage wird sie zunehmend in schlechteres Licht gerückt: sie ist hoffärtig, stolz, boshaft und grausam. Dieses Sagenmotiv einer ruhelosen, nachts durch die Lüfte reitenden wilden Jägerin ist auch aus anderen Gebieten belegt. Eine der bekanntesten Sagen ist jene von der Schwarzen Margarethe, die mit dem dänischen

König Christoph I. (13. Jh.) verheiratet war. Laut Überlieferung lebte sie auf der Weißen Burg Belgard in Pommern. Doch während ihr Vater Krieg gegen die Heiden führte, frönte sie mit dessen Bruder ihrer großen Leidenschaft, der Jagd. Deretwegen soll sie sogar den Sonntag entheiligt haben. Einmal durchschoss sie aus Übermut das Herz der Hl. Jungfrau auf einem Bildstock. Zur Strafe dafür muss sie nun nach ihrem Tod immerfort jagen, und in der Nacht vor dem Margarethentag hofft sie weinend auf Erlösung. – Der in dieser Sage vorkommende Stier ist in den Mythen sowohl ein männliches Fruchtbarkeitssymbol der Natur als auch ein mit dem Mond in Verbindung stehendes Göttinnentier. In den ältesten Mythen werden viele Gottheiten stiergestaltig dargestellt; häufig als Gemahl einer Göttin. Die Stierverehrung im Mithraskult geht auf ältere Mythen der Großen Göttin zurück: Vor der Verehrung Mithras, dem Stier tötenden Erlöser, wurde bereits die Mondgöttin, bei den Griechen die Artemis Tauropolos („Stiertöterin“) verehrt; in Asien tötete die große Kali den Opferstier, und auch zu Ehren der römichen Kybele-Attis (eine ursprünglich hermaphroditische Gottheit) fand ein Stieropfer statt.

104

Die Kröte auf Weißenstein

Eine Frau in Bozen hatte eine Wallfahrt nach Weißenstein versprochen, kam jedoch nie zur Ausführung dieses Gelübdes. Nach ihrem Tode musste sie so lange als Kröte leiden, bis sie ihr Versprechen erfüllte. Als scheußliche Hötsch watschelte sie gegen den berühmten Wallfahrtsort, den sie erst in sieben Jahren erreichen konnte. Als sie das Ziel der Fahrt erreicht hatte und das gnadenreiche Marienbild sah, war sie erlöst und flog in Gestalt einer schneeweißen Taube zum Himmel.

›› Wissenswertes ‹‹

Hötsch = Kröte.

Sehr oft wird von der Verwandlung der Frauen in Kröten berichtet, in deren Gestalt sie auf der Erde so lange herumwandeln und wallfahrten müssen, bis sie ihre Vergehen abgebüßt haben. Auch nicht eingehaltene Wallfahrtsversprechen ziehen schwere Seelenqualen nach sich. Mit der Kröte verbinden wir gerne Hässlichkeit, Ekel und Giftigkeit, gleichzeitig ruft der Anblick einer Kröte auch Mitleid hervor. Da man an die Arme Seele dachte, welche in Gestalt der Kröte umherwandeln könnte, war es verboten, sie zu töten, besonders am Allerseelentag. Das Verwandeln in eine Tiergestalt hängt mit der Vorstellung des irdischen Fortlebens der Seele zusammen. Die Kröte steht wie der Frosch als Symbol für die Auferstehung und gilt in Tirol als geisterhaftes Tier, vor allem wenn sie in der Nähe von Wallfahrtsorten, von Kapellen und Kirchen zu beobachten ist. Besonders an Quatembertagen (Quatember, aus dem lateinischen „quattuor tempora", waren früher auf die vier Jahreszeiten verteilte kirchliche Buß- und Fastentage bzw. -wochen) wandeln die Armen Seelen in Gestalt von Kröten umher. In den Zwölften (Die Nächte der „Zwölften", der zwölf christlichen Weihnachtsfeiertage, und zwar vom Hl. Abend bis zur Nacht vom 5. auf den 6. Jänner, sind, ebenso wie die Quatembertage, gefährliche Geisterzeiten, denn laut Volksglauben steht in dieser Zeit die Tür des Geisterreichs offen) sind sie gefährlich, wahrscheinlich weil sie durch die Rückkehr der Seelen in dieser Zeit ihre dämonische Natur wiedererlangen.

Die Farbe der Kröte zeigt die Größe der Schuld an. Sollte man eine solche Kröte auf ihrer Wallfahrt antreffen, so sollte man sie ziehen lassen, um nicht das gleiche Schicksal zu erfahren.
Fink berichtet, dass in Ritten alte Leute sogar glaubten, dass man das Beten dieser Kröten hören könne. Dort sagte man: „Die wallfahrenden Kröten hummen." – Eine ähnliche Sage aus Meran erzählt von einer Kröte, welche immer wieder am Eingang der Meraner Totengruft gesehen wurde. Eines Tages wurde sie von einem frommen Menschen als Arme Seele erkannt und erlöst. Da verwandelte sie sich – ebenso wie in der angeführten Sage – in eine blütenweiße Taube. Die weiße davonfliegende Taube versinnbildlicht die erlöste Arme Seele, befreit und gereinigt von ihrer Schuld. Daran knüpft der alte Volksglaube der Menschen, welche sich die Seele als Vogel, oftmals als Taube, vorstellten.

Fürstin und Königin

Bunt und facettenreich sind die Sagen um **Königinnen**, **Fürstinnen** und Burgherrinnen. Da sie im Laufe vieler Jahrhunderte entstanden sind, ist auch die Rolle der edlen Frau in den Sagen höchst unterschiedlich; es zeigt sich wieder deutlich, dass die jeweilige Geschichtsepoche gewissermaßen ihre Spuren auch in der Sagenwelt hinterlassen hat. Dass sowohl Geschichtsschreibung als auch das Sammeln und Aufzeichnen von Sagen fast ausschließlich in Männerhänden gelegen ist, ist auch aus den „Ideal"-Beschreibungen der Frauen in vielen Fürstinnen-Sagen ersichtlich. Als besondere Qualitäten der edlen Frau werden demzufolge Treue, Demut, Frömmigkeit, Loyalität dem Manne gegenüber, Selbstaufgabe, Edelmut, Barmherzigkeit und Bescheidenheit genannt.

Doch darf an dieser Stelle nicht unerwähnt bleiben, dass eine Reihe von außergewöhnlichen Frauen aus fürstlichem oder adeligem Geschlecht in der Tiroler Geschichte bleibende Spuren hinterlassen hat. Aus Platzgründen wollen wir nur einige Beispiele aufzählen: Kaiserin Maria Theresia, die große Reformerin im 18. Jh., über welche ihr Erzfeind, Friedrich der Große, einst gesagt haben soll: „Einmal haben die Habsburger einen Mann auf dem Thron, und dann ist es eine Frau." Claudia de Medici (17. Jh.), die „italienische" Landesfürstin von Tirol, nahm als zweifache Witwe bereits mit 28 Jahren die Geschicke des Landes Tirol in die Hand. Eleonore von Schottland (15. Jh.), die kunstsinnige Gattin von Siegmund dem Münzreichen, führte in seiner häufigen Abwesenheit die Regierung und sprach Recht. Verena von Stuben (15. Jh.), die streitbare Äbtissin des Klosters Sonnenburg, kämpfte für ein Leben in Selbstbestimmung und Selbstverwirklichung für sich und zahlreiche adlige Töchter. Margarete von Tirol (14. Jh.), eine der faszinierendsten Frauengestalten Tirols, war klug, schön und mächtig. Theophanu (geboren ca. um 960), Kaiserin des Hl. Römischen Reiches, war eine der einflussreichsten Herrscherinnen des Abendlandes im Mittelalter, welche nach einem heil überstandenen Unfall den Bau der St.-Margareth-Kirche in Lana veranlasst haben soll. Einige Historiker bezeichnen jene Epoche gar despektierlich als „Weiberwirtschaft", weil neben Theophanu damals noch eine Reihe von anderen Frauen eine führende Position in der Politik einnahmen.

Wer heute einen oberflächlichen Blick in die Welt der adligen Frau in diesen vergangenen Jahrhunderten zurückwirft, denkt vielleicht an umworbene

Burgfräulein oder edlen Minnegesang für die Schlossherrin, an eine Schar von Zofen oder kostbare Juwelen. Die Entfaltungsmöglichkeiten dieser Frauen waren jedoch alles andere als leicht, sie variierten zwar je nach Zeitepoche, waren aber auf jeden Fall in eine von Männern bestimmte Ordnung eingebunden. Auch der Familienstand, ledig, verheiratet oder verwitwet, spielte eine Rolle sowie die „Fähigkeit", Nachkommen, wenn möglich männliche, in die Welt zu setzen.

Die Partnerwahl für adlige Töchter und Söhne war eine kalkulierte Angelegenheit. In erster Linie ging es dabei um die Verbesserung des Familienvermögens oder um politisch-strategische Überlegungen oder um beides. Über das weitere Lebensschicksal der Kinder entschieden die väterliche Autorität und oft sogar die erweiterte Adelsfamilie, die Wünsche der Betroffenen selbst spielten bei diesen Entscheidungen keine Rolle. Dies wird in der Sage „Das Liebespaar von Schloss Nanno" aus dem Nonstal im Trentino deutlich, einem Tal, das außerordentlich reich an Burgen und Schlössern ist. Entsprechend viele Burg- und Schlosssagen sind in diesem Tal entstanden und erhalten geblieben.

Hatte eine Frau aus höherem Stand im Mittelalter den Mut, der Stimme ihres Herzens zu folgen und einen Mann niederen Standes zu heiraten, musste sie sich von da an mit der Stellung ihres Ehemannes begnügen. Verliebte sich ein Adliger in eine nichtadlige Frau, war eine Hochzeit nur selten möglich; die Frau nahm den Status einer Mätresse ein. Aus den oben erwähnten Gründen war die sexuelle Toleranz, vor allem Männern gegenüber, zeitweise in den vergangenen Jahrhunderten sehr groß. Die angeführte Sage zu Philippine Welser, die sich jahrzehntelang mit dem Titel „Ferdinands Beiwohnerin" zufriedenstellen musste, zeugt von der schwierigen Situation einer Fürstenfrau bürgerlicher Herkunft.

Große politische Ereignisse wie Kriege, Kreuzzüge und dergleichen zeigten auch in der Tiroler Adelswelt ihre Auswirkungen. Eine der wichtigsten Pflichten der Ritter war der Kriegsdienst, dies führte unter Umständen auch zu längerer Abwesenheit von der schützenden Burg und der Gemahlin. Unzählige Geschichten in ganz Europa erzählen von Treue und Untreue der zurückgebliebenen Ritterfrau; „Die Dame von Hauenstein" ist das Beispiel einer solchen Sage.

Förderung von Kunst und Kultur, Zeitvertreib mit Musik und Poesie wurde auf vielen Höfen großgeschrieben. Die Helden- und Ritterepik fand nicht nur in der Adligenwelt, sondern auch beim einfachen Volk Gefallen. Einige stark gekürzte Ausschnitte aus diesen „Liedern", in welchen königliche Frauen aus dem Tiroler Raum im Mittelpunkt stehen und deren Spuren sich auch in örtlichen Sagen wiederfinden, wurden deshalb mit in dieses Kapitel aufgenommen. Diese Geschichten lassen die einstige machtvolle Stellung auch weiblicher Herrscherinnen erahnen.

Im Mittelalter wurden Mädchen im Alter zwischen 12 und 16 Jahren verheiratet. Die Frau war dem Mann untertan, er verfügte über das von ihr mitgebrachte Geld. Auch die Lage alleinstehender adeliger Frauen war schwierig. Wenn sie nicht heirateten, hatten sie jedoch die Möglichkeit, auf einem Fürstenhof ihre Dienste zur Verfügung zu stellen, z.B. als Kammerjungfer, oder in ein Kloster einzutreten.

Außer den traditionellen monastischen Orden bestand die Möglichkeit des Eintritts in ein Frauenstift. In einem adligen Stift brauchten die Gelübde der Armut und der lebenslänglichen Ehelosigkeit nicht abgelegt zu werden. Neben dem religiösen Gebet und dem karitativen Wirken gab es eine Reihe von Tätigkeiten, die der Selbstverwirklichung der Frauen förderlich waren. Eine andere ordensähnliche Gemeinschaft waren die Beginenhöfe. Aufgrund des Einbringens der jeweiligen Besitztümer und Mitgiften der adligen Frauen waren diese demokratisch organisierten Gemeinschaften wirtschaftlich unabhängig. Die Beginen legten auch stets großen Wert darauf, sich ihren Lebensunterhalt selbst zu verdienen. Vor allem in den Bereichen Handarbeit und Wäsche wurden zahlreiche Beginenhöfe zu wirtschaftlichen Zentren. Auch aus religiöser Sicht entwickelte sich in diesen Gemeinschaften eine gewisse Eigenständigkeit, die sich in der „Frauenmystik" niederschlug. Die zunehmende Selbständigkeit der Beginen führte jedoch zu Konflikten mit Klerus und Handwerkszünften; im Konzil von Vienne (1311/12) wurde deshalb beschlossen, „diese Art zu leben für immer zu verbieten ..." Die älteste Beginengemeinschaft ist aus Bruneck schriftlich belegt. Eine Sage aus dem Kloster Sonnenburg beschließt deshalb dieses Kapitel.

105

Die Frau von Hochgalsaun

Als der Adel im Etschland sich durchaus vor dem Landesfürsten nicht beugen wollte und die treuen Anhänger desselben beraubte und verfolgte, beschloss Friedrich zuerst die Starkenberger zu demütigen. Er zog deshalb vor das Schloss Hochgalsaun, das ihnen gehörte, und belagerte es, da er es wegen seiner Festigkeit nicht im Sturm nehmen konnte. Als im Schlosse die Not aufs Höchste gestiegen war, erflehte die Edelfrau von Hochgalsaun, die eine Schlandersbergerin war, freien Abzug mit dem, was sie tragen könnte. Sie zog alsdann mit ihrem Herrn auf dem Rücken und den wichtigsten Schriften in der Schürze von der Burg herab. Großmütig ließ Friedrich sie ziehen, ließ aber das Schloss von Grund auf zerstören. Diese Tat erinnert gar lebendig an jene Frauen von Weinsberg und an die Frauen von Staupitz, denen Friedrich der Streiter, Herzog zu Sachsen, Landgraf zu Meißen und Landgraf zu Thüringen, in gleicher Weise sein gegebenes Fürstenwort hielt.

›› Wissenswertes ‹‹

Die Burg von Hochgalsaun bei Kastelbell im Vinschgau ist seit 1262 als Eigentum der Herren von Montalban urkundlich nachweisbar. Im 14. Jh. wurde sie zum Hauptsitz der Herren von Schlandersberg, die sich jedoch meistens im nahe gelegenen und bequemeren Ansitz „Kasten" aufhielten. Im Jahre 1423 wurde die Burg vom Grafen von Tirol, Herzog Friedrich IV., der später den Beinamen „Friedrich mit der leeren Tasche" erhielt, endgültig zerstört. In der damaligen Zeit hatten sich zahlreiche aufrührerische Tiroler Adelige zu einem Bündnis gegen den Herrscher zusammengeschlossen, dem Elefantenbund, dem u.a. auch Oswald von Wolkenstein angehörte. Zweck dieses Bundes war der Schutz vor Eingriffen des Landesfürsten in die alten Rechte des Tiroler Adels. Laut Überlieferung musste Herzog Friedrich IV. zwar zähneknirschend, aber voll der Hochachtung für die kluge Starkenbergerin, sie und ihren Gemahl frei abziehen lassen. Heute sind die Burg von Hochgalsaun und Kasten in Privatbesitz.

106

Der Tod der Philippine Welser

Wie man sagt, ist diese schöne Fürstin nicht eines natürlichen Todes gestorben. Ihre Schwiegermutter konnte es ihr nie verzeihen, dass ihr erlauchter Sohn eine gemeine Bürgerstochter geheiratet habe, und hätte sie lieber tot als lebendig gesehen. Deshalb wurden der schönen Philippine, als sie einst im Bade lag, die Adern geöffnet, dass sie verbluten musste. Noch zeigt man im Schlosse Ambras das Badezimmer, in dem dieses geschehen sein soll.

›› Wissenswertes ‹‹

Philippine Welser wurde 1527 in einer wohlhabenden Augsburger Kaufmannsfamilie geboren. 1557 heiratete sie den Kaisersohn und Landesfürsten von Tirol, Erzherzog Ferdinand II., und zwar heimlich, denn eine Hochzeit zwischen Adeligen und Bürgerlichen galt damals als nicht standesgemäß. Als Kaiser Ferdinand I., sein Vater, davon erfuhr, mussten die beiden versprechen, ihre Hochzeit weiterhin geheimzuhalten. Würden aus dieser Ehe Kinder hervorgehen, sollten sie aus der habsburgischen Erbfolge ausgeschlossen werden. So wurden vier Kinder, von denen zwei im Kleinkindalter starben, offiziell von den eigenen Eltern als Waisen bzw. als Findelkinder aufgezogen. Nur wenige Vertraute wussten um die Wahrheit. Zwanzig Jahre lang blieb die Ehe vor der Öffentlichkeit geheim und Philippine Welser musste sich mit dem Titel „Ferdinands Beiwohnerin“ zufriedengeben.

1567 übernahm Ferdinand II. die Regierung Tirols und so zogen sie nach Innsbruck. Auf Schloss Ambras besaß Philippine Welser, die sich zeitlebens mit Kräutern beschäftigte, eine reich ausgestattete Apotheke. Viele kranke und hilfsbedürftige Menschen aus dem einfachen Volk kamen zu ihr. Sie stellte selbst Heilmittel her und hielt ihr Wissen auch in einem Rezeptbuch schriftlich fest. Dieses befindet sich heute in der Wiener Nationalbibliothek. Auch Kochen zählte zu ihren Leidenschaften.

1576 sollte der älteste Sohn Andreas zum Kardinal erhoben werden, wofür er einen Herkunftsnachweis benötigte. Nun endlich entband der Papst seinen Vater des Eides gegenüber dem Kaiser. Ab etwa dem vierzigsten Lebensjahr begannen Philippine Welsers gesundheitliche Beschwerden; sie verstarb 53-jährig im Jahre 1580. Ihr Tod war ein schmerzlicher Verlust für ihren Mann, denn die Ehe zwischen den beiden galt als glücklich und harmonisch. Ihr Grabmal befindet sich in der Silbernen Kapelle der Innsbrucker Hofkirche.

107

Die Dame von Hauenstein

Auf Hauenstein wohnte zur Zeit der Kreuzzüge ein reicher Ritter. Begeistert für die heiligen Stätten in Palästina, zog auch er dorthin. Vor seiner Abreise versah er die Burg mit Lebensmitteln und verriegelte dann das Schloss, in welchem sich nur seine schöne junge Frau mit einer einzigen Magd befand. Eifersüchtig, wie er war, wollte er nicht haben, dass irgendjemand während seiner Abwesenheit, die höchstens ein Jahr dauern sollte, zu seiner jungen Gattin kommen könnte. An kein Eindringen von außen war zu denken und ebensowenig an ein Entkommen von innen.

Die liebenswürdige holde Frau mit der ersten Leibesfrucht trug vergnügt die Einsamkeit und gebar nach einem Vierteljahre ein herziges Knäblein, das dem Vater ganz ähnlich sah. Im Genusse der ersten Mutterfreuden verlief ihr die Zeit schneller, als sie geglaubt hätte, und das Jahr war um, ohne dass der Ritter zurückgekehrt war. Der Nahrungsvorrat neigte sich allmählich seinem Ende zu, und mit Schrecken musste die Arme samt ihrer treuen Magd dem Hungertode entgegensehen. Tag um Tag verrann, und die letzten Lebensmittel waren aufgezehrt.

Eines Tages lehnte die arme Frau tot in der Fensternische; das Kindlein war an ihrer Brust verschmachtet. Drei Tage danach traf ihre Magd dasselbe Schicksal. →

Erst eine Woche später langte der Ritter in sichtlicher Angst auf dem Schlosse an, hoffte auf Leben und fand – drei Leichen. Diesen Anblick konnte er nicht ertragen; er sank tot auf sie hin.

Man bestattete die Toten in der Kirche zu Seis zur letzten Ruhe, die sie jedoch nicht finden konnten. Jeden Freitag Nachmittag um drei Uhr sieht man die Fau mit aufgelöstem Haar nach den Ruinen des Schlosses wandeln, von wo sie dann nach Seis herunterschaut; der Wind trägt ihr die gold'nen Locken ins bleiche Angesicht. – Abends aber, wenn es dunkel wird, sieht man ein Lichtchen am Fenster brennen. Flüsternd und bedeutungsvoll geht es dann von Mund zu Mund: „Das ist die Frau von Hauenstein."

›› Wissenswertes ‹‹

Die Burgruine Hauenstein aus dem 12. Jh., mitten im Walde am Fuße des Schlerns oberhalb von Seis gelegen, ist vor allem als Wohnsitz des spätmittelalterlichen Minnesängers Oswald von Wolkenstein bekannt, der hier 1445 auch gestorben ist. Mehrere bedeutende archäologische Funde wurden in dieser Gegend getätigt, unter anderem das berühmte „Hauensteiner Bronzeschwert" aus der Zeit um 1400 v. Chr. Heute ist die Ruine im Besitz der Diözese Bozen-Trient.

In der Zeit zwischen 1000 und 1300, fast drei Jahrhunderte lang, fanden im Namen der Befreiung des „Heiligen Landes" aus der Hand der Muslime, der „Heiden", mehrere Kreuzzüge der christlichen Völker des Abendlandes statt. Einer der Auslöser war die Zerstörung der Grabeskirche um das Jahr 1000 durch den bedeutenden Kalifen al-Hakim. Die Grabeskirche war eines der größten christlichen Heiligtümer, angeblich über dem Grab Christi errichtet. Die Kreuzzüge waren jedoch nicht nur religiös motiviert, auch strategische und wirtschaftliche Gründe spielten eine wichtige Rolle. Im Namen des „Heiligen Krieges" kam es mitunter auch zu grauenvollen Raubzügen, wie beispielsweise zur brutalen Plünderung der zu jener Zeit hochkultivierten „Weltstadt" Konstantinopel. Die Teilnahme an einem Kreuzzug hatte einen pilgerähnlichen Charakter und war damals sehr populär. Zahlreiche Ritter aus ganz Europa nahmen daran teil. Die sozialen und familiären Folgen für die in der Heimat Zurückgebliebenen und auf die Rückkehr ihrer Angehörigen Bangenden kann man sich leicht vorstellen.

108

Der Garten der Königin

Zwischen den zerklüfteten, engen Hängen des Monte Spinale gegen Grostè und Mondifrà hin öffnet sich, ganz unerwartet und versteckt hinter Felsentrümmern, eine Mulde. Sie scheint wie geschaffen, um sich in eine beschauliche Ruhe zurückzuziehen, geschützt vor neugierigen oder gar heimtückischen Leuten. Es ist eine öde, felsige Gegend, und doch: Aus dem monotonen Grau hebt sich, wie eine Oase inmitten der Wüste, eine kleine grüne Fläche ab. Nicht weit davon entfernt entspringt gurgelnd aus Trümmern und Felsschutt eine Wasserquelle, die mit ihrem frischen Nass den zartgrünen Streifen mit bunten Blumen und würzigen Berggräsern übersät. Und inmitten all dieser Bergkräuter wachsen üppige Zwiebelchen, schmackhaft und scharf. Viele Talbewohnern kennen sie und pflanzen sie zu Hause in ihren Gärten. Diese grüne Mulde wird „Der Garten der Königin" genannt. Aber woher kommt dieser Name?

Eine uralte geheimnisvolle Sage erzählt davon:

Einst, vor langer Zeit, bewegte sich eine lange Schar bewaffneter Krieger durch die dunklen Wälder der Valliana, heute Campiglio genannt. Schweigend und langsam stiegen sie hinauf über die bewachsenen Hänge des Monte Spinale. In ihrer Mitte ritt auf einem edlen Pferd eine vornehme Frau mit königlichem Antlitz. Sie wirkte erschöpft und niedergeschlagen. Ihr Kleid war kostbar, aber stark beschädigt. Sie war umgeben von wachen, schweigsamen Dienern, deren Uniformen ebenso reich und ebenso beschmutzt und zerrissen waren.

Langsam und zögerlich zogen sie, so, als ob sie nicht wüssten, wohin. Die Krieger wirkten entmutigt und verunsichert, während das Gesicht der königlichen Frau, obwohl von Schmerz gezeichnet, Willenstärke und Entscheidungskraft verriet. Doch woher kam dieses Volk? Wer war diese schöne und edle Frau?

Schweigend schritt der Zug dahin; außer den Schritten war nichts anderes zu hören als die Warnpfiffe der Murmeltiere und die knarrende Stimme des Schneehuhns. Die Edelfrau betrachtete mit Wehmut und Bewunderung, die Felsen und Klüfte der Brentagruppe, die tiefen Schluchten und den weißen Schnee der vor ihr aufragenden Cima Tosa.

Immer höher stieg der Zug, immer langsamer, bis zu der versteckt gelegenen Hochfläche. Dort hielten sie inne, labten sich am frischen Quellwasser. Die königliche Frau stieg, beruhigt von der einsamen Stille, von ihrem Pferd und ruhte sich auf der mit Blumen übersäten Wiese aus. Für sie stand fest: Dies war der richtige Ort für ihr Volk, ein sicheres Versteck auch für einen langen Verbleib.

Nachdem sich alle ausgeruht hatten, begann die Arbeit. Mit fieberhaftem Eifer machten sich die Krieger ans Werk. Aus Steinen und Baumstämmen bauten sie Hütten und errichteten Schutzwälle an ausgesetzten Stellen. Diese fruchtbare Erde, vom lebensnotwendigen Wasser gespeist, sollte ihr neuer Wohnort sein. Sie säten Blumen und Kräuter und wahrscheinlich auch diese besonderen Zwiebeln, deren Samen sie mitgebracht hatten.

Nichts ist vom Ausgang dieser abenteuerlichen Besiedelung überliefert. Die Sage berichtet nur, dass es sich um eine verfolgte Königin gehandelt haben soll, über deren Herkunft nichts bekannt ist. Zwar erzählte man sich früher, dass Spuren und Trümmer der Bauten dieser geheimnisvollen Schar hier zu sehen wären, doch Nachforschungen zeigten nur das aus einer Laune der Natur heraus entstandene außergewöhnliche Felsgemäuer.

Doch die Bezeichnung „Der Garten der Königin" haftet für immer an dieser Hochebene. Auch die Zwiebeln blühen jeden Sommer wieder, und sie erinnern mit ihrem kräftig-scharfen Duft an die Gedankenkraft jener Königin, welche hier einst die ersten Samen streute.

›› Wissenswertes ‹‹

Im Laufe der Jahrhunderte kam es immer wieder zu Einfällen fremder Völker in das „Land im Gebirge". Landnahme, Auseinandersetzung mit den Ureinwohnern und deren Flucht vor den Feinden mögen damals oft die dramatische Folge gewesen sein. Diese Sage enthält mutterrechtliche Züge. Die Krieger wurden von einer Königin angeführt und die Ansiedlung erfolgte auf friedvolle Weise (matriarchales Verhalten) und nicht durch Aggression (patriarchales Verhalten). Gärten bildeten laut dem Sagenforscher K.F. Wolff die wirtschaftliche Grundlage der mutterrechtlichen Gesellschaft, ihre Bestellung oblag den Frauen.

Auch Samblàna, die Schneegöttin in den Dolomiten, pflanzte heilkräftige Zwiebeln in einen See am Monte Pelmo (Zwiebelsee), um den Menschen zu helfen.

109

Die Prinzessin im Rosengarten

Auf dem schon mehr erwähnten Jaufen, halbweges von St. Leonhard im Passeiertale zum Jaufenhaus, und eine gute halbe Stunde rechts vom Samensteig seitwärts gegen das Penserjoch zu, pflegte eine wunderschöne Prinzessin einen wunderbar schönen Rosengarten. Aber diese Prinzessin, so schön sie war, war hart von Gemüt und hatte ihre Freude daran, redliche Freier zu necken, und je mehr ein liebendes Gemüt sich kränkte, desto größer war ihre Freude.

Ein edler Ritter, dem das Gleiche widerfuhr, nahm sich die absagende Kälte der Prinzessin so zu Herzen, dass er am „gebrochenen Herzen" starb.

Die Talleute beweinten den edlen Herrn und verwünschten die Prinzessin samt ihrem Rosengarten. Der Himmel hörte den Fluch der Gemeinen – denn droben gilt Prinz und Bauer gleich –, über Nacht wetterte es gewaltig im Gebirge, und als dann ein herrlicher Morgen auffstieg, sah man staunend das Werk der Gerechtigkeit; die Prinzessin in einen Stein verwandelt, und anstatt der Rosen Felsen und ödes Gerölle, mit Moos und Flechten überzogen und kein einziges Alpenblümlein wächst an dieser Stelle des ehemaligen Rosengartens. Ja, wenn Gämsen zufällig nur das Moos fressen, so werden sie von Krankheit ergriffen, magern ab und sterben hin.

›› Wissenswertes ‹‹

Die Rosengarten-Sagen sind in verschiedenen Gegenden Tirols angesiedelt; gleich mehrere davon spielen sich im Meraner Raum ab, in Algund, Plars, Gratsch, wie die obige Sage. Die mittlerweile bekannteste ist jene von König Laurin und seinem Rosengarten am Karerpass. Der Sagenforscher Iganz Zingerle hingegen war überzeugt, dass diese mythische Rosengartensage zum „Meraner" Rosengarten hingehöre. In einer von Adolf Heyl gesammelten Sage ist von einer reichen und schönen Königin am Rosengarten am Karerpass die Rede, welche in Besitz eines wunderschönen Gartens war. Sie wurde von vielen Zwergen bedient. Eine weitere Sage berichtet von einer fremden Prinzessin, die vor ihren Feinden in diesen Rosengarten geflohen war und erst nach vielen Jahren wieder in ihre Heimat zurückkehren konnte. Eine Hexensage aus dem Rosengartengebiet erzählt von der aus einem adligen Geschlecht stammenden Hexe Lomberda oder Langwerda.

Das Sagenmotiv der Prinzessin als Besitzerin eines wunderschönen Rosengartens erinnert auch an Kriemhild aus dem Nibelungenlied, die Herrin über einen herrlichen, von einem Seidenfaden umspannten Rosengarten war. Die Unverletztlichkeit dieses Gartens wurde durch die symbolische Umfriedung durch ein Seidenband dargestellt.

Der Begriff „Rosengarten" erfährt unterschiedliche Deutungen. Neben seiner Interpretation als Jenseitslandschaft, als eine Art Paradiesgarten, wurden im Mittelalter auch Totenäcker und Friedhöfe „Rosengarten" genannt. Auch Schlachtfelder wurden so bezeichnet. Eine durch ein Schwert verursachte Wunde wurde „Rose" genannt. Aus sprachlicher Sicht wird von manchen Forschern vermutet, dass die alte vorrömische Bezeichnung „ruza" für „Schutthalde" zu „Rose" wurde und so in den deutschen „Rosengarten" eingegangen ist. Auch der Name „Laurin" ist Studien zufolge ein vordeutsches Wort und würde so viel wie „Felssturz, Bergwerksschutt oder Geröllhalde" bedeuten.

110

Die Gräfin von Welfenstein

Als es einmal einen Krieg gab und der Welfensteiner in die Schlacht gezogen war, gebar seine Frau mittlerweile mehrere Knäblein zugleich, doch sie schämte sich der armen Wesen. Also beauftragte sie eine Magd, die Neugeborenen zum Eisack hinunterzutragen und dort im Wasser zu ersäufen. Nun ergab es sich, dass der Graf gerade vom Krieg zurückkehrte, als die Magd mit den Kindlein im Schurz den Burghügel hinabging. Auf seine Frage, was sie da im Fürtuch verberge, sagte sie, es handle sich um junge Katzen, die sie im Auftrag der Herrin ersäufen solle. Als der Graf nachschaute und die zwölf Neugeborenen sah, nahm er sie der Magd weg und trug sie heimlich auf die andere Talseite hinüber, wo er die Kleinen mehreren Bauern zur Pflege anvertraute.

Nach siebzehn Jahren, da die Büblein längst groß geworden waren, gab der Graf ein Fest, bei dem er vor allen Leuten seiner Frau die Frage stellte, was einer Mutter gebühre, die ihre Kinder umbringen lasse. „So eine Rabenmutter wäre lebendig einzumauern“, gab ihm die Gräfin zur Antwort. Darauf schrie der Graf: „So eine Rabenmutter bist du!“ Dabei stellte er ihr ihre Söhne vor.

Da verlangte die Frau, zur Sühne lebendig eingemauert zu werden. Einen Hollerzweig solle man ihr in den Mund stecken, würde er grün werden und weiterwachsen, wäre sie selig, würde er aber verdorren, wäre sie verdammt.

Der Holerzweig ist grün geworden, und am Welfensteiner Schloss zeigte man sich in der Vergangenheit einen großen Holunderstrauch.

➤➤ Wissenswertes ◀◀

Vielgeburtssagen sind über ganz Mitteleuropa verbreitet. Bereits Paulus Diaconus erzählt im 8. Jh. eine ähnliche Version von einem langobardischen König in seiner „Historia Langobardorum“.

Laut Überlieferung haben Bauern aus Niederried, einem kleinen Weiler auf der gegenüberliegenden Talseite, die in dieser Sage erwähnten 12 Grafenkinder aufgezogen. Die Höfenamen gehen laut Sage auf die Taufnamen der Grafenkinder zurück: der Mortiner (Martin), der Gorgner (Gregor), der Honsner (Hans), der Woschtner (Sebastian), der Thuminer (Thomas), der Peaterer (Peter), der Maurer (Moritz), der Pauler (Paul), der Ualer (Ulrich), der Luggler (Lukas), der Jörgner (Georg), der Koss (Kassian). In anderen Sagenversionen stehen Welpen anstelle der jungen Katzen. In einer anderen Geschichte um Schloss Welfenstein bei Mauls weist die stolze Gräfin einen armen Bettler ab und muss zur Strafe nach ihrem Tod so lange umgehen, bis aus dem Schutt des verfallenen Schlosses ein Holunderstrauch entsprießt.

Das Schloss Welfenstein bei Mauls steht auf den Resten einer mittelalterlichen Burg aus dem 13. Jh., damals im Besitz des Otto Welf aus dem Geschlecht der Edlen von Welfsberg. Um 1600 war die Burg bereits so verfallen, dass Oswald von Wolkenstein sie als „ain alt zerfallens Burgstall“ bezeichnete. Gegen Ende des 19. Jh. ließ der Innsbrucker Maler Edgar Meyer einen Neubau errichten, im Volksmund „das Zuckerschlössl“ genannt, welches 1918 Opfer eines verheerenden Brandes wurde. Das heutige Schloss ist in Privatbesitz.

111

Das Liebespaar von Castel Nanno

Die Tochter des Schlossherrn von Castel Nanno war jung, anmutig, zugleich wohl erzogen und klug. Wie es im Leben junger Mädchen vorkommt, verliebte sie sich, und zwar in einen jungen Grafen aus der Familie der Grafen von Flavon, welche im Dorf gleichen Namens nicht weit von ihrem Schloss entfernt wohnte.

Ihre Eltern wussten nichts von ihrer Liebe, durften auch nichts erfahren, denn zwischen den Vätern der beiden Liebenden schwelte eine tiefe Feindschaft.

Aber die Liebe macht erfinderisch, und so schafften die zwei Liebenden es eine Zeitlang, sich heimlich in einem dichten Wäldchen unterm Schloss Nanno zu treffen. Eine der Grafentochter treu ergebene Dienstmagd stand während der heimlichen Zusammenkünfte Wache.

Eines Tages jedoch schöpfte der Vater des Mädchens Verdacht. Er beauftragte zwei seiner treuesten Diener, seine Tochter zu überwachen und ihm dann zu berichten. So erfuhr der Graf vom geheimen Treffpunkt der Verliebten. Da er diese Ungeheuerlichkeit kaum glauben konnte, versteckte er sich selbst in der Nähe und musste feststellen, dass seine Diener ihm die Wahrheit gesagt hatten. →

Wutentbrannt kehrte er aufs Schloss zurück. Seinen Dienern befahl er, den Sohn seines Todfeindes zu überwältigen und gefesselt und geknebelt in ein unterirdisches Verlies zu werfen. Hilflos musste seine Tochter dem Ganzen zusehen; ja, sie fiel vor Entsetzen in Ohnmacht, und als sie wieder zu sich kam, befand sie sich in der väterlichen Burg vor den höhnischen Augen ihres Vaters. Schluchzend fragte sie nach ihrem Geliebten. „Ach, der", hohnlachte der Vater, „der befindet sich an einem sicheren Ort, und wenn du willst, kannst du ihm gerne Gesellschaft leisten, im Leben wie im Tod!" „Ich will zu ihm", rief die Unglückliche. „Dem steht nichts im Wege", rief der zornige Vater.

Kurz darauf wurde auch das Mädchen, geknebelt und in Fesseln gelegt, ins Verlies hinuntergebracht. Gemeinsam mit ihrem Geliebten wurde sie an einem dicken eiseren Ring festgebunden.

Nach drei Tagen fand man beide tot. Sie wurden in einer Grube im Verlies begraben, die laut Sage bereits vorher zu diesem Zwecke ausgehoben worden war.

›› Wissenswertes ‹‹

Das Schloss von Nanno, eines der ältesten Dörfer des Nonstales, ist auch Schauplatz weiterer dramatischer Sagen. Leider ist die Burg der Öffentlichkeit nicht zugänglich. Von der mittelalterlichen Burg der Familie Nanno ist nicht mehr viel erhalten. Die Errichtung der heutigen viereckigen Anlage geht auf die mächtige Familie der Madruzzo zurück, die um das 16. Jh. mehr als 100 Jahre lang als Fürstbischöfe von Trient die weltlich-geistliche Macht in ihren Händen hielten. In einem Kellergeschoss befindet sich heute noch ein großer Eisenring, um den sich auch die obige Sage rankt.

Auf der gegenüberliegenden Talseite von Nanno liegen in der Nähe des Dorfes Flavón, verborgen im Gebüsch, die Reste der uralten gleichnamigen Burg. Die Rolle der Grafen von Flavón war richtungsweisend für das Trentiner Mittelalter. Sie waren das erste Trentiner Adelsgeschlecht, dem die Rolle der Advokatur des Fürstbischofes von Trient übertragen wurde, was u.a. die Auferlegung von Gesetzen und Zöllen sowie die Verteidigung des Gebietes beinhaltete. Diese Advokatur war ein vererbliches Amt, wodurch die Grafen von Flavon enorm an Macht gewannen. Dies trug mit dazu bei, dass ein Großteil der Trentiner Lehen in den Besitz der Grafen von Tirol gelangte, wodurch der Grundstein für die spätere Grafschaft Tirol gelegt wurde.

112

Die Wallburg von Mastellina

Einst, vor sehr langer Zeit, da gab es im Val di Sole noch keine großen schönen Dörfer. Die Menschen lebten als herumziehende Jäger oder als Hirten in sicheren Behausungen auf Anhöhen und Hügeln. Zu jener Zeit erhob sich oberhalb von Mastellina die stattliche Wallburg der königlichen Aulasa. Weiter östlich befand sich der düstere Wohnsitz des Prinzen von Eggiano und gegen Westen gelegen die gefestigte Wallburg der Fürsten von Mestriago.

Geheimnisvolles und Gutes erzählten sich die Hirten über die Prinzessin Aulasa: in ihren Räumlichkeiten würden sich die guten Geister der Natur ihr Stelldichein geben, jene, welche für das Grün in der Natur zuständig waren, jene, die den Hirten halfen, die Schafherden zusammenzuhalten, jene, die saftige Gräser für die gezähmten Tiere auf den Weiden wachsen ließen ...

Schön war das Heim der Prinzessin Aulasa. Des Nachts, wenn der Mond rund und voll war, leuchteten die silbernen Dächer ihrer Burg weitum. Nicht nur die einfachen Hirten und Jäger liebten Aulasa, ihre Herrin, auch Prinzen aus dem nahen Nonstal und Fürsten aus dem ferneren Val Camonica kamen angereist und warben um ihre Hand. Dies alles erfüllte die Herzen der Herren von Eggiano und von Mestriago mit Neid und Missgunst. Sie beschlossen, die Pinzessin aus ihrer Burg zu entführen und sie zu zwingen, ihnen das Geheimnis ihres Glücks zu verraten. Eine dunkle regenreiche Nacht, in der alle Hirten lieber in ihren Wohnstätten blieben, war genau richtig für dieses Unterfangen.

Beschwerlich war der Aufstieg auf die Wallburg von Mastellina, und als die beiden endlich die Anhöhe erreicht hatten – fanden sie nur ein paar Mauerreste vor, gepeitscht vom kalten Regensturm; verschwunden war die prachtvolle Burg, Aulasa unauffindbar. Die guten Geister des Berges hatten sie zu sich geholt, in die Sicherheit ihrer funkelnden Grotten im Innern des Berges.

Das Einzige, was heute noch an diese ferne Zeit erinnert, sind die Namen dreier kleiner Dörfer im Val di Sole: Daolasa, Mestriago und Deggiano.

Doch wer in Vollmondnächten – wenn die Bergspitzen der Brenta-Dolomiten in silbernes Licht getaucht sind – diesen geheimnisvollen Ort aufsucht, kann Aulasas weichen Gesang aus dem Innern des Berges heraus vernehmen.

›› Wissenswertes ‹‹

Das kleine Dorf Daolasa mit seinem vorrömischen Namen ist seit dem 12. Jh., Mestriago seit Anfang des 13. Jh. urkundlich belegt. In der Nähe von Deggiano befinden sich auf dem „Colle del Castelir" die Reste einer vermutlich vorgeschichtlichen Wallburg.

113

Die Königinnen von Jochgrimm

Auf Jochgrimm wohnten einst drei Königinnen, deren Höchste den Namen Seeburg hatte. Ihre gastliche Burg war weitum bekannt, und so fanden sich oft Helden aus nah und fern bei ihr ein, um von ihren Abenteuern zu erzählen. Eines Tages waren die drei Riesenbrüder Ecke, Fasold und Ebenrot bei ihr zu Gast. Sie berichteten ihr von den außergewöhnlichen Taten des großen Dietrichs von Bern. Königin Seeburg war davon so beeindruckt, dass sie sich nun nichts sehnlicher wünschte, als ihn von Angesicht zu Angesicht kennen zu lernen. Wer dies schaffe, so sagte sie, würde eine der königlichen Jungfrauen zur Gemahlin bekommen. Da versprach der Riese Ecke ihr, Dietrich auf ihre Burg zu bringen, wenn es sein müsse, auch mit Gewalt. Nun war die wohlhabende Königin in Besitz der teuer erkauften Wunderrüstung des Königs Otnits, des Königs der Lamparten, der vor einer Drachenhöhle in der Nähe Trients den Tod gefunden hatte. Das Panzerhemd dieser Waffenkleidung war aus Gold gefertigt, gehärtet in Drachenblut; der Helm war so hart wie ein Diamant, doch das Unglaublichste war der Schild: Er war mit lauter Schellen besetzt, und wurde er bewegt, ertönte ein liebliches Geläute, das dem ermüdeten Träger neue Kraft schenkte. Diese Rüstung überließ Seeburg dem Riesen Ecke, auf dass er seinen Vorsatz in die Tat umsetzen konnte. Doch Ecke hatte die Kraft Dietrichs unterschätzt. In einem lang andauernden, fürchterlichen Zweikampf fand Ecke trotz seiner Wunderrüstung den Tod. Nach der Bestattung des gewaltigen Recken zog Dietrich nun dessen Rüstung an, band den Kopf des enthaupteten Riesen am Sattel seines Pferdes fest und begab sich nach Jochgrimm. Zu Beginn glaubte Seeburg, Ecke vor sich zu haben, doch als Dietrich ihr den Kopf des Riesen vor die Füße warf, erkannte sie den Irrtum. Entsetzt über den Ausgang dieses Abenteuers fiel sie in tiefe Trauer um Ecke, den strahlenden Riesenjüngling.

›› Wissenswertes ‹‹

Die Sage um die Königin Seeburg ist in dem zum Dietrichepos gehörenden „Eckenlied" aus dem 13. Jh. angesiedelt. Zwar wird in der 1.Strophe als Seeburgs Wohnort Köln am Rhein angeführt, doch im weiteren Handlungsverlauf tauchen immer wieder Tiroler Eigen- und Ortsamen auf, die darauf schließen lassen, dass sich diese Handlung im Tiroler Raum abspielt. Demnach käme mit „Jochgrimm" das am Fuße von Schwarz- und Weißhorn gelegene Jochgrimm in der Nähe Deutschnofens in Frage. Der Name des Riesen Ecke erinnert an das Eggental bei Bozen. Auch gibt es verschiedene Tiroler Riesensagen und Geschichten von Wilden Männern aus dieser Gegend. Ihnen zufolge lebte in Deutschnofen einst ein mächtiges Riesengeschlecht. Bekannt sind u.a. die Deutschnofener Riesen Titsch und Starkwölfl sowie der Riese Grimm, der laut Überlieferung auf dem gleichnamigen Joch gehaust haben soll. Von beiden letzteren Riesen erzählen Sagen, dass sie einen wilden Lindwurm, der das ganze Gebiet unsicher gemacht hatte, getötet hätten. In diesem Zusammenhang sei erwähnt, dass in der in der Nähe gelegenen weltbekannten Bletterbachschlucht versteinerte Spuren verschiedener Saurier gefunden wurden. – Im Eckenlied wird einmal auch der Berg „Nones" erwähnt, der von den Forschern mit dem Nonstal im Trentino gedeutet wird; des Weiteren wird von den im Wald lebenden Wilden Fräulein erzählt, die ebenfalls in der Tiroler Sage beheimatet sind.

Eine Sage bei Zingerle berichtet von drei Hexen, die am Jochgrimm lebten und weit und breit gefürchtet waren. Laut dieser Sage habe es hier einst eine Stadt und einen uralten Verbindungsweg vom Norden nach Venedig und Rom gegeben. Archäologische Funde haben diese Gegend bereits als mittelsteinzeitliche Jägerrast- und Wohnplätze ausgewiesen.

Vom König Otnit oder Ortnit, Herrscher der Lamparten, der auf einer Burg in Garda am Gardasee lebte, erzählt das Wolfdietrich-Epos aus dem 13. Jh.

114

Die Zwergenkönigin von Tirol

Vor langer Zeit lebte in Tirol eine mächtige Königin. Alle Zwerge des Landes waren ihr untertan. Ihr Palast lag bei Jeraspunt im Innern eines Berges, erbaut von den kunstfertigsten Zwergen ihres Königreiches. Gerne hielt Virginal, dies war der Namen dieser jungen Königin, sich aber auch im Wald auf. Und da sie dabei manchmal auch Menschen begegnete, verbreitete sich der Ruf ihrer Schönheit weitum.

Die Zwerge liebten ihre Königin sehr. Nur einer von ihnen, er hieß Elegast, war nicht damit einverstanden, dass sie von einer Frau regiert wurden, die in ihrem Äußeren noch dazu so sehr den Menschen ähnlich war. Die Königin war über seine Dreistigkeit jedoch sehr erzürnt und verwies ihn mit Frau und Kindern aus ihrem Königreich. All sein Bitten um Vergebung war erfolglos. Da beschloss er, sich zu rächen.

Er bat einen heidnischen Fürsten namens Orkise um Hilfe. Dieser riesenhafte Mann besaß ein Pferd, das so schnell wie ein Hirsch laufen konnte, und eine Rüstung, die ihn unverletzbar machte. Das Beste aber war sein Speer, den er so betätigen konnte, dass er den Gesang einer Nachtigall täuschend ähnlich nachahmte. Damit war es ihm ein Leichtes, ahnungslose Menschen anzulocken und gefangenzunehmen.

Mit seinem Heer fiel er in Virginals Königreich ein. Vergeblich leisteten die acht Riesen, welche den Eingang der Höhlenburg von Königin Virginal bewachten, erbitterten Widerstand. Um das Leben ihres Volkes zu retten, blieb Virginal nun kein anderer Ausweg, als sich vor ihm auf die Knie zu werfen und um Gnade für ihr Volk zu flehen. Orkise erklärte sich dazu nur unter einer Bedingung bereit, nämlich dass ihm jedes Jahr eine Jungfrau aus dem Hofstaat der Königin als Opfer für seine Götter überlassen werde. Schweren Herzens willigte die Königin ein.

Jeden Sommer, wenn die kürzeste Nacht herankam, musste ein junges Mädchen das Reich der Zwergenkönigin verlassen. Weitum hörte man bereits Tage zuvor das Wehklagen der Königin und das Weinen der Zwerge. →

Eines Tages kam ein fremder Sänger aus Tirol nach Bern. Er sang am Hof des jungen Königs Dietrich das traurige Lied von der wunderschönen Königin Virginal.

Der alte Waffenmeister Hildebrand war davon schwer beeindruckt, und so überzeugte er den noch unerfahrenen jungen Dietrich, sich gemeinsam mit ihm in die Tiroler Berge aufzumachen, um der Königin Virginal zu Hilfe zu eilen.

Wieder war die Zeit gekommen, da einige Zwerge die schwere Aufgabe hatten, die Jungfrau, auf die das jährliche Los gefallen war, aus dem unterirdischen Königreich an das Tageslicht zu geleiten. Das Tor wurde wieder verschlossen und das Mädchen musste allein den restlichen Weg zum vereinbarten Ort im tiefen Wald zurücklegen, wo der Unhold bereits auf sie wartete.

Der alte Waffenmeister Hildebrand war gerade unterwegs auf Erkundung im Wald, als er dem weinenden Mädchen begegnete, welches ihm unter Schluchzen alles erzählte. Mutig trat der alte Hildebrand dem Riesen entgegen, und nach einem heftigen Kampf gelang es ihm, ihn zu erschlagen.

Er nahm die gerettete Jungfrau hinter sich aufs Pferd und kehrte zu König Dietrich zurück. Als dieser erfuhr, dass das Mädchen eine Dame der Königin Virginal war, war er sehr erfreut darüber, denn er wünschte sich sehr, diese geheimnisvolle, wunderschöne Königin, die über alle Zwerge Tirols regierte und in einem Palast im Innern eines Berges wohnte, kennen zu lernen.

Königin Virginal bekam die glückliche Botschaft vom Tod ihres Feindes von einem Zwerg zugetragen. Nun brannte sie darauf, ihren Retter, den alten Meister Hildebrand, vielmehr aber noch den jungen König Dietrich von Bern, in ihrem Palast willkommenzuheißen. Sie beschloss, ein großes Freudenfest vorzubereiten und schickte einen ihrer besten Vasallen, den Zwerg Bibung aus, um die beiden Helden einzuladen.

Bis diese aber den Hof der Königin erreichten, verging jedoch noch einige Zeit, denn zahlreiche Abenteuer mussten zuerst bestanden werden, doch davon erzählt eine andere Geschichte.

Als Dietrich und Hildebrand endlich im Palast Virginals in Jeraspunt eintrafen, wurde ein Fest gefeiert, das sieben Tage lang dauerte. Köstliches Essen und Trinken, fröhliche Musik, Waffenspiele und vieles mehr erfreute die Gäste. Beim Tanz verliebte sich der junge Dietrich in die schöne Königin. Wie gerne hätte sie ihm vorgeschlagen, bei ihr zu bleiben, aber sie wusste, dass ein Mensch, auch wenn es ein König war, niemals ihr Gemahl werden konnte, denn eine Verbindung zwischen einem irdischen und einem unterirdischen Reich durfte es nie und nimmer geben. Und so kam die traurige Stunde des Abschieds zwischen den beiden. Reich beschenkt kehrten Dietrich und Hildebrand nach Bern zurück.

›› Wissenswertes ‹‹

Das Lied von der Zwergenkönigin Virginal ist vermutlich im 13. Jh. entstanden und gehört zur Dietrich-Epik. Es gibt davon mehrere vollständig erhaltenene Handschriften. Einige Themen aus diesem Heldenepos gehen wahrscheinlich auf ältere Sagen zurück. Der Verfasser ist unbekannt.

Die Handlung spielt größtenteils im Wald und im Gebirge von Tirol; Jeraspunt ist höchstwahrscheinlich Innsbruck, Bern = Verona. Der Namen Orkise erinnert an den Ork, den Orco, einen männlichen Wald- oder Bergunhold in der Tiroler Sage.

Manche ForscherInnen sehen in Virginal eine Saligen-Figur, da sie im Innern eines Berges lebt; auch stehen in einigen österreichischen Sagen die Zwerge im Dienste der Saligen.

115

Die Königin Tresìnga

Tresìnga war die einzige Tochter des Königs von Ragoli. Als er starb, blieb das Königreich ohne männliche Erben und Thronfolger. So bestieg die junge Tresìnga den Thron. Sie war nicht nur schön, sondern auch klug und mutig, und deshalb war sie sich ihrer schwierigen Situation auch sofort bewusst: Würde sie sich mit einem fremden König vermählen, fiele der gesamte Besitz ihres Volkes dem fremden König zu. So entschied sich Tresìnga, auf eine Heirat zu verzichten, um das Reich zu retten.

Ihre Schönheit, vor allem aber ihr Reichtum war weit über die Landesgrenzen hinaus bekannt, und so kamen viele Männer aus den Nachbarländern und hielten um ihre Hand an. Unter ihnen war auch Lavinto, der König von Tuenno, der als stolz, dickköpfig und hochmütig galt. Als all seine Geschenke von Tresìnga abgewiesen wurden, schlugen seine Gefühle für sie in Hass um. Er ließ sein Heer rüsten, um damit nach Ragoli zu marschieren und es mit Gewalt einzunehmen. Als Tresìnga von ihren Botschaftern von seinen Plänen erfuhr, berief sie die Versammlung der Familienoberhäupter ein. Das Volk selbst sollte entscheiden, ob sie von einem fremden König regiert werden oder für ihre Freiheit kämpfen wollten. „Ihr wisst, dass ich geschworen habe, auf eine Heirat zu verzichten. Nun aber liegt die Entscheidung bei euch: Wenn ich Lavinto heirate, wird er euer König, und ihr braucht nicht um euer Leben zu bangen. Wenn wir aber den Kampf gegen ihn aufnehmen, ist unser aller Ende ungewiss. Wollt ihr Tresìnga als Mutter oder Tresìnga als Königin?“ Das Volk von Ragoli zögerte keinen Augenblick: „Wir wollen Tresìnga als Königin!“, riefen alle einstimmig. An der Seite ihrer Königin wollten sie in die Schlacht ziehen und für ihr Reich kämpfen.

Am nächsten Morgen marschierten Soldaten und Bauern, Männer und Frauen, Alt und Jung dem König von Tuenno entgegen. Am Ufer des Tovelsees hatte sein Heer das Nachtlager errichtet. Eine blutige Schlacht begann, sie dauerte tagelang. Das Volk von Ragoli kämpfte mutig und verzweifelt, doch das feindliche Heer erhielt immer wieder neuen Nachschub. Groß war das Sterben unter den Ragolesern, und am Ende fiel auch ihre Königin Tresìnga, angeblich getroffen von einem Pfeil Lavintos. Das Blut der Toten floss in den Tovelsee, so reichlich, dass sich sein Wasser rot färbte. Für lange Zeit zeigte sich das Blut der Toten einmal im Jahr an der Wasseroberfläche des Sees, um an das Morden des Königs von Tuenno zu erinnern, und in den Sommervollmondnächten hört man an seinen Ufern heute noch das Klagen der Königin Tresìnga, die den Tod ihrer treuen Untergebenen beweint.

Bis in die Mitte der sechziger Jahre war der Tovelsee aufgrund einer einzigartigen Erscheinung weitum bekannt: In den Sommermonaten färbte sich sein Wasser an den heißesten Tagen dunkelrot. Dieses eindrucksvolle Schauspiel führte zur Entstehung mehrerer Sagen rund um den Tovelsee, der oft auch der „lago rosso", der „rote See", genannt wurde. In Wirklichkeit ist die Ursache in einer Alge namens „glenodinium sanguineum marchesoni" zu suchen. Da diese Alge mittlerweile in viel schwächerer Konzentration im See vorhanden ist, tritt die Färbung nicht mehr auf. Über dieses Ausbleiben wurde viel geforscht. Mittlerweile weiß man, dass die sommerliche Beweidung einen deutlichen Anstieg von Phosphor und Stickstoff zur Folge hatte, die über den Boden in den See gelangten und der Alge zum Blühen verhalfen. Da ab den sechziger Jahren die Weidewirtschaft stark abgenommen hat, blüht auch diese Alge nicht mehr. Der inmitten des Naturparks Adamello-Brenta (bekannt durch den hier lebenden Braunbären) gelegene See ist nach wie vor von einmaliger Schönheit.

Treséнga heißt der Wildbach, der aus dem Tovelsee entspringt. Auch das zum Tovelsee hineinführende Tal hat diesen Namen. Über den Hintergrund der Sagenfiguren Tresínga und Lavinto (oder Lavinio) ist uns nichts bekannt.

116

Margaretha Maultasch

Margarethas erste Ehe mit dem um fünf Jahre jüngeren Johann von Böhmen war höchst unglücklich. Sie war feurig und stürmisch, Johann geistlos und träge, gegen seine Gattin roh. Ihrem Wunsche, dass sie Mutter werde, konnte er nicht willfahren, da er nach dem damaligen Glauben verhext war. Die junge Fürstin, deren Wahlspruch es war: „Langer Liebesmangel ist meines Herzens Angel", suchte deshalb anderswo jene Genüsse, nach denen sie sich sehnte. Namentlich war sie den schönen Passeirerburschen hold, die sie als Wächter an ihren Hof zog. War sie aber eines derselben überdrüssig, ließ sie nicht selten das Opfer ihrer Lust in den Fällturm zu Tirol werfen. Um nächtlichen Verkehr zu erleichtern, war der Eisenkorb am Erkerfenster der Burg in Meran so eingerichtet, dass er in den Hofraum niedergelassen und der Besucher darin emporgewunden werden konnte. – Aus jenen Zeiten sollen sich viele Privilegien dieses Tales und die Schildhöfe nach der Sage herschreiben. Die Bauern von Passeier waren aber auch der liebenden Gräfin treu ergeben und vertrieben ihren Gemahl aus dem Schlosse Tirol, als Margaretha ihre Abneigung gegen diesen erklärte. Den Freisassen von Goldegg, die durch Schönheit, Größe und Stärke sich auszeichneten, war sie besonders hold und schenkte ihnen viele Privilegien.

In der Nähe des Schlosses Durrnstein hört man oft in der Nacht Musikklänge. Sie sollen von einem Geiste herrühren über den Folgendes erzählt wird:

Am Hofe der Margaretha diente ein Knappe, der wegen seiner Schönheit die Huld seiner Gebieterin in hohem Grade besaß. Ihr Gemahl Johann bemerkte dies und erschoss ihn auf einer Jagd in der Nähe des genannten Schlosses. Seitdem muss der Geist des Armen umgehen.

Nach dem Tode ihres zweiten Gemahls kannte die Gräfin keine Grenzen ihrer Leidenschaft mehr. Sie war der Männer überdrüssig und wandte ihre Liebe einem Maultiere zu, für das sie ein großes Bett anfertigen ließ. Von diesem Tiere wurde sie endlich erdrückt und so endete ihr Leben elendiglich. Dasselbe wird von der schwarzen Margaretha in Schleswig erzählt.

›› Wissenswertes ‹‹

Um Margarete, Gräfin von Tirol mit dem abfälligen Beinamen „Maultasch", ranken sich zahlreiche, zumeist moralisierende Sagen, die vor allem ihren Lebenswandel zum Inhalt haben. Inbegriff einer starken Frau, einer der seltenen weiblichen Herrscherinnen, wurde ihr Bild und ihr Wirken jahrhundertelang von den männlichen Geschichtsschreibern verzerrt. Sie wurde 1318 als Tochter des Heinrich von Tirol-Görz geboren und aus politisch-strategischen Gründen bereits als zwölfjähriges Mädchen mit dem damals achtjährigen Johann Heinrich von Böhmen verheiratet. Sie hatte den Mut, diesem ungeliebten Mann, mit dem sie laut eigenen Angaben die Ehe nie vollzogen hatte, eines Abends, als er von der Jagd zurückkehrte, die Tür nicht mehr aufzumachen, und sich in der Folge selbst einen Mann zu wählen, nämlich Ludwig den Brandenburger. Dieser Skandal erregte in ganz Mitteleuropa großes Aufsehen. Aus politischen Gründen erkannte Papst Clemens VI. die Ungültigkeit der ersten Ehe nicht an, sondern verhängte gegen die beiden den Kirchenbann und über das Land Tirol ein Interdikt. Der Bann wurde erst etliche Jahre später von Papst Innozenz IV. gelöst. Im Scheidungsverfahren gab Margaretes Mann an, von seiner Schwiegermutter verhext worden zu sein, so dass er den ehelichen Pflichten nicht hätte nachkommen können. Seit dem 15. Jh. wird Margarete als hässliche Frau beschrieben, bildlich oft mit einem entstellten Mund dargestellt. In Wirklichkeit soll sie „überaus schön" gewesen sein. Der ihr zugefügte Beiname „Maultasch", dessen Entstehungsursache Gegenstand verschiedener Sagen geworden ist, war im späten Mittelalter Synonym für eine Hure, in der Folge auch die verächtliche Bezeichnung für eine Frau. Auch die Vagina soll früher so umschrieben worden sein.

Margarete überlebte sowohl ihren Ehegatten Ludwig als auch ihren Sohn und Thronfolger Meinhard III. Schlussendlich übergab sie 1363 im Einverständnis mit den Sprechern der Tiroler Bevölkerung das Land Tirol an ihre nächsten Verwandten, die Habsburger. So wurde Tirol österreichisch. Margarete starb 1369 in Wien.

Das Schloss Durrnstein (13. Jh.), heute „Thurnstein", befindet sich in der Nähe von St. Peter/Gratsch bei Dorf Tirol.

117

Der Geist auf der Sonnenburg

Die Sonnenburg bei St. Lorenzen im Pusteral war schon mehrere hundert Jahre ein Nonnenkloster, als die Äbtissin in einen Streit mit dem Bischof von Brixen verwickelt wurde. Die stolzen Nonnen, lauter Töchter der reichsten und vornehmsten Edelherren des Landes, wollten dem Bischof nicht mehr gehorchen, und dieser jagte sie daher aus der Burg. Da war aber eine unter ihnen, welche sagte: „Lieber, als dass ich mich aus den Klostermauern vertreiben lasse, will ich Hungers sterben." Sie floh daher in den Keller und versteckte sich dort, dass niemand sie entdecken konnte. Da blieb sie nun und verhungerte. Aber sie konnte nach ihrem Tode keine Ruhe finden und geht allnächtlich weinend und klagend im verfallenen Gemäuer um.

›› Wissenswertes ‹‹

Verena von Stuben (ca. 1414-1470), „die streitbare Äbtissin" des hochadeligen Nonnenklosters Sonnenburg bei St.Lorenzen im Pustertal, stammte aus einem adligen Geschlecht aus Württemberg. Aufgrund des heftigen Streites mit dem Kardinal und Bischof von Brixen, Nikolaus von Kues, ist sie in die Geschichte eingegangen. Dieser war im päpstlichen Auftrag mit übergroßem Eifer unterwegs, um kirchenreformatorische Pläne in die Tat umzusetzen. Bereits im 12. Jh. hatte die Rechte-Beschneidung der Frauenklöster begonnen, die sich laut kirchlichen Bestimmungen künftig dem männlichen Klerus unterordnen sollten. Auch die Einhaltung strenger Klausur wurde von den Frauenklöstern wie Sonnenburg gefordert. Den bis dahin in Freiheit und Selbstbestimmung lebenden Frauenklöstern wurde auch die Lehre und Diskussion theologischer Inhalte untersagt. Die kluge Äbtissin und ihre Mitschwestern widersetzten sich vehement den Reformplänen des Kardinals. Die Auseinandersetzung zwischen Verena von Stuben und Nikolaus von Kues gipfelte in der „Schlacht von Enneberg", in welcher ca. 50 im Dienst des Klosters von Sonnenburg stehende Männer aus dem Gadertal getötet wurden. Nikolaus von Kues legte den Kirchenbann über die Äbtissin und entkleidete sie ihrer hohen Würde, später verhängte er sogar das Interdikt über Sonnenburg. Fast 10 Jahre lang forderten Verenas Mitschwestern vergeblich ihre Wiedereinsetzung; schlussendlich kehrte sie wieder in ihre deutsche Heimat zurück.

Eine Anekdote erzählt, dass Verena dem Kardinal anlässlich seines Besuches auf Sonnenburg von einer schönen jungen Nonne Kaninchenfleisch auftragen ließ, welchem früher aphrodisierende Kräfte nachgesagt wurden. Aber Cusanus wusste um diese Wirkung und lehnte das Fleisch ab. Es wurde in die Küche zurückgebracht, auf Anordnung der Äbtissin kleingehackt, Fleischklößchen daraus zubereit und dem Kardinal erneut serviert. Diesmal sollen sie ihm gut geschmeckt haben; doch, wie die Geschichte zeigt, brachten die Kaninchenklößchen nicht den gewünschten Erfolg.

Bäuerin und Dirn

„Das machen die 32, und die sieben müssen die fünf erhalten und dann muss auch noch etwas übrig bleiben". So heißt es in dem Tiroler Rätselmärchen „Der gescheite Bauer". Damit gemeint sind die 32 Zähne, die etwas zum Essen haben wollen – sowie die sieben wärmeren Monate, in welchen die Bauern wirtschaften, säen und ernten und so viel einbringen müssen, dass auch die fünf Wintermonate überbrückt werden können, und zudem sollte noch etwas übrig bleiben für Zinsen und Pacht, die es zu zahlen galt.

Das Tiroler Bauernjahr ist stark geprägt durch den jahreszeitlichen Verlauf, doch auch die zahlreichen kirchlichen Feiertage, welche ebenso mit den Zyklen der Natur in Zusammenhang stehen – früher mehr als heute –, haben das bäuerliche Leben wesentlich beeinflusst. Doch zweifelsohne waren für ein gutes Aus- bzw. Einkommen vor allem stets Fleiß und Arbeitseinsatz gefragt. Natürlich gab es auch früher bei den Bauern große Unterschiede, je nach Größe und Lage ihres Besitzes.

Als Tiroler Besonderheit soll an dieser Stelle auch „der geschlossene Hof" erwähnt werden. Bereits im Jahre 1526 verbot die Tiroler Landesregierung die Realteilung, welche eine vielfache Zerstückelung des Besitzes, auch des Hauses, zur Folge hatte; der gesamte Besitz wurde demzufolge nun als Ganzes vererbt. Hoferbe wurde zumeist der älteste Sohn, die jüngeren Geschwister blieben oft als mithelfende Arbeitskräfte mit Wohnrecht auf dem Hof.

Die Bewirtschaftung von Haus und Hof war früher nur durch einen großen menschlichen Arbeitsaufwand möglich; allen voran dem von Bauer und **Bäuerin**, und, je nach Hofgröße, einer kleineren oder größeren Anzahl von Knechten und Mägden, den „Ehehalten", sowie den vorhin genannten Geschwistern des Bauern.

Das „Reich" der Bäuerin war der häusliche Bereich. Dazu gehörten auch der Garten und die Kleinviehzucht. Von den öffentlichen Ämtern und Aufgaben blieb sie zumeist ausgeschlossen, ausgenommen waren der öffentliche Backofen, der Dorfbrunnen, die Spinnstuben usw.

Wurde geheiratet, war die Geburt des ersten Kindes ein wichtiges Familienereignis. Am besten war es, wenn der Familienerbe gesichert war, sprich, wenn ein Sohn auf die Welt kam. Zumeist folgten noch viele weitere Kinder, die von Kindheit an auf dem Hof mithelfen mussten.

Das bäuerliche Jahr beginnt mit Lichtmess (2. Februar). Dies war auch die Schlengglzeit, d.h. die Zeit, in der Knechte und Mägde ihre Arbeitsstelle wechseln konnten oder mussten. Die Vorbereitungen für das neue Arbeitsjahr begannen; Arbeitsgeräte, Pflug, Rechen, Gabeln usw. mussten repariert und einsatzbereit hergerichtet werden und der Mist, der sich in den Wintermonaten angesammelt hatte, wurde auf die Felder gebracht und dort „gebreitet“ oder „geklant“. Diese Arbeit mussten sehr oft die **Dirnen** und Mägde verrichten.

Auch das Setzen von Kartoffeln, Mais und anderen Feldfrüchten war die Aufgabe der Frauen: Sie mussten mit der Haue Löcher hacken, aus ihrem „Fürtuche“ die „Setzknollen“ hineingeben und zuschütten. Um den Acker vor bösen Geistern zu schützen, gab man am Karsamstag geweihte Kohlen und geweihte Palmzweige in die Mitte und an die Ecken des bebauten Ackers Holzkreuze, die im Osterfeuer angebrannt wurden.

Eine weitere Aufgabe im Frühjahr oblag den Mädchen und Buben: die Wiesen „räumen“, d.h. Steine, Äste und größere Reste vom Mistausstreuen wurden weggeräumt.

Dann kam die Bestellung des „kleinen“ Reichs der Bäuerin dran, der Bauerngarten. Laut Tiroler Brauch begann man damit am Gertraudentag (17. März) – nach der Legende war die Hl. Gertaud die erste Gärtnerin –, doch mancherorts musste damit bis Mitte Mai abgewartet werden, wenn die „Eisheiligen“ (Pankraz, Servaz, Bonifaz und „die kalte Sophe“) vorüber waren.

Im Juni folgte die Zeit des Almauftriebes: „Veitstag bricht an, wo man auf die Alm fahrn kann“. Während ein Teil der Dienstboten die auf der Alm anfallenden Arbeiten verrichteten, mussten die anderen Mägde und Knechte sich im Tal vor allem um Heu und Korn kümmern.

Der Sommer war im bäuerlichen Jahresablauf die Zeit, in der am härtesten gearbeitet wurde. Bereits frühmorgens begann die anstrengende Arbeit des Mähens, welche Männersache war. Die Arbeit der Frauen hingegen war es, das frisch gemähte Gras zum Trocknen auszubreiten, dies waren die „Breiterinnen“ oder „Mahdstreuerinnen“.

Für die Heuernte war es wichtig, dass Medardus (8. Juni), der „Heuprunzer“, und Margareta (20. Juli), die „Fetzgreatl“, es gut mit den Bauern meinten, denn, wie eine alte Wetterregel lautet: „Sankt Medardus nass und Regen, bringt den Bauern wenig Segen!“

Bei der Heuarbeit in steilen Gegenden und Wiesen war es im Unterinntal üblich, dass die Frauen über die Röcke Hosen anzogen, in welche sie ihre Kittel hineinsteckten. Mittags versorgte die Bäuerin die hart Arbeitenden mit einem reichhaltigen Essen (z.B. mit Suppe, Türtlen oder Krapfen, Germnudeln, einem Wasserschaff voll Salat, ...), welches oft von jungen Dirnen aufs Feld getragen werden musste. Beim Einbringen des Heues war es die Aufgabe der „Fuderfasserin“, das Heu auf dem Wagen gut aufzustocken. Oft ging es bei der Heuernte lustig zu; auch wenn es anstrengend und ermüdend war, so war man doch noch für manchen Scherz aufgelegt.

Wie wetterabhängig die Bauern waren, zeigen die zahlreichen Wetterwallfahrten im Jahresablauf. Die Trinser Bauern gingen beispielsweise nach St. Magdalena (Gschnitztal), um „Sunne zu beten"; besonders in nassen Sommern wurde diese Wallfahrt nicht selten gemacht. Auch gegen den Wind wurde hier gebetet, man achtete sehr darauf, das „Gatterle" unter der kleinen Kirche wieder zu schließen, denn damit wurde der Wind eingesperrt.

Der Gallitag (Hl. Gallus, 16. Oktober) war ein besonderer Tag im bäuerlichen Jahresablauf; eine Vielzahl der Arbeiten im Freien, wie die Kartoffelernte, welche zu den Aufgaben der Frauen und Kinder gehörte, war nun beendet.

Ab Michaeli, mancherorts um Martini, begann die Zeit des Spinnens und des Flachsbrechelns, einer der wichtigsten Aufgaben der Frauen, denn aus dem „rupfan Tuach" wurden neben den Kleidungsstücken die Bettwäsche und andere Tücher erzeugt. Seltsame Bräuche waren mit dieser Frauentätigkeit verbunden, die an uralte Fruchtbarkeitsrituale erinnern. Kam ein Mann vorbei, trieben die Brechlerinnen mit ihm mutwilligsten Spaß. Er wurde beispielsweise „gekragelt": Wenn er nicht schlagfertig genug auf die verbalen weiblichen Provokationen reagierte, wurde er mit Flachs umwickelt und so lange festgehalten, bis er sich mit Schnaps loskaufte. Bei einer etwas schmerzhafteren Variante wurden dem Burschen Gesicht und Hände mit den stechenden Faserabfällen eingerieben, er dabei mitunter auch wild abgeküsst, wovon er sich sich nur durch eine Geldspende freikaufen konnte. Beim „Höseln" zogen die ausgelassenen Frauen ihm gar gewaltsam die Hose aus und füllten sie mit stoppeliger Spreu, oft scheuten sie auch vor sexuellen Handgreiflichkeiten nicht zurück.

Auch wenn es heißt, „Wenn der Bauer nicht muss, rührt er weder Hand noch Fuß", so gab es auch im Winter einige Arbeiten zu verrichten. Es musste u.a. weiterhin gefüttert, gemolken und Butter gekübelt werden, das „Knollenziehen" war angesagt (d.h. der nach dem Almabtrieb zu Knollen geformte Dünger musste von der Alm in tiefere Lagen herabgeschafft werden), von den Heuschupfen auf höher gelegenen Lagen mussten die Männer mit Schlitten in oft abenteuerlicher Weise das Heu herunterziehen, und besonders die nicht ungefährliche Holzarbeit war angesagt. Die Frauen waren v.a. mit dem Spinnen beschäftigt, oft von frühmorgens bis spätabends, währenddessen sie sich gegenseitig Sagen, Märchen und mancherlei Schwänke bis Anrüchiges erzählten.

Trotzdem – oder zum Glück – war auch die Unterhaltung immer wichtig. Der Volkskundler Ludwig Hörmann hat zu Ende des 19. Jh. errechnet, dass durch die kirchlichen Festtage, Feierabende, Hochzeiten, Taufen, Jahrmärkte usw. im Durchschnitt ein Drittel des Jahres dienstfrei war. Musik, Gesang, Tanz und Sinnlichkeit waren dabei stets wichtige Begleiter. Nur einige Beispiele wollen wir hier anführen: die Feiern zur Schlengglzeit mit gutem Essen für die Dienstboten; die Märkte, wie der „Stega Morscht" (Stegener Markt), der urkundlich bereits 1398 aufscheint, die zahlreichen Tanzstädel, das Faschingstreiben, das Langeswecken, das Scheibenschlagen, der Egetmann-Umzug in Tramin, die Sonnwendfeiern, das Wilde-Mann-Spiel, die Kirchtage, das Krapfenbetteln und Pitschelesingen zu Allerseelen, das „Faule-Weib-Singen“ vor der Hochzeit, das Gassln und Fensterlen u.v.m.

Finden wir im Tiroler Raum auch lokale Unterschiede, so erkennt man doch vielerorts reichhaltige Parallelen. Zahlreiche Tiroler Bauernhöfe liegen in weit vom Dorfkern entfernten Berggebieten; diese Abgeschiedenheit trug mit dazu bei, dass sich Aberglauben und alte Überzeugungen lange halten konnten. Viele der bäuerlichen Bräuche und Traditionen haben bis in die heutige Zeit überlebt und werden gerade in jüngster Zeit wieder mehr gepflegt.

Die schönste dieser Traditionen aber ist aus unserer Sicht das bäuerliche Erzählen, das an den langen Winterabenden während des Spinnens in der warmen Stube, in der Sommerzeit nach dem Heuen auf der Alm und bei unzähligen anderen Gelegenheiten das bäuerliche Leben von Jung und Alt bereicherte. Bäuerinnen und Bauern haben über Generationen hinweg uraltes Sagengut weitererzählt und -gegeben, haben es mit eigenen Erlebnissen verknüpft und dadurch immer wieder neu belebt.

118

Das glückliche Tal

Links vom Dorfe Bach öffnet sich das Seitental Madau. Jetzt ist's ein Alpental, Wetter und Gefahren veranlassten die Bewohner auszuwandern. Doch die Volkssage erzählt, dass hier früher sieben Häuser in ausgedehnten, herrlichen Getreidefeldern gestanden hätten, in welchen sieben glückliche Bauern in patriarchalischem Frieden gelebt, wovon jeder sieben gesegnete Kühe und grüne Wiesen- und Weidegründe mehr als genug gehabt habe. Einer derselben begann vom Pfade der Rechtschaffenheit abzuweichen, daher war's wohl kein Wunder, dass über ihn auch bald das Unglück hereinbrach. Zu grimmer Winterszeit verschüttete eine Lawine dieses Bauernhaus, so dass er und die Seinen nur das nackte Leben retten konnten. Die Nachbarn traten zusammen, bauten im Sommer sein Haus wieder auf und gaben ihm jeder eine Kuh, so dass sie einzeln jetzt jeder sechs Kühe hatten und das gemütliche Leben fortgesetzt werden konnte; denn das Unglück nahm der Getroffene als warnende Prüfung auf; er wurde nun wieder brav und gerecht, wie die andern alle – das Tal war fromm und selig, daher hieß es weitum „das glückliche Tal". Damals lebte im Tale ein altes Mütterchen, welches an den Sonntagen nicht mehr den dreistündigen Weg nach der Pfarrkirche, die in Elbigenalp gestanden, machen konnte, auch sonst schon schwach und gebrechlich war, daher betete es jedes Mal drei Vaterunser dafür. Der Pfarrer von Elbigenalp war ein strenger Seelenhirte und schickte ihr die Aufforderung zu, zum sonntäglichen Gottesdienst zu kommen. Das Mütterchen gehorchte sogleich dem Gebot und wanderte am nächsten Sonntage bei schrecklichem Sturm und Regen den Weg nach der Kirche und stellte sich auch im Widum ein.

Der Pfarrer schalt die Alte wegen Lauheit und fragte, wie viel sie statt sonntäglichem Kirchengang gebetet habe. „Drei Vaterunser!" war die Antwort.

„Und wie viel habt Ihr am Wege hierher und in der Kirche gebetet?", fragte der geistliche Herr weiter. „Auch drei Vaterunser!", antwortete das Mütterchen.

Das dünkte dem strengen Seelenhirten zu wenig. Aber das Weiblein – den Schweiß von der Stirne wischend – sprach: „Es hat alles seine Sach, und es gilt, wie und wann und wo man betet; bei meinem Alter, in unserm Tal drin, bei solchem beschwerlichen Weg und wildem Wetter sind drei Vaterunser mehr wert, als wenn anderswo alle Leute zusammen durchs ganze Tal hinaus beten würden." Das bezweifelte aber der Pfarrer von Elbigenalp, und da hängte das Weiblein zum Zeichen der Wahrheit seinen noch aufgespannten Regenschirm in die Luft, und dieser blieb wirklich in der Luft hängen. Da kam nun alles Volk zusammen, und der Pfarrer und das Volk erkannten, was das glückliche Tal Madau für Leute beherberge und was drei Vaterunser, recht gebetet, wert seien und wirken können; hierauf ging das Weiblein heim, und alle priesen den Herrn, der ihnen das Wunder gezeigt hatte.

›› Wissenswertes ‹‹

Madau ist ein abgelegenes Hochtal im Tiroler Außerfern. Ende des 18. Jh. zählte es noch an die 60 Einwohner, doch bereits wenige Jahrzehnte später verließen die meisten Bewohner dieses Tal. Erst seit 1966 führt eine sehr steile und schmale Straße nach Madau, das heute vor allem von Wanderern und Bergsteigern aufgesucht wird.

Ende des 17. Jh. fiel einem gewaltigen Lawinenabgang der kleine Sohn eines Madauer Bauern zum Opfer, der daraufhin eine Kapelle errichten ließ. Elbigenalp, wohin laut Sage die Leute in dreistündigem Fußmarsch zur Messe gehen mussten, ist der Hauptort des Lechtals.

In dieser Sage stehen sich eine alte fromme Frau, deren Denken und Handeln von einer tiefen Religiosität gekennzeichnet ist, und ein Vertreter der Amtskirche mit seinen kirchlich-institutionellen Vorgaben gegenüber. Die Sage als Ausdruck kollektiver Volksmeinung gibt hier eindeutig der frommen Frau Recht. Sie steht in Einklang mit sich selbst und ihrem Gewissen, lebt ihren Gottesglauben Tag für Tag, so wie das solidarische Verhalten der ganzen Talgemeinschaft Ausdruck gelebter Christlichkeit ist. Deshalb weiß die alte Frau Gott auf ihrer Seite und stellt dies selbstbewusst auch dem Priester gegenüber klar. Die Strapazen, welche die Menschen früher auf sich nehmen mussten, um bei jedem Wind und Wetter dem kirchlichen Gebot des Messebesuches nachzukommen, in den langen Wintermonaten oft noch in stockdunkler Nacht gefährliche Wege beschreiten mussten, sind heute fast nicht mehr vorstellbar. Das Motiv des hängenden Regenschirms und die tiefe Gottesgläubigkeit erinnern an die Lebenslegende um die Hl. Notburga, die ihre Sichel in die Luft hängte (siehe Kapitel Heilige und Maria).

Diese Gegend ist auch Heimat einer weiteren, tatsächlich gelebt habenden außergewöhnlichen Frau: Es ist die aus Buch und Film berühmt gewordene „Geierwally", die in Wirklichkeit Anna Knittel hieß und in Madau im Jahre 1858 siebzehnjährig einen Adlerhorst ausgehoben hat. Sie war Tochter eines Jägers und wiederholte dieses waghalsige Unterfangen nach fünf Jahren sogar noch einmal. Die Filmgeschichte siedelte diese Figur dann im Ötztal an.

119

Die Spinne

Im Dorfe Flies grub eine alte Bäuerin Erdäpfel. Da kroch immer eine Spinne um sie herum. Da sagte das Weib: „Warte nur, wenn dir einmal etwas fehlt, will ich dich pflegen, weil du so zutraulich bist." – Die Bäuerin ging nach getaner Arbeit heim und dachte nicht mehr auf dies Begebnis. Nach vierzehn Tagen kam ein altes Männlein und sagte zur Bäuerin: „Jetzt geh' mit, du hast es meinem Weibe versprochen." – Die Bäuerin erschrak sehr, folgte aber doch dem Männlein, um ihr Wort zu halten. Sie kamen zu einem Wald und da sagte das Männlein: „Jetzt schau' dir die Gegend genau an." – Nun gingen sie weiter und gelangten zu einem großen Palast, worin eine wunderschöne Frau im Wochenbett lag. Die Bäuerin musste die schöne Frau vierzehn Tage lang pflegen und hatte, was sie nur wünschen wollte. Als die Zeit vorüber war, gab ihr das Männlein einen Sack voll Kohlen und begleitete sie bis zum Platze, wo es gesagt hatte: „Jetzt merk' dir die Gegend!" Als sie allein war, dachte sie: „Die Kohlen nehm' ich nicht mit", leerte sie aus und ging zur Heimat. Dort wollte sie ihren Lohn zeigen und lachte dazu. Wie staunten aber alle, als sie hellstes Gold im Sacke fand. Sie kehrte alsbald zurück, um die ausgeschütteten Kohlen zu suchen, fand aber keine mehr.

›› Wissenswertes ‹‹

Sehr oft werden in den Sagen Gegenstände verschenkt, die nach außen hin eigentlich als wertlos erscheinen, sich anschließend aber in Gold verwandeln; v.a. Kohlen kommen bei solchen Erzählungen sehr häufig vor. Um die Kohle, die mit dem uralten Feuerkult in Verbindung steht, ranken sich zahlreiche volksmedizinische und kultische Bräuche. So bestand früher in Tirol der Glaube, dass halbverkohltes Holz aus einem abgebrannten Haus den neuen Hof vor Feuer und Blitz schütze, solche Holz- und Kohlestücke wurden oft dem Mörtel beigemengt und beim Wiederaufbau des Hauses verwendet. In den Kohle-Bräuchen und -sagen können auch ahnenkultische Überreste aus vorchristlicher Zeit vermutet werden, die mit dem Leichenbrand in Zusammenhang stehen. – Ähnlich wie der Frau in der vorliegenden Sage erging es einem Weib in Kitzbühel, welches schneeweiße Kälberzähne gefunden hatte. Um ihren Kindern etwas zum Spielen zu bringen, nahm sie eine Handvoll mit, welche sich allerdings, zu Hause angekommen, als funkelnagelneue Zwanziger herausstellten. Leider fand sie keinen einzigen weiteren Zahn mehr. – Von einem Mädchen wird erzählt, dass es beim Schloss Reifenstein Wasser holen wollte. Aus dem Brunnen rann aber statt des Wassers edler Weizen. Von ihrem Vater gescholten, dass sie nicht mehr genommen hätte, gingen beide zurück, aber da rann nur mehr gewöhnliches Wasser. Zu Hause stellten sie fest, dass sich der Weizen in reinstes Gold verwandelt hatte. – Eine weitere Sage aus Holzgau im Lechtal berichtet in ähnlicher Weise von der Begegnung mit einer Kröte, einer beliebten Erscheinungsform dämonischer Wesen wie Zwerge, Nixen, Hexen oder Teufel. Auch in dieser Geschichte erhält die Helferin für den Pflegedienst nach der Geburt zum Dank einen Sack voll Kohlen, die sie allerdings nicht mit nach Hause nimmt. Zu Hause angekommen findet sie nur noch ein paar Gold-flitter, von dem Schatz jedoch ist keine Spur mehr. – Eine Schweizer Sage erzählt, wie ein Bauer von einer in eine Jungfrau verwandelte Spinne in eine Grotte gelockt wird.

Spinnen spielen im Volksglauben entgegengesetzte Rollen: Einerseits werden sie als Glücksbringer (daher kommt das Sprichwort „einen Groggl in der Tasche haben") und als gutes Omen angesehen, andererseits verkörpern sie das Dämonische und werden sehr oft in Verbindung mit Hexen und dem Teufel genannt. Die Kreuzspinne erhält in Tirol sogar die Rolle des Muttergottestierchens, was wohl auf das Kreuzzeichen auf ihrem Rücken zurückzuführen ist. Der Orientierungssinn der Spinnen gilt im Volksglauben als besonders gut ausgeprägt.

Der Spinne begegnet man auch in vielen Märchen anderer Länder und Kulturen, so übernimmt z.B. der Spinnenmann Anansi in den afrikanischen Volksmärchen die Rolle des schlauen Fuchses. Bei vielen Indianerstämmen gilt sie als Schöpferin von Mensch und Tier und wird als helfendes und gütiges Wesen beschrieben. Sie ist auch ein Merkmal der ägyptischen Schöpfergöttin Neith, die das Universum webte (Weltenspinne, Große Weberin). Auch die Vorstellung von der Verwandlung weiblicher Wesen in Spinnen ist sehr alt. In der griechischen Mythologie wurde die Weberin Arachne, eine Totem-Gestalt der Schicksalsspinnerinnen, von der eifersüchtigen Athene in eine Spinne verwandelt.

120

Die Dirne mit dem Dreikönigküchl

Beim Kafmann im Kafmanntal, dem ehemaligen Linderhofe im Wälschnoven, buk die Bäuerin am Dreikönigsabend Kücheln. Das erste gab sie der Dirn und befahl ihr, dreimal ums Haus zu gehen und das Küchel demjenigen zu geben, der ihr begegnen würde. Als nun die Dirn das dritte Mal ums Haus kam, begegnete ihr der Bauer, und sie gab ihm das Küchel. Die Bäuerin fragte sie, wem sie es gegeben habe, und als die Dirne es sagte, da jammerte die Bäuerin: „O weh, jetzt muss ich meine Sachen zusammenrichten und gehen; ich sterbe dieses Jahr, und du wirst nach mir Bäuerin beim Kafmann." So geschah es dann auch.

Im Kafmanntal ist's unheimlich; da gehen geisterhafte Jungfrauen um, die in den Felslöchern hausen.

›› Wissenswertes ‹‹

Die Schicksalsbefragung anhand von äußeren Zeichen oder Erscheinungen ist ein uralter Brauch. Besonders an bestimmten Abenden und in besonderen Nächten, wie am Festtag des Hl. Andreas (30. November) und des Hl. Thomas (21. Dezember), in den Raunächten und in der Neujahrsnacht wurden verschiedene Bräuche und Handlungen durchgeführt, um so Zukünftiges zu erfahren. Besonders verbreitet waren die Liebesorakel.

In manchen Orten war es z.B. Brauch, dass die Dirn am Allerseelentag dreimal ums Haus laufe, um ihrem Bräutigam zu begegnen. Dass die Frau des Hauses, wie in dieser Geschichte, dabei ihr zukünftiges tragisches Schicksal erfährt, erzählen mehrere Sagen. Von verschiedenen Orten aus dem Wipptal beiderseits des Brenners werden ähnliche Liebes- und Brautorakel wie in der hier angeführten Sage überliefert. So mussten Mädchen am Dreikönigsabend oder auch am Heiligen Abend dreimal ums Haus gehen und in der Hand die ersten an diesem Abend gebackenen Krapfen mit sich tragen. Mancherorts mussten sie dabei völlig nackt sein oder sie durften dabei über keine Türschwelle schreiten, sondern mussten durchs Fenster steigen. Nach der dritten Hausumrundung sahen sie ihren Zukünftigen vor sich.

Auch Burschen führten ähnliche Orakel durch: In der Christnacht mussten sie z.B. ein Scheit aus dem Holzmeiler ziehen; so wie das Holzscheit beschaffen war, ob krumm, astig, dünn oder dick usw., so würde dann auch die „Zukünftige" aussehen.

Über die „geisterhaften" Jungfrauen in Welschnofen und über den uralten, sagenumwobenen Kafmannhof siehe Kapitel Seherin und Prophetin.

121

Der Schütze im hohlen Berg

Drei Tiroler Schützen standen anno neun bei Meran auf einer Felsenhöhle den Bayern und Franzosen gegenüber. Die Kugeln pfiffen hinab und hinan; da brachte auf einmal eine mutige Dirn einen Eimer voll frischer Milch herbei, die Schützen damit zu laben. Sie achtete weder der feindlichen Kugeln noch der Mahnung der Schützen, die gefährliche Stelle zu verlassen. Eine Kugel pfiff und schlug durch den Milcheimer vorn und hinten. Die Dirn steckte die Finger in beide Löcher und rief: „Trinkt, Buabn, wenn noch eine Kugel durchgeht, rinnt die Milch aus." „Barbl, jetzt mach' dich durch, die Franzosen schießen scharf", rief ein Schütze. Er hatte kaum ausgeredet, als ihm eine Kugel in die Brust fuhr. Er war aber ihr Liebster, und die Dirne riss ihm die Joppe auf und wollte das Blut stillen. Jetzt stürmten die Feinde in großer Zahl herauf. Die beiden übrigen Schützen drückten ihre Stutzen ab, und zwei der Angreifer fielen; aber die anderen setzten umso rascher das Stürmen fort. Die beiden Tiroler sprangen über die Felsen und Abgründe, um eine sichere Stelle zu erreichen. Auch die Feinde stürmten vorüber, und Barbl blieb mit ihrem todwunden Friedl allein zurück. Da erschien eine hohe königliche Frau, die Stirne mit einer goldenen Krone geschmückt. Sie sprach dem Mädchen Trost zu, legte Heilkräuter auf die Wunde des Schützen und verband sie. Auf ihren Wink kamen Erdmännlein, hoben den wunden Mann auf und folgten mit ihrer Bürde der vorausschreitenden Gebieterin. Auch die Dirne ging mit dem seltsamen Zuge, der sich langsam dem Talbach entlang fortbewegte, bis sie zu einem blinkenden Ferner kamen. Sie gingen durch den Schlund, woraus der Bach hervorstürzte, und gelangten in einen prächtigen Saal, dessen Wände von Bergkristall glänzten. Dem Eingange gegenüber saß auf einem goldenen Thron der König der Erdmännlein, mit einem Purpurmantel angetan. Der stieg vom Throne herab und trat zu dem wunden Schützen, den die Zwerge auf ein Ruhebett niedergelassen hatten. Nachdem auf seinen Befehl der Verband weggenommen worden war, strich er mit der Hand über die Wunde, und alsbald tat der Schütze die Augen auf. „Barbl", sagte der König, „sei getrost; der Bua wird gsund werden." Die Königin aber reichte der Dirn einen heilsamen Trank; von dem sollte sie ihrem Friedl von Zeit zu Zeit einige Tropfen eingeben. Barbl pflegte nun den Kranken Tag und Nacht, und allmählich genas er wieder unter ihrer eifrigen Pflege. Beide saßen eine Tages Hand in Hand im kostbaren Gemach; durch die kristallenen Wände erblickten sie draußen einen Garten voll Almrosen und Rauten und Edelweiß; die waren viel schöner und voller als die anderen, welche sie sonst auf hoher Alm geklaubt hatten. Endlich kam die Zeit, dass der Schütze, auf die Dirn gestützt, umhergehen konnte; da erlaubte ihnen die Königin, in den Garten hinauszugehen und sich einen Strauß zu klauben. Als dann der Schütze vollkommen hergestellt war, entließ ihn die Königin samt der Dirne, und sie schieden mit Dank von der Königsburg und feierten nach inzwischen eingetretenem Landfrieden ihre Hochzeit.

›› Wissenswertes ‹‹

Diese Sage ist in der Zeit der Tiroler Erhebung gegen die Bayern und die Franzosen um 1809 angesiedelt. Bereits 1805 hatte Österreich die Grafschaft Tirol an Bayern abtreten müssen (Frieden von Preßburg). Die Stagnierung des Wirtschaftslebens, der hohe Steuerdruck und der massive Eingriff ins religiöse Leben im Sinne des aufgeklärten Absolutismus' empörte die Tiroler sehr. So wurden beispielsweise, ähnlich wie unter der Zeit Josephs II., Bittgänge, Prozessionen und das abendliche Glockengeläute verboten, Feiertage abgeschafft, die großen Klöster des Landes konfisziert usw. Das Ausrufen der neuen Staatsverfassung mit dem Ziele der Verwirklichung eines modernen Einheitsstaates brachte das Fass zum Überlaufen. Tiroler Männer wurden nun auch für den bayerischen Militärdienst rekrutiert, da Napoleon von seinen bayerischen Verbündeten Soldaten forderte. So begann der Tiroler Widerstand und daran anschließend die österreichische Kriegserklärung an Bayern und Frankreich.

Diese Sage ist also relativ jung, nämlich „nur" 200 Jahre alt. Trotzdem scheint der magische Glaube um das Vorhandensein überirdischer bzw. unterirdischer Wesen im Volk noch fest verankert zu sein. Zwerge, Zwergenkönig und Jenseitskönigin (Salige?) erinnern an andere im Meraner Raum angesiedelte Sagen vom unterirdischen Zwergen-Königreich mit seinem Rosengarten. In dieser Sage hingegen wachsen im Zaubergarten Alpenrosen und andere seltene Alpenblumen, alte Tiroler Heilpflanzen.

122

Die mutige Hausdirn

Im Wattensertal, das sich mit einundzwanzig Ästen und sechzehn Kaser-Alpen sechs Stunden lang nach dem Hintergrund zieht und mit der Alpe Hochlizum mit zehn Kaserhütten seinen Abschluss findet, liegt, zur Linken des Baches, die schöne Alpe Wotz.

Auf ihr haust zur Winterszeit ein Kasermanndl, das äußerst fleißig und rührig ist und viel rumort, zu Weihnachten aber stiller wird und gegen das Frühjahr zu seinen Abzug nimmt. Bevor dies geschieht, singt zuvor eine Schwarzamsel auf einer nahe der Kaser-hütte stehenden Fichte mehrere Tage lang so schön, dass einer stunden- und tagelang zulosen möchte.

Nun diente im Hause des Bauern, dem diese Alpe gehörte, eine brave Dirne, die aber sehr arm und deren Mutter sehr krank war; die hatte, da das Christfest nahte, alles gar fleißig beschickt, gereinigt, geräuchert, und wie nun am Heiligen Christabend der Rosenkranz gebetet war, schnitt der Bauer den Weihnachtszelten an, verteilte ihn, und ließ sich's mit einigen geladenen Nachbarn wohl schmecken. Da kam die Rede auf die Alm, und die Frage kam auf: Was heute wohl das Kasermanndl droben schaffen möge? Ob selbes auch Weihnachten feiere?

Der Bauer trank vielen Roten und rief in heiterer Festlaune: „Wer von enk die Schneid hat, auf die Wotzer Alm hinaufzugehn und zu schaun, was das Kasermanndl schafft und mir zum Wahrzeichen das Kübelluck und den Wärmer mit herunterbringt, dem geb' i mei schönste Kuah ausm Stall heraus!" –

Aber:

„Die Nachbarn, die Knechte um ihn her,
vernehmens und schweigen still –
und keiner die Kuh gewinnen will" –,

denn das Kasermanndl droben ist kein gutes, und hat schon manchen mit geschwollenem Kopf heim geschickt. Doch die arme Hausdirn fasst sich einen Mut und denkt: „Ich wags in Gottes Namen! Damit hilf i meiner kranken Muatter, i tu's net aus Fürwitz." Und schlägt ein mit dem Zotta-Bauern und fahrt auf die Alm hinauf, zwei Stunden Weges, getrost durch Wind und Schnee.

Droben ist die Kaser hell, alles drin ist blank gescheuert und sauber hergeputzt, das Kasermanndl sitzt feiertäglich am Herd, das Nasenbrennerl dampfend im Maul, und kocht in der Muspfanne ein kohlrabenschwarzes Essen. Die Dirn, wie sie eintritt, knickst gar schön, so gut es eine „gschlechti Menschin" machen kann, und das Manndl winkt ihr zum Herd und zum Mitessen, aber ihr grauelt vor dem Gericht. Darauf spricht das Manndl: „Dirndl, fürcht di net! Mach nur gschleini ein Kritzl Kratzl über die Speis." Jetzt schlug die Dirn das heilige Kreuzeszeichen über die Pfanne, und siehe, da lagen die schönsten Krapfen und Sennenwecken in dem Gefäß, und sie aßen nun beide um die Wette drauf los, das Kasermanndl und des Zotta-Bauern arme Hausdirn. Da fing das Manndl an zu reden: „I woaß schon dein Anliegn, du sollst des Kübelluck und den Wärmer hinunterschaffen. I will dir's gleich gebn, du bist ein braves Dirndl. Und wenn du hinunter kommst, so verlangst du vom Bauer die beste tragete Kuh mitz'sammst dem Kalb, zur Strafe, dass er dich arme Haut bei solcher Kält, Wind und Nebel auffi g'schickt hot."

Der Zotta-Bauer wollte gerade in die Christmette gehen, als die Magd wieder von der Alm mit ihrem Wahrzeichen herunterkam und nun die tragete Kuh begehrte. Er schalt sie aber eine talkete Narrin, dass sie so erzdumm gewesen und auf die Alm gegangen sei und seinen Spaß für bare Münze aufgenommen, und gab ihr nicht eines Pfifferlings Wert, geschweige die Kuh.

Zum anderen Morgen gab es eine sehr traurige Christbescherung auf dem Zotta-Hofe. Die „Robblerin", eine der schönsten Kühe, lag tot im Stalle. Der Bauer wollte sich schier alle Haare ausraufen; diese Kuh war sein Liebling, sie war beim Kuhgefechte stets Siegerin geblieben, daher hieß sie die Robblerin.

„Hättest du sie mir gegeben, wäre sie dir nicht gefallen. Willst du deinen Handschlag mir nicht halten?", fragte die Dirn ihren Herrn, der aber fuhr sie wild und patzig an.

Am nächsten Morgen fand sich die Maierin tot, an ihrer Halskette verschlungen und erhängt. Am dritten Tage fiel die dritte Kuh, und nun erst erweichte sich des Bauern hartes Herz, denn er glaubte, die ganze Herde werde ihm fallen, und nun wollte er sich von der Untreue lösen. Er gab der Dirn die begehrte, trächtige Kuh, die sie nach dem Stalle am Häuslein ihrer Mutter trieb. Da war der Not im selben Häuslein ein Ende, und die Dirne betete Tag und Nacht um die Erlösung und das Seelenheil des Kasermanndls auf der Wotz-Alme.

Nicht weit von den Almen dieser Gegen liegt die Nassen-Dux-Alm; auf derselben haust auch ein Kasermanndl, das sich häufig durch Rufen und Klingeln bemerkbar macht.

›› Wissenswertes ‹‹

zulosen = zuhören, Luck = Deckel, Wärmer = landwirtschaftliches Gerät für die Milchverarbeitung, gschlecht = arm, Nasenbrennerl = Pfeife, „zur Zotta" hieß das am Wattener Berg gelegene Gehöft. – talket = ungeschickt, Stechkuh = jene Kuh, die durch das Stoßen und Stechen mit Hilfe ihrer Hörner alle anderen Kühe besiegt.

Die Alm Wotz liegt im Wattensertal (Wattental) bei Hall in Tirol. – Das Robeln oder Ranggeln ist ein alter Tiroler Männer-Ringsport, wobei ein Gegner den andern zu Boden werfen und versuchen muss, ihn unter sich zu halten. Die Roblerin ist die größte Stechkuh. Beim Almabtrieb erhielt sie den schönsten Kranzschmuck, mitten darin für ihre Unbesiegbarkeit eine „Huifeder", eine krumme Spiel- oder Birkhahnfeder. Die Milchmairin ist die milchertragreichste Kuh. Ihr Schmuck bestand, neben einem Kranz, aus einem Butterkübel oder Rahmmesser. – Laut Volksmeinung musste ein Senner, welcher die Alm unrecht führte, nach dem Tode dort als Kasermandl umgehen, und zwar so lange, bis er seine Taten gebüßt hatte. Hin und wieder trieben sie auch ihren Schabernack mit den Menschen. Um sich vor solchen bösen Geistern, Kobolden und anderen Unholden auf der Alm zu schützen, nahmen die Senner geweihte Kräuter (Dreißgenkräuter), Benediktenpfennige u.s.w. mit.

Das Kasermandl in dieser vorliegenden Sage begegnet dem unschuldigen Mädchen, welches reinen Herzens und mit guten Absichten zu ihm auf die Kaser kommt, freundlich und hilfsbereit. Durch sein reines und mutiges Wesen erlangt es auch für sich selbst mehr als es sich je zu erhoffen gewagt hatte. Im Gegensatz zu den köstlichen Speisen, die in der Walpurgisnacht verspeist und verschenkt werden und die sich dann am nächsten Tag als Mist und Unrat herausstellen, verwandelt das mutige Mädchen durch das Kreuzzeichen das kohlenrabenschwarze Mus in schönste Krapfen und Wecken. Das schwarze Mus steht für die noch abzubüßenden Sünden des Kasermandls, welche aber durch das zutrauliche und „brave" Handeln des Mädchens verschwinden.

Zahlreiche Sagen erzählen vom Büßen der Alm- und Kasmandln und der Almpütze, so z.B. auch die Sage vom „Kopflosen Putz" in Pfitsch, der so lange umgehen musste, bis er seine zu Lebzeiten begangenen Schandtaten und den Überfluss-Frevel abgebüßt hatte.

123

Rosalpina

Auf der Hochfläche von Pinè lag ein schlimmer Zauber. Ein böser Hexenmeister hatte die beiden Seen, den Lago di Serraia und den Lago delle Piazze, in eine schwarze, übel riechende Brühe verwandelt und die Wälder in eine trostlose porphyrne Heidelandschaft. Zu jener Zeit lebte in der Nähe des Serraia-Sees ein junges Mädchen namens Rosalpina. Der Anblick der kranken Natur machte sie von Tag zu Tag trauriger. Da sah sie eines Tages auf der Wasseroberfläche des Sees zahlreiche Blumen im Sonnenlicht funkeln und zart glänzende grüne Gräser dahintreiben. Rosalpina traute ihren Augen nicht. Sie watete in den See hinein, merkte, dass sie nicht geträumt hatte, pflückte das zarte Gras und die duftenden Blumen. So sehr war sie in ihre Beschäftigung vertieft, dass sie auf die verstreichende Zeit vergaß, und plötzlich war sie so müde, dass ihr die Augen zufielen und sie einschlief. Die Strömung trieb sie weiter in den See hinaus.

Am nächsten Morgen entdeckte sie die Herrin des Sees immer noch schlafend, einen Strauß voller Blumen und Gräser an die Brust gedrückt. Der Anblick der im Traum lächelnden Rosalpina bewegte die Fee so sehr, dass sie das Mädchen in ihr Heim brachte, und als Rosalpina endlich erwachte, sagte sie zu ihr: „Bleib doch hier, du sollst es gut bei mir haben." „Das tu ich gerne", antwortete das Mädchen, „aber ich habe eine Bitte. Du musst den bösen Zauber von meinem Land nehmen, damit es wieder so schön wird wie früher." Die Fee erfüllte ihr diesen Wunsch, und Rosalpina blieb bei ihr im See. Nur einmal im Jahr, im Frühling, steigt Rosalpina des Nachts aus dem Wasser. Im Arm hält sie einen großen Behälter voller Samen. Sie schreitet das Seeufer entlang und über die angrenzenden Wiesen dahin, greift tief in ihren Korb und streut die Samen in die Nacht hinein. Duftende Blumen, Ranunkeln, Margeriten, Orchideen und Feldlilien blühen seither auf der Hochfläche von Piné.

›› Wissenswertes ‹‹

Der Lago di Serraia und der Lago delle Piazze liegen auf der Hochfläche von Piné im östlichen Trentino. Dieses Landschaftsgebiet mit seinen vielen kleinen Seen zählte früher zu den schönsten und idyllischsten Gegenden des Trentinos. So verwundert es nicht, dass der Mensch auch hier die Anwesenheit von Feen, Zauberern und anderen Wesen wahrgenommen hat.

Nicht weit vom Serraia-See entfernt befindet sich der bekannteste und meistbesuchte Marienwallfahrtsort des Trentinos, „Madonna di Piné". Laut Legende soll hier 1729/30 die Muttergottes fünfmal dem Hirtenmädchen Domenica Targa erschienen sein. Das verehrte Gnadenbild ist eine Nachbildung der Muttergotteserscheinung von Caravaggio in der Provinz Bergamo. Viele Votivtafeln in der Kirche (ursprünglich der Hl. Anna geweiht), bezeugen die wunderbare Hilfe Mariens.

Zwar sind die Feen und Saligen auch auf der Hochfläche von Piné mittlerweile aus dem menschlichen Wahrnehmungsfeld verschwunden, aber dafür ist das Weiblich-Göttliche in der Gestalt Mariens in Erscheinung getreten und zur Kraftquelle für zahlreiche PilgerInnen geworden. Sowohl in der obigen Sage als auch in der Entstehungslegende des Marienwallfahrtsortes ist ein einfaches bäuerliches Mädchen die Mittlerin zwischen den menschlichen und übermenschlichen/göttlichen Energien.

124

Die tapferen Weiber und Mädchen von Latzfons und Verdings

Es war im Frühling des Jahres 1797. Kaiser Napoleon, der bereits ein Jahr zuvor die Österreicher zum Rückzug aus der Lombardei gezwungen hatte, war mit seinen Truppen auch in Tirol eingefallen. Tapfer setzten sich die Tiroler Schützenkompanien zur Wehr, und auch das Tiroler Volk versuchte verzweifelt, das Vordringen des Feindes zu verhindern. Eine Abteilung französischer Soldaten drang nach Klausen vor, besetzte auch das Kloster Säben. Da rüsteten sich in aller Eile die Landsleute von Pardell, Verdings und Latzfons, denn sie wollten nicht zulassen, dass ihr Land in Feindeshand fiel. Es dauerte nicht lange, und im kleinen Weiler Pardell kam es zu einem hitzigen Kampf. Doch es stand nicht gut um die Bauern.

Vom Verdingser Bühel oberhalb Pardell schauten die Frauen ohnmächtig dem Geschehnis zu. Aber dann beschlossen sie zu handeln. Sie hüllten sich in weiße Mannsmäntel, marschierten in geschlossenen Reihen um den Verdingser Bühel herum, in ihrer Mitte führten sie auf einem Schubkarren ein gefährliches Geschütz mit. Bald kamen sie von der einen, bald von der anderen Seite heran, und das Krachen ihrer gefährlichen Waffe war weitum zu hören.

Als die französischen Soldaten die zahlreichen aufmarschierenden Männer sahen, glaubten sie, die weiß gekleidete österreichische Artillerie vor sich zu haben, die das bedrohliche Geschütz genau gegen sie gerichtet hielt. Und das war noch nicht alles, denn nun prasselte von den Dächern und aus den Hausfenstern auch noch ein gewaltiger Steinregen auf sie nieder, so dass die Franzosen nicht mehr lange überlegten; sie ergriffen Hals über Kopf die Flucht, und ohne sich noch einmal umzusehen, rannten sie durch die Weinberge hinab ins Kloster Säben.

Sie konnten nicht wissen, dass sich unter den weißen Mänteln kein einziges Mannsbild befand; aus der Ferne sahen sie auch nicht, dass das gefährliche Geschütz auf dem hölzernen Schubkarren in Wirklichkeit nur eine Mohnstampfe war, mit der die Bäuerinnen normalerweise den Mohn für die süßen Krapfen zerrieben. Es war auch nicht der bedrohliche Lärm einer Kanone, sondern nur das harmlose Krachen von Böllersalven, wie sie die Tiroler Schützen gerne zum „Salut“ abfeuerten.

Die Bauern aber waren jetzt erst so richtig in Schwung gekommen, sie eilten dem Feinde nach, so schnell sie konnten, beschossen in ihrem Eifer sogar das altehrwürdige Kloster Säben und die Kreuzkirche.

Der Klosterkapellan P. Josef Schweigl machte dem Spektakel ein Ende. Es gelang ihm, einen für die Latzfonser Bauern ehrenvollen Friedensabschluss zustande zu bringen. Darin wurde besiegelt, dass sich auf den Anhöhen von Latzfons und Pardell kein Franzose mehr sehen lassen durfte.

›› Wissenswertes ‹‹

Auch wenn dieses Ereignis auf eine wahre Begebenheit zurückzuführen ist und nicht aus dem Reich der Sage stammt, haben wir uns doch erlaubt, diese Geschichte in unser Buch mit aufzunehmen.

Ähnliche Berichte von todesmutigen Frauen in der Franzosenzeit sind auch aus anderen Tiroler Gegenden bekannt, wie beispielsweise der von Donna Dorotea aus Civezzano im Trentino, die einen französischen Soldaten erschlug, oder jener der tapferen Katharina Lanz, die auf der Friedhofsmauer von Spinges den Feind mit einer Heugabel empfing.

Die tapferen Weiber und Mädchen der Gemeinde Latzfons erhielten einige Jahre später (1804) ein schriftliches Dekret, ausgestellt von der Kaiserlich-Königlichen Hofkanzley, in welchem der „ebenso seltene als rühmliche Beweis ihres Muthes und ihrer treuen Anhänglichkeit gegen Religion, Fürsten und Vatterland das allerhöchste landesfürstliche Wohlgefallen zu erkennen gegeben und gegenwärtiges Belobungsdekret ihnen zum bleibenden Denkmal für ihre Nachkommenschaft ausgefertigt wird ...."

Eine ähnliche Episode ist auch aus dem Lechtal überliefert. Im Dreißigjährigen Krieg waren die Schweden bis nach Elmen im Lechtal vorgedrungen. Auch hier ersannen sich die Frauen eine List: Auf einem Hügel steckten sie Heinzen (Pfähle zum Aufhängen der Korngarben) in großen Mengen auf und bekleideten sie mit Männergewändern. Die Schweden sollen von der großen Männerschar so beeindruckt gewesen sein, dass sie auf und davon liefen. Seitdem dürfen laut Sage die Weiber im Lechtal in der Kirche vor den Männern „zum Opfer" gehen.

125

Das goldene Würmlein

Auf einer Wiese beim Schlosse Brunnenburg hütete ein kleines Mädchen Kühe. Wenn das Vieh ruhig graste, schaute die Hirtin so vergebens in der Wiese herum und wusste selber nicht recht, was sie suchte oder dachte. Aber einmal wurde sie aus diesen Halbträumereien plötzlich aufgeweckt, denn sie sah ein goldenes Würmlein den Berg herabkriechen. Das Mädchen fürchtete sich ganz und gar nicht und ging dem Würmlein nach. Dieses schlängelte sich eine Weile bergab und kroch dann in eine Felsenspalte hinein. Das Mädchen folgte ihm, ging auch in die Felsenspalte und machte nicht kleine Augen, als plötzlich eine goldene Tür aufging und ein großer, glänzender Saal offenstand. Die Pracht in dem Saale hättest du sehen sollen. Der Boden war voller Perlen und anderer Kostbarkeiten, die Wände strahlten von Gold und Silber und waren mit glitzernden Edelsteinen eingefasst. Das Mädchen ging ohne Scheu hinein und durfte sich von den kostbaren Dingen mitnehmen, so viel es nur tragen konnte. Es machte sich auch die Erlaubnis zunutze, packte sich das Fürtuch und alle Taschen voll und ging damit heim. Das arme Hirtenmädchen war jetzt auf einmal steinreich, und was seitdem aus ihm geworden ist, kann ich nicht sagen.

›› Wissenswertes ‹‹

Der Begriff „Wurm" ist bereits für das Althochdeutsche belegt und umfasste ursprünglich alle kriechenden Tiere, also auch Drachen und Schlangen; Letztere werden in Tirol immer noch „Beißwürmer" genannt. Dem Wurm werden ambivalente, dem Menschen nützende und ihn schädigende Eigenschaften zugesprochen. So glaubte man früher, Würmer seien für alle möglichen Krankheiten bei Mensch und Tier verantwortlich; sie waren sogenannte Krankheitsdämonen, gegen welche zahlreiche magische Beschwörungsformeln zur Anwendung kamen. Der Wurm ist wie die Schlange aber auch ein altes Göttinnentier. Aus symbolischer Sicht wird er oft mit dem Tod in Zusammenhang gebracht, da er die Erde zersetzt und in der Erde lebt; dies bringt ihn wiederum mit der Erdgöttin in ihrer Eigenschaft als „Leichenfresserin" in Verbindung. Im übertragenen Sinne ist das in dieser Sage beschriebene Mädchen also reich, weil es, erdverhaftet nach dem Vorbild der großen Göttin, auch dem Tod, der Kehrseite des Lebens, nicht aus dem Weg geht und sowohl die hellen als auch die dunklen Aspekte des Daseins in ihr Leben integriert hat, eine der größten existenziellen menschlichen Aufgaben überhaupt.

Das Schloss Brunnenburg steht auf einem Schuttkegel zwischen Dorf und Schloss Tirol; es ist vermutlich im 13. Jh. entstanden. Um 1900 wurde aus den Ruinen die heutige Burg im neugotischen Stil wieder aufgebaut. Sie beherbergt ein interessantes Bergbauernmuseum und das Ezra-Pound-Literaturzentrum; Besitzer der Burg ist der Volkstumsforscher Siegfried de Rachewiltz, Sohn von Mary de Rachewiltz und Enkel des Dichters Ezra Pound.

126

Der Kranzlwurm

Zu einer Füttererin kam jeden Tag ein Wurm mit einem Kranzl auf dem Kopfe in den Stall. Sie gab ihm morgens und abends Milch in einem Schüsslein. Um Lichtmessen wollte die Magd schlenggeln und am letzten Tage sagte sie abends zum Wurm: „Mein lieber Wurm, leb wohl. Heut' geb' ich dir die Milch zum letzten Mal." – Da legte der Wurm das Kranzl in das Milchschüssele und kroch davon. Die Füttererin nahm das funkelnde Kranzl als Andenken mit und legte es zu ihrem Gelde. Da war nun ein besonderer Segen dabei, denn das Geld nahm nie ab, mochte sie davon nehmen, so viel sie wollte.

➤➤ Wissenswertes ➤➤

In diese Sage aus Gufidaun begegnen wir dem Motiv der gekrönten Schlange, der Schlange mit einem Kranzl. Das Kranzl steht für den Segen und den Reichtum, welcher der Dirn durch ihre Gutmütigkeit und Freundschaft zur Schlange zuteil wird. Auch in Lüsen, auf Nibenal (Nibenol oder Niwenol) kümmerte sich eine gutherzige Dirn um eine Schlange und brachte ihr warme Kuhmilch, bis diese schließlich so zutraulich wurde, dass sie sich sogar abends zu ihr an den Tisch setzte. Auch hier kam mit der Schlange Glück und Segen auf die Alm. Als davon allerdings der Großknecht erfuhr, verjagte er die Schlange; und mit ihr verschwand auch der Segen auf Alm und im Hause.

Laut Marija Gimbutas, Archäologin, ist die Krone seit dem 7. Jahrtausend der Jungsteinzeit das beständige Identifikationsmerkmal der prähistorischen Schlangengöttin. Sie war Lebensspenderin und allwissende Göttin, sorgte u.a. für die Fruchtbarkeit der Kühe und für Milch im Überfluss.

Viele Jahrhunderte später wurde die Göttin dämonisiert, die Schlangenkönigin aus den Ställen vertrieben; es wurde ihr unterstellt, an den Eutern der Kühe zu saugen und sie dadurch ihrer Milch zu berauben.

Um Lichtmess (2. Februar) beginnt das eigentliche Bauernjahr; die Tage werden bereits zunehmend länger und die Sonne stärker, was auch folgender Spruch ausdrückt: „Weihnachten um an' Muggenschritt, Neujahr um an' Hahnentritt, Dreikönig um an' Hirschensprung, Lichtmess um a ganze Stund." Der Lichtmesstag ist der wichtigste Schlenggltag in Tirol, der Tag, an dem die Mägde und Knechte ihren Dienstplatz wechselten, sie „schlenggelten" also von der alten zu einer neuen Arbeitsstelle. War jemand frei, so steckte er sich einen Löffel als Erkennungszeichen an seinen Hut. Vielerorts gab es unterschiedliche Bräuche, die mit Feiern, Abschiednehmen und Ankommen verbunden waren; verschiedenste besondere Speisen wurden bereitet, und es war auch der Tag der Auszahlung. Bei neuen Auftraggebern stellten die Knechte und die Dirnen an diesen Tagen ihre Anliegen und Bedingungen vor, wie z.B. Krapfen für die Beichtzeit, Brennholz, Fleisch für Weihnachten und eine Henne, zudem einige freie Tage für eine Wallfahrt nach Weißenstein. Mit Handschlag wurde die Einstellung bekräftigt.

Auf den „Schlengglhöfen" gab es abends meist eine Feier. Der Abschluss der Schlengglzeit war der 5. Februar (Agathatag). Michaeli (29. September) galt als kleiner Schlenggltag für die saisonalen Dienstboten wie Holzhacker, Senner und Hirten. Lichtmess ist auch ein wichtiger Lostag: „Ist Lichtmess hell und rein, wird a langer Winter sein; wenn es aber sturmt und schneibt, ist der Langes nimmer weit."

127

Das unschuldige Mädchen

Auf dem Dos Trento, einer felsigen Erhebung am Stadtrand von Trient, stand vor längst vergangenen Zeiten eine Kirche, die wahrscheinlich dem Hl. Vigilius und den beiden Heiligen Cosmas und Damian geweiht war. Es wird erzählt, dass sich in den ersten christlichen Jahrhunderten hier die Christen der Stadt getroffen hätten.

Am Fuße dieser Erhebung lebte einst eine kleine Familie: Der Vater war Fischer, die Mutter Weberin, und die einzige Tochter musste auf die Ziege aufpassen. Oft hatte das Mädchen Erwachsene erzählen gehört, dass auf dem Dos ein Schatz vergraben läge, und oft träumte sie davon, ihn eines Tages zu finden. →

Eines Abends stieg sie, wie so häufig, auf den Dos hinauf. Da wurde sie plötzlich so müde, dass ihr die Augen zufielen. Sie erwachte erst gegen Morgengrauen, und da sah sie auf der höchsten Stufe der Kirchenstiege einen glühenden Kohlehaufen. Schon wollte sie davonlaufen, als eine geheimnisvolle Stimme ertönte: „Du brauchst keine Angst zu haben, Mädchen, es kann dir nichts zustoßen. Nimm von den Kohlen so viele du nur tragen kannst, und du wirst Freude, Glück und Zufriedenheit erlangen!" Behände eilte das Mädchen die Stufen hinauf und füllte ihre Schürze bis obenhin mit Kohlen, die, oh Wunder, überhaupt nicht in ihren Händen brannten; dann eilte sie so schnell sie konnte, nach Hause, warf die Kohlen in eine Ecke und erzählte alles der Mutter. Doch da verwandelten sich die Kohlenstücke vor ihrer beider Augen in lauter Barren reinsten Silbers. Auf die Frage der Mutter, ob noch mehr Kohle oben läge, antwortete das Mädchen: „Sicher hab ich noch gute zwei Scheffel voll zurückgelassen, weil ich nicht mehr tragen konnte." Da schickte die Mutter sie mit zwei großen leeren Säcken wieder auf den Dos hinauf, aber der glühende Kohlehaufen war nun verschwunden. Wohl aber fand sie ihre kleine Medaille wieder, die sie am Vorabend oben verloren hatte, und dieselbe geheimnisvolle Stimme ertönte neuerlich: „Liebes Kind, das was du mitgenommen hast, soll und wird dir genügen. Der restliche Schatz ist wieder im Berg versunken und wird erst dann wieder zum Vorschein kommen, wenn zufällig ein geweihtes Stück dort zu Boden fällt, wo du deine Medaille wiedergefunden hast."

Seither sind viele Jahrhunderte vergangen, aber der Schatz wurde nicht mehr gefunden, ja selbst das Wissen um den Schatz auf dem Dos Trento ist verloren gegangen.

›› Wissenswertes ‹‹

Das Naturdenkmal „Dos Trento" erhebt sich wie ein riesiger Pilz aus Fels und Stein am Stadtrand von Trient neben der Autobahn. Die Römer betitelten die Kuppe als „verrucca" (Warze) oder als verrùa viduae (Rücken der Witwe). Bereits im Neolithikum bewohnt, von den Römern befestigt, wurde sie vom römischen Geschichtsschreiber Cassiodorus im 7. Jh. als weltweit einzigartige Festung bezeichnet. Albrecht Dürer hat die Reste der Festung in einem seiner Aquarelle festgehalten. Die Österreicher errichteten 1860 eine Festung, und heute befindet sich auf dem „Dos" ein Denkmal zu Ehren des Trentiner Freiheitskämpfers Cesare Battisti, der von den Österreichern im Jahre 1916 als „Verräter des Kaiserreichs" gehängt worden ist. In den sechziger Jahren kamen bei Ausgrabungen die Reste einer frühchristlichen Kirche, vermutlich aus dem 6. Jh., zum Vorschein.

So ist es nicht verwunderlich, dass ein solch geschichtsträchtiger Ort auch Schauplatz geheimnisvoller Sagen ist. Im Besonderen sind es Schatz-Sagen, die häufig auf uralte Besiedlungs- oder Kultstätten hinweisen, oft werden auch archäologische Funde, beispielsweise römische Münzen, gemacht.

128

Der Faule und die Fleißige

Zur Zeit, als der liebe Herrgott noch auf Erden wandelte, ging er eines Tages mit dem Petrus nach einem Dorfe, wohin beiden der Weg fremd war. Sie begegneten einem Manne, der neben der Straße der Ruhe pflog und fragten, welcher Weg nach dem nächsten Dorfe führe.

Ohne sich vom Boden zu erheben, wies der Gefragte mit dem ausgestreckten Beine die Richtung und sprach: „Dahin geht der Weg." Dabei gebärdete er sich so faul, dass Petrus völlig ärgerlich darüber wurde. Bald darauf kamen die beiden Wanderer zu einem Mädchen, das sich auf dem Felde viel zu schaffen machte. Hier fragten sie nochmals um den rechten Weg.

Gerade das Gegenteil vom früheren Wegweiser, lief diese schnell voran und wich nicht von ihrer Seite, bevor sie ihnen genau erklärt hatte, wohin der kürzeste Weg einzuschlagen wäre.

Das gefiel dem Petrus und er sprach zum Herrn: „Herr, dieser Jungfrau wirst du wohl, weil sie so brav und eifrig ist, einen ebenso braven und arbeitsamen Mann bescheren, nicht wahr?"

„Mitnichten", sprach der Herrgott. „Dieses Mädchen wird gerade jenen Faulen heiraten müssen, der uns mit dem Beine den Weg wies."

„Aber warum denn das?", fiel Petrus in die Rede. „Damit er nicht zugrunde geht, bedarf er eines braven Weibes", sprach ruhig der Erlöser.

›› Wissenswertes ‹‹

Faulheit und Fleiß sind in vielen Märchen, Sagen und Fabeln beliebte Erzählmotive. Oft ist darin die Faulheit negativ und der Fleiß positiv behaftet, wobei eher das faule Mädchen und weniger der faule Mann bestraft wird. Die gesellschaftspädagogische Zielsetzung solcher Geschichten ist unverkennbar. Doch gibt es weltweit zahlreiche Märchen, in denen die weibliche Hauptperson zwar faul, dafür aber schlau ist. Gelingt es ihr beispielsweise, ihren Mann zu überzeugen, dass Flachsspinnen für sie gesundheitsschädigend ist, wird über ihre Faulheit großzügig hinweggesehen, mehr noch: Die Märchenbotschaft ist eindeutig, nämlich dass weibliche Klugheit, gepaart mit Sinn für Witz und Humor, eine Art Ermächtigung darstellt, einem arbeitsreichen Leben aus dem Weg gehen zu dürfen und das Leben zu genießen. Viele Sagen und Märchen mit dem Fleiß- und Faulheitsmotiv ermutigen auch, sich dem gesellschaftlichen Leistungsdruck zu widersetzen. Das Grimm'sche Märchen „Der faule Heinz" ist ein Beispiel für ein solches „Anti-Stress-Märchen", seine zentrale Botschaft ist die Wichtigkeit des Faulenzens im Sinne der psychophysischen Gesundheitsförderung und -erhaltung. Ob die göttliche Entscheidung in der obigen Sage auch der Frau zugute kommt, bleibt allerdings dahingestellt.

129

Mortaso

Vigilius, der glaubenseifrige Bischof von Trient, konnte keinen Seelenfrieden finden. Seine Gedanken beschäftigten sich immerzu mit dem weit von seinem bischöflichen Sitz entfernt gelegenen Rendenatal. Die Einwohner dieses Tales nämlich waren die Einzigen seines ganzen Bistums, die ihre Ohren dem neuen christlichen Glauben verschlossen hielten. Nach wie vor opferten sie ihren heidnischen Göttern, und wehe dem, der sie daran hindern wollte!

Doch Vigilius war entschlossen: Er selbst würde sich ins Rendenatal begeben, um den Menschen dort endlich den richtigen Glauben zu bringen, und würde es auch sein Leben kosten. Lang und mühevoll war der Weg in dieses wilde Tal, reißende Wildbäche mussten überwunden, unheimliche Wälder durchquert und beschwerliche Gebirgspässe überschritten werden.

Endlich war er im Rendenatal angelangt. Dort, inmitten des Tales, befand sich neben dem Sarca-Fluss auf einer von uralten Fichtenbäumen umrahmten Lichtung das Heiligtum des großen Heidengottes Saturn, verehrt in einem hölzernen Standbild.

Als Vigilius dieses Götzenbild sah, konnten ihn seine Begleiter nicht mehr zurückhalten. In überschäumendem Glaubenseifer ging er auf die hölzerne Statue los, schleuderte sie vom Altar, brach Arme und Beine ab, zertrat sie mit den Füßen und riss ihr sogar den hölzernen Kopf ab. Dann warf er die zertrümmerten Teile in den Sarca, stellte sich selbst auf den heidnischen Altar, und mit lauter Stimme verkündete er die christlichen Glaubensworte.

Für eine kurze Zeit, es werden wohl nur wenige Augenblicke gewesen sein, standen die Heiden wie versteinert – zu Tode entsetzt über eine solche Ungeheuerlichkeit, dann aber erwachten sie aus ihrer Unbeweglichkeit. War es ein Wunder, dass sie nun ein heiliger Zorn überfiel? Wortlos bewegte sich die Menschenmenge jetzt auf den Altar zu, allen voran die Frauen, in ihren Händen hielten sie immer noch die soeben aus dem großen Backofen geholten Roggenbrote, denn an diesem Tag war Backtag gewesen; auch ihre Rückenkörbe waren mit Broten gefüllt. Und während die Männer noch nach geeigneten Waffen suchten, Mistgabeln, Spaten, Äxten, nach allem, was sie finden konnten, hatten die Frauen bereits begonnen: Ihre Roggenbrote, hart und kantig, flogen durch die Luft auf den wahnsinnigen Fremden zu, der es gewagt hatte, ein solches Sakrileg zu begehen. Wie gesteinigt stürzte Vigilius vom Podest, lag nun am Boden, und die vor Zorn rasenden Menschen fielen über ihn her, trampelten auf ihm herum und ließen die längste Zeit nicht von ihm ab.

Endlich zerstreute sich die erregte Menschenmenge wieder, kehrte in ihre Häuser zurück. Nur zwei alte Frauen waren übrig geblieben, sie beugten sich über den Fremden, sahen, dass noch Leben in seinem mit dem Tode ringenden Körper war. „Mázzel“! [„Töte ihn“], schrie die eine erbost, doch die andere erwiderte mitleiderfüllt: „El mœur, tas“! [„Er stirbt, schweig!“]

Später kehrten einige Männer zurück, sie warfen die Leiche des Fremden in den Sarca-Fluss, der ihn ein Stück mit sich trug. Dort, neben dem Wildbach, errichteten Christen eine kleine Kirche; sie steht auch heute noch dort und ist dem Märtyrerbischof Vigilius geweiht.

Laut Legende soll der Namen des kleinen Dorfes Mortaso im Rendenatal aus „el-mœur-tas“ abzuleiten sein. Auch erzählt die Sage, dass zur Strafe der Dorfbewohner seit jenem Tag der geknetete Sauerteig für die Roggenbrote nicht mehr aufgehen will, und die gebackenen Brote bleiben flach und zäh.

›› Wissenswertes ‹‹

Mortaso liegt im Rendenatal (bei Judikarien) in der westlichen Trentiner Landeshälfte. Ursprünglich von rätischen und keltisierten Volksstämmen besiedelt, drangen auch in diesem Tal später die Römer ein. Vigilius, Bischof von Trient, soll hier um 400 auf seiner Missionierungsreise getötet worden sein. Einer ähnlichen Legende zufolge soll er mit Holzschuhen („Knospen“) erschlagen worden sein, er wird deshalb ikonografisch oft mit einem Holzschuh in der Hand dargestellt.

Sein Glaubenseifer im Trentino ist auch aus Briefen, die er selbst geschrieben hat, belegt. Darin berichtet er u.a. aus Anaunia (dem heutigen Nonstal), dass die Heiden hier bei einem im Maimonat stattfindenden Fest mit wilden Aufzügen ihre Götzen um ihre Felder trügen, geschmückt mit schreckenerregenden Gewändern, unter dem Geheul teuflischer Gesänge und angetan mit Tiermasken; dies, um von ihren Göttern eine gesegnete Ernte zu erflehen. Drei ins Nonstal geschickte Glaubensboten, die aus Kappadozien stammenden Sisinius, Martyrius und Alexander, wurden ebenfalls von der Bevölkerung getötet, da sie sich u.a. geweigert hatten, Saturn und anderen Göttern zu opfern.

Die Bezeichnung „Heiden“ (germanisch „heidano“ = Bewohner entlegener Waldgebiete) galt ursprünglich all jenen, die zu den Göttern des „pagus“ (lat. „Ort“) beteten, also zu den Göttern ihres Ortes oder Landes. In der Zeit der Christianisierung wurde somit jeder, der nicht an den christlichen Gott glaubte oder sich nicht taufen lassen wollte, „Heide“ genannt. Man unterstellte Heiden auch, dass sie dem Teufel verfallen oder gar geistig zurückgeblieben wären.

130

Das Mädchen aus Fierozzo

Im Schloss von Pergine hatte der Graf zum Fest geladen. Eine besondere Stimmung lag in der Luft, der Graf flüsterte mit dem Aufseher der Schlosswache. Wenige Minuten später öffnete sich die Tür, und herein traten einige seiner Soldaten, in ihrer Mitte führten sie ein junges Mädchen. Ein Raunen ging durch die Reihe der geladenen Gäste, denn eine zarte Schönheit lag auf dem Gesicht des einfachen Bauernmädchens. „Ruhe“, rief der Graf zufrieden lachend, „ihr wollt doch nicht etwa mein kleines Täubchen hier erschrecken, oder?“ Das Täubchen war ein Mädchen aus Fierozzo; am kommenden Morgen sollte ihre Hochzeit mit dem Mann, den sie liebte und der aus demselben Dorf wie sie stammte, stattfinden. Doch vorher verlangte der Graf, was ihm als Herrscher über das

ganze Gebiet zustand: die erste Nacht mit dem jungfräulichen Mädchen zu verbringen; dafür würde er ihr anschließend ganze 100 Taler schenken.
„Komm her zu mir", forderte er das Mädchen mit den melancholischen Gesichtszügen auf, „habt ihr gesehen, liebe Freunde, welch schönes Geschenk ich mir gemacht habe?"

Dann trugen die Diener das Essen auf, köstlichste Speisen, edlen Wein; fröhliche Musik wurde gespielt ... nur das Mädchen saß stumm da, hielt die Augen zu Boden gesenkt, nippte kaum am Weinglas, hielt instinktiv eine Hand schützend vor ihren Körper.

Später zog der Graf sie von ihrem Stuhl hoch und befahl ihr, ihm zu folgen.

Nun war sie ganz allein mit ihm in einem großen Zimmer, ein großes Bett befand sich hier mit samtenen Vorhängen. Sie sah sich um. Durch diese dicken Mauern würde wohl kein Klagelaut, kein Schmerzensschrei nach draußen gelangen. Der Graf riss sie aus ihren Gedanken heraus, ohne Umschweife zog er sie an sich, versuchte, ihr die Bluse vom Leib zu reißen, doch sie hielt immer noch schützend ihre Hand zwischen ihm und ihrem Körper. „Du Unverschämte", rief er, „du wagst es, mir Widerstand zu leisten!" Wutentbrannt schubste er das Mädchen zu Boden und warf sich auf sie.

Was dann passierte, dauerte nicht länger als wenige Augenblicke nur. Ihre vermeintlich den Körper schützende Hand riss aus der Bluse ein scharfes Messer heraus, sie stach dem Grafen damit in die Brust, dort, wo sie sein Herz wusste.

Ein entsetzlicher Schmerzensschrei hallte durch den Raum; gottlob waren die Mauern dick und die Vorhänge aus rotem Samt dicht gewoben. In einer Blutlache lag der Graf am Boden.

Ruhig erhob sich das Mädchen, stolz, den unverschämten Übergriff abgewehrt zu haben. Schnell richtete sie sich die Bluse, rasch durchsuchte sie alle Schubladen und Fächer im Schrank, raffte alles mit, was sie an Schmuck und Geld finden konnte, dann lief sie

die Treppe hinunter, vorbei an den Wachen und Geladenen und rief in gespielter Verzweiflung: „Oh weh, ich Unglückselige, ich bin geschändet, bin entehrt!“

Keiner der halb betrunkenen Gäste hielt sie auf, als sie das Schloss verließ; nur als nach geraumer Zeit der Graf immer noch nicht zurückgekehrt war, wurde die Wache in das sich im oberen Stockwerk befindende Zimmer geschickt.

Unverzüglich machten sich die Soldaten auf, um nach der Mörderin ihres Herrn zu suchen, doch diese war klug, hatte kaum begangene, durch unwegsames Gelände führende Steige benützt, um in ihr Heimatdorf zu gelangen; gemeinsam mit dem sie bereits erwartenden Bräutigam eilte sie zum Pfarrer, um sich heimlich trauen zu lassen.

Dann flüchteten sie über die Berge davon, in Sicherheit. Es wird erzählt, dass die beiden mit Hilfe des dem Grafen entwendeten Schmuckes und Geldes zu Reichtum und Wohlstand gekommen wären, dass sie einen Adelstitel erhalten und ihre Untergebenen zeitlebens respekt- und würdevoll behandelt hätten.

›› Wissenswertes ‹‹

Das „ius primae noctis", zu deutsch „das Recht der ersten Nacht“, ist das Recht eines Feudalherren, bei der Heirat von Menschen, die unter seiner Herrschaft stehen, die erste Nacht mit der Braut zu verbringen. Dieses Recht war aber nie durch königliche Gewalt sanktioniert und noch weniger vonseiten der Kirche. Da geschichtliche Quellen es auch kaum belegen, wird es von vielen Historikern als ein dem Mittelalter zugedichteter Mythos angesehen. Mit Sicherheit kann es als eine Form von Erpressung bezeichnet werden, denn mancherorts ist bezeugt, dass der Bräutigam dieses „Herrenrecht“ durch eine Abgabe ablösen konnte. Doch ist es wahrscheinlich, dass die Bauern in ihrer extremen Bevormundung und Ausgeliefertheit von ihrem Gutsherrn auch solche Übergriffe hinnehmen mussten, wenn sie die verlangten Feudalabgaben nicht leisten konnten. Ein dieser Sage ähnlich gelagerter Fall soll sich um 1194 tatsächlich in Ivrea (Piemont) zugetragen haben, wo Carlo, der Marchese von Monferrato, sich dieses Recht permanent in seinem Territorium herausgenommen haben soll. Eine junge Müllertochter namens Violetta tat so, als ob sie sich seinem Willen beugen würde, tötete ihn aber, schnitt ihm den Kopf ab, warf ihn in die vorbeifließende Dora und zündete das Schloss an. Die gesamte Bevölkerung soll sich anschließend, müde von jahrelangen Schikanen, gegen die Soldaten des Marchese erhoben haben. Nach dreitägigem Kampf seien diese fortgejagt worden und Ivrea wurde eine freie Gemeinde.

Auch im sehenswerten Schloss Sabbionara bei Avio im südlichen Trentino wird im letzten Stockwerk des Hauptturms ein Raum mit wunderschönen profanen erotischen Fresken gezeigt, in welchem der Schlossherr das ius primae noctis ausgeübt haben soll.

Das bereits 845 erstmals schriftlich erwähnte, vermutlich auf einer rätischen Wallburg errichtete Schloss Pergine liegt im Valsugana in der östlichen Trentiner Landeshälfte. Im Mittelalter erhielt die Burg den Charakter einer Festung. Einst im Besitz der Herren von Pergine, fiel es in der Folge Margarete Maultasch und Maximilian I. zu, dann den Fürstbischöfen von Trient. Heute birgt es einen Restaurant- und Hotelbetrieb. Dieses Schloss ist Schauplatz weiterer Sagen, so geht laut Überlieferung beispielsweise eine weiße Frau um, die hier eines gewaltsamen Todes gestorben sein soll. Im Schloss befindet sich auch der berühmte Goccia-Kerker: Hier wurden die Gefangenen einer besonderen Folter unterzogen, nämlich der Tropffolter, welche die Opfer auf qualvolle, langsame Weise zu Tode brachte.

131

Wie die Platzlinerin in Tiers entführt wurde

Eine Platzliner Bäuerin sollte in die Kirche gehen, um aufgesegnet zu werden. Damals war aber der Gang zum Aufsegnen überaus gefährlich, denn es wimmelte im Tal von Unholden, die es besonders arg auf die ungesegneten Wöchnerinnen abgesehen hatten. Es durfte kein Weib vor ihrem Aufsegnen allein vor die Haustür treten. Deshalb wurde die Platzlinerin von ihrer Dirn zur Kirche begleitet. Als sie vor die Kirchenstiege gelangten, blieb die Dirn drei Schritte zurück, und alsogleich war die Bäuerin samt ihrem Kinde verschwunden. Der Bauer und mit ihm das halbe Dorf ging aus, das Weib zu suchen; sie durchstreiften das ganze Tal, allein vergebens. Da sah eines Tages jemand die Platzlinerin hoch oben in einer Felswand; sie rief zu der Person herab und bat sie, ihrem Bauern zu sagen, er solle von da ab am dritten Tage um zwölf Uhr mittags auf einem von ihr näher bezeichneten Platze sein. Dort werde er sie mit dem Kinde sehen und müsse dreimal um sie herumtanzen, erst dann dürfe er auf sie zugehen und sie werde wieder ihm gehören.

Der Bauer begab sich zur bestimmten Stunde auf den bezeichneten Platz, wo auch schon das Weib stand mit dem Kinde auf dem Arm. Er tanzte um sie herum, vergaß aber zu zählen und stürzte sich schon nach dem zweiten Rundtanze auf sein Weib, um es zu fassen. Da schrie die Bäuerin laut auf vor Schmerz und verschwand wieder samt dem Kinde. Der Platzliner hörte sie noch lange schluchzen und klagen, sehen konnte er sie aber nicht mehr.

›› Wissenswertes ‹‹

Im Volksglauben herrschte die Meinung, eine Frau sei durch das Gebären unrein; daher war es lange Zeit Brauch, dass die Wöchnerin zum Pfarrer ging, um sich aussegnen (fürsegnen) zu lassen. Allerdings durfte sie sich nicht alleine auf den Weg machen, denn es bestand große Gefahr, vom Teufel oder anderen dämonischen Wesen geholt zu werden (siehe auch Anmerkungen zu „Die Entführung der Wöchnerin“, Kapitel Riesin und Fangga). Auch viele weitere Sagen haben solche Entführungen zum Inhalt, z.B. wird in Afing erzählt, dass bei der Kindbettwasserle-Quelle eine noch nicht ausgesegnete Wöchnerin entführt wurde, da sie diesen Gang in die Kirche ohne Begleitung unternommen hatte. Oftmals sind die Frauen nicht mehr auffindbar, manchmal besteht die Möglichkeit der Befreiung, so wie auch in dieser Sage aus Tiers. Durch eine Zauberhandlung hätte der Bauer in dieser Sage seine Frau befreien können, was er dann allerdings durch seine Ungeduld und Unkonzentriertheit vermasselte, da er die magische Dreizahl nicht einhielt.

Zu Tanz siehe „Teufel als Tänzer I“ unter dem Kapitel Büßerin und Bestrafte.

132

Das vergessene Kind beim Schatze

Wenn einer sich in der Johannisnacht um zwölf Uhr in den Keller der alten Burg Pretzenberg in Wälschnofen hineinwagt, sieht er dort den Schatz und kann ihn auch leicht bekommen; er braucht nur etwas Geweihtes daraufzuwerfen.

Einmal ging zur bestimmten Stunde ein blutarmes Bauernweib in den Keller und nahm zur größeren Sicherheit ihr kleines Kind mit, denn sie glaubte, die Nähe des unschuldigen Kindes werde allen Zauber verhindern. Der Keller führte aber tief tief in den Berg hinein und als das Weib das Ende des unterirdischen Ganges erreicht hatte, erblickte es einen steinernen Tisch, auf welchem ein Haufen Goldmünzen lag. Sie setzte das Kind auf den Tisch und füllte den Sack, den sie zu diesem Zwecke mitgenommen hatte, mit dem Golde. Auf einmal sah sie im Hintergrunde des Loches eine weiße Gestalt und erschrak so sehr, dass sie eiligst hinauslief. Den Sack, in welchen sie schon ziemlich viele Goldmünzen gesteckt hatte, trug sie mit sich, und so war ihr aus der Not geholfen. Aber das Kind! Ja, das Kind hatte sie vergessen zu nehmen und grämte sich nun so sehr darüber, dass sie trotz des Geldes keinen frohen Augenblick mehr hatte. Sie klagte ihren Jammer dem Geistlichen des Ortes, und dieser riet ihr, übers Jahr in derselben Nacht das Kind zu holen. Das Weib tat es und fand wirklich ihr Kind auf dem gleichen Platze, mit blanken Goldstücken spielend. Sie nahm es geschwind und trug es ungehindert hinaus.

›› Wissenswertes ‹‹

Das Motiv des vergessenen Kindes in unterirdischen Räumlichkeiten wie Keller oder Höhlen ist in vielen Sagen in und außerhalb von Tirol zu finden, wie beispielsweise auch in einer sich in unterirdischen Gemäuern auf Castelfeder bei Auer abspielenden Geschichte. Ähnliche Sagen berichten auch von Kindern, zumeist Mädchen, die in der Wildnis verlorengingen oder sich verirrt haben. Allen gemeinsam ist die völlige Unversehrtheit des wieder aufgefundenen Kindes, das in all dieser Zeit von einer geheimnisvollen Frau betreut und gepflegt wird. Diese Frauengestalt ist eindeutig mit der Percht/Holla oder der Weißen Frau zu identifizieren, welche Beschützerin der Kinder ist.

Laut Volks- und Aberglauben bedarf das Kind aufgrund seiner Vulnerabilität eines besonderen Schutzes, um nicht Opfer über- oder unterirdischer, sprich dämonischer Mächte zu werden; das Auflisten solcher Schutzrituale in den ersten Lebensjahren würde mehrere Seiten füllen. Zum anderen werden dem Kind aufgrund seiner Reinheit und Unschuld aber auch besondere Kräfte zugesprochen, man glaubt es daher geeignet für allen möglichen Zauber, so wie in dieser Sage.

Die Johannisnacht (24. Juni) mit all den sich um sie rankenden Bräuchen ist im Volksglauben eine der magischsten Nächte im Jahresablauf, sie ist die kirchliche Antwort auf das uralte heidnische Feuer-Fest der Germanen, Kelten und Slawen anlässlich der Sommersonnenwende, an welchem zahlreiche Rituale durchgeführt wurden. Die Sonne steht an diesem Tag an ihrem höchsten Stand und besitzt deshalb die größte Kraft im Jahr. In dieser Nacht „blühen“ nicht nur geheimnisvolle Schätze sondern auch das sagenumwobene Farnkraut, welches um Mitternacht seine Samen abwirft. Diese müssen in einem komplizierten Ritual eingesammelt und zum Geld gelegt werden, denn dadurch, so sagt die Überlieferung, nehme dieses trotz aller Ausgaben nie ab. Die in der Johannisnacht geschnittenen Haselruten gäben die besten Wünschelruten ab. Zahlreiche Heilkräuter werden zu dieser Zeit gesammelt.

Johannes der Täufer, der einzige christliche Heilige, der an seinem Geburts- und nicht an seinem Todestag gefeiert wird, hat den großen nordischen Lichtgott Balder/Baldur abgelöst, der von seinem eigenen Bruder getötet wurde. Auch Johannes d.T. ist bekanntlich eines gewaltsamen Todes gestorben: Der Legende nach forderte Salome seinen Kopf auf Anstiften ihrer Mutter Herodias als Belohnung für einen Tanz. Wenn das zu „Johanni“ für die Zubereitung des Johannisöls gepflückte Johanniskraut, auch Balderkraut genannt, zwischen den Fingern zerrieben wird, tritt aus ihm ein roter Saft aus, laut Volksmeinung das Blut des Hl. Johannes.

133

Arnika

In der Nähe der Pale von San Martino lebten in einer einsam gelegenen Behausung mehrere Guane, Wilde Frauen. Sie waren schön anzusehen und den Menschen freundlich gesinnt, schauten auch aus wie diese, nur etwas unterschied sie von ihnen: Einer ihrer beiden Füße war nach hinten gekehrt. Eine der Guane war besonders schön. Einem jungen Burschen aus Primiero war sie schon lange aufgefallen, denn sie hatte wunderschönes Haar, das ihr lang und glänzend weit über den Rücken fiel.

Eines Tages sagte er sich: „Was ist schon so ein kleiner Schönheitsfehler? Ich will sie fragen, ob sie die Meine werden will, ich will nur sie oder keine.“ Und sie sagte ja, aber nur unter der Bedingung, dass er in ihre Behausung ziehe, und, was noch wichtiger sei, dass er niemals ihr Haar berühren dürfe. Er versprach es.

Eine glückliche Zeit begann nun für die beiden; die Frau schenkte nacheinander sechs Kindern das Leben, fünf Buben und zum Schluss noch einem Mädchen, das hatte dasselbe wunderschöne Haar wie ihre Mutter.

Eines Tages hatte der Mann im Dorf zu tun; als er nach Hause zurückkehrte, war es bereits Nacht, und Frau und Kinder schliefen schon. Wie er in die Kammer trat, sah er die Haare seiner Frau wie einen goldenen Wasserfall vom Bett auf den Boden hängen. Ohne zu denken, was er tat, strich er ihr sanft übers Haar. Aber da fuhr die Guana entsetzt aus dem Bett hoch, wurde totenbleich, fing an zu zittern, wurde schmal und schmäler, und schlussendlich löste sie sich, einem dünnen Rauchfaden gleich, in Luft auf. Verzweifelt rief der Mann nach ihr, jedoch vergeblich. Er hatte sein Versprechen gebrochen, wusste, dass er schuld war, dass seine Frau fortmusste. Er weinte die ganze Nacht überm Küchentisch, erst am Morgen, als die Kinder erwachten, fasste er sich. Er musste ja den anfallenden Arbeiten nachgehen, und so trug er den Kindern auf, brav zu sein, bis er später wiederkäme.

Wie staunte er, als er am Abend das Haus aufgeräumt vorfand, die Kinder sauber und ordentlich! Verwundert fragte er sie, wer da so fleißig gewesen sei. „Es war die Mutter", antworteten sie, „die Mutter war den ganzen Tag bei uns, erst vorhin hat sie uns einen Kuss gegeben, und dann ist sie weinend davongegangen."

So ging dies längere Zeit. Eines Tages aber hielt er es nicht mehr aus. Der Wunsch, seine geliebte Frau wiederzusehen, war so groß, dass er eines Morgens nur so tat, als ob er das Haus verließe. In Wirklichkeit versteckte er sich hinter dem großen Backtrog. Es dauerte auch nicht lange, da hörte er das Knarren der Holztür, die vertraute Stimme seiner Frau, die ihre sechs Kinder der Reihe nach beim Namen rief. Als sie gekämmt und gewaschen waren, liefen sie hinaus auf die Wiese, und sie räumte das Haus auf. Aus seinem Versteck konnte der Mann sie genau beobachten, jetzt, da er sie so aus der Nähe sah, schlug sein Herz ihm bis zum Hals vor Sehnsucht nach ihr. Wie konnte es bloß möglich sein, dass all die gemeinsam verbrachten Jahre der Liebe und des Glückes für sie so wenig zählten? Warum nur verzieh sie ihm diesen einzigen Fehler nicht? Hatte sie seine Liebe, seine Zärtlichkeit denn ganz vergessen?

Als sie in die Nähe des Backtrogs kam, sprang er hervor, umschlang sie mit seinen Armen und rief: „Verzeih mir doch, liebe Frau, ich bin todunglücklich ohne dich, ich bitte dich, bleib wieder bei mir!" Die Guana schrie laut auf und unter Schluchzen stieß sie hervor: „Was hast du nur getan! Jetzt darf ich nie mehr wiederkommen!" Sie riss sich von ihm los und lief zur Tür hinaus, eilte über die grüne Wiese davon. Immer wieder verlor sie eines ihrer wunderschönen goldenen Haare, die sich auf der Wiese in seltsame kleine Pflänzchen verwandelten. →

Als die Kinder ihre Mutter davoneilen sahen, liefen sie ihr nach. „Mutter, wart auf uns!“ Aber die Mutter wartete nicht, sie entfernte sich immer weiter und immer schneller, und nur an den auf der Wiese liegenden goldenen Haaren und an den zahlreichen unbekannten grünen Pflanzen konnten die Kinder sehen, in welche Richtung die Mutter davongeeilt war. So gelangten sie bis an den See von Welsperg. Die Mutter konnte doch nicht das Wasser überquert haben? Ganz bestimmt war sie hier irgendwo in der Nähe. Das sahen sie auch an den vielen fremden Pflanzen. „Mutter, Mutter!“, riefen die Kinder, aber nur der Wind und das Echo ihrer verzweifelten Stimmen waren zu hören. Sie warteten viele Stunden, aber vergeblich.

Gegen Abend beschlossen sie, zu ihrem Vater zurückzukehren. Nur das Mädchen blieb allein am Ufer des Sees zurück. Die Mutter würde früher oder später zu ihr zurückkommen, dessen war sie sich sicher. Doch die Zeit verstrich; die Schatten der Nacht wurden länger, bedeckten Almwiesen und Felsen, keine Heuschrecke zirpte mehr, kein Vogelzwitschern war mehr zu hören. Schließlich wurde es ganz dunkel. Das Mädchen zitterte vor Angst. Da, plötzlich, vernahm sie hinter sich ein Geräusch; voller Freude drehte sie sich um, wollte schon „Mamme“ rufen, aber der Ruf erstarb ihr auf den Lippen. Eine bucklige, hässliche Alte stand vor ihr, aber im bleichen Nachtlicht konnte das Mädchen im runzligen Gesicht freundlich blickende Augen erkennen. „Was machst du denn hier allein in der Dunkelheit, Mädchen?“ Sie brach in Tränen aus, erzählte unter Schluchzen, was vorgefallen war. Behutsam strich die Alte ihr übers Haar und sagte: „Hör zu, Mädchen. Einzig und allein die Sterne haben die Kraft, einen solch starken Zauber zu brechen. Komm in der Lorenzi-Nacht hierher, und bei der ersten Sternschnuppe, die du siehst, musst du mit der ganzen Seelenkraft, die du hast, rufen: ‚Sternschnuppe, Sternschnuppe, gleich einer Flamme, mach, dass wiederkommt meine liebe Mamme‘. Und nun hör’ auf zu weinen, geh nach Hause und erzähl’ niemandem davon.“

Mit neuem Mut gestärkt kehrte das Mädchen nach Hause zurück. Von diesem Tag an verrichtete sie die anfallenden Hausarbeiten. Die Anderen glaubten, sie hätte sich nun damit abgefunden, dass die Mutter nicht wiederkam, doch wie hatten sie sich getäuscht! Sie zählte die Tage, und endlich kam die ersehnte Lorenzi-Nacht. Sie bereitete das Abendessen zu, räumte auf und verließ dann heimlich das Haus, ohne dass es jemand bemerkte. So schnell sie konnte, lief sie über die Wiesen, bis zum Lago di Welsperg. Atemlos setzte sie sich ans Ufer und starrte in den funkelnden Sternenhimmel hinauf. Als die erste Sternschnuppe über den Nachthimmel schoss, rief sie, so laut sie konnte, den Spruch, den sie die Alte gelehrt hatte.

Zwei weiche Arme umfingen sie von hinten. Sie drehte sich um, fand sich in den vertrauten Armen ihrer Mutter wieder. Oder war sie es doch nicht? Wo war denn nur ihr langes Haar geblieben? Silbergraue Locken umspielten nun ihr Gesicht; hatte sie denn alle goldenen Haarsträhnen verloren? Nach einer langen innigen Umarmung schaute das

Mädchen um sich, und da sah sie, dass die unbekannten Pflanzen zu goldgelben, kräftig duftenden Blumen erblüht waren.

So ist die Arnika geboren, aus dem Haar einer Guana, sie ist eine der größten Heilpflanzen der Berge, von den Alpenbewohnern hochgeschätzt und viel verehrt.

›› Wissenswertes ‹‹

Diese Sage handelt im Val Canali, einem Seitental des Val Primiero im östlichen Trentino inmitten des Naturparks „Paneveggio-Pale di San Martino", Letzteres ein berühmtes Dolomiten-Bergmassiv. In der Nähe befindet sich auch der europaweit bekannte, von vielen Geigenbauern aufgesuchte „Geigenwald von Paneveggio" („Foresta dei Violini"), denn die hier wachsende Haselfichte ist für den Bau von Musikinstrumenten besonders geeignet.

Der idyllische Lago di Welsperg hat seinen Namen von den „Herren von Welsperg", einst eine der bedeutendsten adeligen Familien Tirols, von denen man um 1500 sagte, dass sie so reich wären, um vom Gardasee bis in die Slowakei immer auf eigenem Boden dahingehen oder -reisen zu können. Auch in Primiero hatten sie Besitzungen.

Einem alten Volksglauben zufolge darf man sich etwas wünschen, wenn man am Nachthimmel eine Sternschnuppe sieht. Am 10. August, der „Lorenzi-Nacht", und den zwei darauffolgenden Nächten sind am Nachthimmel besonders viele Sternschnuppen zu sehen. „Sankt Lorenz kommt in finstrer Nacht, ganz sicher mit Sternschnuppenpracht", sagt eine Bauernregel. Die Magie der Sternschnuppen soll in dieser Nacht besonders stark sein, denn die Sternschnuppen seien die aufblitzenden Tränen des Hl. Laurentius, der aus Liebe zu den Armen einen qualvollen Märtyrertod starb, laut Legende am 10. August 258 auf einem über einem Feuer errichteten Rost.

Die Arnika, auch Bergwohlverleih genannt, ist eine alte Heil- und Zauberpflanze, volksmedizinisch seit dem Mittelalter als Abortivum und bei ausbleibender Menstruation verwendet. Sie wird äußerlich bei Quetschungen, Verstauchungen und Gelenksentzündungen angewendet (Arnikaschnaps) und ist eines der wichtigsten homöopathischen Mittel. Auch im Wetterzauber wurde sie in Form von Räucherungen angewendet.

Die Sagengestalt der Guana wird im Kapitel „Salige" behandelt. Die zentrale Figur dieser Geschichte aber ist das junge Mädchen, welches allein durch seine Liebesfähigkeit und seinen großen Glauben imstande ist, den mächtigen Verbannungszauber, der über ihre Mutter gelegt wurde, zu brechen. Die schöne Botschaft dieser alten Trentiner Sage ist auch heute noch gültig, vielleicht mehr denn je: Es ist einzig und allein die Liebe, welche uns die Kraft verleiht, Wege zu finden und zu gehen, um auch den bösesten Zauber zu besiegen und die größten Hindernisse zu überwinden.

Heilige und Maria

Unzählige Anrufungen und Lobpreisungen spiegeln den Kult und die Verehrung **Mariens**, der „Königin aller **Heiligen**", wider. Allein in Deutschland gibt es mehr als 800 Marienwallfahrtsorte. Ein Großteil der Tiroler Kirchen und Kapellen ist ihr geweiht, viele davon stehen auf alten Kultorten, waren Sitz einer alten Gottheit.
Die mit der Natur stark verbundenen „Heiden" leisteten lange Widerstand gegen die ursprünglich teilweise naturverachtende Haltung des Christentums. Erst im 6. Jh. befahl Papst Gregor der Große, die heidnischen Heiligtümer nicht zu vernichten. Nur die Götzenbilder sollten zerstört werden, die Opferstätten hingegen sollte man mit geweihtem Wasser besprengen und darüber christliche Altäre errichten und Reliquien christlicher Heiliger in die Kirchen bringen. Im Gegensatz zu vorher wurde nun ein „sanfterer" Weg eingeschlagen, um die Menschen von der neuen christlichen Heilslehre und ihren Heiligen zu überzeugen.

Über das Leben Mariens, der meistverehrten christlichen Heiligen und Gottesmutter, erfahren wir einiges aus dem apokryphen Protevangelium des Jakobus: Demzufolge erfuhr die unfruchtbare Anna, die Mutter Marias, von einem Engel, dass sie ein Kind gebären würde, und aus Freude darüber versprach sie es als Opfergabe dem Tempel. Maria war diesen Schriften zufolge ein außergewöhnliches Kind. Bereits mit sechs Monaten machte sie alleine die ersten Schritte. Dreijährig wurde sie in den Tempel gebracht, wo sie vor Freude darüber auf den Altarstufen tanzte; neun Jahre lebte sie hier, „ernährt aus der Hand eines Engels". Mit zwölf, als sie geschlechtsreif wurde, kam sie durchs Los zur Obhut ins Haus des Witwers Joseph, mit sechzehn war sie, die Jungfräuliche, schwanger. Sie brachte Jesus in einer Höhle zur Welt, wurde von einer zweifelnden Hebamme namens Salome auf ihre Jungfräulichkeit hin untersucht, der als Zeichen dieses Frevels die Hand abgefallen sein soll.

Die kirchliche Marienverehrung hat im Osten bereits sehr früh begonnen. Beim Konzil von Ephesus (im Jahre 431), laut Legende Marias letzter Wohnort, wurde entschieden, dass sie den Titel „Gottesgebärerin" tragen dürfe; dieser Beschluss war der Grundstein für die sich nun ausbreitende christliche Marienverehrung.

Die damalige Bischofsversammlung war von einer großen Menschenmasse belagert worden, welche eine Wiedereinführung der alten Göttin verlangte, denn Ephesus war auch die große Kultstätte der göttlichen Artemis/Diana. Maria trat somit an die Stelle dieser und anderer vorchristlicher bis dahin verehrten Muttergottheiten wie Demeter/Ceres, Kybele und vor allem Isis, welche auch die Beinamen „Himmelsherrin", „Totenkönigin", „Heilige Frau und Menschheitsretterin", „Mutter der Natur" usw. trug.

Ab dem 6. Jh. begann sich auch im Abendland der Marienkult auszubreiten. Hier finden sich zahlreiche Parallelen zu germanischen, keltischen und römischen Göttinnen; sehr oft tritt Marias Verehrung im Zusammenhang mit Wasser-, Baum- und Bergkult in Erscheinung. So erscheint Maria in zahlreichen Tiroler Sagen und Legenden, ähnlich wie beispielsweise die römische Diana, in oder unter einem Baum, z.B. in Maria Larch im Gnadenwald bei Absam (Lärche), in Landeck (Fichte), bei der Mariarast-Kapelle auf dem Heinzenberg bei Zell (Baumart unbekannt), als Madonna del Lares (Lärche) bei Bolbeno im Trentino, als Madonna del Frassino (Esche) bei Peschiera del Garda, beim einstigen Muttergottesbaum beim Heroler in Lüsen, beim Kaserer in Steinegg als Gottesmutter in der Lärche, bei Heilig Drei Brunnen bei Trafoi am Ortler (Tanne/Fichte), als Muttergottes von Aufkirchen bei Toblach (Weide), als Madonna della Corona (Linde) auf dem Monte Baldo u.v.a.

Der Kult um heilige Bäume war bei den Rätern sehr verbreitet und hielt sich auch in Tirol sehr lange, weit in die christliche Zeit hinein. Stellvertretend genannt sei hier der legendenumwobene Heilige Baum oberhalb Nauders nahe dem Reschen. Die Verehrung dieser doppelspitzigen Lärche war so groß, dass auf diesem Ort weder geflucht, gelärmt noch gestritten werden durfte. Aus ihr kamen laut Volksmeinung auch die neugeborenen Buben. Unter dem Baum stand ein heidnischer Opferaltar, der vom Hl. Valentin von Rätien (gestorben 475) während seiner Missionierungsreise zerstört wurde; der Heilige Baum hingegen wurde erst im 19. Jh. gefällt. Laut Sage hat hier auch eine Frauendreiheit in einem Schloss gelebt.

Die Verehrung der Frauen-Dreiheit geht mit Sicherheit bis in vorchristliche Zeit zurück, besonders verbreitet war sie bei den Kelten und Römern und hat in vielen alten Tiroler Sagen und Legenden bis heute überlebt. Sie wurde in diesem Kapitel stellvertretend mit der Sage um die Hl. Drei Jungfrauen von Meransen aufgenommen. Auch in den Apokryphen ist von den „Drei Marien" die Rede, die als Erste das leere Grab Christi sahen, und alle drei Töchter der Hl. Anna waren. Die als christliche Version der drei Nornen gedeuteten „Hl. Drei Madlen" Barbara, Margaretha und Katharina erfahren in Tirol große Verehrung. Noch im 11. Jh. kritisierte Burckard von Worms, dass die Menschen immer noch die Drei Parzen ehrten und zu Jahresende für sie den Tisch mit Speis und Trank deckten. Davon übriggeblieben ist in Tirol bis ins 20. Jh. hinein der Speiseopfer-Brauch an die Percht. In verschiedenen europäischen Ländern zogen in der Winterszeit drei Perchten-Frauen von Haus zu Haus und sprachen ihren Segen aus. Sie schrieben die Buchstaben K+M+B an den Türbalken, um das Haus vor bösen Mächten zu schützen. K-M-B (heute für Kaspar, Melchior und Baltarsar; die Abkürzungen stehen ebenso für den Segensspruch „Christus Mansionem benedicat") erinnern auch an die Initialen der Heiligen Frauen Katharina, Margareta und Barbara.

Aber auch in der christlichen Dreifaltigkeit war früher Platz für ein weiblich-göttliches Wesen. In Urschalling am Chiemsee beispielsweise geht auf einem gotischen Kirchenfresko der Hl. Geist bzw. die Hl. Geistin als Frau aus den Kleiderfalten Gottvaters und des Sohnes hervor. Sie ist die bildliche Darstellung von Sophia, der personifizierten Weisheit, die laut Bibel und den gnostischen Schriften gemeinsam mit Gott in der Welt wirkt und bereits bei der Welterschaffung dabei war.

Die Heiligen- und Marienverehrung ist in Tirol mancherorts auch an Gewässern, Quellen und in Sumpfgebieten bekannt, wie z.B. „Unsere Liebe Frau im Moos" in Sterzing, „Maria der Quelle" in Platt im Passeier, „Maria im Moos" in Bozen, der ehemalige „Jungfrauenbrunnen" in Brixen usw. Bereits bei den Venetern, Rätern, Kelten, Römern und Germanen wurden weibliche Gottheiten dem Element Wasser (Quelle, Moor) zugeordnet; das räto-etruskische Quellheiligtum in Moritzing bei Bozen und Dreikirchen bei Barbian sind zwei Beispiele hierfür. In den Tiroler Sagen schimmert diese Form weiblich-göttlicher Verehrung häufig bei Wallfahrts- oder Kirchenentstehungslegenden durch, wie jener von Heiligwasser bei Igls, in verschiedenen Mariensagen aus dem Vinschgau, dem Gnadenbild von Riffian u.a.; auch die in dieses Kapitel aufgenommene Sage von Maria Waldrast weist wasser- und baumkultische Züge auf.

Eine herausragende Stellung nimmt Maria als Mutter der Natur und all ihrer Wesen sowohl in der Legende als auch im Brauchtum ein. Auch hier tritt sie an die Stelle vorchristlicher Göttinnen. Sie wird zur Schöpferin von Blumen und Heilkräutern und erlebt im höchsten christlichen Marienfest „Maria Himmelfahrt" mit dem im germanischen Kultus wurzelnden Kräuterweihe-Ritual ihren Höhepunkt, welches sich in Tirol bis in die heutige Zeit gehalten hat. Viele Pflanzensagen und -legenden ranken sich um Marias Leben; zahlreiche Blumen- und Heilpflanzen erinnern an sie oder sind nach ihr benannt, wie z.B. das Muttergottesschühlein (Frauenschuh), das Unserer Lieben Frauen Bettstroh (Thymian), das Marienblümchen oder Mutterblümchen (Gänseblümchen), die Mariendistel, das Muttergotteskraut (Tausendguldenkraut), das Frauenmantele, die Marienkerze (Königskerze, auch „Himmelbrand" genannt). Diese Letztere gilt als das blühende Zepter der Himmelskönigin: „Unser lieb Frau geht dreimal übers Land, sie trägt den Himmelbrand in der Hand."

Maria gilt auch als Beschützerin von Tieren; Parallelen zur griechischen Göttin Artemis und der Saligengestalt als Herrin der Tiere können hier gezogen werden. Umgekehrt stehen in Volksüberlieferung und Sage bestimmte Tiere in enger Verbindung mit Maria, wie beispielsweise die Kreuzspinne, der man kein Leid antun dürfe, denn sie sei ein „Muttergottestierlein" und bringe Glück; oder das „Pranterle", das Rotschwänzchen, dessen Nest auf keinen Fall ausgenommen werden dürfe, andernfalls schlage im Haus der Blitz ein; auch die Schwalbe, die zu Maria Verkündigung aus dem Süden zurückkehrt und von der man sagt: „Zu Maria Geburt fliegen die Schwalben wieder furt".

Viele der heidnischen heiligen Tage bestehen heute verdeckt in unseren christlichen Feiertagen fort. Die Absicht der christlichen Missionare bestand darin, heidnische Anschauungen in christliche umzulenken. In der vorchristlichen Zeit richtete sich das Denken, auch das religiöse und spirituelle Denken, vielfach nach dem Naturleben aus. Doch auch alle großen kirchlichen Feste und Feiertage sind in dieselbe „heilige", dem Jahreskreislauf der Natur folgende Zeit eingebettet.

Die wichtigsten heidnischen Jahreszeitenfeste waren die Feiern zur Winter- und Sommersonnenwende, die Frühlings- und Herbsttagundnachtgleiche, der Wintervierteltag (im Februar), der Frühlingsvierteltag (im Mai), der Sommervierteltag (im August) und der Herbstvierteltag (im November).

Auch die Marienverehrung, manchmal auch jene anderer weiblicher Heiligen, folgen im Jahresablauf größtenteils diesen Zyklen:

Mariä Lichtmess/Maria Reinigung (2. Februar) ist ein Fest mit uralter Sonnensymbolik, denn um diese Zeit wird die Sonne wieder kraftvoller und wärmer. Bei den Kelten waren es das Fest Imbolc und das Fest der Göttin Brigid, bei welchen die Wiedergeburt des Lichts gefeiert wurde; im Christentum erfolgte deshalb die Festlegung des Namenstages der Hl. Brigitta von Kildare auf den 1. Februar. Der Februar war auch der heilige Monat der römischen Göttin Juno Februata (daher der Monatsname), der Göttin des Liebesfiebers; entsprechend lustvoll und ausgelassen wurde gefeiert. Die Kirche setzte den Hl. Valentin (Valentinstag, Tag der Verliebten) an diese Stelle. Anstatt der heidnischen römischen Fackelläufe führte die Kirche Lichterprozessionen ein.

Maria Verkündigung (25. März) ist die Zeit der Wiedergeburt der Natur nach dem langen Winter. Im alten Rom fand hier eine große Feier zu Ehren der Muttergöttin Kybele statt.

Der ganze Monat Mai ist Maria geweiht. Bei den Kelten (Beltane), Germanen und Römern war dies eine der frohesten Zeiten im ganzen Jahr. Maia war die altitalische Göttin des Wachstums; auch Flora, die römische Göttin der Blumen und des blühenden Getreides, wurde von Ende April bis zum 3. Mai in den Floralia, einer Art Walpurgisnacht, gefeiert.

Mariä Heimsuchung (2. Juli) ist ein wichtiger Tag im Wetterglauben; an diesem Tag ging Maria ihre Base Elisabeth besuchen. Als ein Gewitter ausbrach, suchte sie unter einer Haselnussstaude Zuflucht. Seither gilt die Haselnussstaude Gewitter und Blitz abweisend; in Tirol wird an diesem Tag zum Schutz vor Gewittern ein Zweig an die Haustür oder unters Dach gesteckt.

Der Festtag Maria Schnee (5. August) wird mit einer uralten römischen Legende aus dem 5. Jh. in Verbindung gebracht, derzufolge die Madonna einem römischen Patrizierehepaar erschienen sein und versprochen haben soll, dass ihr Wunsch nach einem Sohn in Erfüllung ginge, wenn ihr zu Ehren eine Kirche errichtet würde, wo am nächsten Morgen Schnee liege (Basilika Santa Maria Maggiore); dieser Marientag wird mit der nordischen Holla/Frau Holle und ihrem Schnee in Verbindung gebracht.

Maria Himmelfahrt (15. August) ist der größte Marienfeiertag. Sie ist Kornmutter, es ist der Tag der Kräuterweihe. Laut Mythos wurde zu dieser Zeit in Rom das Fest der Diana, „Unsere Frau der Ernte“, gefeiert.

Maria Geburt (8. September) wird auch „Kleiner Frauentag“ genannt; die Zeit zwischen Maria Himmelfahrt und Maria Geburt ist eine magische Zeit, die sogenannten „Frauendreißger“, der Zeitraum der vorchristlichen Ernte- und Pflanzenkulte.

Mariä Namen (12. September) kündet das Sommerende an: „An Mariä Namen sagt der Sommer Amen.“

Maria Empfängnis (8. Dezember) erinnert daran, dass ihre Mutter Anna sie ohne den Makel der Erbsünde empfing; ursprünglich ist er als Fest der Hl. Anna im Orient erwähnt.

Weihnachten (24./25. Dezember) ist das Fest der Geburt Christi; Maria übernimmt die Rolle der Sonne- und Lichtgebärerin. Auch Mithras wurde in einer Erdhöhle von der jungfräulichen göttlichen Mutter Erde geboren. Vieles aus dem Kult um den „sol invictus“, die „unbesiegte Sonne“, wurde von der christlichen Religion übernommen, so auch das Fest der Geburt des Gottessohnes Jesu, der wahren Lichtquelle und die Verehrung des neugeborenen Kindes durch die Hirten.

Jungfräuliche Schwangerschaften und Geburten sind aus zahlreichen vorchristlichen Mythen überliefert, denn göttliche Abstammung setzt eine Jungfrauengeburt voraus.

Während also vorchristliche Religionen und Kulturen das Göttliche, und, um genauer zu sein, das Weiblich-Göttliche in erster Linie in Verbindung mit Natur und Landschaft wahrnahmen und verehrten, legte die christliche Lehre ursprünglich die „Heiligkeit" eher als abstrakten Begriff aus und bezog in den ersten Jahrhunderten die in der Natur wirkenden Kräfte nicht mit ein. Doch dies entsprach nicht den Bedürfnissen des von der Natur abhängigen Menschen, der mit Krankheit und Seuchen, Unwettern und Dürreperioden, Ernte und Missernte, Fruchtbarkeit und Unfruchtbarkeit leben musste; er brauchte als Hilfestellung etwas „Konkreteres", etwas Anschauliches und Greifbares: Diese Rolle übernahmen die christlichen Heiligen, sie wurden SchutzpatronInnen und FürsprecherInnen für alle möglichen menschlichen Belange.

Auch im Tiroler Volk ist die Verehrung der Heiligen sehr groß, sie werden bei Krankheit und Tod, Liebe und Fruchtbarkeit bei Mensch, Vieh und Pflanzen, zum Schutz vor bösen Geistern, Dämonen und Unwettern usw. angerufen.

Nicht umsonst wurde früher manchmal von protestantischer Seite provozierend bemerkt, dass die Katholiken ihre Heiligen anbeten würden. Auch Maria, deren göttlicher Schutzmantel Platz für alle Schutzbedürftigen biete, wird als die „geheime Göttin im Christentum" bezeichnet (Christa Mulak).

In diesem Kapitel wurden deshalb sowohl Marien- als auch Heiligenlegenden aus dem Tiroler Raum aufgenommen. Erscheinen sie beim ersten Durchlesen manchmal eher aussageschwach, so ist der mythologische Hintergrund dieser Heiligen umso komplexer, denn zumeist hatten Heilige ja auch die Aufgabe, eine frühere Glaubensgestalt zu ersetzen.

Doch gerade dieser christlichen „Übernahme" verdanken wir es, dass sich uralte kultische Rituale und Bräuche bis in die heutige Zeit gehalten haben, dass das Weiblich-Göttliche in der von Männern regierten Kirche auch weiterhin seinen Platz einnehmen kann und damit ein ganzheitlicheres Gottesbild gegeben ist.

134

Sage vom Jaufental

Das heutige Jaufental war einst viel schöner als jetzt und so sanft aufsteigend, dass ein Weinfass, das man im hintersten Grunde des Tales in Bewegung gesetzt hätte, bis an das äußerste Ende des Tales gerollt wäre, ohne zu zerbrechen.

Da kam aber einmal ein gräuliches Wetter, und das ganze Tal wurde unter Wasser gesetzt. Nur die Kirche, die auf einer Anhöhe stand, war lange Zeit von der Überschwemmung unberührt. Viele Leute hatten sich dahin geflüchtet und läuteten Wetter. Als aber das Wasser auch bis zur Kirche stieg, liefen die Leute davon und retteten sich auf die nahen Berge. Nur der alte Mesner blieb zurück und läutete noch.

Bald sah sich aber auch dieser in größter Gefahr und musste flüchten. Traurig schied er von der Kirche und sprach: „Meine liebe Heilige Ursula! ich kann dir nicht mehr helfen, jetzt musst du dir selbst läuten." Und horch, die Glocken läuteten fort, voller und heller als je, ohne dass ein Mensch sie zog! Auf ihren Wunderklang ließ der Regen nach, die Wolken verzogen sich, das Wasser sank, und die Talbewohner stiegen wieder von den Bergen herab. Aber das Tal war nicht mehr so schön wie früher, denn viele Felsen waren seither nackt, und im Tal blieben Sand und Stein liegen.

›› Wissenswertes ‹‹

Die Hl. Ursula (von lat. „ursus" = Bär, Festtag 21. Oktober), Patronin der Kirche in Jaufental/Mittertal, war laut Legende eine im 4. oder 5. Jh. lebende bretonische Prinzessin, die den Sohn eines heidnischen englischen Königs heiraten sollte. Sie erklärte sich damit einverstanden, wenn er sich taufen ließe und wenn man ihr drei Jahre Zeit gebe, um eine Pilgerfahrt nach Rom unternehmen zu können, begleitet von zehn Jungfrauen. Diesen insgesamt elf Jungfrauen sollten sich auf der Pilgerreise weitere 1000 Jungfrauen anschließen. Als sie mit ihrem Schiff von der römischen Pilgerfahrt zurückkehrten, fanden sie die Stadt Köln von den Hunnen belagert vor. Attila, der Hunnenkönig, hatte bereits von Ursulas Schönheit und Weisheit gehört, er wollte sie daher zur Frau nehmen. Da sie sich verweigerte, wurde sie laut Legende durch einen Pfeilschuss getötet; mit ihr sollen 11.000 Gefährtinnen gestorben sein. Die Hl. Ursula wird seither ikonografisch mit Schiff und Pfeil dargestellt. Der Kult um diese Heilige und ihre Reliquien hat eine weite Verbreitung gefunden, sie zählt zu den populärsten Heiligen überhaupt. – In der romanischen St.-Ursulakirche in Köln findet sich eine Inschrift aus frühchristlicher Zeit (ihre Echtheit ist allerdings nicht gesichert), welche bezeugt, dass hier Jungfrauen das Martyrium erlitten hätten. In Kirchennähe fand man bereits im 12. Jh. eine große Gräberstätte („Ager Ursulanus"), die den Märtyrerkult der 11.000 Jungfrauen aus kirchlicher Sicht noch untermauerte. Tatsächlich aber handelt es sich um ein großes römisches Gräberfeld. Die Zahl 11.000 geht laut Forschung vermutlich auf einen Lesefehler zurück. Höchstwahrscheinlich wurde die lateinische Angabe „XI.M.V." als „11 Milia Virgines" anstatt „11 Martyres Virgines" gelesen; zumal in frühen Quellen nur von 11 Jungfrauen die Rede ist.

In der Heiligenforschung wird die Hl. Ursula mit der vorchristlichen Sachsengöttin Ursel/

Horsel in Verbindung gebracht. Sie war eine Bären- und Mondgöttin, ähnlich der griechischen Artemis, und wurde nicht nur im Kölner Raum hochverehrt; der Kult um die Bärin-Göttin (Bärin als Symbol für die weibliche Urkraft) hielt sich parallel zum Christentum viele Jahrhunderte lang. Sie wurde auch dem Mond gleichgesetzt, und die Sterne, ihre Kinder, entsprächen den 11.000 Jungfrauen. Parallelen können aber auch zu den germanischen Göttinnen Nehalennia und Nerthus gezogen werden, deren Attribut, wie bei der Hl. Ursula, das Schiff ist.

In zahlreichen Tiroler Sagen ist von Glocken die Rede, und auch aus der Tiroler Volkskultur sind sie nicht wegzudenken. Ursprünglich stammt die Glocke vermutlich aus Afrika; man fand sie bereits in römischen Gräbern als Grabbeigabe. Im Alpengebiet ist sie laut Fink erst seit dem 8. Jh. nachweisbar. Glocken sind ein wichtiges Lärminstrument, denn Lärm war immer schon ein Mittel, um Dämonen und Geister abzuwehren. Dieser heidnische Brauch der lärmenden Geisterabwehrung wurde von der Kirche durch die Glockenweihe übernommen; die Kraft der Glocke sollte damit aus der Kraft der christlichen Weihe kommen. Auch die den Almtieren umgehängten geweihten Viehglocken haben ursprünglich diese Aufgabe: Sie sollen die Tiere gegen alle möglichen drohenden Gefahren und vor bösen Geistern schützen. Der Brauch des Wetterläutens ist in Tirol weitum bekannt. Die geweihte Glocke konnte laut Volksglauben so manches Gewitter bannen, zumal die Meinung herrschte, die schlimmen Unwetter würden von einer Hexe herrühren.

Beim Einstellen des Messners, der „rechten Hand des Pfarrers“, wurde besonders darauf geachtet, einen zuverlässigen und achtsamen Mann zu finden. Dafür erhielt er das „Wetterkorn“ oder „Läutkorn“, mancherorts auch die „Wettergarbe“. Vielerorts erinnern heute noch Sagen, Reime und Sprüche an die Funktion der Wetterglocken, wie z.B. bei jener in Teis: „Annamaria hoaß i, olle Wetter woaß i, olle Wetter vertreib’ i und lei im Teiser Turm do bleib i.“

Somit wohnt der christlichen Glocke eine zweifache Kraft inne: jene des Klanges und symbolisch jene der göttlichen Kraft.

135

Die Heilige Notburga

Eine der ältesten Tiroler Burgen war Rottenburg, welche jetzt nur noch in Trümmern die Gegend schmückt. Sie war die Wiege und der Stammsitz eines diese Gegend weithin beherrschenden Dynastengeschlechtes, dessen Ursprung bis in das achte Jahrhundert reicht.

Ein Schutzengel war im 14. Jh. dem Hause zuteil geworden, und zwar in Gestalt einer frommen Jungfrau des Namens Notburga, welche Heinrich I. von Rottenburg und Ottilie, seiner Gemahlin, als Magd diente, und zwar mit der aufopferndsten Treue. Aber auch gegen die Armen war Notburga die Milde selbst; und das war der kargen Herrin Ottilie ein Dorn im Auge; sie wollte nicht einmal dulden, dass die Dienerin die Speisen an Arme gebe, die sie sich selbst vom Munde absparte. So stellte der junge Ritter Notburga zur Rede, als er sie mit gefüllter Schürze auf dem Burghügel antraf. Er fragte sie, was sie in der Schürze trage. Notburga, die den Befehl von der Schlossherrin erhalten hatte, fortan die Überbleibsel der Mahlzeit den Schweinen vorzuwerfen, hatte aber aus Mitleid mit den Notleidenden etwas von ihrem Brot und Wein aufgespart; das wollte sie den Armen bringen. Und der Wahrheit gemäß antwortete sie dem Ritter: „Brot und Wein trage ich", und öffnete voll Unbefangenheit die Schürze. Heinrich aber sah nur Hobelspäne darin und als er von dem Krüglein kostete, schien es ihm, er trinke Lauge. Da war der Ritter noch mehr erbost, denn, so urteilte er, Notburga habe ihn zum Narren gehalten. Mit Schimpfworten jagte er sie vom Schlosse.

Notburga suchte und fand bei einem Bauern im Dörflein Eben beim Achensee Zuflucht, der sie aufnahm, in dessen Haus ihr Walten Segen und Fülle brachte, obgleich die fromme Jungfrau mehr betete als arbeitete. Einst galt es Gras zu schneiden, aber ehe die Arbeit vollendet war, erklang die Feierabendglocke, während die letzten Strahlen der sinkenden Sonne die Gegend vergoldeten. Alsbald beendete Notburga die Arbeit, und darüber wurde der Bauer etwas unmutig und sagte: „Es muss heute zu Ende geschnitten werden." Aber Notburga antwortete nur das eine Wort: „Feierabend!", warf ihre Sichel hoch in die Luft, und siehe, die Sichel blieb hängen auf dem letzten Sonnenstrahl und glänzte hell wie der silberne Mond. Da ließ sie der Bauer gewähren und reicher Segen erfüllte das Haus.

Je mehr bei dem Bauern der Segen wuchs, um so mehr nahm er ab beim Dynasten von Rottenburg. Nach dem Tod seiner Frau Ottilie machte sich deren Geist in Gestalt eines Schweines bemerkbar. Da besann sich Heinrich I. auf Notburga und ließ sie auf die Burg zurückrufen, um ihre Verzeihung zu erbitten. Er gab ihr volle Freiheit in Spendung der Almosen und die Armen und Bedrängten hatten eine liebevolle Mutter an ihr gefunden. Auch eine große Stiftung geschah auf ihre Fürbitte, nach der an einem festgesetzten Tage alljährlich auf St. Georgenberg 500 Arme von Ritter Heinrich von Rottenburg gespeist wurden. Frau Ottilias Geist ward alsbald erlöst. Segen und Friede kehrte mit der heiligen Magd wieder in das Schloss ein. Bald blühte auch auf Rottenburg alles wieder im besten Wohlstand, und eine Reihe von Jahren war Notburga des Hauses wohltuender und segnender Genius. Als aber auch sie ihr Ende herannahen fühlte (nach dessen Eintreten Engel ihre Seele sichtbar in den Himmel trugen), ordnete sie an, dass ihre Leiche auf einen mit zwei Stieren bespannten Wagen gelegt werden sollte, und wo jene – ohne Lenker – sie hinfahren würden, da solle man sie bestatten. Die Tiere fuhren den Leichnam über den Inn, zu einer Kapelle des Heiligen Ruprecht, in welcher in früherer Zeit Notburga oft gebetet hatte; dort begrub man sie nun, und da an ihrem Grabe Wunder geschahen, so wurde sie vom Volke als eine Heilige verehrt und ihr zu Ehren später eine herrliche Kirche erbaut und geweiht, die nun eine besuchte Wallfahrtskirche ist, und zu Eben ob Jenbach steht.

Notburga ist eine der meist verehrten Heiligen Tirols (Festtag am 13. September). Etymologisch wird ihrem Namen die Bedeutung „Schützerin in Gefahr" zugeschrieben. Sie wird als Patronin der Dienstmägde, der Armen und der Bauern sowie des Feierabends und der Sonntagsruhe verehrt. Somit könnte man sie als die Gewerkschafterin unter den Heiligen bezeichnen. Auch für eine glückliche Geburt, für die Fruchtbarkeit und bei Viehkrankheiten wird sie angerufen. Ihre Attribute sind eine Sichel, eine Getreidegarbe und ein Krug, uralte Fruchtbarkeitssymbole; manchmal wird sie auch mit Schlüsselbund, Milchkübel und Broten gezeigt. Ihre Legende setzte sich erst im 17. Jh. durch, daher gibt es auch keine Notburga-Darstellungen aus dem Mittelalter. Bei der Weihung von Kirchen scheint man dieser Volksheiligen, die nie förmlich heilig gesprochen wurde, eher aus dem Weg gegangen zu sein. Erst im Jahre 1862 erhielt die Notburga-Verehrung die offizielle Bestätigung durch Papst Pius IX.

Über das Leben der Notburga gibt es kaum Aufzeichnungen; es wurde aus den Legenden rekonstruiert, v.a. durch den Haller Stiftsarzt Hippolyt Guarinoni. Demnach soll sie um 1265 in Rattenberg am Inn als einfache Frau geboren worden sein und sich zeitlebens für die Armen und Hilfsbedürftigen eingesetzt haben. Bei ihrem Tod im Jahre 1313 wurde sie vor dem Altar der Rupertikirche in Eben am Achensee begraben, die 1434 auf sie umgeweiht wurde. Neben dieser viel besuchten Hauptkultstätte ist auch die Kirche in Hörschwang bei St.Lorenzen im Pustertal ihr geweiht, und in zahlreichen Tiroler Kirchen findet sich ihre Statue. In Eben hielt man ihre Graberde für Mensch und Tier heilsam.

In vielen Sagen und Legenden scheinen Rinder als weisende Tiere auf, sie zeigen die Stelle an, an der eine Kirche oder eine Kapelle errichtet werden soll. Sehr oft gelten auch Vögel als weisende Tiere, so manche Kirche steht heute an einem Ort, der laut Sage von einer Schwalbe oder einer Taube zugewiesen wurde, wie z.B. Heiligkreuz in Abtei, Heiliggeist im Ahrntal, in Albeins, in St. Magdalena in Villnöß u.a.m. Solche Weisungssagen geben Hinweis auf ein hohes Alter der Kultstätte; häufig ist auch von einem Heidentempel die Rede, und bekannterweise wurden viele Kirchen auf vorgeschichtlichen Kultplätzen errichtet.

Zu Beginn des Christentums wurde der christliche Gottesdienst am Sabbat, dem jüdischen Ruhetag, gefeiert; dies wurde in der Folge dann bewusst um einen Tag verschoben. Auch die Sonntagsheiligung wurde der jüdischen Tradition entlehnt. Am „Tag des Herrn", dem Sonntag, durfte/darf man nach christlicher Auffassung keine Arbeiten verrichten. Während in der ersten christlichen Zeit die Sonntagsheiligung freiwillig war, wurde diese mit dem Anerkennen des Christentums als Staatsreligion zur Pflicht für alle.

Die in der Sage erwähnten Rottenburger waren eine Adelsfamilie mit Stammsitz im unteren Inntal. Sie hatten u.a. Besitzungen im Eisacktal, im Südtiroler Unterland und im Trentino. Im 14. Jh. zählten sie in der Grafschaft Tirol zu den politisch einflussreichen Adligen, doch im darauffolgenden Jahrhundert erlosch ihr Geschlecht. Auch ihre Burg ist heute nur mehr eine Ruine.

Eine Sage von der Leuchtenburg bei Kaltern erzählt, dass Notburga oft hierher mitgenommen wurde. Auch hier tat sie den Armen viel Gutes, verteilte Erbsen an sie. Viele davon fielen über den Berg hinunter und gingen im nächsten Frühjahr wild auf. Deshalb gebe es am Mitterberg unterhalb der Ruine Leuchtenburg in Kaltern heute noch viele Erbsen.

136

Die St.-Margareten-Kirche am Kniebos (Kniepass)

Von der Entstehung der Margaretenkirche am Kniebos bei St. Lorenzen im Pustertal erzählt die Sage Folgendes: Von ungefähr begab es sich, dass man in einer abgelegenen, tiefen Höhle jener Gegend auf schroffen Felsen, wohin kaum jemals ein menschlicher Fußtritt gedrungen, das Bildnis der Hl. Margaret gefunden hat. So wundersam und unerklärlich das Dasein der Heiligen in dieser Felsengrotte schien, so schnell und klar schwebte den frommen Nachbarn die Idee vor, der Heiligen Margaret eine Kirche zu bauen. Heinrich Stadler am Stadelhof zu Lothen baute dann im Jahre 1400 wirklich die Kirche am Kniebos. Er selbst ist mit seiner Ehefrau in ritterlicher Tracht im Kirchlein hinter der Türe angemalt zu sehen.

›› Wissenswertes ‹‹

Der eingangs der Sage erwähnte Kniepass (1170 Chniepoz), der gar kein Pass ist, soll laut Hans Fink mit „Knie“ und dem althochdeutschen „pôzan“ (= „schlagen“) zusammenhängen, und würde so viel wie „Anstrengung der Knie in der Steigung“ bedeuten. Die Margarethenkirche am Kniepass kann als Abschluss des Sonnenburger Bezirkes bezeichnet werden, ein uraltes Besiedlungsgebiet mit Funden, die auf die rätisch-etruskische, venetische, keltische und römische Siedlungszeit zuückführen.

Die Hl. Margareta (= „die Perle“, Festtag 13. u. 20. Juli) ist eine sehr verehrte Heilige. Unzählige Kirchen und Kapellen inner- und außerhalb Tirols sind ihr geweiht; die meisten davon befinden sich abseits der geschlossenen Ortschaften; häufig stehen sie an Ufern von Bächen, die aus Schluchten hervortreten, welche laut uralter Überlieferung oft von Drachen und Lindwürmern bewohnt waren.

Zahlreiche Legenden ranken sich um ihre Figur: So soll sie die zum Christentum konvertierte wunderschöne Tochter eines heidnischen Priesters in Antiochia in der südlichen Türkei gewesen sein. Ihr Vater verstieß sie und sie verdiente sich als Schweinehirtin ihren Lebensunterhalt. Als der Stadtpräfekt Olybrius sie begehrte, wies sie ihn zurück, worauf er sie schrecklichen Folterungen unterziehen ließ; schlussendlich wurde sie enthauptet. Als Auslöser für ihr Martyrium wird häufig ihre Schönheit und nicht so sehr ihr Glaube genannt; deshalb wird sie auch mit dem Kummernus-Kult (siehe die Sage „Von der heiligen Kümmernis“) in Verbindung gebracht. In einer Legendenvariante wird sie im Kerker von einem riesigen Drachen verschlungen, dessen Körper sie mit Hilfe des Kreuzes zum Bersten bringt; sie selbst bleibt unverletzt.

In einer anderen Legende tritt sie in Männerkleidern als „Bruder Pelagius“ in ein asketisches Mönchskloster ein, wird dann aber beschuldigt, eine Nonne verführt zu haben, und erst nach ihrem Tod, als entdeckt wird, dass sie eine Frau ist, wird sie rehabilitiert. Auch wird erzählt, dass sie vor diesem Eintritt ins Mönchsleben unter dem Namen Pelagia als göttliche Hure, als Tempelhure, Aphrodite gedient haben soll. Stellvertretend für die große Göttin vollzog sie demzufolge als Priesterin den heiligen sexuellen Ritus, als Zeichen ritueller Fruchtbarkeit und Sexualmagie. Das „Perlentor“ wäre demzufolge der genitale Zugang zur alten Muttergöttin, auch „Schaumgeborene“, „königliche Perle“ oder „Stern des Meeres“ genannt.

Im Alpenraum wird Margareta als vorchristliche Fruchtbarkeitsgöttin gedeutet. Dies wird durch die Forschungen des graubündnerischen Bischofs und Volkstumsforschers Christian Caminada untermauert, der 1931 das rätoromanische St.-Margareta-Lied, die „Sontga Margriata", aufzeichnete, ein uraltes, von den Engadiner Bäuerinnen jahrhundertelang gesungenes Lied.

Die hier als „heilig" besungene Margareta tritt als männlicher Hirte verkleidet in Erscheinung. Doch als man ihre Weiblichkeit, ihre entblößte Brust entdeckt, und ihr Geheimnis nicht respektiert wird, verlässt sie die Alp, und mit ihr verlassen Überfluss und Fruchtbarkeit die Gegend. Der Begriff „heilig" hat im vorchristlichen Sinne mit dem „Mana", der besonderen magischen, einem Wesen oder Ort innewohnenden Kraft zu tun; laut Caminada in diesem Fall die geheimnisvolle Kraft der Alpenfruchtbarkeit. Die in der christlichen Legende als Hirtin beschriebene Heilige wird auch mit der rätischen Göttin Reitia/Reithia/Rätia (ebenfalls „Hirtin" genannt) in Verbindung gebracht, mit der auch Namensähnlichkeit besteht.

Im Christentum zählt Margareta gemeinsam mit Barbara und Katharina als die einzigen weiblichen Heiligen zu den 14 Nothelfern. Das Auftreten dieser Frauendreiheit, bekannt als die „drei heiligen Madln („Margaret mit dem Wurm, Barbara mit dem Turm und Kathrein mit dem Radl sein die drei schönsten Madl."), ist Ausdruck uralter kultischer, im Volk fest verankerter Verehrung. Zusammen mit der Hl. Dorothea sind sie die vier „Virgines capitales", „die wichtigsten Jungfrauen".

Sie gilt als Patronin der Bauern und Hirten, der Jungfrauen, Ammen und Gebärenden, wird u.a. zum Schutz vor Dämonen, bei Unfruchtbarkeit und schweren Geburten angerufen, da sie der christlichen Überlieferung zufolge in ihrer Todesstunde Gott bat, dass jede Frau, die in Kindsnöten ihren Namen anrufe, ein gesundes Kind gebären soll; laut Legende sei ihr dies durch eine aus dem Himmel ertönende Stimme gewährt worden.

Im Volk ist sie als „Wetterfrau" und Beschützerin des Ackerbaus bekannt, als Herrin über den Drachen, der symbolisch für die der Natur innewohnenden Kräfte und der Fruchtbarkeit gedeutet wird. Mancherorts wird sie dargestellt, wie sie den Drachen liebevoll in den Armen hält oder neben sich an der Leine führt. Ihr Tag ist ein gefürchteter Lostag. Wenn es an diesem Tag regnet, regnet es 14 Tage, daher ihr Übername „Fetzgreate". Eine weitere Volksmeinung besagt, dass man zwischen dem 13. und dem 20. Juli keine Schlangen töten soll, weil diese das Weidevieh der Hl. Margareta sind. Auch in der Blumenwelt hat Margareta Aufnahme gefunden: Die Margerite und die Margarethenblume (Gänseblümchen) sind als Liebesorakel-Blumen bekannt; volkstümliche Pflanzennamen wie „Gretl hinter den Stauden" (Jungfer im Grünen), die „faule Gretl" (Erdrauch, eine wichtige Heilpflanze) und die „zottige Gretl" (die wildblühende Federnelke) erinnern an diese Heilige.

137

Die St.-Klara-Birnen

Als die Heilige Klara in der letzten Krankheit lag und ihren Klöstern ein Andenken vermacht hatte, erinnerte man sie an ihr jüngstes Kloster in Brixen und fragte sie, ob sie nicht auch diesem etwas vermachen wolle. Da war es ihr leid, dass sie der jungen Töchter in Brixen vergessen hatte, weil sie so siech war, und sie sprach: „So habe ich doch gar nichts, damit ich sie in Freude versetzen könnte; ach hätte ich doch eine Birne aus dem Garten, die wollt' ich ihnen gerne senden!"

Da war es aber nicht um die Zeit, dass man reife Birnen hatte. Ein Bruder aber ging im Vertrauen auf die Heiligkeit der Jungfrau hinaus in den Garten und sah einen Ast voll zeitiger Birnen, die brach er ab und brachte sie Sankt Klaren. Davon nahm sie eine, lobte Gott und sandte sie ihren Töchtern in Brixen und hieß dieselben von ihr fröhlich grüßen.

Das geschah, und die Töchter Sankt Klaren in Brixen pflanzten mit dem Kern der süßen Frucht in ihrem Garten einen Baum, der ward groß und stark und war alle Jahre voll Blüten und Früchte. Dieser Baum steht noch heute daselbst, und seine Früchte heißt man noch immer Sankt-Klara-Birnen.

›› Wissenswertes ‹‹

Klara von Assisi (1193-1253, Gedenktag 11. August) war die Begründerin des Ordens der „Armen Schwestern". Sie war eine außergewöhnliche Frau. Schon mit 18 Jahren verließ sie gegen den Willen ihrer adeligen Eltern ihre Familie, um wie Franziskus in radikaler Armut zu leben. Für die kirchliche Anerkennung der franziskanischen Lebensform kämpfte sie zeitlebens. Sie war die erste Frau in der Geschichte, welche Ordensregeln für Frauen geschrieben hat. Diese enthielten demokratische Prinzipien, besonderen Wert legte Klara auf die Eigenverantwortung jeder einzelner Schwester. Der von ihr gegründete Klarissenorden erhielt bereits zu Lebzeiten großen Zuspruch; viele Frauen fühlten sich von ihrer religiösen Einstellung angesprochen, sogar ihre Schwester und ihre Mutter folgten ihrem Lebensbeispiel. Bereits zwei Jahre nach ihrem Tode wurde sie heilig gesprochen.

Die seit ihrer Kindheit kränkelnde Hl. Klara ist auf Bildern oft mit einer Monstranz dargestellt; denn beim Einbruch der plündernden Sarazenen nach Assisi soll sie auf dem Krankenbett zur Klosterpforte getragen worden sein, wo sie, im Vertrauen auf Gott, den Feinden die Monstranz entgegengehalten und sie in die Flucht geschlagen haben soll.

Sie ist nicht nur die Patronin der Stickerinnen und Wäscherinnen, sondern eine ausgesprochen moderne Schutzheilige: Aufgrund ihrer Visionen und mystischen Entrückungen – so soll sie beispielsweise einmal von ihrer Klosterzelle aus die Weihnachtsmesse in der Kirche genauestens mitverfolgt haben – wurde sie 1958 von Papst Pius XII. zur Patronin des Fernsehens erklärt.

Die älteste Klarissenniederlassung auf deutschem Boden ist jene in Brixen, erstmals dokumentiert im Jahre 1235. Doch bereits ca. zwei Jahrhunderte später wurde dieses Kloster, wie unzählige andere, vom Reformeifer des Cardinals Nikolaus Cusanus schwer getroffen. Er stellte fest, dass das Klosterleben der Schwestern nicht den kirchlichen Vorgaben entspreche, setzte die Äbtissin ab und übertrug das Amt einer anderen Klosterschwester. Dies hatte die offene Revolte der Schwestern zur Folge, worauf Cusanus Kirchenbann und Interdikt (Verbot aller kirchlichen Amtshandlungen) über das Klarissenkloster legte. Die Klarissin Maria von Wolkenstein, eine Tochter des Minnesängers Oswald, wurde mit einigen anderen Schwestern wegen ihrer Gehorsamsverweigerung sogar eine Zeitlang isoliert. Als es Cusanus endlich gelungen war, sich durchzusetzen, kam es bald darauf zu heftigen Auseinandersetzungen mit dem Tiroler Landesfürsten Erzherzog Sigismund den Münzreichen, der Kardinal wurde sogar gefangengenommen. Daraufhin verhängte der damalige Papst Pius II. über das ganze Land das Interdikt. Ein Großteil des Klerus stand jedoch hinter dem Landesfürsten. In Brixen wurde damals das Interdikt einzig von den Klarissen respektiert, was den Landesfürsten so in Rage brachte, dass er den Nonnen androhte, er werde sie aus der Stadt peitschen oder wie Katzen im Eisack ersäufen lassen, wenn sie es weiterhin einhielten. Tatsächlich mussten sie das Kloster verlassen, sie fanden Unterkunft in deutschen Klöstern. Erst drei Jahre später (1464) konnten sie wieder nach Brixen zurückkehren. Als Lohn für Treue und Gehorsam gewährte der Papst ihnen einen besonderen Ablass, die sog. Trostbulle.

Der in der Sage erwähnte, aus Birnenkernen gezogene Birnbaum steht immer noch im Klostergarten der Klarissen, allerdings ist er aus einem Ableger des ursprünglichen Baumes gezüchtet. Doch, wie uns eine Klarissenschwester mitteilte, würden die St.-Klara-Birnen nicht besonders gut schmecken.

138

Heilige Mutter Anna, du hast uns nit verstanna!

Lange Zeit schon herrschte in Deutschnofen Dürre und Trockenheit und die Bauern erhofften sich Leben spendenden Regen für ihre Felder und Wiesen. Da machten sich die Bewohner in ihrer Not und Hilflosigkeit auf nach Weißenstein, um bei der Heiligen Mutter Anna um Regen zu bitten. Doch angekommen bei der Wallfahrtskirche, begann es plötzlich zu wettern und zu stürmen, jedoch nicht der ersehnte Regen prasselte nieder, sondern es hagelte und schneite. Da blickten sie zum Bildnis der Heiligen Mutter Anna und riefen:

„Hl. Mutter Anna,
du hasch uns nit verstanna:
Wir hab'n gebet'n um an Regn –
Schnee und Schauer hascht du uns geb'n!"

›› Wissenswertes ‹‹

Der Festtag der Hl. Anna, der Mutter Marias und Frau des Joachims, Großmutter von Jesus, wird am 26. Juli gefeiert. Aus den Evangelien erfährt man nichts über ihr Leben, wohl aber erzählt das „Protevangelium" des Jakobus (= Vor-Evangelium, entstanden mindestens ein Jahrhundert nach dem Tode Jesu) von ihr. Demzufolge soll sie dreimal verheiratet gewesen sein, habe trotz ihres betagten Alters und ihrer Unfruchtbarkeit Maria empfangen und dies nur durch einen Kuss des Hl. Joachim.

Im byzantinischen Osten wurde sie bereits im 6. Jh. sehr verehrt, ca. ab dem 8. Jh. gewann sie dann auch im Abendland zunehmend an Bedeutung. Ihr Kult verbreitete sich vor allem im ausgehenden Mittelalter, was sich auch in den zahlreichen Selbdritt-Darstellungen (Anna, Maria und das Jesuskind) aus jener Zeit erkennen lässt. Die Kirche verhielt sich lange Zeit äußerst zurückhaltend diesem Kult gegenüber, erst im 16. Jh. wurde die allgemeine Feier ihres Festes angeordnet.

Oft trägt sie einen grünen Mantel oder eine Matronentracht, manchmal hält sie auch ein Buch in der Hand. Der grüne Mantel steht symbolisch für den Schutz des grünen Grases; als Schutzpatronin der Fruchtbarkeit hielt man den Regen an ihrem Tag für einen Segen. Andernorts sagte man aber auch: „Anna warm und trocken, macht den Bauer frohlocken." Ebenso wurde sie bei Gewittergefahr angerufen. Frauen opferten der Heiligen Kröten-votive und Annahände, Letztere wurden auch sehr erfolgreich von Händlern als Talisman vertrieben.

Die Hl. Anna ist eine große Frauenschutzheilige. Sie ist Heiratsvermittlerin, Patronin der Ehe und der Mütter, der Witwen und der Armen, wird für Kindersegen und eine glückliche Geburt angerufen.

Ab dem 15. Jh. wurde sie eine der wichtigsten Schutzpatroninnen im Bergbau, vor allem für den Abbau von Silber. Als Mutter und Großmutter von Maria (Mond – Silber) und Jesus (Sonne – Gold) wurde sie selbst mit einem Bergwerk verglichen, aus dem diese Edelmetalle hervorgingen. Die Verehrung der Hl. Anna ist deshalb, wie die der Hl. Agatha, in ehemaligen Bergbaugegenden zu finden, wie in dieser Deutschnofner Sage, oder in der Knappenkirche von Rotlahn bei Villanders, in Morgenstätt in Sarnthein u.a.m. Bekannt ist auch die Pusterer Wallfahrt zur Mutter Anna in Ahornach.

Auch bei Fieber, Kopf-, Brust- und Bauchschmerzen wird die Heilige Anna angerufen.

Anna als mythische göttliche Großmutter ist aber bereits schon lange, bevor die christliche Bibel geschrieben wurde, bekannt: als orientalische Göttin Anna, Hannah oder Di-Ana, als Dinah oder Nana bei den Sumerern, als Anat in Kanaan, Anatha in Syrien, als doppelköpfige Anna Perenna oder Jana/Juno, die jungfräuliche Gottesmutter von Mars bei den Römern.

139

Die drei heiligen Jungfrauen I und II

I.

Vor uralten Zeiten ritt ein heidnisch Volk von Morgen her ins Land herein, und der vorderste trug einen Götzen mit drei Köpfen, wie er noch heute zum ewigen Gedächtnis in der guten Stadt Brixen im Standbild zu sehen ist. Sie erschauten drei minnigliche Jungfrauen, so aus königlichem Geschlechte stammten und von fernen Landen in das fromme Tirol gewandert waren, und schienen aufgelegt, sie sonder Glimpf und Zartheit sich ein- und dem Christenglauben abzutun. Es kam aber starkes Fürchten über die Jungfrauen, und sie gedachten, wie sie sich Christo verlobt, und huben sich in Listen von dannen. Die Heiden saßen mit dem Dreikopfe beim Bankett und aßen und tranken und fuhren mit Schall unter die Tische. Derweil stiegen die Königskinder auf den Berg und kamen in ein Dorf, so man Latzfons nennt. Allda lagen sie etliche Zeit still und verborgen und harrten der Dinge in Fasten und Beten und Almosengeben. Denn sie waren über die Maßen reich. Es drang aber die Kunde zum Heidenkönig, dass die schönen Jungfrauen auf Latzfons säßen, und er sandte seine Büttel aus, die sollten sie an seinen Hof bringen. Die Königskinder aber waren vor ihm gewarnt und flohen bei nächtlicher Weile von Latzfons und stiegen einen Berg hinan gen Meransen. Als der Morgen graute, saßen sie gar traurig auf halbem Berge gen Meransen auf einem Stein. Und sie hatten weder Speise noch Wein, sich zu laben, und die Kräfte verließen sie. Als sie lange so dagesessen, sprach die eine: „Christus, mein Herr, nun gedenke, dass du mir aus der Not helfest, und gib mir zu trinken, dass ich nicht zum Spotte der Heiden verdurste!“ Und siehe da, alsbald sprang ein Brünnlein aus dem Felsen, daran sich die Schwestern erlabten. Darauf nach einer

Weile sagte die andere: „Wie haben wir doch nichts zu essen und müssen den Heiden zum Gespött in Unkräften sterben!" Und siehe da, alsbald wuchs ein Kirschbaum empor, der neigte die Äste zu den Königskindern hernieder, und es hing der süßen Kirschen eine Menge daran, so dass sie sich daran erquickten.

Es stieg aber die Sonne höher und höher und brannte aufs Gefelse herab, also dass die Jungfrauen ob der Hitze in Not gerieten. Und es sprach die Dritte: „Unseres Leides wär' ein Teil vergessen, so uns ein kühlend Schattendach vor Sonnenglut Schirm böte." Siehe da, der Baum ließ Äste und Zweige in die Breite wachsen und tat sie weit auseinander, also dass der Platz in dichtem Schatten stand. Des waren die Königskinder froh, sie huben sich alsbald von dannen und stiegen weiter den Berg hinan nach Meransen. Allda fanden sie gastlich Obdach und verblieben in aller Heimlichkeit und unerkannt manches Jahr und waren der Sorge um der frommen Bergleute Wohlergehen untertan.

Aber es ging allmählich ihrer Wundergabe Preis von Mund zu Mund, und es gab bald kein Stüblein, das die Inwohner nicht der Königskinder Milde rühmten.

Wem irgend ein Gebrechen am Leibe zehrte, der ward durch der Frommen Fürbitte von Schaden und Siechtum geheilt, und wessen Kuh von Krankheit oder bösem Zauber niedergeworfen war, der bat die guten Frauen um Hilfe und ging getröstet von dannen.

Darum hielt das Volk sie in großen Ehren und tat sein Bestes, den Frauen zu dienen mit Speise und Trank und aller Notdurft.

Wie aber die Heiden abgezogen und Friede ins Land gekehrt war und ins Reich Germania, da huben die Königskinder ihren Stab und fuhren des Weges weiter und kamen nach

der Stadt Köln, am Rhein gelegen. Allda nahmen sie Herberge und lebten in Ehren und Würden und in Gottseligkeit und blieben der Wundergabe teilhaft bis an ihr selig Ende.

Es hat keine Chronik vom Jahre ihres Ablebens Meldung getan; wohl aber vermeinen einige, die drei Jungfrauen wären nicht vor der wilden Slaven Anzug geflohen, sondern seien, ob ihres christlichen Glaubens aus der alten Stadt Augsburg vertrieben, in die Berge gefahren; wieder andere erzählen, dieselben seien der Christenverfolgung in England entgangen und aus diesem Inselreiche in unser Bergland geflüchtet, und es seien nicht Kirschen gewesen, so ihnen auf der „Jungfernrast" unter Meransen zum Labsal geworden, sondern gar wundersame und kostbare Äpfel. Es gibt auch einige, die da wissen wollen, die drei Jungfrauen seien nicht Schwestern gewesen und nur die mittlere ein Königskind, die beiden andern aber der Prinzessin dienende Mägdlein, und sie wären vom Berge nimmer weg nach Köln oder in eine andere Stadt gezogen, sondern oben auf Meransen entschlafen und begraben, und von ihnen habe der Berg das Christentum.

II.
(Diese Version erzählte man sich in Latzfons)

Es war in uralter Zeit, da brachen Kriegsstürme und Nöte über Wälschland herein und Mord und Brand und Christenverfolgung, und wer heute zu Christo betete, dem ward morgen der Kopf vor den Rumpf gelegt. Das waren schwere Zeiten, und der Väter Sünden wurden schwer gerächt an Kindern und Kindeskindern.

Es lebten aber dazumal drei fromme Schwestern in Italia, die bekannten sich zu Christo, und da sie ihres Bleibens im Heimatland nimmer sicher waren, so machten sie sich heimlich auf den Weg und gingen ins Gebirge. Es stand aber ob dem heutigen Städtlein Klausen eine feste Burg, die das Land weitum schirmte, Säben genannt. Allda saß ein Bischof und waltete der Heidenbekehrung. Darum nahmen die frommen Jungfrauen ob Säben in Latzfons Herberge und pflegten eifrigen Gottesdienst. Das wurden aber alsbald die Latzfonser inne, welche dazumal noch den Götzen opferten. Es ward den Heidenleuten drum nimmer geheuer; sie fanden sich zu den frommen Frauen herüber und drohten den schwachen Mägdlein mit grimmiger Faust. Da tat die Älteste unter ihnen den Mund auf und sprach: „Nun denn, wir heben uns von hinnen, ihr aber höret: Schwere Zeiten voll Not und Kümmernis kommen über euch und eure Kinder, geboren und ungeboren, und sie werden ihre Häupter nimmer zur Ruhe legen, bis sie uns im Grabe gefunden haben und die Unbill sühnen."

Und wie sie diese Worte geredet, schnallten sie ihre Bündel und kamen auf den Berg Meransen. Die Latzfonser hatten aber darauf viele böse Jahre; der Hunger brach in ihr Kirchspiel herein, und schreckbares Siechtum warf Menschen und Tiere nieder. Infolge langen Regens faulte die Ernte, oder es brannte der Sonne Glut lange Wochen auf Flur und Feld hernieder, also dass die Saat versengt ward. →

Da sprachen sie zumal: „Weh uns, wir werden der Tage nimmer froh, seit wir den frommen Jungfrauen also übel gelohnt. Wer uns die Vielholden wieder auf den Berg brächte, dem gäben wir wohl das Beste, des wir gebieten. Wie sollen wir es anfangen, ihnen das Unrecht zu büßen?" Sie gedachten nämlich in ihrer Not der strafenden Worte, so der Jungfrauen älteste vor dem Weggang gesprochen.

Darauf taten die Latzfonser Buße, ließen sich allesamt taufen, einten sich und setzten einen würdigen Gottesmann zu ihrem Führer. Und es lief der Bauer vom Pfluge, der Schmied löschte das Feuer in der Werkstatt aus und schnallte sich den Rücksack um, und der Zimmermann ließ das Beil, so er zum Schneiten gehoben, fallen und sprang auf den Dorfplatz; alle taten sie eine große Wallfahrt mit Fahnen und Kreuz und heiligem Sange und stiegen den Berg hinan gen Meransen, um der frommen Frauen Fürbitte zu erflehen.

Die aber waren nimmer am Leben. Als die Wallfahrer nun von ihren Wundertaten vernahmen, beteten sie mit Inbrunst an der Stätte, wo die Heiligen gelebt und gewandelt, und gingen getröstet von dannen. Sieh' da! Not und Siechtum wichen alsbald von ihnen, und des Glückes Sonne schien wieder auf ihre Heimstatt.

Solches wissen dir die Ältesten in der Gemeinde Latzfons zu sagen.

›› Wissenswertes ‹‹

Sonder Glimpf = ohne Milde, ein nicht korrektes Verhalten. – schneiten (schnoatn) = das Abschneiden der Äste von Laub- und Nadelbäumen.

Über kaum eine andere Tiroler Sagengestalt wurde so viel geforscht und geschrieben – weit über die Tiroler Landesgrenze hinaus – wie über die Hl. drei Jungfrauen von Meransen. Seltsam und geheimnisvoll klingen bereits ihre Namen: Aubet, Cubet und Guerre/Quere oder auch Gewerpet, Ainpet und Barpet, wie sie in einer Urkunde aus dem Jahre 1382 genannt werden. Unterschiedlichste Deutungen wurden in diese Frauen-Dreiergruppe hineininterpretiert: so wären sie vorchristliche Göttinnen, Schicksalsgöttinnen ähnlich den deutschen Nornen, Heilrätinnen, Heilige Mütter, eine Dreifachgöttin, burgundische Prinzessinnen, Salige oder Gefolgsfrauen der Hl. Ursula u.v.m. Mancherorts werden sie auch aufgrund der gemeinsamen Namensendungen „die drei Beten" genannt. Laut H. Ch. Schöll hätten ihre Namen keltische Wortwurzeln; demzufolge wäre Ambet eine Erdgöttin, Borbet eine Sonnengottheit und Wilbet die Mondfrau. Die katholische Kirche versuchte eine Zeitlang, diese Jungfrauen mit den überhaupt nicht christlich klingenden Namen in „Fides, Spes und Caritas" (nach den christlichen Tugenden) umzubenennen.

Wie sehr die Verehrung der Hl. drei Jungfrauen einst verbreitet war, zeigen die zahlreichen Darstellungen und Verehrungsstätten inner- und außerhalb Tirols: beispielsweise in Wielenberg, St.Sigmund und Vierschach im Pustertal, Plawenn im Vinschgau, Klerant bei Brixen, bei der Mühlbacher Klause, in Sterzing, in Obsaurs bei Imst, in Schlehdorf in Bayern, in Cividale i. Friaul, in Worms und Straßburg u.a.

Seit uralten Zeiten werden sie bei unterschiedlichsten Problemen angerufen: bei lang anhaltender Trockenheit, in Kriegsnöten und in Krankheitsfällen bei Mensch und Vieh; zahlreiche Wunder werden ihnen zugeschrieben. Seit 1515 und bis 1906 pilgerten die Latzfonser Männer bei Trockenheit zu Fuß nach Meransen, und, wenn es sein musste, auch dreimal hintereinander: das erste Mal in gewöhnlicher Kleidung, das zweite Mal ohne Hut und Rock, das dritte Mal barfüßig. Aber auch die

Meransner Männer wallfahrten bis in die sechziger Jahre des 20. Jh. zu einer weiteren Frauen-Dreiheit (Maria), nämlich über das „Poschtntol" nach Ehrenburg im Pustertal, um bei der Kornmutter für eine gute Roggenernte zu bitten.

Doch in diesem christlichen Jungfrauenkult lassen sich auch „heidnische" Züge erkennen, und mit Sicherheit reicht die Meransner Jungfrauenverehrung weit in vorchristliche Zeit zurück. Ihre Sagen ranken sich um Quelle, Stein und Baum, Kultobjekte aus vorchristlicher Zeit, wobei vor allem der Steinkult häufig mit weiblichem Göttinnenkult in Verbindung gebracht wird. An dieser Stelle soll auch die uralte Heilig-Baumwallfahrt erwähnt werden, welche die Leute aus Vals einst zur „Linde" bei der Jungfernrast durchführten. Bei einer Visitation im Jahre 1653 wurde sie verboten, da sie „einen Anstrich von Götzenkult habe".

Die Kirche der Hl. drei Jungfrauen steht an einem aus landschaftsmythologischer Sicht beeindruckenden Ort am Rande der Meransner Hochfläche mit einem weiten Umblick; im Hintergrund erhebt sich eine auffallende Berggruppe mit den uralten Namen Gitsch, Fatsch und Gurnatsch. Bei der Renovierung der Kirche stieß man auf Reste einer romanischen Kirchenanlage und in deren Mitte auf einen behutsam umbauten (Kult-)Felsen. Der Wasserlauf auf der Wiese hinter der Kirche und archäologische Funde aus der Meransner Gegend, die bis ins Mesolithikum zurückreichen, unterstreichen die Bedeutsamkeit dieses Ortes. Am uralten Plattenweg über die „Katzenleiter" von Mühlbach nach Meransen findet sich in der Nähe der Jungfernrast „die alte Kuchl", ein weiterer prähistorischer Fundort, und im Felsgewirr oberhalb der Mühlbacher Klause liegt versteckt die „Lange Kirche", eine sagenumwobene Höhle, die so lang sein soll, dass sie bis ins Beinhaus von Meransen hinaufführe. Laut einer Sage aus Latzfons sollen sich die Hl. Drei Jungfrauen hier versteckt haben. Bedauerlicherweise ist diese Höhle vor einigen Jahren aufgrund eines von einem Brandstifter gelegten Waldbrandes größtenteils eingestürzt; ein Hinabsteigen ins Höhleninnere ist wegen der großen Einsturzgefahr nur mehr auf wenige Meter möglich. Auch die Quelle an der Jungfernrast ist wegen einer vor einigen Jahren errichteten Bewässerungsableitung in die tiefer gelegene Gegend versiegt; eine spärliche Wasserzufuhr findet nunmehr über einen unterirdisch verlegten Schlauch statt.

Laut einer Sagenversion haben die Hl. drei Jungfrauen Meransen wieder verlassen und seien über das oberhalb von Meransen gelegene Greiteneck nach Norden weitergezogen. Tatsächlich führt ein uralter Höhenweg vom Pustertal über Meransen und Schalenstein und das Valler Jöchl (prähistorische Fundstelle) in das Eisacktal und weiter zum Brenner.

Auch in Brixen soll laut dem Historiker Joseph Resch „seit unvordenklichen Zeiten die Verehrung der Hl. Drei Jungfrauen in Übung gestanden haben" (1775). Das Vorhandensein eines sagenhaften Jungfrauenbrunnens, dessen Heilwasser bereits im 16. Jh. schriftlich überliefert ist, legt die Vermutung nahe, dass auch in Brixen ein uraltes Frauenquellheiligtum bestanden hat. Bedauerlicherweise wurde der Jungfernbrunnen bei der Überschwemmung von 1882 verschüttet; nur ein in eine Hausmauer eingelassener, ihm gewidmeter Inschriftstein in der Nähe der Adlerbrücke kündet heute noch von ihm.

Ein letztes Element, das auf das hohe Alter dieser Sagen hinweist und ebenfalls mit der heiligen Dreizahl zusammenhängt, ist die Erwähnung der Verehrung eines dreiköpfigen Götzenbildes. Solche Gottheiten sind aus der Religion der Kelten und Veneter und der griechisch/römischen Mythologie bekannt (die dreiköpfige Hekate, die/der dreiköpfige Trumusiate, bei den Venetern und Kerberos, der dreiköpfige Wächter der Unterwelt in Hundegestalt), auch der persische Mithras wurde manchmal dreiköpfig dargestellt. Mancherorts finden sich auch dreigesichtige Christusdarstellungen (z.B. in Neustift); und in den Tiroler Sagen hat der dreiköpfige Riese in Villnöß und in Meransen überlebt.

Vom Riesen Christophorus an der Außenmauer der Meransner Pfarrkirche haben die Meransner Frauen früher mit dem kleinen Rosenkranzkruzifix Mörtel aus der großen Zehe ausgeschabt und in den Germteig gegeben, um ein gutes Aufgehen für die „Küchel" zu bewirken.

140

Von der Hl. Juliana

Seit undenklichen Zeiten haben die Bewohner des Fassatales eine eigene Beschützerin, und dies ist die Hl. Juliana. Seit wann dies so ist, kann man heute gar nicht mehr sagen, es ist schon zu lange her. So sehr verehrten die Fassaner sie, dass sogar die erste Kirche des Tales ihr geweiht wurde.

Diese Stätte nun gewann die Hl. Juliana so lieb, dass sie ihren Platz im Himmel verließ und eine Zeitlang in dieser Kirche lebte. Ein solch heiliges Vorbild in der eigenen Gemeinschaft, im eigenen Tal zu haben, hat natürlich seine Folgen, und so wurde das fassanische Volk so fromm, dass nach dem Tod niemand mehr in die Hölle kam. Dies bereitete dem Teufel große Sorgen, und so beschloss er, der Sache auf den Grund zu gehen, er begab sich selbst ins Fassatal.

Die Fassaner befanden sich gerade in der Kirche, und so musste sich der Teufel vor der Kirchentür gedulden, um die Ursache dieses so fleißigen Messebesuchs zu verstehen. Als die Hl. Juliana dann selbst aus der Kirche trat, war ihm alles klar: Er wusste, würde es ihm gelingen, die Heilige von Gott abspenstig zu machen, hätte dies mit Sicherheit auch entsprechende Auswirkungen auf das Volk. So fing er an, sie zu umschmeicheln, er machte ihr allerlei Versprechen, versuchte mit allen Mitteln, sie von ihrem Wege abzubringen, jedoch vergeblich. Sie befahl ihm, im Namen Gottes und auf der Stelle von ihr zu weichen. Unverrichteter Dinge musste er wieder abziehen, doch sein Zorn darüber, man kann es sich vorstellen, war groß. Er war so groß, dass er buchstäblich in die Luft fuhr, hinauf zur Roda di Vael (Rotwand) im Rosengarten-

massiv, hinein in den Felsen und auf der anderen Seite wieder hinaus. Ein großes Loch entstand im Felsen, man kann es heute noch sehen. Die Fassaner nennen es „l Busc de Sent'Ujana", „das Loch der Hl. Juliana"; die Felsspitze heißt „Croz de Sent'Ujana (2670 m hoch).

›› Wissenswertes ‹‹

Die in der Legenda Aurea beschriebene Vita der angeblich tatsächlich gelebt habenden und um 305 n. Chr. hingerichteten Märtyrerin liest sich spannend und kurzweilig. Juliana übersteht mit himmlischer Hilfe die grausamsten Folterqualen heil und unversehrt, dann gelingt es ihr, den ihr im Kerker in Engelsgestalt erschienenen Teufel zu überwältigen, in Ketten zu legen und ihn schlussendlich in eine Latrine am Marktplatz zu werfen. Daher wird sie zumeist mit dem Teufel an einer Kette hinter sich herziehend dargestellt.

Im Fassatal wurde diese mächtige Frauenheilige vom Volk laut Überlieferung bei allen drohenden Kriegsgefahren und -nöten angerufen; so war sie laut Sage nicht nur imstande, ähnlich der Legende, den Teufel zu verjagen; es gelang ihr auch, die einstürmenden Hunnen aufzuhalten; bei einem Überfall durch die Trevisaner schlug sie einen Verräter aus dem fassanischen Volk eigenhändig mit dem Schwerte zu Boden; und noch 1797 und 1809 jagte sie auch die Franzosen mit kluger List davon.

Die Kirche von Sent'Ujana war viele Jahrhunderte lang ein bekanntes Pilgerziel. Bereits in der Langobardenzeit wurde die Hl. Juliana hier verehrt. Der Sentujànahügel, auch Ciaslir genannt, war in heidnischer Zeit der Mittelpunkt von Fassa. Hier soll sich damals eine von mehreren Ringwällen umgebene Burg befunden haben, in der Hofmitte der Burg soll ein ewiges Feuer gebrannt und ringsherum Abbildungen heidnischer Gottheiten gestanden haben. In unmittelbarer Nähe des Ciaslirs, auf dem Col de Mé (Maihügel), soll ein steinerner, mit Blumen geschmückter Altar gestanden sein, um den herumgetanzt, vor dem gefeiert und Kampfspiele abgehalten worden sein sollen. Im Mai fand alljährlich ein großes Fest statt. Auf dem nahen Col de sas dla Vea sang ein Priester ein Lied, das über viele Generationen hinweg überlebt hat, auch wenn dessen Worte heute nicht mehr verständlich sind:

„Nos do vin bibe vu
A inom de Numa l sas
A nos ton e pabol asá
Pos mort Elis a du.
Ant tina Rez abu
Pepe tor pikol koa
N barat les bot (bez)
Taf kon slap gara."

Ein Zusammenhang mit der räto-etruskischen Siedlungszeit schimmert aus dem Lied durch (Tina/Tinea = die größte etruskische Gottheit und Rezia/Reitia = die räto-venetische Göttin). Numa Pompilius (750-672 v. Chr.) war ein sagenhafter römischer König. Er genoss so hohe Anerkennung, dass er von vielen Nachbarvölkern und -reichen als Schiedsrichter bei Streitigkeiten gerufen wurde. Weitere Informationen im Buch „Märchen und Sagen aus dem Fassatale" von Hugo de Rossi/Ulrike Kindl und „Monographie der Dolomitenstraße" von Karl Felix Wolff. – Aufgrund eines gewaltigen Bergsturzes soll die früher um die Kirche gruppierte Ortschaft zerstört worden und daraufhin die tiefer gelegene Ortschaft Vigo di Fassa entstanden sein. Die heutige über zwei älteren Kirchen erbaute gotische Kirche von St. Ujana stammt aus dem 15. Jh.

Auf Unterschlicht in der Rotwand

Da lebte eine fromme Dirne. Die sagte vor dem Tode: „Liebe Leute, sobald ich gestorben bin, sollt ihr mich auf einen Wagen legen, daran zwei Ochsen spannen und sie frei gehen lassen; wo sie stehen bleiben, dort will ich begraben sein." Sie starb alsbald und man befolgte ihren Willen. Die Ochsen zogen die Leiche lange fort und machten dort Halt, wo jetzt die Kirche zu Lengstein steht; damals war dort nur eine kleine Kapelle. Es wurde nun am bezeichneten Platze ein viereckiges Loch ausgemauert und die Tote hineingelegt. Als vor einigen Jahren die Lengsteiner ihre Kirche restaurierten, fanden sie im seltsamen Grabe die Gebeine der frommen Magd.

➤➤ Wissenswertes ➤➤

Die weisenden Ochsen führen uns zur Lengsteiner Kirche mit der Hl. Ottilia als Kirchenpatronin. Hier wurde bereits im 19. Jh. ein Begräbnisplatz mit vorchristlichen Gräbern, Schmucksachen und einem großen Bronzeschwert gefunden. Wie frühzeitig diese Kirche bereits in hohem Ansehen stand, beweist die Tatsache, dass sie schon 1177 in einem Dokument von Kaiser Friedrich I. schriftlich angeführt wurde.

Diese Heilige (auch Odilie genannt) kam laut Legende blind zur Welt. Ihr Vater wollte sie deshalb töten lassen, doch die Mutter rettete sie, indem sie das Kind in ein Kloster gab. Durch die Taufe soll sie mit zwölf Jahren ihr Augenlicht erhalten haben. Sie wurde Äbtissin und Klostergründerin, unter anderem gründete sie jenes am Odilienberg, dem wichtigsten ellsässischen Wallfahrtsort, auf einem keltischen Kultplatz errichtet, wo sie 720 gestorben sein soll. Hier befindet sich auch eine Heilquelle, die bei Augenleiden aufgesucht wird. Es scheint das Werk der fränkischen Merowinger gewesen zu sein, der um vieles älteren „Lichtgöttin" Lucia die Hl. Ottilie zur Seite gestellt zu haben, so als wolle man sie verdrängen. Ihr Namenstag fällt auf den 13. Dezember, bis zur Einführung des Gregorianischen Kalenders der Tag der Wintersonnwende und der Wiedergeburt des Lichtes.

Auch der hier genannte heilige Bezirk am Ritten weist ähnliche Parallelen auf.

Zur Hl. Ottilia nach Lengstein, der zweitältesten Kirche am Ritten, pilgerten früher Menschen, um Hilfe bei Augenleiden zu erbitten; und es wird wohl kein Zufall sein, dass nicht weit von Lengstein entfernt, nämlich in Unterinn am Ritten, die Hl. Lucia als Kirchenpatronin zu finden ist, die ebenfalls bei Augenkrankheiten angerufen wird. Auf einem nahen Hügel steht das auf einem keltischen Kultplatz gelegene Verena-Kirchlein, in dessen Nähe ein ca. 4000 Jahre alter Figurenmenhir gefunden wurde, genannt „der Menhir von St.Verena". Auch Verena war eine „Heilerin", sie wurde u.a. für männliche Nachkommen und ebenfalls bei Augenleiden angerufen. Eine weitere vorchristliche Kultstätte unweit von Lengstein ist das ebenso in herrlicher Aussichtslage gelegene St.-Andreas-Kirchlein zu Antlass. In ca. 15 Gehminuten gelangt man von Lengstein zum sagenumwobenen Pirchboden, der Geheimnisvolles aus heidnischer Zeit erzählt: Hier hat laut Überlieferung eine weitum bekannte Seherin (im Gegensatz zur blinden! Ottilie) gelebt, hier trafen sich auch die Hexen zu kultischem Tanz und Mahl.

Der Wanderweg führt weiter zum kleinen, in eine Felsnische hineingebauten Kobenkirchlein, das früher von Frauen zwecks Orakelfragen aufgesucht wurde. Der Überlieferung nach stand dieses Kirchlein im Volk einst hoch in Ehren, da man aus einer steinernen Altarplatte die Zukunft in Bezug auf „Ehestandsfreuden" herauslesen konnte. Der Stein hatte farbige Adern, welche je nach der Einbildung der Schauenden verschiedene Figuren bildeten. Er wurde um die Mitte des 19. Jh. entfernt oder übertüncht.

Laut Forschung haben sich auf dem Ritten neben den rätischen Ureinwohnern (Isarken) sowie den Etruskern (der Name „Ritten" leitet sich laut einigen Forschern aus dem Etruskischen ab) auch ligurisch-illyrische Volksstämme angesiedelt (der Menhir von St.Verena untermauert diese Vermutung); und auch die aus dem Osten kommenden Veneter und Kelten haben auf der Rittner Hochfläche ihre Spuren hinterlassen.

Wenn man weiß, dass die Kelten mit dem „Sehen" etwas anderes verbanden – so suchten sie z.B. heilige Quellen auf, um aus ihnen seherische Inspirationskraft zu erlangen, während mit dem Christentum viele Heilquellen zu „Augenwasserlen" für Augenbeschwerden reduziert wurden –, rückt auch dieser heilige Rittner Bezirk mit seinen Augenheiligen und Seherinnen in ein völlig anderes Licht. Die Tatsache, dass der Menhir von St.Verena höchstwahrscheinlich der Mittelpunkt einer megalithischen Kultanlage gewesen ist, unterstreicht die einstige Wichtigkeit dieser Gegend.

Menhire werden als Erscheinungsform der Göttin bezeichnet. Auf bronzezeitlichen Steinstelen in verschiedenen Ländern Europas wird die Leben und Tod bringende Göttin mit Waffen (Schwert oder Dolch – letzterer auch auf dem Menhir von St. Verena abgebildet) dargestellt. Auch Artemis wurde „die Steinerne" genannt.

Zum Schluss sei noch eine Wassersage aus Lengstein angeführt: „Als der selige Hartmann, Bischof von Brixen, der im 12. Jh. lebte, über Lengstein, welches schon damals ein Dorf mit einer Kirche war, nach Eppan und Tirol reiste, da wurde in Lengstein ein Weib, welches ein geschwollenes, blau angelaufenes Gesicht hatte, durch das Wasser, womit sich der Bischof die Hände gewaschen, augenblicklich gesund, wie sie dem frommen Bischof bei seiner Rückreise selbst erzählte."

142

Von der Heiligen Kümmernis

Es war einmal eine Jungfrau, welche die Tochter eines Heidenkönigs gewesen war, der in sündiger Liebe zu ihr entbrannt war. Da flehte sie zu Gott, er möge sie ihrer körperlichen Reize berauben. Darauf wuchs ihr ein Mannsbart, und deshalb, aber auch weil sie Christin geworden war, ließ der Vater ihr den Kreuzestod bereiten, nur dass sie bekleidet starb.

Ein armes, sehr armes Geigerlein spielte ihr ein Trostlied in ihrem seligen Absterben; da warf sie ihm ihren goldenen Schuh als Belohnung hin. Als das Geigerlein den Schuh verkaufen wollte, wurde es für einen Dieb angesehen und zur Richtstätte geführt, hart am Kreuze vorbei, an dem die schuldlos gestorbene Kümmernis hing. Da warf diese dem armen Mann auch ihren zweiten, goldenen Schuh zu, und daran erkannten nun Richter und Volk des Geigerleins Unschuld.

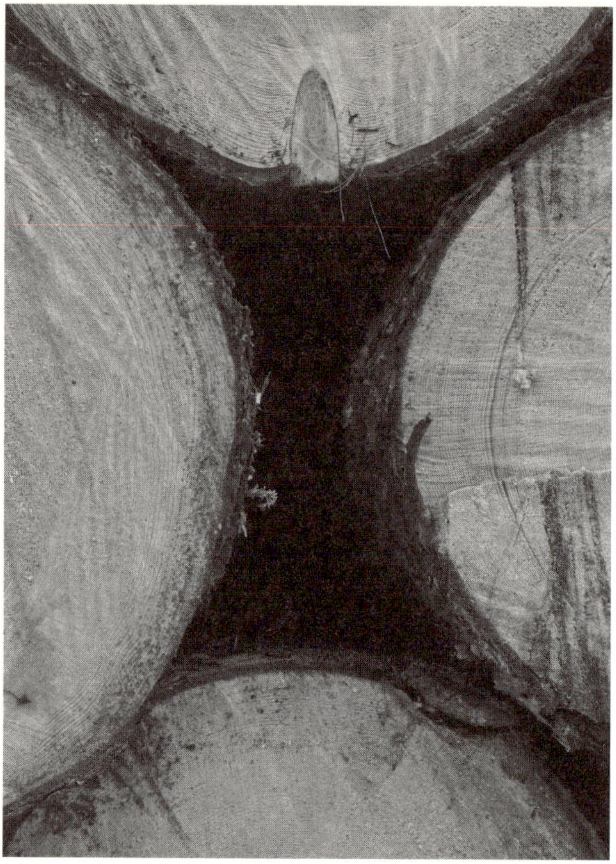

Wissenswertes

Die Hl. Kummernus ist eine umstrittene Volksheilige. Sie wurde in vielen Ländern und unter verschiedenen Namen – z.B. Kümmernis, Ohnkummernus, Commeria, Ontcommer (flämisch), Wilgefortis (iberische Halbinsel), Liberata (Italien) – früher hochverehrt, obwohl sie von der Kirche nie förmlich anerkannt, sondern nur geduldet wurde. Erst ab dem 18. Jh. ist diese Heilige zusehends in Vergessenheit geraten, wurde wohl auch absichtlich von der Amtskirche beiseitegeschoben. Zu ihrer Herkunft und ihrem Hintergrund gibt es unterschiedliche Versionen bzw. Hypothesen. Die gängigste und vor allem in Kirchenkreisen vertretene Interpretation ist jene, wonach die Heilige auf den „Volto Santo" in Lucca, ein seit dem 12. Jh. verehrtes Kruzifix zurückgehe, das den Gekreuzigten beschuht und im langen Gewand (typisch für die romanische Kunstepoche), mit Bart und langem Haar darstellt. Auch das Motiv der Schuhbeschenkung an den Geiger ist beim „Volto Santo" bekannt. Diese Kruzifixverehrung war damals sehr verbreitet. Für Andere handelt es sich um die christliche Umformung antiker hermaphroditischer Gottheiten, die in vielen alten Schöpfungsgeschichten und Mythen überliefert sind, beispielsweise des

Apollon in Frauenkleidern, der Venus Barbata oder der bärtigen Aphrodite. Laut Mythos litten die Römerinnen einmal an einer Krankheit, welche starken Haarausfall zur Folge hatte; als „Gegenmittel" wurde der göttlichen Venus eine Säule errichtet, welche sie halb als Frau und halb als Mann darstellte. Auch auf Zypern, Sizilien und in anderen Ländern wurde eine bärtige Aphrodite (Aphroditos) verehrt. Ein ähnliches Bild wurde ebenso in Pompei gefunden.

Die Hl. Kummernus wird zumeist als gekrönte Jungfrau, oft in einem blauen Kleid mit einem goldenen Gürtel und in goldenen Schuhen dargestellt. Angerufen wurde sie früher vor allem in weiblichen „Angelegenheiten": bei Kinderlosigkeit, bei unglücklichen Ehen, zur Abwehr männlicher Begierde, bei Frauenleiden und auch bei Haarausfall. Ihr nackter Fuß wird als Symbol der Erdverbundenheit und der Fruchtbarkeit gedeutet. Auch in Tirol war ihr Kult einst weit verbreitet. Man opferte ihr früher Wachskröten und Stachelkugeln, Symbole für die Gebärmutter und Gebärmuttererkrankungen. Früher hing ihr Bild häufig über den Betten der bäuerlichen Eheleute, da sie laut Volksglauben Kindersegen und häusliches Glück verlieh.

Mädchen opferten früher ihre Zöpfe der Hl. Kummernus; Ähnliches ist bereits Jahrtausende früher aus Byblos überliefert, wo Frauen ihre langen Haare der Aphrodite/Astarte als Opfer dargebracht haben sollen, bevor sie sich mit dem (fremden) Manne im Tempel liebend vereinten.

Einige Züge dieser Heiligen vermischen sich mit jenen der Hl. Margareta, deren Namenstag sie auch teilt (20. Juli). Jacob de Voragine beschreibt in seiner Legenda Aurea vom 13. Jh., wie während der Folter die wunderschöne Margareta fast unbekleidet aufgehängt wurde. Im Unterschied zur Hl. Kummernus im langen Gewande findet man die Hl. Margareta in manchen alten Darstellungen fast nackt mit ausgebreiteten Armen an einen Baum oder an ein Kreuz gebunden.

Die Hl. Kummernus ist in zahlreichen Orten bzw. Kirchen Tirols zu finden, z.B. in Ridnaun, Schenna, Altenburg bei Kaltern, Schluderns, in der Kapelle beim Gescheibten Turm in Bozen, in Vigo di Fassa u.a. Ein wichtiges Zentrum der Kummernusverehrung war in Südtirol die Lamprechtsburg bei Bruneck; hier wurde ein romanischer Christus zu einem späteren Zeitpunkt zur Kummernus „umgeformt" und bekleidet. Laut dem Volkskundler Hans Fink beteten die Frauen hier zuerst um Fruchtbarkeit, bevor sie sich ins nahe Frauenbad Salomonsbrunn am Eingang zum Antholzer Tal zur Kur begaben. Fink hat einen weiteren interessanten noch zu vertiefenden Forschungsaspekt aufgeworfen; demzufolge findet sich diese „Heilige" häufig in der Nähe von Todesstätten. Beispiele hierfür sind die Gruftkapelle von Axams und die Wiltener Friedhofskapelle in Innsbruck, aber auch bei der Kirche von Lamprechtsburg ist von abgekommenen Friedhöfen die Rede; das Tonignstöckl (Antoniusstöcklein) bei Rasen/Antholz, an dem die Mädchen um einen guten Mann beteten, war früher der Hl. Kummernus geweiht; und in unmittelbarer Nähe wurde ein großes, frühzeitliches Gräberfeld entdeckt. Auch in der Totengruft von Niederolang und in St.Cyrill bei Brixen ist die Kummernus abgebildet; eine Sagenvariante zur Kummernus rankt sich um diesen Ort; und auch hier soll sich laut Überlieferung eine alte Beerdigungsstätte befinden. So scheint die Kummernus früher eine dreifache Fürsprecherin gewesen zu sein: für Mädchen/Jungfrauen, für Frauen/Mütter und für Sterbende/Verstorbene.

143

St. Katharina in der Schart

So heißt eine uralte Kirche, die in der Bucht des Freiberges steht und die ganze Meraner Gegend beherrscht. In den heidnischen Zeiten stand an der Stelle der Kirche ein Tempel, der dem Sonnengotte geweiht war. Die Heiden hatten ihn deshalb dorthin gebaut, weil gerade dort oben die Sonne aufgeht.

›› Wissenswertes ‹‹

Zwar handelt es sich hier um keine Sage, aber da Katharina eine wichtige Tiroler Heilige ist, haben wir diesen Text in das Kapitel der Heiligen mitaufgenommen.

Diese mindestens aus dem 13. Jh. stammende Katharina-Kirche erhebt sich in der Tat auf einem geografisch „heiligen“ Platz, und nicht weit von ihr entfernt, im Dorf von Hafling, steht eine weitere bemerkenswerte Kirche, ebenfalls aus dem 13. Jh., dem Hl. Johannes d. T. geweiht. Es ist kein Zufall, diese beiden Heiligen so nahe beieinander anzutreffen, so wie wir sie auch gemeinsam in Völser Aicha finden. Beide Heiligen werden mit Licht, Sonne und Feuer in Verbindung gebracht. Ihnen geweihte Kirchen befinden sich oft auf aussichtsreichen, sonnenexponierten Höhen. Diese Katharina-Kirche steht vermutlich auch mit anderen uralten Kultplätzen in der Umgebung in einem heiligen Bezug. Nicht umsonst lautet der Volksreim: „St. Ursula auf der Platt (auf dem heiligen Bühel in Pfelders), St. Kathrin in der Schart und St. Vigil aufm Joch (Vigiljoch oberhalb Marling), halten alle Wetter auf und treiben die Hexen ins Loch.“

Heidnische Kultgebiete und Opferstätten waren den christlichen Glaubensboten in den ersten Jahrhunderten der Christianisierung ein Dorn im Auge, doch waren altüberlieferte Bräuche nicht so leicht aus den religiösen Überzeugungen der Menschen zu verdrängen und zu löschen. Viele heidnische Kultplätze wurden mutwillig zerstört; an die Stelle, wo zuvor den örtlichen Gottheiten (Reitia, Diana, Wotan, Saturn u.a.m.) Opfer und göttliche Verehrung dargebracht wurden, errichtete man nun vielerorts christliche Bauten zu Ehren christlicher Heiliger. Aus den Legenden um diese Heiligen lässt sich oft ein deutlicher Bezug zu vorchristlichen Gottheiten herstellen, so wie es auch bei der Hl. Katharina mit dem Rade der Fall ist.

Diese Heilige war laut Legenda Aurea nicht nur ausnehmend schön, sondern außerordentlich klug und gebildet. Weder der römische Kaiser Maxentius noch die 50 besten Philosophen des Landes konnten es mit ihrer Redegewandtheit und Argumentation aufnehmen. Selbst als der Kaiser um ihre Hand anhielt, blieb sie standhaft und überzeugte die Kaiserin, die 50 Philosophen und 200 römische Soldaten von der christlichen Lehre, die allesamt den christlichen Märtyrertod starben. Auch sie selbst wurde qualvollen Martern unterzogen, auf mit spitzen Nägeln versehene Räder gespannt und schlussendlich enthauptet (310 n.Chr.). Laut Legende trugen Engel ihren Leichnam zur Bestattung auf den Berg Sinai. Aus ihren Gebeinen soll Öl ohne Unterlass geflossen sein, „das heilt die Glieder aller, die krank und schwach sind.“ Das Katharinaöl galt in Tirol früher als Allheilmittel (gegen Pest, bei Unterleibs- und Atembeschwerden, Bettnässen, Würmern usw.).

Die Hl. Katharina ist u.a. Schutzpatronin der Gelehrten und Philosophen, der Anwälte und Notare, sie wird in vielen Anliegen, z.B. vor Prüfungen und schweren Entscheidungen, angerufen, auch bei Migräne (da sie enthauptet wurde) und bei Zungenleiden. Ab dem 13. Jh. war sie nach Maria die meistverehrte Heilige.

Der Kathreintag (25. November) war in Tirol lange Zeit ein großer Bauernfeiertag, an dem es hieß: „Alle Räder stehen still!". Alle Arbeiten, besonders jene, die mit Rädern zu tun hatten, durften an diesem Tag im Gedenken an das Martyrium der Hl. Katharina nicht verrichtet werden. An diesem Tag im Jahr wurde das letzte Mal getanzt („St.Kathrein stellt das Tanzen ein"). Von da an wird das Vieh nicht mehr auf die Weide getrieben, die Schafe werden geschoren. Mancherorts wurde den Dienstboten an diesem Tag der Lohn ausbezahlt. In der Steiermark entzündete man dieser Heiligen Feuer und ließ brennende Räder den Berg hinabrollen.

Katharina ist eine der „Drei Heiligen Madln", und damit rückt ihr Kult in die Nähe der Verehrung der vorchristlichen Frauendreiheit, wird von manchen ForscherInnen im gleichen Atemzug wie Einbet, Werbet und Wilbet genannt, da der Name der Letzteren mit „wheel", Rad, zusammenhängen soll.

Das Rad, ein uraltes Symbol der Sonne, ist das Bindeglied zwischen der Hl. Katharina und ihrer vorchristlichen Vorfahrin. Die aus Asien stammende Große Göttin Kali, Göttin des Schicksals und des karmischen Rades, ist auch aus der Gegend des Bergs Sinai (!) als Tänzerin auf dem Feuerrad im Zentrum des Universums überliefert. Auch Fortuna, die römische Glücksgöttin, wird mit einem Rad assoziiert, ihre mythische Vorfahrin hieß Vortumna, „Die, die das Jahr umdreht". Die Kreisbewegung des Rades hatte auch bei den nordischen Völkern eine mystische Bedeutung: Zur Zeit der Wintersonnenwende durften keine Wagenräder rollen, kein Butterfass gedreht werden. Auch bei den Kelten hatte das Rad mit vier Speichen zentrale kultische Bedeutung; dasselbe Symbol wurde bereits in der Bronzezeit in Felsen geritzt und hängt laut Forschern mit dem Sonnenkult zusammen.

Somit ist Katharina Überlieferungsträgerin einer uralten Glaubenswelt und „Erbin" der Rad-Göttin.

144

Das Gewand der Schmerzhaften Muttergottes

In der Kirche in Piano befindet sich eine Statue der Schmerzhaften Muttergottes, welche noch heute von den Gläubigen hochverehrt wird.

Vor langer Zeit erkrankte in Piano eine Fremde schwer. Schwach und blass lag sie in ihrem Bett und fühlte sich dem Sterben nahe. Während ihre kraftlosen Hände den Rosenkranz umklammert hielten, fiel ihr Blick auf das an der Wand hängende Marienbild. Da spürte sie plötzlich, könnte sie das Gewand der Schmerzhaften Muttergottes vom Altar in Piano anziehen, so würde sie wieder gesund werden.

Die Leute vom Dorf brachten es nicht fertig, der Todkranken diesen letzten Wunsch abzuschlagen. So holten sie das Kleid der Muttergottes und brachten es ihr. Und, welch Wunder! Sie hatte das Kleid noch nicht einmal vollends übergezogen, schon spürte sie, wie neue Lebenskraft in ihren Körper zurückkehrte. Das fiebrige Zittern in ihren Armen und Beinen legte sich und ihre blassen Wangen begannen sich wieder zu röten.

Wie im Lauffeuer verbreitete sich dieses Wunder im Dorf. Von überall her eilten die Leute, fanden die dem Tode für nah erklärte Frau in ihrem Bett sitzend vor, wieder aufgeblüht, voller Kraft und Lebensfreude. →

Als sie das Krankenbett ganz verlassen konnte, fertigte sie der Muttergottes zum Dank ein neues Kleid an, ganz aus Seide, sie verzierte es über und über mit den schönsten Stickereien, und jeder ihrer Nadelstiche war ein Gesang der Freude und der Dankbarkeit.

›› Wissenswertes ‹‹

Piano zählt zur Gemeinde Commezzadura im Val di Sole im Trentino. Der Name Val di Sole, auf deutsch „Sulzberg", wird von einigen Forschern mit „sulis", der keltischen Heil- und Wassergöttin, in Verbindung gebracht, von den Römern Minerva genannt. Die berühmten Heil- und Thermalwasserquellen in Pejo und Rabbi im Val di Sole würden diese Hypothese zusätzlich untermauern.

Erzählungen von Wunderheilungen, d.h. Heilungen, die nicht mit den uns verständlichen Naturgesetzen erklärt werden können, sind häufig zu finden. Besonders Maria wird eine große Vielzahl an Wunderheilungen zugeschrieben. So sind im Laufe der Jahrhunderte zahlreiche Marien-Wallfahrtsorte entstanden, an denen Gläubige Trost und Heilung suchten und fanden. Der Glaube an Marias Hilfsbereitschaft ist stark in den Menschen verwurzelt; er wurde v.a. durch den frühmittelalterlichen Marienkult immer stärker. Maria gilt als die Helferin in aller Not, sie wird besonders bei Krankheiten angerufen. Lange Zeit waren auch Marien-Gebetszettel verbreitet, die man bei sich trug, um sich vor allem Bösen zu bewahren, so z.B. das Gebetslied „Unserer Lieben Frauen Traum". Zahlreiche Kirchen und Kapellen sind ihr geweiht, auf Bildstöcklein und Bildnissen finden wir ihr Abbild, und an vielen Orten erzählen Legenden von ihr.

Zahlreiche Wunderheilungen, in erster Linie Krankenheilungen, wurden in Mirakelbriefen festgehalten, oft natürlich auch mit dem Hintergedanken, Pilgerzuspruch zu gewinnen. In der heutigen Zeit werden die sogenannten Wunderheilungen an Wallfahrtsorten (z.B. Lourdes) vonseiten der Kirche genauestens überprüft, bevor sie als solche anerkannt werden. Von religions- und kirchenkritischen Menschen werden Wunderheilungen als unwissenschaftlicher Aberglaube oder als Autosuggestion abgetan.

Das Kleid spielt in den verschiedensten Kulturen und in vielen Bräuchen eine große Rolle. Die Kleider von Göttern und Heiligen wurden seit jeher verehrt; sie wurden als Reliquie aufbewahrt oder man trug kleine Teile bei sich, um seiner großen Heilkraft teilhaftig zu werden. Die Zauberkraft des Kleides hat mit der/dem das Kleid tragenden Heiligen zu tun, in dieser Legende mit Maria. Auch in Maria Einsiedeln versuchte man sich ein Stückchen vom leinenen Unterkleid des Muttergottesbildes abzuschneiden, um dieses bei sich zu tragen und dadurch des Segens Marias sicher zu sein. Bereits bei den Griechen wurden Kleidungsstücke von Heldinnen/Helden und berühmten Personen in den Tempeln verehrt, z.B. in Delphi die Gewänder der Amazonen, der Halsschmuck der Helena usw. Kleider werden auch bei Krankheiten oder zum Dank für das Gesunden geopfert, in der katholischen Tradition dies v.a. der Maria und dem Gottessohn, besonders an Wallfahrtsorten (z.B. Maria Waldrast). Kleideropfer für Götter und Götterbilder sind auch aus vorchristlicher Zeit bekannt.

145

Die Enzian-Madonna

Ein langer Winter war zu Ende gegangen und auf den Almwiesen und Hochweiden des Val di Sole brachte die wieder kräftiger werdende Frühlingssonne den Schnee zum Schmelzen.

Die Leute waren alle noch drunten im Tal in ihren Dörfern. Doch da kam, ganz allein, auf einem schmalen Weg eine Frau daher, gekleidet in einem leuchtend blauen Gewand. Sie war schöner als ein Engel! Sie schritt jedoch mühsam dahin und musste sich zwischendurch immer wieder an einen am Wegrand stehenden Baum anlehnen. Schließlich setzte sie sich an einen Wiesenrand, wo bereits erste Blätter und Kräuter aus dem Boden hervorlugten, um sich auszuruhen. „Ich habe solchen Durst", murmelte sie und blickte sich dabei suchend nach einer Quelle oder einem Wasserrinnsal um. Aber der Almboden war durch die monatelange Schneebedeckung hart und krustig und sog selbst das Schmelzwasser des Schnees gierig in sich auf.

Da verspürte eine kleine zarte Pflanze Mitleid mit der Frau: Mit großer Mühe formte sie aus Stängeln und Blättern einen kleinen Becher und sammelte die von einem Baum heruntertropfenden Wasserperlen darin auf. „Da, trink das Wasser", sagte sie, „es ist zwar wenig, aber mehr hab ich nicht."

Dankbar beugte sich die Frau zum Trinken hinunter, berührte dabei vorsichtig die Pflanze mit ihren Fingern und vereinigte die Blätter zu einer zarten Blüte. Dann berührte sie mit ihrem Kleid die Blumenkrone und ließ kurz ihr blondes Haar darübergleiten.

So ist der Enzian entstanden. Sein Blütenbecher hat die Farbe des leuchtend blauen Kleides der fremden Frau, durchzogen von feinen goldgelben Härchen. Die Frau, ihr ahnt es bereits, war die Muttergottes.

›› Wissenswertes ‹‹

Maria wird auf Abbildungen häufig in einem blauen Kleid oder mit einem blauen Schleier dargestellt; so wird ihr auch der Name „Blaue Frau" zuteil. Oft trägt sie unter einem blauen Mantel ein rotes Kleid, das symbolisch für das (mütterliche) Liebesrot sowie ihren irdischen Anteil steht.

Sehr oft werden Pflanzen nach Maria benannt, auch viele Pflanzensagen und -legenden ranken sich um ihr Leben.

Blau blühende Blumen gelten nicht erst seit der Romantik als besondere Blumen. Sie stehen für Sehnsucht, Liebe, das Streben nach der Einheit mit der Natur und der Unendlichkeit. Auch in der Volksmedizin gelten sie als Zauberkräuter, wie beispielsweise der seltene, blau blühende Kreuz-Enzian. Er wird bereits im 16. Jh. von Hieronymus Bock (1498-1554) beschrieben. Demnach ist die Wurzel dieser Enzianart zu allerlei seltsamen Künsten, besonders in Liebesangelegenheiten und bei Liebeszauber zu verwenden, zumal sie, wie Bock sagte, zerspalten ist „wie ein weiblich glid". Tatsächlich ist die Wurzel kreuzweise in der Mitte durchstochen, was Ursache weiterer Legenden wurde. Die Wurzel des Kreuz-Enzians, auch „Madelgeer" genannt, wurde u.a. gegen Gift, ansteckende Krankheiten und Bisse durch tollwütige Hunde angewandt; man sagte von ihr auch, dass sie den, der sie bei sich trage, bei jedermann beliebt mache. Wie angesehen diese Pflanze einst war, bezeugt der alte Wurzelgräberspruch: „Madelgeer ist aller Wurzel ein Ehr."

Um den Kreuz-Enzian ranken sich verschiedene Sagen. Einer ungarischen Überlieferung zufolge erschien dem Heiligen König Ladislaus zur Pestzeit im Traum ein Engel. Er befahl ihm, einen Pfeil in die Luft zu schießen. Die Pflanze, auf welche der Pfeil fallen würde, könne die kranken Soldaten heilen. Ladislaus befolgte den Rat des Engels; und der Pfeil fiel auf den Kreuz-Enzian, der seither in Ungarn „Kraut des Heiligen Ladislaus, des Königs" genannt wird.

Besonders begehrt war der Kreuz-Enzian im Mittelalter. Durch die kreuzförmige Anordnung der Blattpaare, des Stängel- und Wurzelmarks wurde er zum Symbol für den Kreuzestod von Jesus Christus.

Auch dem gelben und dem punktierten Enzian wird seit jeher eine große Heilwirkung zugesprochen; in Pestzeiten hieß es von ihm: „Esst Enzian und Pimpinell, steht auf, sterbt nicht so schnell!" Der wissenschaftliche Namen „Gentiana" soll vom illyrischen König Gentius (gestorben 168 v. Chr.) herrühren. Laut einer Sage soll der griechische Götterbote Hermes ihn auf diese Pflanze aufmerksam gemacht haben, worauf seine Ärzte aus ihr ein Mittel gegen die Pest herstellten.

146

Das Gnadenbild aus dem Lärchenstock zu Waldrast

Im Jahre 1392 sandte die Große Frau im Himmel einen Engel aus nach Tirol in die Waldrast auf dem Serlesberg. Der trat vor einen hohlen Lärchenstock und sprach zu diesem im Namen der Gottesmutter: „Du Stock sollst der Frauen im Himmel Bild fruchten!" Das Bild wuchs nun im Stock, und ward zuerst am Ostersonnabend von zwei frommen Hirtenknaben, Hänsele und Peterle, aus dem Dorf Mizens erblickt. Verwundert liefen sie hinab zu den Bauern und erzählten: „Gehet auf das Gebirg, da stehet etwas Wunderbarliches im hohlen Stock, wir trauten uns nicht, es anzurühren."

Das heilige Bild wurde nun mit einer Säge aus dem Stock geschnitten und einstweilen nach Matrei gebracht. Da stand es, bis dass ihm eine eigene Kirche zur Waldrast selbst gebaut wurde, dazu bediente sich Unsere Liebe Frau eines armen Holzhackers namens Jakob Lusch aus Matrei. Als der eines Pfinsttags Nacht in seinem Bett lag und schlief, kam eine Stimme, redete zu dreien Malen und sprach: „Schläfst du oder wachst du?" Beim dritten Male erwachte er und fragte; „Wer bist du und was willst du?" Die Stimme sprach: „Du sollst aufbringen eine Kapelle in der Ehre Unserer Lieben Frauen auf der Waldrast." Da sprach der Holzhauer: „Das will ich nit tun." Aber die Stimme kehrte wieder zu der andern Pfinsttagnacht und redete mit ihm in dem Maß als zuvor. Da sprach er: „Ich bin zu arm dazu." Da kam die Stimme zu der dritten Pfinsttagnacht abermals an sein Bett und redete als vor. Also hatte er dreier Nacht keine vor Sorgen geschlafen und antwortete der Stimme: „Wie meinest du's, dass du nicht von mir willt lassen?" Da sprach die Stimme: „Du sollst es tun!“ Da sprach er: „Ich will sel nit tun!“ Da nahm es ihn und hob ihn gerad auf in die Höhe und sagte: „Du sollst es tun, berate dich drum!“ Da gedachte er: „O ich armer Mann, was rat ich, dass ich's recht tue?“ Und sprach, er wollt' es tun, wo er nur die rechte Stätte wüsste. Die Stimme sprach: „Im Wald ist ein grüner Fleck im Moose, da leg dich nieder und raste, so wird dir wohl kundgetan die rechte Stätte.“

Der Holzhauer machte sich auf, legte sich hin auf das Moos und rastete. Wie er entschlafen war, hörte er im Schlafe zwei Glöckel. Da erwachte er und sah vor sich auf dem Flecken, da jetzund die Kirche stehet, eine Frau in weißen Kleidern und hätte ein Kind am Arm, des ward ihm nur ein Blick. Da gedachte er: Allmächtiger Gott, da ist freilich die rechte Statt! Und ging auf die Statt, da er das Bild gesehen hatte, und merkt's aus nach dem, als er vermeinte eine Kirche zu machen, und die Glöckel klungen, bis er ausgemerkt hatte, hernach hörte er sie nicht mehr. Da sprach er: „Lieber Gott, wie soll ich's verbringen? Ich bin arm und habe kein Gut, da ich solchen Bau mit verbringen möge.“ Da sprach wiederum die Stimme: „So geh zu frommen Leuten, die geben dir wohl alsoviel, dass du es verbringst. Und wann es geschiehet, dass man es weihen soll, da wird es stillstehen sechsunddreißig Jahr, darnach wird es fürgäng und werden große Zeichen da geschehen zu ewigen Zeiten.“ Und da er die Kapelle anfangen wollte zu machen, ging er zu seinem Beichtvater und tät ihm das kund. Da schuf er ihn vor den Bischof gen Brixen, da ging er zu fünf Malen gen Brixen, dass ihm der Bischof den Bau und die Kapelle zu machen erlaubte. Das tat der Bischof und ist geschehen am Erchtag (Dienstag) vor St. Pankratius im Jahre 1409. Jakob Lusch erhielt im Jahre 1411 vom Generalvicar zu Brixen einen Sammelbrief, und die anbefohlene Kapelle ward im Jahre 1429 vollendet; nun trat der von der Stimme vorhergesagte Stillstand von 36 Jahren ein, und sie ward erst im Jahre 1465 vom Weihbischof Kaspar von Brixen geweiht.

›› Wissenswertes ‹‹

Glöckel = Glöckchen; „des ward ihm nur ein Blick“ = er sah die Erscheinung nur einen Augenblick.

Maria Waldrast bei Matrei am Brenner, ein Wallfahrtskloster der Serviten, zählt zu den höchstgelegenen Klöstern Europas (1600 m). Es ist ein wahrhaftiger „Ort der Kraft“: eine Stätte, deren besondere positive und heilsame Ausstrahlung nicht nur von den zahlreichen hierher kommenden Pilgern wahrgenommen wird, sondern auch mittels einer fundierten radiästhetischen Untersuchung des Diplomingenieurs und Doktors der technischen Wissenschaften Jörg Purner aus Innsbruck belegt wurde. Die „Waldrast“ liegt am Fuße der „heiligen“ Serles, eines sagenumwobenen weiblichen Bergs, mit dem die Ausstrahlung des Wallfahrtsortes zweifellos in Verbindung gebracht werden kann.

Wie in anderen legendenbehafteten Wallfahrtsorten steht die Marienerscheinung auch hier mit einem Baum in Zusammenhang.

Maria Waldrast wurde früher neben zahlreichen anderen Problemen auch bei Verzauberungen und Teufelsbesessenheit und bei totgeborenen Kindern aufgesucht, die hier durch die Hilfe der Muttergottes noch einmal ein Lebenszeichen gaben und damit getauft werden konnten, um doch noch in den Himmel zu kommen. Im Mirakelbuch von 1759 ist angeführt, dass man Partikel des alten Lärchenbaums in ein Glas Wasser gab und dann trank. Ebenso ist das Darbringen von Kleider- und Wachsopfern, u.a. Wachskröten, schriftlich belegt.

Weitere Besonderheiten dieses Ortes sind die weitum bekannte Heilquelle und ein Schalenstein unterhalb der Kirche. Laut Legende soll Maria auf der Flucht nach Ägypten hier vorbeikommen sein, auf dem Stein gerastet und vom köstlichen Wasser, auch Muetterwasserl genannt, getrunken haben. Der Esel, der sie getragen hat, soll die seltsamen Abdrücke auf dem Stein hinterlassen haben.

Viele Tiroler kommen heute noch regelmäßig hierher, um dieses Quellwasser mit vorzüglicher Qualität in Flaschen abzufüllen. Aber auch die auf dem Weg nach Maria Waldrast gelegenen „Sieben Prünnen“, in deren Nähe der sagenumwobene „Teufelsstein“ steht, ist ein außergewöhnlicher Ort. Diesem aus sieben (!) Quellen geradezu aus der Erde springenden Wasser verdanken laut Legende die Matreier ihre Kinder.

Eine ähnliche Legende rankt sich um die Mariarastkapelle auf dem Heinzenberg bei Zell im Gerlostal. Auch hier wurden einst die neugeborenen Kinder geholt, oberhalb der heutigen Kapelle stand vorher ein uralter Baum. Als man ihn umhackte, hörte man die klagende Stimme der Muttergottes, die im Baum lebte. Hinter der Kapelle befand sich früher auch ein Brunnen.

147

Die Muttergottes von Saalen

Auf dem Rindlerbühel in Saalen im Pustertal erschien die Muttergottes öfters in blauem Gewande den Kindern; besonders gern verkehrte sie mit Hirtenkindern. Einmal pflügte der Tanglbauer, dem der Bühel gehörte, ein uraltes hölzernes Loretobild aus dem Boden und brachte dasselbe in seine Behausung. Aber am andern Tag war das Bild wieder auf dem Rindlerbühel. Als sich das wiederholte, erkannte man, dass die Muttergottes den Rindlerbühel zu ihrem Gnadensitz auserkoren hatte, und der Pfarrer Benedict Achmüller von St. Lorenzen baute 1652 an der Stelle, wo das Bild aus dem Boden gepflügt worden war, die gegenwärtige Wallfahrtskirche.

›› Wissenswertes ‹‹

Maria Saalen bei St.Lorenzen, 1300 erstmals als Weiler Sele genannt, ist einer der zahlreichen Verehrungsorte der Schwarzen Madonna von Loreto (Mittelitalien). Der Kult um die Schwarze Madonna ist seit vielen Jahrhunderten in und außerhalb von Europa weit verbreitet; eine besondere Faszination geht von ihr aus; und in den letzten Jahrzehnten ist sie zu einer Art spiritueller Neuentdeckung geworden. Neben mehreren Pilgerstätten in Frankreich sind vor allem Maria Einsiedeln in der Schweiz, Altötting in Bayern, Tschenstochau in Polen, Oropa in Italien u.a. das Ziel großer Pilgerströme. Bereits seit Jahren beschäftigt sich die Forschung mit der Klärung der Frage des „Warum“ ihrer Schwärze. In letzter Zeit ist man immer mehr davon überzeugt, dass Hintergrund und Ursprung in den antiken schwarzen Fruchtbarkeits- und Muttergöttinnen, die in vielen alten Kulturen verehrt wurden, zu suchen sind. Kybele, Isis und Artemis/Diana sind nur einige Beispiele schwarz dargestellter Gottheiten. Wie so oft, baut das Christentum auch hier auf viel ältere Glaubensvorstellungen auf; doch während die christliche Gottesmutter „nur menschlich“ ist, waren ihre „Vorfahrinnen“ göttlich. Der in der Legende von Saalen geschilderte Muttergottesfund aus der Erde durch den Pflug weist auf archetypische Parallelen mit dem Erd- und Fruchtbarkeitskult alter Göttinnen hin.

An der Außenmauer der Kirche von Maria Saalen ist die Lauretanische Marienlitanei aufgemalt. Diese enthält zahlreiche Titel, mit denen vorher Isis verehrt und besungen wurde. Sie wurde „Mutter Gottes“, „Himmelskönigin, „Unbefleckte“, „Thron der Weisheit“, „Gnadenspenderin“, „Morgenstern“ ... genannt; und, wie später dann Maria, mit Sternen um ihren Kopf und auf einem Halbmond stehend dargestellt. Noch in der Zeit des Urchristentums wurde sie in Rom hochverehrt.

Ephesus war die Heimat der schwarzen, vielbrüstigen Artemis/Diana. Ihr Heiligtum war der größte Tempelbau der Antike und wurde zu den sieben Weltwundern gezählt. In der Apostelgeschichte wird berichtet, wie durch die Verkündigung der neuen christlichen Heilslehre der Artemiskult in Ephesus gefährdet wurde und wie es deshalb aus wirtschaftlichen Interessen (Verkauf von Diana-Statuetten an die Tempelbesucher) zu einem Aufruhr kam. Es war wohl kein Zufall, dass ausgerechnet hier im Jahre 431 das kirchengeschichtlich sehr bedeutende Konzil stattfand, bei welchem entschieden wurde, dass alle bestehenden Kultstätten der Isis und der Kybele in Marienheiligtümer umgewandelt werden sollten. Nun nahm der Marienkult seinen Anfang; 48 Städte haben angeblich damals ihre Schutzgöttin, Jungfrau und Gottesmutter Kybele in die „neue“ Maria umgetauft, die laut Legende auch von Ephesus aus in den Himmel aufgefahren sein soll.

148

Die Heilige Jungfrau vom Farnkraut

Janesel, ein stummer Knabe von zwölf Jahren, hütete im Walde die Herde, als er plötzlich die seligste Jungfrau vor sich sah, die mit der Hand auf das unter einem Kastanienbaume gewachsene Farnkraut deutete, und ihm befahl, denen von Bosentino zu sagen, sie sollen da ein Kapellchen erbauen und ein Madonnenbild zur Verehrung hinsetzen. Maria spricht’s, drückt in einen großen Stein das Zeichen ihrer Hand, und verschwindet. Zugleich löst sich die Zunge des Stummen, das Volk glaubt dem wunderbaren Verkünder, und erfüllt unverweilt, was die Himmelskönigin verlangte. Das Gemälde, so man hierzu verfertigen ließ, stellte Unsere Liebe Frau so vor, wie sie dem Knaben erschienen war, und erhielt von ihrer Stätte den Namen: „Die Heilige Jungfrau vom Farnkraut“.

›› Wissenswertes ‹‹

Diese schöne Heilungsgeschichte rankt sich um den Marienwallfahrtsort „Madonna del Féles“, der von Bosentino aus, zwischen Trient und dem Caldonazzo-See gelegen, in 15 Gehminuten erreichbar ist. Bosentino war, wie die ganze Gegend, bereits in vorrömischer Zeit bewohnt. Etruskische, keltische und römische Siedlungsspuren lassen sich aus den Ortsnamen ableiten; auch eine römische Straße soll am Wallfahrtsort vorbeigeführt haben.

In Kirchennähe befindet sich eine Heilquelle. Laut Überlieferung zogen die Hirten mit ihren Tieren bereits in alter Zeit an diesen Ort, ließen die Schafe trinken, stillten wohl selbst ihren Durst, und so wird es auch der zwölfjährige taubstumme Hirtenknabe Janesel gemacht haben.

Ins Innere der heutigen, mehrmals überbauten kleinen Kirche wurde die Kapelle mit dem wundertätigen Marienfresko mit Jesuskind aus dem 15. Jh. integriert. In einer Nische hinter dem Altar wird heute noch ein Stein gezeigt, in welchem sich die Form einer Hand erkennen lässt, laut Legende jene der Madonna. So sind auch an diesem christlichen Wallfahrtsort ein heiliger Stein und heiliges Wasser vorhanden.

Als im 17. Jh. ringsum die Pest wütete, blieben laut Überlieferung alle Einwohner von Bosentino davon verschont, weil Maria ihre schützende Hand über sie gehalten hatte. Prozessionen und Wallfahrten der Menschen aus der Umgebung zur Madonna del Féles, vor allem bei lang andauernder Trockenheit und Dürre, sind von 1657 bis zu Beginn des 19. Jh. dokumentiert.

In neuester Zeit wurde neben der Kirche der sogenannte „Bezirk der Stille“ errichtet, der zu Meditation und Gebet einlädt.

149

Wallfahrt zur Heiligen Jungfrau Maria in Lavant

Eine Meile unter Lienz, und etwas weniger unter Tristach, am rechtsseitigen Drauufer, hat der kleine Pfarr-, aber große Betfahrtort Lavant sich festgesetzt.

Südwärts vom Dörfchen erhebt sich ein steiler, felsiger Hügel, der zwei Kirchen trägt. Die eine, die ältere, aber kleinere, den heiligen Apostelfürsten Petrus und Paulus geweiht, steht auf der Spitze des Hügels; sie soll aus den Trümmern eines altes Schlosses erbaut worden sein und ward ums Jahr 1485 geweiht. Sie bewahrte einst das Wallfahrtsbild mit anderen Altertümern.

Auf halber Höhe des nämlichen Hügels prangt die zweite oder St.-Ulrichs-Pfarrkirche, wo jetzt das Gnadenbild der Hl. Jungfrau verehrt wird. Dieses wurde nach einer lieblichen Volkssage in einem Gebüsche von Hirten entdeckt, welche Schafe weideten. Die Lämmer und Schafe, welche zuerst an das Mirakelbild kamen, ließen sich rings um das Gestäude auf ihre Vorderfüße nieder, um der Himmelsfrau ihre Huldigung zu bezeigen. Das machte die Hirten aufmerksam auf den verborgenen Schatz, und auch sie sanken voll Ehrfurcht nieder.

Die andächtigen Pilger, welche hier zusammenkommen, die Heilige Jungfrau zu verehren, beten rings umwandelnd an jeder Ecke der Kirche ein bestimmtes Standgebet, um unzählbare Fülle des Ablasses zu gewinnen. Man erzählt nämlich, der einweihende Bischof habe an jeder Ecke einen Hut voll Sand ausgeschüttet, mit der Erklärung, die Anzahl Sandkörner bestimmen die Anzahl der Jahre für die Dauer des Ablasses. Noch zeigt man in der Pfarrkirche ein Horn, womit man einst statt der Glocken das Volk zum Gottesdienst zusammengerufen haben soll.

›› Wissenswertes ‹‹

Die beiden in dieser Sage beschriebenen Kirchen stehen auf einem der markantesten Hügel über dem Lienzer Talboden, der zu den wichtigsten religiösen Kultplätzen Österreichs zählt, ca. zwei Kilometer vom alten Aguntum entfernt. Er ist im Osten und Westen durch einen Bach und im Süden durch eine tiefe Schlucht geschützt, war deshalb ein idealer Siedlungsort. Die Wallfahrtskirche Maria Lavant/St.Ulrich wurde laut archäologischer Forschung auf den Resten einer frühchristlichen Bischofskirche innerhalb einer spätantiken Fliehburg erbaut. Frühchristliche Kirchen, mit Säulen und Marmor prächtig ausgestattet, wurden ab dem 5. Jh. n. Chr. errichtet. Nach der Zerstörung Aguntums 406 n. Chr. musste sich dessen Bischof nach einem anderen Platz für seine Residenz und seine Kirche umsehen. Laut Forschung könnte dies auch Lavant gewesen sein.

Doch reicht die Besiedlungszeit des Kirchbühels weit in vorchristliche Zeit, bis in die Zeit des Endneolithikums zurück, er war sowohl Wohn- als auch als Begräbnisstätte. In späteren Jahrhunderten diente dieser Hügel immer wieder als Rückzugssiedlung vor den aus dem Osten einfallenden Völkern. Um ca. 400 v. Chr. wanderten auch keltische Stämme hier ein, im Lienzer Raum waren es die „Laianci“, von denen die Stadt Lienz ihren Namen geerbt hat.

Auch uralte Sagen ranken sich um die Gegend von Lavant. So war auch in dieses Gebiet einst (1635) das „große Sterben“, die Pest, gekommen. Die Bewohner des Virgentales versprachen deshalb, jährlich ein Widderopfer darzubringen. Und als sie sahen, wie bei Niedermauern ein Widder vom Teufel höchstpersönlich angegriffen wurde und sich erfolgreich gegen ihn durchsetzen konnte, deuteten sie dies als wichtiges Omen. Jahrhundertelang pilgerten sie aus Virgen, Matrei, Zedlach und Prägraten zur Wallfahrtskirche nach Lavant, wo der schönste Widder geopfert wurde. Er wurde versteigert, geschlachtet, sein Fleisch unter die Armen verteilt.

Seit dem 1.Weltkrieg wird diese Prozession zur Wallfahrtskirche Maria Schnee nach Obermauern/Virgen, ebenfalls auf einem alten Kultplatz stehend, durchgeführt. Der Widder darf zuvor zwei Jahre lang nicht geschoren werden, wird sauber gebadet und prächtig herausgeputzt.

Diese Widderopfer-Pozession lässt einen Zusammenhang mit den in vorchristlichen Zeiten weit verbreiteten Tieropfern vermuten. Schafe und Widder wurden in vorchristlicher Zeit oft weiblichen Gottheiten geopfert. Das uralte „heidnische“ Ritual aus Virgen/Lavant wurde demnach, wie so oft, in den christlichen Kult aufgenommen.

Archäologische Grabungen in Welzelach, einer anderen Virgener Fraktion, brachten Steinkistengräber und zahlreiche andere Funde aus dem 6./5. vorchristlichen Jh. zutage. Das berühmteste Stück ist die „Situla von Welzelach“, ein Bronzeeimer, auf dem u.a ein Widderopfer dargestellt ist. Auch die Tatsache, dass laut Sage in der Lavanter Kirche ein Widderhorn gezeigt wird, mit dem man einst zum Gottesdienst rief, ist Hinweis auf uralte kultische Gepflogenheiten, vermutlich aus der Keltenzeit. Es wird angenommen, dass es sich beim gesamten Gebiet um eine uralte Gegend der Frauenverehrung handelt; so wird auch der Name „Matrei“ aus dem vorrömischen „mater“ abgeleitet, der einst weit verehrten göttlichen Mutter „Anna divia Damatria“, der göttlichen Herrin Erd-Mutter.

Die Gewährung verschiedener Ablässe führte besonders seit dem 17. Jh. viele Wallfahrer aus der Umgebung auf den Lavanter Kirchbichl. Die von der Kirche den Sündern hart auferlegten Bußen führten in früheren Jahrhunderten zur Suche nach einer Möglichkeit der Ablösung der Strafen. So begann die Verbreitung des Ablasses vor allem seit dem 11. Jh. Durch den Ablass können zeitliche Sündenstrafen ganz oder teilweise erlassen werden, allerdings wird die Sünde selbst nicht aufgehoben. Die Kirche geht dabei davon aus, dass sie über einen „Gnadenschatz“, durch die überschüssigen Verdienste Jesu und durch die Werke der Heiligen aufgebaut, verfügt. Auch die Toten haben durch die Fürbitte der Gläubigen Anteil daran. Vermindern oder ganz erlassen konnten die Strafen der Papst und Bischöfe. Ein Ablass von einem Jahr bedeutet z.B., dass eine auferlegte Bußhandlung um diesen Zeitraum verkürzt wird. Früher war auch der Ablass-Pfennig in Gebrauch, welcher als Quittung für das geleistete Almosen galt und mancherorts als Amulett diente. Mit der Erfindung der Buchdruckerkunst setzte ein Handel mit sogenannten „Ablassbriefen“ ein. Für Geld konnte man sogar für schwerste und sogar zukünftige Sünden einen Ablass erkaufen. Dieses Ablassgeschäft war derart verbreitet, dass sogar an Banken die Abwicklung der Geldgeschäfte übergeben wurde. Für Martin Luther war dies einer der Beweggründe, seine Thesen aufzustellen. Er bestritt, dass mit dem Verdienst Christi die Bußzeit verringert werden könnte und schon gar nicht durch bare Münze.

150

Maria Weißenstein

Etwa vier bis fünf Stunden im südlich gelegenen Gebirge von der Stadt Bozen, links der Etsch, liegt auf einem hohen waldbewachsenen Felsen in der Pfarre und dem Landgerichte Deutschnofen der sehr berühmte Wallfahrtsort Weißenstein. Die Entstehung der Wallfahrt datiert sich aus dem Jahre 1553 und wird also erzählt:

Herunten im Tale war ein Landgut, von jeher der Weißensteiner Hof genannt, von dem sich ein guter, frommer und einfältiger Bauersmann geschrieben, der um 1550 Besitzer des Hofes war, nämlich Leonhard Weißensteiner. Dieser ist in eine schwere Krankheit geraten, drei Jahre bettlägerig gewesen, und zuletzt von den Sinnen gekommen, also, dass man ihn an Ketten hat legen müssen. Jedermann hatte Mitleiden mit dem guten Manne. Die Mutter der Barmherzigkeit gab dem Betrübten zuzeiten Trost, erschien ihm, nannte ihm den Ort, an welchem sie wolle, dass er ihr eine Kirche auferbauen sollte, welche mit der Zeit durch großen Zulauf und Wunderwerke berühmt sein würde. Sobald aber die Muttergottes verschwunden, ist Leonhard allezeit wieder in seine gewöhnliche Sinnlosigkeit verfallen. Seine Leute hatten auf ihn große Obsicht; aber eines Tages hat er sie betrogen, sich von den Ketten losgemacht, und ist in den nächsten Wald, der kaum eine Viertelstunde von dem Gute entfernt war, geflohen, – da auf die Höhe des Berges geraten, und von derselben tief, doch ohne Schaden, hinuntergefallen. Er kommt zu sich, sitzt auf einem Steine ganz traurig, und indem er umsieht, auf welchem Wege er wieder nach Hause kommen könne, erscheint ihm die Muttergottes abermals, tröstet ihn und verspricht ihm völlige und beständige Gesundheit, sagt ihm auch, nach neun Tagen würden ihn seine Leute an diesem Orte finden, und er werde bis dahin ohne Speise leben, und an den Kräften des Leibes abnehmen. Hat ihn also voll Trostes verlassen.

Inzwischen wird der verlorne Leonhard allenthalben gesucht, und am neunten Tage frisch und gesund von den Seinigen in dem Tale gefunden, die ihn mit Freuden nach Hause begleiten, indem er ihnen nach der Länge erzählt, wie er von der Muttergottes getröstet worden, und die Kapelle aufzubauen mit einem Gelübde sich verbunden. Weil aber die drei Jahre hindurch, so er krank gewesen, auch die Haushaltung darnieder gelegen, und die Äcker und Weinberge hat rückwärts kommen lassen, hat er sich darum also angenommen, dass er des Gelübdes, die Kapelle zu bauen, vergessen, oder vielmehr die Erfüllung von einer Zeit auf die andere verschoben: Ist jedoch von der Krankheit, die er aufs Neue leiden müssen, wieder daran erinnert worden. Er wird daher an den Ort, wo er herabgefallen, und wo man indessen öfters ein ungewöhnliches Licht wahrgenommen, geführt, nimmt eine Haue in die Hand, und will das Fundament oder den Grund zu der Kapelle anfangen. Kaum hat er aber etliche wenige Hiebe getan, so findet er ein von weißem Stein schon gemachtes Marienbild, welches den verblichenen Heiland auf

dem Schoße hält. Wer es verfertiget oder wie es an diesen Ort gekommen, hat man nicht erfahren können.

Leonhard, nun wieder ganz gesund, hat also das Werk fortgesetzt und auch vollendet; er hat das Bild auf den Altar getan, und oft mit einem Glöcklein seinen Hausgenossen und den Nachbarleuten das Zeichen in das Kirchlein gegeben. Noch heutigen Tages wird das Glöcklein im Kirchturm aufbewahrt und beim Anrücken gefährlicher Hochgewitter geläutet.

Zuletzt, nachdem er sich der weltlichen Sachen abgetan, Gott und der Muttergottes treulich gedient hat, ist er in dem Herrn entschlafen.

Nach seinem Tode hat wider alles Vermuten die Andacht mehr und mehr zugenommen, indem man aus den Tälern und von den Bergen haufenweise wallfahren gekommen, also, dass die Kapelle zu eng geworden. Man hat an dieselbe im Jahre 1561 eine größere Kirche anbauen müssen, die aber mit der Zeit wieder zu klein geworden, und da hat man 1638 eine andere, noch größere aufzurichten angefangen, welche aber erst 1654 durch die Opfer der Wallfahrer ganz vollendet, und im Jahre 1673 eingeweiht worden ist.

›› Wissenswertes ‹‹

Der Wallfahrtsort Maria Weißenstein erfuhr auch nach 1673 noch weitere Umbauten und Erweiterungen. Er liegt bei Petersberg am Regglberg unterhalb des Weißhorns und in der Nähe der berühmten Bletterbachschlucht und wird von den Servitenpatres betreut. Im Zuge der Aufklärung ließ Kaiser Joseph II. den Wallfahrtsort im Jahre 1787 aufheben und u.a. sämtliches Kircheninventar versteigern. Damals wurde auch die in der Sage beschriebene alabasterne Marienstatue in die Pfarrkirche von Leifers gebracht, wo sie sich heute noch befindet. Die sog. Auffindungskapelle ist im jetzigen Bau integriert. Maria Weißenstein ist vor Maria Trens der bedeutendste und meistbesuchte Wallfahrtsort Südtirols; zahlreiche Votivtafeln zeugen von der Hilfe und Heilung durch diese Schmerzhafte Muttergottes. Falger berichtet bereits 1846 „von den Mirakeln vieler totgeborener Kinder, die hier zu leben anfingen und getauft werden konnten sowie der Heilung vieler Irrsinniger".

Ein vierstündiger Pilgerweg führt von Leifers übers Brantental nach Weißenstein. Früher war es üblich, dass die Pilger vom Tal einen Stein zur Buße mit herauftrugen und auf einen großen Steinhügel aufschichteten. Das Stein-Mittragen ist auch auf anderen Wallfahrtswegen bekannt, wie beispielsweise zu einem Bildstöckl auf dem steilen Weg von Mühlbach zu den Hl. Drei Jungfrauen nach Meransen.

Diese sich um das Leben des Bauern Leonhard Weißensteiner rankende Sage weist neben der Namensgleichheit noch weitere interessante Verbindungen zum Hl. Leonhard auf. Dieser fränkische Heilige (ca. 500-559) kümmerte sich laut Legende um kranke und hilfsbedürftige Menschen, vor allem aber setzte er sich für die Freilassung Gefangener ein. Er gilt seither u.a. als Schutzpatron all jener, die in Ketten liegen. Auch hilft er, verirrte Menschen und Tiere wiederzufinden.

Da psychisch Kranke früher angekettet wurden, galt die Funktion des Hl. Leonhard als Kettenlöser auch ihnen. Er sollte sie von den Ketten der Krankheit befreien, d.h. ihnen die psychische Gesundheit wiedergeben. Geheilte weihten ihm deshalb ihre Ketten. Auch Leonhard Weißensteiner, der Begründer des Wallfahrsortes Maria Weißenstein, war, wie die Sage berichtet, wiederholt schwer psychisch krank, er verirrte sich deswegen im Wald, wo er erst nach neun Tagen wiedergefunden wurde.

Quellen

Fangga und Riesin

1. Frau Hütt (Frau Hitt)
Quelle: Nacherzählung aus Alpenburg, Johann N. Ritter von: Mythen und Sagen Tirols, unveränderter Neudruck der Ausgabe von 1857, Sändig OHG, Niederwalluf bei Wiesbaden 1971, S. 239, und Brüder Grimm: Deutsche Sagen, Vollständige Ausgabe nach dem Text der 3. Auflage von 1891, buchclub 65, Berlin 1987; Nr. 234, S. 234

2. Die Riesin Melka und ihre Freier
Quelle: Nacherzählung aus Meyer, Martinus: Sagen-Kränzlein aus Tirol, Verlag der Wagner'schen Universitäts-Buchhandlung, Innsbruck, 2. vermehrte Auflage 1884, S. 275

3. Die Langtüttin
Quelle: Zingerle, Ignaz Vinzenz: Sagen aus Tirol, Wagner'sche Universitäts-Buchhandlung, Innsbruck, 2. Auflage 1891, S.110 u. S. 111, Ausschnitt

4. Die Riesentochter
Quelle: Zingerle, Ignaz Vinzenz: Sagen aus Tirol, Wagner'sche Universitäts-Buchhandlung, Innsbruck, 2. Auflage 1891, S. 127

5. Das Ende der Riesin Grostàna
Quelle: Übersetzung und Nacherzählung aus Menapace, Luigi: Leggende del Trentino, Arti Grafiche Saturnia, Trento 1972, S. 71

6. Eine Riesin in Landeck
Quelle: Zingerle, Ignaz Vinzenz: Sagen aus Tirol, Wagner'sche Universitäts-Buchhandlung, Innsbruck, 2. Auflage 1891, S. 621

7. Die wilde Bäuerin in der Girstenmühle
Quelle: Heyl, Johann Adolf: Volkssagen, Bräuche und Meinungen aus Tirol, Verlag der Buchhandlung des Kath.-polit. Pressvereins, Brixen 1897, S. 235 oder Faksimiledruck erschienen unter demselben Titel bei Verlagsanstalt Athesia, Bozen 1989, S. 235

8. Saltthon
Quelle. Zingerle, Ignaz Vinzenz: Sagen aus Tirol, Wagner'sche Universitäts-Buchhandlung, Innsbruck, 2. Auflage 1891, S. 134

9. Die böse Fenkin
Quelle: Hauser, Christian: Sagen aus dem Paznaun und dessen Nachbarschaft, Verlag der Wagner'schen Universitäts-Buchhandlung, Innsbruck 1894, S. 7

10. Die Entführung der Wöchnerin
Quelle: Hauser, Christian: Sagen aus dem Paznaun und dessen Nachbarschaft, Verlag der Wagner'schen Universitäts-Buchhandlung, Innsbruck 1894, S. 12

11. Die Fangga und der Jäger
Quelle: Zingerle, Ignaz Vinzenz: Sagen, Märchen und Gebräuche aus Tirol, Verlag der Wagner'schen Buchhandlung, Innsbruck 1859, S.35

12. Das Kind der Fangga
Quelle: Alpenburg, Johann N. Ritter von: Deutsche Alpensagen, unveränderter und vollständiger Nachdruck der Ausgabe von 1861, neu herausgegeben von Lothar Borowsky Verlag Heinrich Hugendubel München 1977, S. 67

13. Stutz-Förche
Quelle: Alpenburg, Johann N. Ritter von: Deutsche Alpensagen, unveränderter und vollständiger Nachdruck der Ausgabe von 1861, neu herausgegeben von Lothar Borowsky Verlag Heinrich Hugendubel München 1977, S. 68

14. Die wilde Fangga
Quelle: Alpenburg, Johann N. Ritter von: Die Alpenzither aus Tirol, Gedichte und Erinnerungsblätter aus den Jahren 1848 und 1849, Innsbruck 1855, S. 153

15. Die Waldfrauen
Quelle: Zingerle, Ignaz Vinzenz: Sagen, Märchen und Gebräuche aus Tirol, Verlag der Wagner'schen Buchhandlung, Innsbruck 1859, S.34

Perchta/Stampe

16. Frau Berchta in Lajen
Quelle: Zingerle, Ignaz Vinzenz: Sagen aus Tirol, Wagner'sche Universitäts-Buchhandlung, Innsbruck, 2. Auflage 1891. S. 20, Teil 1

17. Die Berchtl bei der Brücke in Virgen
Quelle: Zingerle, Ignaz Vinzenz: Sagen, Märchen und Gebräuche aus Tirol, Verlag der Wagner'schen Buchhandlung, Innsbruck 1859, S. 17

18. Die Gömnacht-Perchtl zu Hechenblaiken
Quelle: Alpenburg, Johann N. Ritter von: Mythen und Sagen Tirols, unveränderter Neudruck der Ausgabe von 1857, Sändig OHG, Niederwalluf bei Wiesbaden 1971, S. 64

19. Der Unschuldigen-Gottesacker
Quelle: Alpenburg, Johann N. Ritter von: Mythen und Sagen Tirols, unveränderter Neudruck der Ausgabe von 1857, Sändig OHG, Niederwalluf bei Wiesbaden 1971, S. 66

20. Die Stampe

Quelle: Heyl, Johann Adolf: Volkssagen, Bräuche und Meinungen aus Tirol, Verlag der Buchhandlung des Kath.-polit. Pressvereins, Brixen 1897, S. 235 oder Faksimiledruck erschienen unter demselben Titel bei Verlagsanstalt Athesia, Bozen 1989, S. 165

21. Frau Berchta bei Villanders

Quelle: Zingerle, Ignaz Vinzenz: Sagen aus Tirol, Wagner'sche Universitäts-Buchhandlung, Innsbruck, 2. Auflage 1891, S. 21

22. Berchtlsagen aus Alpach I und II

Quelle: Zingerle, Ignaz Vinzenz: Sagen aus Tirol, Wagner'sche Universitäts-Buchhandlung, Innsbruck, 2. Auflage 1891. Seite 18, Teil 2
Quelle: Zingerle, Ignaz Vinzenz: Sagen aus Tirol, Wagner'sche Universitäts-Buchhandlung, Innsbruck, 2. Auflage 1891. Seite 19, Teil 4

23. Bertasage aus Folgareit

Quelle: Schneller, Christian: Märchen und Sagen aus Wälschtirol. Ein Beitrag zur deutschen Sagenkunde, Verlag der Wagner'schen Universitätsbuchhandlung Innsbruck 1867, Nachdruck im Georg Olms Verlag, Hildesheim – New York 1976, S. 199

24. Bertasage aus Ronchi bei Ala

Quelle: Schneller, Christian: Märchen und Sagen aus Wälschtirol. Ein Beitrag zur deutschen Sagenkunde, Verlag der Wagner'schen Universitätsbuchhandlung Innsbruck 1867, Nachdruck im Georg Olms Verlag, Hildesheim – New York 1976, S. 201

25. Der eiserne Handschuh

Quelle: Zingerle, Ignaz Vinzenz: Sagen aus Tirol, Wagner'sche Universitäts-Buchhandlung, Innsbruck, 2. Auflage 1891. S. 25

26. Die Stempa

Quelle: Übersetzung und Nacherzählung aus Sebesta, Giuseppe: Fiaba - Leggenda dell' Alta Valle del Fèrsina e carta d'identità delle figure di fantasia, Ediz. Museo provinciale degli usi e costumi della gente trentina – San Michele all'Adige, Arti Grafiche R. Manfrini, Calliano/Trento, 1973, S. 27

27. Die Stampe

Quelle: Nacherzählung aus Petzoldt, Leander (Hsg.): Sagen, Märchen und Schwänke aus Südtirol, gesammelt von Willi Mai, Band I: Wipptal, Pustertal, Gadertal, Tyrolia Verlag Innsbruck-Wien 2000, S. 279

28. Das Kindsmädchen mit dem Kind

Quelle: Menghin, Alois: Aus dem deutschen Südtirol, Verlag von Fr. Plant's Buchhandlung, Meran 1884, S. 10

Seherin und Prophetin

29. Die Jocher Fräulein
Quelle: Heyl, Johann Adolf: Volkssagen, Bräuche und Meinungen aus Tirol, Verlag der Buchhandlung des Kath.polit. Pressvereins, Brixen 1897, S. 410 oder Faksimiledruck erschienen unter demselben Titel bei Verlagsanstalt Athesia, Bozen 1989, S. 410

30. Die Willeweis in Wälschnoven
Quelle: Heyl, Johann Adolf: Volkssagen, Bräuche und Meinungen aus Tirol, Verlag der Buchhandlung des Kath.polit. Pressvereins, Brixen 1897, S. 415 oder Faksimiledruck erschienen unter demselben Titel bei Verlagsanstalt Athesia, Bozen 1989, S. 415

31. Von der Willeweis auf dem Birchboden
Quelle: Heyl, Johann Adolf: Volkssagen, Bräuche und Meinungen aus Tirol, Verlag der Buchhandlung des Kath.polit. Pressvereins, Brixen 1897, S. 271 oder Faksimiledruck erschienen unter demselben Titel bei Verlagsanstalt Athesia, Bozen 1989, S. 271

32. Willeweis
Quelle: Weber, Franz S.: Laurins Rosengarten - Sagen aus den Dolomiten, Verlag Deutsche Buchhandlung Bozen 1914, S. 115

33. Fürweilung
Quelle: Johann Adolf Heyl: Volkssagen, Bräuche und Meinungen aus Tirol, Verlag der Buchhandlung des Kath.polit. Pressvereins, Brixen 1897, S. 272 oder Faksimiledruck erschienen unter demselben Titel bei Verlagsanstalt Athesia, Bozen 1989, S. 272

34. Der Sandwirt
Quelle: Zingerle, Ignaz Vinzenz: Sagen aus Tirol, Wagner'sche Universitäts-Buchhandlung, Innsbruck, 2. Auflage 1891, S. 288

35. Von der Willeweis aus Niederlana
Quelle: Nacherzählung eines Berichtes von Staffler, Walter: Willeweis – Hexenkuchl, in: Der Schlern, Jahrgang 1950, S.36

36. Von der Willeweiß
Quelle: Nacherzählung aus Petzoldt, Leander (Hsg.): Sagen, Märchen und Schwänke aus Südtirol, gesammelt von Willi Mai, Band II: Bozen, Vinschgau und Etschtal, Tyrolia Verlag Innsbruck-Wien 2002, S. 208

37. Die Sibilla von Comano
Quelle: Übersetzung und Nacherzählung aus Brentari, Ottone: Guida del Trentino I, Forni Editore Bologna, Trento 1934, S. 261 und 264; Felicetti, Don Lorenzo: Centoventi leggende del Trentino, Scuola tipografica Arcivescovile "Artigianelli", Trento 1934, S. 208; Borzaga, Giovanna: Leggende del Trentino, Luigi Reverdito Editore 1971, S. 271

38. Die Gannaruna

Quelle: Nacherzählung von „Das Kind im Schatten" aus: Wolff, Karl Felix: Dolomitensagen, Gesamtausgabe, Tyrolia Verlag Innsbruck-Wien-München, 14. erweiterte Auflage 1977, S. 358; Fink, Hans: Dolomitensagen im Eisacktal, Verlag A.Weger, Brixen 1988, Band 43 der Reihe „An der Etsch und im Gebirge", 1988, S. 10 und Heyl, Johann Adolf: Volkssagen, Bräuche und Meinungen aus Tirol, Verlag der Buchhandlung des Kath.polit. Pressvereins, Brixen 1897, S. 605 oder Faksimiledruck erschienen unter demselben Titel bei Verlagsanstalt Athesia, Bozen 1989, S. 605

Salige

39. Die Gämse

Quelle: Zingerle, Ignaz Vinzenz: Sagen aus Tirol, Wagner'sche Universitäts-Buchhandlung, Innsbruck, 2. Auflage 1891, S. 113

40. Die Salgfräulein

Quelle: Zingerle, Ignaz Vinzenz: Sagen aus Tirol, Wagner'sche Universitäts-Buchhandlung, Innsbruck, 2. Auflage 1891, S. 32

41. Die Heilige Frau

Quelle: Übersetzung und Nacherzählung aus Sebesta, Giuseppe: Fiaba - Leggenda dell' Alta Valle del Fèrsina e carta d'identità delle figure di fantasia, Ediz. Museo provinciale degli usi e costumi della gente trentina – San Michele all'Adige, Arti Grafiche R. Manfrini, Calliano/Trento, 1973, S. 110

42. Der Ziegenhirt von Pregossi

Quelle: Schneller, Christian: Märchen und Sagen aus Wälschtirol. Ein Beitrag zur deutschen Sagenkunde, Verlag der Wagner'schen Universitätsbuchhandlung Innsbruck 1867, Nachdruck im Georg Olms Verlag, Hildesheim – New York 1976, S. 215

43. Die Sage vom Schlaraffenlande

Quelle: Zingerle, Ignaz Vinzenz: Sagen, Märchen und Gebräuche aus Tirol, Verlag der Wagner'schen Buchhandlung, Innsbruck 1859, S.31

44. Die Kaiserfrau am Nachtberge

Quelle: Zingerle, Ignaz Vinzenz: Sagen aus Tirol, Wagner'sche Universitäts-Buchhandlung, Innsbruck, 2. Auflage 1891, S. 51

45. Die Wasserfräulein

Quelle: Zingerle, Ignaz Vinzenz: Sagen aus Tirol, Wagner'sche Universitäts-Buchhandlung, Innsbruck, 2. Auflage 1891, S. 101

46. Die Anguana vom Scin-See
Quelle: Übersetzung und Nacherzählung aus Zangrandi, Giovanna: Leggende delle Dolomiti, Nordpress Edizioni, Chiari, 2. edizione 2000, S. 60

47. Die drei Seligen Fräulein ob der Morin im Ötztal
Quelle: Alpenburg, Johann N. Ritter von: Mythen und Sagen Tirols, unveränderter Neudruck der Ausgabe von 1857, Sändig OHG, Niederwalluf bei Wiesbaden 1971, S. 18

48. Die Saligen in Lüsen
Quelle: Zingerle, Ignaz Vinzenz: Sagen, Märchen und Gebräuche aus Tirol, Verlag der Wagner'schen Buchhandlung, Innsbruck 1859, S. 25

49. Von den seligen Leuten bei Brixen
Quelle: Heyl, Johann Adolf: Volkssagen, Bräuche und Meinungen aus Tirol, Verlag der Buchhandlung des Kath.polit. Pressvereins, Brixen 1897, S. 166, Ausschnitt, oder Faksimiledruck erschienen unter demselben Titel bei Verlagsanstalt Athesia, Bozen 1989, S. 166, Ausschnitt

50. Die Saligen an der Rotwand
Quelle: Nacherzählung aus August Kleeberg-Hochnaturns, „Naturnser Sagen" in „Der Schlern", Jahrgang 1931, S. 493

51. Die Ganna aus dem Mittagstal
Quelle: Übersetzung und Nacherzählung aus Alton, Giovanni: Proverbi, tradizioni ed Anneddoti delle valli Ladine Orientali con versione italiana, Stamperia e libreria accademica Wagner, Innsbruck 1881, S. 65

52. Die verjagte Vivana
Quelle: Nacherzählung aus: Rossi, von Hugo, v. Kindl Ulrike (Hsg.): Märchen und Sagen aus dem Fassatale, Istitut cultural Ladin „Majon di fašegn", Vigo di Fassa 1984, S. 178

53. Von den letzten Saligen
Quelle: Meyer, Martinus: Sagen-Kränzlein aus Tirol, Verlag der Wagner'schen Universitäts-Buchhandlung, Innsbruck, 2. vermehrte Auflage 1884, S. 362, Ausschnitt

Von verwunschenen Frauen und Truten

54. Vom Schatz auf Zwingenstein
Quelle: Heyl, Johann Adolf: Volkssagen, Bräuche und Meinungen aus Tirol, Verlag der Buchhandlung des Kath.polit. Pressvereins, Brixen 1897, S. 249, Ausschnitt, oder Faksimiledruck erschienen unter demselben Titel bei Verlagsanstalt Athesia, Bozen 1989, S. 249, Ausschnitt

55. Die verwunschene Königstochter
Quelle: Alpenburg, Johann N. Ritter von: Deutsche Alpensagen, unveränderter und vollständiger Nachdruck der Ausgabe von 1861, neu herausgegeben von Lothar Borowsky Verlag Heinrich Hugendubel München 1977, S. 335

56. Die drei Jungfrauen von Ehrenberg
Quelle: Zingerle, Ignaz Vinzenz: Sagen aus Tirol, Wagner'sche Universitäts-Buchhandlung, Innsbruck, 2. Auflage 1891, S.32

57. Die weiße Frau
Quelle: Zingerle, Ignaz Vinzenz: Sagen aus Tirol, Wagner'sche Universitäts-Buchhandlung, Innsbruck, 2. Auflage 1891, S. 295

58. Der Träger
Quelle: Zingerle, Ignaz Vinzenz: Sagen aus Tirol, Wagner'sche Universitäts-Buchhandlung, Innsbruck, 2. Auflage 1891, S. 317

59. Die Krönlnatter
Quelle: Zingerle, Ignaz Vinzenz: Sagen aus Tirol, Wagner'sche Universitäts-Buchhandlung, Innsbruck, 2. Auflage 1891, S. 325

60. Die Seeschlange
Quelle: Zingerle, Ignaz Vinzenz: Sagen aus Tirol, Wagner'sche Universitäts-Buchhandlung, Innsbruck, 2. Auflage 1891, S. 147

61. Die Frau mit den goldenen Nüssen
Quelle: Zingerle, Ignaz Vinzenz: Sagen, Märchen und Gebräuche aus Tirol, Verlag der Wagner'schen Buchhandlung, Innsbruck 1859, S. 212

62. Das Fräulein auf der Hochburg
Quelle: Zingerle, Ignaz Vinzenz: Sagen aus Tirol, Wagner'sche Universitäts-Buchhandlung, Innsbruck, 2. Auflage 1891, S. 302

63. Die Sage vom Burgstallegg
Quelle: Nacherzählung aus Holzmann, Hermann: Rund um Aldein, in: Reimmichls Volkskalender, Anno Domini 1967, S. 193

64. Die Trude zu Unterholz
Quelle: Alpenburg, Johann N. Ritter von: Mythen und Sagen Tirols, unveränderter Neudruck der Ausgabe von 1857, Sändig OHG, Niederwalluf bei Wiesbaden 1971, S.305

65. Hansl und Franzl
Quelle: Alpenburg, Johann N. Ritter von: Mythen und Sagen Tirols, unveränderter Neudruck der Ausgabe von 1857, Sändig OHG, Niederwalluf bei Wiesbaden 1971, S. 301

66. Die Trude

Quelle: Zingerle, Ignaz Vinzenz: Sagen, Märchen und Gebräuche aus Tirol, Verlag der Wagner'schen Buchhandlung, Innsbruck 1859, S. 347

67. Die angenagelte Trute

Quelle: Heyl, Johann Adolf: Volkssagen, Bräuche und Meinungen aus Tirol, Verlag der Buchhandlung des Kath.polit. Pressvereins, Brixen 1897, S. 289, oder Faksimiledruck erschienen unter demselben Titel bei Verlagsanstalt Athesia, Bozen 1989, S. 289

68. Die große Trude

Quelle: Zingerle, Ignaz Vinzenz: Sagen, Märchen und Gebräuche aus Tirol, Verlag der Wagner'schen Buchhandlung, Innsbruck 1859, S. 426

69. Das Mädchen, das eine Trute gewesen ist

Quelle: Übersetzung und Nacherzählung aus Bellotto, Alfonso (Hsg.): I racconti di Luserna, Circolo Culturale „M. Gandhi" di Luserna, Istituto di Cultura Cimbra „A. Dal Pozzo" di Roana, Vicenza 1978, S. 228

Hexe und Weise Frau

70. Die Hexe mit der hölzernen Rippe

Quelle: Heyl, Johann Adolf: Volkssagen, Bräuche und Meinungen aus Tirol, Verlag der Buchhandlung des Kath.polit. Pressvereins, Brixen 1897, S. 676, oder Faksimiledruck erschienen unter demselben Titel bei Verlagsanstalt Athesia, Bozen 1989, S. 676

71. Die Partschuner Hebamme

Quelle: Heyl, Johann Adolf: Volkssagen, Bräuche und Meinungen aus Tirol, Verlag der Buchhandlung des Kath.polit. Pressvereins, Brixen 1897, S. 295, oder Faksimiledruck erschienen unter demselben Titel bei Verlagsanstalt Athesia, Bozen 1989, S. 295

72. Von den Hexen auf dem Piperbühel

Quelle: Heyl, Johann Adolf: Volkssagen, Bräuche und Meinungen aus Tirol, Verlag der Buchhandlung des Kath.-polit. Pressvereins, Brixen 1897, S. 296 oder Faksimiledruck erschienen unter demselben Titel bei Verlagsanstalt Athesia, Bozen 1989, S. 296

73. Die Hexen und der Schlichterknecht

Quelle: Heyl, Johann Adolf: Volkssagen, Bräuche und Meinungen aus Tirol, Verlag der Buchhandlung des Kath.polit. Pressvereins, Brixen 1897, S. 297, oder Faksimiledruck Heyl, Johann Adolf, Volkssagen, Bräuche und Meinungen aus Tirol, Faksimiledruck der 1897 erschienen Ausgabe, Verlagsanstalt Athesia, Bozen 1989, S. 297

74. Die Hexenfahrt
Quelle: Alpenburg, Johann N. Ritter von: Deutsche Alpensagen, unveränderter und vollständiger Nachdruck der Ausgabe von 1861, neu herausgegeben von Lothar Borowsky Verlag Heinrich Hugendubel München 1977, S. 200

75. Der Hexentanz auf den Gandellen
Quelle: Zingerle, Ignaz Vinzenz: Sagen, Märchen und Gebräuche aus Tirol, Verlag der Wagner'schen Buchhandlung, Innsbruck 1859, S. 297

76. Oh Mander, husch, husch!
Quelle: Heyl, Johann Adolf: Volkssagen, Bräuche und Meinungen aus Tirol, Verlag der Buchhandlung des Kath.-polit. Pressvereins, Brixen 1897, S. 37 oder Faksimiledruck erschienen unter demselben Titel bei Verlagsanstalt Athesia, Bozen 1989, S. 37

77. Die Romhottel
Quelle: Heyl, Johann Adolf: Volkssagen, Bräuche und Meinungen aus Tirol, Verlag der Buchhandlung des Kath.-polit. Pressvereins, Brixen 1897, S. 292 oder Faksimiledruck erschienen unter demselben Titel bei Verlagsanstalt Athesia, Bozen 1989, S. 292

78. Die Schlechtwetterpfanne
Quelle: Heyl, Johann Adolf: Volkssagen, Bräuche und Meinungen aus Tirol, Verlag der Buchhandlung des Kath.-polit. Pressvereins, Brixen 1897, S. 533 oder Faksimiledruck erschienen unter demselben Titel bei Verlagsanstalt Athesia, Bozen 1989, S. 533

79. Die Sage vom Wodansbrunnen
Quelle: Nacherzählung aus Mader Ignaz, „Ortsnamen und Siedlungsgeschichte von Vintl, Weitental, Pfunders“, Schlern-Schriften Nr. 82, Universitäts-Verlag Wagner, Innsbruck, 1951, Erzählung von Josef Oberhofer, „Fuirer“ in Pfunders, S. 130

80. Die drei Schwestern
Quelle: Meyer, Martinus: Schlern-Sagen und Märchen, Verlag der Wagner'schen Universitäts-Buchhandlung, Innsbruck 1891, S. 98

81. Mäusemachen
Quelle: Zingerle, Ignaz Vinzenz: Sagen, Märchen und Gebräuche aus Tirol, Verlag der Wagner'schen Buchhandlung, Innsbruck 1859, S. 302

82. Eine Hexe verwandelt ihren Mann
Quelle: Meyer, Martinus: Sagen-Kränzlein aus Tirol, Verlag der Wagner'schen Universitäts-Buchhandlung, Innsbruck, 2. vermehrte Auflage 1884, S. 264

83. Der Bocherhof
Quelle: Übersetzung und Nacherzählung aus: Sebesta, Giuseppe: Fiaba - Leggenda dell' Alta Valle del Fèrsina e carta d'identità delle figure di fantasia, Ediz. Museo provinciale degli usi e

costumi della gente trentina – San Michele all'Adige, Arti Grafiche R. Manfrini, Calliano/Trento, 1973, S. 46

84. Hexengeschichte aus dem 20. Jahrhundert
Quelle: Pius Mair, geboren 1928, Meransen

Büßerin und Bestrafte

85. Die Entstehung der Marmolata
Quelle: Übersetzung und Nacherzählung aus Felicetti, Don Lorenzo: Centoventi leggende del Trentino, Scuola tipografica Arcivescovile "Artigianelli", Trento 1934, S. 161 eine ähnliche Version auch bei Zingerle, Ignaz Vinzenz: Sagen aus Tirol, Wagner'sche Universitäts-Buchhandlung, Innsbruck, 2. Auflage 1891, S. 368

86. Die Mutter des Heiligen Petrus
Quelle: Übersetzung und Nacherzählung aus Bellotto, Alfonso (Hsg.): I racconti di Luserna, Circolo Culturale „M. Gandhi" di Luserna, Istituto di Cultura Cimbra „A. Dal Pozzo" di Roana, Vicenza 1978, S. 39

87. Der Teufel als Tänzer I
Quelle: Johann Adolf Heyl: Volkssagen, Bräuche und Meinungen aus Tirol, Verlag der Buchhandlung des Kath.-polit. Pressvereins, Brixen 1897, S. 105 oder Faksimiledruck erschienen unter demselben Titel bei Verlagsanstalt Athesia, Bozen 1989. S. 105

88. Der Teufel als Tänzer II
Quelle: Zingerle, Ignaz Vinzenz: Sagen aus Tirol, Wagner'sche Universitäts-Buchhandlung, Innsbruck, 2. Auflage 1891, S. 383

89. Gottesgericht über einen verschwemmten Hof
Quelle: Alpenburg, Johann N. Ritter von: Deutsche Alpensagen, unveränderter und vollständiger Nachdruck der Ausgabe von 1861, neu herausgegeben von Lothar Borowsky Verlag Heinrich Hugendubel München 1977, S.340

90. Noglroath
Quelle: Johann Adolf Heyl: Volkssagen, Bräuche und Meinungen aus Tirol, Verlag der Buchhandlung des Kath.-polit. Pressvereins, Brixen 1897, S. 63 oder Faksimiledruck erschienen unter demselben Titel bei Verlagsanstalt Athesia, Bozen 1989, S. 63

91. Sage von der Pfaffenköchin
Quelle: Nacherzählung aus Mader, Ignaz: Ortsnamen und Siedlungsgeschichte von Vintl, Weitental, Pfunders, Schlernschriften Nr. 82, 1951, Erzählung von Josef Oberhofer, „Fuirer" in Pfunders, S. 129

92. Mädchengestalt am Kalmbach
Quelle: Alpenburg, Johann N. Ritter von: Mythen und Sagen Tirols, unveränderter Neudruck der Ausgabe von 1857, Sändig OHG, Niederwalluf bei Wiesbaden 1971, S. 203

93. Das Knuidlweibele
Quelle: Johann Adolf Heyl: Volkssagen, Bräuche und Meinungen aus Tirol, Verlag der Buchhandlung des Kath.-polit. Pressvereins, Brixen 1897, S. 479 oder Faksimiledruck erschienen unter demselben Titel bei Verlagsanstalt Athesia, Bozen 1989, S. 479

94. Von der eitlen Kellnerin mit der Schlange
Quelle: Johann Adolf Heyl: Volkssagen, Bräuche und Meinungen aus Tirol, Verlag der Buchhandlung des Kath.-polit. Pressvereins, Brixen 1897, S. 158 oder Faksimiledruck erschienen unter demselben Titel bei Verlagsanstalt Athesia, Bozen 1989, S. 158

95. Totenmesse in der Peterskirche
Quelle: Zingerle, Ignaz Vinzenz: Sagen, Märchen und Gebräuche aus Tirol, Verlag der Wagner'schen Buchhandlung, Innsbruck 1859, S. 189

96. Trattla-Pfott
Quelle: Zingerle, Ignaz Vinzenz: Sagen, Märchen und Gebräuche aus Tirol, Verlag der Wagner'schen Buchhandlung, Innsbruck 1859, S. 140

97. Nonnengespenst auf Wolfsthurn
Quelle: Alpenburg, Johann N. Ritter von: Deutsche Alpensagen, unveränderter und vollständiger Nachdruck der Ausgabe von 1861, neu herausgegeben von Lothar Borowsky Verlag Heinrich Hugendubel München 1977, S.293

98. Die Geister der Leuchtenburg
Quelle: Zingerle, Ignaz Vinzenz: Sagen aus Tirol, Wagner'sche Universitäts-Buchhandlung, Innsbruck, 2. Auflage 1891, S. 316

99. Das verlorene Mädel
Quelle: Zingerle, Ignaz Vinzenz: Sagen aus Tirol, Wagner'sche Universitäts-Buchhandlung, Innsbruck, 2. Auflage 1891, S. 283

100. Sterzinger Mooslied
Quelle: Sparber, Prof.Anselm (Hsg): Sterzinger Heimatbuch, Schlernschriften 232, Universitätsverlag Wagner, Innsbruck 1965, S. 560

101. Das Eschenloher Schlossfräulein
Quelle: Nacherzählung aus Zingerle, Ignaz Vinzenz: Sagen, Märchen und Gebräuche aus Tirol, Verlag der Wagner'schen Buchhandlung, Innsbruck 1859, S. 145 und Alpenburg, Johann N. Ritter von: Mythen und Sagen Tirols, unveränderter Neudruck der Ausgabe von 1857, Sändig OHG, Niederwalluf bei Wiesbaden 1971, S. 198

102. Die glühende Sennin
Quelle: Alpenburg, Johann N. Ritter von: Mythen und Sagen Tirols, unveränderter Neudruck der Ausgabe von 1857, Sändig OHG, Niederwalluf bei Wiesbaden 1971, S. 176

103. Die Wilde Jägerin
Quelle: Alpenburg, Johann N. Ritter von: Deutsche Alpensagen, unveränderter und vollständiger Nachdruck der Ausgabe von 1861, neu herausgegeben von Lothar Borowsky Verlag Heinrich Hugendubel München 1977, S.160

104. Die Kröte auf Weißenstein
Quelle: Zingerle, Ignaz Vinzenz: Sagen, Märchen und Gebräuche aus Tirol, Verlag der Wagner'schen Buchhandlung, Innsbruck 1859, S. 138

Fürstin und Königin

105. Die Frau von Hochgalsaun
Quelle: Alpenburg, Johann N. Ritter von: Deutsche Alpensagen, unveränderter und vollständiger Nachdruck der Ausgabe von 1861, neu herausgegeben von Lothar Borowsky Verlag Heinrich Hugendubel München 1977, S. 238 und Zingerle, Ignaz Vinzenz: Sagen, Märchen und Gebräuche aus Tirol, Verlag der Wagner'schen Buchhandlung, Innsbruck 1859, S. 394

106. Der Tod der Philippine Welser
Quelle: Zingerle, Ignaz Vinzenz: Sagen aus Tirol, Wagner'sche Universitäts-Buchhandlung, Innsbruck, 2. Auflage 1891, S.569

107. Die Dame von Hauenstein
Quelle: Menghin, Alois, „Aus dem deutschen Südtirol", Verlag von Fr. Plant's Buchhandlung, Meran 1884, S. 48

108. Der Garten der Königin
Quelle: Übersetzung und Nacherzählung aus: Bolognini, Nepomuceno: Le leggende del Trentino, Arnaldo Forni Editore, Ristampa anastatica dell'edizione di Rovereto 1884 – 1889, S. 45

109. Die Prinzessin im Rosengarten
Quelle: Alpenburg, Johann N. Ritter von: Mythen und Sagen Tirols, unveränderter Neudruck der Ausgabe von 1857, Sändig OHG, Niederwalluf bei Wiesbaden 1971, S. 225

110. Die Gräfin von Welfenstein
Quelle: Nacherzählung aus „Freienfeld", Herausgeber Gemeinde Freienfeld, Verlag Graphic Line, Bozen, 1992, S. 345; Petzoldt, Leander (Hsg.): Sagen, Märchen und Schwänke aus Südtirol, gesammelt von Willi Mai, Band I: Wipptal, Pustertal, Gadertal, Tyrolia Verlag Innsbruck-Wien 2000, S. 204; mündliche Erzählung von Gretl und Werner Fuchs, Sterzing

111. Das Liebespaar von Castel Nanno

Quelle: Übersetzung und Nacherzählung aus Felicetti, Don Lorenzo: Centoventi leggende del Trentino, Scuola tipografica Arcivescovile "Artigianelli", Trento 1934, S. 105

112. Die Wallburg von Mastellina

Quelle: Übersetzung und Nacherzählung aus: Bezzi, Quirino: Racconti e Leggende della Val di Sole, Scuola Tipografica Artigianelli, Trento 1954, S.99

113. Die Königinnen von Jochgrimm

Quelle: Nacherzählung aus Aick, Gerhard: Deutsche Heldensagen II, Verlag Carl Ueberreuter Wien - Heidelberg 1964, S.120; Mudrak, Edmund: Deutsche Heldensagen, Ensslin & Laiblin Verlag, Reutlingen 1955, S. 169; Kralik, von Richard: Das deutsche Götter- und Heldenbuch IV- Dietrich und seine Gesellen, Verlag der Leo-Gesellschaft, Wien 1903; Delago, Hermann: Dolomiten-Wanderbuch, Tyrolia Verlag, Innsbruck-Wien-München, 12. Auflage 1974, S. 44 und/oder Reimmichl-Volkskalender 1967

114. Die Zwergenkönigin von Tirol

Quelle: Nacherzählung aus Aick, Gerhard: Deutsche Heldensagen II, Verlag Carl Ueberreuter Wien - Heidelberg 1964, S.86; Kralik, von Richard: Das deutsche Götter- und Heldenbuch IV – Dietrich und seine Gesellen, Verlag der Leo-Gesellschaft, Wien 1903, S.82; Fährmann, Willi: Deutsche Heldensagen, Thienemann Verlag, Stuttgart-Wien 1993, S. 49

115. Die Königin Tresìnga

Quelle: Übersetzung und Nacherzählung aus: Menapace, Luigi: Realtà e leggenda del Lago Rosso, Strenna Trentina Jahrgang 1934, S. 79; Borzaga, Giovanna: Leggende del Trentino, Luigi Reverdito Editore 1971, S. 197 und Neri, Mauro: Quella terra magica tra i monti, Panorama Ragazzi, Trento 2000, S. 633

116. Margaretha Maultasch

Quelle: Zingerle, Ignaz Vinzenz: Sagen aus Tirol, Wagner'sche Universitäts-Buchhandlung, Innsbruck, 2. Auflage 1891, S. 690

117. Der Geist auf der Sonnenburg

Quelle: Johann Adolf Heyl: Volkssagen, Bräuche und Meinungen aus Tirol, Verlag der Buchhandlung des Kath.-polit. Pressvereins, Brixen 1897, S. 583 oder Faksimiledruck erschienen unter demselben Titel bei Verlagsanstalt Athesia, Bozen 1989, S. 583

Bäuerin und Dirn

118. Das glückliche Tal

Quelle: Alpenburg, Johann N. Ritter von: Deutsche Alpensagen, unveränderter und vollständiger Nachdruck der Ausgabe von 1861, neu herausgegeben von Lothar Borowsky Verlag Heinrich Hugendubel München 1977, S. 161

119. Die Spinne
Quelle: Zingerle, Ignaz Vinzenz: Sagen aus Tirol, Wagner'sche Universitäts-Buchhandlung, Innsbruck, 2. Auflage 1891, Seite 330.

120. Die Dirne mit dem Dreikönigküchl
Quelle: Johann Adolf Heyl: Volkssagen, Bräuche und Meinungen aus Tirol, Verlag der Buchhandlung des Kath.-polit. Pressvereins, Brixen 1897, S. 417 oder Faksimiledruck erschienen unter demselben Titel bei Verlagsanstalt Athesia, Bozen 1989, S. 417

121. Der Schütze im hohlen Berg
Quelle: Johann Adolf Heyl: Volkssagen, Bräuche und Meinungen aus Tirol, Verlag der Buchhandlung des Kath.-polit. Pressvereins, Brixen 1897, S. 482 oder Faksimiledruck erschienen unter demselben Titel bei Verlagsanstalt Athesia, Bozen 1989, S. 482

122. Die mutige Hausdirn
Quelle: Alpenburg, Johann N. Ritter von: Mythen und Sagen Tirols, unveränderter Neudruck der Ausgabe von 1857, Sändig OHG, Niederwalluf bei Wiesbaden 1971, S. 165

123. Rosalpina
Quelle: Übersetzung und Nacherzählung aus Neri, Mauro: Quella terra magica tra i monti, Panorama Ragazzi, Trento 2000, S. 293

124. Die tapferen Weiber und Mädchen von Latzfons und Verdings
Quelle: Nacherzählung aus Michaeler, Otto, Pfarrer: Die tapferen Weiber und Mädchen von Latzfons und Verdings, in: Der Schlern, Jahrgang 1947, S. 100

125. Das goldene Würmlein
Quelle: Zingerle, Ignaz Vinzenz: Sagen aus Tirol, Wagner'sche Universitäts-Buchhandlung, Innsbruck, 2. Auflage 1891, S. 325

126. Der Kranzlwurm
Quelle: Zingerle, Ignaz Vinzenz: Sagen aus Tirol, Wagner'sche Universitäts-Buchhandlung, Innsbruck, 2. Auflage 1891, S. 650

127. Das unschuldige Mädchen
Quelle: Übersetzung und Nacherzählung aus: Felicetti, Don Lorenzo: Centoventi leggende del Trentino, Scuola tipografica Arcivescovile "Artigianelli", Trento 1934, S. 7, auch bei Zingerle, Ignaz Vinzenz: Sagen aus Tirol, Wagner'sche Universitäts-Buchhandlung, Innsbruck, 2. Auflage 1891, S. 331

128. Der Faule und die Fleißige
Quelle: Menghin, Alois: Aus dem deutschen Südtirol, Verlag von Fr. Plant's Buchhandlung, Meran 1884, S. 90

129. Mortaso

Quelle: Übersetzung und Nacherzählung aus: Bolognini, Nepomuceno: Le leggende del Trentino, Arnaldo Forni Editore, Ristampa anastatica dell'edizione di Rovereto 1884 – 1889, S. 7; Felicetti, Don Lorenzo: Centoventi leggende del Trentino, Scuola tipografica Arcivescovile „Artigianelli“, Trento 1934, S. 263, Kurzversion auch bei Zingerle, Ignaz Vinzenz: Sagen aus Tirol, Wagner'sche Universitäts-Buchhandlung, Innsbruck, 2. Auflage 1891, S. 491

130. Das Mädchen aus Fierozzo

Quelle: Übersetzung und Nacherzählung aus Neri, Mauro: Quella terra magica tra i monti, Panorama Ragazzi, Trento 2000, S. 278

131. Wie die Platzlinerin in Tiers entführt wurde

Quelle: Johann Adolf Heyl: Volkssagen, Bräuche und Meinungen aus Tirol, Verlag der Buchhandlung des Kath.-polit. Pressvereins, Brixen 1897, S. 407 oder Faksimiledruck erschienen unter demselben Titel bei Verlagsanstalt Athesia, Bozen 1989, S. 407

132. Das vergessene Kind beim Schatze

Quelle: Johann Adolf Heyl: Volkssagen, Bräuche und Meinungen aus Tirol, Verlag der Buchhandlung des Kath.-polit. Pressvereins, Brixen 1897, S. 386 oder Faksimiledruck erschienen unter demselben Titel bei Verlagsanstalt Athesia, Bozen 1989, S. 386

133. Arnika

Quelle: Übersetzung und Nacherzählung aus Borzaga, Giovanna: Le più belle leggende del Trentino, Ed. Manfrini, Calliano (TN) 1996, S. 154

Heilige und Maria

134. Sage vom Jaufental

Quelle: Zingerle, Ignaz Vinzenz: Sagen aus Tirol, Wagner'sche Universitäts-Buchhandlung, Innsbruck, 2. Auflage 1891, S. 524

135. Die Heilige Notburga

Quelle: Nacherzählung aus Alpenburg, Johann N. Ritter von: Deutsche Alpensagen, unveränderter und vollständiger Nachdruck der Ausgabe von 1861, neu herausgegeben von Lothar Borowsky Verlag Heinrich Hugendubel München 1977, S. 84 und Scheglmann, Maria Aurelia: Tiroler Legenden, Sagen und Volksbräuche, Verlagsanstalt G.J. Manz, Buch- und Kunstdruckerei, München-Regensburg 1928, S. 18

136. Die St.-Margareten-Kirche am Kniebos (Kniepass)

Quelle: Johann Adolf Heyl: Volkssagen, Bräuche und Meinungen aus Tirol, Verlag der Buchhandlung des Kath.-polit. Pressvereins, Brixen 1897, S. 551 oder Faksimiledruck erschienen unter demselben Titel bei Verlagsanstalt Athesia, Bozen 1989, S. 551

137. Die St.-Klara-Birnen
Quelle: Johann Adolf Heyl: Volkssagen, Bräuche und Meinungen aus Tirol, Verlag der Buchhandlung des Kath.-polit. Pressvereins, Brixen 1897, S. 130 oder Faksimiledruck erschienen unter demselben Titel bei Verlagsanstalt Athesia, Bozen 1989, S. 130

138. Heilige Mutter Anna, du hast uns nit verstanna!
Quelle: Nacherzählung aus Weber, P. Beda: Die Stadt Bozen und ihre Umgebung, Verlag J. Eberle (G. Ferrari), Bozen 1849, S. 376

139. Die drei heiligen Jungfrauen I und II
Quelle: Johann Adolf Heyl: Volkssagen, Bräuche und Meinungen aus Tirol, Verlag der Buchhandlung des Kath.-polit. Pressvereins, Brixen 1897, S. 121 oder Faksimiledruck erschienen unter demselben Titel bei Verlagsanstalt Athesia, Bozen 1989, S. 121

140. Von der Hl. Juliana
Quelle: Rossi, von Hugo, v. Kindl Ulrike (Hsg.): Märchen und Sagen aus dem Fassatale, Istitut cultural Ladin „Majon di fašegn“, Vigo di Fassa 1984, S. 105

141. Auf Unterschlicht in der Rotwand
Quelle Zingerle, Ignaz Vinzenz: Sagen aus Tirol, Wagner'sche Universitäts-Buchhandlung, Innsbruck, 2. Auflage 1891, S. 166 und Atz, Karl und Schatz, Adelgott: Der deutsche Antheil des Bisthums Trient, Das Decanat Bozen, Druck und Verlag von Alois Auer & Comp., Bozen 1903 (zitiert unter „Wissenswertes zum Sagenhintergrund), S. 179

142. Von der Heiligen Kümmernis
Quelle: Bearbeitung aus Alpenburg, Johann N. Ritter von: Deutsche Alpensagen, unveränderter und vollständiger Nachdruck der Ausgabe von 1861, neu herausgegeben von Lothar Borowsky Verlag Heinrich Hugendubel München 1977, S. 292

143. St. Katharina in der Schart
Quelle: Zingerle, Ignaz Vinzenz: Sagen, Märchen und Gebräuche aus Tirol, Verlag der Wagner'schen Buchhandlung 1859, S. 386

144. Das Gewand der Schmerzhaften Muttergottes
Quelle: Übersetzung und Nacherzählung aus Bezzi, Quirino: Racconti e Leggende della Val di Sole, Scuola Tipografica Artigianelli, Trento 1954, S. 140

145. Die Enzian-Madonna
Quelle: Übersetzung und Nacherzählung aus Bezzi, Quirino: Lungo le rive del Noce, Editrice Saturnia, Trento 1988, S. 199; Neri, Mauro: Quella terra magica tra i monti, Panorama Ragazzi, Trento 2000, S. 563

146. Das Gnadenbild aus dem Lärchenstock zu Waldrast
Quellen: Brüder Grimm: Deutsche Sagen, Vollständige Ausgabe nach dem Text der 3. Auflage von 1891, buchclub 65, Berlin 1987, S. 318 und Zingerle, Ignaz Vinzenz: Sagen aus Tirol, Wagner'sche Universitäts-Buchhandlung, Innsbruck, 2. Auflage 1891, S. 160

147. Die Muttergottes von Saalen
Quelle: Johann Adolf Heyl: Volkssagen, Bräuche und Meinungen aus Tirol, Verlag der Buchhandlung des Kath.-polit. Pressvereins, Brixen 1897, S. 550 oder Faksimiledruck erschienen unter demselben Titel bei Verlagsanstalt Athesia, Bozen 1989, S. 550

148. Die Heilige Jungfrau vom Farnkraut
Quelle: Falger, Josef Anton: Der Pilger durch Tirol, Verlag von Karl Pfaundler, Innsbruck 1846, S.387 und Zingerle, Ignaz Vinzenz: Sagen aus Tirol, Wagner'sche Universitäts-Buchhandlung, Innsbruck, 2. Auflage 1891, S.492

149. Wallfahrt zur Heiligen Jungfrau Maria in Lavant
Quelle: Falger, Josef Anton: Der Pilger durch Tirol, Verlag von Karl Pfaundler, Innsbruck 1846, 1846, S. 242, Ausschnitt

150. Maria Weißenstein
Quelle: Falger, Josef Anton: Der Pilger durch Tirol, Verlag von Karl Pfaundler, Innsbruck 1846, S. 275, Ausschnitt

Weiterführende Literatur

Aick, Gerhard: Die schönsten Rittersagen des Mittelalters, Verlag Carl Ueberreuter Wien – Heidelberg 1957

Auer, Martin und Wolfsgruber, Linda: Von den wilden Frauen, Verlag für Literatur, Kunst und Musikalien, Bibliothek der Provinz, publication PN 1, keine Jahresangabe

Auer, Ludwig: Heiligen-Legende, Verlag Ludwig Auer-Cassianeum, Donauwörth 1958

Avanzin v. Anton: Neue Tiroler Versionen der Sage vom Tod des großen Pan, in: Der Schlern, Jahrgang 1960

Bächtold-Stäubli, Hanns und Hoffmann-Krayer, Eduard: Handwörterbuch des Deutschen Aberglaubens, Originalausgabe 1927-1942, unveränderter fotomechanischer Nachdruck bei Verlagsgruppe Weltbild, Augsburg 2000

Bauer, Wolfgang und Dümotz, Irmtraud (Hsg.): Lexikon der Symbole, Lizenzausgabe m. Genehmigung der Abi Melzer Productions GmbH, Dreieich für Bertelsmann Reinhard Mohn OHG, Gütersloh, die Europäische Bildungsgemeinschaft Verlags-GmbH, Stuttgart und Die Buchgemeinschaft Donauland, Kremayr&Scheriau, Wien (keine Jahresangabe vorhanden)

Bechstein, Ludwig: Deutsche Märchen und Sagen, Aufbau-Verlag, Berlin 1961

Beckmann, Dieter und Barbara: Das geheime Wissen der Kräuterhexen, Deutscher Taschenbuch Verlag, München 2002

Beyer, Rolf: Die andere Offenbarung – Mystikerinnen des Mittelalters, Gustav Lübbe Verlag, Bergisch Gladbach 1989

Bolognini, Nepomuceno: Nel regno della storia e in quello della leggenda, Memorie Trentine, II edizione dopo il sequestro, Stab. Scotoni e Vitti, Trento 1909

Bonin von, Felix (Hsg.): Schamanismus und Märchen, param-Verlag, Ahlerstedt 2003

Bornhausen, Karl: Der Sonnenstein von Avelengo, in: Der Schlern, Jahrgang 1938

Bornhausen, Karl: Der Dreikopf, in: Der Schlern, Jahrgang 1938

Bravi, Ferruccio: I reto-etruschi, Centro di documentazione storica per l'Alto Adige, Collana della „Clessidra", n. 16, Bolzano 1975

Braun, Wilhelm: Margarete Maultasch, Kitab-Verlag, Klagenfurt – Wien 2007

Bringsvaerd, Tor Age: Die wilden Götter, Verlag Piper, München – Zürich 2004

Brönnle, Stefan: Landschaften der Seele. Landschaften, Geomantie und ihre Auswirkungen auf die menschliche Psyche, Schirner Verlag, Darmstadt 2006

Brüder Grimm: Kinder- und Hausmärchen, Hsg. Hans-Jörg Uther, Eugen Diederichs Verlag, München 1996

Budapest, Zsuzsanna E.: Herrin der Dunkelheit Königin des Lichts, Schirner Verlag, Darmstadt 2006

Büchli, Arnold: Mythologische Landeskunde von Graubünden, Band 3, Desertina Verlag, Disentis 1990

Cambell, Josef: Der Heros in tausend Gestalten, insel taschenbuch, Frankfurt a.M. 1953
Campell, Josef: Die Kraft der Mythen, Albathros, Düsseldorf 2007
Caminada, Christian: Die verzauberten Täler, Walter-Verlag Olten und Freiburg i.B. 1961
Casati, Gianfranco: Leggende dell'Altipiano di Pinè, Casa Editrice Quaderni di Poesia, Milano 1939
Clarus, Ingeborg: Keltische Mythen. Zeugnisse aus einer anderen Welt. Bechtermünz Verlag, Augsburg 1997
Concannon, Maureen: La femmina sacra, Edizioni Arkeios, Roma 2006
Cooper, J.C.: Das große Lexikon traditioneller Symbole, Arkana Goldmann München 2004
Dahn, Therese: Deutsche Heldensagen, Magnus Verlag, Stuttgart/Essen, ohne Jahresangabe
Dähnhardt, Oskar: Natursagen I und II, Gorg Olms Verlag Hildesheim Zürich New York 1983
Dalla Torre, K.W.: Junk's Natur-Führer. Tirol, Vorarlberg und Liechtenstein, Verlag von W.Junk, Berlin 1913
Dal Lago, Bruna und Locher, Elmar: Il Trentino Alto Adige una regione sconosciuta, Newton Compton Edit., Roma 1985
Degasperi, Fiorenzo: Il culto delle acque, Curcu & Genovese, Trento 2005
De Lotto, Enrico: Una divinità sanante a Lagole, a cura del Comune di calalo di Cadore, Web&Graphic Belluno, Giugno 2003
Delug, Karl: Runen – Sagen aus Tirol, Verlag der Wagner'schen k.k. Universitäts-Buchhandlung, Innsbruck 1912
De Rachewiltz, Siegfried: Das Eierschalenrätsel in der Tiroler Sage, in: Der Schlern, Jahrgang 1980
Derungs, Kurt: Kultplatz Zuoz-Engadin, editon amalia, Bern 2001
Derungs, Kurt und Schlatter, Christina, Quellen Kulte Zauberberge, edition amalia, Grenchen b. Solothurn 2005
Devereux, Paul: Der heilige Ort, AT Verlag Baden und München 2006.
Dibona, Dino: Storie, personaggi e racconti leggendari delle Dolomiti, Newton&Compton editori, Roma 2003
Dibona, Dino: Guida insolita ai misteri, ai segreti, alle leggende e alle curiosità delle Dolomiti, Newton&Company, Roma 2000
Di Gesaro, Pinuccia: Le streghe dolomitiche, Praxis 3 Istitut Ladin Micura de Rü, San Martino in Badia 2003
Döbler, Hanns Ferdinand: Magie Mythos Religion, Orbis Verlag, München, 2000
Duerr, Hans Peter: Traumzeit, Syndikat, Frankfurt a.M. 1978
Eliade, Mircea: Das Heilige und das Profane, insel taschenbuch Frankfurt a.M. 1998
Eliade, Mircea: Bilder und Sinnbilder, Walter-Verlag, Olten und Freiburg im Breisgau 1958
Ennen, Edith: Frauen im Mittelalter, Verlag C.H. Beck, München 1999
Felizetti Sorg, Barbara und Felizetti, Paul: Ridnauner Sagenschatz, Ridnauner Hefte 3, 2007

Fink, Hans: Aus der Klausner Sagenwelt, in: Der Schlern, Jahrgang 1972
Fink, Hans, Aus dem Sagenreich von Fassa, in: Dolomiten, 30.08.1988
Fink, Hans: Die Hurl, der Hurla und der Sprauß, in: Der Schlern, Jahrgang 1995
Fink, Hans: Die Stadt Karla-Kerla im Olanger Becken, in: Der Schlern, Jahrgang 1962
Fink, Hans: Eisacktaler Sagen, Bräuche und Ausdrücke, Schlern-Schriften 164, Faksimiledruck des 1957 erschienenen Werkes, Athesia Bozen 2002
Fink, Hans: Eisacktaler Volkserzählungen, Verlag A.Weger, Brixen 1991
Fink, Hans: Ernte-, Korn- und Almdämonen, in: Der Schlern, Jahrgang 1965
Fink, Hans: Salige und Unholde, Verlagsanstalt Athesia, Bozen 1996
Fink, Hans: Verzaubertes Land. Volkskult und Ahnenbrauch in Südtirol. Tyrolia Verlag 1969
Fink, Hans: Zwangseisen für Geisteskranke, in: Der Schlern, Jahrgang 1965
Finsterwalder, Karl: Tiroler Ortsnamenkunde, Universitätsverlag Wagner, Innsbruck 1990
Fischnaler, Conrad: Das Eisacktal in Lied und Sage, Verlag der Wagner'schen Universitätsbuchhandlung, Innsbruck 1883
Forcher, Michael: Kleine Geschichte Tirols, Haymon-Verlag, Innsbruck Wien 2006
Franz, Leonhard C.: Südtiroler Reitia-Inschriften, in: Der Schlern, Jahrgang 1957
Franz, Leonhard C.: Der heilige Leonhard in Geschichte, Glaube und Brauch, in: Der Schlern, Jahrgang 1972
Früh, Sigrid (Hsg.): Der Kult der drei Heiligen Frauen, edition amalia, Bern 1998
Garobbio, Aurelio: Montagne e valli incantate, Cappelli Editore, Bologna 1963
Gatto Chanu, Tersilla: Saghe e leggende delle Alpi, Newton&Compton Editori, Roma 2002
Gebert, Helga: Märchenlexikon, Beltz-Verlag, Weinheim und Basel 1987
Gimbutas, Marija: Die Sprache der Göttin. Zweitausendundeins, Frankfurt am Main, deutsche Erstausgabe 1995.
Göttner-Abendroth, Heide: Die Göttin und ihr Heros, Verlag Frauenoffensive, München 1980
Goebel, Wolfgang und Glöckler, Michaela: Kindersprechstunde, Verlag Urachhaus Johannes M.Mayer, Stuttgart, 10. ergänzte Auflage 1992
Golowin, Sergius: Die Magie der verbotenen Märchen, Band II, Merlin Verlag Hamburg, 1973
Golowin, Sergius: Die weisen Frauen, Goldmann/Sphinx Verlag, Basel, 3. Auflage 1986
Gorfer, Aldo: Le valli del Trentino I und II, Edizioni Manfrini, Calliano, 2° edizione 1983
Granichstaedten-Czerva: Äbtissin Verena und Kardinal Cusa, in: Der Schlern, Jahrgang 1948
Grießmair, Hans, Bewahrte Volkskultur, Südtiroler Landesmuseen, Verlagsanstalt Athesia Brixen 2004.
Grimm Jacob: Deutsche Mythologie, 3 Bände, photomechanischer Nachdruck der 4. Auflage von 1875-78, Akademische Druck- und Verlagsanstalt, Graz – Austria 1968
Gruber, Karl: Die Pfarrkirche von Meransen, Tappeiner Verlag, Lana 1997

Gruber, Karl: Südtiroler Heiligenhimmel, Verlagsanstalt Athesia, Bozen 1991
Gruber Karl und Grießmair Hans: Heilige Orte-Quellen der Kraft, Verlagsanstalt Athesia, Bozen 2007
Gugitz, Gustav: Fest- und Brauchtumskalender, Verlag Brüder Hollinek, Wien 1955
Haid, Hans – Pro Vita Alpina (Hsg.): Mythos Gletscher, loewenzahn Verlag, Innsbruck – Bozen 2004
Haid, Hans: Mythen der Alpen, Böhlau Verlag, Wien Köln Weimar 2006
Haid Hans: Mythos und Kult in den Alpen, Rosenheimer Verlagshaus, Rosenheim 2002
Haid Hans: Wege der Schafe, Tyrolia/Athesia, Innsbruck – Bozen 2008
Haider, Friedrich: Tiroler Brauch im Jahresverlauf, Tyrolia-Verlag, Innsbruck – Wien, Athesia-Verlag, Bozen 1990
Hamp, Vinzenz und Stenzel, Meinrad: Das Alte Testament – vollständige Ausgabe, Paul Pattloch Verlag, Aschaffenburg 1975
Heilfurth, Gerhard: Südtiroler Sagen aus der Welt des Bergbaus – An der Etsch und im Gebirge, Verlag A.Weger, Brixen 1968
Heindrich, Ursula und Heinz-Albert (Hsg. im Auftrag der Europäischen Märchengesellschaft): Die Zeit im Märchen, Königsfurt Verlag, Krummwisch bei Kiel 2005
Heinsohn, Gunnar und Steiger, Otto: Die Vernichtung der Weisen Frauen, Heyne Verlag, München, 3. erweiterte Ausgabe 1989
Hoeniger, Karl Theodor: in „Rundschau über Literatur und Kunst“: zu Karl Felix Wolff „König Laurin und sein Rosengarten“, in: Der Schlern, Jahrgang 1948
Hofer, Karl: Die Heiligen Drei Jungfrauen auf dem Meransnerberge, in: Der Schlern, Jahrgang 1929
Holzmann, Hermann: Pfeifer Huisele, Universitätsverlag Wagner, Innsbruck 1954
Holzmann, Hermann: Wipptaler Heimatsagen, Österreichischer Bundesverlag für Unterricht, Wissenschaft und Kunst, Wien 1948
Hörmann, von Ludwig: Mythologische Beiträge aus Wälschtirol mit einem Anhange wälschtirolischer Sprichwörter und Volkslieder, Druck der Wagner'schen Universitäts-Buchdruckerei, Innsbruck 1870
Hörmann von, Ludwig: Das Tiroler Bauernjahr, Verlag der Wagner'schen Universitäts-Buchhandlung, Innsbruck 1899
Hörmann, von Ludwig: Tiroler Volksleben, Bonz, Stuttgart 1909
Hye, Franz Heinz (Hsg.): Der alte Markt Mühlbach, Schützenkompanie der Marktgemeinde Mühlbach, 1979
Hygen, Anne-Sophie, Bengtsson, Lasse: Felsbilder im Grenzgebiet, Warne Förlag, Sävedalen, Schweden 2000
Innerebner, Georg: Das seltsame Burgstallegg von Aldein, in: Der Schlern, Jahrgang 1954
Jung, C.G. u.A: Der Mensch und seine Symbole, Walter Verlag Zürich und Düsseldorf, 2004
Kalweit, Holger: Das Totenbuch der Germanen, Albatros, Düsseldorf 2006

Kindl, Ulrike: Kritische Lektüre der Dolomitensagen von Karl Felix Wolff, Istitut Ladin, „Micura de Rü“, San Martin de Tor 1983
Kindl, Ulrike: Le Dolomiti nella leggenda, FK-Editrice Fra snelli Keitsch, Verona, IV edizione 2000
Kloft, Hans: Mysterienkulte der Antike, Verlag C.H. Beck, München, 3. Auflage 1999
Knoop, Otto und Asmus, Ferdinand: Volkssagen, Erzählungen, Aberglauben, Gebräuche und Märchen aus dem östlichen Hinterpommern, Verlag Olms, Hildesheim 1987
Köhlmeier, Michael: Die besten Sagen des klassischen Altertums, Piper, München Zürich 2005
Krause, Arnulf (Hsg.): Die Götterlieder der Älteren Edda, Philipp Reclam jun., Stuttgart 2006
Künzl, Ernst: Die Germanen, Verlag Theiss, Stuttgart 2006
LaChapelle, Dolores: Weisheit der Erde, Verlag Neue Erde, Saarbrücken 1978
LaChapelle, Dolores: Geheiligtes Land – geheiligte Sexualität, Neue Erde, Saarbrücken 1990
Langes, Gunther: Burggrafenamt und Meran, Verlagsanstalt Athesia, Bozen, 4. überarbeitete Auflage 1978
Langes, Gunther: Überetsch und Bozner Unterland, Verlagsanstalt Athesia, Bozen, 3. Auflage 1977
Le Pensif, Jaques: Merkwürdige Erlebnisse einer sehr schönen und weit und breit gereisten Tirolerin, Ullstein, Frankfurt – Berlin – Wien 1980
Lunz, Reimo: Archäologische Streifzüge durch Südtirol, Band 1 und 2, Verlagsanstalt Athesia, Bozen 2005 und 2006
Lurker, Manfred: Lexikon der Götter und Dämonen, Alfred Kröner Verlag, Stuttgart 1984
Mahlknecht, Bruno: Südtiroler Sagen. Ausgewählt und bearbeitet von Bruno Mahlknecht. Verlagsanstalt Athesia, Bozen, 2. Auflage 1985
Maier, Bernhard: Die Religion der Germanen, Verlag C.H.Beck, München 2003
Maierbrugger, Matthias: Kärntner Sagenbuch, Verlag Johannes Heyn, Klagenfurt 1979
Mailly von, Anton: Sagen aus Friaul und den Julischen Alpen, Leipzig Dieterich'sche Verlagsbuchhandlung 1922
Mang, Hermann: Krötendarstellungen als Weihegaben, in: Der Schlern, Jahrgang 1924
Marchesini, Roberto, Tonutti, Sabrina: Magia e spiritualità della simbologia animale, De Vecchi Editore, Milano 2000
Marini, Rudolf: Die Verehrung der heiligen drei Jungfrauen Aubet,Cubet und Guerre in Meransen, in: Der Schlern, Jahrgang 1995
Markale, Jean: Die keltische Frau, Goldmann Verlag, München 1986
Martinelli, Maurizio und Paolucci, Giulio: Etruskische Stätten, Scala Florenz 2006
Matscher, Hans: Der Wurzgraber, in: Der Schlern, Jahrgang 1954
Matscher, Hans: Die Dreißgenkräuter, in: Der Schlern, Jahrgang 1950
Mayr, Karl M.: Die Birkenrute von Klobenstein am Ritten und ihre Inschrift, in: Der Schlern, Jahrgang 1958

Mayr Karl M.: Die Inschriften der Votive von Sanzeno, in: Der Schlern, Jahrgang 1950

Mayr, Karl M.: Reitia-Inschrift vom Piperbühel bei Klobenstein am Ritten, in: Der Schlern, Jahrgang 1957

Mayr, Karl M.: Wie hieß die Göttin der Schwefelquellen von Moritzing/Siebeneich bei Bozen im Altertum?, in: Der Schlern, Jahrgang 1965

Menara, Hanspaul: Südtiroler Burgen, Schlösser und Ansitze, Athesia Verlagsanstalt, Bozen 1999

Merci, Lucillo: Volkssagen aus Südtirol, Manfrini Editori, Calliano/Trento 1997

Michaeler Hochw., Otto: Die tapferen Weiber und Mädchen von Latzfons und Verdings, in: Der Schlern, Jahrgang 1947

Monaghan, Patricia: Lexikon der Göttinnen, O.W.Barth-Verlag, Scherz-Verlag, Bern – München – Wien 1999

Mulack, Christa: Die geheime Göttin im Christentum, Kreuz Verlag 1991

Mudrak, Edmund: Deutsche Heldensagen, Ensslin&Laiblin Verlag, Reutlingen 1955

Müller-Ebeling, Claudia, Rätsch, Christian und Storl, Wolf-Dieter: Hexenmedizin, AT Verlag, Aarau, 3. Auflage 2001

Neri, Mauro: Quella terra magica tra i monti, Panorama ragazzi, Tipografia Alcione, Trento 2000

Neri, Mauro: Leggende trentine tra tini e alambicchi, Casa Editrice Panorama, Trento 2004

Neue Zeitschrift des Ferdinandeums für Tirol und Vorarlberg, 12. Bändchen, gedruckt mit Wagner'schen Schriften, Innsbruck 1846, bei: http://books.google.com

Pahlow, M.: Das große Buch der Heilpflanzen. Gesund durch die Heilkräfte der Natur. Bechtermünz Verlag. Lizenzausgabe für Verlagsgruppe GmbH, Augsburg 2001.

Pardeller, Josef: Sagenplätze als vorgeschichtliche Kultstätten im Ortlergebiet, in: Der Schlern, Jahrgang 1949

Pardeller, Josef: Drudensagen aus dem oberen Vinschgau, in: Der Schlern, Jahrgang 1950

Pardeller, Josef: Eigenartiger Opferbrauch, in: Der Schlern, Jahrgang 1949

Pardeller, Josef: Zur Frage der Verwendung der Birkenrute vom Piperbühel, in: Der Schlern, Jahrgang 1960

Paulin Karl: Sagen aus Nordtirol, Wagner'sche Universitätsbuchhandlung, Innsbruck 1933

Paulin Karl: Die schönsten Sagen aus Südtirol, Wagner'sche Universitätsbuchhandlung, Innsbruck 1950

Perger, Anton Ritter von: Deutsche Pflanzensagen, Verlag von August Schaber, Stuttgart und Oehringen 1864

Petzoldt, Leander: Dämonenfurcht und Gottvertrauen. Zur Geschichte und Erforschung unserer Volkssagen. Wissenschaftliche Buchgesellschaft Darmstadt 1989

Petzoldt, Leander: Sagen aus Tirol, Verlag für Sammler, Graz 1976

Pfabigan, Alfred: Die andere Bibel, Eichborn, Frankfurt a.Main 2004

Philips, Ellen und Tölle, Marianne: Die geheimnisvolle Welt der Mythen und Sagen, Band: Riesen und Ungeheuer, Weltbild Verlag, Augsburg 1995
Pollack, Rachel: Im Körper der Göttin, Hugendubel, München 1999
Pogačnik, Marko: Elementarwesen, Knaur, München 1995
Pogačnik, Marko: Schule der Geomantie, Knaur, München 1996
Porter, J.R.: Die verworfenen Schriften, Verlag Katholischs Bibelwerk, Wien 2004
Prayon, Friedhelm: Gli etruschi, il Mulino Universale Paperbacks, Bologna 1966
Pro Cultura (Zeitschrift), Trento, Gennaio-Marzo 1913 und Maggio 1913
Purner, Jörg: Radiästhesie – Ein Weg zum Licht? M&T Edition Astroterra, Zürich/Chur 1988
Rachewiltz, de Siegfried W.: Brot im südlichen Tirol, ARUNDA, Schlanders, 1980
Rainer, Paul: Legenden aus dem Pustertal, Wiener Literarische Anstalt, Wien – Berlin 1920
Rampold, Josef: Bozen, Salten, Sarntal, Ritten, Eggental, Verlagsanstalt Athesia, Bozen, 3.überarbeitete Auflage 1979
Rampold, Josef: Eisacktal, Verlagsanstalt Athesia, Bozen 1969
Rampold, Josef: Pustertal, Verlagsanstalt Athesia, Bozen, 5. überarbeitete Auflage 1987
Rampold, Josef: Vinschgau, Verlagsanstalt Athesia, Bozen, 7. überarbeitete Auflage 1997
Ranke, Kurt (Hrsg.): Enzyklopädie des Märchens, Walter de Gruyter Verlag, Berlin/New York 1999
Ranke-Graves von, Robert: Die weisse Göttin, rowohlts enzyklopädie, Hamburg 2002
Rätsch, Christian: Walpurgisnacht, ATVerlag, Baden und München 2007
Richebuono, Josef: Geschichtlicher Kern dreier ladinischer Sagen, in: Der Schlern, Jahrgang 1973
Rizzi, Giovanni (Hsg.): Schweigende Felsen, SuedMedia,Vahrn/Brixen 2007
Roberti, Giacomo: Cinquecento leggende trentine letterariamente, A.Scotoni, Trento 1934
Rohrecker, Georg: Druiden, Wilde Frauen, Andersweltfürsten, Pichler Verlag, Wien 2002
Romankiewicz, Brigitte: Die schwarze Madonna, Patmos Verlag, Düsseldorf 2004
Rösch, Konstantin und Bott, Kapistran: Das Neue Testament, Verlag Ferdinand Schöningh, München – Paderborn – Wien 1967
Rumpf, Marianne: Perchten, Königshausen&Neumann, Würzburg 1991
Rüttner-Cova, Sonja: Frau Holle – Die gestürzte Göttin, Hugendubel Verlag, München 1998
Savi-Lopez, Marie: Alpensagen, Verlag von Adolf Bonz & Comp., Stuttgart 1893
Schatz, Josef: Wörterbuch der Tiroler Mundarten, Band I und II (Schlernschriften 119 und 120), Universitätsverlag Wagner, Innsbruck 1993
Scherf, Dagmar: Der Teufel und das Weib, Sachbuch Fischer, Frankfurt am Main 1990
Scherf, Gertrud: Zauberpflanzen und Hexenkräuter, BLV Verlagsanstalt, München 2002
Schönweger, Astrid (verantw.) und Madl, Alexandra: „Göttin – Hexe – Heilerin", Broschüre zur gleichnamigen Ausstellung im Frauenmuseum Meran vom 15.05.06-03.11.06
Schreiner, Klaus: Maria, Verlag Anaconda, Köln 2006
Seifarth, Carly: Aberglaube und Zauberei in der Volksmedizin. Bohmeier Verlag, Leipzig 2005

Silvestri, Giuseppe: Leggende e tradizioni della Terza Sponda Anaune, Grafiche Istituto Artigianelli, Trento 1979
Simek, Rudolf: Götter und Kulte der Germanen, 2. Auflage, Verlag C.H. Beck, München 2006
Simek Rudolf: Lexikon der germanischen Mythologie, Alfred Kröner Verlag, Stuttgart 2006
Simrock, Karl: Bertha die Spinnerin, Druck und Verlag v. Heinrich Ludwig Brönner; Frankfurt a.M. 1853
Sheldrake, Rupert: Die Wiedergeburt der Natur, rororoRowohlt, Reinbek bei Hamburg 1994
Steub, Ludwig: Drei Sommer in Tirol, Stuttgart, 1871, Bavarica Reprint im Süddteutschen Verlag München 1977
Storl, Wolf-Dieter: Pflanzendevas – Die Göttin und ihre Pflanzenengel, AT Verlag, Aarau 1997
Storl, Wolf-Dieter: Heilkräuter und Zauberpflanzen zwischen Haustür und Gartentor, AT Verlag Aarau und Baden 2004
Strenna Trentina (Kulturzeitschrift), gebundener Jahrgang von 1907, 1927 und 1943
Streng, Petra und Bakay, Gunter: Bauernerotik in den Alpen, Löwenzahn, Innsbruck 1997
Studi Trentini, Jahrgang 1921
Susin, Guerrino Carlo: Il culto della Dea Madre nella preistoria bellunese, Tiziano Edizioni, Pieve di Cadore 2006
Tessadri, Elena: Le vette solitarie – leggende delle Dolomiti di Brenta, Societá Editrice Internazionale, Torino SEI 1960
Teßmann, Friedrich: Tridentum – Anagnis – Anaunia, in: Der Schlern, Jahrgang 1957
Trapp, Eugen: Kunstdenkmäler Ladiniens, Istitut Ladin Micura de Rü, San Martin de Tor 2003
Trapp, Oswald: Tiroler Burgenbuch I, Verlagsanstalt Athesia Bozen 1976
Turchi, Dolores: Lo sciamanesimo in Sardegna, Newton&Compton editori, Roma 2001
Vernaleken, Theodor: Alpenmärchen, Verlag Lothar Borowsky, ohne Jahresangabe, München, Nachdruck von 1863
Vernaleken, Theodor: Alpensagen, Verlag Anton Pustet, Salzburg Leipzig 1938
Vernaleken, Theodor: Mythen und Bräuche des Volkes in Österreich, Wilhelm Braumüller, Wien 1859
Volgger, Siegfried: Das Klarissen- und Franziskanerkloster in Brixen, Franziskanerkloster Brixen, Ferrari-Auer, Bozen 1996
Voragine, De Jacobus: Legenda Aurea (1263-1273), aus dem Lateinischen übersetzt von Richard Benz, Eugen Diederichs-Verlag, Jena 1925
Walker, Barbara: Das geheime Wissen der Frauen, Arun Verlag, Engerda 2003
Walker, Barbara C.: Die weise Alte, Frauenoffensive, München 2001
Wallnöfer, Louis: Das seltsame Burgstallegg von Aldein, in: Der Schlern, Jahrgang 1954
Wallnöfer, Louis: Die schlafende Riesenfrau „Frau Gant“, in: Der Schlern, Jahrgang 1924

Wallnöfer, Louis: Neue Wallburgen, in: Der Schlern, Jahrgang 1929
Walser-Biffiger, Ursula: Wild und Weise, ATVerlag, Baden – München 1998
Weger, Siegfried und Hölzl, Reinhard: Geheimnisvolles Tirol, loewenzahn, Innsbruck – Bozen 2007
Weingartner, Josef: Die Kunstdenkmäler Südtirols, Tyrolia-Verlag, Innsbruck – Wien – München 1961
Weingartner, Josef: Tiroler Burgen. Ein Führer durch Nord-, Süd- und Osttirol, Tirolia-Verlag, Innsbruck 1962
Wetzel, Christoph: Das große Lexikon der Symbole, Primus Verlag, Darmstadt 2008
Winkler, Robert: Volkssagen aus dem Vinschgau, Verlagsanstalt Athesia, Bozen 1968
Wittig-Oberrauch Traudl: Allerhand Leut', allerhand Sachen. Humorvolles aus Südtirol. Athesia Verlag, Bozen 1987
Wolff, Karl Felix: Monographie der Dolomitenstraße, Verlag der Franz Moser'schen Buchhandlung, Bozen 1908
Wolff, Karl Felix: Die Grundgedanken der Rosengarten-Dichtung, in: Der Schlern, Jahrgang 1965
Wolff, Karl Felix: Fassanische Studien, in: Der Schlern, Jahrgang 1954
Wolff, Karl Felix: Aus Alt-Gröden, in: Der Schlern, Jahrgang 1957
Zaunert, Paul: Deutscher Sagenschatz, Eugen Diederichs, Jena 1921
Zeni, Marte: Leggende delle Dolomiti, Edizioni Generali C.E.S.A. – Arti Grafiche Bertarelli, Roma 1935
Zerling, Clemens: Lexikon der Pflanzensymbolik, AT Verlag, Baden und München 2007
Zingerle, Ignaz: Sitten, Bräuche und Meinungen des Tiroler Volkes, Wagner'sche Universitätsbuchhandlung, Innsbruck, 2. vermehrte Auflage 1871
Zingerle, Ignaz Vinzenz: Sitten, Bräuche und Meinungen des Tiroler Volkes, 2. vermehrte Auflage, Druck und Verlag der Wagner'schen Universitäts-Buchhandlung, Innsbruck 1871, Nachdruck bei Georg Olms Verlag Hildesheim, New York 1978
Zingerle, Oswald: Über verborgene Schätze und ihre Hebung, in: Der Schlern, Jahrgang 1923
Zuffi, Stefano: Die Natur und ihre Symbole, Parthas Verlag, Berlin 2005
Zumstein, Carlo: Schamanismus, Diederichs Kompakt, Heinrich Hugendubel Verlag, München 2001
www.heiligenlexikon.de
www.sagen.at
www.wikipedia.de

Ortsverzeichnis

Stichwortverzeichnis

Margareta Fuchs, geboren 1957, hat in Trient ein parauniversitäres Diplomstudium in der Professionellen Sozialarbeit abgeschlossen, es folgten Zusatzausbildungen in diversen Fachbereichen. In ihrer fast dreißigjährigen Tätigkeit als Sozialassistentin hört(e) sie u.a. unzähligen Menschen in existenziellen Notlagen beim Erzählen beeindruckender Lebensgeschichten zu. Als wildefrau erzählt sie selbst mit viel Temperament und Leidenschaft bei unterschiedlichsten Anlässen Märchen und Sagen aus aller Welt. Zudem bietet sie „sagenhafte" Wanderungen sowie persönlichkeitsstärkende Seminare mit Hilfe von Märchen- und Naturerfahrung an. Ihre besondere Vorliebe gilt dem Aufspüren von sagenumwobenen, in Vergessenheit geratenen geheimnisvollen Plätzen und dem Wiederbeleben von altem Tiroler Heilwissen. Sie lebt mit ihren beiden Töchtern in Brixen.

Kontakte: wildefrau@virgilio.it oder
margareta@maerchen.it

Veronika Krapf, geboren 1974, lebt in Teis/Villnöß. Nach dem Lehramtsstudium der „Biologie und Erdwissenschaften" an der Universität in Innsbruck und weiteren Zusatzausbildungen war sie als pädagogische Mitarbeiterin im Bildungshaus Kloster Neustift für den Aufbau der Umweltwerkstatt Neustift, für diverse Angebote im Erwachsenenbildungsbereich sowie für Projekte im Bereich der Umweltbildung verantwortlich. Seit zwei Jahren ist sie beruflich als Lehrerin tätig.
Seit zehn Jahren beschäftigt sie sich intensiv mit Märchen und Sagen. Mit großer Lust und Freude erzählt sie selbst Märchen und Sagen für Groß und Klein bei allen möglichen Anlässen. Ein weiterer Schwerpunkt ihrer Tätigkeiten liegt im Bereich Natur; so führt sie Natur- und Landschaftsführungen ebenso wie natur- und erlebnispädagogische Aktivitäten durch.

Kontakte: veronika_krapf@hotmail.com oder
veronika@maerchen.it